D0964386

southeast asia
on a shoestring

China Williams, George Dunford, Simone Egger, Matt Phillips, Nick Ray, Robert Reid, Paul Smitz, Tasmin Waby, Matt Warren, Sarah Wintle, Rafael Wlodarski, Wendy Yanagihara, Frank Zeller

BHUTAN

INDIA

BANGLADESH

CHINA

KALAW (p550)
Trekking amid a cool mountain
climate to a tribal village

Myitkyina

BAGAN (p565)
Abandoned Buddhist monuments built
along the mythical Ayeyarwady River

CHIANG MAI (p737)
A bohemian centre and base for
hill-tribe treks into the mountains

Sapa

Mandalay

Fansipan
(3143m)

HANOI

Sittwe

Bagan

Taunggyi

Haiphong

Bay
of
Bengal

20°N

Kalaw

Chiang Rai

Udomxai

Luang Prabang

Gulf of
Tonkin

Hainan
CHINA

Chiang Mai

**MYANMAR
(BURMA)**

LAOS

LUANG PRABANG (p369)
Easy-going ancient capital with
French and Buddhist architecture

Bago

Sukhothai

VIENTIANE

Paksan

Vinh

Pathein

YANGON
(Rangoon)

Udon Thani

Savannakhet

Hué

THAILAND

Danang

BANGKOK (p697)
A steamy disco of a city
where anything goes

Ayuthaya

Ubon
Ratchathani

Hoi An

Paracel
Islands

INDIA

Kanchanaburi

Nakhon Ratchasima
(Khorat)

Pakse

VIETNAM

BANGKOK

Siem Reap

Angkor Wat

CAMBODIA

HOI AN (p871)
An old-world charmer of narrow
streets and hand-tailored silk shops

**ANDAMAN
SEA**

Pattaya

Tonlé
Sap

Nha Trang

Mergui (Myeik)
Archipelago

Ko Chang

Gulf
of
Thailand

**PHNOM
PENH**

Dalat

10°N

Ho Chi Minh City
(Saigon)

ANGKOR (p86)
Man-made wonder of
ancient Hindu-Buddhist temples
that inspire meditation

Ko Pha-Ngan
Ko Samui

Vung Tau

PHUKET (p805)
Silky sand beaches,
buzzing bars and
top-notch diving

Surat Thani

Phu Quoc

SOUTH CHINA
SEA

Spratly
Islands

Nakhon Si Thammarat

Phuket

Hat Yai

Songkhla

Kota Kinabalu

Pulau Langkawi

MT KINABALU (p508)
Ascend into the heavens by scaling
this 4101m-high mountain – half the
height of Mt Everest

Mt
Kinabalu
(4101m)

Banda Aceh

Georgetown
Pulau Penang

Peninsular
Malaysia

BRUNEI

**BANDAR SERI
BEGAWAN**

Sabah

Bukit
Lawang

Ipoh

Taman
Negara

MALAYSIA

Niah

Medan

Berastagi

Danau
Toba

**KUALA
LUMPUR**

Natuna
Islands

MALAYSIA

Kuching

Sarawak

Berau
(Tanjungredeb)

Pulau Simeulue

Melaka

Pulau
Tioman

Anambas
Islands

Putussibau

Pulau Nias

Equator

Sumatra

Pekanbaru

Riau
Islands

SINGAPORE

Pontianak

Kalimantan

Kapuas

Samarinda

0°

Singkep
Islands

TAMAN NEGARA (p479)
A mass of primary jungle,
where you can brave the
creaky canopy walk or
explore bat caves

Bukittinggi

Padang

Pulau Siberut

Jambi

Pulau
Bangka

Balikpapan

Batang

Pangkalanbun

SINGAPORE (p656)
Efficient and tidy, with a
bustling Chinatown, Little India and
loads of shopping

Mentawi
Islands

Musi

Palembang

Pulau
Belitung

Banjarmasin

INDONESIA

GUNUNG BROMO (p205)
Supernatural moonscape of
active volcanoes viewed at the
climax of a predawn trek

BOROBUDUR (p195)
Colossal Buddhist stupa
carved out of volcanic stone

Bandarlampung

Sunda
Strait

Java
Sea

JAKARTA

Madura

INDIAN
OCEAN

Bogor

Bandung

Semarang

Java

Surabaya

Bali Sea

Sumbawa

Borobudur

Solo

Gunung

Mataram

10°S

Yogyakarta

Malang

Bromo

Denpasar

Bali

Lombok

BALI (p207)
Perfect sunsets, giant surf,
scalable volcanoes and
truly 'happy' hours

Christmas Island
AUSTRALIA

100°E

110°E

JAPAN

EAST CHINA
SEA

Tropic of Cancer

TAIWAN

20°N

Batanes
Islands

Luzon Strait

Babuyan
Islands

Laoag

Vigan

Baguio

Luzon

DONSOL (p619)
Snorkelling with whale sharks and
other creatures of the deep

PHILIPPINE
SEA

0 ————— 500 km
0 ————— 300 miles

Polillo
Islands

MANILA

Lucena

Naga

Catanduanes

PHILIPPINES

Mindoro

Sibuyan
Sea

Donsol

Samar

CEBU (p623)
The centre and starting point of a journey
through the unspoilt islands of the Visayas

10°N

Calamian
Group

Panay

Visayan
Sea

Tacloban

Iloilo

Cebu

Leyte

Bacolod

Dinagat

Palawan

Negros

Bohol

Siargao

Bohol Sea

Sulu
Sea

Cagayan de Oro

PALAU

Mindanao

Zamboanga

Davao

PALAWAN (p643)
A frontier island of jagged
mountains, coral-fringed beaches and
underground caves

PACIFIC
OCEAN

Basilan

Jolo

Sulu
Archipelago

Tawi-Tawi

Talaud

Sangir
Islands

Morotai

Celebes Sea

Manado

Halmahera

Waigeo

Equator 0°

Teluk
Tomini

Togean Islands

Maluku
Sea

Halmahera
Sea

Pulau
Biak

Kota Biak

Palu

Pulau
Bacan

Manokwari

Yapen

Jayapura

Poso

Sula Islands

Obi

Teluk
Cenderawasih

Sulawesi

Banggai
Islands

Seram Sea

Misool

Tana
Toraja

Buru

Seram

Puncak Jaya
(5030m)

Papua
(Irian Jaya)

PAPUA
NEW
GUINEA

Pare
Pare

Teluk
Bone

Kota Ambon

Ambon

Banda

Makassar
(Ujung Pandang)

Butung (Buton)

Banda Sea

Kai
Islands

Aru
Islands

Yos
Sudarso

Selayar

Flores
Sea

Komodo

Alor
Islands

Wetar

Leti
Islands

Tanimbar
Islands

Flores

Atauro
Island

Babar
Islands

Ruteng

Ende

Solor
Islands

DILI

Arafura Sea

10°S

Waingapu

Kupang

EAST TIMOR

EAST TIMOR (p125)
Personally congratulate this island
for its hard-won nation status

Rote

West
Timor

Timor Sea

Sumba

Sawu

Sawu Sea

120°E

130°E

140°E

AUSTRALIA

Responsible Travel

At some point on the road you've seen them – the ugly tourists. They step on the culture like a consumed cigarette and return home convinced of their superiority. Whether clueless or callous, irresponsible tourism can adversely affect the local culture.

Alternatively, tourism can be a gift both for the visitor and the host. Tourism provides jobs to communities that would otherwise lose their young people to city factories. Natural environments, such as coral reefs and rainforests, are preserved instead of exploited for resources. Thanks to ethnotourism, hill tribes of Southeast Asia have been spared 'integration' campaigns by majority governments.

In exchange for these immeasurable gifts, you only need to mind your manners and be kind to the environment, even if locals seem unconcerned.

Also see the Responsible Travel sections near the end of individual country chapters for information on specific organisations and p25 for general social etiquette tips.

TIPS TO KEEP IN MIND

- **Ask before you click** Learn to say 'May I take your picture?' in the language of every country you visit.
- **Be a smart shopper** Don't buy souvenirs or eat meals produced from endangered species or flora. Support family businesses, artisans and conscientious guides.
- **Don't be stingy** Be realistic about prices and don't let hustlers and touts make you suspicious of everyone.
- **Don't litter** Hold to the antilitter rules of your home country. Toss those cigarette butts in a rubbish bin, rather than snuffing them out on the beach.
- **Learn the language** Take a course before leaving home or sign up for classes in the countries you visit.
- **Protect coral reefs** Don't touch or step on coral and don't collect pieces as souvenirs.
- **Respect the local culture** Dress appropriately and treat religious centres, no matter how modest, like delicate treasures.

INTERNET RESOURCES

- **www.coralreefalliance.org** Coral-friendly guidelines for divers and news about global reef health.
- **www.ecologyasia.com** Profile of the region's flora, fauna and eco-organisations.
- **www.gunung.com/seasiaweb** Clearing house for links to news and culture of Southeast Asian nations.
- **www.lanna.com/html/tourists.html** Etiquette for tourists visiting hill-tribe communities.
- **www.lomboksumbawa.com/rinjani** Rinjani Trek – award-winning trekking programme that preserves the environment and local culture.

Contents

6

8

10

The Authors

CHINA WILLIAMS
Coordinating Author; Malaysia

That's right, she's named after a country, a really big one. You got a problem with that? Neither does she and so began her fated affair with far-away places. China grew up in South Carolina (USA) and first came to Asia to teach English in Thailand. She now lives in San Francisco with her husband, Matt, and pretends that Asia is just next door.

GEORGE DUNFORD
Singapore

After several Singapore stopovers, George appreciated the chance to explore Little India, slurp down fresh *beehoon* (rice vermicelli) and raise an eyebrow at Haw Par Villa. As well as tackling New South Wales for Lonely Planet's *Australia & New Zealand on a Shoestring*, he's written for the *Big Issue*, *The Age Cheap Eats Guide* and *Australian Traveller Magazine*. While researching this book, George threw out his back (probably from too many Orchard Rd shopping bags), but still enjoyed the club life of MS, rickshaw near-death and even more lip-smacking hawker food.

SIMONE EGGER
East Timor

Too many scintillating secondhand stories sent Simone packing for East Timor. What kind of country includes adventures with a showgirl, commando-turned-honorary-diplomat, health-department policy maker and volunteer musician? Simone discovered first-hand that the world's newest nation is brimming with extraordinary possibilities. Simone keeps one eye on her work as a photojournalist in Melbourne, while the other wanders northward looking for any excuse-ahem-opportunity to revisit this adored region.

MATT PHILLIPS
Cambodia

Matt first dove into Cambodia in 1999 and left smiling and dirty. Getting filthy and enlightened proved addictive and since then, Matt has done his best to feed his habit by travelling through much of Indochina, India, Nepal and some twenty African nations on an independent journey from Cape Town to Morocco. Although he learned his lesson about wearing supportive undergarments while riding camels in the Sahara and horses in Lesotho, it took this trip back into Cambodia's wilds for Matt to realise they are pretty damn important on a moto, too.

LONELY PLANET AUTHORS

Why is our travel information the best in the world? It's simple: our authors are independent, dedicated travellers. They don't research using just the Internet or phone, and they don't take freebies in exchange for positive coverage. They travel widely, to all the popular spots and off the beaten track. They personally visit thousands of hotels, restaurants, cafés, bars, galleries, palaces, museums and more – and they take pride in getting all the details right, and telling how it is. For more, see the authors section on www.lonelyplanet.com.

NICK RAY   Thailand

A Londoner of sorts, Nick comes from Watford, the sort of town that makes you want to travel. He first touched down in Thailand a decade ago and has made frequent forays here in the years since. With a pasty skin, he was always destined for mountains more than beaches and covered Bangkok and all points north for this book. Nick currently lives in Phnom Penh, Cambodia, and has combed every corner of the Mekong region in his work as a guidebook author, tour manager and location scout for TV and film.

ROBERT REID   Myanmar

Moulded and manipulated by Oklahoma (USA) public schools, Robert left with a still-warm journalism degree for a crappy basement apartment on E 2nd St (now Joey Ramone Place) in New York City. Since then he's lived in San Francisco, London and Ho Chi Minh City, where he worked at *Vietnam News* and travelled around Southeast Asia. After Asia, Robert worked at Lonely Planet – as commissioning editor then publishing manager of shoestring guides. He now writes full-time from a Brooklyn apartment with a rare view of trees and gardens.

PAUL SMITZ   Brunei & Malaysian Borneo

Besides a rather dark family secret involving an infatuation with pygmy squirrels, Paul can't claim much prior knowledge of the wilds of Borneo. But previous trips to Indonesia and Malaysia did convince him that there was something to this 'allure of Southeast Asia' stuff, and face-to-face meetings with free-range fauna on previous Lonely Planet trips (most recently in Australia's Northern Territory) had confirmed a passion for nature. So he was super-keen to gaze up at the minarets of Brunei's mosques, disappear into upriver mist in Sarawakian jungle, and sniff the thin air on top of Mt Kinabalu.

TASMIN WABY   Laos

Born in the UK to Kiwi journalists en route to the USA, Tasmin acquired a taste for travel and discovery from a very young age. After dabbling in school teaching, travel writing and guidebook editing, she jumped at the chance to escape the office to research for *Southeast Asia on a Shoestring*. On returning to a physically altered Laos, Tasmin found the people as generous and good-natured as ever – despite living in one of the world's least developed countries.

MATT WARREN   Indonesia

A native of southwestern England, Matt first travelled to Southeast Asia after leaving school, seeing how far he could get through Thailand on $120 (answer: not far). Since then, he returns annually, taking a little more money and a little more experience. After a stint as a reporter on *The Scotsman* in Edinburgh, he now writes for a number of UK national newspapers, filing stories from as far afield as South Africa, Kosovo, Kaliningrad and Cambodia. He has also authored nine other Lonely Planet guides, including the previous edition of *Southeast Asia on a Shoestring*, *Indonesia* and *Thailand*. He lives in London.

SARAH WINTLE
Southern & East Coast Thailand

Sarah jumped at the chance to trade her former marketing role at Lonely Planet to explore the sunny delights of Thailand. Maybe it's symptomatic of going to the same holiday spot as a kid, but this yoga devotee has had wanderlust for years, travelling from New York to Nepal. She thrives in cities but loves the wilderness. Just don't ask her to name her favourite destination – she has loved everywhere – yet she's still fond of going back to her family holiday-haunt to relax and hit the waves. Sarah has also contributed to Lonely Planet's *Australia & New Zealand on a Shoestring*. She is currently based in Bangkok and works for a conservation organisation.

RAFAEL WLODARSKI
Philippines

After completing degrees in marketing and psychology in Melbourne, Rafael vowed never to use either of them and set off on a six-month around-the-world trip. Seven years later and he is yet to come home. Rafael recently spent a year exploring Southeast Asia and has devoted several years to overland travel through the Middle East, the Indian subcontinent and North and South America. He currently calls foggy San Francisco home.

WENDY YANAGIHARA
Vietnam

Curiosity compelled Wendy to live in Ho Chi Minh City for a year, during which she taught English, got schooled, and attained (slightly) higher levels of peace and patience. Wendy has worked on updates of Lonely Planet's *Southeast Asia on a Shoestring*, *Vietnam*, *Japan*, *Best of Tokyo* and *Mexico* guides. Confounded by and enamoured of Vietnam, she currently contemplates its complex psyche from Oakland, California, while dreaming of doing so over a glass of pastis in Saigon.

FRANK ZELLER
Indonesia

Frank was born in Tokyo and grew up in Germany, until his globe-trotting family moved to far sunnier Australia when he was a teenager. After studying journalism, he started work as a newspaper reporter in Sydney, from where he travelled widely through Southeast Asia. Frank's work and his travel itch have since taken him to live in London, Bangkok, Washington, Buenos Aires and Hong Kong.

CONTRIBUTING AUTHOR

Dr Trish Batchelor is a general practitioner and travel medicine specialist who works at the CIWEC Clinic in Kathmandu, Nepal, as well as being a medical advisor to the Travel Doctor New Zealand clinics. Trish teaches travel medicine through the University of Otago, and is interested in underwater and high-altitude medicine, and in the impact of tourism on host countries. She has travelled extensively through Southeast and East Asia and particularly loves high-altitude trekking in the Himalayas.

Destination Southeast Asia

Join a match of beach volleyball in Legian (p215), Bali, Indonesia

If dreaming and waking switched places, you'd be in Southeast Asia. The tropical heat applies a vicelike grip to the land, squeezing out wild sights and smells. As each morning dawns, pots of rice come to the boil and religious devotion begins anew. Saffron-cloaked monks float between shopfronts collecting alms from the faithful, and prayers bellow from the mosques. The earth explodes with fertility, filling the market stands with ambrosial fruits and the horizon with crooked rice paddies. The daily scenes seem improbable, defying gravity and reality, alternating between the cacophony of a rattletrap bus and the deep silence of Buddhist meditation.

Many are lured here by the paradise-kissed beaches where the sun-deprived roast on the sand. The beach mood swings from booze fest to castaway hermitage, and from adventure sport to deep relaxation. The tourist checklist also includes thick jungles filled with storybook creatures, and the wondrous Hindu-Buddhist monuments of Angkor.

Good looks and greatest hits aside, Southeast Asia also lures visitors deep into its heartbeat-paced villages. These are places that balance 21st-century conveniences with a belief in ancient spirits and smiling Buddhas. Here, small children are dazed by your towering height or blinding skin colour, and their families share a simple picnic with you while waiting for a bus. Experiences like these transform a tourist into a backpacker – a collector of experiences not souvenirs. But before discovering the region's power to transform, new arrivals must endure Southeast Asia's roaring cities, so modern that they outpace the future. The dichotomy is part of the courtship, commanding the wakeful awareness of a sleepwalking journey.

HIGHLIGHTS

BEST BEACHES & DIVE SPOTS

Bali (Indonesia) ▪ synonymous with sun and fun, from Kuta's brassy beach scene to Amed's cult of castaways (p207)

Batu Karas (Indonesia) ▪ a surfer's hideaway, just a short detour from the beaten path (p186)

Bantayan Island (Philippines) ▪ unspoiled stretch of blinding sand and little to do but dodge falling coconuts (p629)

Ko Pha-Ngan (Thailand) ▪ something for everybody: quiet beaches, techno parties and 'spring-break' beach cred (p787)

Ko Phi Phi (Thailand) ▪ the prettiest place on earth, promise (p803)

Palawan (Philippines) ▪ no belly rings required on this remote island, one of Jacques Cousteau's favourite dive spots (p643)

Pulau Perhentian (Malaysia) ▪ lounge all day on the beach and never once get hassled, except by the changing tide (p472)

BEST NATURAL WONDERS

Gunung Bromo (Indonesia) ▪ an active volcano and supernatural moonscape best viewed at sunrise (p205)

Halong Bay (Vietnam) ▪ torpedo-shaped limestone mountains aiming out of a jewel-coloured basin (p851)

Cordillera Mountains (Philippines) ▪ a vast bowl-shaped valley of ancient rice terraces and long meditative walks (p614)

Mt Ramelau (East Timor) ▪ bald as a newborn with a beautiful birthing-room view at dawn (p142)

Kinabalu National Park (Malaysia) ▪ within whispering distance of the heavens but compassionately pitched for mere mortals (p508)

Cameron Highlands (Malaysia) ▪ a mellow highland retreat for an expedition through a knotted jungle (p442)

Climb aboard an outrigger canoe and explore the lagoons of El Nido (p645), Palawan, Philippines

Marvel at the elaborate classical Khmer carvings of Banteay Srei (p92), Angkor, Cambodia

BEST ARCHITECTURAL WONDERS

Angkor (Cambodia) ▪ a world wonder of Hindu-Buddhist temples built by the great Khmer kingdom (p86)

Bagan (Myanmar) ▪ a deserted city of ancient temples rippling into the distance like a man-made mountain range (p565)

Borobudur (Indonesia) ▪ a tightly knitted stupa ringed by magnificent mist and mountains (p195)

Petronas Towers (Malaysia) ▪ one of the world's largest skyscrapers with delicate Islamic designs (p431)

Hoi An (Vietnam) ▪ an antique city of narrow streets, squeaky bicycles and lacquered wooden shopfronts wearing scalloped tile bonnets (p871)

BEST CITIES

Bangkok (Thailand) ▪ hands-down the coolest, grittiest, cockiest capital city in the region (p697)

Chiang Mai (Thailand) ▪ a bohemian centre for the culturally curious (p737)

Hanoi (Vietnam) ▪ prim and proper with wide French-inspired avenues and an embalmed Uncle Ho (p831)

Luang Prabang (Laos) ▪ a blushing beauty surrounded by lush emerald forests (p369)

Singapore ▪ efficient and tidy, with a must-see museum and brand-spanking-new hostels (p656)

Catch a cyclo and explore the Old Quarter (p837), Hanoi, Vietnam

Tuck into some local specialities and rural delicacies (p817), Thailand

BEST REASONS TO GET FAT

Khâo nïaw mámûang (Thailand) – luscious golden mangoes slathered in sweetened condensed milk atop a bed of sticky rice

Banh mi (Vietnam) – baguette sandwiches that make the perfect counterbalance to rice overload

Beer Lao (Laos) – the best suds in the region and oh so much more than a breakfast drink

Laksa (Malaysia) – the spicy national noodle dish that captures the taste of an estuary at low tide

Stir-fried critters (Cambodia) – tarantulas, crickets, silk worms and other creepy crawlies that locals call snack food

Garlic stingray (Singapore) – a tasty hawker dish with a whip in the tail

BEST OFF-THE-BEATEN-TRACK PLACES

Muang Sing (Laos) – a sleepy market town with a model eco-trekking programme through the Nam Ha National Protected Area (p391)

Preah Vihear Province (Cambodia) – forgotten temple ruins of the old Angkor trail, where modern machines travel as slow as bygone ox carts (p98)

Mrauk U (Myanmar) – a mini Bagan surrounded by a lively canal-filled village (p577)

Bario & the Kelabit Highlands (Malaysia) – a verdant place for fresh air and jungle wonders (p499)

Baliem Valley (Indonesia) – the stuff of explorers' tales, with thick forests and isolated hunter-gatherer villages (p336)

Visit ethnic Akha villages on an environmentally responsible tour (p391), Muang Sing, Laos

Itineraries

MAINLAND SOUTHEAST ASIA

How long?
1 month-1 year

When to go?
High – Dec-Feb

Low – May-Oct

Budget
US$20 per day

Regional flight
US$70-100

Thailand–Laos–Cambodia–Vietnam–Myanmar

From **Bangkok** (p697), you can bus or train it north on the culture trail to the ancient capitals of **Ayuthaya** (p726) and **Sukhothai** (p732). From here people scurry straight to **Chiang Mai** (p737), but you could take the back-door route along the Burmese border through **Mae Sot** (p736), **Mae Hong Son** (p751) and hippie **Pai** (p750) to reach northern Thailand.

Connect through **Chiang Rai** (p752) to reach the **Chiang Khong–Huay Xai** border crossing (p755) into Laos and boat to **Luang Nam Tha** (p389) or **Muang Sing** (p391) for low-impact ecotours. Bus to the market town of **Nong Khiaw** (p380) and putter down the Nam Ou to charming **Luang Prabang** (p369). Then bus to the **Plain of Jars** (p385) in Phonsavan or the limestone

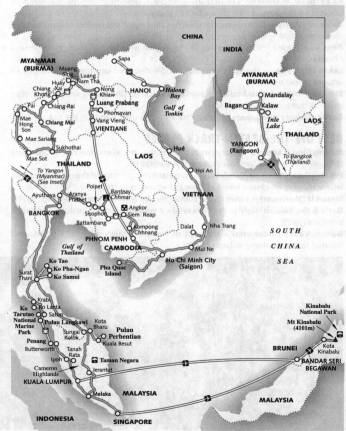

If you're just hitting the highlights, you can whip through all five countries in a dizzying month. But to do it right, give a month each to Laos and Cambodia, where travel is slow. Pick up the pace through Vietnam and Thailand.

mountains of **Vang Vieng** (p366) en route to **Vientiane** (p355), where you can fly to the capital of Cambodia, **Phnom Penh** (p62). Overland routes are also possible (see Mekong River Expedition, p22).

From here fly, bus or boat to **Siem Reap** (p79 and Angkor p86). If overlanding back to Thailand, boat to **Battambang** (p94), bus to **Sisophon** (p93); detour from Sisophon to the temples of **Banteay Chhmar** (p94). Continue on to the border at Poipet and Aranya Prathet and return to Bangkok. Alternatively from Siem Reap, drop south to see the floating village in **Kompong Chhnang** (p98) and bus to Phnom Penh to travel overland to Ho Chi Minh City.

Vietnam's slim shape simplifies travel logistics. Starting in the south at **Ho Chi Minh City** (p891), take a detour to the beaches of **Mui Ne** (p883) or **Phu Quoc Island** (p911). Then bus north through the cool hill station of **Dalat** (p885), to the beaches of **Nha Trang** (p877) and to the colonial ambience of **Hoi An** (p871). Continue by bus to **Hué** (p861) and **Hanoi** (p831), with a diversion to **Sapa** (p857) by train or to **Halong Bay** (p851) by bus. From Hanoi you can fly to other Southeast Asian capitals, including Bangkok.

Count on entering Myanmar by flying to **Yangon** (p534) from Bangkok. Stops along the Burma Trail include the ruins of **Bagan** (p565), trekking in **Kalaw** (p550), **Inle Lake** (p551) and its floating gardens and island monasteries, and the ancient capital of **Mandalay** (p556).

Thailand–Malaysia–Singapore

Bangkok (p697) is a major gateway to the region. From here train or bus south to **Ko Samui** (p783), **Ko Pha-Ngan** (p787) or **Ko Tao** (p781) – a string of beach-bumming islands in the Gulf of Thailand. Bus across the peninsula to the Andaman coast for the limestone peaks of **Krabi** (p800) and world-class rock climbing or the relaxed ambiance of **Ko Lanta** (p799). Need more sand to yourself? Bus and boat to the undeveloped islands of **Ko Tarutao National Marine Park** (p798). Then jump the Thailand–Malaysia border by boat from **Satun** (p797) to **Pulau Langkawi** (p457) and continue by boat to **Penang** (p447). For train or additional bus connections, cross over to the mainland town of Butterworth. Bus to the tranquil hill station of the **Cameron Highlands** (p442), situated around the town of Tanah Rata, and scoot over to the urban sanity of **Kuala Lumpur** (p425), a regional air hub.

If you are on the Gulf Coast side of the peninsula, take a train to the Thai–Malaysian border at Sungai Kolok to **Kota Bharu** (p474), the jumping-off point for the jungle islands of **Pulau Perhentian** (p472). Then take the Jungle Railway from Wakaf Baharu to Kota Bharu and on to **Jerantut** (p478) and boat to the rainforests of **Taman Negara** (p479). Bus south to the historic port town of **Melaka** (p436). Wrap up your mainland wandering in **Singapore** (p656), another major air gateway. From the tip of the peninsula, fly to Borneo through **Bandar Seri Begawan** (p42), the capital of Brunei. On the Malaysian side of the island is towering **Mt Kinabalu** (p508) and the surrounding **Kinabalu National Park** (p508).

How long?
1 month–1 year

When to go?
High – Dec-Feb (west coast), Feb-May (east coast)

Low – May-Oct

Budget
US$20 per day

Regional flight US$30-50

Thailand and Malaysia could monopolise a month with their combined greatest hits. Tack on a few more weeks and you'll have plenty of time to call a little village home, or travel the slow route around dusty corners.

OCEANIC SOUTHEAST ASIA

Indonesia–East Timor–Philippines

How long?
1 month–1 year

When to go?
High – Dec-Feb
(Philippines), May-Sep
(Indonesia & East Timor)

Low – May-Oct
(Philippines), Nov-Feb
(Indonesia & East Timor)

Budget
US$20-25 per day

Regional flight
US$25-100

If you are just dabbling in Indonesia from the mainland, jump the border to Sumatra from Singapore or Malaysia by boat or air. Starting in **Medan** (p261), continue on to the orang-utan park in **Bukit Lawang** (p265) and fly or ferry to the surfer's haven of **Pulau Nias** (p254). In the centre of northern Sumatra, **Danau Toba** (p255) is a huge crater lake. From nearby Padang you can boat or fly to the capital of Jakarta on the island of Java.

If your trip focuses on Indonesia, fly directly to **Jakarta** (p163) and head east. Jakarta charms few, but nearby **Yogyakarta** (p188) is the cultural heart and base for the giant stupa of **Borobudur** (p195). Then bus to **Gunung Bromo** (p205), an active volcano.

Catch the ferry at Ketapang to **Gilimanuk** (p239) in western Bali and bus to **Denpasar** (p210), the regional gateway to the southern belly of Bali. Indo's biggest draws are the resort town of **Kuta** (p213) and surfing meccas of **Bukit Peninsula** (p220) and **Nusa Lembongan** (p229). Bus to **Ubud** (p222), the cultural nexus of the distinctive Balinese arts, and continue to **Padangbai** (p229) for ferries to **Lembar** (p276) in Lombok, or take a quick diversion to the rough-and-tumble beaches of **Lovina** (p233).

Landing on laid-back Lombok, bus to **Senggigi** (p279) and ferry to the northwestern **Gili islands** (p281), then return to the mainland and bus to the sacred volcano of **Gunung Rinjani** (p286). Traipse through **Sumbawa** (p288) en route to the port town of **Sape** (p291) for boats to the Portuguese-influenced island of **Flores** (p292), and the islands of **Komodo** (p291), the stomping grounds of the prehistoric namesake dragons. You'll have to

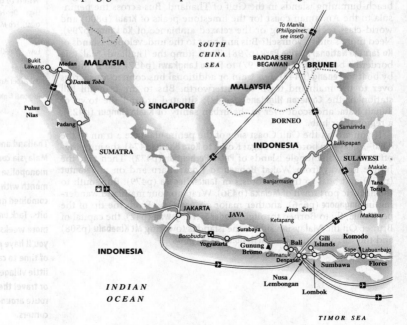

backtrack to Denpasar to fly to Sulawesi or to East Timor to tiptoe into Australia.

On the island of **Sulawesi** (p315), in the **Tana Toraja** (p319) region, Toraja people celebrate fantastical funeral ceremonies. The fast-disappearing forests of Borneo can be accessed by air or sea from Sulawesi to the town of **Balikpapan** (p310). Bus northeast to **Samarinda** (p309), where river trips stab into the lands of the Dayak tribes. Backtrack by bus to the watery canals of **Banjarmasin** (p310). To reach the national parks on the Malaysian side of Borneo, fly from Balikpapan to **Bandar Seri Begawan** (p42) in Brunei.

In Australia's backyard, **East Timor** (p125) is the youngest nation on the planet. Some stops along the way include the capital, **Dili** (p132), the idyllic island of **Atauro** (p138), or a north-coast journey to the old Portuguese village of **Baucau** (p139).

The Philippines is typically a destination unto itself, but you can weave into an island- or mainland-hop by flying from any Southeast Asian capital city. If travelling to or from Indonesia, connect via Brunei for extra savings. **Manila** (p599) is the major gateway. Bus to the hand-hewn rice terraces of **Banaue** (p616) and **Bontoc** (p615) and the perfectly preserved colonial town of **Vigan** (p617). The limestone peaks and quiet beaches of **Palawan** (p643) are a quick flight from Manila, but a world away. Boat south from Batangas to the island of Mindoro to hit **Puerto Galera** (p620) and nearby scuba sites. Ferry on from the port town of **Roxas** (p623) to the resort beach of **Boracay** (p633). Fly from Iloilo to **Cebu** (p623), the dead centre of the archipelago and a transport hub to the Visayan Sea islands, including **Bantayan Island** (p629) and **Malapascua Island** (p629). Many people buy an open-jaw ticket, arriving in Manila and departing from Cebu.

If you've only got a couple of weeks, it's an easy choice: Bali. Or the Philippines. A little bit longer? Jump over to Sumatra or Borneo. For those with bags of time, follow the island chain to East Timor and slip out the backdoor to Australia.

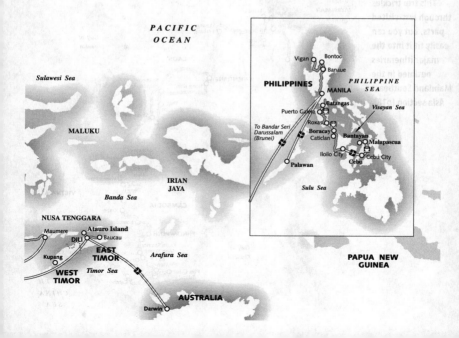

MEKONG RIVER EXPEDITION

How long?
1-2 months

When to go?
River navigation is easiest
Jul-Dec

Budget
US$20 per day

Regional flight
US$50-100

Draining the underbelly of the Asian continent, the Mekong River is justifiably the Father of Waters. Follow this hardworking river in reverse from Vietnam's flat delta to Thailand's hilly interior.

Start in bustling **Ho Chi Minh City** (p891) and bus to **Mytho** (p908), the gateway to the Mekong Delta. Charter a boat to bucolic **Ben Tre** (p909) and bus to the floating markets of **Cantho** (p909). Bus to **Rach Gia** (p910), the jumping-off point to peaceful **Phu Quoc Island** (p911). Ferry back to the mainland and catch a bus to **Chau Doc** (p910), a charming host, before bidding adieu and floating into Cambodia at the **Kaam Samnor–Vinh Xuong** border crossing (p910) all the way to the faded gentility of **Phnom Penh** (p62).

Bus to **Kompong Cham** (p110) and hop on a speed boat for the relaxing journey to **Kratie** (p111), home of the rare freshwater dolphin. Continue by boat north through the rocky rapids to **Stung Treng** (p113), a transfer point into Laos via the **Voen Kham** border crossing (p114) and the 4000 river islands of **Si Phan Don** (p402).

Bus to **Champasak** (p401), a sleepy riverside hamlet, and on to **Savannakhet** (p394), a border crossing into Thailand at **Mukdahan** (p766). Follow the river crook to the quiet hamlets of **That Phanom** (p766) and **Nakhon Phanom** (p767) to charming **Nong Khai** (p767), another crossing point into Laos at **Vientiane** (p355). Alternatively, bus from Savannakhet to Vientiane.

Hop on a bus to bewitching **Luang Prabang** (p369). Pick up the watery route northwest to **Huay Xai** (p393), the border crossing into northern Thailand at **Chiang Khong** (p755). Bus to the Golden Triangle outpost of **Chiang Saen** (p756), then connect through Chiang Rai to continue south to **Chiang Mai** (p737).

This trip trickles through less-visited parts, but you can easily fit it into the major itineraries outlined in the Mainland Southeast Asia section (p18).

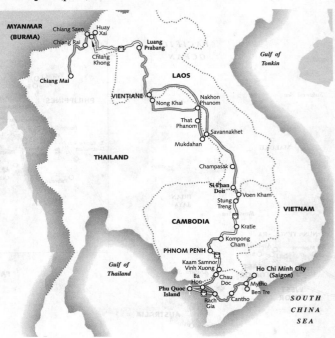

Getting Started

A trip to Southeast Asia is a little more involved than a trip downtown, but plenty of people have filtered in and out of the region without incidence, and even – gasp – without a guidebook. For the low-down on everything from vaccinations to volunteering, check out the Health chapter (p943) and the Southeast Asia Directory (p921). If you read the book cover to cover and still have questions, visit the **Lonely Planet** (www .lonelyplanet.com) website. On the site's 'Thorn Tree' section, you can post any hare-brained questions to tap into the friendly and knowledgeable traveller community; you won't be alone out there.

WHEN TO GO

Southeast Asia is always hot and humid. The mainland countries (Myanmar, Laos, Cambodia, Thailand and Vietnam) tend to share similar weather patterns, enjoying a 'cool' season from December to February (peak months for tourism) and a 'hot' season from March to May. The monsoons last from June to October bringing sudden torrential downpours for an hour or two every day followed just as suddenly by sunshine. In Cambodia and Laos, travel can be disrupted by flooded roads during the monsoon season, otherwise the rains bring a predictable relief from the heat.

Along the Malay peninsula, two monsoons strike: from November to February, the east coast gets all the action; from May to October, the west coast gets soaked. Alternating between the coasts will relieve the drawbacks of inclement weather. The duration of monsoon season varies from year to year.

See Seasons in the Fast Facts box at the start of each country chapter for more information on climate.

Indonesia also gets two monsoons; the best time to visit is from May to September. The rains start in September in Sumatra and head east arriving in East Timor around November/December. April to June is the best time to visit East Timor.

The Philippines shares aspects of both mainland and oceanic climates. Typhoons do occasionally strike the Philippines and Vietnam. The peak typhoon season runs from June to early October, with most occurring in the months of August and September.

There are, of course, regional variations within each country; these are detailed in the respective country chapters' Climate sections. Check out the climate charts on p924.

Large festivals are also factors in plotting an arrival date. Check the respective country Directories for upcoming events that might attract or impede a visit. Businesses tend to close during Muslim Ramadan and Chinese New Year, and everyone goes water-gun crazy during the Buddhist water festival in April.

COSTS & MONEY

Western currencies enjoy a favourable exchange rate with many of the Southeast Asian currencies. If you travel and eat like a local, your daily budget begins to look like Lindsay Lohan – an emaciated US$20 to US$25 a day.

Even if you are strapped for cash, remember to keep prices in perspective. Compared to the average worker in Southeast Asia, your pathetic bank account is the equivalent of a robber baron's. Many of the locals have never left their hometowns, much less travelled to a foreign country, an unimaginable luxury. Granted the 'walking ATM' (everyone wants

WHERE TO START

Try the Net for inspiration and information.

www.cia.gov Know the basic stats by searching the CIA factbook.

http://lonelyplanet.mytripjournal.com Set up your trip blog.

www.seat61.com Plot a rail journey.

www.travelmag.co.uk Dream about future adventures.

WHAT TO TAKE

Here's a challenge: reduce the size of your pack to fit in an overhead aeroplane bin. The reward: the less junk in your trunk, the less of a target you are for touts and con artists.

Camping gear If you plan to do serious (not occasional) camping, trekking or climbing, you should bring the equipment with you from home. Otherwise you can hire items of mediocre quality.

Cash Some small US dollar bills will be useful, especially in Laos, Cambodia and Myanmar; but ATMs and travellers cheques should supply the bulk of funds elsewhere.

Clothes Lightweight, light-coloured, breathable clothes; leave the denim at home. Silk long johns and a fleece for cool climates; rain gear. Line your pack with a plastic bag to keep the contents dry.

Earplugs An indispensable friend for sleeping through your neighbours' drunken fight or the zealous rooster's predawn alert.

Medicine A first-aid kit and any speciality medicines from home. Most countries (Laos and Cambodia are exceptions) have helpful pharmacies and clinics with English-speaking staff. See p944 for advice on stocking a first-aid kit.

Odds & ends Sewing kit, candles, padlock, Swiss army knife, money belt, safety pins, toilet paper, universal sink plug, small torch (flashlight), travel adaptor.

Photocopies of important documents Definitely photocopy your passport, tickets, travellers cheque serial numbers, credit and ATM cards, and pack the copies separately from the originals. Leave a copy at home with a friend, just in case.

Repellent A heavy-duty number is good for sweet-tasting travellers and to ward off bedbugs.

WHAT TO GET THERE

In the large cities, you can buy every imaginable Western product as well as medicines and the following ingenious local products:

Mosquito coils Available at markets, these coils are lit and placed at your feet to discourage a mossie feast.

Powder Available at markets and pharmacies, it does wonders for heat rash and keeps you and your clothes smelling pretty.

Sarong Available at markets, these lightweight cotton 'skirts' can be used as towels, mosquito nets, beach blankets, headgear and general backpacker fashion.

Surgical masks Available at sundry shops, these masks prevent the region's dust- and pollution-induced smoker's cough.

Tiger balm Available at pharmacies, this all-purpose salve relieves headaches, soothes mosquito bites and acts as a bug repellent.

a withdrawal) treatment is frustrating and offensive, but there is no quicker route to a bad time than to get paranoid about being ripped-off. Be a smart shopper, but realise that even in developing countries US$1 doesn't buy everything.

For more information on local currency and exchange rates, see p930 or in the individual country chapters.

LIFE ON THE ROAD

Welcome to your new life. The roosters have been crowing all night, the screaming motorcycles are seemingly doing circles around your bed and the day has already reached a boil. You climb out from under your mosquito net and head down to the shared toilet at the end of the hall.

The mirror is too short, the sink is too low and the whole room needs to be sprayed down with bleach. But this is your second week on the road and you've stopped noticing grout. The toilet is a squat and you precariously balance over the target area. As usual you forgot your toilet paper, so you scoop some water with a shallow bowl from the nearby basin to 'wipe'. Then you take several more scoops of water to 'flush' the toilet and rinse the seat. Now it is time for a shower (cold water for this penny-pincher), a powdering (keeps you cool and sweet smelling) and a desperate search for clean clothes.

Today is the day you pack up and move to the next town. Arriving at the destination station, the bus is flanked by touts all thirsty for your business. First you haggle the transport price to the guesthouse. The driver's price is always inflated with the 'I'm new in town' tax. The guesthouse has a shady yard with chickens scratching around and half-dressed babies playing in the dirt, but the room is dank and noisy, so you thank the testy desk clerk and set off down the road. You use your budget senses to sniff out the best score in town and in a few hours, you're camped out in the shade with a steamy bowl of noodles and a sweaty bottle of beer. Beats the wage-slave life.

CONDUCT

For the first time in your life, you have an extraordinary responsibility: to be an ambassador for your own country as well as the Western world. You can either charm the flip-flops off the Southeast Asians, which is easy to do in these laid-back cultures, or you can leave behind a sour taste for the cash cow of tourism.

So few travellers make an effort to speak the local language or adhere to social customs that the smallest attempts are usually rewarded with genuine appreciation and kindness. Learn how to say 'thank you', 'hello' and 'delicious' in every country you visit. Remember to smile – it expresses tonnes of emotions.

Dress modestly, covering yourself from the shoulders to the knees; this is the number one way to communicate genuine gratitude to your host country. But it's so hot, you might whine. What's funny about this argument is that walking in the shade is a better sun-deflector than showing your belly. Women who dare to wear more will help promote a healthier image of all Western women abroad. Topless sunbathing is also a no-no.

HOW MUCH?
Bottle of beer US$0.50-3
Bottled water US$0.50
Bus ticket US$4-10
Food-stall meal US$1-2
Guesthouse bed US$4-12
Internet access US$0.50-1
Restaurant meal US$5-10
Taxi ride US$3-6

---

10 TIPS TO STAY ON A BUDGET

- To avoid surprises, always ask the price before agreeing to any services.
- Buy souvenirs from craft villages rather than from tourist shops.
- Eat and drink locally at food stalls and markets.
- Go outside the tourist district to buy odds and ends.
- If travelling solo, double up with a fellow traveller to save on room costs.
- Keep a daily diary of expenses.
- Leave expensive electronics and jewellery at home, so you aren't advertising deep pockets.
- Pack light so you can walk to town from the train or bus station.
- Hire a bicycle to get around town to avoid taxi charges.
- Don't book accommodation through an agent; deal directly with the guesthouse or hotel operator.

HOW TO LOOK LIKE A SOUTHEAST ASIA VETERAN

- Crave rice for breakfast.
- Wear your jacket backwards like the motorcycle taxi drivers.
- Use mosquito repellent as deodorant.
- Forsake proper English grammar for local pidgin.
- Walk through a pack of stray dogs without flinching.
- Slip your shoes on and off at a threshold with ease.
- Squat skybomber-style on Western toilets.
- Sit down to a banana pancake breakfast and reach for the fish sauce.
- Be able to recount more than one 'I almost died' story.

For men, resist the urge to strut around without a shirt unless of course you're Brad Pitt, then go ahead.

In Southeast Asia, the feet are the cesspool of the body and the head is the temple. Consider the rules of proper foot etiquette to be like an exotic dance without a partner. Feet for the most part should stay on the ground, not on chairs, tables or bags. Showing someone the bottom of your foot expresses the same insult as flipping them your middle finger. Remove your shoes when entering a home. Don't point your feet towards sacred images or people and follow the locals' lead in sitting in a temple or mosque.

Women aren't allowed to come into contact with monks; this means women can't sit or stand next to them on the bus, pass anything directly to them or touch their belongings. Most mosques have rules about where women can be and how they should be dressed.

For more guidance on how to avoid being a really ugly tourist, see p4 and the countries' respective Culture sections throughout this guidebook.

Some dos and don'ts to remember:
- Ask before taking someone's photograph.
- Bring a gift when visiting someone's home.
- Don't engage in public displays of affection.
- Don't touch people on the head. This is considered rude in Buddhist countries.
- Remove your shoes before entering a home or religious building.
- Don't use your left hand for eating or shaking hands. In many Asian countries, the left hand is used for toilet business.

WHOOPS!

I got excited photographing pythons at a snake temple in Myanmar, which is an OK thing to do. But I became so engrossed in taking the picture that I edged in front of worshippers for the shot, which isn't OK.

Robert Reid

Snapshots

CURRENT EVENTS

The day after Christmas 2004 was a beautiful day, according to eyewitnesses. And Southeast Asia's famous beaches and islands were mobbed during the peak of peak season. Tragic timing or nature's malice, this was also the day of recorded history's second largest earthquake, which triggered a destructive tsunami. Lives and livelihoods were destroyed in 12 countries, including Thailand, Malaysia and Indonesia. (See those individual chapters for country-specific details.)

The post-tsunami emergency effort was perhaps one of the greatest outpourings of global support in recent history. Billions of dollars in international aid, mainly from private donors, was donated to the affected countries. Individuals from across the world and in the countries affected also dug in alongside survivors, removing mud and debris or administering aid to the sick and bereaved. In general the clean-up efforts have been remarkably successful: the feared water-borne epidemics of cholera and the like were averted by quick-acting health measures. The majority of survivors, in all but the most remote areas, received immediate basic necessities.

Once emergency relief progressed to reconstruction, however, the in-fighting and opportunism began. With so much money to be spent, the tsunami-affected governments, often regarded as corrupt, have been accused of cronyism and back-room deals. In Indonesia, the government has been accused of awarding reconstruction contracts to state agencies without reviewing proposals from more reliable private companies. In Thailand, small business owners and fisherfolk fear that proposed environmental restrictions (such as coastal buffer zones and no-development areas) will be used to squeeze out cottage industries and award seaside access to international resorts.

SWEATING IT OUT

During the 1990s, media attention on working conditions in overseas factories of such high-profile companies as Nike and The Gap forced Western nations to consider the ethics of affordable name brands. Aside from China, much of the world's clothing is produced in the factories of Southeast Asia, including the industrialised Indonesian island of Batam.

While concerned consumers often rally to boycott sweatshops, many economics experts conjecture that these campaigns unintentionally harm the economic opportunities of the region's already disadvantaged communities. Organisations, such as **No Sweat** (www.nosweatapparel.com), offer ethical alternatives by encouraging employees to become union members and improving the conditions of factories where goods are made. No Sweat products are made in Indonesia and come with information about workers' conditions.

As competition with China increases, some Southeast Asian countries are hoping to carve out a market niche by taking the 'sweat' out of the sweatshops. With 40% of Cambodia's economy based in textiles, the country is inviting increased monitoring of local factories by the UN to ensure standards are met. Already Cambodia can boast that almost all of its labour force is aged between 19 and 25, while market analysts estimate that 20% of China's workforce is under 16. And more than 60% of buyers of Cambodian products believe that having sweatshop-free clothing is as important as price.

For more information on working conditions in Southeast Asian factories, check out **Asian Labour News** (www.asianlabour.org).

George Dunford

Otherwise, the mainland Southeast Asian countries further from the Indian Ocean disaster garnered few headlines as the Year of the Monkey ceded to the Year of the Rooster. Vietnam and the US celebrated the 30th anniversary of the fall of Saigon with renewed diplomatic promises of trade and tourism. On the backpacker circuit, Vietnam has been open for business for 10 years and continues to develop a thriving middle class.

Continued outbreaks of Avian influenza (bird flu) have affected commercially raised flocks in Thailand and Vietnam. The World Health Organization continues to watch the disease, fearful of a possible epidemic. Bird flu has jumped species and killed 46 people since 2003.

The former backwaters of Laos and Cambodia are enjoying unprecedented levels of prosperity and development as tourists bring in new economic opportunities and as increased trade with China transforms these nations into important commercial crossroads.

Civilian-targeted terrorism in Muslim-majority regions continues to irritate the peace in the Philippines, Indonesia and, to a lesser degree, in southern Thailand. Motives for internal violence in the region vary from the insurgency activity of independence movements, to a more global agenda affiliated with the ongoing conflicts in the Middle East. Despite some promising moves toward democracy, Myanmar remains thoroughly enveloped in its military dictatorship; the most recent leader to lean too far to the West was replaced with a more familiar hardliner.

Lest the news depress, foreign scientists perusing a Laos marketplace spotted a kebab made from a type of rat previously unknown to taxonomists. Commonly known as a rock rat, the animal represents both a new species and a new family of mammals, a rare discovery indeed (the last time a new family was discovered was in the 1970s). In their article in the *New Scientist*, the scientists did not comment on whether the rock rat made a tasty kebab.

HISTORY
Early Kingdoms
As early as 150 BC, China and India interacted with the scattered Southeast Asian communities for trade and tribute. Vietnam, within short reach of China, was a subject, student and reluctant offspring of its more powerful neighbour for over 1000 years. India, on the other hand, conquered through the heart, spreading Hinduism, Buddhism and later Islam across the region, and influencing art and architecture.

Stemming from contact with India, several highly organised states emerged in the region. During the 7th to 9th centuries AD, the Srivijaya empire, with its capital at Palembang in southeast Sumatra, controlled all shipping through the Java Sea. The Srivijaya capital was also a religious centre for Mahayana Buddhism and attracted scholars as well as merchants.

In the interior of present-day Cambodia, the empire of Angkor consumed territory and labour to build unparalleled and enduring Hindu-Buddhist

Want to keep up on current events? Check out the print or online versions of the *International Herald Tribune*, the *Asian Times* and the *Asia Wall Street Journal*. Lonely planet.com/tsunami provides continuing coverage of the post-tsunami recovery effort.

Recommended reading: *Southeast Asia: Past & Present* by DR SarDesai; and *A History of South-East Asia* by DGE Hall.

TIMELINE

2800 BC: Ancestors of modern Southeast Asians begin to migrate south from China	1025: Srivijaya empire is toppled by the Chola kingdom of South India	1565: Spain establishes Cebu and later invades Manila

2800BC	0 AD	700	850	900	1025	1400	1500	1565	1600	1650 AD

Beginning of Time	AD 700: Srivijaya empire emerges in present-day Malaysia and Indonesia and prospers from the India–China shipping trade	AD 802–50: King Jayavarman consolidates the Angkor empire in present-day Cambodia and Thailand	1511: Melaka falls to the Portuguese

---

THE WORLD'S SPICE RACK

Nutmeg, cinnamon, even pepper were once luxuries more prized than gold. Harvested on Indonesia's Spice Islands (Maluku), these goods were used by Europeans for burial rituals, and as flavours and preservatives. Marco Polo and his 1292 account of Asia are often credited with igniting Europe's feverish search for a quick sea passage to the aromatic forests of Indonesia.

---

monuments to its god-kings. Eventually the Angkor empire included most of what is now Thailand, Laos and Cambodia. Angkor's economy was based on agriculture, and a sophisticated irrigation system that cultivated vast tracts of land around Tonlé Sap (Great Lake) was developed. Attacks from the expanding Thai kingdoms contributed to the decline of the empire and the abandonment of the Angkor capital.

The Classical Period, Arrival of Europeans & Imperialism

As the larger powers withered, Southeast Asia entered a classical age of cultural definition and international influence. Regional kingdoms created distinctive works of art and literature, and joined the international sphere as important ports. The Thais, with their capital first in Sukhothai (1219) and later in Ayuthaya (1350), expanded into the realm of the dying Khmer empire and exerted control over parts of Cambodia, Laos and Myanmar (Burma). The Hindu kingdom of Majapahit united the Indonesian archipelago from Sumatra to New Guinea and dominated the age-old trade routes between India and China, starting around 1331. Majapahit's reign continued until the advent of Islamic kingdoms and the emergence of the port town of Melaka (Malacca; established 1402), on the Malay peninsula. Melaka's prosperity soon attracted European interest and it fell first to the Portuguese in 1511, then the Dutch and finally the English.

At first the European nations were only interested in controlling shipping in the region, usually brokering agreements and alliances with local authorities. Centred in Java and Sumatra, the Dutch monopolised European commerce with Asia for 200 years. The Spanish, French and later the English had 'civilisation' and proselytising Christianity on their minds. Spain occupied the loosely related tribes of the Philippine archipelago. Britain steadily rolled through India, Burma and the Malay peninsula. The Dutch grasped Indonesia to cement a presence in the region. And France, with a foothold in Vietnam, usurped Cambodia and Laos, formerly territories of the Thai kingdom, to form Indochina. Although its sphere of influence was diminished, Thailand was the only Southeast Asian nation to remain independent. Credit is frequently given to the Thai kings who Westernised the country and played competing European powers against each other. Another factor was that England and France agreed to leave Thailand as a 'buffer' between their two colonies.

'England and France agreed to leave Thailand as a 'buffer' between their two colonies'

1819: Singapore is founded by British official Thomas Stamford Raffles

1862: France occupies Vietnam

1946: The Philippines wins independence

1949: Indonesia wins independence

| 1700 | 1750 | 1820 | 1860 | 1898 | 1914 | 1920 | 1930 | 1940 | 1945 | 1946 | 1948 | 1949 |

1824: Britain invades Burma capturing the capital Rangoon

1898: The USA annexes the Philippines in the aftermath of the Spanish–American War

1939–45: WWII; Japan occupies much of Southeast Asia

1948: Burma wins independence

MEET SOUTHEAST ASIA'S HISTORICAL HEAVYWEIGHTS

Aung San Burmese revolutionary assassinated in 1947; his daughter Aung San Suu Kyi continues to fight for democracy.
Ho Chi Minh Iconic Vietnamese revolutionary and communist leader.
Lee Kuan Yew Prime minister of Singapore from 1959 to 1990 – from independence to prosperity.
Soekarno Charismatic leader who united diverse Indonesia until a military coup in 1965.

Independence & Beyond

During WWII, European armies deserted Southeast Asia as the Japanese expanded their control throughout the region. After the war, the power vacuums in formerly colonised countries provided leverage for the region-wide independence movement. Vietnam and Indonesia clamoured most violently for freedom, resulting in long-term wars with their respective colonial powers. For the latter half of the 20th century, Vietnam fought almost uninterrupted conflicts against foreign powers. After the French were defeated by communist nationals, Vietnam faced another enemy, the USA, who hoped to 'contain' the spread of communism within the region. Cambodia's civil war ended in one of the worst nightmares of modern times, with the ascension of the Khmer Rouge. It evacuated the cities, separated families into labour camps and closed the country off from the rest of the world. An estimated 1.7 million people were killed by the regime during its brief four-year term (1975–79).

'Cambodia's civil war ended in one of the worst nightmares of modern times'

Many of the newly liberated countries struggled to unite a land mass that shared only a colonial legacy. Dictatorships in Myanmar, Indonesia and the Philippines thwarted the populace's hopes for representative governments and civil liberties. Civilian rioters, minority insurgents and communist guerrillas further provoked the unstable governments, and the internal chaos was usually agitated by the major superpowers: China, the Soviet Union and the USA. With the thawing of the Cold War, Southeast Asia enjoyed renewed stability and vitality thanks to several raging national economies in the 1990s. Singapore became the shining star of the region. Vietnam, Laos and Cambodia opened themselves to foreign trade, regional cooperation and tourism near the turn of the 21st century. Approaching nearly a decade of openness, former Indochina continues to acquire the internal infrastructure of the developed world, while fumbling with the fractures of rapid industrialisation and embedded corruption. Only Myanmar remains cloistered today.

In 1999, East Timor residents voted for independence from Indonesia. A new nation was born after a bloody struggle that involved an international peacekeeping effort. Now emerging out of infanthood, the young nation is struggling to establish a stable economy independent of international aid.

	1957: Independent Malaysia is founded				**1975:** Saigon falls to the North Vietnamese; Khmer Rouge takes over Cambodia			**2004:** Indian Ocean earthquake and tsunami destroys lives and communities in four Southeast Asian countries	
1954	1957	1960	1965	1970	1975	1990	1999	2002	2004
1954: Vietnam defeats the French and disintegrates French Indochina			**1965:** The British retract from Singapore				**1999:** East Timor votes for independence		

THE CULTURE

Like a symphony orchestra, Southeast Asian society is composed of a group acting in concert rather than with the independent, self-determination of Western cultures. Social harmony is ensured by the concept of 'face' – avoiding embarrassing yourself or others. This translates into everyday life by not showing anger or frustration and avoiding serious debates that could cause offence. When the bus breaks down, the passengers calmly file out into the sun and wait for the repairs without causing a scene – in this way an undercurrent of peace is brought to a chaotic situation.

See the Culture sections in country chapters in this book for notes on each country's culture and lifestyle.

> Malaysia, Thailand and the Philippines are in the midst of a cinematic new wave. Keep an eye out for leading filmmakers like Amir Muhammad, Lav Diaz and Pen-ek Ratanaruang, who are flooding international film festivals and art-house cinemas with evocative visual tales of their homelands.

Lifestyle

The diverse countries of Southeast Asia share the unifying characteristics of developing nations. Foreign visitors have varying reactions to this societal progression. Some appreciate the so-called Third World's enduring aspects of community (multigenerational homes, distinct family customs, ancestral villages) that industrialised nations have lost, while others are repulsed by the chasm between their seemingly efficient homelands and the relative poverty and chaos in Southeast Asia. Great disparity between rich and poor, entrenched corruption, and faulty infrastructure are a few of the most uncomfortable differences, although the severity varies within the region. Thailand, Malaysia and Singapore have enjoyed close to 40 years of stable governments and have entered the geopolitical equivalent of young adulthood: an affluent, educated middle class has emerged between the extremes of rich and poor. Laos, Cambodia and Vietnam are still gangly teenagers just beginning to assume adultlike characteristics. Myanmar is in a time warp, caught somewhere between the colonial era and the present.

Population

Within the dominant cultures of Southeast Asia are minority groups that remain in isolated pockets or cultural islands. Regarded as the Jews of Asia, ethnic Chinese filtered into the region as merchants, establishing distinct neighbourhoods within their host communities and perpetuating their mother country's language and customs. Every small town has a Chinatown (typically the business district). In places like Malaysia and Singapore, the Chinese Diaspora has morphed into a distinct entity, frequently termed Straits Chinese, which has merged Chinese and Malay customs, most notably in the kitchen and in conversation. Lunar holidays, such as the Chinese vegetarian festival and the New Year, are celebrated with intense devotion. While most countries derive cultural and commercial strength from Chinese immigrants, in times of economic hardship, especially in Malaysia and Indonesia, ethnic Chinese are frequently targets of abuse for their prosperity. Ethnic Indians from the southern provinces of Tamil Nadu have also settled along the Malay peninsula and remain a distinct group.

> Recommended reading: *Hot Sour Salty Sweet: A Culinary Journey Through Southeast Asia* by Jeffrey Alford; and the *Culture Shock!* series (individual books are available for Thailand, Vietnam, the Philippines etc).

High up in the mountains that run through Myanmar, Laos, northern Thailand and Vietnam, a diverse mix of minority groups, collectively referred to as hill tribes, maintain prehistoric traditions and wear elaborate costumes. Believed to have migrated from the Himalayas or southern China, hill-tribe communities such as the Akha, Karen and Mon, thanks to the geography, were relatively isolated from foreign influences. They were considered a nuisance by lowland governments until hill-tribe trekking became a widespread tourist attraction. Myanmar represents the largest concentration of hill tribes. In the outer areas of Indonesia, such as Kalimantan, Papua, Sulawesi and Sumba, indigenous people practise customs that have entered the global imagination through the glossy pages of *National Geographic*.

Food

Meet Southeast Asia's delectable fruits: jackfruit, a greenish exterior with a rubbery, rich-tasting, yellow flesh; mangosteen, a purplish baseball-sized fruit that opens to reveal a white, juicy interior; rambutan, looks like a reddish Velcro tennis ball covered with hairy spines and a juicy lychee-flavoured flesh.

Southeast Asia's tropical climate creates a year-round bounty. Food is always a cultural celebration that serves as a focal point for family gatherings and daily gossip sessions with coworkers. Many traditional holidays revolve around the harvest, from the religious observances that coincide with the beginning of rice-planting season to the various festivals of an agricultural area's hallmark crop. Food is intrinsically tied to certain Chinese and Muslim religious observances, when the faithful abstain from eating meat or fast during daylight hours. Even the invisible spirits who guide good luck in the Buddhist countries require daily offerings of food to sate their mischievous nature.

Traces of Southeast Asia's cultural parents – India and China – can be detected in the individual nations' cuisines. Myanmar is the best example of this marriage; many of its Indian-inspired curries are more like stews, and some are even served over egg noodles, a Chinese invention, rather than the common staple of rice. Thai, Indonesian and Malay curries have adapted their Indian predecessor with regional flourishes and the addition of coconut milk. Malaysia and its enduring ethnic Indian communities incorporated the roti, an Indian flatbread, and other South Indian dishes into its homegrown menu.

The Chinese donated noodle soups, which have assumed aliases in each country: laksa in Malaysia and Singapore, *pho* in Vietnam or *kŭaytĭaw* in Thailand. Noodle soups are the quintessential comfort food, eaten in the morning, after a night carousing or at midday when pressed for time. In most Southeast Asian countries, chopsticks are used only for this dish.

Vietnam has perfected the cuisine of its culinary professor. Where Chinese cuisine can be bland and oily, Vietnamese dishes are light and refreshing, including delicate spring rolls stuffed with shrimp, mint, basil leaves and cucumbers, which are sold at squat roadside stands. The French imparted a taste for crusty baguettes and thick coffees in former Indochina.

Thailand and Laos share many common dishes, often competing for the honour of spiciest cuisine (Laos wins). Green papaya salad is a mainstay of the two – the Thais like theirs with peanuts, tomatoes and dried shrimp; the Lao version uses pungent fermented fish sauce, crab and lots of chillies. In Laos and neighbouring Thai provinces, the local people eat 'sticky rice' (a shorter grain than the standard fluffy white rice), which is eaten with the hands and usually rolled into balls and dipped into spicy sauces.

As dictated by the strictures of Islam, Muslim communities in Malaysia and Indonesia don't eat pork. Interestingly, nutmeg and cloves, spices so desperately sought after by European traders, are minimally used in Indonesian cooking, regarded as more useful as medicines than flavourings. *Adobo*, a Spanish-inspired stew with local modifications, has come to symbolise Filipino cuisine. In a postcolonial age, Singapore displays its position as a cosmopolitan crossroads with the modern development of Pacific Rim fusion.

Art

Southeast Asia's most notable artistic endeavours are religious in nature and distinctively depict the deities of Hinduism and Buddhism. Both an artistic and architectural wonder, the temples of Angkor in Cambodia defined much of the region's artistic interpretation of Hinduism and Buddhism. The temples' elaborate sculptured murals pay homage to the Hindu gods Brahma (represented as a four-headed, four-armed figure) and Shiva (styled either in an embrace with his consort or as an ascetic), while also recording historical events and creation myths. Statues of Buddha reflect the individual countries' artistic interpretations of an art form governed by highly symbolic strictures. Across mainland Southeast Asia, the Buddha is depicted sitting, standing and reclining – all representations of moments in his life. In Vietnam, representations of the Buddha are more reminiscent of Chinese religious art. Also found decorating many temple railings is the water dragon Naga, which represents the life-giving power of water.

In Indonesia, Malaysia, Brunei and the Philippines, Islamic art and architecture intermingle with Hindu and animist traditions. Every town in Malaysia has a grand fortressed mosque with an Arabic minaret and Moorish tile work. Indonesia is also home to Borobudur, a Buddhist monument that complements the temples of Angkor in religious splendour.

The literary epic of the Ramayana serves as the cultural fodder for traditional art, dance and shadow puppetry throughout the region. In this fantastic tale Prince Rama (an incarnation of the Hindu god Vishnu) falls in love with beautiful Sita and wins her hand in marriage by completing the challenge of stringing a magic bow. Before the couple can live in peace, Rama is banished from his kingdom and his wife is kidnapped by Ravana. With the help of the Monkey King, Hanuman, Sita is rescued, but a great battle ensues. Rama and his allies defeat Ravana and restore peace and goodness to the land.

ENVIRONMENT
The Land

Diverse and fertile, this tropical landmass spans the easternmost range of the Himalayas reaching through northern Myanmar, Thailand, Laos and Vietnam; the rich flood plains of the mighty Mekong River; and the scattered archipelagos of Indonesia and the Philippines, made by crashing tectonic plates and exploding volcanoes.

Indonesia and the Philippines, the world's largest island chains, together contain more than 20,000 islands, some of them uninhabited. The Philippines has 11 active volcanoes; Indonesia at least 120. While the fiery exhausts destroy homes and forests, the ashen remains of the earth's inner core creates fertile farmland.

More regulatory than the seasonal temperature is the seasonal deposit of rain. When the rains come, the rivers transform from smooth looking glasses to watery bulldozers sweeping towards the sea. The dry dustbowl of the deciduous forests that occupy central mainland Southeast Asia spring to life in the rainy season. The tropical forests of the Malay peninsula, Sumatra and Borneo get two monsoon seasons, and like sponges they soak up the moisture to feed their dense canopy and limblike tendrils.

Living as a parasite in the thick jungles, the leafless plant rafflesia sprouts what looks like a cabbage head, which opens some nine months later to reveal one of the world's largest flowers, emitting an unrivalled putrid scent. Other plant species include a huge variety of bamboo and orchids. One of the region's most famous exports, teak, grows in the monsoon forests of Myanmar.

Coastal areas of Southeast Asia are characterised by mangrove trees. Beach and dune forests, which grow along the same coasts above the high-tide line, consist of palms, hibiscus, casuarinas and other tree varieties that can withstand high winds and waves.

> In the Malaysian rainforests, a native plant called *tongkat ali* has been used by the jungle dwellers as a natural form of Viagra, among less erotic applications.

Much of the landmass of Southeast Asia is covered with a thick layer of limestone, the erosion of which yields distinctive limestone towers known as karsts. Fine examples of karsts can be found in Indonesia, Malaysia, Thailand and Vietnam.

Wildlife

Tigers, elephants, Sumatran and Javan rhinoceroses and monkeys once held dominion over the region's forests. Today, these animals are facing extinction due to habitat loss and poaching. Found in Sumatra, the orang-utan is the only great ape species outside of Africa.

But perhaps more impressive is the number of bird species in Southeast Asia. Indonesia's Papua alone has more than 600 species and Thailand more than 1000 (an estimated 10% of the world's total). Large numbers of birds migrate from northern climates, heralding the approach of the monsoons. The Borneo rainforests boast a stunning array of birdlife from the turkey-sized hornbill, represented in local mythology and art, to ground-dwelling pheasants, prized by ancient Chinese traders for their plumage.

The ubiquitous geckos have adapted human habitats as their hunting grounds; they are frequently spotted hanging out around fluorescent lights catching bugs. The shy *tookay* lizard is more frequently heard than seen. In rural areas the lizard croaks its name again and again; the number of recitations has prophetic significance to the local people. Perhaps the star of the Southeast Asian animal theatre is the Komodo dragon, the world's largest lizard, found only on the Indonesian island of Komodo and a few neighbouring islands. A smaller cousin of the Komodo, the monitor lizard hangs out in the cool shade of the Malaysian jungles.

National Parks

The knotted mangrove forests that grow in swampy patches along the coast absorbed some of the 2004 tsunami's punch and in turn protected nearby coastal development.

In recent years there has been a huge increase in the amount of land set aside as national parks and wildlife sanctuaries across Southeast Asia. Thailand leads the way with an astonishing 13% of land and sea under protection (see p693), one of the world's highest ratios (compare this figure with France at 4.2% and the USA at 10.5%). Indonesia and Malaysia also boast fairly extensive national park systems.

Southeast Asia's national parks play an ever-increasing role in the region's tourism industry. Some parks are relatively undisturbed with little infrastructure, but in parks such as Thailand's marine islands, development and profit outstrip environmental protection.

Environmental Issues

Environmental degradation is immediately tangible in Southeast Asia: smoke fills the air as the forests are cleared for more beach bungalows or small-scale farms; major cities are choked with smog and pollution; the waterways are clogged with plastic bags and soft-drink cans; and raw sewage is dumped into turquoise waters. Southeast Asia faces huge challenges from its growing population. Lessons learned from unabated industrialisation by Western countries have little bearing on places struggling for economic prosperity or plagued by corruption.

LAND

The last half of the 20th century saw massive deforestation in Southeast Asia through logging and slash-and-burn agriculture. Indonesia, which contains 10% of the world's remaining tropical forests, is estimated to be losing up to 10,000 sq km of forest per year. Forests in Cambodia, Malaysia, the Philippines and Myanmar are disappearing at similarly alarming rates, earning the region the dubious title of a 'hot spot' for deforestation.

Habitat loss and poaching take a huge toll on Southeast Asia's biodiversity. Rough figures estimate that 15% of land animal species have been lost. As in other parts of the world, large mammals – including tigers, elephants and orang-utans – are the most visible and often the most critically endangered species. The number of plant species lost is probably higher, but precise figures are unavailable because science has yet to catalogue all that the forests have to offer.

WATER

Southeast Asia's coral reefs are regarded as the world's most diverse, claiming more than 600 species of coral. With increased coastal activity and global temperature changes, scientists have determined that 80% to 90% of the region's reefs are in danger of extinction.

The major culprits include dynamite and cyanide fishing, and damage by fishing nets and anchors. Careless divers are also fingered for stepping on, and in turn destroying, coral formations. Runoff from polluted or silt-laden rivers and from rampant coastal development, as well as untreated sewage dumping, are other factors. In recent years, some of the governments of Southeast Asia have made efforts to preserve their reefs by establishing marine parks and other protected zones; however, enforcement is spotty at best.

More swift than human interference was the destruction to coral reefs caused by the 2004 tsunami. It is estimated that between 5% and 13% of Thailand's coral was damaged, primarily by debris that was sucked off the mainland by the retreating waves; reefs growing close to the shore were the worst hit.

Mangrove forests along the coasts have also suffered. Countries such as the Philippines, Thailand and Cambodia have each been losing approximately 2000 sq km of mangrove forest per year. Much of this forest is being cleared for prawn (shrimp) farming and tourism development, but pollution also plays a role.

RELIGION

The dominant religions of Southeast Asia have absorbed many of the traditional animistic beliefs of spirits, ancestor worship and the power of the celestial planets in bringing about good fortune. Southeast Asia's spiritual connection to the realm of magic and miracles commands more respect, even among intellectual circles, than the remnants of paganism in Western Christianity. Thais erect spirit houses in front of their homes, ethnic Chinese set out daily offerings to their ancestors, and Muslims in Indonesia offer prayers to the volcano spirits.

Buddhism

The sedate smile of the Buddhist statues decorating the landscapes and temples summarise the nature of the religion in Southeast Asia. Religious devotion within the Buddhist countries is highly individualistic, omnipresent and nonaggressive, with many daily rituals rooted in the indigenous religions of ancestor worship.

Buddhism begins with the story of an Indian prince named Siddhartha Gautama in the 6th century BC, who left his life of privilege at the age of 29 on a quest to find the truth. After years of experimentation and ascetic practices, he meditated under a Bodhi Tree for 49 days at which point he reached final emancipation, breaking the cycle of birth, death and rebirth.

Monsoon forests occur in regions with a dry season of at least three months. Most trees are deciduous, shedding their leaves in an attempt to conserve water. Rainforests occur in areas where rain falls more than nine months a year. The forests are extremely diverse and dense.

Recommended reading: *Beyond Belief: Islamic Excursions Among the Converted Peoples* by VS Naipaul; *Siddhartha* by Hermann Hesse; *What the Buddha Taught* by Walpola Rahula; *Living Faith: Inside the Muslim World of Southeast Asia* by Steve Raymer.

He returned as the Buddha, or enlightened one, to teach the 'middle way' between extremes. Constant patience, detachment, and renouncing desire for worldly pleasures and expectations brings peace and liberation from suffering. Passion, desire, love and hate are regarded as extremes in the East.

Thailand, Cambodia, Laos and Myanmar practise Theravada Buddhism (Teaching of the Elders), which travelled to the region via Sri Lanka. Vietnam adopted Mahayana (Greater Vehicle) Buddhism, which is also found in Tibet, China and Japan. One of the major theological differences between the two types of Buddhism is the outcome of a devout life. In Theravada, followers strive to obtain nirvana, which can not be accomplished within a single lifetime but over the course of many reincarnations, the final one being a member of the monastic order. In Mahayana, within a single lifetime a lay-person can become a Bodhisattva, who delays nirvana to return to earth just as the Buddha did. Within the Theravada Buddhist countries, the artistic expressions of temple architecture and sculpture define the greatest cultural differences from country to country. Religious art and temples in Vietnam favour Chinese influences over commonalities with its Theravada neighbours.

> Most Vietnamese practice a fusion of Buddhism, Taoism and Confucianism, collectively known as the Triple Religion (Tam Giao).

Islam

In Southeast Asia, Islam bears much of the region's hallmark passivity, lacking the fervour that results from religious persecution. Southeast Asians converted to Islam to join a brotherhood of spice traders and to escape the inflexible caste system of the previous Hindu empires. Malaysia, Indonesia, parts of the Philippines and southern Thailand adopted the Sufi sect of Islam. Revealed by the Prophet Mohammed in the 7th century, 'Islam' is the Arabic word for 'submission', and the duty of every Muslim is to submit to Allah (God). This profession of faith is the first of the Five Pillars; the other four are to pray five times a day, give alms to the poor, fast during Ramadan and make the pilgrimage to Mecca.

> Indonesia is the world's most populous Muslim nation.

With the global rise of fundamentalism, attempts to introduce strict Islamic law (sharia) have increased, especially in Malaysia. Traditionally Southeast Asian Muslim women were never cloistered and never wore full purdah as in the Middle East. This has changed with alarming rapidity, according to non-Muslims in the region. Although the traditional Muslim cultures retain many animistic beliefs and practices, there are periodic cycles of purging Islam of its pagan past.

Despite the region's move towards more devout practices, the Malaysian voting populace recently halted the march toward political Islam. The long-reigning Muslim political party in the Malaysian state of Terengganu was recently voted out of office because they went too far with harsh religious penalties, attempting to outlaw traditional crafts and to introduce death by stoning for adultery. Muslim independence movements, affecting southern Thailand and the southern Philippines, are considered to be more economic than jihadist; typically these are the poorest parts of the respective countries, virtually ignored by the majority government.

> Many Thai, Burmese and Lao young men enter a monastery for a few months to make merit for their ancestors.

Catholicism

Catholicism was introduced to Vietnam by the French and to the Philippines by the Spanish. The Philippines adeptly juggle Spanish, American and Chinese traditions into Catholic festivals, like Christmas when Chinese red lanterns decorate homes while families attend midnight mass and go from house to house carolling. Parts of Indonesia and East Timor are also Catholic due to the Portuguese colonial presence.

Hinduism

Hinduism ruled the spiritual lives of Southeast Asians more than 1500 years ago, and the great Hindu empires of Angkor and Srivijaya built grand monuments to their pantheon of gods. The primary representations of the one omnipresent god include Brahma, the creator; Vishnu, the preserver; and Shiva, the destroyer or reproducer. All three gods are usually shown with four arms, but Brahma has the added advantage of four heads to represent his all-seeing presence. Once Buddhism and Islam filtered across the continent, Hinduism managed to survive on the island of Bali. Within the last 100 years, the influx of Indian labourers to Southeast Asia has bolstered the religion's followers.

Brunei Darussalam

HIGHLIGHTS

- **Kampung Ayer** – chartering a water taxi to get a fish-eye view of these ramshackle water villages (p44)
- **Brunei Museum** – browsing the brilliant Islamic Art Gallery beside the Sungai Brunei (p44)
- **Omar Ali Saifuddien Mosque** – checking out the magnificent minarets of this lagoon-encircled mosque (p44)
- **Off the beaten track** – taking a boat ride to Bangar and trekking in the pristine rainforests of Ulu Temburong National Park (p49)

FAST FACTS

- **ATMs** widespread in central Bandar Seri Begawan (BSB), Seria, Kuala Belait, Jerudong and Muara
- **Budget** US$30-40 a day
- **Capital** Bandar Seri Begawan
- **Costs** cheap room B$30, cheap meal B$3, 2hr bus ride B$6
- **Country code** ☎ 673
- **Famous for** Sultan Sir Hassanal Bolkiah, one of the richest men in the world, and his brother, Prince Jefri Bolkiah, who was sued by the sultan for allegedly misspending US$16 billion of the country's money
- **Languages** Malay, English
- **Money** US$1 = B$1.69 (Brunei dollar)
- **Phrases** *selamat pagi* (good morning), *berapa harganya* (how much is it), *terima kasih* (thank you)
- **Population** 375,000

- **Seasons** high Apr-Sep, low Oct-Mar
- **Visas** not needed for citizens of the UK, Germany and New Zealand (up to 30 days), or US citizens (up to 90 days); most others get a 14-day visa on arrival (see p52 for details)

TRAVEL HINT

Fill up on cheap food at night markets, but be warned that the nutritional value will often be minimal.

OVERLAND ROUTES

From Brunei you can travel west into Sarawak and east into Sabah, both of which are Malaysian states.

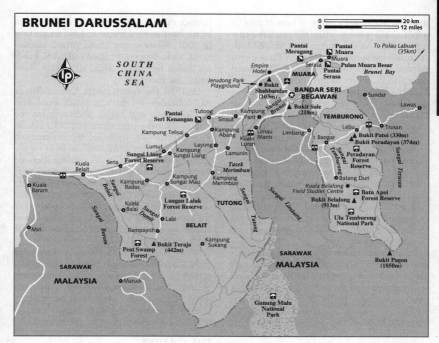

It's one of the smallest countries in the world, but Brunei is also one of the richest. It's a strict Islamic nation with several magnificent places of worship that intimidate with their grand scale and glow powerfully when illuminated at night; yet there's a worldliness and sense of ease about Bruneians that makes it hard not to feel relaxed around them. The capital, Bandar Seri Begawan (BSB), is about as well equipped and orderly as any city within the overheated environs of Southeast Asia can afford to be, yet lining the Sungai Brunei (Brunei River) are stilt villages so lean and deceptively shabby-looking that they seem to be a caricature of the city itself. And while Brunei makes its living by efficiently plundering natural resources from underground, nearly 80% of the country is covered by pristine rainforest threaded by mangrove-lined rivers and walking trails, all of it suffused with a sense of adventure. Such are the contrasts of this intriguing sultanate blessed by a wealth of traditional culture and modernity. Since achieving independence from Britain, it has been known rather fittingly as Negara Brunei Darussalam – Brunei, the Abode of Peace.

CURRENT EVENTS

From the outside, Brunei appears to be an immensely wealthy country with few socio-economic problems: all local education and medical treatment is free, there's no income tax and the government loans cash to all prospective home buyers. But the sources of the sultanate's financial contentment – oil and natural gas – are predicted to run out in the next 30 to 40 years, and when this happens it will have a profound effect on how the next generation of Bruneians live and work. The government, overseen by Sultan Sir Hassanal Bolkiah, is beginning to prepare for this by concentrating on the development of tourism and aquaculture industries.

HISTORY

The first recorded references to Brunei are in documents regarding China's trading connections with 'Puni' in the 6th century AD during the Tang dynasty. Before the region embraced Islam, Brunei was within the boundaries of the Sumatran Srivijaya empire, then the Majapahit empire of Java. It may be hard to believe considering the country's current diminutive size, but in the 15th and 16th centuries the sultanate held sway throughout Borneo and into the Philippines. This lasted up to 1838, when British adventurer (and budding imperialist) James Brooke helped the sultan put down a rebellion from warlike inland tribes. As a reward, the sultan granted Brooke power over part of Sarawak, which in hindsight was a big mistake.

Appointing himself Raja Brooke, James Brooke pacified the tribespeople, eliminated the much-feared Borneo pirates and forced a series of 'treaties' onto the sultan, whittling the country away until finally, in 1890, it was actually divided in half. This situation still exists today – if Bruneians want to get to the Temburong district, they have to go through Sarawak.

Facing encroachment by European land-grabbers, Brunei became a British protectorate in 1888. But it got its own back when oil was discovered in 1929. The development of offshore oil fields in the 1960s really allowed Brunei to flourish. In early 1984 Sultan Sir Hassanal Bolkiah, the 29th of his line, led his country somewhat reluctantly into complete independence from Britain. He celebrated in typically grandiose style by building a US$350 million palace.

The Asian crisis of 1998 (when Thailand's currency nose-dived after too many years of unsustainable growth, sparking similar recessions across Southeast Asia) was a wake-up call for Brunei, with the sultan's personal fortune being considerably depleted. But the greatest shock to the country was delivered by the sultan's younger brother, Prince Jefri, who around the same time managed to go on a US$16 billion spending spree. This included gambling debts that totalled nearly US$25 million – and he was the country's

finance minister! He was eventually reeled in by his brother and forced to hold an auction in 2001, where many of his prized possessions, including gold-plated toilet-roll holders and a helicopter flight simulator, went under the hammer.

In 1998 the sultan's son, Crown Prince Al-Muhtadee Billah, was proclaimed heir to the throne and began preparing for the role as Brunei's next ruler and 30th sultan. That preparation included the 30-year-old prince's wedding in September 2004 to 17-year-old Sarah Salleh, in a ceremony attended by thousands of guests. While Brunei may not be facing the same promise of prosperity that existed when the current sultan took the throne in 1967, it's clear that the sultan sees the crown prince's careful apprenticeship as crucial for the continuing (and absolute) rule of the monarchy.

There was a whiff of reform in November 2004 when the sultan amended the constitution to allow for the first parliamentary elections in 40 years. However, only one-third of parliamentarians will be publicly elected at a yet-to-be-decided date – the rest will still be hand-picked by the sultan.

THE CULTURE

Brunei can be seen as the most Islamic country in Southeast Asia. The sale of alcohol was banned in 1991, stricter dress codes were introduced and, in 1992, Melayu Islam Beraja (MIB; the national ideology that stresses Malay culture, Islam and monarchy) became a compulsory subject in schools. The country is also ruled by an Islamic monarchy. The sultan is head of the religion of the country, and holds the three key cabinet positions: prime minister, defence minister and finance minister.

However, don't expect to find some grim Southeast Asian enclave of fundamentalism. Bruneians are proud of their country, have a high standard of living with many domestic mod-cons, and harbour an international perspective and openness towards visitors. Perhaps it's their Islamic piety and strong cultural identity, in conjunction with wealth and a global outlook, that have given Bruneians an advantage in handling modernity.

Bruneian customs, beliefs and pastimes are very similar, if not identical, to those of the Malays of western Malaysia. *Adat* (social law) governs many local ceremonies,

---

MUST READ

Green Days in Brunei, by Bruce Sterling, is a classic cyberpunk short story (albeit less punkish than the work of contemporaries such as William Gibson), in which programmer Turner Choi slowly comes to grips with this multiracial society and, in the process, himself. You can read it in the collection of Sterling's stories called *Crystal Express*.

particularly royal ceremonies and formal state occasions.

People of Malay heritage and indigenous Kedayan, Tutong, Belait, Bisayah, Dusun and Murut peoples make up approximately 67% of the 375,000-strong population. Iban, Kelabit and other tribes contribute to around 6%, and people of Chinese heritage account for 15% of the population. Westerners, Thais, Filipinos, Indonesians, Indians and Bangladeshis – generally the population of temporary workers – make up the rest.

RELIGION

Although Brunei is a strict Muslim country, with a Ministry of Religious Affairs that fosters and promotes Islam, only 67% of the population is actually Muslim. Buddhists and Christians make up 13% and 10% of the population respectively, and 10% of people have kept their indigenous beliefs.

ARTS

Traditional arts have all but disappeared in modern Brunei. In its heyday, the sultanate was a source of brassware in the form of gongs, cannons and household vessels (such as kettles and betel containers) that were prized throughout Borneo and beyond. The lost-wax technique used to cast bronze declined with the old fortunes of the Brunei sultanate. Brunei's silversmiths were also celebrated. *Jong sarat* sarongs, using gold thread, are still prized for ceremonial occasions, and the art of weaving has survived.

ENVIRONMENT

Brunei consists of two areas, separated by the Limbang district of Sarawak, and covers a total area of just 5765 sq km. The western part of Brunei contains the main towns: BSB, the oil town of Seria (where the sultanate's billionth barrel was filled in 1991)

and the commercial town of Kuala Belait. The eastern part of the country, the rural Temburong district, is much less developed. Away from the coast, Brunei is mainly jungle, with approximately 78% of the country still covered by forest.

Wildlife species found in Brunei are similar to those found in the rest of Borneo. Proboscis monkeys, gibbons, hornbills, deer, monitor lizards, crocodiles and the rare clouded leopard live in the rainforest. Brunei has several recreational parks and forest reserves, plus one national park – the superb Ulu Temburong National Park, a 500-sq-km swathe of protected primary rainforest.

TRANSPORT

GETTING THERE & AWAY
Air

Brunei's sole airport is 10km from the centre of the capital. The national airline, Royal Brunei Airlines, has direct flights between BSB and major Asian destinations such as Jakarta, Bangkok, Hong Kong, Kuala Lumpur and Manila, as well as flights to Kota Kinabalu in Sabah. Malaysia Airlines, Singapore Airlines and Thai Airways also fly into BSB. For sample fares and airline offices in BSB, see p46.

> **DEPARTURE TAX**
>
> There's a departure tax of B$5 when flying to Kuching (in Sarawak Province) or Kota Kinabalu (in Sabah Province), both in Malaysian Borneo, and B$12 to all other destinations.

Being a Muslim airline, Royal Brunei does not serve alcohol on its flights.

Boat

Boats headed to Pulau Labuan in Sabah and Lawas in Sarawak depart from the Serasa Ferry Terminal, 25km northeast of BSB near Muara. There's also a boat that goes from BSB to Limbang in Sarawak. For details on these services, see p46.

Bus & Car

The main overland route to the west is between Kuala Belait in Brunei and Miri in Sarawak. It's also possible to travel south

> **DID YOU KNOW?**
>
> Brunei has a cattle station in Australia that is larger than Brunei itself. The 5986-sq-km station in Willaroo, in the Northern Territory, supplies Brunei with beef and other meat products. The live cattle are brought direct to Brunei from Darwin and slaughtered according to halal practices.

from BSB to Limbang. For information on both routes, see p46.

GETTING AROUND
Boat
The only significant boat service within Brunei connects BSB with Bangar in the Temburong district.

Bus
Brunei isn't a huge place, but outside BSB and off the main routes it's hard to get around without a car. The local bus system within and around BSB is very good and gets you to most places for B$1 to B$2. However, services stop at 6pm and after that you'll have to rely on expensive taxis.

Car
Renting a car is the easiest way to get around Brunei, and Bruneian drivers are quite sane by Southeast Asian standards. It's expensive though (rental starts from B$70 per day) and involves a steep learning curve if you're not used to driving on the left-hand side.

Hitching
Hitching is remarkably easy in Brunei. Chances are you'll stick out your thumb and get a ride instantly, and it's a great way to meet local people. That said, always be careful. Even though Brunei is probably one of the safest places to hitch in Southeast Asia, it's wise to take precautions. Women especially should not hitch alone; if possible, travel with a male companion.

Water Taxi
Most short water-taxi trips cost around B$2, and you can hire your own water taxi for B$20 to B$25 per hour. To flag one down, head out to one of the many jetties jutting onto the river in and around BSB, and simply wave. The city's waterfront is filled with buzzing water taxis, even at night.

BANDAR SERI BEGAWAN

pop 81,500

Bandar Seri Begawan (usually called BSB or Bandar) is the capital of Brunei and is most notable for the absence of the mayhem that most travellers in Southeast Asia expect to greet them upon arrival in any sizable city.

In fact, central BSB introduces itself to the traveller as a quiet, pleasant, greenery-dotted city with a low skyline that's decorated with minarets and neat arrangements of buildings. But despite the city's almost relentlessly tidy character, and the fact that residents are the first to admit there's little to do here at night besides wander dirt-free shopping malls, it's a mistake to dismiss BSB as being unworthy of exploration.

By day you can visit the enigmatic Kampung Ayer, with its tenuous huts and domestic clamour, and take a water taxi downriver to some fine museums. Or, inspired by the calls to prayer that echo across the city at 5am, you can wander around some wonderfully imposing mosques. Bruneians are generally reserved but liven up considerably in conversation, and their friendliness and helpfulness is exceptional.

There are also night markets to ransack and tours into the country's immaculate rainforests to organise. There's simply no excuse not to have a good look around.

ORIENTATION
The centre of BSB lies at the confluence of the Sungai Brunei and Sungai Kedayan, and is compact enough to explore in about an hour. The magnificent Omar Ali Saifuddien Mosque makes a grand landmark on the western edge of the city centre. The post office and tourist information centre are both a short walk north of the bus station along Jl Sultan. Most sights are within walking distance or a short bus or water-taxi ride of the city centre.

GETTING INTO TOWN
BSB's modern airport is 10km northwest of the city. Buses 23, 24 and 38 will get you to/from the airport for B$1. As you leave the terminal, walk diagonally south for 300m to reach the bus stop. Taxis will charge around B$25 for trips between the airport and city centre (the price goes up by at least B$5 after 6pm); taxis are unmetered so agree on the price before getting in.

If you travel into BSB by bus you'll end up at the bus station right in the centre of town. Boats from Limbang (Sarawak) arrive at a jetty off Jl McArthur, also in the centre of town.

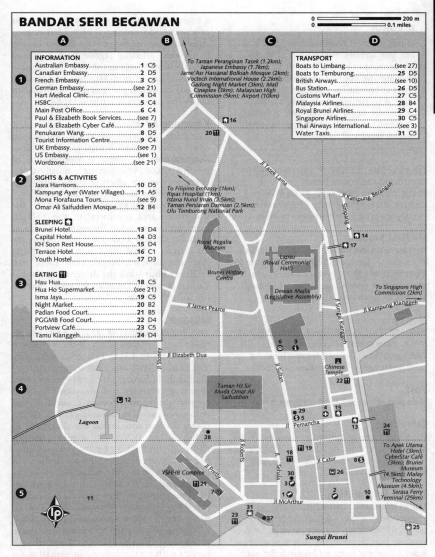

BANDAR SERI BEGAWAN

0 — 200 m
0 — 0.1 miles

INFORMATION
Australian Embassy.....................1 C5
Canadian Embassy.......................2 D5
French Embassy...........................3 C5
German Embassy....................(see 21)
Hart Medical Clinic.....................4 D4
HSBC...5 C4
Main Post Office.........................6 C4
Paul & Elizabeth Book Services...(see 7)
Paul & Elizabeth Cyber Café......7 B5
Penukaran Wang........................8 D5
Tourist Information Centre..........9 C4
UK Embassy...........................(see 7)
US Embassy............................(see 1)
Wordzone...............................(see 21)

SIGHTS & ACTIVITIES
Jasra Harrisons.........................10 D5
Kampung Ayer (Water Villages)..11 A5
Mona Florafauna Tours..........(see 9)
Omar Ali Saifuddien Mosque....12 B4

SLEEPING
Brunei Hotel.............................13 D4
Capital Hotel............................14 D3
KH Soon Rest House..................15 D4
Terrace Hotel............................16 C1
Youth Hostel.............................17 D3

EATING
Hau Hua....................................18 C5
Hua Ho Supermarket.............(see 21)
Isma Jaya..................................19 C5
Night Market............................20 B2
Padian Food Court....................21 B5
PGGMB Food Court..................22 D4
Portview Café...........................23 C5
Tamu Kianggeh.........................24 D4

TRANSPORT
Boats to Limbang...................(see 27)
Boats to Temburong................25 D5
British Airways......................(see 10)
Bus Station...............................26 D5
Customs Wharf.........................27 C5
Malaysia Airlines......................28 B4
Royal Brunei Airlines................29 C5
Singapore Airlines.....................30 C5
Thai Airways International......(see 3)
Water Taxis...............................31 C5

To Taman Peranginan Tasek (1.2km);
Japanese Embassy (1.7km);
Jame'Asr Hassanal Bolkiah Mosque (2km);
Voctech International House (2.2km);
Gadong Night Market (3km); Mall
Cineplex (3km); Malaysian High
Commission (5km); Airport (10km)

To Filipino Embassy (1km);
Ripas Hospital (1km);
Istana Nurul Iman (2.5km);
Taman Persiaran Damuan (2.5km);
Ulu Temburong National Park

Royal Regalia Museum

Brunei History Centre

Lapau (Royal Ceremonial Hall)

Dewan Majlis (Legislative Assembly)

To Singapore High Commission (2km)

Jl James Pearce

Jl Stoney

Jl Elizabeth Dua

Jl Sultan

Taman HJ Sir Muda Omar Ali Saifuddien

Chinese Temple

Jl Tasek Lama

Jl Kampung Berangan

Simpang 2

Jl Sungai Kianggeh

Jl Kampung Kianggeh

Lagoon

Jl Pemancha

To Apek Utama Hotel (3km); CyberStar Café (3km); Brunei Museum (4.5km); Malay Technology Museum (4.5km); Serasa Ferry Terminal (25km)

Jl Cator

Jl Roberts

Jl Sehala

Jl Pretty

YSHHB Complex

Jl McArthur

Sungai Brunei

INFORMATION
Bookshops
Paul & Elizabeth Book Services (☎ 222 0958; 2nd fl, Block B, YSHHB Complex, Jl Pretty) Has a small range of English-language paperbacks.

Wordzone (☎ 223 2764; basement, YSHHB Complex, Jl Pretty) Carries newspapers and there are a few shelves of trashy preloved paperbacks.

Emergency
Ambulance (☎ 991)
Fire (☎ 995)
Police (☎ 993)

Internet Access
Web access will usually cost you B$1 per hour.

ALCOHOL

Brunei is a strict Muslim country that does not sell alcohol. However, non-Muslims are permitted to bring in up to 12 cans of beer and two bottles of liquor for their personal consumption. You must declare any alcohol to customs upon entering Brunei or you risk being charged with trafficking an illegal substance, which is an extremely serious charge.

CyberStar Café (☎ 222 1267; Jl Kota Batu; ☺ 9am-10pm) Opposite Apek Utama Hotel.
Paul & Elizabeth Cyber Café (☎ 222 0958; 2nd fl, Block B, YSHHB Complex, Jl Pretty; ☺ 9.30am-9pm) Centrally located but has temperamental machines.

Medical Services
Hart Medical Clinic (☎ 222 5531; 1st fl, Wisma Setia, 47 Jl Sultan; ☺ 8am-noon & 1-5pm Mon-Sat, 8-11am Sun)
Ripas Hospital (☎ 224 2424; Jl Tutong; ☺ 24hr) A fully equipped, modern hospital across the Edinburgh bridge on the western side of Sungai Kedayan.

Money
HSBC (☎ 225 2222; cnr Jl Sultan & Jl Pemancha) Charges B$15 to change most travellers cheques and has an ATM.
Penukaran Wang (Ground fl, Britannia House, 1 Jl Cator) Next to Rupiah Express; exchanges cash only.

Post
Main post office (cnr Jl Sultan & Jl Elizabeth Dua)

Telephone
Payphones are common in the city centre, and they accept 10c or 20c coins. Phonecards are available from post offices and many retail shops and hotels.

Tourist Information
Tourist information centre (☎ 222 3734; www .tourismbrunei.com; Ground fl, Post Office Bldg, cnr Jl Sultan & Jl Elizabeth Dua) Run under the auspices of Mona Florafauna Tours, the information centre distributes a free *Brunei: A Kingdom of Unexpected Treasures* leaflet, which has a BSB map and bus route details, and the informative free *Traveller Leisure Guide* brochure.

SIGHTS
Omar Ali Saifuddien Mosque
Named after the 28th sultan of Brunei, the **Omar Ali Saifuddien Mosque** (☎ 222 2623; admission free; ☺ nonprayer-time visits 8am-noon, 2-3pm, 5-6pm

& 8-9pm Sat-Wed) was built in 1958 at a cost of about US$5 million. The golden-domed structure stands close to the Sungai Brunei in its own artificial lagoon and is one of the tallest buildings in the city. The mosque is only open to non-Muslims at specified times (outside prayer times). Ask if you can climb the minaret when you visit.

Kampung Ayer
The rustic collective of 30 stilt villages on either side of Sungai Brunei is referred to as **Kampung Ayer**. It's home to a population of around 32,000, who pursue a mostly traditional way of life, albeit in prefab dwellings with plumbing, electricity and colour TV.

Wandering the village plankwalks (try the waterfront area southwest of the YSHHB Complex) or weaving through the maze of stilts in a water taxi (B$2) are highlights. To charter a boat for a tour of Kampung Ayer and the river shouldn't cost more than B$20 per hour – ask the driver to stop off at Taman Persiaran Damuan for great views of the sultan's palace.

Museums
The **Brunei Museum** (☎ 222 3235; Jl Kota Batu; admission free; ☺ 9.30am-4.30pm Sat-Thu, 9-11.30am & 2.30-4.30pm Fri) is 4.5km east of central BSB. The Islamic Art Gallery has some wonderful illuminated (decorated) copies of the Koran, stunning ceramics and glass artefacts and (our favourite) an Ottoman 'decorative boot with compass'. The oil and gas exhibit explains how Brunei found the slick road to riches in the 1920s; the display's hi-tech nature is summed up by the museum brochure: '…parts of the exhibit are in the form of models with electric gadgets'.

Descend the stairs from the car park behind the museum, then turn right to reach the **Malay Technology Museum** (☎ 224 4545; admission free; ☺ 9.30am-4.30pm Sat-Thu, 9-11.30am & 2.30-4.30pm Fri). A pair of rooms here have interesting life-sized re-creations of stilt houses with accompanying information on traditional cultures. The rest of the large building, however, is strangely empty.

Bus 39 will get you out here.

Other Attractions
A fine example of Islamic architecture is **Jame'Asr Hassanal Bolkiah Mosque** (☎ 223 8741; Jl Hassan Bolkiah, Gadong; admission free; ☺ 8am-noon,

2-3pm, 5-6pm & 8-9pm Sat-Wed), the largest mosque in the country. This fabulous sight is in Gadong, a few kilometres northwest of town. Equally photogenic is the **Istana Nurul Iman** (☎ 222 9988; Jl Tutong), the sultan's magnificent palace, which looks particularly impressive when illuminated at night. The Istana is open to the public only at the end of the fasting month of Ramadan and is 2.5km out of town. The best vantage points are from the river and **Taman Persiaran Damuan**, a landscaped park nearby. From BSB, take a water taxi there in the early evening and get off at the park.

Taman Peranginan Tasek is a beautiful forested area with waterfalls and trails. In the early morning or late evening, you may be lucky enough to see some proboscis monkeys. Walk or take a bus past the Terrace Hotel. After passing two sets of traffic lights, turn right and you'll see the entrance.

TOURS

Tours offered from BSB include roaming the waterlogged byways of Kampung Ayer, searching for proboscis monkeys along mangrove-lined rivers and exploring the depths of Ulu Temburong National Park. Prices hinge on the number of paying customers and are far cheaper if there are two or more people. Most three- to four-hour tours cost between B$40 and B$75, while day trips average B$100.

Reputable travel agents:

Jasra Harrisons (☎ 224 3911; jasratvl@brunet.bn; cnr Jl McArthur & Jl Sungai Kianggeh) Good, general travel agent; organises trips to Ulu Temburong. It's also the sales agent for British Airways and Qantas.

Mona Florafauna Tours (☎ 222 3734; Ground fl, Post Office Bldg) Runs BSB's tourist information centre and specialises in outdoor and wildlife tours around the country.

Tours of Ulu Temburong National Park and visits to nearby longhouses (enormous wooden structures on stilts that house tribal communities) can also be organised in Bangar, the main town in the Temburong region. See p48 for details.

SLEEPING

With the exception of the youth hostel, true budget accommodation is a rarity in BSB. You'll just have to grit your teeth and force yourself to enjoy the extra level of comfort afforded by accommodation in the Bruneian capital.

Youth Hostel (Pusat Belia; ☎ 222 2900; Jl Sungai Kianggeh; dm B$10; ✕ ▣) This hostel is part of a youth centre and provides BSB's cheapest accommodation in simple four-bed dormitories. It's often empty but can sometimes fill up with sports groups. Reception is officially open until 10pm but staff are usually occupied elsewhere and it's a minor miracle if you can track anyone down after 5pm. Visitors can use the complex's inviting pool (B$1).

Voctech International House (Seameo Voctech; ☎ 244 7992; www.voctech.org.bn; Jl Pasar Baharu, Gadong; s/d B$40/50; ✕ ▣) Voctech hosts various conferences but also welcomes travellers. The accommodation is excellent, featuring superefficient staff, free transport to and from the airport, and large rooms with a fridge, TV and balcony. An extra B$5 per person gets you breakfast in the on-site café, which serves good, low-priced meals. It's a fair way from the city centre (catch bus 1 or 22), but BSB's lack of nightlife makes that irrelevant, and it's only a short walk from Gadong's huge mall and a terrific night market.

Apek Utama Hotel (☎ 222 0808; Simpang 229, Jl Kota Batu, Kampung Pintu Malim; r B$30; ✕) Established in a one-time government-office building, this friendly and very helpful hotel has good-value rooms and a TV lounge in which to stare vacantly at local soap operas. It's 3km east of town, accessed by bus 39 or by water taxi. Across the parking lot is a good little café.

KH Soon Rest House (☎ 222 2052; 2nd fl, 140 Jl Pemancha; s B$30-35, d B$35-40) Decent budget choice for those seeking a central location, though the stark white paintwork gives it a clinical feel. Rooms are threadbare but huge (a victory for space over substance), and an extra B$5 snags you an attached bathroom.

Other recommendations:

Capital Hotel (☎ 222 3561; 7 Simpang 2, Jl Kampung Berangan; r from B$50; 🖾) Faded place with an un-scrubbed exterior but friendly staff and OK rooms. At the end of an uninviting sidestreet.

Terrace Hotel (☎ 224 3554; www.terracebrunei.com; Jl Tasek Lama; s/d/tw from B$60/65/70; 🖾 🖫) Has very comfortable rooms. Use of a swimming pool and a snooker table are yours once you get past the ugly monochrome exterior.

EATING

Isma Jaya (☎ 222 0229; 27 Jl Sultan; meals B$4-7; 🕑 breakfast, lunch & dinner) The modern, tiled interior of relaxed Isma Jaya makes a nice re-treat from the hot outdoors. Lunchtime often sees the menu of soups, mee and nasi dis-carded in favour of a hearty buffet (B$5.50).

Hau Hua (☎ 222 5396; 48 Jl Sultan; meals B$2.50-10; 🕑 lunch & dinner) Nice, scrupulously clean café that has some reasonable vegetable and bean-curd dishes, a range of fresh juices and a glass cabinet full of cheap takeaway buns.

Portview Café (☎ 223 2555; Jl McArthur; mains B$8-13; 🕑 lunch & dinner) This café is a tourist favour-ite for its outside deck, where you can watch boats thump across choppy Sungai Brunei and dart in and out of Kampung Ayer. The menu is predominantly Malaysian, Chinese and Thai, with an emphasis on seafood. Portview has merged with an Italian res-taurant called Fratini's and offers a separate menu of pastas and pizzas (B$9 to B$25).

If you're staying at Voctech, visit the wonderful **night market** (Jl Kiulap, Gadong; snacks B$1-3; 🕑 dinner) behind Pasar Gadong (a wet market), where you can try kebabs, deep-fried treats and enough sweets to rot every tooth overnight. There's another **night market** (Jl Tasek Lama; 🕑 dinner) serving cheap hawker food, opposite the Terrace Hotel.

The **PGGMB food court** (2nd fl, PGGMB Bldg, Jl Sungai Kianggeh; meals B$1-4; 🕑 breakfast, lunch & din-ner) in the shiny new PGGMB building has a large open-air balcony that overlooks the bustle of Tamu Kianggeh and its surround-ing greenery. Also worth browsing is the **Padian Food Court** (1st fl, YSHHB Complex, Jl Pretty; meals B$2-6; 🕑 lunch & dinner).

Self-caterers can walk across the canal to the local produce market, **Tamu Kianggeh** (Jl Sun-gai Kianggeh; 🕑 breakfast, lunch & dinner), where food stalls are sometimes set up. Supplies can also be bought at **Hua Ho Supermarket** (☎ 223 1120; basement, YSHHB Complex, Jl Pretty; 🕑 10am-10pm).

ENTERTAINMENT

Mall Cineplex (☎ 242 2455; 4th fl, The Mall, Gadong; admission B$4-8) English-language films are part of the programme here. It's located in Gadong's vast shopping plaza.

GETTING THERE & AWAY
Air

The one-way economy air fare between BSB and Kota Kinabalu is roughly B$110, and

---

BORDER CROSSING: INTO MALAYSIA

From the Serasa Ferry Terminal, 25km northeast of BSB near Muara, express boats go to Pulau Labuan in Sabah (B$15, 1½ hours, six departures between 7.30am and 4.40pm). Only one boat departs from Serasa each day for Lawas in Sarawak (B$15, 40 minutes, 11.30am). Check the ferries link on the web-site www.bruneibay.net for the latest schedules from Serasa. Passengers are charged B$1 departure tax at the ferry terminal. For info on getting to BSB from Pulau Labuan see the boxed text, p507.

Boats to Limbang in Sarawak (B$10, 30 minutes) are supposed to make regular departures from the customs wharf (where immigration formalities take place), but the service is highly unreliable and departures are often delayed until more passengers turn up. Buy your ticket from the kiosk on the edge of the Immigration Control Point car park. An alternative to the boat trip is to catch bus 42, 44 or 48 south to Kuala Lurah (B$1, 30 minutes, last departure 5pm) on the Brunei–Sarawak border, from where you can catch another bus (RM5) or taxi (RM15) to Limbang. Note that return boat services from Limbang are as unreliable as those in the other direction and you may have to re-enter Brunei by road; for more on the return trip see the boxed text, p500.

To get to Miri in Sarawak, take a bus to Seria (B$6, two hours) and then buy a combined ticket for the three buses that will take you to Miri (B$11.20, four hours). You change buses in Kuala Belait (B$1 from Seria), cross the river, and switch again at Kuala Baram (Malaysia) for the border. Immigration and customs formalities are taken care of on both sides of the Brunei–Sarawak border. For information on crossing the border in the other direction, see the boxed text, p497.

between BSB and either Kuala Lumpur or Singapore is B$415. Other Asian destinations linked to BSB include Bangkok (B$405), Jakarta (B$330), Manila (B$470), Hong Kong (B$530) and Shanghai (B$840). Discounts and promotions are often offered by **Royal Brunei Airlines** (☎ 221 2222; www.bruneiair.com).

Airline offices or general sales agents in BSB include the following:

British Airways (☎ 224 3911; jasratvl@brunet.bn; Jasra Harrisons, cnr Jl McArthur & Jl Sungai Kiangggeh)

Malaysia Airlines (☎ 222 4141; www.malaysiaairlines .com; 144 Jl Pemancha)

Royal Brunei Airlines (☎ 221 2222; www.bruneiair.com; RBA Plaza, Jl Sultan)

Singapore Airlines (☎ 224 4901; www.singaporeair .com; 1st fl, Wisma Raya Bldg, 49-50 Jl Sultan)

Thai Airways International (THAI; ☎ 224 2991; www.thaiair.com; 4th fl, 401-403 Kompleks Jl Sultan, 51-55 Jl Sultan)

Boat

Boats to Bangar (B$6, 45 minutes, hourly from 7am to 1pm) depart from the Temburong ferry terminal, beside the Arts & Handicraft Centre; the ticket seller will ask you for your passport number and expiry date.

GETTING AROUND
Bus

BSB's reliable bus network operates 6am to 6pm. The bus station is beneath the multistorey car park on Jl Cator. All trips within BSB proper cost B$1. To get to the northwestern suburb Gadong, catch bus 1 or 22.

An express bus (B$2, 40 minutes) departs BSB at 6.30am, 7am, 8.45am, 11.40am, 2pm, 2.30pm and 3.45pm daily for the Serasa Ferry Terminal.

Car

Prices for car rental start at B$70 per day. There are several agencies in town; ask at your hotel. A reasonable, recommended company is **Azizah Car Rentals** (☎ 222 9388; CM11 Cheong's Mansion).

Taxi

Taxis in BSB are all unmetered and you need to negotiate the fare with the driver. A trip across town will usually cost B$10, but rates can climb by as much as 30% after 6pm. Lots of taxis congregate at the bus station, but you may have trouble flagging one down further afield.

Water Taxi

Water taxis are a good way of getting around if your destination is anywhere near the river. Wave them down near the customs wharf, the Tamu Kiangggeh food market or in front of the YSHHB Complex. Fares for short trips shouldn't cost more than B$2 – be firm about this.

AROUND BANDAR SERI BEGAWAN

The serene expanses of forest around BSB, particularly those within the protective borders of Ulu Temburong National Park, make excellent day trips from the Bruneian capital. To the north of the city there are also some nice beaches, a giant amusement park, and a grand hotel that was part of one of the world's most breathtakingly self-indulgent shopping sprees.

BEACHES

Pantai Muara (Muara Beach) is a popular weekend retreat located 2km from Muara town, which is 25km northeast of BSB. The white sand is clean but like many Bornean beaches it's littered with driftwood and other debris. Other beaches around Muara include **Pantai Serasa** and **Pantai Meragang** (also known as Crocodile Beach). If you want solitude, don't go on the weekend.

Get to Muara by express bus (B$2) from BSB. Bus 33 will take you from Muara town to either Pantai Muara or Pantai Serasa for B$1. You'll have to get to Pantai Meragang, 4km west of Muara, under your own steam or hitch a ride.

JERUDONG

The Jerudong area to the northwest of BSB has a couple of sizable distractions.

Jerudong Park Playground (☎ 261 1894; Jerudong; admission & unlimited rides B$15, or admission B$1 & individual rides B$3; ☯ 5pm-midnight Wed-Fri & Sun, 5pm-2am Sat) is a sprawling, decade-old amusement park. Many rides are showing their age but there are a couple of worthwhile thrills, in particular the Pusang Lagi ride, a kind of inverted roller coaster where you're strapped into a seat dangling from a steel rail and flung around at disturbing speeds. The park's main problem is that on most nights it's practically deserted – during our weeknight visit only a handful of rides were open and ride attendants were often in hiding. Try to go on Saturday when the crowds are at their biggest and consequently nearly all the rides should be open.

Also in Jerudong is the **Empire Hotel** (☎ 241 8999; www.empire.com.bn; Muara-Tutong Rd), a prominent (and, to many, painful) reminder of Prince Jefri's scandalous spending habits. The palatial Empire cost US$1.1 billion to build, and it shows – from the oxygen-thin heights of the monumentally lavish lobby to the Jack Nicklaus–designed golf course. The sultan repossessed the hotel from his brother, and the rooms, which start at B$450 (one suite costs B$22,000 per night), are now helping to refill government coffers.

Getting There & Away

Bus 55 travels to Jerudong (B$1) from the BSB bus terminal, passing near the amusement park. From the last stop on the route it's a 25-minute walk along the highway to the Empire. However, the service inconveniently stops running after 5.30pm. A taxi back to BSB will cost around B$30.

A better alternative is the service offered by the tourist information centre (see p44), which will take you to Jerudong and back for B$15 per person (minimum two people) at pre-arranged times and includes a quick detour to check out the interior of the Empire Hotel if requested.

KUALA BELAIT

Kuala Belait is a transit point for buses heading west across the Brunei–Sarawak border to Miri (via Kuala Baram; see the boxed text, p46) and there's really no reason to stay here. The HSBC bank opposite the bus station has an ATM – handy for arrivals from Sarawak.

From Kuala Belait there are regular buses to Seria (B$1) and from there frequent services to BSB (B$6). Up to five buses a day leave for Miri (B$10.20, 2½ hours); the last bus is at 3.30pm.

TEMBURONG

Temburong is the eastern slice of Brunei that is surrounded by a claw of Sarawakian territory. It's a region of lush virgin rainforest reached by a pleasant boat ride from BSB that zips down narrow waterways past feather-shaped nipa palms and mangroves. You can explore Temburong on a tour from BSB (p45), but tours organised in Bangar (see below) are usually far less expensive.

Bangar

Bangar is a small town on the banks of Sungai Temburong that seems perpetually half-asleep, even though it's the administrative centre of (and gateway to) the Temburong district. The **Temburong tourist information centre** (☎ 522 1439; 13 Kedai Rakyat Jati; ⌚ 8am-noon & 1.30-4.30pm Mon-Sat, 8am-noon Sun) provides useful information and books tours. Exiting the boat wharf in Bangar, turn left and you'll find the information centre in the cinnamon-coloured block of offices just before the road bridge.

TOURS

You can visit and stay in one of the Iban longhouses around **Batang Duri**, 17km south of Bangar. Trips to Ulu Temburong National Park work out cheaper the bigger your group is, mainly due to the one-off cost of longboat hire.

Labar Bin Hussin Traditional Crafts (☎ 522 1705, 863 1823; 5 Kedai Rakyat Jati) arranges overnight longhouse stays for B$10 (bring your own food) plus B$30 for transport. For day trips to Ulu Temburong, the estimated per-person cost is B$30 for transport to/from the longboat jetty, B$120 (split between one to five people) for longboat hire and B$5 for admission to the park.

Also organising trips to longhouses and the wild environs of the national park, and quoting similar rates, is the Temburong tourist information centre.

SLEEPING & EATING

Bangar Resthouse (☎ 522 1239; Jl Batang Duri; dm B$10-25; 🅿) This is a government-run complex with hospitable staff and lots of six-bed rooms, each with attached bathroom, a small fridge and TV. Prices are perfect for groups, with one/two people charged B$25/30, and each extra person levied only B$10. From the boat wharf, walk to the bridge, turn right and head 200m to the Jl Batang Duri turn-off – the resthouse is on the corner, signed 'Rumah Persinggahan Keragaan Daerah Temburong'. Bring your own towel and soap.

Youth Hostel (☎ 522 1694, 522 1718; dm B$10) This basic hostel is part of a youth centre and sits in a fenced compound across a side-road from the information centre. It offers bunk beds in fan-cooled rooms and was being renovated at the time of writing. The office is upstairs.

Bangar Restoran (☎ 522 1341; 6 Kedai Pekan Bangar; meals B$2-6; ☼ lunch & dinner) One in a row of four similar coffee shops serving the usual array of quickly plated Malaysian meals. It's in the last row of shops before the road bridge.

Ulu Temburong National Park

The 500-sq-km **Ulu Temburong National Park** (admission B$5) is surrounded by the Batu Apoi Forest Reserve, which covers most of southern Temburong. One of the many pleasures of visiting this stronghold of primary rainforest is that the only access is by longboat. It contains the **Kuala Belalong Field Studies Centre**, a scientific research centre devoted to the study of tropical forests.

It's possible to visit the park on a tour from BSB (see p45) or Bangar (see opposite).

Peradayan Forest Reserve

Fifteen kilometres southeast of Bangar and protected within the **Peradayan Forest Reserve** (admission free) are the peaks of **Bukit Patoi** and **Bukit Peradayan**, which can be reached along walking tracks (bring your own water and trail food). Watch your step on the boardwalks as some of the planks are rotten. The walk through rainforest to Bukit Patoi (5km, one hour) has fine views and starts at the park entrance. Most walkers descend back down this trail but it's possible to continue over the summit and around to Bukit Peradayan (four hours) on a harder, less distinct path.

Inquire about transport to/from the reserve at the information centre in Bangar.

Getting There & Away

Boats to Bangar (B$6, 45 minutes, hourly from 7am to 1pm) depart from the Tembu-rong Ferry Terminal in BSB. The last boat back to BSB leaves Bangar at 3.30pm.

BRUNEI DIRECTORY

ACCOMMODATION

If you're arriving from other countries in Southeast Asia, be prepared for a shock – accommodation in Brunei is expensive. The youth hostel in BSB is the only inner-city option that can truly be called budget. Accommodation in Bangar in the Temburong district is reasonably priced. Except for most hostels and the cheapest hotels, room prices will include an attached bathroom.

ACTIVITIES

Besides swimming at a couple of reasonable beaches to the north of BSB (see p47), the only activity of note in Brunei is walking. Thanks to the sultanate's well-protected tree line, particularly in the Temburong district (opposite), walkers can stride through undisturbed rainforest and up jungle-covered mountain peaks.

BOOKS

For more in-depth coverage of travel in Brunei, grab a copy of Lonely Planet's *Malaysia, Singapore & Brunei* guidebook.

History of Brunei (2002) by Graham Saunders is a thorough, up-to-date history of the sultanate from its beginnings to modern times.

Time and the River (2000) by Prince Mohamed Bolkiah describes the changes to the country as seen through the eyes of the sultan's youngest brother.

By God's Will – A Portrait of the Sultan of Brunei (1989) by Lord Chalfont takes a measured look at the sultan and his dominion.

New World Hegemony in the Malay World (2000) by Geoffrey C Gunn gives an insight into the more contemporary political issues for Brunei and the region.

BUSINESS HOURS

Private offices usually operate from 8am to 5pm on weekdays, and 8am to noon on Saturday. Banking hours are typically 9am to 3pm Monday to Friday and 9am to 11am on Saturday. Government offices open from 7.45am to 12.15pm and from 1.30pm to 4.30pm daily except Friday and Sunday.

BORDER CROSSING: INTO MALAYSIA

It's possible to travel by road from Bangar to Lawas in Sarawak (then by bus to Kota Kinabalu in Sabah), though this 40-minute trip entails an expensive taxi ride. For information on crossing the border in the other direction, see the boxed text, p500.

Most shops open at 10am and close at 9.30pm. During Ramadan, office hours are often shorter. Restaurants typically open around 11am and don't close until after 9pm; cafés open from around 8am.

CLIMATE

Brunei is warm to hot year-round, with heavy (albeit variable) rainfall that peaks from September to January. See the BSB climate chart on p924.

DISABLED TRAVELLERS

The streets of BSB are less embellished with random piles of rubble and the pavements are more even than, for instance, in neighbouring Malaysia. But ramps for wheelchairs and public transport that allows ready access to the mobility impaired are unfortunately still lacking. The standard of accommodation in the capital is such that many hotels have lifts.

DRIVING LICENCE

An International Driving Permit (IDP) is required for driving in Brunei.

EMBASSIES & CONSULATES
Embassies & Consulates in Brunei

For locations of the following embassies and consulates, see the BSB map (p43).
Australia (☎ 222 9435; austhicom.brunei@dfat.gov.au; 4th fl, Teck Guan Plaza, Jl Sultan)
Canada (☎ 222 0043; hicomcda@brunet.bn; 5th fl, Jl McArthur Bldg, 1 Jl McArthur)
France (☎ 222 0960; france@brunet.bn; 3rd fl, 301-306 Kompleks Jl Sultan, 51-55 Jl Sultan)
Germany (☎ 222 5547; prgerman@brunet.bn; 2nd fl, Unit 2.01, Block A, YSHHB Complex, Jl Pretty)
Japan (☎ 222 9265; embassy@japan.com.bn; 33 Simpang 122, Kampung Kiulap)
Malaysia (☎ 238 1095; mwbrunei@brunet.bn; 61 Simpang 336, Jl Kebangsaan)
Philippines (☎ 224 1465; bruneipe@brunet.bn; 17 Simpang 126, Km 2, Jl Tutong)
Singapore (☎ 222 7583; singa@brunet.bn; 8 Simpang 74, Jl Subok)
UK (☎ 222 2231; brithc@brunet.bn; 2nd fl, Unit 2.01, Block D, YSHHB Complex, Jl Pretty)
USA (☎ 222 0384; amembassybrunei@state.gov; 3rd fl, Teck Guan Plaza, Jl Sultan)

Brunei Embassies & Consulates Abroad

Australia (☎ 02-6285 4500; 10 Beale Cres, Deakin, ACT 2600)

Canada (☎ 613-234 5656; 395 Laurier Ave East, Ottawa ON, K1N 6R4)
France (☎ 01 53 64 67 60; 7 Rue de Presbourg, Paris 75017)
Germany (☎ 030-206 07 600; Kronenstrasse 55-58, 10117 Berlin)
Japan (☎ 03-3447 7997; 5-2 Kita-Shinagawa 6-Chome, Shinagawa-ku, Tokyo 141-0001)
UK (☎ 020-7581 0521; 19 Belgrave Sq, London SW1X 8PG)
USA (☎ 202-237 1838; www.bruneiembassy.org; 3520 International Court, Washington DC 2008)

For details of visa requirements, see p52.

FESTIVALS & EVENTS

Hari Raya Aidilfitri Feasting and celebration marking the end of Ramadan (a variable date, based on the Islamic calendar). Sultan's palace is open to visitors.
National Day Parade and procession in central BSB on 23 February.
Sultan's Birthday Marked by fireworks and various processions on 15 July.

FOOD & DRINK

Bruneian cookery is almost identical to Malaysian cuisine, with strong Chinese, Malay and Indian influences. The country also hosts plenty of Western-style restaurants and cafés to please expats, businesspeople and tourists. One traditional Bruneian dish to look out for is *ambuyat*, which is prepared sago served in a gluey mass and eaten with chopsticks.

The preferred liquids in Brunei are also very similar to the choices in Malaysia (see p518), with the exception of anything containing alcohol of course.

At markets and in food courts you can expect to pay from B$1 to B$5, while a simple café meal usually costs from B$4 to B$8.

GAY & LESBIAN TRAVELLERS

Homosexual acts are illegal in Brunei and can be subject to 10 years of imprisonment and a fine of up to B$30,000. Needless to say, whatever gay scene there is in Brunei is rather discreet.

HOLIDAYS

As in Malaysia, the dates of most religious festivals are not fixed as they are based on the Islamic calendar. Fixed holidays:
New Year's Day 1 January
National Day 23 February
Anniversary of the Royal Brunei Armed Forces 31 May
Sultan's Birthday 15 July
Christmas Day 25 December

Variable holidays:
Chinese New Year January/February
Nuzul Al-Quran January/February
Hari Raya Aidilfitri January/February
Isra Dan Mi'Raj February
Anniversary of the Revelation of the Koran April
First Day of Hijrah April/May
Hari Raya Haji June
Hari Moulud (Prophet's Birthday) July/August
Israk Mikraj October/November
1st Day of Ramadan November/December

School holidays take place from mid-November to the beginning of January, and for a week at the end of March, the last two weeks of June and the second week of September.

INTERNET ACCESS

Internet cafés are becoming more common in Brunei and connections are fast. The price per hour is generally B$1.

INTERNET RESOURCES

www.bruneibay.net Plugs programmes for Intrepid Tours and is geared to an upmarket crowd, but has detailed information, including a very useful ferry schedule.
www.brunet.bn/news/bb Website of the *Borneo Bulletin*, the most popular English-language newspaper in Brunei, with plenty of news on the sultanate.
www.tourismbrunei.com Official tourism website, lacking in practical details but has a BSB map and accommodation and travel agency listings.

LEGAL MATTERS

Drug trafficking in Brunei does carry a mandatory death penalty, and being a foreigner will not save you from the gallows. If you do happen to bring alcohol into this strict Islamic country without declaring it to customs and you are caught, you face severe penalties. See the boxed text on p44 for a summary of what visitors are permitted to bring in when it comes to the subject of alcohol.

LEGAL AGE

In Brunei:

- you can begin driving at 18
- heterosexual sex is legal at 14 for males and 16 for females

---

MAPS

The tourist information centre in BSB distributes the free *Brunei: A Kingdom of Unexpected Treasures* leaflet, which has a BSB map and bus route info. The best map of the sultanate is probably the *Road Map and Street Index of Brunei Darussalam*, published by Shell and usually (though not always) available in bookstores.

MONEY

The official currency is the Brunei dollar (B$), but Singapore dollars are equally exchanged and can be used. Banks give around 10% less for cash than travellers cheques.

Brunei uses 1c, 5c, 20c and 50c coins, and notes in denominations of B$1, B$5, B$10, B$50, B$100, B$500, B$1000 and B$10,000.

ATMs are common, and if the banks are closed you can usually find a moneychanger who can also change travellers cheques. Bargaining is reserved for taxis, water taxis and markets (not for food). Credit cards are widely accepted.

Country	Unit	B$
Australia	A$1	1.27
Canada	C$1	1.43
Euro zone	€1	2.03
Japan	¥100	1.47
Malaysia	RM10	4.49
New Zealand	NZ$1	1.18
UK	£1	2.96
USA	US$1	1.69

POST

Postal services in Brunei are quite reliable. BSB's main post office has a poste restante service. Post offices are open from 8am to 4.30pm Monday to Thursday and Saturday, and from 8am to 11am and 2pm to 4pm Friday.

The cost of an airmail postcard to Malaysia and Singapore is 20c; to most other countries in Southeast Asia 35c; to Europe, Africa, Australia and the Pacific 50c; and to the Americas 60c.

RESPONSIBLE TRAVEL

Bruneians are scrupulous about keeping their cities and towns relatively clean, due in no small part to some rigid social standards. It's out in the fragile rainforest that visitors can play their part. Just remember the golden rule when it comes to walking or trekking: if you carry it in, carry it out. This applies to easily forgotten items such as foil, plastic wrapping and tissues. Never bury your rubbish – it may be out of sight, but it won't be out of reach of animals.

TELEPHONE

Brunei has no area codes. The country code is ☎ 673 and the international access code is ☎ 00. Payphones are common in the city centre, and they accept 10c or 20c coins. Phonecards are available from post offices and many retail shops and hotels. There are three types of phone cards: Hallo, JTB and Zippi.

TOILETS

Toilets in Brunei are a mixture of Western-style devices and Asian-style squat toilets, with the latter predominating once you get outside BSB. In rural toilets, toilet paper isn't usually provided. So if using a hose or a bucket of water isn't to your liking, carry your own roll of toilet paper or a packet of tissues.

TOURIST INFORMATION

Brunei's tourist infrastructure isn't well established and at this stage is a cooperative effort between government and private enterprise. Nonetheless, you'll find handy information centres in both BSB and Bangar. The information centre in the capital has plenty of material to look at, and helpful staff.

TOURS

The only practical way of exploring much of the rainforest embedded in Brunei's overgrown south is by taking a tour. A number of tours can be arranged in BSB

(see p45), but generally the tours organised in Bangar (see p48), in the middle of the Temburong district, are less expensive, especially for groups.

VISAS

Countries whose citizens are eligible for visa-free entry for 14 days include Belgium, Canada, Denmark, France, Indonesia, Italy and Japan. Nationals of Germany, Ireland, Malaysia, the Netherlands, New Zealand, Singapore, South Korea and the UK are among those eligible for 30-day visa-free entry. US citizens do not need a visa for visits of up to 90 days. Australians are issued on arrival with a visa valid for a 14-day stay or can apply on arrival for 30-day multiple-entry visas (B$20).

Transit visas valid for 72 hours are apparently also issued to certain travellers, including Australian passport holders. We say 'apparently' because there's no information about such visas online (in fact, Bruneian government websites tend to contradict each other on the subject of visas). Rather, we were told this by an embassy representative. Needless to say, it's best to ring your nearest Bruneian embassy or consulate (see p50) to confirm what visa options are available to you.

There are visa-granting facilities at the borders with Sabah and Sarawak, but the process is time-consuming – it's much easier if you can organise one in advance of your visit.

WOMEN TRAVELLERS

Brunei is a relatively safe country for women travelling on their own. Try to respect local customs and avoid wearing shorts above the knee and sleeveless shirts.

Cambodia

HIGHLIGHTS

- **Temples of Angkor** – marvelling at the world's most spectacular temples and the heart and soul of the Khmer nation – astounding, inspiring and unforgettable (p86)
- **Phnom Penh** – checking the pulse of resurgent Phnom Penh, a crossroads of Southeast Asia's past, present and future (p62)
- **Sihanoukville** – getting happily horizontal on the sands of Cambodia's beach capital, and enjoying its tropical islands, fresh seafood and burgeoning nightlife (p101)
- **Ratanakiri Province** – swimming in a jungle-shrouded volcanic crater, swinging from vines into remote waterfall pools and trekking the uncharted Virachey National Park (p114)
- **Battambang & Around** – playing chicken on the bamboo train and delving into the region's contrasting histories: ancient and recent, brilliant and bloody (p94)
- **Off the beaten track** – taking a 'before' picture of your backside and seeking out Preah Vihear Province's amazing lost jungle temples and rare Angkorian bridges (p98)

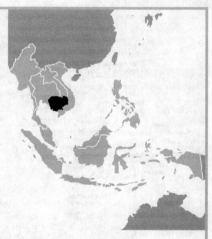

FAST FACTS

- **ATMs** credit-card-compatible ATMs (Visa and MasterCard only) are now in most major cities
- **Budget** US$15-20 a day
- **Capital** Phnom Penh
- **Costs** guesthouse in Sihanoukville US$3-10, 4hr bus ride US$3, draft beer from US$0.50
- **Country code** ☎ 855
- **Famous for** Angkor Wat, Khmer Rouge
- **Languages** Khmer, English, French, Mandarin
- **Money** US$1 = 4111r (riel)
- **Phrases** *sua s'dei* (hello), *lia suhn hao-y* (goodbye), *aw kohn* (thank you), *somh toh* (I'm sorry)
- **Population** 13.5 million
- **Seasons** wet May-Oct, dry Nov-Apr
- **Visas** US$20 for one month; issued at most borders and all airports

TRAVEL HINT

Do as the locals do and buy a *krama* (checked scarf); it's great for sun protection, dust protection, as a towel, as a bandage…anything is possible with the *krama* chameleon.

OVERLAND ROUTES

From Thailand cross into Cambodia's south coast at Krong Koh Kong or further north at Poipet. From Vietnam, convenient buses link Ho Chi Minh City with Phnom Penh. Break the mould and enter Cambodia from Laos in the northeast at Koh Chheuteal Tom, north of Stung Treng.

CAMBODIA

CAMBODIA

You have trusted your eyes your entire life, but visit Cambodia and you just may start to have doubts. How else could you explain the unthinkable splendour of the 9th- to 13th-century Khmer empire's temples, the tropical islands with barely a beach hut in sight and the untold adventures lurking in northern forests? Well, you can cancel your ophthalmologist's appointment, suspend your cynicism and delve into Cambodia's doctrine of disbelief.

Your heart will race at Angkor Wat, one of the world's greatest achievements, only to haltingly derail when faced with the impact of humankind's darkest moments. For after two decades of war and isolation, only now is Cambodia truly starting to recover from the Khmer Rouge's genocidal 1975–79 rule. A visit to sites commemorating their atrocities will paralyse your soul as well as enlighten your mind…you'll never look at the world the same again.

While infrastructure is now making trips to major sights a breeze, explorations to Preah Vihear's astonishing remote jungle temples and Ratanakiri's wildlife-filled forests are something like Cambodia's history: a mix of heaven and hell. How much you enjoy Southeast Asia's last true adventures may depend on which body part you talk to – the key is to never listen to your backside.

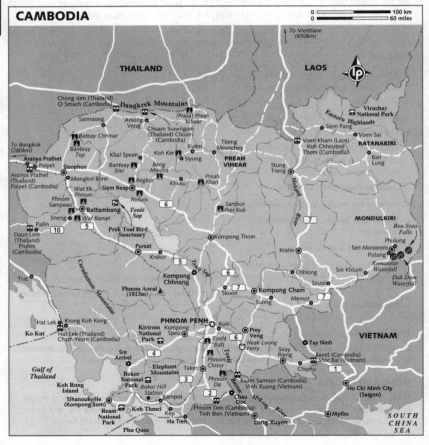

CURRENT EVENTS

Corruption is a word on everyone's lips these days. If you cross into Cambodia by land you may well curse it yourself. Don't say it too loud or you may end like Sam Rainsy, the leader of the opposition party (Sam Rainsy Party) and an outspoken advocate against government corruption. He'd accused Prince Norodom Ranariddh, the leader of the National United Front for an Independent, Neutral, Peaceful & Cooperative Cambodia (Funcinpec), of taking a US$30 million bribe from Hun Sen's Cambodian People's Party (CPP) to form a timely coalition government in mid-2004. On 3 February 2005, the CPP and Funcinpec changed the laws to strip sitting politicians of their parliamentary immunity and promptly charged Sam Rainsy with defamation and arrested two other Sam Rainsy Party politicians. Sam Rainsy quickly fled the country and is currently in exile, appealing to foreign governments to condemn the Cambodian government's repressive tactics. On 10 March 2005, the European Parliament unanimously adopted just such a resolution. The impact of these actions on the electorate and more importantly, Hun Sen's grip on power, remains to be seen.

HISTORY

The good, the bad and the ugly is the easiest way to sum up the history of Cambodia. Things were good in the early years, culminating in the vast Angkor Empire, unrivalled in the region over three centuries of dominance. From the 13th century the bad set in as ascendant neighbours steadily chipped away at Cambodian territory. In the 20th century it turned downright ugly, as a brutal civil war culminated in the genocidal rule of the Khmer Rouge (1975–79) from which Cambodia is still recovering.

Early Years

From the 1st to the 6th centuries, much of present-day Cambodia was part of the kingdom of Funan, whose prosperity was due in large part to its position on the great trade route between China and India. India had the greatest cultural impact and its language, religion and culture was absorbed by Cambodians. A series of small kingdoms then developed, and they unified to create the Chenla empire, the mightiest in the history of Southeast Asia.

Rise and Fall of Angkor

The Khmer empire of the Angkorian era, known for its unrivalled achievements in architecture and sculpture, began under Jayavarman II in 802. During his rule, a new state religion established the Khmer ruler as a *devaraja* (god-king). Vast irrigation systems facilitated intensive cultivation around Angkor, allowing Khmers to maintain a densely populated, highly centralised state that controlled vast swathes of territory across the region. Overstretched outposts, overambitious construction projects and increasingly belligerent neighbours weakened the Angkor Empire. When Thais sacked Angkor in 1432, it was the last straw; the city was abandoned and the capital moved near Phnom Penh. Subsequently, Thai and Vietnamese kingdoms steadily occupied areas of Cambodia, and by the mid-19th century the kingdom was in danger of being squeezed off the map.

Enter the French

Ironically it was the French who preserved the borders, establishing a protectorate from 1864 until independence in 1953. However, the French were more interested in Vietnam's economic potential and left Cambodia to fester. As WWII drew to a close, there were still no universities and only one secondary school!

Independence

A new world emerged from the war and Cambodia's young King Norodom Sihanouk, seeing that colonialism was a dying force, began his crusade for independence, which the French reluctantly granted in 1953. For 15 years King Sihanouk (later prince, prime minister, chief-of-state, king again and now Great Heroic King Sihanouk or His Majesty the King Father since his surprise abdication in 2004) dominated Cambodian politics. The late 1950s and early 1960s were Cambodia's golden years, as the economy prospered while neighbouring countries grappled with domestic insurgencies. However, Sihanouk's erratic and repressive policies alienated both the left and right; the army overthrew him in 1970 and he fled to Beijing. Under pressure from the Chinese, he threw in his lot with Cambodia's weak, indigenous rebels, the Khmer Rouge (French for 'Red Khmer'), boosting their support dramatically.

DID YOU KNOW?

The UN incomprehensibly conferred legitimacy on the Khmer Rouge after its overthrow in 1979, granting it the Cambodian seat at the UN General Assembly until 1991.

Coming of War

From 1969 Cambodia was sucked into the Vietnam conflict. The US secretly began carpet-bombing suspected communist base camps in Cambodia and, shortly after the 1970 coup, American and South Vietnamese troops invaded the country to root out Vietnamese communist forces. They failed and only pushed Cambodia's communists and their Vietnamese allies deep into Cambodia's interior. Savage fighting soon engulfed the entire country, ending only when Phnom Penh fell to the Khmer Rouge on 17 April 1975, two weeks before the fall of Saigon.

Khmer Rouge Takeover

After taking Phnom Penh, the Khmer Rouge, under Pol Pot's leadership, implemented one of the most heinous revolutions the world has ever seen. It was 'Year Zero' and Cambodia was to become a Maoist, peasant-dominated, agrarian cooperative.

During the next four years, hundreds of thousands of Cambodians, including the vast majority of the country's educated people, were relocated to the countryside, tortured to death or executed. Thousands of people who spoke foreign languages or wore spectacles were branded as 'parasites' and systematically killed. Hundreds of thousands more died of mistreatment, malnutrition and dis-

DID YOU KNOW?

Pol Pot, born Saloth Sar in 1925, learnt about radical Marxism in Paris before becoming a school teacher back in Cambodia. Very few people knew of him until he emerged as the public face of the Khmer Rouge revolution towards the end of 1976. Pol Pot died on 15 April 1998, after facing a Khmer Rouge show trial for his crimes. His death perhaps forever robbed the Cambodian people of the chance for truth and justice. Did he jump or was he pushed?

ease. Almost two million Cambodians died between 1975 and 1979 as a direct result of the policies of the Khmer Rouge.

In late 1978 Vietnam invaded and overthrew the Khmer Rouge, who fled westward to the jungles bordering Thailand. In the subsequent chaos, millions of Cambodians set off on foot to find out if family members had survived the apocalypse. Crops wilted during a severe famine in 1979 and 1980 and cruelly killed hundreds of thousands more. Meanwhile, the Khmer Rouge maintained a guerrilla war throughout the 1980s, armed and financed by China and Thailand (and with indirect US support), against the Vietnamese-backed government in Phnom Penh.

A Sort of Peace

In 1991 the warring sides met in Paris and signed a peace accord, which enabled UN-administered elections in 1993. A new constitution was drawn up and adopted, and Norodom Sihanouk once again became king. The government was a volatile coalition of Prince Norodom Ranariddh's Funcinpec and Hun Sen's CPP. Although both were co–prime ministers, the real power was wielded by Cambodia's so-called strongman, Hun Sen, the erroneously named Second Prime Minister, whom the Vietnamese had originally installed. As the bickering intensified, he overthrew First Prime Minister Ranariddh during a July 1997 coup. Ranariddh came back as head of the National Assembly in a later deal.

End of the Khmer Rouge

While hardly a triumph for democracy, the first parliament did witness the Khmer Rouge's eventual death in 1998 after it was decimated by a series of mass defections.

Two decades after the tragic Khmer Rouge revolution, a historic agreement between the UN and the Cambodian government created the first court to bring surviving members to trial, but bureaucratic bickering at home and abroad has stalled its opening. Many Cambodians lament that it's already too late to try Pol Pot, who escaped punishment when he died in 1998.

Cambodia Today

Cambodia is at a crossroads on its journey to recovery from the brutal years of Khmer Rouge rule and must soon choose its path: pluralism, progress and prosperity or intimidation, impunity and injustice. While it's clear the populace want long-term progress, the powerful elite seem stuck on short-term gain.

The mercurial monarch King Sihanouk surprised the world with his unconstitutional passing of the throne to his relatively unknown son King Sihamoni, a former ballet dancer. However, Prime Minister Hun Sen will continue to wear the proverbial crown and wield all the power. Despite losing an eye in the 1975 battle of Phnom Penh, Sen's never lost sight of ultimate power and recently removed parliamentary immunity, enabling him to arrest politicians accusing him of corruption. With a poorly educated electorate and the opposition either on the run or under his thumb, it appears that 'in the country of the blind, the one-eyed man is king'.

THE CULTURE
The National Psyche

While on the surface Cambodia appears to be a nation full of shiny, happy people, a deeper look reveals a country of contradictions. Light and dark, old and new, rich and poor, love and hate, life and death; all are visible on a journey through the kingdom, but most telling is the glorious past set against Cambodia's tragic present.

Angkor is everywhere: on the flag, the national beer, hotel and guesthouse names, cigarettes – it's anything and everything. A symbol of nationhood and fierce pride, it's a fingers-up to the world, stating no matter how bad things have gotten lately, Cambodians built Angkor and it doesn't get better than that. This explains why it's a touchstone for most Cambodians and the fact that Thailand occupied it for more than a century still troubles relations today. Jayavarman VII, Angkor's greatest king, is nearly as omnipresent as his temples, still a national hero for vanquishing the occupying Chams and taking the empire to its greatest glories.

The contrast with the hellish abyss into which Cambodia was sucked by the Khmer Rouge has left a people profoundly shocked. Pol Pot is still a dirty word due to the death and suffering he inflicted. Whenever you hear his name, there'll be stories of endless personal tragedy, of dead brothers, mothers and babies, from which

most Cambodians have never been able to recover. Such suffering takes generations to heal. Meanwhile the country is crippled by a short-term outlook that encourages people to live for today, and not to think about tomorrow because a short while ago there was no tomorrow.

If Jayavarman and Angkor are loved and Pol Pot hated, the mercurial Great Heroic King Sihanouk is somewhere in the middle, the last of the god-kings, who has ultimately shown himself to be human. Many Cambodians love him as the nation's father and his portrait is ubiquitous, but to others he's the man who failed them with his Khmer Rouge association. In many ways, his contradictions are those of contemporary Cambodia. Understand him and what he's had to survive and you'll understand much of Cambodia.

Lifestyle

The defining influences for many older Cambodians are the three Fs: family, faith and food. Family is more than the nuclear family we Westerners know; it's the extended family of third cousins and obscure aunts – as long as there's a bloodline there's a bond. Families stick together, solve problems collectively, listen to elders' wisdom and pool resources. Whether the house is big or small, one thing's for sure – there'll be a big family inside.

Faith is another rock in the lives of many older Cambodians, and Buddhism has helped these Cambodian people to rebuild their shattered lives after waking from the nightmare that was the Khmer Rouge. Most Cambodian houses contain a small shrine to pray for luck and wats fill with the faithful come Buddhist Day. Food is more important to Cambodians than to most Southeast Asians, as they have tasted what it's like to be without. Rice is a staple with every meal and many a Cambodian driver cannot go on without his daily fix.

But to the young generation of teenagers brought up on a steady diet of MTV and steamy soaps, it's a different story. They'll defer to their parents as long as they have to, but what they really want is what teenagers everywhere want – do we need to spell it out? Cambodia is a country undergoing rapid change, but for now the traditionalists are just about holding their own, although the onslaught of karaoke is proving hard to resist.

Population

The 1998 Cambodian census counted 11.8 million people, but it's believed the population now stands at around 13.5 million. With the country's 2.4% birth rate, it should be even higher, but grinding poverty and a poor health-care system have bred disease and led to a depressing infant mortality rate of 96 per 1000 live births, four times that of Thailand or Vietnam. An astounding 40% of the population is under the age of 15.

Officially 96% of Cambodians are described as ethnic Khmer (ethnic Cambodians), suggesting Cambodia is the most ethnically homogeneous country in Southeast Asia. Unofficially it's another story, as there are many more Chinese and Vietnamese in Cambodia than the government ever admits, and a great deal of intermarriage. The Chinese have long played a dominant role in Cambodian commerce. While official estimates put their numbers at around 50,000, it's probably 10 times that. As for the Vietnamese, many immigrated under the French and later during Vietnam's 1980s occupation, and are engaged in fishing and skilled trades across the country.

Cambodia's Cham and Malay Muslims probably account for up to half a million people in the provinces around Phnom Penh. They suffered vicious persecution between 1975 and 1979 and many were exterminated.

Cambodia's diverse *chunchiet* (ethnolinguistic minorities) have traditionally isolated themselves in the country's remote mountainous regions. This suited the Cambodians who were, the truth be told, somewhat afraid of them. Today, *chunchiet* total about sixty to seventy thousand, with the most important groups being the Kreung in Ratanakiri and the Pnong in Mondulkiri.

RELIGION

Theravada Buddhism is the dominant religion in Cambodia and guides the lives of many Khmers. The Khmer Rouge launched an assault on all beliefs but their own, murdering most of Cambodia's monks before being overthrown in 1979. Wats were destroyed or turned into pigsties, but in the past decade there's been a dramatic resurgence in religious worship and Buddhism once again leads the way.

Hinduism flourished alongside Buddhism from the 1st century AD until the 14th century and some elements of it are still incorporated into important ceremonies involving birth, marriage and death.

There is also a significant minority of Cham and Malay people who practise Islam.

ARTS

The fact that centuries-old sculptures, stylised dances and architecture still spellbind the modern visitor speaks volumes.

The Khmer's astounding architecture and sculpture reached its zenith during the Angkorian era, exemplified by Angkor Wat, the many temples of Angkor Thom and the sublime carvings of Banteay Srei. Many of the finest Khmer sculptures are on display at the stately National Museum in Phnom Penh.

Perhaps more than any other traditional art, the royal ballet of Cambodia is a tangible link with the glory of Angkor. Its *apsara* dance is unique to Cambodia, while the court dance has roots in India and Java, with many dances enacting scenes from the Hindu epic the Ramayana, known as the *Reamker* in Cambodia. To see how much traditional dance has blossomed after the apocalyptic Pol Pot years, visit the Royal University of Fine Arts in Phnom Penh (p75).

Like much of Southeast Asia, when it comes to contemporary culture, music rules the roost. This has spawned some homegrown talent like the prolific pop star Preap Sovath, who at the age of 33 has already

---

MUST SEE

The Killing Fields (1984) is a Roland Joffé film about American journalist Sydney Schanberg and his Cambodian assistant during and after the civil war.

recorded over 10,000 songs! You won't need to search for his music, it'll find you – trust us.

While you'll have no clue what he's saying, Nay Krim's comedy antics will likely leave you laughing. He often graces the TVs aboard long-distance buses.

The film industry in Cambodia was given a new lease of life in 2000 with the release of *Pos Keng Kong* (The Giant Snake). A remake of a 1950s Cambodian classic, it tells of a powerful young girl born from a rural relationship between a woman and a snake king. Since its release local directors have turned up production to a dozen films a year.

ENVIRONMENT
The Land
Cambodia covers an area of 181,035 sq km, almost half the size of Italy or Vietnam. The country is dominated by water and it doesn't get much bigger than the Mekong River, cutting through the country from north to south, and the Tonlé Sap (Great Lake), Asia's largest lake. There are three main mountainous regions: the Elephant and Cardamom Mountains in the southwest, the Dangkrek Mountains along the northern border with Thailand, and the Eastern Highlands in the northeast.

The average Cambodian landscape is a patchwork of cultivated rice paddies guarded by numerous sugar palms, the national tree. Elsewhere are grasslands, lush rainforest cloaking the remote areas, and, at higher elevations, unlikely clumps of pines.

Wildlife
Some environmentalists believe what's left of Cambodia's dense jungles hides a host of secrets, including a biodiversity of species as rich as any in Asia. The country's large mammals include tigers, leopards, bears, elephants, wild cows and deer, although exact numbers are unclear due to remote habitats and the impact of hunting. There are several dangerous species of snake, including the king cobra, banded krait and the small haluman.

The many bird species in the country include cormorants, cranes, kingfishers and pelicans, but these often end up in the cooking pot thanks to eagle-eyed kids with catapults. Keen birders should make the boat trip between Siem Reap and Battambang (p85) to glimpse the Prek Toal Bird Sanctuary, which is home to rare water birds such as lesser and greater adjutants, milky storks and spot-billed pelicans.

The Mekong is second only to the Amazon in fish biodiversity and hosts some mighty 3m-long catfish. The rare freshwater Irrawaddy dolphin also inhabits the Mekong north of Kratie.

National Parks
Almost 23% of Cambodia comprises protected areas and national parks, although these are little more than lines on a map – in practice there's very little protection. Four national parks can handle visitors, although facilities at each are pretty limited: huge and unexplored Virachey, in the far northeast, spanning Ratanakiri and Stung Treng Provinces; Kirirom, popular with Khmers, just off the road to Sihanoukville; Ream, a maritime park near Sihanoukville; and beautiful Bokor, a former French hill station near Kampot.

Environmental Issues
Head into the remote northwest or northeast corners of Cambodia and you will soon realise that logging is the biggest threat to the country's environment. Smouldering stumps seem to outnumber trees in some areas of Cambodia and the rainforest that covered almost 75% of the country in the 1960s now covers just 30%.

An emerging environmental threat is the damming of the Mekong River. The financial boom of the numerous mega-projects isn't lost on the United Nations Development

> **DID YOU KNOW?**
>
> During the rainy season from June to October, the Mekong rises dramatically, forcing the Tonlé Sap river to flow northwest into the lake of the same name. During this period, the vast lake swells from around 3000 sq km to almost 13,000 sq km and from the air Cambodia looks like one almighty puddle. As the Mekong falls during dry season, the Tonlé Sap river reverses its flow, and the lake's floodwaters drain back into the Mekong. This unique process makes the Tonlé Sap one of the world's richest sources of freshwater fish – now that's a reversal of fortune!

Programme (UNDP) or the Asia Development Bank (ADB), who've offered to pay for much of the development. Let's hope long-term interests won't be scrapped for short-term profits.

TRANSPORT

GETTING THERE & AWAY

Air

Cambodia is connected by regular air services to its Southeast Asian neighbours. The following prices were quoted by a reputable agent in Phnom Penh. See p76 for details of airline offices in the capital.

LAOS

Vietnam Airlines links Phnom Penh with Vientiane (US$160/310 one way/return), while Lao Airlines connects Vientiane and Siem Reap (US$130/250 one way/return).

MALAYSIA

Malaysia Airlines has daily flights connecting Phnom Penh and Kuala Lumpur (US$280/360 one way/return).

SINGAPORE

SilkAir Singapore with daily flights from the capital Phnom Penh (US$295/420 one way/return) and Siem Reap (US$295/420 one way/return).

> **DEPARTURE TAX**
>
> There's a cheeky departure tax of US$25 on all international flights out of Phnom Penh and Siem Reap.

THAILAND

Bangkok Airways links Bangkok with both Phnom Penh (US$115/160 one way/return) and Siem Reap (US$152/298 one way/return), while Thai Airways only services Phnom Penh (US$150/220 one way/return). President Airlines offers the cheapest daily flights between Bangkok and Phnom Penh (US$105/145 one way/return).

VIETNAM

Vietnam Airlines connects Phnom Penh with Ho Chi Minh City (US$78/140 one way/return) and Hanoi (US$192/360 one way/return). Its daily services also fly from Siem Reap to Ho Chi Minh City (US$120/240 one way/return) and Hanoi (US$192/360 one way/return).

GETTING AROUND

Air

There are now three primary airlines serving domestic routes in Cambodia: President Airlines, Royal Phnom Penh Airways and Siem Reap Airways (see p76 for airline office details).

BORDER CROSSINGS

Cambodia shares one border crossing with Laos (via Stung Treng; see p114) and five crossings with Thailand, although only Poipet (p93) and Krong Koh Kong (p110) are used regularly. The three newly opened and rarely used crossings are: O Smach (C)/Chong Jom (T), connecting Thailand's Surin Province to the remote town of Samraong; Choam (C) Choam Srawngam (T), linking Thailand to the former Khmer Rouge stronghold of Anlong Veng; and Pruhm (C)/Daun Lem (T), which links Pailin to eastern Thailand.

There are three border crossings with Vietnam, via Bavet, Kaam Samnor and Phnom Den (p77).

Thirty-day Cambodian visas are now available at all the land crossings with Thailand and two of the land crossings with Vietnam, but not yet at the Phnom Den(C)/Tinh Bien (V) border or the land crossing with Laos. There are very few moneychanging facilities, so be sure to have some small denomination US dollars handy upon arrival.

Cambodian immigration officers at the land-border crossings have a bad reputation for petty extortion. Travellers are occasionally asked for an 'immigration fee', particularly at the Lao crossing. Charging between 1000B (Thai baht) and 1300B for the US$20 (approximately 800B) visa is more rampant. Some people are even forced to change US dollars into riel at a poor rate. Hold your breath, stand your ground, don't start a fight and remember that not all Cambodians are as mercenary as the men in blue.

DEPARTURE TAX

The departure tax for domestic flights is US$6 from Phnom Penh and Siem Reap, and US$4 from Ban Lung.

The Siem Reap–Phnom Penh route is well lubed with Siem Reap Airways offering up to six flights a day (US$68/105 one way/return) – this usually means you can slide into a seat without much advance notice. President Airlines and Royal Phnom Penh Airways ply the route once daily for US$60 and US$55 (one way), respectively.

Improving roads have reduced the remaining domestic destinations down to only one: Ban Lung. President Airways serves the remote capital of the Ratanakiri Province with several weekly flights from Phnom Penh (US$59/109 one way/return).

Boat

The most popular boat for foreigners runs up the Tonlé Sap from Phnom Penh to Siem Reap. Be warned: the 5½ hour trip can be insanely overcrowded and breakdowns aren't exactly unknown. Less crowded and more stunning are the speedboats between Siem Reap and Battambang. Both trips can be slowed by low water in the dry season and are seriously overpriced now that buses are running the routes for a fraction of the price.

Quite enjoyable and, more importantly, less of a hit to your stash of cash are boats up the Mekong from Kompong Cham to the riverside towns of Kratie and Stung Treng. Riding the Gulf of Thailand's swells between Sihanoukville and Krong Koh Kong is another viable route – this fast boat saves you from sloppy roads in the wet season and costs about the same as the bus.

Bus

A proliferation of sealed roads and improved dirt tracks means buses reach further than ever before. The cities of Stung Treng and Sen Monorom are now easily reachable in a day from Phnom Penh – a feat unfathomable a few years ago. Competition between bus companies is rife along the major routes, causing prices to plummet for comfortable air-con buses to Siem Reap, Poipet, Battambang and Sihanoukville. Phnom Penh

Public Transport (PPPT; formerly Ho Wah Genting) has the most extensive network, which also serves smaller centres like Tonlé Bati, Takeo, Kompong Chhnang, Kompong Cham and Kratie. Hour Lean Transportation's buses are the newest and delve deeper into the northeast covering the provinces of Mondulkiri, Kratie and Stung Treng.

There are no local bus networks in Cambodia, save for a couple of routes to towns near Phnom Penh. Most people use motos (motorcycle taxis) or take the cyclos (bicycle rickshaws).

Car & Motorcycle

Self-drive car hire is a bit of a Mr Bean (loony) option, given the state of roads, vehicles and other drivers (in no particular order). However, guesthouses and travel agencies can arrange a car and driver for anything between US$20 and US$40 a day, depending on the destination. For the sticky roads in the wet season, a 4WD plus driver is more like US$50 to US$80.

While major roads are no less crazy for motorcycles, many of Cambodia's rural and less travelled tracks are primed for two-wheeled exploration. However, forays on motorcycles into the remote and diabolical roads of the northwest and northeast should only be attempted by experienced riders. If you're lacking experience, it's best to hire a motorcycle and driver for those long days in the sand and dirt – it'll set you back about US$15 to US$20 per 24-hour period. In all cases, proceed cautiously as medical facilities are lacking in Cambodia.

Phnom Penh has the best motorbikes, with daily rates ranging from US$3 for 100cc motorbikes to US$7 for 250cc dirt bikes. Sihanoukville and Kampot have a good range with competitive prices. In other provincial towns, it's usually possible to find a 100c motorbike for US$5 a day. In Siem Reap, rental of self-drive motorcycles is currently prohibited.

Local Transport

CYCLO

As in Vietnam and Laos, cyclos are a cheap way to get around urban areas. Being peddled about is a slower, more relaxing way to see the sights, but for everyday journeys cyclos are fast being pushed out of business by motos.

CAMBODIA

Cyclo fares vary wildly depending on negotiating skills, but aim to pay about the same as moto prices.

MOTO

Motos (motorcycle and driver) are a quick way of making short hops around towns and cities. Prices range from 500r to 2000r, depending on the distance and the town. Most journeys are about 1000r – expect to pay double late at night.

It's best to set the price before mounting the moto, as a few drivers may assume you're going to be generous. Most also presume you know the route as well, and this can create complications if they don't speak English – drivers will often just keep going until you tell them to turn, so keep an eye on the route if you don't want to end up in Bangkok or Ho Chi Minh City. The unofficial uniform of the moto driver is the baseball cap.

Since burning flesh doesn't smell very nice and takes a long time to heal, get in the habit of climbing off the moto to your left – this way, you'll step clear of the scorching exhaust pipe.

REMORQUE-KANG & REMORQUE-MOTO

The *remorque-kang* is a trailer pulled by a bicycle, a sort of reverse cyclo. A trailer hitched to a motorcycle is called a *remorque-moto* – the Cambodian equivalent of a local bus. Both are used to transport people and goods and are commonplace in rural areas. They're not seen so much in urban Cambodia, although in places such as Battambang and Kompong Cham the *remorque-kang* acts as a cyclo. Aim to pay the equivalent moto fare.

Share Taxi, Pick-up & Minibus

While vast road improvements across Cambodia have proliferated bus transport, minibuses, pick-up trucks and share taxis are still a crucial part of the equation for those wishing to lose the crowd.

Pick-ups continue to take on the provinces worst roads – squeeze in the air-con cab or, if you feel like a tan and a mouthful of dust, on the back. They leave when seriously full. Much quicker are share taxis, which now run the same bumpy routes during dry season. However, your comfort is directly correlated to the sizes of

the seven backsides shoehorned into the Toyota Camry (vehicle of choice) with you. It it quite possible to buy spare seats to make the journey more comfortable. Arrange pick-ups and share taxis independently, as it's cheaper than going through a guesthouse – haggle patiently to ensure fair prices.

There are almost no metered taxis in Cambodia, save for a couple in the capital.

Minibuses usually travel sealed roads and are the cheapest and most cramped of transportation options. While they offer little in savings, they tend to leave more regularly than other options.

Train

Thanks to new stretches of tarmac, Cambodia's dilapidated rail services are disappearing faster than Smarties in front of a fat kid. The only passenger service still running rattles between Phnom Penh and Battambang.

A lack of maintenance since before the civil war means tracks are more crooked than any Italian mobster. Trains can't travel at more than 20km/h making the 274km Battambang trip last 14 hours. Optimists might say this offers more time to take in the countryside – a lot more time.

Trains are uncomfortable and often overcrowded, but it's possible to sit on the roof, a novelty that many travellers want to try once. Prices are just 15r per kilometre for locals, but foreigner pricing makes the journey to Battambang about US$4.

PHNOM PENH

☎ 023 / pop 1 million

Phnom Penh is at the crossroads of Asia's past, present and future, where extremes of wealth and poverty are a daily diet, and hope and desperation are never far apart. Many cities are captivating, but Phnom Penh is truly unique in its capacity to both charm you and chill you to the core. Sit on the pleasant riverfront, beneath billowing flags and swaying palms, and take in peaceful saffron-clad monks wandering the streets or delve into Tuol Sleng Museum for a disturbing and uncensored look into the darkest side of the human condition.

Much of the city's charm, while tarnished, has managed to survive the violence of its recent past and Phnom Penh seems to be well and truly on the move. Many crumbling French colonial buildings have been tastefully renovated and play home to numerous new eateries and bars.

Many people make the mistake of hitting the road after the obligatory sightseeing circuit is completed, but the city's true appeal is best discovered at leisure.

ORIENTATION

Phnom Penh hugs the western shores of the Tonlé Sap and Bassac rivers, near their convergence with the mighty Mekong River. From the muddy waters, the city radiates outward into a gridlike pattern with the Chrouy Changvar (Japanese Friendship) and Monivong (Vietnam) bridges defining the northern and southern limits respectively. While the centre of town is roughly around Psar Thmei (Central Market), it is the riverfront that's the centre of most travellers' attention.

The major thoroughfares in Phnom Penh run north–south. They're Monivong Blvd (main commercial drag), Norodom Blvd (mostly administrative), Samdech Sothearos Blvd (in front of the Royal Palace) and Sisowath Quay (riverfront wining and dining). The main east–west arteries are Pochentong Blvd in the north; Sihanouk Blvd, which runs past the Independence Monument; and Mao Tse Toung Blvd, in the far south of town, curving northwards in the west of town – the closest thing Phnom Penh has to a ring road.

Apart from main boulevards, there are hundreds of numbered *phlauv* (streets). In most cases, odd-numbered streets run almost north–south, with their numbers rising from the river westwards. Even-numbered streets run east–west and their numbers rise from north to south.

INFORMATION

Bookshops

D's Books (Map p68; www.ds-books.com; 77 Ph 240) Well-stocked with popular albeit tattered titles. There's a second branch near the Foreign Correspondents' Club at 12 Ph 178.

London Book Centre (Map p68; ☎ 214258; 51 Ph 240) The capital's best browsing is at this secondhand bookshop, which gets a steady supply of stock from the UK. Most titles cost around US$5, less with a trade-in.

Monument Books (Map p68; ☎ 217617; 111 Norodom Blvd) Best range of new books in town, with almost everything ever published on Cambodia, but prices are high compared with Bangkok. Also branches at Phnom Penh International Airport and Foreign Correspondents' Club.

Emergency

Ambulance (☎ 119)
English-speaking police (☎ 366841, 012-999999, with fingers crossed) Passers-by may be more helpful.
Fire (☎ 118)
Police (☎ 117)

Internet Access

Internet cafés are everywhere, almost outnumbering moto drivers. Those with card readers and USB connections for digital cameras are more prevalent along the riverfront and in 'NGO-land' just south of Sihanouk Blvd around Ph 57. Healthy competition has dropped prices to 2000r per hour. Burning images to your CD costs about US$1.50; add US$1 if you need a CD.

Laundry

Most guesthouses/hotels around town will happily wash your skanky shirts and other odoriferous attire for about US$1 per kilogram or 500r to 1000r per item. There are plenty of family-run laundry shops – two reliable shops are just south of Royal Phnom Penh Airways on Ph 19 (Map p68).

Medical Services

Calmette Hospital (Map pp64–5; ☎ 426948; 3 Monivong Blvd) Top dog among the local hospitals.

GETTING INTO TOWN

Most buses, pick-ups and taxis arrive near Psar Thmei (New Market, commonly known as Central Market) in the centre of town and it's just a short moto or cyclo ride to guesthouses located anywhere in this small city. Boats from Siem Reap and Chau Doc (Vietnam) arrive at the tourist boat dock near the eastern end of Ph 106, where hundreds of motos wait in ambush. Phnom Penh International Airport is 7km west of central Phnom Penh via Pochentong Blvd. Official taxis and motos cost US$5 and US$2, respectively. A short walk towards town from the airport, you'll find a regular moto for around US$1.

CAMBODIA

PHNOM PENH

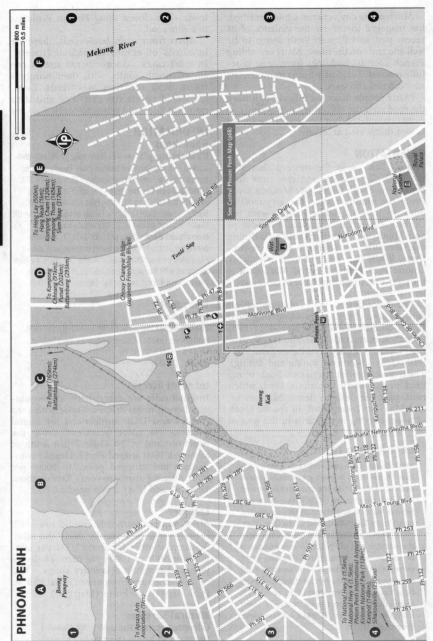

Mekong River

800 m
0.5 miles

To Heng Lay (500m);
Hang Neak (1km);
Kompong Cham (120km);
Kompong Thom (165km);
Siem Reap (317km)

Tonlé Sap Rd.

See Central Phnom Penh Map (p68)

Sisowath Quay

Royal
Palace

National
Museum

Wat
Phnom

Norodom Blvd

Charles de Gaulle Blvd

Chroy Changvar Bridge
(Japanese Friendship Bridge)

Tonlé Sap

Monivong Blvd

Phnom Penh

To Kompong
Chhnang (91km);
Pursat (202km);
Battambang (293km)

Ph 72
Ph 74
Ph 75
Ph 80
Ph 47
Ph 84

To Pursat (165km);
Battambang (274km)

Ph 70

Boeng
Kak

Jawaharlal Nehru (Sihanouk) Blvd

Pochentong Blvd
Ph 112
Ph 118
Ph 122

Kampuchea Krom Blvd

Ph 134

Ph 211

Ph 156

Boeng
Pampoey

To Apsara Arts
Association (1km)

Ph 365

Ph 598
Ph 339
Ph 337
Ph 335
Ph 528

Ph 273

Ph 281
Ph 283
Ph 285
Ph 528
Ph 287
Ph 289
Ph 291

Ph 615

Ph 614
Ph 566

Ph 608

Mao Tse Toung Blvd

Ph 592
Ph 315
Ph 317
Ph 313
Ph 566

Ph 592

To National Hwy 3 (1.5km);
National Hwy 4 (1.5km);
Phnom Penh International Airport (3km);
Kirirom National Park (112km);
Sihanoukville (23km)

Ph 253

Ph 257

Ph 122

Ph 132

Ph 259

Ph 261

CAMBODIA

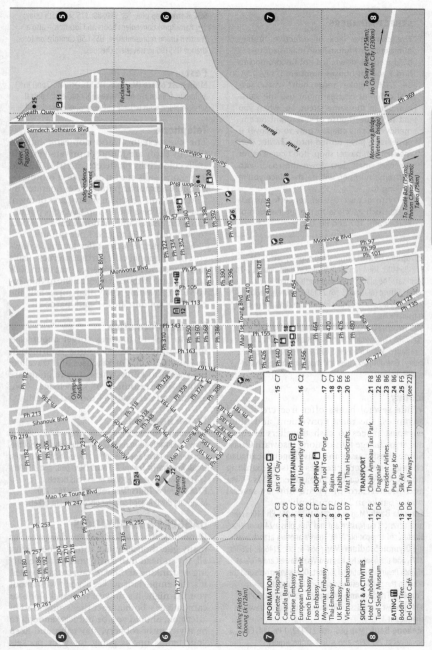

CAMBODIA

STREET NUMBERS

The complete lack of effective house-numbering in Phnom Penh makes addresses hard to track down. It's not uncommon to find a row of houses numbered, say, 13A, 34, 7, 26 – makes sense, huh? Worse, several different houses might use the same number in the same street. So, when you get to a guesthouse or restaurant recommended in this chapter only to discover it appears to have turned into a *prahoc* (fermented fish paste) shop, don't curse us for the bad smell. Just down the road, with the same number, will be the place you're looking for.

Try to get a cross-reference for an address, such as 'close to the intersection of Phlauv (Ph) 107 and Ph 182'.

European Dental Clinic (Map pp64-5; ☎ 211363, 012-854408; 160A Norodom Blvd; ☒ 8am-noon & 2-7pm Mon-Sat) The place to get your teeth sorted.
Naga Clinic (Map p68; ☎ 211300; www.nagaclinic .com; 11 Ph 254; ☒ 24hr) French-run clinic for reliable consultations.
SOS International Medical Centre (Map p68; ☎ 216911; www.internationalsos.com; 161 Ph 51; ☒ 8am-5.30pm Mon-Fri & 8am-noon Sat, 24hr emergency) One of town's best and most expensive medical establishments.

Money

While several banks offer free credit-card advances, the most convenient and often cheapest places to cash travellers cheques are at exchange kiosks along Sisowath Quay. Some guesthouses and travel agents can also change travellers cheques outside banking hours. Credit-card-compatible ATMs (Visa and MasterCard only) are now at several major banks in Phnom Penh.
Canadia Bank (Map p68; ☎ 215286; 265 Ph 110) Free cash advances on MasterCard and Visa, plus a 24-hour Visa/MasterCard-compatible ATM. There's another branch near the **Olympic Stadium** (Map pp64-5; ☎ 214668; 126 Ph 217), and the bank also has two Visa/MasterCard ATMs at Phnom Penh International Airport. One is in arrivals and the other in the public restaurant/snack bar outside.
Foreign Trade Bank (Map p68; ☎ 723466; 3 Ph 114) Lowest commission in town on US dollar travellers cheques at 1%.
Mekong Bank (Map p68; ☎ 217112; 1 Ph 114) Cash advances at 2% here; also a desk at the airport.

SBC Bank (Map p68; ☎ 990688; 315 Sisowath Quay; ☒ 8am-8pm) Convenient hours and location – also a Western Union representative; US$1.50 commission to change US$100 in travellers cheques.

Post

Main post office (Map p68; Ph 13; ☒ 7am-7pm) In a glorious building, it has increasingly successful postal services along with reliable but expensive express mail.

Telephone

The cheapest local and domestic calls in Phnom Penh are found at private kerbside stalls colourfully plastered with 011, 012 and 016. Local calls start from 300r a minute.

There are public phone boxes operated by Camintel and Telstra in many parts of town. Nearby will be a local shop that sells phonecards for pricey international calls – expect to shell out US$2 to US$3 per minute.

Many Internet cafés offer laughably low-cost international calls via the Internet – calls to Europe and North America start from 300r per minute! Although they're cheap they involve an irritating delay that turns half the conversation into 'hello?' and 'pardon?'

Tourist Information

Due to lack of funding, forget about useful government-issued tourist information in Phnom Penh. Guesthouses and travellers who seem to know where they're going are your prime resources of knowledge – oh, and this guidebook isn't too bad either!

Travel Agencies

Hanuman Tourism-Voyages (Map p68; ☎ 218396; www.hanumantourism.com; 128 Norodom Blvd) One of the most reliable travel agencies for air tickets and tour services.
Neak Krorhorm Travel & Tours (Map p68; ☎ 219496; 128 Ph 108) Reasonably priced air and bus tickets.
PTM Travel & Tours (Map p68; ☎ 364768; 200 Monivong Blvd) A good spot for discount flight tickets.

DANGERS & ANNOYANCES

Phnom Penh is by no means as dangerous as many guesthouses make it out to be – after all, if you head into town, you won't be eating or drinking at their restaurant! However, it's still important to keep your wits about you. At night it's unwise to travel alone or carry a bag – both attract the wrong kind of attention. Should you be unlucky enough to be a victim of robbery, stay calm and keep your hands up, as going for your pockets is as good as going for a weapon in the assailant's mind. Since they're usually interested in cash, you may well have your documents and credit cards returned.

When riding a motorcycle don't ignore 'no left turn' signs, as traffic police are only too willing to help you part with cash. They may demand US$20, but if you're patient and smile, a few cigarettes or 1000r should see you on your way.

Begging is a problem in Phnom Penh – have a read of Responsible Travel (p122) for advice on how to help the less fortunate.

SIGHTS

Phnom Penh's attractions offer a stark contrast to the kingdom's history, and stir up a gamut of emotions. The beauty within the National Museum and bejewelled Silver Pagoda will take your breath away, while the horrors of Tuol Sleng Museum and the Killing Fields of Choeung Ek will hit you in the gut and leave you searching for air.

After exploring the dark depths of the city's markets like Psar Thmei and Psar Tuol Tom Pong, head to the thriving riverfront and enjoy a stroll through the vibrant light at sunset.

Royal Palace & Silver Pagoda

The **Royal Palace** (Map p68; Samdech Sothearos Blvd; admission US$3, camera/video US$2/5; 7.30-11am & 2.30-5pm), with its towering tile roofs and ornate gilding, rises upward to dominate the diminutive local skyline. Behind protective walls and beneath shadows of striking ceremonial buildings, it's an oasis of calm with lush gardens and leafy havens like Phnom Mondap. Some of the garden's shrubs would make a coiffed French poodle green with envy. Being the official residence of King Sihamoni, parts of the massive compound are closed to the public.

Within the compound is the extravagant **Silver Pagoda**, the floor of which is lain with five tons of gleaming silver. You can sneak a peek at some of the 5000 tiles near the entrance – most are covered for their protection. Not to be outdone by the floor, an extraordinary Baccarat crystal Buddha sits atop an impressive gilded pedestal. Adding to the lavish mix, and perhaps not wanting to be outdone by the glowing emerald Buddha, is a life-sized, solid-gold Buddha weighing 90kg and adorned with 2086 diamonds,

the largest weighing in at 25 carats. Who takes the cake in the exorbitant Olympics? We'll let you decide.

Photography is not permitted inside the pagoda itself, so the camera prices are a little ambitious – buy some postcards instead.

National Museum

A millennia's worth of masterful Khmer artwork, including the world's finest collection of classical Angkor period (10th to 14th centuries) sculpture, spills out from open-air galleries into an inviting garden and fish-pond-filled inner courtyard of the **National Museum** (Map p68; Ph 13; admission US$3, camera/video US$1/3; 8am-5pm).

One of the most celebrated works is the seated statue of Jayavarman VII (r 1181–1219), his head bowed slightly in a meditative pose. The oldest artefacts are examples of pottery and bronze from the Funan and Chenla empires (4th to 9th centuries AD).

Photography is limited to the courtyard, so don't waste your cash. English- and French-speaking guides are available for a bit of context and there's also a useful exhibition booklet, *The New Guide to the National Museum*, available at the front desk.

The museum used to house a massive and deafening colony of Cambodian freetail bats. Sadly, they flew the coop in 2002.

Tuol Sleng Museum

While walking through the courtyard or down the corridors, with their checked tile floors and cream walls, it's not hard to imagine the site's simple origins as the Tuol Svay Prey High School. However, delving into former classrooms shatters any illusion of normalcy. A single rusty bed and disturbingly gruesome black-and-white photo are all that adorn some rooms, but stand as testament to the unthinkable horrors that happened here. This is one **museum** (Map pp64-5; admission US$2; 8am-5.30pm) where silence doesn't have to be requested – the power of speech is simply lost here.

In 1975 Pol Pot's security forces turned the school into Security Prison 21 (S-21), the largest centre of detention and torture in the country. Almost everyone held here was later executed at the Killing Fields of Choeung Ek (p69). Detainees who died during torture were buried in mass graves inside the prison grounds. During the first part of 1977, S-21

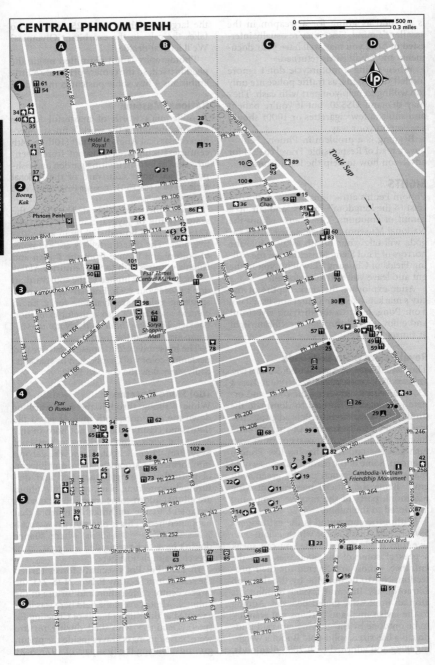

CENTRAL PHNOM PENH

0   500 m
0   0.3 miles

INFORMATION
Australian Embassy....1 C5
Canadia Bank....2 B2
Canadian Embassy....(see 1)
D's Books....3 C5
D's Books....(see 56)
Foreign Trade Bank....4 B2
German Embassy....5 B5
Hanuman Tourism-Voyages....6 D6
Indonesian Embassy....7 C5
Laundry Services....8 C5
London Book Centre....9 C5
Main Post Office....10 C2
Malaysian Embassy....11 C5
Mekong Bank....12 B2
Monument Books....13 C5
Naga Clinic....14 C5
Neak Krorhorm Travel & Tours....15 C2
Philippine Embassy....16 D6
PTM Travel & Tours....17 B3
SBC Bank....18 D3
Singaporean Embassy....19 C5
SOS International Medical Centre....20 C5
US Embassy (open late 2006)....21 B2
US Embassy (until late 2006)....22 C5

SIGHTS & ACTIVITIES
Independence Monument....23 C5
National Museum....24 C4
National Museum Entrance....25 D4
Royal Palace....26 D4
Royal Palace & Silver Pagoda Entrance....27 D4
Seeing Hands Massage....28 B1
Silver Pagoda....29 D4
Wat Ounalom....30 D3
Wat Phnom....31 B2

SLEEPING
Bright Lotus Guesthouse....(see 80)
Capitol Guesthouse III....32 A4
Chantrea Guesthouse....33 A5
Floating Island....34 A1
Grand View Guesthouse....35 A1
Last Home....36 C2
Lazy Fish Guesthouse....37 A2
Lucky Guesthouse II....38 A5
Narin Guesthouse....39 A5
Number 9 Guesthouse....40 A1
Number 9 Sister Guesthouse....41 A2
Okay Guesthouse....42 D5
Renakse Hotel....43 D4
Simon's II Guesthouse....44 A1
Smile Lakeside....(see 37)
Spring Guesthouse....45 A5
Sunday Guesthouse....46 A5
Tat Guesthouse....(see 39)
Washington Guesthouse....47 B3

EATING
Amok Restaurant & Café....48 C6
Bali Café....49 D4
Bayon Market....50 A3
Boat Noodle Restaurant....51 D6
Cantina....52 D3
Chi Cha....53 C2
Curry Pot....54 A1
Dararasmey Restaurant....55 B5
Foreign Correspondents' Club....56 D3
Friends....57 C3
Happy Herb's Pizza....(see 52)
Java Café....58 D5
Khmer Borane Restaurant....59 D4
Kiwi Bakery....60 D2
Lazy Gecko Café....61 A1
Le Café du Centre....62 B4
Lucky Supermarket....63 B6
Lucky Supermarket....64 B3
Mama's Restaurant....65 A4
nature and sea....66 C6
Nike's Pizza House....67 B6
Pencil Supermarket....68 C4
Psar Ta Pang....69 B3
Riverside Bistro....70 D3
Sa Em Restaurant....71 D3
Thai Huot Supermarket....72 A3
Wah Kee Restaurant....73 B5

DRINKING
California 2 Guesthouse....(see 18)
Elephant Bar....74 A2
Elsewhere....75 C5
Ginger Monkey....76 D3
Gym Bar....77 C4
Heart of Darkness....78 B4
Howie's Bar....(see 78)
Memphis Pub....79 C2
Pink Elephant....(see 52)
Rising Sun....80 D3
Riverhouse Lounge....81 C2
Rubies Wine Bar....82 D5
Salt Lounge....83 D3
teukei bar....84 A5

ENTERTAINMENT
French Cultural Centre....(see 62)
Movie Street....85 C6

SHOPPING
NCDP Handicrafts....86 B2

TRANSPORT
Air France....87 D5
Bangkok Airways....88 B5
Boats to Siem Reap & Chau Doc....89 C2
Capitol Tour....90 A4
China Southern Airlines....91 A1
GST....92 B3
Hour Lean....93 C2
Japan Rentals....94 A4
Lao Airlines....95 D5
Lucky! Lucky!....96 B4
Malaysia Airlines....97 A3
Narin Transport....(see 39)
Neak Krorhorm....(see 15)
New! New!....(see 96)
Phnom Penh Public Transport....98 B3
Royal Phnom Penh Airways....99 C4
Shanghai Airlines....100 C2
Share Taxis, Pick-ups & Minibuses....101 B3
Siem Reap Airways....(see 88)
Vietnam Airlines....102 B5

claimed a terrifying average of 100 victims per day.

There's a compelling new photo exhibition examining present-day lives of some S-21 survivors and perpetrators. Also try to catch the documentary film running daily at 10am and 3pm.

A visit here is instrumental in comprehending Cambodia's past and present.

READING UP

For a greater insight into the horror of Tuol Sleng, pick up *Voices from S-21* by David Chandler, a chilling yet incisive account of life in the prison pieced together from the torturers and the tortured.

Killing Fields of Choeung Ek

Rising amid 129 mass graves (43 of which have never been disinterred) is a blinding white stupa that serves as a memorial to the approximately 17,000 men, women and children who were executed here by the Khmer Rouge between mid-1975 and December 1978. Behind the stupa's glass panels, and rising upward shelf by shelf, are over 8000 skulls found during excavations here in 1980 – some of these skulls still bear witness to the fact that they were bludgeoned to death for the sake of saving precious bullets.

Wandering to sounds of joyful children playing at a nearby school and spotting human bone and clothing poking from the churned ground startlingly brings home the

DID YOU KNOW?

In 2005 the government privatised the Killing Fields of Choeung Ek and was paid an undisclosed sum by a Japanese company who'll manage the site and charge admission fees. This has enraged relatives of victims who are sickened by the government trading their murdered loved ones for profit.

striking contrast of Cambodia today to its dark abyss of a recent past.

The **Killing Fields of Choeung Ek** (admission US$2; ⊙ 7am-5.30pm) are 14km southwest of central Phnom Penh, clearly signposted from Monireth Blvd. Return moto rides are about US$4, or it's a pleasant bicycle ride once beyond the city limits.

Wat Phnom

Occupying the city's highest point – don't get too excited, it's just a 27m-high, tree-covered bump – **Wat Phnom** (Map p68; admission US$1) is a quiet, shady and incense-infused respite in the middle of northern Phnom Penh. However, it's not a good place for a picnic, unless the monkeys don't like what you're eating! According to legend, the first pagoda on this site was erected in 1373 to house four Buddha statues deposited here by the waters of the Mekong, discovered by a woman named Penh (thus the name Phnom Penh, literally, Hill of Penh). Besides the temple, you'll find droves of Khmers praying for luck and a few amputees looking for some sympathy and riel.

Independence Monument

Soaring over the city's largest roundabout, with its seemingly countless *nagas* (multi-headed serpents commonly associated with water, fertility, rainbows and creation) is the grand **Independence Monument** (Map p68; cnr Norodom & Sihanouk Blvds), built in 1958. It's now also a memorial to Cambodia's war dead.

Wat Ounalom

The headquarters of the Cambodian Buddhist patriarchate, **Wat Ounalom** (Map p68; Samdech Sothearos Blvd) is the country's pre-eminent centre of Buddhist education and the focal point of the Buddhist faith in Phnom Penh.

There's not much to see, but a stroll through the complex, much of which was heavily damaged during Pol Pot's regime, will let you soak up the palpable and now peaceful ambience.

ACTIVITIES
Massages

'You want massage?' While it's tempting and innocent sounding, most of these offers involve truly wandering hands – yes, most massages are of the naughty variety. For a real and oh-so-rewarding rub, visit the highly skilled blind masseurs of **Seeing Hands Massage** (Map p68; 6 Ph 94; per hr US$4.25). Besides being a fabulous way to relax after a long journey, you're also helping blind Cambodians stay self-sufficient. It's busy, so pop in and make an appointment for later.

Swimming

Dying for a dip? At all costs, don't plunge into Boeng Kak! Several swanky hotels offer pool perusals for reasonable costs – that is, if you make a day of it. The pool at **Hotel Cambodiana** (Map pp44-5; 313 Sisowath Quay) is the most atmospheric, with lovely sun chairs and views of the Tonlé Sap river – prepare to part with US$6 during the week or US$8 on the weekend.

TOURS

The bus company **Capitol Tour** (☎ 217627; 14 Ph 182) and the **Narin Guesthouse** (Map p68; ☎ 982554; touchnarin@hotmail.com; 50 Ph 125) organise city tours including most sights listed earlier for around US$3 without a guide or US$6 with one.

Other popular guesthouses offer similar packages. Note that prices mentioned don't include entrance fees. While these tours may seem cheap and handy, sights like the Killing Fields of Choeung Ek and Tuol Sleng Museum should not be rushed and are best visited independently.

FESTIVALS & EVENTS

Most national holidays (p120) and the Chinese New Year (p119) are celebrated with vigour in Phnom Penh. Festivals focused primarily in the capital city:

Royal Ploughing Ceremony This ritual agricultural festival takes place in early May at a temporary pagoda in front of the National Museum. The noses of the royal oxen are said to predict the success of the upcoming harvest.

WARNING

During large celebrations in Phnom Penh women should watch out for the over-eager attention of young groups of males.

Bon Om Tuk (Water Festival) In late October or November, hundreds of thousands of Cambodians flock to the riverfront to celebrate and watch some 350 boats compete in races on the Tonlé Sap river. The winning boat's 75 paddlers share a whopping US$100 prize.

SLEEPING

Budget options are sprinkled all over town, but Boeng Kak lakefront (sunsets here are not to be missed) and the Psar O Russei area have emerged as popular backpacker haunts. Boeng Kak's wooden guesthouses are perched over water on stilts, a sort of Ko Pha-Ngan without the Gulf of Thailand, while the less atmospheric backstreets south of Psar O Russei house hotel-like guesthouses with a few more creature comforts.

Boeng Kak Area

Rickety wood guesthouses are slowly being replaced by more substantial structures, undermining rumours that this whole area will be pulled down in the next few years as part of Phnom Penh's zealous beautification drive. Most guesthouses have great ambience, with wooden chill-out areas stretching out over the water, and offer very basic rooms at extremely cheap prices – though the odd rodent may come included. Your valuables are best checked in with the owners, as most rooms aren't very secure.

Grand View Guesthouse (Map p68; ☎ 430766; Ph 93; r US$3-8; 🖳) While it's not perched over the lapping lake and thus lacks an atmospheric deck to unwind on, it does offer bright breezy rooms and some great lake views. Snooze in peace here and choose to chill on another guesthouse's deck.

Floating Island (Map p68; ☎ 012-551227; floating island_pp@yahoo.com; 11 Ph 93; r US$3-9; 🖳) Rooms upstairs have windows opening onto the lake, accessing commodities like natural light and fresh air! Flimsy options downstairs save you a couple of dollars, but look into the dark linoleum-walled hallway. Definitely the breeziest terrace in town, it has a great double-decker drinking den for serious sunset views.

Number 9 Guesthouse (Map p68; ☎ 012-766225; Ph 93; s US$2-4, tw US$5-8; 🖳) Despite being laden with copious potted plants, a pool table and many a relaxed traveller, this sprawling and bona fide original lakefront guesthouse is still above water and continuing to please those living on the cheap. Some of the guesthouse's 50-plus rooms are much nicer than others – check out a few.

Simon's II Guesthouse (Map p68; ☎ 012-608892; hongchi72@hotmail.com; Ph 93; r US$10-15; 🖳) This big wedding-cake-style villa is home to the smartest rooms in this part of town, including satellite TV and hot-water showers. Sorry, no fake-wood linoleum lining the walls here!

Lazy Fish Guesthouse (Map p68; ☎ 012-703368; lazyfishlakeside@hotmail.com; 16 Ph 93; r US$2-4) Oh, you love linoleum? Go no further: this mellow lakeside spot's rooms are oozing with it. Further south than the leading spots, this is a quiet alternative with a cool vibe.

Other lakeside options:

Number 9 Sister Guesthouse (Map p68; ☎ 012-424240; Ph 93; s without bathroom US$3, s/tw US$4-5) A quieter and slightly brighter option than its sister Number 9 Guesthouse.

Smile Lakeside (Map p68; ☎ 012-831329; smile_lakeside@yahoo.com; 5 Ph 93; s US$2, tw US$3-4, tr US$5) Another quiet option at the south end of the Boeng Kak area. English and French are spoken here.

Psar O Russei Area

Tat Guesthouse (Map p68; ☎ 012-921211; 52 Ph 125; s/tw without bathroom US$2/4, d US$5-10; 🖳) Below the breezy top-floor restaurant, there's a wide range of good-value rooms – hot showers and cable TV for US$6 is hard to beat. Run by a sweet family, you won't get the hard-sell attitude found at some nearby guesthouses.

Chantrea Guesthouse (Map p68; ☎ 012-944024; 48 Ph 141; r US$5-10; 🖳) The halls are a little dark but the homely rooms are large, squeaky clean and sport TVs. You'll find balconies in some – room 107 is especially nice. Huffing it to the top floor will save you US$1.

Spring Guesthouse (Map p68; ☎ 222155; 34 Ph 111; r US$5-10; 🖳) Nothing homely or atmospheric here – just great value. This slick new maroon tower's rooms are bright, spotless and modern, complete with cable TV. Add US$2 for the privilege of steamy showers.

Sunday Guesthouse (Map p68; ☎ 211623; 97 Ph 141; r US$4-15; 🖳) Rooms here run from the basic fan options at just US$4 to full-blown,

CAMBODIA

SPLURGE!

Renakse Hotel (Map p68; ☎ 215701; 40 Samdech Sothearos Blvd; r incl breakfast US$30-60; 🅿) Lurking beneath the skin of this impressive colonial relic are gorgeous rooms with a perfect mix of old-world elegance and contemporary comfort. Raised platforms made of rich hardwood house comfy cushioned seating areas, and four-poster beds cradle mattresses that will have you gladly sleeping through your alarm. Renovations continue and by the time you arrive, there should be a posh bar and restaurant for your dining pleasure.

hotel-style rooms with TV, hot water and fridge. The friendly English-speaking staff can help with travel arrangements.

Other possibilities:

Capitol Guesthouse III (Map p68; ☎ 211027; 207 Ph 107; s US$4, d US$6-10; 🅿) Decent rooms a stumble away from Capitol Tour's early morning buses.

Lucky Guesthouse II (Map p68; ☎ 218910; 30 Ph 115; r US$6-10; 🅿) Similar feel and value to the Spring Guesthouse.

Narin Guesthouse (Map p68; ☎ 982554; touch narin@hotmail.com; 50 Ph 125; r US$2-7) An old budget favourite that's somewhat on the slide. Ample travel and tour services are on hand.

Around the City

Okay Guesthouse (Map p68; ☎ 012-920556; Ph 258; dm US$1, s US$3-10, d US$5-12; 🅿) With a popular restaurant, appealing garden, great rooms and the best backpacker atmosphere off Boeng Kak, Okay is better than okay – it's a score, so check in here ASAP or you'll leave defeated.

Washington Guesthouse (Map p68; ☎ 986358; cnr Ph 51 & Ph 118; s US$5, d US$7-10; 🅿) Close to Psar Thmei's shopping and transportation links, this friendly guesthouse offers good value. The comfortable yet spartan rooms are clean and include TVs. For some sunshine, ask for one that faces out.

Last Home (Map p68; ☎ 724917; 47 Ph 108; r US$2-8; 🅿) A ramshackle guesthouse with basic rooms that have held their worth for over a decade. It's a short skip from Wat Phnom, riverfront restaurants and the fast boat. It also has a book exchange downstairs.

Bright Lotus Guesthouse (Map p68; ☎ 990446; 22 Ph 178; r US$12-18; 🅿) While a squeeze in

the dollars department, this hotel boasts a most enviable location near the heart of the riverfront. It offers top-floor views of the National Museum, Royal Palace and, if you strain your neck a bit, the riverfront – one set of steps worth climbing.

EATING

You could survive on your guesthouse's reasonably priced and somewhat tasty food, but where's the fun in that? Head to markets and dive into authentic cheap Khmer chow or delve into the city's vast array of quality cosmopolitan eateries.

Unless stated otherwise, restaurants are open for breakfast, lunch and dinner.

Asian

Bali Café (Map p68; ☎ 982211; 379 Sisowath Quay; mains US$2-4) Slip up into this open-air eatery and look over Tonlé Sap river while wrapping your lips around sumptuous *sate ayam madura* (grilled chicken bathing in peanut sauce) or the multitude of other spicy Indonesian staples. For vegetarians, there are several tasty tofu options.

Boat Noodle Restaurant (Map p68; Ph 294; mains 3000-12,000r) New shady and leafy location, same great Thai favourites at an unbeatable price. Service can be a tad tardy if there's a crowd.

Chi Cha (Map p68; ☎ 336065; 27 Ph 110; set meals US$2) This understated Bangladeshi curry house turns out savoury subcontinent selections, including bargain *thalis* (set meals).

Curry Pot (Map p68; Ph 93; mains US$2) Highly rated curries to settle the grumbliest of Boeng Kak's tummies.

Wah Kee Restaurant (Map p68; 296 Monivong Blvd; mains US$1-3; 🕑 dinner) This late-night Chinese spot will quell midnight munchies with authentic tastes of the Middle Kingdom. Spicy beef hotplate or mopo tofu hit the chilli spot.

Khmer

In the evenings, Khmer eateries scattered around town illuminate their beaconlike Angkor Beer signs, hailing locals in for fine fare and wobbly pops (that's beer for the uninitiated). Don't be shy and heed the glowing signs – the food is great and the atmosphere lively. A typical meal will devour a mighty 4000r to 5000r. *Soup chnnang dei* (cook-your-own-soup) is a big thing with

Cambodians and a great idea if there's a group of you dining.

Dararasmey Restaurant (Map p68; 292 Ph 214; mains US$2-6; ☺ dinner) As well as offering the famous soup (US$6 for two serves) it does an excellent *phnom pleung* (hill of fire), a volcano grill for barbecuing your own meats or seafood. Dararasmey is packed with locals every night.

Khmer Borane Restaurant (Map p68; 389 Sisowath Quay; mains US$1.50-3) On the riverfront near the Royal Palace and has perhaps the best selection of old royal recipes in town. Traditional Khmer dishes like fish in palm sugar, pomelo salad or *lok lak* (stir-fried beef) will soon have you realising Khmer cuisine can rival its better-known neighbours.

Amok Restaurant & Café (Map p68; 2 Ph 278; mains US$3-6; set lunches US$3.50; ☺ lunch & dinner) This place is named after one of Cambodia's national dishes – only a wise idea if you can do the dish some serious justice. It hits the mark and then some; the fish *amok* (coconut and lemon grass curry served in a banana leaf) is divine.

Sa Em Restaurant (Map p68; 379 Sisowath Quay; mains US$1-3) This popular no-nonsense choice on the riverfront serves simple Khmer specials beneath its leafy canopy.

The best markets for dining are **Psar Thmei** (Map p68; ☺ breakfast & lunch), **Psar Tuol Tom Pong** (Map pp64-5; ☺ breakfast & lunch) and **Psar O Russei** (Map p68; ☺ breakfast & lunch), which is handy given these are also great shopping venues.

SPLURGE!

Foreign Correspondents' Club (FCC; Map p68; ☎ 724014; 363 Sisowath Quay; mains US$5-8; ☺ breakfast, lunch & dinner) Colonial ambience and aromas of fine fare radiate throughout this cavernous club, which sits high above the riverfront and overlooks both the Tonlé Sap river and the National Museum. It's one of the best places to have that splash-out meal, with flavours from four corners of the globe, including anything from Cambodian curries to wood-fired pizzas or bangers and mash. Thankfully the FCC doesn't require the pretentious press card like other correspondents' clubs around Asia. If the food is beyond the budget, slide in for a happy hour drink between 5pm and 7pm. Prices don't include 10% VAT.

Most dishes cost a paltry 2000r to 3000r. There are also several areas around the city with open-air food stalls during the early evening – try **Psar Ta Pang** (Map p68; cnr Ph 51 & Ph 136; ☺ dinner) for excellent *bobor* (rice porridge) and tasty desserts.

Glitzy Khmer restaurants line NH6 on the east side of the Japanese Friendship Bridge and offer a unique and authentic dining experience for less money than you'd think. Try **Hang Neak** (☎ 369661; NH6; mains US$3-12; ☺ dinner) or **Heng Lay** (☎ 430888; NH6; mains US$3-20; ☺ dinner), which hosts local Charlie Chaplinesque comedians and karaoke stars.

International

Friends (Map p68; ☎ 426748; 215 Ph 13; tapas US$1-2.50) Do sweet potato fries with curry mayonnaise, sun-dried tomato hummus on crispy wonton wafers, and curried pumpkin soup with coriander and garlic croutons tickle your fancy? Enjoy a long list of brilliant tapas in this blissful bolt hole of a restaurant. All proceeds go towards education and job training of street children, so it's dining for a cause.

Boddhi Tree (Map pp64-5; 50 Ph 113; dishes US$1-4) This garden oasis is the perfect antidote to the horrors of the neighbouring Tuol Sleng Museum. Chorizo and vegetable skewers, Khmer curries and big sandwiches – including the tasty combination of roasted aubergine, brie, onion and whole-grain mustard – grace the extensive menu. Enjoy!

Del Gusto Café (Map pp64-5; ☎ 565509; 43 Ph 95; mains US$2-4) A Mediterranean-inspired menu with breads, dips and sprinkles of feta throughout. To shake things up, there's even some sushi to mix. Sink into some wicker, listen to the sounds of jazz, and let your tastebuds dance in this lovingly restored colonial-era villa.

Le Café du Centre (Map p68; Ph 184; mains US$2-4.50) Relish a Nutella-laced crêpe or *croque monsieur* beneath the palms of this gem found hiding in the inner courtyard of the French Cultural Centre. The menu is limited but proceeds go to Mith Samlanh, the NGO running the restaurant Friends.

Lazy Gecko Café (Map p68; 23 Ph 93; mains US$2-5) Boasting 'homemade hummus just like when mum was dating that chap from Cyprus', this Boeng Kak backpacker enclave serves great English pub grub and the full range of comfort food from home.

Java Café (Map p68; ☎ 987420; 56 Sihanouk Blvd; mains US$1.50-4; ☿ breakfast & lunch Tue-Sun) A breezy time machine of a balcony (where did the time go?) and a lunch menu laden with inspired salads, sandwiches and wholesome burgers. Inventive pastas come out to play at dinner.

Riverside Bistro (Map p68; ☎ 213898; 273 Sisowath Quay; mains US$3-7) Take in the riverfront action from your wicker throne and enjoy an eclectic mix of healthy portions from around the world, particularly Central Europe.

Happy Herb's Pizza (Map p68; ☎ 362349; 345 Sisowath Quay; pizzas US$3-5) A copycat inspiring institution with 'happy' (à la ganja) pizzas leaving perma-grins in their wake. Happy enough? The non-'happied' versions won't turn that smile upside down.

Other eateries to scratch that international itch:

Cantina (Map p68; 347 Sisowath Quay; mains US$2-4; ☿ dinner) Tostadas, fajitas and other Mexican favourites.

Mama's Restaurant (Map p68; Ph 111; mains 2000-5000r) Truly cheap eats ranging from shepherd's pie to Thai, French and even African specials.

nature and sea (Map p68; Ph 51; mains 9000-20,000r) Simple spot with sweet and savoury crêpes, salads and fantastic fish and chips.

Nike's Pizza House (Map p68; 160 Ph 63; pizzas US$2-5) Possibly Phnom Penh's best pizzas. Try the 'pineapple porn moan' pizza – silly spelling or pure pleasure?

Self-Catering

Inexpensive restaurants actually offer more savings than self-catering, but for midday snacks or treats from home, supermarkets are perfect. Baguettes are widely available for around 500r and the open-air markets have heaps of fresh fruit and vegetables at fair prices (if you bargain).

Pencil Supermarket (Map p68; Ph 214) It's massive and well stocked – from breads to Bombay Sapphire gin.

Lucky Supermarket (Map p68; 160 Sihanouk Blvd) Home to a serious range of goodies from near and far. There's another in Sorya Shopping Mall (Map p68).

Bayon Market (Map p68; 133 Monivong Blvd) A smaller shop with a surprisingly big stock ranging from local favourites to Gatorade, McVities biscuits and Denmark Crown Butter Cookies.

Thai Huot Supermarket (Map p68; 103 Monivong Blvd) Fridges filled with camembert, brie, roquefort and gouda cheeses. This slice of

French heaven also boasts Bonne Maman jam and creamy chocolate.

Kiwi Bakery (Map p68; ☎ 215784; 199 Sisowath Quay) Now pumping out great cakes and pastries from its new riverfront location.

Another trick is to call at bakeries of five-star hotels, like **Hotel Cambodiana** (Map pp64-5; 313 Sisowath Quay), after 6pm when all cakes are half price.

For after-hours cravings, the Caltex and Total petrol stations found at major junctions have 24-hour shops with imported products.

DRINKING
Cafés

Jars of Clay (Map pp64-5; 39 Ph 155; ☿ Tue-Sat) If the rigours of the Russian Market are too much, a wee walk will have you happily collapsed in this upstairs air-con coffee bar. Frapuccinos, milk shakes and speciality coffees are equally dazzling and affordable. Soon Jars of Clay will be pouring out Phnom Penh's latest liquid craze, bubble tea.

Java Café (Map pp64-5; 56 Sihanouk Blvd; ☿ Tue-Sun) Quality coffees from Earth's four corners. Prices are a little steep at this restaurant (left). Milkshakes are a whopping US$3!

Bars

Hammocks, cheap beers and unbeatable lakefront sunsets make a drink on one of Boeng Kak's guesthouse balconies as pleasurable as it is obligatory. However, the story does not end here!

Luring you off the balconies (with the mosquitos' help) is a plethora of great riverfront and backstreet bars that offer tempting happy hours – drinks are often half price.

Elephant Bar (Map p68; Ph 92) Housed within the luxurious five-star Hotel Le Royal, this bar is the epitome of swank and has two-for-one happy hours between 4pm and 8pm. Play pool and salute the free chips and salsa. Beers cost US$3, cocktails US$4.50, and fancy-pants cocktails US$6, plus 20% tax and service. The Foreign Correspondents' Club (p73) is another posh place made affordable during smiley hours.

Ginger Monkey (Map p68; 29 Ph 178) Striking Angkor-inspired bas-reliefs and carvings act as a backdrop in this unique bar, which also boasts a good location, a lively crowd, and a generous happy hour from 5pm to 9pm with two-for-one cocktails.

Riverhouse Lounge (Map p68; cnr Ph 110 & Sisowath Quay) Located above Riverhouse Restaurant, this lavishly decorated lounge bar is taken over by DJs on weekends. Expats and travellers move to fresh house, drum'n'base and hip-hop beats.

Pink Elephant (Map p68; 343 Sisowath Quay) One in a line of simple riverfront bars that pull punters on evening sessions with cheap drinks and speedy snacks. The shoeshine circus and bookselling bonanza continue through the night but don't hinder large thirsty crowds from gathering.

Salt Lounge (Map p68; 217 Ph 136) Slick, modern and minimalist, this trendy gay cocktail bar thrives on weekends. Straights are welcome too.

Elsewhere (Map p68; 175 Ph 51; ☺ closed Sun) Set in a beautiful French colonial-era villa with lavish gardens, this is the perfect spot to while away a warm evening or late afternoon. Order an 'amnesia' cocktail, settle into the free plunge pool and forget your worries.

Rubies Wine Bar (Map p68; cnr Ph 240 & 19) Warm wood, comfy cushions and a long list of wonderful wines should quench those on the quest for the grape. Glasses of house wine start at US$3.

Gym Bar (Map p68; 42 Ph 178) If you're hankering for a beer, a boisterous bunch and a behemoth screen for the big game, whether it be rugby, football or tennis, this is the spot.

teukei bar (Map p68; Ph 111; ☺ closed Sun) Linger beneath Chinese lanterns and chill to ambient sounds and classic reggae cuts. Small but stiff rum punches are a must. Thankfully, it's stumbling distance from many Psar O Russei guesthouses.

Heart of Darkness (Map p68; 26 Ph 51) The Heart, as locals call it, seems to beat to a different tune these days – now more a nightclub than a bar. It's lost the dark, edgy feel it once had, but remains the place to be and one of Southeast Asia's classic night spots. Quiet before 10pm, it heaves at the hinges come the witching hour. The music is great if you only go once, but the disco diet soon gets repetitive. Be wary of large gangs of rich young Khmers here…some are children of the elite and aren't averse to picking fights with tourists. Their retinue of bodyguards makes it folly indeed to fight back. The Heart usually stays open until the last person leaves.

Other admired establishments with liquid menus:

California 2 Guesthouse (Map p68; 317 Sisowath Quay) Biker bar with the cheapest beer on the riverfront.

Howie's Bar (Map p68; 30 Ph 51) This place is the best bolt hole for those wanting to escape the noise and crowds that threaten to overwhelm the nearby Heart of Darkness.

Rising Sun (Map p68; 20 Ph 178) English pub meets backpacker bar.

ENTERTAINMENT

For the ins and outs on the entertainment scene, check the Friday edition of the *Cambodia Daily* or the latest issues of *Bayon Pearnik* or *Phnom Penh Post*.

Live Music

Live music is pretty limited in Phnom Penh compared with the bigger Asian capitals. The best live music venue right now is the **Memphis Pub** (Map p68; 3 Ph 118), which often looks closed due to the soundproof doors. It has live rock'n'roll from Tuesday to Saturday nights, including Wednesday jam sessions.

Dance

If you want to catch a glimpse of Cambodia's graceful classical dance, you can watch students train at the **Royal University of Fine Arts** (Map pp64-5; Ph 70; ☺ 8-11am Mon-Fri) or **Apsara Arts Association** (71 Ph 598; ☺ 7.30-10.30am & 2-5pm Mon-Sat). Remember, these are schools of learning, not tourist attractions so keep noise levels and flash photography to a minimum. Alternate performances of classical dance and folk dance are held at Apsara every Saturday at 7pm (admission US$5).

Cinemas

The city's burgeoning cinema scene includes little in the way of English films. Most theatres screen budget Khmer films about zombies, vampires and ghosts, or Asian action flicks.

Movie Street (Map p68; Sihanouk Blvd; 1/2/3 tickets US$4/5/6) Private viewing booths with big TVs to watch the latest Hollywood and European titles.

French Cultural Centre (Map p68; Ph 184) Frequent weekday movie screenings in French, usually kicking off at 6pm. Ask for the monthly programme.

CAMBODIA

SHOPPING

There are some great deals in Phnom Penh's lively markets – put on your bartering hats and dive into the fray. **Psar Tuol Tom Pong** (Map pp64-5; cnr Ph 440 & 163), more commonly known as the Russian Market (not to be confused with Psar O Russei!), is packed to the rafters with genuine, and not so genuine, Colombia, Gap and Quiksilver clothes at laughably low prices (no swimsuits ladies). There's also beautiful Cambodian silk, pirated DVDs, CDs and software, and handicrafts. Most markets are open between 6.30am and 5.30pm.

Several stores sell lovely wares to support local organisations striving to improve the lives of Cambodia's disabled community or disenfranchised women. Shops with a cause:

NCDP Handicrafts (Map p68; 3 Norodom Blvd) Exquisite silk scarves, throws, bags and cushions. Other items: *krama*, shirts, wallets and purses, notebooks and greeting cards.

Rajana (Map pp64-5; 170 Ph 450) Beautiful selection of cards, some quirky metalware, quality jewellery, bamboo crafts and a range of condiments from Cambodia. It also has a booth in nearby Psar Tuol Tom Pong.

Tabitha (Map pp64-5; cnr Ph 360 & Ph 51) Premium quality silk with a fantastic collection of bags, tableware, bedroom decorations and children's toys.

Wat Than Handicrafts (Map pp64-5; Norodom Blvd) Similar goods to NCDP. It's set inside Wat Than.

GETTING THERE & AWAY

Air

See p60 for international flights and p60 for domestic flights out of Phnom Penh.

Airlines located around town:

Air France (Map p68; ☎ 219220; www.airfrance.com; Hong Kong Center, Samdech Sothearos Blvd)

Bangkok Airways (Map p68; ☎ 722545; www.bangkokair.com; 61 Ph 214)

China Southern Airlines (Map p68; ☎ 430877; www.cs-air.com/en/; Phnom Penh Hotel, 53 Monivong Blvd)

Dragonair (Map pp64-5; ☎ 424300; www.dragonair.com; A4 Regency Sq)

Lao Airlines (Map p68; ☎ 216563; www.laos-airlines.com; 58 Sihanouk Blvd)

Malaysia Airlines (Map p68; ☎ 426688; www.malaysia-airlines.com; Diamond Hotel, 172 Monivong Blvd)

President Airlines (Map pp64-5; ☎ 993089; www.presidentairlines.com; A14 Regency Sq)

Royal Phnom Penh Airways (Map p68; ☎ 217419; ppenhairw@bigpond.com.kh; 209 Ph 19)

Shanghai Airlines (Map p68; ☎ 723999; www.shanghai-air.com; 19 Ph 106)

Siem Reap Airways (Map p68; ☎ 723963; www.siemreapairways.com; 65 Ph 214)

SilkAir (Map pp64-5; ☎ 426807; www.silkair.com; Himawari, 313 Sisowath Quay)

Thai Airways (THAI; Map pp64-5; ☎ 214359; www.thaiair.com; A15 Regency Sq)

Vietnam Airlines (Map p68; ☎ 363396; www.vietnamairlines.com; 41 Ph 214)

Boat

Several companies take turns offering popular daily fast boats up the Tonlé Sap to Siem Reap (US$18 to US$25, five to six hours), leaving the new tourist boat dock on Sisowath Quay at 7am. Tickets can be arranged through guesthouses or near the dock itself. The boats can be packed like sardines, so it's best to sit on the roof and marinate in plenty of sunscreen. Given the fact that buses to Siem Reap cost US$3.50, it's a very expensive option. See p61 for other rewarding, and less expensive, Cambodian boat journeys.

Bus

Lovely sealed sections of road now connect Phnom Penh with Siem Reap, Battambang and Sihanoukville, making for bountiful bus services. Most currently leave from company offices, which are spread throughout town. The government is slowly but surely developing out-of-town bus stations, so the points of departure may change in time.

Competition ensures that prices are low and differ little between companies.

Phnom Penh Public Transport (PPPT; Map p68; ☎ 210359; Psar Thmei) is the longest-running company and serves Battambang (14,000r, five hours), Kompong Cham (8000r, two hours), Kompong Chhnang (5500r, two hours), Kratie (18,000r, six hours), Neak Luong (5000r, two hours), Poipet (20,000r, eight hours), Siem Reap (14,000r, six hours), Sihanoukville (14,000r, four hours) and Takeo (5000r, two hours).

Following are the companies, their contact details in the capital and the destinations they serve:

Capitol Tour (Map p68; ☎ 217627; 14 Ph 182) Battambang, Bangkok, Poipet, Siem Reap, Sihanoukville.

GST (Map p68; ☎ 012-895550; Psar Thmei) Battambang, Bangkok, Poipet, Siem Reap, Sihanoukville, Sisophon.

Hour Lean (Map p68; ☎ 012-939905; 97 Sisowath Quay) Battambang, Kampot, Kompong Cham, Kratie,

Poipet, Sen Monorom, Siem Reap, Sihanoukville, Stung Treng, Takeo.
Narin Transport (Map p68; ☎ 991995; 50 Ph 125) Siem Reap.
Neak Krorhorm (Map p68; ☎ 219496; 127 Ph 108) Battambang, Poipet, Siem Reap, Sisophon.

For more details on any of these services, see the individual city entries throughout the chapter.

Car & Motorcycle

Self-drive car hire is only for nutters! Guesthouses and travel agencies can arrange a car and driver from US$20 a day, depending on the destination. Motorcycles are a liberating way to see places of interest near Phnom Penh. See p78 for rental details.

Share Taxi, Pick-up & Minibus

With cheap, comfortable and fast buses, and blissful sealed roads heading off in every direction from town, share taxis, pick-ups and minibuses offer little besides flexible departure times to travellers leaving Phnom Penh.

Share taxis to Kampot, Krong Koh Kong and Sihanoukville leave from Psar Dang Kor (Map pp64–5), while minibuses, pick-ups and taxis for most other places leave from near Psar Thmei (Map pp64–5). Vehicles for Svay Rieng and Vietnam leave from Chbah Ampeau taxi park (Map pp64–5).

Train

The last remaining scheduled passenger train service is supposed to leave for Pursat (9900r, eight hours) and Battambang (16,440r, 13 to 15 hours) each odd calendar day (1, 3, 5, etc) at 6.30am, but breakdowns tend to wreak havoc with the timetable.

While more costly, uncomfortable and lengthy than the bus, it's your last chance to experience a rooftop ride on this classic, and soon to be extinct, beast.

GETTING AROUND
Bicycle

Japan Rentals (Map p68; Ph 107; per day US$1), opposite Capitol Guesthouse III, is a perfect place to find some pedal power.

Cyclo

Cyclos are still common, but have lost a lot of business to moto drivers. Costs are generally 1000r for a short trip and 2000r for longer ones, but the guys who hang outside tourist hotspots will pick a number, any number!

Moto

Motos are generally recognisable by the baseball caps favoured by drivers. In areas frequented by foreigners, moto drivers generally speak English and sometimes a little French, making them useful guides as well (US$6 to US$8 per day depending on the destinations). Elsewhere in town it can

---

BORDER CROSSING: INTO VIETNAM

The bus-boat combination via Kaam Samnor (C)/Vinh Xuong (V) is the most scenic way to get between Cambodia and Vietnam, although be aware it links Phnom Penh to Chau Doc in the Mekong Delta, not Ho Chi Minh City. **Capitol Tour** (Map p68; ☎ 963883; off Ph Sivatha) charges just US$6, which includes a bus from Phnom Penh to Neak Luong on the Mekong River and a boat from there to Chau Doc (six to seven hours).

For the adventurous or independent, it can be done for a similar price by first catching a bus from Psar Thmei in Phnom Penh to Neak Luong (4000r), taking a speedboat from there to the border at Kaam Samnor (10,000r), a moto between the borders (4000r), and finally a moto from Vinh Xuong to Chau Doc (US$4).

The run from Phnom Penh to Ho Chi Minh City via Bavet (C)/Moc Bai (V) is less bone-crunching than before, taking between five and six hours. Serious competition means that it's possible to get through-tickets for just US$6 with Capitol Tour or **Narin Transport** (Map p68; ☎ 991995; 50 Ph 125), both running swanky buses. Both involve a change of bus at the border where established Vietnamese companies take over. It can be done independently by using share taxis and local buses, but it's no longer a cheaper option.

The Phnom Den (C)/Tinh Bien (V) crossing, linking Takeo Province with An Giang Province, sits 60km southeast of Takeo town, but has little traffic as it's remote and NH2 is dreadful. You must have a valid Cambodian or Vietnamese visa before making this crossing.

be difficult because eager Khmer-speaking drivers will adamantly nod that they know the destination when they clearly have no clue. If you don't want to end up in Bangkok, pay attention and point directions if necessary.

Most short trips are 1000r and about double that at night. Longer trips will cost more – it's about 2000r from the National Museum to the Russian Market. While it's not necessary to negotiate a price in advance, doing so will quell potential misunderstandings at trip's end.

Motorcycle

The best of the numerous places to rent are **Lucky! Lucky!** (Map p68; ☎ 212788; 413 Monivong Blvd) and nearby **New! New!** (Map p68; ☎ 012-855488; 417 Monivong Blvd). A 100cc Honda costs US$3 to US$4 per day or US$20 per week, and 250cc dirt bikes cost US$7/40 per day/week.

Motorcycle theft is a problem and if the bike goes bye-bye you'll be liable – use a hefty padlock.

Taxi

Phnom Penh has no metered taxis of the sort found in Thailand or Vietnam. **Bailey's Taxis** (☎ 012-890000) and **Taxi Vantha** (☎ 012-855000) offer taxis 24 hours a day, but have a limited number of cars. The airport run costs US$5 and elsewhere taxis charge about US$1 per kilometre.

AROUND PHNOM PENH

TONLÉ BATI

At **Tonlé Bati** (admission US$3, incl drink), you'll find two Angkorian-era temples and a popular lakeside picnic area. Set among flowers and wavering palms, **Ta Prohm** and its bas-reliefs depicting stories of birth, infidelity and murder is much more evocative than the diminutive **Yeay Peau**. Ta Prohm was built by King Jayavarman VII (r 1181–1219) on the site of a 6th-century Khmer shrine. Anyone experienced in Angkor's splendour could survive without a visit, but if Angkor is still on the horizon, make the detour.

It's 2km off NH2, 31km south of Phnom Penh. Grab an hourly PPPT bus (p76) to Takeo and it'll drop you at the turn-off (3000r, one hour).

PHNOM CHISOR

Some spectacular views of the surrounding countryside are offered from the summit of **Phnom Chisor**, although the landscape screams Gobi Desert during dry season. An 11th-century laterite and brick **temple** (admission US$2), with carved sandstone lintels, guards the hilltop's eastern face. Atop its southern stairs, the sacred pool of **Tonlé Om** is visible in the distance below.

It's a 2000r pick-up ride from Tonlé Bati to the Phnom Chisor turn-off on NH2, 57km south of Phnom Penh. From there, a return trip to Phnom Chisor's base by moto is about 6000r. Flag down a PPPT bus back to Phnom Penh (4000r, 1½ hours, hourly).

TAKEO & PHNOM DA

☎ 032 / pop 44,000

Poking its head from hilltop foliage and looking over endless rice paddies is the small laterite temple of **Phnom Da** (admission US$2), in an area that once comprised part of the pre-Angkorian Chenla civilisation's remarkable capital. During the wet season the surrounding land sinks beneath rising waters and Phnom Da is only accessible by speedboat (about US$18 to charter) from **Takeo**, an unremarkable provincial capital. En route, speedboats access Angkor Borei, where there's a small **Chenla Museum** (admission US$1). In dry season take a pick-up to Angkor Borei, then catch a boat to Phnom Da.

Boeung Takeo Guesthouse (☎ 931306; Ph 3; r US$5-10; 🅿) boasts a lakefront location, roomy rooms and clean conditions – just the spot for a night's kip. Rooms with a view are no harder on the pocket.

Restaurant Stung Takeo (Ph 9; meals 3000-6000r; 🕙 breakfast, lunch & dinner), perched on stilts and overlooking the canal to Angkor Borei, is a popular Khmer chow den and the place to fill up before journeying to Phnom Da.

PPPT buses link Takeo to Phnom Penh (5000r, two hours, hourly) between 6am and 4pm. To reach Kampot take a *remorque-moto* to Angkor Tasaom on NH3 before nabbing a share taxi heading south.

KIRIROM NATIONAL PARK

Set amid elevated pine forests, **Kirirom National Park** offers some small waterfalls and decent walking trails. Hook up with a **ranger** (about US$5) for a two-hour hike up to **Phnom Dat Chivit** (End of the World Mountain) where an abrupt cliff-face offers an unbroken view of the western mountain ranges. It's one of the few national parks to have a community tourism programme and proceeds from its educational walks are pumped back into the community. Contact **Mlup Baitong** (☎ 023-214409; mlup@online.com.kh) for details.

Kirirom is 112km southwest of Phnom Penh. It's not easy to access by public transport – Sihanoukville buses can let you off at Kirirom, but you'll have to find a moto for the remaining 25km west. The easiest option is to hire a motorcycle or charter a taxi with others. A large sign marks the turn-off about 85km south of Phnom Penh.

SIEM REAP

☎ 063 / pop 158,000

Having Angkor, one of humanity's most audacious architectural achievements, in its backyard was like sitting on a development time bomb; eventually it had to go BOOM! Siem Reap's borders are currently spilling outward and new guesthouses, hotels and eateries are hitting the scene monthly. Amazingly, the town's core retains its charming rural qualities, with old French shophouses and shady leaf-laden

---

GETTING INTO TOWN

Most arriving by boat aren't surprised by hoards of motos waiting at Phnom Krom dock (11km from town), but they're usually taken aback by the sight of their name on a board being furiously waved by a driver – guesthouses in Phnom Penh pass on or even sell names to guesthouses in Siem Reap! If you follow the sign and stay at that guesthouse, your lift is free. If you choose to stay elsewhere, expect to pay the driver about US$1. Travellers coming independently by road will usually be dropped near Psar Leu in the east of town and from here it's just a short moto ride (2000r) into town. If you're arriving with bus services sold by guesthouses, the bus will head straight to a partner guesthouse. Most guesthouses have a free airport pick-up service – otherwise the 7km ride to town costs US$1 by moto or US$5 for a taxi.

DID YOU KNOW?

The name Siem Reap actually means 'Siamese Defeated', hardly the most tactful name for a major city near Thailand!

boulevards. Those looking for fine fare and lively evenings will be pleasantly surprised with the cosmopolitan flair now lurking beneath the town's pastoral skin.

Unlike the town of Agra that hosts the Taj Mahal, Siem Reap's pleasant atmosphere and array of facilities may actually leave you lingering after your temple experience.

ORIENTATION

Straddling Stung Siem Reap's narrow waters, Siem Reap spreads outward from Psar Chaa, which is the epicentre of ingestion – tasty eats and liquid treats. It's still a small town and easy to navigate, with budget accommodation spread throughout. National Hwy 6 (NH6) runs east–west and cuts the town in two. Street numbering is wholly haphazard, so take care when hunting down specific addresses.

INFORMATION

To keep on top of the constant changes in Siem Reap, pick up a free copy of *Siem Reap Angkor Visitors Guide*, published quarterly. Reviews are linked to advertisers, so take them with a grain of salt.

Bookshops

Some of the cheapest books on Angkor are hawked by local kids and amputees around temples – buying one is a decent way of assisting the disadvantaged.

Lazy Mango (Map p80; ☎ 963875; Bar St) Comprehensive secondhand bookshop with guides, novels and plenty on Cambodia.

Monument Books (Map p80; ☎ 963228; Psar Chaa Area) Great selection of new books on Angkor and Cambodia. More branches at the FCC Angkor (p84) and airport.

Paris Sète (Map p80; Bar St) *Plusieurs livres français*. Can't read French? Then pass on this bookshop.

Emergency

Ambulance (☎ 119)
Fire (☎ 118)
Police (☎ 117)
Tourist Police (Map pp88-9; ☎ 012-969991) Now located at the main Angkor ticket checkpoint.

CAMBODIA

CAMBODIA

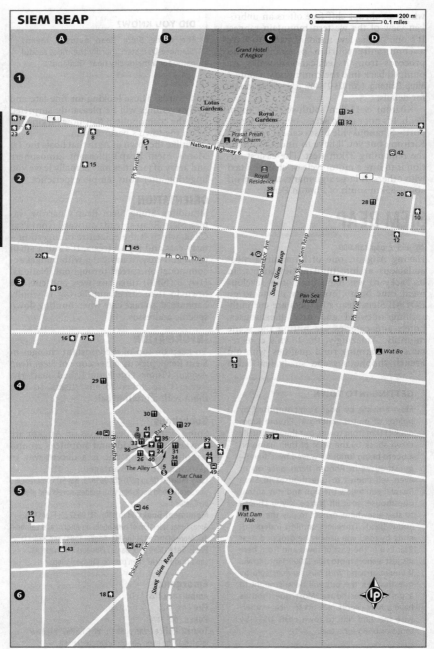

CAMBODIA

Internet Access

Internet access is everywhere, with the highest concentrations of Internet cafés found on Ph Sivatha and around Psar Chaa. Most charge 4000r per hour.

Internet & Email (Map p80; per hr 4000r) Card readers, USB connections and a handy programme to recover those long-lost photo files. Burning images to your CD is US$1.

Medical Services

Naga Medical Centre (Map pp88-9; ☎ 964500; 593 NH6; ☼ 24hr) Best private medical facilities in Siem Reap.

Money

Cambodia Asia Bank (Map p80; ☎ 964741; cnr Ph Sivatha & NH6; ☼ 7.30am-9pm) Cashes travellers cheques at 2% commission. Minimum US$5 charge for credit-card cash advances. Also a booth at the airport.

Canadia Bank (Map p80; ☎ 964808; Psar Chaa) Free credit-card advances and changes travellers cheques in most major currencies at a 2% commission. ATM is Visa/MasterCard-compatible.

Union Commercial Bank (Map p80; ☎ 964703; Psar Chaa) Charges 2% commission for travellers cheques and offers free Visa advances.

Post

Main post office (Map p80; Pokambor Ave; ☼ 7am-5pm) Improving but still sketchy service – ensure your cards are franked or wait until Phnom Penh.

Telephone

The cheapest international calls are via the Internet and start from 400r per minute. Unblemished, yet more expensive, international calls can be made at numerous private booths advertising telephone services – they also offer inexpensive local calls starting from 300r per minute.

Tourist Information

Dumbfoundingly, there's no helpful tourist office for independent travellers in Siem Reap. Talk to smiley backpackers – maybe they know something you don't. The guesthouses are also decent sources of general information.

DANGERS & ANNOYANCES

Compared with Phnom Penh, Siem Reap is pretty safe to stroll around, even by night. However, if you rent a bike don't keep your bag or valuables in the basket – they're easy prey for thieves on passing motorbikes. In more remote locations, such as Kbal Spean or Phnom Kulen, stick to clearly marked trails, as it's potential mine territory.

There are many commission scams run by guesthouses, the worst involving those arriving by bus from Bangkok – see the Bangkok to Siem Reap Bus Scam on p86 for more information. On principle you may want to avoid staying at a guesthouse you're forced to visit, whether by bus, moto or taxi. Booking ahead can alleviate some of these problems.

Begging is prevalent in Siem Reap – have a read of the Responsible Travel section (p122) for advice on how to help the less fortunate.

SIGHTS

For those temple things you may have heard about, see Temples of Angkor (p86).

The **Land Mine Museum** (Map pp88-9; ☎ 012-598951; donations accepted), with extensive details about the types of mines used during the civil war and their continuing destructive capabilities, is of undoubtable educational value to tourists and locals alike. It's part of the **Cambodian Land Mine Museum Relief Fund** (CLMMRF; www.cambodialandminemuseum.org), a Canadian NGO working to reduce land mine casualties and help rehabilitate the wounded. Texas A&M University's architecture department is also helping to design the new museum's home and a nearby rehabilitation facility. The museum's owner, Aki Ra (a former child-soldier for both the Khmer Rouge and Vietnamese) still works occasionally to remove mines that he was once forced to lay. This has drawn the ire of official mine-removal organisations because he doesn't grid the demined area – or is it as others suggest and they're just embarrassed because he removes and defuses mines with only a probing stick and screwdriver for pennies, while they charge almost US$1000 for each mine.

SLEEPING

New guesthouses and hotels are popping up quicker than parts on an adolescent boy accidentally finding himself in the ladies change room. While they're spread throughout town, four areas hold the bulk of quality choices: Psar Chaa, Phlauv Sivatha, NH6 West and the east bank of the river.

Psar Chaa Area

Ivy Guesthouse 2 (Map p80; ☎ 012-380516; r US$6-8) Fronted by a leafy bar and restaurant, this friendly guesthouse sports spotless bathrooms, whitewashed walls and the odd bit of Khmer artwork and silk, something absent in most budget options. There's also a small balcony, complete with hammocks and a TV.

Popular Guesthouse (Map p80; ☎ 963578; chom@camnet.com.kh; s without bathroom US$2-3, s US$5, d US$7-14; ☒) A wide range of clean rooms and a great rooftop restaurant with cheap eats have ensured this backpacker haunt remains – you guessed it – popular. The ever-growing new wing houses extra touches like air-con, TV and hot water.

Red Lodge (Map p80; ☎ 012-707048; www.red lodgeangkor.com; r US$8-12; ☒ ▯) Hidden down the back streets, this modern villa has bright rooms with high ceilings, and a shady sanctuary of cushions and magazines out the back. Throw in free fruit, toast, tea and coffee with free bike rentals and a selection of videos for the TV and you're laughing.

Shadow of Angkor Guesthouse (Map p80; ☎ 964774; Pokambor Ave; r US$8-20; ☒) A breezy French colonial building in a cracking riverfront location. Plank floors, local artwork and balconies grace the air-con options, while fan rooms are more austere and some sadly lack windows.

Phlauv Sivatha Area

Smiley Guesthouse (Map p80; ☎ 012-852955; r US$4-20; ☒) Home to a diverse selection of bright, clean and airy rooms that surround a vibrant pond- and plant-filled courtyard. A big place, but a good place.

Orchidae Guesthouse (Map p80; ☎ 012-939964; s/tw without bathroom US$2/4, s US$5, tw US$6-10; ☒) A great vibe emanates from the thatch-roofed hammock haven out the front. The simple fan rooms downstairs are a little small, but cooler than the wood-lined options found upstairs.

Ecole Hôtelière Sala Bai (Map p80; ☎ 963329; r US$8-25; ☒) The three US$8 standard rooms are bright, breezy and beautiful with silk wall hangings, woven throw pillows and wicker wardrobes. It's run by a school that trains Cambodians for the hospitality industry.

Long Live Angkor Guesthouse (Map p80; ☎ 760286; r US$5-11; ☒) No vibe, but sparkling and new. Fans and TVs throughout and if you want hot water, add US$1.

Naga Guesthouse (Map p80; ☎ 963439; NH6; s/tw without bathroom US$2/3, s & tw US$4-5) This old wooden house is one of town's original guesthouses. Rooms are simple but airy. There's a free pool table in the restaurant.

NH6 West

Jasmine Lodge (Map p80; ☎ 760697; NH6; s/tw without bathroom US$2/3, d US$4-15; ☒) Hospitality, cleanliness and simplicity define this find. The air-con rooms are understandably smarter than the fan options. The staff here are full of Angkor info and serve up choice meals for pennies.

Earthwalkers (Map pp88-9; ☎ 760107; www .earthwalkers.no; off NH6; dm US$4, s/d from US$10/12;

SPLURGE!

Borann L'Auberge des Temples (☎ 964740; www.borann.com; r incl tax US$36-48; 🟦) Settle into a book on your private veranda, wind your way through the tropical garden, gracefully cannonball into the glistening pool or vegetate happily in your gorgeous room, complete with traditional wood furnishings and silk wall hangings. You won't find more for less.

🟦 🖵) A fair hike from town, but a meticulously clean and relaxing joint to unwind in. Set up by fun-loving Norwegians who fell for Cambodia, it's a great source of travel tips and breakfast is on the house.

Chenla Guesthouse (Map p80; ☎ 963233; NH6; s US$3, r US$6-20; 🟦) The new wing is gleaming with polished wood and tiles along with TVs, fridges and hot water. The old wing is cheaper and a little rough around the edges. It's popular with Japanese travellers.

Victory Guesthouse (Map p80; off NH6; r US$5-10; 🟦) More a hotel than guesthouse, this new shiny option has spotless rooms with TVs and offers free laundry.

Apsara Angkor Guesthouse (Map p80; ☎ 012-779678; r without bathroom US$2, r US$5-10; 🟦) Follow the 'bag o'keys' to a room that suits your fancy. US$5 gets you an old but spacious room with a fan and TV.

East Bank of the River

European Guesthouse (Map p80; ☎ 012-582237; r US$5-12; 🟦) Nothing fancy (well if you don't consider the putting green of a hallway upstairs), just simple and sizeable rooms served with a smile. TV rooms start at US$6.

Samnark Preah Riem Guesthouse (Map p80; ☎ 760378; preahriem@camnet.com.kh; r US$5-8) Another friendly family-run option. Vaulted ceilings and walls finely finished in wood give upstairs rooms some serious character, while the downstairs options are stark, but offer more refuge from the heat.

Home Sweet Home Guesthouse (Map p80; ☎ 963245; sweethome@camintel.com; r US$8-15; 🟦) Simple, spacious and spotless rooms, including TVs and, for a couple extra dollars, hot water.

Two Dragons Guesthouse (Map p80; ☎ 012-490005; r US$7-18; 🟦) Next door is this single-

storey option with smart rooms. If you want a boob tube (TV), head elsewhere. The owner runs a renowned Cambodian travel website, so reliable travel information is guaranteed.

Green Town Guesthouse (Map p80; ☎ 964974; r without bathroom US$3, r US$4-12; 🟦) Oodles of inexpensive no-nonsense options. You'll find it cowering behind the luxury Pansea Hotel.

EATING

We wouldn't blame you for eating the odd meal at your guesthouse, but get into the habit and we'll have to come and give you a polite knock upside the head! Indulging in Siem Reap's recent gastronomic extravaganza of Khmer and international flavours won't break the bank and your insides will love you for it.

Unless stated otherwise, restaurants are open for breakfast, lunch and dinner.

Khmer Kitchen Restaurant (Map p80; ☎ 964154; The Alley; mains US$2-3; 🕑 lunch & dinner) Candle-lit tables spill out into the atmospheric alley between Bar St and Psar Chaa and you'll find delectable Khmer and Thai dishes. The pumpkin and coconut soup is sublime, as is the tofu and veg curry. Recent guests include a certain Mick Jagger.

Amok (Map p80; ☎ 012-800309; The Alley; mains US$3-4.50; 🕑 dinner) Just down the alley from Khmer Kitchen, Amok is a small restaurant with a big personality. The emphasis here is Khmer, which is hardly surprising as it's named in honour of Cambodia's national dish.

Blue Pumpkin (Map p80; ☎ 963574; Psar Chaa area; mains US$1.50-5) Plants, wicker chairs and teak umbrellas sit casually out the front while slick all-white fixtures, 'bed seating' and

SPLURGE!

La Noria Restaurant (Map p80; ☎ 964242; mains US$4-6, set lunch or dinner US$5-9) Splash out on a set meal and delve into fine a blend of Khmer and European cuisine, including *samla* (poached fish à la Khmer), gazpacho and delicious brochettes. The restaurant offers *sbei tuoi* (shadow puppet) shows on Wednesday evenings and some of the US$6 ticket goes to a charity supporting local children.

contemporary minimalism boldly stand their ground upstairs. The menu includes light bites, great sandwiches and shakes, and freshly made pastries and ice cream.

Dead Fish Tower (Map p80; Ph Sivatha; dishes US$2-5) Coke-crate lights, tree-trunk tables, comfortable cushions, tasty Thai treats, straws big enough to suck a grape through and a crocodile farm have all found a home in this incredible and eclectic multilevel structure. The owners even brag 'we don't serve dog, cat, rat or worm' – good on them!

Pissa Italiana (Map p80; Bar St; pizzas US$4-9; ⏰ lunch & dinner) Siem Reap's best pizza – bar none. Sounds pricey but one pizza will fill two grumbling tummies. Try 'Cambodia Updated' covered in onions, mushrooms, chillies, bell peppers, basil, egg, pancetta and chorizo.

Chivit Thai (Map p80; 130 Ph Wat Bo; mains US$2-4) Possibly the most atmospheric Thai restaurant, as it's set in a green garden under traditional wooden pavilions. Saunter to a table or sink into a floor cushion and savour some spicy Siamese specials.

Balcony Café (Map p80; Bar St; mains US$2-6) This grand old building houses power shakes and a small selection of Khmer, vegetarian and Western snacks. There's no alcohol served – almost commercial suicide in this town – but 20% of profits go to rural development, so forgive and forget.

Red Piano (Map p80; ☎ 963240; Bar St; mains US$3-5) Now with a commanding balcony overlooking the action on Bar St, there's plenty of space for diners to relax in this restored colonial gem. The menu is a mixed bag of Khmer dishes and a pick-and-mix from beyond.

Arun Restaurant (Map p80; mains US$1.50-3) One of the oldest and best Cambodian restaurants in town – it also lacks the marauding tour groups others attract.

When it comes to cheaper Khmer eats, Psar Chaa (Map p80) has plenty of dishes on display and many more cooked to order. It's a lively and atmospheric place for a local meal at local-ish prices. Alternatively, ask a moto driver for recommendations of the best hole-in-the-walls – these guys are always eating on the cheap.

Other flavoursome feeds:

Banteay Srei Restaurant (Map pp88-9; NH6; mains 4000-10,000r) A bit of a well-kept secret among Khmers for its authentic and understated Cambodian dining.

Ecstatic Pizza (Map p80; ☎ 011-928531; Psar Chaa area; pizzas from US$4) The place to go for 'happy' ganja-topped pizza. Free delivery to guesthouses and hotels.

Jasmine Lodge (Map p80; NH6; mains US$1-2) A stand-out among guesthouse cuisine – Thai and Khmer served.

Taj Mahal (Map p80; Psar Chaa area; curries US$2-5) Probably the town's best Indian restaurant. Liberal portions will fulfil the deepest of curry cravings.

DRINKING

The transformation from the absence of nightlife to the profusion seen today has been a quick one. Psar Chaa's surrounds now crawl with lively bars, with one street even earning the moniker Bar St – dive in, crawl out!

Angkor What? (Map p80; Bar St) A healthy 5pm to 8pm happy hour – with US$5 buckets of Mekong whiskey, Coke and Red Bull, and US$3 Anchor pitchers – lubes things up for later when it's packed and reverberating with cool tunes. Partial proceeds support a local hospital, so drinking here is helping somebody's liver, if not your own.

FCC Angkor (Map p80; Pokambor Ave) Follow wafting tunes beneath the palms and sink into some faux leather for a candle-lit cocktail next to the reflection pool. The landmark 1960s building backs the serene outdoor bar and also makes for a swish place to down a few. Half-price happy hour runs from 5pm to 7pm.

Temple Bar (Map p80; Bar St) Pediments and a Jayavarman VII bust give the exterior a temple feel, but the only worshipping going on here is 'hail the ale'. Popular pavement tables, a generous happy hour from 4pm to 9pm (buy two, get one free) and some alternative rock have quickly earned it a loyal following.

Buddha Lounge (Map p80; Bar St) Opposite the Temple and in a similar vein, the Buddha Lounge is filled with spiritual décor, spirited drinks and loyal followers.

DRINKING WITH A DIFFERENCE!

Butterfly Garden Bar (Map p80; admission US$1; ⏰ 9am-5pm) Spend a mellow afternoon with cool drink in hand and a few dozen fluttering butterflies in sight. It's a quiet colourful garden ensconced in mesh, east of the river.

Linga Bar (Map p80; The Alley) Siem Reap's first and only gay bar welcomes all comers with a laid-back lounge fitout that wouldn't look out of place in any major city. A cracking cocktail list and dance beats are helping to spread the word.

Laundry Bar (Map p80; Psar Chaa) Leave your skanky socks at home and wade into this lavishly decorated night spot for some late-night liquid luxury. One of the few spots with a dance floor, things get busy on weekends or when guest DJs have the house moving.

ENTERTAINMENT

Several restaurants and hotels offer cultural performances during the evening – for many it's the only chance to witness classical Cambodian dance. Unfortunately the shows are either expensive or hardly authentic.

Bayon II Restaurant (Map p80; just north of NH6) A good bet, it offers decent dancing and a buffet dinner for US$11.

Beatocello (Map pp88–9; Jayavarman VII Children's Hospital; 7.15pm Sat) Cello concerts featuring original music and Bach compositions. Entry is free, but donations are welcome; they fund free medical treatment to local children.

SHOPPING

Serious shopping escapades are to be had, whether it be at Psar Chaa, lesser-known markets, souvenir shops or the endless temple jamborees. Buying at the temples is a great way to give back, as many vendors are original Angkor inhabitants' descendents.

Another way to let your shopping dollars do well is to visit shops that support Cambodia's disabled and disenfranchised.

Rehab Craft (Map p80; opposite Psar Chaa) Also known as Made in Cambodia, this place specialises in quality silk products such as wallets, handbags, photo albums and the like. Profits are used to train and employ the disabled community.

Rajana (Map p80; Bar St) Sells quirky wooden and metalware objects, well-designed silver jewellery and handmade cards, as well as local condiments like lemon grass, pepper and coffee. Rajana promotes fair trade and employment opportunities for Cambodians.

Tabitha Cambodia (Map p80; 760650; Ph Sivatha) Home to a beautiful range of silk scarves, cushion covers and throws, the proceeds from which go towards projects like house-building and well-drilling.

Artisans D'Angkor (Map p80; 380354) High-quality reproduction carvings and exquisite silks are sold. Impoverished youngsters are trained in the arts of their ancestors.

GETTING THERE & AWAY
Air

For the lowdown on international destinations from Siem Reap, see p60. For daily domestic flights between Phnom Penh and Siem Reap, see p60.

Airline offices around town:

Bangkok Airways (Map pp88–9; 380191; www .bangkokair.com; NH6)

Lao Airlines (Map pp88–9; 963283; www.laos-air lines.com; NH6)

Malaysia Airlines (Map pp88–9; 964136; www .malaysia-airlines.com; Siem Reap Airport)

President Airlines (Map pp88–9; 963887; www .presidentairlines.com; NH6)

Siem Reap Airways (Map pp88–9; 380192; www .siemreapairways.com; NH6)

Vietnam Airlines (Map pp88–9; 964488; www .vietnamairlines.com; NH6)

Boat

Daily express boats service Phnom Penh (US$18 to US$25, five to six hours), but are overpriced given it's just as fast by road and only US$3.50! Guesthouses usually include transport to the dock at Phnom Krom, 11km south of town, with their tickets. Otherwise expect to pay motos about US$1. Angle for the roof and don't forget to lather on the sunscreen.

Express boats to Battambang (US$15, three to eight hours) pass near Prek Toal Bird Sanctuary on arguably Cambodia's most scenic water route. Low water in the dry season means smaller speedboats make the run, but they often fall prey to sticky mud, making for seemingly endless journeys. Try to ensure the boat driver keeps to a sensible speed, as big waves have proved a major problem for local communities over the years.

Bus

The road to Phnom Penh is now glorious tarmac, making for smooth journeys, whereas the road west to Sisophon and Poipet is still one heck of a bumpy ride. Competition ensures low and consistent pricing among the various bus companies. Most companies pick up at their offices, but

BANGKOK TO SIEM REAP BUS SCAM

While direct Bangkok to Siem Reap bus tickets are cheap and sound convenient, they're anything but. Since bus operators make their real money from Siem Reap guesthouses paying them for bringing guests, their goal is to make the journey as long and uncomfortable as humanly possible. Why? Well, if they dropped you off at an average guesthouse at 4pm, you're likely to search out better accommodation. However if you arrive battered, exhausted and in the dark, you're more likely to succumb to pressure and collapse at their chosen guesthouse.

Some companies are actually secretly using the painful Pruhm/Daun Lem border instead of the much faster (though still painfully bumpy) Poipet/Aranya Prathet crossing! Others also try to 'help' you with your visa, resulting in you being overcharged.

Make travel the adventure it was always supposed to be – book a bus to the border and go it alone from there. Once across, you'll have little trouble finding transport to Siem Reap.

soon buses will depart from the Taxi Park, east of town on NH6.

Neak Krorhorm (Map p80; ☎ 964924; opposite Psar Chaa) offers the most destinations with buses to Phnom Penh (US$3.50, five to six hours), Battambang (US$4, four to five hours), Poipet (US$4, four to five hours) and Bangkok (US$10, 10 to 14 hours).

Other companies with Siem Reap offices and their destinations:

Capitol Tour (Map p80; ☎ 963883; off Ph Sivatha) Phnom Penh, Poipet and Bangkok.

GST (Map p80; ☎ 012-727774; Ph Sivatha) Phnom Penh.

Hour Lean (Map p80; ☎ 760103; Xin Yi Bus office, Ph Sivatha) Phnom Penh.

BOULEVARD OF BROKEN BACKSIDES

Why is the road between Siem Reap and the Thailand border at Poipet still in notoriously bad shape when its condition should be a major priority for trade and tourism? Well, it's rumoured that an unnamed airline is paying an unstated commission to an unnamed political party to indefinitely stall this road's upgrade!

Share Taxi & Pick-up

See the Anlong Veng (p98) and Preah Vihear Province (p98) sections for details on getting to remote temples.

GETTING AROUND

For all the juicy details on how best to explore the temples of Angkor, see p90.

Navigating Siem Reap on foot is pretty straightforward, as it's a relatively small place. If you need to cross town quickly, a moto will cost 1000r – and double that at

night. *Remorque-motos* (with a frilly trailer hitched to the rear) start at US$1.

Motorbike hire is very on-off in Siem Reap. Currently it's off due to several accidents and thefts involving tourists.

TEMPLES OF ANGKOR

Prepare for divine inspiration! The temples of Angkor, capital of Cambodia's ancient Khmer empire, are the perfect fusion of creative ambition and spiritual devotion. Between the 9th and 13th centuries the Cambodian *devaraja* (god-kings) strove to better their ancestors in size, scale and symmetry, culminating in the world's largest religious building, Angkor Wat. The hundreds of temples surviving today are but the sacred skeleton of the vast political, religious and social centre of an empire that stretched from Burma to Vietnam; a city which at its zenith boasted a population of one million when London was a scrawny town of 50,000 inhabitants. The houses, public buildings and palaces were constructed of wood – now long decayed – because the right to dwell in structures of brick or stone was reserved for the gods.

Angkor is the heart and soul of the Kingdom of Cambodia, a source of inspiration and national pride to all Khmers as they struggle to rebuild their lives after the years of terror and trauma. Today, the temples are a point of pilgrimage for all Cambodians and no tourist will want to miss their extravagant beauty when passing through the region.

The 'lost city' of Angkor became the centre of intense European popular and scholarly interest after the publication in the 1860s of

Le Tour du Monde, an account by the French naturalist Henri Mouhot of his voyages. A group of talented and dedicated archaeologists and philologists, mostly French, soon undertook a comprehensive programme of research. Under the aegis of École Française d'Extrême-Orient (EFEO), they made an arduous effort – begun in 1908 and interrupted from the early 1970s by war – to clear away the jungle vegetation that was breaking apart the monuments, and to rebuild the damaged structures, restoring them to something approaching their original grandeur.

The three most magnificent temples at Angkor are the enigmatic **Bayon** in the fortified ancient city of **Angkor Thom**, with its eerie faces staring down; romantic **Ta Prohm**, parts of which are slowly being digested by nature; and the immense **Angkor Wat**, which will send a tingle down your spine as you first cross the causeway. Take your time and spend four to five days, as all these monuments are well worth several visits each and there are dozens of less celebrated but no less rewarding temples to dig around in the area – not literally, mind you, that's best left to the archaeologists!

ANGKOR WAT

Soaring skyward and surrounded by a moat that would make its European castle counterparts blush is Angkor Wat, one of the most inspired and spectacular monuments ever conceived by the human mind.

Some researchers believe a walk from its outer causeway to its inner confines is a symbolic trip back to the first age of the universe's creation. Others point out it also replicates the spatial universe in miniature; the Hindu's mythical Mt Meru represented by the massive central tower, with its surrounding smaller peaks (lesser towers), surrounded in turn by continents (lower courtyards) and oceans (moat). The seven-headed *naga* (multiheaded serpents) along the causeway become an emblematic rainbow-bridge for man to reach the abode of the gods.

Enough of the metaphoric, you say. What do you really need to know? Well, it's the largest religious building in the world and it'll blow your socks off! Not wearing socks? Tighten up those Tevas as they're in for a wild ride!

It was built by Suryavarman II (r 1112–52) to honour Vishnu, his patron deity, and for

> **DID YOU KNOW?**
>
> Much of Thai culture has its links to the Cambodian artisans, dancers and fighters that Thais made off with after they sacked Angkor in 1432. Have a peek at the bas reliefs at Bayon and you'll see something that looks much like the Thai boxing of today. Undoubtedly, this is a seriously sensitive topic between the two cultures and could partly explain their centuries-old rivalry.

use as his funerary temple. The central temple consists of three elaborate levels, each of which encloses a square surrounded by intricately interlinked galleries. Rising 31m above the third level and 55m above the ground is the central tower, which gives the whole ensemble its sublime unity.

Surrounding the central temple complex is an 800m-long series of extraordinarily exquisite **bas-reliefs**. The most celebrated scene, the **Churning of the Ocean of Milk**, is located along the southern section of the east gallery. This brilliantly executed carving depicts 88 *asura* (demons) on the left and 92 *deva* (gods) with crested helmets on the right, churning up the sea to extract the elixir of immortality.

Spend a few hours in awe of this unique place; it's busiest during early morning and in mid-afternoon.

ANGKOR THOM

Five **monumental gates**, each topped by four serene faces of Avalokiteshvara, mark the entrances into the fortified city of Angkor Thom, north of Angkor Wat. Its walls stretch more than 12km and are 6m high and 8m wide every step of the way.

Angkor Thom was built by Angkor's greatest king, Jayavarman VII (r 1181–1219), who came to power after the disastrous sacking of the previous Khmer capital by the Chams.

Behind its walls are some amazing and important monuments, including Bayon, Baphuon, the Terrace of Elephants and the Terrace of the Leper King.

Bayon

Ever get the feeling someone's staring at you? There are 216 gargantuan faces of Avalokiteshvara watching over visitors in this

CAMBODIA

CAMBODIA

TEMPLES OF ANGKOR

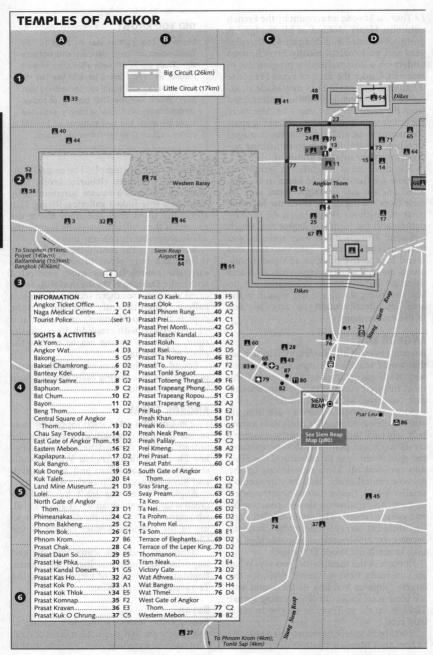

Big Circuit (26km)

Little Circuit (17km)

Western Baray

Siem Reap
Airport

Angkor Thom

Dikes

Dikes

Stung Siem Reap

To Sisophon (91km);
Poipet (140km);
Battambang (159km);
Bangkok (406km)

See Siem Reap
Map (p80)

SIEM
REAP

Psar Leu

Stung Siem Reap

To Phnom Krom (4km);
Tonlé Sap (4km)

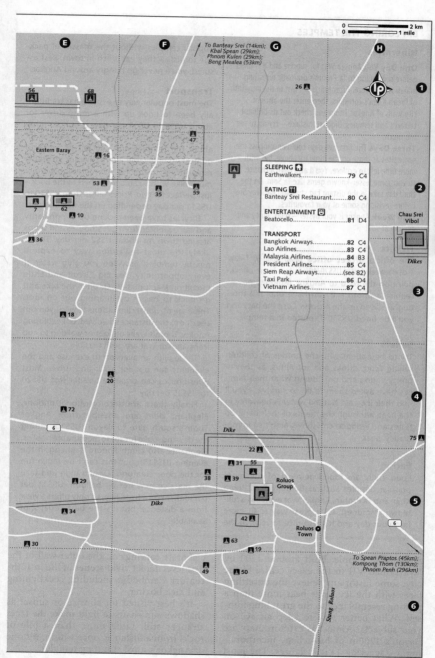

CAMBODIA

SLEEPING 🏠
Earthwalkers.................................**79** C4

EATING 🍴
Banteay Srei Restaurant.........**80** C4

ENTERTAINMENT 🎭
Beatocello....................................**81** D4

TRANSPORT
Bangkok Airways.....................**82** C4
Lao Airlines...............................**83** C4
Malaysia Airlines.....................**84** B3
President Airlines.....................**85** C4
Siem Reap Airways...............(see 82)
Taxi Park....................................**86** D4
Vietnam Airlines......................**87** C4

EXPLORING THE TEMPLES

Itineraries

One Day Visit Angkor Wat for sunrise and a wander before continuing to Ta Prohm's dramatic wrestling match with nature. After lunch get lost in the labyrinth of Preah Khan's corridors, then enter the ancient city walls of Angkor Thom and check out its brilliant terraces and temples. Biggest mistake – trying to see too much.

Three Days The first two days could encompass the same sites as those on the itinerary above, but with more time left to explore. You'll also have a chance to visit some lesser-known gems like Ta Som. On the third day take in the distant but stunning Banteay Srei, before revisiting some of your favourites.

One Week Angkor is your oyster – relax, enjoy and explore at will!

Tickets

The official **ticket office** (Map pp88–9; 1-day/3-day/1-week passes US$20/40/60) is a large checkpoint on the road to Angkor. Multiday passes require a photo – if you have one, it'll thoroughly speed up the process. Lose the pass and you'll be fined US$30 if spotted in a temple.

Sellers

Try to be patient with the hordes of children selling food, drinks and souvenirs, as they're pretty young and only doing what their families have asked them to do to survive – you'll find their ice-cold bottled water is heavenly in the heat, although the merits of their bamboo flutes and wooden crossbows aren't so immediately clear.

Eating

Food stalls are found at most of the more popular temples such as Banteay Srei, Preah Khan and Ta Prohm. Angkor Wat even has a full-blown restaurant. It's a great way to fit more into your day and it's also nice to relax in the popular temples without the masses of package tourists – they eat lunch in town. Rest assured, you'll never go hungry around Angkor.

Transport

The most popular way to explore has traditionally been to hook up with a moto driver for about US$6 to US$8 per day, or a little more if including remote temples. Some know a lot about the temples and can act as de facto guides. An enjoyable alternative for incurable romantics is to opt for the *remorque-moto*, a motorbike with a carriage hitched to the back – just perfect for two. Prices range from US$10 to US$12 per day depending on the destinations.

Bicycles have been picking up in popularity and can be rented from guesthouses and shops around town for about US$2 per day. This is likely the most rewarding way to explore nearby temples, provided you glug water at every opportunity (see Big Circuit and Little Circuit on Map pp88–9). Or ditch the bike and go back to basics by heading out on foot. There are obviously limitations to what you can see due to the distances involved, but exploring Angkor Thom's walls on foot or walking to and from Angkor Wat are both feasible.

Those with an aversion to exercise and the elements can opt for a car and driver. Most guesthouses can organise one for just US$20 to US$25 per day.

Finally there are unconventional options. Elephant rides are possible from Angkor Thom's south gate to Bayon (US$10) during the day and make for some memorable photos. Elephants also climb Phnom Bakheng in the evening (US$15), but this can't be much fun for the poor creatures. Or aim high and take the massive new hot air balloon (US$11 per person). It's on a fixed line, so only offers a view from a distance, but it's the best aerial shot available.

memorable temple. Built around 1200 by Jayavarman VII in the exact centre of the city, some historians believe the unsettling faces with the icy smile bear more than a passing resemblance to the great king himself. What better way to keep an eye on your subjects? Almost as extraordinary are Bayon's 1200m of bas-reliefs, incorporating a staggering 11,000 figures. The most elaborate carvings on the outer wall of the first level depict vivid scenes of life in 12th-century Cambodia, including cockfighting and kick boxing.

It's best visited for sunrise or sunset as shadows and shafts of light make the faces stranger still. Little more than a pile of rocks from a distance, once within, it's one of Angkor's most stunning temples.

Baphuon

Some have called this the world's largest jigsaw puzzle. Painstakingly taken apart piece by piece by a team of archaeologists before the civil war, their meticulous records were destroyed during the madness of the Khmer Rouge. Now, after subsequent years of excruciating research, it's one of the most ambitious restoration projects at Angkor. Adding to the complexity of the jigsaw are 16th-century alterations, including a 70m-long reclining Buddha on the western wall.

Baphuon sits 200m northwest of Bayon and, like Angkor Wat, it's a pyramidal representation of Mt Meru. Construction probably began under Suryavarman I and was later completed by Udayadityavarman II (r 1049–65). It marked the centre of the city that existed before the construction of Angkor Thom.

Terrace of Elephants

Stairways boasting three-headed elephants and retaining walls laden with behemoth-sized bas-reliefs of elephants and mahouts in hunting scenes flank this monumental terrace's central stairway, which is seemingly held up by the outstretched arms of *garudas* (mythical human-birds) and lion-headed figures.

The 300m-long terrace was originally topped with wooden pavilions decorated with golden-framed windows. It was used as a giant reviewing stand for public ceremonies and parades, and served as the king's grand audience hall. It's easy to imagine the overwhelming pomp and grandeur of the Khmer empire at its height in surroundings such as this.

Terrace of the Leper King

The Terrace of the Leper King, just north of the Terrace of Elephants, is a carved 6m-high platform, on top of which stands a mysterious statue. Some believe it's Yama, the god of death, while others think it's Yasovarman, a Khmer ruler who, legend says, died of leprosy.

The front retaining walls are decorated with seven tiers of meticulously executed carvings, including numerous seated *apsara* (dancing girl or celestial nymph). More spectacular still are the evil-looking figures found in the hidden trench behind the front retaining wall. They look as fresh as if they'd been carved yesterday, as they were covered over when the original terrace was enlarged centuries ago.

AROUND ANGKOR THOM

Phnom Bakheng

Built during the reign of Yasovarman (r 889–910), this is the first of Angkor's several temples (including Angkor Wat) designed to represent mythical Mt Meru. While it's still the definitive hilltop location from which to photograph the distant Angkor Wat in the glow of a late afternoon sun, Phnom Bakheng's days as the premier sunset spot are done – sadly it's a circus these days. Quieter spots for sunset are the temples of **Phnom Krom**, overlooking the Tonlé Sap and **Pre Rup**.

Ta Keo

Built by Jayavarman V (r 968–1001), this massive pyramid rises more than 50m, but as it was never finished (perhaps due to the death of the king), it's missing the elaborate carvings seen at other temples. Acrophobes (those with fear of heights) should stick to the eastern stairway.

Ta Prohm

One of the most popular of Angkor's many wonders, Ta Prohm looks like it fell straight out of a film set from *Indiana Jones*; Ta Prohm has recently been used as a set for shooting both *Tomb Raider* and *Two Brothers*. The 12th-century Mahayana Buddhist temple is one of the Angkorian era's largest edifices and has been left much as it looked when the first French explorers set eyes on it more than a century ago. While other major monuments of Angkor have been preserved with a massive programme to clear away the all-devouring jungle, this Buddhist temple has been abandoned to riotous nature and it is quite a riot in some places.

Inside, it's a maze of narrow corridors and crumbling stonework, areas of which are roped off, as the chances of collapse are serious. There are plenty of incredible photo opportunities inside, as the tentacle-like roots of mature trees slowly strangle the stonework. According to inscriptions it took an incredible 80,000 people to maintain the building!

Preah Khan

Preah Khan (Sacred Sword) once housed more than 1000 teachers and may have been a Buddhist university. It's one of Angkor's largest complexes – a maze of vaulted corridors, fine carvings and lichen-clad stonework. Its floor plan resembles Ta Phrom, but it is in a superior state of preservation. Shaped in a cruciform, the southern corridor is a wonderfully atmospheric jumble of vines and stones, while near the eastern entrance there is a curious two-storey structure that would look more at home in Greece than Cambodia.

Preah Neak Pean

Like the ultimate ornamental pond at some Balinese resort, Preah Neak Pean comprises a central tower set in a square pool and four smaller pools laid out symmetrically around the centre, each with an interesting subterranean carved fountain. The temple was originally set in a massive *baray* (reservoir) that fed Preah Khan.

Ta Som

This tiny temple is easy to overlook with so many eminent temptations to choose from, but the eastern gate here has been absolutely overwhelmed by an ancient tree that has sent its intrusive roots on a destructive mission into every nook and cranny. Unlike Ta Prohm, you won't have to wait in line to photograph it.

ROLUOS GROUP

Southeast of Angkor Wat, the monuments of Roluos – which served as the capital of Indravarman I (r 877–89) – are among the earliest large, stone temples built by the Khmer and mark the beginning of classical art. While they can't compete with the major monuments, it's worth visiting these temples for a chronological insight on the evolution of Khmer architectural ingenuity.

Bakong, the grandest of Angkor's earlier temples, was also Indravarman I's baby. Dedicated to Shiva, it's a representation of Mt Meru – something that was copied by many later Angkor creations, including Angkor Wat. The complex consists of a five-tiered sandstone central pyramid, flanked by eight towers of brick and sandstone.

Preah Ko is a direct link to the earlier brick structures of the pre-Angkorian Chenla period, with six brick *prasat* (towers) decorated with carved sandstone and plaster reliefs. It was erected by Indravarman I in the late 9th century.

FURTHER AFIELD

The following temples are beyond the central area of Angkor, but both Banteay Srei and Kbal Spean can be combined together with Angkor if you toss a few more dollars your moto driver's way (US$10 for the day). For a fistful more dollars (US$15 for the day), it's possible to add Beng Mealea to the list. A standard Angkor pass is only good for entry into Banteay Srei and Kbal Spean.

Banteay Srei

Banteay Srei is considered by many to be the jewel in Angkor's artistic crown. At first sight, some are disappointed by its size, but once within its walls it's impossible not to be impressed by the elaborate carvings that adorn the doorways and walls. The carvings are roped off these days. Located about 32km north of Siem Reap, late afternoon or early morning (before the tour buses arrive) is a fine time to visit, as the sun's rays bring out the best in the pink sandstone.

Kbal Spean

The original **River of a Thousand Lingas**, Kbal Spean is home to the most intricate riverbed carvings in the Angkor area and was only 'rediscovered' in 1969. Sadly, its remote location has led to some looting in recent years. There is a small waterfall beneath the carvings, but it's best visited from July to December, as during the dry season the river dries up. It's about 15km north of Banteay Srei and a 30-minute scenic jungle trek from the parking lot.

Beng Mealea

A truly abandoned temple, Beng Mealea makes Ta Prohm look like they just forgot to mow the lawn. Built by Suryavarman II, the man who gave the world Angkor Wat, the layout is remarkably similar to its more famous twin, although this is hard to imagine given the mess it is today. Some jungle has been cleared back for demining and later filming, but it still has a special atmosphere. It's about 70km northeast of Siem Reap on reasonable dirt roads in the dry season, and very unreasonable roads in the wet.

It now costs US$5 to visit Beng Mealea and there are additional small charges for cars and motorbikes – make sure you work out who is paying these in advance.

Phnom Kulen

The famous mountain is one of the most sacred places in Cambodia, and the birthplace of the Khmer empire, after Jayavarman II proclaimed independence from Java in 802. At the mountain's summit (487m) is an ancient reclining Buddha (carved into a massive boulder) and an active monastery, though visitors usually prefer the large waterfall and the impressive carvings found on the riverbed nearby.

It costs a whopping US$20 on top of the US$15 you'll have to fork out for the moto here – quite frankly, it's not worth it. Still interested? It's about 60km from Siem Reap and getting here takes about three hours.

NORTHWESTERN CAMBODIA

Nowhere else in Cambodia, perhaps even in Southeast Asia, is there a region with such an intoxicating mix of history and adventure. Battle Preah Vihear Province's remote jungle paths to sit alone atop immense and inspiring temple complexes, cruise the kingdom's most scenic water route to Battambang, an elegant French colonial town, or wade into the region's recent and painful past as the home of the Khmer Rouge.

POIPET
☎ 054 / pop 45,000

Viva Poipet! Long the cesspit of Cambodia, sadly it's the first place in the kingdom many of you will witness, thanks to the nearby Thailand border crossing from Aranya Prathet. Despite the recent addition of sizeable casinos, there's absolutely no reason to stick around here.

Canadia Bank (☎ 967107; NH5) is not far from the border post and will change travellers cheques.

If bad karma forces you to spend the night, **Ngy Heng Hotel** (☎ 967101; NH5; r US$5-10; ❄) is one of the few cheaper places that isn't taken up with casino employees. Rooms are clean, bright and have TVs.

> ### BORDER CROSSING: INTO THAILAND
>
> When leaving Cambodia walk across the border at Poipet and take a túk-túk (50B per person) or motorcycle taxi (70B) to Aranya Prathet, from where there are two trains (70B, six hours) a day to/from Bangkok and regular air-con buses (180/140B first/second class, five hours, hourly).

Scams abound on transport, so negotiate hard – a share taxi seat should cost 50B to Sisophon (one hour), 150B to Siem Reap (three to four hours) and 100B to Battambang (2½ hours). To dodge the dodgy types, check out Tales of Asia's Cambodia Overland coverage for all the nitty gritty (www.talesofasia.com).

The roads east from Poipet will still shock those arriving from Thailand. Why are they so bad? See Boulevard of Broken Backsides on p86. Times stated are for the dry season – it can take much, much longer in the wet season. Pick-ups are slower, slightly cheaper and much dirtier options.

SISOPHON
☎ 054 / pop 111,700

Most people who've been here never even know it. To them it's just a dusty stop between Poipet and Siem Reap. However, for those in the know, it's the perfect place to base a day trip to the huge temple complex of Banteay Chhmar (p94). It's also the jumping-off point for those heading to Phnom Penh by road via the French colonial town of Battambang (p94).

Cheap guesthouses reside on the road to Siem Reap, the best being **Sara Torn Guesthouse** (NH6 East; s/tw without bathroom 100/150B), with its cosy veranda for kicking back at night. Rooms are spacious, but a little gloomy and flimsy.

Loud karaoke bars plague most of the comfy budget hotels. The **Phnom Svay Hotel** (☎ 012-916995; NH5 west; r US$6-10; ❄), nicknamed the birthday cake by visiting UN and NGO workers thanks to its extravagant exterior, escapes the noisy racket and makes for a fine stay. Fan rooms tend to be the brightest – all have TVs.

For cheap eats, head to the friendly food stalls lining the taxi park. Slightly more sophisticated is **Phkay Proek Restaurant** (NH5; mains

US$1.50-4; 🕒 breakfast, lunch & dinner), next door to the Phnom Svay Hotel. It does a good turn in Thai tastes, plus plenty of Cambodia's most wanted. The cashew nut and chicken stir-fry is particularly good.

After some negotiating, a share taxi seat should cost 60B to Battambang (1¼ hours) and 140B to Siem Reap (two to three hours). For more comfort, you could pay double and have the front seat to yourself. For Poipet transport info see p93. Trains no longer serve Sisophon.

BANTEAY CHHMAR TEMPLE

Vast and remote, the vestiges of **Banteay Chhmar** (admission US$5) linger in the jungle and are a playground for the adventurous. Clamber over rubble strewn with carvings and climb into the shadows of dark corridors. What's left of the massive structure houses some brilliant bas-reliefs, including the famous 32-armed Avalokiteshvaras adorning the rear outer gallery. Sadly, only two Avalokiteshvaras remain, as six were smuggled into Thailand after a brazen act of looting in 1998. The front outer gallery houses a sublime series of bas-reliefs depicting sea battles between the Khmer and Islam empires.

Almost 14km southeast of Banteay Chhmar is **Banteay Top** (Fortress of the Army). Although it's only a wee temple, there's something special about its atmosphere. Set among rice fields, one damaged tower appears partially rebuilt and looks decidedly precarious, a bony finger pointing skyward.

Both temples are best visited as a day trip from Sisophon. Anti-diarrhoeal giant Imodium is rumoured to sponsor the nearby food stalls, so pack a picnic.

NH69 from Sisophon to Banteay Chhmar (two to three hours) ranges from tolerable to bad depending on the season. Arrange a return moto trip in Sisophon (US$10) or take a pick-up to Thmar Puok (5000/3000r inside/outside) and arrange a moto from there (US$5).

BATTAMBANG

☎ 053 / pop 158,100

Nestled along Stung Sangker's banks, Battambang is an elegant riverside town sheltering the best-preserved French-period architecture in the country. The stunning boat trip from Siem Reap lures travellers here, but it's the remarkably chilled atmos-

phere that keeps them lingering. You'd never guess it's the kingdom's second largest city. Battambang's also the ideal base for exploring nearby temples and villages that offer a real slice of rural Cambodia.

Orientation

Battambang is fairly compact and easily negotiable on foot. Most of the restaurants, shops and hotels are on the west bank of the Stung Sangker, within a few blocks of Psar Nat (Meeting Market), which is the town centre.

Information

Numerous Interphone shops south of Psar Nat on the riverfront offer cheap international phone calls. If the delay is putting a stake through your loving, try the private mobile phone booths all over town, which are also best for national calls.

Battambang Referral Hospital (opposite fast boat dock) Has limited services and little English is spoken.

Canadia Bank (☎ 952267; opposite Psar Nat) Offers free Visa and MasterCard cash advances and can change most major currencies or travellers cheques. Home to a Visa/MasterCard-compatible ATM.

Main post office (Ph 1) Not worth the risk – try Phnom Penh or Siem Reap.

Sopheak Web (Ph 3; Internet per hr 3000r, CD burning US$2.50)

Tourist office (near Governor's Residence) Eagerly dishes out info on local sights, though there's little in the way of handouts.

Union Commercial Bank (Ph 1) Offers free Visa cash advances.

Sights

Although it's the pace, not the sights, that seem to keep people here, there are a few things your wandering eyes should ogle. Lazing on the riverbank, in true French fashion, are a series of charming **French shophouses**. Slightly south, the **Battambang**

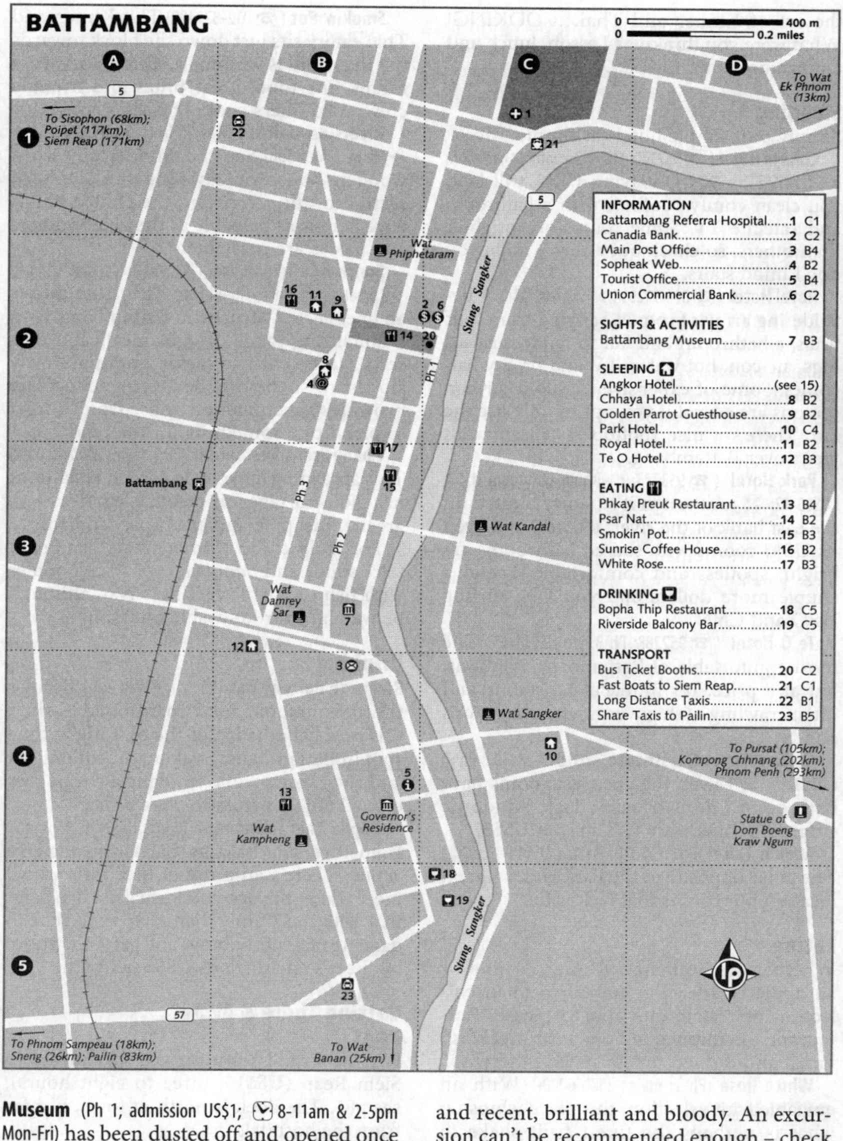
BATTAMBANG
0 400 m
0 0.2 miles
A
B
C
D
1
2
3
4
5
To Sisophon (68km); Poipet (117km); Siem Reap (171km)
To Wat Ek Phnom (13km)
Wat Phiphetaram
Stung Sangker
Ph 1
Ph 2
Ph 3
Battambang
Wat Kandal
Wat Damrey Sar
Wat Sangker
To Pursat (105km); Kompong Chhnang (202km); Phnom Penh (293km)
Governor's Residence
Wat Kampheng
Statue of Dom Boeng Kraw Ngum
To Phnom Sampeau (18km); Sneng (26km); Pailin (83km)
To Wat Banan (25km)
INFORMATION
Battambang Referral Hospital......1 C1
Canadia Bank......2 C2
Main Post Office......3 B4
Sopheak Web......4 B2
Tourist Office......5 B4
Union Commercial Bank......6 C2
SIGHTS & ACTIVITIES
Battambang Museum......7 B3
SLEEPING
Angkor Hotel......(see 15)
Chhaya Hotel......8 B2
Golden Parrot Guesthouse......9 B2
Park Hotel......10 C4
Royal Hotel......11 B2
Te O Hotel......12 B3
EATING
Phkay Preuk Restaurant......13 B4
Psar Nat......14 B2
Smokin' Pot......15 B3
Sunrise Coffee House......16 B2
White Rose......17 B3
DRINKING
Bopha Thip Restaurant......18 C5
Riverside Balcony Bar......19 C5
TRANSPORT
Bus Ticket Booths......20 C2
Fast Boats to Siem Reap......21 C1
Long Distance Taxis......22 B1
Share Taxis to Pailin......23 B5

Museum (Ph 1; admission US$1; ⌚ 8-11am & 2-5pm Mon-Fri) has been dusted off and opened once again. It hosts an attractive but limited collection of fine-carved lintels and an intriguing Mahayana Buddhist boundary stone from the post-Bayon period.

Battambang's surrounding countryside is laced with contrasting histories: ancient and recent, brilliant and bloody. An excursion can't be recommended enough – check out p97 for details.

Courses

Take a lesson at **Smokin' Pot** (☎ 012-821400). First you'll be taught the finer points of purchasing at the open market before delving into the art of Khmer and Thai…COOKING! What were you thinking? Lesson, lunch and a morning of fun for US$7.

Sleeping

Simply put: simple hotels at simple prices.

Chhaya Hotel (☎ 952170; 118 Ph 3; r without bathroom US$3, r US$5-10; ✗) Outlaying US$5 will land you clean comfy confines with a bathroom and satellite TV. Some rooms are brighter than others, so check out a few – hope you don't mind stairs.

Royal Hotel (☎ 016-912034; r US$4-20; ✗) A bewildering array of rooms, ranging from four walls, a bathroom and fan to fancy furnishings, air-con, hot water, TV and breezy balconies. Some of expensive top-floor air-con options are a steal if you opt to only use the fan. There's a nice rooftop restaurant with views over Battambang.

Park Hotel (☎ 953773; r without bathroom US$3, r US$5-12; ✗) Although it's poorly located on the east bank of the river, it's new and even its US$3 rooms with shared bathrooms are bright, spotless and comfortable. Spend a couple more dollars and you'll be surfing HBO and CNN.

Te O Hotel (☎ 952288; Ph 3; s/d US$11/13) The most comfortable of Battambang's options, but at a price. It's immaculate, roomy and often crawling with government delegations and NGOs.

Golden Parrot Guesthouse (☎ 012-284502; Ph 3; r US$3-10; ✗) Even the cheapest rooms have bathrooms, though most lack windows. Brighter rooms with TVs start at US$5.

Angkor Hotel (☎ 952310; Ph 1; r US$11-13; ✗) The polar opposite to the Park Hotel – great location but rooms that lack value.

Eating

Whether it's authentic Khmer cuisine or an apple strudel, Battambang's small collection of restaurants aim to please. Restaurants mentioned are open for breakfast, lunch and dinner, unless stated otherwise.

White Rose (Ph 2; mains 2500-6000r) With an enviable fruit selection, this place whips up what is perhaps the finest fruit shake in Cambodia – heavenly thick and tasty, and only 2000r! The 200-odd Khmer, Chinese and Vietnamese dishes are also palate-pleasing; the fried prawns with fresh green peppercorns over steamed rice especially so. Let's not forget the ice cream!

Smokin' Pot (☎ 012-821400) This Khmer and Thai eatery sits just down the block towards the river, and is winning a faithful following for its fine food, great tunes and friendly crew. Also offers cooking classes (p95).

Riverside Balcony Bar (Ph 1; mains US$2.50-4; ⏰ dinner Wed-Sun) Set in a wonderfully worn wooden house overlooking the southern section of the riverfront, the chilled ambience here is as palpable as the great burgers and pastas are palatable.

Sunrise Coffee House (☎ 953426; mains US$1-3; ⏰ breakfast & lunch, closed Sun) This little café is an unexpected surprise in Battambang, with a tantalising range of light meals and desserts. Have a chicken caesar wrap and slowly sip espresso before devouring chocolate brownies or cinnamon rolls. Don't forget to pick up to something for the road.

Phkay Preuk Restaurant (Ph 3; mains 2000-12,000r) This sprawling Thai-style garden restaurant has no shortage of savoury curries: red, green, pineapple and even spicy Indian.

For truly cheap Khmer treats like *bobor* (rice soup) and *nam ben choc* (rice noodles with fish or curry) visit Psar Nat, although be watchful for 'unusable bits' soup.

Drinking

Riverside Balcony Bar (Ph 1; ⏰ Wed-Sun) Besides the flavoursome food mentioned earlier, this breezy bar is by far the best night-time spot in Battambang. Soak up the moonlight and river views while enjoying a cheap beer or cocktail. It's truly the bee's knees.

Bopha Thip Restaurant (drinks US$2-3) Not far from Riverside Balcony Bar is this massive venue. There's an army of beer girls who'll meet you at the door and usually a live band that gets the Cambodian *rom vong* (circle) dancing moving; be brave and get your groove on. Beer's an atrocious US$3 per bottle.

Getting There & Away

BOAT

For the inside story on the speedboats to Siem Reap (US$15, three to eight hours), see p85. The dock is north of town, not far from the hospital.

BUS & TAXI

The 293km road to Phnom Penh is now the Cambodian equivalent of a motorway, reducing travel times to a mere four or five hours. **Capitol Tour** (☎ 953040), **GST** (☎ 012-727774), **Hour**

Lean (☎ 012-307252) and **Neak Krorhorm** (☎ 012-627299) have various services to the capital departing between 6.30am and 2pm (US$3). They all have ticket booths at the east end of Psar Nat. Capitol Tour and GST also offer buses to Poipet (US$2.50, three hours) and Bangkok (US$10, 10 hours), while Neak Krohorm services Siem Reap (US$4, 4½ hours).

See Sisophon (p93) and Pailin (right) sections for share taxi info between these towns and Battambang. Long-distance taxis leave from NH5, in the town's north, while taxis to Pailin leave from NH57, in the town's south.

TRAIN
The 274km of track between Battambang and Phnom Penh (16,440r, 13 to 15 hours) is home to the country's only remaining passenger service. It's costly and less comfortable than the bus, but the chance to ride the roof of this dying breed might just be worth it. Hopping off at Pursat (6540r, six hours) and catching a bus may keep your sanity and get you to the capital before dark. Trains are 'scheduled' to leave every even calendar day (2, 4, 6, etc) at around 6am.

Getting Around
Most of Battambang is compact enough to comfortably explore on foot. Moto rides are usually 1000r – more at night or if venturing across the river.

AROUND BATTAMBANG
Most destinations following can be combined into an interesting day trip on the back of a moto (US$6 to US$8). Individually, a return moto trip to each sight is about US$4. Particularly helpful English-speaking moto drivers can be found in front of the Chhaya Hotel (Map p95) in Battambang.

A US$2 ticket covers admission to Wat Ek Phnom, Phnom Sampeau and Wat Banan. It can be bought at any of the three sights.

Wat Ek Phnom
Just 13km north of Battambang, standing behind a new and rather impressive 28m-tall Buddha statue is this rather dilapidated Lego-ish looking 11th-century temple. The palm-canopied road that hugs leafy canals and skims village huts is worth the trip here alone, especially in the early morning or late afternoon light.

Phnom Sampeau
This striking limestone outcrop resides 18km southwest of Battambang and has a bit of everything – you'll climb, you'll sweat, you'll admire and you may well cry too. Hike up the rear road to find an old **temple** used as a prison by the Khmer Rouge and two chilling **caves** where evidence of their horrific killing screams on. Climb further and you'll see two massive guns (Russian and German) used by the Vietnamese during the war. Finally, at the summit there's a stunning view over the countryside and a small wat with a golden **stupa**. A massive 38m-high and 112.5m-long Buddha montage is currently being hewn into the outcrop's base. Local children make excellent guides for about 1000r per hour.

Wat Banan
Just 25km south of Battambang, it's your own personal pocket-sized Angkor Wat – climb straight up the 359 stone stairs and enjoy. Locals actually claim it was the inspiration for the most famous of Angkor temples, but its midget-sized five towers suggest they're hopelessly optimistic. Still, it's in impressive shape for its age and its hillside location makes it the most striking and peaceful temple in the area.

On your way back to town ask your driver if you can have a go on Battambang's infamous **bamboo train**. Basically it's a little platform on wheels, powered by a portable motor, but it sure flies; great fun until you meet something coming the other way. Aaaaarrrrrggggghhhhh!

Sneng
This village, 26km down the road to Pailin, is home to **Prasat Yeay Ten**, a 10th-century temple that could pass as an Angkorian toll booth, it clings so closely to the road. The fine lintels have incredibly survived the dual ravages of war and time. Beyond the nearby modern wat are three brick sanctuaries, also with brilliant lintels, making for a bit of a bonanza for temple fans.

PAILIN
☎ 053 / pop 17,800
Pailin has an attractive location amid the foothills of Chuor Phnom Kravanh, but the town itself lacks major attractions unless you know a bit about gemstones or like

CAMBODIA

DON'T STRAY FROM THE PATH!

Pailin is one of the most heavily mined areas in Cambodia so make double sure you don't stray from the path.

---

hanging out with geriatrics responsible for mass murder (Pailin has long been a haven for retired Khmer Rouge leaders). It may see more traffic now that the nearby Thailand border crossing has opened to international traffic.

There are some truly dodgy guesthouses here, but **Guesthouse Ponleu Pich Pailin** (opposite Psar Pailin; r 100B) makes the grade with stark rooms and private bathrooms.

Hang Meas Pailin Hotel (☎ 012-787546; NH57; r US$11-14; ✖) offers smart rooms with satellite TV, fridge and hot shower. There's a decent restaurant attached.

Share taxis to Battambang (200B, two to four hours) regularly ply the bumpy but bearable road.

BORDER CROSSING: INTO THAILAND

Leaving Cambodia, take a share taxi (5000r, one to two hours) from Pailin to the border at Pruhm. From Daun Lem on the Thai side of the border, there are regular minibuses to Chanthaburi (100B, 1½ hours). From there you'll have no problem hopping a bus to Bangkok (148B, four hours).

KOMPONG CHHNANG
☎ 026 / pop 47,100

Kompong Chhnang is a tale of two cities: a bustling riverfront, complete with an interesting floating Vietnamese village, and an old colonial quarter, with its pleasant parks and handsome buildings. Connecting these seemingly opposing halves are two long causeways lined with stilt houses and mazes of narrow walkways – the older unsealed causeway is the more attractive of the two. The rising Tonlé Sap swallows the surrounding lowlands during wet season.

Sohka Guesthouse (☎ 988622; r without bathroom US$3, r US$5-15; ✖) occupies several buildings in a sprawling garden in the south of town. The largest air-con rooms with TV, fridge and hot water can also be rented with fan only for US$8.

Rithesen Hotel (☎ 988632; r US$5-10; ✖) is the only lodging in town that overlooks the Tonlé Sap river, complete with verandas for watching the action below. On the downside the aromas beneath can get pretty strong during dry season.

The central **Meta Pheap Restaurant** (☎ 012-949297; NH5; mains 3000-6000r; ☺ breakfast, lunch & dinner) is across from the Peace Monument and its tasty Khmer and Chinese dishes lure many a Khmer travelling between Phnom Penh and Battambang – take their cue and chow down.

PPPT buses link town to Phnom Penh (5000r, two hours), while you can hop on the many Phnom Penh–Battambang buses to reach Pursat (5000r, two hours) and Battambang (12,000r, three to four hours) via NH5, now a slick, sealed road.

ANLONG VENG
☎ 065

Only 142km north of peaceful Siem Reap is this dusty and isolated town that was long the stronghold of the Khmer Rouge. Anlong Veng finally succumbed to government forces in 1998 and since then the government has been trying to suppress those unhappy with the war's outcome by encouraging both development and an influx of moderate migrants from other parts of the kingdom.

Attractions include military commander **Ta Mok's House** (admission US$1), **Pol Pot's cremation site** and other remarkably dull places catapulted to mildly interesting by their connection with mass murderers. More interesting are the majestic views from the **Dangkrek Mountains** looming over town. Anlong Veng is also the western gateway to Prasat Preah Vihear (opposite).

Phnom Dang Rek Guesthouse (r US$3-5) is pleasant and clean; something no other option here can boast.

Share taxis (15,000, three to five hours) and pick-ups (12,000/8000r inside/outside) regularly ride the roller-coaster dust express (NH67) to Siem Reap.

PREAH VIHEAR PROVINCE

Home to hard-core journeys and rich rewards, this is the province for adventure addicts and those who dream of one-on-one time with mighty Khmer temple complexes. Being the poorest province in Cambodia means infrastructure, though improving, is the kingdom's worst. While sandy ox cart trails and tortuous roads ensure a long, painful, dirty journey, they also guarantee solitude when you want it most, at the temples.

As roads slowly get better, the number of visitors are bound to increase, so say a prayer for your backside now and get out there! The most gratifying trip is one that links Siem Reap and Kompong Thom (the best jumping-off points) via **Koh Ker**, **Preah Khan** and **Prasat Preah Vihear** temple complexes. Throw in some ancient Angkor bridges like **Spean Ta Ong**, and you have one cracking quest.

It's a challenge for highly experienced motorbike riders, so it's definitely not for gung-ho beginners, thanks to seas of sand that swallows Suzukis. Find a good moto driver (about US$15 per day plus petrol) or get a group together and rent a sturdy 4WD with a driver. Carry a hammock and mosquito net and don't *ever* think about it during wet season.

Tbeng Meanchey

☎ 064 / pop 24,400

Tbeng Meanchey is a dusty and seriously out-of-the-way provincial capital that's an important gateway to those rare, brave and admirable souls attempting the overland journey to the glorious temple of Prasat Preah Vihear, 115km to the north. Locals refer to the town as Preah Vihear, a fact that confounds many a foreigner.

The rooms at **Prum Tep Guesthouse** (☎ 012-964645; r US$5–10;) are spacious, comfortable and have satellite TV. Bathrooms include Western-style toilets and it's the only place with air-con, if it's working.

The cheapies with shared bathroom are cells at **27 May Guesthouse** (r 5000-15,000r), but it doesn't come cheaper than US$1.25. It can get noisy here, as it's near the market and taxi park.

The **Mlop Dong Restaurant** (opposite taxi park) has a great range of dishes with prices that won't wilt the wallet. By night, it's the closest thing to a bar in town.

Pick-ups (15,000/7,000r inside/on the back, five hours) and faster share taxis (20,000r) travel the 155km along the horrendous NH64 to Kompong Thom daily.

Prasat Preah Vihear

Occupying the most breathtaking location of all Angkorian temples, **Prasat Preah Vihear**

(admission US$5) is perched atop a mountain escarpment on the border with Thailand, with enormous views across the plains of northern Cambodia 550m below. It was built during the reign of Suryavarman I (c 1002–49) and embellished by successive monarchs, resulting in an impressive series of sanctuaries rising to the cliff's summit. The upper level is the best preserved and hosts some exquisitely carved lintels.

You'll see some incredibly clean Thai tourists, thanks to a stunning stretch of tarmac that Thailand built to the temple's front door – try not to drool or cry when you see it. Just remember, your filth is your passport and you can smile knowing that you've undertaken a modern-day pilgrimage that's easily the equal of any undertaken at the height of the Angkor Empire.

A long day trip here from Anlong Veng by moto (US$15) is feasible; each 103km leg taking about three hours on decent dirt roads. Sporadic pick-ups leave Anlong Veng for nearby Sa Em (10,000r, two hours), from where motos can get you to the escarpment's base (US$3, 40 minutes). Much of the road from Tbeng Meanchey has descended into madness, making the 115km journey a painful five hours – hire a moto (US$15 per day plus petrol) and sleep at a rudimentary **guesthouse** (s 10,000r) below the escarpment.

The road up the escarpment is stupidly steep, with 35% slopes in areas, meaning you'll either have to hike up in the heat for 1½ hours or hire a specialised moto (US$5 return).

Preah Khan

Covering almost 5 sq km, Preah Khan is the largest temple enclosure constructed during the Angkorian period – quite a feat when you consider the competition! Thanks to its arse-end-of-nowhere location, it's

---

ONE STEP BEYOND

Preah Vihear Province is one of Cambodia's most heavily mined provinces and most were laid in the past decade. Do not, under any circumstances, stray from well-trodden paths anywhere in the province, including remote temple sites. Those with their own transport should only travel on roads or trails that locals use regularly.

astonishingly quiet and peaceful. With four enigmatic Bayon-style faces, **Prasat Preah Stung** is perhaps the most memorable of the many temples here. The dramatic *garudas* and delicate elephant carvings clinging to the crumbling remains of **Prasat Damrei**, a few kilometres east, are also worth a peek. Although looters and time have taken their toll at Preah Khan, there's enough rising from the sea of rubble to imagine the complex's former splendour.

The best bet is to stay with one of the friendly families in 'downtown' Ta Seng, the village 4km away. Expect to pay about 10,000r per person with a basic meal.

It's a gruelling five-hour trip from Kompong Thom and Tbeng Meanchey. An amazing, exhaustive and rewarding alternative to is approach along the ancient Angkor highway from Beng Mealea, which is 70km northeast of Siem Reap. You'll cross several splendid Angkor bridges, like the remarkable 77m-long **Spean Ta Ong**, just west of Khvau. Even if you have your own bike, it's still best to hire a knowledgeable moto driver (US$15 per day plus petrol) to help you navigate the countless jungle trails on these three routes.

Koh Ker

Home to almost 30 ancient structures, including the immense seven-tier pyramid of **Prasat Thom**, **Koh Ker** (admission US$10) was the brief 10th-century capital of the Angkor Empire under king Jayavarman IV (r 928–42). Walking past the shattered lion guarding **Prasat Krahom** (Red Temple), you'll soon see the pyramid climbing skyward – the view and breeze at its summit are well worth the steep 40m climb.

For good or bad, Koh Ker represents the future of Preah Vihear's remote temple complexes, with its new road, hefty admission and increasing number of visitors. That said, sufficient word has yet to get out and the future crowds have yet to materialise – hint hint!

If continuing north to Prasat Preah Vihear, spend the night 9km southeast of Koh Ker at **Kohké Guesthouse** (s US$3) in the village of Siyong.

Koh Ker is now only three to four hours or day-trip distance from Siem Reap via Beng Mealea. The 292km return moto trip should be about US$15.

KOMPONG THOM

☎ 062 / pop 74,600

For those exploratory souls wishing to see the pre-Angkorian temples of Sambor Prei Kuk or the remarkable remote temples of Preah Vihear Province, Kompong Thom is a perfect springboard off the popular sealed path (NH6) running between Phnom Penh and Siem Reap. Surrounding this dull and dusty town are endless rice paddies, dirt tracks and glimpses into Cambodia's traditional rural life – something people sticking to the capital and Angkor sadly miss out on.

Sleeping & Eating

You'll find the best snoozing and dining options along NH6.

Arunras Guesthouse (☎ 012-865935; NH6; s US$3-8, tw US$4-8; 🛱) Even this guesthouse's cheapest rooms have TVs and bathrooms. Not all rooms have windows, so scope things out before choosing. The restaurant here, open for breakfast, lunch and dinner, is always packed with itinerants digging into Khmer or Chinese selections (mains 3000r to 6000r). Try the deep-fried honeycomb if it's in season.

Arunras Hotel (☎ 961294; NH6; s US$3-7, tw US$6-12; 🛱) Like its sister next door, this hotel has satellite TVs and bathrooms in all rooms. The renovated double rooms are huge, have smart bathrooms, hot water and even sport master panels on the bedside tables, though there are more switches than lights. It's also proudly home to Kompong Thom's first lift. Its restaurant has the same menu as the guesthouse's, but with fancier décor. In the evenings it becomes the town's only nightclub, with bands belting out Khmer tunes.

Mittapheap Hotel (☎ 961213; NH6; r US$5-10; 🛱) Just over the bridge, this friendly option has bright, albeit slightly dog-eared, rooms with TVs and Kompong Thom's firmest beds.

The **Sen Monorom Restaurant** (mains 3000-8000r; ☺ breakfast, lunch & dinner) offers up traditional Khmer meals, though you should avoid ordering the fried porcupine as it's an endangered species.

Getting There & Away

The numerous buses running along NH6 between Phnom Penh and Siem Reap often drop off or pick up passengers here. A seat to Phnom Penh (2½ hours) or Siem Reap (2½ hours) is about 10,000r.

SAMBOR PREI KUK

This **temple complex** (US$2 donation requested) has the biggest and best bunch of pre-Angkorian temples found anywhere in Cambodia. Formerly a 7th-century Chenla capital called Isanapura, it's now dotted with ancient vestiges and US bomb craters. The best-preserved structure is **Prasat Yeay Peau**, with a solitary tree strangling its east gate like a boa enveloping its prey. Donning elegantly coiffured ringlets, several lion statues guard over the complex's largest remaining structure, **Prasat Tao**. The smaller **Prasat Sambor** is notable for the seven *linga* (phallic symbols) surrounding it. There's a special serenity here in the forest and it's a great prelude to the more famous capital of Angkor.

Take NH6 north, veer right after 5km on NH64 and 11km north is a massive sign. Turn right on a delightful dirt road and it's another 14km; about 30km in total. A return moto trip costs about US$5.

SOUTH COAST

Home to tropical beaches, scenic fishing villages, abandoned colonial-era resorts and several of Cambodia's nascent national parks, the south coast now holds its own among Cambodia's other premier destinations. Taking in these diverse attractions can be done in as little as a week by making a loop between Phnom Penh and Sihanoukville, visiting Kampot, Kep and Bokor along the way. With more time you could find yourself alone on one of the many pristine beaches dotting the coast's undeveloped tropical islands – *The Beach*'s island paradise doesn't exist in Thailand, but it just might exist here.

SIHANOUKVILLE

☎ 034 / pop 77,000

Seeing that Angkor blows minds, the Killing Fields and S-21 squeeze souls, and the roads of the remote north devastate backsides, it's understandable why travellers have now taken to Sihanoukville's stretches of white sand, wavering palms and undeveloped tropical islands. They're the perfect Cambodian cure-all – pure bliss and relaxation. On weekdays it's still even possible to have sections of Sihanoukville's most popular beaches to yourself, though these sands wouldn't qualify as the south coast's finest.

GETTING INTO TOWN

Most buses and share taxis from Phnom Penh, Kampot and Krong Koh Kong stop in the town centre, and from here it's just a moto ride to the most popular guesthouses on Weather Station Hill above Victory Beach or down at Serendipity Beach. Those coming by ferry from Krong Koh Kong will be greeted by motos galore at the port (2km north of town). Aim to pay 3000r to Weather Station Hill, about 5000r to Serendipity Beach.

For a blissful beach-based holiday, you'd still be wiser planting yourself in Thailand or Indonesia.

The influx of those seeking refuge from Cambodia's glorious travelling 'hardships' has led to a boom in the behind-the-beach action, with new bars and eateries seemingly sprouting by the second.

Orientation

Sihanoukville is spread out across a sprawling headland with its mundane city centre set squarely in the middle. To the west is Victory Beach and Weather Station Hill, which comprise the traditional backpackers' hang-out, and to the south is the budding backpacker haven nicknamed Serendipity Beach.

Information

Things are evolving quickly here, so pick up *Sihanoukville Visitor's Guide*, a pocket-sized listings magazine available at local guesthouses and bars, for the latest low-down.

Forget both the unreliable main post office, near the port, and the branch near the market when it comes to postal services. For cheap international phone calls, use an Internet café, or for local calls use one of the private mobile phone booths on the street. Internet access is now possible all over town for only 4000r per hour.

Canadia Bank (☎ 933490; Ph Ekareach) Deals with most currencies, changes travellers cheques at 2% commission, has a credit-card-compatible ATM and offers free MasterCard and Visa cash advances.

Casablanca (near Golden Lions Roundabout) A healthy selection of books for those seeking a literary escape.

Hospital (☎ 933426) Near the Golden Lions Roundabout, but it's rudimentary – head to Phnom Penh if it's serious.

SIHANOUKVILLE

		0	500 m
		0	0.3 miles

INFORMATION
Canadia Bank.............................**1** D5
Casablanca.............................(see 22)
Hospital....................................**2** D6
Union Commercial Bank............**3** D5
Vietnamese Consulate................**4** C4

SIGHTS & ACTIVITIES
EcoSea Dive...........................(see 6)
Scuba Nation.........................(see 21)
Seeing Hands Massage 3..........**5** D5

SLEEPING
Angkor Inn Guesthouse.............**6** D4
Bungalow Village.......................**7** B4
Chan Sovannkiry
  Guesthouse............................**8** C6
Coaster's....................................**9** C6
Coaster's Bungalows.................**10** C6
Da Da Guesthouse....................**11** B4

House of Malibu....................(see 10)
Mealy Chenda Guesthouse.....(see 11)
Nika Guesthouse......................**12** B3
Red Snapper Guesthouse..........**13** C4
Sea Sun Guesthouse................**14** C6
Sea View Villa..........................**15** C6
Sunset Garden Inn....................**16** B4

EATING
Chez Claude............................**17** B5
Espresso Kampuchea..............(see 26)
Indian Curry Pot......................**18** B4
Ku Kai......................................**19** B4
La Paillotte...............................**20** B4
Melting Pot..............................**21** B4
Mick & Craig's Restaurant........**22** C6
Rama Beach Restaurant..........(see 15)
Romduol's Restaurant.............(see 19)
Rose's Place...........................(see 18)
Samudera Market.....................**23** D5

Snake House............................**24** B4
Starfish Bakery.........................**25** D5

DRINKING
Angkor Arms............................**26** D4
Blue Storm...............................**27** D5
Dusk 'til Dawn........................(see 26)
Eden.......................................(see 30)
Le Bar 'Ang............................(see 18)
Occheuteal Beach Shacks........**28** D6
Pet's Place...............................**29** B4
Unkle Bob's.............................**30** C6

TRANSPORT
Capitol Tour.............................**31** D5
GST...**32** D5
GST Motorbike Rental.............(see 32)
Hour Lean.................................**33** D4
Phnom Penh Public Transport....**34** C5
Taxi Park..................................**35** D4

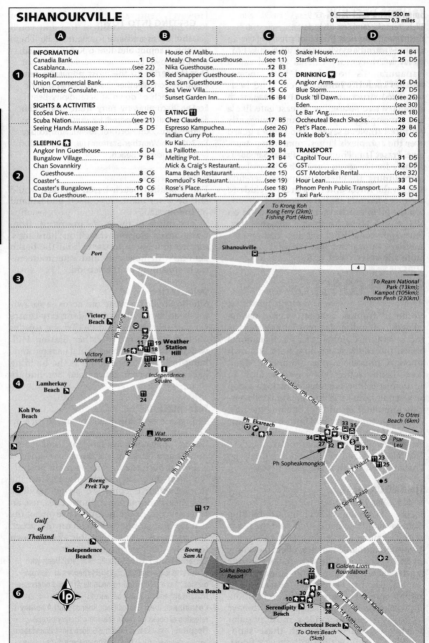

Union Commercial Bank (☎ 933833; Ph Ekareach) Offers free credit-card cash advances.

Vietnamese consulate (Ph Ekareach) Turns out the speediest Vietnamese visas (one month US$30) in Asia: 15 minutes flat!

Dangers & Annoyances

Don't leave valuables on the beach unattended or motorbikes without a hefty padlock, as theft is common. Night robberies have occurred near the port and on the poorly lit areas of Ph Ekareach, so stick together or hook up with a reliable moto driver when heading out on the town alone. Lone women should exercise caution when walking on the beaches after dark, as there's been one high-profile case of rape. Finally, there are deceptively strong currents off Occheuteal, so take care if you're not a decent swimmer.

Sights & Activities

BEACHES

With its north end housing the backpacker haven of Serendipity Beach, the most popular stretch of sand is undoubtedly **Occheuteal Beach**. It's a pretty spot, but it's not always peaceful. Crowds dwindle if you stroll southwards and if you cross the small headland at its southern end you'll be rewarded with **Otres Beach**, a seemingly infinite stretch of vacant white sand. **Victory Beach** is close to the main backpacker ghetto, but it's fairly scruffy and looks onto the port. **Lamherkay**, **Koh Pos**, **Independence** and **Sokha** are other beaches of note; however, much of the latter two is closed to the public.

ISLANDS

There are numerous islands off the coast but, as yet, only **Koh Russei** (Bamboo Island) has some basic bungalows. Many guesthouses offer coastal island boat trips for around US$10, including lunch and snorkelling gear; not quite Mama Hanh's of Nha Trang fame, but fun all the same. A trip out to **Koh Rong** is the best, but you need a group. Overnight trips to the islands cost about US$19 per day.

DIVING

Perhaps due to the subtle art of dynamite fishing in the past, the waters around Sihanoukville are less enviable for underwater action than Indonesia's or Thailand's.

However, venture further to the island of Koh Tang on an overnight trip and you'll get slightly more bang for your buck. There are three reputable dive operators in Sihanoukville:

Chez Claude (☎ 012-824870) Longest-running operator in town, owner Claude knows the local waters as well as anyone.

EcoSea Dive (☎ 012-654104; www.ecosea.com) Offers diving or snorkelling trips and PADI courses.

Scuba Nation (☎ 012-604680; www.divecambodia.com) The first PADI-approved dive centre in Cambodia. French, German and Dutch are spoken.

REAM NATIONAL PARK

The **Ream National Park** (☎ 012-889620) is the backdrop for adventurous and educational guided boat trips through mangrove swamps to deserted beaches on the protected coast. Many guesthouses arrange various trips through the park (about US$15) and the chances of spotting dolphins or monkeys are pretty good. The park is only 13km from Sihanoukville.

MASSAGE

Seeing Hands Massage 3 (Ph Ekareach; per hr US$3) is another outpost of the excellent massage by the blind, pioneered in Phnom Penh.

Sleeping

There are three popular areas for budget accommodation in Sihanoukville: the long-running area centred on Weather Station Hill above Victory Beach, the town centre and the burgeoning Serendipity Beach. Serendipity's land rights and its very name are currently contentious issues, so this area is bound for significant change.

WEATHER STATION HILL

Bungalow Village (☎ 933875; bungalows US$5-10) Occupying a strategic section of the hillside nearer the beach than most, the garden gives this place more charm than many cheapies. The cheaper bungalows are smaller with squat toilets, while the more expensive are bigger and include a balcony with a view.

Sunset Garden Inn (☎ 012-562004; s US$3, d US$4-5) Slightly off the path leading from the beach to backpacker central is this fine and quiet choice. There's a huge, albeit unsheltered, rooftop terrace with glorious views and the clean rooms are good value. All US$5 rooms have satellite TV and some boast sea views.

CAMBODIA

Mealy Chenda Guesthouse (☎ 933472; dm US$2, r US$4-10; 🌀) Sihanoukville's original backpacker guesthouse, it's now huge and hotel-like. Housed below the brilliant ocean-view terrace are cheap rooms in the old block. The new block's rooms are larger, brighter and some offer hot water and air-con. Sadly some smell slightly of cigarettes, so sniff a few before dropping your bags.

Da Da Guesthouse (☎ 012-879527; r without bathroom US$3, r US$5-8; 🌀) Another one of the longer-running places up on the hill, the friendly family here offers a good selection of rooms from the very basic to slightly more sophisticated rooms with TV and bathroom. Possibly the cheapest air-con in town.

Nika Guesthouse (☎ 012-286191; s/tw US$5/6) Rooms are large, bright, squeaky clean and come complete with TVs. Views are available from communal balconies.

SERENDIPITY BEACH
Chan Sovannkiry Guesthouse (☎ 016-891248; d US$6-10, tw US$8-15; 🌀) Atop the dirt road leading from Serendipity, this newish white beast has comfortable rooms and a shared top-floor balcony whose view will ensure your satellite TV sees little action.

Sea Sun Guesthouse (☎ 012-357825; r US$7-13; 🌀) Just up from Chan Sovannkiry and set in a bare garden, these small bungalows offer smart rooms with fan, TV and clean bathrooms. Rooms with ocean views, albeit distant peeks, are no more painful to your pocket. Similar rooms cost over US$30 on the beach itself.

Coaster's (☎ 012-752181; www.cambodia-beach .com; s/d US$7/9) A short stroll from the beach, Coaster's has an atmospheric bar and communal area to go with its no-nonsense rooms. There's a second Coaster's right

down on the beach, where there are fairly ordinary **bungalows** (s/d US$10/15, ste US$25-70) with extraordinary ocean-view verandas.

Sea View Villa (☎ 935555; r US$8-20; 🌀) Laze on the terrace and take in views of the ocean or stumble to the nearby sands and lounge away. The budget rooms are simple and comfortable.

Eden (☎ 933585; r US$8-10) If Adam and Eve were deaf, they'd have stuck around. The beachfront location is great by day, but the night-time beats radiating upward from the bar ensure restless nights, unless of course you crawl upstairs at closing.

TOWN CENTRE
Red Snapper Guesthouse (☎ 012-527043; off Ph Ekareach; r US$5-6) A quiet and secluded place with a more relaxed vibe than other choices in town. The rooms are large and the US$6 options have hot water and TVs.

Angkor Inn Guesthouse (☎ 016-896204; r US$4-5) Cheap and a little bit cheerful, this is a firmly established budget deal. Large TVs and small bathrooms are standard, plus there's the lure of great coffee across the road at Espresso Kampuchea.

Eating
Numerous established eateries flourish on Weather Station Hill, while new restaurants and beachside barbeque shacks are blooming around Serendipity Beach. Unless stated below, all restaurants are open for breakfast, lunch and dinner.

WEATHER STATION HILL
Melting Pot (mains 4000-16,000r) Fruit, yoghurt, muesli and even fresh *pain au chocolat* lure people into this bamboo hut for brekky, while candles, a chilled vibe, quality Western fare and savoury Indian specials, like

dal amritsari (lentils with fruit) and *murg makhini* (succulent chicken in rich butter gravy), draw them in for dinner.

Snake House (☎ 012-673805; mains US$2-5) Can you stomach it? Not the food, but the tables set amid a flourishing reptile house with snakes from all over the world. Dine with a python to your left, a cobra to your right and snakes right underneath your plate…yes they even lurk beneath the glass-topped tables!

Romduol's Restaurant (mains 3000-6000r) Scenic it's not, but the varied assortment of cheap and tasty eats, along with the odd footy match on TV, never fails to draw in the hungry crowds.

La Paillotte (mains US$3-7; ☽ dinner) The daily menus here are sprinkled with French flair and solid seafood selections. You'll find this touch of culinary class set back off the main stretch beneath a thatched roof.

Indian Curry Pot (curries US$2-3) Less ambience than Melting Pot, but it offers a wider range of satisfying curries. The *thalis* and weekend buffets are good value and everything is 100% halal.

Other cheap treats:

Ku Kai (mains US$1-3) Popular wee place specialising in Japanese selections.

Rose's Place (mains 3000-6000r) A hole in the wall with simple Western and Khmer dishes.

SERENDIPITY BEACH

Rama Beach Restaurant (mains US$3-7) A cut above the competition, this place offers low-slung tables on the beach or upright dining under a pavilion, complete with candles in the evening. The menu mixes Asian favourites with tasty pastas, but it's all about the seafood here, including a good selection of shellfish.

Unkle Bob's (mains US$1-6) Sink your feet in the sand, put a beer in your hand and quench both your thirst and hunger beneath the boughs of a mighty creaking tree. The menu is fairly standard and offers Western and Khmer selections.

Mick & Craig's Restaurant (near Golden Lions Roundabout; mains US$2-6) Set under a thatched roof a little way from the beach, it's home to a good selection of breakfasts, including hearty vegetarian options, as well as a serious selection of good Western grub and popular Khmer dishes like *trey choo'im* (fillet of snapper in sweet and sour sauce). Food is served until around 11pm.

TOWN CENTRE

Starfish Bakery (☎ 012-952011; meals US$1-3; ☽ breakfast & lunch) Tucked down a little side street off Ph 7 Makara, this leafy garden café pumps out choice cakes, super shakes and light bites. Better still, it's all in the name of a good cause, as the Starfish Project supports local disadvantaged Cambodians who need a helping hand.

Self-caterers should head to **Samudera Market** (Ph 7 Makara), near Starfish Bakery, which has the best stock of international foods, including cheese, meats and chocolate.

Drinking

The sands of Serendipity are blossoming as a night spot, while Weather Station Hill and the town centre boast many venues knocking out locally brewed Angkor at US$0.50 a glass, the cheapest draught in Cambodia.

Eden (Serendipity Beach) A slight essence of Hat Rin on Koh Pha-Ngan, with candle-lit tables and revellers strewn on the beach, both spilt from its energetic confines. Eden ramps up the amps for full moons and special occasions.

Unkle Bob's (Serendipity Beach) Immediately south of Eden and similar in vibe. It pours out liquid happiness 24 hours a day.

South from here along Occheuteal there are numerous beach shacks that also heave until the early hours. They change names quicker than most of us change underwear, so it's pointless to recommend any by name.

Angkor Arms (Ph Ekareach) Originally a pseudo-pub with darts and draught, it has come on in leaps and bounds, now with outdoor tables for those who want a drink with a breeze.

Dusk 'til Dawn (Ph Sopheakmongkol) Perfect for those lubed up at Angkor Arms and not wanting to end their night till dawn. Its right next door and up a rickety staircase (okay… not so perfect) – mind the stairs!

Le Bar 'Ang, Melting Pot and **Pet's Place** are all on Weather Station Hill and draw a crowd by sundown and often the night shift follows.

The only real nightclub in town is **Blue Storm** (Ph Ekareach; no cover charge), which is packed with young Khmers moving to deafening DJs and VJs on weekends. Drinks are a little pricey.

Getting There & Away

For information on the southern border crossing into Thailand, see p110.

CAMBODIA

BOAT

See p109 for fast-boat services to and from Sihanoukville.

BUS

Capitol Tour (10,000r), GST (14,000r), Hour Lean (12,000r) and PPPT (14,000r) offer numerous daily services to Phnom Penh (four hours) from their offices in town. PPPT and several guesthouses run minibuses to Krong Koh Kong (US$13).

MOTORCYCLE

NH4 to Phnom Penh is busy, boring and dangerous, so riding isn't recommended. However, motorcycles are useful in exploring Kampot, Bokor and Kep. See below for rental details.

SHARE TAXI

Cramped taxis head to Phnom Penh (10,000r, four hours) and Kampot (8000r, two hours) from the new taxi park in the town centre. Buses are clearly the better option to the capital.

TRAIN

Sadly, passenger trains no longer service Sihanoukville.

Getting Around

Bicycles are a pleasant and environmentally friendly way to get around and some guesthouses offer rentals for US$1 to US$2 per day.

With moto drivers having a well-earned reputation for overcharging, it's important to negotiate in advance. From the town centre to Victory or Serendipity Beaches expect to drop about 2000r, while a trip between these beaches is around 3000r. Costs almost double at night.

Numerous guesthouses and restaurants rent 100cc motos for US$3 per day. GST (☎ 933826; Ph Ekareach) rent out slightly newer bikes for US$4 per day, plus larger 250cc trail bikes for US$7 per day, just the medicine for Bokor National Park.

KAMPOT

☎ 033 / pop 37,400

For a place with seemingly little to offer other than being the perfect base to explore nearby caves and Bokor National Park (p108), Kampot manages to charm more

> **DID YOU KNOW?**
>
> In the years before civil war took its toll, no self-respecting French restaurant in Paris would be without Kampot pepper on the table.

than its fair share of visitors with its fine riverside location, laid-back ambience and mix of French legacy architecture.

Information

There's a basic tourist office, but little info is to be had. There are a couple of Internet places near the central roundabout charging 6000r per hour.

Canadia Bank (☎ 932392) Offers free credit-card cash advances and changes most currencies and travellers cheques.

Hospital (☎ 016-877689) Basic, but the only medical facility in town.

Sights & Activities

Remember this is not a town where you come and do, but a place to come and feel. Sit on the riverbank and watch the sun set beneath the mountains or take in some of the town's fine **French architecture**. Oddly enough one of the nicest relics is the **prison**!

About 10km east are the bat-filled caves of **Phnom Chhnork**, one containing a remarkably preserved 7th-century brick temple. Also outside of town are the **Tek Chhouu Falls**, which are really no more than series of not-so-rapid rapids. They're 8km west of town and are filled with bathing locals on weekends.

Sleeping

A regular budget smorgasbord.

Blissful Guesthouse (☎ 012-513024; dm US$2.50, r US$3-5) A lush garden, great chill-out area and popular bar-restaurant make this Kampot's most atmospheric guesthouse. The large rooms are austere but have a few thoughtful trimmings. On the downside the cheapies share a bathroom and only the US$5 rooms have exterior windows.

Long Villa Guesthouse (☎ 012-210820; near Psar Leu; tw US$4-5, q US$6) Run by an extraordinarily friendly Khmer family who go the extra mile to ensure your comfort. The smallish and homely rooms are bright, clean and set in a colonial house that sits back off the road.

Mealy Chenda Guesthouse (☎ 012-831559; dm/s US$2/3, tw US$4-6) Feels cavernous but is full of

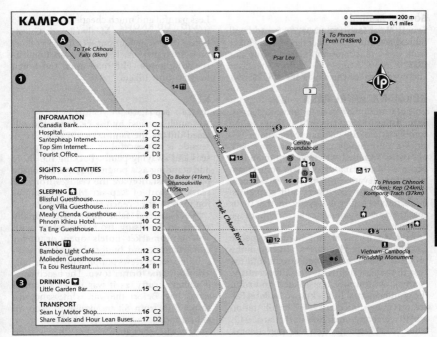

KAMPOT

CAMBODIA

helpful info and travel services. A rooftop restaurant and bar are on order, so it may eventually get some colour in its cheeks.

Ta Eng Guesthouse (☎ 012-330058; dm US$2, s US$3-4, tw US$5) The longest-running backpacker place in town with basic but comfy rooms. The atmosphere is as friendly as the helpful owner, who speaks French and English.

Phnom Khieu Hotel (☎ 012-820923; Central Roundabout; r US$5-10; ✷) This won't win any prizes for character, but when it comes to good rooms at the right prices, it just might. It's spacious and clean, with TV and fridge.

Eating & Drinking
Fine restaurants will keep your stomach seriously satisfied, but the lack of night-life may have your liver screaming for joy. Places mentioned here are open for breakfast, lunch and dinner.

Ta Eou Restaurant (☎ 932422; River Rd; mains 4000-12,000r) Seafood and sunsets are the name of the game here. Sit in the stilted section over the river and crack into some fresh crab laden with tasty green peppercorns. The English-language menu is extensive.

Bamboo Light Café (☎ 012-602661; River Rd; curries US$2-4) Kampot's first Sri Lankan restaurant, Bamboo Light Café brings the spices of the subcontinent to town. Local expats rave about the fine flavours and the setting is slap-bang in the middle of the action on the riverfront.

Several guesthouses serve fine fare along with cold beer, including: **Long Villa Guesthouse** (mains 3000-8000r), with great veg selections like tofu and vegetable curry; **Molieden Guesthouse** (mains US$3-6), which creates town's best pizzas; and **Blissful Guesthouse** (mains US$1-4), for Mexican late-night drinks.

The **Little Garden Bar** (River Rd) has a cosy garden and scenic rooftop deck for a sunset beer, cocktail or glass of vino.

Getting There & Away
Share taxis leave from the old Total station in the southeast of town and ply NH3 to Phnom Penh (10,000r, two hours) and Sihanoukville (8000r, two hours).

A more comfortable and equally cheap option to the capital are the buses of **Hour Lean** (☎ 012-939917).

Getting Around

Sean Ly Motor Shop (☎ 012-944687) rents small motorbikes from US$3 per day and big bikes from US$4, plus cars/minibuses/pick-ups for US$20/25/30. A moto to explore the caves and even Kep for the day is about US$5.

BOKOR NATIONAL PARK

One of Cambodia's premier protected areas, **Bokor National Park** (admission US$5) clings to the southern tip of the Elephant Mountains. Besides a refreshingly cool climate, the park possesses secluded **waterfalls**, commanding ocean views, an abandoned and eerie **French hill station** (elevation 1080m) and exceedingly elusive animals like tigers and elephants. Unfortunately, illegal logging in the 1990s cost the park its chance at a world heritage designation.

At great financial and human expense (many indentured labourers perished in the process), the French forged a road into the area in the first quarter of the 20th century. A small community was created and soon the grand colonial hotel, known as **Bokor Palace**, was inaugurated in 1925. The hill station was twice abandoned: first in the late 1940s when the Vietnamese and Khmer Issarak (Free Khmer) forces overran it while fighting for independence against the French, and again in the early 1970s when it was left to the invading Khmer Rouge. It now has a genuine ghost-town feel, especially when thick mists envelope the skeletons of the original structures.

The picturesque two-tiered drop of **Popokvil Falls**, a peaceful 90-minute walk from the hill station, is best seen in the wet season as it's disappointingly drippy at other times. While in the jungle, remember to stick to well-worn paths and keep an ear out for tigers.

If you'd like to spend the night, the **ranger station** (per bunk US$5) has basic beds. Pack warm clothing, a torch (electricity goes off at about 9pm) and some food as the supplies there are limited.

Getting There & Away

The access road is 7km west of Kampot and from there it's a scenically stunning and horrifically bumpy 25km up to the plateau's first structure, the **black palace**. It's about a two-hour drive from Kampot, making for a perfect day trip. Hiring a 250cc dirt bike and driver for the trip will cost about US$12.

Less painful and much cheaper are the US$6 day trips arranged by Mealy Chenda Guesthouse (p106) in Kampot. For US$6 you get pick-up transport, lunch and an English-speaking guide. The road up is too tough for first-time bikers.

KEP

☎ 036 / pop 11,500

Although ravaged by the civil war and pillaged during the famine of 1979–80, Kep's seaside is as peaceful as ever with lapping seas and swaying palms. Backing the shore and standing as a poignant reminder of the past's devastation are the vestiges from the seaside resort of Kep-sur-Mer, which was founded by the French elite in 1908.

After several false starts, Kep finally seems to be rising from the ashes, with several upmarket hotels open or under construction, and budget bungalows with sublime ocean views popping up on the hillside above the former town. The beach itself is rather scruffy, as it was never a natural sandy bay. Before the war, white sand was shipped in from Sihanoukville to keep up appearances!

Better beaches are found off the coast on islands like **Koh Tonsay** (Rabbit Island), which now has a couple of basic guesthouses. A boat for the day can be arranged from the seafood sellers as you enter town for about US$20, depending on numbers. Guesthouses also arrange boats, starting from US$10 for one to three people.

Sleeping & Eating

Veranda Guesthouse (☎ 012-888619; verandaresort@ mobitel.com.kh; bungalows US$4-15) Elevated walkways and bungalows, each with a shaded veranda and lazy hammock, hover over this hillside resort's verdant gardens and offer stunning views of the ocean below. Bungalows range from small, basic bamboo structures to larger individual pads with striking bathrooms. The lofty, log-furnished restaurant is open to all and specialises in Western fare (mains cost from US$1 to US$4).

Vanna Bungalow (☎ 012-755038; s/d US$7/10) Perched above town and across the track from Veranda, this place has solid, comfortable bungalows at sensible prices. Set in pleasant gardens, there is also a basic restaurant here.

> **SPLURGE!**
>
> **Champey Inn** (☎ 012-501742; champeyinn@ar tsuriyatravel.com; r US$40-60; 🏊) A huge leap in the dollar department, but this stylish spot has a lovely swimming pool and sits almost seaside. The standard rooms surround the pool and have antique furniture with flashes of traditional Chinese-Khmer trimmings. Each room has a wonderful Balinese style open-air bathroom. The deluxe rooms are not worth the extra dough.

Kep Seaside Guesthouse (☎ 012-684241; s US$4, d US$5-7) Best of the budget beachside accommodation, this guesthouse's rooms are big, breezy and some have balconies with sea views. The view from No 10 is worth outlaying US$7. A series of shady hammocks line the rocky shore.

Away from the accommodation, dining is still easy, as there are numerous bamboo shacks along the coast offering fresh seafood, although be sure to agree to a price in advance and make sure the crab is fresh.

Getting There & Away
Kep is just 24km from Kampot, so it's easiest to take a moto (about US$2) or share taxi from there. The Cambodian–Vietnamese border at Ha Tien is not currently open to foreigners.

SRE AMBEL & THE CARDAMOM MOUNTAINS
North of Sihanoukville and located up a river estuary in eastern Koh Kong Province, Sre Ambel is something of a smugglers' port. Plenty of people are passing through on the new road connecting the Thailand border at Krong Koh Kong with Sihanoukville and Phnom Penh, but few ever step off. There's little of interest in the town itself, but lurking nearby is the ultimate wilderness of the Cardamom Mountains.

Downed bridges and rugged logging roads have kept **Puong Roul Waterfall** (one of Cambodia's finest falls, with five big unique cascades plunging down a jungle-covered gorge) a relative secret despite it being only 10km from Sre Ambel. Swimming is an option in the wet season, but heed locals advice about crocodiles. After all, this is the wild, wild Cardamoms.

KRONG KOH KONG
☎ 035 / pop 33,100
Krong Koh Kong (Koh Kong town) is a dusty frontier town of smugglers, gamblers and prostitutes, which acts as a functional stop on the southern overland trail between Thailand and Cambodia. With a new road linking it to the rest of Cambodia, it's no longer necessary to stop the night. For those who have some time to kill, flop on the quiet but scruffy beach east of town or hop on a moto (200B) and head to **Ta Tai Waterfall**, a wide, shallow set of falls spilling over a 4m limestone shelf, some 20km from town on the road to Sre Ambel.

Baht, US dollars and riel are all currencies that are accepted here, so as long as you carry cash you'll be fine. The nearest banks that can deal with credit cards or travellers cheques are in Sihanoukville or Thailand. Internet access is readily available for 120B per hour.

Sleeping & Eating
Phou Mint Koh Kong Hotel (☎ 936221; Ph 1; r US$5-15; 🏊) Occupying a prime position on the riverbank, midway between the boat dock and bridge, this new hotel has huge sparkling rooms with fans and satellite TVs. Some mattresses are hard as nails so poke a few.

Otto's (☎ 963163; Ph 8; r without bathroom 80-120B) Conveniently near the boat dock, this small elevated guesthouse has basic rooms with wafer-thin walls, mozzie nets and prices to match. It's a good spot for reliable travel information and there's a popular Western **restaurant** (mains 60-200B; 🍴 breakfast, lunch & dinner), which serves one of the best bratwurst in Cambodia.

With a garden setting and Thai menu bursting with vegetarian options and fresh seafood, **Baan Peakmai** (cnr Ph 3 & 6; mains 50-150B; 🍴 breakfast, lunch & dinner) is easily the town's most appealing restaurant. For your first or last taste of Khmer cuisine slide into **Samras Angkor Restaurant** (mains 50-150B; 🍴 breakfast, lunch & dinner).

Getting There & Away
Daily buses to Phnom Penh or Sihanoukville both depart around 9am and charge an astounding 500B. Share taxis charge a similar 400B for a seat (space is more accurate, as a whole seat is too much to hope for). Both destinations take about 5½ hours to reach,

---

BORDER CROSSING: INTO THAILAND

Leaving Cambodia, take a share taxi (80B per person) or moto (40B) from Krong Koh Kong over the new bridge to the border at Chong Yeam (C)/Hat Lek (T). Walk across the border where there are minibuses (100B, one hour, every 30 minutes) to Trat for connections to Bangkok or Koh Chang. Slightly cheaper but slower is to take two săwngthăew (small pick-up truck with two benches in the back) – the first to Klong Yai where you change for the second to Trat. Each costs from 30B to 50B.

---

but that can double in the wet season. If the plan to seal the road goes ahead, even dry-season travel times should be reduced significantly.

Fast boats leave daily for Sihanoukville (600B, four hours, 8am). Coming the other way, boats depart Sihanoukville at noon. These boats were designed for rivers, so it can get rough during high winds. With the road as it stands now, use the boat in the wet season and the road in the dry season to avoid the sickening swells.

NORTHEASTERN CAMBODIA

If you feel like riding an elephant through the Modulkiri's forests, swimming in Ratanakiri's jungle-shrouded volcanic crater or glimpsing the sweet breaths of rare freshwater Irrawaddy dolphins in Kratie, the northeast may be for you. While the roads are improving, you'll still end up filthy and feeling like your parents just spanked your butt for putting gum in your kid sister's hair. It's not for everyone, which also means crowds are pleasantly absent.

KOMPONG CHAM

☎ 042 / pop 51,200

Kompong Cham, an important trading post during the French period, sits bruised and battered on the shores of the mighty Mekong. Strangely, this provincial capital's charm resides in its state of decay. This is particularly true south of the massive, Mekong-straddling Japanese bridge, where aged traditional stilted wooden homes hover among decomposing colonial relics. The new bridge and recent move of the Kratie and Stung Treng boat services here from Phnom Penh have made Kompong Cham a crucial travel hub. It makes for an interesting afternoon, but otherwise there's little reason to linger.

Information

ABC Computer (11 Ph Ang Duong; per hr 4000r) Internet access.

Canadia Bank (☎ 941361; Preah Monivong Blvd) Near the market; changes cash and travellers cheques in most currencies and offers free Visa and MasterCard advances.

Sights & Activities

Wat Nokor is an 11th-century Mahayana Buddhist shrine of sandstone and laterite set slap-bang in the centre of an active and slightly kitsch Theravada wat. A peaceful atmosphere pervades the place, which rests about 1km from town, just off the road to Phnom Penh. Equally tranquil is a bike ride or walk on the nearby rural island of **Koh Paen**, which is connected to town in the dry season by an elaborate bamboo bridge – a sight in itself!

Sleeping

One street near the market boasts guesthouses advertising rooms at 5000r, although most rooms are cells and most 'guests' seem to pay by the hour, so it could get oh, ohh, ohhh! so noisy.

Mekong Hotel (☎ 941536; Ph Preah Bat Sihanouk; r US$5-10; 🏋) Still the best all-rounder in town, this hotel has a great riverfront location and vast corridors that are begging for some high-flying ultimate Frisbee action. All rooms come with satellite TV, and ten bucks earns a date with air-con, hot water and a Mekong view.

Thorchakchet Guesthouse (☎ 012-947043; r without bathroom US$2.50, r US$3-4) Set back from the river and away from the ungodly early-morning boat horns is this family-run option. The clean rooms range from small to extra large, and US$4 nabs you a TV. It's a few blocks inland from the Mekong Hotel down a dusty lane.

Bophea Guesthouse (☎ 012-796803; Vithei Pasteur; r US$2-3) Bargain-basement prices found only a block from the river. Think about dropping the extra George Washington for the large rooms that have bathrooms. Conveniently, it also has bicycle rentals (4000r per day).

Eating & Drinking

The cheapest chow is at stop-and-dip food stalls in the market. *Tukalok* (fruit shake) stalls near the police station also do a selection of snacks.

Hao An Restaurant (☎ 941234; Preah Monivong Blvd; mains 5500-10,000r; ☽ breakfast, lunch & dinner) If you get over the pictures of the unhappy and very dead ingredients at the start of the menu, you'll enjoy some great local fish, meats and veggies in an array of special sauces.

Two Dragons Restaurant (Ph Ang Duong; d 4000-8000r; ☽ breakfast, lunch & dinner) A basic place with tasty Khmer staples. You won't see fish *amok* on the menu, but if you ask for it, you'll be justly rewarded.

Mekong Crossing (Vithei Pasteur; meals US$2-4; ☽ lunch & dinner) Grab a frosty beer and while away the hours playing miniature Monopoly and dining on Western treats like toasted sandwiches and burgers.

In the early evening locals gather on the waterfront outside the Mekong Hotel, where a number of stalls sell cheap beers.

Getting There & Away

Phnom Penh Public Transport (PPPT; Preah Monivong Blvd) buses service Phnom Penh (8000r, two hours) and Kratie (15,000r, four hours, 10.30am) along the excellent NH7. To reach Mondulkiri Province, PPPT's Kratie bus can drop you in Snoul (10,000r, 2½ hours) for Hour Lean's noon bus to Sen Monorom (17,000r, 2½ hours). Other options to Phnom Penh include **GST** (Preah Monivong Blvd) buses (7000r), overcrowded minibuses (5000r) and share taxis (10,000r). Travellers going to Kratie on their own motorbikes should consider following the western bank of the Mekong to the Stung Treng district, crossing the river and continuing northward through Chhlong for a really memorable ride.

Fast boats to Kratie (US$7, three hours, 7am) now depart just south of the bridge. From July to around January fast boats go all the way to Stung Treng (US$15, seven hours). Painfully slow cargo boats are cheaper, but follow no regular schedule.

KRATIE

☎ 072 / pop 89,400

Kratie (krach-*eh*) is the best place in Cambodia to glimpse the region's last-remaining freshwater Irrawaddy dolphins. Thanks to the marine life, a pleasant riverside setting

and well-preserved French and Khmer architecture, Kratie is becoming a popular stop on the overland route to Laos or Ratanakiri Province.

Information

There are no facilities for changing travellers cheques or getting credit-card cash advances, so bring US dollars or riel. **Khmer Institute of Democracy** (Rue Preah Suramarit; per hr 4000r) has the town's fastest and cheapest Internet.

Sights & Activities

Just 15km north of town at Kampi, the endangered **Irrawaddy dolphins** are often seen poking through the Mekong's silent surface for a breath of fresh air. The Mekong Dolphin Conservation Project (MDCP) charges US$2 to visit the site plus US$2 to US$3 per person for a boat, depending on the number of passengers. Return trips by moto should cost about US$3. Alternatively, it's an enjoyable 60-minute bike ride to Kampi. Take in a dramatic sunset over the Mekong from **Phnom Sombok** on the way back to town.

Opposite town in the middle of the Mekong is an idyllic slice of rural Cambodia on the island of **Koh Trong**.

Sleeping & Eating

The best budget sleeping and eating options are found in the vicinity of the market. All restaurants mentioned are open for breakfast, lunch and dinner.

Star Guesthouse (☎ 971663; Ph Preah Sihanouk; r US$2-5) Best of the budget bunch with cheap, newly renovated rooms, reliable travel info from knowledgeable English-speaking staff, and a small restaurant with tasty and inexpensive food (mains cost 3000r to 10,000r).

You Hong Guesthouse (☎ 012-957003; 91 Ph 8; r US$2.50-5) One of the newer kids on the block, this guesthouse offers great value for money. The rooms are basic but very clean, and downstairs is a restaurant with great Khmer and Western fare (mains 5000r to 10,000r). Tofu mushroom burgers and tofu curries will have even carnivores happily licking their lips.

Heng Oudom Hotel (☎ 012-276030; Ph 10; s US$3-4, tw US$5-10; ☒) The US$3 rooms lack value and windows, but the remainder are bright, clean and come with satellite TV. There's a communal balcony to take in the market and if you crane your neck, a peek at the river.

While smart, it's a step down in atmosphere from the guesthouses mentioned earlier.

Red Sun Falling (Ph Preah Suramarit; mains US$1-3) A welcome sight on arrival by boat in Kratie, this place has fine furnishings, good music and a small bookshop, setting the tone for a relaxing place to sit and take in Kratie. The menu includes a small selection of Asian food and some Western favourites, including excellent homemade brownies. By night, the bar is the best stocked in town.

Getting There & Away

The 348km road south to Phnom Penh is now entirely surfaced, cutting journey times dramatically. **PPPT** (☎ 012-523400) and **Hour Lean** (☎ 012-535387) each run one bus a day to the capital (18,000r, six hours, 7.30am). More frequent and faster, though less comfortable, are the share taxis to the capital (25,000r, five hours). Hour Lean also serves Stung Treng (22,000r, 3½ hours, around 1pm) along the improving dirt NH7. For Mondulkiri take a share taxi to Snoul (8000r, 1¼ hours) and hop on Hour Lean's noon bus to Sen Monorom (17,000r, 2½ hours).

Other options to Stung Treng are share taxis (US$7.50) and the daily fast boat (US$8, four hours, noon), which runs from July to around January. A year-round fast boat also serves Kompong Cham (US$7, three hours, 10.30am).

MONDULKIRI PROVINCE

Climatically, culturally and visually, Mondulkiri is another world compared with the rest of Cambodia. Its endless grassy hills, dotted with occasional clumps of pines, huddle together against the wind and are home to hardy minority peoples. Half of the sparsely populated province's 35,000 people are from the Pnong minority. Wild animals are more numerous here than elsewhere, including elephants, bears and tigers, although chances of seeing tigers are about as good as winning the lottery. Green grasses or brown brush, messy mud or the dreaded dust, the contrasts between the wet and dry season are stark – take your pick.

Sen Monorom

☎ 073 / pop 7,900
Sen Monorom, the dusty provincial capital, is in reality an overgrown village, a character-filled community hemmed in by hills on all sides. Set at more than 800m, when the winds blow it's noticeably cooler than the rest of Cambodia. The slow pace of life makes it the ideal base to explore the province.

INFORMATION

There are no banks, so carry US dollars or riel. Phone calls are possible from mobiles around town and sporadic Internet access is available at **Arun II Guesthouse** (per hr US$4), on the road to Phnom Penh. The local tourist office is more helpful than most, but Long Vibol, who works for the Red Cross and runs a guesthouse, provides more useful details and can also supply English-speaking guides.

SIGHTS & ACTIVITIES

About 3km northwest of town are **Monorom Falls**, the closest thing to a public swimming pool for Sen Monorom. More enticing falls are found slightly further afield – see opposite for details.

Elephant day-treks can be arranged in nearby Pnong villages such as Putang and Phulung by guesthouses or the local tourist office for around US$25 to US$30 per elephant (two passengers), including moto transport. Bring a comfy pillow to sit on – trust us! It's possible to negotiate an overnight trek from about US$60 per person.

SLEEPING & EATING

Sen Monorom has erratic electricity from around 5am to 10pm only, so a torch is useful for late-night toilet treks. With chilly evening temperatures, hot water is a welcome touch.

Sovankiri Guesthouse (☎ 012-821931; s/tw US$3/5) A short walk down the hill from the airport and home to the Hour Lean buses, its warm, wood-lined singles are large and have their own bathrooms making them the best deal in town.

Holiday Guesthouse (☎ 012-588060; tw/s US$3/5) Across the street from Sovankiri, this palatial pad's twin rooms with shared bathroom are good value. The singles rooms have bathrooms, satellite TVs and a little more room to manoeuvre.

Long Vibol Guesthouse (☎ 012-944647; s US$5, tw US$10-15) Rooms are spaciously spread across the blossoming garden and top dollar gets you hot showers. It's a great source of information on exploring Mondulkiri and a good place to arrange trekking. Its restaurant, open for breakfast, lunch and dinner, is one of the most popular in town, attracting well-to-do Khmers as well as foreigners (mains 3000r to 8000r).

Arun Reah II Guesthouse (☎ 012-856667; bungalows US$5-10) Set at the entrance to town and boasting fine views across the hills of Mondulkiri, this option has seriously sweet bungalows that include bathroom, TV and a torch. Hot-water rooms cost US$8 and the US$10 rooms are cavernous. There's a big restaurant out the front that can be a little quiet, but beer is always available.

Chom Nor Tmei Restaurant (mains 3000-8000r; ☺ breakfast, lunch & dinner) Between the airport and Sovankiri Guesthouse, this Khmer eatery serves up local specials, many flavoured with lemon grass, peanuts, basil or chillies.

GETTING THERE & AWAY

The unthinkable happened in 2005 when scheduled buses linked Sen Monorom with Phnom Penh (32,000r, eight hours). Hour Lean's service leaves for the capital daily at 7am – hop off at Snoul (17,000r, 2½ hours) to make connections to Kratie. Pick-ups also service Snoul (20,000/15,000 inside/outside, three hours). See Getting There & Away under Kratie (opposite) or Kompong Cham (p111) for inbound transportation details.

An adventurous and extremely arduous path connects Sen Monorom with Ban Lung in Ratanakiri Province – hard-core motorcyclists should see Long Vibol Guesthouse for advice.

Flights to Sen Monorom have been suspended since 2000.

GETTING AROUND

Arun Reah II Guesthouse rents out 100cc motorbikes for US$5 per day. Similar bikes at other guesthouses are US$10. If you want a 250cc bike, you'll have to rent it in Phnom Penh (p78).

Around Sen Monorom

The real beauty of the Mondulkiri Province is exploring by motorbike or on foot under your own steam, following small paths into patches of forest that survived mass deforestation in the 1990s. Many visitors end up in *chunchiet* villages, but it's unfair to single any place out, as the influx of visitors could destroy the character. Waterfalls feature prominently around the province, including

the low and wide **Romanear**, 18km southeast of Sen Monorom, and the single drop **Dak Dam Waterfall**, 25km to the city's east. Both are very difficult to find without a guide.

Bou Sraa Falls, a double drop (35m) into a jungle gorge, is one of the largest and most famous waterfalls in Cambodia. This is the one to make for, although the 37km road out here has long been known as the bastard child of the devil himself, involving driving through not one, not two, but three rivers. The authorities plan to improve it, but believe it when you see it. Hire a moto driver for the day or charter a Russian jeep (US$60) with a group.

STUNG TRENG

☎ 074 / pop 27,700

Stung Treng is a real outpost town on the banks of the San and Mekong Rivers, just 50km south of Laos. Travellers heading between Cambodia and Laos often get stuck here for the night, but few hang around for very long as Ratanakiri and Kratie have more to excite.

Information

There are no banks, but Riverside Restaurant can cash travellers cheques. US dollars are best if arriving from Laos. There are several shops with Internet access (12,000r per hr) around the market.

Sleeping & Eating

Riverside Restaurant & Guesthouse (☎ 012-439454; r US$3) Whether just off the boat, bus or bumpy moto, slide in here for fine food and cool drinks on the shady riverfront rooftop and, if you feel so inclined, a night's kip. Rooms are only US$3 and include a basic bathroom. The restaurant, open for breakfast, lunch and dinner, includes Khmer, Thai and Chinese specials to go with the odd international dish (mains 3500r to 10,000r). The staff are a good source of information on Laos, Ratanakiri and Kratie.

Sekong Hotel (☎ 973762; r US$3-15; ✷) This rambling hotel on the riverfront has a dizzying selection of rooms. Cheapest are the big but basic rooms out the back, but for just US$3 or US$4 there's little room to complain. Spend another dollar and you get a TV – US$7 brings hot water.

New World Restaurant (mains 4000-10,000r; ☺ breakfast, lunch & dinner) One block west of the

CAMBODIA

BORDER CROSSING: INTO LAOS

The beautiful river border between Stung Treng Province in Cambodia and Champasak Province in Laos has been open to foreigners since late 2000 and is growing in popularity as an adventurous and cheap way to combine northeastern Cambodia and southern Laos. Have you got your visa? OK, read on...

In theory, if you're armed with a Lao or Cambodian visa, there should be no extra charges at the border, but in reality, Lao immigration asks for US$1 for overtime and Cambodian officials ask for whatever they think they can get away with, from US$1 to US$5 per person. Pay no more than US$1 on either side...and preferably pay nothing! Cambodian immigration is on the western bank of the Mekong; Lao immigration on the east. There's an alternative land border a few kilometres from Voen Kham, known as Dom Krolor on the Cambodian side, which will become more popular in the very near future when the Chinese team completes work on the road to Stung Treng.

Officials have stopped tourists using cheap local slow boats; so when leaving Cambodia it costs US$5 per person for a small speedboat up the Mekong from Stung Treng to Voen Kham. Arriving in Cambodia, there's a 'fixed' price of US$50 per speedboat, which only really takes five people with packs, effectively making it US$10 per person! The boat price includes a stop for Cambodian immigration in either direction.

Transport on the Lao side is very hit and miss for those arriving from Cambodia, but easy when leaving Laos. It's probably going to be necessary to take a motorcycle taxi or *jamboh* (túk-túk) to Nakasong, where there are good public transport connections to points north.

---

market, this new restaurant offers a mix of Asian flavours plus a fair selection of beers to cool your insides.

Cheap food stalls can be found on the riverfront and around the market.

Getting There & Away

An early morning Hour Lean bus leaves for Kratie (22,000r, 3½ hours) and Phnom Penh (40,000r, 10 hours) along NH7. Crowded share taxis head south to Kratie (30,000r) and east to Ban Lung (30,000r, 4½ hours) along a brutal, but supposedly soon to be rebuilt, road. These times are for the dry season; count on much longer during the wet season.

Fast boats run to Kratie (US$8) and Kompong Cham (US$15) from July until about January.

RATANAKIRI PROVINCE

Despite Ratanakiri bursting with a vast diversity of natural attractions and distinct Khmer Loeu (Upper Khmer or *chunchiet*) minorities, few travellers take this bumpy road to paradise – a drastic mistake for many, a just reward for the willing. Swim in clear volcanic lakes, shower under waterfalls, glimpse an elephant or trek in the vast Virachey National Park – it's all up to you. The roads mimic papaya shakes during the

wet season, so the ideal time to explore is December to February. Prepare for a dusty, foul fake tan and orange hair. You didn't think it would be that easy did you?

Ban Lung

☎ 075 / pop 17,000

Dust looms over this quaint capital of Ratanakiri like a thick winter fog over London. However, waterfalls and the kingdom's best swimming pool, lurking in a nearby volcanic crater, will cleanse your skin and soothe your soul. It's also a great place to base your Ratanakiri adventures.

INFORMATION

There are no banks, but travellers cheques can be exchanged for a stiff commission at several guesthouses. Internet access is possible at a local **NGO** (per hr 8000r) and the **post office** (per hr 16,000r). Check out www.yaklom.com for more Ratanakiri info.

SIGHTS & ACTIVITIES
Boeng Yeak Laom

Set amid lush jungle a mere 5km east of town, this cracking **crater lake** (admission US$1) is one of the most serene spots in Cambodia. Get the swimming kit on and make a splash, the bigger the better – the local children will love you for it. There's a small

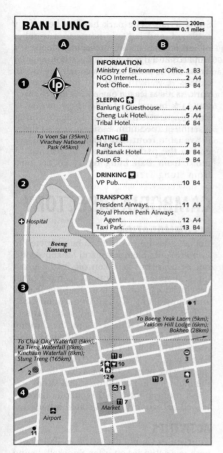

BAN LUNG

0 ———————— 200m
0 ———————— 0.1 miles

INFORMATION	
Ministry of Environment Office..1	B3
NGO Internet.........................2	A4
Post Office............................3	B4

SLEEPING	
Banlung I Guesthouse..............4	A4
Cheng Luk Hotel....................5	A4
Tribal Hotel..........................6	B4

EATING	
Hang Lei.............................7	B4
Rantanak Hotel......................8	B4
Soup 63..............................9	B4

DRINKING	
VP Pub...............................10	B4

TRANSPORT	
President Airways..................11	A4
Royal Phnom Penh Airways	
Agent.............................12	A4
Taxi Park............................13	B4

To Voen Sai (35km);
Virachay National
Park (45km)

Boeng
Kansaign

To Boeng Yeak Laom (5km);
Yaklom Hill Lodge (6km);
Bokheo (28km)

To Chaa Ong Waterfall (5km);
Ka Tieng Waterfall (8km);
Kinchaan Waterfall (8km);
Stung Treng (165km)

Market

Airport

visitors centre (free admission) on the western shore run by **Yeak Loam Community Based Eco-Tourism** (☎ 012-981226; yeak_laom@camintel.com). The centre offers community walks with English-speaking guides (US$3 to US$7 per person depending on numbers), which are an interesting insight into the life of the Tompuon minority, including their relationship with the land. Profits are ploughed back into the community.

A moto here will cost about 2000r, or 8000r if they stick around to drive you back.

Waterfalls

For a power shower, head to **Chaa Ong** (admission 2000r), which is set in a scenic rocky jungle gorge allowing you to clamber straight into the falls. **Ka Tieng** (admission free) is perhaps the most fun, as there are some vines on the far side that are strong enough to swing on for some Tarzan action. Another beautiful waterfall in the neighbourhood is **Kinchaan** (admission 2000r).

These three waterfalls are located separately about 5km to 8km west of town. Although they're signposted en route to Stung Treng, hook up with a local as they're difficult to find.

Trekking

With many local minority villages and attractive areas around Ban Lung, trekking has really started to take off. Figure on US$15 to US$25 a day for a good guide and more for transport, food and lodging along the way. You'll need a group to make it affordable. **Ratanak Hotel** (☎ 974033) arranges the cheapest treks, but make clear arrangements with your guide to ensure you get what you expected. See p116 for trekking options in Virachey National Park.

Ask around town about arranging **elephant treks**, although Mondulkiri is the better choice for a date with Dumbo.

SLEEPING

Cheng Luk Hotel (☎ 012-960323; tw US$5-10; 🅿) Smack in the middle of the action, this hotel offers up bright, clean rooms with satellite TV. Downstairs rooms keep their cool in the daytime heat, but lack windows. Part with US$10 and relish the hot water and air-con.

Tribal Hotel (☎ 974074; tribalhotel@camintel.com; r US$5-25; 🅿) Spread among pleasant gardens, this large complex of wat-like buildings houses a wide range of options. Basic budget rooms, which are clean and comfy, are found in the central and back blocks. If you're in

> **SPLURGE!**
>
> **Yaklom Hill Lodge** (☎ 012-644240; www .yaklom.com; s/d/tr incl breakfast US$10/13/16) Billing itself as Ratanakiri's ecolodge, this place is set amid lush gardens about 6km east of town. It's the most atmospheric option around, with bungalows featuring ethnic minority handicrafts for decoration. There's no electricity during the day, but the fan and lights work at night. The restaurant here serves tasty Thai and Khmer food.

CAMBODIA

need of pampering and the world according to CNN, open your wallet and head for the main building.

Banlung I Guesthouse (☎ 012-532043; s/tw US$3/5) The wood-lined singles are a little dark and you'll have to share a bathroom, but these are the cleanest US$3 options in town. The twins are more comfortable and include TVs and nice bathrooms.

EATING & DRINKING

Ratanak Hotel (mains 3000-10,000r; ☺ breakfast, lunch & dinner) This hotel churns out some of town's finest eats, including the signature *phnom pleung* (hill of fire), a beef and vegetable DIY tabletop barbecue. Ratanak and its VP Pub across the street are the most popular spots for an evening beer.

Soup 63 (mains 5000-8000r; ☺ breakfast, lunch & dinner) Popular with locals for *sach kooang Ratanakiri* (Ratanakiri grilled beef). Although not on the menu, great tofu and veg meals are yours if you ask politely.

Hang Lei (mains 2000-3000r; ☺ breakfast, lunch & dinner) This unmarked eatery on the edge of the market fries up watergrass, pineapple and bell peppers to adorn its filling and oh-so-cheap specials.

GETTING THERE & AWAY

President Airlines (☎ 974098) and **Royal Phnom Penh Airways** (☎ 974147) connect Ban Lung and Phnom Penh (US$59/109 one way/return).

For details of costs to Stung Treng and continuing south overland, see the Stung Treng (p114) and Kratie (p112) entries.

GETTING AROUND

Most guesthouses rent motorbikes (from US$5), as well as pick-ups (US$30) and Russian jeeps (US$40), which both include a driver. A moto for the day ranges from US$6 to US$10, depending on your destinations.

AROUND RATANAKIRI PROVINCE

Located 35km northwest of Ban Lung on the Tonlé Sap, **Voen Sai** is a kaleidoscope community including Chinese, Lao and Kreung villagers. Across the river is an old **Chinese settlement** dating back to the 19th century, a slice of Sichuan, and further downstream several **Lao** and **chunchiet villages**.

Virachey National Park is the largest protected area in Cambodia, stretching east to Vietnam, north to Laos and west to Stung Treng. The park has not been fully explored, and is likely home to a number of larger mammals, including elephants, leopards and tigers. Many guesthouses offer 'treks' in the park, but this usually means an expensive walk in denuded forest near the park, as it's at least a day's walk just to reach the park boundary. Go to the Ministry of Environment Office in Ban Lung to arrange a serious expedition. Easier access to forest is available from **Siem Pang**, at the western end of the park, which can be reached by moto from Ban Lung or by rocket boat from Stung Treng.

CAMBODIA DIRECTORY

ACCOMMODATION

Budget guesthouses used to be restricted to Phnom Penh, Siem Reap and Sihanoukville, but as tourism has taken off in the provinces, there are also options in most other provincial capitals such as Kampot, Kratie and Stung Treng. Costs hover around US$3 to US$5 for a bed. In many rural parts of Cambodia, the standard rate for the cheapest hotels is US$5, usually with attached bathroom and satellite TV, although there may be a few places starting at 10,000r that make more by the hour as brothels than they do by the night – don't count on much sleep!

All rooms quoted in this chapter have attached bathrooms unless stated otherwise.

ACTIVITIES

Tourism in Cambodia is still in its infancy with few activities on offer. Snorkelling and diving are popular in Sihanoukville (p103). Boat trips on rivers and around coastal areas can usually be arranged with locals keen to make some money. Improving roads are seeing an increasing number of cyclists and the horrendous routes remaining are paradise for experienced dirt bikers. Elephant rides and rewarding trekking are both possible in the wilds of Ratanakiri (p114) and Mondulkiri (p112) Provinces.

BOOKS

For in-depth coverage of travel in Cambodia look for Lonely Planet's *Cambodia*.

There's a great selection of books on Cambodia in the better bookshops located in Phnom Penh and Siem Reap, but prices are relatively high. Markets and disabled street-sellers pawn cheap copies of most titles, but we know you wouldn't dream of buying a photocopied Lonely Planet guide!

Angkor
The definitive guidebook to Angkor was long *Les Monuments du Groupe D'Angkor* by Maurice Glaize, first published in the 1940s and available in English as *A Guide to the Angkor Monuments*. It's hard to find, but download it free from the Internet at www.theangkorguide.com.

Among the modern titles, *Angkor: An Introduction to the Temples* by Dawn Rooney is the most popular. Complete with illustrations and photographs, it's a useful, if dry, companion around Angkor. Another popular title is *Angkor: Heart of an Asian Empire* by Bruno Dagens, with the emphasis more on the discovery and restoration of Angkor; it's lavishly illustrated and dripping with interesting asides.

History & Politics
The best introduction to the history of Cambodia is David P Chandler's *A History of Cambodia,* which covers the ups and downs of the Khmers over two millennia. Also by Chandler is *Brother Number One,* the menacing biography of Pol Pot.

Cambodia Year Zero by François Ponchaud is a brutally accurate secondhand account of events between 1975 and 1977. *When the War was Over* by Elizabeth Becker is an insight into life in the last days of Pol Pot's regime, and its aftermath, by one of the few journalists to visit Democratic Kampuchea back in 1978.

There are several harrowing survivor's accounts of life under the Khmer Rouge. *First They Killed My Father* by Luong Ung is the tragic story of destruction, death and disease, as one family is torn apart by the Khmer Rouge. *When Broken Glass Floats*, written by Chanrithy Him, is another astonishing account of Cambodia's darkest days.

Jon Swain's *River of Time* is as much about a personal hell as Cambodia's descent into hell, but it takes us back to an old Indochina and includes the real story behind *The Killing Fields*, in which Swain was played by Julian Sands.

Travel Literature
The classic is Norman Lewis' *A Dragon Apparent* (1951), an account of his 1950 foray into an Indochina that was soon to disappear. It was reprinted by Eland Publishing (2003).

To Asia With Love: A Connoisseur's Guide to Cambodia, Laos, Thailand and Vietnam (2004), an anthology edited by Kim Fay, is a delightful introduction to Cambodia and the Mekong Region for those looking for some inspiration and adventure.

The Coast of Cambodia (2001) by Robert Philpotts is a nice slice of travel literature and a guidebook woven together. He travelled from Krong Koh Kong to Kompong Trach and had a few adventures along the way.

BUSINESS HOURS
Most Cambodians get up very early and it's not unusual to see people out exercising at 5.30am when you're heading home – ahem, sorry, getting up – at that time. Government offices (closed Sundays) theoretically open at 7.30am, break for a siesta from 11.30am to 2pm and end the day at 5pm. However, it's a safe bet that few people will be around early in the morning or after 4pm, as their real income is earned elsewhere.

Banking hours vary slightly depending on the bank, but you can reckon on core weekday hours of 8.30am to 3pm. They're also usually open Saturday mornings.

Local restaurants are generally open from about 6.30am until 9pm and international restaurants until a little later. In this chapter, we consider 7am to 10am breakfast, noon to 3pm lunch and 5pm to 9pm dinner.

CLIMATE
The climate of Cambodia is governed by two monsoons, which set the rhythm of rural life. The cool, dry, northeastern monsoon, which carries little rain, occurs from around November to April. From May to October, the southwestern monsoon brings strong winds, high humidity and heavy rains. Even during the wet season, it rarely rains in the morning – most precipitation falls in the afternoon and, even then, only sporadically. See the Phnom Penh climate chart on p924.

DANGERS & ANNOYANCES
As memories of war grow ever more distant, Cambodia has become a much safer country

CAMBODIA

DRUG WARNING

Watch out for *yama* (known as *yaba* in Thailand), which ominously shares its name with the Hindu god of death. Known as ice or crystal meth back home, it's not just any old diet pill, but home-made meta-amphetamines often laced with toxic substances, such as mercury and lithium. It's more addictive than users would like to admit, provoking powerful hallucinations, sleep deprivation and psychosis.

Also be very careful about buying 'co-caine' in Cambodia. Most of what is sold as coke is actually pure heroin and far stronger than any smack found on the streets back home. Bang this up your hooter and you're in serious trouble – several backpackers die each year.

---

in which to travel, remembering the golden rule – stick to marked paths in remote areas! Check on the latest situation before making a trip off the beaten track, particularly if travelling by motorcycle.

The **Cambodia Daily** (www.cambodiadaily.com) and **Phnom Penh Post** (www.phnompenhpost.com) are good sources for breaking news on Cambodia – check their websites before your arrival.

Mines, Mortars & Bombs

Never, ever touch any rockets, artillery shells, mortars, mines, bombs or other war material. Cambodia is one of the most heavily mined countries in the world with an estimated four to six million of these 'enemies within' littering the countryside. A gentle reminder: *do not* stray from well-marked paths under any circumstances, as even stepping from the roadside in some places could have very nasty consequences.

Mine-clearing organisations are working throughout the country to clear these arbitrary assassins, but even with their pivotal presence, the most common way a landmine is discovered is by a man, woman or child losing a limb.

Theft & Street Crime

Given the number of guns in Cambodia, there's less armed theft than one might expect. Still, hold-ups and motorcycle theft are a potential danger in Phnom Penh and Sihanoukville. See the Dangers & Annoy-

ances section in the Phnom Penh (p66), Siem Reap (p81) and Sihanoukville (p103) sections for more details on theft. There's no need to be paranoid, just cautious. Walking or riding alone late at night is not ideal, certainly not in rural areas.

Pickpocketing isn't a huge problem in Cambodia, but it pays to be careful. Keep your bulk of cash and passport in a belt or pouch beneath your clothing, then hide some dollars in your bag and, lastly, carry a day's spending deep in a pocket – this way you don't have to advertise your main stash every time you need a few dollars.

DISABLED TRAVELLERS

Uneven pavements, potholed roads and, in Angkor, stairs as steep as ladders ensure that Cambodia isn't an easy country in which to travel for most people with mobility impairments. Few buildings have been designed with disabled people in mind, and transport in the provinces is usually very overcrowded, although taxi hire from point to point is at least an affordable option in Cambodia.

On the positive side, Cambodians are usually very helpful towards all foreigners, and local labour is cheap if you need someone to accompany you at all times.

EMBASSIES & CONSULATES
Embassies & Consulates in Cambodia

The following embassies are found in Phnom Penh:

Australia (Map p68; ☎ 213470; 11 Ph 254)
Canada (Map p68; ☎ 213470; 11 Ph 254)
China (Map pp64–5; ☎ 427428; 256 Mao Tse Toung Blvd)
France (Map pp64–5; ☎ 430020; 1 Monivong Blvd)
Germany (Map p68; ☎ 216381; 76-78 Ph 214)
Indonesia (Map p68; ☎ 216148; 90 Norodom Blvd)
Laos (Map pp64–5; ☎ 982632; 15-17 Mao Tse Toung Blvd)
Malaysia (Map p68; ☎ 216177; 5 Ph 242)
Myanmar (Map pp64–5; ☎ 213664; 181 Norodom Blvd)
Philippines (Map p68; ☎ 428592; 33 Ph 294)
Singapore (Map p68; ☎ 360855; 92 Norodom Blvd)
Thailand (Map pp64–5; ☎ 363870; 196 Norodom Blvd)
UK (Map pp64–5; ☎ 427124; 29 Ph 75)
USA (Map p68; ☎ 216436; 27 Ph 240) Moving in late 2006 to Ph 96 between Ph 51 & Ph 61.
Vietnam (Map pp64–5; ☎ 362531; 436 Monivong Blvd)

There's also a handy Vietnam consulate in Sihanoukville (p103).

Cambodian Embassies & Consulates Abroad

Australia (☎ 02-6273 1259; 5 Canterbury Cres, Deakin, ACT 2600)

France (☎ 01-45 03 47 20; 4 rue Adolphe Yvon, 75116 Paris)

Germany (☎ 030-48 63 79 01; Arnold Zweing Strasse, 1013189 Berlin)

Japan (☎ 03-5412 8521; 8-6-9 Akasaka, Minato-ku, Tokyo 1070052)

USA (☎ 202-726 7742; 4500 16th St NW, Washington, DC 20011)

For information on Cambodian visas, see p124.

FESTIVALS & EVENTS

The festivals of Cambodia take place according to the lunar calendar, so the dates vary from year to year.

Chinese New Year The big Chinese community goes wild for the new year in late January or early to mid-February, with dragon dances filling many of Phnom Penh's streets. Also being Tet, the Vietnamese whoop it up too.

Chaul Chnam Held in mid-April, this is a three-day celebration of Khmer New Year, with Khmers dressed to the hilt and hitting wats to worship, to wash away their sins and to toss much water and talc about.

Visakha Puja Celebrated collectively as Buddha's birth, enlightenment and *parinibbana* (passing in nirvana), this festival's activities are centred on wats. The festival falls on the eighth day of the fourth moon (that's May or June to you and me) and is best observed at Angkor Wat, where you can see candle-lit processions of monks.

P'chum Ben This festival falls between mid-September and early October and is a kind of All Souls' Day, when respects are paid to the dead through offerings made at wats.

Bon Om Tuk Held in early November to celebrate the epic victory of Jayavarman VII over the Chams in 1177 and the reversal of the Tonlé Sap river. This is one of the most important festivals in the Khmer calendar and a wonderful, if hectic, time to be in Phnom Penh or Siem Reap.

FOOD & DRINK

It is definitely no secret that Cambodia's neighbouring countries, Thailand and Vietnam, are home to some of the finest food in the world, so it should come as no surprise to discover that Khmer cuisine is also rather special. *Amok* (baked fish with coconut and lemongrass in banana leaf) is sublime and *kyteow* (a rice noodle soup packed with a punch), otherwise known as Cambodia in

a bowl, will keep you going throughout the day.

Rice and *prahoc* (a fermented fish paste that your nose will soon recognise at a hundred paces) form the backbone of Khmer cuisine. Built around these are flavours that give the cuisine its kick: secret roots, welcome herbs and aromatic tubers. Together they give salads, snacks, soups and stews a unique aroma and taste that smacks of Cambodia.

Cambodian meals almost always include *samlor* (soup). *Samlor machou banle* is a popular hot and sour fish soup with pineapple and a splash of spices. Other popular soups include *samlor chapek* (ginger-flavoured pork soup), *samlor machou bangkang* (prawn soup similar to the popular Thai tom yam) and *samlor ktis* (fish soup with coconut and pineapple).

Most fish eaten in Cambodia are freshwater and *trey aing* (grilled fish) is a Cambodian speciality (*aing* means 'grilled' and can be applied to many dishes). Fish is traditionally eaten as pieces wrapped in lettuce or spinach leaves and dipped into a fish sauce known as *tuk trey*, similar to

---

TRAVEL YOUR TASTEBUDS

You're going to encounter food that's unusual, strange, maybe even immoral, or just plain weird. The fiercely omnivorous Cambodians find nothing strange in eating insects, algae, offal or fish bladders. They'll dine on a duck embryo, brew up some brains or snack on some spiders. They'll peel live frogs to grill on a barbecue or down the wine of a cobra to increase their virility.

To the Khmers, there's nothing 'strange' about anything that will sustain the body. They'll try anything once, even a burger.

For obvious reasons avoid eating endangered species.

We Dare You! The Top Five

- crickets
- duck embryo
- durian
- prahoc
- tarantulas

Vietnam's *nuoc mam*, but with ground peanuts added.

Don't drink tap water! Guzzle locally produced drinking water (500r per litre), which is available everywhere or, better yet, filter and/or treat tap water – solving the thousands of empty bottles waste issue. Ice is made from treated water, so enjoy it.

Soft drinks and coffee are found everywhere and a free pot of Chinese-style tea will usually appear as soon as you sit down in local restaurants.

Throughout Cambodia excellent fruit smoothies, known locally as *tukalok*, are omnipresent. Look out for stalls with fruit and a blender – if you don't want heaps of sugar and condensed milk, keep an eye on the preparatory stages.

The most popular beer is the local Angkor, but Anchor, Heineken, Tiger, San Miguel, Stella Artois, Carlsberg and Becks also grace many menus. Cans sells for around US$1 to US$1.50 and glasses of Angkor and Tiger draught are similarly priced.

In Phnom Penh, foreign wines and spirits are sold at bargain prices. 'Muscle wines', something like Red Bull meets absinthe, with names like Hercules, Commando Bear Beverage and Brace of Loma, have been surging in popularity. They contain enough unknown substances to contravene the Geneva Chemical Weapons Convention and should only be drunk with care.

GAY & LESBIAN TRAVELLERS

While Cambodian culture is tolerant of homosexuality, the scene is certainly nothing like that of neighbouring countries. As with heterosexual couples, passionate public displays of affection are considered a basic no-no, so it's prudent not to flaunt your sexuality. That said, same sexes often hold hands in Cambodian society, so it's unlikely to raise eyebrows.

Utopia (www.utopia-asia.com) features gay travel information and contacts, including detailed sections on the legality of homosexuality in Cambodia and some local gay terminology.

HOLIDAYS

Banks, government ministries and embassies close down for public holidays, so plan ahead during these times. Holidays may be rolled over if they fall on a weekend, and some people take a day or two extra during major festivals.

International New Year's Day 1 January
Victory over the Genocide 7 January
International Women's Day 8 March
International Workers' Day 1 May
International Children's Day 1 June
Constitution Day 24 September
Paris Peace Accords 23 October
HM the King's Birthday 30 October to 1 November
Independence Day 9 November
International Human Rights Day 10 December

INSURANCE

Don't visit Cambodia with medical insurance that does not cover emergency evacuation. Limited facilities combined with serious injuries or illness lead to many patients being airlifted to Bangkok (a US$10,000 price tag covered by cheap evacuation insurance).

INTERNET ACCESS

Internet access has spread throughout much of Cambodia. Charges range from 2000r per hour in major cities to US$4 an hour in the smaller provincial capitals.

INTERNET RESOURCES

http://andybrouwer.co.uk A great gateway to all things Cambodian, it includes comprehensive links to other sites and regular Cambodian travel articles.
http://angkor.com When it comes to links, this site has them, spreading its cyber-tentacles into all sorts of interesting areas.
www.lonelyplanet.com Summaries on travelling to Cambodia, the Thorn Tree bulletin board and travel news.
www.mrpumpy.net The definitive website for cyclists passing through Cambodia, it's written with candour and humour.
www.talesofasia.com Up-to-the-minute road conditions and other overland Cambodian travel information.

LEGAL MATTERS

Narcotics, including marijuana, are not legal in Cambodia and police are beginning to take a harder line – the days of free bowls in guesthouses are long gone. However, marijuana is traditionally used in some Khmer food, so its presence will linger on. If you're a smoker, be discreet as police may soon turn the regular busting of foreigners into a lucrative sideline.

Moral grounds alone should be enough to deter foreigners from seeking underage sexual partners in Cambodia, but sadly, in some cases, it's not. Paedophilia is a serious crime and now many Western countries have also enacted much-needed legislation to make offences committed overseas punishable at home.

MAPS

Unless you're looking to head into the wilds on the back of a dirt bike, you won't require additional maps to those in this guidebook. If you need one, the best all-rounder for Cambodia is Gecko's *Cambodia Road Map* at 1:750,000 scale, which has lots of detail and accurate place names. Another popular foldout map is Nelles' *Cambodia, Laos and Vietnam Map* at 1:1,500,000, although the detail is limited.

MEDIA

Magazines & Newspapers

The **Cambodia Daily** (www.cambodiadaily.com) is a popular English-language newspaper, while the **Phnom Penh Post** (www.phnompenhpost.com) offers in-depth analysis every two weeks. Readable magazines include the humorous *Bayon Pearnik* and the travel magazine the *Cambodia Scene*.

Radio & TV

The BBC (100MHz FM) has broadcasts in Khmer and English in the capital.

Most hotels in Cambodia have satellite TV, offering access to BBC World, CNN, Star Sports and HBO.

MONEY

Cambodia's currency is the riel, abbreviated here by a lower-case r written after the sum. The riel comes in notes with the following values: 50r, 100r, 200r, 500r, 1000r, 2000r, 5000r, 10,000r, 20,000r, 50,000r and 100,000r.

Throughout this chapter, each establishment's prices are in the currency quoted to the average punter. This is usually depicted in US dollars or in riel, but in the west of the region it is often in Thai baht. While this may seem inconsistent, this is the way it is done throughout Cambodia and the sooner you get used to thinking comparatively in riel, dollars or baht, the easier your travels will be.

Currency exchange rates at the time this book went to press:

Country	Unit	Riel (r)
Australia	A$1	3081
Canada	C$1	3462
Euro zone	€1	4916
Japan	¥100	3561
Laos	10,000kip	3953
New Zealand	NZ$1	2889
Thailand	10B	1005
UK	UK£1	7262
USA	US$1	4111
Vietnam	10,000d	2585

ATMs

There are now credit-card-compatible ATMs in most major cities (Visa and Master-Card only).

Bargaining

Bargaining is the rule when shopping in markets, when hiring vehicles and sometimes when taking a room. Siem Reap and Angkor aside, the Khmers are not ruthless hagglers and a smile goes a long way.

See Responsible Travel (p122) for appropriate bargaining etiquette.

Cash

There are no banks at Cambodian land-border crossings, so arrive with some US dollars in hand. US dollars are accepted everywhere, so there's not much point exchanging them for riel. Hardened travellers may argue that spending dollars makes things slightly more expensive, but a few lost pennies are worth avoiding the exchange hassle. Hoard riel that you receive in change to pay for motos and such. Those with cash in another major currency can change it in Phnom Penh and Siem Reap.

Credit Cards

Cash advances on credit cards are now available in Phnom Penh, Siem Reap, Sihanoukville, Kampot, Battambang and Kompong Cham. Canadia Bank offers the best service with free MasterCard and Visa cash advances.

Travellers Cheques

Like credit cards, travellers cheques aren't much use when you venture beyond the main tourist centres. Most banks charge a commission of 2% to cash travellers cheques; you'll be given US dollars, not riel. Some hotels and travel agents will also cash travellers cheques after banking hours.

PHOTOGRAPHY & VIDEO

Film and processing are cheap in Cambodia. A roll of 36 exposures costs about US$2. Processing charges are around US$4 for 36 standard prints. Cheap slide film is widely available in Phnom Penh and Siem Reap, but elsewhere it's hard to find.

Many Internet cafés in Phnom Penh, Siem Reap, Battambang and Sihanoukville will burn CDs from digital images using card readers or USB connections. The price is about US$2.50 if you need a CD or US$1.50 if you don't.

Exercise restraint in taking pictures of military installations and convoys.

POST

Post is now routed by air through Bangkok and other regional centres, which has made Cambodia's service faster, though by no means more dependable.

Don't send mail from provinces – stick with Phnom Penh's main post office and make sure postcards and letters are franked before they vanish from your sight. Postcards cost 1500r to 2100r, and a 10g airmail letter from 2000r to 2500r – cross your fingers and hope your mail arrives in two or three weeks.

Phnom Penh's main post office has a poste restante service. Although it now checks identification, don't have anything valuable sent there. It costs 200r per item received.

RESPONSIBLE TRAVEL

Cambodia continues to experience unprecedented growth in tourism and this inevitably brings the bad along with the good. Your goal is a simple one: minimise the negatives and maximise the positives.

There are simple things like bringing a water filter or tablets to treat tap water instead of buying bottled water, thus minimising the growing problem of plastic waste. And if you do buy water, set an example by crushing the plastic container before putting it in the rubbish (trash).

Other actions are not so straightforward, but are even more important – if you do witness suspicious behaviour of tourists with Cambodian children, it's your duty to report it. Child exploitation and sexual abuse is now rightly taken very seriously here and a **hotline** (☎ 023-720555) has been set up to report it.

When bargaining for goods in a market or for a ride on a moto, remember the aim is not to get the lowest possible price, but one that's acceptable to both you and the seller. Coming on too strong or arguing over a few hundred riel does nothing to foster Cambodians' positive feelings towards travellers. Be thankful there's room for discussion in Cambodia, so try not to abuse it.

On the topic of money, Cambodia is an extremely poor country and begging is prevalent in Phnom Penh and Siem Reap. Try not to become numb to the pleas as there's no social security network and no government support. Amputees may also find themselves stigmatised by mainstream society and unable to make ends meet any other way. If you do give – which is viewed positively by Buddhists – keep the denominations small, so expectations don't grow too big. Many amputees now sell books on the street and buying from them may encourage others to become more self-sufficient. Please don't give money to children as they rarely get to keep the money and it only propagates the problem – giving them some food is preferable. A great option in Phnom Penh and Siem Reap is to shop or eat in establishments whose profits benefit street children, disabled people and disenfranchised women – check out Phnom Penh's Eating section (p72) and the Shopping sections under both Phnom Penh (p76) and Siem Reap (p85) for more details.

Looting from Cambodia's ancient temples has been a huge problem over the past couple of decades. Don't contribute to this cultural rape by buying old stone carvings. Classy reproductions are available in Phnom Penh and Siem Reap, complete with export certificates.

Finally, don't forget what the Cambodians have been through in the protracted years of war, genocide and famine. Support local Cambodian-owned businesses; if anyone deserves to profit from the new-found interest in this wonderful country, it's surely the long-suffering Khmers.

SHOPPING

The one item you'll be glad you purchased is the mighty *krama*, a versatile checked cotton scarf worn by Cambodians on their heads, around their necks or around their midriffs – perfect for blocking both sun and dust. Wearing them is an affirmation of identity for many Cambodians. Exquisitely dyed silk or silk-cotton blends are the most sought after for souvenir purposes and the best ones come from Kompong Cham and Takeo Provinces.

Other popular items include antiques, silver, jewellery, gems, woodcarvings, papier-mâché masks, stone copies of ancient Khmer art, brass figurines, oil paintings, silk, sarongs and branded clothing from local factories.

Check out the Phnom Penh (p76) and Siem Reap (p85) Shopping sections for information on buying craft items produced by Cambodian mine victims and disabled and women's groups.

See Responsible Travel (opposite) for appropriate bargaining etiquette.

STUDYING

Organised courses are few and far between in Cambodia. Sadly, the only Khmer language courses on offer are strictly aimed at Phnom Penh's expat community. However, travellers can indulge in Khmer cooking lessons in Battambang (p95).

TELEPHONE & FAX

Brightly numbered private mobile phone booths found on every town's kerbs offer cheap local calls for about 300r a minute. The cheapest international calls are made on Internet phones in cafés and cost 300r to 2000r a minute. Although the price is great, the lengthy satellite delay can be infuriating. More expensive international calls (from US$2 a minute) can be made from public phonecard booths, which are found in major cities.

The cheapest fax services are also via the Internet and cost around US$1 to US$2 per page for most destinations.

TOILETS

Although the occasional squat toilet turns up here and there, particularly in the most budget of budget guesthouses, toilets are usually of the sit-down variety. In remote regions you'll find that hygiene conditions deteriorate somewhat.

The issue of what to do with used toilet paper is a cause for concern. Generally, if there's a wastepaper basket next to the toilet, that is where the toilet paper goes, as many sewage systems cannot handle toilet paper. Toilet paper is seldom provided, so keep a stash with you at all times.

Should nature call in rural areas, don't let modesty drive you into the bushes: there may be land mines not far from the road or track. Stay on the roadside and do the deed, or grin and bear it until the next town.

TOURIST INFORMATION

For independent travellers official tourist information in Phnom Penh and Siem Reap is rather useless. In the provinces it's a different story, with more and more towns ambitiously opening somewhat helpful tourist offices. While the staff have little in the way of brochures or handouts, they'll do their best to tell you about local places of interest and may even drag the director out of a nearby karaoke bar to answer your questions. However, if you've dealt with Malaysian or Singaporean tourist offices, best be lowering your

DOMESTIC TELEPHONE CODES	
Banteay Meanchey	☎ 054
Battambang	☎ 053
Kampot	☎ 033
Kandal	☎ 024
Kep	☎ 036
Kompong Cham	☎ 042
Kompong Chhnang	☎ 026
Kompong Speu	☎ 025
Kompong Thom	☎ 062
Kratie	☎ 072
Krong Koh Kong	☎ 035
Mondulkiri	☎ 073
Oddar Meanchey	☎ 065
Phnom Penh	☎ 023
Preah Vihear	☎ 064
Prey Veng	☎ 043
Pursat	☎ 052
Ratanakiri	☎ 075
Siem Reap	☎ 063
Sihanoukville	☎ 034
Stung Treng	☎ 074
Svay Rieng	☎ 044
Takeo	☎ 032

expectations! Guesthouses and free local magazines are much more useful than tourist offices.

Cambodia has no official tourist offices abroad and it's unlikely that Cambodian embassies will be of much assistance in planning a trip, besides issuing a visa.

TOURS

Despite every English-speaking moto driver in the country claiming to be a tour guide, there are actually few organised tours on offer in Cambodia. The most abundant are city tours of Phnom Penh (p70) and its surrounds, proffered by numerous guesthouses. Tours of the watery variety are available along the island-dotted coast by Sihanoukville's many guesthouses (p103), while organised day trips to Bokor National Park (p108) in the Elephant Mountains can be arranged in Kampot.

VISAS

Most nationalities receive a one-month visa (US$20; one passport-sized photo) on arrival at most land borders (except for those from Laos, and the Phnom Den/Tinh Bien Vietnam crossing) and Phnom Penh and Siem Reap airports. Getting your visa ahead of time will save you being overcharged at the land crossings. Also if you're planning an extended stay, get a one-month business visa for US$25.

Visa extensions are granted in Phnom Penh. Tourist visas can be extended only once for a month, whereas business visas can be extended ad infinitum.

Officially, an extension for one month costs US$30, three months US$60, six months US$100 and one year US$150. However, the police will keep your passport for about 25 days. Strangely enough there's an express, next-day service at inflated prices: one month US$39 (for both tourist and business visas), three months US$80 (only business visas) and so on. You'll need one passport photo for the extension. Overstayers are charged US$5 per day at the point of exit.

Visit the new Immigration Office opposite Phnom Penh International Airport to arrange an extension.

VOLUNTEERING

Cambodia hosts a huge number of NGOs, but most recruit skilled volunteers from home, so opportunities are few and far between. The best way to find out who is working in Cambodia is to hit the **Cooperation Committee for Cambodia** (CCC; ☎ 023-426009; 35 Ph 178, Phnom Penh). This organisation has a handy list of all NGOs, both Cambodian and international.

The **Land Mine Museum** (☎ 012-598951) in Siem Reap and the **Starfish Project** (www .starfishcambodia.org) in Sihanoukville are the notable exceptions when it comes to encouraging volunteers. The museum (p82) works in the area of mine awareness and will eventually have a rehabilitation centre, while the Starfish Project's bakery (p105) helps raise funds for local projects.

WOMEN TRAVELLERS

Women will generally find Cambodia a hassle-free place to travel, although some guys in the guesthouse industry may try their luck occasionally. If you're planning a trip off the beaten trail it would be best to find a travel companion.

Khmer women dress fairly conservatively, and it's best to follow suit, particularly when visiting wats. In general, long-sleeved shirts and long trousers or skirts are preferred. In a skirt and boarding a moto? Do as the Khmer women do and sit side-saddle.

Tampons and sanitary napkins are widely available in major cities and provincial capitals.

WORKING

Job opportunities are limited in Cambodia, partly as Cambodians need the jobs more than foreigners and partly as the foreigners who work here are usually professionals recruited overseas. The easiest option is teaching English in Phnom Penh, as experience isn't a prerequisite at the smaller schools. Pay ranges from about US$5 to US$6 per hour (for the inexperienced) to about US$15 to US$20 per hour for those with a TEFL certificate teaching at the better schools. Places to look for work include the classifieds sections of local English-language newspapers.

East Timor

HIGHLIGHTS

- **Dili** – walking the wonderful waterfront: from the giant Jesus to the hulking port (p134)
- **Atauro Island** – bobbing about in the turquoise waters over the island's lively outlying reef (p138)
- **Hatubuilico & Mt Ramelau** – basking in the bald beauty of this mountain area before hot-footing it up the mountain pre-dawn (p142)
- **Baucau** – being charmed by the second city's pensionable Portuguese architecture, and its cushy beach below (p139)
- **Off the beaten track** – escaping to the stunning isolation of Tutuala and Jaco Island, reached by beaten-up roads (p140)

FAST FACTS

- **ATMs** in Dili
- **Budget** US$20-30 a day
- **Capital** Dili
- **Costs** guesthouse room US$10, around-town taxi US$1, 1500mL bottle of water US$0.50, a beer US$2.50, noodle dish from a local eatery US$1-2
- **Country code** ☎ 670
- **Famous for** its 2002 debut as an independent country
- **Languages** Portuguese (official) & Tetun (official & national)
- **Money** US$ & East Timorese centavos
- **Phrases (Tetun)** *bon dia* (good morning), *botarde* (good afternoon), *bonoite* (good evening/night), *adeus* (goodbye), *obrigadu/a* (m/f) (thank you), *kolisensa* (excuse me)

- **Population** 930,000
- **Seasons** wet Dec-Mar, dry May-Nov
- **Visas** US$30 on arrival

TRAVEL HINTS

Time is a funny thing in East Timor: transport runs to a loose schedule, restaurant meals may take a long time to arrive and that 20-minute bus ride may dissolve into a few hours. If you're travelling between towns, set out early (not later than 7am), try to relax into 'Timor Time' and remember that it's as much about the journey…

OVERLAND ROUTES

Overland travel is possible between East Timor and Indonesian West Timor; see p132 for details.

EAST TIMOR

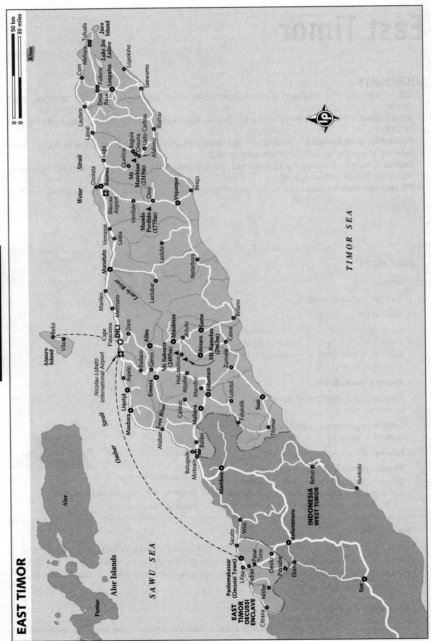

EAST TIMOR

The world's newest nation, East Timor (Timor Lorosa'e in Tetun) is a rare find. It's not every day that a country is newly hatched, handing travellers the reins to steer themselves through its unique physical and cultural landscape. Only recently emerging from a 24-year cultural quash, the country's infrastructure is slowly recuperating after the thorough trashing it endured from departing Indonesian forces in 1999.

Board a bus and bounce along a pocked road (that until recently carried mostly UN vehicles) that's bordered with deserted white-sand bays and brilliant blue water. A colourful reef hugs the coast; from many points you simply walk offshore to see the stunning range of marine life on the island's edge. A journey into the mountainous interior will reveal ruins from East Timor's Portuguese past, hillsides inlaid with religious grottos and topped with crosses, and traditional thatched-roof villages. But what you remember most of East Timor is the East Timorese. Village children run screaming to meet you, and everyone who passes nods a polite greeting – this may be the closest you get to feeling famous.

Nothing in East Timor is gift-wrapped for the traveller: just getting from A to B is an adventure. Travel is something of a pioneering activity here, and the many rewards are waiting to be discovered.

CURRENT EVENTS

The fledgling East Timorese government is not finding nation-building an easy task: there are internal squabbles and serious economic problems associated with running a nation that doesn't, as yet, have a reliable source of income. East Timor's key economic prospect lies in the oil reserves offshore; however, an ongoing sea-boundary dispute with the Australian government is threatening East Timor's earning potential and reinforcing the need for an autonomous industry.

East Timor's tetchy relationship with Indonesia is ongoing. Newspapers trumpeted an alleviation of tensions when the Indonesian president Susilo Bambang Yudhoyono visited East Timor in April 2005. During the visit, he and East Timorese Prime Minister Mari Alkatiri demarcated 96% of their countries' previously porous border. Yudhoyono also laid a wreath at Santa Cruz cemetery to honour the hundreds of East Timorese killed there by Indonesian military in 1991. The visit, however, raised murmurs from unofficial sources criticising the Indonesian tribunal set-up to try military officers and officials for atrocities in East Timor, which had failed to jail any high-ranking Indonesians.

Since 1999 East Timor has been awash with troops and military equipment, UN personnel and their fleets of shiny white 4WDs, plus an international grab-bag of contractors, nongovernmental organisations (NGOs) and assorted aid-organisation personnel. When the majority of these internationals have left, the economic boom associated with such a rush of humanity is bound to crash. Huge hopes ride on tourism to step in and occupy the large number of hotels, restaurants and bars.

The East Timorese know their politicians like the West know their pop stars. Prime Minister Mari Alkatiri is fast losing fans. He was already on the backfoot when he came to power in 2002: having lived in exile during the Indonesian occupation. Being a member of the country's tiny Muslim community and not always seeing eye to eye with the immensely popular President Xanana Gusmão is not winning him any popularity points either. Gusmão was the head of Fretilin, leading the guerrilla struggle against Indonesia from 1978 until his capture and subsequent imprisonment in 1992. Prison in Jakarta, however, soon proved to be a more effective base, with his writings smuggled out of jail.

HISTORY
Portuguese Settle In

Little is known of Timor before 1500 AD, although Chinese and Javanese traders visited the island from at least the 13th century, and possibly as early as the 7th century. Traders searched the coastal settlements for aromatic sandalwood (valued for furniture and incense) and beeswax (for candles). Portuguese traders arrived between 1509 and 1511, but it wasn't until 1556 that a handful of Dominican friars established the first Portuguese settlement at Lifau – in the present-day Oecussi enclave of East Timor – and set about converting the Timorese to Catholicism.

In 1642, Francisco Fernandes led a Portuguese military expedition to weaken the power of the Timor kings. Comprised primarily of Topasses, the 'Black Portuguese' mestizos (people of mixed parentage) from neighbouring Flores, his small army of musketeers settled in Timor, extending Portuguese influence into the interior.

To counter the Portuguese, the Dutch established a base at Kupang in western Timor in 1653. The Portuguese appointed an administrator to Lifau in 1656, but the Topasses went on to become a law unto themselves, driving out the Portuguese governor in 1705.

By 1749 the Topasses controlled central Timor and marched on Kupang, but the Dutch won the ensuing battle, expanding their control of West Timor in the process. On the Portuguese side, after more attacks from the Topasses in Lifau, the colonial base was moved east to Dili in 1769.

The 1859 Treaty of Lisbon divided Timor, giving Portugal the eastern half, together with the north coast pocket of Oecussi – formalised in 1904. Portuguese Timor was a neglected outpost ruled through a traditional system of local chiefs (*liurai*). Control outside Dili was limited and it wasn't until the 20th century that the Portuguese intervened in the interior.

WWII

In 1941 Australia sent a small commando force into Portuguese Timor to counter the Japanese, deliberately breaching the colony's neutral status. Although the military initiative angered neutral Portugal and dragged East Timor into the Pacific War, it slowed the Japanese expansion. The Australian success was largely due to the support they received from the East Timorese, for whom the cost was phenomenal. In 1942 the Portuguese handed control to the Japanese whose soldiers razed whole villages, seized food supplies and killed Timorese in areas where the Australians were operating. In other areas the Japanese incited rebellion against the Portuguese, which resulted in horrific repression when the Japanese left. By the end of the war, between 40,000 and 60,000 East Timorese had died.

Portuguese Pull Out: Indonesia Invades

After WWII the colony reverted to Portuguese rule until, following the coup in Portugal on 25 April 1974, Lisbon set about discarding its colonial empire. Within a few

weeks political parties had been formed in East Timor and the Timorese Democratic Union (UDT) attempted to seize power in August 1975. A brief civil war saw their rivals Fretilin (previously known as the Timorese Social Democrats) come out on top, declaring the independent existence of the Democratic Republic of East Timor on 28 November. But on 7 December the Indonesians launched their attack on Dili.

Indonesia opposed the formation of an independent East Timor and the leftist Fretilin raised the spectre of communism. The full-scale invasion of the former colony came one day after Henry Kissinger and Gerald Ford departed Jakarta, having carefully avoided discussing Indonesia's intentions for East Timor – or so they said. Despite public utterances about the importance of self-determination for the people of East Timor, Australia signalled its reluctance to become bogged down in another futile argument over sovereignty. East Timor and Fretilin were forced to face Indonesia alone.

By the end of 1975 there were 20,000 Indonesian troops in East Timor, and by April in the following year that number had risen to 35,000. Falintil – the military wing of Fretilin – fought a guerrilla war with marked success in the first few years, but weakened considerably thereafter. The cost of the brutal takeover to the East Timorese was huge. International humanitarian organisations estimate that at least 100,000 died in the hostilities and ensuing disease and famine.

By 1989, Indonesia had things firmly under control and opened East Timor to tourism. Then, on 12 November 1991 Indonesian troops fired on protesters gathered to commemorate the killing of an independence activist at the Santa Cruz cemetery in Dili. Captured on film and aired around the world, the severely embarrassed Indonesian government admitted to 19 killings, although it's estimated that over 200 died in the massacre. While Indonesia introduced a civilian administration, the military remained the masters of East Timor. Aided by secret police and civilian Timorese militia to crush dissent, reports of arrest, torture and murder were numerous.

Independence

Timorese hopes for independence remained high, but Indonesia showed no signs of making concessions until the fall of the Soeharto regime. Shortly after taking office in May 1998, Soeharto's successor, President Habibie, suddenly announced a referendum for East Timorese autonomy, much to the horror of the military. On 30 August 1999, East Timor voted overwhelmingly (78.5%) for independence from, rather than autonomy within, Indonesia. Though the Indonesian government promised to respect the results of the UN-sponsored vote, military-backed pro-autonomy Timorese militias massacred, burnt and looted in vicious retribution.

The Indonesian government withered under international condemnation of the scorched-earth campaign, before eventually accepting UN troops into East Timor. The International Force in East Timor (Interfet) landed on 20 September 1999 and quickly controlled the violence, but many Timorese had lost their lives, half a million people were displaced, and the country's infrastructure was devastated. Telecommunications, power installations, bridges, government buildings, shops and houses were destroyed.

The UN Transitional Administration in East Timor (Untaet), established to oversee East Timor during its transition to independence, followed Interfet. Aid and foreign workers flooded into the country. As well as the physical rebuilding, the civil service, police, judiciary, education, health system and so on have all had to be created, and staff recruited and trained from scratch.

The UN successfully handed over government to East Timor less than three years after the independence vote. Independence came, officially, on 20 May 2002 with the inauguration of Falintil leader Xanana Gusmão as president of the new nation, and Mari Alkatiri – long-time leader of Fretilin from exile in Mozambique – as prime minister.

And Then...

In December 2002 Dili was wracked by riots; notably the home of Prime Minister Alkatiri went up in flames. Why? Frustration and discontent are probably the simplest explanations. When East Timor gained independence, its economy was nonexistent. Without any viable industry and no employment potential it was reliant on the sole income of foreign aid.

Despite a general air of dissatisfaction among the population of East Timor, an economy fuelled only by foreign aid became the status quo.

Only a small UN contingent remained in East Timor by mid-2005, and aid workers were completing their projects. East Timor continues to rely on foreign money and struggles to establish an autonomous and viable economy.

Gas and oil deposits in the Timor Sea provide the main potential for East Timor's economy to develop without the assistance of foreign aid. The seabed boundary with Australia is currently in dispute. It's estimated that Australia makes over AUS$1 million per day from a temporary deal granting it access to two-thirds of the oil fields. East Timor argues that the sea border should be in the middle of the two countries – in line with international law. Australia withdrew from the jurisdiction of the international court in relation to maritime boundaries just before East Timor's independence in 2002. The proposed boundary shift has the potential to treble East Timor's current annual oil income.

Tourism has great potential for East Timor's economy, with the government dedicating resources to make it a reality. East Timor is also world renowned for its organic arabica coffee (see p141).

THE CULTURE
The National Psyche

East Timor's identity is firmly rooted in its survival against a history of extreme hardship and foreign occupation. As a consequence of the long and difficult struggle for independence, the people of East Timor are profoundly politically aware – not to mention proud and loyal. While there is great respect for elders and church and community leaders, a residual suspicion surrounding foreign occupiers – most recently in the form of the UN – lurks, as East Timor now struggles for autonomy. Religious beliefs also greatly inform the country's consciousness, where Catholicism cloaks animistic beliefs and practices.

MUST SEE

Punitive Damage (1999) and *In Cold Blood: the Massacre of East Timor* (1992) are documentaries about the Santa Cruz massacre, and its immense influence on independence.

EAST TIMOR

Lifestyle

Most East Timorese lead a subsistence lifestyle: what is farmed (or caught) is eaten, and hopefully there are leftovers to sell or trade. Traditional gender roles are firmly in place, with men tending to much of the physical work, while women tend to family needs. A woman in East Timor will give birth to an average of 7.4 children during her lifetime; she will most likely give birth at home without assistance from a trained health attendant. The infrastructure in East Timor is still limited: the majority of the population does not have access to money, electricity or clean water. While poor in a material sense, the East Timorese are rich in family values and spirituality.

Subsistence farming was severely effected during the Indonesian occupation, with many communities displaced. A family dependent on, for example, fishing, forcibly moved inland could no longer survive with their existing knowledge and practices. The huge death toll in East Timor during WWII and again during the Indonesian occupation was largely due to starvation. Since independence, a slew of NGOs and aid projects have helped communities to establish sustainable agricultural practices.

Population

East Timor has at least a dozen indigenous groups, the largest of which is the Tetun (about 250,000), living around Suai, Dili and Viqueque, as well as in West Timor. The next largest group (around 90,000 people) are the Mambai in the mountains of Maubisse, Ainaro and Same. The Kemak (60,000) live in the Ermera and Bobonaro districts around Maliana. The Bunak (50,000) also live in Bobonaro and their territory extends into West Timor and the Suai area. The Fataluku people (35,000) are famous for their

high-peaked houses in the Lautem district around Lospalos, and to their west is the Makasai (80,000). The other major groups in East Timor are the Galoli (60,000) in the central north around Manatuto and Laleia, and the Tokodede (60,000) along the north coast around Maubara and Liquiçá. To these can be added small groups of mountain people, such as the Idate, Kairui, Lakalei, Naueti and Habu.

East Timor's population is relatively young, with 50% under 15 years old. Life expectancy for East Timorese males is between 55 and 58 (compared to Australia's 85); it's slightly less for females.

RELIGION

It's estimated that about 90% of East Timor's population is Catholic (underpinned by animism). The remainder are Protestant, Muslim and Buddhist. Indigenous religions revolve around an earth mother, from whom all humans are born and shall return after death, and her male counterpart – the god of the sky or sun. These are accompanied by a complex web of spirits from ancestors and nature. The *matan d'ok* (medicine man) is the village mediator with the spirits; he can divine the future and cure illness.

ARTS

Despite 24 years of imposed Indonesian culture, East Timor has its own music and dance, architecture and textiles.

Music & Dance

Almost all Timorese celebrations involve singing and dancing. Timorese traditional music is known as *tebe* or *tebe-dai*. It has changed little since pre-occupation times and is performed on ceremonial occasions. The second generation of music is *koremetan*, which is strongly influenced by country and western, and Portuguese folk. You may also hear contemporary East Timorese rock.

The *likurai* was primarily a Tetun dance used to welcome warriors returning from battle. Women danced with a small drum *(babadok)* tucked under the arm, and would circle the village compound, where heads taken in battle (an ancient practice) would be displayed. Today unmarried women perform it as a courtship dance. The *tebe-dai* dance is a circle dance performed throughout Timor, accompanied by a drum. Your best chance to witness a ceremony is in the villages outside Dili.

Architecture

The traditional houses of East Timor vary from the large conical Bunak houses (deuhoto) in the west to the unique Fataluku houses in the east. The tall, elongated Fataluku houses have stilts supporting a main living room and are topped by a high, tapering thatch roof. Unfortunately many were destroyed, and few remain.

Textiles

Women use simple back-strap looms to weave East Timor's magnificent fabrics (tais). The relatively small looms result in pieces of limited size. They're commonly used as shawls, baby slings or scarfs, and stitched together as clothing. Various regions have their own distinct styles, designs and dye colours. They make souvenirs – see p137.

ENVIRONMENT

Human impact has had severe effects on East Timor's environment. Deforestation is a major concern, with around two-thirds of the country's forests destroyed. Dubious agricultural practices combined with Timor's climate continue to threaten the natural habitat. Air pollution, access to fresh water, unregulated development and waste disposal are major issues currently being tackled. As yet, few areas are formally protected as national parks. Common sense is required when travelling through Timor's delicate ecosystems; see p147 for some hints.

The Land

East Timor (15,007 sq km) consists of the eastern half of the island of Timor, and includes Atauro and Jaco Islands, and the enclave of Oecussi (also known as Ambeno) on the north coast, 70km to the west and surrounded by Indonesian West Timor.

Once part of the Australian continental shelf, Timor fully emerged from the ocean only some four million years ago, and is therefore composed mainly of marine sediment, principally limestone. Rugged mountains, a product of the collision with the Banda Trench to the north, run the length of the island, the highest being Mt Ramelau (2963m) in East Timor. Coastal plains are narrow, and there are no major highland valleys or significant rivers. Rocky, limestone soils and low rainfall make agriculture difficult, resulting in food and water shortages in the dry season.

Wildlife

East Timor is squarely in the area known as Wallacea, a kind of crossover zone between Asian and Australian plants and animals, and one of the most biologically distinctive areas on earth. The numbers of mammals and reptiles in the wild are limited; however, great opportunities exist for spotting birds in East Timor's sky and marine animals in its sea.

Like tropical reefs around the world, East Timor's coral reefs are home to a highly diverse marine life. Manta rays and whale sharks have been encountered along the north coast. Marine mammals include dolphins, whales and dugongs.

More than 240 species of bird have been recorded in the skies over Timor. The Lautem district at the eastern end of the island is noted for its abundance and diversity of birdlife, including honeyeaters, cockatoos, flycatchers and flowerpeckers.

TRANSPORT

GETTING THERE & AWAY
Air

There are three departure points for East Timor's capital Dili: Kupang in Indonesian West Timor, Darwin in Australia's Northern Territory and Denpasar in Bali.

Kakoak Air is East Timor's first commercial airline, flying between Dili and Kupang (US$50, 45 minutes, twice weekly). You can book through **Harvey World Travel** (☎ 331 1140; www.harveydili.com; Dili).

Air North (☎ 8-8920 4000 in Australia; www.airnorth .com.au) flies daily between Darwin and Dili (one way/return plus taxes US$405/480, 1½ hours, twice daily on Monday, Wednesday and Friday). **Merpati** (www.merpati.co.id) flies daily between Denpasar (Bali) and Dili (one way US$250).

DEPARTURE TAX

An international departure tax of US$10 is payable when leaving East Timor.

Bus

For details on crossing the border into Indonesian West Timor, see p137.

GETTING AROUND
Bicycle

For cycling long distances, new bikes can be purchased in Dili for around US$150.

Bad roads, long distances and humid weather conspire to make cycling around the country an endeavour only for the foolhardy, though Dili itself is quite good for cycling.

Boat

Ferry transport is available between Dili and Atauro island (p138) and the Oecussi enclave (p143).

Bus

Mikrolet (minibuses) operate at least daily between most towns, and generally depart early in the morning. Outlying villages are serviced less frequently by *anggunas* – traytrucks where passengers (including the odd buffalo or goat) all pile into the back. Ask locally for departure points.

Car & Motorcycle

Driving in East Timor requires great care: most roads are potholed and singlelane, with livestock crossing at random. Two operators hire out vehicles in Dili: **Rentlo** (☎ 723 5089; rentlo@mail.timortelecom.tp; Fomento-Comoro, Dili) includes 150km free per day in its rentals, and **Thrifty** (☎ 723 1900; timor@rentacar.com.au; Av Sa Bandeira, Dili) includes 100km free per day. A conventional vehicle is fine for around Dili, driving east and west along the north coast, and inland to Maubisse – albeit slowly. Travel further afield requires a 4WD. Rates per day cost from US$30 for a car and US$65 for a 4WD; insurance is optional and limited to your hire vehicle.

Motorcycles are quite handy, breezing over bumps at a respectable pace. Trail bikes and scooters can be rented from **East Timor Backpackers** (☎ 723 8121; Av Almirante Americo Tomas, Dili) for US$10 to US$15 a day.

FUEL

Petrol (gasoline) in Portuguese is *besin,* diesel fuel is *solar;* expect to pay around 68¢ per litre.

Hitching

Hitchhiking is never entirely safe, so it's not recommended. It's not uncommon for locals walking 5km or so into town to ask for a ride. A traveller doing the same would be expected to pay a small sum – usually the price of a *mikrolet* ride.

DILI

pop 100,000

The low-rise capital of Dili is a leisurely city set on the waterfront, sprawling inland in a honeycomb of one-way streets. Pigs, chickens and goats wander head-down about town, especially at the many street markets – where they might equally find a feed or become one. A giant Jesus statue stretches its arms out to Dili, whose buildings still wear the scars from its recent violent history. Dili makes a fabulous base from which to loop out into the country in any direction.

ORIENTATION

Dili sprawls along the waterfront from the airport on the western edge to the Jesus statue at the eastern end of the bay. The central area is reasonably compact, stretching back a few parallel blocks from the waterfront.

Accommodation and restaurant options are spread across town; there's no travellers' hub as such, though the waterfront is understandably popular.

INFORMATION

As yet there's no tourist office. Check out the Internet resources listed on p146 for tourist information.

GETTING INTO TOWN

The standard taxi fare from Nicolau Lobato International Airport, 6km west of town, is US$5 – pricey given that fares around town are US$1 or US$2. Alternatively, you could walk the few hundred metres out to the main road and hail a *mikrolet* (minibus) for around 25¢.

Buses coming from the Batugade land border arrive at the Tasitolu bus terminal, just west of the airport. From here you can catch a *mikrolet* into town.

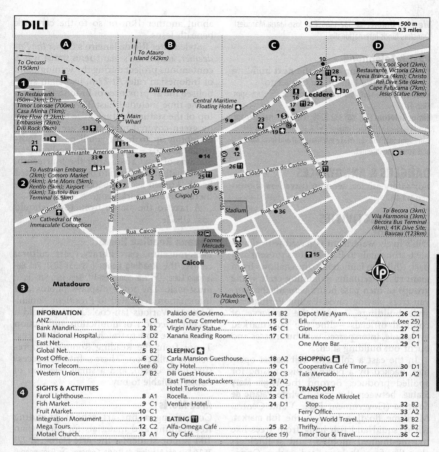

DILI

0 — 500 m
0 — 0.3 miles

To Oecussi (150km)
To Ataturo Island (42km)

Dili Harbour

To Restaurants (50m–2km); Dive Timor Lorosae (700m); Casa Minha (1km); Free Flow (1.2km); Embassies (2km); Dili Rock (9km)

Central Maritime Floating Hotel

To Cool Spot (2km); Restaurante Victoria (2km); Areia Branca (4km); Christo Rei Dive Site (6km); Cape Fatucama (7km); Jesus Statue (7km)

Humanas

Lecidere

Main Wharf

To Australian Embassy (2km); Comoro Market (4km); Arte Moris (5km); Rentlo (5km); Airport (6km); Tasitolu Bus Terminal (6.5km)

Avenida Almirante Americo Tomas

Avenida Alves Aldeia

Rua Formosa

Civpol

Stadium

To Becora (3km); Vila Harmonia (3km); Becora Bus Terminal (4km); 41K Dive Site; Baucau (123km)

Cathedral of the Immaculate Conception

Rua Caicoli

Former Mercado Municipal

Caicoli

Matadouro

To Maubisse (70km)

Rua Circunvalação

INFORMATION	
ANZ	**1** C1
Bank Mandiri	**2** B2
Dili Nacional Hospital	**3** D2
East Net	**4** C1
Global Net	**5** B2
Post Office	**6** C2
Timor Telecom	(see 6)
Western Union	**7** B2

SIGHTS & ACTIVITIES	
Farol Lighthouse	**8** A1
Fish Market	**9** C1
Fruit Market	**10** C1
Integration Monument	**11** B2
Mega Tours	**12** C2
Motael Church	**13** A1

Palacio de Govierno	**14** B2
Santa Cruz Cemetery	**15** C3
Virgin Mary Statue	**16** C1
Xanana Reading Room	**17** C1

SLEEPING	
Carla Mansion Guesthouse	**18** A2
City Hotel	**19** C1
Dili Guest House	**20** C3
East Timor Backpackers	**21** A2
Hotel Turismo	**22** C1
Rocella	**23** C1
Venture Hotel	**24** D1

EATING	
Alfa-Omega Café	**25** B2
City Café	(see 19)

Depot Mie Ayam	**26** C2
Erli	(see 25)
Gion	**27** C2
Lita	**28** D1
One More Bar	**29** C1

SHOPPING	
Cooperativa Café Timor	**30** D1
Tais Mercado	**31** A2

TRANSPORT	
Camea Kode Mikrolet Stop	**32** B2
Ferry Office	**33** A2
Harvey World Travel	**34** B2
Thrifty	**35** B2
Timor Tour & Travel	**36** C2

EAST TIMOR

Emergency
Ambulance (☎ 723 3212)
Fire (☎ 723 0686)
Police (☎ 723 0686)

Internet Access
Internet connections are generally super-fast. See p146 for East Timor–related websites.
East Net (cnr Rua Presidente Nicolau Lobato & Rua Belarmino Lobo; per hr US$5; ☺ 8.30am-12.30am) Photo downloads, CD-burning and web cams.
Global Net (Rua Jacinto de Candido; per hr US$4; ☺ 8.30am-11pm) Photo downloads and CD-burning capabilities.
Timor Telecom (TT; ☎ 332 2245; www.timortele com.tp; Rua Presidente Nicolau Lobato; per hr US$6; ☺ 8.30am-9pm Mon-Fri, 9am-9pm Sat)

Xanana Reading Room (☎ 331 3053; Rua Belarmino Lobo; per hr US$6; ☺ 9am-5pm Mon-Fri, 9am-3pm Sat)

Medical Services
Medical services in East Timor are limited; serious cases may require evacuation to Darwin.
Dentist (☎ 723 3359)
Dili Nacional Hospital (☎ 331 1008; Rua Cicade Viana do Castelo) Just east of Estrada de Bidau.

Money
Banks are generally open between 9am and 3.30pm Monday to Friday.
ANZ (☎ 332 4800; www.anz.com/timorleste; cnr Rua Presidente Nicolau Lobato & Rua Belarmino Lobo) With ATM.
Bank Mandiri (☎ 331 7777; Rua Jose Maria Marques)

Western Union (☎ 332 1586; Rua Jose Maria Marques)
Transfers funds internationally.

Post & Telephone

Both the following are in the next building
along from the Palacio de Govierno.
Post office (Rua Presidente Nicolau Lobato; ⊗ 8am-5pm
Mon-Fri)
Timor Telecom (TT; ☎ 332 2245; www.timortelecom.tp;
Rua Presidente Nicolau Lobato; ⊗ 8.30am-9pm Mon-Fri,
9am-9pm Sat) You can make international and local calls,
and access the Internet.

DANGERS & ANNOYANCES

For safety advice, women travellers should
see p148.

SIGHTS & ACTIVITIES
Waterfront

Dili's lively waterfront is paved with tangible testimonials to East Timor's present and
past. Children launch into the shallows from
giant rusted remains of landing craft, while
groups of men pass hours beneath the banyan trees playing cards. Fading Portuguese-
style buildings – once the preserve of
colonial officials – line the pockmarked
esplanade, interspersed with businesses and
burnt-out building shells.

In the east a colourful **fruit market** operates, backed by a posse of pigs nosing for
spoiled produce. Beyond the **Virgin Mary
Statue**, between the grand white **Palacio de
Govierno** (Government Palace) and Central
Maritime floating hotel is the **fish market**,
where squid and fish hang from trees like
marine-themed mobiles, and stallholders
shoo flies from their un-iced catches. Opposite the wharf, the Indonesian-installed **Integration Monument** represents an angst-ridden
Timorese breaking the chains of colonialism.
Further west, the seaside **Motael Church** is one
of East Timor's oldest institutions. The solar-
powered **Farol lighthouse** beams just beyond.

Cape Fatucama & the Jesus Statue

The coast road crosses a small river at the
far-east end of town, ending where the giant
Christ statue beckons from the tip of Cape
Fatucama (about 7km). There's a sprinkling of foreigner-focused restaurants along
here, as well as some charming grottos and
beaches. **Areia Branca** is the pleasant crescent-
shaped beach before the cape, shaded by
fabulously kitsch giant concrete clams. It's

about another 1km or so to the car park
beneath Jesus.

Styled after Rio de Janeiro's *Christ the Re-
deemer*, Fatucama's giant **Jesus statue** was a
contentious project during the waning years
of Indonesian rule. At 27m, its height symbolised the 27 provinces of Indonesia, which
at the time included East Timor. From the
top of the statue, the turquoise bays backed
by green-covered mountains are stunning.
Climbing up to Jesus, you'll pass 14 individual grottos – representing the Fourteen
Stations of the Cross. After the fourteenth,
a little path leads down to the often-deserted
beach, known as **Jesus Backside beach**, where
there's decent snorkelling.

A taxi to the statue from town should
cost US$2.

Xanana Reading Room

Part museum, part library, part cultural
centre, the **Reading Room** (☎ 331 3053; Rua Belarmino Lobo; ⊗ 9am-5pm Mon-Fri, 9am-3pm Sat) is a
must-visit. The foyer displays photos and
information dedicated to President Xanana
Gusmão. Various fan-cooled rooms hold a
decent selection of nonfiction and fiction
titles. Make time to watch a video about East
Timor from the Reading Room's comprehensive collection. There's Internet access
(per hour US$6), and a small selection of
books available to buy.

Arte Moris

Comprising a fine-art school providing
free training and materials for more than
100 junior students, the **Arte Moris** (☎ 723
3507; Rua dos Martires da Patria, Comoro; ⊗ 9am-noon &
2-6pm Mon-Sat) complex includes two galleries
displaying local artists' work. Upstairs in
the front building is the commercial gallery, while the middle building houses a
permanent collection – functioning in lieu
of an official national gallery. The dramatic-
arts and musical troupe Bibi Bulak is also
on the premises, and it's all set in fabulous
grounds embellished with kooky sculptures.
Travelling west from town, the compound
is over the Comoro bridge, just before the
airport.

Santa Cruz Cemetery

On 12 November 1991 Indonesian soldiers
fired on a peaceful memorial procession at
the Santa Cruz Cemetery. More than 200

civilians died, many of them after they were rounded up and trucked away by the military. Unfortunately for the Indonesian army, one of the people they killed was Kamal Bamadhaj, a New Zealand citizen (and subject of the film *Punitive Damage*), two of the many people they beat up turned out to be American journalists and the bloody attack was filmed by British journalist Max Stahl (whose footage features in the documentary *In Cold Blood*). The massacre at the Santa Cruz Cemetery is cited as a turning point in the independence struggle. The Xanana Reading Room has films available free for viewing, as well as further information.

Snorkelling & Diving

The fringing reef along the entire north coast of East Timor provides spectacular diving and snorkelling opportunities. Many sites are easily accessed by walking in from the beach, with dramatic drop-offs just 10m offshore in parts. The main dive operators are located in Dili, and include the following.

Free Flow (☎ 723 4614; wayneandann@hotmail.com; Av de Portugal) offers guided shore dives, including transport, for US$40. There's also full equipment hire for US$25 per day, plus a full range of Padi courses from US$260.

Dive Timor Lorosae (☎ 723 7092; www.divetimor.com; Av de Portugal) offers day-trip diving around Atauro, including two dives US$100 per person (minimum four people), or US$80 for snorkellers. Shore dives around Dili (including two dives) cost US$75. Padi courses cost US$300.

DILI DIVE & SNORKEL SITES

41K At the 41km post, this offshore wall is legendary.

Christo Rei Midway between Jesus' two carpark-entry points (6km east of Dili).

Dili Rock Just under 10km west of Dili, marked by two rocks.

TOURS

A tour can transport you to places not easily accessible by public transport, and a guide can bridge the language barrier. It's a particularly good option for time-poor travellers, and cost effective if you can rustle up a few friends to join you.

Mega Tours (☎ 723 5199; www.timormegatours.com; Rua Presidente Nicolau Lobato) This slick operation runs tours all over the country. Possible trips include a two-day jaunt through Maubisse to Mt Ramelau (up to four people US$270) and a full-day visiting Ermera – East Timor's coffee-growing region (up to four people US$120).

Vila Harmonia (☎ 723 8265; vilaharmonia@yahoo.com; Av Liberdade Emprensa 418, Becora) This guesthouse is just starting to run eco-tours, including horse-riding and hiking opportunities, in consultation with the villages it visits. Destinations include a sacred waterfall and cave used as a hideout by members of Falintil. Tours are for four nights and cost US$250 per person (minimum of five people).

SLEEPING

Though bountiful, beds in East Timor are no bargain: the influx of UN personnel patronising Dili's hostels set a pricing precedent currently beyond the backpacker budget. As things settle, budget options are gradually surfacing.

East Timor Backpackers (☎ 723 8121; Av Almirante Americo Tomas; dm US$8; ✷) Top or bottom? The usual clincher, that heat rises, doesn't count in the few air-conditioned bunk rooms of this converted home. Each room sleeps from four to six, with just enough floor space for your backpacks. If the pink walls in the lounge area become too loud, retreat to the cushy backyard, off which there's a spick-n-span shared shower block and fully kitted kitchen. The garage keeps a fleet of ex–Australia Post scooters and motorbikes available for hire: per day from US$10.

Vila Harmonia (☎ 331 0548; vilaharmonia@yahoo.com; Av Liberdade Emprensa 418, Becora; dm/s/d US$5/10/13) About 3km from town, this reliable old-timer has been here for over a decade, harbouring international journalists during the Indonesian era. Basic rooms, with bathrooms attached, line-up to form an 'L' around the garden, where a simple (complimentary) breakfast is served. Bicycles are available for hire (US$2), and you're free to use the kitchen.

Venture Hotel (☎ 331 3276; venture_hotel@hotmail.com; Rua Filomena de Camera, Lecidere; dm/s/d US$8/12/22; ✷ ☷) Multicoloured doors attached with sprouting coconuts break the monotony of 99 rooms made from shipping containers. Sometimes, though, comfort conquers character: all rooms are air-conditioned, there's 24-hour power, and a swimming pool with sprinkler rain. Fancier rooms with en suite bathrooms, a sink and fridge cost US$30, including breakfast. There's a restaurant serving Western food (meals US$5 to US$8) and a bar onsite. Sheets are changed daily and they'll launder your clothes for US$4.

Dili Guest House (☎ 723 5755; Av Bispo de Medeiros; s/d US$5/10; 🔀) The cell-like rooms here have seen better days, but they're the cheapest in town and include a bread-and-butter breakfast. One room has air-con, the rest have fans. There's a cupboard-sized kitchen and communal *mandi*-style (scoop shower and toilet) bathroom.

Hotel Turismo (☎ 331 0555; Av dos Direitos Humanos, Lecidere; s/tw/d with breakfast US$35/45/50; 🔀) Everyone knows the Hotel Turismo: This charismatic waterfront doozy has been operating since the Portuguese era. Its fading elegance detracts nothing from its dreamy demeanour: the best rooms have broad balconies opening onto a tended tropical garden. The buffet breakfast of fruit, cereal, and assemble-yourself toasted sandwiches. All rooms are fitted with bathrooms, TVs and air-con.

Carla Mansion Guesthouse (☎ 331 2488; carmen castrence@yahoo.com.au; Rua Geremias do Amaral; r US$20-30; 🔀) This tidy place is a respectable option: with a capacious courtyard encircled by well-tended rooms. Each is generous in size, with a bathroom, TV and air-con. It's held up well, despite being mostly full-up – it has been favoured by UN workers in recent years.

City Hotel (☎ 725 0331; Rua Presidente Nicolau Lobato; s/d US$25/40; 🔀) Rooms here tower four storeys above the ever-popular City Café. Each has a TV, fridge and bathroom. The better rooms have a balcony facing the street, others feature a separate room with a writing desk.

SPLURGE!

Casa Minha (☎ 331 0251; casaminahotel@mail .timortelecom.tp; Av de Portugal; r US$100; 🔀 🔝) Let the coffee kick in from your complimentary breakfast before venturing out the door. Especially if your sumptuous self-contained apartment is positioned near the pool, as it's literally at your doorstep. Located on the waterfront, you'll cop afternoon beach breezes, and can run over to catch the sunsets. (And surrender all your dirty duds – laundry is included.)

Rocella (☎ 723 7993; Rua Presidente Nicolau Lobato 18; r with breakfast US$15; 🔀) There's no chance of you getting out of bed on the wrong side in these teeny rooms: you only have one option. The string of motel-style rooms here all have a bathroom and little fridge. Also onsite is a gallery-shop, bar (open until midnight, and metres from the rooms) and restaurant.

EATING & DRINKING

Most foreign-focused restaurants and cafés serve booze, encouraging many to linger long after they've finished their meal. You can also eat with the locals at one of many street stalls, found at both ends of town: east along the Estrada de Bidau and west on the waterfront along Av de Portugal.

Erli (☎ 724 5293; Rua Formosa; dishes US$1-4; 🕑 lunch & dinner) You get what you're given for dinner at this popular courtyard café. In the evenings there's one special, such as Portuguese-style octopus, which comes in generous portions with rice. By day, whiteboard bread-based menu propped out the front serves as a sign for Erli, located behind the government buildings.

Alfa-Omega Café (☎ 331 7249; Rua Formosa; dishes US$1-2; 🕑 lunch & dinner) The *bain-marie* down the back of this cosy café keeps a medley of dishes to make a budget lunch. (The earlier you arrive, the fresher the dishes.) Alfa also does a decent pizza, plus Mediterranean-inspired meals.

Depot Mie Ayam (Rua Formosa; dishes US$1-2; 🕑 lunch & dinner) Everything tastes better when someone else cooks it, even simple noodles. This little place serves up mounds of simple Indonesian-style dishes, including fried noodles, fried rice and soup.

One More Bar (Rua Governador Filomena da Camara, Lecidere; dishes US$4-9; 🕑 breakfast, lunch & dinner) One More Bar's killer second-storey position, on the waterfront behind the Mary statue, makes it a popular place to linger over a drink or three. The menu's not bad either, ranging from a variety of salads to steaks, with flavours from Asian to Italian. There's a good range of veggie options, as well as seafood and bumper breakfasts.

City Café (☎ 723 1080; Rua Presidente Nicolau Lobato; dishes US$5-9; 🕑 breakfast, lunch & dinner) The blue-uniformed ladies provide excellent service at this popular UN hangout. Sit in or out, day or night: this reliable café can answer most food and drink requirements. The extensive

SPLURGE!

Restaurante Victoria (☎ 725 1901; Rua da Areia Branca, Metiaut; dishes US$5-10; ☒ lunch & dinner) This is simply the best place for a fresh fish barbecue in Dili. Its position just back from the sand, sunsets over the water, and the giant Jesus visible from the corner of your eye, also makes it one of the best locations in town. If you eat out only once in Dili, make it here.

menu includes Portuguese favourites: such as *bacalhau* (cod) any which way, and extends through to Mediterranean and Asian flavours. There's a good range of Australian wines, as well as beers served in big chilled glasses.

Gion (☎ 333 2038; Rua Belarmino Lobo 2; dishes US$3-9; ☒ lunch & dinner) Gion's menu covers all your authentic Japanese favourites: in Japanese, English and pictures. The long windowless room incites intent focus on your sashimi, sushi or tempura. Five-course 'complete sets' are also available.

Cool Spot (Rua da Areia Branca, Metiaut) Join the 'in' crowd at this schmick bar, but never before midnight. Be warned: the music favours Latin grooves, so brush-up on your dance moves.

Self-Catering

There are large food *mercado* (markets) at Comoro, 4km west of the centre, and Becora – about 3km east. You'll find markets on the waterfront in town, as well as in Caicoli, where the old market (*mercado municipal*) building crumbles south of the roundabout. Dili's streets are lined with small shops and stalls selling bottled water and basics, and there are a number of large foreign-owned supermarkets stocked with imported produce, including **Lita** (Av dos Direitos Humanos).

SHOPPING

Tais mercado (Rua Sebastiao da Costa) A *tais* is a piece of East Timorese woven cloth, and each region possesses its own distinct style. This market has *tais* that are from all over the country.

Cooperativa Café Timor (☎ 724 1916; Jl Dr Barros Gomes 16, Lecedere) This office, which promotes and processes local organic coffee on behalf of its members, sells 500gm vacuum-sealed packets of ground coffee (US$5).

GETTING THERE & AWAY

Air

There are no domestic air routes in East Timor; see p131 for details on getting in and out of the country.

Boat

The **ferry office** (☎ 724 0388; Av Almirante Americo Tomas) is open sporadically; however, a regular Saturday service operates from Dili to Atauro island (US$7.50) departing 9am and taking three hours. It returns to Dili on the same day at around 3pm. It also runs twice a week to Oecussi (US$15, 13 hours) departing Thursday and Monday.

The eco-lodge on Atauro operates a community boat departing Dili twice a week; see p138.

Bus

While bus departure points are defined in Dili, they're fairly informal: running to a loose schedule and stopping on demand. Early morning is the best time to travel, and there are fewer services on Sunday.

The Tasitolu depot, west of Nicolau Lobato International Airport, is the hub for destinations to the west of the country. Travelling to the east, to Baucau, Lospalos and Viqueque in particular, buses go from the Becora bus terminal near the Becora market, or you can simply hail a bus heading out on the Baucau road. Try the Camea

BORDER CROSSING: INTO INDONESIA

The three-hour bus ride from Dili to the border town of Batugade costs US$3. You have to walk across the border to Motoain in West Timor, from where a *mikrolet* (minibus) costs less than US$1 to Atambua or a motorcycle taxi costs US$3. From Atambua to Kupang costs about US$3 and takes eight hours. You require an Indonesian visa before crossing the border into West Timor (see p147).

Timor Tour & Travel (☎ 331 7404, 723 2095; Jl 15 Oktober 17) runs a daily service between Dili and Kupang for US$18, which takes 12 hours. The transport is in an air-conditioned minibus and includes pick-up from your accommodation.

For information on getting to East Timor from Kupang, see p273.

EAST TIMOR

Kode *mikrolet* stop beside the *mercado municipal* roundabout for destinations south, such as to Aileu and Maubisse.

GETTING AROUND

See p132 for car-hire options; though it's a compact city and you'll be able to reach most places on foot.

Bicycle

Cycling around Dili is ideal: it's a small city with light traffic and generally cautious drivers. A few bikes are available for rent from Vila Harmonia guesthouse for US$2 per day, and from the self-proclaimed tourist centre downstairs from One More Bar for US$5 per day.

Bus

Minibuses, called *mikrolet,* dart around Dili on designated routes (numbered one to 10) during daylight hours. They stop frequently over relatively short distances, often making a taxi a more efficient option. A *mikrolet* will get you almost anywhere in town for 25¢ or less.

Taxi

There are loads of unmetered taxis around Dili. Almost anywhere around town costs a standard US$1, rising to US$2 for a longer journey (say from Lecidere to Comoro) or any trip at night. It's wise to confirm the price before setting off.

ATAURO

The idyllic island getaway of Atauro is visible from Dili, but a world away. Its lush mountain interior is hemmed by uninterrupted beach and coral reef. The community is comprised of around 8000 people, mostly subsistence fishers and farmers, living in five villages spread across the island. The main centres are along the east coast: Makili, Vila, Beloi (where the public ferry docks) and Bikeli, with Macadade in the mountains. Atauro's isolation made it a natural prison, historically, used by both the Portuguese and Indonesian governments as a place of exile, as well as a natural paradise: spared the violence of '99. Being remote has also contributed to a conservative population: cover up and curb public displays of affection. You're free to do a lot or a little: with stellar walking and snorkelling opportunities (off the pier at Beloi and in front of Tua Koin), or seemingly endless beach to prop on and watch passing outriggers, listening to the attendant rowing songs. Dive Timor Lorosae (p135) takes scuba trips to the surrounding reefs.

Tua Koin (☎ 723 6085; cabin Sun-Thu US$25, Fri & Sat US$30) Eight simple thatched-roof cabins are located on the beach at Vila. Operated by Atauro's NGO, Roman Luan, this ecovillage runs on solar power, recycles grey water and has two bathroom blocks, with compost toilets and separate *mandi* in a gorgeous garden setting. Meals are also provided (for an extra US$11 per day); though not compulsory there are few alternatives. All profits are used to fund community projects, such as schools and water-purification projects. With an outrigger available for use, and walking guides, snorkelling gear and bikes available for hire, Tua Koin is a popular weekend retreat for Dili expats. Bookings are essential, but if you come midweek, you are likely to have all this to yourself.

Getting There & Away

The island of Atauro is 30km directly north of Dili. There's a **ferry service** (☎ 724 0388; Ave Martines da Patria, Dili; US$7.50) from Dili's main wharf to Atauro (three hours) every Saturday at 9am, returning the same day from Atauro at 3pm.

Roman Luan's community boat, the *Maun Alin,* runs from Dili, next to the Central Maritime Floating Hotel, Tuesday and Friday costing US$10 each way. It departs Atauro for Dili Thursday and Sunday, taking around three hours. Departure times vary; ask at Tua Koin at the time of booking.

Keep an eye out for dolphins, which are almost always seen in the waters between the islands.

EAST OF DILI

The stunning coast road east of Dili is in pretty good shape, and traversable with a conventional vehicle. Hugging the waterfront, each curve reveals another 'oh'-inducing beach, with outlying reef providing excellent snorkelling. Colourful corals and reef fish inhabit the waters a short distance offshore at the 41km and 43km marks.

A long bridge spans the Laclo River at **Manatuto**, 64km east of Dili, with its own Jesus statue overlooking town. The road continues another 19km to **Laleia** with a twin-towered pastel-pink church. **Vemasse** is a further 9km and noted for its fortress-like Portuguese construction on the hillside overlooking the town.

BAUCAU

The charming Old Town streets of Baucau, East Timor's second city, zigzag downhill dominated by the ruins of the impressive **mercado municipal**, built during the Portuguese era. Meanwhile the **town market** operates in the next block, with potatoes piled into little pyramids, neat bunches of greens and mounds of maize forming a colourful patchwork on the pavement. A clear spring gushes from the sheer cliff face that backs the Old Town (Kota Lama) and undulates through town, surfacing as the local laundry and bathing spot. Where the road switchbacks right you'll find the fabulous 50m **piscina** (swimming pool; admission 50¢). Continuing downhill you follow the flow of the spring that irrigates paddies and coconut groves punctuated with traditional thatched dwellings before reaching the gorgeous beach at **Osolata** (5km) called Pantai Wataboo. Its white sand is fringed by palms and hemmed by turquoise water.

Historically raffish, Baucau was once the country's international gateway: the first (or last) stop on the '70s hippy trail across Southeast Asia. The UN has used its still-functional airport since the violence of '99, when Baucau was hit particularly hard.

The characterless Kota Baru (New Town) sprung up during the Indonesian era and overlooks the Old Town.

Sleeping & Eating

Hotel Loro-Sae (Old Town; per person US$10) This not-so-inspiring place has basic accommodation with shared *mandi*-style bathrooms. It's located above street level, upstairs from a workshop.

Restaurante Benfika (☎ 724 0913; Rua Principal de Tirilolo, New Town; dishes US$2-4; ☾ lunch & dinner) There are few options for food in Atauro, including this charismatic restaurant which serves a range of meat-based dishes with rice or noodles.

> **SPLURGE!**
>
> **Pousada de Baucau** (☎ 724 1111; Rua de Catedral, Old Town; r US$55; ☒) Luxuriate in colonial charm at the splurge-worthy *pousada* (traditional Portuguese logging): with white bed-linen, whirring ceiling fans, wicker furniture and balconies with sea views. Similar décor flavours the restaurant (dishes US$5 to 10; open for breakfast, lunch and dinner), where a simple beer tastes better than average, seasoned by the surrounds; and Portuguese-influenced meals are on offer.

Restaurante Torres (Old Town; dishes US$2-5; ☾ lunch & dinner) This restaurant does decent fish-and-chips.

Getting There & Away

About three *mikrolet* per day drive the 123km between Dili and Baucau (US$2, three hours). From Baucau *mikrolet* run to Viqueque (US$2, two hours) and Lospalos (US$3, 3½ hours).

SOUTH OF BAUCAU

From Baucau you can head for the hills, taking the lush mountain road south. After 22km the covered mouths of roadside tunnels, which were used by the Japanese as encampments and to stockpile weapons during WWII, are visible. It's another 6km to the village of **Venilale** nestled between Mt Matebian in the east and Mt Mundo Perdido (Lost World) in the west. This mountain region, including the hidden caves in neighbouring **Ossu**, sheltered Fretilin members, such as Xanana Gusmão, working for independence in the waning years of the Indonesian era.

Viqueque, 63km from Baucau, is the centre for the surrounding district of the same name, which is patterned by paddies. The *mikrolet* stops at the heaving market where you can purchase everything from pigeons to palm wine, located in the centre of town. You can stay at Henrique's **guesthouse** (☎ 723 8788; Rua don Jeremias de Lucca; r US$10), which is the terrace house opposite the school (no sign). In the town's north, **Restaurant Luminar** (dishes US$1-2; ☾ lunch & dinner) does decent food.

Mikrolet make runs at least daily between Viqueque and Baucau (US$2, two hours) and on to Dili (US$2, three hours).

EAST TIMOR

If you have a 4WD, you can continue to the coast where the stunning beach at **Beaçu** is slowly swallowing the Portuguese-built customs building. From here it's possible to continue along the coast road – which is so bumpy that attempting to scratch an itchy eye could mean losing it.

EAST OF BAUCAU

About 20km east of Baucau is the coastal village of **Laga**, with a characteristic church and crumbling fort as guardians. From here a road wends south through the mountains to the hill town of **Baguia** (38km) in the shadow of **Mt Matebian** (2315m). Also known as 'Mountain of the Souls' this holy place is topped with a statue of Christ, attracting thousands of pilgrims annually for All Souls Day (2 November) to honour deceased friends and family.

Back on the coast at Lautem (60km east of Baucau), you can detour south to the mountain region of Lospalos (right) or continue east to Com (20km).

At least three *mikrolet* per day run between Baucau and Baguia (US$2, 2½ hours) via Laga.

Com

It's the end of the road when you reach the austere fishing village of Com, 80km from Baucau. The many Dili expats who weekend here would say that the stellar **snorkelling** from the concrete jetty make it a fitting ending.

Just before the jetty is Rosa's **Guesthouse** (s/d US$5/10) with homely rooms and personalised service; meals are also available (US$2 to US$3). The shell-studded **Com Beach Resort** (☎ 332 4227; r US$20-50;) has basic rooms that share a bathroom block, as well as fancier ones with bathrooms; prices are higher on Friday and Saturday. You can hire a snorkel and mask here for US$5 per day. The Resort's **Ocean View Restaurant** (dishes US$4-10; breakfast, lunch & dinner) does everything from basic brekky to a whole roast goat for US$110.

Tutuala & Jaco Island

Travellers speak of Tutuala and Jaco Island with a hushed reverence: the isolation, snorkelling and white-sand stretches making for the ultimate beach experience. It can be a tad tricky without your own

transport. Just past Desa Rasa at Fuiloro, marked by arched ruins, a signposted road leads 34km to **Tutuala** in the island's far east. This pretty village is propped high above the shimmering sea, visible from the cliff at the end of town.

Just before the road ends in Tutuala, a very rough road tumbles 8km downhill to the beautiful white-sand **Pantai Walu**. You can camp here: bring water and food, as you may not see another soul during your stay. Visible offshore is the sacred island of **Jaco**. The water between the beach and the island is a regular thoroughfare for dolphins and the occasional whale, as well as keeping a verdant reef with exceptional snorkelling. Camping on Jaco is prohibited.

If fishermen are ashore, you can negotiate transport to and from the island. To get to Tutuala you could charter a *mikrolet* from Com for around US$10.

Lospalos

Lospalos, home to the Fataluku language group of people, is a practical town, about 25km south of Lautem. This area was a Fretilin stronghold and is severely scarred by the '99 violence. A replica Fataluku-style totem house (*uma-lulik*) stands behind the main street, next to the old market. Opposite is the best accommodation in town: the (unsigned) **Nova Esperança** (per person US$10) with en suite *mandi*-style bathrooms and beds so new they're still wrapped in plastic. You could also check in at the **Welcome Restaurant & Guest House** (dm US$8; breakfast, lunch & dinner) on the main road, which has rudimentary accommodation and decent food (dishes US$3 to US$5).

Mikrolet run at least thrice daily between Lospalos and Baucau (US$3, 3½ hours).

WEST OF DILI

The western pocket of the country is mostly seen via the north coast through the window of a bus, with few travellers disembarking on the journey to the border: where East Timor faces Indonesia, just beyond the border town of Batugade.

There are two routes to discover the west from Dili: the north-coast road is lined with long and lonely beaches, while the inland road will be a hit with coffee junkies.

NORTH-COAST ROAD

Buses to the border travel along the coast road: characterised by black-sand beaches on the ocean-side and vibrant villages on the mountain-side. Plus there are a few coral gardens offshore that inspire many to don a mask-and-snorkel or scuba set.

Thermal water burbles from the seabed 6km short of **Liquiçá**: walk off the shore beside the cemetery to peruse the rays and reef fish that populate that patch of coral. The village itself, 35km west of Dili, warrants a wander for its fine Portuguese architecture and bustling market. You'll recognise **Maubara**, 49km from Dili, by the fort walls and cannons pointing out to sea. The sandy ocean floor slopes away here to a coral bed that attracts its fair share of colourful fish. You could also mingle with the locals in town at Maubara's lively market.

A steady stream of *mikrolet* depart Dili daily stopping at both villages on their way to the border town of **Batugade** (111km); see p137 for further details. These same *mikrolet* then turn inland, travelling 14km to the misty mountain town of **Balibo**. In the main square is Australia Flag House: a community centre with a library and crèche, commemorating five foreign journalists killed by invading Indonesian soldiers in 1975.

Maliana is 26km further inland on the edge of a fertile flood plain. You can stay overnight at **Motel al Jafil** (per person US$5), a few hundred metres east of the church. You can eat for around a dollar at a few shopfronts opposite Maliana's market.

INLAND ROAD

The inland road climbs in from the coast, dipping through a lush valley before reaching **Ermera**, around 60km southwest of Dili. This area has been cultivating coffee since Portuguese times, and is still blanketed by working plantations. Come during harvest (June to August), when the bushes bear their coffee cherries and the area thrums with activity.

Ermera is an easy day trip from Dili, with *mikrolet* regularly departing Dili's Comoro for Ermera (US$1, two hours). With your own wheels, you can bump along the inland road, continuing to Maliana and Balibo before emerging at the coastal border town of Batugade; see left.

SOUTH OF DILI

The thatched roofs of round houses fleck the sides of soaring mountains south of Dili. Nestled in a crest is the mellow mountain town of Maubisse, while the countryside peaks further south, reaching its highest point at Mt Ramelau. Climbing Ramelau makes an excellent adventure, do-able from Dili in three to four days. Those with time credits could continue to the black sands along the south coast.

MAUBISSE

Put your head in the clouds at the lofty mountain town of Maubisse, 70km south of Dili and 1400m up. You'll be sleeping closer to the stars here, and can find a bed

---

COFFEE FOR THE ECONOMY'S COFFERS

East Timor's coffee plants carry more than the weight of their coffee cherries. The industry is one of only a few with the potential to prop the fledgling country's economy.

The Portuguese established fruitful coffee plantations over a century ago. At its peak, coffee accounted for more than half of Portuguese Timor's exports. During the Indonesian years coffee production dwindled down to an almost domestic supply. The industry was further devastated by the destruction of crops and supporting infrastructure (such as roads) in '99. Independent East Timor inherited a lacklustre industry with land divided between an estimated 44,633 farmers working less than a hectare each, independent from any quality-control systems.

Cooperativa Café Timor (CCT, p137), funded by USAid, acts as an export agent for East Timor coffee growers. The co-op ensures a high-quality product: its many individual members united by processing and harvesting standards. East Timor's superior arabica coffee is shade-grown in mountainous districts, such as Ermera, Liquiçá, Bobonaro and Aileu. It's organically grown, which came about by default with most farmers unable to afford chemicals or fertilisers.

Most importantly, East Timor coffee measures up in the cup: described as clean and full-bodied, with a cocoa-and-vanilla character.

at the classic **Pousada de Maubisse** (☎ 332 5023; r US$15 Mon-Thu, US$50-60 Fri & Sat, US$20 Sun) that overlooks town. Its fading grace and gorgeous grounds make for great value during the week, with a restaurant menu offering a variety of Portuguese-inspired dishes (US$8 to US$10). You could also stay with the nuns at Maubisse's elaborate **church** (bed US$10). **Restaurante Sara** (Rua Maubisse; dishes US$2) offers one or two dishes that change daily.

Buses depart from Comoro (Dili) for Maubisse (US$2, three hours) each morning.

HATUBUILICO & MT RAMELAU

Wild roses grow roadside and mountain streams trickle through the precious teeny town of Hatubuilico – at the base of Mt Ramelau. Stay at the **Pousada Alecrim Namrau** (☎ 725 8978; Rua Gruta Ramelau Hun 1; s/d US$10/20) where meals can also be arranged for US$2. The *pousada* (traditional Portuguese lodging) is run by the village *chefe* (chief) who lives next door. He can also arrange a guide (US$5) to get you up the mountain – and up at 3am in time to reach the peak for sunrise.

Hiking from the village to the Virgin Mary statue at the top of Mt Ramelau (2963m) takes around three hours; with a 4WD you can drive 2.5km to a meadow from where it's two hours to the top. The trail leads steadily up, with an open-air 'church' on a plateau at the 2700m mark. From the peak, mountaintops ripple out to the coast visible to the south and north. Sunrise here is humbling: bring a coat though, as early morning temperatures are chilly (about 5°C).

From Maubisse, the Hatubuilico turnoff is at the 81km post; you'll reach the village after 18km. From Maubisse, *anggunas* travel to Hatubuilico on market days: Wednesday and Saturday. The price depends on the number of passengers, but the trip should cost around US$2 and take three hours.

AINARO

Ainaro sits on the crest of a stunning mountain region, 40km southwest of Maubisse. Fittingly for a district capital, the town possesses characteristically charming public buildings and monuments, with a striking church. You can sleep at the simple **Hospedaria & Restaurante Gabmenis** (r US$10) which also has decent meals for US$3.

From Maubisse a *mikrolet* costs US$1.50, and takes an hour.

SAME & BETANO

Same (Sar-may), 43km south of Maubisse, is at the centre of the region's hard-working coffee plantations. Huddled on the fringes are villages set in tall mountain forests. Same is a sizeable town, with a thrumming daily market. The range of sleeping and eating options makes it a good base for exploring the remote south coast.

Hotel & Restaurant Same (Rua Na Raran; r US$25-35) is the schmickest joint in town, with flush toilets in the en suite bathrooms. Otherwise there's **Berlaka** (☎ 725 3182; Rua Mercado Lama; s/d US$12/15) and **Talik** (☎ 723 9882; Rua Kotalala 9; r US$10); the latter with a café offering decent meals for between US$2 and US$4.

The road continues down to the blacksand beach at Betano on the coast. Offshore is the wreck of a WWII ship, and a patch of coral that's worth **snorkelling** over.

Mikrolet run frequently between Maubisse and Same (US$1, one hour), and between Same and Betano (US$1, one hour).

SUAI

The south coast's main town, Suai sprawls 5km inland, dominated by an enormous unfinished cathedral. Capital of the Cova Lima district, Suai is a confusing collection of villages and the centre for offshore oil drilling in the Timor Sea.

The **Eastern Dragon** (dishes from US$5), located between the town centre and the coast, has overpriced rooms and Chinese dishes – such as 'squirrel seafood claypot'. A few shopfronts opposite the market dish-up basic rice and noodle plates for around US$2.

Mikrolet run between Suai and Maubisse, via Ainaro or Same (around US$2, at least three hours).

OECUSSI

Surrounded on three sides by Indonesian West Timor and fronted by the sea, the isolated enclave of Oecussi is politically part of East Timor, but set apart geographically and culturally. Its mostly Dawan population comprises the largest ethnic group in West Timor, and traditional conical-shaped houses dot the hilly landscape.

Oecussi was the first Portuguese colony in Timor. Dominican missionaries settled here as far back as 1556 before abandoning the colony in favour of Dili in 1769. For the most part, the area was the forgotten part of East Timor. It was annexed by Indonesia without resistance in 1976; however, it didn't escape the violence following the independence referendum in '99.

PANTEMAKASSAR

Pantemakassar, also known as Oecussi town, is an idling coastal settlement sandwiched between the hills and the coast. East Timor's occupying forces are represented in a face-off of monuments: in the west stands an Indonesian Integration figure while a Mary statue represents the Portuguese in the east. There's splendid **snorkelling** to be had in the clear waters surrounding the reef about 10m offshore.

The old fort known as **Fatusuba** slowly decays atop the hill 1.5km south of town. In the next block is a fountain and coral grotto housing a statue of the Virgin Mary, which attract more visits from locals, than the fort. **Lifau**, located 5km west of Pantemakassar, is the site of the original Portuguese settlement on Timor; it has a good beach and there is a monument to the first landing.

Pasar Tono, 12km south of Pantemakassar, has a colourful **market** beneath the branches of giant banyan trees. The main produce market in the area, it draws locals dressed in traditional garb who come from all around to stock up and sell their wares.

The fastidiously neat **Restaurant Lily** (Jl Integrasi; r US$7) incorporates a guesthouse with simple tidy rooms that share *mandi* washroom facilities. The restaurant does good grub, such as beef served with fried potatoes and egg (US$5). Find it just off the main grid of streets. The only general store of any size is next door.

GETTING THERE & AWAY

There's a **ferry service** (☎ 724 0388; Av Martines da Paria, Dili) from Dili to Oecussi once a week, typically departing on Thursday morning and arriving in Oecussi 12 to 13 hours later. The return departure is around 5pm the next Friday evening. The fare is US$15 each way. The ferry office in Dili is open sporadic hours. In Pantemakassar the office is close to the landing spot near the Integration Monument.

It's possible to travel overland between Oecussi and Dili, but it requires an Indo-nesian transit visa – for which there is no representative in Oecussi.

EAST TIMOR DIRECTORY

ACCOMMODATION

Accommodation in East Timor averages between US$5 and US$10 for the night: variously charged per person or per room. The majority of places have a bed in a small room with a concrete floor; prices rise to US$20 or US$30 for little luxuries like air-con or en suite bathrooms.

Guesthouse accommodation is most common throughout the country, providing a basic room in a family home, with shared *mandi*-style bathroom – a large concrete basin from which you scoop water to rinse your body and 'flush' the squat toilet. A large number of hotels were purpose built to accommodate the influx of UN and aid workers post-1999. These places are the most likely to have air-con, sit-down loos and in-room power sockets (220V, 50Hz; with no standard socket, so bring a variety of adaptors). The dwindling numbers of foreign workers should lead to accommodation prices coming down.

Outside Dili the guesthouse rules, interspersed with the occasional *pousada* (traditional Portuguese lodging – usually superbly located). The majority of out-of-town places also provide meals: almost always including a coffee-and-bread brekky (free), as well as cooked meals on request. In rural areas, running water and power is only available between 6pm and midnight.

If you find yourself stranded, you can always spend the night with the nuns for around US$10; ask at the town's church. In rural areas where there is little or no commercial accommodation locals usually open their homes to travellers; etiquette would encourage payment (around US$10).

There are no formal camping options in East Timor, though it's not unknown for travellers to pitch a tent in remote areas, such as Tutuala beach.

ACTIVITIES

Though there are few companies offering packaged activities in East Timor, there are loads of opportunities for adventurers with time and their own equipment. The island's interior has networks of limestone caves, and untrafficked roads and tracks are crying out for hardy cyclists.

The main organised activities are diving and snorkelling, with the coral reef that rims most of the island providing plenty of stellar opportunities. Both soft and hard corals play home to a vivid variety of reef fish; and pelagics cruise around spectacular drop-offs just metres offshore. Most sites are on the north coast – with a number in or near Dili – and around Atauro island. Conditions are best during the dry season (March to September), when visibility is at around 20m to 30m. Dive companies offering guided trips, courses and gear hire are located in Dili; see p135.

There are a number of related links with information on diving in East Timor on the **Congo Pages** (www.congo-pages.org).

There are fabulous opportunities for hiking: passing through traditional villages and traversing a variety of terrains. Many happy hikers can claim to have seen the south and north coasts of the country from its highest peak, Mt Ramelau (p142). You can make your own way there or Mega Tours (p135) runs overnight trips from Dili. It's also possible to hike in the steamy interior of Atauro island (p138), as well as to the sacred peak of Mt Matebian (p140) – though the latter requires organising your own transport and guide from Baguia.

BOOKS

Lonely Planet's *East Timor Phrasebook* and *East Timor* guidebook provide comprehensive coverage for travelling in this fascinating fledgling country.

A Woman of Independence by Kirsty Sword Gusmão is the autobiographical account of how this Australian teacher came to be East Timor's first lady. *To Resist is to Win* edited by Sarah Niner is President Xanana Gusmão's biography: featuring speeches, letters, articles, poems and interviews.

East Timor: A Rough Passage to Independence by James Dunn, the Australian consul to Portuguese Timor, is a thorough account of the country's history: from the two years preceding the Indonesian invasion in 1975, through to the violent upheavals of 1999.

Deliverance by Don Greenlees & Robert Garran details the chaotic run-up to the independence referendum.

The Redundancy of Courage by Timothy Mo is a novel whose fictional country's struggle against occupation is a deliberately thinly veiled account of East Timor's actual struggle. This novel was shortlisted for the Booker Prize in 1991.

Hello Missus by Lynne Minion is a lighthearted memoir from a former UN adviser to the East Timorese government, set to a backdrop of *lurv* in the tropical-island paradise.

BUSINESS HOURS

Few places outside Dili keep strict business hours. Shops are typically open 9am to 6pm Monday to Friday, and 9am to noon Saturday. You can usually find a feed at a restaurant between noon and 9pm. Business hours for offices are generally 8am to noon and 1pm to 5pm Monday to Friday.

CLIMATE

East Timor has two seasons: wet (December to April) and dry (May to November). In the dry season the north coast sees virtually no rain; the cooler central mountains and south coast have an occasional shower. When the rains come, they cause floods and landslides, cutting off access to roads. It's common for that slow-moving river you crossed in the morning to become an impassable torrent by the afternoon, after a bout of rain.

Day temperatures are around 30°C to 35°C (85°F to 95°F) year-round in the lowland areas, dropping to the low 20s overnight. In the mountain areas warm-to-hot daytime temperatures drop to a more chilly 15°C (60°F) at night – less at altitude. At the end of the dry season in parts of the north coast the mercury hovers over 35°C; see the climate chart on p924.

The best time to visit is after the wet season from late April to July, when the countryside is green. At the end of the dry, things can become dry and dusty. Travel is certainly possible but difficult during the wet season, when roads and unbridged rivers become impassable.

DANGERS & ANNOYANCES

Malaria and dengue are real concerns for those staying in East Timor for a month or more; take precautions (see p947 and p947). The main risks associated with travel in East Timor are those universal concerns of road safety and petty crime.

The driving is generally passive and traffic is far from dense; however, vehicles and roads are generally in poor condition – made more hazardous by wandering livestock and the lack of street lighting. Theft most frequently occurs from cars, with mobile phones a prime target. Wandering alone on the beach at night is not a good idea, and women travelling solo should take particular care (see p932).

DISABLED TRAVELLERS

There are absolutely no provisions for disabled people in East Timor. Potholed pavements make getting around in a wheelchair problematic, and there are no facilities for sight- or hearing-impaired visitors.

DRIVING LICENCE

Your home-country drivers licence or permit is acceptable in East Timor, as is a valid international drivers licence.

EMBASSIES & CONSULATES
Embassies & Consulates in East Timor

A number of countries have representation in Dili; see p147 for visa information.

Australia (☎ 332 2111; austemb_dili@dfat.gov.au; Av dos Mártires da Pátria) Canadians seeking consular assistance should visit the Australian embassy.

China (☎ 332 5163; chinaembassy2002@yahoo.com; Av Governador Serpa Rosa, Farol)

European Commission (☎ 332 5171; ectimor@arafura .net.au; Rua Santo António de Motael 8, Farol)

Indonesia (☎ 331 7107; kukridil@hotmail.com; cnr Rua Marinha & Rua Governador Cesar, Farol)

Ireland (☎ 332 4880; ireland@arafura.net.au; Rua Alferes Duartre Arbiro 12, Farol)

New Zealand (☎ 332 4982; nzrepdili@bigpond.com; Rua Alferes Duarte Arbiro, Farol)

UK (☎ 331 2652; dili.fco@gtnet.gov.uk; Av de Portugal, Pantai Kelapa)

USA (☎ 332 4684; usrodili@bigpond.com; Av de Portugal, Farol)

East Timorese Embassies & Consulates Abroad

There's only a handful of East Timorese diplomatic representation overseas.

Australia (☎ 02-6260 8800; TL_Emb.Canberra@bigpond .com; 25 Blaxland Cres, Griffith, Canberra, ACT 2603)

European Union (☎ 280 0096; jo_amorim@yahoo .com; Ave de Cortenbergh 12; 1040 Brussels, Belgium)

Indonesia (☎ 021 390 2978; tljkt@yahoo.com; 11th fl, Surya Bldg, Jl MH Thamrin Kav 9, Jakarta 10350)

USA (☎ 202 965 1515; embtlus@earthlink.net; 3415 Massachusetts Ave, NW Washington DC 20007-0000)

FESTIVALS & EVENTS

As a staunchly Catholic country, Christian holidays are celebrated with gusto; see p146 for dates. During any of the major holidays there'll be a church celebration. Easter is particularly colourful, with parades and vigils.

FOOD & DRINK

The food is not what you'll remember most about your visit to East Timor. For many locals, meat added to the staple rice-and-veg dish is a treat. That said, coastal communities do great barbecued fish, flipped straight from the sea to the grill. And veggie dishes, such as coconut rice served with pumpkin flower will have you ordering seconds.

The years of Indonesian and Portuguese rule have flavoured the country's palette, with Indonesian-style fried-noodle dishes and signature Portuguese items such as paõ (bread) and *bacalhau* (codfish) available at many restaurants. But international fare doesn't stop there. The flood of foreigners working with the UN and various aid organisations brought their cuisines with them: In Dili you could splurge on pizza, *pad thai*, sushi or sweet-and-sour chicken, or saw through a steak served with fries.

Dili has the largest choice of restaurants, which exist mainly for the foreign market. Street vendors and hole-in-the-wall type establishments gear their trade to a local market, with a limited menu (usually one or two dishes) and cheaper prices.

Coffee is a speciality in East Timor: it's strong, black and full-bodied – and available everywhere. Bottled drinking water is also readily available; otherwise you should boil tap water before drinking. That milky liquid for sale from street stalls is homebrewed palm wine (*sopi*) that tastes of fermenting palm fruit, which is exactly what it is. Think of it more as a punch (it has one) than a wine. You can buy beer brewed from all over the world – another legacy of the UN.

GAY & LESBIAN TRAVELLERS

There's no organised network for gays and lesbians in East Timor, but it's unlikely that there'll be any overt discrimination.

EAST TIMOR

HOLIDAYS

New Year's Day 1 January
Good Friday March/April
Labour Day 1 May
Assumption 15 August
Consultation Day 30 August
Liberation Day 20 September
All Saints' Day 1 November
Santa Cruz Day 12 November
Immaculate Conception 8 December
Christmas Day 25 December

INTERNET ACCESS

There are plenty of Internet cafés in Dili, with access averaging US$5 an hour. You can forget it outside of Dili.

INTERNET RESOURCES

www.discoverdili.com Publisher of tour and travel information; also available in print (US$2.50) at cafés about town.

www.congo-pages.org Why a site on the Democratic Republic of the Congo should have a sub-section on East Timor is a bit of a mystery, but there's interesting information here, particularly about diving.

www.easttimorpress.com East Timor Press is a locally administrated news site.

www.etan.org The East Timor Action Network is a US-based organisation, with comprehensive web links and loads of information and articles.

www.lonelyplanet.com Succinct summaries on travel in East Timor; check out the Thorn Tree bulletin board.

www.osolemedia.com This unofficial guide to East Timor has decent coverage.

www.timor.com Central source of news regarding East Timor from the World News Network.

www.turismotimorleste.com Official Department of Tourism site.

LANGUAGE

Portuguese and Tetun are East Timor's official languages, with Tetun and 15 other Timorese languages acknowledged by the Constitution as national languages of great importance to the country's heritage.

It's estimated that only 25% of the population speaks Portuguese, while at least 80% speaks Tetun. Most young adults also speak Bahasa Indonesia – the imposed official language from 1975 to 1999. Indonesian has adverse associations: for many families it's a reminder of the malice they suffered during the Indonesian occupation. On the other hand, Portuguese was a symbol of opposition to Indonesian oppression – used clandestinely by the resistance movement, despite being outlawed. Due to the huge UN presence in recent years, English is marginally understood, particularly in Dili. English is also taught in schools.

Any attempts made by travellers to speak Tetun are greatly appreciated. Lonely Planet's *East Timor Phrasebook* is a handy introduction. The Linguistic Institute website at the **National University** (www.shlrc.mq.edu.au/~leccles) publishes bilingual vocab lists and articles.

LEGAL MATTERS

If you are the victim of serious crime go to the nearest police station and, if possible, notify your embassy. The Timorese police force is generally free from corruption. If arrested, you have the right to a phone call and legal representation, which your embassy can help to locate.

Alcohol and tobacco are the only legal drugs: possession and trafficking of illicit drugs carry stiff penalties.

LEGAL AGE

Timorese teens officially attain adulthood when they reach the ripe old age of 17 – when it's legal to vote, drive and shag.

MAPS

The Timorese government's tourism department distributes free *Timor-Leste* country maps (1:750,000), available at the airport. The *Timor Independent Travellers Map* and the *Timor-Leste & Dili Directory* are available for purchase.

MEDIA

Independent East Timor's Constitution guarantees freedom of the press and prohibits mass-media monopolies.

Newspapers

The *Timor Post* and the *Suara Timor Lorosae* are daily local newspapers, mainly in Indonesian but with some news in Portuguese, Tetun and English. Street vendors in Dili sell them. The *East Timor Sun* is a free, weekly, English-language paper that can be found in a few hotels and restaurants in Dili. Disappointingly it usually has more about tourism in Bali than in East Timor.

Radio & TV

Radio is the most important branch of the media, with the national broadcaster Radio de Timor Leste (RTL) and a host of community stations. The Catholic Church's very popular radio station, Radio Timor Kmanek (RTK), is the only community station that has been broadcasting since before the 1999 referendum.

The national public TV station is Televisao de Timor Leste (TVTL), which produces a small amount of local content that's broadcast alongside content from Australia, Portugal and Britain. Some hotels have satellite dishes that pick-up popular Indonesian programmes.

MONEY

The US dollar is the official currency of East Timor. Locally minted centavos coins also circulate, which are of equal value to US cents. Make sure you arrive with some US dollars. You'll need to make all financial transactions in Dili: where ATMs dispense US dollars and banks change travellers cheques. A few establishments in Dili accept credit cards, though there's often a hefty 5% surcharge attached. See p125 for an idea of the daily costs of travel in East Timor.

Country	Unit	US$
Australia	A$1	0.75
Canada	C$1	0.84
euro zone	€1	1.20
Indonesia	10,000Rp	0.98
Japan	¥100	0.86
New Zealand	NZ$1	0.70
UK	£1	1.77

POST

The main post office in Dili (p134) doesn't have poste restante. The mail service is pretty reliable: your postcard will reach its destination, anywhere in the world, for 50¢.

RESPONSIBLE TRAVEL

East Timor is not yet developed for tourism; visitors need to be mindful of the significant impact their behaviour can have on the environment and the population. The majority of East Timorese are highly religious so will appreciate travellers dressing conservatively and eschewing public displays of affection. Indulging in such conduct is thought to be disrespectful and offensive, particularly outside Dili.

Formal protection for geographic areas and species is relatively new, limited, low-profile and under-resourced. You need to be mindful of the impact you have on the environment – there are no signs, rangers or information centres to remind you to 'do the right thing'. And we don't need to remind you not to walk on coral, litter or veer from marked paths, do we?

TELEPHONE

The East Timorese phone network is still recovering from the destruction of the fleeing Indonesians in 1999.

If you're phoning an East Timor number from overseas, the international country code is ☎ 670. When making an international call from East Timor, dial the access code (☎ 0011), the country code, the area code (minus the initial '0') followed by the phone number. There are no area codes in East Timor, and few landline numbers outside Dili. Landline numbers begin with a '3'; mobile numbers start with a '7'. You can make local and international calls from any Timor Telecom office.

A mobile phone is useful in East Timor. You can purchase a SIM card from **Timor Telecom** (www.timortelecom.tp) for US$20, which includes US$10 of calls. Additional prepaid calls can be added in US$15 and US$25 instalments using Timor Telecom phonecards that are readily available from street vendors. The network covers most major towns, as well as Atauro. Timor Telecom has roaming agreements with many operators from 19 countries.

TOURIST INFORMATION

East Timor doesn't yet have a tourist office. In the meantime, ask around – both expats and locals are generally happy to help.

TOURS

Australian adventure-travel operator **Intrepid Travel** (www.intrepidtravel.com) runs excellent 15-day tours of the country for around US$1750.

VISAS

An entry visa (for up to 30 days) is granted to valid-passport holders for US$30 on arrival in East Timor. Visas can be extended

EAST TIMOR

for US$30 a month, if the applicant has a valid reason to do so.

Many backpackers are turning up in East Timor to renew their lapsed Indonesian visas. An Indonesian visa takes five working days to process (so reckon on a week), and costs US$35 for a tourist visa or US$15 for a transit visa. If you're crossing into Indonesian West Timor by land or transiting to Oecussi will need an Indonesian visa.

Go to p145 for a list of embassies and consulates.

VOLUNTEERING

Major volunteer organisations active in East Timor include the following: **Australian Volunteers International** (www.australianvolunteers.com), **UN Volunteers** (www.unv.org) and **US Peace Corps** (www.peacecorps.gov). You may also be able to volunteer with one of the many nongovernment organisations working in the country. See **Fongtil** (www.geocities.com/etngoforum) for a list of relevant NGOs.

WOMEN TRAVELLERS

Women travellers need to be aware of personal security issues, particularly in Dili. Do not walk or take taxis after dark, unless you're in a group. It's wise to avoid dark city stretches where there are not many people. Assault and rape of local women occur too frequently, and there have been reports of attacks on international workers.

Timorese women dress modestly. Women travellers will attract less attention by wearing knee-length or longer clothes, and may want to cover their shoulders. Bikinis are tolerated in only a few locations, such as the popular beaches in Dili. Wearing shorts and a T-shirt is more acceptable beach attire.

Indonesia

HIGHLIGHTS

- **Bali** – partying at Indonesia's veteran resort-island and favourite first stop, offering colourful Hindu culture, sandy beaches, big surf and parties aplenty (p207)
- **Gunung Bromo** – gazing into the guts of Indonesia's sublime volcanic landscape (p205)
- **Gili islands** – living the eternal summer on the best beaches east of Bali (p281)
- **Central Java** – snapping the sunrise from the top of the ancient Buddhist stupa of Borobudur (p195), before trawling the batik markets of bustling Yogyakarta (p193)
- **Komodo** – walking with dinosaurs – or dragons at least – through some of Indonesia's wildest landscapes (p291)
- **Off the beaten track** – heading into the Lost World of Papua's Baliem Valley, a trip into a landscape of thick jungle, dizzy peaks and hidden tribes (p336)

FAST FACTS

- **ATMs** widespread in towns; rare in rural areas
- **Budget** US$15-20 a day
- **Capital** Jakarta
- **Costs** guesthouse in Bali US$5-8, 4hr bus ride US$3-4, beer US$0.70
- **Country code** ☎ 62
- **Famous for** dictators, dragons, sunshine, surf
- **Languages** Bahasa Indonesia and 300 indigenous languages
- **Money** US$1 = 9973Rp (Indonesian rupiah)
- **Phrases** *salam* (hello), *sampai Jumpa* (goodbye), *terima kasih* (thanks), *maaf* (sorry), *satu lagi Bintang* (one more Bintang)
- **Population** 225.3 million
- **Seasons** wet Oct-Apr, dry May-Sep
- **Visas** available on arrival for most nationalities – for details, see p344

TRAVEL HINT

Bahasa Indonesia is one of Southeast Asia's most approachable languages. Pick up a decent dictionary (try Lonely Planet's *Indonesian phrasebook*) and start chattering in the local tongue – a few words will get you a long way.

WARNING

Indonesia has had a volatile few years, with natural disasters and civil unrest impacting on security in large areas of the country. At the time of writing, northern Sumatra, central Sulawesi and areas of Maluku and Papua were high-risk destinations. Most trips to Indonesia are trouble-free, but always keep abreast of developments by reading the papers, surfing news channels on the web, checking your embassy's travel advisories and speaking to locals.

INDONESIA

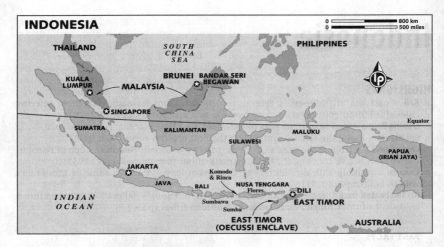

Cascading across the gulf between Asia and Australia, the Indonesian archipelago comes at you like a becak (bicycle rickshaw) without brakes. It is a country where the thrills and spills read like index entries from a modern-day *Odyssey* and where life is both as moreish, and occasionally as hard to swallow, as a bowlful of durian purée. You can stalk dragons on the wild shores of Komodo or hunt Hobbits among the mountains of Flores; witness mock battles on the plains of Sumba or burn the midnight oil in the nightclubs of Bali. Whatever you jot down on your itinerary, a voyage through Indonesia's 17,508 islands is an epic experience, never just a journey.

Give a destination like this to the media and they will have a field day. Stretching nearly 5000km, Indonesia has plenty of dark corners; civil unrest and natural disasters seem to come as standard and many tourists are going elsewhere as a result. But while newsflash Indonesia often looks more like pandemonium than paradise, there is a whole other country out there to discover: one of phenomenal natural beauty and incredible diversity. For those with a backpack and an adventurous streak, this Indonesia is as addictive as any destination in Southeast Asia and promises the kind of backdrops storytellers can only dream about. Forget Homer's *Odyssey,* go live one of your own.

CURRENT EVENTS

Indonesia's little people recently took centre stage when the remains of a new species of human – dubbed *Homo floresiensis,* or less graciously 'Hobbit' – were discovered at Liang Bua on the Indonesian island of Flores. The 1m-tall species lived on the island until as recently as 12,000 years ago and may even have coexisted there with modern humans.

The devastating Boxing Day tsunami of 2004 stole the headlines through to early 2005, however, and reconstruction efforts in northern Sumatra look set to continue for years to come. On the upside, the disaster may yet breathe fresh life into peace talks between Acehnese Free Aceh Movement (GAM) rebels and the Indonesian govern-ment, ending a conflict that has raged there since the 1970s.

In 2004, presidential elections saw Susilo Bambang Yudhoyono oust incumbent Megawati Soekarnoputri from Indonesia's top job. Observers said the election repre-sented the first peaceful transition of power in the country's history.

HISTORY
Beginnings

So, Hobbits may once have roamed the re-mote forests of Indonesia. Discovered on the island of Flores in 2003, the remains of a new species of tiny islander (see the boxed text, p292) have called into question existing theories regarding the origins of Indonesia's human history.

Debate continues, but for now at least, Indonesian civilisation appears to begin with Java man, or *Pithecanthropus erectus*, who made the first tentative steps across the land bridges linking mainland Asia to Java more than a million years ago. Disappointingly, however, these prehistoric pioneers soon vanished into evolutionary obscurity and it wasn't until the 7th century BC that later migrants began laying the groundwork for the small kingdoms that burst onto the scene some 2000 years ago.

Hinduism & Buddhism

If – to quote Dire Straits – money is power, and power is fame, it is hardly surprising that the growing wealth of these early kingdoms soon caught the attention of Indian and Chinese merchants. With them came consumer goods, more money and, most importantly, the dawn in Indonesia of Hinduism and Buddhism.

These religions quickly gained a foothold in the archipelago and soon became central to the great kingdoms of the 1st millennium AD. The Buddhist Srivijaya empire held sway over the Malay Peninsula and southern Sumatra, extracting wealth from its dominion over the strategic Strait of Melaka, while the Hindu Mataram and Buddhist Sailendra kingdoms dominated central Java, raising their grandiose monuments, Borobudur and Prambanan, over the fertile farmland that brought them their prosperity.

Indeed, when Mataram slipped into mysterious decline around the 10th century AD, it was fast replaced with an even more powerful Hindu kingdom. Founded in 1294, the Majapahit empire made extensive territorial gains under its ruler, Hayam Wuruk, and prime minister, Gajah Mada, and while claims that they controlled much of Sulawesi, Sumatra and Borneo now seem fanciful, most of Java, Madura and Bali certainly fell within their realm.

But things would soon change. Despite the Majapahit empire's massive power and influence, greater fault lines were opening up across Indonesia, and Hinduism's golden age was swiftly drawing to a close.

Rise of Islam

With the arrival of Islam came the power, the reason and the will to oppose the hegemony of the Majapahits, and satellite kingdoms soon took up arms against the Hindu kings. In the 15th century, the Majapahits fled to Bali, where Hindu culture continues to flourish, leaving Java to the increasingly powerful Islamic sultanates. Meanwhile, the influential trading kingdoms of Melaka (on the Malay Peninsula) and Makassar (in southern Sulawesi) were also embracing Islam, sowing the seeds that would later make modern Indonesia the most populous Muslim nation on earth.

European Expansion

Melaka fell to the Portuguese in 1511 and European eyes were soon settling on the archipelago's riches, prompting two centuries of unrest as the Portuguese, Dutch and British wrestled for control. By 1700, the Dutch held most of the trump cards, and while the British took advantage of Napoleon's occupation of Holland to establish a brief interregnum under Sir Stamford Raffles between 1811 and 1816, it was the Dutch who retained control of much of Indonesia until its independence 129 years later.

It was not, however, a trouble-free tenancy and while the other European powers toasted new treaties, the Dutch were left to face the guerrilla war launched by Javan Prince Diponegoro in 1825. Finally ending in 1830, when Diponegoro was exiled to Sulawesi, the famously bloody Java War cost the lives of 8000 Dutch troops and devastated Yogyakarta (Yogya), cutting its population by half.

Road to Independence

By the beginning of the 20th century the Dutch had brought most of the archipelago under their control, but the revolutionary tradition of Diponegoro was never truly quashed, bubbling beneath the surface of

INDONESIA

Dutch rule and finding a voice in the young Soekarno. The debate was sidelined as the Japanese swept through Indonesia during WWII, but with their departure came the opportunity for Soekarno to declare Indonesian independence, which he did from his Jakarta home on 17 August 1945.

The Dutch, however, were unwilling to relinquish their hold over Indonesia and, supported by the British, who had entered Indonesia to accept the Japanese surrender, moved quickly to reassert their authority. Resistance was stiff and for four bitter years the Indonesians fought an intermittent war with the Dutch until the Indonesian flag, the *sang merah putih* (Red and White) was finally hoisted over Jakarta's Istana Merdeka (Freedom Palace) on 27 December 1949.

Depression, Disunity & Dictatorship

Unity in war quickly became division in peace, as religious fundamentalists and nationalist separatists became the new bugbears of the fledgling central government. But after almost a decade of political impasse and economic depression, Soekarno made his move, declaring Guided Democracy (a euphemism for dictatorship) with army backing and leading Indonesia into 40 years of authoritarian rule.

Despite moves towards the one-party state, Indonesia's three-million-strong Communist Party (Partai Komunis Indonesia; PKI) was the biggest in the world by 1965 and Soekarno had long realised the importance of winning its backing. But as the PKI's influence in government grew, so did tensions with the armed forces. Things came to a head on the night of 30 September 1965, when Colonel Untung of the palace guard launched an attempted coup. Quickly put down by General Soeharto, the coup was blamed – perhaps unfairly – on the PKI and became the pretext for an army-led purge that left as many as 500,000 communist sympathisers dead. In the ensuing chaos, Soeharto moved to consolidate power and by 1968 had ousted Soekarno and was installed as president.

Soeharto brought unity through repression and reacted to insurgency with an iron fist. In 1975, Portuguese Timor was invaded, leading to tens of thousands of deaths, and separatist ambitions in Aceh and Papua were also met with a ferocious military response. But despite endemic corruption, the 1980s and 1990s were Indonesia's boom years, with meteoric economic growth and a starburst of opulent building ventures transforming the face of the capital.

Soeharto's Fall

As Asia's economy went into freefall during the closing years of the 1990s, Soeharto's house of cards began to tumble. Indonesia went bankrupt overnight and the country found an obvious scapegoat in the cronyism and corruption endemic in the dictator's regime. Protests erupted across Indonesia in 1998 and the May riots in Jakarta left thousands, many of them Chinese, dead. After three decades of dictatorial rule, Soeharto resigned on 21 May 1998.

Passions cooled when Vice-President BJ Habibie took power on a reform ticket, but ambitious promises were slow to materialise, and in November of the same year riots again rocked many Indonesian cities. Promises of forthcoming elections succeeded in closing the floodgates, but separatist groups took advantage of the weakened central government and violence erupted in Maluku, Irian Jaya, East Timor and Aceh. East Timor won its independence after a referendum in August 1999, but only after Indonesian militias had ransacked the country and left thousands dead.

Democracy & Beyond

Against this unsettled backdrop, the promised June 1999 elections passed surprisingly smoothly, leaving Megawati Soekarnoputri and her Indonesian Democratic Party for Struggle (PDI-P) with the lion's share of the vote. Despite this, Muslim alliances moved against her, strong-arming the People's Consultative Assembly into voting Abdurrahman Wahid (Gus Dur) into the presidency and shunting Soekarnoputri into the number two slot.

But Wahid's efforts to undo corruption met with stiff resistance and his presidency fast became a fight for political survival. The battle was soon lost and on 23 July 2001, Soekarnoputri was sworn in as the fifth president of Indonesia, with Hamzah Haz as her deputy.

The first tentative steps towards reform now continue. Soekarnoputri was herself ousted from the presidency in 2004 by

Susilo Bambang Yudhoyono (or 'SBY'), but while there is much work still to be done, the consensus is that Indonesia has finally proved itself to be a workable democracy.

Unfortunately, lack of security and pockets of radicalism – starkly illustrated by the Bali blasts of Octobers 2002 and 2005 – remain the country's biggest bugbears. The fallout from the tragic 2004 tsunami may yet call time on the secessionist conflict in Aceh, and a Helsinki-brokered peace deal was signed in August 2005, committing GAM to decommission hundreds of weapons and the Indonesian government to withdraw thousands of troops and police. At the time of writing, there was a sense of optimism that this time both sides were ready to end a three-decade conflict that has claimed 15,000 lives. But violent squabbling continues in parts of Maluku, Sulawesi and Papua and it remains to be seen whether SBY's tough policies can bring the house into order.

THE CULTURE
The National Psyche
Bhinneka Tunggal Ika, an old Javanese phrase meaning 'They are many; they are one', may be Indonesia's national motto, but in this diverse and disparate archipelago the 'many' and the 'one' aren't always singing from the same hymn sheet. In fact, while the Spartan red and white blocks of the Indonesian flag hint at a solid, unified nation, it is soon clear that the opposite is true.

Some choose to define Indonesia's identity in terms of Java. As home to 50% of the country's 225.3 million people and at the heart of all things economic and political, this little island is arguably the hub of an anachronistic 21st-century empire. But while Java retains the loudest voice, it doesn't speak for every Indonesian and many resent its disproportionate wealth and jealous grip on power.

Others try to define Indonesian psyche in terms of the Pancasila (Five Principles). Expounded by Soekarno in 1945, these lay the philosophical groundwork for the modern Indonesian nation, maintaining that loyalty to the state should supersede ethnic and religious divisions. But while the Pancasila hangs in community buildings across the country, many Indonesians continue to place the interests of their locality and religion above those of their country. This, for now, is unlikely to change.

> **MUST READ**
>
> MC Ricklef's *A History of Modern Indonesia* is a fabulous first stop for those wanting to get a handle on the country's turbulent history.

Indonesia is, in effect, little more than a loose confederacy of peoples, spuriously bound together by a single flag and single language (Bahasa Indonesia). The end of four decades of autocratic rule may have brought new freedoms to everyday Indonesians, but Indonesia is made up of hundreds of ethnic and religious groups and many are now looking to express themselves. Now that East Timor has gone its own way, it remains to be seen whether the concept of a single Indonesia remains strong – and attractive – enough to hold its remaining constituent parts together. Only time will tell.

Lifestyle
The world's most populous Muslim nation is no hard-line Islamic state. Democracy has come of age, secularism is a government-sponsored buzzword and 'liberal' is no longer the expletive it once was. *Reformasi* – a process that refers to updating government processes, as well as anachronistic social attitudes – is gaining ground and trappings of Western living, from baseball caps and mobile phones to doughnuts and Hollywood horror flicks, are sweeping through Indonesian society. TV seems to be playing a significant role in this cultural revolution and you will find a set at the heart of most Indonesian homes. In fact, despite an insufferably bland diet of Western-style soap operas and cleaning product commercials being screened, TV-viewing is one of the country's favourite domestic pastimes.

But trouble is brewing in the shopping mall. The economic crisis of the late-1990s

> **MUST SEE**
>
> Peter Weir's Oscar-winning flick *The Year of Living Dangerously* stars Mel Gibson as a foreign correspondent following the final, turbulent months of the Soekarno regime. It is based on CJ Koch's novel of the same name.

thrust 27% of the population below the poverty line and while the economy has now been stabilised there remains a yawning gulf between the haves and the have-nots. This has led to widespread discontent and a niggling mistrust of the Western-style reforms, propping up, at one extreme, the particularly threatening brand of Islamic fundamentalism behind the 2002 Bali blast. However, these extremes are anathema to most Indonesians and while the process of reform may stall in coming years, its progressive course now seems certain.

Population

The world's fourth-biggest country by population after China, India and the USA, Indonesia is a hodgepodge of more than 300 ethnic groups, ranging from the ethnic Javanese, who account for 45% of the total, to the hill tribes of remote Kalimantan and Papua. Despite its 225.3 million people, however, overpopulation is a phenomenon mainly confined to Java and Bali and much of the archipelago remains largely unpopulated.

Indonesia's population is highly mobile (thanks to a policy of transmigration), with Javanese settlers laying down roots in the four corners of the archipelago and workers from across Indonesia moving to Java to look for work.

Other major ethnic groups: Sundanese (14%), Madurese (7.5%) and coastal Malays (7.5%).

RELIGION

If Indonesia has a soundtrack, it is the muezzin's call to prayer. Wake up to it once and it won't come as a surprise that Indonesia is the largest Islamic nation on earth, with 200 million Muslims (88% of the total population).

But while Islam has the monopoly on religious life, many of the country's most impressive historical monuments, such as the temples of Borobudur and Prambanan, hark back to when Hindu and Buddhist kingdoms dominated Java. These religions have since diminished in popularity, but Hinduism (2% of the population) continues to flourish in Bali, and Christian (8%), Buddhist (1%) and animist (1%) communities also thrive across the nation. Religious clashes in Ambon and Sulawesi and the apparent rise of Islamic fundamentalism have done much to radicalise the image of Indo-

nesian religious life, but most communities coexist in relative harmony.

Although nominally a secular state, religious organisations (some with as many as 40 million members) still wield considerable clout in the corridors of power.

ARTS
Dance

Indonesia has a rich heritage of traditional dance styles. Yogyakarta has its Ramayana ballet, Java's most spectacular dance drama; Central Kalimantan boasts the Manasai, a friendly dance in which tourists are welcome to participate; and Bali has the Barong, Kecak, Topeng, Legong and Baris dances, which are some of the most colourful dances of all.

Literature

Pramoedya Ananta Toer, a Javanese author, is perhaps Indonesia's best-known novelist. His famous quartet of historical realist novels set in the colonial era comprises *This Earth of Mankind, Child of All Nations, Footsteps* and *House of Glass.*

Mochtar Lubis is another well-known Indonesian writer. His most famous novel, *Twilight in Djakarta,* is a scathing attack on corruption and the plight of the poor in Jakarta in the 1950s.

Music

Indonesian music spans everything from thousand-year-old traditional music to high-powered punk pop. Probably the best-known Indonesian musical form is gamelan. Traditional gamelan orchestras are found primarily in Java and Bali. They are composed mainly of percussion instruments including drums, gongs and shake-drums (*angklung*), along with flutes and xylophones.

Theatre

Javanese *wayang* (puppet) plays have their origins in the Hindu epics, the Ramayana and the Mahabharata. There are different forms of *wayang*: *wayang kulit* uses leather shadow puppets, while *wayang golek* uses wooden puppets.

ENVIRONMENT

Things are looking bleak for Indonesia's environment. The country boasts some of the planet's most pristine landscapes, but abuses are rampant and environmental legislation has been largely neglected since the economic crisis of 1997–98.

For more information on Indonesia's environment, visit the **Indonesian Forum for the Environment (WALHI)** (www.eng.walhi.or.id).

The Land

At 1.92 million sq km, Indonesia is an island colossus, incorporating 10% of the world's forest cover and 11,508 uninhabited islands (6000 more have human populations). From the low-lying coastal areas, the country rises through no fewer than 129 active volcanoes – more than any country in the world – to the snow-covered summit of Puncak Jaya (5030m), in Papua. Despite the incredible diversity of its landscapes, however, it is worth remembering that Indonesia is predominantly water; Indonesians refer to the country as Tanah Air Kita (literally, Our Earth and Water). The main islands are Kalimantan (Indonesian Borneo; 539,460 sq km), Sumatra (473,606 sq km), Papua (Indonesian New Guinea; 421,981 sq km), Sulawesi (202,000 sq km) and Java (132,107 sq km).

Wildlife

In his classic study *The Malay Archipelago*, British naturalist Alfred Russel Wallace divided Indonesia into two zones. To the west of the so-called Wallace Line, which runs between Kalimantan and Sulawesi, and south through the straits between Bali and Lombok, flora and fauna resemble those of the rest of Asia, while the species and environments to the east become increasingly like those of Australia. Scientists have since fine-tuned Wallace's findings, but while western Indonesia is known for its (increasingly rare) orang-utans, rhinos, tigers and spectacular rafflesia flowers, eastern Indonesia boasts crocodiles, marsupials and the infamous Komodo dragon.

National Parks

While environmental abuses remain rife, it is only fair to mention that the past decade has seen a rapid increase in the number of national parks and reserves. Indonesian *taman nasional* (national parks) are managed by the Directorate General of Forest Protection and Nature Conservation (PHPA; Perlindungan Hutan dan Pelestarian Alam). Many of Indonesia's national parks are remote and have minimal facili-

---

INDONESIA'S BIGGEST

Biggest Archipelago Covering an area of 1,920,000 sq km, Indonesia's 17,508 islands make up the world's largest archipelago.

Biggest Bang When the west Javan volcano of Krakatau blew itself to smithereens in 1883, policemen on the island of Rodriguez, more than 4600km southwest, reported hearing 'heavy guns'.

Biggest Flowers The world's largest flower, *Rafflesia arnoldi*, often blooms in the thick Sumatran forests near Bukittinggi between August and November.

Longest Insect Stick-insect fans will be delighted to know that the jungles of Borneo – keep an eye out in Kalimantan – are home to the world's longest insects. One specimen of *Pharnacia kirbyi* was a staggering 546mm (21.5in) in length.

Biggest Lizard The Komodo dragon *(Varanus komodoensis)* is the biggest lizard in the world. The largest authenticated specimen was a gift from the Sultan of Bima to a US scientist and measured 3.1m (10ft 2in).

---

ties, but these pockets of pristine wilderness offer the adventurous an invaluable glimpse of the nation's spectacularly diverse flora and fauna. Some of the finest and more accessible parks include Sumatra's Taman Nasional Gunung Leuser (p260) and Lombok's Gunung Rinjani (p286).

For more information on Indonesia's national parks, visit www.geocities.com/Rain Forest/4466.

Environmental Issues

Illegal logging remains one of the greatest threats despite a 2001 law banning the export of timber. The country now has the worst deforestation rate on the planet, with an area the size of Switzerland vanishing every year; 70% of Indonesia's original frontier forests have already gone.

Rapid industrialisation and a booming population are also contributing to Indonesia's pollution crisis. Only 3% of Jakarta's population are connected to a sewer system, and with coastal pollution worsening, as much as 86% of Indonesia's reef area is thought to be at medium or high risk of destruction.

A raft of government initiatives has been tabled to tackle the problem, but while many Indonesians continue to live on the breadline, the environment is likely to remain a secondary concern.

TRANSPORT

GETTING THERE & AWAY
Air
Jakarta in Java and Denpasar in Bali have flights to most major capitals in Asia and further afield. Outside these two major hubs, there are also useful international services from Medan and Padang in Sumatra, Yogyakarta and Surabaya in Java and Manado and Makassar in Sulawesi.

See p173 and p203 for details of major airline offices.

MALAYSIA
There are dozens of flights to Kuala Lumpur from Jakarta and Denpasar. SilkAir also links Kuala Lumpur with Medan (one-way US$84) and Padang (one-way US$125). Malaysia Airlines connects Yogyakarta and Kuala Lumpur (one-way US$188). Garuda flies to Kuala Lumpur from Surabaya (one-way US$193).

SINGAPORE
Apart from the numerous services to/from Jakarta and Denpasar, Garuda links Singapore with Manado (one-way US$500), Medan (one-way US$208) and Surabaya (one-way US$193).

OTHER DESTINATIONS
All other Southeast Asian capitals are easily reached from Jakarta or Denpasar. Merpati runs a useful service between Dili and Jakarta (one-way US$237).

Boat

INTERNATIONAL DEPARTURE TAX

Airport tax for international departures is 100,000Rp.

MALAYSIA
Most sea connections are between Malaysia and Sumatra. The comfortable, high-speed ferries between Penang (Malaysia) and Belawan (near Medan, Sumatra) are one of the most popular ways to reach Indonesia (RM90). There are also ferry connections

---

BORDER CROSSINGS

There are now three possible land crossings to Indonesia. The first is Entikong, between Kalimantan and Tebedu, Sarawak (Malaysian Borneo). Visas were available on arrival at time of writing, but check with your local Indonesian embassy before making the trip (p340).

The border crossing between West and East Timor at Motoain is currently open, however a visa is required in advance when travelling from either East or West Timor. See the boxed text, p273.

The road from Jayapura or Sentani to Vanimo in Papua New Guinea can be crossed, but the situation here is variable, both politically and logistically; you should check the latest situation before making the trip (see also the boxed text, p334). A visa is required in advance if travelling into Indonesia.

---

between Dumai (Sumatra) and Melaka (Malaysia) for 140,000Rp; Pulau Bintan (Sumatra) and Johor Bahru (Malaysia) for 120,000Rp; and Pulau Batam (Sumatra) and Kuala Tungkal (Malaysia) for 80,000Rp.

For east-coast Kalimantan, speedboats depart frequently every morning from Tarakan to Nunukan (82,000Rp) and from Nunukan to Tawau (110,000Rp).

PAPUA NEW GUINEA
Chartering a boat from Jayapura to Vanimo in Papua New Guinea is possible (350,000Rp per person). A visa is required if travelling into Indonesia.

SINGAPORE
Ferries link Singapore with Pulau Batam (S$16) and Pulau Bintan (120,000Rp), both in Sumatra.

GETTING AROUND
Air
The national airline, **Garuda Indonesia** (www .garuda-indonesia.com), operates most major domestic routes using jet aircraft.

Merpati (www.merpati.co.id) is the country's main domestic carrier with an extensive network covering just about everywhere. Bouraq, Lion Air, Mandala, Pelita Air and Jatayu also offer some useful services.

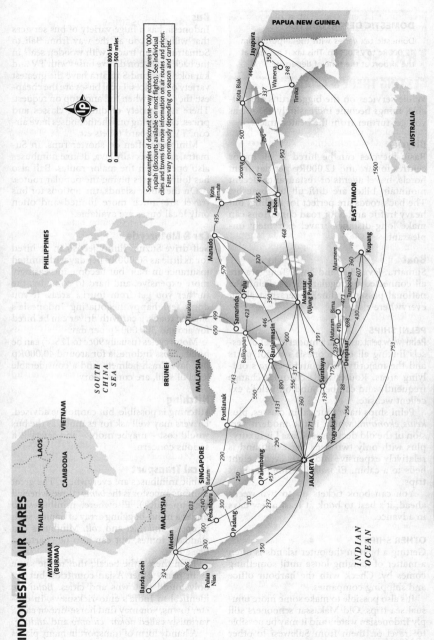

INDONESIAN AIR FARES

Some examples of discount one-way economy fares in '000 rupiah (discounts available on most flights). See individual cities and towns for more information on air routes and prices. Fares vary enormously depending on season and carrier.

PAPUA NEW GUINEA

Jayapura

Wamena 350
348
446
Timika

Kota Biak 337

500
796
952

Sorong 410
655
Kota Ternate
435
Kota Ambon
468

1500

AUSTRALIA

EAST TIMOR

Kupang

Maumere 360
607
Tambolaka 473
Bima 430
Mataram 698
237 Denpasar 753

PHILIPPINES

Manado
320
579
Palu 350
Makassar (Ujung Pandang)
Samarinda 423
446
Tarakan
650 499
Balikpapan 349
Banjarmasin 600
267
391
410
175
88
Surabaya 256
139
Yogyakarta 88

SOUTH CHINA SEA

BRUNEI

MALAYSIA

Pontianak
743
550
890
556 312
360
171
Jakarta

VIETNAM
LAOS
CAMBODIA
THAILAND

MYANMAR (BURMA)

MALAYSIA

SINGAPORE
Batam
290
250
Palembang 457
Pekanbaru 300
Padang 237
633
400
300
Medan
300
350
496
324
Banda Aceh
Pulau Nias

INDIAN OCEAN

0   800 km
0   500 miles

DOMESTIC DEPARTURE TAX

Domestic tax varies with the airport, from 12,000Rp to 25,000Rp. This tax is payable at the airport at the time of departure.

While services on the bigger runs are reliable, things become increasingly chaotic as you get further from the beaten track.

Bicycle

Basic bicycles can be hired in all major centres for around 12,000Rp per day from hotels, travel agents or restaurants; decent mountain bikes are difficult to come by. The back roads are perfect for cycling, but heavy traffic and poor road conditions can make long-distance travel extremely unpleasant.

Boat

Sumatra, Java, Bali and Nusa Tenggara are all connected by regular ferries. Pelni, the national passenger line, covers just about everywhere else.

PELNI SHIPS

Pelni (www.pelni.co.id) has a modern fleet of vessels linking all of Indonesia's major ports and the majority of the archipelago's outlying areas. Routes and schedules change frequently and can be found on Pelni's excellent website.

Pelni ships have four cabin classes, plus *kelas ekonomi,* which is the modern version of the old deck class. Class I is luxury-plus with only two beds per cabin and is relatively expensive and Class IV has eight beds to a cabin. *Ekonomi* is fine for short trips.

You can book tickets up to two weeks ahead; it's best to book at least a few days in advance.

OTHER SHIPS

Getting a boat in the outer islands is often a matter of hanging loose until something comes by. Check with the harbour office and shipping companies.

It's also possible to make some more unusual sea trips. Old Makassar schooners still ply Indonesian waters and it may be possible to travel on them from Sulawesi to other islands, particularly Java.

Bus

Indonesia has a huge variety of bus services that will take you all the way from Bali to Sumatra – from trucks with wooden seats in the back to air-con deluxe buses with TV and karaoke. Java and Sumatra have the greatest variety of services. Local buses are the cheapest; they leave when full and stop on request. There is a variety of different classes and prices, depending on whether buses have air-con, TV, on-board toilets etc.

Minibuses often do shorter runs. In Sumatra, and especially Java, deluxe minibuses also operate on the major routes. Bali also has tourist buses plying the popular routes.

On the other islands, the options for bus travel are much more limited and often only local buses are available.

Car & Motorcycle

Self-drive Suzuki Jimny jeeps can be hired for as little as 80,000Rp per day with limited insurance in Bali, but become increasingly more expensive, and hard to come by, the further you get from tourist areas. If you don't feel happy negotiating Indonesia's chaotic roads, a car with driver can be hired for around 300,000Rp per day.

Motorcycles (usually 90cc to 125cc) can be hired across Indonesia for around 40,000Rp per day. Crash helmets, and a considerable level of skill, are compulsory.

Hitching

Hitching is possible, but cannot be advised. Drivers may well ask for as much as the bus would cost – maybe more – and safety is a serious concern.

Local Transport

Public minibuses are everywhere. The great minibus ancestor is the *bemo* (three-wheeled pick-up truck). Elsewhere, minibuses go under a mind-boggling array of names, such as *opelet, mikrolet* and *colt.* Minibuses run standard routes, but can also be chartered like a taxi.

Then there's the becak; they're the same as in many other Asian countries, but are only found in towns and cities. *Bajaj* are identical to India's auto-rickshaws. In quieter towns, you may find horse-drawn carts, variously called *dokar, cidomo* and *andong.*

A handy form of transport in many places is the *ojek* (motorcycle taxi).

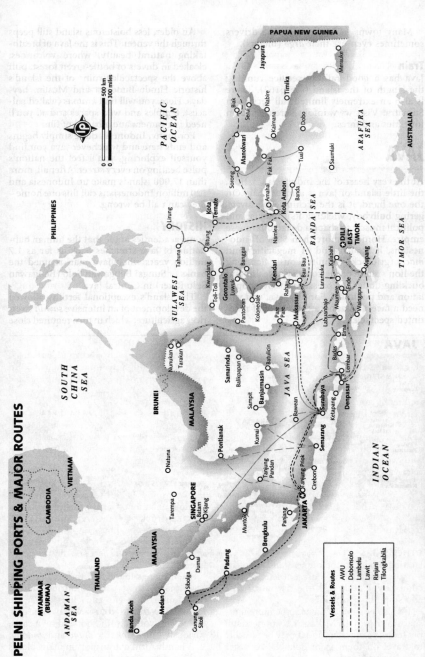

PELNI SHIPPING PORTS & MAJOR ROUTES

Vessels & Routes

AWU
Dobonsolo
Lambelu
Lawit
Rinjani
Tilongkabila

Many towns have taxis and the drivers sometimes even use their *argo* (meters).

Train

Java has a good railway service running the length of the island (see p162). There is also an extremely limited rail service in Sumatra. Visit www.infoka.kereta-api.com for times and fares.

JAVA

At the very heart of the Indonesian nation, the little island of Java is a mixed bag. On the one hand, it is the archipelago's swaggering bullyboy, wielding its financial and political muscle to shape a de facto Javanese empire. Home to more than 50% of Indonesians, it is an island of megacities and *macet* (gridlock), simultaneously flaunting the lion's share of the country's wealth and buckling under the pressures of overpopulation and pollution. For this Java, you will need a face mask and a thick pair of rose-tinted spectacles.

An older, less boisterous island still peeps through the veneer. This is the Java of breathtaking natural beauty, where volcanoes, cloaked in duvets of bottle-green forest, puff above the spectacular ruins of the island's historic Hindu-Buddhist and Muslim heydays. Here, you will find *kratons* (walled palaces), temples and wild spaces and all you'll need is a camera and a bagful of film.

For many, Indonesia quite simply begins and ends here and whichever Java you find yourself exploring, you'll feel the nation's pulse beating on every street. After all, more than 17,000 islands make up Indonesia and 120 million Indonesians call this one home – they can't all be wrong.

HISTORY

Some academics argue that the human habitation of Java stretches back as far as 1.7 million years when Java man roamed the banks of Sungai Bengawan Solo (Bengawan Solo River) in Central Java.

The island's exceptional fertility allowed the development of an intensive *sawah* (wetrice) agriculture, which in turn required close

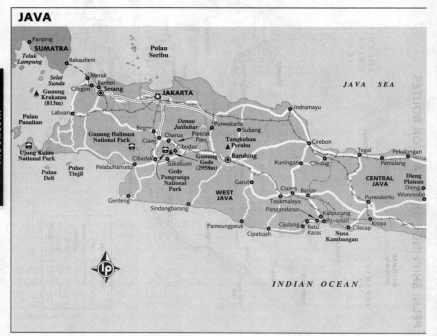

cooperation between villages. Out of village alliances, small kingdoms developed, but the first major principality was that of King Sanjaya, founder of the Mataram kingdom in the beginning of the 8th century. Mataram's religion centred on the Hindu god Shiva, and produced some of Java's earliest Hindu temples on the Dieng Plateau.

The Sailendra dynasty followed, overseeing Buddhism's heyday and the building of Borobudur (probably around AD 780). Hinduism and Buddhism continued to exist in parallel and the massive Hindu Prambanan complex was constructed within a century of Borobudur (c AD 856).

Mataram eventually fell, perhaps at the hands of the Sumatra-based Srivijaya kingdom, but Javanese power revived under King Airlangga, a semi-legendary figure who formed the first royal link between the island and Bali. Airlangga divided his kingdom between his two sons, resulting in the formation of the Kediri and Janggala kingdoms and by the early 13th century, a period of usurpation and conflict had begun.

Out of the ashes, Wijaya established the great Majapahit kingdom and by the reign of Hayam Wuruk (ruled 1350–89), it claimed sovereignty over the entire Indonesian archipelago (probably covering Java, Madura and Bali). Hayam Wuruk's strongman prime minister, Gajah Mada, was responsible for many of Majapahit's territorial conquests.

The Majapahit kingdom went into decline with the death of Hayam Wuruk and Islam moved to fill the vacuum. By the end of the 16th century, it was the Muslim kingdom of Mataram that held sway over central and eastern Java. The last independent principalities, Surabaya and Cirebon, were eventually subjugated, leaving only Mataram and Banten (in west Java) to face the Dutch in the 17th century.

While the Javanese were great warriors, they were prevented from forming effective alliances against the Dutch by internal squabbling. Consequently, most of Java had fallen by the end of the 18th century, although the last remnants of the Mataram kingdom survived as the principalities of Surakarta (Solo)

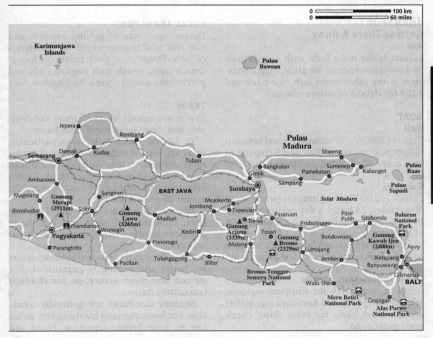

and Yogya (Yogyakarta) until the foundation of the new Indonesian republic.

After independence, Java became the centre of the new Indonesia. And that has led to resentment; to a large extent the rebellions of the Sumatrans, Minahasans and Ambonese in the 1950s and 1960s were reactions to Javanese domination. Furthermore, the abortive communist coup of 1965 started in Jakarta, and some of its most dramatic and disastrous events took place in Java.

Java also dominates economic life in Indonesia. The island has the bulk of Indonesia's industry and it received most of the foreign investment that poured into the country in the 1990s. Java is the most developed part of Indonesia by far, but the effects of the economic crisis have also been felt the most here. Huge numbers of urban workers lost their jobs and rising prices have hit hard right across Java, resulting in sporadic disturbances and riots across the island.

Despite increased security, lasting stability has a habit of eluding the authorities in Java and pockets of militant Islamic fundamentalism remain.

TRANSPORT
Getting There & Away
AIR
Jakarta is the main hub, with connections to destinations across the archipelago. Surabaya is the other main hub. See p173 and p203 for details of airline offices.

BOAT
Bali
Ferries (5000Rp, 30 minutes) travel between Gilimanuk in western Bali and Ketapang in Java every 30 minutes, 24 hours a day.

Sumatra
Ferries (10,000Rp, two hours) operate every 30 minutes, 24 hours a day between Merak in Java and Bakauheni at the southern tip of Sumatra.

Pelni has ships from Jakarta to a number of Sumatran ports; check www.pelni.co.id.

Other Indonesian Islands
Java is a major hub for shipping services. Jakarta (see p173) and Surabaya (see p204) are the main ports for Pelni ships; check www.pelni.co.id.

Getting Around
AIR
As more budget airlines open their doors, flying around Java is becoming an increasingly attractive proposition. Jakarta, Surabaya and Yogyakarta are Java's main airports, but Solo, Bandung, Semarang and even Pangandaran are also serviced by flights.

BUS
Bus travel is often slow and nerve-racking; night buses are a little faster. Trains are often better for the long hauls, but bus departures are much more frequent.

The cheapest and most frequent buses are the big public buses, which are cooled by a blast of sooty air from an open window and seem to stop for passengers every five minutes. Better air-con buses also run the major routes and are often worth paying the extra for.

Small minibuses, called *colt, angkot* or a variety of other names, run the shorter routes more frequently. Door-to-door air-con minibuses (called *travel*) also operate on the major runs. Many hotels can arrange pick-up.

LOCAL TRANSPORT
Dream up a way of getting around, and you will find it somewhere on the streets of Java. *Dokar* – brightly-coloured, horse-drawn carts, awash with jingling bells and psychedelic motifs – are a highlight.

TRAIN
Trains are usually quicker, more comfortable and more convenient than buses.

In Jakarta and Surabaya in particular, there are several stations, some of them far more convenient than others – bear this in mind when choosing your trains. Trains originating in your city of departure are the easiest to get a seat on.

Ekonomi trains are cheapest. They are slow, crowded and often run late. Seats can be booked on the better *ekonomi plus* services.

For a little extra, *bisnis* (business) trains are better and seating is guaranteed. For air-con and more luxury, go for *eksekutif* (executive) trains.

Student discounts are generally available. For basic *ekonomi* trains, tickets go on sale an hour before departure. *Bisnis* and *eksekutif* trains can be booked weeks ahead, and the main stations have efficient, computerised booking offices for *eksekutif* trains.

Try to book at least a day in advance, or a few days beforehand for travel on public holidays and long weekends.

For details of times and prices, check www.infoka.kereta-api.com.

JAKARTA
☎ 021 / pop 9.3 million

America can keep its big apple; Indonesia's capital was never going to be an easy fruit to swallow. Dubbed the 'Big Durian', Jakarta is a chaotic landscape of freeways, skyscrapers, slums and traffic jams; a city of thick skins (you need one to live here) and strong smells. A vast waiting lounge for those queuing up for their share of Indonesia's financial stir-fry, this is a fast-paced city of function rather than form; somewhere to make money and forge political alliances rather than sit back and admire the view. Tourists, as a result, are at a premium.

But just like the big fruit itself, Jakarta rewards those who are prepared to hold their noses and dig in. Pull back the concrete curtain and Indonesia's capital is a microcosm of the bigger nation, containing elements from the four corners of the archipelago. From the steamy streets of Chinatown, through the swanky expat suburbs, to the city's decadent nightclubs, Jakarta is a Pandora's box, filled with all the good and bad of Indonesian life.

Lacking a coherent centre, Jakarta can be a tough city to explore. The old city around Kota offers a clutch of museums and sights, however, as does the area around Freedom Square, which is capped with Soekarno's suspiciously phallic national monument. Sometimes it is best just to accept Jakarta for what it is though and explore the restaurants, clubs and shopping malls that the city does best.

Orientation

Jakarta sprawls 25km from the docks to the southern suburbs. Soekarno's national monument (Monas) in Lapangan Merdeka (Freedom Square) is an excellent central landmark. North of the monument is the older part of Jakarta, which includes the old Dutch area of Kota and the old harbour of Sunda Kelapa. The modern harbour, Tanjung Priok, is several kilometres further

---

GETTING INTO TOWN

Soekarno-Hatta International Airport is 35km northwest of the city at Cengkareng, about an hour away (much longer during peak hours).

There's a Damri bus service (10,000Rp, one hour) every 30 minutes from 3am to 7pm between the airport and Gambir train station.

Alternatively, a metered taxi costs about 60,000Rp, including the airport service charge and the 7500Rp toll-road charges paid on top of the metered fare. These should be organised through the official booths in the arrival terminal.

---

east. The more modern part of Jakarta is to the south of the monument.

Jl Thamrin is the main north–south street of the new city and has Jakarta's big hotels and banks. A couple of blocks east along Jl Kebon Sirih Raya is Jl Jaksa, the cheap accommodation centre of Jakarta.

Information
BOOKSHOPS
QB World Books (Map p164; ☎ 718 7070; Level 3, Plaza Senayan, Jl Asia Afrika; ☯ 9am-7pm) Has a wide range of English-language titles.

CULTURAL CENTRES & LIBRARIES
Australian Cultural Centre (Map p164; ☎ 2550 5555; Australian Embassy, Jl Rasuna Said Kav C15-16; ☯ 9am-4pm Mon-Fri)
British Council (☎ 515 5561; www.britishcouncil.org /indonesia.htm; Level 16, Jakarta Stock Exchange, Jl Jend Sudirman; ☯ 9am-4pm Mon-Thu, 9am-2pm Fri)
Erasmus Huis (Map p164; ☎ 524 1069; www.erasmus huis.or.id; Jl Rasuna Said Kav S-3)

EMERGENCY
Police (☎ 110)

INTERNET ACCESS
Access costs roughly 8000Rp per hour.
Duta Perdana Raya Travel (Map p169; ☎ 314 3310; Jl Jaksa 15A; ☯ 8am-11pm)
Wartel & Warnet Bhumi Bhakti (Map p169; Jl Wahid Hasyim; ☯ 10am-10pm)

INTERNET RESOURCES
www.bartele.com Offers a range of newsletters on everything from security to nightlife.

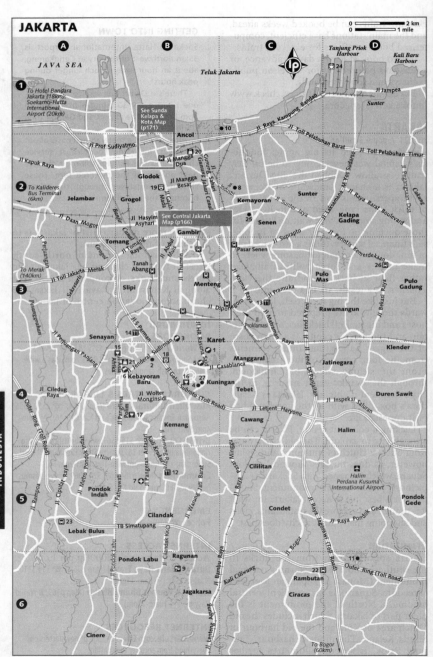

www.expat.or.id A comprehensive guide to all things Jakarta.
www.jakarta.go.id Run by the Jakarta Visitor Information Centre.

MEDIA

The daily *Jakarta Post* (5000Rp) newspaper and monthly *Djakarta!* (20,000Rp) and *Jakarta Kini* (20,000Rp) magazines offer news, reviews and entertainment listings.

For an insight into the city's quirkier side, grab a copy of Daniel Ziv's *Jakarta Inside Out. Bule Gila: Tales of a Dutch Barman in Jakarta*, by Bartele Santema, manager of Bugils bar (see p172) and author of www.bartele.com, is another enlightening read.

MEDICAL SERVICES

SOS Medika (Map p164; ☎ 750 6001; Jl Puri Sakti 10, Kemang; 🕑 24hr)

MONEY

There are banks across town including the following:
Bank Mandiri (Map p169; Jl Wahid Hasyim)
BII (Map p166; Plaza Indonesia, Jl Thamrin)
BNI (Map p169; Jl Kebon Sirih Raya)

POST

Main post office (Map p166; Jl Gedung Kesenian 1; 🕑 8am-7pm Mon-Fri, 8am-noon Sat)

TELEPHONE

Duta Perdana Raya Travel (Map p169; ☎ 314 3310; Jl Jaksa 15A; 🕑 8am-11pm)
Wartel & Warnet Bhumi Bhakti (Map p169; Jl Wahid Hasyim; 🕑 10am-10pm)

TOURIST INFORMATION

Jakarta Visitor Information Centre (Map p169; ☎ 315 4094; www.jakarta.go.id; Jakarta Theatre Bldg, Jl Wahid Hasyim 9; 🕑 9am-5pm Mon-Fri, 9am-1pm Sat) A very useful first stop. There is a second branch in the international arrivals hall of the airport.

TRAVEL AGENCIES

24-Hour Tickets (Map p169; ☎ 3192 3173; Jl Haji Agus Salim 57A; 🕑 9am-8pm Mon-Fri, 9am-5pm Sat)
Robert Kencana Travel (Map p169; ☎ 314 2926; Jl Jaksa 20B; 🕑 24hr)

Dangers & Annoyances

Violent crime, almost unheard of in the rest of the country, is reported, and on the increase, in Jakarta. Avoid disreputable areas, such as Glodok and Kota, after dark, and don't walk the streets alone at night. Muggings by taxi drivers have been reported – stick with the reputable companies. Buses and trains are a favourite haunt of pickpockets. While outbreaks of Avian influenza (bird flu) have been reported in the region, tourists are extremely unlikely to be affected.

Sights & Activities

Many of Jakarta's major sights are north of Jl Jaksa. Most of the grand public buildings – as well as Soekarno's *pièce de résistance*, the Monas – surround Lapangan Merdeka, while the city's historic heart can be found further north around Kota and the old port of Sunda Kelapa.

KOTA   Map p171

Jakarta's history is at its most tangible in Kota, where you will find the remnants of the old Dutch capital of Batavia. **Taman Fatahillah**, the old town square, features some of Jakarta's most venerable buildings and a handful of ho-hum museums. The easiest way to get there from Jl Jaksa is to catch a train to Kota (Jl Stasiun) from Gondangdia

INDONESIA

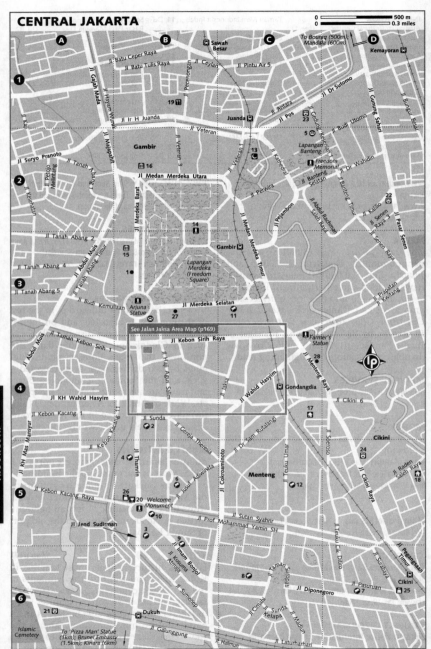

CENTRAL JAKARTA

0 500 m
0 0.3 miles

To Bouraq (500m);
Mandala (600m)

See Jalan Jaksa Area Map (p169)

INDONESIA

station (Jl Cut Nyak Dien). It costs 2000Rp each way and takes about 15 minutes. A taxi from Jl Jaksa will cost around 15,000Rp.

The best way to soak up old glories is to spend the money saved by skipping the museums on a drink at historic **Café Batavia** (☎ 691 5531; Jl Pintu Besar Utara 14; ⏱ 24hr).

The best way to earn your drink, is to explore Kota's quirkier sights on foot. The old Portuguese cannon **Si Jagur** (Taman Fatahillah), or Mr Fertility, opposite the Jakarta History Museum, is perhaps an early version of Soekarno's phallic National Monument. It was believed to be a cure for barrenness because of its suggestive clenched fist and women sat astride it in the hope of bearing children.

Nearby, **Gereja Sion** (Jl Pangeran Jayakarta 1; ⏱ dawn-dusk) is the oldest remaining church in Jakarta. It was built in 1695 outside the old city walls for the 'black Portuguese', who were brought to Batavia as slaves and given their freedom if they joined the Dutch Reformed Church.

More fine Dutch architecture lines the grotty Kali Besar canal, including the **Toko Merah** (Jl Kali Besar Barat), formerly the home of Governor-General van Imhoff. Further north, the last remaining Dutch drawbridge, the **Chicken Market Bridge**, spans the canal.

To the south of Kota, **Glodok** was the old Chinatown of Batavia. Today, it has a steamy, slightly sordid atmosphere, and a stroll through the spitting street kitchens will provide plenty of colour for the day's diary entry.

The area's museums are sold hard in the tourist literature, but their dusty exhibits are rather disappointing. They include the **Jakarta History Museum** (☎ 692 9101; Taman Fatahillah 2; admission 2000Rp; ⏱ 9am-1.30pm Tue-Fri & Sun, 9am-12.30pm Sat), with colonial bric-a-brac in the beautiful old City Hall (1710); the **Wayang Museum** (☎ 692 9560; Jl Pintu Besar Utara 27; admission 2000Rp; ⏱ 9am-1.30pm Tue-Fri & Sun, 9am-12.30pm Sat), with a display of puppets and occasional *wayang* performances; and the **Balai Seni Rupa** (Fine Art Museum; ☎ 690 7062; Taman Fatahillah; admission 2000Rp; ⏱ 9am-1.30pm Tue-Fri & Sun, 9am-12.30pm Sat), with a gallery of modern Indonesian paintings.

SUNDA KELAPA   Map p171
Among the hubbub, floating debris and oil slicks, the old Dutch port is still home to some magnificent Buginese Makassar schooners. Sunda Kelapa is a 1km walk north from Taman Fatahillah or take the unique local transport – a ride on a pushbike's 'kiddie seat' (1500Rp). The **harbour** (admission 1000Rp) is usually a hive of activity.

The early morning **Pasar Ikan** (Fish Market; Jl Pasar Ikan; ⏱ 6am-2pm) is close by. Near the entrance to Sunda Kelapa harbour, one of the old Dutch East India Company warehouses has been turned into the **Museum Bahari** (Maritime Museum; ☎ 669 3409; Jl Pasar Ikan 1; admission 2000Rp; ⏱ 9am-1.30pm Sun-Fri, 9am-12.30pm Sat).

LAPANGAN MERDEKA
Soekarno attempted to tame Jakarta by giving it a central space, **Lapangan Merdeka** (Freedom Square), and topping it with a

INDONESIA

gigantic monument to his machismo, the **National Monument** (Monas; Map p166; ☎ 384 0451; admission 5100Rp; ☒ 8.30am-5pm Mon-Fri, 8.30am-7pm Sat & Sun). The towering, 132m-high column, capped with an illuminated flame, has been ungraciously dubbed 'Soekarno's last erection', but you can whiz up the shaft for impressive views of the smoggy surrounds. The **National History Museum** (Map p166; ☒ 8.30am-5pm Mon-Fri, 8.30am-7pm Sat & Sun), in the base, tells the story of Indonesia's independence struggle in 48 dramatic, overstated dioramas. Admission is included in the Monas entry fee.

'Soekarno's last erection' is the best known, but many of Soekarno's triumphalist monuments have acquired derogatory nicknames over the years. The gentleman at Kebayoran, for example, holding the flaming dish, is now **'Pizza Man'**. You'll find this statue on a roundabout south of the centre en route to Plaza Senayan.

INDONESIAN NATIONAL MUSEUM

The **National Museum** (Map p166; ☎ 386 8171; Jl Merdeka Barat 12; ☒ 8.30am-2.30pm Tue-Thu & Sun, 8.30-11.30am Fri, 8.30am-1.30pm Sat), on the western side of Lapangan Merdeka, is something of an oddity in Jakarta, being a museum that is genuinely worth visiting. There are excellent displays of pottery and ancient Hindu statuary, a huge ethnic map of Indonesia and an equally big relief map on which you can pick out all those volcanoes you have climbed. The museum also features some fascinating fossils (no, really) and examples of costumes and cultural life from across the archipelago.

The **Indonesian Heritage Society** (Map p166; ☎ 386 1551 ext 46; National Museum; ☒ tours Tue-Thu) conducts free tours of the museum.

TAMAN MINI INDONESIA INDAH

A kind of 'whole country in one park' attraction, **Taman Mini Indonesia Indah** (Map p164; ☎ 545 4545; www.jakweb.com/tmii; TMII Pintu 1; admission 6000Rp; ☒ 8am-5pm) is a short bus ride from the Kampung Rambutan bus station, southeast of the city centre (allow 1½ hours from the centre). Exhibits include traditional houses of the 26 provinces of Indonesia and a lagoon 'map' where you can row around the islands of Indonesia. On Sunday mornings there are free cultural performances.

TAMAN IMPIAN JAYA ANCOL

Taman Impian Jaya Ancol (Map p164; ☎ 640 6777; www.ancol.co.id; admission 10,000Rp; ☒ 10am-10pm) is on the waterfront between Kota and Tanjung Priok. This huge amusement complex has an oceanarium, a swimming pool complex, an Indonesian Disneyland and an art market. It also hosts the big gigs when the rock stars come to town.

The big drawcard for locals is **Dunia Fantasi** (Fantasy World; admission extra 50,000Rp; ☒ 11am-6pm Mon-Thu, 11am-8pm Fri-Sun), a mini version of Disneyland, but most visitors find the **Pasar Seni** (Art Market; admission free; ☒ 10am-10pm) of most interest.

To get there, take a train to Kota and then bus 64 or 65 (1500Rp). A taxi will cost around 25,000Rp from Jl Jaksa.

OTHER ATTRACTIONS

To the north of Lapangan Merdeka you can stroll past the gleaming white **Presidential Palace** (Map p166; Jl Medan Merdeka Utara) – beware of the jumpy armed guards. To the northeast is the vast **Mesjid Istiqlal** (Map p166; Jl Veteran 1; ☒ dawn-dusk), one of the grandest mosques in Southeast Asia.

Ragunan Zoo (Map p164; ☎ 780 5280; admission 3000Rp; ☒ 8am-6pm), in the Pasar Minggu district south of the city, has Komodo dragons and orang-utans in not-so-natural surrounds. Take bus 19 from Jl Thamrin. Outbreaks of bird flu have caused the authorities to sporadically close the zoo. While the risk to tourists remains minimal, call ahead to check the latest opening times.

Tours

Jl Jaksa travel agents and the Jakarta Visitor Information Centre (see p165) are the best places to book tours.

Gray Line (☎ 630 8105) offers a 24-hour booking line for pricier tours of destinations further afield, or contact the **Indonesian Heritage Society** (Map p166; ☎ 386 1551 ext 46; Jl Merdeka Barat), at the National Museum, for city tours (100,000Rp).

Festivals & Events

The **Jakarta Anniversary** on 22 June marks the establishment of the city by Gunungjati back in 1527, and is celebrated with fireworks and the **Jakarta Fair**. The latter is a fairground event held at the Jakarta Fair Grounds (Map

JALAN JAKSA AREA

0 ————— 200 m
0 ————— 0.1 miles

INFORMATION
24-Hour Tickets............................1 B4
Bank Mandiri.................................2 A4
BNI Bank.......................................3 C2
Duta Perdana Raya Travel.............4 C3
East Timor Embassy.......................5 A4
Jakarta Visitor Information Centre...6 A4
Robert Kencana Travel...................7 A4
Wartel & Warnet Bhumi Bhakti......8 A4

SLEEPING
Bintang Kejora..............................9 B3
Bloem Steen Homestay...............10 C3

Hotel Margot..............................11 C3
Hotel Tator.................................12 C3
Kresna Homestay.......................13 C3
Nick's Corner Hostel...................14 C3
Wisma Delima.............................15 C2
Yusran Hostel.............................16 C3

EATING
Ali K Baba..................................17 B4
Jasa Bundo................................18 C3
Memories Café...........................19 C3
Pappa Kafe.................................20 C4
Paprika......................................21 C4

Sabang Food Court.....................22 B3

DRINKING
Flanagan's..................................23 A3

SHOPPING
Sarinah Department Store............24 A4

TRANSPORT
British Airways............................25 A3
Continental..............................(see 25)
Qantas....................................(see 25)
Thai Airways International...........(see 25)

---

p164), northeast of the city centre in Kemayoran, from late June until mid-July.

The **Jl Jaksa Street Fair** features Betawi dance, theatre and music, as well as popular modern performances. It is held for one week in August.

Indonesia's **Independence Day** is 17 August and the parades in Jakarta are the biggest in the country.

If you are here in March, keep an eye out for the **Java Jazz Festival** (www.javajazzfestival.com).

Sleeping

JL JAKSA AREA   Map p169

This strip of cheap hotels and restaurants is the main budget accommodation area. It's conveniently located near Jakarta's main drag, Jl Thamrin, and is a 10- to 15-minute walk from Gambir train station. Falling tourist numbers have hit this area hard and standards are slipping – bargain hard!

Kresna Homestay (☎ 3192 5403; Gang I 175; d with shared/private mandi 35,000/50,000Rp) Dark, brooding and a little tumbledown, Kresna is barely big enough to swing a durian in, never mind a cat. 'Dark and brooding' roughly translates as cosy in this instance, however, and the friendly owner adds a little further warmth.

Bloem Steen Homestay (☎ 3192 5389; Gang I 173; s/d with shared mandi 20,000/35,000Rp) Another shoebox, right on Kresna's doorstep, Bloem Steen features no-frills rooms and the faintest whiff of fresh paint. The chatterbox owner is again a plus.

INDONESIA

> **SPLURGE!**
>
> **Hotel Margot** (Map p169; ☎ 391 3830; Jl Jaksa 15; d from 150,000Rp; ☒) A few rotations further up the price escalator, Margot's cleaners are a little heavy-handed with the mothballs. The rooms are spacious and spotless, however, the beds are broad and comfy and there's a lively backpackers bar out front.

Hotel Tator (☎ 3192 3941; Jl Jaksa 37; s/d from 75,000/85,000Rp; ☒) Cleanliness has a downside in this pleasant midranger – the rooms smell of disinfectant. That said, the standards here are about the highest on the block, there's a hip little café down below and the staff aren't strangers to a smile.

Yusran Hostel (☎ 314 0373; Jl Kebon Sirih Barat VI 9; d with shared/private mandi 35,000/50,000Rp) Down a little alleyway opposite the extraordinarily named Piss Salon, this Spartan number offers a few nasty whiffs (drains mostly) of its own. The staff are a bit surly, but it just about passes for the price.

Nick's Corner Hostel (☎ 310 7814; Jl Jaksa 16; dm 20,000Rp, d 50,000-70,000Rp; ☒) You half expect to run into the Minotaur in this underlit, labyrinthine spot. The downstairs rooms are prison-block chic at best, but the upstairs digs are better and brighter, with well-priced air-con in the most expensive.

Wisma Delima (☎ 3190 4157; Jl Jaksa 5; dm/s/d with shared mandi 20,000/30,000/40,000Rp) This has been here since 1969 and today has the ambience of a 19th-century spice clipper: it's hot, rickety and cramped. A minor face-lift has injected a flick of charm into the little eatery downstairs and the rooms are cheap, if a little dreary.

Bintang Kejora (☎ 3192 3878; Jl Kebon Sirih Barat I 52; d with shared/private mandi 40,000/50,000Rp) Trendy new hacienda styling makes this place look like a top choice – from the outside. Unfortunately, the rooms are rather glum by comparison.

CIKINI AREA   Map **p166**
The Cikini area is east of Jl Jaksa, and has a reasonable selection of good (but pricier) guesthouses.

Gondia International Guesthouse (☎ 390 9221; Jl Gondangdia Kecil 22; d 120,000Rp; ☒) Located down a quiet side street off Jl Soeroso, this pleasant spot is just like granny's house, with comfortable rooms, a homely ambience and a small garden area. It is also deathly quiet. Breakfast is included.

Yannie International Guesthouse (☎ 314 0012; Jl Raden Saleh Raya 35; s/d 105,000/120,000Rp; ☒) Cut from similar cloth, this also offers plenty of bang per buck, with well-kept rooms, attentive staff and a few welcome trimmings (like breakfast). There is no sign, just a 'Y' out front.

AIRPORT
Hotel Bandara Jakarta (☎ 619 1964; Jl Jurumudi, Cengkareng; s/d 170,000/190,000Rp; ☒) For a good night's sleep near the airport, this is one of the cheapest options. It doesn't drip style, but does offer free transfers to/from the airport, breakfast is included and the rooms are quiet and comfy if you're trying to face off a dose of jet lag.

Eating
JL JAKSA AREA   Map **p169**
Jl Jaksa's cafés are a little rough and ready, but are your best bet for hooking up with other backpackers. They serve the usual combination of Indonesian and Western food. The next street west of Jl Jaksa, Jl H Agus Salim (also known as Jl Sabang), has a string of cheap to midrange restaurants. Jl Sabang is famed for its satay and dozens of hawkers set up on the street come sundown.

At the southern end of Jl Jaksa, Jl Wahid Hasyim has a number of more expensive restaurants.

Memories Café (☎ 392 8839; Jl Jaksa 17; mains 20,000Rp; ⏰ 24hr; ▣) It's unlikely that memories are made of this (to plagiarise the song), but it is Jl Jaksa's blueprint backpacker café. There's hearty tucker, a bookshop, Internet café, plentiful shenanigans and the typically rickety bamboo décor we have come to know and love.

Jasa Bundo (☎ 390 5607; Jl Jaksa 20A; mains 10,000Rp; ⏰ breakfast, lunch & dinner) For something a little more authentic, this spick-and-span *masakan Padang* (Padang restaurant) cooks up all the old Sumatran favourites.

Pappa Kafe (☎ 3192 3452; Jl Jaksa 41; mains 20,000Rp; ⏰ 24hr) Pappa's looks like it could do with a night off the booze, but the frontier-style atmosphere still draws what crowds there are; the walls are covered in travellers'

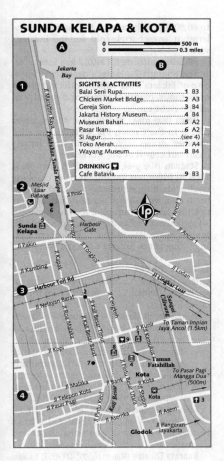

SUNDA KELAPA & KOTA

SIGHTS & ACTIVITIES	
Balai Seni Rupa	1 B3
Chicken Market Bridge	2 A3
Gereja Sion	3 B4
Jakarta History Museum	4 B4
Museum Bahari	5 A2
Pasar Ikan	6 A2
Si Jagur	(see 4)
Toko Merah	7 A4
Wayang Museum	8 B4

DRINKING	
Cafe Batavia	9 B3

SPLURGE!

Cafe Batavia (Map p171; ☎ 691 5531; Jl Pintu Besar Utara 14; mains 50,000Rp; ☮ 24hr; ☒) Ahhh…the good old days. Literally dripping with colonial-era charm and housed in an old Dutch villa in Kota, this is the kind of place that will get you talking like your grandad and consuming the strong stuff like a muscle car at a drag race. The bistro-style food is a triumph of form over content, and a little overpriced, but it looks great and the atmosphere is well worth writing home about.

original purveyors of chic eats – it even starred in the film *Arisan* – this swish spot features topnotch fusion cuisine, stylish décor, immaculately polished glassware and slick service – a real treat.

OTHER AREAS

The expat suburb of Kemang is a good place to head for a range of quality bars and restaurants. The main drag, Jl Kemang Raya, is about 8km south of Jl Jaksa – 20,000Rp in a taxi. There are dozens of places to eat, so just stroll along the road and take your pick.

Taman Ria Senayan (Map p164; Jl Jenderal Gatot Subroto; ☮ breakfast, lunch & dinner) This popular complex has a great selection of stylish restaurants overlooking the lagoon. Wander around to see what takes your fancy – Thai, Balinese, Italian, grills; there's a bit of everything.

Kinara (☎ 719 2677; Kinara Bldg, Jl Kemang Raya 78B; mains 30,000Rp; ☮ lunch & dinner; ☒) As cool as the curries are hot, this is one of Jakarta's most sought-after Indian restaurants. It's the ideal spot to watch the beautiful set sweat into their prawn vindaloo.

Izzi Pizza (Map p164; ☎ 719 2020; Jl Kemang Raya 93A; mains 30,000Rp; ☮ lunch & dinner; ☒) Peddling the kind of pizza that could get Mamma upping sticks and reaching for her passport, getting hooked on Izzi Pizza is, quite literally, easy peasy.

Street food can be picked up at the **night warung** (Map p166; Jl Pecenongan), about 1km north of the National Monument.

Drinking

Jakarta is the most sophisticated, broad-minded and decadent city in Indonesia, with nightlife to match. Bands start around 10pm

scribblings, there's MTV and the food (pancakes, *nasi goreng*, steaks) just about passes the taste test.

Sabang Food Court (☎ 316 0821; Jl H Agus Salim 49; mains 12,000Rp; ☮ lunch & dinner) A big hit with local diners, this basic place is something of a one-stop shop, with all of Indonesia's regional cuisines represented on the menu. There's no sign, so look out for the crowds and the hanging banners.

Ali K Baba (☎ 3193 8147; Jl H Agus Salim 57; mains 25,000Rp; ☮ lunch & dinner; ☒) Arabic music, hubbly-bubbly pipes and Lebanese eats rule the roost at this reliable Middle Eastern outfit.

Paprika (☎ 314 4113; Jl Wahid Hasyim; mains 40,000Rp; ☮ lunch & dinner; ☒) One of Jakarta's

INDONESIA

or 11pm, and continue until 2am or 3am, sometimes later on the weekends, though during the week many places close at 1am.

Most of Jl Jaksa's restaurants take on a lively bar atmosphere about 9pm, but to really get a taste of after-hours Jakarta, you will have to head further afield. Be warned, however, Jakarta's biggest bars are anything but cheap.

Subscribe to the nightlife newsletter at www.bartele.com for the insider's view.

Bugils (Map p164; ☎ 574 7650; Taman Ria Senayan, Jl Jenderal Gatot Subroto; ☽ 11am-late) Given that its name comes from *bule gila*, the Bahasa for 'crazy Westerner', it will come as no surprise that things can really get rolling at this expat favourite. It features pub styling (with a Dutch twist), lashings of continental beer, chips with mayonnaise and plenty of knees-up-Mother-Brown action.

Dragonfly (Map p164; ☎ 520 6789; www.the-dragon fly.com; Graha BIP, Jl Gatot Subroto Kav 23; ☽ noon-late) The name on the tip of everyone's tongue at the moment, Dragonfly is the best thing since draught-beer-and-Bombay mix as far as Jakarta's bar-goers are concerned. It's pricey, but this trendy bar-restaurant serves magic cocktails, delicious Indochinese food and some seriously good looks.

Sportsman's Bar (Map p164; ☎ 720 4731; Jl Palatehani 6-8, Blok M, Kebayoran Baru; ☽ noon-late) Blok M is famed for its raucous – and notoriously decadent – 'girlie bars'. Sportsman's is not one for the faint-hearted and the paying clientele are 98% male, but it remains a Jakarta institution and is well worth a peep. It also shows big-screen sports.

Hotel bars are among Jakarta's most popular hang-outs and fill to bursting at weekends. Current stars:

Burgundy (Map p166; ☎ 390 1234; Jl Thamrin Kav 28-30; ☽ noon-late) Undoubtedly one of Jakarta's swankiest bars, in the Grand Hyatt.

CJ's Bar (Map p164; ☎ 574 7777; Jl Asia Afrika; ☽ noon-late) Wednesday-night favourite, in the Hotel Mulia Senayan.

Flanagans (Map p169; ☎ 323 707; Jl Thamrin; ☽ noon-late) 'Jakarta's finest Irish bar', in the Sari Pan Pacific Hotel.

Clubbing

Jakarta has some sophisticated clubs; many are in the city's five-star hotels. They open around 9pm, but don't really get going until midnight. On weekends they are open to 4am or later. Cover charges range from 25,000Rp

to 60,000Rp. Subscribe to the nightlife newsletter at www.bartele.com for the insider's view.

BATS (Map p166; ☎ 574 8400; Jl Jend Sudirman Kav 1) The Shangri-La Hotel's basement club is one of Jakarta's big-hitters, offering plenty of glamour, plenty of bump-and-grind, and all the right tunes.

Retro (Map p164; ☎ 5296 2828; Jl Gatot Subroto Kav 2-3) In the Crown Plaza Hotel, this slick number draws a young, hip and largely clean-cut crowd at the weekends.

Stadium (Map p164; ☎ 626 3323; Jl Hayum Waruk 111 FF-JJ) Infamous among Jakartan clubbing circles, Stadium represents the 'dark side' of the scene, with drugs, sex and dark corners aplenty. Expect thumping techno, banshee-style dancing and an anything-goes attitude. It stays open all weekend, but take care leaving – this is not Jakarta's safest area.

Entertainment

Check the entertainment pages of the *Jakarta Post*, *Djakarta!* or *Jakarta Kini* for the latest listings.

Taman Ismail Marzuki (TIM; Map p166; ☎ 3193 7325; tamanismailmarzuki@yahoo.com; Jl Cikini Raya 73) Not far from Jl Jaksa, Jakarta's cultural showcase stages everything from Balinese dance to poetry readings. The monthly programme is available from the Jakarta Visitor Information Centre (p165). Events are also listed in the *Jakarta Post*. Prices start at 30,000Rp.

Gedung Kesenian Jakarta (Map p166; ☎ 380 8283; Jl Gedung Kesenian 1) This theatre also has a regular programme of traditional dance and drama, as well as European classical music.

Bharata Theatre (Map p166; ☎ 421 4937; Jl Kalilio 15) Located in Pasar Senen, this stages traditional arts performances.

Wayang kulit and *wayang golek* are occasionally staged at the city's museums – check with the **Indonesian Heritage Society** (Map p166; ☎ 386 1551 ext 46). The various cultural centres, particularly **Erasmus Huis** (☎ 524 1069; www .erasmushuis.or.id; Jl Rasuna Said Kav S-3), which lists its events on its website, also hold regular events.

Shopping

Shopping is a Jakartan speciality. Brandname goods are in profusion and there are handicrafts from across Indonesia. Jakarta also has plenty of shopping centres and markets to explore.

Plaza Indonesia (Map p166; cnr Jl Thamrin & Jl Kebon Kacang Raya; ⊗ 9am-9pm) One of the city's most central shopping malls; it makes a useful landmark.

Sarinah (Map p169; Jl Thamrin; ⊗ 10am-10pm) The 3rd floor of this large department store is devoted to batik and Indonesian handicrafts.

Pasaraya (Map p164; Jl Iskandarsyah II/2; ⊗ 9am-7pm) Housed in Blok M (see opposite), this is in the same vein as Sarinah, but even bigger. Handicrafts can be found on the 4th floor.

Pasar Pagi Mangga Dua (Map p164; Jl Mangga Dua; ⊗ 9am-7pm) This is a huge wholesale market with some of the cheapest clothes, accessories and shoes. Across the road is the Mangga Dua Mall for computers and electronics.

Plaza Senayan (Map p164; Jl Asia Afrika; ⊗ 9am-9pm) Southwest of Jl Jaksa, this is one of Jakarta's glossiest malls, with most of the designer label stores represented.

For arts and crafts, also check out **Pasar Seni** (Art Market; Jl Raya Kampung Bandan; ⊗ 10am-10pm), at Taman Impian Jaya Ancol (see p168), and Jakarta's famous **flea market** (Map p166; Jl Surabaya).

Getting There & Away
Jakarta is the main travel hub for Indonesia, with ships and flights to destinations all over the archipelago. Buses depart for destinations throughout Java and for Bali and Sumatra. Trains are a convenient alternative for many destinations in Java.

AIR
Most flights go from Soekarno-Hatta International Airport, 35km northwest of the city. The departure tax is 100,000Rp on international flights and 20,000Rp on domestic flights, and is payable at check-in.

Domestic airlines serving Jakarta:
Bouraq Airlines (☎ 659 5194; www.bouraq.net; Jl Angkasa 1-3 Kemayoran)
Garuda (Map p166; 24-hr booking line ☎ 0807-1-427832; www.garuda-indonesia.com; Garuda Bldg, Jl Merdeka Selatan 13)
Mandala (☎ 424 6100; www.mandalaair.com; Jl Garuda 76)
Merpati (☎ 654 6789; www.merpati.co.id; Jl Angkasa Blok B/15 Kav 2/3, Kemayoran)

Flying within Indonesia, sample one-way fares include Denpasar (256,000Rp), Surabaya (308,000Rp), Yogyakarta (265,000Rp), Medan (350,000Rp), Makassar (360,000Rp),

Kota Ambon (675,000Rp) and Jayapura (1,500,000Rp). The cheapest fares are subject to early booking and availability and you can expect to pay as much as twice the quoted fares above if you book on the day of travel. See also the air fares chart, p157.

For international flights, the travel agencies on Jl Jaksa are a good place to start looking. International airlines serving Jakarta:
Air Asia (www.airasia.com) The region's budget, web-based airline.
British Airways (Map p169; ☎ 230 0277; www.ba.com; 11th fl, BDN Bldg, Jl Thamrin 5)
Continental (Map p169; ☎ 3193 4417; www.continental.com; Ground fl, BDN Bldg, Jl Thamrin 5)
Malaysia Airlines (Map p164; ☎ 522 9685; www.malaysiaairlines.com; Ground fl, World Trade Center, Jl Jend Sudirman Kav 29-31)
Qantas (Map p169; ☎ 230 0655; www.qantas.com; 11th fl, BDN Bldg, Jl Thamrin 5)
Singapore Airlines (Map p164; ☎ 5790 3747; www.singaporeairlines.com; 8th fl, Menara Kadin Indonesia, Jl HR Kasuna Said, Blok X15 2-3)
Thai Airways International (THAI; Map p169; ☎ 230 2552; www.thaiairways.com; Ground fl, BDN Bldg, Jl Thamrin 5)

BOAT
The **Pelni ticket office** (Map p164; ☎ 421 2893; www.pelni.co.id; Jl Angkasa 18; ⊗ 8am-3pm Mon-Fri, 8am-noon Sat) is 13km northeast of the city centre in Kemayoran. Tickets plus commission can also be bought through designated Pelni agents such as **Menara Buana Surya** (Map p166; ☎ 314 2464; Jl Menteng Raya 29; ⊗ 9am-5pm Mon-Fri, 9am-2pm Sat), in the Tedja Buana building, 500m east of Jl Jaksa. Schedules and prices for all Pelni ferries can also be found on its website; sample fares can be found on the Pelni Shipping Ports & Major Routes map (p159).

Pelni ships all arrive at and depart from Pelabuhan Satu (Dock 1) at Tanjung Priok (Map p164), 13km northeast of the city centre. Take bus p125 from Jl Thamrin, opposite Sarinah department store (1500Rp); allow at least an hour. The bus terminal is at the old Tanjung Priok train station from where it is a 1km walk to the dock, or 2500Rp by *ojek*. A taxi to/from Jl Jaksa will cost around 25,000Rp.

BUS
So many buses leave Jakarta's bus stations that you can usually just front up at the station and join the chaos, though it pays to

book. Travel agencies on Jl Jaksa sell tickets and usually include transport to the terminal. Their prices are a lot higher but save a lot of hassle. Jakarta has four main bus stations, all well out of the city centre.

Kalideres (☎ 541 4996) is 15km northwest of the city centre and has frequent buses to destinations west of Jakarta, such as Merak (14,000Rp, three hours).

Kampung Rambutan (Map p164; ☎ 840 0062) is 18km south of the city and primarily handles buses to destinations south and southeast of Jakarta, such as Bogor (10,000Rp, one hour) and Bandung (30,000Rp, four hours). The trains to Bogor and Bandung are a better alternative.

Pulo Gadung (Map p164; ☎ 489 3742) is 12km east of the city centre and has buses to central and eastern Java, Sumatra and Bali. Most buses to Sumatra leave between 10am and 3pm and include Palembang (125,000Rp, 12 hours) and Bukittinggi (150,000Rp, 24 hours). Headed east, they go to Yogyakarta (80,000Rp, 12 hours), Surabaya (110,000Rp, 18 hours) and Denpasar (240,000Rp, 26 hours).

Lebak Bulus (Map p164) is 16km south of the city and also handles deluxe buses to Yogyakarta, Surabaya and Bali. Most departures are in the late afternoon or evening.

MINIBUS

Door-to-door *travel* minibuses are quick once you leave Jakarta, but can take hours to pick up or drop off passengers in the traffic jams. Jl Jaksa travel agencies, like **Robert Kencana Travel** (Map p169; ☎ 314 2926; Jl Jaksa 20B; ☉ 24hr) can book direct minibuses to Bandung (60,000Rp, three hours), Pangandaran (125,000Rp, 10 hours), Yogyakarta (120,000Rp, 12 hours) and Denpasar (260,000Rp, 24 hours).

TRAIN

Jakarta's four main train stations are quite central, making the trains the easiest way out of the city into Java. The most convenient and important is **Gambir** (☎ 386 2361), on the eastern side of Lapangan Merdeka, a 15-minute walk from Jl Jaksa. Gambir handles express trains to Bogor, Bandung, Yogyakarta, Solo, Semarang and Surabaya. Some Gambir trains also stop at **Kota** (☎ 692 9083), the train station in the old city area in the north. **Pasar Senen** (☎ 421 0164), to the

east, has mostly *ekonomi* trains to eastern destinations. **Tanah Abang** (☎ 314 9872) has trains west to Merak.

Smaller, but useful if you are staying in Jl Jaksa is **Gondangdia**, 500m east of most of the area's guesthouses. From here, there are trains to Bogor and Kota.

For long hauls, the express trains (*bisnis* and *eksekutif*) are far preferable to the *ekonomi* trains and can be booked in advance at the air-con booking offices at the northern end of Gambir train station.

From Gambir, taxis cost a minimum of 15,000Rp from the taxi booking desk. A cheaper alternative is to go out the front to the main road and hail down a *bajaj*, which will cost 7000Rp to Jl Jaksa after bargaining.

For train times and prices, visit www.infoka.kereta-api.com.

Bandung

Parahyangan departs Gambir for Bandung (*bisnis/eksekutif* 40,000/60,000Rp, three hours) every hour or so from 6.30am to 8.30pm. *Eksekutif Argo Gede* (70,000Rp, 2½ hours) leaves Gambir roughly every two hours from 6.35am to 7.20pm.

Bogor

Ekonomi trains to Bogor (3000Rp, 1½ hours) leave Gambir and Gondangdia every 20 minutes or so from 5am to 7pm. Much better express trains leave Gambir hourly from 6.30am to 6pm (*bisnis* 8000Rp, one hour).

Surabaya

Express trains include the *Bima* (*eksekutif* weekday/weekend 180,000/200,000Rp, 13 hours) which departs from Gambir at 6pm, and the luxurious *Argo Bromo Anggrek* (*eksekutif* day/night 200,000/220,000Rp, nine hours), which departs from Gambir at 9.10am and 9.10pm. The *Gumarang* departs Gambir at 6.10pm (*bisnis/eksekutif* 100,000/180,000Rp, 12 hours).

The cheapest train service taking the north-coast route is the *ekonomi Kertajaya* (47,000Rp, 13 hours), which leaves Pasar Senen at 4.45pm.

Yogyakarta & Solo

The most luxurious trains include the *Argo Lawu* (*eksekutif* weekdays/weekends 180,000/200,000Rp, seven hours), which departs from Gambir at 7.50pm, the *Argo*

Dwipangga (*eksekutif* weekdays/weekends 180,000/200,000Rp, seven hours) departing at 8am and the *Bima* (*eksekutif* weekdays/weekends 180,000/200,000Rp, 6¼ hours) departing at 6pm. These trains go to Solo and stop at Yogyakarta, 45 minutes before Solo, but cost the same to either destination.

Cheaper express services to Yogyakarta are the *Fajar Utama Yogya* (*bisnis* 64,000Rp, eight hours) departing from Pasar Senen at 6am and the *Senja Utama Yogya* (*bisnis* 64,000Rp, eight hours) departing Pasar Senen at 8.25pm. The *Senja Utama Solo* goes to Solo (*bisnis* 64,000Rp, 9½ hours) from Pasar Senen at 7.45pm and also stops in Yogyakarta.

The *ekonomi Gayabarumalam* (30,000Rp, 10 hours) starts the run to Solo from Kota at 11.35am.

Getting Around

BUS

Jakarta has a large network of city buses. Ordinary buses cost 1000Rp, express *patas* buses cost 1500Rp and air-con *patas* buses cost 3300Rp. The more expensive buses are generally safer and more comfortable.

Mikrolet and other minibuses also operate in some areas (500Rp to 1500Rp).

The **Jakarta Visitor Information Centre** (Map p169; ☎ 315 4094; www.jakarta.go.id; Jakarta Theatre Bldg, Jl Wahid Hasyim 9; ◷ 9am-5pm Mon-Fri, 9am-1pm Sat) has information on bus routes around Jakarta.

LOCAL TRANSPORT

Bajaj are three-wheelers that carry two passengers (three at a squeeze) and are powered by noisy two-stroke engines. A short ride of a couple of kilometres (such as Gambir train station to Jl Jaksa) will cost 7000Rp, but *bajaj* are not allowed along Jl Thamrin.

TAXI

Metered taxis cost 3000Rp for the first kilometre and 150Rp for each subsequent 100m. Make sure the meter is used.

Bluebird cabs (☎ 794 1234; www.bluebirdgroup .com) are pale blue, can be booked ahead and have the best reputation; do *not* risk travelling with the less reputable firms.

Typical taxi fares from Jl Thamrin: to Kota (15,000Rp), Sunda Kelapa (18,000Rp), Pulo Gadung (20,000Rp), and Kampung Rambutan or Taman Mini (25,000Rp). Any

toll road charges are extra and are paid by the passengers.

It is worth knowing that *argo* means 'meter' and that a *pangkalan* is a 'taxi rank'.

BOGOR

☎ 0251 / pop 715,000

Green, mild and reliably rainy, Bogor shot to notoriety during the British interregnum of Sir Stamford Raffles, offering cool respite for those mad dogs and Englishmen that preferred *not* to go out in the midday sun. These days, this once quiet town is practically a suburb of Jakarta, with the traffic and hubbub to match. But while Bogor itself clogs up with *bemo* and mopeds, the real oasis remains untouched. Planted at the very hub of the city, with *macet* to north, south, east and west, the town's botanical gardens remain – in the words of one upstanding British visitor – 'a jolly fine day out'.

Information

There are *wartel* (telecommunications stalls) across town, and Bogor has plenty of banks, many with ATMs.

BCA (Jl Ir H Juanda 28) Changes money.
Hotel Salak (☎ 340400; Jl Ir H Juanda 8; per hr 10,000Rp; ◷ 8am-9pm) Offers Internet access.
Post office (Jl Ir H Juanda; ◷ 8am-5pm Mon-Fri, 8am-noon Sat)
Tourist office (☎ 642146; Jl Kapten Muslihat; ◷ 8am-5pm) On the western side of the botanical gardens.

Sights

Stealing centre stage are Bogor's botanical gardens, the **Kebun Raya** (www.bogor.indo.net.id /kri; Jl Otto Iskandardinata; admission 5500Rp; ◷ 8am-5pm). It is claimed they are the brainchild of British governor Sir Stamford Raffles, but it was Dutch botanist Professor Reinwardt who did most of the digging, converting the grounds of the Istana Bogor into the gardens that exist today with the help of assistants from London's Kew Gardens. Things can get hectic at weekends, but during the week this is one of West Java's true oases.

The **Istana Bogor** (Presidential Palace), built by the Dutch and much favoured by Soekarno (Soeharto ignored it), stands beside the gardens, and deer graze on its lawns. Visits are by organised tour only – the tourist office may be able to squeeze you into one.

Near the garden entrance, the **Zoological Museum** (Jl Otto Iskandardinata; admission 2000Rp;

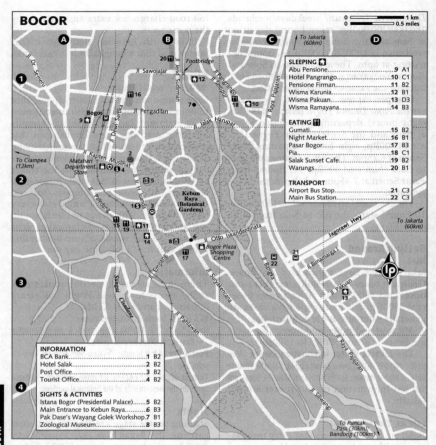

BOGOR

SLEEPING		
Abu Pensione	9	A1
Hotel Pangrango	10	C1
Pensione Firman	11	B2
Wisma Karunia	12	B1
Wisma Pakuan	13	D3
Wisma Ramayana	14	B3

EATING		
Gumati	15	B2
Night Market	16	B1
Pasar Bogor	17	B3
Pia	18	C1
Salak Sunset Cafe	19	B2
Warungs	20	B1

TRANSPORT		
Airport Bus Stop	21	C3
Main Bus Station	22	C3

INFORMATION		
BCA Bank	1	B2
Hotel Salak	2	B2
Post Office	3	B2
Tourist Office	4	B2

SIGHTS & ACTIVITIES		
Istana Bogor (Presidential Palace)	5	B2
Main Entrance to Kebun Raya	6	B3
Pak Dase's Wayang Golek Workshop	7	B1
Zoological Museum	8	B3

8am-4pm Sat-Thu, 8am-noon Fri) has an 'interesting' collection of stuffed animals. Exhibits include a blue whale skeleton, a stuffed Javan rhino and Indonesian rats from Flores. If you have ever heard about the island of Flores having a rat problem, one glance at the showcase will explain why.

If you are interested in seeing a Javanese craftsman at work, Pak Dase makes quality wooden puppets at his **wayang golek workshop** (Lebak Kantion RT 02/VI; 🕑 8am-6pm) among the labyrinthine passages on the west side of the river near Jl Jend Sudirman.

Sleeping

Bogor has some good family-run places; most offer a basic breakfast.

Pensione Firman (☎ 323246; Jl Paledang 48; d with shared/private mandi 40,000/50,000Rp) The décor's a little flaky, but the owner works for the tourist office – helpful if you want the Bogor lowdown – and the rooms are well priced. If one of Bogor's regular thunderstorms is raging, you can also eat here.

Wisma Ramayana (☎ 320364; Jl Ir H Juanda 54; d 65,000Rp) A whiff of Raffles' day remains at this old-school outfit. It is a big hit with Indonesian tourists, so book ahead if you want to lay your head down in one of the spacious rooms.

Abu Pensione (☎ 322893; Jl Mayor Oking 15; d with shared/private mandi 60,000/120,000Rp; 🔀) A hop and a skip from the train station, this scoops top marks for friendliness and help-

> **SPLURGE!**
>
> **Wisma Pakuan** (☎ 319430; Jl Pakuan 12; d from 110,000Rp; 🌀) Bogor's glitziest homestay is well worth the long tramp south from the train station. Prodigal son/daughter welcomes are a standard, the rooms are immaculate and the peaceful ambience should suit anyone here to soak up the hush of the Kebun Raya. Take an *angkot* 6 from the tourist office.

fulness, but slips up on the rooms, which are a little overpriced for the standards on offer. The more expensive rooms do come with air-con though.

Other recommendations:

Hotel Pangrango (☎ 328284; Jl Pangrango 21; d from 110,000Rp; 🌀) Mock-Tudor midranger with a few 'economy rooms'.

Wisma Karunia (☎ 323411; Jl Sempur 33-5; d with shared/private mandi 35,000/45,000Rp) Quiet and homely.

Eating

Salak Sunset Café (☎ 329765; Jl Paledang 38; mains 20,000Rp; 🕒 breakfast, lunch & dinner) Overlooking the river, this pretty spot offers an airy ambience, a decent range of Indonesian and Western fare and a side order of French flair, which drifts in from the adjoining Alliance Française.

Pia (☎ 324169; Jl Pangrango 10; pies 12,000Rp; 🕒 lunch & dinner) Pies may be something of an oddity in Indonesia, but if this little spot is anything to go by, they won't be for long. As well as baking up a mean range of meat pastries, they also specialise in a range of apple-based dishes: apple salad, apple ice cream and even apple-sauce spaghetti.

Gumati (Jl Paledang 28; mains 20,000Rp; 🕒 lunch & dinner) With a colossal open balcony, the views top the menu at this attractive wood and wicker eatery. Using bags of fresh ingredients – check out the chillies on view up front – this is a great spot for feisty Indonesian cooking and Western-style snacks.

Cheap *warung* (food stalls) appear at night along Jl Dewi Sartika and Jl Jend Sudirman and during the day you'll find plenty of *warung* and good fruit at Pasar Bogor, the market close to the main Kebun Raya gates.

Getting There & Away

BUS

Buses to Jakarta depart frequently from the main bus terminal (normal/air-con 7000/10,000Rp). Most go to the Kampung Rambutan station – a little over half an hour via the Jagorawi Hwy toll road, but double that time from Kampung Rambutan to central Jakarta. Some services also go directly to Jakarta's Pulo Gadung bus station and Tanjung Priok harbour.

There are also regular buses to Bandung (normal/air-con 15,000/25,000Rp, 3½ hours) and Pelabuhanratu (normal/air-con 12,000/20,000Rp, 2½ hours). On weekends, buses are not allowed to go via the scenic Puncak Pass (see below) and have to travel via Sukabumi (normal/air-con 20,000/30,000Rp, four hours). **Rama Travel** (☎ 653672) offers air-con, door-to-door minibuses to Bandung (50,000Rp, 3½ hours) and Yogyakarta (125,000Rp, 11 hours), and will collect you from your hotel.

Damri buses head direct to Jakarta's Soekarno-Hatta airport (15,000Rp, 1½ hours) hourly from 4am to 6pm. They leave from Jl Bimamarga 1, near the end of the Jagorawi Hwy toll road.

TRAIN

Trains are the best way to reach Jakarta. Frequent *ekonomi* trains leave for Gambir or Gondangdia (near Jl Jaksa) roughly every 20 minutes until 7pm (3000Rp, 1½ hours). Better *Pakuan* express services to Gambir (8000Rp, one hour) leave less frequently until 6pm.

Getting Around

Angkot (1200Rp) make slow circuits of the gardens, taking in most central locations en route.

PUNCAK PASS

Cool and photogenic, the high **Puncak Pass** between Bogor and Bandung is one of Jakarta's great escapes. While weekenders will find themselves twiddling thumbs in the area's notorious holiday traffic jams, things are quieter during the week when you can easily tramp off into the region's lush hills and tea plantations.

Cibodas is just over the Puncak Pass and is 4km off the main road. It is quieter than **Cisarua**, the other main resort town, and is

INDONESIA

home to the beautiful **Kebun Raya Cibodas** (☎ 0263-512233; admission 4000Rp; 🕑 8am-5pm), which was founded in 1862 for the study of mountain flora, and is a lush, high-altitude extension of Bogor's Kebun Raya.

From April to January, you can also climb **Gunung Gede**, a spectacular 2958m volcanic peak. The PHPA office, opposite the entrance to the gardens in Cibodas, issues permits (5000Rp) and has pamphlets on the national park. The walk from Cibodas takes all day, so start early (usually around 2am) to reach the summit by dawn. PHPA guides to the summit can be hired here for 250,000Rp.

Taman Safari Indonesia (☎ 0251-250000; www.tamansafari.com; Jl Raya Puncak 601, Cisarua; admission 45,000Rp; 🕑 9am-5pm), just east of Cisarua, is a drive-in 'safari park' and rather more pleasant than most Third-World zoos.

The **Gunung Mas Tea Plantation** (☎ 0251-252501; factory tour 5000Rp; 🕑 8am-4pm) is one of Java's oldest plantations and is easily reached by *angkot* (1500Rp) from Cisarua. You can wander through the contoured plantation and watch the pickers in action for free, or tour the factory.

Sleeping & Eating

Accommodation tends to be expensive, though budget places can be found in Cisarua on the Bogor side of the pass, or Cibodas and Cipanas across the pass.

Freddy's Homestay (☎ 0263-515473; Jl Raya Cibodas, Cibodas; d with shared mandi 50,000Rp) The English-speaking owner at this modest bolthole, down a narrow alleyway 500m before the gardens, is one of the best sources of information on the area. The rooms are modest to say the least, but are in keeping with the region's rustic atmosphere.

SPLURGE!

Wisma Tamu (☎ 0263-512233; d 250,000Rp) How often do you get to sleep inside one of the world's prettiest botanical gardens? If the answer is never, here's your chance, in Cibodas. With rooms in a rickety colonial-era villa, Wisma Tamu is the pass's most atmospheric offering, even if it is a little rundown. Come nightfall, you'll only have the bats for company, but this really is class on a budget. Book well ahead.

Bali Ubud (☎ 0263-512051; Jl Raya Cibodas, Cibodas; d 100,000Rp) If Dr Doolittle had a West Javan holiday home, it would look a little like this. Featuring a forest of thick greenery and more pet animals than Taman Safari has wild ones, it's quirky, pretty and fun. Bargain hard though, as the spotty rooms are overpriced.

Kopo Hostel (☎ 0251-254296; Jl Raya Puncak 557; d 35,000Rp) Cisarua's resident cheapie is desperately dowdy, but is the best bet on a budget if you want to sleep this side of the pass.

There's cheap food at the *warung* near the gardens and in the restaurants that line the main road in Cisarua.

Getting There & Away

From Jakarta's Kampung Rambutan bus terminal (20,000Rp, 2½ hours) any Bandung bus (15,000Rp, two hours) can drop you off at the resort towns on the highway (but not on weekends when they aren't allowed to cross the pass). From Bogor (10,000Rp, 1½ hours), frequent buses and *colt* (which travel on Sunday) also ply the highway.

BANDUNG

☎ 022 / pop 2.2 million

Big, burly Bandung comes like a rush of blood to the head after the bottle-green hills of the Puncak Pass. The city has shed the effete charm that once encouraged whimsical travel writers to dub it the 'Paris of the East' and the streets now teem with all the trappings of modern living. But in Bandung, the devil is in the detail, and if you have a good rummage through the concrete sprawl, you will soon be scribbling in your scrapbook. From the city's grand Art Deco buildings to the quirky, fibreglass statues of Jeans Street, from its Sunday morning ram fights to its Sundanese culture, Indonesia's fourth-largest city has a personality to match even the puffing volcanoes that surround it.

Orientation

Bandung's airport is 4km northwest of the city centre, and costs about 30,000Rp by taxi. Regular *angkot* (1500Rp) link the airport and the centre of town.

The city centre runs along Jl Asia Afrika and around the *alun alun* (city square). Most of the budget accommodation is conveniently located around Jl Kebonjati, just south of the train station, while Jl Braga is the place to head for late-night shenanigans.

Information

Bandung Tourist Information Centre (☎ 421 6648; ☼ 8am-5.30pm) At the train station, this office is extremely helpful. There is a second **branch** (☎ 420 6644; Jl Asia Afrika; ☼ 9am -5pm Mon-Sat) on the *alun alun*, but it is often unstaffed.

Bank Mandiri (Jl Merdeka) Has an ATM and exchange facilities. There are other banks with ATMs across town.

Cybernet (☎ 601 4802; Jl Gardujati; per hr 5000Rp; ☼ 1-8pm Mon-Sat) Has Internet access.

Main post office (cnr Jl Banceuy & Jl Asia Afrika; ☼ 8am-7pm Mon-Sat) Opposite the *alun alun*.

RS Boremeus Hospital (☎ 250 4041; Jl Juanda; ☼ 24hr)

Wartel (Jl Kebonjati; ☼ 9am-8pm) International phone calls can be made here.

Sights & Activities

JEANS STREET

Jl Cihampelas, in the north of the city, is to budget denim manufacture what McDonald's is to the hamburger – well, nearly. Lined with jeans stores, which attract their customers with gigantic statues – Superman, Rambo and Aladdin are all here – it is certainly one of Java's most colourful and idiosyncratic streets. And the clothes are cheap, too.

ADU DOMBA

One of Bandung's most popular pastimes is whiling away a Sunday morning watching a traditional adu domba (ram-butting fight). Fights are held between 9am and 1pm and entry is by donation. Check with the Bandung Tourist Information Centre for the latest schedules. At the time of writing, fights were held at Babakan Siliwangi on the first Sunday of the month, Gergerkalong on the second, Moh Toha on the third and Lapangan Arcamanik on the fourth.

MUSEUMS

In 1955, Soekarno, Zhou Enlai, Ho Chi Minh, Nasser and other Third World figureheads congregated in Bandung for the Asia-Africa conference – a second summit was held here in 2005. You can read all about it at the **Museum Konperensi** (Conference Museum) in the **Gedung Merdeka** (Freedom Bldg; ☎ 423 8031; Jl Asia Afrika 65; admission free; ☼ 8am-noon & 1-2pm Mon-Fri).

Given that you are surrounded by volcanoes, you can swot up on your geology homework at Bandung's **Museum Geologi** (Geological Museum; ☎ 720 3205; Jl Diponegoro 57; admission 2000Rp; ☼ 9am-3.30pm Mon-Thu, 9am-1.30pm Sat & Sun). As well as plenty of volcano exhibits, you will be treated to a model skull of Java man.

OTHER ATTRACTIONS

Bandung is noted for its fine Dutch Art Deco architecture. The **Savoy Homann Hotel** (Jl Asia Afrika 112) is worth a look (see the boxed text, below). Also take a peek at the magnificent **Gedung Sate** (Jl Diponegoro), the regional government building, so-called because it's topped by what looks like a satay stick.

Further north, Bandung's **Institute of Technology** (ITB; Jl Ganeca) is one of the most important universities in Indonesia and also has some fine examples of Indo-European architecture. Nearby, **Bandung Zoo** (☎ 250 7032; Jl Taman Sari; admission 5000Rp; ☼ 8am-4pm) is good for a stroll.

Sleeping

Bandung's budget hotels are rather run-down, but Jl Kebonjati, near the train station, is the best place to start looking.

Hotel Surabaya (☎ 436791; Jl Kebonjati 71; d with shared/private mandi 40,000/60,000Rp) With a lick of paint and a good dusting, this could be one of Bandung's most atmospheric hotels – at any price. As it is, it looks rather as though Hotel Surabaya has slipped through a time machine with a rubbish dump and been combined with it in the process. Photographs and knick-knacks hark back to better days, the owner is helpful and friendly, the building is fabulous, but the rooms look like they could collapse at any moment.

Hotel King Garden (☎ 607 3190; Jl Gardujati 81; d from 96,000Rp; ▨) Just around the corner from

---

SPLURGE!

Savoy Homann Hotel (☎ 423 2244; www.savoyhomann-hotel.com; Jl Asia Afrika 112; s/d 475,000/500,000Rp; ▨ ▢ ▨) While you are here, it's worth taking the opportunity to sleep in one of Bandung's monuments to Art Deco. It takes a little imagination to get the feel of the place in its heyday, but this is a good price for a five-star bed and you'll be dozing off in a little piece of history.

INDONESIA

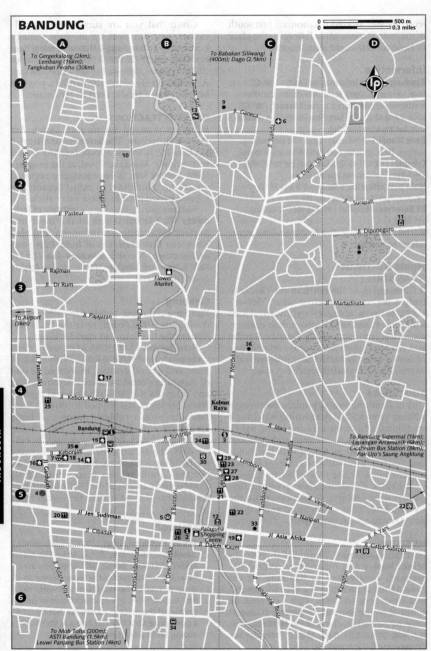

BANDUNG

0 — 500 m
0 — 0.3 miles

To Gergekalong (2km);
Lembang (16km);
Tangkuban Perahu (30km)

To Babakan Siliwangi
(400m); Dago (2.5km)

Jl Taman Sari

Jl Sikajadi

Jl Cipagani

Jl Pasteur

Jl Rajiman

Jl Dr Rum

Jl Pajajaran

Jl Cihampelas

Flower
Market

Jl Ganeca

Jl Ivanda

Jl Dipati Ukur

Jl Surapati

Jl Diponegoro

Jl Martadinata

To Airport
(3km)

Jl Pasirkaliki

Jl Kebon Kawong

Jl Merdeka

Kebun
Raya

Bandung

Jl Sunaraja

Jl Jawa

To Bandung Supermal (1km);
Lapangan Arcamanik (6km);
Cicaheum Bus Station (8km);
Pak Ujo's Saung Angklung

Jl Kebonjati

Jl Gadujati

Jl Lembong

Jl Sumatra

Jl Jen Sudirman

Jl Banceuy

Jl Veteran

Jl Naripan

Jl Lembong

Jl Cibadak

Palaguna
Shopping
Centre

Jl Dalem Kaum

Jl Asia Afrika

Jl Gatot Subroto

Jl Otoiskandardinata

Jl Dewi Sartika

Jl Asama Alyar

Jl Lengkong Besar

Jl Kir Tiyan

To Moh Toha (200m);
ASTI Bandung (1.5km);
Leuwi Panjang Bus Station (4km)

INDONESIA

INFORMATION	Museum Konperensi...............12 B5	Rumah Makan Mandarin.........25 A4
Bandung Tourist Information	Zoo...13 B1	Warung.................................26 B5
Centre...................................1 A4		
Bandung Tourist Information	**SLEEPING** ◘	**DRINKING** ◘
Centre...................................2 B5	By Moritz..............................14 A5	Amsterdam Café....................27 C5
Bank Mandiri...........................3 C4	Hotel Arimbi.........................15 A4	Downtown.............................28 C5
Cybernet..................................4 A5	Hotel King Garden................16 A5	North Sea Bar.......................29 C5
Main Post Office.....................5 B5	Hotel Patradissa....................17 A4	
RS Boremeus Hospital............6 C1	Hotel Surabaya......................18 A5	**ENTERTAINMENT** ◘
Wartel.....................................7 A5	Savoy Homann	Braga Disco...........................30 B5
	Hotel..................................19 C5	Fame Station.........................31 D6
SIGHTS & ACTIVITIES		Rumentang Siang...................32 D5
Gedung Merkeda.................(see 12)	**EATING** ◘	
Gedung Sate (Regional	Hong Kong	**TRANSPORT**
Government Building)...........8 D3	Restaurant..........................20 A5	Garuda.................................33 C5
ITB (Bandung Institute of	London Bakery	Kebun Kelapa Bus Station.......34 B6
Technology).........................9 C1	& Café................................21 C5	Kramatdjati..........................35 A5
Jeans Street...........................10 B2	RM Nusantara......................22 C5	Merpati...............................36 C4
Museum Geologi (Geological	Roempoet.............................23 C5	Pahala Kencana.................(see 35)
Museum).............................11 D2	Royal Siam............................24 B4	Stasiun Hall Angkot Terminal....37 A5

Surabaya, this is a true monster from the outside, but offers some colourful Chinese charm once you are through the door, with chandeliers, technicolour tiles and loads of ostentatious chintz.

By Moritz (☎ 420 5788; Kompleks Luxor Permai 35, Jl Kebonjati; s/d with shared mandi 30,000/40,000Rp) This is a backpackers favourite, but take any recommendations with a pinch of salt. Run by a lively lot, but the rooms would see a Spartan losing sleep, the walls are paper-thin and cleaning appears to be anathema.

Hotel Arimbi (☎ 423 9159; Jl Stasiun Selatan 21-23; s/d 40,000/45,000Rp) The better of the two hotels of his name by the train station, this is slightly closer to the railway, with a coat of fresh yellow paint covering an old villa. The rooms are plain but the staff are friendly.

Hotel Arimbi (☎ 420 2734; Jl Stasiun Selatan 5; s/d 30,000/40,000Rp) The second Arimbi is rough and ready at best, but well placed.

Hotel Patradissa (☎ 420 6680; Jl H Moch Iskat 8; d from 60,000Rp; ◘) This old-timer is a little frumpy and reminiscent of a nursing home, but the bigger rooms are good value. Only the most expensive rooms have air-con.

Eating
Bandung has a number of good Chinese restaurants. On Jl Braga there is a handful of decent cafés and restaurants.

Roempoet (Jl Braga 80; mains 20,000Rp; ◘ dinner) The menu is limited – it pretty much boils down to satay cooked on an open barbecue – but live bands provide some atmosphere and Bandung's trendier set often pops in for a beer and a strum of the guitar.

Royal Siam (☎ 424 1459; Jl Braga 121; mains 30,000Rp; ◘ lunch & dinner; ◘) This air-con eatery whips up some of the city's best Thai food and serves it to tables of pontificating government types. The waiters wear bow ties to keep up the standards, and the service is slick.

London Bakery & Café (☎ 420 7351; Jl Braga 37; ◘ lunch & dinner; ◘) You can quell your sugar cravings here, where sticky cakes and coffee top the menu. It also does savoury mains, but the burgers are famously small.

RM Nusantara (☎ 081-5610 4443; Jl Braga 10; mains 9000Rp; ◘ 24hr) This *au plein air masakan Padang* serves decent Sumatran food from dusk 'til…well…dusk.

Rumah Makan Mandarin (Jl Kebon Kawung; mains 20,000Rp) This is a no-nonsense eatery with seafood specialities and a loyal band of Chinese regulars.

Hong Kong Restaurant (☎ 423 2595; Jl J Sudirman 151; mains 20,000Rp; ◘ breakfast, lunch & dinner) Mirrors, chrome, polished tiles and a gigantic dragon motif provide the backdrop at this striplit spot. The atmosphere is distinctly strange, but the food is reliably good and there's plenty of quirky Chinese razzle-dazzle on the menu for those after something more adventurous.

Bandung Supermal (Jl Gatot Subroto; mains 10,000Rp; ◘ 9am-8pm) In the east of the city, has all the usual food-court favourites.

The best night *warung* are on Jl Cikapundung Barat, across from the *alun alun* near the Ramayana department store. Stalls sell a bit of everything – try the *soto jeroan* (intestinal soup with various medicinal properties), mostly designed to stimulate male libido.

Drinking

Jl Braga is the hub of the city's less cultural pursuits.

North Sea Bar (☎ 420 8904; Jl Braga 82; ☒ 5pm-late) In a colonial-era property daubed with the bar's trademark Popeye motif, this is Bandung's late-night staple, with beer, bar girls and brouhaha aplenty. A becak decorates the bar and you may just need one home – most patrons arrive like Popeye and leave looking more like Olive.

Amsterdam Cafe (Jl Braga 74; ☒ 6pm-late) Next door, Amsterdam offers more of the same.

Downtown (☎ 420 7452; Jl Braga 68; ☒ 10am-2am) The hippest haunt for hustlers, this is a popular pool bar. A table costs 25,000Rp per hour.

Clubbing

Discos (expect a cover charge of 20,000Rp to 40,000Rp) include the Western-oriented **Braga** (☎ 423 3292; Jl Suriaraja 7-9; ☒ 4pm-3am) and the busy dance club **Fame Station** (11th fl, Lippo Centre Bldg, Jl Gatot Subroto 2; ☒ 8pm-late).

Entertainment

Bandung is the place to see Sundanese performing arts. Performance times are haphazard – check with the tourist information centre (p179) for the latest schedules. The tourist information centre also has schedules and programmes for Rumentang Siang and ASTI-Bandung.

Pak Ujo's Saung Angklung (☎ 727 1714; Jl Padasuka 118; performances 35,000Rp) East of the city, Saung Angklung hosts *angklung* (bamboo musical instrument) performances. You can also see the instruments being made. Performances are held most afternoons at 3.30pm.

Rumentang Siang (☎ 423 3562; Jl Baranangsiang 1; performances from 5000Rp) Bandung's performing arts centre hosts *wayang golek* performances, Jaipongan (West Javanese dance), *sandiwara* (traditional Javanese theatre) and *ketoprak* (folk theatre).

ASTI-Bandung (☎ 731 4982; Jl Buah Batu 212; performances from 5000Rp) South of the centre, ASTI is a school for traditional Sundanese arts and hosts a varied cultural programme.

Getting There & Away

AIR

Merpati (☎ 422 2488; www.merpati.co.id; Jl Aceh 65) has daily flights to Jakarta (190,000Rp) and Saturday and Sunday flights to Pangandaran

(199,000Rp). **Garuda** (☎ 0807-1-427832; www .garuda-indonesia.com; Grand Hotel Preanger, Jl Asia Afrika 181) has daily flights to Jakarta (240,000Rp).

BUS

The **Leuwi Panjang bus station** (☎ 522 0768), 5km south of the city centre on Jl Soekarno-Hatta, has buses west to places like Bogor (normal/air-con 15,000/25,000Rp, 3½ hours), Sukabumi (15,000Rp, three hours) and Jakarta's Kampung Rambutan station (30,000Rp, four hours). Buses to Bogor are not allowed to take the scenic Puncak Pass route on weekends. Door-to-door minibuses also go to Bogor (50,000Rp) via Puncak.

Buses east leave from the Cicaheum bus station, on the eastern outskirts of the city. Buses travel to Cirebon (normal/air-con 15,000/25,000Rp, 3½ hours), Garut (6000Rp, two hours), Pangandaran (28,000Rp, six hours) and to Yogyakarta (normal/air-con 35,000/50,000Rp, 10 hours). **Sari Harum** (☎ 607 7065) provides air-con minibuses to Pangandaran (45,000Rp, five hours) – phone to arrange pick-up from your hotel.

For luxury buses to long-distance destinations, **Kramatdjati** (☎ 420 0858; Jl Kebonjati 96) and **Pahala Kencana** (☎ 423 2911; Jl Kebonjati 90) are two upmarket agencies.

TRAIN

The Bandung-Jakarta *Parahyangan* (*bisnis/eksekutif* 40,000/60,000Rp, three hours) is the main service with departures to Jakarta's Gambir train station roughly every hour from 5am to 7.05pm.

The *eksekutif Argo Wilis* leaves Bandung at 7am for Surabaya (165,000Rp, 11 hours). It calls at Yogyakarta and Solo en route. Coming back, it leaves Surabaya at 7am.

For train time and fare information, visit www.infoka.kereta-api.com.

Getting Around

Angkot (1000Rp to 3000Rp) to most places such as Dago, Jl Cihampelas and Tangkuban Perahu, leave from the terminal in front of the train station (Stasiun Hall). Abdul Muis at the Kebun Kelapa bus station is another central terminal, with *angkot* to Cicaheum and Luewi Panjang bus stations. Big Damri city buses (1500Rp) 9 and 11 run from west to east down Jl Asia Afrika to Cicaheum.

Taxis are numerous, but you'll have to bargain hard to get them to use the meter.

TANGKUBAN PERAHU AREA

Thirty kilometres north of Bandung, **Tangkuban Perahu** (literally 'Overturned Boat') is a huge volcanic crater. Legend tells of a god challenged to build a huge boat during a single night. His opponent, on seeing that he would probably complete this impossible task, brought the sun up early and the boat builder turned his nearly completed boat over in a fit of anger.

The huge **Kawah Ratu** (Queen Crater) at the top is impressive, but a warning was issued in 2005 that the volcano may be beginning to stir – check with the **Bandung Tourist Information Centre** (☎ 421 6648) before visiting. Cars can also drive right to the top, so it is a local tourist trap with the usual parade of touts. A park entrance fee of 15,000Rp is payable on arrival.

You can escape the crowds by walking (anticlockwise) around the main crater and along the ridge between the two craters, but parts of it are steep and slippery. Safer and more interesting is the walk to **Kawah Domas**, an active volcanic area of steaming vents and bubbling pools about 1km down from the car park. From here you can follow the trail back to the main road (ask for directions) and flag down a *colt* back to Bandung, or continue to the **Sari Ater Hot Springs Resort** (☎ 0260-471700; admission 9000Rp; ☷ 24hr) at **Ciater**, 8km northeast of Tangkuban Perahu. Guides at Tangkuban Perahu will also offer to lead you to Ciater through the jungle.

You can extend your Tangkuban Perahu trip by walking from the bottom end of the gardens at Maribaya down through a brilliant river gorge (there's a good track) to **Dago**, an exclusive residential suburb of Bandung with a famous **teahouse**. Allow about two hours for the walk to Dago. It's a good spot to watch the city light up and you can then return on the local *angkot*, which run to/from the train station in Bandung.

Getting There & Away

Take a Subang-bound *colt* (8000Rp, 45 minutes) from Bandung's minibus terminal (Stasiun Hall), which will take you, via Lembang, to the park entrance, then take a minibus (5000Rp if full) to the top. Weekends are the best time for finding other passengers to share a minibus, otherwise you'll have to charter one or walk the 4.5km to the top.

PANGANDARAN
☎ 0265

Empty, sweeping beaches, rolling surf, easy access to a national park, bags of budget hotels: on an island not known for its seaside resorts, Pangandaran's CV makes engaging reading. Unfortunately (for the hoteliers at least), few people come here outside the holidays and Pangandaran is one of the quietest major beach resorts in Indonesia. This may change, but for now, this overgrown fishing village, with the sea to east and west and a swathe of jungle to the south, feels like a stride off the beaten track. In short, if you feel like charging your batteries after an overdose of hubbub, this really is the place.

Information

A once-only tourist tax (2500Rp) is charged when entering Pangandaran – keep your ticket safe. In addition to the Telkom office, Pangandaran has plenty of *wartel*.

BNI ATM (Jl Bulak Laut; ☷ 24hr) Opposite the Relax Restaurant.

BRI bank (Jl Kidang Pananjung; ☷ 8am-2.30pm Mon-Fri) Changes money for so-so rates.

CV Sawargi (☎ 639180; Jl Kidang Pananjung; per min 300Rp; ☷ 9am-11pm) Internet access.

Magic Mushroom Books (Jl Pasanggrahan; ☷ 10am-5pm) Books can be bought here.

Main post office (Jl Kidang Pananjung; ☷ 7.30am-3.30pm Mon-Thu, 7.30am-1.30pm Sat) On the main street.

Ocean Pub (☎ 630083; Jl Pamugaran; per min 500Rp; ☷ 9am-midnight) Internet access (also see p185).

PT Lotus Wisata (☎ 639635; lotus_wisata@yahoo .com; Jl Bulak Laut; ☷ 6am-midnight) Useful travel agency with heaps of information on the area.

Telkom office (Jl Kidang Pananjung; ☷ 6am-midnight)

Sights & Activities

Taman Nasional Pangandaran (Pangandaran National Park; ☎ 081-2149 0153; admission 2150Rp; ☷ 6am-4pm), at the southern end of town, is a fabulous stretch of untouched forest with barking deer, hornbills, monkeys and some spectacular white-sand beaches. The **Boundary Trail** offers a pleasant walk through the park – ask the rangers (a guide costs 50,000Rp for two hours) for details. The PHPA is at both entrances to the park.

Pangandaran has big seas and drownings occur – take great care when swimming!

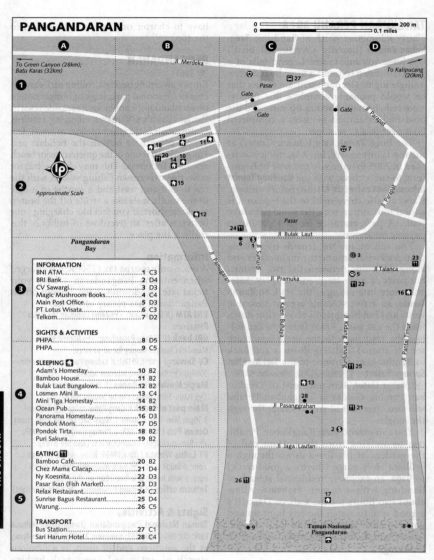

PANGANDARAN

To Green Canyon (28km);
Batu Karas (32km)

To Kalipucang
(20km)

Jl Merdeka

Pasar
Gate
Gate

Gate

Approximate Scale

Pangandaran
Bay

Pasar

Jl Bulak Laut

Jl Pramuka

Jl Talanca

INFORMATION
BNI ATM..................................1 C3
BRI Bank.................................2 D4
CV Sawargi.............................3 D3
Magic Mushroom Books.........4 C4
Main Post Office.....................5 D3
PT Lotus Wisata......................6 C3
Telkom....................................7 D2

SIGHTS & ACTIVITIES
PHPA......................................8 D5
PHPA......................................9 C5

SLEEPING
Adam's Homestay..................10 B2
Bamboo House......................11 B2
Bulak Laut Bungalows...........12 B2
Losmen Mini II......................13 C4
Mini Tiga Homestay...............14 B2
Ocean Pub............................15 B2
Panorama Homestay..............16 D3
Pondok Moris........................17 D5
Pondok Tirta.........................18 B2
Puri Sakura...........................19 B2

EATING
Bamboo Café........................20 B2
Chez Mama Cilacap...............21 D4
Ny Koesnita...........................22 D3
Pasar Ikan (Fish Market)........23 D3
Relax Restaurant...................24 C2
Sunrise Bagus Restaurant......25 D4
Warung.................................26 C5

TRANSPORT
Bus Station...........................27 C1
Sari Harum Hotel..................28 C4

Jl Pasanggrahan

Jl Jaga Lautan

Taman Nasional
Pangandaran

Tours

A host of good-value tours are offered to destinations around Pangandaran, including the Green Canyon (see p186) for 70,000Rp (minimum four people) and walks through the national park (50,000Rp, five hours, minimum four people). Contact **CV Sawargi** (☎ 639180; Jl Kidang Pananjung) for details.

Sleeping

Pangandaran has over 100 places to stay. During the Christmas and Lebaran (the end of Ramadan) holidays, the town is crowded and prices skyrocket. Prices are seasonal and may be higher than quoted here.

The northern end of Jl Pamugaran, on the west beach, is the best place to start looking.

Ocean Pub (☎ 630083; Jl Pamugaran; s/d 70,000/ 75,000Rp) Pick a room with your home country's flag on the door and then tumble the few steps down to the bar. The rooms get noisy if the bar starts filling up, but they are a good buy for the price and it's a good place to make new friends.

Mini Tiga Homestay (☎ 639436; katmaja95@yahoo .fr; s/d 45,000/55,000Rp) Colourful and compact, this cosy little spot off Jl Pamugaran is a hotchpotch of polished wood, psychedelic artwork and trinkets. Run by the same French owner for more than 20 years, it is reliable with a double-decker 'R'.

Puri Sakura (☎ 630552; d from 50,000Rp; 🔀) Someone droning on about how wonderful their hostel is, is never a big selling point, but Puri Sakura, off Jl Pamugaran, is worth the odd boast, with shipshape rooms around a little courtyard. On the downside, there's not much mingling space. The pricier rooms (70,000Rp) come with air-con.

Bamboo House (☎ 639419; s/d 40,000/50,000Rp) This is another Pangandaran old-timer off Jl Pamugaran and a favourite with the rickshaw touts who tend to bring you here if you have no idea where else to go. Rooms are sparse, the mattresses thin, but it scores for friendliness and the decor is cheerful.

Bulak Laut Bungalows (☎ 639377; Jl Pamugaran; d from 55,000Rp; 🔀) This place is something of an oddity, with eccentric Hansel and Gretel styling and a dense garden that explodes into life during the rainy season. Pick from slightly dingy fan rooms, or glossier air-con bungalows (110,000Rp), and watch out for the fish pond if you stagger in late.

Pondok Moris (☎ 639490; Gang Moris 3; s/d 50,000/ 75,000Rp) Small and colourful, this spot is within easy striking distance of the national park and is managed by a beatnik surfie. On the downside, it's so close to the mosque that the call to prayer might as well be coming from your own *mandi* (bathing facility).

Losmen Mini II (☎ 639298; Jl Kalen Buhaya 14; d from 50,000Rp; 🔀) So spotless you can see your face reflected in the floor, this offers a range of rooms from decent fan digs to spacious air-con affairs (150,000Rp). The squeamish may not like the fact that some of the walls are decorated with turtle shells though.

Other recommendations:

Panorama Homestay (☎ 639218; Jl Pantai Timur 197; s/d 45,000/50,000Rp) So-so thatched rooms in a coconut grove.

Pondok Tirta (☎ 639235; Jl Pamugaran 140; s/d 60,000/70,000Rp) Sterile, but ideal for those with a Howard Hughes dirt fixation.

Eating

Pasar Ikan (Fish Market; Komplek Pasar Ikan, Jl Talanca; mains 15,000Rp; 🍴 breakfast, lunch & dinner) Pangandaran is famous for its seafood and this excellent market on the east beach is the place to sample it. There are a dozen little restaurants here – you just pick your fresh fish, pay by the weight and they cook it for you.

Ocean Pub (see left; ☎ 630083; Jl Pamugaran; mains 20,000Rp; 🍴 breakfast, lunch & dinner) The fireworks are missing here, but this bamboo bar-restaurant offers a range of shakes, sandwiches and grills. There's a pool table, some pleasant outdoor seating, a bar for making new mates and a big TV in case you're still on your lonesome by the time your food arrives.

Bamboo Café (Jl Pamugaran; mains 15,000Rp; 🍴 breakfast, lunch & dinner) A few doors up, this follows the same formula as Ocean Pub.

NY Koesnita (☎ 630028; Jl Kidang Pananjung; mains 15,000Rp; 🍴 breakfast, lunch & dinner) Rather more authentic, this Indonesian eatery whips up a good selection of Sundanese and Padang dishes.

Sunrise Bagus Restaurant (☎ 639220; Jl Kidang Pananjung 185; mains 30,000Rp; 🍴 lunch & dinner) Attached to one of the town's more salubrious hotels, this alfresco eatery serves the usual mix of local and international dishes in touristy, wooden surrounds. The food's good, but you do get whiffs of chlorine from the nearby pool.

INDONESIA

Chez Mama Cilacap (☎ 639098; Jl Kidang Pananjung 187; mains 30,000Rp; ☽ breakfast, lunch & dinner) Sporting the biggest sign in Pangandaran, this seafood specialist offers a mean selection of crab dishes under a wooden roof propped up by palm trees.

Relax Restaurant (☎ 630377; Jl Bulak Laut 74; mains 20,000Rp; ☽ breakfast, lunch & dinner) The décor's a little plain in this slightly sterile, Scandinavian-style place, but the food is wholesome and Nordic, it's a good spot for breakfast and you get all sorts of little trimmings, like…wait for it…napkins.

For cheap Indonesian food, the town has dozens of *warung*, especially along the southern end of the western beach.

Getting There & Away

With tourist numbers down in Pangandaran, transport in the area is a bit of a lottery as many services are cancelled when volume is low. All of the below services were operating at the time of writing, but check with a travel agency like **PT Lotus Wisata** (☎ 639635; lotus_wisata@yahoo.com; Jl Bulak Laut) for the latest information.

AIR

Merpati flies twice weekly (Saturday and Sunday) between Pangandaran (Nusa Wiru airport near Batu Karas), Bandung (199,000Rp) and Jakarta (399,000Rp). At the time of writing, Merpati had yet to open an office in Pangandaran, so tickets can be booked through PT Lotus Wisata.

BOAT

An alternative way of getting to/from Pangandaran is the interesting backwater trip between Cilacap and Pamotan. From Pangandaran it starts with a 17km bus trip to Pamotan (4000Rp, 40 minutes), where *compreng* (wooden boats) can be chartered for the scenic journey. The boats hold 15 people and cost 250,000Rp each way. You can organise the boats through PT Lotus Wisata.

On Wednesday, Thursday and Friday, a car ferry travels between Majingklak (20km east of Pangandaran) and Cilacap (7500Rp, three hours). It leaves Majingklak at 8am and Cilacap at 1pm.

At the time of writing, a daily fast service between Kalipucang (15km east of Pangandaran) and Cilacap was also planned

(20,000Rp, two hours). Check with PT Lotus Wisata for the latest.

There are direct buses from Cilacap to Yogyakarta (25,000Rp, five hours) or to Wonosobo (17,000Rp, four hours). The last Yogyakarta bus leaves 9pm. Much easier are the door-to-door services between Pangandaran and Yogyakarta. Bus-ferry-bus services (75,000Rp, 10 hours) are sold all around Pangandaran and will drop you at your hotel in Yogyakarta. But, they are often cancelled because of insufficient numbers.

BUS

Local buses run from Pangandaran's bus station, just north of town, to Tasikmalaya (15,000Rp, three hours), Kalipucang, Pamotan or Majingklak (4000Rp, 40 minutes) and Cilacap (15,000Rp, 2½ hours).

Express buses also leave from here for Bandung (30,000Rp, six hours) and Jakarta (50,000Rp, nine hours). Regular buses also go to Banjar (8000Rp, two hours), where you can pick up connections to Yogyakarta (60,000Rp, nine hours) – you will normally have to change in Purwokerto.

The most comfortable option to Bandung is the twice-daily Sari Harum door-to-door minibus (45,000Rp, five hours). Its office is in the **Sari Harum Hotel** (☎ 639276; Jl Pasanggrahan; ☽ 6am-10pm).

Agencies like PT Lotus Wisata sell tickets for a premium and often include transport to the depot.

BATU KARAS

The little village of **Batu Karas** (admission 1500Rp), 32km from Pangandaran, has one of the best beaches in the Pangandaran area and has become something of a hideaway for surf junkies. The beaches are clean and largely empty and the waves are relatively reliable.

Near the turn-off to Batu Karas, boats take tours for up to five people upriver to **Green Canyon** (per boat 50,000Rp; ☽ 7.30am-4pm), a scenic waterway through a canyon; alternatively, organise a day trip from Pangandaran (see p184).

Sleeping & Eating

Batu Karas caters mainly to surfers and accommodation options are Spartan.

Reef Hotel (☎ 0813-2034 0193; d 100,000Rp; ▣) This offers a few more creature comforts at the other end of the beach.

Kang Ayi Restaurant (☎ 0265-633676; Jl Legok-pari; mains 8000Rp; ☺ breakfast, lunch & dinner) Near Hotel Melati Murni, this offers decent eats by the Batu Karas Surfshop.

The cheapest hotels:

Alana's (Jl Legokpari; d with shared mandi 20,000Rp) Very basic.

Hotel Melati Murni (☎ 0265-633683; Jl Legokpari; s/d 35,000/45,000Rp)

Getting There & Away

Batu Karas can be reached from Pangandaran by bus via Cijulang (10,000Rp, one hour). If you are driving yourself, you can cut 10km off your journey to Batu Karas from Pangandaran by taking a left-hand turn 500m after the bus terminal in Cijulang. This will take you over a beautiful old **bamboo bridge** (toll 1000Rp), an experience in itself.

WONOSOBO

☎ 0286 / pop 25,000

Wonosobo is the main gateway to the Dieng Plateau and has some reasonable budget accommodation; otherwise it's a forgettable place. The **BNI bank** (Jl A Yani) has an ATM and exchange facilities. There's also a centrally located **tourist office** (☎ 321194; Jl Kartini 3; ☺ 7am-2pm Mon-Fri).

Sleeping & Eating

Wisma Duta Homestay (☎ 321674; Jl Rumah Sakit 3; s/d 30,000/50,000Rp) This is the best budget option, with fresh, tidy rooms.

Hotel Sri Kencono (☎ 321522; Jl A Yani 81; d from 50,000Rp; ☒) This spick-and-span spot offers plenty of options from no-frills fan rooms with shared mandi to rather more palatial air-con doubles (150,000Rp).

Asia Restaurant (Jl Kawedanan 43; mains 20,000Rp; ☺ lunch & dinner) Wonosobo's old faithful has high standards, regular locals and a decent range of Indonesian and Chinese cuisine.

Getting There & Away

Wonosobo's bus station is 3km out of town on the Magelang road.

From Yogyakarta, take a bus to Magelang (8000Rp, one hour) and then another bus to Wonosobo (10,000Rp, two hours). **Rahayu Travel** (☎ 321217; Jl A Yani 95) has door-to-door minibuses to Yogyakarta (25,000Rp, three hours). Hotels can arrange pick-up.

Infrequent direct buses run to Cilacap (17,000Rp, four hours). Otherwise take a

bus to Purwokerto (10,000Rp, three hours) and change there. Leave early in the morning to catch the ferry to Majingklak and on to Pangandaran.

Frequent buses to Dieng (5000Rp, one hour) leave from Dieng terminal, 500m west of the town centre, throughout the day.

DIENG PLATEAU

Up in the clouds (it stands at 2000m), the Dieng Plateau is another country: a landscape of marshes, ruined temples, deep green hills and mist. It only takes an hour to get here via the hairpins from Wonosobo, but the humid plains feel light years away when you do reach the top.

In fact, Dieng is the collapsed remnant of an ancient crater. On the swampy plain in front of Dieng village are five Hindu/Buddhist temples that form the **Arjuna Complex**. These temples are thought to be the oldest in Java, predating Borobudur and Prambanan. Though historically important, they are small, squat and not particularly impressive. Another temple nearby is **Candi Bima**; to the south, the small site **museum** (admission free; ☺ 8am-4pm) contains statues and sculpture from the temples.

The plateau's natural attractions and its sense of isolation are the main reasons to visit. From the village, you can do a two-hour loop walk that takes in pretty **Telaga Warna** (Coloured Lake) and **Kawah Sikidang**, a volcanic crater with steaming vents and frantically bubbling mud pools. You can see all the main sights, including the temples, on foot in a morning or afternoon. Other volcanic areas and lakes lie further afield.

It costs 15,000Rp to visit the plateau and temples; there's a small **ticket office** (☺ 8am-6pm) in the village.

The walk to **Sembungan** to see the sunrise from the hill 1km from the village is a popular activity. It's reputed to be the highest village in Java at 2300m. Start at 4am to reach the top 1½ hours later. Dieng Plateau Homestay and Losmen Bu Djono both offer **guides** (per person 40,000Rp).

To really appreciate Dieng, it is worth staying overnight.

Information

The small tourist info office near Losmen Bu Djono has extremely sporadic open times.

BRI bank (8am-2pm Mon-Fri) Near Hotel Gunung Mas, changes US dollars (cash) at poor rates.

Kios Telephone Dian (8am-6pm) Near the BRI bank, calls can be made from here.

Sleeping & Eating

There are only a handful of accommodation choices.

Dieng Plateau Homestay (s/d 30,000/40,000Rp) One of the best options, this has a café, information on Dieng and offers guides.

Losmen Bu Djono (s/d 30,000/35,000Rp) Dieng Plateau is better maintained, but otherwise this offers all the same facilities, including guides.

Hotel Gunung Mas (392417; s/d 80,000/90,000Rp) A little further down the road, this is over-priced and dingy, but it does have hot water.

Getting There & Away

Frequent buses (4000Rp, one hour) run between Dieng and Wonosobo throughout the day.

YOGYAKARTA

 0274 / pop 600,000

If modern Java and its long history sometimes look like uneasy bedfellows, Yogyakarta (pronounced 'Jogjakarta') is the city where the romance burns on. At the heart of the Javanese identity, and the hub of its artistic and intellectual heritage, Yogya (as it is known to its friends) is one of the few Indonesian cities where the modern and the traditional peacefully coexist.

The 21st century is, of course, coming on strong and sitting in the logjam of Jl Malioboro on a Friday afternoon, you might feel like you are right back in the hurly-burly of Jakarta. But still headed by its sultan, whose *kraton* remains the focus of traditional life, modern Yogya is as much a city of batik, gamelan and ritual, as burger bars, *macet* and advertising hoardings. In fact, take a stroll down the crumbling back alleys, and you'll find plentiful snippets from another age.

And if it is all about location, location, location, Yogya's credentials as Java's premier tourist city only improve. With the puffing summit of volcanic Gunung Merapi on one flank, the ancient ruins of Borobudur on the other and the crashing waves of the Indian Ocean to the south, Yogya is a vital pit stop on any itinerary.

> **GETTING INTO TOWN**
>
> Prepaid taxis from a booth in the airport to Yogya, 10km away, cost 25,000Rp. From the main road, only 200m from the terminal, you can get a *colt* into the centre (2500Rp).

Orientation

Jl Malioboro, named after the Duke of Marlborough, is the main street and runs south from the train station, becoming Jl A Yani at the southern end. Most shops are on this street and most cheap accommodation is just off it, in the Sosrowijayan enclave. A second midrange enclave is around Jl Prawirotaman.

The *kraton* is the heart of old Yogya, where you will also find the Taman Sari (Water Castle) and numerous batik galleries.

Information

BOOKSHOPS

Lucky Boomerang (Map p191; 895006; Gang 1; 8am-9pm)

INTERNET ACCESS

Internet cafés are all over town, charging around 5000Rp per hour. They include:

Metro Internet (Map p189; 372364; Metro Guest House, Jl Prawirotaman II 71; 8am-11pm)

Queen Internet (Map p191; 547633; Jl Pasar Kembang 17; 24hr)

MEDICAL SERVICES

Ludira Husada Tama Hospital (Map p189; 513651; Jl Wiratama 4; 24hr)

MONEY

BCA bank (Map p189; Jl Mangkubumi)

PT Haji La Tunrung (Map p191; Jl Pasar Kembang 17; 7.30am-9pm) Open later than most moneychangers.

POST

Main post office (Map p189; cnr Jl Senopati & Jl A Yani; 8am-5pm Mon-Fri, 8am-noon Sat)

TELEPHONE

There are *wartel* across town.

Mendut Wartel (Map p191; Jl Pasar Kembang 49; 8am-10pm)

Telkom office (Map p189; Jl Yos Sudarso; 24hr)

TOURIST INFORMATION

Tourist information office (Map p189; 562000; Jl Malioboro 16; 8am-6.30pm Mon-Sat) This is useful.

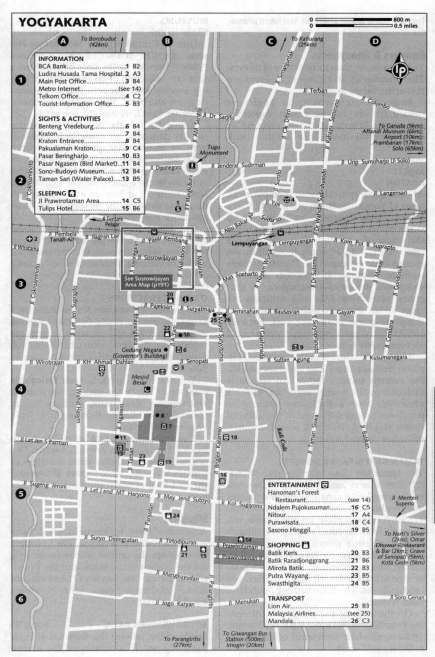

YOGYAKARTA

0 — 800 m
0 — 0.5 miles

To Borobudur (42km)

To Kalurang (25km)

INFORMATION
BCA Bank.........................1 B2
Ludira Husada Tama Hospital.2 A3
Main Post Office...............3 B4
Metro Internet...............(see 14)
Telkom Office..................4 C2
Tourist Information Office....5 B3

SIGHTS & ACTIVITIES
Benteng Vredeburg.............6 B4
Kraton............................7 B4
Kraton Entrance................8 B4
Pakualaman Kraton.............9 C4
Pasar Beringharjo............10 B3
Pasar Ngasem (Bird Market)..11 B4
Sono-Budoyo Museum..........12 B4
Taman Sari (Water Palace)...13 B5

SLEEPING 🏠
Jl Prawirotaman Area..........14 C5
Tulips Hotel....................15 B6

ENTERTAINMENT 📺
Hanoman's Forest
  Restaurant..................(see 14)
Ndalem Pujokusuman..........16 C5
Nitour............................17 A4
Purawisata......................18 C4
Sasono Hinggil.................19 B5

SHOPPING 🛍
Batik Keris.....................20 B3
Batik Raradjonggrang.........21 B6
Mirota Batik....................22 B3
Putra Wayang...................23 B5
Swasthigita.....................24 B5

TRANSPORT
Lion Air.........................25 B3
Malaysia Airlines...........(see 25)
Mandala.........................26 C3

To Garuda (5km);
Affandi Museum (6km);
Airport (10km);
Prambanan (17km);
Solo (65km)

See Sosrowijayan Area Map (p191)

Tugu Monument

Lempuyangan

Gedung Negara (Governor's Building)

Mesjid Besar

To Narti's Silver (2km); Omar Dhuwur Restaurant & Bar (2km); Grave of Senopati (5km); Kota Gede (5km)

To Giwangan Bus Station (500m); Imogiri (20km)

To Parangtritis (27km)

INDONESIA

Tugu train station and the airport also have tourist information counters.

Dangers & Annoyances

Yogya has more than its fair share of thieves. The Prambanan and Borobudur buses are favourites for pickpockets.

Batik salesmen, posing as guides or instant friends, can be a pain, especially around the Taman Sari. Shake them off or endure the inevitable hard sell at a batik gallery.

Sights

KRATON

At the geographical, and metaphorical, heart of Yogya, the **kraton** (Map p189; ☎ 373721; admission 7500Rp; ⌚ 8am-2pm Sat-Thu, 8am-1pm Fri) is the palace of the sultans and effectively the centre of a small, walled city within a city – over 25,000 people live within the greater *kraton* compound. The atmosphere tends to evaporate at weekends when the compound becomes a menagerie of tour buses, screeching kids and dripping ice creams, but it's well worth a visit when things are quieter during the week. For a fee (10,000Rp), a guide will usher you around its sumptuous halls.

The inner court has a **museum** (Map p189) dedicated to Hamengkubuwono IX, the current sultan's father. Admission is included in the *kraton* entry fee, and it's open same hours as the *kraton*. In the inner pavilion, you can see a host of free cultural events staged daily; check with the tourist office for current listings.

TAMAN SARI & PASAR NGASEM

The **Taman Sari** (Water Castle; Map p189; ☎ 0818-0277 0296; Jl Taman; admission 5000Rp; ⌚ 9am-4pm) was a complex of canals, pools and palaces built within the *kraton* between 1758 and 1765 by a Portuguese architect who was allegedly later executed to keep the sultan's hidden 'pleasure rooms' secret. Damaged first by Diponegoro's Java War and then further by an earthquake, it is today a mass of ruins, crowded with small houses and batik galleries. The main bathing pools have been restored.

On the edge of the site is the interesting **Pasar Ngasem** (Bird Market; Map p189; Jl Polowijan; ⌚ 8am-6pm), where thousands of little songbirds are sold daily.

MUSEUMS

Close to the *kraton*, on the northwestern corner of Kraton Sq, the **Sono-Budoyo Museum** (Map p189; ☎ 376775; Jl Trikora 6; admission 7500Rp; ⌚ 8am-1pm Tue-Thu, 8am-noon Fri-Sun) has a first-rate collection of Javanese arts, including *wayang kulit* puppets, kris (traditional daggers) and batik. *Wayang kulit* performances are held here nightly, see p193.

Yogya has plenty of other museums, usually dedicated to some independence hero or military escapade. Dating from 1765, **Benteng Vredeburg** (Map p189; Jl A Yani; admission 5000Rp; ⌚ 8.30am-1.30pm Tue-Thu, 8.30-11am Fri, 8.30am-1pm Sat & Sun) is the old Dutch fort. Now restored, it houses a museum with dioramas showing the history of the independence movement.

The **Affandi Museum** (Jl Solo; admission 5000Rp; ⌚ 9am-2pm Mon-Fri, 9am-1pm Sat), 6km east of the town centre, houses the impressionist works of Affandi, Indonesia's best-known artist.

OTHER ATTRACTIONS

The smaller **Pakualaman Kraton** (Map p189; Jl Sultan Agung; admission 2000Rp; ⌚ 9.30am-1.30pm Tue, Thu & Sun) has a small museum, a *pendopo* (open-sided pavilion), which can hold a full gamelan orchestra, and a curious colonial house.

Yogya's main market, **Pasar Beringharjo** (Map p189; Jl A Yani; ⌚ 8am-5pm), buzzes with life and features cheap batik, clothing and an older section filled to bursting with fruit, veggies and spices.

The main street of **Kota Gede**, 5km southeast of Yogya, is a silverwork centre. This is a must for those after silver jewellery or ornaments. The sacred **grave of Senopati**, the first king of Mataram, can also be seen here.

Sleeping

Accommodation in Yogya is good value and there is a superb choice. The two main enclaves are the central Sosrowijayan area, for the really cheap places, and the Prawirotaman area, 2km south of the *kraton*, for mainly midrange hotels. Most provide a small breakfast.

SOSROWIJAYAN AREA   Map p191

South of the railway line between Jl Pasar Kembang and Jl Sosrowijayan, the narrow

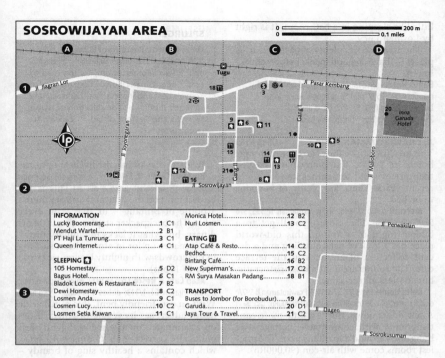

SOSROWIJAYAN AREA

0 — 200 m
0 — 0.1 miles

alleyways of Gang Sosrowijayan I and II have most of the cheap accommodation and eateries. More good places to stay are in other small *gang* (alleys or lanes) in this area.

Hostel standards fluctuate wildly here. Good places may go bad and great places may emerge from the ashes.

Losmen Setia Kawan (☎ 512452; bedhot@hotmail .com; Gang II 58; s/d 35,000/50,000Rp) Looking fresh as a bride's bouquet after a recent face-lift, this is Yogya's current budget favourite. Housed in a brooding old colonial building, with technicolour décor, bags of communal space and tidy rooms, Setia Kawan is a great deal at this price. Book ahead.

Bladok Losmen & Restaurant (☎ 560452; bla dok@yogya.wasantara.net.id; Jl Sosrowijayan 76; d from 60,000Rp; ❄ ♨) It's a bit pricier, but Bladok tops the pops in the area's accommodation stakes, offering a little more gloss, plenty of trimmings and some Eurochic styling for those feeling homesick. Even the cheapest fan rooms are homely and comfy.

Dewi Homestay (☎ 516014; dewihomestay@hot mail.com; s/d 45,000/50,000Rp) Like Tarzan's jungle hideaway, this atmospheric outfit offers a leafy garden, plenty of carved wood and some attractive, bohemian styling. Unlike the King of the Apes, you even get a four-poster bed. It is just off Jl Sosrowijayan.

Monica Hotel (☎ 580598; d from 40,000Rp; ❄) On an alley west of Gang II, Monica looks good in a new coat of salmon-coloured paint. The staff wear matching outfits, some sunlight beams down into the open courtyard and there are rooms to suit most budgets, from basic doubles, to smarter aircon affairs (80,000Rp).

Nuri Losmen (☎ 543654; d with shared/private mandi 25,000/30,000Rp) The rooms look a little downtrodden at this Yogya veteran, but there's a communal balcony for people-watching and some wise-cracking staff. It is down a quiet alley between Gang I and II.

Losmen Lucy (☎ 513429; s/d 30,000/35,000Rp) Just off Gang I, Lucy sports a fresh lick of white paint, slightly saggy beds and an owner who speaks in a bizarre poetic staccato. Lightbulbs are at a premium though and the bathrooms could do with a mop.

105 Homestay (☎ 582896; s/d 35,000/40,000Rp) The rooms here are spotless, even if it is a little like sleeping in a bathroom. It is right by Losmen Lucy.

The area also has plenty of basic, no-frills places – have a good peek before checking in.

Bagus Hotel (☎ 515087; Gang II; s/d with shared mandi 24,000/25,000Rp) Small rooms; low prices.

Losmen Anda (☎ 512452; Gang II; s/d 25,000/30,000Rp) Very cheap; very basic.

JL PRAWIROTAMAN AREA   Map p189

This area used to be the centre for midrange hotels in Yogya, but many have slashed their prices – and sometimes standards – in recent years. There are plenty of bargains to be had.

Mercury (☎ 370846; Jl Prawirotaman II 595; s/d 50,000/75,000Rp) The closest you'll get to a budget night in a *kraton*, this old-world place has a flick of palace styling and a decent collection of antiques in the terrace café. The rooms are a little less aristocratic, but spotless all the same.

Delta Homestay (☎ 372064; Jl Prawirotaman II 597A; d with shared/private mandi from 45,000/70,000Rp; 🏊 🖥) A few doors down, this is a little more contemporary, with comfortable, cottage-style bungalows around a sparkling pool. The priciest rooms come with air-con (90,000Rp).

Metro Guest House (☎ 372364; cafeyg2@idola.net; Jl Prawirotaman II 71; d with shared/private mandi from 50,000/75,000Rp; 🖥) With branches on both sides of the road, Metro is another popular hang-out, with a restaurant, Internet café and plumes of *kretek* (clove cigarette) smoke drifting up from behind the reception desk. The rooms are a bit dingy, but the guesthouse offers free transfers from the bus and train stations.

Also recommended:

Hotel Duta (☎ 372064; www.dutagardenhotel.com; Jl Prawirotaman 1 26; d with shared/private mandi from 50,000/85,000Rp; 🏊) With opulent decor and plentiful fish ponds.

Hotel Sartika (☎ 372669; Jl Prawirotaman I 44A; s/d 40,000/50,000Rp) A decent back-up.

Tulips Hotel (☎ 450137; www.yogyes.com; Jl Tirtodipuran 42; d from 95,000Rp; 🏊 🖥) A Dutch-run midranger.

Eating & Drinking
SOSROWIJAYAN AREA   Map p191

This area boasts a menagerie of cheap eateries. The cheapest places are the *warung* by Tugu train station. Most of the listed restaurants double as bars as the night wears on.

┌───┐

SPLURGE!

Omar Dhuwur Restaurant & Bar (☎ 374952; Jl Mondorakan 252; mains 50,000Rp; 🕐 lunch & dinner) Two kilometres out, on the road to Kota Gede, Omar Dhuwur remains one of Yogya's best and most atmospheric culinary splurges. It offers a wide selection of stylish Western and Eastern dishes in classic, Art Deco surrounds.

└───┘

Jl Sosrowijayan has the liveliest options.

Bintang Café (☎ 374566; Jl Sosrowijayan 54; mains 15,000Rp; 🕐 breakfast, lunch & dinner) This is the busiest joint on the drag and by 9pm there's a bottle of Bintang – or five – on every table. The backpacker staples are a little ordinary, but what it lacks in culinary prowess, it makes up for in atmosphere, sucking in the crowds with nightly live music (from 9pm to 11pm).

Atap Café & Resto (☎ 561922; www.atap.8m.com; Jl Sosrowijayan GT 1/113; dishes 15,000Rp; 🕐 dinner) With an eco-friendly bent, this ramshackle haunt advertises its veggie-oriented dishes on a laminated picture menu. Slightly less politically correct is its *Osama bin Coffee*, which contains a healthy slug of brandy – Mr bin Laden would not approve.

Bladok Restaurant (☎ 560452; Jl Sosrowijayan 76; mains 25,000Rp; 🕐 breakfast, lunch & dinner) The Alpine-style, dark-wood décor gives this little eatery a wholesome air. Dishes are Western-oriented, from fattening schnitzels to hearty fry-ups. See p191.

RM Surya Masakan Padang (☎ 749 2039; Jl Pasar Kembang 55; mains 10,000Rp; 🕐 24hr) Just around the corner from Jl Sosrowijayan, this offers reliable Padang food in authentic (read: net curtains and tiled floors) surrounds. The locals love it, anyway.

Gang I and II are also favourites for cheap eats.

Bedhot (☎ 512452; Gang II; mains 15,000Rp; 🕐 breakfast, lunch & dinner) Backpacker eats in psychedelic surrounds.

New Superman's (☎ 513472; Gang I; mains 20,000Rp; 🕐 breakfast, lunch & dinner) Cheap oriental and Western food beneath the trusted Superman logo.

JL PRAWIROTAMAN AREA   Map p189

Via Via (☎ 386557; www.viaviacafe.com; Jl Prawirotaman I 30; mains 25,000Rp; 🕐 breakfast, lunch & dinner) This chic, travellers-style café brings a little class to the standard package, with stylish furnishings, clocks telling the time in the major world capitals, Belgian beers behind the bar and plenty of well-prepared Western dishes on the menu. It also runs four-hour cookery courses (50,000Rp).

Ministry of Coffee (☎ 747 3828; Jl Prawirotaman I 15A; mains 25,000Rp; ☻ breakfast, lunch & dinner) This contemporary outfit is the place to sip coffee, satisfy your sweet tooth and wax lyrical about the finer points of philosophy (there's a library upstairs if you don't have a dog-eared copy of Nietzsche in your day-pack).

Laba Laba Cafe (☎ 374921; Jl Prawirotaman I 2; mains 15,000Rp; ☻ lunch & dinner) Rather more grungy – *laba laba* means 'spider' – this no-nonsense bamboo bar/eatery has cheap grills and plenty of drunken brouhaha once the Bintang starts flowing.

Entertainment

Dance, *wayang* or gamelan are performed most mornings at the *kraton* (admission free). Check with the tourist office for current listings.

Most famous of all performances is the spectacular Ramayana ballet held in the open air at Prambanan in the dry season (see p195).

Hanoman's Forest Restaurant (Map p189; ☎ 372528; Jl Prawirotaman I; cover charge 15,000Rp) This Prawirotaman eatery has different *wayang* performances at 7pm most nights of the week.

DANCE

Most dance performances are based on the Ramayana.

Purawisata (Map p189; ☎ 380644; Jl B Katamso; tickets 60,000Rp, incl dinner 100,000Rp) The amusement park stages the Ramayana daily at 8pm.

Ndalem Pujokusuman (Map p189; Jl B Katamso 45; tickets 30,000Rp) This theatre hosts performances on Monday and Friday between 8pm and 10pm.

WAYANG KULIT

Leather-puppet performances can be seen at several places around Yogya every night of the week.

Sasono Hinggil (Map p189; tickets 7500Rp) Most of the centres offer shortened versions for tourists but here, in the *alun alun selatan* (south main square) of the *kraton,* marathon all-night performances are held every

second Saturday from 9pm to 5am. Bring a pillow.

Sono-Budoyo Museum (Map p189; ☎ 376775; Jl Trikora 6; tickets 7500Rp) Near the *kraton,* the museum has performances nightly from 8pm to 10pm.

WAYANG GOLEK

Wooden-puppet plays are also performed frequently – the **tourist information office** (Map p189; ☎ 562000; Jl Malioboro 16; ☻ 8am-6.30pm Mon-Sat) has listings of the latest shows.

Nitour (Map p189; Jl KH Ahmad Dahlan 71; tickets 7500Rp) Tourist-oriented shows are staged here at 10.30am daily, except Sunday.

Shopping

Yogya is a great place to shop for crafts and antiques.

Jl Malioboro is one great, long, throbbing bazaar of souvenir shops and stalls selling cheap cotton clothes, leatherwork, batik bags, *topeng* masks and *wayang golek* puppets.

BATIK

Batik in the markets, especially Pasar Beringharjo, is cheaper than in the shops, but you need to be careful about quality and should be prepared to bargain.

Good fixed-price places to try:
Batik Keris (Map p189; ☎ 557893; Jl Malioboro 21; ☻ 9am-9pm)
Mirota Batik (Map p189; ☎ 588524; Jl A Yani 9; ☻ 9am-9pm)

Most of the batik workshops and several large showrooms are along Jl Tirtodipuran, south of the *kraton*. These places cater to tour groups so prices are very high. **Batik Raradjong-grang** (Map p189; ☎ 375209; Jl Tirtodipuran 6A; ☻ 8am-7pm) gives free guided tours of the factory.

SILVERWORK

Silverwork can be found all over town, but head to the silver village of Kota Gede. Fine filigree work is a Yogya speciality.

Narti's Silver (☎ 374890; Jl Tegal Gendu 22; ☻ 9am-6pm) This is a large outlet, and there are dozens of smaller silver shops on Jl Kemesan and Jl Mondorakan, where you can get some good buys if you bargain.

LEATHERWORK

Yogya's leatherwork can be excellent value for money, but always check the quality.

Shops and street stalls on Jl Malioboro are the best places to shop.

Swasthigita (Map p189; ☎ 378346; Ngadinegaran MJ 3/122; ⏰ 9am-4pm) Just north of Jl Tirto-dipuran, this is a large *wayang kulit* puppet manufacturer.

Putra Wayang (Map p189; ☎ 386611; Jl Ngadisuryan; ⏰ 8am-5pm) This place is a smaller affair.

Getting There & Away

AIR

Garuda (Map p191; ☎ 0807-1-427842; www.garuda-indonesia.com; Inna Garuda Hotel, Jl Malioboro) has twice-daily flights to Jakarta (250,000Rp).

Lion Air (Map p189; ☎ 555028; Melia Purosani Hotel, Jl Mayor Suryotomo 31) has cut-price daily flights to Jakarta (88,000Rp), Denpasar (88,000Rp) and Surabaya (139,000Rp) – book ahead.

Mandala (Map p189; ☎ 520602; www.mandalaair.com; Jl Mayor Suryotomo 573A) has daily flights, including Jakarta (160,000Rp), Balikpapan (475,000Rp) and Batam (420,000Rp).

Malaysia Airlines (Map p189; ☎ 557327; www.malaysiaairlines.com; Melia Purosani Hotel, Jl Mayor Suryo-tomo 31) flies to Kuala Lumpur (US$187).

BUS

Yogyakarta's new **Giwangan bus station** (☎ 410015; Jl Imogiri) is 5km southeast of the city centre, on the ring road.

Economy/air-con bus services: Solo (7000/10,000Rp, two hours), Semarang (12,000/20,000Rp, 3½ hours), Purwok-erto (20,000/35,000Rp, 4½ hours), Band-ung (45,000/70,000Rp, 10 hours), Jakarta (40,000/90,000Rp, 12 hours), Surabaya (35,000/55,000Rp, eight hours), Probol-inggo (40,000/60,000Rp, nine hours) and Denpasar (60,000/120,000Rp, 16 hours).

Buses also operate regularly to towns in the immediate area: Borobudur (5000Rp, 1½ hours), Parangtritis (6000Rp, one hour) and Kaliurang (3000Rp, one hour). For Im-ogiri (2000Rp, 40 minutes), take a bus to Panggang and ask the conductor to let you off at the *makam* (graves).

For the long haul trips, tickets for the big luxury buses can be bought at the bus station; it's more expensive but less hassle to check fares and departures with the ticket agencies along Jl Sosrowijayan and Jl Prawi-rotaman. These agencies can also arrange pick-up from your hotel.

You can get to Giwangan on local bus 4 from stops along Jl Malioboro (1000Rp).

MINIBUS

Door-to-door *travel* run to all major cities from Yogya, including Cilacap (60,000Rp, five hours), Surabaya (80,000Rp, eight hours), Jakarta (120,000Rp, 11 hours), Denpasar (150,000Rp, 15 hours), Bromo (100,000Rp, 10 hours) and Pangandaran (100,000Rp, eight hours). Most will pick up from your hotel. For reservations, try **Jaya Tour & Travel** (Map p191; ☎ 586735; Gang II).

TRAIN

Yogya's main **Tugu station** (☎ 512870) is con-veniently central, although some *ekonomi* trains run to/from the Lempuyangan sta-tion 1km further east.

For Jakarta, the *Senja Utama Yogya* (*bisnis* 64,000Rp, eight hours) departs at 8.25pm.

For Solo, the best option is the *Prameks* (*bisnis* 5000Rp, one hour) departing from Tugu at 6.50am, 9.45am, 1pm, 4.10pm and 6.52pm.

To Surabaya, the overnight service run by *Mutiara Selatan* (*bisnis* 80,000Rp, six hours) departs from Tugu at 1am and also travels to Bandung (*bisnis* 80,000Rp, six hours) at 10.35pm if going in the other direction.

For details of all times and prices, visit www.infoka.kereta-api.com.

Getting Around

BUS

Bis kota (city buses) operate on set routes around the city for a flat 1000Rp fare.

LOCAL TRANSPORT

Bicycles (12,000Rp per day) and motor-cycles (40,000Rp) can be hired from travel agents and hotels. Furious bargaining is re-quired with local becak drivers – count on 5000Rp for a short trip.

TAXI

Metered taxis are readily available at 3500Rp for the first kilometre and 1500Rp for subsequent kilometres – try **JAS Taxi** (☎ 373737).

AROUND YOGYAKARTA

Java's biggest drawcards are the Prambanan temple complex and the huge Buddhist stupa at Borobudur – plenty of organised minibus tours from Yogya include visits to the two sites (see above).

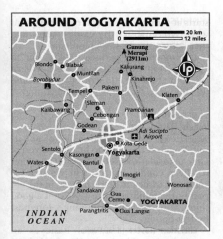

AROUND YOGYAKARTA

Prambanan

The grandest and most evocative Hindu temple complex in Java, **Prambanan** (☎ 0274-496435; admission US$10; �) 6am-6pm, last admission 5.15pm) features some 50 temple sites. The main temples are all in the tourist complex fronting the village on the highway, while others are scattered across the surrounding fields. It is 17km east of Yogya on the Solo road.

The **Shiva Temple** is the largest and most lavish, towering 47 dizzy metres above the valley and decorated with an entire pantheon of carved deities. The statue of Shiva stands in the central chamber and statues of the goddess Durga, Shiva's elephant-headed son Ganesh and Agastya the teacher stand in the other chapels of the upper part of the temple. The Shiva temple is flanked by the **Vishnu** and **Brahma temples**, the latter carrying further scenes from the Ramayana. In the small central temple, opposite the Shiva temple, stands a statue of the bull Nandi, Shiva's mount.

Built in the 9th century AD, around 50 years after Borobudur, the complex at Prambanan was mysteriously abandoned soon after its completion. Many of the temples had collapsed by the 19th century and only in 1937 was any form of reconstruction attempted.

If you are here at the right time, don't miss the great **Ramayana ballet** (tickets from 30,000Rp). Short and long versions of the ballet are performed at 7.30pm alternately from May to October, with the condensed performances taking to the stage year-round. Call Prambanan for more details, or book tickets through travel agents or the **Yogyakarta tourist information office** (☎ 0274-562000; Jl Malioboro 16; �) 8am-6.30pm Mon-Sat).

GETTING THERE & AWAY
From Yogya, take a bus (3000Rp, 30 minutes) from Giwangan bus station – Solo-bound buses also stop here. A bicycle is an ideal way to explore all the temples in the area via the back roads.

Borobudur
☎ 0293
Ranking with Bagan and Angkor Wat as one of the great Southeast Asian monuments, **Borobudur** (☎ 0274-496408; www.borobudurpark.com; admission US$10; �) 6am-5pm) is a truly colossal structure and a poignant epitaph to Java's Buddhist heyday.

The temple, 42km outside Yogya, consists of six square bases topped by three circular ones, and it was constructed at roughly the same time as Prambanan in the early part of the 9th century AD. With the decline of Buddhism, Borobudur was abandoned and only rediscovered in 1814 when Raffles governed Java.

Nearly 1500 narrative panels on the terraces illustrate Buddhist teachings and tales, while 432 Buddha images sit in chambers on the terraces. On the upper circular terraces there are latticed stupas, which contain 72 more Buddha images.

Borobudur is best seen at sunrise, when the crowds are at their smallest and the light at its most spectacular.

The **Mendut Temple** (admission free), 3km east of Borobudur, has a magnificent 3m-high statue of Buddha seated with two disciples. It has been suggested that this image was originally intended to top Borobudur but proved impossible to raise to the summit. It's a fine walk to Mendut and the smaller **Pawon Temple** (admission free); otherwise a *bemo* is 1000Rp.

Knowledgeable guides for Borobudur can be hired (35,000Rp) at the ticket office.

SLEEPING & EATING
Pondok Tingal Hostel (☎ 788245; dm 11,000Rp, d from 50,000Rp; ☒) This midmarket outfit has something for everyone, from basic dorms

to swanky air-con doubles (250,000Rp). The bamboo décor and leafy garden give the place a charisma injection and there's a decent restaurant on-site. It is 1km east of the temple.

Lotus Guest House (☎ 788281; Jl Medang Kamulan 2; s/d 50,000/70,000Rp) Borobudur's veteran hostel has aged rather less gracefully than the monument itself. The rooms are looking rather tatty these days, but the owner is helpful and can whip you up a decent dinner. It is on the eastern side of the temple near the main parking area.

Hotel Bhumisambhara (☎ 788205; Jl Badrawati; s/d 30,000/35,000Rp) Ignore the early morning cock-a-doodle-dos and this is Borobudur's quietest option, with a handful of rooms in a tranquil setting. It is down a quiet alley on the eastern side of the temple complex.

GETTING THERE & AWAY

If you are staying in the Sosrowijayan area of Yogyakarta, the easiest option is to flag down a northbound bus 5 on the corner of Jl Sosrowijayan and Jl Joyonegaran. This will take you to Jombor (1000Rp, 20 minutes), where you can change to a Borobudur bus (5000Rp, 40 minutes). Alternatively, catch a direct bus from Yogya's Giwangan terminal (5000Rp, 1½ hours). The last bus back from Borobudur leaves around 5.30pm.

Kaliurang, Gunung Merapi & Selo

☎ 0274

On the flanks of Gunung Merapi, **Kaliurang** is a pleasant mountain resort, with crisp air and some spectacular views of one of Java's most boisterous volcanoes. It is 26km north of Yogya.

Gunung Merapi is one of Indonesia's most dangerous volcanoes and it erupts with alarming regularity. In November 1994 an eruption killed 69 people; in January 2001, pyroclastic flows and thousands of earthquakes prompted the Volcanology Survey of Indonesia to raise the warning status on the mountain. Advice should be sought before attempting to climb it.

The once popular climb to the summit from Kaliurang has been off limits for quite some time, though you can walk to viewpoints with a qualified guide – contact the owner of Vogels Hostel, **Christian Awuy** (☎ 081-7541 2572), for information and advice. The Vogels tour (per person 50,000Rp) starts at 4am, takes you as far as a viewpoint where volcanic activity can be seen, and then returns to the hostel for 9am.

During quieter periods, it is easier to climb Merapi from **Selo** on the northern side, but at the time of writing, the volcano was off limits from every approach.

SLEEPING

Vogels Hostel (☎ 895208; Jl Astamulya 76; dm/d 9000/40,000Rp) Almost as old as the volcano itself, Vogels is the place to head for if you're after an insider's view of Merapi. The owner has been conducting tours in the area for years and while little has changed in the old part of the building since 1983 (not a good thing), this remains Kaliurang's foremost budget option.

Christian Hostel (d 30,000Rp) Basic as an empty bucket, this nearby Vogels offshoot offers Spartan digs and topnotch Merapi views from the rooftop terrace. You can book it through Vogels.

In Selo, **Pak Auto** (s/d 15,000/30,000Rp) offers basic sleeps and arranges guides.

GETTING THERE & AWAY

Buses (3000Rp, one hour) run direct to Kaliurang from Yogya's Giwangan terminal. For Selo, take a Magelang bus to Blabak (3000Rp) and then a *colt* or bus (3000Rp) onwards. Direct Solo–Magelang buses also pass Selo.

Parangtritis

The best known of the beaches south of Yogya, **Parangtritis** is 27km away. It is a scruffy local resort that is packed on weekends.

Parangtritis is a centre for the worship of Nyai Loro Kidul, the queen of the South Seas, whose mystical union with the sultans of Yogya and Solo requires regular offerings.

Buses (6000Rp, one hour) run regularly from Yogya. Most of Yogya's travel agencies offer day-trips that include Parangtritis.

SOLO

☎ 0271 / pop 525,000

Throughout Indonesia, Solo (also known as Surakarta) is known for its independent thinkers and hot-tempered firebrands. Long rivalling Yogyakarta as the centre of Javanese culture and briefly rising to prominence as capital of the Mataram empire, modern Solo has a penchant for dance, music, *wayang* and, from time to time, political extremism. But while Solo's residents have been known to take to the streets and burn down a shopping mall or two, this is one of Java's friendliest and most engaging cities, offering *kraton,* crumbling back alleys and a thriving arts scene, minus the tourist hordes of Yogyakarta.

Orientation

A metered taxi from the airport, 10km northwest of the city centre, costs 35,000Rp, or take a bus via Kartasura.

Solo's main street is Jl Slamet Riyadi, running east–west through the centre of the city. The train and bus stations are about 2km north of the city centre, while most of the budget accommodation is conveniently clustered around Jl Yos Sudarso and Jl Ahmad Dahlan. The oldest part of Solo is east of here around the Kraton Surakarta and Pasar Klewer.

Information

BCA bank (cnr Jl Dr Rajiman & Jl Gatot Subroto) Has ATM and currency exchange facilities.
Main post office (Jl Jen Sudirman; 🕙 8am-5pm Mon-Fri, 8am-noon Sat) Near the Telkom office.
Surya Internet (☎ 734546; Jl Slamet Riyadi 170; 🕙 9am-6pm Mon-Sat, 9am-1pm Sun)
Telkom office (Jl Mayor Kusmanto; 🕙 7am-6pm) Has Internet access.
Tourist office (☎ 711435; Jl Slamet Riyadi 275; 🕙 8am-4pm Mon-Sat) Central and helpful.

Sights & Activities

KRATON

The Susuhunan of Mataram, Pakubuwono II, moved from Kartasura into his new palace, the **Kraton Surakarta** (☎ 656432; admission 8000Rp; 🕙 8.30am-2pm Sat-Thu), in 1745. Entry is only possible from the northern side, opposite the *alun alun.* A guide leads you through the *kraton* complex to the **Sasono Sewoko museum,** admission included in entry fee to the *kraton,* which has fine silver and bronze Hindu-Javanese figures, Javanese weapons, antiques and other royal heirlooms on display. Many of the *kraton* buildings were rebuilt after a fire in 1985. The distinctive tower known as Panggung Songgo Buwono, used for meditation and built in 1782, is original.

Children's dance practice can be seen here on Sunday from 10am to noon and adult practice from 1pm to 3pm.

Istana Mangkunegaran (☎ 644946; admission 10,000Rp; 🕙 8.30am-2pm Mon-Sat, 8.30am-1pm Sun), the minor palace, was founded in 1757 by a dissident prince, Raden Mas Said. There is a museum in the main hall of the palace behind the beautiful *pendopo,* but the exhibits, which include an extraordinary gold genital cover, are poorly stored.

Guided tours are much less hurried and more informative than at Kraton Surakarta, but the palace is a little ordinary and is fast falling apart. Dance practice is held at the pavilion from 10am to noon on Wednesday.

OTHER ATTRACTIONS

Solo's markets are always worth a browse, especially **Pasar Klewer** (Jl Secoyudan; 🕙 8am-6pm), the multistorey batik market, and **Pasar Triwindu** (Jl Diponegoro; 🕙 8am-5pm), the antique market. The city's back alleys are also worth a wander and chances are you'll be invited into someone's home for a cup of tea and a chat.

Courses

Solo is a centre for traditional Javanese religion and mysticism, and some travellers come here just to meditate. The **tourist office** (☎ 711435; Jl Slamet Riyadi 275; 🕙 8am-4pm Mon-Sat) can steer you in the direction of the many schools. Batik courses are also popular – **Warung Baru** (☎ 656369; Jl Ahmad Dahlan 23) organises one-day batik courses (50,000Rp).

Tours

Many homestays offer excellent bike tours of Solo's cottage industries. For 50,000Rp, a full-day tour takes you through some beautiful countryside to see batik weaving, gamelan making, and tofu, arak and rice-cracker processing. Ask at **Warung Baru** (☎ 656369).

Sleeping

Solo has an excellent selection of homestays.

Cakra Homestay (☎ 634743; Jl Cakra II/15; d with shared/private mandi from 40,000/50,000Rp; 🃏 🖳) Rather more palatial than either of the two *kraton,* this extraordinary hotel occupies one of the city's architectural gems. Hidden away behind an imposing gate, it gets very little custom and while the rooms are basic and echo with early-morning cock crows, Cakra remains Solo's most atmospheric budget bolthole. Air-con costs 70,000Rp.

SOLO

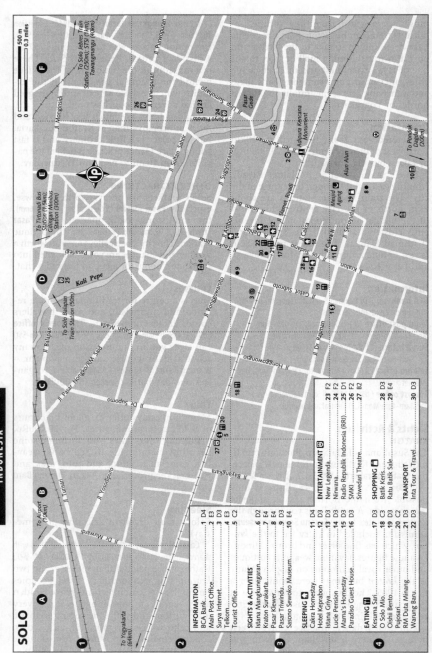

INDONESIA

Istana Griya (☎ 632667; istanagriya@yahoo.com; Jl Ahmad Dahlan 22; d from 50,000Rp; 🔀) More suited to those after the tried-and-tested back-packer format, this is a colourful, cheerful spot with a programme of well-organised tours and a reasonably regular stream of pack-toting guests. There's a little terrace for mingling and a wide range of rooms, including huge, air-con suites (200,000Rp).

Paradiso Guest House (☎ 652960; Kemlayan Kidul 1; d from 35,000Rp) Whitewashed and chintzy, this secure hideaway offers plenty of quiet, spotty rooms and a haphazard garden setting. The wedding-cake architecture is looking a little mouldy, but the rooms are fine for a night's shuteye.

Lucie Pension (☎ 653375; Jl Ambon 12; s/d with shared mandi 25,000/30,000Rp) On a quiet alley near Istana Mangkunegaran, Lucie offers little more than a mat on the floor and a roof above. The owner is a bona fide sweet-heart, but you may as well be camping out in a cardboard box.

Pondok Dagdan (☎ 669324; Jl Carangan Baluarti 42; s/d with shared mandi 25,000/35,000Rp) With an at-mospheric location near Kraton Surakarta, this leafy little number offers a handful of bamboo rooms in a quiet garden.

Mama's Homestay (☎ 662466; Jl Cakra 33; s/d with shared mandi 35,000/45,000Rp) Mama is very old these days and her homestay is looking a lit-tle ramshackle, but the rooms are just about passable if everywhere else is full.

Hotel Keprabon (☎ 632811; Jl Ahmed Dahlan 8-12; d with shared/private mandi from 30,000/42,000Rp; 🔀) This hotel's one-time Art Deco charm is fast fading, but the rooms are still good value and it has the cheapest air-con rooms (55,000Rp) in town.

Eating

Solo is a great place to indulge in street food. Roaming hawkers pack the streets at night advertising their wares by screech-ing, striking buffalo bells or clattering cut-lery. Of the plethora of dishes on offer, try *nasi gudeg* (unripe jackfruit served with rice, chicken and spices) or *srabi* (mini rice puddings served on a crispy pancake with banana, jackfruit or chocolate topping).

O Solo Mio (☎ 727264; Jl Slamet Riyadi 253; mains 35,000Rp; 🕑 lunch & dinner) If you can't be both-ered climbing Gunung Merapi, you can in-stead eat a pizza here that has been cooked on a slab of stone from the mountain. The

décor oozes Mediterranean pizzazz and there's a little yard out back for alfresco dining.

Warung Baru (☎ 656369; Jl Ahmad Dahlan 23; mains 12,000Rp; 🕑 breakfast, lunch & dinner) Solo's veteran backpacker café bakes the best bread in town. The colossal menu is a little ordinary, but you can book tours and get the gossip from mama while you wait for your dinner.

Kesuma Sari (☎ 656406; Jl Slamet Riyadi 111; mains 8000Rp; 🕑 lunch & dinner; 🔀) This sparkling air-con eatery features waiters in crisp white shirts, plenty of Indonesian chicken dishes and gleaming surfaces.

Pujosari (Jl Slamet Riyadi; dishes 10,000Rp; 🕑 24hr) This collection of *warung* next to the tourist office has a sprinkling of just about every-thing.

Other recommendations:

RM Duta Minang (☎ 488449; Jl Slamet Riyadi 66; mains 5000Rp; 🕑 lunch & dinner) For cheap Padang food.

Oishii Bento (☎ 708 7818; Jl Secoyudan 136; mains 15,000Rp; 🕑 lunch & dinner; 🔀) For Japanese fast food.

Clubbing

Hedonists can find a few lively nightspots for an evening of deafening bump-and-grind.

New Legenda (Jl Suryo Pranoto; admission 15,000Rp; 🕑 8pm-2am) Pitch-black, loud and raucous, this has everything you have come to expect from a Javanese nightclub – go get your dancing shoes.

Nirwana (Jl Urip Sumoharjo; admission 15,000Rp; 🕑 8pm-2am) In the same block as New Leg-enda, on the other side, Nirwana adver-tises itself with a lascivious-looking Statue of Liberty and promises more of the same inside.

Entertainment

Solo is an excellent place to see traditional Javanese performing arts. Check the latest schedules with the **tourist office** (☎ 711435; Jl Slamet Riyadi 275; 🕑 8am-4pm Mon-Sat).

Sriwedari Theatre (Jl Slamet Riyadi; tickets 3000Rp) At the back of Sriwedari Amusement Park, this has a long-running *wayang orang* troupe. Performances are staged nightly, except Sunday, from 8pm to 10pm.

Radio Republik Indonesia (RRI) auditorium (☎ 641178; Jl Abdul Rahman Saleh 51; tickets from 5000Rp) The radio auditorium hosts an er-ratic, but eclectic schedule of cultural performances – check with the tourist office for schedules.

Sekolah Tinggi Seni Indonesia (STSI; ☎ 647658; tickets from 5000Rp) The arts academy at the Kentingan campus in Jebres, in the northeast of the city, has dance practice Monday to Thursday from 7.30am to 2pm, on Friday from 7.30am to 11am and on Saturday from 7.30am to noon.

SMKI (☎ 632225; Jl Purwopuran) The high school for the performing arts also has dance practice daily from 8am to noon, except Sunday.

Taman Budaya Surakarta (TBS; ☎ 635414; Jl Ir Sutami 57) The cultural centre, east of the city, holds all-night *wayang kulit* on Friday Kliwon of the Javanese calendar.

Istana Mangkunegaran and Kraton Surakarta also have traditional Javanese dance practice (see p197 for details).

Shopping

Balai Agung (☼ 8am-4pm) On the northern side of the *alun alun,* you can see high-quality *wayang kulit* puppets being made here, and gamelan sets are for sale.

Solo is a major batik centre. You can see the batik process on one of Warung Baru's batik tours (see p197).

Try also the following:

Batik Keris (☎ 643292; Jl Yos Sudarso 62; ☼ 9am-7pm) A fixed-price place.

Pasar Klewer (Jl Secoyudan; ☼ 8am-6pm) This is the cheapest place to buy batik.

Ratu Batik Sale (☎ 667727; Jl Secoyudan 6; ☼ 9am-5pm) Another fixed-price place.

Getting There & Away

AIR

Garuda (☎ 0807-1-427832; www.garuda-indonesia .com; airport) flies daily to Jakarta (450,000Rp). Plane tickets can also be booked at **Inta Tour & Travel** (☎ 654010; Jl Slamet Riyadi 96; ☼ 8am-8pm Mon-Sat, 8am-2pm Sun).

BUS

The Tirtonadi bus station is 2km north of the city centre. Frequent buses go to Prambanan (5000Rp, 1½ hours) and Yogyakarta (normal/air-con 7000/10,000Rp, two hours); and numerous buses go to Surabaya (30,000/40,000Rp, six hours) and Malang (30,000/40,000Rp, seven hours). Agents at the bus station sell tickets for the longer, express routes (eg Jakarta 80,000Rp; Denpasar 110,000Rp).

Homestays and travel agencies also sell tickets for *travel*. A door-to-door service to Bromo (Ngadisiri) costs 130,000Rp.

TRAIN

Solo is on the main Jakarta–Yogyakarta–Surabaya train line. **Solo Balapan** (☎ 714039) is the main station, but some local trains depart from Solo Jebres, further east.

The quickest and most convenient way to get to Yogyakarta is on the *Prameks* (*bisnis* 5000Rp, one hour), which departs from Balapan five times daily at 5.45am, 8.35am, 11.36am, 2.30pm and 5.55pm. These trains start in Jebres 15 minutes earlier.

The *Senja Utama Solo* (*bisnis* 80,000Rp, 9½ hours) departs Balapan for Jakarta at 6pm. The *eksekutif Bima* (200,000Rp, nine hours) leaves Balapan for Jakarta at 8.55pm.

The *Sancaka* (*bisnis/eksekutif* 45,000/ 70,000, Rp 4½ hours) swings through Balapan at 8.14am and 4.59pm on its way to Surabaya from Yogyakarta.

For all times and prices, visit www.info ka.kereta-api.com.

Getting Around

A becak from the train or bus stations into the city centre costs around 5000Rp, and a taxi costs 15,000Rp. Minibus 06 costs 1500Rp to Jl Slamet Riyadi.

Bicycles and motorcycles (motorcycle/ bicycle per day 40,000/15,000Rp) can be hired from homestays.

AROUND SOLO
Sangiran

Prehistoric Java man fossils were discovered at Sangiran, 18km north of Solo, where a small **museum** (admission 7500Rp; ☼ 8am-4pm Tue-Sun) has fossil exhibits. To get there take a Purwodadi bus to Kalijambe (1500Rp) and it's a 4km walk from there (by *ojek* 5000Rp).

Candi Sukuh

This fascinating temple is on the slopes of Gunung Lawu (3265m), 36km east of Solo. Dating from the 15th century, it was one of the last Hindu temples to be built in Java and has a curious Inca-like look. Take a bus to Karangpandan (3000Rp, 30 minutes), then a Kemuning minibus to the turn-off to Candi Sukuh (2000Rp, 20 minutes). On market days the bus goes right to the temple; otherwise it's a 2km uphill walk.

SURABAYA

☎ 031 / pop 2.5 million

The big city of East Java, and Indonesia's second-largest, is a metropolitan colossus, like a clone of Jakarta nurtured in a petri dish and allowed to bloom unchecked on Java's east coast. Frenetic and feisty, Surabaya can feel like a sleeping dragon, a place that could awake into pandemonium at any time. But while the city's smoky streets are intimidating at first, Surabaya does have a gentler, more accommodating face and its shopping malls and extensive Chinatown offer plenty of distractions for avid shoppers and pathological culture vultures alike.

GETTING INTO TOWN

Taxis from Juanda Airport (15km) operate on a coupon system and cost 40,000Rp to the city centre. Damri airport buses (5000Rp) drop off in the city centre and Purabaya bus station.

Information

The BNI and Lippo banks, both on Jl Pemuda, have ATMs.

Main post office (Jl Kebon Rojo; ☺ 8am-6pm Mon-Fri, 8am-noon Sat) North of the centre.

Surabaya City Tourist Office (☎ 567 7219; Jl Adity-warman 110; ☺ 7am-2pm Mon-Fri) About 2km south of the centre, near the zoo.

Transnet (☎ 566 5677; cnr Jl Pemuda & Jl Basuki Rahmat; ☺ 24hr) Internet access.

Sights

Surabaya's crumbling old town is the best place to dip a toe into the city's soul. The streets around **Jembatan Merah** (Red Bridge; Jl Rajawali), where British Brigadier Mallaby was killed during the Battle of Surabaya, have some fine old Dutch architecture. From here you can wander across to **Chinatown**, which bursts into life at night when Jl Kembang Jepun becomes a huge street kitchen known as **Kya Kya** (see p203).

Pasar Pabean (Jl Panggung; ☺ 8am-6pm) is the area's bustling marketplace and the nearby **fish market** (Pasar Ikan; Jl Panggung; ☺ from 8pm), where all the oddities of the sea go on sale come nightfall, makes for a fascinating late-night stroll. Nearby, you will also find the colourful 300-year-old **Kong Co Kong Tik Cun Ong Chinese temple** (Jl Dukuh; admission by donation; ☺ dawn-dusk) and the **Mesjid Ampel**, in the heart of the Arab Quarter. The latter is the most sacred mosque in Surabaya and is approached through Jl Ampel Suci, a narrow, covered bazaar. Plenty of **Makassar schooners** can be seen at the Kalimas wharf north of town.

Sura means 'shark' and *Baya* means 'crocodile'. You can see a statue re-creating the mythical struggle between the two outside the **zoo** (☎ 567 8703; Jl Diponegoro; admission 7500Rp; ☺ 7am-6pm), which has a decent array of animals, including Komodo dragons. The small **MPU Tantular Museum** (☎ 567 7037; Jl Diponegoro; admission 750Rp; ☺ 8am-2pm Tue-Fri, 8am-12.30pm Sat & Sun), opposite the zoo, has so-so archaeological exhibits.

Sleeping

While Surabaya has a reasonable spread of cheap hotels, most cater to Indonesian visitors. In general, you get a lot better value if you are willing to spend a little more.

Plenty of cheap hotels can also be found in the historic area near Kota train station.

Hotel Paviljoen (☎ 534 3449; Jl Genteng Besar 94; s/d 60,000/80,000Rp; ✗) Housed in a flaky Dutch-era villa and run by a bookish owner, this has comfy rooms, a flick of latter-day charisma and a mosquito infestation of almost biblical proportions.

SPLURGE!

Hotel Majapahit Mandarin Oriental (☎ 545 4333; www.mandarinoriental.com; Jl Tunjungan 65; d 475,000Rp; ✗ ☐ ☲) In 1945, returning colonial forces raised the Dutch flag at this colonial-era hotel, an act that sparked the Battle of Surabaya. Still the city's most atmospheric hotel, this opulent outfit is the place to blow the budget and soak up all the glamour of old Surabaya.

Puri Asri (☎ 502 5377; pondokasri@telkom .net; Jl Kalibokor Selatan 108; s/d 140,000/150,000Rp; ✗) In Surabaya's quiet eastern suburbs, this brand-new place is housed in a large, glossy villa with modern amenities and seriously comfy beds. Who knows why they erected a statue of a snake gobbling down a stork in their yard.

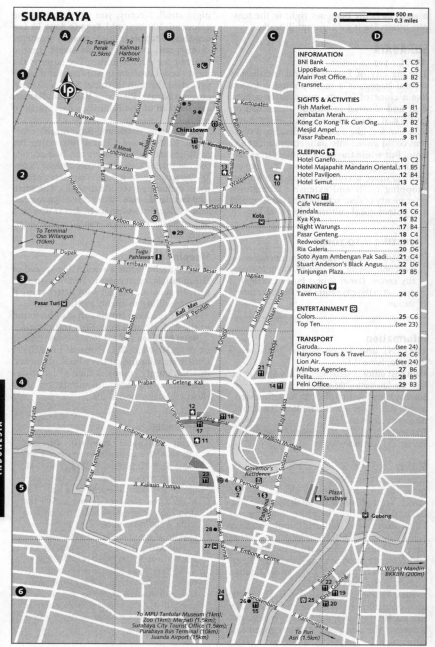

SURABAYA

0 — 500 m
0 — 0.3 miles

INFORMATION

BNI Bank.....................................1 C5
LippoBank...................................2 C5
Main Post Office.........................3 B2
Transnet......................................4 C5

SIGHTS & ACTIVITIES

Fish Market.................................5 B1
Jembatan Merah.........................6 B2
Kong Co Kong Tik Cun Ong.......7 B2
Mesjid Ampel..............................8 B1
Pasar Pabean...............................9 B1

SLEEPING

Hotel Ganefo.............................10 C2
Hotel Majapahit Mandarin Oriental.11 B5
Hotel Paviljoen..........................12 B4
Hotel Semut...............................13 C2

EATING

Cafe Venezia..............................14 C4
Jendala.......................................15 C6
Kya Kya......................................16 B2
Night Warungs...........................17 B4
Pasar Genteng...........................18 C4
Redwood's.................................19 D6
Ria Galeria..................................20 D6
Soto Ayam Ambengan Pak Sadi..21 C4
Stuart Anderson's Black Angus..22 D6
Tunjungan Plaza........................23 B5

DRINKING

Tavern.......................................24 C6

ENTERTAINMENT

Colors..25 C6
Top Ten..................................(see 23)

TRANSPORT

Garuda...................................(see 24)
Haryono Tours & Travel.............26 C6
Lion Air...................................(see 24)
Minibus Agencies......................27 B6
Pelita...28 B5
Pelni Office................................29 B3

To Tanjung Perak (2.5km)
To Kalimas Harbour (2.5km)

Jl Rajawali

Chinatown

Jl Kasuari
Jl Merak
Jl Krem Baral
Jl Indrapura
Jl Sikatan
Jl Cendrawasih
Jl Jembatan Merah
Jl Kembang Jepun
Jl Veteran
Jl Setasiun Kota
Jl Samuda
Jl Waspada
Jl Kertopaten
Jl Palumas
Jl Panggung
Jl Ampel Suci
Jl Dukuh

Kota

To Terminal Oso Wilangun (10km)
Jl Dupak
Jl Kebon Rojo

Tugu Pahlawan

Jl Tembaan
Jl Pahlawan
Jl Pasar Besar
Jl Penghela
Kali Mas
Jl Penelch
Jl Jagalan
Jl Bubutan
Jl Cepu
Jl Semarang

Pasar Turi

Jl Undaan Kulon
Jl Undaan Wetan
Jl Kamboja

Jl Raya Arjuno
Jl Praban
Jl Geteng Kali

Jl Tunjungan
Genteng Besar
Jl Embong Malang
Jl Kaliasin Pompa
Jl Pasar Kembang

Governor's Residence

Jl Walikota Mustajab
Jl Raya Jaksa
Jl Pemuda
Jl Panglima Sudirman
Jl Tegalsari

Plaza Surabaya

Gubeng

Jl Bukuki Rahmat
Jl Embong Cerme

To Wisma Mandiri BKKBN (200m)

Jl Sonokembang
Jl Sumatra
Jl Raya Gubeng
Jl Karimunjawa

To MPU Tantular Museum (1km); Zoo (1km); Merpati (1.5km); Surabaya City Tourist Office (1.5km); Purabaya Bus Terminal (10km); Juanda Airport (15km)

To Puri Asri (1.5km)

INDONESIA

Wisma Mandiri BKKBN (☎ 502 6963; Jl Airlangga 31; d from 60,000Rp; ✖) In front of Airlangga University, these student-style digs are basic, but secure and well mopped. The pricier rooms (85,000Rp) have air-con and it's within easy distance of Gubeng train station.

Hotel Ganefo (☎ 371 1169; Jl Kapasan 169-171; d with shared/private mandi 55,000/65,000Rp; ✖) Oozing the peculiar charms of old Chinatown, this Spartan outfit has cell-like rooms and a seriously atmospheric terrace for sipping tea.

Hotel Semut (☎ 353 1770; Jl Samudra 9; s/d 100,000/113,000Rp; ✖) Offering plenty of decorative Chinese furniture, muzak (we must be heading upmarket) and vaguely stylish rooms, these are some of the best-value digs in the north of town.

Eating

Kya Kya (Jl Kembang Jepun; mains 10,000Rp; ✖ 6-10pm) The name given to the menagerie of street kitchens that stoke up their stoves every night along Chinatown's main drag, Kya Kya is by far the most interesting place for an evening nibble. And if you're not hungry, just bring your camera.

Jendala (☎ 531 4073; Jl Sonokembang 4-6; mains 25,000Rp; ✖ lunch & dinner) Occupying a rambling colonial lodge, with a mellow garden terrace, Jendala's excellent menu runs from cheap local to pricey Western dishes.

Soto Ayam Ambengan Pak Sadi (☎ 532 3998; Jl Ambengan 3A; mains 20,000Rp; ✖ lunch & dinner) Ask a taxi driver for *ayam*, and this is where you will end up. Pak Sadi is Surabaya's answer to KFC's colonel, and you'll find a fabulous array of local chicken dishes on his menu.

Cafe Venezia (☎ 534 3335; Jl Ambengan 16; mains 40,000Rp; ✖ lunch & dinner) Housed in a sprawling Dutch villa, this place has a smorgasbord of dishes (including Korean barbecue) at slightly ostentatious prices. The outside terrace has plenty of class though and there's lots of atmosphere.

The best area for midrange restaurants is south of Gubeng train station along Jl Raya Gubeng. Try the following:

Ria Galeria (☎ 503 3737; Jl Raya Gubeng; mains 35,000Rp; ✖ lunch & dinner) Does Indonesian food.

Redwood's (☎ 503 9316; Jl Raya Gubeng 33; mains 40,000Rp; ✖ lunch & dinner) Offers oriental and fusion specialities.

Stuart Anderson's Black Angus (☎ 502 1400; Jl Raya Gubeng 40; mains 45,000Rp; ✖ lunch & dinner) Serves topnotch US steaks.

You can make your way to **Pasar Genteng** (Jl Genteng Besar; mains 6000Rp; ✖ 9am-9pm) for cheap eats, while **Tunjungan Plaza** (Jl Tunjungan; ✖ 10am-9pm) has a colossal selection of squeaky-clean eateries.

Drinking

Bars at the big hotels are the happening places and often have decent bands performing.

Tavern (☎ 531 1234; Hyatt Regency Hotel, Jl Basuki Rahmat; ✖ noon-1am) A classy, Western-style drinking den.

Clubbing

Colors (Jl Sumatra 81; ✖ 5pm-3am) This lively little venue, in a historic villa, has cheaper beers than the other nightclubs, and a friendly atmosphere. Bands play every night until 2am.

Surabayans are big on discos – try **Top Ten** (Tunjungan Plaza, Jl Tunjungan; ✖ 8pm-3am).

Entertainment

Jendala (☎ 531 4073; Jl Sonokembang 4-6) This restaurant has a varied programme of so-called 'culturetainment' (sometimes dance, sometimes disco, sometimes theatre). Phone for current listings. Also see left.

Getting There & Away

AIR

Surabaya has a few international departures and is an important hub for domestic flights.

The following airlines all operate flights out of Surabaya.

Bouraq (☎ 899 7454; airport)

Garuda (☎ 0807-1-427832; www.garuda-indonesia .com; Hyatt Regency Hotel, Jl Basuki Rahmat 124)

Lion Air (☎ 535 3500; Hyatt Regency Hotel, Jl Basuki Rahmat 124)

Mandala (☎ 561 0777; www.mandalaair.com; Jl Raya Diponegoro 91D)

Merpati (☎ 568 8111; www.merpati.co.id; Jl Raya Darmo 111)

Pelita Air (☎ 534 0303; Jl Basuki Rahmat 16)

Destinations include Kuala Lumpur (one-way US$99), Denpasar (175,000Rp), Jakarta (171,000Rp), Makassar (267,000Rp) and Yogyakarta (185,000Rp).

Haryono Tours & Travel (☎ 532 5800; Jl Panglima Sudirman; ✖ 8am-4pm Mon-Fri, 8am-1pm Sat) can book tickets for all airlines.

INDONESIA

BOAT

Surabaya is an important port and **Pelni** (☎ 355 9950; www.pelni.co.id; Jl Pahlawan 112) ships serve destinations including Makassar, Banjarmasin and Pontianak. Visit the website for details. Boats depart from Tanjung Perak harbour.

Ferries to Kamal on Madura (4000Rp, 30 minutes) also leave every half-hour from here.

BUS

Most buses operate from Surabaya's main Purabaya bus terminal in Bungurasih, 10km south of the city centre. Buses along the north coast and to Semarang depart from the Terminal Oso Wilangun, 10km west of the city.

Buses from Purabaya include Yogyakarta (normal/air-con 35,000/55,000Rp, eight hours), Malang (normal/air-con 10,000/20,000Rp, two hours), Probolinggo (normal/air-con 12,000/22,000Rp, two hours), Banyuwangi (normal/air-con 25,000/35,000Rp, six hours), Solo (normal/air-con 30,000/40,000, six hours), Jakarta (150,000Rp, 18 hours) and Madura.

Luxury long-haul buses also depart from Purabaya. Most are night buses leaving in the late afternoon/early evening. Bookings can be made at the terminal, or travel agencies in the centre of town sell tickets with a mark up.

Door-to-door *travel* operate to Denpasar (125,000Rp, 10 hours), Solo (50,000Rp, six hours) and Yogyakarta (60,000Rp, eight hours). Hotels can make bookings and there are minibus operators on Jl Basuki Rahmat.

TRAIN

Trains from Jakarta, taking the fast northern route via Semarang, arrive at the Pasar Turi train station. Trains taking the southern route via Yogyakarta, and trains from Banyuwangi and Malang, arrive at Gubeng and most carry on to Kota. **Gubeng** (☎ 503 3115) is central and sells tickets for all trains.

Most Jakarta trains leave from **Pasar Turi** (☎ 534 5014), such as the *Gumarang* (*bisnis/ eksekutif* 100,000/180,000Rp, 11 hours), which leaves at 5.05pm. Coming the other way, it departs from Gambir at 6.25pm.

From Gubeng, the slower *Bima* (*eksekutif* 200,000Rp, 13 hours) departs at 6pm for Jakarta, via Yogyakarta, and the *bisnis Mutiara Selatan* (90,000Rp, 13 hours) departs at

4.35pm for Bandung. Coming to Surabaya, they depart at 6pm from Jakarta and 5.05pm from Bandung.

The *Sancaka* is the best day train for Yogyakarta, leaving Gubeng at 7.30am for Solo (four hours) and Yogyakarta (five hours). It costs 45,000/70,000Rp in *bisnis/eksekutif* to either destination and leaves Yogyakarta coming the other way at 4pm.

Apart from services to the main cities, trains leave Gubeng for Malang (4000Rp, two hours) every two hours. The *Mutiara Timur* goes to Banyuwangi (*bisnis/eksekutif* 30,000/45,000Rp, six hours) via Probolinggo at 9.10am.

Getting Around

Surabaya has plenty of air-con metered taxis – **Bluebird** (☎ 372 1234) is the most reliable.

Bemo are labelled A, B, C etc and charge 1500Rp.

AROUND SURABAYA

Scattered around **Trowulan**, 60km southwest of Surabaya on the Solo road, are the ruins of the capital of the ancient Majapahit empire, Java's last great Hindu kingdom. One kilometre from the main Surabaya-Solo Hwy, the **Trowulan Museum** (admission 1000Rp; ♾ 7am-3.30pm Tue-Sun) houses superb examples of Majapahit sculpture and pottery from throughout East Java. Reconstructed temples are scattered over a large area, some within walking distance, though you need to hire a becak to see them all.

The hill resort of **Tretes**, 55km south of Surabaya, is a cool break if you have to kill time in Surabaya, with walks around town and trekking to **Gunung Welirang**.

PPLH Environmental Education Centre (☎ 0321-618752; PPLH@indo.net.id; dm/bungalows 15,000/ 150,000Rp), in a stunning setting near Trawas, a few kilometres northwest of Tretes, is the perfect place to unwind. It mainly caters to groups, but its trekking packages and herbal medicine and ecology courses are open to individuals. There's fine accommodation and a humble but excellent organic restaurant. Take a bus to Pandaan, then a Trawas *bemo* (ask for PPLH) and then take an *ojek*.

PULAU MADURA

Only half an hour from Surabaya by ferry, the rugged island of Madura is famed for its colourful **bull races**, the *kerapan sapi*, which kick off in late August and September and climax with the finals held at Pamekasan. The bulls are harnessed in pairs, two teams compete at a time and they're raced along a 120m course in a special stadium – the bulls can do nine seconds over 100m. Bull races for tourists are sometimes staged at the Bangkalan Stadium, and race practice is held throughout the year in Bangkalan, Pamekasan and Sumenep, but dates are not fixed. The **Surabaya City Tourist Office** (☎ 031-567 7219; Jl Aditywarman 110; ☒ 7am-2pm Mon-Fri) can supply race details.

Pamekasan, the capital of Madura, comes alive in the bull-racing season, but is quiet the rest of the year. **Sumenep**, 53km northeast of Pamekasan, is a more refined, royal town and the most interesting on Madura. You can see Sumenep's 18th-century mosque, and the **kraton** (admission 1000Rp; ☒ 7am-5pm) with its water palace and interesting museum. **Asta Tinggi**, the royal cemetery, is only about 3km from the town centre.

In Pamekasan, **Hotel Ramayana** (☎ 0324-324575; Jl Niaga 55; d 80,000Rp) is a clean, airy option.

In Sumenep, **Hotel Wijaya I** (☎ 0328-662433; Jl Trunojoyo 45-47; d from 30,000Rp; ☒) is the perennial travellers spot, with a range of rooms – some with air-con (70,000Rp) – and a decent buzz.

Getting There & Away

It's only half an hour by ferry (4000Rp) from Surabaya to Kamal, the harbour town on Madura. From the ferry terminal in Kamal, you can take a bus or colt to other main towns, including Bangkalan. Buses also run from Sumenep right through to Surabaya (30,000Rp, five hours).

GUNUNG BROMO
☎ 0335

Gunung Bromo is an active volcano lying at the centre of the Tengger Massif. It is an awesome volcanic landscape and one of the most impressive sights in Indonesia. The massive Tengger crater stretches 10km across and its steep walls plunge down to a vast, flat sea of lava sand. From the crater floor emerges the smoking peak of Gunung Bromo (2329m), the spiritual centre of the highlands. This desolate landscape has a strange end-of-the-world feeling, particularly at sunrise.

Often the whole area is simply referred to as 'Mt Bromo', but Bromo is only one of three mountains within the caldera of the ancient Tengger volcano; it is flanked by the perfect cone of **Batok** (2440m) and the larger **Kursi** (2581m). Further south the whole supernatural moon-likescape is overseen by **Gunung Semeru** (3676m), the highest mountain in Java and the most active volcano in these highlands. The whole area has been incorporated into the **Bromo-Tengger-Semeru National Park**.

A visit to this fantastic volcano is easy to fit in between Bali and Surabaya or Yogyakarta. The usual jumping-off point for Bromo is the town of **Probolinggo** on the main Surabaya to Banyuwangi road. From there, you head to **Ngadisari** or **Cemoro Lawang**, high on the Tengger crater.

Get up at 4.30am or earlier for an easy stroll across to Bromo from Cemoro Lawang. By the time you've crossed the lava plain and started to climb the steps up to Bromo's crater it should be fairly light. Horses can also be hired (40,000Rp). The squat, grey cone of Bromo, only 253 steps high, is not in itself one of the great volcanoes of Indonesia – it is the whole landscape that is breathtaking – but from the top you'll have fantastic views down into the smoking crater and of the sun sailing up over the outer crater. In the wet season, the dawn and the clouds often arrive simultaneously, so at that time of year you might as well stay in bed and stroll across later in the day.

Though Probolinggo is the usual approach, Bromo can also be reached via **Tosari** from the northwest and **Ngadas** from the southwest.

Tours come via Tosari because 4WD vehicles can drive all the way to the base of Gunung Bromo. The main traffic from Tosari, however, is minibus tours via a sealed road right to the top of **Gunung Penanjakan** (2770m) to see the dawn from there. The superb views right across Bromo and the Tengger crater to smoking Gunung Semeru are unsurpassed – this is where those postcard shots are taken.

Gunung Penanjakan can also be reached from Cemoro Lawang, and it's well worth the effort. You can walk (one hour) or take a chartered jeep (100,000Rp) along the road to the **Penanjakan II viewpoint**, itself a spectacular vantage point, but it's worth walking another hour up the steep trail behind this viewing area to Penanjakan proper.

From Malang in the west, it is possible to travel by *mikrolet* to Tumpang, and then by another *mikrolet* to Gubug Klakah, from where you walk 12km to Ngadas. From Ngadas it is 2km to Jemplang at the crater rim, and then three hours on foot (12km) across the floor of the Tengger crater to Gunung Bromo and on to Cemoro Lawang.

Alternatively, from Ngadas it is an 8.5km walk to Rano Pani, where Pak Tasrep runs a homestay and can help organise a climb of Gunung Semeru – off limits at the time of writing due to volcanic activity. It is a full day's walk from Rano Pani to Arcopodo, the camp site on the mountain, and you must be equipped for freezing conditions. The rugged ascent is usually done at 2am the following morning to reach the peak before sunrise.

Information

However you approach Bromo, a 4000Rp park fee is payable at one of the many PHPA checkpoints.

The **PHPA post** (☎ 541038; ☿ 8am-4pm Mon-Fri) in Cemoro Lawang is opposite Hotel Bromo Permai and has information about Bromo.

Festivals & Events

The **Kesada festival** is staged annually by the local Hindu community, when offerings are made to appease Bromo. It fell in September in 2005, but the date changes each year – check with the **tourist office** (☎ 031-567 7219; Jl Aditywarman 110; ☿ 7am-2pm Mon-Fri) in Surabaya.

Sleeping & Eating

CEMORO LAWANG

At the lip of the Tengger crater and right at the start of the walk to Bromo, Cemoro Lawang is the most popular place to stay.

Cafe Lava Hostel (☎ 541020; d with shared/private mandi 60,000/90,000Rp) The gregarious staff scoop the accolades at this friendly and atmospheric travellers hostel. The downstairs café is a great place to hook up with other backpackers and the rooms are tidy, if a little gloomy.

Cemara Indah Hotel (☎ 541019; d with shared/private mandi 30,000/100,000Rp) With some of the best views in town, this is the spot for eager photographers. It's a whole lot less atmos-

> **SPLURGE!**
>
> **Lava View Lodge** (☎ 541009; d 130,000Rp) Five hundred metres outside the village, down a track skirting Bromo Permai, this is another step up the quality ladder, with cosy bungalow rooms and a decent restaurant.

pheric than Cafe Lava, but if you stay here, you won't be spending much time looking around indoors. The pricier rooms have hot water.

Hotel Bromo Permai (☎ 541021; d with shared/private mandi 50,000/150,000Rp; ☒) This is the swankiest place to stay in the village centre, but the rooms are rather ho-hum for the price.

NGADISARI

Another 3km back towards Probolinggo is the tiny village of Ngadisari.

Yoschi's Guest House (☎ 541018; yoschi_bromo@telkom.net; d with shared/private mandi 60,000/100,000Rp) Sporting some extraordinarily kitsch Alpine décor, this is an excellent choice, with oodles of atmosphere, helpful staff and daily tours to the volcano (200,000Rp for four).

PROBOLINGGO

On the highway between Surabaya and Banyuwangi, this is the jumping-off point for Gunung Bromo. Most travellers only see the bus or train station before moving on, but the town has plenty of hotels if you get stuck.

Hotel Bromo Permai (☎ 422256; Jl Panglima Sudirman 237; d 50,000Rp; ☒) This is the most popular travellers hotel, with comfy rooms and an English-speaking owner. It's on the main road close to the centre of town.

Hotel Ratna (☎ 427886; Jl Panglima Sudirman 16; d with shared/private mandi 45,000/200,000Rp; ☒) Further west, Ratna is one of the best in town, with plenty of (fake) colonial charm. The rooms with private mandi come with air-con.

Getting There & Away

Probolinggo's bus station is 5km west of town on the road to Bromo – catch a yellow *angkot* from the main street or the train station for 1200Rp. Normal/air-con buses: Surabaya (12,000/22,000Rp, two hours), Banyuwangi (15,000/25,000Rp, five hours), Yogyakarta (30,000/40,000Rp, eight hours) and Denpasar (40,000/70,000Rp, nine hours).

Green *colt* minibuses from the terminal go to Cemoro Lawang (10,000Rp, two hours) via Ngadisari (7000Rp, 1½ hours) until around 5pm, sometimes later during peak tourist periods. Late-afternoon buses charge more to Cemoro Lawang, when fewer passengers travel beyond Ngadisari. Make sure it goes all the way to Cemoro Lawang when you board.

Probolinggo's train station is 2km north of the centre. The *Mutiara Timur* travels to Surabaya (*bisnis/eksekutif* 30,000/45,000Rp) at 1.25pm. The *Tawang Alun* goes to Banyuwangi (*ekonomi plus* 19,000Rp) at 3.25pm and Malang at 9.37am. The slow *Sri Tanjung* goes to Yogyakarta (*ekonomi* 12,000Rp, 10.40am) via Solo.

Travel agencies in Solo and Yogyakarta book *travel* to Bromo.

BALI

Bali is a brand unto itself, an island that has long outgrown its cramped spot on the map to become the very epitome of the prepackaged paradise. Like a stack of picture postcards, the images are straight from the drawer marked 'Southeast Asian clichés': a technicolour fanfare of golden beaches, ultramarine seas, emerald palm tops and boot-polish suntans. Thrumming along to a soundtrack of late-night shenanigans, breaking waves and chatty souvenir sellers, Bali is Southeast Asia's answer to the Spanish Costas.

Flip the postcard over, however, and you will find that there is plenty to discover behind the predictable, seaside motifs. While much of southern Bali looks like it was designed over cocktail hour at a convention for concrete fetishists, the island also offers a heady mix of untouched wilderness, vibrant Hindu culture and white-knuckle activities. Whether you are here for the suntans, the hangovers, the waves or the culture, Bali is the little isle with everything.

HISTORY

Bali's first prehistoric tourists strolled out of the spume and onto the island's western beaches around 3000 BC. Perhaps distracted by primitive beach life, however, they got off to a relaxed start and it was only in the 9th century that an organised society began to develop around the cultivation of rice.

Hinduism followed hot on the heels of wider cultural development and as Islam swept through neighbouring Java in the following centuries, the kings and courtiers of the embattled Hindu Majapahit kingdom began crossing the straits into Bali, making their final exodus in 1478. The priest Nirartha brought many of the complexities of the Balinese Hindu religion to the island, and established superb sea temples, including Rambut Siwi, Tanah Lot and Ulu Watu.

In the 19th century the Dutch began to form alliances with local princes in northern Bali. A dispute over the ransacking of wrecked ships was the pretext for the 1906 Dutch invasion of the south, which climaxed in a suicidal *puputan* (fight to the death). The Denpasar nobility burnt their own palaces, dressed in their finest jewellery and, waving golden kris, marched straight into the Dutch guns. The rajas of Tabanan, Karangasem, Gianyar and Klungkung soon capitulated, and Bali became part of the Dutch East Indies.

In later years Balinese culture was actually encouraged by many Dutch officials. International interest was aroused and the first Western tourists arrived.

After WWII the struggle for national independence was fierce in Bali. Independence was declared on 17 August 1945 (still celebrated as Independence Day), but power wasn't officially handed over until 27 December 1949, when the Dutch finally gave up the fight. The island languished economically in the early years of Indonesian sovereignty, but Bali's greatest national resource, beauty, was subsequently marketed to great effect. In the years that followed the island's promotion, the tourist industry brought with it all the good (growing prosperity) and bad (massive overdevelopment) of the modern age. It also dragged Bali into the international limelight, making it a target for investors and terrorists alike.

In October 2002 two simultaneous bomb explosions ripped through Kuta, killing 202 people, injuring some 300 others and decimating Bali's tourist industry overnight. The tsunami that devastated northern Sumatra on Boxing Day 2004 indirectly slowed Bali's recovery, a problem further exacerbated by a second spate of tragic bombings in October 2005 (see the boxed text, p208). Many visitors are determined to continue travelling

INDONESIA

THE NIGHTMARE CONTINUES

On 1 October 2005, just days before the third anniversary of the last devastating Kuta bombings, three deadly explosions again tore through Bali's most popular resort. At least three devices, carried by suicide bombers, exploded in Central Kuta and Jimbaran Beach, injuring 90 and killing 26, including three British nationals. Some of the bombers' alleged accomplices were quickly arrested, but the island's economic recovery will remain in jeopardy for many months to come.

to Bali, but the latest incident has raised questions about security on the island.

DANGERS & ANNOYANCES

Persistent hawkers are the bane of most visitors to Bali. The best way to deal with them is to ignore them from the first instance.

You may be offered drugs on the street, particularly in Kuta, but you're unlikely to get a good deal. The government takes the smuggling, use and sale of drugs very seriously, and entrapment by police is a real possibility. Bali's famed *oong* ('magic mushrooms') contain psilocybin, a powerful hallucinogen that can have unpredictable effects.

A different danger exists at the beaches at Kuta and Legian, which are subject to heavy surf and strong currents – swim between the flags.

Scams

Travellers have been stung badly by card-game cons and dodgy holiday 'timeshare' deals. Some have been tricked into paying large amounts for unnecessary repairs to rental cars and motorcycles. Gigolos, 'guides' and friendly locals have persuaded visitors to hand over money to help pay for education expenses and life-saving operations and moneychangers are adept at switching notes at the last minute – a healthy scepticism is your best defence.

TRANSPORT
Getting There & Away
AIR
Domestic Services

Garuda operates many domestic sectors, but tends to be the most expensive option;

Merpati Nusantara Airlines operates to many, more remote destinations. Competition in the market is now fierce and some great deals can be had on the most popular routings. For one-way sample fares see the Indonesian Air Fares map (p157).

Domestic airline offices:

Adam Air (☎ 0361-761104; www.adamair.com; Ngurah Rai airport)

Batavia Air (☎ 0361-254955; Ngurah Rai airport)

Bouraq Denpasar (☎ 0361-241397; Jl Panglima Besar Sudirman); Ngurah Rai airport (☎ 0361-756720)

Garuda Denpasar (☎ 0807-1-427832; www.garuda-indo nesia.com); Ngurah Rai airport (☎ 0361-751011 ext 5228)

Lion Air (☎ 0361-236666; www.lionair.co.id; Ngurah Rai airport)

Mandala Denpasar (☎ 0361-222751; www.mandalaair .com; Jl Diponegoro 98); Ngurah Rai airport (☎ 0361-759761)

Merpati Denpasar (☎ 0800-1-012345; www.merpati .co.id; Jl Melati 51); Ngurah Rai airport (☎ 0361-235358)

Pelita Air (☎ 0361-762248; www.pelita-air.com; Ngurah Rai airport)

International Services

Ngurah Rai airport (DPS; ☎ 0361-751011), a few kilometres south of Kuta, is a major international hub and well connected globally.

Unless stated otherwise, the following airlines are based at the airport:

Air Asia (☎ 0804-1-333333; www.airasia.com)

Air New Zealand (☎ 0361-756170; www.airnew zealand.com)

Cathay Pacific (☎ 0361-753942; www.cathaypacific.com)

Continental (☎ 0361-768358; www.continental.com)

Eva Air (☎ 0361-759773; www.evaair.com.tw)

Garuda Denpasar (☎ 0807-1-427832; www.garuda -indonesia.com); Ngurah Rai airport (☎ 0361-751011 ext 5228)

Malaysia Airlines (☎ 0361-764995; www.malaysiaair lines.com)

Qantas (☎ 0361-288511; www.qantas.com; Grand Bali Beach Hotel, Jl Hang Tuah 1, Sanur)

Singapore Airlines (☎ 0361-768388; www.singapore air.com)

Thai Airways International (☎ 0361-288511; www .thaiairways.com; Grand Bali Beach Hotel, Jl Hang Tuah 1, Sanur)

BOAT
Java

Ferries (5000Rp, 30 minutes) travel between Gilimanuk in western Bali and Ketapang (Java) every 30 minutes, 24 hours a day (see p239).

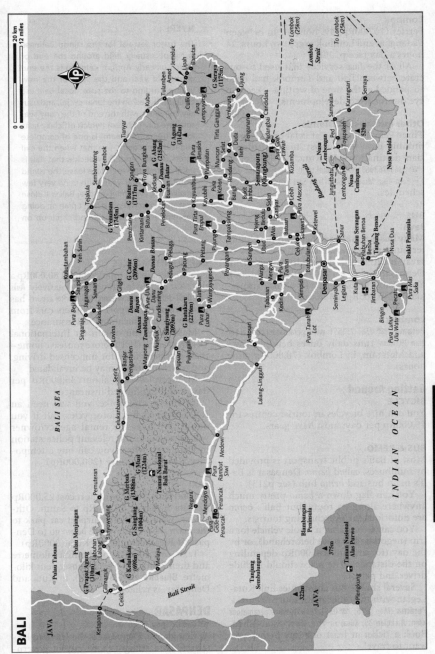

Lombok

Ferries (16,000Rp, 4½ hours) run between Padangbai and Lombok every two hours, 24 hours a day (see p230).

All of the fast services that used to operate between Bali and Lombok had been suspended at the time of writing – keep an eye out for fresh developments.

Other Indonesian Islands

Three Pelni boats stop at Pelabuhan Benoa, linking Bali with most major Indonesian destinations. In Kuta, the **Pelni office** (☎ 0361-763963; www.pelni.co.id; Jl Raya Kuta 288; ⏰ 8am-4pm Mon-Fri, 8am-1pm Sat) has the latest schedules.

BUS
Java

Many buses travel daily between the Ubung terminal in Denpasar and major cities in Java; most travel overnight. Fares from Denpasar: Surabaya (90,000Rp, 12 hours), Yogyakarta (125,000Rp, 16 hours) and Jakarta (240,000Rp, 26 hours).

Lombok

Perama (☎ 0361-751551; www.peramatour.com; Jl Legian 39, Kuta) runs daily buses between Kuta and Mataram, in Lombok (70,000Rp, nine hours).

Getting Around
BICYCLE

You can hire bicycles in tourist centres for 15,000Rp per day; most have gears.

BUS & BEMO

Most of Bali's public transport is provided by minibuses, called *bemo*. Denpasar is Bali's main bus and *bemo* hub (see p213).

You can flag down a *bemo* pretty much anywhere along its route, but Bali's *bemo* are notorious for overcharging tourists.

You can also charter a whole vehicle for a trip (negotiate the price beforehand), or by the day (for around 250,000Rp depending on the distance). The price should include driver and petrol.

Several shuttle bus companies link Kuta-Legian with the other main tourist centres. **Perama** (Map p216; ☎ 0361-751551; www.peramatour .com; Jl Legian 39, Kuta) is the best established. Book a ticket at least one day before you want to travel.

NYEPI

The major festival for the Hindu Balinese is Nyepi, usually held around the end of March or early April. It celebrates the end of the old year and the start of the new year, according to the *saka* (local Balinese calendar based on the lunar cycle), and usually coincides with the end of the rainy season. The day of Nyepi (which officially lasts for 24 hours from 6am) is one of complete and utter inactivity – so that when the evil spirits do descend, they decide that Bali is uninhabited and therefore leave the island alone for another year. With very, very few exceptions, *everything* all over Bali will close or stop during Nyepi, so don't plan on doing anything – bring a book and catch up on some sleep.

CAR & MOTORCYCLE

Four-seater Suzuki Jimnys start at 80,000Rp a day with limited insurance. Alternatively, **Avis** (☎ 0361-282635; www.avis.com; Ngurah Rai airport) has an office at the airport and offers cars from US$40 per day, including full insurance.

Make sure you obtain an International Driving Permit (IDP) before you leave home – there are steep fines for unlicensed driving, and travel insurance may be invalidated.

Motorcycles cost about 35,000Rp per day, including limited insurance.

To hire a motorbike, you will need an IDP endorsed for motorcycles, but if you don't have one, the rental agency/owner will take you to the relevant police station in Denpasar, where you can buy a temporary SIM Turis licence (200,000Rp).

TAXI

Prepaid taxis from the airport cost 25,000Rp to Kuta Beach or 55,000Rp to Sanur. Otherwise, walk across the airport car park to the main road, from where *bemo* go to Denpasar's Tegal terminal via Kuta (2000Rp).

Taxis cost 4000Rp for the first kilometre and then 2000Rp for each subsequent kilometre. **Bluebird** (☎ 0361-701111), in Kuta and Denpasar, is reliable.

DENPASAR
☎ 0361 / pop 370,000

At first glance, Denpasar is the Jekyll to Kuta's Hyde, a straight-faced city of government and bureaucracy, where tourists are anathema and life plods along at a distinctly workaday pace. Although little more than a skip and a jump from Kuta's seafront strip, Denpasar feels a million miles from the razzmatazz of its most boisterous suburb, offering little more than a handful of hotels and nothing in the way of nightlife. But while this is not one of Bali's major tourist drawcards, the island's big city does have a certain mystique, offering a clutch of Hindu temples, Bali's biggest market (Pasar Badung) and, floating through the clouds of acrid exhaust fumes, the faintest whiff of incense.

Orientation
The main street of Denpasar starts as Jl Gajah Mada in the west, becomes Jl Surapati in the centre, then Jl Hayam Wuruk and finally Jl Raya Sanur in the east.

Information
EMERGENCY
Police (☎ 110)

INTERNET ACCESS
Denny's Internet (cnr Jl Diponegoro & Hasanudin; per hr 3500Rp; ☾ 24hr)

MEDICAL SERVICES
Prima Medika (☎ 236225; www.primamedika.com; Jl Pulau Serangan No 9X; ☾ 24hr)

MONEY
There are banks with ATM and exchange facilities across town.
BCA (Jl Hasanudin)
BNI (cnr Jl Gajah Mada & Jl Arjuna)

POST & TELEPHONE
There are *wartel* across town.
Main post office (Jl Raya Puputan; ☾ 8.30am-5pm Mon-Fri, 8.30am-noon Sat) A long way out in the Renon district.

TOURIST INFORMATION
Bali Regional Department of Tourism (☎ 222387; www.balitourismauthority.com; Jl Parman; ☾ 8am-3.30pm Mon-Thu, 8am-1pm Fri) Has a few brochures but little else.
Denpasar Tourist Office (☎ 223602; Jl Surapati 7; ☾ 8am-3.30pm Mon-Thu, 8am-1pm Fri) Deals with Denpasar municipality, including Sanur. It hands out copies of the useful Bali-wide *Calendar of Events*.

TRAVEL AGENCIES
Target Tours (☎ 240967; Jl Diponegoro 75; ☾ 8.30am-4.30pm Mon-Fri, 8.30am-noon Sat) For plane tickets.

Sights & Activities
Denpasar life rotates around Bali's biggest market, **Pasar Badung** (Jl Gajah Mada; ☾ 7am-7pm). The produce on offer is fairly ordinary, but it's a good place to squeeze through the hubbub of day-to-day Denpasar and the best place to get a few colourful snaps.

Taman Budaya (☎ 227176; alleyway off Jl Nusa Indah; admission 2000Rp; ☾ 8am-5pm) is a showcase for Balinese arts, and explodes into life during the major festivals – the Bali Arts Festival in June-July is a must. It's pretty quiet here the rest of the time, but that's a good thing if you fancy escaping the push and shove of the city centre.

The **Museum Negeri Propinsi Bali** (☎ 222680; Puputan Sq; admission 2000Rp; ☾ 8am-3pm Sun-Thu, 8am-noon Fri) is the type of place you'd visit between buses, featuring displays of traditional Balinese bric-a-brac, and a small army of entertaining (for a while) souvenir salesmen.

Opposite the museum, you'll find **Puputan Square**, with its heroic **Catur Mukha statue**. Despite the statue's rather macabre role, commemorating the suicidal stand against the Dutch in 1906, it is a popular local meeting place. The two most important temples are **Pura Jagatnatha** (Puputan Sq; ☾ dawn-dusk), the state temple next to the Museum Negeri Propinsi Bali, and the 14th-century **Pura Maospahit** (☾ dawn-dusk), on an alley off Jl Sutomo.

Sleeping
Nakula Familar Inn (☎ 226446; Jl Nakula 4; s/d 60,000/80,000Rp) Everyone is made to feel 'familiar' at this homely little spot, where the talkative, English-speaking owner will welcome you with open arms and swear blind he's put you up before. The courtyard is a little ramshackle, but the comfy rooms are lovingly swept and polished.

Hotel Merte Sari (☎ 222428; Jl Hasanudin 24; s/d 50,000/70,000Rp) The noise of backfiring *bemo* engines tends to drift through the windows here, but standards are otherwise high at this spotless little outfit.

Hotel Jaya (Djaya) (☎ 222911; Jl Hasanudin 26; d 60,000-100,000Rp; ☒) Next door to Merte Sari,

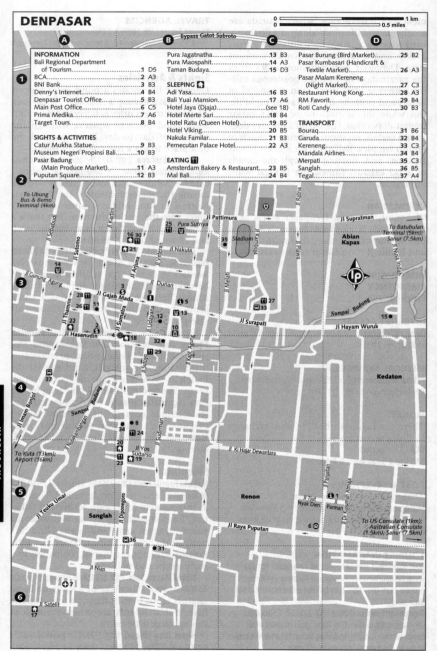

DENPASAR

0 ____ 1 km
0 ____ 0.5 miles

INFORMATION
Bali Regional Department of Tourism	1 D5
BCA	2 A3
BNI Bank	3 B3
Denny's Internet	4 B4
Denpasar Tourist Office	5 B3
Main Post Office	6 C5
Prima Medika	7 A6
Target Tours	8 B4

SIGHTS & ACTIVITIES
Catur Mukha Statue	9 B3
Museum Negeri Propinsi Bali	10 B3
Pasar Badung (Main Produce Market)	11 A3
Puputan Square	12 B3

Pura Jagatnatha	13 B3
Pura Maospahit	14 A3
Taman Budaya	15 D3

SLEEPING
Adi Yasa	16 B3
Bali Yuai Mansion	17 A6
Hotel Jaya (Djaja)	(see 18)
Hotel Merte Sari	18 B4
Hotel Ratu (Queen Hotel)	19 B5
Hotel Viking	20 B5
Nakula Familar	21 B3
Pemecutan Palace Hotel	22 A3

EATING
Amsterdam Bakery & Restaurant	23 B5
Mal Bali	24 B4

Pasar Burung (Bird Market)	25 B2
Pasar Kumbasari (Handicraft & Textile Market)	26 A3
Pasar Malam Kereneng (Night Market)	27 C3
Restaurant Hong Kong	28 A3
RM Favorit	29 B4
Roti Candy	30 B3

TRANSPORT
Bouraq	31 B6
Garuda	32 B4
Kereneng	33 C3
Mandala Airlines	34 B4
Merpati	35 C3
Sanglah	36 B5
Tegal	37 A4

INDONESIA

this is slightly more substantial, with a small interior garden, some comfy, communal meet-and-greet space and a pantheon of ornamental Hindu deities.

Adi Yasa (☎ 222679; Jl Nakula 23B; s/d 35,000/50,000Rp) This old-timer is looking a little hungover these days, with flaking paint and spotty walls. It's cheap though, and the welcomes are as cheerful as ever.

Pemecutan Palace Hotel (☎ 423491; Jl Thamrin 2; d 80,000Rp; ✕) A former royal residence, this is the one spot where you can unload your rucksack in a bona fide palace. Renovations were under way at the time of writing and so things should now be looking shipshape.

Other recommendations:

Bali Yuai Mansion (☎ 228850; Jl Satelit 22; s/d 50,000/60,000Rp; ✕) Way out in Sanglah, homely but a serious hike from the action.

Hotel Ratu (Queen Hotel; ☎ 226922; Jl Yos Sudarso 2-4; d from 50,000Rp; ✕) Pleasant midranger with a spread of rooms.

Hotel Viking (☎ 223992; Jl Diponegoro 120; d 90,000Rp) A flaky back-up.

Eating

Denpasar is no culinary Mecca. The cheapest places are the *warung* at the *bemo*/bus terminals and the markets. Around Pasar Kumbasari (handicraft and textile market) and Pasar Burung (bird market), the *warung* work until about 10pm (after most restaurants in town have closed), while at Pasar Malam Kereneng (Kereneng Night Market) dozens of vendors dish it up till dawn.

Restaurant Hong Kong (☎ 434845; Jl Gajah Mada 99; dishes 20,000Rp; ✕ lunch & dinner) Serving Chinese for the Chinese (read: authentic), expect fluoro lighting, functional décor and some tasty and inventive seafood specialities.

Amsterdam Bakery & Restaurant (☎ 235735; Jl Diponegoro 140; dishes 25,000Rp; ✕ breakfast, lunch & dinner; ✕) You won't find much in the way of atmosphere at this pseudo-Western spot, but it does have the biggest TV in Denpasar, a range of dishes from sticky buns to sizzling steaks and enough waitresses to serve the entire menu simultaneously.

Also try these cheaper places:

RM Favorit (☎ 262439; Jl Mayjen Sutoyo 3; dishes 10,000Rp; ✕ breakfast, lunch & dinner) For cheap and cheerful Indonesian eats.

Roti Candy (☎ 238409; Jl Nakula 31; snacks 5000Rp; ✕ breakfast & lunch) For cakes and bread.

Most of the shopping centre eateries serve a wide variety of cheap Indonesian and Chinese food in hygienic, air-con comfort – try the food court at **Mal Bali** (Jl Diponegoro; dishes 10,000Rp; ✕ 11am-10pm).

Getting There & Around

BEMO

Denpasar is *the* hub for *bemo* transport around Bali. Unfortunately, the city has several confusing terminals and you will often have to transfer between them. Each terminal provides regular connections to the other terminals (2000Rp). The following are the official prices, but tourists often end up paying more.

From Ubung, north of the town centre, *bemo* travel to destinations in northern and western Bali, including Gilimanuk (for the Java ferry; 12,000Rp, 1½ hours), Kediri (for Pura Tanah Lot; 4000Rp, 30 minutes) and Bedugul (for Danau Bratan; 8000Rp, one hour).

From Batubulan, 6km northeast of the city centre, *bemo* head to east and central Bali including Candidasa (9000Rp, one hour), Padangbai (15,000Rp, 1½ hours) and Ubud (9000Rp, one hour).

Tegal, on the road to Kuta, has *bemo* to destinations south, including the airport (5000Rp, 30 minutes), Sanur (5000Rp, 30 minutes) and Kuta (5000Rp, 30 minutes).

Sanglah is a roadside stop, with *bemo* serving Kereneng (2000Rp, 20 minutes) and Pelabuhan Benoa (5000Rp, 30 minutes).

Kereneng, to the east of the centre, has *bemo* to every other terminal and also to Sanur.

BUS

Buses go from Ubung terminal to Surabaya (90,000Rp, 12 hours), Jakarta (240,000Rp, 26 hours) and destinations in Lombok – try **Pahala Kencana** (☎ 410199; Ubung terminal) for air-con services.

TAXI

Taxis can be flagged on the street. Flag-fall is 4000Rp, then 2000Rp per kilometre.

KUTA
☎ 0361

Bali's backpackers and package tourists meet on the promenade of Kuta Beach, a boisterous, fun-filled monument to holiday hedonism. Tourists sizzle in the sunshine by day, gyrate through the happy hours of Jl Legian and Seminyak at night and then stay in bed with their hangovers – and whoever else they might have met over their cocktails – the following morning. A bustling menagerie of surf shops, bars, touts and travellers, Kuta is the place where Indonesia slips on its boldest Bermudas and really lets its hair down.

Kuta's ailing tourist industry was further impacted by the bombings of October 2005, but the local people remain upbeat and recovery seems likely in the mid- to long-term. The nightlife isn't quite as lively as it once was – Seminyak is now the place for that – but good times can still be found.

It is fashionable to disparage Kuta for its tacky resorts and crass commercialism, but the cosmopolitan blend of beach-party hedonism and entrepreneurial energy can be exciting. It's not pretty, but Kuta is rarely dull and even its staunchest critics will find an excuse to order another sundowner somewhere along the way.

Orientation

Prepaid taxis from the airport cost 25,000Rp to Kuta Beach. To get *to* the airport, a metered taxi costs about 15,000Rp. Reliable **Bluebird** (☎ 701111; www.bluebirdgroup.com) taxis can be called in advance.

The *kelurahan* (local government area) of Kuta extends for nearly 8km along the beach and foreshore, and comprises four communities that have grown together.

DID YOU KNOW?

Although the Balinese are nominal Hindus, there are dozens of differences between the way the religion is practised in Bali and India. While the Balinese worship the same trinity of Brahma, Shiva and Vishnu, they also have their own supreme deity, Sanghyang Widi. Additionally, the Balinese never put their trinity on show, employing vacant shrines and empty thrones where Indian Hindus use layers of technicolour iconography. One element of Balinese Hinduism that is impossible to avoid – try not to step on them – are the small offerings placed on the pavement every morning to placate bad spirits and pay homage to the good ones.

Kuta is the original fishing village-cum-budget-beach resort, and has the greatest concentration of tourist businesses, the busiest bit of beach and the worst traffic. Further north, Kuta merges into Legian, which has almost as much commercial activity, and only slightly less traffic. Further north again, Seminyak is less densely developed and has some of the classiest hotels, best restaurants and trendiest nightspots – a focus for long-term visitors and expats. South of Kuta, Tuban has modern shopping centres, upmarket hotels and a good beach.

Jl Legian is the main road running south from Seminyak to Kuta. It is lined with shops, restaurants, moneychangers, *wartel* and Internet cafés. Between Jl Legian and the beach is a tangle of narrow streets, tracks and alleys, with a hodgepodge of cheap hotels, souvenir stalls, *warung*, bars, construction sites and even a few remaining coconut palms.

Information

BOOKSHOPS

There are dozens of second-hand booksellers along Poppies Gang I and II.
Gramedia Books (Map p216; ☎ 769541; www.gramediaonline.com; 1st fl, Discovery Shopping Mall, Jl Kartika Plaza; ☺ 10am-10pm)
Kerta IV Bookshop (Map p216; ☎ 762974; Jl Legian; ☺ 10am-6pm) Has a good range of titles.

EMERGENCY

Police (Map p216; emergency ☎ 110, ☎ 751598; Jl Raya Kuta; ☺ 24hr)

INTERNET ACCESS

There are Internet cafés across Kuta and Legian.
Internet Outpost (Map p216; ☎ 763392; Poppies Gang II; per hr 18,000Rp; ☺ 9am-2am) Offers telephone, Internet, luggage storage and information services.

MEDICAL SERVICES

Bali International Medical Centre (Map p216; ☎ 761263; www.bimcbali.com; Jl Ngurah Rai Bypass 100X; ☺ 24hr) Kuta's biggest and brightest international hospital.
Guardian Pharmacy (Map p216; ☎ 765354; Jl Legian 56; ☺ 8am-10.30pm)

MONEY

Moneychangers are faster, more efficient and open longer hours than banks, and they offer better exchange rates. However, be suspicious of too-good-to-be-true exchange rates, always count your money at least twice in front of the moneychanger, and don't let them touch the money after you've finally counted it. Moneychangers and banks with ATM and change facilities are located all over Kuta-Legian.

POST
Post office (Map p216; ☽ 8am-2pm Mon-Thu, 8-11am Fri & Sat) On an unnamed gravel road, east of Jl Raya Kuta.

TELEPHONE
There are *wartel* across town.
HIS Tourist Information (Map p216; ☎ 758377; Kuta Sq Block C-17; ☽ 10am-10pm)
Internet Outpost (Map p216; ☎ 763392; Poppies Gang II; ☽ 9am-2am)

TOURIST INFORMATION
What's Up Bali (weekly) and *The Beat* (biweekly) are free listings and events guides. Pick them up at restaurants and travel agencies around town.
Badung Tourist Office (Map p216; ☎ 765401; Jl Raya Kuta 2; ☽ 8am-5pm) Has limited information on Kuta, Bali, Nusa Tenggara and Java.
HIS Tourist Information (Map p216; ☎ 758377; Kuta Sq Block C-17; ☽ 10am-10pm) A private tourist information and travel agency outfit.

TRAVEL AGENCIES
The many businesses that advertise themselves as 'tourist information centres' are actually travel agencies selling organised tours, tourist shuttle bus tickets and car or motorcycle rental. They can also book or change airline tickets.
HIS Tourist Information (Map p216; ☎ 758377; Kuta Sq Block C-17)

Sights & Activities
Some of Kuta's biggest thrills roll in 24/7. Yep, whether you are a quivering novice or a seasoned pro, Bali has some great surfing and Kuta is the place to get organised.
Tubes Bar (Map p216; ☎ 753510; Poppies Gang II; ☽ noon-midnight) is a good first stop for information, while **Pro Surf** (Map p216; ☎ 081-2367 5141; www.prosurfschool.com; Grand Istana Rama Hotel, Jl Pantai Kuta; ☽ 9.30am-3.30pm) offers half-day lessons from US$35. Those after the seriously big breakers of G-Land, in Java, can book packages at **Bobby's G-Land Headquarters**

(Map p216; ☎ 755588; www.grajagan.com; Jl Pantai Kuta; ☽ 9am-5pm). Seven-day budget packages, including transfers, start at US$250.

Those after some more mild-mannered waves should head for **Waterbom Park** (Map p216; ☎ 755676; www.waterbom.com; Jl Kartika Plaza; admission US$18.50; ☽ 9am-5pm), where flumes and pools offer plenty of scope for some freshwater splishing and sploshing.

From Kuta you can go sailing, diving, fishing, horse riding or rafting anywhere in the southern part of Bali, and be back in time for dinner. For information and bookings, try **Bali Adventure Tours** (☎ 721480; www.bali adventuretours.com). Bungy freaks can go airborne at **AJ Hackett** (Map p219; ☎ 731144; www.aj-hackett.com/bali; ☽ noon-8pm), where a leap from its 45m tower costs 550,000Rp.

It certainly isn't a tourist attraction, but you will be hard-pressed to walk down Jl Legian without noticing the **Bali Bomb Memorial** (Map p216; cnr Jl Legian & Poppies Gang II). It is a simple and sombre monument, listing the names of those killed by the 2002 blast.

Sleeping
Kuta is the budget accommodation capital of Indonesia, with hundreds of cheapies on and around Poppies Gang I and II. Most places chuck in a simple breakfast.

Rooms in a few of the most basic places start at 35,000Rp, but prices are on the up and most doubles cost 50,000Rp to 100,000Rp. That said, if you're willing to pay the little extra, you will get greater value.

Many places struggle to fill their rooms in low season – always ask for a discount.

CENTRAL KUTA   Map p216
Many cheap places are along the tiny alleys and lanes between Jl Legian and Jl Pantai Kuta, only a short walk from the beach, shops, bars and restaurants.
Kedin's Inn II (☎ 763554; s/d 65,000/85,000Rp; 🏊) A soothing duvet of good karma seems to hang over this tidy little spot, where cosy rooms overlook a blooming garden. Breathe in…and relax. It is just north of Poppies Gang I.
Hotel Sorga (☎ 751897; sorga@idola.net.id; d from 95,000Rp; 🏊) This tip-top outfit injects a little class into the budget hotel formula. Pretend you have joined the jet set while sipping your beer by the pristine pool, before slipping through the colourful garden to bed.

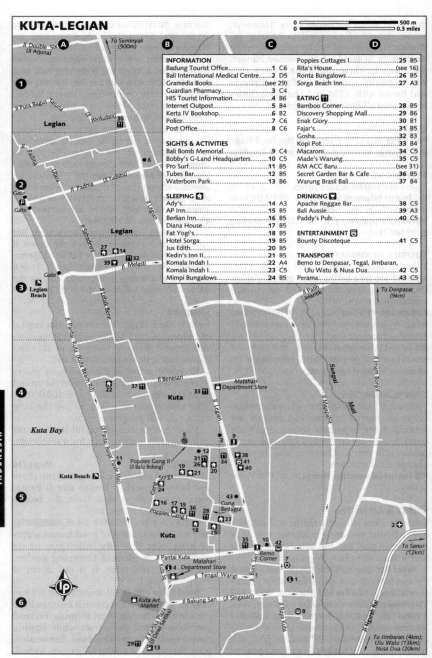

KUTA-LEGIAN

0 — 500 m
0 — 0.3 miles

INFORMATION
Badung Tourist Office..................1 C6
Bali International Medical Centre....2 D5
Gramedia Books....................(see 29)
Guardian Pharmacy.................3 C4
HIS Tourist Information............4 B6
Internet Outpost...................5 B4
Kerta IV Bookshop.................6 B2
Police.............................7 C6
Post Office........................8 C6

SIGHTS & ACTIVITIES
Bali Bomb Memorial................9 C4
Bobby's G-Land Headquarters....10 C5
Pro Surf..........................11 B5
Tubes Bar.........................12 B5
Waterbom Park...................13 B6

SLEEPING
Ady's.............................14 A3
AP Inn............................15 B5
Berlian Inn.......................16 B5
Diana House......................17 B5
Fat Yogi's........................18 B5
Hotel Sorga......................19 B5
Jus Edith.........................20 B5
Kedin's Inn II.....................21 B5
Komala Indah I...................22 A4
Komala Indah I...................23 C5
Mimpi Bungalows.................24 B5

Poppies Cottages I................25 B5
Rita's House....................(see 16)
Ronta Bungalows..................26 B5
Sorga Beach Inn..................27 A3

EATING
Bamboo Corner....................28 B5
Discovery Shopping Mall..........29 B6
Enak Glory........................30 B1
Fajar's............................31 B5
Gosha............................32 B3
Kopi Pot..........................33 B4
Macaroni.........................34 C5
Made's Warung....................35 C5
RM ACC Baru...................(see 31)
Secret Garden Bar & Cafe.........36 B5
Warung Brasil Bali................37 B4

DRINKING
Apache Reggae Bar...............38 C5
Bali Aussie.......................39 A3
Paddy's Pub......................40 C5

ENTERTAINMENT
Bounty Discoteque................41 C5

TRANSPORT
Bemo to Denpasar, Tegal, Jimbaran,
  Ulu Watu & Nusa Dua...........42 C5
Perama..........................43 C5

If you have just arrived, the rooms are the perfect place to do battle with jet lag.

Komala Indah I (☎ 751422; Poppies Gang I; d from 60,000Rp; ⊠) This is a hostel of two halves – there is an extension on Jl Benesari. Both offer a range of pleasant rooms, with a little more hush at Jl Benesari and a little more hubbub at Poppies I. The pricier air-con rooms cost 120,000Rp.

Berlian Inn (☎ 751501; s/d 50,000/60,000Rp) The staff are cheerful, the garden looks like something out of a flower show, but the rooms are rather dowdy at this old-timer. It is just north of Poppies Gang I.

Jus Edith (☎ 750558; s/d 25,000/35,000Rp) Frills? Forget it. Jus Edith offers basic rooms at no-nonsense prices and it does exactly what it says on the tin. It's just south of Poppies Gang II.

Ronta Bungalows (☎ 754246; s/d 30,000/40,000Rp) Just across the road from Jus Edith, this place takes another leaf from the Plain Jane book of hostel design. A recent face-lift has injected a little sparkle, and there's a leafy garden for lounging around in.

AP Inn (☎ 765662; www.apinn.com; Poppies Gang I; d from 100,000Rp; ⊠ ⊠) A few too many mosquitoes have been squashed on the walls of this borderline midranger to say that it still looks sparkling fresh. That aside, you could swing a large cat in the comfy rooms and there's plenty of lounging space around the pool. Air-con rooms cost 150,000Rp.

Fat Yogi's (☎ 751665; fatyogi@telkom.net; Poppies Gang I; d from 70,000Rp; ⊠ ⊠) The staff appear to charge a premium for a smile at this otherwise reliable outfit. There's a wide range of rooms, so you can play at being a convict in a poky cell, or live it up in one of the swankier air-con offerings (150,000Rp).

Diana House (☎ 751605; Poppies Gang I; s/d 45,000/50,000Rp) This modest private house offers humble digs in crumbling surrounds. The rooms are fine for the price.

SPLURGE!

Poppies Cottages I (Map p216; ☎ 751059; info@bali.poppies.net.id; Poppies Gang I; s/d US$60/70; ⊠) With exotically lush gardens and beautiful cottages, complete with alfresco bathrooms and sitting rooms, this is a seriously charismatic top-ender. Book ahead and push for big discounts.

Rita's House (☎ 751760; s/d 40,000/50,000Rp) Right next to Berlian Inn, Rita offers the usual budget staples: fair prices, big smiles, tumbledown surrounds and thin walls.

Mimpi Bungalows (☎ 751848; kumimpi@yahoo .co.sg; s/d 100,000/150,000Rp; ⊠ ⊠) Something of a poor man's Poppies Cottages, Mimpi offers whitewashed thatched cottages in a lush garden setting. Watch out for the cobbled paths if you come in after a night on the tiles though; they can be treacherous. It is just north of Poppies Gang I.

LEGIAN   Map p216

Sorga Beach Inn (☎ 751609; sorga74@hotmail.com; Jl Sahadewa Gang 2; s/d 25,000/50,000Rp) Don't be surprised if you startle the staff here, they don't seem to be expecting guests. The paint job won't be winning any prizes either, but the simple, reasonably priced rooms stand around a shady garden.

Ady's (☎ 759934; Jl Sahadewa Gang 2; s/d 50,000/ 60,000Rp) Nearby, Ady's offers thatch, flowers and a little authentic charm without delving too deeply into your money belt. There's a big garden and the rooms are pathologically tidy.

SEMINYAK   Map p219

Considering all the nightlife here, there's a dearth of cheap places to crash.

Kesuma Sari Beach Bungalows (☎ 730575; d 70,000Rp; ⊠) The sea air has taken its toll on this out-of-the-way little spot. That said, the prices have fallen accordingly and you are guaranteed plenty of peace and quiet. It is down an alley, north of Jl Dhyana Pura.

Blue Ocean Bungalows (☎ 730289; Jl Arjuna; d 120,000Rp) Right opposite the beach, this is a popular haunt for wave slaves and there's even an on-site surfboard repair shop. The central car park is a bit of a turnoff though.

Galaxy Hotel (☎ 730328; Jl Dhyana Pura; d 150,000Rp; ⊠) This red-brick spot is right in the heart of the action and while nightly prices are rather high, it offers colossal discounts for longer stays.

Eating

Restaurants to satisfy every craving abound in the Kuta area, ranging from the basic backpacker eateries in and around Poppies Gang I and II to the chichi bar-restaurants of Seminyak.

Food carts are a little harder to come by, but you'll still find plenty in the **Seminyak night market** (Map p219; cnr Jl Oberoi & Jl Raya Seminyak). Cheap *warung* can be found in the back streets near the main post office.

For a wide range of spick-and-span shopping-mall eateries, head to the 2nd floor of the **Discovery Shopping Mall** (Map p216; Jl Kartika Plaza; mains from 10,000Rp; ☺ lunch & dinner).

SOUTH KUTA   Map p216
Made's Warung (☎ 755297; Jl Pantai Kuta; mains 20,000Rp; ☺ breakfast, lunch & dinner) Creaking woodwork and slow-motion fans bring a flick of colonial-era class to this distinctly Balinese décor at this popular little haunt. The menu bridges the gulf between east and west, offering everything from *nasi goreng* and Balinese fish curries to slap-up breakfasts and tequila shooters.

JL LEGIAN   Map p216
Kopi Pot (☎ 752614; Jl Legian; mains 30,000Rp; ☺ breakfast, lunch & dinner) Bringing a touch of the chintzy English tearoom to a leafy, Balinese setting, this is a top spot for long, lazy breakfasts and a colossal pot of *kopi* (coffee).

Enak Glory (☎ 751091; Jl Legian 445; mains from 20,000Rp; ☺ lunch & dinner) Now more than a quarter of a century old, this is one of Jl Legian's old school fish restaurants, cooking up an *ikan bakar* (grilled fish) in more ways than you can cast a fly line at.

SPLURGE!

Macaroni (☎ 754662; Jl Legian 52; mains 50,000Rp; ☺ breakfast, lunch & dinner) Jl Legian's resident temple of cool features oh-so-trendy lounge music, exotic flowers, hip décor and scrumptious Italian eats. There's wi-fi Internet access for the media savvy, live music every night and a valet to park the motorbike you have just hired.

POPPIES GANG I AREA   Map p216
Secret Garden Bar & Cafe (☎ 757720; Poppies Gang I; mains 20,000Rp; ☺ breakfast, lunch & dinner) A gregarious atmosphere, no-fuss, filling food, ice-cold beer and a pleasant setting make this one of Poppies' flagship eateries. The clientele ranges from boozy expats to dreadlocked surfniks.

Bamboo Corner (Poppies Gang I; mains from 8000Rp; ☺ breakfast, lunch & dinner) Hassle-free breakfasts and backpacker staples, served at hassle-free prices, keep the crowds coming to this Spartan, hole-in-the-wall diner. It's a great spot to order a beer and watch the crowds of Poppies residents pass you by.

POPPIES GANG II AREA   Map p216
You will find a clutch of super-cheap eateries just south of Poppies Gang II.

Warung Brasil Bali (☎ 752692; Jl Benesari; mains 10,000Rp; ☺ breakfast, lunch & dinner) The walls are daubed with frescoes of the traditional Brazilian staples (football, surfing and lounging around by a campfire), a Brazilian flag takes pride of place and the fish dishes are excellent value for money.

Fajar's (mains from 7000Rp; ☺ lunch & dinner) No trimmings, no fuss, just cheap backpacker fare and videos on the TV.

RM ACC Baru (mains from 8000Rp; ☺ lunch & dinner) Right next door to Fajar's, this is a similarly plain local haunt, serving a decent spread of *masakan Padang*.

LEGIAN   Map p216
Gosha (☎ 759880; www.gosharestaurant.com; Jl Melasti; mains 20,000Rp; ☺ breakfast, lunch & dinner) For 'fine food and hospitality, the palace of the king' (their words, not ours), this seafood place offers some fabulously plump lobster, thatch and bamboo décor and plenty of swirly, psychedelic artwork. If bums on seats are the measure, this place comes up trumps, attracting big crowds night after bustling night.

SEMINYAK   Map p219
The expat enclave of Seminyak has dozens of swanky eateries, many serving scrummy food at excellent prices.

Zula Veggie Paradise (☎ 732723; Jl Dhyana Pura 5; dishes 25,000Rp; ☺ breakfast, lunch & dinner; ☒) In a trendy hut with a tin roof, this veggie-oriented diner whips up cakes, sandwiches and a mean wheatgrass juice in super-chilled air-con surrounds.

Zanzibar (☎ 733529; Jl Arjuna; mains 35,000Rp; ☺ breakfast, lunch & dinner) It's not the prettiest kid on the block, but it's right on the beach and you can wash down your pizza and pasta with some dreamy sunset views.

Santa Fe (☎ 731147; Jl Dhyana Pura 11; dishes 30,000Rp; ☺ breakfast, lunch & dinner) This restaurant-meets-bar features live bands, big crowds

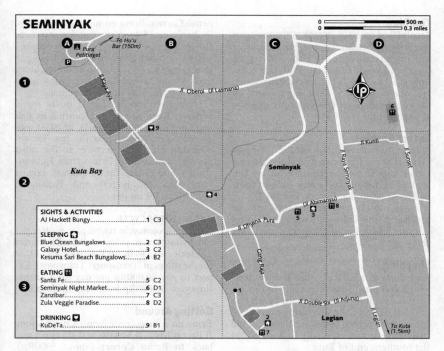

SEMINYAK

0 _____ 500 m
0 _____ 0.3 miles

Kuta Bay

Seminyak

Legian

To Hu'u Bar (150m)

To Kuta (1.5km)

(after 11pm) and a flick of yee-hah road-house atmosphere. Knock down the beers and feast on the Tex-Mex menu into the wee, small hours.

Drinking

The beach is the place to watch the sunset, but most restaurants on Poppies Gang I and II double as lively bars and run happy hours from 6pm to 9pm. From then, there's a bit of a lull, until the clubs start filling up at 11pm – most shut around 4am.

The nightlife scene has shifted slightly since the October 2002 blast and while the party is now slowly returning to Jl Legian, Seminyak has many of the liveliest, late-night venues.

KuDeTa (Map p219; ☎ 736969; www.kudeta.net; Jl Oberoi; ☼ 8am-2am) The coolest address in Bali, KuDeTa is the undisputed king of chic. Trendy eats are served in the restaurant, style gurus linger on the beachside sun loungers and Pete Tong has been known to man the decks. And as if there weren't enough beautiful people here already, more are projected onto giant screens above the cocktail bar.

Hu'u Bar (Map p219; ☎ 736443; www.huubali.com; Jl Oberoi; ☼ 4pm-2am) A little further down the road, this is another of Seminyak's hippest hang-outs, with fancy cocktails, a swimming pool (no, wet T-shirts are not on the menu) and a crowd of groovy model types.

Paddy's Pub (Map p216; ☎ 754046; Jl Legian 66; ☼ noon-4am) The latest incarnation of Paddy's features plenty of low-brow, beer-fuelled shenanigans, raucous parties and cock-fighting shows. For a small fee, they will even pick you up from your hotel.

Apache Reggae Bar (Map p216; ☎ 761210; Jl Legian 146; ☼ 7pm-3am) How many portraits of Bob Marley can you fit in a single room? Come here, and get counting. Hidden behind the restaurant of the same name, this is the spot to let down your dreadlocks and raise the roof for Haile Selassie.

Bali Aussie (Map p216; ☎ 751910; Jl Melasti 69; ☼ 9am-2am) This scruffy, Aussie-style boozer wears a thick coat of graffiti penned by adoring regulars and offers a lively spread of nightly events, from Down Under barbecue evenings (Friday) to its popular Aussie roast-dinner days (Sunday and Wednesday).

INDONESIA

Clubbing

Bounty Discoteque (Map p216; ☎ 752529; New Bounty Mall, Jl Legian; ☯ 24hr) Topping the decks of a giant, prefab galleon, with fully rigged masts and sailor-suited bar staff, this is the upbeat face of the Jl Legian clubbing scene. It's open 24 hours most nights and by midnight things are getting pretty messy – shiver me timbers!

Entertainment

Numerous bar-restaurants around Poppies Gang II show free laser disc video movies. Other bars show live telecasts of cricket, basketball, tennis, and every code of football from Australia, Europe and the USA.

Large hotels and restaurants present tourist-version Balinese dances, but Ubud is a much better (and cheaper) place to see this – see p227.

Shopping

A plethora of small stalls offer T-shirts, souvenirs and beachwear, especially in the 'art markets' on Jl Melasti and at the beach end of Jl Bakung Sari. An increasing number of more sophisticated stores are found on the main streets, and especially in Kuta Sq, at the southern end of Kuta.

Don't be pressured into buying things during the first few days of your stay – shop around for quality and price first. At small shops and souvenir stalls you have to bargain for the best prices.

Pirated DVDs (10,000Rp) and CDs (120,000Rp) do a roaring trade along Poppies Gang I and II.

Getting There & Away

AIR

Plane tickets to destinations across Indonesia and the world can be bought from the airline offices in Kuta and Denpasar. See the airline listings p208.

BOAT

Pelni ferries link nearby Pelabuhan Benoa with destinations throughout Indonesia (see p208).

BUS & BEMO

Public *bemo* travel regularly between Kuta and the Tegal terminal in Denpasar (5000Rp, 30 minutes). The main *bemo* stop in Kuta is on Jl Raya Kuta (Map p216), just east of

Bemo Corner. *Bemo* go south from here to Jimbaran and Ulu Watu, but for anywhere else in Bali you'll have to go via Denpasar.

Lots of travel agencies sell bus tickets to Java, Lombok and Sumbawa, mostly on buses from Ubung terminal in Denpasar – make sure the transfer to Ubung is included.

Numerous tourist shuttle buses travel between Kuta and tourist centres in Bali and Lombok. **Perama** (Map p216; ☎ 751551; www .peramatour.com; Jl Legian 39) is the best-known operator with daily services to the most popular destinations. Prices from Kuta include Ubud (20,000Rp, one hour), Lovina (50,000Rp, 3¼ hours) and Padangbai (30,000Rp, 1¾ hours).

CAR & MOTORCYCLE

Car and motorcycle rental places offer the most competitive prices in Bali. To charter a vehicle, just walk up Jl Legian and listen for the offers of 'Transport? Transport?' Expect to pay 80,000Rp per day for a Suzuki Jimny, or 35,000Rp for a 90cc motorbike.

Getting Around

Bemo do a loop from Bemo Corner along Jl Pantai Kuta, Jl Melasti and Jl Legian and back to Bemo Corner (about 3000Rp). *Bemo* are infrequent in the afternoon and nonexistent in the evening.

A few places hire out bicycles for around 15,000Rp per day.

BUKIT PENINSULA

The southern peninsula, often simply known as Bukit (Hill), is dry and sparsely populated, although it does have some major tourism development.

Just south of the airport, **Jimbaran Bay** is a superb crescent of white sand and blue sea, with a colourful fishing fleet and a few luxury hotels.

On the western side of the peninsula are some of Bali's best surf spots – a road provides access to **Padang Padang** and **Bingin**. At the southwestern tip of the peninsula, **Pura Luhur Ulu Watu** (admission 3000Rp; ☯ 8am-7pm) is an important temple dramatically situated atop sheer cliffs. Enchanting **Kecak dances** (admission 35,000Rp) are held here every night from about 6pm to 7pm. Just before the temple car park, a sign points to **Pantai Suluban**, which has several famous surf breaks.

Nearby, the **Wisnu Kencana Cultural Park** (☎ 0361-703603; www.gwk-bali.com; admission 15,000Rp; ☺ 8am-10pm) features restaurants, theatres and – bizarrely – one of the world's largest statues. The whole complex has been literally hacked out of a limestone quarry, and offers stunning views out to Jimbaran Bay.

Tanjung Benoa
☎ 0361

The peninsula of Tanjung Benoa extends about 4km north from the exclusive **Nusa Dua** resort enclave to the fishing village of **Benoa**. Jl Pratama runs the length of the peninsula and has a better variety of hotels and restaurants than at Nusa Dua. On the beaches, water-sports centres offer diving, snorkelling, parasailing, jet-skiing and water-skiing. You can also hire a speedboat, and cruise on glass-bottom boats.

Near the top of Jl Pratama, several places offer reasonably affordable accommodation, especially when tourist numbers are down. **Pondok Agung Homestay** (☎ 771143; roland@eksadata.com; Jl Pratama; d 120,000Rp; ☒) oozes authentic Balinese charm, with traditional décor, a flower-filled garden and some very comfy rooms. If Kuta's given you a hangover, here's the rescue remedy.

There are plenty of excellent seafood restaurants nearby. Expect to pay around 35,000Rp for mains.

Bemo run from Tegal terminal in Denpasar, via Kuta, to Bualu village (8000Rp). From there, a few *bemo* go north up Tanjung Benoa, mostly in the morning, or you can charter an *ojek* (motorbike taxi).

SANUR
☎ 0361

Sanur is Kuta in a cardigan, offering a gentler, more effete and rather more middle-aged take on the tried-and-tested holiday cocktail of sand, sea and sundowners. Resort hotels are the norm here, but Sanur does cater to backpackers, with a clutch of decent hostels and a few lively bars and restaurants. The beach all but vanishes at high tide and gets very crowded at the weekend, but Sanur remains a pleasant escape from the bump-and-grind of Kuta.

Sleeping
Rooms tend to be a little more upmarket in Sanur, as do the prices.

Flashback's (☎ 281682; www.flashbacks-chb.com; Jl Danau Tamblingan 106; d 150,000Rp; ☒ ☒) It's the trimmings that make Flashback's special: a miniature swimming pool, a pretty (skittish) cat, tea and coffee in the rooms. Run by a cheerful Australian, this is a great little hideaway, with plenty of communal space and some snug, attractively decorated rooms.

There are several cheapies at the northern end of Jl Danau Tamblingan, hidden away behind a row of art shops.

Yulia 1 Homestay (☎ 288089; Jl Tamblingan 38; s/d 60,000/75,000Rp) The owner's bird fetish has got right out of hand at this pleasant little hostel. Half aviary, half hotel, this is a top spot for those who like to wake up to the dawn chorus, and a nightmare for those paranoid about contracting a dose of bird flu. The rooms are spacious and spotless and the garden is awash with colourful flowers.

Yulia 2 Homestay (☎ 287495; Jl Danau Tamblingan; s/d 90,000/100,000Rp) One part Balinese villa, one part Bavarian shooting lodge, this atmospheric spot offers wooden beams, hunting trophies and oodles of quirky charm. There's an excellent bar-café out front.

Coco Homestay (☎ 287391; ketutcoco@hotmail .com; Jl Danau Tamblingan 42; s/d 40,000/50,000Rp) A few doors down from Yulia 1, Coco lacks Yulia's charisma. The rooms are clean, but the setting is dingier and a whole lot more claustrophobic.

Other recommendations:
Ari Accommodation (☎ 289673; Jl Danau Tamblingan 40; s/d 40,000/45,000Rp) Charmless but cheap.
Donna Homestay (☎ 287770; Jl Danau Tamblingan 164; s/d 90,000/100,000Rp) With functional, tidy rooms.
Ida Homestay (☎ 288598; Jl Danau Toba Gang I 4; s/d 80,000/100,000Rp) With a quiet garden setting.

Eating & Drinking
You will find plenty of *warung* and food carts in Sanur. During the day, try the beach bar at the end of Jl Kesuma Sari, at the southern extreme of Jl Danau Tamblingan. Come dusk, things start cooking at Pasar Sindhu (Night Market), at the beach end of Jl Segara Ayu.

Warung Mama Putu (☎ 282025; Jl Kesuma Sari; mains 10,000Rp; ☺ breakfast, lunch & dinner) Mama's is one of a number of cheap and cheerful eateries on this strip of beach. The fresh fish is excellent value, it is choc-a-bloc come nightfall and the sea provides the soundtrack. On the downside, you'll get a very sandy meal if the wind's up.

INDONESIA

Blue Bayou (☎ 081-7080 9234; Jl Kesuma Sari; mains 30,000Rp; 🕒 breakfast, lunch & dinner) Right next to Warung Mama Putu, this offers a little more class, with cushions on the chairs, paint on the walls and pizza and steak on the menu.

Mango Cafe (☎ 288411; Jl Danau Toba 15; mains 25,000Rp; 🕒 breakfast, lunch & dinner) A slightly suspect copy of Botticelli's *Birth of Venus* takes pride of place at this lively venue. The grilled seafood steals the show though, and things get good and lively after dark. Expect everything from *nasi goreng* to ribeye steak.

Lazer Sport Bar (☎ 288807; Jl Danau Tamblingan; mains 25,000Rp; 🕒 breakfast, lunch & dinner) It looks like this bar's had one too many late nights, but it remains a decent spot if you're into loud tunes, big-screen TV, fish and chips and pitchers of beer. It closes when the last person is no longer standing.

Getting There & Away

The *bemo* stops are at the southern end of Sanur on Jl Mertasari, and at the northern end outside the entrance to Grand Bali Beach Hotel. Blue *bemo* go to Denpasar's Tegal terminal; green *bemo* go to Kereneng terminal.

Perama (☎ 081-2366 5317) is at Warung Pojok, a small shop on Jl Hang Tuah at the northern end of town. It runs buses to Kuta (10,000Rp, 20 minutes), Ubud (15,000Rp, 45 minutes), Lovina (50,000Rp, three hours), Padangbai (30,000Rp, 1½ hours) and Candidasa (30,000Rp, 1¾ hours).

UBUD

☎ 0361

Once upon a time, there wasn't a whole lot to do in Ubud but dabble in the arts, and wander whimsically through the bottle-green paddy fields and past the farm ducks (a local speciality). The beating heart of a thriving arts scene, Ubud is the island's most idiosyncratic town, an overgrow\n village where life moves at a sedate waddle and Bali's technicolour Hindu heritage is at its most vivid. With tourists flocking here, Ubud is expanding at breakneck speed and the noise of traffic now competes with the quacking ducks for hegemony over the town's airwaves. But while Ubud is beginning to lose its innocent glow, it remains one of Bali's hottest tickets and an absolute must for those with a passion for island culture.

Orientation

The once small village of Ubud has expanded to encompass its neighbours: Campuan, Penestanan, Padangtegal, Peliatan and Pengosekan. The centre of town is the crossroads near the market and the Ubud palace.

Information

Several banks here have ATMs, and you can also change money at dozens of money changers that have outlets all over town. There are Internet cafés, charging about 250Rp per minute, across town.

BOOKSHOPS

Ganesha Books (Map p223; ☎ 970320; www.ganesha booksbali.com; Jl Raya 73; 🕒 9am-6pm) Has a wide range of new and second-hand titles.
Periplus (Map p226; ☎ 975178; Monkey Forest Rd; 🕒 9am-9pm) For books, magazines and maps.

INTERNET SERVICES

Telephone & Internet Service (Map p226; ☎ 978886; Monkey Forest Rd; per min 200Rp; 🕒 8am-11pm) For Internet and international phone calls.

LIBRARIES

Pondok Pekak Library (Map p226; ☎ 976194; 🕒 9am-8pm) Across the football field from Monkey Forest Rd. Also has a book exchange.

MEDICAL SERVICES

Mua Farma (Map p226; ☎ 974674; Monkey Forest Rd; 🕒 8am-9.30pm) A centrally located pharmacy.
Ubud Clinic (Map p223; ☎ 974911; Jl Raya Compuan 36; 🕒 24hr) Offers round-the-clock medical services.

MONEY

Lippobank (Map p226; Jl Raya Ubud; 🕒 8.30am-2pm Mon-Fri) Has ATM and exchange facilities.

POST

Main post office (Map p223; Jl Jembawan 1; 🕒 8am-6pm)

TOURIST INFORMATION

Tourist office (Map p226; Yaysan Bina Wisata; ☎ 973285; Jl Raya Ubud; 🕒 8am-8pm) This helpful place provides information about many ceremonies and traditional dances.

TRAVEL AGENCIES

HIS (Map p226; ☎ 972621; Monkey Forest Rd; 🕒 10am-6pm) A reliable travel agent.

UBUD AREA

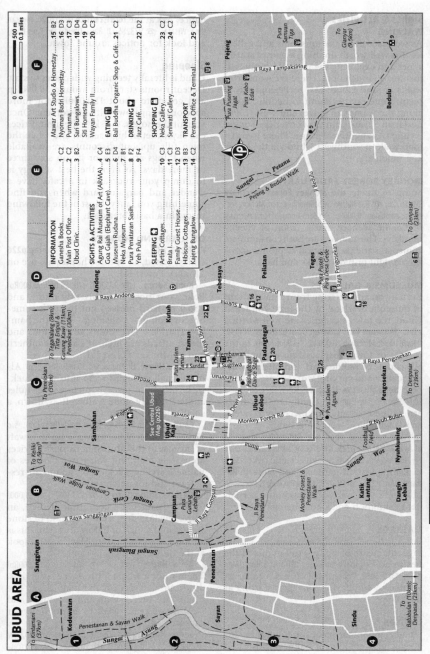

0   500 m
0   0.3 miles

INFORMATION	
Ganesha Books....................	1 C2
Main Post Office.................	2 C2
Ubud Clinic........................	3 B2

SIGHTS & ACTIVITIES	
Agung Rai Museum of Art (ARMA)..	4 C4
Goa Gajah (Elephant Cave)....	5 E3
Museum Rudana..................	6 D4
Neka Museum.....................	7 B1
Pura Penataran Sasih..........	8 F2
Yeh Pulu...........................	9 F4

SLEEPING	
Artini Cottages..................	10 C3
Brata I.............................	11 C3
Family Guest House...........	12 D3
Hibiscus Cottages..............	13 B3
Kajeng Bungalow...............	14 C2

Mawar Art Studio & Homestay....	15 B2
Nyoman Badri Homestay......	16 D3
Purnama...........................	17 D4
Sari Bungalows..................	18 D4
Siti Homestay....................	19 D4
Wayan Family II.................	20 C3

EATING	
Bali Buddha Organic Shop & Café..	21 C2

DRINKING	
Jazz Café..........................	22 D2

SHOPPING	
Neka Gallery.....................	23 C2
Seniwati Gallery................	24 C2

TRANSPORT	
Perama Office & Terminal....	25 C3

INDONESIA

Sights & Activities

WALKING

As well as visiting the museums and galleries it is well worth donning a pair of sturdy shoes and exploring the natural beauty that inspires so much of it. There are wonderful walks around Ubud: east to Pejeng, across picturesque ravines south to Bedulu; north along the Campuan ridge; and west to Penestanan Sayan, with views over the Sungai Ayung (Ayung River) gorge. There is also a loop walk to southwest Ubud via the Monkey Sanctuary.

MONKEY FOREST SANCTUARY

South of town, the **Monkey Forest Sanctuary** (Map p226; ☎ 971304; www.balimonkey.com; Monkey Forest Rd; admission 10,000Rp; ☿ 8am-6pm) offers plenty of Edenic scenery and a troop of cheeky monkeys. The monkeys are both consummate comedians and pathological kleptomaniacs – keep a tight grip on snacks and bags.

MUSEUMS & GALLERIES

Even if you are suffering from a nasty strain of museum overload by the time you reach Ubud, the town's galleries are well worth a visit. **Museum Puri Lukisan** (Map p226; ☎ 971159; Jl Raya Ubud; admission 20,000Rp; ☿ 9am-5pm), in the middle of town, displays fine examples of all schools of Balinese art and offers painting, dance and carving workshops. The superb **Neka Museum** (Map p223; ☎ 975074; admission 20,000Rp; ☿ 9am-5pm), in Campuan, has modern Balinese art and fine pieces by Western artists who have worked in Bali.

Also worth a peek are **Agung Rai Museum of Art** (ARMA; Map p223; ☎ 976659; admission 20,000Rp; ☿ 10am-6pm), which has an eclectic collection in some pleasant gardens, and **Museum Rudana** (Map p223; ☎ 975779; Jl Cok Rai Pudak; admission 20,000Rp; ☿ 9am-5pm), which has both a permanent exhibition and a commercial gallery.

MASSAGE

For a little self-indulgence, sample a massage, manicure or body scrub at one of the health and beauty salons. **Milano Salon** (Map p226; ☎ 973488; Monkey Forest Rd) has a range of weird and wonderful massages, starting at 60,000Rp.

Courses

Ubud is a popular place for courses in languages, arts, cooking or Balinese music and dance. Ask at the **tourist office** (Map p226; Yayasan Bina Wisata; ☎ 973285; Jl Raya Ubud; ☿ 8am-8pm) and look for notices around town.

Sleeping

Ubud is literally teeming with places to stay. Decent rooms start from around 30,000Rp and go up to about 150,000Rp for more spacious bungalows with air-con etc. Once you hit the hotels, the sky's the limit. Prices can skyrocket in high season and when the town fills up, but discounts are available when things are quiet or if you stay three or more days. As ever, the best strategy is to dump your rucksack in a café, have a wander and bargain hard when you find something you fancy. Most of the following throw in a basic breakfast.

ON & AROUND MONKEY FOREST RD   Map p226

Unless stated, all of these homestays are on Monkey Forest Rd.

Kubu Saren (☎ 975704; s/d 55,000/60,000Rp) Poke your nose into this tidy outfit, and you'll be hard-pressed not to catch someone sweeping or polishing – even the bamboo sparkles. The rooms are spacious and the standards are high. It's at the southern end of Monkey Forest Rd.

Arjuna House (Jl Arjuna; s/d 30,000/40,000Rp) Almost small enough to slip into your rucksack, this little place is picturesque, quiet and extremely good value. It is down a small alley off Jl Arjuna.

Canderi (☎ 975054; www.canderirest.com; s/d 100,000/120,000Rp) You can wake up to a waft of incense at this atmospheric outfit. Prices are a little high, but you pay for oodles of Balinese styling, slick décor, an on-site restaurant and topnotch service.

Gayatri Bungalows (☎ 973306; s/d 35,000/50,000Rp) Featuring a collection of cacti, an extremely lazy dog, a congregation of stone statues and a flick of Balinese charm, this is another cheerful option. Have a good look at the rooms, though, as standards vary.

Bella House (☎ 975391; s/d 50,000/60,000Rp) There's not a whole lot to these basic digs, down an alleyway off the main drag. The rooms are bigger than most though, and ideal if you really want to empty out your rucksack and make a mess.

Sadru House (☎ 972630; Jl Arjuna; s/d 40,000/50,000Rp) With plenty of homestay atmos-

INDONESIA

phere, this spot serves a good breakfast from a blackened, smoke-filled kitchen. The rooms are ordinary, but the resident family will make you feel right at home. It is just off Monkey Forest Rd.

Other recommendations:

Merthasaya Bungalows (☎ 974176; s/d 60,000/ 70,000Rp) With a blooming garden.

Pramesti Bungalows (☎ 970843; uni_ pramesti@hotmail.com; s/d 65,000/70,000Rp) Expansive rooms in a coconut grove – hard hats not included.

Rice Paddy Bungalows (☎ 0852-3712 5196; s/d 45,000/60,000Rp) Spotty rooms by a rice paddy.

EAST OF MONKEY FOREST RD

The small streets east of Monkey Forest Rd have numerous family-style homestays, which are quiet but still handy for the town centre.

Shana Bungalows (Map p226; ☎ 970481; Jl Goutama 7; s/d 30,000/40,000Rp) Run by one of Ubud's more green-fingered gardeners, this creaky, old school place offers a handful of thatched rooms in a leafy, flower-filled courtyard. Unfortunately, the bees here seem to have acquired a taste for Bintang beer.

Sania's House (Map p226; ☎ 975535; sania_house @yahoo.com; Jl Karna 7; d from 70,000Rp; ⊠ ▣) Giving the hanging gardens of Babylon a run for their money, this opulent, split-level spot features a range of ornate rooms and a central fountain adorned with a generously proportioned concrete mermaid. The more expensive rooms (250,000Rp) are worth a splurge and come with romantic four-poster beds.

Wayan Family II (Map p223; ☎ 970345; Jl Hanoman; s/d 40,000/50,000Rp) Hidden away on a narrow alley off Jl Hanoman, this popular spot features a hard-haggling owner (discounts are available for the persistent), chicken noises aplenty, a sleepy courtyard for mingling and great value-for-money.

Purnama (Map p223; ☎ 978371; Jl Hanoman; s/d 50,000/60,000Rp) Don't expect much in the way of fireworks, but this homely spot features airy rooms with bamboo beds, a concrete water feature filled with gold fish and a vocal, red parrot.

Other recommendations:

Artini Cottages (Map p223; ☎ 978425; Jl Hanoman; s/d 90,000/100,000Rp; ▣) Midmarket style at reasonable prices.

Brata 1 (Map p223; ☎ 975598; Jl Hanoman; s/d 50,000/70,000Rp) Ordinary, but comfortable.

NORTH OF MONKEY FOREST RD

Suci Inn (Map p226; ☎ 975304; Jl Suweta; s/d 40,000/ 50,000Rp) Bums in beds provide the benchmark here – the full rooms speak for themselves. Central, welcoming and cosy, this is a tried-and-tested favourite and it's worth booking ahead.

Roja's Homestay (Map p226; ☎ 972331; Jl Kajeng 1; s/d 50,000/80,000Rp) Roja's is a typical Ubud homestay, offering all the requisite staples: Balinese brickwork, greenery, incense smells and smiles.

Mawar Art Studio & Homestay (Map p223; ☎ 975086; Jl Raya Ubud; s/d 100,000/150,000Rp) Benefiting from a painter's touch, this working artist's studio offers an exquisite garden setting, decent rooms and a chance to mingle with Ubud's creative types.

Hibiscus Cottages (Map p223; ☎ 970475; hibiscus cottages@hotmail.com; Jl Bisma; s/d 80,000/100,000Rp) There are several little homestays out among the paddy fields off Jl Bisma and this is the cheapest. The courtyard has a slightly scruffy, farmyard feel, but the setting is serene and the rooms are comfortable – if a little overpriced.

Kajeng Bungalow (Map p223; ☎ 975018; Jl Kajeng 29; s/d 70,000/80,000Rp; ▣) The dingy entrance could stand in for Hades, but the layered, riverside setting is impressive, there's a pool – which gets a little murkier every year – and the rooms are perfectly passable.

TEBESAYA   Map p223

East of Ubud, this quiet village comprises little more than a main street, Jl Sukma, which runs between two small streams – the nicest of the rooms overlook the verdant valleys.

Family Guest House (☎ 974054; Jl Sukma; d from 77,000Rp; ⊠) With a garden leafy enough to make even Tarzan feel at home, this Ubud institution offers home-baked bread, lashings of atmosphere, an owner who will never forget your face and rooms for a wide range of budgets.

Nyoman Badri Homestay (☎ 977047; Jl Sukma; d from 50,000Rp) There's heaps of atmosphere here too and if you're nice to Mama, she'll cook you up a feast.

TEGES   Map p223

At the southeastern fringe of the Ubud area, the small community of Teges has a cluster of quiet, passable cheapies.

INDONESIA

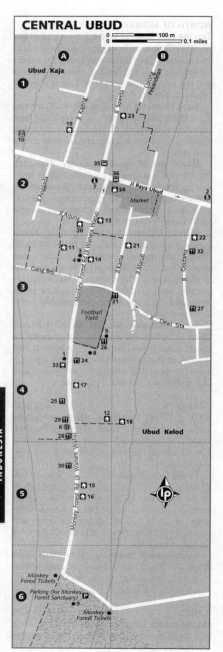

CENTRAL UBUD

Siti Homestay (☎ 978643; s/d 40,0000/50,000Rp) On the quietest little lane in town, Siti serves up a pleasant out-of-the-fray setting, big welcomes and spotty rooms.

Sari Bungalows (☎ 975541; s/d 30,000/34,000Rp) Quacking ducks provide the soundtrack at this otherwise peaceful spot by the paddy fields, and enthusiastic cleaners ensure it remains a reliable bet for a budget.

Eating
Ubud's many restaurants offer the most diverse and delicious food on the island. It's a great place to stretch your budget, and your waistline. For the cheapest meals, a

few food carts congregate on the southern side of the market, but they close early in the evening.

MONKEY FOREST RD   Map p226

All of these restaurants are on, or just off Monkey Forest Rd.

Puteri Minang (☎ 978267; dishes 5000Rp; ☽ lunch & dinner) Frills are at a premium at this Spartan *masakan Padang*, but the locals flock here for tasty eats and it's well worth following them.

Cafe Wayan & Bakery (☎ 975447; cakes 10,000Rp; ☽ breakfast, lunch & dinner) It takes a strong mind – or a peg on the nose – to resist the freshly baked croissant smells that drift out of this pleasant, garden café. Grab a quick coffee up front, or slob out on the terrace out back.

Dian Restaurant (☎ 975587; mains 20,000Rp; ☽ breakfast, lunch & dinner) Reliable as a plate of baked beans, this popular, thatched eatery serves an eclectic mix of Indonesian and international dishes in airy surrounds.

Bumbu Bali 2 (☎ 976698; mains 30,000Rp; ☽ breakfast, lunch & dinner) The decorators sure haven't gone on a charm offensive at this dowdy high-street spot, but there's a good selection of Balinese fare and if you like what you eat, you can enrol in their cookery course (per day 150,000Rp).

Green House (☎ 975236; mains 60,000Rp; ☽ lunch & dinner) The main drag's most fashionable new opening features oh-so-contemporary minimalist design, some topnotch fusion food and a decent dose of gourmet glamour. Sip your cocktail and spend sunset with the swanky set.

JL RAYA & AROUND   Map p223

Bali Buddha Organic Shop & Café (☎ 976324; Jl Jembawan; dishes from 15,000Rp; ☽ breakfast, lunch & dinner) Opposite the post office, Ubud's hip vegetarian temple dishes up a huge spread of wholesome tucker, using organic ingredients from local farmers. There's also a fab shop downstairs selling a smorgasbord of tasty takeaways, or you can phone for home delivery.

JL DEWI SITA & AROUND   Map p226

This small street runs east from Monkey Forest Rd across the top of the football field.

Deli Cat (☎ 971284; Jl Dewi Sita; sandwiches 15,000Rp; ☽ breakfast & lunch) This little slice of the Mediterranean brings all the smells and lip-smacking flavours of rural Italy to a little corner of Ubud's football pitch. Stock up on cheese and sausage at the deli counter or bulk up on a breakfast at a rickety little table out front.

Dewa Warung (Jl Goutama; mains 8000Rp; ☽ breakfast, lunch & dinner) It's not much to look at, but this little spit and sawdust spot is a big hit with backpackers and a great place to catch up on the gossip over a cheap plate of Balinese tucker.

Tutmak (☎ 975754; Jl Dewi Sita; mains 20,000Rp; ☽ breakfast, lunch & dinner) Recently expanding into new digs, this is the place to charge up on coffee, stoke up on sandwiches and salads or simply kick back with a book and views of the football pitch. Don't cheer too loudly though, the tables here are popular with bohemian types discussing Nietzsche.

Warung Biah Biah (☎ 978249; Jl Goutama 13; mains 7000Rp; ☽ breakfast, lunch & dinner) This open-air spot features quirky, high-backed chairs, Louis Armstrong tunes and a cheap-as-chips Balinese menu offering everything from jackfruit with Bali spices (3500Rp) to deep-fried mud snails (8000Rp).

Drinking

No-one comes to Ubud for wild nightlife, but these days a few bars offer after-dinner diversion.

Jazz Café (Map p223; ☎ 976594; Jl Sukma 2; ☽ 5-11.30pm) Serene, smooth and terribly sophisticated, Ubud's classiest after-dark haunt grooves to the sound of a live sax (except Sunday to Monday), serves up a mean selection of cocktails and international cuisine and pulls in a veritable avalanche of punters – book ahead for a table.

Putra Bar (Map p226; ☎ 975570; Monkey Forest Rd; ☽ 4pm-1am) The only real nightspot on Monkey Forest Rd hosts live bands, most of the town's late night bump-and-grind and more than its fair share of reggae fans.

Entertainment

Try to see at least one of the Balinese dances performed in or near Ubud every night. The **tourist office** (☎ 973285) has the latest schedules, and sells tickets (50,000Rp).

Shopping

Pasar Seni (Art Market; Map p226; cnr Jl Raya Ubud & Monkey Forest Rd; ☽ 8am-8pm) The two-storey

INDONESIA

market sells a wide range of clothing, sarongs and souvenirs of variable quality at very negotiable prices, as do many small shops along Monkey Forest Rd and Jl Hanoman.

You can buy paintings at many commercial galleries. **Neka Gallery** (Map p223; ☎ 975034; Jl Raya Ubud; ☯ 9am-5pm) is one of the largest, while **Seniwati Gallery** (Map p223; ☎ 975485; www .seniwatigallery.com; Jl Sriwedari 2B; ☯ 9am-5pm) is a showcase for female artists.

Ubud's main galleries, however, can be expensive. For less expensive art works, look in individual artists' studios.

Getting There & Around

Public *bemo* stop at two convenient points in the centre of town. Small orange *bemo* travel between Ubud and Gianyar (5000Rp, 25 minutes), which has bus and *bemo* connections to most of eastern Bali. Brown *bemo* go to/from Batubulan terminal (9000Rp, one hour), with connections to the other Denpasar terminals (another 2000Rp).

Perama (Map p223; ☎ 973316; Jl Hanoman) has a terminal that is inconveniently located south of town in Padangtegal. It costs 15,000Rp to Sanur (45 minutes); 20,000Rp to Kuta (one hour); 30,000Rp to Padangbai (1¼ hours) and Candidasa (1½ hours); and 50,000Rp to Lovina (2½ hours).

Car and motorcycle rental prices are as cheap as anywhere in Bali. Bicycles cost around 12,000Rp per day, or 10,000Rp per day for longer periods.

AROUND UBUD

In Tampaksiring, just off the main road north of Ubud, **Gunung Kawi** (admission 5000Rp; ☯ 8am-5pm) is a group of large stone memorials cut into cliffs on either side of a picturesque river valley. Believed to date from the 11th century, it's one of the most impressive sights in Bali.

About 2km along the main road to Gianyar is popular **Goa Gajah** (Elephant Cave; Map p223; admission 5000Rp; ☯ 9am-5pm), discovered in the 1920s and believed to have been a Buddhist hermitage. Nearby is **Yeh Pulu** (Map p223; admission 5000Rp; ☯ 8am-6pm), a complex of rock carvings with carved bas-relief. A couple of kilometres north in Pejeng, **Pura Penataran Sasih** (Map p223; admission by donation; ☯ 9am-6pm) houses a bronze drum said to be 2000 years old. A legend tells of it falling to earth as the Moon of Pejeng.

A few kilometres north of Tampaksiring, in the shadow of the Soekarno-era presidential palace, is the holy spring and temple of **Tirta Empul** (admission 5000Rp; ☯ 9am-6pm). An inscription dates the spring from AD 926. There are fine carvings and Garuda on the courtyard buildings. Both sites can be reached by *bemo* (3000Rp) from Ubud.

PURA BESAKIH

Pura Besakih (☎ 0361-222387; admission 3300Rp; ☯ dawn-dusk) is Bali's 'mother temple'. With a photogenic location, 1000m up the flanks of Gunung Agung, the temple is actually a complex of 35 separate, but related, religious structures, which only narrowly escaped destruction during the devastating eruption of Gunung Agung in 1963. Although the architecture is a bit of a disappointment and the inner courtyards are largely closed to visitors, the temple bursts into life during its colourful festivals – particularly during **Odalan**, the temple's anniversary, which falls in the 10th month of the Balinese calendar (usually April). There are plenty of guides offering their 'services' outside but you will have to haggle hard for a good deal.

Most trips to Pura Besakih require a change in Semarapura, about one hour away. Ask the driver to drop you at the temple, rather than the village, which is about 1km south. Transport options evaporate around 3pm and so hiring a private vehicle (ie bringing your own car) is often far more convenient.

GUNUNG AGUNG

Often obscured beneath a thick duvet of mist, Gunung Agung is a relatively infrequent feature of Bali's skyline. When the clouds part, however, Bali's highest and most revered mountain is an imposing sight and is visible from much of southern and eastern Bali.

In fact, Gunung Agung is a relatively moody volcano. A 700m-wide crater marks the mountain's summit and in 1963, Gunung Agung shrank by 126m after a devastating eruption. It now stands 3142m above sea level.

To reach the summit from the village of Besakih (about 1km south of the temple complex) is a very demanding climb – allow at least six hours going up and four hours coming down. Start at midnight to reach the summit for sunrise, before it's enveloped in cloud. You'll need a guide – inquire at the information office at the Pura Besakih car park or contact a guide through **Pondok Wisata Puri Agung** (☎ 0361-23037). Guides ask 150,000Rp to 200,000Rp per person.

A shorter route is from **Pura Pasar Agung** (Agung Market Temple), at around 1500m on the southern slopes of the mountain, which can be reached by a sealed road north from **Selat**. From the temple you can climb to the top in three or four hours, but it's also a pretty demanding trek. You must report to the police station at Selat before you start, and the police will strongly encourage you to take a guide – they'll charge about 200,000Rp, plus the cost of food and transport. The closest accommodation is **Pondok Wisata Puri Agung** (☎ 0361-23037; s/d 80,000/100,000Rp) on the road between Selat and Duda.

SEMARAPURA (KLUNGKUNG)
☎ 0366

Once the centre of an important Balinese kingdom, Semarapura (also known as Klungkung) is the capital of Klungkung regency. Formerly the seat of the Dewa Agung dynasty, the **Semara Pura Complex** (admission 5000Rp; ☻ 7am-6pm) has now largely crumbled away, but history and architecture buffs will enjoy a wander past the **Kertha Gosa** (Hall of Justice) and **Bale Kambang** (Floating Pavilion).

Loji Ramayana Hotel (☎ 21044; Jl Diponegoro; d 50,000Rp) certainly isn't worth getting off the bus for, but remains a passable place to crash if you are stuck here overnight.

Frequent *bemo* and minibuses from Denpasar (Batubulan terminal) pass through Semarapura (9000Rp, one hour) on the way to Padangbai and Amlapura.

NUSA LEMBONGAN

Nusa Lembongan is one of three islands (along with Nusa Penida and Nusa Ceningan) that together comprise the Nusa Penida archipelago. Nusa Lembongan, with its famed surf breaks, white-sand beaches and hotels, is the biggest tourist drawcard and remains a pleasant escape from the hubbub of Bali's south-coast resorts.

Information
The dry season is surfing season, with winds bringing in the waves from the southeast. The Shipwreck, Lacerations and Playground

surf breaks are off the island's west coast, near the little settlement of Jungutbatu.

Most hotels will accept foreign cash from their guests, and some will change travellers cheques (at lower rates than in southern Bali).

Sleeping & Eating
Most of the cheap accommodation is in Jungutbatu, a strip of working beach on the northwest coast.

Johnny's Losmen (d 35,000Rp) Johnny's has been around for almost as long as the island – and it shows. Spartan and spotty, this is simple with a double-decker 'S', but remains something of a rendezvous for visiting backpackers.

Mainski Inn (☎ 0361-24487; d 100,000Rp) Rather more salubrious, Mainski has comfortable, shiny rooms and the fresh looks of a recent face-lift.

Mainski has a decent eatery serving the old favourites.

Getting There & Away
Infrequent public boats (35,000Rp, 1½ hours) leave from the northern end of Sanur Beach, in front of the Ananda Hotel. They land at Jungutbatu and (sometimes) Mushroom Bay. Several companies, including **Bounty Cruises** (☎ 0361-726666; www.balibountycruises.com), run fast boats between Benoa harbour and Nusa Lembongan. Fares start at US$15 each way.

PADANGBAI
☎ 0363

For many travellers, Padangbai is little more than a scribbled entry on the itinerary; the port for ferries to Lombok. In fact, the town curves around a pretty little bay and can make a pleasant stopover in its own right, with plenty of decent hostels and a clean sweep of sand.

Made Homestay (☎ 41441; Jl Silayukti; per hr 10,000Rp; ☻ 9am-9pm) has Internet access and a *wartel*.

Activities
Padangbai has plenty of dive shops offering trips to sites across Bali. With **Water Worxx Dive Center** (☎ 41220; www.waterworxbali.com; Jl Silayukti; ☻ 8am-8pm), two dives at the wreck of the *Liberty* off Tulamben cost US$50, including transfers.

Sleeping

In August especially, hotels can fill up quickly and double their rates. Many of the best homestays are on Jl Silayukti, the beachfront road.

Made Homestay (☎ 41441; mades_padangbai@ hotmail.com; Jl Silayukti; s/d 40,000/60,000Rp; 🖳) The plain 'sea-view' rooms here have 'fine' vistas of the ferry terminal, but there's a decent eatery with chintzy décor, freshly laundered linen on the beds and a nightly film show.

Kerti Beach Inn (☎ 41391; kertibeachinn@yahoo .com; Jl Silayukti 9; s/d 30,000/40,000Rp; 🖳) Just next door, Kerti boasts genuinely pleasant views from its 1st-floor terrace eatery, and bungalow views from its flimsy rattan bungalows.

Padangbai Beach Homestay (☎ 0812-360 7946; Jl Silayukti 14; d from 50,000Rp) Injecting a little class into the Padangbai hotel scene, this midmarket spot has trim lawns, tidy rooms and slightly snooty staff. Pick from poky budget rooms or larger, more regal bungalows (150,000Rp).

Kembar Inn (☎ 41364; Jl Segara 6; d from 40,000Rp; 🐾) Pathological cleanliness comes at the expense of atmosphere at this neat little homestay, where acres of polished tiles smack of a five-star public toilet. That said, there hasn't been a cockroach here since the late 1970s and there are plenty of rooms – from budget to grand air-con affairs (150,000Rp) – to choose from.

Eating

Puri Rai (☎ 41187; Jl Silayukti 7X; mains 15,000Rp; ☙ breakfast, lunch & dinner) Stone statues, the type of drapery that floats around in the background of an R&B video and some stylish furniture bring a whiff of 'Bali chic' to this popular eatery. And its Bali curries (15,000Rp) are pretty good too.

Ozone (☎ 41780; Jl Segara 8; mains 15,000Rp; ☙ breakfast, lunch & dinner) The walls are covered in travellers' scrawlings, portraits of the staff posing proudly and beer advertisements, the food's good and things get a little lively after dark. One way or another, you will end up here eventually.

Warung Marina (Jl Silayukti 20; mains 12,000Rp; ☙ breakfast, lunch & dinner) Opposite Kerti Beach Inn, this tumbledown fish shack has some of the best shark and barracuda in town.

Champion Sport Bar (☎ 0818-0568 6698; Jl Segara; ☙ lunch & dinner) En route to the ferry terminal, this hole-in-the-wall bar stages sports

events on satellite TV – well, when there's power anyway. The coy may want to avert their eyes from the owner's 'erotic' tattoos.

Getting There & Away

From the car park in front of the port, *bemo* go to Amlapura (10,000Rp, 45 minutes), via Candidasa (5000Rp, 20 minutes), and Semarapura (6000Rp, 35 minutes) and Denpasar (15,000Rp, 1½ hours). Tourists are commonly overcharged.

Perama (☎ 41419; www.peramatour.com; Jl Pelabuhan) is based at Cafe Dona and runs tourist buses to Kuta (30,000Rp, two hours), Ubud (30,000Rp, one hour), Candidasa (10,000Rp, 20 minutes) and Lovina (80,000Rp, 3½ hours).

Public ferries between Padangbai and Lembar (Lombok) run every 1½ hours, 24 hours a day (16,000Rp, five hours).

CANDIDASA

☎ 0363

Candidasa's big tourist drawcard, its beach, was washed out to sea when developers got greedy and decided to blow up the protective reef to make cement. Depressing as this may seem, however, Candidasa has more than managed to keep its head above water and remains a pleasant base for those looking to explore Bali's east coast. In fact, so long as you don't mind heading down the coast for a swim, Candidasa is proof positive that there's more to a good seaside resort than an accessible strip of sand.

Orientation & Information

Candidasa is a one-street (Jl Raya Candidasa) town, cut in half by a pleasant lagoon. The area east of the lagoon tends to be a little quieter.

Stroll along the main, seaside strip and you will find plenty of *wartel*, Internet cafés and moneychangers.

Sleeping

Ida's Homestay (☎ 41096; jsidas1@aol.com; Jl Raya Candidasa; d from 110,000Rp) The price tag calls for a bit of a splurge, but this heavenly spot offers Candidasa's most atmospheric digs and plenty of Robinson Crusoe charm. The quirky bungalows look like they have been built out of driftwood and are scattered through a shady, jungle setting. It is west of the lagoon.

Ari Homestay (☎ 0817-970 7339; Jl Raya Candidasa; d from 50,000Rp) Ugly as sin but with a heart of gold, Ari's is proof positive that beauty shines from within. Despite its dodgy roadside face, this popular haunt at the western edge of town offers clean rooms and a friendly Aussie owner who can talk the hind legs off a donkey, charm the spots off a leopard and cook a fabulous fry-up. He will also tell you about the region's best 'secret' beaches.

Temple Cafe & Seaside Cottages (☎ 41629; www.bali-seafront-bungalows.com; Jl Raya Candidasa; d from 50,000Rp; 🐾) Running right down to the sea, this central place has a flower-filled garden, a funky eatery and a room for every budget (to 150,000Rp).

Dewi Bungalows (☎ 41166; Jl Raya Candidasa; s/d 50,000/60,000Rp) East of the lagoon, this quiet spot has a handful of rattan and brick bungalows in a spacious coconut grove.

Eating & Drinking

There are dozens of eateries in Candidasa and you should never be more than a few paces from your favourite dishes. The cheapest places to eat are the food stalls that spring up every evening at the western end of town, where the main road almost crashes into the sea.

Vincent's (☎ 41368; Jl Raya Candidasa; mains 30,000Rp; 🕐 lunch & dinner) With modern art on the walls, slow-moving jazz on the sound system and just about everything else on the menu, this upbeat bar-eatery caters to Candidasa's limited 'it' crowd. Flop into one of the sofas with a cocktail and order up a plate of lobster. It is east of the lagoon.

Artika's (Jl Raya Candidasa; dishes 6000Rp; 🕐 lunch & dinner) Just next door, but at the other end of the price scale, this modest little spot serves a good selection of *masakan Padang*.

Queen's Café (☎ 41655; Jl Raya Candidasa; mains 20,000Rp; 🕐 breakfast, lunch & dinner) This simple wood-and-tin affair is across the road from Artika's and serves pizza, schnitzel, sandwiches, fresh air and a good dose of REM.

Iguana Café (☎ 41973; Jl Raya Candidasa; mains 25,000Rp; 🕐 breakfast, lunch & dinner) Further west, Iguana is a little more salubrious and whips up a good spread of local and seafood dishes.

Getting There & Away

Candidasa is on the main road between Amlapura and Denpasar – there's no terminal,

so hail *bemo* anywhere along the main road (buses probably won't stop).

Perama (☎ 41114; www.peramatour.com; Jl Raya Candidasa) is at the western end of the strip, near Ari Homestay. It runs tourist shuttle buses to Sanur (30,000Rp, 1¾ hours), Kuta (30,000Rp, two hours), Ubud (30,000Rp, 1¼ hours), Lovina (80,000Rp, three hours) and Padangbai (10,000Rp, 20 minutes).

AMLAPURA
☎ 0363

Amlapura isn't worth making a diversion for, but there are worse places to stop if you are already making the trip through eastern Bali. Twenty-first-century hustle and bustle dominates the streets today, but you can catch a glimpse of the fast-fading 'good old days' at the former palace of the Raja of Karangasem, the **Puri Agung Karangasem** (Jl Sultan Agung; admission 3000Rp; 🕐 8am-6pm).

Villa Amlapura (☎ 23246; Jl Gajah Mada; s/d 50,000/ 100,000Rp), around the corner from the palace, is a friendly and slightly eccentric place if you're not in a rush to get back on the road.

Amlapura's bus/*bemo* terminal has regular connections to/from Denpasar (Batubulan terminal; 12,000Rp, two hours) and around the north coast to Singaraja (20,000Rp, 3½ hours).

TIRTA GANGGA
☎ 0363

The village under the volcano, Tirta Gangga (Water of the Ganges) sits in the shadow of Gunung Agung and in the midst of some of Bali's most beautiful scenery. Passed in a gear change and a slow right-hand turn, it's small, isolated and quiet and remains a blissfully serene stopover on the slow road through Bali.

The old **Taman Tirta Gangga** (www.tirtagangga .com; admission 3000Rp; 🕐 7am-6pm) water palace has ornamental ponds and swimming pools – a dip is an extra 6000Rp. The surrounding countryside has sublime rice-field vistas and good trekking possibilities – ask at your hotel for suggestions.

Sleeping & Eating

Most of the hotels will gladly cook up a meal, or the *warung* near the palace are a good bet for cheap eats.

Puri Sawah (☎ 21847; s/d 90,000/100,000Rp) On the Amed side of town, this is Tirta Gangga's most luxurious offering, with photogenic views, comfy bungalows, a trio of friendly (once they get used to you) pooches and the type of garden you'd expect to find David Attenborough tramping through. If you're in your own car, you'll need a run-up to clear the near vertical drive.

Rijasa (☎ 21873; d from 60,000Rp) Right opposite the palace, Rijasa has a spread of digs in a lush, palm-fringed garden. It's also the best spot for local information.

Dhangin Taman Inn (☎ 22059; s/d 30,000/40,000Rp) On the doorstep of the palace and offering a voyeur's glimpse of the grounds, this ramshackle place has so-so rooms, some runaway plants and plenty of faux-wood concrete garden furniture.

Genta Bali Warung (☎ 22436; mains 12,000Rp; ❤ breakfast, lunch & dinner) Clearly courting passing travellers, this Western-style *warung* offers plastic deer statues (no, we don't know why either), bamboo furniture, a funnyman owner and a flick of hippy-chic styling. Food ranges from *nasi campur* (rice with whatever is available; 11,000Rp) to 'spaggetty' (12,000Rp).

Ryoshi (☎ 081-2368 2791; mains 20,000Rp; ❤ breakfast, lunch & dinner) It looks like it has been built from bits of old flotsam, but the views are magical and the Japanese food is as good as it gets in rural Bali.

Getting There & Away

Regular *bemo* and minibuses pass through Tirta Gangga on routes north of Amlapura (2000Rp to Amlapura) – just flag them down.

Perama tourist buses also pass through en route to Lovina (50,000Rp, three hours) or Kuta (40,000Rp, 2½ hours). Try your hotel for tickets.

AMED & THE FAR EAST COAST

☎ 0363

The coast east of Amed is one of Bali's largely forgotten stretches of seaside. Developers are starting to gatecrash the party, but the island's wild east is a far cry from the concrete jungle of the south coast.

Most of the development is around the bays of Jemeluk, Bunutan and Lipah. Facilities are improving and a few hotels and shops offer telephone, Internet and money-changing services. **Euro-Dive** (☎ 23469; www .eurodivebali.com), in Amed, comes well recom-

mended for those wanting to explore the region's many offshore attractions; two-dive packages start at US$45.

Sleeping & Eating

Three Brothers (☎ 23472; s/d 70,000/80,000Rp) The first place you'll come to on the road east of Amed is a tried-and-tested favourite and offers reliable standards, clean rooms and reasonable food.

Amed Cafe (☎ 23473; www.amedcafe.com; d from 80,000Rp; ❤ ☐ ☎) A little further east, Amed Cafe has all the gloss of a major hotel, but offers a range of well-priced budget rooms. There's a restaurant and Internet café over the road.

Aiona Health Garden (mains 20,000Rp; s/d 70,000/ 80,000Rp) Set in a blooming and extremely fragrant herb garden, this is the spot for veggie eats, New Age potions and a serious detox. If you feel invigorated after lunch, you can take the owner's herbal preparations away, or there are rooms for those seriously in need of a detox. It is 2km east of Bunutan.

Further accommodation options around the coast:

Eco-Dive (☎ 23482; d 30,000Rp) Super-basic rattan huts in nearby Jemeluk.

TP Café & Homestay (☎ 23508; s/d 40,000/50,000Rp) In peaceful Lipah, this is an excellent choice.

Waeni (☎ 23515; s/d 50,000/60,000Rp) Spotty rooms, but a stunning cliff-top location over Bunutan.

Getting There & Around

Plenty of minibuses and *bemo* between Singaraja (10,000Rp, three hours) and Amlapura (4000Rp, 40 minutes) go through Culik, the turn-off for Amed. Infrequent *bemo* then link Culik with the resort villages. If you arrive or leave late you may have to charter an *ojek* (per kilometre 2500Rp).

TULAMBEN

☎ 0363

Stay on the shore, and you'll be wondering why anyone visits Tulamben, a no-horse town on the main road west. To answer that question you need to don your scuba gear and head below the surface to the impressive wreck of the US cargo ship *Liberty* – probably the most popular dive site in Bali. Other great dive sites are nearby, and even snorkellers can enjoy the wreck. Inexperienced divers should stick with the most reputable dive operations, such as **Tauch Terminal** (☎ 0361-774504; www.tauch-terminal.com), even if they cost a little more.

Sleeping & Eating
Hotels are spread out along the main road, and most have a restaurant, a dive shop and a variety of rooms.

Puri Madha Bungalows (☎ 22921; s/d 40,000/60,000Rp) Right opposite the wreck, the bungalows here are a little ramshackle. On the upside, there's a cheap dive shop on-site and plenty of bubble-blowing banter in the little café.

Paradise Palm Beach Bungalows (☎ 22910; d from 75,000Rp; 🕱) Back on the main road, this is a far swankier outfit, with a range of bungalows, a dive shop and a lot less rough-and-tumble.

Gandu Mayu (☎ 22912; s/d 45,000/50,000Rp) This is another cheapie.

Rumah Makan Sandya (☎ 22915; mains 20,000Rp; 🕑 lunch & dinner) Also on the main road, this no-nonsense eatery serves up decent grub and travel information from its breezy garden setting.

Getting There & Away
Buses and minibuses pass through Tulamben en route between Amlapura (5000Rp, one hour) and Singaraja (9000Rp, 2½ hours). However, they become much less frequent after 2pm. You may also be able to flag down the once- or twice-daily Perama tourist buses that run between Lovina and Kuta.

SINGARAJA
☎ 0362
Disney fans may be amused to know that Singaraja translates as 'Lion King', but the big city of northern Bali offers little more than a handful of Dutch colonial buildings and an increasingly weathered, oldie-worldie waterfront.

If you are sick, it is also worth knowing that the city is home to the biggest hospital in northern Bali, **RSUP Umum** (☎ 26277; Jl Ngurah Rai; 🕑 24hr).

Most tourists stay at Lovina, about 10km to the west – Singaraja hotels cater mainly to Indonesian travellers.

Wijaya Hotel (☎ 21915; Jl Sudirman 75; d from 50,000Rp; 🕱), on the main road between Denpasar and Lovina, offers right royal welcomes to the handful of tourists that actually stop here. The rooms are spick-and-span and there's a little restaurant for snacks.

Food stalls congregate around the **main market** (cnr Jl Durian & Jl Sawo; 🕑 8am-7pm).

Getting There & Away
Singaraja has three *bemo*/bus terminals. From the main Sukasada terminal, about 3km south of town, minibuses go to Denpasar (Ubung terminal; 15,000Rp, 2½ hours) via Bedugul (5000Rp, one hour) about every 30 minutes from 6am to 4pm.

Banyuasri terminal, on the western side of town, has minibuses for Gilimanuk (8000Rp, two hours) and Lovina (3000Rp, 30 minutes).

The Penarukan terminal, 2km east of town, has *bemo* to Yeh Sanih (4000Rp, 40 minutes) and Amlapura (20,000Rp, 3½ hours) via the coastal road.

Several bus companies have express services to destinations in Java including Surabaya (100,000Rp, 11 hours) and Jakarta (200,000Rp, 24 hours). Travel agencies along the western end of Jl Jen Ahmad Yani sell tickets – try **Pahala Kencana** (☎ 29945; Jl Ahmad Yani 95; 🕑 24hr).

AROUND SINGARAJA
Yeh Sanih
Freshwater springs here are channelled into clean **swimming pools** (admission 3000Rp; 🕑 8am-6pm), set in pleasant gardens. There is frequent public transport from Singaraja.

Gitgit
About 11km south of Singaraja, there is a well-signposted path that goes 800m west from the main road to the touristy waterfall, **Air Terjun Gitgit** (admission 3000Rp; 🕑 8am-5pm). You buy the ticket about halfway down the path. About 2km further up the hill, **Gitgit Multi-Tier Waterfall** (admission 3000Rp; 🕑 8am-5pm) is less spectacular, but it's a nicer walk. You can have a refreshing dip at both falls.

Minibuses between Singaraja and Denpasar will stop at Gitgit.

LOVINA
☎ 0362
Lovina is the north coast's beach-bum magnet, a necklace of villages and black-sand beaches catering to budget travellers with a penchant for sunshine and calm

seas. Always a little rough around the edges, Lovina is still struggling to pick itself up following the tourist lulls that followed the 2002 and 2005 Kuta bombings and the 2004 Indian Ocean tsunami. With hotels struggling to fill their rooms outside July and August, big discounts are now on offer and while partygoers should expect nothing more Bacchanalian than a slow beer at sundown, those after peace and quiet will delight in the region's relative calm.

Information

Kalibukbuk is the focus of the Lovina area, and there are plenty of moneychangers around here. Postal agencies and *wartel* are dotted along the main road.

BCA ATM (cnr Jl Bina Ria & Jl Raya Lovina; ⏱ 24hr)

Mailaku (☎ 41163; Jl Bina Ria; per min 300Rp; ⏱ 8am-11pm) Internet access.

Perama office (☎ 41161; www.peramatour.com; Jl Raya Lovina; ⏱ 7am-10pm) A long trek out in Anturan, this is by far the best source of information, and also has Internet access.

Tourist office (☎ 41910; Jl Raya Lovina; ⏱ 8am-4pm Mon-Sat, until 1pm Fri) Combined with the police station, you are unlikely to find anything more than an unstaffed desk and a pay phone here.

Activities

Keen divers should head to **Spice Dive** (☎ 41509; www.balispicedive.com; Jl Bina Ria, Kalibuk-buk; ⏱ 8am-8pm). It also has an office on the beach, 500m west of Jl Bina Ria.

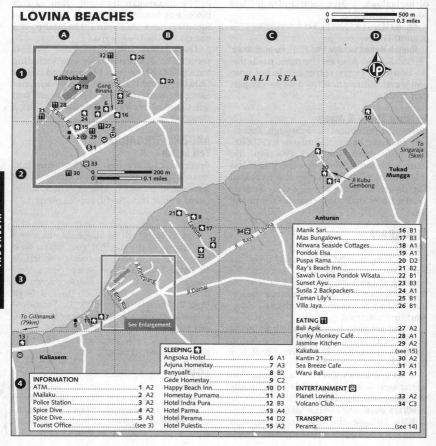

LOVINA BEACHES

SLEEPING	
Angsoka Hotel	6 A1
Arjuna Homestay	7 A3
Banyualit	8 B2
Gede Homestay	9 C2
Happy Beach Inn	10 D1
Homestay Purnama	11 A3
Hotel Indra Pura	12 B3
Hotel Parma	13 A4
Hotel Perama	14 D2
Hotel Pulestis	15 A2
Manik Sari	16 B1
Mas Bungalows	17 B3
Nirwana Seaside Cottages	18 A1
Pondok Elsa	19 A1
Puspa Rama	20 D2
Ray's Beach Inn	21 B2
Sawah Lovina Pondok Wisata	22 B1
Sunset Ayu	23 B3
Susila 2 Backpackers	24 A1
Taman Lily's	25 B1
Villa Jaya	26 B1

EATING	
Bali Apik	27 A2
Funky Monkey Café	28 A1
Jasmine Kitchen	29 A2
Kakatua	(see 15)
Kantin 21	30 A2
Sea Breeze Cafe	31 A1
Waru Bali	32 A1

ENTERTAINMENT	
Planet Lovina	33 A2
Volcano Club	34 C3

TRANSPORT	
Perama	(see 14)

INFORMATION	
ATM	1 A2
Mailaku	2 A2
Police Station	3 A2
Spice Dive	4 A2
Spice Dive	5 A3
Tourist Office	(see 3)

Sleeping

Most of Lovina's cheap accommodation is clustered on side roads to the beach. In high season (July and August), these listed prices can skyrocket, sometimes doubling; out-of-season discounts are likely. The following selection of budget places is listed roughly from east to west, starting about 8km outside Singaraja. Most include breakfast.

TUKAD MUNGGA

Happy Beach Inn (☎ 41017; s/d 50,000/60,000Rp) Right out on a limb, this is one of Lovina's quietest outposts. The beach is pretty much free of masseuses (something of a novelty here), the rooms are comfy and the owner serves up some scrumptious food.

ANTURAN

The little fishing village of Anturan is a bit scruffy, but there's a good community buzz, plenty of hostels and a regular stream of backpackers.

Gede Homestay (☎ 41526; Jl Kubu Gembong; d from 50,000Rp; ✷) It's a fair hike from the beating heart of Kalibukbuk, but Gede remains one of Lovina's most popular backpacker pit stops. The owner is chatty (perhaps too chatty) and friendly, there's a nice little beachside café and there are usually plenty of other travellers to shoot the sea breeze with. Air-con rooms cost 100,000Rp.

Puspa Rama (☎ 42070; agungdayu@yahoo.com; Jl Kubu Gembong; s/d 60,000/70,000Rp) Surrounded by plenty of leafy greenery, the cosy rooms here offer quite a lot more 'posh' for your pound. As well as hot water, you can also expect lampshades and pictures on the walls. On the downside, it lacks Gede's backslapping bonhomie.

Hotel Perama (☎ 41161; peramalovina@yahoo.com; Jl Raya Lovina; d from 35,000Rp; ✷) A little further west, on the main road, the Perama office offers a range of rooms from prison-cell Spartan (with shared bathroom) to comfortable air-con (150,000Rp). There is a 10% discount if you use its bus service.

ANTURAN TO KALIBUKBUK

Jl Laviana has a good collection of hotels, most of which are worth a snoop.

Hotel Indra Pura (☎ 41560; Jl Laviana; s/d 55,000/60,000Rp) The best-looking kid on the block offers warm welcomes and a pretty *Secret Garden* setting. It's a fair way from the beach, but the rooms here are worth every penny.

Mas Bungalows (☎ 41773; mas_bali@hotmail.com; Jl Laviana; d from 80,000Rp; ✷) A talkative miner bird provides the sound effects, a friendly family provides the hospitality and the comfortable rooms provide a good night's sleep. The atmosphere is 'bourgeois' rather than 'backpacker', but there's a café for mingling and the copulating-frog ornaments provide a little light relief.

Also recommended:

Banyualit (☎ 41789; www.banyualit.com; Jl Laviana; d from 100,000Rp; ✷ ☺) Quality midranger with a few economy rooms.

Ray's Beach Inn (☎ 41088; Jl Laviana; s/d 25,000/35,000Rp) Grungy, but cheap.

Sunset Ayu (☎ 41054; Jl Laviana; d from 70,000Rp; ✷)

KALIBUKBUK

A little over 10km from Singaraja, this is the 'centre' of Lovina, with the biggest concentration of hotels, restaurants, services…and touts. Jl Ketepang is the quieter of the two main streets.

On & Around Jl Ketepang

Taman Lily's (☎ 41307; gervanleenen@hotmail.com; Jl Ketepang; s/d 50,000/60,000Rp) The chintzy pink décor is a little unsettling, but this family-run place is as immaculate as Barbie's summerhouse and there's a nice garden for lounging in.

Villa Jaya (☎ 700 1238; Jl Ketepang; d from 100,000Rp; ✷ ☺) It's a little pricy, but you get quite a lot for your money at this glossy new hotel, where there's a swimming pool, sun loungers and some very comfortable rooms.

SPLURGE!

Sawah Lovina Pondok Wisata (☎ 41091; www.paradiseonbali.com; Jl Ketepang; d from 170,000Rp; ✷) If you're up for a splurge, this is the place to tear up the budget. Ideally suited to seclusion seekers, this remote little outfit has a handful of beautifully decorated bungalows in a little patch of Edenic garden. It is down a tight alleyway, on the right if you are heading down Jl Ketepang towards the sea.

INDONESIA

On & Around Jl Bima Ria

Jl Bima Ria is the 'throbbing hub' of Kali-bukbuk. There are plenty of hotels on the small streets running off it.

Manik Sari (☎ 41089; d from 60,000Rp; ☒) The mattresses may be a little thin, but these attractive new digs, with whitewashed walls, flowers and Balinese styling, feel like a splurge at half the price. It is just off Jl Bina Ria and air-con rooms cost 120,000Rp.

Susila 2 Backpackers (☎ 41080; s/d 30,000/40,000Rp) There are only a handful of basic rooms here, and there's not much in the way of communal get-together space, but it's right in the heart of the action and there's access to the pool at the Angsoka Hotel. It is just off Jl Bina Ria.

Pondok Elsa (d from 50,000Rp; ☒) Despite the fabulously baroque styling on the exterior, the bungalows here are rather ordinary on the inside. The cheaper fan rooms are well worth the money though; air-con rooms come in at 100,000Rp. It is just off Jl Bina Ria.

Other recommendations:

Angsoka Hotel (☎ 41841; www.angsoka.com; d from 40,000Rp; ☒ ☒) Big hotel with good facilities and a few cheap rooms.

Hotel Pulestis (☎ 41035; jokoartawan@hotmail.com; Jl Bina Ria; d from 80,000Rp; ☒ ☒) Worth visiting, if only for the surreal, technicolour décor.

Nirwana Seaside Cottages (☎ 41288; Jl Bina Ria; d from 80,000Rp; ☒ ☒) Similar to the Angsoka.

WEST OF KALIBUKBUK

Back on the main road there is a string of cheapies.

Hotel Parma (☎ 41555; Jl Raya Lovina; s/d 30,000/40,000Rp) It's tired and spotty, but it's on the beach and the price is right.

Homestay Purnama (☎ 41043; Jl Raya Lovina; s/d 30,000/35,000Rp) and the even scruffier **Arjuna Homestay** (Jl Raya Lovina; s/d 20,000/35,000Rp) are desperately drab, but very cheap for the area.

Eating & Drinking

Most hotels serve food – just as well if you are staying outside Kalibukbuk. In addition, there are food carts, *warung*, cafés and quite classy restaurants, but not much that's really outstanding. Aspiring chefs should visit the fish market in Anturan and organise a barbecue.

A lot of restaurants have happy hours from about 6pm to 8pm – although they seem to last all day in some places. The vast majority of eateries are in Kalibukbuk.

Waru Bali (Jl Ketepang; mains 18,000Rp; ☺ lunch & dinner) A toss of a beer cap from the beach, this bustling food shack offers a good selection of seafood, plenty of atmosphere and even wine tastings. It also has a happy hour from 6pm to 8pm.

Sea Breeze Cafe (☎ 41138; Jl Bina Ria; mains 15,000Rp; ☺ lunch & dinner) It's more of the same at the Sea Breeze Cafe, where you can catch satellite sports under the bamboo roof and shake your hips along to some live music on Wednesday and Sunday nights (9pm). The menu covers just about everything from chocolate mousse (11,000Rp) to *nasi goreng* (10,000Rp).

Jasmine Kitchen (☎ 41565; mains 30,000Rp; ☺ breakfast, lunch & dinner) Kalibukbuk's resident Thai restaurant is a pleasant affair, with Thai and Western-style seating over two floors. There's bona fide espresso coffee on the menu and the prawn salad in spicy orange and tamarind comes recommended. It is just off Jl Bina Ria.

Bali Apik (☎ 41050; mains 15,000Rp; ☺ lunch & dinner) Some of Lovina's best pizza can be found in this blueprint backpackers café, where you can get a facial (yes, really) while you sip your cocktail, or kick back with a beer and a gigantic two-person rijst-taffel (65,000Rp). It's next door to Jasmine Kitchen.

Kakatua (☎ 41344; Jl Bina Ria; mains 20,000Rp; ☺ lunch & dinner) Presumably named in honour of the pair of cockatoos that spend their days squawking from a cage by the bar, this is one of the main strip's more upmarket diners, serving a generally middle-aged crowd a mix of middle European and Southeast Asian favourites.

Other recommendations:

Funky Monkey Café (Jl Bina Ria; mains 8000Rp; ☺ breakfast, lunch & dinner) For cheap eats on the beach.

Kantin 21 (Jl Raya Lovina; mains 12,000Rp; ☺ lunch & dinner) For fresh juices, grills and a game of pool.

Clubbing

Volcano Club (☎ 41222; Jl Raya Lovina; ☺ 9pm-4am) Sculpted out of cement, like a volcano set from *The Flintstones*, this is Lovina's wildest nightspot. The live bands begin their strumming and wailing around 9pm, while the dark, laser-lit disco (expect techno and thunderous bass lines) kicks off at 11pm. There is a cover charge of 50,000Rp for the disco.

Planet Lovina (Jl Raya Lovina; ☻ 1pm-late) Looking more than a little hungover, this is the quirkiest club in Kalibukbuk itself, with a disco-on-mushrooms ambience, plenty of neon, seriously loud music and rarely more than a handful of punters.

Getting There & Around

From southern Bali, by public transport, you will need a connection in Singaraja, from where there are also air-con buses to Java (see p233 for details). Regular *bemo* go from Singaraja's Banyuasri terminal to Kalibukbuk (about 3000Rp, 30 minutes) – you can flag them down anywhere on the coast road.

At least once a day, **Perama** (☎ 41161; www .peramatour.com; Jl Raya Lovina) links Lovina with Kuta (50,000Rp, 3¼ hours), Sanur (50,000Rp, three hours) and Ubud (50,000Rp, 2½ hours). It also runs services to Padangbai (80,000Rp, four hours) and Candidasa (80,000Rp, 3½ hours), but these are often cancelled when there are too few passengers.

Lovina is an excellent base from which to explore northern and central Bali, and rental prices for cars and motorcycles are quite reasonable. Bicycles can be hired for about 12,000Rp per day.

AROUND LOVINA

About 5km west of Kalibukbuk, a sign points to **Air Terjun Singsing** (Daybreak Waterfall), where you can have a refreshing swim. The falls are sometimes just a trickle in the dry season.

About 10km from Kalibukbuk, near the village of Banjar, a side road leads to **Brahma Vihara Arama**, Bali's only Buddhist monastery. It's a handsome structure with views down the valley and across to the sea. It's about 4km from the main road – you can get an *ojek* at the turn-off.

Not far from the monastery, the **Air Panas Banjar** (Hot Springs; admission 3000Rp; ☻ 8am-6pm) feed several pools where you can soak in the soothing sulphurous water, surrounded by lush tropical gardens.

GUNUNG BATUR AREA
☎ 0366

Volcanic Gunung Batur is a major tourist magnet, offering treks to the summit and spectacular views of Danau Batur (Lake Batur), in the bottom of a huge caldera. Touts and the knots of tourist coaches can detract from the experience, but the area remains one of Bali's great days out. Entry to the area costs 3000Rp per person, plus 1000Rp for a car.

Around the Crater Rim

From the south, **Penelokan** is the first place you'll come to, on the rim of the caldera. There's a brilliant view if it's clear, but be prepared for wet, cold and cloudy conditions, and aggressive souvenir selling. The opulent **Lakeview Restaurant & Homestay** (☎ 51394; d US$30) has brilliant views and comfortable, but very pricey rooms. Big restaurants do buffet lunches for tour groups – small restaurants and *warung* are better value.

Further northwest, the villages of **Batur** and **Kintamani** virtually run together. Batur's **Pura Ulun Danu** (3000Rp; ☻ dawn-dusk) is an important temple, while Kintamani is famed for its colourful **market**. In the middle of Kintamani, **Hotel Miranda** (☎ 0366-52022; s/d 30,000/50,000Rp) is rather mottled, but offers cheap digs. Continue to **Penulisan**, where Bali's highest temple (at 1745m), **Pura Puncak Penulisan** (3000Rp; ☻ dawn-dusk), has a great view to the north coast.

Around Danau Batur

KEDISAN

Kedisan is a quiet village at the bottom of the road from Penelokan. There are fewer guides touting treks here than in nearby Toya Bungkah.

Sleeping

Hotel Surya (☎ 51139; d from 50,000Rp) One of the more opulent outfits near the lake's edge and has plenty of rooms (the best are 120,000Rp) spread across several storeys, a very friendly manager and a little restaurant serving fine views and rice dishes in a basket (just like in a British pub).

Hotel Astra Dana (☎ 081-2466 4047; s/d 40,000/ 50,000Rp) A little further down the road to Toya Bungkah, this is a little cheaper and quite a lot more run-down. On the upside, it is right on the lake.

TOYA BUNGKAH

At the bottom of the steep road that winds down from Penelokan, go left at the T-junction and follow the rollercoaster road

INDONESIA

through the lava fields to Toya Bungkah, the scruffy little village where many visitors begin their ascent of Gunung Batur. There are several sets of hot springs in Toya Bungkah, the most formal – and expensive – of which is the **Natural Hot Spring Swimming Pool** (☎ 51204; admission US$5; ◷ 7am-8pm) in the middle of the village.

Sleeping & Eating

Most of the hotels listed here have restaurants, all with similar menus and prices.

Under the Volcano II (☎ 52508; d from 50,000Rp) The rooms are a little poky at this basic little guesthouse, but the sun visor–toting owner will make you feel welcome and she cooks a mean fish barbecue. Conveniently, her husband is also a trekking guide. It is hidden away down a little alley near the Volcano Breeze Cafe.

Arlina's (☎ 51165; d 70,000Rp) Right on the main road, this no-nonsense spot has some passable bungalows around three sides of a patchy garden.

Under the Volcano (☎ 51166; d 40,000Rp) The lavastone bungalows here look like they might have been in the path of the last eruption, but there's a cheap little eatery, enough space for three to sleep in the rooms and plentiful smiles from the owner. It is also on the main road through town.

Volcano Breeze Cafe (☎ 51824; mains 15,000Rp; ◷ breakfast, lunch & dinner) Down by the lake, this travellers-style café modestly describes itself as 'the fantastic grill house'. 'Fantastic' is a little ambitious, but the food (don't expect giant portions) is OK and the atmosphere is relaxed.

Kios Murni (mains 8000Rp; ◷ breakfast, lunch & dinner) Back towards Kedisan, this is where the locals eat. Expect basic, but authentic, Indonesian cooking.

Trekking Around Gunung Batur

The most popular trek is from Toya Bungkah to the top of Gunung Batur (1717m) for sunrise – a magnificent sight requiring a 4am start from the village. The **Association of Mount Batur Trekking Guides** (HPPGB; ☎ 0366-52362; volcanotrekk@hotmail.com) has the local monopoly and charges from 200,000Rp for one to four people. It has an office in the centre of the village, just down from Amertha's. It is rarely staffed, but someone will soon appear if you loiter with intent.

Getting There & Around

Regular buses go to Kintamani from Denpasar (Batubulan terminal) via Ubud and Payangan (12,000Rp, 2½ hours) – some continue to Singaraja. *Bemo* regularly shuttle back and forth around the crater rim, between Penelokan and Kintamani (1000Rp). Public *bemo* from Penelokan to the lakeside villages go mostly in the morning (4000Rp to Toya Bungkah, 30 minutes).

Perama shuttles between Kintamani and Denpasar are rather sporadic – check with its **Kuta office** (☎ 751551; www.peramatour.com; Jl Legian 39) for the latest schedules.

You can also charter a car from Toya Bungkah to Kuta (200,000Rp, maximum five people) – ask at your hotel.

DANAU BRATAN AREA
☎ 0368

This area of pretty lakes is in the crater of an old, long-extinct volcano. The main village is **Candikuning**, which has a *bemo* stop, a colourful but touristy market and the photogenic **Pura Ulun Danau Bratan** (☎ 21191; admission 3300Rp; ◷ 8am-6pm) lakeside temple. Boat rental, water-skiing and parasailing are available. The **Kebun Raya Eya Karya Bali** (☎ 21273; admission 3500Rp; ◷ 8am-5pm Mon-Fri, 8am-6pm Sat & Sun) botanical gardens, near Candikuning, are a pleasant spot for an afternoon's loafing and offer some reprieve from the sweaty plains below.

Southwest of Danau Bratan is **Gunung Batukaru**, with the remote **Pura Luhur** (admission 3000Rp; ◷ dawn-dusk) perched on its slopes. The road east to **Pacung** has wonderful panoramas.

Interesting trips by road or on foot can be made to the west around **Danau Buyan** and **Danau Tamblingan**.

Further west, **Munduk** is a pretty village perched high on a ridge. There are only a few places to stay in Munduk. **Penginapan Guru Ratna** (☎ 0362-92812; d from 100,000Rp) is the least expensive, with rooms in a lovely old Dutch villa.

Sleeping & Eating

The best budget accommodation is along the road to the botanical gardens.

Pondok Permata Firdous (☎ 21531; Jl Kebun Raya; d 50,000Rp) This functional spot on the gardens' doorstep offers bright bedspreads, shiny headboards and sparkling bathrooms with Western-style toilets.

Depot Makan Mekar Sari (☎ 21193; Jl Kebun Raya; mains 7000Rp; ☀ lunch & dinner) Also en route to the gardens, this bamboo eatery has a good choice of Indonesian and Chinese fare, plastic flowers on the table and a whole load of Bintang behind the bar.

Food stalls at Candikuning market offer cheap eats (mains 7000Rp), and there are food carts further north at the car park overlooking the lake.

Getting There & Away
Plenty of *bemo*, minibuses and buses travel between Denpasar's Ubung terminal (9000Rp, 1¾ hours) and Singaraja's Sukasada terminal (6000Rp, 45 minutes), and stop anywhere along the main road between Bedugul and Pancasari. Some of the **Perama** (☎ 0361-751551; www.peramatour.com) Ubud (30,000Rp, 1½ hours) to Lovina (20,000Rp, one hour) services also stop here.

Public transport to the areas southwest and west of Danau Bratan is very scant.

SOUTHWEST BALI
From Denpasar's Ubung terminal, buses and *bemo* go west to Gilimanuk, via Tabanan and Negara. From this western road, turn north to **Mengwi**, where there's the impressive **Pura Taman Ayun** (admission 3000Rp; ☀ 8am-5pm) water palace and temple. About 10km further north is the monkey forest and temple of **Sangeh** (admission 3000Rp; ☀ 8am-5pm) – watch out, as the monkeys will snatch anything they can. South of the main road, **Pura Tanah Lot** (admission 3300Rp; ☀ dawn-dusk) is spectacularly balanced on a rocky islet. It's probably the most photographed and visited temple in Bali, and is especially touristy at sunset.

The turn-off to the **Medewi** surfing point is well marked on the main road. **Medewi Beach Cottages** (☎ 0365-40029; d from 120,000Rp; ☒ ☒) is pretty upmarket, but has some decent cheaper rooms (90,000Rp) and a pool. Nearby, the unsignposted **Homestay Gede** (s/d 25,000/40,000Rp) has basic rooms.

The beautiful temple of **Pura Rambut Siwi** (admission 3000Rp; ☀ 8am-5pm) is just south of the main road, high on a cliff top overlooking the sea. It's definitely worth a stop.

WEST BALI
Negara
Bullock races are held in nearby Perancak in July and August each year – check schedules with the **Taman Wisata Perancak** (☎ 0365-42173). Otherwise, Negara is a quiet, untouristy town. The best place to stay is **Hotel Wira Pada** (☎ 0365-41161; Jl Ngurah Rai 107; d from 85,000Rp; ☒), where there are pleasant rooms. Many buses and *bemo* stop here.

Taman Nasional Bali Barat
This substantial national park has prolific bird life, with many of Bali's 300 species represented, including the famous *jalak putih* (Bali starling).

The **park headquarters** (☎ 0365-41021; admission 10,000Rp; ☀ 7am-4pm) is at the junction at Cekik. You can arrange a guide here for trekking in the southern part of the park.

There's a visitors centre at **Labuhan Lalang**, in the northwest, where you can get a guide, arrange short treks and snorkel on the reef close to shore. Labuhan Lalang is also the access point for **Pulau Menjangan**, a very popular diving and snorkelling site. A boat to Menjangan costs 250,000Rp for a four-hour trip, and 30,000Rp for every subsequent hour – a boat will take up to 10 people. Hire snorkelling gear from the *warung* here (per four hours about 40,000Rp). Diving trips to the island can also be arranged.

Gilimanuk
Gilimanuk is the terminus for the ferries to/from Java (5000Rp, 30 minutes), which run every half-hour throughout the day and night. There is a bank (with low exchange rates), post office, a *wartel* and a handful of gloomy hotels.

There are frequent buses between Gilimanuk and Denpasar (Ubung terminal; 12,000Rp, 1½ hours), or along the north coast to Singaraja (8000Rp, two hours).

SUMATRA

Lush, enormous and intriguing, Sumatra stretches for 2000km across the equator. Happily, there is a payoff for every pothole along the Trans-Sumatran Highway: volcanic peaks rise around tranquil crater lakes, orang-utans swing through pristine rainforests, and long white beaches offer world-class surf breaks above the surface, and stunning coral reefs below.

Besides natural beauty, the world's sixth-largest island boasts a wealth of natural

INDONESIA

> **WARNING**
>
> An Aceh peace deal spurred by the common suffering brought by the tsunami appeared to have taken hold in late 2005, but stay informed through media reports and your embassy before heading into what was a conflict zone for the better part of three decades.

resources, particularly oil, gas and timber. These earn Indonesia the bulk of its badly needed export dollars, even as their extraction devastates natural habitats. Little of the cash has trickled back to Sumatra, heightening resentment of the political centre in Java – and fuelling a long-running, on-again-off-again rebellion in Aceh, the country's northernmost province.

The Boxing Day 2004 tsunami here and the string of earthquakes that devastated much of Aceh and Pulau Nias brought more tragedy and earned Sumatra the sad distinction of having suffered the worst natural disasters in modern memory. The silver lining was that nature's tectonic fury has led both sides to reach a peace deal that looked promising at the time of writing.

Nearly four times the size of Java, but with less than a quarter of the population, Sumatra can seem quiet after a trip through Indonesia's heartland. As elsewhere in the country, tourists have been thin on the ground for years, even more so since the tsunami.

For the traveller, this makes Sumatra a treasure trove of sights waiting to be rediscovered. Visitors who return before the crowds do are rewarded with tranquillity, low prices and the gratitude of locals who are glad the world hasn't forgotten them.

HISTORY

Mounds of stone tools and shells unearthed north of Medan show that hunter-gatherers were living along the Strait of Melaka 13,000 years ago. But Sumatra had little contact with the outside world until the emergence of the kingdom of Srivijaya at the end of the 7th century. At its peak in the 11th century, it controlled a great slab of Southeast Asia covering most of Sumatra, the Malay Peninsula, southern Thailand and Cambodia. Srivijayan influence collapsed after it was conquered by the south Indian king

Ravendra Choladewa in 1025, and for the next 200 years the void was partly filled by Srivijaya's main regional rival, the Jambi-based kingdom of Malayu.

After Malayu was defeated by a Javanese expedition in 1278, the focus of power moved north to a cluster of Islamic sultanates on the east coast of the modern province of Aceh. The sultanates had begun life as ports servicing trade through the Strait of Melaka, but many of the traders were Muslims from India, and Islam quickly gained its first foothold in the Indonesian archipelago. These traders also provided the island with its modern name – 'Sumatra' is derived from Samudra, meaning 'ocean' in Sanskrit.

After the Portuguese occupied Melaka (on the Malay Peninsula) in 1511 and began harassing Samudra and its neighbours, Aceh took over as the main power. Based close to modern Banda Aceh, it carried the fight to the Portuguese and carved out a substantial territory, covering much of northern Sumatra as well as large chunks of the Malay Peninsula. Acehnese power peaked with the reign of Sultan Iskandar Muda at the beginning of the 17th century.

The Dutch came next and kicked off their Sumatran campaign with the capture of Palembang in 1825, working their way north before running into trouble against Aceh. The Acehnese turned back the first Dutch attack in 1873, but succumbed to a massive assault two years later. They then took to the jungles for a guerrilla struggle that lasted until 1903. The Dutch were booted out of Aceh in 1942, immediately before the Japanese WWII occupation, and did not attempt to return during their brief effort to reclaim their empire after the war.

Sumatra provided several key figures in Indonesia's independence struggle, including future vice-president Mohammed Hatta and the first prime minister, Sutan Syahrir. It also provided the new nation with its fair share of problems. First up were the staunchly Muslim Acehnese, who rebelled against being lumped together with the Christian Bataks in the newly created province of North Sumatra and declared an independent Islamic republic in 1953. Aceh didn't return to the fold until 1961, when it was given special provincial status.

The Sumatran rebellion of 1958–61 posed a greater threat, when the rebels declared their rival Revolutionary Government of the Republic of Indonesia (PRRI) in Bukittinggi on 15 February 1958. The central government showed no interest in negotiations, however, and by mid-1958 Jakarta had regained control of all the major towns. The guerrilla war continued for another three years.

Since the 1970s, Aceh has re-emerged as a trouble spot, with continued calls for greater autonomy and secession from the Indonesian republic. In 1989 the Free Aceh Movement began a low-level uprising against the government, and the armed forces were sent in to 'monitor' the situation.

In 1998 the Indonesian press revealed years of army atrocities in Aceh, prompting armed forces chief General Wiranto to visit the area to apologise. In July 1999, however, an army massacre took place, killing a religious leader and Free Aceh Movement supporters at Lhokseumawe. Another shooting, this time of 40 people, occurred in a crowd at Krueng Geukueh. Over one million people rallied for independence in Banda Aceh on 8 November 1999.

In 2002 an internationally brokered peace deal was signed by both sides, but sporadic violence continued. In May 2003, 30,000 Indonesian troops returned to the province and attacked rebel strongholds. With rampant corruption, a broken economy and an extremely fragile social structure, peace appeared elusive.

The Boxing Day 2004 quake and tsunami (see the boxed text, p266) brought a ray of hope, even as aftershocks continued to terrorise the local population. Both sides concentrated on providing emergency relief, and thousands of foreign aid workers flooded into the region, acting as unofficial observers. Helsinki-brokered talks led to an agreement in August 2005 under which thousands of Indonesian security forces were being withdrawn from the province and GAM agreed to give up hundreds of weapons by the end of the year. At the time of writing, EU and Southeast Asian observers voiced cautious optimism that the three-decade war may have come to an end.

TRANSPORT
Getting There & Away
The international airports at Medan, Padang and Pekanbaru are visa free (see Visas p344), as are the seaports of Nongsa and Sekupang (Pulau Batam), Belawan (Medan), Dumai, Padang, Sibolga and Tanjung Balai (Pulau Karimun).

AIR
Medan is Sumatra's major international airport and has the widest choice of destinations. Malaysian Airlines flies the 40-minute hop from Medan to Penang (US$109) and to Kuala Lumpur (US$84). SilkAir and China Airlines both fly between Singapore and Medan for about US$189. Garuda also flies to Singapore from Medan (US$208) and from Padang (from $178).

Garuda, Merpati, Jatayu, Adam Air, Mandala and Bouraq link Jakarta and Sumatran destinations including Padang, Medan, Pekanbaru, Batam and Palembang.

BOAT
The express ferries between Penang in Malaysia and Medan's Belawan port are the quickest and easiest way to enter Sumatra by water. The crossing from Melaka (Malaysia) to Dumai is another direct route. The route between Singapore and Pekanbaru via Pulau Batam is a popular alternative.

Domestic Services
Pelni (www.pelni.co.id) has ships from Jakarta to a number of Sumatran ports, such as Padang (166,000Rp, 43 hours). For the latest schedules and prices, check the website.

Other boats link Jakarta with Pulau Batam and Pulau Bintan: the islands are only a short ferry ride away from Singapore.

From Merak to Bakauheni, the easiest options are the through buses between Jakarta and destinations in Sumatra, which include the price of the ferry ticket. Ferries (10,000Rp) operate every 30 minutes, 24 hours a day between Merak in Java and Bakauheni at the southern tip of Sumatra. The trip across the narrow Sunda Strait takes two hours. Less frequent fast ferries make the crossing in 40 minutes (15,000Rp).

International Services
Pulau Batam lies just 45 minutes south of Singapore by fast ferry and is a good stepping stone to Sumatra proper. Boats also run from here to other Riau Archipelago islands and to Jakarta.

Frequent ferries run between Singapore's HarbourFront (the former World Trade

INDONESIA

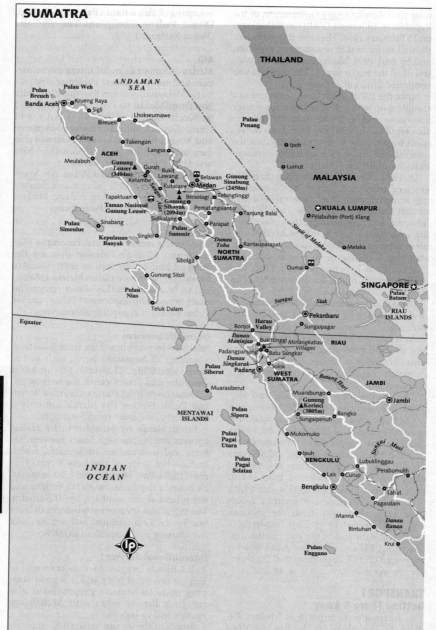

SUMATRA

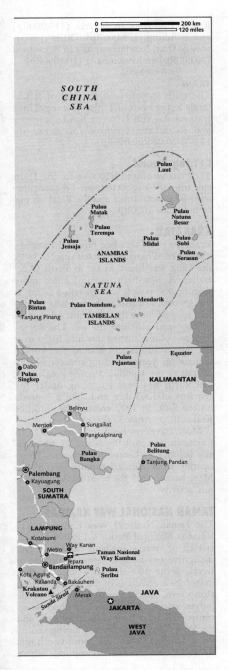

Center) and Pulau Batam's port of Sekupang (S\$16) from 7.30am Singapore time and 7am Indonesian time in both directions. Leave Singapore on the earliest boat to ensure a connection with onward Indonesian ferries that leave from Sekupang for Sumatran destinations such as Pekanbaru.

Getting Around

AIR

An hour on a plane is an attractive alternative to countless hours on a bus. Merpati, Jatayu and the other domestic airlines have a fairly comprehensive network of services between Sumatra's major cities.

BUS

If you stick to the Trans-Sumatran Hwy and other major roads, the big air-con buses can make travel a breeze – which is fortunate since you'll spend a lot of time on the road in Sumatra. The best express air-con buses have reclining seats, toilets and video but run at night to avoid the traffic, so you miss out on the scenery. The non-air-con buses can get very crowded.

Numerous bus companies cover the main routes, and prices vary greatly, depending on the comfort level. Buy tickets direct from the bus company. Agents usually charge 10% more.

Travel on the back roads is a different story. Progress can be grindingly slow and utterly exhausting.

TRAIN

Sumatra has a very limited rail network. The only useful service runs from Bandarlampung in the south to Palembang.

BANDARLAMPUNG

☎ 0721 / pop 743,000

There's not much reason to get off the bus at Bandarlampung, except to use it as a base for visits to Krakatau volcano or Taman Nasional Way Kambas. A town of two parts, Sumatra's fourth-largest city was formed by the union of Tanjungkarang and Telukbetung.

When Krakatau erupted in 1883, almost half of its 36,000 tsunami victims were claimed by the 30m-high wave that funnelled up the Bay of Lampung and devastated Telukbetung. The **Krakatau Monument** is a steel maritime buoy washed up high on a hillside overlooking Telukbetung by the post-Krakatau tidal wave. It's sobering that all below this point was wiped out by the wall of water.

Information

Banks and ATMs are numerous in both Tanjungkarang and Telukbetung.

BCA bank Tanjungkarang (Jl Raden Intan 98) Telukbetung (Jl Yos Sudarso 100)
Central post office (Jl Kotaraja)
FajaNet (Jl Raden Intan 61) Internet access.

Tours

Several travel agents on Jl Monginsidi offer tours to Taman Nasional Way Kambas. They can also arrange tours to Krakatau from $70 a person for a group of four for a bus trip to Kalianda, followed by a boat ride to Krakatau. You may be able to get a cheaper deal from the port (see opposite). The seaworthiness of some boats is questionable – check for life jackets and a two-way radio.

Sleeping

Budget options are seriously limited.

Hotel Purnama (☎ 261448; Jl Raden Intan 77; d from 110,000Rp; ✷) Has good-value rooms.

Passable but perennially dingy hotels:
Hotel Gading (☎ 255512; Jl Kartini 72; d from 66,500Rp; ✷) Slightly better.
Losmen Gunungsari (Jl Kotaraja 21; d 30,000Rp)

Getting There & Away

AIR
Merpati (☎ 260999; Jl Ahmad Yani 19) has daily flights to Jakarta (300,000Rp). **Mahligai Tour and Travel** (☎ 774912; Jl Teuku Umar 11) also sells Adam Air and Sriwijaya flights.

BUS
Rajabasa bus terminal is one of Sumatra's busiest, with a constant flow of departures 24 hours a day, both south to Jakarta and north to all parts of Sumatra. Most people heading north go to Bukittinggi, a long haul that costs from 90,000Rp economy (up to 28 hours) to 270,000Rp for the best air-con services (22 hours). The trip to Jakarta takes eight hours and tickets cost 55,000Rp to 90,000Rp for air-con, which includes the ferry between Bakauheni and Merak.

TAXI
Share taxis can be hired as a pleasant alternative to buses. Reputable **Taxi 4848** (☎ 255388;

Jl Suprapto 26) runs to Jakarta (115,000Rp) and Bandung (175,000Rp). Other companies go from Bandarlampung to Bakauheni (20,000Rp) and Palembang (100,000Rp).

TRAIN
The train station is at the end of Jl Kotaraja in the heart of Tanjungkarang. Three trains a day run between Bandarlampung and Palembang (economy/*bisnis*/*executif* 12,000/30,000/60,000Rp).

Getting Around

Taxis charge a fixed 60,000Rp for the 22km ride from the airport to town. Frequent *opelet* run between town and the Rajabasa bus terminal for 1000Rp.

KRAKATAU

Krakatau is the true bad boy of the world's volcanoes. When it blew itself apart in 1883, the bang was heard as far as Perth (Australia). A 30m-high tsunami killed more than 36,000 people and travelled as far as the Arabian Peninsula. The monster mountain spewed more than 20 cubic kilometres of rock and ash into the air. The 80km-high ash plume turned day into night over the Sunda Straits and altered the world's climate for years, creating sunsets worthy of today's most polluted Asian megacities. The earth has kept rumbling under the remains of Krakatau and, like a B-grade horror flick, in 1927 created the Child of Krakatau, or Anak Krakatau.

Most travellers head to Krakatau from Carita in Java, but the island group actually belongs to Lampung, Sumatra. Tours operate from Bandarlampung (see p243). Make sure to seek the latest advice on seismic activity.

TAMAN NASIONAL WAY KAMBAS

The Taman Nasional Way Kambas (Way Kambas National Park), a 130,000 hectare stretch of steamy lowland rainforest and mangrove coastline, is home to dozens of tigers, some 300 elephants and an estimated 20 individuals of the rare Sumatran rhinoceros. Simple tourist facilities include lodges, wooden pole houses, an observation centre and river boat rides. The park and the Way Kambas elephant training centre, Pusat Latihan Gajah, are about two hours by road east of Bandarlampung, where travel agencies offer a variety of wildlife-spotting trips (these are separate to the Krakatau volcano tours).

KALIANDA

☎ 0727

The small coastal port of Kalianda is the best place to arrange boat trips to Krakatau volcano. Again, check for the seaworthiness of boats and be sure there are life jackets and a two-way radio. Kalianda is 30km north of the Bakauheni ferry terminal. Tours cost about $30 a person, but you may have to charter a whole boat if visitor numbers are low.

Hotel Beringin (s/d 35,000/45,000Rp) has comfortable rooms, Dutch Villa charm and can organise tours to Krakatau.

There are buses that go to Kalianda from Bandarlampung (6000Rp) and Bakauheni (7000Rp).

BAKAUHENI

Bakauheni is the departure point for ferries to Merak, Java. They leave every 30 minutes for the three-hour crossing, a bit less often at night.

Frequent buses depart from outside Bakauheni's terminal building and travel the 90km trip to Bandarlampung (economy/air-con 8000Rp/15,000Rp). If you're planning to stay the night in Bandarlampung, it's worth paying 7000Rp for a seat in one of the share taxis, which will then take you to the hotel of your choice.

PADANG

☎ 0751 / pop 800,000

Sumatra's largest west-coast city has pointed Minangkabau roofs that soar from public buildings, hotels and banks above the sprawling cityscape. While the town centre is the familiar grubby, traffic-choked honk-fest, the city's older south is leafy, tranquil and laid-back. Colourful fishing boats and some old Dutch and Chinese buildings dominate the old harbour on Sungai Batang Arau, with a palm-fringed hillside as a backdrop. The beachside promenade here is just the spot to work off a traditional *masakan Padang* dinner with a sunset stroll.

Orientation

Padang's Teluk Bayur port is 8km east of the centre, the airport is 9km to the north; and Bengkuang bus terminal is inconveniently located in Aie Pacah, about 12km from town – there are a few options for getting into town (see p248). Some boats to the Mentawai islands leave from the old port on the Batang Arau (see p248).

The city centre is easy to negotiate. The busy main street, Jl M Yamin, runs inland from the coast road to the junction with Jl Azizchan. Several hotels and the bus station are on Jl Pemuda, which runs north–south through the western side of town, while the *opelet* terminal and central market are on the northern side of Jl M Yamin.

Information

BOOKSHOPS

Gramedia books (Jl Damar 63)

INTERNET ACCESS

Caroline (☎ 35135; Jl Pondok; per hr 5000Rp) Across the road from SatelitNet.

SatelitNet (☎ 25109; Jl Pondok 79; per hr 5000Rp)

Warposnet Internet café (Jl Azizchan 7) At the post office.

MEDICAL SERVICES

Bunda Medical Centre (☎ 23164; Jl Proklamasi 37; 🕒 24hr)

MONEY

Padang has branches of all the major Indonesian banks – including BCA, BII, BNI and BRI banks – and there are ATMs all over town, including four outside Gramedia Books.

Dipo International Hotel (☎ 34261; Jl Diponegoro 13) There's a 24-hour money-changing service at this seedy hotel.

POST

Main post office (Jl Azizchan 7)

TELEPHONE

Telkom office (Jl Ahmad Dahlan 7) Too far north of the centre to be much use.

Wartel (Jl Imam Bonjol 15H; 🕒 24hr)

TOURIST INFORMATION

Padang City Tourist Office (☎ 34186; Jl Hayam Wuruk 51; 🕒 7.30am-2.30pm Mon-Fri, 7.30am-1pm Sat) Helpful staff have a town map and brochure.

TRAVEL AGENCIES

Ina Tour & Travel (☎ 37925; inatour@pdg.vision.net.id; Jl Diponegoro 13) Attached to Dipo International Hotel, this books tickets for all airlines.

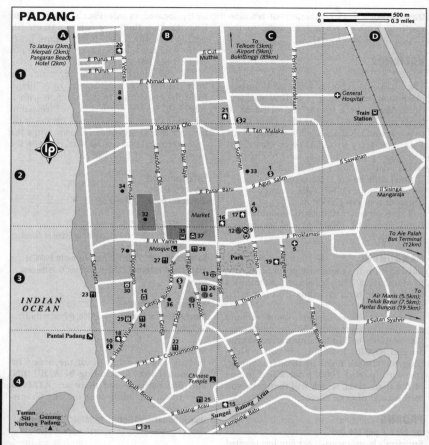

PADANG

Sights & Activities

The **Adityawarman Museum** (☎ 31523; Jl Dipon-egoro; admission 800Rp; ☙ 8am-4pm Tue-Sun) is built in the Minangkabau tradition with two rice barns out the front. West Sumatran-bric-a-brac fans won't be disappointed.

Part of the old Padang–Bukittinggi railway line has been reopened for **tourist trains** (train station ☎ 35954; Jl Stasiun 1). It runs Sunday at 8.20am from Padang up the coast to Pariaman, returning at 1.55pm. Tickets are 6000Rp one-way, 15,000Rp air-con. The train station is east of the city.

Sleeping

Hotel Benyamin (☎ 22324; Jl Azizchan 19; s/d 35,000/45,000Rp; ☒) Down the lane next to Hotel

Femina, this is the best bet in the budget range, with a quiet(ish) location and a nice coat of peach paint on the walls.

Hotel Femina (☎ 34309; Jl Azizchan 15; d from 50,000Rp; ☒) Not the most flash spot in town, the Femina is central, near some good Pa-

SPLURGE!

Batang Arau Hotel (☎ 27400; batangarau@yahoo.com; Jl Batang Arau 33; s/d/tr 350,000/450,000/550,000Rp) Set in an airy colonial building near the Chinese temple, this place has super-stylish rooms, a tempting Mentawai crafts shop and a pleasant little terrace overlooking the old fishing harbour.

INFORMATION		SIGHTS & ACTIVITIES		Simpang Raya.........................**27** B3
ATMs.............................(see 8)		Aditywawarman Museum..........**14** B3		Texano.............................(see 24)
BCA Bank (ATM)......................**1** C2				Texas Fried Chicken..............(see 24)
BII Bank...............................**2** C1		SLEEPING		Warung.............................**28** B3
BNI Bank..............................**3** B3		Batang Arau Hotel..................**15** C4		
BRI Bank..............................**4** C2		Hotel Benyamin....................**16** C2		ENTERTAINMENT
Bunda Medical Centre.............**5** C3		Hotel Femina.......................**17** C2		Matchroom Billiard................**29** B3
Caroline Internet....................**6** B3		Hotel Immanuel....................**18** B4		Taman Budaya Cultural
Dipo International Hotel.........**7** B3		Hotel Sriwijaya.....................**19** C3		Centre...........................**30** B3
Gramedia Books....................**8** B1		New Tiga Tiga.......................**20** B1		
Ina Tour & Travel....................(see 7)		Wisma Mayang Sari...............**21** C1		TRANSPORT
Main Post Office....................**9** C3				Boats to Pulau Siberut.............**31** B4
Moneychanger.......................(see 7)		EATING		Bukittinggi Wisata Express........**32** B2
Padang City Tourist		Apollo................................**22** B4		Garuda.............................**33** C2
Office...........................**10** A4		Beachfront Warung................**23** A3		Mandala............................**34** B2
SatelitNet............................**11** B3		Mirama..............................**24** B3		Opelet Terminal....................**35** B3
Warposnet Interent Café........**12** C3		Modern France Bakery............**25** B4		Silk Air.............................**36** B3
Wartel................................**13** B3		Sari Raso Restaurant..............**26** B3		Taxi Stand.........................**37** B3

dang restaurants and an Internet café, and has good transport information. Air-con rooms cost 80,000Rp.

New Tiga Tiga (☎ 22173; Jl Veteran 33; s/d 49,5000/ 66,000Rp; ❄) This place on a busy main road is faded, with letters missing from the sign, but the bigger air-con rooms (singles/ doubles 66,000/82,500Rp) are reasonable value. Breakfast is included.

Hotel Sriwijaya (☎ 23577; Jl Alanglawas 1; s/d/tr from 25,000/35,000/40,000Rp; ❄) Frills? You must be joking – this is very much a budget option, but the location in a quiet lane near the centre isn't bad.

Hotel Immanuel (☎ 28560; Jl Hayam Wuruk 43; d from 125,000Rp; ❄) Pricier, but worth every extra rupiah for the pleasant southern location near the beach promenade, museum and the old harbour. Rooms are clean, comfy and quiet.

Wisma Mayang Sari (☎ 22647; Jl Sudirman 19; d from 86,250Rp; ❄) Set in a weird-looking modern villa, there are nice rooms with lots of trimmings and a big upstairs terrace. The economy rooms out back are good value.

Eating

The city is famous as the home of *nasi Padang* (Padang food), the spicy Minangkabau cooking that's found throughout Indonesia.

Padang food would have to qualify as the world's fastest fast food. You simply sit down, and almost immediately the waiter will set down at least half a dozen bowls of various curries and a bowl of plain rice. You pay only for what you eat.

Modern France Bakery (☎ 891980; Jl Batang Arau 80; pastries 5000Rp; ❄ breakfast, lunch & dinner) Imitation black forest cake for breakfast? Get a piece and pick a spot by the river.

Apollo (☎ 26355; Jl Cokroaminoto 36A; dishes 20,000Rp; ❄ lunch & dinner) This cheap and cheerful Chinese restaurant has sizzling woks up front and a menu offering everything from chicken and chillies to frogs, sea slugs and abalone.

Mirama (☎ 23237; Jl Gereja 38; dishes 25,000Rp; ❄ lunch & dinner; ❄) Opposite the museum, this stylish air-con joint offers uniformed staff and 'safe' midrange food.

Texas Fried Chicken (☎ 23621; Jl Gereja) Fried-food fans will get their fix next door to Mirama at this place or the attached bakery-café Texano.

Sari Raso (☎ 33498; Jl Karya 3; dishes 8000Rp; ❄ breakfast, lunch & dinner) and **Simpang Raya** (☎ 26430; Jl Bundo Kandung 3; dishes 8000Rp; ❄ breakfast, lunch & dinner) are among the local favourites for Padang food.

Around sunset, head to the beachfront *warung* along the southern end of Jl Samudera for a *nasi goreng*, a banana pancake and a fresh breeze. *Warung* also congregate along Jl Pondok and on Jl M Yamin by the mosque.

Entertainment

Taman Budaya cultural centre (☎ 22752; Jl Diponegoro 31) Stages free dance and theatre performances most Saturday evenings.

Matchroom Billiard (☎ 0751-21919; cnr Jl Diponegoro & Jl Hayam Wuruk; ❄ 11am-2am) For a game of pool and a soft drink, check out the opulent, three-storey Matchroom. The classy blue-felt tables go for 24,000Rp an hour.

Getting There & Away
AIR
Domestic and international prices fluctuate greatly out of Padang, but there are some very competitive rates to Jakarta, which

INDONESIA

make flying a far more attractive option than catching the long-distance bus. These are low-season prices.

SilkAir (☎ 38120; Hotel Bumi Minang, Jl Bundo Kandung 20-28) flies to Singapore on Wednesday and Saturday (one-way US$125). **Jatayu** (☎ 446888; Pangaran Beach Hotel, Jl Juanda 79) flies daily to Pulau Batam (363,000Rp), a short ferry ride from Singapore, as well as to Jakarta (237,000Rp). **Merpati** (☎ 444831; Pangaran Beach Hotel, Jl Juanda 79) flies three times a week to Pulau Batam (300,000Rp).

Garuda (☎ 30737; Jl Sudirman 2) flies to Jakarta (369,000Rp, three times daily); **Mandala** (☎ 38767; Jl Pemuda 29A) also flies to Jakarta (325,000Rp, three times daily) and Medan (300,000Rp, daily).

BOAT

Pelni ships call at Padang's Teluk Bayur port once a month on their way west, and again on the way to Jakarta (17 hours), Surabaya and beyond. The **Pelni office** (☎ 61624) is out at Teluk Bayur, but you can buy tickets from agents around town.

Boats to Pulau Siberut leave from the harbour on Sungai Batang Arau (also known as Sungai Muara), just south of Padang's city centre.

BUS

Every north–south bus comes through here, so there's loads of options, including Bukittinggi (7500Rp, two hours) and various services to Jakarta (air-con/superexecutive 140,000/250,000Rp, 30 hours). Heading north there are regular departures to Parapat (for Danau Toba) (air-con/superexecutive 100,000/180,000Rp, 17 hours) and Medan (air-con/superexecutive 120,000/200,000Rp, 21 hours).

Bukittinggi Wisata Express (☎ 812644; Jl Pemuda 4) offers bus tickets to Medan, Bukittinggi, Dumai and other places.

Getting Around

Airport taxis charge 50,000Rp into town from Tabing airport. The budget alternative is to walk from the airport terminal to the main road and catch any *opelet* heading south (1500Rp). Going to the airport, *bis kota* (city bus) 14A is the best one to get.

Numerous *opelet* and *mikrolet* operate around town out of the Pasar Raya terminal off Jl M Yamin. The standard fare is

3000Rp. *Bendi* (horse-drawn carts) are also common in the city centre.

MENTAWAI ISLANDS
☎ 0751

A longtime surfers' destination, the Mentawais are a remote chain of jungle-covered islands, 85km to 135km west of Padang. The largest island, Siberut, is home to most people, while Sipora, Pagai Utara and Pagai Selatan are sparsely populated and seldom visited.

Buildings on the islands were damaged by the March 2005 quake, though not as much as on other islands, such as Nias.

Trekking is big business on Siberut, which is home to an isolated rainforest people known for their tattooed bodies and filed teeth. Ethnotourism, mostly out of Bukittinggi, has arguably helped restore pride among this community, although much of the cash stays with the outside guides.

Tours

Most travellers take an organised tour, which is far cheaper than chartering your own boat and guide on the island. From Bukittinggi, a 10-day tour costs US$200 to US$300 (see the travel agencies opposite). Shorter trips are poor value given that the travel time will be nearly three days. Trips can also be organised in Padang – check with **Padang City Tourist Office** (☎ 0751-34186; Jl Hayam Wuruk 51; ⏰ 7.30am-2.30pm Mon-Fri, 7.30am-1pm Sat). On the islands, be ready for rain, bland food and malaria.

For surf trips to the Mentawais and other islands, check www.sumatransurfariis.com, www.surfingmentawai.com and www.wavepark.com.

Getting There & Away

Mentawai Express (☎ 751115; Bungus Bay) runs a steel-hull air-con fast boat from Padang's Bungus Bay to Siberut on Thursday at 8am, and to the Mentawai islands' capital Tuapejat on Monday at 10am, with next-day return trips. Tickets (65,000Rp to 75,000Rp) for the five-hour trip sell out early and can be bought at **Rusco Lines** (☎ 21941; Jl Batang Arau 51).

Everyday except Thursday and Sunday, at around 7pm to 9pm, picturesque but flea-infested wooden ships leave from Padang's Batang Arau for the Mentawais, charging from 60,000Rp for the 12 hour-trip.

INDONESIA

The captain may rent you his cabin. **Asimi** (☎ 23321), with its office at the dock, runs to Siberut and Sikabaluan on Monday; to Sikabaluan and Siberut on Wednesday; and to Sioban and Tuapejat on Friday. **Simeulue** (☎ 39312; Jl Arau 7) boats, on the small lane behind Jl Batang Arau, leave for Sioban on Tuesday and Tuapejat on Saturday.

BUKITTINGGI
☎ 0752 / pop 150,000

The cool, quiet hill town of Bukittinggi is the first stop for many travellers heading north from Java, and an easy place to spend a relaxing few days. Perched on the edge of the Sianok canyon at 930m above sea level, it's a charming place with a maze of paths, alleyways and staircases, and views of a trio of volcanoes – Merapi, Singgalang and the distant Sago. Take an afternoon hike up to the old Dutch Fort de Kock in the centre of town to take in some glorious sunset views. That's on a clear day, of course – Bukittinggi has a distinctly European (read: rainy) climate, with the rusty metal roofs to prove it, so take a raincoat, just in case.

Orientation
The town centre is nice and compact, but hilly. The landmark clock tower (Jam Gadang) stands at the southern (top) end of the main street, Jl Ahmad Yani, near the Pasar Atas (market). Walk downhill along Jl Ahmad Yani to get to the main cluster of cheap hotels and restaurants. The footbridge you see overhead connects the old Dutch fort with the hilltop zoo.

Information
INTERNET ACCESS
Access costs about 12,000Rp per hour.
Fifal Internet (☎ 22070; Jl Teuku Umar 10)
Happy Net (Jl Sudirman 5; ☼ 24hr)
Harau Cliff Internet Cafe (☎ 31850; Jl A Yani 134)

MEDICAL SERVICES
Rumah Sakit Sayang Bayi (☎ 627099; Jl Dr A Rivai 15; ☼ 24hr)

MONEY
Banks with ATMs are clustered along Jl A Yani, and travel agents here also change money.
BNI bank (cnr Jl Lenggogeni & Jl M Yamin); branch (Jl A Yani 126)

POST
Main post office (Jl Sudirman 75)

TELEPHONE
International calls can be made from dozens of *wartel*.

TOURIST INFORMATION
Tourist office (Jl Muka Jam Gadang 2; ☼ 8am-3pm Mon-Fri, 8am-noon Sat) Has a few brochures but little else. Opening hours may be shorter than those listed.

TRAVEL AGENCIES
Garuda (☎ 627737; Jl Panorama 2) Has an office in the Hotel Ambun Suri.
PT Maju Indosari (☎ 21671; majutravel@telkom.net; Jl Muka Jam Gadang 17) For planes, buses, motorbikes and cars.
Raun Sumatra (☎ 21133; Jl A Yani 99/110) Organises air travel and jungle and island tours, changes money and cashes travellers cheques.

Sights & Activities
Fort de Kock (Jl Benteng; admission 5000Rp; ☼ 7am-5pm) was built by the Dutch during the Padri Wars in 1835, and this wooded hilltop is a great sunset spot on a clear day. The entry price also gets you into **Puti Bungsu Zoo** (☎ 33306; Jl Minangkabau; ☼ 8am-7pm), across the old footbridge.

Inside the zoo grounds is a museum, the **Rumah Adat Baanjuang** (Jl Minangkabau; ☼ 8am-4pm), which is a fine example of Minangkabau architecture, with two outside rice barns. It has lots of historical and cultural exhibits and a freaky collection of stuffed mutant animals – including what looks like an eight-legged goat.

Japanese Caves & Panorama Park (Jl Panorama; admission 2000Rp; ☼ 8am-8pm) This grid-like set of tunnels was constructed by the Japanese using Indonesian slave labour during WWII and is not for the claustrophobic. The entrance is inside the pretty Panorama Park, which offers views over the 120m-deep Sianok canyon and to Gunung Singgalang.

Tri Daya Eka Dharama Military Museum (Jl Panorama; admission by donation; ☼ 8am-5pm) With an American Harvard B419 plane mounted out the front, this War of Independence museum houses a collection of faded photographs, weapons and memorabilia. It may be open, or it may not.

There is a public **swimming pool** (Jl Kesuma Kodva; admission 1500Rp).

INDONESIA

BUKITTINGGI

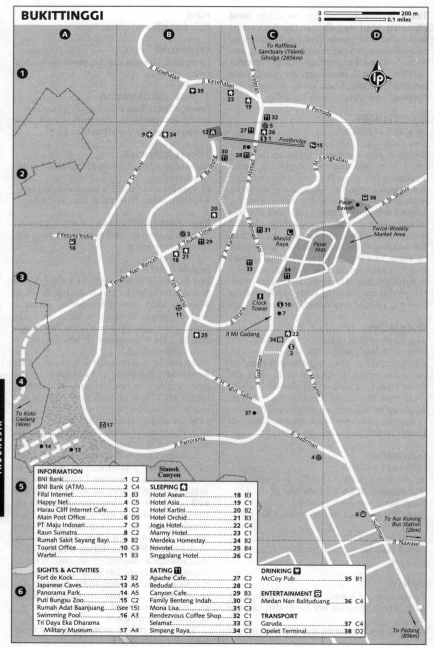

| 0 | 200 m |
| 0 | 0.1 miles |

To Rafflesia
Sanctuary (16km);
Sibolga (285km)

Twice-Weekly
Market Area

To Koto
Gadang
(4km)

Sianok
Canyon

To Aur Kuning
Bus Station
(2km)

To Padang
(89km)

INFORMATION	
BNI Bank..........................1	C2
BNI Bank (ATM)..............2	C4
Fifal Internet...................3	B3
Happy Net......................4	C5
Harau Cliff Internet Cafe..5	C2
Main Post Office.............6	D5
PT Maju Indosari............7	C3
Raun Sumatra.................8	C2
Rumah Sakit Sayang Bayi..9	B2
Tourist Office................10	C3
Wartel.........................11	B3

SIGHTS & ACTIVITIES	
Fort de Kock...............12	B2
Japanese Caves...........13	A5
Panorama Park............14	A5
Puti Bungsu Zoo...........15	C2
Rumah Adat Baanjuang...(see 15)	
Swimming Pool............16	A3
Tri Daya Eka Dharama	
Military Museum........17	A4

SLEEPING	
Hotel Asean.................18	B3
Hotel Asia...................19	C1
Hotel Kartini................20	B2
Hotel Orchid................21	B3
Jogja Hotel..................22	C4
Marmy Hotel................23	C1
Merdeka Homestay........24	B2
Novotel......................25	B4
Singgalang Hotel..........26	C2

EATING	
Apache Cafe................27	C2
Bedudal......................28	C2
Canyon Cafe................29	B3
Family Benteng Indah....30	C2
Mona Lisa...................31	C3
Rendezvous Coffee Shop...32	C1
Selamat.....................33	C3
Simpang Raya..............34	C3

DRINKING	
McCoy Pub.................35	B1

ENTERTAINMENT	
Medan Nan Balituduang...36	C4

TRANSPORT	
Garuda.......................37	C4
Opelet Terminal...........38	D2

INDONESIA

Tours

Almost every hotel, coffee shop and travel agent offers tours to see bullfights, volcanoes or traditional Minangkabau villages. Destinations include the Harau Valley, Danau Singkarak and Danau Maninjau. Six- or 10-day surfing trips to, and village stays on, the Mentawai Islands are popular. For trips to the Mentawai Islands try the Canyon Cafe (right) and the eateries along Jl A Yani to compare what's on offer. Many cafes along Jl A Yani run surfing tours. Check out the Apache Cafe (right) and shop around.

Sleeping

A fair spread of cheapies is clustered at the bottom end of Jl A Yani.

Hotel Kartini (☎ 22885; Jl Teuku Umar 6; d from 60,000Rp) A cute and super-tidy little B&B, decorated with cheesy photo wallpaper and a few bonsai trees. The five rooms have hot showers and Western-style toilets. Breakfast is on the house.

Hotel Orchid (☎ 32684; Jl Teuku Umar 11; d from 45,000Rp) This tiled, three-storey box scoops few points in the style stakes, but it's friendly, clean and secure and has rooms with balconies. The small eatery downstairs is a good spot for info.

Hotel Asean (☎ 21492; Jl Teuku Umar 13B; s/d 30,000/40,000Rp) A few houses up, Asean is equally plain, equally clean and a good spillover if the Orchid should ever be full. It's also a little further from the mosque and its 4am prayer calls.

Merdeka Homestay (☎ 23937; Jl Dr Rivai 20; s/d 30,000/40,000Rp) Set in an old colonial bungalow, this homestay is one of the cheeriest cheapies, with a small café in the garden for communal banter and some pleasant, bright rooms.

Singgalang Hotel (☎ 21576; Jl A Yani 130; d from 50,000Rp) This humble colonial bungalow on the main drag has a three-storey extension filled with large, clean rooms.

Hotel Asia (☎ 625277; Jl Kesehatan 38; d incl breakfast from 90,000Rp) This big, pseudo-opulent place has lots of mirrors and plastic chandeliers. Still, the rooms are spacious, comfy and come with hot water and TV.

Marmy Hotel (☎ 23342; Jl Kesehatan 30; s/d 40,000/50,000Rp) Marmy is a bit musty, but the eight rooms are big, piping-hot water comes as standard and there's a common area and garden for lounging in.

> **SPLURGE!**
>
> **Novotel** (☎ 35000; www.novotel-bukittinggi .com; cnr Jl A Karim & Jl Istana; d from 560,000Rp; 🅿 🛗) This hill-top hotel manages to blend Arabian-Nights–style arches with Minangkabau design elements. The pool area is a quiet retreat, and the airy Anai Bar opens up to great canyon views.

Jogja Hotel (☎ 21142; Jl Yamin 17; s/d/tr with shared mandi 35,000/50,000/80,000Rp) A rock-bottom option. Bukittinggi's oldest hotel dates from 1940 but has preserved only vague echoes of its Art Deco charm under a layer of peach pink.

Eating & Drinking

The travellers' restaurants on Jl Yani feature everything from banana pancakes to the local speciality, *dadiah campur*, a tasty mixture of oats, coconut, fruit, molasses and buffalo yogurt.

Bedudal (☎ 31533; Jl A Yani 95; mains 17,000Rp; ☾ breakfast, lunch & dinner) The friendly guys here make great pizzas, baked potatoes and veggie snacks. A scary wooden warrior stands guard in sunglasses and rapper gear.

Apache Cafe (☎ 0852-6306 5807; Jl A Yani 109; sandwiches 10,000Rp; ☾ breakfast, lunch & dinner) This place serves up more of the same, plus island surf tours and tattoos. There's a Monument Valley wall mural, finished off with a Manchester United clock.

Rendezvous Coffee Shop (☎ 0815-3523 2424; Jl Ahmad Yani; dishes 17,000Rp; ☾ breakfast, lunch & dinner) In this darkish pool, beer and snack spot, a fading Kurt Cobain poster and a battered billiard table set the scene for lagers, loud music and late nights.

McCoy Pub (☎ 32920; cnr Jl Dr Rivai & Jl Kesehatan; drinks 30,000Rp) This pub, attached to the swanky Royal Denai Hotel, has a bored pop band belting out uninspired rock anthems nightly from 10pm to 2am. The Saturday night 40,000Rp cover charge includes a drink.

Canyon Cafe (☎ 23612; Jl Teuku Umar 7A; mains 15,000Rp; ☾ breakfast, lunch & dinner) Owner and jungle guide Mr Wendra will serve up cold beers, good Western and local food and some long travel yarns.

Family Benteng Indah (☎ 21102; Jl Benteng 4; dishes 10,000Rp; ☾ lunch & dinner) Next to the fort, this popular Padang place also offers a panoramic view of town from some out-side tables.

Mona Lisa (☎ 22644; Jl A Yani 58; dishes 10,000Rp; ☯ lunch & dinner) Does pretty good Chinese meals and local fruit platters in hole-in-the-wall surrounds, decorated with Mona Lisa puzzle pictures.

Selamat (☎ 22959; Jl A Yani 19; dishes 6000Rp; ☯ breakfast, lunch & dinner) This clean and busy place serves up a universe of tasty Padang dishes. Ditto **Simpang Raya** (☎ 21910; Jl Minang-kabau 77).

Entertainment

Medan Nan Balituduang (☎ 22438; Jl Perintis Kemer-dekaan 19) These fascinating Minangkabau dance/theatre shows feature graceful danc-ing, colourful costumes, hardcore martial arts and a barefoot broken-porcelain dance that'll make you wince. Nightly shows start at 8.30pm and cost 20,000Rp.

Getting There & Away

The Aur Kuning bus station is about 2km south of the town centre, but easily reached by *opelet* (3000Rp). There are nu-merous local buses to Padang (12,000Rp, two hours) and Danau Maninjau (5000Rp, one hour), as well as frequent services east to Pekanbaru (22,000Rp, six hours) and Dumai (37,000Rp, 10 hours).

All buses travelling the Trans-Sumatran Hwy stop at Bukittinggi. Heading south, you can catch a bus right through to Jakarta from 100,000Rp, up to 250,000Rp for the best air-con services (20 to 36 hours).

The road north to Sibolga and Parapat is twisting and narrow for much of the way. Regular buses take at least 12 hours to Sibolga (60,000Rp). The express air-con buses cut hours off the journey to Parapat by bypass-ing Sibolga. They will get you to Parapat in 14 hours for 110,000Rp. The trip to Medan takes 18 hours and costs from 110,000Rp to 150,000Rp. Ticket prices vary quite a lot between travel agencies, but you can buy tickets from the agencies at the bus station.

If there is demand, **Sikumbang Tur** (☎ 625241; Jl Sultan Syahir 70) may run an evening minivan with hotel pick-up to Padang

If you're arriving in Bukittinggi from the north (Parapat) or east (Pekanbaru), get off the bus near the town centre to save the hassle of an *opelet* ride back from the bus station.

Getting Around

Opelet around Bukittinggi cost 2000Rp. A *bendi* costs from 10,000Rp depending on the distance. Motorcycles are a good way to explore the district and can be hired from travel agencies in Jl Ahmad Yani or coffee shops for around 65,000Rp a day (no insur-ance, no petrol).

AROUND BUKITTINGGI

The silverwork village of **Koto Gadang** is an hour's walk southeast of Bukittinggi through the Sianok canyon. Go through Panorama Park, take the back exit down a series of overgrown steps and the path through the forest is to the left on the first sharp bend.

The bustling small town of **Batu Sangkar**, 41km southeast of Bukittinggi, lies at the heart of traditional Minangkabau country. Five kilometres north, the **Rumah Gadang Pa-yarugung**, at the village of Silinduang Bulan, is a smaller replica of the original palace of the area's rulers.

There is a **rafflesia sanctuary** about 16km north of Bukittinggi, signposted from the village of Palupuh. The rafflesia (the world's biggest flower) normally blooms between August and November, but can flower any time of year. Hotel staff should be able to let you know – and sell you the tour.

DANAU MANINJAU
☎ 0752
Maninjau, 38km west of Bukittinggi, is one of Sumatra's beautiful mountain-crater lakes. On the final descent, the road twists and turns through 44 numbered hairpin bends, offering stunning views over the shimmering blue lake and surrounding hills. Compared with Toba, the lake is quite small (17km long, 8km wide and 480m deep) giv-ing the true feeling of being enveloped in a crater. Maninjau is well set up for travel-lers but remains relatively unspoiled and peaceful, with many visitors preferring it to Bukittinggi as a place to stay.

Orientation & Information

The main village and bus stop is also called Maninjau. It has post and Telkom offices and a BRI bank that changes US dollars.

Cafe Bagoes (☎ 61418; Jl Rasuna Said 6; per hr 20,000Rp) Slow and unreliable Internet access.

Indowisata Travel (☎ 61418) At Cafe Bagoes; sells bus and boat tickets.

Activities

The lake is great for a swim, with warmer and cleaner water than Danau Toba. Some guesthouses hire out dugout canoes or truck inner tubes.

When relaxation becomes too much, many visitors tackle the 70km sealed road that circles the lake. It's about six hours by bicycle or 2½ hours by moped.

There's a strenuous three-hour trek to Sakura Hill and Lawang Top, which have excellent views of the lake. It's easier to do this trek in reverse, catching a Bukittinggi-bound bus as far as Matur and climbing Lawang from there before descending to the lake on foot.

Sleeping

Lakeside bungalows with eateries are strung out north of Maninjau, towards Bayur village, 5km away. Look for the roadside signs and follow the footpaths through the rice paddies.

Arlen (☎ 0815-358 6856; arlen_bungalows@yahoo .com; d 50,000Rp) This beautiful spot is about the furthest out, near Bayur, but well worth the trip. Its eight pleasant bungalows have clean, tiled bathrooms and are set in neatly trimmed gardens. There's a small sandy beach and hammocks from which you can gaze at a little offshore jungle island.

Rizal (☎ 61404; d 25,000Rp) This old favourite, with a stilt restaurant/sun deck among the mangroves, was closed at the time of writing, but owner Rizal was planning to renovate and reopen – so check in town. It's 1km back towards the village.

Lili's (Alex_maninjau@yahoo.com; s/d with shared mandi 20,000/30,000Rp) Still closer to the village, Lili's sports basic cheap bungalows and some very stylish, Tarzan-style 'stilt rooms', set among the trees – no sleepwalkers please.

Palanta Homestay (☎ 61061; s/d 25,000/30,000Rp) On the village outskirts, this concrete hotel offers slightly scruffy and basic sleeps, but the owner will give you a free tube or canoe to play on the lake. There is a *wartel* and café of the same name nearby.

Hotel Tan Dirih (☎ 61263; d from 100,000Rp) This pleasant family-run place is in a different league, with stylish rooms, ironed towels, hot water, TV and a waterside veranda for sunset drinks.

Beach Guest House (☎ 61082; d 30,000Rp) The closest place to town, the Beach Guest House has loads of communal lounging space, rooms with mosquito nets and carpets, and bicycles for rent.

Eating

Cafe Bagoes (☎ 61418; Jl Rasuna Said 6; dishes 12,000Rp; ☻ breakfast, lunch & dinner; 🖳) Right by the bus stop, Bagoes is the heart and soul of Maninjau's somewhat diminished café scene. There's plenty of atmosphere, with dark-wood décor, tourist clutter, Internet access and chessboards aplenty.

Monica Cafe (☎ 61879; Jl Rasuna Said 4; dishes 7000Rp; ☻ breakfast, lunch & dinner) Next door, giving the Bagoes a run for its money, this place sports pop-star posters, a small black-light bar, a comfy roadside terrace and videos on demand. It serves decent meals.

Rama Mini Cafe (Jl Rasuna Said 11; dishes 12,000Rp; ☻ breakfast, lunch & dinner) A little further out, this more traditional-style place offers two-level seating with a view, Indonesian and Western fare and an interesting array of kites on the walls.

Rumah Makan Bundo (☎ 61625; Jl Rasuna Said 10; dishes 7000Rp; ☻ breakfast, lunch & dinner) Padang food fans should head to this local favourite, offering a welcome reprieve for those sick of toasted sandwiches, milkshakes and omelettes.

Maransy Beach (☎ 61264; Jl Raya Maninjau 1; dishes 10,000Rp; ☻ lunch & dinner) This seafood restaurant set on stilts, on the village outskirts, is popular with local families, though the caged animals outside may turn some people off. It also has 14 basic rooms (from 70,000Rp).

Getting There & Around

There are hourly buses between Maninjau and Bukittinggi (5000Rp, one hour) and a daily bus to Padang at 6am (15,000Rp, 3½ hours), which goes via the coast. Hotels and cafés hire out mountain bikes for 25,000Rp a day, and mopeds for 60,000Rp.

Buses travel throughout the day between Maninjau and Bayur.

SIBOLGA

☎ 0631 / pop 200,000

Before the Easter 2005 quake hit Pulau Nias and tourism ground to a halt, Sibolga was the gateway for a small but steady stream of surfers headed to the island. Visitors have long dreaded the small port for its army of predatory touts, though this may be changing. Quake damage was only moderate in Sibolga, compared to Nias.

The **BNI bank** (Jl Katamso) changes money and has an ATM. At **ST Taxi** (☎ 25452; Jl Gendral Ayani 80) friendly, English-speaking Mr Fuady Monte is a great source of information and can arrange charter cars, and transport to Nias. **Hotel Pasar Baru** (☎ 22167; cnr Jl Imam Bonjol & Jl Raja Junjungan; d 50,000-150,000Rp) is clean and has a decent Chinese restaurant.

Merpati has four flights a week to Medan (375,000Rp).

Three ferries leave every evening from Sibolga's Jl Horas port for the overnight trip to Gunung Sitoli (cabin 50,000Rp), and boats run to Teluk Dalam on Tuesday,

Thursday and Saturday (75,000Rp). Twice-monthly Pelni ships sail from Sibolga to Padang and Jakarta.

Trans-Sumatran Hwy express buses bypass Sibolga, but slow public buses run to Bukittinggi (50,000Rp, 12 hours), Padang (60,000Rp, 14 hours) and Medan (50,000Rp, 11 hours).

PULAU NIAS

Known for its surf breaks and traditional villages such as Bawomataluo, Nias was hit twice by major natural disasters within three months (see the boxed text opposite). The seismic events left the main town, Gunung Sitoli, in ruins and thousands homeless across the Bali-sized island. Coral reefs

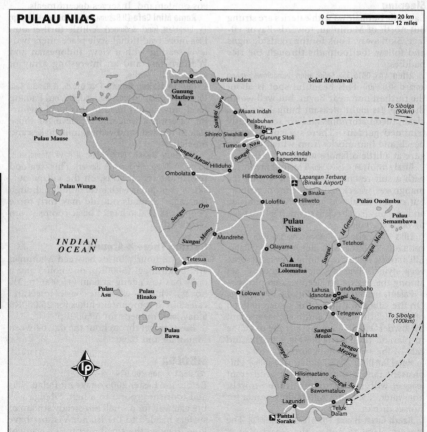

PULAU NIAS

THE PULAU NIAS QUAKE

Pulau Nias felt the fury of nature not once but twice, when the Boxing Day 2004 earthquake and tsunami (p266) were followed by a powerful tremor in Easter 2005. The island weathered the first disaster with relatively few deaths compared to Aceh, because its people remembered the ancient wisdom of running for the hills when the water retreated. Only on the flat south coast did the water wipe out entire villages, such as Sirombu, and the people who lived there.

Three months and many aftershocks later, an 8.7-magnitude quake shook the island, killing more than 830 people. It all but levelled the towns of Gunung Sitoli and Teluk Dalam and utterly demoralised survivors, who were huddling in hillside camps. A 2m-high tsunami wiped out most beach huts on the once famous surf beach of Lagundri and Sorake, where coral reefs were damaged and the surf breaks changed. Around the tiny Hinako islands, the quake actually lifted coral reefs out of the water – so rapidly that marine life was trapped on top. Panicked locals evacuated these islets, fearing they would be swamped by another killer wave.

For updates on aid and rebuilding, check media reports and www.sumatransurfariis.com.

were damaged, and the famous horseshoe bay of Lagundri covered in mud and the debris of beach huts.

The island was a disaster zone at the time of writing, with most brick-and-mortar buildings levelled and people living in hillside camps, facing malaria and other diseases and relying heavily on aid shipments, which at times triggered food riots.

At the time of writing, Gunung Sitoli's hotels were closed, though basic accommodation could be arranged with local families. Electricity was partially restored, and the **BNI bank** (Jl Imam Bonjol) had reopened. Regular phone lines were still down, but cell-phone towers in Gunung Sitoli and Sorake were working.

In Lagundri, 13km from Teluk Dalam, several rooms survived the flood at the Sikomi bungalows and Toho Bar & Restaurant, a longtime surfers' favourite.

There were three daily ferries to Sibolga from Gunung Sitoli, and three vessels per week from Teluk Dalam. **Merpati** (☎ 061-455 1888; Jl Katamso 219, Medan) was flying four times a week from Medan (550,000Rp) to Binaka airport, 20km southeast of Gunung Sitoli.

DANAU TOBA

A gigantic cataract in Sumatra's northern highlands, Danau Toba is a stunning reminder of how truly wild Indonesia's volcanoes can get. Occupying the caldera of a giant volcano that collapsed in on itself after a massive eruption 100,000 years ago, Toba is Southeast Asia's largest lake, covering 1707 sq km and 450m deep. Out of the middle of this huge expanse of blue rises

Singapore-sized Pulau Samosir. Surrounded by steep, mist-shrouded mountains and sandy beaches, this is one of Sumatra's most awesome sights.

PARAPAT
☎ 0625

Parapat has some of the best views in Sumatra – so long as you only face Lake Toba. It is the main departure point for ferries to Pulau Samosir, and the place where you'll first make the acquaintance of Samosir's enthusiastic young guesthouse touts, self-described 'tourist-hunters'.

Orientation & Information

The Trans-Sumatran Hwy (Jl Sisingamangaraja, or simply Jl SM Raja) is lined with shops and restaurants. To get to the passenger ferry dock and main market, follow Jl Pulau Samosir downhill for 1.5km, until it becomes Jl Haranggaol. The car-ferry port to Tomok is 1.5km further southwest around the bay.

Money can be changed at poor rates along Jl Haranggaol.

Sleeping & Eating

Charlie's Guesthouse (☎ 41277; d 30,000Rp; ☺ breakfast, lunch & dinner) Right by the ferry dock and market, Charlie's is a simple and friendly place. English-speaking owner and local recording artist Tongam Sirait likes to jam with guests in his newly renovated World Music Cafe.

Tobali Inn (☎ 41156; Jl Haranggaol 03; s/d/tr 35,000/ 50,000/60,000Rp) Also known as the Toba Nauli Inn, this three-storey budget place up the

INDONESIA

DANAU TOBA

INDONESIA

main drag has 16 mostly airy and light rooms, a souvenir shop and a Bagus Wisata Holidays travel agency desk.

Wisma Gurning (☎ 41165; Jl Nelson Purba 4; d 30,000Rp) A no-frills backpacker option right by the lake, this is close to the harbour and OK for a night. It's on a raised pathway to the left of the ferry dock as you face the lake.

Aek Sere Hotel (☎ 41605; Jl Kebudayaan 17; d from 88,000Rp) For a few dollars more, you can get a clean lakeside bungalow with TV and hot shower here from 110,000Rp. As you face the lake at the dock, turn right and walk five minutes along the pathway.

Mars Family Hotel (☎ 41459; Jl Kebudayaan 1; d from 60,000Rp) From the white-wedding-cake school of architecture, Mars sports a wide range of

quiet and comfy rooms and a smattering of trimmings.

Hong Kong (☎ 41395; Jl Haranggaol 9; mains 20,000Rp; ☺ lunch & dinner) This sparkling Chinese place next to the Tobali Inn is the best bet for a central snack, though restaurants line Jl SM Raja.

Getting There & Away
The bus terminal is on the highway, 2km east of town. Frequent public, non-air-con buses leave in the morning for Medan (20,000Rp, four hours), for Sibolga (40,000Rp, six hours), for Bukittinggi (105,000Rp, 18 hours) and for Padang (130,000Rp, 20 hours). Getting to Berastagi is an adventure in public transport – for details see p261.

ALS runs five daily long-distance buses, misleadingly labelled 'executive' and 'aircon', going to Bukittinggi (120,000Rp) and points east. They bypass Sibolga and travel at night, but the hairpin bends and loud disco music make sleep difficult. Cut out the middle-tout and book ALS tickets directly with **Andilo Nancy** (☎ 41548) at the bus terminal.

At the ferry port, **Bagus Wisata Holidays** (☎ 41747; Jl Pelabuhan 1a) runs tourist minibuses to Medan (55,000Rp) and Sibolga (90,000Rp) and elsewhere on the few days when there are enough passengers.

There were plans to expand Silangit airport, one hour by bus from Parapat, and start regular Merpati flights from Medan. Check locally.

Getting Around
Opelet run a constant loop between the ferry dock and the bus station, via Jl Sisingamangaraja (1000Rp).

PULAU SAMOSIR
☎ 0625 / pop120,000

Perfectly set up for those who want to do nothing, relaxation hotspot Pulau Samosir is a beautiful volcanic island 900m above sea level, cut off from the aches and pains of Sumatran bus travel by a good 8km of deep blue water. The tourism slump has hit hard here, and to describe Tuk Tuk as tranquil would be an understatement. But if you can do without a party scene, then all this means lower prices, and even more relaxation.

If you get bored, scramble over the mountain ridge or hire a moped to check out the west-side Batak villages. Here visitors also find that Samosir isn't really an island but linked to the mainland by a narrow isthmus at the town of Pangururan.

Information
There are no useful banks or ATMs on the island. Exchange rates aren't great, so change money well before you get to Tuk Tuk, and preferably before you get to Parapat.

Bagus Bay (☎ 451287) and **Samosir Cottages** (☎ 41050) guesthouses, both in Tuk Tuk (see Sleeping & Eating, p258), offer international phone services (usually with a 5000Rp fee for collect calls) and slow Internet access at 24,000Rp per hour.

The police post is near the Carolina Hotel, in Tuk Tuk; the post office is in Ambarita. **Gokhon Library** (☎ 451241) Has a book exchange. **Health centre** (☎ 451075) In Tuk Tuk; can cope with grazed knees and little else.

Dangers & Annoyances
Theft has been a problem around Tuk Tuk; try not to leave valuables in your room.

Sights & Activities
TOMOK
Tomok, 5km south of Tuk Tuk, is the main village on the east coast of Samosir and the souvenir-stall capital of the island. Tucked away among the stalls inland and 500m up a path from the road is the **Tomb of King Sidabutar**, one of the last pre-Christian animist kings. It's possible to trek from Tomok to Pangururan on the other side of the island.

AMBARITA
A couple of kilometres north of the Tuk Tuk Peninsula, Ambarita has a group of **stone chairs** (admission 2000Rp; ☻ 8am-6pm) where village matters were discussed and wrongdoers were tried – then apparently led to a further group of stone furnishings where they were beheaded.

SIMANINDO & PANGURURAN
The fine old king's house at Simanindo, 17km north of Tuk Tuk, has been turned into a **museum** (admission 3000Rp; ☻ 10am-4pm). The adjoining replica of a traditional village, surrounded by bamboo-covered ramparts, stages a **Batak dance** (tickets 20,000Rp; ☻ shows 10.30am & 11.45am Mon-Sat, 11.45am only Sun), as long as at least five tourists show up.

From the jetty nearby, you can charter a boat (50,000Rp) to nearby **Pulau Tao**, aka Honeymoon Island, where a small restaurant may or may not be open to serve guests.

Pangururan is the biggest town on the island, but it has nothing of interest, although the nearby villages are peppered with interesting **Batak graves**. Crossing the island back to Tuk Tuk from here, you can visit the hilltop **hot springs**.

TREKKING
There are a couple of interesting treks across the island, though there is little jungle left. Both are well trodden and have overnight options, so you can proceed at your own pace.

INDONESIA

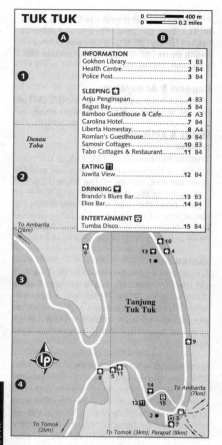

Danau
Toba

To Ambarita
(2km)

Tanjung
Tuk Tuk

To Ambarita
(7km)

To Tomok
(2km)

To Tomok (3km); Parapat (8km)

The shorter trek from Ambarita to
Pangururan starts opposite the bank in
Ambarita. Continue along walking straight
at the escarpment and take the path to the
right of the graveyard. The climb to the
top is hard and steep, taking about 2½
hours. The path then leads to the village
of **Partungkoan (Dolok)**, where you can stay
at Jenny's Guesthouse or John's Losmen for
20,000Rp. From Partungkoan, it takes
about five hours to walk to Pangururan via
Danau Sidihoni.

A longer version of the trek starts from
Tomok. It's 13km from Tomok to Pasanggrahan (Forest House 1), where you can stay
if you wish. From here, you can walk along
the escarpment to Partungkoan.

Sleeping & Eating

Samosir has great-value accommodation,
often in wooden *batak* houses, with hot
showers and attached restaurants (most
are open for breakfast, lunch and dinner).
Competition is fierce, so prices are low. The
ferry will drop you off at or near your guesthouse. East-coast places have sunrise views
and the cleanest water.

TUK TUK

The shoreline is packed with good-value
hotels and *losmen*. The following places are
listed from south to north, in the order the
boat stops.

Liberta Homestay (☎ 451035; s/d 25,000/50,000Rp)
Left of the first ferry stop, this secluded
place has six darkish rooms in stand-alone
Batak cottages, with hot water, balconies
and free nightly frog concerts. Friendly 'Mr
Moon' will greet you with a free drink.

Bagus Bay (☎ 451287; d from 25,000Rp; 🐾 💻)
This place has good-value rooms and a nice
garden, bicycle and moped hire, a book exchange, minigolf, videos, a wartel and Internet access. Traditional Batak dance and
music shows – listen out for the yodelling –
on Wednesday and Saturday at 8.15pm draw
small crowds to its excellent restaurant.

Tabo Cottages (☎ 451318; www.tabo-cottages.com;
d from 40,000Rp; 🐾) Standards are a cut above
the rest here, with a wellness centre, stylish Batak rooms, wholesome veggie fare
and German bakery goodies. Plush air-con
rooms cost as much as 200,000Rp.

Carolina Hotel (☎ 451520; d from 22,000Rp; 🐾)
Posh and popular with moneyed Indonesians, this hotel complex has a great swimming area and bargain bungalows with hot
water on the wooded hillside.

Romlan's Guesthouse (☎ 41557; d with shared/
private mandi 10,000/40,000Rp) This great little
hideaway is set on a rocky east-coast outcrop, with 11 rooms that range from standard to Batak style and from shared *mandi*
to hot shower and balcony.

Anju Penginapan (☎ 451265; d from 25,000Rp) A
labyrinthine hotel complex with a variety of
rooms, great water views and friendly staff.
Facilities here include collect calls, bike hire
and some tip-top pastries.

Samosir Cottages (☎ 41050; d from 25,000Rp;
🐾 💻) The airy bar-restaurant area here,
with billiard and ping-pong tables, is your
best bet to encounter any nightlife. Nice

rooms slope towards the lakeside swimming area, and there is Internet and satellite TV. Air-con rooms cost 50,000Rp.

Bamboo (☎ 451236; d from 10,000Rp) This funky little guesthouse and café has a great view, video nights and serves a chicken curry that has a well-earned reputation. Rooms have mosquito nets and outside hammocks right on the water. Rooms with hot water cost 40,000Rp.

Juwita View (☎ 451217; dishes 12,000Rp) A scramble up the hill from the Carolina Hotel, Juwita's is worth it for the fabulous views and good food, served up on a rocky outcrop. Cooking classes are offered if there is demand.

AMBARITA

Here the party's pretty much over, but if you really want some serious seclusion, there are some quiet guesthouses on the lakeside just north of Ambarita. You may be the first visitor in weeks.

Barbara's (☎ 41230; d from 20,000Rp) and **Thyesza** (☎ 41443; d from 30,000Rp) sit side by side on a nice beach 2km north of the village.

Pizzaria No Name (☎ 0813-7001 3004; ☺ lunch & dinner) A 10-minute walk north, the equally deserted No Name will happily fire up the oven.

PANGURURAN

Hotel Wisata Samosir (☎ 20050; d 25,000Rp) Travellers coming from the west and stuck overnight in Pangururan should check out this hotel.

Drinking

Almost everyone here seems to play guitar and sing, so a good night out can easily creep up on you. Tuk Tuk's once-buzzing nightlife scene, however, has taken a blow. **Samosir Cottages** (see opposite) bar and, across the road, **Brando's Blues Bar** (☎ 451084; beers 16,000Rp; ☺ 9pm-2am) are the only places left for weeknight drinks, music and billiards.

Elios (☎ 451339) On Saturday nights, this unassuming neighbourhood bar has beers, simple cocktails and snacks from 9pm till late (sometimes until sunrise).

Entertainment

Near the Elios bar, Tumba Disco kicks into life until late – even till sunrise if the punters are in.

Getting There & Away
BOAT

Ferries between Parapat and Tuk Tuk (4000Rp, 30 minutes) operate roughly every hour. The last ferry to Samosir leaves at about 7.30pm and the last one back is at about 5.30pm. Tell them where you want to get off on Samosir and you'll be dropped off nearby. When leaving for Parapat, just stand out on your hotel jetty anytime from 7am and wave a ferry down.

There are also car ferries to Tomok from Ajibata, just south of Parapat.

Every Monday and Thursday at 7.30am there's a ferry from Ambarita to Haranggaol (15,000Rp, 2½ hours), from where buses run to Kabanjahe (for Berastagi).

BUS

From Tuk Tuk you can catch a ferry to Parapat, and from there you can travel by bus (see p256 for details on bus travel to/from Danau Toba). There are daily buses from Pangururan to Berastagi (20,000Rp, four hours).

Getting Around

On Tuk Tuk, most people walk or rent a bicycle for about 20,000Rp a day. To get around the island, you can rent a moped with a full tank of petrol for 50,000Rp – preferably from your *losmen* to avoid hassles. There is no insurance, so take care and ask for a helmet. It takes about nine hours to get around the island, so start early.

Regular minibuses run between Tomok and Ambarita (1000Rp), and on to Simanindo (2000Rp) and Pangururan (4000Rp). Services dry up after 3pm. The main road bypasses Tuk Tuk.

BERASTAGI
☎ 0628

If this tiny Karo Highland town were anywhere else, it would see few travellers. The tourism highlight in the one-drag town is a giant sculpture of a cabbage. The slopes of the Karo Highlands, dominated by the volcanic peaks of Gunung Sinabung and Gunung Sibayak, roll away on either side of Berastagi, beckoning to be climbed.

Information

To check email, catch a bus to Kabanjahe, a larger town 14km to the south, with several Internet cafés.

INDONESIA

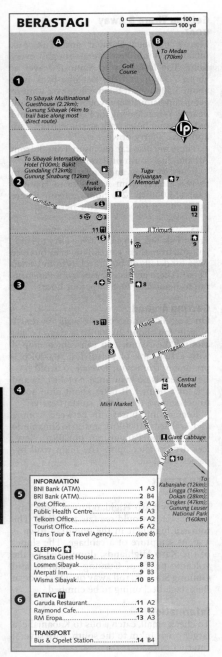

BNI bank (Jl Veteran 22) Has an ATM.
BRI bank (Jl Veteran 84) Has an ATM.
Post office (Jl Gundaling) Also changes money.
Public Health Centre (Jl Veteran)
Telkom office (Jl Gundaling; 24hr) Next door to the post office.
Tourist office (91084; Jl Gundaling; usually 8-10am Mon-Sat) By the central memorial, opens sporadically.
Trans Tour & Travel Agency (91122; Jl Veteran 119) Run by Losmen Sibayak (see opposite). Sells plane and ferry tickets from Medan, as well as local mountain and jungle trips.

Sights & Activities

Nearby volcano, **Gunung Sibayak** (2094m), offers summit views straight out of a tourist brochure, especially during the June–August dry (and trekking) season. Try to avoid weekends, when Medan day-trippers are in force.

You'll need good walking shoes, warm clothes, food and drink. With sudden weather changes, visitors are advised to take a guide. **Erwin** (erwin_sinaga05@yahoo.com) of Wisma Sibayak charges 150,000Rp for a group of three.

The easiest route is to take the track that starts to the northwest of town, 10 minutes' walk past the Sibayak Multinational Guesthouse. The 7km to the top takes about three hours.

Alternatively, you can catch a local bus (2000Rp) to Semangat Gunung at the base of the volcano, from where it's a two-hour climb to the top – the track is narrower and in worse condition than the one from Berastagi.

Another option is to trek through the jungle from the **Panorama Waterfall** on the Medan road, about 5km north of Berastagi. This five-hour walk should not be undertaken without a local guide.

On the way down, it's worth stopping for a soak in the **hot springs** (admission 3000Rp), a short ride from Semangat Gunung on the road back to Berastagi.

Gunung Sinabung (2450m) is a far more demanding climb that takes around 10 hours for the return trip, and is best tackled with a guide.

Berastagi also has plenty of guides offering treks along the well-trodden trails through **Taman Nasional Gunung Leuser**, particularly to Bukit Lawang (three days) or Kutacane (six days).

Map labels (BERASTAGI)

0   100 m
0   100 yd

To Medan (70km)

Golf Course

To Sibayak Multinational Guesthouse (2.2km); Gunung Sibayak (4km to trail base along most direct route)

To Sibayak International Hotel (100m); Bukit Gundaling (12km); Gunung Sinabung (12km)

Fruit Market

Tugu Perjuangan Memorial

Jl Gundaling

Jl Trimurti

Jl Veteran

Jl Veteran

Jl Masjid

Jl Perniagaan

Central Market

Mini Market

Jl Veteran

Giant Cabbage

Jl Udara

To Kabanjahe (12km); Lingga (16km); Dokan (28km); Cingkes (47km); Gunung Leuser National Park (160km)

The villages of **Lingga**, **Dokan** and **Cingkes** offer some fine examples of traditional architecture.

To take a break from it all, relax at the luxury Hotel Internasional Sibayak Berastagi's large **swimming pool** (☎ 91301; www .hotelsibayak.com; Jl Merdeka Berastagi; admission Mon-Fri 8500Rp, Sat & Sun 10,000Rp).

Sleeping

Wisma Sibayak (☎ 91104; Jl Udara 1; d with shared/ private mandi 20,000/50,000Rp) A popular choice, rooms here range from basic with shared *mandi* to hotel-style with private balcony. The friendly staff are right on the ball and there's usually a good crowd with which to spin travellers' yarns.

Losmen Sibayak (☎ 91122; Jl Veteran 119; dm 10,000Rp, d with private mandi 30,000Rp) With its own travel agency and tonnes of maps and information, this place has clean rooms with stone floors and a friendly atmosphere.

Sibayak Multinational Guesthouse (☎ 91031; Jl Pendidikan 93; d from 50,000Rp) An oasis of calm, with spacious rooms, hot showers, great views and a garden for lounging and sun soaking. Catch a Kama *opelet* (1000Rp) from the monument.

Ginsata Guest House (☎ 91441; Jl Veteran; s/d 40,000/50,000Rp) and **Merpati Inn** (☎ 91157; Jl Trimurti 68; s/d 20,000/40,000Rp) have passable rooms in basic surrounds.

Eating

Most of the hotels serve local and Western food, but there are other options:

Raymond Cafe (☎ 0813-6208 1035; Jl Trimurti; mains 10,000Rp; ☼ breakfast, lunch & dinner) Owner Rina serves great vegetarian meals, like Thai pumpkin soup and her very own tofu-heavy special salad, but she doesn't shy away from frying up a mean steak either. Open for breakfast; packed lunches available for trekkers.

RM Eropa (☎ 91365; Jl Veteran 48G; dishes 10,000Rp; ☼ lunch & dinner) Feta and sausage in the window and mouth-watering wok-smells inside. Fries up some excellent Chinese and European fare.

Garuda (☎ 0628-91966; Jl Veteran 8; dishes 10,000Rp; ☼ breakfast, lunch & dinner) This cheery Padang place will serve up a great spread of spicy chicken, fish and vegetable dishes at fair prices. The Indonesian soap operas on TV are free.

Getting There & Away

Frequent buses to Medan (4000Rp, two hours) go from Berastagi's central market. *Opelet* leave here every few minutes for Kabanjahe (1500Rp). Getting to Parapat by public bus (six hours, 15,000Rp) involves changes at Kabanjahe and Pematangsiantar.

Rare tourist buses run to Parapat (50,000Rp, three hours) and Bukit Lawang (45,000Rp, 4½ hours), but you may have to organise enough passengers.

MEDAN

☎ 061 / pop 2.6 million

Tranquillity, peace, clean air: these words aren't commonly associated with Medan, Indonesia's third-largest city. The word *medan* itself can be translated to 'battlefield' – an allusion to the 17th-century struggles here between the Deli and Aceh kingdoms, and an accurate description of modern-day road traffic. As the capital of North Sumatra, this Dutch-era tobacco town is now a polluted, noisy tangle of traffic-choked streets and shopping malls, with few highlights for tourists, but it's a convenient spot to go shopping, book transport or indulge yourself in a dose of fast food.

Orientation

A taxi ride from the airport to the nearby centre should cost 25,000Rp. From the southern bus terminal, the giant Amplas, it's a 6.5km *bemo* ride (5000Rp) into town.

Most hotels are on the north–south thoroughfare Jl Sisingamangaraja (SM Raja), with a cluster of cheapies near the grand mosque.

Parallel to SM Raja, to the west across the railroad tracks, runs Jl Katamso, which changes name further north to Jl Pemuda, then Jl Ahmed Yani and Jl Soekarno-Hatta. This is where you'll find many restaurants, major banks and travel agents.

Information

EMERGENCY

Police (☎ 110)

INTERNET ACCESS

Hokki Bear Internet (☎ 735 6202; Yuki Plaza, SM Raya; per hr 4000Rp; ☼ 10am-9.30pm Mon-Thu, 9.30am-midnight Fri-Sun)

MEDICAL SERVICES

Rumah Sakit Gleneagles (☎ 456 6368; Jl Listrik 6) With English-speaking doctors and a 24-hour ambulance service.

MONEY

ATMs are everywhere, with a string on Jl Pemuda.

BCA (cnr Jl Diponegoro & Jl H Zainal Arifin) Exchanges money.

BII (cnr Jl Diponegoro & Jl H Zainal Arifin) Exchanges money.

Citibank (Jl Imam Bonjol 23; ☒ 8.30am-3pm) Has a 24-hour ATM.

Trophy Tours (Jl Katamso 33D) Exchanges money.

POST

Main post office (Jl Bukit Barisan 1) With fax, photocopy and parcel service.

TELEPHONE

Wartel Maymoon (Jl SM Raya 31/45) One of countless *wartel* in the city.

TOURIST INFORMATION

North Sumatran Tourist Office (☎ 452 8436; Jl Ahmad Yani 107; ☒ 7.30am-4pm Mon-Thu, 7.30am-3pm Fri) Central, with English-speaking staff and city maps.

TRAVEL AGENCIES

Trophy Tours (☎ 415 5666; www.trophytour.com; Jl Katamso 33D)

Sights & Activities

The **Istana Maimoon** (Maimoon Palace; Jl Katamso 66; admission by donation; ☒ 8am-5.30pm) was built by the sultan of Deli in 1888, and the family still occupies one wing. More impressive is the nearby black-domed, Dutch-designed **Mesjid Raya** (Grand Mosque; cnr Jl Mesjid Raya & Jl SM Raja; admission by donation; ☒ 9am-5pm, except prayer times), which has Italian marble and Chinese stained-glass windows.

Sleeping

Most hotels are south on SM Raja, with a cluster of cheap *losmen* around the Mesjid Raya, with all that means for a good night's sleep. On the plus side, they are near the Yuki Plaza on SM Raya, which has ATMs, phone and Internet services – and even a bowling alley and billiard tables.

Hotel Zakia (☎ 732 2413; Jl Sipiso-Piso 10-12; d with shared/private mandi 25,000/32,000Rp) Set on the quiet street directly south of the mosque,

this old travellers' favourite has three floors of rooms with balconies and a courtyard, but the touts can be a pest.

Hotel Deli Raya (☎ 736 7208; Jl SM Raja 53; d from 68,000Rp; ☒) The best of a bad bunch among the SM Raja cheapies, this place has a comfortable lounge area.

Hotel Tamara (☎ 732 2484; d/tr 35,000/40,000Rp) Down the lane near Hotel Deli Raya, this is basic but a little quieter.

Wisma Yuli (☎ 719704; d from 30,000Rp) Nearby, the three-storey Yuli is similar.

Geko'sta Alamanda (☎ 734 3507; Jl SM Raja 59/81B; s/d 35,000/40,000Rp; ☒) The former Gecko's has basic rooms and a small snack restaurant.

Hotel Melati (☎ 736 8021; Jl Amaliun 8; d with shared/private mandi 55,000/95,000Rp; ☒) This mouldy Stalinist-style concrete box hides some clean, good-value rooms. Breakfast included.

Hotel Sri Deli (☎ 736 8387; Jl SM Raja 30; d from 48,000Rp) A touch of Middle-Eastern charm remains. House rules ban unmarried couples and durian.

Ibunda Hotel (☎ 734 5555; Jl SM Raja 31; s/d 100,000/140,000Rp; ☒) Across the road from Sri Deli, this is a more upmarket option with the great Rumah Makan Famili restaurant (see below).

Shahibah Guesthouse (☎ 733 1884; Jl Armada 3; dm/d 50,000/75,000Rp; ☒) South of town, this former cheapie has been renovated into a suburban midranger.

Eating & Drinking

After dark, Jl Ahmad Yani is closed off north of the pink archway at Jl Palang Merah, and the excellent Kesawan Sq night food market springs to life. Also good for Chinese food until after midnight is the **night market** (Jl Semarang) east of the railway line off Jl Pandu.

Rumah Makan Famili (☎ 736 8787; Jl SM Raja 31; dishes from 8000Rp; ☒ breakfast, lunch & dinner) Below the Ibunda Hotel (see above), this cheap, cheery and spotless place enjoys a high turnover that speaks for itself.

Tip Top Restaurant (☎ 453 2042; Jl Ahmad Yani 92; dishes from 15,000Rp; ☒ breakfast, lunch & dinner) This venerable old-world eatery has a streetfront café and ice-cream parlour and an air-conditioned dining room out the back. It serves beef steaks (40,000Rp) and Wiener schnitzel (35,000Rp).

Hash Cafe On On (☎ 451 8516; Jl Mesjid 41; ☒ lunch & dinner) The home of Medan's Hash

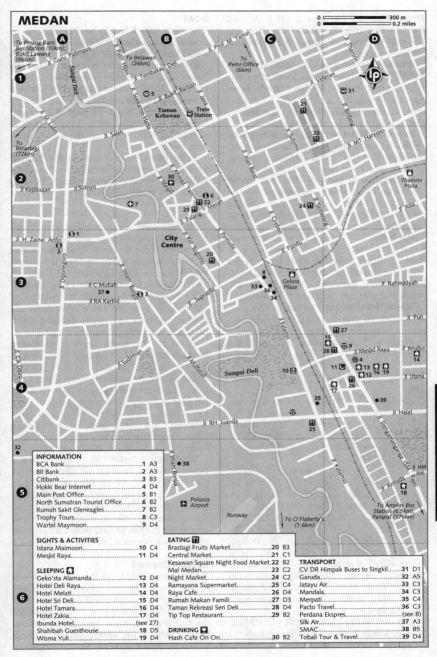

MEDAN

0   300 m
0   0.2 miles

INDONESIA

INFORMATION
BCA Bank	**1** A3
BII Bank	**2** A3
Citibank	**3** B3
Hokki Bear Internet	**4** D4
Main Post Office	**5** B1
North Sumatran Tourist Office	**6** B2
Rumah Sakit Gleneagles	**7** B2
Trophy Tours	**8** C3
Wartel Maymoon	**9** D4

SIGHTS & ACTIVITIES
Istana Maimoon	**10** C4
Mesjid Raya	**11** D4

SLEEPING
Geko'sta Alamanda	**12** D4
Hotel Deli Raya	**13** D4
Hotel Melati	**14** D4
Hotel Sri Deli	**15** D4
Hotel Tamara	**16** D4
Hotel Zakia	**17** D4
Ibunda Hotel	(see 27)
Shahibah Guesthouse	**18** D5
Wisma Yuli	**19** D4

EATING
Brastagi Fruits Market	**20** B3
Central Market	**21** C1
Kesawan Square Night Food Market	**22** B2
Mal Medan	**23** C2
Night Market	**24** C2
Ramayana Supermarket	**25** C4
Raya Cafe	**26** D4
Rumah Makan Famili	**27** D3
Taman Rekreasi Seri Deli	**28** D4
Tip Top Restaurant	**29** B2

DRINKING
Hash Cafe On On	**30** B2

TRANSPORT
CV DR Himpak Buses to Singkil	**31** D1
Garuda	**32** A5
Jatayu Air	**33** C3
Mandala	**34** C3
Merpati	**35** C4
Pacto Travel	**36** C3
Perdana Ekspres	(see 8)
Silk Air	**37** A3
SMAC	**38** B5
Tobali Tour & Travel	**39** D4

House Harriers has moved off Jl Ahmed Yani to this friendly back-street hole-in-the-wall bar, but still draws the occasional athlete-boozer.

O'Flaherty's (Jl Kom Udara Adi Sucipto 8 U-V; ☺ lunch & dinner) This lively Irish pub, south of the airport, is great fun and Medan's hands-down expat favourite. Just make sure to have some spare change left after that last Guinness for the 25,000Rp taxi fare back into town.

Raya Cafe (☎ 734 4485; Jl Sipiso-Piso; dishes 8000Rp; ☺ breakfast, lunch & dinner) In the shadow of Mesjid Raya, this is a simple, covered *warung*, serving good local fare and fruit juices.

Taman Rekreasi Seri Deli (dishes from 5000Rp; ☺ breakfast, lunch & dinner) Opposite the Mesjid Raya, there are up to 20 stalls here dishing up a wide range of seriously cheap Malay specialities.

Mal Medan (Jl MT Haryono) This modern mall has American fast-food joints and a Macan Yaohan supermarket. It feeds into the far more rustic and labyrinthine central market, the Pusat Pasar, which takes up a city block and also has countless food stalls.

Brastagi Fruits Market (Jl Kol Sugiono) This is an upmarket, air-con shop, with a great selection of local and imported tropical fruit.

Ramayana Supermarket (cnr Jl RH Juanda & Jl Katamso) Also has a good range of food.

Getting There & Away

AIR

There are daily international flights to Singapore, Kuala Lumpur and Penang. For details see p241. Airlines with international connections include **Jatayu** (☎ 452 8988; Jl Katamso 62A) and **SilkAir** (☎ 453 7744; Tiara Convention Centre, Jl Cut Mutia).

On domestic routes, **Garuda** (☎ 455 6777; Jl Monginsidi 34A) flies eight times daily to Jakarta (692,000Rp) and daily to Banda Aceh (455,000Rp); **Mandala** (☎ 457 9100; Jl Katamso 37E) connects Medan with Jakarta (510,000Rp) and Padang (375,000Rp); Jatayu flies to Jakarta (500,000Rp), Pekanbaru (320,000Rp), Pulau Batam (400,000Rp) and Banda Aceh (324,600Rp); **Merpati** (☎ 455 1888; Jl Katamso 72) flies to Sibolga (375,000Rp), Pekanbaru (350,000Rp), Pulau Batam (556,000Rp), Pulau Nias (496,000Rp) and Palembang (900,000Rp).

The ominously named **SMAC** (☎ 456 4760, 415 5116; Jl Imam Bonjol 59) flies irregularly to Pulau Simeulue (253,000Rp).

BOAT

The high-speed ferries to Penang can be booked at agencies on Jl Katamso. The **Perdana Ekspres** (☎ 456 6222; Jl Katamso 35C) leaves daily from Penang at 8am and Medan's Belawan port, going the other way, at 11am (tickets RM90). **Pacto Travel** (☎ 451 0081; Jl Katamso 35G) handles tickets for the *Bahagia Ekspres*, which leaves Penang at 9am and Belawan at 10am (RM95). Both companies charge 26,000Rp extra for the bus to Belawan and port tax.

Pelni boats leave Tuesdays for Jakarta. Perdana Ekspres sells tickets. The main **Pelni office** (☎ 662 2526; www.pelni.co.id; Jl Krakatau 17A) is 8km north of the centre.

BUS

There are two main bus stations. Buses to Parapat, Bukittinggi and other southern towns leave from the **Amplas bus station** (Jl SM Raja) 6.5km south of the city centre. Watch your belongings here. ALS charges 40,000Rp for air-con services to Parapat (four hours) and 140,000Rp to Bukittinggi (18 hours). Less reputable companies are cheaper. Almost any *opelet* heading south on Jl SM Raja will get you to Amplas.

Buses to the north leave from **Pinang Baris bus station** (Jl Gatot Subroto), 10km west of the city centre. Get there by taxi (around 25,000Rp) or by *opelet* down Jl Gatot Subroto. There are public buses to both Bukit Lawang (8000Rp, three hours) and Berastagi (6000Rp, 2½ hours) every half-hour between 5.30am and 5pm. Buses to Banda Aceh leave from 8am to 11pm – get tickets from Pinang Baris bus station.

Tobali Tour & Travel (☎ 732 4472; Jl SM Raja 79C) also runs a 'tourist' minibus to Parapat (50,000Rp). **CV DR Himpak** runs two daily minibuses to Singkil (50,000Rp, eight hours), the departure point for boats to the Banyak islands. The buses leave at 9am and 1pm from the **Singkil Raya restaurant** (Jl Bintang 81C), a block northeast of Mal Medan.

Getting Around

Taxi drivers should use the meter but may refuse. Becak drivers (about 1500Rp per kilometre) at the ferry will do almost anything to take you to a particular *losmen* for the commission. Agree on the fare beforehand. *Opelet* cost 2000Rp, maybe double with a backpack.

BUKIT LAWANG

☎ 061 / pop 3,000

A village put on the map by the Bohorok Orang-Utan Viewing Centre, Bukit Lawang suffered a serious blow in November 2003 when a flash flood ripped through it and killed some 280 people. The hamlet is being rebuilt, while villagers wait for the once-booming tourist trade to recover. Despite the scars, Bukit Lawang remains a great place to relax and a base for jungle treks into Taman Nasional Gunung Leuser (Gunung Leuser National Park). The orang-utans are waiting.

Orientation & Information

The bus station is 1km east of town, but minibuses may go to the small square at the end of the road, where a rickety hanging bridge crosses the river to a cluster of hotels. At the square, the **PHPA permit office** (✹ 7am-3pm; tickets 20,000Rp) sells tickets for the orang-utan feeding centre.

Telephone and power lines were still down at the time of writing, though many hotels use mobile phones and have power generators.

The nearby village of Gotong Royong, 2km east of the river, has effectively become the new town centre, with *wartel* and shops but no bank. Near the radio tower, **Valentine Tour and Travel** (☎ 08136-230 2096) changes money, cashes travellers cheques and organises bus, ferry and plane tickets. There is a market at the bus station on Friday, and on Sunday in Bohorok town, 15km away, where you will find the nearest police station and health clinic.

Sights & Activities

BOHOROK ORANG-UTAN VIEWING CENTRE

Twice a day (8.30am and 3pm), visitors can watch rangers here feed bananas and milk to semi-wild orang-utans. The bland fare is meant to encourage the apes to look for other food, often after years of illegal captivity. On a good day, as many as 12 animals show up for a free lunch. From the **PHPA permit office** (tickets 20,000Rp) in town, it's a 30-minute walk up the east bank and a canoe river crossing before a steep path leads to the feeding site.

To learn more about these animals, check out the websites of www.orangutans-sos.org and www.sumatranorangutan.com.

TREKKING

Almost every guesthouse offers jungle treks, from US$10 for a three-hour trek to US$35 for two days, including basic meals, guide fees, camping gear and park permits. River-tubing costs an extra US$5. Most people enjoy their trek, but there have been complaints about ignorant guides damaging the environment and feeding wild orang-utans. Check your guide's licence, talk to the park rangers and ask other travellers. More disturbing are reports of sexual harassment and assault of female travellers. Women, including those in pairs, are advised to join larger groups.

RAFTING

Ecolodge Bukit Lawang Cottages (☎ 0812-607 9983; ecolodge.blc@indo.net.id) organises white-water rafting on the Wampu river for US$40 a day.

Sleeping & Eating

Most *losmen* that survived the flood are on the west bank, across the footbridge. If you don't mind schlepping your backpack uphill for 15 minutes, there are some jungle hideaways with excellent views closer to the feeding centre. Several homestays are also available in Gotong Royong village, about 2km before the road hits the river.

Nora's Homestay (☎ 0813-6207 0656; donipesik@ yahoo.com; d from 15,000Rp) Cheap and friendly, this place has bungalows set above ponds, with a quiet stream running past. It's the perfect place to wash Medan right out of your hair. Ask the bus driver to drop you off 3km before the river.

Jungle Inn (☎ 0813-6243 6238; thejungleinn2000@ yahoo.com; d from 30,000Rp) Across the river from the feeding centre, this quirky place boasts bizarre Tarzan-meets-Hansel-and-Gretel architecture and a decent eatery. Rooms range from very basic to a fairy-tale honeymoon suite (150,000Rp) with its own private waterfall.

Garden Inn (d with shared mandi 25,000Rp) Back downhill, this place also has basic rooms and great views away from the devastation downriver. There are cold beers, tacos and pancakes at the nearby Indra Valley Cafe, which was a guesthouse preflood.

Wisma Sibayak (s/d 30,000/35,000Rp) The first place across the footbridge from the central square, this is a good stop-off for late arrivals, but the dreary rooms let it down.

INDONESIA

Ecolodge Bukit Lawang Cottages (☎ 0812-607 9983; ecolodge.blc@indo.net.id; d from 60,000Rp) Down-river, this resort-like place is set in a well-kept garden at the edge of the forest. It has its own footbridge and a great restaurant. Beds have mosquito nets, and the top-level Orang-Utan Suite comes with open-roofed jungle bathrooms.

Next to Wisma Sibayak, there are basic rooms in the **Yusma Guest House** (d & tr 25,000Rp) and the **Wisma Bukit Lawang Indah** (☎ 0618-828643; d with shared/private mandi 15,000/20,000Rp), which also sports an airy balcony restau-rant. The view across the river is one of village housing being rebuilt by the gov-ernment.

Well-established pizza place **Tony's Restau-rant** (pizza 18,000Rp; ⊙ lunch & dinner) has moved to the bus station. Also at the bus station, you will also find several cheap *masakan Padang*, open for breakfast, lunch and din-ner, with meals for around 5000Rp.

Getting There & Away

Direct buses (6000Rp, three hours) and pub-lic minibuses (8000Rp, two hours) to Med-an's Pinang Baris bus station go at least every half-hour between 5.30am and 5pm. Regular tourist minibuses to Medan and Lake Toba may resume if demand picks up.

BANDA ACEH
☎ 0651

The name Banda Aceh has become synony-mous with the destructive wrath of nature since the 26 December 2004 earthquake and tsunami that killed more than 220,000 people here and along Aceh's west coast. Much of the provincial capital was levelled by the wall of water and the inner city badly damaged by the debris-filled black rivers that crashed through it.

While the devastated north of Banda Aceh will take many years to rebuild, much of the town centre survived the magnitude-9 earthquake and floods. The largely intact grand mosque, the Mesjid Raya Baiturrah-man, still dominates both the skyline and daily life here.

Even before the disaster, the Acehnese were no strangers to suffering. A separatist conflict here has claimed 12,000 lives in 30 years. Clashes between the Indonesian armed forces and the Free Aceh Move-ment (GAM) had kept visitors out since early 2003. The tsunami recovery efforts

---

BOXING DAY TSUNAMI – THE DAY THE SEA ERUPTED

On the morning of Sunday, 26 December 2004, a magnitude-9 underwater earthquake – the world's most powerful in 40 years – triggered a tsunami that hit more than a dozen countries around the Indian Ocean, leaving more than 131,000 people dead or missing, and millions displaced.

Aceh, closest to the epicentre, was by far the worst hit. More than 220,000 people here were killed on 'the day the sea erupted' and a giant wave turned the coastline into a rubble-strewn graveyard.

During the quake, the sea floor bounced up 6m, creating an upsurge of water that, seven hours later, would be felt in Somalia, almost 5000km away.

In West Sumatra, the destruction came within 28 minutes. The initial wave, a half-metre ripple that raced through the ocean at 800km/h, slowed down in shallow coastal waters and rose to a towering 25m. In the most exposed areas, between the west-coast town of Meulaboh and Banda Aceh, towns such as Calang simply disappeared off the face of the earth.

In Banda Aceh, ships came to rest kilometres into the vast death zone, a sea of mud littered with corpses, bricks, trees and twisted vehicles. The seawater levelled palm forests and turned once-lush rice paddies into stagnant puddles of black water. The toxic brew of salt water, sewage and human-made liquids polluted freshwater aquifers.

Like the catastrophe itself, the global aid effort was unprecedented. Australia, Germany, Japan, Spain, the US and other countries sent troops, and global tsunami-aid pledges eventually topped US$5 billion.

World leaders pledged to expand the Pacific network of underwater tsunami sensors to the Indian Ocean. In Aceh villagers started rebuilding their homes amid the rubble. But for the survivors, picking up the pieces is sure to take a lifetime. Many have lost three generations of loved ones – their parents, their spouses and their children.

provided a fresh impetus for peace talks, and the large presence of foreign aid workers helped deter violence. A peace deal appeared to have taken hold in late 2005, but the situation is unpredictable, so check travel advisories and media reports before heading to Aceh.

Orientation & Information
Airport taxis charge 40,000Rp for the 16km ride into town.

Bank Mandiri (Jl Daud Beureueh 15; ⏰ 7.30am-3pm Mon-Sat) Changes money and cashes travellers cheques.

BCA bank (Jl Panglima Polem 38-40) Has an ATM.

Jambo Internet (☎ 31270; cnr Jl Panglima Polem & Jl Nyak Arief; ⏰ 9am-11pm) Internet access.

Post office (Jl Kuta Alam 33) Around the corner from the tourist office, has Internet facilities.

Telkom wartel (Jl Nyak Arief 92) International calls can be made here

Tourist office (☎ 23692; www.acehtourism.com; Jl Chik Kuta Karang 3; ⏰ 8am-2pm Mon-Sat, until noon Fri) This helpful office has maps and brochures.

Sights & Activities
With its brilliant white walls and liquorice-black domes, the **Mesjid Raya Baiturrahman** (Jl Mohammed Jam; admission by donation; ⏰ 7-11am & 1.30-4pm) survived the tsunami intact. The first section of the mosque was built by the Dutch in 1879 as a conciliatory gesture towards the Acehnese after the original mosque had been burnt down.

The **Museum Negeri Banda Aceh** (Jl Alauddin Mahmudsyah 12; admission 800Rp; ⏰ 8.30am-4pm Tue-Thu, 8.30am-noon Fri & Sat) is the site of the Rumah Aceh, a traditional stilt home built without nails.

Sleeping
Many cheap *losmen* were destroyed in the floods and several bigger hotels, including the Kuala Tripa, collapsed in the earthquake. Hotel Wisata remained closed at the time of writing. The following hotels are central, with about 80 rooms each:

Hotel Medan (☎ 21501; Jl A Yani 17; d from 100,000Rp; ⚄) This place has decent rooms and is close to restaurants and the grand mosque.

Hotel Prapat (☎ 22159; Jl A Yani 19; d from 100,000Rp; ⚄) Next door to the Medan, this is a touch rougher.

Hotel Sultan (☎ 21834; Jl A Yani 19-21; s/d 254,000/350,000Rp; ⚄) More upmarket, with its own café and restaurant, this place is a favourite with aid agencies.

Eating
Banda Seafood Restaurant (☎ 740 6085; Jl Panglima Polem 125; ⏰ lunch & dinner) This central restaurant has tasty beef, chicken and vegetable dishes.

Warung Ibu Pocut (☎ 21937; Jl Nyak Adam Kamil IV 41-VII; ⏰ lunch & dinner) Set in an open-sided stilt house, this *warung* offers great local fare with a fresh breeze.

Niagara Cafe (Jl Hasandek 8-9; ⏰ breakfast, lunch & dinner) Has every fruit juice imaginable and a mouth-watering satay stand outside.

There's also a lively night food market, known as the **Rek** (cnr Jl Ahmad Yani & Jl Khairil Anwar).

Getting There & Away
Three airlines fly daily to Medan. Jataju and Adam Air (300,000Rp) each have a morning flight. **Garuda** (☎ 32523; Jl Tengku HM Daud Beureuh 9) has three daily flights to Medan (454,000Rp), connecting to Jakarta (1,400,000Rp). To book flights try **BP Travel** (Jl Panglima Polem 75), where the staff speak English.

From **Terminal Bus Seutui** (Jl Teuku Umar), Kurnia runs 11 daily air-con buses to Medan that leave between 8am and 8pm and take about nine hours. Its downtown office was closed after the flood, so buy tickets at the terminal.

The 240km west-coast road to Meulaboh has been reopened for all-terrain vehicles, though was not yet paved at the time of writing.

Getting Around
Taxis charge 80,000Rp to Krueng Raya (for Pulau Weh). An o*pelet* (aka *labi-labi*) charges only 5000Rp to Krueng Raya from the main **opelet terminal** (Jl Diponegoro) near the flood-damaged Pasar Aceh. Motorised becak require the usual hard bargaining.

PULAU WEH
☎ 0652 / pop 125,000
Weh means 'away from' in Acehnese, and that's what this island is all about. Before WWII it was a more important port than Singapore, but you wouldn't notice today. A laid-back and postcard-pretty coconut island, it has long drawn divers and backpackers. In the 2004 tsunami, the mountainous island was spared the devastation of the mainland. Pulau Weh absorbed many

mainland refugees and became something of an R&R spot for relief workers.

Often just called Sabang, the island has always been a divers' favourite for its spectacular underwater gardens, which survived the tsunami. It was also a popular chill-out stop on the Southeast Asia backpacker circuit before the Aceh civil war reduced, then stopped tourism. Now guesthouse owners and dive masters hope that peace will come, and that the visitors will return.

Orientation & Information

Bypassed by many beach-bound sun seekers, the main town of Sabang is actually a laid-back little port with a lively main street, Jl Perdagangan.

BRI bank (Jl Perdagangan 123) Changes money.

Lumbalumba Dive Centre (☎ 0811-682787; www .lumbalumba.com; Jl Perdagangan 50) Doubles as a tourist office.

Online.Com (☎ 22598; Jl Perdagangan 1) Internet access.

Post office (Jl Perdagangan 66)

Rumah Sakit Umum (☎ 21310; Jl Teuku Umar) Offers medical facilities near Pantai Kasih, about a 30-minute walk from town.

Telkom office (Jl Perdagangan 68; ◷ 24hr) Next door to the post office.

Sights & Activities

Backpacker favourite **Iboih Beach** shelters pretty bungalows set on forested slopes above turquoise waters. The tsunami battered some beachside places here but left the higher huts intact. Just offshore (return by charter boat 15,000Rp) lies the little paradise island of **Pulau Rubiah**, a great snorkelling spot famed for its coral **Sea Garden**.

Around the headland, **Gapang Beach** is good for swimming and has frequent turtle sightings. There are also a few decent beaches around Sabang: **Pantai Kasih** (Love Beach), about a 30-minute walk from town, is a palm-fringed crescent of white sand.

For diving, the Dutch-run **Lumbalumba Dive Centre** (☎ 0811-682787; www.lumbalumba.com; Jl Perdagangan 50), with Gapang and Sabang offices, charges €40 for a day trip with two dives and equipment hire. A beginners' Open Water course is €225. Also recommended, **Rubiah Tirta Divers** (☎ 331119, 0811-685683; www.rubiahdivers.com) charges US$99 for a day trip.

Sleeping & Eating

Dynasty (Jl Perdagangan 54; meals from 10,000Rp; ◷ lunch & dinner) A good eating option is this choice seafood place with a fruit-juice shop to its left.

Murah Raya (☎ 21231; Jl Perdagangan 52; meals from 8000Rp; ◷ lunch & dinner) Has a tasty mix of Acehnese and Indonesian fare.

Harry's Cafe (◷ breakfast, lunch & dinner) For a pancake breakfast or a snack, try Harry's, underneath Losmen Irma.

If you're staying overnight in Sabang, try these reasonable cheapies on Jl Teuku Umar:

Losmen Irma (☎ 21148; Jl Teuku Umar 3; d/tr 30,000/45,000Rp) Has a café (open for breakfast, lunch and dinner) and is good for information.

Pulau Jaya (☎ 21344; Jl Teuku Umar 21-25; s/d 25,000/45,000Rp) Basic but friendly.

Sabang Jaya (☎ 22168; Jl Teuku Umar; s/d 20,000/40,000Rp) Next door, has better rooms but a cooler welcome.

IBOIH

In Iboih, a walking path leads to groups of palm-thatch bungalows, set on the shore and overlooking the water. Rooms start at 30,000Rp. Eric's is a popular spot, as are O'ong and Yulia's bungalows. Communal meals – *ikan bakar* – are served by most *losmen* for 15,000Rp. Arina restaurant here makes lasagne and a mean prawn curry.

GAPANG

One beach along, at the slightly more up-market Gapang, you will find the very comfortable **Gapang Resort** (d 50,000Rp) and **Laguna Resort** (d 85,000Rp), which has a great seaside restaurant (open for breakfast, lunch and dinner). At the end of the beach, the more basic Suykur and the oldish Ramadillo bungalows offer some peaceful seclusion at 30,000Rp per double.

Getting There & Away

A fast ferry to Pulau Weh (25,000Rp, 45 minutes) leaves daily at 1pm from Malahayati port at Krueng Raya, 33km east of Banda Aceh. To get to the port, catch a *bemo* near Pasar Aceh (10,000Rp, 45 minutes). The boat returns from the island's Balohan port, a 20-minute ride from Sabang, to Krueng Raya at 8.30am. A slower car ferry (9000Rp) leaves the mainland at 2pm and takes at least two hours. It leaves Pulau Weh at 8am.

Getting Around

From Balohan port, *bemo* go to Sabang (10,000Rp, 20 minutes). With so few tourists around, you may have to charter a taxi to Iboih and Gapang (200,000Rp, one hour). In the reverse direction, ask the guesthouse owner to arrange 6am or 7am transport to the port, via Sabang.

Mopeds, rented out by many beach bungalows, are a good way to explore the island, but watch those potholed, monkey-infested mountain roads (per day with petrol 50,000Rp to 80,000Rp).

PEKANBARU

☎ 0761 / pop 640,000

Before American engineers struck oil in the area shortly before WWII, Pekanbaru was little more than a sleepy river port on Sungai Siak. Today, it is Indonesia's oil capital and a convenient overnight stop between Singapore and Bukittinggi. Around February and July, acrid smoke from Sumatra's enormous forest fires blankets the town in a thick haze (see boxed text, below).

Orientation & Information

Airport taxis charge 25,000Rp for the 12km trip into town. Most banks and hotels are on Jl Sudirman. The bus station is across town on Jl Nangka.

3Net (Jl Teuku Umar 11; per hr 6000Rp) Internet access.

BCA bank (Jl Sudirman 448) Best place to change money.

Riau Provincial Tourist Office (☎ 858441; Jl Gadah Mada 200; ☯ 8am-4pm Mon-Sat, closed noon-2pm Fri) In a large, white government building.

Santa Maria Hospital (☎ 22213; Jl Ahmed Yani)

FIRE HAZE

In the dry months, Sumatran skies often darken and vendors sell surgical face masks by the roadside. Flights are cancelled, asthma rates go up and the sun becomes a faint orange disc in a soupy, grey sky. Welcome to forest-fire season, a human-made disaster for the health of the people and the planet. Soot clouds rise, mainly from Sumatra and Kalimantan, spewing carbon into the atmosphere and covering much of Southeast Asia in a haze. Some smoke comes from rice field fires, but the major culprits are large logging and plantation companies that illegally clear rainforests.

Sleeping & Eating

Poppie's Homestay (☎ 45762; Jl Cempedak III 11A; d 40,000Rp) A family-run travellers favourite near the bus terminal, with cheery staff and zero-fuss accommodation. Owner Eddie will organise bus trips and local jungle treks.

Hotel Linda (☎ 36915; Jl Tambusai 145; d from 65,000Rp; ✖) Down a small alleyway opposite the bus terminal, this hotel is a little more polished, but still nothing special.

Hotel Anom (☎ 36083; Jl Gatot Subroto 1-3; s/d 75,000/120,000Rp; ✖) Located right in the centre and closer to the ferry, with rooms set around a courtyard.

New Holland Bakery (Jl Sudirman 153; snacks 15,000Rp; ☯ breakfast, lunch & dinner) Serves cakes, pastries, hamburgers and ice cream.

There are other innumerable cheap food places along Jl Sudirman, with evening stalls at the junction with Jl Imam Bonjol.

Getting There & Away

Simpang Tiga Airport is a visa-free entry point.

Batavia (☎ 856031; Jl Sudirman 312) flies to Jakarta for 300,000Rp. **Garuda** (☎ 29115; Hotel Pangeran, Jl Sudirman 371) has the cheapest flights to Singapore at US$75. Merpati, next to Garuda, and **Jatayu** (☎ 855777; Hotel Merdeka, Jl Sudarso 12) both fly to Medan for around 400,000Rp.

By road, frequent buses go to Bukittinggi (from 18,000Rp, five hours) from the Jl Nangka bus station.

For boat trips, the booths at the north end of Jl Sudirman sell speedboat tickets to Pulau Batam. They leave at 8am, take eight hours and cost 125,000Rp. Operator Indomal makes the seven-hour trip to Melaka for 200,000Rp, leaving at 9am.

DUMAI

☎ 0765 / pop 150,000

Most of Pekanbaru's oil exits through Dumai, a dusty industrial port at the end of a 200km-road that follows the pipeline through a landscape of trashed jungle. The only reason to visit Dumai is to use its visa-free port for ferry trips to Melaka, Malaysia. There are two ATMs near the river end of Jl Sudirman.

If you get stuck here, stay at the reasonable *losmen* **Penginapan AA** (☎ 31183; Jl Sudirman 98; d from 40,000Rp; ✖).

INDONESIA

A minibus seat to Pekanbaru is 45,000Rp with operator **Mr W 2002** (☎ 885153; Jl Sudirman 134). It charges 65,000Rp to Bukittinggi and 75,000Rp to Padang.

Ferry company Dumai Express leaves for Melaka at 10am and 1pm (140,000Rp, two hours). Batam Jet leaves at 10.30am (150,000Rp). Get to the port early to clear immigration. Port tax is 3500Rp. Both companies leave for Pulau Batam at 7am for 120,000Rp. Two Pelni ships sail from Dumai to Pulau Bintan, then on to Jakarta.

PULAU BATAM
☎ 0778 / pop 600,000

An ugly cluster of industrial parks and golf courses, Batam hangs like a leech off the underbelly of Singapore, just a short ferry ride from the city-state. Forests have been razed and hillsides levelled to make way for endless, atrocious housing estates, some of them pink. The urban centre, Nagoya, has a sleazy border-town feel to it and is full of karaoke bars and massage joints. Most travellers stay on Pulau Batam about as long as it takes to change ferries.

Orientation & Information

Travellers usually arrive at the Sekupang port by early-morning boat from Singapore, then rush to the domestic terminal next door for Sumatran connections. Most ferries to Pulau Bintan leave from Telaga Panggur in southeast Batam, a 30-minute, whopping 65,000Rp taxi ride away.

Nagoya, in the north, is the island's largest town, a cluster of hotels, shopping centres, fast-food joints and shady discos. The skin-tone Hotel Planet Holiday overlooks the centre, and Jl Imam Bonjol is the main drag, where you will find ATMs and Internet cafés. Addresses are listed by block, not street name. Singapore dollars are accepted everywhere.

The **Batam Tourist Promotion Board** (☎ 322871; ☽ 8am-4pm Mon-Sat, until 1pm Fri) has a small office outside the international terminal at Sekupang.

Sleeping & Eating

Most budget hotels on Pulau Batam double as brothels.

Istana Batam (☎ 455259; Komplek Nagoya Business Centre, Blok VI, 7-8; d 85,000Rp; ❇) If you're stuck here, try the relatively tidy Istana Batam.

Hotel City View (☎ 429022; Block V, 35; d 98,000Rp; ❇) A block to the north, and more up-market.

For a choice of dozens of tempting outdoor food stalls, head south to the Nagoya Food Centre (open for lunch and dinner) across the canal.

Getting There & Away

AIR

Five airlines fly daily to Jakarta. **Lion Air** (☎ 432801; Planet Holiday Hotel; Jl Raja Ali Haji) has the best deals to Jakarta (from 250,000Rp) and Pekanbaru (140,000Rp). **Merpati** (☎ 424000; Hotel Nagoya Plaza, Jl Imam Bonjol) flies to Melaka (US$75) and Indonesian destinations including Pekanbaru (387,000Rp), Padang (470,000Rp), Palembang (509,000Rp) and Pontianak (675,000Rp). **Garuda** (☎ 458620; Jl Imam Bonjol) is in Hotel Goodway and **Bouraq** (☎ 421830; Jl Imam Bonjol, Blok A/3) across from Hotel Harmoni.

BOAT

The main reason travellers come to Pulau Batam from Singapore is for its connections to Pekanbaru on the Sumatran mainland. Boats leave from the domestic wharf next to the international terminal. For Pekanbaru (150,000Rp, eight hours), two boats per day leave Sekupang around 7.30am, so you'll need to catch the very first ferry from Singapore to make it. It's a good idea to change money in Singapore to save time here.

There is also a 7.30am ferry from Sekupang to Dumai (56,000Rp, eight hours).

It is also possible to take a ferry to Tanjung Buton and then a rough four-hour bus ride to Pekanbaru, all for 110,000Rp, but it's hardly worth it because the road is awful.

BORDER CROSSING: INTO SINGAPORE

Flying from Indonesian cities to Pulau Batam is far cheaper than catching a plane directly to Singapore, which is only a short ferry ride away. From Batam's airport, take a 50,000Rp taxi to the Sekupang ferry terminal. From here, 45-minute fast ferries (S$16) leave every half-hour between 7am and 7pm for Singapore's HarbourFront terminal, where visas are issued, on arrival, for many nationalities.

If stuck in Nagoya, **Dumai Express** (☎ 427758; Komplek Lucky Plaza) sells ferry tickets.

To get to Pulau Bintan, take a taxi (50,000Rp) to the Telaga Punggur ferry dock, 30km southeast of Nagoya. Frequent boats leave for Tanjung Pinang (20,000Rp, 45 minutes) from 8.15am to 5.15pm.

Malaysia

From Sekupang there are boats to Kuala Tungkal (80,000Rp), on the Jambi coast in Malaysia. Pelni ships pass through Pulau Batam every four days, on their way to Belawan or Jakarta. Several boats leave daily from Batu Ampar for Johor Bahru (120,000Rp).

Singapore

Ferries shuttle constantly between Singapore's HarbourFront and Sekupang (S$16, 45 minutes). The first ferries leave Sekupang at 7am and Singapore at 7.30am, while the last ferries leave Sekupang at 7.45pm and Singapore at 8.45pm.

Getting Around

A local taxi drop is about 10,000Rp, and an *ojek* ride 5000Rp. Between Nagoya and Sekupang, try to share a taxi. A taxi from Sekupang to Nagoya costs 40,000Rp.

PULAU BINTAN

Pulau Bintan is a quiet retreat after the bulldozer madness of Batam. The old town of Tanjung Pinang (a visa-free entry/exit point) has a charming harbour, and nearby Pulau Penyengat boasts some interesting Muslim ruins. On the east coast lie a string of quiet beaches with several small islands sprinkled offshore.

Tanjung Pinang

☎ 0771 / pop 137,000

Tanjung Pinang, with its busy little harbour and many stilt homes, may be the largest town and administrative centre of the Riau Archipelago, but it retains much of its old-time charm.

INFORMATION

There are several ATMs on Jl Merdeka, and a *wartel* next door to the post office.
BCA bank (Jl Temiang) Change money here.
Bong's Homestay (Lorong Bintan II 20) A good source of information.

Hospital (☎ 313000; Jl Sudirman; ☼ 24hr) South of the town centre.
Post office (Jl Merdeka)
Tanjung Pinang Information Centre (☎ 21284; Jl Merdeka 5; ☼ 7.30am-5pm) Has helpful English-speaking staff, and maps.
WR Internet (Bintan Indah Mall, Jl Pos)

SIGHTS & ACTIVITIES

The old stilted part of town around **Jl Plantar II** is worth a wander – turn left at the colourful **fruit market** at the northern end of Jl Merdeka.

Senggarang is a fascinating village just across the harbour from Tanjung Pinang. The old **Chinese temple** here is held together by the roots of a huge banyan tree. Some 300m beyond lies the **Vihara Darma Sasana** temple complex with large religious sculptures. Boats to Senggarang (3000Rp) leave from the end of Jl Plantar I.

SLEEPING & EATING

Hotel Surya (☎ 21811; Jl Bintan 49; s/d 40,000/45,000Rp) This is good value and clean, with a small courtyard.

Bong's Homestay (☎ 22605; Lorong Bintan II 20; d 35,000Rp) Has been a backpacker favourite since the 1970s.

Johnny's Homestay (Lorong Bintan II 22; d 35,000Rp) Next door, Johnny's takes Bong's overflow.

Ayam Goreng (Bintan Indah Mall, Jl Pos 31; mains 12,000Rp) Good for fried chicken or a burger.

Outdoor restaurants and coffee shops line the front of the volleyball stadium. Try Flipper or **Sunkist** (Jl Teuku Umar 1; snacks 6000Rp).

Pulau Penyengat

This tiny island, a 15-minute *pompong* (small diesel-powered wooden boat) ride (3000Rp) from the main pier, was once the capital of the Riau rajas. It has ruined forts, an old palace and the yellow Sultan Riau mosque.

Beaches

The best beaches on Pulau Bintan, with good snorkelling and some small, attractive offshore islands, are on the east coast at **Pantai Trikora**, some 40km from town. **Beach huts** (60,000Rp) are Spartan and a far cry from Thailand's bungalows. At low tide, the beach becomes a dull mudflat.

South of Teluk Bakau village, try Yasin, which was being renovated at the time of research, or the basic Shady Shark. There

INDONESIA

are no regular public buses, so try to share a minibus (5000Rp per person) or charter a taxi (85,000Rp).

Getting There & Away

Though Pulau Batam is the main link to Sumatra proper, Tanjung Pinang is the jumping-off point to many more remote islands of the Riau Archipelago. It also has links to Singapore and Malaysia. Most services leave from the main pier at the southern end of Jl Merdeka.

Three companies run six weekday services to Tanah Merah, Singapore (120,000Rp) between 7am and 6.30pm, and nine services on weekends, from 6.45am to 6.30pm.

There are six boats a day to Johor Bahru, Malaysia (120,000Rp, two hours). Regular speedboats leave from the main pier for Telaga Punggur on Pulau Batam (20,000Rp, 45 minutes) from 7.45am to 4.45pm daily. Two boats a day go direct to Sekupang (45,000Rp, one hour).

There are two 6am services to Pekanbaru, one bus/boat combination via Tanjung Buton (145,000Rp), the other direct by boat via Sungai Siak (198,000Rp). Both take eight hours and it is worth paying the extra to avoid the bone-shaking four-hour bus journey.

Pelni (☎ 21513; Jl Ketapang 8, Tanjung Pinang) sails to Jakarta (195,000Rp, 28 hours) twice weekly from the southern port of Kijang. You can organise a trip and book with agents on Jl Merdeka.

Getting Around

The bus terminal is 7km out of Tanjung Pinang, an *opelet* ride (3000Rp) along the road to Pantai Trikora, but there are not many buses. Hiring a taxi in Tanjung Pinang is more convenient but it will cost you 85,000Rp to Pantai Trikora. Tanjung Pinang is crawling with *ojek*.

NUSA TENGGARA

As eclectic and diverse as any Indonesian region, the island-chain of Nusa Tenggara takes in Lombok, Sumbawa and Komodo in the west, and Flores, Sumba and West Timor in the east. Generally drier than the rest of the country, and separated from Bali by the deep-sea Wallace's line, its flora and fauna is vaguely reminiscent of nearby Australia.

A remote region with a smorgasbord of sights, Nusa Tenggara lets you party the night away on the sugar-white beaches of Lombok's Gili islands, explore marine life below the waves, watch ancient dragons on Komodo and Rinca, climb rumbling volcanoes over Flores, or photograph Sumba's colourful mock horseback battles.

The trail starts to fade the further you head east, where ferries, bus trips and on-line connections become slower and less frequent. But if you bring time and patience, the rewards are more than worth the effort, especially if you don't mind being

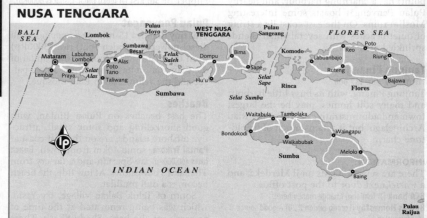

NUSA TENGGARA

the centre of attention. Just get ready for lots of 'hello misters'.

TRANSPORT
Getting There & Away

Denpasar in Bali is the usual jumping-off point for Nusa Tenggara – you can go by ferry or plane across to Lombok, or fly to one of the other islands. Most flights from Nusa Tenggara terminate in Bali, with same-day connections to other parts of Indonesia. See individual island entries for details.

One international gateway into Nusa Tenggara is Mataram, Lombok with SilkAir flights to Singapore. Merpati also flies twice weekly from Kupang to Darwin.

EAST TIMOR VISA RUN

From Nusa Tenggara, hitting Dili in East Timor is the cheapest way to renew your Indonesian visa. Take a bus from Kupang to Atambua (30,000Rp, eight hours), a *bemo* to the Motoain border and a bus to Dili. You may also get a straight Kupang–Dili tourist bus. The 30-day entry visa to East Timor is US$30. Once there, get another 30-day visa at the Indonesian embassy. It will all cost a lot less than flying to Singapore.

Getting Around

The easiest and most popular way to explore Nusa Tenggara is to fly from Bali to Maumere (Flores) or Kupang (West Timor) and island-hop back.

AIR

Merpati covers most destinations in Nusa Tenggara, with **Pelita Air** (www.pelita-air.com) coming in a close second. Garuda, Jatayu and Lion Air also offer services on the biggest routes, mainly to Lombok and Kupang.

Mataram, Kupang and Maumere are the main air hubs and the most reliable places to get a flight. Bima, Labuanbajo, Ruteng and Tambolaka are also serviced by flights. Always book and reconfirm early.

BOAT

Regular vehicle/passenger ferries connect all the main islands, making a loop through the islands from Bali and back fairly easy. From Bali through to Flores, schedules don't vary much, but further east they are subject to sudden change. Boat tours (Perama is a reliable operator) also make the run from Lombok to Flores and back, taking in Komodo and Rinca en route.

Pelni (www.pelni.co.id) has regular connections. Three ships do the round, calling at ports every two weeks. For example, travelling from Java to Papua, the *KM Dobonsolo* was stopping at Jakarta, Surabaya, Denpasar, Kupang, Dili, Ambon, Sorong, Manokwari, Biak and Jayapura. Check the website for details.

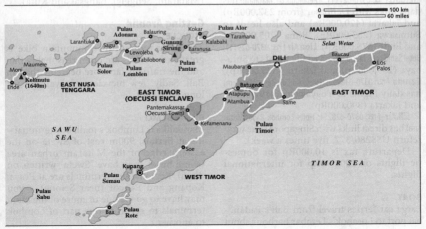

INDONESIA

BUS
Air-con coaches run right across Lombok and Sumbawa, but elsewhere small, slow and very busy minibuses are the only option. They constantly stop to drop off and pick up passengers and will often drive around town for hours until full.

CAR & MOTORCYCLE
A motorcycle is an ideal way to explore Nusa Tenggara, but hiring one is not always easy outside Lombok. Cars with driver/guides are a great option for US$30 a day or more.

LOMBOK

More than just a 'Bali without the crowds', nearby Lombok is Nusa Tenggara's most popular destination; a top spot for sunseekers, surfers, divers and mountain trekkers. Most visitors head to the tiny Gili islands, but beautiful beaches also await on Lombok proper, in the resort stretch of Senggigi, or the southern surf spot of Kuta. Those who've had enough of loafing on the sand can visit a Balinese temple or a traditional Sasak village – or even tackle Gunung Rinjani, the stunning volcano that looms dramatically over Lombok and offers spectacular 360-degree views of the island and the sea.

TRANSPORT
Getting There & Away
AIR
Merpati (☎ 0370-621111; Jl Pejanggik 69, Mataram) has daily links with Denpasar (from 237,000Rp) and Jakarta (420,000Rp) and also heads to Sumbawa (253,000Rp), Bima (705,000Rp) and Ende (875,000Rp). **Lion Air** (☎ 0370-629111; Hotel Sahid Legi, Mataram) has daily flights to Surabaya (239,000Rp) and Jakarta (528,000Rp). **Garuda** (☎ 0370-638259; Hotel Lombok Raya, Mataram) has daily flights to Yogyakarta (419,000Rp) and Jakarta (890,000Rp).

SilkAir (☎ 0370-628254; Hotel Lombok Raya, Mataram) has direct links with Singapore (one way/return US$280/377, five times a week).

Departure tax is 10,000Rp for domestic flights or 100,000Rp for international flights.

BOAT
Large car ferries travel from Bali's Padangbai port to Lombok's Lembar harbour about

every three hours (15,000Rp, 3½ to five hours). The fast Bali–Lombok catamarans are no longer running.

Perama (☎ 635928; Jl Pejanggik 66, Mataram) has five boats and runs a variety of tours between Bali, Lombok and Komodo – provided there are tourists. Perama boats leave Padangbai daily at 1.30pm for Gili Trawangan (180,000Rp), from where small boats connect to Meno and Air. It then sails on to Senggigi (100,000Rp).

From Senggigi, Perama boats leave daily for Gili at 8.30am (50,000Rp) and for Padangbai (100,000Rp) at 9am. From Gili, Perama runs small 7am boats to Bangsal harbour, from where a minibus connects with the 9am Senggigi–Padangbai boat. Meals are provided on board.

From Sumbawa, public ferries from Poto Tano go to Labuhan Lombok, in east Lombok, hourly, 24 hours a day (8000Rp, about 1½ hours).

Three **Pelni** (☎ 637212; Jl Industri 1, Mataram) ships do regular loops through Nusa Tenggara, each one stopping at Lembar about once a fortnight.

BUS
Long-distance public buses go daily from Mataram's Mandalika terminal to Bali and Java in the west, and to Sumbawa in the east. Fares include the ferry crossings.

Perama runs bus/public ferry services between main tourist centres in Bali (Kuta-Legian, Sanur, Ubud etc) and Lombok (Mataram, Senggigi, Bangsal and Kuta).

Getting Around
BICYCLE
Travelling around on a mountain bike is great as the roads are often reasonably flat, and the traffic is far more bearable than in Bali. Sadly, few bicycles are available for long-term rent.

BUS & BEMO
Mandalika is Lombok's main bus terminal – it's at Bertais, 900m east of Sweta on the eastern edge of the Mataram urban area (some buses may have 'Sweta' written on them). Regional bus terminals are at Praya, Kopang and Pancor (near Selong) – you may have to go via one or more of the main terminals to get from one part of Lombok to another.

LOMBOK

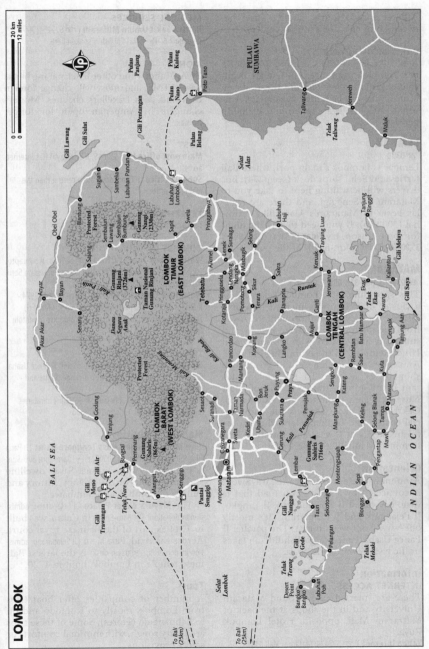

INDONESIA

Perama runs tourist shuttle buses between Lombok's main tourist centres.

CAR & MOTORCYCLE
A Suzuki Jimny costs around 100,000Rp per day, plus insurance, but few are available. Agents in Senggigi are the best bet. Motorcycles can be rented in Senggigi, Ampenan or Cakranegara for around 40,000Rp per day.

LEMBAR
☎ 0370

Lembar is Lombok's main port, where Bali ferries and Pelni ships dock (see p274). Bus drivers will be waiting here to take you to Mataram or Senggigi, and there are regular *bemo* to Mataram's Mandalika terminal (3000Rp). If you need to stay the night for some reason, try **Tidar** (Jl Raya Pelabuhan; s/d 35,000/40,000Rp), 1km north of the port.

MATARAM
☎ 0370 / pop 325,000

This sprawling city, Lombok's largest, is a cluster of four towns merged into one, joined by a busy 10km thoroughfare. Away from the main drag, Mataram is leafy and suburban and dotted with mosques and Hindu temples. In the crumbling old port, Ampenan, some Chinese and Arab-style shophouses survive. To the east, Mataram is the administrative capital of West Nusa Tenggara (Lombok and Sumbawa). Cakranegara, aka Cakra, is the commercial centre, and further inland the colourful market is at Sweta, and the main bus terminal, Mandalika, at Bertais.

Orientation
Ampenan-Mataram-Cakranegara-Sweta is connected by a busy main road that is variously called Jl Yos Sudarso, Jl Langko, Jl Pejanggik and Jl Selaparang. It's mostly one-way, from west to east. The parallel Jl Panca Usaha/Pancawarga/Pendidikan takes traffic back towards the coast.

Information
INTERNET ACCESS
There are Internet cafés around Mataram University and in the shops at the back of Matraram Mall, opposite Hotel Lombok Raya.
Yahoo Internet (☎ 627474; Mataram Mall A11)

MEDICAL SERVICES
Rumah Sakit Umum Mataram (☎ 622254; Jl Pejanggik 6; ☯ 24hr) English is spoken here.

MONEY
BCA, Mandiri and other Jl Selaparang banks have ATMs, and most will change foreign cash and cash travellers cheques. Moneychangers in Ampenan open for longer hours.

POST
Main post office (☎ 632645; Jl Sriwijaya) Has Internet access.
Subpost office (Jl Langko 21) More central than the main post office.

TELEPHONE
Telkom (Jl Langko; ☯ 24hr)

TOURIST INFORMATION
West Lombok Tourist Office (☎ 621658; Jl Suprapto 20; ☯ 8am-2pm Mon-Sat) Marked 'Dinas Pariwisata Seni Dan Budaya', this place has some maps.
West Nusa Tenggara Tourist Office (☎ 635874; Jl Singosari 2; ☯ 8am-3pm Mon-Sat, until 11am Fri) English-speaking staff have maps and organise mountain treks.

TRAVEL AGENCIES
Jatatur (☎ 632878; jatatur@yahoo.com; Jl Panca Usaha Block A 12) English-speaking staff arrange flights and Lombok island tours.
Perama (☎ 635928; Jl Pejanggik 66) Runs minibuses and boats to Bali, the Gilis and Komodo.

Sights & Activities
The **Museum Negeri Nusa Tenggara Barat** (Jl Panji Tilar Negara 6; admission 1000Rp; ☯ 8am-2pm Tue-Sun) is inspired by a traditional Sasak dwelling and has exhibits on the geology, history and culture of Lombok and Sumbawa.

The **Mayura Water Palace** (Jl Selaparang; admission by donation; ☯ 8am-5pm), in Cakra, was built in 1744 as part of the Balinese royal court. Across the road, **Pura Meru** (Jl Selaparang; admission by donation; ☯ dawn-dusk) is the largest Balinese temple in Lombok, built in 1720.

Tours
A number of companies offer boat trips from Lombok, mostly to Komodo and on to Labuanbajo (Flores). Some of these trips are pretty rough, with minimal comforts or safety provisions.

INDONESIA

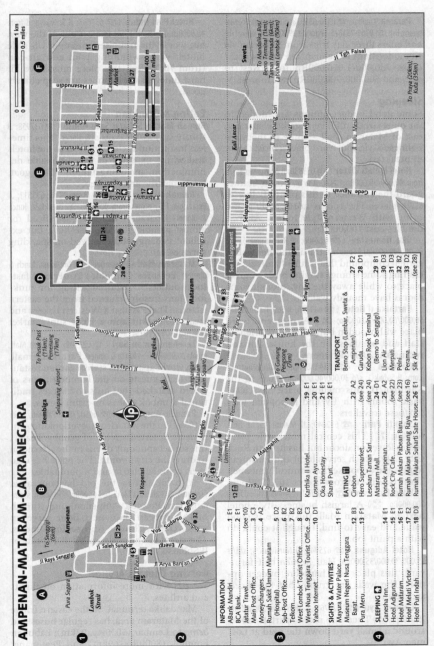

AMPENAN-MATARAM-CAKRANEGARA

INFORMATION
ABank Mandiri	1 E1
BCA Bank	2 E1
Jatatur Travel	(see 10)
Main Post Office	3 C3
Moneychangers	4 A2
Rumah Sakit Umum Mataram (Hospital)	5 D2
Sub-Post Office	6 B2
Telkom	7 B2
West Lombok Tourist Office	8 B2
West Nusa Tenggara Tourist Office	9 C3
Yahoo Internet	10 D1

SIGHTS & ACTIVITIES
Mayura Water Palace	11 F1
Museum Negeri Nusa Tenggara Barat	12 B3
Pura Meru	13 F1

SLEEPING
Ganesha Inn	14 E1
Hotel Adiguna	15 E1
Hotel Mataram	16 E1
Hotel Melati Victor	17 E2
Hotel Puri Indah	18 D3
Karthika II Hotel	19 E1
Losmen Ayu	20 E1
Oka Homestay	21 E1
Shanti Puri	22 E1

EATING
Cirebon	23 A2
Hero Supermarket	(see 24)
Lesehan Taman Sari	(see 24)
Mataram Mall	24 D1
Pondok Ampenan	25 A2
Rock City Cafe	(see 22)
Rumah Makan Pabean Baru	(see 23)
Rumah Makan Simpang Raya	(see 16)
Rumah Makan Suharti Sate House	26 E1

TRANSPORT
Bemo Stop (Lembar, Sweta & Ampenan)	27 F2
Garuda	28 D1
Kebon Roek Terminal (Bemo to Senggigi)	29 B1
Lion Air	30 D3
Merpati	31 D3
Pelni	32 B2
Perama	33 D2
Silk Air	(see 28)

INDONESIA

Perama (Lombok ☎ 0370-635928; Jl Pejanggik 66, Mataram; Bali ☎ 0361-751875; Legian St 39, Kuta) is reliable and offers three-day trips from Mataram via Komodo/Rinca to Labuanbajo. Prices: deck/cabin 750,000/1,050,000Rp from west to east, and 500,000/700,000Rp east to west.

Sleeping

Some good budget options are hidden in the quiet streets off Jl Pejanggik/Selaparang, east of Mataram Mall – some of them are Balinese-style courtyard places; most throw in breakfast.

Hotel Melati Viktor (☎ 633830; Jl Abimanyu 1; s/d from 40,000/50,000Rp; 🔀) Two Hindu statues guard the entrance to this pretty Balinese-style place. The rooms are sparkling and come with Western-style toilets. Air-con doubles cost 100,000Rp.

Oka Homestay (☎ 622406; Jl Repatmaya 5; s/d 35,000/40,000Rp) Nearby, this is another walled garden compound that is full of animals, including some strange singing birds. A great place to while away the day, though some rooms have mouldy walls.

Karthika II Hotel (☎ 641776; Jl Subak I 16; s/d/tr 50,000/60,000/70,000Rp; 🔀) A nice courtyard place with wooden bungalow huts, friendly staff and breakfast on the house. Air-con rooms are 20,000Rp more.

Ganesha Inn (☎ 624878; ganeshainn@hotmail.com; Jl Subak 1; s/d 30,000/40,000Rp) Close to the Karthika II, this mellow place has clean, basic rooms with TV and is popular with Japanese travellers.

Shanti Puri (☎ 632649; Jl Maktal 15; d from 40,000Rp; 🔀) This central motel-style place scores lower on décor but has its own Rock City Cafe, which serves local and European food – and a shop selling comically misspelt T-shirts. Air-con rooms cost 100,000Rp.

Hotel Mataram (☎ 634966; Jl Pejanggik 105; d from 100,000Rp; 🔀) A largish business-style hotel next to Mataram Mall, this place is good value and easy to find, though it could do with a paint job.

Hotel Adiguna (☎ 625946; Jl Nursiwan 9; s/d/tr 25,000/30,000/35,000Rp) Half *losmen*/half farmyard, this place is a hardcore budget option. The walls are grubby but the sheets are clean.

Losmen Ayu (☎ 621761; Jl Nursiwan 20; d from 25,000Rp; 🔀) There are more Spartan rooms around a small yard down the road at Losmen Ayu.

Hotel Puri Indah (☎ 637633; Jl Sriwijaya; d from 45,000Rp; 🔀 🏊) This is a bit out of the way, but worth the trek. Resembling a US-style motel, with swimming pool and air-con (from 70,000Rp), this place must have hit hard times, as these prices are suspiciously good.

Eating & Drinking

Rumah Makan Suharti Sate House (☎ 637958; Jl Maktal 9; satay 9000Rp; 🕑 lunch & dinner) This timeless institution is close to most of the hotels and whips up satay of every possible denomination, including Gurami fish, goat, liver, marrow and chicken.

Rumah Makan Simpang Raya (☎ 633811; Jl Pejanggik 107; dishes from 9000Rp; 🕑 breakfast, lunch & dinner) Character has been sacrificed for almost-pathological hygiene here, but excellent Padang food is served on sparkling surfaces.

Mataram Mall (Jl Pejanggik; 🕑 breakfast, lunch & dinner) Features Lombok's American fast-food outlets – required eating for junk-food fans freshly returned from the eastern islands. There is also a Western bakery and steak restaurant and a Hero supermarket for self-caterers.

Lesehan Taman Sari (☎ 629909; Mataram Mall; meals 20,000Rp; 🕑 lunch & dinner) Part of the mall, yet a world apart, this stylish garden restaurant seats guests on the bamboo floors of stilted thatched-roof huts and serves traditional Lombok dishes on palm leaves.

Pondok Ampenan (☎ 645027; Jl Pabean; beer 12,000Rp) On the waterfront, overlooking Ampenan's deserted stretch of grubby 'beach', this sunset spot only opens in the afternoon to draw the city's youth. The place has cold beer, colonial charm and a pool table.

Also located in the old harbour area, **Cirebon** (Jl Pabean 113; dishes 6000Rp; 🕑 lunch & dinner), near Pondok Ampenan, and Rumah Makan Pabean Baru next door serve up good, cheap Chinese and seafood meals. The street is variously called Jl Pabean or Jl Sudarso.

Getting There & Around

See p274 for more information on flights and airlines.

Mandalika terminal, on the eastern fringe of the Mataram area, has regular buses and *bemo* to Lembar (5000Rp, 22km); Labuhan Lombok (8000Rp, 69km) and Pemenang, for the Gili islands (6000Rp, 31km). The Kebon Roek terminal in Ampenan has *bemo* to Senggigi (3000Rp, 10km).

Bright, new, yellow *bemo* shuttle back and forth between the Kebon Roek and Mandalika terminals (1500Rp).

Perama (☎ 635928; Jl Pejanggik 66) runs buses across Lombok and neighbouring islands.

AROUND MATARAM

About 10km east of Mataram, **Taman Narmada** (admission 1000Rp; ☽ 7am-6pm) is a royal garden laid out as a stylised, miniature replica of Gunung Rinjani and its lake. There are frequent *bemo* from Mandalika terminal which pass the entrance to the gardens.

A few kilometres northwest of Taman Narmada is **Puri Lingsar** (admission by donation; ☽ dawn-dusk), a large temple complex catering for the Bali-Hindu, Islam and Wektu Telu religions. Buy hard-boiled eggs to feed the holy eels.

East of Puri Lingsar, **Suranadi** (admission by donation; ☽ dawn-dusk) has one of the holiest temples in Lombok.

The **Hutan Wisata Suranadi** (admission 3000Rp; ☽ dawn-dusk) is a small forest sanctuary which is OK for short walks and birdwatching.

In Suranadi, **Suranadi Hotel** (☎ 633686; d 175,000Rp; ✷ ✷) is an old Dutch haunt, with tennis courts and a cool spring-fed swimming pool. Nearby, **Pondok Surya** (d 30,000Rp) is casual and friendly, with basic rooms.

SENGGIGI

☎ 0370

Lombok's oldest and most developed tourist area is a picturesque stretch of palm-shaded guesthouses, resorts and beachside cafés in a series of sweeping bays just north of Mataram. The sunsets over the Lombok strait are superb, with Bali's Gunung Agung providing a majestic backdrop. As elsewhere, the downturn in tourism has left the town with a forlorn look outside the peak seasons, but it has also reduced the room rates.

Orientation & Information

Hotels are spread out along nearly 10km of coast, starting 6km north of Ampenan. Restaurants and shops are clustered at the central Senggigi strip, where moneychangers and ATMs can be found. There are *war-*

tel, a post office and a police post near the Sheraton.

Clinic Senggigi (☎ 63210) This small, private clinic near the Senggigi Beach Hotel offers medical service.

Super Star Net Cafe (☎ 693620; Senggigi Plaza B1/05; per hr 18,000Rp) Has high-speed Internet access.

Telkom Near the Pasar Seni (Art Market).

Sights & Activities

On a rocky point south of Senggigi, **Pura Batu Bolong** (admission by donation; ☽ dawn-dusk) is a small Balinese-Hindu temple set on a cliff top that is oriented towards Gunung Agung, Bali's holiest mountain. Legend has it that beautiful virgins were once thrown into the sea from the top of the rock. You'll need to wear a sash to enter the temple.

There's good snorkelling off the point and in the sheltered bay – many hotels and restaurants in central Senggigi hire out mask-snorkel-fin sets for about 20,000Rp per day.

You can organise diving in the Gilis (see p282) or near Kuta (see p287) through **Dream Divers** (☎ 693738, 692047; www.dreamdivers.com), **Dive Indonesia** (☎ 642289; www.diveindonesiaonline.com) and other shops on Senggigi's main drag.

Sleeping

Tough times mean discounts at many places, but some have scrimped on maintenance – always check the room first and make sure the fan works. Breakfast should be on the house.

Sonya Homestay (☎ 693447; s/d with shared mandi 30,000/35,000Rp) A family-run, no-frills place with 10 rooms, this tiny and friendly little homestay is just off the main road and comes well recommended by readers. Free coffee all day.

Raja's Bungalows (☎ 0812-377 0138; d 60,000Rp) Hidden away 250m up a small street and down a narrow alley behind the mosque, the four thatched bungalows here are a secluded tropical delight set in a flower-filled jungle garden.

Ray Hotel (☎ 605599; d from 40,000Rp; ✷) The peach-coloured walls and basic room décors won't win this place any design awards, but the photogenic views from these hillside rooms make up for it. Air-con comes for 20,000Rp more.

Lina Hotel (☎ 693237; s/d from 60,000/75,000Rp; ✷) Fast-fading posh with weather-worn rooms. Rates double with ocean views, but the spectacular sunsets are free from the fab seaside restaurant. The Perama boats for Gili leave from next door.

Hotel Elen (☎ 693077; d from 30,000Rp; ❄) Basic, with predawn mosque wake-up call (it's just north of the mosque). Definitely not for honeymooners. The plastic flowers don't do much to fill the charm vacuum, but the rooms are fine. Air-con rooms cost 60,000Rp.

Batu Bolong Cottages (☎ 693198; bbcresort _lombok@yahoo.com; d from 125,000Rp; ❄) South of the centre, these excellent bungalows on both sides of the road have won a local cleanliness award and come with stylish bamboo furniture and *ikat*-style blankets (*ikat* is cloth in which a pattern is produced

by dyeing individual threads before the weaving process).

Atithi Sanggraha Beach Bungalows (☎ 693070; d 100,000Rp) Overpriced and a little grubby, these bungalows are a long way south of the action, but they front a beautifully deserted sweep of clean sand and coconut palms.

Pondok Siti Hawa (☎ 693414; s/d with shared mandi 25,000/30,000Rp) You want cheap? This is it: an overgrown, farmyard-style place with tiny bamboo cottages, outdoor furniture made from carved-up truck tyres – and a chained-up monkey.

Eating
Super Star Net Cafe (☎ 693620; Senggigi Plaza B1/05; mains 10,000Rp; ☾ breakfast, lunch & dinner) A cyber-

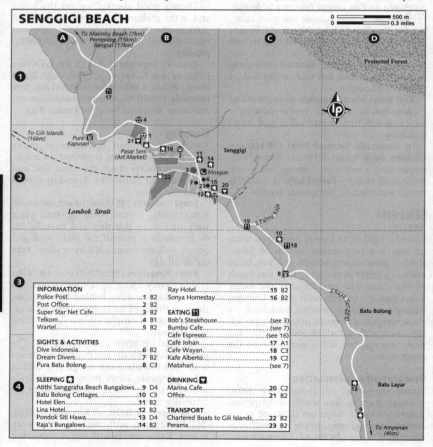

SENGGIGI BEACH

0 — 500 m
0 — 0.3 miles

To Malinbu Beach (7km);
Pemenang (15km);
Bangsal (17km)

Protected Forest

To Gili Islands
(16km)

Pura
Kapusan

Pasar Seni
(Art Market)

Senggigi

Mosque

Lombok Strait

Jl Palma Raja

Batu Bolong

Jl Raya Senggigi

Batu Layar

Batu Layar

To Ampenan
(4km)

café that deserves its name, this funky bamboo joint also serves up some tasty Asian meals, from 7am Super Star breakfasts (22,000Rp) to midnight snacks.

Matahari (mains 35,000Rp; ☺ lunch & dinner) In the centre, this little slice of culinary Mexicana whips up some sizzling Tex-Mex food.

Bumbu Cafe (mains 35,000Rp; ☺ breakfast, lunch & dinner) Next door to Matahari, Bumbu has some surprisingly good Thai fare and excellent seafood dishes.

Cafe Espresso (☎ 693148; cappuccino 10,000Rp; ☺ breakfast, lunch & dinner) This claims to be the first (and only) spot in Lombok to serve real Italian coffee.

Cafe Wayan (☎ 693098; mains 30,000Rp; ☺ breakfast, lunch & dinner) Next to Batu Bolong Bungalows, this tasteful oasis of Balinese calm also serves up some great pizzas, pastas and home-made bread, as well as yummy tandoori chicken breast and avocado shrimp cocktails.

Kafe Alberto (☎ 693039; mains from 30,000Rp; ☺ lunch & dinner) This stylin' outdoor café-cocktail bar blends cutting-edge Italian and fusion cuisine with minimalist Japanese-style garden design and some unbeatable sunset views. It even has tuna sushi and sashimi (35,000Rp).

Cafe Johan (☎ 693722; dishes from 20,000Rp; ☺ lunch & dinner) This little piece of Austria, around the bend 2km north of Senggigi, looked a bit under the weather at the time of writing but planned to renovate and serve up some more hearty Knödel goodness. It also offers pick-up.

Drinking

Senggigi nightlife is low-key when there are few tourists in town. It's busier on Friday and Saturday, when young locals (men and a few women) come up from the Mataram area.

Office (beer 11,000Rp) After a tough day on the beach, why not duck into the Office for a quiet sundowner? Worth it for the name alone, this place behind the art market comes with great food, a pool table, a cockatoo and views of the fishing boats.

Marina Cafe (☎ 693136; admission 10,000Rp) This Hard Rock Cafe clone serves up American bar food, cold beer and live music. On weekend nights, the two-storey place fires up at 10pm and gets rockin' till late. The vodka ice is 40,000Rp.

Getting There & Around

Regular *bemo* travel between Senggigi and Ampenan's Kebon Roek terminal (4000Rp, 10km) – some continue north as far as Pemenang. You can usually wave them down on the main drag.

Perama (☎ 693007) has daily buses across Lombok and daily 8.30am boats to the Gili islands (50,000Rp, 1½ hours). This is highly recommended, if only to avoid the Bangsal touts.

A few places hire out mopeds for 35,000Rp a day plus petrol.

GILI ISLANDS
☎ 0370

In the turquoise waters northwest of Lombok lie three wonderful little specks of jungle-green. They are the coral-fringed Gilis (which just means 'islands'), and these are little slices of paradise that draw a steady stream of sun-bathers, divers and party-animals. The islands are laid-back and beautiful, with few hawkers and no motorised transport. Dogs are banned, but cats are not.

Family-friendly Gili Air is the closest to the mainland, with plenty of homestays dotted among the palm trees. Sleepy Gili Meno, the middle island, is the smallest and quietest, and the place to play Robinson Crusoe.

The reputed 'party island' of Gili Trawangan (population 800) is the farthest out, with the most visitors, the most tourist facilities and the most dishes that contain magic mushrooms.

Information

Each island has shops and/or hotels that will change money, and many midrange hotels and dive shops accept credit cards. There are no banks or ATMs, so it's best to bring rupiah with you. There is mobile phone coverage, and all islands have a *wartel*. Air and Trawangan have tedious but functioning Internet connections at around 400Rp a minute.

The computers at Borubodur restaurant on Trawangan work OK for Internet access.

Ozzy Shop, on Gili Air next door to Abdi Fantastik, has phone and Internet services. **Perama** (☎ 638514) has a small office on Gili Trawangan, by the Art Market and even smaller outlets on Air, at the harbour, and on Meno, in the Casablanca.

Dangers & Annoyances

Don't try to swim between the islands. The currents are strong, and people have died.

In the water, watch out for jellyfish, which can give you a nasty rash.

There are no police on the Gilis, so report any theft to the island *kepala* (head) or Trawangan's Satgas community council. If there is no response, go to a mainland police station. Remember that magic mushrooms and other drugs are illegal, even if they are widely sold.

Cases of sexual harassment have been reported on Gili Air, and single women should be circumspect at night.

If you rent a bicycle on Gili Air, watch out for an annoying small-time scam where a bike part mysteriously disappears during the day, and the owner then fines you a suspiciously standard price when you return the bike. (Handle bar grips are a set 15,000Rp.)

Sights & Activities

The hill in Trawangan's southwest corner is a good spot for sunset-watching. Gili Meno's 2500-sq-metre **Bird Park** (admission 25,000Rp; ☻ 9am-5pm) is home to 300 of our feathered friends, and some confused kangaroos.

The islands' biggest drawcards are under the water. Snorkelling gear can be hired for 25,000Rp per day. Several very professional dive shops charge a uniform US$25 per dive or US$275 for a four-day beginners' course.

On Trawangan, try **Blue Marlin** (☎ 632424; www.diveindo.com), **Manta Dive** (☎ 643649; www.manta-dive.com) or **Dive Indonesia** (☎ 642289; diveindo_senggigi@iname.com). On Gili Air, try **Blue Marlin** (☎ 634387) or **Dream Divers** (☎ 634547; www.dreamdivers.com).

Dynamite fishing has been stamped out, thanks to the eco-trust set up by local dive shops, but the reefs are still recovering from this and warm-water bleaching. Take care when diving and snorkelling and avoid touching or standing on the coral.

Sleeping & Eating

With the tourism downturn, especially Air and Meno can feel very quiet. Everything changes in the high season (July, August and around Christmas) when hotels double or triple their prices. The islands' water – used in hotel bathrooms – is salty-brackish.

GILI AIR

Most low-season action is in the island's southeast, near the boat pier and the popu-

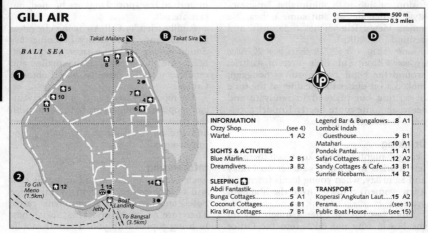

GILI AIR

0 ——— 500 m
0 ——— 0.3 miles

BALI SEA

Takat Malang

Takat Sira

To Gili Meno (1.5km)

Boat Landing

Jetty

To Bangsal (3.5km)

INFORMATION	
Ozzy Shop	(see 4)
Wartel	1 A2

SIGHTS & ACTIVITIES	
Blue Marlin	2 B1
Dreamdivers	3 B2

SLEEPING	
Abdi Fantastik	4 B1
Bunga Cottages	5 A1
Coconut Cottages	6 B1
Kira Kira Cottages	7 B1

Legend Bar & Bungalows	8 A1
Lombok Indah Guesthouse	9 B1
Matahari	10 A1
Pondok Pantai	11 A1
Safari Cottages	12 A2
Sandy Cottages & Cafe	13 B1
Sunrise Ricebarns	14 B2

TRANSPORT	
Koperasi Angkutan Laut	15 A2
Perama	(see 1)
Public Boat House	(see 15)

TOPLESS BATHING

Note that topless (for women) or nude sunbathing is very offensive to the local people, and skimpy clothing is not appreciated away from the beaches.

---

lar swimming beach, but there are many good places scattered around little Gili Air.

Most hostels have their own eateries, but a few restaurants can be found around the island.

Lombok Indah (☎ 08133-956 8324; d 50,000Rp) On the north coast, this new English-run place has comfy bamboo bungalows and great views of both the sunrise and sunset. Mod cons include a pizza oven, DVDs and a glassbottom boat.

Legend Bar & Bungalows (☎ 08123-787254; d 40,000Rp) Next door, this long-running summertime party and barbecue spot has good beach huts, some cheesy coral-and-shell artwork and a laid-back atmosphere. In the off season, it's time for guitar practice and chess.

Sandy Cottages & Cafe (☎ 08123-789832; s/d 40,000/50,000Rp) Lots of communal space and traditional-style accommodation in a flower-filled garden (business motto: 'We mean clean & harmony').

Coconut Cottages (☎ 635365; www.coconuts -giliair.com; d 50,000Rp) Set back from the beach on the east coast, this Scottish-run place has fab, traditional-style bungalows with fans, scattered through idyllic, labyrinthine gardens. They may even have carrot cake.

Kira Kira Cottages (☎ 641021; kirakira cottage@yahoo.co.jp; s/d from 25,000/40,000Rp) Also a bit inland, in a charming garden, there are some stylish cottages here with fresh shower water! Staff serve up tempura and other Japanese snacks.

Abdi Fantastik (☎ 636421; s/d 60,000/70,000Rp) Nearby, this has pleasant – 'Fantastik' is hyperbole – thatched bungalows, set on lawns kept trim by a small herd of cows.

Sunrise Ricebarns (☎ 642370; s/d from 60,000/ 80,000Rp) A large complex on what passes for Gili Air's east-coast main strip, this Scottish-run place has 12 two-storey 'ricebarn' huts. The luxury rooms boast spring beds and 'power showers'.

Safari Cottages (d 30,000Rp) At the time of research the German dive instructor-owner

was planning to add some upmarket bungalows to his thatched cottages, with free mountain bike use for guests. The restaurant does an Indonesian buffet dinner on Friday (30,000Rp).

Matahari (d 50,000Rp) One of the more popular backpacker haunts on the quiet west coast, Matahari boasts plenty of communal seaside chilling space and well-kept cottages in a coconut plantation – watch your head!

Blue Marlin (☎ 634387; dishes from 15,000Rp; ☺ breakfast, lunch & dinner) Has a café with videos and a good selection of post-dive tucker.

Accommodation options **Pondok Pantai** (s/d 30,000/40,000Rp) and the scruffier **Bunga Cottages** (s/d 30,000/35,000Rp) are on either side of the Matahari. They don't see many visitors these days but still have some good-value bungalow sleeps.

GILI MENO

Mellow Meno has more pricey, midrange rooms that don't usually include breakfast. These rooms may not have electricity, which means no fan, so make sure you get a mosquito net. All the guesthouses serve food.

Mallia's Child Bungalows (☎ 622007; s/d 80,000/100,000Rp) With clean, wooden bungalows looking out right over the topnotch beach, this is a great option near the boat landing.

Biru Meno (☎ 08180-365 7322; s/d 50,000/60,000Rp) In a shady southern pine grove, this remote place has a pizza oven and bungalows with comfy cushion terraces.

Amber House (☎ 643676; amber_house02@hotmail .com; d 50,000Rp) Japanese ownership has brought this swish place more than a touch of Zen, with a beautiful garden, immaculate bungalows and an eatery that whips up cappuccino and oven-fresh muffins.

Tao Kombo (tao_kombo@yahoo.com; bungalows 80,000Rp) This jungle bar-travel lodge is run by a French musician committed to bringing nightlife to mellow Meno. It has clean bungalows with open-sky bathrooms and bamboo platforms with mossie nets and safety boxes.

Jali Cafe (mains 15,000Rp; ☺ breakfast, lunch & dinner) Among the pleasant beachfront restaurants near the boat landing is this popular beach-boy haunt.

INDONESIA

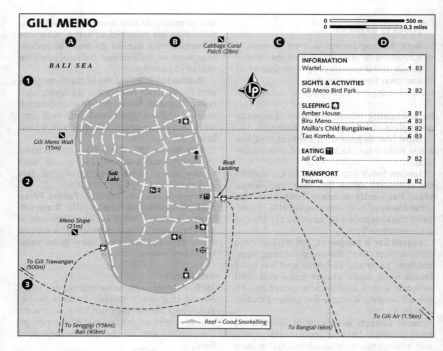

GILI MENO

0	500 m
0	0.3 miles

INFORMATION
Wartel..**1** B3

SIGHTS & ACTIVITIES
Gili Meno Bird Park...........................**2** B2

SLEEPING 🏠
Amber House.....................................**3** B1
Biru Meno..**4** B3
Mallia's Child Bungalows.................**5** B2
Tao Kombo..**6** B3

EATING 🍴
Jali Cafe..**7** B2

TRANSPORT
Perama..**8** B2

BALI SEA

Cabbage Coral Patch (28m)

Gili Meno Wall (15m)

Salt Lake

Boat Landing

Meno Slope (21m)

To Gili Trawangan (500m)

To Senggigi (15km); Bali (40km)

Reef – Good Snorkelling

To Bangsal (6km)

To Gili Air (1.5km)

GILI TRAWANGAN

Party-happy, yet relaxed, Gili T has what it takes to pamper the road-weary back-packer without being in-your-face com-mercial. Dive shops and midrange hotels have brought treats such as saltwater pools, a sushi bar and comfy DVD pavilions to while away a rainy day. Most hotels serve fresh seafood and excellent Western and local dishes. For local food there are *warung* near the boat pier.

Manta Dive (☎ 643649; www.manta-dive.com; d 250,000Rp; 🏊) Even if you don't stay in its up-market and spanking-new Sasak-style bun-galows, you can leave your luggage at this friendly English-run dive shop near the boat pier while you look for a room elsewhere.

TiR na Nog (☎ 639463; d from 100,000Rp; 🏊) Trawangan's barn-like Irish pub and top nightspot now has stylish rooms out the back. The 'Land of Youth' also boasts gen-erous Western meals, pub quizzes, video pavilions and frequent parties.

Big Bubble (☎ 625020; d 100,000Rp; 🏊) The former Tra La La boasts stylish rooms with tiled floors, heavy timber furniture, bedside lamps, coat hangers and hammock-equipped chill-out terraces. It has a swimming pool and a beach volleyball court.

Pondok Lita (☎ 648607; s/d 40,000/50,000Rp) Popular and widely recommended, this modest, family-run place in the village has comfy, safe and spacious rooms around a small courtyard. As everywhere, prices go into orbit in high season.

Aldi Homestay (☎ 0813-3954 1102; s/d 30,000/35,000Rp) It's more of the same from this nearby Pondok Lita clone. Look for the ripped-off logo of the German supermar-ket chain Aldi, which also happens to be the name of the owner's son.

Rhuma Kita (☎ 0813-3953 9176; s/d 40,000/60,000Rp) A block away out the back of the village, this place has a few quiet hide-away bungalows set in a large blooming garden.

Makmur 2 Homestay (☎ 639266; s/d 15,000/20,000Rp) Basic, run-down cottages at bargain-basement prices are the norm here, but at least they're central and a short stagger home from the Irish pub and other spots on the weekly party circuit.

INDONESIA

Coral Beach 2 (s/d 40,000/60,000Rp) A few minutes' walk north of the village, this has basic rooms with mosquito nets. The garden is a bit trashy, but a great sweep of sugar-white sand out the front makes up for it, and the snorkelling is good here.

Blue Beach Cottages (☎ 623849; s/d 150,000Rp) These smart bungalows feature soft furnishings, minibars and verandas. In the seafood eatery, the menu changes as quickly as the day's catch. It's closer to the swimming and sun-bathing beach than the southern places.

Nusa Tiga (d 35,000Rp) On the island's northern tip, these deserted concrete bungalows offer low prices and serious seclusion.

Pondok Santai (s/d 20,000/30,000Rp) On the south coast, with basic, rattan-style digs in an overgrown field, also offers rooms away from it all.

Beachhouse hotel and restaurant (lobster per 100g 25,000Rp; ❤ breakfast, lunch & dinner) Next to the Irish pub, this has a deli and serves seafood barbecue.

Ryoshi sushi bar (18-piece sushi set 59,000Rp; ❤ lunch & dinner) Across the path from the

Beachhouse. Good cafés further north include the Cafe Wayan and Juku.

Rumah Makan Kikinovi (❤ lunch & dinner) Expats swear by this hole-in-the-wall place on the lane just north of the art market.

As sleeping options, the basic **Sandy Beach Cottages** (☎ 625020; d 30,000Rp) and **Pak Majid** (d 30,000-35,000Rp) have clearly seen better days, but they are also right in the fray.

Drinking

Party night rotates along Gili Trawangan through the week under a nonaggression pact between TiR Na Nog, Rudy's Pub and some of the dive shops.

Getting There & Around

Perama (Senggigi ☎ 693007; Gili Trawangan ☎ 638514) operates a fleet of tourist boats to the Gilis – a popular option since it spares you running the Bangsal gauntlet with its army of menacing touts. Boats leave Senggigi for the Gilis at 8.30am (50,000Rp, 1½ to two hours). Perama also sells bus tickets from the Gilis to other points in Lombok and beyond.

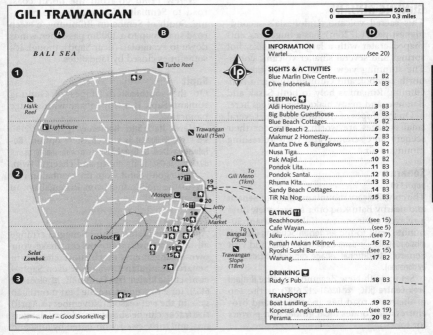

GILI TRAWANGAN

BALI SEA

Turbo Reef

Halik Reef

Lighthouse

Trawangan Wall (15m)

Mosque

To Gili Meno (1km)

Jetty
Art Market

Lookout

To Bangsal (7km)

Selat Lombok

Trawangan Slope (18m)

Reef – Good Snorkelling

0 — 500 m
0 — 0.3 miles

INFORMATION
Wartel.................................(see 20)

SIGHTS & ACTIVITIES
Blue Marlin Dive Centre...................1 B2
Dive Indonesia................................2 B3

SLEEPING
Aldi Homestay..................................3 B3
Big Bubble Guesthouse......................4 B3
Blue Beach Cottages.........................5 B2
Coral Beach 2..................................6 B2
Makmur 2 Homestay.........................7 B3
Manta Dive & Bungalows................. 8 B2
Nusa Tiga.......................................9 B1
Pak Majid.....................................10 B3
Pondok Lita..................................11 B3
Pondok Santai...............................12 B3
Rhuma Kita...................................13 B3
Sandy Beach Cottages....................14 B3
TiR Na Nog...................................15 B3

EATING
Beachhouse.................................(see 15)
Cafe Wayan.................................(see 5)
Juku..(see 7)
Rumah Makan Kikinovi...................16 B2
Ryoshi Sushi Bar...........................(see 15)
Warung.......................................17 B2

DRINKING
Rudy's Pub..................................18 B3

TRANSPORT
Boat Landing...............................19 B2
Koperasi Angkutan Laut................(see 19)
Perama.......................................20 B2

INDONESIA

To get to the Gilis by public transport, take a *bemo* to Pemenang, then get a *cidomo* (horse-drawn cart; 2000Rp) for the last kilometre to the pier at Bangsal, which is inundated with irritating touts suffering Gili envy.

Here the local cartel, the Koperasi Angkutan Laut, runs boats to the islands – 4500Rp to Air, 5000Rp to Meno and 5500Rp to Trawangan. Boats leave when full, so you have to wait until 18 people buy tickets to the same island – try to arrive early. To charter a whole boat from Bangsal costs 88,000Rp to Air, 98,000Rp to Meno and 108,000Rp to Trawangan.

For travel between the islands, an island-hopper makes twice-daily loops starting in Air around 9am and 3pm, charging 15,000Rp between two islands and 18,000Rp between three islands.

Public ferries for the mainland (4000Rp) leave Trawangan around 7am, stopping at the other two islands before making the crossing to Bangsal.

Cidomo rides on the islands are about 5000Rp.

GUNUNG RINJANI

This sacred volcano, Indonesia's second-highest peak (3726m), has a huge crescent-shaped crater with a large green lake, hot springs and several smaller volcanic cones. The stunning view from the rim takes in north Lombok and Gunung Agung in Bali. Gunung Rinjani is holy to both Sasak and Balinese, and many make pilgrimages here.

On the slopes of Gunung Rinjani, several small villages are worth visiting for their scenery and serenity and their refreshing mountain air.

Senaru
pop 1330

The cool, flowery mountain village of Senaru and nearby Batu Koq offer superb views and a relaxed environment. Take a pleasant 30-minute walk to the **Air Terjun Sendang Gila** (admission 2500Rp; ☼ dawn-dusk) waterfalls, and visit Senaru's **traditional village compound** (admission by donation).

Set up with New Zealand help, the **Rinjani Trek Centre** (RTC; ☎ 08681-212 6187) at the top of the main road has great maps and brochures and rotates local guides and porters for tours.

Local women guides also run the half-day **Senaru Panorama Walk** that starts at 8am, and introduces visitors to the village culture in the foothills of Rinjani.

John Adventures (☎ 8175-788081; www.rinjani master.com) offers 'deluxe trips' up the mountain, with thick thermo mats, extra food and toilet tents (three days, US$125) and four-day vulcanology tours (US$180).

Many *losmen* along the main road have basic rooms with breakfast. **Pondok Indah** (d 50,000Rp), the first place you'll pass from Bayan, has sublime views. **Pondok Senaru** (d 70,000Rp) is a cut above the rest and the best option for creature comforts.

To get to Senaru, go first to Anyar and get a local *bemo* from there (3000Rp). After 4pm you'll need to charter a *bemo*.

Sembalun Lawang & Sembalun Bumbung

High on the eastern side of Gunung Rinjani is the remote and beautiful Sembalun valley.

In Sembalun Lawang, Pondok Sembalun and Maria Guest House have simple accommodation (doubles 40,000Rp).

A few *bemo* go from the north coast road to Sembalun Lawang, in the morning. South of Sembalun Bumbung, a steep road snakes up to a 2000m pass, then winds down to Pesugulan (near Sapit), though it's sometimes closed by landslides.

Sapit

On the southeastern slopes of Gunung Rinjani, Sapit is a tiny village with a huge panorama.

Here, **Hati Suci Homestay** (☎ 0367-22197; s/d 40,000/80,000Rp) is the classiest option. **Belelangga Bed & Breakfast** (s/d with shared mandi 30,000/50,000Rp) is its cheap and cheerful twin.

Bemo go to Sapit from the Sembalun valley to the north and from Pringgabaya to the south.

Trekking

Agencies in Mataram and Senggigi arrange all-inclusive treks, but you can make your own arrangements much more cheaply in Senaru, Sembulan Lawang, or even Sapit – contact the **Rinjani Trek Centre** (RTC; ☎ 08681-212 6187). June to August are the best months to go – in the wet season (November to April) the tracks can be slippery and very dangerous, and the views are obscured by mist and cloud. Trekkers were attacked and robbed on the mountain in 2000, but bandit activity had ceased at the time of writing. Check locally to make sure.

The most common trek is to climb from Senaru to Pos III (2300m) on the first day (about five hours of steep walking), camp there and climb to Pelawangan I, on the crater rim (2600m), for sunrise the next morning (about two hours). From the rim, you descend into the crater and walk around to the **hot springs** (two hours) on a very exposed track. The hot springs are a good place to relax and camp for the second night, before returning all the way to Senaru the next day.

The climb to the summit of Gunung Rinjani is very strenuous, and a guide is recommended. Two hours' walk east from the hot springs, at a place called Pelawangan II (about 2900m), a track branches off to the summit. From there, it's a demanding climb (three or four hours) over loose ground to the top (3726m). You go back down to Pelawangan II (two or three hours) and from there west to the lakeside. Alternatively, go east to Sembalun Lawang (five or six hours) to complete a traverse of the mountain.

Sembalun Lawang is also a good starting point, though accommodation and equipment rental is limited. One possibility is to arrange guide, porter and equipment in Senaru, charter a *bemo* to Sembalun Lawang, start trekking from there and stay at Pelawangan II for the first night. Climb Gunung Rinjani for sunrise next morning (if you're keen), then descend to the lakeside and stay there the second night. The next day, walk out via Pelawangan I and down to Senaru, completing an east-to-west traverse.

GUIDES, PORTERS & EQUIPMENT

You can trek from Senaru to the hot springs and back without a guide – the trail is pretty well defined. For other treks, it's best to take a licensed guide. They are available in Senaru, Sembalun Lawang and Sapit for about 70,000Rp a day. Porters charge 50,000Rp per day.

Tent, sleeping bag and stove can be hired in Senaru through the **Rinjani Trek Centre** (RTC; ☎ 08681-212 6187). You'll need solid footwear, several layers of clothing, wet-weather gear, water and a flashlight. It is best to buy food in Mataram or Senggigi, where it's cheaper

and there's more choice, but some provisions are available in Senaru.

Tetebatu

On the southern slopes of Gunung Rinjani, Tetebatu is a lovely, cool mountain retreat. A shady, 4km path from the main road in the village leads to a **Monkey Forest** (admission free). The **Air Terjun Jukut** (admission 1500Rp) waterfall is a steep 2km walk from the car park at the end of the road and is said to increase hair growth.

At the northern end of the road, **Soedjono Hotel** (r 40,000Rp; ⛾) is in a colonial-era building with great views.

Pondok Wisata Mekar Sari, Onong Homestay and Wisma Diwi Enjeni are all fine and are almost identical in standard and price (singles/doubles 30,000/40,000Rp).

KUTA
☎ 0370

Like the alter-ego of its Balinese namesake, Lombok's Kuta Beach is a tranquil stretch of sand and turquoise sea, where surfers and fishermen share the waves and nothing much else happens. Plans for a cluster of resorts amid the rice paddies have fizzled, preserving the laid-back village character of Kuta, which is ringed by dry, rugged hills. The place comes alive only in high season in August and during the annual *nyale* (a type of sea worm) fishing festival during February or March. For the rest of the year, it's a great place to just kick back, relax and watch the water buffalos.

Information

Several places change money, including the Kuta Indah Hotel and **Segara Anak Cottages** (☎ 654846; segarecottages@hotmail.com), which is also a postal agency. There is a small *wartel* in town and several places have Internet access at 500Rp a minute, including **Anda Cottages** (☎ 654836) and Segara Anak Cottages.

Dangers & Annoyances

Women have reported being hassled and spied on, so you should check your room for peepholes.

Activities
SURFING

Good waves break on the reefs off Kuta and east of **Tanjung Aan**. Boatmen will take you out for around 40,000Rp. About 7km east of Kuta is the fishing village of **Gerupak**, where locals may levy a small entry fee at the village gate. There are several potential breaks on the reefs here, and plenty of breaks further out, but nearly all require a boat, at a negotiable 200,000Rp per day.

For surfing tips, repairs and board rentals (25,000Rp per day), visit Ocean Blue surf shop or Surf Shop Island.

Sleeping & Eating

While tourism numbers are down, standards can slip, so have a good look around and bargain hard. Most have their own restaurants; room rates usually include breakfast.

Matahari Inn (☎ 655000; www.matahariinn.com; d from 75,000Rp; ✕ ☎) Worth the splurge and sometimes good for a discount, this hotel-style place with swimming pool has stylish rooms and bungalows set in a garden where stone sculptures are hidden amid bamboo thickets. The best rooms cost 250,000Rp.

Puri Rinjani (☎ 654849; d from 75,000Rp; ✕) This newly refurbished place at the far end of the beach road has brand-new, sparkling bungalows and an open-sided stilt restaurant (open for breakfast, lunch and dinner) with water views and topnotch *ikan bakar*. Air-con rooms cost 135,000Rp.

Anda Cottages (☎ 654836; s/d 30,000/40,000Rp; ☐) Built around a spacious garden, these cottages next door aren't a bad choice, but take a good look as standards vary. The small restaurant (open for breakfast, lunch and dinner) has tasty food and there are Internet facilities.

Segara Anak Cottages (☎ 654846; segare cottages@hotmail.com; s/d 30,000/40,0000Rp) This beachfront place has good rooms and bungalows with mosquito nets. The lively café (open for breakfast, lunch and dinner) has cable TV and Internet access, and the Perama office arranges bus trips.

Sekar Kuning Bungalows (☎ 654856; s/d 25,000/35,000Rp; ☐) Next to the Anda, this is a clean operation with big beds, mosquito nets and small balconies. Larger rooms with fan go for 50,000Rp.

Surfer's Inn (☎ 655582; lombok_hotel@yahoo.com; d from 90,000Rp; ✕ ☎) Brazilian- and Japanese-run, this new beachside place flies a pirate flag, and boasts a swimming pool with an ice-cream bar as well as some eclectic but colourful architecture.

G'day Inn (☎ 655432; s/d 30,000/40,000Rp) A little inland, this five-room place is popular for its tip-top home cooking, which includes free omelettes for breakfast. The English-speaking owners are helpful and offer free surfing lessons.

Lamancha Homestay (d from 30,000Rp) This is a family-run place 100m along the road that runs inland from the beach. The three bungalows here are clean and a reasonable choice if you want to really get away from it all. There's a café next door.

Cafe Riviera (dishes from 12,000Rp ✕ breakfast, lunch & dinner) Opposite the Matahari Inn, Riviera specialises in filling the bellies of hungry surfers. You'll find *warung* and food carts on the esplanade.

Getting There & Away

Infrequent public *bemo* go directly to Kuta from Mataram's Mandalika terminal (6000Rp), but usually you'll have to change in Praya. Travel early or you may get stuck.

Perama (☎ 654846), based at Segara Anak Cottages, has daily 9am tourist shuttle buses to Mataram (two hours) and Senggigi (70,000Rp, 2½ hours), the Gilis (110,000Rp, 3½ hours) and Kuta Beach, Bali (140,000Rp, 6½ hours).

LABUHAN LOMBOK

The only reason to visit this scruffy town is to catch a ferry to Sumbawa (see p274).

Try to arrive early and avoid staying overnight. If you're stuck here, the best option is **Hotel Melati Lima Tiga** (d 40,000Rp) on the road to the port.

Frequent buses and *bemo* travel between Labuhan Lombok and Mandalika terminal (8000Rp).

SUMBAWA

A dry island of rugged peaks and volcanic stumps looming out of the waters between Lombok and Flores, Sumbawa is easily left off travel itineraries. Few people spend longer on the island than the 12 hours it takes to cross in a night bus. But while Sumbawa makes few concessions to travellers, it is the ideal place to head into the unknown and break new trails. With sublime scenery, superb south coast beaches and isolated villages, Sumbawa rewards those who tolerate its uncomfortable buses with a glimpse of an otherwise little-known Indonesia.

TRANSPORT
Getting There & Away
AIR

Merpati flies between Mataram and Sumbawa Besar, but Bima is the main hub with direct flights to Denpasar, Mataram and Labuanbajo, and a (less reliable) hop to Ruteng and Kupang.

BOAT

Ferries from Poto Tano depart for Lombok every two hours around the clock. In the east, Sape is the departure point for daily ferries to Flores. Pelni ships call at Badas port, Sumbawa Besar and go from Bima to Makassar and Bali.

BUS

Big air-con buses run from Mataram right to Bima, where they hook up with smaller shuttles to the Flores ferry at Sape. If you stay in Bima, you may have to leave before dawn to make the Flores ferry.

POTO TANO

The port for ferries to/from Lombok is a straggle of stilt houses beside a mangrove-lined bay, 2km from Sumbawa's single main highway. Most travellers pass straight through to Sumbawa Besar, but you can also head into town, catch a bus to Taliwang, then another 30km south to the superb surf beach at Maluk, a village on the move due to a huge goldmine that has opened nearby. A number of *losmen*, such as **Surya Beach Bungalows** (Jl Pasir Putih; d 40,000Rp) have sprung up here to cater to the tourist trade.

Ferries run regularly between Lombok and Poto Tano; see p274. The through buses from Mataram to Sumbawa Besar or Bima include the ferry fare.

Buses also meet the ferry and go to Taliwang (5000Rp, one hour) and Sumbawa Besar (7000Rp, two hours).

Buses run all day between Taliwang and Maluk (6000Rp, 1½ hours).

SUMBAWA BESAR
☎ 0371 / pop 100,000

Sumbawa Besar is the chief town on the western half of the island. It's a laid-back place where *cidomo* still outnumber *bemo* and the mosques are busy on Friday. The chief attraction is the **Dalam Loka**, the barn-like and crumbling Sultan's Palace, just off Jl Sudirman.

Information

BNI bank (Jl Kartini 10) Has an ATM and changes money.
Gaul Net Café (☎ 626110; Jl Setiabudi 14; per hr 11,000Rp) The last Internet café until Ende.
Post office (Jl Garuda)
Telkom (Jl Setiabudi; ☒ 24hr)
Tourist office (☎ 23714; Jl Bungur 1; ☒ 7am-1pm Mon-Sat, until 11am Fri) About 3km from town, past the post office.

Sleeping & Eating

Hotel Dewi (☎ 21170; Jl Hasanuddin 60; d from 25,000Rp; ☒) Sparkling tiles and a welcoming atmosphere make this a good all-rounder. The cheapest rooms are basic, but air-con comes cheap if you've had your fix of Sumbawan sunshine.

Hotel Tambora (☎ 21555; Jl Kebayan; s/d from 27,500/41,250Rp; ☒) This clean and friendly place is an old travellers' favourite with a wide range of rooms, all the way up to a 253,000Rp suite, a good restaurant (open for breakfast, lunch and dinner) and an ATM next door.

Hotel Suci (☎ 21589; Jl Hasanuddin 59; d 35,000Rp; ☒) The 17 old rooms need a face-lift, but the leafy courtyard setting is pleasant and a swish new wing offers TV and air-con for willing splurgers (doubles 100,000Rp).

Losmen Garoto (☎ 22062; Jl Batu Pasak 48; d 30,000Rp) Class isn't on offer here – the place is all but falling apart, but then it's dirt-cheap, friendly and only a hop and a skip from the sultan's palace.

Rumah Makan Mushin (Jl Wahidin 31; dishes 8000Rp; ☒ breakfast, lunch & dinner) This spotless little café has very tasty Lombok/Taliwang dishes.

Aneka Rasa Jaya (Jl Hasanuddin 14; dishes 20,000Rp; ☒ lunch & dinner) Excellent for Chinese food.

There is a **supermarket** (Jl Sudirman 3).

Warung set up in front of the stadium on Jl Yos Sudarso.

Getting There & Away
AIR

Merpati (☎ 22002; Jl Yos Sudarso 16) flies Thursday and Sunday at 1pm to Mataram (257,000Rp) and on to Denpasar (360,000Rp).

INDONESIA

BOAT

Pelni's *Tatamailau* stops at Badas port, 7km west of Sumbawa Besar, on the way to Sulawesi or Bali. The *Wilis* sails to Labuanbajo, Waingapu and other Nusa Tenggara ports; and in the reverse direction to Surabaya. The Pelni office is at Labuhan Sumbawa, 3km west of town.

BUS

Sumbawa Besar's main long-distance bus station is the Sumurpayung terminal at Karang Dima, 5.5km northwest of town. Some mornings buses to Bima leave from the **Brang Bara station** (Jl Kaharuddin). Fares and journey times from Sumbawa Besar for local buses: Sape (29,500Rp, 7½ hours), Bima (25,000Rp, seven hours), Dompu (20,000Rp, 4½ hours), Taliwang (10,000Rp, three hours), and Poto Tano (7000Rp, two hours). Deluxe, air-con buses run through to Bima and Lombok. Hotels can book them the day before.

PULAU MOYO

Two-thirds of Pulau Moyo, 3km off Sumbawa's north coast, is a reserve noted for its abundant marine life. Boat tours between Lombok and Flores stop on the north of the island. Boats can also be chartered to Tanjung Pasir from Air Bari, 30 minutes north of Sumbawa Besar.

HU'U

Sumbawa's south coast has some beautiful beaches and good surf. The gorgeous white-sand beach of Hu'u, south of Dompu, is Sumbawa's surfing Mecca. Hu'u has about a dozen places to stay, from budget to mid-range. The venerable **Intan Lestari** (huts from 30,000Rp)is one of the original surf camps.

Getting to Hu'u by public transport is a major headache. From Dompu's Ginte bus station take a *bemo* to the hospital, then a *cidomo* to the Lepardi bus station, then an infrequent bus to Rasabau (5000Rp, 1½ hours) and finally a crowded *bemo* to the beach. Most visitors come here by chartered taxi from Bima Airport (an almighty 250,000Rp!).

BIMA & RABA

☎ 0374 / pop 100,000

This sleepy twin city is Sumbawa's main port and the major centre on the eastern end of the island. It's really just a stop on the way through Sumbawa. If you're killing time here, take a walk around the picturesque harbour.

Orientation & Information

Bima's airport is 16km out of town; it's 25,000Rp by taxi.

BNI bank (Jl Sultan Hasanuddin) Changes cash and travellers cheques and has the last reliable ATM until Ende, on Flores.

Tourist office (☎ 44331; Jl Soekarno-Hatta; ⏱ 7am-3pm Mon-Fri, until noon Sat) About 2km east of the town centre in Raba.

Sleeping & Eating

Most hotels are in the middle of Bima, near the market.

Hotel Lila Graha (☎ 42740; Jl Sumbawa 4; d from 60,000Rp; ⊠) The labyrinthine passages here have more types of room than there are names for. The TV boasts English-language cable channels; there's also a restaurant.

Hotel La'mbitu (☎ 42222; d from 71,500Rp; ⊠) Next door to the Lila Graha, this new place is convenient and a touch more upmarket.

Wisma Komodo (☎ 42070; Jl Sultan Ibrahim; d 30,000Rp) Next to the palace, this is a deserted budget option, but only if you don't mind crude graffiti on your bedroom walls.

Rumah Makan Taliwang Perdana (Jl Sultan Hasanuddin; ⏱ breakfast, lunch & dinner) Specialises in zingy Taliwang chicken, and a good bet after the restaurant at Lila Graha.

Pasar (btwn Jl Flores & Jl Sumbawa; ⏱ lunch & dinner) The best bet for varied, supercheap nosh.

Getting There & Away

AIR

Merpati (☎ 44221; Jl Soekarno-Hatta 60) is east of the town centre and flies daily to Mataram (628,000Rp), Denpasar (410,000Rp), Surabaya (585,000Rp) and Jakarta (900,000Rp).

Pelita Air (☎ 43737; Jl Hasanuddin 16) flies three times a week to Denpasar (457,000Rp), Surabaya (650,000Rp), Yogyakarta (771,000Rp), Bandung (1,141,000Rp), Ende (429,500Rp) and Kupang (600,000Rp).

BOAT

Pelni (☎ 42625; Jl Kesatria 2), at Bima's port, has sailings to Java, Lombok and Flores.

BUS

Buses to points west of Bima leave from the central bus station, just south of town. Day buses to Sumbawa Besar cost 10,000Rp. Express, air-con night bus agencies near the station sell tickets to Sumbawa Besar (25,000Rp, six hours) and Mataram (normal/air-con 65,000/95,000Rp, 11 hours). Most buses to Mataram leave around 7.30pm.

Buses to Sape (5000Rp, two hours) depart from Kumbe in Raba, a 20-minute *bemo* ride east of Bima, but they can't be relied upon to meet the early morning ferry to Flores. You may have to charter a predawn *bemo* to Sape (about 100,000Rp, two hours) to make the 8am ferry.

SAPE
☎ 0374

The only real reason to visit Sape is to catch the ferry to Labuanbajo, Flores, from Pelabuhan Sape, the small port 3km from town. Travellers have reported a growing number of scams in the port area. If you are told the ferry is cancelled and then offered a small boat ride to Komodo, think twice. Some of these shaky and dangerous vessels have sunk, with tourists on board.

The **PHPA Komodo information office** (☒ 8am-2pm) is near the port.

For a bed, **Losmen Mutiara** (☎ 71337; d from 25,000Rp), just outside the port entrance, is convenient but noisy. **Losmen Friendship** (☎ 71006; Jl Pelabuhan; d from 20,000Rp) does its name proud and can organise snorkelling trips.

Buses go to Sape (7500Rp, two hours) from the Kumbe terminal in Bima-Raba, though you may have to charter a predawn *bemo* (100,000Rp) to make the 8am ferry to Flores.

Ferries to Labuanbajo (25,000Rp, eight hours) leave **Pelabuhan Sape** (☎ 71075) at 8am Friday to Wednesday and 4pm Thursday. They no longer stop at Komodo.

Ships leave for Sumba (seven to eight hours) on Thursday and Friday at 8pm. Schedules change often and delays are frequent, so be prepared to while the day away at the dock.

KOMODO & RINCA

Desolate and washed by the churning rip tides between Sumbawa and Flores, Komodo and Rinca are stepping-stones back into another time. Ruggedly beautiful and largely unspoilt, these World Heritage sites are home to giant lizards, appropriately known as Komodo dragons.

The only village on Komodo is **Kampung Komodo** on the east coast.

The Loh Liang park headquarters is the gateway to Komodo, with a pier where boat tours drop you off. **Loh Liang** is on the north end of a sheltered bay on the east coast, half an hour's walk north of Kampung Komodo. There are stilted huts (doubles Rp35,000), information centre, cafeteria, snorkelling and several hiking trails (from 2km to 9km).

Quieter Rinca island has a PHPA camp at Loh Buaya. Permits cost 20,000Rp per person. For more information, visit the **PHPA Office** (☎ 0385-41005; www.komodonationalpark.org; Jl Yos Sudarso) in Labuanbajo.

Loh Liang's **PHPA camp** (d from 35,000Rp) has clean wooden cabins. In July/August the rooms may be full, but the PHPA will rustle up spare mattresses. Accommodation on Rinca is similar. The camp restaurants are very basic, so bring supplies.

Getting There & Away

Sape–Labuanbajo ferries no longer stop at Komodo. Instead, operators run expensive

---

DRAGON SPOTTING

Komodo's gargantuan monitor lizards (*ora*) grow up to 3m long and can weigh in at a whopping 100kg. These prehistoric beasts feed on pigs, deer and buffalo. A bite from their septic jaws is almost certain to kill their prey in a few days, through blood-poisoning.

Banu Nggulung, a dry river bed a half-hour walk from Loh Liang, is the most accessible place to see dragons on Komodo. It has been set up like a theatre, though the gruesome ritual of feeding live goats to the reptiles has been stopped. On Rinca, dragons will often congregate near the PHPA post when the rangers are cooking, or guides will take you to their favourite lizard hide-outs.

Spotting dragons is no longer guaranteed, but a few of these fabulous beasties are usually around – especially around watering holes in the June-September dry season. They rarely venture into the midday sun, so get to the islands early. A guide costs 10,000Rp per person.

INDONESIA

three- and five-day tours out of Lombok (see p274). Boats can also be chartered for day trips from Labuanbajo (Rinca return for six people from 250,000Rp, two hours each way; Komodo return from 400,000Rp – this would be a long day trip). Ask at the hotels or around the harbour, but make sure the boat looks seaworthy.

AROUND KOMODO

Most visitors only stay to see the dragons, but Komodo has plenty of other activities, such as walks to **Poreng Valley** and **Loh Sabita**. **Gunung Ara** can be climbed (3½ hours return), and there's good snorkelling at **Pantai Merah** (Red Beach) and the small island of **Lasa**, near Kampung Komodo. The PHPA rents snorkels and masks for 50,000Rp.

FLORES

Wild, green, beautiful Flores feels more like a stride towards the ends of the earth than a step towards Australia. The name – 'flowers' in Portuguese – promises beauty, and Flores more than delivers, offering a dizzying range of volcanoes, pristine offshore beaches and, for those with hangovers from Java, Bali and the Gilis, some great opportunities to unwind. Colonised by the Portuguese, Flores is still largely Catholic, and the island's pot-holed roads and tiny villages are peppered with makeshift shrines and wood and tin churches. The main draw is the coloured volcanic lakes of Kelimutu near Moni. Labuanbajo is a popular place to kick back for a few days and has decent beaches. Bajawa is the place to visit nearby traditional villages.

TRANSPORT
Getting There & Away
AIR

Maumere is Flores' main airport. Ende, Ruteng and Labuanbajo are also serviced by flights that are often cancelled. Book well in advance and always reconfirm.

Merpati flies daily from Maumere to Denpasar and three times a week to Kupang. Other useful flights include Maumere to Waingapu and Tambolaka. Pelita Air flies a regular loop to Kupang and to destinations in Java.

BOAT

Daily ferries connect Labuanbajo with Sape, Sumbawa. From Larantuka, ferries go to Kupang and Pulau Solor and Pulau Alor. From Ende and Aimere, boats will take you to Waingapu.

Pelni ships provide some useful, though rare links, including Labuanbajo–Waingapu, Ende–Waingapu, Ende–Kupang, Maumere–Makassar, Labuanbajo–Makassar and the Larantuka–Kupang link.

Getting Around

The scenic, single-track Trans-Flores Hwy loops and tumbles for 700 paved kilometres from Labuanbajo to Larantuka. Cheap, cramped public buses run regularly (when full), but big air-con luxury buses don't exist on Flores. Many tourists hire a car and driver. Trips start from $30 a day for two passengers, including petrol, or more with more people. You need to negotiate and customise your trip. Ask at the Golo Hilltop (opposite) in Labuanbajo or the Gardena Hotel (p297) in Maumere.

THE LITTLE PEOPLE OF FLORES

The Manggarai people of Flores have long told folktales of child-sized, hairy people with flat foreheads who roamed the island's deep jungles during the times of their distant ancestors. No-one paid them much attention – until September 2003, when archaeologists made a stunning find.

Digging through the limestone cave at Liang Bua, they unearthed a skeleton that was the size of a preschooler but had the worn-down teeth and bone structure of an adult. Six more remains confirmed the theory: The team had stumbled upon a new species of human, *Homo floresiensis*. They unkindly dubbed the 1m-tall pygmy lady 'Hobbit'.

Lab tests brought another surprise: The pint-sized female with the nutcracker jaw, overlength arms and chimp-sized brain lived just 18,000 years ago, a blip on the scale of human evolution. Hobbit-girl and friends may have lived on Flores just 13,000 years ago, practically yesterday in evolutionary terms. Only then did *Homo sapiens* arrive and – being taller, smarter and better at the harsh survival game – decide to vote the little people off the island and into extinction.

The flat, coastal 'Trans-Northern Hwy' now runs from Maumere to Riung.

LABUANBAJO
☎ 0385

More than just a Komodo beachhead, the cute little fishing harbour of Labuanbajo enjoys a beautiful setting and glorious sunsets over countless scattered islands. There is plenty of marine life to be enjoyed, with snorkel and fin, or knife and fork. Whatever your preference, it's a great place to throw away your watch, screw up your schedule and take time out from the road.

Information
The Telkom office is near the tourist office.

BNI bank (Jl Yos Sudarso) Changes money, but does not have an ATM.

BRI bank (Jl Yos Sudarso) Changes money, but also has no ATM.

Post office (Jl Yos Sudarso)

Puskemas Labuanbajo (☎ 41114; Jl Prof WZ Johanes) Offers basic, 24-hour medical care.

Reefseekers (☎ 41443; www.reefseekers.net) One of a few main-street dive shops.

Tourist office (☎ 41170; Jl IY Kasimo; ☯ 8am-2pm Mon-Sat, until 11am Fri) On the airport road.

Tours
Boat tours to Komodo, Rinca and other islands are easily arranged. Many hotels and various 'tourist information centres' organise day trips to Komodo (around 500,000Rp) or Rinca (300,000Rp) for up to six people; gives you about three hours on the island.

A two-day tour to Komodo, Rinca and Kalong for up to eight people starts at around 700,000Rp per person on a fishing boat (sleeping overnight on board). Make sure the boat is not too small – there have been shipwrecks, which the tourists on board were lucky to survive.

For trips via the dragon islands to Lombok, shop around and find out exactly what is included in the price; admission fees, equipment and bus transfers to Mataram may or may not be covered. **Perama** (☎ 41114; Bajo Beach Hotel, Jl Yos Sudarso) boats stop at the islands on their two-day trips to Lombok (deck/cabin 500,000/700,00Rp), which run every six days. They visit Komodo when sailing east and Rinca when heading west. They also stop for snorkelling and offer good food and freshwater showers.

Boats can also be chartered at reasonable rates to Bidadari, Sabola and other small islands for snorkelling. Waecicu Beach is a good place to organise boats.

Sleeping
Competition is cut-throat – rates are extremely variable and negotiable.

Golo Hilltop (☎ 41337; www.golohilltop.com; s/d 60,000/75,000Rp; ❁) You'll be hard-pressed to beat the vistas at Golo Hilltop, where sublime sunsets come as standard. Rooms with air-con start at 120,000Rp. It's 1.5km northeast up the steep coast road, near the cliff-top Paradise Bar.

Gardena Bungalows & Restaurant (☎ 41258; Jl Yos Sudarso; s/d from 40,000/80,000Rp) In a tin-roof town, the Gardena is one of the most attractive places to stay, with a spread of cosy, traditional-style bungalows with views out to the chugging fishing boats.

Chez Felix (☎ 41032; Jl Prof WZ Johanes; s/d 65,000/75,000Rp) With a restaurant (open for breakfast, lunch and dinner) tinkering on a hill a five-minute walk above the harbour, Chez Felix has fab views, fair food and friendly staff.

Hotel Mutiara (☎ 41383; Jl Yos Sudarso; s/d from 30,000/40,000Rp; ❁) A rambling wooden place on the seashore, this is the spot to indulge in some authentic Labuanbajo living. Rooms come with breakfast and maritime smells aplenty. Double the tariff for air-con.

Waecicu Beach Hotel (bungalows per person 50,000Rp) This is one of a number of beach hotels outside the town (most of these hotels are reached by boat, which is free for guests). Waecicu is a 20-minute boat ride north of Labuanbajo.

Eating
Labuanbajo has a few good restaurants specialising in touristy seafood at reasonable prices.

Dewata Ayu (☎ 41304; Jl Yos Sudarso; dishes 20,000Rp; ☯ breakfast, lunch & dinner) This pleasant spot is awash with blooming flowers, Balinese style and romantic charm. The East-meets-West menu features baby shark.

Borobudur (☎ 41215; Jl Yos Sudarso; ☯ breakfast, lunch & dinner) Nearby Borobudur is slightly larger, slightly rougher and ever-so-slightly cheaper.

Rumah Makan Palapa (☎ 41418; Jl Yos Sudarso; mains 10,000Rp; ☯ breakfast, lunch & dinner) This *masakan Padang* does a fine spread of fish dishes.

Getting There & Away

AIR

Merpati (☎ 21147) flies to Denpasar (556,000Rp) five times a week. The flights are direct on Monday at 3pm, Thursday at noon and Saturday at 11am, and via Bima on Tuesday and Friday at 9am. The Merpati office is 1.5km from town and 1km before the airport.

BOAT

The daily Labuanbajo–Sape ferry (25,000Rp, eight hours) usually leaves at 8am. Boats also leave for Sulawesi on Wednesday and Saturday.

The new Pelni terminal is just south of the ferry pier. Its ships sail to Waingapu, Ende, Sabu, Kupang (and Surabaya in the other direction) and Makassar.

BUS

Buses make the trip to Ruteng (20,000Rp, four hours), Bajawa (40,000Rp, 10 hours) and even Ende (65,000Rp, 14 hours). Most leave around 7am.

Buana Mas Transport (☎ 41540; Toko Pulau Mas Elektronik, Jl Soekarno-Hatta) has newer medium-sized buses that run all the way to Maumere (95,000Rp, 19 hours).

A car with a driver starts at 300,000Rp per day, including fuel and all the driver's expenses.

RUTENG
☎ 0385 / pop 100,000

Highland town Ruteng, home to the Manggarai people, is basically just an excuse to get off the bus and nurse sore bottoms. **Compang Ruteng**, 3km southwest, is a semi-traditional village and **Gunung Ranaka** is an active volcano, just outside town.

Information

There is no Internet access in town.
BNI bank (Jl Kartini) Has the best rates.
BRI bank (Jl Sudarso) Note that the ATM here may not work.
Post office (Jl Dewi Sartika 6; ⏰ 7am-2pm Mon-Sat)

Sleeping

Hotel Dahlia (☎ 21377; Jl Bhayangkara; d from 50,000Rp) The top place in town, near the Merlin restaurant, this place has some clean

and good-value economy options, in rooms set around a central garden.

Hotel Rima (☎ 22196; Jl A Yani 14; s/d/tr 40,000/ 50,000/60,000Rp) This comfy, alpine-style place would look more at home in Switzerland. It has snug rooms and a spectacularly kitsch painting of some very bloodthirsty Komodo dragons.

Losmen Agung I (☎ 21080; Jl Waeces 10; d from 50,000Rp) Don't be put off by the scary pink décor in this place, built in colonial style. The staff are cheerful and you won't lose sleep over the rooms. VIP rooms are 75,000Rp.

Hotel Sinda (☎ 21197; Jl Yos Sudarso 26; d with shared/private mandi 30,000/45,000Rp) This hotel is central and a decent stand-by with a nice garden. Rooms are bedraggled, but at least it tries to be backpacker-friendly.

Eating

Ruteng has some good Chinese and seafood restaurants.

Bamboo Den (Jl Motang Rua; dishes 8000Rp; ⏰ lunch & dinner) Serves fried chicken and satay.

Restaurant Merlin (Jl Bhayangkara 14; dishes 10,000Rp; ⏰ lunch & dinner) Cosy and friendly, with Indonesian and European meals.

Getting There & Away

Merpati (☎ 21197) flies five times a week to Kupang (552,000Rp), but services are often cancelled in this foggy town, where a small plane wreck sits rusting in a field as a reminder of the dangers of flying.

Most buses to Labuanbajo (20,000Rp, four hours), Bajawa (20,000Rp, five hours) and Ende (35,500Rp, nine hours) leave around 7.30am and can be hailed on the street.

Buana Mas (☎ 21302; Jl Bhayangkara 14) runs medium-sized buses to both ends of Flores, including Bajawa (25,000Rp), Ende (50,000Rp) and Maumere (70,000Rp).

Puspa Sari has a useful bus that leaves for Bajawa at 4pm (20,000Rp, five hours). Tickets can be booked through hotels or **Agen Pusat** (☎ 21058; Jl Jagu 1).

BAJAWA
☎ 0384

A pleasant little hill town, Bajawa is the centre for the Ngada people, whose traditional villages lie scattered across this plateau beneath the volcanic Gunung Inerie. The old villages have fascinating traditional houses and *ngadhu* – carved poles supporting a conical thatched roof. **Bena**, 19km south of Bajawa, is one of the most spectacular villages. **Bela**, **Nage** and **Wogo** are also interesting. Guides hang out at the hotels and arrange day trips, asking 100,000Rp per person with transport, village entry fees and lunch.

Information

The BNI bank, just off Jl Basuki Rahmat, is the best place to change money, but the ATM was not working at the time of writing.
RSUD Bajawa Hospital (☎ 21030; Jl Diponegoro) Can deal with medical emergencies.
Telkom office (☎ 21218; Jl Soekarno Hatta) The Internet computers were offline at the time of writing.
Tourist office (☎ 21554; Jl Soekarno Hatta; ❧ 8am-2pm Mon-Sat, until 11am Fri) Worth a quick visit.

Sleeping & Eating

Edelweis (☎ 21345; Jl Ahmad Yani 76; d 82,500Rp) Sculpted hedgerows, a fair dose of homely charm and secure but small and spotty rooms are the staple here. Despite the name, there's not a cuckoo clock in sight.

Hotel Korina (☎ 21162; Jl Ahmad Yani 81; d 82,500Rp) Across the road from the Edelweis, this friendly family-run place has a range of clean and comfortable rooms, and a shop and the Lucas Restaurant nearby.

Hotel Kembang (☎ 21072; Jl Marta Dinata 18; d from 75,000Rp) This has plush and clean rooms around a garden, but prices are high for what's on offer. The better 100,000Rp rooms come with carpet and rolls of toilet paper.

Hotel Ariesta (☎ 21292; cnr Jl Diponegoro & Jl Muh Meang; d 60,000Rp) An excellent option in a quiet area, this hotel sports bright rooms and disarmingly friendly staff. The embroidered landscapes on the walls add a cheesy mountain charm.

Hotel & Restaurant Nusantara (☎ 21357; Jl Eltari 10; s/d 25,000/50,000Rp) This has a good eatery (open for breakfast, lunch and dinner), a ping-pong table and 16 so-so rooms at bank-friendly prices.

Hotel Anggrek (☎ 21172; Jl Letjend Haryono 9; s/d 30,000/40,000Rp) This is a good place for a laugh and local gossip, but it can get loud at night. The rooms could do with a few more windows.

Camellia (☎ 21458; Jl Ahmad Yani 74; mains 16,000Rp; ❧ breakfast, lunch & dinner) The liveliest eatery in town, with the calling cards of countless tour groups to prove it. Plastic flowers provide the colour.

Lucas Restaurant (☎ 21340; Jl Ahmad Yani 6; mains 12,000Rp; ❧ breakfast, lunch & dinner) This is a small, carved-wood place, with an English-speaking owner, tour ideas and some tip-top travellers' tucker. Its pork meals rock.

Getting There & Away

The main Watujaji long-distance bus station is 3km south of town, but hotels arrange bus tickets and pick-ups. Buses to Labuanbajo (40,000Rp, 10 hours) leave around 7am. More frequent buses go to Ruteng (20,000Rp, five hours). Buses to Ende (19,000Rp, five hours) leave at 7am and noon.

Small buses and trucks to surrounding villages depart from the Jl Basuki Rahmat terminal.

RIUNG

Riung, on the coast north of Bajawa, is just a mangrove village, but the offshore islands of the **Pulau Tujuh Belas** (Seventeen Islands) marine park have beautiful white beaches and good snorkelling. The park entrance fee is 10,000Rp per person plus 5000Rp per boat. Increasingly expensive boat trips (per boat per day for three to four people 250,000Rp) are easily arranged in Riung, and the nearby **Bugis stilt house community** is worth a visit. Riung is also home to elusive giant iguanas.

Riung has some basic homestays, which charge around 30,000Rp for a bungalow. **Pondok SVD** (d from 100,000Rp; ❣), or 'Missionaries', offers the best rooms in town, with nice touches like soap, towels and flush toilets.

Nur Iklas is popular, because it's near the Bugis harbour with an English-speaking owner. Liberty, Hotel Florida and the somewhat decrepit Tamri Beach offer similarly cheap rooms and basic food. The simple but decent **Murak Muriah** (❧ breakfast, lunch & dinner) is the only restaurant.

Daily buses run between Riung and Bajawa (15,000Rp, 3½ hours), leaving Bajawa at 8am and noon. Buses from Ende (25,000Rp, five hours) go daily at 6am. Otherwise take a bus to Mbay (15,000Rp, 1½ hours) and then a *bemo* to Riung.

ENDE

☎ 0381 / pop 65,000
The south-coast port of Ende is blessed with a fabulous setting: the flattened volcanic cones of Gunung Meja and Gunung

INDONESIA

Iya loom over the city, and crashing breakers roll in from the Sabu Sea and wash over a coastline of blue stones. Ende was once the main Dutch colony, and Soekarno was exiled here in the 1930s.

Information

BNI bank (Jl Gatot Subroto 5) Changes money and has an ATM.

Hospital (☎ 21031; Jl Prof WZ Yohanes)

Telkom office (Jl Kelimutu 5) Has Internet access.

Tourism office (☎ 21303; Jl Soekarno 4; ☿ 8am-1pm Mon-Sat) Has helpful staff.

Sights

You can visit the house Soekarno lived in, now **Musium Soekarno** (Jl Perwira; admission by donation; ☿ 7am-noon Mon-Sat), though his belongings have been cleared out and moved to Jakarta.

Sleeping & Eating

Hotel Ikhlas (☎ 21695; Jl Ahmad Yani 69; s/d/tr from 20,000/30,000/40,000Rp) Welcoming, with a good backpacker buzz. The rooms err on the side of Spartan, but there's plenty of communal sofa space and a café serving blueprint backpacker fare.

Hotel Safari (☎ 21997; Jl Ahmad Yani 65; s/d from 50,000/60,000Rp; ✣) Next door to Ikhlas, this is a glossier place, with better, quieter rooms, but considerably less bonhomie. Add 30,000Rp for air-con.

Hotel Flores (☎ 21075; Jl Sudirman 28; d from 40,000Rp; ✣) A rambling place near the Telkom office with a range of rooms from good-value budget to newly renovated in a lovely pink, all set around an overgrown garden. Air-con rooms cost 75,000Rp.

Restoran Istana Bambu (☎ 21921; Jl Kemakmuran 30; dishes 20,000Rp; ☿ breakfast, lunch & dinner) Near the sea, Bambu serves some topnotch Chinese seafood. It is traveller-friendly, with a big picture of Kelimutu for decoration and a freezer full of Western ice cream.

Minang Baru (☎ 22055; Jl Soekarno 2; dishes 7000Rp; ☿ breakfast, lunch & dinner) This is a central *masakan Padang*, with tasty local fare and plastic flowers.

Getting There & Away

AIR

Merpati (☎ 21355; Jl Nangka) has daily Kupang flights and connections to Bima and to Denpasar.

Pelita Air (☎ 24400; Jl Kelimutu) flies four times a week to Kupang (359,000Rp), Denpasar (666,000Rp) and Surabaya (845,000Rp).

BOAT

A shipwreck had closed off the main port of **Pelabuhan Ipi** (☎ 21007), 2.5km southeast of town, to large vessels at the time of writing, but it was hoped the wreck could be salvaged. (Dharma Lautan Utama's modern *Kirana II* now runs weekly Kupang–Maumere trips.)

ASDP (☎ 22007) still has an office at Pelabuhan Ipi, but its Waingapu boat (35,000Rp, 10 hours) now leaves from Ende's central port. It sails to Sumba on Friday, returns the next day and continues to Kupang (50,000Rp, 16 hours).

Pelni (☎ 21043; Jl Kathedral 2; ☿ 8am-noon & 2-4pm Mon-Sat) sails fortnightly from Ende to Waingapu, Labuanbajo and Sabu, and between Kupang and Benoa.

BUS

Buses to the east leave from Terminal Wolowana, 4km east of town. Most buses to Moni (15,000Rp, two hours) and Maumere (25,000Rp, five hours) leave around 8am. Maumere buses may drop you in Moni, but charge the full Maumere fare.

Westbound buses leave from Terminal Ndao, 5km north of town, to Bajawa (20,000Rp, five hours), Ruteng (50,000Rp, nine hours) and Labuanbajo (70,000Rp, 14 hours).

KELIMUTU

A sunrise trip up sacred Mt Kelimutu (1600m), with its multicoloured crater lakes, is the highlight of any Flores road trip. Minerals in the water account for the weird, ever-changing colour scheme – most recently turquoise, olive and black.

Most visitors head up at 4am from the foothill village of Moni. If enough tourists are around, a truck or minibus will go for 15,000Rp per person. Otherwise it's by *ojek* (50,000Rp) or chartered *bemo* (150,000Rp). The park entry post, halfway up the road, charges a 1000Rp entry fee, if it's staffed.

You can drive back after sunrise or walk the 13.5km down in about 2½ hours. There's a short cut from just beside the entry post, which comes out by the hot springs and waterfall. It's fine going down, but difficult to find in the dark on your way up.

MONI

Moni is a tranquil village set amid rice fields ringed by brooding volcanic peaks, with sea views in the distance. The air is cool, the pace is slow and things are well set up for travellers. About 2km west of Moni is the turn-off to Kelimutu. Moni has no banks and only one telephone. The Monday market is a major local event.

A good day-trip can be made to **Wolowaru**, 13km south of Moni, and on to the traditional villages of **Ranggase**, **Jopu**, **Wolonjita** and **Nggela**, a pleasant four-hour walk one way from Wolowaru, best done with a guide. Ranggase has interesting traditional houses, and Nggela is a noted weaving centre. Moni buses go to Wolowaru and, at 8am, to Nggela.

Sleeping & Eating

Moni is a popular place to stop for a few days and has a cluster of basic, cheap homestays.

Hidayah (d 40,000Rp) At the western entrance to the village, humble Hidayah has a handful of shaky bamboo huts overlooking a brook and pretty rice fields.

Watugana (s/d 40,000/75,000Rp) Down the steps towards the Monday market, this place has concrete rooms and the best free breakfast in Moni: banana pancake *and* fruit salad.

Maria Inn (d from 50,000Rp) This central place is run by a friendly couple and has basic wooden rooms and concrete bungalows (75,000Rp) in a shambolic farmyard setting. Maria whips up a nightly buffet for 25,000Rp.

Amina Moe (d with shared mandi 15,000Rp) Across from the market, this place has dark rooms in the bowels of an expansive family home. The affable owner, Amina, speaks English (nonstop).

Sao Ria Bungalows (d from 50,000Rp) About 1.5km west of Moni, this state-run place has magic rice-paddy views, but the unenthusiastic staff have let room standards slip.

Flores Sare Hotel (☎ 0381-21075; d from 75,000Rp; ✖) Despite the perpetual scaffolding out the front, this courtyard place 1km east of Moni is the local upmarket option.

The homestays provide simple meals, but for variety and good views, check out the cheerful **Bintang Cafe** (mains 20,000Rp; ❧ breakfast, lunch & dinner) and the **Chenty Restaurant & Pub** (❧ breakfast, lunch & dinner) next door.

Getting There & Away

For Ende (10,000Rp, two hours), buses start around 7am. Other buses come through from Maumere or Wolowaru to Ende until about noon. Late buses come through at around 9pm. Many buses and trucks leave on Monday (market day).

For Maumere (15,000Rp, four hours) buses from Ende start coming through around 8am.

MAUMERE

☎ 0382 / pop 75,000

At the end, or the beginning, of most journeys through Flores, the port of Maumere is an almost inevitable addition to the itinerary, and the best place on Flores to organise your trip, cash up and sort out your email. An important mission centre ever since the Portuguese arrived here 400 years ago, Maumere also has strong *ikat*-weaving traditions.

In December 1992, Maumere was devastated by an earthquake and a 20m tsunami that killed thousands. Although many old colonial buildings were destroyed, few obvious scars remain of the disaster.

Orientation & Information

The airport is 3km out, and a taxi there costs 10,000Rp. *Bemo* around town cost 2000Rp.

BNI bank (Jl Soekarno Hatta 4) Changes money.

Comtelnet Cafe (☎ 22132; Jl Bandeng 1; per hr 12,000Rp; ❧ 8am-9.30pm) Has high-speed satellite Internet access.

Danamon bank (Jl Pasar Baru Barat) Has an ATM.

Post office (Jl Pos; ❧ 8am-2pm Mon-Sat)

Telkom office (Jl Soekarno Hatta 5)

Tourist office (☎ 21652; cnr Jl Melati & Jl Wairklau; ❧ 8am-1pm Mon-Sat) This office is of little use.

Sleeping & Eating

Gardena Hotel (☎ 22644; dino_mof@yahoo.com; Jl Patirangga 28; s/d from 50,000/60,000Rp; ✖) Immaculate, with energetic staff and plenty of space, this is a top place to find English-speaking driver/guides. Ask for Dino Lopez or Hironimus Manek. Air-con costs 20,000Rp more.

Hotel Wini Rai (☎ 21388; Jl Gajah Mada 50; d from 49,500Rp; ✖) Close to the Ende bus station, this place has a pretty garden and rooms that range from cheap and dank to air-con luxury (110,000Rp).

Hotel Lareska (☎ 21137; Jl MGR Sugiyo Pranoto 4; s/d 35,000/45,000Rp) Still relatively new, this hotel has a courtyard with clean rooms that are half-decent but very dark.

Hotel Beng Goan I (☎ 21041; Jl Moa Toda 49; d with shared/private mandi 20,000/50,000Rp; 🖾) A popular hang-out for loitering locals, labyrinthine Beng Goan is big and a bit trashy from the outside but has cheap, clean rooms. The pricier rooms come with air-con.

Hotel Senja Wair Bubuk (☎ 21498; Jl Yos Sudarso 81; d 50,000Rp) Near the sea, this shaky old hotel is the picture of maritime decrepitude, where you can sit and watch the paint peel. The rooms are grubby, and electricity only starts at sunset.

The best place for restaurants is around the main drag, Jl Pasar Baru Barat. The following are recommended:

Borobudur (☎ 22351; Jl Soetomo 5; dishes 12,000Rp; 🍽 breakfast, lunch & dinner) Has Mickey Mouse décor – yes, really – and a menu packed with omelettes, toasted sandwiches and steaks.

Suryah Indah (☎ 21374; Jl Raja Centis; mains 20,000Rp; 🍽 breakfast, lunch & dinner) Hard-to-beat Padang grub.

Getting There & Away
AIR
Maumere has the main airport on Flores.

Merpati (☎ 21342; Jl Don Thomas 18) flies daily to Denpasar (473,500Rp), and to Kupang (359,100Rp) on Tuesday, Thursday and Saturday.

Pelita Air (☎ 21732; Jl Sudirman 33) flies on Monday, Wednesday and Friday to the same destinations, at similar prices, as well as to Waingapu (391,000Rp).

BOAT
Pelni (☎ 21013; Jl MGR Sugiyo Pranoto 4) sails fortnightly to Makassar, and to Kalabahi and Kupang in the other direction.

Several private ships run weekly to Kupang (economy 70,000Rp, 16 hours) and Surabaya (215,000Rp, 50 hours), though schedules change depending on cargo, tides and weather. Check **Dharma Lautan Utama** (☎ 21762; Jl Nong Meak 30), which runs the *Kirana II*, or the agent for the Prima Vista and Tirta Kencana ships at the **Hotel Beng Goan I** (Jl Moa Toda 49).

BUS
Buses and *bemo* travel east to Larantuka (20,000Rp, four hours), Geliting, Waiara,

Ipir and to Wodong, and depart from the Lokaria (or Timur) terminal, which is 3km east of town. Buses go west to Ende (25,000Rp, five hours) via Moni (also 25,000Rp, three hours), Bajawa (50,000Rp, 10 hours), Sikka and Ladalero from the Ende (or Barat) terminal, 1.5km southwest of town.

Buses often endlessly cruise town searching for passengers. Hotels can arrange pickup. **Buana Mas Transport** (Hotel Beng Goan, Jl Moa Toda 49) sells bus tickets.

AROUND MAUMERE
The weaving village of **Sikka** lies 27km south of Maumere, and the Catholic seminary in **Ladalero**, 19km from Maumere on the Ende road, has an interesting museum. Along the north coast, seaside bungalows 25km east of Maumere offer snorkelling and island trips. To the west, there are nice deserted beaches, but the best white-sand getaways are the basic bungalows (singles/doubles 15,000/30,000Rp) on **Paga Beach**, an hour's drive towards Ende on the south coast. They serve basic meals and have kerosene lamps at night.

Waiara & Wairterang
East of Maumere, there are some dive resorts and quiet beachside homestays, with palm-fringed beaches, great corals and superb sunsets. To get there, catch a taxi or the Waigatee–Talibura *bemo* from the Lokaria terminal.

Some 13km east of Maumere, Waiara has scuba diving. **Sea World Club** (☎ 0382-21570; www.sea-world-club.com; s/d from US$15/20; 🖾) is worth a splurge, with uniformed staff and CNN on the box.

The nearby **Sao Wisata** (☎ 0382-21555; s/d from 75,000/100,000Rp; 🖾 🖾) resort lets nonguests use its pool for 15,000Rp.

On **Ahuwair beach**, 25km east of Maumere and off the phone grid, the Australian-run **Sunset Cottages** (sunsetcottages@yahoo.co.uk; s/d 20,000/30,000Rp) has beachside bungalows, island trips, *ikat*-weaving and a great banana-coconut-arak cocktail.

A bit further, **Wodong Beach Cottages** (s/d 35,000/40,000Rp) are fine, if deserted. **Ankermi** (☎ 0382-21100; s/d 30,000/35,000Rp) is a mellow place to kick back, with hammocks for well-earned rubber time. The owner's Swiss wife runs a small dive shop.

LARANTUKA

☎ 0383

This little port, a one-time Portuguese en-clave, nestles at the base of the **Ili Mandiri volcano** at the eastern end of Flores. From here, you can see the islands of Solor and Adonara across the narrow strait. It is pri-marily a place to catch ferries.

The BNI and BRI banks both change money, but there are no ATMs.

Sleeping & Eating

Hotel Rulies (☎ 21198; Jl Yos Sudarso 40; s/d/tr from 35,000/60,000/75,000Rp) Homely and well run, this is a good first stop. English is spoken and there are rooms to suit every budget.

Hotel Tresna (☎ 21072; Jl Yos Sudarso 8; d with shared/private mandi 44,000/66,000Rp; 🕃) Nearby, this place is functional, with air-con options (doubles 99,000Rp).

Rumah Makan Nirwana (Jl Niaga; mains 15,000Rp; 🕃 breakfast, lunch & dinner) This is the only real restaurant in town and serves decent Chi-nese meals.

Warung set up in the evening along Jl Niaga.

Getting There & Away

BOAT

Ferries to Kupang (32,000Rp, 15 hours) leave Monday, Wednesday and Friday at 2pm from Waibulan, 4km southwest of Larantuka (by *bemo* 2500Rp). They leave Kupang on Tuesday, Thursday and Sunday afternoons. Ferries can be crowded, so board early to get a seat.

The slow ASDP ferry to Adonara, Lem-bata and Alor leaves every few days (sched-ules vary). More convenient, smaller boats to Adonara, Solor and Lembata leave from the pier in the centre of town. They run to Lewoleba on Lembata (12,000Rp, four hours) at 7am and noon, stopping at Wai-werang (Adonara) on the way.

Pelni ships calls at Larantuka on their Labuanbajo–Papua and Kupang–Makassar trips.

BUS

Regular buses run between Maumere and Larantuka (20,000Rp, four hours). The main bus station is 5km west of town (1000Rp by *bemo*), but you can pick buses up in the centre. Coming into town, buses can drop you in the centre.

SOLOR & ALOR ARCHIPELAGOS

This chain of volcanic islands separated by swift-running, narrow straits lies off the eastern end of Flores and is reached by ferry from Larantuka. Lembata, in the Solor chain, is of most interest and is where the traditional whaling village of Lamalera can be visited.

Lembata

The sleepy main town of Lewoleba is dominated by the ominous smoking of **Ili Api volcano**. Lewoleba has no banks to ex-change money. Stay at the Dutch-owned **Lile Ile homestay** (s & d 20,000Rp), halfway be-tween the ferry wharf and town, or the central **Hotel Lewoleba** (☎ 41012; Jl Awololong 15; s/d 30,000/45,000Rp; 🕃).

There are basic rooms at the Pak Ben, Abel Beding and Mama Maria homestays.

On the south coast, **Lamalera** is an isolated whaling village, where locals still hunt the sea mammals using small rowboats and hand-thrown harpoons. Being a small-scale subsistence activity, the hunting is considered legal. Villagers take occasional visitors out on a hunt during the May-October whaling season, but this is dangerous, chartering your own boat is recommended – ask in Maumere's **Gardena Hotel** (☎ 22644; dino _mof@yahoo.com; Jl Patirangga 28).

Two trucks a day take five hours to travel from Lembata to Lamalera along a very poor 65km road (25,000Rp). Regular pas-senger ferries run between Larantuka and Lewoleba.

Ferries to Kalabahi (Alor) depart from Lewoleba every two or three days to Balaur-ing (10,000Rp, four hours) in eastern Lem-bata, where they stop for the night before continuing to Kalabahi (32,250Rp, nine hours) the next morning. Balauring has a *losmen*.

Alor

☎ 0386 / pop 170,000

Alor, a remote, rugged and beautiful island within sight of East Timor has more than 50 linguistically different tribal groups. It is famed for its all-night *lego-lego* dances, in which participants enter a trance-like state, and for its strange *moko* drums (see the boxed text, p300). There is also excel-lent diving, best arranged in Kupang (see Tours, p301).

INDONESIA

ALOR'S STRANGE MOKO DRUMS

Thousands of hourglass-shaped bronze drums known as *moko* have been found mysteriously buried all over Alor. They were once traded for human heads and are still highly prized in wedding dowries, sometimes indebting a family for a generation. Researchers believe the drums hail from Vietnam's ancient Dongson culture and were brought by spice traders. Locals say *moko* grew from the earth.

Kalabahi is the chief town and ferry port. Bring enough cash as rates are appalling. The central **Hotel Adi Dharma** (☎ 21280; Jl Martadinata 12; d from 35,000Rp), near the pier, is the best bet, with great views. For tonnes of great information, check out www.alor-island.com, which was set up by German aid group GTZ.

Merpati (☎ 21041) has a 12-seater that flies daily to Kupang (370,000Rp), twice on Wednesday and Sunday. The airport is 10km from town.

The ferry to Kupang (35,000Rp, 20 hours) leaves on Sunday at noon, and Saturday at noon coming the other way. Ferries to Lewoleba and Larantuka (34,800Rp, 20 hours) leave Thursday and Sunday at 8am, and they depart Larantuka Friday and Monday at 2pm. There is also a Tuesday ferry to Atapupu (16,750Rp, nine hours), from where buses run to Kupang.

Pelni ships *Awu* and *Sirimau* also call fortnightly at Kalabahi and sail to Kupang (46,000Rp, 10 hours).

WEST TIMOR

Mountainous and dry, West Timor is a region of contrasts, where some of Indonesia's poorest villagers huddle around Kupang, the 'big city' of eastern Nusa Tenggara. The turbulent events surrounding East Timor's independence pulled the tourist trail out from under West Timor's feet. Few travellers now make it this far, unless they are headed for East Timor or Darwin (Australia).

But from the hot, noisy streets of Kupang to the dry, jagged interior, this is a wild, idiosyncratic region at the very edges of the Indonesian identity. With strong animist beliefs, some Timorese have barely been touched by Indonesian national culture and, in parts, even Bahasa Indonesia remains a foreign tongue.

TRANSPORT
Getting There & Away
AIR

A good way to explore Nusa Tenggara is to fly directly from Bali to Kupang with Merpati or other airlines and then island-hop back. Merpati has also resumed twice-weekly flights from Kupang to Dili and to Darwin, Australia (see opposite).

BOAT

The Perum **ASDP** (☎ 0380-838830; Jl Suprato), based in Kupang, has regular car-and-passenger ferries throughout East Nusa Tenggara. Ferries run from Kupang to Larantuka (Flores), Kalabahi (Alor), Rote and Waingapu (Sumba) via Sabu. From Atapupu, near Atambua in West Timor, a ferry runs once a week to/from Kalabahi. The routes are fairly constant but schedules are constantly changing – check on arrival in Kupang.

Pelni passenger ships *Awu*, *Dobonsolo*, *Sirimau*, *Tatamailau* and *Wilis* connect Kupang with Maumere, Ende, Kalabahi, Larantuka, Sabu and onward destinations.

Getting Around

The good main highway is surfaced all the way from Kupang to East Timor, though the buses are of the cramped, crowded, thumping-disco variety found throughout Nusa Tenggara. Away from the highway,

---

WEST TIMOR SECURITY

In the violent chaos that followed East Timor's 1999 independence, pro-Jakarta militiamen killed three foreign UN workers in the border town of Atambua. Almost five years on, the UN lowered its danger index from Phase IV (Iraq level) to Phase III, allowing normal aid programmes to resume. However, tensions remain, and Australians, especially, may face resentment following their country's military intervention in East Timor. Foreigners were evacuated from Atambua during riots in early 2005.

---

roads are improving but can be impassable in the wet season.

KUPANG
☎ 0380 / pop 210,000
Kupang is the biggest city on the island and capital of Nusa Tenggara Timur (NTT). Compared with the sedate little towns on Flores and Sumba, Kupang feels like a booming metropolis. It's not a bad place to hang around – Captain Bligh did, after his *Bounty* misadventures.

Orientation
Kupang's El Tari airport is 15km east of the city centre. Taxis in cost about 50,000Rp. By public transport, turn left out of the terminal and walk 1km to the junction with the main highway, from where a *bemo* to the city costs 3000Rp. Around town, *bemo* cost 2000Rp.

Information
Kupang is a good place to change money.
BNI bank (Jl Sumatera) Has good rates and an ATM.
Main post office (Jl Palapa 1) Accepts poste restante mail and has Internet facilities.
NTT Tourist Office (☎ 821540; Jl El Tari 338; ☼ 7am-3pm Mon-Thu) Out in the sticks near the bus station.
Telkom office (Jl Urip Sumohardjo 11) Also has Internet facilities.

Sights
Kupang's **Museum NTT** (Jl El Tari; admission free; ☼ 8am-3pm Mon-Sat) is worth a look for its collection of crafts and artefacts from across the province.

Tours
Many fascinating traditional villages can be visited in West Timor, but Indonesian, let alone English, is often not spoken, so a local guide is necessary (around 70,000Rp per day).
Some tour companies:
Dive Alor (☎ 821154; www.divealor.com; Jl Raya El Tari 19) Australian-run, arranges dives around Timor and Alor.
Nusafin (☎ 821086; Jl Sudirman 48)
Pitoby Tours (☎ 832700; Jl Sudirman 136)

Sleeping
Pantai Timur Hotel (☎ 831651; Jl Sumatera; s/d 60,000/90,000Rp; ✷) Recent renovations have given this place a face-lift and the rooms are comfortable, clean and (almost) classy, with TV. Air-con doubles cost 140,000Rp.

SPLURGE!
Maya Beach Hotel (☎ 832169; Jl Sumatera 31; d 115,000Rp; ✷) Back opposite the Pantai Timur Hotel, this offers good value (with all the trimmings) for midrange money, if you fancy a splurge.

Hotel Susi (☎ 822172; Jl Sumatera 37; d 55,000Rp; ✷) Cheap concrete doesn't last long in tropical heat and here is the proof. Still, it's near the water and you can always upgrade to air-con (65,000Rp).
Hotel Laguna Inn (☎ 833559; Jl Kelimutu 36; s/d 30,000/40,000Rp; ✷) You wouldn't want to spend too long hanging out in the boxy rooms here, but they're fine for forty winks and are some of the cheapest in town.
Hotel Marina (☎ 822566; Jl Ahmad Yani 79; d from 45,000Rp; ✷) Welcoming and central, this has a wide range of rooms.

Eating & Drinking
Dog meat *(RW)* is something of a speciality in Kupang's *warung*, the best of which are around the Kota Kupang *bemo* terminal.
Depot Nelayan (Jl Mohammed Hatta 14; mains 20,000Rp; ☼ lunch & dinner) This simple place specialises in Chinese food and grills up a mean *ikan bakar*.
Silvia Steakhouse (Jl Beringin 3; steaks 30,000Rp; ☼ lunch & dinner) The best place to satisfy carnivorous cravings, Silvia offers a kaleidoscope of juicy cuts and cold beer.
Tanjung Restaurant (Jl Timor Timur; ☼ lunch & dinner) This classier affair is causing quite a stir with its Manado cuisine.
L'Avalon (Jl Sumatera) This tiny beachside bar offers some interesting clientele, plenty of booze and wads of useful tourist information.

Getting There & Away
AIR
Merpati (☎ 833833; Jl Ahmad Yani 66) flies to Dili (US$50) on Friday and Sunday at 1pm, and to Darwin, Australia (US$250) on Tuesday and Saturday at 12.45pm. It also has direct flights to Denpasar (829,900Rp), Tambolaka (556,000Rp), Maumere (359,100Rp), Alor (391,000Rp), Ende (381,000Rp) and Jakarta (753,600Rp to 1,637,800Rp).
Star Air (☎ 882040; airport) services are often cheaper, where there are flights to Denpasar

www.lonelyplanet.com

KUPANG

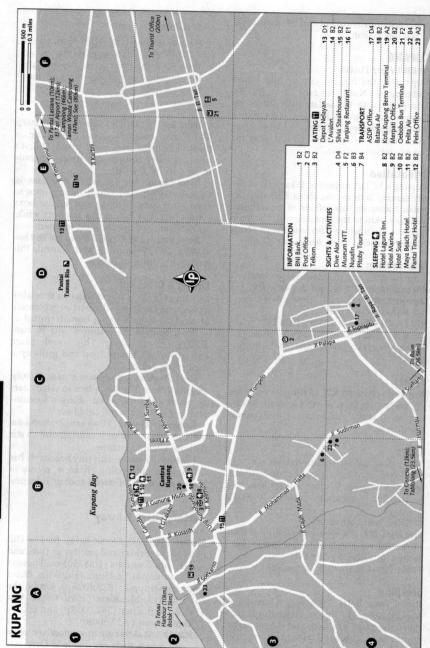

INFORMATION	
BNI Bank	1 B2
Post Office	2 C3
Telkom	3 B2

SIGHTS & ACTIVITIES	
Dive Alor	4 D4
Museum NTT	5 F2
Nusafin	6 B3
Pitoby Tours	7 B4

SLEEPING	
Hotel Laguna Inn	8 B2
Hotel Marina	9 A2
Hotel Susi	10 B2
Maya Beach Hotel	11 B2
Pantai Timur Hotel	12 B2

EATING	
Depot Nelayan	13 D1
L'Avalon	14 B2
Silvia Steakhouse	15 B2
Tanjung Restaurant	16 E1

TRANSPORT	
ASDP Office	17 D4
Batavia Air	18 B2
Kota Kupang Bemo Terminal	19 A2
Merpati Office	20 B2
Oebobo Bus Terminal	21 F2
Pelita Air	22 B4
Pelni Office	23 A2

(430,000Rp), to Surabaya (625,000Rp) and Jakarta (842,000Rp). A number of other domestic airlines also operate out of Kupang, among them **Pelita Air** (☎ 831763; Jl Sudirman) and **Batavia Air** (☎ 830555; Jl Ahmad Yani 73).

BOAT

Pelni (☎ 824357; Jl Pahlawan 3) goes from Kupang to Ende, Kalabahi, Larantuka and Sabu, and ships continue on to many other ports, including those in Sulawesi, Maluku and Papua. Pelni ships leave from Tenau, 10km west of Kupang.

Ferries leave from Bolok, 13km west of Kupang. ASDP has ferries to Larantuka (14 hours), Kalabahi (16 hours) and Ende (16 hours). The Ende ferry continues on to Waingapu (Sumba) and another ferry runs to Kupang–Sabu–Waingapu. Sailings are once or twice a week.

Several larger cargo ships also make twice-monthly trips all the way to Surabaya via ports such as Maumere. Schedules are forever changing – good hotels have the latest schedules.

BUS

Long-distance buses depart from the Oebobo bus station, which is located out near the museum – take a *bemo* 10. Departures include: Soe (20,000Rp, three hours), Niki Niki (18,000Rp, 3½ hours), Kefamenanu (25,000Rp, 5½ hours) and Atambua (35,000Rp, eight hours). *Bemo* to villages around Kupang go from the Kota Kupang Bemo Terminal.

Timor Tour and Travel (Kupang ☎ 881543; Jl TimTim 8; Dili ☎ 670-332 2095; Jl 15 Oktober 17) runs a daily two-way shuttle minibus service with hotel drop-off between Kupang and Dili for US$18. Vehicles are switched at the border.

AROUND KUPANG

Pantai Lasiana, 10km east of town, is a half-decent stretch of sand. **Tablolong**, 27km southwest of Kupang, has a better beach. The small islands of **Pulau Semau** and **Pulau Kera**, just off the coast, are more interesting, and some hotels run day tours.

The small village of **Baun**, 30km south of Kupang in the hilly Amarasi district, is an *ikat*-weaving centre, with a few Dutch buildings. You can visit the *rumah raja*, the last raja's house, now occupied by his widow.

Camplong, which is 46km from Kupang on the Soe road, is a cool, quiet hill town. One kilometre east of the town, the **Taman Wisata Camplong** is a forest reserve that has some caves and a spring-fed swimming pool. As an accommodation option, the church-run **Wisma Oe Mat Honis** (☎ 0380-850006; d 30,000Rp) has good rooms.

ROTE

Rote (also spelled Roti) is Indonesia's southernmost island, with long ties to Timor. Rote is only four hours by ferry from Kupang and receives a steady trickle of surfers in search of the excellent break at **Nemberala**. The west-coast beach is superb, and Nemberala has several cheap *losmen* (Mr Tomas Homestay is the most popular), from 25,000Rp with meals. The **Nemberala Beach Resort** (s/d 60,000/100,000Rp) is more upmarket. You can also stay in the main town of **Baa**.

ASDP ferries run between Kupang and Rote (four hours) daily. Ferries dock at Pantai Baru, from where waiting buses will take you to Baa (1½ hours) or Nemberala (3½ hours).

SOE

☎ 0368

It's on the road from Kupang to Soe that Timor's proximity to Australia becomes most obvious, as the route passes through a landscape reminiscent of the Aussie bush. The town itself is of little interest but the surrounding area is very traditional, and the thatched, beehive-shaped houses of the Dawan people are dotted everywhere. Soe is an excellent place to arrange tours to villages nearby.

The **tourist information centre** (☎ 21149; Jl Diponegoro) can arrange guides, but make sure you change money before arriving as rates are poor.

Sleeping

Hotel Anda (☎ 21149; Jl Kartini 5; s/d 25,000/40,000Rp) A bit run-down, this has to be the most eccentric *losmen* in Indonesia, with gaudy statuary and a dazzling paint job at the front, and a huge, home-made replica of a warship at the back.

Hotel Cahaya (☎ 21087; Jl Kartini 7; s/d 25,000/45,000Rp) A good bet if Hotel Anda is full, and just next door.

INDONESIA

Getting There & Away

The Haumeni bus station is 4km west of town (by *bemo* 3000Rp). Regular buses run from Soe to Kupang (20,000Rp, three hours), Kefamenanu (15,000Rp, 2½ hours) and Oinlasi (10,000Rp, 1½ hours), while *bemo* cover Niki Niki (5000Rp) and Kapan (4000Rp).

AROUND SOE

On market days in the towns, villagers come from miles around, many wearing traditional dress. At the markets, *ikat* weaving and crafts can be found. The Tuesday market at **Oinlasi**, 51km from Soe, is one of the largest, and the Wednesday market at **Niki Niki**, 34km east of Soe, is just as lively and easier to reach.

The main attraction around Soe is **Boti**, a traditional village presided over by a self-styled raja. Christianity never penetrated here, and the raja maintains strict adherence to *adat* (tradition). The village is used to tourists and even gets the occasional tour bus. Buses run to Oinlasi, from where it is 12km on foot along a bad road to Boti. It is best to take a guide who speaks the local dialect. You can stay overnight with the **raja** (r incl meals 50,000Rp).

North of Soe are the **Oehala Waterfall**, the cool hill town of **Kapan**, and **Fatumenasi**, surrounded by highland forest and traditional villages.

KEFAMENANU
☎ 0388

Kefamenanu (Kefa), 217km from Kupang, is cool and quiet with a few colonial buildings. On the outskirts of town, 1.5km south of the bus station, **Maslete** is an interesting traditional village. **Temkessi**, 50km northeast of Kefa, is a more spectacular traditional village, but is very isolated. Kefa is also the gateway to the poor and isolated East Timorese enclave of Oecussi. One of the few overnight options here is the **Hotel Ariesta** (☎ 31007; Jl Basuki Rachmat; d with shared/private mandi 44,000/66,000Rp; ✹).

ATAMBUA
☎ 0389

Atambua is the major town on the overland Dili–Kupang route and a likely stopping point if you are making the visa run over to East Timor (see the boxed text, p273).

Atapupu, 25km away, is a port with a weekly ferry to Kalabahi (Alor). The area around Atambua is home to the matrilineal Tetum (or Belu) people. **Betun**, 60km south of Atambua, has *losmen* and can be used as a base for visiting traditional villages.

In 2000, after East Timor's independence, three UN workers were murdered here by pro-Jakarta militia, and riots broke out in 2005. Ask around in Kupang before travelling here.

In Atambua, stay at the central **Hotel Kalpataru** (☎ 21351; Jl Gatot Subroto 3; s/d with shared mandi 35,000/50,000Rp).

Timor Tour and Travel (☎ 22292; Jl Sukarno 43) arranges shuttle buses to Kupang and Dili.

SUMBA

Local legend recounts how humankind first made landfall on earth by clambering down a giant celestial ladder and touching down on Sumba. Whatever the truth, Sumba remains one of Indonesia's most enigmatic islands. Situated off the archipelago's main sweep, in the Sabu Sea, the former Sandalwood Island has been largely isolated from the cultural forces that make up the Indonesian identity. It remains an ideal destination for those looking to leave the beaten track far behind them.

Known for its large, decorated stone tombs and traditional houses, Sumba is

---

PASOLA FESTIVAL – SUMBA AT WAR

The thrilling, often gruesome mock battles between spear-hurling horsemen during Sumba's Pasola festival are a must for travellers passing through Nusa Tenggara in February and March. The high-energy pageant aims to placate the spirits and restore harmony with the spilling of blood though, happily, blunt spears have been used in recent decades to make the affair less lethal. The ritualistic war kicks off when a sea worm called *nyale* washes up on shore, a phenomenon that also starts the planting season. Call Waingapu or Waikabubak hotels to find out the latest schedules. The festival is generally held in the Lamboya and Kodi districts in February, and at Wanokaka and Gaura in March.

composed of a kaleidoscope of linguistic groups, the leftovers of the small warring tribes that were clashing until the 20th century. These conflicts are still recalled every year during western Sumba's Pasola festivals, when mock battles between mounted warriors often descend into more authentic melees – in 1992, two villages ended up going to war, leaving several dead.

Though Christianity has made inroads, Sumba's isolation has helped preserve some of the country's most ancient animist traditions. You might still see some older people with filed teeth – jagged white teeth were once considered ugly.

TRANSPORT
Getting There & Away
AIR
Merpati flies to Kupang and Denpasar three times a week from Waingapu, and less frequently from Tambolaka in West Sumba. Check changing schedules and book as far ahead as possible.

BOAT
Waingapu is well serviced by ASDP ferries from Ende and Aimere on Flores. Ferries also run to/from Kupang via Sabu.

Pelni has useful services between Ende and Waingapu, and Labuanbajo and Waingapu, and long-distance hops to Lombok and Denpasar.

WAINGAPU
☎ 0387 / pop 25,000
Long forming a centre for the trade in dyewoods, timber and the island's highly prized horses, Waingapu is Sumba's largest town and makes a good base for exploring the surrounding villages.

Orientation & Information
Waingapu has two centres: the older, northern one focuses on the harbour, while the southern one is around the main market and bus station, about 1km inland. *Bemo* from the airport into town, 6km away, cost 2000Rp.

There are no ATMs or Internet access in Waingapu.

BNI bank (Jl Ampera) Near the market.

Post office (Jl Hasanuddin) Located in the old section of the town.

Telkom office (Jl Tjut Nya Dien)

Sleeping & Eating
Most hotels are in the new part of town, near the bus station. Cheap rooms are rare.

Hotel Merlin (☎ 61300; Jl Panjaitan 25; s/d from 88,000/110,000Rp; ✕) Merlin magics up better service and is the top hotel in town. If you really want to splurge, the VIP rooms (132,000Rp) are fit for visiting village warlords. Staff also organise transport.

Hotel Kaliuda (☎ 61264; Jl WJ Lalaimentik 3; s/d 55,000/66,000Rp) Of Waingapu's scattering of cheapies, this is about the best bet, with reasonable rooms and English-speaking staff.

Hotel Sandle Wood (☎ 61887; Jl Panjaitan 23; d with shared/private mandi 66,000/99,000Rp; ✕) This place is pricey, but it stands in leafy grounds and hefty discounts are there for the taking.

Rumah Makan Mini Indah (Jl Ahmad Yani 27; dishes 9000Rp; ☉ breakfast, lunch & dinner) This is a simple place but has very tasty food.

Rumah Makan Nazareth (Jl WY Lalaimentik; mains 15,000Rp; ☉ lunch & dinner) Serving Chinese food, this is the best in town.

Getting There & Away
AIR
Merpati (☎ 61323; Jl Soekarno 4) flies three times a week to Kupang (490,000Rp), and three times weekly to Denpasar (528,500Rp) and on to Surabaya (754,400Rp). There is a weekly flight to Bima (328,300Rp).

BOAT
Schedules change frequently, so check at the **ASDP office** (☎ 61963; Jl Adamalik 85).

A ferry leaves Waingapu for Aimere on Tuesday at 9am (28,000Rp, six hours) and returns from Aimere to Waingapu the same day at 4pm. A ship also leaves Waingapu for Ende (28,000Rp, 13 hours) on Thursday at 4pm and returns from Ende on Friday at 9am. Ferries also run to Sabu (32,000Rp, 17 hours) on Saturday at noon, arriving Sunday at 5am and continuing to Kupang. Pelni ships leave from the Dermaga dock to the west of town (by *bemo* 3500Rp). One ship links Waingapu with Bima and Surabaya, or Larantuka, Kupang and Papua. Another route is from Benoa (Bali) via Lembar (Lombok) to Waingapu, and on to Ende and Kalabahi.

BUS
Buses to Waikabubak (30,000Rp, five hours) leave at 8am, noon and 3pm. Book at the hotels or the agencies opposite the

bus station. Buses also head southeast to Melolo, Rende and Baing.

AROUND WAINGAPU

Several traditional villages in the southeast can be visited from Waingapu by *bemo*. The stone ancestor tombs are impressive, and the area produces some of Sumba's best *ikat*. Almost every village has a visitors book, and a small donation is expected.

Just 3km south of central Waingapu, a few hundred metres west of the airport road, **Prailiu** is the central village of the old Lewa Kambero kingdom and a busy *ikat*-weaving centre.

Melolo, an unspectacular village on the main road, 62km southeast of Waingapu, is easily reached by bus, and from here infrequent *bemo* run to nearby traditional villages.

Located about 7km away from Melolo, **Praiyawang** has a massive raja's tomb (you can stay in the royal Sumbanese house opposite – but remember you are a guest), good *ikat* and many traditional houses. **Um-abara** and **Pau**, 4km from Melolo, have several traditional Sumba houses and tombs, and are also noted weaving centres. These villages are a 20-minute walk away from the main road – the turn-off is 2km northeast of Melolo.

Some 70km from Waingapu, **Kaliuda** has some of Sumba's best *ikat*. Take a Baing bus, get off at Ngalu, and walk 3km to Kaliuda.

There's good surf between May and August at **Kalala**, about 2km from Baing, off the main road from Melolo. An Australian has **bungalows** (fax 0387-61333; www.eastsumba.com; full board per person US$35) on the wide, white-sand beach (Mr David's) and on the southern Manggudu island. Buses from Melolo run to Baing.

Perhaps Sumba's most beautiful beach is at **Tarimbang**, on the coast south of Lewa. Most visitors are surfers, attracted by the break out on the reef, and there are two homestays – the **Bogenvil** (full board per person 50,000Rp) is the best. Buses run to Tarimbang from Waingapu (25,000Rp, four hours) in the morning.

WAIKABUBAK

☎ 0387

At the greener end of Sumba, Waikabubak is a neat little town peppered with traditional houses and old graves. Interesting

traditional villages such as **Kampung Tarung**, up a path next to Tarung Wisata Hotel, are right within the town. One of the spectacular attractions of West Sumba is the **Pasola**, the mock battle held near Waikabubak each year (see the boxed text, p304).

The **tourist office** (☎ 21108; Jl Teratai 1; ⏰ 8am-3pm Mon-Sat, until 1pm Fri) is on the eastern outskirts of town and the **BNI bank** (Jl A Yani) can change money.

Sleeping & Eating

Hotel Aloha (☎ 21245; Jl Sudirman 26; s/d 55,000/60,000Rp) Hotel Aloha is a popular place that pulls in the crowds – when they're here – with sparkling rooms and oodles of tourist information. If you're planning on getting hitched, it is also the local wedding-cake manufacturer.

Hotel Artha (☎ 21112; Jl Veteran 11; s/d 30,000/60,000Rp) The mellow garden courtyard is a bonus here, but the helpful staff scoop a couple of gold stars too.

Tarung Wisata Hotel (☎ 21332; Jl Pisang 26; s/d 30,000/35,000Rp) This is Sumba's cheapest hotel, but there's not a whole lot else to celebrate.

Hotel Manandang (☎ 21197; Jl Pemuda 4; dishes 20,000Rp; ⏰ breakfast, lunch & dinner) This has the best restaurant in town.

Warung congregate around the mosque on the main drag.

Getting There & Away

The **Merpati agent** (☎ 21051; Jl Ahmad Yani 11) is above a shop. The airport is at Tambolaka, 42km north. Merpati usually has a minibus. There are two flights a week to Denpasar (534,500Rp) and Kupang (556,000Rp) and a weekly flight to Ende (418,000Rp).

The bus station is central. Buses run to Waingapu (30,000Rp, five hours), Anakalang (5000Rp, 40 minutes), Wanokaka (5000Rp), Lamboya (3500Rp) and Waitabula (10,000Rp, one hour).

AROUND WAIKABUBAK

At **Anakalang**, 22km east of Waikabubak, some large tombs are right beside the highway, though the more interesting villages are south of town past the market. **Kabonduk** has some fine tombs, and then it's a pleasant 15-minute walk across the fields and up the hill to **Matakakeri** and the original ancestral village for the area, **Lai Tarung**, which has impressive tombs and great views. A festival honouring the ancestors is held every year around June.

Located directly south of Waikabubak is the Wanokaka district, which is a centre for the **Pasola Festival** in March. **Waigali** and **Praigoli** are interesting traditional villages. The south coast has some fine beaches, particularly **Pantai Rua**, with basic homestays, and **Pantai Morosi**.

On the west coast, the coastal village of **Pero** has accommodation at Homestay Stori. It is a popular base for visiting the very traditional nearby villages. Not all are friendly, eg steer clear of Tosi village. From Waikabubak, direct buses go to Waitabula and *bemo* go to Pero from there.

KALIMANTAN

Kalimantan covers the largest chunk of the mist-shrouded rainforest island of Borneo, the world's third-largest. This Edenic wilderness has been home for millennia to indigenous Dayaks, who travelled in river canoes and hunted with bows and arrows in thick mountain jungles that sheltered orang-utan, and it has one of the highest species diversities on earth.

Sadly, the oil, timber and plantation industries are plodding ever inwards, and chainsaws and bulldozers are fast replacing the forests with factories, mines and cities. While the buildings of Balikpapan, Pontianak and

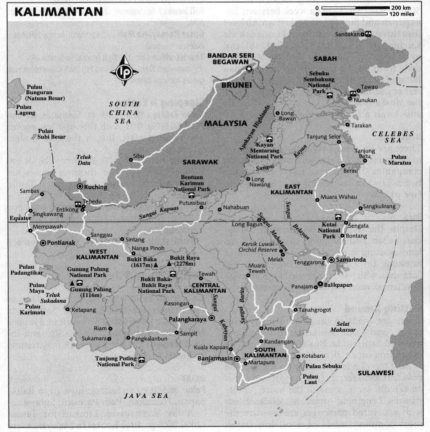

KALIMANTAN

INDONESIA

Banjarmasin are headed slowly skywards, the deep interior is becoming ever more distant and difficult to reach.

But even if the days of the wild Borneo of naturalist Alfred Wallace and novelist Joseph Conrad are numbered, Kalimantan is still good for an adventure for those who bring the time, energy and money to search out the green heart of Borneo.

TRANSPORT
Getting There & Away
AIR
Garuda flies daily from Balikpapan via Jakarta to Singapore (US$160) and Kuala Lumpur (US$130), and to Taipei (US$360). Royal Brunei flies from Balikpapan via Denpasar to Bandar Seri Begawan (US$217). SilkAir has two flights a week between Balikpapan and Singapore. Malaysian Airlines flies three times a week from Pontianak via Kuching to Kuala Lumpur (RM268) and to Singapore (RM286). Batavia Air flies daily from Pontianak via Kuching to Pulau Batam (432,000Rp), near Singapore. To the rest of Indonesia, Garuda and Merpati have the most connections, but Bouraq, Mandala and Awair also fly into Kalimantan.

BOAT
There are shipping connections to Java and to Sulawesi with Pelni and other shipping companies. To Malaysia, fast boats run between Tarakan and Nunukan in Kalimantan (see p156).

BUS
Despite the long land border with Malaysian Sabah and Sarawak, the only official land crossing is the visa-free entry point of Entikong (in Kalimantan) near Tebedu (in Sarawak), which is usually used for Kuching–Pontianak travel (10 hours by express bus).

Getting Around
There are roads in the areas around Pontianak, and from Banjarmasin to Balikpapan and Samarinda. Bus routes seem to be expanding on an almost monthly basis.

Boat travel is fast becoming a thing of the past, but local ferries (*feri sungai* and *kapal biasa*) still serve some of the more remote villages. *Long bots* – narrow wooden boats with a covered passenger cabin – are the most common mode of accessing Dayak

areas, but speedboats also ply the Barito, Kapuas, Pinoh, Kahayan and Kayan rivers.

Merpati, DAS and some smaller carriers have flights into the interior.

TARAKAN
☎ 0551 / pop 200,000
Tarakan, close to the Sabah border, is just a stepping stone to other places. It was the site of bloody fighting between Australians and Japanese at the end of WWII. Unless you have a deep interest in Japanese blockhouses, the only reason to come here is to cross to Tawau in Malaysia.

Orientation & Information
Taxis (25,000Rp) and public minibuses (4000Rp) go to the airport (5km).

BNI bank (Jl Yos Sudarso) Changes money and has an ATM.

Gusar Ramayana Mall (Jl Sudirman) There is Internet access in the mall.

Tourist office (☎ 32100; Jl Jendral Sudirman 76; ☼ 8am-4pm Mon-Thu, 8-11am Fri) Staff can recommend guides for trips inland.

Sleeping & Eating
Hotel Taufiq (☎ 21347; Jl Yos Sudarso 26; s/d from 70,000/80,000Rp; ☒) With tidy, spotless rooms and smiling staff, this is the best budget haunt in town.

Barito Hotel (☎ 21212; Jl Sudirman 129; s/d from 75,000/85,000Rp; ☒) The cheapest rooms are with shared bathroom. A good bet if Taufiq is full.

Rumah Makan Cahaya (Jl Sudirman; dishes from 15,000Rp; ☼ breakfast, lunch & dinner) Plates up tempting octopus.

Food stalls (THM Plaza, cnr Jl Yos Sudarso & Jl Sudirman) Are plentiful.

Getting There & Away
AIR
Kal-Star (☎ 51578; Jl Sudirman 9) heads daily to Balikpapan (650,000Rp) and Samarinda (499,300Rp). **DAS** (☎ 51011; Barito Hotel, Jl Sudirman 129) flies to Samarinda (549,000Rp) and inland. **Merpati** (☎ 33444; Jl Sudirman 9) may resume its flights to Balikpapan.

BOAT
Pelni (☎ 51169; Jl Yos Sudarso) ships go to Balikpapan, Nunukan, Pare Pare and Sulawesi.

A fast ferry leaves Tarakan for Tawau (2000.000Rp, three hours) in Malaysia every morning, except Sunday, when the border is closed.

SAMARINDA

☎ 0541 / pop 600,000

As oil is to Balikpapan, so timber is to Samarinda. It's another trading port on one of Kalimantan's mighty rivers, and a good place to arrange trips up Sungai Mahakam – budget travellers should base themselves here rather than in Balikpapan.

Information

ATMs can be found at a number of banks.
BNI bank (cnr Jl Sebatik & Jl Panglima Batur) Changes only US dollars (cash and travellers cheques).
Meganet (☎ 748541; Hotel MJ, Jl Khalid 1) Has 24-hour Internet access.
Post office (cnr Jl Gajah Mada & Jl Awang Long)
Tourist office (Kantor Parawisata; ☎ 32100; Jl Sudirman 22; ☸ 7.30am-4.30pm Mon-Thu, 8-11am Fri) This is a useful office.

Sleeping & Eating

Hotel Hidayah II (☎ 741712; Jl Hahlid 25; d from 50,000Rp; ✺) Sporting a face-lift, this is one of the best-looking budget options.

  Hotel Hidayah I (☎ 731261; Jl Mas Tumenggung; d from 90,000Rp; ✺) The same as Hidayah II, but with more of an urban buzz. Air-con costs 25,000Rp extra.

  Aida (☎ 742572; Jl Mas Tumenggung; d from 110,000Rp; ✺) Next door and marginally cleaner, Aida has a coffee shop that attracts guides pitching for business.

  Mesra Indah shopping centre (Jl Hahlid; ☸ breakfast, lunch & dinner) Mesra Indah has fast food and a supermarket.

  Lezat (Jl Mulawarman; dishes 13,000Rp ☸ lunch & dinner) Serves up tip-top Chinese fare.

  Samarinda's chief gastronomic wonder is the *udang galah* (giant river prawns) found in the local *warung*. The Citra Niaga hawker centre off Jl Niaga is great for these.

Getting There & Away

AIR

DAS (☎ 735250; Jl Gatot Subroto 92) has expensive and heavily booked flights to the interior. They head to Tarakan (501,000Rp), Melak (336,500Rp) and other destinations.

BOAT

Pelni (☎ 741402; Jl Sudarso 76) goes to Pare Pare (125,000Rp, 21 hours), Surabaya (292,000Rp,

2½ days), as well as to Toli-Toli (131,000Rp), to Tarakan (161,500Rp) and to Nunukan (222,000Rp).

  A ferry goes twice a week to Pare Pare (75,000Rp, 21 hours). The *Teratai* leaves every two days for Berau (90,000Rp, 27 hours). Check with the harbour master at the **Kantor Mangkurat agency** (Jl Yos Sudarso 2).

  Boats up the Mahakam leave from the southwestern Sungai Kunjang ferry terminal. Boats are infrequent, leave around sunrise and service Tenggarong (20,000Rp, 2½ hours), Melak (1000,000Rp, 19 hours), Long Iram (150,000Rp, 30 hours) and – sometimes – Long Bagun (350,000Rp).

BUS

From Samarinda, you can head west to Tenggarong or south to Balikpapan. The long-distance bus station is on the north side of the river, 2km upstream from the bridge.

  Daily buses go to Tenggarong (10,000Rp, one hour), Balikpapan (14,000Rp, two hours) and Kota Bagun (15,000Rp, three hours), where you can catch boats going upriver.

SUNGAI MAHAKAM

Samarinda is probably the best jumping-off point for visits to the Dayak tribes of East Kalimantan. Some of these places are easily reached on the longboats that ply Sungai Mahakam from Samarinda and Tenggarong all the way to Long Bagun, 523km upriver.

  Most people head upriver to **Tanjung Isuy** on the shores of Danau Jempang, with its touristy **Louu Taman Jamrot** (Jl Indonesia Australia; d 60,000Rp), a longhouse/craft centre and tourist hostel. Group tourists flock here for performances of Kenyah, Kayan and Banuaq dancing. Nearby, **Mancong** has another slightly touristy **longhouse** (d 60,000Rp), where it is possible to stay. To get to Danau Jempang, take a longboat from Samarinda to Muara Muntai first, and spend the night there before getting a boat to Tanjung Isuy.

  Melak, 325km from Samarinda, is the biggest town on the upper river and famous for what remains of its 20-sq-km **Kersik Luwai Orchid Reserve** (where the black orchid grows) which was badly damaged by fire. The **Penginapan Rahmat Abadi** (Jl Piere Tendean; d 60,000Rp) and Penginapan Flamboyan are the best places to stay.

Long Iram, 409km and 33 hours from Samarinda, is the end of the line if the river is low. Long Iram is a quiet village and you can explore the nearby lake. Try **Penginapan Wahyu** (Jl Soewondo 57; r per person 60,000Rp).

Further upriver are more longhouses between **Datah Bilang** and **Muara Merak**, including the Bahau, Kenyah and Penan settlements. The end of the line for regular longboat services is **Long Bagun**, or **Long Apari** if the conditions are right. The journey from Samarinda can take three days.

If you want to start your trip from the top, DAS flies three times a week (500,000Rp) to **Data Dawai**, an airstrip near Long Lunuk, although you will need to book weeks in advance.

Duta Miramar Tours and Travel (☎ 738037; Jl Sudirman 20, Samarinda) can book river tours.

BALIKPAPAN
☎ 0542 / pop 440,000

A gateway city that can leave a hole in your pocket, Balikpapan is an air-conditioned boom town that has become rich on oil money. It's far from an unpleasant place, sporting some of the best food and undoubtedly the liveliest nightlife in Kalimantan, but it's not cheap, with little to see.

Orientation & Information
A taxi from Sepinggan airport is 22,000Rp.

There are plenty of banks with ATMs. The **post office** (☎ 733585; Jl Sudirman 6) has an Internet service.

Sleeping & Eating
Hotel Aida (☎ 731857; Jl Sudirman Complex Cemera 44; d/tr from 75,000/115,000Rp; ✱) This is a fair bet, with TV and air-con in the best rooms.

Hotel Ayu (☎ 425290; Jl Gunung Kawi; d from 90,000Rp; ✱) A newish place; not a bad choice.

Bondy's Restaurant (☎ 424438; Jl Ahmad Yani; grilled fish 50,000Rp; ✆ lunch & dinner) Seafood and hearty serves of Western fare in an open courtyard.

Frielanda (☎ 424312; Jl Pranoto; ✆ lunch & dinner) A cheaper option, offering sizzling Chinese seafood.

Drinking
Joy's Bar (Jl Sudirman) Joy's Bar is good for an expat booze-up.

Borneo Pub (Dusit Balikpapan; ☎ 420155, Jl Sudirman) Borneo Pub is another popular R&R spot for oil workers and jungle-weary visitors, with live entertainment till the early hours.

Getting There & Away
AIR
Bouraq (☎ 731475; Jl Sudirman 13) has daily flights to Makassar (from 446,000Rp). **Merpati** (☎ 424452; Jl Sudirman 32) has three weekly flights to Surabaya (745,000Rp) and **DAS** (☎ 423286; Jl Ahmad Yani 33) flies to Banjarmasin (from 349,000Rp).

Also check:

Garuda (☎ 422300; Jl Ahmad Yani 14)
Kal-Star (☎ 731350; Jl Sudirman 86A)
SilkAir (☎ 730800; Gran Senyiur Hotel, Jl ARS Mohamad 7) Flies to Singapore (US$400).

BOAT
Pelni (☎ 424171; Jl Yos Sudarso 76) sails to Makassar (109,500Rp), Pare Pare, Pantoloan, Surabaya and beyond.

Kharma Kencana (☎ 422194; Kampung Baru dock) has a ferry to Mamuju (80,000Rp, 16 hours) and **Tanjung Selamat Express** (☎ 734516; Jl Monginsidi 4) leaves twice a week for Pare Pare (100,000Rp, 24 hours).

BUS
Buses to Samarinda (11,500Rp, two hours) leave from the northern Batu Ampar bus terminal. Buses to Banjarmasin (67,000Rp, 12 hours) leave from the bus station across the harbour. Take a route 5 taxi from Jl Sudirman to Jl Monginsidi and charter a speedboat to the other side.

BANJARMASIN
☎ 0511 / pop 800,000

At first glance it might not look like much, but get out on the canals of Banjarmasin and it quickly becomes one of Indonesia's most stunning cities. With its maze of waterways and other nearby attractions, Banjarmasin is the only city in Kalimantan worth lingering in; it's known as 'River City' and has floating markets.

Orientation & Information
The airport is 26km from town (50,000Rp by taxi). To get there, take a *taxi kota* from Jl Pasar Baru to the Km 6 terminal, then a Martapura-bound *colt*, and get off at the branch road leading to the airport and walk (1.5km).

There are a BCA bank, BNI bank and Telkom office in town.

Borneo Homestay (☎ 57545; borneo@banjarmasin .wasantara.net.id) In a laneway off Jl Hasanuddin 33, this is the best place for travel information and to book tours. Also see p312.

LippoBank (Jl Pangeran Samudera) Cashes travellers cheques.

Post office (☎ 57600; Jl Pangeran Samudera) Has Internet access.

South Kalimantan Tourist Office (☎ 274252; Jl Pramuka 4; ⏰ 7.30am-2.30pm Mon-Thu, 7.30-11.30am Fri) About 6km out of town, this office is helpful and arranges guides for trekking.

Tourist office (☎ 52982; Jl Panjaitan 34; ⏰ 8am-2pm Mon-Thu, Fri & Sat 8-11am)

Sights & Activities

Banjarmasin's major attractions are its canals and its **Pasar Kuin** and **Pasar Lokbaintan floating markets** (⏰ 5-9am). It's possible to tour the waterways of Banjarmasin in a *klotok* (motorised canoe) for around 15,000Rp per hour.

In the middle of Banjarmasin, the **Mesjid Raya Sabilal Muhtadin** (Jl Sudirman), a mosque with a copper-coloured dome and minarets with lids and spires, is the Banjarmasin most impressive building, especially on the inside.

It's also worth taking a boat from the pier at the end of Jl Pos to the nearby river island of **Pulau Kembang**, home to a tribe of long-tailed macaques.

BANJARMASIN

Sleeping

Borneo Homestay (☎ 57545; borneo@banjarmasin
.wasantara.net.id; s/d 33,000/44,000Rp) Good information, tours and a rooftop lounging area
have made this a travellers favourite, though
some guests complain about slipping service. It's in a laneway off Jl Hasanuddin 33.

Hotel Kalimantan (☎ 54483; Jl Haryono MT 106;
d with shared/private mandi 40,000/60,000Rp; ✖) Kalimantan draws Indonesian travellers and
remains a good place to pick up on the local
vibe. Air-con rooms cost 140,000Rp.

Hotel SAS (☎ 53054; Jl Kacapiring Besar 2, off Jl
Pangeran Samudera; d from 140,000Rp; ✖) An altogether more salubrious option, the outlying
SAS has generous, comfy rooms and a buffet breakfast.

Hotel Kertak Baru (☎ 54638; Jl Haryono MT 1; d
from 85,000Rp; ✖) More of the same.

Eating & Drinking

A local speciality is *ayam panggang* (roasted
chicken in sweet soy), but fish and freshwater cray hold pride of place in Banjar
cuisine.

Kaganangan (Jl Pangeran Samudera 30; dishes
15,000Rp; ✖ lunch & dinner) A cheap-eats bonanza, offering a range of local dishes –
they all come at once and you pay for what
you eat.

Rama Steak House (Arjuna Shopping Centre, Jl
Lambung Mangkurat; steaks 50,000Rp; ✖ lunch & dinner)
Flying the flag for Western fare, the place to
satisfy severe carnivorous cravings.

Banjarmasin's excellent array of *kueh*
(cake) includes deep-fried breads from the
canoe *warung* at the floating markets –
3000Rp for a bellyful.

For a hot, aromatic brew, try the tea stalls
near Jl Katamso.

Getting There & Away

AIR

Garuda (☎ 66203; Hotel Istana Barito, Jl Haryono MT)
and **Merpati** (☎ 66203; Jl Ahmad Yani KM2) fly to
Jakarta (890,000Rp). **DAS** (☎ 52902; Jl Hasanuddin 6) flies to Pangkalanbun (477,000Rp) and
Pontianak (550,000Rp). **Bouraq** (☎ 264005; Jl
Ahmad Yani 343) has daily flights to Surabaya
(312,900Rp) that connect to Balikpapan
(349,000Rp) the next day.

BOAT

Pelni (☎ 53077; Jl Martadinata 10) departs for Surabaya or Semarang every two days. **Dharma**

Kencana (☎ 414833; Jl Yos Sudarso 8) also has a
ferry to Surabaya (120,000Rp, 20 hours),
near the Trisakti Pinisi harbour.

River boats go twice a week from the Pasar
Lima wharf to Marabahan (15,000Rp, four
hours) and Negara (20,000Rp, 12 hours).

BUS

Buses and *colt* depart frequently from the
Km 6 terminal in the southeast for Martapura and Banjarbaru. Air-con night buses
to Balikpapan (85,000Rp, 12 hours) leave
daily around 5pm.

AROUND BANJARMASIN

Banjarbaru, on the road from Banjarmasin
to Martapura, has an interesting **museum**
(☎ 0511-92453; Jl Ahmad Yani 36; admission 2000Rp;
✖ 8.30am-1.30pm Tue-Sun, until 11am Fri) with a
collection of Banjar and Dayak artefacts,
and statues excavated from ancient Hindu
temples in Kalimantan.

The diamond fields of **Cempaka** (✖ closed
Fri), 43km south of Banjarmasin, make a
fascinating excursion. The miners labour
in muddy holes – often up to their necks
in water – sifting for gold, diamonds and
agates. Take a Banjarmasin–Martapura *colt,*
and ask to get off at the huge roundabout
just past Banjarbaru. From here take a green
taxi to Alur, and walk the last 1km from the
main road to the diamond digs.

The large Friday market at **Martapura** is a
photographer's paradise – brightly dressed
Banjar women haggle over a cornucopia of
exotic fruit (*colt* 15,000Rp, 45 minutes).

PONTIANAK

☎ 0561 / pop 490,000

Pontianak is a sprawling, industrial city
that sits on the equator and astride the
confluence of Sungai Landak and Sungai
Kapuas Kecil rivers. Like Banjarmasin, it
really needs to be seen from the river and
canals to be appreciated, but few travellers
hang around.

Orientation & Information

Airport taxis into town cost 50,000Rp
(15km).

BNI bank (Jl Tanjungpura) Changes money and has an
ATM.

Kalimantan Barat Tourist Office (☎ 742838;
Jl Sutoyo 17; ✖ 8am-2pm Mon-Thu, 8-11.30am Fri) Also
has Internet access.

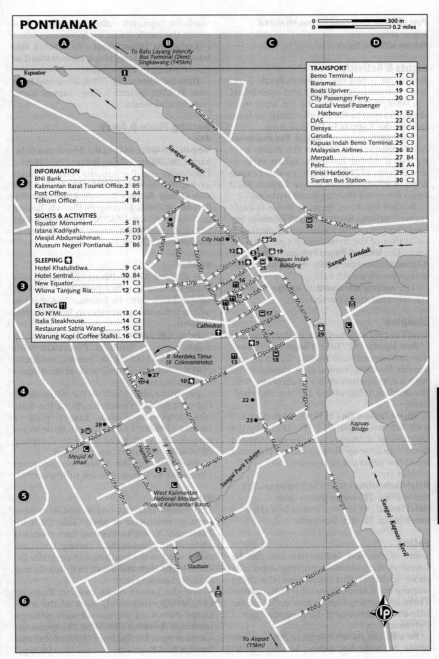

PONTIANAK

0	300 m
0	0.2 miles

INFORMATION
BNI Bank	**1** C3
Kalimantan Barat Tourist Office	**2** B5
Post Office	**3** A4
Telkom Office	**4** B4

SIGHTS & ACTIVITIES
Equator Monument	**5** B1
Istana Kadriyah	**6** D3
Mesjid Abdurrakhman	**7** D3
Museum Negeri Pontianak	**8** B6

SLEEPING 🏠
Hotel Khatulistiwa	**9** C4
Hotel Sentral	**10** B4
New Equator	**11** C3
Wisma Tanjung Ria	**12** C3

EATING 🍴
Do N'Mi	**13** C4
Italia Steakhouse	**14** C3
Restaurant Satria Wangi	**15** C3
Warung Kopi (Coffee Stalls)	**16** C3

TRANSPORT
Bemo Terminal	**17** C3
Biaramas	**18** C4
Boats Upriver	**19** C3
City Passenger Ferry	**20** C3
Coastal Vessel Passenger Harbour	**21** B2
DAS	**22** C4
Deraya	**23** C4
Garuda	**24** C3
Kapuas Indah Bemo Terminal	**25** C3
Malaysian Airlines	**26** B2
Merpati	**27** B4
Pelni	**28** A4
Pinisi Harbour	**29** C3
Siantan Bus Station	**30** C2

To Batu Layang Intercity Bus Terminal (2km); Singkawang (145km)

Equator

Sungai Kapuas

Sungai Landak

City Hall

Kapuas Indah Building

Cathedral

Jl Merdeka Timur (Jl Cokroaminoto)

West Kalimantan National Mosque (Mesjid Kalimantan Barat)

Mesjid Al Jihad

Stadium

Kapuas Bridge

Sungai Parit Tokaya

Sungai Kapuas Kecil

To Airport (15km)

INDONESIA

Post office (Jl Sultan Abdur Rahman 49) Also has Internet access.

Telkom office (Jl Teuku)

Sights & Activities

Pontianak is best seen from its **canals**. *Sampan* (rowboats; 25,000Rp) and speedboats (50,000Rp) can be hired by the hour from the docks next to the ferry terminal, or from behind the Kapuas Indah Building.

The 18th-century **Mesjid Abdurrakhman** royal mosque was built in the Malay style by Syarif Abdul Rahman, sultan of Pontianak from 1771 to 1808. It's a short canoe trip (10,000Rp) across Sungai Kapuas Kecil from the *pinisi* (fishing boat) harbour.

Behind the royal mosque is the sultan's former palace, **Istana Kadriyah** (admission free; 8.30am-6pm). Now a museum, it displays a collection of the royal family's personal effects. The **Museum Negeri Pontianak** (☎ 747518; Jl Ahmad Yani; admission 2000Rp; 8am-3pm Tue-Sun) is also worth a swift look.

The **equator monument** is to the north of the city centre, across the river.

Sleeping

Don't expect any bargains in Pontianak.

New Equator (☎ 732092; Jl Tanjungpura 91; d with shared/private mandi 40,000/70,000Rp;) In a busy, central location, rooms here should come with a complimentary set of earplugs. Still, the bedding is laundered and the staff ebullient.

Wisma Tanjung Ria (☎ 734622; Jl Rahadi Usman 1; d with bathroom 75,000Rp;) This is run by the Indonesian military – note the cannons out front – and the spotless rooms would stand up to the general's inspection.

Also try:

Hotel Khatulistiwa (☎ 736793; Jl Diponegoro 56; d from 66,000Rp;) Another passable option.

Hotel Sentral (☎ 737444; Jl Merdeka Timur 232; d from 99,000Rp;) Nice, clean rooms.

Eating

Some of the best Indonesian fare can be found at the countless *warung*, especially those lining Jl Pattimura, and the night *warung* on Jl Sudirman and Jl Diponegoro. There are *warung kopi* (coffee stalls) on the side streets between Jl Tanjungpura and Jl Pattimura.

Do n'Mi (☎ 746767; Jl Pattimura 200; cakes from 3000Rp; breakfast, lunch & dinner) Sets the benchmark for topnotch cake and coffee – just watch the locals queue up in droves.

Restaurant Satria Wangi (☎ 737961; Jl Nusa Indah II; lunch & dinner) Has a smorgasbord of gut-bursting Chinese dishes.

Italia Steakhouse (☎ 733720; Jl Nusa Indah II 109; steaks 50,000Rp; lunch & dinner) Serves hamburgers and steaks.

Getting There & Away

AIR

Merpati (☎ 768936; Pontianak Mall, Jl Teuku) flies to Jakarta (290,000Rp), Pulau Batam (290,000Rp), Balikpapan and Banjarmasin. Other airlines in Pontianak include **DAS** (☎ 734383; Jl Gajah Mada 67) and **Deraya** (☎ 737670; Jl Gajah Mada 197). **Garuda** (☎ 734986; Jl Tanjungpura) flies via Jakarta to Singapore for US$320. **Malaysian Airlines** (☎ 737327; Hotel Mahkota Kapuas, Jl Sidas 8) flies to Kuching (519,300Rp).

BOAT

The Coastal Vessel Passenger Harbour is the main long-distance port. The City Passenger Ferry runs to Siantan bus station, where you pick up services to the main bus station.

Pelni (☎ 748124; Jl Sultan Abdur Rahman 12) ships regularly connect Pontianak with Jakarta (170,000Rp, 36 hours), Surabaya (197,000Rp, 40 hours) and several Kalimantan ports.

For other ships, ask at the entrance to the port on Jl Pa'kasih, north of the Kartika Hotel. The *Kapuas Express* goes to Jakarta (380,000Rp, 20 hours) three times a week. Daily jet boats travel to Ketapang (80,000Rp, six hours) on the coast.

Riverboats for the 800km journey from Pontianak to Putussibau are now a rarity.

BUS & BEMO

Pontianak's intercity bus station is in Batu Layang, northwest of town. Take the City Passenger Ferry to Siantan bus terminal and a white *bemo* to Batu Layang. For short rides, head to the bustling and centrally located bemo terminal between Jl Juanda and Jl Sisingamangaraja.

For the longer hauls over to Kuching (100,000Rp, 10 hours), most of the midrange hotels in Pontianak can arrange bookings. **Biaramas** (☎ 765018; Jl Diponegoro 165) leaves at 9pm for Kuching (100,000Rp) and Bandar Seri Begawan, Brunei (400,000Rp).

Getting Around

Public *opelet* run routes throughout town and cost a standard 1300Rp regardless of the distance. Taxis can be flagged down or picked up from ranks by Garuda or the road entrance to Kapuas Indah. There are becak aplenty. Motorised canoes depart from the river by the Kapuas Indah building. A trip across to Siantan costs 1500Rp per person or 10,000Rp to charter.

SULAWESI

To some the bizarrely contorted island of four mountainous peninsulas resembles a tropical orchid. Sulawesi – once known as Celebes – certainly gave early seafararers grey hair, but it has delighted generations of travellers and divers since. Jungles, beaches, underwater volcanoes and mysterious mountain villages make it a tropical playground for adventure tourists, while the buzzing port of Makassar showcases the country's rich maritime history. Tana Toraja, with its strange celebratory funeral parties, remains Sulawesi's biggest attraction.

TRANSPORT
Getting There & Away
AIR

Garuda, Merpati, Bouraq, Mandala and Pelita Air all service domestic routes to Sulawesi, mostly via Makassar. SilkAir flies from Manado to Singapore (US$256), and so do Singapore Airlines and Garuda (around US$500).

BOAT

Makassar is a major hub for the Pelni network, with more than a dozen liners stopping here. A number of other Sulawesi ports are serviced by Pelni. See www.pelni .co.id for details.

MAKASSAR (UJUNG PANDANG)
☎ 0411 / pop 1.5 million

In southwestern Sulawesi, this thriving port city is the home of Indonesia's magnificent Bugis schooners. New container handling and other dock facilities have done much to rejuvenate Makassar's role as eastern Indonesia's premier port. Makassar has long played a key role in the region's history. Dominating eastern Indonesia as part of the powerful kingdom of Gowa in the 16th century, revolting against the central government in the 1950s and today maintaining its reputation as a centre for the independent-minded and the staunchly Islamic, Makassar is a big city with big ideas.

Orientation

Hasanuddin airport is 22km to the east, 40,000Rp by taxi or 8000Rp by *pete-pete (bemo)*. Most of the action takes place in the west of this huge city, near the sea. The port is in the city's northwest; Fort Rotterdam is in the centre of the older commercial hub.

Information
INTERNET ACCESS
Cybercafé (☎ 322664; 3rd fl, cnr Jl Kajaolalido & Jl Ahmad Yani) Above Pizza Ria.

MEDICAL SERVICES
Rumah Sakit Pelamonia (☎ 324710; Jl J Sudirman 27)

MONEY
Banks with ATMs on Lapangan Karebosi include BCA and BNI.

POST
Main post office (☎ 323180; Jl Slamet Riyadi 10) Has an Internet centre.

TELEPHONE
There are *wartel* across town.
Legend Hostel (☎ 328204; Jl Jampea 5G)
Wartel Lumbung (☎ 319849; Jl Serui)

TOURIST INFORMATION
Sulawesi Tourism Information Centre (Dinas Kebudayaan & Pariwisata; ☎ 872336; Jl J Sudirman 23; ◷ 8am-4pm Mon-Sat)

Sights & Activities
Fort Rotterdam (☎ 321305; Jl Pasar Ikan; admission by donation; ◷ 8am-4pm) dates from 1545 and has been renovated. Inside the fort, **Museum Negeri La Galigo** (☎ 321305; admission 1700Rp; ◷ 8am-12.30pm Tue-Sun) has assorted bric-a-brac from Tana Toraja.

Bugis schooners dock at **Pelabuhan Paotere** (admission 500Rp), a becak ride north from the city centre. The **fish market** is nearby.

Taman Anggrek CL Bundt (Clara Bundt Orchid Garden; ☎ 322572; Jl Mochtar Lutfi 15; admission by donation) contains exotic hybrids, some 5m high,

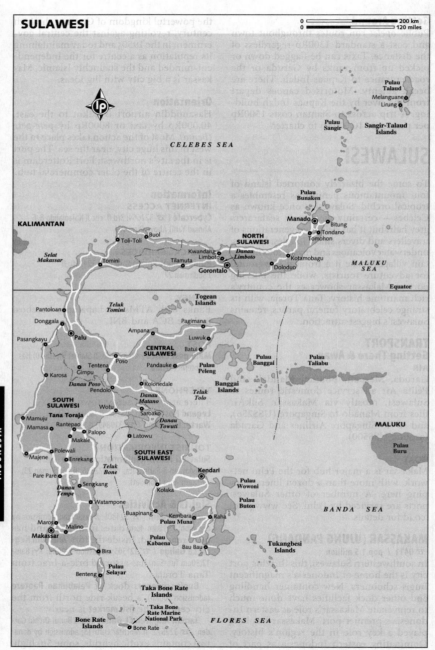

SULAWESI

0 _____ 200 km
0 _____ 120 miles

CELEBES SEA

KALIMANTAN

Toli-Toli
Buol
Kwandang
Limboto
Danau
Limboto
Tilamuta
Tomini
Gorontalo
Doloduo
Kotamobagu
Tondano
Tomohon
Manado
Bitung
NORTH SULAWESI

Pulau Bunaken

Selat Makassar

MALUKU SEA

Equator

Pulau Talaud
Melangguane
Lirung
Sangir-Talaud Islands
Pulau Sangir

Pantoloan
Donggala
Pasangkayu
Palu
Teluk Tomini
Ampana
Pagimana
Togean Islands
Luwuk
Batui
CENTRAL SULAWESI
Pandauke
Pulau Peleng
Banggai Islands
Pulau Banggai
Pulau Taliabu

Karosa
Tentena
Gimpu
Poso
Danau Poso
Pendolo
Kolonedale
Danau Matano
Teluk Tolo
Saroako
Danau Towuti
Wotu
Latowu

SOUTH SULAWESI
Mamuju
Tana Toraja
Mamasa
Rantepao
Palopo
Makale
Polewali
Majene
Enrekang
Pare Pare
Sengkang
Danau Tempe
Watampone
SOUTH EAST SULAWESI
Kendari
Kolaka
Pulau Wowoni
Pulau Buton

Pulau Taliabu

MALUKU

Pulau Buru

Maros
Makassar
Malino
Bira
Pulau Selayar
Benteng
Buapinang
Kembara
Pulau Muna
Raha
Pulau Kabaena
Bau Bau
Tukangbesi Islands

BANDA SEA

Taka Bone Rate Islands
Bone Rate Islands
Taka Bone Rate Marine National Park
Bone Rate

FLORES SEA

INDONESIA

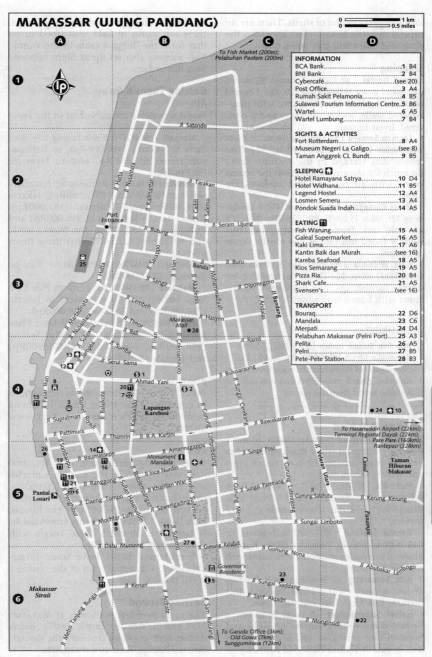

MAKASSAR (UJUNG PANDANG)

0 — 1 km
0 — 0.5 miles

INFORMATION
BCA Bank...**1** B4
BNI Bank...**2** B4
Cybercafé...(see 20)
Post Office..**3** A4
Rumah Sakit Pelamonia.....................**4** B5
Sulawesi Tourism Information Centre.**5** B6
Wartel..**6** A5
Wartel Lumbung..................................**7** B4

SIGHTS & ACTIVITIES
Fort Rotterdam....................................**8** A4
Museum Negeri La Galigo...............(see 8)
Taman Anggrek CL Bundt..................**9** B5

SLEEPING 🏠
Hotel Ramayana Satrya.....................**10** D4
Hotel Widhana....................................**11** B5
Legend Hostel.....................................**12** A4
Losmen Semeru...................................**13** A4
Pondok Suada Indah..........................**14** A5

EATING 🍴
Fish Warung...**15** A4
Galeal Supermarket...........................**16** A5
Kaki Lima...**17** A6
Kantin Baik dan Murah...................(see 16)
Kareba Seafood...................................**18** A5
Kios Semarang....................................**19** A5
Pizza Ria..**20** B4
Shark Cafe...**21** A5
Svensen's...(see 16)

TRANSPORT
Bouraq..**22** D6
Mandala..**23** C6
Merpati...**24** D4
Pelabuhan Makassar (Pelni Port)......**25** A3
Pelita...**26** A5
Pelni..**27** B5
Pete-Pete Station...............................**28** B3

To Fish Market (200m);
Pelabuhan Paotere (200m)

Jl Satando

Jl Hatta
Jl Nusantara
Jl Kalimantan
Jl Tarakan
Jl Caddi
Jl Saleno

Port
Entrance

Jl Seram Ujung

Jl Butung
Jl Sarappo
Jl Irian
Jl Banda
Jl Buru
Jl Mohammadyah

Jl Sangir
Jl Akademis
Jl Diponegoro
Jl Bandang

Jl Lembeh
Jl Timor
Makassar
Mall
Jl Hasyim
Jl Andalas

Jl Bali
Jl Sumba
Jl Cokroaminoto
Jl Ramli

Jl Sulawesi
Jl Serui Sama

Jl Bulusaraung

Jl Ahmad Yani
Lapangan
Karebosi

Jl Gunung Cerekang
Jl Sungai Cerekang

Jl Supratman

Jl Pattimura
Jl Slamet Riyadi
Jl Balakota
Jl Thamrin
Jl R A Kartini
Jl Bawakaraeng

To Hasanuddin Airport (22km);
Terminal Regional Dayak (22km);
Pare Pare (160km);
Rantepao (328km)

Jl Sombaopu
Jl Baumassepe
Jl Amannagappa
Monument
Mandala
Jl Ince Nurdin
Jl Sungai Poso

Jl Veteran Utara

Jl Ranggong
Jl Sultan Hasanudin
Jl Bolokmbangan
Jl Gunung Merapi
Jl Sungai Paremang

Taman
Hiburan
Makasar

Pantai
Losari
Jl Penghibur
Jl Daeng Tompo
Jl Khairlan War
Jl Jendral Sudirman
Jl Sawengading
Jl Gunung Latimojong
Jl Gunung Safahutu
Jl Kerung Kerung

Jl Mochtar Lutfi
Jl Sutoro
Jl Sungai Limboto

Jl Datu Museng
Jl Gunung Kelabat
Jl Gunung Nona

Governor's
Residence
Jl Abubakar Lambogo

Makassar
Strait
Jl Kenari
Jl Arifate
Jl Sam Ratulangi
Jl Sungai Saddang
Jl Sarif Alqadri

Jl Metro Tanjung Bunga
Jl Monginsidi

To Garuda Office (3km);
Old Gowa (7km);
Sungguminasa (12km)

INDONESIA

and a huge collection of shells. There are no official opening hours – just knock on the door and Clara will give you a tour.

Sleeping

Legend Hostel (☎ 328203; Jl Jampea 5G; dm/s/d with shared mandi 15,000/29,000/35,000Rp) Legend remains the best travellers inn, with map-covered walls, warm welcomes and a cluttered, lived-in feel.

Losmen Semeru (☎ 310410; Jl Jampea 28; d with shared/inside bathroom 35,000/45,000Rp; ✷) The motorbikes stacked in the corridor don't do much for the atmosphere, but the rooms come with air-con and the surfaces are clean.

Hotel Ramayana Satrya (☎ 442478; Jl Bawakaraeng 121; s/d/tr 75,000/85,000/125,000Rp; ✷) It's an epic trek from the centre, but this slightly faded midranger has a wide range of rooms.

Hotel Widhana (Jl Botolempangan 53; s/d with breakfast 60,000/72,000Rp; ✷) This is dark, with even darker furnishings, but the comfy rooms come with bonus trimmings like TV.

> **SPLURGE!**
>
> **Pondok Suada Indah** (☎ 312857; Jl Sultan Hasanuddin 12; s/d 135,000/165,000Rp; ✷) Expect oodles of mock-colonial style, baroque furniture, plastic chandeliers and very comfortable rooms from this place.

Eating & Drinking

Shark Cafe (Jl Penghibur 79; snacks 15,000Rp; ◔ lunch & dinner) A giant great white shark model takes pride of place among the tasty juices, rotis and shakes served here.

Pizza Ria (☎ 336336; 2nd fl, cnr Jl Ahmad Yani & Jl Kajaolalido; pizza 16,000Rp; ◔ lunch & dinner) This Pizza Hut clone has a very handy delivery service.

Kareba Seafood (☎ 326062; Jl Penghibur 10; seafood dishes 15,000Rp; ◔ lunch & dinner) Kareba Seafood serenades seafood aficionados with nightly live music.

Kios Semarang (Jl Penghibur; meals 15,000Rp; ◔ lunch & dinner) Near Kareba Seafood, this features fine frogs legs and top views.

Galael Supermarket (Jl Sultan Hasanuddin 1; ◔ lunch & dinner) Has outlets of KFC and Svensen's ice cream, as well as cheap Indonesian eats at Kantin Baik dan Murah.

At night along Jl Metro Tanjung Bunga, there are scores of *kaki lima* (food carts) that form the 'longest table in the world'. Fish *warung* also set up at night opposite Fort Rotterdam.

Getting There & Away

AIR

Flight schedules are published in the *Fajar* newspaper.

Merpati (☎ 442471; Jl Bawakaraeng 109) flies daily to Jakarta (490,000Rp), to Balikpapan (from 517,500Rp) and to Jayapura (952,000Rp).

Garuda (☎ 465 4747; Jl Petarrani 18) has daily services to Manado (352,500Rp), Jakarta (636,300Rp) and Denpasar (391,000Rp). It also flies to Jayapura (1,216,000Rp) and Pulau Biak (1,152,000Rp) five times a week, and to Timika (1,256,700Rp) three times a week.

Bouraq (☎ 452506; Jl Veteran Utara) flies to Surabaya (347,000Rp).

Mandala (☎ 314888; Komp Latanete Plaza D5, Jl Sungai Saddang) has daily services to Jakarta (710,000Rp) and Ambon (528,000Rp).

Pelita Air (☎ 319222; Hotel Golden Makassar, Jl Pasar Ikan 51-52) flies to Jakarta (772,700Rp), Serong (990,500Rp), Manukwari (1,820,900Rp) and Ternate (840,00Rp).

BOAT

Pelni (☎ 331401; Jl J Sudirman 38) has connections to countless destinations across Indonesia from Makassar, its main port. Check www.pelni.co.id.

BUS

Buses heading north leave from Terminal Regional Dayak, in the eastern suburbs, and head towards Pare Pare (20,000Rp, three hours) and to Rantepao (normal/air-con 40,000Rp/55,000Rp, eight hours).

Alam Indah (☎ 586717; Jl Perintis Kemerdelaan Km 8) has clean buses to Tana Toraja with sleeper-seats for 60,000Rp.

Southbound buses leave from Terminal Gowa, 10km southeast of the centre, a 3000Rp *bemo* ride.

Getting Around

The main *pete-pete* station is at Makassar Mall, and the standard fare is 2000Rp. Becak drivers kerb-crawl for custom – the shortest fare is 3000Rp. Taxis run on meters.

TANA TORAJA

Famed for their traditional longhouses with soaring, boat-shaped roofs, the animist highland villages of Toraja Land have long been Sulawesi's top attraction. The somewhat morbid drawcard is the 'funeral season', around July and August, when buffalo sacrifices, all-night dances and colourful ceremonies are staged to ensure a smooth passage into the afterlife for those who have died in the previous months. The bodies are later laid to rest in cliff-side caves, guarded by wooden effigies of the dead which stare silently out into the jungle.

The capital, Makale, and Rantepao, the largest town, are the main centres. *Bemo* link the surrounding villages, but many roads are terrible, and walking is often easier. All the interesting places are scattered around the lush green countryside around Rantepao.

Rantepao
☎ 0423

Rantepao, with few sights of its own, is a comfortable base for exploring Tana Toraja.

Not to be missed is the **Pasar Bolu**, the market 2km northeast of town. It is the prime social event for everyone in the valley and peaks on main market day, once every six days.

INFORMATION

BNI bank (Jl Ahmad Yani) Changes money and has an ATM, but rates are much lower than in Makassar. The best rates are from moneychangers.

Post office (☎ 21014; Jl Ahmad Yani) Next to Telkom.

Rumah Sakit Elim (☎ 21258; Jl Ahmad Yani 68) Has very basic medical facilities.

Telkom office (Jl Ahmad Yani; ☻ 24hr)

Tourist office (☎ 25210; Jl Ahmad Yani 62A; ☻ 8am-2pm Mon-Sat, until noon Fri) This office is useful.

Warnet Petra (Jl Andi Mappanyukki 46) Internet services.

SLEEPING

Rantepao has dozens of clean, good-value hotels. In the July-August high season, tour groups arrive, hotel prices skyrocket, and many homes open their doors to visitors.

Wisma Irama (☎ 21371; Jl Abdul Gani 16; s/d 50,000/75,000Rp) With a pretty garden, relatively modern rooms and (sporadic) hot

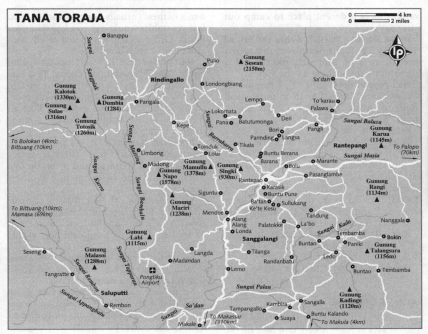

TANA TORAJA

TORAJA CULTURE

Architecture

Traditional *tongkonan* houses – shaped like boats or buffalo horns, with the roof rearing up at the front and back – are the enduring image of Tana Toraja. They are similar to the Batak houses of Sumatra's Danau Toba and are always aligned north–south, with small rice barns facing them.

A number of villages are still composed entirely of these traditional houses, but most now have corrugated-iron roofs. The houses are painted and carved with animal motifs, and buffalo skulls often decorate the front, symbolising wealth and prestige.

Burial Customs

Toraja generally have two funerals – one immediately after the death, and a second, more elaborate ceremony after enough cash has been raised. To deter the plundering of the generous burial offerings, the Toraja started to hide their dead in caves or on rocky cliff faces. You can often see *tau tau* – life-size, carved wooden effigies of the dead – sitting in balconies on rock faces, guarding the coffins.

Funeral ceremonies are the region's main tourist attraction. The more important the deceased, the more buffalo must be sacrificed: one for a commoner, as many as 24 for a high-ranking figure. And the animals aren't cheap: a medium-sized buffalo costs several million rupiah.

Ceremonies & Festivals

The end of the rice harvest, from around May onwards, is ceremony time in Tana Toraja. These festivities involve feasting and dancing, buffalo fights and *sisemba* kick-boxing. Guides around Rantepao will take you to ceremonies for a negotiable price.

---

water, this is a decent place to camp out a few days.

Wisma Morton (☎ 21675; Jl Abdul Gani 16A; s/d 75,000/100,000Rp) Right next door, this sports three storeys of topnotch rooms and a rooftop café for soaking up the views.

Pia's Poppies Hotel (☎ 21121; s/d/tr 45,000/65,000/75,000Rp) A 15-minute stroll south of town, friendly Pia's has wacky rooms with aquariums.

Hotel Pison (☎ 21344; Jl Pongtiku; s/d 50,000/75,000Rp) Next door, equally nice Pison sells itself on the back of its 'spring mattresses'. Rooms also come with hot water and private balconies.

Wisma Surya (☎ 21312; Jl Monginsidi 36; d 75,000Rp) Back in town, this place has been renovated, and smiley staff also scoop a few gold stars. Breakfast is included.

Wisma Maria 1 (☎ 21165; Jl Sam Ratulangi 23; s/d 30,000/50,000Rp) Rooms with hot water are 20,000Rp more. Breakfast included.

Wisma Monika (☎ 21216; Jl Sam Ratulangi 36; s/d 35,000/50,000Rp) Also good for a night's sleep.

EATING & DRINKING

Many of the eateries around Rantepao serve Torajan food. A local speciality is *pa'piong*,

a mix of meat (usually pork or chicken) and leaf vegetables smoked over a low flame for hours. Order a couple of hours in advance and enjoy it with black rice.

Mart's Cafe (☎ 25732; Jl Sam Ratulangi 44A; dishes from 20,000Rp; ☀ breakfast, lunch & dinner) This café has plenty of style and prices to match, but the trademark East-meets-West tourist menu includes some excellent Torajan tucker, as well as familiar Western fare for those missing home.

Restaurant Mambu (☎ 21134; Jl Sam Ratulangi 34; dishes 15,000Rp; ☀ lunch & dinner) This busy eatery has lashings of character and plates up fine Torajan food and belly-bursting Western breakfasts.

Riman Restoran (☎ 23626; Jl Andi Mappanyukki 113; mains 25,000Rp; large beer 12,500Rp; ☀ lunch & dinner) A delicious line in local cuisine can be washed down with ice-cold beer at this place.

Gazebo Restoran (Jl Andi Mappanyukki 96; pa'piong 30,000Rp; ☀ lunch & dinner) Just over the road, Gazebo cooks up a mean *pa'piong*.

Small *warung*, such as **Saleko Cafe** (Jl Andi Mappanyukki; dishes 8000Rp; ☀ breakfast, lunch & dinner), offer first-class *ikan bakar* for considerably less than the restaurants.

GETTING THERE & AROUND

Bus companies are clustered in the town centre around Jl Andi Mappanyukki. For the 330km trip to Makassar (40,000Rp), check **Litha** (☎ 21204) and **Batutumonga** (☎ 21018). Even more buses head to Pare Pare (25,000Rp, five hours).

To the north, buses travel to Pendolo (60,000Rp, 10 hours), to Tentena (75,000Rp, 12 hours), to Poso (85,000Rp, 13 hours) and to Palu (100,000Rp, 20 hours).

Kijang leave constantly, going to Makale (4000Rp, 20 minutes), and will drop you at the signs for Londa, Tilanga or Lemo, from where you can walk.

From Terminal Bolu, 2km northeast of Rantepao, frequent vehicles go east to Palopo (12,000Rp, two hours) for the sights in that direction, and regular *bemo* and *Kijang* go to all the main villages, such as Lempo (near Batutumonga).

Motorcycles can be rented from the main street tour agencies for 40,000Rp per day.

AROUND TANA TORAJA

Countless villages are within fairly easy reach on day trips. If you stay overnight in private homes, pay your way with money or gifts. Guides aren't essential – the Toraja are friendly and used to tourists. For organised tours (as well as treks and rafting) try **Indo Sella** (☎ 25210; Jl Suloara 113) and **PT Panorama Indah** (☎ 25276; Jl Sam Ratulangi 40) in Rantepao.

South of Rantepao

Karasik (1km from Rantepao) is on the outskirts of town, just off the road leading to Makale. The traditional houses are arranged in a square, erected some years ago for a single funeral.

Just off the main road, southeast of Rantepao, **Ke'te Kesu** (6km) is famed for its woodcarving. On the cliff face behind the village are some cave graves and some very old hanging graves – the rotting coffins are suspended from an overhang.

Off to the side of the main road, in **Sullukang** (7km), there's a run-down shack on a rocky outcrop, which contains several derelict *tau tau* (life-size, carved wooden effigies of the dead), almost buried under the foliage. There are also *rante* (large stone slabs planted in the ground) here, one of which is about 4m high.

About 2km off the Rantepao–Makale road, **Londa** (6km) is an extensive burial cave, one of the most interesting in the area. There are a number of coffins containing bones and skulls. Kids hang around outside with oil lamps to guide you for around 10,000Rp.

There are several springs in the Toraja area, and **Tilanga** (cold water; 10km) is one of the prettiest. It's an attractive walk along the muddy trails and through the rice paddies from Tilanga to Lemo – ask directions along the way.

Lemo (11km) is among the largest burial areas in Tana Toraja. The sheer rock face has dozens of balconies for *tau tau*. The biggest balcony has a dozen figures – like spectators at a sports event. There would be even more if they weren't in such demand by unscrupulous antique dealers. A *bemo* from Rantepao will drop you off at the road leading up to the burial site, from where it's a 15-minute walk.

East of Rantepao

Marante (6km) is a fine, traditional village and right by the road east to Palopo. Further off the Palopo road, **Nanggala** (16km) has a grandiose traditional house with 14 rice barns. *Bemo* from Rantepao take you straight there or drop you off on the main road, from where it's a 1.5km walk.

North & West of Rantepao

Gunung Singki (2km) is a small hill just outside Rantepao with a panoramic view.

Sa'dan (12km) is a weaving centre and textile market further to the northeast.

From the pleasant village of **Batutumonga** (20km), you can see a large part of Tana Toraja. The views are even more stunning from the summit of **Gunung Sesean**, a 2150m peak towering above the village. Most *bemo* stop at **Lempo**, an easy walk from Batutumonga.

In Batutumonga, rooms are available in **Mama Siska's Homestay** (d 50,000Rp), **Mentirotiku** (☎ 0811-422260; s/d 50,000/70,000Rp) and **Betania Homestay** (d 50,000Rp), which is very basic, but has sublime views.

There are more cave graves and beautiful scenery at **Lokomata** (26km), just a few kilometres west past Batutumonga.

The return to Rantepao is an interesting and easy trek down the slopes through tiny

INDONESIA

villages to **Pana**, with its ancient hanging graves. The path ends at **Tikala**, where regular *bemo* go to Rantepao.

Pangli (7km), **Bori** (6km) and also **Pangala** (35km), noted for its dancers, are also of interest. The three-day, 59km trek from **Mamasa** in the west to Bittuang is popular. There are plenty of villages en route with food and accommodation (bring some gifts). For a three-day trek try this: day one, Mamasa to Timbaan (23km); day two, Timbaan to Paku (20km); day three, Paku to Bittuang (16km).

There's no direct transport from Rantepao to Mamasa because roads are appalling. You can travel to Bittuang from Makale by *Kijang* or *bemo*. The only direct transport from Tana Toraja to Mamasa is a bus, which runs from Makale three times a week.

PENDOLO

A road bears eastwards from Rantepao to Soroako on the shores of Danau Matano in Central Sulawesi. Midway along this road is the village of Wotu, where the Trans Sulawesi Hwy veers north to the small village of Pendolo on the southern bank of beautiful **Danau Poso**.

The lake and its lovely beaches are the main attractions. You can swim, take boat rides or go for walks.

Rustic **Pendolo Cottages** (Jl Ahmad Yani 441; s/d 40,000/60,000Rp) is near the boat landing and about 1km east of the village. Readers give this place rave reviews. The modern **Homestay Masamba** (Jl Pelabuhan; d 60,000Rp) has an excellent eatery overlooking the water.

There are daily ferries across the lake to Tentena on the northern side.

TENTENA
☎ 0458

This lakeside village lacks Pendolo's fine beaches, but is larger, prettier and has better accommodation. There has been some sectarian violence in Tentena – see the Warning boxed text, right.

Hotel Victori (☎ 21392; Jl Diponegoro 18; s/d from 65,000/125,000Rp; 🌊) is peaceful, with a convivial outdoor sitting area and good information. Breakfast is included. The restaurant at **Hotel Pamona Indah Permai** (☎ 21245; Jl Yos Sudarso 25; d from 60,000Rp) serves the town's famous *sugili* (giant eels), which are netted north of the covered bridge.

Buses make the run to Poso (15,000Rp) in about two hours.

POSO
☎ 0452

As central Sulawesi's second-largest city, Poso's main attractions are its banks, which can change foreign currency. Some good beaches can be found outside town, and **Lembomawo**, 4km south of Poso, is renowned for its ebony carving.

Sectarian tension has erupted into sporadic rioting in recent years, when warring Christian and Muslim gangs have rampaged through Poso and surrounding towns (see the Warning boxed text, below).

Information

Poso is the last chance for Togean- or for Tentena-bound travellers to change travellers cheques.

BNI bank (Jl Yos Sudarso)
Tourist office (☎ 21211; Jl Kalimantan 15; 🕗 8am-3pm Mon-Sat, until 11am Fri) Vaguely useful.

Sleeping

Losmen Lalang Jaya (☎ 22326; Jl Yos Sudarso; d 65,000Rp) Creaky, atmospheric and conveniently located next to the port, this is a decent first stop.

Losmen Alugoro (☎ 21336; Jl Sumatera 20; s 40,000-110,000Rp, d 50,000-175,000Rp; 🌊) Borderline modern, with a wide range of tidy rooms.

WARNING

Many countries advise their nationals to avoid Sulawesi – especially the Poso area, which has suffered sectarian violence since 1998. A 2001 peace deal was followed by shootings, bombings and church attacks in December 2004. Buses carrying tourists have been attacked. In April 2005, both sides agreed to another peace deal, but whether it will hold remains to be seen.

South Sulawesi has also suffered sectarian violence. Four people died in a bomb attack on a café in Palopo in 2004. Check latest travel advisories before going.

In late May 2005, twin explosions ripped through the morning market in the mainly Christian town of Tentena, near Poso, killing at least 20 people and wounding 40.

Getting There & Away

Check at the port for the current details of boats going to the Togean Islands via Ampana.

From the bus terminal, about 800m north of the post office, there are regular buses to Palu (32,000Rp, six hours), Tentena (8500Rp, two hours), Ampana (25,000Rp, five hours), Rantepao (90,000Rp, 13 hours) and Makassar (110,000Rp, 20 hours).

PALU

☎ 0451 / pop 280,000

Set in a rain shadow for most of the year, Central Sulawesi's capital is one of the driest places in Indonesia. The main reason to visit Palu is to arrange the 100km-trip to trek the remote **Taman Nasional Lore Lindu**.

Orientation & Information

Palu's airport is 7km east of town, 25,000Rp by taxi.

Balai Taman Nasional Lore Lindu office (☎ 23439; Jl Tanjung Manimbayan 144) The next stop for those headed to the park, where guides are compulsory.

Tourist office (☎ 455260; Jl Dewi Sartika 91; ☼ 7.15am-4pm Mon-Sat, until 11.30am Fri) Has city maps and trekking tips.

Sleeping & Eating

Purnama Raya Hotel (☎ 423646; Jl Wahidin 4; s/d 25,000/35,000Rp) This is clean and reasonable value. The manager moonlights as a local guide.

Hotel Andalas (☎ 422332; Jl Raden Saleh 50; s/d 65,000/75,000Rp; ❄) More expensive, but with air-con, and a good bet if Purnama Raya is full.

Rumah Makan Kerinci (Jl Kartini; dishes 8500Rp; ☼ breakfast, lunch & dinner) A large *masakan Padang* crowd-pleaser.

Night *warung* congregate in a noisy, fragrant throng along Jl Raja Moili.

Getting There & Around

Merpati (☎ 423341) has flights to Makassar (281,000Rp), Surabaya (666,000Rp), Jakarta (783,000Rp) and Jayapura (1,607,000Rp).

Bouraq (☎ 427795) has flights to Makassar (193,000Rp), Surabaya (457,000Rp) and Balikpapan (292,000Rp).

Pelni (☎ 421696; Jl Kartini 96) and other large vessels dock at Pantoloan, 22km north of Palu. There is another Pelni office at Pantoloan. Smaller ships dock at Wani, 2km

past Pantoloan. Pelni sails to Kalimantan and other parts of Sulawesi.

Buses depart from Terminal Masomda heading to Poso, Palopo, Rantepao, Gorontalo and Manado.

Minibuses and shared taxis to places like Pantoloan (for Pelni boats) and Donggala (for Tanjung Karang) leave from Terminal Manonda.

DONGGALA

☎ 0457

Donggala's main attractions are the coral reefs at **Tanjung Karang**, north of town. The reef off the Prince John Dive Resort (the only dive centre – see below) is a delight for snorkellers and for beginner divers.

Towale, 12km southwest of Donggala, is another top snorkelling spot.

Sleeping

Prince John Dive Resort (☎ 71104; d from US$30) A superb splurge for any keen diver. There's a soda-white beach, and the salubrious bungalows have sensational views.

Harmoni Cottages (☎ 71573; s/d with full board 100,000/175,000Rp) Private cottages situated right on the beach for early morning paddles.

Natural Cottages (s/d 60,000/120,000Rp) Set in Robinson Crusoe surrounds.

Getting There & Away

From Palu, you can catch a shared *taksi* to Donggala for 7500Rp. It's another 30 minutes on foot to the beach or charter a *Kijang* for around 25,000Rp.

AMPANA

☎ 0464

Ampana is the stepping-off point for ferries and chartered boats to the Togean Islands.

If you need to stay overnight, try **Hotel Oasis** (☎ 21058; Jl Kartini 5; dm/d 30,000/80,000Rp) or **Losmen Irama** (☎ 21055; Jl Kartini 11; s/d 35,000/50,000Rp).

Marina Cottage (☎ 21280; d 77,000Rp) at Labuhan, 10 minutes east by *bendi*, has a decent restaurant (open for breakfast, lunch and dinner) with sublime sunsets.

Twice a week a ferry chugs off to Gorontalo via the Togean port of Wakai (25,000Rp, 2½ hours), Katupat, Malenge and Dolong. Three other boats also sail almost daily to Wakai. Depending on demand, they may also sail on to other Togean destinations.

Ampana is on the main road from Poso (35,000Rp, five hours by bus). For Luwuk (50,000Rp, eight hours), get a *bemo* connection in Bunta.

TOGEAN ISLANDS

This remarkably diverse archipelago of coral and volcanic isles is the only place in Indonesia where you can find all three major reef types – atoll, barrier and fringing – in one location.

Getting Around

Transport within the Togeans is a headache. Regardless of where you stay, you need boats to get around and to reach swimming and snorkelling spots. A convenient (but not cheap) solution is to try to charter a boat from Ampana for a few days. Charters are not hard to arrange in Wakai, Bomba and Kadidiri. For public boats between islands, ask your homestay or anyone around the village about the current timetables.

Bomba

This tiny outpost at the southeastern end of Pulau Batu Daka has nearby reefs and plenty of bats (in the caves behind the village), but few travellers.

Homestay Tondongi Reef (d 60,000Rp) is one of the most extraordinary places in the Togeans, built in the Bajau style out in the ocean, and 10 minutes from Bomba. Of other sleeping options, **Losmen Poya Lisa** (d 50,000Rp) is the most conservative, with a pleasant village setting; and **Poya Lisa Cottages** (cottages 50,000Rp) is perched on a tiny island, near the beach.

Wakai

The Togeans' largest settlement is a departure point for Pulau Kadidiri and the best place to stock up on supplies.

DID YOU KNOW?

The Togeans are one of the last remaining habitats of coconut crabs, the world's largest terrestrial arthropod. The crabs, weighing up to 5kg and as much as 90cm across, once scuttled across islands throughout the western Pacific and eastern Indian Oceans, but humans have eaten them to the verge of extinction. If you see them on the menu, consider opting for the *nasi goreng*.

Wakai Cottages (d 50,000Rp) is mellow, ideal for sunbaking and sleeping, while **Rumah Makan Cahaya Sidrap** (d with shared mandi 35,000Rp) has cheap rooms and decent tucker.

Pulau Kadidiri

The *in* place in the Togeans has a perfect beach, dozens of cheap bungalows, supreme snorkelling and superb diving further out. Trekking and other activities can be arranged.

Black Marlin Cottages (☎ 0435-831869; www .blackmarlindive.com; d from 85,000Rp; 🏊) is a grandish resort that hogs the beach and has a range of topnotch bungalows, with Western bathrooms and complimentary sea views. **Pondok Lestari** (d with shared mandi 75,000Rp) is cheerful, but a little mottled and only a whisker cheaper than Black Marlin.

Katupat

Katupat is the main village on the Togean Islands. Good beaches can be found around the island and new accommodation is springing up all the time.

Fadhila Cottages (cottages 75,000Rp), on Tomken island, offers excellent food and superb snorkelling, while **Bolilangga Indah** (cottages 50,000Rp), on Bolilangga island, is the choice of wannabe castaways.

Malenge

Pulau Malenge is remote, but has great snorkelling near the village.

Malenge Indah (cottages 55,000Rp) and **Lestari** (cottages 60,000Rp) sits nicely over the water.

MANADO

☎ 0431 / pop 520,000

Flattened by a series of devastating earthquakes in 1844, Manado had its last major face-lift under the Dutch, who rebuilt the city to make it, in the words of naturalist Alfred Wallace, 'one of the prettiest in the East'. Wallace's words are sadly misleading these days and the capital of North Sulawesi is now little more than a whirlwind of buzzing *mikrolet* and busy streets. Manado is well stocked though, and remains a good place to explore the area or dip into its famed regional Minahasan cuisine.

Orientation

Mikrolet from Sam Ratulangi airport go to Paal 2 terminal, where you change to another for Pasar 45 (the central *mikrolet* terminal) or elsewhere in the city (2000Rp). Taxis from the airport to the city (13km) cost 50,000Rp, if they use the meter.

Along Jl Sam Ratulangi, the main road running north–south, you'll find restaurants, hotels and supermarkets. The esplanade, Jl Piere Tendean, is a surprisingly dreary thoroughfare, although some new developments are springing up.

Information

Manado is packed with banks; the BNI bank has an ATM at the airport.

BCA bank (Jl Sam Ratulangi) Good for changing money.

Cyber Cafe Manado (Jl Sam Ratulangi 23) Internet access, at the post office.

Main post office (Jl Sam Ratulangi 23)

North Sulawesi tourism office (☎ 851723; Jl Diponegoro 111; ⊗ 8am-2pm Mon-Sat) Has maps and a more useful counter at the airport.

Rumah Sakit Umum (☎ 853191; Jl Monginsidi, Malalayang) Offers medical services.

Telkom office (Jl Sam Ratulangi 4)

Festivals & Events

Festivals include the **Tai Pei Kong** festival at Ban Hiah Kong temple in February; the **Pengucapan Syukur** (Minahasan Thanksgiving Day) in June to August; the **Bunaken** festival in July; the **Anniversary of Manado** on 14 July; traditional **horse races** in the second week of August; and the **Anniversary of North Sulawesi** province on 23 September.

Sleeping

Manado Bersehati Hotel (☎ 855022; Jl Sudirman 20; d from 77,500Rp; ✕) Set back from the main road, this pleasant Minahasan-style hotel offers a good dose of hush. The outside is all wood and fairy lights and the rooms are small, but spotless.

Hotel Anggrek (☎ 851970; Jl Kartini 5; s/d 80,000/120,000Rp; ✕) Sprawling and kitsch, this has lots of 1950s-style maroon and dark-wood décor. The rooms are clean and the setting is central.

Rex Hotel (☎ 851136; Jl Sugiono 3; s 50,000-70,000Rp, d 60,000-85,000Rp; ✕) Rex is welcoming and offers air-con at knockdown prices. The cheaper rooms are stuffy though.

Hotel Minahasa (☎ 862559; minahasahotel@hotmail.com; Jl Sam Ratulangi 199; s/d from 90,000/120,000Rp) The city's last bastion of colonial cool, Hotel Minahasa has comfy rooms and a whiff of Art Deco style. The friendly manager speaks Dutch and English.

Eating & Drinking

Manado is a Mecca for adventurous diners, especially at the night *warung* along Jl Piere Tendean. Regional delights include spicy *kawaok* (fried 'forest rat'), tough, gamey *rintek wuuk* (spicy dog meat), *lawang pangang* (stewed bat) and *tinutuan* (vegetable porridge).

Rumah Makan Green Garden (☎ 870089; Jl Sam Ratulangi 52; ⊗ lunch & dinner) This venerable institution has the biggest fish collection this side of Sea World – much of which ends up in the pot. It also serves an excellent array of Asian specialities and 24 different fruit juices.

Rumah Makan Minang Putra (☎ 852982; Jl Sarapung 7; dishes 10,000Rp; ⊗ lunch & dinner) In a peculiarly Alpine building, this is a popular local haunt, serving a smorgasbord of point-and-pick Indonesian favourites.

Dolphin Donuts (☎ 859840; Jl Sam Ratulangi 51; cappuccino 10,000Rp; ⊗ breakfast, lunch & dinner) Sweet-tooths and caffeine cravings are best satisfied here.

To eat well out of town, stop at the row of restaurants in the Lokon foothills, just before Tomohon, south of Manado. Food and views at **Tinoor Jaya** (dishes 12,000Rp) are excellent.

Entertainment

Studio 21 Cinema (☎ 856725; Jl Sam Ratulangi; 15,000Rp) Has four screens showing Western flicks.

Getting There & Away

AIR

These have useful services out of Manado:

Bouraq (☎ 841470; Jl Serapung 27B)

Garuda (☎ 852154; Jl Diponegoro 15)

Merpati (☎ 842000; Jl Sudirman 44)

SilkAir (☎ 863744; Jl Sarapung 5)

International connections include SilkAir's three weekly flights to Singapore. Merpati flies to spots including Jakarta (556,000Rp), Makassar (320,000Rp) and Kota Ternate (435,000Rp).

BOAT

Pelni (☎ 862844; Jl Sam Ratulangi 7) has several large boats calling at the deep-water port

INDONESIA

of Bitung, 55km from Manado, serving Balikpapan, Kota Ternate, Ambon and Gorontalo.

Smaller, uncomfortable boats from Manado tend to call at ports along the coast and go north to Tahuna (Pulau Sangihe) and Lirung (Talaud Islands), or over to Ternate and Ambon.

BUS

From Karombasan terminal, 5km south of the city, buses go to Tomohon (3000Rp) and destinations south; from Malalayang terminal, they go to Gorontalo (50,000Rp, eight hours) and even Makassar (195,000Rp, 48 hours); and from Paal 2 terminal, at the eastern end of Jl Martadinata, public transport runs to Bitung (5000Rp) and the airport (4000Rp).

Getting Around

Manado appears to have more *mikrolet* than people. Destinations are shown on a card in the front windscreen. There are various bus stations around town for destinations outside Manado – get to any of them from Pasar 45. For a cab, call **Dian Taxi** (☎ 851010).

PULAU BUNAKEN

When divers die, they go to Bunaken. At least that's what some of this tiny island's hardcore fans claim. Surrounded by some spectacular coral, Bunaken has become something of an institution in the last decade, with dozens of cheap hotels popping up. Rubbish is not an uncommon sight now, even at 30m – but Bunaken remains an idyllic getaway.

The going rate for dive excursions is around US$20 per dive and US$10 for equipment hire. Check out **Two Fish Divers** (☎ 0811-432805; www.twofishdivers.com), **Sulawesi Divequest** (☎ 0812-441 7676; www.sulawesi-dive -quest.com), **Bastiano's** (☎ 0431-853566; www.bas tianos.com) and **Froggies** (☎ 0812-430 1356; www .divefroggies.com).

The Bunaken park fee is 50,000Rp per day or 150,000Rp for an annual pass.

Sleeping & Eating

There are a number of places to stay on Pantai Liang to the west, and on Pantai Pangalisang near Bunaken village. Liang is the better of the two. Prices here include

three meals a day but are spectacularly high compared to elsewhere in Indonesia.

PANTAI LIANG

The popularity of the coral drop-off, 100m offshore, created a building boom along this beach. Most hotels quote rates for full board, and all these places come with their own eateries.

Papa Roa (☎ 0431-850434; full board per person 120,000Rp) The simple wooden bungalows here have an idyllic setting at the end of the beach, surrounded by mangroves and boulders.

Nelson's Cottages (☎ 0431-856288; full board per person 125,000Rp) Heading down the beach, these are a tad ramshackle, but still on the comfortable side.

Panorama Cottages (☎ 0812-447 0420; full board per person 60,000Rp) Up the steps at the opposite end of the beach from Papa Roa, Panorama has a fab cliff-top setting.

Bastiano's Resort & Dive Centre (☎ 0431-853566; www.bastianos.com; full board per person US$25) The digs here are borderline luxurious, with a terrace for lounging, a well-stocked bar for boozing and a TV for switching off.

Froggies (☎ 0812-430 1356; www.divefroggies.com; full board per person from €20) Another place that's seriously worth a splurge for those after topnotch creature comforts.

PANTAI PANGALISANG

Daniel's Homestay (☎ 0812-447 1188; s/d 60,000/ 120,000Rp) There are basic wooden bungalows, in a pleasant mangroves and flower setting.

Lorenso Cottages (s/d 60,000/120,000Rp) Next door, this is smaller and countless decibels quieter, though a bit run-down.

Two Fish Divers (☎ 0811-432805; s/d 100,000/ 150,000Rp) Another 150m on, Two Fish lacks the charm of Daniel's, but the diving is well recommended and it also gets lively.

Getting There & Away

Boats leave the fishing harbour in Manado daily at 2pm (25,000Rp, one hour), except Sunday. The return from Bunaken is at 8am. A charter costs about 250,000Rp one-way.

TOMOHON

The Minahas Highland's extraordinary cuisine is served in a string of restaurants on a cliff overlooking Manado, just a few kilometres before Tomohon.

Between Tomohon and Lahendong, there's the extensive **Lahendong hot springs**.

Happy Flower Homestay (☎ 352787; Jl Rungku Dusun 1; s/d 35,000/45,000Rp) is justifiably applauded, with quirky bamboo architecture and oodles of charm. From Manado, take a Tomohon-bound bus and get out at the Gereja Pniel church, a few kilometres before Tomohon. Take the path opposite the church (a sign reads 'Volcano Resort'), walk 300m, cross a stream and look for the homestay tucked away in trees to the right.

BITUNG
☎ 0438 / pop 150,000
Bitung is the chief port of Minahasa and lies to the east of Manado. Despite its spectacular setting, the town is not very attractive. The **Pelni office** (☎ 35818) is in the harbour compound.

The **Samudra Jaya** (☎ 21167; Jl Sam Ratulangi 2; d 50,000Rp) is cheap and central.

Bitung is 55km from Manado. *Mikrolet* depart regularly from Manado's Paal 2 terminal. The *mikrolet* drops you off at the Mapalus terminal just outside Bitung, where you catch another *mikrolet* for the short trip into town.

MALUKU

Scattered across the most remote corner of this vast archipelago, Maluku (the Moluccas) has played a part in history that far outweighs its meagre size. As the only spot on earth

IS IT SAFE?

Many governments advise against travel to Maluku, a flashpoint of sectarian violence, with sporadic shootings and bomb blasts. The conflict has left more than 5000 Muslims and Christians dead since 1999. The anniversary of the failed 1950 declaration of a self-styled South Maluku Republic – 25 April – is a dangerous day, when religious violence has broken out in the past. In 2004 riots, dozens died and hundreds were injured. Airport and harbour officials in Ambon have at times turned tourists back.

Search Google News and the trilingual www.malra.org/posko for updates.

where cloves and nutmeg grew, these fabled 'Spice Islands' were famed for centuries as the place where money grew on trees.

These days, the ships have upped anchor and the traders have shut up shop, leaving this necklace of tiny islands, peppered with pristine beaches and dramatic coral reefs, to become a distant backwater once again.

Sadly, the calm has not lasted. The islands were devastated by a spate of bloody communal fighting that erupted between Christians and Muslims in 1999. While the adventurous will find Maluku a fantastically rewarding and hospitable place to travel, a close eye should always be kept on the latest security developments.

TRANSPORT
Getting There & Around
Provincial capital Kota Ambon is connected by air to Jakarta, Makassar, Biak, Sorong and Denpasar by Merpati, which also flies daily between Kota Ternate and Manado (Sulawesi).

Maluku is well connected to the rest of Indonesia via Pelni. Check the latest schedules at www.pelni.co.id. Perintis ships cover the more remote Maluku islands. Local passenger boats operate from Ambon.

PULAU AMBON
Pulau Ambon is Maluku's main island and transport hub. It was hit hard by the sectarian troubles that started in 1999, and most visitors only pass through en route to the Banda islands or Ternate.

Kota Ambon
☎ 0911 / pop 300,000
Maluku's trade and transport centre still bears the scars of the sectarian clashes, the latest in 2004, and is the site of sporadic political violence. Few travellers hang around.

INFORMATION
Maluku Tourist Bureau (☎ 312300; diparmal@ ambon.wasantara.net.id; Jl Jendral Sudirman; ⏰ 8am-2pm Mon-Sat) Is useful.
Rumah Sakit Umum (☎ 353438; Jl Dr Kayado 60/21) Medical services.

SLEEPING & EATING
Wisma Game (☎ 353525; Jl Ahmad Yani 35; d 99,000Rp; ❄) Glitzy it is not, but this is a reasonable place with air-con if you need it.

MALUKU (MOLUCCAS)

Penginapan Beta (☎ 353463; Jl Wim Reawaru; d 90,000Rp; ⊠) If Game is full, this has an English-speaking owner and secure rooms. Air-con rooms cost 120,000Rp.

For cheap eats, there are *warung* near the Batu Merah market.

GETTING THERE & AWAY
Mandala (☎ 344205; Jl Kapitan Ulupaha) flies daily to Jakarta (1,018,000Rp) and Makassar (468,000Rp). **Merpati** (☎ 353161; Jl Ahmad Yani 19) flies Tuesday to Kota Ternate (655,000Rp) and occasionally, Bandaneira (116,000Rp), although at the time of writing flights had been suspended. **Lion Air** (☎ 344205; Jl Wr Supratman) flies daily to Makassar (from 300,000Rp), Denpasar (from 900,000Rp),

and via Jakarta (from 700,000Rp) to Singapore (US$104). Schedules change frequently.

Pelni (☎ 342328) has an office opposite the Pattimura Memorial and boats leave from the main city port.

Smaller boats to just about every island around Maluku leave from the small-boat harbour between Ambon Plaza and the Pasar Mardika ruins.

Ojek (per hour 15,000Rp) are often more convenient and cheaper than buses.

BANDA ISLANDS
Small islands – big history: the storied Bandas, or Nutmeg islands, have over the centuries drawn Chinese, Arab and Javanese traders as well as Portuguese, Dutch and

English colonists, all chasing the valued spice that came from this isloated chain of 10 volcanic islands. Tinkering on the edge of some spectacular undersea drop-offs and coral gardens, the islands in the 1990s became the destination everyone wanted to keep a secret. In the last couple of years, tourist numbers have fallen dramatically, so if you missed out the first time, now is the time to rediscover this little piece of paradise.

Bandaneira
☎ 0910

The main port of the Banda islands, situated on Pulau Neira, is a pleasantly sleepy town of colonial-era buildings and blooming flowers.

SIGHTS & ACTIVITIES
Bandaneira is perfect for aimless wandering. Built by the VOC (Dutch East India Company) in 1611, the imposing fort **Benteng Belgica** stands above Bandaneira and offers staggering views of local volcano **Gunung Api**.

Benteng Nassau, built by the Dutch in 1609 (on the stone foundations laid, but later abandoned, by the Portuguese in 1529), stands below. Neither fort has an admission fee or opening times.

> ### SNORKEL OR DIVE?
>
> Despite massive potential, limited demand means that there's only one dive operator in the Bandas – at Bandaneira's **Hotel Maulana** (☎ 21023; per double dive from US$90). Snorkelling is a better way to view coral gardens and drop-offs that are unusually close to the shore. One of the best drop-offs is just off Ai village on Pulau Ai but many more can be reached by chartering a boat. Masks and fins are available for hire from 15,000Rp per day, but try to bring your own.

SLEEPING & EATING
Vita (☎ 21332; d from 50,000Rp; ✗) Hardly the cheapest option, but the English-speaking owner is savvy with snorkelling opportunities, and the rooms face the looming Gunung Api.

Pondok Wisata Flamboyan (☎ 21233; Jl Syahir; s/d from 35,000/50,000Rp) Flamboyant by name but not by nature, this is nevertheless one

of the best deals on the island. It's 30,000Rp extra for full board.

Delfika (☎ 21027; Jl Gereja Tua; s/d from 35,000/50,000Rp; ✗) This has a fab setting in a colonial-era house, and more expensive air-con rooms (doubles 120,000Rp).

Most guesthouses serve good bargain fare. There are also basic eateries near the port.

GETTING THERE & AROUND
The Bandas are difficult to reach, and air routes have been suspended. Pelni liners sail from Ambon to Bandaneira. Longboats, speedboats and canoes can be rented at the fish market.

Other Islands
Pulau Banda Besar is the biggest of the islands and the most important historical source of nutmeg. You can still visit **nutmeg groves** at the **Kelly Plantation** or wander around the ruinous fort **Benteng Hollandia**.

Pulau Hatta has an incredible coral-encrusted vertical drop-off only metres from tiny Lama village. **Pulau Ai** is easier to reach and also has fabulous coral gardens, drop-offs and beaches. On Ai, **Pondok Wisata Weltvreden** (d 50,000Rp) and **Revenge** (d with shared mandi 50,000Rp) offer accommodation.

GETTING THERE & AWAY
Passenger longboats ply the route between Bandaneira and Pulau Banda Besar (2000Rp) and Pulau Ai (5000Rp). To get to isolated Pulau Hatta, you'll have to charter a sturdy boat for a day trip at about 300,000Rp for the day. The trip one way should take two to three hours.

PULAU TERNATE & TIDORE
Hovering off the shores of the uniquely shaped Pulau Halmahera, the volcanic cone of Ternate is North Maluku's gateway and transport hub. Nearby Pulau Tidore, Ternate's age-old rival, is a relaxed island of villages and empty beaches. While Ternate saw some trouble during 1999 to 2000, it is now business as usual.

Kota Ternate
☎ 0921 / pop 150,000

With air connections to Manado, Kota Ternate is an ideal place to stopover for a few days.

INDONESIA

ORIENTATION & INFORMATION

The airport is close to Kota Ternate – 25,000Rp for a share taxi, or a 3000Rp *bemo* from the main road near the terminal. The city is small enough to walk around.

BNI bank (Jl Pahlawan Revolusi) Has some of the best rates in Maluku and an ATM.

Takoma (☎ 327175; Jl Hasanuddin) Internet access.

Tourist office (☎ 22760; Jl Kamarudin 10; ☼ 7.30am-1pm Mon-Sat, until 11am Fri) Is useful.

SIGHTS

Built around 1250, **Keraton Sultan** (☎ 21166; Sultan's Palace; admission by donation; ☼ 8am-noon) is 2km north of town, just back from Jl Sultan Baballuh, the airport road. It's now a museum.

The **Benteng Oranye** fort, in the centre of town, is also worth a peek.

SLEEPING & EATING

Hotel Sejathara (☎ 21139; Jl Salim Fabanyo 21; d with shared/private mandi 38,500/66,000Rp) This friendly place is one of the best cheap options.

Hotel Indah (☎ 22284; Jl Bosoiri; d from 55,000Rp; ☒) A fair back-up if Sejathara is full.

Rumah Makan Jailolo (Jl Pahlawan Revolusi 7; mains 20,000Rp; ☼ lunch & dinner) Tasty point-and-pick meals in cheerful, hygienic surrounds.

GETTING THERE & AROUND

Merpati (☎ 21651; Jl Bosoiri 10) flies to Ambon (660,000Rp) and Manado (from 286,000Rp).

Every two weeks, the Pelni liners link Kota Ternate with Bitung (101,000Rp), Sorong, Papua (140,000Rp) and Ambon (118,000Rp).

Around Pulau Ternate

Built in 1512 by the Portuguese, and restored by the Dutch in 1610, **Benteng Tolukko** is one of the better forts on the island. Near Bastiong, the 1540 Portuguese **Benteng Kalamata** has been over-restored, but the setting is spectacular.

Not far from Takome in the west is **Danau Tolire Besar**, a stunning, deep volcanic lake. A trail from the main road leads to the lake, which is believed to have crocodiles, and even the wreckage of a WWII plane.

Completely dominating the island, **Gunung Api Gamalama** has erupted fiercely many times over the centuries, most recently in late 1994. With a guide and some effort, you can trek to the top in a few hours. Ask for advice at the tourist office.

Pulau Tidore

Pulau Tidore, the centre of the Central Halmahera district, is more appealing than Pulau Ternate but doesn't have the facilities of its more developed neighbour.

In and around **Soasio**, the capital, are some hot springs, beaches, an interesting market and **Gunung Kiematubu**, which can be climbed or explored. Between Rum and Soasio are the compelling but decrepit **Benteng Tohula** fort and the engaging (but often closed) **Sultan's Memorial Museum**. Soasio has a couple of *losmen*, of which **Johra Penginapan** (☎ 61295; Jl FK Siepo; d 35,000Rp) is the cheapest.

Access is by frequent speedboat (5000Rp) from Bastiong port in Ternate.

PAPUA

One of the planet's last truly wild places, the former Irian Jaya is remote, mountainous and covered in 400,000 sq km of almost impenetrable forest. A land of knife-blade peaks (many permanently snowcapped), 250 designated cultural subgroups, 500 languages and negligible infrastructure, Papua is a vast region where tribal ways survive and the modern world is confined to a scattering of coastal towns.

WEST PAPUA'S HIDDEN WAR

Ever since Indonesia took over Irian Jaya from the Dutch in 1963, an independence movement has been active in what is now called Papua. The Indonesian army (TNI) has been accused of brutal repression of Papua's tribal people. In early 2005 the TNI announced it would boost troop strength to 50,000 in its counterinsurgency campaign against the Free Papua Organisation (OPM). Human rights abuses were recently reported in Puncak Jaya, Mulia and Torikara in the Central Highlands. Visitors are advised to stay away from street protests. Foreigners were kidnapped in West Papua in 2002.

Papua, the Indonesian side of the island of New Guinea, was only acquired from the Dutch in 1963. Indonesian mining and transmigration have not gone unopposed, and the independence movement, known as the Free Papua Organisation (OPM), remains active. Concessions have now been made to the Papuans, but the situation remains precarious and visitors should keep abreast of events.

VISITOR PERMITS (SURAT JALAN)

Within 24 hours of arrival in Papua, visitors must obtain a *surat jalan,* a permission to travel, from the local police station *(polres).* They are easiest to get in Kota Biak and Jayapura and should be ready within one hour. Bring three passport photos, three copies of the photo page in your passport and three copies of the passport page with the Indonesian visa on it. Police will charge a flexible 'administration fee' of around 5000Rp.

List every conceivable place you might want to visit, as it might be difficult to add them later, outside the large cities. As you travel around Papua, you are supposed to have the document stamped in local police stations. It is worth keeping a few photocopies of the permit in case police or hotels ask for them.

TRANSPORT
Getting There & Around
AIR

Papua is reasonably well connected with the rest of Indonesia and unless you have a lot of time, flying is the only way to travel once you are there. The transport centres are Sorong, Biak and Jayapura, so you may spend some time in these places waiting for connections.

Merpati is the main carrier throughout Papua, but flights are regularly cancelled and seats double-booked. Possible alternatives are the missionary services, **Mission Aviation Fellowship** (MAF; Sentani ☎ 0967-91109; Jl Misi Sentani; Wamena ☎ 0969-31263; Jl Gatot Subroto) and **Associated Missions Aviation** (AMA; ☎ 0967-591009; Jl Misi Sentani, Sentani), which will take tourists if they have the room.

There are no scheduled air services into Papua New Guinea (PNG).

BOAT

There are good Pelni connections with the rest of Indonesia and destinations across Papua. For the latest schedules, visit www.pelni.co.id.

Because there are no scheduled boats between Papua and PNG, the best way to get between the two is to charter a boat from Jayapura (ask around the port at Hamadi near Jayapura) to Vanimo (from 350,000Rp per person, minimum of three).

BUS

Roads are like gold dust in Papua and in most areas simply don't exist. You won't be getting very far by bus.

JAYAPURA
☎ 0967 / pop 185,000

If Indonesia has tamed anywhere in Papua, Jayapura is it. Largely populated by Javans and other non-Papuans, the provincial capital has the look and atmosphere of countless other Indonesian cities. For tourists, it is little more than a gateway, but Jayapura enjoys a pleasant seaside setting and it's a good place to regroup and get organised.

Orientation

Jayapura airport is at Sentani, 36km from Jayapura, and 90,000Rp by taxi.

Just about everything you will need in Jayapura is confined to Jl Ahmad Yani and, parallel to it, Jl Percetakan.

Information

BII bank (Jl Percetakan 22) Changes money and has an ATM.
PNG consulate (☎ 531250; Jl Percetakan 28; ☒ 8am-noon & 1-4pm Mon-Fri) Issues one-month tourist visas (225,000Rp) to PNG.
Police station (☎ 534161, 533462; Jl Ahmad Yani; ☒ 7am-3pm Mon-Fri) If you are going to need a *surat jalan,* the 'Satuan IPP' office here is the place to get it.
Post office (Jl Sam Ratulangi) Has an Internet centre.
Rumah Sakit Umum (☎ 533616; Jl Kesehatan; ☒ 24hr) Offers medical services.
Telkom office (Jl Sam Ratulangi)
Tourist office (☎ 583024; Jl Raya Abepura; ☒ 7.30am-3pm Mon-Fri) A *bemo* ride from Jayapura, but don't waste your time.

Sights & Activities

Along the Sentani–Abepura *bemo* route, two places are worth a look. The **Waena Museum Negeri** (Jl Abepura, Waena; admission 750Rp; ☒ 8am-4pm Tue-Sat, 11am-4pm Sun) has Papuan artefacts. Inside Cenderawasih University, the **Museum Loka Budaya** (Jl Abepura, Abepura; admission by donation; ☒ 7.30am-4pm Mon-Fri) displays Asmat carvings.

Pantai Hamadi was the site of an American amphibious landing in 1944. The beach is nice, and there are rusting WWII wrecks

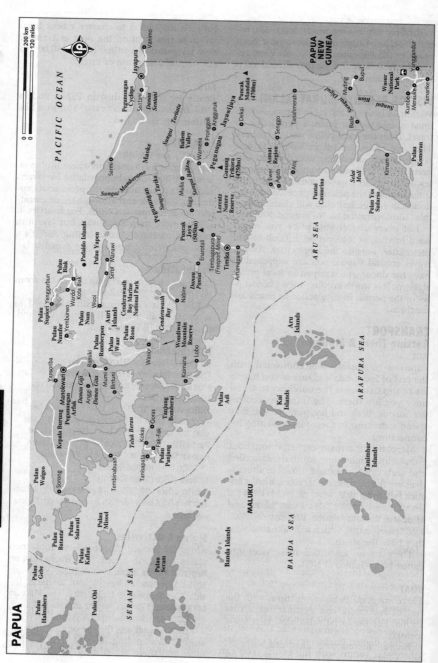

PAPUA

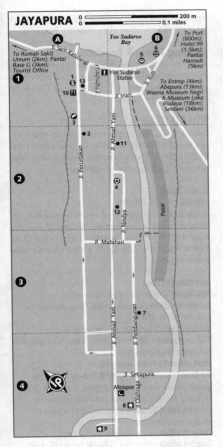

also try **Dani Sangrila Tours & Travel** (☎ 531060; danisa@jayapura.wasantara.net.id; Jl Pembangunan 19).

Sleeping & Eating

Hotel Kartini (☎ 531557; Jl Perintis 2; s/d with outside bathroom 44,000/66,000Rp; ❄) This is the best of a bad bunch, but you may need earplugs. Air-con rooms are 77,000Rp.

Hotel Jayapura (☎ 533216; Jl Olahraga 4; d 45,000Rp) The dark, fan-only rooms here are cheap and OK, but they can get infernally hot and hellishly noisy.

Hotel 99 (☎ 535689; Jl Argapura 2; d with shared mandi 55,000Rp; ❄) This overlooks the harbour, but you'll be hard-pressed to get a view. Air-con rooms are 110,000Rp.

Hotel Dafonsoro (☎ 531104; Jl Percetakan 20; s/d 198,000/253,000Rp) The rooms may be pricey, but the Fantasi Restaurant here, open for breakfast, lunch and dinner, is Jayapura's best all-round eatery. Dishes cost from 12,000Rp to 40,000Rp.

Night *warung* can be found along Jl Ahmad Yani.

Getting There & Away
AIR

Merpati (☎ 533111; Jl Ahmad Yani 15) flies to Kota Biak (446,000Rp), Timika (474,000Rp), Makassar (1,271,000Rp), Surabaya (1,491,000Rp) and Jakarta (1,500,000Rp). Merpati also has regular flights to Wamena, in the Baliem Valley.

Garuda (☎ 522222; Bank Papua Bldg, Jl Ahmad Yani) flies daily to Kota Biak (369,000Rp), Timika

and a statue nearby. The town has a bustling market, and several places to stay. **Pantai Base G**, known locally as Tanjung Ria, is another famous WWII site. The beach is a 15-minute walk from where the regular *bemo* drops you off.

Tours
Flights to the Baliem Valley cost 925,000Rp. Several good travel agencies can arrange local diving and sightseeing trips, as well as tours to the Baliem Valley and Asmat region.

Bucen Tours (☎ 536317; bucentours@yahoo.com) offers a five-day trip to Wamena and around for two people (twin share) for US$750, including flights, English-speaking guide and three-star rooms with full board. You can

INDONESIA

> ### BORDER CROSSING: INTO PAPUA NEW GUINEA
>
> To enter PNG by land, you need to get a visa (one-month tourist visa 225,000Rp) at the **PNG consulate** (☎ 0967-531250; Jl Percetakan 28; ☻ 8am-noon & 1-4pm Mon-Fri) in Jayapura, which may take a couple of days. The occasional bus (90 minutes) leaves for the border (which is open 9am to noon and 1pm to 4pm), though a taxi or *ojek* may be quicker. You must get stamped out, within 24 hours of your departure, at the Immigration Office opposite the Dafonsoro Hotel in Jayapura, not at the border itself, and pay a 50,000Rp 'fee'. The border itself is crossed on foot. On the PNG side, there's usually some vehicle hanging around that will take you to Vanimo. You can also book a taxi in advance through **Visser Car Rentals** (☎ 675-857 1366) in Vanimo.

(348,000Rp), Makassar (1,364,500Rp), Denpasar (1,498,700Rp) and Jakarta (1,576,500Rp).

Missionary service **Associated Missions Aviation** (AMA; ☎ 0967-591009; Jl Misi Sentani, Sentani) is based in Sentani. Large groups may be able to charter a small AMA plane to points such as Ilega (8,800,000Rp).

BOAT

Pelni (☎ 533270; Jl Argapuro 15) sails to Kota Biak fortnightly. The port is about 800m east of the Yos Sudarso statue.

Perintis boats also leave Jayapura every week or so, and stop at Serui, Nabire, Kota Biak and Manokwari – they normally leave from the main Pelni port. Other smaller boats to Sarmi, Serui, Nabire and Kota Biak leave from the small boat harbour along Jl Sam Ratulangi.

SENTANI
☎ 0967

Sentani, next to Jayapura's airport (36km from Jayapura) and near the shores of the magnificent **Danau Sentani**, is quieter, cooler (marginally) and more convenient than Jayapura.

The small town is compact, with most facilities on Jl Kemiri Sentani Kota. **Hotel Semeru** (☎ 591447; Jl Yabaso; d 80,000Rp; ☒) has

spotless and quiet air-con rooms. There are plenty of *rumah makan* (eating houses).

Getting There & Around
Getting to Sentani from Jayapura involves taking three different *bemo*. *Ojek* are much more convenient and can be hired for about 15,000Rp per hour.

PULAU BIAK
Small Biak, an important part of the battle for the Pacific in WWII, has numerous remnants of those horrific days, and is also a major Indonesian naval base.

Kota Biak
☎ 0981 / pop 100,000
Kota Biak, the only real town on the island, is a relaxed, compact place and the ideal base for exploring nearby attractions. The Frans Kaisiepo airport is a short bemo ride from town.

INFORMATION
BNI bank (Jl Imam Bonjol 23) Has an ATM
Danamon Bank (Jl Imam Bonjol) Across the road from BNI, also has an ATM.
diBiak.Com (Jl Sudirman 4) Internet access.
Police station (☎ 21810, 21657; Jl Diponegoro) An easy place to get permits.
Post office (Jl Prof M Yamin 59)
PT Biak Irian Wisata Tours & Travel (☎ 23196; paradise@biak.wasantara.net.id; Hotel Arumbai, Jl Selat Makassar 3) Offers tours, treks and travel information.
Rumah Sakit Umum (☎ 21294; Jl Sri Wijaya) For medical emergencies.
Telkom office (Jl Yos Sudarso 1; ☻ 24hr)
Tourist office (☎ 21663; Jl Prof M Yamin; ☻ 8am-2.30pm Mon-Fri) Opposite the post office.

SLEEPING & EATING
Hotel Maju (☎ 21841; Jl Imam Bonjol 45; s/d 55,000/70,000Rp; ☒) The guests vote with their feet here, the best cheapie in town with small, quiet rooms. Rooms with air-con are 125,000Rp.

Hotel Sinar Kayu (☎ 21333; Jl Sisingamangaraja 89; d 80,000Rp; ☒) Rooms range from the dark and noisy to the clean and comfortable.

Hotel Dahlia (☎ 21851; Jl Selat Madura 6; d with outside/inside bathroom 65,000/70,000Rp) Good, but haunted by the lingering whiff of rambutan.

Purama Restaurant (☎ 220221; Jl Monginsidi 7; mains 15,000Rp) Airy, with bum-breaking wooden chairs and fair food.

KOTA BIAK

```
0                    200 m
0                    0.1 miles
```

To Rumah Sakit
Umum (2.2km)

INFORMATION
BNI Bank...1 C2
Danamon Bank...................................2 C3
diBiak.Com..3 B3
Police Station......................................4 B2
PT Biak Irian Wisata Tours & Travel...5 C3

SLEEPING 🏠
Hotel Dahlia...6 C3
Hotel Maju..7 C3
Hotel Sinar Kayu..................................8 A1

EATING 🍴
Pasar Inpres...9 A2
Pasar Lama..10 B2
Purama Restaurant............................11 B2
Rumah Makan Nirwana......................12 B3

TRANSPORT
Garuda..13 B3
Pelni...14 A2

Bemo/Bus Terminal
Jl Teuku Umar
Ojek Stand
Jl Erlangga
Jl Sisingamangaraja
Djponegoro
Jl Selat Makassar
Port
Jl Sudirman
Yapen Strait
Jl Selat Madura
Jl Ahmad Yani
Jl Monginsidi
Fish Market
Jl Imam Bonjol
Jl Pramuka
Mosque

To Gua Binsari (5km);
Bosnik (16km)

To Telkom (200m); Main Post
Office (1.5km); Tourist Office (1.5km);
Airport (2.5km); Merpati (2.5km)

Rumah Makan Nirwana (☎ 21506; Jl Sudirman 5; cakes 6000Rp; ❤ breakfast, lunch & dinner) Dishes up decent pastries, roti and *kue-kue* (cakes).

Warung congregate at **Pasar Inpres** (Jl Erlangga) and **Pasar Lama** (Jl Selat Makassar).

GETTING THERE & AWAY
Kota Biak is one of Papua's transport hubs.

Merpati (☎ 21213; Jl Prof M Yamin, airport) flies daily to Nabire (446,000Rp), to Jayapura (336,000Rp) and Manokwari (425,000Rp) four days a week, and also to Makassar (721,000Rp) three times a week.

Garuda (☎ 25737; Jl Sudirman 3) flies five times a week to Jayapura (369,000Rp), Makassar (1,157,000Rp) and Jakarta (1,447,000Rp). A flight via Jakarta to Singapore costs US$300.

Pelni (☎ 23255; Jl Sudirman 37) liners stop in Biak and continue to Jayapura (116,000Rp), Manokwari and further afield. Perintis boats also regularly stop in Kota Biak.

AROUND PULAU BIAK
While Kota Biak isn't that exciting, the island does have several interesting places to justify a stopover, and they can all be visited in day trips from the city. *Bemo* and buses leave regularly from the main market. Chartered *bemo* cost around 30,000Rp per hour.

Actually a tunnel, **Gua Binsari** (admission 10,000Rp; ❤ 7am-5pm) is a Japanese cave that provides a chilling impression of a WWII battle. There is a small **museum** next door. Take a *bemo* heading towards Bosnik, which can drop you 800m away.

On the way to Bosnik, the **Taman Burung & Anggrek** (Bird & Orchid Park; admission 5000Rp; ❤ 7.30am-3pm Mon-Sat) is about as close as you will get to a bird of paradise.

Bosnik, another famous WWII site, with boats to the beautiful **Padaido Islands**, has a small market and a lovely **beach**. It's an easy 30 minutes by regular *bemo* (6000Rp).

Although Pulau Biak and the nearby Padaido Islands boast some of the best scuba diving in Indonesia, the local diving industry is not well developed.

Papua Diving (☎ 0411-401660; www.papua-diving.com; Jl Gunung Gamalama 3) is based in Sorong, but this remains one of Papua's top operators.

INDONESIA

CENDERAWASIH BAY

Stretching from Manokwari to the far east of Pulau Yapen, and incorporating the **Cenderawasih Bay Marine National Park** (Taman Laut Teluk Cenderawasih), the Cenderawasih Bay region is easily Papua's most underrated area. With outstanding **diving** and **trekking**, wildlife, deserted beaches and isolated islands, its potential is, however, still hindered by limited transport.

Manokwari

☎ 0986 / pop 100,000

The first place in Papua to be inhabited by missionaries, Manokwari is easy to get around and well connected. Nearby there's **trekking** in the Pegunungan Arfak (Arfak Mountains), the Anggi Lakes and islands such as Pulau Rumberpon. The **tourist office** (☎ 212030; Jl Merdeka) is a useful first stop for loads of information.

In Manokwari itself, an easy 5km walk takes you through the lush **Taman Gunung Meja** (Table Mountain Park), with butterflies and a Japanese WWII memorial. A good beach, **Pasir Sen Babai** is easy to get to, and a canoe trip to **Pulau Mansinam** is a real must.

Cheap sleeps include **Losmen Apose** (☎ 211369; Jl Kota Baru 4; d from 50,000Rp; ✱), opposite the Merpati office; and **Hotel Arfak** (☎ 213079; Jl Brawijaya 8; d from 72,000Rp; ✱), the old Dutch Marines Officers' mess.

Merpati (☎ 211153; Jl Kota Baru 39), weather permitting, flies four times a week to Kota Biak (424,000Rp) and to Jayapura (391,000Rp), and flies twice a week to Anggi (58,500Rp). All four **Pelni** (☎ 215167; Jl Siliwangi 24) liners servicing the north coast make stops in Manokwari.

Anggi Lakes

Set 2030m high in the Pegunungan Arfak, the twin lakes of Danau Giji and Danau Gita offer the visitor exquisite scenery and wildlife, and some excellent walking and swimming.

Guides are essential for the two- and three-day hikes and can be organised at the district office in the transmigrasi town of **Ransiki** (which can be reached by taxi from Manokwari but may be cut off in the rainy season), where the hikes start. The office in Ransiki doubles as a guesthouse. Bring your own food for the hike.

BALIEM VALLEY

For the explorers who believed there were no more surprises up the world's sleeve, the 1938 'discovery' of the Baliem Valley was proof positive that pockets of the planet remained hidden from view, even in the aviation age. Nearly seven decades on, little has changed, and while the rest of Indonesia thunders into the information age, local Dani men are still more likely to be seen sporting a *horim* (penis gourd) than a mobile phone.

The Danis maintain their polygamous marriage system and a man may have as many wives (bought with pigs) as he can afford. Grass skirts usually indicate that a woman is unmarried and one of the more unusual, but increasingly outdated, customs is for women to amputate part of their fingers when a close relative dies.

For several days every August, Wamena and nearby villages host a spectacular tourist festival with pig feasts, mock wars and traditional dancing.

Wamena

☎ 0969 / pop 8500

The main town in the Baliem Valley, Wamena is a dusty sprawl. Although there's not much in the town itself, it's a good base for exploring the surrounding area. Wamena is expensive – a consequence of having to fly everything in from Jayapura.

ORIENTATION & INFORMATION

Wamena is easy enough to walk around. There's no shortage of becak – until it rains. The BRI and Mandiri banks have ATMs.

Bank Papua (Jl Trikora 45) Has lousy rates.

Dirgantara Tour & Travel (☎ 34530; Hotel Anggrek, Jl Ambon 1) Is an agent for Trigana Air Service.

Post office (Jl Timor) Central.

Rumah Sakit Umum (☎ 31152; Jl Trikora) Offers basic medical facilities.

Tourist office (☎ 31365; Jl Yos Sudarso 73) The office is unmarked – look for the Indonesian flag – and of limited use.

Warnet Victory (☎ 31127; Jl Ahmad Yani 49) Internet service.

SLEEPING & EATING

There are some cheap sleeping alternatives – mostly Dani-style huts – in villages near Wamena (see Trekking, opposite).

Hotel Syahrial Makmur (☎ 31306; Jl Gatot Subroto 51; d 70,000Rp) Only two minutes' walk south of the airport, this is the cheapest place in Wamena. Room standards vary.

Wamena Hotel (☎ 31292; Jl Homhom; d 180,000Rp) Welcome seclusion and greenery come into the equation here, but you may have to holler to locate a receptionist.

Hotel Anggrek (☎ 34530; Jl Ambon 1; d 130,000Rp) This has very welcome hot water. The price is high, but it gets points for comfort and cleanliness.

Nayak Hotel (☎ 31067; Jl Gatot Subroto; s/d 120,000/150,000Rp) Often disconcertingly empty, Nayak offers reasonably swish rooms near the airport.

Rumah Makan Mas Budi (Jl Pattimura; dishes from 15,000Rp; ☾ lunch & dinner) Draws travellers with its tasty fare and then sends them packing with its terribly tinny karaoke machine.

Kantin Bu Lies (Jl Gatot Subroto; meals from 10,000Rp; ☾ lunch & dinner) Next to the airport and good for simple Indonesian food.

For a basic meal there are Padang-style places on Jl Sulawesi, behind the market. These open for breakfast, lunch and dinner.

Wamena is officially a 'dry area', so no alcohol is available.

SHOPPING
Readily available souvenirs include *noken* string bags (15,000Rp to 35,000Rp); *suale* (head decorations) often incorporating an entire squashed parrot; the inevitable *horim* (10,000Rp to 60,000Rp); and *kapak* (black-stone axe blades) upward from 40,000Rp. Bargaining is the order of the day.

GETTING THERE & AROUND
Merpati (☎ 31488; Jl Trikora 41) flies between Jayapura and Wamena (from Wamena 303,000Rp, from Jayapura 403,000Rp) 12 times a week, but you should book early and reconfirm.

Trigana Air Service (☎ 31611; airport terminal) plies the same route (from Wamena 395,000Rp, from Jayapura 460,000Rp) and flies to Mulia, Karubaga and Bokondini.

AROUND THE BALIEM VALLEY
Trekking is the best (and most expensive) way to dip into valley life, but you can also see most of the traditional people and customs, mummies, markets, scenery and wild pigs during day trips from Wamena, Jiwika and Kurima.

Trekking
This is great trekking country, but travel light as the trails are rough and hard-going. It's normally cold at night, and it often rains, so bring trekking clothes and gear. You can buy food, water and cooking equipment in Wamena, although it is comparatively expensive.

Staying in village huts, or the homes of local families – the best bet outside Wamena – should cost about 30,000Rp per person per night.

GUIDES
In Wamena, would-be guides will latch onto you as soon as you arrive, and can be persistent. They sometimes refuse to finish the trek until they're paid more than initially agreed. Before committing, speak to other travellers and plan the route you would like to follow.

Prices vary, but according to the tourist office, non-English-speaking/English-speaking guides should cost about 50,000/100,000Rp per day; and a porter around 50,000Rp.

Getting Around
From Wamena, hopelessly overcrowded *taksi* go as far south as Yetni (18km, 20 minutes); as far north, on the western side of the valley, as Pyramid (35km, 45 minutes) and as far north on the eastern side as Manda. To go anywhere else, you can also try to hire *taksi* from the relatively central **'Misi' taksi terminal** (Jl Ahmad Yani) for a negotiable 30,000Rp per hour.

Central & South Baliem Valley
Virtually a 'suburb' of Wamena, **Wesaput** is an easy stroll across the airport. The only museum in the valley, the **Palimo Adat Museum** (admission by donation; ☾ 8am-4pm Mon-Sat), with its limited collection of local artefacts, is at the end of the trail. On the way, **Wio Silimo Tradisional Hotel** (r per person 50,000Rp) is one of the best Dani-style places around.

Behind the museum, a swinging bridge leads to **Pugima**, a flat one-hour walk away. Pugima isn't that exciting, but the trail goes past some charming Dani villages and scenery. At the end of Jl Yos Sudarso, **Sinatma** has good walks around Sungai Wamena, a market and a swinging bridge.

The road south passes through the village of **Hitigima**. An hour or so on foot from

Hitigima (you will need to ask directions or take a guide) are some saltwater wells. The road south stops a few kilometres short of **Kurima**, a good base in the south where you can ask around for a **bed** (per person 35,000Rp). From Kurima, there's more great trekking to places like **Hitugi**, a few hours away. A popular two- or three-day trek is Wamena-Kurima-Hitugi-Pugima-Wamena.

East Baliem Valley

Near **Pikhe**, the northern road crosses mighty Sungai Baliem and passes **Aikima**, which is notable for its 270-year-old **Werapak Elosak mummy** (admission 5000Rp; ☼ dawn-dusk). The route from Aikima to Jiwika is an interesting, flat three- to four-hour walk. **Suroba**, a serene village set 20 minutes off the main road, is worth a stop to admire the countryside and the intricate hanging bridges. **Jiwika** is another good base and **Sumpaima**, 300m north of Jiwika, is home to the 280-year-old **Wimontok Mabel mummy** (admission 5000Rp; ☼ dawn-dusk), the best of its kind near Wamena.

At the turn-off in Jiwika to Iluwe, **Lauk Inn** (d 60,000Rp) is the only proper accommodation outside Wamena and comes well recommended. Otherwise, rooms or **traditional huts** (per person 25,000Rp) are available in most villages.

North of Jiwika, the **Gua Kotilola** (admission 5000Rp; ☼ 8am-4pm Mon-Sat) caves are worth a peek; ask to be dropped off because there is no sign. In **Wosilimo**, the **Gua Wikuda** (admission 5000Rp; ☼ 8am-4pm Mon-Sat) are more interesting. An hour's walk west of Wosilimo, **Danau Ane-gerak** has fishing and some huts to stay in. From Wosilimo, a trekking trail continues to, and beyond, Pass Valley. Also popular is the one- to two-day trek from Wosilimo to Pyramid via Meagaima and Pummo.

Public transport continues north to **Manda**, where there is more pretty countryside and hut-style sleeps. From Manda, treks start to the Wolo Valley.

West Baliem Valley

There isn't a great deal on this side of the valley for trekking, but it's worth a *bemo* trip anyway as far as **Pyramid**, a graceful missionary village with churches, a theological college and a bustling market. You may be able to stay at **Kimbim**.

From Pyramid, popular treks go to **Kelila** in the north and to **Pietriver** in the west. If trekking, take the trail from Kimbim to Pummo and along Sungai Baliem to Wamena through Muai, rather than the dull, direct Pyramid–Wamena road.

INDONESIA DIRECTORY

ACCOMMODATION

Hotel, *losmen, penginapan, wisma:* there are several words for somewhere to lay a weary head and options to suit every budget in most Indonesian towns.

Cheap hotels are usually very basic and with tourist numbers down over recent years, standards tend to be lower than in many other tourist destinations. In compensation, a simple breakfast is often included. Traditional washing facilities consist of a *mandi*, a large water tank from which you scoop *cold* water with a dipper. Climbing into the tank is very bad form! Rooms are assumed to come with a private *mandi* (bathing facility) in this chapter, unless otherwise specified. The air-con symbol (❄) denotes whether air-con rooms are available, otherwise rooms are assumed to come with a fan.

Accommodation prices in Indonesia vary considerably and are at their highest in July and August and the period following Ramadan, when the whole country puts fasting aside and packs its bags for a holiday. Bali is more expensive on the whole, but finding rooms for 40,000Rp a night is possible wherever you are.

ACTIVITIES

Diving, trekking, surfing, rafting; the list is endless in Indonesia and while plenty of cowboys are on the prowl, you will usually be able to find world-class operators in all of the major sites.

Diving

Indonesia is an Aladdin's cave for divers, although visibility is often limited during the wet season (roughly October to April). Many schools offer courses accredited by PADI, NAUI, BSAC etc but remember to bring your certification if you are already qualified.

Highlights include Flores (p292) and the Gili islands (p281) in Nusa Tenggara, Pulau Seribu, Cimaja and Karimunjawa in Java,

Amed (p232) and Lovina (p233) in Bali, Pulau Bunaken (p326) and the Togean Islands (p324) in Sulawesi, Pulau Weh (p267) in Sumatra, the Banda Islands (p328) in Maluku and Pulau Biak (p334) in Papua.

Surfing

Indonesia has waves that will send most surfers weak at the knees. Traditionally June through August offers the most consistent waves, but beaches can get busy and local surfers territorial during this time. If you are just starting out, courses are run throughout Bali, but veterans will never run out of challenges. While shops across Bali and in the hot spots of Java will stock most surfing accessories, including a wide range of boards, you will have to bring your own gear if you are planning on surfing off the beaten track.

Highlights include Pulau Nias (p254) in Sumatra, Cimaja (near Pelabuhanratu) and G-Land (in Taman Nasional Alas Purwo; see Sights & Activities, p215) in Java, Nusa Dua (p221) and Hu'u (p290) in Sumbawa.

Trekking

Despite massive potential, trekking is far less established in Indonesia than it is in, say, Thailand. Local guide services are developing where demand exists, however, and the national parks offer some exciting opportunities.

In Java, trekking is largely confined to shorter treks up volcanoes. Trekking in Bali is similarly restricted to volcanoes, such as Gunung Batur (p237). Gunung Rinjani (p286) on Lombok is one of Indonesia's best and most popular treks (from two to five days).

The Baliem Valley (p336) in Papua is also one of Indonesia's better known walking destinations and Tana Toraja (p319) has plenty of fabulous trekking opportunities through Sulawesi's spectacular traditional villages.

BOOKS

Lonely Planet's *Bali & Lombok* and *Indonesia* guides explore the country in more detail, and Lonely Planet's *World Food Indonesia* is the perfect guide for backpacker gourmets. Lonely Planet also produces the *Indonesian phrasebook*, and *Healthy Travel: Asia* for the lowdown on keeping healthy during your travels.

An excellent history from c 1200 is *A History of Modern Indonesia* by MC Ricklefs. *Nathaniel's Nutmeg* by Giles Milton offers a fascinating account of the battle to control trade from the Spice Islands.

The Malay Archipelago by Alfred Russel Wallace is the 1869 classic of this famous naturalist's wanderings throughout the Indonesian archipelago. Pramoedya Ananta Toer is Indonesia's best-known novelist. Look for the novels *This Earth of Mankind, Child of All Nations, Footsteps* and *House of Glass*.

BUSINESS HOURS

Government offices are *generally* open Monday to Friday from 8am to 4pm – with a break for Friday prayers from 11.30am to 1.30pm – and Saturday until noon. Go early if you want to get anything done.

Banks are open Monday to Friday, usually from 8am to 4pm. In some places banks open on Saturday until around 11am. Foreign exchange hours may be more limited and some banks close their foreign exchange counter at 1pm. Moneychangers are open longer hours.

CLIMATE

Indonesia is hot year-round, with wet and dry seasons. Coastal areas are often pleasantly cool, and it can get extremely cold in the mountains.

Generally, the wet season starts later the further southeast you go. In North Sumatra, the rain begins to fall in September, but in Timor it doesn't fall until November. In January and February it can rain often. The dry season is basically from May to September. The odd islands out are those of Maluku (the Moluccas), where the wet season is the reverse, running from May to September.

See the regional climate charts (p924).

DANGERS & ANNOYANCES

If you have only been reading about Indonesia in the newspapers, you may have a fairly grim view of the archipelago. Terrorism, natural disasters, political upheaval: the list of dangers is long and, for those involved in the Bali blast of 2002 and the tsunami of 2004, terrifyingly real. But while Indonesia does have more than its fair share of woes, only the tiniest number of travellers actually run into trouble here.

INDONESIA

The key to safe travel, however, is to keep abreast of current developments. At the time of writing, areas of Central Sulawesi, Aceh, Papua and Maluku were higher risk destinations, but keep an eye on media reports, check the safety situation with your embassy in Jakarta and, perhaps most importantly, go enjoy yourself.

Violent crime is very rare in Indonesia, but theft and scams (particularly in Bali) can be a problem. If you are mindful of your valuables and take the usual precautions, the chances of being ripped off are small.

See also p925 for information on the risks associated with recreational drug use, and p165 for an update on Avian influenza (bird flu).

DISABLED TRAVELLERS

Laws covering the disabled date back to 1989, but Indonesia has very few dedicated programmes, and is a difficult destination for those with limited mobility. Bali, with its wide range of tourist facilities, and Java are the easiest destinations to navigate.

EMBASSIES & CONSULATES
Embassies & Consulates in Indonesia

Australia Jakarta (Map p164; ☎ 021-2550 5555; Jl Rasuna Said Kav C15-16); Denpasar (☎ 0361-241118; Jl Hayam Wuruk 88B)

Brunei (☎ 021-3190 6080; 7 Jl Tanjung Karang, Jakarta 10230)

Canada (Map p164; ☎ 021-2550 7800; 6th fl, World Trade Centre, Jl Jend Sudirman Kav 29-31, Jakarta)

East Timor (☎ 021-390 2978; tljkt@yahoo.com; 11th fl, Surya Bldg, Jl MH Thamrin Kav 9, Jakarta 10350)

France (Map p166; ☎ 021-314 2807; Jl Thamrin 20, Jakarta)

Germany (Map p166; ☎ 021-390 1750; Jl Thamrin 1, Jakarta)

Japan (Map p166; ☎ 021-324308; Jl Thamrin 24, Jakarta)

Malaysia (☎ 021-522 4947; Jl Rasuna Said Kav X/6 1, Jakarta)

Myanmar (Map p166; ☎ 021-314 0440; Jl H Augus Salim 109, Jakarta)

Netherlands (☎ 021-525 1515; Jl Rasuna Said Kav S-3, Kuningan, Jakarta)

New Zealand (Map p166; ☎ 021-570 9460; 23rd fl, BRI II Bldg, Jl Jend Sudirman Kav 44-46, Jakarta)

Papua New Guinea (Map p164; ☎ 021-725 1218; 6th fl, Panin Bank Centre, Jl Jend Sudirman 1, Jakarta)

Philippines (Map p166; ☎ 021-315 0119; Jl Imam Bonjol 6-8, Jakarta)

Singapore (Map p164; ☎ 021-520 1489; Jl Rasuna Said, Block X/4 Kav 2, Jakarta)

Thailand (Map p166; ☎ 021-390 4052; Jl Imam Bonjol 74, Jakarta)

UK (Map p166; ☎ 021-315 6264; Jl Thamrin 75, Jakarta)

USA Jakarta (Map p166; ☎ 021-3435 9000; Jl Medan Merdeka Selatan 4-5); Denpasar (☎ 0361 233605; Jl Hayam Wuruk 188)

Vietnam (Map p166; ☎ 021-310 0358; Jl Teuku Umar 25, Jakarta)

Indonesian Embassies & Consulates Abroad

Countries with an Indonesian embassy:

Australia (☎ 02-6250 8600; 8 Darwin Ave, Yarralumla, ACT 2600)

Canada (☎ 613-724 1100; 55 Parkdale Ave, Ottawa, Ontario K1Y 1E5)

France (☎ 01 45 03 07 60; 47-49 Rue Cortambert 75116, Paris)

Germany (☎ 030-478 070; Lehrter Str 16-17, 10557 Berlin)

Japan (☎ 03 3441 4201; indonesian-embassy.or.jp; 5-2-9 Higashi Gotanda, Shinagawa-Ku, Tokyo)

Netherlands (☎ 0703-10 81 00; 8 Tobias Asserlaan, 2517 KC Den Haag)

New Zealand (☎ 04-475 8697; 70 Glen Rd, Kelburn, Wellington)

Papua New Guinea (☎ 251 116; 1 + 2/410 Kiro St, Sir John Guise Dr, Waigani)

UK (☎ 020-7499 7661; 38 Grosvenor Sq, London W1K 2HW)

USA (☎ 202-775 5200; 2020 Massachusetts Ave NW, Washington DC 20036)

FESTIVALS & EVENTS

Although some public holidays have a fixed date, the dates for many events vary each year depending on Muslim, Buddhist or Hindu calendars. National public holidays are:

New Year's Day 1 January
Idul Adha February/March
Muharram (Muslim New Year) March/April
Hindu New Year (Nyepi) March/April
Good Friday March/April
Ascension of Christ April/May
Waisak Day April/May
Mohammed's Birthday May/June
Independence Day 17 August
Ascension of Mohammed October
Lebaran (Idul Fitri) December
Christmas Day 25 December

Independence Day is the biggest event, with parades and celebrations held throughout the country.

The Muslim fasting month of Ramadan requires that Muslims abstain from food, drink, cigarettes and sex between sunrise and sunset. Many bars and restaurants close and it is important to avoid eating or drinking publicly during this time. For the week before and after Lebaran (Idul Fitri), the festival to mark the end of the fast, transport is often fully booked and travelling becomes a nightmare – plan to stay put at this time. Ramadan and Idul Fitri move back 10 days or so every year, according to the Muslim calendar.

Nyepi in Bali marks the Hindu New Year, and though it is preceded by festivals, virtually all of Bali closes.

With such a diversity of people in the archipelago there are many other local holidays, festivals and cultural events.

The *Indonesia Calendar of Events* covers holidays and festivals throughout the archipelago. You may be able to pick a copy up from overseas Garuda Airlines offices or an embassy. The Indonesian embassy in the Netherlands lists events on its well-updated website (www.indonesia.nl; the link is under Events).

FOOD & DRINK

A *rumah makan* (literally, eating house) is the cheaper equivalent of a *restoran*, but the dividing line is often hazy. The cheapest option of all is the *warung*, a makeshift or permanent food stall, but again the food may be the same as in a *rumah makan*. With any roadside food it pays to be careful about the hygiene. The *pasar* (market) is a good food source, especially the *pasar malam* (night market). Mobile *kaki lima* (food carts) serve cheap snack foods and meals.

As with food in the rest of Asia, Indonesian food is heavily based on rice. *Nasi goreng* is the national dish: fried rice, with an egg on top in *istimewa* (deluxe) versions. *Nasi campur,* rice with whatever is available, is a *warung* favourite, often served cold. The two other real Indonesian dishes are gado gado and satay (*sate* in Bahasa Indonesia). Gado gado is a fresh salad with prawn crackers and peanut sauce. It tends to vary a lot, so if your first one isn't so special try again somewhere else. Satay are tiny kebabs served with a spicy peanut dip.

Padang food, from the Padang region in Sumatra, is popular throughout Indonesia. In a Padang restaurant *(masakan Padang),* a bowl of rice is plonked in front of you, followed by a whole collection of small bowls of vegetables, meat, fish and eggs. Eat what you want and your bill is added up from the number of empty bowls. In Sumatra, food can be spicy enough to burn your tongue.

Bottled water and soft drinks are available everywhere, and many hotels and restaurants provide *air putih* (boiled water) for guests. The iced juice drinks can be good, but take care that the water/ice has been boiled or is bottled.

Indonesian tea is fine and coffee is also quite good. Local beer is good – Bintang is Heineken-supervised and costs from around US$1 for a large bottle. Bali Brem rice wine is really potent, and the more you drink the nicer it tastes. *Es buah,* or *es campur,* is a strange concoction of fruit salad, jelly (Jello) cubes, syrup, crushed rice and condensed milk. And it tastes absolutely *enak* (delicious).

GAY & LESBIAN TRAVELLERS

Gay travellers in Indonesia will experience few problems, especially in Bali. Physical contact between same-sex couples is acceptable and homosexual behaviour is not illegal – the age of consent is 16. Immigration officials may restrict entry to people who reveal HIV positive status. Gay men in Indonesia are referred to as *homo* or *gay*; lesbians are *lesbi.*

Indonesia's transvestite/transsexual *waria* – from *wanita* (woman) and *pria* (man) – community has always had a very public profile.

Indonesia's first Gay Pride celebration was staged in Surabaya in 1999.

For some background and listings of gay-friendly bars, restaurants and even dive shops in Indonesia, visit www.utopia-asia.com/tipsindo.htm.

INTERNET ACCESS

Internet cafés continue to sprout up across Indonesia and many post offices have a Warposnet, which is a privately contracted Internet service. Rates and server speeds vary: expect to pay between 6000Rp and 15,000Rp per hour.

INTERNET RESOURCES

The web is a rich resource for travellers. **Lonely Planet** (www.lonelyplanet.com) has succinct summaries to most places on earth, postcards from other travellers, the Thorn Tree bulletin board, travel news and updates, and links to useful travel resources.

Some other interesting sites:

http://coombs.anu.edu.au/WWWVLPages /IndonPages/WWWVL-Indonesia.html Australian National University's links site, the 'granddaddy' of links to everything Indonesian.

http://indonesia.elga.net.id A good general introduction to Indonesia with a range of links.

www.antara.co.id The official Indonesian news agency; searchable database.

www.cia.gov/cia/publications/factbook/geos/id .html For all the facts and figures.

www.dfat.gov.au/geo/indonesia/index.html Continuously updated website of the Australian Government.

www.expat.or.id Information, advice and links to the expatriate community.

www.thejakartapost.com Website of Indonesia's English-language daily.

www.tourismindonesia.com Indonesia's official tourist information site.

LEGAL MATTERS

Drugs, gambling and pornography are illegal, and it is an offence to engage in paid work, or stay in the country for more than 60 days on a tourist pass.

Despite claims of reform, corruption is still widespread. Police often stop motorists on minor or dubious traffic infringements in the hope of obtaining bribes. The best advice is to remain calm, keep your money in your pocket until it is asked for and sit through the lecture – it is unlikely more than 50,000Rp will be demanded.

In case of an accident involving serious injury or death, the best advice is to drive straight to the nearest police station as an angry mob may soon gather.

MAPS

Locally produced maps can be good but are often surprisingly inaccurate. Periplus produces excellent maps of most Indonesian cities and regions.

MEDIA

Newspapers

The English-language press is limited mostly to the daily *Jakarta Post* (5000Rp). Two of the leading Indonesian-language newspapers are the Jakarta dailies *Pos Kota* and *Kompas*. Expensive and out-of-date foreign newspapers are available in most major cities.

Radio & TV

Radio Republik Indonesia (RRI) is the national radio station and broadcasts 24 hours in Indonesian from every provincial capital.

Thanks to satellite broadcasting, TV can be received everywhere in Indonesia. You'll see plenty of Indonesians gathered around the TV set of any hotel – they are among the world's foremost TV addicts. Televisi Republik Indonesia (TVRI) is the government-owned Indonesian-language TV station, which is broadcast in every province.

MONEY

ATMs

ATMs are numerous in Indonesia and you could travel through the main tourist areas of Bali, Java and Sumatra without ever setting foot inside a bank. Major regional cities, such as Makassar, Kupang and even Jayapura, also have ATMs that accept Visa, MasterCard or Cirrus cards, but always carry cash or travellers cheques as well as ATMs vanish once you step off the beaten track.

Bargaining & Tipping

Bargaining is required in markets and for transport where prices are not fixed. Tipping is not a normal practice in Indonesia but is often expected for special service.

Credit Cards

MasterCard and Visa (and linked services such as Cirrus and Maestro) are the most widely accepted plastic cards.

Many cards can be used to debit from your savings account rather than racking up credit. Transaction fees may be charged by your home bank and can be ridiculously high, so withdraw as much cash as possible at a time – check with your bank. Always check the transaction record to ensure the correct amount has been debited.

Credit cards can also be used at big hotels, exclusive restaurants and shops.

Currency

The unit of currency in Indonesia is the rupiah (Rp). Coins of 25, 50, 100 and 500 rupiah are in circulation in both the old silver-coloured coins and the newer bronze-coloured coins. A coin of 1000Rp is also minted but rarely seen, and the 25Rp coin has almost vanished. Notes come in 1000, 5000, 10,000, 20,000 50,000 and 100,000 rupiah denominations.

Exchanging Money

The roller-coaster ride that the rupiah took during the monetary crisis seems to have levelled out at about 9973Rp to US$1. For the latest exchange rates check www.xe.com.

Exchange rates vary markedly – the more remote the place, the worse the rates. Jakarta and Bali have the best rates in Indonesia. Elsewhere, eg in the small cities of Papua or Nusa Tenggara, you may be getting 20% less.

US dollars are the most widely accepted foreign currency and usually have the best exchange rate – this is especially so outside the major tourist areas. If you're going to be in really remote regions, carry sufficient cash with you as banks may be scarce or only accept certain varieties of travellers cheques.

Moneychangers are open longer hours and change money (cash or cheques) much faster than the banks. In places like Bali, they offer extremely competitive rates, but Kuta moneychangers are notorious for short-changing.

Country	Unit	Rupiah (Rp)
Australia	A$1	7289
Canada	C$1	8400
euro zone	€1	11,711
Japan	¥100	8456
Malaysia	RM10	26,409
New Zealand	NZ$1	6843
Singapore	S$1	5859
Philippines	P100	18,267
Thailand	100B	24, 233
UK	UK£1	17,426
USA	US$1	9973

POST

The postal service in Indonesia is generally good and the poste-restante service at *kantor pos* (post offices) is reasonably efficient in the main tourist centres. Expected mail always seems to arrive, eventually.

RESPONSIBLE TRAVEL

Indonesia is a conservative, largely Muslim country and while bikinis and Speedos are tolerated in the beach resorts of Bali, try to respect local clothing traditions wherever possible.

Many bus tours and treks pass through traditional villages. Remember that some villages are inundated with tourists, so act respectfully, introduce yourself to the *kepala desa* (village head) first and offer a small donation – 5000Rp is usually enough – if you are asked to sign the visitors book.

A little Bahasa Indonesia will also get you a long way. Not only will it allow you to dig deeper into the community you are staying in, it may also save you a few pence when dealing with market stall owners, hoteliers and becak drivers.

Bargaining is a must in Indonesia, but learn when to draw the line. Losing your temper will only push prices up and remember that a few pence or cents may make a great deal of difference to the other party.

Indonesia's environment is becoming increasingly vulnerable. Divers and snorkellers should try to avoid touching or standing on coral reefs, trekkers should take all disposable waste away with them and souvenirs made from endangered species should be left well alone – apart from anything else, you may end up at the sharp end of the local customs official.

TELEPHONE

International calls are easy to make from private booths in Telkom offices and privately run *wartel* (*warung telekomunikasi,* or telecommunications stalls). Reverse-charge calls can be made from Telkom offices free of charge, though private *wartel* usually don't offer the service, or charge for the first minute or so.

Many Telkom offices have Home Country Direct phones (press one button for connection to your home country operator), which are also found in terminals at big airports, some big hotels, tourist restaurants etc.

The public phones here are either coin phones, chip-card phones (sold at Telkom offices, *wartel,* supermarkets and other retail outlets) and the rarer credit-card phones. Most chip-card phones support International Direct Dialling, coin phones do not.

It's cheaper to ring on weekends and public holidays, when a 25% to 50% discount applies, or on weekdays from 9pm to 6am for Asia and Oceania, or midnight to 7am for North America, Europe and Africa.

The country code for Indonesia is ☎ 62; the international access code varies from *wartel* to *wartel* (ask the friendly face behind the counter).

TOILETS

Public toilets are few and far between, but you will find them in bars, restaurants, public buildings and train and bus terminals. Expect to squat.

TOURIST INFORMATION

The usefulness of tourist offices varies greatly from place to place. Those in places that attract lots of tourists, like Bali or Yogyakarta, provide good maps and information, while offices in the less-visited areas may have nothing to offer at all. Wherever you are, signs are not always in English – look for *dinas pariwisata* (tourist office).

The **Directorate General of Tourism** (Map p166; ☎ 021-383 8000; www.tourismindonesia.com; Jl Merdeka Barat 16-19, Jakarta) has its headquarters in Jakarta, but it is really more of a coordinating body than a helpful source of information.

VISAS

A visa is required to enter Indonesia. Citizens of Australia, Canada, Japan, New Zealand, South Africa, the UK, the US and most European countries, can apply for a 30-day tourist visa on arrival at 14 designated airports and 21 seaports (see www.indonesianembassy .org.uk for a full list). It costs US$25 and you will need to show an onward or return ticket. If your country is not on the visa-on-arrival list, or you need a 60-day visa, you will have to apply for your visa before you leave home.

The best answer to the ticket-out requirement is to buy a return ticket to Indonesia or to include Indonesia as a leg on a through ticket. Cheap, popular options for satisfying the requirement are Medan–Penang and Singapore–Jakarta tickets.

In addition to (sometimes in lieu of) an onward ticket, you may be asked to show evidence of sufficient funds. The magic number is US$1500. Travellers cheques are best to flash at immigration officials.

Tourist passes are not extendable. You may get a few extra days in special circumstances, but *never* simply show up at the airport with an expired visa or tourist pass and expect to be able to board your flight – the penalty for an overstay of 60 days or more is a five-year prison sentence!

Indonesia requires that your passport is valid for six months following your date of arrival.

Travel Permits

For political and bureaucratic reasons, foreigners must obtain a travel permit known as a *surat jalan* before they can visit many places in Papua, including the Baliem Valley. See Visitor Permits (Surat Jalan), p331, for details.

WOMEN TRAVELLERS

Indonesia is a Muslim society and very much male oriented. However, women are not forced to wear purdah, and generally enjoy more freedom than in many more orthodox Middle Eastern societies.

Travelling alone is considered an oddity – women travelling alone, even more of an oddity – and it is certainly tougher-going for a woman travelling alone in isolated regions. Nevertheless, for a woman travelling alone or with a female companion, Indonesia can be easier than some other Asian countries.

Plenty of Western women travel in Indonesia either alone or in pairs – most seem to enjoy the country and its people, and get through the place without any problems. Dressing modestly can help you avoid being harassed.

Laos

HIGHLIGHTS

- **Luang Prabang** – unmissable Unesco-listed French colonial streets and delicately decorated centuries-old Buddhist wat (p369)
- **Muang Sing** – responsible low-impact treks to Akha villages or lush Nam Ha National Protected Area (p391)
- **Si Phan Don** – a lazy maze of shady islands and rocky islets, home to the rare Irrawaddy dolphin (p402)
- **Wat Phu Champasak** – Khmer-era temple ruins perched above the Mekong valley (p402)
- **Off the beaten track** – remote limestone caves of Vieng Xai sheltered revolutionaries before the communist takeover (p388)

FAST FACTS

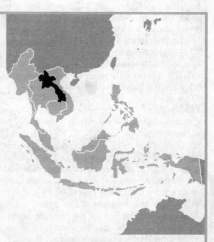

- **ATMs** one in Vientiane with international facilities
- **Budget** US$20 a day
- **Capital** Vientiane
- **Costs** city guesthouse US$4-10, 4hr bus ride US$1.50, Beer Lao US$0.80
- **Country code** ☎ 856
- **Famous for** tragically being one of the most bombed nations on earth
- **Languages** Lao and ethnic dialects
- **Money** US$1 = 8267 kip
- **Phrases** *sábqai-dīi* (hello), *sábqai-dīi* (goodbye), *khàwp jąi* (thank you)
- **Population** 5.6 million
- **Seasons** high season Dec-Feb & Jul-Aug; dry Nov-Apr, wet May-Oct
- **Visas** 15- or 30-day tourist visas are available in advance in Thailand, China, Vietnam or Cambodia. On-the-spot 15-day visas are available for US$30 with two photos on arrival in Vientiane, Luang Prabang and Pakse international airports, and when crossing the border from Thailand, China and Vietnam.

TRAVEL HINT

Flat tyres, breakdowns and unexpected detours are a feature of Laos bus travel; take plenty of provisions and share them round.

OVERLAND ROUTES

Landlocked Laos has multiple entry points from Thailand and Vietnam, one from China, and an unofficial crossing from Cambodia; see p351 for details.

LAOS

LAOS

0 _____ 200 km
0 _____ 120 miles

CHINA

MYANMAR
(BURMA)

Mekong River

Mengla

Phongsali

Tay
Trang

Dien
Bien Phu

Son La

HANOI

Muang
Sing

Boten

Xieng Kok

Luang
Nam Tha

4

Nong
Khiaw

Sam
Neua

Sop Hao

Vieng Xai

Nam Xoi

Udomxai
(Muang Xai)

3

1

Pak
Mong

Hua Muang

Na Maew

Huay Xai

2

Nam Tha

Pak Ou

1

Vieng
Thong

Chiang
Khong

Pak Beng

Luang
Prabang

Xieng
Ngeun

Nam Khan

Muang Kham

6

Nong
Haet

Nam Khan

Gulf of
Tonkin

Sainyabuli

Phu Khun

7

Phonsavan

Nam Can

VIETNAM

Kasi

13

Muang
Khun

Phu Bia
(2819m)

Nam Ngum

Vang
Vieng

Ang Nam
Ngum

6

Nam San

Paksan

Cau Treo

Vinh

SOUTH
CHINA
SEA

Phon Hong

Beung
Kan

Mekong River

Kham
Keut

Kaew
Neua

Pak Lai

VIENTIANE

13

Nong Khai

8

Lak
Sao

Kaen
Thao

Chiang
Khan

Udon Thani

13

Nakhon
Phanom

Tha Khaek

12

Dong Hoi

23

Sepon

Lao
Bao

Dong Ha

Mukdahan

Savannakhet

9

9

Khe Sanh

Hué

THAILAND

Se Pon

23

Se Don

Salavan

Se Kong

Ubon
Ratchathani

Vang
Tao

Sekong
(Muang
Lamam)

Se Kaman

Nakhon
Ratchasima

Chong Mek

Pakse

Champasak

Attapeu
(Samakhi Xai)

18

18

13

Si Phan
Don

Se Kong

Siempang

BANGKOK

Voen Kham

CAMBODIA

Stung Treng

Gulf of
Thailand

Travellers utter a distinct 'ahhh' when they arrive in Laos, like kicking back in a hammock after a long hot day. No teeming, smoggy metropolis, no aggressive entrepreneurialism, this is Southeast Asia's most relaxing country to travel in.

In the north, rugged terrain of emerald mountains and dramatic limestone peaks, criss-crossed with rivers, makes travel impossibly slow. Flat as a pancake and sprinkled with palm trees, the languid south is the quasi market garden of Laos; separated from the economic powerhouse of Thailand by the massive Mekong River.

After 30 years of communist inertia, Laos is hurrying to play catch-up with its neighbours. And while economic reforms have spawned a new urban elite, sporting Tiger Woods attire and polyphonic mobile phones, for the rest of the country subsistence village life remains virtually unchanged since the French sidled in more than a hundred years ago.

CURRENT EVENTS

After years of political isolation, Laos has re-invented itself as the crossroads state. Major highways are being built between China and Thailand and Vietnam and locals hope to make a buck – somehow – from the passing traffic.

Opening up to foreign influences has its challenges, not just for the regime. Concern about the environmental impact of hydroelectric dams in Laos and in neighbouring China and the degradation caused by the continued logging of Laos' forests is also shared by the international community. The future of the Mekong, hanging between the competing interests of the six Greater Mekong Subregion signatories (Cambodia, China, Laos, Myanmar, Thailand and Vietnam), is also on the negotiating table.

Currently public education campaigns and the distribution of condoms at guesthouses are a first step towards combatting the spread of HIV. Tighter border controls were introduced in late 2005 to check the spread of Avian influenza (bird flu). And, as with many developing countries, the fight against people trafficking is an ongoing challenge in Laos, where poverty and a lack of opportunities create an especially vulnerable population.

Rural poverty – and the skyrocketing scrap-metal trade – has also seen rising unexploded ordnance (UXO) fatalities. A lasting legacy of the US-led Secret War, UXOs are another factor in Laos' slow development: land is virtually unusable until it's cleared – an expensive and time-consuming process.

Finally, forced resettlement of villages, and the consequential social disruption and poverty, and government attempts to stop slash-and-burn cultivation techniques, are also controversial conversation topics.

(However, you won't find many Lao nationals prepared to discuss any of these, as political dissent is strictly forbidden.)

HISTORY

The nation we know as Laos is a foreign invention. Before the French, British, Chinese and Siamese drew a line around it and the French added a silent 's' to 'Lao', it was a collection of disparate principalities subject to an ever-revolving cycle of war, invasion, prosperity and decay.

Before foreign intervention, the closest Laos came to nationhood was in the 14th century, when Khmer-backed Lao warlord Fa Ngum conquered Wieng Chan (Vientiane), Xieng Khuang, a chunk of northeastern Thailand (which is still mainly ethnically Lao), Muang Sawa (Luang Prabang) and eastwards to Champa and the Annamite Mountains.

It was Fa Ngum who gave his kingdom the title still favoured by travel romantics and businesses – Lan Xang, or (Land of a) Million Elephants. He also made Theravada Buddhism the state religion and adopted the symbol of Lao sovereignty that remains in use today, the Pha Bang Buddha image, after which Luang Prabang is named.

Lan Xang waxed and waned under other kings (commemorated today in street names such as Samsenthai and Setthathirat), reaching its peak in the 17th century when it was the dominant force in Southeast Asia. By the 18th century, Lan Xang had crumbled, falling under the control of the Siamese, who

---

MUST READ

Laos: Culture & Society, edited by Dr. Grant Evans, contains a series of academic essays that will deepen your understanding of the history, culture and politics of Laos.

coveted much of modern-day Laos as a buffer zone against the expansionist French.

It was to no effect. Soon after taking over Annam and Tonkin (modern-day Vietnam), the French negotiated and treatied Siam into relinquishing all territory east of the Mekong, and Laos was born.

France had a fairly dim view of Laos' usefulness and did virtually nothing for the country, except permit opium production to flourish and allow its colonial administrators to become renowned for their lotus-eating lifestyle.

Laos' diverse ethnic make-up and short history as a nation-state meant nationalism was slow to form. The first nationalist movement, the Lao Issara (Free Lao), was created to prevent the country's return to French rule after the invading Japanese left at the end of WWII. In 1953 France granted full sovereignty, but 20 years of chaos followed as Laos became a stage on which the clash of communist ambition and USA anxiety over the perceived Southeast Asian 'domino effect' played itself out.

A period of shifting alliances and political mayhem saw multiple parties with multiple agendas settle into two factions: the Pathet Lao supported by the North Vietnamese, Chinese and Soviets, and the right-wing elite backed by the US government, which saw Laos rather disproportionately as the crucial Southeast Asian 'domino'.

From 1965 to 1973, the US devastated eastern and northeastern Laos with nonstop carpet bombing to counter the presence of the North Vietnamese in the country. The campaign intensified the war between the Pathet Lao and the Royal Lao armies and if anything, increased domestic support for the communists. The US withdrawal in 1973 saw Laos divided up between Pathet Lao and non–Pathet Lao, but within two years the communists had taken over and the Lao People's Democratic Republic (PDR) was created under the leadership of Vietnamese protégé Kaysone Phomvihan.

Around 10% of Laos' population fled, mostly into Thailand. The remaining opponents of the government – notably tribes of Hmong (highland dwellers) in Xieng Khuang and Luang Prabang – were suppressed, often brutally.

The Lao government quickly recognised the shortcomings of the socialist experiment and since the 1980s socialism has been softened to allow for private enterprise and foreign investment (but not political dissent of course). Laos entered the political family of Southeast Asian countries known as Asean in 1997, two years after Vietnam.

In 2004 the USA promoted Laos to Normal Trade Relations, cementing the end to a trade embargo in place since the communists took power in 1975. The Lao government has set its goal to haul Laos out of the Least Developed Country bracket by 2020. While still heavily reliant on foreign aid, Laos has committed to income-generating projects in recent years in a bid to increase its prosperity.

A perceived détente – two prisoners of conscience known to Amnesty International were released in 2004 – has raised hope among many expats that things are changing in their homeland. Meanwhile, others continue to campaign from afar over allegedly continuing human rights abuses.

THE CULTURE

While Laos has historically been influenced by both Vietnamese and Khmer culture, its strongest cultural and linguistic links are with Thailand. Those links have begun to reassert themselves in a distinctly modern way, with Thai music and Thai TV an almost ubiquitous presence in the country.

Similarities between Thailand and Laos are evident in cultural mores. Touching another person's head is taboo, as is pointing your feet at another person or at a Buddha image. Strong displays of emotion are discouraged. As in Thailand, the traditional greeting gesture is the *nop* or *wâi*, a prayerlike placing together of the palms in front of the face or chest, although in urban areas the handshake is becoming more commonplace.

Socially, Laos is very conservative and regular waves of prohibition sweep the land in response to the perceived menace of bourgeois liberalism seeping over the border from Thailand and the West.

For all temple visits, dress neatly and take your shoes off when entering religious buildings. You should also take off your shoes when entering people's homes and many guesthouses and shops. Shorts or sleeveless shirts are considered improper dress for both men and women. A free booklet *Do's & Don'ts in Laos* produced by the Lao National Tourism Authority (p357) comically describes how to dress and behave in a way that will not offend or encourage irresponsible behaviour among the young and impressionable.

Lao people are generally very laid-back and unassuming, and appreciate others being the same. They love a celebration (and a dirty joke), and at festival time you'll see the characteristic Lao diffidence dissolve as if by magic (or by *lào-láo* aka rice whisky) into bawdy boisterousness. Many are also very superstitious; belief in spirits and ghosts is almost universal.

The communist era has had a marked effect upon the Lao national consciousness. The government has been at pains to encourage national pride and a 'Lao' identity, despite the fact that more than 30% of the country is made up of non-Lao-speaking non-Buddhist hill tribes with little connection to traditional Lao culture. Government education also ensured that knowledge of the outside world was very limited, though Thai TV is changing that.

Men dominate Lao public life, but you don't have to be in the country long to see who is really running the show. All over Laos you'll see women staffing offices and running businesses. It is still expected, however, that they organise the family and run the home while the husband gets drunk with his mates!

MUST SEE

By independent American documentary maker Jack Silberman, *Bombies* (2001) critically examines the legacy of the US-lead Secret War in Laos through the experiences of those people dealing with the unexploded ordnance (UXOs) scattered throughout the country today.

RELIGION

Most lowland Lao are Theravada Buddhists and many Lao males choose to be ordained temporarily as monks, typically spending anywhere from a month to three years at a wat. After the 1975 communist victory, Buddhism was suppressed, but by 1992 the government had relented and it was back in full swing, with a few alterations. Monks are still forbidden to promote *phî* (spirit) worship, which has been officially banned in Laos along with *sâiyasaat* (folk magic).

Despite the ban, *phî* worship remains the dominant non-Buddhist belief system. Even in Vientiane, Lao citizens openly perform the ceremony called *sukhwǎn* or *bạsî*, in which the 32 *khwǎn* (guardian spirits of the body) are bound to the guest of honour by white strings tied around the wrists (you'll see many Lao people wearing these).

Outside the Mekong River valley, the *phî* cult is particularly strong among tribal Thai, especially the Thai Dam. *Mâw* (priests) who are trained to appease and exorcise troublesome spirits preside at important Thai Dam festivals and other ceremonies.

The Khamu and Hmong-Mien tribes also practise animism; the latter group also adds ancestral worship. Some Hmong groups recognise a pre-eminent spirit that presides over all earth spirits; others follow a Christian version of the 'cargo cult' and believe Jesus Christ will arrive in a jeep, dressed in combat fatigues.

ARTS

Lao art and architecture can be unique and expressive, and most is religious in nature. Distinctively Lao is the Calling for Rain Buddha, a standing image with a rocket-like shape. Wat in Luang Prabang feature *sǐm* (chapels), with steep, low roofs. The typical Lao *thâat* (stupa) is a four-sided, curvilinear, spirelike structure.

Traditional Lao art has a more limited range than its Southeast Asian neighbours, partly because Laos has a more modest history as a nation-state and partly because successive colonists from China, Vietnam, Thailand, Myanmar and France have run off with it.

Upland crafts include gold- and silver-smithing among the Hmong and Mien tribes, and tribal Thai weaving (especially among the Thai Dam and Thai Lü peoples).

Classical music and dance have been all but lost in Laos, although performances are occasionally held in Luang Prabang and Vientiane.

Foot-tapping traditional folk music, usually featuring the *khaen* (Lao panpipe), is still quite popular and inspires many modern Lao tunes. Increasingly, though, soppy heartbreak Thai pop and its Lao imitations are the music of choice.

ENVIRONMENT

Laos' 236,800 sq km of rugged geography, and small population, means this is the least changed environment in Southeast Asia. Unmanaged vegetation covers an estimated 85% of the country, and 25% of Laos is primary forest.

Sadly this is under threat. In 1993 the government set up 18 National Biodiversity Conservation Areas (NBCAs), later renamed National Protected Areas (NPAs), comprising a total of 24,600 sq km, or just over 10% of the land. An additional two were added in 1995 (taking the total coverage to 14% of Laos). International consulting agencies have also recommended another nine sites, but these have yet to materialise. Despite these conservation efforts, illegal timber felling and the smuggling of exotic wildlife are still significant threats to Laos's natural resources.

Nonetheless, most Lao still live at or just above subsistence level, consuming far fewer of their own natural resources than the people of any developed country.

Laos' forest cover means it has a greater concentration of wild animals than neighbouring Thailand, though the two countries share many native species. The pristine forests, mountains and rivers of Laos harbour a rich variety of creatures, including an estimated 437 kinds of bird and, in southern Laos alone, an incredible 320 different fish species.

While most conservation areas are in southern Laos, for most foreign travellers, Nam Ha NPA in the northern province of Luang Nam Tha is the most accessible and popular wilderness area to visit (see p389).

There are also wild elephants, jackals, bears, leopards, tigers, deer and, most famously, the Irrawaddy dolphin. Irrawaddy dolphins are the most seriously endangered of Laos' creatures. Their habitat is concentrated in the southern Mekong particularly around Si Phan Don, where you have the best chance of sighting them. Experts say the remaining hundred or so will disappear unless gill-net fishing on the Cambodian side of the border is halted or controlled.

TRANSPORT

GETTING THERE & AWAY
Air
There are currently no intercontinental flights to Laos. You can enter or exit Laos by air at Vientiane (from or to Cambodia, China, Thailand and Vietnam), Luang Prabang (Cambodia, Thailand and Vietnam) or Pakse (Cambodia).

Lao Airlines, Thai Airways International (THAI), Bangkok Airways and Vietnam Airlines all operate flights into the country. All fares listed in this chapter are one-way.

Bangkok Airways (Map p372; ☎ 071-253334; www
.bangkokair.com; 57/6 Th Sisavangvong,
Ban Xiengmuan, Luang Prabang)
Lao Airlines (Map p358; ☎ 021-212051;
www.laos-airlines.com; Th Pangkham, Vientiane)
THAI (Map pp354-5; ☎ 021-216143; www.thaiairways
.com; Th Pangkham, Vientiane)
Vietnam Airlines (Map p358; ☎ 021-217562; www
.vietnamairlines.com; 1st fl, Lao Plaza Hotel,
Th Samsenthai, Vientiane)

CAMBODIA
Lao Airlines flies regularly from Vientiane to Siem Reap (US$155) via Pakse, and Phnom Penh (US$139). Tourist visas are available on arrival at airports in Cambodia for US$20 (plus one passport photo) for most nationalities.

CHINA
Lao Airlines and China Yunnan Airlines fly between Vientiane and Kunming (US$139).

DEPARTURE TAX

Departure tax is US$10, payable in US dollars, baht or kip (cash only) at the airport. At overland crossings, the exit fee should be 5000 kip. Domestic airport tax is also 5000 kip.

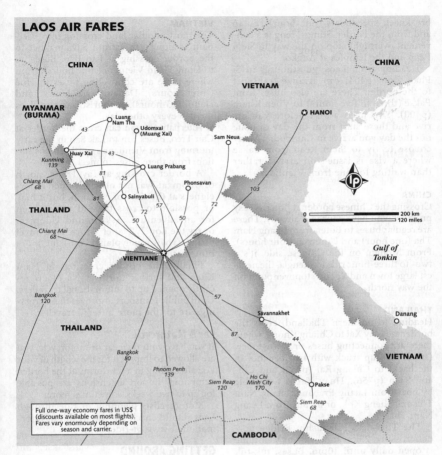

LAOS AIR FARES

Full one-way economy fares in US$ (discounts available on most flights). Fares vary enormously depending on season and carrier.

THAILAND
Lao Airlines and THAI fly from Bangkok to Vientiane (US$80, daily). Bangkok Airways flies to Luang Prabang (US$120, daily), sometimes stopping en route at Sukhothai in Thailand. Lao Airlines also flies to Chiang Mai (US$88, Tuesday, Friday and Sunday) from Luang Prabang.

VIETNAM
Lao Airlines and Vietnam Airlines fly between Vientiane and Hanoi (US$103, daily) and Ho Chi Minh City (US$170, daily).

Border Crossings
Laos has open land borders with Cambodia, China, Thailand and Vietnam, but the situation at all of them is prone to change without warning. Under current rules, a 15-day tourist visa is available on arrival at all international checkpoints (except at the Cambodian border), but this can change rapidly, so check the situation before leaving. For more information on transport options and specific border information, see the boxed text in relevant town sections.

CAMBODIA
The border at Voen Kham is not an official international checkpoint, but travellers have been crossing here without excessive incident for a while. The nearest main town in Cambodia is Stung Treng (p113), from where passenger ferries (three hours) and

LAOS

breakneck speedboats (one hour) run to and from the border. Stung Treng is a convenient overnight stop on the way to Siem Reap and the temples at Angkor.

Heading from Laos, guesthouses in Si Phan Don (p404) can arrange transport to the border. There are also buses from Pakse (three to five hours) to Voen Kham (p400). You need a visa before you arrive and these start from the day of issue not the day you arrive in Cambodia. Many choose to fly to Siem Reap from Pakse where a visa is issued on arrival rather than waiting for one from Vientiane.

CHINA

Crossing the Chinese border at Boten is easy provided you have your visa already. There are regular buses to Boten from Luang Nam Tha (one hour) and Udomxai (four hours). From Mohan, on the Chinese side, it's a two- to three-hour ride to Mengla, the nearest large town and a good stopover point on the way north.

THAILAND

Heading to northern Thailand, cross the border at Huay Xai to Chiang Khong, where there are connecting buses or săwngthăew (small pick-up truck with two benches in the back) to Chiang Rai (p752) and Chiang Saen (p756). Huay Xai is accessible by boat from Luang Prabang, Luang Nam Tha and Xieng Kok, or by bus from Luang Nam Tha.

The Thai–Lao Friendship Bridge border crossing, 25km southeast of Vientiane is open daily until 10pm. Buses, túk-túk and tourist minibuses run from the capital to the bridge almost every hour. From Nong Khai there are regular buses and trains to Bangkok.

Travellers passing through from Vietnam or exiting Laos from the south can cross the Mekong to Thailand either at Tha Khaek or Savannakhet. There are frequent buses on the Thai side of these crossings to Bangkok.

In the far south, you can walk across the border at Vang Tao, an hour west of Pakse by bus or săwngthăew. On the Thai side, Chong Mek is a small, lively market town from where you can take a bus to Ubon Ratchathani (two to three hours), then hop on a bus or train to Bangkok.

VIETNAM

The most popular land crossing into Vietnam is along Rte 9 from Savannakhet to the border crossing at Lao Bao. Buses go to Dong Ha in Vietnam (nine hours), from where there are connecting buses to Hué (three hours), Danang (six hours) and Hanoi (15 hours). A tourist bus also does the trip every other day.

Alternatively you can cross the border at Cau Treo. Buses run to Lak Sao in the early morning from Vientiane's northern bus station; from there buses connect to Vinh.

A border crossing at Tay Trang, north of Udomxai, was not officially open to foreigners at the time of research, but it may be possible to cross there if you're keen for an adventure. Ask around Udomxai or try the Lonely Planet Thorn Tree travel forum (www.lonelyplanet.com) for more information.

Finally, the border crossings at Nam Khan and further north at Na Maew recently opened up to international travellers. Until public transport improves these crossings are for the more intrepid traveller.

Car & Motorcycle

If you have your own car or motorcycle, you are allowed to import it for the length of your visa after filling in a few forms at the border. Temporary import extensions are possible for up to two weeks, sometimes more.

Motorcyclists planning to ride through Laos should check out the wealth of information at www.gt-rider.com.

GETTING AROUND
Air

Lao Airlines (Map p358; ☎ 021-212051; www.laos -airlines.com; Th Pangkham, Vientiane) handles all domestic flights in Laos. Purchasing tickets using credit cards carries an additional surcharge. Schedules are unreliable and during holiday seasons it can be very difficult to get a seat to some destinations, so book ahead.

Safety records for Lao Airlines aren't made public, and many international organisations and Western embassies advise staff not to use this airline. The international flights and busy domestic routes such as Vientiane–Luang Prabang and Vientiane–Pakse are probably as safe as any (ie accidents can happen), but flying into Sam

Neua for example, where the descent is tricky and the conditions unpredictable, is not for timid air travellers.

Always reconfirm your flights a day or two before departing as undersubscribed flights may be cancelled, or you could get bumped off the passenger list.

Bicycle

The light and relatively slow traffic in most Lao towns makes for favourable cycling conditions. Bicycles are available for rent in major tourist destinations, costing around 10,000 kip per day for a cheap Thai or Chinese model. For long-distance cyclists, bicycles can be brought into the country usually without any hassle, and if the mountainous north proves too challenging, a bus will always pick you up along the road.

Boat

With the main highway upgrading process almost complete in Laos, the days of mass river transport are as good as over. Sadly, most boat services today are geared at tourists, pushing prices up.

The most popular river trip in Laos – the slow boat between Huay Xai and Luang Prabang – remains a daily event. From Huay Xai (p393), boats are often packed, while from Luang Prabang (p379) there's usually a bit of leg room. Other popular journeys – between Pakse and Si Phan Don, or between Nong Khiaw and Luang Prabang – are no longer regular, so you'll have to charter a boat.

River ferry facilities are quite basic and passengers sit, eat and sleep on the wooden decks. It's a good idea to bring something soft to sit on. The toilet (if there is one) is an enclosed hole in the deck at the back of the boat.

For shorter river trips, such as Luang Prabang to the Pak Ou caves, you can easily hire a river taxi. The héua hang nyáo (long-tail boats), with engines gimbal-mounted on the stern, are the most typical, though for a really short trip (eg crossing a river) a héua phai (rowboat) or a small improvised ferry will be used.

Along the upper Mekong River, between Luang Prabang and Huay Xai and between Xieng Kok and Huay Xai, Thai-built héua wái (speedboats) – shallow, 5m-long skiffs with 40HP outboard engines – are common.

These are able to cover a distance in six hours that might take a river ferry two days or more. They're not cheap but some ply regular routes, so the cost can be shared among several passengers. For some, a ride on these boats is a major thrill. For others, it's like riding on a giant runaway chainsaw, a nightmare that can't end soon enough. Speedboats, as well as being deafeningly loud, kill and injure people every year. They tend to flip and disintegrate on contact with any solid floating debris, which is in plentiful supply during the wet season.

Bus & Săwngthăew

Long-distance public transport in Laos is either by bus or săwngthăew (literally 'two rows'; converted pick-ups or trucks with two wooden benches down either side). The public transport system in Laos is steadily improving with more services and more options at least on the main north–south route, Rte 13.

The majority of main highways in Laos are now either in a reasonable condition or being upgraded. The worst exceptions are Rte 3 between Huay Xai and Luang Nam Tha, Rte 1 between Vieng Thong and Nong Khiaw, though these are slowly being upgraded. Despite these improvements, road trips in Laos can still be a test of endurance, especially in the northeast where there is barely a straight stretch of road to be found.

Car & Motorcycle

Chinese- and Japanese-made 100cc step-through scooters can be rented for 64,000 kip to 80,000 kip per day in Vientiane, Vang Vieng, Savannakhet, Pakse and Luang Nam Tha. No licence is required. Try to get a Japanese bike if you're travelling any distance out of town. In Vientiane, it's also possible to rent dirt bikes for around US$20 per day. Motorcycle tours of Laos are offered by **Asian Motorcycling Adventures** (www .asianbiketour.com).

Car rental in Laos is expensive, unless you are staying within urban areas, but it's a great way of reaching remote places. In Vientiane, **Asia Vehicle Rental** (AVR; Map p358; ☎ 021-17493; avr@loxinfo.co.th; Th Samsenthai) has sedans, minibuses, 4WDs and station wagons, with or without drivers, from around US$70 per day, not including fuel.

VIENTIANE

To Ban Nong Buathong (1km)

Muang Sikhottabong

Th Nong Douang

Muang Chanthabuli

Th Nong Buathong

Th Phon

Th Thong Khan Kham

Th Dong Mlang

Th Sidamduon

Th Souphanuvong

To Wattay International Airport (2km)

Th T2

21

10

To Marina (500m);
Kiaw Liaw Pier (12km);
Vang Vieng (156km);
Luang Prabang (380km)

Th Luang Prabang

Wat Khounta

15

19

22

Three Elephants Statue

18

Th Sithan

Mekong River Commission

Th Khun Bulom

Th Samsenthai

Th Setthathirat

Th Lan Xang

Th Dong Palan

12   1

2

Wat Ban Fai

Th Fa Ngum

Th Mahasot

See Central Vientiane Map (p358)

Nong Chan

17

Wat Si Muang

Wat Phia Wat

Th Khu Vieng

Mekong River

Don Chan
(size varies with river height)

Th Tha Deua

3

20

UNICEF

Th Si Amphon

4

Wat Ammon

Wat

THAILAND

To Tha Deua (16.5km);
Xieng Khuan
(Buddha Park, 20.5km)

INFORMATION
Australian Embassy.....................1	D2
Australian Embassy Clinic.............2	D2
Cambodian Embassy....................3	D5
Chinese Embassy.........................4	D5
German Embassy..........................5	E5
Indonesian Embassy.....................6	E1
Malaysian Embassy.......................7	E2
Myanmar Embassy........................8	E5
Singaporean Embassy....................9	E2
Thai Embassy..............................10	D2
Vietnamese Embassy....................11	E2

SIGHTS & ACTIVITIES
Patuxai.....................................12	D2
Pha That Luang.........................13	F1
Sokpaluang Swimming Pool.........14	E5
Thongbay Guesthouse.................15	B2
Wat Sok Pa Luang......................16	E5

EATING
Vegetarian Buffet......................17	D3

DRINKING
Sunset Sala Khounta...................18	A2

ENTERTAINMENT
D*Tech.....................................19	B2

TRANSPORT
China Yunnan Airlines.................20	D5
China Yunnan Airlines...........(see 22)	
Northern Bus Station..................21	A1
THAI..22	B2

LAOS

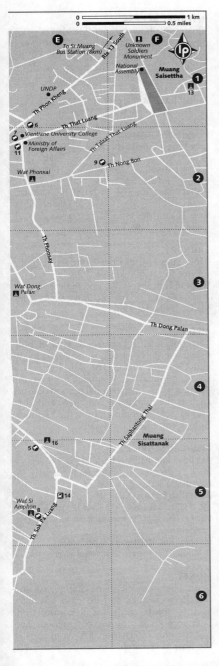

Hitching

Hitching is possible in Laos, but it's never entirely safe and it's definitely not recommended for women as the act of standing beside a road and waving at cars might be misinterpreted! If you are hitching, recognise that you are taking a small but potentially dangerous risk. In any case, public transport is inexpensive and will pick you up almost anywhere. Otherwise long-distance cargo trucks or cars with red-on-yellow number plates (private vehicles) are also a good bet.

VIENTIANE

☎ 021 / pop 201,000

Vientiane's eclectic aesthetic means that neighbourhoods of traditional wood houses and avenues of colonial mansions are mixed with damp inner-city concrete structures, dotted with the odd communist monolith. It's not the most attractive city in Southeast Asia, but its location on a bend of the Mekong and the lack of high-intensity traffic noise more than make up for that. Since opening up to international investment, Vientiane has been slowly evolving. In 2004, it enjoyed the honour of hosting the Asean Summit, placing it firmly on Southeast Asia's diplomatic map. The city may reveal its beauty less readily than Luang Prabang, but spend a few days visiting its unusual sights, sampling its excellent food and enjoying a Beer Lao at sunset by the river, and you'll soon be won over.

HISTORY

Vientiane's peaceful demeanour belies a turbulent history. Over the 1000 or so years of its history, it's been smashed up, pushed around and looted by successive Vietnamese, Burmese, Siamese, Khmer and French conquerors. The French cemented Vientiane's status as a capital city when they took over the protectorship of Laos in the late 19th and early 20th centuries, although the Pathet Lao briefly considered moving the capital to Vieng Xai but then relented and stuck with Vientiane, and the city began a rapid transformation from notorious den of vice to austere socialist outpost. Today, with new high-rise developments and the building of Laos' first multistorey

LAOS

air-conditioned shopping mall, Vientiane surpasses its reputation as a village of villages and presents a modernised face for the 21st century.

ORIENTATION

The three main streets parallel to the Mekong – Th Fa Ngum, Th Setthathirat and Th Samsenthai – form the central inner city of Vientiane and are where most of the budget guesthouses, bars and restaurants are located. Nam Phu is the best inner-city landmark if you're catching a taxi or túk-túk into town. Heading northeast at a 90-degree angle to Th Setthathirat is the wide tree-lined boulevard of Th Lan Xang, where you'll find the Talat Sao (Morning Market) and the Patuxai monument. Heading further north from Patuxai is Th That Luang, which is home to a number of foreign embassies and is crowned by the magnificent golden Pha That Luang, Laos' most distinctive structure.

INFORMATION

BOOKSHOPS

Kosila Bookshop 1 (Map p358; ☎ 241352; Th Chanta Khumman; ⏱ 9am-5pm Mon-Fri) Shelves are stocked with secondhand fiction and old travel guides selling for around 80,000 kip.

Kosila Bookshop 2 (Map p358; ☎ 241352; Th Nokeo Khumman; ⏱ 9am-5pm Mon-Fri) Secondhand novels, a few literary classics and used travel guides. Books in English, French and Japanese bought, sold and exchanged.

Vientiane Book Centre (Map p358; ☎ 213031; Th Pangkham; ⏱ 8.30am-5.30pm Mon-Fri, 8.30am-4pm Sat) As well as secondhand and antique books, it sells international news magazines, academic texts and old NGO reports.

CULTURAL CENTRES

Centre Culturel et de Coopération Linguistique (French Cultural Centre; Map p358; ☎ 215764; www .ambafrance-laos.org/centre in French; Th Lan Xang; ⏱ 9.30am-6.30pm Mon-Fri, 9.30am-noon Sat) Surrounded by manicured lawns, the centre has a library, a large selection of newspapers and magazines from around the Francophone world, French and Lao language lessons, and a popular lunchtime café.

EMERGENCY

Ambulance (☎ 195)
Fire (☎ 190)
Police (☎ 191)
Tourist Police (Map p358; ☎ 251128; Th Lan Xang)

INTERNET ACCESS

Illustrating how competition drives prices down, Internet access in Vientiane is pretty quick and pretty cheap (100 kip per minute). The busier the place, the slower the network, so choose your time and your Internet shop accordingly.

Fastnet Internet (Map p358; ☎ 020-549 2677; Th Samsenthai; per min 100 kip; ⏱ 8am-11pm; 🖳) As the name suggests, good Internet access. Overseas Internet calls available too.

Lane Xang Internet Services (Map p358; ☎ 241012; Th Setthathirat; per min/hr 100/5000 kip; ⏱ 8am-11pm) Spacious and rarely busy. Desks of differing heights, space for laptops and clean toilet facilities.

PlaNet Online (Map p358; ☎ 241251; Th Setthathirat; per min 100 kip; ⏱ 8am-11.30pm; 🖳) Also has a large-screen TV often tuned to the BBC. You can burn photo cards onto CD for 20,000 kip.

LAUNDRY

Most guesthouses offer same-day laundry service for 10,000 kip per kilo.

House of Fruit Shakes (Map p358; Th Samsenthai; per item 500-4000 kip; ⏱ 7am-9pm) Do your laundry at this popular drinking spot (p363).

MEDIA

Laos' only English-language newspaper, published five times a week, is the government-run *Vientiane Times*. The *Bangkok Post* is sold at minimarts in Vientiane from around 4pm each day. International news magazines such as the *Economist*, *Newsweek* and *Time* are also sold at minimarts and the Vientiane Book Centre (left) for details.

MEDICAL SERVICES

Aek Udon International Hospital (☎ 0066 4234 2555). If you're seriously wounded seek an emergency evacuation to this hospital in Thailand.

Australian Embassy Clinic (Map pp354-5; ☎ 413603; Th Mahosot; ⏱ 8.30am-12.30pm & 2-5pm Mon-Fri) Citizens of Commonwealth countries can access treatment here.

Mahasot Hospital (Map p358; ☎ 214023; Th Mahosot) Come here for treatment of minor ailments.

MONEY

Several banks in Vientiane change cash and travellers cheques and do cash advances against credit cards for a commission. Banque pour le Commerce Extérieur Lao had the only international ATM in Laos at the time of research.

Banque pour le Commerce Extérieur Lao (Map p358; ☎ 213200; cnr Th Pangkham & Th Fa Ngum; ☉ 8.30am-5pm Mon-Fri) Good rates for travellers cheques. ATM accessible on weekends too.

Joint Development Bank (Map p358; ☎ 213535; Th Lan Xang; ☉ 8.30am-4pm Mon-Fri) Charges lower commission on cash advances against credit cards.

Lao Development Bank (Map p358; ☎ 213300; Th Setthathirat; ☉ 8.30-11.30am & 2-4pm Mon-Fri)

Siam Commercial Bank (Map p358; ☎ 227306; Th Lan Xang; ☉ 8.30am-4pm Mon-Fri)

POST

Post, Telephone & Telegraph (PTT; Map p358; cnr Th Lan Xang & Th Khu Vieng; ☉ 8am-noon & 1-5pm Mon-Fri, 8am-noon Sat) Stamps, poste restante and (slow) Internet services available here.

TELEPHONE

International call phonecards can be purchased from the PTT (above) and minimarts. Cheaper Internet calls can be made at Internet shops (opposite).

TOILETS

All established restaurants have a toilet (WC) available for customers, and midrange and top-end hotels usually have one on the ground floor (in case of an emergency!). A fee of around 1000 kip (the going price for a pee around the country) is charged for use of the WC at the bus station and post office.

TOURIST INFORMATION

Lao National Tourism Authority (NTAL; Map p358; ☎ 212251; Th Lan Xang; ☉ 8am-noon, 1-4pm Mon-Fri) Located in a large office with postered information about Laos' wildlife, as well as excursions beyond the capital. Free copies of the official *Lao National Tourism Administration Guide*, with listings and editorial commentary in both English and French (recommended reading). The staff speak some English.

TRAVEL AGENCIES

A-Rasa Tours (Map p358; ☎ 213633/4; www .laos-info.com; Th Setthathirat; ☉ 8.30am-5pm Mon-Sat) Organises onward bus tickets in Laos, or to Vietnam and Thailand; books train tickets from Nong Khai to Bangkok; arranges visas and Laos visa extensions; and will happily answer travellers' queries.

Boualian Travel 1 (Map p358; ☎ 213061, 020-551 1646; Th Samsenthai) Books bus tickets; organises tours, visas and Laos visa extensions; hires bicycles for 15,000 kip per day; and sells antiques and souvenirs.

Boualian Travel 2 (Map p358; ☎ 020-5511646; Th Pangkham) Ditto.

SIGHTS
Pha That Luang

The beautiful golden **Pha That Luang** (Great Sacred Stupa; Map pp354-5; Th That Luang; admission 2000 kip; ☉ 8am-4pm Tue-Sun) is the most important national monument in Laos, a symbol of both the Buddhist religion and Lao sovereignty. An image of the main stupa appears on the national seal. Legend has it that Ashokan missionaries from India erected a *thâat* here to enclose a piece of Buddha's breastbone as early as the 3rd century BC. Construction began again in 1566 and, over time, four wat were built around the stupa. Only two remain, Wat That Luang Tai to the south and Wat That Luang Neua to the north. The latter is the monastic residence of the Supreme Patriarch of Lao Buddhism. A high-walled cloister with tiny windows surrounds the 45m stupa. The base of the stupa is designed to be mounted by the faithful, with walkways around each level and connecting stairways. The cloister measures 85m on each side and contains various Buddha images.

SCAMS

Many travellers have fallen victim to the Vientiane–Hanoi bus scam. Agents, often guesthouses, sell tickets for 'air-con tourist coaches' – despite the photo you're shown when purchasing your ticket, these can turn out to be rattletraps or minivans packed to the limit. These trips often include a long wait at the border and we've received reports of drivers phoning ahead to hook you up with hotel touts at your destination. Fantastic! There is no need to use these agents and there are better, cheaper ways of getting to Vietnam (see p364). If you are set on the overnight bus trip to Hanoi, check with other fellow travellers or look on www.lonelyplanet.com/thorntree for recommendations. If one company is booked out the day you want to leave, try another: they don't share information on seat availability. Finally, these buses are often late picking you up from your guesthouse, so prepare for an anxious wait…

LAOS

CENTRAL VIENTIANE

LAOS

0 _____ 0.2 miles
0 _____ 400 m

F

16 🛆

15 🛆
5 ●
10 🛆
9 🛆

Th Sylom

Th Hatsady

Th Khu Vieng

That Dam
(Black Stupa)

Th Phai Nam

Th Bartholomie

21 ●

11 ●

Talat Sao

64 ●

7 ●
19 ●

68 ●

Catholic
Church

Entrance
Gate to Embassy

8 ●

17 ✚

Haw Pha
Kaew

Th Samsenthai

E

25 ●

23 ●

Th Phai Nam

Th Pangkham

6 ●

Th Heng Boun

Th Kai Huang

National
Stadium

69 ●

24 ●

Nam
Phu

65 ●
59 ●

52 ●
3 ●

28 ●
60 ●
4 ●
58 ●

20 ●

27 ●

Th Lan Xang

Th Chanta Khumman

National
Library

Colonial
Villas

Presidential
Cabinet

Presidential
Palace

Promenade

D

C

39 ●
37 ●
29 ●

35 ●
41 ●
36 ●

42 ●

Th Khun Bulom

Th Saigon

Th Phom Penh

Th Hanoi

Th Hengboun

Wat Hai
Sok

Lao National
Culture Hall

Th Nokeo Khumman

48 ●
56 ●
1 ●
18 ●
13 ●
14 ●
54 ●
38 ●
61 ●
63 ●
12 ●
33 ●

Th Wat Xieng Nyeun

45 ●
46 ●
22 ●
2 ●

67 ●

Th Pangkham

Th Manthatulat

Th Fa Ngum

53 ●

Wat Xieng
Nyeun

B

44 ●

49 ●
32 ●
43 ●
40 ●

Wat Ong
Teu Mahawihan

Wat In
Paeng

31 ●

Th Setthathirat

Th Nolam

Th François Ngin

Th Chao Anou

Th In Paeng

Th Khun Bulom

26 ●
34 ●
50 ●
55 ●
30 ●

Haw
Kang

Wat
Chanthabuli

57 ●
47 ●

51 ●

Mekong River

Don Chan
(size varies with
river height)

A

Th Sihom

Th Luang Prabang

1

2

3

4

The temple is the site of a major festival held in early November (see p361). Pha That Luang is about 4km northeast of the city centre at the end of Th That Luang. It's a decent walk but shared túk-túks go this way, or you can hire a bike. The best time to visit is late afternoon to catch the reflected setting sun.

Wat Si Saket

Built in 1818 by King Anouvong (Chao Anou), **Wat Si Saket** (Map p358; cnr Th Lan Xang & Th Setthathirat; admission 2000 kip; ☯ 8am-noon & 1-4pm, closed public holidays) is the oldest temple in Vientiane and is well worth visiting, even if you've overdosed on temples already. Chao Anou was educated in the Bangkok court and was more or less a vassal of the Siamese state. Wat Si Saket was constructed in the early Bangkok style, but it is surrounded with a thick-walled cloister similar to the one that surrounds Pha That Luang and its grounds are shaded with coconut, banana and mango trees. Its stylistic similarity may have motivated the Siamese to spare this monastery when they crushed Chao Anou's rebellion, although they razed many others. The French restored the temple between 1924 and 1930. Wat Si Saket has several

unique features. The interior walls of the cloister are riddled with small niches that contain more than 2000 silver and ceramic Buddha images. More than 300 seated and standing Buddhas of varying age, size and material (wood, stone and bronze) rest on long shelves below the niches. Most of the images are from 16th- to 19th-century Vientiane, but a few hail from 15th- to 16th-century Luang Prabang. A Khmer-style Naga Buddha is also on display, brought from a Khmer site at nearby Hat Sai Fong.

Patuxai

Vientiane's haughty Arc de Triomphe replica is an imposing if slightly incongruous sight, dominating the commercial district around Th Lan Xang. Officially called **Patuxai** (Victory Monument; Map pp354-5; Th Lan Xang; admission 2000 kip; ☯ 8am-5pm), but more commonly known by locals as *anusawali*, it commemorates the Lao who died in pre-revolutionary wars. It was built in 1969 with cement donated by the USA for the construction of a new airport, hence expats refer to it as 'the vertical runway'. The entrance fee allows you to climb the stairway through the bare, cavernous interior to the top of the monument, with views over

LAOS

Vientiane. Beneath the arch, a small outdoor café sells snacks. To the north, musical fountains, lit up at night, draw families and street vendors to enjoy the spectacle.

Lao National History Museum

Housed in a well-worn classical mansion originally built in 1925 as the French governor's residence, the **Lao National History Museum** (Map p358; ☎ 212462; Th Samsenthai; admission 3000 kip; ⏲ 8am-noon & 1-4pm) was formerly known as the Lao Revolutionary Museum. Rooms near the entrance feature cultural and geographical exhibits. Inner rooms are dedicated to the 1893–1945 French colonial period, the 1945–54 struggle for independence, the 1954–63 resistance to American imperialism, the 1964–69 provisional government, and the 1975 communist victory. Many of the displays are now in English as well as Lao. If you get museum-fatigue, you can keep your ticket and come back later the same day.

Xieng Khuan (Buddha Park)

In a grassy field by the Mekong River, 25km southeast of Vientiane, **Xieng Khuan** (Buddha Park; off Th Tha Deua; admission 5000 kip, camera 2000 kip; ⏲ 8am-sunset), as the name suggests, is a park full of Buddhist and Hindu sculptures, a monument to one eccentric man's bizarre ambition. Xieng Khuan was designed and built in 1958 by Luang Pu (Venerable Grandfather) Bunleua Sulilat, a yogi-priest-shaman who merged Hindu and Buddhist philosophy, mythology and iconography into a cryptic whole. The concrete sculptures at Xieng Khuan (which means Spirit City) include statues of Shiva, Vishnu, Arjuna, Avalokiteshvara, Buddha and just about every other Hindu or Buddhist deity imaginable. These, as well as a few secular figures, were all supposedly cast by unskilled artists under Luang Pu's direction.

Buses passing here (3000 kip, 45 minutes) leave the Talat Sao terminal every 30 minutes during the day. You could charter a sǎwngthǎew for 50,000 kip return. Some people visit the park (which is 10km beyond the Thai–Lao Friendship Bridge) on their way out of Laos. If you need some exercise, it's a decent cycle – the road is relatively flat – but the traffic to the bridge is heavy.

ACTIVITIES
Bowling

Bright lights and the high-pitched clatter of wooden pins await you at the **Lao Bowling Centre** (Map p358; ☎ 218661; Th Khun Bulom; per game with shoe hire 20,000 kip; ⏲ 9am-midnight). Even before its 'official' closing time, it may look deserted, but entry is on the right side of the building. As well as good old-fashioned bowling, pool tables, beer, and refreshments are available.

Cooking Classes

Courses at the **Thongbay Guesthouse** (Map pp354-5; ☎ 242292; www.thongbay.laopdr.com; Ban Nong Douange; US$10) are organised on demand and start at 10am or 3pm. A half-day class includes a trip to the market before you cook up a storm, then feast on your culinary creations for lunch or dinner.

Gym & Aerobics

If all that Beer Lao is taking its toll, get thyself to the conveniently located, small street-level gym at the **Tai-Pan Hotel** (Map p358; ☎ 216906; Th François Nginn; per visit 40,000 kip).

Massage & Herbal Saunas

For a traditional massage experience, head to **Wat Sok Pa Luang** (Map pp354-5; Th Sok Pa Luang; ⏲ 1-7pm). Located in a semirural setting (*wat pàa* means 'forest temple') the wat is famous for herbal saunas (10,000 kip) and massages (30,000 kip). It's about 3km from the city centre, but túk-túk drivers all know how to get there.

In the centre of town, **White Lotus Massage & Beauty** (Map p358; ☎ 217492; Th Pangkham; ⏲ 10am-10pm) is a slightly upmarket day spa offering oil massage and traditional Lao-style massages (40,000 to 60,000 kip) in a green, serene environment. The full-body oil massage pays particular attention to sore neck and shoulders – divine!

Meditation

Foreigners are welcome at a regular Saturday afternoon sitting at Wat Sok Pa Luang (above). The session runs from 4pm until 5.30pm with an opportunity to ask questions afterwards.

Swimming

For serious lap swimming, there's the 25m-long **Sokpaluang Swimming Pool** (Map pp354-5;

☎ 350491; Th Sok Pa Luang; admission 6000 kip; ☺ 9am-8pm Tue-Sun), which also has a children's paddling pool and change rooms.

Yoga

To regain your balance look for signposted information on yoga classes in shop windows around Nam Phu.

FESTIVALS & EVENTS

The **That Luang Festival** (Bun Pha That Luang), held in early November, is the largest temple fair in Laos. On the morning of the full moon, hundreds of monks from across the country assemble to receive alms. The festival peaks with a colourful procession between Pha That Luang (p357) and Wat Si Muang. Fireworks cap off festivities in the evening, and are followed by more hours of merriment around town.

Another huge annual event is **Bun Nam** (River Festival) at the end of Buddhist lent in October, when boat races are held on the Mekong River. Rowing teams from all over the country, as well as from Thailand, China and Myanmar compete, and the riverbank is lined with food stalls, temporary discos, carnival games and beer gardens for three nights.

Vientiane also knows how to celebrate the new year, three times a year. The riverbank is the focus of celebrations on 31 December for the **International New Year**, and again for **Vietnamese Tet-Chinese New Year**, usually in February, then once more in mid-April for **Pii Mai** (Lao New Year). For more information on these events, see p410.

SLEEPING

Not surprisingly, in the capital city rents are high and low-cost accommodation options are limited. Anywhere that's cheap and clean fills up very quickly. After that, anywhere cheap and icky fills up too. You may be forced to fork out a bit, at least on your first night, and take a room for more than you'd hope. But you can eat cheap in Vientiane and you can always move into a less expensive place in the morning.

Syri 1 Guest House (Map p358; ☎ 212682; Th Saigon; r US$6-10; ⊠) In a relatively quiet location, this old pink and green house, with high ceilings and a couple of communal spaces to chill out in, is the best budget option in town. Not all rooms have windows to the outside world, but they all have character.

Joe Guest House (Map p358; ☎ 241936; joe_guesthouse@yahoo.com; Th Fa Ngum; r US$5-13; ⊠) In an excellent location opposite the Mekong. The family owners are very hospitable, and breakfast, lunch and dinner are served in the downstairs restaurant. This is a good option for solo women travellers, but try and book ahead in the high season.

Saysouly Guest House (Map p358; ☎ 218383; saysouly@hotmail.com; Th Manthatulat; r US$5-15; ⊠) Blue shuttered windows and doors, and a shared upstairs balcony, add some charm to this simple three-storey guesthouse. Rooms are clean and neat.

Khamvongsa Guest House (Map p358; ☎ 223257; souriyo_a@hotmail.com; Th Khun Bulom; r US$4-7; ⊠) An unexpected treat in the heart of the city: wooden traditional-style buildings in a peaceful setting, with shared cold-water bathrooms. In the main building, rooms have air-con, and hot-water shared bathrooms. It's a bit of a hike from Nam Phu so call this place ahead of time to make sure there's room.

KPP Guest House (Map p358; ☎ 218601; Th Chao Anou; r US$5-8; ⊠) Rooms here are spread over several small shophouses. Some don't have natural light; ask for one with a window.

Syri 2 Guest House (Map p358; Th Setthathirat; r US$3-10; ⊠) Not exceptional, but it fills up quickly. Also offers laundry service and bicycles for rent. A few doors from Blue Sky (p363) if you're wandering up Setthathirat and wondering how much further…

Mixok Guest House (Map p358; ☎ 251606; Th Setthathirat; r US$4-6) Rooms in reasonable condition. Blankets available for cooler nights. Fills up by midday during the high season, mostly due to its very convenient location.

LAOS

If you don't mind splashing out a bit, the following places are worth the extra kip.

Dragon Lodge (Map p358; ☎ 250112; dragonlodge2002@yahoo.com; Th Samsenthai; r US$12-24; ✸) Ambient music, a relaxed atmosphere in the downstairs bar and good service result in many emails to Lonely Planet raving about this place. Some rooms come with reading lights (a novelty in Laos), and the information boards are packed with useful tips if you've just arrived. Also runs air-con minibuses to Vang Vieng (US$5) and organises onwards visas – all good news if you're feeling lazy.

Vayakorn Guest House (Map p358; ☎ 241911; Th Nokeo Khumman; r US$12-15; ✸) Spacious rooms, cleaned daily. All with private bathrooms, hot water, satellite TV – and, wait for it – a telephone! (You can always dial reception for free.) Newspapers and magazines available downstairs.

Orchid Guest House (Map p358; ☎ 252825; Th Fa Ngum; r US$13-15; ✸) Opposite the Mekong with a tiled rooftop to watch the sunset over Vientiane. Staff are friendly and the rooms are generously sized. Small TVs have BBC but no movie channels.

More low-cost accommodation options around the centre include the following:

Praseuth Guest House (Map p358; ☎ 217932; Th Samsenthai; r US$5-7; ✸) One room has a private bathroom, the rest are shared. Staff are helpful.

Sabaidee 1 Guest House (Map p358; Th Setthathirat; dm US$1.50, r US$3-5) Central location. Backpack-sized lockers in each dorm room, plus more lockers in the downstairs foyer. Bring your own sleeping bag or sleeping bag inner.

Sabaidee 2 Guest House (Map p358; ☎ 242894, Th Saigon; dm US$1.80, r US$3-4) Signs in the bathroom politely ask guests to help keep the place clean. Quieter than the first Sabaidee.

EATING

Vientiane's expat community has a lot to answer for: the dining options in Vientiane are so varied you can suffer serious option-paralysis, especially if you've been in the middle of nowhere for weeks. Close to Nam Phu are a number of popular eating spots for homesick *falang* with plenty of pizza and pasta on offer plus Tex-Mex, Indian, Chinese, Japanese – even Russian. Vegetarians won't be disappointed either. And of course there's the night market – for those on a strict budget you've probably already

shelled out too much for a room already, so it's time to take to the streets.

Ban Anou night market (Map p358; off Th Chao Anou; ⏱ 5-10pm) Up Th Chao Anou, Vientiane's Chinatown district, turn right before the T-junction and behold a short street lined with food vendors selling *ping kai* (barbecue chicken on a stick), *làap* (spicy salad), curries, noodles and other delights. Specify your price (3000 kip was enough for a decent feed at the time of research) and add 1000 kip for some *khào nío* (sticky rice).

Open-air riverside food vendors (Map p358; Th Fa Ngum; ⏱ 5-11pm) Numerous stands serve fresh Lao- and Chinese-influenced dishes. Beyond Th Fa Ngum, more open-air Lao eateries continue all the way up to Sunset Sala Khounta (opposite). If it's popular with locals, it's probably good. Take your pick.

Vegetarian Buffet (Map p358; ☎ 020-566 6488; Th Saysetha; lunch buffet 15,000 kip, meals 5000-15,000 kip; ⏱ lunch & dinner Mon-Sat) One of several buffets doing an excellent all-you-can-eat vegetarian buffet, with an à la carte menu for dinner. A gastronomic godsend for any vegetarian who's survived on stir-fried vegetables with sticky rice for too long. Head east along Th Setthathirat to Th Saysetha (a Honda store on the left side marks the street). Turn left and the restaurant is a few doors along with a wooden front.

Khop Chai Deu (Map p358; ☎ 223022; Th Setthathirat; meals 30,000-50,000 kip; ⏱ lunch & dinner; ✸) The most popular *falang* hang-out in town. You can dine out on modern Lao, Chinese, Indian or Western, followed by lashings of over-priced Beer Lao (14,000 kip a bottle outside of happy hour!), a game of pool and live music.

Sabaidee Restaurant (Map p358; ☎ 214278; Th Setthathirat; meals 15,000-40,000 kip; ⏱ breakfast, lunch & dinner) Also popular, and just down the road from Khop Chai Deu; the mixed menu includes Thai dishes. At night, the beer-garden setting is illuminated with red and yellow fairy lights: you can't miss it.

Sticky Fingers Café & Bar (Map p358; ☎ 215972; Th François Nginn; meals 40,000-60,000 kip; ⏱ breakfast, lunch & dinner Sun-Sat; ✸) Owned and operated by Aussie expats; the staff are friendly, newspapers and magazines make a thankful diversion for solo diners, and the food is delicious. During happy hour, on Wednesday and Friday nights, 'Stickies' heaves with NGO workers letting off steam.

Riverside Restaurant (Map p358; Th Fa Ngum; meals 10,000-30,000 kip; ☺ lunch & dinner) On the banks of the Mekong, serving delicious Asian cuisine with tantalising descriptions: anyone for stir-fry frog with hot basil (highly recommended; mind the bones) or whipping tiger salad?

Taj Mahal (Map p358; ☎ 020-561 1003; Th Manthatulat; meals 10,000-40,000 kip; ☺ lunch & dinner) In a quiet side street just behind the National Cultural Hall. Friendly service and excellent Indian curries. Note: raita is listed under drinks.

Kitchen Tokyo (Map p358; ☎ 214924; Th Chao Anou; meals 15,000-50,000 kip; ☺ lunch & dinner) Treat yourself to an Asahi accompanied by sashimi (shipped in from Thailand), tempura, gyoza, nori rolls and yakitori – not what you'd expect to be eating in one of the world's least developed countries. Ask for the upstairs private dining room.

Chinese Liao-ning Dumpling Restaurant (Map p358; ☎ 240811; Th Sihom; meals 8000-12,000 kip; ☺ breakfast, lunch & dinner) This neon-lit restaurant on the edge of Chinatown serves great dumplings as well as wok-tossed meat and vegetables.

Katusha Restaurant (Map p358; Th Fa Ngum; meals 15,000-45,000 kip; ☺ lunch & dinner) After one-too-many shots of vodka, you may find yourself planning your own personal revolution over a bowl of borscht, shaliks, *plov* (pilaf) and *pelmeni* (meat dumplings).

Tex-Mex Alexia (Map p358; ☎ 241349; Th Fa Ngum; meals 20,000-45,000 kip; ☺ 9.30am-11pm) Despite mumblings from expats and travellers alike, Tex-Mex Alexia is always busy. With a corner location in the heart of the downtown action, it's hard not to join the throngs for a taco or two. The upstairs pool table is another vote-buyer.

Blue Sky (Map p358; ☎ 216368; cnr Th Setthathirat & Th Chao Anou; meals 14,000-30,000 kip; ☺ breakfast, lunch & dinner) Similar set-up to Tex-Mex Alexia, ie on a corner with lots of street-side seating. The DVD cinema upstairs is an attractive option if you want a Hollywood fix for dessert.

Nazim (Map p358; ☎ 223480; Th Fa Ngum; ☺ lunch & dinner) Another popular Indian option, due to its location.

Excellent breakfast and lunchtime options include the following, but with so many cafés, crêperies and bakeries to choose from, this list is by no means exhaustive.

PVO (Map p358; ☎ 020-551 5655; Th Samsenthai; meals 5000-20,000 kip; ☺ breakfast & lunch) Crunchy baguettes with juicy fresh salad, cheese and pâté. The *bo bûn* (cold Vietnamese noodle dish) is delicious. A top choice for lunch and to take-away.

JoMa Bakery Café (Map p358; ☎ 215265; Th Setthathirat; meals 16,000-30,000 kip; ☺ breakfast, lunch & dinner Mon-Sat; ☒) A sleek operation with delicious breakfasts available all day, and newspapers to peruse. Sister outlet JoMa is in Luang Prabang.

Just for Fun (Map p358; ☎ 213642; Th Pangkham; meals 15,000-35,000 kip; ☺ breakfast, lunch & dinner Mon-Sat) A playful place with excellent vegetarian – and carnivore – dishes. Specialises in Thai food. Also sells fair-trade honey, a selection of teas and delicious homemade cheesecake. Yum.

DRINKING
Cafés
Life, Coffee, Break (Map p358; ☎ 214781; Th Pangkham; coffee 8000-20,000 kip; ☺ 7am-9pm) Coffee from Laos and almost every other corner of the globe, served hot or ice-cold. Snacks, sandwiches and shakes also available. The '70s retro interior and jovial staff make this a great place to recharge on some high-voltage caffeine.

House of Fruit Shakes (Map p358; Th Samsenthai; fruit shakes 4000-7000 kip; ☺ 7am-9pm) *The* premium fruit-shake shop in Vientiane, although next door is good too. Seasonal highlights include anything with strawberry from December to February or anything with passionfruit from May to July.

Bars
Sunset Sala Khounta (Map pp354-5; ☎ 251079; on the riverfront; ☺ 1-11pm) Shipwrecked on the river bank, this charming bar is, as the name would suggest, the best place in

---

BEER SHOPS

If an establishment looks like a restaurant, but inside there's only men sitting around drinking beer and there's no sign of a kitchen or menu, you have probably stumbled on one of Laos' 'special' beer shops where a bottle of draught is sometimes followed by an appointment with a friendly lady whose affections come at a price.

PARTY FOR YOUR RIGHT TO PARTY

Vientiane is a happening town, there's no doubt about that. But the party is rarely in the same place for long, thanks to the often-strict local police. If you really want to kick up your heels, ask someone (trustworthy, of course!) if they know what's happening. Expat house parties seem to be on every other weekend, and a new face can make a welcome change, or your guesthouse owner might be throwing a wedding (a rowdier and less formal affair than a traditional Western wedding reception) where a couple more guests won't be a problem.

More-established venues, where distortedly loud sounds will damage your head almost as much as that last shot of rice whisky:

D*Tech (Map pp354-5; ☎ 213570; Th Samsenthai; ⏰ 8pm-late) Located behind the Novotel, with a Filipino expat outfit playing Top 40 covers.

Marina (☎ 216978; Th Luang Prabang; ⏰ 8pm-1am) Currently a very popular spot, where you can shake your booty to some Thai pop.

Vientiane for a sunset beer – served with salty bar snacks. A sign hanging over the wooden door marks the spot. It's a bit of a hike; you'll work up a thirst.

Khop Chai Deu (Map p358; ☎ 223022; Th Setthathirat; ⏰ noon-midnight; 🗷) When youngsters from neighbouring *bâan* (villages) hit Vientiane, they're a little awestruck by the bright lights and bright smiles of this mostly *falang* hangout. See p362 for more.

Déjà Vu (Map p358; ☎ 020-561 0735; Nam Phu; ⏰ 8pm-midnight; 🗷) A white interior washed with coloured lights reflecting dozens of bottles of spirits makes a stark contrast with the dusty world beyond. Cool music, cool ambience and a cool cocktail list all raise the bar. If you have daiquiri tastes but a beer budget, you can probably only afford to linger over one or two drinks: enjoy 'em.

Sticky Fingers Café & Bar (p362), Tex-Mex Alexia (p363) and Blue Sky (p363) are also popular spots for a few drinks, too.

ENTERTAINMENT

Lao Traditional Show (Map p358; ☎ 242978; Th Manthaturath; 70,000 kip; ⏰ shows 8pm) For those looking for a cultural experience, there are performances of traditional dance, love songs, and music nightly to an entirely foreign audience.

Centre Culturel et de Coopération Linguistique (French Cultural Centre; Map p358; ☎ 215764; www.ambafrance-laos.org/centre; Th Lan Xang; ⏰ 9.30am-6.30pm Mon-Fri, 9.30am-noon Sat) The centre runs a year-round programme of events such as musical performances and English-subtitled films and documentaries. Details are published on fliers out the front and in the *Vientiane Times*.

Check the *Vientiane Times* and fliers on shop windows around Nam Phu for info on public one-off events.

SHOPPING

Vientiane's labyrinthine **Talat Sao** (Morning Market; Map p358; Th Lan Xang; ⏰ 7am-5pm) sells everything from Lao silks, 'Firkenstocks' and jewellery, to white goods, electronics and bedding. At the time of writing, construction had begun on the new Talat Sao Shopping Mall, a modern shopping complex and multistorey carpark that will replace the bustling goods market. The project, expected to be completed by 2009, is planned in three stages so trade can continue around the construction zone.

Numerous handicraft and souvenir boutiques are dotted around the streets radiating from Nam Phu, none of them offer any real bargains. **Camacrafts** (Mulberries; Map p358; ☎ 241217; www.mulberries.org; Th Nokeo Khumman; ⏰ 10am-6pm Mon-Sat) is a not-for-profit company that contributes to villages through training and resource preservation practices. It sells naturally dyed clothing, weavings, bed spreads and cushion covers. Or try **Mixay Boutique** (Map p358; ☎ 216592; Th Setthatharit; ⏰ 9am-8pm), a multistorey shop full of objects of beauty, with a second gallery-workshop around the corner where you can see a weaving loom in action.

GETTING THERE & AWAY
Air

Lao Airlines (Map p358; ☎ 212051; www.laos-air lines.com; Th Pangkham), **THAI Air** (Map pp354-5; ☎ 251041; www.thaiair.com; M&N Bldg, Th Luang Prabang) and also **Vietnam Airlines** (Map p358; ☎ 217562; www.vietnamairlines.com; 1st fl, Lao Plaza Hotel, Th Samsenthai) are the main carriers for Vientiane.

Boat
It's possible to take a slow cargo boat to Luang Prabang (US$26, upstream four days to one week). Ferries leave from Kiaw Liaw Pier, 3.5km west of the fork in the road where Rte 13 heads north in Ban Kao Liaw. Go to the Kiaw Liaw Pier to reserve a spot the day before. Boats make several stops and passengers typically sleep on board.

Bus & Săwngthăew
The **northern bus station** (Map pp354–5; ☎ 260255; Th T2), a 5000 kip túk-túk ride from the centre of town, is the main departure point for domestic and international buses. Buses leave here for everywhere from Phongsali in the far north to Attapeu in the south, and Ho Chi Minh City (HCMC). The station was the target of a bomb attack in August 2003, so visitors are advised to monitor current events and exercise caution.

The northern **Si Muang Bus Station** (Map pp354–5; Th Tha Deua) is where the more expensive **KVT** (☎ 242101) and **Laody** (☎ 242 102) buses head south to Pakse, via Tha Khaek and Savannakhet.

The other key departure point is the **Talat Sao bus station** (Map p358; ☎ 216507; Th Mahasot) from where buses run to destinations within Vientiane Province and south. This is also where the Thai–Lao International Bus begins its trip across the Thai–Lao Friendship Bridge to Nong Khai (see the boxed text, right).

Up-to-date bus-fare information is published in the *Vientiane Times*.

NORTHERN LAOS
Buses for Luang Prabang (60,000 kip, 11 hours, seven daily at 7am, 9am, 11am, 1.30pm, 4pm, 6pm and 7pm; VIP 75,000 kip, nine hours, three daily at 6.30am, 9am and 7.30pm); Phonsavan (60,000 kip, 12 hours, three daily at 6.30am, 9.30am and 4pm; VIP 80,000 kip, 10 hours, one daily at 7am); Udomxai (85,000 kip, 16 hours, two daily at 6.30am and 2pm) depart from the northern bus station.

From Talat Sao, regular buses head to Vang Vieng (15,000 kip, three to four hours) until 3pm. After that, săwngthăew leave from a truck station 7km west of Vientiane. Seats on air-con minibuses to Vang Vieng (US$5, 1½ hours) can be purchased from guesthouses and travel agents around town.

SOUTHERN LAOS
Buses leave Talat Sao for Savannakhet (45,000 kip, 10 hours, eight daily from 5.30am to 9.30am) and Pakse (70,000 kip, 15 hours, nine daily from 10am to 4pm), stopping for a break in Tha Khaek on the way through. VIP buses to Pakse, including an overnighter, leave Si Muang Air Bus Station. Tickets can be purchased from travel agents in Vientiane.

GETTING AROUND
Bicycle & Motorcycle
Bicycles can be rented for 15,000 kip per day from tour agencies and guesthouses in the city centre: you'll see them lined up on the street, ready to go. Scooters cost around US$6 to US$8 per day. Shop around for one in good condition (your safety depends on it). Without insurance, most hirers expect you to pay to replace the bike if it is seriously damaged or stolen. Read the fine print before signing any contracts and ask your guesthouse to lock your bike inside overnight.
Boualian Travel 1 (Map p358; ☎ 213061; Th Samsenthai; bicycle per day 15,000 kip; ☺ 8am-6pm)
KT Shop (Map p358; ☎ 020-561 4201; ktbikerental@yahoo.com; Th Wat Xieng Nyeun; scooters/motorcycles per day US$8/20)
PVO (Map p358; ☎ 020-551 5655; Th Samsenthai; scooters per day US$7) Hire scooters at this eatery.

BORDER CROSSING: INTO THAILAND
The Thai–Lao Friendship Bridge is 20km southeast of Vientiane. The border is open between 6am and 10pm and the easiest way to cross is on the comfortable Thai–Lao International Bus (10,000 kip, 90 minutes), which leaves Vientiane's Talat Sao bus station at 7.30am, 10.30am, 3.30pm and 6pm. From Nong Khai, it leaves at the same times (30B). The border crossing is easy, with visas issued on arrival in both countries (see p414). Alternative means of transport between Vientiane and the bridge include túk-túk (50,000 kip), or the regular public bus 14 from Talat Sao (5000 kip) between 6.30am and 5pm. At the bridge, shuttle buses ferry passengers between immigration posts every 20 minutes or so. On the Thai side you can take a túk-túk between the bridge and the bus or train station, or if you have time, walk.

Túk-túk

Standard trip costs are posted inside túk-túks, which makes haggling difficult though not impossible. Túk-túks standing in a queue on a street corner won't leave the stand for less than the price already agreed with the other drivers (ie approximately 5000 kip for 1km to 2km; 10,000 kip for 2km to 4km). You're better off trying a free-roaming túk-túk (one driving along the street) where a bit of fare negotiation is possible. You can also flag down a shared túk-túk (one with passengers already in it) that is heading in the direction you want to go. A journey in a shared túk-túk will cost you around 2000 to 5000 kip depending on your destination.

AROUND VIENTIANE

VANG VIENG

023 / pop 25,000

Tucked next to the Nam Song and amid stunning limestone peaks, Vang Vieng is a place travellers either love or loathe. The main reason people stop here is to enjoy the outdoor recreation on offer – tubing, kayaking, cycling, caving and rock climbing. The main street has been unfavourably compared to Bangkok's Khao San Rd, and indeed if you walk away and look back at it by night it's about as incongruous as Las Vegas in the Nevada desert. If you're not really interested in reruns of *Friends* played on rotation and at high volume don't despair, beyond the main drag are a number of excellent guesthouses where the only noise you'll hear at night is something akin to silence.

Orientation & Information

Buses stop east of a large patch of tarmac that was the airstrip. Head west into town, then turn right to reach the main concentration of guesthouses, restaurants and bars. Parallel to the main street are a basic provincial hospital and several more restaurants, plus a few newer bungalow-style guesthouses along the river. For any serious health concerns, get to Vientiane for an ambulance pick-up to Thailand.

Banque pour le Commerce Extérieur Lao (☎ 5114480; ⏰ 8.30am-3.30pm Mon-Sun) Just west of Xayoh Café, does exchanges and cash advances.

BKC Bookshop (☎ 511303; ⏰ 7am-7pm) Sells a small selection of secondhand novels, old guidebooks and hand-drawn – and coloured-in – tourist maps.

PlaNet Online (☎ 511209; per min 300 kip; ⏰ 8am-11pm) Internet access, CD burning, international Internet phone calls. Organises onward visas.

Post office (☎ 511009; ⏰ 8.30am-3.30pm Mon-Fri) Beside the old market.

Dangers & Annoyances

Vang Vieng has its fair share of thefts, many by fellow travellers. Take the usual precautions, and do not leave valuables lying around near caves. Be aware that there have been a few drownings here in recent years, and there are many ways you can improve your safety while enjoying Vang Vieng's attractions (see the boxed text Safety Tips from the Expert, p408). The other trouble that tends to find travellers is the law. Police are adept at sniffing out spliffs, especially late at night. Getting caught can be expensive, with police usually issuing a US$500 on-the-spot fine. And, no, they don't take plastic, nor will they issue a receipt.

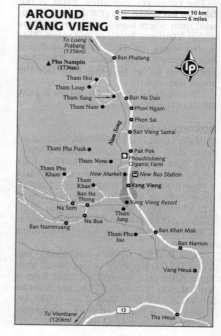

AROUND VANG VIENG

0 — 10 km
0 — 6 miles

To Luang Prabang (135km)

Ban Phatang

▲ Phu Nampin (1736m)

Tham Hoi
Tham Loup
Tham Sang
Tham Nam

Ban Na Dao
Phon Ngam
Phon Sai
Ban Vieng Samai

Tham Pha Puak
Pak Pok
Tham None
Phoudindaeng Organic Farm

Tham Phu Kham
New Market
New Bus Station

Tham Khan
Vang Vieng

Ban Na Thong
Na Som
Vang Vieng Resort

Na Bua
Tham Jang

Ban Nammuang
Tham Pha Jao
Ban Khan Mak

Ban Namon

Vang Heua

To Vientiane (120km)

13

Tha Heua

Sights & Activities

CAVES

The caves around Vang Vieng are generally open from dawn to dusk and with the addition of signs in English there are now entrance charges and, although not strictly compulsory, guide fees. Guides lead you by torchlight, but it's wise to bring your own for back-up. You can buy a local map from BKC Bookshop (opposite) and at several guesthouses. There's someone trying to make a quid at every turn around Vang Vieng, so take plenty of small notes and a sense of humour.

The most famous cave, **Tham Jang** (admission 9000 kip) south of town, was used as a hideout from marauding Yunnanese Chinese in the early 19th century. A set of stairs leads up to the main cavern entrance. There's also a cool spring at the foot of the cave. Follow the signs from the Vang Vieng Resort.

Another popular cave is **Tham Phu Kham** (admission 4000 kip). To reach it, cross the **bamboo footbridge** (toll 2000 kip) near the Hotel Nam Song, then walk or pedal 6km along a scenic, unsealed road to Ban Na Thong, from where you have to walk 1km to a hill on the northern side of the village: follow the signs. It's a tough final 200m climb through scrub forest to the cave.

The **Tham Sang Triangle** is a popular halfday trip that's easy to do on your own and takes in Tham Sang plus three other caves within a short walk of each other. Begin this odyssey by riding a bike or taking a săwngthăew 13km north along Rte 13, turning left a few hundred metres beyond the barely readable Km 169 marker. A rough road leads to the river, where a boatman will ferry you across to Ban Tham Sang (5000 kip return). **Tham Sang** (admission 1000 kip), meaning 'Elephant Cave', is a small cavern containing a few Buddha images and a Buddha 'footprint', plus the elephant-shaped stalactite that gives the cave its name. It's best visited in the morning when light enters the cave.

From here a signed path takes you 1km northwest through rice fields to the entrances of **Tham Loup** and **Tham Hoi** (combined admission for both caves 3000 kip). Tham Hoi reportedly continues about 3km into the limestone and an underground lake. About 400m south of Tham Hoi, along a well-used path, is the highlight of this trip, **Tham Nam** (admission 5000 kip). This cave is about 500m long and a tributary of the Nam Song flows out of its low entrance. In the dry season you can wade into the cave, but when the water is higher you can take a tube in. Dragging yourself through the tunnel on the fixed rope is 'tiring good fun' – boom, boom. From Tham Nam an easy 1km walk brings you back to Ban Tham Sang.

KAYAKING

Kayaking is another popular pursuit. All-day trips (US$8 to US$12 per person) typically take you down a few rapids and include visits to caves and villages. Kayaking trips to Vientiane, advertised around town for about US$15, involve paddling for half a day then going the rest of the way by road. Though all guides are supposed to be trained, many are not. Before using a cheap operator, check guides' credentials (see the boxed text, p408).

ROCK CLIMBING

Wildside Green Discovery (☎ 511230; www.green discoverylaos.com; Th Luang Prabang) operates guided rock-climbing courses for novices (around US$30 per day) up Vang Vieng's dramatic limestone cliffs. If you're a climber you can DIY, but permits (US$5 per day for a group) must be obtained from the Green Discovery office in Vang Vieng.

TUBING

Tubing down the Nam Song is one of Vang Vieng's biggest attractions and there are dozens of tube rental places in shops and guesthouses around town. Prices are fixed at 30,000 kip, which includes the túk-túk ride to the launch point 3km north of town. The trip can take two or more hours depending on river conditions and how many of the makeshift bars you stop off at en route! Of course it's pretty stupid and dangerous to tackle the rapids intoxicated, see p408 for more on water safety.

Sleeping

There are so many guesthouses in Vang Vieng they're doing each other out of business. Here are some of the better options.

Riverside Bungalows (☎ 511035, 020-352 3426; r US$3.50-12; ⚡) This is situated just north of town where the river bends to the west. To get there take the last street to the left.

Riverside's friendly owner, set on making sure everyone has a good time, means this is a good choice. The basic bamboo bungalows all have balconies and shared bathrooms, or you can move upmarket and take a room with private bathroom and air-con.

Maylyn Guest House (☎ 020-560 4095; r US$3-5.50) West of the bamboo footbridge across the Nam Song. The bamboo bungalows with shared bathrooms in a lush garden setting may be spartan, but you have to love the peaceful atmosphere. Show your receipt from the bridge toll for a reimbursement before you get a day pass. To get there follow the westerly road south, pass the hospital and school, and then take the fork down to the river bank. A sign points the way from there.

Vang Vieng Orchid (☎ 020-220 2259; r US$5-10; 🐾) A fairly newish three-storey place on the banks of the Nam Song, it has 20 clean, spacious rooms, 12 with views over to Don Khang and the karst peaks beyond. Walk down through the old market and turn right (north), then it's another 50m on the left.

Dok Khoun 1 Guest House (☎ 511032; r US$3-7; 🐾) Right in the centre of town between the old market and Th Luang Prabang, Dok Khoun is an oldie but a goodie. It's spread over three tall buildings.

Phoudindaeng Organic Farm (☎ 511220; www.laofarm.org; r US$3-6) Around 3km north of town on the banks of the Nam Song, this farm, which grows mulberry trees and organic fruits and vegetables, offers accommodation in dorms or small private rooms with shared bathroom. The attached restaurant (meals 10,000 to 15,000 kip), open for lunch and dinner, makes delicious organic dishes. See the website for directions.

Several more guesthouses, about 250m south of Xayoh Café, are also worth a look if the others are all full. Try the following:

Kianethong Guest House (☎ 511069; r US$4-6; 🐾) Down a side road and away from the action, this newish two-storey concrete building may lack character, but it's cool in the heat of the day, with tiled floors and fans.

Malany Guest House (☎ 511083; Th Luang Prabang; r US$5-10; 🐾) A four-storey monster set back from the street, with clean but unremarkable rooms. Staggering distance from Vang Vieng's restaurants and TV bars.

Nana Guest House & Restaurant (☎ 511036; r US$3-5; 🐾) Nana's is welcoming and the balcony is a good place to chill out. The rooms could do with bit of sprucing up, but for the money this is a good option not too far from the centre.

Eating

Most of Vang Vieng's restaurants produce a varied selection of cuisines including Lao, Thai, Chinese, Western and Rasta. Following are a few decent eateries that have so far resisted Vang Vieng's *Friends* phenomenon. Please also note: in most of Southeast Asia, including Vang Vieng, the word 'happy' before 'pizza' does not mean, as one traveller discovered, extra pineapple.

Nokeo (meals 6000-20,000 kip; 🕑 lunch & dinner) Nokeo has been around for years. It serves consistently good Lao dishes at prices even locals can afford. It's on the corner opposite the old market.

Sunset Restaurant (☎ 511096; meals 20,000-50,000 kip; 🕑 breakfast, lunch & dinner) On the river, this is an ideal spot for breakfast, lunch and sundowners. The menu ranges from Western breakfasts to Lao cuisine.

Xayoh Café (☎ 511088; meals 20,000-40,000 kip; 🕑 breakfast, lunch & dinner) A typically Western menu – pizza, pasta, burgers and chips – similar to what's on offer at the Vientiane branch.

Organic Farm Café (☎ 511174; meals 10,000-25,000 kip; 🕑 breakfast, lunch & dinner) Innovative dishes, an alliterative menu and Laos-famous mulberry shakes make this an excellent choice. Also does water-bottle refills. See left for more about the farm.

VOLUNTEERING IN VANG VIENG

Mr Thi at the Phoudindaeng Organic Farm welcomes those who wish to stay for a week or more and are keen to lend a hand. The days of WWOOFing have gone, but there is still plenty of work for anyone who has the initiative and patience to hang around and to muck in wherever they're needed. Mr Thi's enthusiasm for community development has seen the building of a community centre, a library and the establishment of a free school bus for local children. Teaching at the local school is perhaps the most valuable contribution visitors can make. Teaching local children offers a great opportunity to interact with Lao youngsters and hand something back to the community.

Jamie Thomas, Herefordshire, UK

Fathima Restaurant (☎ 511198; meals 10,000-25,000 kip; ✍ lunch & dinner) A popular Indian restaurant, just east of the old market square, with a decent vegetarian selection.

Restaurant Luang Prabang Bakery (☎ 511145; meals 7000-30,000 kip; ✍ breakfast, lunch & dinner) Strong coffee and tasty muesli set you up for the day. Also makes baguettes (eat-in or takeaway) and sticky pastries.

Thank You Restaurant (meals 10,000-15,000 kip; ✍ breakfast, lunch & dinner) Selling the usual pizza, pasta and fried food, but a little further away from the main concentration of restaurants, with a friendly vibe.

Drinking

With its corner location, pool table, indoor and outdoor seating, and easy atmosphere, Xayoh Café (opposite) is a popular drinking spot.

A more 'underground' vibe is found at the strip of bars competing for trade on **Don Khang**. Many serve slightly chilled Beer Lao and spirits from hastily built bamboo bars. Late-night revellers are drawn to the island by the bonfires, hammocks, music, conversation – and the threat of a police bust. It's a good spot for a progressive drinking party; by getting up and moving along you can share your custom around. Yes, we know it's hard to make your feet move.

Getting There & Away

From the airstrip bus stop (soon to be replaced by a newer bus terminal north of town), buses leave for Luang Prabang (55,000 kip, six to seven hours, five daily), Vientiane (15,000 kip, four to five hours, almost every hour until dark) and Phonsavan (55,000 kip, eight to nine hours, one daily at 8am).

Tickets for minibuses and VIP buses with air-con, travelling direct to Vientiane (US$5, three hours) or Luang Prabang (US$7, six to seven hours) are sold at guesthouses, tour agencies and Internet cafés in town.

Getting Around

The township is small enough to walk around with ease. Bicycles can be rented for around 10,000 kip per day. A few places hire scooters for US$8 per day. A túk-túk up to the organic farm or the Tham Sang Triangle costs around 10,000 kip per person.

NORTHERN LAOS

Home to the various Hmong who originally migrated here from Tibet and southwestern China, Laos' mountainous north is popular with travellers for its spectacular scenery and traditional village life, which was isolated from the modern world until relatively recently. To learn more about the culture and customs of different ethnic groups, a trip to Muang Sing's Guide Services Office (p391) is recommended; from there stay overnight in a village to experience first-hand the realities of subsistence farming life. The slow upgrading of roads has made travel in the north less arduous, although you still can't get anywhere very quickly – patience is the key to travelling here.

LUANG PRABANG

☎ 071 / pop 26,000

Stunning Luang Prabang is a dream location for any travel photographer. Its incredible collection of French colonial architecture, dotted with delicately decorated Buddhist wat and surrounded with emerald green mountains, is the postcard-perfect illustration of historic Indochina. Since Unesco placed the city on its World Heritage list in 1995, restoration works and a tourism boom have seen the once sleepy riverside city getting slowly gentrified. Thankfully, the city's development has been heavily regulated and as a result, Luang Prabang has retained its characteristic charm and sense of isolation that sets it apart from any other city in the world.

Orientation

Most of Luang Prabang's tourist attractions are in the old quarter, on the peninsula bounded by the Mekong and Nam Khan rivers. Dominating the centre of town, Phu Si is an unmissably good landmark. The majority of restaurants, tour companies and Internet cafés line Th Sisavangvong, while more accommodation options and eateries can be found in the streets running from Th Sisavangvong to the Mekong and Nam Khan rivers. The old quarter is easily covered on foot, but hiring a bicycle is an excellent way to explore the city and its attractions.

LAOS

Information

BOOKSHOPS

L'Étranger Books & Tea (booksinlaos@yahoo.com; Th Kingkitsarat; ⏰ 7am-10pm Mon-Sat, 10am-10pm Sun; books per hr/day 20,000/50,000 kip) Fiction and nonfiction, in English and French, is available to buy, rent or exchange. Books and magazines (rare commodities in Laos) are loaned to locals for free. If you'd like to donate a book drop it in, or send one to PO Box 148, LPB, Laos. Also serves lots of tea (p378).

INTERNET ACCESS

You won't have any trouble getting online. Internet shops are dotted along Th Sisavangvong and charge between 150 and 200 kip per minute.

P&T Shop Internet & Email (Th Sisavangvong; per min/hr 200/9000 kip; ⏰ 7am-11pm) Simple facilities in a shopfront with reasonably quick Internet access. Fresh fruit shakes available while you type.

Planet Online (☎ 218972; planet.laopdr.com; cnr Th Sisavangvong & Th Sisavang Vatthana; per min 200 kip; ⏰ 8.30am-10pm) Plentiful and fast connections, but keyboards needed new alphabet stickers when we were there; challenging for those who cannot touchtype.

MEDICAL SERVICES

Lao-China Friendship Hospital (☎ 252049; Th Setthathirat) All-new and eerily deserted. About 5km south off Th Naviengkham, after the stadium (a 10,000 kip túk-túk trip). A large white tower signals the spot. Serious cases need to be flown to Thailand.

Pharmacie (Th Sakkarin; ⏰ 8.30am-8pm) Stocks basic medicines. Open daily, although closes sometimes for a few hours on weekends.

MONEY

Banque pour le Commerce Extérieur Lao (☎ 252983; Th Sisavangvong; ⏰ 8.30am-5pm Mon-Fri, 8.30am-3.30pm Sat & Sun) Will change travellers cheques and cash including Thai baht; US, Australian and Canadian dollars; euros; and UK pounds. Open weekends, but cash advances available weekdays only.

Lao Development Bank (Th Sisavangvong; ⏰ 8.30am-noon & 2-3.30pm) Good exchange rates.

POST

Post office (cnr Th Chao Fa Ngum & Th Kitsarat; ⏰ 8.30am-3.30pm Mon-Fri, 8.30am-noon Sat & Sun)

TELEPHONE

Internet shops along Th Sisavangvong offer long-distance Internet calls. You can make regular international calls from the post office with a phonecard.

TOURIST INFORMATION

Department of Commerce & Tourists (☎ 212019; Th Wisunalat) Stocks a few brochures. Opening hours are erratic.

Unesco World Heritage office (www.unesco.org; Th Sakkarin; ⏰ 8.30am-4.30pm Mon-Fri) An anteroom in an old French customs house at the northeastern tip of the peninsula contains posted public information on the Unesco project in Luang Prabang.

TRAVEL AGENCIES

Diethelm Travel (☎ 212277; ditralpt@laotel.com; Th Xieng Thong) Books air tickets, organises cars with guides.

Willing Service Co (☎ 020-577 2485; Th Sisavangvong; ⏰ 8am-6pm) Organises trips to Pak Ou, Tat Kuang Si and villages. Books plane and bus tickets and provides information on onward travel.

Sights

ROYAL PALACE MUSEUM

A good place to start a tour of Luang Prabang, especially if you're interested in local history, is the **Royal Palace Museum** (☎ 212470; Th Sisavangvong; admission 20,000 kip; ⏰ 8-11.30am & 1.30-4pm, last entry 3.30pm, closed Tue). The palace was originally constructed beside the Mekong River in 1904 as a residence for King Sisavangvong and his family. When the king died in 1959 his son Savang Vattana inherited the throne, but shortly after the 1975 revolution he and his family were exiled to northern Laos (never to be heard from again) and the palace was converted into a museum. Various royal religious objects are on display in the large entry hall, as well as rare Buddhist sculptures from India, Cambodia and Laos. The right front corner room of the palace, which opens to the outside, contains the museum's most prized art, including the Pha Bang, the gold standing Buddha after which the town is named. The murals on the walls in the king's former reception room, painted in 1930 by French artist Alix de Fautereau, depict scenes from traditional Lao life. Each wall is meant to be viewed at a different time of day, according to the changing light. Footwear can't be worn inside the museum, no photography is permitted and you must leave bags with the attendants. A dress code declares that foreigners must not wear shorts, T-shirts or sundresses.

MARKETS

Luang Prabang's main market, the newly built **Phousy Market** (Th Phothisarat; ⏰ 6am-5pm),

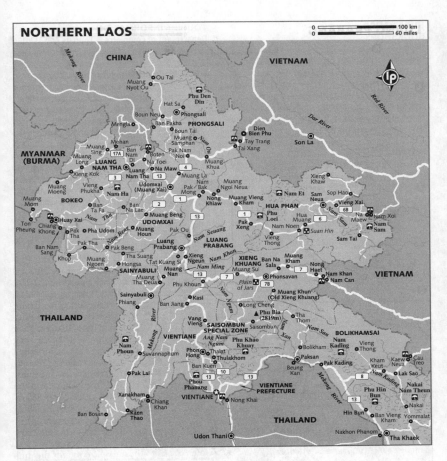

NORTHERN LAOS

which is located just a few kilometres south of the town centre, is heaving with vendors selling an impressive array of hardware and cookware and mountains of fresh produce. To get there, follow Th Chao Fa Ngum south towards Tat Kuang Si. You'll see the market is situated on the left at a major intersection.

At sundown, Th Sisavangvong is closed to traffic between the Royal Palace and Th Kitsalat for the **Hmong Night Market** (4.30-10pm). Lao textiles, handicrafts, jewellery, traditional medicine and antique weavings, mulberry-paper lanterns, mass-produced T-shirts and other souvenirs are all sold here at stalls often manned by tough little negotiators aged 12.

PHU SI

The temples on the slopes of **Phu Si** (admission 10,000 kip; 8am-6pm) are all of relatively recent construction, but the climb up to the temples is well worth it for the superb views – especially near sunset. An admission fee is collected at the northern entrance near Wat Pa Huak. At the summit is That Chomsi, the starting point for a colourful Pii Mai (Lao New Year) procession. Behind the stupa is a small cave-shrine sometimes referred to as Wat Tham Phu Si. Around the northeast flank are the ruins of Wat Pha Phutthabaht, which was originally constructed in 1395 during the reign of Phaya Samsenthai on the site of a Buddha footprint.

LUANG PRABANG

WAT XIENG THONG

Near the northern tip of the peninsula formed by the Mekong and Nam Khan rivers, **Wat Xieng Thong** (off Th Sakkarin; admission 10,000 kip; 🕗 8am-5pm) is Luang Prabang's most magnificent temple. Built by King Setthathirat in 1560, it remained under royal patronage until 1975. Like the royal palace, Wat Xieng Thong was placed within easy reach of the Mekong River. The *sim* (main sanctuary) represents classic Luang Prabang temple architecture, and its rear wall features an impressive tree-of-life mosaic. Inside, richly decorated wooden columns support a ceiling that's vested with *dhammacakka* (dharma wheels). Near the compound's eastern gate stands the royal funeral chapel. Inside are an impressive 12m-high funeral chariot and various funeral urns for each member of the royal family. The exterior of the chapel features gilt panels depicting erotic episodes from the Ramayana.

WAT WISUNALAT (WAT VISOUN)

To the east of the town centre and originally constructed in 1513 (which makes it the oldest continually operating temple of Luang Prabang) is **Wat Wisunalat** (Wat Visoun; Th Wisunalat; admission 5000 kip; 🕗 8am-5pm). It was

rebuilt in 1898 following an 1887 fire started by a marauding gang of Yunnanese robbers known as the Black Flag Haw. Inside the high-ceilinged *sim* is a collection of wooden Calling for Rain Buddhas and 15th- to 16th-century Luang Prabang *sima* (ordination stones). In front of the *sim* is That Pathum (Lotus Stupa), which was built in 1514.

OTHER TEMPLES

In the old quarter, the ceiling of **Wat Xieng Muan** (admission free; 🕗 8am-5pm) is painted with gold *naga* (mythical serpent-beings) and the elaborate *háang thien* (candle rail) has *naga* at either end. With backing from Unesco and New Zealand, the monks' quarters have been restored as a classroom for training young novices and monks in the artistic skills needed to maintain and preserve Luang Prabang's temples. Among these skills are woodcarving, painting and Buddha-casting, all of which came to a virtual halt after 1975.

Across the Mekong from central Luang Prabang are several notable temples. You'll disembark from your ferry across the Mekong near **Wat Long Khun** (admission 5000 kip; 🕗 8am-5pm). The wat features a portico of 1937 vintage, plus older sections from the

LAOS

18th century and a few fading Jataka murals. When the coronation of a Luang Prabang king was pending, it was customary for him to spend three days in retreat here before ascending the throne. A restoration project, completed in 1995 by the Department of Museums & Archaeology with the assistance of the École Française d'Extrême Orient, has brought new life and beauty to the monastery buildings.

Wat Tham Xieng Maen (admission 5000 kip; 8am-5pm) is in a 100m-deep limestone cave, Tham Sakkarin Savannakuha, a little to the northwest of Wat Long Khun. At the top of a hill peaceful **Wat Chom Phet** (admission free; 8am-5pm) offers undisturbed views of the Mekong.

Activities

Cycling is one of the more popular ways to enjoy Luang Prabang. Bicycles can be rented from numerous guesthouses and shops around Th Sisavangvong. The old quarter can be easily covered in half a day, taking in temples and other sights. It doesn't take much effort to get out of town either: head south past Phousy Market and into the hills (watch out for punctures on rocky roads).

After the two-day boat ride from Huay Xai, or the seemingly endless road journey from the south, you've definitely earned a Lao-style massage or sauna, so indulge yourself.

Lao Red Cross (☎ 252856; Th Wisunalat; sauna 15,000 kip, massage per hr 30,000 kip; 3.30-9pm) Offers traditional herbal sauna and hour-long massages to help raise money for the Red Cross' charitable activities.

Mekong Massage (Th Khem Khong; per hr 40,000-50,000 kip; 10am-10pm) Excellent traditional Lao body massages, plus oil body or foot massage, all by friendly well-trained staff. The upstairs space is subtly lit and plays relaxing music.

Somchit Lao Traditional Massage (☎ 252610, 020-577 2956; Ban Mano; per hr 30,000 kip; 8am-6pm) A couple of kilometres from the centre opposite Wat Manolom. Vigorous massage administered by the blind or disabled.

Courses

Attend a half-day cooking course at **Tum Tum Cheung Restaurant & Cooking School** (☎ 252019; Th Sakkarin). You can choose which meal you want to learn, then you're taken to the Phousy Market to buy ingredients, before returning to prepare authentic Luang Prabang cuisine under supervision. The highlight is eating your creation, washed down with a glass of sweet rice wine. Classes are US$10 per person. Register your interest in the book out the front. If you prefer to leave the cooking to the experts, Tum Tum Cheung (p377) also has its own restaurant.

Tours

Trekking and other adventure activity tours near Luang Prabang are starting to hit saturation point. There are a number of outfits vying for your kip and without the controls imposed in the north in the Luang Nam Tha Province, it is starting to get a bit hectic on some trails. Overnight stays in villages, trekking in the forest, kayaking on the river and mountain biking tours are all available. Groups sizes vary as does the language skills and cultural knowledge of guides, so gather as much information as you can from operators, and travellers who have been on recent trips, before signing up.

New-comer to the Luang Prabang outdoor excursions scene and run by Canadian and Lao husband-and-wife owners, **White Elephant** (☎ 254481; white_elephant_adventures@yahoo.ca; Th Sisavangvong; trips per day from US$20) has moved in next door to the firmly established Tiger Trails. Its excursions combine rafting, kayaking, trekking and cycling with an overnight stay in a nearby village. Tours are set at a maximum of six people with two guides. Despite the name, this outfit doesn't do elephant trips.

Geared towards low-impact tourism, and a popular outfit with good reports from travellers, **Action Max Laos** (☎ 253489, 020-561 6053; www.actionmaxasia.com; Ban Xieng Mouan; all-incl guided trek 1-/3-day US$25/65) offers combination trips including trekking, cycling, river trips and elephant riding. French and English guides are available.

Wildside Green Discovery (☎ 212093; www.greendiscoverylaos.com; Th Sisavangvong; per day US$35) specialises in all-inclusive guided white-water rafting on the Nam Seuang, plus treks from one- to four-days through the forests and villages around Luang Prabang.

You won't miss the ubiquitous **Tiger Trails** (☎ 252655, 020-557 0221; www.tigertrail-laos.com; Th Sisavangvong) advertising in the main street. Similar all-inclusive trips, with different routes to the aforementioned outfits, are available with local guides. The German owner can be contacted by phone if you have any queries before making a booking.

Finally, the local outfit **Lao Youth Travel** (☎ 253340; www.laoyouthtravel.com; Th Sisavangvong; per day US$20) takes groups kayaking on the Nam Khan and does overnight treks to villages.

If you're not keen on outdoor pursuits, Action Max Laos (opposite) hosts historical tours of the town with Unesco support.

Festivals & Events

The two most important annual events in Luang Prabang are **Pii Mai** (Lao or Lunar New Year) in April, when Luang Prabang gets packed out with locals as well as tourists (book accommodation well in advance), and boat races during **Bun Awk Phansa** (End of the Rains Retreat) in October. See p410 for more.

Sleeping

Accommodation in Luang Prabang is not cheap, but there are a few guesthouses that cater to travellers wanting a simple clean room without the froufrou. Rooms at the lower end come with shared bathroom, cold water and a fan; the prices go up with hot water, air-con and private bathroom. Prices here are indicative and are more negotiable in the low season. The best budget options are a short walk from the main historic district or if you're completely shattered, a túk-túk to any of these shouldn't cost more than 5000 kip.

Khounsavanh Guest House (☎ 212297; Th Thornkham; r 60,000-120,000 kip; 🕸) In a quiet location with a large green lawn at the front, this is one of better budget options in Luang Prabang. Beds are in the main building with wood walls and shared bathroom, or across the street in the new house where facilities are more upmarket. The staff are friendly and helpful, and Mr Hong's Coffeeshop & Restaurant (p377) is across the street.

Jaliya Guest House (☎ 252154; Th Pha Mahapatsaman; r 25,000-120,000 kip; 🕸) Behind the main building sits an L-shaped row of small motel-style rooms opening onto a grassy garden area, which catches the afternoon sunshine. Rooms at the lower end of the range come with shared bathrooms. At the top end, rooms have private bathrooms, TV and air-con. Bicycles are available to hire.

Thavisouk Guest House (☎ 252022; Th Pha Mahapatsaman; r 70,000-100,000 kip) A guesthouse with the lot. Undergoing renovations at the time of research, Thavisouk already has massage,

hairdressing, Internet, laundry and ticket-booking services. A restaurant and garden were also being built. The friendly owner speaks French and English.

Mano Guest House & Restaurant (☎ 253112; manosotsay@hotmail.com; Th Pha Mahapatsaman; r 80,000-120,000 kip; 🕸) The small rooms in this building are basic but adequate. The terrace restaurant has a convivial atmosphere, and it's a great spot to meet others. Many rave about this place, but on our visit the service was unexceptional.

Near the Mekong and the centre, prices are a little steeper.

Rattana Guest House (☎ 252255; Ban Ho Xiang; r 100,000 kip; 🕸) This homely cluttered guesthouse has ten large and very clean rooms with fans or air-con. The upstairs rooms are quieter. There's a pleasant outdoor sitting area, a few couches inside by the reception desk, and a clothesline for drying laundry. The owners drop the room rates during the low season months.

View Khen Khong (☎ 213032; Th Khem Khong; r 150,000 kip; 🕸) Across the road from the Mekong, this neat little guesthouse is run by a friendly family who speak limited English. All rooms come with private hot-water bathroom and are cleaned daily. It's moving into the midrange category, but well worth the extra money for clean sheets and the wooden shuttered windows.

Suankeo Guest House No 2 (☎ 252804; Ban Ho Xiang; r 40,000-60,000 kip; 🕸) A white two-storey building with blue shutters and an upstairs terrace. Large and cool with a 1950s boarding-school vibe. All rooms come with shared bathroom.

Chaliny Guest House (☎ 252377; Th Khem Khong; r 80,000-100,000 kip; 🕸) Got the thumbs up from those staying there, and every time we visited every room was full. Laundry service and bike hire are also available. A great location and friendly staff.

Phousi Guest House II (☎ 253717; Th Khem Khong; r 60,000-80,000 kip) Extremely laid-back. The Phousi empire may be suffering from its own success, with two restaurants and two guesthouses all within a block of each other. The food was great, but our room was in dire need of a lick of paint and the bathroom was crying for a decent scrubbing brush. Nonetheless, the location and price means this is a good option, especially if you've just got off a boat!

SPLURGE!

If you are intending to indulge yourself once during this trip, the **Villa Santi Resort** (☎ 253470; www.villasantihotel.com; r US$70-100; ✖ 🍴) is not a bad place to do it. To make the most of your stay arrive early and leave as late as possible – even the foyer is a great place to read a book for a few hours. Located about 6km south of town en route to Tat Kuang Si, the sounds of braying ponies and laughing children in a neighbouring village are all that interrupt an otherwise peaceful sojourn. Surrounded by luxurious gardens with water lilies and fountains, 50-odd rooms in newly built double-storey Lao-style buildings feature soft king-sized beds, balconies overlooking rice fields, cable TV, in-room Lao massages and huge deep bathtubs to soak the grit from your pores. At the time of research a giant swimming pool was not yet complete. A minibus regularly shuttles between the town centre, the airport and the resort. This is handy at dinnertime – apart from the all-you-can-eat buffet breakfast, you may prefer to eat in town.

In and around the old quarter budget options are also limited, but at the following you will get what you pay for.

Vatthanaluck Guest House (☎ 212838; off Th Sakkarin; r 70,000-100,000 kip) Located just behind the Villa Santi Hotel, this is a reasonably clean guesthouse with a good central location, and is also popular with Thai travellers. The owner is helpful and bicycles are available for rent.

Chittana Guest House (☎ 020-567 2243; off Th Sakkarin; r 40,000-80,000 kip) Down an alley running to the Nam Khan, this small guesthouse in an excellent location fills up quickly in the high season. First in, first served.

Sokxai Guest House (☎ 254309, 020-557 1559; sokxaigh@yahoo.com; Th Sakkarin; r 120,000-250,000 kip; ✖) This clean and relatively new seven-room guesthouse has an upstairs balcony over looking Wat Sop. Free coffee and tea is served in the morning. The triple room is good value if you're a travelling threesome.

More budget options are found 300m east of Phu Si down a rocky lane running to the Nam Khan.

Cold River (☎ 252810; off Th Phommatha; r 40,000-70,000 kip) Small rooms in a higgledy-piggledy guesthouse. If it's not too busy the affable owners will cook dinner for everyone who wants it, for a small charge. Free bananas and drinking water are on hand in the downstairs reception area. Larger upstairs rooms have river views. The shared outside seating area and small garden buzzes with family and friends teaching backpackers to speak Lao.

Sysomphone Guest House (☎ 252453; off Th Phommatha; r 40,000-60,000 kip) Across the laneway from Cold River. Simple, reasonably clean rooms in a decent guesthouse run by a lovely family. Breakfast is available. Gates close at midnight.

Merry Guest House 1 & 2 (☎ 252325; off Th Phommatha; r 50,000-100,000 kip) A promising name, but the service here wasn't exactly happy. Merry 1 is right on the Nam Khan, Merry 2 is closer to the main road. Renovations were underway, which may see room rates rise. Make sure you get a receipt if you pay for a night, as communication between the staff and the English-speaking owner seemed to be an issue.

Eating
Luang Prabang has its own unique cuisine – consider trying one of the local specialities, no matter how unnerving they sound. A local favourite, *jaew bawng* is a thick condiment made with chillies and dried buffalo skin. *Âw lám* is a soup made with dried meat, mushrooms, eggplant and a bitter-spicy root (roots and herbs with bitter-hot effects are a force in Luang Prabang cuisine). The perfect accompaniment to a bottle of Beer Lao is *khái pâen*, dried river weed is fried in seasoned oil, topped with sesame seeds and served with *jaew bawng*. Other delicacies include *phák nâm*, a delicious watercress that's unique to Luang Prabang. Salad Luang Prabang is a savoury arrangement of *phák nâm*, sliced boiled eggs, tomatoes and onions with a tasty dressing.

For dining on a strict budget, Th Chao Phanya Kang between Th Kitsalat and the river closes to vehicles at night transforming into a bustling **night food market** (🌛 dinner) with a large array of food stalls. Sample some Luang Prabang specialities at one of the open-air wooden bench tables.

Lining the Mekong are numerous **riverside restaurants** (breakfast, lunch & dinner), often with kitchens in a namesake guesthouse across the street, serving delicious Lao fare at good prices, with excellent sunset views and a lanterns-and-fairy-lights festive atmosphere.

CAFÉS

Luang Prabang boasts a steadily improving café scene, where good coffee, crunchy baguettes stuffed with cheese or *jambon* (ham), and sticky pastries will tempt anyone's inner Francophone.

Le Café Ban Vat Sene (Th Sakkarin; meals 10,000-30,000 kip; breakfast, lunch & dinner) In a gorgeously restored colonial building decorated with Lao antiques and wicker furniture. There are plenty of newspapers, espressos and Lao coffees to linger over, and an assortment of pastries, sandwiches and pizzas to tempt you.

JoMa Bakery Café (252292; Th Chao Fa Ngum; meals 12,000-25,000 kip; breakfast, lunch & dinner, closed Sun;) Everything about JoMa shows considerable thought and care: from the bright yellow Vespa out front to the process for ordering and paying for food. Breakfast-sets include coffee (cappuccinos come with cinnamon sprinkles) or juice. The lunch menu includes quiche, muffins, pizza, pasta, sandwiches and salads. There's a sister JoMa in the capital.

Luang Prabang Bakery (253 497; Th Sisavangvong; meals 8000-25,000 kip; breakfast & lunch) The location guarantees this place does a roaring trade all day. Service is attentive, but for a bakery café the baguettes we sampled were disappointingly stale. Still, the newspapers, pastries and the street-front seating *kind of* made up for it (can you tell we're still very disappointed with those baguettes?). Everyone else seemed to be enjoying themselves!

Also recommended:

Café des Artes (Th Sisavangvong; meals 10,000-30,000 kip; breakfast, lunch & dinner) Serves Western food for homesick punters.

Scandanvian Bakery (Th Sisavangvong; meals 5000-15,000 kip; breakfast, lunch & dinner)

RESTAURANTS

Restaurants competing for the foreigner dollar are concentrated on Th Sisavangvong, with slightly more upmarket, but still affordable, options further afield.

Tum Tum Cheung Restaurant & Cooking School (252019; Th Sakkarin; meals 10,000-30,000 kip; lunch & dinner) Renowned for its excellent cooking classes (p374), the Lao food here is top notch. It's a short walk north from the centre, in a quieter *bâan* next to Wat Khili. The wooden building opens out to the street, making this an excellent venue for lunch as well as dinner.

Yongkhoune Restaurant (Th Sisavangvong; meals 10,000-20,000; breakfast, lunch & dinner) This restaurant is located in a superb people-watching location on the main road, and is packed with *falang* in the high season. The service was somewhat forgetful – 'errr, about that sticky rice?' could be heard from more than one table – but when it came, the stir-fry was delicious, the chicken curry with potatoes was hearty and tasty... and the sticky rice? Very fresh!

Mr Hong's Coffeeshop & Restaurant (253533; Th Thornkham; meals 8000-18,000 kip; breakfast, lunch & dinner) Super-friendly Mr Hong draws a steady clientele with a menu of reasonably priced Lao and Thai dishes with plenty of vegetarian options to choose from, plus potent cocktails and a lazy cinema room: Mr Hong knows what the backpacker wants.

Maly Lao Food (252013; Th Phu Vao; meals 10,000-30,000 kip; lunch & dinner) Excellent Lao food worth the trek from town, specialising in *làap* made with buffalo, deer or fish, *tôm jaew pqa* (spicy fish and eggplant soup), *kaeng awm* (a very bitter and hot stew) and *sáa* (minced fish or chicken salad with lemon grass and

> ### SPLURGE!
>
> **Restaurant Brasserie L'Elephant** (252482; Ban Wat Nong; meals 30,000-160,000 kip; lunch & dinner) On a corner near Wat Nong Sikhunmeuang, this elegant restaurant with wooden floors, wide verandas and subdued lighting is *the* spot for a special dining experience. The sumptuous French menu gives European dishes a local touch: boneless quail comes stuffed with Luang Prabang mushrooms and red fruit forest sauce; wild boar terrine is served with green peppers and cognac. You won't find food this good at these prices too often, so why not slip on your Sunday best and spoil yourself rotten. The plonk is good too, but it ain't cheap. Bon appétit!

ginger). Also on hand is homemade liquor – if you haven't tried *láo-láo* yet, get into it.

Samsara (Th Sisavangvong; meals 15,000-40,000 kip; ⊙ lunch & dinner) A chichi interior and table settings; even the menu is an object of beauty. But the modern Indochinese dishes, although a happy change from the standard Lao fare, did not match up to the expectations raised by the 'look' – or the prices.

Of course there are dozens more eating options in Luang Prabang, including these:

Dragon Girl (☎ 020-5673788; Th Khem Khong; meals 15,000; ⊙ dinner) A top recommendation for steamboat, by the river, under the stars.

Nao's Place (☎ 253497; Th Sisavangvong; meals 8000-25,000 kip; ⊙ breakfast, lunch & dinner) Western food is a speciality here.

Nazim (Th Sisavangvong; meals 10,000-25,000 kip; ⊙ breakfast, lunch & dinner) For a taste of south India.

Nisha (Th Sisavangvong; meals 10,000-20,000 kip; ⊙ breakfast, lunch & dinner) Also competing on the south-Indian-curry-and-naan front.

Drinking

L'Étranger Books & Tea (booksinlaos@yahoo.com; Th Kingkitsarat; ⊙ 7am-10pm Mon-Sat, 10am-10pm Sun) Twenty-five different teas are available in the upstairs café of this funky little bookstore (p370), gallery and minicinema.

Khob Chai & Ban Aphay (☎ 020-997 0106; www .explore-laos.com; Th Kingkitsarat; ⊙ noon-late) Laos' first openly gay bar (formerly called Cruisin' Gate until local officials decided that was perhaps inappropriate) is nestled in a curve in the road, not far from the Nam Khan. The crowd is mixed; 'straight' people are welcome too. Across the road is the newer restaurant, bar and beer garden owned by the same partnership. The food is mainly Western, burgers-and-chips style meals, but the upbeat atmosphere and occasional live music draws locals here. Gay travellers note there are guesthouse rooms available above Khob Chai, inquiries to the owner, Uffe.

Hive Bar (hive_bar@yahoo.com; Th Kingkitsarat; ⊙ 5pm-late) Also on the northeast side of Phu Si, the aptly named Hive Bar consists of a honeycomb of brick-lined, candle-lit rooms and corridors, plus a cluster of alfresco tables out the front. Enjoy tapas and an amusing list of drinks based on home-brewed liquors while listening to a mix of trance, trip-hop and tribal beats. Two-for-one spirits from 5pm to 9pm will surely help you 'bee happy' (their pun, not ours).

Maylek Pub (cnr Th Pha Mahapatsaman & Th Setthathirat; ⊙ 5-11pm) Stylishly decorated with modern furniture, Maylek's fully stocked bar includes hard-to-find-in-Laos drinks such as Bailey's Irish Cream, making it a popular choice for travellers staying in the area. Snacks are available if you're peckish.

Martin's Pub (Th Phommatha; ⊙ 8am-midnight) Small, but not very cosy, Martin's was taken over by new owners in late 2004. By day it's more of a café, at night spirits and beer are consumed with loud pop and rock. A small beer-garden area with low cushioned stools offers a reprieve. It had not taken off at the time of research, but the fickle trends of bar popularity the world over could mean it's hugely popular next year.

Entertainment

Royal Ballet Theatre (☎ 253705; Royal Palace Museum, Th Sisavangvong; admission US$6-15; ⊙ shows 6pm Mon, Wed & Sat) Here you can attend performances of different episodes of the 600-year old Ramayana ballet, plus traditional dances of Lao ethnic minorities such as the Phoo Noi and Hmong people.

If you want to kick back and get entertained Hollywood-style, there are several 'minicinemas' with new-release DVDs.

Le Cinema (tickets 20,000 kip; ⊙ 6pm-midnight) Has a decent selection. Follow the signs off Th Sisavangvong and down a laneway.

Mr Hong's Coffeeshop & Restaurant (☎ 253533; Th Thornkham; ⊙ breakfast, lunch & dinner) Has a large cinema room where you can drink and eat dinner (p377) while watching a flick.

L'Étranger Books & Tea (booksinlaos@yahoo.com; Th Kingkitsarat; ⊙ 7am-10pm Mon-Sat, 10am-10pm Sun) This bookstore (p370) shows a regular programme of films and documentaries in its upstairs café at night.

Shopping

Luang Prabang has become a shopping mecca. Dozens of handicraft and souvenir stores line Th Sisavangvong and neighbouring streets. Villagers from far and wide transport their wares to Luang Prabang where it's possible to sell to a steady stream of foreigners for a decent dollar. Bargain-hunters may be disappointed. The better dressed seem to be asked for more per item – so you need to haggle unashamedly. Of course there's no point resenting being asked to pay a fair price. The Hmong Night Market (p371) on Th Sisavangvong has stalls selling similar goods as shops, but without the additional overheads and middlemen.

During the day, a short row of stalls can be found along the Nam Khan close to the north end of Th Kingkitsarat. Around 4pm the villagers here pack up and set up again at the Hmong Night Market.

Also check out **OckPopTok** (☎ 253219, 020-570148; www.ockpoptok.com; Ban Vat Nong; ◷ 8.30am-9pm), a quality handicrafts gallery and workshop selling naturally dyed Lao silk and cotton in modern and traditional styles, as well as clothes and other decorative items. Its informative brochure explains weaving techniques, how to judge the quality of a weaving, and the meaning behind animal motifs used in Lao designs. There is a second branch located on Th Sisavangvong.

Getting There & Away

AIR

Lao Airlines (☎ 212172; www.lao-airlines.com; Th Pha Mahapatsaman) flies from Luang Prabang to Vientiane (US$57, daily) and Huay Xai (US$43) and to Chiang Mai in Thailand (US$88; Tuesday, Friday, Sunday). Flights to Phonsavan, Luang Nam Tha and Udomxai had been cut from schedules at the time of research.

Bangkok Airways (☎ 253334; www.bangkokair .com; Th Sisavangvong) flies from Luang Prabang to Bangkok (US$120). **Siem Reap Airways** (www.siemreapairways.com) goes direct from Luang Prabang to Siem Reap (US$120); bookings through travel agents.

BOAT

Huay Xai & Pak Beng

Slow boats northwest to Huay Xai (US$15) depart 8am. Long-distance ferries stand by the Mekong the day before from where you can start buying tickets, or from a travel agent in town. The trip takes two days with an overnight stop in Pak Beng, roughly halfway between Huay Xai and Luang Prabang. From Pak Beng (US$7.50, 10 to 12 hours) it's also possible to take the bus northeast to Udomxai.

White-knuckle speedboats up the Mekong leave from Ban Don, a 7km 10,000-kip shared túk-túk ride from the centre, to Pak Beng (US$16, three hours) and Huay Xai (US$26, six hours), but it's a trip you take at your own risk.

Nong Khiaw

Although it is quicker by road, many travellers charter a boat for the beautiful seven-hour trip up the Nam Ou to Nong Khiaw for around US$100 for up to 10 people. You can inquire about these trips at the Navigation Office in Luang Prabang or with the travel agents in town, who will post a list of names outside their office where you can join a trip.

Vientiane

Cargo boats to Vientiane have become less frequent since Rte 13 was sealed, but it's still possible to hop on a ferry for the three-day downstream trip for around US$24. Check the chalkboard outside the Navigation Office for departures.

BUS

A number of agents in town sell public bus tickets at marked-up prices, claiming to reserve you a seat, but in reality you can turn up early at the bus station and buy a ticket on the spot for less. BTW: there are no reserved seats!

There are three main bus terminals in Luang Prabang. The northern bus terminal is 6km from town (a 10,000 kip túk-túk ride), while the southern terminal is 3km south of the town centre (5000 kip by túk-túk). A third terminal, on the road to Tat Kuang Si, serves buses going to Sainyabuli Province.

Vientiane & Vang Vieng

Buses leave the southern terminal for Vientiane (60,000 kip, 11 hours, six daily) stopping in Vang Vieng (50,000 kip, seven hours) en route. Travel agents also sell tickets on VIP express buses to Vientiane (75,000 kip, nine hours).

Udomxai, Luang Nam Tha & Nong Khiaw

Buses and sǎwngthǎew leave the northern bus terminal for Udomxai (30,000 kip, five hours, three daily at 8am, 9am and 10am), Luang Nam Tha (60,000 kip, nine hours, one daily at 6pm) and Nong Khiaw (35,000 kip, four to five hours, three daily at 8am, 9am and 10am). Alternatively catch a morning sǎwngthǎew to Pak Mong (15,000 kip, two to three hours) and catch another sǎwngthǎew to these destinations from there.

Xieng Khuang & Hua Phan

There is one direct bus to Phonsavan (70,000 kip, eight hours, daily at 8am). Buses going on to Sam Neua from Vientiane pass through Luang Prabang once a day at around 1pm going the long route north on Rte 13, then east on Rte 1 through Nong Khiaw.

Getting Around

From the airport a túk-túk ride will cost around 10,000 kip, though túk-túk drivers have become accustomed to charging foreigners special tourist prices. Bicycles (10,000 kip per day) are available from many guesthouses and rental shops around town. At the time of research, police had banned the hiring of motorcycles to tourists, reportedly due to the number of accidents we *falang* seem to get into – but the positive reduction in noise pollution was a blessing! Before this, they were about US$10 per day. A túk-túk will take you to sights beyond Luang Prabang for around US$5 per person, depending on the competition around and your powers of playful persuasion.

AROUND LUANG PRABANG

Pak Ou

About 25km by boat from Luang Prabang up the Mekong River, at the mouth of the Nam Ou, are the famous caves at Pak Ou. The two caves in the lower part of a limestone cliff are crammed with a variety of Buddha images, a kind of graveyard where unwanted images are placed. If you go by boat, most trips will involve a stop at small villages along the way. Quite popular is a stop at Ban Xang Hai, or what boatmen call the 'Whisky Village', a now- tourist-dominated village that specialises in producing large jars of *lào-láo*. An enthusiastic collection of boatmen congregates below the Royal Palace Museum touting for Pak Ou passengers. A six- to seven-hour trip including stops at the Whisky Village costs around US$5 per person. Trips can also be arranged through guesthouses and tour operators.

Tat Kuang Si

This beautiful spot 32km south of Luang Prabang features a wide, multitiered waterfall tumbling over limestone formations into a series of cool, turquoise-green pools. The lower level of the falls has been turned into a public park with shelters, picnic tables and food vendors. A trail ascends through the forest along the left side of the falls to an idyllic second tier, which is usually very private except for thousands of butterflies, and has a pristine swimming hole. Entry to the falls site is 15,000 kip. Pak Ou boatmen do the return trip to Tat Kuang Si for around US$5 per person, plus US$2 for the túk-túk ride to reach the falls at the other end. Exercise junkies can also get to Tat Kuang Si by road by bicycle. Túk-túks can be chartered for about US$10 return.

LUANG PRABANG PROVINCE

Nong Khiaw (Muang Ngoi)

Nestled next to the looming limestone cliffs of Phu Nang Nawn (Sleeping Princess Mountain), Nong Khiaw is a quiet market town on the banks of the Nam Ou. The location is stunning, but most backpackers only stop for a short break before catching a boat further north. Those who do decide to stay and explore this area are rewarded with good walks to a nearby cave and Hmong villages, and the friendly guesthouses, on both sides of the river, are markedly less busy than the bungalow huts of Muang Ngoi Neua.

SIGHTS & ACTIVITIES

There are great **trekking** opportunities around Nong Khiaw. You can walk by yourself to **Tham Pha Tok**, a cave where villagers hid out during the Second Indochina War. To get there, walk 2.5km east of the bridge, then look for a clearly visible cave mouth in the limestone cliff to your right (it's about 100m from the road). Longer treks to Hmong and Khamu villages are arranged by the Sunset Guest House for around US$10 per day. You can also try your hand at **traditional river fishing** with nets in the wide rocky shallows of the Nam Ou. Ask at Bamboo Paradise for more info.

SLEEPING & EATING

Sunset Guest House (r 30,000-40,000 kip) On the eastern side of the river in Ban Sop Houn, south of the bridge, this friendly guesthouse is the best set-up in town. The basic bamboo-thatch rooms come with shared bathroom, and there's a superb shady veranda with reclining cushions, river views and decent food.

Bamboo Paradise (r 20,000 kip) To the right of Sunset, this is another good-value option, where the mattresses-on-floor bungalows face the river and visitors are encouraged to brush up on their Lao language skills while they stay.

Sunrise Guest House (r 20,000-30,000 kip) Of a similar standard to Sunset and Bamboo with basic rattan rooms; its location right next to the bridge offers great mountain and river views.

Phayboun Guest House (r 20,000-60,000 kip) On the west side, Phayboun has rooms, including one triple, in a two-storey building. Rooms come with bathrooms and mosquito netting on the windows.

Manypoon Guest House (r 20,000 kip) A friendly place, with good-value rooms in an attractive house, and a good communal upstairs balcony.

As well as at guesthouse restaurants, there are plenty of eating options, both near the boat landing and on the main road. **Bouavieng Restaurant** (meals 5000-15,000 kip; ☾ breakfast, lunch & dinner) and **Manyphong Restaurant** (meals 5000-15,000 kip; ☾ breakfast, lunch & dinner) both serve similar menus of basic Lao food plus Western breakfasts.

GETTING THERE & AWAY
Boat
Regular boats to Muang Ngoi Neua depart until 3pm (13,000 kip, one hour). Tickets are bought at a small office near the boat landing 100m south of the bridge via a dirt road lined with shops.

The journey between Nong Khiaw and Luang Prabang is one of the most spectacular river trips in Laos, passing through dramatic limestone peaks, over rapids and past disgruntled water buffalo. Chartering a boat costs US$100 for the six-hour trip, but this can be negotiated depending on the season, the number of passengers and your driver. To collect enough passengers to make it viable, some travellers put up a list at the ticket office in Nong Khiaw or in Muang Ngoi Neua; or collect people arriving for the morning bus.

Bus & Săwngthǎew
From Luang Prabang, buses and săwngthǎew to Nong Khiaw (35,000 kip, four to five hours) leave the northern bus station. A public bus leaves Nong Khiaw for Luang

Prabang at 8am from outside the post office on the west side of the bridge. Săwngthǎew to Luang Prabang also leave regularly when full.

If you're heading east, you can catch a săwngthǎew as far as Muang Vieng Kham (15,000 kip, three hours), where you change vehicles for Sam Neua (30,000 kip, six hours), Nam Noen (15,000 kip, three hours), or Phonsavan (75,000 kip, 12 hours). These leave when full – arrive early.

For Udomxai, catch one of the regular săwngthǎew (18,000 kip, two hours) to the Rte 1 and Rte 13 junction town of Pak Mong, where buses and săwngthǎew (20,000 kip, one hour) heading northwest from Luang Prabang will pick you up.

Muang Ngoi Neua
After an hour puttering along an almost deserted stretch of the Nam Ou, arriving at Muang Ngoi Neua is a slightly surreal experience. Until a few years ago, this was a small Lao village like any other, dependent on the river for its livelihood and largely cut off from the outside world. Today it is wall-to-wall guesthouses, and tourism has become the mainstay of the local economy. Despite its undeniable strangeness, Muang Ngoi Neua is a relaxing, scenic place to hang out and a good base for trekking into the surrounding hills or frolicking in the river.

INFORMATION
Generators provide electricity to guesthouses and restaurants until around 10pm. There's no Internet or telephone facilities, so it's wise to let anxious loved ones know you may be out of range (some travellers come for a couple of days, but stay a couple of weeks). You can exchange US dollars at Lattanavongsa on the main road, behind the guesthouse of the same name, for unexceptional rates. A couple of pharmacies sell basic medicines; for anything serious get yourself back to Luang Prabang.

SIGHTS & ACTIVITIES
Trekking is one of Muang Ngoi Neua's attractions. From the main street turn east at Kaikeo Restaurant, then follow the path through the large schoolyard and into an area of secondary forest. An admission fee, by donation, will be collected here by a volunteer from town (between dawn and dusk).

After a 5km walk along a path passing rice fields you come to a stream running into **Tham Kang**, a popular spot for spear-fishing. After another five minutes on the same trail you arrive at another cave, **Tham Pha Kaew**. Beyond the caves you can continue on to villages **Huay Bo** (one hour, 3km, 1½ hours), **Huay Sen** (1½ hours) and **Ban Na** (another 20 minutes, 1km). It's also possible to organise a **village stay** if you want to experience something less touristy, although this is also popular so be prepared to walk back again if there's no room at the inn.

Run by a former village school teacher, **Muang Ngoi Tour Office** (7-8am & 6-7pm) is located behind the main street 300m south of the boat landing – look for the signs directing you. From here you can organise small-group treks to Hmong and Khamu villages for around US$8 per day including food and drinks. The school teacher also runs one- or two-day **fishing trips**.

To the left of the boat landing, is **Lao Youth Travel** (7.30-10.30am & 1.30-6pm), which organises overnight treks (from US$10 per day) or will take you up the river with a tube (from 15,000 kip) from where you can amble back.

SLEEPING

There are roughly a dozen guesthouses in the village all doing a roaring trade for half the year. There's little to differentiate between them in terms of price or standard. Most feature bungalows with river views, shared cold-water bathrooms, squat toilets and small restaurants.

Sunset Guest House & Talee 2 (r 20,000 kip) Run by one family, this was the most southerly guesthouse at the time of writing and therefore tucked away from the sounds of generators at night. Hastily built bamboo bungalows stand side-by-side along the river, all with mattresses on the floor, mosquito nets, river views and hammocks. Food and beers ordered here are run back from Kaikeo Restaurant while you wait.

Sainamngoi Bungalows (r 10,000 kip) At the south end of the main street turn left. Cheap and simple bungalows built down the hill all look out at the Nam Ngoi, a tributary of the Nam Ou. Another quiet and relaxing setting away from it all.

Phetdavanh Guest House (r 20,000 kip) The 10 rooms available here are in a sturdy two-storey building on the main street. Clean sheets and clean bathrooms make this a comfortable choice, but you don't get to laze on hammocks and watch the river traffic. If the sound of scurrying visitors at midnight gives you insomnia, this could be a better option for you.

Lattanavongsa Guest House & Restaurant (r 50,000 kip) At the top of the hill leading from the boat landing, sturdy new bungalows with attached bathrooms make this the most expensive accommodation in the village – and with time, more may follow suit.

Other options:

Aloune Guest House & Restaurant (r 10,000 kip) In the main cluster of bungalows halfway along the main street.

Bou Pha Guest House, Bungalows & Restaurant (r 20,000 kip) Simple huts overlooking the river. Photos of backpackers having fun line the restaurant walls.

Kham's Place Bungalows & Restaurant (r 10,000 kip) Again simple bungalows. The restaurant also boasts cold beer.

Ning Ning (r 20,000 kip) On the left when you come up from the boat landing, but lacks great river views.

Shanti Guest House (r 10,000 kip) Small bungalows facing the river; the owner's daughter is a character and seems to run the place. Also has a restaurant.

EATING

No-one comes to Muang Ngoi Neua for its excellent restaurant scene. Accessible only by river, options are limited. Food designed for Western palates rarely hits the mark – the ubiquitous banana pancakes look more like cake than crêpes. However, reclining on cushions in this sociable laid-back atmosphere should make any dining experience a pleasure.

Sengdala Bakery (meals 5000-15,000 kip; breakfast, lunch & dinner) With reasonably fast and friendly service, it makes rice, noodles, curries, soup and salads. Water-bottle refills are also available for 1000 kip per litre.

Nicksa's Restaurant (meals 8000-15,000 kip; lunch & dinner) Overlooking the Nam Ou with a kitchen garden planted on the banks below, Nicksa's is a great spot for an afternoon beer. Bright lights and music mark it out at night.

Sky Restaurant (meals 7000-15,000 kip; breakfast, lunch & dinner) Private cushioned spaces covered by peaked thatched roofs make this a cosy option. On the west side of the main street.

Kaikeo Restaurant (5000-15,000 kip; breakfast, lunch & dinner) A couple of doors east of the main intersection this is a great breakfast spot (where you can watch local kids hurrying off to school, ball of sticky rice in hand). There's a mix of tables and cushioned seating.

Shanti Restaurant (8000-15,000 kip; ☺ breakfast, lunch & dinner) The Shanti restaurant has a similar menu to others with similar cushioned seating, but the owner's daughter steals the show. Also offers accommodation.

Bamboo Restaurant (8000-15,000 kip; ☺ breakfast, lunch & dinner) Lao and Western food served at tables with chairs.

Lattanavongsa Guest House & Restaurant (meals 7000-15,000 kip; ☺ breakfast, lunch & dinner) Serves the usual fare but at tables with chairs and away from the main street. Also offers accommodation.

GETTING THERE & AWAY

Boats to Nong Khiaw leave at 8.30am, 9.30am and 1pm (13,000 kip, one hour). Heading north, it's possible to charter a boat to Muang Khua (boat US$50, five hours) where you change to a boat to Hat Sa (another five hours, US$50) or to a bus back down to Udomxai (25,000 kip, four hours, two daily). From Hat Sa you catch a bus for the final leg along an unsealed road to Phongsali (20,000 kip, two hours). If you have to stay overnight in Hat Sa there's a guesthouse with beds for around 10,000 kip.

XIENG KHUANG PROVINCE

Virtually every town and village in Xieng Khuang Province was bombed between 1964 and 1973. Today the awesome beauty of the mountains and valleys of this province is tragically overshadowed by the denuded hills and valleys pockmarked with bomb craters, where little or no vegetation grows. This remains the province most heavily contaminated with UXO in Laos; walking off paths is extremely inadvisable.

Most visitors come to Xieng Khuang to visit the mysterious Plain of Jars, but there are also several fascinating sites relating to the war open to tourists. Rte 7 from Phu Khun (intersecting with Rte 13 between Luang Prabang and Vang Vieng) is now sealed, making travel to Phonsavan by road a lot quicker.

Phonsavan

☎ 061 / pop 57,000

A sprawling collection of wide streets and concrete shophouses, Phonsavan has little aesthetic appeal except for the ubiquitous collections of war scrap that decorate guesthouses and restaurants. However, it's a comfortable base for exploring the surrounding area and the locals are known to give foreigners a warm welcome.

INFORMATION

Diethelm Travel Laos (☎ 213200; chansmon@laotel .com; Rte 7) Opposite the old bus station; books plane tickets back to Vientiane, and organises tours of the province if you want to create your own sightseeing itinerary. You'll need a few people to make the costs manageable.

Hot Net (Rte 7; per min 500 kip; ☺ 8am-10pm) A few doors along from the post office; has slow Internet connections.

Lao-Mongolian Friendship Hospital (☎ 312166) Five hundred metres west of the Maly Hotel. Medical

---

AN ENDURING LEGACY

Between 1964 and 1973, the USA conducted one of the largest sustained aerial bombardments in history, flying 580,344 missions over Laos and dropping two million tons of bombs, costing US$2.2 million a day. Around 30% of the bombs dropped on Laos failed to detonate, leaving the country littered with unexploded ordnance (UXO).

For people all over eastern Laos (the most contaminated provinces are Xieng Khuang, Salavan and Savannakhet), living with this appalling legacy has become an intrinsic part of daily life.

Since the British Mines Advisory Group (MAG) began clearance work in 1994, only a tiny percentage of the quarter of a million pieces, encompassing 120 different kinds of ordnance, in Xieng Khuang and Salavan has been removed. MAG's work is now supplemented by the UN-administered UXO Lao, but even at the current rate of clearance it will take more than 100 years to make the country safe.

The **Mines Advisory Group Office** (☎ 312459; www.magclearsmines.org; Rte 7; ☺ 8am-4pm Mon-Fri) has information on UXO-clearing projects in Laos including the Plain of Jars (p385). Donations are greatly appreciated.

emergencies will need to be taken to Vientiane for possible transfer to Thailand.

Post office (Rte 7; 8am-4pm Mon-Fri)
On the eastern corner of the town triangle opposite the dry goods market.

SLEEPING

There are numerous accommodation options in Phonsavan so even in the high season you'll have no trouble finding a place to stay.

Kong Keo Guest House (020-551 6365; www .kongkeojar.com; r 60,000-80,000 kip) Kong's guesthouse is like no other in Phonsavan. It's a few hundred metres off Rte 7 across the old air field (a small sign points the way, or ask a local – it won't be hard to find someone who knows Mr Kong). Rooms are in the main three-storey building or in bungalows with attached cold-water bathrooms. Solar panels mean there is lukewarm water in the evening.

Vinh Thong Guest House (312047; Rte 7; r 20,000-30,000 kip) On a street corner located just a few hundred metres from the centre of town is this delightful family-run guesthouse. The thatched rooms are fairly clean, and some are with attached cold-water bathrooms. Inside there is plenty of information about the area, plus a mural and topographical map.

Phoukham Guest House (Rte 7; r 20,000-40,000 kip) Opposite the old bus station, the modern two-storey Phoukham Guest Househas lots of war junk in the foyer adding a sense of history otherwise absent. Reasonably soft beds and private bathrooms are a plus. You can also get onward visas and make Internet phone calls or download digital photos to disk.

Dok Khoun Guest House (312189, 020-563 4792; Rte 7; r 30,000-80,000 kip) A well-run guesthouse on the main road, with hot water in some rooms and tiled floors. Laundry service is available for 10,000 kip per kilo and onward visas can be arranged. You'll need your own sleeping bag and earplugs (it's next to Phonsavan Nightclub).

Vanealoun Guest House (312070; Rte 7; r 50,000 kip) Despite the cell-like rooms, this is another good option for its cleanliness and electric hot-water showers. It even has shampoo satchels in each bathroom; very swish! The tiled floors are cool, and rooms come with fan. Doors close at 11pm.

EATING

There are a number of reasonable dining options in Phonsavan from the day-time-only fresh produce market to Indian, Korean, Lao or Western food.

Siwitmay Restaurant (211344; Rte 7; barbecue per table 15,000 kip; dinner) About 1km west of the triangle, you can indulge in all-you-can-eat Korean-style steamboat. At the time of research there was talk of moving the venue, so check the location before you trek off with your posse.

China Restaurant (312220; Rte 7; meals 10,000-20,000 kip; lunch & dinner) Fried rice, Chinese dumplings, spicy eel slices…an excellent option if your tastebuds desperately desire something other than Lao or Lao-style Western cuisine. Dining is inside off the busy main street.

Nisha (020-569 8140; Rte 7; meals 8000-20,000 kip; lunch & dinner) For vegetarians, who haven't many options in these more remote parts of the country, Indian curries are a gift from Ganesh. It's on the left as you head east.

Kong Keo Guest House (020-551 6365; www .kongkeojar.com; dishes 8000-20,000 kip) Even if you're not staying, this is a great place to eat if you want to meet fellow travellers. The service can be errr… a little forgetful, but you're in Laos: sip a beer by the fire – in a former bomb casing – while sitting cross-legged on cushions soaking up the convivial atmosphere. Try the excellent rice-paper rolls.

Fresh food market (6am-5pm) Located one block south of Rte 7, the market has an undercover section with numerous noodle stands, for a delicious and inexpensive noodle meal. Fresh fruit and vegetables, deep-fried bananas, sticky rice-balls, slippery noodle spring rolls and other culinary treasures also await.

ENTERTAINMENT

For a small town in the middle of Laos, Phonsavan knows how to party. The tourist authority's 'DIY Phonsavan' fact sheet recommends politely crashing a wedding party, provided you're happy to give a monetary gift in a white envelope to the couple. Turning up uninvited is unlikely to offend your hosts, but neglecting to contribute to the gift-giving would be more than a faux pas (and will probably ensure foreigners are no longer welcomed!). Weddings are usually large affairs with the entire neighbourhood invited, live music, dancing and plenty of *lào-láo* going down. The peak wedding season is November to March.

Other options:

Fifa (Rte 7; 7pm-1am) You can attempt to watch football or rugby on cable TV if you're not distracted by the locals dancing, drinking and flirting under flashing disco lights.

Phonsavan Nightclub (Rte 7; 8pm-midnight) Karaoke and live bands play a mixture of Lao, Thai, Chinese and Vietnamese pop to entertain local youth.

GETTING THERE & AWAY

Lao Airlines (312027; www.laos-airlines.com; Phonsavan airport) flies to Phonsavan from Vientiane (US$50, daily). The old bus and săwngthăew station is above the main triangle intersection. At the time of research, buses departed from here then did a pick-up at the new bus station, 3km west along Rte 7. There are regular direct buses to Vientiane via Vang Vieng (70,000 kip, 12 to 13 hours, three daily), Luang Prabang (60,000 kip, eight hours), Sam Neua (50,000 kip, eight hours, two daily) and Udomxai (70,000 kip, 13 hours, one daily).

The roads on these routes are now sealed and in good condition. If you're planning a loop around towards Nong Khiaw, take the Sam Neua bus and get off at Nam Noen (where it's possible to stay the night if you want to) at the junction of Rte 6 and Rte 1 for săwngthăew or buses heading west.

Plain of Jars

The Plain of Jars is a large area extending around Phonsavan from the southwest to the northwest where huge jars of unknown origin are scattered about in dozens of groupings. There are three main sites for visitors to wander around, which have been largely cleared of UXO.

Site 1 is 10km southwest of Phonsavan and is the largest, featuring 250 jars mostly between 1m and 3m tall and weighing between 600kg and one tonne. There's an undercover rest area at this site, where you can buy snacks and drinks – plus read comprehensive information boards provided by Unesco on the jars and the UXO-clearing project here.

Two other jar sites are accessible by an unsealed road from Phonsavan and have fewer jars, but much better views. **Site 2**, about 25km south of town, features 90 jars spread across two adjacent hillsides. Vehicles can reach the base of the hills, then it's a short, steep walk to the jars.

More impressive is 150-jar **Site 3**, which is also known as Hai Hin Lat Khai, located about 10km south of Site 2. This site is on a scenic hilltop near the charming village of Ban Sieng Di, where there's also a small monastery containing the remains of Buddha images damaged in the war. The site is a stiff 2km walk across rice paddies and up a hill.

TOURS

Officially, vehicles must be 'registered' to visit the sites, meaning you have to go on a tour. It seems inconvenient, but there are a number of tours available. Tours can be arranged in Phonsavan, which is notable for its excellent English-speaking guides.

Organised tours to the jars are often extended to include other interesting sites, including a crashed US Thunder Chief 105 plane, a Russian tank, Viet Cong bunkers, the US Lima S 108 airstrip supposedly used for drug running, and hot springs. Trips can also be arranged to the Tham Piu cave, about 60km east, where 400 local people were killed in a US bombing raid.

From upmarket Maly Hotel, **Sousath Travel** (312031; sousathp@laotel.com) runs tours to the jars for US$50 (up to four people). For a bit more, you can choose a programme that takes you to Sites 2 and 3, with stops along the way at Ban Sieng Di near Site 3 and a Hmong village in the area of Muang Kham.

Phou Kham (312121) runs good individually tailored tours costing around US$50 for a car with a guide visiting any of the sites around Phonsavan.

BORDER CROSSING: INTO VIETNAM

If you don't want to backtrack it is possible to cross the Vietnamese border at Nam Khan. To get there, you can either hire a private vehicle with a group from Phonsavan, or catch a săwngthăew to Nong Haet and then another to Nam Khan. Public transport from Nam Can (on the Vietnamese side) to Hanoi or to Vinh is a little scarce; be prepared to wait. For up-to-date traveller information on this new border crossing, check out Lonely Planet's online Thorn Tree travel forum (www.lonelyplanet.com).

> **JARS OF THE STONE AGE**
>
> The purpose of these possibly 2000-year-old jars remains a mystery and without any organic material – such as bones or food remains – there is no reliable way to date them. Archaeological theories and local myth suggest the enigmatic jars were used for burial purposes – as stone coffins or urns – or maybe for storing *lào-láo* (rice whisky) or rice?
>
> In the 1930s, pioneering French archaeologist Madeline Colani documented the jars in a 600-page monograph *Mégalithes du Haut Laos (Megaliths of Highland Laos)*, concluding that they were funerary urns carved by a vanished people. Colani found a human-shaped bronze figure in one of the jars at Site 1, as well as tiny stone beads in the area. Today the whereabouts of these cultural artefacts is unknown.
>
> The relief of a human figure carved onto Jar 217 at Site 1 – a feature Colani missed – lends weight to the sarcophagi theory. Whether they were used for cremation or in a burial practice where a person is 'distilled', reinforces various theories on the pattern of human migration here over the last two millennia.
>
> Aerial photographic evidence suggests that a thin 'track' of jars may link the various jar sites in Xieng Khuang, and some researchers hope future excavations will uncover sealed jars whose contents may be relatively intact. Unfortunately, excavations will take some time while UXOs are slowly removed from the area.

Tours from **Kong Keo Guest House** (☎ 020-551 6365; www.kongkeojar.com; off Rte 7) have also received good reports. A car with driver and guide costs around US$8 per person, depending on the size of the group. The first stop is the fresh food market where you're expected to buy your own provisions for the day.

GETTING THERE & AWAY
It is possible to charter a săwngthăew from Phonsavan to Site 1, 10km from the centre, for 50,000 kip return, including waiting time, for up to six people.

HUA PHAN PROVINCE
Rugged and beautiful, Hua Phan is unlike any other province in Laos. Although home to 22 different ethnic groups including Yao, Hmong, Khamu, Thai Khao and Thai Neua, the influence of the Vietnamese is evident. The province's high altitude means the climate can be cool – even in the hot season – and forested mountains are shrouded in mist. Road journeys to Hua Phan are memorably scenic; described by one local as 'a journey of a million turns'. Now that the border to Vietnam is open to foreigners, you no longer have to turn around and go all the way back again. With improved public transport across the border to Hanoi, this remote part of Laos will hopefully see visitor numbers increase over the coming years.

Sam Neua
☎ 064 / pop 46,800
There is an unmistakable 'frontier' feeling to Sam Neua. Men in military caps and jackets nurse coffees and cigarettes, wrapped up against the morning chill, and pick-up trucks piled high with local villagers, crates of chilli sauce or striped bags stuffed with goods pass through. It's one of the least touristy provincial centres in Laos. While the town offers little in terms of sights, the riverside market is fascinating – all manner of freshly slaughtered or harvested delicacies, as well as textiles, jewellery and consumer goods are sold here. In mid-December, local ethnic groups take part in all-important courtship games and festivities during a **Hmong Lai Festival**.

INFORMATION
Hua Phanh Tourist Office (☎ 312567; ⏱ 8am-3.30pm Mon-Fri) Located 200m north of the bus station. The staff, who speak a little English, have a few dusty pamphlets on hand and can arrange vehicles around the province to more remote sites such as Suan Hin (Sao Hin Tang), a stone garden often likened to Britain's Stonehenge.

Lao Development Bank (☎ 312171; ⏱ 8am-4pm Mon-Fri) On the main road 400m north of the bus station on the left; exchanges cash and travellers cheques.

Post office (⏱ 8am-4pm Mon-Fri) In a large building directly opposite the bus station. A telephone office at its rear offers international calls using a phonecard and is open the same hours.

SLEEPING & EATING

The block between the bus station and the Nam Xam is where the reputable guesthouses and a few restaurants can be found, all within a short walking distance. Accommodation is of a similar standard: multistorey buildings with a sitting area and a pot of tea on each floor, rooms with or without an attached bathroom, and reasonably clean although hard beds to kip in.

Shuliyo Guest House (☎ 312462; r 30,000-50,000 kip) Turning right from the bus station, this is the first place you come to. The family owners speak almost no English, so this is your chance to practise your Lao (or signing skills). The rooms on the top floor come with shared bathroom – on the ground floor. The electric hot-water tanks in each bathroom provide only five minutes of water at a moderate pressure, so be kind to your roommate and have a quick shower.

Phatphousay Guest House (☎ 312943; r 40,000-50,000 kip) On a dark laneway running parallel with the river, this is another family-run guesthouse with clean rooms, twin or double beds, with or without an attached bathroom.

Bounhome Guest House (☎ 312223; 020-234 8125; r 35,000-40,000 kip) The distinguishing feature of this multistorey guesthouse directly opposite Phatphousay is the balcony on each floor. Otherwise the standards are similar to the rest and the price differences are a little inexplicable.

Khaem Xam (☎ 312111; r 30,000-60,000 kip) Located on the corner next to the bridge and opposite the river, the tiled fan-cooled rooms with or without bathrooms here have long been a popular choice for foreign travellers and travelling businessmen. The attached restaurant does simple Lao dishes that are hearty and filling.

Dan Nao Muang Xam Restaurant (☎ 314126; meals 10,000-20,000 kip) At the end of the laneway and a few doors west of Khaem Xam, this is the best eatery in a town that's not winning any gourmet awards. The basic Lao menu also includes Western-style breakfasts, excellent fried rice, fresh baguettes and tender beef salad.

Chittavanh Restaurant (☎ 312265; meals 8000-20,000 kip) On the river road between the bridge and the market is another good option, with a short menu of fried meat and fish, soups and fried rice. It's popular for breakfast or dinner and warming glasses of *lào-láo*.

Mitsampanh Restaurant (☎ 312151; meals 10,000-30,000 kip) In the laneway, a few doors north of Phatphousay Guest House, this restaurant does reasonable Lao food for good prices, but unfortunately it doesn't have much on offer for vegetarians.

At lunchtime, the market is a source of all sorts of delights including bamboo-leaf-wrapped curry with rice, noodle soups, and creepy-crawlies plucked straight from the river, for the adventurous diner!

GETTING THERE & AWAY

Lao Airlines flies to and from Sam Neua from Vientiane (US$72, twice a week). The descent through the Nam Xam valley is tricky; the mountains are frequently shrouded in mist.

There are three main bus departures daily all heading for Vientiane (120,000 kip, 24 hours). The first leaves at 7.30am and arrives in Vientiane at 6am the next day, going via the southern route through Phonsavan (50,000 kip, eight hours), on a good but very winding sealed road. The second leaves at 8am via Rte 1 through Muang Vieng Thong (30,000 kip), Nong Khiaw (60,000 kip) and down through Luang Prabang (70,000 kip, 15 hours), arriving in Vientiane around midnight. If you're heading for Udomxai, take this bus and change to a săwngthăew at Pak Mong. This is a slow, uncomfortable trip, especially in the wet season. The third option is the VIP express bus (130,000 kip) leaving Sam Neua at midday and arriving in Vientiane around 5am.

BORDER CROSSING: INTO VIETNAM

Buses to Na Maew on the Vietnam border depart from Sam Neua at 7am (20,000 kip, three hours) passing through Vieng Xai on the way. Get to the bus station early to ensure a seat. The crossing here was opened to international visitors in January 2004. At the time of research transport on the other side was scarce, but with more travellers making the journey this will pick up. It's a long winding journey from Nam Xoi in Vietnam to Hanoi.

Vieng Xai (Pathet Lao Caves)

In a narrow valley of limestone peaks are caves that served as the elaborate homes and shelters of the Pathet Lao leaders and their followers for more than a decade before their victory in 1975. The caverns are virtually unassailable by land or air, but the area was still heavily pounded by American bombs. Today, the most historically significant caves, named after the leaders who lived in them, are open to tourists.

This is a fascinating and peaceful town to spend a day or two. A wooden board in front of the market features a map of Vieng Xai.

You must report to the **Kaysone Phom Vihan Memorial Tour Cave Office** (☎ 064-314321; ☒ 8am-noon & 1.30-4pm), a 2km walk from the bus station, to pay the caves entrance fee of 10,000 kip, plus 10,000 kip for a guide who will take you to the caves and let you in. It's another 2000 kip to take a camera.

At the time of writing two guides spoke English. A dozen caves at three different sites are open for visitors and tours take two to three hours. The leaders' caves feature multiple entrances, bedrooms, offices, and emergency rooms fitted with steel doors and equipped with large Russian oxygen machines in case of a chemical attack. Many of the caves are now fringed by magnificent gardens, making them look more like holiday grottoes than scenes of war and hardship.

Tham Than Souphanouvong, named after the Red Prince, has a crater from a 500lb bomb near the entrance that has been concreted as a war relic. **Tham Than Kaysone**, named after former president and Pathet Lao leader, has the most to look at, with original beds, clothing, office equipment, books, a portrait of Che Guevara and a politburo meeting room. **Tham Than Khamtay** is the most spectacular of the caves, where up to 3000 Pathet Lao rank and file would hide out.

SLEEPING & EATING

Government Hotel (☎ 064-314356; r 10,000-30,000 kip) The best location in town by a small lake. The shared bathrooms come with small electric hot-water tanks. Rooms with up to three beds have mosquito nets. Leather armchairs line up on the red-tiled veranda and a small restaurant serving simple meals, with notice, is downstairs.

Naxay Guesthouse (☎ 064-314336, 020-576 4729; r 10,000-20,000 kip) Clean rooms in a rickety wooden house with lino floors. The cold-water bathrooms are in a nearby building. Hot water is provided in a thermos.

Next to the Naxay, a small **restaurant** (☎ 064-314336; meals 10,000 kip) does Korean-style steamboat, heating coals in an empty bombshell out the front.

GETTING THERE & AWAY

A bus leaves Sam Neua for Vieng Xai at 6am (7000 kip, 40 minutes), or săwngthăew leave almost every hour when full until mid-afternoon. From Vieng Xai, săwngthăew for Sam Neua leave the market almost hourly until 5pm.

UDOMXAI PROVINCE

This rugged province is wedged between Luang Prabang, Phongsali, Luang Nam Tha, Bokeo and Sainyabuli, with a small section that shares a border with China's Yunnan Province. It is home to 23 ethnic minorities, mostly Hmong, Akha, Mien, Phu Thai, Thai Dam, Thai Khao, Thai Lü and Thai Neua. The Yunnanese presence continues to intensify with the influx of Chinese skilled labourers working in construction, as well as tradespeople from Kunming, the capital of Yunnan.

Udomxai

☎ 081 / pop 80,000

During the Second Indochina War the regional capital became the centre for Chinese troops supportive of the Pathet Lao. Today it's a booming Laos–China trade centre riding on imported Chinese wealth. Despite the enthusiasm of the staff at the tourist office, the town is not particularly exciting. But its position at the crossroads of Rtes 1, 2 and 4 means it's difficult to avoid if you're travelling to Luang Nam Tha or Phongsali.

INFORMATION

Banque pour le Commerce Extérieur Lao (☎ 211260; Rte 1; ☒ 8.30am-4pm) Changes US dollars, Thai baht or Chinese yuan into kip.

Lao Development Bank (☎ 312059; Rte 4; ☒ 8.30am-3.30pm) Also changes US dollars, Thai baht or Chinese yuan into kip.

Oudomsay Provincial Tourism Office (☎ 211797; ☒ 8am-4.30pm Mon-Fri, 8am-noon Sat) Located just up the hill from the bridge.

Post office (⊗ 8am-4pm Mon-Fri, 8am-noon Sat) You can make international calls here with a phonecard.

Udomxai Travel (☎ 212020; travel_kenchan@yahoo .com; Rte 1) For tours to local attractions such as the Houay Nam Kat Reserve find Mr Kenchan O'Phetsan at this travel agency, located next to the bus station.

SLEEPING & EATING

Saylomyen Guest House (☎ 211377; off Rte 1; r 30,000-50,000 kip) To find this guesthouse, turn right at the main intersection about 800m north of the bus station; it's well signposted. The main building has clean rooms with shared bathroom. In a newer construction next door, rooms have attached bathrooms – all with hot water. Great views can be enjoyed from the top floor of the main building.

Bouakhao Guest House (☎ 312269; Rte 1; r 30,000-40,000 kip) A modest two-storey guesthouse, around 25m from the new bus terminal in the direction of Luang Prabang.

Linda Guest House (☎ 312147; Rte 1; r 40,000-50,000 kip) Has 14 fan rooms in a three-storey, ornate building on the main street. If full, there's another branch, Linda 2, on Rte 4, behind the Kaysone Monument, with the same prices and amenities.

Thanousin Restaurant (☎ 312235; Rte 1; meals 5000-25,000 kip) Conveniently located near the junction of Rtes 1 and 2; has seating indoors and out.

Pholay (☎ 312324; Rte 1; meals 10,000-30,000 kip) Located next to a petrol station, Pholay is another reliable place to eat, with an extensive menu of Chinese and Lao food.

GETTING THERE & AWAY

Lao Airlines runs an irregular flight from Udomxai over to Vientiane (US$72). The Chinese-built bitumen roads that radiate from Udomxai are in fair condition (except for the road to Pak Beng) and the city is the largest land-transport hub in the north. The bus terminal at the southwestern edge of town has buses to and from Luang Prabang (30,000 kip, five hours, three daily), Nong Khiaw (24,500 kip, three hours, one daily), Pak Beng (26,500 kip, four hours, two daily), Luang Nam Tha (26,000 kip, three to five hours, three daily), Boten (23,000 kip, four hours, two daily), Phongsali (50,000 kip, eight hours, one daily) and Vientiane (ordinary 90,000 kip, 15 hours; VIP 100,000 kip, 14 hours).

LUANG NAM THA PROVINCE

Virtually destroyed during the Indochina War, Luang Nam Tha has been revived as a commercial node between Thailand, China and Laos. The selection of the province for the experimental Nam Ha Ecotourism Project means that tourism has taken off here, with travellers spreading the word on the low-impact trekking tours out of Luang Nam Tha and Muang Sing. The district is on the cusp of considerable change with the new Hwy 3 from China to Thailand set to alter the dynamic of village life as Laos reinvents itself as an important crossroads state between two of the world's fastest growing economies.

Luang Nam Tha
☎ 086 / pop 35,400

Luang Nam Tha is actually two towns set in a wide flat river valley. The new town, which has the main bus station and the bulk of guesthouses, restaurants and facilities, lies 7km to the north of the old town – where you find the airport and Nam Tha boat landing. Although the town itself is not particularly appealing for most travellers, the surrounding mountains and rices fields have a number of Thai Dam, Khamu and Thai Lü villages that can be visited by bicycle.

INFORMATION
Banque pour le Commerce Extérieur Lao
(⊗ 8.30am-3.30pm Mon-Fri) Opposite the Lao Telecom Office on the main road; offers cash advances on Visa for 2% commission as well as exchanges of cash and travellers cheques.

KNT.com (☎ 211066; per min 500 kip; ⊗ 8am-11pm) Internet connections, downloading digital photos and international phone calls. Also sells an informative not-to-scale local map for 3000 kip.

Lao Development Bank (☎ 312232; ⊗ 8.30am-noon & 2-3.30pm Mon-Fri) Next to KNT.com; exchanges cash and travellers cheques.

Lao Telecom Office (⊗ 8am-noon & 1-5pm) Located on the main road.

Luang Namtha Provincial Tourism Office
(☎ 211534, 020-568 6952; namhacenter@hotmail.com; ⊗ 8am-noon & 2-5pm) One block east of the post office. Possibly the best tourism office in the country; the headquarters of the Nam Ha Ecotourism Project (see p390).

Post office (☎ 312007; ⊗ 8am-noon & 1-4pm Mon-Fri) On the main north–south road, in front of the disused dry-goods market.

LAOS

SIGHTS & ACTIVITIES

The **Luang Nam Tha Museum** (admission 5000 kip; ☺ 8.30-11.30am & 1.30-3.30pm Mon-Fri) contains a collection of local anthropological artefacts, such as ethnic clothing and Khamu bronze drums, along with a display chronicling the revolution.

Most people come to Luang Nam Tha for the **trekking** and **rafting** opportunities around the Nam Ha National Protected Area (NPA). Tours follow strict guidelines on group sizes and frequency, limiting the impact of tourism on villages. Profits from trips go back into the local economy. Travellers should note that it is illegal to go trekking in the Nam Ha NPA with unlicensed guides.

Nam Ha Ecotourism Project (☎ 312047; namha guides@hotmail.com; ☺ 8am-noon & 2-5pm) treks range from one to three days, costing around US$10 per day. The provincial tourism office has information on trips as well as excellent brochures on responsible tourism, local flora and fauna, different ethnic minorities living in neighbouring villages, customs, etiquette and suggested further reading for those who are keen to know more.

Wildside Green Discovery (☎ 211594; www .greendiscoverylaos.com), two doors south of Manychan Guest House-Restaurant, runs one- to four-day kayaking and rafting trips on the Nam Ha for around US$30 per day, depending on the group numbers.

SPLURGE!

The **Boat Landing Guest House & Restaurant** (☎ 312398; www.theboatlanding.com; r with breakfast US$28-45), 7km south of town and about 150m off the main road, is a quiet ecolodge next to the Nam Tha boat landing. Spacious wooden bungalows in landscaped gardens feature private verandas and bathrooms with solar-heated showers. Water is provided in refillable containers and there's loads of information and tips on how to minimise your impact on the environment and help the local economy. This is an excellent stopping-off point on a cycling tour of the valley, or for a predeparture breakfast before taking the boat to Huay Xai (meals go for between 9000 and 45,000 kip). Payment is in cash only, but can be made in kip, baht, yen, US dollars and euros. Highly recommended.

For those who want to go it alone, hire a bicycle or scooter (opposite) and head off to nearby villages, an excellent day-long excursion. Places of interest within easy cycling distance include two 50-year-old wat, **Wat Ban Vieng Tai** and **Wat Ban Luang Khon**, near the airfield; a hill-top stupa, **That Phum Phuk**, about 4km west of the airfield; a small **waterfall** about 3km northeast of town past **Ban Nam Dee**; plus a host of **Khmu**, **Lenten**, **Thai Dam** and **Thai Lü** villages dotted along dirt roads through rice fields. Before you take off it's worth stopping in at the Luang Namtha Provincial Tourism Office (p389) to get information on visiting villages. A good map of the area is sold at KNT.com (p389).

Alternatively, you can join a guided mountain-bike tour of the Nam Tha valley from the **Boat Landing Guest House** (☎ 312398; www.theboatlanding.com) for around US$10 per day. Ten percent of profits go to grassroots development projects in the region.

SLEEPING & EATING

Pheng Thavy Guest House (☎ 312232; r 35,000-45,000 kip) Located south of town on the main road, this nicely decorated wooden building has good rooms with hot showers. There's an excellent balcony area, *foosball* (tabletop football), Internet connections and tour information and bookings. Look for the old Loumai Guest House sign out the front.

Luang Namtha Guest House (☎ 312087; r 40,000-80,000 kip) A bit of a hike from the bus station, head north when you get off the bus – it's 1.5km up this back road, on the left. Thatched bamboo bungalows with attached cold-water bathrooms sit next to a large man-made pond ringed by palm trees, creating a kind of caravan-park aesthetic. More rooms, with solar-heated showers, are available in the main building.

Bus Station Guest House (☎ 211090; r 35,000-45,000 kip) As the name suggests, close to the bus station, but a great choice for early morning departures. Despite images of roaring engines and diesel fumes, it's actually a quiet motel-style place set around a lawn, one block east behind the food vendors. Not all of the 19 rooms, with attached bathrooms, have hot water.

Keosouphone Guest House (☎ 211979; r 30,000 kip) Diagonally across from the bus station and opposite the market, this three-storey building has clean rooms with shared bathroom. Laundry service is available for only 10,000 kip per kilo.

Manychan Guest House-Restaurant (☎ 312209; r 30,000-50,000 kip) A good central option, with fan-cooled rooms on the pleasant wooden upper floor, and a quiet sitting area. Rooms are clean and spartan. Doors close at 10pm.

Palanh Guest House (☎ 312439; r 40,000-60,000 kip) A small simple guesthouse on the main road, just beyond the Indian restaurant. Eight rooms, seven with attached bathrooms, are available.

There are a few specialised eateries in town, including the following.

Panda Restaurant (☎ 211304, 020-560 6549; meals 8000-25,000 kip) Two blocks east of the bus station, Panda has lots of Western and generic Asian dishes, and reasonably quick service.

Yumana Restaurant (☎ 211529; meals 10,000-15,000 kip) On the main north–south road, you'll find this restaurant serving excellent Indian curries. In fact, we'll go as far as saying that you won't find better Indian in Laos. We hope that's still true when you get there!

Aonvilai Restaurant (meals 8000-20,000 kip) Aonvilai may have an amusing menu with 'fist curry' and 'chicken much room', but the food is authentically tasty. It's close to a number of guesthouses on the main north–south street.

GETTING THERE & AWAY

Lao Airlines (☎ 312180; www.laos-airlines.com; Luang Nam Tha airport) flies to Luang Nam Tha from Vientiane (US$81, Monday, Wednesday, Saturday). Charter boats down the Nam Tha to Huay Xai leave from the **boat landing** (per boat US$110; ☻ 8am-4pm), 7km south of town on the Nam Ha. Sign up before your departure to share the charter costs for this two-day trip. In the high season a boat leaves almost every day, depending on passenger numbers. An additional 30,000 kip covers food and lodgings in Ban Khon Khum on the way down. Bring sun protection, plus plenty of water and snacks.

The bus station is opposite the morning market. Buses to Vientiane (110,000 kip, 20 hours) via Luang Prabang leave at 7am and 8.30am. For Udomxai (26,000 kip, three to five hours) departures are at 7am, 8.30am, noon and 2.30pm (if there are enough passengers).

Buses and săwngthăew to Huay Xai (60,000 kip, eight to 10 hours, two daily) leave at 7am and 9.30am. Hwy 3 is being upgraded; the current road is in poor condition. Săwngthăew leave for Muang Sing throughout the day until around 3pm (8000 kip, one to two hours). The winding road to Muang Sing is sealed the whole way and passes through hills of monsoonal forest.

GETTING AROUND

Bicycles (10,000 kip per day), mountain bikes (15,000 kip per day) and not-in-exemplary-condition scooters (80,000 kip per day) are for rent at **Yook Mai** (☎ 312183; ☻ 7am-6pm), north of the Manychan Guest House-Restaurant. Other guesthouses and shops hire bicycles for 10,000 kip.

Muang Sing
☎ 081

Muang Sing is ethnically diverse, a Thai Lü and Thai Neua cultural nexus as well as a trade centre for Thai Dam, Akha, Hmong, Mien, Lolo and Yunnanese. Since the Guide Services Office was set up to regulate the once exploitative trekking business, trips into the beautiful Nam Ha National Protected Area (NPA) have improved substantially. If you're keen to visit ethnic minorities on a socially and environmentally responsible tour, this is possibly your best bet in Southeast Asia.

Muang Sing follows a quadratic grid pattern. A map of the old city is on display in the Guide Services Office (below).

INFORMATION
The small **Lao Development Bank** (☻ 8am-noon & 2-3.30pm Mon-Fri) is opposite the old market on the main street and exchanges US dollars, baht and yuan. The **post office** (☻ 8am-4pm Mon-Fri) is next door.

SIGHTS & ACTIVITIES
Most people come to Muang Sing to trek in the Nam Ha NPA. Treks can only be organised through the **Guide Services Office** (☎ 020-570 8318; ☻ 8-11am & 1.30-5pm), located in a small wooden building signposted off the main street. Even if you're not trekking, pop in for information on Muang Sing from the English-speaking staff. One- to three-day treks, including food, water and

---

PUM PAO

Throughout Laos, particularly in the north, you'll see large boxes on the side of the road, divided into square recesses, with a small coloured balloon inside each one. The idea of this extremely popular game, known as *pum pao*, is that you pay a small fee, collect three darts and hurl them at the balloons from about 5ft away. If you can burst three balloons with three darts, you get a prize, which can be food, sweets or beer. Sounds simple? It should be, but the flights on the darts have been tampered with so you have virtually no control over their direction!

---

lodgings cost around US$10 per day. The office has descriptions of upcoming treks on the wall, with forms attached where you sign up for the trip of your choice. Drug use is banned on these treks. Guides include former farmers, teachers, policemen and agricultural workers. A breakdown of how your money is spent is posted on the wall.

In a beautiful Lao-French wooden building further north on the main street, the **Muang Sing Exhibitions Museum** (admission 5000 kip; 8.30am-4.30pm Mon-Fri, 8.30-11.30am Sat) displays traditional textiles, woven baskets, handicrafts, amulets and cymbals all with dusty signs in simple English. A photographic exhibition 'The Last Guardians of the Mountains' is dedicated to the hill tribes of the area represented in honest up-close black-and-white portraits.

Next to Sing Charean Hotel, a small family-run **traditional massage & sauna** (sauna/massage 10,000/30,000 kip) has been set up in a bamboo thatched building, with the herbal sauna located out the back.

SLEEPING & EATING

Guesthouses in Muang Sing are pretty average. There are a number of large and not overly hospitable options on the main road just north of the old market, with rooms of a similar standard and price. If you're only crashing for one night and have an early trekking departure these are fine, check out a few and find the best bed for the night. If you're staying in Muang Sing for a few days, it's worth heading beyond the main street for better options – and atmosphere!

Saengdeuane Guest House (☎ 212376; r 30,000-50,000 kip) At the far north end of town, this guesthouse offers great views of the mountains from the main building's rooftop. In the garden out the back are two thatched bungalows with cold-water bathrooms. Beyond these, a newer building houses several spotlessly clean rooms with attached hot-water bathrooms. The owner occasionally puts on a Lao-style barbecue for 30,000 kip per person.

Adima (☎ 212372; r 40,000-60,000 kip) Down a dirt track off the road to the Chinese border, Adima is 8km north of Muang Sing in a quiet rural setting near Yao and Akha villages. Rooms range from basic thatch bungalows with shared bathroom, to brand new brick houses with tiled floors. The restaurant serves reasonably good Lao and European food. There are good walks in the area that you can follow with a map available at the guesthouse.

Stupa Mountain Lodge & Restaurant (☎ 020-568 6555; stupamtn@laotel.com; r 80,000 kip) Stupa, set on a hillside 5km south of Muang Sing, consists of five very comfortable wooden bungalows with attached hot-water showers, big verandas and a large restaurant on stilts. To get there, ask to be dropped at Ban Tinthat on the săwngthăew trip from Luang Nam Tha. On top of the hill 500m behind the guesthouse is the impressive golden Chieng Theung stupa.

Many guesthouses have restaurants that are generally reasonable but unremarkable.

Daen Neua Guest House & Restaurant (☎ 212369; meals 6000-15,000 kip) This guesthouse serves good Lao food inside its large street-front restaurant.

Viengsay Guest House & Restaurant (☎ 212372; meals 8000-15,000 kip) Close to the old market and also offers a decent menu, which includes Western-style breakfasts.

Morning market (6-8am) Fresh fruit and vegetables as well as local delicacies can be bought here. To get there turn left (west) at the exhibitions building and right (north) two blocks up. Fŏe (rice noodle) stands are bustling early in the morning, or Laos' ubiquitous roaming baguette vendors sell fresh rolls with condensed milk for breakfast.

GETTING THERE & AROUND

Săwngthăew for Luang Nam Tha leave from the bus station by the morning market,

---

SCAMS

Like any well-travelled route, the Huay Xai to Luang Prabang river journey now has a collection of entrepreneurs trying to make money for nothing. Of course, there's no need to lose your cool, but yes you're getting taken for a ride, literally and figuratively. Some travellers are told, by official-looking men toting official-looking invoice books that they have to pay for 'insurance' before their boat will depart. This is a scam. We've heard from people who haven't paid who experienced no problems – and don't you have travel insurance already anyway?

Before arriving in Pak Beng, hotel touts may board your boat preselling rooms in guesthouses because 'everything else in town is full'. On rare occasions, guesthouses have been known to fill up in Pak Beng, but there's no need to prepurchase a bed without seeing it first. These are, no doubt, overpriced: better to check out what is available in town before handing over your cash.

---

stopping at the bus stop at the old market, six times a day from 8am to 3pm (15,000 kip, one to two hours). Heading southwest, sǎwngthǎew bound for Xieng Kok on the Burmese border (19,000 kip, three to four hours) depart at 9.30am, 11am, 1pm and 2pm. From Xieng Kok it's possible to charter a boat down the Mekong to Huay Xai.

Bicycles are available to rent (5000 kip per day) from several shops on the main road, for journeys to local villages.

BOKEO PROVINCE

Laos' smallest province, wedged between the Mekong River border with Thailand and Luang Nam Tha Province, is a popular entry point for travellers from Thailand. Despite its small size and tiny population, it is home to 34 different ethnic groups, second only to Luang Nam Tha for ethnic diversity.

Huay Xai

☎ 084 / pop 15,500

Huay Xai is a busy riverside town, centred on vehicle- and passenger-ferry landings from Chiang Khong in Thailand, and trade in Chinese goods. The town has undergone a minor construction boom in recent years

and many guesthouses have sprung up to cater for tourists waiting to catch the boat to Luang Prabang or cross to Thailand. A bridge across the Mekong, originally mooted back in 1997, should be constructed in time for the completion of the Hwy 3 upgrade, expected to be finished by 2008.

INFORMATION

The **Lao Development Bank** (8.30am-3.30pm Mon-Fri), opposite Arimid Guest House, is 200m up the hill from the slow-boat landing. The **post office** (8am-4pm Mon-Fri) also contains a telephone office.

SLEEPING & EATING

Arimid Guest House (☎ 211040; Ban Huay Xai Neua; r 50,000-120,000 kip) This is a friendly well-run place, offering a series of pleasant thatched bungalows with hot-water showers. The husband-and-wife owners are helpful and speak English and French.

BAP Guest House (☎ 211083; Th Saykhong; r 25,000-50,000 kip) This guesthouse, which also has friendly and helpful staff, is just up the main road from the Chieng Khong boat landing. It's the best place to pick up information about boats to Luang Nam Tha or tickets to Luang Prabang, including a túk-túk ride to the landing. All rooms come with fan and hot-water shower.

Sabaydee Guest House (☎ 211751; Th Saykhong; r 50,000 kip) Located around 100m north of BAP Guest House, Sabaydee has 14 clean rooms, all with attached hot-water showers.

Savanh Bokeo Guest House (Th Saykhong; r 30,000-40,000 kip) There are rooms with shared facilities and up to four beds in an old wooden house.

Along Th Saykhong, there is a dozen open-air rice and noodle stands. Overlooking the Mekong passenger ferry landing, **Khem Khong Restaurant** (☎ 211064; meals 8000-30,000 kip) does delicious Lao dishes.

GETTING THERE & AWAY

Lao Airlines (☎ 211026; www.laos-airlines.com; Huay Xai airport) flies to Huay Xai from Vientiane (US$81, Monday and Saturday) and to Luang Prabang (US$43) and Luang Nam Tha (US$43) with enough passengers.

An early-morning bus (70,000 kip, eight to 10 hours) and regular sǎwngthǎew to Luang Nam Tha via Vieng Phukha leave the bus station, about 2km south of the boat

LAOS

landing. Until the new Hwy 3 is finished, this is a jangling, dusty ride, which is slower and tougher in the wet season.

Some travellers take a two-day boat trip (US$110 per boat split between passengers, plus 30,000 kip for food and accommodation) from here to Luang Nam Tha, stopping off at Ban Khon Khum or Ban Na Lae for the night. In the dry season this small river can be very shallow; you may be asked to hop out and walk through the shallows carrying the canoe for a while! Check the situation locally or visit Lonely Planet's online Thorn Tree forum (www.lonelyplanet .com) before signing up. Also note the boats are uncovered so bring sun protection. Ask at BAP Guest House for more information.

An assortment of long-distance slow boats go to Luang Prabang (US$15 per person) from the boat landing at the north end of town. The two-day trip stops for one night in Pak Beng (which is also accessible by road from Udomxai). To secure a ticket, go to the boat landing in the afternoon before you travel, or you can purchase a ticket through your guesthouse. It is wise to see the boat in person before you purchase: some boats are enclosed, with no view out and 80 or more people plus their cargo packed inside, making it a cramped, uncomfortable (and for some an unforgivable) experience.

For any journey take plenty of water and food supplies. Keep a sleeping bag or towel separate from your pack as the wooden benches lose their novelty value very, very quickly.

Speedboats to Luang Prabang (US$26, six hours) leave from the landing 2km south of town. Life jackets and crash helmets should

be provided (and are sometimes needed). This is not the safest transport south, and in the dry season no-one but crazy *falang* will get in a speedboat. Fatalities are not uncommon.

SOUTHERN LAOS

Tourism is much less developed in southern Laos than in the north, with only a few areas visited by travellers heading to and from Vietnam and Cambodia. Most visit the Unesco-listed Khmer ruins at Wat Phu Champasak and dreamy Si Phan Don (Four Thousand Islands). However, the lush fertile highlands of the Bolaven Plateau, with its coffee plantations and dramatic waterfalls, and the faded charms of Savannakhet are also must-sees on a tour of the south.

SAVANNAKHET PROVINCE
Savannakhet
☎ 041 / pop 124,000
Super-friendly Savannakhet is a fascinating city on the cusp of considerable change. Tree-lined streets and French architecture suggest how important this town was a couple of centuries ago, but decaying façades tell a different post-independence story. The crumbling colonial buildings, some sheltering food vendors, others overgrown with weeds or strung up with clotheslines, have a ghostly charm that has been lost in the gentrification of Luang Prabang. Several kilometres north of the centre, Laos' second international bridge, due to be completed in 2006, may mean that Savannakhet's status as an important trade hub is revived.

INFORMATION
Internet Access
Phitsamay Internet (☎ 215478; Th Si Muang; per 20 min/hr 2000/6000 kip; ☽ 8am-9.30pm; ✉) In a room beyond the photocopiers, with the best rates.
Silconet Internet (☎ 213560; Th Ratsavongseuk; per min 200 kip; ☽ 9am-10pm) Large shop with excellent facilities, including cold drinks, tea and instant coffee.
SPS Furniture Shop Internet (☎ 212888; Th Khanthabuli; per min 200 kip; ☽ 10am-10pm) Opposite the plaza with plenty of terminals.

Money
The following two banks, located in close proximity to each other, have exchange

---

BORDER CROSSING: INTO THAILAND

The ferry ride to Chiang Khong costs 10,000 kip and the Thai border is open 8.30am to 5pm. Visas are issued on arrival on either side. At weekends or during their lunch hour, Lao immigration officers charge an additional 10,000 kip 'overtime'.

Boats from Pak Beng almost always arrive just a little too late to make the border crossing to Thailand as do buses from Luang Nam Tha. So make sure you're not on the last day of your Laos visa, or you'll be charged for overstaying.

counters. You can also exchange money next to the immigration office that is at the ferry pier.

Banque pour le Commerce Extérieur Lao (☎ 212226; Th Ratsavongseuk; ☻ 8.30am-4pm)

Lao Development Bank (☎ 212272; Th Udomsin; ☻ 8.30-11.30am & 1.30-3.30pm)

Post

Post office (☎ 212205; Th Khantabuli; ☻ 8am-noon & 1-5pm) A couple of blocks south of the plaza.

Telephone

Telephone office (☎ 212047; Th Khantabuli; ☻ 8am-10pm) Behind the post office. Overseas calls available using a phonecard.

Tourist Information

Savannakhet Provincial Tourism Office (☎ 214203; savannakhetguides2@yahoo.com; Th Ratsaphanith; ☻ 8am-noon & 1.30-4pm) Has hand-drawn maps of town, brochures and photos with descriptions of nearby sites. Also runs one- to five-day guided treks to NPAs in the region leaving on different days of the week with a minimum number of participants. Guides speak some English.

SIGHTS & ACTIVITIES

At the time of research the **Savannakhet Provincial Museum** (Th Khantabuli; admission 5000 kip; ☻ 8-11.30am & 1-4pm Mon-Sat) was not open for visitors, although you can still see an American combat aircraft in the grounds that doubles as a jungle-gym for local kids. When open, displays dedicated to political

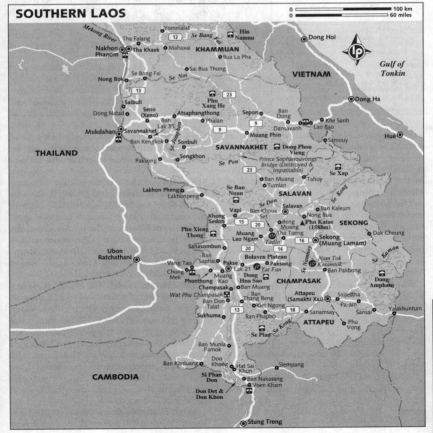

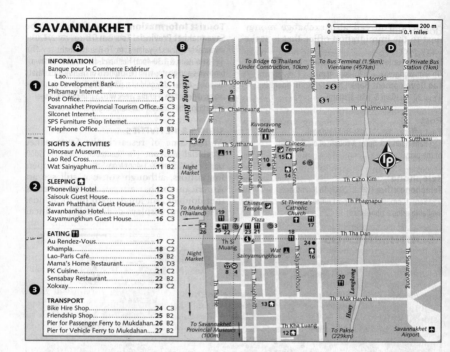

SAVANNAKHET

0 — 200 m
0 — 0.1 miles

INFORMATION
Banque pour le Commerce Extérieur
Lao...1 C1
Lao Development Bank.....................2 C1
Phitsamay Internet...........................3 C2
Post Office.......................................4 C3
Savannakhet Provincial Tourism Office..5 C3
Silconet Internet..............................6 C2
SPS Furniture Shop Internet..............7 C2
Telephone Office.............................8 B3

SIGHTS & ACTIVITIES
Dinosaur Museum.............................9 B1
Lao Red Cross.................................10 C2
Wat Sainyaphum.............................11 B2

SLEEPING
Phonevilay Hotel..............................12 C3
Saisouk Guest House........................13 C3
Savan Phatthana Guest House..........14 C2
Savanbanhao Hotel.........................15 C2
Xayamungkhun Guest House............16 C3

EATING
Au Rendez-Vous..............................17 C2
Khampla...18 C2
Lao-Paris Café.................................19 B2
Mama's Home Restaurant................20 D3
PK Cuisine.......................................21 C2
Sensabay Restaurant........................22 B2
Xokxay..23 C2

TRANSPORT
Bike Hire Shop.................................24 C3
Friendship Shop...............................25 B2
Pier for Passenger Ferry to Mukdahan.26 B2
Pier for Vehicle Ferry to Mukdahan..27 B2

Mekong River

To Bridge to Thailand
(Under Construction, 10km)

To Bus Terminal (1.5km);
Vientiane (457km)

To Private Bus
Station (1km)

Th Ratsavongseuk
Th Udomsin
Th Udomsin
Th Chaimeuang
Th Chaimeuang
Kuvoravong
Statue
Th Sisavangyong
Th Tha He
Th Sutthanu
Chinese
Temple
Th Sutthanu
Th Kouvoravong
Th Ratsaphanith
Th Phetsalat
Th Saenna
Th Caho Kim
Th Khanthabuli
Th Phagnapui
Night
Market
To Mukdahan
(Thailand)
Chinese
Temple
St Theresa's
Catholic
Church
Th Tha Dan
Plaza
Th Si
Muang
Th Si
Muang
Wat
Sainyamukhun
Th Saiyamonkhoun
Th Tha Dan
Th Sisavangyong
Night
Market
Th Tha He
Th Tatsaphanith
Huay Longkong
Th Mak Hayeha
To Savannakhet
Provincial Museum
(100m)
Th Kha Luang
To Pakse
(229km)
Savannakhet
Airport

leader Kaysone Phomvihane, who was born
only 1km away, filled much of this small
museum. To gain access to the collection
try the curator's house – a wooden building
in the southwest corner of the School of
Medicine compound.

The nostalgia-evoking exhibits at the **Dinosaur Museum** (☎ 212597; Th Khantabuli; admission
1000 kip; ☒ 8am-noon & 1-4pm Mon-Fri) inspire a
certain childlike wonderment at prehistoric
times. Savannakhet Province is home to five
dinosaur sites. This is a well-presented little
museum with an enthusiastic curator.

The oldest and largest monastery in
southern Laos, **Wat Sainyaphum** (Th Tha He) was
originally built in 1542, although most of
what stands today is from the last century.
The grounds are large and include a couple
of centuries-old trees; the one by the northern gate is colourfully decorated with a small
shrine at its base.

Lao Red Cross (☎ 214670; Th Phetsalat; ☒ 10am-
9pm) offers traditional herbal sauna (15,000
kip) plus vigorous Lao-style massages
(25,000 kip). Money raised, coupled with
donations from the government, Médecins

Sans Frontières and Unicef, helps fund
AIDS-prevention workshops and care for
those in the province infected with HIV.

SLEEPING

Saisouk Guest House (☎ 212207; Th Phetsalat;
r 25,000-50,000 kip; ☒) A few blocks south of
the centre, this large wooden house is spotlessly clean. Photos of the family adorn the
upstairs dining room. One room comes
with air-con and private bathroom. Showers are cold-water only. Gates are locked at
11pm. Highly recommended.

Savanbanhao Hotel (☎ 212202; Th Saenna;
r 45,000-90,000 kip; ☒) Plenty of rooms, all with
private bathroom and electric hot water.
Also hires scooters for US$8 per day, more
if you want to leave the city. Pushbikes are
available on weekends (when the local kids
aren't using them to get to school). So, why
does this large concrete compound have
four identical buildings in four corners with
what look like servants quarters behind
each? You'll have to ask Mr Pohn!

Savan Phatthana Guest House (☎ 213955; Th
Saenna; r 30,000-50,000 kip) An OK option if next

LAOS

door is full, or you're on a tighter budget. The rooms, off a wide corridor, are a little musty. All have attached cold-water bathrooms without sinks.

Xayamungkhun Guest House (☎ 212426; Th Ratsavongseuk; r 35,000-80,000 kip; ❄) In one of the last colonial-era buildings still being used as a guesthouse, Xayamungkhun has spacious, clean rooms and an inviting atmosphere. The downstairs sitting area has a shelf full of secondhand books to peruse.

Phonevilay Hotel (☎ 212284; Th Phetsalat; 35,000-70,000 kip; ❄) In a garden setting not far from Saisouk Guest House, the cheaper rooms come with attached cold-water bathrooms.

EATING

Mama's Home Restaurant (☎ 231592; off Th Mak Haveha; meals 5000-15,000 kip; ❄ breakfast, lunch & dinner) A few blocks from the centre but well worth the trek. Follow the signs from the canal and bring a torch if it's after dark. Literally in Mama's home replete with photos of her kids on the walls. Mama likes to make her meals a little special – a salad sandwich comes stuffed with hot crinkle cut chips (fries). You can catch up on some cable TV news, or watch a film – you just have to ask.

Khampla (☎ 212882; Th Saiyamonkhoun; meals 30,000-50,000 kip; ❄ dinner) A large lantern-lit beer-gardenesque restaurant with live music on weekends. An eclectic menu includes spicy soups and fondues as well as Lao-style steamboat, the ultimate shared dining experience.

Lao-Paris Café (☎ 212792; Th Si Muang; meals 8000-25,000 kip; ❄ breakfast, lunch & dinner) Across the road from the ferry terminal, but unable to make the most of its location, this is nonetheless a popular *falang* eating option. Dining is at wooden tables inside and out. The menu covers both Lao and French food. The service is sometimes quick, sometimes indifferent.

Sensabay Restaurant (Th Si Muang; meals 5000-20,000 kip; ❄ breakfast, lunch & dinner) Your best bet for breakfast, with a whole range of travellers' favourites from pancakes, baguettes, and muesli with fruit salad and yoghurt, to generic Asian staples. A sign out front proclaims 'the food here is clean' (we didn't see the kitchen, but the food tasted clean to us).

Au Rendez-Vous (☎ 213181; Th Ratsavongseuk; meals 3000-35,000 kip; ❄ breakfast, lunch & dinner) A small restaurant on the busiest road in town, serving a range of Chinese, Vietnam-

ese and international dishes. Service can be sluggish, but who's in a hurry anyway?

For a Lao-style dinner on a budget try the riverside vendors both north and south of the ferry pier, plus the following restaurants on the plaza.

PK Cuisine (☎ 212022; Th Si Muang; meals 10,000-25,000 kip; ❄ lunch & dinner) Decent Thai cuisine.

Xokxay (☎ 213122; Th Si Muang; meals 8000-25,000 kip; ❄ lunch & dinner; ❄) Serves Chinese and Vietnamese dishes.

GETTING THERE & AWAY

Lao Airlines (☎ 212140; www.laos-airlines.com; Savannakhet airport) flies twice weekly to Savannakhet from Vientiane (US$57).

Buses to Vientiane (45,000 kip, eight to 10 hours) leave from the bus terminal at the north end of town every hour until 6pm. A VIP express bus leaves the private bus station (60,000 kip, six to seven hours) at 11am. For Tha Khaek, frequent săwngthăew (20,000 kip, two to three hours) depart all morning, enabling you to stop for a few hours to break up the journey to Vientiane. All public buses heading north go via the bus station on the outskirts of Tha Khaek.

Heading south, regular buses (35,000 kip, five hours) depart all morning for Pakse. A tourist bus to Dong Ha in Vietnam leaves from the Savanbanhao Hotel (US$12, nine hours) at 7.30am.

GETTING AROUND

A túk-túk to the bus station or just about any location around Savannakhet costs 5000 kip per person. Bicycles can be rented from the **Friendship Shop** (☎ 213026; Th Si Muang; per day 10,000 kip; ❄ 8am-7pm) or a **bike hire shop** (☎ 213149, 020-565 8379; Th Ratsavongseuk; per day 10,000 kip; ❄ 8am-6pm) two doors north of Xayamungkhun Guest House.

BORDER CROSSING: INTO THAILAND

Ferries to Mukdahan in Thailand (12,000 kip) depart (almost one an hour) on weekdays from 9.10am to 4.30pm. There are four ferries on Saturday and two on Sunday. From Mukdahan regular buses depart for Bangkok (seven hours). Just ask any túk-túk driver for the 'Bangkok bus'. Once the bridge is complete, you'll probably be able to catch a bus all the way to Bangkok from here.

Pakse

☎ 031 / pop 66,000

On Rte 13, Laos' north–south highway, close to the border of Thailand and the second bridge spanning the Mekong, Pakse is the transport hub of the south. By day, activity centres on the old quarter, the four bus stations and the markets. At night, the pace slows significantly and Pakse can be a little tame (read: dull). Besides dining at one of the reasonably good restaurants in town, there is very little to do but get a good night's sleep. The town does retain a few pockets of French-era character, but an absence of urban planning has seen most of Pakse's charm lost and potential views of the mighty Mekong or gentler Se Don are not capitalised on.

ORIENTATION

Central Pakse is bound by the Mekong to the south; the north and west by the Se Don. Rte 13 cuts through the northern edge of town. On and below Rte 13 towards the Mekong are most of Pakse's guesthouses, shops and restaurants. Heading west across

Se Don takes you to the northern bus terminal. The southern bus station and market are 8km in the opposite direction.

INFORMATION

Emergency

Hospital (☎ 212018; cnr Th 10 & Th 46)
Police (☎ 212145; Th 10)

Internet Access

@d@m's Internet (☎ 213435; www.pakse.info; Rte 13; per min 300 kip; ☻ 10am-10pm) Fast connections, but the extra expense per minute – even if time is calculated more accurately than elsewhere – was sending customers to other outlets.

Lankham Internet (☎ 212125; Rte 13; per min 200 kip; ☻ 8am-11pm) A little lapse about time-keeping, but reasonable computers.

Vandersa Internet Service (☎ 212982; Rte 13; per min 200 kip; ☻ 8am-11pm) Internet plus fruit shakes, the perfect combination!

Money

If you're stuck in Pakse on the weekend with no funds, your only option for exchanging cash and travellers cheques or getting a cash

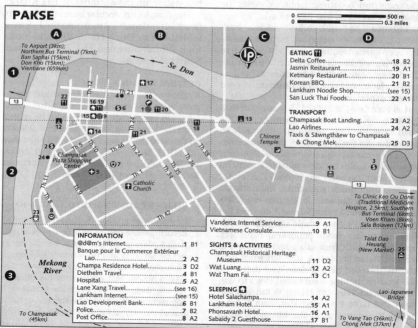

PAKSE

0 — 500 m
0 — 0.3 miles

To Airport (3km);
Northern Bus Terminal (7km);
Ban Saphai (15km);
Don Kho (15km);
Vientiane (659km)

Se Don

To Champasak
(45km)

Mekong
River

To Vang Tao (36km);
Chong Mek (37km)

To Clinic Keo Ou Done
(Traditional Medicine
Hospice, 2.5km); Southern
Bus Terminal (6km);
Voen Kham (8km);
Sala Bolaven (12km)

Talat Dao
Heuang
(New Market)

Lao-Japanese
Bridge

Chinese
Temple

Champasak
Plaza Shopping
Centre

Catholic
Church

EATING
Delta Coffee.............................18 B2
Jasmin Restaurant......................19 A1
Ketmany Restaurant...................20 B1
Korean BBQ..............................21 B2
Lankham Noodle Shop............(see 15)
San Luck Thai Foods...................22 A1

TRANSPORT
Champasak Boat Landing............23 A2
Lao Airlines..............................24 A2
Taxis & Săwngthăew to Champasak
& Chong Mek...........................25 D3

INFORMATION
@d@m's Internet.........................1 B1
Banque pour le Commerce Extérieur
Lao..2 A2
Champa Residence Hotel..............3 D2
Diethelm Travel...........................4 B1
Hospital.....................................5 A2
Lane Xang Travel....................(see 16)
Lankham Internet...................(see 15)
Lao Development Bank.................6 B1
Police..7 B2
Post Office..................................8 A2
Vandersa Internet Service.............9 A1
Vietnamese Consulate.................10 B1

SIGHTS & ACTIVITIES
Champasak Historical Heritage
Museum..................................11 D2
Wat Luang................................12 A2
Wat Tham Fai............................13 C1

SLEEPING
Hotel Salachampa.......................14 A2
Lankham Hotel...........................15 A1
Phonsavanh Hotel.......................16 A1
Sabaidy 2 Guesthouse.................17 B1

advance, all for a hefty commission, is at **Champa Residence Hotel** (☎ 212120; Rte 13), 2km east of the centre.

Otherwise:

Banque pour le Commerce Extérieur Lao (☎ 212770; Th 11; ☑ 8.30am-3.30pm Mon-Fri) Good rates and does cash advances.

Lao Development Bank (☎ 212168; Rte 13; ☑ 8.30am-3.30pm) Exchanges travellers cheques and cash.

Post

Post office (☎ 212293; cnr Th 1 & Th 8; ☑ 8am-noon & 1-5pm)

Travel Agencies

Diethelm Travel (☎ 212596; dtlpkz@laotel.com; Th 21) Around the corner from Sabaidy 2 Guesthouse. Organises tours to the Bolaven Plateau and Wat Phu Champasak.

Lane Xang Travel (☎ 212281, 020-225 5176; www.lane xang-travel.com; Th 14) Sign up on the whiteboard for trips to the Bolaven Plateau, Si Phan Don or Wat Phu Champasak. Organises visas, and books buses to Stung Treng or Vientiane.

SIGHTS & ACTIVITIES

There are 20 wat in town, the largest are **Wat Luang**, featuring ornate concrete pillars and carved wooden doors and murals, and **Wat Tham Fai**, which has a small Buddha footprint shrine in its grounds.

The **Champasak Historical Heritage Museum** (Rte 13; admission 3000 kip; ☑ 8-11.30am & 1-4pm) documents the history of the province, with historical photos and ethnological displays. Some exhibits have captions in English, for others you'll have to let the pictures tell the story.

For a vigorous Lao massage (albeit slightly distracted by pressing mobile-phone calls) **Clinic Keo Ou Done** (Traditional Medicine Hospice; ☎ 251895; ☑ 4-9pm Mon-Fri & 10am-9pm Sat) can be found down a road off to the right, 100m before the Km 3 marker east along Rte 13.

For something different, **Sala Bolaven** (☎ 020-580 0787; Km 12 Rte 16; ☑ 9am-4pm) offers free tastings and sells produce exported to Europe through the Fair Trade network. Try jams, iced tea, Lao Bia (palm beer), local wine and coffee. To get here take Rte 13 to the southern bus station and follow the road to the left towards Paksong. It's a 12km slightly uphill (downhill on the way home!) bike ride, or a 10,000 kip túk-túk ride. The newish shop has outdoor seating and at the time of research there was talk of opening a small kitchen down the track.

SLEEPING

Sabaidy 2 Guesthouse (☎ 212992; Th 24; r 15,000-42,000 kip) Set in a quiet street in an old French colonial neighbourhood off Rte 13 is probably Pakse's best guesthouse. The dark wooden rooms are basic but clean, and shared bathrooms come with hot- or cold-water facilities. The owners and staff are helpful and knowledgeable. The garden courtyard is a good spot to relax or hook up with others heading north or south. Also runs tours to the Bolaven Plateau, serves home-cooked dishes and hires bikes and scooters.

Lankham Hotel (☎ 213314; latchan@laotel.com; Rte 13; r 50,000-100,000 kip; 🕸) A deservedly popular four-storey monolith, the Lankham is big and impersonal, but the rooms are clean and all have their own bathroom. Its location on the main road means rooms in the front get traffic noise; windows onto the corridor mean you hear early-risers leaving. Downstairs is one of Pakse's best noodle shops. Also rents bikes.

Phonsavanh Hotel (☎ 212482; cnr Rte 13 & Th 12; r 20,000-30,000 kip) Once one of the only guesthouses in Pakse, the Phonsavanh now looks like a dusty prison compared to its young competitors. But basic fan rooms with or without cold-water bathrooms still attract a lot of budget travellers.

Hotel Salachampa (☎ 212273; Th 10; r from US$10; 🕸) A little bit more upmarket, the Lao-themed units next to the more expensive colonial building are decent and good-value if you're sharing. Clean white sheets, attached hot-water bathrooms, and a soft bed can make a night in Pakse just that bit less disappointing.

EATING

San Luck Thai Foods (☎ 020-561 6409; Th 11; meals 10,000-30,000 kip; ☑ lunch & dinner) The menu is so big (there are eight varieties of pad thai) it could drive you to tears of indecision, but whatever you choose it'll be freshly cooked and completely delicious. Dining is either in the large front restaurant, or on the decking out the back overlooking the Se Don. BYO mosquito repellent.

Jasmin Restaurant (☎ 251002; Rte 13; meals 8000-35,000 kip; ☑ breakfast, lunch & dinner) A welcoming little shophouse eatery and a popular travellers hang-out. The close outdoor seating and a congenial atmosphere encourages shared dining. The food is OK, with plenty of vegetarian options. If you like your curries spicy make that clear when you order. Also sells bus tickets to Stung Treng and Vientiane.

Other good options in the centre:

Delta Coffee (☎ 212488; Rte 13; meals 15,000-30,000 kip; ☺ breakfast, lunch & dinner) Serves Italian and Thai food, French or Lao-made wines, plus a variety of locally produced coffee made to order.

Ketmany Restaurant (☎ 212615; Rte 13; meals 10,000-30,000 kip; ☺ lunch & dinner; ☒) Lit up like Christmas, Ketmany serves decent Chinese and international dishes.

Korean BBQ (☎ 212388; Th 24; meals 10,000-23,000 kip; ☺ dinner) Popular with Pakse residents for its steamboat, a delicious do-it-yourself cookfest. Get there early and preferably with a posse.

Lankham Noodle Shop (☎ 213314; Rte 13; soup 8000 kip; ☺ breakfast, lunch & dinner) Packed in the early mornings with Lao slurping *fŏe* on their way to work.

GETTING THERE & AWAY
Air
Lao Airlines (☎ 212252; www.laos-airlines.com; Th 11; ☺ 8am-4pm Mon-Fri) flies to Pakse daily to and from Vientiane (US$87 one way). Flights

from Pakse to Siem Reap on Wednesday, Friday and Sunday (US$68) are a good option if you've come this far without a Cambodian visa.

Boat
Regular local boat services run from Pakse to Don Khong via Champasak (US$3 going south, US$5 coming north, six to 10 hours), leaving at 8am from near the junction of the Se Don and the Mekong. You'll be dropped in Ban Hua Khong, a small village near the north tip of Don Khong. From there a túk-túk (1000 kip per person, 12km) or motorcycle taxi (1500 kip) will take you around to Muang Khong where plenty of guesthouses are located. Boats heading back to Pakse usually leave Ban Hua Khong between 6.30am and 8am and take about 11 hours.

Bus & Săwngthăew
Express VIP buses to Vientiane (US$14.50, nine hours) leave daily around 8pm, some boasting air-con and an on-board toilet; tickets can be bought from offices at Champasak Plaza Shopping Centre for **Thongli Company** (☎ 212831, 020-552 7484), **KVT** (☎ 212228), or cheaper (US$9) and slower **Laody Transport Company** (☎ 020-564526). The latter stops at Savannakhet (US$3.50, four hours), Tha Khaek (US$5.50, six hours), and Paksan (US$6.50, eight hours).

VIP buses depart from the northern terminal, 7km north of town on Rte 13 for Vientiane (US$9, nine hours) at 5.30am and 8pm. If you have plenty of time, public buses rattle off to Vientiane (US$7, 16 to 18 hours) about every hour between 7.30am and 4.30pm, stopping wherever you want (and many places you don't) along the way.

For transport south and east, go to the southern terminal, 8km south of town on Rte 13 and a 5000 kip túk-túk ride away. To Champasak buses (US$1.30, two hours, two daily) depart at 10am and noon. Other departures include: Don Khong (US$3, three hours) at 8am and 10am; Tat Lo (US$1.20, two hours) at 9am; and Ban Nakasang for Don Det and Don Khon (US$2, three to four hours) at 7am, 8.30am, 10am and 11.30am. Săwngthăew and pick-up trucks also leave the southern bus station regularly between about 7am and 3pm for Champasak (US$1, two hours), Don Khong (US$3,

---

BORDER CROSSING: INTO THAILAND

The crossing at Vang Tao (Laos) and Chong Mek (Thailand) is the busiest in southern Laos and is open from 5am to 8pm daily. From Pakse, săwngthăew (8000 kip, 75 minutes) and battered taxis run between Talat Dao Heuang (New Market) and Vang Tao regularly from about 4am until 6pm. When your transport stops, walk about 300m up the hill to the building with the green roof, where you'll be stamped in and can buy or sell kip at the exchange office.

Walk through the throngs of traders and small-time smugglers loitering around the border, then about 40m to Thai immigration, who will issue your visa. Continue about 500m to the end of the stall-lined street to the bus station and find a săwngthăew to Phibun (B30, one hour). It will drop you at a point where another săwngthăew will soon pick you up for the trip to Ubon Ratchathani (B30, one hour). Buses leave Ubon regularly (including overnight) for Bangkok, and there are several trains as well, including an overnight sleeper.

three hours), Ban Nakasang (US$2, three to four hours) and Voen Kham (US$2.50, three to four hours).

Regular sǎwngthǎew and pick-ups leave Talat Dao Heuang (New Market) for the Thai border (see the boxed text, opposite).

GETTING AROUND

Pakse's main attractions are accessible by foot. Bicycles (10,000 kip per day) and scooters (US$8 to US$10 per day) can be hired from **Sabaidy 2 Guesthouse** (☎ 212992; Th 24) and **Lankham Hotel** (☎ 213314; latchan@ laotel.com; Rte 13).

Bolaven Plateau

The fertile Bolaven Plateau (Phu Phieng Bolaven in Lao) rises 1500m above the Mekong valley – a beautiful claw-shaped highland fortress of forests, rivers, waterfalls and plantations. The plateau is a centre for several Mon-Khmer ethnic groups, including the Alak, Laven, Ta-oy, Suay and Katu. The Alak and Katu arrange their palm-and-thatch houses in a circle. They are well known in Laos for a water buffalo sacrifice, which they perform yearly, usually on a full moon in March (also see p402). The area wasn't farmed intensively until the French planted coffee, rubber and bananas here. Today the Laven, Alak and Katu tribes have revived cultivation and it's here that the distinctive Lao coffee is grown.

TADLO

Cool and peaceful, the broad 10m-high Tadlo falls and Seset River are surrounded by forests and villages inhabited by the Katu and Alak. This is a popular spot for day treks, elephant riding and of course swimming. Although the recent guesthouse boom gives the area a resortlike feel, the nearby local village is still distinctly Lao.

Activities

Most travellers spend their time **swimming** around Tadlo and Tadhang, reading, walking in the surrounding forest, and generally relaxing with the sounds of constantly tumbling waterfalls. Tadhang, a few hundred metres along, has a deep swimming hole and is also a popular local fishing spot.

Other activities include **trekking** in the forest either on your own (stick to the track) or with a guide from Tim's Guest

House & Restaurant to surrounding villages and waterfalls. Guided treks start at 30,000 kip per person. For more information and maps ask at Tim's. Both Tadlo Lodge and Tim's Guest House & Restaurant organise **elephant rides** through the forest and streams, costing 50,000 kip for 1½ hours. Tim's also hires out bikes for 8000 kip per hour to cycle to local villages.

Sleeping & Eating

Tim's Guest House & Restaurant (☎ 214176; www .tadlo.laopdr.com; r 25,000 kip) This is by far the best set-up in Tadlo, with comfortable bungalows, ceiling fans, shared hot-water bathrooms and Internet facilities. The restaurant serves breakfast, lunch and dinner (meals 6000 to 15,000 kip). Tim's also offers water-bottle refills (1000 kip), transport to the main road (3000 kip) and a book exchange. The English-and French-speaking owner has travel information in a neighbouring hut.

Sephaseuth Guest House & Restaurant (☎ 214185; r 40,000-60,000 kip) There are five clean – although a little gloomy – rooms here, in a wooden building by the river. The attached restaurant, serving breakfast, lunch and dinner (15,000 to 30,000 kip for a meal), is a popular spot in the afternoon.

Saylomyen Guest House (020-227 5542; r 30,000 kip) The cheapest river views from simple huts with fans and shared bathrooms.

Getting There & Away

From Pakse, buses heading for Salavan drop you at the Tadlo turn-off (just ask for Tadlo). They leave at 7am, 9am, 10am, 11am and 1pm (12,000 kip, 1½ hours). From the turn-off just after the bridge, it's a 2km walk (or a 3000 kip túk-túk ride) to Tadlo. Leaving Tadlo, get to the bridge early to catch a Pakse bus.

Champasak

☎ 031

Once the capital of a Lao kingdom, Champasak is now a lazy one-street town. The main road runs parallel to the river then turns inland and makes its way to the dramatic mountainside location of Wat Phu Champasak. Most visitors use the town as a base for visiting the ruins, although some choose to see the ruins on a day trip from Pakse. Champasak boasts great views of the Mekong's riverside beaches and a serene atmosphere. Activity centres on the ferry wharf and, at the other end of town, at Wat Phu Champasak. Guesthouses are mainly found near the fountain.

This town cranks it up every year when pilgrims from near and far amass for **Bun Wat Phu Champasak**. During this three-day Buddhist festival (usually February) worshippers wind their way up and around Wat Phu Champasak, praying and leaving offerings; bands play traditional and modern music; young and old dance together; and Thai boxing, comedy shows and cockfights all add to the entertainment. Stands selling food and drink do a roaring trade along the road from town to Wat Phu and accommodation in town is booked out weeks in advance.

SIGHTS
Overlooking the Mekong valley, **Wat Phu Champasak** (admission 30,000 kip; ⏰ 8am-4.30pm) is one of the most impressive archaeological sites in Laos. It's divided into lower and upper parts and is joined by a steep stone stairway. The whole site is earmarked for restoration, but progress appears to be very slow.

The lower part consists of two ruined palace buildings at the edge of a large square pond, itself split in two by a causeway, used for ritual ablutions. The upper section is the temple sanctuary itself, which once enclosed a large Shiva phallus. Some time later the sanctuary was converted into a Buddhist temple, but original Hindu sculpture remains in the lintels. Just north of the Shivalingam sanctuary you'll find the elephant stone and the enigmatic crocodile stone. The *naga* stairway leading to the sanctuary is lined with *dok jampa* (jacaranda) trees. The upper platform affords spectacular views of the Mekong valley below.

As well as Bun Wat Phu Chamapasak, in February each year, a ritual water buffalo sacrifice to the ruling earth spirit for Champasak, Chao Tengkham, is performed each year. The blood of the buffalo is offered to a local shaman who serves as a medium for the appearance of this spirit.

SLEEPING & EATING
Champasak has a number of good guesthouses strung along its main road, most of which have bedrooms with fans.

Vong Phaseud Guest House (☎ 920038; r 15,000 kip) A popular and friendly place on the river

with plain rooms and a small but social restaurant area serving up good Lao food with fantastic views over the Mekong. Crack a Beer Lao and watch the river slide through a dozen colour changes before nightfall.

Khampoui Guest House (r 15,000-20,000 kip) It's not on the river, but this new place, just south of the roundabout, has the cleanest, most modern budget rooms in town. Rooms in the main house have shared bathrooms.

Dokchampa Guest House & Restaurant (☎ 020-206248; r 15,000 kip) On the southwest corner of the fountain. Gloomy and could-be-cleaner rooms, but cheap and popular, with good food.

GETTING THERE & AWAY
From Pakse, regular buses and săwngthăew leave between 7am and 3pm (10,000 kip, two hours).

To get south to Ban Nakasang (for Don Det) or Muang Khong (on Don Khong) by road, catch a morning ferry from Ban Phaphin (2km north of Champasak) over the Mekong to Ban Muang (2000 kip). On the other side hop on a săwngthăew, or motorcycle taxi (3000 kip) to Ban Lak 30 (an intersection on the main road where a couple of small road-side stalls sell food and drink). There, you can flag down one of the regular buses or pick-up trucks heading south.

For Pakse (15,000 kip, two hours), several buses and săwngthăew depart between 6.30am and 8am.

GETTING AROUND
Bicycles can be rented from guesthouses for 10,000 kip per day for the 8km ride to Wat Phu Champasak. A túk-túk will take you there and back for around 30,000 kip.

Si Phan Don (Four Thousand Islands)
☎ 031
Si Phan Don, where the Mekong fans out forming an intricate network of channels, rocks, sandbars and islets 14km wide, is one of nature's marvels. At night the river is dotted with the lights of fishermen bobbing in the river, while during the wet season the coconut and betel palm–studded islands are alight with fireflies. Water buffalo wade in the shallows, in the morning women wash clothes and children in the river, and steady flows of longtail boats glide back and forward from the mainland. Si Phan Don is

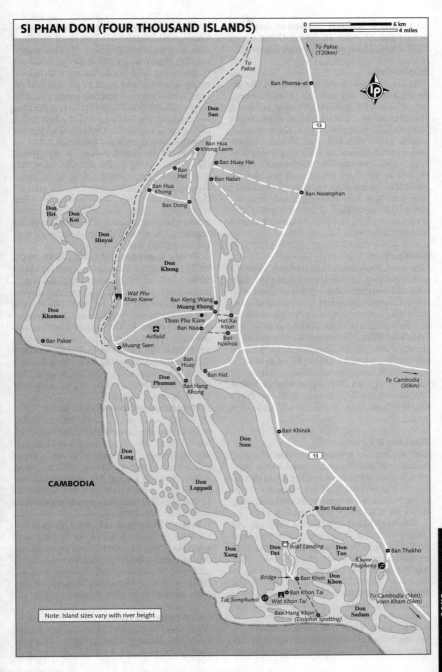

SI PHAN DON (FOUR THOUSAND ISLANDS)

0 ___ 6 km
0 ___ 4 miles

To Pakse

To Pakse
(120km)

Ban Phonsa-at

13

Don
San

Ban Hua
Khong Laem

Ban Huay Hai

Ban
Hat

Ban Nalan

Ban Hua
Khong

Ban Nasenphan

Ban Dong

Don
Het

Don
Koi

Don
Hinyai

Don
Khong

Wat Phu
Khao Kaew

Don
Khamao

Ban Xieng Wang
Muang Khong

Tham Phu Kiaw

Hat Xai
Khun

Ban Pakse

Ban Naa

Ban
Nokhok

Airfield

Muang Saen

Ban
Huay

Ban Hat

Don
Phuman

Ban Hang
Khong

To Cambodia
(30km)

Ban Khinak

Don
Som

13

Don
Long

CAMBODIA

Don
Loppadi

Ban Nakasang

Boat Landing

Don
Xang

Don
Det

Don
Tao

Ban Thakho

Khone
Phapheng

Bridge

Ban Khon

Don
Khon

To Cambodia (5km);
Voen Kham (5km)

Tat Somphamit

Wat Khon Tai

Ban Khon Tai

Ban Hang Khon
(Dolphin Spotting)

Don
Sadam

Note: Island sizes vary with river height

LAOS

also home to the rare Irrawaddy dolphins, which can be seen at the southern tip of Don Khon, plus two impressive waterfalls.

DON KHONG

The largest and most populous of the islands, Don Khong lacks the magical scenery of its neighbours to the south; however, it's an excellent choice if you're after a more 'authentic' experience. The 32km round-island cycle through rice fields, villages and a small huddle of hills in the north is highly recommended for its absence of traffic and an excellent paved road (thank you, President Khamtai Siphandone). The island also boasts a few interesting old temples, the added advantage of 24-hour electricity (coming soon to the islands further south) and virtual silence after nightfall.

Information

One road back from the river, 400m south of the Muang Khong town square the **Agricultural Promotion Bank** (8.30am-3.30pm Mon-Fri) exchanges travellers cheques and cash for high commission and poor rates. Better to come prepared with kip from Pakse. The **telephone office** (8am-noon & 2-4pm Mon-Fri) is directly west of the boat landing. The **post office** (8am-noon & 2-4pm Mon-Fri) is next door to Done Khong Guest House, just south of the bridge. In 2005 **Alpha Internet** (per min 1000 kip; 7am-9pm), 100m north of Pon's Guest House, brought the world wide web to the island.

Sleeping & Eating

Don Khong has a good collection of guesthouses and as it is not tremendously busy even in the high season, finding a bed should not be a problem. Here are a few good options, but there a several more dotted among these, all of a similar standard and price.

Villa Khan Khong (213539; r 50,000 kip;) For a touch of affordable elegance you can't do better than this excellent, well-run teak mansion one block back from the boat landing. All rooms have smooth old-wood floorboards plus attached cold-water bathrooms. There are irresistible lounging areas inside and on the undercover veranda. Scooters and rusty pushbikes are available for hire.

Pon's Guest House (214037; r 50,000-10,000 kip) With 19 very clean rooms all with hot water and shiny tiled floors, this is a popu-

lar choice for backpackers and tour groups. Casual and friendly Mr Pon is an excellent source of local information. He also organises day trips south to Don Khon to see the dolphins, or he'll hook you up with a boat going wherever you want to go. The restaurant, which serves breakfast lunch and dinner (meals 8000 to 20,000 kip), is on decking overlooking the Mekong and the fish specialities are a highlight. Order ahead for the mouthwatering *mak pai* (steamed fish).

Done Khong Guest House & Restaurant (214010; r 50,000-150,000 kip;) Another good choice opposite the river, family-run Done Khong's small concrete rooms are clean and cool with attached cold-water bathrooms. The downstairs restaurant serves excellent noodle dishes. It's open for breakfast, lunch and dinner, and meals cost between 8000 and 25,000 kip.

Mekong Guesthouse (213668; r 20,000-200,000 kip;) Along the dirt road by the river about 500m south of the boat landing, this guesthouse's more secluded location may appeal to you. The rooms in the main house have the most aesthetic appeal, but the cheaper ones are out back. The attached restaurant, which is open for breakfast, lunch and dinner (meals from 5000 to 35,000 kip), boasts Canadian and Lao food. You can get yourself a Canadian-style pancake with a Tim Horton's coffee (but don't expect it to taste like it does back home!).

Phoukhong Guesthouse & Restaurant (213673; r 30,000 kip) Next door to Pon's with a similar outdoor decking overlooking the Mekong, but substantially jazzed-up with red and yellow fairy lights and wagon wheels, this is another good dining option with a mixed Asian menu. It's open for breakfast, lunch and dinner, and meals cost from 7000 to 15,000 kip. The adequate, small rooms come with cold-water bathrooms.

Souksan Restaurant (212071; meals 15,000-50,000 kip; breakfast, lunch & dinner) Opposite upmarket Souksan Hotel and overlooking the river, the spotlessly clean and enormous kitchen here serves good Chinese food or, for those who are seriously homesick for it, a full roast dinner with mashed potatoes.

Getting There & Away

From Don Khong to Pakse, the bus leaves from the Muang Khong town square at around about 8am (15,000 kip, five hours).

Done Khong Guest House runs a minivan direct to Pakse leaving at 8am (50,000 kip, 3½ hours).

If you're heading south to Cambodia, Pon's Guest House arranges transport to the border for 50,000 kip. Otherwise, cross the river to Hat Xai Khun, catch a săwngthăew to the main road and wait for the Pakse–Voen Kham bus, which passes through around 10.30am.

For Don Det, organise a ride on a boat taking people on a day trip to see the Irrawady dolphins (try Pon's Guest House, 30,000 kip one way) or negotiate with the boat drivers near the bridge (you'll need to employ your Lao language skills).

Getting Around

Bicycles can be rented for 15,000 kip per day from guesthouses along the river road or from Alpha Internet. Villa Khan Khong has motorcycles for US$10 per day. Buses, motorcycle taxis or túk-túks run irregularly from Ban Hua Khong to Muang Khong and Ban Huay, from where the car ferry departs.

DON DET & DON KHON

Despite a major tourism boom (the daily sounds of building construction jangle against the peaceful twittering of birds), these steamy islands 16km south of Don Khong have managed to retain their beauty and charm. The two islands are connected by a railway bridge (the only line the French ever laid in Laos) and are traversed by narrow shady paths, which makes them ideal for walking and cycling. Don Det has the bigger backpacker scene (avoid the main bungalows strip if you want an early night). Don Khon is slightly more upmarket in terms of accommodation options, but it's the better island for exploring by day.

Electricity is supposed to arrive on the islands in 2006. Until then, a handful of generators provide power by night and locals have to make the trip across to the mainland every day for provisions (with rising oil prices this isn't as romantic as it sounds). Once it does arrive, you can help protect the islands from becoming the south's answer to Vang Vieng by voting with your feet if anyone thinks a TV bar is a great business idea.

Information

It's possible to change US dollars cash at several guesthouses on the island. **Bungalow Souksan** (☎ 020-227 0414) also exchanges travellers cheques with passport ID for a poor rate and high commission (in other words come here with enough money to see you through your stay if you can). At the time of research, Internet access was available for the truly addicted for 1500 kip per minute using a solar-powered laptop via a mobile phone.

Sights & Activities

For many, the word 'rare', before 'dolphin', can turn a trip to see the **Irrawaddy dolphins** into a minipilgrimage. They say you have a better chance of seeing these playful mammals in the dry season, either early or late in the day. Some people get lucky and view them up-close; others only see a few pale domes poking out of the water.

The easiest way to get to the sand bar viewing area is to join an organised half-day trip (for around 50,000 kip); sign-up on one of the whiteboards along Sunrise Blvd. Others charter a boat from the pier at Kong Ngay (around 25,000 kip per person). Alternatively, walk or ride to the beach at Ban Hang Khon and try your luck seeing the dolphins from there.

Another must-do-if-you're-motivated, is to **walk** or hire a **bicycle** for the day and explore the dirt pathways circumnavigating and crisscrossing Don Det and Don Khon. The defunct **railway line** (a little rocky on a bike: don't be shocked if you get a puncture and have to walk home) takes you to a French loading pier at the southern end of Don Khon. You can also visit the French-built **concrete channels** on the eastern edge of the Don Khon (head northwest from the railway bridge then turn south about 1km along), or the dramatic **Tat Somphamit** waterfalls (go under the railway bridge then follow the road southwest for around 2km). There's a charge of 5000 kip per day to cross the bridge.

Admirers of waterfalls will like **Khone Phapheng**. Although less dramatic than Tat Somphamit, it is considered the largest (by volume) in Southeast Asia and is therefore a boast-worthy sight to visit. Entry is 10,000 kip and the falls are often included on the itinerary of dolphin-viewing day trips.

Tubing and **kayaking** are both possible around the islands, either organised for you, or do-it-yourself. Tubes are available for hire at a number of guesthouses. Lazing in a tube by the small beach at the northern tip of Don Det is another popular way to pass the day. See p943 for information on water-borne parasites in the tropics.

A **pool table** (per hr 10,000 kip) under a thatched roof at Mr Sidae Bungalows, halfway along Sunrise Blvd, gets a workout in the afternoon and evenings. On weekends the island pool competition (entry 5000 kip) sees the winner take all.

Sleeping & Eating

The Lao know a good idea when they see one and now dozens of what look at first like identical guesthouses have mushroomed along the banks of Don Det – less so on Don Khon. Most feature basic stilted wooden or bamboo thatched bungalows with mosquito nets, hammocks and shared bathrooms, and cost between 10,000 and 80,000 kip per night.

So which one do you choose? Following is a list of some of the better, or cheaper, options, but in the high season you may have to stay where you can. Thatched roofs are cooler, detached bungalows are more private, two windows are better than one, and almost all have shared bathroom and cold water. Also note, with the pace of change in Laos, by the time you arrive on the islands something brighter and cleaner than what we have suggested may have been erected.

Bungalow Souksan (020-227 0414; Don Det; r 20,000-80,000 kip) On the northern tip of the island, these sturdily built and well-maintained wooden bungalows were the best available at the time of research. The shared bathrooms with cold-water showers are spotlessly clean and concrete paths lined with low hedges added to the orderly ambience. Solar-powered lights meant it was quieter at night than 'outside' the grounds. The gates are locked at 11.30pm and the bungalows closer to the river were further from neighbouring guesthouse generators. The attached restaurant serves Chinese food and a range of cocktails and uses purified water.

Mama Tanon Café, Restaurant & Guesthouse (020-227 4293; Don Det; r 10,000-20,000 kip) Bungalows, in a wooden building with a tin roof, are attached so forget about privacy, but the communal balcony over the river, with hammocks, is an ideal spot to relax and meet other like-minded folk. The Rasta-themed restaurant is open for breakfast, lunch and dinner, and serves meals priced from 7000 to 15,000 kip. With lots of 'special' dishes, it's popular, even for those not staying in the guesthouse.

Miss Noy's Guesthouse & Restaurant (020-233 7112; Don Det; r 20,000 kip) Built around a grassy square in a prime location, these bungalows have thatched roofs and windows to keep them reasonably cool by day. A sheltered hammock platform by the river is good, as are the vegetarian options on the menu. Meals in the restaurant cost from 7000 to 20,000 kip. Also blessed with a throne-style toilet.

Seng Chan's Bungalows (Don Det; r 15,000 kip) Great value bungalows right on the river, costing less than the competitors, yet with clean bathrooms, and two beds per room. Also hires bicycles for 8000 kip per day.

Mr Pan & Madame Fuang Bungalows (Don Det; r 10,000 kip) These are simple bungalows on the river. This is the cheapest place to plonk your stony-broke self on Don Det, but unfortunately a hammock doesn't come with your hut.

Mr Oudomsouk Bungalows (Don Det; r 20,000 kip) The standout feature of this row of bungalows all with two beds and thatched roofs is that food and drink is served to you on your balcony. Can you get any lazier?

For a more secluded stay, head north along the river road towards the railway bridge where a few more guesthouses are interspersed with family homes and kitchen gardens.

Mr Phao's Guest House (Don Det; r 20,000 kip) In the process of being rebuilt after a clumsy candle fire, this guesthouse has two new bungalows and a couple of the originals all on the river facing west with sunset views.

Santiphab Guest House & Mekong Restaurant (Don Det; r 20,000 kip) The Santiphab is a long way from the action, but its location next to the railway bridge makes it a hive of activity during the day as walkers and cyclists stop off to revive. Well-built bungalows are spaced out and face Don Khon. In the spirit of diversifying business, the Mekong Restaurant (serving meals priced from 6000 to 18,000 kip) does German schnitzel, as well as the usual island fare.

Across the river on Don Khon there are not many budget options although a few exist if Don Det really isn't what you were

---

BORDER CROSSING: INTO CAMBODIA

Once at the Cambodian border, you'll almost certainly be asked for anything up to US$10 in 'administration fees' by the guards. It may take a lot of patience to haggle this down, but since it's not an official crossing you don't really have much bargaining power. Fees tend to be a lot lower on the Cambodian side and once there vehicles, ferries or speedboats run to Stung Treng.

---

hoping for. **Mama Dam Restaurant & Guest House** (Don Khon; r 20,000 kip) has simple rooms close to the bridge and serves meals from 10,000 to 25,000 kip.

Getting There & Around

From Pakse, buses and săwngthăew to Ban Nakasang for Don Det and Don Khon leave the southern bus station every hour until 1pm (20,000 kip, four to five hours). From the boat landing it's a 5000 kip trip to Don Det; more if you have fewer passengers. When the river is low and fewer trips are being made, it's harder to get a boat to go further around to Don Khon, so prepare to negotiate.

For buses and săwngthăew back to Pakse, get across to Ban Nakasang early to be sure of a seat and some legroom. If you're heading to Cambodia, most guesthouses will arrange transport to the border for 15,000 to 20,000 kip per person.

LAOS DIRECTORY

ACCOMMODATION

There's no shortage of accommodation in Laos where even the smallest town will have a guesthouse or a village homestay option. The standard of guesthouses has risen in the last few years, as have prices. Guesthouses usually advertise rates in either US dollars or kip and many also accept payment in Thai baht.

Accommodation is cheapest in the rural north and far south, where it's still possible to find a US$2 bungalow in backpacker spots like Muang Ngoi Neua and Si Phan Don. In larger towns like Vientiane, Luang Prabang, Savannakhet, Pakse and Luang Nam Tha, expect to pay a minimum of 50,000 kip for a budget room with shared bathroom and around 80,000 kip for a room with a bathroom or air-con.

ACTIVITIES
Cycling

Laos' relatively peaceful roads are a haven for cyclists. It's easy to bring your own bicycle into Laos if you're on a long-distance trip and if cycling up mountains in the north gets too much, you can flag down a bus. Laos' main towns all have bicycle-rental shops. Note that it is wise to tie your bag in your basket when riding in town. While theft isn't a particular problem in Laos, if the opportunity presents itself you could lose your day-pack to a passing motorcyclist. Mountain-bike tours are run from Luang Nam Tha (see Boat Landing Guest House, p390) and Luang Prabang (see Tours, p374).

Kayaking & Rafting

Kayaking and white-water rafting have taken off here and Laos has several world-class rapids, as well as lots of beautiful, although less challenging, waterways. Unfortunately, the industry remains dangerously unregulated and you should not go out on rapids during the wet season unless you are completely confident of your guides and equipment. **Wildside** (www.wildside.com) is the most professional kayaking and rafting outfit in the country and should be your first stop for advice.

Rock Climbing

Currently there is only one organised rock-climbing operation in Laos, run by **Green Discovery** (☎ 023-511440; www.greendiscoverylaos.com) in the karst cliffs around Vang Vieng. Experienced rock climbers also organise climbing expeditions in Southeast Asia. Contact clubs in your home country to find out more.

Trekking

Laos' large areas of wilderness are a trekker's dream. Fortunately, responsible travel has taken root in Laos and some of the country's adventure tour companies are keen to avoid repeating the damage wreaked on Thailand's hill tribes by the tourism industry there. The most popular areas for trekking are Luang Nam Tha (p390), Nong Khiaw (Muang Ngoi, p380), Luang Prabang (see Tours, p374) and the Bolaven Plateau (p401).

SAFETY TIPS FROM THE EXPERT

Professionally managed kayaking and rafting trips are a great way to experience the wonderful environments of Laos yet it is important to ensure you go with outfitters who are equipped and prepared should something go wrong. The following questions will help you identify who to trust.

- Do your tours have all of the relevant safety equipment such as life jackets, throw ropes, a first-aid kit and helmets?
- Can I see your first-aid kit, boats and throw bag?
- How long is the pretrip safety briefing and practice session?
- Are your guides trained in basic first aid (discuss CPR) and river rescue? By whom?
- Is the lead guide fluent in English? How long has he or she been leading paddle tours?

All rivers possess inherent risks and in the interests of safety, caution should be maintained. Several tourists have drowned while tubing on the Nam Song during the rainy season. From late May to October strong whirlpools and eddy lines appear in several sections of the river; these can flip people off tubes and make swimming to safety extremely difficult.

Even if you are a confident swimmer wear a lifejacket. When tubing always look well ahead for obstructions such as trees or branches in the river; water sifts through such obstructions, tubers don't. Take evasive action early to avoid being caught in a 'strainer' or scraped over rocks. Do not try to dangle your feet or stand up in fast-flowing water. Foot entrapment can easily occur and in swift water this can be fatal.

Stay together so that you can help your friends if they have trouble. Several unnecessary drownings on the Nam Song have occurred when friends arrived too late to give a helping hand.

The caves of Vang Vieng are fascinating and delicate ecosystems that should be enjoyed yet treated with respect and caution. It is strongly recommended to go caving with guides. This is relatively cheap and will ensure that you go directly to the most interesting caves. Cave exploration without a guide is not recommended. If you do it always report to friends or a guesthouse when and exactly where your group plans to go caving and when you expect to come back. Caving without a guide requires an absolute minimum of three separate forms of light per person. Go deep into caves at your own risk. Tourists have been lost in Vang Vieng caves for days on end and several have perished when search parties could not locate them.

Finally, please promote sustainable ecotourism by paying the signposted fees to cave minders; encouraging locals to use flashlights (torches) rather than candles; not smoking or urinating in caves; and not touching formations, which soon become degraded due to the chemical reactions with human sweat.

Mick O'Shea, certified white-water kayaking expert and expedition leader,
First Descent of Mekong River Source to Sea, 2004

Tubing

Something of a Lao phenomenon, 'tubing' simply involves inserting yourself into an enormous tractor tube inner and floating down a river. Vang Vieng is the tubing capital of the country (p367) with Muang Ngoi Neua (p381) and Si Phan Don (p405) popular runners-up.

BOOKS

Lonely Planet's *Laos* has all the information you'll need for extended travel in Laos. Lonely Planet also publishes the *Lao Phrasebook*, an introduction to the Lao language.

For some light predeparture reading have a look at *Another Quiet American*, where Brett Dakin shares his sometimes very funny experiences and insights into Laos from an outsider's perspective. *Stalking the Elephant Kings: In Search of Laos*, by Christopher Kremmer, is incredibly well researched and an excellent choice for history fans. Harder to track down, *The Ravens: Pilots of the Secret War of Laos* by Christopher Robbins is a good introduction to the other war going on in Southeast Asia in the 1970s which many Lao still remember all too vividly.

BUSINESS HOURS

Government offices are typically open from 8am to noon and 1pm to 4pm, Monday to Friday. Banking hours are generally 8.30am to 4pm Monday to Friday. Shops have longer hours and are often open on weekends. Restaurants typically close by 10pm and bars stay open until around midnight.

CLIMATE

Laos has two distinct seasons, May to October is wet and November to April is dry. The coolest time of year is November to January and the hottest is March to May. The lowlands of the Mekong River valley are the hottest, peaking at around 38°C in March and April and dropping to a minimum of around 15°C in the cool season. Up in the mountains of Xieng Khuang and Sam Neua, cool season night-time temperatures can drop to freezing and even in the hot season it can be pleasant.

The wettest area of the country is southern Laos, where the Annamite mountain peaks get more than 3000mm of rain a year. Luang Prabang and Xieng Khuang receive less than half that amount of rain and Vientiane and Savannakhet get from 1500mm to 2000mm.

See the Vientiane climate chart on p924.

CUSTOMS

Customs inspections at ports of entry are very lax as long as you're not bringing in more than a moderate amount of luggage. You're not supposed to enter the country with more than 500 cigarettes or 1L of distilled spirits. Of course, all the usual prohibitions on drugs, weapons and pornography apply.

DANGERS & ANNOYANCES

Urban Laos is generally safe. You should still exercise ordinary precautions at night, but your chances of being robbed, mugged, harassed or assaulted are much lower than in most Western countries. There are significant dangers around the country, however. For the latest travel warnings for Laos, check government travel advisories on the Internet.

Shootings have plagued Rte 13 between Vang Vieng and Luang Prabang since the '75 revolution. Rte 7 between Phu Khun and Phonsavan has also had a spot of trouble in the past.

In 2003 the security situation deteriorated. Ambushes in and around Sam Neua in Hua Phan province, bombings in Vientiane and attacks on public transport in southern Laos caused considerable anxiety for travellers and locals alike. While there have been no recent incidents of serious civil unrest that have affected tourists, the population of Laos is not exactly happily and peacefully governed by the current administration so be sure to stay abreast of the political situation before – and while – travelling in Laos.

In the eastern provinces, particularly Xieng Khuang, Salavan and Savannakhet, UXO is a hazard. Never walk off well-used paths.

DISABLED TRAVELLERS

Laos has virtually no facilities to meet the needs of disabled travellers. Urban pavements are full of hazards and public transport is often cramped. Any trip to Laos will require considerable forward planning. Many international organisations, such as **Mobility International USA** (☎ 541 343 1284; www.miusa.org; PO Box 10767, Eugene OR, USA), have resources, information and tips on travelling with disabilities.

EMBASSIES & CONSULATES
Embassies & Consulates in Laos

Visas can be obtained in your home country through the Lao embassy or consulate. See p414 for more details.

Australia (Map pp354-5; ☎ 021-413610; Th Nehru, Ban Phonxay, Vientiane)

Cambodia (Map pp354-5; ☎ 021-314952; Th Tha Deua Km 2, Ban Phonxay, Vientiane)

China (Map pp354-5; ☎ 021-315105; Th Wat Nak, Ban Wat Nak, Vientiane)

France (Map p358; ☎ 021-215253; Th Setthathirat, Ban Sisaket, Vientiane)

Germany (Map pp354-5; ☎ 021-312111; Th Sok Pa Luang, Vientiane)

Indonesia (Map pp354-5; ☎ 021-413900; Th Phon Kheng, Ban Phonsaat, Vientiane)

Malaysia (Map pp354-5; ☎ 021-414203; Th That Luang, Vientiane)

Myanmar (Map pp354-5; ☎ 021-314991; Th Sok Pa Luang, Vientiane)

Philippines (☎ 021-315179; Th Salakokthan, Vientiane)

Singapore (Map pp354-5; ☎ 021-412477; Th Nong Bon, Vientiane)

Thailand (Map pp354-5; ☎ 021-214582; Th Phon Kheng, Vientiane)

UK (☎ 021-413610; Th Nehru, Ban Phonxay, Vientiane)

USA (Map p358; ☎ 021-212581; Th Bartholomie, Vientiane)

Vietnam Pakse (Map p398; ☎ 031-212058; Th 24); Vientiane (Map pp354-5; ☎ 413400; Th That Luang)

Lao Embassies & Consulates Abroad

Australia (☎ 02-6286 4595; 1 Dalman Cres, O'Malley, ACT 2606)

China Beijing (☎ 01-532 1224; 11 Sanlitun Dongsie Jie, Beijing 100600); Kunming (☎ 0871-317 6623; Room 3226, Camelia Hotel, 154 East Dong Feng Rd, 650041)

France (☎ 01-45 53 02 98; 74 Av Raymond Poincaré, 75116 Paris)

Germany (☎ 030-890 60647; hong@laos/botschaft.de; Bismarckallee 2A, 14193 Berlin)

Japan (☎ 03-5411 2291; 3-3-21 Nishi Azabu, Minato-ku, Tokyo)

Sweden (☎ 08-668 5122; Hornsgaten 82-B1 TR 11721, Stockholm)

USA (☎ 202-332 6416; 2222 S St NW, Washington, DC 20008)

FESTIVALS & EVENTS

The Lao Buddhist Era (BE) calendar calculates year one as 638 BC, so AD 2006 is 2644 BE according to the Lao Buddhist calendar. Festivals are mostly linked to agricultural seasons or historic Buddhist holidays.

FEBRUARY

Magha Puja (Makkha Busaa; Full Moon) This is held on the full moon of the third lunar month. It commemorates a speech given by Buddha to 1250 enlightened monks who came to hear him without prior summons. Chanting and offerings mark the festival, culminating in the candle-lit circumambulation of wat throughout the country.

Vietnamese Tet-Chinese New Year This is celebrated in Vientiane, Pakse and Savannakhet with parties, deafening nonstop fireworks and visits to Vietnamese and Chinese temples. Chinese- and Vietnamese-run businesses usually close for three days.

APRIL

Pii Mai (Lunar New Year) This festival begins in mid-April (the 15th, 16th and 17th are official public holidays) and practically the entire country comes to a halt and celebrates. Houses are cleaned, people put on new clothes and Buddha images are washed with specially purified water. Later the citizens take to the streets, drink lots of beer and dowse one another with water. Expect to get very, very wet.

MAY

International Labour Day 1 May is a public holiday.

Visakha Puja (Visakha Busaa; Full Moon) Falling on the 15th day of the sixth lunar month (usually in May), this is

considered the day of the Buddha's birth, enlightenment and *parinibbana* (passing into nirvana).

Bun Bang Fai (Rocket Festival) One of the wildest festivals in Laos, a pre-Buddhist rain ceremony celebrated alongside Visakha Puja, involving huge home-made rockets, music, dance, drunkenness, cross-dressing, large wooden penises and sometimes a few incinerated houses.

JULY

Khao Phansaa (Khao Watsa; Full Moon) Late July is the beginning of the traditional three-month rains retreat, when Buddhist monks are expected to station themselves in a single monastery.

SEPTEMBER/OCTOBER

Awk Phansaa (Awk Watsa; Full Moon) Celebrating the end of the three-month rains retreat.

Bun Nam (Water Festival) Held in association with Awk Phansaa. Boat races are commonly held in towns on the Mekong, such as Vientiane, Luang Prabang and Savannakhet.

NOVEMBER

That Luang Festival (Bun That Luang; Full Moon) Takes place at Pha That Luang in Vientiane in early November. Hundreds of monks assemble to receive alms and floral votives early in the morning on the first day of the festival. There is a colourful procession between Pha That Luang and Wat Si Muang.

DECEMBER

Lao National Day Held on 2 December, this public holiday celebrates the 1975 victory of the proletariat over the Royal Lao with parades and speeches.

FOOD & DRINK
Food

Lao cuisine lacks the variety of Thai food and foreigners often limit themselves to a diet of noodles, fried rice and the ubiquitous 'travellers' fare' that has swept Southeast Asia (fruit pancakes, muesli, fruit shakes…) But there are some excellent Lao dishes to try.

The standard Lao breakfast is *fŏe* (rice noodles), which are usually served floating in a bland broth with some vegetables and a meat of your choice. The trick is in the seasoning, and Lao people will stir in some fish sauce, lime juice, dried chillies, mint leaves, basil, or one of the wonderful speciality hot chilli sauces that many noodle shops make, testing it along the way, before slurping it down with chopsticks in one hand and a spoon in the other.

Làap is the most distinctively Lao dish, a delicious spicy salad made from minced beef, pork, duck, fish or chicken, mixed with fish sauce, small shallots, mint leaves, lime juice, roasted ground rice and lots of chillies. Another famous Lao speciality is *tạm màak hung* (known as *som tam* in Thailand), a salad of shredded green papaya mixed with garlic, lime juice, fish sauce, sometimes tomatoes, palm sugar, land crab or dried shrimp and, of course, chillies by the handful.

Most Lao food is eaten with *khào nío* (sticky rice), which is served up in a small wicker container. Take a small amount of rice and, using one hand, work it into a walnut-sized ball before dipping it into the food. When you've finished eating, replace the lid on the container. Less often, food is eaten with *khào jâo* (plain white rice), which is eaten with a fork and spoon.

In rural areas, where hunting is more common than raising animals for food, you're likely to encounter some exotic meats. Apparently these are delicious: wild boar, wild fowl, wild dog and wild squirrel. Monitor lizard and bush rat might take some getting used to.

In main centres, French baguettes are a popular breakfast food. Sometimes it's eaten with condensed milk or with *khai* (eggs) in a sandwich that contains Lao-style pâté and vegetables. When they're fresh, they're superb.

Alcoholic Drinks

The Lao Brewery Co produces the ubiquitous and excellent Beer Lao. Imported beers are also available in cans. Lao Bia – a dark, sweetish palm beer made in Savannakhet – is an interesting brew and is sold mostly around southern and central Laos in small bottles with a distinctly antique-looking label.

Lào-láo (Lao liquor, or rice whisky) is a popular drink among lowland Lao. Strictly speaking, *lào-láo* is not legal but no-one seems to care. The government distils its own brand, Sticky Rice, which is of course legal. *Lào-láo* is usually taken neat, sometimes with a plain water chaser.

In a Lao home the pouring and drinking of *lào-láo* takes on ritual characteristics – it is first offered to the house spirits, and guests must take at least one offered drink or risk offending the spirits.

In rural provinces, a weaker version of *lào-láo* known as *lào hái* (jar liquor) is fermented by households or villages. *Lào hái* is usually drunk from a communal jar using long reed straws. It's not always safe to drink, however, since unboiled water is often added to it during and after fermentation.

Nonalcoholic Drinks

Water purified for drinking purposes is simply called *nâam deum* (drinking water), whether it's boiled or filtered. All water offered to' customers in restaurants or hotels will be purified and bottles of purified water are sold everywhere.

Lao coffee is usually served very strong and sweet enough to make your teeth clench. If you don't want sugar or sweetened condensed milk, ask for *kạa-fáe dạm* (black coffee).

Chinese-style green or semicured tea is the usual ingredient in *nâam sáa* or *sáa láo* – the weak, refreshing tea traditionally served free in restaurants. The black tea familiar to Westerners is usually found in the same places as Lao coffee and is usually referred to as *sáa hâwn* (hot tea).

GAY & LESBIAN TRAVELLERS

Like Thailand, Laos has a very liberal attitude towards homosexuality, but a very conservative attitude to public displays of affection. Gay couples are unlikely to be given frosty treatment anywhere. Unlike Thailand, Laos does not have an obvious gay scene, but in Vientiane's late-night clubs you'll see plenty of young gay Lao whooping it up with everyone else. Luang Prabang boasts Laos' first openly gay bar, with the rainbow-coloured gay pride flag flying in a few places around town. See p412 for information on relations with Lao nationals.

HOLIDAYS

Aside from government offices, banks and post offices, many Lao businesses do not trouble themselves with weekends and public holidays. Most Chinese- and Vietnamese-run businesses close for three days during Vietnamese Tet and Chinese New Year in February.

Most businesses are closed for the following holidays.

Pii Mai (Lunar New Year) 15, 16 and 17 April
Labour Day 1 May
Lao National Day 2 December

INTERNET ACCESS

In Vientiane, there are dozens of Internet places with rates at a standard 100 kip per minute. Further from Vientiane, the slower and more expensive connections become. At press time, reasonably priced Internet was available in most tourism centres outside Vientiane, including Vang Vieng, Luang Prabang, Savannakhet, Pakse and Luang Nam Tha; plus Phonsavan, Udomxai, Don Khong and most recently on Don Det (where Internet can be slow and expensive).

INTERNET RESOURCES

www.cia.gov/cia/publications/factbook/geos /la.html An encyclopaedic overview of the country.

www.global.lao.net/laoVL.html Comprehensive site with features on Lao culture, art, government and political issues.

www.laosguide.com This well-organised site compiles news stories about Lao PDR and the overseas Lao community from many online news services.

www.laos-travel.net Travel information and news, with a slick design.

www.uxolao.org & www.magclearsmines.org Information regarding ongoing mine-clearing work in Laos.

www.vientianetimes.com Not affiliated with the newspaper of the same name. Its tag-line, the Gateway to Democracy, says it all.

www.visit-laos.com Not the official tourist authority site, but more helpful than many of its offices!

LEGAL MATTERS

There is virtually nothing in the way of legal services in Laos. If you get yourself in legal strife, contact your embassy in Vientiane, though the assistance it can provide may be limited.

AS USEFUL AS TOILET PAPER

Be aware when getting US dollars from banks. There are many old notes in circulation that are in such a bad state that no one will accept them, including the bank that gave them to you. Check all your notes at the counter and ask for any old ones (usually in the middle of the pile) to be replaced. Similarly old kip notes that are torn in half and taped up or dotted with holes, although still legal tender, are sometimes rejected by shops. Check your notes and don't accept any that look too dodgy to pass on to anyone but unsuspecting foreigners.

It's against the law for foreigners and Lao to have sexual relations unless they're married. Travellers should be aware that a holiday romance could result in being arrested and deported.

MAPS

An excellent road map of Laos, with city maps of Vientiane, Luang Prabang, Vang Vieng, Muang Sing and Luang Nam Tha, is produced by motorcycle tour company **Golden Triangle Rider Ltd** (www.gtrider.com).

MEDIA

Laos' proximity to Thailand means Thai satellite TV, which also runs BBC and CNN, is the main source of uncensored world news for many Lao. Two official foreign-language newspapers, the English *Vientiane Times* and the French *Le Rénovateur,* are available at minimarts in Vientiane. Thailand's English-language dailies, the *Bangkok Post* and the *Nation,* are also found in guesthouses and cafés frequented by foreigners.

Lao Airline's *Laos Magazine* looks like it was put together by a high-school student in the 1960s, but has some useful listings and sometimes runs interesting cultural features.

MONEY

Prices in this chapter are quoted in kip or US dollars as they are on the ground, but payment can be generally made in either kip, dollars or Thai baht.

ATMs

There is one ATM in Laos with international facilities in Vientiane (see p356).

Bargaining

Almost everything for sale in Laos can be bargained over and although more upmarket shops have fixed prices it never hurts to suggest an alternative. Lao people are not usually aggressive hagglers and a quiet, gentle bargaining technique works much better than arm-waving melodramatics.

There is a two-tier price system in Laos and foreigners often pay more for goods and services than locals (foreign residents are charged up to 10 times more for utilities, so it's not just tourists being asked for more!). In more heavily touristed areas the concept of overcharging tourists has caught on, particularly among túk-túk drivers; but generally in Laos price differences are not worth getting angry about, unless you are being dramatically ripped off.

Black Market
The days of favourable black market money-changing are over and the best exchange rates are usually available in banks, though most guesthouses and many travel agents will change dollars and baht cash at bank rates.

Cash
The only legal currency is the Lao kip, but three currencies are in everyday use: the kip, US dollar and Thai baht. Pretty much anywhere in Laos will accept any of these currencies, or combinations of all three, as payment. Kip come in denominations of 500, 1000, 2000, 5000, 10,000 and new 20,000 kip notes.

Credit Cards
Visa cards are becoming more widely accepted these days and many travel agents, up-market guesthouses, restaurants and shops in tourist areas accept them. MasterCard and Amex are much less common. Cash advances on Visa cards are available in some regional centres but not all so plan ahead.

Exchanging Money
US dollars and Thai baht can be exchanged all over the country. US-dollar travellers cheques can be exchanged in most provincial capitals and attract a better rate than cash. Banks in Vientiane and Luang Prabang change UK pounds, euro, Thai baht, Japanese yen, and Canadian, US and Australian dollars.

The best overall exchange rate is usually offered by Banque pour le Commerce Extérieur Lao. The only advantage of licensed moneychangers is longer opening hours. Exchange rates are as follows:

Country	Unit	kip
Australia	A$1	6376
Cambodia	1000r	2718
Canada	C$1	6819
Euro zone	€1	10,661
Japan	¥100	7710
New Zealand	NZ$1	5859
Thailand	10B	2114
UK	UK£1	15,557
USA	US$1	8267
Vietnam	10,000d	6821

Travellers Cheques
Banks in all provincial centres will exchange US-dollar travellers cheques. If you are changing cheques into kip there is usually no commission, but changing into dollars attracts a minimum 2% charge.

POST
Postal services from Vientiane are generally reliable, the provinces less so. If you have valuable items or presents to post home, there is a **Federal Express** (Map p358; ☎ 021-223278; ☼ 8am-noon & 1-5pm Mon-Fri, 9am-noon Sat) office inside the main post office compound in Vientiane.

RESPONSIBLE TRAVEL
In terms of tourism, Laos is very young and the rapid growth in the country's popularity has taken Lao society a little by surprise. Travellers and locals both raise two main tourism concerns over and over again.

The first is drugs. As Laos opened up to tourism, it gained a reputation as a free-for-all drug haven. It isn't. While opium-use has traditionally been sanctioned only for the elderly, attitudes to drugs like marijuana are not very liberal. There is a strong feeling that widespread opium- and marijuana-use by travellers, who are often seen as wealthy and cool by young Lao, is having a negative influence and drawing them into trouble from which they have little means of escape.

Many are also concerned that the exploitative and intrusive Thai-style hill-tribe trekking business is spilling over into Laos. There seems to be a simple solution: the Nam Ha Ecotourism Project, run from Luang Nam Tha town and Muang Sing, has set up treks with strict guidelines to limit the impact and maximise the economic benefits of trekking to villages (p390). So far the signs are good: it's a project worth supporting. A similar experiment is being conducted by the Savannakhet Provincial Tourism Office (p395).

STUDYING
There are no formal opportunities to study in Laos, but if you are passionately keen to learn more about this country, consider setting up your own study exchange, or develop a research topic, through your home university. Short courses in cooking are available in the capital and informal Lao language lessons are advertised in Vientiane.

TELEPHONE

Laos' country code is ☎ 856. To dial out of the country press ☎ 00 first.

Mobile Phones

If you bring an overseas mobile phone to Laos you can buy a sim card from GMS providers such as Tango for around US$5 and then purchase credits. But at the time of research coverage was limited to Vientiane province, Luang Prabang, Savannakhet and Pakse, where international SMSing is possible.

Mobile phone numbers in Laos have the prefix ☺ 020 followed by seven digits.

Phonecards

Phonecards for domestic calls can be bought at telephone offices and minimarts for use at the increasing number of public phones in provincial towns. International calls can be made from fixed landlines using an international phonecard.

TOURIST INFORMATION

The Lao National Tourism Authority maintains offices throughout Laos. Travel agencies and tour companies like Wildside Green Discovery, Diethelm and Lane Xang Travel are also excellent sources of information, often staffed by English speakers.

VISAS

On-the-spot 15-day tourist visas (US$30 with two passport photos) are available at Vientiane's Wattay International Airport, Luang Prabang International Airport, Pakse International Airport, the Thai–Lao Friendship Bridge at Nong Khai, the Thai border at Huay Xai, Savannakhet, Pakse and the Boten border with China in Luang Nam Tha.

However, the Lao government can be very fickle about its visa regulations and prices. It has cancelled all automatic visas without warning in the past so check the current situation before trying to enter the country. Lao consulates and travel agents in Vietnam, China, Cambodia and Thailand all issue visas and will be able to advise on the latest border crossing situation.

Once in Laos it is easy to obtain a visa extension costing US$1 per day (from the immigration office in Vientiane; Map p358) up to a maximum of 30 days. Elsewhere,

guesthouses and travel agents in provincial centres offer visa extension services for around US$2 to US$3 per day. Your passport will be sent to Vientiane, so it can take up to five days depending on how far from the capital you are. If you overstay your visa, you must pay a fine at the immigration checkpoint upon departure. The fine is US$10 for each day over the visa's expiry date.

VOLUNTEERING

It's not easy to find short-term volunteer work in Laos, however, one place you can walk in off the street is the Phoudindaeng Organic Farm in Vang Vieng (see p368). Occasionally groups seeking assistance from foreigners, such as the teachers' college in Luang Prabang or the orphanage in Phonsavan, will advertise at *falang* hang-outs like restaurants, tourist offices or guesthouses. If you're keen to contribute to the country in any small way, ask around for ideas or projects you can join.

WOMEN TRAVELLERS

Women travellers rarely get hassled in Laos, but it does occur. In fact, you are more likely to be troubled by aggressive Western 'guru' male travellers (you know, the ones who have unravelled the spiritual mysteries of existence and are willing to share them with you in exchange for an invitation to your room) than you are by Lao men. Apart from wandering darkened streets alone at night of course, the main potential danger areas are guesthouses and long-distance buses. Picking a guesthouse run by women will dramatically reduce your chances of trouble. Some women have also been hassled on overnight bus trips, particularly the bus to Vietnam from Vientiane. The best way to combat this threat is to travel in a group and stay alert.

WORKING

Compared to other countries in the region, finding work in Laos is relatively simple. There are an inordinate number of development organisations in Laos (160 at last count), where foreigners with skills can find employment. The old standby of teaching English is always an option and schools in Vientiane are often hiring. Ask around.

Malaysia

HIGHLIGHTS

- **Taman Negara** – balancing like a monkey on the creaky jungle-canopy walk (p479)
- **Pulau Perhentian** – snorkelling among technicolour schools of fish in the crystal-clear water (p472)
- **Mt Kinabalu** – scaling the formidably high granite bulk of Mt Kinabalu (p508)
- **Cameron Highlands** – sipping a freshly snipped brew of full-bodied Highlands tea (p442)
- **Gunung Mulu** – watching bats stream out of the world's biggest cave maw (p498)
- **Off the beaten track** – tracking wild orang-utans beside Sungai Kinabatangan (p513)

FAST FACTS

- **ATMs** widespread, limited on islands
- **Budget** US$13 a day
- **Capital** Kuala Lumpur (KL)
- **Costs** dorm bed RM10, three meals RM18, two beers RM14, 4hr bus ride RM20
- **Country code** ☎ 60
- **Famous for** beautiful island beaches, orang-utans, number of variations on laksa and a perplexing devotion to the durian
- **Languages** Bahasa Melayu (official), Chinese (Hakka & Hokkien dialects), Tamil, English
- **Money** US$1 = RM3.77 (ringgit)
- **Phrases** *selamat pagi* (good morning), *terima kasih* (thank you)
- **Population** 24 million
- **Seasons** dry Apr-Oct, wet Nov-Mar (Malay peninsular regions; east coast – Nov-Mar, west coast – May-Oct)
- **Visas** people of most nationalities visiting Malaysia are presented with a 30- to 90-day visa on arrival

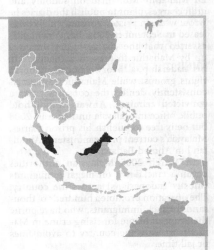

TRAVEL HINT

Malaysians can be ruthless when it comes to queuing at ticket counters. Get close to the counter and surge forward at the first possible opportunity.

OVERLAND ROUTES

From Peninsular Malaysia, you can head into Thailand and Singapore. From Sarawak, you can enter Indonesia (Kalimantan) and Brunei. Brunei can also be entered from Sabah.

Malaysia has a marvellous knack for soothing your senses. The hassles here are few, the landscapes – from intensely beautiful islands and mountains to the verdant forests and jungles in between – are appealingly diverse, and most of the inhabitants would have to be asleep to be more laid back. Arriving here from the communal chaos of other Southeast Asian destinations, you can breathe a deep, slow sigh of relief before ambling around the well-preserved architecture of old colonial towns like Melaka, plunging into the thick of virgin jungles in Sarawak, or eating your way across food courts stocked with multi-ethnic dishes.

Don't presume this means that Malaysia lacks intrigue or excitement. Its complex but surprisingly harmonious cultural make-up gives it a great social life, and some prominent eccentricities – its technology-crazy shopping malls sell cutting-edge goods, but the sound systems of bars and cafés are trapped in a 1980s twilight zone in which REO Speedwagon still reigns supreme. And travellers quickly adopt the adventurous spirit in Borneo, where they sail down remote jungle rivers looking for apes and elephants, climb craggy high-altitude peaks, and pay their respects to tribespeople deep in the interior of this wild island.

CURRENT EVENTS

In 2006, former deputy PM Anwar Ibrahim, jailed in 1998 by then prime minister Dr Mahathir Mohamad on sodomy and graft charges, plans to publish the diaries he wrote while in prison. Anwar, who was released in September 2004, has consistently asserted that the charges were dreamed up by Mahathir to prevent a challenge to his leadership, a theory echoed by human rights groups, while Mahathir has just as consistently denied the conspiracy. As a convicted criminal, Anwar cannot hold public office in Malaysia until at least 2008 but he is free to publish his prison diaries. Malaysia's current prime minister is Abdullah bin Ahmad Badawi.

In March 2005 Malaysian authorities began a crackdown on illegal immigrants (mostly Indonesians) across the country. The operation prompted hundreds of thousands of such immigrants, who have borne the brunt of blame for rising crime in Malaysia, to leave the country to avoid fines or jail time.

HISTORY

The earliest evidence of human life in the region is a 40,000-year-old skull found in Sarawak's Niah Caves. But it was only around 10,000 years ago that the aboriginal Malays, the Orang Asli (see p418 for more information), began moving down the peninsula from a probable starting point in southwestern China.

By the 2nd century, Europeans were familiar with Malaya, and Indian traders had made regular visits in their search for gold, tin and jungle woods. Within the next century Malaya was ruled by the Funan empire, centred in what's now Cambodia, but more significant was the domination of the Sumatra-based Srivijayan empire between the 7th and 13th centuries.

In 1405 the Chinese admiral Cheng Ho arrived in Melaka with promises of protection from the Siamese encroaching from the north. With Chinese support, the power of Melaka extended to include most of the Malay peninsula. Islam arrived in Melaka around this time and soon spread through Malaya. Melaka's wealth and prosperity attracted European interest and it was taken over by the Portuguese in 1511, then the Dutch in 1641 and the British in 1795.

In 1838 James Brooke, a British adventurer, arrived to find the Brunei sultanate fending off rebellion from inland tribes. Brooke quashed the rebellion and in reward was granted power over part of Sarawak. Appointing himself Raja Brooke, he founded a dynasty that lasted 100 years. By 1881 Sabah was controlled by the British government, which eventually acquired Sarawak after WWII when the third Raja Brooke realised he couldn't afford the region's upkeep. In the early 20th century the British brought in Chinese and Indians, which radically changed the country's racial make-up.

Malaya achieved *merdeka* (independence) in 1957, but it was followed by a period of instability due to an internal Communist uprising and an external confrontation with neighbouring Indonesia. In 1963 the north Borneo states of Sabah and Sarawak, along with Singapore, joined Malaya to create Malaysia. In 1969 violent interracial riots broke out, particularly in Kuala Lumpur, and hundreds of people

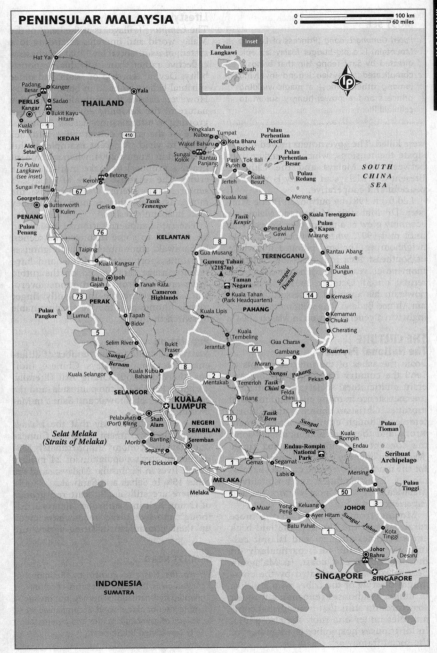

PENINSULAR MALAYSIA

0 — 100 km
0 — 60 miles

Inset
Pulau Langkawi
Kuah

Hat Yai

Padang Besar
Kangar
PERLIS
Kangar
Sadao
Bukit Kayu Hitam
Kuala Perlis
THAILAND
Yala

KEDAH
410

Alor Setar
To Pulau Langkawi (see inset)

Sungai Petani
Keroh
Betong
67

Georgetown
Butterworth
Kulim
PENANG
Pulau Penang
Gerik
4
Tasik Temengor

Taiping
76
KELANTAN

Kuala Kangsar
8

Batu Gajah
Ipoh
Tasik Kenyir

Tanah Rata
Cameron Highlands
Gua Musang
Gunung Tahan (2187m) ▲

Pengkalan Kubor
Tumpat
Wakaf Baharu
Kota Bharu
Bachok
Sungai Kolok
Rantau Panjang
Pasir Puteh
Tok Bali
Jerteh
Kuala Besut
Pulau Perhentian Kecil
Pulau Perhentian Besar
Pulau Redang

SOUTH CHINA SEA

Kuala Krai
3
Merang
Kuala Terengganu
Pengkalan Gawi
Pulau Kapas
Marang
TERENGGANU
Rantau Abang

73
PERAK
Tapah
Bidor

Taman Negara
Kuala Tahan (Park Headquarters)
Kuala Lipis
PAHANG
Kuala Dungun
3
14
Kemasik

Pulau Pangkor
Lumut
5
Selim River
Bukit Fraser
Jerantut
Kuala Tembeling
64
Gua Charas
Gambang
Maran
Kemaman
Chukai
Cherating
Kuantan

Sungai Bernam
Kuala Selangor
Kuala Kubu Baharu
8
Mentakab
Temerloh
2
Tasik Chini
Triang
Sungai Pahang
Pekan

SELANGOR
Pelabuhan (Port) Klang
Shah Alam
KUALA LUMPUR
NEGERI SEMBILAN
Seremban
10
Tasik Chini
Felda Chini
12

Selat Melaka (Straits of Melaka)
Morib
Banting
Sepang
Port Dickson
11
Tasik Bera
Sungai Rompin
Kuala Rompin
Endau
Pulau Tioman

Seribuat Archipelago

1
Gemas
Segamat
Endau-Rompin National Park
Labis
Mersing
Pulau Tinggi

MELAKA
Melaka
5
Muar
Yong Peng
Keluang
50
Jemaluang
JOHOR
3

Batu Pahat
Ayer Hitam
Sungai Johor
Kota Tinggi
1
Johor Bahru
Desaru

INDONESIA
SUMATRA
SINGAPORE
SINGAPORE

MUST SEE

Puteri Gunung Ledang (Princess of Ledang Mountain) is a big-budget Malaysian epic directed by Saw Teong Hin that brings a complicated Malaysian legend involving (among other things) a magic-wielding princess and a power-hungry sultan to celluloid life.

were killed. The government moved to dissipate the tensions, which existed mainly between the Malays and the Chinese. Present-day Malaysian society is relatively peaceful and cooperative.

Led from 1981 by outspoken Prime Minister Dr Mahathir Mohamad, Malaysia's economy grew at a rate of over 8% per year until mid-1997, when a currency crisis in neighbouring Thailand plunged the whole of Southeast Asia into recession. After 22 momentous years, Dr Mahathir Mohamad retired on 31 October 2003. He handed power to his anointed successor, Abdullah bin Ahmad Badawi, who went on to convincingly win a general election in March 2004.

THE CULTURE
The National Psyche

From the ashes of the interracial riots of 1969 the country has forged a more tolerant multicultural society, exemplified by the coexistence in many cities and towns of mosques, Christian churches and Chinese temples. Though ethnic loyalties remain strong and there are undeniable tensions, the concept of a much-discussed single 'Malaysian' identity is gaining credence and for the most part everyone coexists harmoniously. The friendliness and hospitality of Malaysians is what most visitors see and experience.

Moving from the cities to the more rural parts of the country, the laid-back ethos becomes stronger and Islamic culture comes to the fore, particularly on the peninsula's east coast. In Malaysian Borneo you'll be fascinated by the communal lifestyle of the tribes who still live in jungle longhouses (enormous wooden structures on stilts that house tribal communities under one roof, see also p491). In longhouses hospitality is a key part of the social framework.

Lifestyle

The *kampung* (village) is at the heart of the Malay world and operates according to a system of *adat* (social law) that emphasises collective rather than individual responsibility. Devout worship of Islam and older spiritual beliefs go hand in hand with this. However, despite the mutually supportive nature of the *kampung* environment, and growing Westernisation across Malaysia, some of the more conservative attitudes refuse to yield. A recent example of this occurred in August 2004, when parliament heard a proposal to make marital rape a crime. The response of one of Malaysia's senior Islamic clerics was to oppose the move, asserting that women must obey their husband's desires.

The rapid modernisation of Malaysian life has led to some incongruous scenes. In Sarawak, some ramshackle longhouses and huts sport satellite dishes and have recent-vintage cars parked on the rutted driveways out front. And almost everywhere you go people incessantly finger mobile phones as if they're simply unable to switch them off.

Population

Malaysians come from a number of different ethnic groups: Malays, Chinese, Indians, the indigenous Orang Asli (literally, 'Original People') of the peninsula, and the various tribes of Sarawak and Sabah in Malaysian Borneo.

It's reasonable to say that the Malays control the government while the Chinese dominate the economy. Approximately 85% of the country's population of 24 million people lives in Peninsular Malaysia and the other 15% in Sabah and Sarawak.

There are still small, scattered groups of Orang Asli in Peninsular Malaysia. Although most of these people have given up their nomadic or shifting-agriculture

MUST READ

Into the Heart of Borneo by Redmond O'Hanlon is the account of this cheerfully ill-prepared naturalist's journey into the remote interior of the island, accompanied by several idiosyncratic guides and a perpetually bewildered British poet.

> **DID YOU KNOW?**
>
> The *bomoh*, the Malay equivalent of a witch doctor, remains an important part of daily life for many rural communities in Malaysia. Even politicians have been known to consult them.

techniques and have been absorbed into modern Malay society, a few such groups still live in the forests.

Dayak is the term used for the non-Muslim people of Borneo. It's estimated there are more than 200 Dayak tribes in Borneo, including the Iban and Bidayuh in Sarawak and the Kadazan in Sabah. Smaller groups include the Kenyah, Kayan and Penan, whose way of life and traditional lands are rapidly disappearing.

RELIGION

The Malays are almost all Muslims. But despite Islam being the state religion, freedom of religion is guaranteed. The Chinese are predominantly followers of Taoism and Buddhism, though some are Christians. The majority of the region's Indian population comes from the south of India and are Hindu and Christian, although a sizeable percentage are Muslim.

While Christianity has made no great inroads into Peninsular Malaysia, it has had a much greater impact in Malaysian Borneo, where many indigenous people have been converted and carry Christian as well as traditional names. Others still follow animist traditions.

ARTS

It's along the predominantly Malay east coast of Peninsular Malaysia that you'll find Malay arts and crafts, culture and games at their liveliest. Malaysian Borneo is replete with the arts and crafts of the country's indigenous peoples.

Arts & Crafts

A famous Malaysian Bornean art is *pua kumbu*, a colourful weaving technique used to produce both everyday and ceremonial items.

The most skilled woodcarvers are generally held to be the Kenyah and Kayan peoples, who used to carve enormous, finely detailed *kelirieng* (burial columns) from tree trunks.

Originally an Indonesian craft, the production of batik cloth is popular in Malaysia and has its home in Kelantan. A speciality of Kelantan and Terengganu, *kain songket* is a handwoven fabric with gold and silver threads through the material. *Mengkuang* is a far more prosaic form of weaving using pandanus leaves and strips of bamboo to make baskets, bags and mats.

Kelantan's silversmiths specialise in filigree and repoussé work – Kota Bharu is a silverworking centre. Brasswork is an equally traditional skill in Kuala Terengganu.

Dance

Menora is a dance-drama of Thai origin performed by an all-male cast dressed in grotesque masks; *mak yong* is the female version. The upbeat *joget* (better known around Melaka as *chakuncha*) is Malaysia's most popular traditional dance, often performed at Malay weddings by professional dancers.

Rebana kercing is a dance performed by young men to the accompaniment of tambourines. The *rodat* is a dance from Terengganu and is accompanied by the *tar* drum.

Music

Traditional Malay music is based largely on the *gendang* (drum), of which there are more than a dozen types. Other percussion instruments include the *gong, cerucap* (made of shells), *raurau* (coconut shells), *kertuk* and *pertuang* (both made from bamboo), and the wooden *celampang*.

Wind instruments include a number of types of flute (such as the *seruling* and *serunai)* and the trumpet-like *nafiri*, while stringed instruments include the *biola, gambus* and *sundatang*.

The *gamelan*, a traditional Indonesian gong-orchestra, is also found in the state of Kelantan, where a typical ensemble will comprise four different gongs, two xylophones and a large drum.

> **WEB TIP**
>
> The best source of information on what's currently going on in the Malaysian arts scene is **www.kakiseni.com**.

ENVIRONMENT

Malaysia has attracted significant criticism for its logging practices, which are believed to have destroyed more than 60% of the country's rainforests. Though logging wreaks untold ecological damage and has caused the displacement of many tribal people, the priority seems to be the generation of at least US$4.5 billion per year for big business. Another growing phenomenon, particularly in Sabah, is the palm-tree plantation, where vast swathes of land are razed and planted with trees that yield lucrative palm oil. Malaysia has also undertaken construction of the highly controversial Bakun Dam in Sarawak, scheduled to become Southeast Asia's biggest dam in 2006 when it will drown hundreds of square kilometres of virgin rainforest and will have forced up to 10,000 indigenous people from their homes. In equally bad environmental news, much of the power generated at Bakun looks likely to go into a giant aluminium smelter slated to be built in Sarawak by 2007.

The Land

Malaysia covers 329,758 sq km and consists of two distinct regions. Peninsular Malaysia is the long finger of land extending south from Asia and is mostly covered by dense jungle, particularly the mountainous northern half. The peninsula's western side has a large fertile plain running to the sea, while the eastern side is fringed with sandy beaches. Malaysian Borneo consists of Sarawak and Sabah, both states covered in thick jungle and with extensive river systems. Sabah is crowned by Mt Kinabalu (4101m), the highest mountain between the Himalayas and New Guinea.

Wildlife

Malaysia's ancient rainforests, climatic stability, plentiful rainfall and tropical-greenhouse heat have endowed it with a cornucopia of life forms. In Peninsular Malaysia alone there are over 8000 species of flowering plants, including the world's tallest tropical tree species, the *tualang*. In Malaysian Borneo, where hundreds of new species have been discovered in the past decade, you'll find the world's largest flower, the rafflesia, measuring up to 1m across, as well as the world's biggest cockroach. Mammals include elephants, rhinos (extremely rare), tapirs, tigers, leopards, honey bears, *tempadau* (forest cattle), gibbons and monkeys (including, in Borneo, the bizarre proboscis monkey), orang-utans and scaly anteaters (*pangolins*). Bird species include spectacular pheasants, sacred hornbills and many groups of colourful birds such as kingfishers, sunbirds, woodpeckers and barbets. Snakes include cobras, vipers and pythons.

National Parks

Malaysia's 19 national parks cover barely 5% of the country's land mass. The country's major national park is Taman Negara, on the peninsula, while Gunung Mulu and Kinabalu are the two main parks in Sarawak and Sabah respectively. Especially on Borneo, the rarity and uniqueness of local flora and fauna is such that scientists – from dragonfly experts to palm-tree specialists – are regular visitors and vocal proponents of new parks and reserves both on land and in the surrounding waters. The Malaysian government created one such marine reserve around Pulau Sipadan in 2005 and is considering submitting the island and its heavenly waters for World Heritage listing.

TRANSPORT

This section of text is divided into two separate parts, dealing first with Peninsular Malaysia and then with Malaysian Borneo.

PENINSULAR MALAYSIA
Getting There & Away
AIR

The gateway to Peninsular Malaysia is the city of Kuala Lumpur, although Pulau Penang and Johor Bahru (JB) also have international connections. Singapore is a handy arrival/departure point, as it is just a short trip across the Causeway from JB and generally has more international connections. Malaysia Airlines is the country's main airline carrier.

Some airlines with offices in KL:

Aeroflot (Map p431; www.aeroflot.ru/eng; ☎ 03-2161 0231; 17 Wisma Kia Peng, Jl Perak)

Air India (☎ 03-2142 0166; www.airindia.com; Angkasaraya Bldg, 123 Jl Ampang)
British Airways/Qantas (☎ 1800 881 260; www.british airways.com; 8th fl, West Wing, Rohas Terkasa, 8 Jl Perak)
Cathay Pacific Airways (☎ 03-2078 3377; www .cathaypacific.com; Suite 22.01, 22nd fl, Menara IMC, 8 Jl Sultan Ismail)
China Airlines (☎ 03-2142 7344; www.china-airlines .com; Amoda Bldg, 22 Jl Imbi)
Garuda Indonesian Airlines (☎ 03-2162 2811; www.garuda-indonesia.com; Suite 19.03, 19th fl, Menara Citibank, Jl Ampang)
Japan Airlines (☎ 03-2161 1722; www.jal.com; 20th fl, Menara Citibank, Jl Ampang)
Lufthansa (Map p431; ☎ 03-2161 4666; www .lufthansa.com; 18th fl, Kenanga International Bldg, Jl Sultan Ismail)
Malaysia Airlines (Map p431; ☎ 1300 883 000; 03-2161 0555; www.malaysiaairlines.com); Bangunan MAS (☎ 03-7846 3000; Jl Sultan Ismail); KL Sentral Station (☎ 03-2272 4260)
Royal Brunei Airlines (Map p431; ☎ 03-2070 7166; www.bruneiair.com; Menara UBN, 10 Jl P Ramlee)
Royal Phnom Penh Airways (www.rlppairways.com)
Singapore Airlines (☎ 03-2692 3122; www.singa poreair.com; Wisma SIA, 2 Jl Dang Wangi)
Thai Airways International (THAI; ☎ 03-2031 2900; www.thaiairways.com; 30 Wisma Goldhill, 67 Jl Raja Chulan)
Vietnam Airlines (www.vietnamairlines.com)
Virgin Atlantic (☎ 03-2143 0322; www.virgin-atlantic .com; 25th fl, Central Plaza, Jl Sultan Ismail)

Brunei
You can fly from KL to Bandar Seri Begawan. Because of the difference in exchange rates, it's around 40% cheaper to fly to Brunei from Malaysia than vice versa.

Cambodia
Flights between KL and Phnom Penh are available with Malaysia Airlines and Royal Phnom Penh Airways.

Indonesia
It's a short hop from Pulau Penang to Medan in Sumatra. To Java, the cheapest connections are from Singapore. Discounts are sometimes available on flights from Bali to Singapore.

Malaysian Borneo
Flights are available from JB and KL to Kota Kinabalu (KK) in Sabah and to Kuching in Sarawak.

Philippines
You can fly with Malaysia Airlines from KL to Cebu/Manila.

Singapore
Malaysia Airlines and Singapore Airlines sometimes make seats available on flights between KL and Singapore at discounted rates on a first-come, first-served basis. Malaysia Airlines also connects Singapore to Langkawi and Penang.

Thailand
There are flights between Bangkok and KL.

Vietnam
Malaysia Airlines and Vietnam Airlines operate flights from KL to Ho Chi Minh City and Hanoi.

BOAT
There are no services connecting the peninsula with Malaysian Borneo.

Indonesia
The main ferry routes between Peninsular Malaysia and Sumatra are Georgetown–Medan and Melaka–Dumai.

The popular crossing between Georgetown and Medan is handled by two companies that, between them, have services most days of the week. The boats actually land in Belawan in Sumatra, and the journey to Medan is completed by bus (included in the price). Indonesian visa requirements have changed recently for arrivals in Belawan. See p454 for full details of this route.

Twice daily high-speed ferries run between Melaka and Dumai in Sumatra. Dumai is now a visa-free entry port into Indonesia for citizens of most countries. See p441 for details.

You can also take a boat from the Bebas Cukai ferry terminal in JB (see p461) direct to Batu Ampar and Tanjung Pinang, both in Sumatra. And you can take a ferry from Kukup, in Johor, to Tanjung Balai in Sumatra.

Singapore
There are several ferry connections from Malaysia to Singapore, but most people cross by road via the Causeway. The main ferry crossing is between JB in Malaysia, and Changi, Singapore. High-speed

MALAYSIA

catamarans run between Pulau Tioman, Malaysia, and the Tanah Merah ferry terminal in Singapore. Small boats also ply between Pengerang in Johor and Changi. For further information see p661.

Thailand
Regular daily boats run between Pulau Langkawi (p459) and Satun (p798) in Thailand. There are customs and immigration posts here, although it's an expensive entry/exit point. Get your passport stamped on entry.

BUS & TRAIN
Thailand
On the western side of Peninsular Malaysia, you can travel by bus from Alor Setar to the border crossing at Bukit Kayu Hitam. There's also a train passing through Padang Besar and then heading north into Thailand bound for Hat Yai. For details of both routes, see p459.

On the peninsula's eastern side you can bus it from Kota Bharu to the border town of Rantau Panjang; see p477.

Singapore
At the southern tip of Peninsular Malaysia you can cross into Singapore from Johor Bahru (see p460).

Getting Around
AIR
Malaysia Airlines (☎ 1300 883 000; www.malaysia airlines.com.my) is the country's main domestic

operator, linking major regional centres on the peninsula and on Pulau Langkawi. It will change flight reservations on the spot in any of its offices, free of charge. **Pelangi Air** (☎ 06-317 4175) is a small regional airline that has useful services to Ipoh and Langkawi; reservations can be made through Malaysia Airlines. The Malaysian Air Fares map (p422) details key local routes and one-way economy fares.

Air Asia (☎ 1300 889 933; www.airasia.com) is a no-frills airline offering super-cheap domestic flights. It helps if you're vertically challenged but flights in Malaysia are quick and you can cover more of the country than if you travelled by road. Air Asia flies to/from KL to Langkawi, Pulau Penang, Kota Bharu and Kuala Terengganu, plus smaller destinations.

Tiny **Berjaya Air** (☎ 03-2145 2828; www.ber jaya-air.com) has flights between KL, Pulau Tioman and Pulau Pangkor.

BOAT
Boats and ferries sail between the peninsula and offshore islands. Some ferry operators are notoriously lax about observing safety rules and local authorities are often nonexistent. If a boat looks overloaded or otherwise unsafe, do not board it.

BUS
Peninsular Malaysia has an excellent bus system. Public buses do local runs and a variety of privately operated buses generally handle

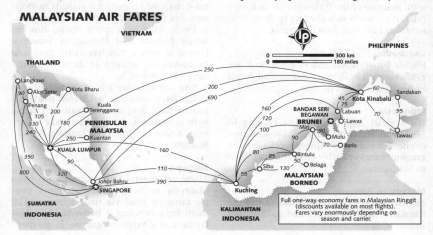

MALAYSIAN AIR FARES

Full one-way economy fares in Malaysian Ringgit (discounts available on most flights). Fares vary enormously depending on season and carrier.

the longer trips. In larger towns there may be several bus stations. Local and regional buses often operate from one station and long-distance buses from another; in other cases, KL for example, bus stations are differentiated by the destinations they serve.

Buses are an economical form of transport, reasonably comfortable and seats can be reserved, though on major runs you can often just turn up and get on the next bus. On many routes there are air-con buses, which usually cost just a few ringgit more than regular buses.

Ekspres, in the Malaysian context, often means indeterminate stops. To make up this time many long-distance bus drivers tend to think of the *lebuhraya* (highway) as their personal Formula One track.

CAR

Driving in Peninsular Malaysia is a breeze compared to most Asian countries; the roads are generally high quality, plenty of new cars are available and driving standards aren't too hair-raising. Road rules are basically the same as in Britain and Australia. Cars are right-hand drive and you drive on the left side of the road. However, you should be constantly aware of the hazards posed by stray animals and numerous motorcyclists.

Unlimited-distance rental rates for a 1.3L Proton Saga, the cheapest and most popular car in the country, cost from around RM130/870 per day/week, including insurance and collision-damage waiver.

HITCHING

Hitching is never entirely safe in any country and we don't recommend it. True, Malaysia has long had a reputation for being an excellent place to hitchhike but, with the ease of bus travel, most travellers don't bother. On the west coast, hitching is quite easy but it's not possible on the main *lebuhraya*. On the east coast, traffic is lighter and there may be long waits between rides.

LOCAL TRANSPORT

Local transport varies but almost always includes local buses and taxis. In many Peninsular Malaysian towns there are also bicycle rickshaws. While these are dying out in KL and have become principally a tourist gimmick in many Malaysian cities,

---

REAR VIEWS

When it comes to the interior decoration of their motor vehicles, every Malaysian driver is an artist at heart. Glance out the window of your bus and you'll look down on plastic flower gardens flourishing along a car's back shelf, mini-shrines to favourite deities on the dashboard or platoons of cartoon characters like Garfield stuck fast to passenger-side windows. But it's in the garnishing of rear-view mirrors that Malaysians really outdo themselves. Following is just some of the stuff we saw dangling in front of drivers:

- fluffy dice the size of bricks
- large plastic skulls
- orchards of plastic fruit
- baby dummies
- chattering dolls
- CDs
- old sunglasses

---

they are still a viable form of transport elsewhere. Indeed, in places like Georgetown, with its convoluted and narrow streets, a bicycle rickshaw is probably the best way of getting around.

TAXI

You'll be hard pressed to find a taxi with an operational meter in Malaysia and, except where pre-purchased coupons are involved or where drivers have agreed on a standard route fare, you will inevitably have to negotiate with the driver. On their worst days, taxi drivers will charge extortionate amounts. Don't be afraid to turn down a fare you think is too high and walk over to the next taxi to ask what they charge, or to negotiate a fairer price. Even better, ask at your hotel or a visitors centre about reasonable fares.

Long-distance (or share) taxis are an expensive way to travel. They work on fixed fares for the entire car and will head off when a full complement of passengers (usually four people) turns up. Between major towns you have a reasonable chance of finding other passengers without having to wait too long; otherwise, you'll have to charter a whole taxi at four times the single fare.

TRAIN

Peninsular Malaysia has a modern, comfortable and economical railway service that has basically two lines. One runs from Singapore to KL, to Butterworth and on into Thailand. The other line, known as the Jungle Railway, cuts through the interior of Malaysia linking Gemas, Taman Negara with Kota Bharu, a transit town for Pulau Perhentian.

Passes

The privatised national railway company, **Keretapi Tanah Melayu** (KTM; ☎ 03-2267 1200, 2773 1430; www.ktmb.com.my), offers a tourist Rail Pass for five days (adult US$35), 10 days (adult US$55) and 15 days (adult US$70). This pass entitles the holder to unlimited travel on any class of train but does not include sleeping-berth charges. Rail passes are available only to foreigners and can be purchased at KL, JB, Butterworth, Pelabuhan (Port) Klang, Padang Besar, Wakaf Baharu and Butterworth train stations. You have to do an awful lot of train travel to make it worthwhile.

Services & Classes

Peninsular Malaysia has three main types of rail services: express, limited express and local trains. Express trains are airconditioned and generally 1st and 2nd class only, and on night trains there's a choice of berths or seats. Limited express trains may have 2nd and 3rd class only but some have 1st, 2nd and 3rd class with overnight sleepers. Local trains are usually 3rd class only, but some have 2nd class.

Express fares to/from KL: to Butterworth (from RM17), Ipoh (from RM10), JB (from RM33) and Jerantut (from RM18).

MALAYSIAN BORNEO
Getting There & Away
AIR

The main airport for Sarawak is in Kuching, while for Sabah it's in Kota Kinabalu. **Malaysia Airlines** (☎ 1300 883 000; www.malaysiaairlines.com .my) has flights linking both cities with KL, though flying from JB is the cheapest way to reach Sarawak. **Air Asia** (☎ 1300 889 933; www.air asia.com) offers bargain-basement flights on the same routes. **Royal Brunei Airlines** (www .bruneiair.com) flies between Kota Kinabalu and Bandar Seri Begawan (BSB), in Brunei).

There are also weekly flights between Kuching and Pontianak in Kalimantan (Indonesia), and between Tawau in Sabah and Tarakan in Kalimantan.

BOAT

You can travel by boat from Limbang in Sarawak to Brunei (see p500). Boats also make the run between Brunei and Pulau Labuan in Sabah (see p507), where you can catch boats onward to KK. Boats head from Tawau in Sabah to Nunukan in Kalimantan and then on to Tarakan (see p514). Passenger ferries run between Sandakan and Zamboanga in the Philippines (see p512).

BUS

Sarawak shares borders with Kalimantan and Brunei. Regular buses run between Kuching and the Indonesian city of Pontianak via the visa-free entry point between Tebedu and Entikong (for details see p488), and you can also catch buses from Miri across the Bruneian border into Kuala Belait (see p497).

Getting Around
AIR

Malaysia Airlines (☎ 1300 883 000; www.malaysiaair lines.com.my) has a comprehensive network of Bornean flights, including a rural air service which consists of 18-seater Twin Otter aircraft. Flying is sometimes the most practical means of reaching a remote area, one example being Bario up in the highlands. During school holidays (mid-May to mid-June and late October to early December) it can be nearly impossible to get a seat on any flight into the interior at short notice.

BOAT

There are no ferry services between Malaysian Borneo and the peninsula. Travel on the larger rivers, such as the Rejang and Baram, is accomplished in fast passenger launches known by the generic term *ekspres,* which carry around 100 people. Travel on smaller, squeezier waterways is mainly by longboat (often motorised). Be prepared to pay for your longboat experience, as fuel isn't cheap in remote areas. It's best to organise a group to share costs.

BUS & CAR

Travellers arriving from elsewhere in Malaysia will be pleasantly surprised by the relative sanity of Bornean drivers (bus and minivan drivers excepted of course). The main road in Sarawak winds from Kuching to the Brunei border and is sealed all the way, and an estimated 70 bus companies negotiate part or all of this route.

The main destinations in Sabah – from Beaufort in the southwest to Tawau in the southeast – are linked by a reasonable system of roads. There's no highway linking Sarawak and Sabah.

See p423 for an idea of starting prices for car rental.

TAXI
See p423 for the lowdown on Malaysian taxis.

TRAIN
In Sabah there's a narrow-gauge railway line that can transport you from KK south to Beaufort and then through Sungai Pegas gorge to Tenom. The trip through the gorge is the worthwhile bit; for more information see p506.

KUALA LUMPUR

☎ 03 / pop 1.4 million

Kuala Lumpur (KL) is a city of trees and skyscrapers, balancing a modern metropolis in a jungle landscape. Magnificent Islamic high-rises ringed by an island of trees tower over multilane highways, while small-scale commerce clogs cramped Chinatown and Little India. KL has matured from a tin-mining frontier into an affluent capital where careers and cars careen ambitiously forward. Malaysia's unique twist on multiculturalism is strongly pronounced in the capital city. Here the ethnic triumvirate (Chinese, Indian and Malay) mingle in the workplace but maintain their separate cultural orbits.

For a first-time touchdown in Asia, KL is a baby pool. Transport from the airport is effortless, scams are minimal, and the city is more humane than Southeast Asia's other megacities.

ORIENTATION
Merdeka Square is the traditional heart of KL. Southeast across the river, the banking district merges into Chinatown, popular with travellers for its budget accommodation and lively night market.

East of Merdeka Square is Masjid Jamek, at the intersection of the Star and Putra Light Rail Transit (LRT) lines. Jl Tun Perak, a major trunk road, leads east to the long-distance transport hub of the country, the Puduraya bus station.

To the east of Puduraya bus station, around Jl Sultan Ismail, the Golden Triangle is the modern, upmarket heart of the new KL.

The transport-hub KL Sentral station (and the KL City Air Terminal) is in the Brickfields area, southeast of the centre.

(Continued on page 429)

GETTING INTO TOWN

The efficient KLIA Ekspres (adult one way/return RM35/65, 28 minutes, every 15 minutes from 5am to 1am) spirits you to/from the airport (KLIA) to KL Sentral train station. This is without doubt the easiest way to travel to/from the airport.

If you have more time than money, catch the express bus (RM14, 45 minutes, hourly from 7am to 9pm) from the KLIA bus terminal (ground level, Block C of the covered car park) to Chan Sow Lin station on the Star Light Rail Transit (LRT) line, which will deliver you to various central KL destinations. Build in a lot of time for traffic.

Taxis from KLIA operate on a fixed-fare coupon system. Purchase a coupon from a counter at the arrival hall and use it to pay the driver. Standard taxis cost RM60 to RM70.

If your hotel isn't near an LRT station, consider hopping one of the airport coaches (RM20) that shuttle passengers between designated hotels in KL to the airport; schedules vary. Ticketing offices are on the ground floor of KLIA complex. For transport die-hards, airport coaches (RM20) also connect KLIA to Chan Sow Lin station on the Star LRT (about one hour). These buses depart for the airport every 30 minutes from 5am to 10.30pm and 6.15am to 12.30pm in the opposite direction.

MALAYSIA

KUALA LUMPUR

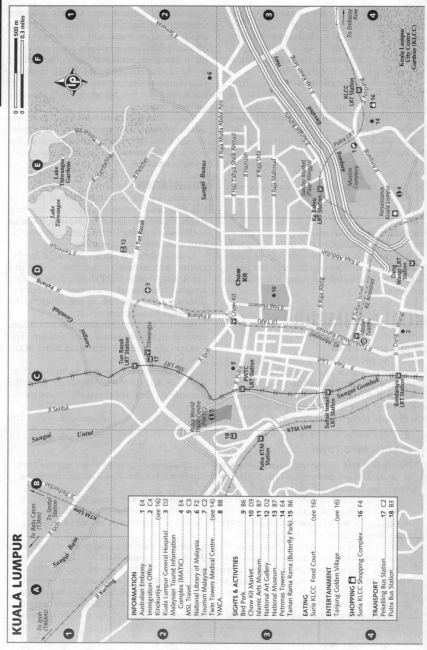

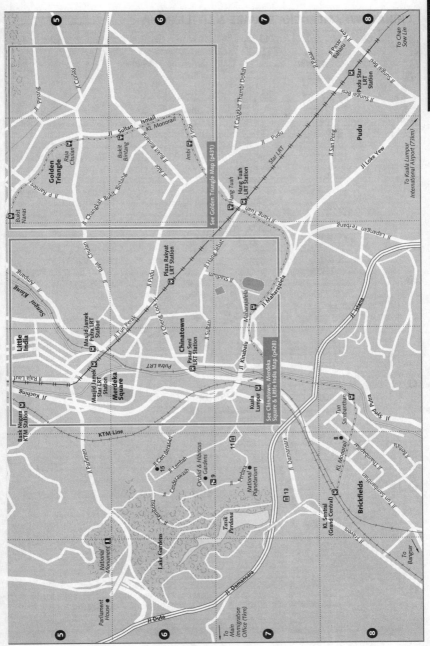

MALAYSIA

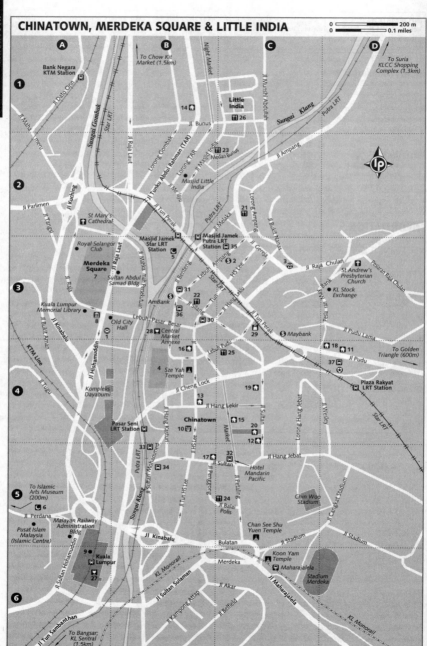

CHINATOWN, MERDEKA SQUARE & LITTLE INDIA

(Continued from page 425)

INFORMATION
Bookshops
Kinokuniya (Map pp426–7; ☎ 2164 8133; 4th fl, Suria KLCC Shopping Complex)

MPH Bookstores (Map p431; ☎ 2142 8231; Ground fl, BB Plaza, Jl Bukit Bintang) Also a branch at Mid Valley Megamall.

Silverfish Books (☎ 2284 4837; www.silverfishbooks .com; 67-1 Jl Telawi 3, Bangsar) Publisher of contemporary Malaysian literature.

Emergency
Fire (☎ 994)
Police & ambulance (☎ 999)

Immigration Offices
Immigration Office – City Centre Branch (Map pp426–7; ☎ 2698 0377; Kompleks Wilayah, cnr Jl Dang Wangi & Jl TAR)

Main Immigration Office (☎ 2095 5077; Block I, Pusat Bandar Damansara) Visa extensions. 1km west of Lake Gardens.

Internet Access
Internet shops turn over frequently but are usually replaced by another nearby. Try Jl Sultan or the streets surrounding Kota Raya shopping centre in Chinatown (both on Map p428). Rates per hour start at RM2.

Libraries
National Library of Malaysia (Map pp426–7; ☎ 2687 1700; www.pnm.my; 232 Jl Tun Razak)

Medical Services
Kuala Lumpur General Hospital (Map pp426–7; ☎ 2615 5555; Jl Pahang)

Twin Towers Medical Centre (Map pp426–7; ☎ 2382 3500; Lot 401 F&G, 4th fl, Suria KLCC Shopping Complex)

Money
Banks and ATMs are concentrated around Jl Silang at the northern edge of Chinatown. Moneychangers are located in shopping malls, along Lebuh Ampang and near Klang bus station on Jl Sultan (see Map p428).

Post
Main Post Office (Map p428; JL Raja Laut; ⏰ 8.30am–6pm Mon-Sat) The office is closed on the first Saturday of the month. Poste restante mail is held at the information desk on the 2nd floor.

Telephone
Phonecards are widely available in KL but finding a compatible public phone is a challenge, especially if you leave KL. Shops in Chinatown and on Jl Bukit Bintang have pay-per-call IDD-STD phones. Call ☎ 103 for local directory inquiries and ☎ 108 for the international operator.

Telekom Malaysia (Map p428; Jl Raja Chulan; ⏰ 8.30am-4.30pm Mon-Fri, 8.30am-12.30pm Sat) Calls can be made here.

Tourist Information
Malaysian Tourist Information Complex (Matic; Map pp426–7; ☎ 2164 3929; 109 Jl Ampang; ⏰ 9am–midnight) KL's largest and most useful tourist office; it also holds regular cultural performances.

Travel Agencies
For discount airline tickets, long-running and reliable student-travel agencies include:
MSL Travel (Map pp426–7; ☎ 4042 4722; msl@po.jaring .my; 66 Jl Putra)
STA Travel (Map p431; ☎ 2143 9800; stakul@po.jaring .my; Lot 506, 5th fl, Plaza Magnum, 128 Jl Pudu)

MALAYSIA

STREET FASHION

The diversity of Malaysian fashion makes Western wardrobes look like government-issued uniforms. Walking the streets, you might pass a Muslim woman framed by a tropically coloured headscarf and a flowing full-length skirt and blouse (*baju kurung*). Turn a corner and pass a Chinese woman wearing a catwalk miniskirt and a tank top. Following close behind is an older Indian woman wrapped tight in a sari. She and her daughter, in jeans and flip-flops, both wear bindis (the Hindu forehead dot); the mother's is red to denote being married, and the daughter's matches her outfit. In just one block, the street fashions have spanned continents and time periods and no one has given another a disapproving look.

SIGHTS
Colonial District   Map p428

Hugging Sungai Klang between Jl Tun Perak and Jl Kinabalu is Kuala Lumpur's colonial district. The symbolic heart is **Merdeka Square** (Jl Raja Laut), a formal parade ground around which dutifully pose the architectural legacies of Malaysia's successive conquerors, both Islamic and European. Fittingly, the nation's independence was proclaimed here in 1957. Further south is the **old railroad station** (Jl Hishamuddin), a fanciful castle of Islamic arches and spires.

The **National History Museum** (☎ 2694 4590; 29 Jl Raja; admission free; ☷ 9am-6pm) will instil a sense of Malaysian pride in a new arrival, plus the 2nd-floor view of Merdeka Square is stunning. Take the Putra LRT to Pasar Seni station.

Masjid Jamek (Jl Tun Perak; admission free; ☷ 8.30am-12.30pm & 2.30-4pm) is a tranquil creation built in 1907 and set in a grove of palm

WHATTA BARGAIN!

Keep an eye out for Mydin Wholesale Emporiums, which are located in most Malaysian cities. These clearing-house stores carry odd lots at deep discounts. Stock varies, but past bargains have included big jugs of water, toiletries and Islamic paraphernalia. A handy location in Kuala Lumpur is the **branch** (Map p428) on Jl Tun Perak.

trees; headscarves and robes are provided at the gate. It's closed during Friday prayers (11am to 2.30pm). To get here take the Star or Putra LRT to Masjid Jamek station.

Masjid Negara (National Mosque; Jl Perdana; admission free; ☷ 9am-6pm Sat-Thu, 2.45-6pm Fri) is one of Southeast Asia's largest mosques. The main dome is an 18-pointed star, symbolising the 13 states of Malaysia and the five pillars of Islam. Remove shoes and dress conservatively. The Putra LRT to Pasar Seni station will get you here.

Chinatown   Map p428

Circuitous streets and cramped chaos create a pressure-cooker of sights and sounds. **Jl Petaling** is a bustling street market selling souvenirs, like 'authentic' Paul Frank and cheap Birkenstocks and Levis. Chinatown is accessed on the Putra LRT to Pasar Seni station or on the KL Monorail to Maharajalela station.

Chinese **coffee shops** are along Jl Penggong and Jl Balai Polis. You'll spot temples and shophouses in the side streets – check out KL's principal Hindu temple, **Sri Mahamariamman Temple** (Jl HS Lee).

Near the city's original market and gambling sheds is **Central Market** (Jl Cheng Lock; ☷ 10am-10pm), a refurbished Art Deco building that sells Malay crafts and art. The neighbouring pedestrian zone is often littered on weekends with snacking teenagers and their discarded trash.

Little India   Map p428

Little India has all the feel of a bazaar. The sari shops and the shopping women along **Jl Masjid India**, the district's main street, are swathed in vibrant colours: sherbets, turquoise and vermilions. Meanwhile Indian pop blasts through tinny speakers, and musky incense and delicious spices flavour the air. The district swings into full spectacle during the Saturday *pasar malam* (night market). Little India is reached on the Star or Putra LRT to Masjid Jamek station.

Golden Triangle

A forest of high-rises, the Golden Triangle is central KL's business, shopping and entertainment district. A package tourist-ghetto emerges along the western end of Bukit Bintang. Several nightspots hang out along Jl Sultan Ismail and Jl Ramlee.

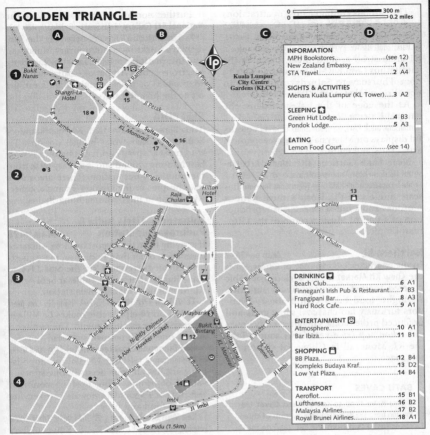

GOLDEN TRIANGLE

0 ——— 300 m
0 ——— 0.2 miles

Sitting on a forested hill, **Menara Kuala Lumpur** (Kuala Lumpur Tower; Map p431; ☎ 2020 5448; Jl Punchak; adult RM15; �) 9am-10pm, last tickets 9.30pm) is the fourth-highest telecommunications tower in the world. Visitors can ride the lift right up to the viewing deck (276m) for superb panoramic views, superior to those from the Petronas Towers. Take the KL Monorail to Bukit Nanas station.

Formerly the world's tallest skyscrapers (until Taipei 101 took over the title in 2004), the twin **Petronas Towers** (Map pp426-7; Jl Ampang; www.petronas.com.my/petronas; admission free; �) 10am-12.45pm & 3-4.45pm Tue-Sun) serve as the elegant headquarters of the national petroleum company. This steel-and-glass monu-

ment weaves together traditional Islamic symbolism with modern sophistication. First-come, first-serve tickets are available for visiting the 41st-floor Skybridge that connects the two towers; tickets are issued at 8.30am and 15-minute visits start at 10am. To get here, take the Putra LRT to KLCC station.

Lake Gardens & Around   Map pp426-7

Escape from the heat and concrete to this inner-city garden district at the western edge of central KL. Intrakota bus 21C from the Jl Sultan Mohammed bus stop, or buses 21B, 22, 48C and F3 from Chinatown will take you there. It is also a 20-minute walk from Masjid Jamek (opposite).

The gardens contain a host of attractions such as the **Bird Park** (☎ 2273 5423; adult RM22; ◷ 9am-7.30pm) and **Taman Rama Rama** (Butterfly Park; adult RM10; ◷ 9am-6pm). You can take a leisurely stroll around them, or catch the shuttle bus (adult RM1; operating 9am to 6pm Thursday to Saturday and noon to 3pm Friday) that does a loop of the area.

At the edge of the Lake Gardens, the **National Museum** (Muzium Negara; ☎ 2282 6255; Jl Damansara; adult RM1; ◷ 9am-6pm) boasts colourful displays on Malaysia's history, economy, arts, crafts and culture.

Near Lake Gardens, the **Islamic Arts Museum** (Muzium Kesenian Islam Malaysia; ☎ 2274 2020; Jl Lembah Perdana; adult RM8; ◷ 10am-6pm Tue-Sun) has scale models of the world's most famous mosques and a full-scale interior reproduction of a typical Muslim room of the Ottoman Empire.

Northern KL   Map pp426–7

In the characterless expanse of Chow Kit is the **Chow Kit Market** (Jl TAR), a claustrophobic covered market selling ordinary sundries. At night, food takes centre stage – vendors furiously fan charcoal satay grills and practiced professionals juggle steamy bowls of *beehon sup* (rice-vermicelli soup). Take the KL Monorail to Chow Kit station for this place.

BATU CAVES

If you have time to spare, **Batu Caves** (admission free; ◷ 8am-8pm) is a system of three caves just 13km from the capital. The most famous is Temple Cave, because it contains a Hindu shrine reached by a straight flight of 272 steps. Almost a million pilgrims come here every year during Thaipusam (January/February) to engage in or watch the spectacularly masochistic feats of the devotees. Dark Cave can be explored on a spelunking tour with the **Malaysian Nature Society** (☎ 03-4022 5124; www.mns.org.my).

From Chinatown, take Intrakota bus 11D (RM1.20, 30 minutes) from the stop in front of the Bangkok Bank on Jl Tun HS Lee, or Cityliner bus 69 (RM1.20) from Medan Pasar, near the HSBC bank. Bus 11D also stops along Jl Raja Laut in the Chow Kit area. During Thaipusam special trains and buses run to the caves.

Further north near Lake Titiwangsa, the **National Art Gallery** (Balai Seni Lukis Negara; ☎ 4025 4990; Jl Temerloh, off Jl TAR; admission free; ◷ 10am-6pm) displays works by contemporary Malaysian and international artists. Take any Len Seng bus from Lebuh Ampang (Chinatown area, Map p428) or from along Jl Raja Laut; get off at the hospital stop.

SLEEPING

Travellers complain that KL has some of Southeast Asia's worst budget options. Tis true, most are pretty grim. Chinatown is your best hunting ground and is an easy walk from the Puduraya bus station. There are only a few cheapies in the Golden Triangle, otherwise home to international hotel chains.

Chinatown, Little India & Puduraya bus station   Map p428

If arriving from the airport or a long-distance bus station other than Puduraya, these guesthouses can be reached via the Star LRT to Plaza Rakyat, Putra LRT to Pasar Seni or the KL Monorail to Maharajalela station.

Le Village (☎ 2026 6737; 99A Jl Tun HS Lee; dm/r RM10/30) Lots of ethnic chic makes Le Village an easy-going establishment. The common area is one of Chinatown's cosiest.

Red Dragon Backpacker's Hostel (☎ 2078 9366; 83 Jl Sultan; dm 12, r RM40-60; ☒) This monopolising giant has all your needs in one spot – a variety of rooms, a big upstairs common area, lots of TVs and a sidewalk café serving Western food and beer.

Lee Mun Guest House (☎ 2078 0639; 5th fl, 109 Jl Petaling; dm/s RM9/20, d RM25-35; ☒) You could say this skeletal cheapie has personality. Rooms and shared baths are tidy, dorms are icky. Up high, cool breezes sneak in at sunset.

Anuja Backpackers Inn (☎ 2026 6479; anuja@sgsmc .com; 1st-3rd fl, 28 Jl Pudu; r RM25-40; ☒) A cramped pressure cooker, but conveniently located opposite Puduraya bus station.

Puduraya Hotel (☎ 232 1000; 4th fl, Puduraya Station, Jl Pudu; s RM105, d RM115-125; ☒) From Puduraya bus station, catch the lift to reception on the 4th floor. Spacious, ageing rooms have sweeping views of the city.

Coliseum Hotel (☎ 2692 6270; 100 Jl TAR; s/d RM28/38; ☒) With its famous old planters' restaurant and bar downstairs, the Coliseum has a potent sense of colonial history. Rooms are huge, without bathrooms (some have sinks), and come with heritage-style furnishings. Though shabby, it's a KL institution.

Pudu Hostel (☎ 2078 9600; puduhostel@hotmail .com; 3rd fl, Wisma Lai Choon, 10 Jl Pudu; dm/s/d RM12/30/40; ☺ 24hr; ☒) This hostel got a superb write-up in a previous edition and when the loyal readers came, it promptly took a nose dive. Only one plus remains: it is terribly convenient to the Puduraya bus station.

Also recommended:

Backpackers Travellers Lodge (☎ 2031 0889; 1st fl, 158 Jl Tun HS Lee; dm RM10, r RM25-60; ☒)

Backpackers Travellers Inn (☎ 2078 2473; back packer_inn@hotmail.com; 60 Jl Sultan; dm RM10, r RM25-50; ☒)

SPLURGE!

Even the shoestring Nazis couldn't fault you for opting for the obvious value of mid-range hotels in Chinatown. Most run week-day promotions making comfort even more affordable. Both options can be reached via the Putra LRT to Pasar Seni station.

Hotel China Town Inn (Map p428; ☎ 2078 4008; www.chinatowninn.com; 52-54 Jl Petaling; r RM80-108; ☒) Rooms are quiet with spacious bathrooms and cable TV.

Swiss Inn (☎ 2072 3333; 62 Jl Sultan; r RM115; ☒ ☒) A professional hotel for jet-lag recovery. Silent crypts and cable TV.

Golden Triangle   Map p431

These guesthouses can be reached via the KL Monorail to Bukit Bintang station.

Pondok Lodge (☎ 2142 8449; pondok@tm.net.my; 3rd fl, 20 Jl Changkat Bukit Bintang; dm/s/d RM20/45/55; ☒) A spacious, mellow retreat, Pondok has airy common lounges, a rooftop sitting area and a real 'home' feel.

Green Hut Lodge (☎ 2142 3339; thegreenhut.com; 48 Tengkat Tong Shin, off Jl Changkat Bukit Bintang; dm/d RM25/50; ☒) New and shiny, this all air-con spot has all sorts of add-ons, including a sun deck and kitchenette.

EATING

All the food groups – Indian, Chinese, Malay and Western fast food – abound in the Malaysian capital.

Chinatown & Little India   Map p428

In the morning, grab a marble-topped table in one of the neighbourhood's coffeeshops

(kedai kopi) for a jolt of joe spiked with condensed milk. The midday meal can be slurped down at stalls that line Jl Sultan serving all the you-name-it noodles, from prawn or *won ton mee* (Chinese-style egg noodles served with stuffed wontons) to *laksa lemak* (white rounded noodles served with coconut milk, also called curry laksa). Jl Petaling market is closed to traffic in the evenings and Chinese restaurants set up tables beside all the action.

Little India is your best hunting ground for a slap-up Indian curry sopped up with flaky *roti canai* (Indian-style flaky flat bread, also known as 'flying dough').

Fatt Yan Vegetarian Restaurant (☎ 2070 6561; cnr Jl Tun HS Lee & Jl Silang; meals RM12; ☺ lunch & dinner) Herbivores will approve of this Buddhist Chinese restaurant that eschews meat on religious principles.

Old China Café (☎ 20725915; 11 Jl Balai Polis; meals RM8-15; ☺ dinner) Granted it's a tourist spot, but one that nails the 1920s Sino fantasy of shadow-casting ceiling fans, time-worn antiques and a soundtrack of sparrow sopranos. Baba Nonya (descendants of Chinese Straits settlers who intermarried with Malays) dishes are hit and miss.

Bilal Restoran (☎ 2078 0804; 33 Jl Ampang; meal for 2 RM12-15; ☺ breakfast, lunch & dinner) No points for ambience, but Bilal, north of Chinatown, is highly popular for its South Indian–Muslim dishes.

Restoran Yasin (☎ 2698 2710; 141 Jl Bunus; meals RM3.50-7; ☺ breakfast, lunch & dinner) A locals' institution serving incredibly tasty South-and North-Indian fare.

Restoran Wilayah Baru (29 Lebuh Pudu; meals RM2-5; ☺ breakfast, lunch & dinner) An excellent China-town eatery with cheap Indian-Malay food.

A busy **food court** (Jl Masjid India) gobbles up a big block. Little India's **Saturday night market** (Lorong TAR) has sensational tucker and a great atmosphere.

Golden Triangle & KLCC

When it's hot out, head to central KL's air-con shopping centres for international and local food. Jl Nagsari, off Jl Changkat Bukit Bintang (Map p431), is lined with Malay food stalls and open-air restaurants. Jl Alor, one street northwest of Jl Bukit Bintang has a carnival-like night market of Chinese hawker stalls. Take the KL Monorail to Bukit Bintang to reach these.

Suria KLCC Shopping Complex (Map pp426-7; ☎ 2382 2828; Jl Ampang; meals RM10-20; ❤ lunch & dinner) This upscale shopping centre has a 2nd-floor food court which is a good introduction to the diversity of Malaysian cuisine. Best reached by the Putra LRT to KLCC station.

Lemon Food Court (Map p431; Low Yat Plaza; meals RM4-8; ❤ lunch & dinner) Lemon Food Court has sizzling hot plates, mouth-watering aromas and a more proletariat ambience than hoity-toity KLCC. Take the KL Monorail to Bukit Bintang.

DRINKING

Drinking in Malaysia is no budget activity (around RM10 per bottle) and drinks at 'proper' bars are nearly double in price. The cheapest places to imbibe are Chinese eateries or open-air hawker stalls.

The intersection of Jl Sultan Ismail and Jl P Ramlee forms a Texas-sized watering-hole complex with lots of freshly pressed patrons. Wear your best club gear and prepare to unload a handsome handful of ringgit.

Reggae Bar (Map p428; ☎ 2272 2158; 158 Jl Tun HS Lee) Travel halfway around the world and find the unofficial Bob Marley cult, oh joy! Here you'll find endless tracks of the Jamaican bard, drink promotions and a lot of backpackers.

Heritage Station Bar (Map p428; ☎ 2272 1688; Jl Sultan Hishamuddin) Use the all-purpose excuse of needing a drink to wander around the colonial-era train station and the booze-dispensing bar of the Heritage Station Hotel, a trunk-travellers' lodge auspiciously situated beside the railroad tracks.

Finnegan's Irish Pub & Restaurant (Map p431; ☎ 2284 9024; 6 Jl Telawi Lima) This is a first-

rate place for a knees up with live ESPN sports coverage, enthusiastic staff, stout and a decent menu.

Beach Club (Map p431; ☎ 2166 9919; Jl P Ramlee) Start the crawl at this paradise-themed bar which is stranded in an asphalt oasis. This spot solves the old question about what to bring to a deserted island: a big city, of course.

Hard Rock Cafe (Map p431; ☎ 2715 5555; Ground fl, Wisma Concorde, 2 Jl Sultan Ismail) Sounds like a cop-out, but this international chain really is one of the best places in town for local and regional live music.

CLUBBING

Bar Ibiza (Map p431; ☎ 2713 2333; 924 & 926 Jl P Ramlee; cover RM25 Sat & Sun) Don't tell the KL-ers this, but nightlife in the capital city is stuck somewhere in the early 1990s. But after bar-hopping down the *jalan* (street), you might be amazed how well a big-screen TV attracts the technocrati.

Atmosphere (Map p431; ☎ 2145 9198, www.twelvesi.com; 12 Jl Sultan Ismail; cover RM25; ❤ 9pm-3am Thu-Sat) Centrepiece of the sleek two-storey and high profile TwelveSI complex, this up-to-the-minute multi-tier club wills clubbers on with house and techno.

NIGHTLIFE GURUS

To keep up with the clubbers, check out the latest in **KLue** (www.klue.com.my; RM5) or **Juice** (www.juiceonline.com; free).

ENTERTAINMENT

Tanjung Golden Village (Map pp426-7; ☎ 7492 2929; www.tgv.com.my; 3rd fl, Suria KLCC Shopping Complex) The latest Bollywood and Hollywood blockbusters can be viewed in the arctic atmosphere of KL's most convenient multiscreen cinema.

Actors Studio Theatre (☎ 2694 5400; www.theactorsstudio.com.my; 3rd fl, New Wing, Bangsar Shopping Centre, 285 Jl Maarof; tickets RM25-45) This well-regarded company hosts contemporary Malaysian plays and adaptations of classic theatre performances. Workshops are also offered – see p521.

Regular cultural performances and shows are held at the **Malaysian Tourist Information Complex** (MATIC; Map pp426-7; ☎ 2164 3929, 2163 3667; 109 Jl Ampang; adult RM5; ❤ 3-3.45pm Tue, Thu, Sat &

GAY & LESBIAN BARS

Liquid (Map p428; ☎ 2078 5909; Central Market Annexe; admission RM10; ❤ 10pm-3am Thu, Fri & Sat) KL's most famous and funkiest gay venue, this sophisticated bar in the Central Market Annexe draws an international and local crowd of young dancers. It's not cheap, but it is very smooth and the ultimate chill-out bar.

Frangipani Bar (Map p431; ☎ 2144 3001; 25 Jl Changkat Bukit Bintang) Above the restaurant of the same name, this seductive bar attracts a stylish gay and straight crowd.

Sun) and the **Central Market** (Map p428; ☎ 2274 6542; admission free; ⊙ 7.45pm Sat & Sun).

SHOPPING

Jl Petaling in the heart of Chinatown has cheap clothes, copy watches, pirated CDs and a smattering of crafts; bargain very, very hard. More of the same can be found at Chow Kit Market (Map pp426–7). Over in Little India, Jl Masjid India is the place to shop for saris, Indian silks, carpets and other textiles.

Kompleks Budaya Kraf (Map p431; ☎ 2162 7459; Jl Conlay; 10am-6pm) This place has a large selection of handicrafts.

Suria KLCC Shopping Complex (Map pp426-7; ☎ 2382 2828; Petronas Twin Towers) This is a gleaming, fashion-conscious shopping complex, at the foot of the Petronas Towers.

BB Plaza (Map p431; Jl Bukit Bintang) Everyone comes here to enjoy a market informality and load up on all the teenage essentials.

GETTING THERE & AWAY

Kuala Lumpur is Malaysia's principal international arrival gateway and it forms the crossroads for domestic bus, train and taxi travel.

Air

Kuala Lumpur International Airport (KLIA; ☎ 8777 8888; www.klia.com.my; Pengrus Besar) is a flamboyant structure, 75km south of the city centre at Sepang. Many airlines service this airport, but the country's international airline, Malaysia Airlines, is the major carrier. See p422 for more on domestic routes and costs. For information on international routes see p420.

Bus

Most long-distance buses operate from the **Puduraya bus station** (Map p428; Jl Pudu), just east of Chinatown. A few travellers have reported being robbed late at night, so stay alert. The tourist police and information counters are right inside the main entrance. The left-luggage office is at the back. From Puduraya, buses go all over Peninsular Malaysia, including the east coast, Singapore and Thailand. The only long-distance destinations that Puduraya doesn't handle are Kuala Lipis and Jerantut (p478), which leave only from Pekeliling bus station.

Pekeliling (Map pp426-7; ☎ 4042 7256; Jl Tun Razak) and **Putra** (Map pp426-7; ☎ 4042 9530; Jl Putra) bus stations in the north of the city handle a greater number of services to the east coast. Buses at these stations often have seats available when Puduraya buses are fully booked.

Typical fares and journey times travelling from KL:

Destination	Fare (RM)	Duration (hr)
Cameron Highlands	14	3½
Georgetown (Penang)	24	5
Ipoh	13	3
Johor Bahru	20	4
Kota Bharu	26	10
Kuala Terengganu	30	7
Kuantan	17	4½
Lumut	16	4
Melaka	9	2½
Mersing	20	5½
Singapore	25	5½

Taxi

The long-distance taxi stand is on the second floor of the **Puduraya bus station** (Map p428; Jl Pudu). Fixed whole-taxi fares: Cameron Highlands (RM140), Melaka (RM140) and Penang (RM240). Do your homework about prices before dealing with taxi drivers who are unscrupulous about ripping-off tourists.

Train

KL is the hub of the **KTM** (☎ 2267 1200; www .ktmb.com.my) national railway system. The long-distance trains depart from KL Sentral (Map pp426–7). The **KTM information office** (⊙ 6.30am-10.30pm) in the main hall can advise on schedules and check seat availability. There are daily departures for Butterworth, Wakaf Baharu (for Kota Bharu), Johor Bahru, Thailand and Singapore. Most express-train seats can be booked up to 60 days in advance.

Not to be confused with the intercity long-distance line is the KTM Komuter, which links central KL with the Klang Valley and Seremban.

GETTING AROUND

KL has a sophisticated and extensive public transport system to make it easier to hop between neighbourhoods. See Getting Into Town (p425) for information for airport arrivals.

MALAYSIA

Bus

Of the many local bus companies, **Intrakota** (☎ 7727 2727) and **Cityliner** (☎ 7982 7060) are the largest. Local buses leave from many of the bus terminals around the city, including **Puduraya bus station** (Map p428; Jl Pudu), Klang bus station, the Jl Sultan Mohammed bus stop south of the Central Market, and from along Medan Pasar and Lebuh Ampang near the Masjid Jamek LRT stations. These bus stops are marked on Map p428. The maximum fare is usually 90 sen or RM1 for destinations within the city limits; try to have correct change ready when you board.

Taxi

Taxis in KL do have meters but, according to one driver, the meters haven't been used in nine years because the fares are outdated and don't reflect current costs. As a result, you have to bargain. Ask at your hotel about fares before heading to a taxi stand, since the price doubles when a tourist approaches. Standard trips around town start at RM5.

Train

KL's pride and joy is a user-friendly light rail transit (LRT) system, which is composed of the **Star** (☎ 4294 2550) and **Putra** (☎ 7625 8228) lines. Fares range from RM1 to RM2.80 and trains run every 15 minutes from 6am to midnight.

The **KL Monorail** (☎ 2267 9888) is a 16km-elevated single-track train convenient for hops between Chinatown and the northern areas of Bukit Bintang and Chow Kit. Fares are RM1.20 to RM2.10 and trains run every 15 minutes from 6am to midnight.

KTM Komuter (☎ 2272 2828), not to be confused with the long-distance KTM service (see p435), links Kuala Lumpur with outlying suburbs and the historic train station.

KL Sentral station, in the Brickfields area 1km south of the historic Old Railway Station, is the central transit station for all train-based travel in Kuala Lumpur. Other interchange stations include the following: Masjid Jamek (Map p428), transfer between Star and Putra LRT; Hang Tuah and Titiwangsa (Map pp426–7), transfer between KL Monorail and Star LRT; Bukit Nanas (Map p431), transfer between KL Monorail and Putra LRT; Tasik Selatan, transfer between KTM Komuter and Star LRT.

PENINSULAR MALAYSIA – WEST COAST

The west coast of the Malay peninsula has long entertained foreign visitors since the monsoon trade winds first blew the sailing ships bound for India or China into the protected passage of the Strait of Melaka. This exposure to the world beyond has created a cosmopolitan populace, fluent in English, well travelled and ethnically diverse. Mellifluously named Melaka and Penang are historical legends, born during the spice trade when commerce played matchmaker to cultures and customs. Offering a restorative elixir to Asia's tropical heat is the cool climate of the Cameron Highlands. The low-key beach destinations of Pulau Langkawi and Pulau Pangkor aren't as stunning as their east coast rivals, but pleasant alternatives to the zombie procession.

MELAKA
☎ 06 / pop 648,500

It isn't just an accident of geography that has made the port city of Melaka such a desired possession. It exudes a sultriness not usually found in modest Malaysia and must have cast an intoxicating spell on its historical suitors – Chinese royalty, Portuguese seafarers, Dutch traders, and English colonists. Like a well-trained courtesan, Melaka excels in the arts of beauty and food.

Today visitors from Singapore come to soak up Melaka's atmospheric past, an activity that creates parody rather than authenticity. Watching the lines around famous food shops or frantic haggling over 'Baba Nonya' baubles will delight a voyeur relieved that the tourist machine is aimed at another target. Striking off into the alleys you'll find lots of spots where real life is unconcerned with tourists – the closet-sized blacksmith shops, or the unlikely neighbours of a Hindu shrine, Islamic mosque and Chinese temple.

Melaka received its first royal patron in the 14th century when Parameswara, a Hindu prince from Sumatra, chose it as a favoured port for resupplying trading ships. In 1405 Admiral Cheng Ho arrived bearing gifts from the Ming emperor and the promise of protection from Siamese enemies. Chinese

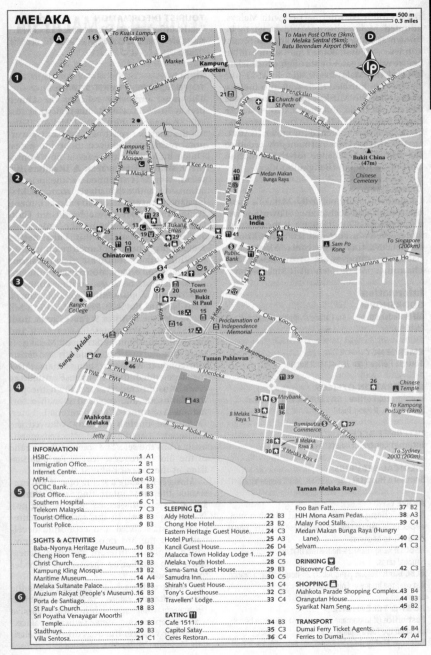

MELAKA

0 _____ 500 m
0 _____ 0.3 miles

settlers followed, intermarried with Malays, adopted Malay customs and came to be known as Baba Nonya, and later as Straits Chinese or Peranakan. This cosmopolitan centre was the gateway through which Islam entered the Malay peninsula. In 1511, the Portuguese muscled their way into the city and ended the Muslim domination of the eastern sea trade. But promiscuous Melaka rarely remained faithful to one master and soon the Dutch marched into town in 1641. In 1795 Melaka was permanently ceded to the British in exchange for the Sumatran port of Bencoolen (Bengkulu today).

Orientation

Chinatown is undoubtedly Melaka's most interesting and scenic area. Town Square, also known as Dutch Square, is the centre of a preserved museum district. Further north is Melaka's tiny Little India. Most backpacker guesthouses are in the newer, less charming, part of town off Jl Melaka Raya.

Information
BOOKSHOPS
MPH (Ground fl, Mahkota Parade shopping complex; Jl Merdeka)

EMERGENCY
Tourist Police (☎ 285 4114; Jl Kota)

IMMIGRATION OFFICES
Immigration office (☎ 282 4958; 2nd fl, Wisma Persekutuan, Jl Hang Tuah)

INTERNET ACCESS
Internet Centre (Jl Bunga Raya)

MEDICAL SERVICES
Southern Hospital (☎ 283 588, 169 Jl Bendahara)

MONEY
Moneychangers are scattered about town, especially near the guesthouses off Jl TMR and Chinatown.
HSBC (Jl Hang Tuah) 24-hour ATMs that accept international cards.
OCBC Bank (Lorong Hang Jebat) 24-hour ATM at a branch just over the bridge in Chinatown.

POST & TELEPHONE
Post office (Jl Laksamana) A small post office can be found off the Town Square.
Telekom Malaysia (☙ 8am-5pm) East of Bukit St Paul.

TOURIST INFORMATION
Tourist Office (☎ 281 4803; www.melaka.gov.my; Jl Kota; ☙ 8.45am-5pm, closed 12.15-2.45pm Fri) Opposite Christ Church.

Sights
TOWN SQUARE & BUKIT ST PAUL

The most imposing relic of the Dutch period in Melaka is **Stadthuys** (Town Sq; adult RM2; ☙ 9am-6pm Sat-Thu, 9am-12.15pm & 2.45-6pm Fri), the massive red town hall and governors' residence. Believed to be the oldest Dutch building in the East, it now houses the **Historical, Ethnographic & Literature Museums**, which is included in the price of admission and exhaustively recounts Malaysian history and literary development. Facing the square is the bright-red **Christ Church** (1753), completing the geographic and cultural fantasy that this is just another Dutch village beside a tamed river.

While other Southeast Asian nations may have ruins from deceased Hindu empires, Malaysia bears yet another conqueror's sacred monuments. From Stadthuys, steps lead up Bukit St Paul, which is a hill topped by the ruins of **St Paul's Church**, built in 1521 by a Portuguese sea captain, and overlooks the famous Strait of Melaka. It took the Portuguese a month to divide and conquer Melaka's sultan rulers. After the siege ended, the Portuguese ousted the city's Muslim traders, tore down the primary mosque and replaced it with a fort named A Famosa ('The Famous'). Later, Dutch and English invaders followed the Portuguese paradigm and attacked mercilessly from the sea. The sole surviving relic of the old Portuguese fort is **Porta de Santiago**, at the foot of Bukit St Paul.

Along Jl Kota are a string of cultural museums, the most interesting is the **Muzium Rakyat** (People's Museum; ☎ 282 6526; adult RM2; ☙ 9am-6pm Tue-Sun). In this buffet collection of Malaysia's social and economic development is the 3rd floor Beauty Museum, which explores different cultures' obsessions with mutilating themselves in order to look good.

A short walk east of Bukit St Paul is the **Melaka Sultanate Palace** (☎ 282 7464; adult RM2; ☙ 9am-6pm Wed-Mon), which houses a massive wooden replica of a Melaka sultan's palace.

Further west on the quayside is the **Maritime Museum** (☎ 283 0926; admission RM2; ☙ 9am-

6pm Wed-Mon), housed in a re-creation of the Portuguese sailing ship, the *Flora de la Mar*, which sank off the coast while transporting Malayan booty back to Europe.

CHINATOWN

Melaka's Chinatown is wonderfully preserved; perhaps a little pickled in parts. Jl Tun Tan Cheng Lock is lined with ornate mansions built by Peranakan (Baba Nonya) rubber tycoons. But the primary tourist attraction is Jl Hang Jebat (Jonker Street), which is lined with antique stores, a weekend market and clan houses where the neighbourhood's senior citizens come to show off their karaoke prowess. Wander the small side streets where family shophouses are linked by veranda walkways, creating dramatically framed views of street life: a bare-bellied patriarch in his warehouse–living room, a wizened trishaw driver blaring outdated dance hits from his portable radio, or an earth-toned Chinese temple decorated with sensual dragons.

Baba-Nonya Heritage Museum (☎ 283 1273; 48-50 Jl Tun Tan Cheng Lock; adult RM8; ⏰ 10am-12.30pm & 2-4.30pm Wed-Mon) is a captivating museum set in a traditional Peranakan townhouse in Chinatown.

Cheng Hoon Teng (Qing Yun Ting, Green Clouds Temple; Jl Tukang) is Chinatown's most famous temple, dating back to 1646. It's Malaysia's oldest Chinese temple and all materials used in its building were imported from China.

VILLA SENTOSA

After sampling Melaka's Chinese and European heritage, don't overlook the city's Malay family tree. **Villa Sentosa** (☎ 282 3988; www.travel.to/villasentosa; 138 Kampong Morten; admission by donation; ⏰ 9am-1pm & 2-5pm Sat-Thu, 2.45-5pm Fri) is a private museum on the Melaka River in Kampung Morten. Tours led by family members include a visit to the ancestral *kampung* home, dating from the 1920s, filled with Malay handicrafts and interesting architectural adaptations for surviving the tropics before air-conditioning.

Sleeping

JL TAMAN MELAKA RAYA (JL TMR)

Melaka's guesthouse ghetto occupies the western terminus of Jl Taman Melaka Raya (Jl TMR), a charmless complex of shophouses, more Chinese banquet restaurants than Chinese families and tacky neon bars. From the bus station, take town bus 17 (50 sen) or a taxi (RM12 to RM15).

Many places are Muslim-run and owners strongly request that no pork or non-halal Chinese food is brought onto the premises. Obviously beers are not for sale, but most guesthouses allow BYO and drinking on the premises.

Travellers' Lodge (☎ 226 5709; 214B Jl Melaka Raya 1; s RM16-33, d RM35-50; ⏲) Surprising for a place with pushy bus station touts, Traveller's Lodge is phenomenally clean. The lodge is well run, with friendly staff and lots of extras (rooftop sitting area, kitchen, movies).

Kancil Guest House (☎ 281 4044; kancil@machinta .com.sg; 177 Jl Parameswara; dm RM12, r RM28-38) Kancil is a distinctive family-run guesthouse with a quiet, relaxed atmosphere. It's clean, with shared bathrooms, heaps of sitting areas and a lush garden at the back. Over its 15 years, travellers from far-flung destinations have painted murals on the walls, which gives Kancil a personalised feel. Laundry services and bike hire are available.

Shirah's Guest House (☎ 286 1041; 207-209 Jl Melaka Raya 1; dm RM12, s RM18-20, d RM22-40; ⏲) Lots of Mediterranean colours and a mellow vibe makes Shirah's a handsome find. The three-bed dorm is a humane alternative to the usual bunker. Doubles are excellent value.

Also recommended:

Malacca Town Holiday Lodge 1 (☎ 284 8830; 148B-149B Jl TMR; s RM16-18, d RM18-20, tr RM27-30) Rooms on the main thoroughfare can be noisy.

Melaka Youth Hostel (Asrama Belia Youth Hostel; ☎ 282-7915; 341A Jl Melaka Raya 3; dm RM12, r RM20-50) Rooms are clean and the bed sheets have met and tumbled with bleach.

Samudra Inn (☎ 282 7441; 348B Jl Taman Melaka Raya 3; dm/s RM10/22, d RM28-35; ⏲) Basic Samudra is clean and quiet.

CHINATOWN

Because of restrictive taxes, Melaka's most scenic section of town can't afford to bed backpackers. There are, however, a number of exceptions. Take town bus 17 to Town Square (70 sen). A taxi should cost RM10 to RM12.

Sama-Sama Guest House (☎ 012-305 1980; www .sama-sama-guesthouse.com; 26 Jl Tukang Besi; dm RM10, r RM20-35) Scatterbrained Sama-Sama has big rooms arranged around an interior courtyard of cool breezes and stray views of tiled rooftops. The front common area is filled with a retired pool table, an eclectic record collection and lazy cats; the neighbourhood characters assemble here after sunset. Treat it kindly as many travellers will be disappointed to find that their secret cocoon has found its way into the Lonely Planet.

Tony's Guesthouse (☎ 012-688 0119; 24 Lorong Banda Kaba; r RM15) Some people discover Tony's only after a sleepless night at Eastern Heritage. The bedsheets and bathrooms don't get as much attention as they should, but you'll likely have the place to yourself.

Chong Hoe Hotel (☎ 282 6102; 26 Jl Tukang Emas; r RM25-45; ❄) This Chinese-run hotel occupies a little lane behind all the action on Jonker Street.

Eastern Heritage Guest House (☎ 283 3026; 8 Jl Bukit China; r RM18-22) In a superb 1918 building, Eastern Heritage looks good from the outside. But the guts aren't as endearing: noise thunders in from the main drag and readers have complained about rude management. Its location is somewhat redeemable.

SPLURGE!

Aldy Hotel (☎ 283 3232; www.aldyhotel.com .my; r RM110-130; ❄) Still bearing that fresh-from-the-factory smell, Aldy is a multistorey number near Town Square. The bathrooms are big enough to sprawl out in and there are real beds, cable TV and a rooftop Jacuzzi.

Hotel Puri (☎ 282 5588; www.hotelpuri .com; 118 Jl Tun Tan Cheng; r RM130-150; ❄) This street is filled with traditional Perana-kan mansions that have been converted into hotels. By and large, the lobbies are always lovely – delicate ironwork, winding staircases, colourful tiles. But because of demand, the same artistic sensibilities don't usually make their way into the rooms. Hotel Puri, however, is one of the better options in the line-up.

Eating

The city's fabled Baba Nonya cuisine distinguishes itself from Penang's Malay-Chinese hybrids by favouring Indonesian flavours, like sweet, rich coconut milk. In Melaka the Portuguese might have wreaked havoc on civic order, but it built up a tradition for cakes and seafood, most obvious in the Eurasian dish of devil's curry. Then there are the immigrant contributions of Indian curries and the versatile Chinese noodle dishes.

Hawker stalls around the lively Jl TMR roundabout are a good bet for the regional version of laksa.

Capitol Satay (☎ 283 5508; 41 Lorong Bukit China; meals RM5-10; ❄ closed Monday) A third-generation family-run business, Capitol is enough to make you move to Melaka. It is famous for satay *celup* (a Melaka adaptation of satay steamboat). Stainless steel tables have a bubbling vat of satay sauce in the middle, which is regularly replenished. You dunk skewers of okra (ladies' finger) stuffed with fish, tofu, Chinese sausage, chicken, pork, prawns, bok choy, and side dishes of pickled egg with pickled ginger.

HJH Mona Asam Pedas (Jl Kota Lakshamana; meals RM15-30; ❄ dinner) Tucked back behind the southwestern side of Chinatown is a string of open-air restaurants serving *ikan asam pedas* (spicy tamarind fish). The food orgy doesn't start until nightfall and then continues until the wee hours of the morning.

Foo Ban Fatt (40 Jl Tukang Besi; meals RM5-10; ❄ breakfast & lunch) Specialising in Hakka cuisine, this basic shop lures neighbours with its meatball soup flavoured with *petai*, a vegetable regarded for its medicinal properties.

Medan Makan Bunga Raya (btwn Jl Bunga Raya & Jl Bendahara; ❄ breakfast, lunch & dinner) When you hear the sound of the meat cleaver, you've reached 'Hungry Lane,' known for Indian-style curry-pork rice and *gula melaka* (palm-sugar) during the day. At night more stalls pop up.

Ceres Restoran (256 Jl Taman Melaka Raya 3; meals RM5-10; ❄ lunch & dinner) At this health-food spot, unpolished rice is mixed with other whole grains creating a toothy accompaniment for big plates of vegetable stir-fries. Other gut-friendly options include granola, whole grain bread, and lots of takeaway snacks.

Cafe 1511 (☎ 286 0151; 52 Jl Tun Tan Cheng Lock; meals RM7; ❄ lunch & dinner Thu-Tue) Next to the Baba-Nonya Heritage Museum is this Peranakan café sporting a high ceiling, original tiles, lovely carved screens and a mishmash of decorative objects from Southeast Asia. Nonya favourites are served up.

Selvam (☎ 281 9223; 3 Jl Temenggong; meals RM7; ❄ breakfast, lunch & dinner) This Little India eatery has a loyal band of local patrons.

There's a choice range of tasty and cheap curries and roti, plus a Friday afternoon vegetarian special (RM5).

Kampong Portugis (dinner) In the eastern part of the city, 3km from Town Square, is a small community claiming mixed Portuguese-Indian ancestry. Often hyped as a mini-Lisbon, this otherwise nondescript neighbourhood caters to the curious tourists with food stalls and a few clunky Eurasian restaurants. On weekend evenings, Restoran de Lisbon (meals RM25) is known for chilli crabs and devil curry. Any other time of the week, Medan Portugis has food stalls, serving many of the same dishes at seaside tables. Take town bus 17 to Kampong Portugis and walk toward the sea; coming back to town, hop off the bus at Mahkota Parade Shopping Centre before it speeds onto the flyover.

Drinking

During the weekend night market on Jonker Street, the Chinese food shops have beer promotions, providing great people-watching seats. Medan Portugis, in Kampong Portugis (see above), has cheap beers and sunset views. The alleys in the backpacker ghetto off Jl TMR have lots of watering troughs.

Discovery Cafe (3 Jl Bunga Raya; meals RM8-15) Situated by the river in the centre of town the Discovery is a popular place for travellers; it's an excellent café-bar with cold beer and mixing locals. It's open late, there's Internet access and outside seating.

Melaka's midweek nightlife is slow but heats up on Saturday night. If you're a karaoke fiend, there are innumerable bars in the alleyways off Jl TMR.

Clubbing

Sydney 2000 (284 3299; 16-22 Jl Melaka Raya 15; 9pm-4am) You could try this place, which can be heard before you see it. Sydney fills up on Saturday and pumps till late.

Shopping

A wander through Chinatown will have you wishing for more room in your pack.

Orangutan House (282 6872; www.charlescham .com; 59 Lorong Hang Jebat) Doubling as a gallery, this place sells colourful works by young local artist Charles Cham.

Syarikat Nam Seng (94 Jl Kampung Pantai) Right before the intersection of Jl Kampung Hulu,

look for the shop crowded with recently cut tree trunks. The craftsmen inside fashions these raw materials into wooden cutting boards – just what you need to really make your pack heavy.

Mahkota Parade Shopping Complex (282 6151; Lot B02, Jl Merdeka) Melaka's biggest shopping centre is full of hip affordable boutiques where Malaysia dabbles in fashionista fetish. Plus it has life-saving air-conditioning.

Getting There & Away

Melaka is 144km from KL and 224km from Johor Bahru.

BUS

Melaka's local bus station, express bus station and taxi station are all combined into the massive **Melaka Sentral** (Jl Panglima Awang), roughly 5km north of Town Square. Because Melaka is a popular weekend destination, make advance bus reservations for Singapore and Kuala Lumpur.

The following long-distance destinations can be reached from Melaka: KL (RM7.90, two hours, hourly from 8am to 7.30pm), Georgetown (RM30, eight hours, two daily), Ipoh (RM25, five hours, two daily), Jerantut (RM14.10, five hours, one daily), Johor Bahru (RM12.30, three hours, hourly 8am to 11am and 1pm to 6pm), Kota Bharu (RM32, 10 hours, five daily), Kuala Terengganu (RM27.30, nine hours, five daily), Kuantan (RM18, five hours, two daily), Mersing (Rm14.80, 4½ hours, four daily) and Singapore (RM13.75, 4½ hours, hourly 8am to 11am and 1pm to 6pm).

If you're hustling back to KL International Airport, you can bypass KL by taking

---

BORDER CROSSING: INTO INDONESIA

High-speed ferries make the trip from Melaka to Dumai (p269), in Sumatra, twice daily at around 9.30am and 3pm (one-way/return RM80/129, 1¾ hours). **Madai Shipping** (284 0671; Jl PM2) and **Tunas Rumpat Express** (283 2506; Jl PM2) have ticket offices near the jetty (which is on Jl Quayside). Travellers will need a visa to enter Dumai (for more information see the Indonesia Directory, p344).

MALAYSIA

a Seremban-bound bus (RM4.70, 1½ hours, every 30 minutes) and then catch a local bus (RM5) to KLIA; give yourself plenty of time, though.

Getting Around
Town bus 17 runs every 15 minutes from the Melaka Sentral bus station to Town Square, Mahkota Parade Shopping Complex, Taman Melaka Raya (50 sen) and Medan Portugis (80 sen).

Melaka is a walking and cycling city. Bicycles can be hired at some guesthouses for around RM7 per day; there are also a few bike-hire outfits around town.

A trishaw should cost around RM10 for any one-way trip within the town, but you'll have to bargain. Taxis charge around RM8 to RM10 within a 5km radius with a 50% surcharge between 1am and 6am.

CAMERON HIGHLANDS
☎ 05

Just high enough to mingle with the clouds, Cameron Highlands is a cool and picturesque retreat from the tropical lowlands. Altitude-loving tea plantations form emerald-coloured corduroy vests along the peaks of stout pyramid-shaped mountains. Cottage variety flowers bow in the gentle wind, scattering sweet perfume as the morning fog collects in big teardrops. In the fertile valleys, the obedient fruits of the harvest – bulbous cabbage heads, blushing strawberries, vibrant roses – wait patiently to be picked.

A major highlight on the backpacker trail, Cameron Highlands is Malaysia's best-known and most extensive hill station, dating back to the English colonial days. Sitting at an altitude of 1300m to 1829m, Cameron Highland's undeveloped forests are nature's equivalent of a playground jungle gym. A network of steep trails are crisscrossed by thick roots turning a 'walk' into an all-fours crawl. The cool weather tempts visitors to exertions normally forgotten at sea level. In addition, there are colourful temples, apiaries, rose gardens and lush green tea plantations where visitors are welcome to try the local brew.

Orientation & Information
The Cameron Highlands stretches along the road from the town of Ringlet, through the main towns of Tanah Rata, Brinchang and beyond to smaller villages to the northeast.

Tanah Rata is the main Highland town where you'll find budget accommodation and other essentials. Most guesthouses offer Internet access for around RM5 an hour.

Dobi Highlands Laundry (62A Persiaran Camellia 3)

Gil's Tourist Information (☎ 017-550 8326; main bus station, Jl Besar; ☼ roughly 8.30am-9.30pm) Gil, affiliated with Golden Highlands Adventure Holidays, is a likeable character and can offer tourist advice.

Maybank (Jl Mentigi) The only bank/moneychanger in Tanah Rata.

Yam Tourist Information (☎ 019-611 0242; Jl Besar) The friendly and knowledgeable Yam has added this tiny kiosk onto the front of his cobbler's stall, next to Restaurant Kumar. Operating hours are erratic, but he's happy to answer queries by phone.

Sights & Activities
Taking in a jungle stroll is thoroughly enjoyable and is often the best way to reach some of the area's other tourist attractions. Most walks and sights can be accessed by the local bus, a rattler that chugs up and down the main highway.

Visiting one of the tea plantations is another must. The rolling hills are carpeted with hectares of green and occasionally speckled with tea-pickers wading between the rows snipping the tender green tips. **Sungai Palas Boh Tea Estate** (Gunung Brinchang Rd, Brinchang; admission free; ☼ 8.30am-4.30pm Tue-Sun) is the easiest plantation to visit on your own. Tours are free and the tea rooms out the back offer grand vistas. Take the local bus from Tanah Rata bus station north of Brinchang toward Kampung Raja. In between is a tourist strip of strawberry farms, cactus gardens and butterfly farms; hop off at the roadside vegetable stands and follow the intersecting road.

Boh Tea Estate (Boh Rd Habu, Ringlet; admission free; ☼ 8.30am-4.30pm) below Tanah Rata, 8km from the main road, is also open to the public. It's only a 45-minute walk from the end of jungle Trail 9A, which you can pick-up outside of Tanah Rata.

Sam Poh Temple (Brinchang; admission by donation; ☼ 8.30am-6pm) is a typically Chinese kaleidoscope of Buddha statues, stone lions and incense burners. It's accessible from Tanah Rata – take Trail 3, near the golf course, and then connect to Trail 2.

When you head out on a trail, go in pairs, take drinking water and rain gear.

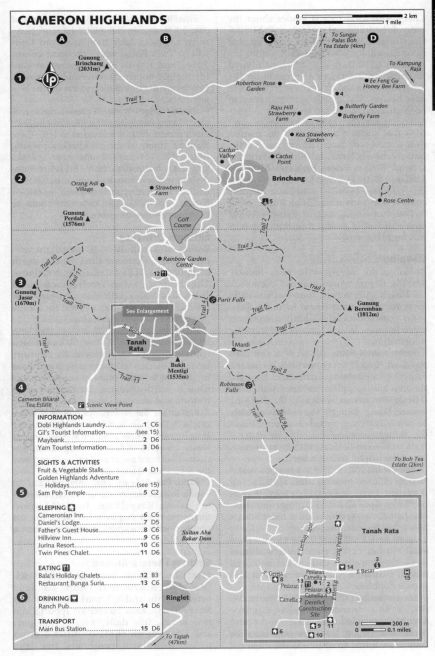

CAMERON HIGHLANDS

0   2 km
0   1 mile

Gunung Brinchang (2031m)

To Sungai Palas Boh Tea Estate (4km)

To Kampung Raja

Trail 1

Robertson Rose Garden

Ee Feng Gu Honey Bee Farm

4

Raju Hill Strawberry Farm

Butterfly Garden
Butterfly Farm

Kea Strawberry Garden

Cactus Valley

Cactus Point

Brinchang

Orang Asli Village

Strawberry Farm

5

Rose Centre

Gunung Perdah (1576m)

Golf Course

Trail 2

Trail 3

Trail 10

Trail 11

Rainbow Garden Centre

12

Trail 3

Trail 10

Gunung Jasar (1670m)

Parit Falls

Trail 4

Trail 5

Gunung Beremban (1812m)

Trail 7

Jl Besar

See Enlargement

Tanah Rata

Mardi

Trail 6

Bukit Mentigi (1535m)

Trail 8

Trail 13

Robinson Falls

Cameron Bharat Tea Estate

Scenic View Point

Trail 9

Trail 9A

To Boh Tea Estate (2km)

INFORMATION
Dobi Highlands Laundry.............................1 C6
Gil's Tourist Information....................(see 15)
Maybank...2 D6
Yam Tourist Information...........................3 D6

SIGHTS & ACTIVITIES
Fruit & Vegetable Stalls.............................4 D1
Golden Highlands Adventure
  Holidays...(see 15)
Sam Poh Temple...5 C2

SLEEPING
Cameronian Inn..6 C6
Daniel's Lodge..7 D5
Father's Guest House..................................8 C6
Hillview Inn...9 C6
Jurina Resort..10 C6
Twin Pines Chalet......................................11 D6

EATING
Bala's Holiday Chalets..............................12 B3
Restaurant Bunga Suria............................13 C6

DRINKING
Ranch Pub..14 D6

TRANSPORT
Main Bus Station.......................................15 D6

Sultan Abu Bakar Dam

Ringlet

To Tapah (47km)

Tanah Rata

7

Jl Lembah Asar

Lorong Perdah

14

3

Gereja

Pesiaran Camellia 3

13

Pesiaran 1

Pesiaran 2

Jl Besar

15

Camellia 2

Camellia 4
Derelict Construction Site

Jl Mentigi

6

9   11

10

0   200 m
0   0.1 miles

Check with local tourist guides about the state of the trails and recommended walks. Guesthouses in Tanah Rata often employ informal guides who lead daily walks. Inexperienced walkers would be well advised to employ the services of a guide on the longer trails; in recent years, several people have become lost. Single women have also been attacked in remote areas.

Tour operators offer a variety of daytrips that include a visit to a tea plantation, strawberry farm, flower and cactus nursery, honey farm and butterfly farm for around RM15. **Golden Highlands Adventure Holidays** (☎ 491 4478; main bus station; tours RM15-100; ☽ 8.45am & 1.45pm) runs popular half-day countryside tours from Tanah Rata.

Tours operating out of Father's Guest House include a good jungle-flora trip perfect for plant nerds.

Sleeping

Bookings are advisable in peak holiday periods (April, August and December). Laid-back guesthouse touts will usually meet your bus upon arrival in Tanah Rata. Most guesthouses have libraries, common video lounges, Internet access and trekking information.

Father's Guest House (☎ 491 2484; www.fathers place.cjb.net; PO Box 15, Tanah Rata; dm RM8-10, r RM20-80) Father's greatest strength is its scenic grounds, set on a hill a couple of minutes' walk from Jl Besar surrounded by views of the changing sky and flower gardens. The old bunker-style Nissen huts are surprisingly comfortable and the dorm has a summer-camp camaraderie. It's a family-run business with lovely owners who offer helpful tourist advice.

Hillview Inn (☎ 491 2915 17 Jl Mentigi; s RM30, d RM35-88) Perched high on a hill, Hillview Inn is carpeted and impeccably clean. Rooms on the 1st floor all have balconies and share real bathrooms (rather than a toilet with a hose) that have hot water.

Jurina Resort (☎ 491 5522; 819 Jl Mentigi; r from RM50) Further uphill, past Hillview, Jurina is another excellent choice. It has a well tended garden, a well-mannered host and spruce doubles.

Cameronian Inn (☎ 491 1327; 16 Jl Mentigi; dm RM7, r RM25-60) In a converted bungalow, Cameronian has basic windowless rooms and a busy communal sitting area. It's popular with couples as dorms are cramped and dark.

Twin Pines Chalet (☎ 4912169; twinpinech@hotmail .com; 2 Jl Mentigi; dm RM8, r RM20-45) The party scene seems to have migrated from Daniel's to Twin Pines, where the local guides, guests and lots of guitars gather around the nightly bonfire to serenade the moon. Rooms are big but dank and the dorms lack windows.

Daniel's Lodge (☎ 491 5823; danielslodge@hotmail .com; 9 Lorong Perdah; dm RM7, s RM18-30, r RM20-35) On a recent visit, it was hard to tell where Daniel's stood in the backpacker pecking order. The concrete rooms were Spartan and clean, but eerily empty. Travellers have definitely been spooked away, but it was unclear if the boycott was based on fact or fiction. One noticeable deterrent could be the shanty-town neighbours.

Eating & Drinking

Eating in Tanah Rata is incredibly self-explanatory. There are three blocks' worth of options – Malay, Indian and Chinese. The cheapest food in Tanah Rata is found at a row of Malay stalls along Jl Besar, near the bus station. Keep an eye out for locally produced strawberry ice cream.

Bala's Holiday Chalet (☎ 491 1660, btwn Tanah Rata & Brinchang; ☽ lunch & dinner) A local Highlands tradition is tea time with the requisite beverage, scones and jam; many guesthouse in town offer this midday meal but this place is worth checking out because of its historic and wooded setting.

Restaurant Bunga Suria (66A Persiaran Camellia 3; meals RM2-9; ☽ lunch & dinner) No traveller should miss Suria's banana-leaf meal, a locals' hangout with lots of vegetarian options. There are sweet and savoury roti and the samosa and lassi are delicious.

Ranch Pub (Jl Besar) The only real bar in Tanah Rata is this place, in the same building as the Kavy Hotel. Its 'Wild West' theme may not inspire a hoedown but it's popular with backpackers and also has a pool table.

Getting There & Around

From Tanah Rata, buses go to/from KL (RM13 to RM20; four hours; six daily between 8am and 4.30pm). Another bus leaves Tanah Rata bound for Ipoh (RM5; two hours, five daily, 8am to 5.30pm) and Georgetown (RM19). Buses also go to Tapah (RM4.20, two hours, five daily

8am to 5.30pm), the transfer point for Singapore (RM45, seven hours, 10.30am and 9.30pm). Book tickets at the bus station. For east coast destinations, connect through Ipoh (below).

Local buses run from Tanah Rata to Brinchang (RM1, roughly hourly from 6.30am to 6.30pm) and less frequently to Kampung Raja (RM2.40), passing butterfly attractions and the turn-off to Sungai Palas Estate.

Taxi services from Tanah Rata include Ringlet (RM15), Brinchang (RM5), Sungai Palas Boh Tea Estate (RM15) and Boh Tea Estate (RM20). For touring around, a taxi costs RM18 per hour, or you can go up to Gunung Brinchang and back for RM60.

IPOH
☎ 05

Many travellers pass through Ipoh ('ee-po'), primarily using it as a transit hub for the Cameron Highlands or Pulau Pangkor. The 'City of Millionaires' made its fortune from the tin mines of the Kinta Valley. All travellers should take care at night as Ipoh has a prostitution problem.

Orientation & Information

Many of Ipoh's streets have been renamed and some may still be known by the old names. These include Jl CM Yussuf (formerly Jl Chamberlain), Jl Bandar Timah (formerly Jl Leech), Jl Dato Maharajah Lela (formerly Jl Station), Jl Sultan Idris Shah (Jl Clarke) and Jl Panglima Bukit Gantang Wahab (Jl Kelab). Ipoh's 'Old Town' is west of Sungai Kinta, New Town is east.

The two banks listed here are near the clock tower.

HSBC (Jl Dato Maharajah Lela)

Perak Tourist Information Centre (☎ 241 2957; Jl Tun Sambanthan; ⏰ 8am-1pm & 2-4.30pm Mon-Thu, 8am-12.15pm & 2.45-4.30pm Fri, 8am-1pm Sat)

Standard Chartered Bank (Jl Dato Maharajah Lela)

Sights

Ipoh's **Old Town** showcases elegant colonial architecture and the **train station** (known locally as the 'Taj Mahal') is magnificent.

There are spiritual Buddhist cave-temples on the outskirts of the city, including **Perak Tong** (⏰ 8am-6pm), 6km north on the road to Kuala Kangsar, and **Sam Poh Tong** (⏰ 8am-4.30pm), a few kilometres to the south. Both are easily accessible by local bus.

Sleeping

Decent budget places are in short supply in Ipoh. You're better off with a midrange option.

Sun Golden Inn (☎ 243 6255; 17 Jl Che Tak; r RM40; ✸) This simple spot has a fashion-fearless owner who will be eager to bargain on rates.

New Caspian (☎ 255 1221; Jl Ali Pritchay; r RM55) One of the town's better options, New Caspian is run by a nice couple and rooms have TV and mould-free baths. A discreet arrow in each room points to Mecca.

Grand View Hotel (☎ 243 1488; 36 Jl Horley; r RM70-80; ✸) One of the smarter midrange places, with clean, brightly furnished rooms in a quiet area near the city centre; the hotel is aptly named.

Eating & Drinking

Perak state's tin mines attracted Chinese labourers, who in turn populated the state capital with renowned Chinese food, including the famous dish Ipoh *kway teow* (rice-noodle soup). Ipoh's regional variation of curry laksa is another treat, merging Chinese barbecue pork with an Indian-style curry.

FMS Bar & Restaurant (☎ 253 7678; 2 Jl Sultan Idris Shah; dishes from RM7; ⏰ lunch & dinner) An excellent Chinese restaurant in a beautifully restored colonial building on the edge of the Padang (town square). Seafood and beancurd dishes are winners and there's a small saloon-style bar downstairs.

Kedai Makanan Lok Wee Koi (cnr Jl Mustapha Al-Bakri & Jl Raja Musa Aziz; ⏰ breakfast, lunch & dinner) This is a typical Chinese coffeeshop hosting several different hawker noodle stalls; try the famed *kway teow* or curry laksa here.

Medan Selera Dato Tawhil Azar (Jl Raja Musa Aziz; ⏰ dinner) This large open-air food stall around a small square is a good spot for a Malay meal in the evening.

Miners' Arms (8 Jl Dato Maharaja Lela; meals RM4-7; ⏰ dinner) This popular British-style pub also serves grills and steak dinners.

Getting There & Away

Ipoh is 205km north of KL and 164km south of Butterworth. The **long-distance bus station** (Medan Goreng) is south of the train station and the city centre, a taxi ride from the main hotel area should be RM5 to RM7.

Destinations and standard fares: Alor Setar (RM14.50, four hours, two daily), Butterworth (RM9, three hours, five daily), Hat Yai in Thailand (RM33, nine hours, one daily), Johor Bahru (RM35, eight hours, two daily), Kota Bharu (RM21.70, seven hours, one daily), KL (RM15, three hours, hourly), Lumut (RM4.60, two hours, frequent), Melaka (RM19.30, five hours, three daily) and Tanah Rata (RM5, two hours, frequent). There is also an Ipoh–KLIA (KL International Airport) express service (RM42, three hours, four departures from 6am to 7.30pm). From the airport, the Ipoh-bound bus makes four trips from 7.30am to 6.30pm.

The local bus station is northwest of the long-distance station on the other side of the roundabout. Local buses depart from here for outlying regions close to Ipoh, such as Kuala Kangsar.

Ipoh's **train station** (☎ 254 7987) is on the main Singapore–Butterworth line. The train to KL (*ekonomi*/2nd class RM10/18) leaves at 1.05am, arriving at 7.11am; in the opposite direction, a daily train heads to Butterworth (*ekonomi*/2nd class RM9/17) at 1.15am, arriving at 6.10am, before continuing to Hat Yai in Thailand.

LUMUT
☎ 05

Lumut is the departure point for Pulau Pangkor. **Tourism Malaysia** (☎ 683 4057; Jl Sultan Idris Shah; ☷ 9am-5pm Mon-Fri, 9am-1.45pm Sat) is midway between the jetty and the bus station. Next door you'll find a moneychanger offering better rates than on Pulau Pangkor, and Maybank further down the street.

If you get marooned, there are reasonable **Chinese hotels** (Jl Titi Panjang; r RM40) on the road leading out past the bus station, as well as on the waterfront road near the jetty.

Direct buses run to/from KL (RM16, four hours, three daily), Butterworth (RM10.50, five hours, three daily), Johor Bahru (RM40, 10 hours, four daily), Melaka (RM20, seven hours, two daily) and Kuantan (RM25, five hours, one daily). There are no direct buses from Lumut to the Cameron Highlands; take a bus to Ipoh (RM4.60, two hours, hourly), then transfer to Tanah Rata.

The Pulau Pangkor pier is an easy walk from the bus station. Boats run every 30 minutes and cost RM10.

PULAU PANGKOR
☎ 05 / pop 25,000

Just a half day's journey from Kuala Lumpur, Pulau Pangkor is a delightful *kampung* island with a jungle-clad interior and pristine beaches. It doesn't make much noise along the traveller's grapevine but is an excellent diversion if burning up a few days before a flight home.

Pangkor's piece of history, the foundations of a **Dutch fort** dating from 1670, is 3km south of Pangkor Town at Teluk Gedong.

Ferries from Lumut stop on the eastern side of the island at Sungai Pinang Kecil (SPK) and then Pangkor Town, where you'll find banks, restaurants and shops.

Beaches

The main beaches are on the west coast. Travellers, especially women, should take care on Pulau Pangkor, especially on empty stretches at the island's northeastern side and south of Pangkor Town.

Five minutes' walk north of Teluk Nipah, **Coral Bay** is the best beach on this side of the island, with clear, emerald-green water, due to the presence of limestone.

Pasir Bogak is a swimming beach favoured by holidaying Malaysians, and gets crowded during holidays. It's narrow, with white-sand and mostly midrange accommodation.

A popular backpacker haven, **Teluk Nipah** is north of Pasir Bogak. This is a scenic beach with offshore islands, a variety of budget accommodation and a lively atmosphere.

Sleeping
TELUK NIPAH

Most accommodation is set on access roads between the beachfront road and the jungle – a blessing in disguise when the local kids start racing their motorcycles along the main drag.

Nazri Nipah Camp (☎ 685 2014; dm RM10, r RM15-40) The party place where empty beer cans will greet early risers. This is the cheapest on the island with simple A-frames and more comfortable chalets with bathroom.

Seagull Beach Resort (☎ 685 2878; r RM40-80; ☷ ☐) A friendly guesthouse in a quiet spot back from the road. The prices are slowly outpacing the quality of the rooms, though. Small, basic huts are cramped, and the pricier air-con doubles are preferable. There's a restaurant on-site.

Mizam Resort (☎ 685 3359; r RM30-50; 🔀) A hidden gem set well back from the beach, at the very edge of the jungle. It's a quiet place, and the rooms all come with TV and attached bathroom.

Ombak Inn (☎ 685 5223; r RM40-70; 🔀) A sweet little place with a variety of options, from basic A-frame huts to sparkling fan/air-con bungalows with attached bathrooms. The owners are quick with a joke.

PASIR BOGAK

The atmosphere here is lacking compared to Teluk Nipah, and fewer overseas travellers stay here.

Coral View Beach Resort (☎ 685 2163; r from RM70; 🔀) Formerly Khoo Holiday Resort starts at the western end of the beach. The main building of this resort is a rather ugly concrete conglomeration, but the simple wooden chalets with bathroom on the steep slope behind are great deals with views across the ocean to Pulau Pangkor Laut.

Lambaian Beach Resort (☎ 685 4020; r from RM70; 🔀) North of the intersection, this hotel was closed for upgrades at the time of research, although the on-site manager was enthusiastic about keeping budget rooms available.

Eating & Drinking

Several of Teluk Nipah's guesthouses have restaurants, though outside high season (November to March), these often close down. Most restaurants serve alcohol. There are also some basic food stalls at the beach.

Takana Juo Restoran (TJ's; dishes from RM6; 🕒 breakfast, lunch & dinner) By far the most popular eatery, and deservedly so, this is a family-run Indonesian restaurant at the bungalows of the same name. TJ's cooks up delicious, cheap food, though staff certainly take their time serving it. It's open breakfast to dinner and is regularly full, so you'll need to get there early.

Tiger Beer Garden (Teluk Nipah) On the main road just down from the Hornbill Beach Resort, this place has a few outdoor tables where you can drink a beer and watch the sunset.

Getting There & Away

Berjaya Air (☎ 685 5828; www.berjaya-air.com) flies to/from KL's Subang airport (RM230), daily except on Tuesday and Thursday.

In the high season, ferries (return RM10, 45 minutes, every 30 minutes from 7am-8pm) run to and from Lumut and Pangkor Town.

Getting Around

There are no public buses but pink mini-bus taxis operate between 6.30am and 9pm. Fares are set for the entire vehicle to/from the jetty in Pangkor town and go to Pasir Bogak (RM4), Teluk Nipah (RM10) and around the island (RM35 to RM45).

Motorcycles (RM30) and bicycles (RM15) can be rented in Pangkor town and at main beaches.

BUTTERWORTH

This mainland town is the jumping-off point for Pulau Penang. The Butterworth–Penang ferry jetty (RM0.60; every 20 minutes from 5.30am to 12.30pm) is conveniently located next to the train and bus station. Fares for the ferry are charged only for the journey from Butterworth to Georgetown (on Penang); returning to Butterworth on the mainland is free.

The **train station** (☎ 323 7962) is next to the jetty and bus station. There is a nightly train to KL (economy/2nd class/berth RM17/30/40) at 9.30pm, arriving at 7.30am the next morning. In the opposite direction, there is a daily train to Hat Yai, Thailand (2nd class/berth RM36/36) at 6.10am, arriving at 10.15am Thai time (one hour behind). There is also an international express train leaving Butterworth at 2.20pm and arriving in Hat Yai at 7.25pm and Bangkok at 12.50pm the next day. Times and fares vary.

The bus station is next to the jetty and train station. Buses depart from Butterworth to the following destinations: Johor Bahru (RM35, 12 hours, six daily), KL (RM25, five hours, hourly), Kota Bharu (RM20, seven hours, two daily), Kuala Terengganu (RM30, 10 hours, two daily), Kuantan (RM10.50, 12 hours, six daily), Melaka (RM28, 12 hours, two daily) and Singapore (RM45, nine hours, two daily).

PULAU PENANG

Think globalisation is a new phenomenon? Reach back into the history of Penang to see the rise and fall of one of the world's mightiest corporations, the East India Company. Back when the distinction between governments, armies and companies was less precise, the British-based juggernaut sailed into the harbour and took over the 28-sq-km island as its first settlement on the Malay peninsula, a strategic move intended to break Dutch Melaka's monopoly of the spice trade.

What evolved on the formerly unpopulated 'Betel Nut Island' was a bustling port. Entrepreneurs of every imaginable ethnicity, most notably Chinese, flocked to this new land of opportunity, creating wealth and cultural hybrids. Like many company towns, Penang wilted after the collapse of the British empire, and continues to decline as a player on the international trading floor.

Penang's loss of prestige only sweetens its appeal to a world-rover. In the commercial centre of Georgetown, the modern world inhabits the narrow streets and crumbling mercantile buildings like a family reunion. The elders' faded glory hovers over the exuberance of the next generation. Beyond Georgetown's heat and decay are beach resorts, such as Batu Ferringhi (p456), and the sleepy Malay fishing village of Teluk Bahang (p456).

Georgetown
☎ 04

Cramped and chaotic, central Georgetown is an obstacle course of daily life. Dodging in and out of traffic and across open drains

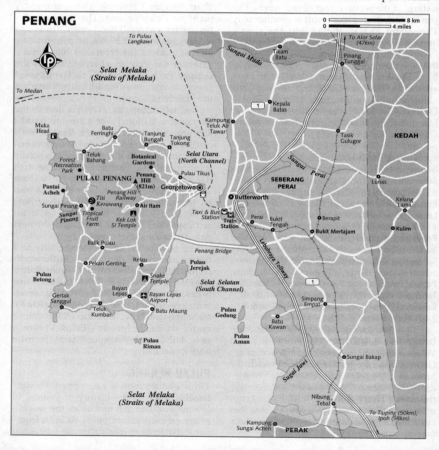

PENANG

0 —————— 8 km
0 —————— 4 miles

To Pulau Langkawi
To Alor Setar (47km)

Selat Melaka (Straits of Melaka)

To Medan

Tikam Batu
Pinang Tunggal
Sungai Muda

Kepala Batas

Kampung Teluk Air Tawar

Tasik Gulugor

KEDAH

Muka Head
Batu Ferringhi
Tanjung Bungah
Tanjung Tokong

Selat Utara (North Channel)

Teluk Bahang
Botanical Gardens

Forest Recreation Park

Pulau Tikus

PULAU PENANG
Penang Hill (821m)

Penang Hill Railway

Georgetown

Butterworth

SEBERANG PERAI

Sungai Perai

Lunas

Pantai Acheh
Titi Kerawang
Air Itam

Sungai Pinang
Tropical Fruit Farm
Kek Lok Si Temple

Taxi & Bus Station
Train Station
Perai
Bukit Tengah

Kelang Lama

Berapit

Bukit Mertajam

Kulim

Balik Pulau

Penang Bridge

Pekan Genting
Relau

Pulau Jerejak

Lebuhraya Tollway

Snake Temple

Selat Selatan (South Channel)

Pulau Betong

Bayan Lepas
Bayan Lepas Airport

Pulau Gedung

Simpang Empat

Gertak Sanggul
Teluk Kumbar
Batu Maung

Batu Kawan

Pulau Aman

Pulau Rimau

Sungai Bakap

Selat Melaka (Straits of Melaka)

Nibung Tebal

To Taiping (50km); Ipoh (98km)

Kampung Sungai Acheh

PERAK

Sungai Jawi

turns walking into a full-contact sport. When you can shift your concentration away from ground-level, you'll notice Georgetown's charms: atmospheric shophouses, elaborate temples and sagging colonial grandeur. It's a grazing city, showcasing the culinary offspring of the island's unique cultural intermingling. Off the island, Georgetown is often referred to as Penang (Pinang).

ORIENTATION
Georgetown is at the northeastern corner of Pulau Penang. Central Georgetown is compact and easily navigated on foot. Many of Georgetown's oldest mosques, temples and churches can be found at, and around, Lebuh Pitt (also called Jl Masjid Kapitan Keling). Following Jl Penang southwest, you'll reach Kompleks Komtar (Kompleks Tun Abdul Razak), the island's transport hub and shopping centre.

INFORMATION
Branches of major banks and 24-hour ATMs are concentrated around Kompleks Komtar and around Lebuh Pantai and Lebuh Downing, near the main post office, while Internet access is widely available on Lebuh Chulia and Lebuh Cintra (rates start at RM1 per minute). You can stock up on reading supplies at the host of cheap secondhand bookshops.

General Hospital (☎ 229 3333; Jl Residensi)
HS Sam Book Store (☎ 262 2705; 473 Lebuh Chulia)
Immigration Office (☎ 261 5122; 29A Lebuh Pantai)
Loh Guan Lye Specialist Centre (☎ 228 8501; 19 Jl Logan)
Penang Tourist Guides Association (☎ 261 4461; 3rd fl, Kompleks Komtar, Jl Penang; ☺ 10am-6pm Mon-Sat) Excellent tourist office, but hard to find; look for signs near the McDonald's on the 3rd floor.
Popular Bookshop (☎ 263 6122; Kompleks Komtar)
Tourism Malaysia (☎ 262 0066; 10 Jl Tun Syed Sheh Barakbah; ☺ 8am-4.30pm Mon-Thu, 8am-12.15pm & 2.45-4.30pm Fri, 8am-1pm Sat)

DANGERS & ANNOYANCES
While generally a safe place to wander, Georgetown has its seamy side. Travellers have been mugged at Love Lane and other dimly lit side-streets, so take care around this area if you're out late, and take a taxi or trishaw to your accommodation. Motorcycle snatch thieves are also a problem, so take care of shoulder bags and purses.

GETTING INTO TOWN
Penang's Bayan Lepas International Airport is 18km south of Georgetown. Yellow Bus 83 runs to/from the airport (RM1.50, one hour, hourly from 6am to 9pm) with stops at Pengkalan Weld, Komtar and Lebuh Chulia.

If arriving via the Butterworth-Penang ferry, exit toward Pengkalan Weld and catch any Kompleks Komtar–bound bus (RM1, 15 minutes, frequent) to reach accommodation in Chinatown.

SIGHTS & ACTIVITIES
Cheong Fatt Tze Mansion
A magnificent lavender mansion, **Cheong Fatt Tze Mansion** (☎ 262 5289; Lebuh Leith; adult RM10; ☺ tours 11am & 3pm Mon-Fri, 11am Sat & Sun) was built in the 1880s by Cheong Fatt Tze, a local Hakka merchant-trader who left China as a penniless teenager and eventually established a vast financial empire, earning himself the sobriquet 'Rockefeller of the East'.

The 38-room mansion blends Eastern and Western influences and promotes good feng shui by sitting on a 'dragon's throne' – a mountain (Penang Hill) behind, and water (the Channel) in front. It has Art Nouveau stained-glass windows, elaborate wrought ironwork and a superb glazed-tile roof adorned with ceramic motifs.

Check out this mansion at night when it's colourfully lit and looks the stuff of fairy tales.

Heritage Trail
You can follow the Heritage Trail walking tours, that take in Georgetown's historic colonial architecture and some temples and mosques in Chinatown – pick up a pamphlet showing the routes at the tourist offices.

There's also a free **shuttle bus** (☺ 7am-7pm Mon-Fri, 7am-2pm Sat) that runs between the jetty and Kompleks Komtar, winding its way through Georgetown's colonial core. Pick up a brochure at the **Penang Tourist Guides Association** (☎ 261 4461; 3rd fl, Kompleks Komtar, Jl Penang; ☺ 10am-6pm Mon-Sat) for a copy of the route.

Temples & Mosques
In honour of the goddess of mercy, good fortune, peace and fertility the **Kuan Yin Teng** (Lebuh Pitt; admission by donation; ☺ 9am-5pm) was

MALAYSIA

GEORGETOWN

built in the early 19th century by the first Hokkien and Cantonese settlers in Penang. It's usually buzzing with worshippers burning paper money.

Dedicated to Mar Chor, the patron saint of seafarers, **Hainan Temple** (Lebuh Muntri; admission by donation; 🕑 9am-5pm) was completed in 1895. Remodelling in 1995 has refreshed its distinctive swirling dragon pillars and brightened the ornate carvings.

Built by Penang's first Indian-Muslim settlers, the yellow **Kapitan Keling Mosque** (Lebuh Pitt) has a single minaret in an Indian-influenced Islamic style. This building is best appreciated from the street.

Khoo Kongsi (Lebuh Cannon; adult RM5; 🕑 9am-5pm), near the end of Lebuh Pitt, is a colourful mix of dragons, other statues, paintings, lamps, coloured tiles and carvings; it dates from 1906. A *kongsi* is a clan house, a building that's partly a temple and partly a meeting hall for Chinese of the same clan or surname.

Other Sights

Fort Cornwallis (Lebuh Light; adult RM3; 🕑 9am-7pm) was built on Georgetown's cape, the historic landing of the city's founder Captain Francis Light in 1786. An old cannon dating back to 1603 has finally found a permanent home here after a few centuries of being stolen from one conqueror after another.

Penang Museum (🕿 261 3144; Lebuh Farquhar; adult RM1; 🕑 9am-5pm Sat-Thu) is one of the best-presented museums in Malaysia. In front is a bronze statue of Captain Light, and excellent exhibits on the ground floor illustrate the customs and traditions of Penang's various ethnic groups – Indian, Chinese, Baba Nonya, etc – with impressive appreciation for diversity. Upstairs is the history gallery.

SLEEPING

Georgetown has plenty of cheap accommodation, mainly clustered in Chinatown along Lebuh Chulia, Love Lane and Lebuh Leith. During holidays, most notably Chinese New Year (January/February), hotels fill up very quickly and prices can become ridiculously inflated; if you intend to stay at this time, book in advance.

Swiss Hotel (🕿 262 0133; 431F Lebuh Chulia; r RM20) Well run and great value, the Swiss is set back from Lebuh Chulia in an Art Deco–style hotel. The operators are a little gruff, but who can expect friends at this price. The ground-floor rooms are a little dank.

75 Travellers' Lodge (🕿 262 3378; 75 Lebuh Muntri; dm RM7, s RM15-18, d RM18-40; 🔀) A travellers' favourite, 75 is run by Mr Low, an exceptionally friendly and helpful owner. We've spotted a few complaints in travellers' logs along the trail about this one, but a recent visit found clean baths and decent rooms.

Oasis Hotel (🕿 263 9710; 23 Love Lane; r RM18-30; 🔀) Beds aren't the usual thin spread and baths are church-camp clean.

Cathay Hotel (🕿 262 6271/6272; 22 Lebuh Leith; r RM50-70; 🔀) Recapture the romance of the colonial era in this gracefully ageing diva.

High-ceilinged rooms will make you feel oh-so demure and other character details (note euphemism for 'needing a coat of paint') will put this hotel in your budget. You may remember seeing it in the 1995 film *Beyond Rangoon*.

Pin Seng Hotel (☎ 261 9004; 82 Love Lane; r RM20-25) Tucked down a tiny alley off Love Lane, Pin Seng is nothing flash but rooms are clean and there's a sink in each room.

Olive Spring (☎ 264 4641; 302 Lebuh Chulia; dm RM8, r RM30) Folks dig the outgoing guesthouse operator, who is usually found chewing the fat in the downstairs café. But the rooms aren't much with musty carpet and a few echo chambers right on busy Lebuh Chulia. Shared baths are sparkly clean.

100 Cinta Street (☎ 264 3581; 100 Lebuh Cintra; r RM20) What an architectural charmer – lots of wooden fretwork, stained glass and Chinese antiques, like an ornate human-sized bird cage. Skip the dorms, which are just a few beds in a spare corner of a common hallway and always lock your door as security here is a joke.

D'Budget Hostel (☎ 263 4794; 9 Lebuh Gereja; dm RM7, s RM15-20, d RM20-25, tr RM25-30; ⊠) Cheap and close to the ferry terminal, D'Budget doesn't have much in the way of character, except of course the backpacking veterans who return like migrating swallows. The rooftop deck is a perfect place to watch night fall over Georgetown. Doors lock at 1am.

SPLURGE!

Eastern Oriental (☎ 222 2000; www.e-o-hotel.com; 10 Lebuh Farquhar; ste from RM400-500; ⊠ ⊠) It really is a pipe dream to think that you can spend a night in this legendary grand dame. But you can wander over in your best safari suit for a sunset drink on the seaside terrace. You're in good company here too – Rudyard Kipling, Noel Coward and Somerset Maugham were just some of the famous faces who passed through its doors.

Cheong Fatt Tze Mansion (☎ 262 5289; www.cheongfatttzemansion.com; 14 Lebuh Leith; r from RM250; ⊠) This is an exclusive and unique owner-hosted homestay, which is also one of the city's premier tourist attractions. The opulently furnished suites are individually styled, and each comes with a personal valet.

EATING

Penang cuisine is legendary: Indian, Chinese, and Malay purveyors jostle with one another for affection from a constantly snacking populace. Along with Melaka, Penang boasts the indigenous fusion of Baba Nonya cuisine. Penang's Baba Nonya dishes differ from Melaka's by drawing more sour notes from nearby Thailand, but the term is so amorphic that often any hybrid is attributed to or adopted by Malaysia's respective ethnic groups.

Chinese

In the morning, an umbrella village of food stalls sets up across from Chowrasta Bazaar near the vegetable sellers. Here you'll find vendors dexterously folding and stuffing slippery *chee cheong fun* (broad rice noodles filled with prawns or meat); watching the dish's creation is much easier than wrestling the noodles into your mouth (good luck).

At night, Lebuh Kimberly drains the electrical grid with riotously lit hawker stalls where simple ingredients are transformed into Chinese delicacies.

Lebuh Cintra is lined with bustling Chinese noodle and dim-sum joints.

Hsaing Fast Food (97 Lebuh Cintra; meals RM2-6; ⊗ breakfast & lunch) Point and choose from the array of seafood, meat and vegetarian fare displayed tantalisingly in stainless steel trays. As with any of these 'fast food' eateries it's best to arrive noon-ish when the dishes are fresh.

Wen Chang (63 Lebuh Cintra; meals RM2-5; ⊗ breakfast & lunch) Extremely popular lunch spot with enthusiastic staff. Piles of steamed white rice and tender chicken cooked and flavoured in Hainanese style served with a herbal broth.

Sin Kuan Hwa Cafe (cnr Lebuh Chulia & Cintra; meals RM2-5; ⊗ breakfast & lunch) Another of Georgetown's excellent Hainanese chicken-rice purveyors.

Ng Kee Cake Shop (☎ 261 2229; 61 Lebuh Cintra; cakes RM0.60-3; ⊗ breakfast & lunch) Pick up your long-distance bus and train snacks here. Ng Kee has a range of sweet treats such as tiny cakes sweetened with coconut and the addictive *kacang* (nut bars): peanut, sesame seed and honey.

Kedai Makanan De Tai (Lebuh Cintra; RM2-4; ⊗ breakfast, lunch & dinner) Packed early in the morning with customers craving dim sum, this place has an air-conditioned back room where you can revive with a refreshing cane juice. Duck lovers can order with confidence.

Sim Sun Fook (105 Lebuh Cintra; meals RM4-10; ☺ breakfast & lunch) This morning dim-sum house is not as crowded as De Tai, making it much easier for a clueless round-eye to get a seat. Order a pot of tea and wait for the bamboo trays of mystery meat dim-sum to make their rounds. The deep-fried wontons are made more delicious with dollops of mayonnaise.

Malay & Nonya

You'll have to venture outside Chinatown for Penang's signature Malay and Baba Nonya dishes. Lorong Baru, just off Jl Macalister, has a row of food stalls whipping up satay; things don't start sizzling until nightfall. Lorong Swatow, off Jl Burma, is known for the decadent dessert of ABC.

Esplanade Food Centre (Jl Tun Syed Sheh Barakbah; meals RM3-6; ☺ dinner) This is Penang's best hawker centre, as much for the delightful sea breezes as the Malay stalls serving laksa asam, *pasembur* (a vegetable-and-fish salad topped with a sweet and spicy gravy) and radioactive-coloured bowls of ABC and cendol. The more restaurant-like Chinese section features seafood and icy-cold beer.

Medan Selera (Jl Macalister; meals RM4-6; ☺ dinner) This covered food centre makes grazing through Penang's legendary menu effortless. Everything is here – laksa, Hokkien mee, rojak, *char kway teow*. Order from the vendor and pay when it arrives.

Kek Seng Café (Jl Penang; ☺ breakfast, lunch & dinner) Folks agree that this shop, between Jl Burma and Jl Macalister, does the best laksa asam in town.

Indian

Georgetown's Little India is along Lebuh Pasar, Lebuh China and the side streets between Lebuh Penang and Lebuh Pitt. Several small restaurants and food stalls serve cheap North (Muslim) and South Indian (vegetarian) food. Lebuh Tamil, off Jl Penang, is an easygoing alley for a shady respite of Indian and Malay dishes or a cup of *teh tarik* ('pulled tea,' tea with frothy milk). On a no-name alley off Jl Penang, near Restoran Yasmeen, is a concentration of *nasi kandar* (pre-made dishes to accompany rice) stalls.

Meena Cafe (118 Lebuh Penang; meals RM2.50-6; ☺ breakfast & dinner) Friendly staff serve up tasty Indian food. Mutton and fish curries are fragrantly delicious and the *masala thosai* (spicy potato filling wrapped in a rice-and-lentil crepe) is as enticing as the blackcurrant and mango lassi.

PENANG MUST EATS

Penang is known as the hawker capital of Malaysia and most of the city's specialities – claiming mixed Malay and Chinese extraction – are best fetched from a portable cart or food centre.

Cendol Garishly coloured green strands (made from sweetened pea flour) are layered with crushed ice, coconut milk and brown-sugar syrup. The related dessert of ABC is the shepherd's pie of sweets, with shaved ice, ice cream, flavoured sugar water, beans and tapioca balls.

Char kway teow Medium-width rice noodles are stir-fried with egg, vegetables, shrimp and Chinese sausage in a dark soy sauce.

Chee cheong fun A popular dim sum dish, these are broad, paper-thin rice noodles that are steamed and rolled around a filling of prawns served with an oily, chili dipping sauce.

Curry mee Curly egg noodles (*mee*) are served in a spicy coconut-curry soup, garnished with bean sprouts, prawn, cuttlefish, cockles, beancurd and mint.

Hokkien mee A busy and spicy pork-broth soup crowded with egg noodles, prawns, bean sprouts, kangkong, egg and pork.

Laksa asam Also known as Penang laksa, this is a fish-broth soup spiked with a sour tang from tamarind paste (*asam*) and a mint garnish; it's served with thick, white rice noodles (laksa).

Rojak A fruit and vegetable salad tossed in a sweet-tamarind-and-palm-sugar sauce and garnished with crushed peanuts, sesame seeds and chillies.

Won ton mee This is a Cantonese clear-broth soup of wheat-and-egg noodles swimming with wontons (rice-paper dumplings stuffed with shrimp), vegetables and *char siew* (barbecued pork); the regional twist adds *belacan* (fermented shrimp paste).

Sri Ananda Bhawan (☎ 264 4204; 55 Lebuh Penang; meals RM3-6; ☻ breakfast & dinner) A neighbourhood favourite for banana-leaf meals. You can stay cheap and vegetarian with the basic set-up automatically brought out by a platoon of workers. To explore the menu, add a few side dishes, like pepper chicken. Chase away the fire in your belly with a lassi and call yourself a lucky eater.

Krsna Restaurant (☎ 264 3601; 75 Lebuh Pasar; meals RM5-10; ☻ breakfast & dinner) Sweaty and busy, this vegetarian South Indian spot does a great *oothaban*, like a vege-filled pizza you eat with your hands (your right hand, that is).

DRINKING

Amidst Penang's ancient shophouses is the renovated row of Jl Penang where nouveau bistros and lounges show off their multilingual sophistication.

Blue Diamond Hotel & Cafe (☎ 261 1089; 422 Lebuh Chulia) This guesthouse in a formerly grandiose mansion hosts a nightly beer garden with various appearances by self-described 'guitar men'.

20 Leith St (20 Leith St) A historic bar with a festive, upbeat atmosphere. Jaunty fairy lights and glowing red Chinese lanterns are strung up in the convivial front beer garden. It's a mix of locals and foreigners who are equally fascinated by the high-energy entertainment. Happy hour is 4pm to 9pm.

Jim's Place Café (☎ 653 6963; 433 Lebuh Chulia) A long-time character on the Chulia strip,

Jim now has his own place, serving cheap, cold beer, and lots of unsolicited advice.

Coco Island Travellers Corner (273 Lebuh Chulia) Under the Hong Ping Hotel, Coco Island is a big backpackers' pub stuck in an 1980s aesthetic (at least the look is hip again?). Flashing neon lights, locals cruising for a lonely foreign friend, and a gruff waitress make a potent cocktail.

CLUBBING

Lush (the Garage, 2 Jl Penang) A contemporary nightclub with slick minimalist design in stark tones of red, grey and black. DJs and nightly promotions are a fun diversion to the usual backpacker night sweats.

Slippery Senoritas (SS; the Garage, 2 Jl Penang) In the same complex, Slippery Senoritas is brasher than Lush but is still good for a laugh, and the Tom Cruise *Cocktail*esque show put on by the bar staff is mesmerising.

GETTING THERE & AWAY

See Butterworth (p447) for information about reaching the island of Penang from the mainland, and for long-distance train and bus travel.

Advance bookings on long-distance trains can be made at the **Railway Booking Office** (Pengkalan Weld), near the Butterworth-Penang ferry jetty.

Air

Airline offices that have connections to Pulau Penang:

Air Asia (☎ 644 8701; www.airasia.com; ground fl, Kompleks Komtar) To and from KL one-way/return RM50/100.

Malaysia Airlines (☎ 262 0011; www.malaysiaairlines.com; Menara KWSP, Jl Sultan Ahmad Shah) To/from KL RM330.

Singapore Airlines (☎ 226 6211; www.singaporeair.com; Wisma Penang Gardens, Jl Sultan Ahmad Shah) To/from Singapore RM600.

Thai Airways International (THAI; ☎ 226 6000; www.thaiair.com; Wisma Central, 41 Jl Macalister) To/from Bangkok RM830.

Boat

There are a million different company names floating around for the ferry service between Pulau Langkawi and Penang. All the offices are clustered together and all put you on the same boats, so listing the company names here would be a gratuitous

---

BORDER CROSSING: INTO INDONESIA

Travellers can skip over to the Indonesian island of Sumatra from Pulau Penang via ferry. There are several ferries each way in the morning, and times can change, but generally ferries depart Georgetown at 8.30am and return at 10.30am (one-way/return RM90/160); the trip takes 4½ to five hours. The boats leave from Georgetown's Swettenham jetty and land in Belawan where the remaining journey to Medan is completed by bus (included in the price). Buy tickets the day before to verify departure times. Upon arriving at Belawan port, most nationalities will need to pay US$25 per person fee for a month-long Indonesian visa.

attempt to rationalise our job. But for the sticklers, you'll be in good hands with **Super Fast Ferry Ventures** (☎ 262 0802), **Langkawi Ferry Services** (LFS; ☎ 264 2088) and **Ekspres Bahagia** (☎ 263 1943), all in the PPC Building on Pesara King Edward.

They run daily ferries from Georgetown to Langkawi (one-way/return RM40/75, 2½ hours). Boats leave at 8.30am, 8.45am and 2.45pm, returning from Langkawi at 11.30 am, 2.30pm, and 5.30pm. Check the times the day before, as schedules vary. Also note that ferries to Langkawi depart the jetty off Pesara King Edward near the clock tower.

Bus

Buses to all major towns on the peninsula leave from both Georgetown and Butterworth. Several long-distance bus services leave from Kompleks Komtar in central Georgetown.

There are daily buses to Ipoh (RM12, three hours, hourly), KL (RM23, five hours, hourly), Kuantan (RM37, eight hours, one daily), Melaka (RM30, seven hours, two daily), and Singapore (RM45, nine hours, two daily).

There are also bus and minibus services to Thailand: Hat Yai (RM20), Krabi (RM38), Phuket (RM60), and Ko Samui (RM55). The minibuses usually don't go directly to some destinations so there are significant waiting times. Train is usually quicker.

GETTING AROUND

Penang has a good public transport system that connects Georgetown with the rest of the island.

Bus

There are several local bus stops in Georgetown. Kompleks Komtar and Pengkalan Weld, in front of the Butterworth–Penang jetty, are two of the largest stops. Fares within Georgetown are under RM1, points beyond are RM1 to RM2 depending on the destination (exact change required).

For around RM5 you can do a circuit of the island by public transport.

Motorcycle & Bicycle

You can hire bicycles from shops at Lebuh Chulia, Batu Ferringhi (13km northwest of Georgetown) and some guesthouses. Bicycles cost RM10, and motorcycles start at

---

USEFUL BUSES IN PULAU PENANG

You can catch TransitLink (TL), Yellow Bus (YB), Hin Bus (HB) and Sri Negara city buses from the Pengkalan Weld stop, near the Butterworth–Pulau Penang jetty or Kompleks Komtar. Most of the TransitLink buses also have stops along Lebuh Chulia.

Air Itam (transfer point for Penang Hill) TL 1, 101, 351, 361; YB 85;

Batu Ferringhi HB 93; TL 202

Bayan Lepas Airport YB 83

Chinatown TL 1, 101, 351, 361; YB 85

Penang Hill Railway TL 1, 130, 351; YB 85; Mini 21 from Air Itam

Teluk Bahang HB 93; TL 202

RM20 to RM25 per day. Remember that if you don't have a motorcycle licence, your travel insurance probably won't cover you in the case of an accident.

Taxi

You'll need to bargain for a fair fare. Typical taxi rates around town are RM3 to RM6. Other fares include Batu Ferringhi (RM15), Penang Hill/Kek Lok Si Temple (RM10) and Bayan Lepas airport (RM23).

Trishaw

Bicycle rickshaws are an ideal way to negotiate Georgetown's backstreets and cost around RM1 per kilometre but, as with taxis, agree on the fare before departure. For touring around, the rate is about RM25 per hour.

AROUND PULAU PENANG

Take a break from Georgetown's intensity with a day trip to the nearby beaches, fishing villages or tranquil Penang Hill.

Penang Hill

Once a fashionable retreat for the city's elite, Penang Hill (800m) provides cool temperatures and spectacular views. There are pretty gardens, an old-fashioned kiosk, a restaurant and a hotel, as well as a lavishly decorated Hindu temple and a mosque at the top. Penang Hill is particularly wonderful at dusk as Georgetown, far below, starts to light up.

From Kompleks Komtar, or at Lebuh Chulia, you can catch one of the frequent

TransitLink buses (1, 101, 351 or 361) or Yellow Bus 85 to Air Itam. From Air Itam, walk five minutes to the funicular railway (adult/child RM4/2; 30 minutes; every 15 to 30 minutes from 6.30am to 9.30pm) where long queues may await, or take the half-hourly TransitLink shuttle bus 8. The energetic can get to the top by an interesting three-hour trek, starting from the Moon Gate at the Botanical Gardens.

Kek Lok Si Temple, the largest Buddhist temple in Malaysia, stands on a hilltop at Air Itam, near Penang Hill. Construction started in 1890, took more than 20 years, and was largely funded by donations. To reach the entrance, walk through the souvenir stalls until you reach the seven-tier, 30m-high **Ban Po Thar** (Ten Thousand Buddhas Pagoda; admission RM2). The design is said to be Burmese at the top, Chinese at the bottom and Thai in between.

Batu Ferringhi
☎ 04

Following the coastal road east will lead you to Batu Ferringhi, a graceful curved bay lined with resorts on one end and guesthouses on the other. The eastern end has a sleepy village ambience, which is more appealing than the less-than-paradise-perfect sand and sea. The 2004 tsunami grazed this portion of Penang, causing minimal property damage and flooding. Locals say the beach sands got a much needed polish from the hungry waves.

SLEEPING
Low-key guesthouses are clustered together opposite the beach, and most will give discounts for multiday stays.

Shalini's Guest House (☎ 881 1859; 56 Batu Ferringhi; s/d from RM30/40; ✖) An old, two-storey wooden house with a friendly, family atmosphere. Rooms are basic but neat and some have balconies.

Baba Guest House (☎ 881 1686; 52 Batu Ferringhi; r RM30-50; ✖) A tidy family home with plain rooms, most with shared bathrooms. The dearer air-con rooms come with a refrigerator and shower.

ET Budget Guest House (☎ 881 1553; 47 Batu Ferringhi; r RM20-60; ✖) Another double-storey house with basic rooms, most with common bathroom. The pricier air-con rooms come with TV and shower.

Ali's Guest House (☎ 881 1316; 53 Batu Ferringhi; r RM30-65; ✖) A simple budget place with a popular beachside bar and restaurant at the front, though travellers have complained of rude and unhelpful staff.

Ah Beng (☎ 881 1036; 54C Batu Ferringhi; r RM20-30; ✖) Small but comfortable rooms, some with sea-facing balconies.

GETTING THERE & AWAY
Hin Bus 93 (half-hourly), TransitLink 202 (hourly) and Minibuses 31A and 88A from Kompleks Komtar take around 30 minutes to reach Batu Ferringhi and cost RM2.

Teluk Bahang
☎ 04

If you're looking to get off the beaten path, you don't need to do a 10-hour bus ride to escape the circuit. Just east of Batu Ferringhi, Teluk Bahang is a sleepy Malay fishing village that has faded out of the backpacker radar. There isn't a lot to do in Teluk Bahang and that's the point. Many return travellers come to Teluk Bahang to practice a devout regime of destination-less strolls and grazing at roadside stalls.

The main road cuts south at the village and passes several garden attractions, including the **Tropical Fruit Farm** (☎ 866 5168; tours RM20; ☯ 9am-5pm), which raises over 140 types of tropical and sub-tropical fruit trees, native and hybrid. To get here, take the infrequent Yellow Bus 76, which runs between Balik Pulau and Teluk Bahang four times a day. Ask the driver where to get off.

SLEEPING
Miss Loh's Guest House (☎ 885 1227; 159 Jl Teluk Bahang; dm/s/d from RM8/20/30; ✖) Set amidst a fruit orchard, this is the kind of place where you can put down roots and watch the days drip by like molasses. Before arriving at the guesthouse, stop in to see Miss Loh, who can be found at a former sundries shop (look for building No 159) near the roundabout.

Rama Guest House (☎ 885 1179; r RM8-15) Take a right at the roundabout to reach an equally quirky and charming guesthouse run by wiry Mr Rama. His wife will make you coffee in the morning and Mr Rama's big heart will make you feel like a rescued stray.

Fisherman Village Guest House (☎ 885 2936; r from RM20) In Kampong Nelayan, a 20-minute walk from Teluk Bahang, this place offers simple, tidy rooms in a family home.

GETTING THERE & AWAY
Hin Bus 93 runs from Georgetown every half-hour all the way along the north coast of the island as far as the roundabout in Teluk Bahang, as does the hourly Transit-Link bus 202.

ALOR SETAR
☎ 04

For transport reasons, you'll pass through the capital of Kedah state. Alor Setar (*allo-star*) is north of Butterworth on the main road to the Thai border and is the transfer point to Kuala Kedah, the port town for ferries to Pulau Langkawi. This region is conservative and not accustomed to seeing shockingly white foreigners. To better fit in with Islamic dress norms, wear clothes that cover your elbows and knees.

Grand Jubilee Hotel (☎ 733 0055; 429 Lebuhraya Darul Aman; r RM40-50; ❄) is a white concrete box, set back from the road, opposite the Hotel Samila, offering plain but clean rooms with fan or air-con.

Getting There & Away
BUS
The bus station is 3.5km outside the town centre. Buses serve the following destinations: Ipoh (RM14.20, three daily, four hours), Johor Bahru (RM45.65, 10 hours, one daily), Kota Bharu (RM22.50, two daily, six hours), Kuala Lumpur (RM25, hourly, six hours), Kuala Terengganu (RM37, 10 hours, one daily), Kuantan (RM37, 10 hours, one daily), Melaka (RM35, eight hours, two daily).

To reach Langkawi, take a local Kuala Kedah–bound bus (RM6, 15 minutes, frequent) to the ferry jetty. A shuttle bus (70 sen) connects the town centre with the bus station; a taxi will cost RM6.

TRAIN
The **train station** (☎ 731 4045; Jl Stesyen) is a 15-minute walk southeast of town. The daily northbound train to Hat Yai, Thailand, (2nd class/berth RM36/45) leaves at 8.15am, arriving at 10.15am Thai time (an hour behind Malaysia). In the opposite direction, the train to KL (economy/2nd class RM20/31) departs at 7pm, reaching the capital at 7am the following morning. There is also an international express train that leaves Alor Setar at 4pm and arrives in Hat Yai at 7.25pm and Bangkok at 1pm the next day. The southbound train leaves Alor Setar at 11.30am and terminates in Butterworth at 1.30pm (economy/2nd class RM18/31).

KUALA PERLIS
☎ 04

This small port town in the extreme northwest of the peninsula is a departure point for ferries to Pulau Langkawi. Several hotels sit directly opposite the jetty, including **AZ Motel** (☎ 019-402 1861; 5 Persiaran Putra Timur 1, Jl Kampung Perak; r RM63-75; ❄).

The bus and taxi stations are behind the row of shophouses across from the jetty. A limited number of destinations are served from Kuala Perlis' bus station; these include Butterworth (RM7.20, four daily), Kuala Lumpur (RM18, frequent) and Kuantan (RM30, one daily). For other destinations, take a taxi (RM10) to the larger bus station in Kangar, which has buses bound for Alor Setar (RM2.50) and the border town of Padang Besar (RM2.15).

Ferries depart for Kuah, on Pulau Langkawi (RM15; every hour between 8am and 6pm).

PULAU LANGKAWI
☎ 04

The island of Langkawi is almost perfect: it is blessed by a generous stole of blonde sand, a thick jungle crown, and magical legends that explain the mysteries of its geography. Now the 'but' – thanks to its 1986 designation as duty-free zone, it suffers from a midriff of commercialism bulging with concrete shopping centres and artificial tourist attractions better suited to the mainland.

Despite its identity crisis, Langkawi is still a tranquil but pricey paradise for travellers who leapfrog across from Thailand. Vacationing Malaysians are Langkawi's primary fan base and former prime minister Dr Mahathir even lobbied to move the state capital from Alor Setar to Langkawi.

Orientation
The Langkawi archipelago comprises 99 islands, of which Pulau Langkawi is the largest and most visited. It sits 30km off the

GETTING INTO TOWN

Coupon-fare taxis run to/from Kuah jetty to Pantai Cenang (RM16).

coast from Kuala Perlis and 45km from the Thai border town of Satun. In the southeast corner is Kuah, the major town and the arrival point for ferries. On the west coast are Pantai Cenang (cha-*nang*), a lively beach strip mainly in the mid-budget range. Accommodation is cheaper on adjacent Pantai Tengah. During the monsoons here (May to October), jellyfish make swimming a problem.

Information

The only banks are at Kuah, which are open Monday to Friday. Moneychangers are tucked in and around the duty-free shops at Kuah. **Tourism Malaysia** (☎ 966 7789; Jl Persiaran Putra, Kuah; ⏰ 9am-1pm & 2-6pm) offers comprehensive information and advice about the island.

Sleeping

Accommodation on Pulau Langkawi is overpriced. Rates drop considerably in the off season between March and October. Upon arriving in Langkawi, touts swarm the disembarking ferry passengers, spruiking for hotels for which their company receives a commission, which will be built into your nightly rate.

PANTAI CENANG

The following places are grouped on either side of the main road and are listed here in south-to-north order. Most budget options are across the road from the beach.

My Guest House (☎ 012-4755 5812; dm RM15, r RM35) The only guesthouse on the beach is a homely spot with lots of tidy communal spaces. Look for the 'My Dobi Laundry' sign across from Nadias Inn.

Amzar Motel (☎ /fax 955 8513; r RM35-60; ⚡) Characterless rooms huddle around a court in a close approximation of an American motel court.

AB Motel (☎ 955 1300; abmotel@hotmail.com; r RM60-120) A range of chalets with the cheapest garnering a view of the main road. The breezy communal sitting area facing the beach is lovely.

Sandy Beach Resort (☎ 955 1308; r RM30-80; ⚡) Gulp, those tatty A-frames that are usually a shoestringer's best friend are a whopping RM80. The cheaper rooms land you in a multistorey hotel.

Malati Tanjung (☎ 955 1099; r RM40-100) Simple beach chalets, some with a minibar and TV, with clean bathrooms, steps away from the beach.

PANTAI TENGAH

For cheap sleeps right on the beach, head to Pantai Tengah. The options here are listed in south-to-north order.

Sugary Sands (☎ 955 3473; r RM35-65) A terrific option with reasonably priced chalets facing the beach.

Tanjung Malie (☎ 955 1891; r RM35) This cluster of little beach huts is within sunstroke-stumbling distance to the beach.

Green Hill Beach Resort (☎ 955 1935; r RM40-120; ⚡) Just after the headland that separates the two beaches, this resort has basic wooden huts.

Eating

Pantai Cenang has the most eating options. Langkawi's proximity to Thailand means that the Thai penchant for fiery chillies has found its way into local dishes.

Breakfast Bar (⏰ breakfast & lunch) If the morning meal doesn't mean rice, Breakfast Bar has the usual suspects of eggs, toast, beans and weak, milky coffee.

Champor-Champor (meals RM7-25; ⏰ lunch & dinner) With an emphasis on Thai food, this splurge-worthy option serves Asian-Western cuisine, including vegetarian options, in an intimate garden setting with candles and twinkling fairy lights.

Rasa Restaurant (meals RM3-25; ⏰ lunch & dinner) No alcohol here, instead try some of the sumptuously fresh fruit juices or a mocktail. Flashy orange shirts worn by the staff add a colourful touch, and this cosy restaurant makes a fantastic Thai-style curry.

Ras Saujana (meals RM3-15; ⏰ lunch & dinner) This open-air restaurant masters the *nasi* and *mee* variations so well that locals grow visibly hungry just thinking about the menu.

Laksa stall (meals RM3-5; ⏰ lunch) Across from Underwater World, this place is where the national noodle dish is served in the northern (*utara*) regional style, a fiery, fishy concoction.

Next door to the Breakfast Bar is a *roti canai warung* where locals jump-start the day with thick coffee, *nasi lemak* (coconut rice wrapped in banana leaf) and flying bread (a poetic term to describe the acrobatic kneading process used to make *roti canai*).

Drinking

Nearly all hotels have bars and most restaurants serve alcohol.

Oasis Pub (☎ 955 8236; Pantai Tengah; meals RM3-30) South of Underwater World, this is a breezy beach bar with an oh-so-tropical ambience and fancy cocktails. It serves North Indian and Western food, and then turns into a regular party venue after the dinner plates have been cleared.

Reggae Café (Pantai Cenang) Recently, this place has dominated the beach nightlife with live bands.

Across from Underwater World, the Irish Bar is the place to go for a pint of Guinness and a game of darts.

Getting There & Away

AIR

Malaysia Airlines (☎ 966 6622; Langkawi Fair shopping mall), to/from KL RM240, and **Air Asia** (☎ 955 7751), to/from KL RM200, have 10 flights every day. Malaysia Airlines also flies to/from Pulau Penang (RM90, daily).

SilkAir (☎ 955 9771; www.silkair.com) flies to/from Singapore (RM800, four times a week).

BOAT

All passenger ferries to/from Langkawi operate out of Kuah.

From about 7am to 7pm, regular ferries operate roughly every hour in either direction between Kuah and the mainland ports of Kuala Perlis (RM12, 45 minutes) and Kuala Kedah (RM15, one hour).

Daily ferries also run between Kuah and Georgetown on Pulau Penang (one-way/return RM40/75, 2½ hours), departing from Georgetown at 8.30am, 8.45am and 2.45pm and departing Kuah at 11.30am, 2.30pm and 5.30pm. Check at the jetty as times do vary.

Getting Around

There is no public transport on the island. Car hire is excellent value starting at RM70 per day for a newish Kancil or RM30 for a motorbike; travellers say that cheaper rates

---

BORDER CROSSING: INTO THAILAND

There are several options for crossing the Malay-Thai border on the west coast.

Bukit Kayu Hitam (Malaysia)–Sadao (Thailand) Buses from Alor Setar (p457) go to this border crossing. You'll have to take a minibus on the Thai side of the border to the transport hub of Hat Yai (p793).

Langkawi (Malaysia)–Satun (Thailand) Travellers can cross from the island of Langkawi to the mainland town of Satun, Thailand, with **Langkawi Ferry Services** (LFS; ☎ 966 1125), which makes four daily runs between 9.30am and 5pm (RM20, approximately one hour).

Padang Besar (Malaysia) – Kanger (Thailand) Trains travelling south and north pass through these border towns. In Malaysia, Alor Setar (p457) is the closest transport hub for train passengers heading to Langkawi. Hat Yai (p793) is the closest transport hub on the Thai side.

See p797 for information on travelling to/ from Satun's port and bus station.

---

can be found at the jetty, but most places to stay also hire cars. Beware of cows and buffalo, random cyclists and motorbikes. A few places also rent mountain bikes for RM15 per day.

Otherwise, taxis are the main way of getting around. Fixed fares for the entire vehicle (which can be split between passengers) cost the following from the Kuah jetty: Kuah town (RM4), Pantai Cenang (RM16) and Pantai Tengah (RM18).

PENINSULAR MALAYSIA – EAST COAST

Malaysia's east coast is a napping beauty with a sunrise view of the South China Sea. Wooden *kampung* houses squat amid coconut groves and rubber plantations, unconcerned that modern Malaysia is obsessed with terrace houses and mobile phones. Predominantly Malay Muslim, the east coast has elegantly mellowed Islam's inflexible tendencies, embracing compassion over rigid idealism. From this softer approach, Christianity's long-standing rival becomes a work of art. The daily call to prayer emanates from the landscape as if the earth's mute materials have found a voice. Framed Koran verses decorate the postage-stamp houses like ancient talismans, and the skull-capped, white-clad school boys racing their bicycles look like mission-bound angels.

Easy-going and unhurried, the east coast is the ideal place to recover from road fatigue. Sprinkled off the coast are Pulau Perhentian, with arguably the best beaches in the region, and mellow Pulau Tioman. Mainland Cherating is another low-key recovery room. And even the unimpressive transit towns, like Kuantan and Kota Bharu, lack the chaos of the west-coast cities.

JOHOR BAHRU
☎ 07

You'll pass through this state capital (known as JB) if travelling to/from peninsular Malaysia and Singapore. Most Malaysian buses only have service to Johor Bahru where you'll transfer to a local Singapore-bound bus, stopping for border formalities en route. JB is connected to Singapore by the 1038m-long Causeway. There is little reason to hang around, unless you are a fan of underdog cities. The immigration office is across from Merlin Tower, which is surrounded by a walkable downtown of midrange hotels, food shops and banks.

Tourism Malaysia (☎ 222 3590; www.johortourism.com.my; 5th fl, Jotic Bldg, 2 Jl Air Molek; ☉ 8am-4.30pm Mon-Thu, 8am-12.15pm & 2.45-4.30pm Fri, 8am-12.45pm Sat) is walking distance from Merlin Tower, ask for directions to the Jotic Building.

The finest museum of its kind in Malaysia, **Muzium Diraja Abu Bakar** (☎ 223 0555; adult US$7; ☉ 9am-5pm Sat-Thu) conveys the wealth and privilege of the sultans. Tickets are payable in ringgit at a bad exchange rate; the ticket counter closes at 4pm.

Sleeping & Eating

Shoestringers may consider skipping a night in JB for there is little in the way of genuine budget accommodation.

Footloose Homestay (☎ 224 2881; 4H Jl Ismail; dm/d RM12/24) This is the only budget option in Johor Bahru. Travellers should take note that Lonely Planet has received a letter claiming that a female traveller was sexually assaulted while staying here.

Fortuna (☎ 223 3210; Jl Meldrum; r RM66; ☒) A passable multistorey hotel with friendly desk clerks and decent rooms.

There are good hawker venues, including the daily **Pasar Malam** (Night Market; Jl Wong Ah Fook) outside the Hindu temple. The **Tepian Tebrau food centre** (Jl Abu Bakar) is famous for its excellent seafood.

Getting There & Away
AIR

JB is well served by Malaysia Airlines and flights to other places in Malaysia are much cheaper than from Singapore. But most domestic flights connect through KL, a four-hour bus ride away. **Malaysia Airlines** (☎ 334 1011; 1st fl, Menara Pelangi Bldg, Jl Kuning, Taman Pelangi) is 2.5km north of the city centre.

JB's airport is 32km northwest of town at Senai.

BOAT

In Johor Bahru ferries leave for Singapore and Indonesia. See the boxed text, opposite, for more information.

BUS & TAXI

Most people travel from Johor Bahru to Singapore by bus; see boxed text, opposite, for more information.

Johor Bahru's long-distance bus station is Larkin station, 5km outside of the centre. Buses run to/from Larkin to all parts of Malaysia, including Melaka (RM12.50, three hours, hourly), Kuala Lumpur (RM20.30, four hours, hourly), Ipoh (RM35, seven hours, one daily) and Butterworth (RM45, twelve hours, one daily), Mersing (RM17, three hours, four daily), Kuantan (RM17.90, five hours, four daily), Kuala Terengganu (RM30, nine hours, two daily) and Kota Bharu (RM35, 10 hours, two daily). Long-distance taxis also leave from Larkin (there's a price list at the stand).

A taxi across the Causeway to the Queen St terminal in Singapore should cost about RM10 per person. A taxi from central JB to the bus station should cost RM6.

TRAIN

Daily trains depart JB (RM33 to RM66) at 9.20am, 4.15pm and 10pm for Kuala Lumpur. It is also possible to change at Gemas (RM21 to RM38) and board the 'jungle train' for connections to Jerantut (for

---

BORDER CROSSING: INTO SINGAPORE & INDONESIA

To Singapore

There are frequent buses between Singapore's Queen St bus station and JB's Larkin bus station, 5km north of the city. Most convenient is the air-con Singapore–Johor Bahru Express (RM2.40, one hour, every 10 minutes from 6.30am to midnight). Alternatively, there's city bus 170 (RM1.70). Both buses stop at the Malaysian and Singapore immigration check points; disembark from the bus with your luggage, go through immigration and re-board on the other side (keep your ticket). There's also a bridge that connects Tanjung Kupang in Malaysia with the suburb of Tuas in Singapore, but it's a minor entry point and most traffic will use the Causeway.

There are also trains to Singapore, but it's more convenient to take a bus or taxi.

To Indonesia

The Johor Bahru International Ferry Terminal at Kompleks Bebas Cukai, about 2km east of the Causeway, has services heading to Indonesia. The easiest way to get to the jetty is by taxi (RM6) or take city bus 170 from Larkin to the city centre and then transfer to a Stulang/Duty Free Zone bus. At the complex, **Sriwani Tours and Travel** (☎ 221 1677; Kompleks Bebas Cukai, 88 Jl Ibrahim Sultan, Stulang Laut) handles tickets to most destinations. There are departures to Batam Centre (adult one-way RM50, hourly from 7.50am to 6.40pm) and Sekupang (RM50, 8.30am and 12.20pm departures), both port towns on the Indonesian island of Batam. Boats also go to Tanjung Pinang (adult one-way RM65, hourly from 8.15am to 5.30pm), a port town on the Indonesian island of Bintan. Both Indonesian arrival ports have connecting services to mainland towns on other islands.

Taman Negara) and Kota Bharu. See Jungle Railway (p477) for more information.

WALKING

It is possible to walk to/from Singapore across the Causeway (25 minutes).

MERSING

☎ 07

Mersing is a small fishing town on the east coast of Peninsular Malaysia. It's the main departure point for boats to Pulau Tioman. **Mersing Tourist Information Centre** (☎ 799 5212; Jl Abu Bakar; ⏰ 8am-1pm & 2-4.30pm Mon-Thu, 8am-noon & 2.45-4.30pm Fri, 8am-12.45pm Sat) has information about Mersing and Pulau Tioman.

Sleeping & Eating

East Coast Backpacker's Hotel (☎ 012-736 2120; rockyanwar2002@hotmail.com; 43A Jl Abu Bakar; dm/s/d RM10/20/25) If you're looking for a friendly welcome in Mersing, this efficient and backpacker-oriented hotel gets the thumbs up – cheap beds, informative and helpful staff and a relaxed ambience.

Omar's Backpackers' Hostel (☎ 799 5096, 019-774 4268; Jl Abu Bakar; dm/d RM8/20) A cheap and popular travellers' den. Fan doubles and four-bed dorms are clean, there's a balcony and the

owners can offer local knowledge. Phone ahead in peak season (June to September).

There are several places around town for *roti canai* and *kopi* (coffee).

Restoran Al-Arif (44 Jl Ismail; meals RM7) Serves tasty Indian food; one of the best in town.

Restoran Laut Yong Seng (Jl Ismail; meals RM3) Offers pre-made Chinese dishes, and is popular with lunching construction workers.

Getting There & Away

Long-distance buses depart from Plaza R&R, near the jetty. Purchase tickets at the ticket booths at Plaza R&R. Destinations include Johor Bahru (RM7.50, three hours, two daily), Kuala Lumpur (RM19.50, six hours, five daily), Kuantan (RM10.60, five hours, two daily), Kuala Terengganu (RM22.10, nine hours, two daily), Butterworth (RM45, eleven hours, one daily) and Ipoh (RM37.20, nine hours, one daily).

See p464 for information on ferries to Pulau Tioman.

PULAU TIOMAN

☎ 09

Pulau Tioman is a bit of an oxymoron – it is one of the tropic's best beach destinations without a beach. All the island fantasies can be indulged here: falling asleep to the music of the surf, watching the sun sink into the horizon, swimming with neon-coloured fish. Everything, except carefree strolls along silky smooth sand because Tioman's beaches are variously divided between good sunbathing patches and rocky coral deposits. So why do people come to Tioman? It's proximity to Singapore is one bonus, the coral gardens are another and the mood is so mellow that many people don't notice its shortcomings. Certainly other beaches are forgiven for more grievous deficiencies.

During the east-coast monsoon, from approximately November to March, boat service to the island is infrequent or suspended. If you plan to visit Tioman during this time, call the tourist office in Mersing for weather conditions and ferry schedules as the monsoon season often varies.

Orientation & Information

Most budget accommodation is clustered on Air Batang (ABC) and Salang on the northern end of the west coast. Salang has the best sand and swimming, but the accommodation options tend to be more expensive and the mood is more expan-

---

TIOMAN SCAMS

Oh those tenacious entrepreneurs have cooked up a good one for Tioman-bound travellers arriving in the jumping-off port town of Mersing. The Mersing-bound bus is supposed to stop at the bus station near the jetty, but instead foreigners are 'advised' to get off at a travel agent office in town. The agent sells standard boat tickets (no loss to the traveller here), but accommodation rates can often be doubled, turning what would otherwise be a great budget hut into an overpriced disappointment. If you're worried about finding accommodation, call the guesthouse directly to reserve a room, but don't rely on a middle man.

We haven't tried this, but for readers who support healthy competition, try refusing to get off the bus at the travel agent's office. If the bus driver obliges and delivers you to the jetty, you can freely choose which ferry company to buy a ticket from.

---

sive with sunbathing-oiled crowds and night-time beer sloshing. In sharp contrast, ABC is like a charming Malay village with one narrow footpath linking family businesses to each another. There is a healthy disregard for time, schedules and being in a rush.

Connected to ABC by a footpath over a rocky headland, Tekek is the island's main village, where you'll find a bank, telephones, Internet access and a post office. The duty-free shop at the airport in town sells beer cheaper than water.

On the east coast of the island, Juara has a beautiful beach and affordable accommodation, but it is difficult to reach and a little isolating for social types. See p464 for transport details.

Sights & Activities

According to one guesthouse operator, you come to Tioman for what's under the water, not above. Most places rent snorkelling gear and you can join day-trips to Pulau Tulai, better known as Coral Island, where you can swim with nibbling fish and aloof sharks.

Openwater dive courses cost around RM750, and two dives with equipment rental around RM160. Try **B&J Diving Centre** (☎ 419 5555; www.divetioman.com; Salang & ABC).

There's a fantastic 7km walk that crosses the island's waist from Tekek to Juara (carry plenty of water). It takes around 2½ hours, is steep in parts and starts about 1km north of the jetty in Tekek. Near the top of the hill, you pass a small waterfall and the jungle is awesome.

Power Batik (www.welcome.to/rikkipower; ABC), a tiny batik workshop, is run by Rikki Power, a Malaysian artist with a fine-art background. Sarongs cost from RM65.

Sleeping & Eating

From June to August, when the island swarms with visitors, accommodation becomes tight. Either side of these months it's a buyer's market. If you want to secure a room before arriving, call the guesthouse operator directly rather than going through a booking agent.

Most restaurants, with similar menus, are attached to chalet operations. ABC, Tekek and Salang all have small convenience stores.

AIR BATANG (ABC)

The northern end of the beach is somewhat rocky and poor for swimming; the southern end, near Nazri's Place, has the better beach.

ABC Bungalows (☎ 419 1154; chalet RM35-120; ❄) North of the jetty, this place offers a variety of chalets set in well-tended grounds. Bathrooms are clean and modern and chalets have verandas with views to the hill. It also does a fresh fish barbeque and is the favourite drinking spot for locals.

Nazri's II (☎ 419 1375; s RM25-30, d RM60-100; ❄) Also known as Nazri's Beach Cabanas, this roomy outfit is one of the best options, providing large and clean bungalows with sea views, towards the northern end of ABC.

Mawar Resort (☎ 419 1153; r from RM25) Claiming a pretty strip of sand, Mawar is an excellent cheapie with clean bungalows facing the water. It's south of the jetty.

My Friend's Place (☎ 419 1150; r RM15-50) One of the cheapest places on Tioman with a wide range of top-value rooms. South of the jetty.

Mokhtar's Place (RM15-20) Little rickety shacks lend a true-grit ambience to island living here. South of the jetty.

Nazri's Place (☎ 419 1329; r RM80; ❄) South of the jetty, this friendly place has undergone some upgrades to boost it into the upper budget range. ABC's prettiest stretch of beach is right outside your door and rooms have real double-decker beds.

SPLURGE!

Bamboo Hill Chalets (☎ 419 1339; chalets RM70-120; ❄) Set high on a cliff on the northern end of the beach, Bamboo Hill has a stupendous location surrounded by slices of jungle alongside a waterfall and a pool. Return guests swear this is a better deal than nearby Panuba Resort. These well-kept chalets (six in all) are almost always full, so call ahead.

SALANG

The small bay at Salang has a beautiful beach and excellent water. With its restaurants and nightlife, Salang is the most social beach strip on Tioman. The government has recently built a hulking Medan Selera to house the wooden stalls that used to dot the beach. Intended to 'clean up' the beach

PULAU TIOMAN

0 ——— 5 km
0 ——— 3 miles

Pulau Tulai (Coral Island)

Bukit Kerayung Kecil (390m)
Bukit Kerayung Besar (409m)
Salang
Jetty

Monkey Bay
Monkey Beach
537m
Panuba
Jetty
Air Batang (ABC)
Dungung

SOUTH CHINA SEA

Air Batang Bay

Mosque
Bukit Parang Panjang (488m)
Pulau Rengis
Jetty
Airstrip
Tekek

Bunut
Juara
Jetty

Paya
Gua Teh Angin (945m)

Gunung Kajang (1038m)

Jetty
Genting

Bukit Seperok (958m)

To Mersing (51km)
Nipah
Nenek Semukut
Waterfall

Batu Siran (753m)
Mukut
Asah
Jetty

---

for tourists, it's a successful eyesore and a source of snickering for locals.

Pak Long Chalet (☎ 419 5000; www.paklong tioman.com; r RM30-50; ❄) Next door to Salang Pusaka, this cosy spot has straightforward chalets that exceed expectations thanks to the maternal mood of the outgoing owner.

Salang Pusaka (☎ 419 5317; salangpusaka@yahoo .com; chalet RM45-100; ❄) Formerly Khalid's Place, this complex is tucked behind the lagoon and the new Medan Selera. The garden is attractive, but the rooms are showing some age.

Salang Sayang Resort (☎ 419 5020; chalet RM60-80) This is a popular place, formerly Zaid's Place, with an attractive garden and restaurant. It claims the prettiest patch of beach and the price is more a reflection of location than interior amenities.

Salang Beach Resort (☎ 799 2337; r RM80-110; ❄) Go past Salang Indah to reach this northernmost resort. The chalets are attractively situated on the hillside facing the water, but you'll have to walk back to the jetty to get some sand and surf.

Salang Indah Resort (☎ 419 5015; r RM25, chalet RM50-150; ❄) Sprawling north of the jetty, this resort is the biggest of the bunch, with a huge restaurant facing the sea, a bar, a shop and a wide variety of mediocre accommodation. The beach on this end is rocky.

JUARA

For now, Juara's beach is excellent, practically deserted during the shoulder seasons. This is a place for serious relaxation, since there is little to do except swim and laze away under the coconut trees. Once the interior road is finished (they said in 2005), the town criers are convinced that Juara will shed its peaceful ambience for high-rolling resort life. We'll have to wait and see.

Rainbow Chalets (☎ 419 3109; r RM20-50) Multicoloured bungalows hold a staring contest with the ocean. The affiliated Bushman Café is a great place to grab a meal after hiking through the jungle; the friendly owner has lots of left-wing opinions about paradisal tourism.

River View Place (☎ 419 3168; chalet RM20) North of the jetty, River View Place has simple A-frame chalets (with mosquito nets) and can offer cheap, long-stay options.

Juara Mutiara Resort (☎ 419 3159; chalet RM25-60; ✴) South of the jetty this extensive resort has largish, characterless chalets on and off the beach and there's a sizeable restaurant.

Getting There & Away

Berjaya Air (☎ 419 1303; www.berjaya-air.com), with offices at Berjaya Tioman Beach Resort (about half way up the west cost) and at the airstrip, has daily flights to/from KL (one-way/return RM214/428) and Singapore (RM150/300).

Mersing is the ferry port for Tioman. Several companies run boat services to the island; tickets can be bought around Mersing town or at the jetty near R&R Plaza. There are usually five to six departures throughout the day between 7am and 5pm, but specific departure times vary with the tides. Regular ferries (RM30, two to three hours) leave from the Mersing jetty and drop off passengers in south to north order on the island. Speedboats (RM35, 90 minutes) make a harrowing, white-knuckled ride from the same jetty. Many green-faced arrivals swear they'll never set foot on another speedboat and promptly book a return trip on the regular boat or by air.

Getting Around

Getting around the island is, for the moment, problematic. You can walk from ABC to Tekek in about 20 minutes. But you'll need to charter a boat through a guesthouse or restaurant to travel between ABC and Salang (RM20).

Boats from Mersing don't travel to Juara; you'll have to get off at Tekek and then hire a minivan (RM25 for four people); fares to Juara are highly negotiable so use your best bargaining skills.

KUANTAN

☎ 09

Many travellers find themselves on an overnight stopover in Kuantan, the state capital, as it's the main transit point between Taman Negara and Pulau Tioman. Kuantan's star attraction is **Masjid Negeri**, the east coast's most impressive mosque, which presides regally over the *padang* (city square). At night it's a magical sight with its spires and lit turrets.

Information

Banks are clustered at Jl Bank and there are plenty of ATMs around Jl Haji Abdul Aziz (the continuation of Jl Mahkota).

CH Internet Centre (G013, ground fl, Block A, Kuantan Centre Point, Jl Haji Abdul Rahman)

Dobi Laundry Service (Jl Tekok Sisek)

Hamid Bros Books (☎ 516 2119; 23 Jl Mahkota) Licensed moneychanger and English-language bookseller.

Immigration office (☎ 573 220; Kompleks Khedm, Bandar Indera Mahkota)

Main post office (Jl Haji Abdul Aziz) Near the soaring Masjid Negeri.

Telekom Malaysia (☎ 513 9191; 168 Jl Besar)

Tourist information centre (☎ 516 1007; Jl Mahkota; ⏰ 9am-10pm Mon-Thu, 2-5pm & 2.45-5pm Fri, 9am-1pm & 2-5pm Sat) Near the local taxi stand.

Sleeping

There are no guesthouses to be found in Kuantan, only multistorey hotels of questionable cleanliness.

Hotel Baru Raya (☎ 513 9746; 134-136 Jl Besar; r RM45) After checking out all of Kuantan's seedy hotels, this place is a relative charmer. A decent room, a lumpy bed and a squat toilet provides almost incomparable luxury for the price. Rooms facing the street can be noisy, but the staff is friendly and helpful.

KUANTAN

Hotel Meian (☎ 552 0949; 2nd fl, 78-80 Jl Telok Sisek; s RM18, r RM20-25; ❄) Some of the rooms are a little noisy and some are a little small and some of the bedsheets are threadbare, but this is just a one-night stand.

Hotel Makmur (☎ 514 1363; 1st & 2nd fl, B14 & 16, Lorong Pasar Baru 1; r RM25-38; ❄) Makmur is a good option if staying overnight for a bus connection.

Hotel Classic (☎ 516 4599; 7 Jl Besar; r RM75-85; ❄) River-view rooms are spacious with a TV, and the bathrooms, with steaming hot water, are bigger than some dorms. The threadbare sheets could do with an upgrade, but the Classic really is a classic and there are terrific views of Masjid Negeri from the balcony. Rates include breakfast.

Eating
Sampan (Jl Bukit Ubi; meals RM2-4; ❄ lunch) A group of Chinese food stalls serving a range of meals. Try the herbal chicken noodle soup, which has natural ingredients to boost your 'vitality'.

Restoran Paruvathy (☎ 514 3140; 75 Jl Bukit Ubi; meals RM1.50-4; ❄ breakfast, lunch & dinner) Stupidly cheap *masala dosai* and *chapati thali* (flat unleavened bread with small amounts of curry) are delicious dinner options. Paruvathy is patronised by a loyal group of regulars and serves vegetarian curries.

Taj Point (☎ 512 1074; Lorong Tun Ismail 4; meals RM2-6; ❄ breakfast, lunch & dinner) Tasty vegetarian and meat curries where you sop up the gravy with piping hot, flaky roti. On

Sunday, ask for sweet *acol* (cashews in a sweet tomato jam laced with rose-water).

New Yee Mee Restoran (21-22 Jl Haji Abdul Aziz; meals RM2-5; ☯ lunch & dinner) Chinese food at its best – this restaurant has a group of hawker kitchens, each cooking a specific dish such as noodle soup. Top spot for a beer too.

Kafe Seri Tjantek Art Bistro (☎ 967 2021; 46 Jl Besar; dishes RM20; ☯ dinner) West meets East at this modern Malay restaurant. In a 1928 converted shophouse, Tjantek is something different: stylish, with an emphasis on art. There's a range of pastas, cooling salads, sizzling steaks, and imported coffee and tea.

Kemaman Kopitiam (Jl Tun Ismail; dishes RM5-10; ☯ breakfast & lunch) Wondering where cosmopolitan Kuantan hangs out? Across from Mega Mall of course. A steady stream of suits and cell phones file into this spacious coffeeshop situated according to feng shui principles. The local brew is a special blend from the nearby town of Kemaman.

Food stalls can be found along the riverbank across from Hotel Baru Raya, and at the **central market** (Jl Bukit Ubi).

Drinking

Boom Boom Bistro & Bar (☎ 552 5184; 236 Jl Telok Sisek; ☯ 6.30pm-3am Tue-Sun) Near the Mega View Hotel, this lively bar has sports TV, pool, occasional live music, draught Tiger beer and local and Western dishes.

Bistro Kuantan (Jl Besar) Along the river behind Mega View Hotel, this is an alfresco bar, with a huge TV screen for live sports events.

Getting There & Away

AIR

Malaysia Airlines (☎ 531 2123; www.malaysiaairlines .com.my; Lapangan Terbang Sultan Hj Ahmad Shah) has direct flights to KL (RM246, five daily). **Kuantan airport** (☎ 538 2923; Lapangan Terbang Sultan Hj Ahmad Shah) is 15km from the city centre; take a taxi (RM20).

BUS & TAXI

There are three bus stations in Kuantan. Long-distance buses obviously operate from the **Terminal Makmur** (Jl Stadium). Services include KL (RM14.30, 4½ hours, seven daily), Mersing (RM10.60, 3½ hours, three daily), JB (RM17.90, five hours, four daily), Kuala Terengganu (RM11.50, three hours, two daily), Kota Bharu (RM20.60,

seven hours, frequent), Jerantut (RM10.50, 3½ hours, five daily), Melaka (RM17.60, five hours, two daily) and Butterworth (RM32.50, eight hours, two daily).

Northbound local buses operate out of a **local bus station** (Jl Besar) near the river, these include services between Cherating (RM3) and Marang (RM8). There is also an **intra-city bus station** (cnr Jl Pasar & Mahkota) for destinations within Kuantan town.

There are two **long-distance taxi stands** – one on Jl Stadium in front of the long-distance bus station, and the other on Jl Mahkota near the local bus station. Destinations and costs (per car) include Mersing (RM120), Cherating (RM40), and Jerantut (RM120); but fares were set to increase at the time of writing.

TASIK CHINI
☎ 09

If you're sick of shuffling through the 'trail', consider chasing down a jungle adventure at Tasik Chini, a series of 12 linked lakes surrounded by thick jungle and fringed with pink lotus blossoms (blooming in June to September). Along the shores live the Jakun people, an Orang Asli (indigenous) tribe. It's not that easy to reach scenic Taski Chini and it is a popular domestic attraction, so to avoid the crowds arrive during the week. You can also visit the lake as part of a group tour from Cherating for around RM70 per person.

Across the lake at Kampung Gumum, **Rajan Jones Guest House** (r RM18) is about 10 minutes' walk up the main road and offers extremely basic accommodation. Rajan speaks excellent English, is knowledgeable about the Orang Asli and can arrange a spectrum of activities. Grab a brochure with directions to the guesthouse from the Kuantan tourist information centre (p464).

Getting There & Away

The best way to get to Tasik Chini is to take a bus from Kuantan's **local bus station** (Jl Mahkota) to Felda Chini (Chini Village; RM5, two hours, six daily from 8am to 5.30pm) or Pekan (RM3.60, four daily from 11am to 5.45pm). From Felda Chini, hire a private car or motorcycle (around RM5, 10 minutes).

A taxi direct from Kuantan is around RM70 to the resort or Kampung Gumum.

CHERATING
☎ 09

Over the years Cherating has had several incarnations: backwater *kampung*, backpacker bohemia, and more recently an R&R stop for young families and overworked city slickers. Cherating's faded past as a travellers' pick-up scene adds a sense of melancholy, since the young and available crowds have migrated north, but Cherating retains its original 'lost in time and place' ambience. Even getting to this place feels like stepping off the map. The Kuantan–Terengganu bound bus drops travellers off by a few wooden shacks and a cicada-filled wilderness. This is surely nowhere, how delightful.

Cherating's beach is a shallow C-curve along the energetic South China Sea. During the monsoon season here (November to March), storms kick up surfable waves, especially good for beginners as there are no underwater head-splitters.

Batik workshops are enormously popular, and part of the Cherating experience. **Matahari Chalets** (☎ 581 9835) has the largest artists' studios, but other workshops have sprung up along the same road. A batik sarong starts at around RM40.

There are also myriad adventures on the river – kayaking, spotting monkeys and river otters, fishing trips, etc.

Information

There are no banks in Cherating; the two travel agents on the main road, Travelpost and Badgerlines, will change travellers cheques and cash, but the rates are poor.

Badgerlines Information Centre (☎ 581 9552; ⊙ 9.30am-12.30pm, 2.30-4pm & 8-10pm) offers boat service, overseas telephone service, mini postal service and Internet access. Travelpost Travel Agency arranges ticketing, bicycle and vehicle hire, Internet, tourist information and nature tours.

Sleeping

Cherating has a 'strip' where most of the restaurants and guesthouses congregate. Foreigners tend to gravitate to the guesthouses on the west side of town and Malaysian holidayers, on the east side. On weekends, teenagers from Terengganu like to buzz through town on their wheezy motorcycles.

Payung Guest House (☎ 019-917 1934; r RM30-35) Sturdy wooden bungalows set in a leafy garden with a riverside aspect. Payung's owners are mad surfers and also run Lelaut Sports and rents kayaks.

Mimi's Guest House (☎ 019-904 5251; r RM30-35) Surf boards and wet suits are more prolific than the usual array of beer bottles and ashtrays at this little colony. The polished wooden huts are tidy but tiny. It is directly across the street from Rhana Pippins.

Shadow of the Moon at Half-Past Four (☎ 581 9186; r RM35-40) At this sylvan retreat, reality seems permanently on pause and the resident characters seem suspiciously like escapees from the pages of a well-worn novel. Spacious chalets hide amid the trees, a favourite hunting ground for nocturnal monkeys and wild boars, and a guest walking to town will be chaperoned by the manager's trustworthy dogs.

Matahari Chalets (☎ 581 9835; chalets RM20-25) On the road between the beachfront and the main highway, Matahari has fan-only chalets with a balcony, fridge and mosquito net. The bathrooms do little to inspire personal hygiene.

Maznah's Guest House (☎ 581 9072; chalets RM20-25) Between Matahari and the main highway is Maznah's, run by a rotund butterball of a woman who will greet you breathlessly. She has several basic, spacious A-frames in varying stages of renovation, and guests are welcome to cook their own breakfast.

Eating & Drinking

At the western tail-end of the strip are a row of concrete food stalls, serving *roti canai* and Malay specialities. Most of the Chinese-run restaurants serve beer and there are two bars in town.

Amie's Café (☎ 581 9700; ⊙ breakfast & lunch, Thu-Mon) Directly across from the Malay food stalls, Amie's brings the health food of the Hawaiian islands to a kindred location. Sink your teeth into homemade brown bread, combat any tummy trouble with herbal tonics and pique your senses with coriander-spiked omelettes and sandwiches.

Restoran Duyong (☎ 581 9578; dishes RM3-10; ⊙ dinner) Through the Cherating Beach Mini Motel is this excellent eatery, built on stilts over the beach. It's a highly convivial spot and the menu specialises in seafood,

Western and Thai fare. Thoroughly recommended are the Thai green curries and Chinese dishes.

Cherating Lagoon Seafood Restaurant (dishes RM5-15; 🕑 dinner) Across from the horse stables, this blaring Chinese restaurant might lure you because of the cheap Chang beer, but dabble in the substantial sustenance of fresh seafood.

Pop Inn Steakhouse & Pub (🕑 lunch & dinner) Live bands play on weekends at this place next door to Restoran Duyong, and there's also a pool table. Pop Inn makes a promising start to your evening.

Rhana Pippins Bar (🕑 dinner) With a beautiful position right on the beach, across from Ranting Resort, Rhana's has lengthy happy hours (3pm to midnight). It becomes crowded around midnight and peaks at around 2am.

Deadly Nightshade Bar (🕑 lunch & dinner) This is the restaurant and bar portion of the Shadow of the Moon guesthouse, east of Residence Inn Cherating, where all the guests converge at a communal table to feast over devil curry (a Eurasian speciality) made of wild boar, and listen to the manager spin epic war stories.

Getting There & Away
Cherating doesn't have a bus station, but any Kuantan–Terengganu bus will drop off passengers at the turn-off to the village road. Oddly, they won't pick you up from the main highway. Instead you'll need to wave down a local bus bound for Kemaman (where you can catch another bus to Terengganu) or Kuantan. Buses run every 30 minutes (RM3, 1¼ hours).

MARANG
☎ 09
Marang, a fishing village at the mouth of Sungai Marang, was once a favourite stopover for travellers making their way along the east coast. Unfortunately, much of the town's traditional charm has fallen victim to characterless development. The main reason to come here is to catch a ferry to Pulau Kapas, 6km offshore. Both Marang and Pulau Kapas can be explored as daytrips from Kuala Terengganu.

If you're around on Sunday, check out the excellent **Sunday Market**, which starts at 3pm near the town's jetties.

Directly across the jetty to Pulau Kapas is **Nusantara Hostel** (☎ 013 980 7385; dm RM10), a good option for an overnight stay.

A 15-minute walk from the jetty is **Island View Resort** (☎ 618 2006; Jl Kg Paya; r RM25-40; 🐱), which has a clutch of ageing chalets and several large cages full of chirpy birds across from the shore.

Over the bridge to the southeast, **Anguillia Beach House Resort** (☎ 618 1322; a_beach@tm .net.my; r from RM50; 🐱) is a quiet place with a range of chalets under palm trees on a sheltered stretch of beach. Call from the bus stop for a pick-up.

Getting There & Away
There are regular local buses to/from Kuala Terengganu (RM1.50). For long-distance buses, there's a **ticket office** (☎ 618 2799; Jl Tanjung Sulong Musa) near the town's main intersection. There are buses to/from Kuala Lumpur (RM25.80, two daily), JB (RM28.70, two daily), and Kuantan (RM11.50, two daily) via Cherating.

PULAU KAPAS
☎ 09
Fans of Kapas contend that it is a beach without a beach scene. That is of course when it isn't overrun with day-trippers during holidays and at weekends; otherwise, the island is likely to be very quiet. Kapas also has the usual (and utterly splendid) postcard-perfect physique – clear water and powdery white-sand beaches. All the accommodation is clustered together on two small beaches on the west coast, but you can walk around the headlands to quieter beaches.

Note that accommodation on the island shuts down during monsoon season (November to March).

There is only one budget accommodation option on Kapas, **Lighthouse** (☎ 019-215 3558; dm/d RM15/35), which has rustic rooms in one elevated longhouse under the trees. It's basic but very sociable.

Recently transformed and rechristened into a higher budget range is **Kapas Beach Chalet** (☎ 017-936 0750; r RM50-75), formerly known as the humble Zaki Beach Chalet.

It is also possible to camp on some of the isolated beaches at the northern and southern ends of the island, but bring your own food and water.

Getting There & Away

Six kilometres offshore from Marang, Kapas is reached by boats in mere minutes from Marang's main jetty. Tickets (slow boat RM15, speed boat RM25) can be purchased from any of the agents nearby. Boats depart when four or more people show up. Be sure to arrange a pick-up time when you purchase your ticket. You can usually count on morning departures at around 8am and 9am.

KUALA TERENGGANU

☎ 09

Standing on a promontory formed by the South China Sea, Kuala Terengganu offers a glimpse into a typical Malaysian town. As the state capital of Malaysia's oil-producing state, Terengganu has money (the lunching housewives are fittingly bejewelled) but still retains the laid-back spirit of a former fishing village.

Kuala Terengganu is a convenient staging post to nearby attractions such as Tasik Kenyir, Pulau Kapas and Pulau Redang. Note that official business in Terengganu is closed on Friday and Saturday in observance of the Islamic holiday.

Information

Jl Sultan Ismail is the commercial hub of the town and home to most of the banks. Internet shops are along Jl Tok Lam.

Hospital Terengganu (☎ 623 3333; Jl Sultan Mahamud)
Immigration office (☎ 622 1424; Wisma Persekutuan, Jl Sultan Ismail)
Moneychanger (Jl Sultan Ismail) Next to the Terengganu Hotel.
Mr Dobi Laundry (☎ 622 1671; Jl Masjid Abidin) Around RM3.50 per kg.
State Tourist Office (☎ 622 1553; Jl Sultan Zainal Abidin; ☼ 9am-5pm Sat-Thu)
Tourism Malaysia (☎ 622 1433; Menara Yayasan Islam Terengganu, Jl Sultan Omar; ☼ 9am-5pm Sat-Thu)

Sights

Kuala Terengganu's compact **Chinatown** is along Jl Bandar. It comprises the usual array of hole-in-the-wall Chinese shops, hairdressing salons and restaurants, as well as a sleepy **Chinese temple** and some narrow alleys leading to jetties on the waterfront.

The **central market** (cnr Jl Kg Cina & Jl Banggol; ☼ 8am-5pm Sat-Thu) is a lively, colourful spot, and the floor above the fish section has a wide collection of batik and *kain songket* (handwoven fabric). Across from the market is a flight of stairs leading up to **Bukit Puteri** (Princess Hill), a 200m hill with city vistas and the remains of a fort. **Istana Maziah** (Sultan's Palace; Jl Masjid Bidin) and **Zainal Abidin Mosque** (Jl Masjid Bidin) are not camera shy.

Kompleks Muzium Negeri Terengganu (Terengganu State Museum; ☎ 622 1444; adult RM5, ☼ 9am-5pm) claims to be the largest in the region and attractively sprawls over landscaped gardens along Sungai Terengganu. Traditional architecture, fishing boats and textiles comprise the bulk of the collection. The museum is 5km from Terengganu; take minibus 10 (80 sen).

In the middle of Sungai Terengganu, **Pulau Duyung Besar** carries on the ancient boat-building tradition handed down for generations; the village is good for a day of wandering and snacking. Take the local ferry (60 sen) from the jetty near Restauran Terapung across Bukit Puteri.

Sleeping

Travellers Inn (☎ 626 2020; 77A Jl Sultan Sulaiman; dm RM8, r RM18-36; 🗷) This is the best, and only, budget option in town, affiliated with the attached Ping Anchorage travel agency, which organises accommodation to nearby resort islands (see p471) and various sightseeing tours. You can also grab a Western-style breakfast or beer from its Travellers Cafe.

Awi's Yellow House (☎ 624 5046; dm/d RM6/15) A unique guesthouse built on stilts over Sungai Terengganu, on Pulau Duyung Besar, a 10-minute ferry ride across the river from Terengganu. It may be a little rustic for some, but it's a friendly and relaxed place.

Seri Malaysia Hotel (☎ 623 6454; www.seri malaysia.com.my; 1640 Jl Balik Bukit; r RM85-110; 🗷) Excellent standby rates can be found here and some rooms have river views. Air-con rooms have comfortable double beds and a TV that plays English movies. Rates include a buffet breakfast.

Seaview Hotel (☎ 622 1911; 18A Jl Masjid Abidin; r RM45-65; 🗷) A cheap, standard midrange place that has clean rooms with TVs, but no sea views.

Eating

Terengganu has several regional specialities, such as *nasi dagang* (glutinous rice

cooked with coconut milk and served with fish curry) and *keropok lekor* (deep-fried fish crackers), that draw food enthusiasts from across the country.

Batu Buruk Food Centre (Jl Pantai Batu Buruk; ☽ lunch & dinner) This is a great outdoor food centre near the beach; don't leave without trying their famous *ais-krim goreng* (fried ice cream).

Restoran Golden Dragon (☎ 622 3034; 198 Jl Kg Cina; dishes RM3-6; ☽ lunch) Self-serve your own lunch where you can point and choose from delicious green-bean and chilli salad, roast pork, spinach salad and sweet 'n' sour dishes.

Sahara Tandoori (☎ 623 7777; Jl Air Jernih; dishes RM3-7; ☽ lunch) Tasty snacks such as banana

fritters and *roti canai* are served at popular Sahara. Be sure to try *abok abok*, a glutinous rice treat sweetened with coconut sap and wrapped in a banana leaf.

Warung Simpang Toku (Jl Simpang Toku; ☽ lunch) Outside the town centre, this busy open-air shop is famous for its sweet and spicy *nasi dagang* and local interpretation of laksa. Minibus 19 shuttles down this street after passing the state museum.

Pasir Panjang (cnr Jl Sultan Mahamud & Jl Pantai Batu Buruk; ☽ breakfast & lunch) This crowded roadside stall, across from the sports ground, is the connoisseurs' stop for adoring and consuming Malay cakes and desserts.

Kak Yah (Jl Losong; ☽ lunch) Just past the fresh fish market beside the Sultan Mahmud bridge is this famous *keropok lekor* factory that has earned the owner a BMW and a fancy house. To reach it take minibus 19 to here.

There's a **night market** (beachfront) every Friday evening, and Chinatown's outdoor hawker centre, divided into Chinese and Malay sections, is also worth a graze.

Drinking

Yes Café (Jl Air Jemih) Terengganu's answer to nightlife – food, booze and karaoke all under one roof. Before delving into the fermented juice, try the corner stall where a mad-scientist of fruit juices concocts astounding varieties of blended drinks.

Restoran Ocean (☎ 623 9156; Jl Sultan Zainal Abidin; dishes from RM6) This big Chinese restaurant is also a fun place for a beer and a side of dinner.

Getting There & Away

The main taxi stand is at Jl Masjid Abidin across from the main bus station.

AIR

Malaysia Airlines (☎ 622 1415; www.malaysiaairlines .com.my; 13 Jl Sultan Omar) has direct daily flights to/from Kuala Lumpur (RM180). **Air Asia** (☎ 631 3122; www.airasia.com; Menara Yayasan Islam, Jl Sultan Omar) also has flights to KL (from RM65, two daily). A taxi to/from the **airport** (☎ 666 3666), located 13km northeast of the town centre, costs around RM20.

BUS

The **main bus station** (Jl Masjid Abidin) serves as a terminus for all local buses. Some long-distance buses depart from here as well, but most use the **express bus station** (Jl Sultan Zainal Abidin), in the north of town. There is talk of a new express bus station, but nothing concrete yet.

At the main bus station, there are services to/from Marang (RM1.50, 30 minutes, every half hour from 6.30am to 6.30pm) and Kuala Besut (RM7, 2½ hours, hourly).

From the express bus station, there are regular services running to/from Johor Bahru (RM31, nine hours, two daily), Ipoh (RM37, 10 hours, two daily), Kuala Lumpur (RM25, seven hours, five daily), Kuantan (RM12, four hours, three daily), Melaka (RM28, nine hours, one daily), Mersing (RM22, seven hours, two daily) and Kota Bharu (RM9, three hours, seven daily).

MERANG

☎ 09

The gateway to Pulau Redang, the sleepy little fishing village of Merang (*mer*-ang; not to be confused with Marang, further south) is one of the few remaining villages to have escaped development. There is little of interest to do in the village but to wander around watching the age-old traditions of *kampung* life: harvesting coconuts, repairing fishing nets and gossiping about neighbours.

SPLURGE! RESORT GETAWAYS AROUND TERENGGANU

Although roughing it has its own unique charms, you'll periodically need a hot shower and air-con to reclaim a non-sweaty state. If comfort calls, the dreaded word 'resort' has come to your rescue. Near Kuala Terengganu are a handful of resort attractions that most backpackers skip because prices outpace their daily budget. Luckily **Ping Anchorage** (☎ 626 5020; www.pinganchorage.com; 77A Jl Sultan Sulaiman) acts as a clearing house for unsold rooms, offering inclusive three-day, two-night packages that start at RM250 to RM300. The price breakdown comes within a comfortable margin of going at it alone, plus you get air-conditioning. Here are the various locations Ping has packages for:

Pulau Redang is one of the largest and most beautiful of the east-coast islands. Redang is one of nine islands that form a protected marine park, and it is considered one of the best dive spots in the world thanks to its ancient coral gardens and good visibility. Hawksbill and green turtles nest on parts of the island and leatherbacks are occasionally spotted feasting on jellyfish. Accommodation options range from international class hotels to air-con chalets.

Tasik Kenyir is a huge lake dotted with over 340 islands and surrounded by a national park of ancient forests and an elephant colony. Exploring waterfalls and caves, kayaking and canoeing are high on the list of Kenyir's attractions. Accommodation is aboard a houseboat, floating chalets or lakeshore resorts. Ping also arranges day-trips.

The best place to stay is **Kembara Resort** (☎ 653 1770; kembararesort@hotmail.com; dm/d/chalets from RM10/30/60; ✉ 🖳), about 500m south of the village (follow the signs from the main road). There are air-con chalets and Internet access, and a common kitchen is available for those who bring their own food. The resort also organises various river safaris.

Merang is best reached from Terengganu. There are daily buses from the main bus station in Kuala Terengganu to Merang (RM2).

KUALA BESUT

The primary jetty town for boats to Pulau Perhentian is Kuala Besut (bee-su), south of Kota Bharu. It is a sleepy fishing village with a handful of collaborating boat companies and a small bus station.

But you probably won't arrive at Kuala Besut because taxi drivers get paid higher commissions to take travellers to the upstart jetty of **Tok Bali**, just across the river. Only one company (Symphony) operates out of Tok Bali, and at the time of writing they only had one boat that made one, sometimes two, trips in each direction. There are promises of more boats in the indeterminate future. Getting to the island from Tok Bali doesn't pose much of a problem, give or take an hour or two of 'tropical' time delay. Returning to the mainland is where things get tricky; your Symphony ticket is only good on Symphony boats, which aren't as numerous or as frequent as Kuala Besut–bound boats. If you get taken to Tok Bali, buy a one-way ticket, leaving yourself the option of returning to Kuala Besut, so god forbid, you aren't trapped in paradise. For more information see p474.

Most Kota Bharu guesthouses arrange shared taxis to Kuala Besut (RM28) or Tok Bali (RM24); the fare can be split between four people. There is also the infrequent local bus 639 (RM4, 2½ hours, two daily), but it doesn't present much of a savings over splitting a taxi. Taxis also pick-up passengers at the Wakaf Bahru train station (RM35).

From Kuala Besut's small bus station, you can travel to Kuala Lumpur (RM7, eight hours, two daily) and to the transport hubs of Jerteh (RM1.50, every 20 minutes) and Pasir Puteh (RM1.50, every 20 minutes). To reach Kuala Terengganu (RM7, 2½ hours, hourly), go to the main highway, and wave down a southbound bus (this really does work, we've tried it).

PULAU PERHENTIAN

☎ 09

The Perhentian Islands, composed of Pulau Besar (Big Island) and Kecil (Small Island), are Malaysia's showpiece islands. This is a paradise of expansive white-sand beaches, turquoise-blue water and a jungle-fringed interior refreshingly undeveloped – no cars, no high-rises, and no mainland hassles.

Both islands have their strong points: many travellers head to Kecil, which is one of the best backpacker beaches in mainland Southeast Asia; while others prefer quieter Besar (Big Island), with its higher accommodation standards.

The best time to visit is from March to mid-November. The Perhentians close for the monsoon season, but usually reopen around Chinese New Year in February. Dates vary depending on the whim of the monsoons.

There are no banks on the Perhentians. Generators are the source of power and are run during limited hours. There are no public phones on Pulau Perhentian; they're all mobiles. If you're desperate you can make international calls for a heart-stopping RM15 per minute.

Diving & Snorkelling

Dive operators on the island contend that the Perhentians offer all the underwater delights of the east coast of Thailand without the 'dive-factory' feel. Classes are smaller and more relaxed than the dive diva of Ko Tao. A four-day openwater course starts at RM850 and is pro-rated for various initiation steps. For the surface skimmers, guesthouses arrange snorkelling trips around the island (RM30 to RM50).

Sleeping, Eating & Drinking

On Pulau Kecil (Small Island), Long Beach has the biggest range of budget chalets and 'nightlife' (that means two beachfront bars). In the high season (usually from late May to early September), finding accommodation here can be tough, so book ahead or arrive early. Accommodation on Pulau Besar (Big Island) is more upmarket and usually includes air-con and an attached bathroom; but the beaches aren't as pretty as Kecil.

Alcohol is available in a few bars and hotel restaurants on both islands, though it's not openly displayed and you will have to ask for it.

PULAU PERHENTIAN KECIL

A trail over the narrow waist of the island leads from Long Beach to smaller Coral Bay (sometimes known as Aur Bay) on the western side of the island. It's a 15-minute walk along a foot-path through the jungle interior (watch for monitor lizards). Coral Bay has a smaller beach strip that's littered with coral (still gorgeous) and a more chilled ambience; it also faces the west for an uninterrupted view of the brilliant sunsets.

There are also a number of small bays around the island, each with one set of chalets, and often only accessible by boat.

Matahari Chalets (☎ 019-956 5756; Long Beach; chalets RM30-80) In a shadeless complex, Matahari has solidly built, clean chalets and a buddy atmosphere; but pick an abode away from the generator.

Lemon Grass Chalet (☎ 012-900 8393, 019-982 8393; Long Beach; chalets RM20-30) Perched against the rocky headlands, Lemon Grass has new wooden shacks sporting new sheets (holy wow!) and frontier-rustic baths. Don't overlook the views from the café.

Chempaka Chalets (☎ 010-985 7329; Long Beach; r RM20-60) Run by the ever-cheerful Musky, Chempaka forms the beach's prerequisite shanty town complete with scrap-metal huts and naked children. The spontaneous parties and beach barbecues make this a lively, sociable place.

Panorama Chalets & Restaurant (☎ 010-934 0123; Long Beach; r RM35-55) Well-shaded chalets are expansive and comfortable with a fresh lick of paint and basic baths, but the share bathrooms are so-so. Restaurant dishes are from RM5 to RM10.

Maya Beach Resort (☎ 019-937 9136; Coral Bay; r RM40-50) The central Maya Beach Resort has fine A-frames on the beach, and even the spots off the beach have a sea view.

Fatimah Chalets (☎ 019-963 0391; Coral Bay; dm/d from RM10/40) You'll be serenaded by the resident guitar man at this 'feeling groovy' spot.

Aur Bay Chalets (☎ 010-985 8584; Coral Bay; r RM40-60) Aur Bay Chalets provides basic accommodation set back from the sea, with a small restaurant attached.

Suria Resort (☎ 697 7990; www.suriaresorts.com; Coral Bay; r RM50-150; ❄) At the southern edge of the beach, Surai Resort has spotless modern chalets in a great location. The polished huts are more deserving of the term 'chalet'. Check the website for room promotions.

D' Lagoon Chalets (☎ 019-985 7089; r RM25-50) This place is on Teluk Kerma, a small bay on the northeastern side of the island. There are longhouse rooms and chalets, as well as a more unusual treehouse for all those budding Tarzans and Janes (RM25).

Mira Chalets (☎ 010-964 0582; r RM30-50) On the southwest coast is this adventurous choice on a small secluded beach, with the jungle right behind. There are just eight rickety chalets set amid banana and coconut trees, in a location Robinson Crusoe would have been proud to call home.

PULAU PERHENTIAN BESAR

The beaches on Besar are rockier than on Kecil, but a little hunting can usually turn up a smooth patch of sand. Of the three main beaches, the sand surrounding the Perhentian Island Resort is the rockiest, heading south the sand is less cluttered, and finally Teluk Dalam, a secluded bay with a long stretch of shallow beach, is just silken. An easily missed track leads from behind the second jetty over the hill to Teluk Dalam.

It's possible to camp on the beach south of the Government Resthouse; this area is busy at long weekends.

The options here are listed from north to south.

Reef (d RM70) This is a basic, laid-back place with 11 simple chalets set back from the beach.

Paradise Island Resort (☎ 019-981 1852; r RM30-60; ❄) Next along is a friendly place with big, but musty-smelling, chalets and the novel addition of screens on the windows.

Mama's Place (☎ 010-981 3359; r RM60-95) The last place on this section of beach offers a choice of reasonably comfortable chalets, most with seaviews.

New Cocohut (☎ 697 7988; r RM30-80; ❄) Over the headland there's another stretch of beach with smoother sand. The first place here has a choice of accommodation including beachside chalets and a two-storey longhouse, which has vistas from the upstairs balcony.

Abdul's (☎ 010-983 7303; r RM50-80) Clambering over the next headland brings you to a quiet beach where you'll find this popular place with fan chalets and attached bathrooms.

Flora Bay Resort (☎ 697 7266; www.florabayresort .com; Teluk Dalam; r RM50-150; ﹡) This is a big, appealing place set back from the beach. Note, though, that prices rise by 20% on weekends.

Fauna Beach Chalets (☎ 697 7607; Teluk Dalam; r RM40-50) The next place along is more basic.

Getting There & Around

Pulau Perhentian is 21km off the coast. Both speedboats (RM60 return, 30 minutes,) and slow boats (RM40 return, 1½ hours) run several times a day from Kuala Besut to the Perhentians, from 8am to 3pm. In the other direction, speedboats depart from the islands daily at around 8am, noon and 4pm; slow boats leave hourly from 8am to noon. Note that you can board a speedboat in either direction with a slow-boat ticket if you pay the RM10 fare difference. See Kuala Besut (p472) for more information about the competing jetty of Tok Bali.

When the waves are high on Long Beach, you'll be dropped off or picked up on the other side of the island at Coral Bay. Also, guesthouse operators on Kecil now charge RM2 for ferry pick-ups and drop-offs.

The easiest way to island (or beach) hop is by boat. Posted fares and boat operators usually camp out under a shady coconut tree. From island to island, the trip costs RM10.

KOTA BHARU

☎ 09

In the northeastern corner of the peninsula, Kota Bharu is a shy state capital still surprised to see such exotic creatures as Westerners. In this pocket, the population is homogenous, predominately Malay Muslim, making the city and the state of Kelantan a stronghold for Malay culture and Islamic scholarship. Most visitors just pass through en route to Pulau Perhentian, but there are some interesting cultural attractions to burn away a few hours.

Information

Banks and ATMs are scattered around town; the Maybank moneychanger (near Jl Padang Garong and Jl Mahmud), near the central market, is usually open till 7pm. Internet shops can be found in the alleys between Jl Doktor and Jl Kebun Sultan.

General Hospital (☎ 748 5533; Jl Hospital)

Immigration office (☎ 748 212; Jl Temenggong)

Muda Osman (☎ 744 8010; 101 Jl Buluh Kubu) English-language books and stationery.

Tourist Information Centre (☎ 748 5534; Jl Sultan Ibrahim; ☉ 8am-1pm & 2-4.30pm Mon-Thu, 8am-12.15pm & 2.45-4.30pm Fri, 8am-12.50pm Sat)

Sights & Activities

Kota Bharu's main attraction is its **central market** (Jl Padang Garong), housed in a modern octagonal building where traders sell fresh produce, spices, basketware and other goods. You might come to observe the locals, but the locals are more than happy to look at you.

For a dose of Malay tradition, head to the cultural centre, **Gelanggang Seni** (☎ 744 3124; Jl Mahmud; admission free; ☉ 3.30-5.30pm Mon, Wed & Sat, 9pm-midnight Wed & Sat), for top spinning, *seni silat* (martial arts), shadow puppetry, kite making etc. Playing chicken-feather-ball is truly entertaining. Check with the tourist information centre, as opening and performance times vary.

Exhibits at the **Muzium Negeri Kelantan** (☎ 748 2266; Jl Hospital; adult RM2; ☉ 8.30am-4.45pm Sun-Thu) combine an eclectic array of artefacts, including traditional instruments, kites and shadow puppets.

Other museums are clustered around Padang Merdeka (Independence Square). **Istana Jahar** (Royal Customs Museum; ☎ 748 2266; Jl Hilir Kota; adult RM3; ☉ 8.30am-4.45pm Sun-Thu) exhibits royal rites of passage and traditional ceremonies, such as circumcision and engagement, from birth to death; this may not sound that engaging, but wandering around the scenic building gives a glimpse into Malay Muslim architecture. **Muzium Islam** (☎ 744 0102; Jl Sultan; admission free; ☉ 8.30am-4.45pm Sun-Thu) is also worth a look and **Istana Batu** (☎ 748 7737; Jl Hilir Kota; adult RM2; ☉ 8.30am-4.45pm Sun-Thu) has displays on royal history.

Sleeping

Most people arrive in Kota Bharu on an overnight bus at an unseemly hour. Dazed and confused, they fend off the taxi drivers and stagger off in the direction of a guesthouse. In this state, any guesthouse will do;

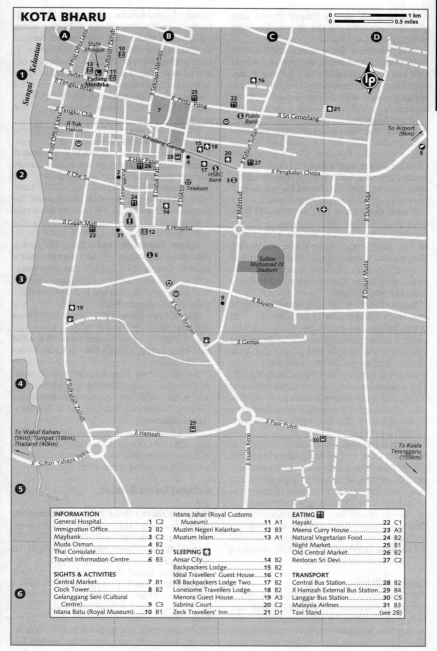

KOTA BHARU

0 — 1 km
0 — 0.5 miles

if you plan on staying longer than a day, consider auditioning the more charming outlying guesthouses.

Ideal Travellers' Guest House (☎ 744 2246; 3954F Jl Kebun Sultan; dm/s/d RM7/15/20) In a private house, down an alley off Jl Pintu Pong, Ideal is an absolute winner. Spacious rooms are airy, some with a leafy aspect, and the bathrooms are clean. There's a shady backyard reading area.

Zeck Travellers' Inn (☎ 743 1613; 7088G Jl Sri Cemerlang; dm/s/d RM7/15/20; 🞩) An oasis just 10 minutes' walk from the city, Zeck's is relaxed, clean and quiet with a range of decent-sized rooms. The turn-off from Jl Sri Cemerlang is easy to miss; keep an eye out for the outgoing group of boys selling sugar cane.

Menora Guest House (☎ 748 1669; 3338D Jl Sultanah Zainab; r RM15-38; 🞩) Menora's prime attraction is its rooftop garden with views of the city, Sungai Kelantan and beyond. There's one room on the rooftop that has its own one-air shower. Inside, there are a variety of clean rooms. Note that the gate is locked at 11.30pm.

Sabrina Court (☎ 744 7944; sabrinacourt@hotmail .com; 171-81 Jl Padang Garong; r RM25-39; 🞩) This centrally located hotel has basic, slightly rundown, but perfectly comfortable rooms; you can even stay in one of the fan-only 'Lonely Planet' rooms (no relation!).

Ansar City (☎ 747 4000; Jl Maju; s/d RM70/100; 🞩) The otherwise nondescript hotel rooms at Ansar are noteworthy because of the hotel's Islamic environment. Verses from the Koran decorate the hallway and an arrow in each room points to Mecca.

Backpackers Lodge (☎ 943 8002; Jl Padang Garong; dm/s/d RM8/15/28) and **KB Backpackers Lodge Two** (☎ 747 0125; 1872A Jl Padang Garong; dm/s RM8/18, d RM20-22) are two similarly named spots that verge on grungy but redeem themselves with their central location, which is so close to the drop-off for long-distance buses that you hardly have time to worry about pre-dawn no-goods. Also recommended is **Lonesome Travellers Lodge** (☎ 959 3680; 375 Jl Dato Perdana 3; dm/s/d RM8/15/20).

Eating & Drinking

Night Market (cnr Jl Datok Pati & Jl Pintu Pong; 🕓 dinner) For a bonanza of regional Malay and Indian specialities, at hawker prices, head to this vibrant market. Here you will find *ayam percik* (marinated chicken on bamboo

skewers), *nasi kerabu* (rice tinted blue with herbs, mixed with coconut, fish, vegetables and spices), squid-on-a-stick, sweet banana and savoury *murtabak* (thick Indian pancake stuffed with onion, egg, chicken, mutton or vegetables), and a bewildering array of cakes. Prayer always pulls rank over food and at prayer time (roughly between 7pm and 7.45pm) everyone is chased out of the market.

Old Central Market (cnr Jl Datok Pati & Jl Hilir Pasar; meals RM2-4; 🕓 breakfast & lunch) The old market has blocks worth of food vendors with mouth-watering trays of pre-made curries and stir-fries. Just point and gulp.

Restoran Sri Devi (☎ 746 2980; 4213F Jl Kebun Sultan; dishes RM3-6; 🕓 breakfast, lunch & dinner) As popular with locals as it is with tourists, this is a great place for an authentic banana-leaf curry and a mango lassi.

Natural Vegetarian Food (☎ 746 1902; 2848 Jl Ismail; dishes from RM3.50; 🕓 lunch) Serves exactly what it says on the sign; you can help yourself to as much as you like from the all-vegetarian buffet, and wash it down with a glass of wheatgrass juice.

Meena Curry House (☎ 743 0173; 3377 Jl Gajah Mati; dishes RM3-7; 🕓 lunch & dinner) If you're looking to expand your Western palate, try the fish-head curry. There's also meat and vegetable curries.

Hayaki (Jl Pintu Pong; dishes RM3-19; 🕓 lunch) A glossy lunch spot that serves chicken rice and *nasi kandar*. The main reason you come here is for the icy blended fruit drinks – truly refreshing.

As Kota Bharu is a conservative Muslim city, alcohol is not widely available, but there are several Chinese restaurants around town that serve beer.

Getting There & Away

AIR

Malaysia Airlines (☎ 744 7000; www.malaysiaairlines .com.my; Jl Gajah Mati) is opposite the clock tower. There are direct flights to/from KL (RM200). **Air Asia** (☎ 746 1671; www.airasia.com) has flights to KL from RM81. The **airport** (Lapangan Terbang Sultan Ismail Petra) is 9km from town. You can take bus 9 from the **old central market** (Jl Hilir Pasar); a taxi costs RM15.

BUS

There are three bus stations in Kota Bharu. Local buses depart from the **central bus** station (Jl Padang Garong), also known as the state-run SKMK bus station. Most long-distance buses will drop off passengers near here, but do not depart from here. All long-distance companies serving Kota Bharu have ticket agents nearby. When buying your ticket, verify which long-distance terminal the bus departs from. Most Transnacional long-distance buses depart from **Langgar bus station** (☎ 748 3807; Jl Pasir Puteh), in the south of the city. All the other long-distance bus companies operate from the external **bus station** (Jl Hamzah).

A few handy local buses include bus 639 to Kuala Besut (for boats to Pulau Perhentian; RM4, 2½ hours, two daily), bus 9 to Kota Bharu airport (RM1, every 20 minutes), and buses 19 and 27 travel to Wakaf Baharu (RM1). Note that some of these routes may be identified by destination rather than number.

Long-distance destinations include Butterworth (RM20, seven hours, one daily), Ipoh (RM21.50, eight hours, five daily), Johor Bahru (RM35, 10 hours, five daily), Kuala Lumpur (RM26, 10 hours, hourly), Kuala Terengganu (RM7, three hours, two daily), and Kuantan (RM20, seven hours, five daily).

TAXI
The taxi stand is on the southern side of the central bus station. Taxi costs are quoted here per car (which can be split between four passengers): Wakaf Baharu (RM10), Kota Besut (RM28), Tok Bali (RM24). Taxi drivers in KB are uncharacteristically aggressive for Malaysia; do your homework on fares before soliciting. Most guesthouses arrange shared taxis, especially for early morning departures.

BORDER CROSSING: INTO THAILAND

If you are travelling to Thailand from the east coast, you should catch local bus 29 from Kota Bharu (RM3, every 30 minutes) to the Malaysian border town of Rantau Panjang. From here, you can walk across the border to the Thai town of Sungai Kolok (p797), where Bangkok-bound trains leave at 11am and 2pm (though times can vary – local guesthouses can provide updated information).

TRAIN
The nearest **train station** (☎ 719 6986) to Kota Bharu is at Wakaf Baharu, on the Jungle Railway line (see below). For travel to/from Thailand, use the train station in Rantau Panjang; see left for more information.

PENINSULAR INTERIOR

A thick band of jungle buffers the two coasts from one another. Within the middle is Taman Negara, the peninsula's most famous national park, and the Jungle Railway, an engineering feat.

JUNGLE RAILWAY
This line trundles into the mountainous, jungle-clad interior, stopping at every little ramshackle *kampung*, packing in chattering school children and headscarfed women lugging oversized bundles. Travellers' reports range from sheer awe of the natural splendour and amusement with the local camaraderie to boredom and irritation with faulty air-conditioning in the carriages and dirty windows. If you're in good company and have a lot of time, then there are worse ways to travel between Pulau Perhentian and Taman Negara. Ask around to get a better gauge for your personal preference.

The northern terminus is Tumpat, but most travellers start/end at Wakaf Baharu, the closest station to the transport hub of Kota Bharu. The train departs from Wakaf Baharu on its southbound journey at 6am. It reaches Jerantut (p478), the jumping-off point for Taman Negara, anywhere from eight to 11 hours later (RM12.60). The train continues south to Gemas (RM19.20), meeting the Singapore–KL train line.

There are also express trains that travel at night, but that would defeat the purpose of seeing the jungle. There is a daily express train that leaves Wakaf Bahru at 6pm and arrives in KL at 7.25am the following day. There is also a daily express train to Singapore (RM32) leaving at 7pm and arriving at 9am the following day.

Northbound trains leave Gemas at 7.45am, reaching Jerantut at 12pm and arriving at Wakaf Bahru at 9.30pm.

Note that the KTM railway company changes its schedule every six months, so it pays to double-check departure times.

MALAYSIA

JERANTUT

☎ 09

Jerantut is the first of several stepping stones to Taman Negara. It is a good spot to pick up supplies, change money, and overnight if you've missed a transit connection. Most guesthouses are affiliated with travel agencies that offer transfer services to nearby Kuala Tembeling jetty (where boats leave for the national park), ferry services to Kuala Tahan (the base camp village for Taman Negara) and tours of the park.

Hotel Sri Emas (☎ 266 4499; www.taman-negara .com; Jl Besar; dm RM8, r RM15-38; 🔀) is backpacker central, and can make full arrangements for your trip to Taman Negara. The hotel runs minibus transport to the park or Kuala Tembeling jetty. It provides free pick-up from the train station. Rooms are average and some cleaning products wouldn't go astray, but it's cheap and it's open 24 hours.

Another backpacker favourite is **Greenleaf Guesthouse** (1st fl, Jl Diwangsa; dm RM10, r 20-30; 🔀), open 24 hours, with free pick-up and drop-off to the train and bus station, luggage storage, etc. It is across from the bus station near the AM Finance bank.

Jerantut Traveller's Inn (☎ 266 6845; www .taman-negara-island.com; Tingkat Satu; dm RM10, r RM25-35; 🔀) is only 300m from the bus station. This guesthouse is affiliated with SPKG travel agency.

The food stalls between the market and train station are surprisingly good. Cheap *kedai kopi* can be found along Jl Besar and in the buildings across from the bus station.

Getting There & Away

BOAT

River ferries make the scenic journey between Kuala Tembeling, 16km north of Jerantut, and Kuala Tahan. Several ferry companies sell tickets at the jetty, if you arrive independent of arranged transport from Jerantut. In most cases, though, travel agents sell combination tickets that include transfer from Jerantut to the jetty and ferry to Kuala Tahan.

For information on ferries to Kuala Tahan, see p482.

BUS & TAXI

The bus station and taxi stand are in the centre of town.

The trickiest part of negotiating Jerantut is getting from the bus station to the Kuala Tembeling jetty (where boats leave for Taman Negara). The path of least resistance is to follow the representative from NKS/Hotel Sri Emas (left) who meets arriving buses and trains for minibus transfers (RM5) from Jerantut to Kuala Tembeling. If you want to resist the herding, go to **Nusa Camp's office** (☎ 266 2369; Jl Diwangsa), which is next door to the KFC across the street from the bus station; they are a well-regarded company that arranges transfer to the jetty, ferry services and lodging at the park. Lastly, beware of touts at the train and bus stations who tell you there are no boats running from Tembeling to the park; they're only trying to get you to take their very expensive alternatives.

There is a local bus between Kuala Tembeling and Jerantut bus station (signed as 'Kerambit', RM1.50, 45 minutes, 8.15am, 11.15am, 1.45pm and 5.15pm departures), but the times are not pegged to boat departures or arrivals (see p482 for ferry times); the return bus leaves Kuala Tembeling at 10am, 1pm and 3.30pm.

You can also skip the boat journey and hop on a Kuala Tahan–bound bus (signed as 'Latif', RM6, one to two hours, 5.30am and 1pm departures); Kuala Tahan is the base camp village for Taman Negara.

If you've exhausted all other methods, you can hire a taxi to Kuala Tembeling (RM16) or to Kuala Tahan (RM60) for the entire car.

When you are ready to get the hell out of Jerantut, there are buses to/from KL's Pekeliling bus station (RM10.85, 3½ hours, four daily) via Temerloh. If you miss the bus to KL, buses go every hour to Temerloh (RM4, one hour), from where there are more connections to KL and other destinations. If you're itching to get to Pulau Tioman, you'll have to catch a bus to Kuantan (RM10.50, 3½ hours, three daily) and then a bus to Mersing.

You can also take a bus from Jerantut to Melaka (RM15.10, five hours, one daily). Long-distance taxis go to Temerloh (RM30), KL (RM120) and Kuantan (RM100).

TRAIN

Jerantut is on the Jungle Railway (Tumpat-Gemas line; see p477). The **train station** (off Jl Besar) is just behind Hotel Sri Emas. For the famed jungle view, catch the northbound local train at 12.10pm (RM13). If you opt to skip the view, a daily northbound express train leaves Jerantut at 2am (RM15 to RM20, four hours).

For southbound trips, there is a midnight express train leaving Jerantut for Sentral KL (RM18 to RM22, seven hours), 1am express train for Singapore (RM14 to RM20, seven hours), and an 8.40am local train for Singapore (RM9 to RM14, nine hours). Another local southbound train leaves at 3.30pm terminating at Gemas (RM6 to RM10; four hours), where you can catch an inconvenient 2am Singapore (RM24 to RM30) or KL train.

TAMAN NEGARA
☎ 09

Taman Negara is a mass of primary jungle over 130 million years old and sprawling across 4343 sq km. You can trek through deep jungle, join the crowds braving the creaky canopy walk, spot a colony of bats asleep in a musty cave, or spend the night in the great outdoors hoping to spot a famous nocturnal animal.

Some visitors leave the park cursing that they haven't stared down an elusive elephant or tiger. Sightings are extremely rare and require backcountry trekking. For the lightweight naturalist (and that includes most of us), a night in one of the park's observation hides will introduce furless humans to smaller creatures like deer, snakes, 'small' big cats, tapirs, and insects, spiders and beetles enormous enough to spawn sci-fi movie plots. And lot's of creepy jungle noises.

The best time to visit the park is in the dry season between February and September. During the rainy season, leeches are an unwelcome welcoming committee.

Orientation & Information
Kuala Tahan is the base camp for Taman Negara. It has accommodation, mini markets and floating barge restaurants. Directly opposite Kuala Tahan, across Sungai Tembeling, is the entrance to the national park, Mutiara Taman Negara Resort and the park headquarters located at the Wildlife Department, behind the resort's restaurant.

You must pay a RM1 entrance fee and an optional RM5 camera permit at the **Wildlife Department** (☎ 266 1122; ✆ 8am-7pm Sat-Thu, 8am-12pm & 3-7pm Fri). The reception desk also provides basic maps, guide services and advice.

Internet access is painstakingly slow and expensive. **RiverNet Station** (per hr RM8) has the most PCs and it's workable. There are no banks in Taman Negara.

Sight & Activities
HIDES & SALT LICKS
Animal observation hides (bumbun) are built overlooking salt licks and grassy clearings, which attract feeding nocturnal animals. You'll need to spend the night in order to see any real action. There are several hides close to Kuala Tahan (Tabing and Kumbang hides being the most popular) and Kuala Trenggan that are a little too close to human habitation to attract the shy animals. Even if you don't see any wildlife, the jungle sounds are well worth it – the 'symphony' is best at dusk and dawn.

PLANNING FOR TAMAN NEGARA

Stock up on essentials in Jerantut. If it's been raining, leeches will be out in force. Mosquito repellent, tobacco, salt, toothpaste and soap can be used to deter them, with varying degrees of success. A liberal coating of insect spray over shoes and socks works best.

Everyday clothes are suitable around Kuala Tahan, but wear long sleeves and long pants when hitting the trails. Covering up will protect you from insects and brambles. Take plenty of water, even on short walks, and on longer walks take water-purifying tablets to sterilise stream water.

Sturdy boots are essential; lightweight, high-lacing canvas jungle boots that keep out leeches can be hired from the camping-ground office. Camping gear can also be hired at Kuala Tahan jetty or Mutiara Taman Negara resort.

Taman Negara: Malaysia's Premier National Park written by David Bowden (available in the bigger bookshops of Kuala Lumpur, or online) is an excellent resource, with detailed route maps and valuable background information.

Hides need to be reserved at the Wildlife Department (per person per night RM5) and they are very rustic with pit toilets. Some travellers hike independently in the day to the hides, then camp overnight and return the next day; while others go to more far-flung hides that require some form of transport and a guide; the Wildlife Department can steer you in the right direction. For overnight trips you'll need food, water and a sleeping bag. Rats on the hunt for tucker are problematic, so hang food high out of reach.

Some of the following hides can be reached by popular treks (see below).

Bumbun Blau & Bumbun Yong On Sungai Yong. From the park headquarters, it's roughly 1½ hours' walk to Bumbun Blau (3.1km), which sleeps 12 people and has water nearby, and two hours to Bumbun Yong (4km). You can visit Gua Telinga along the way. Both hides can also be reached by the riverbus service (see p482).

Bumbun Cegar Anjing Once an airstrip, this is now an artificial salt lick, established to attract wild cattle and deer. A clear river runs a few metres from the hide. 1½ hours' walk from Kuala Tahan, after rain Bumbun Cegar Anjing may only be accessible by boat (per four-person boat RM40). There are bunks for eight people at the hide.

Bumbun Kumbang From the park headquarters, it's roughly five hours' walk to Bumbun Kumbang. Alternatively, take the riverboat service up Sungai Tembeling to Kuala Trenggan from Kuala Tahan (per four-person boat RM90, 35 minutes), then walk 45 minutes to the hide. Animals most commonly seen here are tapirs, rats, monkeys and gibbons, and occasionally elephants. The hide has bunks for 12 people.

Bumbun Tahan Roughly five minutes' walk from the park headquarters. There's little chance of seeing any animals, apart from monkeys and deer at this artificial salt lick.

TREKKING

Clambering over tree roots through steamy jungle is a primary activity at Taman Negara. There are treks to suit all levels of motivation, from a half-hour jaunt to a steep nine-day tussle up and down Gunung Tahan (2187m). Night treks have had mixed responses: some people spot an assortment of nocturnal species, and others only reflections from curious eyes. It's unanimous, however, that the guides are excellent.

Popular do-it-yourself treks, from one to five hours, include the following:

Bukit Teresik From behind the Canopy Walkway a trail leads to the top of this hill from which there are fine views across the forest. Steep and slippery in parts. Return trip is approximately one hour.

Canopy Walkway (admission RM5; 11am-2.45pm Sat-Thu, 9am-noon Fri) Anyone who says walking isn't an adrenalin sport has never been suspended on a hanging rope bridge constructed of wooden planks and ladders elevated 45m above the ground; come early to avoid long waits in line.

Gua Telinga From the park headquarters, roughly 1½ hours' walk (2.6km). Think wet: a stream runs through this cave (with sleeping bats) and a rope guides you for the strenuous 80m half-hour trek – and crawl – through the cave. Return to the main path through the cave or take the path round the rocky outcrop at its far end. From the main path, it's 15 minutes' walk to Bumbun Blau hide or you can walk directly back to Kuala Tahan.

Kuala Trenggan The well-marked main trail along the bank of Sungai Tembeling leads 9km to Kuala Trenggan. This is a popular trail for those heading to Bumbun Kumbang.

Lubok Simpon Popular swimming hole. Near the Canopy Walkway, take the branch trail that leads across to a swimming area on Sungai Tahan.

Longer treks, which require a guide, include the following:

Gunung Tahan For the gung-ho, Gunung Tahan, 55km from the park headquarters, is Peninsular Malaysia's highest peak (2187m). It takes nine days at a steady pace, although it can be done in seven. Guides are compulsory (RM500 for seven days, plus RM50 for each day thereafter). Try to organise this trek in advance through the Wildlife Department (p479).

Rentis Tenor (Tenor Trail) From Kuala Tahan, this trek takes roughly three days. Day one: take the trail to Gua Telinga, and beyond, for about seven hours, to Yong camp site. Day two: a six-hour walk to the Renuis camp site. Day three: cross Sungai Tahan (up to waist deep) to get back to Kuala Tahan, roughly six hours' walk, or you can stop over at the Lameh camp site, about halfway.

OTHER ACTIVITIES

Many travellers sign up for tours to an Orang Asli settlement. Tribal elders give a general overview and you'll learn how to use a long blowpipe and start a fire.

Catch-and-release fishing is allowed along Sungai Keniam. The sport fish known locally as *ikan kelah* (Malaysian mahseer), a cousin of India's king of the Himalayan rivers, is a prized catch. You'll need a fishing licence, transport and a guide; go to the **Wildlife Department** (266 1122; 8am-7pm Sat-Thu, 8am-12pm & 3-7pm Fri) for more information.

Tours

Guides who are licensed by the Wildlife Department have completed coursework in forest flora, fauna and safety and are registered with the department. But often the Kuala Tahan tour operators offer cheaper prices than the Wildlife Department, although there is no guarantee that the guide is licensed. Guides cost RM150 per day (one guide can lead up to 12 people), plus a RM100 fee for each night spent out on the trail.

Consider booking tours *after* you arrive in Kuala Tahan. Talk to fellow travellers about which tour operators are doing a good job since a recommendation by a certain guidebook can cause quality to deteriorate. Readers have also complained that certain tour operators will promise a particular tour, but only be able to fulfil a portion of the planned itinerary upon arrival.

Sleeping & Eating

Guesthouses are listed here in south-to-north order. Malay food (dishes for around RM3 to RM10) is available from barge restaurants floating on Sungai Tembeling, at a couple of places attached to guesthouses and at the **Mutiara Taman Negara Resort** (☎ 266 3500; dishes from RM15-50; 🔀).

KUALA TAHAN

Ekoton Chalets (☎ 266 9897; tamannegara@hotmail .com; dm RM13-20, r RM70-90; 🔀) Run by the same mob as Sri Emas (in Jerantut), Ekoton has generous-sized dorms, but travellers complain that the wooden, air-con chalets have seen better days.

Agoh (☎ 019-928 0414; d RM40) This dusty collection of chalets doesn't make much of an impression at first. Take a closer look, though. Those aren't corrugated metal shacks, but an artistic façade mimicking tree bark, and the baths are brand-spanking new.

Tembeling River Hostel & Chalets (☎ 266 6766; dm RM10, chalets RM35-50) Follow the river bank to simple Tembeling, which has a high perch over the river activities. Four-bed dorms, with fan and mosquito net, are all a vagabond really needs. There's also a restaurant.

Liana Hostel (☎ 266 9322; dm RM10) A barracks-like but clean hostel, Liana creeps up the river bank and devotes its spare time to worshipping Bob Marley.

Teresek View Motel (☎ 266 9177; dm RM10, r RM30-100; 🔀) The modern Teresek building

strangely reminiscent of a mosque occupies the 'centre' of Kuala Tahan, a small intersection of two main roads incongruously busy for the otherwise quiet hamlet. A lot of weighted-down packs claim a roadside chalet or dorm out of exhaustion, not out of inherent value.

Tahan Guesthouse (☎ 266 7752; dm RM19, r RM40) Don't give up at Teresek View, follow the zig-zag in the road to this bright and cheerful house with a comfortable front-yard sitting area.

Durian Chalet (☎ 266 8940; r RM25-50) Go past Tahan Guesthouse, past the rubber tapping farm, and veer left just as you smell this chalet's namesake fruit. It is far enough from town that the silvery stars and moon bid you goodnight, and jungle noises rouse you from sleep. The simple chalets reflect the owners' personal fastidiousness and have lots of extras to make you feel like a budget princess. There's a restaurant with a simple Malay menu.

NUSA CAMP

Nusa Camp (☎ 266 3043/2369; dm RM15, r RM55-110) Fifteen minutes up Sungai Tembeling from Kuala Tahan, this is a quieter accommodation option. Much more of a 'jungle camp', there is a range of accommodation here for most budgets. The clean, spacious double cottages with a fan and bathroom are the best value.

Drinking & Entertainment

Mutiara Taman Negara Resort (☎ 266 3500; beers RM8) Kuala Tahan is dry, so if you're after a beer you'll have to cross over to this resort. After dark in Kuala Tahan, the no-name restaurant, third from the left facing the park headquarters, has a mellow campfire atmosphere and welcoming locals usually strumming guitars, singing and playing cards. It's also popular with guides.

Getting There & Away

Getting to Taman Negara involves a lot of transfers: bus or train to Jerantut (p478), minibus to Kuala Tembeling, river boat to Kuala Tahan. It is an all-day affair, but the languid boat ride up the undeveloped river will soothe any sweaty bus frustration. If you're pressed for time in either direction, you can also take a taxi or a minibus from Jerantut to Kuala Tahan (see p478).

BOAT

The river jetty for Taman Negara–bound boats is in Kuala Tembeling, 18km north of Jerantut.

Boats depart Kuala Tembeling every day at 9am and 2pm (and an additional 2.30pm departure on Friday). On the return journey, boats leave Kuala Tahan at 9am and 2pm (and 2.30pm on Friday). The journey takes three hours upstream and two hours downstream. One-way fares are RM22. Note that the boat service is irregular during the November-to-February rainy season.

BUS & TAXI

See p478 for details on buses and taxis from Jerantut to Kuala Tembeling.

There are several daily minibus shuttles direct from Kuala Lumpur to Kuala Tembeling jetty (RM25 to RM30). NKS leaves from **Hotel Mandarin Pacific** (Jl Petaling, Chinatown, KL), and Nusa Camp leaves from **Swiss Inn** (Jl Sultan, Chinatown, KL).

A local bus travels from Kuala Tahan to Jerantut (RM6, one to two hours, 7.30am and 3pm daily). The bus stop is on the access road to the main highway, around the corner from the row of sundry stalls.

Getting Around

There is a cross-river ferry (RM1) that shuttles passengers across the river from Kuala Tahan to the park and Mutiara Taman Negara Resort. It will also pick up and drop off folks at the trailhead for Gua Telinga, across a small tributary from the resort.

Nusa Camp's floating information centre in Kuala Tahan runs scheduled riverboat services upriver to Bumbun Blau/Bumbun Yong (one-way/return RM7/10; two daily), Kuala Terenggan (RM10; two daily). Check with the information desk for times and prices, as they vary considerably by season. Keep in mind that these regularly scheduled riverboat services run pretty much on time during the peak season, but may be dropped entirely during the rainy season.

In addition to the riverbus, you can also charter a boat for considerably more – Bumbun Blau (RM60) and Kuala Trenggan (RM90). You can arrange private boat trips at the Wildlife Department (p479), at the resort or at the restaurants in Kuala Tahan (the latter are usually 10% cheaper).

MALAYSIAN BORNEO – SARAWAK

Its name conjures up vivid images of little-explored jungle, intimidating wildlife and tribespeople living in the shadows of fantastically remote mountains, yet Borneo remains such an enigma that many people struggle to locate it on a map and are unaware that the island is shared by three countries – Malaysia (the states of Sarawak and Sabah), Brunei, and Indonesia (the Kalimantan province). A trip to Sarawak is a wonderful opportunity to demystify Borneo and replace imaginative speculation with the much more captivating reality.

The pleasures of visiting Sarawak include exploring the charming, waterfront state capital, Kuching; surging up the Batang Rejang in a high-powered riverboat to stay the night in isolated longhouses; winging your way into the mountainous interior to relax in highland towns; trekking through the peak-ringed jungles of Gunung Mulu and other superb national parks; and having laidback locals sit next to you in cafés and parks and engage you about politics or your home 'country'. Best of all, Sarawak runs on 'rubber time' – time here stretches and makes a mockery of tight schedules, and you're invited to do the same.

KUCHING

☎ 082 / pop 496,000

Kuching is a busy yet seductively laidback city, a mixture of administrative centre, waterfront beauty, suburban sprawl, marketplace commerce and colonial relic. The blandest part of town is the upscale tourist centrifuge around the Hilton but most other areas have an intriguing character: the waterfront promenade that invites indolence; the orderly businesses of pedestrianised Jl India; shopfronts squeezed along Main Bazaar and fronted by wildly dipping sidewalks; the river criss-crossed by *tambang* (small river boats); aromatic food courts; even the jam of buses near the mosque. Put aside at least a few days to explore and enjoy this delightful Southeast Asian city.

MALAYSIA

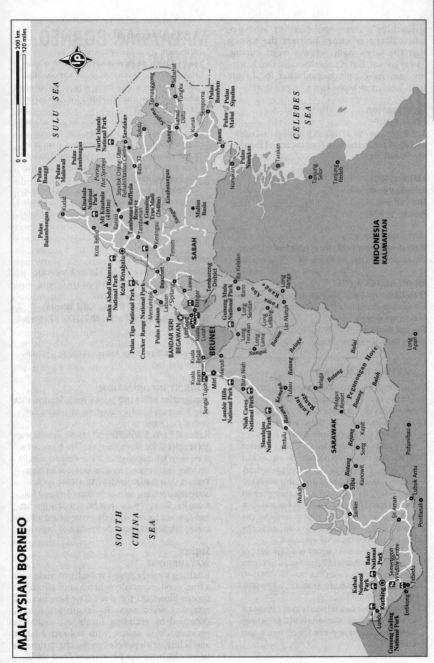

MALAYSIAN BORNEO

Kuching's overpopulation of stumpy-tailed Bornean felines bolsters the theory that the city's name comes from *kucing*, Malay for cat. But it's also thought that Kuching may have been named after local fruit trees known as *mata kucing* (cat's eye).

Information

BOOKSHOPS
Red Bookshop (☎ 241168; 68 Jl Wayang) Has English-language fiction and books on Bornean flora and fauna, plus Sarawak maps.

EMERGENCY
Ambulance (☎ 999)
Fire (☎ 994)
Police (☎ 999)

INTERNET ACCESS
Waterfront Cyber Café (☎ 243680; Sarawak Steamship Bldg, Main Bazaar; per 10 min RM1; ☉ 9am-5.30pm)

MEDICAL SERVICES
Chan Clinic (☎ 240307; 98 Main Bazaar; ☉ 8am-noon & 2-5pm Mon-Fri, 9am-noon Sat) Good place for treating minor travel ailments.
General Hospital (☎ 257555; Jl Hospital) For emergencies and major ailments only.

GETTING INTO TOWN

Kuching International Airport's battered old terminal is 12km south of the city centre. Sarawak Transport Co's (STC) green-and-cream bus 12A does a circuit that takes in the airport, while Chin Lian Long's (CLL) blue-and-white bus 8A does a direct airport to city run. The fare on either bus is 90 sen. To walk to the airport bus stop, exit the terminal and turn right. Minivans also swing by the stop and can transport you to town for about RM3. A coupon-fare taxi between Kuching airport and the city centre costs RM17.50. Buy coupons at the counter at the terminal entrance.

The express-boat wharf is 6.5km east of town in the suburb of Pending. To get from there into town, catch CLL bus 1A (RM1, 40 minutes) from outside Khatulistiwa (p488). Taxis cost RM20.

The express bus station is 5km southeast of the city centre. Numerous STC buses run between station and city for 60 sen. A taxi costs RM15.

VISAS & PERMITS

Although it's a Malaysian state, Sarawak is semi-autonomous and has its own immigration controls. On arrival most nationalities will be given a visa for a stay of between one and three months, valid for Peninsular Malaysia as well.

If you plan to visit Belaga or any of the longhouses above Kapit on the Rejang or Baleh Rivers, you must obtain a permit in Kapit (see p492). Similarly, you need to get a permit in Miri before visiting Bario in the Kelabit Highlands (see p496).

These permits aren't always checked but they're free and easy to obtain, and worth getting just in case officials are on the ball when you visit.

MONEY
There are plenty of ATMs in Kuching.
Majid & Sons (☎ 422402; 45 Jl India) A licensed moneychanger dealing in cash only.
Maybank (☎ 416889; Jl Tunku Abdul Rahman).
Standard Chartered Bank (☎ 252233; Jl Padungan)

POST
Main post office (Jl Tun Abang Haji Openg; ☉ 8am-4.30pm Mon-Sat)

TOURIST INFORMATION
Immigration office (☎ 245661; 2nd fl, Sultan Iskandar Bldg, Jl Simpang Tiga) For visa extensions. Located 3km south of the centre.
National Parks & Wildlife (☎ 248088; Sarawak Tourism Complex, Jl Tun Abang Haji Openg) The main counter of the visitor information centre is also a contact point for this office, which makes park accommodation bookings.
Visitors information centre (☎ 410944; www .sarawaktourism.com; Sarawak Tourism Complex, Jl Tun Abang Haji Openg; ☉ 8am-6pm Mon-Fri, 8am-4pm Sat, 9am-3pm Sun) Located in the old courthouse and with extremely helpful staff. Pick up the free *Kuching Tourist Map*.

Sights
WATERFRONT
Kuching's lovely paved waterfront makes for a fine stroll, especially when a cool afternoon breeze blows off the river. The benches and retaining walls along its length are usually occupied by reclining locals. At night the promenade is ablaze with colourful lights and is busy with people buying cheap dinners or snacks from the permanent food stalls.

KUCHING

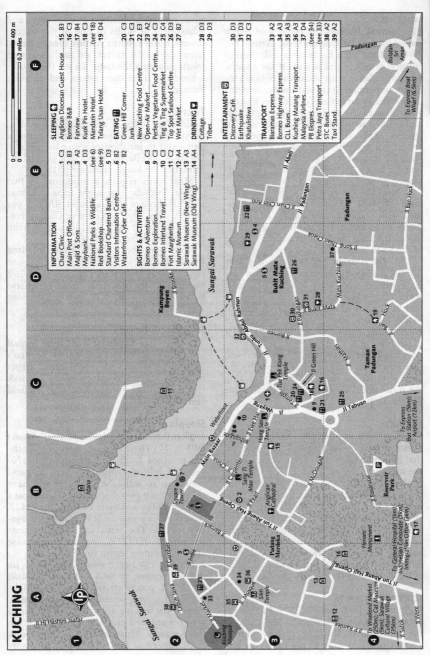

400 m
0.2 miles

To Express Boat
Wharf (6.5km)

Bulatan
Sri
Aman

Padungan

Padungan

Ban Hock

Sungai Sarawak

Kampung
Boyen

Bukit Mata
Kuching

Padungan

Taman
Padungan

To Express
Bus Station (5km);
Airport (12km)

Green Hill

Waterfront

Main Bazaar

Istana

Sungai Sarawak

Jl Hj Hashim Jaafar

Reservoir
Park

Heroes'
Monument

Padang
Merdeka

Anglican
Cathedral

Tua Pek Kong
Temple

Hong San
Temple

Hiang
Thian Siang
Temple

Mao Temple

Kuching
Mosque

Sikh
Temple

Mosque

Jl Tun Abang Haji Openg

Jl Tun Abang Haji Openg

To Weekend Market (250m);
Cat Museum (5km); Sarawak
Cultural Village (35km)

To General Hospital (1km);
Indonesian Consulate (3km);
Immigration Office (6km)

Jl P Ramlee

Jl Satok

MALAYSIA

MUSEUMS

The **Sarawak Museum** (☎ 244232; www.museum
.sarawak.gov.my; Jl Tun Abang Haji Openg; admission free;
🕑 9am-5.30pm) has a fascinating collection of
cultural artefacts and is a must for anyone
wanting to learn more about the region's indigenous peoples. It consists of two sections
connected by an ornate footbridge. The old
wing houses the main ethnology exhibits
and is filled with tribal masks, totem poles,
fetishes, explanations of tattooing and body
art, and a walk-in longhouse. The newer
wing has temporary exhibits and is slated to
one day host a 'History Museum'. The landscaped grounds are a good place to loiter.

Behind the newer wing is the **Islamic Museum** (☎ 244232; Jl P Ramlee; admission free; 🕑 9am-
6pm), with magnificent examples of Islamic
interior decoration and architecture, including an intricate model of Jerusalem's Dome
of the Rock inlaid with mother-of-pearl.

The **Cat Museum** (☎ 446688; Kuching North
City Hall, Jl Semariang; admission free; 🕑 9am-5pm)
is crammed with kitty kitsch (figurines,
stuffed fauna like the ultra-cute leopard cat
etc) in honour of an animal prominent in
Malay folklore. Some find the museum an
entertaining distraction, while others find it
as fascinating as a furball. Petra Jaya Transport bus 2C or 2D (80 sen, 20 minutes) will
take you to the base of a hill topped by the
large shuttlecock-shaped building housing
the museum; it's a steep uphill climb from
the bus stop.

MARKET

Kuching has a wonderfully chaotic **weekend
market** (Jl Satok; 🕑 late afternoon Sat, 5am-noon Sun)
that inhabits a labyrinth of side-streets along
the southern edge of Jl Satok. The smells of
fresh herbs, fruits and meats compete with
the scent of delicious fried foods like pancakes to pull you every which way. But if
you're reasonably tall (by Malaysian standards), don't go charging through the stalls
or you'll impale yourself on one of the low-
hanging umbrellas or awnings. Saturday afternoon is the best time to visit, when throngs
of locals snap up the freshest goods.

FORT MARGHERITA

Built by Charles Brooke in 1879, **Fort Margh-
erita** (admission free; 🕑 9am-5pm Tue-Sun) guarded
the approach to Kuching against pirates.
There's precious little to see here now bar

some menacing muskets in glass cases and
a basketful of skulls in one of the watchtowers, but it's worth visiting for the views,
from the main turret, of multicoloured
rooftops across the river. To get there, take
a *tambang* from the eastern end of Main
Bazaar.

Tours

Besides day trips in and around Kuching,
many travel agents also offer trips to national
parks and to longhouses along the Skrang,
Lemanak and Rejang rivers. For general information on longhouses, see p515.

Most tours require a minimum of two
people. Two-day/one-night trips to Lemanak longhouses cost around RM390 per
person. Day trips to Gunung Gading National Park cost from RM140, and to Bako
National Park from RM160.

Tour operators include **Borneo Interland
Travel** (☎ 413595; www.bitravel.com.my; 1st fl, 63 Main
Bazaar), **Borneo Exploration** (☎ 252137; 1st fl, 76 Jl
Wayang) and the generally more expensive
Borneo Adventure (☎ 245175; www.borneoadventure
.com; 55 Main Bazaar).

Festivals & Events

The three-day **Rainforest World Music Festival**
(www.rainforestmusic-borneo.com) unites Borneo's
indigenous tribes with international artists
for a musical extravaganza in the Sarawak
Cultural Village outside Kuching. It's held
annually in July.

Sleeping

Anglican Diocesan Guest House (☎ 414027; Jl Pearl; r
RM18-28; 🈯) There are fine views over Kuching rooftops from this atmospheric, 170-
year-old hilltop refuge. It's kept in good
condition so wannabe penitents will have
to create their own discomfort. Twins cost a
bargain RM18 and there's a triple for RM23.
Access is via a gate on Jl Pearl, but it's usually locked. The genial caretaker suggests
you scream 'HELLO!' over the traffic noise
and he'll wander down to admit you.

Fairview (☎ 240017; www.geocities.com/the_fair
view; 6 Jl Reservoir; dm RM20, s RM50-60, tw RM100;
🈯 🖳) If you're in the mood for high-
ceilinged rooms, serenity and colonial ambience, try this big roomy house set on its
own begardened plot across the road from
the Sarawak Museum and a short walk
from Reservoir Park. Each pair of comfy

SPLURGE!

Telang Usan Hotel (☎ 415588; www.telang
usan.com; Jl Ban Hock; s/tw/d RM90/120/140; ❄)
This well-appointed hotel is owned and
managed by indigenous Orang Ulu, which
makes it unique in Kuching; for more on
these tribespeople, see p490. It's relatively
expensive but very comfortable and special
rates are often available; the price of twins
can drop to RM90. The hotel has a Dayak-
themed coffee house.

upstairs rooms shares a large bathroom,
while downstairs you'll find broadband Internet access.

Borneo B&B (☎ 231200; bidasbuan@yahoo.com;
3 Jl Green Hill; dm RM16-18, s RM24-28, d RM40-55; ❄)
Tucked away around the corner from Chin
Heng Café is this impressively friendly and
comfortable place, barely a year old at the
time of writing. Room prices include breakfast and free DVDs. The RM55 double is
worth considering as it has cooking facilities and a small fridge.

Kuok Pin Hotel (☎ 462822; 10 Jl Green Hill; r RM25-
50; ❄) This hotel is clean and welcoming,
though the scorpions sitting despondently
in a glass case at reception are an odd touch.
The cheapest rooms are small, fan-cooled
and use a shared bathroom.

Mandarin Hotel (☎ 418269; 6 Jl Green Hill; r RM50;
❄) This place near Kuok Pin has well-kept
rooms, friendly staff and a laundry service.

Eating
There are numerous Chinese eateries along
Carpenter St whipping up delicious cheap
treats like *tau hu* (fishball soup), including
a food court opposite Sang Ti Mao Temple
that has another Chinese temple acting as
its rear wall.

Top Spot Seafood Centre (Jl Padungan; meals
RM4-35; ❄ breakfast, lunch & dinner) An excellent
rooftop plaza with acres of tables and a
penchant for seafood. Order anything from
abalone to banana prawns or numerous varieties of fish, and chase it down with a
cold bottle of Tiger. To get here, climb the
stairs leading from Jl Padungan to Tapanga
restaurant, and keep heading upstairs from
there.

Perfect Vegetarian Food Centre (☎ 424733;
Jl Green Hill; meals RM2-4; ❄ breakfast, lunch & din-

ner) This place dishes out numerous veggie
staples and faux-meat concoctions. Feeling a bit sluggish from the night before?
Try the laksa for a spicy wake-up call. Another treat is the *mee jawa* (noodles with
pumpkin gravy).

Open-Air Market (Jl Market; meals RM1.20-5; breakfast, lunch & dinner) Actually a covered market offering lots of Chinese and Malay food. Feast
on pork buns, *siow bee* (tasty steamed dumplings), wonton soup or plain fried rice.

New Kuching Food Centre (Jl Chan Chin Ann; meals
RM5-40) Visit at night and take a table on the
lit-up concrete apron across the road, from
where you can look out over the river as you
chew great seafood. Meal costs are often
determined by the weight of the key ingredient (eg crab is priced in 100g helpings).

Green Hill Corner (Jl Temple; meals RM2-4;
❄ breakfast, lunch & dinner) Three food counters
crank out the meals at this popular eatery, with dishes varying depending on
the time of day. For a refreshing noodle-
and-soup combination, try the excellent
wonton *mee*.

Junk (☎ 259450; 80 Jl Wayang; mains RM18-40;
❄ dinner Wed-Mon) The Junk's expensive
Westernised menu includes pasta, Caesar
salad and steak and is popular with travellers pining for a taste of home. Eat in the
low-lit interior or soak up the fumes of
passing traffic at an outside table.

The daily waterfront **wet market** (Jl Gambier)
is where you can pick up freshly unloaded
vegetables, fruit and seafood. Also handy
for self-caterers is **Ting & Ting Supermarket**
(☎ 423987; Jl Tabuan).

Drinking
Several drinking dens line Jl Bukit Mata.

Cottage (☎ 412679; 16 Jl Bukit Mata) Attempts
to re-create the atmosphere of a dark-
timbered English tavern (the stained glass
is going a little far, guys) and has Kilkenny
on tap and a pool table.

Tribes (☎ 424708; Jl Albell; ❄ 7pm-1am Mon-Sat)
Descend into Tribes' tropical décor via
the rotunda outside the Holiday Inn. Admission (RM20) is charged from 9.30pm
and entitles you to one drink and a performance from the resident Malay (often
Kuching-based) pop group. Worthwhile
if you feel like sampling the syrupy local
mainstream music, but not for its overpriced drinks alone.

Clubbing

Earthquake (☎ 256225; Jl Bukit Mata; admission free) The images of collapsing buildings on the walls here mimic what happens when the club's young fans drink too much and start dancing atop the bar (usually very late on Friday and Saturday nights).

Khatulistiwa (☎ 415604; Jl Tunku Abdul Rahman; ☉ nightclub 7pm-1am) This three-storey waterfront complex has a 24-hour ground-floor café (meals RM6 to RM22), an exuberant disco (admission free) on the second floor with an outdoor balcony, and several pool tables on the floor above. The dance floor starts getting a workout around 11pm.

Discovery Café (☎ 238829; Jl Padungan) Has an outdoor terrace and a dim, poky interior layered with spilt drinks, where patrons try to harness a collective drunken energy. DJs do their thing on Wednesday, Saturday and Sunday (admission free).

Getting There & Away

AIR

Malaysia Airlines (☎ 1300 883 000; www.malaysiaair lines.com.my; 215 Jl Song Thian Cheok) flies between Kuching and KL (RM160), from where there are numerous onward connections. There are also several flights daily from Kuching to Johor Bahru (RM110) and Singapore (RM390).

Within Malaysian Borneo, from Kuching there are regular flights to Sibu (RM55), Bintulu (RM80), Miri (RM100), Kota Kinabalu (RM135) and Labuan (RM120).

Air Asia (☎ 1300 889 933; www.airasia.com; Ground fl, Wisma Ho Ho Lim, No 291 Jl Abell) has numerous daily flights to KL at bargain-basement prices (from RM80).

BOAT

Express Bahagia (☎ 410076) and **Express Sejahtera** (☎ 256736) boats run to and from Sibu (RM36, 4½ hours), departing from the express boat wharf in Pending. Express Bahagia leaves at 8.30am daily. At the time of writing Express Sejahtera had just resumed operation after months of suspended services and their schedules were not yet fixed.

BUS

Long-distance buses depart the **express bus station** (Jl Penrissen), 5km southeast of the centre. There are regular services to Sibu

---

> **BORDER CROSSING: INTO INDONESIA**
>
> From the express bus station, there are services to Pontianak (RM45, nine hours, four departures daily between 7am and noon) in Kalimantan. Buses cross at the Tebedu–Entikong border. It's a visa-free entry point into Indonesia for citizens of most nationalities, but check with the Indonesian Consulate in Kuching before leaving.

(RM40, seven hours, eight departures daily between 6.30am and 10pm); the overnight bus departing at 10pm is a good option for saving a night's accommodation, though it deposits you at Sibu's long-distance bus station at 5am, two hours before public buses start running into town. Buses also run from Kuching to Bintulu (RM60, 10½ hours, nine departures daily between 6.30am and 10pm).

The main long-distance bus companies listed below also have counters at the express bus station:

Biaramas Express (☎ 456999; Jl Khoo Hun Yeang)
Borneo Highway Express (☎ 232201; Jl P Ramlee)
PB Ekspres (☎ 232201; Jl P Ramlee)

Getting Around

For information on travelling into Kuching from the airport, express boat wharf or express bus station, see Getting Into Town (p484).

Kuching is easily navigated on foot. There's a dearth of pedestrian crossings on busy roads, but just do as the locals do and walk across thoroughfares wherever you like with a calm, unflinching authority.

Tambang ferry passengers across Sungai Sarawak. From 6am to 10pm the fare is 30 sen; outside these times it's RM1.

The City Tram (actually a bus) does a hop on, hop off circuit of inner-city Kuching. Between 10am and 4pm the route involves seven stops, including the Sarawak Museum and the visitors centre. The night service (7pm to 9pm) only makes four stops. The service is free but you need to have one of the passes distributed by most hotels. The tram is often sidelined for 'maintenance'.

There are taxi ranks at the market and express bus station. Most short trips around town cost between RM6 and RM10.

AROUND KUCHING
Semenggoh Wildlife Centre

The **Semenggoh Wildlife Centre** (☎ 082-618423; www.sarawakforestry.com; Penrissen Rd; admission RM3; ☺ 8am-5pm) attempts to rehabilitate orang-utans, gibbons, hornbills and other creatures that have been orphaned or illegally caged. Time your visit to coincide with orang-utan feeding times (9am to 10am and 3pm to 4pm) to see the star attractions close up. Sometimes as many as four to five of the animals congregate to eat and show off for the cameras, but sometimes none show up.

Semenggoh is 20km south of Kuching. Take STC bus 6, 6A, 6B or 6C from opposite Kuching's post office (RM2, 45 minutes, eight departures daily from 7am to 2pm). The bus will drop you off at the access road; pay admission at the kiosk then walk the remaining 1km to the centre. The last bus back to Kuching passes Semenggoh at 3.30pm. To travel Kuching–Semenggoh by taxi costs RM30.

Bako National Park

Lying between the mouths of Sungai Sarawak and Batang Bako is the unspoilt promontory of **Bako National Park** (☎ 011-225049; admission RM10; park office ☺ 8am-5pm), an exceptionally beautiful spot where rocky headlands are indented with clean beaches. Bako is famous for its wildlife, including bright green (and highly venomous) pit vipers and the rare proboscis monkey, which means it's often filled with visitors. The **Lintang Trail** (5.25km, 3½ hours) is an undulating loop of the promontory's interior that links up with other trails – combine it with the side-trail to **Telok Paku** (45 minutes return), which offers your best chance of seeing the elusive proboscis.

Register for the park upon arrival at the boat dock in Bako Bazaar. From Bako Bazaar it's a 20-minute boat ride to **park headquarters** (Telok Assam), where there's accommodation and a cafeteria.

The **hostel** (dm/r RM16/45) has cooking facilities and four rooms with four beds in each. Also available are **lodges** (r RM55), each with a pair of two-bed rooms, and **chalets** (r RM105), each with a pair of three-bed rooms. All accommodation is fan-cooled and has shared bathrooms.

The **camping ground** (camp sites RM5) is a swamp for much of the year and has a shower block. Bring your own utensils, sheets, sleeping bags and toiletries. Note that resident monkeys are apt to steal anything that's not nailed down.

Make accommodation bookings in advance through **National Parks & Wildlife** (☎ 248088; Sarawak Tourism Complex, Jl Tun Abang Haji Openg), based at Kuching's information centre.

The park cafeteria sells cheap meals and basic provisions.

GETTING THERE & AWAY

From Kuching, take a bus to Bako Bazaar in Kampung Bako, then charter a boat to the park. Petra Jaya bus 6 (RM1.50, 45 minutes, departures hourly from 7am to 6pm) leaves from near Kuching's open-air market. The last bus back to Kuching leaves Kampung Bako at 5pm. A taxi from Kuching to Bako Bazaar costs RM30.

The pleasant boat ride from Bako Bazaar to the park headquarters costs RM40 each way for a group of up to five people. Note the boat's number and be sincere when you agree to a pick-up time. If you want to share another boat back, tell park headquarters your boat number and they will cancel your original boat.

Kubah National Park

The walking trails that weave through the dense rainforest of **Kubah National Park** (☎ 082-231033; admission RM10; park office ☺ 8am-5.15pm) expose you to a beguiling tangle of foliage inhabited by both the largest and smallest species of squirrel in the world and (after it rains) a healthy population of leeches. The park also has 90-plus species of palm. Follow the **Main Walk** to Rayu Waterfall (return three hours).

You can stay in the park's simple **hostel** (dm RM15), which has cooking facilities; bring your own food and drink. Book through **National Parks & Wildlife** (☎ 248088; Sarawak Tourism Complex, Jl Tun Abang Haji Openg) at Kuching's information centre.

Kubah is 20km west of Kuching. Kuching Matang Transport bus 11 (RM1.80, 40 minutes, departures mostly early morning) will drop you at the park's access road, from where it's a 400m uphill walk to the park entrance. On the days they choose to run, minivans depart when full from an alleyway adjacent to the Kuching Matang Transport bus stop, charging RM2 for the trip to Kubah. The last bus back to Kuching passes Kubah around 4.30pm. A taxi from Kuching to Kubah should cost RM35.

Gunung Gading National Park

The chief attraction at **Gunung Gading National Park** (☎ 082-35714; admission RM10; park office ☷ 8am-5pm) is the **rafflesia**, the world's largest flower. Before heading to the park, call the rangers or ask at Kuching's information centre whether any rafflesias are blooming. The flower takes nine months to mature but blooms only for around five days, so if you hear one has just unfurled itself, hightail it to Gunung Gading. Visitors must be guided by park rangers at a cost of RM20 per hour for a group of up to five people. November to January (in the rainy season) are the peak blooming months.

Gunung Gading has many **walking trails** and a **natural swimming pool** close to the park office that's popular with locals.

To get there, catch a bus (60 sen) to Kuching's express bus terminal (almost any STC bus passing the stop opposite the post office will take you there), then take STC bus EP7 to Lundu (RM8.30, two hours, departs 8am, 11am, 2pm and 4pm). From Lundu, take a minivan or taxi (RM5) to the park.

BATANG REJANG

The Batang Rejang is the main 'highway' of central Sarawak, a waterway where most of the state's inland trade is conducted. A boat ride up the muddy Rejang is a memorable experience. Sections of the river and surrounding jungle are blanketed by mist early in the morning, while longboats and riverside dwellings appear and disappear with enigmatic abruptness. Unfortunately the river is often choked with logging detritus, forcing boats to steer a hazardous course. Logs regularly thud off boat hulls and occasional churning rapids also add to the excitement.

The Iban are the major ethnic group around Kapit, with a population three times greater than the Orang Ulu ('Upriver People') who live further up the Rejang and Baleh Rivers. Orang Ulu is a catch-all term for a number of different tribal groups, including the Kenyah, Kayan, Bukitan, Lahanan and the semi-nomadic Penan. A huge number of Orang Ulu have recently been displaced by the Bakun Dam; for more on this controversial project, see p420.

Many indigenous people still live in communities centred on a longhouse, a large structure raised above the ground on stilts that provides shelter for villagers under its long roofline. Longhouses carved out of jungle timber with few modern embellishments still exist, but nowadays it's the norm to see corrugated-iron roofs, the odd satellite dish and Western clothes hung out to dry. A visit to one of the longhouses scattered along the Rejang's banks and tributaries (see opposite) is one of the highlights of a trip to Sarawak.

The best time for a trip up the Rejang is in late May/early June. This is the time of **Gawai**, the Dayak harvest festival, when longhouses are busy with feasts and traditional dancing and welcome visitors. The only hotel accommodation along the river is in Kanowit, Song, Kapit (p492) and Belaga (p493).

Anyone travelling upriver beyond Kapit needs a permit (see p492).

SIBU

☎ 084 / pop 201,000

Sibu is the gateway to the Batang Rejang, making it a major transit point for travellers and the nexus of trade between the coast and the upriver hinterland. It's a rough-looking jumble of low-rise buildings overshadowed by the undistinguished modernity of the enormous Wisma Sanyan mall, and has nothing to rival Kuching in the charm stakes. But the locals are mostly just as friendly as their counterparts in Sarawak's capital.

Information

Emergency (☎ 999)
Hospital (☎ 343333)
Police (☎ 336144)
Visitor Centre (☎ 340980; www.sarawaktourism.com; 32 Jl Tukang Besi; ☷ 8am-5pm Mon-Fri) This office provides information about upriver trips out of Song, Kapit and Belaga. It's also open 8am to 12.45pm on the second and fourth Saturday of each month.
Wisma Sanyan (Jl Morshidi Sidek) There are several Internet cafés on the 4th floor here.

Sights

Scale the seven-storey waterfront **Kuan Yin pagoda** (Jl Temple; admission free) to see just how uninspiring Sibu's cityscape is, not to mention the impenetrable muddiness of the Batang Rejang. Also check out the birds' nests in the eaves of the top level. Get a key from the ground-floor counter to unlock the stairwell gate.

Tours

Sazhong Trading & Travel Services (☎ 336017; www.geocities.com/sazhong; 4 Jl Central) is located at the Villa Hotel and can help if you're stuck for a hotel, looking for a longhouse tour or need to book airline tickets.

Sleeping

Unless you want to sleep in a hovel or a brothel, a good rule of thumb in Sibu is not to stay anywhere costing less than RM30 per night (with the exception of several places listed below).

Hoover Lodging House (☎ 334490; Jl Pulau; dm/s/tw RM15/20/30; ☒) The accommodation offered in the administration building of the Methodist church is excellent value for money. Most rooms have high ceilings and attached bathrooms. You can also safely store gear here while travelling upriver.

Villa Hotel (☎ 337833; 2 Jl Central; s/d RM35/40; ☒) A rustic hotel with simple, scuffed rooms and some truncated beds that may be problematic for taller travellers. But it's centrally located and welcoming. Reception always seems to be cheerfully embroiled in light-hearted chaos.

River Park Hotel (☎ 316688; 51 Jl Maju; r RM70-100; ☒) Official room rates here are quite steep, but discounts to as low as RM50 are often offered, which makes this place a viable option. Rooms are nothing special but are bigger and cleaner than most of the other local accommodation, and lie opposite a tiny bit of greenery.

Holiday Hotel (☎ 317440; 14 Jl Tan Sri; r RM25-30; ☒) One of the few lodging houses around the bus station that doesn't need a red light outside. Your worn-out room comes with a panorama of back-street squalor.

Eating & Drinking

In the late afternoon a host of food stalls set up near the concrete **SMC Market** (Jl Channel). Some of the waterfront Chinese *kedai kopi* open around dawn, handy if you're catching an early boat.

Sri Meranti (☎ 337996; 1st fl, 58 Jl Kampong Nyabor; meals RM6-18; ☽ lunch & dinner) Good Thai and Malay dishes such as fish-head curry are offered at this well-established restaurant. The large outdoor patio is a mixed blessing – you can sit outside to enjoy the breeze, but that breeze is often supplied by traffic streaming down Sibu's busiest thoroughfare.

Soon Hock Café (cnr Jl Temple & Bank; meals RM2-3; ☽ breakfast & lunch) This café is just down the street from the pagoda and serves some simple veggie-centric fare. Note that meat dishes are also served here, so make sure you know what you're ordering.

Little Roadhouse (☎ 319384; Jl Causeway; meals RM5-19; ☽ closed Mon) Mellow 1st-floor pub serving good *tom yum* soup and chicken claypot, plus pasta and steak. Perch on the tiny balcony with a beer or cocktail and watch Sibu life pass by below.

Getting There & Around
AIR

Malaysia Airlines (☎ 1300 883 000; www.malaysiaair lines.com.my; 61 Jl Tuanku Osman) has several flights daily from Sibu to Bintulu (RM85), Kuching

---

VISITING A LONGHOUSE

The main reason to travel upriver is to visit a longhouse. The Iban and Orang Ulu are generally hospitable, but without an introduction they aren't going to invite you into their homes. Turning up unannounced is not just bad manners; it can, in certain circumstances, be a minor catastrophe, particularly if there has been a recent death or during certain rituals.

Longhouse tours can be arranged in Kapit (p492) and Belaga (p493). Visiting a longhouse independently is much harder and requires patience and flexibility. You'll need to stay in towns visited regularly by tribal people and try to strike up conversations with them. Belaga is probably the best option – hang around the wharf when boats are being loaded/unloaded and try your luck.

If you are invited to a longhouse (including on a tour), it's etiquette to bring a small gift for your hosts. Sharing is an important local custom, so food is good as it can be shared with longhouse residents at mealtimes. Noodles, coffee and sugar are all OK but avoid too many sweets as tooth decay is rife among local children. Items from your home country (caps, toys etc) are also well received, as is tobacco.

MALAYSIA

(RM55), Miri (RM130), Kota Kinabalu (RM200) and KL (RM185). **Air Asia** (☎ 1300 889 933; www.airasia.com; Jl Keranji) has dirt-cheap flights between Sibu and both KL and Johor Bahru.

BOAT

Boats leave from the **River Express Terminal** (☎ 339936) at the western end of the Rejang Esplanade. **Express Sejahtera** (☎ 321424) and **Express Bahagia** (☎ 319228) run boats to Kuching (4½ hours), at 7.30am and 11.30am respectively. Both companies charge RM36 for the trip and have booths at the terminal.

Getting to Kapit is the first leg of the journey up the Batang Rejang. Several boats motor the 140km from Sibu to Kapit (RM20, three hours, departures between 6am and 1.45pm). One express boat leaves daily for Belaga (RM45, seven hours) at 5.45am.

BUS

Bus companies have ticket stalls at the **long-distance bus station** (Sungai Antu) and around the local bus station on the waterfront. Starting from 7am, local buses run regularly from the long-distance station into town (60 sen).

Buses run between Sibu and Kuching (RM40, seven hours, regular departures between 6.30am and 10pm), Miri (RM40, 7½ hours, departures roughly hourly from 6am to 10pm) and Bintulu (RM20, 3½ hours, departures roughly hourly from 5.30am to 6pm).

KAPIT

☎ 084 / pop 8200

This heat-stung river-town dates back to the days of the white raja and lives to trade. Wander the busy docks and market stalls to see what upriver people are selling and buying. Modern-day Kapit is also an administrative centre, which explains the incongruous District Office Building on the waterfront.

You can peek behind the 125-year-old white planks of historic **Fort Sylvia** (☎ 799171; Jl Kubu; admission free; ☒ 10am-noon & 2-5pm Tue-Sun) or inquire at hotels about tours to local longhouses, but otherwise there's little reason to linger.

Information

Goodtime Cyber Centre (354 Jl Yong Moh Chai; per hr RM3) Internet access.

Hyperlink Cyber Station (1st fl, 17 Ting Kat Jl Tan Sit; per hr RM3) A noisy Internet cafe.
Kapit Hospital (☎ 796333; Jl Hospital)
Police station (☎ 796222; Jl Selirik)
Public Bank (Jl Wharf) Has an ATM and changes travellers cheques.

PERMITS

A permit is required for travel upriver past Pelagus Resort to Belaga or anywhere up the Baleh River system. These are free, valid for one week and swiftly issued by the **Pejabat Am** (Resident's Office; ☎ 796445; 1st fl, State Government Complex, Jl Penghulu Nyanggau; ☒ 8am-12.30pm & 2-5pm Mon-Thu, 8-11.40am & 2.30-5pm Fri). The form asks for your cholera vaccination expiry date, but this isn't checked as such vaccinations are no longer required for international travel. The office is also open 8am to 1pm on the second and fourth Saturday of each month.

Sleeping & Eating

Food stalls set up in the evening at the night market, by the wet market at the western end of town. A triangular covered hall off Jl Penghulu Nyanggau also has food stalls.

River View Inn (☎ 798600; krvinn@tm.net.my; 10 Jl Tan Sit Leong; s/tw RM40/45; ☒) On the western edge of Kapit's modest town square, this is probably the cleanest place in town. Rooms lack the damp smell so common in Sarawakian places to stay. Many also lack windows, so inspect your room before signing in if this matters to you.

New Rejang Inn (☎ 796600; 104 Jl Teo Chow Beng; r RM50-60; ☒) Spotless five-storey inn a block off the waterfront. 'Deluxe' twins cost RM10 more than standard rooms only because they're a little bigger, so you're better off sticking to the cheaper rooms.

Ark Hill Inn (☎ 796168; Jl Penghulu Gerinang; s RM35-65, tw RM55-70; ☒) This place looms over the western end of town, opposite Kapit's covered market. The cheaper rooms are OK for the price, even if reception staff are a little dismissive. Ask for a northwestern corner room to view river activities.

Kong Hua Café (1 Jl Wharf; meals RM2-5; ☒ breakfast, lunch & dinner) A reliable array of cooked-to-order meals are available here at the Kong Hua, across the street from New Rejang Inn. The laksa is excellent and they'll sometimes whip up eggs and toast for breakfast.

Orchard Restaurant (☎ 797228; 64 Jl Tiong Ung Hong; meals RM5-15; ⊗ lunch & dinner) This jovial restaurant's bright yellow interior and large tables make a refreshing change from the cramped monochrome interiors of most Bornean cafés. The chef can guide you through the menu, which includes fresh seafood, mixed vegetables and super-salty seaweed soup.

Getting There & Away

Express boats depart Kapit for Sibu (RM20, three hours) between 6.30am and 2.30pm daily; they leave from the wharf opposite the new district office building. A boat sets off on the 170km journey to Belaga (RM25, four hours) at 9am daily, departing the wharf opposite the town square. When the river is too low for express boats, small speedboats skim up to Belaga (RM50).

BELAGA

☎ 084 / pop 2500

Belaga is a small, friendly community on the Rejang's upper reaches, surrounded by ridges covered in jungly forest and often wreathed in mist. It's a very laidback place where excitement peaks with children playing badminton in the laneways at dusk. There are several longhouses upriver and tribal people are regular visitors.

Belaga's local agent for **Malaysia Airlines** (☎ 461512; 4 Belaga Bazaar; per hr RM5) provides Internet access. Belaga has no banks so get cashed up beforehand.

You need a permit to reach Belaga by river from Kapit; see opposite. The permit covers travel as far as the Bakun Dam area, an hour upstream.

A few locals organise **jungle treks** which often include a visit to the impressive Pasang Rapids and are usually arranged in conjunction with **longhouse stays**. A three-day/two-night trip typically costs an all-inclusive RM100 per person per day. Longhouses close to Belaga (such as Uma Aging and Uma Kahei) are mostly Kayan, but Uma Neh is a Kejaman longhouse and Long Semiang is a Lahanan longhouse within a 30-minute boat ride of Belaga. It's possible to visit a longhouse independently from Belaga, but you need to be invited (you can't invite yourself); see Visiting A Longhouse (p491).

The eponymous owner of **Daniel's Corner** (☎ 461997, 013-848 6351; udiontheroad@yahoo.com; 34 Jl Bato Luhat) is an enthusiastic, reliable organiser of visits throughout the area; email him beforehand to discuss possibilities. It would be easy to let Daniel organise your entire stay, but don't forget to sound out other Belagans for their suggestions.

Sleeping & Eating

Belaga Hotel (☎ 461244; 14 Belaga Bazaar; s/d RM30/35; ⊗) Plain, well-kept rooms and a decent coffee shop downstairs are the main characteristics of this hotel, located in the two-storey block facing the dock. Get a room with a bathtub to soak any cares away.

Hotel Sing Soon Huat (☎ 461307; 26 New Bazaar; r RM35-45; ⊗) This hotel is in the block behind Belaga Hotel and has similar tiled-floor rooms and facilities, except for the bathrooms, some of which make a shoebox seem spacious.

Hock Chiang Inn (☎ 461258; 1 Belaga Bazaar; r from RM35; ⊗) Many rooms here are considerably brightened by the hotel's location on the corner of a block, as opposed to being sandwiched between other buildings. The downstairs café (meals RM2.50 to RM6) is open for breakfast and lunch and is a good place to enjoy a morning *kopi* and engage with talkative locals.

Lai Bin Ong Café (☎ 461309; Jl Bato Luhat; meals RM2.5-6.50; ⊗ breakfast & lunch) Locally hunted animals like wild boar and mouse deer (or chevrotain) occasionally make the menu here. The café is sometimes frequented by Kayan and Kenya people.

Getting There & Away

Belaga's tiny airstrip is 20 minutes downriver of town by longboat (RM10). There are twice-weekly flights (Wednesday and Saturday) between Belaga and Bintulu (RM50, one hour). Contact **Malaysia Airlines** (☎ 461512; 4 Belaga Bazaar).

For information on boats from Kapit, see left.

Several 4WDs negotiate logging roads to Bintulu (RM50, 4½ hours). Make arrangements the night before through Daniel's Corner (above) or ask at your hotel. If you're headed for Batu Niah, ask to be dropped off at the highway and flag down the next Niah-bound bus (you'll probably be charged around RM10).

BINTULU

☎ 086 / pop 102,800

Bintulu is a convenient way-station for travellers and doesn't make a great first impression, with its traffic jams and the rubbish washed up on the foreshore. But for a different perspective on the city catch a *tambang* across the river and explore the traditional fishing village of **Kampong Jepak**, sheltered by a roofline of tightly packed corrugated-iron. There's also a colourful **Chinese temple** (Main Bazaar) near the waterfront.

Star Internet (Jl Law Gek Soon; per hr RM3) is one block inland from the riverside *pasar utama* (main market). Take the stairwell beside HSBC Bank to the 2nd floor.

Get medical care at **Bintulu Hospital** (☎ 331455; off Lebuh Raya Abang Galau). The main **police station** (☎ 312531; Jl Tun Hussein Onn) is 3km north of the centre.

Hong Leong Bank (☎ 332393; Lebuh Raya Abang Galau), opposite the waterfront *pasar tamu* (jungle-produce market), changes cash and travellers cheques.

Sleeping & Eating

You can stay in hotels on or near Jl Keppel for as little as RM15 per night, but saggy beds and dubious hygiene will be your lot. Bintulu's midrange hotels are a better bet.

Eden Inn (☎ 315150; Jl Abang Galau; r RM40-45; ❄) Arguably the best deal in town, recently renovated and with each room now sporting a bright new colour scheme, TV and attached bathroom. It's open 24 hours.

Sea View Inn (☎ 339118; 254 Taman Sri Dagang; r RM40-50; ❄) Relaxed hotel with a cheap café downstairs. The higher priced 'deluxe' rooms look out over the water, where human traffic flows continuously on and off unkempt riverboats.

Riverfront Inn (☎ 333111; 256 Taman Sri Dagang; s RM65-85, d RM70-100; ❄) Desperate for the feel of carpet instead of tiles under your toes? Longing for a towel instead of a wafer-thin washcloth? Craving a minibar? Then splurge on one of the cheaper rooms here. Its Western-style café (meals RM5 to RM18) is open all day, and is good for people-watching.

Famous Mama Café (☎ 336541; 10 Jl Somerville; meals RM2-5.50; ☽ lunch & dinner) A perpetually busy café churning out tasty halal Indian and Malaysian dishes. Try the *roti canai*.

The *pasar tamu* and the top floor of the *pasar utama* have dozens of **food stalls** (meals RM2-5) and there are cheap kedai kopi along Jl Masjid.

Getting There & Around

AIR

Bintulu airport is 24km west of the centre. A taxi there costs RM30.

Malaysia Airlines (☎ 1300 883 000; www.malaysiaairlines.com.my; Jl Masjid) flies between Bintulu and Kota Kinabalu (RM145), Kuching (RM80), Miri (RM90) and Sibu (RM85). Malaysia Airlines Twin Otters fly twice weekly to Belaga (RM50).

BUS

The long-distance bus station is 5km north of town. Travel between the two by local bus or taxi (RM8).

There are frequent daily services between Bintulu and Kuching (RM60, 10½ hours), Miri (RM20, 4½ hours) and Sibu (RM20, 3½ hours). The main bus companies are **Biaramas Express** (☎ 339821), **Borneo Express** (☎ 314460) and **Lanang Road Bus Company** (☎ 338518).

CAR

The sidestreet between Li Hua Plaza and Welcome Inn is where you'll find 4WDs bound for Belaga (RM50, 4½ hours).

NIAH CAVES NATIONAL PARK

☎ 085

The massif that provides a stunning backdrop to the village of Batu Niah hints at the rocky splendour of **Niah Caves National Park** (☎ 737454; admission RM10; ☽ park office 8am-5pm). Underneath the park's limestone seal is the aptly named **Great Cave**, one of the world's largest and strung with an astonishing network of bamboo poles enabling Penan workers to collect swiftlet nests, the key ingredient of the famous birds-nest soup. If you negotiate the cave's boardwalk during the nest-harvesting season, you'll see pinpoints of Penan flashlights probing distant recesses of the cavern.

Humans have probably lived around the caves for 40,000 years. The discovery of rock art and small canoe-like coffins (death ships) within the greenish walls of the **Painted Cave** indicate that it was once a burial ground.

You can pay admission at the national park office, beside Sungai Niah which is some 3km from Batu Niah. Walk there by following the path signposted from the northern end of town (same end as the jetty) – the path passes a red Chinese temple, then shadows the river. Alternatively, catch a boat or taxi (both RM10). From the park office, ride the ferry across the river (the fare is 50 sen between 7am and 5pm, then RM1 until 7.30pm), then follow the 3km boardwalk to the caves. Bring footwear that grips or risk slipping on the caves' treacherous mud- and guano-caked boardwalk.

Sleeping & Eating

There are several decent places to stay in compact Batu Niah. Numerous similar-standard Chinese and Malay cafés are scattered throughout the village.

Niah Cave Hotel (☎ 737726; 155 Batu Niah Bazaar; s/d RM25/38; ☒) The simple, clean rooms here all share bathrooms at the end of the hall. The beds are eerily reminiscent of an old hospital ward, though this doesn't make them any less comfortable.

Niah Cave Inn (☎ 737333; 621 Batu Niah Bazaar; s/d from RM60/70; ☒) Despite the unfortunate connotations of its name, this is a sturdy, high-quality hotel. It's the first hotel you'll see as the bus chugs into town. The 'economy' rooms lack windows but are very comfortable.

Ming Kee Seafood Restaurant (☎ 737472; 622 Batu Niah Bazaar; meals RM4-11; ☒ breakfast, lunch & dinner) An airy restaurant beside Niah Cave Inn serving delicious meals. The menu is dominated by oceanic fare like fish, squid and sea cucumbers, but also includes chicken (in the form of 'chicken porridge', no less), deer and lots of vegetable dishes.

At the national park office are more choices, including a **hostel** (dm/r RM16/45) with comfortable fan-cooled dorms. Utensils for self-caterers and bedding are provided. **Camping** (camp sites RM5) is another option. The park has a canteen with a good range of meals and provisions.

Getting There & Away

Batu Niah is 11km west of the Miri–Bintulu highway. Express buses briefly stop at the junction, which has a small market and a few shops, but from there you'll have to make your own way to Batu Niah.

From Bintulu, **Suria** (☎ 086-335489) runs to Batu Niah (RM11, two hours, five departures daily between 6am and 3.30pm) from Jl Masjid in front of Li Hua Plaza. From Miri, **Suria** (☎ 085-430416) heads to Batu Niah (RM10, 1¾ hours, six departures daily between 6.30am and 4pm) from Miri bus station. From Batu Niah, buses head to Miri and Bintulu roughly between 7am and 4pm.

LAMBIR HILLS NATIONAL PARK

Although **Lambir Hills National Park** (☎ 085-491030; admission RM10; ☒ park office 8am-5pm) doesn't have the spectacular scenery of Niah and Mulu, it does offer **jungle trails** (including the Tree Tower suspended walk) and **swimming**, and is an easy day trip from Miri.

When we visited, most of the park was closed due to recent flooding and restorative work on walking trails, such as the popular route to Latak Waterfall, had not yet begun. Check that trails are open before you visit.

The park's fan-cooled **chalets** (r RM50) have two bedrooms, each with four bunks. Air-conditioned **chalets** (r RM100) also have two rooms, equipped with either three single beds or one single and one double bed. There's also **camping** (camp sites RM5) but there are no cooking facilities, just a canteen selling basic provisions.

The park office, canteen and accommodation are situated beside the highway 30km south of Miri. From Miri, any bus (RM3, 35 minutes) bound for Bekenu or Batu Niah can drop you here. A taxi from Miri costs RM40.

MIRI

☎ 085 / pop 177,800
Miri is a boomtown obsessed with the proceeds of oil and logging and has an appealing small-city feel. It's mainly a stopover for travellers en route to longhouses on Sungai Baram or the caves of Niah, or who are catching flights into the Sarawakian interior. But Miri has recently rebranded itself the 'Resort City' and adopted the seahorse as its mascot, in the hope of exploiting its proximity to some fine offshore reefs and luring curious divers.

Information

There are plenty of ATMs around town.

Cyber Corner (1st fl, Wisma Pelita Tunku, Jl Padang; per 20 min RM1; 9am-8pm) Internet access.

Cyber World (1st fl, Wisma Pelita Tunku, Jl Padang; per 20 min RM1; 10am-8pm) Internet access.

Maybank's Forex Booth (☎ 438467; ground fl, Centre Point Commercial Centre, Jl Melaya) Changes travellers cheques and offers cash advances on credit cards.

Miri Hospital (☎ 420033; off Jl Cahaya)

National Parks & Wildlife (☎ 434184) This office shares the main counter at the visitors centre and books accommodation for Gunung Mulu, Niah Caves and Lambir Hills National Parks.

Pejabat Residen (☎ 433203; Jl Kingsway; 8am-12.30pm & 2-5pm Mon-Fri, 8am-12.45pm Sat) Before visiting Bario, get a free travel permit here. Besides your passport, you may also be asked for the white card stamped by officials when you entered Sarawak.

Police station (☎ 433222; Jl Kingsway) In the city centre.

Visitors centre (☎ 434181; vic-miri@sarawaktourism .com; 452 Jl Melayu; 8am-6pm Mon-Fri, 8am-4pm Sat) Miri's excellent visitor centre provides city maps, transport schedules and information on accommodation and tours.

Sights & Activities

Consider visiting the **Lian Hia San (Lotus Hill) Temple** (Jl Jee Foh Utama) in the suburb of Krokop. It's the biggest Taoist temple in Southeast Asia. You can't go inside but it makes an impressive sight. Bus 44 goes to Krokop; ask the driver where to get off.

To investigate the little-explored Miri-Sibuti reef system, contact **Tropical Dives** (Seridan Mulu Tours; ☎ 414300; www.tropical-dives.com; 1 Lobby Arcade, Parkcity Everly Hotel, Jl Temenggong Datuk Oyong Lawai). Day trips involving two dives cost from around RM300.

Sleeping

Brooke Inn (☎ 412881; brookeinn@hotmail.com; 14 Jl Brooke; s/d RM40/45;) Raja Brooke would have given his entrepreneurial approval to this hospitable, well-kept establishment and its conveniently central location. All rooms have televisions and also telephones, so loved ones back home can pester you at inconvenient hours.

Highlands (☎ 422327; maran_telian@kelabit .net; 2nd fl, Block 9, 1271 Jl Sri Dagang; dm RM25, tw & d RM50;) Newish hostel boasting modern steel-frame bunks, good facilities and convenient access to a bar one floor down. It has a cosy communal feel, as opposed to the compartmentalised anonymity of a budget hotel, and organises tours beyond Miri. It's on the waterfront a block off Jl Bendahara.

Richmond Inn (☎ 413289; 243 Jl Setia Raja; r RM50-80;) This hotel has spacious rooms and willing staff. The ambience can be affected by the basement karaoke club, however, so take a top-floor room to avoid the noise of frayed vocal chords. Upper-floor rooms have a small fridge.

Tai Tong Lodging House (☎ 411498; 19 Jl Cina; dm/s RM12/25) Bare bones but clean accommodation near the local bus station. The 'dorm' is a collection of bunks in the hallway – very cheap, but offering little in the way of security. The hotel's entrance is on Jl Bendahara.

Treetops Lodge (☎ 482449; www.borneo-holidays .com/sgh.htm; Siwa Jaya; dm RM20;) Modelled on a longhouse and situated on a tree-shaded plot near the beach 40km south of Miri, this is a good place to hang out. An extra RM5 gets you breakfast, and other meals can be arranged. Catch local bus 13 from Miri to the end of the line, where you can either walk the remaining 1.5km to the lodge or arrange a lift.

Eating

Nyonya's Family Café (☎ 016-884 8384; 21 Jl Brooke; meals RM2.50-7; lunch & dinner) This cheerful café has declined the plastic chairs and bland aesthetic of standard budget cafés in favour of flowery wall tiles, wooden seats, faux-marble tabletops and a colourful paint job. It's a great place with a small, tasty menu. Look for the yellow banner with red lettering out front.

Bilal Restaurant (☎ 418440; 250 Jl Persiaran Kabor; meals RM2-6; lunch & dinner) A busy Indian eatery, one of many similarly styled places on pedestrianised Jl Persiaran Kabor. Eat tasty varieties of *dosai* (rice and lentil crepes), *rojak* (vegetables or fruit salad in spicy peanut sauce) and *murtabak* (filled pancakes) while downing a *lassi* (yogurt-based drink).

Chatterbox Coffee House (☎ 432432; ground fl, Mega Hotel, 907 Jl Merbau; meals RM9-30; breakfast, lunch & dinner) Relaxed Western-style oasis serving lots of Malaysian and Chinese meals, plus steaks, burgers and some pastas. The delicious food is balanced out by abominable piped muzak.

The small **Taman Seroja food centre** (JI Brooke; meals RM2-10; ☺ lunch & dinner), located near the Brooke Inn, serves cheap Malaysian food and a small selection of Western meals (the latter at dinner only). There is also another convenient **food centre** (JI Cina; meals RM2-6; ☺ lunch & dinner) near the waterfront markets.

Drinking

Discovery Bistro & Pub (☎ 433450; 513 JI Merbau) This pub is big and breezy, a novelty in Sarawakian bar culture, and has outdoor decking and an upstairs balcony where you can swill RM9 spirits and RM12 cocktails. Bar staff go crazy when a Whitney Houston song comes on; sad, but true.

Pelita Commercial Centre (cnr JI Miri Pujut & Sehati) Those keen on a pub crawl might consider catching a taxi to this warren of small bar-lined streets 3km north of the centre. Anyone with an aversion to disco glitterballs, karaoke and expats need not apply for the experience.

Getting There & Away

AIR

Miri is well served by **Malaysia Airlines** (☎ 1300 883 000; www.malaysiaairlines.com.my), which has Twin Otter services to Bario (RM70), Lawas (RM70), Limbang (RM65), Marudi (RM50), and Gunung Mulu (RM90). Larger aircraft fly direct to Bintulu (RM90), Sibu (RM130), Kuching (RM100), Pulau Labuan (RM50) and Kota Kinabalu (RM70). Book flights to/from Bario (one flight daily) or Mulu (two flights daily) as far in advance as possible.

Air Asia (☎ 1300 889 933; www.airasia.com) does cheap flights between Miri and both KL and Johor Bahru. The small regional airline **Hornbill Skyways** (☎ 611066) flies between Miri and both Bario and Gunung Mulu.

BUS

Major bus companies serving Miri include **Suria** (☎ 430416), **PB Ekspres** (☎ 435816) and **Biaramas Express** (☎ 414999). Suria has six buses leaving between 6.30am and 4pm for Batu Niah (RM10, 1¾ hours) from Miri's long-distance bus station.

From the local bus station, beside the visitors centre, bus 1A (RM4, 45 minutes) takes you to the wharf in Kuala Baram for Marudi-bound boats.

> ### BORDER CROSSING: INTO BRUNEI
>
> The ticket office at the local bus station sells a combined ticket (RM13) for travel on bus 2 (departs 7am, 10am, 1pm and 3.30pm) from Miri to the border crossing at Sungai Tujoh, and then on another bus from the border to Kuala Belait. Including the drudgerous immigration formalities, the Miri–Kuala Belait trip takes about 2½ hours.
>
> For information on crossing the border in the other direction, see p46.

Getting Around

Bus 33 (70 sen) leaves regularly from the local bus station for the long-distance bus station, 4km north of the centre. Buses 28 and 30 run frequently between the local bus station and the airport from 6am to 7pm (RM1.20, 20 minutes). Heading into town, the airport bus stop is to the left of the terminal as you exit.

Taxis from the airport to the city centre run on a coupon system (RM14).

MARUDI

☎ 085 / pop 1400

Marudi is a small town lodged on Sungai Baram. It's upriver of Kuala Baram, which lies north of Miri. Visitors pass through on their way to nearby longhouses or Gunung Mulu.

A short walk uphill from the jetty is the Brooke outpost of **Fort Hose**, a white-washed structure built in 1898 and now boarded up. Travel beyond Marudi to upriver **longhouses** is pleasant and rewarding, at least once you get to Long Lama. Locals in Marudi can help arrange a visit, but get preliminary advice from the Miri visitors centre.

The **Public Bank** (JI Kapitan Lim Ching Kiat) has an ATM.

At the edge of town is the big yellow **Mayland Hotel** (☎ 755106; JI Nakhoda Abang Matasim; s/d RM35/45; ☒), with a surprisingly ornate pillared foyer and some strange wooden buttresses on upper-floor ceilings. Rooms are very comfortable and great value for the price.

A block back from the waterfront, near the town square, is **Zola Hotel** (☎ 755311; JI Kapitan Lim Ching Kiat; r RM35; ☒), which has rough edges but is in reasonable condition.

Getting There & Away

The local Malaysia Airlines agent is **Tan Yong Sing** (☎ 755480; www.malaysiaairlines.com.my; 60B Jl Kapitan Lim Ching Kiat). Twin Otter flights go to Bario (RM55, four flights daily), with weekly departures to Miri (RM29, two to five departures daily).

There are express boats from Marudi to Kuala Baram (RM20, three hours, departures roughly hourly between 7am and 3pm). Late-afternoon arrivals at Kuala Baram's jetty may find they've missed the last Miri-bound bus and will have to catch a minivan (RM12) or a taxi. An express boat heads upriver from Marudi to Long Terawan (RM20; 3½ hours; 11am) for Gunung Mulu National Park; a speedboat costs RM32.

GUNUNG MULU NATIONAL PARK

Gunung Mulu National Park (☎ 085-433561; www.mulupark.com; admission RM10; ☼ park office 8am-5pm) is the centrepiece of Sarawakian wilderness, a World Heritage–listed park blanketed by rainforest and riven by a network of underground passages stretching 51km. This subterranean world is occupied by 27 species of bat and houses Deer Cave, with the world's biggest cave entrance, and the Sarawak Chamber, the largest cavern yet discovered. Things are no less spectacular on the surface, where strangler figs, wild orchids and pitcher plants thrive. Striding along the forest boardwalks, you may come across tiny pygmy squirrels, tree lizards or assemblies of Raja Brooke's bird-wing butterflies fluttering their large green-streaked wings. And high up on the slopes of Gunung Api are the amazing limestone spikes known as the Pinnacles.

Bring plenty of cash as there are no ATMs or credit card facilities.

Sights & Activities

The park's two major mountains, **Gunung Mulu** and **Gunung Api**, are visited on four- and three-day treks respectively. The cost of trekking guides depends on the distance covered and the number of trekkers. For a group of five trekking to the **Pinnacles** over three days and two nights, a guide costs RM400; to the summit of Gunung Mulu it's RM1000. The Pinnacles trek also involves a short longboat ride; the return fare for a group of one to four people is RM350.

In a bit of bureaucratic overkill, you must pay for a guide (RM4) to accompany you along the easy 3km boardwalk from park headquarters to the awesome maw of **Deer Cave**. The guide then leads you through the cave and adjoining **Langs Cave**. From about 5pm, you may see some of Deer Cave's three million wrinkle-lipped bats emerge to form twisting ribbons in the sky. Tours depart park headquarters at 1.30pm and 2.30pm daily.

You must also be accompanied by a guide (RM4) to see the impressive underground river in **Clearwater Cave** and the captivating stalactites of **Wind Cave**. However, it's deemed OK to walk to these caves solo from park headquarters via a 4km plank-and-concrete walkway (allow one hour) that at one point winds through the lovely narrow passages of **Moonmilk Cave**. You can also get to Wind Cave, where tours begin at 9.30am and 10.30am daily, by boat (one-way/return RM15/25).

You'll need a torch (flashlight) for both tours. These can be hired for RM4 (plus RM10 deposit) from Café Mulu (see below).

Sleeping & Eating

Due to the park's popularity it's best to pre-book your accommodation, which can be done through National Parks & Wildlife agents in Kuching (p484) or Miri (p496). If you arrive without having booked, you might find all the park accommodation is taken and your only other option is an expensive room (if available) at the nearby Royal Mulu Resort.

Park accommodation is in the form of comfortable above-ground lodges. There's an 18-bed **hostel** (dm RM15) and two- to four-bed rooms in **chalets** (r RM50-120; ☒); cheaper rooms are fan-cooled.

There are no cooking facilities. Noodle and rice meals, egg and pancake breakfasts and snacks are served on the wide veranda at **Café Mulu** (meals RM4-9; ☼ breakfast, lunch & dinner). There's also a pair of café-bars across the suspension bridge from park headquarters.

Getting There & Around

Malaysia Airlines (☎ 1300 883 000; www.malaysiaairlines.com.my) flies in direct from Miri (one-way/return RM100/200) and Kota Kinabalu (one-way/return from RM200/390). **Hornbill**

Skyways (☎ 455737) also flies between Mulu and Miri. Book as early as possible and note that cancellations due to bad weather are not uncommon. The park office is a half-hour walk from the airstrip, or minivans can shuttle you to/from the terminal for RM3/5.

To get to the park via boat (a much longer trip), catch an express boat from Marudi to Long Terawan (RM20; 3½ hours; 11am daily); a speedboat will cost RM32. To charter a boat from here to Gunung Mulu (two hours) costs around RM250 for one to four people.

Another option is the **Headhunters' Trail**, a route once taken by Kayan war parties intent on raiding communities in the Limbang district. The three-day trail can be done in either direction but is usually followed from Gunung Mulu down to Long Berar, Sungai Terikan, Medamit and finally Limbang. Talk to tour operators in major cities or staff at **Parks & Wildlife** (☎ 085-434184) about this possibility.

BARIO & THE KELABIT HIGHLANDS
☎ 085

Bario is a small, languid settlement of 800 people (and 10 cars) in a sublime valley 1500m up in the Kelabit Highlands, a remote region alongside the border with Kalimantan. This is one of Sarawak's real get-away-from-it-all destinations, being far removed from urban congestion and awash with fresh air and the indigenous hospitality of the Kelabit people. There are few things more relaxing than sitting on a porch and watching drifts of the feather-light rain locals call 'Bario snow'. If you're feeling active, embark on a highland trek taking in longhouses and abundant flora and fauna.

To visit Bario and trek into the surrounding countryside, you need a permit from the Pejabat Residen in Miri; see p496. There are no banks or credit card facilities in the highlands so bring plenty of cash.

Activities
Guided treks ranging from overnight excursions to a five-day highlands loop can be organised through Bario accommodation providers. If possible, make arrangements a few days before your visit. Going rates for guides (and porters if you need them) start at RM65 per day for a solo trekker and

RM40 per person per day for two or more walkers. To stay overnight in a longhouse, expect to pay RM40 per person (including food). Camping may work out cheaper, but you'd probably need a porter to carry the equipment. If the trip involves river travel, you'll pay anything from RM50 per person for short trips up to RM150 for a one-way ride to the Kalimantan border.

Sleeping & Eating
All Bario accommodation options give you a choice between a bed-only price and a package deal that includes all meals (utilising Bario's famous long-grain rice) and transport. Those opting only for a bed can buy supplies at local shops and can also usually pay for individual meals (RM7 to RM15).

Bariew Backpacker Lodge (☎ 791038; www .ebario.com; bed/package RM20/55) An excellent homestay in a modern wood-lined house with plenty of places to lounge. Most rooms have two to four beds; there's one double. Follow the main road through Bario and as it dog-legs past the old airport; the lodge will be on your left.

Labang Longhouse (☎ 418396; ncb@yahoo.com; bed/package RM20/60) Stay in this splendid, decade-old longhouse – one of the ground-floor planks is a staggering 15m long. The owner is an expert on the Sarawakian environment and will happily engage you on local wildlife and conservation issues. Follow the road heading east to Pa Ukat for 1km beyond Bario.

Other options:

De Plateau Lodge (www.kelabit.net/websites/munney /deplateau.html; bed/package RM15/50) White-timber house surrounded by a lovely garden, 2km east of Bario; stick left when the road forks.

Nancy Harris Homestay (☎ 791074; nancyharriss@ yahoo.com; bed RM15-20, package RM40) Recently renovated, friendly homestay near Bariew Backpacker Lodge.

Getting There & Around
The only way into Bario is by air, an exhilarating flight that exposes you to the ugly ribs of logging roads in lowland Sarawak before sweeping past thickly forested hills into a beautiful mountain valley. **Malaysia Airlines** (☎ 1300 883 000; www.malaysiaairlines .my) has at least one flight daily between Miri and Bario (return flight RM145, 50 minutes).

Communication between the Malaysian Airlines office in Bario and Malaysian Airlines offices elsewhere is haphazard, so reconfirm your flight out of Bario as soon as you arrive. Flights are often booked out well in advance and are dependent on the weather; cancellations aren't uncommon.

Small regional airline **Hornbill Skyways** (☎ 611066) also flies between Miri and Bario.

It takes 25 minutes to walk into Bario from the airport. Turn left at the T-junction.

LIMBANG
☎ 085 / pop 3700

The riverbanks of the small district centre of Limbang are lined with rickety stilt houses. You may pass through here on your way to/from Brunei. Limbang is also one end of the **Headhunters' Trail**, a backdoor route to Gunung Mulu (for more on the trail, see p498).

Sleeping & Eating

Decent accommodation in town is confined to midrange hotels.

Best Continental Inn (☎ 215600; 26 Jl Wong Tsap En; s/tw RM40/45; ✷) Diagonally opposite the wharf is this hotel with well-maintained, reasonably priced rooms. It shouldn't be judged by the state of the hallway carpet.

BORDER CROSSING: INTO BRUNEI

Boats between Limbang and Bandar Seri Begawan (BSB) in Brunei (RM20 or B$10, 30 minutes) are infrequent in either direction and may not run after early afternoon.

From outside the riverfront immigration post, a minivan departs when it has enough passengers for Kuala Lurah (RM5, 45 minutes) on the Bruneian border; from here you catch a local bus to BSB (B$1, 30 minutes). The minivan driver isn't always in attendance but stay near the vehicle and eventually he'll turn up. If you're the only passenger and you want to leave for the border immediately, the driver won't budge for less than RM20. This service is far preferable to using local taxis, which can charge upwards of RM40 for the trip to Kuala Lurah, and to the local Limbang–Kuala Lurah bus service, which runs infrequently.

For details on coming in from Brunei, see the boxed text, p46.

Mariner Inn (☎ 212922; 1371 Jl Buangsiol; s/tw RM50/55; ✷) Beside the river a few hundred metres from the wharf (turn left as you exit immigration) is a small grouping of hotels, the best of which is this one.

Kuali Coffee House (☎ 216700; ground fl, Purnama Hotel, Jl Buangsiol; meals RM3-12; ✷ breakfast & lunch) This is the place to go if you miss French toast and club sandwiches.

There's also a cheap **food court** (Limbang Plaza) adjoining the Purnama Hotel.

There are food stalls on the 1st floor of the waterfront market and a cluster of cheap cafés a block from the river, behind the grimy Muhibbah Inn.

Getting There & Around
AIR

Malaysia Airlines (☎ 1300 883 000; www.malaysiaairlines.com.my) has Twin Otter flights to Miri (RM65) and Kota Kinabalu (KK; RM75). The airport is 4km south of the town centre, a RM10 taxi ride.

BOAT

An express boat goes to Lawas daily at 7.30am (RM23, 30 minutes). The express boat to Pulau Labuan in Sabah leaves at 8.30am daily (RM23, two hours).

LAWAS
☎ 085 / pop 1080

Lawas is a transit town for trips to/from the Temburong district of Brunei and for flights to Miri. It has several basic hotels with rooms costing around RM35.

Ngan Travel Services (☎ 285570; Lot 455, 2 Jl Liaw Siew Ann) is the Malaysia Airlines agent. There are several **Malaysia Airlines** (www.malaysiaairlines.com.my) flights each week to Miri (RM70) and KK (RM75). The airport is 2km from town.

BORDER CROSSING: INTO BRUNEI

The road trip to Bangar in Brunei's remote Temburong district will likely entail an expensive taxi ride. From Bangar, it's a 45-minute boat trip to Bandar Seri Begawan. For information on crossing the border in the other direction, see Border Crossing: into Malaysia (p46).

The boat from Lawas to Serasa Ferry Terminal departs at 9.30am daily (RM25, 40 minutes).

An express boat to Limbang (RM23, 30 minutes) leaves between 8am and 9am; check the schedule at the wharf. Boats to Labuan (RM25, two hours) usually leave at 9am daily, but this schedule changes often.

Buses head to Kota Kinabalu in Sabah (RM20) at 7.30am and 1.30pm daily.

MALAYSIAN BORNEO – SABAH

Sabah is settled comfortably on the northern tip of Borneo and has acquired an enviable reputation among international nature-lovers thanks to the self-conscious antics of orang-utans at Sepilok, the wildlife (from proboscis monkeys to pygmy elephants and crocodiles) roaming the banks of the remote Sungai Kinabatangan, and the profoundly beautiful underwater world beneath Pulau Sipadan. Travellers also have access to some of Borneo's best beaches, tangled jungle trails, the busy urbanity of Kota Kinabalu and serene rural locales where cares can be washed away in rivers and hot springs. Sabah's most prominent feature is Mt Kinabalu, a towering collection of granite peaks where trekkers get a rare chance to feel like mountaineers.

KOTA KINABALU

☎ 088 / pop 270,000

Sabah's capital is a vigorous city bordered to the west by the South China Sea, which sweeps beyond the islands of Tunku Abdul Rahman National Park, and to the east by the tall foothills of the verdant Crocker Range. The city's scenic location imprints itself on the minds of travellers, as does its abundance of eateries and markets, its relative wealth (the neat innercity blocks corral Borneo's largest population of shiny big 4WDs) and the ocean smells that break over the surprisingly barren, rock-strewn waterfront. The downtown area of KK (as everyone calls it) is dominated by several boxy malls and hotels, and is big enough that a few areas have an isolated edge to them after dark. However, there's little edginess in the homogenous suburbs that wander aimlessly along the coast for several kilometres.

VISAS & PERMITS

Sabah is semi-autonomous and, just like Sarawak, has its own immigration controls. On arrival most nationalities will be given a visa for a stay of between one and three months (also valid for Peninsular Malaysia).

A permit is needed to climb Mt Kinabalu; pay when you arrive at Kinabalu National Park headquarters; see p508.

Information

EMERGENCY
Ambulance (☎ 999)
Fire (☎ 994)
Police (☎ 999, 212222; Jl Dewan)

INTERNET ACCESS
KK's cybercafés charge between RM3 and RM5 per hour.
Net Access Internet Café (Jl Pantai; ⏰ 9am-2am)
Print Shop (☎ 248399; 63 Jl Gaya; ⏰ 8am-7pm Mon-Sat) Superfast access.
Touch & Surf (cnr Jl Labuk & Datuk Saleh Sulong; ⏰ 9am-12.30pm Mon-Sat, 9am-9pm Sun)

MEDICAL SERVICES
Queen Elizabeth Hospital (☎ 218166; Jl Penampang)

MONEY
You'll find numerous moneychangers on the ground floors of Centre Point and Wisma Merdeka; shop around for the best rates.
Maybank (☎ 250557; 9 Jl Pantai) One of many centrally located banks with an ATM.

POST
Post Office (☎ 210855; Jl Tun Razak; ⏰ 8am-4.30pm)

TOURIST INFORMATION
Immigration office (☎ 280700; 4th fl, Wisma Dana Bandang, Jl Tunku Abdul Rahman; ⏰ 8-11.30am & 2-4.30pm Mon-Fri, 8am-1pm Sat)
Sabah Parks (☎ 211881; Lot 1-3, ground fl, Block K, Sinsuran Kompleks, Jl Tun Fuad Stephen; ⏰ 8am-1pm & 2-4.30pm Mon-Thu, 8-11.30am & 2-4.30pm Fri, 8am-12.50pm Sat) Good source of information on the state's parks. Books accommodation on Pulau Tiga, an island south of KK surrounded by its own national park and where one series of *Survivor* was filmed.
Sabah Tourism Board (☎ 212121; www.sabahtour ism.com; 51 Jl Gaya; ⏰ 8am-5pm Mon-Fri, 8am-4pm Sat, 9am-4pm Sun) An excellent source of information.

GETTING INTO TOWN

Kota Kinabalu's modern international airport is 7km southwest of the centre. Minivans leaving from the main terminal charge RM2, while minivans or local buses that pass the airport bus stop (turn right as you leave the terminal and walk for 10 minutes) charge RM1. Taxis heading from the terminal into town operate on a system of vouchers (RM14), sold at a taxi desk on the terminal's ground floor.

The bus stations servicing northern Sabah and southern Sabah (plus Sarawak) and the terminal for boats arriving from Pulau Labuan are all within walking distance of the city centre.

Tanjung Aru train station is 5km south of the centre. Minivans or buses returning from the airport pass the station, or catch a taxi into town for RM7.

Sutera Sanctuary Lodges (☎ 243629; www .suterasanctuarylodges.com; Lot G15, ground fl, Wisma Sabah, Jl Haji Saman; ۩ 9am-6.30pm Mon-Fri, 9am-4.30pm Sat, 9am-3pm Sun) Books accommodation in Kinabalu National Park (including Poring Hot Springs and Mesilau) and on Manukan Island in Tunku Abdul Rahman National Park.

Tourism Malaysia (☎ 248698; www.tourism.gov.my; ground fl, 1 Chester St; ۩ 8am-4.30pm Mon-Thu, 8am-noon & 1.30-4.30pm Fri) Geared towards travel throughout Malaysia. The office is also open 8am to 2.45pm on the second and fourth Saturday of each month.

Sights

The main building of the **Sabah Museum** (☎ 253199; Jl Kebajikan; admission RM5; ۩ 9am-5pm Sat-Thu) is modelled on a Rungus longhouse and is an ethnographic treat, exhibiting traditional items like ceramics and colourful wedding costumes from many of Sabah's 30 indigenous groups. In a separate building is the **Sabah Art Gallery**, while off the car park is the fascinating **Heritage Village**, with recreations of longhouses. Bus 13 can drop you on Jl Penampang, where there's a footbridge and a path leading uphill to the museum, saving you a long walk around the corner – the footbridge gate is often locked for some reason, but it's easy to climb around.

The **Central Market** (Jl Tun Fuad Stephen) is in two sections: the waterfront area sells fish and the area bordering Jl Tun Fuad Stephen sells fruit and vegetables. Next door is the **Handicraft Centre** (Jl Tun Fuad Stephen), jammed with craft, textile and jewellery stalls. At the small adjacent **fruit market**, drain a coconut for RM0.50. A section of Jl Gaya is closed to traffic on Sunday morning to accommodate the stalls of KK's popular **Gaya St Fair** (۩ 7am-1pm Sun).

Tours

The ground floor of Wisma Sabah is infested with tour operators conducting day trips around KK and excursions elsewhere in Sabah.

Riger Travel & Tours (☎ 221888; Lot G08, Wisma Sabah, Jl Haji Saman) does rafting trips on Sungai Kiulu (easy, grades I and II; from RM150) and Sungai Padas (medium, grades III and IV; from RM180); minimum of two people required.

Several operators show experienced divers nearby waters from RM200 for two dives.

Sleeping

North Borneo Cabin (☎ 272800; www.northborneo cabin.com; 74 Jl Gaya; dm/tw RM20/50; ▯) There's a lot to like about one of KK's newest hostels: spotless rooms, free Internet and breakfast, and a small homely lounge. It's not a big place but there's no risk of cabin fever here due to the downtown location, and it's open 24 hours.

Borneo Backpackers (☎ 234009; www.borneo backpackers.com; 24 Lorong Dewan, Australia Pl; dm RM25-30; ⊠ ▯) Pleasant three-storey hostel, one of three backpackers crowded together around Australia Pl (so-named because Australian soldiers camped here on arrival in 1945). Dorms have six to 10 beds and can get pretty crowded; there's one room with two beds (singles/doubles RM40/60). There's also a teensy communal area and a rooftop deck.

Backpacker Lodge (Lucy's Homestay; ☎ 261495; http://welcome.to/backpackerkk; 25 Lorong Dewan, Australia Pl; dm/d RM18/40) Another Australia Pl hostel, this is a small, cluttered place where you really feel as if you're staying in someone's home. It has a pair of large dorms and several doubles; room prices include breakfast.

Tropicana Lodge (☎ 270284; 1st fl, 9 Lorong Dewan, Australia Pl; dm RM20-25; ⊠) Arguably the least appealing of the Australia Pl trio, though breakfast is included in the price and there's

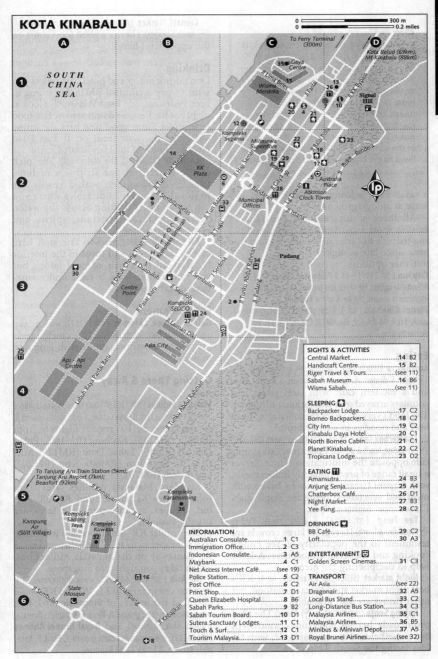

KOTA KINABALU

0 _____ 300 m
0 _____ 0.2 miles

SOUTH CHINA SEA

To Ferry Terminal (300m)

Kota Belud (69km); Mt Kinabalu (88km)

Gaya Centre

Jl Lima Belas

Wisma Merdeka

KK Bypass

Signal Hill

Jl Pantai

Kompleks Segama

Milimewa Superstore

Touch & Surf

KK Plaza

Jl Haji Saman

Jl Tun Fuad Stephens

Jl Tun Razak

Beach St

Gaya St

Jl Sembilanbelas

Kompleks Sinsuran

A B C D E F G H

Jl Pantai

Jl Datuk Chong Thian Vin

Jl Duapuloh

Jl Pasar Baru

Centre Point

Jl Sapuloh

Kompleks SEDCO

Jl Sembulan

Sentosa

Jl Laiman Diki

Asia City

Jl Tugu

Municipal Offices

Jl Bandaran

Jl Istana

Jl Dewan

Atkinson Clock Tower

Australia Place

Jl Tunku Abdul Rahman

Padang

Jl Padang

Api - Api Centre

Lebuh Raya Pantal Baru

Jl Tunku Abdul Rahman

To Tanjung Aru Train Station (5km);
Tanjung Aru Airport (7km);
Beaufort (92km)

Jl Kemajuan

Kompleks Karamunsing

Kampung Air (Stilt Village)

Kompleks Sadong Jaya

Kompleks Kuwasa

Jl Tuaran

State Mosque

Jl Penampang

Jl Sembulan

Jl Kebajikan

INFORMATION
Australian Consulate	**1** C1
Immigration Office	**2** C3
Indonesian Consulate	**3** A5
Maybank	**4** C1
Net Access Internet Café	(see 19)
Police Station	**5** C2
Post Office	**6** C2
Print Shop	**7** D1
Queen Elizabeth Hospital	**8** B6
Sabah Parks	**9** B2
Sabah Tourism Board	**10** D1
Sutera Sanctuary Lodges	**11** C1
Touch & Surf	**12** C1
Tourism Malaysia	**13** D1

SIGHTS & ACTIVITIES
Central Market	**14** B2
Handicraft Centre	**15** B2
Riger Travel & Tours	(see 11)
Sabah Museum	**16** B6
Wisma Sabah	(see 11)

SLEEPING 🛏
Backpacker Lodge	**17** C2
Borneo Backpackers	**18** C2
City Inn	**19** C2
Kinabalu Daya Hotel	**20** C1
North Borneo Cabin	**21** C1
Planet Kinabalu	**22** C2
Tropicana Lodge	**23** D2

EATING 🍴
Amansutra	**24** B3
Anjung Senja	**25** A4
Chatterbox Café	**26** D1
Night Market	**27** B3
Yee Fung	**28** C2

DRINKING 🍷
BB Café	**29** C2
Loft	**30** A3

ENTERTAINMENT 🎭
Golden Screen Cinemas	**31** C3

TRANSPORT
Air Asia	(see 22)
Dragonair	**32** A5
Local Bus Stand	**33** C2
Long-Distance Bus Station	**34** C3
Malaysia Airlines	**35** C1
Malaysia Airlines	**36** B5
Minibus & Minivan Depot	**37** A5
Royal Brunei Airlines	(see 32)

MALAYSIA

a small back balcony on which to eat and stare at an overgrown ridge.

All three aforementioned Australia Pl hostels sport security doors, perhaps hinting that it's not wise to wander around this area alone late at night.

Other options:

City Inn (☎ 218933; 41 Jl Pantai; s/d RM50/55; ❄) Affordable option for when the hostels are full. The entrance is around the back of the building.

Planet Kinabalu (☎ 319168; planetkinabalu@hotmail .com; 1st fl, 98 Jl Gaya; dm RM18) Cheap, central, but distinctly dingy.

Eating

Amansutra (SEDCO Sq, Jl Kampung Air 4; meals RM3.50-8; ☽ lunch & dinner) A cross between a *kedai kopi* and a modern café, with steel tables and counters arrayed over that familiar tiled floor. The food's very good: try the *soto daging* (lean beef and noodles in a tangy broth).

Chatterbox Café (☎ 272588; Jl Gaya; meals RM2.50-7; ☽ breakfast, lunch & dinner) Fuel up at this simple café opposite the information centre. Serves a small range of predominantly Indian meals, with *biryani* (steamed rice oven-baked with meat and vegetables) being the staple dish. Closes most nights at 7pm.

Yee Fung (☎ 312042; Jl Gaya; meals RM3-6; ☽ breakfast & lunch) Its regular large crowds are testament to the popularity of Yee Fung's cooking and convivial atmosphere. Ask for help in deciphering the menu.

Night market (SEDCO Sq, Jl Kampung Air 4) KK's best night market specialises in seafood, but other dishes are also available.

Anjung Senja (meals RM3-7; ☽ dinner) The tiled promenade here is sometimes windswept but nonetheless very atmospheric, with tables facing the South China Sea.

Central Market (Jl Tun Fuad Stephen; meals RM2-6; ☽ lunch & dinner) There's a good food court on the upper level here.

Drinking

Don't drink in top-end hotel bars unless you want to pay a criminal RM16 for a mug of beer. Pedestrianised **Beach St** is worth a look at night but has become dominated by fast-food enterprises. Some good new bars are strung out along the waterfront off Jl Tun Fuad Stephen, south of the Handicraft Centre.

Loft (☎ 270387; 12 The Waterfront) The pick of the waterfront bar strip – a mellow, friendly drinking den with a sturdy bar to slouch on and outside tables where you can watch boats drifting across the water. Serves cocktails, mocktails, spirits and some international beers.

BB Café (☎ 233882; Beach St) The staff here can be indifferent and most of the interior is taken up by a pair of pool tables, but you can grab an outside table under vine-covered lattices.

Entertainment

Golden Screen Cinemas (☎ 212322; www.gsc.com .my; Jl Laiman Diki; tickets RM5-8) This cinema reels off plenty of mainstream English-language movies.

Getting There & Away

AIR

Malaysia Airlines (☎ 1300 883 000; www.malaysiaairlines .com; Jl Limabelas 11th fl Gaya Centre; Jl Bukit Nenas Ground fl, Kompleks Karamunsing) has regular flights to/from Bintulu (RM145), Kuching (RM160), Pulau Labuan (RM45), Lahad Datu (RM125), Miri (RM70), Sandakan (RM60), Sibu (RM200) and Tawau (RM70).

Standard Malaysia Airlines fares from Johor Bahru/KL are around RM200/250, but cheaper advance-purchase fares are usually available.

The regular KK–Singapore fare is RM690, so it's cheaper to fly to Johor Bahru and cross the Causeway on the Malaysia Airlines bus, which takes you right into Singapore.

Air Asia (☎ 1300 889 933; www.airasia.com; 94 Jl Gaya) has cheap fares to KL. Within KK you'll also find the offices of **Dragonair** (☎ 254733; www.dragonair.com; ground fl, Block C, Kompleks Kuwasa, Jl Tunku Abdul Rahman) and **Royal Brunei Airlines** (☎ 242193; www.bruneiair.com; ground fl, Block B, Kompleks Kuwasa, Jl Tunku Abdul Rahman).

BOAT

Passenger boats leave for Pulau Labuan (RM31, 1½ hours) from the ferry terminal north of the city centre; from Labuan, there are connecting services to Brunei (see p507). Boats leave roughly at 8am, 10am, 1.30pm and 3pm, but double-check schedules at the terminal.

For information on boats to Tunkul Abdul Rahman National Park, see right.

BUS

Air-conditioned express buses heading to Mt Kinabalu and major towns on the east coast leave from the **long-distance bus station** (Jl Tunku Abdul Rahman). This is also the place to catch minivans to northern destinations like Kudat and the 7.30am bus to Lawas in Sarawak (RM20). You'll be greeted by touts upon reaching the bus lot – most are helpful and will guide you to the right bus. Myriad companies service the main routes and many have metal shacks where you can check current schedules and make advance bookings.

The large lot opposite Wawasan Plaza is a busy **minibus and minivan depot** (Jl Kemajuan) servicing destinations south of KK.

Bus departures are frequent in the early morning but dwindle later in the day.

TAXI

Several share-taxis do a daily run between KK and Ranau, passing the start of the short side-road to the Kinabalu National Park office. You can be dropped off at either destination for between RM10 to RM15. Share-taxis also head north to Kudat (RM20).

Most share-taxis depart opposite the long-distance bus station. Before you get in, agree on the price and check how many passengers they have as they only leave when full.

TRAIN

A railway line runs from KK's **Tanjung Aru train station** (☎ 262536), 5km south of the city centre, down to Beaufort (RM4.80, two hours, departures 9.50am and 1.40pm, 1.40pm only Sunday) and Tenom (RM7.50, four hours, departure 7.45am).

Getting Around

Minibuses marked 'Putatan' run regularly to the airport (RM2) from the minibus station (bay 17) opposite Wawasan Plaza;

alternatively, the minibuses can drop you off at the airport access road (RM1), from where it's a five-minute walk to the airport. Local buses departing the local bus stand can also drop you off at the access road (RM1). Taxis head to the airport for RM14. Note that Air Asia flights depart from the old airport building, now called Terminal 2; specify this to taxi or minibus drivers when heading out there.

Minivans and local buses headed to the airport also pass the train station. A taxi from the city should cost RM7.

Also see the boxed text Getting Into Town (p502).

Some members of KK's large taxi population are metered but most are not, in which case negotiate a fare before heading off. There are several hubs where taxis congregate, including outside the **Milimewa Superstore** (Jl Lintas). Most trips around town cost about RM5.

TUNKU ABDUL RAHMAN NATIONAL PARK

It's a short boat ride from KK to **Tunku Abdul Rahman National Park** (admission RM10), which comprises the serene offshore islands of Gaya, Mamutik, Manukan, Sapi and Sulug. These islands have some of Borneo's best beaches, crystal-clear waters and a wealth of marine life. The best, most easily reached stretch of sand is on Manukan, though you share it with guests of the local resort. Snorkels can be rented (RM10) at the KK ferry terminal.

Sleeping & Eating

You can **camp** (camp sites per person RM5) on Sapi, Mamutik and at a new place on Gaya called Teluk Malohom. Park permits and camping fees are paid on arrival at each island. Four-/ six-person tents (RM30/40) can be rented from national parks offices.

Luxury, restaurant-equipped resorts are located on Gaya and Manukan. Snacks and drinks are sold on Sapi, but for camping on Sapi or Mamutik bring your own water.

Getting There & Away

Boats to the islands are arranged inside the waiting room at KK's ferry terminal. Sign up for your chosen destination and then take a seat until there are enough passengers (usually eight) to depart. Services run from 7am to 6pm daily but it's best to catch a boat in the morning, as it's much harder to make up boat numbers in the afternoon.

Return fares to Mamutik, Manukan and Sapi are RM14. You can also buy two-/three-island passes for RM24/34. The resort on Gaya operates a ferry (RM10 each way) roughly every 1½ hours from 8am to 11pm, though services are often nonexistent between 1.30pm and 6pm. There were no services to Sulug at the time of writing.

TAMBUNAN RAFFLESIA RESERVE

High up in the forested Crocker Range, 60km east of KK beside the highway to Tambunan, is the **Tambunan Rafflesia Reserve** (admission free; 8am-noon Sun-Fri), an open-air incubator for one of the world's biggest flowers. The rafflesia is a parasitic plant that (taking its cue from *Alien*) hides within its host until bursting into enormous bloom.

Due to the area's unpredictable weather, the reserve only opens in the morning and you must pay for a guide to lead you to the flowers, each of which only blooms for around five days. Guide costs depend on the number of sightseers, but you may be charged up to RM30 per person. To ensure your money and time are well spent, ask at KK's information centre (p501) whether rafflesias are blooming before you come out here. The reserve is also open 9am to noon on the second and fourth Saturday of each month.

Take a Tambunan- or Keningau-bound bus from KK to the reserve (RM10, one hour). From the reserve, southbound travellers can catch a passing bus to Keningau (RM8, one hour), then on to Tenom (RM5, one hour). You could catch a bus from the reserve only as far as Tambunan (RM5, 30 minutes), but there's little reason to stop here unless you want to head north to Ranau (RM12, two hours) on a tricky mountain road.

BEAUFORT

☎ 087 / pop 48,000

Beaufort is a quiet provincial town on Sungai Padas. It has a certain dilapidated charm but most visitors are drawn more by local opportunities for white-water rafting. See p502 for information on rafting trips out of KK.

Heading south to Lawas in Sarawak, you'll pass through Sipitang, which has cheap accommodation and early morning boats to Labuan.

Sleeping & Eating

Beaufort Hotel (☎ 211911; 19-20 Lo Chung Park, off Jl Pasar Awam; s/d RM36/45;) This is a central, very clean option with good-sized rooms and some upper-floor windows yielding views over town.

Mandarin Inn (☎ 212800; s/d 35/45;) This slightly shabbier alternative is located over the bridge on an unsignposted street fronting the river.

Restoran Al Rahmat (Jl Pasar Awam; meals RM2.50-4; breakfast & lunch) Situated in the same block as Beaufort Hotel is one of the friendliest places in town. They have a habit of piling the food up on your plate.

Getting There & Away
BUS & MINIVAN

Lucky Express (☎ 016-837 3223) buses depart for KK (RM8.20, 1½ hours) several times between 9am and 5.30pm daily. A minibus departs for Menumbok (RM5.50, one hour) at 1.20pm daily, while other minibus services head to Sipitang (RM5, 1½ hours) at 10.45am, 1.45pm and 6.30pm. All these services depart from outside the train station.

Minivans depart when full from the block opposite the market and cost several ringgit less than the equivalent buses (ie to KK costs about RM5).

TRAIN

Beaufort can be reached (slowly) from KK via the Sabah State Railway line, which then winds its way (even more slowly) east across the slopes of thickly forested hills alongside the boulder-strewn Sungai Padas to Tenom. The history of this narrow-gauge line has been plagued by safety concerns, but the Beaufort–Tenom trip is definitely worth taking. Economy/1st-class tickets for the two-hour Beaufort–Tenom ride cost RM2.20/7.60; 1st-class involves a ride in a small *relkar*, similar to a minibus on rails. Buy tickets at Beaufort's **train station** (☎ 211518). Standard *penumpang* (passenger) trains depart Beaufort at 7.45am and 3.55pm daily Monday to Saturday, and at 7am, 7.45am and 1.50pm Sunday; *relkar* depart 8.30am daily Monday to Saturday and at noon on Sunday.

Train services to KK (economy/1st class RM4.80/15) depart at 10am, 12.45pm and 5pm daily Monday to Saturday, and at 10am and 4.20pm on Sunday.

PULAU LABUAN

☎ 087 / pop 76,000

Off the coast from Menumbok is the small island of Labuan, the main jumping-off point for Brunei. It's a tax haven (the Malaysian version of the Canary Islands), hence Bandar Labuan is an uninspiring place full of expensive 'duty-free' shops and overpriced hotels. The island does have interesting **WWII sites** and a couple of decent **beaches**, information on which is available at Labuan's **tourist information centre** (☎ 423445; www.labuantourism.com.my; cnr Jl Dewan & Berjaya; ⏰ 9am-5pm), but most travellers transit as quickly as possible.

Sleeping & Eating

Budget accommodation in Labuan is of poor quality. Midrange hotels are a better option.

Melati Inn (☎ 416307; U0061 Jl Perpaduan; s/d RM45/50; 🉑) A peach-coloured place with rooms that are a little worse for wear, but the rates are probably the best in town for somewhere that's not a fleapit. Jl Perpaduan runs inland from the waterfront, close to the wharf.

Global Hotel (☎ 425201; U0017 Jl OKK Awang Besar; s/d RM69/99; 🉑) This hotel has very clean rooms and good amenities, and throws in free transport to the airport, though solo travellers may not find this enough compensation for the cramped singles.

Federal Hotel (☎ 411711; Jl Bunga Kesuma; s/d from RM50/65; 🉑) The interior of this place is OK, even though the exterior looks fire-singed.

Restoran Seri Malindo (☎ 416072; Jl Dewan; meals RM3-10; ⏰ breakfast, lunch & dinner) Open-air restaurant set on a hangar-sized expanse of paving, a good place to join in the bustle of local mealtimes. Your ears, however, will be assailed by its choice of muzak: the ubiquitous (and dreadful) Malay pop.

Choice Restaurant (☎ 418086; U0104 Jl OKK Awang Besar; meals RM2-6; ⏰ lunch & dinner) A good-value, modern Indian-Malay eatery with tasty *murtabak* and *biryani*. A relaxed place for lunch or dinner.

LA Coffeebean Restaurant (☎ 411800; J8 Complex, U0054 Jl OKK Awang Besar; meals RM3.50-10; ⏰ lunch & dinner) More like a pub than a restaurant, with drinkers lounging at outside tables and a big-screen TV blaring MTV. But besides mugs of Tiger, you can also get Malay meals, steaks and chops.

Getting There & Away

Malaysia Airlines (☎ 1300 883 000; www.malaysiaairlines.com.my) has flights to KK (RM45), KL (RM245), Kuching (RM120) and Miri (RM50). **Air Asia** (☎ 1300 889 933; www.airasia.com) has cheap flights to KK twice a day.

Passenger ferries connect Labuan with KK (RM31, 1½ hours), departing at 8.30am, 10.45am, 1pm and 3pm. Express boats to Limbang in Sarawak (RM23, two hours) leave at 12.30pm and 2.30pm daily. Boats to Lawas (RM25, two hours), also in Sarawak, depart at 12.30pm daily.

A 50 sen departure tax is charged at the ferry terminal. A brand new terminal was about to open beside the old one at the time of research.

> ### BORDER CROSSING: INTO BRUNEI
>
> Numerous express boats (RM24, 1½ hours) go to the Serasa Ferry Terminal located 25km northeast of BSB near Muara in Brunei, departing between 8.30am and 3pm. For information on doing this route in the other direction, see p46.

TENOM

☎ 087 / pop 38,000

Tenom is a relaxed, greenery-fringed rural town where you'll get dizzy from returning all the passing hellos from friendly Murut and Dusun people. Watch football matches on the central *padang* (field) on Sunday afternoons.

Taman Pertanian Sabah (Sabah Agricultural Park; ☎ 737952; www.sabah.net.my/agripark; Taman Pertanian Sabah WDT28; admission RM25; ⏰ 9am-5.30pm Tue-Sun), 15km southeast of Tenom, is Eden for those interested in tropical horticulture. Highlights include the largest collection of orchid species in Southeast Asia, walking trails in the surrounding hills, a bee centre and a museum explaining how various plants are used and cultivated. Local buses take you here for RM2.

Sleeping & Eating

Hotel Sri Perdana (☎ 734001; 77 Jl Tun Mustapha; s/d from RM35/40; ✷) Singles are on the small side here and connecting doors admit the sounds of your neighbour's TV, but this is still a good-value place. Advertises 'Special Decoration', which may explain the glittering pineapple in a glass case at reception.

Orchid Hotel (☎ 737600; 58 Jl Tun Mustapha; s/d/tw/tr from RM33/45/50/60; ✷) Another dependable option on the main street, with variously sized cheap rooms.

Taman Pertanian Sabah (Sabah Agricultural Park; ☎ 737952; www.sabah.net.my/agripark; Taman Pertanian Sabah WDT28; dm RM15-25, camp site RM10) The cheapest accommodation is out at the park, where there's a large hostel dorm.

There are plenty of *kedai kopi* selling basic Chinese food. Food stalls set up in the evening in the car park down the main road from the *padang*, selling lots of low-nutrient fried foods.

Getting There & Away

Minivans depart Tenom for Keningau (RM5, one hour) and KK (RM15, 3½ hours). The **Nui Luk express bus** (☎ 264315) heads to KK (RM16) from beside the train station at 7am, 8am, noon and 4pm daily.

From Tenom you can ride part of Borneo's sole railway line through a splendid river-gouged valley to Beaufort. Penumpang/*relkar* tickets cost RM2.20/7.60 and can be bought at Tenom's **train station** (☎ 735514), located across the *padang* from Jl Tun Mustapha. Passenger trains depart Tenom for the two-hour trip at 8am and 2.50pm daily Monday to Saturday, and at 8am, noon and 2.30pm Sunday; *relkars* depart 6.40am daily Monday to Saturday and 7.25am Sunday.

KUDAT

☎ 088 / pop 56,000

Kudat is a quiet port town on a small peninsula in Sabah's far north. It has a noticeable Filipino flavour and the surrounding countryside is home to tribal cousins of the Kadazan, one of Borneo's Dayak tribes. The road here from **Kota Belud**, where Sabah's biggest, most colourful and overhyped market takes place each Sunday, is lined with palm plantations. There are fine **beaches** west of town and it's possible to visit Rungus **longhouses** near the highway, but you'll need a car or taxi to reach them.

Hotel Sunrise (☎ 611517; Jl Ibrahm Arshao; s/d RM40/50; ✷) has clean rooms and is a convenient option as arriving minivans drop you near its front door. They have budget doubles for RM30 but we were unable to assess them.

Malaysia Airlines (☎ 1300 883 000; www.malaysiaairlines.com.my) has several flights each week from Kudat to KK (RM70) and Sandakan (RM75).

Minivans regularly make the trip to KK (RM15, 3½ hours) via Kota Belud (RM10, two hours).

KINABALU NATIONAL PARK

Sabah's main attraction is the highest mountain between the mighty Himalayas and Mt Puncak Jaya in Papua – **Mt Kinabalu**, towering 4101m above northern Borneo. Thousands of people of all ages climb Mt Kinabalu every year, but it's a long hard climb (and an equally taxing descent) that leaves the majority of its conquerors leg-sore for days afterwards. The summit trail wriggles up through gradually thinning stands of coniferous and montane oak forests and past alpine meadows, terminating on the mountain's barren granite massif. Climbing the mountain can seem rather pointless when you find yourself wearily clinging to a rope on a rocky incline in chilly 4am darkness. But it's also a dizzying accomplishment to be perched on the summit in golden light, looking down on surrounding peaks and cloud-shrouded Bornean wilderness.

Spend a day exploring the well-marked trails around park headquarters.

Orientation & Information

The Kinabalu park headquarters is located 88km from KK.

Bring your own toiletries, warm wet-weather gear and a set of dry clothes for the stopover at Laban Rata. Also bring sufficient drinking water and energising snacks, plus a torch for the pre-dawn summit ascent (hired at the park for RM5).

PERMITS & GUIDES

Park entry costs RM15 for adults. A climbing permit (RM100) and insurance (RM3.50) are compulsory.

Guides are compulsory for the summit trek. The collective guiding fee for one to three climbers tackling the trail from Timpohon Gate is RM70, for four to six climbers it's RM75, and for seven to eight climbers it's RM80. Porters can be hired to carry a maximum load of 10kg; for one to three climbers the cost is RM60, for four to six it's RM80, and for seven to eight climbers it's RM90. The guiding and porter fees are higher if the trek involves the Mesilau Trail.

Pay all fees at park headquarters before you climb.

The Climb

Climbing Mt Kinabalu is a two-day exercise for most people. The acclimatisation is important as the mountain is high enough for altitude sickness. You'll climb to Laban Rata the first day, a 6km walk which can take anywhere from 3½ to six hours depending on your fitness level. The next morning you hit the trail around 2.30am and spend the next 2½ to four hours scaling the 2.7km trail to the summit at Low's Peak, ideally in time for sunrise. Then you pick your way back down to park headquarters.

The official Mt Kinabalu trail begins at Timpohon Gate; leave no later than 11am to make Laban Rata in good time. A second, slightly longer and less crowded option is the **Mesilau Trail**, which begins at Mesilau Nature Resort (20km by road east of park headquarters) and links up with the main trail at Layang Layang.

The climb is uphill 99% of the way – an unrelentingly steep path up large dirt steps and over piled rocks. The trail becomes even steeper as you approach the summit, disappearing altogether on fields of slippery granite. A couple of sections here require that you haul yourself up using thick ropes. Every step can be a struggle as you suck oxygen from the thin air, and on our climb we encountered more than a few people who were either unable or unwilling to push themselves to the summit.

The secret to climbing Mt Kinabalu is stamina. Take it slowly. Many start briskly then have to take frequent and increasingly longer rest breaks, while others just keep trudging along.

Dawn on the summit is often an all-too-brief glimpse across Borneo at 6am before the clouds roll in along the mountainous spine. Sometimes the summit is covered in cloud already; at other times the sun shines through till 10am or later.

Sleeping & Eating

Advance bookings through **Sutera Sanctuary Lodges** (Map p503; ☎ 243629; www.suterasanctuary lodges.com; Lot G15, ground fl, Wisma Sabah, Jl Haji Saman) in KK are all but essential. Sutera handles bookings for all accommodation around park headquarters and at Laban Rata, Mesilau Nature Resort and Poring Hot Springs. If you turn up without a reservation, you risk finding all lodgings at this very popular park are full.

PARK HEADQUARTERS

Medang Hostel (dm RM12) and **Menggilan Hostel** (dm RM12) have dormitory accommodation. Both are clean, comfortable and have cooking facilities and a fireplace-warmed dining area. Each unit at **Nepenthes Lodge** (unit RM290) sleeps four people.

The canteen-style **Restoran Kinabalu Balsam** (meals RM3-12; ☼ breakfast, lunch & dinner) offers basic but decent fare you can munch on an outside deck. It also has a small, well-stocked shop.

LABAN RATA

Laban Rata Resthouse (dm RM34, hut dm RM17) This resthouse has four- and six-bunk rooms equipped with heaters, and sporadic hot-water showers in common bathrooms. You can also stay near the resthouse in unheated huts with basic cooking facilities.

Resthouse Restaurant (☼ 2-3am & 7.30am-7.30pm) Laban Rata's only eating option (besides self-catering) is this place, which presents overpriced buffets for its captive clientele: light breakfasts (served pre-dawn) cost RM14, while breakfast/dinner costs RM17/22 respectively. There's also a separate, limited menu (RM10 to RM21).

Getting There & Around

Express buses and minivans travelling between KK and Ranau or Sandakan pass the park turn-off, from where it's 100m uphill to the park. Air-con express buses (RM15, three hours) leave from KK's long-distance bus station four times daily, starting at 7.30am; minivans (RM10) depart the same station.

If you're heading back towards KK, minivans pass the park headquarters until mid-afternoon, but the best time to catch one is between 8am and noon. The park has a minivan that can be hired for RM65 to take up to six people to Poring Hot

Springs. By public bus it's RM5 to Ranau, then RM10 to Poring.

The return fare for the bus from park headquarters to Timpohon Gate is RM5.

RANAU

☎ 088 / pop 49,800

Ranau is a collection of concrete shop blocks in a lovely green valley on the route between KK and Sandakan. There's a busy Saturday **tamu** (night market).

Bank Simpanan Nasional (Jl Kibarambang) has an ATM. Internet access is available at **Max. com** (Jl Kibarambang; per hr RM2; ☒ 10am-9pm), beside Milimewa Superstore.

Sleeping & Eating

Kinabalu View Lodge (☎ 879111; 1st fl, Tokogaya Bldg, Lorong Kibarambang; r RM65-80; ☒) Treat yourself to a room at this lodge, especially if you've just endured Mt Kinabalu. It's a new place with spacious rooms, appealing décor and fluffy pillows not yet flattened by the weight of too many heads.

Rafflesia Inn (☎ 879359; 1st fl, Block E, Sedco Bldg; s/d/tw from RM25/30/35; ☒) If you'd rather a budget place, the same owners run this spartan but well-kept place.

Restaurant Double Luck (☎ 879246; Jl Kibarambang; meals RM6-10; ☒ breakfast, lunch & dinner) This is not the cheapest eatery in town but has the best food, friendly staff and ice-cold beer. Ask for a filled omelette for breakfast or try the tofu claypot for a veggie treat.

Getting There & Away

Just off Jl Pekan is a parking lot full of taxis. The next lot down from here is where you catch minivans to Tambunan (RM12, two hours) and Keningau (RM15, 2½ hours) – these traverse a hazardous mountain road – and to KK (RM15, 3½ hours). Services to KK pass the entrance to Kinabalu National Park (RM5). To charter a minivan to Poring Hot Springs costs RM30. Minivans also line up along the main street.

Catch express buses to Sandakan (RM20, four hours, departures hourly between 9am and 1pm) from the highway bus stop, about 150m from Restaurant Double Luck.

PORING HOT SPRINGS

Poring Hot Springs (☎ 088-879248; admission RM15; ☒ visitors centre 9am-4.30pm) lies within Kinabalu National Park some 43km from park head-

quarters and 19km north of Ranau. If you arrive here directly after climbing Mt Kinabalu, you can use your national park entry ticket to gain admission to Poring (and vice versa).

Steaming, sulphurous water is channelled into pools and tubs in which visitors relax their tired muscles after summitting Mt Kinabalu. The weathered outdoor tubs are free but are often either occupied or painfully slow to fill (test the taps before choosing one). Consider renting an indoor tub (per hour RM15); these fill quickly and give you private soaking time.

The other features include **walking trails**, a **tropical garden** (admission RM3; ☒ 9am-4pm), **butterfly farm** (admission RM4; ☒ 9am-4pm) and a 41m-high **canopy walkway** (admission RM5; ☒ 6.30am-5.30pm).

Sleeping & Eating

Reserve accommodation in advance through **Sutera Sanctuary Lodges** (☎ 088-243629; www.sute rasanctuarylodges.com; Lot G15, ground fl, Wisma Sabah, Jl Haji Saman) in KK.

Kelicap Hostel (dm RM12) and **Serindit Hostel** (dm RM12) have clean, spacious kitchens with gas cookers. Free blankets and pillows are provided. A **camping ground** (camp sites RM6) is available for tent-equipped visitors.

The **Rainforest Restaurant** (meals RM6-20; ☒ breakfast, lunch & dinner) is a breezy place overlooking the water slide and serves plenty of Western meals. There are also inexpensive eating places opposite the spring's entrance.

Getting There & Away

Kinabalu National Park's main office has a minivan that can be hired for RM65 to take up to six people to Poring Hot Springs.

From outside Poring Hot Springs visitors centre, minivans can be chartered for around RM30 to transport you to Ranau. Public buses to Ranau cost RM10.

SANDAKAN

☎ 089 / pop 223,000

At first Sandakan seems merely a chaotic commercial centre with traffic-choked streets and grimy buildings. But wander the smaller streets near the waterfront to get revealing glimpses of multistorey residences overflowing with laundry and local life. Sandakan sits at the entrance to a beautiful, island-studded bay, efficiently exploited for its seafood.

Travellers use Sandakan primarily as a base for trips to the Sepilok Orang-Utan Rehabilitation Centre and up Sungai Kinabatangan.

Information

Cyberjazz (2nd fl, Centre Point Mall, Jl Pelabuhan; per hr RM4; ☻ 9am-8pm Mon-Sat, 9am-7pm Sun) Get online here.

Emergency (☎ 999)

HSBC Bank (Lebuh Tiga) Has an ATM and is open Saturday morning.

Police (☎ 212222; Lebuh Empat)

Post office (off Jl Leila; ☻ 8am-4.30pm Mon-Sat) At the western end of town.

Sandakan Cybercafé (☎ 216158; 3rd fl, Wisma Sandakan; per hr RM4; ☻ 9am-5pm) Internet access.

Sandakan Hospital (☎ 212111; Lapulk Rd)

Standard Chartered Bank (Lebuh Tiga) Another bank with an ATM that opens Saturday morning.

Tan Seng Huat Moneychanger (☎ 213364; 35-B Jl Tiga; ☻ 8.30am-9pm) Changes cash.

Tourist information centre (☎ 229751; Lebuh Tiga; ☻ 8am-1pm & 2-4.30pm Mon-Fri) Opposite the municipal government building, this office has extremely helpful staff. It's also open 8am to 12.30pm on the second and fourth Saturday of each month.

Sights

Sandakan Memorial Park (Batu 8, Sandakan-Ranau Rd; admission free; ☻ 9am-5pm) marks the former site of an infamous WWII Japanese prisoner of war camp and the starting point of the 'death marches' to Ranau. (These three marches took place early in 1945 when, in the face of the imminent arrival of the Allies, the Japanese forced their prisoners to walk 250km through jungle to Ranau. Out of the 1577 prisoners subjected to the 'death marches', over half died on the walks and the rest – excepting a half-dozen Australians who escaped – were dead of disease, starvation or violence within six months.) To get there catch any local bus (RM1.30) marked Batu 8 (Km12) or higher; a taxi costs RM15.

Forty kilometres offshore is the 1740-hectare **Turtle Islands National Park** (admission RM10), which is one of the world's few sea-turtle sanctuaries. The park has three islands – Selingan, Bakungan Kecil and Gulisan – and visits, including accommodation, must be arranged through travel agencies or **Crystal Quest** (☎ 212711; cquest@tm .net.my; Jl Buli Sim Sim).

Tours

In Sandakan you can arrange to meet some magnificent wildlife along Sungai Kinabatangan (p513). A reputable budget operator is **Uncle Tan's** (☎ 531639; www.uncletan.com; office at SUDC Shoplots, Mile 16, Jl Gum Gum), which offers two-night stays at a riverside jungle camp for an all-inclusive RM240 per person. The basic accommodation comprises mattresses under mosquito nets in raised, open-fronted huts; bring all toiletries. When not snoozing in a hammock, drinking warm beer or shouting at thieving macaques, you'll be looking for animals on boat cruises and hikes. To reach Uncle Tan's office from Sandakan, catch a bus to Batu 16. Travellers heading on to Semporna can be directed from the jungle camp on to a bus bound for Lahad Datu, rather than backtracking to Sandakan.

Also reputable but much more upmarket is **Wildlife Expeditions** (☎ 219616; www.wildlife -expeditions.com; Room 903, 9th fl, Wisma Khoo Siak Chiew), which runs the Sukau River Lodge and has a base price of around RM320 per night.

Before committing to an operator (besides the two recommended above), get feedback from other travellers and ask plenty of questions at Sandakan's tourist information centre.

It's also possible to head partway up the Kinabatangan using local transport and to track down accommodation and tours in Sukau; see p513.

Sleeping

May Fair Hotel (☎ 219855; 24 Jl Pryer; s/d RM36/45; 🛇) This hotel is a great budget deal, with immaculate, spacious rooms that each have a DVD player; ransack their DVD collection at no charge. Avoid the rooms adjacent to reception, however, unless you want to become overly familiar with the owner's taste in movies.

Hotel London (☎ 216371; 10 Jl Empat; s/d/tr RM40/50/60; 🛇) Rooms here are OK but some could do with a little airing out. Those on the 1st and 2nd floors come with bathtubs and there's a rooftop garden to relax in.

Eating

For no-frills food, try one of the stalls in the waterfront market near the local bus station. A night market sets up outside the post office each evening and there are more Malay food stalls at the western end of Jl Coastal.

MALAYSIA

Penang Curry House (☎ 226675; Lebuh Dua; meals RM2-7; ☽ breakfast, lunch & dinner) Bustling little place offering tasty curries and a warm welcome. It's squeezed in among a raft of shopfronts near the intersection with Jl Dua.

Restoran Modern II (☎ 211008; Jl Pryer; meals RM2-4; ☽ breakfast & lunch) This café always looks freshly scrubbed, and tightly spaced ceiling fans keep the room relatively cool. Slide into a booth or grab a table facing the hubbub of the market.

Getting There & Away

AIR

Malaysia Airlines (☎ 1300 883 000; www.malaysiaair lines.com.my) flies direct to KK (RM60) and Tawau (RM95). There are also Twin Otter flights to Kudat (RM75).

Air Asia (☎ 1300 889 933; www.airasia.com) has several direct flights daily from KL to Sandakan (RM100).

BUS

The long-distance bus station is inconveniently located in a large parking lot at Batu 2½, 4km north of town. Most buses (and all minivans) head off in the morning. Schedules are posted at bus company booths at the station.

Most express buses to KK (RM25, six hours) leave between 6.30am and 2pm and pass the turn-off to Kinabalu National Park headquarters (RM25). There are also buses to Ranau (RM25, four hours), Lahad Datu (RM15, 2½ hours) and Tawau (RM30, 5½ hours) regularly between 6.30am and 5pm. There's a bus to Semporna (RM30, 4½ hours) at 8am; if you miss it, take a bus or minivan to

---

BORDER CROSSING: INTO PHILIPPINES

The boats operated by **Weesam Express** (☎ 212872) take 12 hours to sail to Zamboanga in the Philippines, departing 7am Wednesday and Friday. Operating bigger, more comfortable boats on this route, but taking 16 hours, is **Timmarine** (☎ 224009), which sails at 5pm Tuesday and Friday. Both operators leave from Karamunting jetty, 4km west of town, where immigration formalities take place. Economy fares start around RM210. For information on boats going the other way see p595.

Lahad Datu, from where there are more frequent minivans to Semporna.

Getting Around

The airport is 11km from town. The airport bus (RM1.20, departures roughly every half-hour from 6am to 5pm) departs from in front of **Yen Boutique** (Lebuh Dua), near the corner of Jl Pelabuhan. A coupon-fare taxi from the airport to the city centre costs RM17.50; going the other way, taxis charge RM15.

Local buses service central Sandakan from the long-distance bus station. A taxi for the same short trip should cost RM5, but lately drivers seem to have conspired to charge foreigners an overblown RM10.

The **local bus station** (Jl Pryer) and **minibus station** (Jl Coastal) are both on the waterfront. To get to Karamunting jetty, take a Pasir Putih bus (90 sen).

SEPILOK ORANG-UTAN REHABILITATION CENTRE

☎ 089

Sepilok is one of only four orang-utan sanctuaries in the world and is one of Sabah's major tourist attractions. The apes are brought here to be rehabilitated into forest life and at feeding times (usually 10am and 3pm) some of these fascinating animals usually swing into view along suspended ropes and clamber onto a feeding platform. Unfortunately, Sepilok's rampant popularity results in big crowds of yabbering tourists wielding digital cameras like weapons – do as the rangers ask and keep quiet during feedings.

At Sepilok you should also be able to view the endangered **Sumatran rhinoceros** (admission RM10; ☽ 9am-noon Mon-Thu, 9-11.30am Fri), though the exhibit's future was in doubt when we visited. The surrounding reserve has **nature trails** varying in length from 250m to 5km.

Information

Morning and afternoon programmes are posted at the **visitor centre** (☎ 531180; soutan@ po.jaring.my; admission RM30; ☽ visitor centre 9am-noon & 2-4pm Sat-Thu, 9-11.30am & 2-4pm Fri, ticket counter 9-11am & 2-3.30pm). The centre tries to charge an extra RM10 for use of cameras, which is annoying when you've already paid a hefty admission fee. However, this is practically impossible to enforce.

Informative videos are screened at 8.30am, 11am, noon and 3.30pm. There are free lockers for your valuables; orangutans have occasionally souvenired tourist belongings.

Sleeping & Eating

Sepilok Resthouse (☎ 534900; imejbs@tm.net.my; dm RM18, r RM45-65; 🔀) This comfortable, popular place is closest to the centre entrance. It's clean and has a nice yard to relax in. Breakfast is included in the price.

Sepilok Jungle Resort (☎ 533031; www.borneo-online.com.my/sjungleresort; dm RM18, r RM40-120; 🔀 🏠) This resort is a 10-minute walk from the centre, set in garden-decorated grounds where hornbills and other birds are commonly sighted. Rooms priced at RM65 or higher have air-con and there's an on-site café.

Caféteria (meals RM2.50-6; 🕐 breakfast & lunch) The visitor centre's cafeteria has the usual rice and noodle dishes, plus cheap omelettes, burgers and sandwiches.

Getting There & Away

The blue Labuk bus marked 'Sepilok Batu 14' takes you directly to the rehabilitation centre (RM2, 45 minutes) from Sandakan's local bus station. Minivans also make the trip every hour or so. A taxi costs RM25.

Regular buses marked 'Batu 14' or higher can drop you at the turn-off to Jl Sepilok, 1.5km from the centre. Just ask the driver and remind him as you get closer; the fare is 40 sen, or RM1.50 from the town centre.

Returning from Sepilok, the last bus leaves for Sandakan around 4.30pm.

SUNGAI KINABATANGAN

The wide, mud-clotted Sungai Kinabatangan is Sabah's longest river. Some stretches of the river, particularly the upper reaches, have been devastated by logging or the clearing of jungle for plantations. But elsewhere, its shallow depths and shores are teeming with wildlife.

Short of trekking into Borneo's interior, a visit to the Kinabatangan is one of the best ways to observe the island's wild animals close up. Visitors usually get to see orangutans and elusive proboscis monkeys, crocodiles, bearded pigs, pythons, bats that sleep during the day in funnel-shaped leaves, monitor lizards, frogs, myriad bird species including kingfishers and hornbills, and of course the ubiquitous macaque. If you're very lucky, you may even encounter pygmy elephants.

You need experienced guides to show you around and point out the animals hiding in trees, bushes, on riverbanks, above your head and under your feet. A couple of Sandakan-based outfits transport you to jungle camps and lodges and from there take you on boat rides and hikes to meet the locals; see p511.

There are also several accommodation and tour possibilities in **Sukau**, located on the Kinabatangan 135km southeast of Sandakan. One option that's been recommended by several travellers is **Sukau B&B** (☎ 230269; dm RM20), also called Esry B&B, which offers free breakfasts and can cook extra meals for RM10. Getting to Sukau is a mini-adventure in itself; ask at Sandakan's information centre for an update on transport options.

SEMPORNA & PULAU SIPADAN

☎ 089 / pop 91,900

Though not a particularly appealing town, Semporna does have a lively waterfront market and a mosque attractively framed against the waters of the Celebes Sea.

Most of Semporna's visitors are en route to/from Pulau Sipadan, a small island 36km offshore that's regarded as one of the world's best dive sites. Divers take exhilarating plunges off a 600m limestone wall, while snorkellers can expect to have sea turtles and other marine creatures glide under them. Since the beginning of 2005 Sipadan has been under Parks & Wildlife management and there's no longer any accommodation or dive operators on the island.

There's a ATM-equipped branch of Maybank opposite the mosque.

Tours

Most of the Semporna-based operators conducting diving and snorkelling tours to Sipadan, Mabul and nearby islands have offices located beside the entrance to Dragon Inn. The most reliable of these operators are **North Borneo Dive** (☎ 942788; borneo_tours@hotmail.com; Jl Causeway) and **Uncle Chang** (☎ 781002; unclechang99@hotmail.com; Jl Causeway). Another good choice in operator is **Scuba**

Junkie (☎ 785372; www.scuba-junkie.com; Lot 36, Block B, Semporna Seafront), situated on the road leading past the market. Day trips involving three dives (usually two at Sipadan and one at Mabul) cost between RM220 and RM240, plus RM60 equipment hire. Snorkelling costs around RM150, plus RM20 for equipment rental. All trips include lunch and can normally be arranged the day before, though sometimes groups book out available slots.

Sleeping & Eating

Dragon Inn (☎ 781088; www.dragoninnfloating.com .my; 1 Jl Custom; dm/r from RM15/70; ☒) An impressive-looking complex consisting of buildings raised above the harbour on stilts (you can see the water rippling between the floorboards of your room) and connected by a disorienting number of walkways. Dorms are in a longhouse and each have about 20 beds. The inn's restaurant is expensive but has ocean views and is ideal for a post-Sipadan drink.

Damai Travellers Lodge (☎ 782011; s/d from RM30/45; ☒) A clean budget hotel down the street from the mosque, and not far from the bus station. The cheap 'economy' rooms are fan-cooled and have no TV, but retain an attached bathroom.

The food stalls next to the fish market are cheap. If you buy seafood at the market, a couple of these places can cook it for you.

Getting There & Away

Minivans congregate at a station in the town centre and travel to Lahad Datu (RM15, two hours), Sandakan (RM30, 4½ hours) and KK (RM45, 10 hours). Minivans heading to Tawau (RM7, 1½ hours) depart from a separate station only a few minutes' walk away; just ask for directions.

TAWAU

☎ 089 / pop 245,000

Tawau is a port for travel across the nearby border to the Indonesian province of Kalimantan. If you have queries or difficulties, visit the **Indonesian consulate** (☎ 772052; Jl Apas; ☽ 8am-1pm Mon-Fri). The road trip to Tawau from either Lahad Datu or Semporna reveals how palm-tree plantations, harvested for palm tree oil, are choking the landscape of East Sabah. There's Internet access at **Cyberland** (Jl Musantara; per hr RM2; ☽ 9am-11pm).

Sleeping

Hotel Soon Yee (☎ 772447; 1362 Jl Stephen Tan; s/d RM30/34; ☒) Excellent budget hotel, a much better bet than the lodging houses (mostly brothels) around the local bus station. Opt for a quieter back room.

Loong Hotel (☎ 765308; 3868 Jl Abaca; r from RM50; ☒) Situated alongside wooden houses in a quiet street in the town's northwest. Standard rooms are nothing special but the family room (RM70) has four single beds and is ideal for a group.

Eating

Tawau is famed for its fine, inexpensive seafood, supplied by the waterfront markets. There are enclaves of cheap food stalls at the seaside end of Jl Nusantara and at night around the central market.

Restoran Aul Bismillah (☎ 764675; Jl Bunga Tan Jung; meals RM2-6; ☽ breakfast, lunch & dinner) Cheerful, no-fuss restaurant that's good for catching the breeze coming in off the ocean and serves good meals, like tofu curry.

Getting There & Away

Malaysia Airlines (☎ 1300 883 000; www.malaysia airlines.com.my) has flights between Tawau and both KK (RM70) and Sandakan (RM95).

Several express buses to KK (RM50, 10 hours) leave around 7am and again around 7.30pm from a lot just south of Sabindo Plaza, off Jl Chen Fook. Land Cruisers also depart from here between 7.30am and 8am for the long journey over rough roads to Keningau (RM70, 11 hours).

Road transport for other destinations departs from the block next to Sabindo Plaza, off Jl Dunlop. There are frequent services to Semporna (RM7, 1½ hours), Lahad Datu (RM15, two hours) and Sandakan (RM28, 5½ hours).

BORDER CROSSING: INTO INDONESIA

Boats leave the customs wharf (next to the fish market) for the Indonesian province of Kalimantan. Tickets can be purchased from a half-dozen booths and shops near the wharf entrance. There are several departures daily for Pulau Nunukan (RM25, 1½ hours), from where you can continue to the mainland Kalimantan town of Tarakan.

MALAYSIA DIRECTORY

ACCOMMODATION

Accommodation in Malaysia costs slightly more than elsewhere in Southeast Asia. And note that you'll pay more for a place to stay in Malaysian Borneo than in Peninsular Malaysia, and that beach accommodation is generally more expensive than mainland digs.

A dorm bed costs anywhere from RM7 to RM20, fan-only rooms with a share bathroom RM17 to RM30, and rooms with air-con and attached bathroom RM35 to RM55. Bathrooms are often a hand-held shower head above a toilet, usually with cold water.

Midrange accommodation usually offers a separate bathroom (sometimes a bath), inner-spring mattresses, TV, phone and air-con; prices range from RM60 to RM100. Places tending towards the upmarket (the ones trying to attract more sophisticated clientele by posting 'No Durian' signs) are often just as idiosyncratic as budget places, so you don't always get what you pay for.

Note that in Malaysia, 'single' often means one bed, as opposed to one person, and 'double' means two beds, or what we would call a twin. If you're after a double bed, just say 'one big bed'.

Check-out times are usually 11am or noon for hostels and guesthouses and from around noon until 3pm for hotels. See p517 for a warning about theft in guesthouses.

Camping

Many of Malaysia's national parks have camping grounds and will permit camping in nondesignated sites once you are into the back country. There are also many lonely stretches of beach, particularly on the peninsula's east coast, which are ideal for camping. Likewise, it is possible to camp on uninhabited bays on many of Malaysia's islands.

Hostels & Guesthouses

Rock-bottom accommodation is found at hostels and guesthouses (called backpackers) that cluster around tourist hot spots. These places often book tours and offer laundry services and transport. Staying at a backpackers is the best way to meet and exchange tips with fellow travellers.

In cities, most backpackers are on the top floors of multistorey buildings where lifts are about as conspicuous as a Bornean rhino. At beaches and smaller towns, accommodation ranges from A-frame chalets with a fan and attached bathroom to rooms in a private house.

Hotels

Chinese-run hotels are the cheapest, offering spartan rooms with a bed, chair, table, wardrobe and sink. The showers and toilets (sometimes Asian squat-style) may be down the corridor but are usually clean. Ultrabudget options will only have a *mandi* (dip shower, ie bucket and water).

Budget hotels can sometimes be terribly noisy as they're often on main streets and the walls rarely reach the ceiling – the top is simply meshed or barred in, which is great for ventilation but terrible for privacy.

In Malaysia there's a 5% government tax (+; plus) that applies to hotel rooms. Additionally, there's a 10% service charge (++; plus plus) in more-expensive places. Cheap Malaysian hotels generally quote a net price inclusive of the government tax, but double-check the total price before checking in.

Longhouses

Longhouses are the traditional dwellings of the indigenous peoples of Borneo. These communal dwellings are raised above the ground and may contain up to 100 individual family 'apartments' under one long roof. The most important area of a longhouse is the common veranda, which serves as a social area and sometimes as sleeping space.

Travellers used to talk about there being two types of longhouse: 'tourist longhouses' and 'authentic longhouses'. However, the distinction has become more and more blurred over the years – more tours to more longhouses are now offered, and longhouse communities are becoming increasingly modernised. The fact is that a tour can still be a good way of experiencing longhouse life and meeting the residents. If you're going to go it alone, it's essential that you're familiar with the etiquette involved; for more on this, see p491.

ACTIVITIES

Caving

Malaysia's limestone hills are riddled with caves. Some are easily accessible and can be visited without any special equipment or preparation, while others are strictly for experienced spelunkers. There are caves on the peninsula and dotted around Malaysian Borneo, including one of the world's premier caving destinations: Gunung Mulu (p498).

Climbing

Sabah's Mt Kinabalu (p508) is an obvious choice for those interested in mountain climbing, but it isn't the only Malaysian mountain worth climbing. Sarawak's Gunung Mulu (p498) is a challenging four-day climb and, on the peninsula, there are overnight climbs in Taman Negara National Park (p480).

Cycling

Malaysia is one of the best places in Southeast Asia for bike touring. Perhaps the most popular route heads up the east coast of Peninsular Malaysia via relatively quiet roads, but some may prefer the hillier regions of the peninsula's interior or Malaysian Borneo.

Diving & Snorkelling

Malaysia has many beautiful dive sites, decorated with shipwrecks, intricate coral formations and gloriously colourful marine life. It's also one of the cheapest places in the world to learn how to dive, with a four-day open-water course costing around RM800. Including equipment hire, snorkelling costs from RM160 and three dives cost from RM250. Prime spots include Pulau Perhentian (p472), Pulau Redang (p471) and Pulau Tioman (p462), but the best site of all is the spectacular limestone abyss off Pulau Sipadan (p513).

Trekking

Despite intense logging, Malaysia is still home to some of the world's most impressive stands of virgin tropical jungle. Almost all of Malaysia's national parks offer excellent jungle trekking, including Taman Negara (p480) and the Cameron Highlands (p442) on the peninsula, and Gunung Mulu National Park (p498) in Sarawak.

BOOKS

Lonely Planet's *Malaysia, Singapore & Brunei* has all the information you'll need for extended travel to these countries. Lonely Planet also publishes the *Malay Phrasebook,* an introduction to the Malay language.

Although *Lord Jim* is based on the exploits of absconding seaman AP Williams, Joseph Conrad's tale of derring-do on the South China Seas also recalls the real-life story of Raja Brooke of Sarawak. Wallow in tales of life in Malaysia (and Singapore) during colonial times by reading *Malaysian Stories,* penned by short-story master Somerset Maugham.

For glimpses of traditional village life, try to track down the translations of fine Malaysian writers offered in the Oxford University Press paperback series, Oxford in Asia: Modern Authors.

A work of contemporary Malaysian fiction (in English) that's wholeheartedly recommended is KS Maniam's *The Return.* Maniam shines a light on the Indian Malaysian experience through his character's search for a home on returning from being educated abroad. For more modern Malaysian fiction, including plays and poetry, keep an eye out for books published by KL-based **Silverfish Books** (www.silverfishbooks.com).

Budding explorers should read *Stranger in the Forest,* Eric Hansen's account of a remarkable half-year journey across Borneo on foot, and Redmond O'Hanlon's marvellous *Into the Heart of Borneo. Mountains of Malaysia – A Practical Guide and Manual* by John Briggs is essential reading for anyone intending to do a lot of local mountain walking.

BUSINESS HOURS

Government offices are usually open from 8am to 4.15pm weekdays. Most close for lunch from 12.45pm to 2pm, and on Friday the lunch break is from 12.15pm to 2.45pm for Friday prayers at the mosque. Saturday hours are usually 8am to 12.45pm.

Bank hours are normally 10am to 3pm on weekdays and 9.30am to 11.30am on Saturday. Shop hours are variable but are generally 9am to 6pm Monday to Saturday. Major department stores, shopping malls and Chinese emporiums open from around 10am until 9pm or 10pm daily.

In the more Islamic-minded states of Kedah, Perlis, Kelantan and Terengganu, government offices, banks and many shops close on Friday and on Saturday afternoon.

CLIMATE

Malaysia is hot and humid year-round. The temperature rarely drops below 20°C, even at night, and usually climbs to 30°C or higher during the day.

It rains throughout the year. Peninsular Malaysia gets heavier rainfall from September to March, with the east coast bearing the full brunt of the monsoon rains from November to February. Rainfall on the west coast peaks slightly during the May to October monsoon. Malaysian Borneo also gets the northeast and southwest monsoons, but they are less pronounced and rain tends to be variable.

Cold-weather gear is needed for Mt Kinabalu and the hill stations.

See the climate charts (p924).

DANGERS & ANNOYANCES

In general Malaysia is very safe, with physical attacks being uncommon. However, the usual travel precautions apply, such as restraining your urge to go wandering around seedy areas alone late at night. Credit-card fraud is a growing problem so only use your cards at established businesses and guard your credit-card numbers. The snatching of bags by thieves on motorcycles is a recurring crime in KL and Penang's Georgetown, so keep bags away from the roadside in these areas. In seedy areas like Ipoh and KL's Golden Triangle, male travellers may be harassed to buy pirated porn DVDs, drugs or the services of prostitutes.

A disturbingly high incidence of theft occurs in guesthouse dorms. Sometimes this involves an outsider sneaking in and other times it involves fellow travellers. Don't leave valuables or important documents unattended. Also consider packing a small sturdy padlock for when you stay at places like cheap beach chalets.

See p522 for issues specific to women travellers.

Rabies is an ever-present problem in Malaysia – treat any animal bite very seriously. Leeches can be a nuisance after heavy rain on jungle walks; see p479 for tips on discouraging them.

DISABLED TRAVELLERS

For the mobility impaired, Malaysia can be a nightmare. In most cities and towns there are often no footpaths, kerbs are very high, construction sites are everywhere and pedestrian crossings are few and far between. Budget hotels almost never have lifts. On the up side, KL's modern urban railway lines are at least reasonably wheelchair-accessible.

Both Malaysia Airlines and Keretapi Tanah Melayu (KTM, the national railway service) offer 50% discounts on travel for disabled travellers.

EMBASSIES & CONSULATES
Embassies & Consulates in Malaysia

For locations of these and other embassies, see individual city maps. Embassies are in KL unless otherwise indicated. Most embassies are located east of the city, along Jl Ampang.

Australia Kuala Lumpur (Map pp426-7; ☎ 03-2146 5555; 6 Jl Yap Kwan Seng); Kota Kinabalu (Map p503; ☎ 088-267151; 10th fl, Suite 10.1, Wisma Great Eastern, 65 Jl Haji Saman)

Brunei (☎ 03-2161 2800; 19-01 Tingkat 19, Menara Tan & Tan, Jl Tun Razak)

Canada (☎ 03-2718 3333; 7th fl, Plaza OSK, 172 Jl Ampang)

France (☎ 03-2162 0671; Pesuruhjaya Tinggi Perancis, Jl Ampang)

Germany (☎ 03-2175 1666; Jl Tun Razak)

Indonesia Kuala Lumpur (☎ 03-2142 1151; 233 Jl Tun Razak); Georgetown (☎ 227 4686; 467 Jl Burma); Kuching (☎ 082-241734; 111 Jl Tun Abang Haji Openg); Kota Kinabalu (☎ 088-219110; Jl Kemajuan); Tawau (☎ 089-772052; Jl Apas)

Ireland (☎ 03-2161 2963; 5th fl, The Ampwalk, 218 Jl Ampang)

Japan (☎ 03-2142 7044; 11 Persiaran Stonor)

Netherlands (☎ 03-2161 0148; 7th fl, The Ampwalk, 218 Jl Ampang)

New Zealand (Map p431; ☎ 03-2078 2533; 21st fl, Menara IMC, 8 Jl Sultan Ismail)

Philippines (☎ 03-2148 9989; Jl Changkat Kia Peng)

Singapore (☎ 03-2161 6277; 209 Jl Tun Razak)

Thailand Kuala Lumpur (☎ 03-2148 8222; Jl Ampang); Kota Bharu (☎ 744 0867; Jl Pengkalan Chepa); Georgetown (☎ 226 8029; 1 Jl Tunku Abdul Rahman)

UK (☎ 03-2148 2122; 185 Jl Ampang)

USA (☎ 03-2168 5000; 376 Jl Tun Razak)

Malaysian Embassies & Consulates Abroad

For a full list of Malaysian embassies and consulates abroad, check out www.tourism.gov.my.

Australia (☎ 02-6273 1543; mwcnbera@aucom.com.au; 7 Perth Ave, Yarralumla, ACT 2600)

Brunei (☎ 238 1095; mwbrunei@brunet.bn; 61 Simpang 336, Jl Kebangsaan, Bandar Seri Begawan BS 4115)

Canada (☎ 613-241 5182; mwottawa@istar.ca; 60 Boteler St, Ottawa, Ontario K1N 8Y7)

France (☎ 01 45 53 11 85; mwparis@wanadoo.fr; 2, bis rue Benouville, 75116 Paris)

Germany (☎ 030-885 7490; mwberlin@compuserve.com; Klingelhofer Strasse 6, 10785 Berlin)

Indonesia (☎ 21-522 4947; mwjakarta@indosat.net.id; 1-3 Jl HR Rasuna Said, Jakarta 12950)

Japan (☎ 03-3476 3840; mwtokyo@malaysia.or.jp; 20-16, Nanpeidai-cho, Shibuya-ku, Tokyo 150 0036)

Netherlands (☎ 070-350 6506; mwthehague@euro net.nl; Rustenburgweg 2, 2517 KE, The Hague)

New Zealand (☎ 04-385 2439; mwwelton@xtra.co.nz; 10 Washington Ave, Brooklyn, PO Box 9422, Wellington)

Singapore (☎ 6235 0111; 30 Hill St 02-01)

Thailand (☎ 02-679 2190; mwbangkok@samart.co.th; 35 Sth Sathorn Rd, Tungmahamek Sathorn, Bangkok 10120)

UK (☎ 020-7235 8033; mwlondon@btInternet.com; 45-46 Belgrave Sq, London SW1X 8QT)

USA (☎ 202-572 9700; malwash@kln.gov.my; 3516 International Court NW, Washington, DC 20008)

FESTIVALS & EVENTS

There are many cultures and religions co-existing in Malaysia, which means there are many occasions for celebration throughout the year.

Some of the major events:

Thaipusam (January/February) One of the most dramatic Hindu festivals, in which devotees honour Lord Subramaniam with acts of amazing physical resilience. Self-mutilating worshippers make the procession to the Batu Caves outside KL.

Gawai Dayak (late May/early June) Festival of the Dayaks in Sarawak, marking the end of the rice season. War dances, cock fights and blowpipe events all take place.

Dragon Boat Festival (June to August) Celebrated in Penang.

Moon Cake Festival (September) Chinese festival celebrating the overthrow of Mongol warlords in ancient China with the eating of moon cakes and the lighting of colourful paper lanterns.

Festival of the Nine Emperor Gods (October) Involves nine days of Chinese operas, processions and other events honouring the nine emperor gods.

Fire-walking Ceremonies (October/November) Held in KL and Penang

Ramadan (October/November) This major annual Muslim event is connected with the 30 days during which Muslims cannot eat, drink, smoke or have sex from sunrise to sunset.

Deepavali (November) The Festival of Lights, in which tiny oil lamps are lit outside Hindu homes, celebrates Rama's victory over the demon King Ravana.

FOOD & DRINK
Food

Mealtime in Malaysia is a highly social event and the food strongly reflects the country's Malay, Chinese and Indian influences. You can feast at hawker stalls for RM1 to RM3. A meal in a restaurant costs around RM4 to RM12.

There are less culinary choices outside the cities, where staple meals of *mee goreng* (fried noodles) and *nasi goreng* (fried rice) predominate. Vegetarian dishes are usually available at both Malay and Indian cafés, but are hardly sighted at *kedai kopi*. You can also find an excellent selection of fruits and vegetables at markets.

Roti canai (flaky flat bread dipped in a small amount of dhal and potato curry) is probably the cheapest meal (from 80 sen) but don't let price completely limit your diet. Try a bit of everything, from delicious won ton soup and seafood laksa to the freshly caught and cooked wild cat or mouse deer you may be offered at a longhouse. Speaking of sweets, halfway between a drink and a dessert is *ais kacang*, an old-fashioned snow-cone, but the shaved ice is topped with syrups and condensed milk, and it's all piled on top of a foundation of beans and jellies (sometimes corn kernels). It sounds and looks gross but tastes terrific.

Drink

Tap water is safe to drink in many cities but check with locals if you're unsure.

With the aid of a blender and crushed ice, delicious concoctions like watermelon juice are whipped up in seconds. Lurid soybean drinks are sold at street stalls and soybean milk is also available in soft-drink bottles. Medicinal teas are a big hit with the health-minded Chinese.

Alcohol isn't popular with the Muslim population and incurs incredibly high taxes. A mug of beer at a *kedai kopi* will cost around RM6, and around RM12 to RM15 at bars and clubs. Anchor and Tiger beers are popular, as are locally brewed Carlsberg and Guinness. Indigenous people have a soft spot for *tuak* (rice wine), which tends to revolt first-timers but is apparently (so we're told) an acquired taste. Another rural favourite is the dark-coloured spirit *arak*, which is smooth and potent.

GAY & LESBIAN TRAVELLERS

Conservative political parties and religious groups make a regular habit of denouncing gays and lesbians in Malaysia, a country where homosexuality is punishable by imprisonment and caning. Fortunately, these groups remain on the fringe and outright persecution of gays and lesbians is rare. Nonetheless, while in Malaysia, gay and lesbian travellers (particularly the former) should avoid behaviour that attracts unwanted attention. See right for some useful websites.

HOLIDAYS

Although some public holidays have a fixed annual date, Hindus, Muslims and Chinese follow a lunar calendar, which means the dates for many events vary each year. Chinese New Year is the year's most important celebration for the Chinese community and is marked with dragon dances and street parades. Families have an open house, unmarried relatives (especially children) receive *ang pow* (money in red packets), businesses traditionally clear their debts and everybody wishes you a 'kong hee fatt choy' (a happy and prosperous new year).

Hari Raya Puasa marks the end of the month-long fast of Ramadan with three days of joyful celebration. This is the major holiday of the Muslim calendar.

During Hari Raya Puasa and Chinese New Year, accommodation may be difficult to obtain, many businesses may be closed and transport can be fully booked.

National holidays:

New Year's Day 1 January
Chinese New Year January/February
Hari Raya Haji March/April
Awal Muharam April/May
Wesak Day April/May
Labour Day 1 May
Agong's (King's) Birthday 1st Saturday in June

Birth of the Prophet June/July
National Day 31 August
Hari Raya Puasa November
Deepavali November
Christmas Day 25 December

INTERNET ACCESS

Internet access is widespread and available at numerous Net cafés, backpackers and shopping malls, generally on fast broadband connections. In cities, rates range from RM2 to RM6 per hour; on islands and in remote areas, rates skyrocket (and speed plummets) to around RM7 to RM10 per hour.

INTERNET RESOURCES

http://gayguide.net/Asia/Malaysia Comprehensive resource that highlights gay and lesbian hot spots worldwide, with excellent links.

www.lonelyplanet.com Succinct summaries on travelling to Southeast Asia, and the Thorn Tree bulletin board; including the Travel Links site for other useful travel resources.

www.malaysiakini.com Practically Malaysia's only independent daily news source, with uncensored features and commentaries.

www.tourism.gov.my The official government site for tourist information, with events calendars, regional links, background information and listings of domestic and international tourist offices.

www.utopia-asia.com/tipsmala.htm, www .utopia-asia.com/wommala.htm Personal accounts from gays and lesbians living in Malaysia.

LEGAL MATTERS

In any of your dealings with the local police forces, it pays to be deferential. Minor misdemeanours may be overlooked, but don't count on it and don't offer anyone a bribe.

Drug trafficking in Malaysia carries a mandatory death penalty. Even possession of tiny amounts of drugs for personal use can bring about a lengthy jail sentence and a beating with the *rotan* (cane).

LEGAL AGE

In Malaysia:

- The legal age for voting is 21.
- You can begin driving at 18.
- Heterosexual sex is legal at 16.
- To legally buy alcohol you must be 21.

MAPS

The best map for Peninsular Malaysia is the 1:650,000 *West Malaysia* map produced by Nelles Verlag. Nelles also produces *Malaysia,* which shows both Peninsular Malaysia and Malaysian Borneo. Periplus produces an excellent series of Malaysia city and state maps, including *Johor, Kuala Lumpur, Melaka, Penang, Sabah* and *Sarawak.*

Tourism Malaysia's *The Map of Malaysia* has useful distance charts and inset maps of many major cities.

MEDIA

Malaysia has newspapers in English, Malay, Chinese and Tamil. The *New Straits Times* is the main English-language publication, while *Borneo Post* focuses more on issues relevant to Sabah and Sarawak. Foreign magazines are widely available.

There's a variety of radio stations in Malaysia, broadcasting in Bahasa Malaysia, English and various Chinese and Indian languages and dialects. The number of English stations is highest around KL, while radio wave pickings are scarce in Malaysian Borneo.

Malaysia has two government TV channels (RTM 1 and 2) and two commercial stations. Programmes range from local productions in various languages to Western imports.

The government tightly controls the main media outlets, often pursuing critics through the courts. The main newspapers tend to parrot the official line and the less said about news on Malaysian TV channels, the better.

MONEY

For information on costs and money, see Fast Facts (p415).

The Malaysian ringgit (RM) consists of 100 sen. Coins in use are one, five, 10, 20 and 50 sen, and RM1; notes come in RM1, RM2, RM5, RM10, RM50 and RM100. Locals sometimes refer to the ringgit as a 'dollar'.

In September 1998 Malaysia fixed the ringgit at RM3.80 to US$1. In 2005 the end of the currency peg was announced, but the national bank intervenes to maintain the stability of the ringgit. Ultimately the ringgit is still pegged, but on a 'moving' basis. It's currently RM3.77 to US$1 (the rate for other currencies remains variable).

Bargaining & Tipping

Bargaining is not usually required for everyday goods in Malaysia, but feel free to bargain when purchasing souvenirs, antiques and other tourist items, even when the prices are displayed. Transport prices are generally fixed, but negotiation is required for trishaws and taxis around town or for charter.

Tipping is not common in Malaysia.

Exchanging Money

The US dollar is the most convenient currency to take to Malaysia, but you'll have no problems changing other major currencies either.

Banks are efficient and there are plenty of moneychangers in main centres. Credit cards are widely accepted and many ATMs accept international key cards, Visa and MasterCard. Some banks are also connected to networks such as Cirrus, Maestro and Plus.

Exchange rates are as follows:

Country	Unit	Ringgit (RM)
Australia	A$1	2.75
Brunei	B$1	2.21
Canada	C$1	3.15
euro zone	€1	4.41
Indonesia	10,000Rp	3.77
Japan	¥100	3.16
New Zealand	NZ$1	2.57
Philippines	P100	6.90
Singapore	S$1	2.21
Thailand	100B	9.15
UK	£1	6.54
USA	US$1	3.77

POST

There are poste restante services at all major post offices, which are open from 8am to 5pm daily except Sunday and public holidays (closed on Friday and public holidays in Kedah, Kelantan and Terengganu districts).

Aerograms and postcards cost 50 sen to send to any destination. Letters weighing 10g or less cost 55 sen to Asia, Australia and New Zealand, 90 sen to the UK and Europe, and RM1.10 to North America.

You can send parcels from any major post office, although the rates are fairly high (from RM20 to RM35 for a 1kg parcel, depending on the destination).

RESPONSIBLE TRAVEL

Numbers of the leatherback turtle, which nests on Peninsular Malaysia's east coast, have declined by an incredible 98% since the 1950s, and sightings of these turtles at Rantau Abang have dropped from almost one thousand back in the 1984 season to just three in 2002. While the collection and sale of leatherback eggs have been banned since 1988, in coastal markets it's common to see hundreds of eggs of the smaller green, hawksbill and olive ridley turtles, all of which have suffered a marked decline in their populations. Don't buy turtle eggs, turtle meat or anything made from turtle shell. Also make sure your litter doesn't end up on beaches or in oceans.

Try to buy local handicrafts and souvenirs in preference to mass-produced items, so that the money goes to local communities where possible.

STUDYING

Several of Malaysia's cultural centres offer classes in traditional Malaysian handicrafts. Kota Bharu and Cherating are the best places to get a hands-on feel for batik, puppet making and kite making. Kuala Lumpur is the place to study Bahasa Malaysia, and cooking courses are occasionally offered in Penang. Ask at local tourist offices to see what's on offer when you're in town.

Actors Studio Academy (Map p428; ☎ 03-2697 2797; www.theactorsstudio.com.my; Lot 19, Plaza Putra) This academy in the underground Plaza Putra at Merdeka Square in KL has workshops on everything from modern choreography and classical Indian dance to Chinese orchestral music.

YMCA (Map pp426-7; ☎ 03-2274 1439; 95 Jl Padang Belia) This Brickfield's hostel and community centre offers a variety of short- and long-term language classes in Bahasa Malaysia, Hindi, Thai, Mandarin, Cantonese and Japanese, as well as courses in martial arts.

TELEPHONE
International, STD & Local Calls

International direct dial (IDD) phone calls and operator-assisted calls can be made from any private phone. The access code for making international calls to most countries is ☎ 00. For information on international calls, dial ☎ 103. For operator-assisted calls, dial ☎ 108. Phone calls to Singapore are STD (long-distance) rather than international.

To make an IDD call from a pay phone, look for a Telekom pay phone marked 'international' (with which you can use coins or Telekom phone cards; dial the international access code and then the number). However, these phones are often in disrepair and frustratingly difficult to find.

Alternatively, you can buy the phonecards of other companies (such as Uniphone and Cityphone) and look for the corresponding pay phone. But there's no guarantee you'll find phones belonging to the same company in the next town you visit and your card may then be useless. The best option is to make a pay-per-minute call from a shop with an IDD-STD phone or at the Telekom office.

The card phones mentioned above all allow STD calls. Local calls cost 10 sen for three minutes.

Mobile Phones

If you have arranged 'global roaming' facilities with your home provider, your GSM digital phone will automatically tune into one of the region's digital networks. If not, and you are carrying your phone with you, the simplest way to go mobile is to buy a pre-paid SIM card on arrival in the country.

TOILETS

Western-style toilets are slowly replacing the Asian squat-style toilet in many towns, hence the doors of some newly installed sit-down toilets carry a poster with a diagram instructing locals not to squat on top of the toilet seat. A hose to be used as a bidet is in most toilets; cheaper places have a bucket of water and a tap. Toilet paper (and soap) are rarely provided.

Public toilets in shopping malls and at transport depots are usually staffed by attendants and cost 10 sen to 20 sen to use; an extra 10 sen often gets you a dozen sheets of toilet paper.

TOURIST INFORMATION

Domestic tourist offices are usually helpful and can often (but not always) provide specific information on accommodation, attractions and transport. Within Malaysia there are also various state tourist-promotion organisations, which often have more information about specific areas.

Tourism Malaysia (Map pp426–7; ☎ 03-2615 8188; www.tourism.gov.my; 17th fl, Putra World Trade Centre, 45 Jl Tun Ismail, Kuala Lumpur) has a network of overseas offices, which are useful for pre-departure planning. These include the following:

Australia Sydney (☎ 02-9299 4441; 2nd fl, 171 Clarence St, NSW 2000); Perth (☎ 08-9481 0400; MAS Bldg, 56 William St, WA 6000)

Canada (☎ 604-689 8899; 1590-1111 West Georgia St, Vancouver V6E 4M3)

France (☎ 01 42 97 41 71; 29 Rue des Pyramides, 75001 Paris)

Germany (☎ 069-28 37 82; Rossmarkt 11, 60311 Frankfurt-am-Main)

Japan Tokyo (☎ 03-3501 8691; 5F Chiyoda Biru, 1-6-4 Yurakucho, Chiyoda-ku, Tokyo 100); Osaka (☎ 06-6444 1220; 10th fl, Cotton Nissay Biru, 1-8-2 Utsubo-Honmachi, Nishi-ku, Osaka 500-0004)

Singapore (☎ 02-6532 6321; 01-01 B/C/D, 80 Robinson Rd, Singapore 068898)

Thailand (☎ 02-631 1994; Unit 1001 Liberty Sq, 287 Silom Rd, Bangkok 10500)

UK (☎ 020-7930 7932; 57 Trafalgar Sq, London WC2N 5DU)

USA Los Angeles (☎ 213-689 9702; 818 West 7th St, Suite 804, Los Angeles, CA 90017); New York (☎ 212-754 1113; 120 East 56th St, Suite 804, New York, NY 10022)

TOURS

Reliable tours of Peninsular Malaysia and Malaysian Borneo are run regularly by international operators:

Exodus (www.exodus.co.uk)
Explore Worldwide (www.explore.co.uk)
Intrepid Travel (www.intrepidtravel.com.au)
Peregrine Adventures (www.peregrine.net.au)

VISAS

Visitors must have a passport valid for at least six months beyond the date of entry into Malaysia. Nationals of most countries are given a 30- to 90-day visa on arrival.

Commonwealth citizens (except those from India, Bangladesh, Sri Lanka and Pakistan) and citizens of Austria, Belgium, the Czech Republic, Denmark, Finland, France, Germany, Hungary, Iceland, Ireland, Italy, Japan, Luxembourg, the Netherlands, Norway, Slovak Republic, South Africa, South Korea, Sweden, the USA and most Arab countries should not require a visa for a visit of less than three months.

Citizens of many South American and African countries do not require a visa for a

visit not exceeding one month. Most other nationalities are given a shorter stay-period or require a visa. Citizens of Israel cannot enter Malaysia.

Sabah and Sarawak are semi-autonomous and treated in some ways like separate countries. Your passport will be checked on arrival in each state and a new stay-permit issued, usually valid for 30 days. Travelling directly from either Sabah or Sarawak back to Peninsular Malaysia, however, there are no formalities and you do not start a new entry period, so your 30-day permit from Sabah or Sarawak remains valid. You can then extend your initial 30-day permit, though it can be difficult to get an extension in Sarawak.

For more information (albeit scant), see the website of the **Malaysian Ministry of Foreign Affairs** (www.kln.gov.my). For listings of embassies and consulates in Malaysia, and of Malaysian embassies and consulates abroad, see p517.

VOLUNTEERING

For volunteering opportunities, check out online directories like **Volunteer Abroad** (www.volunteerabroad.com), which detail conservation and community programmes, or charity organisations like **Raleigh International** (www.raleigh.org.uk/volunteer/nonuk.html).

WOMEN TRAVELLERS

Foreign women travelling in Malaysia can expect some attention outside the bigger centres, though a lot of it will just involve stares from locals unfamiliar with (or curious about) Westerners. Sometimes there will be crass Bahasa banter from men to contend with, but the norm appears to be frank but not aggressive scrutinisation. It helps if you dress conservatively by wearing long pants or skirts and loose tops. Western women are not expected to cover their heads with scarves (outside of mosques that is).

Peninsula Malaysia's west coast is fairly easygoing, but on the peninsula's east coast and in Malaysian Borneo women may find it more comfortable to cover their shoulders and midriffs. It isn't appropriate to sunbathe topless on beaches.

Tampons and pads are widely available, especially in big cities, and over-the-counter medications are also fairly easy to find.

Myanmar

HIGHLIGHTS

- **Bagan** Thousands of ancient temples with hidden stairways and peeling murals on a 42-sq-km plain crossed by bike or horse cart (p565)
- **Inle Lake** A pristine lake amid mountains, home to floating villages, monasteries and gardens (p551)
- **Kalaw** Myanmar's trekking HQ, and something of a backpacker scene, with longhouse overnighters looming in the hills (p550)
- **Mandalay's neighbours** The biggest lure of Burma's last capital's biggest lure: the four ancient cities nearby, including Amarapura and its famed teak bridge (p563)
- **Off the beaten track** The allure of 'real life' in a river town such as Katha (p572) or Pakokku (p572)

MYANMAR

FAST FACTS

- **ATMs** none
- **Budget** US$12-20 a day
- **Capital** Yangon
- **Costs** guesthouse US$3-8, 4hr bus ride US$1.50-2.50, beer US$1
- **Country code** ☎ 95
- **Famous for** jade, opium, Aung San Suu Kyi
- **Languages** Burmese, English
- **Money** US$1 = about K950 (kyat) = 1FEC
- **Phrases** *min găla ba* (hello), *thwa-ba-oun-meh* (goodbye), *chè zù bèh* (thanks)
- **Population** about 52 million
- **Seasons** cool Nov-Feb, hot Mar-May, wet Jun-Oct
- **Visas** around US$20 for 28 days, issued by Myanmar embassies and consulates

abroad. These can be extended in Yangon (only) for a cost of US$36 (see p586).

TRAVEL HINTS

Many visitors fill a 28-day visa going between the 'big four' – Yangon, Inle Lake, Mandalay and Bagan. Don't try to cram too much in – travel takes lots of time here. If you're flying out, you can easily overstay your visa five or so days, at a penalty of $US3 per day (see p587).

OVERLAND ROUTES

You can presently enter Myanmar from Ruili in China, Mae Sai in Thailand and Ranong in Thailand. See p531 for more.

MYANMAR

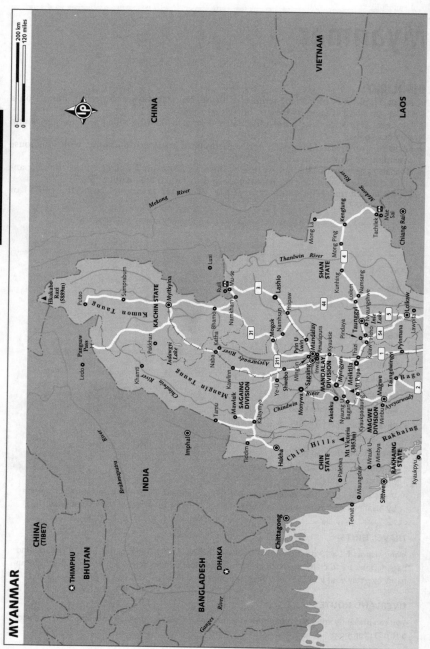

MYANMAR

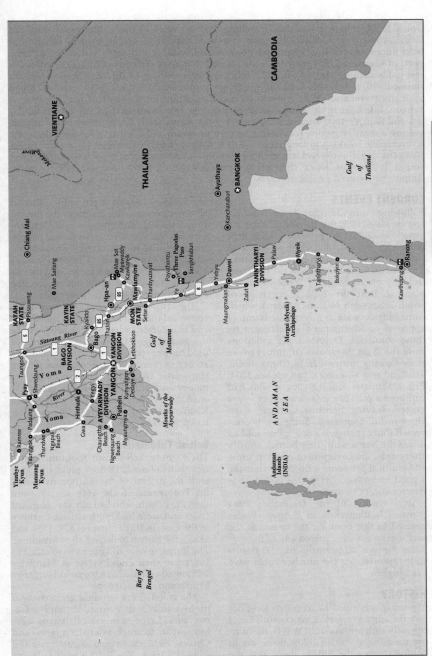

Going to Myanmar is like time-travelling back 50 years or more. Men wear skirt-like *longyi*, women and kids blot *thanaka* (powdered bark make-up) on their faces, spat-out betel juice congeals into blood-like pools on sidewalks – and that's just at Yangon airport. In Myanmar, holy men are more revered than rock stars (or government officials), and golden stupas marking Buddha relics dot every hilltop in this kite-shaped country rimmed with mountains. Isolated by a long-running military junta, Myanmar is skipped by many travellers. Those who do go usually venture on a circuit of the 'big four' – Yangon, Inle Lake in the cool Shan mountains, the last Burmese royal capital of Mandalay, and Bagan's 4000 ancient temples facing the Ayeyarwady River. Other treats include visiting a massive golden rock teetering on a mountain edge, drifting for days along the Ayeyarwady, trekking to longhouses outside Kalaw, and DIY surprises in random towns along the way. But the real trip-making encounters come with the people, who often greet you as 'brother' or 'sister' right off and rush to return a K500 note you drop – they're simply the sweetest people on earth.

CURRENT EVENTS

Following Aung San Suu Kyi's third arrest in May 2003, the US and Europe led sanctions against the military government (which prompted international banks to close up and run – there are none now). Tony Blair signed the UK onto the tourism boycott in February 2005. Myanmar plans to host the 2006 Association of South-East Asian Nations (Asean), which some outsiders see as a symbolic stamp of approval of Myanamar's government by those countries. Despite trade sanctions from the West, Myanmar continues to see trade flowing in freely from China, India, Thailand and Singapore. In October 2004, Prime Minister Khin Nyunt – who had authored a plan towards democracy – was sacked, leaving hardline General Than Shwe in full command. Some locals celebrated ('*any* change is good'); one told us it was the 'same wine, new bottle'. Shortly afterwards, the government released some 400 political prisoners – no doubt to make a good impression before the Asean conference comes to town.

Real reports of the December 2004 tsunami bottlenecked in Yangon. Places covered in this book on the coast felt the earthquake but were spared any of the tsunami damage. Apparently over 50 deaths were reported, but the number could have been higher.

HISTORY

Myanmar was ruled by iron fists long before the current regime took control. From the early 19th century until WWII, the hungry machine of British colonialism was in control. Before the British, there were the monarchs, who came to power by killing off all other persons with claims to the throne. If we trace the conflicts back to the 9th century, we find the Himalayan Bamar people, who comprise two-thirds of the total population, at war with the Tibetan Plateau's Mon. The fight went on for so long that by the time the Bamar came out on top, the two cultures had effectively merged.

The 11th-century Bamar king Anawrahta converted the land to Theravada Buddhism, and inaugurated what many consider to be the golden age of Myanmar's history. He used his war spoils to build the first temples at Bagan. Succeeding generations put up stupa after stupa, but the vast amount of money and effort poured into them weakened the region. The Mongol raider Kublai Khan ransacked Bagan in 1287 and hastened Myanmar's decline.

British Colonialism

There's not much known about the centuries that followed. History picks up again with the arrival of the Europeans – first the Portuguese, in the 16th century, and then the British, who had already colonised India and were looking for more territory in the East. In three moves (1824, 1852 and 1885), the British took over all of Myanmar. The Burmese king and queen were exiled to India and their grand palace at Mandalay was looted and used as a barracks to quarter British and Indian troops.

The colonial era wrought great changes in Myanmar's demographics and infrastructure. Large numbers of Indians were brought in to work as civil servants, and Chinese were encouraged to immigrate and stimulate trade. The British built railroads and ports, and many British companies became wealthy trading in teak and rice. The Burmese chafed under colonialism. A nationalist movement grew, and there were demonstrations, often led, in true Burmese fashion, by Buddhist monks. Two famous nationalist monks, U Ottama and U Wizaya, died in a British prison and are revered to this day.

WWII & Early Independence

During WWII, the Japanese, linked with the Burmese Independence Army (BIA), drove the British out of Myanmar and declared it an independent country. But the Japanese were able to maintain Burmese political support for only a short time before their harsh and arrogant conduct alienated the Burmese people. Towards

SHOULD YOU GO?

Lonely Planet believes anyone thinking of going to Myanmar must ask themself this complicated question first.

Myanmar is ruled by an oppressive military regime. Some refugee and human-rights groups urge foreigners not to visit Myanmar, believing that tourism legitimises the government and contributes to its coffers. Others reversed their stance in recent years. National League for Democracy (NLD) general secretary Aung San Suu Kyi (see p528), urged outsiders to boycott Myanmar during the government's 'Visit Myanmar Year 1996' campaign, in which forced labour of tens of thousands (maybe more) were used to rebuild infrastructure and some sites such as Mandalay Palace. Suu Kyi asked visitors to 'visit us later', saying that visiting at the time was 'tantamount to condoning the regime'.

It's worth pointing out that much of the criticism is directed toward package tourists, who spend the most money and stay in expensive joint-venture hotels that are potentially in cahoots with the government. Western package tourists and backpackers brought in US$25 million in 2003, possibly 12% of which went to the government. (This compares with US$655 million in natural-gas exports that year.) Obviously the less you spend, the less that 12% figure will be. A pro-NLD, pro-tourism Yangon resident told us, 'Don't come in with your camera and only take pictures. We don't need that kind of tourist. Talk to those who want to talk. Let them know of the conditions of your life.'

If You Go

Here are a few ways to minimise the money that goes to the government:

■ Avoid government-run hotels (often named for the city, eg Mrauk U Hotel) and stay in cheap family-run guesthouses (see p579 for more).

■ Try to avoid government-run services: Myanmar Travel & Tours (MTT) is the government-operated travel agency, Myanma Airways is the government airline, nearly all buses are independent, while IWT ferries are government-controlled.

■ Spread your money – don't fill all your needs (food, beer, guides, taxi, toilet paper) at one source (eg a guesthouse).

■ Buy handicrafts directly from artisans.

■ Try to get off the beaten track a bit, including towns not covered in this book.

■ Read about Myanmar – see p580 for some book suggestions. It's important to know a bit about Ne Win's coup, the events of 1988 and Aung San Suu Kyi before coming.

About this Chapter

We believe travellers to Myanmar should support private tourist facilities wherever possible. We've not reviewed any restaurants, hotels or shops known to be government-run. We flag any government-run services (such as ferries or MTT travel agents).

Read Lonely Planet's expanded 'Should You Go?' coverage in the Myanmar guidebook or get the free download at www.lonelyplanet.com/worldguide/destinations/asia/myanmar.

the end of the war, the Burmese switched sides and fought with the Allies to drive out the Japanese.

Bogyoke Aung San emerged from the fog of war as the country's natural leader. An early activist for nationalism, then defence minister in the Burma National Army, Aung San was the man to hold the country together through the transition to independence. When elections were held in 1947, Aung San's party won an overwhelming majority. But before he could take office, he was assassinated by a rival, along with most of his cabinet. Independence came in 1948, but with Aung San's protégé U Nu at the helm. Ethnic conflicts raged, and chaos ensued.

Ne Win's Coup

In 1962 General Ne Win led a left-wing army takeover and set the country on the 'Burmese Way to Socialism'. He then nationalised everything, including retail shops, and quickly crippled the country's economy. By 1987 it had reached a virtual standstill, and the long-suffering Burmese people decided they'd had enough of their incompetent government. In early 1988, they packed the streets and there were massive confrontations between pro-democracy demonstrators and the military that resulted in an estimated 3000 deaths over a six-week period. Once again, monks were at the helm. They turned their alms bowls upside down (the Buddhist symbol of condemnation) and insisted that Ne Win had to go. He finally did, in July 1988, but he retained a vestige of his old dictatorial power from behind the scenes.

The 1989 Election

The shaken government quickly formed the ill-sounding Slorc (State Law and Order Restoration Council), declared martial law and promised to hold democratic elections in May of 1989. The opposition, led by

Bogyoke Aung San's charismatic daughter, Aung San Suu Kyi, organised an opposition party, the NLD. Around the same time, Slorc changed the country's official name from the Union of Burma to the Union of Myanmar, claiming 'Burma' was a vestige of European colonialism.

While the Burmese population rallied around the NLD, the Slorc grew increasingly nervous. They placed Aung San Suu Kyi under house arrest and postponed the election. In spite of this and other dirty tactics, the NLD won over 85% of the vote. Slorc, the sore losers, refused to allow the NLD to assume their parliamentary seats and arrested most of the party leadership. Most were later released.

Aung San Suu Kyi was awarded the Nobel Peace Prize in 1991 and was finally released from house arrest in July 1995. She was arrested again in 2000 and held in her home until the UN brokered her unconditional release in May 2002. She was re-arrested in May 2003 and remains under house arrest. She continually refuses offers of freedom in exchange for exile from the country and, despite an ongoing debate in the pro-democracy movement over future strategy, her stature throughout Myanmar is as great as ever.

The difficulties facing Myanmar today are manifold. The economy is a shambles. HIV/AIDS is rampant. The ceasefires with most of the rebellious ethnic groups are tenuous. Cynics say that with such troubles, only rulers as oppressive as the current regime are capable of holding the country together. Others hope for change from within. Leaders, concerned about their image abroad and the economic sanctions that have hobbled them, are making signs of moving towards more internationally acceptable governance. The feared old hardliner, Ne Win, finally died in December 2002 aged 91.

THE CULTURE
The National Psyche

Religion, language and customs differ from region to region. For the majority, Buddhism is the guiding principle and life centres on the monastery. A typical Burmese values meditation, gives alms freely and sees his or her lot as the consequence of sin or merit in a past life. The social ideal for most

---

MUST READ

Living Silence: Burma under Military Rule, by Christina Fink (2001), is a very readable account of Myanmar's military years, and offers humanising glimpses into both sides of the conflict.

Burmese citizens is a standard of behaviour commonly termed *bamahsan chin* (or 'Burmese-ness'). The hallmarks of *bamahsan chin* include showing respect for elders, acquaintance with Buddhist scriptures and discretion in behaviour towards the opposite sex. Most importantly, *bamahsan chin* values the quiet, subtle and indirect over the loud, obvious and direct. Burmese also love a good laugh, and puns are considered a very high form of humour.

Lifestyle

Most people in Myanmar lack just about every material thing, get abysmal healthcare and have scant chance for advancement, since the government holds the economy in its fist and doesn't play fair. Higher education gets disrupted every time there's a hint of unrest in the country, as the government shuts down the universities. The banks are under government control, so savings can be (and have been) wiped out at the whim of the rulers. Nominally, Burmese people have relative economic freedom, but just about any business opportunity requires bribes or connections. The small wealthy class (made up for the most part of military officers and government officials, or those with close ties to them) has modern conveniences, good medical treatment, fancy, well-fortified homes and speedy cars. (You are in an officers' neighbourhood when all the houses look new and luxurious.) Peaceful political assembly is banned and citizens are forbidden to discuss politics with foreigners – though many relish doing so as long as they're sure potential informers aren't listening.

Population

The population is made up of – by some counts – 135 ethnic groups indigenous to Myanmar, including the Bamar (or Burman, around 68%), Shan (9%), Kayin (or Karen, 7%), Rakhaing (4%), Mon (less than 3%), Kachin (less than 3%), Chin (less than 3%) and Kayah (1%). There are still quite a few Indians and Chinese in Myanmar, but only a sprinkling of other foreigners and immigrants.

RELIGION

About 87% of Myanmar's citizens are Theravada Buddhists. There is also a strong belief in *nat* (guardian spirit beings), and many of

> **MUST SEE**
>
> *Burmese Harp* by Japanese director Kon Ichikawa (1956) is a classic anti-war film told from the perspective of a Japanese soldier disguised as a Buddhist monk.

the hill tribes are Christian. Smaller Hindu and Muslim communities are common throughout the country.

Buddhism

For the average Burmese Buddhist everything revolves around the merit (*kutho*, from the Pali *kusala*, meaning 'wholesome') one is able to accumulate through rituals and good deeds. One of the more typical rituals performed by individuals visiting a stupa is to pour water over the Buddha image at their astrological post (determined by the day of the week they were born) – one glassful for every year of their current age plus one extra to ensure a long life.

Every Burmese male is expected to take up temporary monastic residence twice in his life: once as a *samanera* (novice monk), between the ages of five and 15, and again as a *pongyi* (fully ordained monk), sometime after the age of 20. Almost all men or boys under 20 years of age participate in the

> **DOS & DON'TS**
>
> ■ Don't touch anyone's head, as it's considered the spiritual pinnacle of the body.
>
> ■ Don't point feet at people if you can help it, and avoid stepping over people.
>
> ■ Burmese women don't ride atop pick-ups as it can be insulting to men beneath them.
>
> ■ Hand things – food, gifts, money – with your right hand, tucking your left under your right elbow.
>
> ■ Dress modestly when visiting religious sites – no shorts, tight clothes or sleeveless shirts.
>
> ■ Take off your shoes when entering temple precincts – usually including the long steps up to a hilltop pagoda.

MYANMAR

shinpyu (novitiation ceremony) – for which their family earns great merit.

Though there is little social expectation to do so, a number of women live monastic lives as *dasasila* ('ten-precept' nuns). Burmese nuns shave their heads, wear pink robes and take vows in an ordination procedure similar to that undergone by monks.

Nat Worship

Buddhism in Myanmar has suppressed, but never replaced, the pre-Buddhist practice of *nat* worship. The 37 *nat* figures are often found side by side with Buddhist images. The Burmese *nats* are spirits that can inhabit natural features, trees or even people. They can be mischievous or beneficent.

The *nat* cult is strong. Mt Popa (p571) is an important centre. The Burmese divide their devotions and offerings according to the sphere of influence: Buddha for future lives, and the *nat* – both Hindu and Bamar – for problems in this life. For example, a misdeed might be redressed by offerings made to the *nat* Thagyamin, who once a year records the names of those who perform good deeds in a book made of gold leaves. Those who do evil are recorded in a book made of dog skin.

ARTS

Burmese fine art, at the court level, has not had an easy time since the forced exile of the last king, Thibaw Min. Architecture and

---

BURMA OR MYANMAR?

The government changed most of the country's geographical names after 1988's uprising, in an attempt to purge the country of the vestiges of colonialism, and to avoid exclusive identification with the Bamar ethnic majority. ('Burma' is actually an English corruption of 'Bamar', and never has been the name of the country locally – at least since Marco Polo dropped by in the 13th century!) So Rangoon switched to Yangon, Pagan to Bagan, Irrawaddy River to Ayeyarwady River and so on.

In this book, 'Myanmar' is used in text to describe the country's history and people. 'Burmese' refers to the language, the food and the Bamar people.

---

art were both royal activities which have floundered and faded without royal support. On the other hand, Burmese culture at the street level is vibrant and thriving.

Marionette Theatre

Yok-thei pwe, or Burmese marionette theatre, was the forerunner of Burmese classical dance. Marionette theatre declined following WWII and is now mostly confined to tourist venues in Mandalay and Bagan.

Music

Traditional Burmese music relies heavily on rhythm, and is short on harmony, at least to the Western ear. Younger Burmese listen to heavily Western-influenced sounds – you're likely to hear Burmese-language covers of your favourite oldies. A few Burmese rock musicians, such as Lay Phyu of the band Iron Cross, produce good compositions of their own. **Myanmar Future Generations** (www.mm-fg.net) is an anonymous rap collective that post politically charged songs online.

Pwe

The *pwe* (show) is everyday Burmese theatre. A religious festival, wedding, funeral, celebration, fair, sporting event – almost anything can be a good reason for a *pwe*. Once under way, a *pwe* traditionally goes on all night, which is no strain – if an audience member gets bored at some point during the performance, they simply fall asleep. Ask a trishaw driver if one is on nearby.

Myanmar's truly indigenous dance forms are those that pay homage to the *nat* (guardian spirit beings). In a special *nat pwe*, one or more *nat* are invited to possess the body and mind of a medium; sometimes members of the audience seem to be possessed instead, an event that is greatly feared by most Burmese.

ENVIRONMENT

Myanmar covers an area of 671,000 sq km – that's roughly the size of Texas or France. From the snow-capped Himalaya in the north to the coral-fringed Mergui (Myeik) Archipelago in the south, Myanmar's 2000km length crosses three distinct ecological regions: the Indian subregion, along the Bangladesh and India borders;

the Indochinese subregion in the north, bordering Laos and China; and the Sundaic subregion, bordering peninsular Thailand. Together, these regions produce what is quite likely the richest biodiversity in Southeast Asia.

At the moment, deforestation by the timber industry poses the greatest threat to wildlife habitats. Optimistically, about 7% of the country is protected by national parks and other protected areas. Wildlife laws are seldom enforced, partly due to corruption. While many animals are hunted for food, tigers and rhinos are killed for the lucrative overseas Chinese pharmaceutical market.

TRANSPORT

GETTING THERE & AWAY

Air

All international flights arrive to the crummy Yangon airport (RGN), except flights from Chiang Mai direct to the palatial and sparkling Mandalay airport (MDL). The most common route, by far, is via Bangkok (a good place to pick up cheap tickets to Myanmar). From here a one-way ticket to Yangon is about US$90 or US$100. Flights also connect Yangon with Kolkata, Delhi, Dhaka, Hong Kong, Kuala Lumpur, Kunming and Singapore.

It's important to reconfirm outgoing flights from Myanmar for all airlines other than Thai Airways and SilkAir. You do not need to show onward tickets to enter Myanmar.

The following airlines have regular links to (and offices in) Yangon.

Air China (☎ 01-505024; www.airchina.com, www
.airchina.com.cn/en/index.jsp; airline code CA; B13/23
Narnattaw Rd, Kamayut Township) To/from Kunming.

Air Mandalay (Map p536; ☎ 01-525488; www.airman
dalay.com; airline code 6T; 146 Dhamma Zedi Rd) Connects
Mandalay with Chiang Mai (about 5000B one way).

Biman Bangladesh Airlines (Map p540; ☎ 01-
275882, 240922; www.bimanair.com; airline code BG;
106-108 Pansodan St) To/from Bangkok and Dhaka.

Indian Airlines Limited (Map p540; ☎ 01-253598;
http://indian-airlines.nic.in; airline code IC; 127 Sule Paya
Rd) To/from Bangkok and Kolkata.

Malaysia Airlines (Map p540; ☎ 01-241007; www
.malaysiaairlines.com; airline code MH; 335 Bogyoke Aung
San Rd) To/from Kuala Lumpur.

Myanmar Airways International (MAI; Map p540;
☎ 01-255260; www.maiair.com; airline code 8M; 123
Sule Paya Rd) To/from Bangkok, Delhi, Hong Kong, Kuala
Lumpur and Singapore.

SilkAir (Map p540; ☎ 01-255287; www.silkair.com;
airline code MI; 339 Bogyoke Aung San Rd) To/from
Singapore.

Thai Airways International (THAI; Map p540;
☎ 01-255499; www.thaiair.com; airline code TG; 339
Bogyoke Aung San Rd, 1st fl) To/from Bangkok and
Chiang Mai.

Border Crossings

Most of Myanmar's borders are closed. The following sections outline when and how you can cross into Myanmar by land. You *cannot* reach Myanmar by sea or from Bangladesh, India or Laos.

FROM MAE SAI, THAILAND

You can cross from the northern Thai town of Mae Sai to dreary Tachilek (p554). A US$5 day pass (paid on the spot) allows you travel within 5km; a US$10 14-day pass allows you travel to Kengtung and Mong La. Only if you already possess a 28-day tourist visa will you be able to travel farther into the country by air only (not by land).

FROM RANONG, THAILAND

Travel agents in Ranong can arrange 28-day visas, allowing you to cross into Kawthoung (p549). You can enter for two days with a US$5 'day pass'.

FROM RUILI, CHINA

You can come into Myanmar from China, but you cannot exit to China from Myanmar. To come from China, you must possess a 28-day tourist visa – you can get one at the Myanmar Consulate in Kunming's **Myanmar Consulate** (☎ 0871-371-6609; Camelia Hotel, Bldg No 3; ⏰ 8.30am-noon & 1-4.30pm Mon-Fri) for Y185 to Y285.

To cross from Ruili (20 hours from Kunming), you must book a multiday 'package trip' to go from Mu-Se, Myanmar (at

---

DEPARTURE TAX

Have the US$10 departure tax – in US dollars, not kyat – in hand when leaving the country.

the border), and on to Lashio (northeast of Hsipaw; p555) for about Y1400 – about the same price as a one-way flight to Mandalay from Kunming.

GETTING AROUND

Travel here takes time, but roads are often surprisingly less rough than in parts of Laos, Cambodia or Vietnam. Much of the country, unfortunately, is off-limits (chiefly places not covered here, including Chin State and much of Shan State), though nothing keeps you from stopping in villages between places listed in this chapter and looking about.

Air

Four airlines – three private companies and the government-run Myanma Airways – ply Myanmar's skyways (and 66 airstrips).

Yangon offices for the carriers follow:

Air Bagan (☎ 1-514741, 513322; www.airbagan.com; airline code AB; 56 Shwe Taung Gyar St, Bahan) Privately run domestic carrier.

Air Mandalay (Map p536; ☎ 01-525488; www .airmandalay.com; airline code 6T; 146 Dhammazedi Rd) Singapore/Malaysia joint venture.

Myanma Airways (MA; Map p540; ☎ 01-374874, 277013; 104 Strand Rd) The government's airline.

Yangon Airways (Map p540; ☎ 1-383106; www .yangonair.com; airline code HK; MMB Tower, 5th fl, 166 Upper Pansodan St) Thai joint venture.

One-way tickets are half the return fare and should be bought at least a day in advance. You'll need to have your passport, a passport copy (often) and US dollars (or FEC, see p585) handy to pay for the ticket. Travel agencies tend to sell tickets for slightly less than airline offices. All prices should include the US$3 insurance fee. There's no domestic departure tax.

GOVERNMENT TRANSPORT

Be aware that the government profits from your use of transport services that it owns and/or runs. You may choose to avoid the following government companies:

- Inland Water Transport (IWT)
- Myanma Airlines (domestic)
- Myanma Five Star Line (MFSL; ships)
- Myanma Railways

MA's fleet is a bit tatty and has a dodgy record, and schedules are approximate at best – though prices are often US$10 or US$20 less than the other carriers.

Boat

There are 8000km of navigable river in Myanmar. Boats can travel from the delta north to Bhamo even in the dry season, and in the wet they can reach Myitkyina on the Ayeyarwady. Other important rivers include the Twante Canal, which links the Ayeyarwady to Yangon, and the Chindwin, which joins the Ayeyarwady a little above Bagan. The main drawback is speed: boats typically take three to four times as long as road travel.

Most ferries are operated by the government's Inland Water Transport (IWT).

The Mandalay–Bagan service is very popular among travellers. A ferry or express ferry runs daily. If you take the slower local boats, this trip can be extended to Pyay or even all the way to Yangon. Probably the best long-haul river trip – in season – is north of Mandalay, drifting south from Bhamo (p572) or Myitkyina (p572). The nicest short trip is between Mawlamyine and Hpa-An (p548).

The government's Myanma Five Star Line (MFSL) travels very infrequently and irregularly from Yangon's MFSL Passenger Jetty (south of Strand Rd), heading north to Sittwe and south to Kawthoung. Ask at MTT or call the **MFSL office** (Map p538; ☎ 01-295279; 132-136 Thein Byu Rd) in Yangon.

Bus

Some of the long-distance buses are new and comfortable. Most of the others are packed to the ceiling with people and goods and are often hours late. They break down often, and the roads are so bad in most places that two vehicles travelling in opposite directions can't pass without pulling off the road. On the other hand, bus travel is cheap and frequent, and you're bound to meet local people. Long-haul buses make a rest stop every few hours. Buy your ticket as far as possible in advance so you don't get stuck sitting on a sack in the aisle. On minibuses, beware of the back seat – on Myanmar's rough roads, you'll be bounced around like popcorn. Have a blanket for air-con or trips through mountains.

MAJOR PUBLIC TRANSPORT ROUTES

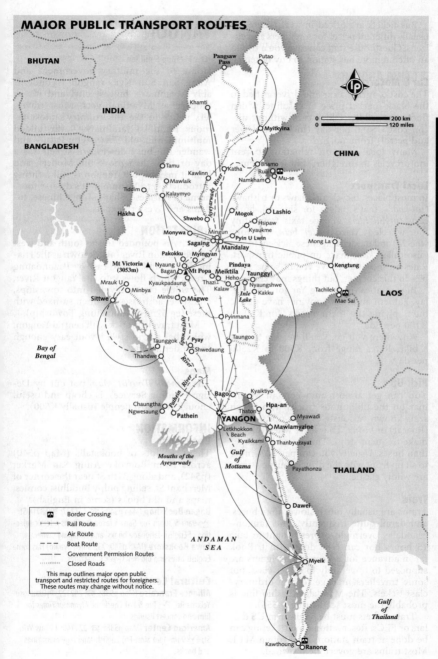

MYANMAR

Border Crossing
Rail Route
Air Route
Boat Route
Government Permission Routes
Closed Roads

This map outlines major open public
transport and restricted routes for foreigners.
These routes may change without notice.

Bus tickets are priced in kyat. There are usually different prices for foreigners and citizens. Guesthouse staff can save you a trip to an often remote bus station to buy tickets.

Car & Motorcycle

The cost of hiring a car and driver is tied to the black-market price of gasoline, which fluctuates wildly. Older cars without aircon cost US$50 per day (including driver and petrol) from Yangon.

Many locals remain reluctant to rent motorcycles to foreigners, but it happens.

Local Transport

In most places, bicycle rickshaws or trishaws (*sai-kaa* – that's pidgin for sidecar), horse carts *(myint hlei),* vintage taxis *(taxi),* tiny four-wheeled Mazdas (*lei bein,* or 'four wheels') and modern Japanese pick-up trucks (also called *kaa*) make up public transport. Rates are negotiable. We've put some samples in this chapter, but things may change.

Bigger cities (including Yangon, Mandalay, Pathein and Mawlamyine) have public buses plying the main streets, for K10 to K100 per ride.

Anywhere you go, you'll be able to rent a bike. Rates range from K500 to K2500 per day.

Pick-Up

You can get almost anywhere in Myanmar on the ubiquitous trucks with bench seats known variously as pick-ups, *lain-ka* (linecar) or *hi-lux.* They leave when full and make frequent stops. They're a bit cheaper than buses. Usually you can pay 50% more to sit up front with the driver. Journey times are wildly elastic.

Train

Trains are usually much slower than buses, and derail quite frequently. The Yangon–Mandalay overnight express ought to take 15 hours but can take double that. Book far in advance for a sleeper. Foreigners are supposed to travel only in upper class, but some travellers manage to buy ordinary-class tickets. The Mandalay–Lashio line is probably the most scenic ride (p556).

Train tickets must be paid for in US dollars or FECs. Reservations and ticketing can be done at train stations or through MTT. Most trains are government owned.

YANGON

☎ 01 / pop 5 million

Home to the military government and Aung San Suu Kyi, Yangon is undeniably Myanmar's biggest city, and it's as modern as Myanmar gets. Most travellers pause to see the country's most famous Buddhist landmark – the gilded multimillennia-old Shwedagon Paya – and wander the busy downtown streets for a day or two, then move on. Modern and loud it may be, but Yangon is still a fitting introduction to Myanmar. It's diverse too – home to Burmese, Shan, Mon, Chinese, Indians and Western expats.

ORIENTATION

The city is bounded to the south and west by the Yangon River (also known as the Hlaing River) and to the east by Pazundaung Creek, which flows into the Yangon River. The whole city is divided into townships, and street addresses are often suffixed with these (eg 52nd St, Botataung Township).

Most travellers stick with central Yangon, which has a grid-style layout easy enough to wander about.

Maps

The *Yangon Tourist Map*, put out by Design Printing Services, is cheap and useful enough for most people (usually K500).

INFORMATION
Bookshops

There are lots of bookstalls (Map p540) across from Bogyoke Aung San Market (p542), and along 37th St near the corner of Merchant St, selling pulpy Buddhist comics, maps and old books (some in English).

Bagan Bookshop (Map p540; ☎ 377227; 100 37th St; ☺ 9am-5.30pm Tue-Sun) A favourite for its eclectic selection of English-language books, and engaging owner.

Inwa Bookstore (Map p540; 232 Sule Paya Rd) Has some English titles and old *Newsweek* magazines.

Cultural Centres

Alliance Francaise (Map p538; ☎ 282122; Pyidaungsu Yeiktha Rd; ☺ Tue & Fri) Check the *Myanmar Times* for film and concert listings.

American Center (Map p538; ☎ 223140; 14 Taw Win St; ☺ 9am-4pm Mon-Fri) English-language magazines and books.

British Council Library (Map p540; ☎ 2953000;
80 Strand; ⊗ 8.30am-8pm Mon-Fri, 8.30am-4.30pm Sat)
Excellent collection of English-language Burmese-history
books located in the UK embassy.

Emergency
Your embassy may also be able to assist in
an emergency.
Ambulance (☎ 192)
Fire (☎ 191)
Police (☎ 199)
Red Cross (☎ 295133)

Internet Access
Many guesthouses offer email. It's usually
cheaper to go to an Internet café.
Cyber World II (Map p540; Nay Pyi Daw Cinema, 246-
248 Sule Paya Rd; per hr K1000) This place is in a central
location.

Medical Services
City Mart Supermarket (Map p538; cnr Anawrahta Rd
& 47th St) Well-stocked place (tampons available) that
includes a pharmacy.
International SOS Clinic (24hr alarm centre ☎ 667879;
37 Kaba Aye Paya Rd) On the ground floor of the Renaissance
Inya Lake Hotel on the east bank of Inya Lake, this is your best
bet in Yangon if you want medical attention.

Money
Yangon usually has the best exchange rate in
the country. Touts around Sule Paya or the
northern end of the adjacent Mahabandoola
Garden offer the best rates, but are known to
short-change stacks of kyat. Don't hand over
your bills before counting all the kyat. Your
guesthouse is a safer option. The Central
Hotel, near the Bogyoke Aung San Market,
has particularly good rates – changing usually occurs in the next-door teashop.

In a pinch, a couple of top-end hotels
(such as the Sedona Hotel; p539) accept
credit cards.

Post
DHL office (Map p540; Traders Hotel, 223 Sule Paya
Rd; ⊗ 8am-6pm Mon-Fri) To ship or receive anything
valuable, go here.
Main post office (Map p540; Strand Rd; ⊗ 7.30am-
6pm Mon-Fri)

Telephone
Central Telephone & Telegraph office (CTT; Map
p540; cnr Pansodan St & Mahabandoola St) Has overseas
calls for US$5 to US$7 per minute.

Tourist Information
Myanmar Travel & Tours (MTT; Map p540;
☎ 275328; 77/91 Sule Paya Rd; ⊗ 8.30am-5pm)
Government-run travel agency which offers free maps and
can help extend visas.

Travel Agencies
More useful than MTT are privately run
travel agencies. They're good for hiring a
car, checking on travel permits to closed
areas, or extending a visa.
Good News Travel (Map p540; ☎ 5019044;
good-news@mptmail.net.mm; 4th fl, FMI Centre, 380 Bogyoke Aung San Rd) Very well-run agency, though usually
geared to high-end travellers.
New Horizons Travels & Tours (Map p536;
☎ 542949; tun@mptmail.net.mm; 64 B2R Shwe Gon
Plaza) Worth the taxi here. They book trips with overseas
groups and are quite responsible.
Santa Maria Travel & Tours (Map p540; ☎ 254625;
www.myanmartravels.net; 195B 32nd St)

DANGERS & ANNOYANCES
Many travellers report being overcharged
double or triple the correct amount when
buying bus tickets from the kiosks around
Aug San Stadium in Yangon. Moneychangers on the street are less likely to
run away than slip in a few torn (therefore
useless) bills.

SIGHTS
Shwedagon Paya
Myanmar's most famous (and loved) landmark, the gilded **Shwedagon** (Map p536; admission US$5; ⊗ 5am-10pm) rises like a shining
golden eye 98m from its base, a couple
of kilometres north of the centre. Dating
back 2500 years – if legend is to be believed – Shwedagon is Yangon's one clear
must-see attraction. Every good Buddhist
in Myanmar tries to make at least one pilgrimage here in their lifetime; many do for

---

GETTING INTO TOWN
Walk past taxi stands in the airport terminal (about 15km north of the centre) and
negotiate with drivers outside. It's US$3 or
US$4 anywhere in Yangon; have small bills
handy. Most buses arrive at the Highway
Bus Centre (Aung Mingalar Bus Terminal),
a few kilometres northeast of the airport; a
taxi to town should be US$4.

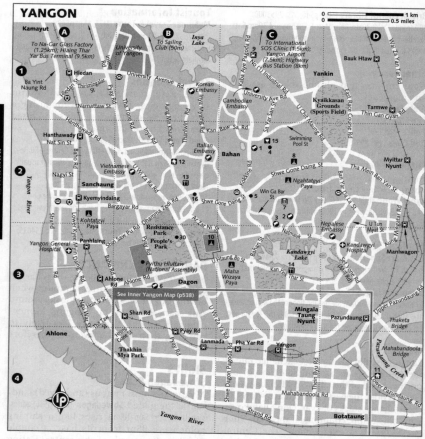

YANGON

See Inner Yangon Map (p538)

the **Shwedagon festival** in February to March (see p582). Any national festival quickens the pulse here too.

The compound, with its main stupa and 82 other buildings, is astounding any time of day, but the evening and sunrise – when slanting light enlivens the gilding – is the most magical.

The *paya* ('holy one', a religious monument) is said to be built upon the hill where Buddha relics have been enshrined, including eight hairs of the Buddha. In the 15th century, Queen Shinsawbu gilded it with her own weight in gold, beaten to gold leaf. Her son-in-law offered four times his own weight and that of his wife's. By 1995, the *zedi* (stupa) had re-

portedly accumulated 53 metric tonnes of gold leaf. The top of the spire is encrusted with more than 5000 diamonds and 2000 other stones.

In the compound's northwestern corner is a huge bell that the British managed to drop into the Yangon River while trying to carry it off. Unable to recover it, they gave the bell back to the Burmese, who refloated it using low-tech lengths of bamboo.

The US$5 entrance fee supposedly goes to pagoda upkeep. There is a lift large enough to accommodate a wheelchair. To get there, either take packed bus 37 from the east side of Mahabandoola Park, or hop in a taxi (about K1000 one way).

INFORMATION	
Bangladesh Embassy	1 C2
German Embassy	2 C2
Japanese Embassy	3 C2
Mahasi Meditation Centre	4 C2
New Horizons Travels & Tours	5 C2
Thailand Embassy	6 B3
SIGHTS & ACTIVITIES	
Bogyoke Aung San Museum	7 C2
Chaukhtagyi Paya	8 C2
Sedona Hotel	9 C1
Shwedagon Paya	10 B3
SLEEPING	
Motherland Inn II	11 D4
Winner Inn	12 B2
EATING	
Café Dibar	13 B2
Sandy's Myanmar Cuisine	14 C3
DRINKING	
Mr Guitar Café	15 C2
Patty O'Malleys	(see 9)
TRANSPORT	
Air Mandalay	16 B2

Other Sights

One of Yangon's top *paya*, the slightly kitschy, riverside **Botataung Paya** (Map p538; Strand Rd; admission US$2) is named for 1000 military leaders who escorted Buddha relics from India 2000 years ago. Its *zedi* is, unusually, hollow, so you can walk through it. There are good river views nearby.

If you can't get to Bago, the reclining Buddha at **Chaukhtatgyi Paya** (Map p536; Shwe Gone Daing St) is nearly as impressive.

You can't visit Aung San Suu Kyi's present home, but you can see where she grew up at the **Bogyoke Aung San Museum** (Map p536; ☎ 541359; Bogyoke Aung San Museum St, Bahan Township; admission US$3; 10am-3.30pm Tue-Sun), dedicated to her father, the independence leader who was assassinated in 1947. It's behind the Japanese embassy, just north of Kandawgyi Lake.

The **Na-Gar Glass Factory** (☎ 526053; 152 Yawgi Kyaung St, Hlaing Township; admission free; 9.30-11am & 12.30-3.30pm) is fun to explore. They made the mesmerising eyes for a reclining Buddha in Yangon's Chaukhtatgyi Paya. Most drivers aren't familiar with it, so getting there requires some patience. Tell them it's in Hlaing (lie-eng) Township.

For the best 360-degree views of Yangon, ride the (free) lift to the top of the **Sakura Tower** (Map p540; cnr Bogyoke Aung San & Sule Paya Rds).

For more sights see the walking tour (below).

ACTIVITIES

The Yangon Hash House Harriers walk or run at 4pm Saturday from the **Sailing Club** (132 Inya Rd) on Inya Lake. If you aren't familiar with Hashers, they're the drinkers with the running problem.

Good strolling grounds can be found at **Kandawgyi Lake** (Map p536), north of the city centre. About 3km north, **Inya Lake** (Map p536) has little chance for shade, but is five times larger – and not far from **Suu Kyi's home** (54 University Ave).

The **YMCA** (Map p538; ☎ 294128; Mahabandoola Rd; beginners 7-9am Tue, Thu & Sat, experienced 3-5pm Mon, Wed & Fri) offers first-rate kickboxing instruction.

DOWNTOWN WALKING TOUR

Downtown's by-the-grid streets (Map p540), lined with majestic government buildings from the British era, is the best (and only) real place to wander the capital by foot. One way around is starting at 2200-year-old **Sule Paya**, a big-time Buddhist traffic circle with an unusual octagonal shape. Just east is golden **City Hall** and, further east, the **Immigration Office** (Mahabandoola Rd), once a mammoth department store.

Continuing east, the **High Court Building** (Pansodan St) is on the right – the nation's top-mamma court. Take Pansodan St south to Strand Rd, the last road before the Yangon River. To the left is the colonial stand-out **Strand Hotel**, with an air-conditioned bar if you want a break, and the **British Council Library** (p535).

West on the Strand, you'll pass the 1915 **Customs House** and the colonnaded **Law Court**. Head north to the popular **Mahabandoola Garden** (admission K50), a slightly faded park home to the Independence Monument (and some shade). Just north is the Sule Paya. Walking west, through the chaotic Indian and Chinese quarters, there's a great **pedestrian bridge** for photos of Yangon traffic. Then wander north to **Bogyoke Aung San Market**.

MYANMAR

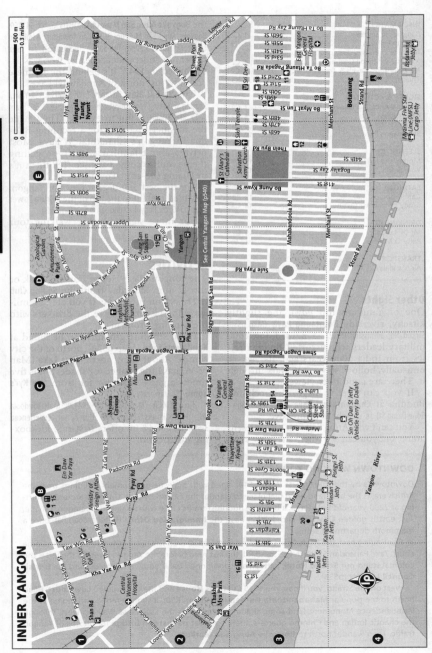

INNER YANGON

If you're hankering for some **swimming**, top-end hotels allow dips for a few dollars; one of the nicest is at the **Sedona Hotel** (Map p536; ☎ 666900; 1 Kaba Aye Pagoda Rd, Inya Lake; admission US$5). Or try the **Yangon Swimming Club Pool** (Map p538; U Wi Za Ya Rd), next to the He & Me Food Centre.

SLEEPING

For cheap sleeps (and the best of Yangon anyway) stay downtown or nearby, where you won't need a taxi every time you do something. Off season you may be able to bargain. All prices include free breakfast.

Motherland Inn II (Map p536; ☎ 291343; www.myanmarmotherlandinn.com; 433 Lower Pazundaung Rd; s US$7-9, d US$9-13; 🔀 🖥) A kilometre east of the centre, Mother is deservedly popular with the backpacker core. Three tiers of rooms come with and without private bathroom, with fan or air-con. Rooms are basic, but quite clean, and there's a free airport shuttle running twice daily.

White House Hotel (Map p540; ☎ 240780; whitehouse@mptmail.net.mm; 69/71 Kon Zay Dan St; s/d from US$5/10; 🔀) Rooftop hammocks (and beer and good views) reward those willing to make the steep climb up. The rooms are clean but oddly shaped, with shards of glass decorating walls. The more expensive rooms have private bathroom. Staff are helpful with travel arrangements, and breakfast is better than average.

Haven Inn (Map p538; ☎ 295500; phyuaung@mptmail.net.mm; 216 Bo Myat Tun St; s/d US$10/15; 🔀) Probably worth the extra dollars, Dr Htun's five well-furnished rooms get booked ahead in high season – try for No 101, the largest. No rooms have windows, but all have private bathroom and air-con, and Dr Htun is quite welcoming.

Three Seasons Hotel (Map p538; ☎ 293304; phyuaung@mptmail.net.mm; 83/85 52nd St; s/d US$12/20; 🔀) For just a few more dollars than Haven, the Three Seasons (run by the same family as Haven) is popular with 30-something couples, offering a little more comfort (high ceilings, wood floors) in a house-style building east of the centre. Breakfast sprawls. It's quiet at night.

Garden Guest House (Map p540; ☎ 253779; 441-445 Mahabandoola St; s US$4-6, d US$6-10; 🔀) and **Mahabandoola Guest House** (Map p540; ☎ 248104; 93 32nd St; s/d with shared bathroom US$3/5), both fronting Sule Paya, are grubbier cheapies.

Other recommended places in the centre include:

SPLURGE!

The **Central Hotel** (Map p540; ☎ 241007; www.myanmartravelinformation.com/central hotel; 335-357 Bogyoke Aung San Rd; s/d US$30/35; 🔀 🖥), just east of the Bogyoke Aung San Market, looks like a big-playing midranger; the rooms are large and clean, but nothing too fancy. But for the price, it gets you closest to swishy comfort for minimal extra money. The moneychangers downstairs have good rates.

Outside the centre, walkable distance from Shwedagon Paya or Inya Lake, the **Winner Inn** (Map p536; ☎ 535205; www.winnerinnmyanmar.com; 42 Thanlwin Rd; r US$20 & 25; 🔀 🖥) is a low-slung building attached to a four-storey wing with great-value rooms, complete with private bathroom, fridge and satellite TV. The dining room overlooks the garden.

MYANMAR

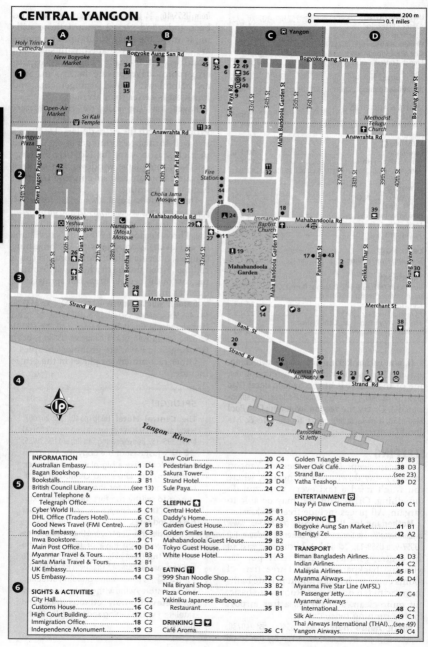

CENTRAL YANGON

0 — 200 m
0 — 0.1 miles

INFORMATION

Australian Embassy	**1** D4
Bagan Bookshop	**2** D3
Bookstalls	**3** B1
British Council Library	(see 13)
Central Telephone & Telegraph Office	**4** C2
Cyber World II	**5** C1
DHL Office (Traders Hotel)	**6** C1
Good News Travel (FMI Centre)	**7** B1
Indian Embassy	**8** C3
Inwa Bookstore	**9** C1
Main Post Office	**10** D4
Myanmar Travel & Tours	**11** B3
Santa Maria Travel & Tours	**12** B1
UK Embassy	**13** D4
US Embassy	**14** D4

SIGHTS & ACTIVITIES

City Hall	**15** C2
Customs House	**16** C4
High Court Building	**17** C3
Immigration Office	**18** C3
Independence Monument	**19** C3
Law Court	**20** C4
Pedestrian Bridge	**21** A2
Sakura Tower	**22** C1
Strand Hotel	**23** D4
Sule Paya	**24** C2

SLEEPING 🏠

Central Hotel	**25** B1
Daddy's Home	**26** A3
Garden Guest House	**27** B3
Golden Smiles Inn	**28** B3
Mahabandoola Guest House	**29** B2
Tokyo Guest House	**30** D3
White House Hotel	**31** A3

EATING 🍴

999 Shan Noodle Shop	**32** C2
Nila Biryani Shop	**33** B1
Pizza Corner	**34** B1
Yakiniku Japanese Barbeque Restaurant	**35** B1

DRINKING 🍷

Café Aroma	**36** C1

Golden Triangle Bakery	**37** B3
Silver Oak Café	**38** D3
Strand Bar	(see 23)
Yatha Teashop	**39** D2

ENTERTAINMENT 🎭

Nay Pyi Daw Cinema	**40** C1

SHOPPING 🛍

Bogyoke Aung San Market	**41** B1
Theingyi Zei	**42** A2

TRANSPORT

Biman Bangladesh Airlines	**43** D3
Indian Airlines	**44** C2
Malaysia Airlines	**45** B1
Myanma Airways	**46** D4
Myanma Five Star Line (MFSL) Passenger Jetty	**47** C4
Myanmar Airways International	**48** C2
Silk Air	**49** C1
Thai Airways International (THAI)	(see 49)
Yangon Airways	**50** C4

Daddy's Home (Map p540; ☎ 252169; 107 Kon Zay Dan St; r per person US$4-10) Good bare-bones choice.

Golden Smiles Inn (Map p540; ☎ 373589; myathiri@mptmail.net.mm; 644 Merchant St; s US$5-8, d US$8-12; 😵) Eight rooms, balcony hangout.

Tokyo Guest House (Map p540; ☎ 287143; 200 Bo Aung Kyaw St; r with shared bathroom US$6; 😵) Tiny, well-kept rooms.

YMCA (Map p538; ☎ 294128; 263 Mahabandoola Rd; s US$8-10, d US$16-19; 😵) Large, spare rooms. New wing in the works. The entrance is off Mahabandoola Rd.

EATING

Yangon has Myanmar's nicest restaurants, most of which loom to the north of the centre on various embassy rows or around the lakes. In the centre, sidewalk stalls are the cheapest eats in town. Many places close by 9pm.

Bamar & Shan

The best night out in Yangon takes in the open-air **barbecue grills** (Map p538; 19th St; 😵 after 5pm) in Chinatown, between Mahabandoola and Anawrahta Sts. Point at the skewers you want – mostly meat, some fish and artichokes and bean curd (about K150 each) – and down Myanmar Beer as it gets cooked up. Pre-buy some sweets (or crickets and the like) on the **snack stalls** (Mahabndoola) around the corner for dessert.

Feel Myanmar Food (Map p538; ☎ 725736; 124 Pyidaungsu Yeiktha St) Feel is best at lunch, when locals and foreign-embassy staff pack the dining room for buffet-style meals.

999 Shan Noodle Shop (Map p540; 130B 34th St; noodle dishes K400) This teensy eatery behind City Hall has an English-language menu for such superb Shan meals as *hkauq sweh* (thin rice noodles in slightly spicy chicken broth).

Maw Shwe Li Restaurant (Map p538; ☎ 221103; 316 Anawrahta Rd, Lanmadaw Township) Another good Shan eatery west of the city centre. Shan specialities include *pei pot kyaw* (sour bean condiment) and *hmo chawk kyaw* (fried mushrooms).

Other Asian

Yakiniku Japanese Barbeque Restaurant (Map p540; ☎ 374738; 357 Shwe Bontha St; barbecue dishes K1000; 😵 lunch & dinner) Near the Bogyoke Aung San Market, Yakiniku offers gas-fired grills at tables for DIY meals of meat and fish.

Singapore's Kitchen (Map p538; ☎ 226297; 524 Strand Rd; 😵 lunch & dinner) One of Yangon's best Chinese restaurants, with an open kitchen and tables that spill onto the footpath during fair weather. It's between 12th and Phoone Gyee Sts. A 10% service charge is added to the bill.

Along Anawrahta Rd, west of Sule Paya Rd, are a number of super-cheap Indian biryani shops (*keyettha dan bauk* in Burmese) and at night roti-and-dosa makers set up on sidestreets. All-you-can-eat thali meals or biryani cost K200 to K300. **Nila Biryani Shop** (Map p540; Anawrahta Rd) is one of the most popular.

Western

Pizza Corner (Map p540; ☎ 254730; pizza K2000-2800) Pizza Hut–style joint a block from Bogyoke Aung San Market. Lights are bright and the décor is American fast food to the hilt but the veggie and meat pizzas are tasty. Pasta and fried chicken are also on the menu.

50th Street Bar & Grill (Map p538; ☎ 298096; 9-13 50th St; pizzas US$7) A real expat hangout, complete with pool table, overseas newspapers and overpriced Cokes (US$2).

'MOUTH-WATERING SNACKS'

Myanmar *tha yei za* (literally 'mouth-watering snack') come in an eye-popping array of cheap bite-sized snacks that line 'night markets' in Yangon and all around the country. Makeshift desserts come in the form of multicoloured sticky-rice sweets, poppyseed cakes, banana puddings and the like. Others test local claims that 'anything that walks on the ground can be eaten':

- *wek thaa douk htoe* (barbecue stands) – sidewalk stools selling graphic, sliced-up pig parts; about K20 per piece
- *pa-yit kyaw* (fried cricket) – sold on skewers or in a 10-pack for about K400
- *bi-laar* (beetle) – prepared like crickets; local tip is 'suck the stomach out, then chew the head part'
- *thin baun poe* (larva) – insect larva, culled from bamboo, are lightly grilled and served still wriggling

MYANMAR

Pizzas, sandwiches, pastas, salads are all fine. There are half-price drinks 5pm to 8pm Monday to Thursday and 4pm to 9pm Friday and Sunday. Lunches during the week are half price.

Café Dibar (Map p536; ☎ 006143; 14/20 Thanlwin Rd; mains K3000) North of the centre, Café Dibar is a cosy Italian bistro – one of several inviting, slightly posher eateries on the strip. The seafood pizza and lasagne are excellent.

DRINKING
Cafés & Teashops

Café Aroma (Map p540; Sule Paya Rd; ⏱ 8am-11pm) If you need a damn good cup of coffee, this is the Starbucks of Yangon, with espresso and snacks.

Golden Triangle Bakery (Map p540; 641 Merchant St) This place brings in beans from northeast of Mandalay. A cappuccino is K500.

Sei Taing Kya Teashop (Map p538; cnr Anawrahta Rd & 51st St) Teashops, like everywhere in Myanmar, are buzzing snack stops all day. This local chain serves first-quality tea, *mohinga* (rice noodles with fish) and other snacks.

Yatha Teashop (Map p540; 352 Mahabandoola Rd) A popular Indian-style teashop between Seikkantha Stand 39th St.

Bars

Paling in comparison to Bangkok's booze (plus) scene, Yangon is nevertheless as 'sceney' as Myanmar gets. Expat-oriented places – mostly north of the centre – are quite pricey. See local listings – the *Myanmar Times* is a good start – for more recommendations. If you're counting kyat, some sidewalk stalls or 'beer gardens' can fix you up with a bottle of Myanmar Beer for about K1000.

Mr Guitar Café (Map p536; ☎ 550105; 22 Sa Yar San St; ⏱ 6pm-midnight) Burmese rock and pop stars often drop by this dark café-bar, founded by famous singer Nay Myo Say. Live folk music goes on from 7pm to midnight daily. Drinks are expensive; an imported beer is about US$4.

Silver Oak Café (Map p540; ☎ 299993; 83/91 Bo Aung Kyaw St) This is one of the few centres of gay nightlife in the city. There's live music almost every night. The bar Patty O'Malleys at the **Sedona Hotel** (Map p536; ☎ 666900; 1 Kaba Aye Pagoda Rd, Inya Lake) is another gay-friendly scene.

50th Street Bar & Grill (Map p538; ☎ 298096; 9-13 50th St) Some buzzes are born here, particularly at happy hours.

Strand Hotel (Map p540; Strand Rd; ⏱ 11am-11pm) The bar at the Strand booms on Friday – happy hours runs 5pm to 7pm daily.

ENTERTAINMENT

Nay Pyi Daw Cinema (Map p540; Sule Paya Rd; tickets K800) Watch Western films, subtitled in Burmese, here. Get in early for the funny government propaganda reels.

SHOPPING

Bogyoke Aung San Market (Scott Market; Map p540; Bogyoke Aung San Rd; ⏱ 8am-6pm Tue-Sun) This labyrinthine, 70-year-old market has the largest selection of Burmese handicrafts you'll find in Yangon: jewellery, *longyi*, shoes, bags and pretty much anything else.

Theingyi Zei (Map p540) This is the market for everyday housewares and textiles, and it extends four blocks east to west from Konzaydan St to 24th St, and north to south from Anawrahta St to Mahabandoola Rd. Theingyi Zei is renowned for its traditional Burmese herbs and medicines.

GETTING THERE & AWAY
Air

See p531 for information on international air services and carriers based in Yangon, and airline offices. See p532 for details on domestic flights, which leave from the same airport.

Boat

On the Yangon River waterfront, which wraps itself around southern Yangon, four main passenger jetties service long-distance ferries head up the delta towards Pathein or travel north along the Ayeyarwady River to Pyay, Bagan and to Mandalay.

When you purchase a ticket for a particular ferry from government-run **Inland Water Transport** (IWT; Map p538; ☎ 284055) at the back of **Lan Thit St jetty** (Map p538; ☎ 284055), be sure to ask which jetty your boat will be leaving from.

Bus

Yangon has two main bus stations: the Highway Bus Centre (aka Aung Mingalar Bus Terminal) serves the most destinations, while the **Hlaing Thar Yar Bus Terminal** (Hwy No 5, Yangon–Pathein Rd) serves the Delta.

The Highway Bus Centre is a confusing array of various bus companies in a dusty lot, southwest of the Yangon airport.

The Hlaing Thar Yar Bus Terminal is 45 minutes (at least) west of the centre on the other side of the Hlaing River.

Guesthouses can help with tickets. Bigger companies with bus-ticket offices opposite the Central Train Station include **Kyaw Express** (☎ 242473), **Sun Moon Express** (☎ 642903) and **Transnational Express** (☎ 249671). A longtime bus company **Leo Express** (☎ 252001) is here too, though it often inflates ticket prices out of Yangon.

Several buses to Pathein (K2500, three to four hours), Chaungtha Beach (K5000, six to seven hours) and Ngwesaung Beach (K5000, five hours) leave from the Hlaing Thar Yar Terminal from the early morning to 1pm. The comfiest ones leave early on.

Train

The 716km-long trip from Yangon to Mandalay is the only train trip most visitors consider. The express trains are far superior to the general run of Burmese trains. Upper class has reclining seats and is quite comfortable. Reserve sleepers several days in advance. Get advance tickets at the **Yangon train station** (Map p538; ☎ 274027; ⏱ 6am-4pm).

BUS FARES

Sample fares and information about for buses leaving the Highway Bus Centre include:

Destination	Fare	Duration	Departure Times
Bagan	K6500	14hr	3pm
Bago	K500-1000	2hr	frequent
Kyaikto (for Golden Rock)	K2500	4½hr	morning
Hpa-An	K4000	8hr	6.30-8pm
Mawlamyine	K3000	6hr	evening
Mandalay	K6000	12hr	4.30-6pm
Taunggyi (Kalaw & Inle Lake)	K6000	20hr	afternoon
Thandwe (Ngapali)	K4500	17hr	afternoon

GETTING AROUND
Bus

Over 40 numbered city bus routes – on dodgy old pick-ups and newer Japanese or Korean buses with air-con – connect the townships of Yangon. Some can be quite crowded, but midday pops across the centre (for example) beat a taxi. Tickets cost K5, K10 or K20.

A few good routes include:
- Bogyoke Aung San Market to Mingala Zei (near Kandawgyi Lake) – pick-up 1
- Sule Paya to Pyay Rd (University of Yangon; near Inya Lake) to airport – blue bus 51, 52 and air-con bus 51
- Sule Paya to Highway Bus Centre – bus 43, 45, 51
- Sule Paya to Hlaing Thar Yar Bus Station – bus 54, 59, 96
- Sule Paya to Shwedagon Paya – bus 37, 43, 46

Taxi

Licensed taxis carry red licence plates, though there is often little else to distinguish a taxi from any other vehicle in Yangon. The most expensive are the *car-taxis*

TRAIN FARES

Destination	2nd class	1st class	Sleeper	Duration	Departure Times
Bagan	US$11	US$34	US$34	19hr	8.30am, 10am
Kyaikto (for Golden Rock)	US$4	US$9	n/a	8hr	7am, 10pm
Mandalay	US$13	US$30-38	US$50	14hr	7 daily
Thazi	US$10	US$26	US$34	12hr	7 daily

(usually older), midsized Japanese cars. Fares are highly negotiable; trips around the central area shouldn't cost above K1000. Sule Paya to Shwedagon Paya runs at about K1200 or K1500. Late at night, expect to pay more. A taxi for the day is US$15 to US$30.

Trishaw

Trishaws aren't permitted on the main streets from midnight to 10am, and you'll see far fewer trishaws or bicycles in Yangon than anywhere else in Myanmar. Rides cost about K250 to K500.

CENTRAL MYANMAR

The bulk of Myanmar's flat, dusty, rice-producing dry zone – between Yangon, Bagan and Inle Lake – is filled with some appealing lesser-seen towns bursting with history and some of the friendliest locals. Most require overnighting, others provide good fodder for heading north in steps.

BAGO

☎ 052 / pop 48,000

Eighty kilometres north of Yangon (en route to Inle Lake or Mandalay), Bago is something of a Buddha World, with giant monuments popping up in the plain. Bago sees some travellers, but mostly just during the day (or on their way to the Golden Rock; p547). Founded in AD 573 by the Mon, Bago's days as a major river-port town were lost when the river changed course and ass-kicking Burmese king Alaungpaya destroyed it in 1757.

Sights

A US$10 ticket covers entrance to Shwethalyaung, Shwemawdaw Paya, Mahazedi Paya, Kyaik Pun Paya and the Kanbawzathadi Palace, but ticket checkers quit work at 4.30pm. All other sights listed have free admission. Camera fees are enforced. A new 70m Buddha is scheduled to be added to the scene by 2006.

SHWETHALYAUNG & AROUND

Shwethalyaung is a 55m reclining Buddha image that's 9m longer than the one at Wat Pho in Bangkok and has a sweet, lifelike face. The jewelled soles of the feet are particularly beautiful. A mural tells the temple's melo-dramatic story, which began in AD 994.

Just before the Shwethalyaung is the re-constructed **Maha Kalyani Sima** (Hall of Or-dination) and a curious quartet of standing Buddha figures.

Carry on beyond the Shwethalyaung and you soon come to **Mahazedi Paya**, where men (only) can climb to the top for fine views. Just beyond is **Shwegugale Paya**, with a tunnel lined with 64 seated Buddha images.

SHWEMAWDAW PAYA & AROUND

Rebuilt after an earthquake in 1930, the Shwemawdaw Paya is 14m higher than Shwedagon Paya in Yangon. Note the large chunk of the *zedi's* spire (which was toppled by an earthquake in 1917) resting at the northeastern corner of the *paya*. The stupa, reached by a covered walkway lined with stalls, sees most worshippers during the **full-moon festival** at Tagu (March/April).

Beyond the Shwemawdaw Paya is **Hintha Gon Paya**, a hilltop shrine guarded by mythi-cal swans. You get great Bago views without paying the US$10.

KHA KHAT WAIN MONASTERY

One of the top-three biggest *kyaung* (Bud-dhist monasteries) in Myanmar, this is a bustling hive of 1200 monks, and an es-pecially welcoming one. Tourists tend to come to watch the 10.30am lunch – you'll find it's more relaxed at other times of the day.

KANBAWZATHADI PALACE & MUSEUM

This Mon-style palace, just south of Shwe-mawdaw Paya, was the home of a 16th-century Taungoo king. The excavated walls are the only authentic 16th-century arte-facts. Everything else is a reproduction, similar to the palace in Mandalay.

Sleeping

Bago has plenty of decent rooms at rock-bottom prices. Most include breakfast.

> **SPLURGE!**
>
> **Bago Star Hotel** (☎ 23766; 11-13 Kyaikpon Pa-goda Rd; s/d US$24/30; ⌘) Bago's nicest hotel, on the same road as Kyaik Pun Paya, has wooden bungalows with all-hours air-con. The OK pool does the job.

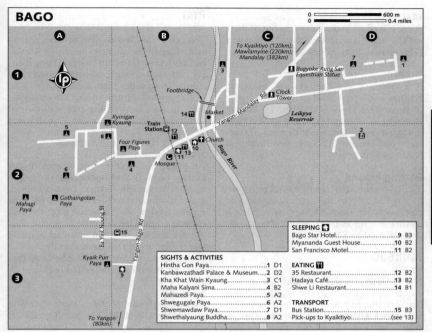

BAGO

SIGHTS & ACTIVITIES
Hintha Gon Paya..............................1 D1
Kanbawzathadi Palace & Museum.....2 D2
Kha Khat Wain Kyaung...................3 C1
Maha Kalyani Sima..........................4 B2
Mahazedi Paya................................5 A2
Shwegugale Paya............................6 A2
Shwemawdaw Paya........................7 D1
Shwethalyaung Buddha...................8 A2

SLEEPING
Bago Star Hotel...............................9 B3
Myananda Guest House...................10 B2
San Francisco Motel........................11 B2

EATING
35 Restaurant................................12 B2
Hadaya Café..................................13 B2
Shwe Li Restaurant.........................14 B1

TRANSPORT
Bus Station....................................15 B3
Pick-ups to Kyaiktiyo.................(see 13)

Myananda Guest House (☎ 22275; 10 Yangon-Mandalay Rd; r US$4-10; ✷) A cheery, well-run place with noisy, roadside rooms. The cheapest rooms are fan-cooled and there's a clean shared bathroom. A good local guide, Mr Han, hangs out here.

San Francisco Motel (☎ 22265; 14 Yangon-Mandalay Rd; s/d US$5/8; ✷) Quieter than its neighbours, it has simple spotless rooms, some with balcony. Rooms in the new (west) wing are a bit brighter.

Eating & Drinking
In the centre of town near the market are a number of food stalls, including some good Indian biryani stalls. Beer stations are near the bridge on the Main Rd.

Shwe Li Restaurant (194 Strand St; dishes from K900) Half a block north of the main road, this homey, wood-floored gem is good for Shan or Indian curries.

Hadaya Café (Yangon-Mandalay Rd; ⊙ 24hr) Opposite the Emperor Hotel, this teashop has a good selection of pastries.

35 Restaurant (Yangon-Mandalay Rd; dishes K1000) This friendly lil' shabby place has cheap Bamar, Chinese and European dishes – plus 'goat fighting balls' (goat 'nads).

Getting There & Away
BUS & PICK UP
Buses from Yangon (K500 to K1000, two hours) depart approximately hourly from 6am from Yangon's Highway Bus Centre. Pick-ups to Bago (K300, front seat K500, up to four hours) depart frequently from Yangon's **Tha-khin Mya Pan-gyan Gate terminal** (Map p538; Strand Rd).

Hadaya Café can help get you on a Yangon bus heading north. To Mandalay, buses arrive around 7pm; you'll have to pay the full fare (K5000) for the 12-hour ride.

Air-con buses to Nyaungshwe (Inle Lake) leave around 1.30pm (K2000, 16 hours), arriving at 4.30am.

To reach Bagan, take a Mandalay-bound bus to Meiktila and catch a ride the next morning to Nyaung U.

Pick-ups east to Kyaikto (for Golden Rock) leave from Hadaya Cafe (K500, five hours). Buses go from near the Emperor Hotel (K800 to K1000).

MYANMAR

TAXI
Some travellers make a day trip out of Bago with a hired car from Yangon. One-way rides should cost US$15 or US$20.

TRAIN
A couple of evening trains (presently 6.50pm and 9pm) head daily to Mandalay (ordinary/1st class US$11/29, 14 hours), stopping in Taungoo (US$4/8; four hours), though it can be tricky getting a seat. Trains leave for Yangon (US$2/5, two hours) at 5am and 8am.

Getting Around
Trishaw is the main form of local transport in Bago. A trip in the central area should cost no more than K300. A wise idea is getting one for the day, which should cost about K2500 to K3000.

TAUNGOO
☎ 054

A one-time powerful kingdom, and now a quiet spot passed in the night on buses between bigger places, Taungoo nevertheless gets high marks from those who do stop a spell at one of the country's best guesthouses. And it's hard to beat a day on a bike soaking up palm shade in coffee country in the surrounding countryside. Taungoo is just under half way from Yangon to Mandalay.

In town, **Shwesandaw Paya** (1597) is the biggest pilgrimage spot. Several other Buddhist sites are on and around the 'royal lake'. The old moat is on the town's west side.

Up in the Karen mountains, **Seinnyay Forest Camp** is a popular elephant camp that some tour groups pop by. The guesthouse arranges trips for about US$40 per person, which is actually less than half of the Yangon rate.

Myanmar Beauty Guest House II, III & IV (☎ 23270; Pauk Hla Gyi St; fourdoctors@mptmail.net .mm; r US$8-25; 🏊) are three teak houses with poster beds, hot showers and wide-open views of the rice paddies. It's just north of the bridge, south of town.

Heading north or south on air-con buses you'll pay the full fare. Most stop at Golden Myanmar Restaurant, in the centre. Local buses go to Yangon (K1700) and Mandalay (K2000) around 6pm.

PYAY
☎ 053

Though roads leading to Yangon, Bagan and Ngapali Beach meet here, few travellers are tempted to stop in Pyay. Poor Pyay. It's laid back enough, with river views and nearby ruins older than Bagan's.

The central statue of Aung San on horseback is 2km west of the bus station, just south of the main market, and a block east of the Ayeyarwady.

Sights
Atop a hill in the centre (and nicer than your average pagoda), **Shwesandaw Paya** is actually a metre taller than Shwedagon Paya in Yangon, and – it's insisted – dates from 589 BC. The double golden *hti* (umbrella) atop the *zedi* represent peace between the Mon and Burmese; the second was put up when Burmese leader Alaungpaya captured the city in 1755. Facing the *paya* from the east is **Sehtatgyi Paya** (Big Ten Storey), a giant seated Buddha.

Sleeping
Myat Lodging House (☎ 21361; 222 Bazaar St; s US$8-10, d US$10-12, tr US$16-18; 🏊) This small backstreet guesthouse has well-loved, but simple rooms (green carpet, writing desks) a block from the Pyay 'action'. The extra US$2 for rooms gets you private bathroom, hot water and satellite TV. Ask for the Pyay map.

Aung Gabar Guesthouse (☎ 21400; 1462 Bogyoke Rd; s/d US$3/6) Pyay's cheapest bed isn't bad. Small rooms with shared bathroom are basic (concrete floors, fan) but clean (and lighter than the dark hall suggests).

Eating
Pyay Star Restaurant (cnr Bogyoke Rd & Pyay-Yangon Rd; dishes K1000) Overlooking the Aung San statue, this is a buzzing beer hall with upstairs balcony and pretty good Chinese food.

Hline Ayar (Strand Rd; dishes from K800; 🕙 breakfast to dinner) On the river just west, this place shows its years, but the food is quite good and there are open-deck seats facing the Ayeyarwady.

Getting There & Away
BOAT
Ferry routes on the Ayeyarwady stop and start in Pyay. A couple of weekly ferries go to Yangon (US$8; two or three days) and Mandalay (US$12; six or seven days).

The **IWT Office** (☎ 24503; The Strand; ☽ 9am-5pm Mon-Fri) can help with tickets and times.

BUS
The highway bus station, 2km east of the centre, sends frequent buses to Yangon (K1550; six hours). No direct buses go to Bagan; at research time, a lone 9.30am bus left for Magwe (K1800, seven or eight hours), where you're likely required to stay overnight – ask a trishaw driver to take you to Rolex Guest House, if so. A few morning buses leave Magwe for Nyaung U (K2500, four to five hours). To reach Thandwe (near Ngapali Beach), bus to Taunggok (K2500 to K4000, eight or nine hours) around 6pm, where you can catch a bus or pick-up to Thandwe (four or five hours).

TRAIN
A single train connects Pyay with Yangon in 12 hours.

AROUND PYAY
About 8km east of Pyay, **Thayekhittaya** (Sri Ksetra; admission US$4; ☽ 8am-5pm) is a sprawling oval-shaped walled city of the enigmatic Pyu, who ruled here, oh, 1500 years ago. The only real way around the site is by ox cart (K3000), which takes a 12km loop in three hours. Few sites stand – the 46m cylindrical Bawbawgyi Paya is the finest – but the trip is fun, and you can wander about farming villages to reach a few remote pagodas the driver will point out. From the centre of Pyay, pick-ups go to the bus station, where eastbound buses go within 2km of the site. A return taxi to the site is about K4000 or K5000. You can bike to the site, but not around it.

West of the road to Yangon, about 14km south of Pyay, **Shwemyetman Paya** (Paya of the Golden Spectacles) is home to a large, white-faced, seated Buddha – with giant gold-plated glasses on! Hop on a local Yangon-bound bus or south-bound pick-up, and get off in Shwedaung town.

SOUTHEASTERN MYANMAR

This slender seaside spit of unknown turf is often left off travellers' itineraries, but it's worth venturing beyond the Golden Rock at Kyaikto for some off-the-beaten-track adventure. Highlights include the superb boat ride between Mawlamyine and Hpa-an. Some travellers enter Myanmar from Ranong, Thailand, to Kawthoung (and the nearby Mergui [Myeik] Archipelago), a flight or boat ride from the rest of Myanmar.

KYAIKTIYO (GOLDEN ROCK)
☎ 035
Of all things to make you scratch your head, this is one of the most intriguing: a giant, gold-leafed boulder teetering on the very edge of a cliff on Mt Kyaikto. Legend says Kyaiktiyo (Golden Rock) marks the spot of a Buddha hair donated by a hermit in the 11th century. Apparently, the king surfaced it from the bottom of the sea and brought it to this spot via a boat that subsequently turned to stone (see it 300m away). There's no denying the power of the place – or the improbability of a boulder that just won't tip. Pilgrims pour in, particularly during the cooler months between October and March. It's a magical place to detour to.

Some travellers try this on a day trip from Yangon; don't. You need more time to get any enjoyment out of it. Plan on a night here or in Bago.

Orientation
The town of Kyaikto is 9km away from the foot of Mt Kyaikto. The village of **Kinpun**, sometimes referred to as 'base camp', is a collection of restaurants and guesthouses right at the foot of Mt Kyaikto, and the most common starting point up.

Seeing the Rock
There are two ways up to see the Rock: hiking 11km from Kinpun (four to six hours one way), or trucking then walking. Most

---

SPLURGE!

Spend the sunset or sunrise with the Golden Rock, by staying up top. **Golden Rock Hotel** (Yangon ☎ 01-502479; grtt@goldenrock.com.mm; s/d US$38/45, bungalows US$43/58; ▓) is among lush vegetation, but a 40-minute walk to the top. Rooms at **Mountain Top Inn & Restaurant** (s/d US$38/45) are disappointingly basic, but it's perfectly positioned at the mountaintop.

do the latter. Packed trucks from Kinpun (K500, K1000 front seat) ply upwards from 6am to 7pm, stopping for a fascinating 45-minute walk from the stupa. You'll be joined on the steep, paved path by a moving party of pilgrims and monks. Side trails offer more exploration that can soak up a day.

Locals may offer to carry you up in a sedan-chair for US$5 to US$7. Men only are permitted to walk along a short chasm-spanning bridge to the boulder itself.

There is a US$6 entrance fee collected at the **MTT office** (☽ 6am-6pm).

Sleeping & Eating

Only a few guesthouses in Kinpun accept foreigners; all rates include breakfast.

Sea Sar Guest House (s US$3-10, d US$6-20; ✖) Cuddly touts point you here – and that's not a bad thing, it's the best place. Pricier rooms are small bungalows with private bathroom.

Pann Myo Thu Inn (s US$3-6, d US$6-12; ✖) You can't swing your elbows far for fear of wall-made bruises. Mid-priced rooms, however, have wood floors and furniture (and air-con) – better than the more expensive 'modern' ones.

Because Kinpun is always crowded with pilgrims, Chinese and Bamar restaurants line the main street. They are virtually indistinguishable in quality, menu and price. Restaurants at the 'splurge' hotels have the same knock-out views.

Getting There & Away

Buses en route from Yangon to points further south stop in Kyaikto. There are buses between Yangon and Kyaikto (K2500, 4½ hours) leaving from Yangon's Highway Bus Centre. The bus stop in Kyaikto is across from Sea Sar Guest House, where you can get a bus to Bago (K1700, three hours) or pick-up (K1000, three hours).

Pick-ups head south to Hpa-An and Mawlamyine (K1500, front seat K2500, five hours) from 6am to 1pm.

A direct train from Bago to Kyaikto leaves at 4.30am daily (US$7; 2½ hours).

Pick-ups connect Kinpun and Kyaikto (K500), or you can walk the 11km.

MAWLAMYINE
☎ 057

Busy and big (it's Myanmar's third-largest city), Mawlamyine shows little of its colo-

nial glory. Most buildings of this mainly Mon town are modern Chinese-style jobs facing the Thanlwin River. The bridge, completed in 2004, offered long-overdue connections with the north. The main reason to come is the five-star boat ride up to Hpa-an (opposite).

The **Mon Cultural Museum** (cnr Baho & Dawei Jetty Rds; admission US$2) has a modest selection of Mon pieces. For good views, amble up the tallest stupa (to the south of the ridge), **Kyaik-thanlan Paya**, or other nearby pagodas. The mosques in town are the nicest buildings, particularly the green-and-turquoise **Kaladan Mosque**. The central **zeigyo** (market; South Bogyoke Rd), on the west side of the road, features a few 'fallen off the boat' black-market goods.

About 14km outside town, **Pa-Auk-Taw-Ya Kyaung** (☎ 032-22132; www.paauk.org; c/o Major Kan Saing, 653 Lower Main Rd) is one of the largest meditation centres in Myanmar.

A picturesque isle off the city's northwestern end is **Shampoo Island** (Guangse Kyun), reached by boat for K1000.

The best place to stay is **Breeze Rest House** (Lay Hnyin Tha; ☎ 21450; 6 Strand Rd; s US$4-8, d US$8-15; ✖). Upstairs rooms have a balcony.

Getting There & Away
BOAT

Double-decker ferries from the Hpa-an jetty in Mawlamyine leave on a gorgeous trip amid limestone mountains and sugar-cane fields for Hpa-an (US$2; five hours) between noon and 2.30pm daily, depending on tide and water level.

BUS

Several overnight buses connect Mawlamyine with Yangon (K3000, six or seven hours). Pick-ups to Hpa-an (K300, two hours) leave from the *zeigyo* hourly from 8am to 3pm.

TRAIN

The train station is north of the river in Mottama. Two daily express trains connect Mottama with Yangon (upper-class seat US$17; nine hours), stopping in Bago. Presently trains leave at 10am and 7pm.

SETSE

A brown-sand beach south of Mawlamyine, Setse has been popular since the colonial days. It has shallow surf and Casuarine trees. Stay in basic beachside bungalows at **Ngwe Moe Guesthouse** (s/d US$10/18). Plan a day ahead for a pick-up from Mawlamyine (K300, 2½ hours), which often lingers a while in Kyaikkami.

HPA-AN
☎ 058

The green, village-like capital of Kayin State is dotted with tall palms and backed by curious hills that seem to rise out of nowhere. The best thing to do is climb the concrete steps up **Mt Zwegabin** (722m). The walk up isn't gorgeous, but the views are – plus if you get there before noon the monastery offers a free lunch (rice, orange, tea), in time too for the 11am monkey feeding. Watch your rice!

Neither of the licensed accommodation options are knockouts. Rooms at **Soe Brothers Guest House** (☎ 21372; 46 Thitsa Rd; s/d US$4/6) have windows, shared bathrooms and no mosquito nets. Around the corner, **Parami Hotel** (r per person US$5 & US$22) has nets – its US$22 rooms have private bathroom.

The boat to Mawlamyine leaves at 7.30am. The bus to Yangon's Highway Bus Centre (K2000, 10 to 11 hours) leaves at 6pm. Pick-ups to Kyaikto (K800) leave from the central green mosque.

KAWTHOUNG

Myanmar's southernmost tip is just across the Pagyan River from Ranong, Thailand, but feels like a half-century time warp away. The waterfront is lined with teashops and moneychangers – and touts offering boat trips to Thailand. At **Cape**

Bayinnaung (Victoria Point), the statue of King Bayinnaung (who invaded Thailand in the 16th century) points a sword towards Thailand.

Activities

The offshore **Mergui (Myeik) Archipelago** – one of Myanmar's most beautiful places, and almost completely unexplored – features 4000 islands. These islands are home to 'sea gypsies', as the nomadic Salon people are called. Phuket-based tour groups offer high-priced diving and kayaking trips; also ask at **Moby Dick Tours** (☎ 4410129; www.mobydick-myanmar.com) for overnight trips to islands.

Sleeping & Eating

Cheap rooms aren't particularly good. **Kawthoung Motel** (☎ 51046; Bogyoke Rd; r 800B; ✷), 500m up from the jetty, has simple rooms with cold-water private bathroom. Cheaper, and more basic, is **Tanintharyi Guest House** (☎ 51748; Garden St; r 400B).

The place for food or beer is **Moby Dick Restaurant** (dishes 50B; ◷ 10am-11pm).

Getting There & Away

Foreigners can't go from here into Myanmar's 'mainland' by road. Government-run Myanma Airways flies to Yangon (US$145), stopping in Mawlamyine.

Boats from Ranong (Thailand) cost 250B. Private ferries go north to Myeik (US$25, 6½ hours) at 5.30am daily. MFSL ferries to Yangon are less regular.

INLE LAKE & SHAN STATE

The heart of giant Shan State centres on Inle Lake, which is nearly as popular as Bagan for visitors. Much of the gorgeous state itself – mysterious, rebellious, mountainous – remains closed off, though treks open up rural areas (including ethnic villages where you can sleep) to visitors in ways unrivalled elsewhere. Conflicts with ethnic rebels and the government along the Thai border continue to this day, fuelled by the profitable cash crop of opium. Ask locally for the latest situation before making plans to venture into rural areas.

BORDER CROSSING: INTO THAILAND

Boats hop between here and Ranong (p811), 10km away, regularly from about 6am to 4.30pm (150B, 40 minutes).

If leaving here, odds are you'll have to pay a US$25 'fee' to the Myanmar Travel and Tours office. It can be difficult leaving if your visa has expired.

If you visit Kawthoung as a day visitor, you must pay US$5 for a 'day pass', which allows two nights. If you have a valid Myanmar visa in advance, you can travel further into Myanmar.

MYANMAR

Some travellers bound for here stop in Meiktila or Thazi, nearby bus and train links; see p571.

KALAW
☎ 081

Set 1320m up, on the roly-poly west edge of the Shan Plateau, Kalaw is Myanmar's trekking HQ and gets more and more high-raised thumbs among backpackers than Inle Lake, to the east. Actually it's possible to hike between the two (about 45km), on mountains dotted with Palaung, Pa-O, Intha and Shan villages – it's a popular activity.

Trekking

Half-day to five-day treks are the main reason to stop in Kalaw. An array of local guides can tailor itineraries based on demands. At high season, it can be group following group in some areas; in the wet season, paths get miserably muddy. Licensed guides in Kalaw charge US$5 to US$8 per day for overnight hikes, a dollar less for day hikes. It's possible to stay in longhouses in mountain villages; Viewpoint is a mountaintop home of a Nepali family where you can stay for about K1500 (including meals).

If you want to walk between Kalaw and Inle Lake, guesthouses can arrange to send ahead any of your belongings not needed for the hike. Have good shoes and warm clothing for the cool evenings.

When visiting villages, it's better to contribute cash to the monastery's *sayadaw* (head teacher) than hand out gifts of any kind.

Sleeping

Breakfast comes with your room. Electricity in Kalaw is even sketchier than elsewhere.

Golden Lily Guest House (☎ 50108; golden lily@myanmar.com.mm; 5/88 Nat Sein Rd; s/d US$3/6; 🖳) This family-owned backpacker favourite has cosy, wood-finished rooms with private bathroom. The owner's brother Robin is a good guide. Internet connection is slow.

Golden Kalaw Hotel (☎ 50311; 66 Nat Sein Rd; s/d US$4/6) Lily's neighbour is just as good, with clean agreeable rooms and a hangout lobby.

Parami Motel (☎ 50027; Merchant Rd; s US$3-6, d US$6-10) Parami is a friendly, family-run place (a block from the market) with a variety of room options. Cheaper rooms have shared bathrooms.

New Shine Hotel (☎ 50028; newshine@myanmar .com.mm; 21 Union Rd; s US$18-24, d US$24-36) Two modern buildings (with some wicker details) offer a little more comfort.

Eating & Drinking

Everest Nepali Restaurant (Aung Chantha Rd; dishes from K1000; 🕑 breakfast, lunch & dinner) Good chapatis and fresh juice in a backpackery setting.

Sam's Family Restaurant (dishes K1000, vegetable dishes K500) White tablecloths and candlelight give a surprisingly romantic vibe for its Chinese and Bamar meals.

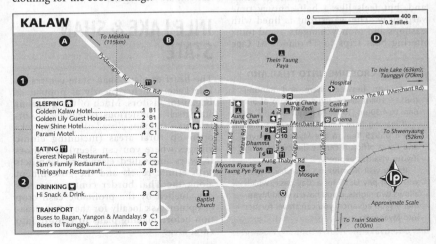

KALAW

SLEEPING 🏠
Golden Kalaw Hotel...........................1 B1
Golden Lily Guest House..................2 B1
New Shine Hotel...............................3 C1
Parami Motel.....................................4 C1

EATING 🍴
Everest Nepali Restaurant................5 C2
Sam's Family Restaurant..................6 C2
Thirigayhar Restaurant....................7 B1

DRINKING 🍸
Hi Snack & Drink..............................8 C2

TRANSPORT
Buses to Bagan, Yangon & Mandalay..9 C1
Buses to Taunggyi...........................10 C2

To Meiktila (115km)
Pyidaungsu Rd
(Union Rd)
Thein Taung Paya
To Inle Lake (63km); Taunggyi (70km)
Hospital
Kone The Rd (Merchant Rd)
Aung Chang Tha Zedi
Central Market
Cinema
Aung Chan Naung Zedi
Merchant Rd
Nat Sein Rd
Thirimingalar Rd
Zatila Rd
Yatana Rd
Dhamma Yon
Aung Chantha Rd
Zigyo Rd
Station Rd
To Shwenyaung (52km)
Myoma Kyaung & Hsu Taung Pye Paya
Aung Thabye Rd
Mosque
Baptist Church
Approximate Scale
To Train Station (100m)
0   400 m
0   0.2 miles

Thirigayhar Restaurant (Union Rd; mains K2000; ☺ breakfast, lunch & dinner) Occasional tour groups stop here for Shan, Indian or Western dishes, but its cottage set-up is the most charming location in Kalaw.

Hi Snack & Drink (Aung Chantha Rd) A very local, all-wood bar featuring beer and impromptu guitar concerts.

Getting There & Away
Many buses pass through Kalaw (heading towards Bagan, Yangon, Mandalay and Taunggyi), so it may be easier to stop here first, then leave the region from Inle Lake or Taunggyi to the east. A guesthouse should be able to help you get on a bus passing through.

Yangon-bound buses from Taunggyi pass by in the evening (K7000, about 15 hours). A spot on a Taunggyi bus to Bagan or Mandalay costs about K5000. A bus to Shwenyaung (the Inle Lake junction) costs K3000 and takes three hours. A taxi to Meiktila is about US$25.

PINDAYA
A 20km scenic road between Kalaw and Heho (home of the 'Inle airport') leads to touristy **Pindaya Caves** (admission US$3), where 8000 Buddha images form a labyrinth throughout the chambers of the caves. The condensation on the 'perspiring Buddhas' is rubbed on the face for good luck. **Myit Phyar Zaw Gji** (Taunggyi ☎ 081-22158; 317 Zaytan Quarter; s/d US$12/20) is the cheapest place to stay.

From Kalaw, take a local bus to Aung-ban (K150) and catch another to Pindaya (K550) – leave early and allow a full day. A lone bus connects Taunggyi (K1500) daily. It's easier to hire a taxi from Kalaw for US$15 to US$20.

INLE LAKE
☎ 081

'Inle' – with its cooler temperatures and blurry distinction between earth and water – has beckoned travellers since Myanmar opened to tourism. Uncertain shorelines and high hills ring the 22km shallow lake, which is filled with Intha folks fishin' and propelling flat-bottomed boats with their feet. Locals needing to borrow noodles from next door don't walk – they can't! – so they take the ol' canoe out.

In September and October, the **Phaung Daw U festival** runs nearly three weeks and is followed by the **Thadingyut festival** – one of Myanmar's greatest events (see p582).

Always cooler, Inle gets downright cold at night in January and February.

Orientation & Information
There are many villages in and around Inle Lake, but **Nyaungshwe** is the biggest and the one with budget accommodation. The transport hub at **Shwenyaung** is 13km away. **Taunggyi** is the main town in the area, east of Nyaungshwe.

To enter the Inle Lake zone, tourists are required to pay a US$3 entry fee at the **MTT office** (Strand Rd, Nyaungshwe) on the water.

Sights & Activities
THE LAKE
The best way to experience the lake is to play like a tourist and take a full-day **motorboat tour**. Any guesthouse – or any bloke with a boat near the MTT office – can arrange one for roughly K6000 to K8000 (and up). They'll take you by the touristy **floating gardens of Kela**, **Nga Phe Kyaung** (nicknamed 'jumping cat' monastery) and whichever village market is on that day. They'll also take you to artisans' shops, where weaving, blacksmithing and jewellery-making happens. The workshops are interesting and you're not obligated to buy anything, but if you'd rather skip them, tell your boatman. Cloth is a good buy here.

Another option – away from the package-tourist frenzy and MTT fee – is a self-guided **canoe trip** through the villages on the lesser-seen north end of the lake. A *nat* shrine is opposite Nanthe village, south of Nyaungshwe. Rates range from K500 per hour. You can arrange for one in the canal or near the MTT office.

IN NYAUNGSHWE
The **Museum of Shan Chiefs** (Third St; admission US$2; ☺ 9.30am-3.30pm Tue-Sun), in an impressive teak-and-brick mansion, was once the palace of the last Shan *sao pha* (chieftain). There are many Shan furnishings and costumes, plus a teak-floored audience hall in the north wing, to see.

There are plenty of Buddhist sites around town (see Map p552). The oldest is **Yadana Man Aung Paya**, with a step-spired stupa and 'you will be old/sick' cased figures outside.

MYANMAR

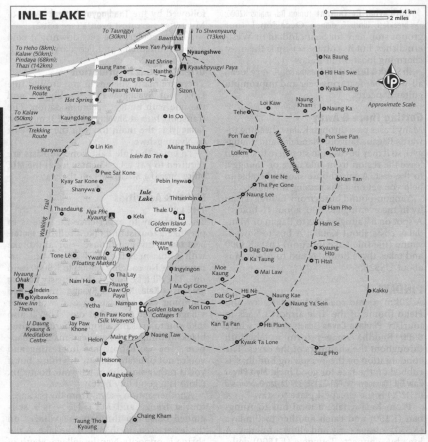

INLE LAKE

0 — 4 km
0 — 2 miles

To Taunggyi (30km)
To Shwenyaung (13km)
Bawrithat
Shwe Yan Pyay
To Heho (8km); Kalaw (50km); Pindaya (68km); Thazi (142km)
Nat Shrine
Nyaungshwe
Paung Pane
Nanthe
Kyaukhpyugyi Paya
Taung Bo Gyi
Na Baung
Trekking Route
Nyaung Wan
Sizon
Hti Han Swe
Hot Spring
Kyauk Daing
To Kalaw (50km)
Kaungdaing
In Oo
Loi Kaw
Naung Kham
Naung Ka
Approximate Scale
Trekking Route
Tehe
Kanywa
Lin Kin
Maing Thauk
Pon Tae
Pon Swe Pan
Inleh Bo Teh
Loilem
Wong ya
Pwe Sar Kone
Kyay Sar Kone
Pebin Inywa
Ine Ne
Kan Tan
Shanywa
Tha Pye Gone
Inle Lake
Thitseinbin
Naung Lee
Thandaung
Nga Phe Kyaung
Kela
Thale U
Ham Pho
Golden Island Cottages 2
Ham Se
Nyaung Win
Kyaung Hto
Zayatkyi
Dag Daw Oo
Ka Taung
Tone Lè
Ywama (Floating Market)
Ti Htat
Ingyingon
Moe Kaung
Mai Law
Nyaung Ohak
Tha Lay
Nam Hu
Phaung Daw Oo Paya
Ma Gyi Gone
Hti Nè
Naung Kae
Kakku
Indein
Nampan
Dat Gyi
Naung Ya Sein
Kyibawkon
Yetha
Golden Island Cottages 1
Kon Lon
Shwe Inn Thein
In Paw Kone (Silk Weavers)
Kan Ta Pan
Hti Plun
U Daung Kyaung & Meditation Centre
Jay Paw Khone
Naung Taw
Kyauk Ta Lone
Helon
Maing Pyo
Saug Pho
Hsisone
Magyizeik
Taung Tho Kyaung
Chaing Kham
Mountain Range
Walking Trail

OTHER ACTIVITIES

You can always dip in water hot enough to scorch Satan's butt at the **hot spring** (public/private bathing US$1/3; ☼ 7am-5pm), which is close to the Intha village of Kaungdaing. Rent a *longyi* for bathing for K200, private rooms are US$2. A boat comes here from Nyaungshwe (K800 each way). It is possible to take your bike and cycle here on a bumpy, hour-long ride.

Guided **day treks** can usually be arranged through guesthouses for approximately US$5 per day. There is a good, but quite rugged, all-day trip that leads to the monastery of **Koun Soun Taungbo** and to a nearby cave, passing two Pa-O villages on the way.

Sleeping

Nyaungshwe is teeming with good budget rooms. All include breakfast and rent bicycles unless otherwise noted.

Aquarius Inn (☎ 29352; 2 Phaung Daw Pyan Rd; s/d US$6/12) Excellent value, the quiet and friendly Aquarius has several cosy and warm all-wood rooms, plus a small library.

Remember Inn (☎ 29257; remember@myanmar .com.mm; Haw St; s US$4-10, d US$8-12; ☐) Popular with both backpackers and taxi drivers. Remember seems to be tapped into the commission network. Cheapest rooms – decked in bamboo – are the best deals.

Viewpoint Hotel (☎ 29062; s/d US$7/14) This hotel's unique location just over the bridge on the other side of the canal is a mixed

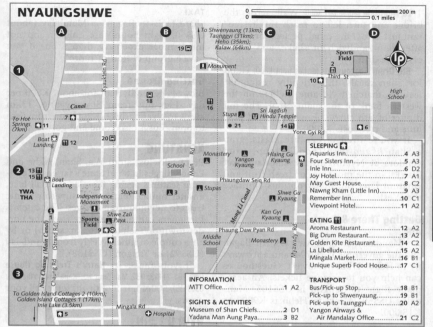

NYAUNGSHWE

0   100   200 m
0   0.1 miles

MYANMAR

blessing: sleeping over the water is fun, but morning boats serve as dependable alarm clocks. Rooms have balconies.

May Guest House (29417; 85 Myawady Rd; s/d US$6/12) Look for the small yellow building opposite Hlaing Gu Kyaung down a quiet side street. Snug rooms are squeaky clean, with hot-water shower and a small veranda.

Inle Inn (29016; Yone Gyi Rd; s/d US$8/12) This long-time inn on the eastern side of town is

SPLURGE!

If you want to sleep on – or 'over' to be more precise – the lake, the best deals are offered at **Golden Island Cottages 1** and **2** (Taunggyi 081-23136, Yangon 01-549019; www .gicmyanmar.com; s US$35-60, d US$40-70;), in Nampan and Thale U respectively. The main lodge is connected to 'island' cottages by elevated walkways over the water. Newer rooms are much nicer. Nampan has better lake views, but Thale U is quieter. The operation is run as a Pao-O collective, benefiting the local community.

quiet and has a pleasant garden sitting area out back. Bamboo bungalow rooms are best.

Four Sisters Inn (29190; 105 Nan Pan Qtr; s/d US$7/12) A quiet guesthouse between the canal and rice paddies; it's about 1km south of the village.

Joy Hotel (29083; Jetty Rd; s US$4-8, d US$5-9) On a narrow, quiet canal west of the market, the Joy Hotel feels pleasantly isolated.

Nawng Kham (Little Inn; 29195; Phaung Daw Pyan Rd; s/d US$5/10) Seven basic carpeted rooms arranged around a pleasant garden with atmospheric views of the nearby *zedi*.

Eating & Drinking

Unique Superb Food House (3 Myawady Rd; chicken fricassee K2000) A few tables face a garden; filet mignon is K2000, cream of carrot soup K500.

Golden Kite Restaurant (Yone Gyi Rd; dishes K1000; breakfast, lunch & dinner) The king of pasta and pancakes, the chef learned his thing from a pal in Bologna.

Aroma Restaurant (Chaung Rd; dishes from K1000; lunch & dinner) Modest canalside restaurant that pumps out stunningly good Indian food.

La Libellude (apple tart K600) Walk across the bridge and turn left to reach this restaurant just across the canal, perfect for a late-afternoon sandwich or shake, and watch canal life drift by.

Big Drum Restaurant (dishes from K800) Good for Shan meals, this friendly restaurant features thatched A-frame shelters on the western bank of the main canal. The full dinner of fish curry, bean soup, fried peanuts and rice costs K1000.

If you're tired of egg breakfasts, grab a Shan *hkauq-sweh* (noodle soup) from vendors at Nyaungshwe's **Mingala market** (Main Rd) in the morning, or fresh fruit and whatnot later on. Many options embrace the West.

Getting There & Away
AIR
Air Mandalay, Yangon Airways, Air Bagan and the government-run Myanma Airways fly to Heho, 41km northwest. Guesthouses can help you to arrange tickets. An aeroplane flight to Yangon is US$105, Mandalay US$50. A taxi to Heho is K9000 to K15,000.

BUS & PICK-UP
You can catch buses leaving Taunggyi at the Shwenyaung junction: the bus to Bagan (K7000, 12 hours) passes by at 5am; buses to Mandalay (K5000 or K6000, eight to 12 hours) go from 6pm to 8pm; and night buses to Yangon (K7000, 16 to 20 hours) stop around noon.

Pick-ups ply these routes but take much more time. Be prepared for cold travelling in January.

BORDER CROSSING: INTO THAILAND

You can cross the border from Tachilek into Mae Sai in Thailand. It's not a problem leaving here as long as your visa hasn't expired.

Dreary Tachilek is about three to four hours from Kengtung on a paved road. It's much cheaper going to Tachilek (about K4000 by bus, K7500 by Toyota 'van'), than the other direction (generally US$6 and US$14 respectively). The border is open roughly 6am to 6pm weekdays, 6am to 9pm weekends.

TAXI
Share taxis to Bagan or Mandalay (about US$50, eight hours) are quicker and not much more expensive than a bus if you have a group of four or more.

Getting Around
Bicycles generally rent for about K500 per day. Pick-ups from Shwenyaung, 13km away, to Nyaungshwe (K200) run from 6am to 6pm. Buses also come and go.

KENGTUNG
Practically lost amid Wa, Shan, Akha and Lahu villages in Shan State's far east, Kengtung features ageing temples, a small lake, a water-buffalo market and superbly scenic treks to neighbouring villages. The catch is foreigners can only get here from the border town of Tachilek (163km south) or by air a couple of times weekly from Mandalay (US$92) or Yangon (US$138).

If you make it, **Harry's Trekking House** (☎ 101-21418; 132 Mai Yang Rd, Kanaburoy Village; r US$3-15), 500m north of town, serves all your needs.

PYIN U LWIN
☎ 085
Up in the foothills northeast of Mandalay (in northern Shan state), this former British hilltown – called Maymyo during the British era – is a welcome 7°C cooler than Mandalay and lined with more British-era buildings than most places in the country. It's more about biking past blooming trees, or hanging with a locally made espresso, than anything heavy-duty. You can also ride on cute pony-led miniature wagons – like the Wells Fargo days of the American West.

Domestic travellers pour in during the hottest months (March through May).

Orientation & Information
Pyin U Lwin is spread out. The highway between Mandalay and Hsipaw passes through the main road.

You can get online across from the bus stand at **Shwe Htay Internet** (Main Rd; per min K25; ⏲ 8am-9pm).

Sights
A few kilometres to the west of the town's centre, 436-acre **National Kandawgyi Gardens** (☎ 22130; admission K2000, camera/video fee K200/

K1000; ☼ 8am-5pm) is a lovely area run by a Singapore joint-venture company, with an inviting pool facing a small lake.

In town, the **Purcell Tower** – which was a gift from Queen Victoria – still chimes to the tune of Big Ben. The **market** is filled with local strawberry jam and wine, plus pullover-makers leaning over old sewing machines.

The best way to fill a day is visiting the **Anisakan Falls** (admission free), a 45-minute hilly hike from the village of Anisakan (8km south of Pyin U Lwin). The falls are nice; it may be easiest to go with a guide (K15,000 including taxi). You can take a pick-up to Anisakan from the main road in Pyin U Lwin for K300.

Sleeping

Few hotels in the centre are licensed for foreigners. The most relaxing deals – many are midrangers – are south and southwest of town. All rates include free breakfast.

Grace Hotel 1 (☎ 21230; 114A Nann Myaing Rd; s/d US$5/10) A walkable couple of blocks south-east of the main strip, this hotel has a garden out front and basic rooms with private bath.

Golden Dream Hotel (☎ 21302; 42/43 Main Rd; s US$3-4, d US$6-8) Run by a pleasant Indian family, this walk-up hotel above a pullover shop has old but clean rooms.

Dahlia Motel (☎ 22255, 09-204-4153; s US$5-12, d US$10-18) This great traveller-oriented motel – a couple of kilometres southwest of the centre – is run by an outgoing 'rock-and-roll Muslim' (translation: 'drinks beer, eats pork sometimes') who can help arrange day treks to Shan villages (US$8). The older rooms are the best deals.

Eating

Many very basic Chinese restaurants are on the side streets north and south of the main road.

Golden Triangle Café & Bakery (☎ 24288; Mandalay-Lashio Rd; sandwiches & pizza K1400-1800; ☼ breakfast, lunch & dinner) The best snack or coffee spot is this surprising bakery, which brews espresso for K400.

Getting There & Away

Pyin U Lwin sees limited bus services. By far the easiest way to or from Mandalay or Hsipaw is by share taxi. A small share-taxi stand on the main road, 200m east of the clock tower, arranges taxis to Mandalay (K3500,

two hours) and Hsipaw (K4500, three hours). Most go from 7am to 2pm or 3pm.

Pick-up trucks, lingering near Purcell Tower, go to Mandalay (K1000). A pick-up to Hsipaw (K2000) leaves at 6am from the banyan trees across from the taxi stand.

The train station is north of the main road, 1km east of the taxi stand.

HSIPAW
☎ 082

Three hours northeast of Mandalay, Hsi-paw is a lovely laid-back highland town with DIY trekking potential, a bustling riverside morning market and a knack for stretching out some travellers' day-by-day itineraries.

Bawgyo Paya Pwe is held in February/March (see p582).

Sights & Activities

The **Shan Palace** (suggested donation US$1; ☼ 4pm) at the northern end of town, built in 1924, is home to the nephew of the last prince of Hsi-paw, and his wife. The gracious couple show guests the mansion's memorabilia and tell its story, which is intertwined with Shan State's. (This same story is the topic of *Twilight over Burma: My Life as a Shan Princess*, a memoir by Austrian-American Inge Sargent.)

The **popcorn factory** north of town uses an alarmingly explosive technique to make the snack. It's tricky to find. Ask around.

For a great sunset, walk to either **Five Buddha Hill** or **Nine Buddha Hill**. Cross the bridge on the Lashio road, walk 200m and look for a path leading to both hills.

Boat trips along the Dokhtawady can be arranged through Mr Charles (below) or Nam Khae Mao Guest House (p556) for about US$5 per person.

Talk to **Mr Book**, who runs a bookshop on the main road and gives out hand-drawn maps of outlying-area hikes. He can also organise tubing in summer.

Sleeping

Mr Charles Guest House (☎ 80105; 105 Auba St; s US$3-6, d US$6-15) A bustling and popular spot north of town. The common veranda has hosted many a beer-soaked sit session. Mr Charles often leads three-hour morning trips to a village or nearby waterfall. The higher-priced rooms here have private bathroom.

Nam Khae Mao Guest House (☎ 80088; nkmao @myanmar.com.mm; 134 Bogyoke Rd; r with shared bathroom US$3, s/d with private bathroom US$7/10) Next to the clock tower, this friendly place is starting to crumble a bit.

Eating
The market stalls have Hsipaw's best food. Across from 'Mr Food' on the main road, **Burmese Cuisine** (curry K300) is a row of pots filled with tasty curries – including a sublime pumpkin. Mr Food (aka Law Chun) gets swamped with foreign travellers for its English-language menu and noodle and rice dishes.

Getting There & Away
Bus service here can be dodgy – the mightbreak-down kind of dodgy. Buses leave Hsipaw at 6am for Mandalay (K2300), stopping in Pyin U Lwin. Buses also head to Lashio (K600, two hours), 72km northeast.

Most people go by share taxi to or from Mandalay (K6000 per person, three hours). Taxis to Lashio cost K3000.

The train route toward Mandalay (ordinary/1st class US$3/6, 10½ hours) goes by the Gokteik Gorge and is revered as one of Myanmar's most beautiful rides, though the carriages can rock like a horse. The train leaves Hsipaw (allegedly; it's often late) at 9.30am.

MANDALAY

☎ 02
Founded as capital of the Burmese empire in 1861, Mandalay served as the setting for the last kings of Burma, who wore their shiny gems here till the British stormed in and took over in 1885 – a largely uncontested conflict.

Not all visitors to Myanmar's second city (young at under 150) fall in love with its one-way grid of streets that sprawl east of the Ayeyarwady and south of Mandalay Hill, essentially the only bump in the flat city-scape. But its walkable downtown is filled with cheap guesthouses, and day trips to the nearby ancient cities (p563) are too good to pass up. The town has been booming lately from new Chinese-run businesses and it is whispered that the red, green and white trades – rubies, jade and heroin – fuel the economy as well. Alongside these commercial endeavours you're more than likely to encounter a totally different side of life as more than three out of five of Myanmar's population of Buddhist monks live here.

ORIENTATION
Lower numbered streets run east–west, counting from north to south. The north–south running streets are numbered 60 and above, higher streets to the west. The fastest cross-city thoroughfares are 35th St and 80th St. The city centre, called 'downtown' by English-speaking locals, runs roughly from 21st to 35th Sts, 80th to 88th Sts. Street addresses usually include cross streets; in Mandalay (as in this text), '66th St, 26/27' means '66th St between 26th and 27th Sts'.

MTT sells a Mandalay map for K100.

INFORMATION
Internet Access
Many guesthouses have a lone computer offering Internet for K1000 or K1500 per hour. Other downtown email outlets include:
Micro-Electronics Email Service (Map p559; 83rd St, 23/24; per hr K1000; ☯ 9am-8.30pm)
Winner (Map p559; 83rd St, 24/25; per hr K1000; ☯ 8am-8pm)

Medical Services
Main Hospital (Map p557; 30th St, 74/77)

Money
Exchange rates in Mandalay are just a little worse than in Yangon, but better than elsewhere.
Kyaw Kyaw Aung Email (Map p559; 27th St, 80/81; ☯ 9am-6pm) Has a poor Internet connection, but cashes American Express travellers cheques at a 20% commission.
Sedona Hotel (Map p557; cnr 26th St & 66th St) This joint venture is the only business that accepts credit cards.

Post
DHL Express office (Map p559; ☎ 39274; 22nd St, 80/81)
Main post office (Map p559; 22nd St, 80/81; ☯ 9.30am-3pm)

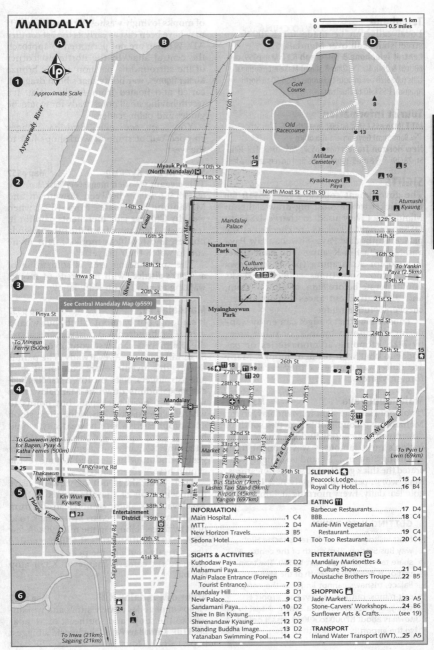

MANDALAY

MYANMAR

See Central Mandalay Map (p559)

See Central Mandalay Map (p559)

0 .... 1 km
0 .... 0.5 miles

Approximate Scale

Ayeyarwady River

Golf Course

Old Racecourse

Military Cemetery

Myauk Pyin (North Mandalay)

10th St
11th St

North Moat St (12th St)

Mandalay Palace

Nandawun Park

Culture Museum

Myainghaywun Park

Kyauktawgyi Paya

Atumashi Kyaung

To Yankin Paya (2.5km)

Canal
14th St
16th St
18th St
Inwa St
20th St
Shweta
22nd St

Pinya St

Bayintnaung Rd

Fort Moat

East Moat St

12th St
14th St
16th St
19th St
21st St
23rd St
24th St
25th St

26th St
27th St
28th St
29th St
30th St
31st St
32nd St
33rd St
34th St
35th St
36th St
37th St
38th St
39th St
40th St
41st St

Mandalay

To Mingun Ferry (500m)

To Gawwein Jetty for Bagan, Pyay & Katha Ferries (500m)

Thakawun Kyaung

Kin Wun Kyaung

Entertainment District

Yangyiaung Rd

Thissa Yarzar

Sidaw-Myo-Pyo Rd

New Tu Chaung Canal

Yay Ni Canal

To Pyin U Lwin (69km)

Market

To Highway Bus Station (7km); Lasho Taxi Stand (9km); Airport (45km); Yangon (697km)

To Inwa (21km); Sagaing (21km)

INFORMATION

Main Hospital	1	C4
MTT	2	D4
New Horizon Travels	3	B5
Sedona Hotel	4	D4

SIGHTS & ACTIVITIES

Kuthodaw Paya	5	D2
Mahamuni Paya	6	B6
Main Palace Entrance (Foreign Tourist Entrance)	7	D3
Mandalay Hill	8	D1
New Palace	9	C3
Sandamani Paya	10	D2
Shwe In Bin Kyaung	11	A5
Shwenandaw Kyaung	12	D2
Standing Buddha Image	13	D2
Yatanaban Swimming Pool	14	C2

SLEEPING

| Peacock Lodge | 15 | D4 |
| Royal City Hotel | 16 | B4 |

EATING

Barbecue Restaurants	17	D4
BBB	18	C4
Marie-Min Vegetarian Restaurant	19	C4
Too Too Restaurant	20	C4

ENTERTAINMENT

| Mandalay Marionettes & Culture Show | 21 | D4 |
| Moustache Brothers Troupe | 22 | B5 |

SHOPPING

Jade Market	23	A5
Stone-Carvers' Workshops	24	B6
Sunflower Arts & Crafts	(see 19)	

TRANSPORT

| Inland Water Transport (IWT) | 25 | A5 |

Telephone

Local calls can be made for K200 from street stands all over Mandalay.

Central Telephone & Telegraph (CTT; Map p559; cnr 80th St & 26th St; 7am-8.30pm) Make international calls (US$3.20 per minute to Europe, US$4.50 to North America, US$1.40 to Thailand).

Tourist Information

MTT (Map p557; ☎ 60356; cnr 68th St & 27th St; 9am-5pm) Government-run office

New Horizon Travels (Map p557; ☎ 60767; 122 36th St, 78/79; 8am-5.30pm) Helps find drivers and guides.

SIGHTS

The government collects a flat US$10 fee for a ticket to see most big-draw sights in Mandalay. (They used to charge US$3 to US$5 *per sight.*) Tickets are checked at the palace, Kuthodaw Paya, Shwenandaw Paya and Shwe Ta Bin Kyaung. The same ticket is good for Amarapura (p563) and Inwa (p563) too. Sometimes collection desks don't operate before 8am, or after 4.30pm, and alternative entrances bypass ticket-checkers. Nudge nudge.

Those on a strict budget can enjoy wandering downtown by foot, or other areas by bike, stopping at monasteries or pagodas to chat with resident monks. Many are quite welcoming as they receive few foreign visitors.

Mahamuni Paya — Map p557

If you only see one sight in Mandalay, go for Mahamuni, a couple of kilometres south of downtown. Its central Buddha image – the nation's most famous – was brought from Rakhaing State in 1784, and is so highly venerated the thick gold leaf obscures its features. Male worshipers (only) apply new layers of gold leaf daily. Every morning at 4am, a team of monks lovingly washes the image's face. It may have been cast as early as the 1st century AD. Women are not permitted to approach the central altar. In the northwest corner of the surrounding pavilion are six bronze **Khmer figures**, war booty that's been dragged, carted and floated from Angkor Wat. It's worth having small notes ready for would-be guides and palm-readers.

You can see new Buddha images chipped out of stone at workshops just to the west.

> **GETTING INTO TOWN**
>
> Most visitors arrive at the ramshackle Highway Bus Station, 7km south of the centre. A share taxi to town is about K2500. The train station is downtown, south of the Mandalay Palace; trishaws cannot linger at the entry/exit ramps, but are nearby. The airport is a staggering 45km from the centre. A taxi to town is about K7000 to K9000 (less if going *to* the airport).

Shwe In Bin Kyaung — Map p557

This elegant wooden **monastery** (Teak Monastery; cnr 89th St & 38th St) between downtown and Mahamuni Paya, dates from 1895, when wealthy Chinese jade merchants paid for it. It's lovely, free, away from the other pagoda hordes, and toothless monks might invite you to watch their prayer.

The surrounding area is something of a **'monk's district'**, with hundreds of monks walking to and fro on leafy lanes.

Mandalay Hill — Map p557

It's a long, hot barefoot climb, but what a view. Two hundred and thirty metres above the plain, you can rest your eyes on the Shan hills and the Ayeyarwady. The path is lined with souvenir sellers, cold-drink guys and astrologers. Near the top, a **standing Buddha image** points down at Mandalay. He's not saying 'head back pal', but points to where – legend says – Buddha once stood and prophesied where a great city would be built – got a pen? – in the Buddhist year 2400 (the Roman equivalent of 1857), the year Mindon Min decided to move the capital here.

Tuck your shoes out of view or leave them with one of the attendants (K100). An elevator/escalator combo leads up from a halfway point reached by switchback road built by forced labour in the mid-'90s. A few gates lead up; the best is the lion-guarded one, directly south of the peak.

There's a camera charge of K350 atop the hill.

Around Mandalay Hill — Map p557

Heaps of pagodas draw visitors and worshipers to the south and southeast of Mandalay Hill. **Kuthodaw Paya** (the 'world's biggest book') draws tour buses for its 729 slabs

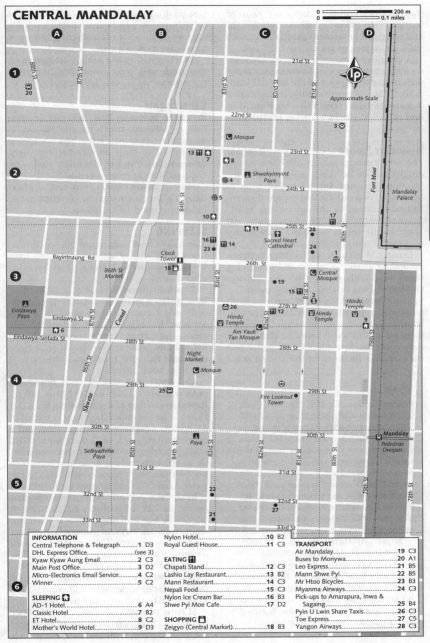

CENTRAL MANDALAY

MYANMAR

that retell the Tripitaka canon. It's included in the US$10 ticket (see p558). Nearby, the more haggard **Sandamani Paya** has more such slabs and is free to get in.

A couple of hundred metres south, the intricately carved wooden **Shwenandaw Kyaung**, the only surviving part of the original Mandalay Palace, is worth seeing. It was moved outside the palace walls following King Mindon's death. It's included in the US$10 ticket (see p558).

Mandalay Palace   Map p557

The royals moved palaces like chess pieces, on the advice of their celestial advisors. Mindon Min, the second-to-last king of Myanmar, ordered the old palace dismantled and moved to this sprawling, moat-guarded central spot from Amarapura, just 11km to the south, in 1861. Thibaw Min occupied it until the Brits came.

During WWII, fierce fighting between occupying Japanese forces and advancing British and Indian troop resulted in fires that burned the original to the ground.

The **new palace** (⏱ 7.30am-5pm) was built using concrete, aluminium and forced labour. It's not exactly authentic – though there's a useful watchtower to climb. The only entry for foreigners is along the east wall, and it's included in the US$10 ticket

(see p558). Most of the interior – restricted to visitors – is a leafy army barracks. Most visitors, and locals remembering the work to rebuild it, skip a visit.

You can walk along a shady **promenade** on the south wall, near downtown, to admire the original walls close up for free.

Other Sights

Yatanaban Swimming Pool (Map p557; admission K200; ⏱ 5am-6pm), north of the palace, is an outdoor pool that's the best cheap dip in town. The kid's pool features a slight urine-addled tint, but the main pool – an Olympic-size number – is fine.

Hilltop **Yankin Paya** is 3km east of Mandalay Palace. See maps for other pagodas, fodder for good DIY exploits.

SLEEPING

Mandalay's best budget options – all downtown – fill up by afternoon in the high season (October to March). Breakfast is included at all.

Royal Guest House (Map p559; ☎ 65697; 41 25th St, 82/83; s US$3-7, d US$6-10; ❄) Hands down best-run budget guesthouse in town, its rooms are small but brightly done and sparklingly clean. The management is very friendly and helpful and will serve *mohinga* (rice noodles with fish) for breakfast if you ask. It fills first; book ahead.

AD-1 Hotel (Map p559; ☎ 34505, 09-69-71116; Eindawya Sintada St; s US$3, d US$6; ❄) A bit removed from other downtown deals, the AD-1 Hotel is in the most 'kept real' quarter of Mandalay – between Eindawya Paya and a crazy market, on a brick lane with shops selling monk gear. The 27 rooms are a little scruffed up, but are clean and cute, with sky-blue tiles and private bathrooms and hot water. There's a rooftop deck for brekkie.

Nylon Hotel (Map p559; ☎ 66550; nylon@mptmail .net.mm; cnr 25th St & 83rd St; s US$3-5, d US$6-10; ❄ 🖳) A big building above a generator shop, with an array of rooms (most have air-con, some have TVs; all have private bathroom and hot water). Rooms on the fourth and fifth floors get views (No 401 is a good cheapie up there). Internet is K1000 per hour. Staff sometimes add commission to things like taxis or toilet paper.

ET Hotel (Map p559; ☎ 65006; 129 83rd St, 23/24; s/d from US$5/8; ❄) A friendly guesthouse near the Shan district, with basic rooms, private

---

SPLURGE!

Peacock Lodge (Map p557; ☎ 33411, 61429; 5 Myaypadethar St, off 61st St, 25/26; s/d US$12/18; ❄) Lost in the backlanes east of the palace walls, the Peacock offers village-like peace, and the owners treat you like part of the family. Guests are likely to be offered a whisky over a leisurely afternoon chat in the photo-filled TV room. The seven rooms have nice wood floors, and do fill in peak season. Bicycles are available. A library of old books includes a 1938 Mandalay phonebook (lots of British names in there).

Royal City Hotel (Map p557; ☎ 31805; 130 27th St, 76/77; s/d from US$13/18; ❄) A bit pricier (and a couple of steps up in comfort), this stylish hotel, run by the Royal Guest House folks, offers big rooms with air-con, TV, private bathroom and serious views from its wood-framed windows. Breakfast is served on the outdoor/indoor roof garden.

bathroom with hot water, and a book swap downstairs. Most rooms have TV; cheaper ones have fan.

Classic Hotel (Map p559; ☎ 32841; 59 23rd St, 83/84; s/d US$8/16; ✿) Tidy rooms with TV, air-con and private bathrooms with hot showers; it's a bit pricier than ET Hotel around the corner, without a real jump in quality.

Mother's World Hotel (Map p559; ☎ 33627; 58 79th St, 27/28; s/d US$10/18; ✿) The street's a little trashy (behind the train station), but the hotel has well-kept carpeted or green-tiled rooms with Chinese-style woodwork; single room No 506 has full views of Mandalay Hill and the Shan hills.

EATING & DRINKING

'Mandalay' means 'sleazy beer joints and disco' in Burmese. Just joking. There's good food here, but not much in the night to conjure. Sit and write a poem, you heathen.

Downtown

Lashio Lay Restaurant (Map p559; No 65 23rd St; dishes K300-K400; ✿ breakfast, lunch & dinner) The best food downtown – and one of a couple of Shan eateries nearby – Lashio Lay is a two-floor spot with blazing fans and a dozen pots of Shan dishes that come with rice (several veggie options).

Chapati Stand (Map p559; cnr 27th St & 82nd St; meals under K300; ✿ dinner) For people-watching and price, nothing beats this unnamed open-air stand. Veggie or meat curries come with piping-hot chapatis. There's a mixed crowd: *longyi*, skullcaps, turbans and Kathmandu backpacks.

Nepali Food (Map p559; 81st St, 26/27; dishes K900; ✿ breakfast, lunch & dinner) Cute purple-on-purple curry house serves no meat, no alcohol and no eggs. *Thali* (three curries, chapati, rice and dahl) is a super deal.

Nylon Ice Cream (Map p559; 173 83rd St, 25/26; ✿ breakfast, lunch & dinner) The de facto meeting place for locals and downtown-based travellers. A scoop of ice cream is K200. A Myanmar Beer – stay or go – is K1000.

Shwe Pyi Moe Café (Map p559; 25th St, 80/81; tea K80; ✿ breakfast & lunch) Downtown's best teashop serves good tea, and cooks up *ei-kyar-kwe* (long, deep-fried pastries; K70) and banana pancakes (K180).

Mann Restaurant (Map p559; 83rd St; dishes K600-K800; ✿ breakfast, lunch & dinner) This bare-bones

Chinese restaurant is a longtime backpacker standby; a Ms Tiger rep serves a fair share of red-faced locals.

Around Town

Too Too Restaurant (Map p557; 27th St, 74/75; meals K800; ✿ lunch & dinner) Hole-in-the-wall heartbreaker for tasty Burmese pick-and-point pots of curries – catfish, prawn, chicken, veggie. Best at lunch.

Marie-Min Vegetarian Restaurant (Map p557; 27th St, 74/75; dishes K600-1400; ✿ breakfast, lunch & dinner, closed May) This traveller-oriented Indian restaurant serves all-veggie meals. Plenty of choice in the chapati meals (aubergine dip with vegetables is good), and the lassis are made with purified water. It's down a lane mid-block.

BBB (Map p557; ☎ 25623; 292 76th St, 26/27; dishes K3000; ✿ breakfast, lunch & dinner) No more rice! This two-floor bamboo lodge cranks the air-con, pipes in ESPN on the telly, and sells all the sorts of things you might miss (pasta, burgers, barbecue chicken).

Hoist that bottle of Myanmar Beer high, over your chosen skewers of pork, chicken, whole fish or veggies (spiced bean curd, lady fingers) at Mandalay's lively (at night) strip of open-air **barbecue restaurants** (Map p557; 30th St, 65/66). A full meal with beer runs around K3000 or K4000.

ENTERTAINMENT

Moustache Brothers Troupe (Map p557; 39th St, 80/81; donation K2500; ✿ 8.30pm) Performing in the home of the banned trio, this colourful troupe has celebrated traditional Burmese folk opera for over three decades. The show is quite in your face, and pretty cornball, as relayed atop a miniwood-crate stage, with a dozen or so plastic chairs a metre away. The once famous troupe is now banished from public performances, and its original shtick in Myanmar has shifted to English. The night meanders through slapstick, political satire, Myanmar history, traditional dance and music, and how to tie up your *longyi*. Lu Maw's English is pretty good – he's particularly fond of expressions like 'cat out of the bag' – though if you speak English as a second language you may struggle a bit. T-shirts are K5000. Drop by any time to chat.

Mandalay Marionettes & Culture Show (Map p557; ☎ 34446; 66th St, 26/27; admission K3500; ✿ 8.30pm) The worthwhile hour-long shows

MYANMAR

in this small theatre feature marionette episodes of *zat pwe* (re-creation of Buddhist tales) and *yama pwe* (tales from the Indian epic Ramayana); all the while the soundtrack comes from a floor-plopped crew of drum-banging traditional musicians. New puppets are sold at decent prices.

SHOPPING

Crafts are a big deal in Mandalay, where you can pick up marionettes (new and old) for a few dollars, as well as *kalaga* (a traditional tapestry) and other antiques.

Sunflower Arts & Crafts (Map p557; 27th St, 74/75) Part of Marie-Min Vegetarian Restaurant (p561) features two showrooms of old wood and bronze doo-dads and some anatomically correct (read: dangling genitalia) puppets (new ones are US$3 and up, antiques US$10 and up). Mandalay Marionettes (see p561) also sells puppets.

Zeigyo (Map p559; 84th St, 26/28) Encompasses two large modern buildings, packed with plenty of Myanmar-made items (including handicrafts) that spill onto the surrounding sidewalks.

Jade market (Map p557; admission US$1; 7am-5pm) Amid the 'monk district', this market features dozens of stalls and tables where locals get serious over rock. Beware of fakes.

Vendors outside the Mahamuni Paya (p558) sell handicrafts and Buddhism tidbits. The stone-carvers' workshops, just west of the pagoda, are cheaper if you're looking for a little stone elephant or Buddha.

GETTING THERE & AWAY

See p564 for details on pick-ups and other transport to Amarapura, Inwa, Sagaing and Mingun.

Air

Mandalay sees daily services to and from Yangon (US$96 to US$102), Nyaung U (for Bagan; US$42 to US$46) and Heho (for Inle Lake; US$42 to US$50), as well as flights to Kengtung, Bhamo and Myitkyina. Air Mandalay, Bagan Air, Yangon Airways and Myanma Airways serve Mandalay.

Downtown offices include the following (domestic fares can be purchased at travel agents too):

Air Mandalay (Map p559; ☎ 31548; 82nd St, 26/27; 9am-5pm Mon-Fri, 9am-1pm Sat)

Myanma Airways (Map p559; ☎ 35221; 81st St, 25/26; 9am-2pm)

Yangon Airways (Map p559; ☎ 31799; 81st St, 25/26; 9am-5pm)

Boat

The **Inland Water Transport office** (IWT; Map p557; ☎ 36035; 35th St; 10am-2pm) sells tickets for Ayeyarwady boats. Gawwein Jetty is to the west of the centre.

Destination	Fare	Duration	Departures
Bagan (slow boat)	US$10	15hr	5.30am (Sun & Wed)
Bagan (express boat)	US$16	9hr	6am (Mon, Tue & Thu-Sat)
Bhamo	US$9/24/54	2-3 days	5.30am (Tue, Fri & Sun)

Bus

Mandalay's dusty Highway Bus Station sees a mind-numbing array of daily options for transport. You can arrange tickets to Yangon at small stands downtown, including **Leo Express** (Map p559; ☎ 39323; cnr 83rd St & 33rd St), at **Mann Shwe Pyi** (Map p559; ☎ 88267; cnr 32nd St & 83rd St) and at **Toe Express** (Map p559; ☎ 64926; 32nd St).

At the time of research, a 5.30am bus left a new bus station just a couple of kilometres east of the Highway Bus Station for Pyin U Lwin and Hsipaw and Lashio (K2300 flat rate). Buses for Monywa (K1000 and up; four hours) leave from a small **downtown station** (Map p559; off 88th St, 21/22). Some Monywa-bound drivers refuse to take on foreigners.

Taxi

The easiest way to Pyin U Lwin is via share taxi (about K5000 per person, 1½ hours). Check at your guesthouse or at the **taxi stand** (Map p559; cnr 27th & 83rd Sts). The Highway Bus Station has a **Lashio taxi stand** (☎ 80765) that sends cars to Hsipaw (K8000, five hours) or Lashio (K8000, six hours).

Train

Mandalay's modern (largely bare) train station features, just inside the main (east) entrance, an **MTT office** (☎ 22541; 9.30am-6pm), which sells tickets at 10% commission. You *might* be able to buy tickets from tellers directly upstairs.

At research time, seven trains a day left for Yangon (via Thazi, Taungoo and Bago). The quickest trains were No 6 Down, No 15 Up and No 17 Up (taking about 12 hours); these left at 3.15pm, 5.15pm and 6.30pm respectively. Others took 14 to 16 hours. Ordinary tickets ran US$11 to US$15, first class US$30 to US$35 and sleepers US$45 or US$50.

Trains also leave for Nyaung U (Bagan; ordinary/first class US$4/9, seven hours) at 10pm. Two daily trains go to Myitkyina (US$10/27, 24 hours). One morning train goes northeast to Pyin U Lwin (US$2/4, three hours) and Hsipaw (US$3/6, 10 hours).

GETTING AROUND

Try not to shop with a driver, as you may be paying way more based on commission deals drivers work out with shop owners.

Bicycle & Motorcycle

There are several central places to rent bicycles, including **Mr Htoo Bicycles** (Map p559; 83rd St, 25/26; per day K1000; ⏰ 8am-7pm). Marie-Min Vegetarian Restaurant (p561) can rent a motorcycle for K7500 per day.

Bus

Mandalay's city buses are almost always crowded, particularly during the 7am to 9am and 4pm to 5pm rush hours.

Taxi

White taxis and 'blue taxis' (which are teensy Mazda pick-ups) whisk folks around Mandalay most hours. Prices are negotiable. A ride from downtown to the Bagan jetty is about K2000. A full-day trip by blue taxi to nearby attractions is about K15,000.

Trishaw

The familiar back-to-back trishaws are the usual round-the-town transport. Count on K200 to K500 for a short ride, or K1000 for a longer one – say, from the Mandalay Hill to downtown. Bargain. At night, expect to pay more.

AROUND MANDALAY

For many, the reason to stick around Mandalay is daytripping to the four 'ancient cities' nearby. Lesser-seen Monywa is a good alternate route from Mandalay to Bagan via Pakokku.

AMARAPURA

The short-term capital 11km south of Mandalay – the 'City of Immortality' – is famed for its1.2km-long teak **U Bein's Bridge** leading to **Kyauktawgyi Paya** and small **Taungthaman** village with tea and toddy shops. At 200 years old, the bridge sees lots of life along its 1060 teak posts, with monks and fishers commuting to and fro. A popular sunset activity is renting a **boat** (about K1500) to drift by as the skies turn orange, or watching it from a waterside beer station.

Just west is the **Ganayon Kyaung**, where hundreds of monks breakfast at 11am. Resist the temptation to thrust a camera in their faces as some travellers do.

The highway is about 1km west of the bridge; ask the pick-up driver to direct you. It's possible to bike from Mandalay in about 45 minutes.

Technically Amarapura is part of the Mandalay US$10 ticket (see p558), but at research time no-one checked for it here, so it wasn't necessary to pay to see the bridge.

INWA

Cut off by rivers and canals, Inwa (called Ava by the British) served as the Burmese capital for nearly four centuries. Admission is included in the US$10 Mandalay ticket. **Horse carts** (K2500 for two people) lead a three-hour loop around Inwa's handful of

MYANMAR

MANDALAY BUSES & FARES				
Destination	**Fare**	**Duration**	**Departures**	**Type of Bus**
Bagan	K4200	8hr	9am, 2pm & 9pm	local
Meiktila	K600	3hr	frequent	local
Taunggyi (to Inle)	K4500	10-12hr	6pm	air-con
Yangon	K4500	12-15hr	5.30pm	air-con

sights. Aside the road, villagers till soil or bathe in ponds in an area picturesquely dotted with abandoned temples.

The finest sight is the happily unrenovated **Bagaya Kyaung**, a teak monastery supported by 267 posts. The 27m **Nanmyin** watchtower seriously leans; look for the breast-shaped Kaunghmudaw Paya in the distance, across the river about 10km west of Sagaing. **Maha Aungmye Bonzan** (aka Ok Kyaung) is a brick-and-stucco monastery dating from 1822.

Take a pick-up to the Inwa junction. From here it's 1km south to the water, where you can catch a ferry to Inwa.

SAGAING

Across the Ava Bridge from the Inwa junction, the stupa-studded hilltops of Sagaing loom over the Ayeyarwady. With 500 stupas, and more monasteries, Sagaing is where stressed Myanmar Buddhists come to relax and meditate; some monks invite visitors to stay. Sagaing is also known for silver shops and guitars.

The highlight is a kilometre north of the market and highway, up and around **Sagaing Hill** (admission US$3); some locals know free ways up, but the admission fee also gets you into Mingun. Trees hang over stone steps leading past monasteries to the top. **Tilawkaguru** (donation K500), near the southwest base, is a mural-filled cave temple dating from 1672. There are great views above, and pathways lead all the way to the water for the adventurer.

Asekhan Fort, a couple of kilometres south of Ava Bridge, was the site of a minor 1886 battle with the British. A small cemetery – for three fallen Brits – is just south.

One block northeast of the market is **Happy Hotel** (☎ 072-21420; s/d from US$8/15; ✗).

SEEING THE ANCIENT CITIES 101

Mingun is reached by boat (see right). Frequent go-when-packed **pick-ups** (Map p559; cnr 29th St & 84th St) from Mandalay stop by Amarapura (30 minutes) and the Inwa junction (40 minutes) before reaching Sagaing (45 minutes). It's K100 during the day, K200 after dark. For shoestringers pool kyat for a 'blue taxi' – which costs about K10,000 or K15,000 for a full day. Seeing the three in one day is a bit rushed, but do-able.

Pick-ups start/stop near the market. Sagaing is spread out. A trishaw driver can show you around for about K2500 for half a day.

MINGUN

Up and across the Ayeyarwady from Mandalay, **Mingun** (admission US$3) is fun to visit. The boat trip drifts peacefully for 11km, and a half dozen sights face the water, all peppered with ample opportunities for noodles, art and postcards. The 50m **Mingun Paya** – just the earthquake-cracked base of an intended 150m monster stupa – is an impressive pile of bricks you can climb up. Just north is the **Mingun Bell**, the world's largest uncracked bell. It's worth pressing 200m north to the white, wavy-terraced **Hsinbyume Paya**.

A government-run riverboat to Mingun (K1500, one to two hours) departs from the west end of 26th St in Mandalay at 9am daily, returning at 1pm. If you miss it, you can negotiate a ride for about K7000. Admission to Mingun includes Sagaing.

MONYWA

☎ 071

This scrappy trade town, 136km west of Mandalay, is missed by most visitors, but has knockout sights nearby. About 20km south, **Thanboddhay Paya** (admission US$3; ☼ 6am-5pm) bursts with carnival shades of pink, orange, yellow and blue. Inside are over half a million Buddhas filling nooks and crannies. About 4km east is a Buddha frenzy in the foothills – a 90m reclining Buddha and a construction of a standing Buddha (to be the world's second tallest by 2006). It's far easier to visit by taxi.

Across the Chindwin River and 25km west, the 492 **Hpo Win Daung Caves** (admission US$2) occupy a mountain shaped like a reclining Buddha. There are many carved Buddhas, with streams of light beaming through holes in the walls. Plus monkeys. It's best to go with a guide. Boats for here leave on the Monywa jetty (a whopping K1500 each way) to a jeep stand (K5000 for five people).

Shwe Taung Tarn Hotel & Restaurant (☎ 21478; 70 Station Rd; r per person US$5-8; ✗) offers surprisingly comfy rooms in the back building, with wood floor, air-con and TV. There's excellent food.

Getting There & Away

Hourly buses leave for Mandalay (K700, four hours) from the station, 1.5km south of the centre. For information on going the other way see p562. Four daily buses go to Pakokku (K600, 4½ hours) en route to Bagan. There are no passenger ferries.

BAGAN REGION

BAGAN

☎ 02 & 061

If you put all of Europe's medieval cathedrals on Manhattan island – plus a few extra – you'd start to get a sense of the ambition of the temple-packed plain of Bagan. Home to 4400 temples built mostly 800 or more years ago, Bagan rivals Angkor Wat as one of Southeast Asia's most remarkable sites. The temples are smaller than Cambodia's, but nearer each other – leading to great vistas and sunsets. On any given day, some passageways are stuffed with travellers (and hawkers), while others nearby are empty.

History

Bagan was born when King Anawrahta took the throne by force in 1044. In short order he unified the country, founded Theravada Buddhism and began building Bagan's first temple, the grand Shwezigon. The hubristic Anawrahta coveted the sacred Buddhist scriptures (the Tripitaka) held by the very Mons who enlightened him. When they refused to hand them over, he took them by force. Anawrahta was eventually killed by a wild buffalo, but his line ruled for 200 years. This was Bagan's golden age, a period of furious temple building. Things began to go bad under the decadent King Narathihapati, who built the gorgeous Mingalazedi pagoda but bankrupted the city, leaving it vulnerable to attack by Kublai Khan, in 1287.

The city was crushed again in 1975, when an earthquake measuring 6.5 on the Richter scale damaged many of Bagan's important structures.

Bagan's most recent upheaval happened in 1990, when the government forcibly rooted up the residents of Old Bagan and planted them in undeveloped land 5km to the south (now New Bagan).

BAGAN TELEPHONE CODES

These are a little crazy. The Bagan area has two area codes: ☎ 061 and ☎ 02. You may see some old numbers beginning with the borrowed Pakokku code (☎ 062), which were assigned in the rush for new telephone numbers as more businesses opened since 2000. All old numbers that start with ☎ 062 have been switched to ☎ 02. All local numbers are five digits. To add to the fun, any old numbers that previously began with 70 changed to 67, meaning the old number ☎ 062-70999 is now ☎ 02-67999.

Orientation

The massive Bagan Archaeological Zone stretches 42 sq km and is home to the 'towns' of Nyaung U, Old Bagan, Myinkaba, New Bagan and a few others. By far most independent travellers base themselves at the northeast corner of the zone at Nyaung U (home to the bus station, and 5km north of the airport and train station). About 4km west, Old Bagan's hotels – amid the bulk of the temples – cater to tour groups; 3km south is New Bagan, with a few more midrange offers. Well-paved roads connect them, with dirt paths venturing off-road to the temples.

Just east of the bus station is the unnamed 'restaurant row' where you'll find plenty of places to eat.

In town, 'Main Rd' is used (locally and in text) to refer to the main strip, which runs along the Bagan-Nyaung U Road east of the bus station, and along the Anawrahta Rd from the market to the Sapada Paya.

The Map of Bagan (K500), found at most guesthouses, is very useful.

Information

All foreign visitors to the Bagan Archaeological Zone must pay a US$10 entrance fee, technically lasting as long as you'd like to stay.

Nyaung U is home to most traveller services, including a post office and Internet access.

Ever Sky Information Service (Map p570; ☎ 061-60146; Nyaung U; ☯ 7am-9.30pm) This place in restaurant row helps arrange cars, trips and guides, plus it has a small bookstore.

Internet Stand (Map p570; Main Rd, Nyaung U; Internet access per hr K1000; ☯ 8am-8pm)

MYANMAR

Myanmar Travel & Tours (Map p567; MTT; ☎ 061-60277, 02-67418; New Bagan; ⏱ 8.30am-4.30pm) Government-run tourist office just north of New Bagan.

RMCG Computer Centre (Map p570; Main Rd, Nyaung U; Internet access per hr K2500; ⏱ 7am-9pm) Burns digital camera shots onto CD for US$2.

Sleeping

All prices include breakfast. Old Bagan's joint-venture hotels are geared to bigger wallets and as a result are not covered here.

NYAUNG U

Eden Motel (Map p570; ☎ 02-67078; Main Rd; s US$4-10, d US$10-15; ✷) This motel has 18 great-value, air-conditioned rooms, all with private bathroom. The older complex has cheaper rooms, and the better ones really (bamboo walls, wood floors, cranking air-con). Newer rooms (across the street) have TV and more space.

Pann Cherry Guest House (Map p570; ☎ 061-60075; Main Rd; s $US3-4, d US$6-8) Closest to the bus station, Pann has basic rooms with a bed, fan, screen window and four walls – but it's clean and cheap.

Shwe Na Di (Map p570; ☎ 061-60409; Main Rd; r per person US$3; ✷) This formerly unlicensed guesthouse offers basic rooms with new air-con units and cold-water attached bathroom.

May Kha Lar Guest House (Map p570; ☎ 061-60306, 02-6706; Main Rd; s/d from US$6/10; ✷) A step up in comfort, this well-kept, three-storey guesthouse has bright, clean rooms with air-con,

---

SPLURGE!

If you want a pool, you can pay a few dollars to jump in at a fancy Old Bagan hotel's pool or stay at one of these Nyaung U places.

Thante Hotel (Map p570; ☎ 02-67317, Yangon ☎ 1-664424; nyaunguthante@mptmail.net .mm; Main Rd; s/d US$30/35; ✷ ✥) South of the market, the Thante offers roomy bungalows on shady grounds with a pleasant swimming pool (US$3 for nonguests). Rooms come with satellite TV and deck chairs on a small porch.

Golden Express Hotel (Map p570; ☎ 02-67101; geh@myanmar.com; Main Rd; s US$12-25, d US$18-30; ✷ ✥) A couple of kilometres west of town, Express has four price ranges, a lovely pool (US$3 for nonguests), and a practically private pagoda nearby.

---

ceiling fan and screen windows. The pricier rooms with TV have wooden floors.

Inn Wa Ga (Map p570; ☎ 02-67125; Main Rd; s/d US$3/6; ✷) A stone's throw from the market, the Wa Ga offers simple fan-cooled rooms on the main floor, and air-con with huge windows upstairs.

New Park Hotel (Map p570; ☎ 061-60322; 4 Thiripyitsaya; s US$6-7, d US$10-12; ✷) For a bit more quiet, this two-complex 20-room hotel – one of a few porched ones in the leafy back lanes near the 'restaurant row' – is worth an extra dollar or two.

NEW BAGAN

Bagan Beauty Hotel (Map p567; ☎ 061-60351; Main Rd; s/d US$3/6; ✷) This friendly blockhouse cheapie is clean but no diva. Its 12 simple rooms have hot showers, twin beds and wrinkled vinyl floors.

Kyi Kyi Mya Guest House (Map p567; ☎ 02-67037; Main Rd; s/d US$6/12; ✷) Next to the Beauty, Kyi Kyi Mya rents its 10 basic rooms with air-con to foreigners (and discourages them from its fan-cooled rooms). It's cute enough from the outside, but probably not worth the extra kyat from Beauty.

Bagan Central Hotel (Map p567; ☎ 02-67141; Main Rd; s US$10-15, d US$15-20; ✷) Good-value rooms in stone-covered units with hot water, armoire, wood floors and twin beds, all set around courtyard with tables for open-air breakfast. Cheaper rooms are the best deals if you can cope without TV.

Thiri Marlar Hotel (Map p567; ☎ 02-67370; thirimarlar@mptmail.net.mm; s/d US$20/25; ✷) This excellent-value mini splurge, a couple of blocks from the road to Old Bagan, has 21 often-filled rooms (with twin or double beds and private bathroom) set around teak walkways facing a leafy courtyard with a bamboo coffeehouse. Bar and breakfast deck up top.

Eating
NYAUNG U

Bagan action centres on Nyaung U – either along the main street or the unnamed 'restaurant row'. Pizza reigns at most, but you'll find a motley crew of Asian foods (Burmese, Chinese, Thai and Indian) at many too.

Pho Cho (Map p570; restaurant row; dishes from K1000; ⏱ breakfast, lunch & dinner) Best for its Thai, Pho Cho may not be 100% authentic, but it's good. The vegetable salad is a particularly good deal, coming hot and on a platter.

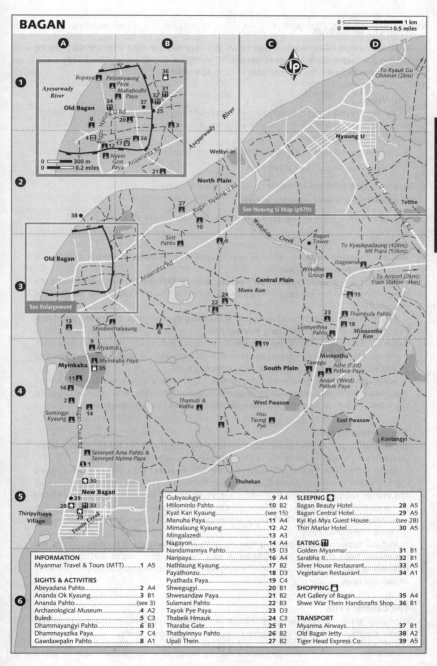

BAGAN

MYANMAR

TEMPLES OF BAGAN

With more temples than tourists on most days, you can easily find a spare temple top or decaying mural to take in alone in Bagan (Map p567). This section groups some of the more popular (and impressive) ones. See p571 for info on getting around.

Top Views

It's sacrilege to pick some temple views over others (*so* many are good), but some get the props for sunset viewing and others (including big temples like Ananda) are disqualified because their top terraces are closed.

- Dhammayangyi Pahto – The Central Plain
- Shwesandaw Paya – The Central Plain
- Mingalazedi – Around Myinkaba
- Buledi ('Temple 394') – The North Plain
- Pyathada Paya – The Central Plain (has a giant open terrace for viewing)

Old Bagan

This 2km counterclockwise circuit takes in sites within old city walls. The hearty could take it in by foot, otherwise hire a bike.

North of the ho-hum **Archaeological Museum** (Nyaung U–Old Bagan Rd), the 60m **Gawdawpalin Pahto** – one of the fine late-period temples – was rocked by the 1975 earthquake but has been reconstructed.

About 200m south, a dirt road leads past **Mimalaung Kyaung** (note the *chinthe*, a half-lion, half-guardian deity) and **Nathlaung Kyaung** (the only remaining Hindu temple at Bagan) to Bagan's highest temple, **Thatbyinnyu Pahto** (Omniscience Shrine), with two white boxy storeys, surrounded by diminishing terraces and rimmed with spires, built in 1144. A couple of hundred metres south you can climb up on old bits of the city wall.

Some 200m north of the temple is **Shwegugyi**, a 1131 temple with corncob *sikhara* (Indian-style temple finial) atop and stucco carvings inside. Back north on the Nyaung U–Old Bagan Rd, you'll find the 9th-century **Tharaba Gate**, the former eastern entry to the walled city.

The Northern Plain

The bulk of 'Bagan' fills the broad space between Nyaung U and Old Bagan; these sites are (roughly) west to east between the two paved roads between the two.

About half a kilometre east of Thatbyinnyu, the 52m **Ananda Pahto**, with its golden *sikhara* top and gilded spires, is probably Bagan's top cat. Finished in 1105, the temple has giant Buddha images facing each of the four entranceways. On the full moon of the month of Pyatho (between mid-December and mid-January), a three-day *paya* festival attracts thousands.

Just northwest is **Ananda Ok Kyaung**, with colourful murals (some with Portuguese traders) detailing 18th-century life.

Midway between Old Bagan and Nyaung U, **Upali Thein** features brightly painted and big murals from the early 18th century. Across the road, the spot of the terraced 46m **Htilominlo Pahto** was picked by 1218 by King Nantaungmya, who used a 'leaning umbrella' to pick the spot.

The Central Plain

Ramblings in this wide pocket (roughly south of Anawrahta Rd between Nyaung U and New Bagan) sometimes lead past goat-herders, 2km away from paved roads.

South of Thatbyinnyu, the 11th-century five-terraced **Shwesandaw Paya** (1057) is a graceful white pyramid-style pagoda with 360-degree views – packed for sunset, empty during the day. Note the original *hti* lying to the south (toppled by the quake). Half a kilometre south, the ever-visible, walled **Dhammayangyi Pahto** has two encircling passageways – the inner one intentionally filled; it's believed King Narathu was such a bastard that the workers ruined it after his assassination in 1170. Ceilings tower – bat noises echo down from the darkness.

One kilometre east, the broad two-storeyed **Sulamani Pahto** (1181) is one of Bagan's prettiest – with lush grounds and carved stucco. Just 150m east, **Thabeik Hmauk** looks like a mini-Sulamani, but without the hawkers *and* you can climb up the top.

Around Myinkaba

The area around Myinkaba village – south of Old Bagan – is chock full of sites. Of the most popular is **Mingalazedi** (1274), with three receding terraces lined with 561 glazed tiles and tasty views of the nearby river and east toward the plain.

Just north of town, **Gubyaukgyi** (1113) sees a lot of visitors for its richly coloured paintings inside – a torch (flashlight) helps. In town, the modern-looking **Manuha Paya** (1059) was built by the captive Mon king. Note the four giant Buddha images that are seemingly too large for the enclosure – symbolic of Manuha's discontent with his prison life. Stairs in the back lead above the reclining Buddha. Just south, **Nanpaya**, from the same era, is a cave-style shrine, possibly once a Hindu shrine (note the three-faced Brahma on the pillars).

About 400m south of town, the Sinhalese-style stupa of the 11th-century, **Abeyadana Pahto**, was likely built by King Kyanzittha's (waiting) Bengali wife and features original frescoes. Across the road, **Nagayon** (its corncob *sikhara* top possibly a prototype to Ananda) has some tight stairs leading up to the roof.

South Plain

This rural stretch is accessed via the road from New Bagan to the airport, or by dirt roads from the Central Plain. About 3.5km east of New Bagan, **Dhammayazika Paya** (1196) is unusual with its five-sided style. It's quite made over – with lush grounds and lavish attention from worshippers. A dirt road leads 2km to Dhammayangyi.

An excellent cluster of sites is about 3km east. North of the road, **Tayok Pye Paya** has good westward views of the site. To the south, 13th-century **Payathonzu**, a small complex of three interconnected shrines, gets much attention for its murals.

About 200m north, same-era **Nandamannya Pahto** features the 'temptation of Mura' murals – in the form of topless women reaping no response from a meditating Buddha. (It's often locked; ask at Payathonzu for the 'keymaster'.) Just behind, the **Kyat Kan Kyaung** has been a cave-style monastery for nearly 1000 years.

Around Nyaung U

In town, the gilded bell of **Shwezigon Paya** (1102) is considered by many to be the prototype for many Myanmar pagodas. The 37 pre-Buddhist *nat* were endorsed by the Bamar monarchy here. A yellow compound located on the east side (called '37 Nats' in English) features figures of each.

From the Nyaung U jetty, you can negotiate a fun boat trip (about K4000) to see temples just off the Ayeyarwady: **Thetkyamuni** and **Kondawgyi Pahto** are about 1km north; the **Kyauk Gu Ohnmin** cave temple (dating back close to a thousand years) was supposedly the start of a tunnel intended to go 18km – only 50m is accessible nowadays.

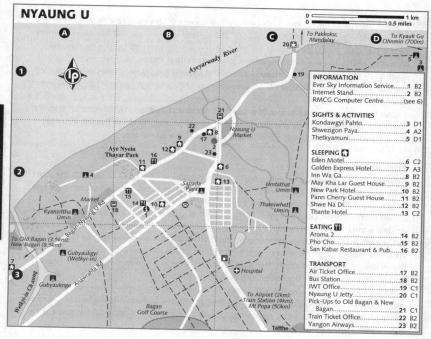

NYAUNG U

Aroma 2 (Map p570; restaurant row; dishes K1500-3500; ☼ lunch & dinner) Often lively outdoor setting with some of Myanmar's best Indian food; curries come as dollops on banana-leaf plates.

San Kabar Restaurant & Pub (Map p570; Main Rd; pizza K2400-3600, pasta K1600-3600; ☼ breakfast, lunch & dinner) The birthplace of Bagan pizza, the San Kabar's streetside candlelit courtyard fills nightly with travellers seeking tomato sauce and thin-crust pies.

OLD BAGAN

During the day, Old Bagan's eateries are the closest tummy-filling spots to the heart of the temples.

Sarabha II (Map p567; dishes K1200-6000; ☼ lunch & dinner) Of the two Sarabhas back to back, the one away from the road is more quiet. Staff offer cold towels for your dusty face. Food is mostly Asian, but there's spaghetti too.

Golden Myanmar (Map p567; buffet K1500; ☼ lunch & dinner) Simple roadside Burmese eatery with shaded seats on a brick floor and a 'buffet' of meat curries with a table-full of condiments and 'bean stick' dessert.

About 250m west of the gate are several eateries including Vegetarian Restaurant.

NEW BAGAN

Tour groups (mostly) stop at a few atmospheric riverside restaurants during the day. All like to plug nightly puppet shows and the expensive river prawn and fish (from K4000), but you can get fried rice for K800 on the main road in town at the Silver House Restaurant (not on menu; ask).

Shopping

Shwe War Thein Handicrafts Shop (Map p567; ☎ 061-67032; dsavariau@mptmail.net.mm; ☼ 7am-9pm Oct-Mar) In Old Bagan, this shop, just east of Tharabar Gate, is a treasure trove of Myanmar trinkets and one of the region's best souvenir shops.

The town of Myinkaba is the lacquerware HQ – it's the best in the country. Several family-run workshops sell traditional pieces, better quality than offerings by hawkers around temples. One good choice is **Art Gallery of Bagan** (Map p567; ☎ 061-60307).

Getting There & Away

Most travel services arrive and depart at Nyaung U. Ask at **Ever Sky** (Map p570; ☎ 061-60146; Nyaung U; ☒ 7am-9.30pm) or your guest-house about hiring a share taxi. A ride to Inle is about US$75, Mandalay US$50.

AIR

Regular services connect Bagan with Yan-gon (US$93), Mandalay (US$45) and Heho (US$65). On Nyaung U's main road, an **air ticket office** (Map p570; ☎ 02-67406, 09-204-2001; ☒ 9am-5pm) sells domestic tickets for Air Mandalay, Yangon Airways and Air Bagan. The government-run Myanma Airways of-fice is in Old Bagan.

BOAT

The Shwe Kein Nayi Express ferry leaves for Mandalay at 5.30am (US$16, 12 hours, five days a week). More visitors opt to drift downriver from Mandalay. The slow boat (US$10, two nights, twice weekly) goes to Mandalay (US$10, two nights) or downriver to Pyay (US$9, two nights). Most boats leave from the Nyaung U jetty (Map p570), a kilometre northeast of the market; some stop and start in Old Bagan (Map p567) depending on the tide and time of year.

From the Nyaung U jetty local ferries go to Pakokku (K1000, 2½ hours), where you can catch a bus to Monywa (p564).

BUS

Local buses to Mandalay (K4000, eight hours), via Meiktila, leave at 7am and 9am from the bus station in Nyaung U (Map p570). Here you can catch a 3pm air-con bus to Yangon (K6500, about 15 hours) or a 5am local bus to Taunggyi (K6000, 10 to 12 hours). Local buses also go to Yangon for K2500. Book tickets two days in advance in peak season.

PICK-UP

Pick-ups to Mt Popa leave from the Nyaung U bus station. Tiger Head Express Co (Map p567) sends daily pick-ups from New Bagan to Taunggyi (K1000, 10 hours) at 3am.

TRAIN

Presently two morning trains leave from Mandalay (ordinary/1st class US$4/9, 10½ hours) and there's an evening train to Yan-gon (US$11/31, 20½ hours). The train sta-tion is 4km southeast of Nyaung U. You can also get tickets at a train station office on the main road in Nyaung U.

Getting Around

Bicycles are a fine way to see Bagan. Take water though, as some patches are not near vendors. The going rate from guesthouses is K500 per day in Nyaung U, double that in New Bagan.

A horse cart isn't a bad way to orient yourself on day one. It's about K5000 or K6000 per day for up to four people.

A pick-up runs between Nyaung U and New Bagan, stopping in Old Bagan and Myinkaba. A ride costs K200. A taxi for the day runs about US$20.

AROUND BAGAN

Mt Popa

This 1520m-high monastery-topped hill – which is visible from Bagan on a clear day (if you look to the right end of the moun-tains to the west) – offers gee-whiz views of the plain, and more importantly, it's Myanmar's most important centre for *nat* worship. The trip up is worth it if you have at least two full days for Bagan itself. The 30-minute climb up goes past mon-keys and many pilgrims (including slow-stepping *yeti* hermits). The **Mahagiri shrine**, at the foot of the mountain, features a display of the 37 *nat*. Festivals include the full moon of **Nayon** (May/June) and **Nadaw** (November/December). Up the hill, you can swim at the posh, Singapore JV **Popa Mountain Resort** (☎ 02-69168; r from US$50; ☒) for US$2.

It's possible to visit by pick-up from Nyaung U (K200), often with a change in Kyaukpadaung. Far easier is getting a slot in a share taxi for US$5 per person. Ask the driver to point out remnants of the petrified forest.

Meiktila & Thazi

If you find yourself in Meiktila while travel-ling the Bagan-to-Inle corridor, the **Honey Hotel** (☎ 21588; Pan Chan St; s US$5-10, d US$8-15; ☒) is a converted mansion on the shores of Lake Meiktila.

Thazi, the rail junction, has a place li-censed for foreigners: **Moon-Light Rest House** (☎ Thazi 56; r from US$3; ☒).

Pakokku

An alternate route between Bagan and Monywa goes by this lazy, very real town on the west bank of the Ayeyarwady. Stay at **Mya Yatanar Inn** (☎ 062-21457; 75 Lanmataw St; r per person K3500), a down-home mansion on the water run by a priceless 70-something couple.

UPPER AYEYARWADY

The river is life in Myanmar, and the action is up way north of Mandalay in Kachin State, home to some great long-haul river adventuring on the Ayeyarwady. Most travellers train or fly north – to Myitkyina or Bhamo – and drift south on ferries with locals and plenty of time to discover the little things.

Much of the area away from the river is closed to foreigners.

MYITKYINA

☎ 074

The Kachin capital – near China – mainly lures folks to start southward boat trips, or drop by Kachin villages in the area. Rice grown here is considered Myanmar's best.

Snowland Tours (☎ 23498; snowland@mptmail .com.mm; ☺ closed Sun) can provide tours of the region.

Several Buddhist sites are in the area, though many locals are Christian. About 14km north is **Praying Mountain**. The modest **Kachin State Culture Museum** (Youngyi Rd; admission US$2; ☺ 10am-3pm Tue-Sun) is 3km from the centre.

The **YMCA** (☎ 23010; mka-ymca@myanmar.com .mm; 12 Myothit Rd; s US$5-7, d US$6-12; ☒ ☐) is the most traveller-friendly and savvy place in town, though the water pressure's iffy, and some ants occupy rooms too. The Internet's pokey at best.

Getting There & Around

Government-run Myanma Airways flies to and from Mandalay (US$70).

Sometimes 'fast boats' to and from Bhamo (K8000, seven hours) are restricted for foreigners. Pick-ups on the 188km road between Bhamo and Myitkyina leave from near the Y at 8.30am. Have passport copies ready for checkpoints.

A blanket is mandatory for nights on the train to and from Mandalay (1st-class/sleeper US$27/US$40, 25 to 50 hours).

A shop behind the Y can rent motorcycles (per day K6000).

BHAMO

☎ 074

More charming than Myitkyina, the river town of Bhamo, 186km south, features a bustling daily market, drawing Lisu, Kachin and Shan folk from around the countryside. The old Shan city walls of **Sampanago** – rubble, really – are located 3km north of town. Rather interesting **Kachin villages** can be visited.

Most unexpected is the **homemade helicopter** made by Sein Win, who was inspired by James Bond flicks; ask about it at the **Friendship Hotel** (☎ 50095; yonekyi@baganmail.net .mm; r from US$5).

MA flies here from Mandalay (US$50) twice weekly. Lower/upper deck seats on the ferry to Mandalay are US$9/24. The trip takes 1½ days. Fast boats to Katha (ordinary/1st class K3500/10,000, five to seven hours) are excellent value.

KATHA

This appealing river town will mean more to you if you've read George Orwell's *Burmese Days*. Georgie, who was stationed here in 1926–7, based his novel on this setting. The old **British Club**, around which much of the novel swirls, is now an agricultural co-op. The tennis court mentioned in the novel is still in use.

Opt for the road-facing upstairs rooms at the basic **Ayeyarwady Guest House** (Strand Rd; r K3000) for river views.

The ferry south to Mandalay (deck/cabin US$7/42, around 24 hours) goes three times weekly. It's also possible to bus to Mandalay (K3500, 12 hours). The nearest train station is 25km west at Naba.

BEACHES & THE DELTA

It's not just the Buddhist sites that draw travellers to Myanmar's shores – increasingly, it's the shores themselves. The sprawling coastline has some tasty slices of sand. Rather remote Ngapali Beach (p575) is the finest, but Chaungtha Beach (p574) and Ngwesaung Beach (p574) are easier to reach from Yangon (both via the appealing delta town of Pathein). Government officials have their eyes on the tourist appeal of these places more intently than much of Myanmar, but there are private alternatives.

During the monsoon season (mid-May to mid-September) heavy rains blanket the coast and chase away most travellers.

The earthquake that kick-started the December 2004 tsunami was felt at these places, but no damage was sustained.

PATHEIN

☎ 042 / pop 300,000

On the way to Chaungtha or Ngwesaung beaches from Yangon, in the heart of the delta, compact but big Pathein is a great town to stop in for some real-deal local mingling and to pick up a parasol to protect you from the rays. The wide, scenic Pathein River curves through town, bringing in constant action.

Pathein is about 120km west of Yangon.

Sights

Pathein's claim to fame is the 'umbrellas' – actually parasols for the sun, not rain – made in the couple of dozen parasol workshops

scattered in the northern part of the city, particularly around the Twenty-Eight Paya, off Mahabandoola Rd. They're made in various colours, and some are painted with nature motifs; saffron-coloured ones are waterproofed. You can pick one up for a couple of thousand kyat. The **Shwe Sar Umbrella Workshop** (☎ 25127; 653 Tawya Kyaung Rd; ☼ 8am-5pm) is a good place to watch them being made.

Shwemokhtaw Paya, in the centre of Pathein near the riverfront, is a huge, golden, bell-shaped stupa. The *hti* consists of a top tier made from 6.3kg of solid gold, a middle tier of pure silver and a bottom tier of bronze. The seated Buddha in the southern shrine supposedly floated here on a raft from Sri Lanka.

Settayaw Paya is perhaps the most charming of the several lesser-known *paya* in Pathein. The *paya* compound wraps over a couple of green hillocks dotted with a number of well-constructed *tazaung* (shrine buildings).

Sleeping

Electricity ebbs and flows (mostly ebbs).

Paradise Guest House (☎ 25055; 14 Zegyaung Rd; r US$10; ☒) The nicest place for the buck.

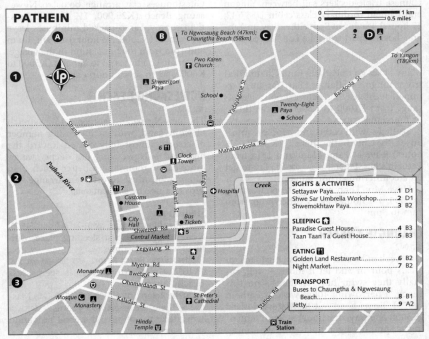

PATHEIN

To Ngwesaung Beach (47km);
Chaungtha Beach (58km)

To Yangon (180km)

Pwo Karen Church

Shwezigon Paya

School

Twenty-Eight Paya

School

Pathein River

Clock Tower

Mahabandoola Rd

Creek

Customs House

Hospital

City Hall

Bus Tickets

Shwezedi Rd
Central Market

Zegyaung St.

Myenu Rd

Monastery

Bwetgyi St

Ohnmardandi St

Mosque

Monastery

Kaladan St.

St Peter's Cathedral

Station Rd

Hindu Temple

Train Station

SIGHTS & ACTIVITIES
Settayaw Paya......................................1 D1
Shwe Sar Umbrella Workshop..........2 D1
Shwemokhtaw Paya............................3 B2

SLEEPING
Paradise Guest House.........................4 B3
Taan Taan Ta Guest House................5 B3

EATING
Golden Land Restaurant....................6 B2
Night Market.......................................7 B2

TRANSPORT
Buses to Chaungtha & Ngwesaung
　Beach...8 B1
Jetty..9 A2

MYANMAR

Alongside a canal, a block from the central market, Paradise rooms are modern, with TVs and friendly staff.

Taan Taan Ta Guest House (☎ 22290; 7 Merchant St; s US$5-7, d US$6-10; ❄) Simple, clean rooms with private bathroom in this central, five-storey hotel.

Eating

Night market (Strand Rd) This particularly worthy, riverside market is a teen flirt zone and a veritable smorgasbord of treats: crisp, delicate coconut crêpes spread with just-sweet-enough jaggery syrup, potato and banana fritters, fresh fruit, scissor-cut noodles, rice and peanuts steamed in bamboo.

Golden Land Restaurant (Merchant St; mains K2000; ❂ lunch & dinner) Just north of the clock tower, Golden Land sets up dinner tables outside among the trees. It is pricier than the others but blessedly quiet. Good for a beer away from the street noise.

Getting There & Away

BOAT

Chinese triple-deckers sail between Yangon and Pathein (ordinary class/cabin US$7/42, 17 hours), leaving at 5pm either way. In Yangon, boats depart from the Lan Thit St jetty.

BUS

Many buses go to Pathein (and Chaungtha) from Yangon's Hlaing Thar Yar bus terminal, most leaving before noon. Tickets range from K1000 to K3000 for the three- or four-hour trip.

Stuffed – with cargo and people – minibuses to Chaungtha Beach (K2500, 2½ hours) leave at 7am, 11am and 1pm from Pathein's **bus station** (Yadayagone St). Try to get on a comfier bus from Yangon.

Shwe Min Than buses go to Ngwesaung (K2500, 1½ hours) every other hour from 7am to 3pm.

CHAUNGTHA BEACH
☎ 042

On weekends and holidays, busloads of locals pour in and let it loose – well, actually they swim fully clothed – on this beach, a harrowing 40km west of Pathein (p573). Boats head out to **Whitesand Island** (K3000 one way, one hour) at 8am, returning at 5pm. It's a good place for swimming

and snorkeling, though 'Three Tree Island' might have been a more apt name. The **market** (❂ 6-9am) is a lively vestige of life here before tourism – great when the fish come in.

Sleeping & Eating

Chaungtha – give it props – has the cheapest places to stay of Myanmar's beach towns, though most places poke into mid-range. Some places close between mid-May and mid-September.

Shwe Hin Tha Hotel (☎ 24098, Yangon ☎ 1-650588; s US$5-18, d US$10-25; ❄) The only cheapie on the beach. Cheapest rooms are small blue bungalows with private porch facing the courtyard.

Several budget places away from the beach are worth a look, including **Win Villa** (s/d US$3/6), a teak-style home with balcony and no-frill rooms. A good one near the village is **Discovery Inn** (s/d US$3/6).

Food's found at all guesthouses and hotels and around the village main street.

Getting There & Away

Guesthouses can arrange boats to Ngwesaung Beach (K25,000, 1½ hours). Less-than-roomy, cargo-packed minibuses leave for Pathein (K2500, 2½ hours) at 7am, 11am and 1pm from the bus station in the village. Better air-con buses go to Yangon (K5000 to K6000, six to seven hours) at 7am.

NGWESAUNG BEACH
☎ 042

The 'new Ngapali' – a gorgeous 15km stretch of white sand, with an increasing number of resorts almost fully geared toward the high end – Ngwesaung has deeper water, more elbow room and a better beach than Chaungtha. Most resorts can arrange day trips to a nearby **elephant camp**.

Sleeping

Golden Sea Resort (Yangon ☎ 01-241747; s/d US$15/20) Ngwesaung's cheapest sleeping place, with small wood bungalows.

Silver View Beach Resort (☎ 581100, ext 318; s/d US$20/25; ❄) Motel-like, it seems less 'beachy' than rest.

Yuzana Resort (☎ 581100; r US$25-50; ❄) Massive – there are some 133 rooms – with a hangar-like reception and a good restaurant on the terrace.

Getting There & Away

Regular buses connect Chaungtha with Pathein (K2500, 1½ hours) and several buses leave for Yangon (K5000, five hours).

There are no roads to Chaungtha. You can boat (K25,000, 1½ hours) or go by bus via Pathein (K2500, two hours), which leaves every other hour between 7am and 3pm.

NGAPALI BEACH

☎ 43

In southern Rakhaing State – accessed by long-haul buses from Yangon via Gwa or Pyay – Myanmar's best beach boasts 3km of palm-backed white sand facing the turquoise Bay of Bengal. It's increasingly leaning toward big-money tourism, but it's beautiful and quiet, and the seafood is some of the country's best food.

Sights & Activities

Anyone can set you up on a half-day **snorkel trip** (US$12 to US$15 including boat, mask and snorkel for up to five people). The coral's OK – there are some cones to swim around – but plenty of brightly coloured fish will keep you company.

The fishing village south of the beach (with drying fish lay on bamboo mats) is **Jade Taw**, easily reached by foot. Farther south (by road) is **Lontha**, home to a hilltop stupa (go left at the market crossroads and follow the water) with superb views.

Sleeping

All but the Grand include free breakfast.

Linn Thar Oo Lodge (☎ 42333, Yangon 1-229928; www.linntharoo-ngapali.com; s/d from US$15/20) A sprawling old standby with 42 bungalows of various conditions now edges its prices along with midrange neighbours. Power runs 1pm to 3pm and 5pm to 10pm. Most rooms face the water. It's near the north end of the beach.

Royal Beach Hotel (☎ 42411, Yangon 1-243880; royalngapali@myanmar.com.mm; r US$15-40) Near the south end, this nice midranger has five price ranges in its shady, compact complex amid a small forest of palms. Rooms have wood floors, mosquito nets and private bathrooms. Power runs limited hours unless you opt for a US$35 or US$40 room with 24-hour generator power.

Grand Resort (s/d US$6/10) Just north of the main strip, Ngapali's only surviving chea-

pie is far from Myanmar's comfiest – and certainly no 'resort' – but the simple rooms (concrete floor, buzzing light bulb, mattress on floor), with OK bathrooms attached, are on the water.

Eating

Only hotels have food or drink on the water. Along the road just inland are some superb open-air, family-run restaurants. Squid – sometimes flattened in 'filet' style – with garlic and ginger sauce is particularly good. Crab, squid or barracuda is about K2000, tiger prawn K3500. **Moonlight** (200m north of Royal Beach) is an excellent choice.

Getting There & Around

Visitors reach Ngapali via the **Thandwe Airport** (☎ 42611), 5km north of the beach, or the Thandwe bus station, 9.5km northeast. Flights to Yangon cost US$72 to US$80; it's about US$10 cheaper to Sittwe.

Long-distance bus services to and from Yangon take 17 or 18 hours, leaving around 3pm, and cost K4500. **Ye Aung Lan** (☎ 43500) sends buses along the smoother route (via Gwa). **Aung Thit Sar** (☎ 43499) goes via Pyay (K4500, 12 hours) along a stomach-churning trip over the mountains – often in buses filled with bags of dried fish. Buses will pick you up from your guesthouse. Alternatively, a pick-up from Ngapali leads to Thandwe (K200, 45 minutes), where you'll have to take a trishaw to the station.

There is no bus service north to Sittwe, but you can take a boat from Taunggok, reached by pick-up or the Pyay bus from Thandwe. See p577 for more information.

Guesthouses rent bikes for about K2000 per day.

WESTERN MYANMAR

Enigmatic Western Myanmar, home to the (very) proud Rakhaing, can feel islandlike considering its inaccessibility. Port town Sittwe is reached by air or boat; once there the ruins of Mrauk U are reached by a boat ride inland. The Rakhaing people (snubbed by the government as 'Burmese') gush over their own culture and language. You'll likely hear a couple retell, with fresh anger, how the Mahamuni Buddha image (north of Mrauk U) was nicked by the Burmese and moved to Mandalay in 1784.

The Muslim population, known as the Rohingya, is frequently in conflict with the Buddhist majority. Tension erupted into riots in 2001, and 20 were killed. The government doesn't recognise the Rohingya as full citizens, and many have moved across the border to Bangladesh as refugees.

See p575 for information on Ngapali Beach, which is in southern Rakhaing State.

SITTWE
☎ 043 / pop 200,000

Primarily a hurry-and-leave transit point en route to Mrauk U, Sittwe (once called Akyab) nevertheless has a smashing waterfront location and more attractions than many such-sized towns. About 30% is Muslim, with the central Jama Mosque the most historic (and lovely) religious site in town.

Information

There's sketchy web access at a lone **Internet stand** (Main Rd; per hr K4500; ⏰ 8am-9pm).

Sights

A busy port town for generations, Sittwe's best attractions hover where the wide Kaladan meets the Bay of Bengal. In the centre, the morning **fish market** kicks off at 6am, with thousands of fish splashed on the stone pier. About 2km south (via the Strand) is the **Point** (admission K50, per bicycle K50), a land projection with big-time sunset views and a café selling coconuts and beer. There are fees for photography.

In the centre, the **Rakhaing State Cultural Museum** (Main Rd; admission US$2; ⏰ 10am-4pm Tue-Sat) features a Mrauk U model, many artefacts of the era, and watercolours of traditional wrestling moves. There are English signs.

Watch for **fruit bats** taking off at dusk. Hundreds sleep off the daylight in trees at the university, about 200m south of the museum.

A couple of hundred metres north of the centre, the **Maka Kuthala Kyaungdawgyi** (Large Monastery of Great Merit; Main Rd; admission free) features an interesting collection of relics, notes and golf trophies in an old British-colonial mansion.

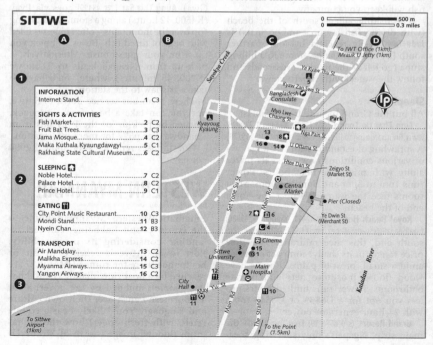

SITTWE

Sleeping

The budget options are disappointing. Electricity runs from 7pm to 11pm at best.

Palace Hotel (☎ 21657; 5 Main Rd; s/d US$5/10) Thin-mattress beds with mosquito nets and occasional power for *either* a fan or a hanging fluorescent bulb.

Prince Hotel (☎ 21395; Yangon 1-286701; www .mraukuprincehotel.com; 27 Main Rd; s US$5-15, d US$10-20; ✴ 💻) Most rooms are small and dingy, but they come with brekky. You can get air-con in the more expensive room.

Noble Hotel (☎ 23558; 45 Main Rd; noble@myanmar .com.mm; s/d with breakfast US$25/35; ✴) Midrange choice across from the museum, with all-hours air-con and satellite TV.

Eating

Ask for Rakhaing specialities – lots of seafood, with spice – at restaurants for the best dining.

Mondi stand (bowl K150; ☯ breakfast & lunch) The best cheapie is this place on the airport road a couple of blocks inland from the Main Rd (across from City Hall). Mondi is the tasty local variant of Burmese *mohinga* (with chillies, not peanuts).

Nyein Chan (dishes K1000-2000; ☯ breakfast, lunch & dinner) On the perpendicular road adjacent to City Hall is a stretch of good family-style Burmese/Chinese restaurants, including this one offering a 15-prawn-filled Rakhaing curry soup worth savouring.

City Point Music Restaurant (The Strand; dishes K1000-2000; ☯ breakfast, lunch & dinner) Just south of the market, this eatery has a live music man at night and a spot on the river.

Getting There & Away

Roads to Sittwe are restricted for travellers.

AIR

Air Mandalay (☎ 21638; U Ottama St) and **Yangon Airways** (☎ 24102) fly to Yangon (US$105) via Thandwe (US$75) most days. The government's **Myanma Airways** (☎ 23157; Main Rd; ☯ 9am-5pm) is US$15 or US$20 cheaper. The airport is 2.5km southwest of the centre; go outside the gate to get cheaper trishaws into town.

BOAT

To reach Ngapali or Yangon, **Malikha Express** (☎ 23441; Main Rd; ☯ 9am-5pm) sells fast-boat tickets to/from Taunggok (US$40, eight hours) three times weekly. From Taunggok,

buses or pick-ups go to Pyay or Thandwe (Ngapali). Buy tickets in advance.

See p579 for information on boat services to and from Mrauk U.

MRAUK U

☎ 043

Reached by a relaxing 65km boat ride northeast from Sittwe, Mrauk U – the ancient capital of the Rakhaing – is smaller than Bagan but more alive. You'll see shepherds leading their flocks past curved hillocks dotted with temples, and refuse fires add a mysterious haze to the timeless setting. A huge **pagoda festival** is held in mid-May.

Mrauk U (m'yawk-oo) served as the Rakhaing capital from 1430 to 1784, when the Brits moved it to Sittwe. It was a ripe time, with kings hiring Japanese samurais as bodyguards and the naval fleet of 10,000 boats terrorizing neighbouring countries from the Bay of Bengal.

It's worth reading up. Tun Shwe Khine's *A Guide to Mrauk U* or U Shwe Zan's *The Golden Mrauk U: An Ancient Capital of Rakhine* are only available in Yangon.

Sights

Over 150 temples and the town mingle over a 7-sq-km, canal-sliced area. Foreigners must pay US$10 to visit, plus a K1000 'donation' for (tacky) fluorescent lights in some temples. Payment can be made at the Shittaung temple.

PALACE SITE & AROUND

Little is left but crumbling walls of the central palace, which is located just east of the market. Apparently astrologers advised King Minbun to move his home here in 1429 to shun 'evil birds' at his Launggret palace. Inside the western walls, the Department of Archaeology's **museum** (admission free; ☯ 11am-3pm Mon-Fri) has pre-restoration photos, a site model and a replica of the Shittaung pillar.

On a hill just north, the 18th-century **Haridaung** pagoda has nice westward views.

NORTH GROUP

The main sites of Mrauk U are clustered beyond the **Shittaung** (Shrine of the 80,000 Images), the most complex of the surviving temples. Built in 1535, the pagoda has a maze-like floor plan. An outer chamber

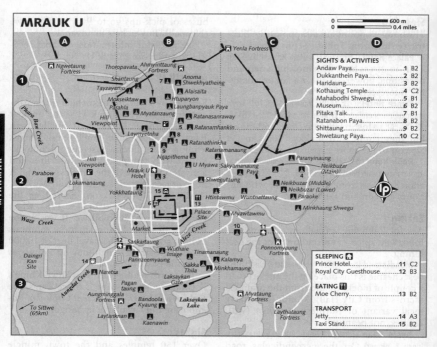

MRAUK U

SIGHTS & ACTIVITIES
Andaw Paya	1 B2
Dukkanthein Paya	2 B2
Haridaung	3 B2
Kothaung Temple	4 C2
Mahabodhi Shwegu	5 B1
Museum	6 B2
Pitaka Taik	7 B1
Ratanabon Paya	8 B2
Shittaung	9 B2
Shwetaung Paya	10 C2

SLEEPING
Prince Hotel	11 C2
Royal City Guesthouse	12 B3

EATING
Moe Cherry	13 B2

TRANSPORT
Jetty	14 A3
Taxi Stand	15 B2

(the far left door at the entry hall to the east side) passes 1000 sculptures; the inner chamber coils to a dead end, passing a 'Buddha footprint' on the way – supposedly the halls get 'cooler' as you go (symbolic of Buddha's teachings). On the outer walls, you may find some rather pornographic renderings of local figures.

Just north is the 16th-century **Andaw Paya** and beyond the **Ratanabon Paya**, a stupa dating from 1612 and survivor of a WWII bomb.

CHIN STATE EXCURSIONS

Once-popular excursions to inland Chin State from Mrauk U – a bargain at roughly US$60, compared to government rates to Chin State from Bagan – were suspended in October 2004. The trips – taking in traditional Chin villages (famously where women with web-like tattoos on their faces live) – may start up again, though rumours abound of insurgent clashes and a Yangon entrepreneur trying to 'buy a village' to corner the tourism market.

Across the road west from Shittaung, the bunker-like **Dukkanthein Paya** (1571), set amid a green field, is the most impressive of the batch: watch for Mrauk U's 64 traditional hairstyles on sculptures on the coiling path leading to a sun-drenched Buddha in the inner chamber.

Farther north of Ratanabon, hilltop **Mahabodhi Shwegu** (1448) features 280 *jakata* (stories of the Buddha's past lives) – including animal love acts! – on its narrow entry walls. About 200m north, the compact and ornate **Pitaka Taik** (1591) is the last remaining library at Mrauk U.

EAST GROUP

East of the Palace walls, the temples are spaced farther out – some temples stand on hilltops with good vantage points. One of Mrauk U's highlights is located 2km east. The massive **Kothaung Temple** (Shrine of the 90,000 Images) was named by King Minbun's son to beat out pop's 80,000 images at Shittaung. Much of the temple is in fragments – at the time of research there were crews busy at work restoring it – but the accessible outer passageway is lined with thousands of evocative bas reliefs of Buddha images (some headless); 108 stupas once dotted the presently bare temple-top.

SOUTH GROUP
Amid confusing – and quite interesting – village backlanes, this area has a number of pagodas. Mrauk U's best view is at the **Shwetaung Paya** (Golden Hill Pagoda; 1553), which is southwest of the palace. Trails up get lost under vegetation at times, so it is best return before dark. Views of the Chin Hills and the river to the west justify the scrapes.

To the north, **Laksaykan Gate** leads to the eponymous lake, a water source.

Sleeping
Royal City Guesthouse (☎ 23808-19; d $7-10, bungalow US$15) A couple of hundred metres north of the jetty, this friendly riverside guesthouse has ceiling-free shared bathroom and rooms just big enough for a bed (with mosquito net) and small table. Free breakfast.

Prince Hotel (☎ 01-4410150, Yangon 1-286701; www.mraukuprincehotel.com; r US$15-20) Southeast of the centre (and a bit remote), this leafy complex of seven bungalows used to be dark and dreary, but fixed itself up (somewhat) in 2004. Bamboo details fill the rooms, each with private bathroom. Staff have made up a nice map to use.

A small guesthouse next door to the Royal was under renovation at research time.

Eating
Moe Cherry (dishes K1000-2000, beer K1500; ☻ lunch & dinner) On the road east of the palace, this traveller-focused two-storey restaurant serves a few meals nightly (there's no menu; just ask). The cauliflower dish was a knockout and there's also some spicier Rakhaing-style curries. The restaurant – uprooted here from west of the palace by the government in 1998 – can help arrange car service.

A couple of basic Chinese restaurants are near the market in the town centre.

Getting There & Around
The only way to Mrauk U is by boat. The two-tier government-run Inland Water Transport (IWT) runs to Mrauk U from Sittwe (US$4, six to seven hours), leaving three mornings a week from a jetty 1km

north of Sittwe's centre. Other days you can catch a small 'private boat' (US$10, four to five hours) at 7am or 2.30pm. **Nawarat Shwe Pyi Thar** (☎ 23159) runs enclosed 'fast boats' (US$20, three hours), leaving at 2.30pm.

At the time of research, boats left from Mrauk U at 8am from the jetty, 1km south of the market.

Note: seven people (including five Italian tourists) were killed in December 2004 when an unexpected storm overturned a fast boat after dark.

A horse cart around the temples is US$8 to US$10 per day. You can rent a bike for about K2000 per day. The taxi stand (they're jeeps) is on the north side of the palace.

MYANMAR DIRECTORY

ACCOMMODATION
Hotels and guesthouses are a bit more expensive in Myanmar than in neighbouring countries. In places with choice, you can often find a plain room – some concrete floors, squashed mosquitos left on the walls, and cold-water shower down the hall – and for US$4 to US$6 per person you'll usually score yourself breakfast. Another dollar or two might get you air-con, hot water, even TV.

Nearly all hotels and guesthouses quote prices in US dollars. Most accept kyat at a slightly disadvantageous rate (say K1000 to the dollar, instead of the K950 exchange rate). Prices listed are during peak season (roughly October to March); some may drop a dollar (or be haggled down) off-season.

All accommodation supposedly must be licensed to accept foreign guests. You'll

---

GOVERNMENT HOTELS

The big question many travellers ask themselves in Myanmar regards avoiding government-run hotels. Government officials get their fingers in the pockets of top-end and joint-venture hotels, rarely touching guesthouses. Full-on government hotels often are named for the destination (eg Mrauk U Hotel in Mrauk U) and fly the national flag outside. Generally 10% of what you spend at any guesthouse goes to the government. The less your bunk costs, the less is passed on.

need to show your passport, but you get to keep old of it. Sometimes unlicensed guesthouses will say they're 'full' rather than explaining. In out-of-the-way towns, some local guesthouses will put you up. Prices are about US$2 and conditions are basic.

ACTIVITIES

Barefoot hikes up pagoda-top hills (such as Mandalay Hill; p558) or biking around a town are the most common activities, but there are other ways to break a sweat too.

Cycling

If you bring your own spare parts and bike, you can take to Myanmar's highways (popular stretches are between Mandalay and Bagan, via Myingyan; or the hilly terrain from Mandalay to Hsipaw). Roads are actually smoother than some Southeast Asian countries. The brutal hot season may deflate your cycling dreams in a jiff though.

Diving & Snorkelling

Unfortunately, there's not much underwater action in Myanmar for the budget traveller. You can snorkel past colourful fish and a coral tower or two off Ngapali Beach (p575) or Chaungtha Beach (p574). The more spectacular Mergui (Myeik) Archipelago, near Kawthoung (p549), is generally accessible via expensive live-aboard cruises operating out of Thailand (see p811).

Trekking

Treks between Kalaw and Inle Lake (p550) take in an overnight stay in a longhouse. Other excellent opportunities are outside Hsipaw (p555) and Kengtung (p554).

BOOKS

Even more than with most countries, it's wise to read up before arriving in Myanmar. Pick up Lonely Planet's *Myanmar* for more comprehensive coverage, or the helpful *Burmese phrasebook*.

Other top books:

- *From the Land of Green Ghosts: A Burmese Odyssey* by Pascal Khoo Thwe (2002). A recent literary memoir of a Karenni tribesman escaping post-1988 chaos to study literature at Cambridge.
- *Trouser People* by Andrew Marshall (2002). The author follows the footsteps

of a scrappy Scot who introduced football to hill tribes in the late 19th century.

- *Burmese Days* by George Orwell (1934). The classic sweat-stained novel of the last lonely days of Britain's colonial grip; available around the country.
- *The Glass Palace* by Amitav Ghosh (2001). The best recent novel, intertwining a motley crew of locals (Indians, Chinese, Burmese) amid lushly retold historical events.
- *Freedom from Fear & Other Writings* by Aung San Suu Kyi (1995). A collection of essays.

BUSINESS HOURS

Government offices are generally open from 8am to 4.30pm Monday through Friday. Private shops are open about 9.30am to 6pm or later daily. Restaurants usually open from 7am to 9pm or 10pm.

CLIMATE

November through February is the best time to visit. Temperatures can get quite cold in the hills, close to freezing in Kalaw for example. From mid-February, it gets increasingly hot – April being the 'cruellest month', as per TS Eliot, until rains douse the land from mid-May through mid-October. See climate charts (p924).

CUSTOMS

Immigration officers at Yangon airport are often a smiley lot. Even customs seems relatively cheerful. However, you must declare foreign currency in excess of US$2000 as well as electronic goods such as iPods, radios and cameras. Laptops could arouse some suspicion that you're a journalist or political activist. Have a back-up explanation ready.

Technically, antiques cannot be taken out of the country, though it's not often checked.

DANGERS & ANNOYANCES

It's likely the only time a local will be running with your money or belongings is returning it to you if you've dropped it. Theft is quite rare, but don't tempt fate in this poor country by flashing valuables or leaving them behind.

A few bomb incidents have occurred in recent years. In December 2004, a couple of small bombs exploded in Yangon (supposedly planted by the Vigorous Burmese Student Warriors), injuring one person. Areas around the Myanmar–Thai border – rife with the drug trade – can be dangerous (and off-limits) areas to explore.

Talking politics with locals can potentially endanger them, so be discreet. A taxi driver taking you to see the area of Aung San Suu Kyi's house can get into trouble too. Generally let a local dictate the conversation. In private places, and some teashops, some will be quite frank. Don't force an issue.

Power outages can be an annoyance, as can mosquitos.

SCAMS

The only real scams are dodgy money-changers slipping in torn notes and drivers or guides getting a commission for purchases at shops they take you to.

DISABLED TRAVELLERS

It's a tricky country for mobility-impaired travellers. Wheelchair ramps are virtually unheard of and transport is crowded and difficult even for the fully ambulatory.

DRIVING LICENCE

You won't need a driving licence to ride a bicycle, and your national one should do if you plan to rent a motorcycle around town. Technically you'll need to have an International Driving Permit, and apply with the Road Transport Administration Department for Yangon if you plan to drive a car (though this is not easy to arrange).

EMBASSIES & CONSULATES

For visa information, see p586.

Embassies & Consulates in Myanmar

Myanmar is usually a good place to get visas for other countries. Sometimes you can pay with kyat. Countries with diplomatic representation in Yangon include:

Australia (Map p540; ☎ 01-251810, 251809; 88 Strand Rd)
Bangladesh (Map p536; ☎ 01-515275; 11B Thanlwin Rd, Kamayut Township)
Canada Affairs handled by Australian embassy
China (Map p538; ☎ 01-221281; 1 Pyidaungsu Yeiktha Rd)

France (Map p538; ☎ 01-212523, 212532; 102 Pyidaungsu Yeiktha Rd)
Germany (Map p536; ☎ 01-548951; 32 Natmauk Rd)
India (Map p540; ☎ 01-282933; 545-547 Merchant St)
Indonesia (Map p538; ☎ 01-254465, 254469; 100 Pyidaungsu Yeiktha Rd)
Japan (Map p536; ☎ 01-549644; 100 Natmauk Rd)
Laos (Map p538; ☎ 01-222482; A1 Diplomatic Quarters, Taw Win Rd)
Malaysia (Map p538; ☎ 01-220249; 82 Pyidaungsu Yeiktha Rd)
New Zealand Affairs handled by UK embassy
Singapore (☎ 01-559001; 238 Dhama Zedi Rd)
Thailand (Map p536; ☎ 01-224550; 73 Manaw Han St)
UK (Map p540; ☎ 01-256918; 80 Strand Rd)
USA (Map p540; ☎ 01-379880; 581 Merchant St)

For other embassies and consulates, see individual city maps.

Myanmar Embassies & Consulates Abroad

Australia (☎ 02-6273 3811; 22 Arkana St, Yarralumla, ACT 2600)
Bangladesh (☎ 02-60 1915 89B Rd No 4, Banani, Dhaka)
Canada (☎ 613-232 6434/46; Apt 902-903, 85 Range Rd, The Sandringham, Ottawa, Ontario K1N 8J6)
China (☎ 010-6532 1584/6; 6 Dong Zhi Men Wai St, Chaoyang District, Beijing 100600)
France (☎ 01-42 25 56 95; 60 rue de Courcelles, 75008 Paris)
Germany (☎ 30-206 1570; Zimmerstrasse 56, 10117 Berlin)
India (☎ 11-688 9007/8; 3/50F Nyaya Marg, Chanakyapuri, New Delhi 110021)
Israel (☎ 03-517 0760; 26 Hayarkon St, Tel Aviv 68011)
Italy (☎ 06-854 3974, 858 63343; Viale Gioacchino Rossini, 18, Int 2, 00198 Rome)
Japan (☎ 03-3441 9291; 8-26, 4-chome, Kita-Shinagawa, Shinagawa-ku, Tokyo 140-0001)
South Korea (☎ 02-792-3341; 723-1/724-1 Hannam-Dong Yongsam-ku, Seoul 140-210)
UK (☎ 020-7499 8841; 19A Charles St, London W1X 5DX)
USA (☎ 202-332 9044/5/6; 2300 S St NW, Washington, DC 20008)

FESTIVALS & EVENTS

Traditionally Myanmar follows a 12-month lunar calendar, so most festival dates cannot be fixed on the Gregorian calendar. Most festivals in Myanmar are on the full moon of the Burmese month in which they occur, but the build-up can go for days. Besides Buddhist holy days, some Hindu, Muslim and Christian holidays and festivals are also observed.

MYANMAR

MYANMAR

January
Independence Day 4 January. A major public holiday marked by a seven-day fair at Kandawgyi Lake in Yangon, and countrywide fairs.

February/March
Union Day 12 February. Celebrates Bogyoke Aung San's short-lived achievement of unifying Myanmar's disparate racial groups.

Bawgyo Paya Pwe Held the day after the Tabaung full moon, this is one of the oldest and largest Shan festivals.

Shwedagon Festival This is the largest *paya* festival in Myanmar and takes place on the full moon.

Armed Forces Day 27 March. This event is celebrated with parades and fireworks. Since 1989 the government has made it a tradition to pardon a number of prisoners on this day.

March/April
Full-Moon Festival The Tagu full moon is the biggest event of the year at Shwemawdaw Paya in Bago.

April/May
Buddha's Birthday The full moon also marks the day of the Buddha's enlightenment and the day he entered nirvana. Thus it is known as the 'thrice blessed day'. One of the best places to observe this ceremony is at Yangon's Shwedagon Paya.

Thingyan (Water Festival) Celebrates the Burmese New Year with a raucous multiday water fight. Traditional Burmese restraint goes out the window. It is impossible to go outside without getting drenched so you may as well join in. Leave cameras inside. Businesses close and many buses do not run. It's a favourite with children and teenagers but many adults check into meditation centres until the insanity's over.

Workers' Day 1 May. Although the government renounced socialism in 1989, Myanmar still celebrates May Day.

June/July
Buddhist Lent Start of the Buddhist Rains Retreat (aka 'Buddhist Lent'). Laypeople present monasteries with new robes, since during the three-month Lent period monks are restricted to their monasteries. This is the traditional time for young men to temporarily enter the monasteries.

July/August
Martyr's Day 19 July. Commemorates the assassination of Bogyoke Aung San and his comrades on 19 July 1947. Wreaths are laid at his mausoleum, north of Shwedagon Paya in Yangon.

Wagaung Festival Lots are drawn to see who will have to provide monks with their alms. If you're in Mandalay, try to get to Taungbyone, about 30km north, where there is a noisy, seven-day festival to keep the *nat* happy.

September/October
Boat Races This is the height of the wet season, so boat races are held in rivers, lakes and even ponds all over Myanmar. The best place to be is Inle Lake.

Festival of Lights (Thadingyut) Celebrates Buddha's return from a period of preaching. For the three days of the festival, all Myanmar is lit by oil lamps, fire balloons, candles and even mundane electric lamps.

October/November
Tazaungdaing Another 'festival of lights', particularly celebrated in the Shan State. In Taunggyi there are fire-balloon competitions. In some areas there are also speed-weaving competitions during the night. The biggest weaving competitions occur at Shwedagon Paya in Yangon.

Kathein A one-month period at the end of Buddhist Lent during which new monastic robes and requisites are offered to the monastic community. Many people simply donate cash; kyat notes are folded and stapled into floral patterns on wooden 'trees' called *padetha* and offered to the monasteries.

December
Christmas Day 25 December. Despite Myanmar's predominantly Buddhist background, Christmas Day is a public holiday in deference to the many Christian Kayin (Karen).

Kayin New Year December/January. Considered a national holiday, when Karen communities throughout Myanmar celebrate by wearing their traditional dress and by hosting folk dancing and singing performances. The largest celebrations are held in the Karen suburb of Insein, just north of Yangon, and in Hpa-an.

Ananda Festival December/January. Held at the Ananda Pahto in Bagan at the full moon.

FOOD & DRINK
Food
Mainstream Burmese cuisine represents a blend of Bamar, Mon, Indian and Chinese influences. If you're coming in from Thailand or Vietnam or Malaysia, you may be a bit disappointed. Some travellers search out Chinese restaurants after a few Burmese meals.

A typical meal has *htamin* (rice) as its core, eaten with a choice of *hin* (curry dishes), most commonly fish, chicken, prawns or mutton. (Beef and pork are less popular, being considered offensive to most Hindus and Buddhists.) Soup is always served, along with a table full of condiments (including pickled veggies as dipping sauces). Usually they'll refill bowls as you eat – so come hungry.

Outside of Rakhaing State (near Bangladesh), most Burmese food is pretty mild in terms of chilli power. Most cooks opt for a simple masala of turmeric, ginger, garlic, salt and onions, plus plenty of peanut oil and shrimp paste. Usually *balachaung* (chillis, tamarind and dried shrimp pounded together) or the pungent *ngapi kyaw* (spicy shrimp paste with garlic) is on the table for your own adding. Almost everything in Burmese cooking is flavoured with *ngapi* (a salty paste concocted from dried and fermented shrimp or fish).

Noodle dishes are most often eaten for breakfast or as light snacks between meals. By far the most popular is *mohinga* (moun-hinga), rice noodles served with fish soup and as many other ingredients as there are cooks.

Shan khauk-swe (Shan-style noodle soup; thin wheat noodles in a light broth with meat or tofu) is a favourite all over Myanmar, but is most common in Mandalay and the Shan State. Another Shan dish worth seeking out is *htamin chin* (literally, sour rice – a turmeric-coloured rice salad).

See p541 for examples of snacks found in street markets around Myanmar.

The seafood along the coasts, particularly grilled squid in Ngapali Beach, is particularly good. See p962 for more food vocabulary.

Drink

Only drink purified water. Be wary of ice. Widely available 1L bottles of water (often cooled) cost K150 or K200.

Burmese tea, brewed in the Indian style with lots of condensed milk and sugar, is cheap. Most restaurants will provide as much weak Chinese tea as you can handle – and it's free. Teashops – Myanmar's best hangouts – are a good place to drink safely boiled tea and munch on inexpensive snacks like *nam-bya* and *palata* (flat breads) or Chinese pastries. Ordering isn't as easy as in restaurants. Ask for *lahpeq ye* (tea with a dollop of condensed milk); *cho bouk* is less sweet, and *kyauk padaung* is very sweet.

Locally produced colas (such as Fantasy, Max and Star) run about K150 per bottle, compared to the (rare) bottle of Coke for K700. Sugarcane juice is a very popular street-side drink.

Hey, there's beer too! Myanmar Beer (about K1000 or K1500 for a bottle) is the best local brew – rather light, but not any less tasty than Tiger Beer, you'll find.

Mandalay Beer is a bit dodgy. Yangon has all the bars. Elsewhere open-air barbecue restaurants and 'beer stations' embrace a steady crew of red-faced local drinkers. It's fine to buy a bottle to take to the guesthouse, or sit at a restaurant and get plastered.

GAY & LESBIAN TRAVELLERS

Lesbians and gays are generally accepted without comment in Burmese culture (in fact local women walking with foreign men raise more eyebrows). Yangon has the most active gay 'scene', particularly at the Silver Oak Café (p542) on the Strand or Patty O'Malleys pub at the Sedona Hotel (p539). It's OK to share rooms, but public displays of affection – for anyone – are frowned upon.

HOLIDAYS

Major public holidays:

Independence Day 4 January
Peasants Day 2 March
Armed Forces Day 27 March
Workers' Day 1 May
National Day late November/early December
Christmas Day 25 December

INTERNET ACCESS

Access to the Net is on the rise here. It's about K1000 per hour, though at places like Bagan, Ngapali Beach and Inle Lake it costs K3000. The government, however, restricts Web-based email sites such as Hotmail and Yahoo. Email accounts that end in something other than '.com' – such as www.online.ie – are at times easier to access. Sites such as www.bbc.co.uk, www.nytimes .com and www.espn.com were available at research time.

There are two ISPs – a government-run dial-up and a private broadband service (now run by the military we hear).

INTERNET RESOURCES

Here are a few useful sites:

Irrawaddy (www.irrawaddy.org) Website of a Bangkok-based publication. It focuses on political issues, but covers many cultural news topics.

Mizzima (www.mizzima.com) A nonprofit news service organised in 1998 by Burmese journalists in exile.

Myanmar Home Page (www.myanmar.com) Provides a funny government dictum, and two local English-language papers, including the useful *Myanmar Times* (for entertainment listings, flight schedules).

MYANMAR

Myanmar Travel Information (www.myanmar travelinformation.com) Includes train and airline schedules (though these date quickly).
Online Burma/Myanmar Library (www.burmalibrary .org) Comprehensive database of books on Myanmar.

LEGAL MATTERS

Myanmar has no individual judiciary branch. If you engage in political activism (ie handing out pro-democracy leaflets as some Westerners have), illegally cross the border into the country, or get caught with drugs, you have no legal recourse. We've heard of a French traveller bribing his way out of a heroin-possession arrest. Political activists are less likely to make deals.

MAPS

The best map found outside Myanmar is Periplus Editions' 1:2,000,000 *Myanmar Travel Map*; you can find it at **MapLink** (www .maplink.com). Around Myanmar you'll find regional maps made by Design Print Services (DPS). Its *Tourist Map of Myanmar* is sometimes free at the Yangon Airport (otherwise it costs up to K1000). DPS also prints maps for Yangon, Mandalay and Bagan.

MEDIA
Magazines

You can get old copies of *Newsweek* and *Time* at **Inwa Bookstore** (Map p540; 232 Sule Paya Rd, Yangon).

Newspapers

The government-line-toeing *New Light of Myanmar* is hilarious, in its Orwellian propaganda way (watch for anti-West poems). Far more useful is the *Myanmar Times* (which has an Australian editor), with an international flights schedule and entertainment listings. Both are scarce outside Yangon.

Radio

All legal radio and TV broadcasts are state controlled. Radio Myanmar broadcasts news in Burmese, English and eight other national languages three times a day. Only music with Burmese-language lyrics goes out on the airwaves.

Many Burmese listen to Burmese-language broadcasts from the Voice of America and the BBC for news from the outside world.

TV

TV Myanmar (MRTV) operates from 5pm to midnight (at the mercy of the local power source). Check out the 9.15pm national news, when a newscaster coldly reads the censored news before a mural of a power plant. English Premiership games often get broadcasted.

Many hotels have satellite TV, if only in the lobby. CNN and the BBC are available on these sets and there seems to be no censorship by the government.

MONEY

Kyat, dollars, FEC (see opposite) – lots of money to reckon with here. Kyat covers the little things (bottles of water, renting a bike, some rice), while dollars (or fading FEC notes) are usually requested for ferries, air tickets, hotels and museums. While inflation has skyrocketed in recent years – nearing 50% in 2003 alone! – costs in US dollars don't fluctuate much. Be sure to bring what US dollars you'll need (the euro is increasingly being accepted). Crisp, new US$100 bills attract the best exchange rates. Small bills, however, are useful for guesthouses, most of which price rooms in dollars rather than kyat.

ATMs

Myanmar has no ATMs (cash points).

Bargaining

Essentially anything you're quoted is up for negotiating. Exceptions are transport (other than taxis) and museum and other entrance fees. We found a craft item could often be purchased for half the first offer. Guesthouses and hotels may drop fares when quiet, or if you're planning a longer stay. Ask.

Cash

Myanmar's everyday currency, the kyat (pronounced chat, and abbreviated K) is divided into the following banknotes: K1, K5, K10, K15, K20, K45 (seriously), K50, K90 (no joke), K100, K200, K500, K713 (actually this one's a lie, sorry) and K1000.

DOLLARS VS KYAT

Prices in this book follow local usage: dollars when locals ask for them, kyat otherwise. Note some strict museum and ferry folks will insist on dollars.

Credit Cards

If you're looking for a credit-card bailout, get yourself to Bangkok; very very few upmarket hotels accept them here – and no-one else does. Before the banking crisis in 2003, American Express, Visa and JCB credit cards were accepted.

Exchanging Money

Offers to 'change money' nearly outnumber *longyi* in this country. Essentially the only reasonable way to get kyat is via the 'black market' – meaning from guesthouses, shops, travel agencies or less reliable blokes on the street. Some won't accept US dollar bills starting with the serial numbers 'CB'. The airport exchange counter at research time offered K450 for the dollar, while in Yangon rates were about K950.

Only US dollars and euros can be exchanged in Myanmar. Baht can be exchanged only at the border with Thailand. The exchange rates here are based on those used in the streets of Myanmar; other sources differ considerably from this.

Many travellers do the bulk of their changing in Yangon, where rates are a little higher than elsewhere. Count your money before handing over dollars, and don't change in the street. Honest exchangers won't mind you counting. Generally kyat are banded in stacks of 100 K1000 bills. If you want to look like a naive uninformed tourist by all means change at a government bank or airport.

Foreign Exchange Certificates (FEC)

In 2003, the government stopped requiring visitors to change US$200 worth of Foreign Exchange Certificates (FEC) upon arrival. The FEC, pegged 1:1 to the US dollar, is still accepted at hotels and for many tourism-related services such as ferries or air tickets.

Tipping & Bribes

Minor bribes – called 'presents' or 'tea money' in Burmese English – are part of everyday life in Myanmar. Extra compensation is expected for the efficient completion of many standard bureaucratic services, such as a visa extension.

Tipping, as it is known in the West, is not the rule in any but the fanciest hotels and restaurants. Rounding up a restaurant bill is certainly appreciated.

Travellers Cheques

In Yangon, you can cash travellers cheques at some upscale hotels for a 3% to 10% commission. Also, a lone shop in Mandalay (p556) cashes cheques for a – are you sitting down? – 20% commission.

PHOTOGRAPHY & VIDEO

Some Internet cafés can burn digital photos onto a CD for about K1000, but you should have your own adapter. Colour print film (mostly Kodak and Fujifilm) are widely available in most towns. Some sights, including some pagodas, charge a camera fee of K100 or so. Avoid taking photos of military facilities, uniformed individuals, road blocks, bridges, NLD offices and Aung San Suu Kyi's house.

POST

You can send a postcard (K75) or letter (K80) to anywhere in the world from post offices, which stay open roughly 9.30am to 3.30pm Monday through Friday. For bigger (or dearer) packages, **DHL Worldwide Express** (Yangon ☎ 01-664423; Traders Hotel; 223 Sule Paya Rd; Mandalay ☎ 02-39274) send packages to anywhere but the USA (restricted due to sanctions). A 0.5kg package to Europe or Canada is about US$65, Australia is US$50.

RESPONSIBLE TRAVEL

See 'Should You Go?' (p527).

STUDYING

Most outside students in Myanmar are getting busy with *satipatthana vipassana,* or insight-awareness meditation. Yangon is the meditation HQ, with several centres; but Sagaing (p564) is another good place to find opportunities. Often food and lodging are provided at no charge, but meditators must follow eight precepts (including no food after noon, as well as no music, dancing, jewellery or perfume). It's for the experienced only. Daily schedules are rigorous – sometimes nonstop practice from 3am to 11pm.

For practice sessions of less than one month, a tourist visa suffices. For longer terms, it's necessary to apply for a 'special-entry visa', which you cannot apply for while in Myanmar on a tourist visa. Applicants must receive a letter of invitation from a centre. The process takes eight to 10 weeks.

MYANMAR

For further information, contact these centres:

Chanmyay Yeiktha Meditation Centre
(☎ 01-661479; www.chanmyay.org; 55A Kaba Aye Paya Rd, Yangon) Second location outside town.

International Meditation Centre (☎ 01-535549; 31A Inya Myaing Rd, Yangon)

Kyaswa Kyaung (☎ 72-21541; ulkyaswa@myanmar .com.mm, mettadana@aol.com; Sagaing)

Mahasi Meditation Centre (Map p536;
☎ 01-541971; http://mahasi.com; 16 Thathana Yeiktha Rd, Bahan Township, Yangon) Myanmar's most famous centre.

Panditarama Meditation Centre (☎ 1-535448; panditarama@mptmail.net.mm; http://web.ukonline .co.uk/buddhism/pandita.htm; 80A Than Lwin Rd, Bahan Township, Yangon) Second branch outside town.

There is useful information on meditation centres at www.rainbow2.com/burma and http://web.ukonline.co.uk/buddhism /meditate.htm.

TELEPHONE

Local calls can be made cheap or for free from guesthouses. Domestic long distance is cheap from a Central Telephone & Telegraph (CTT) office or from phone stalls on the street. International calls – made at a CTT office or from guesthouse – run about US$4 or US$5 per minute to Australia or Europe, an extra dollar to call North America. Some smaller towns still use manual switchboards, which can be a hoot to see in action.

Mobile Phones

Myanmar has no mobile-phone service. If you're carrying one, however, be sure to declare it upon arrival.

Phone Codes

To call Myanmar from abroad, dial your country's international access code, then ☎ 95 (Myanmar's country code), the area code (less the 0) and the five- or six-digit number. To dial long distance within Myanmar, dial the area code (including 0) and the number.

TOILETS

In many places, toilets are often squat jobs, generally in a cobweb-filled outhouse reached by a dirt path behind a restaurant. In guesthouses and hotels, you'll find Western-style sit-down flushers. Toilet paper is widely available and should not be flushed.

TOURIST INFORMATION

Myanmar Travel and Tours (MTT; www.myanmars .net/mtt) is part of the Ministry of Hotels & Tourism (MHT), the official government tourism organ in Myanmar. Its main office is in Yangon (p535) and there are also offices in Mandalay, Bagan and Inle Lake. It steers visitors to government-run services, but can be useful in terms of gauging prices and getting info on travel restrictions.

VISAS

Passport holders from Asean countries, China, Bangladesh and Russia do not need to apply for visas to visit Myanmar. All other nationalities do. A tourist visa's validity expires 90 days after issue and only allows a 28-day, single-entry visit. It costs US$20. You'll need three passport-sized photos for the process.

There are also 28-day business visas (US$30) and 28-day special visas (US$30) for former Myanmar citizens (which can be extended for three to six months once in Yangon, for US$36). A multiple-entry business visa is US$150. There are also meditation visas (US$30) for those going for that purpose.

At research time, the online **e-Visa service** (www.visa.gov.mm) was suspended. Previously anyone planning to enter Myanmar overland must have had a visa obtained directly through a Myanmar consular service (p581).

At research time, travel agencies along Bangkok's Khao San Rd specialized in getting quick tourist visas for Myanmar. Rates depended on turnaround times, which always aren't met: visa in one day 1800B, two days 1600B and three days 1100B. The process at the Bangkok embassy takes at least a day. Show up early.

Visitors from Thailand can get very short-term 'visas' that allow minimal travel in border regions of Myanmar; see p941.

Applications

Myanmar's embassies and consulates abroad are scrupulous in checking out the backgrounds of visa applicants. Consider declaring another profession if you're any of the following: journalist, photographer, editor, publisher, motion-picture director or producer, cameraperson, videographer or writer. Otherwise you're likely to be rejected!

Extensions

At the time of research, it was possible to extend a tourist visa by an additional 14 days (only) beyond its original 28-day validity in Yangon only. The process costs US$36 and usually takes about three days. A travel agent can help through the bureaucracy; MTT can too, with an extra charge of US$2. You'll need two copies of your passport and visa, two passport-sized photographs and a recommendation letter from your hotel. The process cannot be started in advance or from elsewhere in Myanmar.

Overstaying Your Visa

Another option, if you want just a few more days, is overstaying your visa. Check with a Yangon agent before your visa's up, but at research time there's generally little hassle to overstay *if* you're leaving from the Yangon or Mandalay airports. Be prepared to spend at least 20 minutes with some paperwork, and to pay US$3 per day, plus a US$3 'registration fee'. Try to have correct change handy. Many travellers have overstayed up to seven days without incident.

If you're leaving overland to Thailand on an expired visa, it's best to enlist help from a travel agency before popping up at the border. In one case, an extra US$35 fee was lopped onto the US$3-per-day penalty to cross to Ranong, Thailand.

VOLUNTEERING

You'll have plenty of chances to help locals with English over tea. Some foreigners have been able to volunteer as English teachers at monasteries. In November 2004, seven foreigners doing so at Mandalay's Phaungdaw Kyaung were deported, though this was likely a repercussion of the monastery's connection with ousted prime minister Khin Nyunt.

WOMEN TRAVELLERS

Women travelling alone are more likely to be helped than harassed. In some areas, you'll be regarded with friendly curiosity (and asked, with sad-eyed sympathy, 'Are you only one?') because Burmese women tend to prefer to travel en masse. At the more remote religious sites, a single foreign woman is likely to be 'adopted' by a young Burmese woman, who will take you by the hand to show you the highlights. In some sites, such as Mandalay's Mahamuni Paya (p558), 'ladies' are not permitted to the central altar, as signs indicate.

You can get tampons at upmarket shops in Yangon and Mandalay.

WORKING

Surprisingly, work permits in Myanmar are not totally impossible to get these days. Your first steps would be to arrange some sponsorship from a local company and have a persuasive reason to be there – some kind of business development, for example. Seek out expats in Yangon for more information.

Philippines

HIGHLIGHTS
- **Cordillera region** Trekking through immense rice terraces around Banaue and Batad in Luzon's rugged north (p614)
- **Visayas & south** Easing down to small-island life on Siquijor (p638), Bantayan (p629), Malapascua (p629) and Camiguin (p642)
- **Beach resorts** Swimming or diving every day and sampling seafood and San Miguel beer every night in Puerto Galera (p620) and Boracay (p633)
- **Biggest fish** Snorkelling with whale sharks near tiny Donsol in South Luzon (p619)
- **Off the beaten track** Exploring sunken WWII wrecks and hidden lagoons in the Calamian group of islands, particularly around Busuanga (p646)

FAST FACTS

- **ATMS** common though routinely 'offline' in cities and popular resorts
- **Budget** US$20-25 a day
- **Capital** Manila
- **Costs** island cottage US$5-11, 4hr bus ride US$2-3, beer US$0.40
- **Country code** ☎ 63
- **Famous for** shoe-loving Imelda Marcos, diving, infinite beach-fringed isles
- **Languages** Filipino (Tagalog), English, 11 regional languages and 87 dialects
- **Money** US$1 = P54.79 (peso)
- **Phrases** hello (nonverbal: raise eyebrows while tilting head upwards), *paálam* (good-bye), *salámat* (thanks), *iskyu* (sorry)
- **Population** 86.2 million, including between seven and 10 million Filipinos working overseas

- **Seasons** dry season Oct-May, wet Jun-Sep
- **Visas** free, 21-day visa given on arrival; extensions up to 59 days cost US$37 and are available in major cities

TRAVEL HINT

Try to fly into Manila and out of Cebu, or vice versa, and save yourself lots of backtracking.

MINI-ITINERARY

From **Manila** (p599) head north to **Banaue** (p616) and **Sagada** (p615) or **Vigan** (p617), back to Manila and then either to **South Luzon** (p617) or to **Mindoro** (p620) and **Boracay** (p633), from where you can island-hop to **Cebu** (p623). From Cebu, you can either head back to **Manila** via Palawan's **Puerto Princesa** (p643), **El Nido** (p645) and the **Calamian Group** (p646) or shoot for **Siquijor** (p638), **Camiguin** (p642) or **Siargao** (p641) and fly out of Cebu.

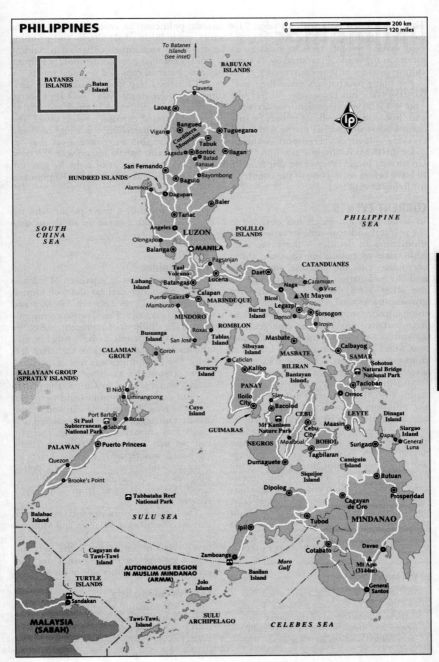

PHILIPPINES

This is southeast Asia with an edge: 7106 islands; politicians as crooked as the pristine coastline; steaming jungles; scorching volcanoes; monolithic whale sharks and grinning card sharks; resolute treasure hunters; ex-headhunters; and some of the last remaining pirates in the world. Flavoured by its Spanish and US colonial past, contemporary Filipino culture marks a unique convergence of Christianity, baseball caps and mystical spirits.

Not many backpackers make the trans–South China Sea leap from Thailand's banana-pancake trail, but those who do feel like conspirators let in on Asia's best-kept secret. This is a land where ancient rice-terrace amphitheatres lie concealed in thick mountains, and thousands of far-flung islands lie in wait for the intrepid explorer's beach towel. The oceans boast world-class diving with a kaleidoscope of fish patrolling sprawling reefs and creaking shipwrecks. Transport connections are extensive, but in remote areas may require intestinal fortitude and affinity for the Filipino maxim *bahala na*: go with the flow. Gregarious locals everywhere dispense smiles like they're going out of style. Be sure not to leave before seeing one of the country's spirited festivals and sampling the Filipino zeal for living *la vida loca*.

CURRENT EVENTS

In some ways not much has changed in the political and economic structure of the Philippines in decades – the same clannish circle of politicians runs the show, corruption cuts the potential for growth, and the population boom continues. On the other hand the economy has been growing by around 5% for 10 years, and more job opportunities locally and overseas have curtailed poverty. The emergence of an ambitious, well-organised middle class that won't put up with national leaders as murky as ousted president Joseph Estrada is a sign of another shift in Filipino society.

Muslim insurgency, in this predominantly Christian country, has long affected the Philippines' south. After 11 September 2001, US Special Forces teamed up with the Filipino army to combat a radical group on Basilan Island calling itself Abu Sayyaf, which specialises in kidnappings and bombings. Nationalists and left-wing groups decried the return of the Americans. A brief rebellion enacted by disgruntled soldiers in 2003 showed that at least part of the army isn't too happy about the never-ending conflict either. While President Gloria Macapagal-Arroya has been extending the olive branch in recent years, it would be a brave person who bet on peace breaking out in the south any time soon.

HISTORY
First Filipinos

Recent discoveries in northern Mindanao might push the earliest date of human habitation back to between 100,000 and 400,000 years ago. The Negrito communities of the Philippines represent one of the oldest Asian peoples, and probably also the shortest (most are less than five feet tall). The Philippines was one of the earliest centres of the Austronesian migration wave, which started in China, skipped to Taiwan and the Philippines and swept out as far as New Zealand, Hawaii and Madagascar. Outrigger canoes safely carried new crops and animals such as pigs, and you can bet that a proto-cockfighting fanatic on board was tenderly holding his prize rooster. Boat travel still helps to define Filipino life. A *barangay*, or neighbourhood, derives its name from *balangay*, a type of sailboat.

The Indian Brahmi script that was adapted and used by tribes in Palawan and Mindoro indicates some Indian cultural influences that go back millennia. But in the 16th century, a new player in the islands' fortunes arrived – from the other side of the world.

Spanish Colonialists

In 1519 Ferdinand Magellan set off from Europe with instructions to sail around the world, claim anything worth claiming and extend Spain's spice empire into the Pacific region. Reaching the Islamic Sultanate of

Cebu in 1521, Magellan managed to convert a number of people to Christianity before he was killed by Chief Lapu-Lapu on Mactan Island.

In 1565 the Spanish returned. Miguel de Legazpi stormed the island of Cebu and established the first permanent Spanish settlement. Then, in 1571, the headquarters were relocated to Manila and from there the Spanish gradually took control of the entire region. The colony, however, never became very profitable for Spain.

The Spanish aimed to convert the *Indios* (Filipinos) to Catholicism, their fortified churches defended priests and converts from Chinese and Moro piracy. The *frialocracia* (friar-ocracy) came to run local administration such as the police, hospitals and schools while the Filipinos were left with little except toil and the Virgin Mary. Luzon's Cordillera Mountains and the Muslim south remained free of Spanish rule.

Decline of Spanish Rule

A combination of bad weather and English forces defeated the Spanish Armada in 1588, and the Spanish empire began a long, slow decline. There were over 100 revolts and peasant uprisings against the Spanish before they finally sealed their fate in 1896 by executing the writer José Rizal for inciting revolution. A brilliant scholar and poet, Rizal had worked for independence by peaceful means. His death galvanised the revolutionary movement.

With aid from the USA, already at war with Spain over Cuba, General Aguinaldo's revolutionary army drove the Spanish back to Manila. American warships defeated the Spanish fleet in Manila Bay in May 1898, and independence was declared on 12 June 1898.

American Rule

Unfortunately for the revolutionaries, the American intervention was just a stepping stone towards a new colonial regime. Today, American English, American food and a more obviously corrupt form of American politics (presidency, congress and senate) still exist, but the American presence, or 'tutelage', in the Philippines was always intended to be temporary. The first Philippine national government was formed in 1935 with full independence pencilled in for 10 years later.

> **RIZAL'S TOWER OF BABEL**
>
> The Philippines' answer to Gandhi, writer and gentle revolutionary Dr José Rizal could read and write at the age of two. He grew up to speak more than 20 languages, 18 of them fluently, including English, Sanskrit, Latin, French, German, Greek, Hebrew, Russian, Japanese, Chinese and Arabic. His last words were *consummatum est!* (It is done!).

This schedule was set aside when Japan invaded the islands in WWII. The Americans sustained heavy casualties before finally overcoming the Japanese during the bloody Battle for Manila in 1944. The devastation of the Philippines during the war was profound.

Independence

Independence was granted in 1946, though America continued to exert influence and maintained a vast military presence at Subic Bay Naval Base and Clark Field Airbase, which remained until 1991.

During the early years of independence the Philippines bounced from one ineffectual leader to another until Ferdinand Marcos was elected in 1965. With a nod and wink from the US he took a *datu*-style (local chieftain) approach to government and marched the Philippines towards dictatorship, declaring martial law in 1972. Violence, previously widespread, was curtailed, but the Philippines suffered from stifling corruption and the economy became one of the weakest in an otherwise booming region.

The 1983 assassination of Marcos' opponent Benigno 'Ninoy' Aquino pushed opposition to Marcos to new heights. Marcos called elections for early 1986 and the opposition united to support Aquino's widow, Corazon 'Cory' Aquino. Both Marcos and Aquino claimed to have won the election, but 'people power' rallied behind Cory Aquino, and within days Ferdinand and his profligate wife Imelda were packed off by the Americans to Hawaii, where the former dictator later died.

Politics & Unrest

Cory Aquino managed to hang on throughout numerous coup attempts. With weak

PHILIPPINES

central control, human-rights abuses by the police and army flared as they never had under the reign of Marcos. The resurgent New People's Army (NPA), pushing for a communist revolution, fought the army and police across much of the countryside, especially in Negros and Bicol (the south Luzon region) where pockets of resistance still exist. Meanwhile in the south the Moro National Liberation Front (MNLF), provoked in part by the migration of poor Christians onto tribal and Muslim lands, was fighting for an independent Muslim state.

Fidel Ramos, Imelda's cousin, was elected in 1992 and carried out some much-needed repairs on the economy, encouraged foreign investment and took steps to end the NPA guerrilla war. In 1996 a peace agreement was signed with the MNLF and the Autonomous Region in Muslim Mindanao (ARMM) was created. Only three provinces voted to join the ARMM, making the Christian domination of the rest of Mindanao even more apparent. A faction, calling itself the Moro Islamic Liberation Front (MILF), split from the MNLF and continued the fight.

In 1998 Ramos was replaced by B-grade movie actor Joseph 'Erap' Estrada, who promised to redirect government funding towards rural and poor Filipinos. Unfortunately, Erap spent most of his time redirecting government funding towards his own coffers and was impeached two years later. What followed was a kind of middle-class revolt, which was called EDSA 2 (EDSA was the Manila ring road where the demonstrators gathered and EDSA 1 had been the overthrow of Marcos). The diminutive vice-president Gloria Macapagal-Arroyo (GMA), the daughter of the former president Diosdado Macapagal, took the reins and was re-elected in 2004 on the basis of continued promises to fight against corruption.

MUST READ

America's Boy – the Marcoses and the Philippines by James Hamilton-Paterson examines the personalities and politics surrounding America's imperialistic diversions in the archipelago.

THE CULTURE
The National Psyche

Everyone from Muslim sultans to Catholic priests to American generals has had a turn at shaping Filipino life, but isolated mountain and coastal villages still remain relatively untouched. People often say the Philippines is too Westernised, but the cathedrals and shopping malls are only the most visible aspects of a unique Asian society.

In the countryside, the rhythms of life are surprisingly resilient. They centre on the sea, rivers and fields. In the hinterland, spirits reside in forest groves. A villager might be possessed by a wandering spirit, causing them to commit strange acts. Urban Filipinos can consult an incredible range of services to commune with the supernatural: faith healers, psychics, fortune-tellers, tribal shamans, self-help books and evangelical crusaders all can help cast away ill-fortune.

Filipino society is characterized by strong religious faith, respect for authority, high regard for *amor proprio* (self-esteem) and smooth interpersonal relationships. Filipinos are a passionate lot, whether they are belting out a Tom Jones classic or asserting their regional allegiances. Filipinos from Cebu think Samar people are backward, while Samar people think Cebuanos are conceited, and everybody distrusts the dominant Tagalog speakers around Manila. Filipino politicians know that all politics is local, and rule like the old *datu* chieftains, settling disputes, offering land to new families, strengthening alliances and doing favours.

Lifestyle

The hub of national life in the Philippines is Manila, and Manila is two cities – Tokyo or New York from the 3rd storey up (in apartment blocks and skyscrapers), but Jakarta or Mumbai at street level. The well-educated and moneyed inhabitants of the upper storeys might have a blend of Chinese and European ancestry – some old families speak perfect Spanish. They, and the emerging urban professionals below them, cross paths at vast air-con shopping malls or text each other on Nokias.

Family links sprawl far beyond the usual Western limits in the Philippines, so cousins of cousins attend weddings, anniversaries and overseas departures. Identity is deeply embedded in this web of kinship. Graduations are another big ritual – education is a massive business here, and a passport into well-paid overseas jobs such as nursing, engineering and IT. Women play a significant role in everyday Filipino life and have excellent access to jobs and education.

Officially, 7.4 million people work overseas (9% of the population), but the true figure might be 10 million or more. Whole families live off the income of one father or sister in Europe or the Gulf. Villagers and country people without that source of income have it much tougher. Work might only be seasonal and an early marriage and lots of kids is typical for a country Filipina. Farmers growing copra, bananas, tobacco and rice are at the mercy of broken roads, old ships and the weather. The NPA squeezes revolutionary taxes from everyone, from sari-store owners to mobilephone companies, in some regions.

It's an uncertain life for many. On Palawan and Mindanao in particular, migrant farmers and settlers are leaving the crowded islands and trying their hand at farming in isolated pockets of land claimed only by tribal tradition, not by official land title from Manila. Further out on the fringes of the cash economy are dwindling numbers of forest communities, such as the Negritos.

Population

The population of the Philippines is estimated to be 86 million and growing by 1.6 million every year. Filipino families are large, averaging five children. The people are mainly of the Malay race although there's a sizable and economically dominant Chinese minority and a fair number of *mestizos* (Filipinos of mixed descent). Pre-Malayan communities include the Negritos, who now form the Irayan Mangyan tribes from the mountainous interior on Mindoro, and the Tagbanua on Palawan.

SPORT

Sports play a big part in Filipino life – basketball is *the* sport of the Philippines. You can catch a game in just about every town square and you'll often be invited to participate. In Manila, you may be able to see the sport of *jai alai*, or *pelota*, imported from the Basque region of Spain. The local game has a colourful history of match fixing and illegal gambling.

THE SEARCH FOR SPOILS

Legends of buried treasure flourish in the Philippines. The most famous urban myth talks of Yamashita's Horde, a cache of bullion sunk on a WWII Japanese ship, which Ferdinand Marcos claimed to have found. Modern-day Indiana Jones types, including ex-Japanese soldiers and CIA operatives, supposedly still scour the country's remote regions in search of plunder.

RELIGION

The Philippines is the biggest Christian country in Asia – over 90% of the population identify themselves as Christian, and over 80% identify as Catholic. The largest religious minority is the Muslims (5%), who live chiefly in the Autonomous Region in Muslim Mindanao (ARMM). Filipino Muslims belong to the mainstream Sunni sect, and while many groups combine tribal and Muslim law and customs in their daily lives, others have become more orthodox.

The Catholic church has made a big comeback from its unpopularity at the end of the Spanish era. Catholic celebrations such as local saints' days are adapted from pre-Christian festivals for local deities. These are a part of the Filipino calendar, no matter what sect people belong to. The Catholic bishops wield real influence, and the church sometimes thunders from above on topics like contraception.

MANILA GALLEONS

For 250 years Spanish governors, priests and traders set forth across the Pacific in 'Manila galleons' from the Mexican Pacific port of Acapulco, Manila's lifeline to Spanish power. The Spanish traded Mexican gold and silver for the wealth of Asia: spices, Chinese porcelain, brocade silks, jade, ivory, gems and lacquer goods taken for the markets in Europe and North America. The ships were a bounty for European and local pirates, and even today the Sulu Sea can be a risky area for international cargo. Many ships went down in storms or foundered on reefs, and stories of lost galleons laden with riches abound.

> **MUST SEE**
>
> *Crying Ladies* (2003), directed by Mark Meily, is an intimate film about the last professional mourners of Manila's Chinatown.

American evangelical churches such as Jehovah's Witnesses, Mormons (Church of Latter-Day Saints) and various brands of Southern Baptists all have a high profile. Others are involved in folk practices such as faith healing (where illusionists extract chicken meat rather than tumours from patients in scalpel-free operations), and blessings with spells that might be delivered in a mix of Latin, Tagalog and local phrases.

For a taste of local spiritualism, check out the stalls selling herbal remedies and amulets near Quiapo church in Manila, or the faith healers in Baguio.

ARTS

Cinema

The Filipino film industry began at the turn of the 20th century and today the country is Southeast Asia's most prolific film-making nation. Cinemas are popular and inexpensive. Most show a mix of imported blockbusters and brassy local films – tough cop movies with starlets and guys with great hair in romantic roles. It's no coincidence that former president Joseph Estrada made his name playing a gun-toting good guy. The Philippines also produces a lot of animation, often for Japanese manga movies or US productions.

Dance

Among the most beautiful traditional dances in the Philippines are *tinikling* (bamboo or heron dance) and *pandanggo sa ilaw* (dance of lights); the best-known Filipino-Muslim dance is *singkil* (court dance). You will also often see performances of the Filipino variations of the Hispanic dances *habanera*, *jota* and *paypay* (the fan dance).

Music

The *kundiman*, a bittersweet combination of words and music, is one of the best-loved traditional modes of musical expression in the Philippines. The modern composers Nicanor Abelardo and Francisco Santiago have taken this tradition to new heights by combining modern musical forms with ancient folklore and music.

Traditional instruments include the *kulintang gong* or chime found in North Luzon, and the *kutyapi*, an extremely demanding, but hauntingly melodic, two-stringed lute, commonly found in Mindanao.

Manila and many smaller cities and towns have spawned lively rock scenes, with power ballads and heavy metal among some of the favourites.

ENVIRONMENT

As with much of the government, the budget of the Department of Environment & Natural Resources (DENR) is never quite what it seems once the system of corruption and paybacks bites. The Philippines has excellent environmental laws on its books, but they just aren't enforced. Only 3% of the reefs are in a pristine state, and 60% have been severely damaged.

The biggest culprit of reef damage is silt, washed down from hills and valleys cleared of their original forest cover. Incredibly short-sighted techniques for making a few extra bucks include dynamite and cyanide fishing.

The uncontrolled harvesting of seashells for export, particularly in the Visayas, is another problem. Don't go buying souvenirs made from shell or coral (souvenirs made from farmed oyster shells are an exception).

Floods, most recently in 2004, are exacerbated by the uncontrolled deforestation of much of the country. Serious lip service is given to the issue by the government but the situation remains mostly unchanged.

The Land

Most of the Philippine islands are volcanic in origin, and active volcanoes, such as the Taal and Mayon Volcanoes in Luzon, grumble regularly. The volcanoes may be tempestuous, but they do provide excellent soil. The plains north of Manila and the sugar belt around Negros are incredibly fertile.

Wildlife

The country's flora includes well over 10,000 species of trees, bushes and ferns, including 900 types of orchid. About 10% of the Philippines is still covered by tropical rainforest. Ironically, some forests in Mindanao,

Negros, Samar and Bohol still exist only because of the presence of insurgent armies.

Endangered animal species include the rare mouse deer, the tarsier (a pocket-sized, wide-eyed primate), the tamaráw (a species of dwarf buffalo) of Mindoro, the Palawan bearcat and the flying lemur. As for the national bird, only about 100 haribons, or Philippine eagles, remain in their natural habitat in Mindanao.

There's an unbelievable array of fish, seashells and corals, as well dwindling numbers of the *duyong* (dugong, or sea cow). If your timing's just right you can spot *butanding* (whale sharks) near Donsol (p619) in South Luzon.

National Parks

There are numerous national parks in the Philippines, but many are off limits. Perhaps the most accessible park is St Paul Subterranean National Park (p644) on Palawan.

Samar's Sohoton Natural Bridge National Park (p640) has impressive limestone formations in a protected cave system, and Tubbataha Reef National Park (p644), near Puerto Princesa, offers fantastic diving in untouched reefs.

TRANSPORT

GETTING THERE & AWAY
Air

Unless you fly in with Philippine Airlines (PAL), which uses the tidy new Centennial Terminal II, you'll have to fight your way through Ninoy Aquino International Airport (NAIA). Expect disorganisation, long queues and diabolical transport connections to the city.

If you're heading south, a much better option is to fly into Cebu City's Mactan International Airport with Cathay Pacific, Malaysia Airlines or Singapore's regional feeder airline, SilkAir. You could also fly into Davao in Mindanao from Singapore and from Manado in Indonesia, but given recent troubles in Davao it's not currently advisable.

CHINA
China Southern Airlines (www.cs-air.com) flies from Beijing to Manila. **Cathay Pacific** (www.cathaypacific.com) flies from Hong Kong to Manila and to Cebu.

INDONESIA
Philippine Airlines (PAL; www.philippineair.com) has direct flights between Jakarta and Manila, but if you fly via Brunei with **Royal Brunei Airlines** (www.bruneiair.com) it's cheaper.

Bouraq Airlines (www.bouraq.net) flies between Davao, in the south of Mindanao, and Manado in the north of Sulawesi for around US$220/350 one way/return

MALAYSIA
Malaysia Airlines (www.malaysiaairlines.com) has flights between Kuala Lumpur and Manila, and between Kuala Lumpur and Cebu. You can also fly between Manila and Kota Kinabalu in Sabah.

SINGAPORE
Philippine Airlines has flights between Singapore and Manila. **SilkAir** (www.silkair.com) also flies between Singapore and Cebu.

THAILAND
The competition on the route between Bangkok and Manila is fierce, so you can score a good deal if you look around.

Boat

Although there are plenty of shipping routes within the Philippines, international services are scarce. To Indonesia, all ferry services leave from ports in southern Mindanao. One route is from General Santos to Bitung, the port for Manado in northern Sulawesi (US$25, 36 hours, once a week), with EPA Lines. There are also services from Zamboanga to Sandakan in the Malaysian state of Sabah with Aleson Lines (from P1100, 17 hours, twice weekly) or with an SRN fast boat (P3300, eight hours, once a week). At present, travel in this region is not recommended (see p640). For information on boats between Sabah in Malaysia and Palawan, see p643.

GETTING AROUND
Air

There's an extensive domestic network, but most flights leave from either Manila or Cebu, and there aren't many flights

---

DEPARTURE TAX

International departure tax is P550, and is payable only in cash (peso or US$).

PHILIPPINES AIR FARES

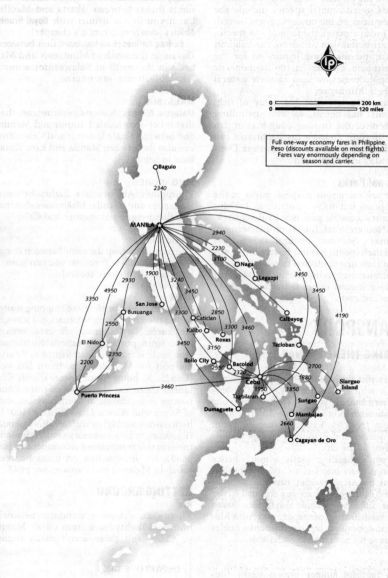

0 — 200 km
0 — 120 miles

Full one-way economy fares in Philippine Peso (discounts available on most flights). Fares vary enormously depending on season and carrier.

Baguio
2340

MANILA

2940
2230
3100 Naga
Legazpi 3450

3450

1900
2930 3240
3450
San Jose
Busuanga 3300 Caticlan 2850 Calbayog
2550 Kalibo 3300 3460
El Nido Roxas Tacloban
2350 3150
Iloilo City Bacolod 2700
2200 3450 2550 2320 1880
Cebu Siargao Island
Puerto Princesa 3460 1950 1850
Tagbilaran Surigao
Dumaguete Mambajao
2660
Cagayan de Oro

3350
4950
3350

4190

between other cities. Competition is vigorous and it's well worth checking a few airlines to find the best fare. A two-hour journey from Manila to Cebu might be only P1800 with a promotional fare, which compares pretty well with paying for a comfortable cabin and meals on a 22-hour ferry ride.

Philippine Airlines has the biggest and generally the newest fleet, though its fares tend be a little higher than those of its competitors. Student-card holders under 25 years and passengers over 60 years receive a 20% discount. In Manila, all PAL flights leave from the Centennial Terminal II.

Other domestic services leave from Manila's domestic terminal. Air Philippines and Cebu Pacific are the biggest competitors, while Asian Spirit and Seair tend to cover more obscure destinations with smaller aircraft.

Domestic departure taxes vary – generally P100 from Manila, and less at other airports.

Limited promotional seats, with discounts of up to 50% off regular fares, are offered by most airlines, but these go quick so it pays to book well in advance. There are express offices for the airlines at their respective terminals; you can also book online. PAL is at Centennial Terminal II; the other airlines listed are at Manila's domestic terminal:

Air Philippines (☎ 02-855 9000; www.airphils.com)
Asian Spirit (☎ 02-851 8888; www.asianspirit.com)
Cebu Pacific (☎ 02-636 4938-45; www.cebupacificair.com)
Philippine Airlines (PAL; ☎ 02-855 8888; www.philippineair.com)
Seair (☎ 02-884 1521; www.flyseair.com)

Boat

If boats are your thing, this is the place for you. The islands of the Philippines are linked by an incredible network of ferry routes, and services are generally fast, frequent and cheap. The vessels used range from tiny, narrow outrigger canoes (known locally as *bangca*, or pumpboats), to luxury passenger catamarans and vast multidecked ships like the WG&A SuperFerry. There are often several boats a day covering the major routes, though boats to minor destinations are less frequent.

The jeepney of the sea, the *bangca*, comes sometimes with a roof, sometimes without.

Bangcas ply regular routes between islands and are also available for hire per day for diving, sightseeing or just getting around. The engines on these boats can be deafeningly loud, and they aren't the most stable in rough seas, but on islands like Palawan the *bangca* can be preferable to travelling overland.

For the most part, ferries are an easy, enjoyable way to hop between islands, but accidents are not unknown. Follow your instincts – if the boat looks crowded, it is, and if sailing conditions seem wrong, they are. Pumpboats during stormy weather are especially scary.

Ferry prices vary widely, but as a guide, the average fare between Manila and Cebu City is around P1100, depending on which class you take, and between Manila and Puerto Princesa fares start at about P900. Inquire about student discounts: some shipping lines give 20% or 30% off.

Most of the long-haul services out of Manila and Cebu are provided by the ocean liners of Negros Navigation, Sulpicio Lines and WG&A, all of which have booking offices in major towns. Useful Manila offices are:

Negros Navigation (Map pp600-1; www.negrosnavigation.ph; ☎ 02-245 5588; Pier 2, North Harbor)
Sulpicio Lines (Map pp600-1; ☎ 02-245 0616; www.sulpiciolines.com; Pier 12, North Harbor)
WG&A SuperFerry (Map pp600-1; ☎ 02-528 7000; www.superferry.com.ph; Pier 15, South Port)

Bus

Philippine buses come in all shapes and sizes, from rusty boxes on wheels to luxury air-con coaches. Bus depots are dotted throughout towns and the countryside, and most buses will stop if you wave them down. Destinations are marked on the front of the bus. Terminals are usually on the outskirts of town, but tricycle drivers should know where they are.

There are extremely regular services from Manila to most other towns in Luzon, and on sealed roads elsewhere in the islands (eg the coastal roads around Cebu, Negros and Panay). Generally, more services run in the morning – buses on unsealed roads may run only in the morning. Most buses follow a fixed schedule but may leave early if they're full – take care if there's only one bus a day!

Buses from Manila to major cities such as Baguio usually run until late at night.

PHILIPPINES

You should also look out for air-con L-300 or FX minibuses, which are used in many parts of the Philippines as rivals to regular buses. However, you may have to play a waiting game until the vehicles are full.

Local Transport

JEEPNEY

The first jeepneys were modified army jeeps left behind by the Americans after WWII. They have been customised with Filipino touches like chrome horses, banks of coloured headlights, radio antennae, paintings of the Virgin Mary and neon-coloured scenes from action comic books. Modern jeepneys are built locally from durable aluminium and stainless steel, but are faithful to the original design.

Jeepneys form the main urban transport in most cities and compliment the bus services between regional centres. Within towns, the starting fare is usually P5 to P5.50. You can pay anywhere along the way: just pass your money up to the front and the correct change will invariably be passed back to you.

The list of destinations written on the side of the jeepney will often give a more accurate picture of the route than the signboards in the window. Try to avoid being the sole passenger on a jeepney, as the driver may decide that it's not worth completing the journey and drop you off in the middle of nowhere.

KALESA

Kalesa are two-wheeled horse carriages found in Manila's Chinatown, Vigan (North Luzon) and Cebu City (where they're known as *tartanillas*). In Manila they seem to exist solely to help tourists part with large sums of money, so be careful to agree on a fare before clambering aboard. You can pay anywhere between P200 and P800 for a 20-minute ride – happy bargaining!

GEMS OF THE PHILIPPINES

This is our completely subjective list of the best and strangest in this incredible country.

Favourite Small Mercies

■ The widespread distribution of what is probably the cheapest beer in the world

■ When ships broadcast prayers blessing your journey, complete with swelling choir

■ All-you-can eat buffets after 18-hour boat trips

Most Tragically Popular Karaoke Songs

■ *I Will Always Love You*, Whitney Houston

■ *Dancing Queen*, Abba

■ *Wind Beneath My Wings*, Bette Midler

Most Challenging Moments

■ Roosters with dysfunctional circadian rhythms crowing at 3am

■ The Filipino penchant for any machine that spews diesel exhaust fumes

■ Maniacal drivers who feel invincible because their window is plastered with 'God bless this trip' stickers

Worst Times to Run Out of Film

■ While glued to a hammock on Bantayan's blindingly white Santa Fe beach

■ At the rice terrace amphitheatre in Batad as the sun sets

■ When savouring the view from any volcano you have just spent 10 hours climbing

TAXI

Manila taxi drivers are more reliable than they used to be, but there are still some rogue drivers out there. Most will turn on the meter, but even if they do it's worth checking to see that it's working. It's easy to charter a taxi for a couple of hours of a day to do some sightseeing with a modicum of comfort. To avoid paying whatever the driver thinks you can pay, a day's driving (eight hours) should be around P2000, or P250 per hour.

Taxi drivers at airports rarely agree to use the meter – you may have to settle on a fixed price. You generally don't have this problem going *to* an airport.

The flagfall in Manila, Cebu and Baguio is P30; after that it's P2.50 per 300m.

TRICYCLE

Found in most cities and towns, the tricycle is the Philippine rickshaw – a little, roofed sidecar bolted to a bicycle or motorcycle. Locals will pay as little as P5 for a short trip, but the ride will often stop to pick up other passengers en route. Motorcycle tricycles routinely ask elevated fees in tourist centres so feel free to haggle. You can also charter one for about P100 per hour.

In some areas, you may also find *habal-habal* – motorcycles with an extended rear seat (literally translated as 'pigs copulating,' after the level of intimacy attained when sharing a seat with four people). These charge roughly the same as tricycles and are better on unsealed roads.

MANILA

☎ 02 / pop 11.2 million

Manila's moniker as the 'Pearl of the Orient' couldn't be more apt – its cantankerous shell reveals its jewel only to those resolute enough to pry. No stranger to hardship, the city has endured every disaster both man and nature could throw at it, and yet today the chaotic 600-sq-km city gives the term 'sprawling metropolis' a run for its money. Gleaming skyscrapers pierce the hazy sky, mushrooming from the grinding poverty of expansive shantytowns. The congested roads snarl with traffic, but like the overworked arteries of a sweating giant, they are what keep this modern metropolis alive. The tourist belt of Ermita and Malate flaunts an unin-

hibited nightlife that would make Bangkok's go-go bars blush, and the gleaming malls of Makati foreshadow Manila's brave new air-conditioned world. The determined will discover Manila's tender soul, perhaps among the leafy courtyards and cobbled streets of serene Intramuros, where little has changed since the Spanish left. Or it may be in the eddy of repose arising from the generosity of one of the city's 11 million residents.

HISTORY

The Spanish brushed aside a Muslim fort here in 1571 and founded the modern city as a mercantile centre and the capital of their realm. They named it *Isigne y Siempre Leal Ciudad* ('distinguished and ever-loyal city'), but the name Manila (from *Maynilad,* derived from a local term for a mangrove plant) soon became established. The Spanish lived in the walled city of Intramuros while the natives settled outside the walls. After being razed to the ground during WWII, the city grew exponentially during the post-war era as migrants left the countryside for new opportunities. Explosive growth slowly devoured 17 surrounding cities, which were eventually consolidated into Metro Manila in 1976.

ORIENTATION

Although it sprawls a great distance along Manila Bay, the core of Metro Manila is the area surrounding the mouth of the Pasig River. The main accommodation and dining districts are Ermita and Malate (Map pp602–3), which lie just south of Rizal Park (Map pp602–3), and the old walled city of Intramuros (Map p606).

Makati (Map pp600–1) is the business hub of the Philippines, or rather it is where much of the nation's wealth vanishes to.

On the northern side of the river (Map pp600–1) you'll find Binondo (Manila's old Chinatown), Quiapo and North Harbor, the departure point for many interisland ferries. The airport is about 10km south of the centre in Parañaque (Map pp600–1).

To reach the business district of Makati or the huge shopping centres in Ortigas, you'll need to take a Metrorail train or bus along the ring road known as Epifanio De Los Santos Ave (EDSA). This road runs

(Continued on page 604)

PHILIPPINES

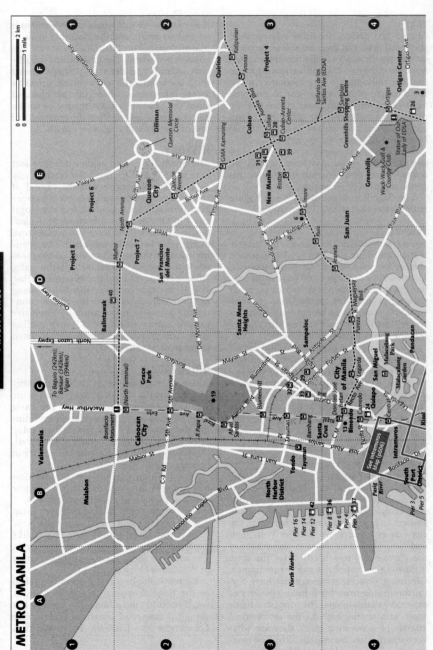

METRO MANILA

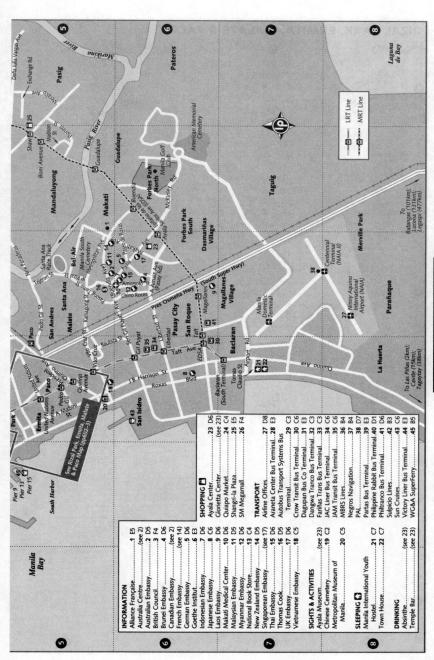

PHILIPPINES

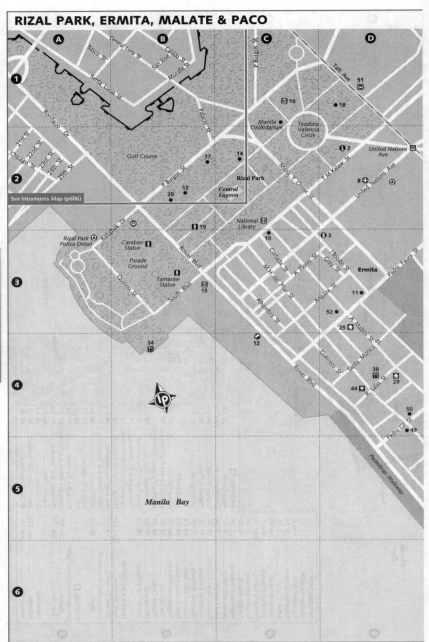

RIZAL PARK, ERMITA, MALATE & PACO

See Intramuros Map (p606)

Manila Bay

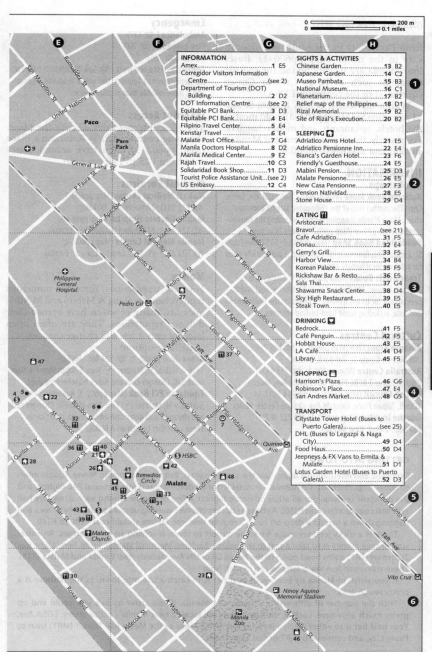

INFORMATION

Amex	1 E5
Corregidor Visitors Information Centre	(see 2)
Department of Tourism (DOT) Building	2 D2
DOT Information Centre	(see 2)
Equitable PCI Bank	3 D3
Equitable PCI Bank	4 E4
Filipino Travel Center	5 E4
Kenstar Travel	6 E4
Malate Post Office	7 G4
Manila Doctors Hospital	8 D2
Manila Medical Center	9 E2
Rajah Travel	10 C3
Solidaridad Book Shop	11 D3
Tourist Police Assistance Unit	(see 2)
US Embassy	12 C4

SIGHTS & ACTIVITIES

Chinese Garden	13 B2
Japanese Garden	14 C2
Museo Pambata	15 B3
National Museum	16 C1
Planetarium	17 B2
Relief map of the Philippines	18 D1
Rizal Memorial	19 B2
Site of Rizal's Execution	20 B2

SLEEPING

Adriatico Arms Hotel	21 E5
Adriatico Pensionne Inn	22 E4
Bianca's Garden Hotel	23 F6
Friendly's Guesthouse	24 E5
Mabini Pension	25 D3
Malate Pensionne	26 E5
New Casa Pensionne	27 F3
Pension Natividad	28 E5
Stone House	29 D4

EATING

Aristocrat	30 E6
Bravo!	(see 21)
Cafe Adriatico	31 F5
Donau	32 E4
Gerry's Grill	33 F5
Harbor View	34 B4
Korean Palace	35 E5
Rickshaw Bar & Resto	36 E5
Sala Thai	37 G4
Shawarma Snack Center	38 E5
Sky High Restaurant	39 E5
Steak Town	40 E5

DRINKING

Bedrock	41 F5
Café Penguin	42 F5
Hobbit House	43 E5
LA Café	44 D4
Library	45 F5

SHOPPING

Harrison's Plaza	46 G6
Robinson's Place	47 E4
San Andres Market	48 G5

TRANSPORT

Citystate Tower Hotel (Buses to Puerto Galera)	(see 25)
DHL (Buses to Legazpi & Naga City)	49 D4
Food Haus	50 D4
Jeepneys & FX Vans to Ermita & Malate	51 D1
Lotus Garden Hotel (Buses to Puerto Galera)	52 D3

PHILIPPINES

(Continued from page 599)

from Pasay City in the south to Caloocan City in the north (Map pp600–1). Buses into Manila are usually bound for specific terminals such as Pasay City or Cubao (northeast of the centre on EDSA).

Within the tourist belt, A Mabini St and M Adriatico St (Map pp602–3), hold most of the hotels, restaurants and moneychangers. Fortunately, this is also the centre of Manila's student and alternative nightlife.

INFORMATION
Bookshops
National Book Store (Map pp600-1; 665 Rizal Ave, Santa Cruz) The mother ship of the Philippines' largest bookstore chain. Major Manila shopping centres, including the convenient Robinson's Place (Map pp602-3), have branches.

Solidaridad Book Shop (Map pp602-3; 531 Padre Faura St, Ermita) This famous leftie bookshop is particularly good for titles on local history and politics.

Tradewinds Books (Map p606; 3rd fl, Silahis Arts & Artifacts Center, 744 General Luna St, Intramuros) Worth seeking out for its assortment of books on the Philippines and Asia, including some hard-to-find volumes.

Cultural Centres
Alliance Française (Map pp600-1; ☎ 895 7585; 209 Nicanor Garcia St, Bel-Air II, Makati)
Australia Centre (Map pp600-1; ☎ 757 8135; 23rd fl, Tower 2 RCBC Plaza, 6819 Ayala Ave, Makati)
British Council (Map pp600-1; ☎ 914 1011-14; 10th fl, Taipan Place, Emerald Ave, Ortigas Center, Pasig)
Goethe Institut (Map pp600-1; ☎ 722 4671; 687 Aurora Blvd, New Manila)

Emergency
Ambulance (☎ 117)
Fire brigade (☎ 160)
Police (☎ 166)
Tourist assistance unit (☎ 524 1728/1660) Based at the Department of Tourism, this unit is available 24 hours and is more reliable than regular police.

Internet Access
There are Internet cafés all over the place; shopping centres such as Robinson's Place (Map pp602–3) often have several. Rates vary from P25 to P40 per hour.

Medical Services
Makati Medical Center (Map pp600-1; ☎ 815 9911; 2Amorsolo St, Makati)
Manila Doctors Hospital (Map pp602-3; ☎ 524 3011; 677 United Nations Ave, Ermita)
Manila Medical Center (Map pp602-3; ☎ 523 8131-65; 1122 General Luna St, Ermita)

Money
For cash transactions, there are numerous moneychangers along A Mabini and M Adriatico Sts, many of which have earned their dubious reputations. They are often open late, but only a few will change cheques.

Reliable options:
Amex (Map pp602-3; ☎ 524 8681/8682; 1810 A Mabini St, Malate; ☯ 9am-5.30pm Mon-Fri, 9am-noon Sat) Changes cash and Amex travellers cheques.
Equitable PCI Bank (Map pp602-3; Robinson's Place, Adriatico St, Malate; ☯ 9am-3pm Mon-Fri) Changes cash and cheques, and gives cash advances on credit cards. There's another branch on A Mabini St.

GETTING INTO TOWN

Domestic and international flights use the same runways, but three terminals: Ninoy Aquino International Airport (NAIA); Centennial Terminal II (for all domestic and international PAL flights); and the domestic terminal (for all other domestic flights). A line of booths around each departure hall sells taxi coupons (around P350). A cheaper option involves walking upstairs to the arrivals area and flagging down a taxi on a drop-off run – a regular ride into Malate should cost P100 to P140.

There is a tricky jeepney route from the airport to town, involving several changes. An easier way to save money is to take a taxi to the nearby Baclaran Metrorail station. From here, Light Rail Transport (LRT) trains head north to the Pedro Gil or UN Ave stations near Ermita and Malate (P15). These trains can feel like a sardine can in rush hour.

If you arrive in Manila by boat, your best bet is to catch a taxi into town, as the harbour is a pretty rough area.

With the number of different bus stations in Manila, if you arrive by bus you could end up pretty much anywhere. Luckily, most terminals are located near Manila's major artery, EDSA Ave. Your best bet is to either catch a jeepney along EDSA Ave or the Metro Rail Transit (MRT) train to Pasay City, and continue by LRT or taxi from there.

Thomas Cook (Map pp600-1; ☎ 816 3701; cnr Sen Gil Puyat Ave & Tindabo St, Makati; ☻ 8.30am-5.30pm Mon-Fri, 8.30am-12.30pm Sat) Changes Thomas Cook travellers cheques (obviously), and is another reliable place to exchange cash.

Post
Malate Post Office (Map pp602-3; ☎ 450 8353; Pilar Hidalgo Lim St; ☻ 8am-noon & 1-5pm Mon-Fri) A friendly local post office conveniently close to Malate.
Manila Central Post Office (Map p606; ☎ 527 0085/0079; ☻ 8am-noon & 1-5pm Mon-Fri, 8am-noon Sat) This imposing, neoclassical building north of Intramuros handles most postal transactions, including poste restante. It's between the Jones and MacArthur Bridges,

Telephone
Phone calls can be made from many hotels and from the numerous offices of PLDT, BayanTel, Smart Telecom and Globe Telecom. Phone cards are sold at convenience stores everywhere.

Toilets
Shopping centres and fast-food chain restaurants are the best places to head for relief; they're generally pretty clean.

Tourist Information
Department of Tourism (DOT; Map pp602-3; ☎ 525 2000) There's a helpful office in the vast DOT building at the Taft Ave end of Rizal Park. There are also smaller DOT offices at Manila's Ninoy Aquino International Airport and the Centennial Terminal II.

Travel Agencies
Filipino Travel Center (Map pp602-3; ☎ 528 4504/4507; www.filipinotravel.com.ph; cnr Adriatico St & Pedro Gill St, Ermita) Established, full-service agency that books tours and accommodation and arranges tickets for most domestic travel needs and international flights.
Kenstar Travel (Map pp602-3; ☎ 524 1211-6; 635 General Malvar St, Malate) Offers quite good rates for international air tickets.
Rajah Travel (Map pp602-3; ☎ 523 8801; cnr A Mabini St & Kalaw St, Ermita) Also reputable, this place can handle anything from tickets to visa extensions.

DANGERS & ANNOYANCES
Manila can be a pretty sketchy place, particularly after dark. The touristed areas of Ermita, Malate and Makati are considered some of the safer areas, but even here it pays to be careful after dark. See also p649.

SIGHTS
Intramuros   Map p606
A spacious borough of wide streets, leafy plazas and lovely colonial houses, the old walled city of Intramuros was the centrepiece of Spanish Manila. At least it was until WWII, when the Americans and Japanese levelled the whole lot. Only a handful of buildings survived the firestorm; over 100,000 Filipino civilians were not so lucky.

The Spanish replaced the original wooden fort with stone in 1590, and these walls stand much as they were 400 years ago. They're still studded with bastions and pierced with gates (puertas). The golf course, however, is a relatively new addition. At the mouth of the Pasig River you'll find **Fort Santiago** (admission P40; ☻ 8am-6pm Tue-Sun), fronted by a pretty lily pond and a small visitors centre that hands out simple maps and information. During WWII the fort was used as a prisoner-of-war camp by the Japanese. The **Rizal Shrine** and the **Rizal Museum** (admission by donation; ☻ 8am-6pm Tue-Sun) contain personal effects and other items relating to the national hero, José Rizal, including an original copy of his last poem, penned as he awaited execution. The museum houses brilliantly presented translations of some of his famous works.

The most interesting building to survive the Battle of Manila is the church and monastery of **San Agustin** (General Luna St). This appealing church is where the last Spanish governor of Manila surrendered to the Filipinos in 1898. The interior is truly opulent and the ceiling, painted in 3D relief, will make you question your vision. The former Augustinian monastery next door is now an excellent **religious museum** (General Luna St; admission P65; ☻ 9am-noon & 1-6pm). **Casa Manila** (cnr Real St & General Luna St; admission P40; ☻ 9am-noon & 1-6pm Tue-Sun) is a beautifully restored, three-storey Spanish colonial mansion filled with antiques. It's also possible to wander around the gardens and decadent shops and restaurants of the surrounding **Plaza Luna Complex** for free. Nearby, the flashy **Bahay Tsinoy Museum** (cnr Anda & Cabildo Sts; admission P100; ☻ 1-5pm Tue-Sun) uses vivid dioramas and photographs to tell the story of the Chinese in Manila.

Also of interest is the grand Romanesque **Manila Cathedral** (cnr Postigo St & General Luna St;

INTRAMUROS

0 ———— 200 m
0 ———— 0.1 miles

Pasig   River

INFORMATION
Immigration Office...........................**1** C1
Intramuros Visitors Center...............**2** B2
Manila Central Post Office...............**3** C1
Tradewinds Books.............................**4** C3

SIGHTS & ACTIVITIES
Bahay Tsinoy Museum......................**5** C2
Casa Manila.....................................**6** C3
Fort Santiago...................................**7** A2
Manila Cathedral.............................**8** B2
Plaza de Roma..................................**9** B2
Plaza Luna Complex.....................(see 6)
Religious Museum.......................(see 12)
Rizal Museum.................................**10** A2
Rizal Shrine....................................**11** A2
San Agustin Church........................**12** C3

TRANSPORT
Buses, Jeepneys & FX to Makati & Pasay
   City...**13** D2
Jeepneys & FX to Quiapo & Santa
   Cruz..**14** D2

⌚ 6.30am-5.30pm), which is a Vatican-funded
reconstruction of the cathedral destroyed
in WWII, and the sixth church on this site.
The gilded altar and stained-glass, rosette
windows are spectacular and there's an
enormous organ at the rear. The cathedral
faces onto the **Plaza de Roma**, once used as a
bullfighting ring.

It's easy to catch a jeepney, bus or FX
from the stops on nearby P Burgos St.

Rizal Park   Map pp602–3
One of the precious few bits of green in
Manila, the 60-hectare Rizal Park (also
known as Luneta) offers urbanites a place
to decelerate among ornamental gardens
and a whole pantheon of Filipino heroes.

On Sunday afternoon you can watch martial arts displays here, including the Filipino
school of *arnis*, a style of stick-fighting.

Located at the bay end of the park are the
Rizal Memorial and the **site of Rizal's execution**.
The **planetarium** is flanked by a **Japanese garden** (admission P5) and a **Chinese garden** (admission
P5), which are favourite meeting spots for
young couples. At the Taft Ave end there's
a gigantic pond with a three-dimensional
relief map of the Philippines.

The collection at the splendid **National
Museum** (Museum of the Filipino Peoples; Map pp602–3;
T Valencia Circle, Rizal Park; admission P100, free Sun;
⌚ 9am-5pm Wed-Sun) includes excellent dis-
plays on the wreck of the *San Diego*, a
Spanish galleon from 1600, plus lots of

artefacts and musical instruments from the pre-Hispanic era.

There's a jeepney and FX stop nearby on Taft Ave, where you can pick up a ride to Ermita and Malate.

Museums

As well as the offerings in Intramuros and Rizal Park, Manila has plenty of other interesting museums.

The **Ayala Museum** (Map pp600-1; Makati Ave, Makati; admission P120; ☉ 10am-6pm Tue-Sun) tells the story of the Filipino quest for independence through dioramas, and has exhibitions by contemporary artists. The **Metropolitan Museum of Manila** (Map pp600-1; BSP Complex, Roxas Blvd; admission P50; ☉ 10am-6pm Mon-Sat) is in the Central Bank Complex and features an avarice-inducing collection of pre-Hispanic gold.

A great place for both little and grown-up kids is the **Museo Pambata** (Children's Museum; Map pp602-3; cnr Roxas Blvd & South Blvd, Ermita; admission P60; ☉ 8am-noon & 1.30-5pm Tue-Sat, 1-5pm Sun), with lots of hands-on stuff to learn with.

Chinese Cemetery

Boldly challenging the idea that you can't take it with you, the mausoleums of wealthy Chinese in the **Chinese Cemetery** (Map pp600-1; Rizal Ave Extension or Aurora Blvd; admission free; ☉ 7.30am-7pm), in the north of Santa Cruz, are fitted with flushing toilets and crystal chandeliers. Entry is free; hiring a guide (P300) will let you into the best tombs. To get here take a 'Monumento' jeepney to Aurora Blvd (where Rizal Ave becomes Rizal Ave Extension) and walk east to F Heurtes St, which leads to the south gate. Abad Santos is the closest LRT station.

SLEEPING
Hostels

Manila International Youth Hostel (Map pp600-1; ☎ 832 2112; 4227-9 Tomas Claudio St, Parañaque; dm/d P200/700; ☒) This hostel is 3km north of the international airport. It has clean sheets and pleasant staff, and is a good place to meet fellow travellers and Filipino students. Discounts are available for members.

Guesthouses

Manila's budget accommodation centres around Ermita and Malate, but even the cheapest rooms can feel a bit overpriced.

Friendly's Guesthouse (Map pp602-3; ☎ 0917 333 1418; cnr Adriatico & Nakpil Sts; dm/s P250/320; d P420-470; ☒) Captained by the affable and informative Benjie, this place is the pick of the litter. Located in an apartment building above the street-level mayhem, it has an air-con dorm, neat, small fan rooms, a green balcony and comfortable communal lounge. There's free tea and coffee, bag lockers, kitchen and laundry facilities, and best of all, free wine 'appreciation' on Saturday nights.

Pension Natividad (Map pp602-3; ☎ 521 0524; 1690 MH del Pilar St, Malate; dm P280, d P650-980; ☒) Set around a private courtyard, this is a sociable family affair popular with Peace Corps volunteers and long-termers. There's an inexpensive coffee shop serving yummy breakfasts and snacks, and luggage lockers.

Town House (Map pp600-1; ☎ 854 3826; 31 Bayview Dr, Parañaque; dm P180, d P300-950; ☒) Conveniently close to the airport, but inconveniently far from central Manila, the Town House has a leafy rooftop patio and smiling owners. The fan rooms share communal bathrooms.

Malate Pensionne (Map pp602-3; ☎ 523 8304; 1771 Adriatico St, Malate; dm P300, d P600-1300; ☒) Located off Adriatico St, behind Starbucks (frappe-latte anyone?), this long-established wooden pension has a quiet courtyard and cosy lounge. The better air-con doubles come with cable TV and private bathrooms.

New Casa Pensionne (Map pp602-3; ☎ 522 1740; cnr Pedro Gil St & Leon Guinto St, Ermita; s P380-550, d P490-780; ☒) You will be well looked after by the matronly staff in this small, secure place. Most of the tidy rooms share a bathroom.

SPLURGE!

Adriatico Arms Hotel (Map pp602-3; ☎ 524 7426; 561 J Nakpil St, Malate; d P1500-1800; ☒) This small boutique hotel is smack-bang in the heart of trendy Nakpil St. The rates are surprisingly low for the location and the snazzy rooms.

Sky High Restaurant (Map pp602-3; ☎ 524 1726; 463 Remedios St, Malate; mains P250-380; ☉ to 11.30pm) While the décor subscribes to the severe 'Chinese Restaurant' school of interior design, the seafood experience here is exceptional. A decadent seafood dish with vegetables and rice will set you back around P440.

Mabini Pension (Map pp602-3; ☎ 523 3930; 1777 A Mabini St, Ermita; d P550-900; 🏵) A big choice of mellow, quaint rooms in an old Mabini mansion.

Adriatico Pensionne Inn (Map pp602-3; ☎ 404 2300/3430; 1612 Adriatico St, Malate; d P580-930; 🏵) The nice little garden and free breakfast and laundry may help you overlook some of cramped rooms in this inn. All combinations of fan/air-con and shared/private bathroom are available.

Hotels

Stone House (Map pp602-3; ☎ 524 0302; 1529 A Mabini St; d P250-900; 🏵) This chic new place offers a contemporary habitat for style-savvy backpackers. There is a small, elegant bar downstairs and while the budget rooms are nondescript, the better doubles are excellent value and come with a squillion cable-TV channels.

Bianca's Garden Hotel (Map pp602-3; ☎ 526 0351; 2139 Adriatico St, Malate; d P800-2000; 🏵 🏵) Just south of Remedios Circle, Bianca's pays homage to the best of '80s Palm Springs living. All the huge rooms contain native furniture and works of art.

EATING

At first glance it's easy to be blinded by the neon of ubiquitous Western fast-food joints, but look closely and you'll find lots of local barbecue stands and cheerful modern Filipino bistros, as well as Chinese, Japanese, Thai and numerous other regional cuisines. Many meals are meat-centric, but Korean and Chinese restaurants will often have dishes to feed hungry vegetarians.

Filipino

Malate's label as the city's 'it' destination means that cheap Filipino fare is becoming scarce. The best option in the tourist belt is the string of cheap canteens on Santa Monica St in Ermita (Map pp602-3), which offer *adobo* with rice and other Filipino favourites for about P70.

Gerry's Grill (Map pp602-3; ☎ 522 1334; 556 Remedios Circle; mains P85-190) One of the better and smaller Manila chains of restaurants serving up well-prepared Filipino standards in a convivial atmosphere.

Aristocrat (Map pp602-3; ☎ 524 7671; cnr Roxas Blvd & San Andreas St; mains P200-340; 🕑 24hr) The hospital mess-hall feel is compensated for by Filipino classics like grilled *bangus* (milkfish) and pork knuckles, served here for over 60 years.

Harbor View (Map pp602-3; ☎ 524 1532; South Blvd, Rizal Park; mains P180-340) This is a laidback place at the end of a pier jutting well into Manila Bay near Quirino Grandstand. There's a wide range of fresh seafood to enjoy with the golden sunset and some amber refreshments.

Cafe Adriatico (Map pp602-3; ☎ 525 2509; 1790 Adriatico St, Malate; mains P190-390) A Malate institution and the forerunner to the area's cultural renaissance, Cafe Adriatico expertly fuses Filipino and Spanish gastronomy. Musicians enthusiastically serenade tables on weekends.

Asian

For a great budget meal, try popping into one of the dozens of simple Chinese and Korean eateries, serving dim sum, *congee* (rice porridge) and steamed rice with toppings.

Rickshaw Bar & Resto (Map pp602-3; ☎ 521 6129; 1723 Adriatico St, Malate; mains P80-140) The peppy staff in this spotless eatery are deft at serving inexpensive dim sum (starting at P70). A bowl of noodles will set you back P80, while a rice-and-topping set, served with soup and iced tea, costs P120.

Shawarma Snack Center (Map pp602-3; ☎ 525 4541; 45 Salas St; snacks P45-65, meals P70-150; 🕑 24hr) Scrumptious Middle Eastern snacks and meals, from falafel to grilled goat meat. Sit and watch the world go by while smoking a flavoured tobacco water-pipe for P150.

Korean Palace (Map pp602-3; ☎ 521 6695; cnr Adriatico St & Remedios St, Malate; mains P200-380; 🕑 10am-2am) This is one of the best Korean restaurants in town, with a meal of marinated meat or seafood, side dishes and rice costing about P240.

Sala Thai (Map pp602-3; ☎ 522 4694; 866 Nakpil St, Malate; mains P100-180; 🕑 to 10pm Mon-Sat) The granddaddy of Manila's Thai restaurants, the dishes here are authentic and the prices sensible .

Western

Fast-food outlets notwithstanding, there are loads of other Western restaurants.

Steak Town (Map pp602-3; ☎ 522 2632; 1738 Adriatico St, Malate; mains P250-400) The Disneyesque wild-west theme in this long-standing steakhouse is a surprisingly big hit. Main courses come with soup and garlic bread, and unlimited helpings from a salad bar plus tea or coffee.

Bravo! (Map pp602-3; ☎ 303 3508; cnr Nakpil St & Adriatico St, Malate; mains P300) One of a stylish new breed of Italian restaurants, with moody lighting and friendly staff. There are many variations on a thin-crust pizza, all tastily garnished with herbs and spices.

Donau (Map pp602-3; ☎ 521 0701; cnr General Malvar & Adriatico Sts, Malate; meals P200-300) This is the place to satisfy that bratwurst craving with good-value German cuisine. Worth visiting for the four-course dinner special alone (around P260).

For plentiful, cheap snacks and Filipino fast food you can always duck into any shopping mall's food court. Robinson's has dozens of options on the third floor.

DRINKING

Malate's J Nakpil St and Maria Y Orosa St are the epicentre of a thriving, student-led nightlife scene. The life-cycles of the ephemeral bars, clubs and karaoke joints in the area seem to be shorter than a fruit-fly's, but at least there's no shortage of variety. Whatever you're into, be it Whitney Houston, dwarves, Pearl Jam or gay bars, there's a good chance you'll find something that tickles your fancy within walking distance of Remedios Circle. Male travellers will get many insistent offers to visit a different type of bar or nightclub, in the expectation that you'll hook up with girls euphemistically called GROs – 'guest relations officers'.

Bedrock (Map pp602-3; ☎ 522 7279; 1782 Adriatico St; ⏰ 6pm-4am) Bedrock hosts quality loud bands and has friendly staff, never mind that they're dressed like the Flintstones. Good place to meet people, particularly on packed weekends.

Hobbit House (Map pp602-3; ☎ 521 7604; A Mabini St; admission P100-150; ⏰ to 3am) Around before the *Lord of the Rings* revival, this folk-music club is run by a collective of dwarves, and is actually pretty dignified. There aren't many places in the world where you can listen to Filipino bands cover Bob Dylan classics while vertically challenged servers pour you drinks.

Café Penguin (Map pp602-3; ☎ 303 7355; 604 Remedios St; ⏰ 6pm-2am Tue-Sat) This vibrant bar-cum-gallery has been the hangout of artists and bohemians for nearly two decades.

Library (Map pp602-3; ☎ 522 2484; 1179A Adriatico St; ⏰ 7pm-2am Sun-Thu, to 4am Fri & Sat) A tiny stand-up-comedy and karaoke bar that draws a mixed gay/straight crowd. This place can be high on the sleaze factor.

LA Café (Map pp602-3; MH del Pilar St; ⏰ 24hr) An infamous dive that's a throwback to Malate's seedier past. There's live music, billiards, cheap food and drinks, a rowdy expat crowd and lots of GROs. Hushed dark corners abound.

For some *über*-hip bar action, you may need to grab a cab (P60) to the malls of the Makati district. Current popular spots include **Temple Bar** (Map pp600-1; ☎ 757 4813; Greenbelt 2, Ayala Center, Makati; ⏰ 5pm-2.30am Sun-Tue, 5pm-4am Wed-Sat), home to a 3.5m Buddha and popular with the post-college crowd, and **Absinthe** (Map pp600-1; ☎ 757 4967; Greenbelt 3, Ayala Center, Makati; ⏰ 6pm-late Mon-Sat), one of the best places to see and be seen.

ENTERTAINMENT

Check fliers around Malate and weekend entertainment supplements in the newspapers for big club events and concerts. *Colors* and *Manila Nightlife* magazines are full of ideas. Live concerts (often promotions for a beer or cigarette company) are sometimes held on outdoor stages on J Nakpil St (Map pp602-3). On Saturday nights the road is closed to traffic and becomes a catwalk for the young, hip and slightly drunk. For free entertainment, you shouldn't miss the pedestrian walkway along Roxas Blvd (Map pp602-3) as it turns into a veritable 'battle of the bands' after sunset. There's an abundance of streetside restaurants, hip live bands and throngs of ambling Filipinos.

KARAOKE & COVERS

Many Filipinos head for karaoke bars on their nights off and you'll be strongly encouraged to participate if you come along. Karaoke singing is a serious affair, and no matter how bad the singer, everyone gets respect. It's not uncommon for bus passengers to join in a sing-along for a particularly popular power ballad. Live music is also popular; most towns have live music bars with local talent belting out flawless cover versions of classic rock and recent hits.

Manila's 200 movie screens are dominated by imported blockbusters. All the shopping centres have multiscreen, air-con cinemas – there are seven screens in Robinson's Place (Map pp602–3) – and most show at least one Tagalog film. Admission is P80 to P120.

SHOPPING

Shopping for handicrafts in Manila can be a little sad – you could be forgiven for thinking that all tourists buy are cheesy paintings of technicolour sunsets. For something a little more interesting, the market area around Quiapo church (Map pp600–1), particularly under the Quezon St overpass, sells basketware, shell-work, amulets and other handicrafts.

Shopping for discounted brand name goods is a much happier affair. Robinson's Place (Map pp602–3) has several outlet stores, but you're better off heading to the monolithic malls of Makati and Ortigas. The biggest and 'best' are the vast Ayala Center (Map pp600–1) and Glorietta Center (Map pp600–1), in Makati, and the mighty SM Megamall (Map pp600–1) and Shangri-la Plaza (Map pp600–1). Harrison's Plaza, (Map pp602–3), just south of Malate, is a little more downmarket.

San Andres Market (Map pp602–3; ☑ 24hr) is one endless fruit-stall selling exotic delicacies like durians (with that distinctive open-drain aroma).

GETTING THERE & AWAY
Air

Most international airlines have offices at the NAIA terminal, as well as satellite offices in Makati. PAL is based at Centennial Terminal II. Domestic airlines have offices at the domestic terminal and booking agents dotted around town. See Transport (p595) and Philippines Air Fares (Map p596) for details on airlines and domestic flights.

Boat

There are a number of departures from both North and South Harbor in Manila to many of the Philippines' main islands. WG&A, Negros Navigation and Sulpicio Lines are the biggest companies (see p597). Schedules are often advertised in the English-language Manila newspapers, and travel agencies in Malate and Ermita sell ferry tickets.

A taxi from Malate to North Harbor should cost about P70 and to South Harbor P50, but you stand little chance of getting a metered ride back to town. The harbour area is pretty rough, so it's probably better to take a taxi rather than risking the circuitous jeepney trip via Divisoria.

Bus

Confoundingly there's no single long-distance bus station in Manila. The terminals are mainly strung along EDSA, with clusters in Pasay City to the south and Cubao, including the Araneta Center Bus Terminal (Map pp600–1) to the north. There is another big group of terminals at the intersection of Taft Ave and Gil Puyat Ave (Buendia) in the south. Heading into Manila, most buses will just have 'Cubao', 'Pasay' or 'Buendia' on the signboard. It may sound confusing but it's easier than it looks – tell a taxi driver which city you want to visit, and he'll usually take you to the right bus terminal.

There are several air-con buses to Legazpi via Naga City leaving around 7pm daily from in front of the **DHL office** (Map pp602–3; Pedro Gil St, Malate). You can book tickets from the nearby **Food Haus** (Map pp602–3; Pedro Gil St, Malate) booking desk. Fares are about P450 to P610 to Naga City and P780 to Legazpi.

For Puerto Galera on Mindoro, there are daily private buses from the **Citystate Tower Hotel** (Map pp602–3; A Mabini St) connecting with the ferry (P500 for bus and ferry), and from the **Lotus Garden Hotel** (Map pp602–3; A Mabini St) to connect with another boat to Puerto Galera (P410/790 one way/return).

The following is a list of major bus companies and depots:

NORTHBOUND Map pp600–1
Autobus Transport Systems (☎ 735 8098; cnr Tolentino St & España St, Sampaloc) Autobus has buses to Banaue and Vigan.
Dangwa Tranco (☎ 731 2879; 1600 Dimasalang St, Sampaloc) Dangwa has buses every two hours to Baguio.
Fariñas Trans (☎ 743 8580; 1238 AH Lacson St, Sampaloc) Services to Vigan.
Partas (☎ 725 1740; Aurora Blvd, Cubao) To Vigan via San Fernando (La Union).
Philippine Rabbit (☎ 734 9836, EDSA, Balintawak) Frequent buses to Baguio and Vigan.
Victory Liner (☎ 727 4688; EDSA, Cubao) To Baguio.

SOUTHBOUND   Map pp600-1

Crow Transit (☎ 804 0623; cnr EDSA & Taft Ave)
Buses to Nasugbu and Tagaytay.
JAC Liner (☎ 928 6140; Taft Ave, Pasay City) JAC has buses to Batangas.
JAM Transit (☎ 925 1758; Taft Ave, Pasay City) JAM also heads to Batangas.
Philtranco (☎ 851 8075; cnr EDSA & Apelo Cruz St) Philtranco has services to Legazpi and Naga (Bicol), Tacloban (Samar) and all the way to Cagayan de Oro (Mindanao).

GETTING AROUND
Bus

The most useful routes for travellers are the buses that run along EDSA. These pass through Makati and Cubao, where you'll find many of the major shopping centres and bus terminals. There are also buses to Makati from Gil Puyat Ave in Pasay City and from Quezon Ave in Quiapo. Destinations are displayed in the bus window. Fares are P6 to P15 on regular buses, and P9 to P20 on air-con services.

Jeepney

Heading south from Ermita/Malate along MH del Pilar St, jeepneys to Baclaran pass close to many of the southbound bus terminals and also provide easy access to the southern end of EDSA, where you can pick up buses to the northbound bus terminals and Makati.

Going north from Ermita/Malate along A Mabini St, jeepneys head off in various directions from Rizal Park (Map pp602–3): 'Divisoria' jeepneys take the Jones Bridge, passing close to the immigration office (Map p606); 'Santa Cruz' and 'Monumento' jeepneys take the MacArthur Bridge, passing the main post office; and 'Quiapo' and 'Cubao' jeepneys take the Quezon Bridge, passing the Quiapo church and markets (Map pp600–1).

Toyota FX vans, sometimes with a classy 'Mega-Taxi' sign, follow similar routes to jeepneys, with fares around P15 for a few blocks to P30 for longer hauls.

Taxi

If the driver relents and uses the meter, air-con sedan taxis are a fairly economical way to travel to remote places like the airport, the harbours or the numerous bus terminals.

Train

There are three elevated railway lines in Manila. The LRT runs from Baclaran in Pasay City along Taft and Rizal Aves to Monumento in Caloocan City. Of the two Metro Rail Transit (MRT) lines, one follows EDSA from Taft Ave in Pasay City to North Ave in Quezon City, and the second runs east from Quiapo along Ramon Magsaysay and Aurora Blvds to Cubao and beyond.

During rush hour these trains can get mosh-pit crowded and pickpockets can be a problem, but for the rest of the day there's a good chance of getting a seat and enjoying an air-conditioned ride above the snarling street traffic below. Rides start at P12 on the LRT and P9 on the MRT lines. You can also get multiple-trip tickets. Trains run from 5.30am to 10.30pm daily.

AROUND MANILA

There are several worthy excursions that offer opportunities to escape Manila's snarling traffic. Taal volcano is the country's terrestrial femme fatale, as dangerous as it is beautiful, while the spirits of fallen WWII soldiers supposedly haunt the historic Corregidor Island. Weekenders from the capital can overwhelm Manila's nearby destinations so it's best to visit during the quieter weekdays.

CORREGIDOR

Jealously guarding the mouth of Manila Bay, this tiny island is where General MacArthur is said to have uttered 'I shall return' as he fled the invading Japanese. He was eventually true to his word, and day-tripping Filipinos have also been heeding his call: Corregidor's rusty WWII relics are now a big tourist draw. The Malinta tunnels, which once housed an arsenal and a hospital, penetrate the island's rocky heart and there's a small museum displaying leftover uniforms and weapons.

Most visitors book boat and tour packages for around P1400. The main operators are the **Corregidor Visitors Information Centre** (Map pp602-3; ☎ 02-550 1347) and **Sun Cruises** (Map pp600-1; ☎ 02-831 8140; www.corregidorphilippines.com) – you can book directly with them or through most Manila travel agencies.

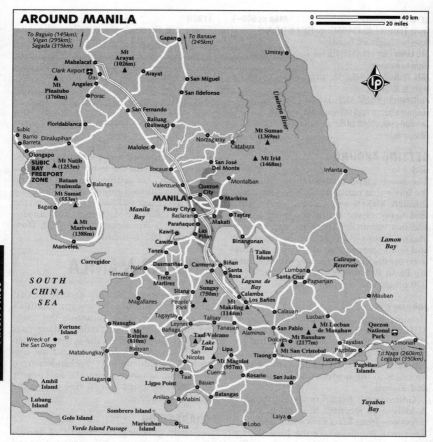

AROUND MANILA

PHILIPPINES

TAAL VOLCANO & TAGAYTAY

Don't be fooled by the small size of this bubbling island mound – Taal's sudden and violent eruptions have claimed more than their fair share of lives. Resting on the rim of an ancient 30km caldera, the noticeably cool town of **Tagaytay** has outstanding views of the area and is an easy day trip from the

DE JA VU

If canoe trips though the jungle-bordered river to Corregidor's Pagsanjan Falls feel eerily familiar, it may be because this was one of the locations for Francis Ford Coppola's *Apocalypse Now*.

capital. This area is an emerging retreat for wealthy Manilenos; that is until it's obliterated by Taal's next eruption. The DOT-operated **Tagaytay Picnic Grove** (admission P30), 8km from Tagaytay on the road to People's Park, easily wins the best-vista accolade. In the summer months, Tagaytay buzzes with festivals, fruit stalls and a never-ending supply of local *buko* (coconut) pie that would make Gilligan's Mary-Anne re-think her recipe.

If you wish to get closer to the action, you can charter *bangcas* to the Taal Lake Island from **Talisay**, on the lake's northeastern shore, for around P800 to P1200 return. As protection against sharp, high grass and volcanic stones, you should wear long trousers and suitable shoes. The walk to and from the main crater, filled by a toxic yellow pool, takes about two hours.

For Tagaytay, take a Crow Transit bus (see p610) from Manila bound for Nasugbu (P70, one hour). To get from Manila to Talisay, first take a JAM Transit bus marked 'Lemery' or 'Batangas' as far as Tanauan (P80, one hour), then a jeepney from the public market to Talisay (P17, 30 minutes). Talisay is also easily reached from Batangas.

From Tagaytay, jeepneys to Leynes (P22) leave from the road to the People's Park, about 8km east of town. Tricycles run along the shore to Talisay.

BATANGAS
☎ 043/pop 248,000
Batangas is primarily an industrial town, and its main attraction is the port for the beach resorts at Puerto Galera on Mindoro. A short jeepney ride west of Batangas there are several dive resorts at Anilao, while the well-preserved historical town of Taal, birthplace of several Filipino heroes and patriots, lies a little further up the coast.

Ferries to Puerto Galera, Sabang Beach and White Beach leave regularly throughout the day from Batangas pier at the end of Rizal Ave. Competition is fierce, and prices can range from P100 to P170 depending on the boat. There are also regular boats to Calapan (P100, two hours) in northern Mindoro and San Jose (P320, 12 hours) in southern Mindoro.

JAM Transit (p610) has frequent buses directly to the Batangas pier (P136, three hours) from Buendia in Pasay City, Manila (Map pp600–1). If you're heading to Lake Taal, pick up a Pasay-bound JAM bus from the terminal in Batangas town.

NORTH LUZON

The north of Luzon is home to the rugged Cordillera mountains, a temperate region that is the tribal soul of the Philippines. Those who can brave the butt-numbing journeys needed to get there will be rewarded with thriving forests, trekking opportunities and delightful villages carrying forth traditions from eons past. Near Banaue, the extraordinary rice terraces of the Ifugao people are considered an engineer-ing feat on par with the pyramids. The colonial centre of Vigan, in the northwestern coastal Ilocos region, boasts a colonial hub that is the country's best-preserved vestige of its Spanish heritage.

BAGUIO
☎ 074 / pop 335,964
Since the 1900s, the pine forests of Baguio (1450m) have revived travellers from Manila with a refreshing change of cool mountain air. Used by the US as a summer capital, this alpine town at the foot of the Cordilleras attracts the rich and indolent for a spot of social and romantic sport in the hot season. Artists and students also flock here and invigorate the town's active nightlife.

As well as being a pleasant, and necessary, stopover on the way to Sagada and the mountain regions beyond, this is a good spot to pick up handicrafts or that perfect trinket for uncle Bob back home. Baguio is famed for its faith healers and 'psychic surgeons', who perform operations removing offending internal organs with their bare (sleight-of) hands. The city centres on the expansive Burnham Park, and the market and Dangwa Tranco bus terminal are north of the centre on Magsaysay St. Baguio seems to be getting too popular for its own good, and downtown traffic is often at gridlock – you're best to walk short distances.

Information
Session Rd hosts several Internet cafés, banks, and telephone offices. The surly tourist office (☎ 446 3434; Lake Dr, Burnham Park; ⏰ 8am-6pm) has maps and brochures, some free and others costing P40.

Sights
The city market, north of Burnham Park, shouldn't be missed – it's an infinite warren of stalls selling everything from soap to fresh-grilled chicken foetus. You can also pick up all manner of mass-produced handicrafts, including basketwork, textiles, woodcarvings and jewellery (cheap silver is a local speciality), as well as strawberries and wild honey.

Tam-awan Village (☎ 446 2949; Long-long Rd, Pinsao) is a cultural centre in the northwest of Baguio, with eight Ifugao homes reconstructed on a ridge – tam-awan means 'vantage point'. The village preserves the arts of the Cordillera, and if you call ahead you can learn

PHILIPPINES

indigenous dance, music and the martial art *arnis*. To get here, take a taxi or a Quezon Hill–Tam-awan or Tam-awan–Long-long jeepney (P5.50) from the city market.

Sleeping

The breezy climate can get a bit chilly in the evenings. Rooms here can fill up quickly so it's a good idea to book ahead.

Red Lion Pub/Inn (cnr Upper General Luna Rd & Wood Rd; s/d P400/600) Fifteen minutes southeast of the market, this notable newcomer boasts everything a weary traveller needs: a restaurant, a pub and a patio with sweeping views. All the remodelled rooms have private bathroom and come with a breakfast fry-up.

Tam-Awan Village (☎ 446 2949; tamawan@skyinet .net; Long-long Rd, Pinsao; s/d P500/900) Seven traditional *nipa* (a kind of palm) huts were transplanted here from the mountains to accommodate travellers. Everything is authentic, except for the electricity and lights. The huts share bathroom facilities.

YMCA (☎ 442 4766; Post Office Loop; dm P300) Next to the post office, the roomy dorms here share a spiffy new bathroom and are central but mercifully quiet.

> **SPLURGE!**
>
> **Burnham Hotel** (☎ 442 2331; 20 Calderon St, Baguio; d P1000-1400) Beautifully adorned with local handicrafts and staffed by a lively, informative family, this graceful choice is well worth a couple of extra pesos.

Eating

Kusima ni Ima Restaurant (Legarda Rd; set meals from P95-175) Exotic specialities like frogs stuffed with chicken and pork, frog *adobo* (salty stewed frog) and *camaru* (deep-fried cricket stew with garlic) are served here at Kusima ni Ima Restaurant. Salty stewed frog – yummy...

Red Lion Pub/Inn (cnr Upper General Luna Rd & Wood Rd; mains P65-210) Red Lion Pub/Inn serves up well-prepared Western classics and San Miguel on tap to a regular crowd of grumbling expats. Renowned for its lip-smacking rack-o-ribs (P210).

In the evenings, Perfecto St (near Burnham Park) turns into a freeway of street-stalls barbecuing pretty much everything under the sun.

Drinking & Entertainment

Rumours (56 Session Rd; ☺ 11am-2am Mon-Fri, 4pm-2am Sat & Sun) An intimate bar that is blissfully pop-music free. This is the place to gather with friends and listen to sultry jazz and other ambient sounds.

For live music try **Alberto's Music Lounge** (Carino St; ☺ 7pm-5am), an arena-sized venue with local talent strutting their stuff, or **Gimbal's** (Legarda Rd; ☺ 6pm-3am), which stages thunderous rock bands for students and yuppies alike.

Getting There & Away
AIR
Asian Spirit (www.asianspirit.com) has flights from Manila to Baguio (P2340, four weekly). Jeepneys to the airport, which lies south of the town, leave from Mabini Rd, between Session Rd and Harrison Rd.

BUS
You can get from Manila to Baguio (around P320, eight hours) with Victory Liner, Philippine Rabbit and Dangwa Tranco (see p610).

Many bus lines depart from the **Dangwa Tranco terminal** (Magsaysay Rd) behind the Central Mall. From here, buses leave every morning to Sagada (P190, seven hours) and Bontoc (P185, 6½ hours).

To Banaue, KMS lines have one morning and two evening buses, all leaving from near Rizal Park (P360, eight to 10 hours).

CORDILLERA MOUNTAINS

At 1500m above sea level and a world away from the Philippines' lazy beaches, the Cordilleras are comprised of a rugged, sloping landscape slashed by rivers and the occasional sorry excuse for a road. Its valleys conceal several tribal groups, many with a savage past, which were mostly ignored by successive colonisers. While here, you can hire local guides, trek to villages in the area and observe traditional customs, such as elaborate marriage and burial rituals.

The spectacular **rice terraces** near Banaue were hewn out of the solid rock by local tribes, including the Ifugao, some 2000 to 3000 years ago. These mountains were tamed using primitive tools and an ingenious irrigation system – legend has it that the Igorot god Kabunyan used the resulting steps to visit his people on earth. Many of the original terraces survive, their snaking walls providing the backdrop for what must be the most remarkable sunset in the Philippines. Reaching 1500m high in places, if laid end to end the terraces would stretch halfway around the world.

Be sure to bring some warm clothing, as the altitude of most towns will make you brrr. Travel in the Cordillera Mountains can be exhilarating but it requires patience, and ideally a pillow to sit on. The twisting roads are rough, dusty affairs that become mudpits bisected by the occasional landslide in the July to September wet season. The Halsema Hwy between Baguio and Bontoc is the highest road in the Philippines, reaching 2255m in places, and offers amazing views of the Cordillera. The trip takes about seven hours and from Bontoc you can make side trips to places like Sagada, or continue to Banaue, the main town for rice terrace adulation. There is also a bus from Baguio to Banaue (see opposite) that skirts the southern edge of the Cordillera, but this takes up to 10 hours.

BONTOC
pop 23,880

This is the region's transport hub and the capital of Mountain Province. You're likely to see tribal people strolling the streets of this wild-west, frontier town. It's possible to trek from Bontoc to the villages of the Igorot people, who build their rice terraces with stone dykes, or to the villages of the war-like Kalinga people to the north. Pine's Kitchenette (opposite the Town Plaza) is a good source of information on the region and can arrange guides for around P500 to P800 per day.

There are two Dangwa Tranco buses and numerous D'Rising Sun buses every morning between Bontoc and Baguio (P185, eight hours). D'Rising Sun buses do this trip all day from beside the town hall. To Banaue, jeepneys and buses leave every two or three hours until 4pm (P100, 2½ hours). Jeepneys to Sagada (P30, one hour) leave until 5pm from near the Eastern Star Hotel.

There is no direct bus between Manila and Bontoc. The best way to get here is to catch a Banaue-bound bus and then continue by jeepney.

SAGADA
pop 11,090

Sagada (1477m) is a delightfully laid-back village where you can fall asleep to the sound

> **DID YOU KNOW?**
>
> The Kalinga people, indigenous to the areas north of Bontoc, were head-hunters until they signed a peace pact with the government in the 1950s. Descendants of the signees must, to this day, perform rituals in order to refrain from their anti-social activities and keep the accord.

of chickens and cicadas rather than cars and karaoke. It's home to hearty Igorot mountain folk and is set amid jagged rock formations that slice through Sagada's rich fir forests. Adventurers will find loads to explore in the area, including the eerie **burial caves** and **hanging coffins**, an underground river system, waterfalls and the imposing **Mt Polis**. Vivid photographs of tribal life from the 1930s to 1950s, taken by local photographer **Eduardo Masferré**, hang in many establishments. The town is renowned for its weaving.

Guides can be arranged at the tourist information centre in the town hall, just below the bus depot. One guide (with a lamp) will cost around P400 to the caves or P1200 for an all-day trip up Mt Polis. Visitors must pay a P10 environmental protection fee.

Every Saturday there is a colourful tribal market on the main street.

Sleeping

There are several basic guesthouses in town, and hot water for showers can be provided if you order it the evening before.

Green House (s/d P170/300) A few pleasant, small, traditional rooms are available in this private home, run by the genial 'aunty'. It's on the right, downhill from the town hall.

Olahbinan Resthouse (s/d/tr P200/350/500) It's wood from floor to ceiling inside this immaculately kept, rambling house, located behind the Sagada Igorot Inn. The rooms are basic but spotless.

St Joseph's Resthouse (dm P150, d P300-1500) A slightly creepy old convent set in a garden overlooking the town. There are some cosy cottages; the cheaper rooms are shoeboxes.

Eating

There's a surprisingly big range of quality eating options in Sagada.

Yoghurt House (mains P65-120) A local gallery and craft museum as much as a restaurant,

Yoghurt has a lip-smacking menu offering spicy Indian curries, filling pastas and its trademark yogurt muesli breakfasts (P85).

Log Cabin (mains P80-150; ⊙ dinner) The fireplace dining here hits the spot on those chilly evenings. On Saturdays you can pull out that old tuxedo – there's a decadent buffet prepared by the resident French chef (P250).

Shamrock (mains P65-125; ⊙ breakfast & dinner) Next to the town hall, this cheerful little bar and restaurant turns into a boisterous after-dinner hideout.

Getting There & Away

Buses from Bontoc to Sagada depart until 5pm (see p615). You can also catch a bus here from Baguio (p614).

Dangwa Tranco and Lizardo buses leave Sagado for Baguio (P190, seven hours) each morning until about 10am. Jeepneys to Bontoc (P30, one hour) leave between 6am and noon.

BANAUE

☎ 074 / pop 24,856

Banaue (1200m) is the jump-off point for surrounding rice terraces, towering steps carved out of the hillsides over 2000 years ago by the Ifugao people. Banaue itself isn't much more than a landslide of greyish buildings clinging to the mountainside, but the views of the Banaue valley and surrounding mountains are inspiring. The little **market** in the lower part of town is worth a gander and sells some interesting handicrafts from the villages that pepper the area. Two kilometres north you will find the main **lookout point**, where you can ogle terraces to your heart's content as Ifugao villagers in traditional garb pose for photographs, for a fee. Some of the most striking examples of terrace engineering, however, are to be found around the village of Batad (right), several hours hike from Banaue.

Information

The tourist office is opposite the plaza and can help organise guides for trekking and transport to terraces and nearby villages. Hotels also sell good little maps of Banaue's surroundings for P10. You can change money at the Banaue Hotel or the moneychanger in the main market area.

Sleeping

Banaue View Inn (☎ 386 4078; dm/d P150/700) This inn boasts a birds-eye view of the Cordillera Mountains and has shipshape rooms. Karen, the owners' daughter, is a great source of information.

Sanafe Lodge & Restaurant (☎ 386 4085; dm/s/d P150/600/750) Wood panelling is the theme here and the small rooms are homey. The barstools precariously perched over the Banaue valley are the best place in town to throw back a few.

Spring Village Inn (☎ 386 4037; s/tr/d P500/600/1300) The cheery rooms here have wooden floors and some have verandas. It's situated just south of town.

Getting There & Away

You can catch a bus to Banaue from Baguio (p614) or Bontoc (p615).

From Banaue you can get back to Baguio either via Bayombong or on the much more scenic route via Bontoc (p615), where you'll have to change buses. There is one 7am bus and two 5pm buses to Baguio via Bayombong with KMS and Ohayami lines (P295 to P360, eight to 10 hours). Buses to Bontoc depart all day from the market (P100, 2½ hours).

Autobus Transport Systems has a bus to Manila at 5.30pm (P342, eight hours), which leaves Manila at 10pm in the reverse direction. If you miss the direct bus, take a jeepney to Solano (P73), just before the Banaue turn-off, and pick up one of the several buses plying the Manila–Tuguegarao route.

BATAD

pop 1100

To really see the Ifugao **rice terraces** in all their glory, you'll need to trek up to Batad (900m) – nestled halfway up an imposing amphitheatre of rice fields. Most of the inhabitants still practise traditional tribal customs in what must be one of the most serene, picture-perfect villages to grace the earth. Batad is a two-hour, often steep, walk after a 12km jeepney or tricycle ride from Banaue.

A 45-minute walk beyond the village itself, over a steep saddle, is the gorgeous 25m-high **Tappiya Waterfall** and swimming hole.

Sleeping

Accommodation in Batad is rustic; only a few places have electricity or running water. Rather than being a disadvantage, this, and the distinct absence of any kind of engine, is a big part of the town's appeal. There's a mini-village of hotels on the ridge above Batad. They can provide blankets to take the edge off the chilly nights.

Hillside Inn, Rita's Mount View Inn, and Simon's Inn all have restaurants and rooms for P100. They're all simple, clean and homely, but Rita's wins our hearts with its all-round charm.

Getting There & Away

You can get a jeepney (P60) or tricycle (P250 to P300) 12km of the way to Batad from Banaue, but you still have to walk the rest of the way. If you're taking a tricycle to Batad for a day trip, it's a good idea to get the driver to wait for you or you may be stranded. Most drivers will ask for P500, but don't pay the full fare until you return. Jeepneys leaves Banaue when full, between 7am and 9am.

VIGAN

☎ 077 / pop 46,450

Originally a thriving pre-colonial trading post, Vigan became an important centre of culture and politics once the Spanish took the reins. Spared much of the physical destruction wreaked by WWII, Vigan today is the best-preserved planned Spanish town in Asia. Walking among the narrow, cobbled streets of the historical mestizo district with only the clip-clop of horse-drawn *kalesa* (two-wheeled carts) for company will make you want to re-live a past you never actually lived. After being razed several times by earthquakes, the **Cathedral of St Paul** (Plaza Salcedo) was rebuilt in 1641, bigger and better, in a style known as 'earthquake baroque'. It was a successful technique, and the church is now one of the oldest and biggest in the Philippines.

If possible, try to make it here during the Town Fiesta in the third week of January.

Sleeping

It's worth paying a little extra to stay in one of Vigan's charismatic colonial homes. Many of the pricier rooms include breakfast.

Villa Angela (☎ 722 2914; 26 Quirino Blvd; d P850-1600; 🏠) This magnificent place has a living room looking much as it would have in the 18th century. The quarters have high ceilings and old-fashioned beds.

> **FUSION ARCHITECTURE**
>
> Many of the surviving colonial houses in Vigan were erected by wealthy Chinese merchants and display a unique mix of Filipino, Spanish and Chinese influences.

Grandpa's Inn (☎ 722 2118; 1 Bonifacio St; d P500-1200; 🏠) Two rooms here have beds in *kalesa* carriages. It has lots of character, a clutter of antiques and a modern café open until midnight.

Vigan Hotel (☎ 722 1906; Burgos St; d P495-1395; 🏠) There's some nice rooms in a snug older building here.

Eating

Café Leona (Mena Crisologo St; dishes P120-280) Just off Plaza Burgos, Café Leona serves terrific Ilocano and Japanese specials. It's popular and stays open late.

Evening **street stalls** (Plaza Burgos) serve cheap snacks such as *empenadas* (deep-fried tortillas with shrimp, cabbage and egg) and *okoy* (shrimp omelettes).

Getting There & Away

The trip from Manila takes about eight hours with Philippine Rabbit (p610; around P350), which also has hourly buses to Baguio (P220, five to six hours). Buses from San Fernando (La Union) to Laoag also stop in Vigan. From Vigan to San Fernando it's P160 (three hours). There's no public transport over the rugged Cordillera to Bontoc or Sagada.

SOUTH LUZON

Not many travellers make it to Bicol (as this region is known) but the countless bays, rampant greenery and plentiful peaks provide lots of opportunities to get intimate with nature. Mt Mayon, near the town of Legazpi, is a faultless volcano cone encircled by flourishing pineapple plantations. Remote beaches await the arrival of the determined backpacker in the Caramoan peninsula. The sleepy village of Donsol, meanwhile, acts as a regular playground for colossal whale sharks. You'll want to pay extra attention to the news before you go, as the area is prone to natural disasters

PHILIPPINES

of biblical proportions – floods, typhoons and showers of ash and molten rock are not uncommon. Sporadic NPA guerrilla activity can also be an issue.

The Pan-Philippine or Maharlika Hwy runs right through Bicol down to Matnog on the southern tip, from where ferries cross to Samar. Long-haul buses between Manila and Leyte or Mindanao stop at all major towns.

NAGA

☎ 062 / pop 159,850

Naga is as young and vibrant as its student population, and the city's claim to fame is September's **Peñafrancia Festival**, when it throws a spirited procession in honour of the region's patroness, the Virgin of Peñafrancia. People flock to Naga around this time and hotels can fill to bursting. The rest of the year, life in this clean little city centres on a pleasant double plaza that bursts into life after sundown. Strolling Filipinos turn the plaza into the town's communal loungeroom and street-food vendors set up shop to feed the hungry masses. Check out the huge central market, and be sure to sample some pili nuts (a local favourite) served salted, raw or candied.

The **Kadlagan Outdoor Shop** (☎ 472 3305; kadlagan@yahoo.com; 16 Dimasalang St) hires out tents and other camping gear. Under the guidance of Jojo Villareal, this place is a great source of information on treks and other outdoorsy stuff in the area. Kadlagan also arranges camping trips for groups of up to 20 people.

Sleeping

Naga seems to have cornered the market on small, windowless rooms.

Golden Leaf Hotel (☎ 471 6507; Misericordia St; s P250-450, d P300-600; 🔊) Positively gleaming new rooms are a welcome change to Naga's usual musty offerings. Cross the Panganiban Dr bridge then take the second left.

Hotel Mirabella (☎ 811 5656; Panganiban Dr, s/d P545/645; 🔊) Also just over the Panganiban bridge, Mirabella has a small selection of simple, clean rooms – all with air-con.

Aristocrat Hotel (☎ 473 8832; Elias Angeles St; s P240-595, d P295-731; 🔊) A cavernous, convoluted place that feels like an aged carnival fun-house. The rooms vary greatly from small and dank to large and comfy.

Eating

If you catch the Magsaysay jeepney from Peñafrancia Ave, after five minutes you will come to a huddle of swish new restaurants.

Coco Leaf (Magsaysay Ave; mains P65-120) This place is popular with resident Peace Corps volunteers and serves well-prepared local dishes.

Chili Pepper's (Magsaysay Ave; mains P75-160) Unfortunately not as spicy as the name suggests, but the famous barbecue pork rib combo (P140) is worth digging into.

New China Restaurant (General Luna St; mains P120) Back in town, this restaurant serves excellent Chinese and is usually packed at breakfast time.

Great local food is also available from the busy food stalls around Plaza Rizal.

Getting There & Away

A flight from Manila to Naga costs P2230. Most long-haul buses from Manila (around P450, eight hours) to destinations further south stop in Naga; see p610. Local buses make frequent runs to Legazpi (P90, two hours).

CARAMOAN PENINSULA

A circuitous, four-hour journey from Naga towards the Pacific Ocean brings you to the picturesque Caramoan Peninsula. About 4km from Caramoan town is **Gota Beach**, a stretch of sugary, fine sand that can look the Philippines' best beaches square in the eye. Several beach-lined limestone islets, known as the Malarad Islands, doze just offshore. Rent a *sibid-sibid* (small fishing boat) and paddle from island to island.

You can ask locals about hiring a fishing boat in Caramoan town. There are small eateries where you can buy meals, and two hotels on the peninsula. Caramoan town's small **Rex Inn** (d P300) has basic rooms with fan while **La Casa Roa** (☎ 054-811 5789; s P700, d P900-1200; 🔊) is the newer, nicer and pricier of the two. The peninsula is best enjoyed outdoors and you're better off camping on Gota Beach; just be sure to bring camping gear from Naga.

To strike out to the peninsula on your own, firstly take a bus or jeepney from the central terminal in Naga to Sabang (P50, two hours). From Sabang, there are morning boats to Guijalo (P100, two hours) – this is the best bit of the trip. You can hire your own boat for P2000. From Guijalo, it's a 10-minute jeepney or tricycle ride to Caramoan town.

There are a couple of direct morning jeepney services between Naga and Caramoan.

LEGAZPI

☎ 052 / pop 184,130

Charm is in short supply in Legazpi, but with the towering cone of Mt Mayon hogging the horizon no-one seems to really notice. The useful provincial **tourist office** (☎ 482 0712; Rizal St) is by Albay Astrodome in the Regional Centre. The **Ibálong Festival** in October is quite lively, while the **Magayong Festival** in May lasts the whole month.

Sleeping

Legazpi Tourist Inn (☎ 480 6147; V&O Bldg, 3rd fl; s P400-510, d P510-550; ✷) These are the best moderately priced digs in town. This modern place is clean, has a small café and lots of mirrors, and, most importantly, a waterfall in the lounge.

Tropical Tours Apartelle (☎ 482 0463; benjy santiago@hotmail.com; Pag-asa, Rawis; d P850; ✷) This is the place for a spot of comfort once you've reached Legazpi. There's apartment-style rooms, hot showers, TV, a garden restaurant and tours to Mayon and Donsol. It's signposted down a side street on the western edge of Rawis, about 15 minutes from the town centre.

Catalina's Lodging House (☎ 480 7841; 96 Peñaranda St; s P180-400, d P210-550; ✷) If you can find it behind the After Six eatery, this place has rooms ranging from very cheap and basic to less cheap and basic.

Eating

Chinese cuisine is all the rage in Legazpi, but local specialities such as the fiery *kilawan* (marinated mackerel) are worth perusing.

Waway Restaurant (Peñaranda St; meals P120) On the northern side of town, this place is known for local dishes and has an excellent buffet.

Four Seasons (Magallanes St; dishes P130-170) This gleaming upstairs restaurant has good Chinese dishes.

Getting There & Away

Philippine Airlines (PAL; www.philippineair.com) flies here daily from Manila for P2940.

The main bus terminal is at the Satellite Market, halfway between Albay and the port district. Several companies run daily buses to and from Manila (from P300/600 for ordinary/air-con, 11 hours). There are daily ordinary buses to and from Naga (P90, 2½ hours) and Donsol (P55, two hours). You can also catch jeepneys to Donsol (P50) from the Shell station in nearby Daraga.

MT MAYON

Bicolanos hit the nail on the head when they named this monolith – *magayon* is the local word for 'beautiful'. The impossibly perfect slopes of the volcano's cone rise to 2451m above sea level and tower over the flat plains and surrounding plantations. The spirit of the mountain is an old king whose beloved niece ran away with a young buck – the grumpy old man's pride still erupts every 10 years or so. Lately his temper is getting worse and the eruptions are becoming more frequent. The last lava flows were recorded in 2004.

Though subject to weather, and obviously to flows of rather unpleasant molten lava, it's possible to climb the mountain in under three days. You don't need to be an experienced mountain climber, but you should be in good shape. Guides can be arranged through the **DOT** (☎ 482 0712) and **Bicol Adventure and Tours** (☎ 480 2266; bicoladve nture@digitelone.com; Ste 20, V&O Bldg) in Legazpi. Both charge around US$100 for two days and one night (up to two people) with a guide and food. Either place should register you with the relevant authorities.

DONSOL

Large numbers of whale sharks, or *butanding*, have taken a liking to the fishing village of Donsol, about 50km south of Legazpi. Every year this sleepy, almost catatonic,

---

COCKSURE GAMBLERS

Heavy male drinking and bonding occur over gambling – on anything from *sabong* (cockfights) to horse racing. But *sabong* are what Filipino men get most excited about. All over the country, every Sunday and public holiday, irritable and expensive fighting birds are let loose on one another. The cockpits are full to bursting and the audience is high with excitement – as much as P100,000 may be wagered on a big fight. All this plus cheap booze, lots of guns, pimps, players and prostitutes make for an interesting life for police.

community plays host to travellers hoping to swim with the silver-speckled marine leviathans, some of which grow up to 18m in length. Though never guaranteed, spottings of these graceful beasts are common between January and May. The Worldwide Fund for Nature (WWF) helps run the well-organised tours and provides alternate employment for local fishermen. The **Butanding Festival** happens around April every year and has boat races, traditional dances and a life-size replica of the festival's namesake (on wheels).

To go on a spotting safari, pop into the new **visitors centre** (☎ 0927 233 0364; Dancalan Rd; ☼ 7.30am-5pm), 4km from town (P15 by tricycle). Staff will arrange a boat, spotter and a Butanding Interaction Officer (BIO) for you. Total cost is P2500 per day (for up to seven people) plus a P300 registration fee for the season. These fees let the local government to thwart illegal fishing of these glorious sharks. You reserve a seat by leaving a message for Salvador Adrao at the visitors centre.

Sleeping

Santiago Lodging House (d P300) This makeshift place opposite the town hall is basically a homestay with the Santiago family – you also can use the kitchen. The friendly owner used to be a local teacher.

Visitor's Inn (Rizal St; per person P250; ☼) These tidy rooms take the cake as the cheapest air-con accommodation in the Philippines. There's also a communal living room. To get here, walk east past the market and turn right down Rizal St.

Amor Farm Beach Resort (Dancalan Rd; d P400-600; ☼) Has well-kept cottages spread around an immaculate palmtree garden, facing a black-sand beach in Dancalan Bay, 3km from Donsol. A tricycle from Donsol costs P15.

Getting There & Away

Jeepneys frequent the Donsol–Legazpi road (P50, two hours) from 6am to 3pm, or there are ordinary buses from Legazpi (P55, two hours).

MINDORO

Untamed, a near-impenetrable interior and remote bays may make for a stark contrast to the bar-hopping scene of Puerto Galera, but that's Mindoro in a nutshell. Inland

mountains shelter both loin-clothed Mangyan tribes and NPA revolutionaries, while the north's secluded resorts harbour holidaying diving aficionados.

The island's comely beaches around Puerto Galera and first-rate scuba-diving opportunities in the surrounding Unesco-protected marine reserve are the big tourist draw. Sabang is the area's party and dive headquarters, while at White Beach and Aninuan Beach, on a more attractive part of the coastline, visitors concentrate on more languorous activities. Bring enough cash – the nearest ATM to the beaches is in Calapan, which is over two hours' journey away. For something off this well-beaten path, make a beeline for the west coast's **Apo Reef**, where the world-class underwater action involves plenty of sharks and stingrays.

Getting There & Away

Asian Spirit (www.asianspirit.com) flies to San Jose daily (P1900), but it's easier and quicker to get to Puerto Galera by travelling by boat and by bus.

The usual bus and ferry route to Mindoro is from Batangas in Luzon to Puerto Galera. JAM Transit (p610) has super-frequent buses directly to Batangas pier from Pasay City in Manila (P136, three hours) – make sure the bus is going to the pier rather than the downtown terminal.

Ferries and outriggers operate between Batangas and Puerto Galera or Sabang until about 4pm. The crossing takes one to two hours, and costs between P100 for outriggers and P170 for swanky air-con fast catamarans.

If you're heading south, you can continue travelling from Roxas on Mindoro's southeast coast to Caticlan on Panay (for Boracay) either directly or via Tablas Island. These boats are strictly fair-weather options.

PUERTO GALERA

☎ 043 / pop 26,076

Puerto Galera (*pwair*-toe gal-*air*-ah) is the main port for the surrounding resorts and is where most of the fastcraft from Batangas dock, but most people don't stay overnight. The pier area is separated from the town by a hill, where the bumpy road to Sabang Beach starts. The restaurants by the pier are good for a meal if you're waiting for a ferry.

PUERTO GALERA BEACHES

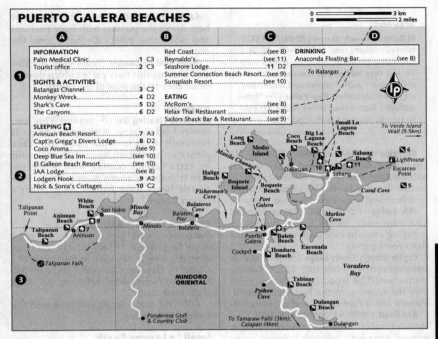

INFORMATION
Palm Medical Clinic...............................**1** C3
Tourist office..**2** C3

SIGHTS & ACTIVITIES
Batangas Channel.................................**3** C2
Monkey Wreck.....................................**4** D2
Shark's Cave...**5** D2
The Canyons...**6** D2

SLEEPING
Aninuan Beach Resort...........................**7** A3
Capt'n Gregg's Divers Lodge...............**8** D2
Coco Aroma.......................................(see 9)
Deep Blue Sea Inn............................(see 10)
El Galleon Beach Resort...................(see 10)
JAA Lodge...(see 8)
Lodgers Nook.......................................**9** A2
Nick & Sonia's Cottages........................**10** C2

Red Coast...(see 8)
Reynaldo's...(see 11)
Seashore Lodge...................................**11** D2
Summer Connection Beach Resort....(see 9)
Sunsplash Resort................................(see 10)

EATING
McRom's...(see 8)
Relax Thai Restaurant ....(see 9)
Sailors Shack Bar & Restaurant.........(see 9)

DRINKING
Anaconda Floating Bar.......................(see 8)

Information
Palm Medical Clinic (☎ 442 0250) This is just out of
Puerto Galera proper, on the road to Sabang.
Tourist office (☎ 287 3051; Muelle pier) This office can
help organise vehicle hire (from P1000/2000 per day for a
tricycle/jeepney) or a local guide (around P800 per day).
There's a board advertising pumpboat fares outside.

Getting There & Away
There are fastcraft and outrigger boats to/
from Batangas all day (P100 to P170), see
also opposite. You can also charter a *bangca*
to Sabang (P200) or White Beach (P500).

Jeepneys leave for Sabang Beach (P15)
from just above the wharf (when full). Tricycles charge a steep P150 for a special ride.

Heading west, there are regular jeepneys to
White Beach (P15) and Talipanan (P20) from
the wharf. You can catch one of the frequent
jeepneys to Calapan (P65, two hours) from
the petrol station 500m south of town.

AROUND PUERTO GALERA
The name Puerto Galera typically refers to
the strip of beaches formed by the scruffy
Sabang Beach and the prettier shores of Small

and Big La Laguna. Accommodation can
also be found on the more secluded sands of
White Beach, Aninuan Beach and Talipanan
Beach, all further west along the coast.

Sabang Beach
☎ 043
It is impossible to walk on Sabang's shrinking
beach without tripping over a dive school,
guesthouse or restaurant. Drinking and underwater pursuits are the activities of choice
with plenty of establishments offering variations on this theme. A dive with all equipment costs about US$20 to US$28 while an
open-water course will set you back US$250
to US$300. Snorkel and fin hire is P200 a day.
Rates drop significantly in the low season.

SLEEPING
Many sleeping options come with kitchens – perfect for satisfying those midnight
munchies.

   Seashore Lodge (☎ 287 3021; d P700-1200; ❄)
This is a small compound with balconied
huts surrounded by brimming flora. The
better huts have fridges, bathtubs and TV.

> **SPLURGE!**
>
> **El Galleon Beach Resort** (☎ 0917 814 5170;
> tommy@asiadivers.com; d US$31-41; ✗ ⚏)
> First-class, poolside, hut-style rooms with
> TV and ritzy bathrooms feature at this re-
> sort. There's also a stylish restaurant and
> a groovy bar called **The Point** (⊗ 10am–
> midnight), with ocean views and a CD col-
> lection as colourful as the cocktails.

Reynaldo's (☎ 0917 489 5609; d P500-800; ✗)
On the hill above Tina's and away from the
hubbub, Reynaldo's rooms are in the midst of
jovial Filipino families. The rooms are edged
by foliage and some have great sea views.

JAA Lodge (☎ 0919 640 2040; d P600-800)
The enormous rooms here have comfy
lounging areas to kick back in after a hard
day's coral gazing.

Capt'n Gregg's Divers Lodge (☎ 0917 540 4570;
captngreggs@gmx.net; d P600-1200; ✗) A Sabang
institution. The wood-lined rooms, right
over the water, earn the best-view plaudit.
There's also a dive centre and a restaurant.

Red Coast (☎ 0919 810 4009; d P600-1300) Two
rows of solid, brightly painted cottages
around a garden – all with balcony, bathroom and fan. The pricier cottages have a
kitchen and TV.

EATING
McRom's (Sabang Beach) Serves up sizzling local
and Western dishes. It's popular with expats in the know.

> **BEST PUERTO GALERA DIVE SITES**
>
> ■ The Canyons – teeming with all types of
>   coral and fish life
>
> ■ Batangas Channel – drift dive with regu-
>   lar stingray and reef-shark sightings
>
> ■ Shark's Cave – spy on sleeping white-
>   tip and leopard sharks; hammerheads
>   and whale sharks sometimes make an
>   appearance
>
> ■ Verde Island Wall – one of the best wall
>   dives in the country
>
> ■ Monkey Wreck – a sunk cargo boat
>   now home to batfish and snapper (for
>   advanced divers)

Capt'n Gregg's (Sabang Beach) The restaurant
here draws the punters with huge portions
and tables that practically hover over the
ocean.

Relax Thai Restaurant (Sabang Beach) It's also
worth trying this tasty place hidden down a
small alley to the west of the centre.

DRINKING
Anaconda Floating Bar (⊗ 9am-late) This bar,
moored off Sabang, is the place to go if
you really want to drink like a fish. Take
plenty of protection against the sun and
be extra careful coming back – the return trip always seems more wobbly. Free
shuttle boats leave from Capt'n Gregg's
Divers Lodge.

GETTING THERE & AROUND
Bangcas come and go from Sabang's central
shore to Batangas (P140) all day. You can
charter a *bangca* for trips to Puerto Galera
(P200) or elsewhere. Jeepneys and tricycles
to Puerto Galera head off from the steep
main road inland.

Off-road motorcycles can be rented for
around P700 a day.

Small La Laguna Beach
☎ 043
Around the headland and a stone's throw
from Sabang, the nicer and more laid-back
Small La Laguna Beach has a clean strip
of sand.

Great, roomy huts surround an immaculate garden at **Sunsplash Resort** (☎ 0917 459
8639; d P700-1200; ✗), where you can really
soak up the hush.

Deep Blue Sea Inn (☎ 0917 450 4969; dbs@batangas
.i-next.net; d P1000-1500; ✗) has funky, rattan-
lined rooms stacked all the way up the steep
hill. There's a relaxed seaside restaurant.

A rambunctious Filipino family
runs the spartan **Nick & Sonia's Cottages**
(☎ 0917 373 8156; d P700-1000; ✗), located behind
Action Divers.

White Beach
☎ 043
A short hop by *bangca* or jeepney west of
Puerto Galera, White Beach offers a reprieve from the go-go bars and heartfelt
flipper-talk of Sabang. Its wide, sandy thoroughfare is a popular spot to catch some
UV rays, whack a volleyball and dodge the

small legion of determined hawkers plying the waterfront. A few dive shops sprinkle the area, and eating and accommodation options are plentiful.

SLEEPING & EATING

Rates here vary greatly, depending on the time of year and mood of the owners.

Summer Connection Beach Resort (☎ 0920 230 5098; s P500-800, d P600-1000; 🔀) A seemingly random collection of very tidy little huts strewn around the far end of the beach.

Coco Aroma (☎ 0919 472 8882; s/d/tr P800/ 1000/1500) Neat, all-wood cottages on a peaceful section of sand. The owner has decked out some of the rooms with Japanese panache.

Lodgers Nook (☎ 0915 540 0315; d P500-1000; 🔀) This place has rudimentary cabanas facing the water as well as an open-air billiard hall and volleyball courts.

All the resorts have their own restaurants, and you can also try the pleasant Sailors Shack Bar & Restaurant.

Aninuan Beach

☎ 043

Further west from White Beach is the even more appealing Aninuan Beach. **Aninuan Beach Resort** (☎ 0920 226 8808; aninuanbeachresort@yahoo .com; d P900-1800) has pretty rooms, each with a small balcony right on the pristine cove. Tuck into decent seafood dishes (P150 to P300) at sand-side tables. There is little to do here but worship the sun.

ROXAS

☎ 043 / pop 38,889

Roxas (*raw*-has) is a dusty little spot with ferry connections to Caticlan (the jumping-off point from Boracay). Active types can take a day trip and walk to the villages of the Mangyan tribes from Mansalay, further south from Roxas.

The only respectable option in town is **Tropical Lodge** (☎ 0921 502 1477; d P350), conveniently located near the ferry terminal in Dangay, 3km south of Roxas. Breezy, new rooms have an interesting concrete-and-rattan motif.

Buses to Calapan (P130, three to four hours) leave from Morente St near the plaza. L-300 vans also cover the route (P150, three hours). In the reverse direction, buses and vans to Calapan depart from in front of the main market in Roxas. There are frequent jeepneys from Calapan to Puerto Galera.

Ferries to Caticlan (P230, four daily, five hours) leave from Dangay, a P5 ride from town. There are also three boats a week to Odiongan on Tablas (around P140, five hours).

CEBU

Surrounded on all sides by the Philippine isles and dotted with palm-fringed fishing villages, Cebu is the island heart of the Visayas. Cebuanos are proud of their heritage – it is here that Magellan sowed the seed of Christianity and was pruned for his efforts at the hands of the mighty chief Lapu-Lapu. The island's booming metropolis, Cebu City, is a transport hub to pretty much anywhere you may wish to go. Moalboal's Pescador Island placed Philippine diving on the world map, while the Malapascua marine scene boasts encounters of the thresher-shark kind. On northern Bantayan's flawless beach, meanwhile, it seems that strenuous activity of any kind is a foreign concept.

Getting There & Away

AIR

There are international flights into Cebu's Mactan International Airport from half a dozen points in Asia with Cathay Pacific, SilkAir and Malaysian Airlines.

A huge domestic network connects Cebu City with major Philippine centres (see p596). All the major Philippine airlines service these routes, though schedules tend to be fractious. The terminal fee is P100.

BOAT

Most of the long-haul ferries from Manila to ports in the southern islands stop in Cebu City, including WG&A SuperFerry and Sulpicio Lines. Fastcraft such as SuperCat and Oceanjet have speedy connections to Bohol, Panay, Negros, Mindanao and Leyte. Plenty of slow ferries also follow in their wake. Tourist offices, and even travel agencies, can't keep up with the changing schedules; the best source of info is the weekly schedule in the *Sun Star* newspaper.

Shipping companies in Cebu City:
Cebu Ferries (☎ 032-232 1181; www.cebuferries.com; Pier 4, North Reclamation Area) To Bohol, Leyte & Mindanao.

PHILIPPINES

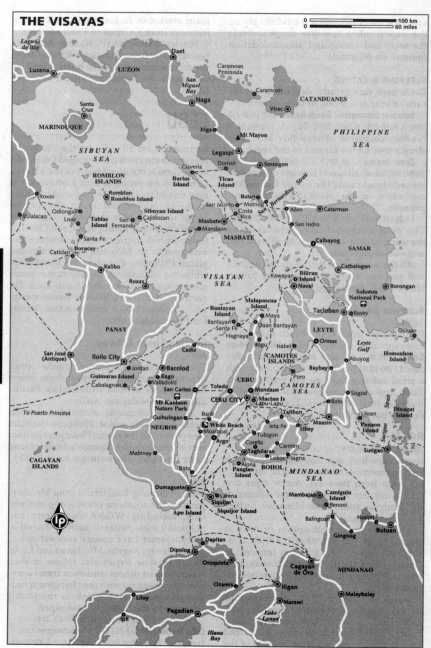

THE VISAYAS

0 — 100 km
0 — 60 miles

Cokaliong Shipping Lines (☎ 032-232 7211-18; D Serging Osmeña Ave, North Reclamation Area) To Bohol, Panay and Mindanao. Boats depart Pier 1.

George & Peter Lines (☎ 032-254 5404; GP Bldg, cnr Arellano Blvd & V Gullas St) To Panay and Mindanao. Boats depart Pier 2.

Lite Shipping Corporation (☎ 032-253 7776; 14 GL Lavilles St) To Bohol and Leyte. Boats depart Pier 1.

Palacio Shipping (☎ 032-255 4538; cnr Mabini St & Zulueta St) To Bohol, Siquijor and Negros. Boats depart Pier 1.

Oceanjet (Map p626; ☎ 032-255 7560; oceanjet@ skyinet.net; Pier 1, North Reclamation Area) To Bohol, Leyte and Camiguin.

Sulpicio Lines (☎ 032-232 5361; www.sulpiciolines .com; Sulpicio Go St, Reclamation Area) To Manila, Leyte and Mindanao. Boats depart Pier 4.

SuperCat (☎ 032-234 9630-34; www.supercat.com.ph; Pier 4, North Reclamation Area) To Bohol, Negros, Siquijor, Leyte and Mindanao.

Super Shuttle Ferry (☎ 032-232 3150; 38 Gorordo Ave) To Ormoc and Camiguin. Boats depart Pier 1.

Trans-Asia Shipping Lines (Map p626; ☎ 032-254 6491; www.transasiashipping.com; cnr MJ Cuenco Ave & Quezon Blvd) To Bohol, Panay, Leyte and Mindanao. Boats depart Pier 5.

WG&A SuperFerry (☎ 032-233 7000; www.superferry .com.ph; Pier 4, North Reclamation Area) To Manila and Mindanao.

CEBU CITY
☎ 032 / pop 805,937

Compared to Manila's full-throttle exuberance, Cebu seems happy running along in second gear. One of the first stops on Spain's conquest agenda, Cebu lays claim to everything old – including the oldest street (Colon St), the oldest university and the oldest fort. The superb transport links to the rest of the Philippines, however, are the city's biggest attraction.

Cebu's downtown district (Map p626) is its smoggy mercantile nucleus where you will find many sights, while uptown (Map p627) is a little greener and has the better accommodation options.

Information
There are plenty of Internet cafés around town, particularly near the student haunts of uptown.

Bureau of Immigration (☎ 345 6442; cnr Burgos St & Mandaue Ave) Behind the Mandaue Fire Station, opposite the Mandaue Sports Complex, 6.5km northeast of town. You can extend a 21-day visa to 59 days here for P2020 in about an hour; just bring your passport.

Cebu Doctors Hospital (Map p627; ☎ 253 7511; Pres Osmeña Blvd) Near the Capitol Building.

Central post office (Map p626; Quezon Blvd) Opposite Fort San Pedro.

Department of Tourism Downtown (Map p626; ☎ 254 2811; LDM Bldg, Legazpi St); Mactan Airport (☎ 340 8229) The downtown office is near the Fort. There are also counters at the international and domestic arrivals terminals at the airport.

HSBC Bank (Ayala Mall) There are several branches of the major Philippine banks in Cebu City, including this one with an ATM.

National Bookstore (Map p627; General Maxilom Ave) A good smattering of books, magazines and maps.

Visayas Community Hospital (☎ 253 3025; Osmeña Blvd)

Sights
Fort San Pedro (Map p626; Legazpi Extn; admission P20; ☻ 8am-noon & 1-5pm Tue-Sun) was built in 1565 as a defence against marauding pirates. This gently crumbling ruin served as the nucleus of Spanish settlement and houses artefacts from old Spanish galleons. The golden-cloaked **Santo Niño statuette** is the *pièce de résistance* at **Basilica Minore del Santo Niño** (Map p626; Pres Osmeña Blvd), built in 1740. Magellan apparently gave this image of the child Jesus to Queen Juana of Cebu on her baptism in 1521. It's the oldest religious relic in the country, and you can pick up a copy of your very own at stalls selling gaudy religious iconography around the basilica.

In the central Pari-an district, the impressive **Casa Gorordo Museum** (Map p626; 35 L Jaena St; admission P70; ☻ 8.30am-noon & 1-4pm Tue-Sun) is a beautifully restored home dating from the mid-19th century.

> **GETTING INTO TOWN**
>
> Taxis between Cebu City and Mactan International Airport cost around P200. A cheaper option is to take a tricycle (if you can find one) to Lapu-Lapu city and pick up a jeepney into town from there.
>
> To get into town from the ports, catch one of the jeepneys that pass by the piers and go to downtown Cebu City. Change at Pres Osmeña Blvd for a jeepney going Uptown. Similarly, from either bus station you can also catch a jeepney heading downtown and change at Pres Osmeña Blvd.

PHILIPPINES

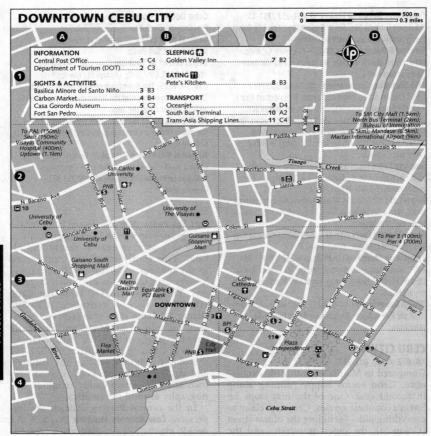

DOWNTOWN CEBU CITY

0 — 500 m
0 — 0.3 miles

INFORMATION
Central Post Office.....................1 C4
Department of Tourism (DOT).........2 C3

SIGHTS & ACTIVITIES
Basilica Minore del Santo Niño.........3 B3
Carbon Market.........................4 B4
Casa Gorordo Museum..................5 C2
Fort San Pedro........................6 C4

SLEEPING
Golden Valley Inn.....................7 B2

EATING
Pete's Kitchen........................8 B3

TRANSPORT
Oceanjet.............................9 D4
South Bus Terminal...................10 A2
Trans-Asia Shipping Lines.............11 C4

PHILIPPINES

For a chaotic frontal assault on the senses, don't miss out on a visit to the the **Carbon Market** (Map p626; Quezon Blvd). Here you will find everything from fruit to chicken gizzards to all manner of unidentifiable organic material.

Overlooking the town is a magnificent **Taoist Temple**, where you can worship, enjoy great views and have your fortune read all at the one place. To get there, take a Lahug jeepney from uptown and get off at the posh Beverly Hills district – you then have a 1.5km walk uphill. A taxi there is about P150.

Mactan Island, where Magellan reluctantly met his maker, is now the site of Cebu's airport.

Sleeping
UPTOWN
Map p627

Villa de Mercedes (☎ 253 3320; 366 Orchid St; d P545-695, tr P665-875; 🖭) Down a hushed street on the edge of town, this place has balconies with great views of the northern hills. Standard rooms are large and no frills while the better rooms have TV.

Jasmine Pension (☎ 254 2686; cnr Jasmine St & Don Gil Garcia St; s P380-450, d P420-480; 🖭) Located in a pretty yellow building with a North Asian feel, Jasmine has a few spacious, wood-lined rooms – some with fab retro black-tile bathrooms.

Pensionne La Florentina (☎ 231 3318; 18 Acacia St; s P450-580, d P650) In an attractive, older building around the corner from Kukuk's,

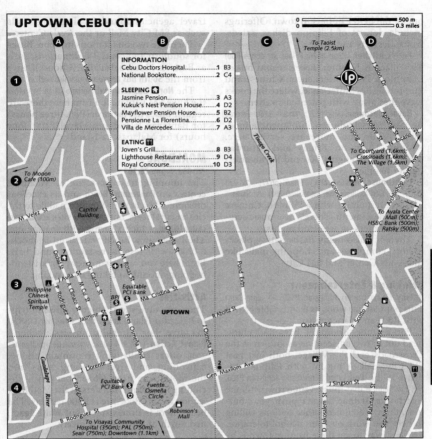

UPTOWN CEBU CITY

INFORMATION	
Cebu Doctors Hospital	1 B3
National Bookstore	2 C4

SLEEPING	
Jasmine Pension	3 A3
Kukuk's Nest Pension House	4 D2
Mayflower Pension House	5 B2
Pensionne La Florentina	6 D2
Villa de Mercedes	7 A3

EATING	
Joven's Grill	8 B3
Lighthouse Restaurant	9 D4
Royal Concourse	10 D3

this pension offers peace and seclusion. The shady communal veranda out the front is a good place to get intimate with San Miguel's fine merchandise.

Mayflower Pension House (☎ 255 2800; Villalon Dr; s P260-480, d P380-630, tr P500-780; ✗) It's amazing what a lick of paint can do to a place. The very green, very clean, spartan rooms at this secure pension are not too shabby. There is a convenient convenience store downstairs.

Kukuk's Nest Pension House (☎ 231 5180; kukuks _nest80@hotmail.com; 157 Gorordo Ave; s P200, d P300-500; ✗) The cheaper rooms here are a little musty and have weathered bamboo furniture – BYO air-freshener. There's a popular outdoor bar-restaurant where the theme is beer and girls (not necessarily in that order).

DOWNTOWN   **Map p626**
Golden Valley Inn (Map p626; ☎ 253 8660; 155A Pelaez St; s P600, d P700-1100; ✗ ▯) If you must stay in the hazy, carbon-monoxide fog of downtown, treat yourself to the relative luxury of air-con, TV and hot water in every impeccable room. There's a café downstairs.

Eating
Mooon Cafe (cnr E Osmeña St & J Diaz St; meals P60-110) A seriously hip Mexican-styled place with interesting local art garnishing its warm adobe walls. Also serves pizza and pasta. Find it just west of the Capitol building.

Joven's Grill (Map p627; cnr Pres Osmeña Blvd & Jasmine St; all-you-can-eat P120) A great place to gorge after an extended journey, this is

PHILIPPINES

one of the better buffets in town. Offerings include dozens of Filipino dishes, salads, fruits, desserts and drinks.

Pete's Kitchen (Map p626; Pelaez St; dishes P60) This place is brighter, breezier and busier than most. Pete's offers cheap Chinese and Filipino dishes buffet-style, where the cooks wave flies away with patented swatters.

Royal Concourse (Map p627; ☎ 231 3160; Gorordo Ave; meals P90-240) Filipino and Japanese food, mixed grills and more are served here. Around 10pm on Friday and Saturday night, the disco lights descend for an after-dinner boogie.

Lighthouse Restaurant (Map p627; ☎ 233 2383/2386; Gen Maxilom Ave; meals P80-200) A Spanish-style restaurant with a Filipino, Chinese and Japanese menu. There's live music serenading punters on weekend nights.

There are also many flashy eating places in hotel complexes and shopping malls like the Ayala Center and SM City.

Drinking & Entertainment

Ratsky (Ayala Center; admission P150; ☽ 6pm-3am) This popular bar woos its fashionable crowd with R&B and dance music.

For a smorgasbord of bars and clubs, head out to two adjacent areas known as the Crossroads and the Village, both just past SM City mall. A big hit with Filipino students is the **Courtyard** (Crossroads; admission P100; ☽ 8pm-4am), a live-music venue rowdy till the wee hours. If that doesn't push your buttons, there are endless other options willing to help you work on your alcohol tolerance. The best way to get there from uptown is by taxi (P60).

Getting There & Away

Most of the long-haul ferries (see p623) leave from Pier 4, on the northern extension of Osmeña Blvd, where you'll also find the terminal for SuperCat fastcraft to Bohol, Siquijor, Negros and Leyte. WG&A SuperFerry vessels to Manila leave from Pier 6.

There are several daily departures to Bohol, Siquijor, Leyte and Negros costing between P400 to P700 on fastcraft and around P300 on slower boats. More distant destinations have at least four to six connecting services a week; expect to pay around P500 to P600 for an economy berth to Mindanao or Iloilo and upwards of P1100 to Manila. Tickets are easily purchased at travel agencies found in shopping malls such as SM City Mall or the Ayala Center.

There are two bus stations in Cebu. Buses for southern and central destinations, such as Bato via Moalboal (P70, 2½ hours), leave from the **South bus terminal** (Bacalso Ave).

The **North bus terminal** (Soriano St) is beyond the huge SM City mall. From here there are regular buses to Hagnaya (P80, three hours) for Bantayan Island and Maya (P100, four hours) for Malapascua Island.

MOALBOAL

☎ 032 / pop 26,383

The jumping traveller scene at Moalboal centres on **Panagsama Beach** and its excellent offshore scuba action. You can paddle to the closest coral reefs, but the best sites are at **Pescador Island**, which swarms with marine life. The Panagsama Beach waterfront is chock-a-block with resorts, restaurants and bars. From here you can organise day trips, island-hopping, mountain biking or kayaking.

Activities

There are dive shops aplenty offering trips to Pescador Island and other sites for US$20 per dive. For adrenalin junkies, Jochen's **Planet Action** (☎ 474 0068; www.action-philippines.com) offers challenging mountain-biking, canyoning, and river-climbing tours into the mountains from US$35 per day – including lunch and transfers in the Mad Max 'action truck'. Bike hire is P300 per day. The beach here is nonexistent, but **White Beach**, just north of Moalboal, is lovely.

Sleeping

There are two clusters of accommodation in Moalboal, reached by separate roads.

Mollie's Place (☎ 0917 254 7060; d P275-675; ☒) Dirt-cheap, snug rooms with fan and common bathroom are available here, along with much roomier air-con abodes.

Sunshine Lodge (☎ 474 0049; sunshinepension@yahoo.com; d P500-600; ☒) Sunshine has a clear pool, a Swiss restaurant and cottages with bathroom and fan. You'll find it on the southern part of the beach.

Love's Lodge (☎ 474 0140; loveslodge@hotmail.com; d P600-1400; ☒) The great rooms here are set around a manicured putting-green lawn, some with prime sunset views. The more expensive deluxe boudoirs have hot water, air-con and breakfast included.

Pacitas (☎ 0919 206 2637; d P350-1000; ⌘)
The fan cottages, each with a small lounge,
are excellent value at this rambling Moalboal institution. Sleep may be elusive on
rowdy Saturday nights.

Eating
There are dozens of eateries along the beach
strip. New on the scene is **Moti** (mains P70-
180), a popular Indian number with a comfy,
cushioned loft ideal for sunset adulation.
Seaside (mains P120) serves Filipino favourites
and is famed for its barbecue fish, and **Last
Filling Station** (breakfast P85-110) serves a satisfying morning fry-up.

Drinking
Panagsama Beach throngs with life once
the fins are drying. The current favourite is
the Chilli Bar – drawing patrons with beer,
billiards and a boisterous crowd. Lloyd's
Music lounge takes over when other's shut
down, while Pacita's Saturday-night discos
have taken on legendary status.

Getting There & Around
Regular ABC and Albines buses to Bato
from Cebu's South bus terminal pass
through Moalboal (nonair-con P70, 2½
hours). Several 'disco buses', popular with
holidaying students and with painfully loud
sound-systems, also run up the coast.

A tricycle to Panagsama Beach from
Moalboal cost P25 (P35 at night).

BANTAYAN ISLAND
☎ 032
Bantayan plays host to a section of unspoilt seashore that quietly rivals the best
beaches in the country. A long stretch of
powdery sand divides the turquoise waters and the palm-lined village of Santa Fe,
where boats from Cebu pull in. There is
very little to do in this disturbingly quiet
community but dodge the occasional
falling coconut. Ten minutes walk from
town, inside a snazzy resort, **Ogdong Cave**
(admission P50) opens into a small freshwater
swimming hole. Much off the island is
scrubby farmland, but **Bantayan town**, the
main settlement, is a fine Spanish town
with the obligatory old church, a cinema,
Internet access and a branch of the Allied
Bank. The island's wild **Holy Week** festivities (March/April) attract big crowds.

Sleeping
Most of the accommodation is spread out
along the pearly-white sand near Santa Fe.

Budyong Beach Resort (☎ 438 5700; s P400,
d P700-1300; ⌘) This resort has charming,
shady *nipa* huts with balconies facing a
perfect, private beach.

Sugar Beach Resort (d P350-600) Great budget
beach shacks under swaying palm trees.
There is no phone or restaurant, but the
smiling sisters minding the huts will happily cook anything you wish – as long it
involves fish and rice. This is a great place
to meet picnicking Filipino families.

Fairview Lodge (☎ 0919 612 8459; d P200-600;
⌘ ⌘) Located 100m beyond Ogdong Cave
and just 200m from Paradise beach, this
new resort has bargain-basement luxury
rooms and cottages inside an imposing
turquoise building. The panorama you get
from the balcony is unparalleled. Guests
can also rent motorbikes for only P150
per day.

Getting There & Around
There are several boats between Hagnaya
and Santa Fe (P10 to P100, 25 minutes to
two hours) on Bantayan until 6.30pm.

A boat also leaves Bantayan town for
Cadiz (P150, four hours) on Negros every
other morning.

There are regular buses to Hagnaya (P80,
three hours) from the North bus terminal
in Cebu; you'll need to leave before 2pm to
connect with the last boat to Bantayan.

Jeepneys and tricycles run between Santa
Fe and Bantayan town (P15). A short pedal-
tricycle is about P20.

MALAPASCUA ISLAND
The prospect of diving with majestic thresher sharks attracts travellers to
this petite island off Cebu's northern
tip. Though the big fish are increasingly
difficult to spot, Malapascua's diminutive blonde beaches and laid-back island
ambience offer plenty of reasons to stick
around. All this may soon change: developers and decision-makers on high aim
to transform Malapascua into Philippine
tourism's magnum opus. Free of cars and
tricycles, you can easily walk around the
island in a day, stopping in at the **lighthouse** on the northern tip and at the island's sole village of Logon.

Sleeping

There are several resorts strung out both behind and along the beach.

White Sands (☎ 0927 318 7471; s/d P400/600) These new shady huts sit right on the sand of a picturesque cove behind Bounty Beach, near the village.

Logon Beach Resort (☎ 0920 553 9847; d P800-1000) A cheerful place high on a rocky outcrop overhanging a tiny, private cove. *Nipa* huts have balconies with the best sunset views in Malapascua. To get here turn left after White Sands and follow the sign.

Borggren Cottages (☎ 0927 331 3809; d P300) This little family place has a few well-furnished huts at one of the best rates in town. It's behind Cocobana Beach Resort.

Eating & Drinking

Ging-Ging's Flower Garden (meals P60) A big selection of cheap, tasty, filling favourites and the cheapest beer in town (P25). Enough said.

La Isla Bonita Restaurant (dishes P120-220) This is still the best restaurant on the island, with an array of Greek, Thai and Indian dishes – and, of course, pizza.

Sunsplash Bar (☉ 7am-late) This lazy, open-air bar and restaurant has pool tables and sofas. Despite the floating bar and the 'drink for your country' shooter-drinking competitions, it stays mellow *most* of the time.

Maldito's (☉ 24hr) A huge Filipino-style entertainment complex, complete with scantily-clad waitresses, may seem out of place in Malapascua – but that's considered progress. There's a club, bar and restaurant with Internet access.

Getting There & Away

The scheduled boat from Maya (P75, 20 minutes to one hour) to Malapascua leaves when full. To avoid travelling on Filipino time and spending several hours at the docks, pay a little extra to have the boat leave early. There are regular buses to Maya from Cebu's North bus terminal.

Ordinary buses to Cebu's North terminal depart fairly regularly from Maya (P100, four hours). Otherwise, take a 20-minute jeepney (P10) or tricycle (P50) to Daan Bantayan and catch a bus from there (P90, 3½ hours).

BOHOL

Bohol is a short hop from Cebu. It's difficult to reconcile its bloody history with the relaxed isle of today. It's here that Francisco Dagohoy led the longest revolt in the country against the Spaniards from 1744 to 1829. The Chocolate Hills, rounded mounds resembling chocolate drops, are the big tourist magnet. Bohol also has fair beaches, endearing little primates, coral cathedrals and lush jungle, ripe for exploration, around the town of Loboc. Diving on Panglao Island is excellent, and marine-mammal devotees can go dolphin- and whale-spotting near Pamilacan Island.

Getting There & Away

Tagbilaran is the main gateway, with the island's airport and main port. There is a plethora of boats to and from Cebu City and connections to Mindanao, Negros and Siquijor; see opposite.

TAGBILARAN

☎ 038 / pop 95,485

Tagbilaran is a busy port that serves as the transport hub for most the island's attractions. There's a ridiculously large number of tricycles here, many of which seem to spend the night drag racing though the streets. The **tourist office** (☎ 235 5497) is by the market on the main road.

Sleeping

Casa Juana (☎ 411 3331; CP Garcia Ave; s/d P300/500; ❂) These utilitarian rooms win the best-value ribbon – they all come with air-con and private bathroom.

Nisa Travelers Inn (☎ 411 3731; CP Garcia Ave; s P200, d P250-600) A friendly and spacious place, with a timber balcony and simple restaurant.

Taver's Pension House (☎ 411 4896; tavers@moz com.com; Remolador St; s/d from P600/750; ❀) This has all the creature comforts. The central rooms are clean and quiet, with cable TV, hot water and telephone.

Eating

JJ's Dimsum Restaurant (☎ 411 3306/3331; CP Garcia Ave; meals P60) Good Chinese is served up here, cheaply and en masse. You can have great fried fish and tofu for two to three people for P100 while peso-pinchers can order the budget meal combo for P60.

Joving's Seafood Restaurant (main wharf; meals P80-180) Precariously perched on gnarled mangrove stilts, this place does Filipino-style seafood well. You can also buy *kalamay*, a local sugar and coconut speciality, from vendors on the pier.

Getting There & Away

There are daily flights on **Asian Spirit** (www .asianspirit.com) connecting Tagbilaran with Manila and Cebu (see p596).

Several fast boats run daily to and from the jetty at the northern end of town connecting Tagbilaran with Cebu (P480, 1½ hours), Dumaguete (P510, 2½ hours), Siquijor (P645, three hours) and Dapitan (P780, three hours). There are also slower connections to Cagayan de Oro (P480 economy, eight hours) every other day.

Buses to everywhere on the island leave from the Integrated bus terminal in Dao, north of town. Minibuses (P5) run here from the city market on Carlos P Garcia St.

AROUND TAGBILARAN

Near the village of **Sikatuna**, in a *barangay* (neighbourhood) known as Canapnapan, is the **Tarsier Visitors Center** (☎ 0912 516 3375; requested donation P20; ☺ 8am-4pm) where you can visit the saucer-eyed tarsiers, probably the world's cutest micro-primates. The centre has tons of information, a captive breeding programme and a wildlife sanctuary. A small patch of forest beside the centre allows for guided walks and discreet ogling of several mature tarsiers. You can catch a bus or jeepney to Sikatuna (P15, 30 minutes) from the Dao terminal and ask to be dropped off at the Tarsier Centre.

Be sure not to miss **Nuts Huts Retreat** (☎ 0920 846 1559; dm P200-350, d P400-550), 3km north of **Loboc** village. This riverside refuge

is a backpacker Shangri-la of cottages and hammocks smack in the middle of dense, verdant forest. The gracious Belgian hosts are a mine of information on the region and have created an eco-haven from which you can explore the surrounding area by boat, mountain bike or on foot. To get there, catch a Loboc-bound bus (P20) and get off at the Nuts Huts sign. It's a 15-minute walk from the road.

Nature lovers can also grab a jeepney to **Baclayon** (P6), 6km east of Tagbilaran, and organise boats for dolphin- and whale-watching trips with **Pamilacan Island Dolphin & Whale Watching Tours** (☎ 038-540 9279; around P2000 for 6-8 people).

PANGLAO ISLAND

☎ 038

When you've had enough of Tagbilaran's trillion tricycles, head for the open spaces and lovely beaches of Panglao Island, connected to the city by bridge. **Alona Beach**, on the southwest coast, is a fine sliver of white sand intermittently speckled with bronze bodies. It's also a major diving destination, with several dive shops offering trips to the black coral forest of **Balicasag Island** and the dive sites at **Cabilao Island**, 30km northwest, which often see hammerhead sharks and dolphins. Dives average US$18 to US$24.

On the northeast coast, you can make a detour to the interesting **Hinagdanan Cave** at Bingag (it's on the bus route back to Tagbilaran). You can change money and get cash advances on major credit cards at the Credit Card Payment Centre, near the Alona Kew White Beach Resort.

Sleeping & Eating

Alona Beach is wall-to-wall *nipa* guesthouses, bars and dive shops.

DID YOU KNOW?

The tarsier is considered the smallest primate on earth. These funny creatures grow to between 8cm and 16cm in length, can move their large ears independently of each other, rotate their head 180 degrees and jump 20 times their body length. But they're not very good at chess – each of their enormous eyes is bigger than their entire brain.

Safety Stop (☎ 502 9058; hut P500) A few nice, two-storey *nipa* huts with two double beds are available behind this popular bar.

Hippocampus (☎ 0916 273 1089; cottage P400) Formerly part of Alonaville, this little farm of nondescript cottages is in a central beach location.

Peter's House (☎ 502 9056; d P450-550) The huts here have great views; they're in a large *nipa* complex where divers spin yarns. Rooms are reserved for divers during the high season.

Alonaland (☎ 502 9007; P450-1300; 🞨) A good option 50m walk from the beach (through Alona Tropical). Accommodation ranges from basic *nipa* huts to air-con cottages with kitchens. There's a pool table and sensibly priced beer.

Trudy's Place (meals P60-110) This place right on the beach is one of the best budget Filipino eateries around, but either get here early or bring your knitting for the long wait.

Getting There & Around

Buses (P20, 45 minutes) leave when full from the market at the Dao terminal. You can get here by tricycle for around P150 or taxi for P200. To explore the area at your own pace, you can hire off-road motorbikes for P500 per day.

CHOCOLATE HILLS

An interesting quirk of nature, the **Chocolate Hills** (admission P10) consist of over 1200 conical hills, up to 120m high. They were supposedly formed over time by the uplift of coral deposits and the effects of rainwater and erosion. Since this explanation cannot be confirmed, the local belief that they are the remnants of a battle between two giants may one day prove to be correct. In the dry season, when the vegetation turns brown, the hills are at their most chocolaty.

St Jude buses make the winding trip to Carmen (4km north of the Chocolate Hills) hourly from the Dao terminal in Tagbilaran (P40). *Habal-habal* (motorcycle taxis) will take you up to the Chocolate Hills viewing point from Carmen (P30), or the Chocolate Hills turn-off (P10). A more fun method is to take a *habal-habal* in and around the hills; a 1½-hour ride costs P150.

PANAY

Though overshadowed by its brightest star Boracay, Panay has plenty to offer the plucky traveller. Green hills roll into endless rice fields, and crumbling forts and watchtowers intermittently dot the landscape. Panay's many thatch-hut villages huddle the curving shore all the way south to the meandering river of Iloilo city.

Most tourists pass through the island en route to Boracay, off Panay's northwestern tip. The stunning beach here lives up to most people's expectations, but it's a stretch of paradise you will have to learn to share with others.

Getting There & Away

The main airport is at Iloilo City in the south, but there's also a string of smaller airports at Caticlan (for Boracay), Kalibo and Roxas. There are flights to Panay from Manila and Cebu (see p596).

Iloilo is a major stop on the north-south boat route. There are regular ferries from Cebu, Manila, Negros and several ports in Mindanao.

ILOILO CITY

☎ 033 / pop 409,294

Iloilo city is an agreeable stopover on the Visayan island-hopping itinerary. Straddling the lazy Iloilo River, this busy urban expanse retains some of its colonial glory in the architecture of the **Jaro** district and the nearby coral **Molo Church**. The **Museo Iloilo** displays interesting tapestries, furniture and memorabilia, and January's **Dinagyang Festival** fills the streets with revellers. Iloilo City is noted for its *jusi* (raw silk) and *piña* (pineapple fibre) weaving.

Information

Iznart St and JM Basa St form the main drag, where there are plenty of banks and ATMs. The helpful **tourist office** (☎ 335 0245; Bonifacio Dr) is next to the Museo Iloilo.

Sleeping

Pensione del Carmen (☎ 338 1626; General Luna St; s P550-650, d P650-750; 🞨) This graceful family home is owned by the equally gracious Carmen. Rooms have hot water, air-con and TV. Guests can use the kitchen and

PHILIPPINES

fridge and there's a breezy communal balcony overlooking the river.

Family Pension House (☎ 335 0070; General Luna St; s P250-375, d P350-575; ❄) A spirited, popular place in an old building with polished floorboards and clean, fair-priced rooms. Only the 'budget' rooms are a bit lacklustre. There's an airy restaurant upstairs.

Eros Traveller's Pensionne (☎ 337 1359; General Luna St; s P280-380, d P345-510; ❄) Another cheapie worth considering is this place, opposite St Paul's Hospital, with clean, but mostly windowless, rooms.

Eating

Mundo Ristorante (☎ 509 3721; General Luna St; meals P65-160) This tastefully decorated and cheery little Italian gem has a few quiet riverside tables – the ultimate first-date location. It's next to Residence Hotel.

Marina (☎ 320 1230; Iloilo Diversion Rd; meals P55-180) An open-air, *nipa* restaurant with great river vistas, just over the northern side of the bridge. Marina does genuine Filipino food with a seafood edge.

Ted's Old Timer Lapaz Batchoy (General Luna St; meals P50-60; ⏰ 24hr) The local specialties of *bihon batchoy* (soup noodles with beef and crunchy pork), and *sotanghon batchoy* (much the same, but meatier and crunchier) are expertly doled out here.

Getting There & Away

There are regular flights connecting Iloilo with Manila and Cebu City (see p596). The airport is about 4km away, and a taxi there is about P70.

Several daily fastcraft make the hop from Iloilo to and from Bacolod on Negros (P140 to P220, one to two hours).

Milagrosa J Shipping Lines (☎ 033-335 0955; Jarcel Bldg, La Puz Norte) has a weekly service that runs between Iloilo City and Puerto Princesa in Palawan (economy P550, 26 hours) via Cuyo.

From the **Ceres Liner terminal** (Rizal St) there are many buses from Iloilo City to Kalibo (P157, four hours) and several buses to Caticlan (P220, five hours).

CATICLAN

☎ 036

Caticlan is a lazy fishing hamlet where the main attractions are its transport hubs – the port for Boracay, the nearby bus terminal and the airport (2km away, P30 by tricycle). If you arrive late and must stay in town, the **Casimero Lodging House** (☎ 288 7027; d P400-600) will happily provide you with rundown, cramped, concrete rooms at inflated prices. See the Boracay (p635) and Roxas (p623) sections for more transport details.

BORACAY

☎ 036

Boracay's famed White Beach is where the crystal, turquoise waters of the Visayan Sea meet blinding, snow-white sand. The sand, in turn, meets a small bungalow jungle of development – needed to sustain the throng of visitors that flock to this island paradise. On Boracay you can try your hand at a stupendous array of sporting pursuits including, but not limited to, jet-skiing, horse-riding, windsurfing, kite-surfing, sailing, kayaking, scuba diving, snorkelling, paragliding, mountainbiking, yoga, bowling, tennis and golf. There is also plenty on offer for those who consider drinking and dining as sporting pursuits.

A line of swaying palms successfully hides much of the build-up, preserving some fine beach vistas, and a sandy pedestrian highway runs its length. Three 'Boat Stations' are spaced out along White Beach – simply patches of beach where *bangcas* drop off and pick up passengers. Walking is the best way to get around (Boracay is only 9km long by 1km wide), but tricycle drivers will vie for your custom if your legs give out.

Information

Bank of the Philippine Islands Has an ATM at D'Mall accepting MasterCard and Cirrus.

Boracay Tourist Center (⏰ 8am-noon) Offers Internet access and money-changing facilities, and sells plane and ferry tickets.

Bureau of Immigration (Villa Camilla; ⏰ 1-5pm Mon, 9am-noon & 1-5pm Tue & Wed) This office, near Boat Station 3, does visa extensions in 15 minutes for P2020.

Don Ciriaco Senares Tirol Snr Memorial Hospital (☎ 288 3041) Off the main road, behind Boat Station 2.

DOT (☎ 288 3689; ⏰ 8am-noon & 1-5pm Mon-Fri) Friendly and informed. In D'Mall shopping arcade in front of Boat Station 2.

Metrobank (Boracay Main Rd) Has an ATM taking Visa cards.

Metropolitan Doctors Medical Clinic (☎ 288 6357) Near Boat Station 1. Has Manila-trained doctors and gets good reviews.

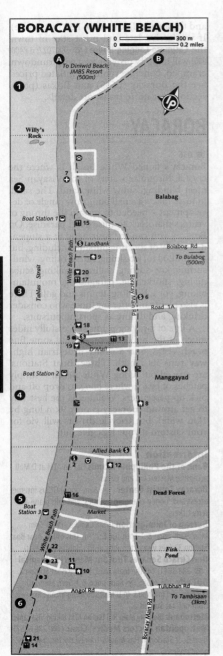

BORACAY (WHITE BEACH)

Sleeping

Hoteliers on Boracay make their money during the brief high season from November to May, when prices for accommodation rise astronomically. As Boracay gradually sprints upmarket, real budget places are getting thinner on the ground, but with 240 lodging options at last count, you're bound to find something. The better-value places are hidden down narrow paths away from the water (beach-side huts cost 50% to 100% more). You can bargain big discounts off these prices in the low season.

Melinda's Garden (☎ 288 3021; melindasgarden@ hotmail.com; d P800-1400) A hidden jewel down a pathway off the beach, Melinda's Garden features some splendid cottages located around a sheltered garden. It lends out beach towels and mats, it has a great restaurant and, in addition, it employs thoughtful staff.

Orchids (☎ 288 3313; orchidslynn@hotmail.com; d P800-2000; 🖳) Near Melinda's, this is a nifty collection of *nipa*-lined rooms and garden cottages nicely decked out with bamboo goodies.

INFORMATION
Bank of the Philippine Islands	**1** A3
Boracay Tourist Center	**2** A5
Bureau of Immigration	**3** A6
Don Ciriaco Senares Tirol Snr Memorial Hospital	**4** B4
DOT	**5** A3
Metrobank	**6** B3
Metropolitan Doctors Medical Clinic	**7** A2

SLEEPING 🏠
Du Berry	**8** B4
Fiesta Cottages	**9** A3
Melinda's Garden	**10** A6
Orchids	(see 10)
Roy's Rendevous	**11** A6
St Vincent Cottages	**12** B5

EATING 🍴
Blue Berry	**13** B3
Pizzeria Floremar Ristorante Italiano da Mario	**14** A6
Real Coffee & Tea Cafe	**15** A2
Restaurante Banza	**16** A5
Thai Castles Restaurant	**17** A3

DRINKING 🍸
Bom Bom Bar	**18** A3
Hey Jude	**19** A4
Jay-Jay's Movie Bar	**20** A3
Red Pirates	**21** A6

TRANSPORT
Asian Spirit	**22** A5
PAL	**23** A6
Seair	(see 5)

Roy's Rendezvous (☎ 288 3403; d P700-1000; ☒) Next door to Orchids, Roy's has similar cottages around a more sunlit garden, and the ultimate budget luxury – remote-controlled fans.

JMBS Resort (☎ 288 3934; Diniwid Beach; d P700-800) There is a low-key atmosphere at this resort, which has decent cottages and an awesome open-plan loft. It's further north of Boat Station 1 on the secluded Diniwid Beach, a stone's throw from the action on White Beach, but much quieter.

On the northern part of White Beach, set back from the sand, we couldn't spot the difference between **St Vincent Cottages** (☎ 288 5674; d P800-1500; ☒) and **Fiesta Cottages** (☎ 288 3818; d P800-1500), both with hushed, plain huts set around big square lawns. If you are really pinching pesos, **Du Berry** (☎ 0919 5894349; d P400-800) offers large, satisfactory rooms with shared bathroom along the busy main road.

Eating

There's a plethora of reasonably priced eating options on Boracay – strolling around the Vegas-lit beach at night you will be assaulted by smells and invitations. There are also cheap snack bars, juice bars and *turo turo* (point-point) stalls to be checked out in D'Mall.

Pizzeria Floremar Ristorante Italiano da Mario (pizza & pasta P120-180, other meals P150-250) The authentic Italian chequered-tablecloth dining experience – on the beach surrounded by swaying palms.

Thai Castles Restaurant (meals P190-295) Very good Thai cuisine is served here in a series of bamboo pavilions. There are plenty of cushions and the loft is a good place to lounge away a hot afternoon.

Real Coffee & Tea Cafe (snacks P80) This café has, believe it or not, real coffee and real tea as well as yummy sandwiches, fresh fruit shakes and baked goods like mother used to make.

Blue Berry (mains P50-100) Dirt-cheap eatery with a never-ending menu. It's in a small but flamboyant space in D'Mall.

Drinking

Boracay has no shortage of bars, from peaceful, beachfront cocktail affairs, where you can sip a mai-tai while you watch the sunset, to throbbing discos that run late into the night.

SPLURGE!

Restaurante Banza (☎ 288 5167; meals P240-620) This is one of the best restaurants on the island. Convivial Portuguese owner-chef Antonio serves the freshest seafood, with an emphasis on quality, flavour, oil and garlic. If you have a sweet tooth, the coconut and cinnamon cakes (both P120) are delicious.

Red Pirates (☺ 5pm-2am) A funky new establishment at the far south end of the beach. It has its own elaborate driftwood forest where you can kick back to the hum of ambient beats. Look for the Red Pirate ship.

Jay-Jay's Movie Bar (☺ 10am-2am) Leaping across the digital divide, Jay-Jay's plays DVDs nightly and has a ludicrously extensive collection of MP3 files.

Bom Bom Bar (☺ 5pm-2am) Towards Boat Station 1 at the northern end of the beach, Bom Bom has excellent music and a chilled island vibe.

Hey Jude (☺ 9am-2am) Slick New York–style bar with serious drink mixology credentials.

Getting There & Away

AIR

The quickest (and most expensive) way to Boracay from Manila is to fly to Caticlan with **Asian Spirit** (www.asianspirit.com) or **Seair** (www.flyseair.com) for P3240. **PAL** (www.philippineair.com), Cebu Pacific and Air Philippines all fly to Kalibo airport in northern Panay (see p596), where air-con buses meet the flights and run to Caticlan.

PAL, Seair and Asian Spirit all have offices along the beach in Boracay.

BOAT

MBRS Lines (☎ 02-241 8497; Pier 8, North Harbour, Manila) has boats leaving three times a week from Manila to Caticlan (P900 to P1200, 14 hours). The craft waits just offshore at Caticlan and you have to scramble along gangplanks onto outriggers.

Outriggers cover the 20-minute hop between Caticlan and Boracay all day (P20) and into the night (P30). During the southwestern monsoons, from June to November, outriggers land on the east coast at Tambisaan or Bulabag, a P7 tricycle ride from White Beach.

PHILIPPINES

Getting Around

This compact island is perfect to explore on foot. Tricycles cost about P7 for short trips, mountain bikes can be hired for around P150 per hour and motorcycles for about P250 per hour.

NEGROS

Negros is the sweet tooth of the Philippines, heart of the country's sugar production. Leviathan steam locomotives are still used to transport saccharine cargo around the island. Split in two by intimidating mountains, its unspoilt coastline and natural finery earn it some traveller kudos. The Kanlaon volcano is being touted as the next big thing in volcano scrambling, while Apo Island, near the lovely town of Dumaguete, offers plenty of escapades for both divers and rock climbers.

BACOLOD

☎ 034 / pop 518,023

Although Bacolod lacks anything in particular to hold a traveller's interest, its wide, green backstreets, colourful market and good budget-accommodation options make it worthwhile calling 'round. The quiet municipality is centred on the city plaza. Locals masquerade in grinning masks for October's **MassKara Festival** and in April/May there's the Panaad crafts festival, which is the culmination of several weeks of neighbourhood fiestas.

Information

Around the plaza you'll find the Negros Navigation and WG&A offices, some banks, Internet cafés and the **tourist office** (☎ 435

MYSTERIES OF THE BABAYANS

The diminutive Negrito people of Panay's mountainous interior are called the Ati. There are perhaps 5000 Ati living in scattered hamlets, but you'll more likely see them begging in Iloilo City or on Boracay – they're a highly marginalised group. Their spiritual leaders were female shamans, Babayans, interacting with the human world and the shadowy spirit world, with an influence that could cause illness, depression or even death.

1001), which has first-hand information about climbing, or avoiding, Mt Kanlaon.

Here you can arrange guides from the Negros Mountaineering Club (NMC) for the intense three- to four-day trek to Mt Kanlaon's 2465m-high peak – the highest point in the central Philippines. Expect to pay around P5000 to P6000 each (minimum two people) for guides, food, camping equipment and transport.

Sleeping

Pension Bacolod (☎ 433 3377; 11th St; s P100-450, d P205-560; 🅿) Near the Ceres North bus terminal, this peaceful place is the incarnation of an alpine chalet and offers excellent value for money with large, cool rooms.

Rosita's Hometel (☎ 434 5136; cnr Mabini St & San Sebastian St; d P300-500; 🅿) is painted a forcibly cheery baby-blue and yellow, and has plain, clean generous rooms, while **Star Plus Pension House** (☎ 433 2948-9; cnr Lacson St & Rosario St; s/d P310/475; 🅿) is clean and well maintained, with room service available from the café.

Eating

Inaka Japanese Restaurant & Sushi Bar (cnr 21st St & Lacson St; meals P85-240) If you're hankering for flavours from the land of the rising sun, there's excellent Japanese provisions here – with plenty for both carnivores and veggies. It's near the funky bar district along 20th, 21st and 22nd streets.

University Courtyard (La Salle Ave) This place, opposite University Saint La Salle, has cafés, bars, pastry shops and Internet cafés as well as bookshops and clothing outlets.

Manokan Country (meals about P55; 🕒 24hr) Near the city plaza in the Reclamation Area, this is a complex of cheap chicken-barbecue restaurants which also sell beer.

Getting There & Away

PAL (www.philippineair.com) and **Cebu Pacific** (www.cebupacificair.com) both fly to Bacolod from Manila (P3300) and Cebu (P2320).

The main port is on reclaimed land, west of the centre. Sea Angels, Bullet Express and Weesam Express all have regular fastcraft to and from Iloilo (P140 to P220, one to two hours) on Panay.

From the northbound **Ceres Liner terminal** (Lopez Jaena St) there are several buses every morning to Cebu City (P300, seven hours) via San Carlos–Toledo. Ordinary buses also run from here to Dumaguete (P220, seven hours) via San Carlos (P105, 3½ hours) in the north of the island.

The Public South bus terminal has ordinary Ceres Liner buses that go to Dumaguete via the faster southern route (P172, five hours).

Getting Around

A taxi from the airport to the city plaza shouldn't be more than P50; alternatively, you can take a jeepney. A tricycle to the port costs P5 from the city plaza, while a taxi is around P40. To get to the Ceres Liner terminals, take a 'Shopping' jeepney from city plaza for P5, or grab a taxi (P50).

DUMAGUETE

☎ 035 / pop 118,713

Dumaguete is a leafy, prosperous little city that bustles with energy, mostly emanating from its sprawling Silliman University campus. The university's **Anthropology Museum** (Hibbard Ave; admission P12; ☷ 8am-noon & 2-5pm Mon-Fri) is worth a look if you can find the custodian to let you in. On the far side of the campus you'll find the **Silliman University Marine Laboratory** (admission P10; ☷ 8am-noon & 2-5pm Mon-Fri), with breeding pens full of turtles, crocodiles, clams and indigenous fish – the crocodiles are fed twice a week at 2pm (chicken, in case you were wondering). The city's pleasant, tree-lined promenade buzzes with night-time activity; be sure to check out the bizarre statue of flailing nuns.

Orientation & Information

Dumaguete centres on Rizal Park, which is surrounded by several banks, the town hall and the post office. The main drag, Perdices St, runs up to the Silliman University campus, where there are several Internet cafés.

The chatty staff at **city tourist office** (☎ 225 0549; City Hall, Santa Catalina St) are very helpful.

Sleeping

Harold's Mansion Tourist Inn (☎ 225 8000-01; haroldsmansion@yahoo.com; 205 Hibbard Ave; s P300, d P385-1089; ☷) This is a big, efficiently run, powder-green hotel 10 minutes' walk from the main shopping area. There's enough room for you to swing two cats in the immaculate doubles.

Vintage Inn (☎ 225 1076; Legazpi St; s P220-440, d P330-605; ☷) Centrally located opposite the market, this is a reasonable budget option. The better doubles have hot water. Jeepneys and buses heading north stop just around the corner from here.

Private Garden Resort (☎ 225 0658; privategardenresort@yahoo.com; Noreco Rd, Mangnao; d P500-800; ☷ ☐) Practically a holiday destination unto itself, this resort is on the coast, out of the hullabaloo of the city but still within a P10 tricycle ride. The wonderful, big rooms are decorated with backlit crafts and all have kitchens. There's motorbike rental (P600 per day), Internet and pool tables. Head 3km south from town and turn left at the Shell service station.

Eating

Why Not (☎ 225 4488; Rizal Blvd; meals P150; ☷ to 2am) This tourist magnet is a one-stop-shop – it has a restaurant, deli, bar, pool hall, Internet café and disco. The pizzas (P140 to P180) are great, and it's worth visiting for the salad-bar alone (P2.50 per 10g), a welcome reprieve from the usual meatfest.

Chin Loong Restaurant (☎ 422 6933; cnr San Jose St & Rizal Blvd; meals P50-160) Near Why Not, with big servings of tasty Chinese and Filipino victuals on the menu. The 'special dinner', birds-nest soup, fried rice, chop suey, two mains and a soft drink, is only P135.

Evening **food stalls** (Rizal Blvd) at the top end of Rizal Blvd serve excellent tempura fish and squid balls (P5 per stick). There are several groovy **cafés** (Silliman Ave) catering to students opposite the university.

Getting There & Away

Cebu Pacific (www.cebupacificair.com) and **Air Philippines** (www.airphils.com) fly daily from Manila to Dumaguete for P3450.

Fast ferries go to and from Cebu city (P600, 3½ hours), Larena (P270, one hour) on Siquijor Island and Tagbilaran (P510, two hours) on Bohol. The wharf is near the junction of Rizal Blvd and Silliman Ave. From the nearby port of Sibulan there are pumpboats to Lilo-an on Cebu island (P30, 30 minutes), from where there are buses to Cebu City. A tricycle to anywhere in town, including the main wharf, will cost P5.

For the fastest connection to Bacolod, take a Ceres Liner bus via Mabinay (P172, five hours) from the **Ceres terminal** (South Rd).

HUBBLE BUBBLE, TOIL & TROUBLE

Herbalists from all over the country meet annually in the *barangay* (neighbourhood) of **San Antonio** to prepare an all-powerful healing brew. A large cauldron is filled with coconut oil, roots, herbs, insects and other secret ingredients while *mananameal* (medicine men) gather in a circle murmuring incantations. This all takes place on black Saturday in the belief that with the death of Christ, supernatural entities roam the earth and share their healing powers.

SIQUIJOR
☎ 035 / pop 87,110

Spooky little Siquijor is renowned as much for its witches and healers as for the friendliness of its inhabitants. With your own transport you can circumnavigate the island in a day and explore beaches, colonial relics, waterfalls, caves and charming villages. The most popular beaches are at **Sandugan**, 6km north of the port of Larena, and along the west coast at **Solangon**, 9km from the capital Siquijor town. The marine reserve near Sandugan gets many divers' tails wagging.

Sleeping

Kiwi Dive Resort (☎ 0917 361 5997; www.kiwidiveresort.com; dm P180, d P450-790) On Sandugan Beach, this long-timer offers dives (US$22) and hires out motorbikes (P490 per day). The dorms are plain but the huts are very nice, with lots of thoughtful extras. They accept credit cards.

Islander's Paradise (☎ 0919 446 9982; www.islanders6226.com; d P300-600) Next to Kiwi's, this place features simpler huts – the big difference being the prime, beachfront real estate.

SPLURGE!

Coral Cay Resort (☎ 0919 269 1269; scoralcayresort@yahoo.com; d P750-2400; 🗷 🗩) This resort is on a perfect stretch of white-sand beach at Solangon, 3km from the town of San Juan. The lavish rooms come with all the fixin's, like bamboo furniture and private bathrooms. There's jeepney tours, a pool, mountain-bike rental, pool tables, plenty of palm trees and the only thatch-hut gym we have ever seen.

The staff here are exceptionally friendly and helpful.

Luisa & Son's Lodge (s/d P150/250) If you must stay in Larena, this place is near the wharf. The paper-thin walls and intersection location mean that you'll have to enter a coma to get any rest.

Getting There & Around

There are several daily fastcraft between Dumaguete on Negros and Larena (P270, one hour) and between Dumaguete and Siquijor town (P200, one hour). There are also boats from Siquijor to Cebu (P760, four hours) and Tagbilaran on Bohol (P645, three hours).

Jeepneys run regularly to Siquijor town (P15) and San Juan (P25) from Larena market, uphill from the port. Sandugan is a short tricycle ride in the other direction.

SAMAR

This largely unspoilt, and frequently wet, tropical island is home to wild beaches and even wilder forested hinterlands. It's here in 1521 that Magellan planted his first footstep, on the island of Homonhon, on his way to claim the Philippines for the Western world. Tourist development is a far-off dream, there are no ATMs and transport can be uncomfortable and sporadic at best. For fanatical surfers, the eastern seashore offers a coastline of unexplored breaks facing the onslaught of Pacific currents – getting there is the only problem.

Samar is a stepping stone linking the Philippines' eastern islands, with boat connections to southern Luzon and Mindanao, and the excellent Pan-Philippine Hwy linking Leyte to Samar. Be mindful of periodic NPA activity in the island's interior. Samar's star attraction, **Sohoton National Park**, is near Basey in southern Samar and is best accessed from Tacloban on Leyte (see p640).

Getting There & Away

Asian Spirit (www.asianspirit.com) flies from Manila to Calbayog for around P3100.

Samar lies on the epic bus route from Manila to Davao, so it's possible to get aircon buses from Calbayog or Catbalogan to Manila (P1207 to P1332, 25 to 30 hours) getting off anywhere in Southern Luzon, to

Tacloban (P80 to P120, two to three hours) on Leyte and further on to Mindanao.

There are a number of ferries daily between Matnog on Luzon and Allen (P65, one hour) or San Isidro (P75, 1½ hours) on Samar.

CALBAYOG

☎ 055 / pop 160,248

Calbayog is a transit town whose claim to 'fame' is its ranking as the Philippines' 19th oldest city. There are some pretty coastal views along the road to Allen.

Sleeping & Eating

Eduardo's Tourist Hotel (☎ 209 2407; Pajario St; d P300-1200; 🔀) By default, this is the best option in town – all rooms have air-con and TV. The attached Chinese restaurant is probably the best in town.

San Joaquin Inn (Nijaga St; d P400-650) This decidedly average place is near the market and has a rooftop restaurant.

Getting There & Away

There are a couple of daily Philippine Eagle buses and several jeepneys between Catarman and Calbayog, via Allen (P120, four hours). Several ordinary buses a day go from Catbalogan to Calbayog (P65, two hours). Buses and jeepneys to Allen leave from the Capoocan bus terminal, a P15 tricycle ride from the centre of town.

LEYTE

Like Samar, Leyte has tourist potential that is yet to be realised. A rugged, almost impassable ridge lined with extinct volcanoes traverses the island's length. This is where General MacArthur fulfilled his promise to return, with help from Allied forces, at the tail end of WWII.

PAL, Cebu Pacific and Air Philippines fly to Tacloban from Manila daily (P3450).

Buses to Mindanao run from Tacloban to Liloan in the south of the island (P140, four hours); from there a ferry takes you across to Lipata (P130, 3½ hours), 10km north of Surigao.

The Pan-Philippine Hwy runs right through Leyte and Samar. Philtranco buses run all the way from Manila to Tacloban daily, via Catbalogan and Calbayog on Samar, but

it's a harrowing 28 hours of crazy driving (P920/1375 standard/air-con).

The major port on Leyte is Ormoc, from where there are fast boats to Cebu. Buses go hourly between Tacloban and Ormoc (P80, two hours).

TACLOBAN

☎ 053 / 242,683

Birthplace of the 'Rose of Tacloban', Imelda Marcos, Tacloban is an industrious town and Leyte's main metropolis. **Red Beach** (its WWII code name) is where MacArthur began his campaign to oust Japanese forces from the Philippines. Grab a 'Palo' jeepney to get there.

There are a couple of ATMs and a surprising number of Internet cafés. The **tourist office** (☎ 321 2048) is at the Leyte Hotel, north of the town.

Northwest of Tacloban, **Biliran Island** has some splendid beaches and waterfalls.

Sleeping

Welcome House Pension (☎ 321 2739; Santo Niño St; s/d from P200/350; 🔀) This bright new place has an assortment of rooms. Simple digs have fan and shared bathroom while the better ones have TV and air-con.

Rosvenil Pensione (☎ 321 2676; Burgos St; s/d P370/550; 🔀) Located in a great rambling house with a pleasant garden out front. The neat rooms all have air-con and TV.

Eating

Tacloban is famous for delicious cakes such as *binagol*, a sticky confection wrapped in banana leaves and baked in a coconut shell.

Seafood in Tacloban is worth pursuing; try the **San Pedro Bay** (meals P180) restaurant at Leyte Park Resort Hotel; it's in a colossal thatch hut at the end of the pier. **Socsargen Grill** (meals P70-140), next to Rosvenil Pensione, gets excellent reviews and does a roaring trade in freshly grilled meats and fish.

Getting There & Around

Long-haul ferries run to and from Manila and Cebu from the **wharf** (Bonifacio St).

From the **waterfront bus terminal** (Quezon Ave), ordinary buses run south to Ormoc (P80, two hours) and north to Catbalogan (P80, two hours) and Calbayog (P120, 3½ hours). There are also buses to Kayawan and Naval on Biliran Island (around P120, 2½ hours), and jeepneys to Basey in Samar (P15) for Sohoton National Park.

A tricycle to anywhere in town should cost P5.

SOHOTON NATURAL BRIDGE NATIONAL PARK

Named for a magnificent stone bridge connecting two mountain ridges, this national park has an expansive cave system, subterranean rivers, waterfalls and limestone formations. The area was supposedly used as a Stone Age burial site.

Tours of the park can be arranged by contacting **Mr Corales** (☎ 053-276 1151) in Basey. For the Panhulugan cave tour you will need to charter a boat (P700, for five to seven people), pay P150 for a guide (plus P200 for kerosene lighting) and fork out another P150 for entry to the park. If you just want to hike to the Sohoton natural bridge, a guide from Basey is P200. The jeepney from Tacloban to Basey is P15, but you must arrive before 8am to make the boat. In Basey, you can stay in the nondescript rooms of the **DENR Guest House** (d P300-400).

ORMOC

☎ 053 / 186,623

Ormoc is little more than the springboard for boats to Cebu. The violin-shaped **Lake Danao** makes a good day trip for a cool freshwater swim. Keep your eyes peeled; it's said to be the habitat of the giant eel. To get there catch a jeepney from the main bus station (P25).

Sleeping & Eating

Budget sleeping options in Ormoc leave a lot to be desired.

Don Felipe Hotel (☎ 255 2460; cnr Bonifacio St & Imelda Blvd; s/d from P360/420; 🅿) Has a pretty standard offering of frill-free rooms on the waterfront opposite the pier. There's a decent coffee shop.

Pongos Hotel (☎ 255 2540; Bonifacio St; s P216-420, d P336-600; 🅿) This place hasn't been refurbished since the Marcos era – but the sheets have probably been changed.

For inexpensive meals, try the busy **Zenaida's Fast Food** (Rizal St; meals P65) and **Chito's Chow Bar** (meals P60) on the waterfront. There are plenty of bakeries and fruit stalls in town.

Getting There & Away

Conveniently, the bus terminal is just over the road from the port. Several fast ferries go to and from Cebu daily (P580, two hours), as do slower craft (P280, five hours). Buses run north to Tacloban (P80, two hours) and south to destinations in Mindanao. A tricycle around town is P5.

MINDANAO

The sprawling region of Mindanao has equal measures of dazzling scenery and political unrest. Central, southern and western Mindanao, and much of the Sulu Archipelago, is the scene of ongoing hostilities between separatists and government forces. Travel to these areas is considered risky; consult local sources for the latest situation.

Islam had established a footing on the island long before the arrival of the Spanish. Today, Muslim-dominated areas contest their subjugation to outside authorities. The Moro Islamic Liberation Front (MILF) is the main organisation fighting for autonomy, but in recent years the more militant Abu Sayyaf has been grabbing headlines. Abu Sayyaf has vied for the government's attention with indiscriminate violence, foreigner kidnappings and, more recently, bombings – including a ferry bombing in 2004 and explosions in Davao, General Santos and Manila in 2005. American 'advisers' and Filipino troops have battled Abu Sayyaf in the Sulu region intermittently since 2002.

The northeastern coast of Mindanao is generally considered as safe as anywhere else in the country. Once here you will find first-rate surfing on Siargao and a peaceful island-life existence on Camiguin.

Getting There & Away

All the big Philippine airlines (p595) provide services to Mindanao from Cebu City and Manila. Most major cities in Mindanao

WARNING

Before you head off to Mindanao, make sure your destination and travel route are safe. Your embassy and local news sources are likely to be more honest about the situation than tourist offices.

are serviced, including Cagayan de Oro, Surigao and Siargao Island (see p596).

WG&A, Negros Navigation and Sulpicio Lines (p597) all have long-haul services from Manila to Cagayan de Oro via Cebu or Dumaguete (around P2000, 35 hours). There are also long-haul boats to Surigao.

There are also smaller ferries to Bohol and Siquijor.

SURIGAO & SIARGAO ISLAND
☎ 086

Siargao Island, near Surigao city, is sprinkled with coves, villages, languid beaches and some outstanding surf. It's a wonder this place has slipped under the tourist radar for so long. The community of **General Luna** (GL) is home to surfing breaks that rank among the top five in the world; when the conditions are right, that is. These clean, fast swells host the **Siargao International Surfing Cup** every October. GL itself scoops the prettiest town in the Philippines award, and if braving the ocean's washing machine is not your thing, you can spend days exploring nearby waterfalls and caves or discovering palm-fringed islands.

The best spot for surfing is Tuazon point near the Cloud Nine resort. Boards can be rented in GL for about P200 per day.

Sleeping & Eating
Dexter Pension House (☎ 232 7526; San Nicolas St; s/d P150/300; ⌘) If you need to stay the night in Surigao, this place near the Plaza has passable, nondescript rooms in a (relatively) quiet building down an alley.

Bleached-out surfer types flock to the coast north of General Luna, within paddling distance of the popular breaks. All these resorts can organise day tours and boat trips. Many other places mushroom in the high surfing season (July to November), when prices can almost double.

Cloud Nine (☎ 0918 564 5981; d P600-800) Right by the surfers' boardwalk, the charming Cloud Nine has comfortable, fan-cooled *nipa* huts with bathrooms. There's a great restaurant here.

Jungle Reef Resort (☎ 0919 809 5774; d P350) This provides excellent, roomy, beachside A-frame bungalows and its own restaurant.

Ocean 101 Beach Resort (meals P100) This restaurant nearby gets rave reviews from ravenous surfers.

Jadestar Lodge (☎ 0919 234 4367; d P300-600) On the south side of GL, you'll find the seriously chilled Jadestar, which has alluring cottages around a meticulous beach garden and can whip up filling, delicious meals upon request.

Getting There & Away
Asian Spirit (www.asianspirit.com) flies three times a week between Cebu and Surigao (P1880) while **Seair** (www.flyseair.com) flies twice a week between Cebu and Siargao Island (P2700).

Cokaliong Shipping Lines has boats to Cebu most nights (P450 economy, 10 hours). Some of the big WG&A, Negros Navigation and Sulpicio boats (p597) also travel here from Manila.

There are two boats daily to Liloan (P130, 3½ hours) on Leyte from Lipata, about 10km northwest of Surigao. To get to Tacloban, catch the Liloan boat and continue by bus (P140, four hours).

Buses run from the Integrated bus terminal on the outskirts of Surigao. There are numerous air-con services to Cagayan de Oro (P335, six hours) via Butuan and to Davao (P450, eight hours).

The marathon Philtranco bus route passes through Surigao on its way from Davao to Manila via the regions of Leyte, Samar and Bicol – this option is strictly for masochists.

Getting Around
Several daily fastcraft leave Surigao for Dapa on Siargao (P210, one hour) from the **main wharf** (Borromeo St), south of the centre. On Siargao, jeepneys run from Dapa to General Luna (P15), or you can take a *habal-habal* (motorcycle taxi) for P50. Ask the driver for 'GL'.

CAGAYAN DE ORO
☎ 088 / pop 578,456

A spick-and-span, progressive city, Cagayan de Oro is a lively university town that's well connected to Cebu and the rest of Mindanao. The **tourist office** (☎ 726 394; Velez St) is south of the city centre. Head south or west of this city and you risk being caught up in conflict between the government and local rebel groups. The highway up the coast to Surigao is generally safe, though you should keep an eye on local news.

PHILIPPINES

The main drag is formed by T Neri St and Abejuela St, which are separated by a string of small parks.

The **Xavier University Folk Museum** (Museo de Oro; Corrales Ave; admission P10; ⏰ 8.30-11.30am & 2.30-5pm Tue-Fri, 8.30-11.30am Sat) houses artefacts from Muslim-Bukidnon culture.

Sleeping

Ramon's Hotel (☎ 857 4804; Burgos St; d P500-700; ✗) This relatively new, central hotel has a top setting, with the best-value rooms overlooking a river. There's a scenic balcony attached to the restaurant.

Nature's Pensionne (☎ 857 2274; T Chavez St; d P550-840; ✗) This has nice, clean rooms with air-con, private bathroom, TV and hot water.

Parkview Hotel (☎ 857 1197; cnr T Neri & General Capistrano Sts; d P275-495; ✗) An organised place that has economical rooms – check out a few as many boast brick-wall views.

Eating & Drinking

There's a variety of student hangouts serving beer and pizza on Velez St, south of T Neri St.

Bigby's Café (cnr Hayes St & Tiano Brothers St; meals P150) Serves dependable Western food to both locals and homesick expats in a snug, old-school diner setting.

Consuelo (Corrales Ave; all-you-can-eat P115) A popular buffet with an abundance of dishes – a great place to re-fuel after a 14 hour boat trip.

X-Cite Bar is a popular evening student watering hole opposite the Dynasty Court Hotel.

Getting There & Around

There is at least one flight daily from Cagayan de Oro to Manila (P4190) and Cebu (P2660).

There are long-haul boat services to Cebu (P515, 12 hours), plus smaller boats to Bohol (P420, nine hours) and sometimes to Siquijor Island. 'Pier' jeepneys sprint the 5km to the pier.

All bus services going to Davao and Zamboanga should be considered risky. There are regular air-con services northbound to Surigao (P335, six hours) via Butuan.

The airport is about 10km west of town (P130 by taxi). The main bus terminal is on the edge of town, beside the Agora Market (take a 'Gusa' or 'Cugman' jeepney from town). By taxi it's P60.

CAMIGUIN

☎ 088

Camiguin is a friendly little island packed with seven volcanoes, waterfalls, hot and cold springs and even an underwater cemetery which slid into the sea following an 1871 earthquake (you'll need to don scuba gear to see it). Its undulating landscape, with cloud-tipped volcanoes as a continuous backdrop, makes it a great place to strike out on your own and explore, either by foot or by using motorised transport. There's a couple of offshore, pearly-sand isles perfect for acting out Robinson Crusoe fantasies.

Seair (www.flyseair.com) flies here twice a week from Cebu (P1850) or you can catch a regular boat from Balingoan in Mindanao to Benoni (P70, 1½ hours) on Camiguin. Frequent buses run to Balingoan from Cagayan de Oro (P80 1½ hours).

Mambajao

☎ 088 / pop 33,110

In this shady capital of Camiguin, life rarely gets out of first gear. The Philippine National Bank can change US dollars and there's Internet access at the Shell petrol station. The Camiguin **tourist office** (Provincial Capitol building) has free maps of the island.

Enigmata (formerly Tarzan's Nest; ☎ 387 0273; dm P150-200, d P600-800; ⛵), near Mambajao, is a hippyesque artist hangout. It has a fantastic treehouse resort built around a towering hardwood tree. The rooms are veritable open-plan apartments swathed in murals and artwork. There's also a little pool and a good restaurant. The dirt road here turns off the highway about 2km east of Mambajao.

Around Mambajoe

The best budget resorts are on the black-sand beaches around the island's northern point, between 4km and 6km west of Mambajao. There are jeepneys every one to two hours (P6), or you can hire a tricycle or motorbike taxi for a negotiable P50 to P100 to get to any of the resorts. You can rent motorbikes for around P350 per day.

Green Tropical Pub (⏰ Tue-Sun; meals P80-130), just west of Mambajao, is an open restaurant with pizzas and Thai and Filipino dishes served with commanding ricefield vistas.

Bug-Ong

Several kilometres west along Camiguin's ring road lies the small township of Bug-Ong, home to a few resorts.

Jasmine by the Sea (☎ 387 9015; d P300-500) has cosy garden cottages with sea-view balconies. There are mountain bikes for hire for P150 per day, and both the Western and Filipino food gets great reviews.

Seascape (☎ 0916 876 9707; d P500) is right next to Jasmine, with big, austere bungalows on a quiet stretch of beach.

Agoho

Keep heading west for another kilometre and you'll come to the village of Agoho.

Camiguin Seaside Lodge (☎ 387 9031; cottages P500) has thoughtfully decked out cottages with a comfortable veranda on which to sit and watch the fishermen ply their trade. There's a big restaurant area.

PALAWAN

Palawan is fast becoming a haven for nature buffs and intrepid adventurers. Drifting on the Philippines western edge, this long sliver of jungle is one of the country's last ecological frontiers. The Amazonian interior is barely connected by a few snaking roads that will make your fillings jingle, and the convoluted coast is comprised of one breathtaking bay after another. Puerto Princesa is the energetic capital from where you can explore nearby Sabang, with its famous underground river, and Port Barton, a nice stretch of beach popular with weary travellers. Towering limestone cliffs shelter the northern community of El Nido, and the Calamian group of islands offer up plenty of island beaches and unbeatable diving to those who make the effort to get there.

Only the road between Puerto Princesa and Roxas is sealed, and the infrequency of transport can test a Zen master's patience – seafaring *bangcas* are a popular way of avoiding dusty inland routes.

Getting There & Away

PAL, Seair and Air Philippines fly daily between Manila and Puerto Princesa, and Cebu Pacific also flies from Cebu to Puerto Princesa (see p595 for contact details). Seair has very useful hopping routes – Manila, Coron,

El Nido, Puerto Princesa – but schedules seem to change daily. One 'hop' costs from P2100 to P2930 (see p596). The airport departure tax from Puerto Princesa is P40.

WG&A sails from Manila to Puerto Princesa twice a week, once directly (P1715, 27 hours), and once via Coron (P1270, 14 hours). Milagrosa J Shipping sails between Puerto Princesa and Iloilo (P495, 26 hours) via the Cuyo Islands.

There is a reliably irregular cargo boat between Brooke's Point, south of Puerto Princesa, and Sabah in Malaysia.

PUERTO PRINCESA

☎ 048 / pop 183,256

Puerto is more like a village on diesel steroids than a city, but in amongst its hustle and bustle lie some quiet sidestreets and several quality sleeping and dining options. Rizal Ave is the main east-west drag, extending from the port in the west to the airport. The small **Palawan Museum** (Rizal Ave; admission P20; ⊙ 9am-5pm Mon-Sat) is worth a look; it's beside the city plaza. Be sure to stock up on cash as this may be your last chance in Palawan to use an ATM or get a decent exchange rate.

Information

There are branches of the Equitable PCI Bank and Philippine National Bank on Rizal Ave with ATMs; they also give cash advances on credit cards. There are half a dozen or so Internet cafés on Rizal Ave. The main **post office** (Burgos St) is just off Rizal Ave.

There's a **city tourist office** (☎ 433 2983) at the airport, and a provincial **tourist office** (☎ 433 2968; Provincial Capitol, Rizal Ave) at the corner of Fernandez St.

The **Bureau of Immigration** (☎ 433 2248; Rizal Ave; ⊙ 8am-noon & 1-5pm Mon-Fri) is upstairs in a white building next to the Palawan Hotel. Visa extensions take about 30 minutes and cost P2020 for up to 59 days.

WARNING

Malaria is an issue in rural areas. Use the mosquito nets provided by most guesthouses and coat yourself with insect repellent at dusk. Minuscule, stinging sandflies (aptly named *nik-niks*) delight in biting exposed skin and can be a curse on some western beaches.

Sleeping

Banwa Art House (☎ 434 8167; Liwanag St; dm P150, s P300-500, d P350-500) This place oozes charm from every artisan craft adorning its walls. There's a groovy bamboo lounge, surrounded by a waterfall of vines, that plays excellent tunes. It's located near the corner of Mendoza and Rizal Sts.

Casa Linda Tourist Inn (☎ 433 2606; Trinidad Rd; casalind@mozcom.com; s P400-650, d P500-750; ✹) Slightly upmarket, this splendid place off Rizal Ave is wall-to-wall bamboo and has a big, tranquil garden courtyard with (bamboo!) reading gazebo.

Moana Hotel (☎ 434 4753; Rizal St; moanatel@moz com.com; d P650-850; ✹) Just out of the airport towards town, this hotel has comfy rooms surrounding a pool, and a great Italian restaurant. There is also a dive shop on site.

Eating

Kalui Restaurant (369 Rizal Ave; meals P120; ☽ dinner Mon-Sat) For possibly the best Filipino food in the country try this elegant restaurant, about 1km from the airport towards town. It serves huge five-course seafood feasts for P275, incorporating various catch-of-the-day combinations plus tropical fruit desserts.

Neva's Place (D Manga St; meals P40-100) Great budget Filipino food as well as pastas and gourmet pizzas served in a blissful garden. It's near the Children's Park.

Vegetarian House (cnr Burgos & Manalo Sts; mains P60) Yes you read that correctly. This is a rarity of a restaurant in the meat-mad Philippines, but don't expect peace, love and mungbeans – just a big range of tasty faux-meat dishes in austere surrounds.

MEGA-SPLURGE!

To really blow the budget, cast off on an epic seven-day diving trip 200km southeast into the Sulu Sea to **Tubbataha Reef National Park**. This place was one of Jacques Cousteau's favourite underwater retreats. There's been no dynamite fishing at Tubbataha, and it's reputed to have some of the most pristine reefs left in the country. **Moana Dive Centre** (☎ 434 5198; moanatel@mozcom .com) can arrange trips on one of the several boats heading there for around US$800 per person, unlimited dives included!

You can slurp delicious soup at the numerous **Vietnamese restaurants** (pho noodle soup P25-50) along Rizal Ave, catering to boat people who settled here.

Getting There & Around

The main bus terminal is at the San Jose market 6km north of town, to get there grab a multi-cab (mini-jeepney) from anywhere along Rizal St (P7).

From Puerto Princesa there are buses south to Quezon (P160, four hours) and to most northern destinations. There are several daily buses to Roxas (P156) and at least two morning buses to El Nido (P300, eight hours).

Jumbo jeepneys also run between Puerto Princesa, Sabang and Port Barton.

The set tricycle rate into town is P40, but if you flag down a ride from the road out front it's only P7. Off-road motorbikes can be hired for P700 per day.

SABANG

☎ 048

Tiny Sabang has a long expanse of beach and is famed for the impressive 8km underground river in **St Paul Subterranean National Park** – a highlight of Palawan. This navigable river winds under limestone and marble cliffs through a spectacular cave before emptying into the sea. From the beach in Sabang you can either take a boat to the mouth of the river for P600 (up to six people), or take a two-hour hike along the **monkey trail** through the beautiful jungle of the national park. Be sure to pay the P200 park entry fee at the pier before you set off.

Sleeping & Eating

There are several places to stay by Sabang Beach, all with restaurants.

Blue Bamboo (☎ 0918 646 7179; d P100-350; mains P75-150) This beach has some truly rustic micro-huts and nicer, intricate and airy bamboo cottages – all with sea views. Located 400m left past the pier.

Dab Dab (☎ 0910 843 9606; d P400-500; mains P95-155) Just before Blue Bamboo, this place has art-deco native cottages with some bonus personal touches.

Mary's Cottages (☎ 0920 432 1139; d P250-450; mains P45-90) Recently re-opened, with simple huts right on its own perfect bay. It's at the far end of the beach; turn right at the pier.

Getting There & Away

The dirt track out to Sabang is butt-smacking, but worth the effort. There are early morning jeepneys and buses from Puerto Princesa to Sabang (P90, 2½ hours).

In the high season (and even then demand permitting) weekly *bangcas* make the (relatively) smoother journey from Sabang to El Nido (P1500, around seven hours) with drop-offs, but not pick-ups, in Port Barton (P800, three hours).

NORTH PALAWAN
Port Barton

☎ 048

People find themselves unable to leave Port Barton, and only partly because of the town's poor transport links. Set on a small, attractive cove, the area has some fine islands in the bay and good snorkelling, but most people spend their days reading and hammock-hopping. Port Barton shuts down in the low season.

SLEEPING & EATING

Port Barton has several beachside options.

Elsa's Beach Cottages (☎ 0920 368 4745; d P300-500) This place is run by a particularly friendly family and has snug, native-style cottages. The restaurant serves a mean shrimp curry (P150).

Swissipini Lodge (☎ 0921 616 5671; d P300-700) There's a range of clean, huddled cottages, some with beach views, in this well-run place. There is a dive-shop 'castle' on site and they do cash advances.

El Dorado Sunset Cottages (☎ 433 2110; d P350-550) Over the creek at the northern end of town, El Dorado has a lively bar run by Dan from Chicago, and nine clean cottages with frilly extras. There's real coffee and a great range of cocktails.

GETTING THERE & AWAY

There is a single morning jeepney going to and from Puerto Princesa (P160, four hours). You can get off at San Jose and charter a motorcycle taxi for a steep P700 to Port Barton.

El Nido

☎ 048

Concealed in a cove on Palawan's north-western tip and punctured by immense limestone cliffs, El Nido is the island's

Aladdin's Cave. The friendly town clings to the bay's small, grey beach and graciously integrates the swelling number of backpackers and expats that find their way here. The edible nests of the tiny swiftlets that inhabit the cliffs give the town its name. There's some good diving and snorkelling, and limitless possibilities for exploring the islands, lagoons and perfect beaches of the **Bacuit Archipelago**. **Corong-Corong**, just across the rocky headland, also has a good beach.

INFORMATION

Considerably more useful that the tourist office is **El Nido Boutique & Art Shop** (☎ 048 5509), near the wharf. Run like Swiss clockwork by Judy, the boutique arranges boat trips, treks, kayak and bike hire, offers folders on everything to do in the area, sells airline tickets and gives cash advances on Visa cards. Oh, and they sell art and food.

ACTIVITIES

Palawan Divers (☎ 0916 777 6917; 2 dives P2000) has boat trips to surrounding islands.

Snorkelling and island-hopping trips to the Bacuit Archipelago cost P350 to P450 including lunch.

SLEEPING

Many resorts are clustered on the beach in town.

El Nido Cliffside Cottages (☎ 0919 785 6625; d P350-500) On the road to Corong-Corong beach and enveloped by the eerie cliffs, this tranquil place has clean courtyard bungalows. The smiling service is no extra charge.

Tandikan Cottages (☎ 0917 961 3232; d P500-600) Neat, but slightly older bungalows, all with verandas right on the town's beach.

Gloria's & Rico's (☎ 0921 622 7938; d P400-600) Run by the tetchy Gloria and her son. The nicer rooms upstairs have a balcony overlooking the bay.

Lualhati Cottage (☎ 0919 319 6683; d P200-350) A little further up from Cliffside, this simple guesthouse has straightforward rooms around a family garden. It's under the guidance of the fascinating Mr Lualhati, who used to train American soldiers in jungle combat and work for Philippine intelligence. Currently he offers great massages.

PHILIPPINES

THE PERFECT BEACH

There's a rumour that the island described in Alex Garland's backpacker classic The Beach was somewhere in the Calamian island group (Garland set the book in Thailand, but admits that the real island was somewhere in the Philippines).

EATING & DRINKING

Squidos (Quezon St; mains P100-160) Try this spot for Filipino and Western food with a hint of French.

Ric Son's Restaurant (mains P60-150) This place seems to be popular for breakfast – and most other meals.

The beach side Blue Karrot Bar and the Shipwrecked Bar are both lively places for a drink and do bar snacks. They are on the main street near the wharf.

GETTING THERE & AROUND

Seair (www.flyseair.com) flies from El Nido to Manila, Busuanga and Puerto Princesa (see p596). The only way to the airport is by tricycle for a non-negotiable P150 (we smell tricycle mafia).

There are also two cargo boats a week to Manila (P800, 30 hours). They're old boats but they're under no pressure to meet a schedule by heading into a storm, so they're fairly safe. From Manila, boats leave from the end of Pier 2 in North Harbour – ask the taxi driver for Isla Putingbato. Call **San Nicholas Shipping** (☎ 02-245 2830) for information. A weekly boat from **Ateinza Shipping Lines** (☎ 02-243 8845) also leaves for Coron (P650, nine hours) from Liminangcong, 1½ hours south of El Nido.

AFRICAN SAFARI?

In 1976, several kinds of endangered African animals were brought from Kenya to a wildlife reserve on Calauit Island. Today, visitors can see giraffes, impala, zebras and gazelles roaming wild. The most economical way to get there involves renting a motorbike from Coron town and riding up to Quezon (two hours), from where you can rent a boat (P200) for the short hop across to Calauit. Entry to the island is P300.

High season *bangcas* wade down to Sabang (P1500, about seven hours), with drop-offs in Port Barton (P1000, four hours).

Several morning busses make the transPalawan journey to Puerto Princesa (P300, eight hours).

Busuanga Island – Coron
pop 22,711

Some of the most beautiful isles in the Philippines lie here, scattered halfway between Mindoro and Palawan. The Calamian Group Islands hold as much allure above water as they do below it. Several WWII wrecks make for exhilarating dives and beaches fringe rocky islands where crystal-clear lagoons loll concealed within.

The Japanese shipwrecks dotting the area provide sanctuary to a magnificent variety of fish and coral and are regarded as among the world's premier wreck dives. Coron Island has an incredible dive at **Barracuda Lake** (admission P75), where the clear water gets scorching hot as you descent through its swirling, volcanic thermals. You can also go for a dip in Coron Island's unspoiled **Lake Cayangan** (admission P200), home to the petite and elusive Tagbanua people. The Swagman office on the highway changes cash and cheques.

ACTIVITIES

Many dives at Coron are less than 30m, but some of the best sites are reserved for advanced divers. A dive with all equipment costs US$16 to $US20.

Boat trips to Coron Island usually include snorkelling, as well as a visit to Coron Island's lakes, and cost around P1100 for up to 10 people. There are **hot springs** a short tricycle ride from town (P100 return). Several places hire out sea kayaks for around P250 and motorbikes for P500.

SLEEPING & EATING

A P5 tricycle ride from the Coron town wharf will bring you to the central market area, half of which is perched on bamboo stilts.

Seadive Resort (☎ 0918 400 0448; www.seadive resort.com.ph; d P300-700; ☒) A three-storey monolith on the sea accessed by a long walkway, this place has it all – decent rooms, restaurant, bar, Internet and a busy dive shop. It can organize island-hopping and kayak and motorbike rental.

L&M Pe Sea Lodge & Restaurant (☎ 0921 354 9693; d P200-800; 🌂) Built out over the water just west of the market, this is a warm and friendly cheapie with quality food. The tiny top-floor room has unbeatable panoramic views.

Krystal Lodge (☎ 0910 686 6757; d P200-1200) This great place is a maze of bamboo walkways ending in rooms that range from passable boxes to airy, deluxe 'apartments' jutting well out to sea. There's an inviting restaurant where you can arrange day trips around the islands.

Bistro Coron (meals P85-195) A cheap, French bistro on one of the Philippines' most isolated islands – it works for us. The French chef whips up mouthwatering delights to enthusiastic regulars. The tenderloin steak in black pepper sauce with sautéed herb potatoes (P195) is a must.

GETTING THERE & AWAY

Seair and Asian Spirit fly from Manila to little YKR airport on the northern side of Busuanga Island (P2930) and provide chartered jeepneys for the one-hour trip to Coron town (P150). You can book Seair flights at **Coron Tours** (☎ 0920 909 8639; Real St). **Asian Spirit** (☎ 0921 691 4579) is on the national highway.

PHILIPPINES DIRECTORY

ACCOMMODATION

Accommodation in the Philippines ranges from plush beachside bungalows to stuffy hotel shoeboxes, and everything in between. Prices vary considerably depending on where you are and at what time of year you are there. In much of the country expect to pay about P250 for a room with shared bathroom and fan; with private bathroom, P400 is fairly typical. The rooms in Manila are the worst value; a dingy single with shared bathroom can cost as much as P600. Batad, on the other hand, has charming rustic quarters with priceless views for only P100. Most rooms have electrical outlets accepting two flat, parallel prongs and pumping out 220 volts at 50–60Hz.

Resort accommodation, in popular destinations like Boracay and Puerto Galera, is a little more expensive. Many resorts offer native-style *nipa* (palm-leaf) huts, with or without attached bathroom. Beachfront huts cost more than huts set back from the water, and almost all rates double during the high season from November to April. During Filipino holidays like Holy Week (Easter) and Christmas, Filipinos embark on a mass exodus from the cities, and rooms at popular spots become scarce. The prices quoted in this book are all high-season prices.

ACTIVITIES

Scuba diving is the most popular adventure activity in the Philippines, but there is also a small surf scene, and windsurfing and mountain biking are growing in popularity.

Cycling

If you bring your own bicycle, there are excellent cycling opportunities on the quieter islands though, as elsewhere, you should beware of lunatic drivers. Spare parts are available in major cities and even small villages have repair shops catering to the local tricycle drivers. The most accessible mountain-biking area is Moalboal, on Cebu, which has several bike-hire companies that can organise guided trips into the remote interior of the island.

Diving

Despite the popularity of dynamite fishing, the Philippines still boasts some topnotch dive sites. The WWII shipwrecks at Coron (Busuanga Island) offer outstanding wreck dives, while the impressive reefs around Puerto Galera (Mindoro), El Nido and Puerto Princesa (Palawan), Siquijor and Apo Islands (Negros), Alona Beach (Bohol) and Moalboal and Malapascua Island (Cebu) offer a more traditional fish-and-coral environment. Beginners should head for the dozens of competitive scuba schools in Puerto Galera or Boracay.

Generally, it costs certified divers about US$18 to US$26 for a dive with all equipment. Open-water diving courses go for about US$300.

Surfing

The top surfing destination in the Philippines is Siargao Island, off the northeast coast of Mindanao. In the right weather conditions, the waves here can be Hawaiian in scale. Cloud Nine, the best surfing spot on the island, is the setting for the annual Siargao International Surfing Cup held in October.

There is also Surf Beach at San Juan, near San Fernando (La Union) on the west coast of Luzon. Samar's east coast boasts some very impressive breaks, though many are unexplored and inaccessible to all but the most determined board-heads.

Trekking

This is possible just about anywhere – the entire archipelago is criss-crossed with paths and trails, though they're not always clearly marked. With the right planning, a trek can avoid practically all contact with cobbles, asphalt and exhaust fumes. Volcano climbing is a local speciality, though some of the more notoriously active ones are probably best avoided; insurance companies might not pay out for lava-burn claims.

Windsurfing

The island of Boracay is the Philippine mecca for windsurfers. The best conditions for both beginner and advanced levels can be found on the east coast.

BOOKS

Lonely Planet publishes *Philippines*, the pintsized *Filipino (Tagalog) Phrasebook*, and for the mask-and-flippers fans there's *Diving & Snorkelling Philippines*. If you want to brush up on some recent history, Stanley Karnow's Pulitzer Prize–winning effort *In Our Image* takes an intriguing look at the US relationship with its biggest colony. *Ants for Breakfast – Archaeological Adventures among the Kalinga,* by James M Skibo, is a tasty work of asides and insights gleaned from fieldwork among the Kalinga people of the Cordilleras.

BUSINESS HOURS

Government offices and public authorities, including tourist offices, are generally open from 8am to 5pm Monday to Friday, often with a break from noon to 1pm. Banks usually open from 9am to 3pm. To be safe, it's best to visit embassies and consulates between 9am and noon on weekdays. Airline offices are usually open from 9am to 5pm on weekdays and 9am to noon on Saturday. Airport offices are also open on Sunday. Depart-

ment stores and shopping centres are usually open from 10am to around 9pm at night. Businesses first open their doors between 8am and 10am. Unless otherwise noted, restaurants are typically open for breakfast from 8am to 10am, lunch from 11am to 2pm and dinner from 6pm to around 10pm.

CLIMATE

The Philippines is hot and humid throughout the year, with a January–June dry period and a July–December wet period. During the wet season the islands are prone to flooding, leading to an annual displacement of people living in low-lying areas. January, February and March are probably the best months for a visit, as it starts to get hotter after March and the heat peaks in May.

From May to November the islands are often battered by savage typhoons, which are characterised by strong winds and rainstorms of almost cataclysmic proportions. During a typhoon, flights may be grounded, ferries can stop running and even road transport can grind to a halt. See also the climate charts (p924).

CUSTOMS

The usual rules apply; personal effects, 200 cigarettes or two tins of tobacco, and 2L of alcohol are free of duty. Illicit drugs, firearms and pornography are forbidden, as is the export of coral, mussels and certain types of orchid, and animal products such as turtle shells and python skins. The amount of foreign currency taken out upon departure can't exceed the sum brought in on arrival.

DANGERS & ANNOYANCES

The Philippines has a few pitfalls for the unwary. Mindanao (the central and southwest regions in particular) and the Sulu archipelago are the scene of clashes between the army and US 'advisers' on one side and the Abu Sayyaf terrorist group and the Moro Islamic Liberation Front (MILF) on the other. There have been bombings and other civil disturbances in Davao, General Santos and even Manila. The north coast of Mindanao is generally pretty safe, but check with your embassy and local news sources before heading off. Across the country NPA rebels occasionally stage attacks on police stations and military personnel, though they don't seem to bother tourists, unlike Abu Sayyaf rebels.

Bus companies, shipping lines and even airlines in the Philippines are legendary for their cavalier attitude to safety. There have been a number of high-profile shipping and aviation disasters in recent years. As a general rule, the most popular routes are safer, while the craziest drivers and more dilapidated vehicles are reserved for obscure regional itineraries.

As for annoyances, you'll probably find you don't share the Filipino enthusiasm for roosters, particularly when the little beasts wake you for the 15th time in one night. Just as inescapable is the wail of karaoke. Most hotels are within earshot of a karaoke bar or restaurant, so pack a pair of earplugs. In some cities, heavy air-pollution may make you feel like you've been sucking on a bus exhaust after taking a 20-minute stroll.

In the prostitution hotspots of Angeles, Subic Bay, Sabang Beach on Mindoro, and parts of Manila, any single male is likely to be viewed as a potential customer. If you're not looking for this kind of 'entertainment', the constant offers can be quite demoralising.

DISABLED TRAVELLERS

Steps up to hotels, tiny cramped toilets and narrow doors are the norm almost everywhere in the Philippines. Lifts, if present, are often out of order, and boarding any form of rural transport, from jeepneys to *bangcas* (pumpboats), is likely to be fraught with difficulty.

On the other hand, most Filipinos are more than willing to lend a helping hand,

and do so without ingratiating themselves in an embarrassing way. The cost of hiring a taxi for a day and possibly an assistant as well is not excessive.

EMBASSIES & CONSULATES
Embassies & Consulates in the Philippines

Most embassies and consulates are among the bright lights and shiny skyscrapers of Makati in Manila. Most of the office blocks here require you to leave a piece of photo ID with the security guard on the door.

Australia (Map pp600–1; ☎ 02-757 8100; 23rd fl, Tower 2 RCBC Plaza, 6819 Ayala Ave, Makati)
Brunei (Map pp600–1; ☎ 02-816 2836; 11th fl, BPI Bldg, Ayala Ave, cnr Paseo de Roxas, Makati)
Canada (Map pp600–1; ☎ 02-857 9000; 6th fl, Tower 2, RCBC Plaza 6819 Ayala Ave, Makati)
France (Map pp600–1; ☎ 02-857 6900; 16th fl, Pacific Star Bldg, cnr Gil Puyat Ave & Makati Ave, Makati)
Germany (Map pp600–1; ☎ 02-892 4906; 6th fl, Solid Bank Bldg, 777 Paseo de Roxas, Makati)
Indonesia (Map pp600–1; ☎ 02-892 5061; 185 Salcedo St, Makati)
Japan (Map pp600–1; ☎ 02-551 5710; 2627 Roxas Blvd, Pasay City)
Laos (Map pp600–1; ☎ 02-852 5759; 34 Lapu-Lapu St, Magallanes, Makati)
Malaysia (Map pp600–1; ☎ 02-817 4581; 107 Tordesillas St, Makati)
Myanmar (Map pp600–1; ☎ 02-817 2373; Xanland Bldg, 152 Amorsolo St, Makati)
New Zealand (Map pp600–1; ☎ 02-891 5358; 23rd fl, BPI Buendia Center, Gil Puyat Ave, Makati)
Singapore (Map pp600–1; ☎ 02-751 2345; 35th fl, Tower 1, Enterprise Center, 6766 Ayala Ave, Makati)

SCAMS

Manila, in particular, has a fine tradition of con artists, rip-off merchants and pickpockets. Thankfully, most rely on guile, so violent crime isn't so common.

Beware of people who claim to have met you before, particularly in Ermita. Confidence tricksters hit on solo travellers, particularly new arrivals, and invite them home. The situation ends with the traveller being drugged and robbed. Never leave your drink unattended in bars and clubs. People who approach you on the street to change money at high rates can nail you with really good amateur-magician card tricks – turning P1000 into P100 with sleight-of-hand. There are also phoney police officers and other unofficial 'officials'; a favourite scam is to ask to check your money for counterfeit notes, only to hand it back with notes missing or replaced with fakes.

Several of the *kalesa* (two-wheeled horse-drawn cart) drivers around Ermita and Intramuros can be hard work as well – prices can change suddenly. Just make sure you agree on the price before setting off. If you're taking a taxi, some people recommend writing down the licence plate number just in case you've hired the type that drives off with your luggage.

Thailand (Map pp600-1; ☎ 02-815 4220;
107 Rada St, Makati)
UK (Map pp600-1; ☎ 02-816 7116;
15th fl, LV Locsin Bldg, 6752 Ayala Ave, Makati)
USA (Map pp602-3; ☎ 02-528 63000;
1201 Roxas Blvd, Ermita)
Vietnam (Map pp600-1; ☎ 02-524 0364;
554 Vito Cruz St, Malate)

Philippine Embassies & Consulates Abroad

For Philippine diplomatic offices in Southeast Asia, see the relevant country chapter.
Australia (☎ 02-6273 2535; www.philembassy.au.com; 1 Moonah Place, Yarralumla, ACT 2600)
Canada (☎ 613-233 1121; http://www.philcongen-toronto.com/; Ste 606, 130 Albert St, Ottawa, ON KIP5G4)
France (☎ 01 44 14 57 00; ambaphilparis@wanadoo.fr; 4 Hameau de Boulainvilliers, 75016 Paris)
Germany (☎ 030-864 9500; www.philippine-embassy .de; Uhlandstrasse 97, 10715 Berlin)
Japan (☎ 03-5562 1600; www.tokyope.org; 5-15-5 Roppongi, Minato-ku, Tokyo 106-8537)
New Zealand (☎ 04-472 9848; embassy@wellington -pe.co.nz; 50 Hobson St, Thorndon, Wellington)
UK (☎ 020-7937 1600; www.philemb.org.uk; 9A Palace Green, Kensington, London W8 4QE)
USA (☎ 202-467 9300; www.philippineembassy-usa.org; 1600 Massachusetts Ave NW, Washington DC 20036)

FESTIVALS & EVENTS

Every Filipino town manages to squeeze in at least one fiesta a year, accompanied by frenzied eating, drinking and merrymaking. Some of the most lively fiestas and festivals are listed here:

January
Vigan Town Fiesta Luzon's Spanish colonial gem commemorates St Paul in the third week of January.

April/May
Panaad Held in Bacolod on Negros, Panaad is a crafts festival as well as the culmination of several weeks of neighbourhood fiestas in Bacolod.

September
Peñafrancia In the third week of September thousands of devotees make a pilgrimage to Naga in southeastern Luzon for the celebration of the Virgin of Peñafrancia, the Bicol region's patron saint.

October
MassKara On the weekend nearest 19 October, Bacolod on Negros goes joyfully crazy with the 'Many Faces Festival', which sees participants wearing elaborate, smiley-face masks and dancing in the streets.

December
Lantern Festival On the closest Saturday to Christmas, a number of truly gigantic Christmas lanterns are paraded through San Fernando (Pampanga) in Luzon; the lanterns remain on display until January.

FOOD & DRINK
Food

The native cuisine blends a number of influences, particularly from China and Spain, with the main flavours being ginger, tamarind, onion, vinegar, soy sauce and herbs like bay leaves rather than Asian spices. *Turo turo* (point-point) restaurants are everywhere – they display their food in cafeteria-style glass cases and you simply point-point to your order.

Favourite Filipino snacks and dishes:
Arroz Caldo Thick rice soup with chicken, garlic, ginger and onions.
Bangus Milkfish, lightly grilled, stuffed and baked.
Kare-Kare Meat (usually intestines) in coconut sauce.
Lechon Spit-roast baby pig with liver sauce.
Lumpia Spring rolls filled with meat or vegetables.
Mami Noodle soup, like *mee* soup in Malaysia or Indonesia.
Menudo Stew with vegetables, liver or pork.
Pancit Stir-fried *bihon* (white) or *canton* (yellow) noodles with meat and vegetables.
Pinangat A Bicol-region vegetable dish laced with hot peppers.
Pinakbet Vegetables with shrimp paste, garlic, onions and ginger.
Torta Fried eggplant and egg.

Drink

Stick to bottled water; it's sold everywhere and will set you back around P15 to P25. Tea is served in Chinese restaurants; elsewhere instant coffee rules, except in the top-end hotels, where imported beans are often used.

Other nonalcoholic drinks:
Buko juice Young coconut juice with floating pieces of jelly-like flesh.
Calamansi juice A refreshing cordial made from lime juice, credited with curative effects.
Gulaman A sweet concoction made from water, ice, sweet syrup and chunks of agar jelly.
Halo-halo A tall, cold glass of milky crushed ice with fresh fruit and ice cream.
Iced tea Probably the most popular drink after soft drinks, made with real brewed tea, lemon juice and sweet syrup.

San Miguel is very palatable and is one of the cheapest beers in the world at around P18 per bottle. San Miguel also brews a beer called Red Horse; it's ludicrously strong so make sure you are close to home when you order your 1L bottle. Carlsberg and other foreign brands are increasingly present. Tanduay rum is the national drink, and amazingly cheap at around P20 for 375ml – it's usually served with coke. Approach *tuba* with caution – it's a strong local 'wine' made from fermented coconut. There's also *basi*, made from sugarcane juice.

Go to p963 for more on food and drink vocabulary.

GAY & LESBIAN TRAVELLERS

Bakla (gay men) and *binalaki* (lesbians) are almost universally accepted in the Philippines. There are well-established gay centres in major cities, but foreigners should be wary of hustlers and police harassment. Remedios Circle in Malate, Manila, is the site of a June gay-pride parade and the centre for nightlife. For up-to-date information on gay life in the Philippines, you can check out the **Utopia Asian Gay & Lesbian Resources** (www.utopia-asia.com) and the **Asian Gay Guide** (www.dragoncastle.net).

HOLIDAYS

Offices and banks are closed on public holidays, although shops and department stores stay open. Good Friday is the only day when the entire country closes down – even public transport stops running, and PAL remains grounded. The public holidays are:

New Year's Day 1 January
Maundy Thursday, Good Friday & Easter Sunday March/April
Araw ng Kagitingan (Bataan Day) 9 April
Labour Day 1 May
Independence Day 12 June
All Saints' Day 1 November
Bonifacio Day (National Heroes Day) 30 November
Christmas Day 25 December
Rizal Day 30 December
New Year's Eve 31 December

INTERNET ACCESS

Surprisingly fast Internet cafés are sprouting with reckless abandon all over the Philippines, particularly in towns with a high school or university. Shopping centres usually have at least one cybercafé and rates tend to be around P20 to P40 per hour. Many big-city cafés offer file-transfer and CD-burning facilities. The most expensive place to surf might be El Nido on Palawan (P100 per hour) while places such as Cebu and Baguio are a bargain at around P15 per hour.

INTERNET RESOURCES

www.dfa.gov.ph The Department of Foreign Affairs site has lists of Philippine embassies and consulates abroad, as well as foreign embassies and consulates in the Philippines. It also lists current Philippines visa info.

www.lakbay.net This site has lots of useful Philippines links, as well as some shipping and bus schedules, and an online air-ticket booking service.

www.divephil.com Offers a lot of general information about diving and dive sites in the Philippines and is a good resource for scuba enthusiasts.

www.filipinolinks.com This vast directory has an extensive set of links relating to all aspects of the country.

www.philnews.com This has a fantastically thorough pile of local news and views, and includes links to all the main daily newspapers.

www.tourism.gov.ph This official tourism site (called WOW! Philippines) is a good place to start, but it has a slightly fabricated feel.

www.travel.state.gov Mildly paranoid but useful travel information and advisories are available from the US State Department. The US is said to have the best Western intelligence-gathering network in the Philippines.

LANGUAGE

Filipino (or Tagalog) is one of the country's two official languages, alongside English. It belongs to the Malayo-Polynesian family of languages, which spreads from Hawaii to Madagascar. Tagalog was renamed Filipino in officialdom to make it more acceptable to people outside the language's heartland around Manila. Cebuano (Visaya) is spoken throughout many of the central islands. Most Filipinos speak good English, making it one of the easiest countries in the region for communication. See the Language chapter for some useful Tagalog phrases (p963).

DID YOU KNOW?

One of the first major email viruses was invented and unleashed by a Filipino IT student in 1999. It seems very Filipino that it was called the 'I love you' virus.

LEGAL MATTERS

Corruption is an issue in the Philippines. If you are arrested, your embassy may not be able to do anything more than provide you with a list of local lawyers and keep an eye on how you're being treated. Drugs in particular are an absurd risk; penalties range from long prison terms to death. Even being caught with marijuana for personal use can mean jail. The *shabu* (crystal methamphetamine) epidemic is a real problem, and official attitudes on drugs are very tough indeed.

If you have something stolen and need to get a police report for your insurance company, it's not a good idea to take your watch or other valuables with you when you visit the police station. Things often 'go missing'. Get some advice from your hotel owner or manager before going to a police station – it might be easier if someone accompanies you.

MAPS

The Nelles Verlag *Philippines* map is a good map of the islands at a scale of 1:1,500,000. More useful to the traveller are the excellent locally produced *E-Z Maps*, which cover Manila, Makati, Quezon City, Baguio, Boracay, Cebu, Davao and Palawan, for about P80 to P100 per map.

MEDIA
Magazines & Newspapers

There are about 20 major national and regional English-language newspapers, from the staid *Manila Bulletin* to the openly seditious *Philippine Daily Inquirer*. Well-stocked newspaper stands can be found in towns and cities all over the country, though all papers have a heavily Manila-centric world view. The Philippines prints lots of glossy magazines – *Mega* and *Metro* are fashion/lifestyle glossies, heavily patterned after the American *Vanity Fair*. *Newsbreak* and *Graphic* present weekly news summaries along with columns on a variety of topics.

LEGAL AGE

- you can begin driving at 16
- voting age is 18
- drinking is allowed from 18
- sex is legal at 18

Radio & TV

Radio and TV operate on a commercial basis. There are 22 TV channels and seven of these broadcast from Manila, sometimes in English, sometimes in Tagalog, and usually in a hybrid combination of the two. There are plenty of provincial radio stations, as well as big Manila broadcasters like DZMM (630 kHz), run by the TV network ABC-CBN.

Many hotels offer cable TV with international channels as part of their service. Look for the Viva Cinema channel for hours of Filipino classics – no subtitles, alas. Lighthearted, glitzy entertainment such as beauty pageants and dubbed Latin American soap operas like *The Rich Also Cry* keep housewives in tears.

MONEY

The unit of currency is the peso (or piso), divided into 100 centavos. Banknotes come in denominations of five, 10, 20, 50, 100, 500 and 1000 pesos. The most common coins are 10 and 25 centavos, and one and five pesos.

ATMs

There are ATMs located in cities and towns throughout the country, but they often go offline (especially on Fridays and weekends). You stand your best chance during banking hours from 9am to 3pm on weekdays. The Maestro/Cirrus network is most readily accepted, followed by Visa/Plus cards, then by American Express (Amex). The most common, and least unreliable, ATMs belong to Equitable PCI Bank (PCI), Philippine National Bank (PNB) and Bank of the Philippine Islands (BPI). Most ATMs have a P5000 per-transaction withdrawal limit, which can be a pain if you are being slapped with high fees back home. The HSBC ATMs in Manila and Cebu let you take out up to P20,000 per transaction.

Bargaining

When shopping in public markets or even shops, Filipinos try to get a 10% discount. They almost always succeed. Foreign customers will automatically be quoted a price that is around 20% more than normal or, in places that deal mainly with tourists, up to 50% more.

Cash

Exchanging travellers cheques can be like pulling teeth, and Philippine ATMs are notoriously unreliable. Emergency cash in US dollars can help get you back to civilisation if you run out of pesos on an isolated island. Other currencies, such as pound sterling or euro, are more difficult to change outside of the bigger cities.

'Sorry, no change' becomes a very familiar line. Stock up on notes smaller than P100 at every opportunity.

Credit Cards

Major credit cards are accepted by many hotels, restaurants and businesses. Most Philippine banks will let you take a cash advance on your card; be sure to bring identification and some patience. Watch out for scams like taking your card into a back room at a shop to run it off a few extra times.

Exchanging Money

There are no particular hassles with exchanging or carrying pesos. US dollars are preferred and accepted everywhere. Moneychangers are much faster than the banks and give a better rate for cash, but can be dodgy, in Manila in particular. Ask the hotel front desk to recommend a local moneychanger. The rate varies with the size of the bill – US$50 and US$100 bills are best.

Exchange rates are as follows:

Country	Unit	Peso (P)
Australia	A$1	42.20
Canada	C$1	45.04
euro zone	€1	70.77
Indonesia	10,000Rp	57.64
Japan	¥100	50.96
Malaysia	RM1	14.42
New Zealand	NZ$1	38.74
UK	UK£1	102.95
US	US$1	54.79

Travellers Cheques

We don't recommend bringing travellers cheques as banks here seem to have a vendetta against them. Without exception you will need your passport and the original receipts and you may find that banks and moneychangers will only change cheques between 9am and 10am, or only at limited branches. You stand the best chance with Amex US-dollar cheques – other companies and denominations may not be changeable.

Of the banks, the best bet is usually the Equitable PCI Bank, but the Philippines National Bank is also useful. In Makati, Manila, you can rely on the huge HSBC and Citibank on Ayala Ave. The rate is usually a little lower than for cash.

POST

The postal system is generally quite efficient, but mail from the provinces can take weeks to reach Manila, let alone the outside world. Wait until you get back to the capital if you're sending anything internationally. Poste restante is available at the main post office in all major towns. Hours vary widely, but you can usually count on post offices being open from 8am to noon and 1pm to 5pm Monday to Friday.

Airmail letters (per 20g) within the Philippines cost P17 (ordinary, three weeks), P21 within Asia, P21 to Australasia and the Middle East, and P22 to Europe and North America. Aerograms and postcards cost P11 to anywhere.

RESPONSIBLE TRAVEL

As in other Asian countries, always allow locals a way of extracting themselves from an awkward situation. Publicly dressing down a Filipino is a surefire way to stir up trouble. Most Filipinos love having their photo taken, but tribespeople in rural areas in particular might resent it if you snap away without asking.

The Philippines is home to 100 or so cultural groups, and while it is rather adventurous to trek to a tribal village, you have to be a little more cautious. It might just be a fleeting visit for you, but the impression you make could be long remembered. Courtesies like asking to meet the village headman before staying overnight, not flaunting your (relative) wealth and keeping a sense of humour when faced with deeper than average curiosity all go a long way toward bridging the cultural gaps.

Filipinos are generally modest people. Bikinis and skimpy trunks are fine for the main resorts, but swimming costumes should be more conservative at local beaches and swimming holes.

The Philippines is one of the biggest sextourism destinations. Something like 70% of tourists are single men, quite a number of whom visit hot spots like Angeles, though every big city and quite a few smaller places cater to this business. Among the major sex-tour operators are the Japanese Yakuza. Most prostitutes come from impoverished provincial families and are easy prey for the girlie-bar trade, which takes a majority cut of their earnings in exchange for bare-essential living arrangements and protection from the police. Other Filipinas are forced into prostitution abroad by crooked recruitment agencies, which promise young women legitimate work and then sell them to prostitution cartels. Although prostitution is officially illegal, few foreigners have been prosecuted.

End Child Prostitution and Trafficking (Ecpat; www.ecpat.org) is a global network of organisations that works to stop child prostitution, child pornography and the traffic of children for sexual purposes.

TELEPHONE

The country code for the Philippines is ☎ 63. The international dialling code is ☎ 00. For local area codes, dial the first zero when calling from within the Philippines.

You won't find land lines everywhere in the Philippines, though mobiles are starting to appear deep in the provinces. In an emergency try the nearest police station. Directory assistance numbers are complicated by the fact that different phone companies have separate directories. For the PLDT directory call ☎ 187 (P3 per minute) nationwide.

International calls are simple in comparison. They can be made from many hotels or from one of the many offices of PLDT, BayanTel, Smart Telecom or Globe Telecom. PLDT and BayanTel offer flat rates for international calls for US$0.40 per minute. For reverse-charge calls, a flat fee of anything from P20 to P50 is charged.

Mobile Phones

Mobile phones are the biggest thing here since watches, and half the country spends much of the time furiously texting the other half. You sometimes see road signs warning against texting at pedestrian crossings.

Locally bought mobile phones (starting at around P3000) can be funded with prepaid cards and have the cheapest international call rates. You can bring your own GSM phone, but the overseas roaming charges

can make it expensive. Globe and Smart are the biggest carriers and provide reception even in far-flung places. Philippine mobile phone numbers all begin with 09.

TOILETS

Toilets are commonly called a 'CR', an abbreviation of the delightfully euphemistic 'comfort room'. Public toilets are virtually nonexistent, so aim for one of the ubiquitous fast-food restaurants should you need a room of comfort. The more expensive places have sit-down toilets, while simpler places (beach-hut compounds, for example) may have squat toilets.

TOURIST INFORMATION

The Department of Tourism (DOT) office in Manila has tons of brochures and information (not always up-to-date) on various regions. Regional DOT offices also offer huge racks of brochures and local maps.

Tourist Offices Abroad

Australia (☎ 02-9283 0711; gjones@pdot.com.au; 1st fl, Philippine Centre, 27-33 Wentworth Ave, Sydney, NSW 2000)

Canada (☎ 416-924 3569; info@wowphilippines.ca; 151 Bloor St, West Suite 1120, Toronto ON M5S 1S4)

France (☎ 01 42 65 02 34; dotpar@wanadoo.fr; c/o Philippine Embassy, 4 Hameau De Boulainvilliers 75016, Paris)

Germany (☎ 069-20893; phildo-fra@t-online.de; Kaiserhofstrasse 7, D-60313 Frankfurt)

Japan (☎ 03-5562 1583; dotjapan@gol.com; c/o Philippine Embassy, 5-15-5 Roppongi, Minato-ku, Tokyo 106-8537)

Singapore (☎ 6738 7165; philtours_sin@pacific.net.sg; 6-11 Orchard Towers, 400 Orchard Rd, Singapore 238875)

UK (☎ 0207-835 1100; tourism@pdot.co.uk; Cultural & Tourism Office, 146 Cromwell Rd, London SW7 4EF)

USA Los Angeles (☎ 213-487 4525; pdotla@aol.com; Ste 216, 3660 Wiltshire Blvd, CA 90010); New York (☎ 212-575 7915; pdotnycl@aol.com; 556 Fifth Ave, NY 10036)

VISAS

Visa regulations vary with your intended length of stay. The easiest procedure is to simply arrive without a visa, in which case you will be permitted to stay for up to 21 days. As usual, your passport must be valid for at least six months beyond the period you intend to stay. If you obtain a visa overseas it will usually allow a 59-day stay – fees vary from place to place but are around US$35. If you already have a visa when you arrive, make sure the immigration officers know this or your passport will still be stamped for just 21 days.

It is easy enough to extend your visa. Bureau of Immigration offices in provincial cities are usually the quickest – the **Bureau of Immigration** (Map p606; ☎ 02-527 3248; Magallanes Dr, Intramuros, Manila; ◷ Mon-Fri 8am-noon & 1pm-5pm) head office is crowded and slow. To extend a 21-day visa to 59 days costs P2020. You need to photocopy the details page of your passport plus the page with the old visa, and it takes under an hour to get through the paperwork in regional offices. You could also pay only P1520 and wait two weeks for a visa extension from the Manila office, but it's hardly worth it. For up-to-date visa information visit the **Lonely Planet** (www.lonelyplanet.com) website.

A FAMILY AFFAIR

Volunteering in the Philippines has been like joining a large Filipino family – people here have welcomed me and been a constant source of support. I have learned more about contemporary Filipino culture and attitudes than I could have ever imagined possible.

Brian Houle, Volunteer

VOLUNTEERING

Major volunteer organisations active in the Philippines include **Australian Volunteers International** (www.australianvolunteers.com), **UN Volunteers** (www.unv.org), the **US Peace Corps** (www.peacecorps.gov) and the UK-based **Voluntary Service Overseas** (www.vso.org.uk). Many projects centre on conservation and deprived city neighbourhoods.

WOMEN TRAVELLERS

Many male Filipinos think of themselves as irresistible macho types, but can also turn out to be surprisingly considerate, and especially keen to show their best side to foreign women. They will address you respectfully as 'Ma'am', shower you with friendly compliments and engage you in polite conversation. In Filipino dating culture, striking up a private conversation is seen as a major step towards something more intimate, whereas in the Western world this is not taken as particularly significant.

Filipinas rarely miss the chance to ask personal questions out of curiosity – about your home country, family, marital status and so on. It's worth packing a few stock answers to these questions in your luggage for cheerful distribution.

Tampons are fairly widely available but it's a good idea to stock up.

Singapore

HIGHLIGHTS

- **Little India** – soaking up the bustling colourful vibe that could be downtown Mumbai (p667)
- **Lau Pa Sat** – chowing down in a vibrant yet Victorian-style hawker centre (p673)
- **Clarke Quay** – drinking at the city's best bars (p674) or taking an evening cruise on a boat adorned with lanterns (see p670)
- **Asian Civilisations Museum** – discovering the region's diverse arts and history from manga to Mandarin (p666)
- **Changi Prison Museum & Chapel** – witnessing how POWs survived WWII and visiting the original handmade church (p669)
- **Off the beaten track** – relaxing in the Botanic Gardens, an ideal picnic spot and a sanctuary from Orchard Rd shopping (p667)

FAST FACTS

- **ATMs** widespread
- **Budget** US$25 a day
- **Costs** hostel dorm bed S$15-20, 4hr bus ride S$2-3, beer S$8
- **Country code** ☎ 65
- **Famous for** long-term leader Lee Kuan Yew, Tiger balm, Tiger beer and a downright weird Merlion statue
- **Languages** English, Mandarin, Malay, Tamil
- **Money** US$1 = S$1.69 (Singaporean dollar)
- **Phrases** *ni hao ma?* (how are you?), *zai jian* (goodbye), *xie xie* (thanks), *dui bu qi* (sorry)
- **Population** 4.24 million
- **Seasons** wet Nov-Jan, dry Feb-Oct

- **Visas** most travellers get a 30-day tourist visa on arrival. See p683 for more.

TRAVEL HINT

Museums are free on Friday nights after 6pm (Singapore Art Museum) or 7pm (Asian Civilisations Museum).

OVERLAND ROUTES

Take the Causeway across to Johor Bahru in Malaysia, or cross the bridge at Tuas to Tanjung Kupang in Malaysia.

If you want a crash course in Asia, squeaky clean Singapore is it. Where else could you take a rickshaw to Chinatown or jump on a bumboat (motorised sampan) for a wild night out at the globally glam Clarke Quay? Or hop on the MRT to Little India for all the saris and spice you can handle? Or find Malay culture in Kampung Glam, or wartime relics at Changi chapel and the Battle Box? And you can do it all in a safe and scenic city that is one of the most affluent in Asia.

Singaporeans have two unifying passions: eating and shopping. Even on the tightest budget you'll end up doing more of both than you planned. Luckily, hawker centres dish up affordable cuisine that is as diverse as the Lion City's many inhabitants. The shopping Mecca Orchard Rd and the latest tech toys that obsess Singaporeans may do more serious damage to your credit cards. Fortunately government initiatives to create lush green pockets of parkland give you a place to catch your breath.

CURRENT EVENTS

Although not hit by the devastating 2004 Boxing Day tsunami, Singaporeans felt the impact on neighbours such as Indonesia and Malaysia, and subsequently gave more than S$170 million in aid, as well as serving as a UN base for aid.

Socially, Singapore has loosened its famously prim laws. Bungee jumping and late-night drinking are now common, and the controversial new casino (euphemistically called an integrated resort) is the first of its kind on the island.

HISTORY

Malay legend reckons that a Sumatran prince spotted a lion while visiting the island of Temasek, and based on this good omen he founded a city there called Singapura (Lion City). Records of Singapore's early history are patchy; originally it was a tiny sea town squeezed between powerful neighbours Sumatra and Melaka.

Singapore broke onto the world stage when Sir Thomas Stamford Raffles arrived in 1819 to make the island a bastion of the British Empire. It prospered as a trade hub for Southeast Asia, and attracted large-scale immigration of Chinese workers.

The glory days of the Empire came to an abrupt end on 15 February 1942, when the Japanese invaded Singapore. For the rest of WWII the Japanese harshly ruled the island, jailing Allied prisoners of war (POWs) at Changi Prison and killing thousands of locals, particularly Chinese. Although the British were welcomed back after the war, the Empire's days in the region were numbered.

The socialist People's Action Party (PAP) was founded in 1954, with Lee Kuan Yew (see Singapore's Own Eminem, right) as its secretary general. Lee led the PAP to

victory in elections held in 1959, and hung onto power for over 30 years. Singapore was kicked out of the nascent federation of Malaysia in 1965, but Lee made the most of one-party rule, and pushed through an ambitious industrialisation programme and a strict regulation of social behaviour and identity. By the time of his retirement as prime minister in 1990, Lee had created a tech-savvy nanny state.

His immediate successor, Goh Chok Tong, relaxed things a little, relaxing laws such as the banning of chewing gum and bungee jumping. In 2004 Goh stepped down and Lee Hsien Loong (Lee Kuan Yew's son) took over the top job. Lee Hsien Loong's leadership appears to be similar to the approach of his predecessor, and there are plans for a casino in the city.

THE CULTURE

Affluent Singaporeans enjoy a lifestyle that fuses technology and tradition. You'll see teenage girls on the Mass Rapid Transit (MRT) texting for the latest Chinese horoscope at thumb-throbbing speeds while boys listen to Indian hip-hop on MP3 players.

The Chinese majority (76.7% of the population) are Buddhists or Taoists, and Chinese customs and superstitions dominate

---

SINGAPORE'S OWN EMINEM

Singapore's influential first prime minister, Lee Kuan Yew, should be confident that his son, Lee Hsien Loong, the current prime minister, will keep the country safe and sound. However, he still holds a place in cabinet as Minister Mentor (or MM to the amusement of locals) and exerts significant behind-the-scenes power.

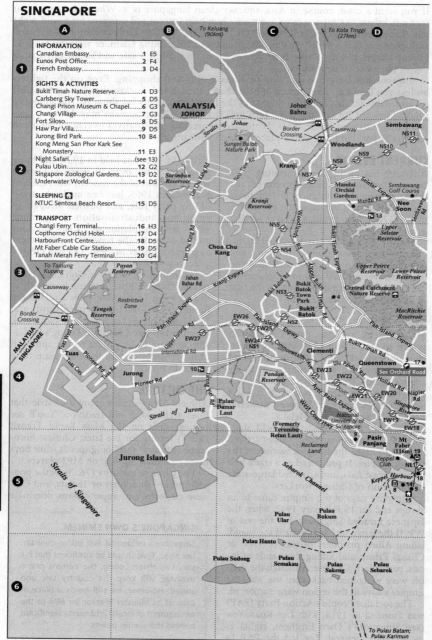

SINGAPORE

INFORMATION
Canadian Embassy	1	E5
Eunos Post Office	2	F4
French Embassy	3	D4

SIGHTS & ACTIVITIES
Bukit Timah Nature Reserve	4	D3
Carlsberg Sky Tower	5	D5
Changi Prison Museum & Chapel	6	G3
Changi Village	7	G3
Fort Siloso	8	D5
Haw Par Villa	9	D5
Jurong Bird Park	10	B4
Kong Meng San Phor Kark See Monastery	11	E3
Night Safari	(see 13)	
Pulau Ubin	12	G2
Singapore Zoological Gardens	13	D2
Underwater World	14	D5

SLEEPING
NTUC Sentosa Beach Resort	15	D5

TRANSPORT
Changi Ferry Terminal	16	H3
Copthorne Orchid Hotel	17	D4
HarbourFront Centre	18	D5
Mt Faber Cable Car Station	19	D5
Tanah Merah Ferry Terminal	20	G4

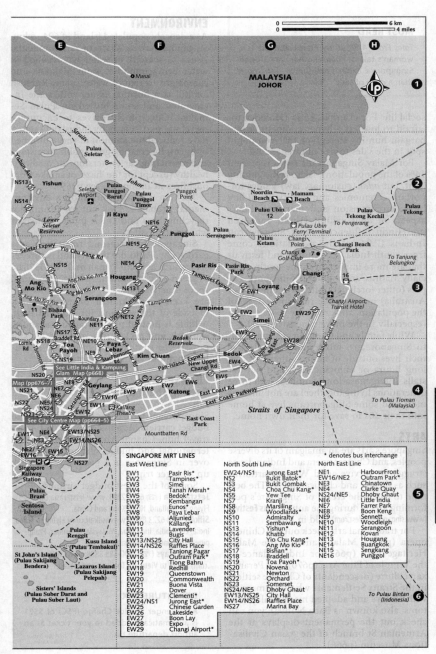

SINGAPORE MRT LINES
* denotes bus interchange

East West Line
EW1	Pasir Ris*
EW2	Tampines*
EW3	Simei
EW4	Tanah Merah*
EW5	Bedok*
EW6	Kembangan
EW7	Eunos*
EW8	Paya Lebar
EW9	Aljunied
EW10	Kallang*
EW11	Lavender
EW12	Bugis
EW13/NS25	City Hall
EW14/NS26	Raffles Place
EW15	Tanjong Pagar
EW16	Outram Park*
EW17	Tiong Bahru
EW18	Redhill
EW19	Queenstown
EW20	Commonwealth
EW21	Buona Vista
EW22	Dover
EW23	Clementi*
EW24/NS1	Jurong East*
EW25	Chinese Garden
EW26	Lakeside
EW27	Boon Lay
EW28	Expo
EW29	Changi Airport*

North South Line
EW24/NS1	Jurong East*
NS2	Bukit Batok*
NS3	Bukit Gombak
NS4	Choa Chu Kang*
NS5	Yew Tee
NS7	Kranji
NS8	Marsiling
NS9	Woodlands*
NS10	Admiralty
NS11	Sembawang*
NS13	Yishun*
NS14	Khatib
NS15	Yio Chu Kang*
NS16	Ang Mo Kio*
NS17	Bishan*
NS18	Braddell
NS19	Toa Payoh*
NS20	Novena
NS21	Newton
NS22	Orchard
NS23	Somerset
NS24/NS5	Dhoby Ghaut
EW13/NS25	City Hall
EW14/NS26	Raffles Place
NS27	Marina Bay

North East Line
NE1	HarbourFront
EW16/NE2	Outram Park*
NE3	Chinatown
NE4	Clarke Quay
NS24/NE5	Dhoby Ghaut
NE6	Little India
NE7	Farrer Park
NE8	Boon Keng
NE9	Sennett
NE10	Woodleigh
NE11	Serangoon
NE12	Kovan
NE13	Hougang
NE14	Buangkok
NE15	Sengkang
NE16	Punggol

social life. For example, *kiasu* (Hokkien for 'afraid to lose') is a hyper-competitive and bargain-hunting stereotype that you might spot in the sales frenzy of Orchard Rd.

For Malay Singaporeans (who represent 14% of the population), Islam is the guiding light, but *adat* (customary law) guides important ceremonies and events, including birth, circumcision and marriage. Many aspects of *adat* exhibit Hindu and even pre-Hindu influences. Most Singaporean Indians (7.9% of the population) come from south India, so customs and festivals that are more important in the south, especially Madras, are popular in Singapore. Expats (other foreigners, often from the UK or Australia) make up the remaining 1.4% of the population, and are a very visible group (especially in the more expensive bars).

While family and tradition are important to Singaporeans, most young people live their lives outside of home, either working long hours or enjoying bars and hawker stalls. Intergenerational families (with three generations living together) are not uncommon, and some Singaporeans live at home into their 30s to save for their own home.

ARTS

Singapore's arts are an amalgam of its diverse peoples, and Chinese opera and Indian dance struggle to survive amid Western artforms such as theatre and classical music. The best time to catch the cream of Singapore's performing arts is during the annual **Arts Festival** (www.singaporeartsfest.com) held in June.

For traditional arts check out the Chinese opera (p678), Malay dance at the Malay Heritage Park (p667) or Indian dance at the Temple of Fine Arts (p670). For Peranakan culture (descendants of Chinese settlers in the Straits Settlements who intermarried with Malays and adopted many Malay customs, also known as Baba Nonya), you can check out the permanent displays at the Armenian St branch of the Asian Civilisations Museum (p666).

ENVIRONMENT

As a densely populated island of 604 sq km, Singapore has its share of environmental issues. A scarcity of water has resulted in water being imported from Malaysia and campaigns to reduce water usage. Rubbish landfill is a burning issue, with some incinerated and some buried on Pulau Semakau. Government drives to encourage recycling, particularly by industrial estates, have reduced the amount of waste dumped or burnt. By creating good public transport and restricting car ownership, air quality is healthy (except for the 'haze' of smoke from bushfires in Indonesia, see p269).

To help out with Singapore's environmental problems, look out for prominent recycling bins and catch public transport whenever possible.

Singapore has a proud reputation as a garden city. Parks dot the city and nature reserves such as Bukit Timah make up 3326 ha of green oasis around the island. This small space is actively used by Singaporeans who are keen to walk, fish or wildlife-spot. Outside of the zoo and Jurong Bird Park, wildlife is limited to long-tailed macaques, squirrels and geckos in parks, but it's still possible to spot flying lemurs and reticulated pythons in more remote spots.

TRANSPORT
Getting There & Away
AIR
Singaporeans have enthusiastically taken to budget carriers. As a major Southeast Asian travel hub, Changi Airport hosts most international and budget airlines, so a stopover in Singapore is a good way to break up a longer trip.

Some of the latest budget airlines:

Jetstar Asia (☎ 6822 2288; www.jetstarasia.com) Flying to Thailand, Hong Kong and China.

SilkAir (☎ 6223 8888; www.silkair.com) Flying to China, India, Cambodia, Indonesia, Malaysia, Myanmar, Philippines, Thailand and Vietnam.

Tiger Airways (☎ 1800-388 8888; www.tigerairways .com) Flying to Vietnam, Thailand and Macau.

DEPARTURE TAX

A Passenger Service Charge (PSC) of S$21 is automatically added to your ticket as an airport departure tax.

Valuair (☎ 6220 8258; www.valuair.com.sg) Flying to Hong Kong, Bangkok, Jakarta and Perth.

The bigger airlines:

British Airways (Map pp676-7; ☎ 6589 7000; www.qantas.com.sg; 06-05 Cairnhill Pl, 15 Cairnhill Rd)

Lufthansa (Map pp676-7; ☎ 6835 5933; www .lufthansa.com; 05-01 Palais Renaissance, 390 Orchard Rd)

Malaysia Airlines (Map pp664-5; ☎ 6336 6777; www .sg.malaysiaairlines.com; 02-09 Singapore Shopping Centre, 190 Clemenceau Ave)

Qantas (Map pp676-7; ☎ 6589 7000; www.qantas .com.sg; 06-05 Cairnhill Pl, 15 Cairnhill Rd)

Singapore Airlines (Map pp676-7; ☎ 6223 8888; www .singaporeair.com; Level 2, Paragon Bldg, 290 Orchard Rd)

Internal flights within Malaysia are often cheaper from Johor Bahru with a Malaysia Airlines connecting bus service (S$12) from Singapore's **Copthorne Orchid Hotel** (Map pp658-9; 214 Dunearn Rd).

BOAT

Ferries from Singapore regularly connect to Malaysia and the Indonesian islands of the Riau archipelago. The main departure point for ferries to Indonesia is the HarbourFront Centre, next to HarbourFront MRT station (Map pp658–9), where you'll find the agents **Penguin** (☎ 6271 4866; www .penguin.com.sg), **Sea Flyte** (☎ 6270 0311; www.sea flyte.com) that has return trips to Batam for S$20, and **Berlian** (☎ 6272 2192; www.avipclub .com/sg/berlian).

The **Tanah Merah ferry terminal** (Map pp658-9; ☎ 6542 7102) south of Changi Airport handles ferries to Pulau Bintan in Indonesia and Pulau Tioman in Malaysia. To get here take the MRT to Bedok and then bus 35. A taxi from the city is around S$13.

Changi ferry terminal (Map pp658-9; off Changi Coast Rd) and the pier at Changi Village, both north of Changi Airport, have ferries to Malaysia. To get to Changi ferry terminal, take bus 2 to Changi Village and then a taxi.

BUS

For Johor Bahru, both the air-con express bus (S$2.40) and the public SBS bus 170 (S$1.10) depart every 15 minutes between 6.30am and 11pm from the **Queen St bus terminal** (Map p668; cnr Queen & Arab Sts). Bus 170 can be boarded anywhere along the way, such as on Rochor, Rochor Canal or Bukit Timah Rds. Share taxis to many places

in Malaysia also leave from the Queen St bus terminal.

The buses stop at the Singapore checkpoint – keep your ticket and hop on the next bus that comes along after you've cleared immigration. You'll go through the same process at Malaysian immigration and customs across the Causeway. The bus continues (your ticket is still valid) to the Johor Bahru bus terminus on the edge of town.

If you are travelling beyond Johor Bahru, it is easier to catch a long-distance bus straight from Singapore, but there is a greater variety of bus services from Johor Bahru and fares are cheaper.

In Singapore, long-distance buses to Melaka and the east coast of Malaysia leave from (and arrive at) the **Lavender St bus terminal** (Map p668; cnr Lavender St & Kallang Bahru), a 500m walk north from Lavender MRT station. For destinations north of Kuala Lumpur, such as Thailand, buses leave from the **Golden Mile Complex** (Beach Rd), a 500m walk south of Lavender MRT station.

TRAIN

Malaysian company **Keretapi Tanah Melayu Berhad** (☎ 6222 5165; www.ktmb.com.my) operates

---

BORDER CROSSING: INTO MALAYSIA & INDONESIA

A 1km-long Causeway in the north, at Woodlands, connects Singapore with Johor Bahru in Malaysia. To the west another bridge connects the suburb of Tuas with Tanjung Kupang in Malaysia. Immigration procedures on both sides of the bridges are straightforward.

When travelling into Malaysia by train, passports are checked by Malaysian immigration at the Singapore train station (officially part of Malaysia) but *not* stamped. This should not be a problem when you leave Malaysia if you keep your train ticket and immigration card.

Boats connect Singapore to Pulau Tioman in Malaysia once the monsoon is over.

Ferries and speedboats run between Singapore and Pulau Bintan in the Riau island group in Indonesia. Immigration is straightforward, though expect to pay for an Indonesian visa (US$20 for three days) at the other end.

three air-conditioned express trains daily from Singapore to Kuala Lumpur (S$12.50, six to seven hours) with connections on to Thailand.

Getting Around

BICYCLE

Singapore has few hills, but rush-hour traffic will present a challenging journey for all but the most seasoned trishaw driver. Along the east coast there are good paths, but elsewhere there are few dedicated cycling routes.

Bicycles can be hired from **Treknology Bikes** (Map pp676-7; ☎ 6732 7119; 01-02 Tanglin Pl, Tanglin Rd; 24-hr hire S$35; ☉ 11am-7.30pm Mon-Sat, 11.30am-3.30pm Sun).

BOAT

You can charter a bumboat (motorised sampan) to take a tour up the Singapore River or to visit the islands around Singapore. For boats to the islands, you usually pay no more than S$5 depending on how many people are in your group. **Singapore River Cruises** (☎ 6336 6111) and **Singapore Explorer** (☎ 6339 6833; www.singaporeexplorer.com .sg) both charge adult/child S$5/3 from Boat Quay to Clarke Quay.

There are regular ferry services from the HarbourFront Centre to Sentosa (ferry tickets can be bought at HarbourFront Centre) and the other southern islands, and from Changi Village to Pulau Ubin. You can also take river cruises, or boat cruises around the harbour (see p670).

BUS

Fares start from 60c (70c for air-conditioned buses) for roughly the first 3.2km, and rise to a maximum of S$1.20 (air-con buses S$1.50). There are also a few flat-rate buses. When you board the bus drop the exact money into the fare box, as no change is given.

Ez-link cards (see Mass Rapid Transit, right) can be used on all buses. You'll need to flash the card in front of the card reader when boarding the bus and once again when leaving. If you forget, you'll be charged the maximum fare for your bus journey next time you use your card.

There are a couple of tourist bus services: the **SIA Hop-On** (☎ 65-6734 9923; http://www.singapore air.com/saa/en_UK/content/promo/ssh/hop-on_bus _index.jsp; 1-day Singapore Airlines passengers/nonpassengers S$3/6) takes in much of the town; and

Singapore Explorer (☎ 6339 6833; www.singapore explorer.com.sg; 1 day S$10) – tickets can be bought from the bus driver of the service or at hotels. **City Buzz** (☎ 1800-767 4333; www.citybuzz.com .sg) costs S$5 for a day's hop-on, hop-off bussing, taking in most city sites.

CAR

Renting a car in Singapore is easy, but with dreamlike public transport and parking a nightmare, there's no need. Expensive surcharges make it pricey to take a rental car into Malaysia, plus they're cheaper there anyway.

MASS RAPID TRANSIT

The ultramodern Mass Rapid Transit (MRT) subway system is the easiest, quickest and most comfortable way to get around. The system operates from 6am to midnight, with trains at peak times running every three minutes, and off-peak every six minutes.

Single-trip tickets cost from 80c to S$1.80, but it's cheaper and more convenient to buy a S$15 Ez-link card from any MRT station. This electronic card, which includes S$10 of value (you'll get back the S$3 deposit and any remaining value on the card when you return it), can be used on all public buses (and at McDonald's restaurants) and can easily be topped up at ticket machines in MRT stations or at McDonald's. Fares using an Ez-link card range from 60c to S$1.65. Cards can be read through your wallet or purse when you tap it on the ticket gate sensor upon entering and leaving an MRT station.

A tourist day-ticket (S$10), giving you 12 rides on buses and trains, and valid for one day's travel, can be bought from MRT stations and bus interchanges.

TAXI

The three major cab companies are **City Cab** (☎ 6552 2222), **Comfort** (☎ 6552 1111) and **SMRT** (☎ 6555 8888; www.smrttaxis.com.sg).

Fares for most companies start from S$2.40 for the first kilometre, then 10c for each additional 220m. There are various surcharges, eg for late-night services, airport pick-ups and bookings. You can flag down a taxi any time or use a taxi rank (there are signs in English).

TRISHAW

Bicycle trishaws congregate at popular tourist places, such as Raffles Hotel, the pedestrian mall at Waterloo and Albert Sts, Clarke Quay and the end of Sago Lane. Always agree on the fare beforehand, and expect to pay around S$50 for half an hour.

ORIENTATION

The Singapore River cuts the city in two: south is the central business district (CBD), and to the north of the river are the hepped-up areas of Clarke and Robertson Quays, with the popular dining area, Boat Quay, to the river's south. To the southwest, Chinatown adjoins the CBD.

North of the river is the colonial district and further north again are Little India and Kampung Glam, the Muslim centre of the city. Northwest of the colonial district is Orchard Rd, Singapore's premier shopping centre.

To the west, the predominantly industrial area of Jurong contains a number of tourist attractions. Heading south you'll find the recreational island of Sentosa.

Eastern Singapore has some interesting suburbs (such as Geylang and Katong), a major beach park and Changi Airport. The central north of the island has much of Singapore's remaining forest and the zoo.

INFORMATION
Bookshops

Borders Wheelock Pl (Map pp676-7; ☎ 6235 7146; 01-00 Wheelock Pl)

Kinokuniya (www.kinokuniya.com.sg) Orchard Rd (Map pp676-7; ☎ 6737 5021; 03-10/15 Ngee Ann City, 391 Orchard Rd); River Valley Rd (Map pp664-5; 03-50 Liang Court, 177C River Valley Rd); Victoria St (Map p668; 03-09/12 Parco Bugis Junction, 200 Victoria St)

Select Books Tanglin Rd (Map pp676-7; ☎ 6732 1515; www.selectbooks.com.sg; 03-15 Tanglin Shopping Centre, 19 Tanglin Rd) Specialises in Southeast Asian titles.

Sunny Books Scotts Rd (Map pp676-7; ☎ 6733 1583; 03-58/59 Far East Plaza, 14 Scotts Rd; ⊙ 10am-8pm Mon-Sat, 11am-6pm alternate Sun) Secondhand books.

Emergency

Ambulance (☎ 995)
Fire (☎ 995)
Police (☎ 999)

Internet Access

Hostels regularly offer free Internet with accommodation; there are loads of other places to get online (for around S$5 per hour).

GETTING INTO TOWN

Changi Airport, about 20km from the city centre, is served by the Mass Rapid Transit (MRT). From Changi to City Hall is only S$1.35 (26 minutes, trains every seven minutes).

Public bus 36 leaves for the city approximately every 10 minutes between 6am and midnight, and takes just 20 minutes. Make sure you have the right change (S$1.50) when you board.

Taxis from the airport pay a supplementary charge (S$3 to S$5 depending on time) on top of the metered fare, which is around S$12 to most places in the city centre.

Chills Cafe (Map pp664-5; ☎ 6883 1016; 01-07 Stamford House, 39 Stamford Rd; ⊙ 9am-midnight)

Cyberia (Map pp676-7; ☎ 6732 1309; 02-28 Far East Shopping Centre, 545 Orchard Rd; ⊙ 9am-11.30pm)

Mega Cybernet (Map pp664-5; ☎ 6227 0887; 04-16 Pearl Centre, 100 Eu Tong Sen St; ⊙ 11am-11.30pm)

SCS Cybercafé (Map pp664-5; ☎ 6226 2567; www.scs .org.sg; 53/53A Neil Rd; ⊙ 10am-5pm Mon-Fri)

Laundry

Many hostels have washing machines that you can use (usually S$5 per load).

Washy Washy (Map pp676-7; 01-18 Cuppage Plaza, 5 Koek Rd; ⊙ 10am-7pm) Charges around S$10 per load.

Medical Services

Raffles SurgiCentre (Map p668; ☎ 6334 3337; www .raffleshospital.com; 585 North Bridge Rd; ⊙ 24hr)

Singapore General Hospital (Map pp664-5; ☎ 6321 4311; Block 1, Outram Rd; ⊙ 24hr)

Tanglin Clinic (Map pp676-7; ☎ 6733 4440; 04-20 Tanglin Shopping Centre; ⊙ 9am-5.30pm Mon-Fri, 9am-1pm Sat)

Money

Moneychangers can be found in every shopping centre, and many do not charge fees on foreign money or travellers cheques.

DECIPHERING ADDRESSES

Many Singaporean shops, businesses and residences are in high-rise buildings, so addresses are often preceded by the floor number, then the shop or apartment number. For example, 05-01 The Heeren, 260 Orchard Rd, is outlet number 01 on the 5th floor of the Heeren building.

CITY CENTRE

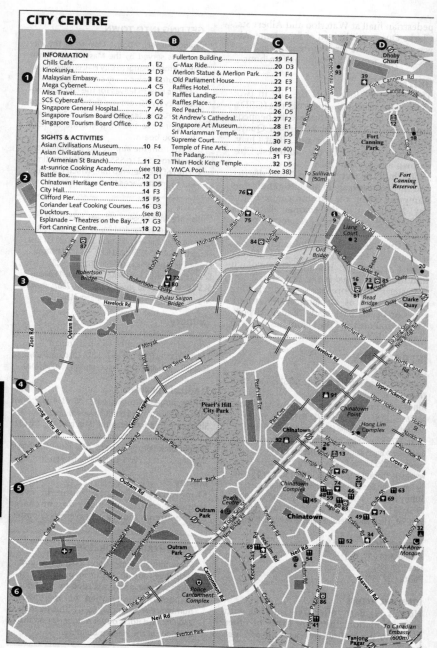

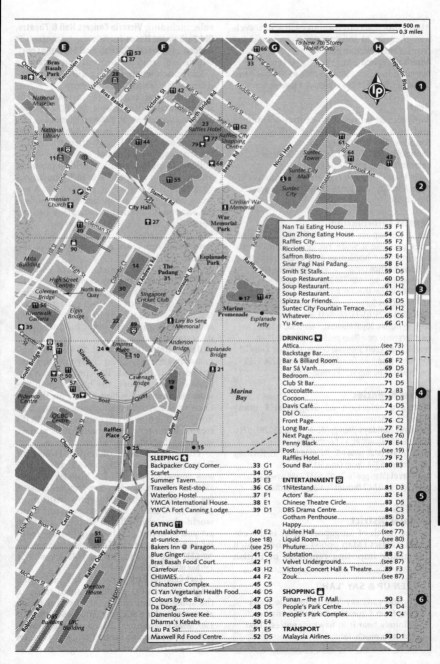

Many shops accept foreign cash and travellers cheques at lower rates than you'd get from a moneychanger.

American Express Changi Airport (☎ 6543 0671, Terminal 2) Tangs Plaza (☎ 6735 2069; 01-02 Tangs Plaza, 320 Orchard Rd; ☒ 9.30am-8.30pm) A good option.

Post

Most tourist information centres sell stamps and post letters. Large post offices can be found at the following places:

Changi Airport (Map pp658-9; 024-39, Terminal 2)

Comcentre (Map pp676-7; 31 Exeter Rd)

Lucky Plaza (Map pp676-7; 02-09 Lucky Plaza, Orchard Rd)

Ngee Ann City (Map pp676-7; 04-15 Takashimaya, 391 Orchard Rd)

Tourist Information

Most Singapore Tourism Board (STB) offices provide a wide range of services, including tour bookings and event ticketing.

STB head office Orchard Spring Lane (Tourism Court; Map pp676-7; ☎ 1800-736 2000; 1 Orchard Spring Lane; ☒ 8.30am-5pm Mon-Fri, 8.30am-1pm Sat)

STB branches Suntec City (Map pp664-5; ☎ 1800-332 5066, 6333 3825; 01-35/37/39/41 Suntec City, 3 Temasek Blvd; ☒ 8am-6.30pm Mon-Sat, 9am-6.30pm Sun); Liang Court Shopping Centre (Map pp664-5; ☎ 6336 7184; Level 1, Liang Court Shopping Centre, 177 River Valley Rd; ☒ 10am-10pm); Inn Crowd (Map pp668; ☎ 6296 9169; Inn Crowd, 73 Dunlop St; ☒ 10am-10pm)

Travel Agencies

Here's a selection of Singapore's many travel agencies:

Jetabout Holidays (Map pp676-7; ☎ 6822 2288, 6734 1818; 06-05 Cairnhill Pl; 15 Cairnhill Rd)

Misa Travel (Map pp664-5; ☎ 6538 0318; 03-106 Hong Lim Complex, 531A Upper Cross St)

STA Travel (Map pp676-7; ☎ 6737 7188; www.sta travel.com.sg; 07-02 Orchard Towers, 400 Orchard Rd)

SIGHTS
Colonial District

To the north of Singapore River is the colonial district (Map pp664–5), where you'll find many imposing remnants of British rule, including **Victoria Concert Hall & Theatre**, **Old Parliament House** (now an arts centre), **St Andrew's Cathedral**, **City Hall** and **Supreme Court**, which are arranged around the **Padang**, a cricket pitch where players still don the traditional whites for the odd game.

Nearby, the state-of-the-art **Asian Civilisations Museum** (Map pp664-5; ☎ 6332 7789; www.nhb.gov.sg/acm/acm.shtml; 1 Empress Pl; adult S\$5, child & concession S\$2.50; ☒ 1-7pm Mon, 9am-7pm Tue-Thu, Sat & Sun, 9am-9pm Fri) has 10 thematic galleries that explore different aspects of Asian culture, from the Islamic world to Japanese anime. At the **Armenian St branch** (Map pp664-5; ☎ 6332 3015; 39 Armenian St; adult S\$3, child & concession S\$1.50; ☒ 1-7pm Mon, 9am-7pm Tue-Thu, Sat & Sun, 9am-9pm Fri) permanent displays include Peranakan culture, Chinese ceramics and Buddhist artefacts. A combined ticket for both branches costs adult S\$6, child and concession S\$3.

The spiky, round metallic roof of **Esplanade – Theatres on the Bay** (Map pp664-5; ☎ 6828 8222; www.esplanade.com; 1 Esplanade Dr) has earned it the nickname of the 'big durian'. It attracts Singaporeans for its performing arts space, arts library and shops, but mostly for its restaurants.

Raffles Hotel (Map pp664-5; ☎ 6337 1886; www.raffles.com; 1 Beach Rd) is best enjoyed with a languid drink in the Long Bar (p675), but if you *must* explore history, the hotel's small **museum** (admission free; ☒ 10am-7pm) is on the 3rd floor in the attached shopping centre. The hotel itself is open to all comers, though it's treated like a temple to the Empire, and no shorts and sandals are allowed.

Three blocks west of Raffles Hotel, the **Singapore Art Museum** (Map pp664-5; ☎ 6332 3222; www.museum.org.sg/sam; 71 Bras Basah Rd; adult/child S\$3/1.50; ☒ noon-6pm Mon, 9am-6pm Tue-Thu, Sat & Sun, 9am-9pm Fri) is in St Joseph's Institution, a former Catholic boys' school, and hosts world-class exhibitions, though for local art you're better off checking out the regular exhibitions at the **Substation** (Map pp664-5; ☎ 6337 7800; www.substation.org; 45 Armenian St; ☒ box office 4-8.30pm Mon-Fri).

Fort Canning Park is on the site of Raffles' original botanical garden; guided tours of the spice garden can be arranged through **at-sunrice cooking academy** (Map pp664-5; ☎ 6336 3307; www.at-sunrice.com) based in the monumental **Fort Canning Centre** (Fort Canning Park; Cox Tce), the former barracks dating from 1926.

OPEN UP & SAY 'LAH'!

Singaporeans say 'lah' to indicate everything from a question to excitement. You'll definitely hear it in hawker centres: 'That costs too much, lah!'

Keeping it military, the **Battle Box** (Map pp664-5; ☎ 6333 0510; 51 Canning Rise; adult/child S$8/5; ☽ 10am-6pm Tue-Sun) is a warren of 26 underground rooms and tunnels that once served as a British base during WWII. A lengthy audio-visual exhibition tells the story of the fall of Singapore in 1942.

CBD & the Quays

South of the river is the CBD, the financial pulse of Singapore. Once the city's vibrant heart, **Raffles Place** (Map pp664-5) is now a rare patch of grass surrounded by the gleaming towers of commerce. At the river mouth into the harbour is the kooky **Merlion statue** (Map pp664-5), a lion/fish icon that could only have been dreamed up in the 1960s by a tourism board keen to create an artificial mascot.

You can hire a boat at **Clifford Pier** (Map pp664-5) for a pleasant harbour cruise or ogle the **Fullerton Building** (Map pp664-5), the former general post office re-invented as an *über*-swanky hotel. Further south along the waterfront is **Lau Pa Sat** (Map pp664-5; 18 Raffles Quay), a hawker centre that occupies the old Telok Ayer Market building, a spectacular cast-iron doily.

The hot new address along Singapore River is **Clarke Quay** (Map pp664-5), a redeveloped area drowning in bars and loaded with restaurants. **Boat Quay** (Map pp664-5) and **Robertson Quay** (Map pp664-5) are known for their nightspots and eateries. Riverside walkways link the quays, or you can take a bumboat tour between them.

Chinatown

Bustling Chinatown is crammed with stalls, eateries and tradition, all beautified by extensive conservation efforts. Resplendent with rooftop dragons, the highlight is **Thian Hock Keng Temple** (Map pp664-5; ☎ 6423 4626; 158 Telok Ayer St; ☽ 7.30am-5.30pm), Singapore's most ancient Hokkien building. Also on the temple trail, the **Sri Mariamman Temple** (Map pp664-5; ☎ 6223 4064; 244 South Bridge Rd; ☽ 7.30-11.30am & 5.30-8.30pm) is Singapore's oldest Hindu house of worship, recognisable by the pantheon of gods, fierce lions and bored cows piled onto its roof.

For a peek into the past, **Chinatown Heritage Centre** (Map pp664-5; ☎ 6325 2878; www.chinatownheritage.com.sg; 48 Pagoda St; adult/child S$8/4.80; ☽ 10am-7pm) is crammed with interactive, imaginative

displays. Got history overload? Keep your ticket stub so you can return the same day.

Little India & Kampung Glam

With a waft of spice and a Bollywood beat, Little India is a world away from the rest of Singapore. **Sri Veeramakaliamman Temple** (Map p668; ☎ 6293 4634; 141 Serangoon Rd; ☽ 8am-12.30pm & 4-8.30pm), dedicated to the goddess Kali, is one of Little India's most popular temples.

Further out is the **Sakaya Muni Buddha Gaya Temple** (Map p668; ☎ 6294 0714; 366 Race Course Rd; ☽ 8am-4.45pm), a Thai Buddhist place of worship that's popularly known as the Temple of 1000 Lights. It houses a 15m-high seated Buddha, plus many a lightbulb.

Worth avoiding are the seedy alleyways behind **Desker Rd** that house Singapore's dodgiest brothels.

Southeast of Little India is Kampung Glam, Singapore's Muslim quarter. Here, especially along North Bridge Rd, you'll find Malaysian and Indonesian shops, and the golden-domed **Sultan Mosque** (Map p668; ☎ 6293 4405; 3 Muscat St; ☽ 5am-8.30pm), the biggest mosque in Singapore; the entrance gets crowded with mopeds and empty shoes at Friday prayer time.

Istana Kampung Glam is the former Malay palace before colonisation, which was recently transformed into the **Malay Heritage Park** (Map p668; ☎ 6391 0450; www.malayheritage.org.sg; 85 Sultan Gate; admission S$3, cultural show S$8; ☽ 10am-6pm Tue-Sun, 1-6pm Mon). The park is a celebration of Malay culture and includes a small museum and vibrant dance and cultural show (at 10am, 11.30am and 3.30pm).

Orchard Road Area

Let's face it: Orchard Rd is all about shopping (see p679). Sure you could pretend to be getting some culture at the **Istana** (President's Palace; Map pp676-7; ☎ 6737 5522; www.istana.gov.sg; Orchard Rd) but as it's only open on selected public holidays, you may as well keep spending.

When you're over the shops, the serene **Singapore Botanic Gardens** (Map pp676-7; ☎ 6471 7361; www.nparks.gov.sg; 1 Cluny Rd; admission free; ☽ 5am-midnight) is an ideal spot to rest and revive. Strictly for flower fans, the **National Orchid Garden** (Map pp676-7; ☎ 6471 7361; adult S$5, child & concession S$1; ☽ 8.30am-7pm) is inside the gardens and boasts over 60,000 unique plants.

LITTLE INDIA & KAMPUNG GLAM

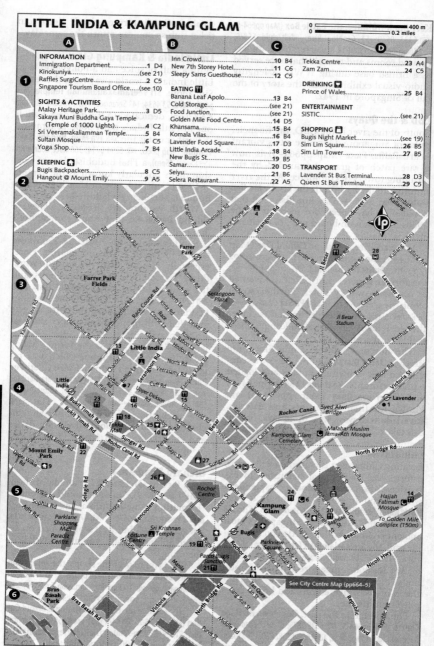

0 — 400 m
0 — 0.2 miles

INFORMATION
Immigration Department................................1 D4
Kinokuniya...(see 21)
Raffles SurgiCentre.......................................2 C5
Singapore Tourism Board Office...............(see 10)

SIGHTS & ACTIVITIES
Malay Heritage Park.....................................3 D5
Sakaya Muni Buddha Gaya Temple
(Temple of 1000 Lights)...........................4 C2
Sri Veeramakaliamman Temple.................5 B4
Sultan Mosque...6 C5
Yoga Shop...7 B4

SLEEPING
Bugis Backpackers...8 C5
Hangout @ Mount Emily..............................9 A5

Inn Crowd...10 B4
New 7th Storey Hotel.................................11 C6
Sleepy Sams Guesthouse...........................12 C5

EATING
Banana Leaf Apolo......................................13 B4
Cold Storage...(see 21)
Food Junction...(see 21)
Golden Mile Food Centre..........................14 D5
Khansama...15 B4
Komala Vilas...16 B4
Lavender Food Square................................17 D3
Little India Arcade......................................18 B4
New Bugis St...19 B5
Samar...20 D5
Seiyu...21 B6
Selera Restaurant..22 A5

Tekka Centre..23 A4
Zam Zam..24 C5

DRINKING
Prince of Wales..25 B4

ENTERTAINMENT
SISTIC..(see 21)

SHOPPING
Bugis Night Market....................................(see 19)
Sim Lim Square...26 B5
Sim Lim Tower...27 B5

TRANSPORT
Lavender St Bus Terminal..........................28 D3
Queen St Bus Terminal..............................29 C5

East Coast & Changi

East of the city is the **Changi Prison Museum & Chapel** (Map pp658-9; ☎ 6214 2451; www.changi museum.com; 1000 Upper Changi Rd North; admission free; guided tour S$8; ☺ 9.30am-5pm), commemorating POWs who were interned by the Japanese during WWII. There are exhibits and the haunting original church, complete with messages from families of former POWs.

Further east the sleepy **Changi Village** is the jumping-off point for the rural retreat of **Pulau Ubin**. Boats (one-way S$2, from 6am to 11pm) depart for the island regularly and once there you can hire a bicycle to explore this last undeveloped pocket of Singapore. Bus 2 from the city centre will take you to Changi Village, or take the MRT to Tampines and get bus 29.

Northern & Central Singapore

In the far north of the island, beside the Upper Seletar Reservoir, is the excellent **Singapore Zoological Gardens** (Map pp658-9; ☎ 6269 3411; www.zoo.com.sg; 80 Mandai Lake Rd; adult/child S$14/7; ☺ 8.30am-6pm), which has 4000 animals housed in open areas, including endangered white rhinos, Bengal white tigers and even polar bears. Next door is the **Night Safari** (Map pp658-9; ☎ 6269 3411; www.nightsafari .com.sg; adult/child S$15.45/10.30; ☺ 7.30pm-midnight), a 40-hectare forested park where you view nocturnal animals, including tigers, lions and leopards, as they come alive at night.

Also worth exploring is the sprawling **Kong Meng San Phor Kark See Monastery** (Map pp658-9; ☎ 6453 4046; 88 Bright Hill Dr; ☺ 7am-6pm), mainly for the monumental halls of worship and the Pagoda of 10,000 Buddhas, but also for the traditional Buddhist crematorium. Bus 410 (with the white-plated sign) runs here from Bishan MRT station.

Southern & Western Singapore

For a beautiful view walk up 116m **Mt Faber** (Map pp658–9), then catch the **cable car** (☎ 6270 8855; www.cablecar.com.sg; adult/child S$8.50/ 3.90; ☺ 8.30am-9pm) to the HarbourFront Centre or continue across to Sentosa Island.

Building **Haw Par Villa** (Map pp658-9; ☎ 6872 2780; 262 Pasir Panjang Rd; admission free; ☺ 9am-7pm) – with its grotesque depictions of Chinese mythology's goriest moments – was a strange way for the Haw Par brothers to blow the fortune made from Tiger balm, but the site makes for a good afternoon.

Jurong Bird Park (Map pp658-9; ☎ 6265 0022; www.birdpark.com.sg; 2 Jurong Hill; adult/child S$14/7; ☺ 8am-6pm) offers impressive enclosures and beautifully landscaped gardens for over 8000 birds. Get here on bus 194 or 251 from Boon Lay MRT station.

Sentosa Island

The plastic fantastic of **Sentosa** (Map pp658-9; ☎ 1800-736 8672; www.sentosa.com.sg; admission S$2; ☺ 7am-midnight) is a tourist magnet, with attractions including **Underwater World** (☎ 6275 0030; www.underwaterworld.com.sg; adult S$17.30; ☺ 9am-9pm), an aquarium that has you diving with dugongs; historic military base **Fort Siloso** (adult S$8; ☺ 10am-6.30pm); and **Carlsberg Sky Tower** (admission adult S$10; ☺ 9am-9pm), which offers city panoramas. The artificial **beach** is pleasant, with volleyball and water sports to keep you busy until the free **Magical Sentosa** laser light–and-music show (5pm, 5.30pm, 7.40pm and 8.40pm) kicks off in the evening – the best show is after dark.

There are many ways of getting to Sentosa, including bus, cable car (see left) and ferry from HarbourFront; the easiest is to take the MRT to HarbourFront station, then walk across the causeway or hop on the shuttle bus.

ACTIVITIES

Bukit Timah Nature Reserve (Map pp658-9; ☎ 1800-468 5736; www.nparks.gov.sg; ☺ 8.30am-6pm) is the only large area of primary rainforest left in Singapore and has some easy **walking** and **mountain-biking** trails. Pulau Ubin also has a few good **walking** and **cycling** trails. For off-road action, **Detour Outdoors** (☎ 6243 1174; www .detouroutdoors.com; 16 Siglap Plain, 1-/2-day tours S$75/130) runs bike tours to Bintan that explore the dense jungles of the nearby island.

For swimming there are good **beaches** on Sentosa and Pulau Ubin, or you can do a few laps at the **YMCA pool** (Map pp664-5; ☎ 6336 6000; www.ymca.org.sg; 1 Orchard Rd). The eatery **Whatever** (Map pp664-5; ☎ 6221 0300; www.what ever.com.sg; 31 Keong Saik Rd; 2-hr class S$25) offers drop-in Ashtanga and Hatha yoga classes, while the **Yoga Shop** (Map p668; ☎ 6296 6566; www .the-yoga-shop.com; 4 Kerbau Rd) offers free Raja yoga classes.

For a real adrenaline rush, strap yourself into the **G-Max Ride** (Map pp664-5; ☎ 9385 0697; River Valley Rd; adult/student S$30/25; ☺ 5-9pm) for a bungee bounce over scenic Clarke Quay.

SINGAPORE

COURSES

The best cookery courses are offered by **at-sunrice cooking academy** (Map pp664-5; ☎ 6336 3307; www.at-sunrice.com; Fort Canning Centre; half-day courses S$60). Their half-day **Spice Garden Walk** (S$30) takes you through the garden to identify the best Asian cookery ingredients, plus there's a morning tea. Another excellent cookery course is run by Asian fusion restaurant **Coriander Leaf** (Map pp664-5; ☎ 6732 3354; www.corianderleaf.com; 02-03 3A River Valley Rd; 1-day courses S$100), which teaches eight classic Singaporean recipes.

You can join traditional Indian dance classes at the **Temple of Fine Arts** (Map pp664-5; ☎ 6339 0492; www.templeoffinearts.org/sg; 02-11 Excelsior Hotel & Shopping Centre, 5 Coleman St; classes from S$60).

TOURS

For a leg-stretching tour, the well-informed **Original Singapore Walks** (☎ 6325 1631; www.singaporewalks.com; half-day adult/child S$18/12) offers good tours of Chinatown, Little India and the colonial area. **Ducktours** (☎ 6338 6877; www.ducktours.com.sg; Galleria, Suntec City; 1-hr tour adult/child S$33/12; ☼ 10am-6pm) offers fun-filled amphibious jaunts around the city that take in the Padang before hitting the water around Marina Bay.

Cruises

Bumboat cruises depart from several places along the Singapore River, including Clarke Quay, Raffles Landing and Boat Quay, as well as Merlion Park and the Esplanade Jetty on Marina Bay, running between 8.30am and 10.30pm.

Singapore Explorer (☎ 6339 9833; www.singaporeexplorer.com.sg) offers trips in glass-top boats (adult/child S$15/6) or traditional bumboats (S$12/6). **Singapore River Cruises** (☎ 6336 6111; www.rivercruise.com.sg) has 30-minute bum-

---

SPLURGE!

Red Peach (Map pp664-5; ☎ 6324 1250; 66-68 Pagoda St; 30 min/1hr S$30/90) Beat the heat of Pagoda street with an escape at this day spa that specialises in Chinese massage. Tired tootsies (and the rest of the body) are catered for with a special foot reflexology massage (30 min/1hr S$38/68). Best of all you can take tea in a private room afterwards and flip through polo magazines while catching up on expat gossip.

---

boat tours (S$12/6) and 45-minute tours (S$15/8). Take a night tour and admire the atmospheric red Chinese lanterns dangling from the boat's canopies.

A host of operators have harbour cruises departing from Clifford Pier, just east of Raffles Place. **Fairwind** (☎ 6533 3432) offers *towkang* (Chinese-junk) cruises (one-hour cruises S$15), as well as lunch and dinner cruises.

FESTIVALS & EVENTS

Singapore's multicultural population celebrates an amazing number of festivals and events. **Chinese New Year** (January/February) is the major festival. Look out for parades throughout Chinatown and festive foods in shops.

In March and April the month-long **Singapore Food Festival** (www.singaporefoodfestival.com) celebrates eating, and is held at hawker centres and gourmet restaurants. During the **Great Singapore Sale**, held around July, merchants drop prices to boost Singapore's image as a shopping destination. Singapore's performing arts community dances, acts and performs up a storm during the **Arts Festival** (www.singaporeartsfest.com) held every June.

For details on public holidays in Singapore, see p681.

SLEEPING

Bunking down in the booming colonial district is certainly convenient for the big sights and Orchard Rd, but Chinatown and Little India will give you insights into other cultures. Staying on Sentosa is a little out of the way for everything except, well, Sentosa.

Colonial District

Waterloo Hostel (Map pp664-5; ☎ 6336 6555; www.waterloohostel.com.sg; 4th fl, Catholic Centre Bldg, 55 Waterloo St; dm S$23, s S$53-68, d S$58-69; ☒ ☐) This tidy Catholic-run outfit has dorms that sleep eight, or other spacious rooms (you'll pay more for ones with attached bathrooms). Breakfast is included in the price.

New 7th Storey Hotel (Map pp664-5; ☎ 6337 0251; 229 Rochor Rd; dm S$17, d S$52-75; ☒ ☐) This well-run hotel has good four-bed dorms, some with access out onto scenic balconies. Doubles (shared or private bathroom) are spacious and clean and have individual TVs. Bike rental (per hour from S$3.50) is a bonus.

YMCA International House (Map pp664-5; ☎ 6336 6000; www.ymca.org.sg; 1 Orchard Rd; dm/s/tw/tr S$25/80/90/115; ❑ ❑ ❑) If you're after extra facilities (pool, gym and squash courts, anyone?) and free breakfast, this well-located place will do the trick. Dorms are spacious and other rooms are hotel-style and include fridges and en suites.

YWCA Fort Canning Lodge (Map pp664-5; ☎ 6338 4222; reservations@ywcafclodge.org.sg; 6 Fort Canning Rd; dm S$51, s/tw from S$136/159; ❑) With facilities similar to YMCA International House (plus a bonus rooftop tennis court), this is a dependable place to stay. It's girls-only in the five-bed dorms, which include air-con, TV and attached bathrooms, but stylish standard rooms are open to all.

Backpacker Cozy Corner (Map pp664-5; ☎ 6338 8826, 6224 6859; www.cozycornerguest.com; 490 North Bridge Rd; dm/s S$15/45; ❑ ❑) The rooftop bar is cool, but paying for extras isn't.

Chinatown & the Quays

Summer Tavern (Map pp664-5; ☎ 6535 6601; www.summertavern.com; 31 Carpenter St; dm S$20; ❑ ❑) Handy for the Quays, it compensates for tight dorms with free Internet and a relaxed bar/common area downstairs.

Travellers Rest-stop (Map pp664-5; ☎ 6225 4812; www.atravellersreststop.com.sg; 5 Teck Lim Rd; dm/s/d/tw S$18/35/55/60; ❑ ❑) Clean and exuberantly friendly, this well-located hostel has small common areas and kitchens. Doubles come with en suites and TVs. The cheery owners also offer personal Chinatown tours.

Little India & Kampung Glam

Hangout @ Mount Emily (Map p668; ☎ 6438 5588; www.hangouthotels.com; 10a Upper Wilkie Rd; dm S$35, d & tw S$88; ❑ ❑) For state-of-the-art hostelling you can't beat the Hangout. Clean, modern rooms with dorm beds (not bunks) are a treat, plus there's free Internet, gym and breakfast. The Pigout café is cheap for other meals, too. The only downside is the up-hill hike – not too easy with a hefty bag.

Inn Crowd (Map p668; ☎ 6296 9169; www.the-inncrowd.com; 73 Dunlop St; dm/d S$18/48; ❑ ❑) Freshly renovated, the Crowd has moved around the corner, but it keeps the friendly vibe of its smaller operation in Campbell Lane. Rates include breakfast, use of a locker and free Internet access, in its comfy ground-floor lounge that includes TV and DVD. It even holds luggage long term.

CAMPING

The **National Parks Board** (☎ 6391 4488; www.nparks.gov.sg; 18-01/08 Gateway West, 150 Beach Rd) administers several free camp sites around the island, including at East Coast Park and Pasir Ris Park. You need a permit to camp but these can usually be obtained on the spot. For East Coast Park go to Carpark C3 near McDonalds. The permits are free but you'll need to pay a small fee to use the barbecue pits or shower facilities.

Sleepy Sams Guesthouse (Map p668; ☎ 9277 4988; www.sleepysams.com; 55 Bussorah Rd; dm/s/d S$25/39/65; ❑) A great downstairs common space in the heart of Kampung Glam more than compensates for tight dorms upstairs. Singles and doubles are linked to dorms by thin divider walls, so they're not particularly quiet. All rates include free Internet, breakfast and massive barbecues on Thursday and Friday nights.

Prince of Wales (Map p668; ☎ 6299 0130; www.pow.com.sg; cnr Dunlop & Madras Sts; dm/d S$18/30) Good-value rooms above the pub, especially with a free beer!

Bugis Backpackers (Map p668; ☎ 6338 5581; www.bugisbackpackers.com; 162B Rochor Rd; dm/d S$16/36; ❑ ❑) Large rooms crammed with beds and minikitchens; it's in a central location.

Sentosa Island

NTUC Sentosa Beach Resort (Map pp658-9; ☎ 6275 1034; www.ntucclub.com; 30 Imbiah Walk; kampung huts/r from S$24/98; ❑ ❑ ❑) Beachside, Sentosa's budget accommodation options are small, air-con wooden huts that sleep up to three people and have shared bathrooms. Book months ahead to score a spot on the weekends, but during the week it's easy enough.

SPLURGE!

Scarlet (Map pp664-5; ☎ 6511 3303; 33 Erskine Rd; d S$180; ❑ ❑ ❑) Definitely for romantic couples, this boutique hotel is the place for a Singapore fling. Rooms are plushly decorated in individual colour schemes and include extras such as deep baths and DVDs. Breakfast in the opulent café, Desire, is included if you can get out of bed for it.

EATING

It's all about eating in Singapore, with affordable hawker cuisine (usually S$3 to S$5 per dish) a national obsession. Every Singaporean has their favourite hawker who specialises in a particular dish, so you can build mix-and-match banquets with Indian, Cantonese and Malay dishes, plus there's plenty of vegetarian options (if not whole stalls). Prices increase once you sit down in a restaurant, and if you're dining by the river expect to pay around S$20 for mains. See Food (p681) for dishes you can sample.

Colonial District

RESTAURANTS

at-sunrice (Map pp664–5; ☎ 6336 3307; Fort Canning Centre; mains S$4–6; ☺ 11am-9pm) This self-serve restaurant is in a quiet spot in the leafy surrounds of Fort Canning Park, and serves great-value, tasty Asian meals.

Annalakshmi (Map pp664–5; ☎ 6339 9993; 02-10 Excelsior Hotel & Shopping Centre, 5 Coleman St; ☺ lunch & dinner) A good vegetarian restaurant where you 'eat as you like, give as you feel'. It's run by volunteers and profits help to support various Indian arts foundations and charitable causes. You can also see traditional Indian dance here presented by the Temple of Fine Arts (p670).

Soup Restaurant (Map pp664–5; ☎ 6333 9388; 39 Seah St; ☺ lunch & dinner Mon-Sat, lunch Sun) Specialises in MSG-free, double-boiled herbal soups (all under S$12) and luscious Samsui ginger chicken (entrée/main S$13/24). Other branches include **Chinatown** (Map pp664–5; ☎ 6222 9923; 25 Smith St; ☺ lunch & dinner), **Suntec City** (Map pp664–5; ☎ 6333 9886; B1-059 Suntec City; ☺ lunch & dinner) and **DFS Galleria Scottswalk** (Map pp676–7; ☎ 6333 8033; 25 Scotts Rd; ☺ lunch & dinner).

Colours by the Bay (Map pp664–5; ☎ 6835 7988; 01-13A/G Esplanade Mall, 8 Raffles Ave; mains S$10–20; ☺ 11.30am-11pm) This is no food court, but offers the variety of one. Comprising seven different restaurants, you can sit at one and order from any of the others.

CHIJMES (Map pp664–5; 30 Victoria St) also has several restaurants all at the upper end of the price bracket, but often offering good-value set meals or deals. Try **Carnivore** (☎ 6334 9332; 01-29A, CHIJMES; all you can eat S$39; ☺ lunch & dinner), a barbecue flesh-feast where you cut your own meat from the spit and add a salad if you must.

FOOD CENTRES

Try the following:

Raffles City (Map pp664–5; 3rd fl, 252 North Bridge Rd)

Food Junction (Map p668; 200 Victoria St) In the basement of Seiyu.

Bras Basah Food Court (Map pp664–5; 232 Victoria St; ☺ 7am-9pm)

Nan Tai Eating House (Map pp664–5; Blk 262 Waterloo St)

New Bugis St (Map p668; New Bugis St)

Suntec City Fountain Terrace (Map pp664–5; Suntec City Mall, 3 Temasek Blvd)

SELF-CATERING

The supermarket **Cold Storage** (Map p668; www .coldstorage.com.sg; Seiyu Department Store, 200 Victoria St) has several branches across the city. If you can't find what you want here, try the French hypermarket **Carrefour** (Map pp664–5; Suntec City Mall).

CBD & the Quays

RESTAURANTS

Ricciotti (Map pp664–5; ☎ 6533 9060; B1-49/50 The Riverwalk, 20 Upper Circular Rd; mains S$6–12; ☺ 10am-10pm Mon-Fri, 9am-10pm Sat & Sun) Affordable wines (per glass S$5 to S$7) and an authentic Italian menu are the big drawcards of this riverside deli-style café. Apart from the pricey, but worthwhile gelato (S$9), meals are relatively cheap, such as the lunchtime panini (S$6.50 to S$9).

Yu Kee (Map pp664–5; ☎ 6337 7525; cnr Liang Seah St & North Bridge Rd; mains S$3–7; ☺ 7am-11pm Sun-Thur, 7am-2pm Fri & Sat) It's traditional hawker in fast-food style at this always-packed corner spot that does great duck rice (S$3). Friday and Saturday nights see a devoted crowd of cab drivers and clubbers slurping down the katong laksa (S$3) to stay awake.

Dharma's Kebabs (Map pp664–5; ☎ 6239 0980; 40 Boat Quay; meals S$7–15; ☺ lunch & dinner Mon-Sat) Not just the humble kebab is given the Indian treatment by veteran chef Dharma Nand. Great onion bhaji burgers or huge prawn shaslicks offer good-value grub, and the place has nice views.

Saffron Bistro (Map pp664–5; ☎ 6536 5025; 50 Circular Rd; mains S$8–17; ☺ lunch & dinner) Just one street back from the river, this nook offers a modern take on classic tandoori cuisine with healthy low-oil dishes.

Sinar Pagi Nasi Padang (Map pp664–5; ☎ 6536 5302; 13 Circular Rd; meals S$4–6; ☺ 9am-1am Mon-Fri, 12pm-4am Sat) For spicy, simple Indonesian with red-hot sambals and plenty of fish, you can't go past this down-to-earth place. For the unadventurous, it also does Western meals.

FOOD CENTRES

Lau Pa Sat (Map pp664-5; 18 Raffles Quay) Famous for its renovated Victorian market building, you can also sample from more stalls that set up on Boon Tat St nightly.

Chinatown
RESTAURANTS

Whatever (Map pp664-5; ☎ 6221 0300; www.whatever.com.sg; 20 Keong Saik Rd; meals S$5-11; ☻ 8am-11pm) Skip the New Age bookstore at the front and head for the breakfast treats (banana crepes, anyone?), or go for mains such as organic spaghetti or brown-rice curries at this healthy eatery.

Da Dong (Map pp664-5; ☎ 6221 3822; 39 Smith St; mains S$12-20, yum cha S$2.80-4.80; ☻ 7am-11pm) Grab a serve of the celebrated dim sum from the steamer trolleys that are wheeled to your table in old-school Chinese style. Quick service and excellent food have made this a local legend.

Damenlou Swee Kee (Map pp664-5; ☎ 6221 1900; 12 Ann Siang Rd; mains S$10-15) A long-running family restaurant, famed for its *ka shou* (fish-head noodles); dine on the Peranakan-style ground floor, or phone ahead for a table on the roof with a postcard view across Chinatown.

Qun Zhong Eating House (Map pp664-5; ☎ 6221 3060; 21 Neil Rd; mains under S$10; ☻ 11.30am-3pm & 5.30-9.30pm Thu-Tue) Join the queue outside for the yummy handmade dumplings, interesting Chinese-style pizza and red bean–paste pancakes.

Ci Yan Vegetarian Health Food (Map pp664-5; ☎ 6225 9026; 2 Smith St; mains S$4-6; ☻ 12pm-10.30pm) Delicious concoctions of tofu and steamed veggies pour out of this place, all served on hearty brown rice for the fibre-conscious.

Spizza for Friends (Map pp664-5; ☎ 6224 2525; 29 Club St; pizzas S$15-18; ☻ lunch & dinner) Popular with expats for its thin-crust pizza, there's a few good gourmet options as well.

FOOD CENTRES

Apart from the outdoor stalls set up along Smith St each night, try following:

Chinatown Complex (Map pp664-5; cnr Sago & Trengganu Sts; ☻ 24hr)

Maxwell Rd Food Centre (Map pp664-5; cnr South Bridge & Maxwell Rds; ☻ 24hr) Excellent; famous for the chicken rice at stall 10.

Little India
RESTAURANTS

Khansama (Map p668; ☎ 6399 0300; 166A Serangoon Rd; mains S$6-10) Here, plates are piled high with traditional tandoori food, so expect spicy with good veggie options. Sweet tooths should try the *barwan binfi* (ladyfinger bananas stuffed with dry masala).

Komala Vilas (Map p668; ☎ 6293 6990; 76-78 Serangoon Rd; mains S$5-10; ☻ 7am-10.30pm) This restaurant has terrific, inexpensive vegetarian food served on the traditional banana leaf. The *dosa* (lentil-flour pancakes) have become the fast food of Little India. Goodies from its **sweet shop** (82 Serangoon Rd) make a tasty dessert.

Banana Leaf Apolo (Map p668; ☎ 6293 8682; www.bananaleafapolo.com; 54-58 Race Course Rd; meals from S$6; ☻ 10am-10pm) Specialises in fish-head curry (S$18 to S$26) but it also does cheap *thalis*; there's also a plusher **branch** (Map p668; 66-68 Race Course Rd; ☻ 11am-11pm) that serves North Indian cuisine.

Selera Restaurant (Map p668; ☎ 6338 5687; 15 MacKenzie Rd; meals S$8-15; ☻ 10.30am-10.30pm) This little corner place packs a punch with kick-arse curry puffs that attract fans for miles. Grab a cuttlefish ball for a weird taste sensation.

FOOD CENTRES

Lavender Food Square (Map p668; Jl Besar; ☻ 24hr)
Little India Arcade (Map p668; Serangoon Rd; ☻ 7am-late)
Tekka Centre (Map p668; cnr Serangoon & Buffalo Rds; ☻ 10am-10pm)

Kampung Glam

RESTAURANTS

Samar (Map p668; ☎ 6398 0530; cnr Baghdad & Bussorah Sts; mains S$8-16, shisha S$14; ✆ lunch & dinner) Arabic traditions don't get much swankier than this, with great bread and dips, meat-based meals and Muslim tunes. You can try a hookah pipe packed with three kinds of *shisha* (flavoured tobacco) or pause for a calming mint tea.

Zam Zam (Map p668; ☎ 6298 7011; 699 North Bridge Rd; murtabak S$4; ✆ 7am-11pm) This is the best place to sample *murtabak* (flaky flat bread stuffed with mutton, chicken or vegetables).

FOOD CENTRES

Golden Mile Food Centre (Map p668; 505 Beach Rd; ✆ 10am-10pm) offers a wide range of local specialities, while across the road in the **Golden Mile Complex** (✆ 10am-10pm) you'll find many Thai food stalls.

Orchard Road Area

RESTAURANTS

Echizen (Map pp676-7; ☎ 6738 0711; B1-12/13 Orchard Point, 160 Orchard Rd; sushi S$1-3; ✆ 10am-10pm) For a cheap inner-city munch, catch the sushi train at this Japanese joint that has cheap daily specials.

Din Tai Fung (Map pp676-7; ☎ 6836 8336; B1-03/06 Paragon Bldg, 290 Orchard Rd; mains S$8-17; ✆ 10am-10pm) Specialising in noodles, this place serves up Thai beef and chicken varieties. The plump dumplings also make a great snack.

DRINKING DICTIONARY

The many bars of Singapore use confusing lingo to describe their many offers and specials. Here's a quick rundown:

- One-for-one: buy one get one free.
- Housepour: selected drinks determined by each bar at lower prices, much like house spirits.
- Free housepour: drinks are free…once you've paid the cover charge.
- Happy hour: usually several hours between 6pm and 9pm when drinks are half-price.
- Crazy hour: one hour when drinks are extremely cheap, often quarter-price.
- Ladies night: free drinks for girls, which strangely attracts a lot of boys.

Bakers Inn @ Paragon (Map pp676-7; ☎ 6333 6647; 02-09 Paragon Bldg, 290 Orchard Rd; snacks S$4-8; ✆ 10.30am-10.30pm Sun-Thu) From focaccias to handmade ice-cream to soufflés, this is a boutique bakery that has great desserts and snacks. There's another outlet at Raffles Place.

FOOD CENTRES

Basements of most malls and department stores have food courts. Try the following:
Cuppage Terrace (Map pp676-7; 160 Orchard Rd; ✆ 10am-10pm)
Great Treat (Map pp676-7; 100 Orchard Rd; ✆ 10.30am-10pm) Good for Thai.
Newton Food Centre (Map pp676-7; Scotts Rd; ✆ 24hr) Outdoor dining and excellent garlic stingray.
Takashimaya Food Village (Map pp676-7; Takashimaya, Ngee Ann City, 391 Orchard Rd; ✆ 10am-10pm)

SELF-CATERING

Tanglin Market Place (Map pp676-7; Tanglin Mall, 163 Tanglin Rd; ✆ 10am-10pm) A great grocery store.

Bread Talk (Map pp676-7; www.breadtalk.com; B1-11/12 Paragon Bldg, 290 Orchard Rd; ✆ 7am-10pm) A popular bakery chain, with several outlets around Orchard Rd; also in the City Link Mall and Parco Bugis Junction.

DRINKING

Drinking is pricey in the Lion City, with a beer costing at least S$5 and wine generally too expensive to bother with. Luckily, many bars offer cheap deals (to translate confusing signs, see the Drinking Dictionary, left). The main party places include Mohamed Sultan Rd, Clarke and Boat Quays, and Emerald Hill Rd just off Orchard Rd. Most bars open from 5pm daily until at least midnight Sunday to Thursday, and 2am on Friday and Saturday.

Colonial District

CHIJMES (Map pp664-5; 30 Victoria St) There's a wide selection of bars, and charming outdoor areas and, often, live music.

Post (Map pp664-5; ☎ 656 877 8135; The Fullerton Singapore, 1 Fullerton Sq) For a drink in decorous surrounds, Post delivers a modish bar that retains the fittings from the original post office.

Raffles Hotel (Map pp664-5; ☎ 6337 1886; raffles@raffles.com; 1 Beach Rd) It's a compulsory cliché to sink a Singapore Sling (S$16, or

S$25 with a souvenir glass) in the **Long Bar** (⊙ 11am-late), plus it will supply you with peanuts to de-shell and eat while you swill. A more sophisticated sip can be obtained at the Bar & Billiard Room, a large space where you would expect to see monocles or spats.

CBD & the Quays

Cocoon (Map pp664-5; ☎ 6557 6268; 01-02 3A Merchant Court, River Valley Rd) Easily the coolest of Clarke Quay's bars, Cocoon is tricked-out with silk curtains, terracotta warriors and reclining sofas for a relaxed drink.

Attica (Map pp664-5; ☎ 6333 9973; 01-03 3A Merchant Court, River Valley Rd; ⊙ 5pm-3am Mon-Sun) This place is known for its solid tunes and laid-back drinking.

Boat Quay has many expat options, including the traditionally British **Penny Black** (Map pp664-5; ☎ 6538 2300; 26/27 Boat Quay) and the Canadian-inspired late-opener, **Bedroom** (Map pp664-5; ☎ 9009 7424; www.thebedroombar.com; 68 Circular Rd; ⊙ 5pm-6am).

The Mohamed Sultan Rd area (MS as seasoned bar-hoppers call it) is the spot for a bar crawl, though bars have a cover charge (around S$10) after 9pm on Fridays and Saturdays. Begin at kooky **Coccolatte** (Map pp664-5; ☎ 6735 0402; www.coccolatte.com; 01-09 Gallery Hotel, Robertson Quay), where they play electroclash and hip-hop to get your party started. Further along are **Front Page** (Map pp664-5; ☎ 6238 7826; 17/18 Mohamed Sultan Rd), and the adjoining **Next Page** (Map pp664-5; Mohamed Sultan Rd), which is good for serious drinking in big comfy chairs; or take the stairs up to **Dbl O** (Map pp664-5; ☎ 6735 2008; www.dbl-o.com; 01-24 Robertson Walk, 11 Unity St; admission S$25; ⊙ 5pm-3am Mon-Sat), heaven for its full-sized pool tables, Top 40 dance music and S$3 drinks (once you've forked out the cover charge). At the end of the road, **Sullivans** (Map pp664-5; ☎ 6737 1760; 262-4 River Valley Rd) is a grungy bar with one of the longest happy hours in town (3pm to 9pm).

Chinatown

Tanjong Pagar Rd has an active gay and lesbian bar scene (see p678) and welcomes drinkers regardless of their sexuality.

The sophisticated bars of Club St are housed in attractive, restored shophouses (many are closed Sunday).

Davis Café (Map pp664-5; ☎ 6220 9390; 28 Smith St) Attracts a backpacker crowd; there are drink deals and partying, with views of hawker stalls below.

Backstage Bar (Map pp664-5; ☎ 6227 1712; 13A Trengganu St; ⊙ 7pm-2am Sun-Thu, 7pm-3am Fri & Sat) At this gay and lesbian hangout, there are similar views as at Davis Café.

Bar Sá Vanh (Map pp664-5; ☎ 6323 0503; 49a Club St) Pop into Sá Vanh, or No 49A, to get a feel for the street's swankiness.

Club St Bar (Map pp664-5; ☎ 6227 9527; 87 Club St) More relaxed (especially with prices) is this bar, with a casual vibe and an international crowd.

Little India

Prince of Wales (Map p668; ☎ 6299 0130; www.pow.com.sg; cnr Dunlop & Madras Sts) The drinking scene in Little India is quiet, but fortunately the POW has drink specials and regular live local and Australian bands.

Samar (Map p668; ☎ 6398 0530; cnr Baghdad & Bussorah Sts; shisha S$14) For non-alcoholic libation, such as tea or a hookah pipe, try this place.

Orchard Road Area

Dubliner (Map pp676-7; ☎ 6735 2220; 165 Penang Rd) Housed in a colonial plantation mansion, this pub offers a surprisingly snug spot to down Irish beers with a mature crowd.

Emerald Hill Rd has a collection of bars in the renovated terraces just up from Orchard Rd. Flanking Rouge (p678) are the **Acid Bar** (Map pp676-7; ☎ 6738 8828; 180 Orchard Rd) and the seriously cool **Alley Bar** (Map pp676-7; ☎ 6738 8818; 2 Emerald Hill Rd). **No 5** (Map pp676-7; ☎ 6732 0818; 5 Emerald Hill Rd) has a chilli vodka with a mean reputation, while **Ice Cold Beer** (Map pp676-7; ☎ 6735 9929; 9 Emerald Hill Rd) is a raucous spot with a challenging range of chilled brews.

CLUBBING

Club culture is purely about dance in Singapore and tough penalties are meted out for drug possession. Cover charges for clubs are around S$15 to S$25, and this includes at least one drink.

Zouk (Map pp664-5; ☎ 6738 2988; www.zoukclub.com.sg; 17 Jiak Kim St) The stayer of the Singapore scene still nabs top-name DJs such as Dimitri from Paris and Carl Cox. It's actually three clubs in one, plus a wine bar, so go the whole hog and pay the full

ORCHARD ROAD

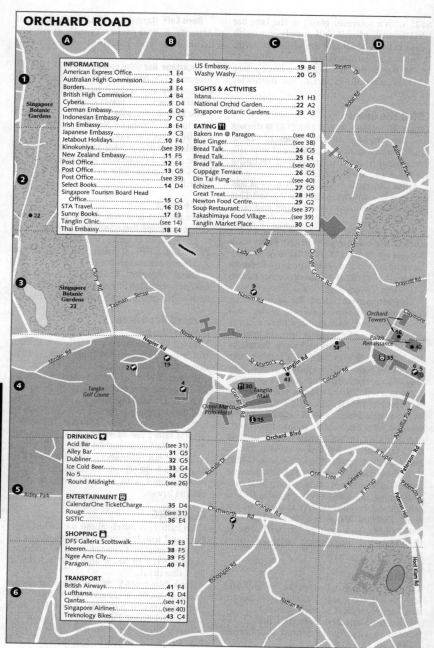

INFORMATION
American Express Office.................**1** E4
Australian High Commission.........**2** B4
Borders...**3** E4
British High Commission...............**4** B4
Cyberia..**5** D4
German Embassy..............................**6** D4
Indonesian Embassy........................**7** C5
Irish Embassy..................................**8** D4
Japanese Embassy............................**9** C3
Jetabout Holidays.........................**10** F4
Kinokuniya..................................(see 39)
New Zealand Embassy...................**11** F5
Post Office.....................................**12** E4
Post Office.....................................**13** G5
Post Office..................................(see 39)
Select Books...................................**14** D4
Singapore Tourism Board Head
  Office...**15** C4
STA Travel.....................................**16** D3
Sunny Books..................................**17** E3
Tanglin Clinic.............................(see 14)
Thai Embassy.................................**18** E4

US Embassy.....................................**19** B4
Washy Washy..................................**20** G5

SIGHTS & ACTIVITIES
Istana..**21** H3
National Orchid Garden.................**22** A2
Singapore Botanic Gardens...........**23** A3

EATING 🍴
Bakers Inn @ Paragon................(see 40)
Blue Ginger.................................(see 38)
Bread Talk....................................**24** G5
Bread Talk....................................**25** E4
Bread Talk..................................(see 40)
Cuppage Terrace............................**26** G5
Din Tai Fung...............................(see 40)
Echizen..**27** G5
Great Treat....................................**28** H5
Newton Food Centre......................**29** G2
Soup Restaurant..........................(see 37)
Takashimaya Food Village............(see 39)
Tanglin Market Place......................**30** C4

DRINKING 🍷
Acid Bar......................................(see 31)
Alley Bar......................................**31** G5
Dubliner..**32** G5
Ice Cold Beer.................................**33** G4
No 5...**34** G5
'Round Midnight.........................(see 26)

ENTERTAINMENT 🎭
CalendarOne TicketCharge............**35** D4
Rouge..(see 31)
SISTIC...**36** E4

SHOPPING 🛍
DFS Galleria Scottswalk.................**37** E3
Heeren...**38** F5
Ngee Ann City...............................**39** F5
Paragon...**40** F4

TRANSPORT
British Airways...............................**41** F4
Lufthansa.......................................**42** D4
Qantas...(see 41)
Singapore Airlines.......................(see 40)
Treknology Bikes............................**43** C4

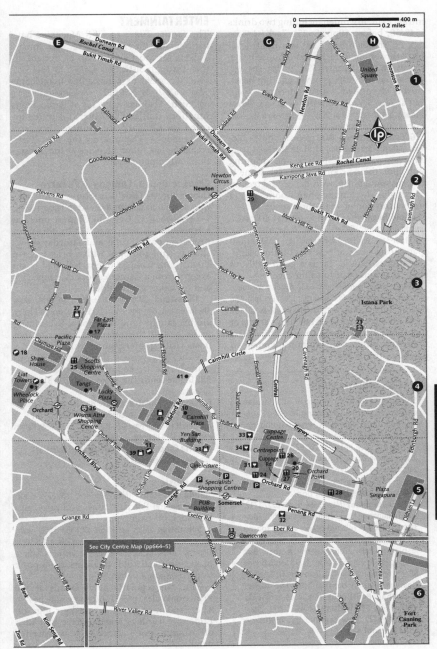

entrance (men/women including two drinks S$45/38; before 10pm S$25). **Zouk** (admission S$25; 7pm-3am Wed, Fri & Sat) is a multi-level party throbbing to techno and house beats. Spacey **Phuture** (admission S$25; 7pm-3am Wed, Fri & Sat) has hip-hop, grooves and big beats. Plushly decorated with modern art (yep, that's *The Scream* on the wall) is **Velvet Underground** (admission S$35; 9pm-3am Tue-Sat), with a more artsy crowd.

Gotham Penthouse (Map pp664-5; 6339 5595; www.gothampenthouse.com; 03-01 3A Merchants Court, Clarke Quay; admission S$25) Dark and dripping with cool, the new kid on the club scene is making some noise, with dance and techno tracks plus the loungy Shag Room – good luck in this cooler-than-thou space.

Liquid Room (Map pp664-5; 6333 8117; www .liquidroom.com.sg; Gallery Hotel, 76 Robertson Quay; 11pm-3am Sun-Fri, 11pm-4am Sat) This small space hosts some of best DJs on the island. Downstairs, Sound Bar is a good chill-out space that looks out onto the river.

Rouge (Map pp676-7; 6732 6966; www.rouge club.com; 2F Peranakan Pl, 180 Orchard Rd; 7pm-3am Wed-Sat) Luxurious yet intimate, this space hosts an eclectic mix of DJs at a variety of nights, from downbeat to afro-latin beats to techno, often with a choose-your-own jukebox from iPods.

GAY & LESBIAN CLUBS

Singapore has a thriving gay and lesbian club scene, particularly along Tanjong Pagar Rd. For more details of what's going on, check out www.fridae.com.

Happy (Map pp664-5; 6227 7400; www .happy.com.sg; 01-04, 29 Tanjong Pagar Rd; 9pm-2am Mon-Sat) The dancing queen of Tanjong Pagar, it has occasional cabaret shows and regular disco, techno and pop.

Backstage Bar (Map pp664-5; 6227 1712; 13A Trengganu St; 7pm-2am Sun-Thu, 7pm-3am Fri & Sat) A relaxed place, with a roomy balcony to spy on Chinatown's streets. Its lesbian-friendly sibling is the **Actors' Bar** (Map pp664-5; 6533 2436; 13/15 South Bridge Rd; 5pm-2am Mon-Thu, 5pm-3am Fri & Sat), a classy two-storey bar that hosts live music.

Gotham Penthouse (Map pp664-5; 6339 5595; 03-01 3A Merchants Court, Clarke Quay; admission S$25) also has wild gay nights on Sundays until 4am.

ENTERTAINMENT

The *Straits Times* and *I-S Magazine* have listings for movies, theatre and music. Tickets for most events can be bought either through **Sistic** (Map pp676-7; 6348 5555; www.sistic.com.sg) or **CalendarOne TicketCharge** (Map pp676-7; 6296 2929; www.ticketcharge.com .sg). Sistic also has agencies at Parco Bugis Junction, Raffles City, the STB office located on Orchard Rd, Suntec City, and Esplanade – Theatres on the Bay; TicketCharge has other agencies at the Substation and Funan Centre.

Chinese Opera, Comedy & Theatre

Chinese Theatre Circle (Map pp664-5; 6323 4862; www.ctopera.com.sg; 5 Smith St; tickets through SISTIC; 1-/2-hr show S$20/35) Get into Chinese opera at a teahouse session organised by this non-profit company. Friday and Saturday shows start at 7pm and 8pm with a brief talk (in English) on Chinese opera, followed by an excerpt from a Cantonese opera. Lychee tea and tea cakes are included.

1Nitestand (Map pp664-5; 6334 1954; www .the1nitestand.com; gigs S$50; 01-15 3A Valley Rd) There are big laughs (and occasional live music) to be had at this quayside favourite that hosts visiting international comedians.

Other big venues that feature various comedy, theatre and musical acts:

DBS Drama Centre (Map pp664-5; 6733 8166; 20 Merbau Rd)

Esplanade – Theatres on the Bay (Map pp664-5; 6828 8222; www.esplanade.com; 1 Esplanade Dr)

Jubilee Hall (Map pp664-5; 6331 1732; 3rd fl, Raffles Hotel Arcade; 328 North Bridge Rd)

Victoria Concert Hall & Theatre (Map pp664-5; 6345 8488; Empress Pl)

Live Music

'Round Midnight (Map pp676-7; 6737 1507; 43A Cuppage Tce) For jazz, blues and salsa, gigs here kick off from 9pm.

Substation (Map pp664-5; 6337 7800; www .substation.org; 45 Armenian St; box office 4-8.30pm Mon-Fri) This eclectic alternative arts space plays host to all kinds of events, from punk to performance poetry.

You can regularly catch bands at the Prince of Wales (p675) and Alley Bar (p675). The Esplanade has free outdoor gigs on Fridays, Saturdays and Sundays that kick off around 7pm – check their website for details.

SHOPPING

No longer a bargain destination (Singaporeans jet over to Hong Kong for that), shopping remains an essential part of a trip to Singapore. Prices for clothing, electronics and books are relatively cheap, but prices for CDs and DVDs are what you'd pay at home (unless you find a rare pirate retailer).

Orchard Rd is packed with ultramodern shopping centres, including the **Heeren** (Map pp676-7; ☎ 6733 4725; www.heeren.com.sg/; 260 Orchard Rd) that has hip young stores such as **DCP Streetwear** (☎ 6834 2651; 02-09A/10 The Heeren) famous for its Slurping Ape T-shirts, and funky Asian-inspired **Paperdoll** (☎ 6270 3626; www.paperdoll.com.sg; 03-14 The Heeren). The swanky **DFS Galleria Scottswalk** (Map pp676-7; ☎ 6229 8100; www.dfsgalleria.com; 25 Scotts Rd) is strictly duty-free shopping, with perfumes, boutique wear and luxury goods, but it makes nice window-shopping. Other good places to browse include the **Paragon** (Map pp676-7; ☎ 6738 5535; 290 Orchard Rd) and **Ngee Ann City** (Map pp676-7; ☎ 6733 0337; 391 Orchard Rd) with its high-fashion focus.

In Chinatown, **People's Park Complex** (Map pp664-5; 1 Park Cres) and **People's Park Centre** (Map pp664-5; 110 Upper Cross St) sell almost everything, but beware of tourist prices. **Bugis Night Market** (Map p668; New Bugis St) has cheap T-shirts, bags and other bargains.

Sim Lim Square (Map p668; ☎ 6332 5839; 1 Rochor Canal Rd) and **Funan – the IT Mall** (Map pp664-5; ☎ 6337 4235; 109 North Bridge Rd) sell computers, software, camera gear and MP3 players. Also try **Sim Lim Tower** (Map p668; ☎ 6295 4361;

10 Jl Besar), a mammoth electronic centre with everything from mobile accessories to computers to audio and video gear.

For affordable handicrafts, wandering Arab St in Kampung Glam and Chinatown's Pagoda, Smith and Temple Sts is worthwhile, though Chinatown has several touts keen to tailor you a suit (see 'Top 5 Touts' Calls', left). Little India has plenty of options, with Serangoon Rd offering gold, saris, incense and an array of Bollywood music and DVDs.

SINGAPORE DIRECTORY

ACCOMMODATION

Hostels are booming in Singapore, so expect competitive prices (usually around S$20) and loads of facilities, including free Internet, breakfast and laundry use. Cheaper hotel rooms (S$50 to S$70) are cramped, often windowless, with shared facilities (and where private facilities are available, they're listed as separate prices). Most places offer air-con rooms, with cheaper fan rooms. Most establishments will quote net prices, which include all taxes. If you see +++ after a price it means you'll need to add on 10% service charge, 5% GST and 1% government tax. All room prices quoted in this chapter include all taxes, and unless otherwise stated prices do not include bathrooms.

ACTIVITIES

If Singapore had a national sport it would be shopping, so athletic types will be disappointed by Singapore. There's some good walking trails in Bukit Timah Nature Reserve (see p669). Cycling is uncommon, though along the beach near Changi is popular. Swimmers can try Sentosa's beaches (p669), which are well designed for volleyball and sunbathing. The YMCA pool (p669) is a good lap pool with a view of the city.

To find out more on sports and activities in Singapore check www.ssc.gov.sg.

BOOKS

For almost every visitor, Lonely Planet publishes a guidebook: foodies love *World Food: Malaysia & Singapore*; for quick visits there's *Best of Singapore*; for longer visits it may be worth investing in *Malaysia,*

TOP 5 TOUTS' CALLS

Sure they may be annoying sometimes, but if you listen hard touts can often be very witty in their attempts to get you into their stores. Here's the five best we've heard:

- 'I'll make you long pants for short price.'
- 'Here's my business card so you can send me Christmas cards.'
- 'You have beautiful English skin, like fish and chips.'
- 'Why pay so much, lah? My brand also the same for less!'
- 'Would you like a ride in my air-conditioned helicopter?' (from a rickshaw driver).

Singapore & Brunei or *Singapore* city guide; and for budget trips, the book in your hands is the last word.

Can't get enough of Raffles the man? *In the Footsteps of Stamford Raffles* (also titled *The Duke of Puddledock*) by Nigel Barley is a cheery history about the man who put Singapore on the world map. *Saint Jack* by Paul Theroux is an American pimp's road to Damascus, painting a vivid picture of Singapore's raffish past.

For contemporary books, *Foreign Bodies* and *Mammon Inc.* by Hwe Hwe Tan are modern morality tales of Singaporean youth. *Notes from an Even Smaller Island* by Neil Humphries is a witty observation of Singapore through the eyes of a cheeky Englishman.

BUSINESS HOURS

Government offices are usually open from Monday to Friday and on Saturday morning. Hours vary, starting at around 7.30am to 9.30am and closing between 4pm and 6pm. On Saturday, closing time is between 11.30am and 1pm.

Shopping malls are open from 10am to 10pm daily; most small shops in Chinatown close Sundays, though Sunday is the busiest shopping day in Little India. Banks are open from 9.30am to 3pm weekdays (and until 11.30am on Saturday).

Singapore's food centres and hawker stalls open various hours (some 24 hours), but regular restaurants open for lunch from noon to 2.30pm and then for dinner from 6pm to 10.45pm.

CLIMATE

November to January is the wettest time; however, temperature (uniformly humid) and rainfall are steady year-round. See p924 for climate charts.

CUSTOMS

You can bring in 1L of wine, beer or spirits duty-free. Electronic goods, cosmetics, watches, cameras, jewellery (but not imitation jewellery), footwear, toys, arts and crafts are not dutiable; the usual duty-free concession for personal effects, such as clothes, applies. Duty-free concessions are not available if you are arriving from Malaysia or if you leave Singapore for less than 48 hours.

Toy currency and coins, obscene or seditious material, gun-shaped cigarette lighters, pirated recordings and publications, and retail quantities of chewing gum are prohibited. If you bring in prescription drugs you should have a doctor's letter or a prescription confirming that they are necessary.

DANGERS & ANNOYANCES

The most annoying aspect of Singapore is its tough laws, but, thankfully, crime is minimal. Pickpockets have been known to operate in Chinatown, Little India and other tourist areas, so look after your valuables in these areas. See also Legal Matters on p682.

DISABLED TRAVELLERS

Wheelchair travellers can find Singapore difficult, though shopping malls and hotels usually have lifts. The hi-tech nature of phones means that TTY phones and other aids for the hearing-impaired are available. Check out *Access Singapore,* a useful guidebook for the disabled, which is available from STB offices, or contact the **National Council of Social Services** (☎ 6336 1544; www.ncss.org.sg).

DRIVING LICENCE

To drive in Singapore you'll need your home driver's licence and an international permit from a motoring association in your country.

EMBASSIES & CONSULATES
Embassies & Consulates in Singapore

The following embassies, consulates and high commissions are in Singapore:

Australia (Map pp676-7; ☎ 836 4100; www.australia .org.sg; 25 Napier Rd)

Canada (Map pp658-9; ☎ 6325 3200; www.cic.gc.ca; IBM Towers, 80 Anson Rd)

France (Map pp658-9; ☎ 6880 7800; www.france.org .sg; 101-103 Cluny Park Rd)

Germany (Map pp676-7; ☎ 6737 1355; 14-01 Far East Shopping Centre, 545 Orchard Rd)

Indonesia (Map pp676-7; ☎ 6737 7422; 7 Chatsworth Rd)

Ireland (Map pp676-7; ☎ 6238 7616; www.ireland .org.sg; 541 Orchard Road, ☎ 08-00 Liat Towers)

Japan (Map pp676-7; ☎ 6235 8855; www.sg .emb-japan.go.jp; 16 Nassim Rd)

Malaysia (Map pp664-5; ☎ 6235 0111; 30 Hill St 02-01)

New Zealand (Map pp676-7; ☎ 6235 9966; www
.nzembassy.com/home.cfm?c=28;
15-06/10 Ngee Ann City, 391 Orchard Rd)
Thailand (Map pp676-7; ☎ 6737 2644; www.thai
embsingapore.org; 370 Orchard Rd)
UK (Map pp676-7; ☎ 6424 4200; www.britain.org.sg;
100 Tanglin Rd)
USA (Map pp676-7; ☎ 6476 9100; http://singapore
.usembassy.gov/index.shtml; 27 Napier Rd)

Singaporean Embassies & Consulates Abroad

For a list of Singaporean missions abroad
see www.visitsingapore.com/publish/stb
portal/en/home/about_singapore
/travellers__essentials/foreign___singa
pore.html#0001218, which also has a full
list of foreign embassies and consulates
in Singapore.
Australia (☎ 02-6273 3944; 17 Forster Cres, Yarralumla,
ACT 2600)
France (☎ 01-45 00 33 61; 12 Square de l'Ave Foch,
Paris 75116)
Germany (☎ 030-226 3430; Friedrichstrasse 200, 10117
Berlin)
Indonesia (☎ 021-520 1489; Blk X/4 Kav 2, Jl Rasuna
Said, Kuningan, Jakarta 12950)
Malaysia (☎ 03-2161 6277; 209 Jl Tun Razak, Kuala
Lumpur 50400)
New Zealand (☎ 04-470 0850; 17 Kabul St, Khandallah,
PO Box 13-140, Wellington)
Thailand (☎ 02-286 2111; 9th & 18th fls, Rajanakam
Bldg, 183 South Sathorn Rd, Bangkok)
UK (☎ 020-7235 8315; 9 Wilton Cres, Belgravia, London)
US (☎ 202-537 3100; 3501 International Pl, NW,
Washington DC 20008)

For information on Visas, see p683.

FOOD & DRINK

As a multicultural trading centre, Singapore has a table so full of great eating options that it's buckling at the legs. While
Singaporeans claim as their own the delicious Hainanese chicken rice, Chinese
stir-fried *beehoon* (rice vermicelli) and the
Indo-Malay breakfast favourite, *roti par-
atha* (flaky, flat bread served with curry),
most of their cuisine is imported with
new twists. Unmissable local innovations
include chilli crab (stir-fried with tomato
and chilli) and gruesomely tasty fish-head
curry. Be warned that desserts could involve the sickly sweet durian – an acquired
taste that's banned on the MRT.

GAY & LESBIAN TRAVELLERS

Despite homosexuality being technically
illegal, the gay community is acknowledged as an important part of the Lion
City's cultural life. Public displays of affection will usually draw a few disapproving looks, though same-sex hand-holding
is possible.

Law-makers are slow to come to the
party, with ministers mumbling about dubious connections between the spread of
HIV and dance events, refusing to licence
events as they are 'contrary to the public
interest'. There's also no official recog-
nition of gay and lesbian groups, such
as **People Like Us** (www.plu.sg), a group that
lobbies for homosexual interests. A good
web resource is the Asia-wide **Fridae** (www
.fridae.com), which has a fantastic guide to
Singapore's hot spots. See also the boxed
text on p678.

HOLIDAYS

The following days are public holidays.
Many are based on the lunar calendar, and
their dates are variable.
New Year's Day 1 January
Chinese New Year January/February
Thaipusam January/February
Good Friday March/April
Hari Raya Haji April/May
Vesak Day April/May
Labour Day 1 May
National Day 9 August
Hari Raya Puasa October/November
Deepavali October/November
Christmas Day 25 December

INTERNET ACCESS

You'll have no problem finding places to
get online, and many hostels offer free Internet – some even have zippy broadband
connections. Expect to pay S$5 per hour in
Internet cafés.

INTERNET RESOURCES

www.asia1.com.sg Website of Asia One, the company
that owns Singapore's newspapers; has links to the *Straits
Times*, the *New Paper* and the *Business Times*.
www.gov.sg Singapore Government website with all the
official info you could wish for on the island state.
www.talkingcock.com Singapore's favourite satirical
website that has a quirky take on the island.
www.visitsingapore.com Singapore Tourism's site,
with plenty of links to things to see and do.

LEGAL MATTERS

The law is extremely tough in Singapore, but also relatively free from corruption. Possession of drugs means a long jail term and a beating, with trafficking punishable by death. There are big fines for smoking in all public places, jaywalking, eating on the MRT and littering.

MAPS

The Official Map of Singapore, available free from the STB and hotels, is excellent. Periplus and Lonely Planet also produce maps.

MEDIA

English dailies include the Straits Times (which includes the Sunday Times), the Business Times and the New Paper. Free publications with events information, such as Where Singapore, I-S Magazine, Think, Banter and Juice, are available at tourist offices, most major hotels and several restaurants, cafés and bars. Also useful is the gossipy Eight Days (a weekly TV and entertainment magazine) and Today (free from Monday to Friday, 50c on the weekend).

MONEY

The unit of currency is the Singaporean dollar, which is made up of 100 cents. Singapore uses 1c, 5c, 10c, 20c, 50c and S$1 coins, while notes come in denominations of S$2, S$5, S$10, S$50, S$100, S$500 and S$1000; Singapore also has a S$10,000 note – not that you'll see many. For more details on costs in Southeast Asia, see p23.

Banks and ATMs are everywhere. Exchange rates vary from bank to bank and some charge a service fee on each exchange transaction – usually S$2 to S$3, but it can be more, so ask first.

Exchange rates at time of press:

Country	Unit	S$
Australia	A$1	1.24
Canada	C$1	1.43
euro zone	€1	1.99
Indonesia	10,000Rp	1.69
Japan	¥100	1.43
Malaysia	RM1	0.44
New Zealand	NZ$1	1.16
Philippines	100P	3.12
Thailand	100B	4.13
UK	UK£1	2.92
USA	US$1	1.70

Contact details for credit-card companies in Singapore:

American Express (☎ 6299 8133)
Diners Card (☎ 6294 4222)
JCB (☎ 6734 0096)
MasterCard & Visa (☎ 1800-345 1345)

POST

Post in Singapore is among the most reliable in Southeast Asia. Postcards cost 50c to post anywhere in the world, but letters start at 70c to Australia, New Zealand and Japan, or S$1 to Europe or the USA. Post offices are open from 8am to 6pm Monday to Friday, and 8am to 2pm Saturday. Call ☎ 1605 to find the nearest post office branch, or check www.singpost.com .sg. Letters addressed to 'Poste Restante' are held at the **Eunos Post Office** (Map pp658-9; ☎ 6741 8857; 10 Eunos Rd), next to the Paya Lebar MRT.

RESPONSIBLE TRAVEL

Recycling and using public transport are two of the best ways to conserve Singapore's fragile environment. For more advice on responsible travel, see p4.

TELEPHONE
International Calls

To call Singapore from overseas, dial your country's international access number and then dial 65, Singapore's country code, before entering the eight-digit telephone number.

Calls to Malaysia are considered to be STD (trunk or long-distance) calls. Dial the access code 020, followed by the area code of the town in Malaysia that you wish to call (minus the leading zero) and then your party's number. Thus for a call to 346 7890 in Kuala Lumpur (area code 03), you would dial ☎ 020 3 346 7890. Call ☎ 104 to get assistance with Malaysian area codes.

LEGAL AGE

- voting begins at 21
- drinking is allowed at 18
- you can begin driving at 18
- heterosexual sex is legal at 16

Local Calls

From public phones, local calls cost 10c for three minutes. There are no area codes in Singapore; telephone numbers are eight digits unless you are calling toll-free (☎ 1800).

Mobile Phones

Mobile phone numbers in Singapore start with 9. If you have 'global roaming', your GSM digital phone will automatically tune into one of Singapore's two digital networks, MI-GSM or ST-GSM. There is complete coverage over the whole island, even in the deepest MRT tunnels. Rates are variable but quite reasonable in comparison with other countries in the region. SMS is particularly cheap, so Singaporeans communicate by messaging.

You can buy a SIM card (usually S$20) or a 'disposable' mobile from most post offices and 7-Eleven stores, from Singtel, Starhub and MI.

Phonecards

Local phonecards are widely available from 7-Eleven stores, post offices, Telecom centres, stationers and bookshops, and come in denominations of S$5, S$10, S$20 and S$50. Most phone booths take phonecards, and some take credit cards, with only a few booths around that still take coins. For more details see www.singtel.com.

TOILETS

Generally toilets in Singapore are clean and well-maintained, though they might vary between the sit-down and squatting types. In some hawker centres you may pay have to pay a small fee (between 10c and 50c).

VISAS

Citizens of British Commonwealth countries (except India) and citizens of the Republic of Ireland, Liechtenstein, Monaco, the Netherlands, San Marino, Switzerland and the USA do not require visas to visit Singapore. Citizens of Austria, Belgium, Denmark, Finland, France, Germany, Iceland, Italy, Japan, Korea, Luxembourg, Norway, Spain and Sweden do not require visas for stays up to 90 days for social purposes.

You will be given a 30-day visitor's visa if you arrive by air, and a 14-day visa if you are arriving by land or sea. Extensions can be applied for at the **Immigration Department** (Map p668; ☎ 6391 6100; 10 Kallang Rd), one block southwest of Lavender MRT station.

For details of embassies and consulates, see p680.

VOLUNTEERING

Singapore serves as a base for many NGOs working throughout Southeast Asia, but most of these recruit skilled volunteers from their home countries. In Singapore itself the **National Volunteer & Philanthropy Centre** (www.nvpc.org.sg) coordinates a number of community groups, including an extensive database of grassroots projects, such as education, environment and multi culturalism.

WOMEN TRAVELLERS

There are few problems for women travelling in Singapore. In Kampung Glam and Little India skimpy clothing may attract unwanted stares, so consider wearing long pants or skirts and loose tops. Tampons and pads are widely available across the island, as are over-the-counter medications.

Thailand

HIGHLIGHTS

- **Southern islands** – diving under the waters at Ko Tao (p781), raving the night away on Ko Pha-Ngan (p787) and then flopping on the beaches of Ko Samui (p783)
- **Chiang Mai** – dosing up on Thai culture in this welcoming walled city, a sophisticated base to study Thai cooking, traditional massage or meaningful meditation (p737)
- **Phuket** – luxuriating in the silky sand, sublime seas and divine seafood on the biggest and boldest of Thailand's islands (p805)
- **Pai** – tuning in and dropping out at this laid-back land of lotus-eaters – head to the hills, run the river or join the nightshift (p750)
- **Khao Yai National Park** – getting back to nature at luscious Khao Yai, one of the world's finest national parks, home to *that* waterfall from the film *The Beach* (p762)
- **Off the beaten track** – marooning yourself on empty beaches and witnessing the fire-ball sunsets melting into the horizon at Ko Tarutao National Marine Park (p798)

FAST FACTS

- **ATMs** widespread
- **Budget** US$11-15 (500-650B) a day
- **Capital** Bangkok
- **Costs** guesthouse in Bangkok (US$5-10; 200-400B), 4hr bus ride (US$2.50-5; 100-200B), rice and curry (US$0.75; 20-30B)
- **Country code** ☎ 66
- **Famous for** blissful beaches, devilish chillies, you lady boy!
- **Language** Thai
- **Money** US$1 = 41B (baht)
- **Phrases** sà wàt dii (hello), kà rú naa (please), khàwp khun (thank you)
- **Population** 62 million
- **Seasons** high Nov-Feb, low Mar-Jun, monsoon Jul-Oct
- **Visas** 30-day visa-free entry for most nationalities

TRAVEL HINT

Don't just dream about 'real' Thailand – live it. Skip the 'discount' buses departing from the tourist ghettos and hop aboard a rót thamádaa (ordinary bus) that carries the country's extraordinary characters. This is Amazing Thailand.

OVERLAND ROUTES

Thailand shares land borders with Cambodia, Laos, Malaysia and Myanmar. Buses are best for Cambodia, crossing the Mekong by boat or bridge is more common for Laos, while comfortable trains and sleeper buses run to Malaysia. The Myanmar border is sensitive and for day-trippers only.

Thailand is *the* destination in Southeast Asia. All roads lead to Bangkok and most travellers begin their journey of discovery in this fabled country, the perfect balance between East and West. Foreign yet familiar, adventurous and accessible, rich in culture but cheap to chill out in, Thailand has the right blend for backpackers. Whether riding the Skytrain through Bangkok, trekking to a minority village or digging around the ruins of lost civilisations, life in Thailand is one long trip.

Thailand is also a land of plenty. The rice paddies glitter with greens you've never seen before, the warm seas bear a bounty of marine life and the gardens are dripping with fresh fruits – some familiar friends, others so exotic they look like jewels. Food is so plentiful that a *rót khěn* (vendor cart) is as much a part of the landscape as the horizon.

Thailand's ancient past was riddled with conflict; empires rising and falling as invaders came and went. But with a dose of luck, Thailand has entered the modern age in better shape than most. As its neighbours fell to European powers or ripped themselves apart in civil wars, Thailand remained independent and united. Thailand has welcomed the Western world on its own terms to become one of the most accessibly exotic locations on the globe.

It might be the saffron robes of a monk travelling on the Metro, it could be the sensuous smell of the spices drifting up from a curry or it may be seeing the sun come up over a tropical island (when you haven't been to bed), but at some point the Thai experience enters the soul. From here on, the hardest part of the trip is working out how much longer you can extend your stay and how long it will be before you return.

CURRENT EVENTS

Prime Minister Thaksin Shinawatra is a larger-than-life personality in Thailand. After a landslide win in the 2001 elections, the populist billionaire boosted his majority in the 2005 elections and his Thai Rak Thai (Thais Love Thais) party now dominates the political scene. It has not all been plain sailing for this political tycoon, who has managed to alienate large sections of the intelligentsia with his CEO style of leadership.

First came the war on drugs and a controversial shoot-to-kill policy towards suspected drug dealers in an effort to thwart the country's growing methamphetamine (*yaa bâa* or 'crazy drug') problem. Bodies soon piled up as extrajudicial and revenge killings exploded. The war lingers on today and has proved a popular way to rekindle support among the conservative majority in Thailand.

The drugs war is his, but the separatist war in the south is not. Some elements of the minority Muslim community want more autonomy – even a separate state – for their people and are willing to fight for it. Thaksin responded in typically tough fashion and sent in the army. The casualties mounted on both sides and it soon became apparent that the carrot might work better than the stick. Now dialogue and discussion are on the agenda, but it remains a simmering cauldron of tension.

Disease has been a big topic of discussion over the past few years. First came SARS and an attempted cover-up in Thailand, which damaged the country's image. More recently, Avian influenza (bird flu) has been breaking out at regular intervals and has claimed some lives.

Thaksin's popularity was plummeting in 2004, but on 26 December 2004 tragedy struck along the Andaman coast of Thailand. A powerful earthquake off the coast of Sumatra in Indonesia unleashed a tsunami that swallowed a number of resorts along the Thai coast. Thousands died and the tourism industry went into a reverse from which it is only just recovering. Thaksin immediately flew to the affected areas and was widely hailed for his proactive role in rallying a rapid response from the government. Check out the boxed text on p803 for more on the tsunami and its aftermath.

HISTORY
Rise of Thai Kingdoms

It is believed that the first Thais migrated southwest from modern-day Yunnan and Guangxi, China, to what is today known as Thailand. They settled along river valleys and formed small farming communities that eventually fell under the dominion of the expansionist Angkor Empire of present-day Cambodia. What is now southern Thailand, along the Malay peninsula, was under the sway of the Srivijaya empire in Sumatra.

THAILAND

THAILAND

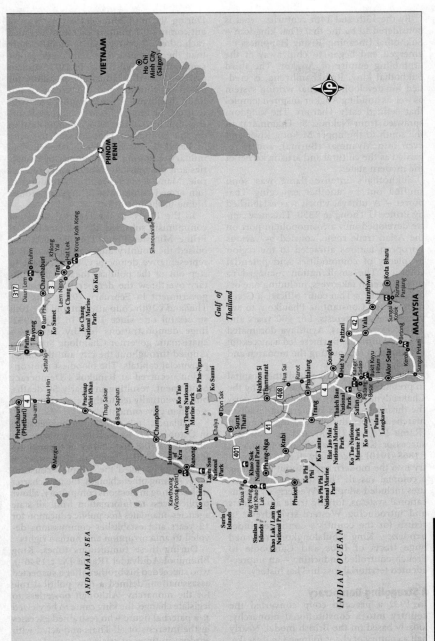

By the 13th and 14th centuries, what is considered to be the first Thai kingdom – Sukhothai (meaning 'Rising Happiness') – emerged and began to chip away at the crumbling empire of Angkor. The third Sukhothai king, Ramkhamhaeng, is credited for developing a Thai writing system as well as building Angkor-inspired temples that defined early Thai art. The kingdom sprawled from Nakhon Si Thammarat in the south to the upper Mekong River and even into Myanmar (Burma), and is regarded as the cultural and artistic kernel of the modern state.

Sukhothai's intense flame was soon snuffed out by another emerging Thai power – Ayuthaya, which was established by Prince U Thong in 1350. This new centre developed into a cosmopolitan port on the Asian trade route, courted by various European nations attracted to the region by plenty of commodities and potential colonies. The small nation managed to thwart foreign takeovers, including one orchestrated by a Thai court official, a Greek man named Constantine Phaulkon, to advance French interests. For 400 years and 34 successive reigns, Ayuthaya dominated Thailand until the Burmese led a successful invasion in 1765, ousting the monarch and destroying the capital.

The Thais eventually rebuilt their capital in present-day Bangkok, established by the Chakri dynasty, which continues to occupy the throne today. As Western imperialism marched across the globe, King Mongkut (Rama IV, r 1851–68) and his son and successor King Chulalongkorn (Rama V, r 1868–1910) successfully steered the country into the modern age without becoming a colonial vassal. Their progressive measures included adopting Western-style educational systems, forging trade agreements and introducing Western-style dress. In return for the country's continued independence, King Chulalongkorn returned huge tracts of Laos and Cambodia to French-controlled Indochina – an unprecedented territorial loss in Thai history.

A Struggling Democracy

In 1932 a peaceful coup converted the country into a constitutional monarchy, loosely based on the British model. Nearly half a century of chaos followed in its wake.

During the mid-20th century, a series of anticommunist military dictators wrestled each other for power, managing little more than the suppression of democratic representation and civil rights. In 1973, student activists staged demonstrations calling for a real constitution and the release of political dissidents. A brief respite came, with reinstated voting rights and relaxed censorship. But in October 1976, a demonstration on the campus of Thammasat University in Bangkok was brutally quashed by the military, resulting in hundreds of casualties and the reinstatement of authoritarian rule. Many activists went underground to join armed communist insurgency groups hiding in the northeast.

In the 1980s, as the regional threat of communism subsided, the military-backed Prime Minister Prem Tinsulanonda stabilised the country and moved towards a representative democracy. Not content to step out of the political theatre, the military overthrew the democratically elected government in February 1991. This was Thailand's 19th coup attempt and the 10th successful one since 1932. In May 1992, huge demonstrations led by Bangkok's charismatic governor Chamlong Srimuang erupted throughout the city and the larger provincial capitals. The bloodiest confrontation occurred at Bangkok's Democracy Monument, resulting in nearly 50 deaths, but it eventually led to the reinstatement of a civilian government.

Thailand's 16th constitution was enacted in October 1997 by parliamentary vote. Because it was the first charter in the nation's history not written under military order, it is commonly called the 'people's constitution'. Among other changes, the new charter makes voting in elections compulsory, allows public access to information from all state agencies, mandates free public education for 12 years and establishes commissions devoted to anticorruption and human rights.

During these tumultuous times, King Bhumibol Adulyadej (Rama IX, r 1946–), who succeeded his brother after a suspected assassination, defined a new political role for the monarchy. Although powerless to legislate change, the king came to be viewed as a paternal figure who restrained excesses in the interests of all Thais and acted with wisdom in times of crisis.

Economic Roller Coaster

During the 1990s, Thailand was one of the so-called tiger economies, roaring ahead with one of the world's highest growth rates – 9% at its peak. It was poised to join the ranks of Hong Kong, Singapore and other more industrialised nations of the Pacific Rim. But unabated growth soon imploded, sending Thailand and its neighbours into a regional currency crisis in 1997. The Thai baht dived to an all-time low – roughly 40% against the US dollar. The freewheeling boom days were over and the country entered a nearly three-year recession. The International Monetary Fund (IMF) provided a US$17.2 billion rescue package in the form of short-term loans, with the stipulation that the Thai government follow IMF's prescriptions for recapitalisation and restructuring.

Thailand's convalescence has progressed remarkably well with more sustainable economic growth (a healthy 6.3% in 2004, so say the economists) enabling an 'early exit' from the IMF's loan package back in mid-2003.

However, the tourism-dependent side of the economy has taken several sucker punches in the past few years, including the outbreak of SARS in 2003, bird flu in 2004 and the devastating waves of the tsunami that pounded the Andaman coast on 26 December 2004.

THE CULTURE

Thais are master chatters and for a Westerner they have a shopping list of questions: where are you from, how old are you, are you married, do you have children? Occasionally they get more curious and want to know how much you weigh or how much money you make; these questions to a Thai are matters of public record and aren't considered impolite. They also love to dole out compliments. Foreigners who can speak even the most basic Thai are lauded for being linguistic geniuses. And the most reluctant smile garners heaps of flattery about your ravishing looks. Why do some foreigners come to Thailand and never leave? Because Thais know how to make visitors feel like superstars.

The National Psyche

Thais are laid-back, good-natured people whose legendary hospitality has earned their country a permanent place on the global travel map. Paramount to the Thai philosophy of life is *sànùk* (fun) – each day is celebrated with food and conversation, foreign festivals are readily adopted as an excuse for a party and every task is measured on the *sànùk* meter.

The Thai-on-Thai culture is a lot more mysterious to unravel. Whole books are dedicated to the subject and expats spend hours in speculation. A few guiding principles are *nâa* (face) and elder-junior hierarchy. Like many Asian cultures, Thais believe strongly in the concept of 'saving face' – that is, avoiding confrontation and endeavouring not to embarrass themselves or other people. All relationships in Thai society are governed by connections between the elder and the junior, following simple lines of social rank defined by age, wealth, status and personal and political power. The elder of the table always picks up the tab. The junior in the workplace must do all the elder's menial chores and is not encouraged to participate in meetings or decision-making. The Western mindset is so different in this regard that it becomes something of a handicap in Thai society.

Delving deeper into the serious side of Thailand, the culture's fundamental building blocks are family and religion. Take all the pressures that your parents put on you

---

DID YOU KNOW?

- His Majesty Bhumibol Adulyadej, on the throne for more than 60 years, is the longest-reigning king in Thai history, as well as the longest-reigning current monarch worldwide.

- It is illegal to step on money in Thailand, as the king's image is on all coins and notes.

- The minimum daily wage in Bangkok and surrounding provinces is 175B (US$4.50).

- According to the *Bangkok Post*, there is an estimated 120,000 stray dogs in Bangkok.

- Thailand is 543 years ahead of the West, at least according to the Thai calendar that measures from the beginning of the Buddhist Era (in 543 BC).

THAILAND

WHY WÂI?

Traditionally, Thais greet each other not with a handshake but with a prayer-like palms-together gesture, known as a *wâi*. If someone *wâi's* you, you should *wâi* back (unless *wâi*-ed by a child or a serviceperson). The placement of the fingertips in relation to the facial features varies with the recipient's social rank and age. The safest, least offensive spot is to place the tips of your fingers to nose level and slightly bow your head.

about a career, education, a future spouse and multiply that by 10 – now you are approaching the environment of your Thai peer. Young Thais from poor families are also expected to support the family financially. Many do so with side jobs; they sell sweets from their front porch, run small Internet cafés or sell orange juice to tourists. For a culture that values having a good time, they work unimaginably long hours, usually wearing a beaming smile.

Religion and the monarchy, which is still regarded by many as divine, are the culture's sacred cows. You can turn your nose up at fish sauce or dress like a retrohippy, but don't insult the king and always behave respectfully in the temples. One of

Thailand's leading intellectuals, Sulak Sivarak, was once arrested for describing the king as 'the skipper' – a passing reference to his fondness for sailing. Pictures of the king, including Thai currency and stamps, are treated with deference as well.

Lifestyle

Thailand has a split personality – the highly Westernised urban Thais in major cities, and the rural farming communities more in tune with the ancient rhythms of life. But regardless of this divide, several persisting customs offer us a rough snapshot of daily life. Thais wake up early, thanks in part to the roosters who start crowing sometime after sunset. The first events of the day are to make rice and to sweep the floor and common spaces – very distinct smells and sounds. In the grey stillness of early morning, barefoot monks carrying large round bowls travel through the town to collect their daily meals from the faithful. Several hours later, business is in full swing; the vendors have arrived at their favourite corner to sell everything imaginable, and some things that are not, and the civil servants and students clad in their respective uniforms swoop in and out of the stalls like birds of prey.

A neat and clean appearance complements Thais' persistent regard for beauty.

ARE YOU A DEEP-FRIED FARÀNG?

Faràng is the word that Thais use for foreigners. It is derived from the word for French (*faràngsèht*) and can be merely descriptive, mildly derogatory or openly insulting, depending on the situation. When kids yell it as they pass by on bikes, it is usually the first, as if they were pointing out a big truck. You can graduate to the last category by being clueless or disrespectful toward the culture. Here are some tips on how to avoid the label:

- Before every movie and in bus and train stations, when the national anthem is played you are expected to stand with your arms by your side.
- Don't lick stamps, which usually bear an image of the king, or your fingers – to the Thais only animals lick things.
- Don't get angry, yell or get physically violent; keep your cool and things will usually work out in your favour.
- Feet are the lowest and 'dirtiest' part of the body in Thailand. Keep your feet on the floor, not on a chair; never touch anyone or point with your foot; never step over someone (or something) sitting on the ground. Take your shoes off when you enter a home or temple.
- Dress modestly and don't sunbathe topless.
- Woman aren't allowed to touch or sit next to a monk or his belongings. The very back seat of the bus and the last row on public boats are reserved for monks.

Despite the hot and humid weather, Thais rarely seem to sweat and never stink. Soap-shy backpackers take note: if you don't honour the weather with regular bathing you will be the sole source of stench on the bus. Thais bathe three or four times a day, more as a natural air-conditioner than as compulsive cleaning. They also use talcum powder throughout the day to absorb sweat, and as one Thai explained, 'for freshy'.

Superficially, eating makes up the rest of the day. Notice the shop girls, ticket vendors or even the office workers: they can be found in a tight circle swapping gossip and snacking (or *gin lên*, literally 'eat for fun'). Then there is dinner and after-dinner and the whole seemingly chaotic, yet highly ordered, affair starts over again.

Population

About 75% of citizens are ethnic Thais, further divided by geography (north, central, south and northeast). Each group speaks its own Thai dialect and to a certain extent practises customs unique to its region or influenced by neighbouring countries. Politically and economically the central Thais are the dominant group. People of Chinese ancestry make up more than 10% of the population, many of whom have been in Thailand for generations. Ethnic Chinese probably enjoy better relations with the majority population here than in any other country in Southeast Asia. Other large minority groups include the Malays in the far south, the Khmers in the northeast and the Lao, spread throughout the north and east. Smaller non-Thai-speaking groups include the colourful hill tribes living in the northern mountains.

SPORT
Muay Thai (Thai Boxing)

The wild musical accompaniment, the ceremonial beginning of each match and the frenzied betting around the stadium – almost anything goes in this martial sport, both in the ring and in the stands.

Bouts are limited to five three-minute rounds separated by two-minute breaks. Contestants wear international-style gloves and trunks (always either red or blue) and their feet are taped. All surfaces of the body are considered fair targets and any part of the body except the head may be used to

> **MUST SEE**
>
> Seek out *Satree Lek* or *Iron Ladies*, which tells the true story of a transvestite volleyball team that won the men's national championships in 1996. A huge hit internationally, it is also the second-biggest grossing film in Thai cinematic history.

strike an opponent. Common blows include high kicks to the neck, elbow thrusts to the face and head, knee hooks to the ribs and low crescent kicks to the calf. A contestant may even grasp an opponent's head between his hands and pull it down to meet an upward knee thrust. Punching is considered the weakest of all blows and kicking merely a way to 'soften up' one's opponent; knee and elbow strikes are decisive in most matches.

Matches are held every day of the year at the major stadiums in Bangkok (see p716) and the provinces. There are about 60,000 full-time boxers in Thailand.

Tàkrâw

The most popular variation of *tàkrâw*, sometimes called Siamese football, is best described as volleyball for the feet. Using a *lûuk tàkrâw* (rattan ball), players assemble on either side of the net, using similar rules to volleyball except that only the feet and head are permitted to touch the ball. Like gymnasts the players perform aerial pirouettes, spiking the ball over the net with their feet. Another variation has players kicking the ball into a hoop 4.5m above the ground – basketball with feet, but without a backboard!

The traditional way to play *tàkrâw* is for players to stand in a circle and simply try to keep the ball airborne by kicking it, like hacky sack. Points are scored for style, difficulty and variety of kicking manoeuvres.

RELIGION

Alongside the Thai national flag flies the yellow flag of Buddhism – Theravada Buddhism (as opposed to the Mahayana schools found in East Asia and the Himalayas). Country, family and daily life are all married to religion. Every Thai male is expected to become a monk for a short period in his life, since a family earns great merit

THAILAND

when a son 'takes robe and bowl'. Traditionally, the length of time spent in a wat is three months, during the Buddhist lent *(phansǎa)*, which begins around July and coincides with the rainy season, or when an elder in the family dies.

More evident than the philosophical aspects of Buddhism is the everyday fusion with animist rituals. Monks are consulted to determine an auspicious date for a wedding or the likelihood of success for a business. Spirit houses *(phrá phuum)* are constructed outside buildings and homes to encourage the spirits to live independently from the family, but to remain comfortable so as to bring good fortune to the site. The spirit houses are typically ornate wat-like structures set on a pedestal in a prominent section of the yard. Food, drink and furniture are all offered to the spirits to smooth daily life. Even in commerce-crazy Bangkok, ornate spirit houses eat up valuable real estate and become revered shrines to local people.

Roughly 95% of the population practises Buddhism, but in southern Thailand there is a significant Muslim minority community.

ARTS
Music
TRADITIONAL

Classical central Thai music features an incredible array of textures and subtleties, hair-raising tempos and pastoral melodies. Among the more common instruments is the *pìi*, a woodwind instrument with a reed mouthpiece; it is heard prominently at Thai boxing matches. A bowed instrument, similar to examples played in China and Japan, is aptly called the *saw*. The *ránâat èhk* is a bamboo-keyed percussion instrument resembling the Western xylophone, while the *khlùi* is a wooden flute. This traditional orchestra was originally developed as an accompaniment to classical dance-drama and shadow theatre, but these days it can be heard at temple fairs and concerts.

In the north and northeast there are several popular wind instruments with multiple reed pipes, which function basically like a mouth-organ. Chief among these is the *khaen*, which originated in Laos; when played by an adept musician it sounds like a rhythmic, churning calliope organ. It is used chiefly in *mǎw lam* music. The *lûuk thûng*, or 'country' (literally, 'children of the fields') style, which originated in the northeast, has become a favourite throughout Thailand.

MODERN

Popular Thai music has borrowed much from the West, particularly its instruments, but retains a distinct flavour. The best example of this is the famous rock group Carabao. Recording and performing for more than 20 years now, Carabao has crafted an exciting fusion of Thai classical and *lûuk thûng* forms with heavy metal.

Another major influence on Thai pop was a 1970s group called Caravan. They created a modern Thai folk style known as *phleng phêua chii-wít* (songs for life), which features political and environmental topics rather than the usual moonstruck love themes.

Sculpture & Architecture

On an international scale, Thailand has probably distinguished itself more in traditional religious sculpture than in any other art form. Thailand's most famous sculptural output has been its bronze Buddha images, coveted the world over for their originality and grace.

Architecture, however, is considered the highest art form in traditional Thai society. Ancient Thai homes consist of a single-room teak structure raised on stilts, since most Thais once lived along river banks or canals. The space underneath also serves as the living room, kitchen, garage and barn. Rooflines in Thailand are steeply pitched and often decorated at the corners or along the gables with motifs related to the *naga* (mythical sea serpent), long believed to be a spiritual protector.

MUST READ

Like a ripe mangosteen, you won't put down Alex Garland's 1997 novel *The Beach* until you've devoured it. A tale of island-hopping backpackers trying to carve out their own private paradise, this is essential reading for any Thailand trip beginning in a Th Khao San fleapit. A glossy Hollywood film based on the novel and starring Leonardo DiCaprio was released in 2000.

Temple architecture symbolises elements of the religion. A steeply pitched roof system tiled in green, gold and red, and often constructed in tiered series of three levels, represents the Buddha (the Teacher), the Dhamma (Dharma in Sanskrit; the Teaching) and the Sangha (the fellowship of followers of the Teaching).

Theatre & Dance

Traditional Thai theatre consists of six dramatic forms: *khŏhn,* formal masked dance-drama depicting scenes from the Ramakian (the Thai version of India's Ramayana) and originally performed only for the royal court; *lákhon,* a general term covering several types of dance-dramas (usually for nonroyal occasions), as well as Western theatre; *lí-keh* (likay), a partly improvised, often bawdy folk play featuring dancing, comedy, melodrama and music; *mánohraa,* the southern-Thai equivalent of *lí-keh,* but based on a 2000-year-old Indian story; *năng,* or shadow plays, limited to southern Thailand; and *hùn lŭang* or *lákhon lék* puppet theatre.

ENVIRONMENT

Thailand's shape on the map has been likened to the head of an elephant, with its trunk extending down the Malay peninsula. The country covers 517,000 sq km, which is slightly smaller than the US state of Texas. The centre of the country, Bangkok, sits at about 14° north latitude – level with Madras, Manila, Guatemala and Khartoum. Because the north–south reach spans roughly 16 latitudinal degrees, Thailand has perhaps the most diverse climate in Southeast Asia.

The Land

The country stretches from dense mountain jungles in the north to the flat central plains to the southern tropical rainforests. Covering the majority of the country, monsoon forests are filled with a sparse canopy of deciduous trees that shed their leaves during the dry season to conserve water. The landscape becomes dusty and brown until the rains (from July to November) transform everything into a fecund green. Typically, monsoon rains are brief afternoon thunderstorms that wet the parched earth and add more steam to a humid day.

As the rains cease, Thailand enters its 'winter', a period of cooler temperatures, virtually unnoticeable by a recent arrival except in the north where night-time temperatures can drop to 13°C. By March, the hot season begins with little fanfare and the mercury climbs to 40°C or more at its highest, plus humidity.

In the south, the rainy season lasts until January, with months of unrelenting showers and floods. Thanks to the rains, the south supports the dense rainforests more indicative of a 'tropical' region. Along the coastline, mangrove forests anchor themselves wherever water dominates.

Thailand's national flower, the orchid, is one of the world's most beloved parasites, producing such exotic flowers that even its host is charmed.

Wildlife

Thailand is particularly rich in bird life: more than 1000 resident and migrating species have been recorded and approximately 10% of all world bird species dwell here. Thailand's most revered indigenous mammal, the elephant, once ran wild in the country's dense virgin forests. Since ancient times, annual parties led by the king would round up young elephants from the wild to train them as workers and fighters. Integral to Thai culture, the elephant symbolises wisdom, strength and good fortune. White elephants are even more auspicious and by tradition are donated to the king. Sadly, elephants are now endangered having lost their traditional role in society and much of their habitat.

National Parks

Despite Thailand's rich natural diversity, it's only in recent decades that most of the 96 national parks and 100 wildlife sanctuaries have been established. Together these cover 13% of the country's land and sea area, one of the highest ratios of protected to unprotected areas of any nation in the world.

The majority of the preserved areas remain untouched thanks to the **Royal Forest Department** (www.forest.go.th/default_e.asp), but a few – notably Ko Phi Phi, Ko Samet and Ko Chang – have allowed rampant tourism to threaten the natural environment. Ironically, the devastating tsunami had one positive effect in Ko Phi Phi, washing away the

THAILAND

worst of the developments and allowing the island to be reborn again. Poaching, illegal logging and shifting cultivation have also taken their toll on protected lands.

Environmental Issues

Like all countries with a high population density, there is enormous pressure on Thailand's ecosystems: 50 years ago about 70% of the countryside was forest; by 2000 an estimated 20% of the natural forest cover remained. In response to environmental degradation, the Thai government has created a large number of protected areas since the 1970s. It is now illegal to sell timber felled in Thailand, and the government hopes to raise total forest cover to 40% by the middle of this century.

Air and water pollution are problems in urban areas. The passing of the 1992 Environmental Act was an encouraging move by the government, but standards still lag centuries behind Western nations.

Thailand is a signatory to the UN Convention on International Trade in Endangered Species (CITES). Forty of Thailand's 300 mammal species are on the International Union for Conservation of Nature (IUCN) list of endangered species. As elsewhere in the region, the tiger is one of the most endangered of large mammals. Tiger hunting or trapping is illegal, but poachers continue to kill the cats for the lucrative overseas Chinese pharmaceutical market. Around 200 wild tigers are thought to be hanging on in the national parks of Khao Yai, Kaeng Krachan, Thap Lan, Mae Wong and Khao Sok.

Corruption impedes the government's attempts to shelter species coveted by the illicit global wildlife trade. The Royal Forest Department is currently under pressure to take immediate action in those areas where preservation laws have gone unenforced, including coastal zones where illegal tourist accommodation has flourished.

TRANSPORT

GETTING THERE & AWAY

Thailand has six international airports: Bangkok, Chiang Mai, Phuket, Ko Samui, Sukhothai and Hat Yai. Most international flights arrive and depart from Bangkok's international airport.

Leading international airlines operating out of Thailand:

Air Asia (airline code AK; ☎ 0 2515 9999; www.airasia .com; hub Bangkok)

Bangkok Airways (airline code PG; ☎ 0 2265 5678; www.bangkokair.com; hub Bangkok)

Thai Airways International (airline code TG; THAI; ☎ 0 2280 0060; www.thaiair.com; hub Bangkok)

For more international and domestic options out of Bangkok, see p718.

It is possible to fly return from Bangkok to the US, Europe and Australia for less than US$1000. Cheaper indirect options are available, particularly via Hong Kong, Taiwan and Japan to the US, or via the Middle East to Europe.

DEPARTURE TAX

Departure tax on international flights is 500B, which is paid before passing through immigration.

GETTING AROUND
Air

Thailand's major domestic carrier is Thai Airways International (THAI) with Bangkok Airways behind it running a close second, but there has been an explosion of no-frills budget airlines serving popular routes in recent years, making for some dirt-cheap deals for the vigilant traveller. The most useful routes for shoestringers are Mae Hong Son–Chiang Mai, Ko Samui–Bangkok and Phuket–Bangkok – in each case a bus ride of eight to 15 hours is condensed to a one-hour hop. But there are also some amazing deals available on the Bangkok–Chiang Mai route, because competition is fierce. Book your tickets several days in advance for all domestic air travel.

Leading airlines for domestic routes include the following:

Air Andaman (☎ 0 2229 9555)

Air Asia (☎ 0 2515 9999; www.airasia.com)

Bangkok Airways (☎ 0 2265 5678; www.bangkokair .com)

Nok Air (☎ 1318; www.nokair.com)

Orient Thai (☎ 0 2267 3210; www.orient-thai.com)

Phuket Air (☎ 0 2679 8999; www.phuketairlines.com)

Thai Airways International (THAI; ☎ 0 2280 0060; www.thaiair.com)

Bicycle

Bicycles are available for rent in many areas; guesthouses often have a few for rent at only 30B to 50B per day. Just about anywhere outside Bangkok, bikes are the ideal form of local transport because they're cheap, nonpolluting and keep you moving slowly enough to see everything. Carefully note the condition of the bike before hiring; if it breaks down, you are responsible and parts can be expensive.

See p813 for information on bicycle touring in Thailand.

Boat

Being a riverine people, Thais have colourful boats of traditional design. With a long graceful breast that barely skims the water and a tail-like propeller, longtail boats are used as island-hoppers, canal coasters and river ferries. Small wooden fishing boats, brilliantly painted, sometimes shuttle tourists out to nearby islands. Longer trips to the islands of Ko Pha-Ngan and Ko Tao are undertaken by slow yet determined cargo boats through the dark of night. Boat schedules are subject to change depending on weather conditions and demand.

Bus

The Thai bus service is widespread, convenient and phenomenally fast – nail-bitingly so. While private companies usually bag unsuspecting travellers, you're better off with companies operating out of the government bus station. These buses cater to the Thai community, making them more culturally engaging and safer for your belongings. Starting at the top, VIP buses are the closest you will come to being pampered like a rock star. The seats recline, the air-con is frosty and your very own 'air hostess' dispenses refreshments and snacks. Various diminishing classes of air-con buses begin to strip away the extras until you're left with a fairly beat-up bus with an asthmatic cooling system. Incredibly punishing but undeniably entertaining are the 'ordinary' buses. These rattletraps have fans that don't work when the bus has come to a stop, school-bus sized seats and a tinny sound system that blares the driver's favourite music. The trip is sweaty, loud and usually involves as many animals and babies as adult passengers. At stops

BORDER CROSSINGS

Thailand enjoys open and relatively safe border relations with Malaysia, Cambodia and Laos. Myanmar's internal conflicts require a restricted border that is subject to frequent closings and shifting regulations. Along the Thailand–Cambodia border, there are small border crossings that have opened up recently, but see little traffic due to roller-coaster roads on the Cambodian side. The Chong Jom–O Smach border connects Surin Province with Siem Reap, but is very remote on the Cambodian side. There is another remote crossing that links Si Saket Province with the former Khmer Rouge stronghold of Anlong Veng, but access is tough on both sides of the border. For all other crossings, specific information appears throughout the chapter.

along the way, vendors walk the aisles selling food, everyone throws their rubbish out the window and the driver honks at every passer-by hoping to pick up another fare. It's a real trip!

For long distance trips, check out schedules and/or purchase tickets the day before. Visit www.transport.co.th for bus routes and timetables in English.

Car & Motorcycle

Cars, 4WDs or vans can be rented in Bangkok and large provincial capitals. Check with travel agencies or hotels for rental locations. Always verify that the vehicle is insured for liability before signing a rental contract, and ask to see the dated insurance documents. If you have an accident while

ALWAYS LOOK ON THE BRIGHT SIDE...

'Always look on the bright side...' unless you happen to be on a Thai bus. If you get on board and everyone has clustered to one side, don't celebrate that you've scored a whole row. Thais instinctively know where the sun will be at all times of the day. The deserted side of the bus will be the side that gets bleached by the sun for the entire trip. Banish the urge to populate virgin territory and join the dark side for the day.

THAILAND

driving an uninsured vehicle, you're in for some major hassles.

Thais drive on the left-hand side of the road – most of the time. Like many places in Asia, every two-lane road has an invisible third lane in the middle that all drivers feel free to use at any time. Passing on hills and curves is common – as long as you've got the proper Buddhist altar on the dashboard, what could happen? The main rule to be aware of is that 'might makes right' and smaller vehicles always yield to bigger ones.

Motorcycle travel is a popular way to get around Thailand. Dozens of places along the guesthouse circuit rent motorbikes for 150B to 300B a day. It is also possible to buy a new or used motorbike and sell it before you leave the country – a good used 125cc bike costs around 40,000B. If you've never ridden a motorcycle before, stick to the smaller 100cc step-through bikes with automatic clutches. Motorcycle rental usually requires that you leave your passport.

Hitching

It is uncommon to see people hitching alongside the highway, since bus travel between towns is fairly inexpensive and reliable. Hitching becomes a better option in the country where public transportation isn't available. If you get dropped off by a bus outside a national park or historical site, you can catch a ride along the remainder of the road with an incoming vehicle. Just remember to use the Asian style of beckoning: hold your arm out towards the road, palm-side down and wave towards the ground.

Local Transport

Rarely does anyone get stuck anywhere in Thailand, but it is also impossible to escape the hungry drivers who have mastered the most irritating phrase in the English language, 'Hey you, where you go?' A literal translation from the typical Thai inquiry, this phrase will drive you to the edge of insanity, but keep in mind that most don't intend offence, they only want to make a living.

SĂAMLÁW & TÚK-TÚK

Săamláw (also written samlor), meaning 'three wheels', are pedal rickshaws, and you'll see them in a few towns in the northeast and in Chiang Mai. These are good for relatively short distances, but expect to pay

a little more if you take one further afield, as it is all human powered. Then there are the motorised săamláw, called túk-túk because of the throaty cough their two-stroke engines make. In Bangkok especially, túk-túk drivers give all local transporters a bad name. The worst cases are unscrupulously greedy – exorbitantly inflating the fares or diverting passengers to places that pay commissions.

You must bargain and agree on a fare before accepting a ride, but in many towns there is a more-or-less fixed fare anywhere in town.

SĂWNGTHĂEW

Săwngthăew (literally, two benches) are small pick-ups with a row of seats down each side. In some towns, săwngthăew serve as public buses running regular routes for fixed fare. But in tourist towns, you'll also find săwngthăew performing the same function as túk-túk, transporting people to and from the bus station or to popular attractions for a bargained fare.

Train

All rail travel originates in Bangkok and radiates out, forming the following four spurs: Ayuthaya–Phitsanulok–Chiang Mai; Khorat–Surin–Ubon Ratchathani; Nakhon Ratchasima (Khorat)–Khon Kaen–Nong Khai; and Hua Hin–Surat Thani–Hat Yai. The government-operated trains (www.railway.co.th) in Thailand are comfortable and moderately priced, but rather slow. On comparable routes, the buses can often be twice as fast, but the relatively low speed of the train means you can often leave at a convenient hour in the evening and arrive at your destination at a pleasant hour in the morning. Very useful condensed railway timetables are available in English at the Hualamphong train station in Bangkok. These contain schedules and fares for all rapid and express trains, as well as a few ordinary trains.

CLASSES & COSTS

First-, 2nd- and 3rd-class cabins are available on most trains, but each class may vary considerably depending on the type of train (rapid, express or ordinary). First class is typically a private cabin. Second class has individually reclining seats or padded bench seating; depending on the train some cabins have air-con. Non-air-conditioned, 3rd class is spartan and cheap with shared wooden-bench seating.

Ordinary trains only have the most basic version of 3rd class and stop at every itsy bitsy station. Express and rapid are, well, faster making fewer stops, but there is a 60B surcharge for express trains and 40B for rapid trains. Some 2nd- and 3rd-class services are air-con, in which case there is a 70B surcharge. For the special-express trains that run between Bangkok and Padang Besar (Malaysia) and between Bangkok and Chiang Mai, there is an 80B to 100B surcharge (or 120B if a meal is included).

Overnight trains have sleeping berths in 1st and 2nd class. The charge for 2nd-class sleeping berths is 100B for an upper berth and 150B for a lower berth (or 130B and 200B, respectively, on a special express). For 2nd-class sleepers with air-con add 250/320B for upper/lower. No sleepers are available in 3rd class.

All 1st-class cabins come with individually controlled air-con. For a two-bed cabin the surcharge is 520B per person.

RESERVATIONS

Trains are often heavily booked, so it's wise to reserve your place well ahead, especially for long-distance trips. At **Hualamphong Station** (☎ 0 2220 4334) in Bangkok, you can book trains on any route in Thailand. The advance booking office is open from 8.30am to 4pm daily. Seats, berths or cabins may be booked up to 60 days in advance. Visit www.railway .co.th for train timetables in English.

BANGKOK

pop 6 million

Ladies and gentlemen, fasten your seatbelts. You are now entering Bangkok, a city that is always on the move. Ancient temples in the shadow of space-age shopping malls, soaring skyscrapers towering over tumbledown hovels, *über*-cool cafés and restaurants surrounded by simple street stalls, Bangkok is an interchange of the past, present and future, and a superb subject for any urban connoisseur. It's your decompression chamber, softening the landing in another world, familiar enough to feel like a hot

> **DON'T MISS...**
> - wandering the grounds of Wat Phra Kaew and the Grand Palace
> - taking a ride on the Skytrain
> - pub-crawling along the infamous Th Khao San
> - catching cool breezes on the Chao Phraya river ferry

version of home, exotic enough to point the way to adventures ahead. Delve beneath the elevated highways and skyways and you'll find a small village napping in the narrow soi with an unmistakable *khwaam pen thai* (Thai-ness).

The capital of Thailand was established at Bangkok in 1782. But the name Bangkok, baptised by foreigners, actually refers to a small village within the larger beast. The Thais call their capital Krung Thep, or City of Angels, a much shortened version of the very official and very long tongue-twister of *Krungthep mahanakhon amonratanakosin mahintara ayuthaya mahadilok popnopparat ratchathani burirom udomratchaniwet mahasathan amonpiman avatansathit sakkathattiya witsanukamprasit.*

ORIENTATION

The Mae Nam Chao Phraya divides Bangkok from the older city of Thonburi, where the Southern Bus Terminal and the Thonburi (Bangkok Noi) train station are located.

Bangkok can be further divided into east and west by the main railway line, which feeds in and out of Hualamphong station. Sandwiched between the western side of the tracks and the river is the older part of the city, crowded with historical temples, bustling Chinatown and the popular travellers' centre of Banglamphu. This section of town is less urban, relatively speaking, with low-slung residential homes and shops built along the *khlong* (canals; also written *khlawng*).

East of the railway line is the new city, devoted to commerce and its attendant temples of skyscrapers and shopping centres. Th Phra Ram I feeds into Siam Sq, a popular shopping district, and eventually turns into Th Sukhumvit, a busy commercial centre. Between Siam Sq and Sukhumvit,

THAILAND

Th Withayu shelters many of the cities foreign embassies. South of these districts, Th Silom is another concentration of high-rise hotels and multinational offices.

This simple sketch of Bangkok's layout does a real injustice to the chaos that the city has effortlessly acquired through years of unplanned and rapacious development. Street names are unpronounceable, compounded by the inconsistency of romanised Thai spellings. Street addresses are virtually irrelevant as the jumble of numbers divided by slashes and dashes are a record of lot distribution rather than sequential order along a block. Soi (lanes) can't be trusted as they change course more frequently than unfettered rivers.

In short, you will need a good map and a lot of patience. Lonely Planet publishes a handy-sized *Bangkok City Map*. If you plan to use Bangkok's very economical bus system, you should buy the *Tour 'n' Guide Map to Bangkok Thailand*. *Nancy Chandler's Map of Bangkok* is a colourful schematic map of the usual attractions, popular restaurants and other tips from Nancy Chandler, a long-time Bangkok resident. Another contender on the market, *Groovy Map's Bangkok by Day Map 'n' Guide* and combines an up-to-date bus map, sightseeing features, and a short selection of restaurant and bar reviews.

INFORMATION
Bookshops

The bookshops in Bangkok are among the best in Southeast Asia. Options include the following:

Aporia Books (Map p709; 131 Th Tanao, Banglamphu) Used books.

Asia Books Th Sukhumvit (Map pp704-5; Soi 15);
Th Ploenchit (Map pp704-5; 3rd fl, Central World Plaza);
Th Silom (Map pp704-5; 3rd fl, Thaniya Plaza);
Th Ratchadamri (Map pp704-5; Peninsula Plaza);
Th Phra Ram I (Map pp704-5; Siam Discovery Center) Books on anything and everything.

Shaman Books (Map p709; 71 Th Khao San, Banglamphu) Huge selection of used books.

Emergency

Bangkok does not have an emergency phone system staffed by English-speaking operators.

Tourist Assistance Centre (☎ 0 2281 1348;
🕑 8am-midnight) A division of the Tourism Authority of Thailand (TAT) dealing with tourist safety.

GETTING INTO TOWN

Bangkok's Don Muang Airport (Map pp700–1) is 25km north of the city centre. A fairly economical shuttle bus (100B) runs four designated routes into town from 6am to 12.30am. A1 connects to Silom, A2 to Th Khao San (in Banglamphu), A3 to Th Sukhumvit and the A4 to Hualamphong station.

Touts try to steer all arriving passengers towards one of their expensive 650B limousine services or to the flat-rate taxis. Ignore them and buy a ticket from the public taxi booth located near the kerb right outside the arrival hall. Fares differ according to destination; most destinations in central Bangkok cost from 200B to 300B.

The cheapest way to get into town is the train, as there is a station across the street from the airport. Trains run frequently between 4.40am and 9.45pm, take about 45 minutes to one hour and terminate in central Hualamphong station. Tickets cost 10B for ordinary trains. But then you still need to arrange transport from the station!

Once you know where you are going, you are in a position to exploit the public bus system. Located just a few steps outside the airport there is a highway that leads straight into the city. Air-con bus 29 (16B, runs 24 hours) goes to the Siam Sq and Hualamphong areas. Air-con bus 4 (16B, runs from 5.45am to 8pm) works its way to Th Silom and across the river to Thonburi. Air-con bus 513 (16B, runs from 4.30am to 9pm) is a good option for Th Sukhumvit–bound travellers. Air-con bus 510 (16B, runs from 4am to 9.30pm) goes from the airport all the way to the Southern Bus Terminal located in Thonburi.

Confusingly enough, by the time you read this, **Suvarnabhumi International Airport** (www .suvarnabhumiairport.com/en/index.htm) may be up and running and most international flights will operate out of here. It is likely to open some time in 2006, and a similar range of transport options will be available as at Don Muang.

Tourist police (☎ 1155; ☿ 24hr) English-speaking police to assist tourists in trouble.

Immigration Office
Bangkok Immigration Office (Map pp704-5; ☎ 0 2287 3101; Soi Suan Phlu, Th Sathon Tai; ☿ 9am-noon & 1-4.30pm Mon-Fri, 9am-noon Sat)

Internet Access
Internet cafés are ubiquitous. Rates vary depending on concentration and affluence of cyber junkies. Cheapest access is found in the back streets around Th Khao San where it starts at around 30B an hour. Siam Sq is the next best bet, but places around the Th Sukhumvit and Silom areas are considerably more expensive. Connections are surprisingly slow and are frequently lost mid-click.

Internet Resources
Bangkok Recorder (www.bangkokrecorder.com) Online magazine on music trends (the indie revolution), nightlife (curfew crackdowns) and other vexing capital questions.
Bangkok Thailand Today (www.bangkok.thailand today.com) Solid tips on shopping, nightlife, dining and sightseeing, with an emphasis on the river and Ko Ratanakosin.
Khao San Road (www.khaosanroad.com) News, reviews and profiles of Bangkok's famous tourist ghetto.

Libraries
Besides offering an abundance of reading material in English, Bangkok's libraries make a peaceful escape from the heat and noise.
National Library (Map pp704-5; ☎ 0 2281 5212; cnr Th Samsen & Th Si Ayuthaya) Foreign-language books and magazines; membership free.
National Museum (Map p709; Th Na Phra That) History, art and culture of Thailand.
Neilson Hays Library (Map pp704-5; ☎ 0 2233 1731; 195 Th Surawong; ☿ 9.30am-4pm Tue-Sat, 9.30am-2pm Sun) The oldest English-language library in Thailand. Next to the British Club on Th Surawong.

THÀNŎN & SOI

Throughout this book, *thànŏn* (meaning 'street') is abbreviated as 'Th'. A soi is a small street or lane that runs off a larger street. The address of a site located on a soi will be written as 48/3-5 Soi 1, Th Sukhumvit, meaning off Th Sukhumvit on Soi 1.

Media
There is a ton of free rags available in Bangkok to stay ahead of what is cool and what is not in this dynamic city. Pick up a copy of *Bangkok Metro* or *BK Magazine* for listings, reviews and what's on.

Medical Services
There are several outstanding hospitals in Bangkok with English-speaking staff:
Bangkok Adventist (Mission) Hospital (Map pp704-5; ☎ 0 2281 1100; 430 Th Phitsanulok)
Bangkok Christian Hospital (Map pp704-5; ☎ 0 2634 0560; 124 Th Silom)
Bumrungrad Hospital (Map pp704-5; ☎ 0 2253 0250; 33 Soi 3, Th Sukhumvit)

Money
Thai banks have currency exchange kiosks in many parts of Bangkok, although a large number of exchange kiosks are concentrated in the Th Sukhumvit, Th Khao San, Siam Sq and Th Silom areas. Hours sometimes vary, but most kiosks are open from 8am to 8pm daily. Regular bank hours in Bangkok are 10am to 4pm. ATMs are located everywhere.

Post
Main post office (Map pp704-5; Th Charoen Krung; ☿ 8am-8pm Mon-Fri, 8am-1pm Sat & Sun) Poste restante and a packing service for sending parcels home. Branch post offices throughout the city also offer poste restante and parcel services.

Telephone
Communications Authority of Thailand (CAT; Map pp704-5; Th Charoen Krung; ☿ 24hr) Next to the main post office.
Telephone Organisation of Thailand (TOT; Map pp704-5; Th Ploenchit) International faxes and calls.

Tourist Information
Bangkok Tourist Division (Map p709; ☎ 0 2225 7612; www.bangkoktourist.com; 17/1 Th Phra Athit; ☿ 9am-7pm)
Tourism Authority of Thailand (TAT; www.tourism thailand.org) main office (Map pp704-5; ☎ 0 2250 5500; 4th fl, 1606 Th Phetburi Tat Mai; ☿ 8.30am-4.30pm); airport information desk (☎ 0 2504 2701; Arrival Hall, Terminal 1, Bangkok International Airport; ☿ 8am-midnight) To get to the main office, take air-con bus 512, microbus 10 and ordinary buses 11, 38, 58, 60, 72, 99 and 113 or walk from Asoke Skytrain station.

THAILAND

THAILAND

GREATER BANGKOK

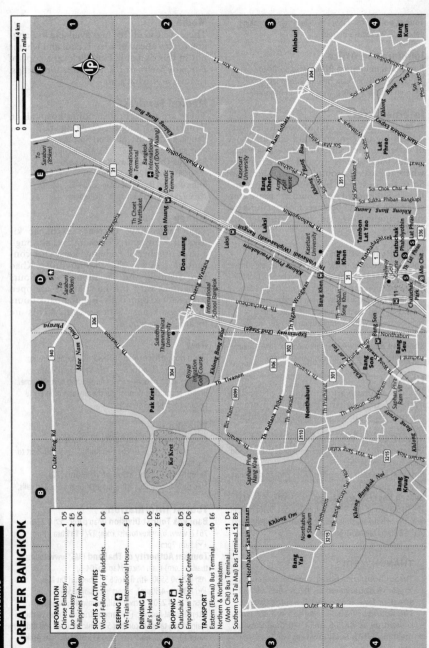

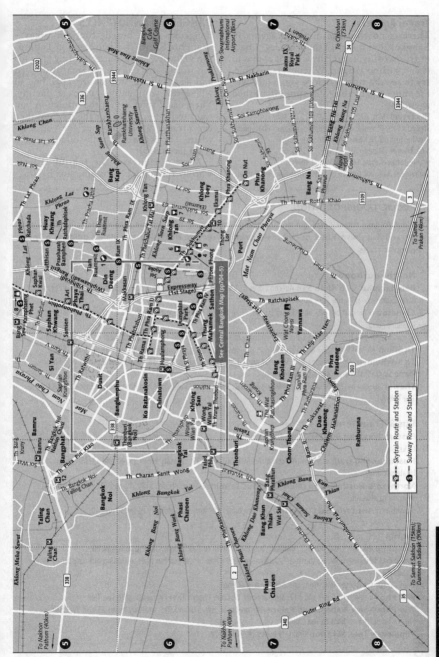

Travel Agencies

There is no shortage of travel agents in Bangkok, but not all of them are legitimate or trustworthy, especially when it comes to cheap airline tickets. Whenever possible, try to see the tickets before you hand over the money. Try the following established agencies:

IBS Travel (Map p709; ☎ 0 2810 1219; 108/11 Th Khao San) One of the most reliable options in backpackersville, just off Th Khao San near Susie Pub.

STA Travel (Map pp704–5; ☎ 0 2236 0262; www.statravel.com; 14th fl, Wall St Tower, 33/70 Th Surawong) Bangkok branch of an international institution.

DANGERS & ANNOYANCES

Bangkok's most heavily touristed areas – Wat Phra Kaew, Th Khao San, Jim Thompson's House – are favourite hunting grounds for professional con artists. Smartly dressed and slick talking, not all are Thai, but all will speak your native language fluently. Their usual spiel is that the attraction you want to visit is closed for the day and they can arrange a bargain tour for you elsewhere. This is the bait for the infamous gem scam (see p815).

More obvious are the túk-túk drivers who are out to make a commission by drag-

---

PUBLIC TRANSPORTATION

Want to save money and get around town like a local? Then ignore those pesky túk-túk drivers and flag down a bus, or better yet catch a river taxi. Here is an at-a-glance guide to a few popular spots.

Neighbourhoods

Banglamphu & Th Khao San Air-con buses 511 and 512; ordinary buses 3, 15, 30, 32 and 53; Chao Phraya River Express boat to Tha Phra Athit.

Chinatown Air-con bus 507 or ordinary bus 53; Chao Phraya River Express boat to Tha Ratchawong; Metro to Hualamphong.

Siam Sq Air-con buses 508, 515 and 529; ordinary buses 15, 16, 25 and 40; Skytrain to Siam or National Stadium.

Th Silom Air-con buses 502 and 505; Skytrain stations Sala Daeng, Chong Nonsi and Surasak; Metro to Silom.

Th Sukhumvit Air-con buses 501, 508, 511 and 513; ordinary buses 2, 25, 38 and 40; Nana, Asoke and Phrom Phong Skytrain stations; Metro to Sukhumvit.

Thewet Air-con buses 505 and 506; ordinary buses 3, 16, 30, 32, 33 and 53; Chao Phraya River Express boat to Tha Thewet.

Bus & Train Terminals

Eastern (Ekamai) Bus Terminal Air-con buses 508, 511 and 513; ordinary buses 25 and 40; Skytrain to Ekamai.

Hualamphong train station Air-con buses 501, 507 and 529; ordinary buses 25, 40 and 53; Metro to Hualamphong.

Northern & Northeastern (Moh Chit) Bus Terminal Air-con buses 510, 512 and 513; ordinary bus 3; Skytrain to Mo Chit.

Southern Bus Terminal (Thonburi) Air-con buses 507 and 511; ordinary buses 30 and 40.

Sights

Lumphini Park Air-con bus 507; ordinary bus 15; Skytrain to Ratchadamri; Metro to Lumphini.

National Museum Across the street, Sanam Luang is a hub for several bus lines, including ordinary buses 30, 32 and 53.

Wat Arun Cross-river ferry from Tha Tien, near Wat Pho.

Wat Pho Air-con buses 508 and 512; ordinary bus 32; Chao Phraya River Express boat to Tha Tien.

Wat Phra Kaew & the Grand Palace Air-con buses 508, 512 and 515; ordinary buses 25 and 32; Chao Phraya River Express boat to Tha Chang.

Vimanmek Teak Mansion Ordinary buses 18, 70 and 72.

ging you to a local silk or jewellery shop, even though you've requested an entirely different destination. In either case, if you accept an invitation for 'free' sightseeing or shopping, you're quite likely to end up wasting an afternoon or – as happens all too often – losing a lot of money.

SIGHTS

The cultural gems of Bangkok are found in Ko Ratanakosin, the oldest and holiest part of town. For good old-fashioned wandering, sample the commercial chaos of Chinatown; to escape the heat and congestion, explore the Mae Nam Chao Phraya.

Ko Ratanakosin Area

Bordering the eastern bank of the Mae Nam Chao Phraya, this area is a veritable Vatican City of Thai Buddhism, filled with some of the country's most honoured and holy sites: Wat Phra Kaew, the Grand Palace and Wat Pho. These are also the most spectacular tourist attractions the city has to offer and a must for even the most unmotivated students of culture and history. Many Thais make religious pilgrimages here, so remember to dress modestly (clothes to elbows and knees) and behave respectfully (remove shoes when instructed). And for walking in the grounds, wear shoes with closed toes and heels, not sandals.

Wat Phra Kaew (Map pp704-5; ☎ 0 2623 5500; Th Na Phra Lan; admission 200B; ⏰ 8.30-3.30pm), also known as the Temple of the Emerald Buddha, is an architectural wonder of gleaming, gilded *chedi* (stupas) seemingly levitating above the ground, polished orange and green roof tiles, mosaic-encrusted pillars and rich marble pediments. The highly stylised ornamentation is a shrine to the revered Emerald Buddha, which is housed in the main chapel. Actually made of jasper, the Emerald Buddha has endured an epic journey from northern Thailand, where it was hidden inside a layer of stucco, to its present home. In between it was seized by Lao forces and carried off to Luang Prabang and Vientiane, where it was later recaptured by the Thais.

Within the same grounds is the **Grand Palace**, the former royal residence. Today the Grand Palace is used by the king only for certain ceremonial occasions such as Coronation Day; the king's current residence is Chitlada Palace in the northern part of the city. The exteriors of the four buildings are worth a swift perusal for their royal bombast, but their interiors are closed to the public. The intrigue and rituals that occurred within the walls of this once-cloistered community are not always evident to the modern visitor. A fictionalised version is told in the trilogy *Four Reigns,* by Kukrit Pramoj, about a young girl named Ploi, growing up in the Royal City. The admission fee also includes entry to Vimanmek Teak Mansion (p707), near the Dusit Zoo.

Nearby **Wat Pho** (Map pp704-5; ☎ 0 2221 9911; admission 20B; ⏰ 8am-5pm) sweeps the awards for superlatives: it's the oldest and largest temple in Bangkok, dating from the 16th century; it houses the country's largest reclining Buddha; and it has the biggest collection of Buddha images in the country. The *big* attraction is the stunning reclining Buddha, 46m long and 15m high, illustrating the passing of the Buddha into final nirvana. The figure is modelled out of plaster around a brick core and finished in gold leaf. Mother-of-pearl inlay ornaments the eyes and feet, and the feet display 108 different auspicious *láksànà* (characteristics of a Buddha). See p708 for information on Wat Pho Thai Massage School.

The **National Museum** (Map p709; ☎ 0 2224 1370; Th Na Phra That; admission 40B; ⏰ 9am-4pm Wed-Sun), reportedly the largest in Southeast Asia, offers visitors an overview of Thai art and culture, a useful stepping stone to exploring the ancient capitals of Ayuthaya and Sukhothai. On the downside, the labelling isn't exactly illuminating and there is no air-conditioning to help you keep your cool on a hot day. Try the free guided tour (on Wednesdays at 9.30am in English, French and German) to put some perspective on the collection.

Wat Arun (Map pp704-5; ☎ 0 2466 3167; Th Arun Amarin; admission 20B; ⏰ 9-5pm) is a striking temple, named after the Indian god of dawn, Aruna. It looms large on the Thonburi side of the Mae Nam Chao Phraya, looking as if it were carved from granite; a closer inspection reveals a mosaic of porcelain tiles covering the imposing 82m Khmer-style *praang* (spire). The tiles were left behind by Chinese merchant ships no longer needing them as ballast.

CENTRAL BANGKOK

See Banglamphu Map (p709)

THAILAND

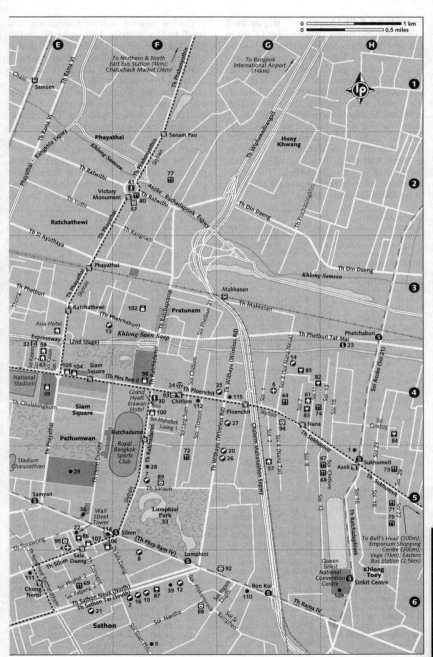

Chinatown & Phahurat   Map pp704–5

Gleaming gold shops, towering neon signs in Chinese characters, shopfronts spilling out on to the sidewalk – welcome to Chinatown, the epicentre of Bangkok's bustling commercial cult. The neighbourhood's energy is at once exhilarating and exhausting. Slicing through the centre of the district, the famous **Sampeng Lane** (Soi Wanit) runs roughly parallel to Th Yaowarat and is jam-packed with the useful and the useless, but all at bargain prices. On the corner of Th Yaowarat and Th Chakrawat is **Thieves Market** (Nakhon Kasem), so named for the 'hot' items once sold here. The neighbourhood is fun to explore at night when it is lit up like a Christmas tree.

On the western side of Chinatown is a small Indian district, known as Phahurat. Th Chakraphet is popular for its Indian restaurants and shops selling Indian sweets.

Wat Traimit (☎ 0 2623 1226; cnr Th Yaowarat & Th Charoen Krung; admission 20B; ☻ 9am-5pm) shelters a 3m-tall, 5.5-tonne, solid-gold Buddha image – an impressive sight, even in the land of a million Buddhas. This gleaming figure was once covered in stucco, but during efforts to move it in the 1960s, the figure fell, cracking the stucco and revealing the treasure inside. The covering was probably intended to hide it during one of Burma's many invasions. Located near Hualamphong station, this temple's English

THAILAND

name is, surprise surprise, Temple of the Golden Buddha.

Mae Nam Chao Phraya

Once upon a time, Bangkok was called the 'Venice of the East'. Canals, not roads, transported goods and people, and the mighty Mae Nam Chao Phraya (Chao Phraya River) was the superhighway leading to the interior of the country. All life centred on these vast canal networks and Thais considered themselves *jâo náam* (water lords). Times have changed, but you can observe remnants of urban river life by boarding a Chao Phraya River Express boat at any *thâa* (pier). This is also one of the more pleasant commuting options in Bangkok and is used by a healthy cross-section of the populace, from uniformed school children to saffron-robed monks.

Just across the river in the area known as Thonburi, **Khlong Bangkok Noi** train station provides a quick escape from Bangkok's modern madness. The further into the *khlong* you venture, the better the rewards, with teak houses on stilts and plenty of greenery. Longtail tourist boats depart regularly from Tha Chang, next to Silpakorn University, to the town of **Bang Yai** (Map pp700-1; 60B return; 🕑 8am-3pm Mon-Fri).

Foreigners also had a presence on the river during the bygone shipping era. Two Dutch sea captains built the majestic **Oriental Hotel** (Map pp704-5; ☎ 0 2659 9000; www.mandarinoriental.com; 48 Soi Oriental, Th Charoen Krung), an attraction in its own right. Somerset Maugham and Joseph Conrad were among the Oriental's famous guests. You can toast those literary giants in the hotel's Author Wing café or the riverside bar; dress smartly.

Other Attractions   Map pp704–5

Jim Thompson's House (☎ 0 2216 7368; Soi Kasem San 2, Th Phra Ram I; adult/child 100/50B; 🕑 9am-5pm) is the beautiful house of the American entrepreneur Jim Thompson, who successfully promoted Thai silk to Western markets. After a long career in Thailand, he mysteriously disappeared in 1967 in Malaysia's Cameron Highlands; the reason remains unknown and many suspect foul play. Atmospherically sited on a small *khlong*, his house was built from salvaged components of traditional Thai houses. In addition to remarkable architecture, his collection of

Thai art and furnishings is superb. Admission proceeds go to Bangkok's School for the Blind.

Vimanmek Teak Mansion (☎ 0 2628 6300; foreigner/Thai 100/50B, free with Grand Palace ticket; 🕑 9.30am-4pm), in the serene Dusit Palace grounds, is reputedly the world's largest golden teak building. In the early 20th century Rama V lived in this mansion of graceful staircases, octagonal rooms and lattice walls. The interior contains various personal effects of the king, and a treasure-trove of early Ratanakosin art objects and antiques.

Lumphini Park (cnr Th Phra Ram IV & Th Ratchadamri; 🕑 5am-8pm) offers a shady respite from the city's noise and traffic; the afternoon drop-in aerobics class is great free entertainment whether or not you join the synchronised crowd.

Although religion and commerce may seem diametrically opposed, Thai Buddhism is a flexible faith, as witnessed by the numerous and popular shrines built in front of huge shopping centres and hotels throughout Bangkok. Outside Grand Hyatt Erawan Hotel, the **Erawan shrine** (San Phra Phrom; cnr Th Ratchadamri & Th Ploenchit) is dedicated to

---

FREE STUFF

Despite Bangkok's consumer frenzy, you can soak up city life without spending a baht. In the evenings, breakdancers practise their moves on the elevated walkway between the Siam Sq Skytrain station and the various shopping malls. This walkway has become an urban park with cuddling couples, as well as an unsanctioned bazaar with sellers displaying their wares and keeping an eye out for the police.

The narrow lanes of **Little Arabia** (Map pp704-5; Soi 3, Th Sukhumvit), a Middle Eastern transplant that feels like a modern medina, comes complete with lively cafés and smoky *sheesha* (water pipe) bars.

More spectacular and synchronised are the evening aerobics classes that occur in **Lumphini Park** (Map pp704–5) and also in **Santichaiprakan Park** (Map p709; Th Phra Sumen, Banglamphu). The combination of the techno beat, setting sun and crowd of bouncing bodies attracts almost as many onlookers as participants.

the Hindu deity of creation and is credited for bringing good fortune and lottery winnings to many of the faithful. If a wish is granted, the wishmaker repays the favour by hiring musicians and dancers to perform in front of the shrine.

Wat Benchamabophit (cnr Th Si Ayuthaya & Th Phra Ram V; admission 20B; ☼ 8am-5.30pm), built under Rama V in 1899, is made of white Carrara marble and is a stunning example of modern temple architecture. The real treasure here is a rear courtyard containing a large collection of Buddha images from all periods of Thai Buddhist art. Wat Ben is diagonally opposite Chitlada Palace. Buses 503 (air-con) and 72 stop nearby.

A small Hindu Shiva temple, **Sri Mariamman (Maha Uma Devi) Temple** (☼ 5am-8pm) sits on the corner of Th Pan and Th Silom.

COURSES
Cooking
One of the best ways to crack Thailand's lengthy menu is to take a cooking course. **Thai House** (Map pp700-1; ☎ 0 2903 9611; www.thaihouse.co.th; Bang Yai, Nonthaburi; programme 3550-16,650B) Set in a homely traditional teak house about 40 minutes north of Bangkok by boat. Choose from a one- to three-day programme, which includes preparing Thai standards (*tôm yam*, pad thai and various curries). There are also cooking and lodging packages available.

Language & Culture
AUA Language Centre (Map pp704-5; ☎ 0 2252 8170; www.auathai.com; 179 Th Ratchadamri) One of the most popular places to study Thai, the American University Alumni school is also one of the largest private language institutions in the world.

Chulalongkorn University Continuing Education Centre (Map pp704-5; ☎ 0 2218 3908; www.cec .chula.ac.th; 5th fl, Vidhyabhathan Bldg, 12 Soi Chulalongkorn, Chulalongkorn University; course US$950) The most prestigious university in Thailand offers a two-week intensive Thai studies course called Perspectives on Thailand. The 60-hour programme includes classes in Thai culture, history, politics, art and language.

Siri Pattana Thai Language School (Map pp704-5; ☎ 0 2286 1936; YWCA, 13 Th Sathon Tai) This place offers Thai language courses and preparation for the *paw hòk* exam, required for teaching in Thai public schools.

Massage
Wat Pho Thai Massage School (Map pp704-5; ☎ 0 2221 3686; watpottm@netscape.net; 392/25-28 Soi Phenphat 1, Th Maharat; course 7000B) Affiliated with Wat Pho, this massage school offers two 30-hour courses – one on general Thai massage, the other on massage therapy – that you attend for three hours per day for 10 days, or two hours per day for 15 days. Other coursework includes a 15-hour foot massage (3600B) and longer one- to three-year programmes that combine Thai herbal medicine with massage for a full curriculum in Thai traditional medicine. Some knowledge of Thai will ease the communication barrier for all of these courses.

Meditation
Wat Mahathat (Map p709; ☎ 0 2222 6011; Th Maharat) This 18th-century wat opposite Sanam Luang provides meditation instruction daily at Section 5, a meditation hall near the monks' residences. Some of the Thai monks here speak English, and there are often Western monks or long-term residents available to interpret. Contact the **Buddhist Meditation Centre** (☎ 0 2623 5881), affiliated to Wat Mahathat, for information on meditation centres or English-speaking teachers.

World Fellowship of Buddhists (Map pp700-1; ☎ 0 2661 1284; www.wfb-hq.org; Soi 24, Th Sukhumvit) At the back of Benjasiri Park, next to the Emporium, this is a centre for information on Theravada Buddhism. It also sells a handy booklet listing meditation centres throughout Thailand.

Muay Thai (Thai Boxing)
Jitti's Gym Thai Boxing & Homestay (Sor Vorapin; Map p709; ☎ 0 2282 3551; www.thaiboxing.com; 13 Soi Krasab, Th Chakraphong; courses per day/week/month 500/3000/10,000B) In Banglamphu near Th Khao San, this school specialises in training foreign students (women and men); fees include daily training sessions, plus accommodation and evening meals.

TOURS
ABC Amazing Bangkok Cyclists (☎ 0 2712 9301; www.realasia.net; 1000B; ☼ 1-6pm) Discover another side to Bangkok on a cycling tour through Thonburi. The trip starts with a longtail boat ride across the river and includes a slice of village life in the city.

FESTIVALS & EVENTS
Chinese New Year Thai-Chinese celebrate the lunar new year in February or March, with a week of house-cleaning, lion dances and fireworks. Festivities centre on Chinatown.

Kite-Flying Season In March, during the windy season, colourful kites battle it over the skies of Sanam Luang and Lumphini Park.

Songkran Held from 13 to 15 April, the celebration of the Thai new year has morphed into water warfare with high-powered pistols and lots of talc being launched at suspecting and unsuspecting participants around Th Khao San. Prepare to be soaked or stay away.

Royal Ploughing Ceremony His Majesty the King commences rice-planting season with a royal-religious ceremony at Sanam Luang, in early May.

Loi Kràthong A beautiful festival where on the night of the full moon in early November, small lotus-shaped boats made of banana leaf containing a lit candle are set adrift on the river.

King's Birthday On 5 December locals celebrate their monarch's birthday with lots of parades and fireworks.

SLEEPING

Bangkok possesses arguably the best variety and quality of budget places to spend the night of any Asian capital city, which is one of the reasons why it's become such a popular destination for roving world travellers. Due to the geographic spread of places,

narrow the options by working out where you want to base yourself.

Where there are backpackers, there you will find Th Khao San wannabes. The guesthouse rooms come in every shape and size from cheap cells to fancy frills; the late-night bars are loud and the constant pedestrian traffic is an attraction in itself. Banglamphu, the neighbourhood surrounding Th Khao San, is a sedate residential area with better-value guesthouse options. The drawback is that Banglamphu is far removed from central Bangkok, so trips to other parts of town take some time.

The Siam Sq area is centrally located and on both Skytrain lines. Accommodation in Siam Sq is more expensive than

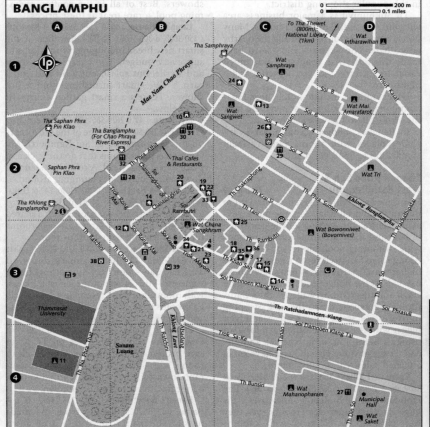

BANGLAMPHU

Banglamphu, but then so is the real estate in this popular shopping district.

Th Sukhumvit is a major business area with only a handful of budget hotels. Many hotels attract sex tourists visiting the nearby go-go bars. The Skytrain and Metro have made this otherwise congested area much easier to traverse, but taxi travel is still a nightmare.

Other options include hotels near Hualamphong train station or somewhere near the airport if you have an early flight.

In Bangkok, budget accommodation includes places with rooms ranging from about 100B to 750B per night.

Thanon Khao San & West Banglamphu   Map p709

If you are on a tight budget, head straight to the soi around Th Khao San, the main travellers' centre. It is getting a little gentrified of late, and there are some superb options with swimming pools along Soi Rambutri. Along Khao San itself room rates tend to be higher than smarter places just a few blocks beyond. At the budget end, rooms are quite small and the dividing walls are thin. Bathrooms are usually down the hall. Stepping up the price scale, rooms are a smidgen bigger with real walls; another leap forward brings a bathroom, a hot shower and aircon. Some of these guesthouses have small attached cafés with limited menus.

Rambuttri Village Inn (☎ 0 2282 9162; 95 Soi Rambutri; s 290-400B, d 380-650B; ⚄ ▢ ⚄) The Holiday Inn of budget guesthouses, this huge place has super-clean rooms – yes, they were cleaning the tile grout with a tooth-

brush when we were here – with hot-water showers. Best of all is the rooftop swimming pool, a rare treat at these prices.

Lamphu House (☎ 0 2629 5861; Soi Rambutri; s 150-300B, d 300-580B; ⚄ ▢) Another of the smart new breed of lodgings with rooms to suit every budget. The cheapies are small and sterile, but splash out a bit and you'll earn a TV, smart furnishings and a hot shower. There's a smart garden courtyard café below.

My House (☎ 0 2629 5861; 37 Soi Chanasongkran; s 150-190B, d 250-500B; ⚄) One of the old-timers on this continuation of Soi Rambutri, My House has plain rooms that do the trick as a place to rest your head. A reliable restaurant downstairs encourages lounging around.

Bella Bella House (☎ 0 2629 3090; 74 Soi Chanasongkran; s 170B, d 220-490B; ⚄) This big, modern guesthouse has cheaper rooms with a shared bathroom and some larger air-con rooms for those parting with 400B or more.

Khao San Palace Inn (☎ 0 2282 0578; Th Khao San; r 280-530B; ⚄) Just a stone's throw off Th Khao San – don't try it, you might hurt someone – this is one of the smarter places, with rooms that don't resemble a prison cell. Fan rooms have private bathroom, while air-con rooms include TV and hot water.

Prakorb's House (Th Khao San; s/d 120/250B) One of the reliable cheapies on Th Khao San proper, Prakorb's has simple clean rooms with shared bathroom. The restaurant downstairs has a good reputation for a coffee fix after a night on the town.

Ranee's Guest House (☎ 0 2282 4072; 77 Trok Mayom; s/d 120/200B) Escape from the madness on the main road, with a stroll down

THAILAND

this pedestrian alley to Ranee's. The rooms are much of a muchness, like many in Banglamphu, but the bakery downstairs has some of the best croissants and pastries in the area.

Other places worth considering:

Baan Sabai (☎ 0 2629 1599; Soi Rambutri; s 170B, tw 270-500B; 🗷) The name means cosy house and it's aptly named for its relaxed atmosphere. Popular bar attached.

Chada Guest House (☎ 0 2629 3372; Th Khao San; s/d 140/180B; 🖳) A Khao San original if you want to live the budget life to the max, or should that be to the min?

Classic Inn (☎ 0 2281 7129; Th Khao San; s 250-390B, d 300-450B; 🗷) Smart rooms verging on the hotel-like if you need a comfort fix.

East Banglamphu & Thewet

Delving deeper into Banglamphu brings more bang for your baht. The places off Th Samsen are close to Tha Saphan Ram VIII, where you can catch the river taxi. Further north on Th Samsen is the area called Thewet, near the National Library.

Villa Guest House (Map p709; ☎ 0 2281 7009; Soi 1, Th Samsen; d 250-500B) Tucked away down a small alley is this old teak house wrapped in a leafy garden. The atmospheric rooms are furnished in period pieces and antiques, but it's shared bathrooms all the way. Book ahead.

River Guest House (Map p709; ☎ 0 2280 0876; Soi 3/Soi Wat Samphraya, Th Samsen; r 130-160B) Tucked away down a mazelike soi and not particularly well signposted, seclusion is the name of the game. Cheap rooms mean a faithful following.

Other places to consider in this area:

Bamboo Guest House (Map p709; ☎ 0 2282 3412; Soi 1, Th Samsen; s/d/tr 150/220/330) Quiet pad with a large communal area out the front.

Taewez Guest House (Map pp704-5; ☎ 0 2280 8856; riverside soi, cnr Th Samsen & Th Si Ayuthaya; s 150B, d 250-300B; 🗷) Chatty staff, lively service and a friendly vibe.

Hualamphong   Map pp704–5

Hotels near the train station are cheap, but the area is so noisy that the traffic along Th Phra Ram IV has to be heard to be believed. Exercise a lot of street smarts around the station, which is crawling with razor artists, scammers and low-lives.

Sri Hualamphong Hotel (445 Th Rong Meuang; d 200B) Along the eastern side of Hualamphong station, this Chinese-run hotel is a creaky old spot with a grand staircase and terrace seating. The partitioned rooms are flimsy to say the least. Share bathrooms only.

Krung Kasem Srikung Hotel (☎ 0 2225 0132; 1860 Th Krung Kasem; d 550B; 🗷) West of the station, Krung Kasem is worth the extra investment, as it is a well-managed business hotel. Large, clean rooms have TV, air-con and hot water.

Siam Square   Map pp704–5

Siam Sq is a microcosm of this megacity: supermodern shopping centres, nonstop traffic jams and a simple village with traveller-friendly facilities hidden in the small soi off Th Phra Ram 1.

Bed & Breakfast Inn (☎ 0 2215 3004; Soi Kasem San 1; s/d 400/500B; 🗷) This friendly spot has the real

THAILAND

deal on air-con rooms with hot-water bathroom attached. It doesn't stop there – as the name suggests, breakfast is included.

White Lodge (☎ 0 2216 8867; 36/8 Soi Kasem San 1; s/d 400/500B; 🕱) Another Soi Kasem San stalwart. The rooms are fairly small here, but there are lots of conversation-inducing common areas.

Wendy House (☎ 0 2216 2436; www.wendyguesthouse.com; Soi Kasem San 1; s/d from 700/800B; 🕱) This is teetering on the edge of expensive, but the rooms are the smartest in this strip and the service more than a cut above average.

Thanon Sukhumvit   Map p709

North of Th Phra Ram IV and east of the railway line, Th Sukhumvit is a major commercial artery, with several enclaves of long-term expats. Most hotels are out of the budget traveller's price range, but it provides a change of scene after an overdose of Banglamphu.

Atlanta (☎ 0 2252 1650; 78 Soi 2, Th Sukhumvit; r 353-590B; 🕱 🖳) Simply put, the Atlanta is a Bangkok institution. The lobby hasn't changed in decades and oozes timeless chic. Check out the old-fashioned writing desks from the days before Internet and the jungle-landscaped swimming pool. This is the only hotel in the area that loudly and proudly forbids sex tourists. But the run-down rooms could use renovation. The classy coffeeshop offers a crash course in Thai cuisine, plus the hotel offers some great guidance on attuning to Thai culture.

Suk 11 (Map pp700-1; ☎ 0 2253 5927; www.suk11.com; dm/s/d 250/450/500B; 🕱) Escape from the chaos of Sukhumvit down Soi 11 to Suk 11, one of the only genuine budget places in this part of town. Top value, especially as breakfast comes free in the leafy courtyard. Advance reservations required.

Airport

Finding decent, moderately priced accommodation in the airport area is difficult. Most of the hotels charge nearly twice as much as comparable hotels in the city.

We-Train International House (Map pp700-1; ☎ 0 2967 8550; www.we-train.co.th; 501/1 Mu 3, Th Dechatungkha, Sikan, Don Muang; dm 200B, r from 400B) Run by a nonprofit women's group, We-Train offers a free airport pick-up. Download a map and directions from the hotel's website if making your own way.

EATING

No matter where you go in Bangkok, food is never far away. The variety of places to eat is simply astonishing and defeats all but the most dogged food samplers in their quest to say they've tried everything. Street surfing the stalls may be the cheapest option, but don't neglect to explore the city's food courts in the shopping centres, as these are the indoor versions (pollution free and air-conditioned) of the city's outdoor markets.

While Thai food may be sufficiently exotic, Bangkok offers an incredible international menu thanks to its many immigrant communities. Chinatown is naturally a good area for Chinese food and the Phahurat quarter around Th Silom is Little India, where cubicle-sized Indian restaurants turn out the best of the subcontinent. In the crowded bazaarlike area of Little Arabia, just off Th Sukhumvit, there is Muslim cuisine from every far flung corner of the region. Western cuisine, ranging from Italian to Mexican, is prepared in the latest, greatest way for power diners or as pub grub to keep the homesickness at bay.

Vegetarians are onto a good thing in Bangkok. In addition to all of the veggie-speciality spots, Indian and Muslim restaurants frequently have veggie options, as do most Thai and Chinese restaurants. During the vegetarian festival in October, the whole city goes mad for tofu, and stalls and restaurants indicate their nonmeat menu with yellow flags.

Banglamphu & Thanon Khao San   Map p709

Th Khao San is lined with restaurants, but the prices tend to be higher and the quality somewhat lower than in the surrounding streets of Banglamphu. Serial snackers can survive by surfing up and down the many street vendors here. For a cheap and authentic meal, leave Khao San behind and head to the stalls along Soi Rambutri or Th Chakraphong. Fresh seafood barbecues are now a big hit on Soi Rambutri, washed down with dirt-cheap Beer Chang at 50B a go.

Khrua Nopparat (Th Phra Athit; dishes 60-100B; ⏰ lunch & dinner) Thai bohemians gravitate to the cafés and restaurants along Th Phra Athit, Bangkok's answer to Greenwich Village. Khrua Nopparat is not as trendy as some, but that leaves them free to concentrate on the food. The dishes are small, so don't shy away from the Thai tradition of over-ordering.

Hemlock (☎ 0 2282 7507; 56 Th Phra Athit; dishes 80-200B; ✆ lunch & dinner) This welcoming place has an eclectic menu including *miang kham* (tea leaves wrapped with ginger, shallots, peanuts, lime and coconut flakes) and *náam phrík kháa* (spicy dipping sauce served with vegetables and herbs) – dishes not easily found elsewhere.

Je Hoy (Soi 2, Th Samsen; dishes 50-100B; ✆ dinner) This old-timer is an open-air Chinese-Thai restaurant that draws a steady crowd to sample its Hokkien specials, such as *puu phàt phŏng kà-rìi* (crab stir-fried with curry powder and egg). Point to the seafood and watch the cook work wonders in the wok.

Arawy (152 Th Din So; dishes 35B; ✆ breakfast, lunch & dinner) When it comes to genuine vegetarian delights, Arawy is one of the best Thai restaurants in the city. Pre-prepared point-and-eat dishes keep it simple. The restaurant was inspired by ex-Bangkok governor Chamlong Srimuang's strict vegetarianism. The roman-script sign reads 'Alloy' and it is opposite the Municipal Hall.

Also worth seeking out:

Roti-Mataba (cnr Th Phra Athit & Th Phra Sumen; dishes 50-80B; ✆ breakfast, lunch & dinner) Stop here for the flavours of India. First come, first served in this tiny eatery.

Ton Pho (☎ 0 2280 0452; Th Phra Athit; dishes 60-100B; ✆ breakfast, lunch & dinner) Overlooking the Mae Nam Chao Phraya, this is a great spot for authentic Thai standards. No roman-script sign.

Hualamphong, Chinatown & Phahurat   Map pp704–5

Hualamphong Food Centre (Hualamphong Station; dishes 30-60B; ✆ breakfast, lunch & dinner) In most countries, station food is the blandest of the bland, but in Thailand the vendors know the importance of fulfilling their customers' needs before a long journey. Stop here for a top selection of Thai, Chinese and Indian dishes.

Royal India Restaurant (392/1 Th Chakraphet; dishes under 80B; ✆ breakfast, lunch & dinner) Hidden away down a dark alley across from the ATM Shopping Centre, Royal India has long been considered one of the best North Indian restaurants in town. Staying in Khao San and feeling lazy? Check out the smart new

restaurant (on Soi Rambutri; open for breakfast, lunch and dinner), set around a pond in the grounds of Rambuttri Village Inn.

Other options:

ATM Food Centre (Th Chakraphet, Phahurat; ✆ breakfast, lunch & dinner) Indian food centre on the top floor, plus Indian food stalls in the nearby alley.

Hong Kong Noodles (Th Phra Ram IV; dishes 30-80B; ✆ breakfast, lunch & dinner) Just outside Hualamphong Metro station, this air-conditioned place has slick Chinese food.

Siam Square   Map pp704–5

Food vendors on Soi Kasem San 1 do a brisk business of feeding hungry clockwatchers and lounging *faràng*; they are masters at communicating with hand gestures.

Mahboonkrong Food Centre (MBK; southwestern cnr of Th Phra Ram I & Th Phayathai; ✆ breakfast, lunch & dinner) The 7th-floor food court in this shopping centre is one of the busiest in the city, thanks to an assortment of tasty dishes that compete with the best on offer in the streets below.

> **SPLURGE!**
>
> **Le Lys** (Map pp704–5; ☎ 0 2652 2401; 75 Soi 3, Soi Lang Suan; dishes 80-200B; ✆ lunch & dinner) Le Lys prepares classic Thai dishes, such as *kaeng phèt mǔu yâang bai chá-om* (roast pork curry with acacia leaves), easily selected from a menu accompanied by appetising photos. In a breezy colonial-style house, this is a great escape from the bustle of Bangkok beyond.

Thanon Sukhumvit   Map pp704–5

Cabbages & Condoms (☎ 0 2229 4610; Soi 12, Th Sukhumvit; dishes 100-200B; ✆ lunch & dinner) This restaurant is the ideal introduction to Thai food for anyone still fine-tuning their chilli-radar. Instead of after-meal mints, diners get packaged condoms: 'Our food is guaranteed not to cause pregnancy.' All proceeds go towards sex education/AIDS prevention programmes, run by the Population & Community Development Association (PDA).

Al-Hussain (1/4 Soi 3/5, Th Sukhumvit; dishes 100-200B; ✆ breakfast, lunch & dinner) Just off Th Sukhumvit and Soi 3 (Soi Nana Neua), there is a winding maze of cramped sub-soi known as 'Little Arabia', where the number of

THAILAND

Map pp704–5

SPLURGE!

Maha Naga (Map pp704–5; ☎ 0 2662 3060; 29, Th Sukhumvit; dishes 300-700B; ☺ lunch & dinner) Although children of Thai and Western parents are usually destined for pop-stardom in Bangkok, it is not always the same story with fusion restaurants. Maha Naga is the exception to the rule, with feisty flavours such as deep-fried prawn rolls served with plum sauce and crispy vermicelli, scallops in Thai-style gravy and pork chops topped with *sôm-tam* (papaya salad).

Middle Eastern and African residents make Thais seem like the foreigners. This openair café has a colourful table of subtly spiced curries and dhal (curried lentils). Air-con inside, street action outside.

Tamarind Café (☎ 0 2663 7421; 27 Soi 20, Th Sukhumvit; dishes 100-250B; ☺ breakfast, lunch & dinner) Try the Tamarind for divine desserts and one of the most creative vegetarian menus in town. This artistic space, home to the F-Stop Gallery of photographs, includes a sweeping bar, making for hard choices; should you take the innovative fruit shake or the ice-cold beer?

Larry's Dive Center, Bar & Grill (☎ 0 2663 4563; Soi 22, Th Sukhumvit; dishes 95-175B; ☺ breakfast, lunch & dinner) The extensive American and Tex-Mex fare here includes salads, quesadillas, nachos, chilli, spicy chicken wings and Larry's food guarantee: 'Served in 30 minutes, or it's cold.' There's an attached dive shop, should you get the urge to go snorkelling in a nearby *khlong*.

Also recommended:

Crepes & Co (☎ 0 2653 3990; 18/1 Soi 12, Th Sukhumvit; dishes 140-280B; ☺ breakfast, lunch & dinner) Crêpes of all kinds, European-style breakfasts and a nice selection of Mediterranean dishes.

Mrs Balbir's (☎ 0 2651 0498; 155/18 Soi 11/1; dishes 150-250B; buffet lunch 150B; ☺ breakfast, lunch & dinner) Mrs Balbir has been teaching Indian and Thai cooking for many years.

Thanon Silom & Thanon Surawong

Map pp704–5

The small soi on the western end of Th Silom and parallel Th Surawong are home to an active Muslim and Indian community, which provides visiting business folk with the taste of home.

Naaz (Soi 43, Saphan Yao; dishes 50-70B; ☺ breakfast, lunch & dinner) Pronounced 'Naat' in Thai, this neighbourhood café is often cited as having the richest *khâo mòk kài* (chicken biryani) in the city. Dabble with a dessert, as the house speciality is *firni*, a Middle Eastern pudding spiced with coconut, almonds, cardamom and saffron.

Muslim Restaurant (1356 Th Charoen Krung; dishes under 40B; ☺ breakfast, lunch & dinner) This faded old restaurant may not look all that, but it has been feeding various Lonely Planet authors for more than 20 years. Near the intersection of Th Charoen Krung and Th Silom, the assortment of curries and *rotii* is displayed in a clean glass case for easy pointing and eye-catching allure.

Ban Chiang (☎ 0 2236 7045; 14 Soi Si Wiang, Th Surasak; dishes 90-150B; ☺ lunch & dinner) Ban Chiang pays homage to the fiery cuisine of the northeast. Occupying a restored wooden house with simple décor, get acquainted with the taste of Isan by trying *yam plaa duk foo* (fried shredded catfish salad).

Also well worth a diversion south towards the river are the food vendors on Soi 20 (Soi Pradit), off Th Silom near the mosque. The street throngs with office workers at lunchtime and the smells are divine.

SPLURGE!

Eat Me Restaurant (Map pp704–5; ☎ 0 2238 0931; Soi Phiphat 2, Th Convent; dishes 150-400B; ☺ dinner) One of Bangkok's best fusion restaurants, Eat Me conjures up creativity with a luscious tuna tartare, glass-noodle spring rolls and five-lettuce salad. The chic décor is accented by rotating exhibits of modern Thai artists. This is a place to be seen.

Greater Bangkok

Map pp704–5

Both of the following places are easily accessible by riding the Skytrain to Victory Monument.

Pickle Factory (☎ 0 2246 3036; 55 Soi 21, Th Ratwithi; dishes 150-200B; ☺ dinner) Occupying a 1970s-vintage Thai house, the Pickle Factory creates a dinner-party mood with indoor sofa seating and outdoor tables around a swimming pool – the perfect place to chill out for an evening. The menu includes creatively topped pizzas like Chiang Mai sausage and holy basil paste with wing beans.

Victory Point (Th Phayathai & Th Ratwithi; dishes 25-50B; ⊗ dinner) Lining the busy round-about is a squatters' village of stalls known collectively as 'Victory Point'. Near the fairy lights is a beer-and-food garden with live music. Order a pitcher and a few plates of the zesty Thai classics for a thoroughly satisfying meal.

DRINKING

Officially Bangkok has a curfew of 1am for bars and 2am for clubs, and this is quite strictly enforced at most establishments. The Khao San area is the exception, where guesthouses and restaurants let the drinks flow, but disguise them in plastic cups. Most short-term travellers passing through stick around Khao San, where the carnival atmosphere keeps drinkers entertained till dawn. There are also some great bars in the surrounding soi, as this area is now attract-ing as many Thais as tourists. If you can rouse yourself from a Beer Chang–stupor, brave a pub crawl in such nightspots as Th Silom–Patpong or Th Sukhumvit.

The Khao San area is a cheap place to warm up for a night out, thanks to the proliferation of street bars. Sometimes they are stalls, sometimes VW camper vans with the roof hacked off, but all of them offer dirt-cheap beer and 'very strong' cocktails. Throw in the informal draught beer stands and you are never more than a few metres from an alcoholic drink.

Sunset Street (Map p709; Th Khao San) Wander down this paved alley for a sophisticated selection of bars and clubs. This is where the Thai crowd comes to party and there is a beautiful Franco-Chinese house at the rear with a beer garden.

Gullivers Traveller's Tavern (Map p709; Th Khao San) This place pulls the punters as the night wears on. Downstairs is mayhem most nights, but upstairs is usually quieter with a couple of pool tables.

Bangkok Bar (Map p709; 149 Soi Rambutri) This small shopfront is home to smooth samba beats and a cosy bar where mixed *faràng* and Thai couples hunker down away from the madness nearby. It is next door to Sawasdee House, a guesthouse with a 24-hour bar.

Baghdad Café (Map p709; Soi 2, Th Samsen) Just over Khlong Banglamphu is this *sheesha* bar for puffing pungent fruit tobacco on Arabic water pipes. A nice change from Arabic tra-dition is that alcohol is also available.

Susie Pub (Map p709; Soi 11, Th Khao San) In an alley off the northern side of Khao San, this pub pulls in the Thai university students celebrating birthdays. The bar is beautifully done, but drink prices are ambitious given the bargains on offer on the street.

About Studio/About Cafe (Map pp704-5; ☎ 0 2623 1742; 418 Th Maitrichit) A lounge-chic lair, About Studio successfully combines gallery space with social space. Hours are erratic, so call ahead. There is no sign in English, but it will be the only place on the block with a crowd.

Bull's Head (Map pp700-1; Soi 33/1, Th Sukhumvit) One of many British pubs in the Sukhumvit area, the Bull's Head is a beautiful galleried bar that looks like it has been shipped in from London. This is a popular stop for stand-up comedians touring Asia, plus there are quiz nights.

Cheap Charlie's (Map pp704-5; Soi 11, Th Sukhumvit) For the cheapest beer this side of Khao San, check out Cheap Charlie's, a no-frills beer stall. Expat workers stop off on the way home and there is plenty of standing room on the soi, if few seats. On a sub-soi off Soi 11, look for the 'Sabai Sabai Massage' sign and lots of red-nosed foreigners.

Vertigo (Map pp704-5; ☎ 0 2679 1200; 21/100 Th Sathon Tai, Banyan Tree Hotel) Definitely not for Cheap Charlies, this sky-high, open-air bar will quite literally take your breath away. From ground level, the elevator delivers you to the 59th floor where you emerge above the roar of Bangkok traffic far below. Expensive, but the view is priceless.

CLUBBING

High-powered cocktails and high heels are the name of the game in the dance and lounge clubs in the City of Angels. The fickle beautiful people are constantly on the move, leaving behind the stylish car-casses to tourists and working girls. The cover charge ranges from 500B to 600B and usually includes a drink. Don't even think about showing up before 11pm.

Bed Supperclub (Map pp704-5; ☎ 0 2651 3537; 26 Soi 11, Th Sukhumvit) So it's in and out of fashion with the beautiful people, but who cares – for the first-time visitor this is a place to be. Lounge like a lizard on the beds before unleashing yourself on the dancefloor.

THAILAND

Q Bar (Map pp704-5; ☎ 0 2252 3274; Soi 11, Th Sukhumvit) This Ho Chi Minh City refugee is a minimalist two-storey club of high-octane cocktails, including absinthe and 40 varieties of vodka. Check out the dance moves, some of which are straight off a go-go stage. To find it, take Soi 11 all the way to the end and hang a left. No sandals and no shorts.

Narcissus (Map pp704-5; ☎ 0 2258 2549; 112 Soi 23, Th Sukhumvit) A Romanesque temple to techno and trance, Narcissus demands you to be young, beautiful and conspicuously consuming. International DJs regularly turn the tables here.

Tapas (Map pp704-5; Soi 4, Th Silom) Mix it up Moroccan style at this Th Silom dance club. The drapes and décor are straight out of Marrakesh, but the tunes are jazz, Latin and other world grooves.

Also recommended are **Lucifer** (Map pp704-5; Patpong Soi 1, Th Silom) and a string of nearby dance clubs on Soi 2 and Soi 4 (Soi Jaruwan), both parallel to Soi Patpong 1 and 2, off Th Silom, that attract a mixed clubbing crowd.

ENTERTAINMENT
Live Music
Saxophone Pub & Restaurant (Map pp704-5; ☎ 0 2246 5472; 3/8 Th Phayathai) A must on the Bangkok music scene, Saxophone is home to the soothing sounds of reggae, rock, blues and

jazz, with a German beer-cellar look about it. Grab a perch in the 2nd-floor alcoves. Accessible via Skytrain to Victory Monument station.

Ad Here the 13th (Map p709; 13 Th Samsen) Just over the Khlong Banglamphu bridge, this lively hole-in-the-wall bar has a talented house band that bangs out the blues from 10pm nightly and cold beer that keeps on flowing. The regulars are really regular here so you should make some friends.

Brown Sugar (Map pp704-5; Th Sarasin) Jazz up your life by dropping in on this popular club near Lumphini Park. On Sunday nights, the serious musicians touring the luxury hotels come here to jam.

Radio City (Map pp704-5; ☎ 0 2266 4567; Soi Patpong 1) Head here after bargaining your pants off at the Patpong night market. Grab a drink on the patio to watch the haggling or duck inside for covers of your favourite rock-and-roll hits. The Thai Elvis here is a legend in his own lifetime.

Muay Thai (Thai Boxing)
Lumphini Boxing Stadium (Map pp704-5; Th Phra Ram IV; ☺ bouts 6pm Tue, Fri & Sat, also 5pm Sat), near Lumphini Park, and **Ratchadamnoen Boxing Stadium** (Map pp700-1; Th Ratchadamnoen Nok; bouts 5pm Mon, Wed & Thu, 6pm Sun), near the Democracy Monument, both host popular *muay*

BANGKOK A GO-GO

'We don't come to Thailand for the ruins', was an overheard insult delivered by a veteran sex tourist to an unsuspecting backpacker. True enough, many male visitors come solely for the women or, in some cases, the men. The shopping venues for potential partners occupy a whole subset of Bangkok's nightlife, from massage parlours and go-go clubs to pick-up bars.

Patpong (Soi Patpong 1 & 2, Th Silom), Bangkok's most famous red-light district, has mellowed a lot over the years and now draws more sightseers than flesh-seekers. The open-air tourist market on Patpong 1 has drawn much of the attention away from erotica. There are still a handful go-go bars that have morphed into a circus of ping-pong shows for tourists and couples. Avoid bars touting 'free' sex shows as there are usually hidden charges and when you try to ditch the outrageous bill the doors are suddenly blocked by muscled bouncers.

The gay men's equivalent can be found on nearby Soi Thaniya, Soi Pratuchai and Soi Anuman Ratchathon. Along with male go-go dancers and 'bar boys', several bars feature live sex shows, which are generally much better choreographed than the hetero equivalents on Patpong.

Soi Cowboy (btwn Soi 21 & Soi 23, Th Sukhumvit), a single-lane strip of 25 to 30 bars, claims direct lineage to the post–Vietnam War '70s, when a black American ex-GI nicknamed 'Cowboy' was the among the first to open a self-named go-go bar off Th Sukhumvit.

Nana Plaza (Soi 4/Soi Nana Tai, Th Sukhumvit) is a three-storey place that's quite literally a strip-mall, complete with its own guesthouses, and used almost exclusively by female bar workers for illicit assignations. The 'female' staff at Casanova consists entirely of Thai transvestites and transsexuals – this is a favourite stop for foreigners visiting Bangkok for sex re-assignment surgery.

GAY & LESBIAN BANGKOK

Bangkok's gay community is loud, proud and knows how to party. A newcomer might want to visit the website of **Utopia** (www.utopia-asia.com), a great resource for news and happenings in Thailand and Southeast Asia. **Anjaree** (☎ 0 2477 1776) is a lesbian group that organises social events and community outreach programmes.

Babylon Bangkok (Map pp704-5; ☎ 0 2213 2108; 50 Soi Atakanprasit, Th Sathon Tai; ⊙ 5am-11pm) A four-storey gay sauna, Babylon Bangkok has been described as one of the top 10 gay men's saunas in the world. Facilities include a bar, roof garden, gym, massage room, steam and dry saunas, and spa baths. The spacious, well-hidden complex also has accommodation.

Vega (Map pp700-1; ☎ 0 2258 8273, 0 2662 6471; Soi 39, Th Sukhumvit) This lesbian-owned pub-restaurant features live music and dancing, while upstairs there's karaoke. On Friday and Saturday nights local lesbian celebrities sometimes stop by.

Patpong Soi 2 and Soi 4 have the highest concentration of gay dance clubs in the city. DJ Station and JJ Park are just some of many clubs that pack narrow Soi 2 with late-night energy. DJ Station also boasts *kàthoey* (transvestite) cabaret. Chill out at Expresso, beside the waterfall wall, for a bird's-eye view of the pretty boys. On Soi 4, Telephone, Bangkok's oldest gay bar, has a 'telephone' by which patrons can get to know one other. Across the street the Balcony has prime people-watching tables.

thai fights. The cheapest seats are 500B for the outer circle, 800B for the middle circle and 1500B for ringside. This is for eight to 10 fights of five rounds each; the last three are the headliner events when the stadiums fill up. Aficionados say the best-matched bouts are reserved for Tuesday night at Lumphini and Thursday night at Ratchadamnoen. Always buy tickets from the ticket window, not from a hawker hanging outside the stadium.

Ratchadamnoen stadium can be reached via air-con bus 503 and ordinary bus 70. Lumphini stadium can be reached via ordinary bus 47.

Thai Classical Dance

Chalermkrung Royal Theatre (Map pp704-5; Sala Chaloem Krung; ☎ 0 2222 0434; cnr Th Charoen Krung & Th Triphet) In this Thai art-deco building at the edge of the Chinatown–Phahurat district, Chalermkrung provides a striking venue for *khǒhn* (dance-drama based on the Ramayana epic) performances. When it opened in 1933, the royally funded Chalermkrung was the largest and most modern theatre in Asia, with state-of-the-art film-projection technology and the first chilled-water air-con system in the region.

National Theatre (Map p709; ☎ 0 2224 1342; Th Na Phra That; admission 20-200B) Near Saphan Phra Pin Klao, the National Theatre hosts performances of the traditional *khǒhn*. The theatre holds performances on the last Friday and Saturday of each month, but call ahead for confirmation.

Maneeya Lotus Room (Map pp704-5; ☎ 0 2282 6312; 518/5 Th Ploenchit) Sponsors dinner-theatre performances of Thai classical dance; the food is nothing special, but the prices are reasonable (200B to 500B).

To see some examples of Thai classical dancing for free, hang out at **Lak Muang Shrine** (Map pp704–5), near Sanam Luang, or **Erawan Shrine** (Map pp704–5), next to Grand Hyatt Erawan; dancers are hired in thanks for the shrines' mystical assistance in picking winning lottery numbers.

SHOPPING

Bangkok is not the place for recovering shopaholics, as the temptation to stray from the path is overwhelming. From mesmerising markets to state-of-the-art shopping centres, shopping in Bangkok sets the pulse racing in even the most ardent of antishoppers.

WARNING: THE GEM SCAM

Unless you really know your stones, Bangkok is no place to seek out 'the big score'. Never accept an invitation from a friendly stranger to visit a gem shop, as you will end up with an empty wallet and a nice collection of coloured glass. See Scams (p815) for more on this.

Markets

Phenomenal bargains are on offer at the city's informal markets. Most are an odd assortment of plastic toys, household goods, copy clothing and some knock-off designer watches and bags. Even more interesting are the food markets where food-savvy Thais forage for brightly coloured tapioca desserts, spicy curries and fruits that look like medieval torture devices.

Chatuchak Market (Map pp700-1; Th Phanonythin; ⊗ 8am-6pm Sat & Sun) Chatuchak is the mother of all markets. It sprawls over a huge area with 15,000 stalls and an estimated 200,000 visitors a day. Deep in the bowels of the market, you'll forget that it is daylight. Everything is sold here, from live chickens and snakes to handicrafts and antiques to aisles and aisles of clothes. Everyone leaves here with empty wallets, armfuls of plastic bags and thoroughly exhausted – it's great fun. North of central Bangkok off Th Phahonyothin, air-con buses 502, 503, 509, 510, 512 and 513, ordinary bus 77 and a dozen others serve the market. The Skytrain runs direct to Moh Chit station, which looks over the market.

Other recommendations:

Banglamphu Day Market (Th Chakkraphong, Th Tanao & Th Tani) Clothes, foodstuffs and household goods.

Patpong Soi 2 Night Market More popular than the ping-pong shows these days.

Th Khao San Night Market T-shirts, artwork, souvenirs and traveller ghetto gear.

Shopping Centres   Map pp704–5

Central World Plaza (cnr Th Ploenchit & Th Ratchadamri) Boasting eight floors of air-conditioned escapism, the plaza's lifeblood is the Zen department store, which is dotted with high-end fashion brands.

Siam Center (cnr Th Phayathai & Th Phra Ram I) Thailand's first shopping centre, Siam Center opened its doors in 1976 and has aged well. It features designer and brand-label clothing shops, electronics and food outlets galore. There's more of the same at the Siam Discovery Center, connected to Siam Center by an enclosed pedestrian bridge.

Mahboonkrong (MBK; cnr Th Phayathai & Th Phra Ram I) Thai teenagers worship this shopping centre, just across the road from Siam Sq. Small, inexpensive stalls and shops sell mobile phone accessories, cheap T-

shirts, wallets and handbags, plus there is the midrange Tokyu department store.

River City Shopping Complex (Th Charoen Krung) Almost worshipped as a museum, River City contains a number of high-quality art and antique shops on its 3rd and 4th floors. **Acala** (shop 312) is a gallery of unusual Tibetan and Chinese artefacts. **Old Maps & Prints** (☎ 0 2237 0077, ext 432; shop 432) has one of the best selections of one-of-a-kind rare maps and illustrations with a focus on Asia.

GETTING THERE & AWAY
Air

Bangkok acts as the air travel hub for Thailand and mainland Southeast Asia. Some airline offices with representation in Bangkok:

Bangkok Airways (Map pp704-5; ☎ 0 2265 5555; www.bangkokair.com; Queen Sirikit National Convention Centre, 99 Th Viphavadi Rangsit)

Cathay Pacific Airways (Map pp704-5; ☎ 0 2263 0606; www.cathaypacific.com; 11th fl, Ploenchit Tower, 898 Th Ploenchit)

Garuda Indonesia (Map pp704-5; ☎ 0 2679 7371; www.garuda-indonesia.com; 27th fl, Lumphini Tower, 1168/77 Th Phra Ram IV)

Lao Airlines (Map pp704-5; ☎ 0 2236 9822; www.lao-airlines.com; Silom Plaza, 491/17 Th Silom)

Malaysia Airlines (Map pp704-5; ☎ 0 2263 0520; www.malaysiaairlines.com; 20th fl, Ploenchit Tower, 898 Th Ploenchit)

Myanmar Airways International (Map pp704-5; ☎ 0 2261 5060; www.maiair.com; 8th fl, 54 BB Bldg, Soi 21/Asoke, Th Sukhumvit)

Singapore Airlines (Map pp704-5; ☎ 0 2236 0440; www.singaporeair.com; 12th fl, Silom Centre Bldg, 2 Th Silom)

Thai Airways International (THAI; Map pp704-5; ☎ 0 2232 8000, reservations ☎ 0 2280 0060; www.thaiair.com; Empire Bldg, 485 Th Silom)

Vietnam Airlines (☎ 0 2655 4137, reservations ☎ 0 2280 0060; www.vietnamair.com; 7th fl, Ploenchit Center Bldg, Soi 2, Th Sukhumvit)

For a list of mainly domestic airlines, see p694. International and domestic flights currently use Bangkok's Don Muang International Airport, 25km outside the city. Just to confuse things, the new Suvarnabhumi International Airport will be up and running during the lifetime of this book and most international flights will operate out of here. Find more information at www .suvarnabhumiairport.com/en/index.htm.

Bus

Buses departing from the government bus station are recommended over those departing from Th Khao San and other tourist areas, due to a lower incidence of theft and greater reliability. The Bangkok bus terminals (all with left-luggage facilities) are as follows:

Eastern Bus Terminal (Ekamai; Map pp700-1; ☎ 0 2391 2504; Soi 40/Soi Ekamai, Th Sukhumvit) Pattaya, Rayong, Chanthaburi and Trat (mainland departure points for boats Ko Samet and Ko Chang).

Northern & Northeastern Bus Terminal (Moh Chit; Map pp700-1; ☎ 0 2936 3659 for northern routes, ☎ 0 2936 2841 for northeastern routes; Th Kamphaeng Phet) All northern and northeastern cities including Chiang Mai, Nakhon Ratchasima (Khorat), as well as central destinations such as Ayuthaya, Lopburi and Aranya Prathet (near the Cambodian border). The terminal's near Chatuchak Park.

Southern Bus Terminal (Sai Tai Mai; Map pp700-1; ☎ 0 2435 7192; cnr Hwy 338 & Th Phra Pin Klao, Thonburi) Nakhon Pathom, Damnoen Saduak, Kanchanaburi, Hua Hin, Surat Thani, Phuket, Hat Yai and all points south.

Train

There are two main train stations in Bangkok. **Hualamphong station** (Map pp704-5; general information ☎ 02220 4334, advance booking ☎ 0 2220 4444; Th Phra Ram IV) handles services to the north, northeast and most of the services to the south. **Thonburi station** (Bangkok Noi; Map

---

BORDER CROSSING: INTO CAMBODIA

Anyone undertaking the Angkor pilgrimage into Cambodia will want to cross over the Thai–Cambodian border at Aranya Prathet–Poipet. Most people start this run from Bangkok, which makes for an epic journey: start out early, bring a lot of snacks and practise Buddhist calm. Frequent daytime buses and two trains per day connect Bangkok with Aranya Prathet (five hours), and from Poipet (p93) buses go to Siem Reap (p79; three to six hours). To travel between the two border towns, you must take a túk-túk (motorised rickshaw) or săwngthăew (small pick-up). If the ticket offered to you on Th Khao San sounds too good to be true, it is; they are setting you up for a ride on the Bangkok to Siem Reap Bus Scam (see p86 for more details on avoiding this).

---

pp700-1) handles Kanchanaburi and some services to the south. If you're heading south, check which station you need.

GETTING AROUND

The main obstacle to getting around Bangkok is the troubling traffic, which adds a half-hour to an hour delay to daytime outings, depending on the route. See p702 for handy routes to popular destinations.

Boat

Slow barges being pulled by determined tug boats, kids splashing around the river banks, majestic Wat Arun rising in the distance like a giant lingam – all these sights are courtesy of the inexpensive and convenient river taxis, which ply a regular route along the Mae Nam Chao Phraya. The **Chao Phraya River Express** (☎ 0 2623 6001-3) operates between Tha Wat Ratchasingkhon in south central Bangkok northwards to Nonthaburi Province. There are four boat lines: two express lines (indicated by yellow or orange flags), the local line (without a flag) and the tourist line. Express boats stop at certain piers during morning and evening hours (usually 6am to 9am and 3pm to 7pm) and cost 10B to 25B, depending on the destination. Local boats stop at all piers from 6am to 7.40pm, and fares range from 6B to 10B, plus small boats ply back and forth across the river for 2B per trip.

See p702 for the closest *thâa* to your destination.

Bangkok Metropolitan Authority operates two **Khlong Taxi** (5-8B; ☉ 6am-7pm) routes along the canals: Khlong Saen Saep (Banglamphu to Bang Kapi) and Khlong Phasi Charoen in Thonburi (Kaset Bang Khae port to Saphan Phra Ram I). The Khlong Saen Saep canal service is the most useful one for short-term visitors as it provides a traffic-free trip between Siam Sq and Banglamphu. In Siam Sq, the pier (Tha Ratchathewi) is by the bridge next to the Asia Hotel; in Banglamphu (the last stop on the line) the pier is near Wat Saket and Phra Samen Fort. If travelling from Banglamphu to Siam Sq, it is really easy to miss the stop, so let the person sitting next to you know that you want 'See-yahm Sa-quare'. The canals make the Chao Phraya river look like a mountain spring, so try not to get splashed.

Bus

The Bangkok bus service is frequent and frantic, so a bus map (*Tour 'n' Guide Map to Bangkok Thailand*) is an absolute necessity. Don't expect it to be 100% correct though, as routes change regularly.

Fares for ordinary buses vary according to the type of bus: from 3.50/4B (red/green buses) to 5B (white-and-blue buses) for any journey under 10km. There are also the cream-and-blue air-con buses that start at 8B but jump to 20B on longer trips. Orange Euro 2 air-con buses are 12B for any distance, while white-and-pink air-con buses cost 25B to 30B. The least crowded are the red microbuses, which stop taking passengers once every seat is filled, and cost a 25B flat fare (have exact change ready).

Metro

The first line of Bangkok's subway or underground (depending on your nationality!) opened in 2004 and is operated by the **Metropolitan Rapid Transit Authority** (MRTA; www.mrta.co.th). Thais call it the Metro, which no doubt pleases the French. The line connects the railway station of Bang Sue with Chatuchak (Skytrain interchange to Mo Chit), Sukhumvit (Skytrain interchange to Asoke), Lumphini Park, Silom (Skytrain interchange to Sala Daeng) and terminates at Hualamphong station.

Trains operate from 5am to midnight and cost 14B to 36B, depending on distance. Future extensions will connect Hualamphong to Chinatown and Thonburi.

Motorcycle Taxi

Motorcycle taxis typically camp out at the beginning of a residential soi to transport people the last few kilometres home. Since the corners are always overstaffed, drivers will gladly take you anywhere for the right price. Fares for a motorcycle taxi are about the same as túk-túk fares except during heavy traffic, when they may cost more. Riding on the back of a speeding motorcycle taxi in Bangkok traffic is a close approximation to an extreme sport.

Skytrain

The ultramodern elevated **Bangkok Mass Transit System Skytrain** (BTS; ☎ 0 2617 7300; www.bts.co.th) arrived at just the right time to rescue Bangkok from choking traffic jams. Okay, the jams are still there, but everyone smart enough to use the Skytrain can consider themselves rescued. The Skytrain offers a new perspective on the city from on high, plus you get to sit in air-conditioned comfort.

Trains run frequently from 6am to midnight along two lines. The trains are labelled with their final destination and handy maps in the stations explain the layout. Free maps also outline the system, and friendly English-speaking ticket vendors are old-hands at helping confused *faràng*.

The Sukhumvit Line starts at Mo Chit station, near Chatuchak Market and the Northern & Northeastern Bus Terminal and eventually swings east along Th Sukhumvit with plenty of stations along this popular strip. The Silom line runs from the National Stadium station, near Siam Sq, through the popular Th Silom area to Saphan Taksin on the banks of the Mae Nam Chao Phraya. The two lines share an interchange at Siam station and there are Skytrain interchanges with the newer Metro at Silom and Asoke.

Fares vary from 10B to 40B, and machines only accept coins (get change from the ticket windows). There are a variety of stored-value tickets for one-day and multi-day unlimited trips; inquire at the stations.

Taxi

Fares for metered taxis are always lower than those for nonmetered taxis; look for ones with signs on top reading 'Taxi Meter'. Don't be shy about asking the driver to use the meter; sometimes they 'forget'. In tourist haunts they may refuse to use the meter; just find another taxi. Fares should generally run from 50B to 100B. In most large cities, the taxi drivers are seasoned navigators familiar with every out-of-the-way neighbourhood or street. However, this is not the case in Bangkok where, if you succeed in correctly pronouncing your destination, the taxi driver might still stare vacantly at your map. To ensure that you'll be able to return home, grab your hotel's business card, which will have directions in Thai.

Túk-Túk

You must fix fares in advance for túk-túks and they are only really sensible for shorter trips, if at all. Many have seemingly graduated from the Evel Knievel school of driving and that doesn't always work with three wheels on a sharp bend! Some travellers swear by túk-túk, others have a hard time bargaining a fair price – it all depends on your patience and a winning smile. Beware of túk-túk drivers who offer to take you on a sightseeing tour for 10B or 20B – it's a touting scheme designed to pressure you into purchasing overpriced goods.

AROUND BANGKOK

If you're tied to Bangkok for several days but feel the urge for some fresh air, take a day trip to some of the nearby attractions.

DAMNOEN SADUAK FLOATING MARKET

The image is iconic. Wooden canoes laden with multicoloured fruits and vegetables, paddled by Thai women wearing indigo-hued clothes and wide-brimmed straw hats: this is the realm of postcards. The reality reveals a scene of commercial chaos, more souvenir stalls than market vendors, more tourists than locals. But like all jamborees, it can still be fun. The action takes place on the water and the key is to get here early before the big buses arrive.

The smart money says arrive in Damnoen Saduak the night before and crash at the conveniently located **Noknoi Hotel** (Little Bird; ☎ 0 3225 4382; s/d 220/350B) and get up at 7am to see the market while the light is good, the sun forgiving and the tourists absent. By 9am the hordes from Bangkok arrive and the atmosphere drains away.

You can hire a boat from any pier that lines Th Sukhaphiban 1, which is the land route to the floating market area. The going rate is 150B to 200B per person, per hour. If the boat operator wants to charge you more, keep shopping.

Damnoen Saduak is 105km southwest of Bangkok. Air-con buses 78 and 996 (65B, two hours, every 20 minutes from 6.30am to 9pm) go direct from Bangkok's Southern Bus Terminal to Damnoen Saduak.

NAKHON PATHOM

Nakhon Pathom, 56km west of Bangkok, claims to be the oldest city in Thailand, but the only clue to its longevity is the **Phra Pathom Chedi**, originally erected in the early 6th century by the Theravada Buddhists of Dvaravati. The contemporary bell-shaped structure was built over the original in the early 11th century by the Khmer king, Suryavarman I of Angkor. This alteration created the world's tallest Buddhist monument, 127m high. Sitting in the middle of town, Phra Pathom Chedi makes for a pleasant stroll or interesting sketching subject. Opposite the *bòht* (central sanctuary) is a **museum** (admission 20B; ☯ 9am-4pm Wed-Sun), which contains some Dvaravati sculpture. In November, there's the **Phra Pathom Chedi Fair** that packs in everyone from fruit vendors to fortune-tellers.

Air-con buses 997 and 83 (35B, one hour, frequent) leave from Bangkok's Southern Bus Terminal to Nakhon Pathom. To return to Bangkok, catch one of the idling buses from Th Phayaphan on the canal side of the road a block from the train station. Bus 78 to Damnoen Saduak Floating Market (left) leaves from the same stop.

Two trains daily (7.45am and 1.45pm) depart Thonburi (Bangkok Noi) station for Nakhon Pathom (3rd class 14B, about 1¼ hours). Returning to Thonburi there are also two departures (8.55am and 4.20pm). There are also connections with Hualamphong, but the journey takes longer.

SAMUT PRAKAN'S ANCIENT CITY

Samut Prakan's claim to fame is the **Ancient City** (Muang Boran; ☎ 0 2323 9253; www.ancientcity .com; adult/child 300/200B; ☯ 8am-5pm), alleged to be the world's largest outdoor museum. Around 12km south of the city centre, it is home to 109 scaled-down replicas of Thailand's most famous historic sites, including some that no longer survive. Visions of Las Vegas and tiny tacky treasures may spring to mind, but the Ancient City is architecturally sophisticated and a preservation site for classical buildings and art forms. For students of Thai architecture or even for those who want an introduction to the subject, it is definitely worth the trip. It is also a good place for leisurely walks or bicycle rides (50B rental), as it's rarely crowded.

Ordinary bus 25 (3.50B) and air-con buses 507, 508 and 511 (16B) ply regular routes between central Bangkok and Samut Prakan. The trip can take up to two hours depending on traffic. Ancient City is 33km from Bangkok along the Old Sukhumvit

Hwy. From Samut Prakan take a green minibus 36 (6B), which passes the entrance to Ancient City; sit on the left-hand side of the bus to spot the 'Muang Boran' sign. To return to town, cross the main highway and catch white săwngthăew 36 (5B).

CENTRAL THAILAND

The fertile plains of central Thailand are the geographic and cultural heart of the country. Along the banks of life-giving Mae Nam Chao Phraya, the cultural and military identity of the early Thai nation is known to have evolved in the ancient capitals of Suk-hothai and Ayuthaya. Once known as the Siamese language, today the region's dialect is considered standard Thai. Featuring history, superb scenery and easy adventures, central Thailand is fast becoming a must for travellers.

KANCHANABURI

pop 61,800

West of Bangkok, Kanchanaburi is blessed with an idyllic location, nestled in between rugged limestone peaks and the pretty Mae Nam Khwae (Kwai River). The peaceful atmosphere belies the town's tragic past as the site of a WWII prisoner-of-war camp and the infamous Bridge over the River Kwai. Today visitors come to pay their respects to fallen Allied soldiers or discover for themselves more about the town's dark past. But Kan, as locals call it, is also a great place to relax at riverside guesthouses or venture to nearby natural attractions.

Information

Check out www.kanchanaburi-info.com for general information on town and around. Several major Thai banks can be found around Th Saengchuto near the market and bus terminal. There are plenty of places to get online along Th Mae Nam Khwae.

Post office (Th Saengchuto)

TAT office (☎ 0 3451 1200; Th Saengchuto; ⏰ 8.30am-4.30pm) Near the bus terminal, it provides information on trips beyond Kanchanaburi, as well as bus and train schedules.

Thanakarn Hospital (☎ 0 3462 2358) Best-equipped place for foreigners.

Tourist police (☎ 0 3451 2668) Several locations around town.

Sights

THAILAND–BURMA RAILWAY CENTRE

Before you head out to the Kwai River Bridge, get a little history under your belt at this **museum** (☎ 0 3451 0067; 73 Th Jaokannun; adult/child 60/30B; ⏰ 9am-5pm). Professional exhibits outline Japanese aggression in Southeast Asia during WWII and their plan to connect Yangon (in Burma) with Bangkok via rail for transport of military supplies. Captured Allied soldiers as well as Burmese and Malay captives were transported to the jungles of Kanchanaburi to build 415km of rail – known today as the Death Railway because of the many lives (more than 100,000 men) the project claimed.

KANCHANABURI ALLIED WAR CEMETERY

Across the street from the Thailand–Burma Railway Centre, the **Kanchanaburi Allied War Cemetery** (Th Saengchuto; admission free; ⏰ 7am-6pm) is a touching gift from the Thai people to remember the POWs, mainly from Britain and Holland, who died on their soil.

KWAI RIVER BRIDGE
(DEATH RAILWAY BRIDGE)

While the story made famous by the film *The Bridge on the River Kwai* is one of endurance, heroism and suffering, the span itself is just an ordinary bridge with an extraordinary history. A bit of imagination and some historical context will help to enliven a visit to the bridge, which was a small but strategic part of the Death Railway to Burma. Engineers estimated that construction would take five years, but the human labourers were forced to complete the railway in 16 months. Allied planes destroyed the bridge in 1945 but later repairs restored the span; the bomb damage is still apparent in the pylons closest to the riverbanks.

During the first week of December there's a nightly sound-and-light show put on at the bridge. It's a pretty impressive scene, with simulations of bombers and explosions and fantastic bursts of light. The town gets a lot of tourists during this week, so book early.

The bridge is roughly 3km from the town centre and the best way for you to reach it is by bicycle. You can also catch a săwngthăew (5B) going north along Th Saengchuto, but it isn't obvious when to get off; if you get to the Castle Mall, you've gone too far. There

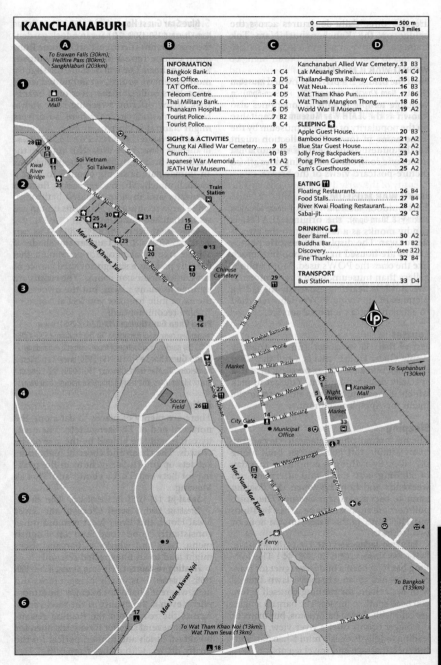

KANCHANABURI

0 — 500 m
0 — 0.3 miles

INFORMATION
Bangkok Bank.................................1 C4
Post Office.....................................2 D5
TAT Office.....................................3 D4
Telecom Centre.............................4 D5
Thai Military Bank..........................5 C4
Thanakarn Hospital........................6 D5
Tourist Police................................7 B2
Tourist Police................................8 C4

SIGHTS & ACTIVITIES
Chung Kai Allied War Cemetery......9 B5
Church...10 B3
Japanese War Memorial................11 A2
JEATH War Museum.....................12 C5

Kanchanaburi Allied War Cemetery.13 B3
Lak Meuang Shrine.......................14 C4
Thailand–Burma Railway Centre....15 B2
Wat Neua....................................16 B3
Wat Tham Khao Pun.....................17 B6
Wat Tham Mangkon Thong...........18 B6
World War II Museum...................19 A2

SLEEPING
Apple Guest House.......................20 B3
Bamboo House.............................21 A2
Blue Star Guest House..................22 A2
Jolly Frog Backpackers..................23 A3
Pong Phen Guesthouse.................24 A2
Sam's Guesthouse........................25 A2

EATING
Floating Restaurants.....................26 B4
Food Stalls...................................27 B4
River Kwai Floating Restaurant......28 A2
Sabai-jit......................................29 C3

DRINKING
Beer Barrel..................................30 A2
Buddha Bar.................................31 B2
Discovery..............................(see 32)
Fine Thanks.................................32 B4

TRANSPORT
Bus Station..................................33 D4

To Erawan Falls (30km);
Hellfire Pass (80km);
Sangkhlaburi (203km)

Castle Mall

Kwai River Bridge

Soi Vietnam
Soi Taiwan

Th Saengchuto

Th Mae Nam Khwae

Mae Nam Khwae Yai

Soi Rong Hip Oi

Th Chaokunen

Train Station

Chinese Cemetery

Th Ban Neua

Th Tesaban Bamrung

Th Kratai Thong

Th Hiran Prasat

Market

Th Bovon

Th Pakpraek

Th Khu Meuang

Th U Thong

Night Market

Kanakan Mall

Market

Th Lak Meuang

Soi Khwae

Soccer Field

City Gate

Municipal Office

Th Wisuttharangsi

Th Pak Praek

Th Saengchuto

Mae Nam Mae Klung

To Suphanburi (130km)

Ferry

To Bangkok (139km)

Th Chukkadon

Mae Nam Khwae Noi

To Wat Tham Khao Noi (13km);
Wat Tham Seua (13km)

Th Sala Klang

THAILAND

are also three daily departures across the bridge on the Kanchanaburi–Nam Tok train.

WORLD WAR II MUSEUM

Near the bridge is a privately owned **museum** (Th Mae Nam Khwae; admission 30B; ⏱ 9am-6pm), a veritable temple to kitsch, sometimes also known as the **JEATH War Museum** to capitalise on the popularity of another museum by the same name in town. The collection might be the oddest assortment of memorabilia under one roof, but the building does afford picture-postcard views of the bridge.

JEATH WAR MUSEUM

This outdoor **museum** (Th Pak Phraek; admission 30B; ⏱ 8.30am-6pm), the original JEATH, is run by monks as a testament to the atrocities of war. The displays of historic photographs are housed in a bamboo hut, much like the ones the POWs used. More a photo gallery than museum, it isn't very informative, but it is heartfelt, especially the fading pictures of surviving POWs who returned to Thailand for a memorial service.

Courses

Test of Thai (Th Saengchuto) Run by friendly Apple Guest House, this is a full-day Thai cooking course (900B per person), held in a specially designed kitchen. You get to pick which dishes you want to make from the menu for Apple's restaurant.

Sleeping

The most atmospheric places to stay are the many simple raft guesthouses built along the river. Everything is conducive to a day of chilling out until mid-afternoon on weekends and holidays when the floating karaoke bars and discos fire up. The noise polluters are supposed to be in bed by 10pm but Thai time, in this case, runs an hour or two behind.

Jolly Frog Backpackers (☎ 0 3451 4579; 28 Soi China, Th Mae Nam Khwae; s 70B, d 150-290B; 🕸) The Jolly Frog has long been a budget magnet for travellers thanks to an expansive lawn littered with deck chairs for sunning yourself before you head south to the sea. The bargain singles are cells with shared bathrooms, but many of the bigger rooms offer a river view. The soi leading to Jolly Frog is a mini Khao San with Internet, massage and travel agents.

Blue Star Guest House (☎ 0 3451 2161; 21 Th Mae Nam Khwae; d 150-450B; 🕸) Set in a lush garden, the wooden huts here feel part of some Robinson Crusoe retreat more than downtown Kanchanaburi. The real deal are the slightly more expensive rooms, set in knotted wood bungalows built over the river on a boardwalk, many offering sweeping river views. No commissions are paid here, so drivers might claim it is closed.

Bamboo House (☎ 0 3451 2532; 3-5 Soi Vietnam, Th Mae Nam Khwae; r 200-500B; 🕸) Moving towards the bridge, this small guesthouse has an immaculate lawn big enough to host a football match. The budget rooms float on the water and involve a shared bathroom, while large rooms with ablutions on tap are set in thatched bungalows.

Apple Guest House (☎ 0 3451 2017; 52 Soi Rong Hip Oi; r 250-500B; 🕸) Set under the shade of a huge tree (a mango, not an apple), this friendly pad has a straightforward choice of fan-cooled or air-con rooms. The rooms are as same as many places, but the owners go the extra mile to make you feel at home.

Also recommended:

Pong Phen Guesthouse (☎ 0 3451 2981; www .pongphen.com; 5 Soi Banglated, Th Tha MaKam; r 120-430B; 🕸) Big garden, good range of rooms and still expanding.

Sam's Guesthouse (☎ 0 3451 5956; www.samsguest house.com; Th Mae Nam Khwae; r 150-600B; 🕸) One of the old favourites, the leafy garden is a homely hideaway.

Eating

There are plenty of places to eat along the northern end of Th Saengchuto. The quality can usually be judged by the size of the crowds. The cheap and cheerful night market sets up on Th Saengchuto in the parking lot between Th U Thong and Th Lak Meuang.

Sabai-jit (28-45/55 Th Saengchuto; dishes 40-80B; ⏱ breakfast, lunch & dinner) Close to the River Kwai Hotel, this lively local restaurant has consistently good food and an English menu. Beer and whisky at bargain prices might lead to an unexpected session!

Floating restaurants (Th Song Khwae; dishes 100-150B; ⏱ dinner) It is worth taking a lucky dip here, where it's hard not to enjoy the atmosphere, even if the quality of the food varies. Across the road from the floating restaurants are several smaller food stalls open for breakfast, lunch and dinner; perfect for the thrifty drifter, with dishes from 50B.

THAILAND

River Kwai Floating Restaurant (☎ 0 3451 2595; 415 Th Mae Nam Khwae; dishes 50-200B; ☺ breakfast, lunch & dinner) Anyone visiting the infamous bridge should consider a short stop here for refreshment. The menu is huge if a little pricey, but the view doesn't come more iconic than this for a sunset beer.

Most of the popular guesthouses have restaurants churning out the greatest hits from banana pancakes to *tôm yam*. The food at **Apple Guest House** (☎ 0 3451 2017; 52 Soi Rong Hip Oi; ☺ breakfast, lunch & dinner) is a cut above the rest, but it lacks a river view.

Drinking

Beer Barrel (Th Mae Nam Khwae) Lost in a forest of trees, this outdoor beer garden of gigantic wooden tables is the right remedy after a harrowing day of history in town. The music kicks in around sunset and the crowds drift in. Unfortunately, so do the mosquitoes.

Buddha Bar (Th Mae Nam Khwae) There is a whole strip of small bars opposite the 7-Eleven, but most are about pink lights and pretty girls. Buddha Bar is the not-so-zen exception – it's more of a biker's haunt, rocker's bar and hard-drinking club.

Fine Thanks (2/8 Th Song Khwae) This glitzy glass palace has a popular outdoor garden for watching big sports events. Don't be put off by the giant boots and short skirts of the waitresses; the owner obviously has a strange taste in uniforms.

Discovery (Th Song Khwae) Located right next door to Fine Thanks, Discover is the oldest disco in Kanchanaburi, and is packed to the gunnels with locals each and every weekend. A few bold *faràng*, warmed up on whisky, join in the jamboree. There is nothing as effective as cutting some dodgy dance moves to earn yourself the respect of strangers.

Getting There & Away

Kanchanaburi's bus station is on Th Saengchuto, near Th Lak Meuang and the TAT office.

Bus trips go to Bangkok's Southern Bus Terminal (air-con 62B to 79B, three hours, every 15 minutes until 7pm), Nakhon Pathom (ordinary 28B, 1½ hours), Ratburi (36B, 2½ hours), Sangkhlaburi (90B, five hours), and Suphanburi (35B, 2½ hours), for connections to Ayuthaya.

Kanchanaburi is on the Thonburi (Bangkok Noi)–Nam Tok train line. The **train station** (Th Saengchuto) is 500m from the river. There are only two trains a day originating from Thonburi (25B). West of Kanchanaburi to Nam Tok, the train travels a portion of the Death Railway (17B, two hours, three departures daily).

Getting Around

Săamláw within the city cost 30B a trip. Regular săwngthăew in town are 5B to 10B and ply Th Saengchuto, but be careful you don't accidentally 'charter' one – these are a rip-off at 500B an hour.

There are plenty of places hiring motorbikes along Th Mae Nam Khwae. The going rate is 150B to 250B per day and it's a good way of getting to the rather scattered attractions around Kanchanaburi.

Bicycles can be rented from most guesthouses for around 50B a day.

AROUND KANCHANABURI

Most of the popular guesthouses in town offer tours that take in the main attractions around Kanchanaburi. Shop around for the best deal.

Erawan National Park (☎ 0 3457 4222; admission 200B per person; ☺ 8am-4pm) is the home of the seven-tiered **Erawan Falls**, which makes for a refreshing day trip; bring along a swimsuit for a plunge in some of the enticing pools. To get yourself to the park take an early morning bus (26B, 1½ hours, hourly from 8am) from Kanchanaburi to the end of the line, from where you will have to walk a couple of kilometres to the waterfall trail. The last bus back to Kanchanaburi leaves at 4pm.

Carved out of unforgiving mountain terrain, the section of the Death Railway called **Hellfire Pass** (suggested donation 30-100B; ☺ 9am-4pm) was so named for the unearthly apparitions cast by the nightly fires of the labouring POWs. Today a 4km-long trail follows the old route with some remnants of the rail line still intact. Located near Km Marker 66 on Sai Yok–Thong Pha Phum road, Hellfire Pass can be reached by a Sangkhlaburi-bound or Thong Pha Phum-bound bus (27B, 1½ hours, last bus back at 4pm); use the Thai script for 'Hellfire Pass' that is printed on the TAT-distributed map to inform the attendant of your destination.

THAILAND

SANGKHLABURI & THREE PAGODAS PASS

Northwest of Kanchanaburi is a legal day-trip crossing into Myanmar at Three Pagodas Pass (Chedi Sam Ong). The village on the Myanmar side has been the scene of firefights between minority insurgents and the Burmese government; both parties want to control the collection of 'taxes' levied on smuggling. In 1990, the Burmese government regained control of the area, rebuilt the bamboo village in wood and concrete and renamed it Payathonzu. A row of souvenir shops and the three pagodas, which are rather inconspicuous, are all the town offers. The trip is more for bragging rights of being in Myanmar rather than a rewarding excursion. At the time of writing the border was open to foreigners.

Sleeping

P Guest House (☎ 0 3459 5061; www.pguesthouse.com; 8/1 Mu 1; s/d from 150/200B; 🌐) These attractive, spacious bungalows have verandas along a slope overlooking the lake, making it worth the 1km walk from the bus stop. Shared bathrooms are cleaner than average here. P does packages (850B) that include rafting on the lake and elephant riding, as well as a room for one night. It also rents kayaks and motorcycles.

Burmese Inn (☎ 0 3459 5146; www.sangkhlaburi .com; r 120-400B) Set in a flourishing garden, this guesthouse is perched on a lagoon with views of the wooden bridge that crosses to the Mon village, about 800m south from the Sangkhlaburi bus station. Cheaper rooms are a bit-bare bones and involve a shared bathroom.

BORDER CROSSING: INTO MYANMAR

It is sometimes possible to make a day trip into Myanmar at Three Pagodas Pass. It requires an overnight pause in Sangkhlaburi, 203km north of Kanchanaburi, where you get a temporary exit stamp from **Thai immigration** (☎ 0 3459 5335), close to the bus station near the post office. Frequent săwngthăew can take you the remaining 18km to the border where you pay US$10 to enter Myanmar for one day only; you're not allowed to travel further than 1km from the border (open from 6am to 6pm).

Getting There & Away

To travel from Kanchanaburi to Sangkhlaburi, take ordinary bus 8203 (90B, five hours, 6am, 8.40am, 10.20am and noon) or the air-con bus (151B, four hours, 9am and 1.30pm).

A minivan service to Kanchanaburi via Thong Pha Phum (118B, three hours, six daily from 7.30am to 4.30pm) leaves Sangkhlaburi from near the market.

If you go by motorcycle or car, you can count on about three to four hours to cover the 203km from Kanchanaburi to Sangkhlaburi. Alternatively, you can make it an all-day trip and stop off in Ban Kao (a museum displaying Neolithic artefacts), Meuang Singh (the remains of a 13th-century Khmer shrine of the Angkor Empire) and Hellfire Pass. Be warned, however, that this is not a trip for an inexperienced motorcycle rider. The Thong Pha Phum to Sangkhlaburi section of the journey (74km) requires sharp reflexes and previous experience on mountain roads. This is also not a motorcycle trip to do alone, as stretches of the highway are practically deserted.

From Sangkhlaburi, there are hourly săwngthăew (30B, 40 minutes) to Three Pagodas Pass all day.

AYUTHAYA

pop 81,400

In their race to reach the Gulf of Thailand, three rivers (Mae Nam Lopburi, Chao Phraya and Pa Sak) converge to form the island of Ayuthaya, the former Thai capital, named after the home of Rama in the Indian epic Ramayana.

The rivers formed both a natural barrier to invasion and an invitation to trade. From 1350 to 1767, Ayuthaya was the cultural centre of the emerging Thai nation. Throughout Ayuthaya's domination of central Thailand, Asian and Western foreign powers eyed up this strategic city and successive Thai kings had to foil coups and play foreign powers off against one another. But the river defences were unable to repulse persistent attacks by the Burmese. After two years of war, the capital fell; the royal family fled to Thonburi, near present-day Bangkok, and the Burmese looted the city's architectural and religious treasures.

Today a modern city has sprung up around the holy ruins. Life revolves around the river, which acts as transport, bath and kitchen sink for its residents. The holiday of **Loi Krathong** – held on the proper full-moon night, when tiny votive boats are floated on rivers as a tribute to the River Goddess – is celebrated with great fanfare in Ayuthaya.

Information

ATMs are abundant, especially along Th Naresuan near Amporn Shopping Centre. The Internet shops on and around Soi 1, Th Naresuan, offer the cheapest deals.

Main post office (Th U Thong)
Nakorn Sri Ayutthaya Hospital (☎ 0 3524 1027)
TAT office (☎ 0 3524 6076; 108/22 Th Si Sanphet; ⏲ 9am-5pm) Distributes an Ayuthaya tourist map and bus schedule.
Tourist police (☎ 0 3524 1446, emergency ☎ 1155; Th Si Sanphet)

Sights

A Unesco World Heritage site, Ayuthaya's historic temples are scattered throughout this once magnificent city, and along the encircling rivers. The ruins are divided into two geographical areas: ruins 'on the island', in the central part of town between Th Chee Kun and the western end of Th U Thong, which are best visited by bicycle; and those 'off the island' on the other side of the river, which are best visited on an evening boat tour (from 250B; book through guesthouses) or by bicycle. Getting a handle on the religious and historical importance of the temples is difficult to do without some preliminary tutoring. **Ayuthaya Historical Study Centre** (☎ 0 3524 5124; Th Rotchana; adult/student 100/50B; ⏲ 9am-4.30pm Mon-Fri, 9am-5pm Sat & Sun) has informative, professional displays that paint an indispensable picture for viewing the ancient city. Also purchase the *Ayuthaya* pamphlet (15B) for sale at Wat Phra Si Sanphet's admission kiosk.

There are also two national museums in town. The building that houses the **Chantharakasem National Museum** (Map pp728-9; admission 30B; ⏲ 9am-4pm Wed-Sun) is a museum in itself. King Rama IV had this palace rebuilt and established as a museum in 1936. The less charming but larger **Chao Sam Phraya National Museum** (cnr Th Rotchana & Th Si Sanphet; admission 30B; ⏲ 9am-4pm Wed-Sun) has a first-

WHAT'S A WAT?

Planning to conquer Thailand's temples and ruins? With this handy guide, you'll be able to sort out your wats from your what's that:

chedi – large bell-shaped tower usually containing five structural elements symbolising (from bottom to top) earth, water, fire, wind and void; relics of Buddha or a Thai king are housed inside the *chedi;* also known as a stupa

praang (prang) – towering phallic spire of Khmer origin serving the same religious purpose as a *chedi*

wat – temple monastery

wíhǎan – main sanctuary for the temple's Buddha sculpture and where laypeople come to make their offerings; classic architecture typically has a three-tiered roofline representing the triple gems: Buddha (the teacher), Dharma (the teaching) and Brotherhood (the followers)

Buddha Images

Elongated earlobes, no evidence of bone or muscle, arms that reach to the knees, a third eye: these are some of the 32 rules, originating from 3rd-century India, that govern the depiction of Buddha in sculpture. With such rules in place, why are some Buddhas sitting and others walking? Known as 'postures', the pose of the image depicts periods in the life of Buddha:

reclining – exact moment of Buddha's enlightenment

sitting – Buddha teaching or meditating: if the right hand is pointed toward the earth, Buddha is shown subduing the demons of desire; if the hands are folded in the lap, Buddha is turning the wheel of law

standing – Buddha bestowing blessings or taming evil forces

walking – Buddha after his return to earth from heaven

class collection of gold artefacts in a secure room upstairs.

Most of the temples are open from 8am or 9am until 5pm or 6pm daily.

ON THE ISLAND

The most distinctive example of Ayuthaya architecture is **Wat Phra Si Sanphet** (admission 30B) thanks to its three bell-shaped *chedi* that taper off into descending rings. This site served as the royal palace from the city's founding until the mid-15th century, when it was converted into a temple.

THAILAND

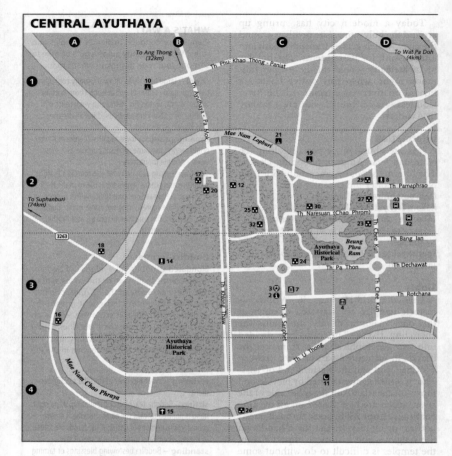

CENTRAL AYUTHAYA

Although the grounds are now well tended, these efforts cannot hide the ravages of war and time. The surrounding buildings are worn through to their orange bricks, leaning to one side as gravity takes its toll. The complex once contained a 16m-high standing Buddha covered with 250kg of gold, which was melted down by the Burmese conquerors.

The adjacent **Wihaan Phra Mongkhon Bophit** houses a huge bronze seated Buddha, the largest in Thailand.

Wat Phra Mahathat (admission 30B) has one of the first Khmer-style *praang* built in the capital. One of the most iconic images in Ayuthaya is the Buddha head engulfed by tentacle-like tree roots.

OFF THE ISLAND

The main *wíhǎan* of **Wat Phanan Choeng** (admission 30B) contains a 19m-high sitting Buddha image, which reportedly wept when the Burmese sacked Ayuthaya. The temple is dedicated to Chinese seafarers and on weekends is crowded with Buddhist pilgrims from Bangkok who pay for saffron-coloured cloth to be ritually draped over the image.

Wat Chai Wattanaram used to be one of Ayuthaya's most overgrown lost-city ruins, with stately rows of disintegrating Buddhas. Today, some harsh restoration work (and the wonders of modern cement) has produced a row of lookalike brand-new Buddhas. It is still a lovely temple and a photogenic subject for sunset photo shoots.

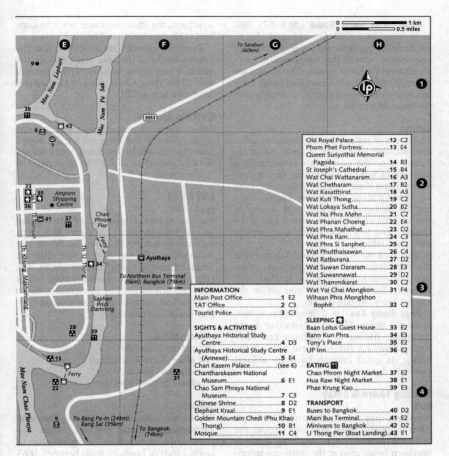

The **Golden Mountain Chedi** (Phu Khao Thong) lies to the northwest of the city and has a wide view over the flat country. Also to the north is the **elephant kraal**, a restored version of the wooden stockade once used for the annual roundup of wild elephants. To the southeast, **Wat Yai Chai Mongkon** has a massive ruined *chedi*, which contrasts with surrounding contemporary Buddha statues.

Sleeping

Bann Kun Phra (☎ 0 3524 1978; bannkunpra@ai-ayutthaya.com; 48/2 Th U Thong; dm 150B, s/d 250/350B) If it is atmosphere in abundance you seek, then this stylish old teak house is calling. The rooms are rustic, verging on basic for the money, and bathrooms are shared, but the riverbank location is superb. Downstairs is an authentic restaurant with a cracking little terrace for nightly breezes.

Tony's Place (☎ 0 3525 2578; 12/18 Soi 8, Th Naresuan; r 160-500B;) Tony's Place has been around almost as long as some of the temples, but keeps drawing the faithful thanks to a healthy selection of rooms and a lively restaurant and bar. Cheaper rooms have shared bathroom, while life at the top brings a virtual suite, lounge and all.

UP Inn (☎ 0 3525 1213; 20/1 Soi Thaw Kaw Saw; s 180-200B, d 250-500B) Just up the road from Tony's, UP is set in a smart, modern villa with shiny, bright clean rooms. The friendly family know their stuff: tourist information on tap, bikes for rent and boat tours are all available.

Baan Lotus Guest House (☎ 0 3525 1988; 20 Th Pamaphrao; r 300B) An old teak home set in huge gardens, this a quiet, homely guesthouse where the owners just can't do enough for their guests. The rooms are large, the bathrooms larger and some have balcony views. Walk slowly, as dogs guard the place in numbers.

Eating

The range of restaurants can come as a disappointment after living it up in Bangkok. Eating in at the guesthouse is normally a dull option, but the riverside terrace restaurant at Bann Kun Phra is worth a visit, even for those staying elsewhere. Tony's Place has the best general menu, with a reliable mix of Thai and Western dishes and is the closest thing to a backpacker bar, complete with pool table.

The Hua Raw and Chao Phrom night markets, both on Th U Thong, have Muslim-style *rotii* as well as popular Thai wok-wonders. Strike for here if you are in the market for a bargain dinner.

Phae Krung Kao (Th U Thong; dishes 60-100B; ☽ lunch & dinner) Floating restaurants are a popular fixture in Ayuthaya and Phae Krung Kao, on the southern side of the bridge, is good enough to draw a local crowd in droves.

Getting There & Away

BUS

Ayuthaya has two bus terminals. Buses from the south, west and east stop at the main **bus terminal** (Th Naresuan). Long-distance northern buses stop at the northern terminal, 5km east of the centre.

Frequent buses run between the main terminal and the airport (39B, 1½ hours) and Bangkok's Northern & Northeastern Bus Terminal (ordinary/air-con 41/64B, two hours) from about 5am to 7pm. Minivans to Bangkok (45B, two hours) leave from Th Bang Ian, just south of the main bus terminal, every 20 minutes between 5am and 5pm. Passengers are dropped off at Bangkok's Victory Monument.

TRAIN

The trains to Ayuthaya leave Hualamphong station in Bangkok (3rd-class 15B, 1½ hours) almost hourly between 6am and 10pm, usually stopping at Don Muang Airport. From Ayuthaya, the train continues north to Lopburi (13B, one hour) and beyond.

From Ayuthaya's train station, on the eastern banks of the Mae Nam Pa Sak, the quickest way to reach the old city is to walk west to the river, where you can take a short ferry ride across (2B).

Getting Around

Bikes can be rented at most guesthouses (50B). Túk-túk can be hired for the day to tour the sites (200B per hour); a trip within the city should be about 20B or about 30B to the station.

LOPBURI

pop 57,600

For the visitor, Lopburi is of interest for its fine juxtaposition of ancient brick ruins and not-so-ancient shophouses, hotels and restaurants. It's one of the few cities in Thailand that actually feels as old as it is (since at least the Dvaravati period, 6th to 11th centuries AD). The town is also home to a resident troop of mischievous monkeys that keeps things lively.

Information

Hospital (☎ 0 3641 1250)
Post office (Th Phra Narai Maharat)
Tourist police (☎ 0 3641 1013)
TAT office (☎ 0 3642 2768; Th Phraya Kamjat)

Sights

The former palace of King Narai, **Phra Narai Ratchaniwet** (Th Sorasak; ☽ 7.30am-5.30pm), opposite Lopburi Asia Hotel, is a good place to begin a tour of Lopburi. Built between 1665 and 1677, it was designed by French and Khmer architects, creating an unusual blend of styles. Inside the grounds is the **Lopburi National Museum** (admission 30B; ☽ 8.30am-noon & 1-4pm Wed-Sun), which contains an excellent collection of Lopburi period sculpture, as well as an assortment of Khmer, Dvaravati, U Thong and Ayuthaya art, plus traditional farm implements.

Opposite the San Phra Kan, near the Muang Thong Hotel, **Prang Sam Yot** (Sacred Three Spires; admission 30B; ☽ 8am-6pm) represents classic Khmer-Lopburi style and is a Hindu-turned-Buddhist temple. Originally, the three towers symbolised the Hindu trinity of Shiva, Vishnu and Brahma. Now two of them contain ruined Lopburi-style Buddha images.

Directly across from the train station, **Wat Phra Si Ratana Mahathat** (admission 30B; ☻ 7am-5pm Wed-Sun) is a large 12th-century Khmer temple that's worth a look.

Sleeping & Eating

Lopburi Asia Hotel (☎ 0 3661 8893; cnr Th Sorasak & Th Phraya Kamjat; r 200-300B; ✷) Overlooking Phra Narai Ratchaniwet, this old Chinese hotel has large rooms, the more expensive ones with air-con. Ask to see a room first, as some are in a better state than others.

White House Garden Restaurant (Th Phraya Kamjat; dishes 60-120B; ☻ lunch) Opposite the TAT office, the White House offers a range of Thai-Chinese specialties. Generous portions and high-quality vegetarian dishes keep the punters coming.

The **central market** (Th Ratchadamnoen & Th Surasongkhram), just north of the palace, is a great place to pick up *kài thâwt* or *kài yâang* (fried or grilled chicken) with sticky rice for a long trip further north. In the evenings a night market sets up along Th Na Phra Kan, with some great little treats for compulsive snackers.

Getting There & Away

Ordinary buses leave from Ayuthaya (40B, 1½ hours, every 10 minutes) or from Bangkok's Northern & Northeastern Bus Terminal (ordinary/air-con 62/85B, three hours, every 20 minutes). For Kanchanaburi, take a bus to Suphanburi (38B, 2½ hours) and change. The scenery is beautiful along this route.

By train you can reach Lopburi by local train from Ayuthaya (3rd class 13B, one hour) or by express train from Bangkok (64B, 1½ hours). One way of visiting Lopburi on the way north is to take the train from Ayuthaya (or Bangkok) early in the morning, leave your gear at the station while you look around, then continue north on the night train.

Getting Around

Săamláw go anywhere in old Lopburi for 30B. Săwngthăew run a regular route between the old and new towns for 5B per person.

PHITSANULOK

pop 100,300

Many travellers prefer to use vibrant Phitsanulok as a base for visiting the ancient city of Sukhothai as it has more charm and better grazing options. Phitsanulok is often abbreviated as 'Phi-lok'. The town's own attractions include **Wat Phra Si Ratana Mahathat** (known locally as Wat Yai), which contains Phra Phuttha Chinnarat, one of the most beautiful and revered Buddha images in Thailand.

Information

Internet shops dot the streets around the railway station and on the western bank of the river.

Bangkok Bank (35 Th Naresuan) ATM, plus after-hours exchange window.

Post office (Th Phuttha Bucha)

Pra Buddha Chinnaraj Hospital (☎ 0 5371 1303)

TAT office (☎ 0 5525 2742; 209/7-8 Th Borom Trailokanat; ☻ 8.30am-4.30pm)

Sleeping

Phitsanulok Youth Hostel (☎ 0 5524 2060; phitsanulok@tyha.org; 38 Th Sanam Bin; dm/s/d/t 120/200/300/450B) Phi-lok's youth hostel is brimming with backpackers during high season. Old teak furniture gives the rooms character, but they generally lack windows. There is a friendly café here and breakfast is included in the rates. HI membership is mandatory (temporary one-night memberships are 50B). The manager is a great source of information on Phi-lok and beyond. The hostel is 1.5km east of the city centre; take a săamláw (30B).

Lithai Guest House (☎ 0 5521 9626; Th Phayalithai; r 200-360B; ✷) With sixty bright and light rooms strung out over three floors, the Lithai feels more like an apartment block than a guesthouse. Prices vary based on amenities like hot water, TV, air-con and fridge. Rooms on the 4th floor with wood floors and shared bathrooms are the best deal.

London Hotel (☎ 0 5522 5145; 21-22 Soi 1, Th Sailuthai; d 100-150B) Near Th Phuttha Bucha, this old wooden Chinese converted shopfront house looks like it comes from another era. Rooms are basic with shared bathroom only, but the owners are house-proud. Walk here from the train station; turn left on the main road, then take the first right on to Th Sailuthai.

Eating

Phitsanulok is a market crossroads for the country's vegetable industry and gets the pick of the harvest. A good sampler dish is *phàt phàk ruam* (stir-fried vegetables). Sniff out this and other veggie dishes at the **food stalls** (dishes 20-40B), just west of London Hotel near the cinema.

In the night market along the river, a couple of **street vendors** (dishes 40-80B; ☾ dinner) specialise in preparing *phàk bûng lawy fáa*, which translates as 'flying vegetable' – referring to the 'air' the dish catches as it's tossed in the wok. It's all about the preparation, like watching a cocktail waiter in full flow, as the dish is a fairly standard water spinach stir-fried in soya bean sauce and garlic.

Floating restaurants on the Mae Nam Nan are a hit at night. The old favourite of **Phae Fa Thai** (Th Wangchan; dishes 30-80B) fulfils the senses as much as the stomach with its dinner river cruise; pay a small fee to board the boat and order away from the menu – there is no minimum charge.

Pa Lai (Th Phuttha Bucha; dishes 20-30B) This noodle shop has become a local legend thanks to its famous *kǔaytǐaw hâwy khàa* (literally, legs-hanging rice noodles). The name comes from the way customers sit on a bench facing the river, with their legs dangling below.

Drinking

Along Th Borom Trailokanat near the Pailyn Hotel is a string of popular, rockin' Thai pubs. **Jao Samran** (Th Borom Trailokanat) features live Thai-folk and pop with food from 6pm and music from 8pm.

The most happening nightspot in town is the **Phitsanulok Bazaar** (Th Naresuan), where several pubs and dance clubs are clustered in a hedonist's mall. It doesn't get started until at least 9pm, but it is heaving by midnight.

Getting There & Away

Thai Airways International (THAI; ☎ 0 5525 8020; www.thaiair.com; 209/26-28 Th Borom Trailokanat) offers daily connections between Phitsanulok and Bangkok.

Phitsanulok is a major junction between the north and northeast. Most buses stop at the government bus station on Hwy 12 about 1.5km from the town centre. Buses for Bangkok depart from private bus company offices in the town centre on Th Ekathotsarot, south of the train station.

Available bus trips include Bangkok (aircon 185B to 250B, six hours), Chiang Mai (ordinary/air-con 140/196B, five hours), Sukhothai (ordinary/air-con 24/33B, one

hour, every 30 minutes from 6am to 6pm), Kamphaeng Phet (ordinary/air-con 43/60B, two hours) and also Khon Kaen (ordinary 130B, air-con 153B to 203B, five hours).

The train station is located in the centre of town on Th Ekathotsarot and Th Naresuan. Trains to Bangkok (1st/2nd/3rd class 324/159/69B, ordinary eight to nine hours, rapid seven hours) are a more convenient option, since Bangkok's train station is in the centre of the city.

Trains north to Chiang Mai (1st/2nd/3rd class 269/122/52B, five hours) usually depart in the afternoon.

Getting Around

City buses run between the town centre and the airport (bus 4) or bus terminal (bus 1) for 4B. The TAT office distributes a local bus route hand-out. The terminal for city buses is south of the train station on Th Ekathotsarot near the AmPm store. Sǎamláw rides within the town centre should cost you around 20B to 30B per person.

Run by the TAT, the Phitsanulok Tour Tramway (PTT) lets you see all the sights in one day. The tram leaves from Wat Yai at 9am, costs 20B and stops at fifteen sights before returning to Wat Yai at 3pm.

Motorcycles can be rented at **PN Motorbike** (☎ 0 5524 2424; Th Borom Trailokanat). Rates are 200B per day for a 125cc motorbike.

SUKHOTHAI
pop 39,800

The Khmer empire extended its influence deep into modern-day Thailand before a formidable rival arose in 1257 to undermine the distant throne's frontier. Naming its capital Sukhothai (Rising Happiness), the emerging Thai nation flourished militarily, claiming lands as far north as Vientiane, and culturally, developing a Thai alphabet as well as distinctive architecture and art. All this was accomplished in 150 years before Sukhothai was superseded by Ayuthaya to the south. If you can only digest one 'ancient city', Sukhothai should top the list; the ruins here are better preserved and less urban than those at Ayuthaya (see p727).

While the old city will charm the pants off anyone, the modern town of Sukhothai (12km from the ruins) doesn't quite live up to the atmosphere of its illustrious ancestor. It is a standard provincial town, big on con-

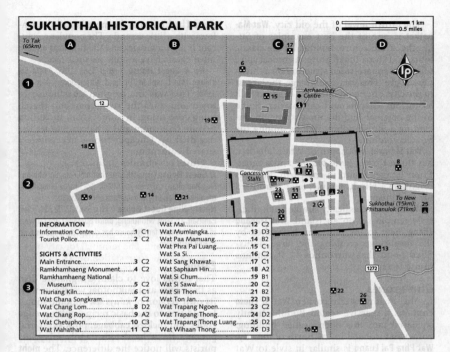

SUKHOTHAI HISTORICAL PARK

INFORMATION	
Information Centre	1 C1
Tourist Police	2 C2

SIGHTS & ACTIVITIES	
Main Entrance	3 C2
Ramkhamhaeng Monument	4 C2
Ramkhamhaeng National Museum	5 C2
Thuriang Kiln	6 C1
Wat Chana Songkram	7 C2
Wat Chang Lom	8 D2
Wat Chang Rop	9 A2
Wat Chetuphon	10 C3
Wat Mahathat	11 C2

Wat Mai	12 C2
Wat Mumlangka	13 D3
Wat Paa Mamuang	14 B2
Wat Phra Pai Luang	15 C1
Wat Sa Si	16 C2
Wat Sang Khawat	17 C1
Wat Saphaan Hin	18 A2
Wat Si Chum	19 B1
Wat Si Sawai	20 C2
Wat Sii Thon	21 B2
Wat Ton Jan	22 D3
Wat Trapang Ngoen	23 C2
Wat Trapang Thong	24 D2
Wat Trapang Thong Luang	25 D2
Wat Wihaan Thong	26 D3

crete and crowds, and small on atmosphere and attractions. Many travellers opt for Sukhothai as a day trip from nearby Phitsanulok (p731), as the bright lights of the big city can prove irresistible.

Information

There are banks with ATMs scattered around the central part of New Sukhothai, plus one in Old Sukhothai. Internet is common in New Sukhothai and some guesthouses offer access. The tourist police maintain an office in the Sukhothai Historical Park, opposite the Ramkhamhaeng National Museum.

Post office (Th Nikhon Kasem, New Sukhothai; 8.30am-noon Mon-Fri, 1-4.30pm Sat & Sun) Has an attached international phone office.

TAT office (Th Prawet Nakhon; 9am-5pm Mon-Fri) North of the River View Hotel in New Sukhothai.

Sukhothai Historical Park

The original capital of the first Thai kingdom was surrounded by three concentric ramparts and two moats bridged by four gateways. Today the remains of 21 historical sites can be seen within the old walls,

plus 70 sites within a 5km radius. The ruins are divided into five zones and there is a 30B admission fee for each zone; the central zone is 40B, plus 10B if you ride in on a bicycle. Invest in the 150B ticket that includes entrance to all sites and associated museums.

A lot of the religious symbolism here is lost on a Westerner; see What's a Wat? (p727) for a beginner's dip into this complicated realm.

The historical park (or *meuang kào*: 'old city') is best reached from town by săwngthăew (10B, every half hour from 6am to 6pm) leaving from Th Jarot Withithong near the Mae Yom, across the street from the 7-Eleven. Bicycles (20B) are essential for getting around the park and can be rented at the gate.

CENTRAL ZONE

Ramkhamhaeng National Museum (admission 30B; 9am-4pm) provides an introduction to Sukhothai history and culture and is a good place to begin exploring. If only it were air-conditioned there would be a lot more 30B scholars.

THAILAND

The crown jewel of the old city, **Wat Mahathat** is one of the best examples of Sukhothai architecture, typified by the classic lotus-bud stupa that features a conical spire topping a square-sided structure on a three-tiered base. This vast assemblage, the largest in the city, once contained 198 *chedi*, as well as various chapels and sanctuaries. Some of the original Buddha images remain, including a 9m standing Buddha among the broken columns.

Wat Si Sawai, just south of Wat Mahathat, has three Khmer-style *praang* and a moat. From images found in the *chedi*, this was originally a Hindu temple, later retrofitted for Buddhism.

Wat Sa Si is a classically simple Sukhothai-style temple set on an island. **Wat Trapang Thong**, next to the museum, is reached by the footbridge crossing the large, lotus-filled pond that surrounds it. It remains in use today.

OTHER ZONES

In the northwestern corner, **Wat Si Chum** contains a massive seated Buddha tightly squeezed into this open, walled building. Somewhat isolated to the north of the city, **Wat Phra Pai Luang** is similar in style to Wat Si Sawai. **Wat Chang Lom**, to the east, is surrounded by 36 elephants. **Wat Saphaan Hin** is a couple of kilometres west of the old city walls on a hillside and features a large Buddha looking back to Sukhothai.

Sleeping

At the bus station a small sǎwngthǎew mafia has emerged to promote guesthouses that pay commissions. If you're set on a particular guesthouse, don't believe them when they say the place is closed or dirty – always check yourself.

Ban Thai (☎ 0 5561 0163; guesthouse_banthai@ yahoo.com; Th Prawet Nakhon; d 150-250B) Looking over the Mae Nam Yom, Ban Thai offers a warm welcome to all. All the rooms are in smart shape and the shared bathrooms are not something to fear. The pretty bungalows include a private bathroom and share a small garden. Ban Thai is also the local oracle on things to see and do in the Sukhothai area.

Garden House (☎ 0 5561 1395; toonosman@yahoo .com; 11/1 Th Prawet Nakhon; r 120B, bungalows 200-300B; ☒) Take your pick from cheapies with a

shared bathroom or the more homely bungalows with a little veranda. The popular restaurant is big on movies and the fun staff ensure most guests have a smile on their face.

No 4 Guest House (☎ 0 5561 0165; 140/4 Soi Khlong Mae Lamphan, Th Jarot Withithong; s & d 150-450B) This was the original guesthouse in town and does the rustic bamboo-thatch bungalow thing in some style, including private bathroom and a balcony to let the day drift by. Cheaper rooms necessitate a shared bathroom.

Other possibilities in town:

JJ Guest House (jjguesthouse@hotmail.com; Soi Khlong Mae Ramphan; s/d from 200/250B; ☒) Large bungalows, friendly staff and fresh baguettes and croissants.

Ninety-Nine Guest House (☎ 0 5561 1315; 234/6 Soi Panitsan, Th Jarot Withithong; dm/d 80/150B) Not far west of No 4, this teak family house has cheap, clean rooms with shared bathroom.

Eating

Thai towns love to claim a signature dish as their own and Sukhothai weighs in with its own version of *kǔaytiaw* (noodle soup). In addition to the basic recipe, cutting-edge cooks add pickled cabbage, pork skins and peanuts for a local twist. Only *kǔaytiaw* purists will notice the difference. The **night market** (Th Jarot Withithong & Th Rat Uthit), near the Mae Nam Yom bridge, and the **municipal market** (btwn Th Rat Uthit & Th Ratchathani) are purveyors of this and other quick eats.

Evening meals centre on the series of open-air restaurants south of Chinnawat Hotel just off Th Nikhon Kasem.

Dream Cafe (Th Singhawat; dishes 80-150B) This compelling café is a treasure-trove of 19th-century Thai antiques. The food is no slouch either, with a yummy selection of sandwiches and pastas, as well as tasty Thai food.

Sukhothai Suki-Koka (Th Singhawat; dishes 30-90B; ☯ lunch & dinner; ☒) If you're starting to miss a spot of cooking with all this eating out, try the Thai-style sukiyaki here, a local cook-your-own soup. Also turns out Thai food and Western staples.

Getting There & Away

Sukhothai airport is 27km outside town off Rte 1195. **Bangkok Airways** (☎ 0 5563 3266; www .bangkokair.com) operates two flights daily connecting Sukhothai with Bangkok and Chiang Mai, and Luang Prabang in Laos.

The bus station is 4km northwest of the town centre on Hwy 101. Options include Bangkok (ordinary/air-con 142/199B, seven hours, hourly 7am to 11pm), Chiang Mai (ordinary/air-con 122/171B, six hours, frequent), Phitsanulok (ordinary/air-con 24/33B, one hour, every 30 minutes from 6am to 8pm), Sawankhalok (ordinary 16B, hourly), Si Satchanalai (ordinary/air-con 27/38B, one hour, hourly) and Tak (ordinary/air-con 31/43B, 1½ hours, hourly).

Getting Around

From the bus station a chartered săwngthăew should cost 30B to any guesthouse. When returning to the bus station, catch a public săwngthăew (6B) in front of the 7-Eleven on Th Jarot Withithong. Across the road is the stop for buses to the old city (10B).

SI SATCHANALAI-CHALIANG HISTORICAL PARK

Set amid rolling mountains, Si Satchanalai and Chaliang were a later extension of the Sukhothai empire. The park (admission 40B, plus 50/10/30B per car/bicycle/motorcycle; 8.30am-5pm) encompasses ruins of the old cities of Si Satchanalai and Chaliang, 56km north of Sukhothai.

Climb to the top of the hill supporting Wat Khao Phanom Phloeng for a view over the town and river. Wat Chedi Jet Thaew has a group of stupas in classic Sukhothai style. Wat Chang Lom has a *chedi* surrounded by Buddha statues set in niches and guarded by the fine remains of some elephant buttresses. Walk along the riverside for 2km or go back down the main road and cross the river to Wat Phra Si Ratana Mahathat, a very impressive temple that has a well-preserved *praang* and a variety of seated and standing Buddhas.

The Si Satchanalai–Sukhothai area was famous for its beautiful pottery, much of which was exported. The Indonesians were once keen collectors, and some fine specimens can be seen in the National Museum in Jakarta. Much of the pottery was made in Si Satchanalai. Rejects, buried in the fields, are still being discovered. Several of the old kilns have been carefully excavated and can be viewed along with original pottery samples at the Si Satchanalai Centre for Study & Preservation of Sangkhalok Kilns (admission 30B). So far the centre has opened two phases of its construction to the public: a site in Chaliang with excavated pottery samples and one kiln; and a larger outdoor site, 2km northwest of the Si Satchanalai ruins. The exhibits are very well presented despite the lack of English labels.

Si Satchanalai-Chaliang Historical Park is off Rte 101 between Sawankhalok and new Si Satchanalai. From Sukhothai, take a Si Satchanalai bus (ordinary/air-con 27/38B, one hour) and ask to get off at *meuang kào* (old city). The last bus back leaves around 4pm.

KAMPHAENG PHET

pop 27,500

Kamphaeng Phet (Diamond Wall) previously played a role as an important front line of defence for the Sukhothai kingdom. It's a nice place to spend a day or so wandering around the ruins and experiencing a small northern provincial capital that sees few tourists.

The Kamphaeng Phet Historical Park (0 5571 1921; admission 40B, plus 10/20B per bicycle/motorcycle; 8am-5pm) contains a number of temple ruins and the very fine remains of a long city wall. Wat Phra Sri Iriyabot features the shattered remains of standing, sitting, walking and reclining Buddha images. Wat Chang Rop (Temple Surrounded by Elephants) is just that – a temple with an elephant-buttressed wall.

Sleeping & Eating

Three J Guest House (0 5571 3129; threejguest@hotmail.com; 79 Th Rachavitee; r 200-400B;) The congenial host of this relatively new bungalow set-up for backpackers, Mr Charin, is happy to pick up guests from the bus terminal. Each of the bungalows is unique and the cheaper ones share a clean bathroom. Bicycles and motorbikes are available for rent.

Teak Tree Guest House (0 1675 6471; Soi 1 Th Chakungrao; s/d 170/250B) Next to the old city wall, the Teak Tree Guest House is the original guesthouse in town – just three fan rooms set in a tidy wooden house on stilts with shared hot-water bathroom. Open high season only.

A small night market gets set up every evening in front of the provincial offices, near the old city walls, and there are some cheap restaurants near the roundabout.

Getting There & Away

The government bus station is located across the river from town and is served by the following destinations: Bangkok (ordinary/air-con 125/165B), Sukhothai (45B, 1½ hours), Phitsanulok (ordinary/air-con 43/60B, two hours) and Tak (35B).

MAE SOT

Mae Sot is a kaleidoscope of colourful people, befitting its position as a major border town between Thailand and Myanmar. Strolling the streets reveals an interesting ethnic mixture – Burmese men in *longyi* (sarongs), Hmong and Karen women in traditional hill-tribe dress, bearded Indo-Burmese men and Thai army rangers. Shop signs along the streets are in Thai, Burmese and Chinese. A population of Western doctors and NGO aid workers attests to the human cost of an unstable border. For more than a decade, refugee camps have provided a short-term safety net for people fleeing clashes between ethnic minorities and the central Burmese government. The border is also a hotbed of smuggling – be it gems, drugs or even human beings – although these activities remain below the radar of the average visitor.

Information

There are several banks with ATMs in the town centre.

DK Book House (Th Intharakhiri) Attached to the DK Mae Sot Square Hotel, it has good maps.

Southeast Asia Tours (Th Intharakhiri) Internet access and international calls.

Tourist police (☎ 0 5553 3523, 0 5553 4341; Th Asia) One block east of the bus terminal.

Sleeping

No 4 Guest House (☎ 0 5554 4976; 736 Th Intharakhiri; dm/s/d 50/80/100B) Based in a large teak house hidden from the road, No 4 is a well-managed place with plenty of tourist information. All rooms have little more than mattresses on the floor, but have shared hot-water bathrooms. Donations of clothes and medicines are accepted here for distribution at the camps.

Green House Guest House (☎ 0 5553 3207; 406/8 Th Intarahakhiri; dm/s/d from 80/150/200B) Run by a welcoming local family, this place has an enticing combination of generously proportioned rooms, plenty of info and a central

location. Upstairs rooms have hardwood floors and are well worth the short climb.

Eating

The day market intersects with Th Prasat Withi near Siam Hotel and extends for several winding blocks to a covered area surrounded by simple Burmese food counters. A favourite local snack is *krabawng jaw* (Burmese for 'fried crispy'), a sort of vegetable tempura. While you tuck into your curry, other customers might stop in for a nip of the under-the-counter hooch.

Food stalls set up at night along Th Prasat Withi. Several Burmese-Indian shops, opposite the mosque, serve curries, *khâo sawy* (chicken curry with noodles) and tasty samosas (in the morning).

KCB Snack Shop (Th Intharakhiri; dishes 35-75B; ✆ breakfast, lunch & dinner) This friendly place past Soi Ruam Jai is a good spot to find out about volunteering opportunities at the nearby refugee camps.

Drinking

For a night on the town Mae Sot style, head to the bars on the western end of Th Intharakhiri. A current favourite is **Crocodile Tear** (Th Intharakhiri), featuring an extensive selection of mixed drinks, live music and many drunken travellers; but most of the places along here have pool tables and the drinks keep flowing.

Getting There & Away

Phuket Air (☎ 0 5553 1440; www.phuketairlines.com; Mae Sot Airport) connects Mae Sot with Bangkok daily. It also flies to Chiang Mai several days a week.

BORDER CROSSING: INTO MYANMAR

Frequent sǎwngthǎew (10B) go to the Burmese border across the Mae Nam Moei, 6km from Mae Sot, to Myawaddy. This border periodically closes due to fighting, but currently foreigners are allowed to do a day-crossing into Myawaddy, a fairly typical Burmese town, for a fee of US$10. The Pan-Asian Hwy (Asia Rte 1) continues from here west to Mawlamyine (Moulmein) and Yangon – and eventually Istanbul – but that adventure still sits in the 'some day' category. The border is open 6am to 6pm.

The government bus station, which is located just off Th Asia, handles transport to Bangkok (air-con/VIP 310/480B, nine hours). For travel to any other destinations, it is best to change in Tak (ordinary/air-con 44/50B), which offers smooth connections to points in the north such as Lampang and Chiang Mai. You can also travel the western rim of Thailand by catching a bus or săwngthăew to Mae Sariang (160B, six hours) for transport to Mae Hong Son.

NORTHERN THAILAND

The peaks and valleys of northern Thailand are the guardians of an abundance of natural and cultural attractions that make it a must for most travellers traversing throughout the kingdom. These ancient mountains cascade across northern Thailand, Myanmar and southwest China, where Yunnanese trading caravans of mule-driven carts once followed the mountain ridges all the way to the sea. Centuries before, another group, considered to be the original Thais, followed a similar route into the lush river valleys of what is modern-day Thailand. Eventually the independent state known as Lanna Thai (Million Thai Rice Fields) emerged here; its modern descendants maintain a distinct northern culture that is not easily diluted by the passage of time. Other wanderers, like the autonomous hill-tribe peoples, traversed the range, limited only by altitude rather than political boundaries.

Travellers trek through the wilderness towards hill-tribe villages hoping to find out what they lost when life became as easy as flip of a switch. Places along twisting mountain roads, small towns awaken to a thick morning fog, offering the simple pleasures of reflective walks and breathtaking vistas.

CHIANG MAI
pop 1.6 million
To Thais, Chiang Mai is a national treasure – a cultured symbol of nationhood. For visitors, it's a cool place to kick back and soak up some of the Thai-ness that may have been missed on the beaches of the south coast. The climate is forgiving,

bookshops outmuscle synthetic shopping centres, and the region's unique cultural heritage is worn as proudly as its vibrant hand-woven textiles. For culture vultures, Chiang Mai forms a playground, with classes in Thai language, cooking, meditation and massage.

The old city of Chiang Mai is a neat square bounded by moats and remnants of a medieval-style wall built 700 years ago to defend against Burmese invaders. A furious stream of traffic flows around the old city, but inside narrow soi branch off the clogged arteries into a quiet world of charming guesthouses, leafy gardens and friendly smiles.

Orientation
Th Moon Muang, along the east moat, is the main traveller centre. Intersecting with Th Moon Muang, Th Tha Phae runs east from the exterior of the moat towards the Mae Nam Ping. Once it crosses the river, the road is renamed Th Charoen Muang and eventually arrives at the main post office and train station.

Finding your way around Chiang Mai is fairly simple. A copy of Nancy Chandler's *Map Guide to Chiang Mai* is a good investment if you plan extensive exploration of the city. Pick up a copy at bookshops or guesthouses.

Information
BOOKSHOPS
DK Book House (Th Kotchasan) New books on history, culture and travel in the region.
Gecko Books (☎ 0 5387 4066; Th Chiang Moi Kao) Largest choice of used books in the city.
Shaman Bookstore (☎ 0 5327 5272; 2 Soi 1, Th Kotchasan; ☺ 9am-8pm) Inexpensive used books, plus travel and some spirituality.
Suriwong Book Centre (☎ 0 5328 1052; 54 Th Si Donchai) Best selection of new books in town.

EMERGENCY
Tourist police (☎ 0 5327 8798, 24hr emergency ☎ 1155; Th Chiang Mai-Lamphun; ☺ 6am-midnight) Near the TAT office, Chiang Mai's tourist police enjoys a good reputation.

IMMIGRATION OFFICE
Immigration office (☎ 0 5320 1755; off Rte 1141/ Th Mahidon) The place to get visa extensions, located near the airport.

CENTRAL CHIANG MAI

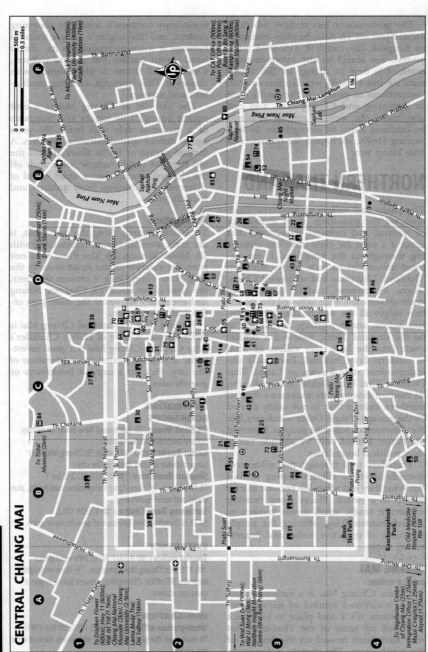

INTERNET ACCESS

Internet cafés are everywhere.

Chiang Mai Disabled Center (☎ 0 5321 3941; www.infothai.com/disabled; 133/1 Th Ratchaphakhinai; per hr 20B) A nonprofit organisation funding services for the disabled. Provides Internet access, bicycle rental and massages.

INTERNET RESOURCES

Chiang Mai Online (www.chiangmai-online.com) Basic background on Chiang Mai, along with comprehensive accommodation listings.

City Life (www.chiangmainews.com) Articles on local events, culture and art, plus current news.

MEDIA

Chiangmai Mail Weekly newspaper, good for local news.
City Life Popular with residents and tourists; articles on local culture and politics, and events listings.

MEDICAL SERVICES

Chiang Mai Ram Hospital (☎ 0 5322 4861; Th Bunreuangrit) The most sophisticated hospital in town.
Malaria Centre (☎ 0 5322 1529; 18 Th Bunreuangrit) Does free blood checks for malaria.

McCormick Hospital (☎ 0 5324 1311; Th Kaew Nawarat) The best-value place for minor treatment.

MONEY

All major Thai banks have several branches throughout Chiang Mai, many of them along Th Tha Phae, and there is no shortage of ATMs around town.

POST

Main post office (Th Charoen Muang) East of town; there's also a handy branch at the airport.

TELEPHONE

Overseas calls can also be made from one of the private offices along Th Tha Phae.
CAT office (Th Charoen Muang; ◷ 7am-10pm) Behind the main post office.

TOURIST INFORMATION

TAT office (☎ 0 5324 8604; 105/1 Th Chiang Mai-Lamphun; ◷ 8am-4.30pm) On the east banks of Mae Nam Ping, it has a list of registered trekking guides, plus maps and brochures.

THAILAND

Dangers & Annoyances

Many travellers have reported that their belongings (particularly credit cards) stored at Chiang Mai guesthouses have gone walkabout while they are trekking. Most guesthouses recommend you take such sensitive items with you, but be sure that you are travelling in safe areas as there are occasional incidents of whole trekking groups being robbed in the jungle. You can't win on this one, so before you stow your bags, make an itemised list of all belongings, including travellers cheques, and note your credit card balance. See p742 for more crafty scams.

Sights

TEMPLES

Chiang Mai has more than 300 temples – almost as many as Bangkok, which is a far larger city. The temple architecture here is markedly different from other parts of Thailand. Notice the intricate woodcarvings and colourful murals; these are hallmarks of the Lanna period (13th and 14th centuries). Three-tiered umbrellas adorning the tops of the temples, Singha lions guarding the entrances and high-base *chedi* are all Burmese influences imported into the city by wealthy teak merchants when they migrated to this important trade centre.

Wat Phra Singh (☎ 0 5381 4164; Th Singarat; ☉ 6am-6pm) is the real star amid the inner-city's soaring stupas, and a perfect example of Lanna architecture. Established in 1345, this wat contains murals depicting Lanna customs and dress, as well as a scripture repository. It is also the focal point for Songkran (Water Festival) festivities in mid-April.

Wat Chiang Man (☎ 0 5337 5368; Th Ratchaphakhinai; ☉ 6am-6pm) is the oldest wat within the city walls and was erected by King Mengrai, Chiang Mai's founder, in 1296. Two famous Buddha images (Buddha Sila and the Crystal Buddha) are kept here in the *wíhǎan* to the right of the main *bòht*. The Crystal Buddha is believed to have the power to bring seasonal rains.

Wat Chedi Luang (☎ 0 5327 8595; Th Phra Pokklao; ☉ 6am-6pm) contains the ruins of a huge *chedi* that collapsed during an earthquake in 1545. A partial restoration has preserved the *chedi* 'ruined' look while ensuring it doesn't crumble further. The venerable Emerald Buddha, now housed in Bangkok's Wat Phra Kaew, occupied the eastern niche here in 1475.

Wat Jet Yot (☎ 0 5321 9483; Superhighway; ☉ 6am-6pm) is modelled somewhat imperfectly on the Mahabodhi Temple in Bodhgaya, India. The seven spires represent the seven weeks Buddha was supposed to have spent in Bodhgaya after his enlightenment. Find it near the National Museum, 1.5km northwest of town.

Wat Suan Dok (☎ 0 5327 8967; Th Su; ☉ 6am-6pm) contains a 500-year-old bronze Buddha image and colourful *jataka* murals showing scenes from Buddha's past lives. Scenic sunsets are the temple's biggest attraction, especially for shutterbugs. A 'monk chat' from 5pm to 7pm Monday, Wednesday and Friday is hosted, free of charge, on the grounds, for foreigners to meet and chat with novice monks studying at the monastic university. It's 1km west of town.

Wat U Mong (☎ 0 5327 3990; Soi Wat U Mong; ☉ 6am-6pm) is a forest temple dating from Mengrai's rule and has a fine image of the fasting Buddha. Brick-lined tunnels in an unusual-looking large, flat-topped hill were supposedly fashioned around 1380 for a clairvoyant monk; some are still open for exploration. Resident foreign monks give talks in English on Sunday afternoon at 3pm by the lake. It's 4km west of town.

CHIANG MAI NATIONAL MUSEUM

Lanna history and art works are documented at the **Chiang Mai National Museum** (☎ 0 5322 1308; Hwy 11/Superhighway northern loop; admission 30B; ☉ 9am-4pm Wed-Sun), 500m past Wat Jet Yot, northwest of town. Buddha images, northern Thai handicrafts and pottery fill the halls.

TRIBAL MUSEUM

If you decide against trekking through the hill-tribe villages, check out the worthwhile **Tribal Museum** (☎ 0 5321 0872; Th Chotana; admission free; ☉ 9am-4pm Mon-Fri, slide & video shows 10am-2pm), at Ratchamangkhla Park north of the city. This renovated museum houses a large collection of artefacts and other displays on the various cultural nuances and ethnic backgrounds of the hill tribes in Thailand.

CHIANG MAI NIGHT BAZAAR

Chiang Mai's leading tourist attraction is in fact the legacy of the original Yunnanese trading caravans that stopped here along the ancient trade route between Simao (in

China) and Mawlamyine (on Myanmar's Indian Ocean coast). Today commerce is alive and well, sprawling over several blocks on Th Chang Khlan from Th Tha Phae to Th Si Donchai, towards the river. Made up of several different covered areas, ordinary glass-fronted shops and dozens of street vendors, the market offers a huge variety of Thai and northern Thai goods. Some buys include Phrae-style *sêua mâw hâwm* (blue cotton farmer's shirt), northern and northeastern Thai hand-woven fabrics, *yâam* (woven shoulder bags) and hill-tribe crafts – many tribespeople set up their own stalls here, while the Akha wander around on foot.

Activities

ROCK CLIMBING

Chiang Mai Rock Climbing Adventures (☎ 0 6911 1470; www.thailandclimbing.com; 55/3 Th Ratchaphakhinai; day trips per person 1500-200B, multiday intensives 5500-9500B) organises climbs of the limestone cliffs called Crazy Horse Buttress, behind Tham Meuang On, about 20km east of Chiang Mai.

TREKKING

Chiang Mai is one of the most popular places in Thailand to arrange a trek. Many guesthouses and lots of travel agents are looking for a slice of action in this 'competitive' (read cutthroat) business and it pays to shop around before signing up. Most treks include visits to minority villages, some jungle action, plus the option of rafting or elephant rides. See p748 for more on trekking in northern Thailand.

Courses

BUDDHIST MEDITATION

Northern Insight Meditation Centre
(☎ 0 5327 8620; watrampoeng@hotmail.com; Wat Ram Poeng; admission free) Ten- to 26-day individual intensive courses in *vipassana* (insight meditation) are taught by a Thai monk or nun, with Western students or bilingual Thais acting as interpreters.

Wat Suan Dok (☎ 0 5327 3105/20/49; Th Suthep; admission free) An English-language introduction to Buddhist meditation from Sunday afternoon to Monday morning, with an overnight stay at the monastery, 4km west of town.

COOKING

Cooking classes are a big hit in Chiang Mai and typically include an introduction to Thai herbs and spices, a local market tour, cook-

ing instructions and a recipe booklet. Plus you get to eat the delicious Thai food you cook – everything from Chiang Mai–style chicken curry to steamed banana cake. Cooking classes usually cost 700B to 1000B a day.

We've heard consistently good things about the following places:

Baan Thai (☎ 0 5335 7339; www.cookinthai.com; 11 Soi 5, Th Ratchadamnoen) Lunch and dinner courses.

Chiang Mai Thai Cookery School (☎ 0 5320 6388; www.thaicookeryschool.com; 1-3 Th Moon Muang) Owned by a famous Thai TV chef.

Gap's Thai Culinary Art School (☎ 0 5327 8140; gap_house@hotmail.com; Gap's House, 3 Soi 4, Th Ratchadamnoen)

Jungle Survival Cooking Course (☎ 0 5320 8661; www.smilehousechiangmai.com; Smile House, 5 Th Ratchamankha) Learn how to live in the wild using only your wits.

LANGUAGE

American University Alumni (AUA; ☎ 0 5327 8407; aualanna@loxinfo.co.th; 73 Th Ratchadamnoen; 30/60hr course 2700/3500B) The basic AUA Thai course consists of three levels with 60 hours of instruction. There are also 30-hour courses in 'small talk', reading and writing, and northern Thai dialect.

Chiang Mai Thai Language Center (☎ 0 5327 7810; cmat@loxinfo.co.th; 131 Th Ratchadamnoen; 30hr course 2200B) Thai language courses from beginners to advanced.

Payap University (☎ 0 5330 4805, ext 250-1; intpros@payap.ac.th; Th Kaew Nawarat; 60/120hr course 6000/12,000B) Intensive Thai language courses at beginning, intermediate and advanced levels. Conversational skills, reading and writing, and Thai culture.

MUAY THAI (THAI BOXING)

Lanna Muay Thai (Kiatbusaba; ☎ 0 5389 2102; www.lannamuaythai.com; 64/1 Soi Chiang Khian; day/month courses 250/7000B) A boxing camp northwest of town that offers authentic *muay thai* instruction to foreigners as well as Thais. Lanna-trained *kàthoey* boxer Parinya Kiatbusaba triumphed at Lumphini stadium in Bangkok in 1998. Part of his opening routine, when the boxers pay homage to their trainers, included a flamboyant show of putting on make-up.

TRADITIONAL MASSAGE

More visitors learn the art of Thai massage in Chiang Mai than anywhere else in Thailand. Tuition starts at around 3500B for 10 days. The following places are recommended for their massage classes:

Ban Nit (☎ 0 1180 9769; Soi 2, Th Chaiyaphum; day/week courses from 1000/3500B; ⊕ 10am-4.30pm)

A unique, one-on-one course in deep-tissue, nerve and herbal massages. Most students live in and eat meals with Nit and her family.

Lek Chaiya (☎ 0 5327 8325; www.nervetouch.com; 25 Th Ratchadamnoen; 5-day course 4000B) Khun Lek, a Thai woman who has been massaging and teaching for more than 40 years, specialises in *jàp sên* (similar to acupressure) and the use of medicinal herbs.

Old Medicine Hospital (OMH; ☎ 0 5327 5085; 78/1 Soi Siwaka Komarat, Th Wualai; courses 3500B) Just south of town, the OMH curriculum is very traditional, with a northern-Thai slant. There are two 11-day courses a month year-round, except for the first two weeks of April. Classes tend to be large during the months of December to February, but smaller the rest of the year.

Festivals & Events

Flower Festival The mother of Chiang Mai festivals, including parades, the Queen of the Flower Festival beauty contest and plenty of flower-draped floats. It's held in the first week of February.

Songkran (Water Festival) Think you can handle a water pistol? Chiang Mai is the place to find out, as it is water-world here in mid-April.

Winter Fair Held from late December to early Jan, this is a big event in the Chiang Mai calendar, with all sorts of activities and interesting visitors from the hills.

Sleeping

Most of the leading guesthouses are clustered on either side of the east moat. If you're having problems finding a room during peak periods (December to March and July to August), stop by the TAT office and pick up a free copy of *Accommodation in Chiang Mai*.

Most guesthouses make their 'rice and curry' from running trekking tours and reserve rooms for those customers. Usually a guesthouse will inform you in advance how many days (usually two to three) the room is available for nontrekkies, but to avoid surprises, check first.

SPLURGE!

Top North Hotel (☎ 0 5327 9623; www.top northgroup.com; 41 Th Moon Muang; r 550-900B; 🞩 🞩) This big hotel, near Pratu Tha Phae, has large, smart rooms with amenities like TV and fridge. The big pool out front is the main draw. The same gang runs the **Top North Guest House** (☎ 0 5327 8900; 15 Soi 2, Th Moon Muang; r 300-600B; 🞩 🞩), another of the few guesthouses to boast a pool.

MORE CRAFTY SCAMS

Bus or minivan services from Th Khao San in Bangkok often advertise a free night's accommodation in Chiang Mai if you buy a Bangkok–Chiang Mai ticket. What usually happens on arrival is that the 'free' guest-house demands you sign up for one of the hill treks immediately; if you don't, the guesthouse is suddenly 'full'. Sometimes they levy a charge for electricity or hot water. The better guesthouses don't play this game.

The most atmospheric places are tucked away into narrow soi where pedestrians outnumber vehicles, and most will arrange free transport from the bus station with advance warning.

SK House (☎ 0 5321 0690; www.sk-riverview.com; 30 Soi 9, Th Moon Muang; r 300-600B; 🞩 🞩 🞩) Delivering hotel standards at guesthouse prices, the smart fan rooms with attached hot-water bathroom are well worth the money here. There is a large swimming pool in a central courtyard and doubling your money brings air-con and satellite TV.

Grace House (☎ 0 5341 8161; 27 Soi 9, Th Moon Muang; s/d 150/250B) Set in a bustling location of shops and restaurants, Grace has clinically clean rooms set above a great little health-food shop with creative coffees and teas and vegetarian specials.

Bow Chiangmai House (☎ 0 5321 1707; bow rins@yahoo.com; 15 Soi 9, Th Moon Muang; r 300-400B; 🞩) Located opposite SK House, this smart new guesthouse has thoughtfully equipped rooms with more furnishings than you'd expect at this price. Check out the rooftop veranda for a view over Chiang Mai.

Golden Fern Guest House (☎ 0 5327 8423; www .goldenfern.com; 20 Soi 8, Th Phra Pokklao; r 250-450B; 🞩) Golden Fern keeps its rooms pretty full thanks to a reputation for slick service and a commitment to cleanliness. Set in a converted apartment building, it has 30 rooms.

Banana Guest House (☎ 0 5320 6285; 4/9 Th Ratch-aphakhinai; dm 80B, r 100-200B) Near Chiang Mai Gate, this budget crash pad has earned a cult following over the years. Basic sleeping but plenty of fun: satisfied visitors have scrawled their approval all over the walls of the lounge.

Smile House (☎ 0 5320 8661; smile208@loxinfo
.co.th; 5 Soi 2, Th Ratchamankha; r 300-450B; 🕸) Smile
House has rooms in an old Thai house
surrounded by smart modern blocks. This
house once served as the 'safe house' of infamous Shan-Chinese opium warlord Khun
Sa whenever he came to Chiang Mai.

Eagle House 2 (☎ 0 5341 8494; 26 Soi 2, Th Ratwithi;
dm 60B, r 180-360B) The nicer of the Eagle House
twins; the lush garden here encourages calm.
The rooms are fairly standard, but this place
has a good reputation for treks.

Pun Pun Guest House (☎ 0 5324 3362; 321 Th
Charoenrat; d 225B) Settled upon the shores of
the Mae Nam Ping, there is a choice here
between tidy bungalows with shared bath
(175B) or smarter rooms with hot-water
bathrooms attached in a Thai-style house.

Also recommended out of the hundreds
of other options:

Awana Sleep & Swim Guesthouse (☎ 0 5341 9005;
Soi 1, Th Ratchadamnoen; s/d 300/400B; 🕸 💷) One of
the cheapest places with a pool.

Supreme House (☎ 0 5322 2480; 44/1 Soi 9,
Th Moon Muang; s/d 120/180B) Small, popular place that
doesn't push treks.

Your House Guest House (☎ 0 5321 7492;
8 Soi 2, Th Ratwithi; r 160-260B; 🕸) Wide range of
rooms including air-con indulgence from 350B.

Eating

Indulge your intestines in Chiang Mai
as the food here is top drawer. You can
become a disciple of northern cuisine at
one of the age-old institutions, or chase up
some comfort food from home.

THAI
Chiang Mai is famed for its fine *khâo sawy*.
The oldest area for this dish is the Jin Haw
(Yunnanese Muslim) area around the Ban
Haw Mosque on Soi 1, Th Charoen Prathet,
not far from the night market.

Khao Soi Islam (Soi 1, Th Charoen Prathet;
dishes 20-40B; 🕘 breakfast, lunch & dinner) A reliable
choice for *khâo sawy*, this place also serves
Muslim curries and a good goat biryani.
There is no roman-script sign out the front.

Heuan Phen (☎ 0 5327 7103; 112 Th Ratchamankha;
dishes 30-120B; 🕘 breakfast, lunch & dinner) This famous local eatery suffers from a split personality. The outdoor eating area out front
is just a like any other local canteen, but the
northern and northeastern menu is one of
the strongest in town. At night, the alter ego
emerges – a lovely old teak house behind
with tropical plants and antique furnishings. Well worth the detour.

Aroon (Rai) Restaurant (☎ 0 5327 6947; 45 Th
Kotchasan; dishes 40-80B; 🕘 breakfast, lunch & dinner)
Almost a warehouse for dining, this huge
open-fronted place has a solid selection of
precooked northern Thai curry dishes and
a good *kaeng kàrìi kài* (chicken curry). It's
situated on the eastern side of the moat,
south of Th Tha Phae; head upstairs at
night to catch the breeze.

Heuan Sunthari (☎ 0 5325 2445; 46/2 Th Wan
Singkham; dishes 40-90B; 🕘 lunch & dinner) Northeast
of the old town, the menu of northern, central
and Isan cuisine draws a crowd here, but so
does the rustic riverfront setting. But the real
pulling power is the owner, famous northern

NORTHERN CUISINE

Thanks to northern Thailand's cooler climate, your dreaded or beloved vegetables from home –
like broccoli and cauliflower – might make an appearance in a stir-fry or bowl of noodles. Untrans-
latable herbs and leaves from the dense forests are also incorporated into more regional dishes,
imparting a distinct flavour of mist-shrouded hills. Even coffee grows here, and with a little luck
you can find a chewy cup of arabica, although somewhere in that mythical handbook on foreigners that all Thais read, Nescafé is the *faràng* prescription. Day-market vendors sell blue sticky rice,
which is dyed by a morning-glory-like flower and topped with a sweetened egg custard that will
rot a whole row of teeth.

Showing its Burmese, Chinese and Shan influences, the north prefers curries that are more
stewlike than the coconut-milk curries of southern and central Thailand. Sour notes are enhanced
with the addition of pickled cabbage and lime, rather than the tear-inducing spiciness favoured
in most Thai dishes. The most famous example of northern cuisine is *khâo sawy*, a mild chicken
curry with flat egg noodles, which is comforting on a cool foggy morning. A Burmese expat, *kaeng
hang-leh*, is another example of a northern-style curry and is accompanied by sticky rice, which
is eaten with the hands.

Thai singer Soontaree Vechanont, who performs nightly. No roman-script sign.

Also recommended is the busy **Somphet market** (Th Moon Muang), north of Th Ratwithi, which sells cheap takeaway Thai food and northern-style sausages. **Pratu Chiang Mai night market** (Th Bamrungburi) has plenty of tables where people make an evening of eating and drinking.

Kalare Food Centre (dishes 20-50B; ☼ breakfast, lunch & dinner), opposite the main night market building, is a food court with lots of Thai dishes and free Thai classical dancing.

INTERNATIONAL

Art Cafe (☎ 0 5320 6365; cnr Th Tha Phae & Th Kotchasan; dishes 50-120B; ☼ breakfast, lunch & dinner; ☒) The strategic location opposite Pratu Tha Phae ensures this place a steady clientele. The global menu includes stops along the way in Italy and Mexico, plus a healthy dose of Thai to ensure there is something for everyone.

Da Stefano (☎ 0 5387 4189; 2/1-2 Th Chang Moi Kao; dishes 100-200B; ☼ lunch & dinner) This little trattoria delivers authentic Italian cuisine at a price that won't break the bank. Great seafood pastas, professional antipasto and one of the better wine lists in town.

Indian Restaurant Vegetarian Food (☎ 0 5322 3396; Soi 9, Th Moon Muang; dishes 20-60B; ☼ breakfast, lunch & dinner) For a slice of the subcontinent, try this friendly, family-owned place that serves cheap and cheerful vegetarian thalis and Indian staples. The owners offer popular Indian cooking classes.

Jerusalem Falafel (☎ 0 5327 0208; 35/3 Th Moon Muang; dishes 40-80B; ☼ breakfast, lunch & dinner Sat-Thu) The falafel is fast becoming Thailand's most popular adopted dish and this hole-in-the-wall does a good range of Middle Eastern favourites.

Zest (☎ 0 5321 3088; Th Moon Muang; 50-150B; ☼ breakfast, lunch & dinner) Sitting in a pukka position in front of the Top North Hotel, this classy alfresco café has substantial sandwiches and a drinks menu to stick around for. It's a good place to watch the world of Chiang Mai go by.

VEGETARIAN

Chiang Mai has a huge choice of vegetarian food thanks to its reputation for all things healthy and holistic.

AUM Vegetarian Restaurant (☎ 0 5327 8315; 65 Th Moon Muang; dishes 30-70B; ☼ breakfast, lunch & dinner)

AUM is almost as old as the hills around Chiang Mai. It does Thai and Chinese favourites with not a scrap of meat in sight. Upstairs is a laid-back lounge with low tables.

Vegetarian Centre of Chiang Mai (☎ 0 5327 1262; 14 Th Mahidon; dishes 10-15B; ☼ breakfast, lunch & dinner) Sponsored by the Asoke Foundation, this cafeteria offers the cheapest Thai vegetarian food this side of the street vendors. The restaurant is south of the southwestern corner of the city wall.

Biaporn (Soi 1, Th Si Phum; dishes 20-40B; ☼ breakfast, lunch & dinner) Within stumbling distance of the guesthouse ghetto, this blink-and-you'll-miss-it place has a limited menu of vegetarian classics at the right price.

Drinking

The ale flows fast and furiously at the strip of bars along Th Moon Muang near the Pratu Tha Phae. It's a familiar sight: lots of sweaty *faràng*, cheap beer and lots of neon. Some of the best bar-restaurants with live music are on the east bank of the Mae Nam Ping.

Riverside Bar & Restaurant (☎ 0 5321 1035; Charoenrat; dishes 60-200B) One of the old-timers on the banks of the Mae Nam Ping, this rambling barn of a bar draws a sophisticated crowd thanks to endless river views, two live bands and an expansive international menu. Jugs of beer outnumber glasses – always a sign of the good times.

Brasserie (☎ 0 5324 1665; 37 Th Charoenrat) The diners drift off around 10pm or so and the drinkers drift in. The layered terrace spills down to the river's edge, great for knocking back a bottle of wine. Inside, famous Thai guitarist Khun Took plays some superb covers, including Hendrix, Cream, Dylan, Marley and other gems from the good ol' days of rock and roll.

THC (19/4-5 Th Kotchasan) The marijuana motif says it all. This place is so chilled out it's horizontal. Occupying a rooftop overlooking the old city, there is a rave up here every Sunday and beers daily.

Pinte Blues Pub (33/6 Th Moon Muang) Breaking all records for bar life expectancy, this tiny place has been banging out the blues for more than 20 years. Don't come expecting fancy-pants drinks here – it's beer all the way.

UN Irish Pub (24/1 Th Ratwithi) Un-Irish Pub perhaps, as there is no Guinness on tap and only the most subtle of Emerald Isle touches. Still, it's spacious place with a popular upstairs balcony for watching the night unfold on Th Rathithi below. Regularish live music.

Drunken Flower (end of Soi 1, Th Nimanhaemin) The posh end of town, this is where you will find well-heeled Thais and the local expat crowd of NGO workers. Live music at weekends and a dangerous selection of drinks.

Drunk Studio (☎ 0 9997 7037; 32/3 Th Atsadathon) An alternative, industrial bar near Talat Kamthiang, this is Chiang Mai's unofficial headquarters for live alternative music. Thai bands play grunge, hardcore, nu-metal and *phêua chîiwít* (Thai 'songs for life') nightly.

Near Eagle House 2, in what at first glance is just a dusty car park, there is a cluster of low-key garden bars turning out cheap beers and cool tunes. The original and still the most popular, Rasta Café has a soundtrack of reggae, dub, African and Latin.

Entertainment

Major Cineplex (☎ 0 5328 3939; Central Airport Plaza, 2 Th Mahidon) is the best cinema spot in town. Every Sunday at 3pm, **Chiang Mai University** (☎ 0 5322 1699; Th Huay Kaew; admission free), 1.5km northwest of the old town, presents a different foreign film in the main auditorium of the Art & Culture Centre.

Shopping

Long before tourists began visiting the region, Chiang Mai was an important centre for handcrafted pottery, weaving, umbrellas, silverwork and woodcarvings, and today it's still the country's number-one source of handicrafts. The **Pratu Chiang Mai night market** (Th Bamrungburi), on the southern edge of town, is a great place to bargain like a local. A former royal cremation grounds, Warorot Market (also locally called Kat Luang, or Great Market) is the oldest market in Chiang Mai. It's a good spot for Thai fabrics, cooking implements and prepared foods (especially northern Thai foods).

Getting There & Away

AIR

Regularly scheduled international flights arrive at **Chiang Mai International Airport** (☎ 0 5327 0222) from the following cities: Kunming (China), Singapore, Taipei (Taiwan), Vientiane and Luang Prabang (Laos), Yangon and Mandalay (Myanmar).

Domestic routes include Bangkok, Chiang Rai, Mae Hong Son, Mae Sot, Nan,

Phitsanulok, Phrae, Phuket and Sukhothai. Worthwhile options include the short hop to Mae Hong Son with Thai Airways International and the discount flights to Bangkok with Air Asia and Nok Air, almost as cheap as a VIP bus.

Airlines operating out of Chiang Mai:

Air Asia (☎ 0 2515 9999; www.airasia.com)
Air Mandalay (☎ 0 5381 8049; www.air-mandalay.com)
Bangkok Airways (☎ 0 5321 0043; www.bangkok air.com)
Lao Airlines (☎ 0 5322 3401; www.lao-airlines.com)
Mandarin Airlines (☎ 0 5320 1268; www.mandarin -airlines.com)
Nok Air (☎ 1318; www.nokair.com.th)
Orient Thai (☎ 0 5392 2159; www.orient-thai.com)
SilkAir (☎ 0 5327 6459; www.silkair.com)
Thai Airways International (THAI; ☎ 0 5321 1044; www.thaiair.com)

BUS

There are two bus stations in Chiang Mai: **Arcade bus station** (eastern end of Th Kaew Nawarat), northeast of town, handles Bangkok and most long-distance cities, while **Chang Pheuak bus station** (Th Chang Pheuak), north of the town centre, handles buses to Fang, Tha Ton, Lamphun and destinations within Chiang Mai Province. From the town centre, a túktúk or chartered săwngthăew to the Arcade bus station should cost about 40B; to the Chang Pheuak bus station get a săwngthăew at the normal 10B per person rate.

Destination	Class	Fare (B)	Duration (hr)	Frequency
Bangkok	VIP	322-470	10	several daily
Chiang Rai	ordinary	77	3	frequent daily
	air-con	139		
Khon Kaen	ordinary	243	12	regular daily
	air-con	340-437		
Mae Hong Son	ordinary	143	8	regular daily
	air-con	257	5	
Mae Sai	ordinary	95	4	regular daily
	air-con	171		
Mae Sariang	ordinary	78	5	7 daily
	air-con	140		
Mae Sot	ordinary	134	6	2 daily
	air-con	241		
Nan	ordinary	128	6	5 daily
	air-con	179-230		
Pai	ordinary	60	4	5 daily
	air-con	80		
Phitsanulok	ordinary	140	6	hourly
	air-con	196		7am-3pm

TRAIN

The **train station** (☎ 0 5324 5363; Th Charoen Muang) is on the eastern edge of town. There are four express trains and two rapid trains per day between Chiang Mai and Bangkok (1st/2nd class 593/281B, fare without surcharges). Advance booking is advised. Transport to the station via săwngthăew should cost 20B.

Getting Around

Airport taxis cost 100B. Pick up a ticket at the taxi kiosk just outside the baggage-claim area, then present the ticket to the taxi drivers outside arrivals. The airport is only 3km from the city centre. You can charter a túk-túk or red săwngthăew from the centre of Chiang Mai to the airport for 50B or 60B.

Plenty of red săwngthăew circulate around the city with standard fares of 10B per person, but drivers often try to get you to charter (60B or less). If you're travelling alone, they typically ask for 20B. The săwngthăew don't have set routes; you simply flag them down and tell them where you want to go. Túk-túks only do charters at 30B for short trips and 40B to 60B for longer ones. Chiang Mai still has loads of săamláw, especially in the old city around Talat Warorot. Săamláw cost around 20B to 30B for most trips.

You can rent bicycles (30B to 50B a day) or 100cc motorcycles (from 100B to 200B) to explore Chiang Mai. Bicycles are a great way to get around the city:

Chiang Mai Disabled Center (☎ 0 5321 3941; www .infothai.com/disabled; 133/1 Th Ratchaphakhinai) Bicycle rental to assist Chiang Mai's disabled community

Contact Travel (☎ 0 5327 7178; www.activethailand .com; 73/7 Th Charoen Prathet; per day 200B) Top notch, 21-speed mountain bikes.

BORDER PATROLS

In an effort to stop the smuggling of drugs and other contraband, staffed patrol posts search all vehicles headed towards the Burmese border. Police usually board public buses, sniff around a bit, give the evil eye to boys wearing make-up and perfunctorily check everyone's ID or passport. *Faràng* are usually ignored, but if you don't want trouble, don't look for it. And stuff that souvenir opium pipe deep inside your bag.

AROUND CHIANG MAI
Doi Suthep

Perched on a panoramic hilltop, **Wat Phra That Doi Suthep** (30B) is one of the north's most sacred temples. The site was 'chosen' by an honoured Buddha relic mounted on the back of a white elephant; the animal wandered until it stopped (and died) on Doi Suthep, making this the relic's new home. A snaking road ascends the hill to a long flight of steps, lined by ceramic-tailed *naga*, that leads up to the temple and the expansive views of the valley below. Watching the sunset from up here is an institution.

About 4km beyond Wat Phra That Doi Suthep are the palace gardens of **Phra Tamnak Phu** (admission free; ⏱ 8.30am-12.30pm & 1-4pm Sat, Sun & holidays), a winter residence for the royal family. The road that passes the palace splits off to the left, stopping at the peak of Doi Pui. From there, a dirt road proceeds for a couple of kilometres to a nearby **Hmong village**, which is well touristed and sells handicrafts.

Săwngthăew to Doi Suthep leave from Th Mani Nopharat and Th Chotana for the 16km trip (40B up, 30B down); for another 10B, you can take a bicycle up with you and zoom back downhill.

Bo Sang & San Kamphaeng

The 'umbrella village' of **Bo Sang** (Baw Sang) is 9km east of Chiang Mai. It's a picturesque though touristy spot where the townspeople engage in just about every type of northern Thai handicraft, including making beautiful paper umbrellas.

About 5km further down Rte 1006 is **San Kamphaeng**, which specialises in cotton and silk weaving.

Frequent buses to Bo Sang (6B) and San Kamphaeng (8B) leave from Chiang Mai near the main post office on the northern side of Th Charoen Muang. White săwngthăew (6B) leave from the Chang Pheuak bus station and make the trip to either destination.

Doi Inthanon

The highest peak in the country, **Doi Inthanon** (2595m), and the surrounding **national park** (admission 200B) can be visited as a day trip from Chiang Mai. There are some impressive waterfalls and popular picnic spots on the road to the summit. Between Chiang Mai and Doi Inthanon, the small town of Chom Thong has a fine Burmese-style temple, **Wat Phra That Si Chom Thong**, where 26-day *vipassana* meditation courses are available.

Buses to Chom Thong (23B) leave from inside Pratu Chiang Mai at the south moat, as well as from the Chang Pheuak bus station in Chiang Mai. From Chom Thong there are regular săwngthăew to Mae Klang (15B), about 8km north. Săwngthăew from Mae Klang to Doi Inthanon leave almost hourly until late afternoon and cost 30B per person.

Lampang & Around

Lampang is like a low-key, laid-back little Chiang Mai. Like its larger sibling, Lampang was constructed as a walled rectangle and boasts magnificent temples, many of which were built from teak by Burmese and Shan artisans. Lampang is also known throughout Thailand as Meuang Rot Mah (Horse Cart City) because it's the only town in Thailand where horse-drawn carriages are still used as transport.

SIGHTS & ACTIVITIES
Temples

The old town's fine structures include **Wat Si Rong Meuang**, **Wat Si Chum** and **Wat Phra Kaew Don Tao** (one of the many former homes of the Emerald Buddha, now residing in Bangkok's Wat Phra Kaew) on the bank of the Mae Nam Wang, north of town.

In the village of Ko Kha, about 18km to the southwest of Lampang, lies **Wat Phra That Lampang Luang**, arguably the most beautiful wooden Lanna temple in northern Thailand. It is an amazing structure with walls like a huge medieval castle. To get here, catch a blue săwngthăew south on Th Praisani to the market in Ko Kha (10B), then take a Hang Chat–bound săwngthăew (5B) 3km north to the entrance of Wat Phra That Lampang Luang. A motorcycle taxi from Ko Kha to the temple costs approximately 30B.

Thai Elephant Conservation Center

At one time in Thai society, elephants were war machines, logging trucks and work companions. The automobile has rendered the elephant jobless and orphaned in the modern world. The **Thai Elephant Conservation Center** (☎ 0 5422 9042; www.changthai.com; admission 50B; ✆ public shows 10am & 11am daily, 1.30pm Fri, Sat & holidays Jun-Feb) attempts to remedy this by promoting ecotourism, providing medical care and training young elephants.

The centre offers elephant rides (from 200B for 15 minutes) and elephant bathing shows. The animals appreciate a few pieces of fruit – 'feels like a vacuum cleaner with a wet nozzle', reported one visitor. Travellers can sign on for a one-day mahout course (1500B) or a three-day programme (4000B).

To reach the camp, take a bus or săwngthăew from Lampang's main bus station bound for Chiang Mai and get off at the Km 37 marker. Free vans shuttle visitors the 2km distance between the highway and the centre.

Pasang

Only a short săwngthăew (10B) ride south of Lamphun, Pasang is a centre for cotton weaving. Near the wat is a cotton-products store called Wimon (no roman-script sign), where you can watch people weaving on looms or buy floor coverings, cotton tablecloths and other utilitarian household items. You'll also find a few **shops** (opposite Wat Pasang Ngam) near the main market in town.

SLEEPING & EATING

Riverside Guest House (☎ 0 5422 7005; riverside family@yahoo.com; 286 Th Talat Kao; r 250-500B; ✖) Sometimes you just have to give yourself a little tender loving care, and this elegantly restored teak house is the place to do it. Smart rooms and stylish surrounds make it a fine place to relax by the river. Italian, French, English and Thai are spoken.

Riverside Bar & Restaurant (☎ 0 5422 1861; 328 Th Thip Chang; dishes 40-190B; ✆ lunch & dinner) Set in a rambling old teak structure on the river, this is *the* place to be in Lampang. It serves vegetarian and northern Thai dishes as well as pastries and ice cream. If you're not in the market for a meal, come for the well-stocked bar and soak up the live music till midnight.

Pet Yang Hong Kong (Th Boonyawat; dishes 25-34B; ✆ breakfast, lunch & dinner) Come to Pet Yang for some very tasty roast duck with rice or noodles (note that it closes at 6pm). There

TREKKING TO THE CORNERS

One of the most popular activities from Chiang Mai, Chiang Rai or Mae Hong Son is to take a trek through the mountains to observe the region's traditional hill-tribe villages. The term 'hill tribe' refers to ethnic minorities living in mountainous northern and western Thailand. The Thais refer to them as *chao khǎo*, literally meaning 'mountain people'. Each hill tribe has its own language, customs, mode of dress and spiritual beliefs. Most are of semi-nomadic origin, having migrated to Thailand from Tibet, Myanmar, China and Laos during the past 200 years or so, although some groups may have been in Thailand for much longer. The Tribal Research Institute in Chiang Mai recognises 10 different hill tribes, but there may be up to 20 in Thailand. The institute estimates the total hill-tribe population to be around 550,000. Lonely Planet's *Hill Tribes Phrasebook* gives a handy, basic introduction to the culture and languages of a number of the tribes.

Be an Informed Trekker

For the hill-tribe groups of Southeast Asia, tourism is a mixed blessing. It has helped to protect these cultures from widespread dismantling by majority governments, but has also contributed to the erosion of traditional customs through continued exposure to outside influences. Because trekking is big business, some villages have become veritable theme parks with a steady supply of visitors filtering in and out, creating exactly the opposite environment to the one trekkers hope to find, and eroding the fabric of the village.

Do your homework before you sign up for a trek. Find out if the tour group will be small, if the guide speaks the hill-tribe language and can explain the culture, and how many other groups will visit the village on the same day. Also find out if the village has a voice in its use as an attraction and whether it shares in the profits.

Remember that these villages are typically the poorest in the region, and what you consider to be your 'modest' belongings might be viewed as unthinkable luxuries to your hosts. While it is impossible to leave the community unaffected by your visit, at least respect their culture by observing local taboos:

- Dress modestly no matter how hot and sweaty you are.

- Don't take photographs unless permission is granted. Because of traditional belief systems, many individuals and even whole tribes may object strongly to being photographed. Always ask first, even if you think no one is looking.

- Show respect for religious symbols and rituals. Don't touch totems at village entrances, or any other object of obvious symbolic value, without asking permission. Unless you're asked to participate, keep your distance from ceremonies.

- Don't use drugs; set a good example to hill-tribe youngsters by not smoking opium or using other drugs.

- Don't litter while trekking or staying in villages; take your rubbish away with you.

- Don't hand out sweets and refrain from giving out other forms of charity (like pens and money) to children, as this encourages begging and undermines the parents' ability to be breadwinners for their families. Talk to your guide beforehand about materials the local school or health centre may need in order to benefit the community as a whole.

Hill-Tribe Communities

Akha (Thai: I-kaw)
Population: 48,500
Origin: Tibet
Present Locations: Thailand, Laos, Myanmar, Yunnan (China)
Economy: rice, corn, opium
Belief Systems: animism, with an emphasis on ancestor worship

Distinctive Characteristics: The Akha wear headdresses of beads, feathers and dangling silver ornaments. Villages are set along mountain ridges or on steep slopes 1000m to 1400m in altitude. They are among the poorest of Thailand's ethnic minorities and tend to resist assimilation into the Thai mainstream. Like the Lahu, the Akha often cultivate opium for their own consumption.

Hmong (Thai: Meo or Maew)

Population: 124,000
Origin: southern China
Present Locations: southern China, Thailand, Laos, Vietnam
Economy: rice, corn, opium
Belief Systems: animism
Distinctive Characteristics: Hmong tribespeople wear simple black jackets and indigo trousers with striped borders, or indigo skirts, and silver jewellery. Most women wear their hair in a large bun. They usually live on mountain peaks or plateaus. Kinship is patrilineal and polygamy is permitted. They are Thailand's second-largest hill-tribe group and are numerous in Chiang Mai Province.

Karen (Thai: Yang or Kariang)

Population: 322,000
Origin: Myanmar
Present Locations: Thailand, Myanmar
Economy: rice, vegetables, livestock
Belief Systems: animism, Buddhism or Christianity, depending on the group
Distinctive Characteristics: The Karen have thickly woven V-neck tunics of various colours (unmarried women wear white). They tend to live in lowland valleys and practise crop rotation rather than swidden (slash and burn) agriculture. Kinship is matrilineal and marriage is endogamous (ie only within the tribe). There are four distinct Karen groups: White Karen (Skaw Karen), Pwo Karen, Black Karen (Pa-o) and Kayah. These groups combined are the largest hill tribe in Thailand, numbering a quarter of a million people, or about half of all hill-tribe people. Many Karen continue to migrate into Thailand from Myanmar, fleeing Burmese government persecution.

Lahu (Thai: Musoe)

Population: 73,000
Origin: Tibet
Present Locations: southern China, Thailand, Myanmar
Economy: rice, corn, opium
Belief Systems: theistic animism (supreme deity is Geusha), Christianity

Distinctive Characteristics: Lahu wear black-and-red jackets, with narrow skirts for women. They live in mountainous areas at about 1000m. Their intricately woven yâam (shoulder bags) are prized by collectors. There are four main groups: Red Lahu, Black Lahu, Yellow Lahu and Lahu Sheleh.

Lisu (Thai: Lisaw)

Population: 28,000
Origin: Tibet
Present Locations: Thailand, Yunnan (China)
Economy: rice, opium, corn, livestock
Belief Systems: animism with ancestor worship and spirit possession
Distinctive Characteristics: The women wear long multicoloured tunics over trousers and sometimes black turbans with tassels. Men wear baggy green or blue pants that are pegged in at the ankles. They often wear lots of bright colours. Lisu villages are usually in the mountains at about 1000m. Premarital sex is said to be common, along with freedom in choosing marital partners. Patrilineal clans have pan-tribal jurisdiction, which makes the Lisu unique among hill-tribe groups (most tribes have power centred at the village level with either the shaman or a village headman as leader).

Mien (Thai: Yao)

Population: 40,000
Origin: central China
Present Locations: Thailand, southern China, Laos, Myanmar, Vietnam
Economy: rice, corn, opium
Belief Systems: animism with ancestor worship and Taoism
Distinctive Characteristics: Women wear black jackets and trousers decorated with intricately embroidered patches and red fur-like collars, along with large dark-blue or black turbans. They tend to settle near mountain springs at between 1000m and 1200m. They have been heavily influenced by Chinese traditions and use Chinese characters to write the Mien language. Kinship is patrilineal and marriage is polygamous.

are a few other rice and noodle shops in this area.

GETTING THERE & AWAY

From Chiang Mai, buses to Lampang (ordinary 25B, air-con 50B to 65B, two hours, every half-hour) leave from the Arcade bus station and also from next to Saphan Nawarat in the direction of Lamphun. Buses also depart for Lamphun (29B).

You can also travel to Lampang from Chiang Mai by train (2nd/3rd class 37/15B, two hours).

PAI

pop 3000

The hippy trail is alive and well in Pai, a flashback to stories from the '70s and counterculture colonies in Kabul and Kathmandu. Pai emerged from nowhere in a cool, moist corner of a mountain-fortressed valley along a rambling river. Foreigners stumbled through here on their way to somewhere else and realised Pai was a mountain paradise of easy living. A steady scene has since settled in with the town's more permanent population of Shan, Thai and Muslim Chinese. The town itself can be explored in a matter of minutes, but the real adventure lies along the paths in the hills beyond.

Information

Pick up a copy of the *Pai, Soppong, Mae Hong Son Tourist Map* (20B) for extensive listings. Several places around town offer Internet services and they all charge around 40B per hour.

Krung Thai Bank (Th Rangsiyanon) Has an ATM and foreign-exchange service.

Siam Used Books (Th Rangsiyanon) Best place for second-hand books in town.

Activities

All the guesthouses in town can provide heaps of information on local trekking and a few offer guided treks for as little as 600B per day if there are no rafts or elephants involved.

Thai Adventure Rafting (TAR; ☎ 0 5369 9111; www.activethailand.com; Th Charongkham; per person 2000B) has two-day, white-water rafting trips on the Mae Nam Pai from Pai to Mae Hong Son. The main rafting season runs July to December. Cheaper river activities include

tubing; tubes can be hired for 50B around town.

Thom's Pai Elephant Camp Tours (☎ 0 5369 9286; Th Rangsiyanon; 1-/3-hr rides per person 300/500B) offers jungle rides year-round from Thom's camp near the hot springs, which include a soak in the camp's hot-spring-fed tubs afterwards.

The Pool (50B; ☒ 10.30am-8.30pm) Need to cool off and chill out? Sun yourself on the deck, sip a drink and take a dip at this refreshing swimming pool.

Pai Traditional Massage (☎ 0 5369 9121; Th Sukhapiban 1; ☒ 4.30am-8.30pm Mon-Fri, 8.30am-8.30pm Sat & Sun; massage per hr 150B, sauna 60B) has very good northern Thai massage, as well as a sauna where you can steam yourself in *sàmŭn phrai* (medicinal herbs).

Sleeping

From December to March it can be difficult to find a room. The most atmospheric guesthouses are spread along the banks of the Mae Nam Pai and they number in the dozens.

Pai River Hill Guesthouse (☎ 0 5369 8230; r 100B) Spilling down a hill towards the banks of the Mae Nam Pai, these basic bungalows come with an expansive view above or a river breeze below. The creaky bamboo restaurant offers big views over town. Take the first left after the bridge from the road to the hot springs.

Pai River Lodge (☎ 0 9520 2898; south of Th Ratchadamnoen; s/d 120/200B) The lengthy lawn is a draw here, ringed by typical A-frame huts (with share bathrooms) and a couple of smarter options. The chill-out lounge and diner is a good place to catch up on life around Pai. Riverbank relaxation guaranteed.

Golden Hut (☎ 0 5369 9949; Mae Pai; dm 50B, r 100-300B) Occupying a prime piece of riverfront, the Golden Hut pulls in the punters thanks to a wide range of rooms from cheap dorms to top-drawer options with a hot shower. The tree houses are pretty wild at 100B, although not if you are planning a drink-up. A green garden, wooden walkways and a sociable restaurant complete the picture.

Star House (☎ 0 9559 6065; Mae Pai; r 60-350B) Across the river from the Golden Hut via a rickety old bridge, a new guesthouse village is springing up. Star shines bright over here, with a good range of cheapies with shared bathroom running to 150B and some smarter options for a guaranteed bathroom. Check out the personal pavilions overlooking the river. Perfect.

Sun Hut (☎ 0 5369 9730; 28/1 Ban Mae Yen; s/d from 200/250B) This eclectic collection of zodiac-inspired bungalows is one of the more tranquil places around Pai. Bungalows and huts are well spaced, and more expensive bungalows have a porch and oodles of charm. The turn-off for Sun Hut is signposted about 3km from town on the road to the hot springs.

Eating & Drinking

There are an incredible number of places to get a good feed in Pai. Many of the riverfront guesthouses are capitalising on their location with rustic restaurants built on stilts near the water.

All About Coffee (☎ 0 5369 9429; Th Chaisongkhram; dishes 35-65B; ☾ breakfast, lunch & dinner) Anyone in search of a creative coffee kick need look no further than here. Sandwiches are made with delicious homemade bread and the salads are crisp. It closes at 6pm.

Ban Benjarong (Th Rangsiyanon; dishes 40-100B; ☾ lunch & dinner) For a good range of Thai dishes as a prelude to a night on the town, this place delivers. Partly open-air, it is less of a beer garden than its neighbours. Bag a table with views of the rice paddies out the back.

Ting Tong (Th Ratchadamnoen; ☾ 5pm-2am) The motto here is 'lazy days, crazy nights' which pretty well sums up Pai for many. Seek some soul mates at this bohemian garden bar, a refuge for hard drinkers rather than the health conscious.

Bebop Restaurant & Music (Th Rangsiyanon; ☾ 6pm-1am) Wait till the midnight hour and you can be sure half of Pai is at the Bebop. Live bands perform every night, playing old covers, country and western and rockin' originals. Get here early if you want a seat, get here late if you want to dance.

Getting There & Away

The **bus stop** (Th Chaisongkhram) is in a dirt lot in the centre of town. All buses that stop here follow the Chiang Mai–Pai–Mae Hong Son–Mae Sariang loop in either direction. Buses to Chiang Mai (air-con/ordinary 84/60B, four hours) and Mae Hong Son (air-con/ordinary 74/53B, four hours) leave

five times daily. The road is savagely steep and snaking; grab a window seat and ride on an empty stomach if motion sickness is a problem.

MAE HONG SON
pop 8300

Hemmed in by mountains on all sides, Mae Hong Son feels like the end of the road, but sees its fair share of foreigners thanks to the daily flights from Chiang Mai. Many travellers skip the sales pitch in Chiang Mai in favour of the localised trekking scene in Mae Hong Son, Thailand's far northwestern provincial capital. The town's population is predominantly Shan, but the feel is more a Thai town than minority mountain getaway. Head down to the shores of Nong Jong Kham (Jong Kham Lake) to escape the bustle of the busy streets.

Information

Most of the banks on Th Khunlum Praphat have ATMs. Internet access is widely available in the town centre but connections can be slow.

Post office (Th Khunlum Praphat)
Sri Sangwarn Hospital (☎ 0 5361 1378; Th Singhanat Bamrung)
TAT office (☎ 0 5361 2982; Th Khunlum Praphat; ☾ 8.30am-4.30pm Mon-Fri) Across from the post office.
Thai Airways International (THAI; ☎ 0 5361 1297; www.thaiair.com; 71 Th Singhanat Bamrung)
Tourist police (☎ 0 5361 1812, emergencies ☎ 1155; Th Singhanat Bamrung; ☾ 8.30am-9.30pm) To report thefts or lodge complaints against trekking companies or guesthouses.

Sights & Activities

Wat Jong Klang and **Wat Jong Kham** (south of Nong Jong Kham) are the focal point of the **Poi Sang Long Festival** in March, when young Shan boys are ordained as novice monks. The boys are carried on the shoulders of friends or relatives and paraded round the wat under festive parasols.

Guesthouses in town arrange **treks** to nearby hill-tribe villages, as well as **whitewater rafting** on the Mae Nam Pai. Reliable operators include:

Nam Rim Tours (☎ 0 5361 3925; Th Khunlum Praphat) Funny, professional and knowledgeable.
Sunflower Café (Th Udom Chaonithet) Consistently good feedback.

Sleeping & Eating

Friend House (☎ 0 5362 0119; 20 Th Pradit Jong Kham; r 100-400B) If you're looking for a friend, you have come to the right place. Clean, efficient and deservedly popular, this guesthouse provides large rooms in a teak house. Head upstairs for a lake view. Shared hot-water showers.

Palm House Guest House (☎ 0 5361 4022; 22/1 Th Chamnansthit; r from 250B; 🔀) Palm House offers a healthy dose of VFM (value for money), a family-run pad with airy rooms and power showers. Upstairs are some fine views of the lake and its temples.

Johnnie House (Th Pradit Jong Kham; d 200B) Another established crash pad near Nong Jong Kham, it has cheaper rooms that are a little threadbare with shared bathrooms, but construction is underway to up the game. There's a popular little traveller restaurant, too.

Salween River Restaurant (☎ 0 5361 2050; dishes 35-80B; 🕙 breakfast, lunch & dinner) Salween is the place to come for hill tribe coffee, *pain au chocolat,* vegetarian dishes and Shan specialties like *kài òp* (baked Shan chicken casserole). The friendly owners are a rich source of information and it's a popular hang-out for volunteers.

Sunflower Café (Th Udom Chaonithet; dishes 40-100B; 🕙 breakfast, lunch & dinner) A fine place to while away some time, Sunflower offers freshly baked breads, serious soups and salads, and popular pizzas. Near the post office, it is also a reliable place to arrange treks.

Lakeside Bar & Restaurant (Th Pradit Jong Kham; buffet 59B; 🕙 lunch & dinner) With a sharp setting on the shores of the lake, this restaurant has a popular daily buffet. By night, it livens up and slowly but surely the drinkers outnumber the diners. There's live music until midnight most nights.

Mae Si Bua (Thai Yai Food; Th Singhanat Bamrung; dishes 15-35B) Near the tourist police, this simple shop turns out delicious Shan and northern Thai food.

Getting There & Away

Mae Hong Son is 368km from Chiang Mai, but the terrain is so rugged (and beautiful) that the trip takes at least eight long sweaty hours. For this reason, many people fly to or from Chiang Mai with **Thai Airways International** (THAI; ☎ 0 5361 2220; www.thaiair.com; Th Singhanat Bamrung), which has four flights daily.

The **airport** (☎ 0 5361 2057; Th Nivit Pisan) is near the centre of town.

The **bus station** (Th Khunlum Praphat) is near the Siam Hotel. There are two routes from Mae Hong Son: the northern route is faster by about an hour, but the southern route includes more bathroom stops. Buses travelling south from Mae Hong Son stop at Mae Sariang (ordinary/air-con 78/140B, four hours, five daily), while buses heading north stop at Pai (ordinary/air-con 53/74B, four hours, seven to eight daily). Both eventually reach Chiang Mai (ordinary/air-con 143/257B).

THA TON & AROUND

In the far northern corner of Chiang Mai Province, Tha Ton is the launching point for river trips to Chiang Rai. The ride down Mae Nam Kok is a big hit with tourists and the villages along the way are geared up to groups, but it remains a relaxing route to avoid the bone-rattling buses for a day. Tha Ton is little more than a boat dock with a few guesthouses and souvenir stands, so come equipped with money and other sundries.

Guesthouses line the main road into town on either side of the river. **Chan Kasem Guest House** (☎ 0 5345 9313; d 90-300B) is the nearest spot to the boat dock, and has simple rooms with shared bathroom in the old house and smarter rooms in a brick block. There's also an atmospheric restaurant on the river.

Buses from Chiang Mai (70B, four hours, six departures daily) leave Chang Pheuak starting at 6am, which is the only departure that will arrive in time for the 12.30pm boat to Chiang Rai. From Tha Ton, yellow sǎwngthǎew run north to Mae Salong (50B, 1½ hours, departures every 30 minutes) and south to Fang (12B, 40 minutes).

Chiang Rai–bound boats taking up to 12 passengers leave from the pier in Tha Ton at 12.30pm only (250B, three to five hours). Six-person charters are available for 1700B between 7am and 3pm. Many travellers like to do the trip in stages, stopping in minority villages along the way. Guesthouses in Tha Ton can arrange combination rafting and trekking trips ending in Chiang Rai.

CHIANG RAI

pop 40,000

Leafy and well groomed, Chiang Rai is more liveable than visitable, lacking any major tourist attractions except being a gateway to

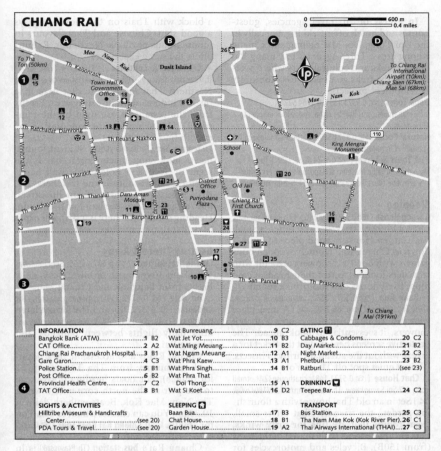

CHIANG RAI

INFORMATION						
Bangkok Bank (ATM)	1 B2	Wat Bunreuang	9 C2	EATING		
CAT Office	2 A2	Wat Jet Yot	10 B3	Cabbages & Condoms	20 C2
Chiang Rai Prachanukroh Hospital	3 B1	Wat Ming Meuang	11 B2	Day Market	21 B2
Gare Garon	4 C3	Wat Ngam Meuang	12 A1	Night Market	22 C3
Police Station	5 B1	Wat Phra Singh	13 A1	Phetburi	23 B2
Post Office	6 B2	Wat Phra Kaew	14 B1	Ratburi	(see 23)
Provincial Health Centre	7 C2	Wat Phra That				
TAT Office	8 B1	Doi Thong	15 A1	DRINKING		
		Wat Si Koet	16 D2	Teepee Bar	24 C2
SIGHTS & ACTIVITIES						
Hilltribe Museum & Handicrafts		SLEEPING		TRANSPORT		
Center	(see 20)	Baan Bua	17 B3	Bus Station	25 C3
PDA Tours & Travel	(see 20)	Chat House	18 B1	Tha Nam Mae Kok (Kok River Pier)	26 C1
		Garden House	19 A2	Thai Airways International (THAI)	27 C3

the Golden Triangle and an alternative spot for arranging hill-tribe treks. Of late, Chiang Rai has become more popular with well-heeled international conventioneers than with those lacking an expense account.

Information

Chiang Rai has a good number of banks, especially along Th Thanalai and along Th Utarakit. Internet access is readily available around town.

CAT office (cnr Th Ratchadat Damrong & Th Ngam Meuang; 7am-11pm Mon-Fri)

Chiang Rai Prachanukroh Hospital (0 5371 1303)

Gare Garon (869/18 Th Phahonyothin; 10am-10pm) Second-hand English books, plus coffee, tea and handicrafts.

Post office (Th Utarakit) South of Wat Phra Singh.

TAT office (0 5371 7433; 448/16 Th Singkhlai; 8.30am-4.30pm)

Tourist police (0 5371 1779)

Sights & Activities

In the mid-14th century, lightning struck open the *chedi* at **Wat Phra Kaew** (cnr Th Trairat & Th Reuang Nakhon), thus evealing the much-honoured Emerald Buddha hiding inside.

Hilltribe Museum & Handicrafts Center (0 5374 0088; www.pda.or.th/chiangrai; 620/1 Th Thanalai; admission 50B; 9am-6pm Mon-Fri, 10am-6pm Sat & Sun), run by the nonprofit PDA, displays clothing and the history of major hill tribes. PDA also organises hill-tribe treks.

THAILAND

In excess of 20 travel agencies, guest-houses and hotels offer trekking, typically in the Doi Tung, Doi Mae Salong and Chiang Khong areas. Three agencies in Chiang Rai operate treks and cultural tours where profits from the treks go directly to community development projects:

Dapa Tours (☎ 0 5371 1354, 0 1764 5221; info@dapatours.com) Run by Akha, specialises in tours to Akha areas.

Natural Focus (☎ 0 5371 5696; natfocus@loxinfo.co.th) Specialises in nature tours.

PDA Tours & Travel (☎ 0 5374 0088; 620/1 Th Thanalai, Hill Tribe Museum & Handicrafts Center) Culturally sensitive tours led by PDA-trained hill-tribe members.

Sleeping

Garden House (☎ 0 5371 7090; 163/1 Th Banphaprakan; s 100B, d 140-200B) Tucked away down a small soi, Garden House is good place to hunker down in Chiang Rai. Homely wooden bungalows with open-air showers are a hit with travellers looking to rest their heads. Good food, lively tunes and motorbike rental.

Baan Bua (☎ 0 5371 8880; baanbua@yahoo.com; 879/2 Th Jet Yot; s/d from 180/200B; ✖) A small place with just 10 large, spotless rooms with hot showers, it's essential to book ahead. The protective screens here are just the ticket for a breeze without the attendant army of insects. It's in a quiet spot off Th Jet Yot.

Chat House (☎ 0 5371 1481; chathouse32@hotmail .com; 3/2 Soi Saengkaew, Th Trairat; dm/s/d 60/180/200B; ✖) Set in an old Thai house with a flourishing garden, the friendly Chat offers small, clean rooms that are fine for forty winks, plus cheaper rooms with shared bathrooms (from 150B). Bicycles and motorcycles for rent, plus guided treks offered.

Eating & Drinking

The **day market** (off Th Utarakit) is a real maze; explore the eats on offer to put together a cheap lunch. Near the bus station, the **night market** (off Th Phahonyothin) is a must for dining thanks to a huge local crowd and more stalls than a Bangkok food court. Older Thais and foreigners are drawn to the food and beer garden for northern Thai dance performances, while younger Thais prefer the acoustic guitar stage. That's entertainment and it's free.

Phetburi (Th Banphaprakan; dishes 30B; ✖ breakfast, lunch & dinner) Near the clock tower, this no-nonsense rice-and-curry shop is chock-

a-block with Thais on the move – always a good sign. Chinese and Thai flavours in mountainous portions. Next door, Ratburi offers the same experience.

Cabbages & Condoms (☎ 0 5374 0784; 620/1 Th Thanalai; dishes 35-90B; ✖ breakfast, lunch & dinner) Northern Thai food is the diet here in a relaxed indoor-outdoor eating area. Profits from the restaurant are used by the non-profit PDA to make sure condoms are as easy to find as cabbages.

Teepee Bar (Th Phahonyothin) Student lounge meets junk shop meets reggae bar is the scene at Teepee: a hole-in-the-wall hangout for local dreadheads and travellers. Yes, it is as small as it looks from the street, but regulars extend the hand of friendship. Heading south from here is a string of expat bars that draw a mixed crowd.

Getting There & Away

Chiang Rai Airport (☎ 0 5379 3555; Superhighway 110), about 10km north of town, fields daily flights from Bangkok and Chiang Mai.

Air Asia (☎ 0 5379 3545; www.airasia.com), **Air Andaman** (☎ 0 5379 3726) and **Thai Airways International** (THAI; ☎ 0 5477 1179; www.thaiair.com) all offer daily flights between Bangkok and Chiang Rai.

Chiang Rai is also accessible by a popular boat journey from Tha Ton (see p752 for details). For boats heading upriver, go to the pier in the north corner of town at Tha Nam Mae Kok. Boats embark daily at 10.30am. You can charter a boat to Tha Ton for 1600B. Call **Chiang Rai Boat Tour** (☎ 0 5375 0009) for further information.

Chiang Rai's **bus station** (Th Prasopsuk) is in the heart of town. Bus services connect Chiang Rai with Bangkok (air-con 370B to 452B, VIP 700B, 10 hours), Chiang Mai (ordinary/air-con 77/139B, four hours, hourly 6am to 5pm), Chiang Khong (ordinary 42B, three hours, hourly 7am to 5pm), Chiang Saen (ordinary 25B, 1½ hours, every 15 minutes 6am to 6pm) and Mae Sai (ordinary/air-con 25/37B, one hour, every 15 minutes 6am to 6pm).

GOLDEN TRIANGLE & AROUND

The three-country border between Thailand, Myanmar and Laos forms the legendary Golden Triangle, a mountainous frontier where the opium poppy was once an easy cash crop for the region's ethnic minorities.

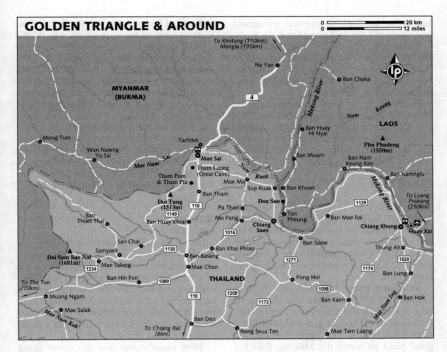

GOLDEN TRIANGLE & AROUND

As early as the 1600s, opium joined the Asian trade route along with spices and natural resources. The world soon had an opium addiction, but the drug and its derivatives, morphine and heroin, weren't outlawed in the West until the early 20th century. While Myanmar and Laos are still big players in worldwide opium production, Thailand has successfully stamped out its cultivation through crop-substitution programmes and aggressive law enforcement. Today the region's sordid past is marketed as a tourist attraction, and curious onlookers soon find that souvenirs of opium pipes and Golden Triangle T-shirts are the main success story of the substitution programme.

Chiang Khong
pop 9000

Chiang Khong is an important market town for local hill tribes and for trade with northern Laos. It is quite a lively little community and a lot of travellers pass this way between Thailand and Laos. Nearby are several villages inhabited by Mien and White Hmong.

Si Ayuthaya, Kasikornbank and Siam Commercial Bank all have branches in town with ATMs and foreign-exchange services.

Bamboo Riverside Guest House (☎ 0 5379 1621/9; sweepatts@hotmail.com; 71 Mu 1 Hua Wiang; dm 70B, r 150-250B) is a great introduction to Thailand or somewhere to leave for Laos on a high. It has bamboo-thatched dorm rooms as well as private rooms, all with fan and attached hot shower. The owner ensures a

BORDER CROSSING: INTO LAOS

From the Mekong River village of Chiang Khong, you can cross into the Lao village of Huay Xai; ferry boats make the passage for 40B. Fifteen-day Lao visas are available on arrival for US$30. From Huay Xai (p393), you can catch boats to Luang Prabang or minivans to Vientiane. See p352) for more information on transport within Laos. Buses connect Chiang Khong with Chiang Rai and Chiang Mai to the south, and you can travel southeast to Nong Khai.

THAILAND

bohemian atmosphere and the restaurant has views of Laos and good food.

Buses depart hourly for Chiang Rai (42B, three hours, 4am to 5pm) and Chiang Saen (50B, two hours). Daily buses to Bangkok (ordinary/air-con/VIP 382/491/573B, nine hours) leave in the evening.

Boats taking up to 10 passengers can be chartered up the Mekong River from Chiang Khong to Chiang Saen for 1800B. Boat crews can be contacted near the customs pier behind Wat Luang, or further north at the pier for ferries to Laos.

Chiang Saen
pop 55,000

Since it isn't in the officially marketed 'Golden Triangle', Chiang Saen is still a sedate little town on the Mekong River. You can while away a day exploring ruins of the long-extinct Chiang Saen kingdom, visiting the small national museum or watching the boat traffic.

Gin's Guest House (☎ 0 5365 1023; 71 Mu 8; bungalows 200-250B, r 300-700B), on the north side of town (about 1.5km north of the bus terminal), is a friendly and secluded place with solid rooms. The upper terrace is a good place to watch the Mekong flow by. Mountain-bike and motorcycle rentals are available.

Cheap noodle and rice dishes are available at food stalls in and near the market on the river road, and along the main road through town from the highway, near the bus stop. A small night market sets up each evening at the latter location and stays open until around midnight.

Chiang Saen is most easily reached via Chiang Rai (ordinary 25B, 1½ hours, frequent departures). Sǎwngthǎew go to Mae Sai (30B, one hour) and Chiang Khong (50B, two hours).

Six-passenger speedboats go to Sop Ruak (one way/return 400/700B, 30 minutes) or Chiang Khong (one way 1500B, 1½ hours), but be ready to bargain.

Sop Ruak

Busloads of package tourists converge on Sop Ruak's 'Welcome to the Golden Triangle' sign to pose proudly for photos. It is an all-out tourist trap, lacking the romance people might hope to find in such an infamous place.

House of Opium (admission 30B; ⏰ 7am-7pm), in the centre of town, is worth a peek. It's a small museum telling the story of opium culture, and is the cheaper alternative to the **Opium Exhibition Hall** (☎ 0 5378 4444; www.goldentrianglepark.com; admission 300B), an ultraflash exhibition hall on the history and production of opium, as well as the debilitating effects of the drug. It is located about 1km beyond Sop Ruak on the road to Mae Sai.

Sop Ruak is 9km from Chiang Saen, and sǎwngthǎew and share taxis cost around 10B; these leave every 20 minutes. It's an easy bicycle ride from Chiang Saen to Sop Ruak; guesthouses in Chiang Saen can arrange rentals.

Mae Sai
pop 25,800

Thailand's northernmost town, Mae Sai, is a handy launch pad for exploring the Golden Triangle and Mae Salong. The frontier town is a busy trading post for gems, jewellery, cashews and lacquerware, and also forms a legal border crossing into Myanmar. Many travellers make the trek here to extend their Thai visa or to tick Myanmar off as a destination on their global travel map.

Most guesthouses line the street along the Mae Nam Sai to the left of the border checkpoint.

Mae Sai Guest House (☎ 0 5373 2021; 688 Th Wiengpangkam; s 100-150B, d 200-500B) is a bungalow village that includes riverfront berths

---

BORDER CROSSING: INTO MYANMAR

In peaceful times, foreigners may cross from Mae Sai into Tachilek, Myanmar. The border is open 8am to 5pm daily, except when fighting erupts between the Burmese central government and Shan minority groups; ask about current conditions before making the trip to Mae Sai.

To extend your stay in Thailand, get stamped out of Thailand before crossing the border. At the Myanmar border you will be expected to pay a US$5 fee.

Foreigners are permitted to cross the border to Tachilek (the town opposite Mae Sai) and continue to Kengtung or Mengla; see the Myanmar chapter for regulations and border fees regarding this overland option (p586).

with porches over the water. It is overseen by friendly, enthusiastic staff. Its riverside restaurant serves tasty Thai and Western dishes and you can keep one eye on Myanmar while you dine. It's about 150m beyond what seems like the end of Th Sailomjoi.

Northern Guest House (☎ 0 5373 1537; 402 Th Tham Pha Jum; r 120-350B; ☒) is on the banks of the Nam Ruak – the sign has about a dozen names for this popular guesthouse set in spacious gardens. Chose from rustic huts to modern air-con rooms in a two-storey building by the river. The on-site restaurant is open for breakfast, lunch and dinner, and offers room service.

Mae Sai has a **night market** (Th Phahonyothin) with an enticing mix of Thai, Burmese, Chinese and Indian dishes.

The **bus station** (☎ 0 5364 6437; off Th Phahonyothin) is 3km from the border or 1km from the immigration office. For information on crossing into Myanmar, see opposite.

Buses connect Mae Sai with Bangkok (air-con 374B to 481B, VIP 685B, 12 hours, regular departures). Other services include Chiang Mai (ordinary/air-con 95/171B, four to five hours, regular departures) and Chiang Rai (ordinary/air-con 25/37B, one hour, frequent departures). The bus to Tha Ton (36B) and Fang (45B) leaves at 7am and takes two hours.

The Chiang Rai–bound bus makes stops along the way where you can pick up sǎwngthǎew to Mae Salong or Sop Ruak. Tell the attendant your final destination and they will alert you for your stop.

Mae Salong
pop 10,000

Built along the spine of a mountain, Mae Salong was originally settled by the 93rd Regiment of the Kuomintang Nationalist Party (KMT), which fled from China after the 1949 Chinese revolution. Crossing into northern Thailand with their pony caravans, the ex-soldiers and their families re-created a society that was much like the one they left behind in Yunnan. Chinese language rather than Thai is more frequently spoken here, and the land's severe inclines boast tidy terraces of tea and coffee plantations.

An interesting **morning market** (☉ 5-7am) convenes at the T-junction near Shin Sane Guest House. The market attracts town residents and many tribespeople from the surrounding districts. Most of the guesthouses in town can arrange **horseback treks** around the area.

Shin Sane Guest House (Sin Sae; ☎ 0 5376 5026; r 50-300B) is Mae Salong's original guesthouse, and the cheapies are as cell-like as you'd expect for such few baht. It has reliable information on trekking and a small restaurant.

Akha Mae Salong Guest House (☎ 0 5376 5103; Th Mae Salong; dm/s/d 50/100/150B), next door to Shin Sane, is run by a friendly Akha family. Handicrafts are made and sold in the reception area.

To get to Mae Salong, take a Chiang Rai–Mae Sai bus and get off at Ban Basang (ordinary 15B, 1½ hours). From there, sǎwngthǎew climb the mountain to Mae Salong (50B per person, one hour). Yellow sǎwngthǎew follow the scenic road west of the village to Tha Ton (50B).

NAN
pop 24,300

Nan was a semi-autonomous kingdom until 1931 and it still retains something of its former isolation and individuality. Surveying the town's distinctive **temples** and visiting the **National Museum** (☎ 0 5477 2777, 0 5471 0561; Th Pha Kong; admission 30B; ☉ 9am-4pm Mon-Sat) help to pass an unhurried day. Many visitors stop in Nan only long enough to arrange a trek into mountainous **Doi Phu Kha National Park** and the adjacent hill-tribe villages of the Thai Lü, Htin, Khamu and Mien people.

Information

There are several banks with ATMs on Th Sumonthewarat. Internet services are available around town for 40B per hour.

Post office (Th Mahawong) In the centre of town.

Tourist information centre (☉ 8am-5pm) Opposite Wat Phumin.

Activities

Fhu Travel Service (☎ 0 5471 0636, 0 1287 7209; www.fhutravel.com; 453/4 Th Sumonthewarat) offers treks to minority villages. They have been leading tours for almost two decades, and are a professional, honest and reliable organisation. Trekking tours start from 700B for a day. Fhu also offers white-water rafting trips, kayaking trips and elephant tours.

Sleeping

Nan Guest House (☎ 0 5477 1849; 57/16 Th Mahaphrom; d 200B) This centrally located, converted home has reasonable rooms, including cheaper ones with shared bathrooms (single/double 100/150B). Tours and bus information are available here. It's just off Th Mahaphrom, near the THAI office.

Amazing Guest House (☎ 0 5471 0893; 25/7 Th Rat Amnuay; s/d/tr 150/200/250B) Things are very homely here, in this quiet self-contained house a little way out of the town centre. The rooms are small and bathrooms are shared, but the water is hot and there's a relaxing garden.

Eating

You can buy Nan's famous golden-skinned oranges from the **day market** (cnr Th Khao Luang & Th Jettabut) as well as takeaway food like *sôm-tam* (papaya salad). At night, vendors set up along the banks of the Mae Nam Nan to bring nourishment to the masses.

Da Dario (☎ 0 5475 0258; 37/4 Th Rat Amnuay; dishes 60-100B; ✆ dinner Tue-Fri, lunch & dinner Sat & Sun) Next to Amazing Guest House, Da Dario is an Italian-Thai restaurant that makes delicious pizza, minestrone and other treats. Prices are reasonable and the service impressive.

Yota Vegetarian Restaurant (Th Mahawaong; dishes 10-30B; ✆ breakfast & lunch) This is one of the best deals in town, and *the* best if you're vegetarian. Once the food runs out, it's all over rover.

Getting There & Away

Air Andaman (☎ 0 5471 1222) offers services that connects Nan with Chiang Mai (four flights weekly) or Bangkok (daily). Air Andaman offers free transport between Fahthanin Hotel and the airport. **PB Air** (www .pbair.com) also has flights from Bangkok (four flights weekly).

The government bus station is located roughly 500m southwest of town on the highway to Phrae. Buses travel between Nan and Bangkok (air-con 300B to 387B, VIP 600B, 10 to 12 hours). There are also services available to Chiang Mai (ordinary 128B, air-con 179B to 230B, six to seven hours, four daily), to Chiang Rai (air-con 110B, six to seven hours, 9.30am) and to Phrae (ordinary/air-con 44/62B, 2½ hours, frequent departures).

NORTHEASTERN THAILAND

Kiss goodbye to the tourist trail, as the northeast is a trip back in time to old Thailand. Rice fields stretch as far as the eye can see in every direction, haphazardly divided by earthen paths and punctuated by tired, sun-beaten trees and lonely water buffaloes submerged in muddy ponds. During the wet season the land is so vivid with tender rice shoots that your eyes ache, but in the dry season the land withers to the texture of a desert. Traditional culture is the rich lifeblood of the Lao, Thai and Khmer people, coursing as deliberately as the mighty Mekong River.

Also referred to as Isan, the northeast is Thailand's least-visited region, as it lacks a well-developed tourist infrastructure. Few towns boast a backpacker scene and fewer have mastered English as a second language. Travelling the wide arc of the Mekong River between the Laos gateways of Nong Khai and Mukdahan is an inviting array of small towns, best visited during a local festival when music, dancing and food are out in force. Elsewhere, the ancient Angkor kings left behind magnificent temples on their far-flung frontier, part of a holy road connecting Angkor Wat with present-day Thailand.

NAKHON RATCHASIMA (KHORAT)

pop 2 million

Thailand's second-largest city, Nakhon Ratchasima, which goes by the nickname 'Khorat', is a slow burner with little evident charm for the whistle-stop visitor. Development has buried much of its history, but unlike other Thai metropolises, Khorat has a genuine core. This is the gateway to Isan and a real city where tourism takes a backseat to real life. Khorat is also a handy base for exploring the nearby Khmer ruins of Phimai or Khao Yai National Park.

Information

There are banks galore in Khorat, all with ATMs and exchange services.

Post office (Th Jomsurangyat; ✆ 8am-5pm Mon-Fri, until noon Sat)

Ratchasima Hospital (☎ 0 4426 2000; Th Mittaphap)

TAT office (☎ 0 4421 3666; Th Mittaphap; ⏱ 8.30am-4.30pm) On the western edge of town, beyond the train station.

Tourist police (☎ 1155) Opposite bus station No 2, north of the city centre.

T-Net (1st fl, The Mall, Th Mittaphap; per hr 20B; ⏱ 10am-10pm) Internet access.

Sights

In the city centre is the defiant statue of **Khun Ying Mo** (Thao Suranari Memorial), a local heroine who led the inhabitants against Lao invaders during the reign of Rama III (r 1824–51). A holy shrine, the statue receives visitors offering gifts and prayers or hiring singers to perform Khorat folk songs. The steady activities of the devotees make for a lively cultural display.

For a dose of Khmer and Ayuthaya art, visit **Mahawirawong National Museum** (☎ 0 4424 2958; Th Ratchadamnoen; admission 10B; ⏱ 9am-4pm), housed in the grounds of Wat Sutchinda.

Sleeping

Sakol Hotel Korat (☎ 0 4424 1260; Th Atsadang; r 150B; ☒) This hotel shows a little more attention to detail than most of the cheapies. The bright rooms are good value, given they include a bathroom, and you can upgrade to air-con for 400B.

Doctor's House (☎ 0 4425 5846; 78 Soi 4, Th Seup Siri; r with shared bathroom 180B) More of a homestay than a guesthouse, this house is a real residence, local family and all. The five rooms are airy and spacious, but it is not for party animals as the owner locks the gate at 10pm.

Tokyo Hotel (☎ 0 4424 2788; Th Suranari; r 250B; ☒) Occupying a strategic location near bus station No 1, the Tokyo Hotel has a monopoly on fly-by-night types. A recent renovation has smartened things up here, although more on the outside than in! Air-con is available at 350B.

Eating & Drinking

Khorat is overflowing with tasty Thai and Chinese restaurants, particularly along Th Ratchadamnoen near the Thao Suranari Memorial and western gate to central Khorat.

Thai Phochana Restaurant (142 Th Jomsurangyat; dishes 40-120B; ⏱ breakfast & lunch; ☒) A slice of old Khorat, this atmospheric wooden house is popular for its mixture of Thai and local specialities, including *mìi khorâat* (Khorat-style noodles) and *yam kòp yâang* (roast frog salad). The *kaeng phèt pèt* (duck curry) is a winner.

Kai Yang Seup Siri (Th Seup Siri; dishes 20-40B; ⏱ lunch) Anyone staying at the Doctor's House should make for this place on Th Seup Siri. It is the top spot in town for *kài yâang* (grilled spiced chicken) and *sôm-tam*. Other Isan restaurants nearby fill the dinner void once this place closes.

Cabbages & Condoms (☎ 0 4425 8100; 86/1 Th Seup Siri; mains 60-120B; ⏱ lunch & dinner; ☒) A little out of the way, unless you are staying at the Doctor's House; at least you won't forget the name. It has a leafy terrace to indulge in a carefully crafted menu of Thai and Western favourites. Like the original eatery in Bangkok, this is dining for a cause to help the PDA.

Hua Rot Fai Market (Th Mukkhamontri; ⏱ 6-10pm), located near the Khorat train station, is a lively place to head after dark. Slower paced are the **night food stalls** (Th Phoklang) that set up

---

ISAN CUISINE

The food of hard-working farmers who have honed their tolerance for peppers as well as their sinewy muscles against exhaustion, Isan cuisine is true grit. The holy trinity of the cuisine – *kài yâang* (grilled chicken), *sôm-tam* (papaya salad) and *khâo nĭaw* (sticky rice) – are integral to the culture and reminisced like lost lovers by displaced Isan taxi drivers in Bangkok. Early in the morning a veritable chicken massacre is laid out on an open grill, sending wafts of smoke into the dry air as free advertising. Beside the grill is a huge earthenware *khrók* (mortar) and wooden *sàak* (pestle) beating out the ancient rhythm of *sôm-tam* preparation: in go grated papaya, sliced limes, peppers, sugar and a host of preferential ingredients. People taste the contents and call out adjustments: more *náam plaa* (fish sauce) or *plaa rá* (fermented fish sauce, which looks like rotten mud). Everything is eaten with the hands, using sticky rice to help offset the chilli burn. Isan food is almost flammable, with a fistful of potent peppers finding their way into every dish, especially *láap*, a super-spicy salad originating from Laos.

THAILAND

NAKHON RATCHASIMA (KHORAT)

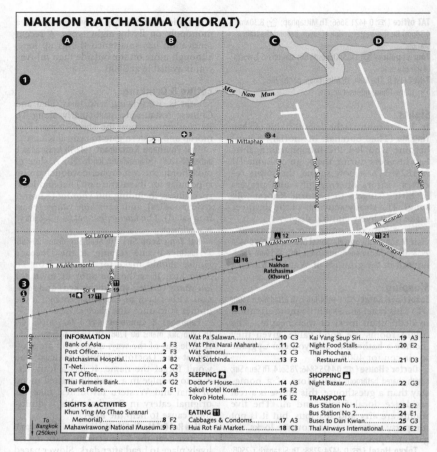

INFORMATION
Bank of Asia	1 F3
Post Office	2 F3
Ratchasima Hospital	3 B2
T-Net	4 C2
TAT Office	5 A3
Thai Farmers Bank	6 G2
Tourist Police	7 E1

SIGHTS & ACTIVITIES
Khun Ying Mo (Thao Suranari Memorial)	8 F2
Mahawirawong National Museum	9 F3

Wat Pa Salawan	10 C3
Wat Phra Narai Maharat	11 G2
Wat Samorai	12 C3
Wat Sutchinda	13 F3

SLEEPING
Doctor's House	14 A3
Sakol Hotel Korat	15 F2
Tokyo Hotel	16 E2

EATING
Cabbages & Condoms	17 A3
Hua Rot Fai Market	18 C3

Kai Yang Seup Siri	19 A3
Night Food Stalls	20 E2
Thai Phochana Restaurant	21 D3

SHOPPING
Night Bazaar	22 G3

TRANSPORT
Bus Station No 1	23 E2
Bus Station No 2	24 E1
Buses to Dan Kwian	25 G3
Thai Airways International	26 E2

beside the Chinese temple and offer a good range of Thai and Isan cuisine.

Try your hand at street surfing along the open-air bars that are dotted about the **night bazaar** (Th Manat). Local drinkers are pretty friendly here and you might end up on a pub crawl you didn't expect.

Shopping

Light up your life with a wander through the Th Manat **night bazaar** (Th Manat), which is so well lit you'll need shades. Anything and everything is available on this strip and you don't have to bargain as hard as in Bangkok. Several Khorat-style **silk shops** (Th Ratchadamnoen) can be found close to the Thao Suranari Memorial.

Getting There & Away

Khorat has two bus stations: **No 1** (Th Burin) serves Bangkok's Northern & Northeastern Bus Terminal and provincial destinations; **No 2** (Th Chang Pheuak) serves all others.

Buses travel from Khorat to Bangkok (ordinary/air-con 96/157B, four to five hours, frequent departures daily), Nong Khai (ordinary/air-con 110/220B, six hours, several departures daily), Phimai (40B, one hour, frequent departures between 5.30am and 10pm) and also to Ubon Ratchathani (ordinary/air-con 149/260B, six hours, regular departures daily).

The **train station** (Th Mukkhamontri) is on the western side of the city. Destinations like Bangkok, Surin and Buriram are all more

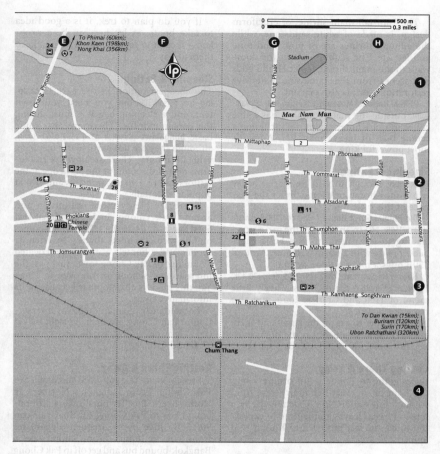

To Phimai (60km);
Khon Kaen (198km);
Nong Khai (356km)

Stadium

Mae Nam Mun

Th Chang Phuak

Th Chang Pheuak

Th Suranari

Th Mittaphap

Th Phonsaen

Th Buriri

Th Suranari

Th Ratchadamnoen

Th Chumphon

Th Chakri

Th Prajak

Th Manat

Th Yommarat

Th Phonlan

Th Tharaobosura

Th Phoklang Chinese Temple

Th Yothana

Th Atsadang

Th Jomsurangyat

Th Wachara...

Th Chumphon

Th Kudan

Th Mahat Thai

Th Chainarong

Th Saphasit

Th Ratchanikun

Th Kamhaeng Songkhram

To Dan Kwian (15km);
Buriram (120km);
Surin (170km);
Ubon Ratchathani (320km)

Chum Thang

conveniently reached by train than bus. Up to seven trains a day connect Khorat with Bangkok's Hualamphong train station (2nd/3rd class 110/50B), plus there are six services on to Ubon Ratchathani (2nd/3rd class 213/138B).

Getting Around

Local buses and sǎwngthǎew ply fixed routes through Khorat. Get onto sǎwngthǎew 1 (Th Phoklang–Mukhamontri) or onto 2 (Th Jomsurangyat–Th Mukhamontri) to reach the train station or the TAT office from the town centre. Local bus 15 hits both bus stations and can be picked up on Th Ratchadamnoen. Túk-túks and motorbike taxis are also available if you feel the need for speed.

PRASAT HIN PHIMAI

When the Angkor Empire was at its height, present-day northeastern Thailand was an important regional centre for the Khmers. An ancient laterite highway, lined with temples, linked Prasat Hin Phimai with the heart of the empire at Angkor in Cambodia. The Phimai temple, along with the other Khmer monuments in this part of Thailand, predates the Angkor Wat complex.

Originally started by Khmer King Jayavarman V in the late 10th century and finished by King Suryavarman I (r 1002–49), **Prasat Hin Phimai** (admission 40B; ☉ 6am-6pm), 60km northeast of Khorat, projects a majesty that transcends its size.

THAILAND

The 28m-tall main shrine, of cruciform design, is made of white sandstone, while the adjunct shrines are of pink sandstone and laterite. The sculptures over the doorways to the main shrine depict Hindu gods and scenes from the Ramayana. Extensive restoration work is also evident.

Phimai National Museum (admission 30B; ☼ 9am-4pm), outside the main complex, has a fine collection of Khmer sculpture, including a serene bust of Jayavarman VII, Angkor's most powerful king.

Sleeping & Eating

It is easy enough to visit Phimai as a day trip from Khorat, but some prefer the easy pace of this little town.

Old Phimai Guest House (☎ 0 4447 1918; dm/s/d 80/130/150B; 🖳) In an alley off the main street leading to the ruins, this is a basic backpacker place with a warm welcome. Around 350B buys a bit of air-con action.

Baiteiy Restaurant (☎ 0 4447 1725; dishes 30-40B; ☼ breakfast, lunch & dinner) Offers a lively little menu of Thai and Chinese food, and also rents out bicycles.

It's cheaper to eat on the street and there are sizzling woks aplenty at the night market, just north of the regular day market.

Getting There & Away

Buses going to Phimai (40B ordinary bus, one hour or so, every half hour) leave from Khorat's bus station No 1. Catching the 8am bus to Phimai leaves ample time to explore the ruins; the last bus back to Khorat is at 6pm.

KHAO YAI NATIONAL PARK

Up there with the world's finest national parks, **Khao Yai** (☎ 0 3731 9002; adult/child 200/100B) includes one of the largest intact monsoon forests in mainland Asia. The park has more than 50km of trekking trails, many of them formed by the movement of wildlife. Elevations range from 100m to 1400m, where the western edge of Cambodia's Dangrek mountain range collides with the southern edge of the Khorat Plateau.

Somewhat inaccurate trail maps are available from the park headquarters. It's easy to get lost on the longer trails, so it's wise to hire a guide (200B). In nearby Pak Chong, several guesthouses can offer tours starting from 1000B with an overnight stay.

If you do plan to trek, it is a good idea to take boots, as leeches can be a problem – mosquito repellent does help to keep them at bay.

Sleeping & Eating

The cheapest option in the park is **camping** (per person 30B) but you need your own tent, and a sleeping bag is a must during the cooler months. There are also some basic **bungalows** (Bangkok ☎ 0 2562 0760; 800B), although they are not particularly inspiring value for money. There are now five restaurants dotted throughout the park; one at the visitors centre, two at campsites and two at popular waterfalls.

There are plenty more options in and around Pak Chong, including **Green Leaf Guest House** (☎ 0 4436 5024; r 200B), which comes highly recommended thanks to friendly service and a homely atmosphere. Located 7.5km out of Pak Chong town, just past the international school on the way to Khao Yai, this place is also popular because of its informative tours.

Located near the main highway intersection in Pak Chong is a buzzing **night market** (☼ 5-11pm) purveying a delicious range of Thai and Chinese food.

Getting There & Away

To reach Khao Yai, you need to connect to Pak Chong. From Bangkok's Northern & Northeastern Bus Terminal take a Khorat-bound bus to Pak Chong (ordinary/air-con 90/150B, three hours, frequent departures from 5am to 10pm). From Khorat take a Bangkok-bound bus and get off in Pak Chong (ordinary/air-con 28/65B, one hour).

From in front of the 7-Eleven store in Pak Chong, you can catch a săwngthăew to the park gates for 10B. You may also be able to take a direct bus from Bangkok at certain times of the year – inquire at the Northern & Northeastern Bus Terminal.

You can also easily access Pak Chong by train from Ayuthaya (2nd/3rd class 58/26B, three hours) and Khorat (2nd/3rd class 50/20B, 1½ hours).

PHANOM RUNG HISTORICAL PARK

Spectacularly located atop an extinct volcano, the elegantly restored temple of **Prasat Hin Khao Phanom Rung** (☎ 0 4463 1746; admission 40B; ☼ 6am-6pm) is the most impressive of all

THAILAND

Angkor monuments in Thailand. Dating from the 10th to 13th centuries, the complex faces east towards the sacred capital of Angkor in Cambodia. It was first built as a Hindu monument and features sculpture relating to the worship of Vishnu and Shiva. Later the Thais converted it into a Buddhist temple.

One of the most striking design features at Phanom Rung is the promenade leading to the main entrance. The avenue is sealed with laterite and sandstone blocks and flanked by sandstone pillars with lotus-bud tops. The avenue ends at the first and largest of three *naga* bridges. These *naga* bridges are the only three that have survived in Thailand. The central *prasat* (tower) has a gallery on each of its four sides, and the entrance to each gallery is itself a smaller incarnation of the main tower. The galleries have curvilinear roofs and windows with false balustrades. Once inside the temple walls, check out the galleries and the *gopura* (entrance pavilion), paying particular attention to the lintels over the doors. The craftsmanship at Phanom Rung represents the pinnacle of Khmer artistic achievement, on a par with the bas-reliefs at Angkor Wat in Cambodia.

The Sanctuary Phanomrung, by Dr Sorajet Woragamvijya, is an informative booklet on sale near the entrance to the complex. Several English-speaking guides also offer their services at the complex – fees are negotiable. Downhill from the main sanctuary is a visitors centre that houses a scale model of the area, as well as some artefacts from the site.

Sleeping

Phanom Rung can be undertaken as a day trip from Khorat, Buriram, Nang Rong or Surin. Although Buriram is closest, the selection of accommodation is miserable, making other towns more attractive options. The pick of a poor pack in Buriram is the **Thai Hotel** (☎ 0 4461 1112; 38/1 Th Romburi; r 250-400B; 🛠), but that's hardly a glowing endorsement. In the small village of Nang Rong, **Honey Inn** (☎ 0 4462 2825; 8/1 Soi Ri Kun; s/d 200/250B) is a homestay run by a local school teacher who speaks English. Bathrooms are shared, and motorbikes are available for rent (250B), which is handy for Phanom Rung. See Nakhon Ratchasima (Khorat) (p759) or Surin (right) for other options.

Getting There & Away

From Khorat, take a Surin-bound bus and get off at Ban Ta-Ko (air-con/ordinary 60/35B), which is well marked as the turn-off for Phanom Rung. Likewise, from Surin take a Khorat-bound bus to Ban Ta-Ko.

Once in Ban Ta-Ko, it is time for multiple choice. At the Ban Ta-Ko intersection you can wait for a săwngthăew that's going as far as the foot of Phanom Rung (20B), 12km away, or one that's headed south to Lahan Sai. If you take a Lahan Sai truck, get off at the Ban Ta Pek intersection (10B). From Ban Ta Pek, take a motorcycle taxi (50B) the rest of the way or book a return trip with wait time for about 150B.

It's easier from Buriram. From here, Chanthaburi-bound buses stop at Ban Ta Pek (ordinary 30B, one hour); you can then continue by motorcycle taxi as suggested.

From Nang Rong, catch a săwngthăew to Ban Ta-Ko and continue from there. Or for more freedom, rent a motorcycle from the Honey Inn for 250B.

SURIN

pop 41,200

Sleepy Surin goes wild in November during its annual **Elephant Roundup**, drawing huge numbers of foreign visitors. Elephant races, tug-of-war and a spot of soccer – these tuskers sure have a diverse repertoire.

Culturally, the town of Surin is a melting pot of Lao, Khmer and Suay (a minority elephant-herding tribe) cultures, resulting in an interesting mix of dialects and customs. Surin silk is renowned; it's worn by the college-educated professional and the illiterate vegetable-seller alike.

Sights

Surin is best enjoyed as a base for day-tripping to nearby attractions. To see Surin's elephants during the low season, visit **Ban Tha Klang** in Tha Tum District, about 60km north of Surin. Many of the performers at the annual festival are trained here and there are two-hour **shows** (☎ 0 1966 5284; admission 200B) every Saturday at 9am. Silk weaving can be observed at several local villages, including **Khwaosinarin** and **Ban Janrom**. You can also visit **Phanom Rung**, and other minor Angkor temples.

As an evening reward, Surin's main attraction is a pedestrian-only **night market**

THAILAND

(Th Krung Si Nai) that delivers healthy doses of eating and people-watching.

Sleeping & Eating

During the elephant roundup, accommodation vacancies shrink and rates triple; book well in advance.

Pirom's House (☎ 0 4451 5140; 242 Th Krung Si Nai; s/d 100/150B) At Surin's one and only guesthouse, host Pirom offers a warm welcome at his atmospheric (read: basic, with shared bathrooms) teak home. Pirom is a mine of information on the surrounding area. The guesthouse may move during the lifetime of this book – call Pirom's mobile (☎ 0 9355 4140) to check.

New Hotel (☎ 0 4451 1341; 6-8 Th Thanasan; r 200B; ✿) Just across from the train station, this pad has clean rooms of varying sizes and shapes. Air-con rooms are 350B a pop.

Petmanee 1 (dishes 50-80B; ✿ breakfast, lunch & dinner) Down a small soi across from Wat Salaloi, Th Thesaban 4, this famous *sôm-tam* shop has won national competitions for its local variation of the papaya salad, using a native herb. Don't speak Thai? No problem, tick the fourteenth item on the menu. Or ask a friendly Thai for help if you want something more substantial. Good luck.

Also recommended are the **municipal market** (Th Krung Si Nai), near Pirom's House, for *khâo phàt* (fried rice) and the **night market** (Th Krung Si Nai) for *khanŏm jiin* (curry noodles served with a huge tray of veggies) and *hǎwy thâwt* (batter-fried mussels).

Getting There & Away

The **bus terminal** (Th Chit Bam Rung) is one block from the train station. Destinations include Bangkok (air-con/VIP 250/385B, eight

> ### BORDER CROSSING: INTO CAMBODIA
>
> Foreigners are able to cross the border from Chong Jom in Thailand to O Smach in Cambodia. There are five buses a day from Surin to Chong Jom (30B, two hours). Once on the Cambodian side, it is possible to arrange a taxi on to Siem Reap (US$30, five to seven hours). Alternatively, head to Samraong (US$5, 30 minutes) and arrange local transport from there to Siem Reap or Anlong Veng.

hours, regular departures), Ubon (air-con 188B, four hours, frequent departures) and Khorat (air-con 115B, four hours, frequent departures).

These destinations, however, are more convenient by train (Bangkok 2nd/3rd class 210/80B). The **train station** (intersection of Th Nong Toom & Th Thawasan) is centrally located.

UBON RATCHATHANI

pop 115,300

Although it is one of the bigger cities in the region, Ubon still retains a small-town feel and is easily traversed by foot. Through something as simple as workday attire, Ubon stays true to its values, with middle-class professionals donning traditional silks from local weavers rather than the latest foreign imports.

With the Thai–Lao border crossing at nearby Chong Mek open to foreigners, Ubon (not to be confused with Udon Thani) has been receiving many more travellers who are finding it a good place to decompress after the relatively rustic conditions of southern Laos.

Information

Bangkok Bank (Th Suriyat) One of many banks in town.
MD.Com (221 Th Kheuan Thani; ✿ 11am-10pm) Internet access near the post office.
Post office (Th Si Narong)
Saphasit Prasong hospital (☎ 0 4526 3043; Th Saphasit)
TAT office (☎ 0 4524 3770; 264/1 Th Kheuan Thani; ✿ 8.30am-4.30pm) Helpful place opposite Sri Kamol Hotel; provides maps and advice on outlying attractions.
Tourist police (☎ 0 4524 5505, emergency ☎ 1155; Th Suriyat) Behind the police station.

Sights

Housed in a former palace of the Rama VI era, west of the TAT office, **Ubon National Museum** (☎ 0 4525 5071; Th Kheuan Thani; admission 30B; ✿ 9am-4pm Wed-Sun) is a good place to delve into Ubon's history and culture before exploring the city and province.

Across the Mae Nam Mun in the Warin Chamrap District is **Wat Pa Nanachat Bung Wai** (Ban Bung Wai, Amphoe Warin, Ubon Ratchathani 34310), which is directed by an Australian abbot and populated by European, American and Japanese monks. Write in advance for information about overnight stays and meditation classes.

Pastel-coloured silks displaying Lao influences are unpacked like contraband along the streets near Ubon's hotel districts; the making of these and other handicrafts can be observed in the nearby villages of **Ban Khawn Sai**, **Ban Pa-Ao** and **Khong Jiam**.

Festivals & Events

Ubon's **Candle Festival**, usually held in July, is a grand parade of gigantic, elaborately carved wax sculptures that are a celebration of Khao Phansa, a Buddhist holiday marking the start of the monks' retreat during the rainy season.

Sleeping

Rates and availability shoot up during the Candle Festival.

River Moon Guesthouse (☎ 0 4528 6093; Th Si Saket; s/d 120/150B) Travellers arriving from Laos will appreciate the calm and tranquillity at River Moon, a flashback to island life in Si Phan Don. The rustic bungalows have more function than flair, and bathrooms are shared, but the atmosphere is laid-back. Find it across the river from central Ubon in the Warin Chamrap District, near the train station.

New Nakornluang Hotel (☎ 0 4525 4768; 84-88 Th Yutthaphan; r 150-200B) The heart of old Ubon is blessed with some attractive Indochinese architecture that the French left behind from Hanoi to Phnom Penh. The New Nakornluang is not that new, but a comfortable option near some classic buildings.

Tokyo Hotel (☎ 0 4524 1739; 178 Th Uparat; old bldg r 250B, new bldg d 500B; ▨) The best of the budget deals in the centre of town, the Tokyo has some old cheapies that are starting to show their age. Flash the cash and opt for the swish new rooms with TV and textbook trim.

Eating & Drinking

Kai Yang Wat Jaeng (☎ 0 1709 9393; Th Suriyat; dishes 20-50B; ◷ breakfast, lunch & dinner) Spit and sawdust Thai-style. It may be a simple shack, but it is considered by those in the know to do the best *kài yâang* (grilled Lao-style chicken). The chicken is sold from 9am to 2pm only, after which it's curries only. Seek it out one block north of Wat Jaeng.

Indochine (☎ 0 4524 5584; Th Saphasit; dishes 50-150B; ◷ lunch & dinner) Near Wat Jaeng, this old teak house has been swallowed by vines

and creepers. Downstairs you'll find excellent Vietnamese food until 6pm when the action moves upstairs to the Intro Pub until midnight. There's live music that joins the nightshift.

Chiokee (☎ 0 4525 4017; Th Kheuan Thani; dishes 20-60B; ◷ breakfast, lunch & dinner) East meets West at this popular spot, with Chinese-Thai décor and bright white tablecloths. Professional breakfasts, including Thai, Chinese and Western, plus coffee with a kick to start the day.

Also worth sniffing out are Ubon's two night markets: one by the river near the main bridge, and the other near the bus station on Th Chayangkun.

U-Bar (☎ 0 4526 5141; 97/8-10 Th Phichit Rangsan; ◷ 6pm-2am) This is as hip as it gets in Isan, a full-on bar club to see and be seen in, for young Thais at least. Upstairs is a slow-paced terrace balcony, where there is often live music and it heaves at the hinges from 10pm most nights.

Getting There & Away

Thai Airways International (THAI; ☎ 0 4531 3340-4; www.thaiair.com; 364 Th Chayangkun) has three daily flights from Bangkok to Ubon. **Air Asia** (☎ 0 2515 9999; www.airasia.com) has a cheaper daily flight between Ubon and Bangkok.

Ubon's **bus terminal** (☎ 0 4531 2773; Th Chayangkun) is located at the far northern end of town, 3km from the centre. Local buses 2 and 3 can drop you off near the TAT office. Chartered transport is more like 100B into town.

Buses link Ubon with Bangkok's Northern & Northeastern Bus Terminal (ordinary/air-con 200/300B, nine hours, hourly 6am to midnight), with Buriram (ordinary/air-con 65/150B, four to five hours), with Khorat (ordinary/air-con 149/260B, six hours), Mukdahan (ordinary/air-con 60/110B, three hours) and with Surin (ordinary/air-con 75/88B, three hours).

The **train station** (☎ 0 4532 1004; Th Sathani) is located in Warin Chamrap, south of central Ubon. Use local bus 2 to cross the Mae Nam Mun into Ubon (5B). There are a couple of night trains in either direction connecting Ubon and Bangkok (express 2nd/3rd class 301/175B, express 2nd-class sleeper 401B). Express trains also stop in Surin and Khorat, but not necessarily at convenient times!

MUKDAHAN

pop 34,300

Looking across to the Lao city of Savanna-khet, Mukdahan is a well-oiled revolving door between the two countries. A popular Thai-Lao market, with a few Vietnamese traders for good measure, sets up along the river near the border checkpoint, nicknamed **Talat Indojin** (Indochina Market). It is a pretty enough town today, but looks set for big changes come the completion of the new bridge across the Mekong, cementing its status as a trading crossroads between Bangkok and Danang and all points in between.

There are a couple of cheap if cheerless to stay places near the pier. **Hua Nam Hotel** (☎ 0 4261 1137; 36 Th Samut Sakdarak; r 220-280B; ☒ ▣) has been to self-improvement classes in recent years and offers good-value rooms, plus bicycles for hire. **Hong Kong Hotel** (☎ 0 4261 1143; 161/1-2 Th Phitak Santirat; d 180B) remains second in the pecking order, as the large rooms are sagging at the seams.

Mukdahan's main bus terminal is on Rte 212, north of town. Take a yellow sǎwngthǎew (5B) from the fountain near the 7-Eleven on Th Samut Sakdarak for a cheap connection to the centre.

Mukdahan is serviced by buses coming from Bangkok's Northern & Northeastern Bus Terminal (ordinary/air-con/VIP 202/382/590B, 12 hours, several departures daily), Nakhon Phanom (ordinary/air-con 40/72B, two hours, hourly until 5pm) via

That Phanom (ordinary/air-con 20/40B, one hour) and Ubon Ratchathani (ordinary/air-con 60/110B, three hours, several daily).

For information on crossing into Laos, see below.

THAT PHANOM

This place might have been forgotten to the world were it not for the looming spire of **Wat Phra That Phanom**, a badge of Isan identity and an icon in the region. Next in line as an attraction is the riverfront promenade – a decaying path where residents' lives spill out from their houses, transforming the road into a playground or chicken coop. A lively Lao market gathers by the river from 8.30am to noon on Monday and Thursday.

The original backpacker pad, **Niyana Guest House** (☎ 0 4254 1450; 110 Moo 14 Th Rim-khong; d/t 120/140B), has moved house; but it's still a chaotic yet charming place. The owners are very friendly and the information flows freely, but the rooms are pretty basic and the bathrooms are shared in what is more of a homestay than a guesthouse. Find it near Wat Hua Wiang at the northern end of town.

There are regular buses from Th Chayangkun to Mukdahan (ordinary/air-con 20/40B, one hour, hourly until 5pm), Ubon Ratchathani (ordinary/air-con 65/140B, three hours, hourly) and Nakhon Phanom (ordinary/air-con 38/21B, one hour, hourly).

BORDER CROSSINGS: INTO LAOS

Chong Mek to Pakse

Chong Mek is the only place in Thailand where you can cross into Laos by land (that is, you don't have to cross the Mekong). The southern Lao city of Pakse is about an hour away by road, but the actual Lao border town is Vang Tao. To reach Chong Mek from Ubon, catch a Phibun bus (25B) from the bus terminal near Warin market between 5am and 3.30pm and change to a sǎwngthǎew bound for Chong Mek (25B). Two daily air-con buses run directly from Chong Mek to Bangkok and vice versa. They leave Chong Mek at 5pm and arrive at the Northern & Northeastern Bus Terminal in Bangkok at about 6am the next day. Lao immigration may try and levy an 'overtime' charge if you arrive at the border after 4pm.

Mukdahan to Savannakhet

Foreigners may cross the Mekong by ferry (50B). The ferry departs hourly between 9am and 4.30pm Monday to Friday; on weekends the schedule is limited to just a few crossings. The ferry pier in Mukdahan is at the foot of Th Song Nang Sathit, to the left of the immigration office. However, by the time you are reading this a bridge should be spanning the Mekong, no doubt with a border bus shuttling visitors back and forth.

NAKHON PHANOM

pop 31,700

In Sanskrit, Nakhon Phanom means 'city of hills', but they must be talking about the ones across the Mekong River in Laos. The striking views aside, it's a somnolent town with a smart riverfront promenade, a few graceful French colonial buildings and not a whole lot else.

Renu Nakhon, a village south of Nakhon Phanom on the way to That Phanom, is renowned for its daily handicraft market (simply huge on Saturday).

Information

Cyberspace (☎ 0 4251 3633; Th Sunthon Wijit; 🕙 10am-9pm) Riverfront Internet access.

Immigration office (☎ 0 4251 1235; Th Sunthon Wijit; 🕙 8.30am-4.30pm Mon-Fri)

Post office (cnr Th Ratchathan & Th Sunthon Wijit)

TAT office (☎ 0 4251 3490; cnr Th Sala Klang & Th Sunthon Wijit; 🕙 8.30am-4.30pm)

Festivals & Events

Usually in late October (on the full moon of the 11th lunar month), Nakhon Phanom celebrates **Wan Phra Jao Prot Lok** by launching *reua fai* (fire boats) on the Mekong. The boats carry offerings of cakes, rice and flowers and are illuminated in a spectacular display, plus there are longboat races during the day.

Sleeping & Eating

Rarely is a 'Grand' hotel that grand in provincial Thailand, and Nakhon Phanom's **Grand Hotel** (☎ 0 4251 1526; cnr Th Si Thep & Ruamjit; d 160-180B) is no exception. A block south of Wat Okaat, the rooms here are comfortable enough to rest your head though.

Most of the town's better Thai and Chinese restaurants are along the river on Th Sunthon Wijit. **Golden Giant Catfish** (☎ 0 1421 8491; 259 Th Sunthon Wijit; mains 25-80B; 🕙 breakfast, lunch & dinner) is housed in a rambling wooden house, run by two old matriarchs, with good views, plenty of character and some delicious Chinese specialties.

Getting There & Away

The **bus terminal** (Th Fuang Nakhon) is east of the centre. From here, buses head to Nong Khai (ordinary/air-con 109/171B, five hours, 10 daily); Udon Thani (ordinary/air-con 90/120B, four hours, hourly until 3pm) via

---

> ### BORDER CROSSING: INTO LAOS
>
> Foreigners are permitted to cross by ferry from Nakhon Phanom to Tha Khaek, a two-hour bus ride from Savannakhet. Stop by the immigration office, across the street from the Indochine souvenir market, for an exit stamp before boarding the ferry (50B) across the river. Once in Laos, you'll need to pay an entry tax of 50B. Mukdahan (see opposite), however, is a more convenient border crossing for Savannakhet.

Sakon Nakhon (ordinary/air-con 40/60B, 1½ hours); and Mukdahan (ordinary/air-con 40/72B, two hours, hourly until 5pm) via That Phanom (ordinary/air-con 21/38B, one hour). **999 VIP** (☎ 0 4251 1403), with offices at the bus terminal, has air-con (319B, 13 hours, five daily) and super VIP (635B, 13 hours, twice daily) buses to Bangkok. For information on crossing into Thailand from Tha Khaek, see above.

NONG KHAI

pop 61,500

Time ticks past slowly in charming Nong Khai and many travellers find themselves staying here longer than expected. Nestled on the banks of the Mekong River, Nong Khai is the perfect preparation for understanding the unhurried pace of Laos, the town's neighbour and cultural parent. The soaring Thai–Lao Friendship Bridge connects Nong Khai with the Lao capital, Vientiane, creating one of the busiest border points between the two countries and ensuring the town is a hot stop on the travellers' map of Thailand.

Information

There is no shortage of banks with ATMs in town, while cash machines remain a rarity in Laos. For a wealth of information on Nong Khai and the surrounding area, visit www.mutmee.net.

Hornbill Bookshop (☎ 0 4246 0272; Th Kaew Worawut; 🕙 10am-7pm) On the soi leading to Mut Mee Guest House, it has new and used English-language books, plus Internet access.

Immigration office (☎ 0 4241 2089; 🕙 8.30am-4.30pm Mon-Fri) On the road leading to the Thai-Lao Friendship Bridge, south of the bus stop. Visa extensions.

Nong Khai Hospital (☎ 1669; Th Meechai) For medical emergencies.

Post office (Th Meechai)

TAT office (☎ 0 4246 7164; ◯ 8.30am-4.30pm) In a row of shops next to the Thai–Lao Friendship Bridge checkpoint.

Tourist police (☎ 0 4224 0616, emergency ☎ 1155; Th Meechai)

Sights

Sala Kaewkoo (admission 10B; ◯ 7.30am-5.30pm) is a surreal spiritual and sculptural journey into the mind of a mystic Shaman of Lao descent. This park offers a potpourri of the Hindu and Buddhist pantheon of deities; and the immense statues offer some freaky photo opportunities. While the motivations for its 20-year construction were undoubtedly spiritual, the end result is a masterpiece of mysterious modern art for the casual browser. The gardens are in the grounds of Wat Khaek, 5km southeast of town. It is easily reached by bicycle from Nong Khai; Mut Mee Guest House distributes handy maps.

Talat Tha Sadet (Th Rimkhong) follows the river, obscuring the view with stalls selling crusty French baguettes, silks, souvenirs, kitchen utensils and, if you look really hard, possibly the kitchen sink.

In an effort to preserve an ancient art and stem the migration of young women to the bright lights of the big city, **Village Weaver Handicrafts** (☎ 0 4242 2651; Soi Jittapunya, Th Prajak), a nonprofit organisation, established a village weaving cooperative. It sells high-quality fabrics and ready-made clothes. The *mát-mìi* (hand-dyed) cotton is particularly fine here. Visitors are welcome to watch the weaving process.

Sleeping

Mut Mee Guest House (☎ 0 4246 0717; www.mutmee. net; 111/4 Th Kaew Worawut; dm 90B, r 320-600B; ◻) Overlooking the mighty Mekong, the Mut Mee is one of those rare guesthouses that has become a destination in itself. The dorms are bare bones, but the rooms are good value (especially those with shared bathrooms for 120B to 280B) and there is even one air-con indulgence in the owner's house. Retreat here for some reflection before or after an adventure in Laos. The pedestrian soi verges on a traveller ghetto, with bookshops, Internet access and yoga available. Mut Mee is a reliable spot for traveller info.

Sawasdee Guest House (☎ 0 4241 2502; Th Meechai; d 300B; ◻) A little slice of history, the Sawasdee is housed in a classic Indochine-era shophouse. The rooms don't quite match the romantic exterior, but fan rooms with shared bathroom are keenly priced at 100/140B for singles/doubles, and the air-con is a steal at 300B. This hotel has a pretty plant-filled courtyard leading to the small but clean rooms.

Chongkohn Guesthouse (☎ 0 4246 0548; 649 Th Rimkhong; s/d 100/160B) The sleepy riverfront road is lined with small guesthouses, among them the go-slow Chongkohn, a converted home with 2nd-floor rooms and shared bathrooms. Try and bag a room at the back for views of Laos.

Eating

The riverside restaurants are the most atmospheric in town and there is a whole cluster of them on Th Rimkhong.

Nong Naen Pla Phao (Th Rimkhong; dishes 50-150B; ◯ breakfast, lunch & dinner) This lively little Lao-style restaurant turns out delicious salt-baked *plaa châwn* (river fish) stuffed with herbs, plus *kài yâang*, *kaeng lao* (Lao-style bamboo-shoot soup), grilled sausage and grilled prawns. The dining area includes free river views.

Udom Rod Restaurant (☎ 0 4241 3555; Th Rimkhong; mains 30-80B; ◯ lunch & dinner) Another authentic eatery on the popular riverfront strip, Udom Rod draws a crowd around sundown to soak up the views. It's a rambling, creaky old place, but the food is temptingly priced.

Daeng Namnuang (☎ 0 4241 1961; Th Banthoengjit; mains 30-60B; ◯ breakfast, lunch & dinner; ◻) The house speciality at this little eatery is *năem neuang* – spicy pork sausages that are rolled up in rice wrappers with lettuce leaves, star fruit and veggies, and then dipped in various condiments. A hive of buzzing activity, the air-con sure helps on a hot day. It closes at 7pm.

For a bargain bite, check out the evening vendors on Th Prajak, who stoke up their woks each night between Soi Cheunjit and Th Hai Sok.

Also recommended:

Mut Mee Guest House (dishes 40-100B; ◯ breakfast, lunch & dinner) Best guesthouse food in town, including a healthy vegetarian selection and lots of company.

Thai Thai (cnr Th Prajak & Soi Vietnam; dishes 50-150B;

breakfast, lunch & dinner) Thai and Chinese standards, but at least it's open all night.

Drinking

Crawling along Th Rimkhong, the riverfront road, there is no shortage of *faràng*-style pubs with cocktail specials. For something a little more Thai, follow the road past Talat Tha Sadet (keep going, don't give up) until it delivers full views of the Mekong River. This is the domain of neon-lit restaurant-bars churning out dinner and drinks to a Thai crowd of all ages.

Mittraphaap Bar (Th Kaew Worawut) Welcome to the Wild East. This is a good introduction to Thai country bars if you have just arrived from Laos. Thais can't get enough of the cowboy thang and this bar offers live music, hard drinking and occasional wobbly dancing. On a full tank, you could wander over to the Thai-Lao Riverside Hotel disco to cut some moves on the dance floor.

Getting There & Away

Nong Khai's main **bus terminal** (☎ 0 4241 1612) is just off Th Prajak, by the Pho Chai market, about 1km from the riverfront guesthouses. Services link Nong Khai to Bangkok (air-con/VIP/Super VIP 273/351/545B, 11 hours, eight daily); Udon Thani's No 2 bus terminal (40B, one hour, hourly), a transfer point to other destinations; Khon Kaen (140B, four hours, regular departures); Si Chiangmai (22B, 1½ hours); and Loei (84B, six hours, frequent departures).

The **train station** (☎ 0 4246 4513; Hwy 212) is 1.5km from town, near the bus stop for transport to Laos. Nong Khai is at the end of the railway line that runs from Bangkok

---

BORDER CROSSING: INTO LAOS

Nong Khai is the most popular land border crossing between Thailand and Laos. Shuttle buses (10B, every 10 minutes from 6am to 9.30pm) depart for the border from a bus station near Nong Khai's train station at the corner of Hwy 212. The bridge is open from 6.30am to 9.30pm. To reach the bus stop from town, take a túk-túk (50B). Once across the bridge, it is 22km to Vientiane. There are also four direct buses a day to Vientiane from Nong Khai's bus terminal (80B, one hour).

---

through Khorat, Khon Kaen and Udon Thani. When making the long trip to or from Bangkok, most people opt for a sleeper train. There are two night trains out of Bangkok and one departing Nong Khai daily. Fares range from 318/183B for a 2nd-/3rd-class seat to 1117B for a first-class sleeper cabin.

NONG KHAI TO LOEI

You've hit all the highlights, now it is time to enjoy the easy life. Cradled by the meandering Mekong River, little villages slumber in the shade of Laos' voluptuous hills. With a visit to **Si Chiangmai**, **Sangkhom**, **Pak Chom** or **Chiang Khan**, the day's most pressing business is to stroll the riverside road with no particular destination in mind. The crowds usually hurry on to more famous spots, leaving the family guesthouses quiet, friendly and cheap (around 100B).

LOEI & AROUND

Loei is little more than a brief base to prepare your adventures into the more remote pockets of the country beyond. **Phu Kradung National Park** (☎ 0 4287 1333; reserve@dnp.go.th; admission 200B; 8.30am-4.30pm Oct-Jun), about 75km to the south, encloses a bell-shaped mountain blessed with unhindered sunrise and sunset views. The climb to the summit takes about four hours if you're in shape. Being the northeast's version of a 'spring break' destination, the park fills up with guitar-toting college students during school holidays and weekends.

Dan Sai's three-day **Spirit Festival**, usually in June, is a curious cross between the drunken revelry of Carnival and the spooky imagery of Halloween. On the second day of the festival, villagers don elaborate masks to transform themselves into ghosts, and down shots of *lâo khǎo* (rice whisky) to get themselves drunk. The colourful and rowdy group then parades through town to the local temple for more processing until they stagger home to sleep it off. Dan Sai is 80km west of Loei.

Sleeping & Eating

LOEI

Friendship Guest House (☎ 0 4283 2408; Th Charoenrat; d 150B) The only real guesthouse in town, Friendship has the cheapest digs around, but the rooms are basic with a capital B and bathrooms are shared.

Sun Palace Hotel (☎ 0 4281 5714; Th Charoenrat; d 330-400B; 🗙) It is worth shelling out some shekels for the Sun Palace, which offers meticulously clean rooms, hot water and satellite TV. Near the main post office, the hotel is midway between town and the bus station.

Charcoal Restaurant (☎ 0 4281 5675; Th Nok Kaew; mains 30-90B; 🕒 lunch & dinner) Locals flock in droves after dark and the beers go down well amid a whirlwind of eager servers. The spicy Thai dishes come in generous portions and there's a limited English-language menu.

Also worth seeking out are the **night market** (cnr Th Ruamjai & Th Charoenrat), for cheap eats and local specialities like *khài pîng* (toasted eggs), and the morning vendors, selling *kha-nŏm pang mǔu* (mini-baguette pork sandwiches).

PHU KRADUNG NATIONAL PARK

A **visitors centre** (☎ 0 2562 0760; 🕒 7am-3pm) at the base of the mountain distributes detailed maps and rents **tents** (100B) and **A-frame huts** (200B). Amazing but true, after walking for hours you will find a friendly vendor at the top of the mountain eager to flog you food; life at the top is pricey, but it beats hauling it up the mountain yourself.

DAN SAI

Few people stop in Dan Sai outside the festival season and so the accommodation options availiable are extremely limited within the town itself. The **information centre** (☎ 0 4289 1094; Th Kaew Asa; 🕒 8am-5pm Mon-Fri) can arrange basic homestay accommodation from 100B per person.

Getting There & Around

Loei **bus station** (Highway 201) is roughly 500m west of the town centre; hired transport to get you into town costs about 5B per person or 30B for a charter. Routes include Bangkok's Northern & Northeastern Bus Terminal (air-con 250B to 350B, 10 hours), Udon Thani (ordinary/air-con 60/110B, four hours, five daily) and Nong Khai (ordinary 84B, six hours, four daily).

To get youself to Phu Kradung National Park from the Loei bus station, take a Khon Kaen–bound bus (35B, 1½ hours, every half-hour from 6am until 6.30pm) to the town of Phu Kradung. From there, hop on a săwngthăew (10B) to the visitors centre at the base of the mountain, 7km away.

There is no admission after 3pm. The last bus back to Loei leaves around 6pm.

Buses between Loei and Dan Sai (45B, two hours) depart almost hourly during the day.

UDON THANI & AROUND
pop 227,200

Udon Thani is never going to draw visitors in big numbers, with the charms of Nong Khai to the north and the student-driven sophistication of Khon Kaen to the south. Sprawling Udon Thani is too big to be charming and too conservative to be cultured. It boomed on the back of the Vietnam War, exploding into life as US air bases opened nearby. These days, with the bases closed, it feels a little like the city is still searching for something to fill the vacuum.

Why make the trip? For skeletons of the past. Fifty kilometres east, **Ban Chiang** is one of the earliest prehistoric cultures known in Southeast Asia, and the site's **excavation pit** (at Wat Pho Si Nai; admission 30B; 🕒 8.30am-5pm) displays 52 human skeletons, in whole or in part. More artefacts can be viewed at Ban Chiang's **national museum** (admission 30B; 🕒 9am-4.30pm).

Information
Banks are spread liberally across town.
Aek Udon International Hospital (☎ 0 4234 2555; www.aekudon.com; 555/5 Th Pho Si)
Post office (Th Wattananuwong)
T & A Net Corner (☎ 0 4232 9123; 124/8-9 Th Sri Suk; 🕒 11am-10pm) Internet access.
TAT office (☎ 0 4232 5406; Th Thesa; 🕒 8.30am-4.30pm)
Tourist police (☎ 0 4224 0616, emergency ☎ 1155; Th Thesa) Next to the TAT office.

Sleeping & Eating
Accommodation in Udon Thani is entirely in high-rise hotels of varying quality. The best of the bunch includes **Chai Porn** (☎ 0 4222 1913; 209-211 Th Mak Khaeng; d 180-250B; 🗙), a friendly spot with spartan rooms, and **King's Hotel** (☎ 0 4222 1634; Th Pho Si; r 190-200B), a Vietnam War–era hangover which offers cheap fan rooms.

Clinging to the banks of the Nong Prajak reservoir, **Rabiang Phatchani** (Th Suphakit Janya; mains 30-80B; 🕒 lunch & dinner) whips up a sorted selection of local dishes in simple surrounds. Head here for sundown when the views look best.

The big draw at **Steve's Bar** (☎ 0 4224 4523; www.stevesbarudon.com; 234/25 Th Prajak Silpakorn; ☻ lunch & dinner) is the big Sunday roast, best served in front of English Premiership football, and shown on a very impressive 50-inch screen.

Getting There & Away

Thai Airways International (THAI; www.thaiair.com) and **Nok Air** (www.nokair.co.th) have several daily flights to Bangkok. **Air Asia** (☎ 0 2515 9999; www.airasia.com) connects Udon twice daily with Bangkok.

Udon has two bus stations. **Bus terminal No 1** (off Th Sai Uthit), near the Charoen Hotel in the southeastern part of town, serves Bangkok (air-con/VIP 251/500B, 10 hours, hourly), Khon Kaen (air-con 110B, 2½ hours, hourly) and Khorat (air-con 142B, 4½ hours).

Bus terminal No 2 (near Th Pho Si & Hwy 201) is on the northwestern outskirts of the city next to the highway and serves Loei (ordinary/air-con 60/110B, four hours, five daily) and Nong Khai (40B, one hour, hourly).

To reach Ban Chiang, take a sǎwngthǎew from the morning market on Th Pho Si to Ban Chiang (25B, 40 minutes); they run from late morning until around 3.45pm. Returning to Udon Thani from Ban Chiang, sǎwngthǎew stop running at 10.30am! Instead, take a túk-túk (50B) to the highway at Ban Pulu, and flag a bus on the Sakon Nakhon–Udon Thani route.

Trains from Udon Thani's **train station** (east end of Th Prajak Silpkorn) travel to Bangkok (1st/2nd/3rd class 459/220/95B, plus applicable sleeper chargers), taking nine or so hours. Take a sleeper for this long trip.

STRING-TYING CEREMONY

To occupy yourself on those long, boring bus rides, do a survey of Thais wearing thin yellow or white strings round their wrists. In rural villages in Isan, elders and family members assemble to tie *bai sǐi* (sacred thread) as a bon voyage measure. The strings act as leashes for important guardian spirits and ensure safety during a trip. Some people believe that the strings must fall off naturally rather than be cut off, but this can take weeks, turning sacred thread into stinky thread.

Nong Khai (3rd class 11B, one hour) is also accessible by train.

KHON KAEN

pop 145,300

It's not the big cities that draw visitors to Isan, but Khon Kaen might just be the exception thanks to a vibrant energy that is shifting the skyline and diversifying the dining scene. Home to the northeast's largest university, the city is youthful, educated and on the move. It also makes a sensible base for exploring nearby silk-weaving villages and scattered Khmer ruins, and is a gateway to the northeast from Phitsanulok and Sukhothai.

The town's only tourist attraction is the well-curated **Khon Kaen National Museum** (☎ 0 4324 2129; Th Lang Sunratchakan; admission 30B; ☻ 9am-noon & 1-5pm Wed-Sun), which features ancient art and artefacts.

Information

It's hard to walk around Khon Kaen without bumping into an ATM or bank.

Internet (Th Si Chan; per hr 15B; ☻ 10am-midnight) Near the Sofitel Hotel.

Khon Kaen Ram Hospital (☎ 0 4333 3900; Th Si Chan)

Lao consulate (☎ 0 4324 2856; 191/102-3 Th Prachasamoson) Southeast of the city centre, it issues 30-day visas for Laos in three days. Get one on arrival instead!

Post office (cnr Th Si Chan & Th Klang Meuang)

TAT office (☎ 0 4324 4498; 15/5 Th Prachasamoson; ☻ 8.30am-4.30pm)

Tourist police (☎ 0 4323 6937, emergency ☎ 1155; Th Prachasamoson) Next door to TAT.

Vietnamese consulate (☎ 0 4324 2190; 65/6 Th Chatapadung) Issues visas in three days.

Festivals & Events

Khon Kaen's biggest annual event is the **silk and phùuk sìaw festival**, which runs over a period of 12 days and nights from late November to early December. Centred on Ratchadanuson Park and the Provincial Hall, the festival celebrates the planting of the mulberry tree, which is an essential step in the production of silk. Also considered particularly important is *phùuk sìaw* (friend-bonding), a reference to the *bai sǐi* ceremony in which sacred threads are tied round one's wrists to give spiritual protection; see the boxed text, left. Music, folk dancing and food, and all things Isan, are major highlights.

Sleeping & Eating

Si Monkon (☎ 0 4323 7939; 61-67 Th Klang Meuang; r 120-200B; ✖) This wooden pad has some ramshackle charm, but the walls are thin for light sleepers. Air-con is available for 300B.

Saen Samran Hotel (☎ 0 4323 9611; 55-59 Th Klang Meuang; s/d 150/200B; ✖) Reputedly Khon Kaen's oldest hotel (not always a good claim to fame), Saen Samran is an ageing wooden building with a certain charm and character. Fan rooms are clean and air-con kicks in at 350B.

First Choice (☎ 0 4333 3352; 18/8 Th Phimphaseut; r 150-200B; ✖) On its way to becoming the town's first backpacker hostel, the rooms are spartan but certainly cheap. Downstairs is a traveller-friendly eatery, serving the usual selection of shakes and snacks.

Em Oht (Th Klang Meuang; dishes 30-50B; ⚇ breakfast, lunch & dinner) Em Oht is a popular place to sample some Isan fare, including the signature breakfast: *khài kàthá* (eggs served in a pan with local sausages) with a cup of real coffee to wash it down.

Heuan Lao (☎ 0 4324 7202; 39 Th Phimphaseut; mains 40-140B; ⚇ lunch & dinner; ✖) Housed in an elegant old wooden villa, this restaurant is piled with antique bric-a-brac and serves mouthwatering Thai and Isan dishes. There's a verdant garden for alfresco dining or a dose of air-con to hide away in. It's open till midnight. No roman-script sign.

Well worth a visit is Khon Kaen's lively **night market** (Th Reun Rom), the heart and soul of budget dining in town. Find it next to the air-con bus station, between Th Klang Meuang and Th Na Meuang.

Shopping

Khon Kaen is a good place to buy handcrafted Isan goods such as *mát-mìi* cotton and silk, silverwork and basketry. **PK Prathamakhan Local Goods Center** (☎ 0 4322 4080; 79/2-3 Th Reun Rom), just west of Th Na Meuang, is a local handicraft centre with a small museum. Also good are **Rin Mai Thai** (☎ 0 4322 1042; 412 Th Na Meuang) and **Klum Phrae Phan** (☎ 0 4333 7216; 131/193 Th Chatapadung), the latter run by the Handicraft Centre for Northeastern Women's Development.

Getting There & Away

The **airport** (☎ 0 4323 6523/8835; off Hwy 12) is a few kilometres west of the city centre. **Thai Airways International** (THAI; ☎ 0 4322 7701;

www.thaiair.com; Sofitel Hotel, 9/9 Prachasumran) flies three times daily between Bangkok and Khon Kaen. **Air Asia** (☎ 0 2515 9999; www.airasia .com) flies daily to and from Bangkok.

Khon Kaen has two bus stations: the **ordinary bus terminal** (Th Prachasamoson) is a five-minute walk northwest of Th Klang Muang, while the **air-con bus terminal** (Th Klang Meuang) is in the town centre near the night market.

Buses travel to and from Bangkok (aircon 259B, seven hours, every half-hour from 7am to 11pm), Chiang Mai (air-con 394B, 12 hours, 8pm and 9pm), Khorat (ordinary 70B, three hours) and Nong Khai (air-con 140B, four hours, six daily).

Khon Kaen is on the Bangkok–Khorat–Udon Thani railway line, but buses are much faster along this section. Track down information from Khon Kaen **railway station** (☎ 0 4322 1112).

EAST COAST

The ideal jaunt from jostling Bangkok, Thailand's east coast is a popular and increasingly upmarket stretch favoured for its convenience to the capital. For pure escapism, the more stunning and affordable southern destinations win out, but the east coast's charms (candle-lit beach dining, healthy strips of sand and smooth transfers) mean it's always busy.

KO SAMET

Every thriving metropolis should have a Ko Samet nearby – somewhere close enough for a quick escape, yet worlds away for the urbanite to hang loose. A favourite weekend getaway for young Thais, Ko Samet is equally popular with travellers getting their last sun and sand before being whisked home. While there's no comparison with its southern counterparts, low-key Ko Samet is perfect for a couple of days of cheery abandonment, and enjoys better weather during the rainy season than many islands. There's a massage to be had under every shady tree; sarong sellers ply the beach and lobstertanned tourists frolic. It's been a **national park** (admission 200B) since 1981, and there are walking trails all the way to the southern tip of the island, as well as a few cross-island trails, but it does have problems with litter and overcrowding.

Information

Internet (Ao Hin Khok; per min 2B; ☺ 9am-midnight)
Internet access and international calls; it's between Samed
Grand View Resort and Reggae Pub & Karaoke.

Ko Samet Health Centre (☎ 0 3864 4123;
2/2 Moo 4 Phe Mang Rayong; ☺ 8.30am-4.30pm)
For minor medical problems.

Siam City Bank (Th Nadaan) There are no banks on
Ko Samet, but this ATM is located at the 7-Eleven near
the national park entrance. There's another ATM at the
7-Eleven near the ferry.

Tourist information (☎ 0 3864 4240;
☺ 7am-midnight) Conveniently located near the pier.

Sleeping & Eating

In the northeast part of the island, Ao Hin
Khok and Ao Phai (*ao* means 'bay') is the
main place for seafood-eating, novel-reading
and email-sending. The further south you
go, the more Thai and isolated it becomes.

Naga Bungalows (Ao Hin Khok; d 700B; ☐ ☒)
Has a mish-mash of bamboo and gaudy
concrete bungalows, with the shared bathroom versions going for 350B. Naga has a
bakery (get 'em while they're fresh!), billiards table, book exchange and nightly
DVD flicks. On Saturdays from 6pm to
9.30pm, there's a vegetarian buffet (120B
per person). Reputedly, the poste restante
service is not the most reliable.

Tok's Little Hut (☎ 0 3864 4072; Ao Hin Khok;
d 300-350B) Solid, albeit scruffy, pale blue
wooden huts. Bungalows one to 10 are the
best bet. The bar's 'wasted nights' leave little
to the imagination.

Jep's Bungalows (☎ 0 3864 4112; Ao Hin Khok;
www.jepbungalow.com; d 600B) Next door to Tok's,
it has no-frills bungalows climbing up a hill.
Its shaded restaurant is a smart operation –
look for the star paper lanterns. Cheaper
rooms (400B) share bathrooms.

Silver Sand Resort & Restaurant (☎ 0 3864 4074;
www.silversandresort.com; Ao Phai; d from 400B; ☒)
This place has had a major overhaul in
recent years and its simple concrete bungalows now look like poor cousins compared with the Cape Cod–style versions.
There's a juice, crêpe and espresso bar.
It can get busy here, especially when it's
'full moon party' time, and bucket cocktail
concoctions reign.

Tub Tim Resort (☎ 0 3864 4025; tubtimresort@yahoo
.com; 13/15 Moo 4, Tumbol Phe, Ao Phutsa; d from 500B;
☒) Tub Tim has been running for 20 years
and remains as popular as ever. Thatched

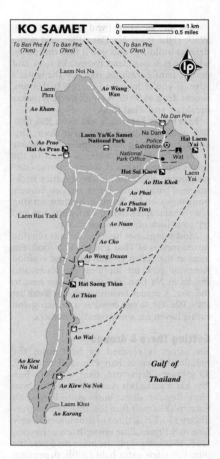

KO SAMET

bungalows are set over an expansive area.
Newer, pricier bungalows are positioned
closest to the beach. The restaurant is an
all-round pleaser.

Nuan Bungalows (Ao Nuan; d from 500B) A quieter option suited to nature-lovers, this is
the sole occupant of private Nuan beach.
Charming castaway-style bungalows, with
mosquito nets and shared bathrooms, are
tucked amid gardens and rocky outcrops.
There's a bohemian restaurant with outdoor
seating and good vegetarian options.

AO WIANG WAN

Get away from the tourist ghetto and consider quiet and pretty Ao Wiang Wan in the
island's north as a base.

THAILAND

Lung Ritt Bungalow (☎ 0 3864 4032; d 1000B) Walk right from Na Dam Pier past some derelict buildings and you'll find this place, which has some clean rooms, in twin and double configurations, right by the water's edge. If you're happy to share a bathroom, rooms drop to 500B. A small kitchen makes breakfast and Thai food.

Baan Praguy Kaew (☎ 0 9603 2609; s 200B, d300-500B, tw 800B) Located right next door, this equally appealing and friendly guesthouse is on stilts over the water – listen to the waves lapping below. Cheaper rooms (single/double 200/300B) share the nice rock-inspired bathrooms. There are two homely bungalows and a humble kitchen serving tasty Thai staples. Borrow a fishing rod and try your luck off the rickety jetty.

Most bungalows have restaurants offering mixed menus of Thai and traveller food. Eat local at the cheap noodle bars and seafood joints or pick up supplies like water and snacks in Na Dan, the small village next to the pier. A reader recommends **Bay Watch Bar** (☎ 0 1826 7834; Ao Vong Duean) as a drinking and eating haven for world-weary travellers.

Getting There & Around
Ko Samet is reached by boat from the mainland town of Ban Phe (50B one way, 45 minutes, departures 6am to 6pm). Ban Phe has a small bus station beyond the boat piers. Regular, direct buses go to Bangkok's Eastern (Ekamai) Bus Terminal (air-con/ordinary 150/125B, three to four hours, hourly 5am to 8.30pm). Blue săwngthăew to Rayong (15B, 45 minutes) ply the main road near the pier. For a few extra baht (200B, depending on the number of people) private boat charters can drop you elsewhere on the island.

Săwngthăew on the island cost from 10B to 100B per person, depending on how far you're going and the number of passengers. From the pier, reaching some locations furthest south can cost 300B to 500B if there are only one to two people travelling.

CHANTHABURI & TRAT
There's an earthiness about these two provincial towns, which are enveloped by palm trees and plantations. While travellers use them mostly for swift connections to Ko Chang or the Cambodian border, if you stop to catch your breath in sleepy Trat, you'll get a feel for small-town living. East

of Trat, as Thailand merges with Cambodia, a number of little-known beaches, including **Hat Sai Si Ngoen**, **Hat Sai Kaew**, **Hat Thap Thim** and **Hat Ban Cheun**, are worth a look.

Information
In Trat, **Tratosphere Bookshop** (23 Th Kluarimklong; books 70-200B; ☀ 8am-10pm), run by a friendly Frenchman, is a handy place to pick up your next read or get travel tips on the area.

Sleeping & Eating
Ban Jaidee Guesthouse (☎ 0 3952 0678; 67-69 Chaimongkol, Trat; d 120-150B) A traditional Thai place, this is the best pad in town with glossy polished floors, lounge area, clean shared bathrooms with hot water, and welcoming staff. Breakfast is available.

Pop Guest House (☎ 0 3951 2392; 1/1 Th Thana Charoen, Trat; d 250-400B; 🖵) South of all the hubbub in and out of Trat, Pop has sparkly newer abodes, garden-fringed bamboo bungalows, outdoor dining pavilions and transfer bookings. Cheaper singles/doubles with shared bathroom go for 80/120B. The restaurant here serves dishes from 40B to 70B.

Friendly Guest House (☎ 0 3952 4053; 106 Th Lak Meuang, Trat; s/d 60/100B) Friendly is just that. Small rooms have wafer-thin walls and rock-hard beds, and bathrooms are shared.

Trat's municipal market is in the centre of town and will satisfy your nutritional needs cheaply. On the Trat river, northeast of town, is a smaller night market that sells seafood.

Getting There & Away
Bangkok Airways (in Bangkok ☎ 0 2265 5555; www.bangkokair.com) has two daily flights to Trat (around 1800B, 50 minutes); the airport is 40km from town and a taxi to or from the airport will cost around 300B (depending on how many people are catching a ride).

Chanthaburi has the larger **bus station** (Th Saritidet), with connections to Khorat (air-con 260B, seven hours), Aranya Prathet (air-con 200B, eight hours) and east coast towns. Buses going to Bangkok's Eastern (Ekamai) Bus Terminal stop in Chanthaburi en route to Trat (air-con/ordinary 221/170B, five to six hours, six departures daily from 6.30am to 5.30pm). Between Chanthaburi and Trat, ordinary buses (60B, 1½ hours) and share taxis (100B) are also happy to have you.

THAILAND

BORDER CROSSINGS: INTO CAMBODIA

Hat Lek to Krong Koh Kong

You have two transport options for getting to the Cambodian border from Trat. The most direct way is to take an air-con minibus from Trat to the border town of Hat Lek (100B, one hour, departures every hour, 6am to 6pm), which leaves Trat's Th Sukhumvit in front of the municipal market. Motorcycles and taxis are available from Hat Lek across the border to Krong Koh Kong (50B). From Krong Koh Kong, there is only one boat per day to Sihanoukville (600B, four to five hours, departing at 8am). If you want to get from Trat to Sihanoukville in one day, you should be on the 6am minibus from Trat to Hat Lek and at the border with passport in hand as soon as it opens at 7am. This border crossing closes at 5pm.

Another alternative for reaching the border is to take a blue sǎwngthǎew or share taxi (ordinary/chartered 35/400B, 45 minutes) from Trat to Khlong Yai. You can find transport at the back of Trat's municipal market. From Khlong Yai, take another sǎwngthǎew to Hat Lek (ordinary/chartered 30/200B, 16km); motorcycle taxis also make this journey (50B).

Chanthaburi to Pailin

Foreigners can cross the border from Daun Lem in Thailand to Pruhm in Cambodia. To travel this way independently, first take a minibus from Chanthaburi to Daun Lem (100B, 1½ hours). Cross the border and then arrange a share taxi into Pailin (200B for the whole car, 50B per person). From Pailin it is possible to connect with Battambang (200B, four hours) by share taxi on a real joker of a road.

To get to Ko Chang from Trat, take a sǎwngthǎew (30B) to the pier in the village of Laem Ngop (10 to 20 minutes). Scores of sǎwngthǎew line Trat's main road, fishing for customers; keep shopping if you're quoted 'charter' prices (150B).

Transport options for crossing over the border into Cambodia are detailed in the boxed text, above.

KO CHANG

Just a few years back, Ko Chang was an outpost near 'war-torn' Cambodia where hippies revelled in some of Southeast Asia's best untamed forests and isolated coast. Then the world caught up.

Ko Chang has lost its virginity – its virgin forest that is. This **national park** (admission 200B) was once undeveloped and lacking modern amenities like 24-hour electricity, souvenir stands and ATMs. Under the government's new plan for the island, backpackers are *out* and luxury tourists are *in*: spiffy air-con set-ups are swiftly replacing cheap bungalows. But if you fancy spending your time in Ko Chang trekking to mountainous waterfalls or catching dazzling views while whizzing by on a motorbike, don't despair, this sprawling island still fits the bill.

Most of the development of Ko Chang is located on the west coast, although the east coast is sure to catch up sometime very soon. Ferries arrive and depart from the mainland at the northern tip of the island. Ban Bang Bao is a traditional fishing village in the south built on a series of piers over the water.

Information

Internet cafés are plentiful on the island and access charges average 2B per minute.

Ko Chang Hospital (☎ 0 3958 6131; Ban Dan Mai) Near the police headquarters.

Police (☎ 0 3958 6191; Ban Dan Mai) There are also police based near KC Grande Resort.

Post office (🕙 9am-4.30pm Mon-Fri) Near the ferry terminal at Ban Khlong Son.

Siam Commercial Bank (Hat Sai Khao; 🕙 8.30am-3.30pm) Also has an exchange window that stays open until 8pm.

Sleeping & Eating

KC Grande Resort (☎ 0 3955 1199; www.kckohchang.com; d 300-450B) Starting at the northern end of the island at pretty Hat Sai Khao (White Sand Beach), KC is one of the island's originals with plenty of decent, closely positioned bamboo bungalows, resort facilities and a busy restaurant.

Chaichet Bungalows (☎ 0 3955 1070; www
.kochangchaichet.com; Ao Khlong Phrao; d 600B; ✖)
Craving some comfort and solitude?
Further south, Chaichet has clean concrete bungalows with ocean views on a
coconut-shaped bay ringed by brooding
mountains. There's a great dining area set
among Chaichet Bungalows' mangroves,
serving dishes from 30B to 200B. Couples
will love this place.

Bang Bao Cliff Cottages (☎ 0 1864 1471; Bang
Bao; d 200B) Set on the far side of the cove
from Bang Bao fishing village, play cubby-
house at this secluded spot, which has rustic
bungalows (with shared bathrooms) built
on a shady hillside – some of which have
superb views. The guesthouse's chilled-out
restaurant overlooks a rocky cove.

Nature Beach Resort (☎ 0 3955 8027;
d 400-600B) Set on Ko Chang's Hat Tha Nam
(Lonely Beach), this resort boasts good-
looking bungalows and a classy Mediterranean chic meets Thai-style restaurant
(dishes 45B to 55B).

Tree House Lodge (www.treehouse-kohchang.de;
d 150-250B; dishes 45-70B) If you're after a lazy,
village-like atmosphere, the Tree House
Lodge will please for its seclusion and simple stilt bungalows. There's a great deck
where you can feast on Indian dahl or kick
back with a book. It's often full.

Menus at all the bungalows on Ko Chang
are pretty similar. There are several small
eateries (dishes 40B) along the eastern side
of the main road in Hat Sai Khao.

Also worth trying out are the seafood
restaurants located on the pier at Ban
Bang Bao, including **Chow Lay** (☎ 0 1917 9084;
seafood priced by weight; ✖ lunch & dinner), or get
your hippy shakes at the **Chai Shop** (☎ 0 6842
8568; shakes 35B). The nearby **Bangbao Delight
Bakery Cafe** (takeaways 15-25B) makes a swag of
homemade goodies to feed your face with,
including doughnuts.

Getting There & Around

From the pier in Laem Ngop, boats go
to Ko Chang (100B return, one hour, departures hourly) from 7am to 5pm. The
schedule is reduced to about every two
hours in the low season. From Ko Chang's
pier (either Tha Dan Kao or Ao Sapparot),
sǎwngthǎew will be waiting to take you to
any of the various beaches along the west
coast (30B to 80B).

SOUTHERN THAILAND

Beach lovers unite! Any fully fledged itinerary through Southeast Asia will surely feature southern Thailand's dreamy beaches, renowned islands and world-class dive sites.

A thin ribbon of land divides the Gulf of
Thailand to the east from the sun-drenched
Andaman Sea in the west. On either side are
famous islands and beaches where residents
of northern latitudes escape cruel winters.
In southern Thailand, you're not a Londoner or Swede but that universal species:
sunworshipper.

Everyone comes here in search of paradise: consider coming here outside the peak
season (November to April) and you'll have
a better chance of finding it footprint-free.

The Gulf Coast island standouts (Ko Tao,
Ko Pha-Ngan and Ko Samui) are affordable
with simple beachfront bungalows attracting hammock heroes wanting to go a deeper
shade of brown. Along the way, there's a
string of lesser-known pit stops including
Cha-am and friendly Prachuap Khiri Khan.

The Andaman Sea coast is the stuff of
dreams. Phuket, the country's largest, most
populous and most visited island, is Hollywood on the Andaman. Pinch yourself at the
watery wonders of Ko Phi Phi, marvel at Krabi's sculpted limestone mountains, admire
interesting architecture in old Phuket town
or chill out on cloud nine in Ko Lanta.

Deeper south the geography is flanked by
glossy palm trees and rubber plantations.
It's pure cultural exchange here: Thai-ness
fuses with Malay, Indian and Chinese influences in an intoxicating stir-fry of colour,
culture and tradition. The brightly coloured
wats are soon outnumbered by fortresslike
mosques. Southern Thais speak a dialect
that confounds even visitors from other
Thai regions. Diction is short and fast and
the clipped tones fly into the outer regions
of intelligibility. In the provinces nearest
Malaysia, many Thai Muslims speak Yawi,
an old Malay dialect.

Following the tragic tsunami of December 2004, which wreaked despair and destruction along the region's Andaman coast
(see p803), southern Thai hospitality is
more welcoming than ever. Beware: you're
dealing with a potential lifelong addiction
once you delve south.

CHA-AM

pop 48,600

A low-key seaside town located 40km south of Phetburi, Cha-am specialises in old-fashioned Thai fun: jet skis pull banana boats with teams of laughing Thai students behind, shop vendors sport tropical shirts, fully clothed locals float on inner tubes, and families scoot around on tricycles. Whereas Hua Hin, 26km further south, could be described as a pseudosophisticated elder sibling, Cha-am is more like the coy teenager.

Sleeping & Eating

Cha-am is a big weekend destination, so from Friday to Sunday expect a 20% to 50% increase on most prices listed here. Accommodation on Th Ruamjit is opposite the casuarina-lined waterfront promenade. There are no grass huts in sight.

Nirundorn Resort (☎ 0 3247 1038; 247/7 Th Ruamjit; d 250-300B; ✷) Housed in a modern building, the clean, monotone rooms have cable TV and fridge, while cheaper rooms (200B) share bathrooms. Breakfast is served downstairs (70B); caffeine addicts will be chuffed to find cappuccino.

Memory House (☎ 0 3247 2100; cha_ammemory@yahoo.com; 200 Th Ruamjit; d from 300B; ✷) In the same vein as Nirundorn, this guesthouse has comfortable rooms with hot water, cable TV and fridge. Free maps of the town are available here.

Jolly & Jumper (☎ 0 3243 3887, 0 7970 4367; www.jolly-jumper.info; 274/2-3 Th Ruamjit; s/d from 150/300B; ✷) This is a clean place run by an eccentric Dutch duo. Rooms are large with frilly furnishings. More expensive rooms come with air-con. Satisfy steak cravings (150B to 200B) at the popular restaurant and bar filled with all things elephant-related. Dishes here are 60B to 200B.

Anantachai Guesthouse (☎ 0 3243 3396; 235/8-9 Th Ruamjit; d from 300B; ✷) The rooms at this corner-side hotel are ordinary with soft beds. At least the rooms at the front feature sea views; all of them have TV. There's a cheap restaurant on the ground floor (dishes from 25B).

Poom Restaurant (☎ 0 3247 1036; 274/1 Th Ruamjit; dishes 40-350B) Poom has a large outdoor patio and specialises in seafood; it's very popular among visiting Thais.

Getting There & Away

Most ordinary and air-con buses stop in the town centre on Phetkasem Hwy. Some private air-con buses to and from Bangkok conveniently go all the way to the beach, stopping at a small bus station a few hundred metres south of the Th Narathip intersection.

The frequent bus services going to and from Cha-am include Bangkok (air-con/ordinary 113/95B, three hours), Phetburi (ordinary 25B, 40 minutes) and Hua Hin (ordinary 20B, 30 minutes).

The **train station** (Th Narathip) is inland, west of Phetkasem Hwy and a 20B motorcycle ride from the beach. There are daily services to Cha-am from three stations in Bangkok: Hualamphong (3.50pm), Sam Sen (9.27am) and Thonburi (7.15am, 1.30pm and 7.05pm). Tickets cost from 80B to 193B. Cha-am isn't listed on the English-language train schedule.

HUA HIN

pop 48,700

Most likely to win the tidiest town award, sweet-as-pie Hua Hin, 230km from Bangkok, is a sanitised version of Thailand for the masses. The longtime retreat of Thai

---

SOUTHERN CUISINE

The dishes of southern Thai are as flamboyant and seductive as its award-winning beaches. Blessed by the bounty of the sea and the region's abundant rainfall, southern cuisine is effortlessly delicious and morbidly spicy. Dishes like *khâo mòk kài* (chicken biryani) and other standard curries are a brilliant yellow colour (thanks to the liberal use of turmeric), and represent a geographic map of the region's Chinese, Malay and Indian influences. Of Chinese-Malay heritage, *khanŏm jiin nâam yaa* is a dish of thin noodles doused in a fish curry sauce. A large tray of green vegetables to accompany the dish is prominently displayed at the communal table – a helpful signal to the illiterate traveller.

Malay-style *rotii kaeng* is a fluffy flat bread served with a curry dip; order another if you like to watch the hooded Muslim women slap the dough into a gossamer circle, then toss it into a spitting wok.

royalty, it feels like the town is on constant alert for the King himself, presenting clean streetscapes and groomed beaches. Chock-a-block with modern restaurants, tailors, masseurs and souvenir shops, it's probably the easiest and safest southern Thai coastal retreat, favoured by families and oldies who frequent the colossal beachfront resorts hogging the nicest stretches of sand. Nonetheless, this quiet spot possesses steady weather and a certain finesse – just like Thai cuisine minus the spice.

Sleeping

Accommodation in Hua Hin tends to be a bit on the expensive side due to its proximity to Bangkok.

Pattana Guest House (☎ 0 3251 3393; huahin pattana@hotmail.com; 52 Th Naresdamri; d 200-525B) Go for comfort at Pattana, the town's most intimate option. Located down a narrow alley, Pattana has cosy rooms in a secure converted teak house surrounded by a peaceful garden.

Memory (☎ 0 3251 1816; 108 Th Naresdamri; s/d from 150/200B; 🏠) You forfeit water views here, but you gain spiffy rooms and cheap rates. Tightwads rejoice!

All Nations Guest House (☎ 0 3251 2747; 10-10/1 Th Dechanuchit; s/d from 150/250B; 🏠) Owned by a very friendly Canadian-Thai couple, this place is popular with backpackers. The rooms are clean and have shared bathrooms. Downstairs is an open-air restaurant and bar with a pool table.

Fulay (☎ 0 3251 3145; www.fulay-huahin.com; 110/1 Th Naresdamri; s/d from 300/400B; 🏠) Clean and breezy, Fulay is a touch reminiscent of England's Brighton Beach, with midrange, moderate-sized rooms that open out to a jetty over the water. The big score is the room at the far end of the strip.

Euro Hua-Hin City Hotel (☎ 0 3251 3130; euro _huahinhotel@yahoo.com; 5/15 Th Srasong; d & tw with air-con 800B; 🏠) This is actually a hostel and a super-clean one at that, just a stone's throw from the train station. Cheap fan rooms start from 130B.

Au-Sa Guesthouse (☎ 0 3253 0363; 5/8 Th Aumnuaysin; d 600B; 🏠) Gleams with cleanliness, and all rooms have TV and fridge.

Eating & Drinking

Hua Hin is noted for seafood, especially *plaa mèuk* (squid), *puu* (crab) and *hǎwy* (clams).

In the centre of town, the colourful **Chatchai Market** (Th Phetkasem & Th Dechanuchit) feeds hordes of hungry visitors night and day. At the **night market** (cnr Th Dechanuchit & Th Phetkasem), there's a smorgasbord of food stalls equipped with well-seasoned woks and display cases packed with fruits of the sea. It's barely possible to break 100B for a bellyful of feasting.

Monsoon Restaurant & Bar (☎ 0 3253 1062; monsoon@cscoms.com; 62 Th Naretdamri; dishes 100-350B, tapas 65-110B; 🕐 lunch & dinner) Step back into 1920s Thailand at stylish Monsoon. You might not be able to afford to pay attention to the menu, but a drink (perhaps a 'Hua Hin Lover'?) perched at the chic bar is a perfect after-dinner mint.

For more serious drinkers, check out the gaudy bars on Soi Bintaban, off Th Naretdamri.

Getting There & Around

Buses to Bangkok (air-con 128B, three hours, departures hourly) leave from next to the Siripetchkasem Hotel.

All other buses leave from the regular **bus station** (Th Liap Thang Rot Fai), 400m from the train station. Buses travel to/from Prachuap Khiri Khan (ordinary 50B, two hours, frequent departures daily between 6.30am and 4pm), Chumphon (air-con 125B, four hours, hourly 7am to 2am), Surat Thani (air-con 210B, seven hours, 13 daily between 8am and 1.30am) and Phuket (VIP/ air-con 755/305B, 11½ hours, 12 daily between 9am and 1.30am).

The impressive **train station** (end of Th Damnoen Kasem) services Bangkok (2nd class 302B to 332B, 3rd class 104B).

Sǎamláw from the train station to the beach cost 50B to 70B; from the bus station to Th Naretdamri, 50B to 70B; and from Chatchai Market to the fishing pier, 20B.

PRACHUAP KHIRI KHAN

pop 27,700

Roughly 80km south of Hua Hin, this small town retains an unhurried pace. Consider mellow Prachuap (pronounced 'pra-*juap*') if you're looking for somewhere to break up the long trip to the island beaches or are desperate to escape your Khao San compatriots.

The bus dumps you off in the centre of town – not a pushy motorcycle taxi or foreigner in sight. If you arrive in the heat of the day, it might even feel like a ghost town. At the base of Prachuap is a sparkling blue bay sprinkled with brightly coloured fishing boats. To the north is **Khao Chong Krajok** (Mirror Tunnel Mountain), topped by a wat with spectacular views; the hill is claimed by a clan of monkeys who supposedly hitched a ride into town on a bus from Bangkok to pick up some mangoes. There isn't much else to do except walk along the waterfront promenade or explore nearby **Ao Manao** (Lime Bay) and **Ao Noi** (Little Bay).

Sleeping & Eating

Yuttichai Hotel (☎ 0 3261 1055; 115 Th Kong Kiat; d from 160B) Run by a smiley family, this place is close to the bus station and night market. There's some beautiful timber flooring (and some gaudy laminate) throughout, and old-style rooms are big enough to stretch your legs. Tuck into cheap breakfasts, exotic coffees and ice creams.

Suk Sant Hotel (☎ 0 3261 1145; 11 Th Suseuk; s/d from 300/350B; ✺) You'll have to forsake all architectural taste at this monstrous pink building near the waterfront promenade (Th Chai Thaleh), but you'll be rewarded with lovely views (in the fan rooms only). Very basic but clean rooms.

At the foot of Th Thetsaban Bamrung is a small **night market** (Th Chai Thaleh) that's good for seafood.

Pan Phochana Restaurant (☎ 0 3261 1195; 40 Th Chai Thaleh; dishes 40-120B; ✷ breakfast, lunch & dinner) Near Suk Sant Hotel, it's famous for its *hàw mòk hǎwy* (ground fish curry steamed in mussels on the half-shell).

Vegetarian café (☎ 0 3261 1672; dishes around 23B) Noncarnivores may prefer to shuffle on down to this blink-and-you'll-miss-it café on the same street as a Suk Sant Hotel (no roman-scipt sign). There's no menu but the friendly women running the kitchen will happily wok-up something.

Getting There & Away

Buses to and from Bangkok, Hua Hin, Cha-am and Phetburi stop on Th Phitak Chat, near Yuttichai Hotel. Regular buses stop a block away near Inthira Hotel.

Services run to Bangkok (air-con/ordinary 176/140B, five hours), Hua Hin (ordinary 50B, two hours, frequent departures between 6.30am and 4pm) and Chumphon (ordinary 70B, four hours), the transfer point for Surat Thani buses and boats to the Samui islands.

The **train station** (end of Th Kong Kiat) is a block from Th Phitak Chat. Heading south and north, there are several afternoon departures to Bangkok (2nd class 195B to 245B, 3rd class 118B), Hua Hin (19B to 79B) and also to Chumphon (2nd class air-con 34B to 278B).

CHUMPHON

pop 480,000

Roughly 500km from Bangkok, Chumphon marks out where southern Thailand really begins in terms of dialect and religion. Chumphon is a revolving door for travellers going to or coming from Ko Tao (p781). The transition from arriving in Chumphon to getting a boat ticket to Ko Tao is painless. Travel agencies are within spitting distance of the bus station and provide all sorts of free amenities (such as luggage storage, shower and toilet).

Farang Bar (☎ 0 6943 5105, 0 7750 1003; farang bar@yahoo.com; Th Tha Tapao; s/d 150/160B; ▯) has a motto – 'if it can be done…we will do it' – and they certainly cater to travellers with spartan (fan only) accommodation, a bar and travel agency, plus cable TV for mindless diversion. You can stock up on food supplies for the slow boat at the small **night market** (Th Krom Luang Chumphon).

There are three daily boats to Ko Tao from Chumphon pier. Speed and express boats (400B, 1½ to two hours) leave in the morning around 7am (leave Chumphon town at 6am) to Ko Tao, catamarans leave at 1pm (500B to 550B, 1½ hours) and the ferry (250B, six hours) departs at midnight. Transport to the pier, 14km from Chumphon, is included in the fare.

Buses arrive at and depart from Chumphon's **bus station** (Th Paramin-mankar). Destinations include Bangkok (air-con 320B to 211B, seven hours, nine daily), Ranong (air-con 90B, three hours, hourly) and Surat Thani (air-con 130B, three hours, hourly).

The **train station** (Th Krom Luang Chumphon) is within walking distance of the centre of town. Destinations include Bangkok (2nd class 310B to 390B, 3rd class 202B to 252B, 7½ to nine hours, 11 daily), Surat Thani (35B, two to 3½ hours, 11 daily) and Hat Yai (80B, six to 8½ hours, five daily). Northern- and southern-bound trains have several afternoon departures.

SURAT THANI

pop 125,500

This busy port is of interest to most travellers only as a jumping-off point for the islands off the coast. If you arrive in Surat by train or bus in the morning you'll have no problem making a connection with one of the day express boats.

Sleeping & Eating

If you need a place to stay, check out **Ban Don Hotel** (☎ 0 7727 2167; 268/2 Th Na Meuang; d from 200B; ⊠), the best budget value in Surat, with small yet extremely clean rooms. The entrance is through a Chinese restaurant – quite good for inexpensive rice and noodle dishes. **Thai Tani** (☎ 0 7727 2977; Th Talat Mai; s/d 240/300B) is across the street from the local bus station. If you get stuck at the train station, which is in nearby Phun Phin, try **Queen** (☎ 0 7731 1003; 916/10-13 Th Mahasawat; s/d 180/260B; ⊠). It is round the corner from the train station on the road to Surat Thani. Look at a couple of rooms as quality varies.

The market near the bus station has cheap provisions. Stalls near the bus station specialise in hearty *khâo kài òp* (marinated baked chicken on rice). The **night market** (Th Ton Pho) is the place for fried, steamed, grilled or sautéed delicacies.

Getting There & Away

Be wary of dirt-cheap combo tickets to the islands sold on Th Khao San in Bangkok – they often have extra surcharges, invalid legs or dubious security. For the Bangkok–Surat Thani trip, it is recommended that you use buses departing from government bus stations or ask an island survivor to advise of a reliable travel agent.

AIR

There is a twice-daily service to Bangkok on **Thai Airways International** (THAI; ☎ 0 7727 2610; www.thaiair.com; 3/27-28 Th Karunarat).

BOAT

There are three piers located in and around Surat Thani: Ban Don, in the centre of town, receives the night ferries; Tha Pak Nam (Tha Thong pier), 5km from Surat Thani, receives **Songserm's** (☎ 0 7728 6340) express boats; and Don Sak, 60km from central Surat Thani, receives the car-passenger ferries and **Seatran** (☎ 0 7727 5060; www.seatranferry .com; 136 Th Na Meuang) express boats.

For travellers heading to Ko Samui, there are various options. Seatran offers bus-ferry combinations (150B, 3½ hours, departures every hour between 5.30am and 5.30pm) leaving from the bus station in Surat Thani and boarding a car ferry at Don Sak pier. Seatran's bus-express boat combinations (250B) also leave from the bus station in Surat Thani and board at Don Sak pier at 8.30am and 2.30pm. **Raja Ferry** (☎ 0 7747 1151) also leaves from Don Sak (84B, 1½ hours, departures every hour between 6am and 6pm). A night ferry (150B, six hours, departing at 11pm) leaves from Ban Don pier.

To Ko Pha-Ngan, Raja Ferry (160B, 2½ hours, four departures daily) leaves from Don Sak. Songserm's express boat (250B, 3½ hours, departing once daily at 8am) leaves from Tha Pak Nam. The night ferries (200B, seven hours, departing at 11pm) leave from Ban Don pier. **Pha-Ngan Tour** (☎ 0 7720 5799) does a bus-ferry combination for this service (240B).

To Ko Tao, night ferries (500B, seven to eight hours, departing at 11pm) and express boats (500B, five hours, one morning departure) leave from Ban Don pier.

BUS & MINIVAN

There are three bus stations in Surat Thani: **Talat Kaset 1** (off Th Talat Mai & Th Na Meuang) for local and provincial destinations, including Chumphon and the Surat Thani train station; **Talat Kaset 2** (btwn Th Talat Mai & Th That Thong) for air-con minivans and towns outside the province; and the new station outside town for Bangkok-bound buses. The travel agencies also run cramped minivan services to popular tourist destinations; these are usually faster, but have unreliable departure times and tickets tend to cost 50B to 100B more.

Buses travel to and from Bangkok (air-con 350B to 590B, 10 to 11 hours), Chumphon (ordinary 80B, three hours), Hat Yai (air-con 295B, four to five hours), Krabi (ordinary 80B, three to four hours, hourly) and Phuket (air-con/ordinary 105/170B, seven hours). Minvans also run to Hat Yai (180B) and Krabi (120B).

TRAIN

The train station is in Phun Phin, 14km from Surat Thani. Destinations include Bangkok (2nd class sleeper 498B to 748B,

---

MEDITATION WITH THE MONKS

About 60km north of Surat Thani, Chaiya is one of the oldest cities in Thailand, dating back to the Srivijaya empire, and home to Wat Suanmok (Wat Suan Mokkhaphalaram), a forest wat founded by Ajahn Buddhadasa Bhikkhu, arguably Thailand's most famous monk. At the affiliated International Dharma Hermitage (IDH), across the highway 1.5km from Wat Suanmok, resident monks hold English-language guided meditation retreats in the first 10 days of every month. Anyone is welcome to participate; the cost is 1500B (150B per day for 10 days; non-refundable), which includes meals. Advance registration is not possible; simply arrive in time to register on the morning of the final day of the month preceding the retreat. Be prepared for deep, meditative silence that lasts for 10 days.

Wat Suanmok is 7km from Chaiya and not visible from the highway. Chaiya is on the railway line only 20km north of Surat Thani. Săwngthăew leave from Surat Thani's Talat Kaset 2 bus station (30B, one hour) until late afternoon.

2nd class 368B to 478B; 3rd class 227B to 297B, 12 hours); there are several afternoon and evening departures for northern-bound trains. For destinations south of Surat Thani, there are several early morning departures, but seats tend to sell quickly.

Getting Around
Orange buses (10B, departures every 15 minutes) depart from Talat Kaset 1 local bus station, which is within walking distance of the Ban Don pier, for the train station. Orange săwngthăew (30B, departures every 15 minutes) leave from Talat Kaset 1 to Don Sak pier, but most island tickets include transport to the pier. Taxis from the train station in Phun Phin to town cost about 100B.

KO TAO
pop 5000

Mountainous Ko Tao perches on a ledge of coral reefs like a sunbathing turtle (*tao* means 'turtle'). The island is famous as a diving and snorkelling mecca thanks to the water's high visibility, abundant coral and diverse marine life. The absence of traditional package tourists keeps prices low, but in the popularity contest with the other Gulf Coast islands, Ko Tao is catching up.

Whether you're an aspiring diver on a cheap certification mission, a new-age spa junkie or just an all-round sun lover, everyone finds a little of what they want on Ko Tao.

Orientation & Information
Only 21 sq km in area, Ko Tao lies 45km north of Ko Pha-Ngan. Boats dock at the Mae Hat pier, on the west coast. Mae Hat has a small collection of travel services, Internet cafés, post and money-exchange facilities, but no presence of a Thai community unaffiliated with the tourist trade. North of Mae Hat is the diver headquarters of Hat Sai Ri. The nondiving crowd generally scatters to the other beaches and coves on the south and east coast. These are reached along treacherous unsealed roads that cut through the interior of the island. Hat Sai Ri also has traveller facilities and services.

Activities
Ko Tao's best **diving & snorkelling** sites are offshore islands or pinnacles, including White Rock, Shark Island, Chumphon Pinnacle, Green Rock, Sail Rock and Southwest Pinnacles. About 40 dive operators eagerly offer their services to travellers. The larger dive operators aren't necessarily better than the smaller ones, and will often take out bigger groups of divers. These operators usually have more than one office around the island (like at Mae Hat and at Hat Sai Ri).

Rates are similar everywhere, and typically cost 800B per dive to 5400B for a 10-dive package. An all-inclusive introductory dive lesson costs 1600B, while a four-day, open-water PADI certificate course costs around 8000B – these rates include gear, boat, instructor, food and beverages. Any bungalow or dive shop can arrange snorkelling day trips around the island for 400B. If you just want to rent a snorkel, mask and fins it will cost you around about 100B for the day.

Sleeping & Eating

Food can be expensive on Ko Tao as there are no community markets or nontourist-related vendors. Except for Hat Sai Ri, which has an assortment of restaurants, you are a captive to the guesthouse kitchens. If you're not on the mango-shake and banana-pancake train, now is the time to get on board or go hungry.

HAT SAI RI & AROUND

This is the island's longest stretch of beach, and the most populated, with a string of busy cafés, restaurants and simple (largely overpriced) accommodation. Some guesthouses are affiliated with a dive company and don't accept customers who aren't enrolled in a course.

In-Touch Bungalow (☎ 0 7745 6514; Hat Sai Ri; d 300-500B) A 15-minute walk from the pier, In-Touch boasts an ultra-chilled-out restaurant and bar with eclectic décor, knock-out spring rolls and icy shakes. Dishes here are 40B to 200B. The rooms are a little dark, but the staff are as sweet as can be.

Sai Ree Cottages (☎ 0 7745 6374; nitsairee@hotmail .com; Hat Sai Ri; d 250-500B; 🖵) You've now hit the heart of Sai Ri, where the collection of miniature A-frame huts forms a kind of munchkin village. Of all the lacklustre accommodation options, Sai Ree Cottages is the least offensive with older-style thatched-roof bungalows ringing a grassy lot. There's a popular restaurant serving dishes from 40B to 90B.

Simple Life Villa (☎ 0 7745 6142; d 600B, tw 400-500B) Don't expect anything flash here and try and get a room away from the noisy

---

> ### SPLURGE!
>
> Lash out at **View Point Resort** (☎ 0 7745 6444; www.kohtaoviewpoint.com; Chalok Baan Kao; d 200-1300B, tw 250B; 🗙) set amid tropical gardens. Billed as 'a fusion of architecture and nature', the more expensive architecturally designed rooms combine Thai and Balinese styles with linen drapes, massive beds, even bigger decks and views of the ocean from the shower! A quiet vibe prevails despite a chugging generator near the idyllic stilt restaurant, which serves dishes from 40B to 70B. Cute cheapie rooms are available too.

---

bar. There's a busy on-site dive operation, and a party-animal atmosphere prevails.

Also recommended:

Queen Resort (☎ 0 7745 6001; moo_mmm@hotmail .com; Hat Sai Ri; d from 350B; 🗙) Mid-priced rooms aren't bad, but quality varies more than the tides. Cheaper rooms (200B) share bathrooms.

D.D Hut Bungalows (☎ 0 7745 6077; deedee_hut@ hotmail.com; d 250-600B) Consider these dishevelled fibro and/or concrete bungalows if you're on a tight budget. Also serves dishes from 30B to 170B.

CHALOK BAAN KAO BAY

A crowded but good-looking bay favoured by the young and carefree, it might just be your version of paradise.

JP Resort (☎ 0 7745 6099; d from 500B; 🗙 🖵) A clean and comfortable set-up with 28 seaview bungalows. Tiled rooms are bright and fresh surrounded by manicured gardens. It's one of the island's better deals.

HAT TAA TOH

The Thai-run **Freedom Beach** (☎ 0 7745 6596; Haad Taa Toh Klaang; d 300B) is a little slice of heaven. There's a small selection of old-school bungalows positioned on a ridge. The casual restaurant has stellar views (dishes from 45B to 60B). Pale-skinned travellers will delight in the shady protection offered by small trees on the tiny beach below, not to mention the translucent water.

AO LAEM THIAN & AO TANOT

Through the dense jungle canopy along roads better suited for water drainage, you reach the northeast cape of Laem Thian and its small rocky cove.

Laem Thian Bungalows (☎ 0 7745 6477; ping pong_laemthian@hotmail.com; d 350-1000B) Having done a trekking trip before you try negotiating the steep steps here will serve you well. The lone occupier of this cove has ultrabasic huts and dim share bathrooms. The reception/dining area is crying out for a makeover, but you'll probably spend your days snorkelling and hardly notice. Ring ahead for pick-up from Ban Mae Hat pier.

Further south, Ao Tanot is a pretty cove surrounded by huge limestone rock formations and a sandy beach. Here you have a handful of guesthouses making an amenable compromise between isolation and socialisation.

Poseidon Bungalows (☎ 0 7745 6733; poseidon kohtao@hotmail.com; Ao Tanot; d 250-600B) Simple backpacker-friendly bungalows set in a natural garden full of bougainvillea and cacti. Most of the bamboo and hardwood retreats will give you glimpses of the sea. Dishes here are 40B to 250B.

Diamond Bungalows (☎ 0 7745 6591; diamond _tanote@hotmail.com; 40/7 Ao Tanot; d 600B; 🖳) Cute octagonal huts are stylish and breezy but are needy of shade and are a tad too closely packed. The Diamond restaurant serves dishes from 40B to 80B.

Black Tip Diver Resort (☎ 0 7745 6488; www.blacktip-kohtao.com; d 800-1350B; 🕸) You can't miss this resort's white faux Greek Islandsesque headquarters. Black Tip is primarily geared towards divers (expect 50% off room rates if you do a dive course), but there are decent wood bungalows with thatch roofs and stone bathrooms (including doubles that share bathrooms for 500B). Pick-ups from Ban Mae Hat pier are available.

HAT SAI DAENG

Coral View Resort (☎ 0 7745 6482; www.coralview .net; Hat Sai Daeng; d 500-900B) On the southern coast in stunning Hat Sai Daeng, Coral View has comfortable 'grown-up' bungalows, plus original bamboo ones, sea views and one of the best two-tier restaurants on the island. Coral View is run by a friendly Australian-Thai couple, and if you call in advance and make a reservation, they will pick you up at the Ban Mae Hat pier.

New Heaven Nature Huts (Hat Sai Daeng; d 400 -500B) Run by a quirky crew, this rustic ensemble blends nicely into the hilltop. Dishes in the restaurant average 50B to 110B.

Drinking

At night, the action centres on Hat Sai Ri's bars, a mix of diving and suntanning afterglow. The crowds bulk up during some of the weekly parties, advertised on fliers posted throughout the village. Because travel between beaches is difficult, people staying on the east or south coast tend to hang out in their guesthouses recounting the day's adventures.

Getting There & Away

There is only one pier in Ko Tao. To reach Surat Thani, take an express boat (500B,

five hours, one morning departure) or night ferry (500B, seven to eight hours, one departure nightly). An additional express boat service does the island jump to Thong Sala on Ko Pha-Ngan (180B to 250B, one to two hours, six departures daily from 9.30am to 3.30pm) and on to Na Thon in Ko Samui (280B to 550B).

Chumphon is another mainland option, reached by express boats (400B, 1½ to two hours, departing from 10.30am to 3pm) and a slow boat (250B, six hours, departing at 10am).

KO SAMUI

pop 39,000

Ko Samui is like a beautiful woman who wears too much make-up. To attract more attention, this natural knockout is packed with glitzy strip malls, a busy airport, manicured resort hotels, late-night discos and souvenir stands. It's like Hawaii's Maui: synonymous with all things resort-chic and touristy. Old-timers from the 1970s Southeast Asia trail brag about how wonderful Samui was before it was 'discovered'.

Hat Chaweng is *the* place to be if you want to eat, drink and beach it with the crowds, but there are several northern options to escape the droves.

Information

Bank of Ayudha (☎ 0 7742 0176; Na Thon; ⏱ 8.30am-3.30pm) Head about 200m from the ferry towards the Police Station and then 50m left. Also has branches at Hat Chaweng and Hat Mae Nam.

Internet (Na Thon; per min 1B) There's a nameless www hub about a 100m up the road adjacent to the ferry terminal office.

Post office (Th Chenwithee, Na Thon; ⏱ 8.30am-4.30pm Mon-Fri, 9am-noon Sat, Sun & public holidays) Go on, mail those postcards! Overseas calls can be made here (from 8am to 8pm).

Samui International Hospital (Chaweng Hospital; ☎ 0 7742 2272) For medical or dental needs.

Tourist information (☎ 07 7420 7202; tatsamui@tat.or.th; Th Malitra Vanitch-roen, Na Thon; ⏱ 8.30am-noon & 1-4.30pm)

Tourist police (☎ 0 7742 1281, 24hr emergencies ☎ 1155)

Sights & Activities

The beaches are beautiful and, naturally, the main attraction. If you tire of the same pitch of land outside your guesthouse, be

THAILAND

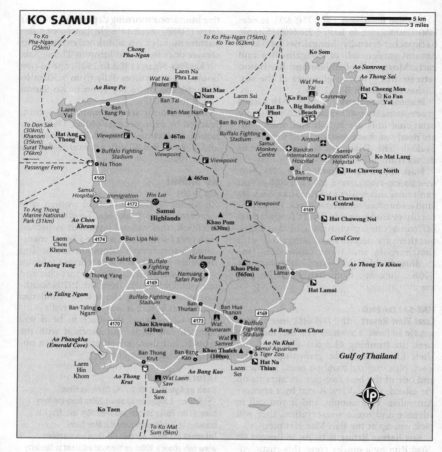

KO SAMUI

sure to set your sights a bit further afield and explore some other stretches of sand. **Chaweng** is famous for a reason – the water is crystal clear and the beach is 6km long; it is also one of the few spots on the island with surf. Receiving second place in the popularity contest, **Lamai**'s waters are calmer thanks to an offshore coral reef. **Bo Phut** arguably has the best sunset view, easily enjoyed at one of the beachfront restaurants in Fisherman's Village. A little further west is the low-key village of **Mae Nam**. The southern end of the island turns into a rocky landscape of small coves and bays that are good environments for snorkelling; you'll need to rent a motorcycle to explore this end.

Ko Samui also has scenic waterfalls in the centre of the island – **Hin Lat**, 3km southeast of Na Thon, and **Na Muang**, 14km southeast of Na Thon.

Near Ban Bang Kao in the south, there's an interesting old *chedi* at **Wat Laem Saw**, while **Wat Phra Yai** (Big Buddha Temple), with its 12m-high Buddha image, is located at the northeastern end of the island, on a small rocky islet joined to the main island by a causeway. The monks are pleased to have visitors, but proper attire (no shorts or sleeveless tops) should be worn on the temple premises.

Several guide companies on Chaweng and Lamai beaches offer kayak trips to **Ang Thong National Marine Park**.

Sleeping & Eating

NA THON

The only reason to stay in Na Thon is for an early morning boat departure or to capitalise on the island's best-value digs (minus the beach).

Samui Mansion (☎ 0 7723 6083; d 350-500B; ⊠) Right near the pier, rooms at this small guesthouse all come equipped with air-con, and clean tiled floors predominate.

Wang Bua Home Guesthouse (☎ 0 7742 0317; 212/7 Th Chonwithi; d from 350B; ⊠) Opposite the Thai Farmers Bank, it's also popular with Thais and astute travellers.

Several restaurants face Na Thon's harbour and offer a combination of Western food and Thai seafood.

Coffee Island (dishes 50-180B; ⏲ 6.30am-10pm) Opposite the new pier, it has a good selection of its namesake as well as bakery goodies.

About Art & Craft (☎ 0 6789 1190; 90/3 Th Chonwithi) This is actually a café serving a healthy line-up: try the pumpkin and tofu salad (100B).

Many travellers fill up on *kŭaytĭaw* and beer at the **night market** (Th Chonwithi), near the pier, before catching the slow boat back to the mainland. The **day market** (Th Thaweeratpakdee), two blocks back from the ferry terminal, is brimming with fresh fruit.

HAT CHAWENG

With its rocking discos and deluxe hotels, crowded Chaweng offers more amusement than relaxation and people come a long way from anywhere to get to this famous beach strip. Fittingly, the accommodation scene in Chaweng is boom or bust. The real cheapies (around 200B) are so decrepit that they should pay you to stay there. Bumping up to the next level, the 400B places offer more creature comforts than an average backpacker needs, but there is very little in between. The northern part of the beach, where the sand begins to taper off, becomes quieter and better value than other parts.

Matlang Resort (☎ 0 7723 0468; matlang@loxinfo .co.th; 154/1 Moo 2; d/tw from 400/600B; ⊠ ⊡) Squeezed in among some flashier places, you'll find quiet Matlang at the pretty far northern end of the beach. You won't be staring into your neighbour's bungalow and no doubt you'll spend time at the gorgeous restaurant (dishes from 60B to 240B).

Your Place Bungalows (☎ 0 7741 3105; 119/21 Moo 2; d from 400B; ⊠) This is a well-run establishment. The bigger and better positioned the bungalow, the more you pay.

Charlie's Hut (☎ 0 7742 2343; d from 300B; ⊠ ⊡) At the southern end of the beach, Charlie's is a maze of A-frame huts set amid palms, qualifying as one of Chaweng's only tolerable budget joints and, as such, it's generally full.

Cosy Guest House (☎ 0 7723 0844, 0 6943 7325; 162/88 Moo 2, Th Bophud; d from 400B; ⊠) About 300m from the ritzy precinct at the northern end of Hat Chaweng, this newish place is a real steal – convenient, clean and friendly. Rooms include TV.

Also recommended:

Dew Drop Hut Bungalow (☎ 0 7723 0551; 14/1 Moo 2; d 400B) Wooden bungalows in a little sliver of a forest.

Chaweng Pearl Cabana (☎ 0 7741 3109; d 350B) Next door to Your Place Bungalows, this collection of tin-roofed bungalows is popular with the fresh-faced set.

At night, restaurants set up romantic candle-lit tables on the beach. You pick your meal from the iced tray of seafood, which is priced by the kilo, and then it hits the barbecue grill. Salty folklore says to pick a fish with unclouded eyes (a sign of freshness) and a fairly small body (a sign of tenderness).

There is also a series of cheap food stalls near nightclub soi, just off the main drag in central Chaweng. As daylight disappears, *kàthoey* fuel up here for a night of female impersonation.

HAT LAMAI

Samui's second-most popular beach is just as busy as Chaweng, but the crowd is younger and less well groomed. Behind the beach, a shopping, eating and low-key girly-bar strip caters to all your needs. A shoestringer could rent a spot right in the midst of the party, but for quieter times head to the northern end of the beach, which at the time of our visit needed a bit of a clean-up.

Beer's House Beach Bungalows (☎ 0 7723 0467; 0 1958 4494; 161/4 Moo 4, Th Maret; d 450-500B) Run by a pleasant Thai couple, this set of chunky bungalows with beach access gets the thumbs-up for no-hassle comfort. Like anywhere, you'll pay a bit more the louder you hear the waves' lullaby. The cheapest rooms (200B) share bathrooms.

Spa Samui Resort (☎ 0 7723 0855; www.spasamui .com; s/d from 500/800B; ☒ ⬛) Unblock your chakras or join a meditation group at Spa Samui, which specialises in health programmes (from 300B a day) and treatments (150B to 650B). Stay near the resort's 'village' or beachfront. The busy kitchen, open for breakfast, lunch and dinner, prepares holistic food like seaweed soup (40B) and scrambled tofu (85B) – no *seriously*, this is fabulous vegetarian cuisine and it must annoy the fasters in residence. Most dishes cost from 30B to 280B.

Utopia Bungalow (☎ 0 7723 3113; www.utopia -samui.com; 124/105 Moo 3 Maret; d incl breakfast from 500B; ☒ ⬛) A reliable choice, this smooth operation offers clean but dull rooms, leafy surrounds and a beach restaurant (dishes 60B to 140B).

New Hut Bungalows (☎ 0 7723 0437, 0 9874 6033; d 400-500B) Tide-side dining and A-frame birdhouses with fans and mattresses on the floor. Rooms with shared bathrooms (300B) seem to do it for most budget beach-bums. The restaurant serves dishes from 45B to 100B.

Also recommended:

No Name Bungalow (☎ 0 7745 8116; 173/3 Moo 4 Marat; d from 300B; ☒ ⬛) Near New Hut Bungalows, this Japanese-run set of fibro shacks is an OK base.

Sea Breeze Bungalows (☎ 0 7742 4258; seabreeze _bungalow@yahoo.com; 124/3 Moo 3 Maret; d 250-400B; ☒) At the busy southern end, Sea Breeze has fan-cooled wooden bungalows in shady grounds.

HAT BO PHUT (BIG BUDDHA BEACH)

Many visitors to Ko Samui are prepared to sacrifice the picture-perfect contours of crowded Hat Chaweng for the slower pace of bohemian Bo Phut. It's particularly

---

SPLURGE!

If you've won the lottery on your travels, or perhaps you're about to say 'bon voyage' to Thailand, you may just be able to justify a stay at the exclusive **Zazen Boutique Resort & Spa** (☎ 0 7742 5177; www.samuizazen .com; 177 Moo 1, Bo Phut; d from 2400B; ☒), a seriously glam resort with massage pavilions by lush ponds, plump silken day beds and exceptional service. Thai-style rooms with all the mod-cons, including DVD player, just scream class.

---

popular with European sun-seekers who don't seem to mind the shallow waters that sometimes verge on the muddy side.

You're better off looking in the 500B range in and around the compact Fisherman's Village, which has several charming restaurants serving Thai and Western food.

Rasta Baby II (☎ 0 1082 0339, 0 9475 7656; 176 Moo 1; d from 200B) If you're adamant about hunting down a bargain, try your luck here. If this place was a hairstyle, it would be a set of dreadlocks. Get comfortable in unpretentious bungalows. Dishes in the restaurant average 40B to 120B.

Big Buddha Beach is the preferred spot for many independent travellers.

Chalee Bungalows (☎ 0 7724 5035; freddy _raymond@hotmail.com; 58/1 Moo 4; d 800B; ☒) This is a lovely nook with well-maintained bungalows boasting personable interiors. The attached Shabash Restaurant & Bar dishes out Indonesian, Indian and Middle Eastern fare.

HAT MAE NAM

If you find yourself lying on the beach wondering what country you're in, it is time to pack up and move to Mae Nam. Although the beach isn't jaw-droppingly beautiful, the surrounding village is a much-needed dose of Thailand. The foreign crowd tends to be calmer, complementing the laid-back Thai community.

Mae Nam Village Bungalows (☎ 0 7742 5151; 129/2 Moo 1, Th Maenam; d 300-400B; ☒) This end of Mae Nam is a good starting point for budget digs. You'll find basic white concrete bungalows here; the ones around 350B to 400B are the best bet.

Finding a Thai meal in Mae Nam is much easier than at other beaches. Grab an iced Thai coffee at the morning market, or a bowl of *khànŏm jiin* (curry noodles and veggies) at the food stalls in the village of Mae Nam. Savour spicy meals at bohemian **Cafe Talay Bar Restaurant** (dishes 100B; ☯ lunch & dinner) positioned near where the beach meets Th Mae Nam. It's a fitting place to soak up the low-key beachside mood; try the zesty and light *yam kûng* (spicy shrimp salad).

Drinking

Ko Samui's nightlife can be summed up with one word: Chaweng. Back behind the main drag, opposite the ocean, is a maze of soi lined with open-air bars with competing stereo systems and gyrating Thai women. An odd mix of depravity and innocence imbues these alleyways. Lonely hearts and content crowds of friends play dominoes with the young garland sellers, while the female bartenders do raunchy pole dances. Although the scene is probably better appreciated by men, women shouldn't feel uncomfortable.

Green Mango (0 7742 2148; Soi Green Mango; admission free; from 10pm) At the nexus of the strip is this slick disco playing hard house and dance anthems that ripens around midnight.

Mint Bar (Soi Green Mango; 6pm-2am) A passing parade of international DJs hits the decks here.

Getting There & Away

Be cautious when using local agents to make mainland train and bus bookings; the bookings don't always get made or are not for the class you paid for. Several travellers have written to complain of rip-offs here.

Bangkok Airways (in Chaweng 0 7742 2512-9) flies about 20 times daily between Ko Samui and Bangkok (one-way 2400B to 3800B). Other destinations include Phuket and Singapore (about twice a day). The **Samui airport** (0 7742 2512; btwn Hat Chaweng & Hat Bang Rak) departure tax is 400B for domestic flights and 500B for international flights.

Na Thon is Ko Samui's main pier for passenger and car ferries to Surat Thani; at other areas such as Hat Bang Rak (Big Buddha Beach), Hat Bo Phut and Hat Mae Nam, there is a seasonal service to Ko Pha-Ngan and Ko Tao. Ferry schedules are subject to change and services decrease during the low season.

Songserm (0 7742 0157; Na Thon pier) runs an express boat (150B, 2½ hours, one daily) to Surat Thani's Tha Thong pier (Tha Pak Nam). **Seatran** (0 7742 6000) runs an express boat (250B, two hours, two departures daily) to Surat Thani's Don Sak pier and a car ferry (150B, 2½ hours, hourly from 5.30am to 6pm) also to Surat Thani's Don Sak pier, and then by bus to central Surat Thani. The night ferry (150B, six hours, departing at 9pm) arrives at the Ban Don pier in Surat Thani.

To get to Ko Pha-Ngan (Thong Sala) there are regular departures from Na Thon pier (four daily), Hat Mae Nam pier (three daily) and Phra Yai pier (four daily); also see p792 for more information.

To reach Ko Tao, take Songserm's speedboat (550B, 1½ hours, two departures daily) from Hat Bo Phut and Hat Mae Nam piers. A slower ferry (380B, 3½ hours, one morning departure) leaves from Hat Mae Nam pier.

For more information contact the **Thai Ferry Centre** (0 7747 1151-2) in Surat Thani.

Getting Around

The island's roads are well sealed, making transportation easy and affordable. Săwngthăew can be flagged down on the island's main road or at the Na Thon pier as the drivers do their loops round the island; from Na Thon to the beaches expect to pay 30B to 50B. It's always a good idea to establish the price beforehand so that you aren't socked with a surprise 'charter'.

You can rent motorcycles on Ko Samui for about 150B to 200B a day; there are numerous outlets. Take it easy on the bikes; every year several *faràng* die or are seriously injured in motorcycle accidents on Samui, and a helmet law is enforced. To deter snatch thieves, don't put valuables in the bike's basket.

KO PHA-NGAN
pop 10,300

Wedged between Ko Tao and Ko Samui, Ko Pha-Ngan is part of backpacking folklore, a place custom-made for hammock swinging and navel gazing. Swaying coconut trees, brooding mountains, ribbons of turquoise water – Ko Pha-Ngan is everything a tropical island paradise should be. While the island is devoid of an airport and the roads remain unruly, it will be spared from full-throttle development; however, the days of 100B beachfront bungalows are rarer with each passing year.

Every sunburnt face you meet in Khao San's bars will tell you of the best beach to head to, and the truth is you're spoilt for choice here and it ain't such a bad idea to move from one beach to the next depending on how much time you have up your cheesecloth sleeve.

Orientation

The island of Ko Pha-Ngan is 100km from Surat Thani and 15km north of Ko Samui. Most boats arrive in the southwestern

THAILAND

KO PHA-NGAN

corner of the island at Thong Sala, a dusty port town of shops and tourist services. In the far southeastern corner is the famed party beach quarter of Hat Rin, divided into Hat Rin Nai (to the west) and Hat Rin Nok (to the east). On the west coast are the quieter outposts of Hat Yao (Long Beach) and Ao Mae Hat. On the northern side is Ao Chalok Lam and its thriving fishing village, as well as Hat Khuat (Bottle Beach), reachable only by boat. Transport around the island is expensive because of rugged terrain and unsealed roads.

Information
Ko Pha-Ngan Hospital (☎ 0 7737 7034) Around 2.5km north of Thong Sala; 24-hour emergency service.

PJ Home (☎ 0 7737 5403; 95/15 Moo 6, Hat Rin; per min 2B) Internet access at this travel agency near Hat Rin's pier.
Police (☎ 0 7737 7114, emergency 191)
Siam City Bank (☎ 0 7737 5476; 9/60 Moo 6, Hat Rin Village; ⏰ 8.30am-3.30pm Mon-Fri) ATM and currency exchange bureau. There are also several banks in Thong Sala.

Sights & Activities
In the eastern part of the island, **Nam Tok Than Sadet** (Than Sadet Falls) has attracted three generations of Thai kings as well as countless *faràng*. Take a longtail boat from Hat Rin to Hat Sadet and walk into the island along the river for 2.5km. The east coast, especially **Hat Thian** and **Ao Thong Nai**

Pan, is lauded as having the best snorkelling and swimming.

At **Wat Khao Tham**, on a hilltop on the southwestern side of the island, 10-day Buddhist meditation retreats are conducted by an American-Australian couple during the latter half of most months. The cost is 4000B. Contact the **wat** (www.watkowtahm.org; PO Box 18, Ko Pha-Ngan, Surat Thani 84280) for information, or preregister in person from 1pm to 2pm the day before the retreat is due to begin. A different preregistration process exists for under 26-year-olds; check the website for more details.

Sleeping

As you get off the ferry in Ko Pha-Ngan, consider this question: do you want to party like a rock star or sleep like a baby? If the former, head straight to Hat Rin; if the latter, pick any other beach *except* Hat Rin.

HAT RIN & AROUND

Ground zero for the monthly full moon parties, Hat Rin is a thriving offspring of Bangkok's Th Khao San. The village is a rabbit warren of shops to keep your baht rolling over, movies on constant rotation, scruffy dogs nipping flees and secondhand bookstores to peruse. This long cape is divided into two beaches: Hat Rin Nok

(Sunrise Beach), along the eastern shore, and Hat Rin Nai (Sunset Beach), along the western shore. Hat Rin Nok is a touch Rio Di Janeiro, with everyone comparing tans. Hat Rin Nai is a little quieter. Accommodation tends to be both expensive (jumping by around 200B a night when everyone is full-mooning) and average because there's a long queue of backpackers drooling to get in.

Same Same Lodge & Restaurant (☎ 0 7904 3923; www.same-same.com; 139/19 Th Ban Tai, Hat Rin Nok; s/d 350/450B) Mighty popular with some readers, Same Same is run by a Thai-Danish couple and caters to shoestringers with 22 clean new rooms, billiards, island trips (500B), cooking classes (800B) and 'warm-up' full moon preludes. You're a short walk to Hat Rin village and the beach from this pink base. The restaurant here serves dishes from 35B to 160B.

Phangan Bay Shore Resort (☎ 0 7737 5224; 141 Moo 6, Hat Rin Nok; s/d from 500/600B; ⊠) Towards the far end of Sunrise Beach, this is the pick of the bunch around here.

Paradise Bungalows (☎ 0 7737 5242; Hat Rin Nok; d & tw from 300B; ⊠) One of the oldest guesthouses on the beach, Paradise started the full moon parties more than a decade ago. Simple cottages line the beach (cheapies at 200B share bathrooms) and crawl up the

---

GET YOUR MOON ON

As the moon reaches its monthly climax, it seems that every other traveller you meet is making the migration to Ko Pha-Ngan and its famous full moon rave party. Under the cover of darkness Hat Rin becomes charged with drug-induced euphoria, and excited glow-torch dancers become hypnotised by the DJs' electro-charged turntables.

And now a word from your mother... Even in paradise you should practise common sense. Readers have reported having valuables stolen from rooms, or being drugged and then robbed. Returning home alone at night is also an invitation for trouble, especially for women. Lonely Planet has received reports of alleged assaults by people 'posing' as longtail boat drivers.

Be careful about going on midnight swims, as Hat Rin has dangerous and unpredictable riptides; drownings have occurred. And don't hop on that handy motorcycle for a little cruising mayhem. Accidents happen.

In January 2005, a speedboat leaving Ko Pha-Ngan's full moon party en route to Ko Samui was overloaded with party-goers and tragically capsized leaving 15 foreigners dead. Don't get on packed boats – or crammed pick-up trucks for that matter.

Even though it seems like the entire island is a drug buffet, narcotics are illegal in Thailand and police enforcement is stepped up during full moon parties. Thai police take this *very* seriously. The going rate for a small pot bust is 50,000B.

Accommodation is slim nearing the actual event, when crowds numbering between 5000 to 8000 people arrive; to secure a pad show up several days early.

Now be safe and have a good time.

cliff for sea views. No points for the junk lying about. You'll pay 50B to 150B for a feed in the restaurant.

Neptune's Villa (☎ 0 7737 5251; neptune1@thaimail .com; Hat Rin Nai; d from 400B; ⌘) At the western end of the beach, this well-tended place has compact, tidy bungalows around a neat garden. Surprisingly, there's a Moroccan restaurant, Marrakech, here too, serving dishes from 80B to 230B. It's open for dinner.

Also recommended:

Sea View Haad Rin Resort (☎ 0 7737 5160; Hat Rin Nok; d 300-800B; ⌘) Dormitory-style budget bungalows are a short stroll from the beach and flashier ones are near the shoreline. For 1000B you get air-con. The restaurant serves dishes from 45B to 120B.

Bongo Bungalows (☎ 0 7737 5269; d from 300B; ⌘) Cheapie seen-better-days bungalows run by so-so interested staff. Restaurant dishes here cost 40B to 160B.

WEST OF HAT RIN

If Hat Rin is a flashy pair of trainers, then the area between Ban Khai and Ban Tai, about 4km west, is a happily weathered sandal. Although the area isn't ideal for swimming, it is within attack-and-retreat range of Hat Rin and you have a better chance of securing beachfront real estate.

Phangan Rainbow Bungalows (☎ 0 7723 8236; www.rainbowbungalows.com; btwn Ban Tai & Ban Khai; d from 100B; ⌘ 🖳) A happy-go-lucky spot with a Thai-Australian couple presiding over the quiet ambience geared towards backpackers. Quality varies according to how much you're willing to spend on your four-walled surrounds. The restaurant here serves dishes from 40B to 110B.

Mac Bay Resort (☎ 0 7723 8443; www.macbay resort.com; btwn Ban Tai & Ban Khai; d from 300B; ⌘) Decent hardwood and concrete bungalows and a welcoming vibe. Meals here cost from 25B to 60B.

Liberty Guesthouse (☎ 0 7723 8171; liberty bantai@hotmail.com; Ban Tai; d 250-400B) Another traveller's haven, with a great pavilion eating area (dishes 40B to 250B). Lino-floored bungalows are simple but homely.

SOUTH WESTERN KO PHA-NGAN

Cookie Bungalows (☎ 0 7737 7499; cookies_bunga lows@hotmail.com; Woktum Bay; d 250-400B; ⌘) North of Thong Sala pier, this is a real find if the happy snaps of past punters are anything to go by. Lush gardens and mango trees envelop nicely spaced bamboo huts.

If the *faràng*-friendly restaurant or rocky cove don't titillate, take a dip in the above-ground pool.

Stone Hill Resort (☎ 0 7723 8654; d from 400B; ⌘) Nearby, this newly opened place comes recommended by a reader. It boasts modern, clean villas with awesome views, and its high-altitude Amsterdam Bar & Restaurant is unique. Try to get the taxi to take you up here, as it's one hell of a steep driveway.

WESTERN KO PHA-NGAN

On the western side of the island, the sealed road extends as far as **Hat Yao**, a long curve of beach round a shallow bay popular with families and couples. **Bay View Bungalows** (☎ 0 7737 4148; Hat Yao; d 300B) commands the rocky headlands with balconied cottages.

Further north on a rutted dirt road, **Ao Mae Hat** is scenic in its own way and the anchored fishermen in their longtail boats break up the monotony of sun, sand and sea. A sandbar connects the beach to a nearby island during low tide and there's wonderful snorkelling in these parts. Stay at well-positioned and quiet **Mae Hat Bay Resort** (☎ 0 7737 4171; Ao Mae Hat; d/tw from 350/400B; ⌘) or **Island View Cabana** (☎ 0 7737 4172; Ao Mae Hat; d 200-300B; dishes 45-120B), which has lots of older-style white bungalows and a busy restaurant. Apart from the sound of wind ruffling the palm trees you'll have few nightly disturbances around here. The **Village Green** (81/7 Moo 8, Hat Chaophao) is a favourite among shoestringers for its tasty Euro-Asian food and Pirate Bar.

NORTHERN KO PHA-NGAN

Travelling the winding road towards Ao Chalok Lam you descend into a verdant valley below mountains the colour of bruised storm clouds. Camped out by the water is the small fishing village of **Ban Chalok Lam**, where residents have seen their island change like a growing child. The road officially stops at Ban Chalok Lam, and to continue on to beautiful and remote Hat Khuat (Bottle Beach), you have to catch a longtail boat.

Sai Thong Resort (☎ 0 7737 4115; Ao Chalok Lam; tw & d 300-600B; ⌘ 🖳) Bungalows here are a bit rough around the edges but they are likeable nonetheless. The real drawcard is the restaurant's views over the sea and its estuary.

Fanta Bungalows (☎ 0 7737 4132; fanta phangan@yahoo.com; Ao Chalok Lam; d from 150B; ❄ 🖳) We're tipping the owner might have been partial to a certain fizzy drink. Here you'll be greeted with basic, rather dark, bungalows with chip-wood interiors and balconies fitted with hammocks. Fanta's restaurant serves dishes from 35B to 100B.

Accessible only via longtail boat, **Hat Khuat** (Bottle Beach) is the current darling of the self-respecting backpacker posse. The thick sandy beach and its glassy water are the main attractions – you'll never want to leave, unless you're chasing a cranking nightlife.

Longtail boats from Ban Chalok Lam to **Hat Khuat** (Bottle Beach) make the trip from dawn till dusk (50B).

Smile Bungalows (☎ 0 1780 2881; d 350-500B) You'll find this supremely orderly set-up at the end of the beach. Expect 28 very clean and neighbourly bungalows and a garden straight out of a Disney film.

Bottle Beach Three (☎ 0 7744 5154; d 350/550B, 2-storey bungalow 850B) Thai pop drawls from the spic 'n' span restaurant (dishes from 40B to 210B), and timber bungalows on the beach strike a good-looking pose. Rendered *Truman Show*–style 'homes' are found at the back of the property. Opting for one of the spiffy new two-storey pads is a good choice if there are two couples together (two double beds; one in the attic).

Also recommended:

Bottle Beach One (☎ 0 7744 5125; d 300-850B; 🖳) Bottle Beach's original cluster of bungalows to suit low, high and in-between budgets. Spotless restaurant: chip sandwich anyone (60B)? Other dishes range from 40B to 220B.

Bottle Beach Two (☎ 0 7744 5156; d 300-350B) About 22 blue crash pads have prime beach frontage. There's a shady eating space – shell chimes mix it with a set of imposing speakers. Run by distracted young staff. Dishes in the restaurant cost from 40B to 180B.

EASTERN KO PHA-NGAN

The Sanctuary (☎ 0 1271 3614; www.thesanctuary-kpg .com; Hat Thian; dm 70B, d 400-1000B) On Hat Thian, health and nature are stressed with a great community feeling. The creatively built restaurant serves vegetarian dishes and seafood. On offer are daily yoga, meditation and full spa treatments (*including* colonic cleansing). Boats from Hat Rin cost 50B; it's a one-hour walk along a rough trail.

In the northeastern corner, **Ao Thong Nai Pan Yai** and **Ao Thong Nai Pan Noi** have well-regarded swimming beaches. The two bays are separated by a steep 20-minute walk over a headland, or a longtail boat ride.

Baan Panburi (☎ 0 7723 8599; www.baanpanburi .bigstep.com; Ao Thong Nai Pan Noi; d from 370B; ❄) If you can afford to stay here, do it! Oodles of character and friendly staff. Bamboo bungalows, set among tropical gardens, average around 570B per night. The restaurant is a classy affair – relish nightly barbecues under romantic fairy lights.

Ta Pong (☎ 0 7744 5079; Ao Thong Nai Pan Noi; d from 150B) Rustic, unshaven-looking bungalows with wooden balconies overlook the beach (number eight has stellar views) and tend to attract an alternative crowd. There's a great bar come meeting place – *the* spot to head for sundowners. Restaurant dishes cost from 40B to 80B.

Star Hut Bungalow (☎ 0 7744 5085; star_hut@ hotmail.com; Ao Thong Nai Pan Noi; d from 220B; ❄) One of this stretch's no-fuss originals. Newer bungalows, some with terrific decks, were being finished off at Star Hut at the time of our visit.

White Sand (☎ 0 7744 5123; Ao Thong Nai Pan Yai; d/tw 500/700B) At the east end of Thong Nai Pan Yai, it has neat bungalows with wooden floors.

Eating & Drinking

For all its strong points, Ko Pha-Ngan isn't known for fabulous cuisine. Virtually all beach accommodation has a simple café with typical *faràng* versions of Thai food, plus the usual muesli/yogurt/banana pancake concoctions. Some safe Thai dishes to order are *khâo phàt* (fried rice) and *kài phàt kà-phrao* (chicken stir-fried with basil). In Thong Sala, you can find *kǔaytǐaw* vendors and food stalls. Waiting for a ferry? The **Yellow Cafe** (opposite the pier; dishes 60-90B) feeds the hungry and idle with baked potatoes, sandwiches and teas.

As the moon begins to wane, Hat Rin's beachside bars are cocktail-in-a-bucket heaven for ragers. Hat Rin's **Backyard** (☽ from 11am) is a popular day club following the full-moon assault. **Outback Bar** (94/25 Moo 6, Hat Rin Village; dishes 40-200B; ☽ 8am-midnight) is a typical pub with boppy tunes and no fewer than 10 TVs. Get your Sunday roast fix here (199B).

THAILAND

After 10pm taxi prices explode making it cheaper for solos or couples to find a room in Hat Rin for the night rather than make the return trip to a distant beach.

Getting There & Around

Most ferries arrive and depart from the pier in Thong Sala, but during the high season there are endless combinations of services between Ko Pha-Ngan's Hat Rin and several beaches on Ko Samui's north coast. Schedules and frequency vary according to the season.

To Surat Thani, there are express boats via Ko Samui (240B, four hours, four departures daily) and night ferries (220B, seven hours, departing at 10pm). These boats leave from Thong Sala on Ko Pha-Ngan, and arrive in Ban Don, Surat Thani.

There are 10 to 11 daily ferry departures between Ko Pha-Ngan and Ko Samui. These boats leave throughout the day from 7am to 4.30pm, take from 30 minutes to an hour and cost 120B to 250B. All leave from either Thong Sala or Hat Rin on Ko Pha-Ngan and arrive either in Na Thon, Mae Nam, Hat Bo Phut or Hat Bang Rak on Ko Samui. If you have a preference, clearly state it when buying a ticket.

Boats to Ko Tao (180B to 250B, one to three hours, six departures from 8.30am to 12.30pm daily) leave from Thong Sala.

Săwngthăew do daytime routes from Thong Sala to Hat Yao, Ban Chalok Lam or Hat Rin for 20B to 100B; travelling solo you'll pay around 250B to get most places on the island. On the northwestern and northeastern coasts, roads are unsealed and the terrain is difficult. Taxis moving around the islands, especially at night, are expensive, ranging from 500B to 1000B. Longtail boats also service Thong Sala, Hat Yao, Hat Rin and other beaches for 50B to 100B.

NAKHON SI THAMMARAT

pop 122,400

Off the tourist trail, Nakhon Si Thammarat is a quintessential southern town. During early Thai history, it functioned as a major hub for trade within Thailand as well as between the western and eastern hemispheres. Clergy from Hindu, Islamic, Christian and Buddhist denominations established missions here over the centuries, and many of their houses of worship are still active today.

Information

Bovorn Bazaar (Th Ratchadamnoen) A small *faràng*-oriented centre with a few restaurants and Internet cafés.
Main post office (Th Ratchadamnoen; ☼ 8.30am-4.30pm Mon-Fri)
Telephone office (☼ 8am-11pm) International service; upstairs in the post office.
TAT office (☎ 0 7534 6515; tatnakon@nrt.cscoms.com; Th Ratchadamnoen; ☼ 8.30am-4.30pm)

Sights

The city boasts the oldest and biggest wat in the south, **Wat Phra Mahathat** (Th Ratchadamnoen), reputed to be over 1500 years old and comparable in size to Wat Pho in Bangkok. The temple is 2km south of town; any săwngthăew chugging south will take you there for a bargain 6B.

To atone for all that mindless sunbathing you did on the islands, pay a visit to the **National Museum** (☎ 0 7534 1075, 0 7534 0419; Th Ratchadamnoen; admission 30B; ☼ 9am-4pm Wed-Sun), 1km south of Wat Mahathat, for its interesting 'Art of Southern Thailand' exhibit.

Thai *năng tàlung* (shadow theatre) was developed in Nakhon Si Thammarat. The acknowledged master of shadow puppets is Suchart Subsin, and you can view a performance at his **workshop** (☎ 0 7534 6394; Soi 3, 110/18 Th Si Thammasok; admission 50B, minimum 2 people; ☼ shows at 8.30am & 5pm). Puppets can also be purchased at reasonable prices.

Sleeping

You're not going to fall in love with the city's budget hotels, but at least you're out of the gutter.

Nakron Garden Inn (☎ 0 7531 3333; 1/4 Th Pak Nakhon; d 445B; ✷) The other choices are rather bleak, so you would be wise to expand your budget and shoot for a tidy room at this hotel.

Thai Hotel (☎ 0 7534 1509; 1375 Th Rajdamneon; d from 220B; ✷) Convenient to the night market and Bovorn Bazaar eats, this place offers secure old-fashioned rooms with TV.

Phetpailin Hotel (☎ 0 7534 1896; 1835/38-39 Th Yommarat; d from 180B; ✷) Simply a place to crash, with dim corridors and spaciously dreary rooms.

Eating

At night the entire block running south of Th Neramit is lined with cheap food vendors preparing *rotii klûay* (banana pancakes), *khâo mòk kài* (chicken biryani) and *mátàbà* (pancakes stuffed with chicken or vegetables).

Hao Coffee (☎ 0 7534 6563; Bovorn Bazaar; dishes 20-100B; ☺ breakfast, lunch & dinner) Select one of 18 international or southern Thai-style coffees ('Hao coffee' on the menu) and sit at a table encasing old collectables like watches and currency.

Getting There & Away

Ordinary, VIP and air-con buses to Bangkok and Phuket depart from the **bus station** (Kra Rom), 1km west of the TAT office. Minivans to Krabi, Phuket and Surat Thani leave from the City Hall area between Th Thanon Jamroenwithi and Th Thanon Ratchadamnoen, while minivans to Hat Yai depart from the Mae Somjit market area on Th Yommarat.

Buses head to Bangkok (VIP/air-con/ordinary 705/454/350B, 10 to 12 hours, 8am, 9am and hourly from 5pm to 7pm), Hat Yai (air-con 73B to 102B, three to four hours, hourly), Krabi (air-con/ordinary 120/65B, three hours), Phuket (air-con/ordinary 200/125B, eight hours) and Surat Thani (air-con/ordinary 95/55B, two hours).

HAT YAI

pop 191,200

If you've just crossed into Thailand from Malaysia, welcome to the Land of Smiles. Hat Yai is southern Thailand's commercial centre where the east and west coast roads and the railway line all meet. It is a steaming pot of ethnicities – made up of Chinese, Muslim and Thai faces – with a dash of debauchery for visitors from Thailand's puritanical southern neighbour. The city, perhaps with the highest concentration of hairdressers and beauticians this side of Bangkok, is one big shopping spree, with customers eyeing gold jewellery and ladies dressed like orchids encased behind glass doors. Like every good border town, Hat Yai knows how to party, especially during its signature holiday of the Chinese New Year in February.

Information

Bangkok Bank (cnr Th Prachathipat & Th Niphat Uthit 3) Currency exchange between 8.30am and 5pm, plus ATM.
Hat Yai Hospital (☎ 0 7423 0800; Th Rattakan)
Immigration office (☎ 0 7425 7019; Th Phetkasem) Near the railway bridge, in the same complex as the tourist police station.

Owen Tour (☎ 0 7423 4173; 49 Thamnoonvithi; per hr 40B; ☺ 8.30am-10pm) Internet access, just round the corner from Cathay Guest House.
TAT office (☎ 0 7424 3747; 1/1 Soi 2, Th Niphat Uthit 3; ☺ 8.30am-4.30pm)

Sleeping

Hat Yai has dozens of hotels within walking distance of the train station.

Louis Guesthouse (☎ 0 7422 0966; 21-23 Thamnoonvithi; d/tw from 300/400B; ✂) An extremely tidy and friendly crash pad near the train station. It's like a shrine to the Thai royal family inside; check out the photo of Elvis playing meet-and-greet with them.

Cathay Guest House (☎ 0 7424 3815; cnr Th Niphat Uthit 2 & Th Thamnoonvithi; s/d 160/200B; 🖳) Still popular with backpackers despite the creepy hallways, Cathay has little cubbyhole-sized rooms and a well-regarded travel agency. The restaurant is open for breakfast (dishes from 22B to 75B).

Hok Chin Hin Hotel (☎ 0 7424 3258; 87 Th Niphat Uthit 1; s/d 180/260B) Unmemorable rooms above a Chinese noodle shop. Dishes in the restaurant cost around 30B.

Eating & Drinking

You can eat your way through three superb ethnic cuisines in a six-block radius. Many Hat Yai restaurants, particularly the Chinese ones, close in the afternoon between 2pm and 6pm. The extensive **night market** (Th Montri 1), across from the Songkhla bus station, specialises in fresh seafood and *khànǒm jiin*.

Muslim Ocha (Th Niphat Uthit 1; dishes 25-120B; ☺ breakfast, lunch & dinner) *Rotii kaeng* everywhich-way, plus daytime rice and curry, soups and vegetarian selections. Opposite King's Hotel.

Dao Thiam (☎ 0 7424 3268; 79/3 Th Thamnoonvithi; dishes 40-80B; ☺ breakfast, lunch & dinner; ✂) Opposite Odean Department Store, this diner is something of a local institution serving reliable Thai-Chinese meals (including meat-free options). Currency from around the world adorns the walls but don't even think about funding the next leg of your trip – it's all framed behind glass.

Vegetable Food (☎ 0 7423 5369; 138/4 Th Thamnoonvithi; dishes 25B) Vegetarians on the hunt will be able to feast themselves silly on Chinese-influenced dishes at this very local haunt, opposite the Prince Hotel. There's a small roman-script sign out the front.

THAILAND

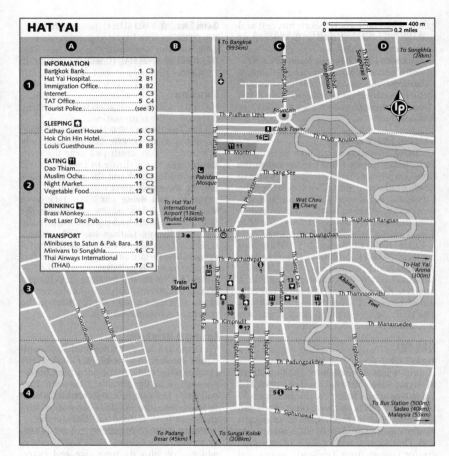

HAT YAI

0 ____ 400 m
0 ____ 0.2 miles

To Bangkok (993km)

To Songkhla (28km)

INFORMATION
Bangkok Bank...........................1 C3
Hat Yai Hospital.......................2 B1
Immigration Office...................3 B2
Internet...................................4 C3
TAT Office................................5 C4
Tourist Police......................(see 3)

SLEEPING
Cathay Guest House..................6 C3
Hok Chin Hin Hotel...................7 C3
Louis Guesthouse.....................8 B3

EATING
Dao Thiam...............................9 C3
Muslim Ocha..........................10 C3
Night Market..........................11 C2
Vegetable Food.......................12 C3

DRINKING
Brass Monkey..........................13 C3
Post Laser Disc Pub................14 C3

TRANSPORT
Minibuses to Satun & Pak Bara...15 B3
Minivans to Songkhla.............16 C2
Thai Airways International
(THAI)...............................17 C3

To Hat Yai International Airport (13km); Phuket (466km)

Th Pratham Uthit
Fountain
Clock Tower
Th Chuti Anuson

Th Rattakan
Th Montri 1
Th Sang See

Th Phetkasem
Pakistan Mosque

Wat Cheu Chang

Th Suphasan Rangsan

Th Phetkasem
Th Duangchan

Th Pratchathipat

To Hat Yai Arena (300m)

Th Rattakan
Train Station
Th Saeng Chan
Th Saocharuson
Th Thamnoonvithi

Khlong Toei

Th Manasruedee

Th Rot Fai
Th Kimpradit

Th Niphat Uthit 1
Th Niphat Uthit 2
Th Niphat Uthit 3

Th Lepsongkran

Th Padungpakdee

Soi 2

To Bus Station (500m); Sadao (40km); Malaysia (53km)

Th Siphunawat

To Padang Besar (45km)

To Sungai Kolok (208km)

THAILAND

Post Laser Disc Pub (☎ 0 7423 2027; 82-83 Th Thamnoonvithi; dishes 40-120B; ❤ lunch & dinner) Whether a farewell or maiden night in Thailand, raise a frothy glass to the house band mumbling its way through English tunes, or join the *kàthoey* headbanging to Guns 'n' Roses – now that's postmodern.

Brass Monkey (☎ 0 7424 5886; 94 Th Thamnoonvithi) This club/billiards hang-out looks like it's ready to party, even though it was deserted when we called in.

Getting There & Around

For information on travelling to Malaysia from Hat Yai, see the boxed text opposite.

Flights to Bangkok with **Thai Airways International** (THAI; ☎ 0 7423 3433; www.thaiair.com;

182 Th Niphat Uthit 1) are available five times daily. There are also daily flights available through THAI from Hat Yai International Airport, 13km west of Hat Yai, to Phuket and Singapore.

The **bus station** (off Th Siphunawat) is roughly 2km east of the town centre. For information on bus routes, fares and frequency, see opposite.

There are also minibus services across the street from the train station to Satun (65B, 1½ hours) and Pak Bara (70B, two hours). Minivans to Songkhla (20B, one hour) also stop at the clock tower on Th Phetkasen. Share taxis to Padang Besar (100B share taxi, 500B private charter, one hour) are well advertised in town.

BORDER CROSSING: INTO MALAYSIA

Hat Yai is the gatekeeper for passage into Malaysia. To hit targets on Malaysia's west coast, you can plough straight through, with the appropriate border formalities, from Hat Yai to Alor Setar, Georgetown and Kuala Lumpur on the railway line, but advance booking is recommended. The Malaysian border town for these trips is Padang Besar. The same towns are accessible by bus from Hat Yai as well.

Padang Besar is the closest border crossing from Hat Yai for a quick boost to your Thai visa. Also, by boat you can travel between Satun to Pulau Langkawi in Malaysia (see p459). To access Pulau Langkawi or Kuala Perlis, on Malaysia's west coast, take a bus from Hat Yai to Satun and then a boat to the islands.

On the east coast, Sungai Kolok–Rantau Panjang is the handiest border crossing for trips onward to Kota Bharu. Sungai Kolok is on the railway line from Hat Yai; buses can do the deed too.

The **train station** (Th Rattakan) is an easy stroll from the centre of town. Destinations include Bangkok (first class air-con/third class 1394/269B), Sungai Kolok (ordinary 3rd class 82 to 102B) and Butterworth, Malaysia (180B to 322B).

It costs 20B to get to town from the bus station on the local săwngthăew. Share taxis to the airport are 180B.

SONGKHLA

pop 86,700

Unwind from your bus journeys and border crossings at low-key Songkhla with its colourful market and its apparently timeless streets (west of Th Ramwithi). This blossoming coastal town, 25km from bustling Hat Yai, is a popular weekend destination. Songkhla's waterfront hosts Malaysian families for the daytime ritual of picnicking in the shade.

Orientation

The minibus from Hat Yai will drop you off on Th Ramwithi in the modern part of town. Just a short walk north along Th Ramwithi, the town does a quick change into a manicured garden of charming colonial architecture and wooded twin hills.

Information

Coffeebucks (25/1 Th Phetchakhiri; per hr 30B; 8am-8pm) Internet access, tucked within a small shopping centre.

Corner Shop (☎ 0 7431 2577; cnr Th Saiburi & Th Phetchakhiri) English-language books, including Lonely Planet guides, and newspapers.

Immigration office (☎ 0 7430 1011; Th Lang Prarum; 8.30am-4.30pm Mon-Fri)

Kasikorn Bank (near cnr Th Chana & Th Platha; 8.30am-3.30pm) There are several banks in town but this is the most convenient.

Post office (near cnr Th Phetchakhiri & Th Wichianchom; 8.30am-4.30pm Mon-Fri, 9am-noon Sat, Sun & holidays)

Songkhla Hospital (☎ 0 7432 1072)

BUSES FROM HAT YAI

Destination	Class	Fare (B)	Duration (hr)	Frequency
Bangkok	VIP	830	14	10 daily
Ko Samui	bus-car ferry	280	7	1 daily
Krabi	air-con	220	5	1 daily
Padang Besar	air-con	40	1½	every 10 min
Pak Bara	air-con	60	2½	6 daily
Phuket	VIP	420	7-9	6 daily
	air-con	320		
	ordinary	180		
Satun	air-con	65	1½-2	frequent
	ordinary	40		
Songkhla	ordinary	14	1	frequent
Sungai Kolok	air-con	150	4	2 daily
Surat Thani	air-con	185	5-6	5 daily
	ordinary	115		

THAILAND

Consulates

Chinese consulate (☎ 0 7431 1494; Th Sadao)
Indonesian consulate (☎ 0 7431 1544; Th Sadao)
Malaysian consulate (☎ 0 7431 1062; 4 Th Sukhum)

Sights

Hat Samila, a municipal beach in the northeast corner of town, is lined with leafy casuarina trees and open-air seafood restaurants. At one end of the beach a sculptured bronze mermaid squeezes water from her hair (similar to the image of Mae Thorani, the Hindu-Buddhist earth goddess). The local people regard the mermaid statue as a shrine, tying the waist with coloured cloth and rubbing the breasts for good luck.

Wander through the breezy halls of polished teak at the **National Museum** (☎ 0 7431 1728; cnr Th Rong Meuang & Th Saiburi; admission 30B; ⏰ 9am-4pm Wed-Sun), housed in a 100-year-old Sino-Portuguese palace. Other rambles in town include a climb up **Khao Tang Kuan**, or a stroll through **Wat Matchimawat** (Th Phattalung), southwest of the town centre, which

has frescoes, an old marble Buddha image and a small museum.

Sleeping

Amsterdam Guest House (☎ 0 7431 4890; 15/3 Th Rong Muang; d 180-220B) Missing home? Across the street from the national museum in a peaceful soi, quirky Amsterdam is decorated like a real house with inviting furniture and wall hangings. Bathrooms are shared. The restaurant, which is open for breakfast and lunch, serves dishes from 40B to 60B.

Songkhla Guest House (☎ 0 1368 5623, 0 6693 6091; d 150-250B) Next door, this is another lovely option. It claims to be 'nice, clean and cheap' and we can't disagree, although bathrooms are shared.

Yoma Guesthouse (☎ 0744 1425; 27 Th Rong Muang; d from 250B; 🕸) Also run by Songkhla Guest House, head here if you want a private bathroom. It also has cheaper rooms with share bathrooms.

Also recommended:

ABC Guesthouse (☎ 0 1678 0329, 0 6290 7744; noysarati123@hotmail.com; 28/14 Th Tanon Ramvitthi; d 250B; 🖳) Rooms without bathroom go for 200B.
Choke Dee Inn (☎ 0 7431 2275; 14/19 Th Suan Mak; d 280-380B; 🕸) This sprightly hotel prides itself on cleanliness. Choke Dee, which means 'good luck', is a little more sterile than the other guesthouses in Songkhla.
Narai Hotel (☎ 0 7444 0589; 14 Th Chai Khao; tw/d 200/150B) A 100 year-old yellow house with well-swept rooms, shared bathrooms and a gated front yard. If you're curious to see how Thais live, this is a good place to experience it.

Eating & Drinking

For cheap food, try the string of seafood places on Th Ratchadamnoen, near Hat Samila. Curried crab claws or fried squid are always a hit. Right at the tip of Songkhla's northern finger are food carts that set out mats in the grassy waterfront park. There's also a seriously good *rotii* vendor on Th Sisuda in the evenings.

Khao Noi Phochana (Th Wichianchom; dishes 30-50B) Near Chok Dee Inn, it has a good lunchtime smorgasbord of Thai and Chinese rice dishes on display. No roman-script sign.

For a relief from the heat, see if you can squeeze in between the tables of Thai teenagers at one of the air-con fast-food restaurants, on the corner of Th Sisuda and Th Platha.

SOUTHERN UNREST

Four of Thailand's southernmost and predominantly Muslim provinces (Songkhla, Yala, Pattani and Narathiwat) go through hot and cold periods that involve the Pattani United Liberation Organization (PULO), a small armed group that, since its formation in 1959, has been dedicated to making a separate Muslim state.

Between 2002 and early 2005 a series of arson attacks, bombings and assaults took place in Pattani, Yala and Narathiwat Provinces. Most attacks were on military posts or police posts; the PULO has an avowed policy not to target civilians or tourists.

Unfortunately the Thai government's heavy-handed military and police response to the 40-year-old Muslim nationalist movement (including the 2004 massacre of 108 machete-armed youths in a Pattani mosque and the suffocation deaths of 78 in brutal arrests in Narathiwat that same year) seem destined to provoke further trouble.

We urge travellers to use caution when travelling in Yala, Pattani and Narathiwat. Avoid military or police installations and avoid road travel at night.

A string of bars just east of the Indonesian consulate is jokingly referred to among local expats as 'The Dark Side'. Not as ominous as it sounds, this strip caters mainly to oil company employees and other Westerners living in Songkhla. Near the Pavilion Songkhla Hotel, on Th Platha, are a few other casual bars worth checking out. As the sun begins to set, **Corner Bier** (Th Sisuda) and **Timber Hut** (Th Sisuda) swell with the town's expat Canadian community.

Getting There & Away

The **bus station** (Th Tao It) is 2km from the town centre. For more options or to travel by train, you must connect to Hat Yai. Destinations include Bangkok (air-con 600B, 14 hours, three departures daily), with stops in Nakhon Si Thammarat and Surat Thani.

Hat Yai minibuses (20B, every 30 minutes from 10am to 10pm) can be picked up in town from in front of Wat Jaeng, on Th Ramwithi, or at the bus station.

SUNGAI KOLOK
pop 39,000

Sungai Kolok, in the southeast, is the border town for crossing over to the east coast of Malaysia (see p795). The town's **TAT office** (☎ 0 7361 2126; 18 Th Asia; ⊙ 8.30am-4.30pm), tourist police and immigration are all at the border. There's another **Thai immigration office** (⊙ 9am-4pm Mon-Fri) in town, near the Merlin Hotel.

The town centre is just a 15B sǎamláw ride from the border or a five-minute walk straight ahead from the train station.

Getting There & Away

When you cross the border from Rantau Panjang in Malaysia, the train station is about 50m straight ahead on the right-hand side, or 20B by motorcycle taxi.

The bus station is another 1km beyond the train station. From here, Bangkok buses (VIP 1090B, air-con 546B to 702B, 17 to 18 hours, three daily) go through Surat Thani (280B air-con, nine to 10 hours).

Minivans to Hat Yai (150B, three to four hours, hourly from 6am to 5pm) leave from near the train station.

Trains from Sungai Kolok to Bangkok include the 11.55am rapid and 2.05pm special express trains (260B to 1493B). Trains to Hat Yai (82B to 126B, four hours) have two morning departures.

SATUN
pop 33,400

Travelling to the deepest western corner of Thailand, you pass woven bamboo huts and harvested fields where villagers' stage football games, plus men dressed in the traditional Muslim garb, headscraved women and onion-domed mosques. With a large Muslim population speaking Yawi, Satun is barely Thailand – it didn't join the country as a province until 1932 and still clamours, along with other southern provinces, for independence.

The town boasts one major attraction: the **Satun National Museum** (☎ 0 7472 3140; Soi 5, Th Satun Thani; admission 30B; ⊙ 9am-4pm Wed-Sun), which gives its visitors a surprisingly thorough introduction to the traditions and folk ways of the Thai-Muslim southern provinces.

Sleeping & Eating

There are just a handful of large dorm-like hotels in Satun, including **Rian Thong Hotel** (Rain Tong; ☎ 0 7472 2518; Th Samanta Prasit; s/d from 250/300B; 🔀) and **Udomsuk** (☎ 0 7471 1006; Th Hatthakam Seuksa; s/d from 150/250B; 🔀). Rooms facing the street at both hotels suck in noise like a vacuum cleaner.

Near the gold-domed Bambang Mosque in the centre of town, there are several inexpensive Muslim shops. Morning coffee can be shared with chatty vegetable sellers at the **day market** (Khlong Bambang), south of town. The **night market** (btwn Th Buriwanit & Th Satun Thani), north of the mosque, provides the pleasurable evening entertainment of eating fluffy *rotii* and watching the communal TV.

Getting There & Away

Minibuses to Hat Yai (65B, 1½ hours) stop at the bus shelter on Th Buriwanit, across from Bangkok Bank.

To get to Pak Bara pier (for boats to Ko Tarutao National Marine Park), take a sǎwngthǎew (20B) from this same bus shelter to the nearby village of La-Ngu, where you can pick up a motorcycle taxi (30B) for the remainder of the trip to Pak Bara. Getting yourself onto the right sǎwngthǎew is a little tricky, so let a Thai waiting at the bus station know where you're headed. The Satun–Pak Bara trip takes 1¾ hours.

THAILAND

Boats to Pulau Langkawi in Malaysia (200B, four departures daily) depart from Tha Tammalang, 9km away. To get to the pier from Satun, take an orange sǎwngthǎew (20B) across the street from Wat Chanathip on Th Buriwanit.

KO TARUTAO NATIONAL MARINE PARK

Isolated, serene and full of rugged gorgeous-ness, Ko Tarutao National Marine Park – a little-known archipelago of 51 islands in the furthest southwestern reaches of Thai terri-tory – is one of those rare places in Thai-land that's far from the madding crowds, devoid of beachfront bars and maxed-out stereo systems. Let's just hope it manages to stay that way.

Admission to the park is 200B for for-eigners, and the park is only 'officially' open from around November to May, depending on the weather patterns during the mon-soon period.

Sleeping & Eating

Of the five accessible islands, park accom-modation is available on mountainous Ko Tarutao and Ko Adang. Looking to do a little tourist activism? Think twice before you sign up for Ko Lipe, the only island in the park open to private development. Please excuse the soapboxing, but consider this: once building restrictions have been removed, development will meet demand and before long Ko Lipe will be just as touristed as other 'national parks', such as Ko Phi Phi, Ko Samet and Ko Chang. If Ko Lipe is a successful moneymaker, then how long will other islands in the park be protected?

Park-managed **accommodation options** (in Pak Bara ☎ 0 7478 3485, 0 7472 9002, in Bangkok ☎ 0 2562 0760; camp sites 30B, 4-person longhouse 500B, 2-/4-person bungalows 600/1200B) on Ko Tarutao island should be booked ahead in peak times, but can also be arranged at the park office in Pak Bara. Tents are available to rent (150B) and can be pitched right on the beach.

On Ko Adang, you'll find longhouse ac-commodation similar to that on Ko Tarutao for 400B (sleeps four).

Before leaving the mainland, load up on food and water supplies as the park shop is limited and the food at **Tarutao Cafe** (☺ breakfast & lunch) is average.

Getting There & Away

From Pak Bara pier, boats go to Ko Taru-tao (one way/return 180/300B, one hour, 10.30am, 3pm, 4.30pm plus another after-noon departure depending on demand), Ko Adang (one way/return 500/900B, 1½ hours, 1.30pm) and to Ko Lipe (one way/return 500/900B, 1.30pm). For up-to-date fast-ferry times call the **Tarutao Speed Boat Ferry Team & Tour** (☎ 0 7478 3055) and for regular-ferry times call **Andrew Tours** (☎ 0 7478 3459), **Adang Sea Tour** (☎ 0 7478 3368) or **Wasana Tour** (☎ 0 7471 1782).

Minibuses (60B to 70B) and vans (80B) to Hat Yai park near the pier, and share taxis will take you to the moon for the right price.

TRANG

pop 69,100

Midway between Krabi and Hat Yai, bus-tling Trang is a cheerful and pleasant Thai town. We love the lolly-coloured Vespas and vintage túk-túks whizzing around the place.

The city's **Vegetarian Festival** taking place in September/October, a frenzied fiesta complete with acts of self-mortification, would be struggling to attract even the most committed of Western activists; see the boxed text opposite.

Information

Should you need to top-up your baht, there's a Bangkok Bank opposite the post office on Th Phra Ram VI, the main strip running east of the train station. Staff at **Chao Mai Tour** (☎ 0 7521 6380; 15 Th Phra Ram VI; per min 1B) travel agency are very helpful and you can jump on the Net here.

Sleeping & Eating

Yamawa (☎ 0 7521 6617; yamawa@cscoms.com; 94 Th Visetkul; d 200B) This budget haven has clean, pleasantly decorated rooms with bamboo interiors.

Ko Teng Hotel (☎ 0 7521 8622; 77-79 Th Phra Ram VI; d from 180B) 'Yes, I have room for you!' is Ko Teng's catch phrase. It feels like a massive school boarding house from the 1950s and offers clean rooms with sparse furnishings.

Look for Trang's speciality, *khànǒm jiin*, at the night market, just east of the provin-cial offices.

Trang is also famous for its *ráan kaa-fae* or *ráan ko-píi* (coffee shops), which are usually run by Hokkien Chinese. These shops serve real filtered coffee. When you order coffee here, be sure to use the Hokkien word *ko-píi* rather than the Thai *kaa-fae*, otherwise you may end up with Nescafé or instant Khao Chong coffee – the proprietors often think this is what *faràng* want. Check out **Yuchiang** (Th Phra Ram VI; dishes 25-50B) opposite Khao Tom Phui.

Sin Ocha Bakery (Th Sathani; dishes 25-50B; ✆ breakfast, lunch & dinner) Near the train station, popular Sin Ocha is the most convenient *ráan ko-píi* around. Simple Thai dishes and breakfast are served (try the oversized muesli with fruit and yoghurt), along with huge coffee drinks (10B to 40B) and teas. Takeaway cakes and biscuits are tempting glucose hits.

Kao Tom Pui (☎ 0 7521 0127; Th Phra Ram VI; dishes 30-50B; ✆ dinner) Run by a gaggle of Thai teenage girls, this simple Thai eatery occupies a corner and has English menus on hand. It's open late.

Wang Boa Restaurant (dishes 30-80B; ✆ breakfast, lunch & dinner) Right next door to the train sta-

---

FOR THE SAKE OF VEGGIES

In a country where not eating meat is tantamount to suicide, vegetarians have something to celebrate during the annual **Vegetarian Festival**, which occurs during the first nine days of the ninth lunar month of the Chinese calendar (usually in late September or early October). While the festival is recognised throughout the country, the southern towns of Phuket, Krabi and Trang elevate it from the pedestrian act of abstinence from meat to inhuman acts of self-mortification – walking on hot coals, climbing knife-blade ladders, and piercing the skin with sharp objects.

More than just a show of wills, participants act as mediums for the nine emperor gods invoked by the festival. In a trancelike state, participants proceed through the streets collecting fruit offered at shopkeepers' altars and adding the objects to the sharpened skewers piercing their cheeks, like a bizarre moustache. The entire atmosphere is one of religious frenzy, with deafening fireworks, ritual dancing, bloody shirt fronts and so on.

---

tion, this casual place is popular with locals and serves Thai and Western dishes. Go on: try the 'Like a Virgin' salad (80B).

Getting There & Away

The **bus station** (Th Huay Yot) is 400m from the centre. Buses travel to Bangkok (VIP 580B to 750B, air-con 490B, 12 to 13 hours, five daily), Hat Yai (ordinary 60B), Satun (air-con/ordinary 100/55B, two hours), Krabi (air-con/ordinary 90/55B, three hours) and Phuket (air-con 189B, five hours).

Share taxis and minibuses also service many of the popular destinations. Most leave from the train station. Minibuses to the nearby beaches (50B) leave from different spots around town.

The **train station** (west end of Th Phra Ram VI) serves only two trains travelling all the way from Trang to Bangkok (175B to 1240B, 16 hours, evening departures).

KO LANTA
pop 20,000

Slip into a beachy existence on Ko Lanta. Don't be put off by the dusty unsealed road slithering down its coastline: you'll soon be greeted with great, flat beaches. The resident Muslim and Thai community don't want to see their island become someone else's to exploit, so there are strict building and development restrictions in place to fend off the big end of town (for the time being anyway). Things are quickly moving upmarket nonetheless.

Pick-up share taxis (30B to 120B) and motorbike hires (200B to 250B per day) are available from Ban Sala Dan, near 7-Eleven in Saladan Village. Saladan's main street is lined with Internet cafés and travel agencies selling onward and upward tickets.

Information

Ko Lanta Hospital (☎ 0 7569 7017)
Post office (✆ 8.30am-3.30pm) In the street southeast of the pier.
Siam Commercial Bank (☎ 0 7568 4577) Opposite 7-Eleven in Saladan village, it has currency exchange from 8.30am and 9.30pm, plus an ATM.

Sleeping & Eating
HAT PHRA AE

Many shoestringers head over to Hat Phra Ae (Long Beach) and the beach is long (surprise, surprise). There's a convenience store, ATM and Internet access in close proximity to the accommodation mentioned below.

The Sanctuary (☎ 0 1891 3055; sanctuary_93@ yahoo.com; d 300-500B) Put some 'om' back into your life at this traveller's utopia. New beachfront bungalows capture sea breezes and there are cheaper cuties. Join a stretchy yoga class in the beachside pavilion from Monday to Saturday (300B per class 300B, or 1000B for four classes). The restaurant (open for breakfast, lunch and dinner) dishes out to-die-for banana fried rice, *rotii* and breakfast burritos for 60B to 200B…mmm.

Reggae House Pub & Restaurant (☎ 0 1091 1201; d 80-150B) A little piece of Jamaica in southern Thailand. Brick tepee-style huts are as cheap as they look. There's nightly bongo drumming and 'jam sessions' in the rambling driftwood bar and restaurant, which is open for breakfast, lunch and dinner (dishes 40B to 80B). Swing by Bob Marley's birthday (6 February) or 22–26 December for annual music festivals. Security isn't great here so watch your valuables.

Nautilus Bungalows (☎ 0 6996 5567; 147 Moo 2; d from 600B; ✷) Next door by a rocky cove, this place is run by a helpful family. You'll find tastefully decorated bungalows with outdoor bathrooms, high wooden beds and roomy decks.

Earth Bar (☎ 0 7265 9662; drinks 50-380B; ☽ nightly) Behind the Sanctuary, Earth Bar projects a cool ambience and dazzling lighting made for after-dusk raging.

HAT KHLONG KHONG

Where Else? (☎ 0 1536 4870; d 200-500B) Backpacker-friendly bungalows. Decent Thai, Indian and vegetarian meals are served in the guesthouse restaurant.

AO KANTIANG

A fine sprinkling of sand on which to rest your travel-weary bones awaits you on Ao Kantiang; with several nearby tour offices providing Internet access and motorcycle hire.

Kantiang Bay View Resort (☎ 0 1787 5192; reekantiang@hotmail.com; d 400-1200B; ✷) Bamboo and pricier modern bungalows with fan or air-con to suit your budget and personal thermostat.

Getting There & Away

Ko Lanta is accessible by bus from Trang (ordinary 90B, two hours, two morning and two afternoon departures) or by minivan from Trang (180B) or Krabi (150B, 1½ hours, three departures). Passenger boats between Ko Lanta's Ban Sala Dan and Krabi's Kong Ka (Chao Fa) pier run from October to April (200B, two hours, two departures daily).

KRABI

pop 89,980

For many, a stop-off in Krabi is part of a well-balanced diet after a rendezvous on the Gulf of Thailand coast or vice versa. In fact, the path from Surat Thani on the Gulf Coast to Krabi (pronounced gra-*bee*) on the Andaman coast is so well oiled that you will find yourself being herded off the ferry into cramped cattle cars for delivery across the peninsula before you can even deliberate.

Krabi Town

Often referred to as if it were a beach destination, Krabi is a jumping-off point for the epically beautiful island of Ko Phi Phi, as well as the popular mainland beaches of Ao Nang, Ton Sai and Rai Leh.

INFORMATION

Almost all of Krabi's budget travel agencies and restaurants offer Internet access for 40B to 60B per hour.

Bangkok Bank (Th Utarakit) ATM and money exchange.
Krabi Hospital (☎ 0 7561 1210) 1km north of town.
Main post office (Th Utarakit; ☽ 8.30am-4.30pm Mon-Fri, 9am-noon Sat & Sun) A telephone office is attached.

SLEEPING & EATING

Chan-Cha-Lay Guesthouse (☎ 0 7562 0952, 0 1817 3387; chanchalay_krabi@hotmail.com; 55 Th Uttarakit; s/d from 300B/400B; ✷ ▢) Very friendly, this is an excellent place to stay with clean, modern rooms (including cheaper ones that share bathrooms) and creative touches. It's no surprise it's popular. The restaurant here is open for breakfast and lunch.

A.Mansion (☎ 0 7563 0511; 12/6 Th Chao Fah; d from 300B; ✷) Don't let the skinny frontage fool you – it's actually a big, efficient hotel-standard place with good-value rooms fitted with TVs.

KR Mansion Hotel (☎ 0 7561 2761; d from 280B; ❌ 🖳) A reliable old favourite with good southern service and clean smallish rooms, including cheaper ones without bathrooms. The rooftop Moon Bar is the place to unwind with a drink in hand.

K Guesthouse (☎ 0 7562 3166; 15-25 Th Chao Fah; d from 300B) This family-run place is in an eye-catching two-storey building made of wood, with a small café (dishes 40B to 60B).

Pull up a pew with the locals at the waterfront night market. The **morning market** (Th Si Sawat & Th Preuksa Uthit), near the Vieng Thong Hotel in the centre of town, has delicious takeaway dishes like *phàt thai* (stir-fried noodles), *khâo màk kài* (chicken biryani) and *khâo kà-pì* (rice with red shrimp paste).

May & Mark (☎ 0 7561 2562; Th Ruen Rudee; dishes 50B; ⏰ breakfast, lunch & dinner) Near Thai Hotel, it offers excellent Thai and Western food, as well as freshly baked bread.

Pizzeria Firenze (☎ 0 7562 1453; 10 Th Khongkha; dishes 100-200B) For those spaghetti napolitano and gelati cravings.

Beaches

Dramatic karst formations soaring from emerald waters like a surreal dreamscape surround the crescent-shaped coves, creating the illusion of islands rather than a peninsula disconnected from the Krabi town by road. These beaches tend to attract a more active crowd of travellers who earn their nightly beers after a day of walking, paddling or other sweaty pursuits. Rock climbing has become a major activity on Hat Ton Sai and Hat Rai Leh. In the low season, from May to October, prices are slashed by nearly half. During the high season, arrive early as competition for rooms is fierce.

AO NANG

The furthest western beach, Ao Nang is connected to Krabi town via Hwy 4203, which parades traffic within arm's length of the shore. On the paved inland side of the road, a string of tourist shops is more reminiscent of beach towns back home than castaway tropical paradises. Favoured by families and the well heeled, Ao Nang emits a comfortable air.

There's a cluster of guesthouses about a block from the beach where Hwy 4203 turns inland.

PK Mansion (☎ 0 7563 7431; pkmansion@hotmail.com; 247/12-15 Moo 2; d & tw from 250B; ❌) At the end of a laneway, PK has big, tiled ('hygienic') rooms and feels secure. Dishes in the PK restaurant cost 50B to 80B.

Yellow Sun Guesthouse (☎ 0 7569 5607; d 200-400B) Opposite Krabi Seaview Resort, it has small, clean nondescript rooms at the rear of a travel agency of the same name.

JHotel (☎ 0 7563 7878; j_hotel@hotmail.com; 23/3 Moo 2; d from 600B; ❌ 🖳) This princely place is very comfortable and rooms have hot water and TV.

Sea Beer (d 150-250B; ❌) Near PK Mansion, Sea Beer has good, if not plain, upstairs rooms with sea views.

Lavinia Restaurant & Bakery (☎ 0 7569 5404; dishes 70-240B; ⏰ breakfast, lunch & dinner) This waterside place claims to be Ao Nang's 'trendsetter' and it's certainly the only place where you can compose your own breakfast and sandwiches.

Somkiat Buri Restaurant (☎ 0 7563 7574; dishes 60-250B) Somkiat Buri cooks up great Thai food but the best reason to come here is the lush, open-sided pavilion where you sit.

75 Million Years Pub (☎ 0 7563 7130; regular cocktails 130B) Appropriately named for the ancient limestone environs, this eclectic mosaic-floored bar has water views and 80B cocktails from 5.30pm to 9pm. It's part of the Pra Nang Inn.

HAT TON SAI

Not to be confused with the Hat Ton Sai on Ko Phi Phi, this beach is the type of place rock climbers in distant lands dream about because it's surrounded by climbing cliffs (with bolts) on all sides. It isn't as spectacular as neighbouring Hat Rai Leh, but remains the cheapest and least-developed beach on Krabi's mainland. Its relative isolation and popularity with a cool young crowd has fuelled an alternative full moon party. No one is in a hurry here.

Tonsai Bay Bungalows (☎ 0 7562 2584; d from 600B; ❌) Near the beach, this sprawling place is a mixture of upmarket (and overpriced) bungalows and older ones with grotty share bathrooms (for 200B to 350B). Set in a forest; a popular choice. The restaurant here serves dishes from 50B to 220B.

Dream Valley (☎ 0 7562 2583; www.krabidir.com /dreamvalresort/index.htm; d from 200B; ❌ 🖳) Sitting among a myriad of trees, Dream Valley has affordable bungalows of rustic bamboo. The air-con choices are presentable.

Andaman Nature Resort (☎ 0 7562 2585; d 200-500B) A climbers' hang-out that offers a variety of bamboo, wood or concrete bungalows – some are crying out for a revamp, but the grungy and sporty don't seem to mind.

HAT RAI LEH

On the very tip of the peninsula, hypnotic Hat Rai Leh is divided into the superior West Rai Leh and the affordable East Rai Leh. The epitome of a honeymoon destination, West Rai Leh has only dream-on resort bungalows that monopolise the stunning scenery. Shoestring accommodation is off a public path in East Rai Leh, whose beach is a muddy mangrove forest unsuitable for swimming. Don't fret, though, the postcard-perfect beaches at West Rai Leh and Tham Phra Nang (south of East Rai Leh) are both open to the public; you just pay less to use them.

Rapala (☎ 0 7562 2586; rapala@loxinfo.co.th; East Rai Leh; d 400-800B; 🖳) Up 48 steps, Rapala has an easy-on-the-eye garden and log cabins with mattresses on glossy floors. Listen to the longtail boats darting across the water from the airy café specialising in Indian fare.

Ya-Ya (☎ 0 7562 2593; East Rai Leh; d 600B; dishes 70-190B) You'll find 80 basic rooms with mini-me toilets and equally dwarfish tables and chairs in treehouselike buildings. Ya-Ya prospers from being next to the public path; sometimes people are willing to pay just to stop searching for a bed.

Getting There & Around

Krabi's airport is 17km northeast of town on Hwy 4. Several airlines service Krabi. **Thai Airways International** (THAI; ☎ 0 7562 2439; www.thaiair.com; Krabi Maritime Park & Spa, Th Utarik) has three daily flights to and from Bangkok (2560B, 1¼ hours). PB Air and Phuket Air also fly to Bangkok, although these flights are more sporadic and depend on demand.

The **bus station** (Talat Kao) is 4km north of Krabi town. Red săwngthăew (20B) deliver passengers from the bus station to town, in front of the 7-Eleven on Th Maharat. Buses

---

KRABI FOR CLIMBERS

Rock climbers from the world over congregate at this climbing mecca to test their strength and endurance on some of the world's most picturesque climbs. But this place isn't just for hardcore rock jocks – there are hundreds of climbs for all abilities. The local guides are only too happy to rope you up, get the adrenaline pumping and scare you silly. The euphoria of reaching the top is complemented by postcard views of 100m cliffs, dense jungle and perfect beaches. An excellent guide for the area is King Climbers' *Route Guide Book*. You can pick this up from most of the climbing shops.

The climbing ranges from steep pocketed walls to muscle-bursting overhanging horrors. The limestone rises directly out of the Andaman Sea with huge stalactites hanging down, requiring interesting acrobatic moves.

If you're after a climbing guide or want to do a course, head for Railay on the east side of Phra Nang. From what we have seen the guides are very friendly, patient and professional. There are numerous climbing schools that provide all equipment. A half-day climb with guide, equipment and insurance costs around 800B, while one-day/three-day climbs cost 1600/5000B.

If you have your own gear, a 60m rope and rope bag to keep the sand off is very useful. It's a sport-climbers' paradise, so just bring your quickdraws and follow the bolts. Alternatively, you can rent sport-climbing equipment for two people (half/full day 600/1000B), which includes harnesses, shoes, a rope, 12 quickdraws, a belay device, a locking karabiner, chalk and a guidebook.

Hat Ton Sai, part of the jagged Laem Phra Nang peninsula, is the real climbing hub where the more advanced climbers tend to strut their stuff; however, the 'Groove Tube' climb is a real favourite of beginners and advanced climbers alike in this area.

If you're after a bit of an adventure, pack a torch and head to Tum Choee cave, which you can see at the northern end of Hat Tham Phra Nang beach. Bats eventually emerge halfway up the huge monolith of Thaiwand Wall. A 25m abseil into the jungle and a 10-minute scramble will bring you to West Hat Rai Leh beach for a well-deserved Chang.

By Melanie Mills and Scott Welch, go-anywhere rock climbers from Melbourne, Australia.

TSUNAMI: SORROW & SURVIVAL IN SOUTHERN THAILAND

tsuna'mi

n. series of long, high sea waves caused by disturbance of ocean floor or seismic movement

26 December, 2004: the wave that shook the world and left more than 220,000 people dead did not spare parts of southern Thailand. Sumatra's monster 9.0-magnitude quake travelled up to 1000km per hour hitting the shores of the Andaman Sea just 60 minutes later, swallowing resorts around Khao Lak and Phuket and pummelling parts of Ko Phi Phi. But the real cost was human life: 5395 dead, 8457 injured and 2932 missing in Thailand alone.

After this monumental tsunami, which struck 12 countries, it's not surprising holiday-makers were fearful of returning to the region. The tragic loss of life and relentless media coverage marred the start of Thailand's 2005 high season. According to the Tourism Authority of Thailand (TAT), 2005 tourist arrivals to the affected area were expected to drop by 55.6%, causing a revenue loss of around 63,033 million baht – or 54% of gross domestic product in the affected area.

However, there is a silver lining. On Phi Phi, a new re-zoning development plan and public beach park were being considered at the time of research. Authorities at Phuket's Patong Beach were also keen to take advantage of the clean slate and curb the number of businesses and vendors operating on the prime beach strip.

By travelling in southern Thailand, you're part of a bigger picture. The killer waves may have struck more than once on that fateful day, but an economic crisis sustained by tourists cancelling or postponing trips would be yet another unfair blow for the locals.

Thanks for coming.

---

travel between Krabi and Bangkok (air-con 357B to 710B, 12 hours, seven daily); Hat Yai (air-con/ordinary 173/96B, four to five hours, hourly), note only the 1pm departure is for the non-air-con service; Phuket (air-con/ordinary 117/65B, three to four hours, hourly); and Surat Thani (air-con/ordinary 140/80B, two to three hours, regular daily departures until 4pm).

White sǎwngthǎew (20B during the day, 50B after 6pm) to Krabi from Ao Nang take about 45 minutes. Longtail boats bounce between Krabi and Hat Rai Leh (70B) and Hat Ton Sai (110B), when enough passengers have accumulated.

KO PHI PHI

Despite the tragic tsunami that swept through Ko Phi Phi Leh in December 2004, if there was to be a contest for one of the planet's most jaw-dropping beauties, Ko Phi Phi would be a frontrunner. Stunning limestone cliffs, translucent water, fine white arcs of sand – Ko Phi Phi is so beautiful it will evoke tears. Shed a few more when you realise that you have to share it with every Speedo on the planet.

The crowds and development belie the fact that Ko Phi Phi (officially named Ko Phi Phi Don) is part of a national marine park. Ko Phi Phi Leh, a satellite island, remains unin-

habited thanks in part to a more profitable business than tourism – harvesting nests of swiftlets for medicinal purposes. Visiting the island is expensive, but just to behold it for a day is worthwhile. Ko Phi Phi was hit particularly hard by the tsunami – virtually every standing structure on the twin bays of Ao Ton Sai and Ao Lo Dalam was destroyed, although much has now been rebuilt.

Activities

The **diving** on Ko Phi Phi is world-class and some think it's even better than Ko Tao. The best months for visibility are December to April, though certain other months (like June and July) see fewer divers and can be less hectic. Where there is diving, there is **snorkelling** too. Shop around for competitive prices and ask for recommendations from other travellers.

Sleeping

Budget accommodation on Ko Phi Phi? Don't kid yourself: there isn't any, although there are a few pockets of relative affordability, especially in the interior of the island. Things get tight during the high season from December to March.

Phi Phi Paradise Pearl Resort (☎ 0 7562 2100; www.ppparadise.com; Hat Yao; d 250-1500B; 🗷) Occupying most of pretty Hat Yao (Long

Beach), these clean beachside bungalows may have been designed by carbon copy, but at least you're near the beach and brilliant snorkelling action. Rates soar if you want air-con. The restaurant here, open for breakfast, lunch and dinner, serves dishes from 40B to 95B.

Phi Phi Long Beach (☎ 0 7561 2217, 0 1510 6451; d 300-1000B) Has cement-floor bungalows devoid of any decorative touches, with cane beds. The best bit? You're near the beach.

Maprao Resort (☎ 0 7562 2486; www.maprao.com; Maprao Ton Deao; d 300-650B, 2-bedroom house 1200B) Off by itself in a little cove at the southeastern end of Hat Hin Khao, Maphrao has thatched A-frame huts hidden in the woods. The beach is rocky, but the place packs a lot of personality.

Phi-Phi Rim Na Villa (☎ 0 1894 2668) This place has opened 24 of its 50 bungalow rooms, which are connected by rickety wooden walkways.

Eating & Drinking

Most of the resorts, hotels and bungalows around the island have their own restaurants. Pre-tsunami, cheaper and often bet-

ter food was available at the restaurants and cafés in Ton Sai village. As Ton Sai recovers, some of the old ones have reopened.

Thai Cuisine (☎ 0 7563 1565; dishes 40-100B) A simple and casual place with natural décor and good ambience, it fills up quickly at night. The kitchen grills up Thai, seafood and breakfast, although the food is nothing special.

Pee Pee Bakery (dishes 40-150) Good breakfasts, pizza, steak and Thai food.

Similarly, Ton Sai's bars are slowly reopening, and most should be up and running by 2007. Two that have opened their doors are Apache Bar, a large, open-air place terraced up from the beach and commanding an impressive view of Ao Ton Sai, and Carlito's Bar, a fairy-lit beachside bar.

Getting There & Away

Ko Phi Phi is equidistant from Phuket and Krabi, but Krabi is the more economical point of departure. Boats run regularly from November to May, but schedules depend on the weather during the monsoon.

From Ton Sai pier in Ko Phi Phi, boats depart for Krabi (200B, 1½ hours, three daily),

---

THE PRICE OF PARADISE

Southern Thailand is at a crossroads. In 2004, Thailand received 11.65 million international tourists, with the majority visiting the south – and this immensely popular area is paying the price for unsustainable levels of development.

Thailand's islands and beaches face a myriad of environmental woes: uncontrolled developments and laissez-faire building controls; declining forests; irresponsible boating and scuba diving; water pollution; waste dumping by hotels and restaurants; and fresh water shortages.

The current 'cash cow' mentality ('a company is a country, a country is a company', according to Thai prime minister, Thaksin Shinawatra) isn't helping. And while Ko Samui has been a pilot for 'green tourism' projects, it is becoming a case of too little, too late.

Near Phuket, the 20,000-year-old reefs of the Similan Islands are attracting increasing numbers of visitors. However, unlike on Ko Phi Phi, there's a growing awareness that overcrowding is actually a turn-off to potential tourists. In 2003, around 50,000 visitors to Similan National Park were recorded. Twelve months on, it had risen to 54,000 visitors. National park authorities claim to be re-evaluating how many tourists are allowed in the park, but a 2004 moratorium on the registration of tourism boats saw the number soar to 126 – from just 40 a year earlier – as operators desperately tried to secure their future tourism operations in the park.

So, when travelling in southern Thailand, think about how you're impacting on the environment. Of course, we're the last ones to discourage travel but it *must* be responsible – after all, it's a privilege to be in this incredible part of the world.

Try to deposit nonbiodegrable rubbish on the mainland rather than on the islands: on Ko Samui alone visitors and inhabitants produce more than 50 tonnes of rubbish a day, much of it plastic. Shorten showers. Request glass water bottles and minimise consumption of plastic bottles. If you don't need a bag for a purchase at a shop, say so. Support genuine ecotourism outfits and suss out the credentials of dive operators.

Phuket (one way 300B to 500B, return 700B to 900B, 1½ hours, five daily) and Ao Nang (250B to 400B, two hours, three daily).

PHUKET
pop 82,800
Phuket (poo-get) reigns supreme as southern Thailand's undisputed tourism king – it's Thailand's rock and roll and it's either your gig or not. And Phuket's popularity isn't just hype. The beaches are wide and luxurious with squeaky clean sand and jade-coloured water. This large teardrop island is largely the domain of package tourists fortressed in minicity resorts that claim huge portions of waterfront property, but backpackers can still enjoy Phuket's vocabulary of seafood, swimming and shopping.

Here is an unorthodox suggestion: don't stay at the beach. Most beach communities are cluttered with lame strip malls and overpriced accommodation. Instead, consider staying in underrated Phuket town, a stylish city of Sino-Portuguese architecture and culinary diversity from the town's bygone days as a stop on the India–China trade route. From Phuket town, public transport radiates out to a buffet of silky sand beaches.

Also note that Phuket's beaches are subject to strong seasonal undercurrents. During the monsoon season from May to the end of October, drowning is the leading cause of death for tourists visiting Phuket. Some, but not all, beaches have warning flags (red flag – dangerous for swimming; yellow flag – rough, swim with caution; green flag – stable).

Information
Bank of Asia (Map p808; Th Phuket) ATM and currency exchange from 8.30am to 6pm. There are several other banks near On On Hotel.
Connect Internet Cafe (Map p808; Th Rasada; per hr 20B; 🕙 11am-1am)
Immigration office (Map p808; ☎ 0 7621 2108) South of town, almost at the end of Th Phuket near Saphan Hin park.
Phuket International Hospital (Map p806; ☎ 0 7624 9400, emergency ☎ 0 7621 0935; Th Charlerm Pra Kiat).
Post office (Map p808; ☎ 0 7621 1020; Th Montri; 🕙 8.30am-4.30pm Mon-Fri, 9am-noon Sat, Sun & public holidays)
South Wind Books (Map p808; ☎ 0 7625 8302; 9 Th Phang-Nga; 🕙 9am-7pm Mon-Sat) Second-hand reads in seven languages; cheap used magazines too.

TAT office (Map p808; ☎ 0 7621 2213; 73-75 Th Phuket; 🕙 8.30am-4.30pm) Distributes a handy guide to local transport fares.

Sights & Activities
BEACHES
Set along the jagged western coast of this 810-sq-km island are the beach communities of **Patong**, **Karon** and **Kata**. All were affected to some extent by the tsunami, but remain majestic sweeps of sand. Their interior villages are a dizzying dose of neon and concrete, good for night-time prowling, but a drag in the noontime sun. Manicured **Hat Nai Han**, at the southern tip of the island, is strictly beach without the diversions of T-shirt shops and pub grub. Rounding the tip towards the east, **Hat Rawai** is a good place to charter boats to nearby islands. Absurdly beautiful **Laem Singh**, north of Patong on the west coast, may be that elusive piece of paradise. On the northwestern coast, **Hat Mai Khao** is part of the Sirinat National Marine Park and the nesting grounds for sea turtles from late October to February.

DIVING
Although there are many, many places to dive around Thailand, Phuket is to-dive-for; it's indisputably the primary centre for the Thai scuba-diving industry and one of the world's top 10 dive destinations. The island is ringed by good to excellent dive sites, including several small islands to the south. Live-aboard excursions (you'll never be content with a dive day trip again) to the fantastic Surin and Similan Islands, or to the Burma Banks, in the Mergui (Myeik) Archipelago off the southern coast of Myanmar, are also possible from Phuket (though these destinations are far away). **Snorkelling** is best along Phuket's west coast, particularly at the rocky headlands between beaches. As with scuba diving, you'll find better snorkelling, with greater visibility and variety of marine life, along the shores of small outlying islands like Ko Hae, Ko Yao Noi and Ko Yao Yai and Ko Raya.

These are dive shops with supplies:
Dive Supply (☎ 0 7634 2513; www.divesupply.com; 189 Th Rat Uthit, Patong) Lots of diving equipment and good service in several languages.
Phuket Wetsuits (☎ 0 7638 1818; Th Chao Fa west, Ao Chalong) Offers both custom- and ready-made wet suits. This place is 2km north of Ao Chalong.

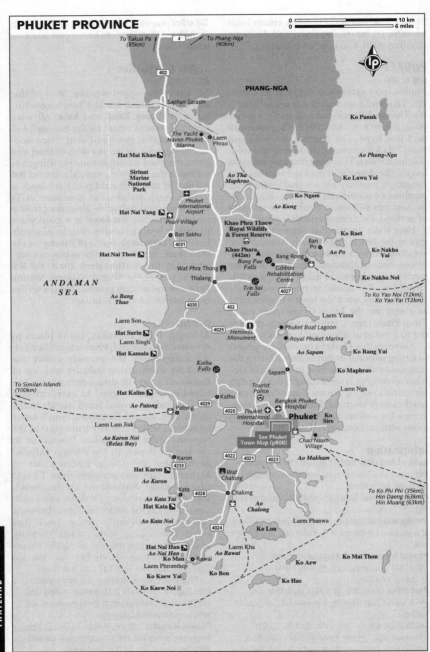

PHUKET PROVINCE

0 — 10 km
0 — 6 miles

To Takua Pa
(85km)
To Phang-Nga
(40km)
4

402

PHANG-NGA

Ko Panuk

Saphan Sarasin

The Yacht
Haven Phuket
Marina
Laem
Phrao

Hat Mai Khao

Ao Tha
Maphrao

Ao Phang-Nga

Ko Lawa Yai

**Sirinat
Marine
National
Park**

Ko Ngam

Ao Kung

Phuket
International
Airport

Hat Nai Yang

Pearl Village

**Khao Phra Thaew
Royal Wildlife
& Forest Reserve**

Ko Raet

Ban
Po

**Ko Nakha
Yai**

Ban Sakhu

4031

**Khao Phara
(442m)**
Bang Pae
Falls
Bang Rong
Gibbon
Rehabilitation
Centre

Hat Nai Thon

Wat Phra Thong

Thalang

Ton Sai
Falls

4027

Ko Nakha Noi

To Ko Yao Noi (12km);
Ko Yao Yai (12km)

*ANDAMAN
SEA*

Ao Bang
Thao

4030

402

4025

Heroines
Monument

Laem Yamu

Phuket Boat Lagoon

Royal Phuket Marina

Ao Sapam

Ko Rang Yai

Laem Son

Hat Surin

Laem Singh

Hat Kamala

Kathu
Falls

Ko Maphrao

Laem Nga

To Similan Islands
(100km)

Hat Kalim

Ao Patong
Patong

Kathu

4029

4020

Sapam

Tourist
Police
Bangkok Phuket
Hospital
Phuket
International
Hospital

Phuket

**Ko
Sire**

Laem Lam Jiak

Ao Karon Noi
(Relax Bay)

See Phuket
Town Map (p808)

Chao Náam
Village

Karon

4233

4022

4021

4023

Ao Makham

Hat Karon

Ao Karon

Kata

4028

Wat
Chalong

Chalong

Ao
Chalong

To Ko Phi Phi (35km);
Hin Daeng (63km);
Hin Muang (63km)

Hat Kata

Ao Kata Yai

Ao Kata Noi

4024

Laem Phanwa

Ko Lon

Hat Nai Han
Ao Nai Han
Ko Man
Laem Phromthep

Ko Kaew Yai

Ko Kaew Noi

Rawai

Laem Kha
Ao Rawai

Ko Bon

Ko Aew

Ko Hae

Ko Mai Thon

THAILAND

PHUKET GIBBON REHABILITATION CENTRE

Near Nam Tok Bang Pae (Bang Pae Falls) is the **Phuket Gibbon Rehabilitation Centre** (Map p806; ☎ 0 7626 0492; www.warthai.org; admission by donation; 🕑 8am-6pm). What's a gibbon you ask? A too-cute monkey with a white-rimmed face that looks like it's covered with shag-carpet. Financed by donations and run by volunteers, the centre cares for gibbons that have been kept in captivity and reintroduces them into the wild. Visitors who wish to help may 'adopt' a gibbon for 1800B, which will pay for one animal's care for a year.

Festivals & Events

Phuket's most important festival is the **Vegetarian Festival** (see boxed text p799), centred on five Chinese temples, including Jui Tui on Th Ranong, and Bang Niaw and Sui Boon Tong temples. The TAT office in Phuket prints a helpful schedule of events for the Vegetarian Festival each year.

Sleeping & Eating

Map p808

PHUKET TOWN

Talang Guest House (☎ 0 7621 4225; 37 Th Thalang; s from 280B, d 300-350B, tr 400-450B; ❄ 💻) Friendly Talang has warehouse-style rooms with dark floorboards, high ceilings and 1960s furniture. A few rooms open out to a breezy gallery. A continental breakfast of coffee, toast and a token banana is included.

On On Hotel (☎ 0 7621 1154; 19 Th Phang-Nga; s/d from 200/280B; ❄ 💻) Phuket's first hotel has a white yesteryear façade. In the common areas are signs of faded glamour, none of which is retained in the rooms that posed as the Khao San flophouse in the filming of *The Beach* (room 38, in fact).

Pengman (☎ 0 7621 1486; 69 Th Phang-Nga; d 120B) You may have dreams filled with noodles and dumplings as the smells from the Chinese restaurant waft upstairs into your shoebox room. Bathrooms are shared.

Phuket cuisine is a mix of Thai, Malay and Chinese with some exceptional twists on the country's standard dishes.

China Inn Cafe (☎ 0 7635 6239; 20 Th Thalang; 🕑 breakfast, lunch & dinner, closed Mon) This stylish café, fashioned from the pages of an interiors magazine, rolls out delicious food in a cute courtyard.

Khanasutra (☎ 0 1894 0794; 18-20 Th Takua Pa; dishes 60-120B; 🕑 lunch & dinner Mon-Sat, dinner Sun) Enjoy some of the best Indian tucker this side of Delhi. You almost expect Bollywood dancers to shimmy out from the 'tent' area. Spicy? You bet!

Ran Jee Nguat (Th Yaowarat; dishes 20B; 🕑 breakfast & lunch) Four doors down from the corner of Th Dibuk, this long-running institution serves up Phuket's most famous dish: *khànŏm jiin náam yaa phuukèt* (Chinese noodles in a puréed fish and curry sauce). It might be helpful to come armed with your Thai phrasebook and to know that there is no roman-script sign out the front.

Nai Yao (☎ 0 7621 2719; Th Phuket; dishes 50-100B) A sidewalk haunt typically filled with Thais. More like a curry than a soup, the speciality dish *tôm yam hâeng* will knock your sweaty sandals off. Other taste sensations include the clams and *hàw mòk thàleh* (steamed seafood curry wrapped in banana leaf).

Barhemian Cafe (☎ 0 9652 4223; 61 Th Talang; 🕑 lunch & dinner) This hip place rules for the local arty set.

The **day market** (Th Ranong), just off Fountain Circle, sells fresh fruit. At night the area is just as crammed with vendors selling grilled skewers of meat and seafood. When you pick out your order, hand it to the vendor so it can be heated up; point to the vats of sauce on the counter if you like spicy dipping sauces.

A few vegetarian shops line Th Ranong east of the garish Jui Tui Chinese temple. **Muslim rotii restaurants** (Th Thalang) huddle near Th Thepkasatri.

HAT PATONG

Going cheap in popular Patong is like slumming in Beverly Hills – you're sure to have hotel envy.

Baan Patong Guesthouse (☎ 0 7634 4152; 3 Th Rat Uthit; d from 300B; ❄) If this four-storey place was in a supermarket isle it would scream 'good value'. And you, the shopper, would check into modern peachy rooms with large beds.

Chanathip Guest House (☎ 0 7629 4087; 53/7 Th Rat Uthit; d from 350B; ❄) Neat rooms have spring mattresses, TV and hot water. Some rooms stare into boring brick walls.

Crown Hostel (☎ 0 7634 2297; nartboon@loxinfo.co.th; 169/3-4 Th Rat Uthit; dm 250-300B, r from 350B; ❄ 💻) Friendly and central, it's geared to

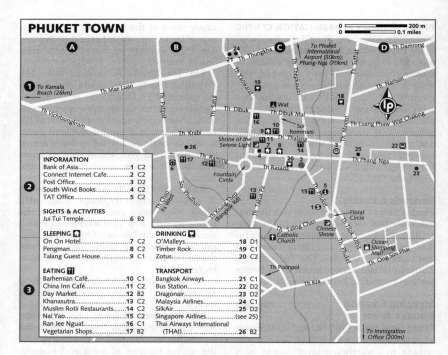

PHUKET TOWN

0 — 200 m
0 — 0.1 miles

backpackers. There are air-conditioned single-sex dormitories plus a communal fridge.

Also recommended:

Simon Laundry (☎ 0 7634 0981; 143/16 Th Rat Uthit; d 350B) Literally above a laundry, rooms are a tad claustrophobic. The builder won't be winning any prizes for his construction, but the ladies running the show are a smiley duo.

Touch Villa (☎ 0 7634 4011; touchvilla@hotmail.com; 151/4 Rat Uthit; d from 250B; 🟦) Rooms have hot water and it's about as quiet as you'll find in the area.

Got a hankering for some seafood but are intimidated by the restaurants packed with platinum-card users? Head on down to Soi Eric, a claustrophobic alley just off Th Bang-La. With barely space to loiter, the cheap seafood stalls (dishes 80B to 100B) feed a rotating crowd of expectant diners, who are rarely disappointed.

HAT KARON & HAT KATA

South of Hat Patong is a string of three beaches: the long golden sweep of Hat Karon; the smaller but equally beautiful Hat Kata Yai (Big Kata), separated by a small headland; and Kata Noi (Little Kata), where you'll find good snorkelling. If you're beach-bound, Karon and classy Kata are better bets than saturated Patong. During the 2004 tsunami, the waves hammered Hat Karon and left a good deal of debris on the beach, which has since been cleaned up. None of the guesthouses or resorts suffered significant damage.

Lucky Guest House (☎ 0 7633 0572; 110/44-45 Th Thai Na, Hat Kata Yai; d from 300B; 🟦) On the southern side of Th Thai Na, Lucky is well-run and spotlessly clean. Bungalows are also available.

Kata On Sea (☎ 0 7633 0594; 96/6 Th Thai Na, Hat Kata Yai; d from 250B; 🟦) This collection of simple bungalows (with fans) gets great views of Phuket's voluptuous hills. Getting to the beach is a bit of a trek, but Th Thai Na is filled with affordable backpacker traps to make the walk entertaining.

Bazoom Hostel (☎ 0 7639 6913; www.bazoom hostel.com; 269/2-3 Patak East, Karon Plaza, Hat Karon; dm 80-120B, d from 2400B; 🟦 💻) Colourful and happening with mixed dorms and double rooms with share bathrooms (but you're literally *in* the dorm). Better rooms have funky window seats, cool bed heads and air-con. Dishes in the Bazoom restaurant (open for breakfast, lunch and dinner) will set you back 50B to 120B.

Ann Guesthouse (☎ 0 7639 8288; berniesbistrobar@hotmail.com; Hat Karon; d from 450B; ✉) At the northern end of Karon about 500m from the roundabout, this Australian-owned guesthouse has clean rooms in concrete blocks plopped down in a fairly deserted strip between several major resort hotel complexes. The restaurant serves dishes from 50B to 275B.

HAT MAI KHAO

Phuket Campground (☎ 0 1370 1579; www.phuketcampground.com; Ao Mai Khao; tent 150-300B, d 600B) This privately operated camping ground rents large, 4-sq-metre tents near the beach, each with rice mats, pillows, blankets and a torch; it also has two-person cabins and a small restaurant. The camping ground is 2km south of the police kiosk in Ban Mai Khao.

Drinking
PHUKET TOWN

The major hotels have discos and/or karaoke clubs.

Timber Rock (Map p808; ☎ 0 7621 1839; Th Yaowarat) A Western-style rock pub with rustic décor, it's one of the most popular live-music venues in town. Arrive after 9pm, although by 10pm it's usually standing room only.

O'Malleys (Map p808; ☎ 0 7622 0170; 2/20-21 Th Montri) This chain Irish pub is good fun and has innovative promotions, such as 'Bring in a Party Photo and Get a Free Beer'. Mexican buffets are sometimes held.

Zotus (Map p808; Th Rasada) There's not much room to dance at this small place, although Thai bands perform on the stage. It caters to the deaf, with very loud, heart-stopping bass beats.

HAT PATONG

A neon-lit zoo after dark, throngs of people graze at watering holes along Th Bang-La. If you think 'Patong' sounds like Bangkok's 'Patpong', you're on to something – it looks like it too. In addition to foamy drinks, the bars serve gyrating girls, gay boys and lady boys.

Molly Malone's (☎ 0 7629 2771; Th Thawiwong) This pub rocks with Irish gigs every night at 9.45pm. There's a good atmosphere, lots of pub food and some great tables out the front from which to admire the ocean and legions of tourist passers-by.

Two Black Sheep (Th Rat Uthit) In the thick of the inland action, next to K Hotel, there's mostly an intimate bar atmosphere here with good live rock music nightly in a trendy, dark space.

Gonzo Bar (Th Bangla) This large bar attracts hordes of *faràng*, who come in part for the bar games. Grab a stool and watch others humiliate themselves while sipping cheap drinks, or lose your inhibitions and join in the fun.

Banana Disco (☎ 0 1271 2469; 96 Th Thawiwong; admission 200B) An Aztec-like theme prevails at this club. It's on the main beach strip and the cover charge includes two drinks.

Getting There & Away
AIR

Phuket international airport (Map p806; ☎ 0 7632 7230) is 30km to the north of the city centre, just off Hwy 402. Thai Airways International, Phuket Air and Air Andaman operate about a heap of daily flights from Bangkok. There are also regular flights to Hat Yai, as well as to international destinations such as Penang, Langkawi, Kuala Lumpur, Singapore, Hong Kong, Taipei and Tokyo.

Taxis ask 340B for the trip from the airport to the city, or for 500B to 600B to the beaches.

Airline offices servicing Phuket include the following:

Air Asia (☎ 0 7635 1428; www.airasia.com)
Bangkok Airways (Map p808; ☎ 0 7622 5033; www.bangkokair.com; 58/2-3 Th Yaowarat)

Dragonair (Map p808; ☎ 0 7621 5734; www.dragonair .com; Th Phang-Nga)

Malaysia Airlines (Map p808; ☎ 0 7621 3749; www .malaysiaairlines.com; 1/8-9 Th Thungkha)

Phuket Airlines (in Bangkok ☎ 0 2679 8999; www .phuketairlines.com; 1168/102 34th-B fl Lumpini Tower Bldg, Rama 4 Rd, Sathorn, Thungmahamek, Bangkok)

SilkAir (Map p808; ☎ 0 7621 3891; www.silkair.com; 183/103 Th Phang-Nga)

Singapore Airlines (☎ 0 7621 3891; www.singaporeair .com; 183/103 Th Phang-Nga)

Thai Airways International (THAI; Map p808; ☎ 0 7621 1195; www.thaiair.com; 78/1 Th Ranong)

BOAT

There are a couple of major boat and ferry operators available to provide services out of Phuket, including **Phuket Boat Lagoon Marina** (☎ 0 7623 9055; www.phuketboatlagoon.com/marina /marina.php; 22/1 Moo 2 Thepkasattri Rd, T Kohkaew A Muang) and **Phuket Island Marina Co Ltd** (☎ 0 7620 6704-5; www.yacht-haven-phuket.com; 141/2 Moo 2 Tumbol Maikhao Thalang).

BUS

Phuket's **bus station** (off Th Phang-Nga) is right in the centre of Phuket town and a comfortable walk to the nearby guesthouses. From Phuket, buses go to Bangkok (VIP 486B to 755B, air-con 378B to 567B, 12 to 15 hours, morning and several evening departures daily), Hat Yai (air-con 210B to 270B, six to eight hours, several morning departures daily), Krabi (air-con 117B, ordinary 65B, three to four hours, departures regularly from 7am to 6.30pm), Phang-Nga (ordinary 36B, 2½ hours, five departures from 10am to 4.30pm), Surat Thani (air-con 170B, ordinary 105B, five to six hours, several daily) and Trang (air-con 189B, ordinary 105B, five to six hours, hourly from 5am to 6.30pm).

Getting Around

When you first arrive in Phuket, beware of the rip-off artists who claim that the tourist office is 5km away, that the only way to get to the beaches is to take a taxi, or that a săwngthăew from the bus station to the town centre will cost you a small fortune.

Săwngthăew depart from Th Ranong, near the market, to different spots on the island between 6am and 6pm. To go around town, the standard fare is 10B; to Hat Patong it's 15B; and to Hat Kata, Hat Karon and Hat Rawai it's 20B. These prices are only for trips originating or terminating in Phuket town; between the beaches you have to haggle.

You can also hire motorcycles almost anywhere for 150B to 200B. Exercise extreme caution as Phuket's roads are windy and accidents claim close to 200 lives on Phuket alone every year.

PHANG-NGA
pop 9700

Fringed by limestone cliffs and the luscious Andaman Sea, you'll go gaga over little Phang-Nga, a scenic day trip or overnighter from Phuket. The biggest attraction is a longtail boat tour through **Ao Phang-Nga**, a widely promoted bay of mangrove forests, 120 mountainous islands and caves virtually melting with waxlike stalactites.

Tours usually include a stop at a Muslim fishing village and James Bond Island (the island rock in *The Man with the Golden Gun*) within Ao Phang-Nga National Marine Park. The tours cost around 950B for two to three hours and can be arranged through tour agencies at the Phang-Nga bus station.

Sleeping & Eating

Phang-Nga Inn (☎ 0 7641 1963; phang-ngainn@png .co.th; 2/2 Soi Lohakit; r 500-1400B; ✖) The most pleasant hotel in town. A converted family mansion, it has 12 homey, quiet rooms. All are comfortably modern and well furnished; there's an eating area in front. It's on a side street off the main road near the centre of town.

Phang-Nga Guest House (☎ 0 7641 1358; Th Phetkasem; r 220-1000B; ✖) The best-value budget digs in town, with 12 clean, neat and pleasant rooms that come in a variety of sizes and prices. Sayan Tours takes its clients here.

Thawisuk Hotel (☎ 0 7641 2100; 77-79 Th Phetkasem; r 150-200B) A rambling, pastel-blue building in the middle of town, it's friendly and offers bright, simple rooms. There's a rooftop with good views.

Several food stalls on the main street sell delicious *khànŏm jiin* (thin wheat noodles) with chicken curry, *náam yaa* (spicy ground-fish curry) or *náam phrík* (sweet and spicy peanut sauce).

Cha-Leang (☎ 0 7641 3831; dishes 40-90B) This is one of the best and most popular restaurants in town, cooking up well-priced seafood dishes – try the 'clams with basil leaf and chilli' or the 'edible inflorescence of banana plant salad'. There's a simple but pleasant back patio.

Phang-Nga Satay (184 Th Phetkasem; dishes 20-60B) A tiny shack that specialises in Malay-style satay – try the shrimp version.

Getting There & Away

Frequent Phuket-bound buses (36B to 65B) run until 8pm and take 1½ to 2½ hours depending on who's at the wheel. Buses depart from the **bus station** (Th Phetkasem) in Phang-Nga.

KHAO SOK NATIONAL PARK

When your head starts to sizzle from endless sunbathing, head to the refreshing jungles of Khao Sok National Park. Conveniently wedged between Surat Thani to the east and Phang-Nga to the west, it's littered with clear streams and swimming holes sitting by limestone cliffs. Adding to its credentials, the Khao Sok rainforest is a remnant of a 160-million-year-old forest ecosystem that is believed to be much older and richer than the forests of the Amazon and central Africa – at least according to Thom Henley, author of *Waterfalls and Gibbon Calls*.

The best time of year to visit Khao Sok is in the dry season (December to May), when there are fewer blood-sucking leeches. In January and February, a wild lotus (*Rafflesia kerri meyer*), the largest flower in the world, bursts into bloom emitting a rotten-meat stench that attracts pollinating insects.

The **park headquarters & visitors centre** (☎ 0 7739 5139; www.dnp.go.th; admission per day 200B) are 1.8km off Rte 401, near the 109km marker.

Sleeping & Eating

Near the visitors centre you can pitch your own **tent** (camp site for 2 people 60B, tent & bedding hire 225-405B) or rent **bungalows** (1-4 people 800B, 5-8 people 1000B). At picturesque Chiaw Lan Lake, park-managed substations have **floating raft houses** (☎ 0 7739 5139; 2/4/6 people 400/800/1200B).

Off the main road are several private guesthouses that can organise day and overnight trips in the area.

Morning Mist Resort (☎ 0 9971 8794; www .morningmistresort.com; d 350-700B) Family-run

Morning Mist has clean river bungalows and cheaper mountainside ones too. A restaurant filled with hanging lanterns and romantic fairy lights serves terrific food for breakfast, lunch and dinner (dishes 45B to 60B); try the *matsaman* curry or slurp down a sapodilla shake. The cocktails look wickedly good.

Our Jungle House (☎ 0 9909 6814; ourjungle house2005@yahoo.de; d 600-800B) Catering for small groups and independent travellers, this place has some super treehouse bungalows by the river and serves good food priced from 50B to 120B, making it deservedly popular.

Art's River Lodge (☎ 0 7276 3933; d 450B-1200B) A peaceful place with a tasteful selection of old- and new-style bungalows. A traditional Thai building perched by the river houses the idyllic restaurant (dishes 55B to 95B); come here around 5pm to feed the monkeys.

Also recommended:

Freedom Resort (☎ 0 7739 5157; freedomresort@ yahoo.com; 200 Moo 6; d 200B, tent hire 50B; 🖩 🖳) Australian-run with barbecues and a relaxed vibe. For 500B you get air-con. Dishes in the restaurant range from 45B to 70B.

Khao Sok Rainforest Resort (☎ 0 7739 5136; d 400-600B) A tranquil spot with tiled bungalows reminiscent of the cartoon show, *The Flintstones*. You'll pay 45B to 85B for a feed in the restaurant.

Getting There & Away

To get to the national park, take a Takua Pa–Surat Thani bus; tell the driver 'Khao Sok'. Khao Sok (50B, one hour, nine daily) is 40km from Takua Pa (on the west coast) and almost 100km from Surat Thani (on the east coast).

RANONG

pop 24,500

This small and friendly provincial capital has a bustling fishing port and is separated from Myanmar only by Pak Chan, the estuary of Mae Nam Chan (Chan River). Burmese residents from nearby Kawthoung (Ko Song; also known as Victoria Point) easily hop across the border. The city is also a gateway to Kawthoung and Thahtay Island, and many expats (and a growing number of switched-on travellers) pass through on quick trips across the border to renew their visas.

Information

Most of Ranong's banks are on Th Tha Meuang (the road to the fishing pier), near the intersection with Th Ruangrat. Many have ATMs. The main post office is on Th Chonrau near the intersection of Th Dap Khadi. The CAT telephone office is south on Th Phoem Phon.

Chonakukson Bookstore (Th Ruangrat) Near Asia Hotel, it sells English-language books and Phuket Airlines tickets to Bangkok.

Immigration office (☎ 0 7782 2016; Th Ruangrat; ⏰ 8.30am-6pm) Seven hundred metres north of Saphan Pla pier, 4.5km from Ranong centre. Border check for travellers crossing to Myanmar by boat (see the boxed text below).

Sights & Activities

Although there is nothing of great cultural interest in town, Ranong's **hot springs** (Wat Tapotaram; admission free), just outside town, attract Thai and foreign visitors alike.

Because of its close proximity to southern Myanmar, Ranong is a base for **dive trips** to the Burma Banks, within the Mergui (Myeik) Archipelago, as well as the world-class Surin and Similan Islands. Because of the distances involved, dive trips are mostly live-aboard and not cheap. Expect to pay more than US$200 for a two-day/two-night deal.

A couple of dive shops in Ranong can get you started. Try **Aladdin Dive Cruise** (☎ 0 7781 2967; www.aladdindivecruise.de) at Kay-Kai Internet Café or **A-One-Diving** (☎ 0 7783 2984; www.a-one-diving.com; 77 Saphan Pla).

Sleeping & Eating

Kiwi House (☎ 0 7783 2812; www.kiwiorchid.com; d 250B; 💻) Conveniently located near the bus station is this bright yellow travellers pad run by a Thai-New Zealand couple. You'll find clean rooms and bed-bug free beds, although bathrooms are shared. The restaurant serves dishes from 45B to 70B. Pick up a free map of the town here. Information and bookings for trips around Ranong also available.

Also recommended:

Asia Hotel (☎ 0 7781 1113; 39/9 Th Ruangrat; d from 200B; 🍴) An institutional place near the market.

Banggan Bar (☎ 0 9727 4334; Th Ruangrat; d 90B) Near 7-Eleven, this kooky place does cheap drinks, trippy wallpaper and old TVs as tables. Rooms have mattresses on lino flooring and bathrooms are shared.

For inexpensive Thai and Burmese breakfasts, try the **morning market** (Th Ruangrat) or nearby traditional Hokkien coffee shops with marble-topped tables.

Getting There & Away

There are daily flights between Ranong and Bangkok with **Phuket Airlines** (☎ 0 7782 4590; www.phuketairlines.com).

The bus station is on Hwy 4 towards the south end of town, near Kiwi House, although some buses stop in town before going on to the bus station. You can reach Ranong from Bangkok (VIP 520B, air-con 260B to 330B, 10 hours, 8.30am and 8pm), from Chumphon (70/50B air-con/ordinary, hourly departures, three to five hours) and Phuket (ordinary 130B, five to six hours).

BORDER CROSSING: INTO MYANMAR

It is now legal to travel from Ranong, Thailand, to Kawthoung, Myanmar, and from there into the interior of Myanmar – eg Dawei or Yangon – by plane and boat. Road travel north of Kawthoung, however, is forbidden. When the Thai–Myanmar border is open, boats to Kawthoung leave the Saphan Pla (Pla Bridge) pier, about 4.5km from the centre of Ranong. Departures are frequent from around 8.30am until 6pm, and cost 60B to 100B per person. To reach the pier, take săwngthăew 2 from Ranong (7B) and get off at the **immigration office** (☎ 0 7782 2016; Th Ruangrat; ⏰ 8.30am-6pm), 700m north of the pier, to get your passport stamped.

Upon arrival at the Kawthoung jetty, there's a stop at Myanmar immigration. At this point you must inform the authorities if you're a day visitor – in which case you must pay a fee of US$5 for a day permit. Bear in mind when you are returning to Thailand that Myanmar time is half an hour behind Thailand's. Though Thai immigration seems to have changed its hours in order to avoid return hassles, you should double-check when leaving the country. See p586 for visa regulations and border fees.

For an effortless visa run, **Kiwi House** (☎ 0 7783 2812; www.kiwiorchid.com) in Ranong organises a 2½ hour door-to-door service (300B plus your day permit) with departures at 9am, 11am, 1.30pm and 3.30pm daily.

From town, blue săwngthăew 2 passes the bus station.

For information on crossing over into Myanmar, see the boxed text opposite.

THAILAND DIRECTORY

ACCOMMODATION

There is a healthy range of budget accommodation in Thailand, kicking off at around US$2 (80B) for a dorm bed or a cheap single with fan and share bathroom. Make the leap to US$6 (250B) and you get an attached bathroom, while US$10 (400B) will see you enter the air-con league. The cheapest rooms include four walls of varying cleanliness, a bed of varying comfort and a creaking fan. Check out the sanitary standards of the shared bathroom before you make a decision. Although basic, the most comfortable lodging is at 'guesthouses'. Some long-running establishments will make a destination, while others can make you suspicious of all Thai motivations. More impersonal but sometimes the only choice in nontouristy places are the Chinese-run hotels that cater to Thai clientele. The rates run a little higher than budget guesthouses (200B to 350B) and include a private bathroom, TV and sometimes a view. However, communication with the staff will require a lot of hand gestures.

During Thailand's high season (December to February), prices increase and availability decreases. Reservations at most of the small family-run hotels are not recommended as bookings are rarely honoured. Advance payment to secure a reservation is also discouraged as this tends to disappear on arrival.

Practising Buddhists may be able to stay overnight in some temples for a small donation. Facilities are very basic, and early rising is expected. Temple lodgings are usually for men only. Neat, clean dress and a basic knowledge of Thai etiquette are mandatory.

In this chapter, assume that the prices listed are for rooms with a fan and en suite bathroom unless otherwise indicated.

ACTIVITIES

Despite the hot and humid weather, Thailand offers all sorts of athletic escapes. The most popular pursuits include div-

ing, snorkelling and jungle trekking, but cycling, kayaking and rock climbing aren't far behind.

Cycling

Many visitors bring their own bicycles to Thailand. In general, drivers are courteous, and most roads are sealed with roomy shoulders. Grades in most parts of the country are moderate; exceptions include the far north, especially Mae Hong Son and Nan Provinces, where you'll need iron legs. Favoured touring routes include the two-lane roads along the Mekong River in the north and northeast – the terrain is mostly flat and the river scenery is inspiring. The 2500-member **Thailand Cycling Club** (☎ 0 2612 5510; www.thaicycling.com/index_en.html) serves as an information clearing house on bicycle tours and cycle clubs around the country.

Diving & Snorkelling

Thailand's two coastlines and countless islands are popular among divers for warm waters and colourful marine life. The biggest diving centre is still Pattaya, simply because it's less than two hours' drive from Bangkok. Phuket is the second-biggest jumping-off point and has the advantage of offering the largest variety of places to choose from. Reef dives off the coast of Phuket are particularly rewarding – some 210 hard corals and 108 reef fish have so far been catalogued in this under-studied marine zone.

Dive operations have multiplied on the palmy islands of Ko Samui, Ko Pha-Ngan and Ko Tao, all in the Gulf of Thailand. Newer frontiers include the so-called Burma Banks (in the Mergui [Myeik] Archipelago northwest of Ko Surin) and islands off the coast of Krabi and Trang Provinces.

Most of these places have areas that are suitable for snorkelling as well as scuba diving, since many reefs are covered by water no deeper than 2m.

Masks, fins and snorkels are readily available for hire, but quality is often second-rate. Most dive shops can offer basic instruction and NAUI or PADI qualification for first-timers. An average four-day, full-certification course costs around 10,000B, including instruction, equipment and several open-water dives. Shorter, less expensive 'resort' courses are also available.

THAILAND

Kayaking

Exploring the islands and limestone karsts around Phuket and Ao Phang-Nga by inflatable kayak is a whole lot of fun. Typical trips seek out half-submerged caves, which can be accessed at low tide for a bit of on-the-water underground adventure.

Trekking

Trekking is one of northern Thailand's biggest attractions. Typical trekking programmes run for four or five days and feature daily walks through forested mountain areas, coupled with overnight stays in hill-tribe villages to satisfy both ethnotourism and ecotourism urges.

Other trekking opportunities are available in Thailand's larger national parks, including Khao Sok (p811) and Khao Yai (p762), where park rangers may be hired as guides and cooks for a few days at a time. Rates are reasonable.

BOOKS

Lonely Planet titles include *Thailand, Thailand's Islands & Beaches* and *Bangkok*. *Diving & Snorkelling Thailand* is chock-a-block full of colour photos and essential diving information. *Best of Bangkok* is a compact guide that's ideal for short-stay visitors. *World Food Thailand* is a unique culinary guide that takes you to the heart of the kingdom's culture.

Everyone in the City of Angels has a story and author James Eckardt tells it through a series of short stories and interviews with motorcycle drivers, noodle vendors, go-go dancers and heavy hitters in *Bangkok People*.

Meet a prepubescent Thai 12-year-old who lives in Bangkok, lusts after girls and meets the adult world, in the semiautobiographical *Jasmine Nights* by wunderkind SP Somtow. Born in Bangkok, educated at Eton and Cambridge, and now a commuter between two 'cities of angels' (Los Angeles and Bangkok), Somtow's prodigious output includes a string of well-reviewed science fiction/fantasy/horror stories.

What can a 1950s housewife teach you about Thailand? A lot! Author Carol Hollinger writes of her romance with Thai culture in *Mai Pen Rai Means Never Mind* as the atypical wife of an American businessman living in Bangkok.

Celebrated writer Pira Sudham was born into a poor family in northeastern Thailand, and brilliantly captures the region's struggles against nature and nurture. *Monsoon Country* is one of several titles Sudham wrote originally in English.

BUSINESS HOURS

Most government offices are open from 8.30am to 4.30pm weekdays, but often close from noon to 1pm for lunch. Businesses usually operate between 8.30am and 5pm weekdays and sometimes on Saturday morning. Larger shops usually open from 10am to 6.30pm or 7pm, but smaller shops may open earlier and close later. Restaurants keep erratic hours, but most are open from mid-morning to late at night.

Note that all government offices and banks are closed on public holidays.

CLIMATE

Tropical Thailand is warm year-round. The three seasons are: hot (from March to May), rainy (from June to October) and cool (from November to February). Towards the end of the hot season the northeast can get even hotter than Bangkok, although it's a drier heat. In the cool season, night-time temperatures in the north can drop as low as 4°C. Brrrrr!

The rainy season is no reason to put off a visit to Thailand, even though Bangkok is often flooded come September – the whole place is sinking, just like Venice.

See the Bangkok climate chart (p924) for more.

DANGERS & ANNOYANCES

Although Thailand is not a dangerous country, it's wise to be cautious, particularly if travelling alone. Theft in Thailand is still usually a matter of stealth rather than strength; travellers are more likely to have pockets picked than to be mugged. Take care of valuables, don't carry too much cash around and watch out for razor artists who ingeniously slit bags open in crowded quarters.

All travellers should ensure their rooms are securely locked and bolted at night. Inspect cheap rooms with thin walls in case there are strategic peepholes. We receive regular reports of thefts frequently occurring from guesthouses in Bangkok's Th Khao San and on the island of Ko Pha-Ngan.

THAILAND

Take caution when leaving valuables in hotel 'safes', usually a filing cabinet or desk drawer. Many travellers have reported problems with leaving valuables in Chiang Mai guesthouses while trekking, particularly credit cards taking themselves out on shopping sprees. Make sure you obtain an itemised receipt for property left with hotels or guesthouses – note the exact quantity of travellers cheques and all other valuables.

When you're on the road, keep zippered luggage secured with small locks, especially while travelling on buses and trains. Several readers' letters have recounted tales of thefts from their bags or backpacks during long overnight bus trips, particularly on routes between Bangkok and Chiang Mai or Ko Samui.

Thais are friendly and their friendliness is usually genuine. Nevertheless, on trains and buses, particularly in the south, beware of strangers offering cigarettes, drinks or chocolates. Several travellers have reported waking up with a headache to find their valuables have disappeared. Travellers have also encountered drugged food or drink offered by friendly strangers in bars and by prostitutes in their own hotel rooms.

Armed robbery does occur in some remote areas of Thailand, but the risk is fairly low. Avoid going out alone at night in remote areas and, if trekking in northern Thailand, always travel in groups.

There has been widespread unrest in the four southernmost provinces of Thailand during the last few years. Muslim separatists have been clashing with government forces in Songkhla, Yala, Pattani and Narathiwat and while civilians and tourists have not been targetted, there is always the remote possibility of getting caught in the crossfire. The government's response has been pretty heavy-handed and the violence shows no signs of dying down. See the boxed text (p796) for more details.

Penalties for drug offences are stiff these days in Thailand: if you are caught using marijuana, mushrooms or LSD, you face a fine of 10,000B plus one year in prison; for heroin or amphetamines, the penalty can be anywhere from a 5000B to 10,000B fine and six months' to 10 years' imprisonment, or worse. Remember that it is illegal to buy, sell or possess opium, heroin, amphetamines, LSD, mushrooms or marijuana in any quantity.

DISABLED TRAVELLERS

Thailand presents one large, ongoing obstacle course for the mobility-impaired. With its high kerbs, uneven pavements and non-stop traffic, Bangkok can be particularly

---

SCAMS

As old as the hippy trail, the gem scam is still alive and well. Over the years, Lonely Planet has received dozens of letters from victims who've been cheated of large sums of money by buying colourful pieces of glass masquerading as rare gems. Every report Lonely Planet receives follows the same scenario: you, the traveller, are headed to a popular attraction, a friendly local approaches you speaking your native language fluently and tells you that the attraction is closed. You curse Lonely Planet for not telling you and then look imploringly at your new friend who says that there are other interesting attractions nearby and they will arrange a ride for you. Now you are being taken for the proverbial 'ride'. What comes next is a one-day only, super bargain opportunity to learn an expensive lesson. If the price is too good to be true, then a scam is afoot.

The scam has also morphed into deals on clothing and card games. If you happen to become involved in one of these scams, the police (including the tourist police) are usually of little help: it's not illegal to sell gems at outrageously high prices and everyone's usually gone by the time you come back with the police.

Any túk-túk (three-wheeled motorcycle taxi) driver who offers you a ride for only 10B or 20B is a tout who will undoubtedly drag you somewhere else for a commission.

When you land in a bus station, a crowd of touts, as tactful as celebrity paparazzi, jockey for your business. Often these guys are harmless and even helpful, but some are crafty and will steer you to hotels that pay higher commissions rather than long-established places that don't 'tip' the driver. Hence, don't believe them if they tell you the hotel or guesthouse you're looking for is closed, full, dirty or bad – this is all 'tout speak' for no commission.

difficult. Rarely are there ramps or other access points for wheelchairs.

For wheelchair travellers, any trip to Thailand will require advance planning. The book *Exotic Destinations for Wheelchair Travelers* by Ed Hansen and Bruce Gordon contains a useful chapter on seven locations in Thailand. See p928 for organisations promoting travel for special-needs travellers.

DRIVING LICENCE

An International Driving Permit is necessary to drive vehicles in Thailand, but this is rarely enforced for motorcycle hire.

EMBASSIES & CONSULATES

For information on Thai visas, see p821.

Embassies & Consulates in Thailand

For locations of these and other consulates in Thailand, see individual city maps. The following embassies are found in Bangkok:

Australia (Map pp704-5; ☎ 0 2287 2680; 37 Th Sathon Tai)

Brunei (☎ 0 2204 1476; 698 Sukhumvit 71, Soi 42, 16 Phanit Anan Yeak)

Cambodia (Map pp704-5; ☎ 0 2254 6630; 185 Th Ratchadamri)

Canada (Map pp704-5; ☎ 0 2636 0540; 15th fl, Abdul-rahim Bldg, 990 Th Phra Ram IV)

China (Map pp700-1; ☎ 0 2245 7043; 57 Th Ratchadaphisek)

France (Map pp704-5; ☎ 0 2266 8250; 35 Soi 36, Th Charoen Krung); Consulate (Map pp704-5; ☎ 0 2287 1592; 29 Th Sathon Tai)

Germany (Map pp704-5; ☎ 0 2287 9000; 9 Th Sathon Tai)

India (☎ 0 2258 0300; 46 Soi Prasanmit (Soi 23), Th Sukhumvit)

Indonesia (Map pp704-5; ☎ 0 2252 3135; 600-602 Th Phetburi)

Japan (Map pp704-5; ☎ 0 2252 6151; 1674 Th Phet-chaburi Tat Mai)

Laos (Map pp700-1; ☎ 0 2539 6679; 520/1-3 Th Pracha Uthit, end of Soi 39, Th Ramkhamhaeng)

Malaysia (Map pp704-5; ☎ 0 2679 2190; 35 Sth Sathorn Rd, Tungmahamek Sathorn)

Myanmar (Map pp704-5; ☎ 0 2233 2237; 132 Th Sathon Neua)

New Zealand (Map pp704-5; ☎ 0 2254 2530; 19th fl, M Thai Tower, All Seasons Pl, 87 Th Withayu)

Philippines (Map pp700-1; ☎ 0 2259 0139; 760 Th Sukhumvit)

Singapore (Map pp704-5; ☎ 0 2286 2111; 9th & 18th fls, Rajanakam Bldg, 183 South Sathorn Rd)

UK (Map pp704-5; ☎ 0 2305 8333; 1031 Th Withayu)

USA (Map pp704-5; ☎ 0 2205 4000; 120-122 Th Withayu)

Vietnam (Map pp704-5; ☎ 0 2251 5836; 83/1 Th Withayu)

Thai Embassies & Consulates Abroad

Thai diplomatic offices abroad include the following:

Australia (☎ 02-6273 1149; 111 Empire Circuit, Yarralumla, ACT 2600)

Canada (☎ 613-722 4444; 180 Island Park Dr, Ottawa, Ontario K1Y 0A2)

France (☎ 01 56 26 50 50; 8 Rue Greuze, 75116 Paris)

Germany (☎ 030-794 810; Lepsiusstrasse 64-66, 12163 Berlin)

Israel (☎ 972-3 695 8980; 21 Shaul Hamelech Blvd, Tel Aviv)

New Zealand (☎ 04-476 8618; 2 Cook St, Karori, PO Box 17226, Wellington)

UK (☎ 020-7589 0173; 29-30 Queen's Gate, London SW7 5JB)

USA (☎ 202-944 3608; 1024 Wisconsin Ave NW, Washington, DC 20007)

FESTIVALS & EVENTS

Many Thai festivals are linked to Buddhist rituals and follow the lunar calendar. Thus they fall on different dates each year, depending on the phases of the moon. Many provinces hold annual festivals or fairs to promote their specialities. A complete, up-to-date schedule of events around the country is available from TAT offices in each region or from the central Bangkok TAT office.

Businesses typically close and transportation becomes difficult during the following public holidays:

New Year's Day 1 January

Chakri Memorial Day Held on 6 April; to celebrate the founder of the current royal dynasty.

Songkran Festival From 12 to 14 April, Buddha images are 'bathed', monks and elders receive the respect of younger Thais by the sprinkling of water over their hands, and a lot of water is generously tossed about for fun. Song-kran generally gives everyone a chance to release their frustrations and literally cool off during the peak of the hot season. Hide out in your room or expect to be soaked; the latter is a lot more fun.

National Labour Day 1 May

Coronation Day 5 May

Queen's Birthday (Mother's Day) Held on 12 August; festivities occur mainly in Bangkok.

Chulalongkorn Day King Chulalongkorn is honoured on 23 October.

King's Birthday (Father's Day) 5 December
Constitution Day 10 December
New Year's Eve 31 December

Lunar public holidays include:

Magha Puja (Maakhá Buuchaa) Held on the full moon of the third lunar month to commemorate Buddha preaching to 1250 enlightened monks who came to hear him 'without prior summons'. It culminates with a candlelit walk around the *wian tian* (main chapel) at every wat.

Visakha Puja (Wísǎakhà Buuchaa) This event falls on the 15th day of the waxing moon in the sixth lunar month and commemorates the date of the Buddha's birth, enlightenment and passing away. Activities are centred on the wat.

Khao Phansa (Khâo Phansǎa) This marks the beginning of Buddhist 'lent', the traditional time of year for young men to enter the monkhood for the rainy season. It's a good time to observe a Buddhist ordination.

Loi Krathong On the night of the full moon, small lotus-shaped baskets or boats made of banana leaves containing flowers, incense, candles and a coin are floated on Thai rivers, lakes and canals.

FOOD & DRINK

Thai food is a complex balance of spicy, salty, sweet and sour. The ingredients are fresh and light with lots of lemon grass, basil, coriander and mint. The chilli peppers pack a slow, nose-running burn. And pungent *náam plaa* (fish sauce; generally made from anchovies) adds a touch of the salty sea. Throw in a little zest of lime and a pinch of sugar and the ingredients make a symphony of flavours that becomes more interesting with each bite. A relationship with Thai food has a long courtship phase – at first the flavours are too assertive and foreign, the hot too hot, the fish sauce too fishy. But with practice you'll smell rice cooking in the morning and crave a fiery curry instead of dull toast and jam. Now you are 'eating', which in Thai literally means to 'eat rice', or *kin khâo*.

Food
STAPLES & SPECIALITIES
Welcome to a country where it is cheaper and tastier to eat out than to cook at home. Day and night markets, pushcart vendors, makeshift stalls, open-air restaurants – prices stay low because of few or no overheads, and cooks become famous in all walks of life for a particular dish. It is possible to eat well and cheaply without ever stepping foot into a formal restaurant. No

self-respecting shoestringer would shy away from the pushcarts in Thailand for fear of stomach troubles. The hygiene standards are some of the best in the region, and sitting next to the wok you can see all the action, unlike some of the guesthouses where food is assembled in a darkened hovel.

Take a walk through the day markets and you will see mounds of clay-coloured pastes all lined up like art supplies. These are finely ground herbs and seasonings that create the backbone for Thai *kaeng* (curries). The paste is thinned with coconut milk and decorated with vegetables and meat. Although it is the consistency of a watery soup, *kaeng* is not eaten like Western-style soup, but is ladled on to a plate of rice.

For breakfast and for late-night snacks, Thais nosh on *kǔaytǐaw*, a noodle soup with chicken or pork and vegetables. There are two major types of noodles you can choose from: *sên lek* (thin) and *sên yài* (wide and flat). Before you dig into your steaming bowl, first use the chopsticks (or a spoon) to cut the noodles into smaller segments so they are easier to pick up. Then add to taste a few teaspoonfuls of the provided spices: dried red chilli, sugar, fish sauce and vinegar. Now you have the true taste of Thailand in front of you. The weapons of choice when eating noodles (either *kǔaytǐaw* or *phàt thai*) are chopsticks, a rounded soup spoon or a fork.

Not sure what to order at some of the popular dinner restaurants? Reliable favourites are *yam plaa mèuk* (spicy squid salad with mint leaves, cilantro and Chinese celery), *tôm yam kûng* (coconut soup with prawns, often translated as 'hot and sour soup') or its sister dish *tôm khàa kài* (coconut soup with chicken and galangal).

At the simple open-air restaurants there is a standard range of dishes that every cook worth their fish sauce can make. These are the greatest hits of the culinary menu and include the following:

kài phàt bai kà-phrao – fiery stir-fry of chopped chicken, chillies, garlic and fresh basil
khâo phàt – fried rice
phàt phrík thai krà-thiam – stir-fried chicken or pork with black pepper and garlic
phàt thai – fried rice noodles, bean sprouts, peanuts, eggs, chillies and often prawns
phàt phàk khanáa – stir-fried Chinese greens, simple but delicious

EATING ETIQUETTE

Thais are social eaters: meals are rarely taken alone and dishes are meant to be shared. Usually a small army of plates will be placed in the centre of the table, with individual servings of rice in front of each diner. The protocol goes like this – ladle a spoonful of food at a time on to your plate of rice. Dishes aren't passed in Thailand; instead you reach across the table to the different items. Using the spoon like a fork and your fork like a knife, steer the food (with the fork) onto your spoon, which enters your mouth. To the Thais placing a fork in the mouth is just plain weird. When you are full, leave a little rice on your plate (an empty plate is a silent request for more rice) and place your fork so that it is cradled by the spoon in the centre of the plate.

Even when eating with a gang of *faràng*, it is still wise to order 'family style', as dishes are rarely synchronised. Ordering individually will leave one person staring politely at a piping hot plate, and another staring wistfully at the kitchen.

Drink

Water purified for drinking purposes is simply called *náam dèum* (drinking water), whether boiled or filtered. All water offered to customers in restaurants or to guests in an office or home will be purified. Ice is generally safe in Thailand. *Chaa* (tea) and *kaa-fae* (coffee) are prepared strong, milky and sweet – an instant morning buzz.

Thanks to the tropical bounty, exotic fruit juices are sold on every corner. Thais prefer a little salt to cut the sweetness of the juice; the salt also has some mystical power to make a hot day tolerable. Most drinks are available in a clear plastic bag designed especially for takeaway customers; in time you'll come to prefer the bag to a conventional glass.

Cheap beer appears hand-in-hand with backpacker ghettos. Beer Chang and Beer Singha (pronounced 'sing', not 'sing-ha') are a couple of local brands you'll learn to love, although they pack a punch. Thais have created yet another innovative method for beating the heat; they drink their beer with ice to keep the beverage cool and crisp.

More of a ritual than a beverage, Thai whisky (Mekong and Sang Thip brands) usually runs with a distinct crowd – soda water, Coke and ice. Fill the short glass with ice cubes, two-thirds whisky, one-third soda and a splash of Coke. Thai tradition dictates the youngest in the crowd is responsible for filling the other drinkers' glasses. Many travellers prefer to go straight to the ice bucket with shared straws, not forgetting a dash of Red Bull for a cocktail to keep them going.

GAY & LESBIAN TRAVELLERS

Gays won't have a problem travelling in Thailand as the country has a long history of homosexuality. Prominent gay communities exist in large cities like Bangkok and Chiang Mai, and gay pride events are celebrated in Bangkok, Pattaya and Phuket. While public displays of affection are common (and usually platonic) between members of the same sex, you should refrain from anything beyond friendly hand-holding for the sake of social etiquette.

Gay, lesbian and transsexual Thais are generally tolerated, living peaceably in even the most conservative Thai towns. All is not love and understanding, though. Labelled 'sexual deviants', suspected gays are barred from studying to become teachers or from joining the military.

Utopia (www.utopia-asia.com) is a good starting point for more information on Thailand for the gay traveller. Utopia also runs Thailand **tours** (☎ 0 2238 3227; Lobby, Tarntawan Place Hotel, Th Surawong). **Anjaree Group** (☎ 0 2668 2185; PO Box 322, Ratchadamnoen, Bangkok 10200) is Thailand's premier (and only) lesbian society.

HEALTH

By regional standards, Thailand is a relatively healthy country for travel. Pharmacies are widely available in most towns, and pharmacists typically speak some English. The most advanced hospitals are in Bangkok, Chiang Mai, Udon Thani, Hat Yai and Phuket. Recently, many travellers have made special trips to Thailand to receive inexpensive medical and dental care.

Southeast Asian liver flukes (*Opisthorchis viverrini*) are occasionally present in freshwater fish, and when ingested can cause a liver condition known as opisthorchiasis. The main risk comes from eating raw or undercooked fish. In particular, travellers should avoid eating *plaa ráa* (sometimes called *paa daek* in northeastern Thailand), an unpasteurised fermented fish used as an accompaniment to rice in the northeast.

See p943 for more information.

HOLIDAYS

For a list of holidays in Thailand, see Festivals & Events (p816).

INTERNET ACCESS

You can't walk far without tripping over an Internet café in Thailand. Connections tend to be slow and unreliable, but rates are usually cheap (20B to 50B per hour).

INTERNET RESOURCES

www.bangkokpost.com This English-language newspaper posts its entire newspaper content online; check out Bernard Trink's 'Night Owl' column for this dirty old man's unabashed coverage of the go-go bar scene, as well as wit and wisdom.

www.elephantguide.com Find news and reviews of Bangkok restaurants, clubs and events.

www.happycow.net Reviews and contact details on vegetarian restaurants worldwide.

www.hilltribe.org This virtual hill-tribe museum is a good way to learn about the hill tribes of northern Thailand and etiquette in minority villages.

www.nationmultimedia.com Another English-language newspaper that also posts content on the web.

www.tat.or.th Thailand's official tourism website covers major tourist spots and lists licensed tour operators.

www.thaifootball.com The online headquarters of the Thai national football team profiles players and posts news and scores. Great prereading for conversations with taxi drivers.

www.thailand.com Here you'll find a general overview of art, history and culture, as well as destinations.

LEGAL MATTERS

In general, Thai police don't hassle foreigners, especially tourists. One major exception is in regard to drugs (see p814).

If you are arrested for any offence, the police will allow you the opportunity to make a phone call to your embassy or consulate in Thailand, if you have one, or to a friend or relative if not. Thai law does not

---

presume an indicted detainee to be either 'guilty' or 'innocent' but rather a 'suspect', whose guilt or innocence will be decided in court. Trials are usually speedy.

MAPS

Lonely Planet publishes a *Bangkok City Map*, and the Roads Association of Thailand produces a useful bilingual road atlas, *Thailand Highway Map*. Updated every year, it has city maps, distance charts and an index.

MEDIA

Thailand is widely considered to have the freest print media in Southeast Asia, although there is self-censorship in matters relating to the monarchy, and the Royal Police Department reserves the power to suspend publishing licences for national security reasons. The *Bangkok Post* in the morning and the *Nation* in the afternoon are the country's two English-language newspapers.

Thailand has more than 400 radio stations, almost all of them government-owned and -operated. English-language broadcasts of the international news services can be picked up over short-wave radio. The frequencies and schedules appear in the *Post* and *Nation*.

Thailand possesses five VHF TV networks based in Bangkok, all but one government-operated. The single private network, ITV, is owned by the current prime minister, so even this one is a slave to the government line politically.

MONEY

The baht (B) is divided into 100 satang, although 25 and 50 satang are the smallest coins that you're likely to see. Coins come in 1B, 5B and 10B denominations. Notes are in 20B (green), 50B (blue), 100B (red), 500B (purple) and 1000B (beige) denominations of varying shades and sizes.

ATMs

All major Thai banks, which are well distributed throughout the country, offer ATM services; most of the machines will accept international credit and debit cards. ATMs typically dispense 1000B notes that should be broken at 7-Elevens or guesthouses rather than in the market.

LEGAL AGE

- voting starts at 18
- you can begin driving at 18
- sex is legal at 15

THAILAND

Bargaining

Bargaining is mandatory in markets and small family-run stores and with all túk-túk and taxi drivers (unless the cab is metered). By and large it is not appropriate in most hotels or guesthouses unless staff initiate it, but you can ask politely if there's anything cheaper. Always smile and never become frustrated or angry when bargaining.

Credit Cards

Credit cards are widely accepted at upmarket hotels, restaurants and other business establishments. Visa and MasterCard are the most commonly accepted, followed by American Express (Amex) and Diners Club. Cash advances are available on Visa and MasterCard at many banks and exchange booths.

Exchanging Money

Banks give the best exchange rates and hotels give the worst. In the larger towns and tourist destinations, there are also foreign-exchange kiosks that open longer hours, usually from 8am to 8pm. Since banks charge commission and duty for each travellers cheque cashed, use larger cheque denominations to save on commission. British pounds and euros are second to the US dollar in general acceptability.

Exchange rates at the time this book went to press were as follows:

Country	Unit	Baht
Australia	A$1	30
Cambodia	100r	1
Canada	C$1	35
Euro zone	€1	48
Japan	¥100	35
Laos	K1000	4
Malaysia	RM1	11
New Zealand	NZ$1	28
Singapore	S$1	24
UK	£1	72
USA	US$1	41

POST

The Thai postal system is relatively efficient and few travellers complain about undelivered mail or lost parcels. Never send cash or small valuable objects through the postal system, even if the items are insured. Poste restante can be received at any town that has a post office.

RESPONSIBLE TRAVEL

Be aware about having a negative impact on the environment or the local culture. Read p689 for guidance on observing social mores. See p4 for suggestions on treading lightly through Thailand's environment and through tribal peoples' villages.

Despite Thailand's reputation among sex tourists, prostitution was declared illegal in the 1950s. Many of the sex workers are uneducated women or girls from villages who are struggling to support children or who have been sold into the business by their parents. The government does little to enforce antiprostitution laws in cases of consenting adults; however, a jail term of four to 20 years and/or a fine up to 40,000B can be imposed on anyone caught having sex with a person under 15 years of age. If the child is under 13, the sentence can amount to life imprisonment. Many Western countries have also instituted extraterritorial legislation where citizens can be charged for child prostitution offences committed abroad.

The Thai government encourages people to help eradicate child prostitution by reporting child sexual abuse. You can contact **End Child Prostitution & Traffic International** (Ecpat; ☎ 0 2215 3388; www.ecpat.org; 328 Th Phayathai, Bangkok 10400), a global network of organisations that works to stop child prostitution, child pornography and the traffic of children for sexual purposes.

STUDYING

Thai cooking, traditional medicine, language, *muay thai* (Thai boxing): the possibilities of studying in Thailand are endless and range from formal lectures to week-long retreats.

Especially popular are meditation courses for Western students of Buddhism. Unique to Buddhism is the system of meditation known as *vipassana*, a Pali word that roughly translates as 'insight'. Foreigners who come to study *vipassana* can choose from dozens of temples and meditation centres. Thai language is usually the medium of instruction but several places provide instruction in English. Contact details for some popular meditation-oriented centres are given in the city, town and province sections of this chapter. Instruction and accommodation are free at temples, but donations are expected.

Described by some as a 'brutally pleasant experience', Thai massage does not directly seek to relax the body, but instead uses the hands, thumbs, fingers, elbows, forearms, knees and feet to work the traditional pressure points. The client's body is also pulled, twisted and manipulated in ways that have been described as 'passive yoga'. The objective is to distribute energies evenly throughout the nervous system to create a harmony of physical energy flows. The muscular-skeletal system is also manipulated in ways that can be compared to modern physiotherapy. Thailand offers ample opportunities to study its unique tradition of massage therapy. Wat Pho (p708) in Bangkok is considered the master source for all Thai massage pedagogy, although Chiang Mai (p741) boasts a 'softer' version.

Training in *muay thai* takes place at dozens of boxing camps around the country. Be forewarned, however: training is gruelling and features full-contact sparring. Many centres are reluctant to take on foreign trainees. Rates vary from US$50 to US$250 per week, including food and accommodation. The website www.muaythai.com contains loads of information including the addresses of training camps. Also see the Bangkok (p708) and Chiang Mai (p741) sections for information on *muay thai* training programmes in these two cities.

Several language schools in Bangkok and Chiang Mai offer courses in Thai language. Tuition fees average around 250B per hour. See the Courses sections in this chapter for further detail.

TELEPHONE

The telephone system in Thailand, operated by the government-subsidised Telephone Organization of Thailand (TOT) under the Communications Authority of Thailand (CAT), is quite efficient and offers International Direct Dial (IDD) universally. In smaller towns these services are available at the main post office. You can make international calls from public telephone booths with a prepaid phonecard available from 7-Eleven stores. Rates tend to be about the same as the government phone offices. Guesthouses also offer phone services that are considerably more expensive.

Roaming charges are quite reasonable in Thailand for those with mobile phones. There are several cheap international call carriers that offer significant savings on international calls from a mobile: dial out using ☎ 008 or ☎ 009 for a bargain.

The telephone country code for Thailand is ☎ 66. All Thai phone numbers listed in this book are preceded by ☎ 0, but you only need to include the zero when dialling numbers within Thailand. City prefixes were recently integrated into the phone numbers for all calls regardless of their origin.

TOURIST INFORMATION

The **Tourist Authority of Thailand** (TAT; www.tat.or .th) has offices throughout the country, which are helpful for bus schedules, local maps and finding accommodation. Contact information for regional offices is listed under each town.

TAT offices can be found in the following countries:

Australia (☎ 02-9247 7549; Level 2, 75 Pitt St, Sydney, NSW 2000)

France (☎ 01 53 53 47 00; 90 Ave des Champs-Elysées, 75008 Paris)

Germany (☎ 069-138 1390; Bethmannstrasse 58, D-60311 Frankfurt/Main)

Malaysia (☎ 603-216 23480; Suite 22.01, Level 22, Menara Lion, 165 Jl Ampang, 50450 Kuala Lumpur)

Singapore (☎ 235 77901; c/o Royal Thai Embassy, 370 Orchard Rd, 238870)

UK (☎ 020-7925 2511; 3rd fl, Brook House, 98-99 Jermyn St, London SW1Y 6EE)

USA Los Angeles (☎ 323-461 9814; 1st fl, 611 North Larchmont Blvd, LA, CA 90004); New York (☎ 212-432 0433; Suite 281, 61 Broadway, New York, NY 10006)

VISAS

Citizens of 39 countries (including most European countries, Australia, New Zealand and the USA) can enter Thailand visa-free at no charge. See the website of Thailand's **Ministry of Foreign Affairs** (www.mfa .go.th) for the full story. For a longer stay, just leave and re-enter the country at any border point: upon re-entry you get another 30 days, thank you very much. You can also extend the 30-day visa for seven to 10 days at any Thai immigration office for 500B.

With advance planning, a 60-day tourist visa is available from Thai embassies or consulates worldwide (see p816). Application fees are usually US$30 and take up to a week. Contact the embassy for an application form and additional instructions.

The Non-Immigrant Visa is good for 90 days, must be applied for in your home country, costs US$60 and is not difficult to obtain if you are travelling for business, study, retirement or an extended family visit. For anyone planning on staying longer than three months, this is the one to go for.

If you overstay your visa, the usual penalty is a fine of 200B for each extra day, with a 20,000B limit; fines can be paid at any official exit point or in advance at the **Investigation Unit** (☎ 0 2287 3101-10; Immigration Bureau, Room 416, 4th fl, Old Bldg, Soi Suan Phlu, Th Sathon Tai, Bangkok).

Cambodian and Lao visas are now available at most land-border crossings with Thailand and all international airports. For trips to Myanmar, short-visit visas are available for day crossings, but get a visa in advance if you are flying into Yangon. Most visitors to Malaysia do not require a visa.

VOLUNTEERING

Voluntary and paid positions with charitable organisations can be found in the education, development or public health sectors.

Mon, Karen and Burmese refugee camps along the Thailand–Myanmar border often need volunteers. Since none of the camps are officially sanctioned by the Thai government, few of the big NGOs or multilateral organisations are involved here. If this interests you, travel to Mae Sot (p736) and ask around for the 'unofficial' camp locations, or contact **Burma Volunteer Programme** (www.geocities.com/maesotesl), which offers three-month volunteer jobs teaching English or working on human rights issues.

Other volunteer organisations:

Ecovolunteer Programme (www.ecovolunteer.org; per person US$600-800) A network of NGOs working on environmental issues; in Thailand volunteers collect data on mangrove forests, study sea turtles or help run an animal rescue sanctuary.

Habitat for Humanity (www.habitat.org; per person US$2000-3000) One- to three-week house-building trips in northeast Thailand with a charitable organisation founded by former US president Jimmy Carter.

Human Development Foundation (www.fatherjoe .org) A community outreach centre in the Bangkok slum of Khlong Toei; volunteers work on basic medical care, HIV/AIDS education and drug prevention.

WOMEN TRAVELLERS

By and large women are safe travelling in groups or solo through Thailand. Extra caution needs to be exercised at night, especially when returning home from a bar or arriving in a new town late at night. Thais, both men and women, are chatty and will extend the hand of friendship, give you a ride or take you to the disco. Often accepting these invitations are fun experiences, but women should be aware that Thai men don't adhere to their own culture's rules when dealing with foreign women. While hand-holding, hugging or any other public contact between members of the opposite sex is a huge no-no in Thai society, Thai men think it is appropriate to touch (however innocently) foreign women even if the advances aren't encouraged.

Despite Thailand's peaceful nature, rape is a concern. Over the past decade, several foreign women have been attacked while travelling alone in remote areas and there have been several high-profile murders. Still, given the huge tourist numbers visiting Thailand, there is no need to be paranoid.

WORKING

Teaching English is one of the easiest ways to immerse yourself into a Thai community. Those with academic credentials, such as teaching certificates or degrees in English as a second language (ESL) or English as a foreign language (EFL), get first crack at the better-paying jobs at universities and international schools. But there are hundreds of language schools for every variety of native English speaker.

Maintained by an EFL teacher in Bangkok, www.ajarn.com has tips on where to find teaching jobs and how to deal with Thai classrooms, as well as current job listings.

Rajabhat Institute (☎ 0 2628 5281, ext 2906; teerawat23@hotmail.com; Teerawat Wangmanee, Office of Rajabhat Institute, Ministry of Education, Th Ratchadamnoen Nok, Bangkok 10300) has one-year English-teaching positions available in 41 teachers colleges right across the country. These positions pay well by Thai standards, and most students are preparing to be the country's next generation of primary- and secondary-school English teachers.

Vietnam

HIGHLIGHTS

- **Northern mountains** – trekking from rice-terraced Sapa to diverse hill-tribe villages or Vietnam's highest peak, Fansipan (p857)
- **Hanoi** – taking in the French colonial flavour, seeing water-puppet theatre and savouring Vietnamese culinary treats (p831)
- **Halong Bay** – kayaking around the thousands of limestone islands jutting from turquoise waters (p851)
- **Hoi An** – roaming Cham ruins at dawn, sunbathing at midday and sampling local culinary specialities by night, dressed in custom-tailored silk (p871)
- **Mui Ne** – downshifting to the sway of this bay's breezes and dozing on the beach, or kick-starting a kite-surfing obsession (p883)
- **Off the beaten track** – riding Phu Quoc Island's dirt roads to find bliss-out nothingness on tranquil beaches (p911)

FAST FACTS

- **ATMs** in many cities
- **Budget** US$23 a day
- **Capital** Hanoi
- **Costs** guesthouse in Hanoi US$6-12, 4hr bus ride US$4-6, beer US$0.65
- **Country code** ☎ 84
- **Famous for** independence leader Ho Chi Minh, *pho*, conical hats, *Apocalypse Now* and the American War
- **Languages** Vietnamese and ethnic dialects
- **Money** US$1 = 15,700d (dong)
- **Phrases** *xin chao* (hello), *tam biêt* (good-bye), *cam on* (thanks), *xin loi* (sorry), *khong cam on, di bo* (no thanks, I'll walk)
- **Population** 82.7 million
- **Seasons** south hot & wet Apr-Sep, hot & dry Oct-Mar; north hot & dry Apr-Sep, cool & wet Oct-Mar; central coast typhoons Jul-Nov
- **Visas** arrange in advance, with fixed arrival and departure dates; US$35-60 for 30 days

TRAVEL HINT

Persistent vendor or cyclo driver wearing you down? Say no once (with a smile), and move on. Continuing the conversation invites dogged negotiations.

OVERLAND ROUTES

Boats travel the Mekong River between Phnom Penh in Cambodia and Ho Chi Minh City (p910); otherwise, roads cross the Cambodian (p910), Lao (p867) and Chinese (p847 and p857) borders.

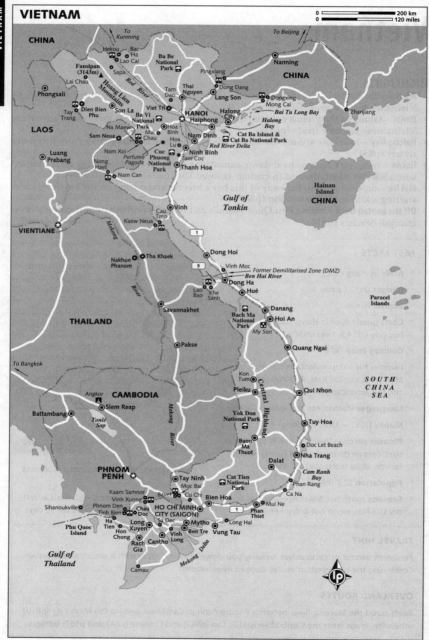

Brace yourself for this ride. Vietnam has more than a dash of the Wild West to it, from the bucking-dragon shape of its geography to an underlying sense of joyful lawlessness. Yes, there is peace in that pagoda, but on the street just beyond, living in the moment is an art mastered by the Vietnamese.

The ebullient, intense people of Vietnam are quick on the draw when it comes to making a deal, and quicker to smile if you can crack a joke. Moving on from yesterday and not worrying too hard about tomorrow – their attitude is all about the now. This is a nation of determined optimists who have weathered war upon war, survived colonialism, a closed society and Communist rule, and come out alive and kicking as an intact culture.

The Vietnamese countryside, from shimmering rice paddies to stunning karst formations, is punctuated with cheerfully patriotic propaganda billboards and populated with workers toiling from dawn to dusk. It's mad, it's loud, it's a little overwhelming – but like the all-encompassing presence of Ho Chi Minh, you'll get used to it.

CURRENT EVENTS

Vietnam exists in a curious state of dichotomy. While the Communist Party is still very much in charge (Vietnamese president Tran Duc Luong is high up in the party), capitalism is the ideology of choice and action. There are the rules, and then there is the national pastime of getting around them. Foreign investors are setting up joint ventures with Vietnamese companies, cultural exchange is exerting international influence over fashion, technology and a new generation, and Vietnam is speeding towards the future with its politics and desires in a delicate balance.

HISTORY
Early Vietnam

The sophisticated Indianised kingdom of Funan flourished from the 1st to 6th centuries AD in the Mekong Delta area. Archaeological evidence reveals that Funan's busy trading port of Oc-Eo had contact with China, India, Persia and even the Mediterranean. Between the mid-6th century and the 9th century, the Funan empire was absorbed by the pre-Angkorian kingdom of Chenla.

Around the late 2nd century when the Hindu kingdom of Champa was putting down roots in the Danang area, the Chinese had conquered the Red River Delta near Hanoi.

Thus began a thousand-year pattern of the Vietnamese resisting the yoke of Chinese rule, while at the same time adopting many Chinese innovations to evolve into today's rice-growing society. The most famous act of resistance during this period (c 200 BC–AD 938) was the rebellion of the two Trung sisters (Hai Ba Trung), self-declared queens of the Vietnamese state, who drowned themselves rather than surrendering to the Chinese.

By the 10th century, Vietnam had declared independence from China and begun almost one thousand years of a dynastic tradition. During this era, the Vietnamese successfully repulsed attacks by the Khmers, Chams, Mongols and Chinese, eventually assimilating the Cham civilisation into Vietnamese society.

Vietnam & the West

As far back as AD 166, Vietnam had contact with Europeans from the Rome of Marcus Aurelius. European merchants and missionaries trickled into the country in the early 16th century, among them the brilliant Alexandre de Rhodes. A French Jesuit missionary, de Rhodes developed the *quoc ngu* script still used for written Vietnamese.

In 1858 a joint military force from France and the Spanish colony of the Philippines stormed Danang after several missionaries were killed. Early the next year, it seized Saigon. By 1883 the French had imposed a Treaty of Protectorate on Vietnam; French rule often proved cruel and arbitrary. Ultimately, the most successful resistance came from the communists – the first Marxist group in Indochina, the Vietnam Revolutionary Youth League, was founded by Ho Chi Minh in 1925.

During WWII, the only group that significantly resisted the Japanese occupation was the Communist-dominated Viet Minh. When WWII ended, Ho Chi Minh – whose Viet Minh forces already controlled large parts of the country – declared Vietnam independent. French efforts to reassert control soon led to violent confrontations and full-scale war.

In May 1954, Viet Minh forces overran the French garrison at Dien Bien Phu.

The Geneva Accords of mid-1954 provided for a temporary division of Vietnam at the Ben Hai River. When Ngo Dinh Diem, the anti-communist, Catholic leader of the southern zone, refused to hold the 1956 elections, the Ben Hai line became the border between North and South Vietnam.

Around 1960, the Hanoi government changed its policy of opposition to the Diem regime from one of 'political struggle' to one of 'armed struggle'. The National Liberation Front (NLF), a Communist guerrilla group better known as the Viet Cong (VC), was founded to fight against Diem.

A brutal ruler, Diem was assassinated in 1963 by his own troops. After Hanoi ordered North Vietnamese Army (NVA) units to infiltrate the South in 1964, the situation for the Saigon regime became desperate. In 1965 the USA committed its first combat troops, soon joined by soldiers from South Korea, Australia, Thailand and New Zealand.

As Vietnam celebrated the Lunar New Year in 1968, the VC launched a deadly surprise offensive (the Tet Offensive), marking a crucial turning point in the war. Many Americans, who had for years believed their government's insistence that the USA was winning, started demanding a negotiated end to the war. The Paris Agreements, signed in 1973, provided for a cease-fire, the total withdrawal of US combat forces and the release of American prisoners of war.

Reunification

Saigon surrendered to the NVA on 30 April 1975. Vietnam's reunification by the communists meant liberation from more than a century of colonial repression, but it was soon followed by large-scale internal repression. Hundreds of thousands of southerners fled Vietnam, creating a flood of refugees for the next 15 years.

Vietnam's campaign of repression against the ethnic-Chinese, plus its invasion of Cambodia at the end of 1978, prompted China to attack Vietnam in 1979. The war lasted only 17 days, but Chinese-Vietnamese mistrust lasted well over a decade.

Transition & Globalisation

With the end of the Cold War and the collapse of the Soviet Union in 1991, Vietnam and Western nations sought *rapprochement*. The 1990s brought foreign investment and Asean membership. The USA established diplomatic relations with Vietnam in 1995, and in 2000, Bill Clinton became the first US president to visit northern Vietnam.

The lingering effects of the 1997 Asian economic crisis, as well as outbreaks of SARS in 2003 and Avian influenza (bird flu) in 2004 and 2005 have meant sluggish growth in tourism numbers over the last few years. Though some visitors to Southeast Asia have rerouted their plans to Vietnam from neighbouring tsunami-affected countries, others are avoiding the region altogether. However, recent years have also seen burgeoning international trade, domestic development and a rise in foreign business visitors. Although the government still appears unreconciled over the direction of economic and political reform, Vietnam is slowly opening to the inevitability of globalisation.

THE CULTURE

The Vietnamese take passionate pride in their national identity, and they have their entire history to back them up. Having defended their sovereignty as a nation from the Chinese to the French, the people's determination and optimism reflect the collective strength and sense of self that keep Vietnam bouncing back.

As in other parts of Asia, life revolves around the family; there are often several generations living under one roof. Poverty, and the transition from a largely agricultural society to that of a more industrialised nation, sends many people seeking fortune to the bigger cities and thus changes the structure of the modern family unit. Women make up 52% the nation's workforce but are generally not in high positions of power.

Vietnam's population is 84% ethnic Vietnamese *(Kinh)* and 2% ethnic Chinese; the rest is made up of Khmers, Chams and

---

MUST SEE

The Quiet American (2002) – see the excellent film, then read the even-better novel by Graham Greene. Wartime intrigue, a love triangle, and intercultural human relationships, set in 1950s Saigon.

members of more than 50 ethnolinguistic groups known as Montagnards (French for 'highlanders').

RELIGION

Over the centuries, Confucianism, Taoism and Buddhism have fused with popular Chinese beliefs and ancient Vietnamese animism to form what's collectively known as the Triple Religion (Tam Giao). Most Vietnamese people identify with this belief system, but if asked, they'll usually say they're Buddhist.

Vietnam has a significant percentage of Catholics (8% to 10% of the population), second in Southeast Asia only to the Philippines.

The unique and colourful Vietnamese sect called Caodaism was founded in the 1920s. It combines secular and religious philosophies of the East and West, and was based on séance messages revealed to the group's founder, Ngo Minh Chieu.

ARTS

Contemporary Arts

It's sometimes possible to catch modern dance, classical ballet and stage plays in Hanoi and Ho Chi Minh City (HCMC). The work of contemporary painters and photographers covers a wide swathe of styles and gives a glimpse into the modern Vietnamese psyche. Check the *Guide* or *Time Out* for current theatre or dance listings in Hanoi and HCMC.

Traditional Arts

ARCHITECTURE

The Vietnamese were not great builders like their neighbours the Khmer, who erected the Angkor temples in Cambodia. Most early Vietnamese buildings were made of wood and other materials that proved highly vulnerable in the tropical climate. The grand exception is the stunning towers built by Vietnam's ancient Cham culture. These are most numerous in central Vietnam. The Cham ruins at My Son (p877) are a major tourist draw.

SCULPTURE

Vietnamese sculpture has traditionally centred on religious themes and has functioned as an adjunct to architecture, especially that of pagodas, temples and tombs.

> **MUST READ**
>
> *Catfish & Mandala* (1999), by Andrew X Pham, is the author's bicycle journey that wheels from Saigon to Hanoi and far beyond. Exquisitely intimate but broadly illuminating.

The Cham civilisation produced exquisite carved sandstone figures for its Hindu and Buddhist sanctuaries. The largest single collection of Cham sculpture is at the Museum of Cham Sculpture (p869) in Danang.

WATER PUPPETRY

Vietnam's ancient art of *roi nuoc* (water puppetry) originated in northern Vietnam at least 1000 years ago. Developed by rice farmers, the wooden puppets were manipulated by puppeteers using water-flooded rice paddies as their stage. Hanoi is the best place to see water-puppetry performances, which are accompanied by music played on traditional instruments. There are also performances in Saigon.

ENVIRONMENT

Environmental consciousness is low in Vietnam. Compounded with rapid industrialisation, deforestation and pollution are burgeoning problems in the country.

Unsustainable logging and farming practices, as well as the USA's extensive spraying of defoliants during the American War, have contributed to deforestation. This has resulted not only in significant loss of biological diversity, but also in the reduction of livelihood options for many Montagnard groups.

The country's rapid economic and population growth over the last decade (demonstrated by the dramatic increase in motorbike numbers and helter-skelter construction) has put additional pressure on the already-stressed environment.

The Land

Vietnam stretches over 1600km along the east coast of the Indochinese peninsula. The country's land area is 329,566 sq km, making it slightly larger than Italy and a bit smaller than Japan.

Of several interesting geological features found in Vietnam, the most striking are the karst formations (limestone regions with caves and underground streams). The northern part of Vietnam has a spectacular assemblage of karst areas, particularly around Halong Bay and Tam Coc.

The country's two main cultivated areas are the Red River Delta in the north and the Mekong Delta in the south. The latter has produced one of the world's great deltas, composed of fine silt that has washed downstream for millions of years.

Wildlife

Because Vietnam has such a wide range of habitats, its fauna is enormously diverse; its forests are estimated to contain 12,000 plant species, only 7000 of which have been identified. Vietnam is home to more than 275 species of mammal, 800 species of bird, 180 species of reptile and 80 species of amphibian. In the 1990s, one species of muntjac (deer) and an ox similar to an oryx were discovered in Vietnam – the only newly identified large mammals in the world in the last 60 years.

Tragically, Vietnam's wildlife is in precipitous decline as forest habitats are destroyed and waterways become polluted. Uncontrolled illegal hunting has also exterminated the local populations of various animals, in some cases eliminating entire species. Officially, Vietnamese government recognises 54 mammal species and 60 bird species as endangered.

The trade in wildlife for export and domestic consumption goes largely unregulated by the government, though laws are in place to protect the animals. Poachers continue to profit from meeting the demand for exotic animals for traditional medicinal purposes and as pets.

Animal welfare is not a priority in the Vietnamese culture, evidenced by the appallingly inadequate conditions for caged wildlife throughout Vietnam.

National Parks

About 3% of Vietnam's total territory is dedicated to national park land. Vietnam has 13 national parks and an expanding array of nature reserves well worth exploring. The most interesting and accessible are: Cat Ba, Ba Be and Cuc Phuong National Parks in the north; Bach Ma National Park in the centre; and Yok Don National Park in the south.

With the help of nongovernmental organisations, including the UN Development Programme and the World Wildlife Federation, the Vietnamese government is taking steps to expand national park boundaries, crack down on illegal poaching and educate and employ people living in national park buffer zones.

TRANSPORT

GETTING THERE & AWAY
Air

Maximise your time and minimise cost and hassle by booking an open-jaw ticket – then you can fly into HCMC and out of Hanoi (or vice versa). These tickets save you from backtracking and are easily arranged in hubs like Bangkok and Hong Kong.

Keep in mind that international flights purchased in Vietnam are always more expensive than the same tickets purchased outside. See the city Getting There & Away sections for further information.

Airlines flying to and from Vietnam within the region often operate codeshare flights with Vietnam Airlines.

Air France (www.airfrance.com) Has daily flights from Bangkok to HCMC and to Hanoi.

Cathay Pacific (www.cathaypacific.com) Flies daily from Hong Kong to HCMC; daily from Hong Kong to Hanoi.

China Southern Airlines (www.cs-air.com/en) Flies direct from Guangzhou (Canton) to HCMC; all other flights arrive via Hanoi.

Lao Airlines (www.laos-airlines.com/) Flies daily between Vientiane and Hanoi.

Malaysia Airlines (www.malaysiaairlines.com) Flies from Kuala Lumpur to HCMC and Hanoi.

Siem Reap Airways (www.siemreapairways.com) Daily flights from Phnom Penh to HCMC.

DEPARTURE TAX

Vietnam's international departure tax is not included in your air fare, so bring US$12 when departing from Tan Son Nhat airport in Ho Chi Minh City (HCMC), and US$14 for Noi Bai airport in Hanoi. Departure tax is US$8 from Danang and Cam Ranh.

Dollars or dong will do, but take small change if paying in dollars. Otherwise, you're likely to get a fistful of (unexchangeable) dong in return.

Singapore Airlines (www.singaporeair.com) Has daily flights from Singapore to both HCMC and Hanoi.
Thai Airways International (THAI; www.thaiair.com) Several daily flights to both HCMC and Hanoi from Bangkok.
Vietnam Airlines (www.vietnamairlines.com) Operates daily flights throughout the region.

Land

There are land-border crossing points from Vietnam into China (see p847 and p857), Laos (see p867) and Cambodia (p910).

GETTING AROUND

Air

Air travel within Vietnam is dominated by **Vietnam Airlines** (www.vietnamairlines.com), while its competitor **Pacific Airlines** (www.pacificairlines .com.vn) offers limited routes between Ho Chi Minh City, Danang and Hanoi. Reasonably priced domestic flights can trim precious travel time off a busy itinerary.

Domestic departure tax of 25,000d is included in the ticket price.

Bicycle

Long-distance cycling is becoming a popular way to tour Vietnam, most of which is flat or moderately hilly. With the loosening of borders in Southeast Asia, more and more people are planning overland trips by bicycle. All you need to know about bicycle travel in Vietnam, Laos and Cambodia is contained in Lonely Planet's *Cycling Vietnam, Laos & Cambodia*.

The main hazard is the traffic, and it's wise to avoid certain areas (notably National Hwy 1). The best cycling is in the northern mountains and the Central Highlands, though you'll have to cope with some big hills.

Purchasing a good bicycle in Vietnam is hit or miss. It's recommended that you bring one from abroad, along with a good helmet and spare parts.

Bicycles can also be hired locally from guesthouses for US$1 or less per day, and are a great way to get to know a new city.

Boat

Commercial hydrofoils connect HCMC with the beach resort of Vung Tau (p906), as well as points in the Mekong Delta. The extensive network of canals in the Mekong Delta makes getting around by boat feasible in the

far south. Travellers to Phu Quoc Island can catch ferries from Rach Gia (p910).

In the northeast, fast and slow boats connect Haiphong with Cat Ba Island (near Halong Bay), and day cruises on Halong Bay are extremely popular.

Bus

Bus drivers rely on the horn as a defensive driving technique. Motorists use the highway like a speedway; accidents, unsurprisingly, are common. On bus journeys, keep a close eye on your bags, never accept drinks from strangers, and consider bringing earplugs. And those plastic bags passed out at the beginning of trips? They're for motion sickness.

LOCAL BUS & MINIBUS

Travelling on the highways, you'll see big public buses of every vintage, packed to the gills with unfortunate souls hanging limp heads or hands out the windows. You can travel on these rattletraps – it's the cheapest way and covers the entire country – but expect breakdowns, lots of stops and overcrowded conditions. It's rubbing shoulders with The People, and a slice of life these foreigners don't experience.

A step up are the express minibuses that go everywhere the public buses go. Run by private companies, they're a bit more expensive but worth it. They'll pick up passengers along the way until full, but the trips are more comfortable and faster than the public buses. It's a good idea to try buying tickets at the station the day before; while not always possible, this reduces your chances of having to bargain with the driver immediately before departure.

The only time we recommend avoiding these buses (and the public ones) is around Tet when drivers are working overtime and routes are dangerously overcrowded.

SURVIVAL TIP

Walk, don't run! When confronted by traffic that stops for no pedestrian – and may sometimes appear to veer towards you – your instinct may be to make a mad dash for it. But the trick is to make eye contact with oncoming drivers as you walk *slowly* across so that they can see and steer around you.

Generally, buses of all types leave very early in the morning, but shorter, more popular routes will often leave at intervals throughout the day, and usually until about midafternoon.

OPEN-TOUR BUS

For the cost of around US$22, the sold-everywhere open ticket can get you from HCMC to Hanoi at your own pace, in air-con comfort. Open-tour tickets entitle you to exit or board the bus at any city along its route, without holding you to a fixed schedule. Confirm your seat the day before departure.

These tickets are inexpensive because they're subsidised by an extensive commission culture. All of the lunch stops and hotel drop-offs give monetary kickbacks to the bus companies. But you're never obligated to stay at the hotel you've been dropped at; if you don't like it, find another.

Although it's convenient and cheap, we're not crazy about the open-tour ticket, as it isolates you from experiencing Vietnam. These vehicles rarely see Vietnamese passengers, since they're tailored to foreign travellers. Also, once you buy the ticket, you're stuck with it and the company you've bought it from ('guaranteed' refunds are not always honoured).

An alternative to the open-tour ticket is to buy individual, point-to-point tickets along the way; though this will cost more, you have the flexibility to take local buses, trains or flights, or to switch open-tour companies.

All companies offering open-tour tickets have received both glowing commendations and bitter complaints from travellers. Your best bet is to ask your fellow travellers about specific routes; look for open tickets at travellers cafés throughout Vietnam.

Car & Motorcycle

PURCHASE

Except for legal foreign residents, buying a motorbike for touring Vietnam is technically illegal. However, so far the authorities seem to be turning a blind eye to the practice. The big issue is what to do with the motorbike when you've finished with it. Some simply sell it back to the shop they bought it from (for less than they paid, of course). Others sell it to another shop or to a foreigner travelling in the opposite direction. But, remember, buying a motorbike is illegal and a crackdown may come at any time.

HIRE

Motorbikes can be hired for US$4 to US$7 per day, depending on the make of the cycle and what region you're in; with a driver, the cost can be up to US$10 per day. Hiring a car with a driver costs about US$35 per day. In smaller towns and cities, you should be fine if you watch how people drive and go with the flow. In HCMC or Hanoi, consider hiring a driver unless you're used to driving in Southeast Asia. Fifteen minutes on a bus travelling National Hwy 1 should convince you to leave the long-distance driving to a local.

Some of the most memorable experiences come from hiring a motorbike guide. In almost any backpacker area, you may be approached by guides armed with books of testimonials from past satisfied customers. If they don't come to you, travellers cafés can often recommend one. Hiring a motorbike guide leaves you free to gawk at daily life and scenery, and guides are experts on their own turf. Many travellers hit it off so well with their guides that they hire them for the long haul. It's a wonderful way to travel, and you'll get an insider's perspective on the country.

Drivers usually charge around US$10 to US$12 per day. If you're undertaking a long trip, you should also expect to pay for meals, in addition to the daily fee (drivers are typically accommodated for free cigarettes and beer) – it's your call.

ROAD RULES

The road rule to remember: small yields to big (always). Traffic cops are there to be paid off (usually). Vehicles drive on the right-hand side of the road (usually). Spectacular accidents are frequent.

When driving Vietnam's on highways, helmets are required by law only for motorbikes (and a necessary accessory if you're fond of your skull).

Never leave a motorbike unattended – if you can't park it where you can keep it in constant view, park it with a motorbike valet (2000d) and don't lose your claim ticket.

Hitching

As in any country, hitching is never entirely safe in Vietnam, and it is not recommended. If you do decide to hitch, keep in mind that drivers will usually expect to be paid for picking you up, so negotiate the fare before getting in.

Local Transport

You'll never have to walk in Vietnam if you don't want to; drivers will practically chase you down the street offering you rides.

At least once during your visit, take a whirl on a *xich lo* (cyclo), a bicycle rickshaw with the chair at the front, the bicycle at the back. They're a pleasant, nonpolluting way to see a city. Generally, cyclo rides should cost 1000d to 5000d per kilometre, or US$5 to US$8 for a day tour.

Xe om or *Honda om* (literally, 'Honda hug'; motorcycle taxi) are faster – made up of a motorbike, a driver and you. Short rides around town typically start at 5000d.

Metered taxis are abundant, but check the meter before you get in and make sure the driver uses it.

Hiring a bicycle is arguably the most fun way to see any city, and an adventure in itself. Hotels and travellers cafés usually hire them out for about US$1 per day.

Train

Vietnam Railways (Duong Sat Viet Nam; ☎ 04-747 0308; www.vr.com.vn) operates the 2600km-long Vietnamese train system that runs along the coast between HCMC and Hanoi, and links the capital with Haiphong and northerly points. Odd-numbered trains travel south; even-numbered trains go north.

The *Reunification Express* chugs along the 1726km journey between Hanoi and HCMC at an average speed of 48km per hour, and takes from 30 to 41 hours. There are five classes of train travel in Vietnam: hard seat, soft seat, hard sleeper, soft sleeper (normal) and soft sleeper (air-con). Conditions in hard seat and soft seat can be rough – it can be even less comfortable than the bus.

The government has changed its pricing policy so that foreigners now pay the same prices as Vietnamese passengers (instead of four times as much). Prices change, but at the time of writing, a ticket for an air-con soft sleeper for the 30-hour fast train from HCMC to Hanoi was around US$60. Flying the same route costs around US$93.

Theft can be a problem, especially on overnight trains. In sleeper cars, the bottom bunk is best because you can stow your pack underneath the berth; otherwise, secure it to something for the duration of the trip. Though trains are sometimes slower than the bus, they're a terrific way to meet local people.

HANOI

☎ 04 / pop 3.5 million

Capital of the Socialist Republic of Vietnam (SRV), Hanoi assumes the role with style and dignity. Sophisticated, modern, and yet coolly romantic, the city is a self-assured blend of French colonial flair and vintage Vietnam. Late-model motorbikes pulse through the intersections of the Old Quarter's labyrinthine streets, and expats and foreign tourists slurp soup on the street alongside old men with goatees and Vietnamese fashion plates in silk and denim.

With a flourishing café culture and lively bar scene, travellers love to while away a few days in the relaxed frenzy of Hanoi (named 'the City in a Bend of a River'). Stroll around Hoan Kiem Lake, take in a museum or two, and treat yourself to a little trinket in one of Hanoi's sweet boutiques.

ORIENTATION

Rambling along the banks of the Red River (Song Hong), Hanoi's centre extends out from the edges of Hoan Kiem Lake. Just to the north of this lake is the Old Quarter, characterised by narrow streets whose names change every block or two. Travellers mostly like to base themselves in this part of town.

Along the western periphery of the Old Quarter, the Hanoi Citadel was originally constructed by Emperor Gia Long. It's now a military base. Further west is Ho Chi Minh's mausoleum, in the neighbourhood where most foreign embassies are found, many housed in classical architectural masterpieces from the French colonial era. Hanoi's largest lake, West Lake (Ho Tay), lies north of the mausoleum.

Street designations in Hanoi are shortened to P for *pho* or Đ for *duong* (both meaning street).

VIETNAM

There are decent city maps for sale at bookshops in Hanoi for around US$1.

INFORMATION
Bookshops
Bookworm (Map pp834–5; ☎ 943 7226; bookworm@fpt.vn; 15A P Ngo Van So; ☼ 10am-7pm Tue-Sun) Hanoi's best selection of new and used English-language books, with a good stock of fiction; Bookworm will buy back books you've bought here for 20% of the price you paid.
Hanoi Bookstore (Map p838; ☎ 824 1616; 34 P Trang Tien) A good place to find souvenir coffee-table books.
Love Planet (Map p838; ☎ 828 4864; 25 P Hang Bac) Trade in used books for other second-hand reads – lots of books in English and several other languages.

Cultural Centres
American Club (Map p838; ☎ 824 1850; amclub@fpt.vn; 19-21 P Hai Ba Trung)
British Council (☎ 843 6780; www.britishcouncil.org/vietnam; 40 P Cat Linh) Next to the Hanoi Horison Hotel.
Centre Culturel Français de Hanoi (Map p838; ☎ 936 2164; alli@hn.vnn.vn; 24 P Trang Tien) In the L'Espace building, opposite the Dan Chu Hotel.
Goethe Institut (Map pp834–5; ☎ 734 2251; www.goethe.de/ins/vn/han/enindex.htm; 56-58 P Nguyen Thai Hoc)

Emergency
Ambulance (☎ 115)
Fire (☎ 114)
Information (☎ 1080)
Police (☎ 113)

Internet Access
There are countless Internet cafés in Hanoi, notably along P Hang Bac (a central cross-street in the Old Quarter); many guest-houses and cafés also provide Internet access. Online access in Hanoi costs around 6000d per hour.

Medical Services
Bach Mai Hospital (Benh Vien Bach Mai; Map pp834–5; ☎ 869 3731; P Giai Phong) Has an international department with English-speaking doctors.
Dental Clinic (☎ 846 2864, 0903-401 919; Van Phuc Diplomatic Compound, 298 P Kim Ma, Ba Dinh District) Take your aching teeth to the dental branch of Hanoi Family Medical Practice.
Hanoi Family Medical Practice (24hr emergency ☎ 843 0748, ☎ 0903-401 919, 0913-234 911; www.vietnammedicalpractice.com; Van Phuc Diplomatic Compound, 298 P Kim Ma, Ba Dinh District) Has a team of international physicians; service is pricey, so make sure your insurance is up-to-date.
Institute of Acupuncture (☎ 853 4253; 40 P Thai Thinh, Dong Da District)
Institute of Traditional Medicine (Map pp834–5; ☎ 826 2850; 26-29 P Nguyen Binh Khiem)
International SOS (Map p838; 24hr emergency ☎ 934 0555, ☎ 934 0555; Central Bldg, 31 P Hai Ba Trung; initial consultations US$55-65) Has a 24-hour clinic with international physicians speaking English, French and Japanese; house calls available for an additional fee.
Vietnam-Korea Friendship Clinic (Map pp834–5; ☎ 843 7231; 12 Chu Van An; initial consultations US$5) Nonprofit clinic reputed to be the least-expensive medical facility in Hanoi; maintains a high international standard.

GETTING INTO TOWN

From Noi Bai airport, Vietnam Airlines' airport minibus (US$2, 45 minutes, 35km) is cheap and easy. It drops you in front of the **airline offices** (Map p838; 1 P Quang Trung) in the Old Quarter. Catch the airport bus at the concrete island across the road as you exit the terminal; buy tickets at the airline offices for a ride to the airport.

Taxis should cost about US$10; some require that you pay the toll for a bridge en route. Ask before agreeing on a price. Buy tickets from the seller at the head of the taxi queue outside the concourse.

The cheapest option is the Hanoi public bus company's service from the airport, which stops at the Daewoo Hotel and then goes on to the Opera House. Line 7 (2500d) departs every 15 to 20 minutes, between 5am and 9pm daily.

From either of Hanoi's train stations, you can walk the 15 to 20 minutes to the Old Quarter where you'll probably want to stay. However, it's worth the 5000d for a xe om (motorcycle taxi) if you have a big pack to haul around after waking from a long train trip. Same goes for Long Bien bus station (Map pp834–5), which is across the street from Long Bien train station.

From other bus stations, a xe om to the Old Quarter should cost 10,000d to 15,000d, depending which station you're coming from.

Money

ANZ Bank (Map p838; ☎ 825 8190; 14 P Le Thai To) Has cash-advance facilities and a 24-hour ATM.

Industrial & Commercial Bank (Map p838; ☎ 825 4276; 37 P Hang Bo) This bank cashes travellers cheques, exchanges US dollars and also gives credit-card cash advances.

Vietcombank P Hang Bai (Map p838; ☎ 826 8031; 2 P Hang Bai); P Tran Quang Khai (Map p838; ☎ 826 8045; 198 P Tran Quang Khai; ✆ 7.30-11.30am & 1-3.30pm Mon-Fri, 7.30-11.30am Sat) The main branch on P Tran Quang Khai is the best bet for all currency exchange services, but there are conveniently located ATMs scattered around the Old Quarter.

Post

Postal kiosks are all over the city, for picking up stamps or dropping off letters.

Domestic post office (Map p838; ☎ 825 7036; 75 P Dinh Tien Hoang; ✆ 7am-8.30pm)

International post office (Map p838; ☎ 825 2030; cnr P Dinh Tien Hoang & P Dinh Le) Only international parcels can be shipped from here (from 7.30am to 11.30am and 1pm to 4.30pm Monday to Friday).

International courier services in Hanoi:

DHL (Map pp834–5; ☎ 733 2086; 49 P Nguyen Thai Hoc)

Federal Express (Map p838; ☎ 824 9054; 6C P Dinh Le)

UPS (Map p838; ☎ 824 6483; 4C P Dinh Le)

Telephone

To make domestic calls, the domestic post office is a reliable bet, but Internet cafés, guesthouses and travellers cafés will let you use their phone for a small fee, usually around 2000d per minute for local calls. Calls outside the local area or to mobile phones will levy a higher rate. Make international calls from the international post office or at Internet cafés offering Internet phone calls.

Travel Agencies

Hanoi has heaps of budget travel agencies, many of which double as cafés offering cheap eats, rooms for rent and Internet access. It is not advisable to book trips or tickets through guesthouses and hotels. Dealing directly with tour operators gives you a much better idea of what you'll get for your money, and of how many other people you'll be travelling with. Seek out tour operators that stick to small groups, and use their own vehicles and guides.

New travel agencies open all the time and existing places have a tendency to change, so shop around. Successful tour operators often have their names cloned by others looking to trade on their reputations, so check addresses and websites carefully. Consider the following places in the Old Quarter (Map p838):

ET Pumpkin (☎ 926 0739; www.et-pumpkin.com; 71 P Hang Bac)

Explorer Tours (☎ 923 0713; explorertours@yahoo .com; 75 P Hang Bo)

Footprint Travel (☎ 826 0879; footprinttravel@yahoo .com; 16 P Hang Bac)

Handspan Adventure Travel (☎ 926 0581; www .handspan.com; 80 P Ma May) At the Tamarind Café. Offers unique trips such as kayaking, and sleep-aboard boat tours on a refurbished junk in Halong Bay.

Kangaroo Café (☎ 828 9931; kangaroo@hn.vnn.vn; 18 P Bao Khanh) The one and only branch – see p843. Uses indigenous local guides on its Sapa trekking tours.

Red River Tours (☎ 826 8427; www.redrivertours .com.vn; 73 P Hang Bo)

Sinh Café 1 & 2 (☎ 828 7552; 18 P Luong Van Can & 52 P Hang Bac) At two locations.

Threeland Travel (☎ 926 2056; www.threeland.com; 8B P Hang Tre)

Vega Travel (☎ 926 0910; www.vega-travel.com; 24A P Hang Bac) Formerly Fansipan Travel, with a different name and the same (good) reliability.

DANGERS & ANNOYANCES

Western women have reported being hassled by young men around town who follow them home. Women walking alone at night are generally safe in the Old Quarter but should always be aware of their surroundings. Catching a *xe om* is a good idea if it's late and you have a long walk home.

Gay men should beware of a scam going on around Hoan Kiem Lake. Scenario: friendly stranger approaches foreigner, offering to take him out. They end up at a karaoke bar, where they're shown into a private room for a few drinks and songs. When the bill is brought in, it's often upwards of US$100. The situation deteriorates from there, ending in extortion. Exercise caution and follow your instincts.

SIGHTS
Vietnam Museum of Ethnology

The wonderful **Vietnam Museum of Ethnology** (Bao Tang Toc Hoc Viet Nam; ☎ 756 2193; Đ Nguyen Van Huyen; admission 10,000d; ✆ 8.30am-5.30pm Tue-Sun)

VIETNAM

CENTRAL HANOI

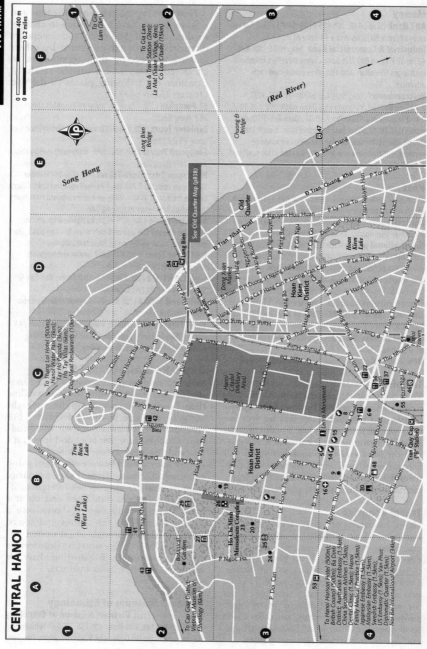

0 ____ 400 m
0 ____ 0.2 miles

To Gia
Lam (2km)

To Gia Lam
Bus & Train Station (2km);
Le Mat (Snake Village, 6km);
Co Loa Citadel (15km)

(Red River)

Song Hong

Long Bien
Bridge

Chuong Đ
Bridge

Đ Bach Dang

See Old Quarter Map (p838)

Old
Quarter

Đ Tran Quang Khai

P Tong Dan

Đ Nguyen Huu Huan

Tran Nguyen Han

P Ly Thai To

Lo Lu

Lo Thach

Long Bien

54

Đ Tran Nhat Duat

Dong Xuan
Market

Hoan
Kiem
Lake

P Hang Chieu

P Nguyen Sieu

P Luong Ngoc Quyen

P Hang Bac

P Cau Go

P Dinh Tien Hoang

P Le Thai To

To Hang Loi Hotel (500m);
Hanoi Water Park (3km);
Ho Tay Villas (6km);
Đ Dog-Meat Restaurants (10km)

Hang Than

Hang Cot

Đ Hang Dau

Hang Than

P Clau

B Xuan

B H Duong

H Ngang

Hang Buom

Hang Dao

Đ Hang Can

P Luong Van Can

P Hang Bo

Hoan
Kiem
District

P Hang Trong

P Hang Khay

P Hang Manh

Hang Ga

Hang Cot

Hang Non District

P Phu Doan

P Hang Su

P Quan Su

P Ba Trieu

P Trang Thi

51

Hanoi
Towers

Nguyen Truong To

P Yen Phu

Chinh

Phan Đinh Phung

Đ Yen Phu

Đ Cua Bac

P Phan Đinh Phung

Ly Nam Đe

P Phung Hung

P Nam Đe

P Đ Thanh

32

36

37

P Pho Nhuom

Phan Boi Chau

Nam Ngu

46

P Nguyen Bieu

Hoang Van Thu

Đ Đang Dung

P Chau Long

P Cua Bac

Hanoi
Citadel
(Military
Area)

P Cua Đong

P Nguyen Ta Phuong

Lenin Monument

8

31

6

55

Nguyen Khuyen

Ngo Si Lien

Tran Quy Cap
(Ga Station)

P P Đuc

Ngo 42

Phan Đinh Phung

Nguyen Thuong

Truc
Bach
Lake

Đ Thanh Nien

Ho Tay
(West Lake)

Hoang Hoa Thu

Ngo Canh Chan

P Quan Thanh

Đ Dang Tat

Đ Đien Bien Phu

Đ Bac Son

Đ Hoang Dieu

15

5

14

9

16

Cao Ba Quat

Nguyen Thai Hoc

Chu Van An

Khuc Hao

Le Hong Phong

Đ Tran Phu

48

30

P Điện Bien Phu

Hoan Kiem
District

19

Đ Hung Vuong

26

P Ngoc Ha

Ho Chi Minh
Mausoleum Complex

23

20

24

25

29

41

43

Botanical
Gardens

27

To Cau Giay District;
Vietnam Museum of
Ethnology (6km)

P Đoi Can

53

P Đoi Can

To Hanoi Horison Hotel (500m);
British Consul (500m); Ba Đinh
District; Australian Embassy (1.5km);
China Southern Airlines (1.5km);
Dental Clinic (1.5km); Hanoi
Family Medical Practice (1.5km);
Japanese Embassy (1.5km);
Swedish Embassy (1.5km); Van Phuc
US Embassy (1.5km); Van Phuc
Diplomatic Quarter (1.5km);
Noi Bai International Airport (34km)

LP (compass logo)

VIETNAM

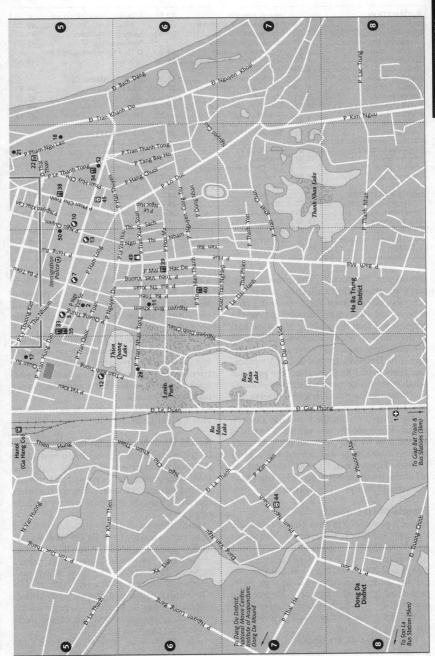

VIETNAM

should not be missed. The museum features an astounding collection of art and everyday objects from Vietnam, with maps, videos and dioramas supplementing the collection. From the making of conical hats to the ritual of a Tay shamanic ceremony, the museum explores Vietnam's cultural diversity. Displays are labelled in Vietnamese, French and English. Even the grounds outside are home to more exhibits; there's also a centre for research and conservation based here.

The museum is in the Cau Giay district, about 7km from the city centre. The trip is 30 minutes by bicycle; a *xe om* ride costs around 20,000d, or you can catch local bus 14 from Hoan Kiem Lake (2500d) and get off at the junction between Đ Hoang Quoc Viet and Đ Nguyen Van Huyen.

Temple of Literature

Hanoi's peaceful **Van Mieu** (Temple of Literature; Map pp834-5; P Quoc Tu Giam; admission with/without guide 20,000/12,000d; 🕙 8am-5pm) was dedicated to Confucius in 1070 by Emperor Ly Thanh Tong, and later established as a university for the education of mandarins. A well-preserved jewel of traditional Vietnamese architecture in 11th-century style with roofed gateways and low-eaved buildings, the temple is a must-visit.

Five courtyards are enclosed within the grounds. The front gate is inscribed with a request that visitors dismount from their horses before entering. There's a peaceful reflecting pool in the front courtyard, and the Khue Van Pavilion at the back of the second courtyard.

In 1484, Emperor Le Thang Tong ordered the establishment of stelae honouring the men who received doctorates in the triennial examinations dating back to 1442. Each of the 82 stelae that stands here is set on a stone tortoise.

The Temple of Literature is 2km west of Hoan Kiem Lake.

Ho Chi Minh Mausoleum Complex

In the tradition of Lenin, Stalin and Mao, the final resting place of Ho Chi Minh is a glass sarcophagus set deep within a monumental edifice. As interesting as the man himself are the crowds coming to pay their respects.

Built despite the fact that his will requested cremation, the **Ho Chi Minh Mausoleum Complex** (Map pp834-5; P Ngoc Ha & P Doi Can; admission free; 🕙 8-11am Sat-Thu) was constructed between 1973 and 1975, using native materials gathered from all over Vietnam. Ho Chi Minh's embalmed corpse gets a three-month holiday to Russia for yearly maintenance, so the mausoleum is closed from September through early December.

All visitors must register and leave their bags and cameras at a reception hall (a free service); brochures (4000d) are optional. You'll be refused admission to the mausoleum if you're wearing shorts, tank tops or other 'indecent' clothing. Hats must be taken off inside the mausoleum building, and a respectful demeanour should be maintained at all times. Photography is absolutely prohibited inside the building.

After exiting the mausoleum, check out the following sights.

Dien Huu Pagoda One of the most delightful in Hanoi.

Ho Chi Minh Museum (Bao Tang Ho Chi Minh; admission 5000d; ⏰ 8-11am & 1.30-4.30pm Sat-Thu) Displays each have a message, such as 'peace', 'happiness' or 'freedom'. It's probably worth taking an English-speaking guide, as some of the symbolism is hard to interpret on your own.

Ho Chi Minh's stilt house Ho's residence, on and off, between 1958 and 1969.

One Pillar Pagoda (Chua Mot Cot) Built by Emperor Ly Thai Tong (r 1028-54) and designed to represent a lotus blossom, a symbol of purity, rising out of a sea of sorrow.

Presidential Palace (admission 5000d; ⏰ 8-11am & 2-4pm Sat-Thu) Constructed in 1906 as the palace of the governor general of Indochina.

Other Museums

The terrific **Women's Museum** (Bao Tang Phu Nu; Map p838; 36 P Ly Thuong Kiet; admission 10,000d; ⏰ 8am-4pm Tue-Sun) includes the predictable tribute to women soldiers, balanced by some wonderful exhibits from the international women's movement protesting the American War. The 4th floor displays costumes worn by the ethnic-minority groups in Vietnam. Exhibits have Vietnamese, French and English explanations.

Hoa Lo Prison Museum (Map p838; ☎ 934 2253; 1 P Hoa Lo; admission 10,000d; ⏰ 8-11.30am & 1.30-4.30pm Tue-Sun) is all that remains of the former Hoa Lo Prison, ironically nicknamed the 'Hanoi Hilton' by US POWs during the American War. The bulk of the exhibits focus on the Vietnamese struggle for independence from France. Tools of torture on display include an ominous French guillotine used to behead Vietnamese revolutionaries; some exhibits have explanations in English and French.

One block east of the Opera House, the **History Museum** (Bao Tang Lich Su; Map pp834-5; 1 P Pham Ngu Lao; admission 15,000d; ⏰ 8-11.30am & 1.30-4.30pm Fri-Wed) is one of Hanoi's most stunning structures. Ernest Hebrard was among the first in Vietnam to incorporate design elements from Chinese and French styles in his architecture; this building was completed in 1932. Exhibits include artefacts spanning Vietnam's long and turbulent history, beginning with the Palaeolithic period.

Old Quarter   Map p838

Hoan Kiem Lake is the liquid heart of the Old Quarter, a good orienting landmark.

Legend has it that in the mid-15th century, heaven gave Emperor Ly Thai To (Le Loi) a magical sword that he used to drive the Chinese out of Vietnam. One day after the war, while out boating, he came upon a giant golden tortoise swimming on the surface of the water; the creature grabbed the sword and disappeared into the depths of the lake. Since that time, the lake has been known as Ho Hoan Kiem (Lake of the Restored Sword) because the tortoise returned the sword to its divine owners.

Ngoc Son Temple (Jade Mountain Temple; admission 2000d; ⏰ 8am-7pm), which was founded in the 18th century, is on an island in the northern part of Hoan Kiem Lake. It's a meditative spot to relax, but also worth checking out for the embalmed remains of a gigantic tortoise of the species said to still inhabit the lake.

Tiny **Thap Rua** (Tortoise Tower), on an islet in the southern part of the lake, is often used as an emblem of Hanoi.

Memorial House (87 P Ma May; admission 5000d; ⏰ 9-11.30am & 2-5pm) is definitely worth a visit. Thoughtfully restored, this traditional Chinese-style dwelling gives you an excellent idea of how local merchants used to live in the Old Quarter.

Bach Ma Temple (cnr P Hang Buom & P Hang Giay; ⏰ 8-11.30am & 2.30-5.30pm) is the oldest temple in Hanoi and resides in a shred of Chinatown in the Old Quarter. Legend has it

---

A DAY IN HANOI

Travellers with one day in Hanoi can spend the morning roaming the Vietnam Museum of Ethnology, then grab some lunch before checking out the Temple of Literature. Stroll by French colonial embassy buildings on P Hoang Dieu, and walk or cycle to the Ho Chi Minh Mausoleum Complex. Finish by hitting a bar or two back in the Old Quarter. Simple, cheap, satisfying.

VIETNAM

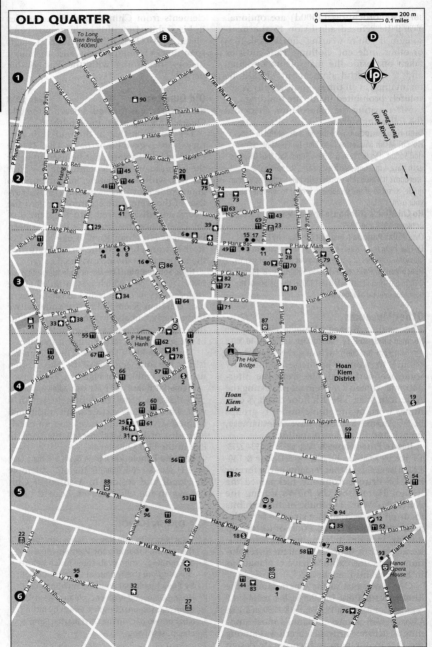

OLD QUARTER

0 —————— 200 m
0 —————— 0.1 miles

To Long Bien Bridge (400m)

Song Hong (Red River)

Hoan Kiem Lake

The Huc Bridge

Hoan Kiem District

Hanoi Opera House

INFORMATION		
American Club	**1**	C6
ANZ Bank	**2**	B4
ET Pumpkin	**3**	C3
Explorer Tours	**4**	B3
Federal Express	**5**	C5
Footprint Travel	**6**	B3
Handspan Adventure Travel	(see 69)	
Hanoi Bookstore	**7**	D6
Industrial & Commercial Bank	**8**	B3
International & Domestic Post Office	**9**	C5
International SOS	**10**	B6
Love Planet	**11**	D5
New Zealand Embassy	**12**	D5
Post Office	**13**	B3
Red River Tours	**14**	A3
Sinh Café 1	**15**	C3
Sinh Café 2	**16**	B3
UK Embassy	(see 10)	
UPS	(see 5)	
Vega Travel	**17**	C3
Vietcombank	**18**	C5
Vietcombank	**19**	D4

SIGHTS & ACTIVITIES		
Bach Ma Temple	**20**	B2
Dan Chu Hotel	**21**	D6
Hoa Lo Prison Museum	**22**	A5
Memorial House	**23**	C2
Ngoc Son (Jade Mountain) Temple	**24**	C4
QT Salon	(see 56)	
St Joseph Cathedral	**25**	B4
Thap Rua (Tortoise Tower)	**26**	C5
Women's Museum	**27**	B6

SLEEPING		
Binh Minh II Hotel	**28**	C3
Camellia Hotel 5	**29**	A2
CoCo Café & Hotel	**30**	C3
Hotel Thien Trang	**31**	B4

Lotus Guesthouse	**32**	B6
Manh Dung Guesthouse	**33**	A3
Nam Phuong	(see 31)	
Real Darling Café	**34**	B3
Sofitel Metropole Hotel	**35**	D5
Spring Hotel	**36**	B4
Stars Hotel	**37**	A2
Tam Thuong Guesthouse	**38**	A3
Thu Giang Guesthouse	(see 38)	
Thuy Nga Guesthouse	**39**	B2
Van Minh Hotel	**40**	B3
Venus Hotel	**41**	B2
Viet Anh Hotel	**42**	C2

EATING		
69 Bar-Restaurant	**43**	C2
Al Fresco's	**44**	C6
Au Lac	(see 52)	
Baan Thai Restaurant	**45**	B2
Baguette & Chocolat	**46**	B2
Cha Ca 66	**47**	A3
Cha Ca La Vong	**48**	A2
Com Chay Nang Tam	**49**	C3
Cyclo Bar & Restaurant	**50**	A4
Dinh Lang Restaurant	**51**	B4
Diva	**52**	D5
Fanny	**53**	B5
Fivimart	**54**	D5
Hanoi Garden	**55**	A4
Intimex	**56**	B5
Kangaroo Café	**57**	B4
Kem Trang Tien	**58**	C6
Khazaana	**59**	D4
La Brique	**60**	B4
La Salsa	**61**	B4
Le Café des Arts	**62**	B4
Little Hanoi 1	**63**	C2
Little Hanoi 2	**64**	B3
Moca Café	**65**	B4
No Noodles Sandwich Bar	(see 36)	
Pepperoni's Pizza & Café	**66**	B4
Pho Bo Dac Biet	**67**	A4
Press Club Deli	(see 52)	

Saigon Sakura	**68**	B5
Tamarind Café	**69**	C2
Tandoor	**70**	C2
Thuy Ta Café	(see 51)	
Trung Tam Thuong Mai	**71**	C3
Whole Earth Restaurant	**72**	C3

DRINKING		
½ Man, ½ Noodle	**73**	C2
Bar Labyrinth	**74**	C2
Bar Le Maquis	**75**	B2
Camellia Café & Bar	**76**	D6
Funky Monkey	**77**	B3
GC Pub	**78**	B4
Highway 4	**79**	D3
Le Pub	**80**	C3
Polite Pub	**81**	B4
Quan Bia Minh	**82**	C3
Spotted Cow	**83**	C6

ENTERTAINMENT		
Centre Culturel Français de Hanoi	**84**	D6
Cinematheque	**85**	C6
Jazz Club by Quyen Van Minh	**86**	B3
Municipal Water Puppet Theatre	**87**	C3
New Century Nightclub	**88**	A5
R&R Tavern	**89**	D4
Terrace Bar	(see 52)	

SHOPPING		
Dong Xuan Market	**90**	B1
Hang Da Market	**91**	A3
Vietnamese House	**92**	B3

TRANSPORT		
Airport Minibus	(see 96)	
Japan Airlines	**93**	D6
Singapore Airlines	**94**	D5
Thai Airways International	**95**	A6
Vietnam Airlines	**96**	B5

that Emperor Ly Thai To prayed at this temple for assistance in building the city walls because they continually collapsed, no matter how many times he rebuilt them. His prayers were finally answered when a white horse appeared out of the temple and guided him to the site where he eventually built his walls. Inside the pagoda is a statue of the honoured white horse, and a beautiful red-lacquered funeral palanquin. Admission is free, but you might drop a few thousand dong in the box for maintenance and preservation.

Stepping inside **St Joseph Cathedral** (P Nha Tho; ☯ 5-7am & 5-7pm) is like being transported to medieval Europe. The cathedral (inaugurated in 1886) is noteworthy for its square towers, elaborate altar and stained-glass windows. The main gate is open when mass is held.

Lenin Park

Early risers should make a point of stopping by **Lenin Park** (Cong Vien Le Nin; Map pp834-5; ☯ 6am-10pm) to work out with like-minded company. At the crack of dawn, elderly ladies practising a form of t'ai chi, young athletes out for a jog and kids of all ages swinging badminton racquets are in full force. Afterwards, refresh yourself with a steamed sweet potato, or weigh yourself on one of the walking, talking scales. It's a wonderful way to see Hanoians at their most relaxed.

ACTIVITIES

Feel like a dip? There are several places for swimming in Hanoi.

Army Hotel (Khach San Quan Doi; Map pp834-5; ☎ 825 2896; 33C P Pham Ngu Lao; day use US$3.50) Big enough to do laps, the pool is open all year.

SPA SPLURGE!

Pay someone to pound and pummel you into jellylike relaxation at the luxuriously low rate of US$4 to US$6 per hour; this rate may also include sauna time.

Dan Chu Hotel (Map p838; ☎ 825 4937; www .danchuhotel.com; 29 P Trang Tien)

Hoa Binh Hotel (Map pp834-5; ☎ 825 3315; kshoabinh@hn.vnn.vn; 27 P Ly Thuong Kiet)

Thang Loi Hotel (Cuban Hotel; ☎ 829 4211; thangloihtl@hn.vnn.vn; Đ Yen Phu)

Or, treat your inner princess (you know she's in there) to a 45-minute facial (US$13) accompanied by a hand-and-foot aromatherapy massage. Ahhh.

QT Salon (Map p838; ☎ 928 6166; 28 P Le Thai To; ◷ 10am-8pm)

Hanoi Water Park (☎ 753 2757; admission 30,000-50,000d) Open from 15 April to November, 5km from the city centre; features a variety of pools and slides.

Thang Loi Hotel (Cuban Hotel; ☎ 829 4211; thangloihtl@hn.vnn.vn; Đ Yen Phu; day use US$1) Near Ho Tay (West Lake), the pool is open from May to September.

COURSES
Language
Hanoi Foreign Language College (Map pp834-5; ☎ 826 2468; 1 P Pham Ngu Lao) is a branch of Hanoi National University. Vietnamese-language tuition varies with class size, but shouldn't cost more than US$7 per lesson.

Music
Seized by a sudden inspiration to learn the 16-stringed zither? Phan Kim Thanh, an award-winning musician and music professor at the Hanoi Conservatory of Music, offers lessons in playing several traditional Vietnamese musical instruments. Get in touch with his English-speaking contact **Mr Do Viet Dung** (☎ 851 6569; dungdoviet@yahoo.com) for more information.

FESTIVALS & EVENTS
Tet (Tet Nguyen Dan/Vietnamese Lunar New Year) A flower market is held on P Hang Luoc during the week preceding Tet, in late January or early February. In addition, there's a colourful two-week flower exhibition and competition, beginning on the first day of the new year, that takes place in Lenin Park (Cong Vien Le Nin) near Bay Mau Lake.

Quang Trung Festival On the 15th day of the first lunar month (February or March), wrestling matches, lion dances and chess games are played at Dong Da Mound in west Hanoi – Dong Da is the site of the uprising against Chinese invaders led by Emperor Quang Trung (Nguyen Hue) in 1788.

Vietnam's National Day Celebrated at Ba Dinh Sq (Map pp834-5) – the expanse of grass in front of the Ho Chi Minh Mausoleum Complex – with a rally and fireworks on 2 September; boat races are also held on Hoan Kiem Lake.

SLEEPING
Make a beeline for the Old Quarter once you land in Hanoi; the majority of Hanoi's budget accommodation lies within 1km of Hoan Kiem Lake. It's often possible to negotiate a discounted room rate if you're travelling alone or plan on staying for a few days, but spend at least one night before committing long-term.

The following places are all on the Old Quarter map (p838).

Camellia Hotel 5 (☎ 828 2376; 81 P Thuoc Bac; d US$10-15; ⬚ ▢) The staff here are friendly and speak good English; there are 16 simple, clean, often windowless rooms. Breakfast and free Internet use is included in the rates. There are four other Camellias around the Old Quarter with similar amenities and prices.

Stars Hotel (☎ 828 1911; 26 P Bat Su; d US$10-15; ⬚) Popular with travellers for its clean, comfortable rooms and friendly service, this place is a stellar deal. The more expensive rooms have balconies, and the room at the top has a lovely view overlooking the tiled roofs in the Old Quarter. Book ahead, as its reputation precedes it and rooms fill fast.

Van Minh Hotel (☎ 926 0150; nngocminh@fpt.vn; 88 P Hang Bac; r US$10-20; ⬚) In addition to pluses like spotless rooms and TV, Van Minh has plentiful hot water so you won't be left cold two minutes into your shower.

Manh Dung Guesthouse (☎ 826 7201; manh dung@vista.gov.vn; 2 P Tam Thuong; r US$6-8; ⬚ ▢) A cosy little spot in a tucked-away alley, this friendly guesthouse is run by a solicitous family who makes guests feel right at home. If it's full, check out the newer branch near Hang Da Market.

Thuy Nga Guesthouse (☎ 826 6053; thuynga hotel@hotmail.com; 24C P Ta Hien; s/d US$10/11) This bright and airy place houses six tiny, spotless rooms; the more expensive ones have balconies but they all come with a smile.

Viet Anh Hotel (☎ 926 1302; www.vietanhhotel .com; 11 P Ma May; r US$8-20; ✗ 🖥) On the upper end of the budget scale, the rooms at this newish, swish minihotel boast polished wood trim and bathtubs. It's centrally located and well worth a look.

Lotus Guesthouse (☎ 934 4197; lotus-travel@ hn.vnn.vn; 42V P Ly Thuong Kiet; r US$6-15; ✗) Sleeping here is akin to curling up in an eclectic little rabbit warren – claustrophobics and larger folk might think twice. Yes, it's on the small side, bearing narrow stairways and a café downstairs with a five-person seating capacity (only a slight exaggeration).

Venus Hotel (☎ 826 1212; venus.hotel@fpt.vn; 10 P Hang Can; d incl breakfast 120,000-150,000d; ✗) Though fraying around the edges, the red carpet gives an aged-decadence feel, and the hotel is clean and secure.

Tam Thuong Guesthouse (☎ 828 6296; three _men_on_business@yahoo.com; 10A1 P Yen Thai; r US$5-7; ✗ 🖥) Travellers have had excellent things to say about this family-run spot, run by low-key, friendly folks.

Thu Giang Guesthouse (☎ 828 5734; thugiangn@ hotmail.com; 5A P Tam Thuong; r US$6-10; ✗ 🖥) Popular with backpackers, this friendly guesthouse is in a narrow alley between P Yen Thai and P Hang Gai. Prices for these modest rooms depend on the size of the room. There's a new branch near Hang Da Market.

Also consider the following:

CoCo Café & Hotel (☎ 824 2229; 49 P Hang Be; r US$10-12; ✗) Rooms don't scream with character but are a decent deal for the basics.

Binh Minh II Hotel (☎ 825 0728; leduan2hotel@ yahoo.com; 31 D Hang Mam; r US$10; ✗) A simple stand-by.

SPLURGE!

Sofitel Metropole Hotel (Map p838; ☎ 826 6919; sofitelhanoi@hn.vnn.vn; 15 P Ngo Quyen; r from US$159; ✗ 🖥 🖳) French colonial dignity marks the spot. Just south of Hoan Kiem Lake, the luxurious Metropole is saturated with character, especially in the original wing, where rooms are floored in wood and furnished with vintage pieces. The hotel's excellent shops and restaurants purvey deli treats and full-course meals; the small pool and 2nd-floor gym help offset your overindulgences.

Real Darling Café (☎ 826 9386; darling_café@ hotmail.com; 33 P Hang Quat; dm US$3, r US$5-12) One of Hanoi's few spots with dorm rooms; staff speak good English.

A handful of family-run hotels cluster near St Joseph Cathedral, boasting a quieter location than north of the lake.

Hotel Thien Trang (☎ 826 9823; thientranghotel24@ hotmail.com; 24 P Nha Chung; d US$10-15; ✗) Try to get a room with windows.

Nam Phuong (☎ 824 6894; 26 P Nha Chung; d US$10; ✗) Clean rooms and helpful staff.

Spring Hotel (☎ 826 8500; spring.hotel@fpt.vn; 8A P Nha Chung; d US$10-15; ✗) Rooms on the upper floors are a bit brighter, but all have large windows and are fairly roomy. Staff here speak good English.

EATING

Hanoi is a gourmand's wonderland, full of restaurants serving regional specialities like *cha ca* (fish braised in broth and served with noodles and fresh dill and peanuts) as well as a broad palette of international cuisine.

The real culinary treasures in Hanoi are its speciality food streets (Map pp834–5). Cam Chi, 500m northeast of Hanoi train station, is an alley crammed full of lively street stalls serving delicious budget-priced food. P Mai Hac De, in the south-central area west of Bay Mau Lake, has several blocks of restaurants running south from the northern terminus at P Tran Nhan Tong. Đ Thuy Khue, on the south bank of West Lake, features a strip of 30-odd outdoor seafood restaurants with pleasant lakeside seating. P To Hien Thanh also specialises in small seafood restaurants, south of the city centre, east of Bay Mau Lake. P Nghi Tam, 10km north of central Hanoi, has 1km of dog-meat restaurants.

Just about anywhere you walk, you'll stumble on wandering street vendors serving *bun cha gio* (rice vermicelli with spring rolls) and tiny shopfronts selling *chao vit* (rice porridge with duck). If you stick with these eateries, it's possible to dine on the streets of Hanoi for less than US$2 a day.

Self-Catering

The following listings are all on the Old Quarter map (p838).

Dong Xuan Market (P Dong Xuan; ⏱ 6am-10pm) Swing by for fresh fruits and veggies and freshly baked baguettes (see p846).

If Western junk food and drinks are what you seek, stop by the following supermarkets for imported picnic fixings and busjourney munchies:

Fivimart (☎ 826 0167; P Tong Dan; ☿ 8.30am-9pm) On the eastern side of Hoan Kiem Lake.

Intimex (☎ 825 6148; 22-32 P Le Thai To; ☿ 8am-7.30pm) Enter at the narrow driveway next to the Clinique shop, on the western side of the lake.

Trung Tam Thuong Mai (7 P Dinh Tien Hoang; ☿ 8am-noon & 1.30-7pm) If you need a spare pair of socks along with your packet of biscuits...

Gourmet takeaway sandwiches featuring toothsome components like tea-smoked salmon and New Zealand lamb can be found at the **Press Club Deli** (☎ 934 0888; 59A Ly Thai To; sandwiches from 45,000d).

Vietnamese
BUDGET

The following listings are all on the Old Quarter map (p838).

Little Hanoi 1 (☎ 926 0168; 25 P Ta Hien; mains 15,000d) This cheap and cosy little eatery in the Old Quarter has become so popular that it's added locations along P Ta Hien.

Dinh Lang Restaurant (☎ 828 6290; 1 P Le Thai To; mains from 25,000d) Come here for the great views over Hoan Kiem Lake; this place also hosts traditional music nightly. It's right above the busy **Thuy Ta Café** (☎ 828 8148; P Le Thai To).

La Brique (☎ 928 5638; 6 P Nha Tho; cha ca 70,000d) Housed in a small brick shopfront, this cosy little Vietnamese seafood speciality place serves cha ca.

Hanoi Garden (☎ 824 3402; 36 P Hang Manh; set dinner around 90,000d; ☿ lunch & dinner) Dine in the elegant building or the open-air courtyard on Hanoi Garden's southern Vietnamese food.

69 Bar-Restaurant (☎ 926 0452; 69 P Ma May; meals from 40,000d; ☿ lunch & dinner) Set in a beautifully restored old Vietnamese house, this restaurant's menu draws on influence beyond Vietnam and is open later than many places in the neighbourhood.

Cha Ca La Vong (☎ 825 3929; 14 P Cha Ca; meals from 50,000d; ☿ lunch & dinner) Another place for cha ca, this one is notable for its longevity – purportedly it's been in continuous operation since 1899. Reservations are required.

Other recommendations:

Cha Ca 66 (☎ 826 7881; 66 P Hang Ga; mains 15,000d; ☿ lunch & dinner) Recommended for cha ca.

Diva (☎ 934 4088; 57 P Ly Thai To; mains around 60,000d; ☿ lunch & dinner) Owned by a former Miss Vietnam, it has an open-air setting and serves Vietnamese and international dishes.

Pho Bo Dac Biet (2 B P Ly Quoc Su; pho 6000d) For special pho bo – classic Vietnamese beef noodle soup.

GOURMET

A superb gourmet meal doesn't have to break the bank. If you time it well, you can also experience some live traditional music into the bargain. The following listings are all on the Central Hanoi map (pp834–5).

EATING WELL, DOING GOOD

Serving a nobler purpose than typical eateries, this trio of Hanoi restaurants takes in disadvantaged people and street kids to train them for higher-end culinary careers. Each admirable enterprise serves tasty cuisine with friendly smiles in pleasant settings, and all provide job placement for their graduates in restaurants all over Vietnam.

Hoa Sua (Map pp834-5; ☎ 942 4448; www.hoasuaschool.com; 28A P Ha Hoi; lunch around 35,000d; ☿ 11am-10pm Mon-Fri) Hoa Sua restaurant serves excellent Vietnamese and international cuisine, and its pastries are to die for (Hoa Sua School also runs Baguette & Chocolat). Breakfast is offered on weekends only, starting at 7.30am. To get there, take P Quang Trung south, cross P Tran Hung Dao and turn right on the second alley called Ha Hoi. It's at the end of the alley.

KOTO (Map pp834-5; ☎ 727 0337; www.streetvoices.com.au; 57 P Cua Nam; mains around 40,000d; ☿ 7.30am-4.30pm) KOTO stands for 'Know One, Teach One', reflecting owner Jimmy Pham's philosophy of mentoring. Australian and Vietnamese comfort foods on the menu include lots of satisfying vegetarian choices.

Baguette & Chocolat (Map p838; ☎ 923 1500; www.hoasuaschool.com; 11 P Cha Ca; sandwiches 23,000d; ☿ 7am-10pm) The café branch of Hoa Sua School, Baguette & Chocolat turns out the best pain au chocolat (7000d) in the country in addition to sandwiches, salads and Vietnamese classics. The no-shoes dining area upstairs is relaxing and intimate, perfect for a snack or light meal.

Brothers Café (☎ 733 3866; 26 P Nguyen Thai Hoc; set lunch/dinner buffet US$6/11.50; ☻ lunch & dinner) A remarkable eatery set in the rear courtyard of an elegantly restored, 250-year-old Buddhist temple. The dinner price includes one drink.

Emperor (☎ 826 8801; 18B P Le Thanh Tong; mains from 40,000d; ☻ lunch & dinner) This indoor-outdoor restaurant has a stunning traditional atmosphere and cosy Chinese-style furniture. Enjoy live traditional dinner music on Wednesday and Saturday nights (7.30pm to 9.30pm).

Seasons of Hanoi (☎ 843 5444; 95B P Quan Thanh; mains from 40,000d; ☻ lunch & dinner) Vietnamese *haute cuisine* in a classic French villa tastefully decorated with Vietnamese and colonial-era antiques.

Nam Phuong (☎ 824 0926; 19 P Phan Chu Trinh; mains 60,000d; ☻ lunch & dinner) An elegant villa setting for dining on authentic Vietnamese cuisine. There's a backdrop of traditional Vietnamese music every night (7.30pm to 9.30pm).

International

Most of the following places are concentrated in the 'Latin Quarter' on the western side of Hoan Kiem Lake, around P Bao Khanh, P Nha Chung and P Nha Tho. They are all on the Old Quarter map (p838).

No Noodles Sandwich Bar (☎ 928 5969; 20 P Nha Chung; sandwiches 30,000d; ☻ lunch & dinner) As the name implies, the sandwich reigns supreme here. Toasted sandwiches come stuffed with goodies such as avocado, chicken salad and mozzarella. Perch on a barstool and enjoy.

Le Café des Arts (☎ 828 7207; 11B P Bao Khanh; ☻ lunch & dinner) Head to this casual café for couscous or cassoulet, and other French classics. Modelled on a Parisian brasserie, it lives up to its name with regular art exhibitions.

Kangaroo Café (☎ 828 9931; kangaroo@hn.vnn.vn; 18 P Bao Khanh; mains 20,000d) This friendly travellers café serves an array of Vietnamese, Western and vegetarian food at backpacker prices. It also pours the biggest cups of coffee in Hanoi.

Pepperoni's Pizza & Café (☎ 928 5246; 29 P Ly Quoc Su; mains 40,000d; ☻ lunch & dinner) Stop by for good, authentic pizza with thick or thin crust, or fill up at lunch with the 25,000d all-you-can-eat pasta and salad bar. There's other Western and Asian food on the menu.

La Salsa (☎ 828 9052; 25 P Nha Tho; ☻ lunch & dinner) Another European place on the trendy strip by St Joseph Cathedral; the food is fabulous. Come here with a small group to sample tapas, or paella (110,000d) on Thursday.

Also try the following:

Al Fresco's (☎ 826 7782; alfresco@fpt.vn; 23L P Hai Ba Trung; ☻ lunch & dinner) Fantastic ribs, pizzas and salads – gigantic portions at reasonable prices.

Cyclo Bar & Restaurant (☎ 828 6844; 38 P Duong Thanh; mains around 60,000d; ☻ lunch & dinner) Hop into one of its converted cyclos and have yourself some casual Vietnamese or French fare; the US$4 set lunch is good value.

Vegetarian

Com Chay Nang Tam (Map pp834-5; ☎ 942 4140; 79A P Tran Hung Dao; mains 10,000d) Famed for veggie creations named for, and remarkably resembling, meat dishes; try the superb 'fried snow balls'. The main branch is nestled in an alley off of P Tran Hung Dao. There's another branch in the Old Quarter, at 79 P Hang Bac.

Tamarind Café (Map p838; ☎ 926 0580; tamarind_café@yahoo.com; 80 P Ma May; mains from 50,000d; ☻ breakfast, lunch & dinner) Dishing out Asian-style vegetarian dishes and rejuvenating fresh-fruit smoothies, this cushion-laden haven also houses Handspan Adventure Travel (p833).

Whole Earth Restaurant (Map p838; ☎ 926 0696; 7 P Dinh Liet; mains 18,000d; ☻ lunch & dinner) Good budget vegetarian fare set along a crowded block full of small cafés and market bustle. The mostly Vietnamese dishes feature mock meat and tofu.

Other Asian Cuisine

Good Chinese and Japanese food in Hanoi tends to be pricey, and the best stuff is usually at upmarket hotels. Some good Old Quarter Asian options (all on the Old Quarter map, p838) include the following:

Baan Thai Restaurant (☎ 828 8588; baanthai95@hotmail.com; 3B P Cha Ca; lunch around 30,000d; ☻ lunch & dinner) One of the longer-running, central Thai restaurants in the Old Quarter, Baan Thai is deservedly popular. There's also a photo-illustrated menu.

Saigon Sakura (☎ 825 7565; 17 P Trang Thi; mains around 60,000d; ☻ lunch & dinner) More than just sushi, the extensive menu features noodle soups, grilled fish and seaweed salads. Prices are reasonable.

Khazaana (☎ 824 1166; khazana@fpt.vn; 41B P Ly Thai To; mains around 40,000d; ☺ lunch & dinner) Another well-established favourite serving excellent North Indian food, the restaurant formerly known as Revival has a comfortable ambience and chilli ratings to gauge spiciness.

Tandoor (☎ 824 5359; 24 P Hang Be; mains around 50,000d; ☺ lunch & dinner) The reasonably priced *thali* (set meal) is a good deal, and it's a cosy spot in the Old Quarter.

Cafés

Check out the slightly manic, fun Vietnamese coffee shops along P Hang Hanh, and watch the motorbikes load and unload from the balconies upstairs. Or try the following (all on the Old Quarter map, p838, unless otherwise specified):

Little Hanoi 2 (☎ 928 5333; 21-23 P Hang Gai; breakfasts 60,000d; ☺ breakfast, lunch & dinner) A well-loved open-air café serving fresh fruit juices, espresso, cocktails and great food – all with amiable and attentive service. Unrelated to Little Hanoi 1.

Moca Café (☎ 825 6334; moca@netnam.vn; 14-16 P Nha Tho; espresso 20,000d; ☺ breakfast, lunch & dinner) Huge windows facilitate prime people-watching while you eat well-priced Vietnamese, Western and Indian food. Or choose the high-ceiling dining space upstairs and enjoy a red Belgian beer.

Kinh Do Café (Map pp834-5; ☎ 825 0216; 252 P Hang Bong; pastries 7000d; ☺ breakfast & lunch) Where Catherine Deneuve took her morning cuppa during the filming of *Indochine* – don't mistake the flashier bakeries nearby for this unassuming place.

Au Lac (☎ 825 7807; 57 P Ly Thai Tol; ☺ lunch & dinner) Sit in the pleasant front courtyard of a French villa and sample some of Hanoi's best coffee while hanging with the local cool kids.

Fanny (☎ 828 5656; 48 P Le Thai To; ice cream 10,000d; ☺ lunch & dinner) Churns out the lushest, yummiest Franco-Vietnamese ice cream in the city. Cool your heels across from Hoan Kiem's lakefront and sample alluring seasonal flavours like *com* (sticky rice), *khoai mon* (taro) or *mang cau* (custard apple).

If locals forget to tell you about their favourite ice-cream shop, the constant mob milling in front of **Kem Trang Tien** (54 P Trang Tien; ice cream 10,000d) should clue you in.

DRINKING

Hanoi has a healthy pub scene, with something for everyone. You'll find these watering holes scattered around the Old Quarter (all listed on the Old Quarter map, p838).

Highway 4 (☎ 926 0639; www.highway4.com; 5 P Hang Tre) Highway 4 is an established gathering point for members of Hanoi's notorious Minsk Motorbiking Club, and a beautifully designed place to discover the mystical, medicinal qualities of Vietnamese *ruou* (rice wine).

Quan Bia Minh (☎ 934 5233; 7A P Dinh Liet) A backpacker favourite, thanks to some of the cheapest Hanoi beer in town. There's a great balcony overlooking Dinh Liet, and a large beer can be had for pocket change (8000d).

Bar Labyrinth (☎ 926 0788; hanoi_labyrinth@yahoo .com; 7 P Ta Hien) Hard to find, easy to love: musical instruments await, in case your muse strikes. Open until the last customer goes home or joins the owner for dancing.

½ Man, ½ Noodle (☎ 926 1943; 52 P Dao Duy Tu) Just down the alley off Labyrinth is this popular hang-out.

Spotted Cow (☎ 824 1028; 23C P Hai Ba Trung) This Aussie pub features intellectual diversions such as darts and frog-racing along with your suds.

Bar Le Maquis (☎ 828 2598; 2A P Ta Hien) Francophiles should head to this cosy, smoky little speakeasy.

Camellia Cafe & Bar (☎ 933 1233; 5 P Hai Ba Trung) Attracting a curious mix of local hipsters and foreigners, Hanoi's after, *after*-hours hang-out never closes. Start with a nightcap and end with brunch.

Le Pub (☎ 926 2104; 25 P Hang Be) Friendly and funky, Le Pub serves up a mean Long Island Iced Tea.

On the western side of Hoan Kiem Lake, P Bao Khanh has a string of bars and coffee shops attracting both locals and foreigners. Most fun and raucous on weekends, the street's filled with motorbikes and image-conscious Hanoians dressed to kill.

GC Pub (☎ 825 0499; 5 P Bao Khanh) This is one of the most laid-back bars around here for folks of all persuasions. There's a pool table and a good crowd.

And nearby:

Funky Monkey (☎ 928 6113; 15B P Hang Hanh) Serious cocktails and a pool table attract more alternative-minded folks.

Polite Pub (☎ 825 0959; 5 P Bao Khanh) The place to watch major sports events.

CLUBBING

The shelf life of Hanoi's discos is short, so ask around about what's hot or not during your visit.

Apocalypse Now (Map pp834-5; P Pham Ngoc Thach, Dong Da District; ☽ 8pm-late) Dropping its old digs and downscale demeanour, Apocalypse continues to pack in the pretty people. There's no cover but the drinks and taxi ride will cost you. Loud, thumping and open late, it's worth the trek if you want to dance the night away.

New Century Nightclub (Map p838; ☎ 928 5285; 10 P Trang Thi; cover US$1-3; ☽ 8pm-late) Still all the rage with hip Vietnamese scenesters out to impress; if you need an excuse to dress to the nines, this is it.

Titanic (Map pp834-5; 42 P Chuong Duong Do; ☽ 5pm-late) A floating nightclub on the Red River, Titanic's relative isolation from residential areas keeps the DJs spinning and clubbers jamming 'til the break of dawn.

ENTERTAINMENT
Cinemas

National Movie Centre (☎ 514 1114; 87 P Lang Ha) The best venue in Hanoi for catching foreign films, more arty than mainstream. It's southwest of the city.

Cinematheque (Map p838; ☎ 936 2648; 22A P Hai Ba Trung) Showing a surprisingly eclectic selection of art-house films, Cinematheque is easily walkable from the Old Quarter.

See also:

Centre Culturel Français de Hanoi (Map p838; ☎ 936 2164; 24 P Trang Tien) For French flicks.

Fanslands Cinema (Map pp834-5; ☎ 825 7484; 84 P Ly Thuong Kiet) Mainstream Western movies.

Live Music

The following listings are on the Old Quarter map, p838.

Terrace Bar (☎ 934 0888; 59A P Ly Thai To) Located at the Press Club, the Terrace Bar has a Friday night happy hour at 6pm, for a decadent start to your evening. Drink specials start at 20,000d, entitling you to sample from roving platters of salmon mousse or olive tapenade crostini while rocking to live music. Fill up on appetisers, then move on.

R&R Tavern (☎ 934 4109; bth@hn.vnn.vn; 49 P Lo Su) Live music here runs the gamut, from a Vi-

etnamese band doing rockin' Allman Brothers classics to classical music performed by the Thang Long String Quartet on Thursday night. This laid-back place welcomes you *and* the horse you rode in on.

Jazz Club by Quyen Van Minh (Cau Lac Bo; ☎ 825 7655; 31-33 P Luong Van Can) Nightly jazz, only here. The owner teaches saxophone at the Hanoi Conservatory and sometimes jams here in the evenings; international jazz acts also appear here.

Traditional Music

You can catch live traditional music daily at the Temple of Literature (p836) or at upmarket Vietnamese restaurants.

Among the restaurants where you can splash out on an upscale meal to the strains of traditional music:

Cay Cau (Map pp834-5; ☎ 824 5346; 17A P Tran Hung Dao) In the De Syloia Hotel.

Nam Phuong (☎ 812 077; 48 Đ Hai Ba Trung; mains 25,000d; ☽ breakfast, lunch & dinner) Has live music from 7.30pm to 9.30pm.

Water Puppetry

Municipal Water Puppet Theatre (Roi Nuoc Thang Long; Map p838; ☎ 825 5450; 57B P Dinh Tien Hoang; admission 20,000-40,000d; ☽ 6.30pm & 8pm daily, 9.30am Sun) The higher admission buys better seats and a cassette of the music; you must pay extra fees to take photos and video.

SHOPPING

Your first shopping encounter will likely be with the kids selling postcards and books.

They're notorious overchargers (asking about triple the going price), so a reasonable amount of bargaining is called for.

The Old Quarter is crammed with appealing loot; price tags signal set prices. And even if you don't need new shoes, take a walk along P Hang Dau (Map p838) at the northeastern corner of Hoan Kiem Lake to gawk at the wondrous shoe market. Larger Western sizes are rare, but for petite feet, great bargains abound.

Handicrafts

If you don't make it up to Sapa, you can find a wide selection of ethnic-minority garb and handicrafts in Hanoi; a stroll along P Hang Bac or P To Tich will turn up a dozen places.

North and northwest of Hoan Kiem Lake around P Hang Gai, P To Tich, P Hang Khai and P Cau Go you'll be tripping over shops offering Vietnamese handicrafts (lacquerware, mother-of-pearl inlay, ceramics), as well as watercolours, oil paintings, prints and assorted antiques – real and fake.

Local artists display their paintings at private art galleries, the highest concentration of which is on P Trang Tien, between Hoan Kiem Lake and the Opera House. The galleries are worth a browse even if you're not buying.

Craft Link (Map pp834-5; ☎ 843 7710; 39-45 P Van Mieu) Make socially conscious purchases at Craft Link, across from the Temple of Literature. It is a nonprofit organisation that buys high-quality tribal handicrafts at fair-trade prices, and it funds community development initiatives for the artisans and villages.

Vietnamese House (Map p838; ☎ 826 2455; 92 P Hang Bac) This small, attractive shop deals in a hodge-podge of old and new treasures.

Markets

Dong Xuan Market (Map p838; P Dong Xuan; ✆ 6am-10pm) With hundreds of stalls, the three-storey market, 600m north of Hoan Kiem Lake, is a tourist attraction in its own right.

Hom Market (Map pp834-5; P Hué) On the northeastern corner of P Hué and P Tran Xuan Soan, this is a good general-purpose market with lots of imported food items.

Hang Da Market (Map p838; Yen Thai) West of Hoan Kiem Lake, Hang Da is relatively small, but good for imported foods, wine,

beer and flowers. The 2nd floor is good for fabric and ready-made clothing.

Silk Products & Clothing

P Hang Gai, about 100m northwest of Hoan Kiem Lake, and its continuation, P Hang Bong, is a good place to look for embroidery such as tablecloths, T-shirts and wall hangings. This is also the modern-day silk strip, with pricey boutiques offering tailoring services and selling ready-to-wear clothing. It's a good place to look for silk ties, scarves and other threads.

Other fashionable streets include the blocks around St Joseph Cathedral (Map p838): P Nha Tho, P Ly Quoc Su and P Hang Trong. Designer boutiques here sell silk clothing, purses, homewares and antiques.

GETTING THERE & AWAY
Air

Hanoi has fewer international flights than HCMC, but with a change of aircraft in Hong Kong or Bangkok you can get anywhere. International airlines with local booking offices include the following:

All Nippon Airways (Map pp834-5; ☎ 934 7237; www.ana.co.jp/eng; 25 P Ly Thuong Kiet)

Cathay Pacific Airways (Map pp834-5; ☎ 826 7298; www.cathaypacific.com; Ground fl, 49 P Hai Ba Trung)

China Airlines (Map pp834-5; ☎ 824 2688; www.china-airlines.com; 18 P Tran Hung Dao)

China Southern Airlines (Map pp834-5; ☎ 771 6616; www.cs-air.com/en; Ground fl, 360 P Kim Ma, Ba Dinh District)

Japan Airlines (Map p838; ☎ 826 6693; www.jal.com/en; 5th fl, 63 P Ly Thai To)

Malaysia Airlines (Map pp834-5; ☎ 826 8819; www.malaysiaairlines.com; 49 P Hai Ba Trung)

Pacific Airlines (Map pp834-5; ☎ 851 5350; www.pacificairlines.com.vn; 100 P Le Duan)

Singapore Airlines (Map p838; ☎ 826 8888; www.singaporeair.com; 17 P Ngo Quyen)

Thai Airways International (THAI; Map p838; ☎ 826 7921; www.thaiair.com; 44B P Ly Thuong Kiet)

Vietnam Airlines (Map p838; ☎ 943 9660; www.vietnamairlines.com; 25 P Trang Thi)

Bus

Hanoi has several main bus stations, each serving a particular area. It's a good idea to arrange your travel the day before you want to leave. The stations are pretty well organised with ticket offices, and printed schedules and prices.

Gia Lam bus station (Ben Xe Gia Lam) is for buses to points northeast of Hanoi, including Halong Bay (35,000d, 3½ hours), Haiphong and Lang Son (30,000d, three hours) near the Chinese border. The station is 2km northeast of the centre. Cyclos can't cross the Red River Bridge, so you'll have to take a motorbike or taxi.

Kim Ma bus station (Map pp834–5; Ben Xe Kim Ma; cnr P Nguyen Thai Hoc & P Giang Vo) is for buses to the northwest regions, including Lao Cai (53,000d, 10 hours) and Dien Bien Phu (100,000d, 16 hours). Tickets should be purchased the day before departure.

Son La bus station (Ben Xe Son La; Km 8, P Nguyen Trai) is for buses to the northwest, including Son La (63,000d, 12 to 14 hours), Dien Bien Phu (100,000d, 16 hours) and Lai Chau. It's southwest of Hanoi, near Hanoi University.

Giap Bat bus station (Ben Xe Giap Bat; Đ Giai Phong) is for points south of Hanoi, including HCMC (49 hours). It's 7km south of the Hanoi train station.

Car & Motorcycle

To hire a car or minibus with driver, contact a travellers café or travel agency. The main roads in the northeast are generally OK, but in parts of the northwest they're awful (you'll need a high-clearance vehicle or 4WD).

A six-day trip in a 4WD can cost US$200 to US$400 (including 4WD, driver and petrol). You should inquire about who is responsible for the driver's room and board – most hotels have a room set aside for drivers, but work out ahead of time what costs are included.

See Tours (p919) for more information on motorbike guides and arrangements.

Train

The main Hanoi train station (Ga Hang Co; Map pp834–5; ☎ 825 3949; 120 Đ Le Duan; ticket office ☒ 7.30-11.30am & 1.30-7.30pm) is at the western end of P Tran Hung Dao. Trains from here go to destinations south. It's best to buy tickets at least one day before departure to ensure a seat or sleeper. Staff at counter 2 speak English.

The place you purchase your ticket is not necessarily where the train departs, so be sure to ask exactly *where* you need to catch your train. For short-distance trains, it's only possible to purchase tickets 30 minutes to one hour before departure, and room for baggage is severely limited.

BORDER CROSSING: INTO CHINA

The busiest border crossing to China is at Dong Dang (open 7am to 5pm), 20km north of Lang Son in northeastern Vietnam. Its nearest Chinese town is Pingxiang. Nanning, capital of China's Guangxi Province, is about four hours by bus or train from the border. The crossing point is known in Vietnamese as Huu Nghi Quan (Friendship Gate). There's a twice-weekly direct Beijing–Hanoi train (US$112, 48 hours).

In the far northeast, the Mong Cai border crossing (open 7.30am to 4.30pm) is just opposite the Chinese city of Dongxing. To use this border, your Chinese visa *must* be issued in Hanoi only. Hydrofoils (US$12, three hours) to China leave Bai Chay in Halong City (p851) at 8am and 1pm.

Tran Quy Cap station (B station; Map pp834–5; ☎ 825 2628; P Tran Qui Cap) is just two blocks behind the main station on Đ Le Duan. Northbound trains leave from here.

Gia Lam station (Nguyen Van Cu, Gia Lam District) has some northbound (Yen Bai, Lao Cai, Lang Son) and eastbound (Haiphong) trains departing from here, on the eastern side of the Red River.

To make things complicated, some of the same destinations served by Gia Lam can also be reached from Long Bien station (Map pp834–5; ☎ 826 8280).

GETTING AROUND
Bicycle

Pedalling around the city is a great way to cover lots of ground without wearing yourself out; and it places you smack in the middle of typical Vietnamese life. Many hotels and cafés offer cycles to rent for about 10,000d per day.

If you want to purchase your own set of wheels, P Ba Trieu and P Hué are the best places to look for bicycle shops.

Bus

Figuring out exactly where Hanoi's 31 bus lines go is a challenge, and service on some lines is infrequent. Still, only walking is cheaper – fares within the city are 2500d. You can pick up city bus-route maps at kiosks around Hoan Kiem Lake; the maps also give bus-stop locations.

Cyclo

Cyclos in Hanoi are wider than the Saigon breed, making them big enough for two to share the fare. Around the city centre, most cyclo rides should cost around 5000d. Longer rides – from the Old Quarter to the Ho Chi Minh Mausoleum Complex, for example – would cost double or triple that. One common cyclo-driver's ploy when carrying two passengers is to agree on a price and then double it on arrival, saying the price was for one person, not two.

The cyclo drivers in Hanoi are less likely to speak English than the ones in HCMC, so take a map, paper and pencil – this way you can write the name of your destination and negotiate the numbers. It's a thankless job, so don't agonise too much over giving your driver that extra few thousand dong.

Motorcycle

Walk 5m down any major street and you'll be bombarded by offers for *xe om*. They should cost about the same as a cyclo.

Though many travellers have rented motorbikes to tour Hanoi, it's not recommended that you drive in the city unless you're used to Vietnamese road rules. If you fervently desire to drive in Hanoi, make absolutely sure to observe driving patterns before revving up.

Taxi

There are several companies in Hanoi offering metered-taxi services for similar rates. Flag fall is 2500d, which takes you 2km; every kilometre thereafter costs around 5000d. Don't pay more than US$10 to go to the airport. Competitors in this business include the following:

Airport Taxi (☎ 873 3333)
City Taxi (☎ 822 2222)
Red Taxi (☎ 856 8686)
Taxi PT (☎ 856 5656)
Viet Phuong Taxi (☎ 828 2828)

AROUND HANOI

PERFUME PAGODA

The **Perfume Pagoda** (Chua Huong; boat journey & admission 35,000d), about 60km southwest of Hanoi by road, is a complex of pagodas and Buddhist shrines built into the limestone cliffs of **Huong Tich Mountain** (Mountain of the Fragrant Traces). The pagoda is a highlight of the area; the scenery resembles that of Halong Bay, though you're on a river rather than by the sea.

Vast numbers of Buddhist pilgrims come here during a festival that begins in the middle of the second lunar month and lasts until the last week of the third lunar month. These dates usually end up corresponding to March and April. Also keep in mind that weekends tend to draw large crowds, with the attendant litter, vendors and noise.

If you want to do the highly recommended scenic river trip, you need to travel from Hanoi by car to My Duc (two hours), then take a small boat rowed by two women to the foot of the mountain (1½ hours).

The main pagoda area is about a 4km walk up from where the boat lets you off. Two bits of advice: be in decent shape, and bring good walking shoes. The path on this two-hour (-plus) climb to the top is very steep in places, and when wet, the ground can get very slippery. Shorts are considered disrespectful at the pagoda; wear long pants and long-sleeved shirts.

Hanoi's travellers cafés (see p833) offer day tours to the pagoda for as little as US$9, inclusive of transport, guide and lunch (drinks excluded). If you're going with a small-group tour, expect to spend around US$14 to US$16. You can also rent a motorbike to get there on your own; it takes around two to three hours to drive.

HANDICRAFT VILLAGES

There are numerous villages surrounding Hanoi that specialise in particular cottage industries. Visiting these villages can make a rewarding day trip, though you'll need a good guide to make the journey worthwhile. Travellers cafés in Hanoi offer day tours covering several handicraft villages.

Bat Trang is known as the ceramic village. You can watch artisans create superb ceramic vases and other masterpieces in their kilns. Bat Trang is located 13km southeast of Hanoi.

So, known for its delicate noodles, mills the yam and cassava flour for noodles. It is in Ha Tay Province, about 25km southwest of Hanoi.

You can see silk cloth being produced on a loom in **Van Phuc**, a silk village 8km southwest of Hanoi in Ha Tay Province.

There's also a small produce market every morning.

Dong Ky survives by producing beautiful, traditional furniture inlaid with mother-of-pearl. It is 15km northeast of Hanoi.

The locals in **Le Mat** raise snakes for the upmarket restaurants in Hanoi, and for producing medicinal spirits. Fresh snake cuisine and snake elixir is available at this village; for around US$6 to US$8 you can try a set meal of snake meat prepared 10 different ways. Le Mat is 7km northeast of central Hanoi.

Other handicraft villages in the region produce conical hats, delicate wooden bird cages and herbs.

BA VI NATIONAL PARK

☎ 034 / elev 1276m

Centred on scenic Ba Vi Mountain (Nui Ba Vi), **Ba Vi National Park** (☎ 881 205; admission 10,000d) boasts more than 2000 flowering plants. There are trekking opportunities through the forested slopes of the mountain, and those who climb up to the summit will be rewarded with a spectacular view of the Red River valley – at least between April and December, when the mist won't obscure the landscape.

At the **Ba Vi Guesthouse** (☎ 881 197; d 120,000-150,000d; 🛠), rooms have private bathrooms, but prices go up about US$2 per room on weekends, when Hanoians trickle into the park. You must have your passport with you to check in here. The restaurant serves great, fresh food (meals 18,000d). You'll want to avoid the toilets here if you can help it.

Ba Vi National Park is about 65km west of Hanoi, and is not served by public transport. Make sure your driver knows you want to go to the park rather than Ba Vi town.

NINH BINH

☎ 030 / pop 53,000

Ninh Binh has evolved into something of a travel hub in recent years. Its sudden transformation from sleepy backwater to tourist magnet has little to do with Ninh Binh itself, but rather with its proximity to Tam Coc (9km; p850), Hoa Lu (12km; p850) and Cuc Phuong National Park (45km; p850).

Although it is possible to visit these sights as a day trip from Hanoi, most travellers prefer to stay overnight in Ninh Binh or the national park to appreciate the scenery at a more leisurely pace. Because Ninh Binh has not yet become a stop for the masses, it's still a low-key, no-hassle base, perfect for a few days of bicycle expeditions.

There's an Internet café about 40m from the train station, and an **Incombank** (Đ Tran Hung Dao, Hwy 1) with an ATM open during banking hours.

Sleeping & Eating

Folks who run guesthouses in Ninh Binh have a reputation for honest, friendly service. All the places listed can arrange tours and hire motorbikes and bicycles. And in case you're headed that way, tours to Sapa can be booked more cheaply here than in Hanoi.

Queen Mini-Hotel (☎ 871 874; 21 P Hoang Hoa Tham; dm US$3, r US$4-12; 🛠) Continuing its tradition of excellence, this minihotel receives raves from travellers about the charming and helpful Mr Luong and his staff. Though only 30m from Ninh Binh train station, it's a quiet place to stay. There's also a restaurant here serving good food.

Xuan Hoa Hotel (☎ 880 970; 31D P Minh Khai; dm US$3, r US$4-12; 🛠) The kind of guesthouse you wish existed in every town. Friendly Mr Xuan makes his guests feel truly cared for, as does his wife Ms Hoa, whose Vietnamese cooking is a treat. Find the hotel 350m south of the main bridge intersecting Hwy 1, on the other side of a small reservoir.

Thuy Anh Hotel (☎ 871 602; 55A P Truong Han Sieu; r US$7-40; 🛠 🖳) Long a family-run backpacker favourite, this place has grown into a busy, clean hotel that pulls in the tour groups. In addition to a large restaurant, there's a rooftop bar and diversions including a dart board and pool table.

Thanh Thuy's Guesthouse (☎ 871 811; tuc@hn .vnn.vn; 128 P Le Hong Phong; r US$5-16; 🛠) This guesthouse is decent value for the price; some balcony rooms have lovely views of the surrounding tile-roofed neighbourhood.

Getting There & Away

Ninh Binh is 93km southwest of Hanoi. Regular public buses leave almost hourly from the Giap Bat bus terminal in Hanoi and make the 2½-hour run for 25,000d. The bus station in Ninh Binh is across the Van River from the post office.

Ninh Binh is also a hub on the north–south open-tour bus route (see p830). Buses from Hué and Hanoi stop for travellers getting off here.

Ninh Binh is a scheduled stop for *Reunification Express* trains travelling between Hanoi and HCMC. Trains to Hanoi take two hours and cost 30,000d.

AROUND NINH BINH
Tam Coc

Known as 'Halong Bay on the Rice Paddies' for its huge rock formations jutting out of rice paddies, Tam Coc boasts breathtaking scenery.

The way to see Tam Coc is by rowboat on the **Ngo Dong River**. The boats row through karst caves on this peaceful and beautiful trip, and take about three hours, including stops. Tickets are sold at the small booking office by the docks. One boat seats two passengers and costs 55,000d per person – this includes the boat ride and entry fee.

Bring a hat to keep the sun off your face, as there's little shade on the water. Be prepared for the rowing ladies to give you the hard sell with their embroidered items, and other boat vendors to push drinks. If you cave in to the pressure of buying a drink for your boat rower, the rower will often sell the drink right back to the vendor for half-price.

Restaurants are plentiful at Tam Coc, and if you want to see where all the embroidery comes from, you can visit **Van Lan village** behind the restaurants. Prices there are cheaper than on the boats.

About 2km past Tam Coc is **Bich Dong**, a cave with a built-in temple. Getting there is easy enough by river or road.

Tam Coc is 9km southwest of Ninh Binh. By car or motorbike, follow National Hwy 1 south and turn west at the Tam Coc turn-off, marked by a pair of tall stone pillars. Travellers cafés in Hanoi (see p833) book inexpensive day trips to Tam Coc (US$12 to US$20).

Hoa Lu

The scenery here resembles nearby Tam Coc, though Hoa Lu has an interesting historical twist. Hoa Lu was the capital of Vietnam under the Dinh dynasty (968–80) and the Le dynasties (980–1009). The site was a suitable choice for a capital city due to its proximity to China and the natural protection afforded by the region's bizarre landscape.

The **ancient citadel** (admission 10,000d) of Hoa Lu, most of which, sadly, has been destroyed, once covered an area of about 3 sq km. The outer ramparts encompassed temples, shrines and the palace where the king held court. The royal family lived in the inner citadel.

There is no public transport to Hoa Lu, which is 12km north of Ninh Binh. Most travellers get here by bicycle, motorbike or car; guesthouses in Ninh Binh can provide basic maps for guidance. Hanoi's travellers cafés (see p833) organise day tours combining visits to Hoa Lu and Tam Coc.

CUC PHUONG NATIONAL PARK
☎ 030 / elev 648m

Cuc Phuong National Park (☎ 848 006; admission 40,000d) is one of Vietnam's most important nature preserves. Ho Chi Minh personally took time off from the war in 1963 to dedicate this national park, Vietnam's first. The hills are laced with many grottos, and the climate is subtropical at the park's lower elevations.

Excellent trekking opportunities abound in the park, including a trek (8km return) to an enormous **1000-year-old tree** (*Tetrameles nudiflora,* for botany geeks), and to a **Muong village** where you can also go rafting. A guide is not essential for short walks, but is recommended for long trips and mandatory for longer treks.

During the rainy season (July to September) leeches are common in the park; the best time to visit is between December and April. Try to visit during the week, as weekends and Vietnamese school holidays get hectic.

One marvellous organisation based in the park is the **Endangered Primate Rescue Center** (www.primatecenter.org; admission free; ⏰ 9-11am & 1-4pm), run by German biologists. The centre is home to around 120 rare monkeys bred in captivity or confiscated from illegal traders. These gibbons, langurs and lorises are rehabilitated, studied and, whenever possible, released back into their native environments or into semiwild protected areas.

Guided tours of the primate centre are free but must be arranged from the main park office. Entry to the centre is free, but consider making a donation, or buying some postcards or a poster to support this critical conservation project.

Sleeping & Eating

The best place to stay, if you want to wake up and trek, is in the centre of the park (18km from the gate). There are rooms in a concrete, cold-water **pillar house** (r US$6) and also a few rooms in the **bungalows** (s/d US$15/25); electricity is generated for four hours in the evenings. Meals in the park centre cost around US$7 per day. Nearby is a huge river-fed swimming pool.

There's another **pillar house** (r US$5) near the park headquarters. **Camp sites** (US$2) are also offered here, but you need to bring your own gear. Rooms in the park's **guesthouse** (d US$15-20) can be reserved by contacting **Cuc Phuong National Park** (☎ 848 006; Nho Quan District, Ninh Binh Province), or its **Hanoi office** (☎ 04-829 2604; 1 P Doc Tan Ap, Hanoi).

Getting There & Away

Cuc Phuong National Park is 45km from Ninh Binh. There is no public transport on this route, but it's a beautiful drive by car or motorbike. Ask for directions or pick up basic area maps at the hotels in Ninh Binh.

NORTHERN VIETNAM

Stretching from the Hoang Lien Mountains (Tonkinese Alps) eastward across the Red River Delta to the islands of Halong Bay, the northern part of Vietnam (Bac Bo), known to the French as Tonkin, includes some of the country's most spectacular scenery. The mountainous areas are home to many distinct hill-tribe groups.

A highly recommended journey from Hanoi is the 'northwest loop'. Head for Mai Chau, followed by Son La and Dien Bien Phu, then north to Lai Chau, Sapa, Lao Cai, Bac Ha and back to Hanoi. The loop route requires a 4WD or motorbike, and you should allow at least a week.

HALONG BAY

Magnificent Halong Bay, with more than 3000 islands rising from the clear, emerald waters of the Gulf of Tonkin, is a Unesco World Heritage site and one of Vietnam's natural marvels. The vegetation-covered islands are dotted with innumerable grottos created by the wind and the waves. Besides the breathtaking vistas, visitors to Halong Bay come to explore the countless caves.

Ha long means 'where the dragon descends into the sea'. The legend says that the islands of Halong Bay were created by a great dragon that lived in the mountains. As it ran towards the coast, its flailing tail gouged out valleys and crevasses; as it plunged into the sea, the areas dug up by its tail became filled with water, leaving only bits of high land visible.

From February through until April, the weather is often cold and drizzly, and the ensuing fog can cause low visibility, although the temperature rarely falls below 10°C. Tropical storms are frequent during the summer months.

To see the islands and grottos, a boat trip is mandatory. It's well worth booking a two- or three-day Halong Bay tour at a travellers café in Hanoi (see p833). The trips are very reasonably priced, starting as low as US$15 per person on a jam-packed 45-seat bus, and rising to around US$35 for a small-group tour on which you can sleep on a junk (recommended!). Three-day tours continue on to Cat Ba Island. Most tours include transport, meals, accommodation and boat tours.

You really couldn't do it any cheaper on your own, but if you prefer travelling independently it's simple enough to do so. Direct buses go from Hanoi to Halong City, as do ferries from Haiphong. From Halong City (see p852) or Cat Ba Island (see p853), you can also arrange tours on Halong Bay on a chartered boat trip.

If you book a tour package, there is always a small chance that the boat trip may be cancelled due to bad weather. This may entitle you to a partial refund, but remember that the boat trip is only a small portion of the cost of the journey.

HALONG CITY
☎ 033 / pop 149,900

With the kind of makeover Halong City has been getting, it will never be Vietnam's beauty queen, but it attracts its fair share of Vietnamese and Chinese tourists, and has a flourishing Thai massage and karaoke scene (read: prostitution).

Orientation & Information

The town is bisected by a bay – the western side is called Bai Chay, just a short ferry ride (5000d) from the eastern side, known as Hon Gai. Accommodation can be found on both sides.

Emotion Cybernet Cafe (☎ 847 354; emotionqn@ hn.vnn.vn; Đ Halong; ☯ 9am-9pm) On the main drag in Bai Chay, about 100m west from the post office.

Post office (☎ 840 000; Đ Halong; ☯ 7.30am-5pm)

Vietcombank (Đ Halong) Offers the usual exchange services and features an ATM.

Tours

You can wrangle a tour the day you arrive in Halong City, at the marina. If you catch a morning bus to Bai Chay from Hanoi, you can easily grab some lunch before heading to the docks to hire a boat. You'll find a lot of Vietnamese and foreign travellers milling around the harbour trying to arrange afternoon tours around the bay.

The **booking office** (☯ 8.30am-5.30pm; 3-4hr tour 30,000d) at the marina (1.5km west of Bai Chay), offers a range of tours at fixed prices. Tickets usually include admission to several caves and grottos on the bay. Day tours are fine, but staying overnight on a boat is recommended. Some drop you at Cat Ba Island, from where you can take a ferry to Haiphong and a bus or train back to Hanoi.

Sleeping

In Bai Chay, the heaviest concentration of hotels is in the 'hotel alley'. Expect to pay US$8 to US$12 for a double room with private bathroom and air-con. Up the hillside from Đ Halong, a couple of hotels with views of the bay provide an interesting alternative.

Bong Lai Hotel (☎ 845 658; d US$10-12; ☒) This is a clean, cheap and friendly place offering simple rooms with super-fine views.

Hai Long Hotel (☎ 846 378; d US$12; ☒) Of a slightly higher standard, this place is a bit bigger with more great views from the rooftop.

Hoang Lan Hotel (☎ 846 504; 17 Đ Vuon Dao; r US$10-12; ☒) Friendly hosts and the usual amenities: hot water, satellite TV and fridge, with the added bonus of a free breakfast.

Thanh Hue Hotel (☎ 847 612; 17 Đ Vuon Dao; r US$10-12; ☒) On the same hill as the Hoang Lan, the climb up is worth it, with views of the sparkling (or misty) bay. Rooms are decent and have balconies.

Eating

The area just west of central Bai Chay contains a solid row of cheap restaurants. Over in Hon Gai, check out the string of local eateries along P Ben Doan. If you're on a tour, meals should be included in the price.

Getting There & Away

Buses from Hanoi leave the Gia Lam station for Bai Chay (35,000d, three hours). From Bai Chay to Hanoi (35,000d, three hours), buses leave from Mien Tay bus station until 2.30pm. Buses to Haiphong (18,000d, two hours) leave from across the road, about 20m east of Mien Tay station. Buses bound for Mong Cai (35,000d, six hours) on the Chinese border leave from Hon Gai bus station.

Slow boats connecting Hon Gai with Haiphong (30,000d, three hours) leave daily at 6.30am, 11am and 4pm. Schedules are prone to change, so always check the times beforehand.

A slow boat connects Hon Gai to Cat Hai Island (30,000d, two hours) but departure times vary. At Cat Hai you can hop on another small ferry to get to Cat Ba Island (30,000d, two hours).

There are also hydrofoils (180,000d, three hours) to Mong Cai leaving daily at 6am, and ferries (70,000d, seven hours) leaving daily at 9am.

CAT BA ISLAND

☎ 031 / pop 7000

The only populated island in Halong Bay, about half of Cat Ba Island was declared a national park in 1986 in order to protect the island's diverse ecosystems and wildlife, including the endangered Cat Ba langur. There are beautiful beaches, numerous lakes, waterfalls and grottos in the spectacular limestone hills, the highest of which rises 331m above sea level.

The island's human population is concentrated in the southern part of the island, around the town of Cat Ba. Cat Ba is still relatively laid-back, although it's mobbed on weekends and holidays, and rates fluctuate accordingly.

Information

There are no banks in Cat Ba town, but there are a few jewellery stores north of the harbour that exchange dollars.

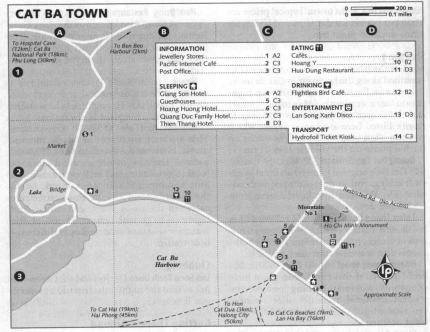

CAT BA TOWN

INFORMATION
Jewellery Stores...............................1 A2
Pacific Internet Café.........................2 C3
Post Office......................................3 C3

SLEEPING
Giang Son Hotel...............................4 A2
Guesthouses...................................5 C3
Hoang Huong Hotel.........................6 C3
Quang Duc Family Hotel..................7 C3
Thien Thang Hotel...........................8 D3

EATING
Cafés...9 C3
Hoang Y..10 B2
Huu Dung Restaurant....................11 D3

DRINKING
Flightless Bird Café........................12 B2

ENTERTAINMENT
Lan Song Xanh Disco.....................13 D3

TRANSPORT
Hydrofoil Ticket Kiosk....................14 C3

To Hospital Cave (12km); Cat Ba National Park (18km); Phu Long (30km)

To Ben Beo Harbour (2km)

Market

Lake   Bridge

Restricted Rd   (No Access)

Mountain No 1

Ho Chi Minh Monument

Cat Ba Harbour

Approximate Scale

To Cat Hai (19km); Hai Phong (45km)

To Hon Cat Dua (3km); Halong City (50km)

To Cat Co Beaches (1km); Lan Ha Bay (16km)

0 ——— 200 m
0 ——— 0.1 miles

Pacific Internet Café (per min 200d; 8am-7pm) On 'hotel alley' in Cat Ba. Has a roomful of terminals.

Post office (7.30am-9pm Mon-Fri) Near the ferry landing on the main drag; international calls can be made from here.

Sights & Activities

Home to various species of monkey, wild boar and hedgehog, **Cat Ba National Park** (admission 15,000d, guide per day 75,000d; dawn-dusk) has a myriad of trekking opportunities. Even though a guide is not mandatory, we definitely recommend it.

There's a very challenging 18km trek (five to six hours) through the park that many enjoy. You need a guide, transport to the trailhead and a boat to return, all of which can be arranged in Cat Ba town. If you're planning on doing this trek, equip yourself with proper trekking shoes, rainwear, a generous supply of water, plus some food. Camping is allowed in the park, but you'll need to bring all your own gear.

To reach the national park headquarters at **Trung Trang**, take a minibus (8000d, 30 minutes, 17km) from Cat Ba for the trip.

All restaurants and hotels should be able to sell you minibus tickets. Another option is to hire a motorbike for about 20,000d one way.

Hospital Cave is the intriguing site that was used as a secret hospital during the American War – another amazing example of Vietnamese engineering born of necessity.

The white-sand **Cat Co beaches** (called simply Cat Co 1, Cat Co 2 and Cat Co 3) are perfect places to lounge around for the day; however, Cat Co 1 and 3 are being transformed into big resorts. Cat Co 2 is the least busy and the most attractive beach, also offering simple accommodation and camping (see p854). To get there, take the wooden cliffside walkway connecting it to Cat Co 1.

The beaches are about 1km from Cat Ba town and can be reached on foot or by motorbike for about 5000d.

Tours

Tours of the island and national park, boat trips around Halong Bay and fishing trips are peddled by nearly every hotel and restaurant in Cat Ba town. Typical prices are US$8 per person for day trips and US$20 for a two-day/one-night trip.

Sleeping

Most of the island's 40 or so hotels are concentrated along the bayfront in Cat Ba town. Room rates fluctuate greatly between high-season summer months (May to September) and the slower winter months (October to April). Listed here are winter prices, which you can often bargain down. The discos on the hill pump up the volume after 11pm.

Quang Duc Family Hotel (☎ 888 231; d 150,000d; ✷) Cat Ba's original family-run hotel keeps on trucking, with rooms equipped with satellite TV. You can hire kayaks here from US$10 per day.

Thien Thang Hotel (☎ 888 568; r US$10; ✷) A swish new place offering midrange standards at budget prices. Satellite TV, big bathrooms and sea-view balconies available.

Hoang Huong Hotel (☎ 888 274; d US$6-12; ✷) Front rooms of this family-run place have enormous windows looking out on the water; communal balconies offer a bird's-eye view of guys gambling on the waterfront promenade.

Giang Son Hotel (☎ 888 214; d US$7-10; ✷) On the western side of town, this big place has some rooms with great views of the rocky outcrop across the harbour. There's a restaurant downstairs serving decent Vietnamese and Western food.

Sleeping on the beach is also possible, if you rent **tents** (30,000d) at the **guesthouse** (r 50,000d) on Cat Co 2. The national park also has a **guesthouse** (r US$10) offshore on Hon Cat Dua (Pineapple Island). If you want to camp here, you'll have to bring your own gear and plan on being self-sufficient for the night. Private boats (90,000d) and accommodation on the island can be arranged at Quang Duc Family Hotel.

Eating & Drinking

A fun dining experience in Cat Ba is the floating seafood restaurants in Cat Ba or Ben Beo harbours, where you choose your own seafood from pens underneath the restaurant. A rowing boat there and back should cost about 15,000d with waiting time; a feast for two should cost around 100,000d. We've heard reports of overcharging, so work out meal prices beforehand.

Huu Dung Restaurant (mains around 25,000d; ☾ lunch & dinner) Also known as the Coca Cola Restaurant due to its former paint job, this popular restaurant is up the hill near Cat Ba's nightclub strip. It serves good fresh seafood.

Hoang Y (mains 35,000d; ☾ lunch & dinner) For a variety of delicious seafood and vegetarian dishes, check out Hoang Y, at the western end of town. This place is always busy.

Flightless Bird Café (☎ 888 517; ☾ from 6.30pm) This hip waterfront spot has darts, movies, music, books and Australian wine (20,000d a glass). The Kiwi owner is a good source of local information, and he'll even make you a packed lunch if you order ahead. Along the waterfront of Cat Ba town, streetside cafés sell the usual sweet iced coffees and cigarettes to go with your front-row plastic seat to low-stakes card games and fishing-boat traffic.

Clubbing

Lan Song Xanh Disco (☾ 7pm-late) Climb up the hill to find the nightclub strip (don't worry, you'll hear it).

Getting There & Around

Cat Ba Island is 133km from Hanoi, 45km east of Haiphong, and 20km south of Halong City. Slow boats (50,000d, 2½ hours) and hydrofoils (70,000/90,000d, 45/75 minutes) travel daily between Cat Ba town and Haiphong. Ask locally about departure times, which change frequently, and show up early if travelling during the high season. There's a hydrofoil ticket kiosk about 100m east of the ferry landing, but you can also buy tickets at the landing a few hours before departure.

An alternative route to Cat Ba is via the island of Cat Hai, which is closer to Haiphong. A boat leaves Haiphong for Cat Hai, makes a brief stop and continues on to the port of Phu Long on Cat Ba Island. Chartered private boats run trips between Cat Ba and Halong Bay; make inquiries at the pier at either end.

Rented bicycles are a bracing way to explore the island. Most hotels can find you a cheap Chinese bicycle; inquire at Flightless Bird Café (above) about mountain-bike rentals.

Motorbike rentals (with or without driver) are available from most of the hotels.

If you're heading to the beaches or national park, pay the 2000d parking fee – this will ensure your vehicle isn't stolen or vandalised.

HAIPHONG
☎ 031 / pop 1.67 million

Haiphong, a busy maritime city with an important seaport and a major industrial centre, is mostly used as a stepping-stone by travellers on their way to Cat Ba Island and Halong Bay. For such a big city – Haiphong is Vietnam's third-most populous – it retains a relaxed feel, shot through with tall colonial-style buildings and tree-lined avenues. Pull up a plastic seat on the pavement and enjoy a sign-language conversation over a plate of *com*.

Information

There are a couple of Internet cafés on P Le Dai Hanh near P Dien Bien Phu.

Main post office (3 P Nguyen Tri Phuong) It's easy to spot, standing on a corner in dignified yellow.

Vietcombank (☎ 842 658; 11 P Hoang Dieu; ☒ closed Sat) Cashes travellers cheques, does cash advances and has an ATM.

Vietnam-Czech Friendship Hospital (Benh Vien Viet-Tiep; ☎ 700 463; P Nha Thuong) In emergencies, get medical help here; otherwise, you're better off heading for Hanoi.

Vietnam Tourism (☎ 745 432; vntourism.hp@bdvn.vnmail.vnd.net; P Dien Bien Phu) Can answer your questions and arrange tours.

Sights & Activities

Though there isn't a whole lot to see in Haiphong, its slow-paced appeal is enhanced by the **French colonial architecture** along the streets between the ferry landing and the Tam Bac bus station. The tree-shaded avenues in this neighbourhood make for a nice stroll if you've got time to kill.

Du Hang Pagoda (Chua Du Hang; 121 P Chua Hang; ☒ 7-11am & 1.30-5.50pm), founded three centuries ago and rebuilt several times since, has architectural elements that look Khmer-influenced. Just as cool is meandering along the narrow alley it's on, **P Chua Hang**, which is buzzing with Haiphong street life.

Sleeping

Duyen Hai Hotel (☎ 842 157; P Nguyen Tri Phuong; r 100,000-200,000d; ☒) This is a good deal – cheaper rooms are small but clean. All rooms come with TV and bathtubs.

Hotel du Commerce (☎ 842 706; 62 P Dien Bien Phu; r US$10-20; ☒) Rooms in this venerable old building are slowly being upgraded, and have high ceilings and huge bathrooms.

Khach San Thang Nam (☎ 745 432; 55 P Dien Bien Phu; d 170,000d; ☒) Great value – this comfortable place has bright, clean rooms and is a 10-minute walk from the ferry landing.

Eating

P Minh Khai offers a good selection of cheap eateries; and most hotel restaurants dish up variations on the fresh seafood available in Haiphong. Also check out P Quang Trung with its many cafés and *bia hoi* (draught beer).

Com Vietnam (☎ 841 698; 4 P Hoang Van Thu; mains 25,000d; ☒ lunch & dinner) A pleasant little Vietnamese restaurant near the post office.

Chie (☎ 821 018; 64 P Dien Bien Phu; meals around US$10; ☒ lunch & dinner) Good Japanese food, if you've got cash to spare.

Getting There & Around

Vietnam Airlines (www.vietnamairlines.com) offers several flights from Haiphong to HCMC and Danang.

Haiphong is 103km from Hanoi; minibuses for Hanoi (25,000d, two hours) leave about every 15 minutes between 4.15am and 7pm from the **Tam Bac bus station** (P Tam Bac), 4km from the waterfront. Buses heading south leave from **Niem Nghia bus station** (Đ Tran Nguyen Han).

You can also take an express local train (22,000d, two hours) to Hanoi from the **Haiphong train station** (Đ Luong Khanh Thien & Đ Pham Ngu Lao) at 6.10pm daily. From Hanoi, trains leave **Tran Quy Cap station** (B station; ☎ 04-825 2628; P Tran Qui Cap) at 5.50am; other trains leave from Long Bien train station several times daily.

BA BE NATIONAL PARK
☎ 0281 / elev 145m

Boasting waterfalls, rivers, deep valleys, lakes and caves, **Ba Be National Park** (Vuon Quoc Gia Ba Be; ☎ 894 014; admission per person 10,000d, per car 10,000d, insurance fee 1000d) is set amid towering peaks. The surrounding area is home to members of the Tay minority, who live in stilt homes. This region is surrounded by steep mountains that reach up to 1554m high. The park is a tropical rainforest area with more than 400 named plant species.

The 300 wildlife species in the forest include bears, monkeys, bats and butterflies and other insects.

Ba Be (Three Bays) is in fact three linked lakes, with a total length of 8km and a width of about 400m. The Nang River is navigable for 23km between a point 4km above Cho Ra and the **Dau Dang Waterfall** (Thac Dau Dang), which is a series of spectacular cascades between sheer walls of rock. The interesting **Puong Cave** (Hang Puong) is about 30m high and 300m long, and passes completely through a mountain. A navigable river flows through the cave.

Renting a boat is *de rigueur*, and costs 40,000d per hour. The boats carry about eight people, and you should allow at least seven hours to take in most sights; an optional guide (recommended) costs US$10 per day. The boat dock is about 2km from the park headquarters.

Sleeping & Eating

Just by the park headquarters are **guesthouses** (☎ 876 131; r US$20) and two-room air-con **cottages** (r US$25). There is also Internet access for 10,000d per hour, and a **restaurant** (dishes 10,000-30,000d), where you can order food about an hour before you want to eat.

The cheapest and most interesting way to stay at Ba Be is in **stilt houses** (per person US$3) in the park's small villages. Food is available in the villages; arrange these homestays at the park headquarters.

Rangers can arrange tours of the park that include the major sights; they can also arrange homestays, trekking, canoeing and other activities along the way. Costs depend on the number of people; if travelling alone, you'll probably pay at least US$25 a day.

Getting There & Around

Ba Be National Park is 240km from Hanoi. Most visitors get here by chartered vehicle from Hanoi; the one-way journey takes about six hours. Most travellers allow three days and two nights for the excursion.

Reaching the park by public transport is possible, but not easy. Take a bus from Hanoi to Phu Thong (30,000d, six hours) via Thai Nguyen or Bac Kan, and from there another bus to Cho Ra (10,000d, one hour). From Cho Ra you will need a motorbike (about 30,000d) to do the last 18km stretch of road.

Some travellers cafés in Hanoi (see p833) offer tours to Ba Be for around US$60.

MAI CHAU

☎ 018 / pop 47,500

Mai Chau is one of the closest places to Hanoi where you can visit a hill-tribe village. The area is a beautiful collection of farms and stilt homes spread out over a large valley. Most of the people here are ethnic White Thai, the majority of whom dress the same as Vietnamese. Traditional weaving is practised here and the beautiful results can be purchased direct from the weaver.

Information

Guides can be hired for around US$5 for a 7km to 8km walk. Staying overnight in White Thai stilt houses and trekking to minority villages further afield can also be arranged. Ask around the Mai Chau villages of Lac or Pom Coong. Be aware that Mai Chau sees a lot of tourists and has all the modern comforts: TVs, toilets and all.

Tourists must pay an admission fee of 5000d to enter Mai Chau.

Sleeping & Eating

Most backpackers prefer to stay a few hundred metres back from the main road in **White Thai stilt houses** (per person 50,000d) in Lac or Pom Coong villages. Most of these homes serve meals for about 20,000d. Reservations are not necessary, but it's advisable to arrive before dark.

The state-run **Mai Chau Guesthouse** (☎ 851 812; r from 120,000d) has basic, clean rooms that are OK for the price. Rooms at the back have wide views of the cultivated valley and the mountains beyond.

Getting There & Around

Mai Chau is 135km from Hanoi and just 6km south of Tong Dau junction on National Hwy 6 (along the Hanoi–Dien Bien Phu route).

There's no direct public transport to Mai Chau from Hanoi, but buses to nearby Hoa Binh (15,000d, two hours) are plentiful. From Hoa Binh you can get a local bus (20,000d, two hours) to Tong Dau junction, where you can hire a *xe om* (5000d) to Mai Chau.

Many travellers cafés and travel agencies in Hanoi (see p833) run inexpensive trips to Mai Chau.

LAO CAI

☎ 020 / pop 100,000

One of the gateways to China, Lao Cai lies at the end of the train line on the Chinese border. The border crossing slammed shut during the 1979 war between China and Vietnam and remained closed until 1993. Its reopening changed Lao Cai into a major hub for travellers journeying between Hanoi, Sapa (38km away) and Kunming.

Information

There is Internet access across from the train station.

BIDV bank (Đ Thuy Hoa) Does currency exchange and has an ATM; it's on the west side of the river, near Lao Cai's bus station.

Post office (☼ 7am-7pm) If you're facing the train station, the post office stands directly to the left.

Sleeping & Eating

Gia Nga (☎ 830 459; P Moi; s & d US$8-10, shower & soap US$1; 🍴) Very clean, and closest to the train station, this is good value. There's also a shower and luggage room for groggy arrival and departure clean-ups.

Thuy Hoa Hotel (☎ 826 805; 118 Đ Thuy Hoa; r US$11-12; 🍴) This smart little hotel is conveniently near the bus station, bank and border. Rooms are spotless and come with IDD phone and TV.

Binh Minh Hotel (☎ 830 085; 39 P Nguyen Hue; d US$7-10; 🍴) Very friendly staff, and clean rooms with all the basics.

Friendly Café (☎ 832 759; 322 Đ Nguyen Hue) If you have some time to kill while waiting for a train, there's good food and friendly folks at this café near the entrance of the train station. Most travellers tend to congregate here to chat and enjoy cheap eats before those long train rides. There is also a row of good, inexpensive eateries clustered near the roundabout directly in front of the train station.

Viet Hoa Restaurant (☎ 830 082; P Phan Dinh Phung; ☼ 11am-10.30pm) Off P Nguyen Hue by the train station, this serves good Vietnamese food and has an English-language menu.

Getting There & Around

Lao Cai is 340km away from Hanoi. Buses (53,000d, 10 hours) leave from the train station, but most travellers prefer to do the journey by train (US$15, 10 to 12 hours). Two trains run daily in each direction. The

---

> **BORDER CROSSING: INTO CHINA**
>
> The Lao Cai–Hekou crossing (open 7am to 5pm) is popular with travellers making their way between northern Vietnam and Yunnan. China is separated from Vietnam by a bridge over the Red River that pedestrians pay a 10,000d toll to cross. The border is about 3km from Lao Cai train station; the short motorbike journey costs 5000d.
>
> The train service running directly from Hanoi to Kunming in China, has been suspended indefinitely since 2002. However, it's possible to take a train to Lao Cai, cross the border into China, and catch a midmorning or overnight sleeper bus (US$11, 12 hours) or train (US$10, 16 hours) from the Chinese border town of Hekou to Kunming.

---

border is 3km from Lao Cai train station; a *xe om* should cost you 5000d.

SAPA

☎ 020 / pop 36,200

The premier destination of northwestern Vietnam, Sapa is a French hill station that was built in 1922. The whole area is spectacular and frequently shrouded in mist. Hilltribe people from surrounding villages don their most colourful costumes and head to the market on Saturday.

Don't forget your winter woollies – Sapa is known for its cold, foggy winters (down to 0°C). The dry season for Sapa is approximately January to the end of June – afternoon rain showers in the mountains are frequent.

Information

A minute on the Internet will cost you about 500d at guesthouses and travel agencies around town. Most hotels will exchange dollars for dong (at worse exchange rates than in Hanoi).

Royal Hotel (☎ 871 313; royalhotel_sapa@yahoo.com; P Cau May) Cashes travellers cheques for a 5% commission.

Sapa Information & Service Centre (☎ 871 975; P Cau May; ☼ 8.30-11am & 1.30-5.30pm) Useful maps (20,000d) of the town and surrounding country can be found here.

Sights & Activities

Surrounding Sapa are the Hoang Lien Mountains, including **Fansipan**, which at 3143m is Vietnam's highest peak. The trek

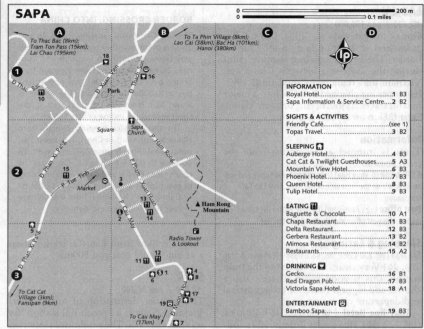

SAPA

0 — 200 m
0 — 0.1 miles

INFORMATION
Royal Hotel.....................................1 B3
Sapa Information & Service Centre...2 B2

SIGHTS & ACTIVITIES
Friendly Café............................(see 1)
Topas Travel..................................3 B2

SLEEPING
Auberge Hotel................................4 B3
Cat Cat & Twilight Guesthouses......5 A3
Mountain View Hotel......................6 B3
Phoenix Hotel.................................7 B3
Queen Hotel...................................8 B3
Tulip Hotel....................................9 B3

EATING
Baguette & Chocolat.....................10 A1
Chapa Restaurant.........................11 B3
Delta Restaurant..........................12 B3
Gerbera Restaurant......................13 B2
Mimosa Restaurant......................14 B2
Restaurants.................................15 A2

DRINKING
Gecko..16 B1
Red Dragon Pub...........................17 B3
Victoria Sapa Hotel......................18 A1

ENTERTAINMENT
Bamboo Sapa................................19 B3

from Sapa to the summit and back can take several days. Treks can be arranged at guesthouses and travel agencies around town, including **Mountain View Hotel** (Ninh Hong Guesthouse; ☎ 871 334; ninhhong@hn.vnn.vn; 54A P Cau May), **Auberge Hotel** (☎ 871 243; auberge@sapadiscovery.com; P Cau May) and **Topas Travel** (☎ 871 331; www.topas-adventure-vietnam.com; 28 P Cau May). Other recommended places to find trekking guides are **Chapa Restaurant** (☎ 871 045; 40 P Cau May) or the **Friendly Café** (at the Royal Hotel; ☎ 871 313; royalhotel_sapa@yahoo.com; P Cau May).

Some of the better-known sights around Sapa include **Tram Ton Pass**, **Thac Bac** (Silver Falls) and **Cau May** (Cloud Bridge), which spans the Muong Hoa River.

Sleeping

Cat Cat & Twilight Guesthouses (☎ 871 387; catcatht@hn.vnn.vn; Đ Phan Xi Pang; s & d US$4-30) On either side of the road leading to Cat Cat village, this perennial favourite continues to receive rave reviews. The terrace restaurant has a gorgeous, sweeping view, as do rooms higher up the hillside. Some rooms have fireplaces, and all have shared balconies.

Mountain View Hotel (Ninh Hong Guesthouse; ☎ 871 334; ninhhong@hn.vnn.vn; 54A P Cau May; s & d US$6-15) Run efficiently by one of Sapa's first female trekking guides, the Mountain View remains a terrific choice with stunning views. If you don't snag a choice spot, console yourself with breakfast on the terrace – akin to a spiritual experience, as you watch mist move over mountain.

Auberge Hotel (☎ 871 243; auberge@sapadiscovery.com; P Cau May; s & d US$6-18; ▢) Though older rooms lost their spectacular views in the building boom, this Sapa stalwart is still a great place to stay and get trekking information. Some rooms have fireplaces, and there's a lovely bonsai garden. The intimate terrace restaurant makes a good gathering spot for dinner.

Baguette & Chocolat (☎ 871 766; Đ Thac Bac; r US$14) Rents out four wonderfully cosy rooms with names like 'Cookies', but book well in advance. Also a great (and worthy) eating spot.

On the southern road heading away from Sapa, there's a row of small, family-run guesthouses. A few you might look into:

Phoenix Hotel (☎ 871 515; Đ Muong Hoa; r US$6-8)
Wood-panelled interior and huge views of Sapa on the exterior.

Queen Hotel (☎ 871 301; Đ Muong Hoa; d US$5-10)
Friendly; cosy rooms with unobstructed views, nice fireplaces and wood floors.

Tulip Hotel (☎ 871 914; 29 Đ Muong Hoa; r US$6-12)
Small, simple, clean with some terrific views.

Eating

Gerbera Restaurant (P Cau May; mains 28,000d; ☺ lunch & dinner) Uphill off P Cau May, this family-run eatery serves good, reasonably priced carnivore dishes of the Vietnamese and Western type, as well as pasta and salads.

Auberge Hotel (☎ 871 243; auberge@sapadiscovery .com; P Cau May; dishes around 12,000d; ☺ breakfast, lunch & dinner) The ever-popular Auberge terrace is a good spot for breakfast, and the inexpensive menu items include several vegetarian options.

Baguette & Chocolat (☎ 871 766; Đ Thac Bac; picnic lunches 32,000d; ☺ breakfast, lunch & dinner) The Sapa satellite of Hoa Sua School (see the boxed text, p842), this is the place for packed lunches for those long treks, and hot chocolate afterwards. All this good eating goes towards a worthy cause, providing valuable career-training for disadvantaged local kids. Also offers accommodation.

There are also several small family-run restaurants serving inexpensive Vietnamese food on P Tue Tinh in the market area.

Other recommendations:

Chapa Restaurant (☎ 871 045; 40 P Cau May; ☺ breakfast, lunch & dinner) A true travellers café; may look crowded but there are tables upstairs.

Delta Restaurant (☎ 871 799; P Cau May; pastas 33,000d; ☺ breakfast, lunch & dinner) Sapa's sole Italian restaurant does good pizzas and pastas.

Mimosa Restaurant (☎ 871 377; P Cau May; mains around 25,000d; ☺ lunch & dinner) Has a similar set-up as the Gerbera.

Drinking

Drinks are cheapest and most often imbibed at the local restaurants and cafés, but the following bars have notable style.

Red Dragon Pub (☎ 872 085; 21 Đ Muong Hoa) Just what Sapa needed, an English pub designed by its British-architect owner. Substantial full breakfasts (65,000d) are served in the tearoom downstairs; upstairs, a classic pub.

Gecko (☎ 871 504; P Thach Son) This French-run bar has a dimly lit, relaxed atmosphere. It also offers European and Vietnamese food, as well as packed lunches for trekkers passing through.

Victoria Sapa Hotel (☎ 871 522; www.victoria hotels-asia.com) Although stylish, drinks cost more here than elsewhere in town.

Entertainment

Bamboo Sapa (Bamboo Sapa Hotel; ☎ 871 075; P Muong Hoa) Take in free traditional hill-tribe music-and-dance shows here on Friday and Saturday from 8.30pm.

Getting There & Away

Sapa's proximity to the border region makes it a possible first or last stop for travellers crossing between Vietnam and China.

The gateway to Sapa is Lao Cai, 38km away on the Chinese border. Minibuses (25,000d, 1½ hours) make the trip regularly until midafternoon; they circle around town from the Royal Hotel to the church. Locals are also willing to take you down the mountain by motorbike for US$4. Minibuses run from Lao Cai to Bac Ha (20,000d, 2½ hours) and leave around 6am and 1pm daily. For those doing the self-drive, Lai Chau is 195km away.

Driving a motorbike from Hanoi to Sapa is a very long trip (380km) – start early. The last 38km is straight uphill, and the rocky road is under major construction.

Cafés in Hanoi offer weekend trips to Sapa for around US$40, but doing it on your own is also fun, and none too challenging. If you're not buying a ticket at the station yourself, shop around for the best deal, as travel agencies charge varying commissions.

Purchasing train tickets in Sapa costs a bit more than at the station in Lao Cai, but assures you a seat on the train. Most hotels and travel agencies around town can book tickets for you.

BORDER CROSSING: INTO LAOS

Tay Trang, near Dien Bien Phu in northern Vietnam, was not officially open to foreigners when last we heard; inquire around Hanoi before heading for the hills. For other border crossings into Laos, see p867.

Getting Around

Downtown Sapa can be walked in 20 minutes. If you've got a spare hour, follow the steps up to the radio tower; from here, the valley views are breathtaking.

For excursions further out, you can hire a self-drive motorbike for about US$5 per day, or take one with a driver for about US$8. Cat Cat village (3km) is an easy downhill walk through green fields and small houses along a winding path.

BAC HA

☎ 020 / pop 70,200

The Sunday market in Bac Ha is where you'll want to stock up on water buffalo, pigs and horses. Once you're all set, you can also browse for bottles of local firewater (made from rice, cassava or corn), or handicrafts made by some of the 10 Montagnard groups living near here – Flower Hmong, Dzao, Giay (Nhang), Han (Hoa), Xa Fang, Lachi, Nung, Phula, Thai and Thulao.

Bac Ha is a less crowded alternative to Sapa, and arriving midweek makes for a relaxing visit. Around 700m above sea level, the highlands around Bac Ha are somewhat warmer than Sapa. But helping keep tourists at bay are the loudspeakers cranking the 'Voice of Vietnam' from 5am to 6am and 6pm to 7pm daily – bring earplugs.

Sights & Activities

BAN PHO VILLAGE

The Hmong villagers in Ban Pho are some of the kindest people you'll meet in Vietnam. Ban Pho is a 7km return trip from Bac Ha. You can take a loop route to get there and back.

Other nearby villages include **Trieu Cai** (8km return), **Na Ang** (6km return) and **Na Hoi** (4km return). Ask at your hotel for directions.

MONTAGNARD MARKETS

Other than the colourful Sunday **Bac Ha market** in town, there are several interesting markets nearby, all within about 20km of each other.

Can Cau market, one of Vietnam's most exotic open-air markets, is 20km north of Bac Ha and just 9km south of the Chinese border. The market runs on Saturday.

Coc Ly market happens on Tuesday, about 35km from Bac Ha. There's a pretty good

road, or you can go by road and river; ask at hotels in Bac Ha to organise trips.

Lung Phin market is between Can Cau market and Bac Ha town, about 12km from the town. It's less busy, and runs on Sunday.

Sleeping & Eating

Room rates tend to increase on weekends, when tourists arrive for a piece of the Sunday-market action.

Sao Mai Hotel (☎ 880 288; r US$7-25; 🖳) The big Sao Mai has clean, pleasant rooms of various vintages; it's popular with group tours and has an outdoor restaurant and bar.

Toan Thang Hotel (☎ 880 444; r 100,000d) Staying in this cute, sturdy wooden house reaps benefits like hot water, rustic character and a less-empty wallet.

Tran Sin Hotel (☎ 880 240; s/d US$8/10) Overlooking the market, the Tran Sin has balconies and mountain views from some rooms. Its restaurant (open for lunch, and dinner until 9pm) is one of the few in town.

Anh Duong Guesthouse (☎ 880 329; d 80,000-100,000d) This friendly place is close to the market, yet far enough from the main road and loudspeakers to be quiet. Rooms are small and bright.

Minh Quan Hotel (☎ 880 222; d 120,000-150,000d) Near the market, this homely spot has comfortable rooms with balconies and views over Bac Ha Market and mountains.

Hotel restaurants serve breakfast, but the Sao Mai Hotel is a good stand-by for eggs and bread, or surprisingly good crêpes. You might also sample the street eats: we suggest the *xoi* (sticky rice).

Cong Phu Restaurant (☎ 880 254; mains around 20,000d; 🕙 lunch & dinner) Central and hospitable, Cong Phu serves tasty low-priced food and has an English-language menu.

Getting There & Around

Buses make the 63km trip from Lao Cai to Bac Ha (40,000d, two hours) at 6.30am and 1pm daily. Buses from Bac Ha to Lao Cai leave at 5.30am and 11.30am.

Xe om make the Lao Cai–Bac Ha run for 100,000d, and Sapa–Bac Ha (110km) for around US$13.

Sunday minibus tours from Sapa to Bac Ha cost around US$10, including transport, guide and trekking to a minority village. On the way back to Sapa you can hop off in Lao Cai and catch the night train to Hanoi.

Bac Ha is 330km (10 hours) from Hanoi. Some cafés in Hanoi offer four-day bus trips to Bac Ha for around US$60, usually with a visit to Sapa included.

CENTRAL COAST

HUÉ

☎ 054 / pop 286,400

Traditionally, Hué has been one of Vietnam's cultural, religious and educational centres. Hué served as the political capital from 1802 to 1945 under the 13 emperors of the Nguyen dynasty. Today, Hué's decaying, opulent tombs of the Nguyen emperors and grand, crumbling Citadel comprise a Unesco World Heritage site. Most of these architectural attractions lie along the northern side of the Song Huong (Perfume River).

For rest, refreshment and recreation, the river's south side is where the action's at.

Information

INTERNET ACCESS

You'll find travellers cafés and Internet cafés along the northern end of Đ Hung Vuong and around the intersection of Đ Nguyen Tri Phuong. Many hotels and travellers cafés also offer Internet access for 6000d to 10,000d per hour.

MEDICAL SERVICES

Hué Central Hospital (Benh Vien Trung Uong Hué; ☎ 822 325; 16 Đ Le Loi) Close to Phu Xuan Bridge.

MONEY

Industrial & Development Bank (☎ 823 361; 41 Đ Hung Vuong) Same services as Vietcombank, sans ATM.
Vietcombank (54 Đ Hung Vuong) Exchanges travellers cheques, processes cash advances and has an ATM. Another convenient branch with a 24-hour ATM on Đ Hung Vuong in front of the Hotel Saigon Morin.

POST

Branch post office (Đ Le Loi) Near the river.
Main post office (14 Đ Ly Thuong Kiet) Has postal and telephone services.

TRAVEL AGENCIES

Café on Thu Wheels (☎ 832 241; 10/2 Đ Nguyen Tri Phuong) Friendly Minh Toan Thu and her brothers run great motorbike tours. Great drinking location too (see p867).
Mandarin Café (☎ 821 281; mandarin@dng.vnn.vn; 3 Đ Hung Vuong) This reliable tour desk is great for

information and tours, as well as good backpacker fare (see p866).
Stop & Go Café (☎ 827 051; 10 Đ Ben Nghe) Another pack of superb motorbike guides is based here, under the direction of silver-haired Mr Do.

Sights & Activities

CITADEL

One of Vietnam's disintegrating treasures is Hué's **Citadel** (Kinh Thanh), the erstwhile imperial city on the northern bank of the Song Huong. Though heavily bombed by the Americans, and much of it now used for agriculture, its scope and beauty still impress.

Construction of the moated Citadel, by Emperor Gia Long, began in 1804. The emperor's official functions were carried out in the **Imperial Enclosure** (Dai Noi, or Hoang Thanh; admission 55,000d; ☺ 6.30am-5.30pm), a 'citadel within the Citadel'. Inside the 6m-high, 2.5km-long wall is a surreal world of deserted gardens and ceremonial halls.

Within the Imperial Enclosure is the **Forbidden Purple City** (Tu Cam Thanh), which was reserved for the private life of the emperor. The only servants allowed inside were eunuchs, who posed no threat to the royal concubines. Nowadays, all are welcome.

ROYAL TOMBS

Set like gems on the banks of the Song Huong, the **Tombs of the Nguyen Dynasty** (☺ 8-11.30am & 1.30-5.30pm) are 7km to 16km south of Hué. Visiting several tombs can be expensive, with *xe om* shuttles and individual admission – if you visit only one, make it Tu Duc or Minh Mang.

Tomb of Tu Duc (admission 55,000d), Emperor Tu Duc's tomb complex, is a majestic site, laced with frangipani and pine trees and set alongside a small lake. The buildings are beautifully designed. Near the entrance, the pavilion where the concubines used to lounge is a peaceful spot on the water.

The **Tomb of Dong Khanh** (admission 22,000d), built in 1889, is the smallest of the Royal Tombs. It's very beautiful and doesn't get many visitors; find it about 500m behind the Tomb of Tu Duc.

Perhaps the most majestic of the Royal Tombs is the **Tomb of Minh Mang** (admission 55,000d), who ruled from 1820 to 1840. This tomb is renowned for its architecture, which blends into the natural surroundings.

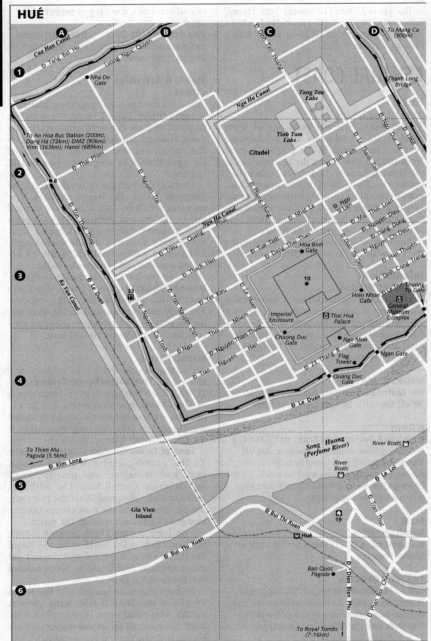

HUÉ

To Mang Ca (300m)

Cua Hau Canal

Đ Tang Bat Ho

Lương Ngoc Quyen

Đ Đinh Tien Hoang

Nha Do Gate

Thanh Long Bridge

Ngu Ha Canal

Tang Tau Lake

Đ Ngo Duc Ke

Đ 1968

Tinh Tam Lake

Citadel

To An Hoa Bus Station (200m);
Dong Ha (72km); DMZ (90km);
Vinh (363km); Hanoi (689km)

Đ Thai Phien

Đ Nguyen Trai

Đ Ton That Thiep

8

Đ Phung Hung

Đ Le Thanh Ton

Đ Tinh Tam

Ngu Ha Canal

Đ Nhat Le

Đ Ngo Si Lien

Đ Mai Thuc Loan

Đ Nguyen Dieu

Đ Dang Dung

Phuc

Đ Triệu Quang

Đ Thach Han

Đ Tue Tinh

Đ Dang Thai Than

Hoa Binh Gate

Đ Doan Thi Diem

Đ Nguyen Chi Dieu

Đ Han Thuyen

Ke Van Canal

Đ Le Duan

33

Đ Tran Nguyen Dan

Đ Yet Kieu

Đ Le Huan

10

Đ Dinh Cong Trang

Đ Le Truc

Thuong Tu Gate

Hien Nhon Gate

General Museum Complex

Imperial Enclosure

Thai Hoa Palace

Đ Nguyen Cu Trinh

Đ Ngo

Nhiem

Tho

Đ Nguyen Thien Thuat

Han

Chuong Duc Gate

Ngo Mon Gate

Ngan Gate

Đ Tran Nguyen

Đ 23 Thang 8

Flag Tower

Quang Duc Gate

Đ Le Duan

To Thien Mu
Pagoda (3.5km)

Đ Kim Long

Song Huong (Perfume River)

River Boats

River Boats

Đ Le Loi

Gia Vien Island

Đ Bui Thi Xuan

19

Đ Tran Thuc

Hué

Đ Bui Thi Xuan

Hué

Bao Quoc Pagoda

Đ Dien Bien Phu

Đ Phan Bội Châu

To Royal Tombs
(7-16km)

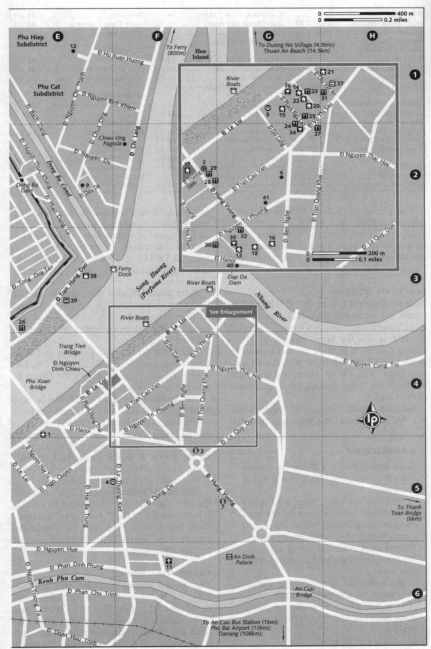

The elaborate, hilltop **Tomb of Khai Dinh** (admission 55,000d), who ruled from 1916 to 1925, stands out from the other tombs for its unique structure. The buildings and statues reflect a distinct mix of Vietnamese and European features.

PLACES OF WORSHIP

Thien Mu Pagoda (Đ Le Duan; ⏰ 7.30-11.30am & 1.30-5.30pm), an octagonal pagoda, is one of the most famous structures in Vietnam. Founded in 1601, it was the home pagoda of Thich Quang Duc, who publicly burned himself to death in 1963 to protest the policies of President Ngo Dinh Diem. Thien Mu is on the banks of the Song Huong, 4km southwest of the Citadel.

Bao Quoc Pagoda (Ham Long Hill, Phuong Duc District; ⏰ 7.30-11.30am & 1.30-4.30pm) was founded

A ROYAL SCAM

Quick, what colour is a 20,000-dong note? And a 5000-dong note? Right: blue and blue. You win!

Or maybe you lose: a ticket seller at one of the Royal Tombs has reportedly been short-changing unwary tourists by placing a (blue) 5000d note underneath a (blue, too) 20,000d note, instead of giving two twenties. Most people wouldn't look twice at two blue notes.

This author didn't, once giving a street kid change for a folded-up 20,000d note. Later, pulling it from her pocket, she found that it was a fiver with the one crucial corner taped on.

in 1670 by Giac Phong, a Chinese Buddhist monk. Monks and students gather to study in the peaceful orchid-lined courtyard behind the sanctuary. To get here, head south from Đ Le Loi on Đ Dien Bien Phu and turn right immediately after crossing the railway tracks.

Notre Dame Cathedral (Dong Chua Cuu The; 80 Đ Nguyen Hue; ⏰ mass 5am & 5pm, Sun 7pm) is a blend of European and Asian architectural elements; this modern cathedral was built between 1959 and 1962.

There are quite a few pagodas and Chinese congregational halls in Phu Cat and Phu Hiep subdistricts, across the Dong Ba Canal from Dong Ba Market.

Dieu De National Pagoda (Quoc Tu Dieu De; 102 Đ Bach Dang; ⏰ 7.30-11.30am & 1.30-4.30pm) was built under Emperor Thieu Tri (r 1841–47). It is one of Hué's three 'national pagodas', once under the direct patronage of the emperor. In the 1960s, it was a stronghold of Buddhist and student opposition to the South Vietnamese government and the war.

Tang Quang Pagoda (Tang Quang Tu) is just down the alley opposite 80 Đ Nguyen Chi Thanh. It is the largest of the three Theravada Buddhist pagodas in Hué, and its distinctive architecture comes from Sri Lankan and Indian influences rather than Chinese.

THANH TOAN BRIDGE

Though the **covered footbridge** itself is a delight, the joy is in the journey. Seven kilometres east of central Hué, it's a tricky little spot to find, but the bicycle or motorbike ride takes you through gorgeous rice paddies and some ornate village homes besides the road.

To get there, head north for a few hundred metres on Đ Ba Trieu until you see the 'Citadel Hotel' sign. Turn right here, then follow the bumpy dirt track for 6km. At the T-junction, turn left towards the market building; just beyond is the bridge.

THUAN AN BEACH

Thuan An Beach (Bai Tam Thuan An), 15km northeast of Hué, is on a lovely lagoon near the mouth of the Song Huong.

Tours

If you have a specific agenda in mind, motorbike guides from local travellers' cafés can do customised day tours of the Royal Tombs, the Citadel, the Demilitarised Zone (DMZ) and surrounding countryside. But the best way to visit the tombs is on a river cruise.

SONG HUONG (PERFUME RIVER) CRUISES

Boat rides down the scenic Song Huong are the 'must-do' of a visit to Hué. Tours costing about US$2 per person typically take in several tombs and Thien Mu Pagoda, and include lunch. Admission to the individual tombs is not included, but you can pick and choose which tombs to visit.

Many restaurants and hotels catering to foreigners arrange these boat tours, and the journey usually runs from 8am to 2pm daily.

DEMILITARISED ZONE (DMZ) TOURS

From 1954 until 1975, the Ben Hai River served as line of demarcation between South Vietnam and North Vietnam. The DMZ, 90km west of Hué, consisted of an area 5km on either side of the demarcation line.

Most of what you can see nowadays in the DMZ are places where historical events happened, and may not be worthwhile unless you're really into war history. To make sense of it all, and to avoid areas where there is still unexploded ordnance, you should take a guide. Day tours from Hué cost around US$15.

Significant sites:

Khe Sanh Combat Base (admission 25,000d) The site of the American War's most famous siege, now on a barren plateau about 130km from Hué.

Truong Son National Cemetery (Nghia Trang Liet Si Truong Son) A memorial to the tens of thousands of North Vietnamese soldiers killed along the Ho Chi Minh Trail.

Row after row of white tombstones stretch across the hillsides, about 105km from Hué.

Vinh Moc Tunnels (admission & guided tour 20,000d) Similar to the tunnels at Cu Chi (p905); 110km from Hué.

Festivals

Festival Hué This biennial cultural festival, to be next held in June 2006 and lasting about a week, features traditional dance and music from Vietnam and other participating countries. Guesthouses are jammed during this time, so plan ahead.

Sleeping

EAST LE LOI

You can find heaps of cheap rooms in the narrow alley off Đ Le Loi between Đ Pham Ngu Lao and Đ Chu Van An.

Mimosa Guesthouse (☎ 828 068; tvhoang4@hotmail.com; 46/6 Đ Le Loi; r US$5-12; ✕) A popular place run by a former French teacher, you should book ahead if you're set on staying here. There are shared garden balconies and the place has a pleasant atmosphere.

Guesthouse Van Xuan (☎ 826 567; 10 Đ Pham Ngu Lao; s US$6, d US$7-8; ✕) This sweet little guesthouse has a lovely shared terrace filled with greenery. Homely rooms come with hot water.

Minh Hien Hotel (☎ 828 725; 3 Đ Chu Van An; r incl breakfast US$10; ✕) Simple hot-water bathroom, IDD, satellite TV.

A Dong Hotel (☎ 824 148; adongcoltd@dng.vnn.vn; 1 Đ Chu Van An; r US$8-10; ✕) Very friendly folks keep this place going. Cute tiles, balconies, IDD phone, TV and hot water round out the amenities.

Guesthouse Hoang Huong (☎ 828 509; 46/2 Đ Le Loi; dm US$2.50, r US$5-10; ✕) This guesthouse is basic and usually full, which is a good sign.

SPLURGE!

Hotel Saigon Morin (☎ 523 526; www.morinhotel.com.vn; 30 Đ Le Loi; r US$50-500; ✕ ▯ ▭) Occupying a prime corner opposite the Trang Tien Bridge on the south bank of the Song Huong, this grand hotel exudes historical charm. Along with the four-star comforts of its guest rooms, the hotel has three restaurants (including a US$1 restaurant), a lovely courtyard café with very reasonably priced bar food, a rooftop bar, and a gourd-shaped swimming pool.

Choose from the ultracheap dorm accommodation or private rooms.

Thanh Thuy's Guesthouse (☎ 824 585; 46/4 Đ Le Loi; r US$4-8; ❄) More expensive rooms at this small family-run place have balconies; all have air-con. Book ahead.

Đ HUNG VUONG

Another cluster of inexpensive rooms is in the narrow alley just west of Đ Hung Vuong, off Đ Nguyen Tri Phuong.

Binh Duong Hotel (☎ 833 298; binhduong1@dng .vnn.vn; 4/34 Đ Nguyen Tri Phuong; dm US$3, r US$6-25; ❄ 🖳) Centrally located in this backpacker alley, the popular Binh Duong is great value. It's clean, with pleasant public sitting-areas and satellite TV. There's another branch on the same street.

Hung Vuong Inn (☎ 821 068; 20 Đ Hung Vuong; r US$10; ❄) Clean and bright, with French bakery goods downstairs. Front rooms have balconies, and all are tidy and well kept.

Hai Dang Hotel (Lighthouse Hotel; ☎ 824 755; thanhtrang5htk@dng.vnn.vn; 43 Đ Hung Vuong; r US$8-15; ❄) Streetside rooms at this clean spot are noisier but have windows to the outside. Prices may be bumped down if the hotel isn't full.

WEST LE LOI

Le Loi Hué Hotel (☎ 822 153; 2 Đ Le Loi; d US$7-17; ❄) In central Hué, location gives this place its edge: it's a 100m walk from the train station. The budget rooms at the back border on dreary, but pricier rooms come with IDD phones and satellite TV.

Eating

SOUTH BANK

Mandarin Café (☎ 821 281; mandarin@dng.vnn.vn; 3 Đ Hung Vuong; breakfast 10,000d; ☽ breakfast, lunch & dinner) At this backpacker magnet, the BLTs,

---

SPLURGE!

Y Thao Garden (☎ 523 018; hoacuchue@dng .vnn.vn; 3 Đ Thach Han; set meals US$7-10) Set in a charmingly decorated house, Y Thao Garden surrounds your supper in Citadel ambience. Sample sumptuous Hué specialities of the vegetarian (and non-) variety. The set menus are beautifully presented and replicate dishes from the Hué royal court. Book ahead to reserve a place at the table.

---

potato salad and banana pancakes are recommended. The owner, Mr Cu, is helpful and cheery – and has consistently improved his services since the first LP mention, a rarity worth noting. Mandarin also gives good information about tours (p861).

Minh & Coco Mini Restaurant (☎ 821 822; 1 Đ Hung Vuong; dishes 5000-50,000d; ☽ breakfast, lunch & dinner) Run by two gregarious sisters, this is a fun place to eat a cheap lunch and watch life go by on busy Đ Hung Vuong.

Xuan Trang Cafeteria (☎ 832 480; 14A Đ Hung Vuong; mains 20,000d; ☽ breakfast, lunch & dinner) There's a good vegetarian selection on Xuan Trang's menu of cheap and delicious food. The bustling crowd is a great recommendation.

Hien's Canteen (Đ Pham Ngu Lao; ☽ breakfast, lunch & dinner) Run by a friendly couple, this place has it all: cheap cuisine, a pool table, cold beer, local information and Internet access.

Tinh Tam (☎ 823 572; 12 Đ Chu Van An; mains from 10,000d; ☽ lunch & dinner) This family place serves excellent and inexpensive vegetarian food. Dishes made with mock meat, such as 'deer' with black pepper and lemon grass, are delish but the noodle soups are also worth trying.

La Carambole (☎ 826 234; la_carambole@hotmail .com; 19 Đ Pham Ngu Lao; mains around 30,000d; ☽ breakfast, lunch & dinner) Mixing it up with French fare and solid Vietnamese stand-bys, La Carambole also offers a good wine list and a fine ambience.

Little Italy (☎ 826 928; littleitalyhue@gmail.com; 2A Đ Vo Thi Sau; mains around 40,000d; ☽ lunch & dinner) Where else do you think you'll find Hué's best Italian food? Pizzas are respectable, pastas are perfectly *al dente*.

Omar Khayyam's Indian Restaurant (☎ 821 616; 10 Đ Nguyen Tri Phuong; curries 30,000-60,000d; ☽ lunch & dinner) One more link in Omar's coastal chain, this small spot dishes out favourites like naan and curry. It fills quickly when tour groups descend, so you may have to wait during peak hours.

Stop & Go Café (☎ 889 106; 4 Đ Ben Nghe; mains 40,000d; ☽ breakfast, lunch & dinner) With a unique bohemian air, this is a great place for a beer, but the meals are a bit overpriced. An excellent place to arrange motorbike tours; it also has rooms for rent.

Dong Tam (☎ 828 403; 48/7 Đ Le Loi; set meals 25,000d; ☽ lunch & dinner) Come here to enjoy bargain Vietnamese veggie cuisine in a low-key garden setting.

NORTH BANK

Lac Thien Restaurant (6 Đ Dinh Tien Hoang; ◷ lunch & dinner) Be deceived not by neighbouring copycats – this is the original deaf-mute restaurant serving up a variety of Hué specialities such as *banh khoai* (pork and prawn crêpes) and other Vietnamese classics.

Dong Ba market (Đ Tran Hung Dao; ◷ 6.30am-8pm) Although the dining conditions aren't ideal, the market is a good place to put together cheap meals, as well as do some shopping.

Drinking

In the evenings, backpackers gather over Huda beers in the cafés along Đ Hung Vuong. If you're looking to party and play a bit of pool, try these spots.

DMZ Bar & Cafe (44 Đ Le Loi) The DMZ is a long-running, popular pool-shooting and dance spot for expats and travellers. It stays open late and keeps the music flowing.

Bar Why Not? (☎ 824 793; 21 Đ Vo Thi Sau) Why not, indeed. This corner place in the East Le Loi neighbourhood mixes respectably potent cocktails. It also serves good bar food and has a pool table.

Café On Thu Wheels (☎ 832 241; 10/2 Đ Nguyen Tri Phuong; ◷ 7am-late) Another popular place to hang, swap stories and throw back a few. It's tiny, but crammed with character, as well as colourful characters. Great motorbike tours are run from here too (p861).

Entertainment

Tropical Garden Restaurant (☎ 847 143; 27 Đ Chu Van An; mains 30,000-80,000d; ◷ dinner) Treat yourself to dinner tunes and sample Hué-style and central-Vietnamese cuisine in the restaurant garden or inside the spacious dining area. Traditional Vietnamese music is performed nightly between 7pm and 9pm.

Shopping

Hué is known for producing the finest conical hats in Vietnam. The city is famous for its 'poem hats', which, when held up to the light, reveal black cut-out scenes sandwiched between the layers of translucent palm leaves.

Hué is also a prime place to look for rice-paper and silk paintings, but the prices initially quoted are usually about four times the actual price. Walking away from a souvenir stall will often bring the bargaining down.

Dong Ba market (Đ Tran Hung Dao; ◷ 6.30am-8pm) Buy everything from machetes to pyjamas at this market, a few metres north of Trang Tien Bridge on the northern bank of the river.

Getting There & Away

AIR
Vietnam Airlines (☎ 823 249; www.vietnamairlines.com; 20 Đ Hanoi; ◷ 7-11am & 1.30-4.30pm) also has a **booking office** (☎ 824 709; 7 Đ Nguyen Tri Phuong; ◷ 7-11am & 1.30-5pm Mon-Sat) in the Thuan Hoa Hotel.

BORDER CROSSING: INTO LAOS

You can cross overland into Laos at four legal border outposts, where 15-day Lao visas are issued on arrival.

A popular route over the Lao Bao crossing (open 7am to 5pm) is by tourist bus from Hué to Savannakhet in Laos. The trip often requires an overnight at Dong Ha. You can travel on local buses from Dong Ha to Lao Bao (20,000d, two hours), and arrive early to catch the daily bus to Savannakhet.

Night buses travel direct between Hanoi and Vientiane, crossing at Cau Treo (open 7am to 5pm). It's also possible to catch a bus from Vinh to Tay Son (10,000d), then a motorbike or minibus (50,000d) to the Cau Treo–Kaew Neua border post. Taxis and trucks then continue on to Lak Sao in Laos.

It's also possible to cross at Nam Can to Nong Haet in Laos, but this is a marathon trek for those willing to wait around for the infrequent public transport. Start in Vinh and aim for Phonsavan in Laos.

Another northern crossing is open at Nam Xoi/Na Maew, connecting Moc Chau in Vietnam to Sam Neua in Laos.

Be aware that unscrupulous travel agencies from Hoi An to Hanoi sell bus tickets purportedly going to various destinations in Laos, when in fact they drop travellers at the Lao border without onward transport. Shop around carefully and talk to other travellers before booking through an agency – or consider taking public transport.

Several flights a day connect Hué to HCMC and Hanoi. Phu Bai airport is 13km south of the city centre and takes about 25 minutes by car. Some hotels arrange share taxis for about US$2 per person. Even better, Vietnam Airlines has a minibus service (25,000d) from its office to the airport, departing about two hours before each flight.

BUS

Hué has three main bus stations: An Cuu, at the southeastern end of Đ Hung Vuong, serves the southern destinations; An Hoa, northwest of the Citadel on Hwy 1, serves northern destinations; and Dong Ba, a short-haul bus station, is next to Dong Ba market.

Tourist minibuses can be booked at most budget cafés and hotels. Minibuses to Danang (108km) and Hoi An leave at 8am daily and cost US$3. The service for the Hué–Hanoi leg of the open-tour trail (see p830) receives the most (and most bitter) complaints from backpackers. Consider taking the train for this route.

Tourist buses to Savannakhet in Laos can be booked from Hué for about US$15. If you take public buses, you'll have to catch one bound for Dong Ha, then transfer to another bus bound for Lao Bao (15,000d, two hours). From Lao Bao, the border post is about 2km; a *xe om* should cost about 10,000d. You'll have to walk the 1km distance between the Vietnamese and Lao border posts.

TRAIN

Hué train station (Ga Hué; ☎ 822 175; 2 Đ Bui Thi Xuan; ⊙ ticket office 7.30am–5pm) is on the south bank of the river, at the southwestern end of Đ Le Loi.

Getting Around

Bicycles (US$1), motorbikes (US$4 to US$7) and cars (US$35 per day, with driver) can be hired from hotels all over town.

Co Do Taxi (☎ 830 830) has air-con vehicles with meters. Cyclos and *xe om* will find you when you need them.

BACH MA NATIONAL PARK

☎ 054 / elev 1450m

Forty-five kilometres southeast of Hué, **Bach Ma National Park** (Vuon Quoc Gia Bach Ma; ☎ 871 330; www.bachma.vnn.vn; admission 10,500d) is a French-era hill station known for its cool weather. There are abundant trekking opportunities through beautiful forests to cascading waterfalls. The park's highest peak, which can be climbed, is 1450m above sea level. From the peak of the summit trail there are sweeping 360-degree views across the stone remains of villas dotted around the nearby hills.

Bach Ma National Park is rich in flora and fauna and is a bird-watcher's paradise. The park is very foggy and wet from July to February and rainy in October and November. The best time to visit is between March and June.

Trails are marked on the national park map, which you receive with your ticket. Further information is found in the *Bach Ma National Park* booklet, available for 12,000d at the park entrance.

Sleeping & Eating

National Park Guesthouse (☎ 871 330; camp site per person 3000d, 6-person tents 80,000d, r 100,000-150,000d) This pleasant guesthouse, rebuilt from one of the old French ruins, sits in the middle of the park. Contact the guesthouse or call the park headquarters to book accommodation. Because meals are prepared to order and require a trip to the market, give at least four hours' advance notice.

There's a canteen near the visitors centre, and those wishing to dine at the summit can make advance orders to eat here.

Getting There & Around

The entrance and visitors centre is at Km 3 on the summit road, which starts at the town of Cau Hai on National Hwy 1. It's another meandering 16km from the gate to the summit, and unless you are willing to walk it (three to four hours; bring lots of water and wear a hat), you'll need to hire private transport from the park.

Eight-passenger 4WDs are available to hire for around 250,000d per same-day return, 350,000d next-day return or 150,000d one-way.

It's most convenient to hire a vehicle to keep with you for the time you spend in the park, especially if you plan to do some trekking. Trailheads are spread along the 16km summit road, and motorcycles and bicycles are not allowed to access this road.

DANANG

☎ 0511 / pop 1.1 million

Danang is Vietnam's fourth-largest city and it forms a mere transit stop for most travellers visiting the Museum of Cham Sculpture. But there are tranquil beaches nearby; and Danang's slow pace and relative dearth of travellers make it easy to take it easy.

Information

INTERNET ACCESS

Internet cafés around town are plentiful; you can find several around Đ Tran Quoc Toan, between Đ Yen Bai and Đ Nguyen Chi Thanh. Most charge around 6000d per hour.

MEDICAL SERVICES

Danang Family Medical Practice (☎ 582 700; 50-52 Đ Nguyen Van Linh) One of Vietnam's most trusted foreign-owned clinics comes to Danang.

Hospital C (Benh Vien C; ☎ 822 480; 35 Đ Hai Phong) The most advanced medical facility of the four in Danang.

MONEY

VID Public Bank (2 Đ Tran Phu)

Vietcombank (140 Đ Le Loi) The only place in town to exchange travellers cheques, and it has an ATM.

POST

Danang domestic & international post offices (Đ Bach Dang)

TRAVEL AGENCIES

An Phu Tourist (☎ 818 366; 5 Đ Dong Da; ☼ 7.30am-4.30pm)

Dana Tours (☎ 825 653; danamarle@dng.vnn.vn; 76 Đ Hung Vuong) With an enlightened attitude compared with other state-run agencies, this is a great place to arrange transport and tours.

Sights & Activities

Danang's jewel is the famed **Museum of Cham Sculpture** (Bao Tang Cham; cnr Đ Trung Nu Vuong & Đ Bach Dang; admission 20,000d; ☼ 7am-5pm). This small, breezy museum houses the finest collection of Cham sculpture to be found anywhere. These intricately carved sandstone pieces come from Cham sites all over Vietnam, and detours should be scheduled for a visit here.

Guides hang out at the museum's entrance; should you hire one, agree on a fee beforehand.

Sleeping

While Danang doesn't offer many budget options, there are a few nice places near the riverfront.

Tan Minh Hotel (☎ 827 456; tanminhhotel@dng .vnn.vn; 142 Đ Bach Dang; d 120,000-150,000d; ⊠) The best of the budget bunch, this small family-run place has clean good-sized rooms with psychedelic-tile floors. Rooms with balconies look onto the river, and all rooms have air-con and hot water.

Guesthouse 34 (Nha Nghi 34; ☎ 822 732; 34 Đ Bach Dang; d 75,000-105,000d; ⊠) There are several basic rooms here – the best deal in Danang – encircling a quiet garden courtyard in front. Air-con rooms have hot water; fan rooms have cold. Find it right on the waterfront.

Bach Dang Hotel (☎ 823 649; bdhotel@dng.vnn .vn; 50 Đ Bach Dang; r US$18-50; ⊠ ⊠) The cheapest rooms at the back face a quiet tree-lined street and have an expansive shared veranda along the front. Spacious rooms come with fridge and satellite TV, and the hotel exudes a faded, postcolonial character worth spending up for.

If you'd like easy access to the beach, consider one of the following places.

Hoa's Place (☎ 969 216; hoasplace@hotmail.com; r US$4-6) A laid-back little gem, this famously cosy spot is near China Beach. Hoa and his wife are superb hosts, the food here is fresh and tasty, and the vibe is comfortably relaxed.

My Khe Beach Hotel (☎ 836 125; r US$12-20; ⊠) Over the last few years, this beach hotel has been renovated to make it a presentable, good choice. Rooms have the usual amenities for this price range, and there's a friendly restaurant on-site.

Eating

Mi Quang (1A Đ Hai Phong; dishes from 5000d; ☼ lunch & dinner) Near the Caodai Temple, this popular lunch place serves deliciously filling bowls of Danang's local speciality, *mi quang* – thick, flat noodles in broth with salad greens stirred through it. It's also open in the evenings, but tends to close on the early side.

Com Chay Chua Tinh Hoi (500 Đ Ong Ich Khiem; dishes from 3000d; ☼ lunch & dinner) This joint is cited by locals as having the best vegetarian food in town; it's just inside the entrance gate to the Phap Lam Pagoda, about 1km

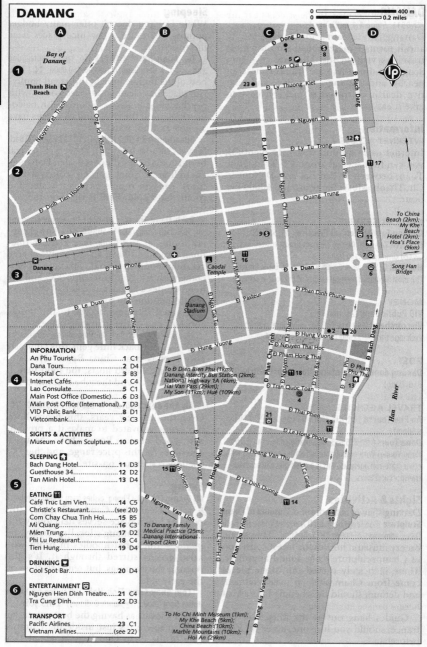

DANANG

0 ——— 400 m
0 ——— 0.2 miles

Bay of Danang

Thanh Binh Beach

Đ Nguyen Tri Thanh

Đ Ong Ich Khiem

Đ Cao Thang

Đ Dinh Tien Hoang

Đ Tran Cao Van

Danang

Đ Hai Phong

Đ Le Duan

Đ Ong Ich Khiem

Đ Dong Da

Đ Tran Qui Cap

Đ Ly Thuong Kiet

Đ Nguyen Du

Đ Ly Tu Trong

Đ Tran Phu

Đ Bach Dang

Đ Quang Trung

Đ Le Loi

Đ Nguyen Chi Thanh

Đ Nguyen Thi Minh Khai

Caodai Temple

Danang Stadium

Đ Ngo Gia Tu

Đ Pasteur

Đ Le Duan

Đ Phan Dinh Phung

Đ Hung Vuong

Đ Hung Vuong

Đ Hung Vuong

Đ Phan Chu Trinh

Đ Nguyen Thai Hoc

Đ Pham Hong Thai

Đ Yen Bai

Đ Tran Phu

Đ Pham Phu Thu

Đ Tran Quoc Toan

Đ Thai Phien

Đ Le Hong Phong

Đ Ong Ich Khiem

Đ Trieu Nu Vuong

Đ Hoang Dieu

Đ Hoang Van Thu

Đ Co Giang

Đ Le Dinh Duong

Đ Nguyen Van Linh

Đ Huynh Thuc Khang

Đ Phan Chu Trinh

Đ Trung Nu Vuong

Han River

Song Han Bridge

To China Beach (2km); My Khe Beach Hotel (2km); Hoa's Place (9km)

To Đ Dien Bien Phu (1km); Danang Intercity Bus Station (2km); National Highway 1A (4km); Hai Van Pass (29km); My Son (31km); Huế (109km)

To Danang Family Medical Practice (25km); Danang International Airport (2km)

To Ho Chi Minh Museum (1km); My Khe Beach (5km); China Beach (10km); Marble Mountains (10km); Hoi An (29km)

VIETNAM

from the city centre. In the streets near the pagoda, there are several other cheap vegetarian shops.

Christie's Restaurant (☎ 824 040; 112 Đ Tran Phu; meals around 50,000d; ☺ lunch & dinner) Christie's dishes up decent burgers, pizzas and pasta, as well as Japanese and Vietnamese food. It's on the 2nd floor of the building that houses the Cool Spot Bar downstairs.

Phi Lu Restaurant (☎ 823 772; 225 Đ Nguyen Chi Thanh; mains 20,000d; ☺ lunch & dinner) You'll find excellent Chinese food here in the busy, banquet-style dining room that's open to the street. The cuisine is tasty and the service efficient.

Café Truc Lam Vien (☎ 582 428; 37 Đ Le Dinh Duong; snacks 15,000d; ☺ lunch & dinner) Old-world Vietnam lies inside the gate – stake out a table under the gorgeously lacquered verandas and sip a fruit shake after drifting through the Museum of Cham Sculpture.

Other spots to try:

Mien Trung (9 Đ Bach Dang) Serving Vietnamese, Chinese and Western dishes, with a good location on the river.

Tien Hung (Đ Tran Phu) A cheap and excellent place to sample dumplinglike *banh cuon* (steamed rice-flour rolls).

Drinking

Cool Spot Bar (☎ 824 040; 112 Đ Tran Phu) A central place to catch a drink, this place has satellite TV and is a hang-out for local expats – but atmospheric it ain't.

Entertainment

Tra Cung Dinh (☎ 35 Đ Tran Phu) Though the coffee and shakes are nonalcoholic in nature, the jazz on tap sets a certain smooth mood.

Nguyen Hien Dinh Theatre (☎ 561 291; 155 Đ Phan Chu Trinh; admission 20,000d; ☺ 7.30–11pm Fri-Sun) Catch traditional Vietnamese music and dance performances here on weekends; you can buy tickets on the day.

Getting There & Away

Danang international airport has flights from Bangkok, Hong Kong and Singapore. **Vietnam Airlines** (☎ 821 130; www.vietnamairlines .com; 35 Đ Tran Phu) has an extensive domestic schedule to/from Danang. **Pacific Airlines** (☎ 886 799; www.pacificairlines.com.vn; 6 Đ Le Loi) also has a booking office in town.

The **Danang intercity bus station** (Ben Xe Khach Da Nang; Đ Dien Bien Phu; ☺ 7-11am & 1-5pm) is 3km from the city centre. Long-distance buses run to Hanoi (87,000d, 16 hours), Hué

(22,000d, three hours), Saigon (104,000d, 24 hours) and nearly anywhere else you might go, including Savannakhet in Laos.

To get to Hoi An, your best bet is to hire a car (around US$10) from a local travel agency, or a friendly neighbourhood *xe om* (around US$6). A stop at the Marble Mountains will cost a bit extra. Travel agencies can also arrange passage on open-tour minibuses (about US$2) running between Hoi An and Danang.

Danang train station (Ga Da Nang) is about 1.5km from the city centre on Đ Hai Phong at Đ Hoang Hoa Tham. Danang is served by all *Reunification Express* trains.

AROUND DANANG

About 10km south of Danang are the immense **Marble Mountains** (admission 10,000d; ☺ 7am-5pm), consisting of five marble outcrops that were once islands. With natural caves sheltering small Hindu and Buddhist sanctuaries, a picturesque pagoda and scenic landings with stunning views of the ocean and surrounding countryside, it's well worth the climb.

China Beach (Bai Non Nuoc), once a rest-and-relaxation post for US soldiers during the American War, is actually a series of beaches stretching 30km north and south of the Marble Mountains. Nearest to central Danang, **My Khe Beach** is well touristed and accordingly has beachside restaurants and roving vendors. Opposite the Marble Mountains is the also-populous **Non Nuoc Beach**, and in between the two are countless spots to explore or spread your beach towel.

For surfers, China Beach's break gets a decent swell from mid-September to December. The best time for swimming is from May to July, when the sea is at its calmest. There's a mean undertow at China Beach, worst in the winter, so take care.

Buses and minibuses running between Danang and Hoi An can drop you off at the entrance to the Marble Mountains and China Beach, and it's easy to find a *xe om* for onward travel. From Danang, it's also possible to reach this area by bicycle.

HOI AN

☎ 0510 / pop 75,800

Like a living museum piece, Hoi An enchants with its beauty and accessible history. Set on the Thu Bon River, Hoi An – or

Faifo, as early Western traders knew it – was an international trading port as far back as the 17th century. Influences from Chinese, Japanese and European culture are well preserved in local architecture and art. Roaming the narrow lanes at night, it's easy to imagine how it might have looked 150 years ago.

Hoi An's charms aren't limited to its exquisite architecture, though; the nearby beach and Cham ruins make excellent expeditions out of town. Returning to Hoi An means that libations and alimentations are never far away.

Information

EMERGENCY

Hoi An Hospital (☎ 861 364; 10 Đ Tran Hung Dao) Serious problems should be taken to Danang.
Hoi An police station (☎ 861 204; 84 Đ Hoang Dieu)

INTERNET ACCESS

Internet cafés are hard to miss in Hoi An. Popular places to check email over a cool drink include the following:
Banana Split Café (☎ 861 136; 53 Đ Hoang Dieu)
Hai's Scout Café (☎ 863 210; 98 Đ Nguyen Thai Hoc)

INTERNET RESOURCES

Hoi An Old Town (www.hoianworldheritage.org) Wondering how to win some hearts in Hoi An? Some etiquette tips.

MONEY

Incombank (9 Đ Le Loi)
Vietincombank (☎ 862 675; 4 Đ Hoang Dieu) Exchanges cash and travellers cheques, gives credit-card cash advances; also has an ATM.

POST

Post office (48 Đ Tran Hung Dao) At the corner of Đ Ngo Gia Tu.

TRAVEL AGENCIES

Small travel agencies are scattered throughout town, and there's a strip of agencies along Đ Tran Hung Dao. Since most offer the same services and tours for similar costs, one cannot be recommended over the other. Competition around here is pretty fierce, so if you want to book something expensive or complicated, check out a few options and then negotiate.

Some of these agencies exchange cash and/or travellers cheques; count your dong carefully before walking out the door.

Dangers & Annoyances

For the most part, Hoi An is very safe at any hour. However, late-night bag-snatchings in the isolated, unlit market are on the rise. Avoid walking around this area alone when the market day is over.

There have also been (extremely rare) reports of women being followed to their hotels and assaulted. Lone women should have a friend walk home with them at night (and don't underestimate the results of yelling your lungs out).

At the My Son ruins, there's a running scam involving motorbike vandalism and extortionist 'repairs' made by the vandals themselves. It's recommended that you hire a driver if you visit independently.

Sights

HOI AN OLD TOWN

Having been named a Unesco World Heritage site, **Hoi An Old Town** (admission 75,000d) now charges an admission fee, which goes towards funding the preservation of the town's historic architecture. Buying the ticket gives you a choice of heritage sites to visit, including an 'intangible culture' option, like a traditional musical concert or stage play. You can also visit these sites, paying as you go, without buying the ticket.

Despite the number of tourists who come to Hoi An, it's still a pretty conservative town – out of courtesy for the residents, visitors should dress modestly (eg sleeved shirts) and carry themselves respectfully when touring the sites, especially in pagodas and temples.

Our list of sites is by no means comprehensive; buying a ticket at the Hoi An Old Town booths will also get you a tourist guide of all the sites.

Quan Cong Temple (24 Đ Tran Phu) is dedicated to Quan Cong and has some wonderful papier-mâché and gilt statues, as well as carp-shaped rain spouts on the roof surrounding the courtyard. Shoes should be removed before mounting the platform in front of Quan Cong.

Tan Ky House (☎ 861 474; 101 Đ Nguyen Thai Hoc; ☾ 8am-noon & 2-4.30pm) is a lovingly preserved house from the 19th century, which once belonged to a Vietnamese merchant. Japanese and Chinese influences are evidenced throughout the architecture. The house is a private home, and the owner – whose family

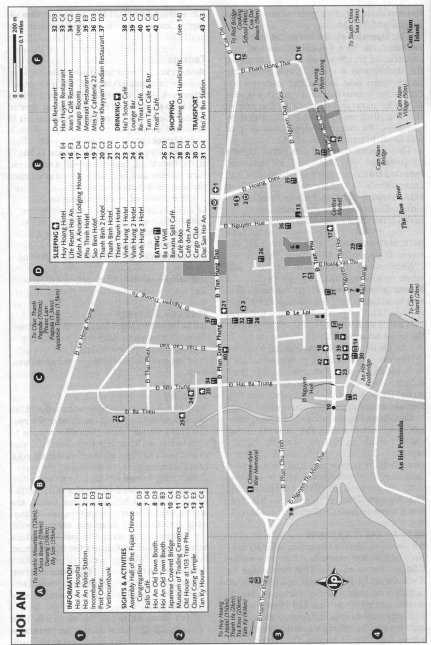

has lived here for seven generations – speaks French and English.

The **Japanese Covered Bridge** (Cau Nhat Ban/Lai Vien Kieu; Đ Tran Phu & Đ Nguyen Thi Minh Khai) was constructed in 1593. The bridge has a roof for shelter and a small temple built into its northern side. According to one story, the bridge's construction began in the year of the monkey and finished in the year of the dog; thus one entrance is guarded by monkeys, the other by dogs (neither pair will confirm or deny this story).

The **Assembly Hall of the Fujian Chinese Congregation** (7.30am–noon & 2-5.30pm) was founded for community meetings; the hall later became a temple to worship Thien Hau, a deity born in Fujian Province in China. Check out the elaborate mural, the unhealthy red or green skin of the statuary, and the replica of a Chinese boat. Remove your shoes at the platform just past the naves. It's opposite 35 Đ Tran Phu.

Showcasing a collection of blue and white ceramics of the Dai Viet period, the **Museum of Trading Ceramics** (80 Đ Tran Phu; 8am–noon & 2-4.30pm) is in a simply restored house; it's delightful. In particular, notice the great ceramic mosaic that's set above the pond in the inner courtyard.

The **Old House at 103 Tran Phu** (103 Đ Tran Phu; 8am–noon & 2-4.30pm) is picturesque with its wooden front and shutters; inside is an eclectic shop where women make silk lanterns. There are ornamental aquarium fish for sale, *and* you can buy shampoo.

Chuc Thanh Pagoda (Khu Vuc 7, Tan An; 8am–6pm) was founded in 1454, making it the oldest pagoda in Hoi An. Among the antique ritual objects still in use are a stone gong, which is two centuries old, and a carp-shaped wooden gong, said to be even older. To get here, go all the way to the end of Đ Nguyen Truong To and turn left. Follow the sandy path for 500m.

ARTS & CRAFTS VILLAGES

All those neat fake antiques sold in Hoi An's shops are manufactured in nearby villages. Cross the An Hoi footbridge to reach the **An Hoi Peninsula**, noted for its boat factory and mat-weaving factories. South of the peninsula is **Cam Kim Island**, where you see many people engaged in the wood-carving and boatbuilding industries (take a boat from the Đ Hoang Van Thu dock).

Cross the Cam Nam bridge to **Cam Nam village**, a lovely spot also noted for arts and crafts.

Courses

Restaurants all over town advertise cooking courses (around US$6 to US$7), in which attendees learn how to make several dishes and then sit down to enjoy the meal they've made. Most courses require a minimum of around four people.

Red Bridge (933 222; www.visithoian.com) offers a reasonably priced half-day course (US$12) that covers it all, beginning with a trip to the local market and including a boat trip down the river to the cooking class.

Other cafés offering cooking courses:

Cargo Club (910 489; www.hoianhospitality.com; 107-109 Đ Nguyen Thai Hoc) The US$20 course, with Ms Trinh Diem Vy, includes a trip to the market. See opposite.

Faifo Café (80 Đ Bach Dang)

Hai's Scout Café (863 210; 98 Đ Nguyen Thai Hoc) See p876.

Mermaid Restaurant (861 527; 2 Đ Tran Phu) See p876.

Festivals & Events

Hoi An Legendary Night Takes place on the 14th day (full moon) of every lunar month from 5.30pm to 10pm. These festive evenings feature traditional food, song and dance, and games along the lantern-lit streets in the town centre.

Sleeping

Tiny Hoi An is awash with accommodation options after a building boom over the past few years. During peak periods – August to October and December to February – you might want to book ahead if you have your heart set on a particular hotel.

Vinh Hung 1 Hotel (861 621; vinhhung.ha@dng .vnn.vn; 143 Đ Tran Phu; d incl breakfast US$15-45;) Set in a classic Chinese trading house, the atmospheric deluxe rooms are decorated with antiques and beautiful canopy beds. All rooms come with the usual modern amenities. Michael Caine used two of these rooms while filming scenes in *The Quiet American*. If this one's full, there are two newer branches with swimming pools. Definitely book in advance if you want to stay at the original.

Thien Thanh Hotel (916 545; 34 Đ Ba Trieu; r US$10-25;) Most of the accommodations here have breezy balconies at the back with views over a rice field. This place is laid-back and friendly, and a short stroll to the town centre.

Phu Thinh Hotel (☎ 861 297; minhthaoha@dng .vnn.vn; 144 Đ Tran Phu; r US$8-15; ✕) Set back from a quiet but central block of Đ Tran Phu, this Chinese-style place has clean and comfortable rooms. Windowless rooms, some with private bathrooms, are on the small side. Aim for pricier rooms above the inviting courtyard. There's a newer branch, with fancier rooms and a pool, on the beach road.

Minh A Ancient Lodging House (☎ 861 368; 2 Đ Nguyen Thai Hoc; r US$7-12; ✕) There should be more places like this in Hoi An, because its three rooms fill up fast. It's a family-owned historic house that feels like a B&B, without the B (breakfast is not included).

Huy Hoang Hotel (☎ 861 453; kshuyhoang1@dng .vnn.vn; 73 Đ Phan Boi Chau; r incl breakfast US$7-25; ✕ ▣) In a choice location right on the riverfront, the Huy Hoang has comfortable rooms and lots of them. The back terrace – framed by hanging plants – is a chilled spot to enjoy a meal on the river.

Thanh Binh Hotel (☎ 861 740; vothihong@dng.vnn .vn; 1 Đ Le Loi; r US$10-25; ✕) This family-run hotel is close to the town centre and has spacious rooms. Try to snag a room overlooking the small park beside the hotel.

Thanh Binh 2 Hotel (☎ 863 715; vothihong@dng .vnn.vn; 1 Đ Nhi Trung; r US$7-20; ✕ ▣ ✈) The newer branch of this hotel has a swimming pool and elegant rooms.

Huy Hoang 2 Hotel (☎ 916 234; kshuyhoang2@dng .vnn.vn; 87 Đ Huynh Thuc Khang; r US$6-15; ✕ ▣)

SPLURGE!

Life Resort Hoi An (☎ 914 555; www.life -resorts.com; 1 Đ Pham Hong Thai; r US$109-276; ✕ ▣ ✈) Elegant but not showy, luxurious without feeling overindulgent, Life Resort provides a mellow riverside haven in the east end of town. Rooms are split-level and have small private terraces overlooking river or garden. Facilities around the colonial-style resort include several restaurants and a pool. Inquire in advance about current promotions, but if rates are too steep, just stop by for a Dutch beer or an exquisite house-made pastry. Or book a spot on its sunset river cruise (US$7), which includes complimentary snacks and a drink.

About a 15-minute walk from the centre, this place is good value with big clean rooms and satellite TV. There's also a garden restaurant.

Sao Bien Hotel (Sea Star Hotel; ☎ 861 589; 15 Đ Cua Dai; r US$8-15; ✕) On the beach road, these rooms have seen better days, but they're clean and perfectly fine. The budget rooms at the top have great views over Hoi An's red-brick roofs.

Eating

Hoi An's restaurants burst with gastronomic delights, three of which are town specialities. Be sure to try *cao lau*, doughy flat noodles mixed with croutons, bean sprouts and greens, topped with pork slices and served in a savoury broth. The real thing can only be had in Hoi An, as the water for *cao lau* noodles must come from Ba Le well. The other two culinary specialities are fried wonton, and 'white rose', a petite steamed dumpling stuffed with shrimp.

Café des Amis (☎ 861 616; 50 Đ Bach Dang; ✆ dinner) Come hungry or risk the disapproval of chef Mr Kim. Every night, he dreams up two set-menu dinners; vegetarian (50,000d) and seafood (60,000d). Five or six courses of consistently delicious dishes will parade across your table, and the chef himself may survey yours to see how you're liking it.

Miss Ly Cafeteria 22 (☎ 861 603; 22 Đ Nguyen Hue; mains 18,000d; ✆ breakfast, lunch & dinner) This true Hoi An institution has some of the best white roses and wonton in town. It closes when empty (that's usually late) and is nearly always crowded.

Cargo Club (☎ 910 489; www.hoianhospitality .com; 107-109 Đ Nguyen Thai Hoc; mains around 40,000d; ✆ breakfast, lunch & dinner) A chilled place, popular for its Vietnamese and international menu, as well as its sunny front terrace, shady upstairs balcony and expansive wood-floored interior. Great for breakfast, but the tempting pastry counter is crowded at all hours.

Mango Rooms (☎ 910 839; mangocafé@yahoo.com; 111 Đ Nguyen Thai Hoc; mains around 30,000d; ✆ lunch & dinner) With a lounge feel and a fusion twist on Vietnamese cuisine, this is a cool spot to take in river breezes and sample something nontraditional. There's another entrance along Đ Bach Dang.

Dac San Hoi An (☎ 861 533; 89 Đ Tran Phu; mains 20,000d; ✆ lunch & dinner) Excellent Hoi An seafood, wonton and *cao lau* are served here with a friendly smile, in an old-school Hoi An structure. Ask for a table upstairs on the balcony.

Mermaid Restaurant (☎ 861 527; 2 Đ Tran Phu; mains 18,000d; ☽ breakfast, lunch & dinner) With a prime people-watching location – screened by hanging foliage – the Mermaid serves fabulous food and has a nice vibe.

Ba Le Well (☎ 864 443; 45/51 Đ Tran Hung Dao; mains 12,000d; ☽ lunch & dinner) Near the famous well is this modest family restaurant of the same name. The house specialities include *thit nuong* (spiced, grilled rolls of pork) and *banh xeo* (stuffed rice crêpe that you wrap in lettuce and herbs and dip in fish sauce).

Omar Khayyam's Indian Restaurant (☎ 910 245; 14 Đ Phan Dinh Phung; ☽ lunch & dinner) Satisfying vegetarian and nonveggie Indian food is served here at reasonable prices.

Han Huyen Restaurant (Floating Restaurant; ☎ 861 462; ☽ lunch & dinner) Moored on the riverside, the setting is soothing and sort of romantic, and the food is good. It's down the road from the Japanese Covered Bridge.

Find a string of good seafood restaurants along riverfront Đ Bach Dang. Some backpacker favourites serving inexpensive Vietnamese and Western food include the following:

Banana Split Café (☎ 861 136; 53 Đ Hoang Dieu; ☽ breakfast, lunch & dinner) Banana split and Internet: order a snack or drink (the fruit shakes are good) and get 10 minutes' Internet access free.

Café Bobo (☎ 861 939; 18 Đ Le Loi; ☽ breakfast, lunch & dinner)

Dudi Restaurant (☎ 861 923; 12 Đ Le Loi; ☽ breakfast, lunch & dinner)

Jean's Café Restaurant (48 Đ Phan Dinh Phung; ☽ breakfast, lunch & dinner)

Drinking

Tam Tam Cafe & Bar (☎ 862 212; tamtam.ha@dng.vnn .vn; 110 Đ Nguyen Thai Hoc) The mainstay of nightlife in Hoi An is this thoughtfully restored tea warehouse. Hoi An's best margaritas are made here, which you can enjoy over a game of pool or an intimate chat on the balcony. There's also a good bar menu, and a small book collection if you're feeling antisocial.

Hai's Scout Café (☎ 863 210; 98 Đ Nguyen Thai Hoc; cocktail specials 35,000d) Lovely tables on the front patio, huge terrace in the back, open early and late, Internet access at the usual rates, cooking classes, cocktail specials, excellent food and real espresso drinks – all in a casual atmosphere.

Treat's Café (☎ 861 125; 158 Đ Tran Phu) A dimly lit bar upstairs and down, with cool CDs in rotation, pool tables and a generous happy hour (4pm to 9pm): what more do you need to get a nice buzz?

Lounge Bar (☎ 910 480; 102 Đ Nguyen Thai Hoc) Stylish silk-cushioned seating and a cool upstairs terrace accent this converted ancient house.

Re-Treat Café (31 Đ Phan Dinh Phung) 'Same same not different', or 'same same but better'? This retreat has good patio seating.

Shopping

Before you even get your bearings in Hoi An, you may find yourself strong-armed with sweetness by a young girl taking you to her 'auntie's' tailor shop, despite an official ban on touts. Tailor-made clothing is one of Hoi An's best trades, and there are more than 200 tailor shops in town that can whip up a custom-tailored *ao dai* (traditional Vietnamese tunic and trousers). Other hot items include handmade shoes and silk lanterns.

Hoi An also boasts a growing array of interesting art galleries, especially on the west side of the Japanese Covered Bridge.

Reaching Out Handicrafts (Hoa Nhap Handicrafts; ☎ 910 168; hoanhap@yahoo.com; 103 Đ Nguyen Thai Hoc; ☽ 7.30am-7.30pm) This notable fair-trade gift shop is worth browsing. It sells handicrafts made by disabled craftspeople from all over Vietnam. The shop employs several local disabled craftspeople, and its profits support community programmes for disabled people locally and throughout Vietnam.

Getting There & Away

All hotels in Hoi An book minibuses to Nha Trang (US$8), Danang (US$2) and Hué (US$4). Buses to Danang via the Marble Mountains depart from the **Hoi An bus station** (Ben Quoc Doanh Xe Khach; 74 Đ Huynh Thuc Khang), 1km west of the town centre.

Getting Around

Motorbike drivers wait to solicit business outside all the tourist hotels. Many hotels also offer bicycles for hire for around US$1 per day.

VIETNAM

AROUND HOI AN

My Son

The Cham ruins at **My Son** (admission 50,000d; ⊙ 6.30am-4.30pm), dating back to the 7th century, are a scenic 35km trip southwest of Hoi An. The ruins are nestled in a lush valley surrounded by hills and the massive Hon Quap (Cat's Tooth Mountain). My Son became a religious centre under King Bhadravarman in the late 4th century and was occupied until the 13th century – the longest period of development of any monument in Southeast Asia. My Son is one of the most stunning sights in the area, and another Unesco World Heritage site.

Day tours to My Son can be arranged in Hoi An for about US$3, not including admission, and there are also trips back to Hoi An by boat. If you want to visit on your own, hire a *xe om* to drive you there early (as in predawn, baby), to beat the tour groups, or in the afternoon. Round-trips should cost about US$6.

Cua Dai Beach

You can sometimes find this white-sand beach deserted on weekdays, though weekends tend to be a little crowded. Palm-thatch huts give shelter and roaming vendors sell drinks and fresh seafood. Swimming is best between April and October.

To get there, take Đ Cua Dai east out of Hoi An about 5km. As is the national standard, motorbike parking should cost 2000d.

SOUTH-CENTRAL COAST

NHA TRANG

☎ 058 / pop 315,200

Seaside Nha Trang's multifaceted personality sparkles with subtlety. You can have your 24-hour debauched party if you want, but you can temper it with snorkelling at reefs rife with sea life, checking out Cham ruins and Buddhist pagodas with fabulous views, or soaking in mineral mud. On the beach, roving vendors offer massages, manicures and lunch. Boat trips come highly recommended, whether you choose the booze cruise or something more sedate.

Nha Trang has a booming fishing industry and is also known for salt production. The weather is usually best between late January and late October.

Information

BOOKSHOPS

Mr Lang's Book Exchange (Đ Tran Phu) Near the War Memorial, stocks a decent collection of used books in several languages.

Shorty's Bar (☎ 810 985; 45 Đ Biet Thu) Books in English, with a pool table if you don't find a good read.

INTERNET ACCESS

Heaps of hotels, travellers cafés and Internet cafés offer web access all over town.

La Fregate Internet (☎ 829 011; fregate@dng.vnn.vn; 4 Đ Pasteur; per minute 100d; ⊙ 8am-noon & 2pm-midnight) Plenty of fast ADSL access.

Thanh's Family Booking Office (2 Đ Hung Vuong) Closer to the town centre.

MEDICAL SERVICES

Hon Chong Hospital (☎ 831 103; Đ Hon Chong) Has a few English-speaking doctors.

Khanh Hoa Provincial Hospital (☎ 822 168; 19 Đ Yersin)

MONEY

Vietcombank Đ Quang Trung (☎ 822 720; 17 Đ Quang Trung; ⊙ Mon-Fri); Đ Hung Vuong (☎ 524 500; 5 Đ Hung Vuong; ⊙ Mon-Fri) Both branches exchange travellers cheques and have ATMs. The Đ Quang Trung branch processes cash advances; and the Đ Hung Vuong branch exchanges cash.

POST

Central post office (☎ 821 271; 4 Đ Le Loi)
Post office (☎ 823 866; 50 Đ Le Thanh Ton)

TRAVEL AGENCIES

Café des Amis (☎ 813 009; 13 Đ Biet Thu) A good place to inquire about 4WD or motorbike tours into the Central Highlands.

Con Se Tre (☎ 811 163; 1006 Đ Tran Phu) Interesting boat tours to Hon Tre (p879); ask about camping on the island. The office is about 1km south of town.

Hanh Cafe (☎ 814 227; hanhcafe@dng.vnn.vn; 26 Đ Tran Hung Dao)

Sinh Cafe (☎ 811 981; sinhcafent@dng.vnn.vn; 10 Đ Biet Thu)

TM Brothers Cafe (☎ 814 556; hoanhaont@dng.vnn .vn; 22 Đ Tran Hung Dao)

Dangers & Annoyances

Though Nha Trang is generally a safe place, be very careful on the beach at night. The best advice is to stay off the beach after dark. We've heard countless reports of rip-offs, mostly instigated by quick-witted working girls who canvass the seaside.

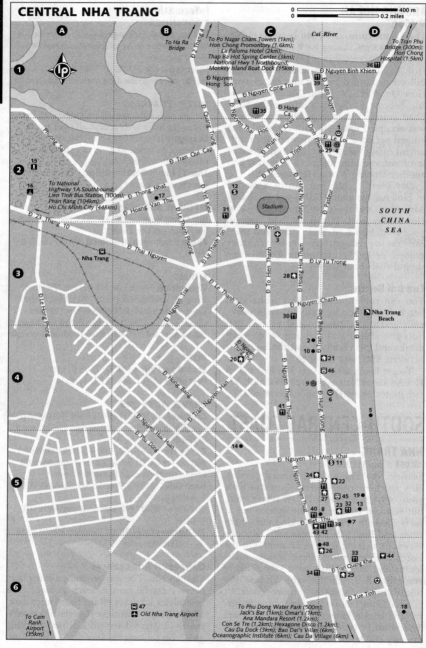

CENTRAL NHA TRANG

0 — 400 m
0 — 0.2 miles

To Ha Ra Bridge

Đ 2 Thang 4

Cai River

To Po Nagar Cham Towers (1km);
Hon Chong Promontory (1.6km);
La Paloma Hotel (2km);
Thap Ba Hot Spring Center (3km);
National Hwy 1 Northbound;
Monkey Island Boat Dock (15km)

To Tran Phu Bridge (300m);
Hon Chong Hospital (1.5km)

Đ Nguyen Binh Khiem

36

39

Đ Nguyen Hong Son

Đ Nguyen Cong Tru

Đ Nga Quyen

35

Đ Hang Ca

Đ Nguyen Thai Hoc

Đ Phan Boi Chau

Đ Dinh Phung

1
Đ Le Loi
29 4

Đ Quang Trung

Đ Tran Qui Cap

Đ Phan Chu Trinh

Đ Truong Nu Vuong

Đ Phuong Sai

15

16

To National
Highway 1A Southbound;
Lien Tinh Bus Station (100m);
Phan Rang (104km);
Ho Chi Minh City (448km)

Đ 23 Thang 10

12
$

Đ Thong Nhat

17

Đ Hoang Van Thu

Đ Yet Kieu

31

Stadium

Đ Pasteur

SOUTH
CHINA
SEA

Đ Le Thanh Phuong

Đ Ly Thanh Ton

Đ Yersin

3

Đ Thai Nguyen

Nha Trang

Đ Le Hong Phong

Đ To Hien Thanh

Đ Hoang Hoa Tham

Đ Ly Tu Trong

Đ Le Thanh Ton

28

Đ Nguyen Chanh

30

Nha Trang Beach

Đ Nguyen Trai

Đ Tran Phu

Đ Hong Bang

Đ Nguyen Thi Thuat

20

2
10
21
46
9
6

5

Đ Tran Nguyen Han

Đ Nguyen Thien Thuat

Đ Hung Vuong

Đ Nguyen Huu Huan

41

Đ Phu Dong

14

Đ Nguyen Thi Minh Khai

11

24
37
22

27

45 19
23 32 13
40 8
Đ Biet Thu
38 7
43 42
48
26

33 44
34 25
Đ Tran Quang Khai

Đ Tue Tinh

18

47
Old Nha Trang Airport

To Cam Ranh Airport (35km)

To Phu Dong Water Park (500m);
Jack's Bar (1km); Omar's (1km);
Ana Mandara Resort (1.2km);
Con Se Tre (1.2km); Hexagone Disco (1.2km);
Cau Da Dock (3km); Bao Dai's Villas (6km);
Oceanographic Institute (6km); Cau Da Village (6km)

Sights

Built between the 7th and 12th centuries on a site used by Hindus for worship, the **Po Nagar Cham Towers** (Đ 2 Thang 4; admission 4500d; 🕙6am-6pm) are 2km north of central Nha Trang on the left bank of the Cai River. From the hill are blue views of the harbour below.

The impressively adorned **Long Son Pagoda** (Chua Tinh Hoi Khanh Hoa; Đ 23 Thang 10; admission free; 🕙sunrise-sunset) is decorated with mosaic dragons covered with glass and ceramic tile. Founded in the late 19th century, the pagoda still has resident monks. At the top of the hill, behind the pagoda, is the **Giant Seated Buddha** visible from town. From where the Buddha sits, you too can contemplate the view of Nha Trang. The pagoda is about 500m west of the train station.

Swimming around in the **Oceanographic Institute** (Vien Nghiem Cuu Bien; ☎ 590 036; adult/child 10,000/5000d, English-speaking guide 30,000d; 🕙7.30am-noon & 1-4.30pm), a French colonial building, are colourful representatives of squirming sea life. Occupying the hall at the back are specimens of less-lively – pickled, actually – marine fish and fowl.

Bao Dai's Villas (Biet Thu Cau Da; ☎ 590 148; baodai@dng.vnn.vn; admission 2000d, restaurant patrons usually free; 🕙8am-10pm) are worth roaming on a slow afternoon, with a scenic lunch spot overlooking the South China Sea. From Nha Trang, take Đ Tran Phu south and turn left, uphill past the cement oil-storage tanks before Cau Da village. The

villas are several hundred metres north of the Oceanographic Institute.

The work of Nha Trang's most acclaimed photographer, Long Thanh, is shown at **Long Thanh Gallery** (☎ 824 875; lvntrang50@hotmail .com; 126 Đ Hoang Van Thu). His striking, luminous black-and-white images capture the essence of Vietnam. **Do Dien Khanh** (☎ 512 202; www.ddk -gallery.com; 126B Đ Hong Bang) is another local shutterbug whose black-and-white portraiture is also worth a look.

BEACHES

Coconut palms provide shelter for sunbathers and strollers along most of Nha Trang's 6km beachfront; beach chairs are available for hire.

Stylish **La Louisiane Café** (☎ 812 948; lalouisiane@dng.vnn.vn; 29 Đ Tran Phu; 🕙7am-midnight) resembles a Western-style beach club. Guests can use the swimming pool and beach chairs here in exchange for patronising the restaurant, bakery or bar.

Hon Chong Promontory, 1.8km north of central Nha Trang, is a scenic collection of granite rocks jutting into the South China Sea. The promontory borders a rustic beach cove lacking the pedicures and massages, but compensating with island views and local colour.

ISLANDS

The nine outlying islands of Nha Trang beckon offshore; hop on one of the boat tours sold all over town. For as little as

US$6, you can join a day tour visiting four islands. Or, cobble together your own trips to various islands.

There's a working fish farm on **Hon Mieu** (Mieu Island) that's also a beautiful outdoor **aquarium** (Ho Ca Tri Nguyen). From there, you can rent canoes, or hire someone to paddle you out to the nearby islands of **Hon Mun** (Ebony Island) or **Hon Yen** (Swallow Island). Rustic bungalows on the island rent for about 90,000d. Ferries to Hon Mieu (5000d) leave regularly throughout the day from Cau Da dock at the southern end of Nha Trang. Catch ferries back to Nha Trang at Tri Nguyen village on Hon Mieu.

Idyllic **Hon Tre** (Bamboo Island) is the largest island in the area. You can get boats to **Bai Tru** (Tru Beach) at the northern end of the island, but it's also recommended to take the day or overnight trips here offered by **Con Se Tre** (☎ 811 163; 1006 Đ Tran Phu). There's great snorkelling and diving off **Hon Mun**, **Hon Tam** and **Hon Mot**.

Activities

DIVING

Nha Trang is Vietnam's premier diving locale, with around 25 dive sites in the area. Visibility averages 15m, but can be as much as 30m, depending on the season (late October to early January is the worst time of year). There are some good drop-offs and small underwater caves to explore, and an amazing variety of corals. Among the colourful reef fish, stingrays are occasionally spotted.

A full-day outing, including two dives and lunch, costs between US$40 and US$60. Dive operators also offer a range of courses, including a 'Discover Diving' programme for uncertified, first-time divers. Consider the following outfits, but shop around:

Blue Diving Club (☎ 825 390; www.vietnamdivers .com; 12B Đ Biet Thu) Owned and operated by French and British divers.

Coco Dive Center (☎ 812 900; www.cocodivecenter .com; 2E Đ Biet Thu) Opened by the talented Ms Minh Xuan, a local swim and karate champion.

Jeremy Stein's Rainbow Divers (☎ 829 946; www .divevietnam.com; 72-74 Đ Tran Phu) At Nha Trang Sailing Club; owner Jeremy Stein is a dead ringer for Chuck Norris.

Octopus Diving Club (☎ 810 629; haison.aaa@dng .vnn.vn; 62 Đ Tran Phu) Brit- and Japanese-run; guides here speak 11 languages between them.

SWIMMING & WATER SPORTS

Mana Mana Beach Club (☎ 512308; manamanavn@vnn .vn; La Louisiane Café, Tran Phu Beach) rents windsurfing, wakeboarding, sea-kayaking catamarans and gives lessons on how to use them. Equipment is state-of-the-art and safety is a priority.

If salt water's not your thing, **Phu Dong Water Park** (admission 20,000d; ☒ 9am-5pm) has water slides, shallow pools and fountains right on the beachfront.

THAP BA HOT SPRING CENTER

Soothing pools of hot mineral-rich mud, hot-spring baths and a massage centre await at **Thap Ba Hot Spring Center** (Suoi Nuoc Nong Thap Ba; ☎ 835 335; www.thapbahotspring.com.vn; tickets 15,000-50,000d; ☒ 8am-8pm Mon-Fri, 7am-9pm Sat & Sun), 2.5km along Đ Son Thuy. There's also a regular swimming pool, a restaurant and simple neat bungalows.

Tours

Mama Linh (☎ 826 693; 2A Đ Hung Vuong) runs island-hopping party boats that run daily, stopping at Hon Mun, Hon Mot, Hon Tam and Hon Mieu (see p879). Tickets are sold from the home office, but you can book almost anywhere around town for an additional commission.

Sleeping

Ha Huong Hotel (☎ 512 069; hahuongnt@dng.vnn.vn; 26 Đ Nguyen Trung Truc; dm US$2, r US$6-15; ☒) With a tiny koi pond and orchids hanging in the courtyard, this friendly hotel is on a quiet street about five minutes' walk from the beach. Rooms are clean, and the air-con ones have satellite TV and balconies.

Sao Mai Hotel (☎ 827 412; saomaiht@dng.vnn.vn; 99 Đ Nguyen Thien Thuat; dm US$2-3, r US$5-10; ☒) The Sao Mai is a good clean budget place with dorm accommodation, one of the few in Nha Trang. It also has a pretty rooftop terrace adorned with potted plants.

Phong Lan Hotel (Orchid Hotel; ☎ 811 647; orchidhotel2000@yahoo.com; 24/44 Đ Hung Vuong; r US$5-10; ☒) This lovely family-run place is in a quiet alley off Hung Vuong, with small clean rooms with TV and fridge. The owners speak French and English.

O-Sin Hotel (☎ 822 902; osinhotel@hotmail.com; 15 Đ Hung Vuong; dm US$2, r US$4-10; ☒) Opt for this branch rather than the older one. The best rooms are upstairs, with air-con and better

---

SPLURGE!

Ana Mandara Resort (☎ 829 829; resvana@
dng.vnn.vn; Đ Tran Phu; bungalows US$236-468;
❄ 🖳 ⚤) The only beachfront digs in the
town, Ana Mandara takes full aesthetic advantage of its location. Flagstone paths wind
around free-standing, wood-raftered bungalows, each of which is outfitted with all
modern comforts and tucked into the tropical landscaping. Two swimming pools and
two restaurants anchor each end of the low-
lying resort, and its Six Senses spa is a hidden haven for massage and other corporeal
pampering. Email ahead to ask about current
promotions; discounts are often available
when the resort is not fully booked.

---

amenities. Staff here are friendly and the
place is just 30m from the beach.

Perfume Grass Inn (☎ 822 433; www.perfume
-grass.com; 4A Đ Biet Thu; r US$10-20; ❄ 🖳) Some
rooms here have ocean views, and the priciest have beautiful wood interiors with bathrooms. Downstairs there's a cosy bar and a
garden restaurant.

Sakura Hotel (☎ 524 669; 1/32 Đ Tran Quang Khai;
r US$8-12; ❄ 🖳) A comfy minihotel on one
of the central but quieter sections of Nha
Trang, the Sakura has rooms equipped with
satellite TV, IDD phone and fridge.

La Paloma Hotel (☎ 831 216; datle@dng.vnn.vn;
1 Đ Hon Chong; r incl breakfast & dinner US$12-20; ❄)
Up the road from laid-back Hon Chong
beach (2km north of town); the staff here
make you feel right at home. Jeep rides to
and from town, the train station and the old
airport are provided for free.

Also recommended:

Huu Nghi Hotel (☎ 826 703; huunghihotel@dng.vnn
.vn; 3 Đ Tran Hung Dao; s/d/tr 75,000/150,000/285,000d)
A time-honoured backpackers haunt; the older rooms are
cheery but the bathrooms could be cleaner.

Thien Tan Hotel (New Sky Hotel; ☎ 816 455;
newskyhotel@dng.vnn.vn; 78 Đ Hung Vuong; r US$7-18;
❄) This sparkly clean minihotel has comfortable, bright
rooms with satellite TV and phone.

Yen My Hotel (☎ 829 064; yenmyhotel@hotmail.com;
22 Đ Hoang Hoa Tham; r US$5-10; ❄) A good budget
place run by the very friendly Mr Duan.

Eating

Central Nha Trang teems with dining
choices too numerous to list here. As always,

taking a meal in the market is a cheap adventure, and **Dam market** (Đ Nguyen Hong Son)
in the north end of town has lots of local
food stalls, including *com chay* (vegetarian food).

Ice-cream fiends will want to make for
Nha Trang's own original-versus-copycat
rivals, the **Banana Split Cafés** (banana split 10,000d)
along the roundabout where Đ Quang
Trung meets Đ Ly Thanh Ton.

VIETNAMESE

Dua Xanh Restaurant (Green Coconut; ☎ 823 687; 189
Đ Nguyen Binh Khiem; mains 35,000d; ☯ lunch & dinner)
This is a pleasant little spot specialising in
great seafood dishes. It has outdoor garden tables in addition to its indoor dining
room, and the owner speaks English and
French. Save room for dessert.

Truc Linh (☎ 820 089; 21 Đ Biet Thu; mains 20,000-
100,000d; ☯ lunch & dinner) Popular and festive,
Truc Linh has a garden setting and indoor-
outdoor seating. You can choose fresh seafood from a table in front of the restaurant
and enjoy a beer while you wait for it to be
prepared to order.

Lac Canh Restaurant (☎ 821 391; 44 Đ Nguyen
Binh Khiem; mains 35,000d; ☯ lunch & dinner) Beef,
squid, giant shrimps and lobsters are
grilled right at your table. This busy eatery
is a long-running favourite in Nha Trang.

Red Star (☎ 812 790; 14 Đ Biet Thu; mains 25,000d;
☯ lunch & dinner) This no-frills place dishes up
excellent seafood; try the crab or clams with
ginger, lemon grass and chilli.

Au Lac Vegetarian Restaurant (28C Đ Hoang Hoa
Tham; mains 12,000d; ☯ lunch & dinner) Near the
corner of Đ Nguyen Chanh, this hole-in-
the-wall looks dumpy but creates excellent
cheap vegetarian soups, rice plates and
special-occasion treats.

Café des Amis (☎ 813 009; 13 Đ Biet Thu; set dinner
50,000d; ☯ breakfast, lunch & dinner) Good vegetarian fare to fill your stomach; interesting art
to feed your eyes.

INTERNATIONAL

Cyclo Café (☎ 524 208; khuongthuy@hotmail.com; 5A
Đ Tran Quang Khai; mains around 30,000d; ☯ breakfast,
lunch & dinner) Run by a local couple with many
years of experience in Nha Trang's restaurant business; this expertise clearly comes
through in the attentive service, excellent
Vietnamese and Italian dishes and pleasing
ambience.

Good Morning Vietnam (☎ 815 071; 19B Đ Biet Thu; mains 20,000-50,000d; 🕙 lunch & dinner) One more link in the Italian-run chain, this establishment does down-home, reasonably priced pizza, pasta and salads, plus some Vietnamese and Thai dishes to spice things up. Upstairs, kick back on cosy Thai cushions to eat or watch movies in the evenings.

El Coyote (☎ 820 202; coyote-nt@caramail.com; 76 Đ Hung Vuong; mains 50,000d; 🕙 lunch & dinner) The only place in Nha Trang for decent Mexican food.

Omar's (☎ 814 489; omarnewdelhi@yahoo.com; 96A/8 Đ Tran Phu; meals around 60,000d; 🕙 lunch & dinner) At the south end of Tran Phu near Jack's Bar, Omar's serves Nha Trang's best Indian food, with lots of vegetarian options.

7C Biergarten (☎ 828 243; 7C Đ Le Loi; mains 23,000d; 🕙 lunch & dinner) Serving Nha Trang's appetite for authentic bratwurst and schnitzel, plus home-baked brown bread and Viet Duc beer on tap (12,000d).

And backpacker favourites:

Candle Light Cafe (☎ 813 133; candlelightcafé2001@ yahoo.com; 6 Đ Tran Quang Khai; mains 25,000d; 🕙 7am-11pm) A warm, bamboo interior and good Vietnamese and Western food.

Thanh Thanh Cafe (☎ 824 413; 10 Đ Nguyen Thien Thuat; dishes 30,000d; 🕙 breakfast, lunch & dinner) There's a nice terracotta patio here, but if you feel like ordering in Thanh Thanh also delivers.

Drinking

Guava (☎ 524 140; www.clubnhatrang.com; 17 Đ Biet Thu; cocktail specials 15,000-25,000d) A little lounge, a little sports bar, a lot of fun. Outside is a tree-shaded patio; inside are cushion-laden sofas as well as a pool table and TVs. Substantial hangover breakfasts are served all day, the happy-hour specials are generous and the crowd is a hip mix of locals and tourists.

Nha Trang Sailing Club (☎ 826 528; www.sailingclubvietnam.com; 72-74 Đ Tran Phu; 🕙 until 4am) Dance the night away, after having a bite to eat – Vietnamese, Japanese or Italian – and partaking in happy hour (usually 8.30pm to 10.30pm) with a game of pool. Always a good time at this venerable beachside late-night hang-out.

Crazy Kim Bar (Kim Dien Bar; ☎ 816 072; 19 Đ Biet Thu) A fun place for a drink, and a great place to volunteer in Nha Trang. Stop by the bar and sign up to give English lessons to disadvantaged local kids during the day.

Jack's Bar (☎ 813 862; jacks_bar_vn@yahoo.com; 96A Đ Tran Phu; 🕙 8am-late) A generous happy hour (6pm to 10pm) gives you plenty of time for some pool, good music and cold beer on the roof terrace overlooking Nha Trang Bay. A full menu is offered from 8am to 10pm.

Entertainment

Vien Dong Hotel (☎ 821 606; 1 Đ Tran Hung Dao; admission free; 🕙 performances 7.30pm) Nightly ethnic-minority song and dance performances.

Hexagone Disco (☎ 826 762; Huong Duong Centre, Đ Tran Phu; 🕙 8pm-midnight) Not exactly a disco inferno, but if you feel like dancing it's down near the Ana Mandara Resort.

Cool Kangaroo (☎ 826 520; 17C Đ Hung Vuong) Free movies in the evening, friendly folks.

Shopping

Many restaurants and bars around town display the works of local photographers and artists, which are usually for sale if something catches your eye.

You'll find a lot of seashells and coral for sale, but their harvestation destroys the beauty and ecology of Nha Trang's reefs. You can discourage this detrimental practice by not buying the dead critters.

Kim Quang (☎ 0913-416 513) Kim Quang's hand-painted T-shirts make great souvenirs; find him working on his creations at Nha Trang Sailing Club every night.

Getting There & Away
AIR

Vietnam Airlines (☎ 826 768; www.vietnamairlines .com; 91 Đ Nguyen Thien Thuat) has flights connecting Cam Ranh airport (35km south of Nha Trang) with HCMC, Hanoi and Danang. To get to the airport, catch a shuttle bus (30,000d) from the old Nha Trang airport terminal, two hours before your flight.

BUS

Minibuses from HCMC to Nha Trang (11 to 12 hours) depart from Mien Dong bus station in HCMC. **Lien Tinh bus station** (Ben Xe Lien Tinh; ☎ 822 192; Đ 23 Thang 10), Nha Trang's main intercity bus terminal, is 500m west of the train station.

Open-tour buses to and from HCMC, Dalat and Hoi An are easy to book at travellers cafés and hotels.

CAR & MOTORCYCLE

A series of roughly parallel roads head inland from near Nha Trang, linking Vietnam's deltas and coastal regions with the Central Highlands.

TRAIN

The **Nha Trang train station** (Ga Nha Trang; ☎ 822 113; ticket office ⏰ 7am-2pm) is conveniently located in the middle of town, opposite 26 Đ Thai Nguyen, but it's usually worth the small commission for the convenience of booking your ticket at a hotel or a travellers café.

Getting Around

The erstwhile Nha Trang airport, from which buses shuttle passengers to Cam Ranh airport, is on the southern side of town. Cyclos go to both the old airport and the train station for about US$1.

Nha Trang Taxi (☎ 824 000) and **Khanh Hoa Taxi** (☎ 810 810) have air-con cars with meters.

Many hotels have bicycle rentals for around US$1 per day.

MUI NE

☎ 062

Far from the madding crowd of HCMC, yet only three hours away, lies an 11km-stretch of beach outside the fishing village of Mui Ne. In the last few years, this out-of-the-way resort strip has seen a boom in construction, but it retains a slow pace and rickety charm.

Orientation & Information

Local addresses are designated by a kilometre mark measuring the distance along Rte 706 from Hwy 1 in Phan Thiet. To mix things up a bit, Rte 706 is also known as Đ Nguyen Dinh Chieu. Small restaurants along the road offer Internet access; the going rate is about 300d per minute.

Hanh Cafe/Ha Phuong Tourist (☎ 847 347; Km 13) Travel arrangements, backpacker grub and Internet access can be found at this travellers café.

Incombank (68 Đ Nguyen Dinh Chieu; ⏰ Sun-Fri) At Tropico Resort, this branch can exchange currency and travellers cheques.

Mui Ne Sailing Club (☎ 847 440; www.sailingclub vietnam.com; Km 13) Has a registered nurse. For serious medical problems, head to HCMC.

TM Brothers Cafe (☎ 847 359; Km 13) About 200m from Hanh Cafe, with similar services.

Sights

You'll smell Mui Ne as you arrive, and you'll see the pungent source in clay vats along the palm-lined road: fish sauce, for which Mui Ne is famous. But Mui Ne is more famous for its enormous **sand dunes**. Be sure to try the sand-sledding. The **Fairy Spring** (Suoi Tien) is a stream that flows through a patch of the dunes and rock formations near town. Also nearby are a **red stream**, **market** and **fishing village**. A 4WD tour of the dunes and nearby sights should cost around US$10 for the day.

On Rte 706 heading towards Phan Thiet, the small **Po Shanu Cham tower** (Km 5; admission

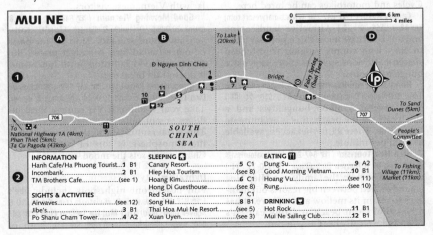

MUI NE

Đ Nguyen Dinh Chieu		To Lake (20km)	Bridge
706	SOUTH CHINA SEA		707

To National Highway 1A (4km); Phan Thiet (5km); Ta Cu Pagoda (43km)

To Sand Dunes (5km)

People's Committee

To Fishing Village (11km); Market (11km)

0 — 6 km
0 — 4 miles

INFORMATION		SLEEPING 🏠		EATING 🍴	
Hanh Cafe/Ha Phuong Tourist...1	B1	Canary Resort....................5	C1	Dung Su.........................9	A2
Incombank....................2	B1	Hiep Hoa Tourism..........(see 8)		Good Morning Vietnam....10	B1
TM Brothers Cafe...........(see 1)		Hoang Kim....................6	B1	Hoang Vu....................(see 11)	
		Hong Di Guesthouse.......(see 8)		Rung..........................(see 10)	
SIGHTS & ACTIVITIES		Red Sun........................7	C1		
Airwaves......................(see 12)		Song Hai........................8	B1	**DRINKING** 🍸	
Jibe's..........................3	B1	Thai Hoa Mui Ne Resort....(see 5)		Hot Rock.......................11	B1
Po Shanu Cham Tower.......4	A2	Xuan Uyen....................(see 3)		Mui Ne Sailing Club.........12	B1

VIETNAM

2000d; ⊙ 7.30-11.30am & 1.30-4.30pm) occupies a hill with sweeping views of Phan Thiet, the river mouth filled with boats and a cemetery filled with candylike tombstones.

Further afield lies Vietnam's largest **reclining Buddha** (49m) at Ta Cu Pagoda. Most visitors take the Austrian-built cable car (50,000d return) to the base of the pagoda, from where the Buddha is a short, but steep, hike. It's also possible to trek two hours up the scrubby mountainside; bring plenty of water and wear a hat. Ta Cu Mountain is just off Hwy 1, 28km south of Phan Thiet.

Activities

The season for windsurfers is from late October to late April. Ask at **Jibe's** (☎ 847 405; www.windsurf-vietnam.com; Km 13, 90 Ð Nguyen Dinh Chieu) for information about local spots. It rents state-of-the-art boards of all sorts, by the hour or day. It also offers kite-surfing and wind-surfing lessons.

Airwaves (☎ 847 440; www.airwaveskitesurfing .com), based at Mui Ne Sailing Club, is another outfit offering lessons and equipment rentals.

Sleeping

Thai Hoa Mui Ne Resort (☎ 847 320; dtp@hcm.vnn .vn; Km 18; bungalows 120,000-150,000d) The friendly proprietors here offer simple bungalows with shared or private bathroom, located around a sandy courtyard full of palms. The clean beach in front has chairs and umbrellas, and there's a shady café with an ocean view. Cycles and motorbikes can be hired here.

Canary Resort (☎ 847 258; www.canaryresort.com; Km 18; r US$5-20; 🌂) Attractive landscaping and a shaded café make this a popular place to stay, with rooms ranging from cheap shared-bathroom spots to more expensive bungalow rooms.

Hong Di Guesthouse (☎ 847 014; hdhongdi@yahoo .com; 70 Ð Nguyen Dinh Chieu; bungalows US$10; 🌂 🖳) With several bamboo bungalows and a small café on the beach, this is an intimate little place. There's Internet access available at 200d per minute.

Hiep Hoa Tourism (☎ 847 262; hiephoatourism@ yahoo.com; 80 Ð Nguyen Dinh Chieu; r US$10-15; 🌂) Calm and bucolic, the family-run Hiep Hoa is sandwiched between big resorts but manages to retain its mellow atmosphere. It has a beautiful clean beach and tiny café. It's often full, so call ahead if you can.

Hoang Kim (☎ 847 689; 140 Ð Nguyen Dinh Chieu; r US$4-15; 🌂 🖳) Cheapest rooms at this amiable guesthouse have shared bathrooms, but pricier ones are a better deal for your budget dollar.

Other recommendations:

Red Sun (☎ 847 387; caféloumi@hcm.vnn.vn; Km 13; r incl breakfast US$8-15; 🌂) Features a shady, brick courtyard.

Song Hai (☎ 847 015; songhairesort@yahoo.com; 72 Ð Nguyen Dinh Chieu; r US$10-15; 🌂) Bamboo-bead curtains and terracotta terrace, plus an in-house restaurant.

Xuan Uyen (☎ 847 476; Km 13.3; r US$8-12; 🌂) Very simple and clean bungalow rooms.

Eating

Most guesthouses run their own cafés serving cheap food, usually with Vietnamese and Western selections. If you tire of your home café, Rte 706 is lined with small family restaurants serving similar dishes at comparable prices. Try the local *com* shops for a plate of rice and fish for a frugal 6000d.

Hoang Vu (Double Wheels Restaurant; ☎ 847 525; Km 12.2; seafood 30,000d; ⊙ lunch & dinner) Within its cosy wood-and-rattan interior, Hoang Vu provides casually attentive service and delicious beautifully presented Vietnamese food at reasonable prices.

Dung Su (☎ 847 310; Km 10; meal around 40,000d; ⊙ lunch & dinner) After choosing your own seafood fresh from the tank (priced per kilo), enjoy authentically prepared local dishes in this stilt-restaurant over the water. Service here is friendly, and it's very popular with Vietnamese visitors.

Good Morning Vietnam (☎ 847 342; Km 11.8; mains 20,000d; ⊙ lunch & dinner) Can't stomach any more seafood? Stop by for pasta or other Italian fare at budget prices. But don't say 'good morning' until lunchtime; it doesn't do breakfast.

Rung (Forest Restaurant; ☎ 847 589; 65B Ð Nguyen Dinh Chieu; mains around 50,000d; ⊙ lunch & dinner) Take your traditional Vietnamese meal indoors or out onto the landscaped terrace. This restaurant is best in the evening, when the atmosphere is sort of romantic and Cham music sets the mood.

Drinking

Fun beachfront nightspots include **Jibe's** (☎ 847 405; www.windsurf-vietnam.com; Km 13, 90 Ð Nguyen Dinh Chieu) and **Mui Ne Sailing Club** (☎ 847 440; www.sailingclubvietnam.com; Km 13), both of which serve great food too. On the other side of the road, **Hot Rock** (Km 12.1) has a pool table and friendly vibes. Many people just gather at guesthouse cafés to swap stories over bottles of Bia 333.

Getting There & Around
From HCMC, the 200km drive to Mui Ne takes three hours. Travellers cafés sell tickets on open-tour buses for about US$6.

Long-distance buses do not stop in Mui Ne, but will drop you on National Hwy 1 at Phan Thiet, where you can catch a *xe om* to Mui Ne (22km) for about 50,000d. A local bus shuttles between Phan Thiet bus station and Mui Ne between 8.30am and 4pm, but it is irregular and slow.

It's best to cruise around Mui Ne on bicycle, which most guesthouses can rent to you for US$1 to US$3 a day.

CENTRAL HIGHLANDS

The Central Highlands covers the southern part of the Truong Son Mountain Range. This geographical region, home to many Montagnards, is renowned for its cool climate, beautiful mountain scenery and innumerable streams, lakes and waterfalls.

DALAT
☎ 063 / pop 130,000
Honeymooners and kitsch-seekers love Dalat. Dotted with lakes and waterfalls, and surrounded by evergreen forests, temperate Dalat is nicknamed the City of Eternal Spring. Days are fine and nights cool at 1475m, and wool hats and scarves abound in the market if you're caught unprepared for the winter nights that can get downright cold.

The economy is based on tourism and agriculture, drawing domestic and foreign visitors with its liveable climate, French-colonial architecture and carnival-like parks and flower gardens.

Information
INTERNET ACCESS
There are several Internet cafés along either side of Đ Nguyen Chi Thanh (Map p888). Rates for Internet use are around 150d per minute.

MEDICAL SERVICES
Lam Dong Hospital (Map p886; ☎ 822 154; 4 Đ Pham Ngoc Thach)

MONEY
These downtown banks exchange cash and travellers cheques and do credit card cash advances.
Agriculture Bank of Vietnam (Ngan Hang Nong Nghiep Viet Nam; Map p888; ☎ 822 535; 22 Hoa Binh Sq) There's another branch on Đ Nguyen Van Troi.
Incombank (Map p888; ☎ 822 496; 46-48 Hoa Binh Sq; ☒ closed Sat)
Vietcombank (Map p888; ☎ 510 478; 6 Đ Nguyen Thi Minh Khai) There's a 24-hour ATM here.

POST
Main post office (Map p886; ☎ 836 638; 14 Đ Tran Phu; ☒ 6.30am-9pm) International phone calls and Internet access are available here.

TRAVEL AGENCIES
Dalat Travel Service (Map p888; ☎ 822 125; ttdhhd@hcm.vnn.vn; 7 Đ 3 Thang 2) Vehicle rentals and local tours with knowledgeable guides.
Hardy Dalat (Map p888; ☎ 836 840; hardydl@hcm .vnn.vn; 66 Đ Phan Dinh Phung) An experienced team of French- and English-speaking tour guides, offering abseiling trips to local waterfalls, trekking, swimming and bird-watching tours.
Phat Tire Ventures (Map p888; ☎ 829 422; www .phattireventures.com; 73 Đ Truong Cong Dinh) Mountain-biking adventures around Dalat, or downhill coasts (actually, there is some pedalling involved) to the coast at Mui Ne.

Sights
Perhaps there's something in the cool mountain air that fosters the distinctly bohemian vibe and un-ironic kitsch in Dalat. Whatever the reasons, Dalat has attractions you won't find elsewhere in Vietnam.

The **Crémaillère** (Map p886; ☎ 834 409; return 75,000d; ☒ departures 8am, 9.30am, 2pm & 3.30pm) is a cog railway, about 500m east of Xuan Huong Lake that linked Dalat and Thap Cham Phan Rang from 1928 to 1964. The line has now been partially repaired and is operated as a tourist attraction. You can ride 8km down the tracks to Trai Mat village, where you can visit the ornate **Linh Phuoc Pagoda**.

Bao Dai's Summer Palace No 3 (Map p886; Đ Le Hong Phong; admission 5000d; ☒ 7-11am & 1.30-4pm) is a sprawling villa constructed in 1933.

VIETNAM

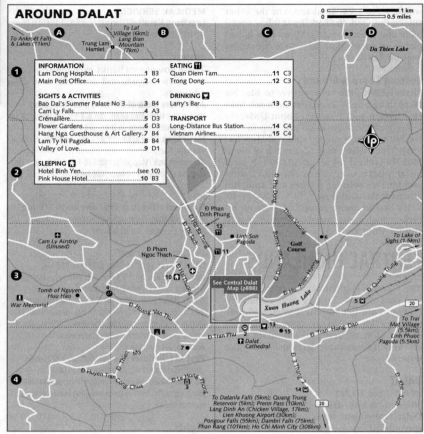

AROUND DALAT

0 ——— 1 km
0 ——— 0.5 miles

INFORMATION
Lam Dong Hospital..........................**1** B3
Main Post Office.............................**2** C4

SIGHTS & ACTIVITIES
Bao Dai's Summer Palace No 3........**3** B4
Cam Ly Falls..................................**4** A3
Crémaillère....................................**5** D3
Flower Gardens..............................**6** D3
Hang Nga Guesthouse & Art Gallery.**7** B4
Lam Ty Ni Pagoda...........................**8** B4
Valley of Love................................**9** D1

SLEEPING
Hotel Binh Yen...........................(see 10)
Pink House Hotel..........................**10** B3

EATING
Quan Diem Tam.............................**11** C3
Trong Dong...................................**12** C3

DRINKING
Larry's Bar....................................**13** C3

TRANSPORT
Long-Distance Bus Station...............**14** C4
Vietnam Airlines.............................**15** C4

To Ankroët Falls & Lakes (11km)
To Lat Village (6km); Lang Bian Mountain (7km)
Trung Lam Hamlet
Da Thien Lake

Cam Ly Airstrip (Unused)
Đ Phan Dinh Phung
Linh Son Pagoda
Golf Course
To Lake of Sighs (1.5km)

Đ Pham Ngoc Thach

Tomb of Nguyen Huu Hao
War Memorial

See Central Dalat Map (p888)

Xuan Huong Lake

Đ Hoang Van Thu

Đ Tran Phu
Dalat Cathedral

Đ Tran Hung Dao
To Trai Mat Village (5.5km); Linh Phuoc Pagoda (5.5km)

Đ Thien My
Đ Huyen Tran Cong Chua
Đ Le Hong Phong

To Datanla Falls (5km); Quang Trung Reservoir (5km); Prenn Pass (10km); Lang Dinh An (Chicken Village, 17km); Lien Khuong Airport (30km); Pongour Falls (55km); Dambri Falls (75km); Phan Rang (101km); Ho Chi Minh City (308km)

The palace is surrounded by landscaped grounds and decked out in the royal colour yellow. Riding a bicycle is a pleasant way to get here, as you pass French colonial houses along the road, which is shaded with pines. Shoes must be removed at the door.

Lam Ty Ni Pagoda (Quan Am Tu; Map p886; 2 Đ Thien My; ☯ 8-11.30am & 1-6.30pm) was founded in 1961; this small pagoda is less famous than Mr Thuc, the Crazy Monk who lives here. He's not so much crazy as artistic, and in fact some call him the Business Monk for the brisk sales of his voluminous collection of self-brushed artwork. A pathway through the pagoda garden is walled in with hanging paintings on paper.

Southeast of central Dalat, **Hang Nga Guesthouse & Art Gallery** (Map p886; ☎ 822 070; 3 Đ Huynh Thuc Khang; admission 5000d; ☯ 8am-7pm) is a funky place that's earned the moniker Crazy House from local residents. It's notable for its *Alice in Wonderland* architecture, where you can perch inside a giraffe or get lost in a giant spider web. You can also stay in one of these kooky, slightly spooky rooms (US$19 to US$60), but book in advance.

At the **Valley of Love** (Thung Lung Tinh Yeu; Map p886; Đ Phu Dong Thien Vuong; adult/child 6000/3000d; ☯ 8am-8pm) you can pose for photos on a pony accompanied by a Vietnamese dude dressed as a cowboy. It's about 5km from **Xuan Huong Lake** (Map p888), where you can rent a paddleboat shaped like a giant swan.

Lake of Sighs (Ho Than Tho; admission 5000d) was enlarged by a French-built dam. The sentimentally named natural lake lies 6km northeast of Dalat. **Horses** (per hr 80,000d) can be hired near the restaurants.

Established in 1966 by the South Vietnamese Agriculture Service, the grounds of the **Flower Gardens** (Vuon Hoa Dalat; Map p886; ☎ 822 151; 2 Đ Phu Dong Thien Vuong; admission 4000d; ☯ 7.30am-4pm) are lovely with blooming Dalat flora – detracting from the beauty are a few caged monkeys.

WATERFALLS

Dalat's waterfalls are obviously at their gushing best in the rainy season but still run during the dry season. We advise skipping Prenn Falls, which is overdeveloped and includes an appalling collection of caged animals on-site.

Datanla Falls (admission 5000d) is southeast of Dalat off Hwy 20, about 200m past the turn-off to Quang Trung Reservoir. It's a nice walk through the rainforest and a steep hike downhill to the falls. Butterflies and birds are abundant.

If you feel that you must have Vietnamese cowboys and stuffed jungle animals in your holiday photos, look no further than **Cam Ly Falls** (Map p886; admission 5000d). This is a popular stop for domestic visitors to Dalat and is notable more for the circus-style ambience than for the waterfall itself.

LANG BIAN MOUNTAIN

With five volcanic peaks ranging in altitude from 2100m to 2400m, **Lang Bian Mountain** (Nui Lam Vien; admission 5000d) makes a scenic trek (three to four hours from Lat village). You might spot some semiwild horses grazing on the side of the mountain, where rhinoceros and tigers dwelt only half a century ago. Views from the top are tremendous.

The nine hamlets of **Lat village**, whose inhabitants are ethnic minorities, are about 12km northwest of Dalat at the base of Lang Bian Mountain.

LANG DINH AN

Also called the Chicken Village, Lang Dinh An is a minority village 17km south of Dalat. It gets its nickname from an enormous concrete **chicken statue** in the middle of the huts. The chicken's presence there is explained by conflicting stories, one about

a romance gone awry, another about the government honouring the industriousness of the village people.

Tours

Witty and knowledgeable, the Easy Riders are an informal crew of local motorbike guides who can whirl you around Dalat on their vintage motorbikes. This is a great way to explore the region, and having a friendly and articulate guide provides a new perspective on the sights. Some travellers get on so well with their guides that they adopt their drivers for the longer haul – it's highly recommended that you test-drive with a day tour before committing to a longer trip. Most speak great English and/or French.

The Easy Riders can be found hanging around the hotels and cafés in Dalat, but they're likely to find you first. Check out their guestbooks full of glowing testimonials from past clients.

Sleeping

Dreams Hotel (Map p888; ☎ 833 748; dreams@hcm.vnn.vn; 151 Đ Phan Dinh Phung; r incl breakfast US$10-15; 🖳) One of the best deals in Dalat, this super-welcoming place has tidy, comfortable rooms, some with balconies. There's free Internet access in the lobby. You can even pay with a credit card.

Pink House Hotel (Mai Nha Hong; Map p886; ☎ 815 667; pink_063@yahoo.com; 7 Đ Hai Thuong; s/d incl breakfast 75,000/180,000d) This pink hotel is excellent value, with spotless rooms and a perky, friendly staff. It's down a quiet alley about 15 minutes' walk from the city centre.

Peace Hotel (Map p888; ☎ 822 787; peace12@hcm.vnn.vn; 64 Đ Truong Cong Dinh; r US$8-15) The Peace Hotel is a longtime favourite with backpackers, and its café downstairs is a popular gathering place for travellers and motorbike guides. There's another villa-style branch up the street known as **Peace Hotel II** (Map p888; 67 Đ Truong Cong Dinh).

Mimosa Hotel (Map p888; ☎ 822 656; 170 Đ Phan Dinh Phung; r US$4-12) Rooms here are tidy and sunny, and some have balconies – a reliable budget stand-by.

Hotel Binh Yen (Map p886; ☎ 823 631; 7 Đ Hai Thuong; r incl breakfast US$4-10) The rooms at this well-priced hotel here are comfortable.

It's also possible to camp at the **Stop & Go Cafe** (Map p888; ☎ 828 458; 2A Đ Ly Tu Trong), the grounds of which are parklike and green.

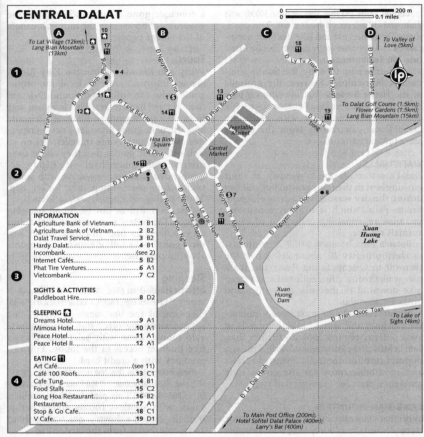

CENTRAL DALAT

INFORMATION
Agriculture Bank of Vietnam..............1 B1
Agriculture Bank of Vietnam..............2 B2
Dalat Travel Service..........................3 B2
Hardy Dalat.....................................4 A1
Incombank...................................(see 2)
Internet Cafés.................................5 B2
Phat Tire Ventures............................6 A1
Vietcombank...................................7 C2

SIGHTS & ACTIVITIES
Paddleboat Hire...............................8 D2

SLEEPING
Dreams Hotel...................................9 A1
Mimosa Hotel.................................10 A1
Peace Hotel...................................11 A1
Peace Hotel II................................12 A1

EATING
Art Café.....................................(see 11)
Café 100 Roofs..............................13 C1
Cafe Tung....................................14 B1
Food Stalls....................................15 C2
Long Hoa Restaurant.......................16 B2
Restaurants...................................17 A1
Stop & Go Cafe..............................18 C1
V Cafe...19 D1

Eating

Along Đ Phan Dinh Phung (Map p888), near the Mimosa Hotel, are several good restaurants serving inexpensive Vietnamese, Chinese and Western food. At night, when the market area has a festive feel, check out the food stalls on Đ Nguyen Thi Minh Khai (Map p888) and the steps leading to the market. Eat cheap noodle soup and steamed sweet potato, and drink hot sweetened soy milk while hunting for bargains.

RESTAURANTS

V Cafe (Map p888; ☎ 837 576; 1 Đ Bui Thi Xuan; mains around 40,000d) A little of this, a little of that – Vietnamese and American-style food is served here in a casual but refined setting,

at very reasonable prices. The atmosphere is friendly and convivial, making it an appealing rendezvous spot.

Quan Diem Tam (Map p886; ☎ 820 104; 217 Đ Phan Dinh Phung; noodle soup 7000d) Be sure to try the delicious *mi hoanh thanh* (yellow-noodle won ton soup) at this long-running Chinese-style noodle-soup shop.

Trong Dong (Map p886; ☎ 821 889; 220 Đ Phan Dinh Phung; mains around 35,000d) House specialities at this superb Vietnamese restaurant include grilled shrimp paste on sugar cane, claypot fish, and minced beef wrapped in *lalot* (betel) leaves. It's not central, but worth the walk.

Long Hoa Restaurant (Map p888; ☎ 822 934; 6 Đ 3 Thang 2; mains 25,000d) Long in vogue with travellers, Long Hoa serves great sautéed dishes and hotpot.

CAFÉS

Café 100 Roofs (Way to the Moon; Map p888; ☎ 822 880; puppy@hcm.vnn.vn; 57 Đ Phan Boi Chau) More of Dalat's wacky sculptural architecture. Have some ice cream inside this labyrinthine café created by a friend and colleague of the Crazy House's architect. Constantly evolving, the wet concrete of the interior even smells like a limestone cave.

Stop & Go Cafe (Map p888; ☎ 828 458; 2A Đ Ly Tu Trong) Dalat poet, artist, gardener and musician Duy Viet graciously serves cakes and croissants with your coffee when you arrive in his living room, and he might even invite you to play a song on his guitar. Stop by, and leave reluctantly.

Cafe Tung (Map p888; 6 Khu Hoa Binh Sq) This famous hang-out of Saigonese intellectuals during the 1950s now has a less lively atmosphere, but it's a good place to have a jolt of hot coffee on a cold Dalat evening, with strains of French music playing softly in the background.

Art Café (Map p888; ☎ 510 089; 70 Đ Truong Cong Dinh; mains 30,000d) Owned by an artist whose work adorns the walls, and whose tables bear white tablecloths and wineglasses, this elegant café offers mostly Vietnamese dishes with a few Western curveballs thrown in for good measure.

Drinking

Larry's Bar (Map p886; ☎ 825 444; 12 Đ Tran Phu) Happy hour (5pm to 7pm) at Larry's Bar also applies to food on the bar menu. Find this cosy little tavern in the basement of the Hotel Sofitel Dalat Palace.

Shopping

Hoa Binh Sq (Map p888) and the market building adjacent to it are the places to go for purchasing ethnic handicrafts from the nearby Montagnard villages. You can find Lat rush baskets that roll up when empty, as well as gourds for carrying water. Nonhandicraft items at rock-bottom prices include quilted, fake-fur-lined alpine jackets imported from China, and lacquered alligators holding light bulbs in their mouths.

One of Dalat's culinary specialities is *mut* (candied fruit), and vendors in the market

will let you sample a bit of something before you buy.

Getting There & Around

Vietnam Airlines (Map p886; ☎ 822 895; www.vietnam airlines.com; 40 Đ Ho Tung Mau) runs daily flights connecting Dalat with HCMC.

Long-distance buses leave from the station on Đ 3 Thang 2 (Map p886), about 1km south of the city centre. Open-tour minibuses to Dalat can be booked at travellers cafés in Saigon, Mui Ne and Nha Trang.

Mountain roads connect Dalat with other Central Highlands towns. For vehicle rentals, visit **Dalat Travel Service** (Map p888; ☎ 822 125; ttdhhd@hcm.vnn.vn; 7 Đ 3 Thang 2).

Full-day tours with local motorbike guides are a great way to see the area, as many of the sights lie outside Dalat's centre. Depending on how far you want to go, expect to pay between US$7 and US$10 for a day tour.

Many hotels offer bicycle and motorbike hire.

AROUND DALAT

The largest waterfall in the Dalat area, **Pongour Falls** (admission 5000d) is about 55km in the direction of HCMC and 7km down a dirt road off the highway. These stepped falls are beautiful anytime but most spectacular during the rainy season when they form a full semicircle.

Dambri Falls (admission 10,000d), 75km from Dalat, are the tallest falls in the area – walking down to feel the spray from the bottom is divine on a hot day. You can take a lift down and trek back up, but don't wander too far upstream if you don't want to see the minizoo of monkeys and reindeer. There's also a good restaurant with mimosa-framed views near the parking lot.

Waterfalls in the Dalat region are best accessed on your own wheels. Those doing long-haul journeys with motorbike drivers can easily detour to the falls on the way to or from Dalat.

BUON MA THUOT

☎ 050 / pop 186,600

The biggest town in the Central Highlands, Buon Ma Thuot is surrounded by coffee plantations and sells superb coffee at lower prices than in Hanoi or HCMC.

Dam San Tourist (☎ 851 234; damsantour@dng.vnn .vn; 212-214 Đ Nguyen Cong Tru) and **Daklak Tourist**

(☎ 852 108; daklaktour@dng.vnn.vn; 3 Đ Phan Chau Trinh) can arrange tours and your travel permits for the Ede, M'nong and Bahnar villages nearby.

Other sights of interest include the **Ethnographic Museum** (☎ 850 426; cnr Đ Nguyen Du & Đ Le Duan; admission 10,000d; ⊙ 7.30-11am & 1.30-5pm Tue-Sun), which has exhibits covering some of the 31 ethnic groups from Dac Lac Province. For amazing views from the hills head to **Lak Lake**, near a M'nong village. Nearby **Yok Don National Park** (Vuon Quoc Gia Yok Don; ☎ 783 049; yokdon@dng.vnn.vn) is home to 38 endangered mammal species. Stunning waterfalls in this area include **Gia Long** and **Dray Nur Falls** along the **Krong Ana River**.

Sleeping & Eating
Good budget choices include the following, all of which are clean and central. The more expensive rooms have air-con and private toilet:

Duy Hoang Hotel (☎ 858 020; 30 Đ Ly Thuong Kiet; r 170,000-200,000d; ✖)

Thanh Binh Hotel (☎ 853 812; 24 Đ Ly Thuong Kiet; r 150,000-170,000d; ✖)

Thanh Phat Hotel (☎ 854 857; 41 Đ Ly Thuong Kiet; r 120,000-180,000d; ✖)

Bon Trieu (33 Đ Hai Ba Trung; mains 20,000d) A good local restaurant known for its delicious beef dishes, Bon Trieu is reasonably priced.

Quan Ngon (☎ 851 909; 72-74 Đ Ba Trieu; mains around 35,000d) This eatery has outdoor seating in a pleasant courtyard garden if you don't fancy the indoor rice-wine-pickled animals watching you eat.

Getting There & Away
Vietnam Airlines (☎ 955 055; www.vietnamairlines .com; 65-67 Đ Nguyen Chi Thanh) connects Buon Ma Thuot with HCMC and Danang. The airport is about 10km from town.

Buon Ma Thuot is served by buses from HCMC, Nha Trang, Dalat, Pleiku, Kon Tum and Danang. National Hwy 27 from Dalat is best travelled by motorbike or 4WD.

PLEIKU
☎ 059 / pop 141,700
Most travellers prefer to skip the market town of Pleiku in favour of Kon Tum, 49km to the north. Local authorities require travel permits outside of Pleiku itself and aren't the most hospitable in the area.

Gia Lai Tourist (☎ 874 571; gialaitourist@hotmail .com; 215 Đ Hung Vuong) can arrange travel permits and tours, including elephant treks. Exchange travellers cheques at **Vietcombank** (☎ 828 593; 12 Đ Tran Hung Dao), as there is nowhere to do so in Kon Tom.

Seven kilometres outside of Pleiku is the deep **Sea Lake** (Bien Ho), a scenic spot. Also in the area are **villages** of the Bahnar and Jarai people.

Sleeping & Eating
Hung Vuong Hotel (☎ 824 270; 2 Đ Le Loi; r US$10-24; ✖) This large hotel has comfortable rooms featuring satellite TV and fridge. Try to get a room facing the back.

Thanh Lich Hotel (☎ 824 674; 86 Đ Nguyen Van Troi; r US$7-15; ✖) Backpackers tend to gravitate towards this centrally located hotel. Some rooms have small terraces.

My Tam (cnr Đ Quang Trung & Đ Le Loi; mains 15,000d) does good local food, while **Nem Ninh Hoa** (80 Đ Nguyen Van Troi; mains 12,000d) turns out Pleiku's best spring rolls.

Getting There & Away
Vietnam Airlines (☎ 823 058; www.vietnamairlines .com; 55 Đ Quang Trung) has flights between Pleiku and HCMC and Danang.

Buses run from HCMC, Buon Ma Thuot and most coastal towns between, and including, Nha Trang and Danang.

KON TUM
☎ 060 / pop 89,800
Kon Tum seems to hold the most thrall for travellers in the area, especially for cyclists, as motorised traffic is light, the scenery fine and the climate pleasant.

Around the edges of town are a couple of **Bahnar villages** within walking distance. Along Đ Nguyen Hue, there's a ceremonial *rong* house – a community hall on stilts – and a **Catholic seminary** with a **hill-tribe museum** on the 2nd floor.

Exchange dollars for dong at **BIDV** (☎ 862 340; 1 Đ Tran Phu). The terrific **Kon Tum Tourist** (☎ 861 626; 2 Đ Phan Dinh Phung) has its booking office in Dakbla Hotel.

Sleeping & Eating
There are only three accommodation options in town, all owned by Kon Tum Tourist. They are all fine, if somewhat overpriced.

KON TUM ORPHANAGES

Several hundred children from diverse ethnic backgrounds reside at Kon Tum's sister orphanages, Vinh Son 1 (behind the wooden church on Đ Nguyen Hue) and Vinh Son 2 (southeast of Vinh Son 1, behind Bahnar village). The friendly nuns at both orphanages welcome visitors who come to share their time and play with the children. Donations of nonperishable food, toys and clothing are always greatly appreciated. Vinh Son 2 receives fewer visitors, but with more kids it has a greater need for attention and donations. If you plan to stay in Kon Tum for a few days, the orphanages may need short-term volunteers – stop by and ask.

Dakbla Hotel (☎ 863 333; 2 Đ Phan Dinh Phung; r incl breakfast US$23-30; ✱) The plushest of the bunch, Dakbla is near the river.

Dakbla Hotel 2 (☎ 863 335; 163 Đ Nguyen Hue; r US$6-10; ✱) Cheaper fan rooms and attentive though non-English-speaking staff.

Quang Trung Hotel (☎ 862 249; 168 Đ Ba Trieu; r US$5-25; ✱) Of a similar standard to Dakbla Hotel 2, the cheapest rooms are Spartan, fan-only cells.

The options for eating and drinking:

Dakbla's (☎ 826 584; 168 Đ Nguyen Hue; mains 30,000d) For local fare, try this popular place.

Eva Cafe (☎ 862 944; 1 Đ Phan Chu Trinh) For hot coffee or cold beer, stop by Eva's atmospheric garden.

Quan Chay 33 Le Loi (33 Đ Le Loi; mains 15,000d) Vegetarians meals.

Getting There & Away

Buses from HCMC take 12 hours along scenic National Hwy 14. Kon Tum's bus station is 13km north of town, but buses often drive through Kon Tum, where they can drop you instead. Kon Tum buses connect with Pleiku, Buon Ma Thuot and Danang.

HO CHI MINH CITY (SAIGON)

☎ 08 / pop 5.38 million

Ho Chi Minh City (HCMC; also known as Saigon) runs a continuous soundtrack loop: mobile phones tweeting, horns honking, screeching metal doors signalling the begin-

ning of another business day. The river of chaotic traffic only ebbs in the wee hours, and soup steams from streetside cauldrons all day and all night. HCMC is nonstop, a city full of pilgrims seeking fortune and open 24 hours a day for the next big thing.

The heart of central HCMC beats in Districts 1 and 3, where stately tamarind trees shade fading French colonial buildings and narrow Vietnamese shophouses. High-rise hotels jostle with towers of commerce near the Saigon River. And everywhere, HCMC residents are on the go. High-society families and poverty-stricken street kids are part of the masses in a city where beauty and ugliness are caught in the same blink of an eye.

ORIENTATION

A sprawl of 16 urban and five rural *quan* (districts) make up the vast geography of HCMC, though most travellers stick to the centre around the Dong Khoi and Pham Ngu Lao neighbourhoods. Cholon, the city's Chinatown, lies southwest of the centre, and the Saigon River snakes down the eastern side.

Wherever you roam, you'll have to cross the street eventually, so go armed with this survival tip: step into the street and walk *slowly* across so that drivers can see you and drive around you. If you lack the nerve, look for locals crossing the street and creep behind.

Street labels are shortened to Đ for *duong* (street), and ĐL for *dai lo* (boulevard).

GETTING INTO TOWN

Tan Son Nhat international airport (Map pp892–3) is 7km northwest of the city centre. If your taxi driver refuses to use the meter, find one who will. The ride into town costs around US$4 (60,000d). The cheapest deal is the 1000d airport bus 152, which goes directly through Dong Khoi and Pham Ngu Lao.

From the Saigon train station (Ga Sai Gon; Map pp892–3), a *xe om* (motorcycle taxi) to Pham Ngu Lao shouldn't cost more than 10,000d.

From Saigon's intercity bus stations, most fares on a *xe om* should be between 10,000d and 20,000d. Public buses (3000d) from the stations stop near Ben Thanh Market, but these cease midafternoon.

HO CHI MINH CITY (SAIGON)

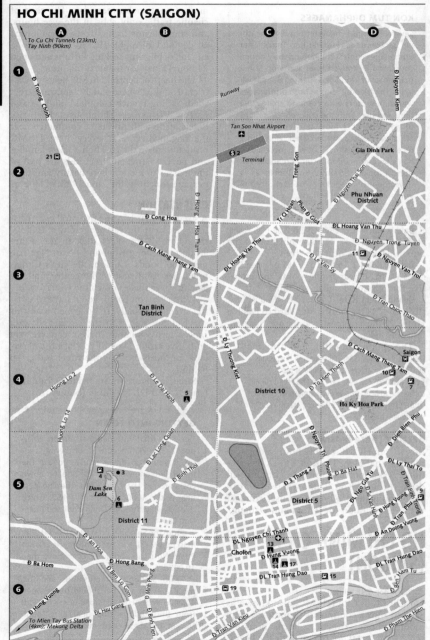

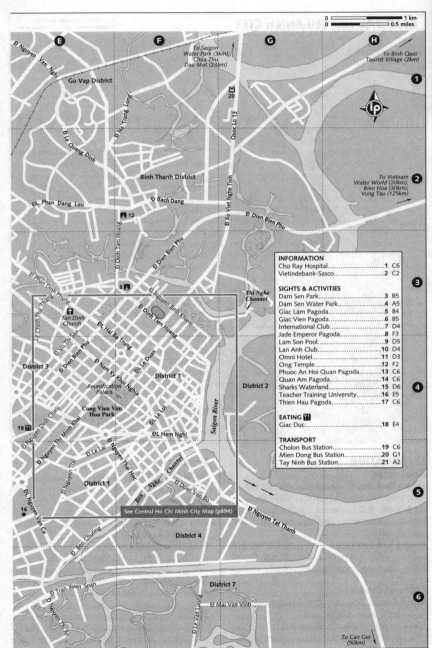

0 _____ 1 km
0 _____ 0.5 miles

Đ Nguyen Van Nghi

E **F** **G** **H**

To Saigon
Water Park (3km);
Chua Thu
Dau Mot (23km)

To Binh Quoi
Tourist Village (2km)

1

Go Vap District

Đ Trang Long

Quoc Lo 13

Đ Le Quang Dinh

Binh Thanh District

To Vietnam
Water World (20km);
Bien Hoa (30km);
Vung Tau (125km)

2

Đ. Phan Dang Luu

Đ Bach Dang

Đ Xo Viet Nghe Tinh

Đ Dien Bien Phu

Đ Dien Bien Phu

Đ Dinh Tien Hoang

12

3

Đ Nguyen Binh Khiem

Đ Dien Bien Phu

Thi Nghe
Channel

Đ Phan Dinh Phung

8

Đ Dinh Tien Hoang

INFORMATION
Cho Ray Hospital.........................1 C6
Vietindebank-Sasco.....................2 C2

Ly Chinh Thang

Tan Dinh
Church

ĐL Hai Ba Trung

SIGHTS & ACTIVITIES
Dam Sen Park..............................3 B5
Dam Sen Water Park.....................4 A5
Giac Lam Pagoda..........................5 B4
Giac Vien Pagoda.........................6 B5
International Club..........................7 D4
Jade Emperor Pagoda....................8 F3
Lam Son Pool...............................9 D5
Lan Anh Club..............................10 D4
Omni Hotel.................................11 D3
Ong Temple................................12 F2
Phuoc An Hoi Quan Pagoda..........13 C6
Quan Am Pagoda.........................14 C6
Sharks Waterland.........................15 D6
Teacher Training University...........16 E5
Thien Hau Pagoda.......................17 C6

District 3

Đ Vo Thi Sau

Đ Dien Bien Phu

Đ Le Duan

Đ Nam Ky Khoi Nghia

District 1

Reunification
Palace

District 2

4

Saigon River

**Cong Vien Van
Hoa Park**

Đ Le Loi

18

Đ Nguyen Dinh Chieu

ĐL Ham Nghi

EATING
Giac Duc.....................................18 E4

Đ Nguyen Thi Minh Khai

Đ Le Lai

Đ Nguyen Thai Hoc

Ben Nghe
Channel

Đ Nguyen Trai

TRANSPORT
Cholon Bus Station......................19 C6
Mien Dong Bus Station.................20 G1
Tay Ninh Bus Station....................21 A2

District 1

Đ Doan Van Bo

16

See Central Ho Chi Minh City Map (p894)

Đ Nguyen Tat Thanh

5

ĐL Nguyen Van Cu

Đ Ben Chuong

District 4

Đ Tran Xuan Soan

District 7

Đ Nguyen Thi

District 7

Đ Mai Van Vinh

6

Đ Le Van Luong

To Can Gio
(50km)

CENTRAL HO CHI MINH CITY

INFORMATION
Bookshops

Fahasa Bookshop Đ Dong Khoi (Map p896; ☎ 822 4670; 185 Đ Dong Khoi); ĐL Nguyen Hue (Map p896; ☎ 822 5446; 40 ĐL Nguyen Hue; ⏰ 8am-5pm) One of the better government-run bookshops, with maps, books and dictionaries.

Phuong Nam Bookshop (Map p894; ☎ 822 9650; 2A ĐL Le Duan; ⏰ 8am-9.30pm) Carries books and magazines in English, French and Chinese, mostly instructional in nature.

Cultural Centres

British Council (Map p894; ☎ 823 2862; www.british council.org/vietnam; 25 ĐL Le Duan)

Idecaf (Institute of Cultural Exchange with France; Map p896; ☎ 829 5451; 31 Đ Thai Van Lung) French culture, language and arts centre.

Emergency

Ambulance (☎ 115)
Fire (☎ 114)
Information (☎ 1080)
Police (☎ 113)

Internet Access

Hundreds of Internet cafés thrive in HCMC – in Pham Ngu Lao (Map p898) you can't swing a dead cat without hitting one. Rates are generally a cheap 100d per minute with a minimum charge of 2000d.

Media

Hotels, bars and restaurants around HCMC carry the free entertainment magazines the *Guide* and *Time Out* (see p917).

There's also an eclectic selection of slightly stale foreign newspapers and magazines – day-old *Le Monde* or last week's *Newsweek* – for sale by the guys standing on the corner of Đ Dong Khoi and ĐL Le Loi (Map p896), across from the Continental Hotel. Bargain down a bit.

Medical Services

Cho Ray Hospital (Benh Vien Cho Ray; Map pp892–3; ☎ 855 4137; 201 ĐL Nguyen Chi Thanh, District 5; consultations from US$4; ☾ 24hr) The largest medical facility in Vietnam, with 24-hour emergency services and excellent, inexpensive care. About a third of the physicians speak English.

Emergency Centre (Map p894; ☎ 829 2071; 125 ĐL Le Loi; ☾ 24hr) Has doctors who speak English and French.

HCMC Family Medical Practice (Map p896; ☎ 822 7848, 24hr emergency ☎ 0913-234 911; www.vietnam medicalpractice.com; Diamond Plaza, 34 ĐL Le Duan; consultations from US$50; ☾ 24hr) One of the best international clinics in Vietnam, with prices to match.

International Medical Center (Map p896; ☎ 827 2366, 24hr emergency ☎ 865 4025; fac@hcm.vnn.vn; 1 Đ Han Thuyen; consultations US$40-80; ☾ 24hr) This nonprofit organisation may be the least expensive Western healthcare centre in the city. Most doctors are English-speaking French physicians.

International SOS (Map p896; ☎ 829 8424, 24hr emergency ☎ 829 8520; 65 Đ Nguyen Du; consultations US$55-65; ☾ 24hr) An international team of docs speaking English, French, Japanese and Vietnamese.

Money

Vietindebank-Sasco (Map pp892–3; ☎ 844 0740), just outside the airport exit, gives the official exchange rate but keeps irregular hours. In case it's closed, have sufficient US dollars in small denominations to get into the city centre. Banks around town include the following:

ANZ Bank (Map p896; ☎ 829 9319; 11 Me Linh Sq) 24-hour ATM.

Fiditourist (Map p898; ☎ 835 3018; 195 Đ Pham Ngu Lao; ☾ 8am-10pm) This establishment keeps late hours in backpackerland, though the rates it offers aren't the best.

HSBC (Hongkong Bank; Map p896; ☎ 829 2288; 235 Đ Dong Khoi) 24-hour ATM, horrendous commission on travellers cheques.

Sacombank (Map p898; ☎ 837 8778; 211 Đ Nguyen Thai Hoc) In backpacker central, has an ATM.

Vietcombank (Map p894; ☎ 829 7245; 29 Đ Ben Chuong) Closed on the last day of every month.

Post

Main post office (Buu Dien Thanh Pho Ho Chi Minh; Map p896; 2 Cong Xa Paris) Saigon's French-era post office is next to Notre Dame Cathedral.

Travel Agencies

You will find the following budget agencies in the backpacker ghetto of Pham Ngu Lao (Map p898):

Delta Adventure Tours (☎ 836 8542; 187A Đ Pham Ngu Lao) Great Mekong Delta tours.

Fiditourist (☎ 835 3018; 195 Đ Pham Ngu Lao)

Kim Travel (☎ 836 9859; 270 Đ De Tham) Longtime tour operators.

Linh Cafe (☎ 836 0643; linhtravel@hcm.vnn.vn; 291 Đ Pham Ngu Lao)

Mekong Tours (☎ 837 6429; mekongtours@hotmail .com; 272 Đ De Tham)

Sinh Cafe (☎ 836 7338; www.sinhcafe.com; 248 Đ De Tham) Well-established backpacker travel pros.

Sinhbalo Adventures (☎ 837 6766, 836 7682; www .sinhbalo.com; 283/20 Đ Pham Ngu Lao) More upmarket, long-running and eminently reliable operators for custom tours.

TM Brothers (☎ 836 1791; huuhanhnguyen@yahoo .com; 288 Đ De Tham)

DANGERS & ANNOYANCES

Although travellers very rarely face any physical danger in HCMC (besides the traffic), the city has the most determined thieves in the country. Drive-by crooks on motorbikes can steal bags off your arm and sunglasses off your face, and pickpockets work all crowds. Beware, too, of the cute children crowding around you, wanting to sell postcards and newspapers.

While it's generally safe to take cyclos during the day, it is not always safe at night – take a metered taxi or *xe om* instead.

SIGHTS

Reunification Palace

Built in 1966 to serve as South Vietnam's Presidential Palace is the **Reunification Palace** (Hoi Truong Thong Nhat; Map p894; ☎ 829 4117; 106 Đ Nguyen Du; admission 15,000d; ⌚ 7.30-11am & 1-4pm). It was towards this building that the first communist tanks in Saigon rushed on the morning of 30 April 1975, the day Saigon surrendered. The building has been left just as it looked on that momentous day.

Enter on Đ Nam Ky Khoi Nghia, where English- and French-speaking guides are on duty.

War Remnants Museum

Documenting the atrocities of war, the **War Remnants Museum** (Bao Tang Chung Tich Chien Tranh; Map p894; ☎ 930 5587; 28 Đ Vo Van Tan; admission 10,000d; ⌚ 7.30-11.45am & 1.30-5.15pm Tue-Sun) is unique, brutal and an essential visit. On display are retired artillery pieces, a model of the tiger cages used to house Viet Cong prisoners, and a heartbreaking array of photographs of the victims of war – those who suffered torture as well as those born with birth defects caused by the USA's use of defoliants. Exhibits are labelled in Vietnamese, English and Chinese.

History Museum

The impressive collection of HCMC's **History Museum** (Bao Tang Lich Su; Map p894; ☎ 829 8146; Đ Nguyen Binh Khiem; admission 10,000d; ⌚ 8-11.30am & 1-4pm Tue-Sun) is housed in a stunning Sino-French building constructed in 1929 by the Société des Études Indochinoises. Display-

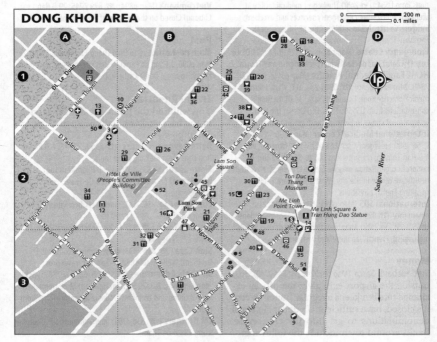

DONG KHOI AREA

ing artefacts from 3300 years of human activity in what is now Vietnam, it's just inside the main entrance to the zoo.

Pagodas, Temples & Churches

For a dose of peace, fortified with architectural appreciation, seek out these places of worship.

CENTRAL HCMC

Notre Dame Cathedral (Map p896; Đ Han Thuyen; mass 9.30am Sun), built between 1877 and 1883, stands regally in the heart of the government quarter. Its red-brick neo-Romanesque form and two 40m-high square towers tipped with iron spires dominate the skyline.

A splash of southern India's colour in Saigon, **Mariamman Hindu Temple** (Chua Ba Mariamman; Map p894; 45 Đ Truong Dinh; 7am-7pm) was built at the end of the 19th century and is dedicated to the Hindu goddess Mariamman. There are only 50 to 60 Tamil Hindus in HCMC, but the temple is also considered sacred by many ethnic Vietnamese and Chinese.

Constructed by South Indian Muslims in 1935 on the site of an earlier mosque, **Saigon Central Mosque** (Map p896; 66 Đ Dong Du; 9am-5pm) is an immaculately clean and well-kept island of calm in the middle of bustling central Saigon. In front of the spar-

A DAY IN SAIGON

Downtown HCMC can be walked in a day, making a loop from **Pham Ngu Lao** (Map p894) to **Ben Thanh Market** (p904), detouring through the **Fine Arts Museum** (p899). The **Reunification Palace** (opposite) and **War Remnants Museum** (opposite) could be followed by dinner and a drink in the **Dong Khoi** (Map p896) neighbourhood.

A day tour on a *xe om* (motorcycle taxi) to points further afield like **Cholon** (below) should cost US$5 to US$10.

kling white-and-blue structure with its four nonfunctional minarets, is a pool for ritual ablutions before prayers. As at any mosque, remove your shoes before entering.

CHOLON

Cholon has a wealth of wonderful Chinese temples including **Quan Am Pagoda** (Map pp892-3; 12 Đ Lao Tu; 8am-4.30pm), founded in 1816 by the Fujian Chinese congregation. The roof is decorated with fantastic scenes, rendered in ceramic, from traditional Chinese plays and stories. The tableaux include ships, houses, people and several ferocious dragons. The front doors are decorated with very old gold-and-lacquer panels.

INFORMATION		EATING 🍴		Q Bar	(see 45)
ANZ Bank	1 C2	Akatombo	17 C2	Saigon Saigon Bar	37 B2
Australian Consulate	2 C2	Angkor Encore Plus	18 C1	Sango Aquarium Cafe	38 C1
Canadian Consulate	3 A2	Annie's Pizza	19 C2	Sheridan's Irish House	39 C1
Continental Hotel	4 B2	Ashoka	20 C1	Underground	40 C3
Fahasa Bookshop	5 C3	Augustin	21 B2	Vasco's Bar	41 C1
Fahasa Bookshop	6 B2	Bo Tung Xeo Restaurant	22 B1		
HCMC Family Medical		Cafe Latin	23 C2	ENTERTAINMENT 🎭	
Practice	(see 43)	Cafe Mogambo	24 C1	Apocalypse Now	42 C2
HSBC	(see 3)	Chao Thai	25 B2	Diamond Plaza Cinema	43 A1
International Medical		Chi Lang Cafe	26 B2	IDECAF	44 C1
Center	7 A1	Fanny	27 B3	Municipal Theatre	45 C3
International SOS	8 A2	Hoi An	28 C1	Tropical Rainforest Disco	46 C3
Japanese Embassy	9 C3	Huong Lai	29 B2		
Main Post Office	10 B1	Indian Canteen	(see 15)	SHOPPING 🛍	
Malaysian Embassy	11 C2	Java Coffee Bar	30 C2	Russian Market (Tax Department	
		Juice Bar	(see 19)	Store)	47 B2
SIGHTS & ACTIVITIES		Kem Bach Dang	31 B3		
Caravelle Hotel	(see 37)	Kem Bach Dang	32 B3	TRANSPORT	
Museum of Ho Chi		Lemongrass	(see 21)	All Nippon Airways	(see 5)
Minh City	12 A2	Mandarine	33 C1	Cathay Pacific Airways	48 C3
Notre Dame Cathedral	13 A1	Quan An Ngon	34 A2	Japan Airlines	49 C3
Renaissance Riverside	14 C2	Restaurant 13	35 C3	Malaysia Airlines	50 A2
Saigon Central Mosque	15 C2	Restaurant 19	(see 35)	Pacific Airlines	51 C3
				Philippine Airlines	(see 50)
SLEEPING 🛏		DRINKING 🍷		Thai Airways International	(see 8)
Rex Hotel	16 B2	Blue Gecko Bar	36 B1	Vietnam Airlines	52 B2

VIETNAM

Nearby, **Phuoc An Hoi Quan Pagoda** (Map pp892-3; 184 Đ Hung Vuong; ☼ 7am-5.30pm) stands as one of the most beautifully ornamented constructions in the city. Of special interest are the many small porcelain figures, the elaborate brass ritual objects and the fine woodcarvings on the altars, walls and hanging lanterns. From outside the building you can see the ceramic scenes, each made up of innumerable small figurines, decorating the roof. This pagoda was built in 1902 by the Fujian Chinese congregation.

One of the most active in Cholon, **Thien Hau Pagoda** (Ba Mieu or Pho Mieu; Map pp892-3; 710 Đ Nguyen Trai; ☼ 6am-5.30pm) is dedicated to Thien Hau, the Chinese goddess of the sea. As she protects fisherfolk, sailors, merchants and any other maritime travellers, you might stop by to ask for a blessing for your next boat journey.

GREATER HCMC

Beautiful **Giac Lam Pagoda** (Map pp892-3; 118 Đ Lac Long Quan; ☼ 6am-9pm) dates from 1744 and is believed to be the oldest in the city. The architecture and ornamentation have not changed since 1900, and the compound is a very meditative place to explore. A *xe om* should cost about 15,000d from central HCMC.

In a semirural setting next to Dam Sen Lake, serene **Giac Vien Pagoda** (Map pp892-3; 247 Đ Lac Long Quan; ☼ 7am-7pm) was founded by Hai Tinh Giac Vien about 200 years ago and has some interesting sculptural adornment. Leading up to the pagoda are a few impressive **monks' tombs**.

Jade Emperor Pagoda (Phuoc Hai Tu or Chua Ngoc Hoang; Map pp892-3; 73 Đ Mai Thi Luu; ☼ 7.30am-6pm) is a gem of a Chinese temple, filled with colourful statues of phantasmal divinities and grotesque heroes. Built in 1909 by the Cantonese congregation, it is one of HCMC's most spectacular pagodas. The statues, which represent characters from both the Buddhist and Taoist traditions, are made of reinforced papier-mâché. To get to the pagoda, go to 20 Đ Dien Bien Phu and walk half a block in a north-west direction.

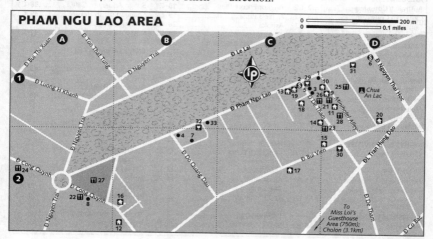

Other Museums

Housed in a beautiful grey neoclassical structure, the **Museum of Ho Chi Minh City** (Bao Tang Thanh Pho Ho Chi Minh; Map p896; ☎ 829 9741; 65 Đ Ly Tu Trong; admission 15,000d; ☑ 8-11.30am & 2-4pm Tue-Sun) was built in 1886 and has displays of artefacts from the various periods of the Communist struggle for power in Vietnam.

The city's **Fine Arts Museum** (Bao Tang My Thuat; Map p894; ☎ 822 2441; 97A Đ Pho Duc Chinh; admission 10,000d; ☑ 9am-4.30pm Mon-Sat) covers art from Vietnam's earliest civilisations, the Oc-Eo and Cham, to contemporary work. The collection represents a good overview of the evolution of Vietnamese aesthetics.

Zoo & Botanical Gardens

Founded by the French in 1864, and a lovely place for a stroll under giant tropical trees is the **Zoo & Botanical Gardens** (Thao Cam Vien; Map p894; ☎ 829 3901; 2 Đ Nguyen Binh Khiem; admission 8000d; ☑ 7am-8pm). Although the animal enclosures are better than the usual standard in Vietnam, we would suggest sticking with the gardens and giving the zoo a miss.

ACTIVITIES
Massage

Most upmarket hotels offer massage service (some more legitimate than others); another option is the **International Club** (Map pp892-3; ☎ 865 7695; 285B Đ Cach Mang Thang Tam; admission 25,000d; ☑ 9am-midnight).

The **Vietnamese Traditional Medicine Institute** (Map p898; ☎ 839 6697; 185 Đ Cong Quynh; per hr 35,000-45,000d, sauna 25,000d; ☑ 9am-9pm) offers no-nonsense, muscle-melting massages performed by blind masseurs.

Swimming

Nonguests can pay an admission fee of US$5 to US$13 per day to use the swimming pools at plush hotels. Local clubs with lower fees:
Caravelle Hotel (Map p896; 823 4999; 19 Lam Son Sq; admission US$13)
International Club (Map pp892-3; ☎ 865 7695; 285B Đ Cach Mang Thang Tam; admission 25,000d; ☑ 9am-midnight) Pool, sauna, steam rooms and gym.
Lam Son Pool (Map pp892-3; ☎ 835 8028; 342 Đ Tran Binh Trong; admission per hr 5000d, after 5pm 6000d; ☑ 8am-8pm) Olympic-sized pool.
Lan Anh Club (Map pp892-3; ☎ 862 7144; 291 Đ Cach Mang Thang Tam; admission 25,000d; ☑ 6am-9pm) There's also a good gym here.
Omni Hotel (Map pp892-3; ☎ 844 9222; 251 Đ Nguyen Van Troi)
Renaissance Riverside (Map p896; ☎ 822 0033; 8-15 Đ Ton Duc Thang)

Water Parks

Saigon Water Park (☎ 897 0456; Đ Kha Van Can; admission 60,000d; ☑ 9am-5pm Mon-Fri, 9am-8pm Sat, 8am-8pm Sun & public holidays) has slides and a wave pool in the suburbia of Thu Duc, north of the centre; shuttle buses (5000d) leave every half-hour from Ben Thanh Market station.

Other water parks:
Dam Sen Water Park (Map pp892-3; ☎ 858 9991; www.damsenwaterpark.com.vn; 3 Đ Hoa Binh; admission 50,000d; ☑ 9am-6pm Mon-Fri, 8am-7pm Sat & Sun)
Sharks Waterland (Map pp892-3; ☎ 853 7867; 600 Đ Ham Tu; admission 20,000-45,000d; ☑ 8am-9pm Mon-Fri, 10am-9pm Sat & Sun) In Cholon.

Yoga

Drop in for hatha yoga classes at **Saigon Yoga** (Map p894; ☎ 910 5181; www.saigonyoga.com; 10F Đ Nguyen Thi Minh Khai; 90min class US$10). Check the website for class times.

VIETNAM

COURSES
Cooking
Vietnamese cooking classes can be arranged by **Expat Services** (☎ 823 5872; vietnamcookery@hcm .vnn.vn).

Language
Teacher Training University (Dai Hoc Su Pham; Map pp892-3; ☎ 835 5100; ciecer@hcm.vnn.vn; 280 Đ An Duong Vuong; private/group class US$4/2.50)
University of Social Sciences & Humanities (Dai Hoc Khoa Hoc Xa Hoi Va Nhan Van; Map p894; ☎ 822 5009; 12 Đ Dinh Tien Hoang; per hr US$2.80) Vietnamese language study in group classes, on a term schedule.

FESTIVALS & EVENTS
Saigon Cyclo Race In mid-March, professional cyclo drivers find out who's fastest; money raised is donated to local charities.
Festival at Lang Ong On the 30th day of the 7th month, people pray for happiness and the health of the country at the Ong Temple in HCMC's Binh Thanh district; plays and musical performances are staged.

SLEEPING
Affordable rooms, cheap eats and cold beer are jam-packed into Saigon's backpacker-land, known as Pham Ngu Lao. Like Bangkok's Th Khao San in miniature, budget travellers will find everything from shoeshines to shoestring tours here.

If you don't really know where you want to stay, turn up in Pham Ngu Lao and proceed on foot. If you don't want to lug your bags around (making you prime prey for touts), drop your gear for a few minutes at one of the travellers cafés. Most won't mind keeping an eye on it for you and they'll be happy to show you the tour programmes they have on offer.

Minihotel Alley is bookended by Đ Bui Vien and Đ Pham Ngu Lao. There are more than a dozen places squeezed into this narrow lane. Most are family-run and the price range hovers around US$6 to US$10 for fan rooms, or about US$12 to US$20 for bigger air-con rooms, some with balconies.

Pham Ngu Lao
The following hotels are all on the Pham Ngu Lao map (p898).

Hong Hoa Hotel (☎ 836 1915; www.honghoavn .com; 185/28 Đ Pham Ngu Lao; r US$13-20; ✖ 🖵) In Minihotel Alley, Hong Hoa has it all: clean rooms, shuttles to and from the airport, free Internet, a convenience store and amiable, helpful staff.

Bi/Bee Saigon (☎ 836 0678; www.bisaigon.com; 185/26 & 185/16 Đ Pham Ngu Lao; r US$10-30; ✖) This pair of cute hotels in Minihotel Alley has amenities like fridges and TVs, and a good restaurant as well.

Nga Hoang (☎ 920 3356; 269/19 Đ Pham Ngu Lao; r incl breakfast US$6-20; ✖) Just off Đ De Tham down a narrow alley, this spotless, family-run guesthouse is a terrific deal. There's satellite TV and the management is friendly.

Hotel 127 (☎ 836 8761; madamecuc@hcm.vnn.vn; 127 Đ Cong Quynh; r US$12-20; ✖) Madam Cuc and her staff consistently give a warm and welcoming reception; her places are clean and outfitted with satellite TV, bathrooms and fridges. Madam Cuc's happy dominion also includes **Hotel 64** (☎ 836 5073; 64 Đ Bui Vien) and **MC Hotel** (☎ 836 1679; 184 Đ Cong Quyen).

Hotel 211 (☎ 836 7353; hotelduy@hotmail.com; 211 Đ Pham Ngu Lao; r incl breakfast US$7-12; ✖) Perking up this large budget establishment are a rooftop terrace and hot water.

Chau Long Minihotel (☎ 836 9667; chaulong minihotel@yahoo.com; 185/8 Đ Pham Ngu Lao; r US$6-10; ✖) Another good choice in Minihotel Alley, the reasonably priced rooms come with hot water, fridge and TV.

Vuong Hoa (☎ 836 9491; thuavu50@hotmail.com; 36 Đ Bui Vien; dm US$3, r US$6-10; ✖) Simple rooms are on offer at this central place run by a very nice couple, who between them can speak English, Japanese and German.

Other recommendations:
Hotel 265 (☎ 836 1883; hotelduy@hotmail.com; 265 Đ De Tham; incl breakfast dm US$3, r US$7-12; ✖) Clean rooms.
Minh Chau Guesthouse (☎ 836 7588; minhchauho@ telhcm.vnn.vn; 75 Đ Bui Vien; 🖵) Offers laundry service, free tea and coffee, and Internet access in the lobby.

SPLURGE!

Rex Hotel (Map p896; ☎ 829 6043; rexhotel@hcm .vnn.vn; 141 ĐL Nguyen Hue; d US$70, ste US$550; ✖) The goofy opulence of the Rex conjures fabulous ambience for crashing in a decadent way. Don't neglect to have a drink on the classic rooftop veranda edged with caged songbirds and animal topiaries. Email ahead to ask about its current promotions; generous discounts are often offered.

Peace Hotel (☎ 837 2025; 272 Đ De Tham; d 105,000-120,000d; ❷) Another good well-established place.

Tan Thanh Thanh Hotel (☎ 837 3595; tanthanh thanh@hcm.fpt.vn; 205 Đ Pham Ngu Lao; dm/s/d incl breakfast US$3/5/10; ❷) It's sometimes possible to trade language lessons for accommodation.

Co Giang

A quieter alternative about 10 minutes on foot from the Pham Ngu Lao area is a string of fine guesthouses on an alley connecting Đ Co Giang and Đ Co Bac. To reach the guesthouses, walk southeast on Đ Co Bac and turn left after you pass the *nuoc mam* (fish sauce) shops. The following entries are on the Central Ho Chi Minh City map (p894).

Miss Loi's Guesthouse (☎ 837 9589; 178/20 Đ Co Giang; r incl breakfast US$6-20; ❷) The first guesthouse in the neighbourhood is probably still the best. Lovely Miss Loi cultivates a family atmosphere with her warm staff and homely set-up.

Guest House California (☎ 837 8885; guesthouse -california-saigon@yahoo.com; 171A Đ Co Bac; r US$12-16; ❷) This may be the only guesthouse in Saigon with a kitchen where you can cook your own meals. It's low-key, neat and clean and also rents out reliable bicycles and motorbikes.

Ngoc Son (☎ 836 4717; ngocsonguesthouse@yahoo .com; 178/32 Đ Co Giang; r US$6-9; ❷) Run by a gentle family, the quiet Ngoc Son has rooms with cable TV and fridge. It, too, has wheels for hire for your city excursions.

EATING

Dining on the cheap in Saigon is more a challenge of the what, rather than the where. Noodle soup is available all day long at street stalls and hole-in-the-wall shops everywhere. A large bowl of beef noodles costs 5000d to 10,000d. Just look for the signs with the words *pho* or *hu tieu*. Don't eat meat? Look for the magic word *chay* (vegetarian) tacked on the end.

Banh mi (sandwiches) with a French look and a very Vietnamese taste are sold by street vendors. Fresh baguettes are stuffed with something resembling pâté (don't ask) or soft French cheese and cucumbers seasoned with soy sauce, and cost 5000d to 10,000d.

Markets always have a vast dining area, often on the ground floor or in the basement. Clusters of food stalls can be found in Ben Thanh (Map p894) and Thai Binh (Map p898) Markets.

Đ Pham Ngu Lao and Đ De Tham form the axis of Saigon's budget eatery haven, where travellers cafés dish out backpacker cuisine and book tours on the side.

Self-Catering

Simple, dirt-cheap meals can be cobbled together from street stalls and markets with fresh fruits and vegetables, baguettes baked daily and soft French cheese.

You'll find Western-style junk food along Đ De Tham in Pham Ngu Lao, or at **Hanoi Mart** and **Co-op Mart** (Map p898; Đ Cong Quynh; ❧ 8am-8pm), just down the street from each other, west of the traffic circle near Thai Binh Market.

Vietnamese

Hardcore budget travellers could subsist exclusively on 5000d bowls of *pho*, but spending less frugally will have you feasting on a wider variety of Vietnamese deliciousness.

Huong Lai (Map p896; ☎ 822 6814; jins@hcm.fpt.vn; 38 Đ Ly Tu Trong; set dinner US$5-7; ❧ lunch & dinner) In an airy loft, the owner serves up beautifully presented Vietnamese dishes, while the staff – formerly disadvantaged youth – receive valuable job training. Flavoursome food, perfect service and the sunlit wood-floored room add up to a wholly satisfying experience. Supporting such a worthy cause is the icing on the cake.

Quan An Ngon (Map p896; ☎ 829 9449; 138 Đ Nam Ky Khoi Nghia; mains 10,000-60,000d; ❧ lunch & dinner) Two people can sample a spread of regional Vietnamese treats for US$5 to US$6. Poke around the outside edge first, where cooks at individual stations make their specialities, and see if anything flirts with your appetite.

Banh Xeo Dinh Cong Trang (Map p894; ☎ 824 1110; 46A Đ Dinh Cong Trang; mains 17,000d; ❧ lunch & dinner) Famous city-wide for its *banh xeo*, a crispy Vietnamese rice crêpe filled with bean sprouts, prawns and pork. A haystack of greens is served alongside; break up the *banh xeo*, wrap it in a lettuce leaf with herbs, and dip into fish sauce.

Bo Tung Xeo Restaurant (Map p896; ☎ 825 1330; 31 Đ Ly Tu Trong; mains 30,000d; ❧ lunch & dinner) The house speciality is Vietnamese barbecue: tender marinated beef, which you grill over a charcoal brazier at your table.

Other places to try:

ABC Restaurant (Map p894; ☎ 823 0388; 172H Đ Nguyen Dinh Chieu; soups 8000d; ✉ breakfast, lunch & dinner) Join seriously chic Saigonese for late-night *pho* until 4am.

Restaurant 13 (Map p896; Đ Ngo Duc Ke; ✉ lunch & dinner) Next door to Restaurant 19, highly popular with locals and expats.

Restaurant 19 (Map p896; ☎ 829 8882; 19 Đ Ngo Duc Ke; ✉ lunch & dinner) Tasty variations on Hanoi's *cha ca* (braised fish).

International

Augustin (Map p896; ☎ 829 2941; 10 Đ Nguyen Thiep; mains 50,000d; ✉ breakfast, lunch & dinner) Many consider this Saigon's best cheap French restaurant, serving great bistro-style food.

Cafe Mogambo (Map p896; ☎ 825 1311; 20 Đ Thi Sach; mains 35,000d; ✉ lunch & dinner) Polynesian décor, juicy burgers, tacos and even goulash – this is a restaurant, pub and minihotel.

Cafe Latin (Map p896; ☎ 822 6363; 19-21 Đ Dong Du; mains 60,000-150,000d; ✉ lunch & dinner) Vietnam's first tapas bar, with freshly baked bread, a respectable wine list and several appealing vegetarian options.

Cafe Havana (Map p894; ☎ 827 9682; 25B Đ Tran Cao Van; mains around 30,000d; ✉ lunch & dinner) Cuban cocktails, wood-fired pizza and a breezy outdoor terrace beckon the weary visitor – and there's a chance to catch live music here.

Other restaurants to try:

Annie's Pizza (Map p896; ☎ 823 9044; 45 Đ Mac Thi Buoi; pizzas around 55,000d; ✉ lunch & dinner) Long-running popular pizza joint that delivers.

SPLURGE!

A gourmet Vietnamese dinner will cost you about US$10 at these swank places:

Mandarine (Map p896; ☎ 822 9783; 11A Đ Ngo Van Nam; ✉ lunch & dinner) Traditional dishes drawing from southern, central and northern Vietnamese cooking styles, and live traditional music performances in a plush atmosphere.

Hoi An (Map p896; ☎ 823 7694; hoian.hcm@hcm.fpt.vn; 11 Đ Le Thanh Ton; ✉ dinner) A lovely Chinese-style place with an antique motif. Central Vietnamese and imperial Hué-style dishes are the house specialities.

Lemongrass (Map p896; ☎ 822 0496; 4 Đ Nguyen Thiep; ✉ lunch & dinner) This is classical, flavourful Vietnamese cuisine served with low-lit ambience.

Good Morning Vietnam (Map p898; ☎ 837 1894; 197 Đ De Tham; mains around 50,000d; ✉ breakfast, lunch & dinner) Authentic northern Italian pasta and pizza.

L'en Tête (Map p894; ☎ 821 4049; 139 Đ Nguyen Thai Binh; dishes around 100,000d; ✉ lunch & dinner) A new contender with knockout artwork and pricey French food, this is a great place for a drink off the tourist track.

Other Asian

Angkor Encore Plus (Map p896; ☎ 829 8814; 28 Đ Ngo Van Nam; mains around 45,000d; ✉ lunch & dinner) Wonderful Khmer cuisine, now cooking in a new central, yet out-of-the-way, little haven of pretty décor and authentic flavours.

Chao Thai (Map p896; ☎ 824 1457; 16 Đ Thai Van Lung; mains around 45,000d; ✉ lunch & dinner) Lunch sets are good value, with some of Saigon's best Thai food.

Ashoka (Map p896; ☎ 823 1372; 17A/10 Đ Le Thanh Ton; lunch buffet 75,000d; ✉ lunch & dinner) The halal lunch buffet is a great deal at this excellent Indian place.

Asian Kitchen (Map p898; ☎ 836 7397; 185/22 Đ Pham Ngu Lao; mains 18,000d; ✉ lunch & dinner) Budget Indian, Japanese and vegetarian, in Minihotel Alley.

Indian canteen (Map p896; 66 Đ Dong Du; dishes 7000d; ✉ lunch & dinner) For really cheap Indian food, you have to seek out a local favourite: the canteen behind the Saigon Mosque.

Akatombo (Map p896; ☎ 824 4928; 36-38 Đ Hai Ba Trung; meals 50,000d; ✉ lunch & dinner) Delicious ramen, sashimi and traditional Japanese food at affordable prices.

Vegetarian

For the best bowl of vegetarian *pho* in Saigon, stop by the corner of Đ Ba Huyen Thanh Quan and the narrow alley southeast of Xa Loi pagoda (Map p894). Several vegetarian shopfronts cluster around the alley; look for the hand-painted sign that says *pho chay*.

Tin Nghia (Map p894; ☎ 821 2538; 9 ĐL Tran Hung Dao; mains 8000d; ✉ lunch & dinner) It doesn't look like much from the outside, but the kitchen turns out delicious traditional Vietnamese vegetarian fare.

Dinh Y (Map p898; ☎ 836 7715; 171B Đ Cong Quynh; mains 7000d; ✉ breakfast, lunch & dinner) Run by a friendly Cao Dai family, Dinh Y serves wonderful, inexpensive vegetarian dishes – from noodle soups to savoury claypot mushrooms.

Zen (Map p898; ☎ 837 3713; 185/30 Đ Pham Ngu Lao; mains 12,000đ; ⏰ breakfast, lunch & dinner) Good cheap veggie food in a mellow family atmosphere in Minihotel Alley.

Original Bodhi Tree (Map p898; ☎ 837 1910; 175/4 Đ Pham Ngu Lao; mains 12,000đ; ⏰ breakfast, lunch & dinner) Make a beeline for the Original in the alley east of Minihotel Alley. The food is excellent and very cheap.

Giac Duc (Map pp892–3; ☎ 835 6161; 492 Đ Nguyen Dinh Chieu; ⏰ lunch & dinner) Dine with the monks on Taiwanese mock meat prepared a hundred different ways.

Cafés

These cafés are all on the Dong Khoi map (p896).

Java Coffee Bar (☎ 823 0187; 38-42 Đ Dong Du; smoothies 35,000đ) Espresso bar, roasted veggie sandwiches, even smoothies made with silken tofu. This place is chic and relaxed, with the comfiest chairs ever.

Juice Bar (☎ 829 6900; 49 Đ Mac Thi Buoi) The plain name belies its fabulousness. This refreshing oasis features freshly squeezed fruit juices, including wheatgrass. For the less virtuous, it's also a cool spot for cocktails.

Fanny (☎ 821 1633; 29-31 Đ Ton That Thiep; ice cream 6000-15,000đ) Luscious Franco-Vietnamese ice cream in local and classic flavours, in a stylish restored French villa.

Kem Bach Dang (☎ 829 2707; 26 & 28 ĐL Le Loi; ice cream 15,000đ) A remodelled, air-conditioned branch faces its open-air, streetside sibling across Đ Pasteur. Watch the ebb and flow of traffic at this busy corner over *kem trai dua* (ice cream in a young coconut).

Chi Lang Cafe (☎ 824 2489; cnr Đ Dong Khoi & Đ Le Thanh Ton; coffee 6000đ) Parklike and central, this long-running outdoor café is a pleasant spot to put your feet up with a lemon soda on a hot afternoon.

DRINKING

Saigon's nightlife depends on government whims – some seasons, everything shuts down by midnight. Other times, you can party down till dawn.

Pham Ngu Lao Area   Map p898

Lost in Saigon (169 Đ Pham Ngu Lao; ⏰ from 5pm) The walls of this longtime backpacker hang-out are covered in mural art, and the draw of good drinks, pool and excellent burgers means the place is always humming.

Sahara Bar (☎ 837 8084; 277 Đ Pham Ngu Lao; ⏰ 9am-late) One of the more stylish places along Pham Ngu Lao, the Sahara Bar is a good place to shoot some pool and grab a bite to eat.

Go$_2$ Bar (☎ 836 9575; 187 Đ De Tham; ⏰ 8am-late) You can't miss the retro colour scheme screaming from the corner of Đ Bui Vien and Đ De Tham. Drinks are reasonably priced and the location is bang in the centre of backpackerland.

Allez Boo Bar (☎ 837 2505; 187 Đ Pham Ngu Lao; ⏰ noon-late) Watch the backpackers trundle by from this busy bamboo-walled corner.

Guns & Roses Bar (207 Đ Pham Ngu Lao) Dark, divey and decibel-icious, this closet packs them in till late. There's a pool table in back there somewhere.

Dong Khoi Area   Map p896

Blue Gecko Bar (☎ 824 3483; 31 Đ Ly Tu Trong; ⏰ 5pm-late) Shoot some pool, watch sports on TV or just enjoy the fun crowd, often composed largely of Aussies.

Underground (☎ 829 9079; 69 Đ Dong Khoi) Spacious and hopping, and as the name implies, UK-inspired. It's even located underground, in the basement of the Lucky Plaza building. Great happy hour.

Sango Aquarium Cafe (☎ 829 3189; 21 Đ Thai Van Lung; ⏰ 10am-midnight) Drink like a fish at Sango, where you can commune with marine critters up close – as in, they lie underneath your drink on the aquarium countertops. (Be nice and take your grilled fish upstairs.)

Sheridan's Irish House (☎ 823 0973; 17/13 Đ Thanh Ton; ⏰ 11am-midnight) A traditional Irish pub that's been beamed straight from the backstreets of Dublin, Sheridan's showcases live music some nights and good times every night.

Vasco's Bar (☎ 824 3148; 16 Đ Cao Ba Quat; ⏰ 10am-late) The expat crowd converges here on weekend nights; drinks don't come cheap but it's undeniably hip.

Saigon Saigon Bar (☎ 823 4999; 19 Lam Son Sq; ⏰ 2pm-midnight) Posh cocktails served with a classic Saigon view are here, on the 10th floor of the Caravelle Hotel. Happy hour is from 4pm to 8pm.

Q Bar (☎ 823 3479; 7 Lam Son Sq; ⏰ 6pm-midnight) For a more subterranean experience, there's *über*-chic Q Bar right across the way from Saigon Saigon Bar.

VIETNAM

CLUBBING

Ask around locally for the latest, besides the following established joints (on the Dong Khoi map, p896).

Apocalypse Now (☎ 824 1463; 2C Đ Thi Sach) For a study in the seamier side of international relations, Apocalypse Now is a late-night stand-by for dancing the night away.

Tropical Rainforest Disco (Mua Rung; ☎ 825 7783; 5-15 Đ Ho Huan Nghiep; cover US$4) One of the hottest dance spots in the city centre for the younger crowd. The cover charge entitles you to one free drink.

Vasco's Bar (☎ 824 3148; 16 Đ Cao Ba Quat; ☺ 10am-late) Vasco's (see p903) hosts live music on Thursday, Friday and Saturday.

ENTERTAINMENT

There are water-puppetry performances at the **History Museum** (Map p894; ☎ 829 8146; Đ Nguyen Binh Khiem; admission 10,000d; ☺ 8-11.30am & 1-4pm Tue-Sun). Schedules vary, but shows tend to start when about five or more people show up. Also check out the schedule of performances at the **War Remnants Museum** (Map p894; ☎ 930 5587; 28 Đ Vo Van Tan; admission 10,000d; ☺ 7.30-11.45am & 1.30-5.15pm Tue-Sun).

Theatre, live music and films around the Dong Khoi area (Map p896):

Diamond Plaza Cinema (☎ 825 7751; 34 Đ Le Duan) Sometimes screens films in English; call ahead for details.

Idecaf (Institute of Cultural Exchange with France; ☎ 822 4577; 31 Đ Thai Van Lung; ☺ 8pm Tue) Weekly screenings of French films.

Municipal Theatre (Nha Hat Thanh Pho; ☎ 829 9976; Lam Son Sq) Plays and musical performances.

SHOPPING

Among the tempting wares to be found in Saigon are embroidered-silk shoes, knock-off Zippo lighters engraved with fake soldier poetry and toy helicopters made from Tiger beer cans. Boutiques along Đ Le Thanh Ton and Đ Pasteur sell hand-made ready-to-wear fashion cheaper than you'll find in Hanoi. In Pham Ngu Lao, shops sell ethnic-minority fabrics, handicrafts, T-shirts and various appealing accessories.

Ben Thanh Market (Cho Ben Thanh; Map p894) This is the best place to start. Part of the market is devoted to normal everyday items like bitter melon and laundry detergent, but the lucrative tourist trade also has healthy representation. This means you need to be alert to sticky fingers.

Đ Dong Khoi (Map p896) This is one big arts-and-crafts tourist bazaar, but prices can get outrageous – negotiate if no prices are posted.

Russian Market (Tax Department Store; Map p896; cnr Đ Le Loi & Đ Nguyen Hue) No longer the dowdy but charming cavern of vendors and bargains it was before its face-lift, there are still a few deals in there. Worth a look for clothes in Western sizes without the boutique mark-ups.

GETTING THERE & AWAY

Air

All Nippon Airways (Map p896; ☎ 822 4141; www .ana.co.jp/eng; 114A Đ Nguyen Hue)

Cathay Pacific Airways (Map p896; ☎ 822 3203; www.cathaypacific.com; 58 Đ Dong Khoi)

Japan Airlines (Map p896; ☎ 821 9098; www.jal .com/en; 115 Đ Nguyen Hue, 17th fl)

Malaysia Airlines (Map p896; ☎ 824 4223; www .malaysiaairlines.com; 235 Đ Dong Khoi)

Pacific Airlines (Map p896; ☎ 823 1285; www .pacificairlines.com.vn; 2 Đ Dong Khoi)

Philippine Airlines (Map p896; ☎ 827 2105; www .philippineairlines.com; 229 Đ Dong Khoi)

Singapore Airlines (Map p894; ☎ 823 1588; www .singaporeair.com; 29 ĐL Le Duan, Ste 101)

Thai Airways International (THAI; Map p896; ☎ 822 3365; www.thaiair.com; 65 Đ Nguyen Du)

Vietnam Airlines (Map p896; ☎ 832 0320; www .vietnamairlines.com; 116 ĐL Nguyen Hue)

Boat

Cargo ferries serving the Mekong Delta depart from the **Bach Dang jetty** (Map p894; Đ Ton Duc Thang). Costs for these ferries are negotiable; after asking how long it will take to your desired destination, ask yourself how much you're willing to pay for such a trip. Also departing from here are hydrofoils to Vung Tau (US$10, one hour 20 minutes, nine daily).

GAY & LESBIAN HCMC

Though outright 'out' venues don't exist, Saigon's popular bars and clubs are generally gay-friendly and have mixed scenes.

Lost in Saigon (Map p898; 169 Đ Pham Ngu Lao; ☺ from 5pm) is a good place to start. Check out **Apocalypse Now** (Map p896; ☎ 824 1463; 2C Đ Thi Sach) if you're into clubbing.

Bus

Intercity buses depart from and arrive at several stations around HCMC. Local buses (around 3000d) to the intercity bus stations leave from the station opposite Ben Thanh Market (Map p894). There are four useful bus stations around the city:

Cholon bus station (Ben Xe Cho Lon; Map pp892-3; Đ Le Quang Trung) Convenient buses to Mytho and other Mekong Delta towns; one street north of Binh Tay Market.

Mien Dong bus station (Ben Xe Mien Dong; Map pp892-3; ☎ 829 4056) Buses to places north of HCMC; in Binh Thanh district, about 5km from central Saigon on National Hwy 13.

Mien Tay bus station (Ben Xe Mien Tay; ☎ 825 5955) Even more buses to points south of HCMC, but located about 10km southwest of Saigon in An Lac.

Tay Ninh bus station (Ben Xe Tay Ninh; Map pp892-3; ☎ 849 5935) Buses to Tay Ninh, Cu Chi and points northeast of HCMC, located in Tan Binh district.

Car & Motorcycle

Travellers cafés can arrange car rentals (US$35 per day with driver); Pham Ngu Lao generally offers the lowest prices. This is also the neighbourhood to look for motorbike rentals (US$4 to US$7 per day).

Train

Saigon Railways Tourist Services (Map p898; ☎ 836 7640; 275C Đ Pham Ngu Lao) A convenient place to purchase tickets.

Saigon train station (Ga Sai Gon; Map pp892-3; ☎ 824 5585; 1 Đ Nguyen Thong; ⏰ 7.15-11am & 1-3pm)

GETTING AROUND
Bicycle

Bicycles are available for hire from many budget hotels and cafés, especially around Pham Ngu Lao.

Car & Motorcycle

If you're brave (or kind of stupid), it's a thrill a minute driving here. Motorbikes are available for hire around Pham Ngu Lao for US$4 to US$7 per day. Make sure to give it a test drive before plunking down your cash; you'll usually be asked to leave your passport or yellow customs slip as collateral.

Hiring cars is also possible, although it's only economical if you split the cost between several people. Ask about rentals at travellers cafés.

Cyclo

Cyclos are the most interesting way of getting around town, but avoid them at night and always agree on fares beforehand.

Taxi

Hail taxis on the street. If you don't find one straight away, ring up and one will be dispatched in less time than it takes to say 'Ho Chi Minh'. Companies include the following:

Ben Thanh Taxi (☎ 842 2422)
Mai Linh Taxi (☎ 822 2666)
Red Taxi (☎ 844 6677)
Saigon Taxi (☎ 842 4242)
Vina Taxi (☎ 811 1111)

AROUND HO CHI MINH CITY

CU CHI TUNNELS

The **tunnel network** (admission 65,000d) at Cu Chi became legendary during the 1960s for its role in facilitating Viet Cong control of a large rural area only 30km from Saigon. At its height, the tunnel system stretched from Saigon to the Cambodian border. In the district of Cu Chi alone, there were more than 200km of tunnels. After ground operations targeting the tunnels claimed large numbers of casualties and proved ineffective, the Americans turned their artillery and bombers on the area, transforming it into a moonscape.

Parts of this remarkable tunnel network have been reconstructed and two sites are open to visitors; one near the village of Ben Dinh and the other at Ben Duoc. During guided tours of the tunnel complex, it's possible to actually descend into tunnel entrances as well as into the tunnels themselves. Although some sections have been widened, others remain in their original condition. If you can fit into the narrow passageways, you'll gain an empathetic, if claustrophobic, awe for the people who spent weeks underground.

Day tours operated by travellers cafés charge around US$4 per person (transport only); most include a stop at the Caodai Great Temple in Tay Ninh. Public buses going to Tay Ninh can drop you in Cu Chi; however, since the tunnel complex is about

15km outside town, you'll have to hire a motorbike to get to the tunnels.

TAY NINH

☎ 066 / pop 41,300

Tay Ninh town, capital of Tay Ninh Province, serves as the headquarters of one of Vietnam's most interesting indigenous religions, Caodaism (see p827). The **Caodai Great Temple** was built between 1933 and 1955. Victor Hugo is among the Westerners especially revered by the Caodai; look for his likeness at the Great Temple.

Tay Ninh is 96km northwest of HCMC. The Caodai Holy See complex is 4km east of Tay Ninh. One-day tours from Saigon, including Tay Ninh and the Cu Chi Tunnels, cost around US$4. Public buses to Tay Ninh leave from the Mien Tay station in HCMC.

VUNG TAU

☎ 064 / pop 161,300

A quick getaway from HCMC, Vung Tau drones with bass-thumping action on the weekends as Saigonese visitors motor into town. Weekdays, however, are blissfully dead, with kilometres of empty beaches. The business of oil-drilling here means the azure horizon is marred by oil tankers, and the population flecked with expats. It's a commercialised beach resort, but it's easy enough to escape the seedy karaoke scene.

Information

International SOS (☎ 858 776; Đ Le Ngoc Han; 24hr) Initial medical consultations cost US$55 to US$65.

Le Loi Hospital (☎ 832 667; 22 Đ Le Loi)

OSC Vietnam (☎ 852 008; osc-tours@hcm.vnn.vn; 9 Đ Le Loi) Offers tour bookings and tourist maps of Vung Tau.

Post office (☎ 851376; 80 Đ Ba Cu)

Vietcombank (☎ 852 024; 27-29 Đ Tran Hung Dao; 7.30-11am & 1.30-4pm Mon-Fri)

Sights & Activities

Atop Small Mountain (Nui Nho), a **giant Jesus** (admission free, parking 2000d; 7.30-11.30am & 1.30-5pm) waits with arms outstretched to embrace the South China Sea – showing off the swallows' nests in his armpits. At his foot is a sad collection of monkeys and snakes in small cages.

The nearby **lighthouse** (admission 2000d; 7am-5pm) boasts a spectacular 360-degree view sans imprisoned animals. From the ferry

dock on Đ Ha Long, take a sharp right on the alley north of the Hai Au Hotel, then roll on up the hill.

Pagodas dot the length of Đ Ha Long, but prim **Hon Ba Pagoda** sits offshore on an islet accessible only at low tide.

Along the downtown waterfront, you'll find café-bars on the hillside facing the ocean. On weekends, you stand the best chance of hearing local amateurs belting out the ballads *du jour*, backed by live bands. It's like karaoke, only…good.

Sleeping

There's a guesthouse strip at Back Beach.

Thien Nhien (☎ 853 481; 145A Đ Thuy Van; d 100,000-200,000d;) This airy, friendly guesthouse is very clean; some rooms have balconies, aircon and ocean views.

Song Bien (☎ 523 311; 131A Đ Thuy Van; d 120,000-150,000d;) Chinese-style décor brightens this very clean and comfortable place; some rooms have big ocean views.

My Tho Guesthouse (☎ 832 035; 47 Đ Tran Phu; s/d 90,000/120,000d) With simple rooms, this is the sweetest little guesthouse on the peninsula, about 2km north of central Vung Tau in a quiet area called Mulberry Beach (Bai Dau). The warm couple running the guesthouse serve delicious, cheap home-cooked meals on the cosy terrace, and offer free laundry services, cycle hire and friendly conversation. From the centre, take Đ Quang Trung going north, which turns into Đ Tran Phu.

Eating & Drinking

BACK BEACH

The road along Back Beach, Đ Thuy Van, is crammed with *com* shops and seafood restaurants.

Quan Com Dai Duong (☎ 816 108; 27 Đ Thuy Van; mains 15,000d; lunch & dinner) A small family-run place serving seafood at reasonable prices.

Dai Loc (☎ 858 124; 170 Đ Hoang Hoa Tham; mains 15,000d; lunch & dinner) Serves both Vietnamese and Western food in a friendly atmosphere.

MULBERRY BEACH

Mulberry Beach's main road has several good seafood places down on the water.

Cafe 11 (11 Đ Tran Phu; lunch & dinner) Has low thatch huts shading two-lover canvas chairs for intimate chats. Cheap *com* (5000d) is served on the terrace above; below, behold barnacled rocks and basket boats.

Quan Tre Bamboo (7 Đ Tran Phu; mains 40,000d; ☺ lunch & dinner) Head here if you're hankering for lobster or a cocktail with a view of the giant Mary with baby Jesus statue, best enjoyed from the upstairs terrace.

BB Bar/Whispers Restaurant (☎ 856 028; 13-15 Nguyen Trai; ☺ until midnight) Local expats start their evening here for the well-prepared Western food and pool tables in a noisy, lively setting.

Getting There & Away

From Mien Dong bus station in HCMC, aircon minibuses (25,000d, two hours, 128km) leave for Vung Tau throughout the day until around 4.30pm.

Should convenience outweigh cost in your mind, catch a **Vina Express hydrofoil** (HCMC ☎ 829 7892, Vung Tau ☎ 856 530) to Vung Tau (US$10, 80 minutes) at Bach Dang jetty in HCMC. Boats leave every two hours starting at 6.30am, but check in HCMC for the latest schedule. In Vung Tau, the boat leaves from Cau Da pier, across from the Hai Au Hotel.

From the **Vung Tau bus station** (192A Đ Nam Ky Khoi Nghia) to Mulberry Beach or Back Beach, a *xe om* should cost around 10,000d.

Getting Around

Vung Tau is easily traversed on two wheels. Guesthouses can arrange bicycle hire; motorbikes cost US$4 to US$7 per day. Or, just make eye contact with that cyclo or *xe om* driver on the corner.

LONG HAI

☎ 064

The fishing village of Long Hai has little to offer besides its rustic beach – which might be all you need. If you require nightlife (or, well, daylife), head to Mui Ne (p883) instead.

Outside Long Hai are a few interesting sights, although you'll likely need to hire a guide from Vung Tau to find them. **Chua Phap Hoa**, a peaceful pagoda set in a forest with lots of wild monkeys, has some good trails nearby for short treks.

At Minh Dam, which is 5km from Long Hai, there are **caves** with historical connections to the Franco–Viet Minh and American Wars. Nearby there's a **mountaintop temple** with great panoramic views of the coastline.

You could also indulge for a day at **Anoasis Beach Resort** (☎ 868 227; www.anoasisresort.com.vn; day passes Mon-Fri US$6, Sat & Sun US$10; ☒). The grounds of this luxury resort were once home to another of Emperor Bao Dai's villas. Day passes entitle nonguests to full use of the recreational facilities, which include swimming pool, tennis courts, billiards, ping-pong and a lovely stretch of private beach.

Sleeping & Eating

Palace Hotel (☎ 868 364; d 140,000d) Flanked by frangipani trees, the Palace (on the corner of Rte 19 and the road past Thuy Lan) has a decaying grandeur that is spookily appealing. Enormous rooms are fan-only and a bit musty but worth a look, with wide windows looking down the palatial terraced stairs.

Huong Bien Hotel (☎ 868 430; bungalows 120,000-180,000d; ☒) Down a signposted dirt driveway off Rte 19, Huong Bien has simple concrete bungalows among palms and casuarinas. Most have private bathroom and fan, some have air-con, and all nestle right on the beach.

Guesthouse 298 (☎ 868 316; d 100,000-180,000d; ☒) Rooms are clean and comfortable, with hot water; the cheapest rooms are fan-only. It's at the dead-end of Rte 19.

There's a cluster of good beachside restaurants called Can Tin 1, 2 and 3 near Guesthouse 298. Across from the Palace Hotel, **Thuy Lan** (meals 12,000d; ☺ lunch & dinner) is also good (and clean), as is the seaside **Vinh Quang** (meals 12,000d; ☺ lunch & dinner), near the Huong Bien Hotel.

Getting There & Around

Long Hai is 124km from HCMC, about a two-hour journey by car. There are some Long Hai–HCMC buses (30,000d, three hours) from Mien Dong station, though not many. Backpacker cafés in HCMC can also organise trips here.

The 30km road between Vung Tau and Long Hai is not served by any public transport; a *xe om* ride should cost around 45,000d.

Roam around on foot, or find *xe om* around the guesthouse area.

MEKONG DELTA

The Mekong Delta vibrates with colour – bright-green rice shoots, yellow and electric-pink incense sticks drying along roadsides. So, too, the rhythm of life along Mekong byways buzzes with slow but constant energy. A trip into the nation's rice basket is a glimpse into the life of Vietnam's agricultural workforce, which feeds the nation on this life-sustaining river.

After winding its way from its source in Tibet, the Mekong River meets the sea in southernmost Vietnam. This delta-plain is lush with rice paddies and fish farms. Once part of the Khmer kingdom, the Mekong Delta was the last part of modern-day Vietnam to be annexed and settled by the Vietnamese.

By far the easiest and cheapest way to see the Delta is by taking a cheap tour (one to three days) with a backpacker café in Ho Chi Minh City. It's also possible to travel independently – though more expensive, sometimes confusing and time-consuming, this option gives you maximum flexibility.

MYTHO

☎ 074 / pop 169, 300

Gateway to the Delta, Mytho is an easy day trip from Saigon. But if this is only the first stop on your Delta exploration, press on a little further to Ben Tre, where boat tours are cheaper and the town has a less-trafficked charm.

In Mytho, river-boat tours can be booked at the main riverfront office of **Tien Giang Tourist** (Cong Ty Du Lich Tien Giang; ☎ 873 184; 8 Đ 30 Thang 4; ⏰ 7am-5pm). Boat tours cruise past pleasant rural villages and are the highlight of a visit to Mytho. Depending on what you book, destinations usually include a coconut-candy workshop, a honey-bee farm and an orchid garden. Also of interest are several islands in the area.

Hiring a boat with a big group makes these local-government tours economical; on your own, they're expensive at US$25 for two to three hours. Significantly cheaper independent guides may approach you on the riverfront near **Cuu Long Restaurant** (☎ 870 779; Đ 30 Thang 4; mains 25,000d). Keep in mind that these guys operate illegally and, though enforcement is erratic and unlikely, there's a

small risk that you or they may be fined by zealous river cops.

Sleeping

Rang Dong Hotel (☎ 874 400; 25 Đ 30 Thang 4; s/d US$8/12; ✕) The big rooms here are one of the better deals in town. Rang Dong is centrally located along the waterfront, with its sidewalk cafés and *xe om* galore.

Song Tien Hotel (☎ 872 009; 101 Đ Trung Trac; r US$7-16; ✕) The Song Tien has clean, comfortable rooms with TV, fridge and shared balconies overlooking both town and channel.

Trade Union Hotel (Khach San Cong Doan; ☎ 874 324; congdoantourist@hcm.vnn.vn; 61 Đ 30 Thang 4; r US$7-12; ✕) With a central location near the boat landing, this big busy place has river views from some of the rooms. Air-con rooms come with a fridge.

Eating

Chi Thanh (☎ 878 428; 19 Đ Ap Bac; mains 20,000d; ⏰ lunch & dinner) A tidy spot for good Chinese and Vietnamese dishes, Chi Thanh has menus in English.

Hu Tieu 44 (44 Đ Nam Ky Khoi Nghia; soups 6000d; ⏰ 5am-noon) Try Mytho's speciality, *hu tieu my tho*, a rice-noodle soup full of fresh vegetables, pork, chicken and dried seafood in a rich broth.

Hu Tieu Chay 24 (24 Đ Nam Ky Khoi Nghia; soups 3000d; ⏰ 6-9am) Happily, there's a delicious vegetarian version, too. Most Vietnamese people have *hu tieu* for breakfast, so eat early.

Getting There & Around

Buses leaving from the Cholon bus station in HCMC drop you right in Mytho (10,000d, two hours). Buses to other Mekong destinations depart from Mytho bus station (Ben Xe Khach Tien Giang), several kilometres west of town. From the city centre, take Đ Ap Bac westward and continue on to National Hwy 1.

Slooow cargo ferries depart from HCMC's Bach Dang jetty. Bring your own food and water and negotiate a price with the ferry captain if he agrees to take you. A ride to Mytho might cost you around 20,000d.

To get to Ben Tre, head west for 1km on Đ 30 Thang 4 – which turns into Đ Le Thi Hong Gam – to the Ben Tre ferry terminal. The ferry charges 1000d for passengers and 6000d for motorbikes.

Mytho is small and walkable; expeditions out of town can be arranged on boat or *xe om*.

BEN TRE

☎ 075

Famous for its *keo dua* (coconut candy), Ben Tre is a bucolic 20-minute ferry ride from Mytho. Located away from the main highway, it receives far fewer visitors than Mytho and makes a lovely stop on a Mekong tour.

HCMC-bound minibuses leave daily from the petrol station on Đ Dong Khoi, but they don't run on a fixed schedule. Ask at a local hotel for the latest word.

A few hotels and family-run restaurants face the tiny Truc Giang Lake.

Thao Nhi Guesthouse (☎ 860 009; Hamlet 1, Tan Thach Village; d US$10; ✕) Small and intimate Thao Nhi is outside of town in an orchard setting. The in-house restaurant dishes up an excellent elephant-ear fish served with rice paper and fresh greens.

Dong Khoi Hotel (☎ 822 501; 16 Đ Hai Ba Trung; r US$10-35; ✕) Prices here veer towards the midrange, but you pay for spotless rooms with bathrooms. It's popular for wedding parties, as it has the most upmarket restaurant in town.

Phuong Hoang Hotel (☎ 821 385; 28 Đ Hai Ba Trung; r US$10; ✕) More central to town is the lakeside Phuong Hoang, a 10-room mini-hotel that's decent value.

Your best bet for cheap eats is at the market near the waterfront, where you'll find a myriad of food stalls.

CANTHO

☎ 071 / pop 330,100

Home of the Ho Chi Minh Tin Man statue, Cantho is a major Mekong hub and a prime base for exploring some **floating markets**.

Cai Rang is the biggest floating market in the Mekong Delta, 6km from Cantho towards Soc Trang. Though the lively market goes on until around noon daily, show up before 9am for the best photo opportunities. You can hire boats on the river near the Cantho market. Cai Rang is one hour away by boat, or you can drive to Cau Dau Sau boat landing, where you can get a rowed **boat** (per hr around 50,000d) to the market, 10 minutes away.

Less crowded and less motorised is the **Phong Dien** market, with more stand-up

rowboats. It's best between 6am and 8am. Twenty kilometres southwest of Cantho, it's easy to reach by road and you can hire a boat on arrival.

Tours of the markets and canals in the area can be arranged by the friendly staff at **Cantho Tourist** (☎ 821 852; 20 Đ Hai Ba Trung).

Sleeping & Eating

Hien Guesthouse (☎ 812 718; hien_gh@yahoo.com; 118/10 Đ Phan Dinh Phung; r US$4-10; ✕) A bona fide travellers' place, Hien is family-run and warm. It's tucked down a narrow and quiet alley a few minutes' walk from the city centre. Rooms are basic but immaculate, and the owner is an excellent source of local travel information. Dependable motorbikes can be hired here.

Huy Hoang (☎ 825 833; 35 Đ Ngo Duc Ke; r 80,000-150,000d; ✕) Another popular spot for the backpacker crowd, the Huy Hoang is centrally located and has nice views from the common balcony.

Phuong Hang Hotel (☎ 814 978; 41 Đ Ngo Duc Ke; d 70,000-120,000d; ✕) You'll find clean well-furnished rooms here and friendly service to boot.

Restaurant alley (Đ Nam Ky Khoi Nghia) Want to slip away from the tourist scene on the riverfront? Situated in an alley between Đ Dien Bien Phu and Đ Phan Dinh Phung, this alley has about a dozen local restaurants scattered on both sides of the street.

You'll find several other popular eateries along the riverfront strip, across from the huge silver Uncle Ho statue:

Mekong (☎ 821 646; 38 Đ Hai Ba Trung; mains 20,000d; ✕ breakfast, lunch & dinner) Always packed and stays open late (until 2am).

Nam Bo (☎ 823 908; 50 Đ Hai Ba Trung; mains 25,000-50,000d; ✕ lunch & dinner) Housed in a restored French villa and serving excellent European and Vietnamese food.

Nam Phuong (☎ 812 077; 48 Đ Hai Ba Trung; mains 25,000d; ✕ breakfast, lunch & dinner)

Getting There & Around

Buses and minibuses from HCMC leave the Mien Tay station (35,000d, five hours). The Cantho bus station is at Đ Nguyen Trai and Đ Tran Phu, about 1km north of town.

Xe loi (motorbikes with two-seater carriages on the back) cost 3000d for rides around town. Most guesthouses also hire out bicycles.

VIETNAM

CHAU DOC

☎ 076 / pop 100,000

Close to the Cambodian border, shyly charming Chau Doc houses mosques, pagodas and temples, including the cave temples at **Sam Mountain**.

War remnants near Chau Doc include **Ba Chuc**, the site of a Khmer Rouge massacre with a bone pagoda similar to that of Cambodia's Choeung Ek memorial; and **Tuc Dup Hill**, where an expensive American bombing campaign in 1963 earned it the nickname Two Million Dollar Hill. It's also possible to visit fish farms set up underneath floating houses on the river.

Bring a stash of dong to Chau Doc, as there isn't anywhere to exchange travellers cheques. A good place to start for local travel information is the tourist desk at the Vinh Phuoc Hotel.

Sleeping & Eating

Vinh Phuoc Hotel (☎ 866 242; 12-14 Đ Quang Trung; r US$4; ❄) A smashing deal: excellent local travel information, decent budget rooms and a backpacker restaurant, all for a bargain price.

Ngoc Phu Hotel (☎ 866 484; 17 Đ Doc Phu; r US$6-10; ❄) Even the fan rooms at this large liveable place have hot water, TV and fridge. Friendly staff and a central location round out the pluses.

Delta Adventure Inn (☎ 861 249; deltaadventureinn@hotmail.com; r US$7-15; ❄) Though 4km outside of Chau Doc near Sam Mountain, the cottages, communal hut and restaurant here are worth considering. It provides free shuttles into town and back from 6am to 10pm.

Good local eateries include **Bay Bong** (☎ 867 271; 22 Đ Thuong Dang Le; mains 25,000d; ☽ lunch & dinner) with excellent hotpots and soups, and **Thanh Tinh** (☎ 865 064; 13 Đ Quang Trung; mains 15,000d; ☽ lunch & dinner) for tasty vegetarian sustenance.

Getting There & Around

Sinh Cafe (Vietnam) and Capitol Tours (Cambodia) have a slow boat (US$8, six to seven hours) departing Chau Doc around 8.30am. Boats coming from Phnom Penh arrive in Chau Doc around 2.30pm. Fast boats (US$12, four hours) operated by the **Victoria Chau Doc Hotel** (☎ 865 010) and **Hang Chau 2 Hotel** (☎ 868 891) have the advantage of a completely hassle-free border crossing –

BORDER CROSSING: INTO CAMBODIA

Two popular border crossings near Chau Doc can get you into Cambodia: by road at Moc Bai (to Bavet on the Cambodian side); or by river at Vinh Xuong (to Kaam Samnor). Both crossings issue one-month Cambodian visas on arrival.

Crossing at Moc Bai is easily done on buses going from Ho Chi Minh City (HCMC) to Phnom Penh (US$6, seven hours).

A more scenic way to go is by boat. Travel agencies in Chau Doc sell boat-plus-bus trips to Phnom Penh (US$8, six hours including border check).

There's a third crossing at Tinh Bien, but it's more remote – you're best off sticking with the two former routes.

---

neither you nor your bags have to show up at customs.

Hydrofoil services between bucolic Hon Chong (also known as Binh An, about 100km from Chau Doc) and Phu Quoc Island were suspended at the time of research but it's possible that they will resume. Ask around in Chau Doc or phone the friendly folks at **Relax Restaurant** (☎ 077-759 942) in Binh An to see if a new schedule has been established.

Buses to Chau Doc depart HCMC's Mien Tay station (40,000d, six hours).

RACH GIA

☎ 077 / pop 172,400

Rach Gia's port is perched on a rivermouth opening onto the Gulf of Thailand, making it a jumping-off point for Phu Quoc Island. It's a prime smuggling hub, due to its proximity to Cambodia, Thailand and the great wide ocean. The centre of town sits on an islet embraced by the two arms of the Cai Lon River; the north side has your getaway options out of town.

Information

This is your last chance to exchange money before Ha Tien.

Kien Giang Tourist (Cong Ty Du Lich Kien Giang; ☎ 862 081; 12 Đ Ly Tu Trong) The provincial tourism authority.

Rach Gia Internet Café (130 Đ Nguyen Trung Truc) Has a pretty fast connection.

Vietcombank (☎ 863 178; 2 Đ Mac Cuu) Has a 24-hour ATM.

Sleeping & Eating

Lan Huong Guesthouse (☎ 867 628; 3 Đ Tu Do; r 50,000d) Buy a beer downstairs and watch boats come down the river from the shared balcony. Very basic, tiny fan-only rooms come supercheap. There are shared toilet and bathroom facilities at this place near the port.

Phuong Hong Guesthouse (☎ 866 138; 5 Đ Tu Do; d 60,000-120,000d; 🛇) Also near the port, this simple place has en suite bathrooms and is run by nice people.

Kim Co Hotel (☎ 879 610; 141 Đ Nguyen Hung Son; r 160,000-200,000d; 🛇) With a cheery, colourful interior, this hotel offers amenities closer to the midrange. Find it on the islet in the centre of town.

Cheap, tasty Vietnamese food is sold from food stalls along Đ Hung Vuong between Đ Bach Dang and Đ Le Hong Phong. Other places to try:

Ao Dai Moi (☎ 866 295; 26 Đ Ly Tu Trong; mains 12,000d) *Ao dai* is the traditional Vietnamese tunic and trousers, and *moi* means new - this place is run, fittingly, by a tailor. Very good morning *pho* and won ton soup.

Hung Phat (☎ 867 599; 7 Đ Nguyen Du; meals 25,000d) It does excellent sweet-and-sour soups and a good vegetarian fried rice.

Tay Ho (☎ 863 031; 6 Đ Nguyen Du; meals 25,000d) Good Chinese and Vietnamese food can be had here.

Getting There & Away

Vietnam Airlines flies once daily between HCMC and Rach Gia. There's also a daily morning flight from Rach Gia to Phu Quoc Island. You'll have to catch a *xe om* or *xe loi* from the airport to Rach Gia.

Hydrofoils (130,000d, 3½ hours), leaving at 8.30am and 1.30pm, zip from Rach Gia to An Thoi on Phu Quoc Island. Stop by the Rach Gia **hydrofoil terminal** (☎ 879 765) the day before, or phone ahead to book a seat.

Buses from HCMC (40,000d, six to seven hours) leave for Rach Gia from Mien Tay bus station in An Lac. Night buses leave Rach Gia between 7pm and 11pm. Minibus touts also sell tickets for rides straight from the boat landing; don't pay more than 70,000d for a ride to HCMC. The **minibus terminal** (Ben Xe Ha Tien; Đ Tran Quoc Toan) offers daily express services to Long Xuyen, Sa Dec and HCMC. The **main bus station** (Ben Xe Rach Soi; 78 Đ Nguyen Trung Truc) in Rach Soi, 7km south of Rach Gia, connects to Cantho, Dong Thap, Ha Tien, Long Xuyen and HCMC.

PHU QUOC ISLAND

☎ 077 / pop 52,700

Mind the Ps and Qs of Phu Quoc: Peace and Quiet. You'll find both on undeveloped white-sand beaches running for miles, and natural springs tucked inside the last large stand of forest in southern Vietnam. The island's wild beauty is beginning to draw more travellers, but Phu Quoc is still sleepily off the mainland march up the coast.

Most beachside accommodation options are south of Duong Dong town on the western side of the island. Addresses outside of Duong Dong's centre are designated by the kilometre mark south of town. Bring a torch to navigate the road and beach at night.

One of the more famous English-speaking guides around Phu Quoc is **Tony** (☎ 0913-197 334), who speaks with an idiosyncratic, Don Corleone–style accent. He can arrange guides and transport.

Sights & Activities

Deserted white-sand beaches run for kilometres, allowing for contemplation of a blue horizon, or your belly button. **Bai Sao** and **Bai Dam**, just north of Bai Kem (closed to the public), are lovely ones on the south end of the island. **Bai Thom**, on the northeastern end, is a narrower strip of sand near a fishing village.

About 90% of Phu Quoc Island is protected forest. The mountainous northern half of the island, where the trees are most dense, has been declared a **forest reserve** (Khu Rung Nguyen Sinh). You'll need a motorbike to get into the reserve, and as there are no real trekking trails, you'll need a guide anyway. In the centre of the island, just east of the guesthouse coast, are two hot springs, **Suoi Da Ban** (admission 2000d) and **Suoi Tranh**. In the dry season they're more moonscape than waterway.

The **An Thoi Islands** – 15 islands and islets at the southern tip of Phu Quoc – can be visited by chartered boat (US$40 per day), and it's a fine area for swimming, snorkelling and fishing.

Diving and snorkelling in Phu Quoc are just taking off, with few crowds and a more pristine marine environment than along the coast. Stop by the **Rainbow Divers** (☎ 0913-400 964; Km 1.5) desk at the Rainbow Bar on the beach.

VIETNAM

Sleeping

Nam Phuong Guesthouse (☎ 846 319; Km 1.5; r US$7-8, bungalows US$15) This popular place has several bungalows near the beach and a breezy café.

Thanh Hai (☎ 847 482; Km 1.7; d US$8) A kind, gentle family runs this peaceful place a short walk from the beach.

Nhat Lan (☎ 847 663; Km 1.7; d US$8-12) Another nice family offers comfortable concrete bungalows here that come with excellent hammocks.

Beach Club (☎ 980 998; Km 2.7; r US$8-15) Further down the beach is this friendly, foreign-run spot.

Thousand Stars Resort (Khu Du Lich Ngan Sao; ☎ 848 203; hungthanhphuquoc@hcm.vnn.vn; Km 3; d US$14, bungalows US$20-40; ✗) Find a beautiful beach here, with delightful plaster animals welcoming guests along the entry path. Great place for drinks or a seafood dinner at sunset.

Eating & Drinking

Most guesthouses have their own lively cafés or restaurants in-house; wander along the beach until you find somewhere appealing.

Mai House (☎ 847 003; Km 1.7; mains around 40,000d; ✗ lunch & dinner) This pretty resort restaurant has a raised dining area next to the beach, a good place for a more upscale dinner.

Le Bistrot (☎ 982 200; Km 1.7; mains around 30,000d; ✗ lunch & dinner) Good French food, good times, Dalat wine, plus a pool table – run by a friendly French-Vietnamese couple.

Rainbow Bar (☎ 0903-177 923) The hottest place to hang after dark. It's open-air, with a pool table and good music in a garden setting.

Getting There & Around

Vietnam Airlines has four daily flights (US$60 return) to Phu Quoc from HCMC, and daily flights from Hanoi, Danang, Hué and Nha Trang. A *xe om* from the airport to guesthouses south of town should be around 10,000d.

Hydrofoils from Rach Gia (p911) and Hon Chong (p910) arrive in Phu Quoc daily. Ticket offices line the road into Duong Dong town, selling tickets for fast boats from Phu Quoc.

Ferries (66,000d, eight hours) chug from Rach Gia to Phu Quoc. Slow boats between Phu Quoc and mainland Ha Tien are considered risky and are not recommended.

Xe om rides from An Thoi harbour to Duong Dong cost about 30,000d. The island's middle road from An Thoi to Duong Dong is paved, but dirt is the colour of the island's other roads. If you rent a motorbike, wear long trousers and sturdy shoes; spills are common on the sandier roads.

VIETNAM DIRECTORY

ACCOMMODATION

Accommodation is at a premium during Tet (late January or early February), when the country is on the move and overseas Vietnamese flood back into the country. Prices can rise by 25%. Christmas and New Year represent another high season, but to a lesser extent than Tet.

Family-run guesthouses are usually the cheapest option, with private bathrooms and rates ranging from around US$5 to US$15. Some places offer dorm beds for US$2 to US$3 per person, with shared bathroom. Guesthouse accommodation is generally plentiful, and discounts are negotiable if you plan to stay for a few days or are travelling alone.

A step up from the guesthouses, mini-hotels typically come with more amenities: satellite TV, minifridges and IDD phones. Rates often include a free continental breakfast, and as with smaller guesthouses, some discounts can be negotiated. Although mini-hotel rates can be as high as US$20 to US$25, it's still fairly easy to find rooms for around US$10. Rates often go down the more steps you have to climb; that is, upper floors are cheaper.

ACTIVITIES

Vietnam's roads and rivers, sea and mountains, provide ample opportunity for active adventures. Travel agencies and travellers cafés all over the country can arrange local trips, from kayaking on Halong Bay to trekking up Fansipan to kite-surfing in Mui Ne.

Cycling

The flatlands and back roads of the Mekong Delta are wonderful to cycle through and observe the vibrant workaday agricultural life. Another spot well away from the insane traffic of National Hwy 1 is Hwy 14, winding through the Central Highlands. Arrange mountain-biking tours in the northern mountain at **Handspan Adventure Travel** (Map p838; 04-926 0581; www.handspan.com; 80 P Ma May, Hanoi); and stop by **Sinhbalo Adventures** (Map p898; ☎ 08-837 6766, 08-836 7682; www.sinhbalo .com; 283/20 Đ Pham Ngu Lao) in HCMC to meander the Mekong Delta or further afield.

Diving & Snorkelling

Vietnam has several great dive destinations for underwater exploration. Long established, with many dive sites, is beachside resort Nha Trang (p877). A notable emerging dive destination is Phu Quoc Island (p911), with fewer visitors and a more pristine environment.

Kayaking

For an even closer look at those limestone crags, it's now possible to paddle yourself around Halong Bay. Inquire around travel agencies in Hanoi to arrange Halong Bay kayaking trips.

Trekking

The most popular region for trekking is the northwest – notably around Sapa (p857), which includes Vietnam's tallest mountain, Fansipan. There's also good trekking in the jungle of Cuc Phuong National Park (p850). The trekking trails in Bach Ma National Park (p868) are improving, but you may still need a guide. The trek up Lang Bian Mountain (p887) in Dalat also gets good reviews.

Water Sports

Mui Ne (p883) is Vietnam's best shoreline for kite-surfing and windsurfing fiends.

Nha Trang (p877) is another good locale for windsurfing, sailing or wakeboarding. The area around China Beach, south of Danang, also gets passable surf between September and December.

BOOKS

Lonely Planet's *Vietnam* guide provides the full scoop on the country. If you're interested in cuisine and the culture behind it, sink your teeth into *World Food Vietnam*. The *Vietnamese Phrasebook* is practical and helps pass the time on long bus rides. If you prefer cycling it, put *Cycling Vietnam, Laos & Cambodia* into your panniers.

For travel inspiration and commiseration, contemporary tales of Vietnamese journeys include *Hitchhiking Vietnam* (1998), Karin Muller's story detailing a fairly tumultuous seven-month journey through Vietnam. A more light-hearted narrative is *Sparring with Charlie: Motorbiking down the Ho Chi Minh Trail* (1996), by Christopher Hunt.

One of the finest books about the American War written by a Vietnamese is *The Sorrow of War: A Novel of North Vietnam* (1996) by Bao Ninh.

BUSINESS HOURS

Offices and other public buildings are usually open from 7am or 8am to 11am or 11.30am and from 1pm or 2pm to 4pm or 5pm. Banks tend to be open during these hours, and until 11.30am on Saturday. Post offices are generally open from 6.30am to 9pm. Government offices are usually open until noon on Saturday and closed Sunday. Most museums are closed on Monday. Temples are usually open all day, every day.

Many small, privately owned shops, restaurants and street stalls stay open seven days a week, often until late at night.

CLIMATE

Vietnam's south is tropical but the north can experience chilly winters – in Hanoi, an overcoat can be necessary in January.

The southwestern monsoon blows from April or May to October, bringing warm, damp weather to the whole country, except those areas sheltered by mountains, namely the central part of the coastal strip and the Red River Delta.

See the Hanoi climate chart (p924).

CUSTOMS

Though you're probably not travelling on a shoestring in order to support your antique-collection mania, keep in mind that customs may seize suspected antiques or other 'cultural treasures', which cannot legally be taken out of Vietnam. If you do purchase authentic or reproduction antiques, be sure to get a receipt and a customs clearance form from the seller.

DANGERS & ANNOYANCES

Since 1975 many thousands of Vietnamese have been maimed or killed by rockets, artillery shells, mortars, mines and other ordnance left over from the war. *Never* touch any war relics you come across – such objects can remain lethal for decades, and one bomb can ruin your whole day.

Violent crime is still relatively rare in Vietnam, but petty theft is definitely not. Drive-by bag snatchers on motorbikes are not uncommon, and thieves on buses, trains and boats stealthily rifle through bags or haul them off altogether. Skilled pickpockets work the crowds.

One strong suggestion, in particular for HCMC, is to not have anything dangling off your body that you are not ready to part with. This includes cameras and any jewellery. When riding a *xe om*, sling shoulder bags across the front of your body. On public buses, try to stow your bag where you're sitting; on trains, secure it to something if you have to leave it.

DISABLED TRAVELLERS

Vietnam poses many technical challenges for the disabled traveller, some of which include the lack of lifts; a steeplechase of kerbs, steps and uneven pavements, where they exist; plus problematic squat toilets in narrow stalls.

Nonambulatory Vietnamese people get around in hand-pumped vehicles or specially tricked-out motorbikes, while the poorest of the poor are simply hand-pulled or self-propelled on boards outfitted with wheels. Foreigners can get around in a hired car with driver and/or guide, which is not prohibitively expensive due to the low cost of labour.

Travellers with crutches or canes should do fine, and can usually find ground-floor rooms. Those who have vision, hearing or speech impairments might want to hire a guide or travel with a companion in order to get around.

Check out Lonely Planet's **Thorn Tree** (http://thorntree.lonelyplanet.com) to connect with other travellers; searching the Southeast Asia branch will yield the best results.

Vietnam-veteran groups that organise tours to Vietnam might also have some good travel tips, or seek advice from the organisations listed in the Southeast Asia Directory (p928).

DRIVING LICENCE

International driving licences are not valid in Vietnam. If you have a motorcycle licence, you must have the document translated into a Vietnamese equivalent in order for it to be officially recognised. In practice, most foreign residents and visitors drive without a licence.

EMBASSIES & CONSULATES

Visas can be obtained in your home country through the Vietnamese embassy or consulate. See p932 for more details.

Embassies & Consulates in Vietnam

Australia Hanoi (☎ 04-831 7755; 8 Duong Dao Tan, Ba Dinh District); HCMC (Map p896; ☎ 08-829 6035; 5th fl, 5B Đ Ton Duc Thang)

Brunei (☎ 04-943 5195; 27 Quang Trung St, Hoan Kiem, Hanoi)

Cambodia Hanoi (Map pp834-5; ☎ 04-942 4789; arch@fpt.vn; 71A P Tran Hung Dao); HCMC (Map p894; ☎ 08-829 2751; cambocg@hcm.vnn.vn; 41 Đ Phung Khac Khoan)

Canada (www.dfait-maeci.gc.ca/vietnam) Hanoi (Map pp834-5; ☎ 04-734 5000; 31 P Hung Vuong); HCMC (Map p896; ☎ 08-827 9899; 10th fl, 235 Đ Dong Khoi)

China Hanoi (Map pp834-5; ☎ 04-845 3736; eossc@hn.vnn.vn; 46 P Hoang Dieu); HCMC (Map p894; ☎ 08-829 2457; chinaconsul_hcm_vn@mfa.gov.cn; 39 Đ Nguyen Thi Minh Khai)

France Hanoi (Map pp834-5; ☎ 04-943 7719; www.ambafrance-vn.org; 57 P Tran Hung Dao); HCMC (Map p894; ☎ 08-829 7231; www.consulfrance-hcm.org; 27 Đ Nguyen Thi Minh Khai)

Germany Hanoi (Map pp834-5; ☎ 04-845 3836; www.hanoi.diplo.de; 29 P Tran Phu); HCMC (Map p894; ☎ 08-829 1967; 126 Đ Nguyen Dinh Chieu)

Indonesia (Map pp834-5; ☎ 04-825 3353; komhan@hn.vnn.vn; 50 P Ngo Quyen, Hanoi)

Japan Hanoi (☎ 04-846 3000; www.vn.emb-japan.go.jp; 27 P Lieu Giai, Ba Dinh District); HCMC (Map p896; ☎ 08-822 5314; 13-17 ĐL Nguyen Hue)

Laos Hanoi (Map pp834-5; ☎ 04-825 4576; 22 P Tran Binh Trong); HCMC (Map p894; ☎ 08-829 7667; 181 Đ Hai Ba Trung); Danang (Map p870; ☎ 0511-821 208; 12 Đ Tran Quy Cap)

Malaysia Hanoi (☎ 04-831 3400; mwhanoi@hn.vnn.vn; 16th fl, 6B P Lang Ha, Ba Dinh District); HCMC (Map p896; ☎ 08-829 9023; Ste 1208, Me Linh Point Tower, 2 Đ Ngo Duc Ke)

Myanmar (☎ 04-845 3369; Bldg A3, Van Phuc Diplomatic Quarter, P Kim Ma, Ba Dinh District, Hanoi)

Netherlands (Map p894; ☎ 08-823-5932; 29 Đ L Le Duan, HCMC)

New Zealand Hanoi (Map p838; ☎ 04-824 1481; nzembhan@fpt.vn; 5th fl, 63 P Ly Thai To); HCMC (Map p894; ☎ 08-822 6907; 5th fl, 41 Đ Nguyen Thi Minh Khai)

Philippines (Map pp834-5; ☎ 04-943 7873; hanoipe@dfa.gov.ph; 27B P Tran Hung Dao, Hanoi)

Singapore (Map pp834-5; ☎ 04-823 3965; www.mfa .gov.sg; 41-43 P Tran Phu, Hanoi)

Thailand Hanoi (Map pp834-5; ☎ 04-823 5092; thaconho@hcm.vnn.vn; 63-65 P Hoang Dieu); HCMC (Map p894; ☎ 08-932 7637; thaconho@hcm.vnn.vn; 77 Đ Tran Quoc Thao)

UK (www.uk-vietnam.org) Hanoi (Map p838; ☎ 04-936 0500; 4th fl, 31 P Hai Ba Trung); HCMC (Map p894; ☎ 08-829 8433; 25 Đ Le Duan)

USA (http://usembassy.state.gov/vietnam) Hanoi (☎ 04-772 1500; 7 P Lang Ha, Ba Dinh District); HCMC (Map p894; ☎ 08-822 9433; 4 ĐL Le Duan)

Vietnamese Embassies & Consulates Abroad

Australia Canberra (☎ 02-6286 6059; vembassy@ webone.com.au; 6 Timbarra Cres, O'Malley, ACT 2606); Sydney (☎ 02-9327 2539; tlssyd@auco.net.au; 489 New South Head Rd, Double Bay, NSW 2028)

Canada (☎ 613-236 0772; www.vietnamembassy -canada.ca; 470 Wilbrod St, Ottawa, ON K1N 6M8)

China Beijing (☎ 010-6532 1125; vnaemba@mailhost .cinet.co.cn; 32 Guanghua Lu, 100600); Guangzhou (☎ 020-8652 7908; Jin Yanf Hotel, 92 Huanshi Western Rd)

France (☎ 01 44 14 64 00; 62-66 Rue Boileau, 75016 Paris)

Germany (☎ 228-357 021; Konstantinstrasse 37, 5300 Bonn 2)

Hong Kong (☎ 22-591 4510; 15th fl, Great Smart Tower, 230 Wan Chai Rd, Wan Chai)

Japan Tokyo (☎ 03-3466 3311; 50-11 Moto Yoyogi-Cho, Shibuya-ku, 151); Osaka (☎ 06-263 1600; 10th fl, Estate Bakurocho Bldg, 1-4-10 Bakurocho, Chuo-ku)

UK (☎ 020-7937 1912; 12 Victoria Rd, London W8 5RD)

USA Washington (☎ 202-861 0737; www.vietnam embassy-usa.org; 1233 20th St NW, Ste 400, DC 20036); San Francisco (☎ 415-922 1707; www.vietnamconsulate -sf.org; 1700 California St, Ste 430, CA 94109)

FESTIVALS & EVENTS

Vietnam's major festival is Tet – see p916 for details.

Ngay Mot & Ngay Ram Pagodas are packed with Buddhist worshippers on the first and 15th days of the lunar month; and tasty, cheap vegetarian meals are served around them.

Tiet Doan Ngo (Summer Solstice) Human effigies are burnt to satisfy the need for souls to serve in the God of Death's army, on the fifth day of fifth lunar month.

Trung Nguyen (Wandering Souls Day) On the 15th day of seventh lunar month, offerings are presented to the ghosts of the forgotten dead.

Mid-Autumn Festival On the night of 15 August, children walk the streets carrying glowing lanterns, and people exchange gifts of mooncakes.

FOOD & DRINK
Food

One of the delights of visiting Vietnam is the cuisine; there are said to be nearly 500 traditional Vietnamese dishes. Generally, food is superbly prepared and very cheap...and you never have to go very far to find it.

FRUIT

Aside from the usual delightful Southeast Asian fruits, Vietnam has its own unique *trai thanh long* (green dragon fruit), a bright fuchsia-coloured fruit with green scales. Grown mainly along the coastal region near Nha Trang, it has white flesh flecked with edible black seeds, and tastes something like a mild kiwifruit.

MEALS

Pho is the Vietnamese name for the noodle soup that is eaten at all hours of the day, but especially for breakfast. *Com* are rice dishes. You'll see signs saying *pho* and *com* everywhere. Other noodle soups to try are *bun bo Hué* and *hu tieu*.

Spring rolls (*nem* in the north, *cha gio* in the south) are a speciality. These are normally dipped in *nuoc mam* (fish sauce), though many foreigners prefer soy sauce (*xi dau* in the north, *nuoc tuong* in the south).

Because Buddhist monks of the Mahayana tradition are strict vegetarians, *an chay* (vegetarian cooking) is an integral part of Vietnamese cuisine.

SNACKS

Street stalls or roaming vendors are everywhere, selling steamed sweet potatoes, rice porridge and ice-cream bars even in the wee hours. There are many other Vietnamese nibbles to try:

Bap xao Fresh, stir-fried corn, chillis and tiny shrimp.

Bo bia Nearly microscopic shrimp, fresh lettuce and thin slices of Vietnamese sausage rolled up in rice paper and dipped in a spicy-sweet peanut sauce.

Hot vit lon For the brave. Steamed, fertilised duck egg in varying stages of development (all the way up to recognisable duckling), eaten with coarse salt and bitter herb.

Sinh to Shakes made with milk and sugar or yogurt, and fresh tropical fruit.

SWEETS

Vietnamese people don't usually end meals with dessert, which isn't to say they don't have a sweet tooth. Many sticky confections are made from sticky rice, like *banh it nhan dau*, made with sugar and bean paste and sold wrapped in banana leaf.

Most foreigners prefer *kem* (ice cream) or *yaourt* (yogurt), which is generally of good quality.

Try *che*, a cold, refreshing sweet soup made with sweetened black bean, green bean or corn. It's served in a glass with ice and sweet coconut cream on top.

Drink
ALCOHOLIC DRINKS

Memorise the words *bia hoi*, which mean 'draught beer'. Similar to this is *bia tuoi*, or 'fresh beer'. Quality varies but it's generally OK and supercheap (3000d per litre!). Places that serve *bia hoi* usually also have cheap food.

Several foreign labels brewed in Vietnam under licence include BGI, Tiger, Fosters, Carlsberg and Heineken. National and regional brands – cheaper, and typically lighter than light – include Halida, Huda, Saigon and Bia 333 *(ba ba ba)*.

NONALCOHOLIC DRINKS

Whatever you drink, make sure that it's been boiled or bottled. Ice is generally safe on the tourist trail, but not guaranteed elsewhere.

Vietnamese *cà phê* (coffee) is fine stuff and there is no shortage of cafés in which to sample it. Try seeking out the fairy-lit garden cafés where young couples stake out dark corners for smooch sessions.

Foreign soft drinks are widely available. An excellent local treat is *soda chanh* (carbonated mineral water with lemon and

sugar) or *nuoc chanh nong* (hot, sweetened lemon juice).

GAY & LESBIAN TRAVELLERS

Vietnam is pretty hassle-free for gay travellers. There's not much in the way of harassment, nor are there official laws on same-sex relationships (although the government considers homosexuality a 'social evil'). Vietnamese same-sex friends often walk with arms around each other or holding hands, and guesthouse proprietors are unlikely to question the relationship of same-sex travel companions. But be discreet – public displays of affection are not socially acceptable whatever your sexual orientation.

Check out **Utopia** (www.utopia-asia.com) to obtain contacts and useful travel information. Some of the interesting content includes details on the legality of homosexuality in Vietnam and local gay terminology.

HOLIDAYS

The Lunar New Year is Vietnam's most important annual festival. The Tet holiday officially lasts three days, but many Vietnamese take the following week off work, so hotels, trains and buses are booked solid – and most everything else shuts down. If visiting Vietnam during Tet, memorise this phrase: *Chúc mùng nam mói!* (Happy New Year!). Smiles in response are guaranteed. Vietnamese public holidays are:

Tet (Tet Nguyen Dan) 18 February 2007 (Year of the Pig), 7 February 2008 (Year of the Rat)

Liberation Day 30 April; in 1975 Saigon surrendered to Hanoi-backed forces on this date.

International Workers' Day 1 May

Ho Chi Minh's Birthday 19 May

National Day 2 September; commemorates the proclamation of the Declaration of Independence of the Democratic Republic of Vietnam by Ho Chi Minh in 1945.

INTERNET ACCESS

Internet access is available throughout Vietnam, sometimes in the most surprising backwaters. Faster ADSL connections are becoming more widespread.

The cost for Internet access ranges from about 100d to 500d per minute.

INTERNET RESOURCES

www.vietnamadventures.com Full of practical travel information, this website features monthly adventures and special travel deals.

LEGAL MATTERS

Most Vietnamese never call the police, preferring to settle legal disputes on the spot (either with cash or fists). If you lose something really valuable like your passport or visa, you'll need to contact the police. Otherwise, it's better not to bother.

The Vietnamese government is seriously cracking down on the burgeoning drug trade. You may face imprisonment and/or large fines for drug offences, and drug trafficking can be punishable by death.

MAPS

Basic road maps of Vietnam and major cities such as Hanoi, Saigon, Hué and Nha Trang are readily available. For most other destinations, it's slim pickings.

MEDIA
Magazines & Newspapers

The English-language *Vietnam News* is published daily and will do at a pinch.

Of more interest are the monthly *Vietnam Economic Times* (VET) and the weekly *Vietnam Investment Review* (VIR). VET's free insert, the *Guide*, is an excellent source of leisure information and can be picked up in hotels, bars and restaurants in larger cities. VIR's free supplement, *Time Out*, is another good rag for finding what's on in Ho Chi Minh City and Hanoi.

Radio & TV

Foreign radio services such as the BBC World Service, Radio Australia and Voice of America can be picked up on short-wave frequencies.

Vietnamese TV broadcasts little of interest to foreigners, but satellite dishes are everywhere, and many hotels now offer Hong Kong's Star TV, BBC, CNN and other channels.

MONEY

Vietnam's official currency is the dong (d). Banknotes come in denominations of 200, 500, 1000, 2000, 5000, 10,000, 20,000, 50,000, 100,000 and 500,000. Plastic banknotes are now in circulation, so in addition to the new 500,000 notes, there are two different types each of 50,000 and 100,000 notes. Adding even more confusion to the mix, the government has also begun minting small-denomination coins (from 200 to 5000).

US dollars and euros are the easiest currencies to exchange.

Be very careful with money – travellers cheques and large-denomination notes belong inside a money belt or secret pocket stash.

ATMs

ATMs can be found in most bigger cities nowadays, with Vietcombank having the widest network. All ATMs dispense cash in dong only.

Bargaining

For *xe om* and cyclo trips, as well as anywhere that prices aren't posted, you'll be expected by the locals to bargain. In high-tourist areas, you may be quoted as much as five times the going price, but not everyone is trying to rip you off. In less-travelled areas, foreigners are often quoted the Vietnamese price (you'll still want to bargain a bit).

Bargaining politely usually invites reciprocal good-faith negotiation; getting belligerent gets you nowhere. If you can't agree on a price, thanking the vendor and walking away sometimes brings about a change of heart. When it's a matter of a few thousand dong, don't drive too hard a bargain.

Cash

The US dollar acts as a second local currency. Hotels, airlines and travel agencies all normally quote their prices in dollars, due in part to unwieldy Vietnamese prices (US$100 is around 1,600,000d). For this reason, we quote some prices in US dollars. For the best exchange rate, you should pay in dong.

Credit Cards

Visa, MasterCard and American Express (Amex) credit cards are accepted in most cities at high-end hotels, restaurants and shops. Getting cash advances on credit cards is also possible, but you'll be charged between 1% and 5% commission.

Exchanging Money

If you need to exchange money after hours, jewellery shops will exchange US dollars at rates comparable to, or even slightly better than, the banks.

Exchange rates are as follows:

Country	Unit	Dong (d)
Australia	A$1	11,630
Cambodia	1000r	3870
Canada	C$1	13,350
Euro zone	€1	18,620
Japan	¥100	13,460
Laos	K1000	1529
New Zealand	NZ$1	10,893
Thailand	B100	38,706
UK	£1	27,679
USA	US$1	15,890

Tipping

Tipping isn't expected in Vietnam, but it's enormously appreciated. Many travellers take up a collection (each contributing a few dollars) for their tour guides and drivers, after multiday tours or for outstanding service. For someone making under US$50 per month, the cost of your drink can equal half a day's wages.

Travellers Cheques

Travellers cheques in US dollars can be exchanged for local dong at certain banks; Viet-combank is usually a safe bet, although they will charge a commission of 1% if you exchange cheques for dong. Most hotels and airline offices will not accept travellers cheques.

PHOTOGRAPHY

Vietnam's gorgeous scenery and unique character make prime subject matter for memorable photographs.

Inspiration will surely strike when you see a row of colourfully dressed hill-tribe women walking to market, but remember to maintain an appropriate level of respect for the people and places you visit. Please use common courtesy and ask permission before snapping a photo of someone; if permission is refused, respect that person's wishes.

Colour-print film can be found virtually everywhere; slide film is available in HCMC and Hanoi. Processing is fairly cheap, from around US$3 per roll for prints. It's recommended that you process slide film elsewhere. Photo-processing shops and Internet cafés in bigger cities can burn digital photos onto CDs for you inexpensively.

POST

International postal service from Vietnam is not unreasonably priced when compared with most countries, though parcels mailed from smaller cities and towns may take longer to arrive at their destinations. Be aware that customs will inspect the contents before you ship anything other than documents, so don't show up at the post office with a carefully wrapped parcel ready to go. It will get eviscerated on the table.

Take your letters to the post office yourself and make sure that the clerk franks them while you watch so that someone for whom the stamps are worth a day's salary does not soak them off and throw your letters away.

Poste restante works in the larger cities but don't count on it elsewhere. There is a small surcharge for picking up poste restante letters. All post offices are marked with the words *buu dien*.

RESPONSIBLE TRAVEL

'When in Rome…' the saying goes, but if Romans are tossing plastic bags into the ocean it doesn't mean you should, too. You can make a difference with your example: pack out your own trash and pick up what you can of others'.

Buying coral, limestone or dried sea life encourages such harvestation to meet the demand, meanwhile killing the living ecosystems that travellers visit to enjoy. In the same vein, sampling 'exotic' meats like muntjac, seahorse or bat may seem culinarily adventurous, but many of these species are endangered. Help preserve vulnerable species by not eating them.

When travelling in hill-tribe areas, refrain from giving away candy and pens to children, which only encourages a reliance on begging. Instead, donate school supplies to local schools or support the local economy by purchasing goods from the craftspeople themselves.

A growing crisis in Vietnam is the accelerating spread of HIV/AIDS. For the protection of others and yourself, please practise safe sex.

STUDYING

To qualify for a student visa, you need to study at a bona fide university (as opposed to a private language centre or with a tutor). Universities require that you study

10 hours per week. Lessons usually last for two hours per day, for which you pay tuition of around US$5.

Decide whether you want to study in northern or southern Vietnam, because the regional dialects are very different. See Courses in Hanoi (p840) or HCMC (p900) for school listings.

TELEPHONE

The cheapest and simplest way to make an International Direct Dial (IDD) call is to dial ☎ 17100 plus the country code and phone number. These calls cost about 20,000d per minute to most countries. Vietnam's country code is ☎ 84.

In HCMC and Hanoi, it's possible to make reverse-charge calls at the main post offices. The telephone booking desk has a list of toll-free numbers you can call for a nominal fee, to connect with an international operator or long-distance service.

Useful numbers:

Directory assistance (☎ 116)
General information (☎ 1080)
International operator (☎ 110)
International prefix (☎ 00)
Time (☎ 117)

For mobile phones, Vietnam uses GSM 900/1800, which is compatible with most of Southeast Asia, Europe and Australia but not with North America. If you have a compatible phone, you can buy a SIM card with a local number in Vietnam. Mobilephone service providers like VinaPhone and MobiFone sell prepaid phonecards in denominations of 30,000d and up.

Calls to mobile phones cost more than to local numbers. Mobile phone numbers start with the digits ☎ 0903, ☎ 0913 or ☎ 0908.

TOILETS

Most hotels have the familiar Western-style sit-down toilets, but squat toilets in varying states of refinement exist in some cheap hotels and public places like restaurants and bus stations. Hotels usually supply a roll, but you'd be wise to keep a stash of toilet paper with you while travelling.

As public toilets are scarce, ask and ye shall usually receive the blessing to use the toilet at a nearby hotel, restaurant or shop – again, BYOTP (bring your own toilet paper).

TOURIST INFORMATION

Tourist offices in Vietnam have a different philosophy from the majority of tourist offices worldwide. These government-owned enterprises are really travel agencies whose primary interest is turning a profit.

Though travellers cafés have a similar agenda, they're generally a better source of information and offer cheaper ways of getting to where you're going. Hitting up your fellow travellers for information is an excellent way to get the latest, greatest scoop on the where and how.

TOURS

Motorcycling in Vietnam's wild northern territory is unforgettable. If you're not confident riding a motorbike yourself, it's possible to hire someone to drive you. Four-wheel drive trips in the north are also highly recommended, though the mobility of travelling on two wheels is unrivalled.

While it's possible to organise a motorcycling trip on your own, hiring a guide will certainly make the trip run smoothly and get you places you'd never discover from a cursory scan of a map.

The 125cc Russian-made Minsk is the best overall cycle for touring the north. The daily hire cost for a Minsk is around US$7. Foreign guides charge considerably more than local Vietnamese guides, but are worth every dong.

Explore Indochina (☎ 0913-524 658; www.explore indochina.com) is run by Digby and Dan, two excellent foreign guides (from Australia and the UK, respectively) with years of experience behind them. After dark, try tracking them down at Highway 4 in Hanoi (p844).

Free Wheelin Tours (☎ 04-747 0545; www.free wheelin-tours.com) is another reputable company established by Fredo (Binh in Vietnamese), a French-Vietnamese expat. He speaks French, English and Vietnamese and is one of Hanoi's top foreign motorbike guides. He also has Vietnamese guides on call.

VISAS

People of all nationalities require a visa to enter the country, and while Vietnamese bureaucracy is legendary, completing the visa application is pretty painless. You'll need at least one passport-sized photo to accompany the visa application.

Tourist visas are valid for a single 30-day stay and enable you to enter and exit the country via any international border (make sure to specify this when arranging your visa). Depending on where you acquire it, prices for single-entry tourist visas cost around US$30 to US$60. Cambodia, where your visa application can be processed on the same day, is the most convenient place in Southeast Asia to get a Vietnamese visa. Bangkok is another popular place, as many travel agents offer cheap packages including both an air ticket and a visa.

If you plan to spend more than a month in Vietnam or travel overland between Laos, Vietnam and Cambodia, it's possible to get a three-month multiple-entry visa. These are not available from all Vietnamese embassies but can be picked up for US$70 in Cambodia and for US$85 in the USA.

Business Visas

There are several advantages in having a business visa: such visas are usually valid for three or six months; they can be issued for multiple-entry journeys; you are permitted to work in Vietnam; and the visas can be extended with relative ease. The notable disadvantage is cost, which is about four times as much as a tourist visa.

Getting a business visa tends to be easier once you've arrived in Vietnam; most travel agencies can arrange one for you, sponsor and all.

Visa Extensions

If you've got the dollars, they've got the rubber stamp. Visa extensions cost around US$20, but go to a travel agency to get this taken care of – turning up at the immigration police yourself usually doesn't work. The procedure takes one or two days (one photo is needed) and is readily accomplished in major cities like Hanoi, HCMC, Danang and Hué.

Official policy is that you are permitted one visa extension only, for a maximum

of 30 days. Be on the lookout for sudden changes to these regulations.

VOLUNTEERING

15 May School (www.15mayschool.org) A school in HCMC for disadvantaged children, which provides free education and vocational training.

Idealist.org (www.idealist.org) Look up volunteer opportunities with nonprofit organisations worldwide.

Street Voices (www.streetvoices.com.au) Donate your skills, time or money to help give street children career opportunities. Street Voices' primary project is KOTO restaurant (see p842); check its website to see what you can do to help in Vietnam or Australia.

WOMEN TRAVELLERS

While it always pays to be prudent (avoid dark lonely alleys at night), foreign women have rarely reported problems in Vietnam. Most Vietnamese women do not frequent bars on their own; be aware that you may receive unwanted – though usually harmless – advances if drinking or travelling alone. When travelling on overnight trains it's a good idea to travel with a companion to keep an eye on your bags when you use the toilet, and on each other if you have any overly friendly strangers sharing your compartment.

Some Asian women travelling with Western men have occasionally reported verbal abuse from Vietnamese people who stereotype them as prostitutes. However, with the increase of foreign tourists visiting the country, locals are becoming more accustomed to seeing couples of mixed ethnicity.

WORKING

At least 90% of foreign travellers seeking work in Vietnam end up teaching English, though there is some demand for French teachers too. Pay can be as low as US$2 per hour at a university and up to US$15 per hour at a private academy.

Jobs in the booming private sector or with NGOs are usually procured outside of Vietnam before arriving.

It's best to arrange a business visa if you plan to job hunt (see p919).

Southeast Asia Directory

CONTENTS

This chapter includes general information about Southeast Asia. Specific information for each country is listed in the Directory section at the back of each country chapter.

ACCOMMODATION

The accommodation listed in this guidebook occupies the low-end of the price and amenities scale. 'Bare bones', 'basic' and 'simple' typically mean that the room has four walls, something that resembles a bed and a fan (handy for keeping mosquitoes at bay). In the cheapest instances, the bathroom is usually shared. Most places geared to foreigners have Western-style toilets, but multistorey hotels that cater to locals usually have Asian squat toilets. Air-con, private bathroom and well-sealed rooms are treated as 'splurges' in this guidebook. Camping is not a widespread option.

It is imperative to be a smart shopper when looking for a room. Always ask for the price first, then ask to see a room for cleanliness, comfort and quiet. Don't feel obligated to take a room just because the clerk climbed up five flights of stairs or because the place is mentioned in Lonely Planet. Sometimes the quality of a guesthouse plummets after gaining a mention in Lonely Planet, but this can be corrected by diligent travellers who exercise their own judgment.

If the price is too high, ask if they have anything cheaper. Don't use the price listed in Lonely Planet as a bargaining chip. Unless it is the low season, most hotels don't bargain over their rates. Once you've paid for a room there is no chance of a refund, regardless of the size of the rat that scurried across the floor. This is why it is recommended to pay per day rather than in bulk, but be courteous and pay first thing in the morning to keep staff from resorting to pushiness. Settle your bill the night before if you are catching an early bus out of town; most hotels and guesthouses do not staff their desks from midnight to 6am.

Unless you are staying at one of the mid- to top-end hotels, advance reservations (especially with advance deposits) are not advised. For budget places, don't rely on an agent to make bookings; the price will mysteriously double to pay the extra outstretched hand.

ACTIVITIES

Ocean sports and jungle trips are the major outdoor activities that the Southeast Asian nations offer. If you're beyond a beginner, consider bringing required gear from home, as equipment here can be substandard.

Diving & Snorkelling

Southeast Asia is a diving and snorkelling paradise. Operators are plentiful in popular tourist spots and offshore reefs are accessible and beautiful. In Indonesia, Bali is the diving superstar, but there are countless small islands and reefs between Flores, Timor, Komodo and Maluku (see p338 for details).

There's some diving on the west coast of Malaysia, but it's better on the east coast where the islands of Pulau Tioman (p461), Pulau Redang (p471) and Pulau Perhentian (p472) are just some of the possibilities. There are also sites in Malaysian Borneo.

In Thailand, Phuket (p805) attracts well-heeled divers from across the globe to its nearby islands, including Ao Phang-Nga and the world-famous Similan and Surin Islands in the Andaman Sea. Some of the inland reefs on Thailand's west coast were roughed up in the 2004 tsunami. In the Gulf of Thailand off the east coast, the popular islands of Ko Samui (p783), Ko Pha-Ngan (p787) and Ko Tao (p781) all have dive outfits that tend to be cheaper.

Many beach resorts rent out masks, snorkels and fins, and novices will require little outlay. But if you intend to do a lot of snorkelling it's worth bringing your own equipment: rental gear is not always of good quality and it soon becomes more economical to buy rather than rent. If you've never seen Southeast Asia's jewel-hued waters before, just about anywhere will seem amazing. A few noteworthy spots for snorkelling include Lovina (p233) in Bali and the Gili islands (p281) on Lombok, in Indonesia; Tioman and Perhentian islands on Malaysia's east coast; and Ko Pha-Ngan and Ko Tao in Thailand.

Opinions vary about whether Southeast Asia is a reputable spot to gain diving certificates; the island of Ko Tao in Thailand is regarded as one of the cheapest, but dive operators in other locations complain that Ko Tao is a dive factory, just passing people through the machine.

Surfing

Indonesia is the biggest surfing destination in Asia. For years surfers have been carting their boards to isolated outposts in search of long, deserted breaks. Kuta (p213) in Bali is a famous spot, but there's surf right along the south coast of the inner islands – from Sumatra through to Sumbawa, and Sumba across to Papua. Pulau Nias (p254), off the coast of Sumatra, is another beloved spot, but the 2004 earthquake and tsunami have caused significant infrastructure damage on the island; investigate the progress of recovery before planning a visit.

RESPONSIBLE DIVING

Please consider the following tips when diving and help preserve the ecology and beauty of reefs:

- Never use anchors on the reef and take care not to ground boats on coral.

- Avoid touching or standing on living marine organisms or dragging equipment across the reef. Polyps can be damaged by even the gentlest contact. If you must hold on to the reef, only touch exposed rock or dead coral.

- Be conscious of your fins. Even without contact, the surge from fin strokes near the reef can damage delicate organisms. Take care not to kick up clouds of sand, which can smother organisms.

- Practise and maintain proper buoyancy control. Major damage can be done by divers descending too fast and colliding with the reef.

- Take great care in underwater caves. Spend as little time within them as possible as your air bubbles may be caught within the roof and thereby leave organisms high and dry. Take turns to inspect the interior of a small cave.

- Resist the temptation to collect or buy coral or shells or to loot marine archaeological sites (mainly shipwrecks).

- Ensure that you take home all your rubbish and any litter you may find as well. Plastics in particular are a serious threat to marine life.

- Do not feed fish.

- Minimise your disturbance of marine animals. *Never* ride on the backs of turtles.

SAFETY GUIDELINES FOR DIVING

Before embarking on a scuba diving, skin diving or snorkelling trip, carefully consider the following points to ensure a safe and enjoyable experience:

- Get a current diving certification card from a recognised scuba diving instructional agency (if scuba diving).
- Be sure you are healthy and feel comfortable diving.
- Obtain reliable information about physical and environmental conditions at the dive site (eg from a reputable local dive operation).
- Be aware of local laws, regulations and etiquette about marine life and the environment.
- Dive only at sites within your realm of experience; if available, engage the services of a competent, professionally trained dive instructor or dive master.
- Be aware that underwater conditions vary significantly from one region, or even site, to another. Seasonal changes can significantly alter any site and dive conditions. These differences influence the way divers dress for a dive and what diving techniques they use.
- Ask about the environmental characteristics that can affect your diving and how local trained divers deal with these considerations.

Trekking

Trekking in Southeast Asia isn't on the same mountain scale as in Nepal, but the more demure peaks are home to many minority hill-tribe villages, which host overnight trekking parties. The northern Thai cities of Chiang Mai (p741), Mae Hong Son (p751) and Chiang Rai (p753) are very popular with prospective trekkers, turning Dr Livingstone fantasies into package tour realities.

Muang Sing (p391) in Laos has developed an award-winning ecotourism project for visits to local ethnic minority villages. The treks to Gunung Rinjani (p286) in Indonesia have earned similar praise for preserving the environment and local culture. The mountain village of Sapa (p857) in Vietnam is another base for organised hill-tribe journeys.

Malaysia has some excellent national parks, including Taman Negara (p479), Sarawak's Gunung Mulu National Park (p498) and the summit of 4101m-high Mt Kinabalu (p508), which is one of the region's highest peaks.

In Indonesia, it's easy to organise treks through Sumatra's jungles in Berastagi (p259) or Bukit Lawang (p265). Java's volcanic peaks, like Gunung Merapi (p196), can be a taxing climb, while spectacular Gunung Bromo (p205) is more of a stroll. Gunung Batur (p238) and Gunung Agung volcanoes (p228) in Bali are popular day trips. Indonesia's outer regions, particularly Papua (p330) and Sulawesi (p315), offer more adventurous jungle-trekking opportunities.

In the Philippines, the Mt Mayon volcano (p619) is an interesting climb, although recent eruptions have made things more dangerous. You can also arrange walks around Banaue (p616) in North Luzon.

BATHING

Most hotels and guesthouses do not have hot-water showers, though places in the larger cities or in colder regions may have hot-water options for an extra charge.

Many rural people bathe in rivers or streams. If you choose to do the same be aware that public nudity is not acceptable. Do like the locals do and bathe with some clothing on.

At basic hotels in rural towns the bathrooms usually have a large jar or cement trough filled with water for bathing purposes. A plastic or metal bowl is used to sluice water from the jar or trough over the body – don't jump in the trough!

BOOKS

See the country chapters for recommended reading about each country (fiction and nonfiction), and the Snapshots chapter (p27) for books covering the whole region's history and culture.

For more detailed information on a specific area or country, refer to the large range of travel guidebooks produced by Lonely Planet. Titles to look for include: *Bali & Lombok; Cambodia; East Timor; Indonesia; Laos;*

Malaysia, Singapore & Brunei; Myanmar (Burma); Philippines; Thailand; Thailand's Islands & Beaches; and *Vietnam.* Travellers wanting to really dig beneath a city's surface should keep an eye out for *Bangkok* and *Singapore.*

If you're looking to indulge a passion for underwater exploration, you might like to check out *Diving & Snorkeling in Bali & Lombok* or *Diving & Snorkeling in Thailand.* If, on the other hand, you have a passion for simply indulging, you can't do better than *World Food Thailand, World Food Indonesia, World Food Malaysia & Singapore* or *World Food Vietnam.*

Also of interest to travellers who like to get chatty are Lonely Planet's phrasebooks, which include the *Burmese Phrasebook, East Timor Phrasebook, Hill Tribes Phrasebook, Indonesian Phrasebook, Lao Phrasebook, Malay Phrasebook, Filipino (Tagalog) Phrasebook, South-East Asia Phrasebook, Thai Phrasebook* and *Vietnamese Phrasebook.*

BUSINESS HOURS

In the Buddhist countries of Southeast Asia businesses are typically open seven days a week. In the Muslim countries some businesses close during Friday afternoon prayers. Refer to the Directory in individual country chapters for more details.

CLIMATE

With the exception of northern Myanmar, all of Southeast Asia lies within the tropics. This means that regardless of when you visit, the weather is likely to be warm or even downright hot. High humidity is also common, with few areas far enough inland to enjoy thoroughly dry weather. Of course, temperatures are much cooler in the mountains.

Broadly speaking, there are two main weather patterns in the region: that of mainland Southeast Asia and that of oceanic Southeast Asia. A brief description of these patterns is provided in this section, but be sure to check the country chapters of this book, as there are significant regional variations.

Mainland Southeast Asia (Three-Season Countries)

Cambodia, Laos, Vietnam and the northern and central regions of Thailand and Myanmar generally have a relatively cool dry sea-

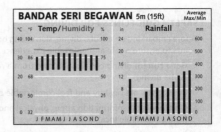

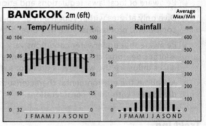

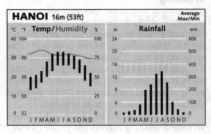

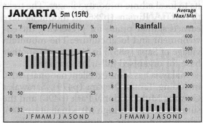

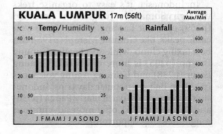

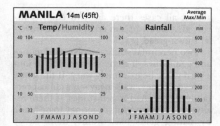

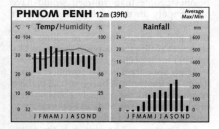

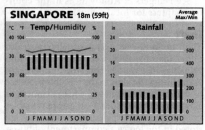

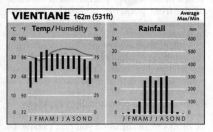

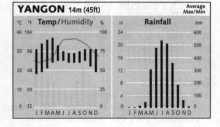

son starting from November to late February, followed by a hot dry season from March to May, and then a hot rainy season that starts sometime in June and peters out during September or October. Fortunately, even during the rainy season it seldom rains all day and travel is possible over most of the region.

Oceanic Southeast Asia (Two-Season Countries)

The climates of southern Thailand, southern Myanmar, Brunei, Indonesia, Malaysia and Singapore are governed by two monsoons: one from the northeast, which usually falls between the months of October and April; and one from the southwest, which usually falls between the months of May and September. Rain is usually heavier during the northeast monsoon. However, neither of these monsoons is severe enough to preclude travel; often, you will find better weather simply by crossing from one side of the island or country to the other.

The climates of the Philippines and Maluku (Indonesia) are more complex and share aspects both of mainland and of oceanic climates.

Typhoons

Most of Southeast Asia lies off the track of tropical cyclones (typhoons). However, typhoons do occasionally strike the Philippines and Vietnam. Peak typhoon season runs from June to early October, with most occurring in the months of August and September.

CUSTOMS

Customs regulations vary little around the region. Drugs and arms are strictly prohibited – death or a lengthy stay in prison are common sentences. Pornography is also a no-no. Check the Customs sections in the Directory of the country chapters for details on duty-free allowances.

DANGERS & ANNOYANCES
Drugs

The risks associated with recreational drug use and distribution have grown to the point where all travellers should exercise extreme caution even in places with illicit reputations. Easy-going Bali now has a jail just down the road from Kuta Beach, where a number of travellers are enjoying the tropical climate much longer than they had intended. In

Indonesia you can actually end up behind bars because your travel companions had dope and you didn't report them. A spell in a Thai prison is true Third World torture; in Malaysia and Singapore, possession of certain quantities of dope can lead to hanging.

The death penalty, prison sentences and huge fines are given as liberally to foreigners as to locals – no-one has evaded punishment because of ignorance of local laws or citizenship to a country with more relaxed standards. And don't think that your government can save you here; it can't.

With heightened airline security after the 11 September 2001 attacks in the USA, customs officials are zealous in their screening of both luggage and passengers.

Prostitution & Sex Tourism

Prostitution, including child prostitution, is unfortunately common in parts of Southeast Asia. Most of the women and children who work in this industry are forced to by conditions of poverty. Others, including most child prostitutes, are actually sold into the business by relatives. These sex slaves are either trafficked overseas or forced to cater to domestic demand and local sex-tourism operators.

Fear of contracting HIV/AIDS from mature sex workers has led to increasing exploitation of (supposedly as yet uninfected) children. Unicef estimates that there are close to one million child prostitutes in Asia – one of the highest figures in the world. Those who aren't put off by the stark realities of child prostitution in Southeast Asia should keep in mind that penalties in the region for paedophiles are severe, and other countries around the world – including Australia, New Zealand, a number of European countries and the USA – now prosecute and punish citizens for paedophilia offences committed abroad.

For more information about groups working to end this exploitation, visit the website of **End Child Prostitution & Trafficking** (Ecpat; www .ecpat.net). This is a global network that works to stop child prostitution, child pornography and the trafficking of children for sexual purposes.

Scams

Every year we get hundreds of letters and emails from hapless travellers reporting that they've been scammed in Southeast Asia. In almost all cases there are two culprits involved: a shrewd scam artist and the traveller's own greed.

Two perennial scams involve card games and gemstones. If someone asks you to join a card game be extremely wary. If the game involves money, walk away – it's almost certainly rigged. As for gemstones, if there really were vast amounts of money to be made by selling gems back home, more savvy businesspeople than yourself would have a monopoly on the market already. Don't believe the people who say that they support their global wanderings by re-selling gemstones; in reality they support themselves by tricking unsuspecting backpackers.

These are only the most common scams. There are many more, but almost all of them revolve around the unlikely scenario of a local presenting you with an opportunity to save or make lots of money.

See Dangers & Annoyances in the country chapters for local scams.

Theft

Theft in Southeast Asia is usually by stealth rather than by force. Keep your money and valuables in a money belt worn underneath your clothes. Be alert to the possible presence of snatch thieves, who will whisk a camera or a bag off your shoulder. Don't store valuables in easily accessible places like packs that are stored in the luggage compartment of buses, or the front pocket of backpacks. Be especially careful about belongings when sleeping in dorm rooms.

Violent theft is very rare but occurs from time to time – usually late at night and after the victim has been drinking. Be careful walking alone late at night and don't fall asleep in taxis.

Always be diplomatically suspicious of over-friendly locals. Don't accept gifts of food or drinks from someone you don't know. In Thailand, thieves have been known to drug travellers for easier pickings.

Finally, don't let paranoia ruin your trip. With just a few sensible precautions most travellers make their way across the region without incident.

Trouble Spots

The global rise of civilian terrorism has gained momentum in Southeast Asia since the shocking 2002 Bali nightclub bombings.

The subsequent 2005 bombing of a Bali restaurant shows that the once-peaceful island is still a vulnerable target. The threat is highest in parts of Indonesia, Thailand and the Philippines where separatist groups and other fringe networks have been most active, but caution should be exercised elsewhere. Trouble spots can crop up almost anywhere, often with very little warning – make sure you get the most up-to-date information on local conditions before setting off (and even while you're on the road). The governments of most countries issue travel warnings for their citizens; you can find online travel advisories in Lonely Planet's **Travel Ticker** (www .lonelyplanet.com/travel_ticker) or visit the travel warnings page on the website of the **US State Department** (www.travel.state.gov).

The local English-language newspapers available in most parts of Southeast Asia are also good sources of information. At the time of writing, the following areas were considered trouble spots.

INDONESIA
According to the US State Department, Indonesia has several active cells of Jemaah Islamiyah (JI), a militant Islamic group suspected of having links to Al-Qaeda. This group is believed to have orchestrated the 2002 Bali nightclub bombings, in which 202 people, mainly foreign tourists, were killed. The Muslim cleric believed to be the group's spiritual leader, Abu Bakar Bashir, was found guilty of conspiring the 2002 Bali attacks and sentenced to 2½ years in prison by an Indonesian court, a sentence highly criticised by Australia and USA as being too lenient. Four other suspects were charged and convicted for carrying out the attack and have been sentenced to death or life imprisonment. Three years later, Bali was targetted once again when three bombs exploded in a food court and Kuta town square, killing 20 civilians, mainly Indonesians, and injuring hundreds of others. Initial evidence suggests that suicide bombers were responsible for the blasts and JI tops the list of suspects, but no arrests have been made at the time of writing. The motivations are also unconfirmed, but the timing of the attacks coincide with a massive gas price-hike, the start of Ramadan, and the third anniversary of the 2002 Bali bombings. Other attacks with possible links to

JI include the 2004 bombing of the Australian embassy and the 2003 bombing of the Marriott Hotel in Jakarta. While no-one can predict when or where another attack will occur, be aware that targets range from political to domestic to religious, and have been scattered throughout the most populous islands of the archipelago.

Nonhumanitarian travel to Sumatra's northern province of Aceh is still rare because of the devastation to infrastructure caused by the 2004 earthquake and tsunami, as well as long-running separatist tensions (although in August 2005 a Helsinki-brokered peace deal was signed by the Free Aceh Movement and the government, giving a sense of optimism that there may be an end to the three-decade-long conflict). Check latest reports for security updates and travel restrictions. Other potentially violent areas, where leisure travel is discouraged, include parts of Papua, formerly known as Irian Jaya; of Maluku, especially the capital city; and of central Sulawesi.

PHILIPPINES
Imperatively speaking, avoid travel in Mindanao and Sulu archipelago. Insurgency activities of the Islamic rebel group Abu Sayyaf have included kidnappings, beheadings and killings of foreigners and local civilians. Terrorist activities have been ongoing with bombing incidents at airports, on public buses and in ferry terminals in the southern Philippines and Manila.

The New People's Army (NPA), the military arm of the outlawed communist party, remains active throughout the country and has issued threats against foreign interests in the country, although recent attacks have been limited to Filipino public officials. In 2002 an American was shot and killed on the slopes of Mt Pinatubo, located in an area of rebel activity.

THAILAND
The predominately Muslim southern provinces of Narathiwat, Yala, Pattani and Songkhla have long experienced periods of unrest between Islamic separatist groups and the central Thai government. Since 2002 violence has re-emerged in the region, beginning with attacks on public schools, government officials and police posts. After the recent escalation of attacks on

civilian targets and the raiding of an army weapons cache in 2004, the central Thai government was forced to recognise the existence of organised separatist militants, previously dismissed as bandits. In early 2005, the major transit hub of Hat Yai airport and a supermarket were bombed, followed by an explosion in the Sungai Kolok train station, a border-crossing point between Thailand and Malaysia. While the Thai government has stepped up efforts to apprehend perpetrators, attacks are expected to continue and venture further into civilian territory, especially into the previously peaceful province of Songkhla. Western governments have issued travel warnings to citizens travelling overland between Thailand and Malaysia.

The entire Thai–Myanmar border experiences periodic clashes between the Burmese army, Thai border patrols and the minority Shan State rebels. When conflicts arise the borders are closed and travel into affected areas is restricted.

DISABLED TRAVELLERS

Travellers with serious disabilities will likely find Southeast Asia a challenging place to travel. Even the more modern cities are very difficult to navigate for the mobility- or vision-impaired. In general, care of a person with a disability is left to close family members throughout the region and it's unrealistic to expect much in the way of public amenities.

International organisations that can provide information on mobility-impaired travel include the following:

Mobility International USA (☎ 541-343 -1284; www.miusa.org; PO Box 10767, Eugene, OR 97440, USA)

Royal Association for Disability & Rehabilitation (Radar; ☎ 020-7250 3222; www.radar.org.uk; 12 City Forum, 250 City Rd, London EC1V 8AF, UK)

Society for Accessible Travel & Hospitality (SATH; ☎ 212-447-7284; www.sath.org; 347 Fifth Ave, Suite 610, New York, NY 10016, USA)

DISCOUNT CARDS

The International Student Identity Card (ISIC) is the official student card accepted in Southeast Asia, with moderate success. Some domestic and international airlines provide discounts to ISIC cardholders, but because knock-offs are so readily available the cards carry little bargaining power.

DISCRIMINATION

By and large most Southeast Asian countries are homogeneous (or at least the majority thinks so), creating fairly rigid attitudes towards ethnicities, based solely on skin colour. White foreigners stand out in a crowd. Children will point, prices will double and a handful of presumptions will precede your arrival. In general, these are minor nuisances or the exotic elements of travel. If you are a Westerner of Asian descent most Southeast Asians will assume that you are a local until the language barrier proves otherwise. With the colour barrier removed, many Western Asians are treated like family and sometimes get charged local prices. Many Asians might mistake people of African heritage with fairly light complexions for locals or at least distant cousins. People with darker complexions will be regarded as foreign as whites, but with the extra baggage of Africa's inferior status in the global hierarchy. Mixed Asian and foreign couples will attract some disapproval, especially in Thailand where sex tourism suggests that the Asian partner is a prostitute. See also Gay & Lesbian Travellers (opposite) and Women Travellers (p932) for more information.

DRIVING LICENCE

Parts of Southeast Asia, including Malaysia, Indonesia and Thailand, are good spots for exploring by car and motorcycle. If you are planning to do any driving, get an International Driving Permit (IDP) from your local automobile association before you leave your home country; IDPs are inexpensive and valid for one year. In some countries (eg Malaysia) your home driving licence is sufficient, but elsewhere (eg Indonesia and Thailand) an IDP is required.

ELECTRICITY

Most countries work on a voltage of 220V to 240V at 50Hz (cycles); note that 240V appliances will happily run on 220V. You should be able to pick up adaptors in electrical shops in most Southeast Asian cities.

EMBASSIES & CONSULATES

It's important to realise what your own embassy – the embassy of the country of which you are a citizen – can and can't do to help you if you get into trouble.

Generally speaking, it won't be much help in emergencies if the trouble you're in is remotely your own fault. Remember that you are bound by the laws of the country you are in. Your embassy will not be sympathetic if you end up in jail after committing a crime locally, even if such actions are legal in your own country.

In genuine emergencies you might get some assistance, but only if other channels have been exhausted. For example, if you need to get home urgently, a free ticket home is exceedingly unlikely – the embassy would expect you to have insurance. If you have all your money and documents stolen, it might assist with getting a new passport, but a loan for onward travel is out of the question.

Most travellers should have no need to contact their embassy while in Southeast Asia, although if you're travelling in unstable regions (eg parts of Indonesia) or really going off the trail, it may be worth letting your embassy know – be sure to let them know when you return. In this way valuable time, effort and money won't be wasted looking for you while you're relaxing on the beach somewhere in a different country.

For details of embassies in Southeast Asia see the Directory in the country chapters.

FESTIVALS & EVENTS

Most Southeast Asian holidays revolve around religious events and typically provide an excellent display of the country's culture, food and music. Businesses are usually closed and travelling is difficult, so plan ahead.

Vietnamese Tet & Chinese New Year Probably one of the loudest festivals on the planet; it is celebrated countrywide in Vietnam and in Chinese communities throughout the region in February, with fireworks, temple visits and all-night drumming.

Easter Week In March or April, the Christian holiday of Easter is observed in the Philippines, Indonesia and East Timor.

Thai, Lao & Cambodian New Year The lunar New Year begins in mid-April, and in addition to religious devotion, the citizens take to the streets dowsing one another with water.

Buddhist Lent At the start of the monsoonal rains in June or July, the Buddhist monks retreat into monasteries in Myanmar, Laos and Thailand. This is the traditional time for young men to visit the monasteries.

Ramadan Observed in Malaysia, Indonesia, Brunei and southern Thailand during October, November or December, the Muslim fasting month requires that Muslims abstain from food, drink, cigarettes and sex between sunrise and sunset.

Christmas In December, various local celebrations occur in the Philippines, East Timor and Indonesia.

GAY & LESBIAN TRAVELLERS

The Philippines, Thailand and Laos have the most progressive attitudes towards homosexuality; the Philippines even has legislation against gay discrimination. While same-sex displays of affection are part of most Asian cultures, be discreet and respectful of the local culture. Extra vigilance should be practised in Vietnam, where authorities have arrested people on charges of suspected homosexual activities. Police harassment and imprisonment is also a possibility in Muslim countries. Modern Singapore still enforces its colonial-era antisodomy laws regardless of gender.

Check out **Utopia Asian Gay & Lesbian Resources** (www.utopia-asia.com) and **Rainbow** (www.rainbowquery.com) for more information on gay and lesbian travel in Asia.

INSURANCE

A travel insurance policy to cover theft, loss and medical problems is a necessity. There's a wide variety of policies available, so check the small print. For more information about the ins and outs of travel insurance, contact a travel agent or travel insurer.

Some policies specifically exclude 'dangerous activities', which can include scuba diving, motorcycling and even trekking. A locally acquired motorcycle licence is not valid under some policies. Check that the policy covers ambulance rides, emergency flights home and repatriation of a body.

Also see p943 for further information. For info on car and motorcycle insurance see the Car & Motorcycle sections in the relevant country chapters.

INTERNET ACCESS

You can access email and Internet services in all countries of the region, except Myanmar, where you can only use email from certain providers (but not Hotmail or Yahoo) and only surf a limited number of websites. Access points in Southeast Asia vary from Internet cafés to post offices and guesthouses (see the Internet Access section in the country chapters for further details). The cost is generally low.

LEGAL MATTERS

Be sure to know the national laws before unwittingly committing a crime. In all of the Southeast Asian countries, using or trafficking drugs carries stiff punishments that are enforced even if you're a foreigner.

If you are a victim of a crime, contact the tourist police, if available; they are usually better trained to deal with foreigners and foreign languages than the regular police force.

MAPS

Country-specific maps are usually sold in English bookstores in capital cities. Local tourist offices and guesthouses can also provide maps of smaller cities and towns.

MONEY

Most experienced travellers will carry their money in a combination of travellers cheques, credit/bank cards and cash. You'll always find situations in which one of these cannot be used, so it pays to carry all three.

ATMs

In fairly large cities ATMs are widespread and most networks talk to overseas banks, so you could withdraw cash (in the local currency) directly from your home account. But before banking on this option review the individual country's Money section for specifics; Cambodia and Laos are virtually ATM-free.

Use your card only when you are dealing with cash machines, not for point of sale purchases. Having your credit-card number stolen is a real concern, and you will have more consumer protection with a credit card (which is paid after the purchase) than an ATM card (which deducts the cost at the time of purchase). Talk to your bank before heading out about compatibility with foreign ATMs and surcharges.

Bargaining & Tipping

Most Southeast Asian countries have inherited the art of bargaining from ancient Indian traders. Remember that it is an art not a test of wills, and the trick is to find a price that makes everyone happy. Bargaining is acceptable in markets and souvenir shops, where fixed prices aren't displayed. As a beginner, tread lightly by asking the price and then asking if the seller can offer a discount. The price may creep lower if you take your time and survey the object. If the discounted price isn't acceptable give a counter offer but be willing to accept something in the middle. Once you counter you can't name a lower price. Don't ask the price unless you're interested in actually buying it. If you become angry or visibly frustrated then you've lost the bargaining game.

Tipping is not a standard practice but is greatly appreciated.

Cash

Having some cash (preferably US dollars) is handy, but is risky too; if you lose it, it's gone.

Credit Cards

For a splurge at a nice hotel or a crazed shopping spree in Singapore, a credit card is your best friend; keep careful tabs on purchases as fraud is a concern.

Exchanging Money

Currency exchange is generally straightforward throughout the region. In Vietnam, Cambodia and Myanmar, US dollars in cash are readily accepted at hotels and on some transport; you'll need local currency to buy smaller items. See the individual country chapters for more details.

Other major currencies, such as the euro and the Australian dollar, are easy to change in the main centres; it's when you start getting away from regularly visited areas that your currency options become more limited.

Travellers Cheques

Travelling with a stash of travellers cheques can help if you hit an ATM desert. Get your cheques in US dollars and in large denominations, say US$100s or US$50s, to avoid heavy per-cheque commission fees. Keep careful records of which cheques you've cashed and keep this information separate from your money, so you can file a claim if any cheques are lost or stolen.

PASSPORT

To enter many countries your passport must be valid for at least six months from your date of entry, even if you're only staying for a few days. It's probably best to have at least a year left on your passport if you are heading off on a trip around Southeast Asia.

Testy border guards may refuse entry if your passport doesn't have enough blank pages available. Before leaving get more pages added to a valid passport (if this is a service offered by your home country), or once on the road, you can apply for a new one in most major Southeast Asian cities.

PHOTOGRAPHY
Airport Security
X-ray machines that claim to be film-safe generally are. You are advised to have very sensitive film (1000 ISO and above) checked by hand. *Never* put your film in your checked baggage – the X-ray machines used to check this luggage will fog your film.

Film & Equipment
Print film is readily available in cities and larger towns across Southeast Asia. The best places to buy camera equipment or have repairs done are Singapore, Bangkok or Kuala Lumpur.

If you're after some tips, check out Lonely Planet's *Travel Photography: A Guide to Taking Better Pictures*, written by internationally renowned travel photographer, Richard I'Anson.

For those travelling with a digital camera, most Internet cafés in well-developed countries allow customers to transfer their images from the camera to an online email account or storage site. Before leaving home, find out if your battery charger will require a power adapter by visiting the website of the **World Electric Guide** (www.kropla.com/electric.htm). Also be aware that the more equipment you travel with, the more vulnerable you are to theft.

Photographing People
You should always ask permission before taking a person's photograph. Many hill-tribe villagers seriously object to being photographed, or they may ask for money in exchange; if you want the photo, you should honour the price. See Responsible Travel in each country chapter's Directory for more information.

POST
Postal services are generally reliable across the region. Of course, it's always better to leave important mail and parcels for the big Asian centres such as Bangkok, Singapore, Kuala Lumpur and Jakarta.

There's always an element of risk in sending parcels home by sea, though as a rule they eventually reach their destination. If it's something of value, it's worth considering air freight – better still, register the parcel or send it by courier. Don't send cash or valuables through government-run postal systems.

Poste restante is widely available throughout the region and is the best way of receiving mail. When getting people to write to you, ask them to leave plenty of time for mail to arrive and to print your name very clearly. Underlining the surname also helps.

SOCIAL PROBLEMS
The disparity between rich and poor is one of Southeast Asia's most pressing social concerns. Few of the region's countries have established social nets to catch people left homeless or jobless by debt mismanagement or larger problems associated with rapid industrialisation. Most destitute people migrate to the cities to do menial labour at barely subsistence wages or sell their bodies for more handsome profits. The attendant problems of displaced citizens include drug abuse, HIV/AIDs, and unsanitary and dangerous shanty towns. Because of the Buddhist belief in reincarnation, the prevailing political wisdom is that the poor are fated to suffer because of wrongdoings committed in previous lives.

STUDYING
There are a variety of courses available throughout the region, from language, meditation and massage to *muay thai* (Thai boxing) and cooking, and from formal programmes sponsored by international agencies to informal classrooms run in homes. **Council on International Educational Exchange** (☎ 888-268-6245; www.ciee.org/study) arranges study-abroad programmes in language, art and culture in Thailand and Vietnam, hosted in local universities. The University of Texas at Austin maintains a useful website, **Study Abroad Asia** (http://asnic.utexas.edu/asnic /stdyabrd/StdyabrdAsia.html), which lists universities that sponsor overseas study programmes in Southeast Asia. Also visit Lonely Planet's **Travel Links** (www.lonelyplanet.com/travel_links), and see the individual country Studying sections for more information.

TELEPHONE

Phone systems vary widely across Southeast Asia. For international calls, most countries have calling centres (usually in post offices) or public phone booths that accept international phonecards. Each country's system is different, so it's a good idea to check the Telephone sections of the country chapters before making a call.

You can take your mobile phone on the road with you and get respectable coverage in major population centres. Not all mobile phones, especially those from the USA, are outfitted for international use. Check with your service provider for global-roaming fees and other particulars.

Fax services are available in most countries across the region. Try to avoid the business centres in upmarket hotels – tariffs of 30% and upwards are often levied on faxes and international calls.

TOILETS

Across the region, squat toilets are the norm, except in hotels and guesthouses geared towards tourists and international business travellers.

Next to the typical squat toilet is a bucket or cement reservoir filled with water. A plastic bowl usually floats on the water's surface or sits nearby. This water supply has a two-fold function: toilet-goers scoop water from the reservoir with the plastic bowl and use it to clean their nether regions while still squatting over the toilet; and a bowl full of water poured down the toilet takes the place of the automatic flush. More rustic toilets in rural areas may simply consist of a few planks over a hole in the ground.

Even in places where sit-down toilets are installed, the plumbing may not be designed to take toilet paper. In such cases, the usual washing bucket will be standing nearby or there will be a waste basket in which you place used toilet paper.

Public toilets are common in department stores, bus and railway stations and large hotels. Elsewhere you'll have to make do; while on the road between towns and villages it's acceptable to go discreetly behind a tree or bush. Of course, in land mine-affected countries like Laos and Cambodia, stay on the roadside and do the deed, or grin and bear it until the next town.

TOURIST INFORMATION

Most of the Southeast Asian countries have government-funded tourist offices with varying capacities of usefulness. Better information is sometimes available through guesthouses and your fellow travellers than through the state-run tourist offices. See the individual country chapter Tourist Information sections for contact information and overseas branches.

VISAS

Visas are stamps in your passport that permit you to enter a country and stay for a specified period of time. Visas are available to people of most nationalities on arrival in most Southeast Asian countries, but rules vary depending on the point of entry. See the respective country Directory.

Get your visas as you go rather than all at once before you leave home; they are often easier and cheaper to get in neighbouring countries and visas are valid within a certain time period, which could interfere with an extended trip.

Procedures for extending a visa vary from country to country. In some cases, extensions are nearly impossible, in others they're a mere formality. See the Visas sections in the individual country chapters for further information. And remember the most important rule: treat visits to embassies, consulates and borders as formal occasions and look smart for them.

In some Southeast Asian countries you are required to have an onward ticket out of the country before you can obtain a visa to enter. In practice, however, as long as you look fairly respectable, it's unlikely that your tickets will be checked.

VOLUNTEERING

For long-term commitments in health, agriculture or education, contact **Voluntary Service Overseas** (VSO; ☎ 020-8780 7200; www.vso.org.uk); **VSO Canada** (☎ 613-234 1364; www.vsocan.org); **Overseas Service Bureau** (OSB; ☎ 03-9279 1788; www.australianvolunteers.com) or the **US Peace Corps** (☎ 800-424-8580; www.peacecorps.gov) for placement in one of the Southeast Asian countries.

WOMEN TRAVELLERS

While travel in Southeast Asia for women is generally safe, solo women travelling in Muslim areas have reported some negative reception. In conservative Muslim areas, local women rarely go out unaccompanied and are usually modestly dressed (including headscarves). Foreign women who enter these areas without observing local customs infrequently incur backlash either as sexual or anti-Western aggression.

Keep in mind that modesty in dress is culturally important across all Southeast Asia. In conservative Muslim areas, you can cut your hassles in half just by tying a bandanna over your hair (a minimal approximation of the headscarf worn by most Muslim women). Other causes for commotion are the ever-popular midriff T-shirts that inadvertently send the message that you're a prostitute. At the beach, save the topless sunbathing for home or the nude-magazine spread rather than this conservative region of the world.

When travelling through Buddhist countries, solo women should be equally on guard especially when returning home late at night or arriving in a new town at night. While physical assault is rare, local men often consider foreign women as being exempt from their own society's rules of conduct regarding members of the opposite sex.

Treat overly friendly strangers, both male and female, with a good deal of caution.

Many travellers have reported small peepholes in the walls and doors of cheap hotels, some of which operate as boarding houses or brothels (often identified by their advertising 'day use' rates). If you can afford it, move to another hotel or guesthouse.

Use common sense about venturing into dangerous-looking areas, particularly alone or at night. If you do find yourself in a tricky situation, try to extricate yourself as quickly as possible – hopping into a taxi or entering a business establishment and asking them to call a cab is often the best solution.

Finally, you can reduce hassles by travelling with other travellers. This doesn't necessarily mean bringing a friend from home; you can often pair up with other travellers you meet on the way.

WORKING

Teaching English is the easiest passport for supporting yourself in Southeast Asia. For short-term gigs, the large cities like Bangkok, Ho Chi Minh City and Jakarta have a lot of language schools and a high turnover. **Payaway** (www.payaway.co.uk) provides a handy online list of language schools and volunteer groups looking for recruits for its Southeast Asian programmes.

Transitions Abroad (www.transitionsabroad.com) and its namesake magazine cover all aspects of overseas life, including landing a job in a variety of fields. The website also provides links to other useful sites and publications.

Transport

This chapter gives an overview of the transport options for getting to Southeast Asia, and getting around the region once you're there. For more specific information about getting to (and around) each country, see the country chapter's Transport sections.

GETTING THERE & AWAY

Step one is to get to Southeast Asia, and flying is the easiest option. The only overland possibility from outside the region is from China into Myanmar, Vietnam or Laos.

AIR
Tickets

The major Asian gateways for cheap flights are Bangkok, Singapore and Denpasar (Bali). Bangkok and Penang (in Malaysia) are good places to shop for onward tickets and tickets around the region.

To research and buy a ticket on the Internet, try these services:

Cheapflights (www.cheapflights.com) No-frills website with a number of locations.

Lonely Planet (www.lonelyplanet.com) Use the Trip-Planner service to book multistop trips.

OneTravel (www.onetravel.com) Another with a number of locations.

Travel.com (www.travel.com.au) There is also a New Zealand version (www.travel.co.nz).

RTW & CIRCLE ASIA TICKETS

Consolidators and online search engines offer cheap tickets to the region. If Asia is one of many stops on a worldwide tour, consider a round-the-world (RTW) ticket, which allows a certain number of stops within a set time period as long as you don't backtrack; for more information, talk to a travel agent.

Circle Asia fares are offered by various airline alliances for a circular route originating in the USA, Europe or Australia and travelling to two destinations in Asia, including Southeast and East Asia. Prices usually start at US$2000. Before committing, check out the fares offered by the budget regional carriers to see if the circle pass provides enough of a saving. Contact the individual airlines or a travel agent for more information.

From Asia

If you are flying in from India to Southeast Asia, most large cities with a tourist industry have bucket shops that can sell cheap tickets to any destination you can dream of. Many flights originating or departing for the USA change planes in East Asia; ask your travel agent about extending a stopover.

From Australia

The best place to look for cheap fares is in the travel sections of weekend newspapers,

---

THINGS CHANGE...

The information in this chapter is particularly vulnerable to change. Check directly with the airline or a travel agent to make sure you understand how a fare (and ticket you may buy) works and be aware of the security requirements for international travel. Shop carefully. The details given in this chapter should be regarded as pointers and not as a substitute for your own careful, up-to-date research.

such as the *Age* in Melbourne and the *Sydney Morning Herald*.

Two well-known agencies for cheap fares:
Flight Centre (☎ 133 133 using local area code; www .flightcentre.com.au) Has dozens of offices throughout Australia.
STA Travel (☎ 1300 733 035 Australia-wide; www.sta travel.com.au) Has offices in all major cities and on many university campuses.

From Canada

It is cheaper to fly from the west coast than it is to fly from the east. Canadian air fares tend to be higher than those sold in the USA. The *Globe & Mail*, the *Toronto Star*, the *Montreal Gazette* and the *Vancouver Sun* carry travel agency ads and are good places to look for cheap fares. **Travel CUTS** (www.travelcuts.com) is Canada's national student travel agency and has offices in all major cities.

From Continental Europe

France has a network of student travel agencies, including **OTU Voyages** (www.otu.fr), which can supply discount tickets to travellers of all ages. General travel agencies in Paris include **Nouvelles Frontières** (☎ 08 25 00 07 47; www.nouvelles-frontieres.com; 21 ave des Gobelins) or **Voyageurs du Monde** (☎ 08 92 68 83 63; www.vdm .com; 55 rue Sainte Anne).

In Switzerland, **SSR Voyages** (☎ 058 450 4020; www.ssr.ch; Ankerstrasse 12, Zurich) specialises in student, youth and budget fares; there are also branches of this organisation in other major Swiss cities.

In the Netherlands, **NBBS Reizen** (☎ 0900 1020 300; www.nbbs.nl; Rokin 66, Amsterdam) is the official student travel agency.

From New Zealand

The *New Zealand Herald* has a helpful travel section. **Flight Centre** (☎ 0800 243 544; www.flight centre.co.nz) has a large central office in Auckland and many branches throughout the country. **STA Travel** (☎ 0508 782 872; www.statravel .co.nz) has offices in Auckland as well as in Hamilton, Palmerston North, Wellington, Christchurch and Dunedin.

From the UK

Advertisements for many travel agencies appear in the travel pages of the weekend broadsheets, such as the *Independent* and the *Sunday Times*.

For students or travellers under 26, popular travel agencies in the UK:
STA Travel (☎ 08701 600 599; www.statravel.co.uk) Has offices throughout the UK; the website has an online directory of STA Travel websites and offices throughout Europe.
Trailfinders (☎ 0845 058 5858; www.trailfinders.co.uk)

From the USA

Ticket promotions frequently connect Asia to San Francisco and Los Angeles, New York and other big cities. The *New York Times*, the *Los Angeles Times*, the *Chicago Tribune* and the *San Francisco Examiner* all produce weekly travel sections in which you will find a number of travel agency ads and fare promos.

For qualifying travellers, contact the US offices of **STA Travel** (☎ 800 781 4040; www.sta travel.com).

LAND

The land borders between Southeast Asia and the rest of Asia include the frontier that Myanmar shares with India and Bangladesh, and the Chinese border with Myanmar, Laos and Vietnam. Of these, it is possible to travel overland from China into Myanmar (but not vice versa) and in either direction between China and Laos, and China and Vietnam. See the Transport sections in the Myanmar (p531), Laos (p350) and Vietnam (p828) chapters for more information.

An unreliable option is the road leading from Indonesia's Jayapura or Sentani towards Vanimo in Papua New Guinea, which can be used depending on the current political situation. See p156 for more information.

SEA

Ocean approaches to Southeast Asia from your home continent can be made aboard cargo ships plying various routes around the world. Ridiculously expensive and hopelessly romantic, a trip aboard a cargo ship is the perfect opportunity to finally write that novel that never writes itself. Ships are usually open for two to eight non-crew members, who have their own rooms and eat meals with the crew. Prices vary widely depending on departure point but start at around US$5000.

Charter boats can transport you from Papua New Guinea to Papua (formerly Irian Jaya) in Indonesia.

GETTING AROUND

AIR

Air travel can be a bargain within the region, especially from transit hubs like Bangkok, Singapore and Kuala Lumpur. No-frills regional carriers, like **Air Asia** (www.airasia.com), have made travelling between capital cities cheaper than taking land transport in some cases. Air routes between Southeast Asian countries are listed in the Transport sections of each country chapter.

A little caution is necessary when buying tickets from travel agents. Carefully check the tickets to make sure that the dates meet your specifications and confirm with the airline as soon as possible. Favourite tricks include tickets with limited validity (when you've been told the tickets are valid for one year). Get recommendations from fellow travellers or ask for a list of licensed agents from the country's tourist office.

Most airports in Southeast Asia charge a departure tax, so make sure you have that final necessary bit of local currency left.

Approximate intra-Asia fares are shown on the Southeast Asian Air Fares map (p936).

Air Passes

National airlines of Southeast Asian countries frequently run promotional deals from select Western cities or for regional travel. **Airtimetable.com** (www.airtimetable.com) posts seasonal passes and promotions.

An ongoing deal is the Asean Air Pass, offered through cooperating airlines for travel in Southeast Asia; coupons cost US$130. Visit **Thai Airways International** (THAI; www.thaiair .com) for more details.

BICYCLE

Touring Southeast Asia on a bicycle has been gaining more and more supporters. Many long-distance cyclists start in Thailand and head south through Malaysia to Singapore. Road conditions are good enough for touring bicycles in most places, but mountain bicycles are recommended for forays off the beaten track.

Vietnam is a great place to take a bicycle – traffic is relatively light, buses take bicycles

SOUTHEAST ASIAN AIR FARES

Full one-way economy fares in US$ (discounts available on most flights). Fares vary enormously depending on season and carrier.

0 — 1000 km
0 — 600 miles

and the entire coastal route is feasible, give or take a few hills. Indonesia is a more difficult proposition. Distances in Sumatra, congested roads in Java, hills in Bali and poor road conditions on the outer islands all conspire against it, although that won't deter dedicated cyclists. In Laos and Cambodia, road conditions can impede two-wheeling, but light traffic, especially in Laos, makes peddling more pleasant than elsewhere.

Top-quality bicycles and components can be bought in major cities like Singapore but, generally, 10-speed bicycles and fittings are hard to find (impossible in Vietnam). Bring your own. Bicycles can travel by air; check with the airline about extra charges and shipment specifications.

BOAT

Ferries and boats make trips between Singapore and Indonesia, Malaysia and Indonesia, and Thailand and Malaysia. Typically, guesthouses or travel agents sell tickets and can provide updated departure times. Be sure to check the visa regulations regarding border crossings at port cities. While Malaysia and Thailand won't be a problem for most visitors, Indonesia has varying requirements for different points of entry.

BUS

In most cases, land borders are crossed via bus, which either travel straight through the two countries with a stop for border formalities or require a change of buses at the appropriate border towns. Bus travellers will enjoy a higher standard of luxury in Thailand, Philippines and Malaysia, where roads are well-paved, reliable schedules exist and, sometimes, snacks are distributed. Be aware that theft does occur on some long-distance buses departing from Bangkok's Th Khao San (in Banglamphu) heading south; keep all valuables on your person, not in a stowed locked bag.

Local buses in Laos, Cambodia and Vietnam are like moving sardine cans, but that is part of the charm.

CAR & MOTORCYCLE

What is the sound of freedom in Southeast Asia? The *'put-put'* noise of a Honda Dream motorcycle. Convenient for getting around the beaches or touring in the country, motorcycles are available for hire or purchase,

---

> ### MOTORCYCLE TIP
>
> Most Asians are so adept at driving and riding on motorcycles that they can balance the whole family on the front bumper or even take a quick nap as a passenger. Foreigners unaccustomed to motorcycles are not as graceful. If you're riding on the back of a motorcycle remember to relax. For balance hold on to the back bar, not the driver's waist. Tall people should keep their long legs tucked in as most drivers are used to shorter passengers. Women (or men) wearing skirts should always ride side-saddle and collect longer skirts so that they don't catch in the wheel or drive chain. Now enjoy the ride.

---

but require a lot more investment and safety precautions than many visitors realise.

It is advisable to hire a car or motorcycle in a certain locality rather than depend upon it for regional travel. You could hit Thailand and Malaysia by car pretty easily and enjoy well-signposted, well-paved roads. Road conditions in Laos and Cambodia vary, although sealed roads are slowly becoming the norm.

See p928 for driving licence laws.

Hire

There are Western car-hire chains camped out at Southeast Asian airports, capital cities and major tourist destinations. On many tourist islands, guesthouses and locals will hire motorcycles for an affordable rate.

Insurance

Get insurance with a motorcycle if at all possible. The more reputable motorcycle-hire places insure all their motorcycles; some will do it for an extra charge. Without insurance you're responsible for anything that happens to the bike. To be absolutely clear about your liability, ask for a written estimate of the replacement cost for a similar bike – take photos as a guarantee. Some agencies will only accept the replacement cost of a new motorcycle.

Insurance for a hired car is also necessary. Be sure to ask the car-hire agent about liability and damage coverage.

(Continued on page 942)

TRANSPORT

TRANSPORT

SOUTHEAST ASIAN BORDER CROSSINGS

If you have the time, you can travel overland through the specified border points listed here (note we haven't listed any connections between Laos and Myanmar as those borders are closed). The border crossings are listed alphabetically in order of the countries' names; the following abbreviations are used for conven-ience: B (Brunei), ET (East Timor), C (Cambodia), I (Indonesia), L (Laos), M (Malaysia), My (Myanmar), P (Philippines), S (Singapore), T (Thailand) and V (Vietnam).

Be aware of border closing times, visa regulations and any transport scams by asking your fellow travellers before making a long-

BORDER CROSSINGS

TRANSPORT

distance trip, or by referring to the relevant country's Transport section and the specific entries on the border towns.

BRUNEI

From Malaysia

Brunei forms a C-clamp between the Malaysian states of Sarawak and Sabah. In Sarawak, buses

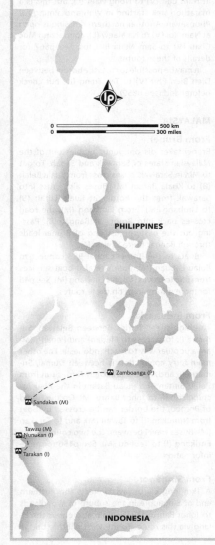

enter the sultanate from Kuala Baram (M) to Kuala Belait (B; see p497), Limbang (M) to Kuala Lurah (B) and Bangar (B; see p500). All roads feed into the Brunei capital of Bandar Seri Begawan, known as BSB. From the state of Sabah, Lawas (M) connects with Bangar (B) and on to BSB by boat (p500). You can also connect to BSB from Pulau Labuan (M) – see p507.

CAMBODIA

From Laos

The only border passage to Cambodia is at Voen Kham (L). Confusingly there are two Cambodian posts that service this crossing, which connects Si Phan Don in southern Laos to Stung Treng (C): one on the river (Koh Chheuteal Thom) and one on the new road to Stung Treng (Dom Kralor) – see p351 for details.

From Thailand

The border at Aranya Prathet (T) to Poipet (C) – see p719 for details – is frequently used to travel between Bangkok (T) and Siem Reap (C). Along the coast, crossings can be made from Hat Lek (T) to Krong Koh Kong (C) by road (see p775). There are also three recently opened crossings in remote areas: Chong Jom (T) in Surin Province to O Smach (C), leading to Samraong (see p764); Choam Sa-Ngam (T) to Choam (C) leading to the former Khmer Rouge stronghold of Anlong Veng (though these routes are rarely used by travellers and road conditions on the Cambodian side are substandard); and in the southeast Daun Lem (T) to Pruhm (C) leading to Pailin (see p775 for more information).

From Vietnam

There are three border-crossing options: the road border at Moc Bai (V) to Bavet (C) for quick passage between Ho Chi Minh City and Phnom Penh, two Mekong River crossings from the delta town of Vinh Xuong (V) to Kaam Samnor (C), and the remote Tinh Bien (V) to Phnom Den (C) crossing. See p910 for details.

EAST TIMOR

From Indonesia

The Motoain (I) to Batugade (ET) border crossing (between East Timor and Indonesian West Timor) is open and serviced by bus. See p273 for details.

INDONESIA

From East Timor

The Batugade (ET) to Motoain (I) border crossing between Indonesian West Timor and East Timor is open and serviced by bus. See p137 for more information.

From Malaysia

The high-speed ferries between Penang (M) and Belawan, Sumatra (I) are a popular way to reach Indonesia and to access Medan (p454). The other main ferry connection is between Melaka (M) and Dumai, Sumatra (I) – see p441). Daily ferries run from Johor Bahru (M) to Pulau Bintan and Pulau Batam in the Riau Archipelago (I) – see p461). On the island of Borneo, the border can be crossed by boat from Tawau (M) to Nunukan (I) – see p514. Buses travel between the two countries via Tebedu (M) and Entikong (I) – see p488. Fast boats also run between Tarakan (M) and Nunukan (I).

From Singapore

Ferries run from Singapore to the Riau Archipelago (I). See p661 for details.

LAOS

From Cambodia

Voen Kham (L) is the only active border post with Cambodia. Koh Chheuteal Thom (C), on the Mekong River, and Dom Kralor (C), on the new road to Stung Treng (C), service Voen Kham and link Cambodia with southern Laos' Si Phan Don area. See p114 for more information.

From Thailand

From northern Thailand, cross the border by boat at Chiang Khong (T) to Huay Xai (L; p755). The most popular crossing is done from Nong Khai (T) across the Thai–Lao Friendship Bridge to Vientiane (L; p769). From the northeast, travellers have the option of crossing the Mekong River at Nakhon Phanom (T) to Tha Khaek (L; p767) or at Mukdahan (T) to Savannakhet (L; p766).

In eastern Thailand, you can cross by land at Chong Mek (T), near Ubon Ratchathani, to Vang Tao (L), an hour west of Pakse – see p766.

From Vietnam

You can travel overland by bus between the central city of Dong Ha (V) and the southern Laos province of Savannakhet via Lao Bao (L). Further north there is another land border at Cau Treo (V) to Kaew Neua (L). The nearest Vietnamese city, Vinh, is about 80km from the border and on the Lao side it's about 200km from the border to Tha Khaek, just opposite Nakhon Phanom in Thailand. It's also possible to cross at Nam Can (V) to Nong Haet (L), but this is a marathon trek starting in Vinh and aiming for Phonsavan. Another northern crossing is open at Nam Xoi (V) to Na Maew (L), connecting Moc Chau (V) to Sam Neua in Laos. See p867 for details of these routes.

It may be possible to cross the border between Dien Bien Phu (V) to Tay Trang (L), but check beforehand (see p859).

MALAYSIA

From Brunei

Brunei takes discontiguous nibbles out of the Malaysian states of Sarawak and Sabah. To get to Miri in Sarawak, buses cross from Kuala Belait (B) to Kuala Baram (M). Buses also cross into Sarawak from the border at Kuala Lurah (B) to Limbang (M). From Limbang (M), the road crosses back into Brunei at Bangar (B). Passing out the easternmost end of Brunei leads through Bangar (B) to Lawas (M).

Boats to the Brunei capital BSB connect to Pulau Labuan (M); there are also boat services from BSB to Lawas (M) and Limbang (M). See p46 for more information on these routes.

From Indonesia

The high-speed ferries between Belawan, Sumatra (I; for access to Medan) and Penang (M) are a popular way to reach Indonesia. The other main ferry connection is between Dumai, Sumatra (I) and Melaka (M). Daily ferries run from Pulau Bintan and Pulau Batam in the Riau Archipelago (I) to Johor Bahru (M). On the island of Borneo, the border can be crossed by boat from Nunukan (I) to Tawau (M), and to Tarakan (M). Buses travel between the two countries via Entikong (I) to Tebedu (M). See p156 for more information.

From Singapore

A 1km-long causeway connects the northern end of Singapore in the suburb of Woodlands to Johor Bahru (M); the train also enters the island via this route. To the west another bridge connects Singapore (in the suburb of Tuas) with Tanjung Kupang (M). Boats also connect Singapore to Pulau Tioman (M) once the monsoon is over. See p661 for details.

From Thailand

On the west coast, the crossing between Satun (T) to Pulau Langkawi (M) is made by boat. On the east coast, Sungai Kolok (T) to Rantau Panjang (M) is a dusty land crossing for travel between Kota Bharu (M) and Pulau Perhentian (M). The major transit hub in Thailand, Hat Yai, and Penang–Butterworth in Malaysia, receive bus and rail traffic through the borders at Kanger (T) to Padang Besar (M) or Sadao (T) to Bukit Kayu Hitam (M) – see p795. Betong (T) to Keroh (M) is also a land crossing open to foreigners, although it offers little advantage over other points.

MYANMAR

From Thailand

There are two legitimate crossings: Mae Sai (T) to Tachilek (My; p756) and Ranong (T) to Kawthoung (My; see p812). To enter Myanmar you must have a valid visa or buy a day pass at the border. These land routes are usually used to renew a Thai visa. There are also two day-pass points: Mae Sot (T) to Myawaddy (My; p736) and Sangkhlaburi (T) to Payathonzu (My; p726).

PHILIPPINES

From Malaysia

Passenger ferries run between Sandakan in Malaysian Borneo (M) and Zamboanga (P) – see p512 for more information.

SINGAPORE

From Indonesia

Ferries run from Pulau Bintan and Pulau Batam in the Riau Archipelago (I) to Singapore. See p156 for details.

From Malaysia

A 1km-long causeway in Johor Bahru (M) connects to the northern end of Singapore in the suburb of Woodlands; the train also enters the island via this route. To the west another bridge connects Tanjung Kupang (M) with the suburb of Tuas (S). In season, boats also connect Pulau

Tioman (M) to Singapore. See p461 for more information.

THAILAND

From Cambodia

The border at Poipet (C) to Aranya Prathet (T) is frequently used to access Siem Reap (C) or Bangkok (T); see p93. Along the coast, crossings can be made from Krong Koh Kong (C) to Hat Lek (T) by road (p110). There are also three recently opened crossings: from the remote town of Samraong through O Smach (C) to Chong Jom (T) in Surin Province; from the former Khmer Rouge stronghold of Anlong Veng through Choam (C) to Choam Srawngam (T; see p60); and from the southwest town of Pailin through Pruhm (C) to Daun Lem (T). See p98 for details.

From Laos

Heading to northern Thailand, cross the border by boat at Huay Xai (L) to Chiang Khong (T); p394. The most popular crossing is from Vientiane (L) across the Thai–Lao Friendship Bridge to Nong Khai (T) – see p365. From the south, travellers have the option of crossing the Mekong River at Tha Khaek (L) to Nakhon Phanom (T) or at Savannakhet (L) to Mukdahan (T); p397. In the far south, you can cross by land at Vang Tao (L), an hour west of Pakse, to Chong Mek (T), near Ubon Ratchathani (p400).

From Malaysia

On the west coast, the crossing between Pulau Langkawi (M) and Satun (T) is made by boat. Hat Yai, the major transit hub in Thailand, receives bus and rail traffic from Malaysia (usually Penang) through the border at Padang Besar (M) to Kanger (T), or Bukit Kayu Hitam (M) to Sadao (T). See p459 for details of these routes. On the east coast, Rantau Panjang (M) to Sungai Kolok (T) is a dusty land crossing between Kota Bharu (M) and Pulau Perhentian (p477). Keroh (M) to Betong (T) is also a land crossing open to foreigners, although it offers little advantage over other points.

From Myanmar

There are two legitimate crossings: Mae Sai (T) to Tachilek (My; p531) and Ranong (T) to Kawthoung (My; p531). Be sure to have a valid Myanmar visa when exiting and be prepared for unexpected charges from Myanmar officials at the border when crossing into Thailand.

TRANSPORT

VIETNAM

From Cambodia

There are three border-crossing options for travel between Vietnam and Cambodia: the road border at Bavet (C) to Moc Bai (V); the Mekong River crossing at Kaam Samnor (C) to Vinh Xuong (V); or the remote crossing of Phnom Den (C) to Tinh Bien (V). See p77 for more information.

From Laos

You can travel overland by bus between the southern Laos province of Savannakhet and central Vietnamese city of Dong Ha via the border crossing at Lao Bao (L). Further north there is another land border from Kaew Neua (L) to Cau Treo (V). See p352 for more information. The nearest Vietnamese city of any importance, Vinh, is about 80km from the border and on the Lao side it's about 200km from the border to Tha Khaek, just opposite Nakhon Phanom in Thailand.

It's also possible to cross at Nong Haet (L) to Nam Can (V), but this is a marathon trek starting in Phonsavan and aiming for Vinh (see p385). Another northern crossing is open at Na Maew (L) to Nam Xoi (V), connecting Sam Neua to Moc Chau – see p387. It may be possible to cross the border between Tay Trang (L) and Dien Bien Phu (V), but check beforehand (p352).

(Continued from page 937)

Road Rules

Drive carefully and defensively; lives are lost at astounding rates on Southeast Asian highways. Remember too that smaller vehicles yield to bigger vehicles regardless of circumstances – might makes right on the road. The middle of the road is typically used as a passing lane, even if there is oncoming traffic. And the horn is used to notify other vehicles that you intend to pass them.

Safety

Always check a machine thoroughly before you take it out. Look at the tyres for treads, check for oil leaks, test the brakes. You may be held liable for any problems that weren't duly noted before your departure. When driving a motorcycle, wear protective clothing and a helmet. Long pants, long-sleeved shirts and shoes are highly recommended as protection against sunburn and as a second skin if you fall. If your helmet doesn't have a visor then wear goggles, glasses or sunglasses to keep bugs, dust and other debris out of your eyes.

HITCHING

Hitching is never entirely safe in any country in the world and is not recommended. Travellers who decide to hitch should understand that they are taking a small but potentially serious risk. People who do choose to hitch will be safer if they travel in pairs and let someone know where they are planning to go.

LOCAL TRANSPORT

Because personal ownership of cars in Southeast Asia is limited, local transport within a town is a roaring business. For the right price, drivers will haul you from the bus station to town, around town, around the corner, or around in circles. The bicycle rickshaw still survives in the region, assuming such aliases as săamláw in Thailand and cyclo in Vietnam. Anything motorised is often modified to carry passengers – from Thailand's obnoxious three-wheeled chariots known as túk-túk to the altered US Army jeeps (jeepneys) in the Philippines. In large cities, extensive public bus systems either travel fixed routes or do informal loops around the city picking up passengers along the way. Bangkok, Kuala Lumpur and Singapore can also boast state-of-the-art light-rail systems that make zipping around town feel like time travel.

TRAIN

For intercountry travel, the *International Express* train travels from Thailand all the way through the Malay Peninsula, ending its journey in Singapore. Trains also serve the Thai border towns of Nong Khai (a border crossing into Laos) and Aranya Prathet (a border crossing into Cambodia).

Health   Dr Trish Batchelor

CONTENTS

Health issues and the quality of medical facilities vary enormously depending on where and how you travel in Southeast Asia. Many of the major cities are now very well developed, although travel to rural areas can expose you to a variety of health risks and inadequate medical care.

Travellers tend to worry about contracting infectious diseases when in the tropics, but infections are a rare cause of serious illness or death in travellers. Pre-existing medical conditions such as heart disease, and accidental injury (especially traffic accidents), account for most life-threatening problems. Becoming ill in some way, however, is relatively common. Fortunately, most common illnesses can either be prevented with some common-sense behaviour or be treated easily with a well-stocked traveller's medical kit.

The following advice is a general guide and does not replace the advice of a doctor trained in travel medicine.

BEFORE YOU GO

Pack medications in their original, clearly labelled, containers. A signed dated letter from your physician describing your medical con-ditions and medications, including generic names, is a good idea. If carrying syringes or needles, be sure to have a physician's letter stating their medical necessity. If you have a heart condition, bring a copy of your ECG taken just before travelling.

If you take any regular medication, bring a double supply in case of loss or theft. In most Southeast Asian countries, excluding Singapore, you can buy many medications over the counter without a doctor's prescription, but it can be difficult to find some of the newer drugs, particularly the latest antidepressants, blood-pressure medications and contraceptive pills.

INSURANCE

Even if you are fit and healthy, don't travel without health insurance – accidents do happen. Declare any existing medical conditions you have – the insurance company *will* check if your problem is pre-existing and will not cover you if it is undeclared. You may require extra cover for adventure activities such as rock climbing. If your health insurance doesn't cover you for medical expenses abroad, consider getting extra insurance. If you're uninsured, emergency evacuation is expensive – bills of more than US$100,000 are not uncommon.

Find out in advance if your insurance plan will make payments directly to providers or reimburse you later for overseas health expenditures. (In many countries doctors expect payment in cash.) Some policies offer a range of medical-expense options; the higher ones are chiefly for countries that have extremely high medical costs, such as the USA. You may prefer a policy that pays doctors or hospitals directly rather than you having to pay on the spot and claim later. If you have to claim later, make sure you keep all documentation. Some policies ask you to call (reverse charges) a centre in your home country, where an immediate assessment of your problem is made.

VACCINATIONS

Specialised travel-medicine clinics are your best source of information; they stock all available vaccines and will be able to give specific recommendations for you and your trip. The doctors will take into account factors such as past vaccination history, the length of your trip, activities you may be undertaking and underlying medical conditions, such as pregnancy.

Most vaccines don't produce immunity until at least two weeks after they're given, so visit a doctor four to eight weeks before departure. Ask your doctor for an International Certificate of Vaccination (otherwise known as the yellow booklet), which will list all the vaccinations you've received.

Recommended Vaccinations

The World Health Organization (WHO) recommends the following vaccinations for travellers to Southeast Asia:

Adult diphtheria and tetanus Single booster recommended if you haven't had one in the previous 10 years. Side effects include a sore arm and fever.

Hepatitis A Provides almost 100% protection for up to a year; a booster after 12 months provides at least another 20 years' protection. Mild side effects such as headache and a sore arm occur in 5% to 10% of people.

Hepatitis B Now considered routine for most travellers. Given as three shots over six months. A rapid schedule is also available, as is a combined vaccination with Hepatitis A. Side effects are mild and uncommon, usually headache and a sore arm. Lifetime protection occurs in 95% of people.

Measles, mumps and rubella (MMR) Two doses of MMR are required unless you have had the diseases. Occasionally a rash and flu-like illness can develop a week after receiving the vaccine. Many young adults require a booster.

Polio In 2002, no countries in Southeast Asia reported cases of polio. Only one booster is required as an adult for lifetime protection. Inactivated polio vaccine is safe during pregnancy.

Typhoid Recommended unless your trip is less than a week long and only to developed cities. The vaccine offers around 70% protection, lasts for two to three years and comes as a single shot. Tablets are also available, however, the injection is usually recommended as it has fewer side effects. A sore arm and fever may occur.

Varicella If you haven't had chickenpox, discuss this vaccination with your doctor.

The following immunisations are recommended for long-term travellers (more than one month) or those at special risk:

Japanese B Encephalitis Three injections in all. A booster is recommended after two years. A sore arm and headache are the most common side effects. A rare allergic reaction comprising hives and swelling can occur up to 10 days after any of the three doses.

Meningitis Single injection. There are two types of vaccination: the quadrivalent vaccine gives two to three years' protection; the meningitis group C vaccine gives around 10 years' protection. Recommended for long-term backpackers aged under 25.

Rabies Three injections in all. A booster after one year will then provide 10 years' protection. Side effects are rare – occasionally a headache and a sore arm.

Tuberculosis (TB) A complex issue. Long-term adult travellers are usually recommended to have a TB skin test before and after travel, rather than vaccination. Only one vaccine is given in a lifetime.

Required Vaccinations

The only vaccine required by international regulations is for yellow fever. Proof of vaccination will only be required if you have visited a country in the yellow-fever zone within the six days before entering Southeast Asia. If you are travelling to Southeast Asia from Africa or South America you should check to see if you require proof of vaccination.

MEDICAL CHECKLIST

Recommended items for a personal medical kit:

- antibacterial cream, eg Muciprocin
- antibiotic for skin infections, eg amoxicillin/Clavulanate or Cephalexin
- antibiotics for diarrhoea, such as Norfloxacin or Ciprofloxacin; for bacterial diarrhoea Azithromycin; for giardiasis or amoebic dysentery Tinidazole
- antifungal cream, eg Clotrimazole
- antihistamine – there are many options, eg Cetrizine for daytime and Promethazine for night
- anti-inflammatory such as Ibuprofen
- antiseptic, eg Betadine
- antispasmodic for stomach cramps, eg Buscopa
- contraceptives
- decongestant, eg Pseudoephedrine
- DEET-based insect repellent
- diarrhoea treatment – consider an oral rehydration solution (eg Gastrolyte), diarrhoea 'stopper' (eg Loperamide) and antinausea medication (eg Prochlorperazine)
- first-aid items such as scissors, plasters, bandages, gauze, thermometer (but not one with mercury), sterile needles and syringes, safety pins and tweezers
- indigestion medication, eg Quick Eze or Mylanta

- iodine tablets (unless you are pregnant or have a thyroid problem) to purify water
- laxative, eg Coloxyl
- migraine medication – sufferers should take personal medicine
- paracetamol
- Permethrin to impregnate clothing and mosquito nets
- steroid cream for allergic or itchy rashes, eg 1% to 2% hydrocortisone
- sunscreen and hat
- throat lozenges
- thrush (vaginal yeast infection) treatment, eg Clotrimazole pessaries or Diflucan tablet
- Ural or equivalent if you're prone to urine infections

ONLINE RESOURCES

There is a wealth of travel health advice on the Internet. For further information, **Lonely Planet** (www.lonelyplanet.com) is a good place to start. The **World Health Organization** (www.who.int/ith) publishes a superb book called *International Travel & Health*, which is revised annually and is available online at no cost. Another website of general interest is **MD Travel Health** (www.mdtravelhealth.com), which provides complete travel health recommendations for every country and is updated daily. The **Centers for Disease Control and Prevention** (CDC; www.cdc.gov) website also has good general information.

FURTHER READING

Lonely Planet's *Healthy Travel – Asia & India* is a handy pocket-size book that is packed with useful information, including pretrip planning, emergency first aid, immunisation and disease information, and what to do if you get sick on the road. Other recommended references include *Traveller's Health* by Dr Richard Dawood and *Travelling Well* by Dr Deborah Mills – check out www.travellingwell.com.au.

IN TRANSIT

DEEP VEIN THROMBOSIS (DVT)

Deep vein thrombosis (DVT) occurs when blood clots form in the legs during plane flights, chiefly because of prolonged immobility. The longer the flight, the greater the risk. Although most blood clots are re- absorbed uneventfully, some may break off and travel through the blood vessels to the lungs, where they may cause life-threatening complications.

The chief symptom of DVT is swelling or pain of the foot, ankle or calf, usually but not always on just one side. When a blood clot travels to the lungs, it may cause chest pain and difficulty in breathing. Travellers with any of these symptoms should immediately seek medical attention.

To prevent the development of DVT on long flights you should walk about the cabin, perform isometric compressions of the leg muscles (ie contract the leg muscles while sitting), drink plenty of fluids and avoid alcohol and tobacco.

JET LAG & MOTION SICKNESS

Jet lag is common when crossing more than five time zones; it causes insomnia, fatigue, malaise or nausea. To avoid jet lag try drinking plenty of (nonalcoholic) fluids and eating light meals. Upon arrival, seek exposure to natural sunlight and readjust your schedule (for meals, sleep etc) as soon as possible.

Antihistamines such as dimenhydrinate (Dramamine) and meclizine (Antivert or Bonine) are usually the first choice for treating motion sickness. Their main side effect is drowsiness. A herbal alternative is ginger, which works like a charm for some people.

IN SOUTHEAST ASIA

AVAILABILITY OF HEALTH CARE

Most capital cities in Southeast Asia now have clinics that cater specifically to travellers and expats. These clinics are usually more expensive than local medical facilities, but are worth utilising, as they will offer a superior standard of care. Additionally, they understand the local system and are aware of the safest local hospitals and best specialists. They can also liaise with insurance companies should you require evacuation. Recommended clinics are listed under Information in the capital city sections of country chapters in this book.

It is difficult to find reliable medical care in rural areas. Your embassy and insurance company are good contacts.

Self-treatment may be appropriate if your problem is minor (eg traveller's diarrhoea),

---

AVIAN INFLUENZA (BIRD FLU)

In 2003 and 2004, five Southeast Asian countries (Cambodia, Indonesia, Laos, Thailand and Vietnam), plus China, Japan and South Korea, reported an outbreak of Avian influenza (bird flu). The strain in question, known as 'Influenza A H5N1' or simply 'the H5N1 virus', was a highly contagious form of Avian influenza that has since spread as far as Turkey to the west. Throughout the region, government officials are scrambling to contain the spread of the disease, which wreaks havoc with domesticated bird populations.

While the Avian influenza virus usually poses little risk to humans, there have been several recorded cases of the H5N1 virus spreading from birds to humans. Since 1997, there have been about 250 reported cases of human infection, with a fatality rate of about 30%. The main risk is to people who directly handle infected birds or come into contact with contaminated bird faeces or carcasses. Because heat kills the virus, there is no risk of infection from properly cooked poultry.

There is no clear evidence that the H5N1 virus can be transmitted between humans. However, the main fear is that this highly adaptable virus may mutate and be passed between humans, perhaps leading to a worldwide influenza pandemic.

Thus far, however, infection rates are limited and the risk to travellers is low. Travellers to the region should avoid contact with any birds and should ensure that any poultry is thoroughly cooked before consumption.

---

you are carrying the appropriate medication and you cannot attend a recommended clinic. If you think you may have a serious disease, especially malaria, do not waste time – travel to the nearest quality facility to receive attention. It is always better to be assessed by a doctor than to rely on self-treatment.

Buying medication over the counter is not recommended, as fake medications and poorly stored or out-of-date drugs are common.

The standard of care in Southeast Asia varies from country to country:

Brunei General care is reasonable. There is no local medical university, so expats and foreign-trained locals run the health-care system. Serious or complex cases are better managed in Singapore, but adequate primary health care and stabilisation is available.

Cambodia There are a couple of international clinics in Phnom Penh, and one in Siem Reap, that provide primary care and emergency stabilisation.

East Timor No private clinics. The government hospital is basic and should be avoided. Contact your embassy or insurance company for advice.

Indonesia Local medical care in general is not yet up to international standards. Foreign doctors are not allowed to work in Indonesia, but some clinics catering to foreigners have 'international advisers'. Almost all Indonesian doctors work at government hospitals during the day and in private practices at night. This means that private hospitals often don't have their best staff available during the day. Serious cases are evacuated to Australia or Singapore.

Laos There are no good facilities in Laos; the nearest acceptable facilities are in northern Thailand. The Australian Embassy Clinic treats citizens of Commonwealth countries.

Malaysia Medical care in the major centres is good, and most problems can be adequately dealt with in Kuala Lumpur.

Myanmar Local medical care is dismal and local hospitals should only be used in desperation. There is an international medical clinic in Yangon. Contact your embassy for advice.

Philippines Good medical care is available in most major cities.

Singapore Excellent medical facilities, and it acts as the referral centre for most of Southeast Asia.

Thailand There are some very good facilities in Thailand, particularly in Bangkok. After Singapore this is the city of choice for expats living in Southeast Asia who require specialised care.

Vietnam Government hospitals are overcrowded and basic. In order to treat foreigners, a facility needs to obtain a special licence, and so far only a few have been provided. The private clinics in Hanoi and Ho Chi Minh City should be your first port of call. They are familiar with the local resources and can organise evacuations if necessary.

INFECTIOUS DISEASES
Cutaneous Larva Migrans

Risk All countries except Singapore.

This disease, caused by dog hookworm, is particularly common on the beaches of Thailand. The rash starts as a small lump, then slowly spreads in a linear fashion. It is intensely itchy, especially at night. It is easily treated with medications and should not be cut out or frozen.

Dengue
Risk All countries.

This mosquito-borne disease is becoming increasingly problematic throughout Southeast Asia, especially in the cities. As there is no vaccine available it can only be prevented by avoiding mosquito bites. The mosquito that carries dengue bites day and night, so use insect-avoidance measures at all times. Symptoms include high fever, severe headache and body ache (dengue used to be known as breakbone fever). Some people develop a rash and experience diarrhoea. Thailand's southern islands are particularly high risk. There is no specific treatment, just rest and paracetamol – do not take aspirin as it increases the likelihood of haemorrhaging. See a doctor to be diagnosed and monitored.

Filariasis
Risk All countries except Singapore.

This mosquito-borne disease is very common in the local population, yet very rare in travellers. Mosquito-avoidance measures are the best way to prevent this disease.

Hepatitis A
Risk All countries.

A problem throughout the region, this food- and water-borne virus infects the liver, causing jaundice (yellow skin and eyes), nausea and lethargy. There is no specific treatment for hepatitis A; you just need to allow time for the liver to heal. All travellers to Southeast Asia should be vaccinated against hepatitis A.

Hepatitis B
Risk All countries.

The only sexually transmitted disease that can be prevented by vaccination, hepatitis B is spread by body fluids, including sexual contact. In some parts of Southeast Asia, up to 20% of the population carry hepatitis B, and usually are unaware of this. The long-term consequences can include liver cancer and cirrhosis.

Hepatitis E
Risk All countries.

Hepatitis E is transmitted through contaminated food and water and has similar symptoms to hepatitis A, but is far less common. It is a severe problem in pregnant women and can result in the death of both mother and baby. There is currently no vaccine, and prevention is by following safe eating and drinking guidelines.

HIV
Risk All countries.

HIV is now one of the most common causes of death in people under the age of 50 in Thailand. The countries with the worst and most rapidly increasing HIV problem are Cambodia, Myanmar, Thailand and Vietnam. Heterosexual sex is now the main method of transmission in these countries.

Influenza
Risk All countries.

Present year-round in the tropics, influenza (flu) symptoms include high fever, muscle aches, runny nose, cough and sore throat. It can be very severe in people over the age of 65 or in those with underlying medical conditions such as heart disease or diabetes; vaccination is recommended for these individuals. There is no specific treatment, just rest and paracetamol.

Japanese B Encephalitis
Risk All countries except Singapore.

While rare in travellers, this viral disease, transmitted by mosquitoes, infects at least 50,000 locals each year. Most cases occur in rural areas and vaccination is recommended for travellers spending more than one month outside of cities. There is no treatment, and a third of infected people will die while another third will suffer permanent brain damage. Highest-risk areas include Vietnam, Thailand and Indonesia.

Leptospirosis
Risk Thailand and Malaysia.

Leptospirosis is most commonly contracted after river rafting or canyoning. Early symptoms are very similar to the flu and include headache and fever. The disease can vary from very mild to fatal. Diagnosis is through blood tests and it is easily treated with Doxycycline.

Malaria
Risk All countries except Singapore and Brunei.

For such a serious and potentially deadly disease, there is an enormous amount of misinformation concerning malaria. You must get expert advice about whether your trip actually puts you at risk. Many parts of Southeast Asia, particularly city and resort areas, have minimal to no risk of malaria, and the risk of side effects from the prevention tablets may outweigh the risk of getting the disease. For most rural areas, however, the risk of contracting the disease far outweighs the risk of any tablet side effects. Remember that malaria can be fatal. Before you travel, seek medical advice on the right medication and dosage for you.

Malaria is caused by a parasite transmitted by the bite of an infected mosquito. The most important symptom of malaria is fever, but general symptoms such as headache, diarrhoea, cough or chills may also occur. Diagnosis can only be made by taking a blood sample.

Two strategies should be combined to prevent malaria – mosquito avoidance and antimalarial medications. Most people who catch malaria are taking inadequate or no antimalarial medication.

Travellers are advised to prevent mosquito bites by taking the following steps.

- Use a DEET-containing insect repellent on exposed skin. Wash this off at night, as long as you are sleeping under a mosquito net. Natural repellents such as citronella can be effective, but must be applied more frequently than products containing DEET.
- Sleep under a mosquito net that is impregnated with Permethrin.
- Choose accommodation with screens and fans (if not air-conditioned).
- Impregnate clothing with Permethrin in high-risk areas.
- Wear long sleeves and trousers in light colours.
- Use mosquito coils.
- Spray your room with insect repellent before going out for your evening meal.

There are a variety of medications available. Derivatives of **Artesunate** are not suitable as a preventive medication. They are useful treatments under medical supervision.

The effectiveness of the **Chloroquine and Paludrine** combination is now limited in most of Southeast Asia. Common side effects include nausea (40% of people) and mouth ulcers. Generally not recommended.

The daily **Doxycycline** tablet is a broad-spectrum antibiotic that has the added benefit of helping to prevent a variety of tropical diseases, including leptospirosis, tick-borne disease, typhus and melioidosis. The potential side effects include photosensitivity (a tendency to sunburn), thrush in women, indigestion, heartburn, nausea and interference with the contraceptive pill. More serious side effects include ulceration of the oesophagus – you can help prevent this by taking your tablet with a meal and a large glass of water, and never lying down within half an hour of taking it. It must be taken for four weeks after leaving the risk area.

Lariam (Mefloquine) has received much bad press, some of it justified, some not. This weekly tablet suits many people. Serious side effects are rare but include depression, anxiety, psychosis and seizures. Anyone with a history of depression, anxiety, other psychological disorders, or epilepsy should not take Lariam. It is considered safe in the second and third trimesters of pregnancy. It is around 90% effective in most parts of Southeast Asia, but there is significant resistance in parts of northern Thailand, Laos and Cambodia. Tablets must be taken for four weeks after leaving the risk area.

Malarone is a combination of Atovaquone and Proguanil. Side effects are uncommon and mild, most commonly nausea and headache. It is the best tablet for scuba divers and for those on short trips to high-risk areas. It must be taken for one week after leaving the risk area.

A final option is to take no preventive medication but to have a supply of emergency medication should you develop the symptoms of malaria. This is less than ideal, and you'll need to get to a good medical facility within 24 hours of developing a fever. If you choose this option the most effective and safest treatment is Malarone (four tablets once daily for three days). Other options include Mefloquine and Quinine, but the side effects of these drugs at treatment doses make them less desirable. Fansidar is no longer recommended.

Measles

Risk All countries except Singapore and Brunei.

Measles remains a problem in some parts of Southeast Asia. This highly contagious bacterial infection is spread via coughing and sneezing. Most people born before 1966 are immune as they had the disease in childhood. Measles starts with a high fever and rash and can be complicated by pneumonia and brain disease. There is no specific treatment.

Meliodosis
Risk Thailand only.

This infection is contracted by skin contact with soil. It is rare in travellers, but in some parts of northeast Thailand up to 30% of the local population is infected. The symptoms are very similar to those experienced by tuberculosis sufferers. There is no vaccine but it can be treated with medications.

Rabies
Risk All countries except Singapore and Brunei.

Still a common problem in most parts of Southeast Asia, this uniformly fatal disease is spread by the bite or lick of an infected animal – most commonly a dog or monkey. You should seek medical advice immediately after any animal bite and commence postexposure treatment. Having pretravel vaccination means the postbite treatment is greatly simplified. If an animal bites you, gently wash the wound with soap and water, and apply iodine-based antiseptic. If you are not prevaccinated you will need to receive rabies immunoglobulin as soon as possible.

Schistosomiasis
Risk Philippines, Vietnam and Sulawesi (Indonesia).

Schistosomiasis is a tiny parasite that enters your skin after you've been swimming in contaminated water – travellers usually only get a light infection and hence have no symptoms. If you are concerned, you can be tested three months after exposure. On rare occasions, travellers may develop 'Katayama fever'. This occurs some weeks after exposure, as the parasite passes through the lungs and causes an allergic reaction – symptoms are coughing and fever. Schistosomiasis is easily treated with medications.

STDs
Risk All countries.

Sexually transmitted diseases most common in Southeast Asia include herpes, warts, syphilis, gonorrhoea and chlamydia. People carrying these diseases often have no signs of infection. Condoms will prevent gonorrhoea and chlamydia but not warts or herpes. If

after a sexual encounter you develop any rash, lumps, discharge or pain when passing urine, seek immediate medical attention. If you have been sexually active during your travels, have an STD check on your return home.

Strongyloides
Risk Cambodia, Myanmar and Thailand.

This parasite, transmitted by skin contact with soil, is common in travellers but rarely affects them. It is characterised by an unusual skin rash called *larva currens* – a linear rash on the trunk that comes and goes. Most people don't have other symptoms until their immune system becomes severely suppressed, when the parasite can cause an overwhelming infection. It can be treated with medications.

Tuberculosis
Risk All countries.

While rare in travellers, medical and aid workers and long-term travellers who have significant contact with the local population should take precautions. Vaccination is usually only given to children under the age of five, but adults at risk are recommended pre- and post-travel TB testing. The main symptoms are fever, cough, weight loss, night sweats and tiredness.

Typhoid
Risk All countries except Singapore.

This serious bacterial infection is spread via food and water. It gives a high and slowly progressive fever, headache and may be accompanied by a dry cough and stomach pain. It is diagnosed by blood tests and treated with antibiotics. Vaccination is recommended for all travellers spending more than a week in Southeast Asia, or travelling outside of the major cities. Be aware that vaccination is not 100% effective so you must still be careful with what you eat and drink.

Typhus
Risk All countries except Singapore.

Murine typhus is spread by the bite of a flea, whereas scrub typhus is spread via a mite. These diseases are rare in travellers. Symptoms include fever, muscle pains and a rash. You can avoid these diseases by following general insect-avoidance measures. Doxycycline will also prevent them.

TRAVELLER'S DIARRHOEA

Traveller's diarrhoea is by far the most common problem that affects travellers – between 30% and 50% of people will suffer from it within two weeks of starting their trip. In over 80% of cases, traveller's diarrhoea is caused by a bacteria (there are numerous potential culprits), and therefore responds promptly to treatment with antibiotics. Treatment will depend on your situation – how sick you are, how quickly you need to get better, where you are etc.

Traveller's diarrhoea is defined as the passage of more than three watery bowel-actions within 24 hours, plus at least one other symptom such as fever, cramps, nausea, vomiting or feeling generally unwell.

Treatment consists of staying well hydrated; rehydration solutions such as Gastrolyte are the best for this. Antibiotics such as Norfloxacin, Ciprofloxacin or Azithromycin will kill the bacteria quickly.

Loperamide is just a 'stopper' and doesn't get to the cause of the problem. It can be helpful, for example, if you have to go on a long bus ride. Don't take Loperamide if you have a fever, or blood in your stools. Seek medical attention quickly if you do not respond to an appropriate antibiotic.

Amoebic Dysentery

Amoebic dysentery is very rare in travellers but is often misdiagnosed by poor quality labs in Southeast Asia. Symptoms are similar to bacterial diarrhoea, ie fever, bloody diarrhoea and generally feeling unwell. You should always seek reliable medical care if you have blood in your diarrhoea. Treatment involves two drugs: Tinidazole or Metronidazole to kill the parasite in your gut and then a second drug to kill the cysts. If left untreated, complications such as liver or gut abscesses can occur.

Giardiasis

Giardia lamblia is a relatively common parasite in travellers. Symptoms include nausea, bloating, excess gas, fatigue and intermittent diarrhoea. 'Eggy' burps are often attributed solely to giardiasis, but work in Nepal has shown that they are not specific to this infection. The parasite will eventually go away if left untreated but this can take months. The treatment of choice is Tinidazole, with Metronidazole being a second option.

ENVIRONMENTAL HAZARDS
Air Pollution

Air pollution, particularly vehicle pollution, is an increasing problem in most of Southeast Asia's major cities. If you have severe respiratory problems speak with your doctor before travelling to any heavily polluted urban centres. This pollution also causes minor respiratory problems such as sinusitis, dry throat and irritated eyes. If troubled by the pollution, leave the city for a few days and get some fresh air.

Diving

Divers and surfers should seek specialised advice before they travel, to ensure their medical kit contains treatment for coral cuts and tropical ear infections, as well as the standard problems. Divers should ensure their insurance covers them for decompression illness – get specialised dive insurance through an organisation such as **Divers Alert Network** (DAN; www.danseap.org). Have a dive medical before you leave your home country; there are certain medical conditions that are incompatible with diving, and economic considerations may override health considerations for some dive operators in Southeast Asia.

Food

Eating in restaurants is the biggest risk factor for contracting traveller's diarrhoea. Ways to avoid diarrhoea include eating only freshly cooked food, and avoiding shellfish and food

---

DRINKING WATER

- Never drink tap water.
- Bottled water is generally safe – check the seal is intact at purchase.
- Avoid ice.
- Avoid fresh juices – they may have been watered down.
- Boiling water is the most efficient method of purifying it.
- The best chemical purifier is iodine. It should not be used by pregnant women or those with thyroid problems.
- Water filters should also filter out viruses. Ensure your filter has a chemical barrier such as iodine and a small pore size, eg less than four microns.

that has been sitting around in buffets. Peel all fruit, cook vegetables, and soak salads in iodine water for at least 20 minutes. Eat in busy restaurants with a high turnover of customers.

Heat

Many parts of Southeast Asia are hot and humid throughout the year. For most people it takes at least two weeks to adapt to the hot climate. Swelling of the feet and ankles is common, as are muscle cramps caused by excessive sweating. Prevent these by avoiding dehydration and excessive activity in the heat. Take it easy when you first arrive. Don't eat salt tablets (they aggravate the gut), but drinking rehydration solution or eating salty food helps. Treat cramps by stopping activity, resting, rehydrating with double-strength rehydration solution and gently stretching.

Dehydration is the main contributor to heat exhaustion. Symptoms include weakness, headache, irritability, nausea or vomiting, sweaty skin, a fast, weak pulse, and a normal or slightly elevated body temperature. Treatment involves getting out of the heat and/or sun, fanning the person and applying cool wet cloths to the skin, laying the person flat with their legs raised, and rehydrating them with water containing a quarter of a teaspoon of salt per litre. Recovery is usually rapid and it is common to feel weak for some days afterwards.

Heat stroke is a serious medical emergency. Symptoms come on suddenly and include weakness, nausea, a hot dry body with a body temperature of over 41°C, dizziness, confusion, loss of coordination, seizures and eventually collapse and loss of consciousness. Seek medical help and commence cooling by getting the person out of the heat, removing their clothes, fanning them and applying cool wet cloths or ice to their body, especially to the groin and armpits.

Prickly heat is a common skin rash in the tropics, caused by sweat being trapped under the skin. The result is an itchy rash of tiny lumps. Treat by moving out of the heat and into an air-conditioned area for a few hours and by having cool showers. Creams and ointments clog the skin so they should be avoided. Locally bought prickly-heat powder can be helpful.

Tropical fatigue is common in long-term expats based in the tropics. It's rarely due to disease and is caused by the climate, inadequate mental rest, excessive alcohol intake and the demands of daily work in a different culture.

Insect Bites & Stings

Bedbugs don't carry disease but their bites are very itchy. They live in the cracks of furniture and walls and then migrate to the bed at night to feed on you. You can treat the itch with an antihistamine.

Lice inhabit various parts of your body but most commonly your head and pubic area. Transmission is via close contact with an infected person. Lice can be difficult to treat and you may need numerous applications of an antilice shampoo such as Permethrin. Pubic lice are usually contracted from sexual contact.

Ticks are contracted after walking in rural areas. They are commonly found behind the ears, on the belly and in armpits. If you have had a tick bite and experience symptoms such as a rash at the site of the bite or elsewhere, or fever or muscle aches, you should see a doctor. Doxycycline prevents tick-borne diseases.

Leeches are found in humid rainforest areas. They do not transmit any disease but their bites are often intensely itchy for weeks afterwards and can easily become infected. Apply an iodine-based antiseptic to any leech bite to help prevent infection.

Bee and wasp stings mainly cause problems for people who are allergic to them. Anyone with a serious bee or wasp allergy should carry an injection of adrenaline (eg an Epipen) for emergency treatment. For others, pain is the main problem – apply ice to the sting and take painkillers.

Most jellyfish in Southeast Asian waters are not dangerous, just irritating. First aid for jellyfish stings involves pouring vinegar onto the affected area to neutralise the poison. Do not rub sand or water onto the stings. Take painkillers, and if you feel ill in any way after being stung seek medical advice. Take local advice if there are dangerous jellyfish around and keep out of the water.

Parasites

Numerous parasites are common in local populations in Southeast Asia; however, most of these are rare in travellers. The two rules for avoiding parasitic infections are to wear shoes and to avoid eating raw food, especially fish, pork and vegetables. A number of parasites are transmitted via the skin by walking barefoot, including strongyloides, hookworm and cutaneous *larva migrans*.

Skin Problems

Fungal rashes are common in humid climates. There are two common fungal rashes that affect travellers. The first occurs in moist areas that get less air, such as the groin, armpits and between the toes. It starts as a red patch that slowly spreads and is usually itchy. Treatment involves keeping the skin dry, avoiding chafing and using an antifungal cream such as Clotrimazole or Lamisil. *Tinea versicolor* is also common – this fungus causes small, light-coloured patches, most commonly on the back, chest and shoulders. Consult a doctor.

Cuts and scratches become easily infected in humid climates. Take meticulous care of any cuts and scratches to prevent complications such as abscesses. Immediately wash all wounds in clean water and apply antiseptic. If you develop signs of infection (increasing pain and redness), see a doctor. Divers and surfers should be particularly careful with coral cuts as they can be easily infected.

Snakes

Southeast Asia is home to many species of both poisonous and harmless snakes. Assume that all snakes are poisonous and never try to catch one. Always wear boots and long pants if walking in an area that may have snakes. First aid in the event of a snakebite involves pressure immobilisation via an elastic bandage firmly wrapped around the affected limb, starting at the bite site and working up towards the chest. The bandage should not be so tight that the circulation is cut off, and the fingers or toes should be kept free so the circulation can be checked. Immobilise the limb with a splint and carry the victim to medical attention. Do not use tourniquets or try to suck the venom out. Antivenin is available for most species.

Sunburn

Even on a cloudy day sunburn can occur rapidly. Always use a strong sunscreen (at least factor 30), making sure to reapply after a swim, and always wear a wide-brimmed hat and sunglasses outdoors. Avoid lying in the sun during the hottest part of the day (10am to 2pm). If you become sunburnt, stay out of the sun until you have recovered, apply cool compresses and take painkillers for the discomfort. One percent hydrocortisone cream applied twice daily is also helpful.

WOMEN'S HEALTH

Pregnant women should receive specialised advice before travelling. The ideal time to travel is in the second trimester (between 16 and 28 weeks), when the risk of pregnancy-related problems is at its lowest and pregnant women generally feel at their best. During the first trimester there is a risk of miscarriage and in the third trimester complications such as premature labour and high blood pressure are possible. It's wise to travel with a companion. Always carry a list of quality medical facilities available at your destination and ensure you continue your standard antenatal care at these facilities. Avoid rural travel in areas with poor transportation and medical facilities. Most of all, ensure travel insurance covers all pregnancy-related possibilities, including premature labour.

Malaria is a high-risk disease during pregnancy. WHO recommends that pregnant women do *not* travel to areas with Chloroquine-resistant malaria. None of the more effective antimalarial drugs are completely safe in pregnancy.

Traveller's diarrhoea can quickly lead to dehydration and result in inadequate blood flow to the placenta. Many of the drugs used to treat various diarrhoea bugs are not recommended in pregnancy. Azithromycin is considered safe.

In the urban areas of Southeast Asia, supplies of sanitary products are readily available. Birth control options may be limited so bring adequate supplies of your own form of contraception. Heat, humidity and antibiotics can all contribute to thrush. Treatment is with antifungal creams and pessaries such as Clotrimazole. A practical alternative is a single tablet of Fluconazole (Diflucan). Urinary tract infections can be precipitated by dehydration or long bus journeys without toilet stops; bring suitable antibiotics.

TRADITIONAL MEDICINE

Throughout Southeast Asia, the traditional medical systems are widely practised. There is a big difference between these traditional healing systems and 'folk' medicine. Folk remedies should be avoided, as they often involve rather dubious procedures with potential complications. In comparison, traditional healing systems such as traditional Chinese medicine are well respected, and aspects of them are being increasingly utilised by Western medical practitioners.

All traditional Asian medical systems identify a vital life force, and see blockage or imbalance as causing disease. Techniques such as herbal medicines, massage and acupuncture are used to bring this vital force back into balance, or to maintain balance. These therapies are best used for treating chronic disease such as chronic fatigue, arthritis, irritable bowel syndrome and some chronic skin conditions. Traditional medicines should be avoided for treating serious acute infections such as malaria.

Be aware that 'natural' doesn't always mean 'safe', and there can be drug interactions between herbal medicines and Western medicines. If you are using both systems ensure you inform each practitioner what the other has prescribed.

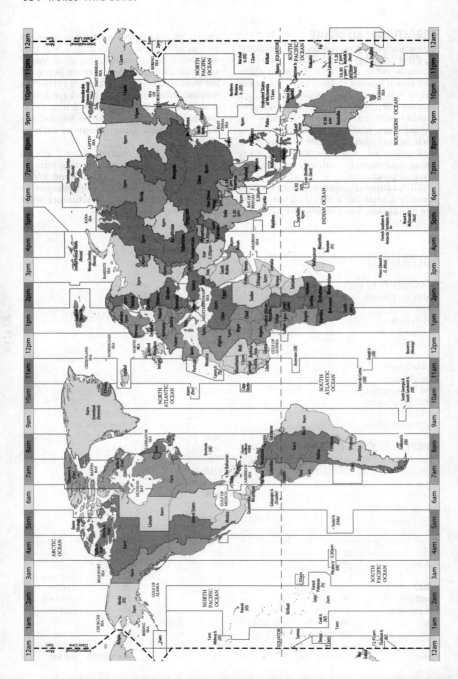

Language

Language

CONTENTS

CAMBODIA (KHMER)

ACCOMMODATION

Where is a (cheap) hotel?	sahnthaakia/ohtail (thaok) neuv ai naa?
Do you have a room?	niak mian bantohp tohmne te?
How much is it per day?	damlay muy th'ngay pohnmaan?

I'd like a room ...	kh'nyohm sohm bantohp ...
for one person	samruhp muy niak
for two people	samruhp pii niak
with a bathroom	dail mian bantohp tuhk
with a fan	dail mian dawnghahl
with a window	dail mian bawng-uit

CONVERSATION & ESSENTIALS

The Khmer language reflects the social standing of the speaker and subject through various personal pronouns and 'politeness words', many based of the subject's age and sex in relation to the speaker. Foreigners aren't expected to know all of these forms; the easiest and most general personal pronoun is *niak* (you), which may be used in most situations, with either sex. It comes at the beginning of a phrase.

Hello.	johm riab sua/sua s'dei
Goodbye.	lia suhn hao-y
See you later.	juab kh'niath'ngay krao-y
Yes.	baat (used by men)
	jaa (used by women)
No.	te
Please.	sohm

Thank you.	aw kohn
You're welcome.	awt ei te/sohm anjœ-in
Excuse me/I'm sorry.	sohm toh
Pardon?	niak niyey thaa mait?
Hi. How are you?	niak sohk sabaay te?
I'm fine.	kh'nyohm sohk sabaay
Where are you going?	niak teuv naa?

(NB This is a very common question used when meeting people, even strangers; an exact answer is not necessary.)

Do you speak English?	niak jeh phiasaa awngle te?
I understand.	kh'nyohm yuhl
I don't understand.	kh'nyohm muhn yuhl te

EMERGENCIES – CAMBODIA

Help!	juay kh'nyohm phawng!
Call a doctor!	juay hav kruu paet mao!
Call the police!	juay hav polih mao!

Are there any land mines in this area?	neuv m'dohm nih mian miin reu te?
Where are the toilets?	bawngkohn neuv ai naa?

FOOD & DRINK

restaurant	resturaan/phowjuhniiyathaan
food stall	kuhnlaing luak m'howp
market	p'saa
I'm a vegetarian.	kh'nyohm tawm sait
beef	sait kow
chicken	sait moan
fish	trei
coffee	kaafe
boiled water	tuhk ch'uhn
milk	tuhk dawh kow
tea	tai
sugar	skaw

NUMBERS

1	muy	11	dawp muy
2	pii	12	dawp pii
3	bei	16	dawp bram muy
4	buan	20	m'phei
5	bram	21	m'phei muy
6	bram muy	30	saamsuhp
7	bram pii	40	saisuhp
8	bram bei	100	muy roy
9	bram buan	1000	muy poan
10	dawp	one million	muy lian

LANGUAGE

SHOPPING & SERVICES

I'm looking for the ...	kh'nyohm rohk ...
Where is a ...	... neuv ai naa?
bank	th'niakia
hospital	mohntii paet
market	p'saa
post office	praisuhnii
police station	poh polih/
	s'thaanii nohkohbaal
public telephone	turasahp saathiaranah
public toilet	bawngkohn saathiaranah

What time does it open?	wia baok maong pohnmaan?
What time does it close?	wia buht maong pohnmaan?

TIME & DAYS

What time is it?	eileuv nih maong pohnmaan?
in the morning	pel pruhk
in the afternoon	pel r'sial
in the evening	pel l'ngiat
today	th'ngay nih
tomorrow	th'ngay s'aik

Monday	th'ngay jahn
Tuesday	th'ngay ahngkia
Wednesday	th'ngay poht
Thursday	th'ngay prohoah
Friday	th'ngay sohk
Saturday	th'ngay sav
Sunday	th'ngay aatuht

TRANSPORT

Where is the ...?	... neuv ai naa?
airport	wial yohn hawh
bus station	kuhnlaing laan ch'nual
bus stop	jamnawt laan ch'nual
train station	s'thaanii roht plœng

What time does the ... leave?	... jein maong pohnmaan?
bus	laan ch'nual
plane	yohn hawh/k'pal hawh
train	roht plœng

Directions

Is it far?	wia neuv ch'ngaay te?
Is it near?	wia neuv juht te?
Go straight ahead.	teuv trawng
Turn left ...	bawt ch'weng
Turn right ...	bawt s'dam

EAST TIMOR (TETUN)

Tetun is the most widely spoken lingua franca in East Timor. Originally spoken on the south coast of Timor, a form of Tetun was brought to Dili by the Portuguese in the late 18th century. Although Portuguese was nominated East Timor's official language after East Timor gained independence, Tetun became the national language with the intention of making it co-official with Portuguese.

PRONUNCIATION

j	as the 's' in 'pleasure' (sometimes as the 'z' in 'zebra')
r	trilled
x	as the 'sh' in 'ship' (the more traditional, Portuguese-style spelling is **ch**, but it's always pronounced as 'sh'); sometimes pronounced as the 's' in 'summer'

ACCOMMODATION

I'm looking for a ...	Hau buka hela ...
guesthouse	losmen/pensaun
hotel	otél

Do you have any rooms available?	Ita iha kuartu ruma mamuk?

I'd like ...	Hau hakarak ...
a single room	kuartu mesak ida
to share a room	fahe kuartu ida

CONVERSATION & ESSENTIALS

Hello.	Haló. (pol)/Olá. (inf)
Goodbye.	Adeus.
Yes.	Sin/Diak/Los.
No.	Lae.
Please.	Favór ida/Halo favór/ Faz favór/Por favór.
Thank you (very much).	Obrigadu/a (barak).
You're welcome.	La (iha) buat ida./(De) nada.
Excuse me.	Kolisensa.
What's your name?	Ita-nia naran sa/saida?
My name is ...	Hau-nia naran ...
Do you speak English?	Ita koalia Inglés?
I don't understand.	Hau la kompriende.

EMERGENCIES – EAST TIMOR

Help!	Ajuda!
Call a doctor!	Bolu dotór!
Call the police!	Bolu polísia!
I'm lost.	Hau lakon tiha.
Where are the toilets?	Sintina iha nebé?

FOOD & DRINK

breakfast	matebixu; han dadér
lunch	han meudia
dinner	jantár
I'm a vegetarian.	Hau (ema) vejetarianu.
bread	paun
butter	manteiga
chicken	nan manu
eggs	manutolun
fish	ikan
fruit	aifuan
milk	susubén
pepper	pimenta
salt	masin
sugar	masin midar (lit: sweet salt)
vegetables	modo tahan
water	be
mineral water	be minerál
boiled water	be tasak/nono
bottled water	ákua; be botir
tea	xa
(Timorese) coffee	kafé (Timór)
beer	serveja

NUMBERS

Larger numbers are given in Tetun, Portuguese or Indonesian.

	Tetun	Portuguese
0	nol	zero
1	ida	um/uma
2	rua	dois/duas
3	tolu	três
4	hat	quatro
5	lima	cinco
6	nen	seis
7	hitu	sete
8	ualu	oito
9	sia	nove
10	sanulu	dez
11	sanulu-resin-ida	onze
12	sanulu-resin-rua	doze
20	ruanulu	vinte
100	atus ida	cem
1000	rihun ida	mil

SHOPPING & SERVICES

Where is a/the ...?	... iha nebé?
bank	banku
general store	loja
market	basar/merkadu
post office	koreiu; kantor pos
public telephone	telefone públiku; wartel
toilet	sintina/WC

What time does ... open/close?	Tuku hira maka ... loke/taka?
How much is it?	Folin hira?

TIME & DAYS

What time is it?	Tuku hira (ona)?
(It's) one o'clock.	Tuku ida.
today	ohin
tonight	ohin kalan
tomorrow	aban
yesterday	horseik

Monday	segunda
Tuesday	tersa
Wednesday	kuarta
Thursday	kinta
Friday	sesta
Saturday	sábadu
Sunday	dumingu

TRANSPORT

When does the ... leave/arrive?	Tuku hira maka ... ba/to?
bus	bis/biskota
minibus	mikrolet
plane	aviaun

bus station	terminál bis nian
road to (Aileu)	dalan ba (Aileu)

Directions

Go straight ahead.	Los deit.
To the left.	Fila ba liman karuk.
To the right.	Fila ba liman los.
near	besik
far	dok

INDONESIA (BAHASA)

ACCOMMODATION

guesthouse	losmen
bathroom	kamar mandi
bed	tempat tidur
toilet	WC (way say)/kamar kecil

Is there a room available?	*Adakah kamar kosong?*
May I see the room?	*Boleh saya melihat kamar?*
one night	*satu malam*
two nights	*dua malam*

CONVERSATION & ESSENTIALS

Good morning.	*Selamat pagi.*
Good day.	*Selamat siang.*
Good afternoon.	*Selamat sore.*
Good evening/night.	*Selamat malam.*
Goodbye. (to person staying)	*Selamat tinggal.*
Goodbye. (to person going)	*Selamat jalan.*
How are you?	*Apa kabar?*
I'm fine.	*Kabar baik.*
Please.	*Tolong.*
Thank you (very much).	*Terima kasih (banyak).*
Yes.	*Ya.*
No.	*Tidak/Bukan.*
Excuse me.	*Maaf/Permisi.*
I don't understand.	*Saya tidak mengerti.*
Do you speak English?	*Bisa berbicara bahasa Inggris?*

EMERGENCIES – INDONESIA

Help!	*Tolong!*
Call a doctor!	*Panggil dokter!*
Call the police!	*Panggil polisi!*
I'm lost.	*Saya kesasar.*
Go away!	*Pergi!*

FOOD & DRINK

beef	*daging*
chicken	*ayam*
crab	*kepiting*
egg	*telur*
fish	*ikan*
food	*makanan*
fried noodles	*mie goreng*
pork	*babi*
potato	*kentang*
prawns	*udang-udang*
rice with odds & ends	*nasi campur*
fried rice	*nasi goreng*
white rice	*nasi putih*
soup	*soto*
mixed vegetables	*sayur-sayuran*
fried vegetables	*cap cai*
beer	*bir*
coffee	*kopi*
drinking water	*air minum/air putih*

milk	*susu*
orange juice	*air jeruk*
tea with sugar	*teh manis/teh gula*
tea without sugar	*teh pahit*

NUMBERS

1	*satu*	10	*sepuluh*
2	*dua*	11	*sebelas*
3	*tiga*	20	*duapuluh*
4	*empat*	21	*duapuluh satu*
5	*lima*	30	*tigapuluh*
6	*enam*	50	*limapuluh*
7	*tujuh*	100	*seratus*
8	*delapan*	1000	*seribu*
9	*sembilan*	2000	*duaribu*

one million	*sejuta*

SHOPPING & SERVICES

Where is a/the ...?	*Dimana ...?*
bank	*bank*
post office	*kantor pos*
tourist office	*dinas pariwisata*
public telephone	*telepon umum*
public toilet	*WC umum*

How much is it?	*Berapa harganya ini?*
expensive	*mahal*
open/close	*buka/tutup*

TIME

When?	*Kapan?*
At what time ...?	*Pada jam berapa ...?*
today	*hari ini*
tonight	*malam ini*
tomorrow	*besok*
yesterday	*kemarin*

TRANSPORT

What time does the ... leave/arrive?	*Jam berapa ... berangkat/tiba?*
bus	*bis/bus*
boat	*kapal*
train	*kereta api*

bus station	*setasiun bis/terminal*
ticket	*karcis/tiket*

Directions

I want to go to ...	*Saya mau pergi ke ...*
How far?	*Berapa jauh?*
near/far	*dekat/jauh*
straight ahead	*terus*
left/right	*kiri/kanan*

LANGUAGE

LAOS (LAO)

TONES

Lao is a monosyllabic, tonal language, like various dialects of Thai and Chinese. Many identical phonemes or vowel-consonant combinations are differentiated by tone only. The word *sao*, for example, can mean 'girl', 'morning', 'pillar' or 'twenty', depending on the tone.

Variations in the speaker's pitch are relative to their natural vocal range, so that one person's low tone is not necessarily the same pitch as another person's.

low tone – produced at the relative bottom of your conversational tonal range – usually flat level, eg *dji* (good)

mid tone – flat like the low tone, but spoken at the relative middle of the speaker's vocal range. No tone mark is used, eg *het* (do)

high tone – flat again, but at the relative top of your vocal range, eg *heúa* (boat)

rising tone – begins a bit below the mid tone and rises to just at or above the high tone, eg *sǎam* (three)

high falling tone – begins at or above the high tone and falls to the mid level, eg *sâo* (morning)

low falling tone – begins at about the mid level and falls to the level of the low tone, eg *khào* (rice)

ACCOMMODATION

hotel	hóhng háem
guesthouse	hǎw hap kháek
room	hàwng
toilet	sùam

Do you have a room?	míi hàwng baw?
single room	hàwng náwn tjang diaw
double room	hàwng náwn tjang khuu

How much ...?	... thao dǫi?
per night	khéun·la
per week	qathit·la

(I/we) will stay two nights.	si phak sǎwng khéun
May (I/we) look at the room?	khaw beng hàwng dâi baw?

CONVERSATION & ESSENTIALS

Greetings/Hello.	sábqai·dji
Goodbye. (general farewell)	sábqai·dji

Goodbye. (said by person leaving)	láa kawn (lit: leaving first) pǫi kawn (lit: going first)
Goodbye. (said by person staying)	sǫhk dji (lit: good luck)
How are you?	sábqai·dji baw?
I'm fine.	sábqai·dji
Please.	kálunaa
Thank you (very much).	khàwp jǫi (lǎi lǎi)
Excuse me.	khǎw thôht
Do you speak English?	jâo páak pháasaa qngkít dâi baw?
I don't understand.	baw khào jǫi

FOOD & DRINK

chicken	kai
crab	pǔu
fish	pqa
pork	mǔu
shrimp/prawns	kûng
fried rice with ...	khào (phát/khùa) ...
steamed white rice	khào nèung
sticky rice	khào nío
fried egg	khai dǫo
plain omelette	jeun khai
fried potatoes	mán falang jeun
fried spring rolls	yáw jeun
plain bread (usually French-style)	khào jìi
boiled water	nâam tǫm
cold water	nâam yén
hot water	nâam hâwn
soda water	nâam sah·dqa
ice	nâam kâwn
weak Chinese tea	nâam sáa
hot Lao tea	sáa hâwn
no sugar (a request)	baw sai nâam·tqan
coffee	kqa·féh
orange juice/soda	nâam màak kîang
plain milk	nâam nóm
yoghurt	nóm sòm
beer	bja
rice whisky	lào·láo

LANGUAGE

NUMBERS

0	sŭun	12	síp·sǎwng
1	neung	13	síp·sǎam
2	sǎwng	20	sáo
3	sǎam	21	sáo·ét
4	sìi	22	sáo·sǎwng
5	hàa	30	sǎam·síp
6	hók	100	hâwy
7	jét	200	sǎwng hâwy
8	pàet	1000	phán
9	kâo	10,000	meun (síp·phán)
10	síp	100,000	sǎen (hâwy phán)
11	síp·ét	one million	lâan

SHOPPING & SERVICES

Where is a/the ...?	... yùu sǎi
bank	thanáakháan
hospital	hóhng mǎw
pharmacy	hâan khǎai yqa
post office	pqi·sá·nǐi/hóhng sǎai
stupa	thâat

open	pòet
closed	pít
How much is it?	thao dqi?

TIME & DAYS

today	mêu nǐi
tonight	khéun nǐi
tomorrow	mêu eun
yesterday	mêu wáan nǐi

Monday	wán jqn
Tuesday	wán qngkháan
Wednesday	wán phut
Thursday	wán phahát
Friday	wán súk
Saturday	wán sǎo
Sunday	wán qathit

TRANSPORT

Where is the ...	... yùu sǎi?
bus station	sathǎanii lot pájqm tháang
bus stop	bawn jàwt lot pájqm tháang
taxi stand	bawn jàwt lot thaek·sǐi

What time will the ... leave?	... já àwk ják móhng?
boat	heúa
bus	lot
minivan	lot tûu
taxi	lot thâek·sǐi
samlor (pedicab)	sǎamlâw
tuk-tuk (jumbo)	tuk·tuk

How much to ...?	pqi ... thao dqi?

Directions

I want to go to ...	khàwy yàak pqi ...
How far?	kqi thao dqi?
far/not far	kqi/baw kqi
Turn left.	líaw sâai
Turn right.	líaw khwǎa
Go straight ahead.	pqi seu·seu

MALAYSIA (BAHASA)

ACCOMMODATION

hotel	hotel
losmen	losmen
room	bilik
bed	tempat tidur
expensive	mahal

Is there a room available?	Ada bilik kosong?
How much is it per night/person?	Berapa harga satu malam/orang?
May I see the room?	Boleh saya lihat biliknya?

CONVERSATION & ESSENTIALS

Good morning.	Selamat pagi.
Good day. (around midday)	Selamat tengah hari.
Good evening.	Selamat petang.
Good night.	Selamat malam.
Goodbye. (to person staying)	Selamat tinggal.
Goodbye. (to person leaving)	Selamat jalan.
Yes.	Ya.
No.	Tidak.
Please.	Tolong/Silakan.
Thank you (very much).	Terima kasih (banyak).
You're welcome.	Kembali.
Sorry/Pardon.	Maaf.
Excuse me.	Maafkan saya.
Do you speak English?	Bolehkah anda berbicara bahasa Inggeris?
I don't understand.	Saya tidak faham.

EMERGENCIES – MALAYSIA

Help!	Tolong!
Call a doctor!	Panggil doktor!
Call the police!	Panggil polis!
I'm lost.	Saya sesat.
Go away!	Pegi/Belah!

FOOD & DRINK

without meat	tanpa daging
vegetables only	sayur saja
fish	ikan
chicken	ayam
egg	telur
pork	babi
crab	ketam
beef	daging lembu
prawns	udang
fried rice	nasi goreng
boiled rice	nasi putih
rice with odds & ends	nasi campur
fried noodles	mee goreng
soup	sup
fried vegetables	cap cai
potatoes	kentang
vegetables	sayur-sayuran
drinking water	air minum
orange juice	air jeruk/air oren
coffee	kopi
tea	teh
milk	susu
sugar	gula

NUMBERS

1	satu	10	sepuluh
2	dua	11	sebelas
3	tiga	12	dua belas
4	empat	13	tiga belas
5	lima	20	dua puluh
6	enam	21	dua puluh satu
7	tujuh	30	tiga puluh
8	delapan	100	seratus
9	sembilan	1000	seribu

one million	sejuta

SHOPPING & SERVICES

Where is a/the ...?	Di mana ada ...?
bank	bank
hospital	hospital
post office	pejabat pos
public toilet	tandas awam
tourist office	pejabat pelancong

What time does it open/close?	Pukul berapa buka/tutup?
How much is it?	Berapa harganya ini?

TIME & DAYS

When?	Bila?
How long?	Berapa lama?
today	hari ini
tomorrow	besok
yesterday	kelmarin

Monday	hari Isnin
Tuesday	hari Selasa
Wednesday	hari Rabu
Thursday	hari Kamis
Friday	hari Jumaat
Saturday	hari Sabtu
Sunday	hari minggu

TRANSPORT

What time does the ... leave?	Pukul berapakah ... berangkat?
bus	bas
train	keretapi
ship	kapal
boat	bot

Directions

How can I get to ...?	Bagaimana saya pergi ke ...?
Go straight ahead.	Jalan terus.
Turn left/right.	Belok kiri/kanan.
near/far	dekat/jauh
here/there	di sini/di sana

MYANMAR (BURMESE)

TONES & PRONUNCIATION

Like Thai, Lao and Vietnamese, Burmese is a tonal language, where changes in the relative pitch of the speaker's voice can affect meaning. There are three basic tones in Burmese:

high tone – produced with the voice tense and high-pitched; indicated by an acute accent, eg *ká* (dance)

high falling tone – starts with the voice high, then falling; indicated by a grave accent, eg *kà* (car)

low tone – the voice is relaxed and remains low; indicated by no accent, eg *ka* (shield)

Three other features important to Burmese pronunciation are:

LANGUAGE

a stopped syllable – with a high pitch, the voice is cut off suddenly to produce a glottal stop (similar to the 'non' sound in the middle of the exclamation 'oh-oh'); it's indicated in this guide by a 'q' after the vowel, eg *kaq* (join)

a weak syllable – only occurs on the vowel a, and is pronounced like the 'a' in 'ago'; indicated by a 'v' accent, eg *ălouk* (work)

aspirated consonants – pronounced with an audible puff of breath; indicated by a following apostrophe, eg *s'i* (cooking oil)

ACCOMMODATION
hotel	ho·the
guesthouse	tèh·k'o·gàn
May I see the room?	ăk'àn cí·bayá·ze?

How much is ...?	... beh·lauq·lèh?
one night	tăyeq
two nights	hnăyeq
a single room	tăyauq·k'an
a double room	hnăyauq·k'an

CONVERSATION & ESSENTIALS
Hello.	min·găla·ba
How are you?	k'ămyà (m)/shin (f) ne·kaùn·yéh·là?
I'm well.	ne·kaùn·ba·deh
Have you eaten?	t'ămin sà·pì·bi·là?
I have eaten.	sà·pì·ba·bi
Thanks.	cè·zù·bèh
Thank you.	cè·zù tin·ba·deh
You're welcome.	keiq·sá măshí·ba·bù
Yes.	houq·kéh
No.	măhouq·p'ù
Do you speak English?	k'ămyà (m)/shin (f) ìn·găleiq·zăga lo pyàw·daq·thălà?
I don't understand.	nà·màleh·ba·bù

FOOD & DRINK
Is there a ... near here?	di·nà·hma shí·dhălà?
Chinese restaurant	tăyouq·s'ain
food stall	sà·thauq·s'ain
restaurant	sà·daw·s'eq
Shan noodle stall	shàn·k'auk·swèh·zain

breakfast	măneq·sa
lunch	né·leh·za
dinner	nyá·za
snack/small meal	móun/thăye·za

beef	ămèh
bread	paun·móun
butter	t'àw·baq
chicken	ceq·thà
coffee	kaw·fi
water	ye
boiled cold water	ye·jeq·è
bottled water	thán·ye
egg (boiled)	ceq·ú·byouq
egg (fried)	ceq·ú·jaw
fish	ngà
hot (spicy)	saq·deh
pork	weq·thà
noodles	k'auq·s'wèh
rice (cooked)	t'ămìn
soup	hìn·jo
sugar	thăjà
plain green tea	lăp'eq·yeh·jàn
toast	paun·móun·gin
vegetables	hin·dhì·hìn·yweq
vegetarian	theq·thaq·luq

NUMBERS
1	tiq/tă	10	(tă)s'eh
2	hniq/hnă	11	s'éh·tiq
3	thòun	12	s'éh·hniq
4	lè	20	hnăs'eh
5	ngà	35	thòun·zéh·ngà
6	c'auq	100	tăya
7	k'ú·hniq/ k'ú·hnă	1000	(tă)t'aun
8	shiq	10,000	(tă)thàun
9	kò	100,000	(tă)thèin/lakh

one million	(tă)thàn

SHOPPING & SERVICES
Where is a/the ...?	... beh·hma·lèh?
bank	ban·daiq
hospital	s'è·youn
market	zè
pharmacy	s'è·zain
post office	sa·daiq

Where can I buy ...?	... beh·hma weh·yá·mălèh?
Do you have ...?	... shí·là
How much is ...?	... beh·lauq·lèh?
expensive	zè·cì·deh
cheap	zè·pàw·deh

LANGUAGE

TIME & DAYS

today	*di·né*
tomorrow	*mǎneq·p'yan*
yesterday	*mǎné·gá*

Monday	*tǎnìn·la·né*
Tuesday	*in·ga·né*
Wednesday	*bouq·dǎhù·né*
Thursday	*ca·dhǎbǎdè·né*
Friday	*thauq·ca·né*
Saturday	*sǎne·né*
Sunday	*tǎnìn·gǎnwe·né*

TRANSPORT

Where is the ...?	*... beh·hma·lèh?*
bus station	*baq·sǎkà·geiq*
railway station	*bu·da·youn*
riverboat jetty	*thìn·bàw·zeiq*

When will the ... leave?	*... beh·ǎc'ein t'weq· mǎlèh?*

bus	*baq·sǎkà*
train	*mì·yǎt'à*
riverboat	*thìn·bàw*
taxi	*ǎhngǎ·kà*
rickshaw/sidecar	*s'aiq·kà*
bicycle	*seq·bein*
motorcycle	*mo·ta s'ain·keh*

Directions

How do I get to ...?	*... ko beh·lo thwà·yá·dhǎlèh?*
Is it nearby?	*di·nà·hma·là?*
Is it far?	*wè·dhǎlà?*
straight (ahead)	*téh·déh*
left/right	*beh·beq/nya·beq*

PHILIPPINES (FILIPINO)

ACCOMMODATION

camping ground	*kampingan*
guesthouse	*báhay pára sa nga turist*
cheap hotel	*múrang hotél*
price	*halagá*

Do you have any rooms available?	*May bakánte hó ba kayo?*
How much for one night?	*Magkáno hó ba ang báyad pára sa isang gabi?*

CONVERSATION & ESSENTIALS

Hello.	*Haló.*
Good morning.	*Magandáng umága.*
Good evening.	*Magandáng gabí.*
Welcome/Farewell.	*Mabúhay.*
Goodbye.	*Paálam.*
Thank you.	*Salámat hô.*
Excuse me.	*Mawaláng-galang nga hô.*
Yes.	*Oó.*
No.	*Hindí.*
Do you speak English?	*Marunong ba kayóng mag-Inglés?*
I don't understand.	*Hindí ko hô náiintindihán.*

EMERGENCIES – PHILIPPINES

Help!	*Saklolo!*
Where are the toilets?	*Násán hô ang CR?*
Go away!	*Umalís ka!*
Call ...!	*Tumawag ka ng ...!*
a doctor	*doktór*
the police	*pulís*

FOOD & DRINK

breakfast	*almusal/agahan*
lunch	*tanghalian*
dinner	*hapunan*
snack	*meryenda*

I'm a vegetarian.	*Gulay lamang ang kinákain ko.*
(cup of) tea	*(isang tásang) tsaá*
beer	*serbésa*
boiled water	*pinakuluáng túbig*
coffee	*kapé*
food	*pagkaín*
milk	*gátas*
restaurant	*restorán*
salt	*ásin*
sugar	*asúkal*
vegetables	*gulay*
water	*túbig*

NUMBERS

English numbers are often used for prices.

1	*isá*	9	*siyám*
2	*dalawá*	10	*sampú*
3	*tatló*	11	*labíng-isá*
4	*apát*	12	*labíndalawá*
5	*limá*	20	*dalawampú*
6	*ánim*	30	*tatlumpú*
7	*pitó*	100	*sandaán*
8	*waló*	1000	*isáng libo/sanlíbo*

LANGUAGE

SHOPPING & SERVICES

Where is a/the ...?	Saán hô may ...?
bank	bangko
market	palengle
post office	pos opis
public telephone	telépono
public toilet	CR/pálikuran

How much?	Magkáno?
too expensive	mahál

TIME & DAYS

What time is it?	Anong óras na?
today	ngayon
tomorrow	búkas
yesterday	kahápon

Monday	Lunes
Tuesday	Martes
Wednesday	Miyérkolés
Thursday	Huwebes
Friday	Biyernes
Saturday	Sábado
Sunday	Linggó

TRANSPORT

Where is the ...?	Násaan ang ...?
bus station	terminal ng bus
train station	terminal ng tren
road to ...	daan papuntang ...

What time does the bus leave/arrive?	Anong óras áalis/ dárating ang bus?

Directions

Is it far from/near here?	Maláyó/malápit ba díto?
straight ahead	dirétso lámang
to the right	papakánan
to the left	papakaliwá

THAILAND (THAI)

TONES & PRONUNCIATION

Thai is a tonal language, where changes in pitch can affect meaning. The range of all five tones is relative to each speaker's vocal range, so there's no fixed 'pitch' intrinsic to the language. The five tones of Thai are:

low tone – a flat pitch pronounced at the relative bottom of the vocal range, eg *bàat* (baht – the Thai currency)

level or mid tone – pronounced flat, at the relative middle of the vocal range, eg *dii* (good); no tone mark is used

falling tone – pronounced as if emphasising a word, or calling someone's name from afar, eg *mâi* (no/not)

high tone – pronounced near the relative top of the vocal range, as level as possible, eg *máa* (horse)

rising tone – sounds like the inflection used by English speakers to imply a question, eg *sǎam* (three)

The 'ph' in a Thai word is always pronounced like an English 'p', not as an 'f'.

ACCOMMODATION

I'm looking for a ...	phǒm/dì-chǎn kam-lang hǎa ...
guesthouse	bâan phák (kèt háo)
hotel	rohng raem
youth hostel	bâan yao-wá-chon

Do you have any rooms available?	mii hâwng wâang mǎi?

I'd like (a) ...	tâwng kaan ...
bed	tiang nawn
single room	hâwng dìaw
double room	hâwng khûu
room with two beds	hâwng thîi mii tiang sǎwng tua
ordinary room (with fan)	hâwng tham-má-daa (mii pát lom)

How much is it ...?	... thâo rai?
per night	kheun lá
per person	khon lá

CONVERSATION & ESSENTIALS

When being polite, a male speaker ends his sentence with *khráp* and a female speaker says *khâ*; it's also the common way to answer 'yes' to a question or show agreement.

Hello.	sà-wàt-dii (khráp/khâ)
Goodbye.	laa kàwn
Yes.	châi
No.	mâi châi
Please.	kà-rú-naa
Thank you.	khàwp khun
You're welcome.	mâi pen rai/yin-dii
Excuse me.	khǎw à-phai
Sorry. (forgive me)	khǎw thôht
How are you?	sa-bai dii rěu?
I'm fine, thanks.	sa-bai dii
I don't understand.	mâi khâo jai
Do you speak English?	khun phûut phaa-sǎa ang-krìt dâi mǎi?

FOOD & DRINK

I'd like...	khăw ...
I'm allergic to...	phŏm/dì-chăn pháe ...
I don't eat ...	phŏm/dì-chăn kin ... mâi dâi
rice	khâo
rice noodles	kŭaytĭaw
meat	néua sàt
chicken	kài
fish	plaa
seafood	aahăan tháleh
pork	mŭu
beer	bia
coffee	kaafae
tea	chaa
milk	nom jèut
water	náam
ice	náam khăeng

NUMBERS

1	nèung	9	kâo
2	săwng	10	sìp
3	săam	20	yîi-sìp
4	sìi	21	yîi-sìp-èt
5	hâa	30	săam-sìp
6	hòk	100	nèung ráwy
7	jèt	1000	nèung phan
8	pàet	10,000	nèung mèun

SHOPPING & SERVICES

I'm looking for ...	phŏm/dì-chăn hăa ...
a bank	thá-naa-khaan
the market	ta-làat
the post office	prai-sà-nii
a public toilet	hâwng nám săa-thaa-rá-ná
the telephone centre	sŭun thoh-rá-sàp
the tourist office	săm-nák ngaan thâwng thîaw
When does it open?	ráan pòet kìi mohng?
When does it close?	ráan pìt kìi mohng?
I'd like to buy ...	yàak jà séu ...
How much is it?	thâo rai?

TIME & DAYS

What time is it?	kìi mohng láew?
It's (8 o'clock).	pàet mohng láew
When?	meua-rai?
today	wan níi
tomorrow	phrûng níi
yesterday	mêua waan
Monday	wan jan
Tuesday	wan ang-khaan
Wednesday	wan phút
Thursday	wan phá-réu-hàt
Friday	wan sùk
Saturday	wan săo
Sunday	wan aa-thít

TRANSPORT

What time does the ... leave/arrive?	... jà àwk/thĕung kìi mohng
boat	reua
bus	rót meh/rót bát
(intercity) bus	rót thua
plane	khrêuang bin
train	rót fai
I'd like ...	phŏm/dì-chăn yàak dâi ...
a one-way ticket	tŭa thĭaw diaw
a return ticket	tŭa pai klàp
airport	sa-năam bin
bus station	sa-thăa-nii khŏn sòng
bus stop	pâai rót meh
train station	sa-thăa-nii rót fai
ticket office	tûu khăi tŭa

Directions

Where is ...?	... yùu thîi năi?
Can you show me (on the map)?	hâi duu (nai phăen thîi) dâi mái
How far?	klai thâo rai?
near	klâi
far	klai
(Go) Straight ahead.	trong pai
Turn left.	líaw sái
Turn right.	líaw khwăa

VIETNAM (VIETNAMESE)

There are differences between the Vietnamese of the north and the Vietnamese of the south; where different forms are used in this guide, they are indicated by 'N' for the north and 'S' for the south.

TONES & PRONUNCIATION

There are six tones in Vietnamese, each of which is represented by a different diacritical mark. Depending on the tones, the word *ma* can mean 'ghost', 'mother', 'which/but', 'tomb', 'horse' or 'rice seedling'. The six tones of Vietnamese are:

mid tone – produced at the relative middle of your voice range. No tone mark is used, eg ma (ghost)

high-rising tone – begins high and rises sharply, eg má (mother)

low-falling tone – begins low and falls lower, eg mà (which/but)

low-rising tone – begins low, dips lower, then rises sharply, eg mả (tomb)

high-broken tone – begins above middle, dips, then rises sharply, eg mã (horse)

low-broken tone – begins low then falls sharply, eg mạ (rice seedling)

đ	with a crossbar, as the 'd' in 'did'
d	without a crossbar, as 'z' (north) and as 'y' (south)
gi	as 'z' (north) and as 'y' (south)
ng	like the '-nga-' in 'long ago'
nh	as the 'ni' in 'onion'
ph	as an 'f'
r	as 'z' (north) and 'r' (south)
s	as 's' (north) and 'sh' (south)
tr	as 'ch' (north) and 'tr' (south)
th	as a strongly aspirated 't'
x	as the 's' in 'sit'
ch	as a 'k'
ô	as the 'o' in 'obey'
ơ	as the 'er' in 'fern'
ư	between the 'i' in 'sister' and the 'u' in 'sugar'

ACCOMMODATION

Where is a (cheap) ...?
đâu có ... (rẻ tiền)?	dow káw ... (rảir dee·èn)?
camping ground	
đất trại	dút trại
hotel	
khách sạn	kát sạn
guesthouse	
nhà khách	nyà kát

air-conditioning
máy lạnh	máy lạng
bathroom	
phòng tắm	fòm dúm

hot water
nước nóng	nur·érk nóm
toilet	
nhà vệ sinh	nyà vạy sing

I'd like (a) ...
Tôi muốn ...	doy moón ...
single room	
phòng đơn	fòm dern
room with two beds	
phòng gồm hai	fòm gòm hai
giường ngủ	zur·èrng ngóo

How much is it ...?
Giá bao nhiêu ...?	zá bow nyoo ...
per night	
mọt đêm	một dem
per person	
mọt ngừơi	một ngừ·ee

CONVERSATION & ESSENTIALS

There are many different forms of address in Vietnamese, depending on a person's age, sex, social position and how well the speaker knows them. Using an unsuitable term can cause misunderstanding and even embarrassment. The safest way to address people is: *ông* (to a man of any status), *anh* (to a young man), *bà* (to a middle aged or older woman), *cô* (to a young woman) and *em* (to a child).

Hello.	Xin chào.	sin jòw
Goodbye.	Tạm biệt.	dụm bee·ẹt
Please.	Làm ơn.	làm ern
Thank you.	Cảm ơn.	kảm ern
Excuse me.	Xin lỗi.	sin lõ·ee
Yes.	Vâng. (N)	vang
	Dạ. (S)	yạ
No.	Không.	kom

How are you?
Có khỏe không?	káw kwảir kom

Fine, thank you.
Khỏe, cảm ơn.	kwảir kảm ern

I (don't) understand.
Tôi (không) hiểu.	doy (kom) hẻe·oo

Do you speak English?
Bạn có nói được	Bạn káw nóy dur·ẹrk
tiếng Anh không?	tíng ang kom

LANGUAGE

EMERGENCIES – VIETNAM
Help!
   Cứu tôi!   cúr·oo doy
I'm lost.
   Tôi bị lạc đường.   doi bẹe lạk dur·èrng
Where's the toilet?
   Nhà vệ sinh ở đâu?   nyà vạy sing ér dow
Leave me alone!
   Thôi!   toy!

Call ...!
   Làm ơn gọi ...!   làm ern gọi ...
   a doctor
     bác sĩ   bák sẽe
   the police
     công an   gom an

FOOD & DRINK
I'm a vegetarian.
   Tôi ăn chay.   doy un chay

bread	*bánh mì*	bán mèe
steamed rice	*cơm trắng*	kerm cháng
noodles	*mì*	mèe
beef	*thịt bò*	tịt bàw
chicken	*thịt gà*	tịt gà
fish	*cá*	ká
pork	*thịt heo*	tịt hay·o
mineral water	*nước khoáng/*	nur·érk kwáng/
	nước suối (N/S)	nur·érk sóo·ee
tea	*chè/trà* (N/S)	jàir/chà
coffee	*cà phê*	kà fay
milk	*sữa*	sữr·a
beer	*bia*	bi·a
ice	*đá*	dá

NUMBERS
1	*một*	mọt
2	*hai*	hai
3	*ba*	ba
4	*bốn*	bón
5	*năm*	num
6	*sáu*	sów
7	*bảy*	bảy
8	*tám*	dúm
9	*chín*	jín
10	*mười*	mùr·ee
11	*mười một*	mùr·ee mọt
19	*mười chín*	mùr·ee
20	*hai mươi*	hai mur·ee
21	*hai mươi mốt*	hai mur·ee mót
22	*hai mươi hai*	hai mur·ee hai

30	*ba mươi*	ba mur·ee
90	*chín mươi*	jín mur·ee
100	*một trăm*	mọt chum
200	*hai trăm*	hai chum
900	*chín trăm*	jín chum
1000	*một nghìn* (N)	mọt ngìn
	một ngàn (S)	mọt ngàn
10,000	*mười nghìn* (N)	mùr·ee ngìn
	mười ngàn (S)	mùr·ee ngàn
one million	*một triệu*	mọt chee·ọo
two million	*hai triệu*	hai chee·ọo

SHOPPING & SERVICES
I'm looking for ...
   Tôi tìm ...   doy dìm ...
   a bank
     ngân hàng   ngun hàng
   the hospital
     nhà thương   nyà tur·erng
   the market
     chợ   jẹr
   the post office
     bưu điện   bur·oo dee·ẹn
   a public phone
     phòng điện thoại   fòm dee·ẹn twại
   a public toilet
     phòng vệ sinh   fòm vạy sing
   tourist office
     văn phòng hướng   vun fòm hur·érng
     dẫn du lịch   zũn zoo lịt

How much is this?
   Cái này giá   kái này zá
   bao nhiêu?   bow nyoo
It's too expensive.
   Cái này quá mắc.   kái này gwá múk

TIME & DAYS
What time is it?
   Mấy giờ rồi?   máy zèr ròy?
It's ... o'clock.
   Bây giờ là ... giờ.   bay zèr là ... zèr

now	*bây giờ*	bay zèr
today	*hôm nay*	hom nay
tomorrow	*ngày mai*	ngày mai
Monday	*thứ hai*	túr hai
Tuesday	*thứ ba*	túr ba
Wednesday	*thứ tư*	túr dur
Thursday	*thứ năm*	túr num
Friday	*thứ sáu*	túr sów
Saturday	*thứ bảy*	túr bảy
Sunday	*chủ nhật*	chỏo nhụt

LANGUAGE

TRANSPORT

What time does the (first)... leave/arrive?

Chuyến `... (sớm nhất)	chwee·én ... (sérm nhút)
chạy lúc mấy giờ?	chạy lóop máy zèr
boat	
tàu/thuyền	tòw/twee·èn
bus	
xe buýt	sair béet
plane	
máy bay	máy bay
train	
xe lửa	sair lử·a

Directions

Where's ...?

ở đâu ...?	èr dow ...

I want to go to ...

Tôi muốn đi ...	doy móon dee ...

Can you show me (on the map)?

Xin chỉ giùm	sin chée zòom
(trên bản đồ này).	(tren bản dò này)

Go straight ahead.

Thẳng tới trước.	tủng dér·ee trur·érk

Turn left.	*Sang trái.*	sang trái
Turn right.	*Sang phải.*	sang fái
at the corner	*ở góc đường*	èr góp dur·èrng
at the traffic	*tại đèn giao*	tại dèn zow
lights	*thông*	tom
far	*xa*	sa
near (to)	*gần*	gùn

LANGUAGE

Glossary

ABBREVIATIONS

B – Brunei
C – Cambodia
ET – East Timor
I – Indonesia
L – Laos
M – Malaysia
My – Myanmar (Burma)
P – Philippines
S – Singapore
T – Thailand
V – Vietnam

ABC (M) – Air Batang
adat (B, I, M, S) – customary law
alun alun (I) – main public square of a town
andong (I) – four-wheeled horse-drawn cart
anggunas (ET) – tray-trucks where passengers (including the odd buffalo or goat) all pile into the back
angkot – see *bemo*
ao (T) – bay, gulf
ao dai (V) – traditional Vietnamese tunic and trousers
APEC – Asia-Pacific Economic Cooperation
apsara (C) – dancing girl, celestial nymph
argo (I) – meters
Asean – Association of Southeast Asian Nations
asura (C) – demon

bâan (T) – house, village; also written as 'ban'
Baba Nonya – descendents of Chinese settlers in the Straits Settlements (Melaka, Singapore and Penang) who intermarried with Malays and adopted many Malay customs; also written as 'Baba Nyonya'
bajaj (I) – motorised three-wheeled taxi
balangay (P) – sailboat
Bamar (My) – Burmese ethnic group
bangca (P) – local outrigger, pumpboat
barangay (P) – community with a local government
batik (I, M) – cloth coloured by waxing and dyeing process
BE (L, T) – Buddhist Era
becak (I) – bicycle rickshaw
bemo (I) – three-wheeled pick-up truck, often with two rows of seats down the side
bendi (I) – two-person horse-drawn cart
benteng (I) – fort
bis kota (I) – city bus
bisnis (I) – business class on buses, trains etc
boeng (C) – lake

BSB (B) – Bandar Seri Begawan
bukit (B, I, M, S) – hill
bumboat (S) – motorised *sampan*
bun (L) – festival
buu dien (V) – post office

Caodaism (V) – Vietnamese religious sect
CAT (T) – Communications Authority of Thailand
Cham (V) – ethnic minority descended from the people of Champa, a Hindu kingdom dating from the 2nd century BC
chedi (T) – see *stupa*
chunchiet (C) – ethnolinguistic minorities
cidomo (I) – horse-drawn cart
CITES – Convention on International Trade in Endangered Species of Wild Fauna & Flora
colt – see *opelet*
CPP (C) – Cambodian People's Party
CTT (My) – Central Telephone & Telegraph
cyclo (V) – pedicab

datu (P) – traditional local chief, head of village
DENR (P) – Department of Environment & Natural Resources
deva (C) – god
devaraja (C) – god king
DMZ (V) – Demilitarised Zone
dokar (I) – two-wheeled horse-drawn cart
DOT (P) – Department of Tourism
duong (V) – road, street; abbreviated as 'Đ'

EAEC – East Asian Economic Caucus
Ecpat – End Child Prostitution & Trafficking
ekonomi (I, M) – economy class on buses, trains and other transport
eksekutif (I, M) – executive (ie 1st) class on buses, trains and other transport

falang (L) – Western, Westerner; foreigner
faràng (T) – Western, Westerner; foreigner
FEC (My) – Foreign Exchange Certificate
Funcinpec (C) – National United Front for an Independent, Neutral, Peaceful & Cooperative Cambodia

gamelan (I, M) – traditional Javanese and Balinese orchestra with large xylophones and gongs
gang (I) – alley, lane
gua (M) – cave
gunung (I, M) – mountain

hàat (T) – beach; also written as 'hat'
habal-habal (P) – motorcycle taxi

HCMC (V) – Ho Chi Minh City
héua hang nyáo (L) – longtail boat
héua phai (L) – rowboat
héua wái (L) – speedboat
Holy Week (P) – week preceding Easter Sunday, a time of festivities in Christian countries
Honda om (V) – motorbike taxi
hti (My) – umbrella, decorated top of a pagoda

IDP – International Driving Permit
ikat (I) – cloth in which a pattern is produced by dyeing individual threads before the weaving process
IMF – International Monetary Fund
Interfet (ET) – International Force in East Timor
istana (B, I, M, S) – palace

jalan (B, I, M, S) – road, street; abbreviated as 'Jl'
jataka (T) – stories of the Buddha's past lives, often enacted in dance-drama
JB (M) – Johor Bahru
jeepney (P) – wildly ornamented public transport, originally based on WWII US Army Jeeps
Jl (B, I, M, S) – abbreviation for *jalan*

kaa (My) – city bus
kain songket (M) – fabric woven with gold/silver thread
kaki lima (I) – mobile food stall; food courts
kalaga (My) – tapestry embroidered with silver threads and sequins
kalesa (P) – two-wheeled horse-drawn cart
kampung (B, I, M, S) – village; also written as 'kampong'
kantor pos (I) – post office
karst – limestone region with caves, underground streams, potholes etc
káthoey (T) – transvestite, transsexual
kedai kopi (M) – coffee shop
khâen (L) – panpipe; also written as 'khaen'
khǎo (T) – hill, mountain; also written as 'khao'
khlong (T) – canal; also written as 'khlawng'
khwǎn (L) – guardian spirits of the body
KK (M) – Kota Kinabalu
KL (M) – Kuala Lumpur
KLIA (M) – Kuala Lumpur International Airport
klotok (I) – motorised canoe
ko (T) – island
koh (C) – island
kongsi (M) – Chinese clan organisations, also known as ritual brotherhoods, heaven-man-earth societies, triads or secret societies; meeting house for Chinese of the same clan
kota (M) – fort, city
krama (C) – checked scarf
kraton (I) – palace
kris (I) – traditional dagger
KTM (M) – Keretapi Tanah Melayu; national rail service
kyaung (My) – Buddhist monastery

labuan (M) – port
lákhon (T) – dance drama
lí-keh (T) – popular form of folk dance-drama; also written as 'likay'
longhouse (M) – enormous wooden structure on stilts that houses a tribal community under one roof
longyi (My) – wraparound worn by women and men
losmen (I) – basic accommodation
LRT (M) – Light Rail Transit

mae nam (T) – river
MAF (I) – Mission Aviation Fellowship
MAI (My) – Myanmar Airways International
mandi (I, M) – bathing facility
masjid (B, M) – mosque
mát-mii (T) – cloth made of tie-dyed silk or cotton thread; also written as 'mat-mii'
merdeka (I, M) – independence
mesjid (I) – mosque
mestizo (P) – person of Filipino-Spanish or Filipino-American descent
meuang (T) – city
MHT (My) – Ministry of Hotels & Tourism
mikrolet – see *opelet*
MILF (P) – Moro Islamic Liberation Front
MNLF (P) – Moro National Liberation Front
Montagnards (V) – highlanders, mountain people; specifically the ethnic minorities inhabiting remote areas of Vietnam
moto (C) – motorcycle taxi
MRT (S) – Mass Rapid Transit; metro system
MTT (My) – Myanmar Travel & Tours
muay thai (T) – Thai boxing
myint hlei (My) – horse cart

nâam (L, T) – water, river
naga (C, L, T) – mythical serpent-being
nákhon (T) – city
nǎng (T) – shadow play
nat (My) – spirit-being with the power to either protect or harm humans; Myanmar's syncretic Buddhism
Negrito (P) – ancient Asian race distinguished by their black skin, curly hair and short size
NGO – nongovernmental organisation
NLD (My) – National League for Democracy
Nonya – see *Baba Nonya*
nop (L) – palms-together greeting, see *wâi*
NPA (L, P) – National Protected Area; New People's Army
NTAL (L) – National Tourism Authority of Laos
Nyonya – see *Baba Nonya*

ojek (I) – motorcycle taxi
opelet (I) – small minibus
Orang Asli (M) – Original People, Malaysian aboriginal people

padang (M, S) – open grassy area
PAL (P) – Philippine Airlines
pantai (B, I, M) – beach
pasar (I, M) – market
pasar malam (I, M) – night market
paya (My) – holy one, often applied to Buddha figures, *zedi* and other religious monuments; see *stupa*
PDI-P (I) – Indonesian Democratic Party for Struggle
Pelni (I) – national shipping line
pendopo (I) – open-sided pavilion
penginapan (I) – simple lodging house
Peranakan – a combination of Malay and Chinese cultures of pre-Colonial Singapore; see also *Baba Nyonya*
Ph (C) – abbreviation for *phlauv*
phlauv (C) – road, street; abbreviated as 'Ph'
phleng phêua chii-wít (T) – songs for life, modern Thai folk songs
PHPA (I) – Perlindungan Hutan dan Pelestarian Alam; Directorate General of Forest Protection & Nature Conservation
pinisi (I) – fishing boat
polres (I) – local police station
pongyi (My) – Buddhist monk
pousada (ET) – traditional Portuguese lodging
praang (T) – Khmer-style tower structure, found on temples; see also *chedi; stupa*
prasat (C, T) – tower, temple
psar (C) – market
pulau (B, I, M) – island
pwe (My) – show, festival

quan (V) – urban district
quoc ngu (V) – Vietnamese alphabet

raja (I, M) – king
Ramakian (T) – Thai version of the *Ramayana*
Ramayana – Indian epic story of Rama's battle with demons
remorque-kang (C) – bicycle-pulled trailer
remorque-moto (C) – motorcycle-pulled trailer
roi nuoc (V) – water puppetry
rót thamádaa (T) – ordinary bus
rumah makan (I) – restaurant, food stall

săamláw (T) – three-wheeled pedicab; also written as 'samlor'
sabong (P) – cockfight
sai-kaa (My) – bicycle rickshaw
sampan (I, M, S) – small boat
săwngthăew (L, T) – small pick-up truck with two benches in the back; also written as 'songthaew'
sima (L) – ordination-precinct marker
Slorc (My) – State Law & Order Restoration Council
soi (T) – lane, small street
STB (S) – Singapore Tourism Board

Straits Chinese – the modern descendants of *Baba Nonya*
stung (C) – river
stupa – religious monument, often containing Buddha relics
sungai (B, I, M) – river; also written as 'sungei'
surat jalan (I) – visitor permit

taman (I, M) – park
taman nasional (I) – national park
tambang (M) – double-oared river ferry; small river boats
tamu (M) – weekly market
tartanilla – see *kalesa*
tasik (M) – lake
TAT (T) – Tourism Authority of Thailand
tatseng (L) – subdistrict
teluk (I, M, S) – bay; also written as 'telok'
Tet (V) – lunar New Year
Th (L, T) – abbreviation for *thànŏn*
thâa (T) – ferry, boat pier; also written as 'tha'
thâat (L) – Buddhist *stupa*, reliquary; also written as 'that'
THAI (T) – Thai Airways International
thànŏn (L, T) – road, street, avenue; abbreviated as 'Th'
tongkonan (I) – traditional house with roof eaves shaped like buffalo horns
tonlé (C) – river, lake
tukalok (C) – fresh-fruit smoothie
túk-túk (L, T) – motorised *săamláw*

UDT (ET) – Timorese Democratic Union
UN – United Nations
UNDP – United Nations Development Programme
Untaet (ET) – United Nations Transitional Administration in East Timor
UXO (C, L) – unexploded ordnance

vipassana (My, T) – insight awareness meditation

wâi (L, T) – palms-together greeting
wartel (I) – telephone office
warung (I, M) – food stall
wat (C, L, T) – Buddhist temple-monastery
wayang kulit (I) – shadow-puppet play enacting tales from the *Ramayana*
wayang orang (I) – dance-drama enacted by masked performers, recounting scenes from the *Ramayana*
wíhăan (T) – sanctuary, hall, dwelling
wisma (I, M) – guesthouse, lodge; office block, shopping centre
WWF – World Wide Fund

xe om (V) – see *Honda om*

yâam (T) – woven shoulder bag

zedi (My) – see *stupa*

Behind the Scenes

THIS BOOK

This is the 13th edition of *Southeast Asia on a Shoestring*. The 1st edition was written by Tony and Maureen Wheeler in 1975, funded by the cult success of their first guidebook, *Across Asia on the Cheap*, a compilation of journey notes put together way back in 1973. As the scope of the book grew, so did the need to share the load: this edition is the work of 13 authors. Coordinating author extraordinaire China Williams led an expert team: George Dunford, Simone Egger, Matt Phillips, Nick Ray, Robert Reid, Paul Smitz, Tasmin Waby, Matt Warren, Sarah Wintle, Rafael Wlodarski, Wendy Yanagihara and Frank Zeller. This guidebook was commissioned in Lonely Planet's Melbourne office, and produced by the following:

Commissioning Editor Kalya Ryan
Coordinating Editors Carolyn Boicos, Gina Tsarouhas
Coordinating Cartographer Corey Hutchison
Coordinating Layout Designer Yvonne Bischofberger
Managing Cartographer Corie Waddell
Assisting Editors Monique Choy, Pete Cruttenden, Andrea Dobbin, Laura Gibb, Liz Heynes, Kate James, Helen Koehne, Anne Mulvaney, Maryanne Netto, Lauren Rollheiser
Assisting Cartographers Barbara Benson, Hunor Csutoros, Dianna Duggan, James Ellis, Jacqui Saunders
Assisting Layout Designers Tom Delamore, Laura Jane, Wibowo Rusli,
Cover Designer Wendy Wright
Indexers Yvonne Bischofberger, Laura Jane, David Kemp, Wibowo Rusli, Jacqui Saunders
Project Managers Eoin Dunlevy, Glenn van der Knijff, Fabrice Rocher
Language Content Coordinator Quentin Frayne, Branislava Vladisavljevic
Thanks to Dave Burnett, Sally Darmody, Rebecca Lalor, Adriana Mammarella, Wayne Murphy, Mary Neighbour, Darren O'Connell, Stephanie Pearson, Helen Rowley, Suzannah Shwer, Andrew Weatherill, Gabrielle Wilson, Celia Wood

THANKS from the Author

China Williams Malaysia rocks – it is full of smart, funny people who speak English fabulously. Thanks to John Khoo in Penang, Alex Lee and Mazlina in Kuala Terengganu, the wacky owners of Sama Sama Guesthouse in Melaka, the sweet ticket agent in Marang, Asrul Abdullah in Taman Negera, countercultural Absamat and chatty Abdul Hadi Othman on Pulau Tioman, and to Tourism Malaysia's well-organised staff. Thanks to Kalya Ryan for sending me to such a great place, the contributing authors and the unsung heroes of LP's staff. Thanks most to my hubby who moved me across the country so that the flight time to Asia is more humane.

George Dunford A spicy *dosa* for my wonderful travelling companion Nikki. A serve of *kaya* toast for China Williams for all her hard coordinating work. A Tiger beer for Helen P and Sanchia Draper for local contacts. A heartfelt thank you to Gary Lim for showing me a night or two on Clarke Quay. Thanks also to James Chong and Cyril Wong for their tips and advice. A nod to Daniel Chi, Malcolm Davies and Hai for their insights into their own little corners of the Lion City. A generous serve of *beehoon* to Simon Richmond for his work on previous editions, a swinging Singapore Sling for Kalya Ryan for in-house hard yards, plus a sobering *kopi* for Wing Commander David Nelson for sorting out insurance. Thanks most of all to Marge Tiyce, who passed away during research for this book – we remember you with love.

Simone Egger Many thanks to Sarah Moon, Kevin Bailey and Pedro Lebre; with a cherry on top to Jorge Torterolo and Simon King.

Matt Phillips Thanks to Georgina for your devotion, understanding and love; Kalya for your support and giving me the chance to revisit another love – Cambodia; my Mum for opening her heart and door to craziness – yet again; Dad and Vikki for always believing in me; Pam for being my most ardent supporter; Margaret, Eunice, Alex, Bonnie, Lizzy and Rose for keeping me in their thoughts; Andrew for his unbelievable generosity in Phnom Penh; Nick for his insider tips and enthusiasm; my wonderful friends in Vancouver for always looking out for me; and the generosity of wonderful Cambodians who helped along the way.

Nick Ray A huge thanks to my wonderful wife Kulikar Sotho and my young son Julian Ang Ray, aka Mr J, for indulging me the time to travel to

Thailand to research this book. Your love and support is invaluable. Thanks also to the many family and friends who have indulged me over the years, none more so than Mum and Dad. Thanks also to many good people in Thailand for help, including the many authors who have contributed to the knowledge bank over the years, especially Joe Cummings, China Williams and Steve Martin.

Robert Reid Thanks to Kalya Ryan for offering the work, Michael Grosberg for cohortmanship on the *Myanmar* book, China Williams for scrapping together this one, and Mai for tolerating the mess.

Paul Smitz Big thanks to all the Malaysians, Bruneians and backpackers who gave me advice, companionship and grooming tips during my research, including those who wrote in to Lonely Planet. In particular, thanks to André and Alice for lighting up Belaga and for the inspiring tales of Hope St; Hannah and Robin, for great company at Bako and for not taunting me from the KL Hilton; Graham and David, for porchfront chats in Bario; Syriá, for the highly knowledgeable guiding at Gunung Mulu; Mary and Jeff, for bad one-liners and smoky nights on the Kinabatangan and beyond; and finally to Buffalo Gandhi in Kota Belud, because legends have to start somewhere. Thanks also to co-author China Williams for enjoying herself way too much in Peninsular Malaysia, to Kalya Ryan for fine commissioning and for flying to KL just to spy on me, and to Corie Waddell for never being at her desk when I call. Special thanks to the enigmatic woman who should just do what Eric Clapton requests and unplug him.

Tasmin Waby Despite this being a small chapter in a big book there is a number of people to thank for making it all happen. Thanks to all the welcoming people of Laos (whose names I never asked) for sharing your food, bus seats and experiences with me. Thanks to the following people for your assistance on this project: Glenn Hunt, Paul Cannon, Lorraine Bramwell, Jan Barrish, Mick O'Shea, Samantha Giannikos, Mr Souliyavong Sihijamphon or 'Bobby', Mr Soneathith Souliyavong aka 'Viet', Ms Khamsavey, Mr Sonepasird Soukaseum, Dara and Amarine, Bruce Evans, Holly Schauble, Kalya Ryan, Carolyn Boicos, Gina Tsarouhas, Liz Heynes, Suzannah Shwer, Mary Harrington and Sharna Smith. To my fellow travellers, thanks for your company and your tips: Alison Murphy, Nicola Brunelli, Crystal Fletcher, Seb from Chester, Rick and Bee from Bangkok, Jamie of Herefordshire, and Tom and Erin. Finally, thanks to the mates

who kept the emails coming from home while I was on the road; Judith and Dugald for keeping me sane during the write-up in Melbourne; my father, the late Ross Waby, for inspiring and encouraging; and, finally, my mum and brother, plus my partner in absurdity, Hugh McNaughtan, thanks for everything.

Matt Warren Big thanks go to Gerhard for his help and hospitality in Jakarta, Hansjorg and Tomoka for the comfy beds, Nam for the biggest meal I have ever eaten, Alex and Li Anne for the Seminyak nights and Lina, with the keen eye for a knalpot. Most of all, a huge thank-you to Becky, just for being there.

Sarah Wintle Thank you to my gorgeous assortment of family and friends for keeping me inspired. Thanks a million to Kalya Ryan and hats-off to the behind-the-scenes Lonely Planeteers, Anna Bolger, Adrian Campbell and authors Joe Cummings, China Williams and Becca Blond. Big thanks to Stacey Hanson for her free-flowing advice and spurring me on to tackle a mega chocolate sundae in Bangkok. Thank you to Mr Somkiat and Mrs Supree Siricharoenlarp, Laksamee Prakongsin, Vipasai Niyamabha of *The Nation,* and Ying at Baan Panburi, Ko Pha-Ngan. Tourism Authority of Thailand (TAT) staff – including Natapat Achariyachai in Phuket, Soraya Homchuen in Bangkok, Pongsak Kanittanon and Melanie McCoy in Sydney – gave me helpful low-downs. Thumbs-up to Melanie Mills and Scott Welch, and hugs to Chelsea Mannix. A special shout out to the Lonely Planet readers who were generous with their Thailand tip bits. Foremost thanks to the people of Thailand who continually wow me with their limitless grace and generosity.

Rafael Wlodarski A million thanks goes out to the good people who smoothed my speedy path through the Philippines: Gabriel and Benjie in Manila, Salvador in Donsol, Lee in Boracay, Jochen in Moalboal, Jojo in Naga, Luke and Rick in North Luzon, Linda and Martin all over the place, DOT offices far and wide and the countless bus-stop barbecue stands that kept me alive. Thanks to China Williams for sharing a burrito and some wisdom back home, and Lonely Planet's Kalya Ryan for never-ending answers to never-ending questions. Special thanks goes out to the ongoing support of Suzanna, Brent and Stan.

Wendy Yanagihara Warm thanks and cool glasses of *nuoc mia* to my extended family in Saigon: Diem and Adrien, the Bo family and the Le family. My profound gratitude goes once again to Le Van

Sinh for so generously sharing with me his expertise, energy and laptop. Special thanks and shout-outs to Arnaud and Nhu for putting me up and José for setting things straight on Phu Quoc, to Quinn and Darren in Nha Trang for more news and booze, to Mr Binh in Hoi An, the charismatic Xuan Hoa duo in Ninh Binh, Thanh at Cuc Phuong, Son in Hanoi and Maite, Christian and Aitor for all the spaghetti and salsa dancing. Lastly, thank you to all the travellers who doled out good advice and told even better tales.

Frank Zeller Many thanks to Rita and Armin for their support, Adi and friends for their inspiration, Karl and Amy for their hospitality, the Padang surfer gang for their help and Dino for an excellent road trip.

OUR READERS

Many thanks to the hundreds of travellers who used the last edition and wrote to us with helpful hints, useful advice and interesting anecdotes:

A David Abrey, Kyle Acierno, Brooke Alexander, Kelly Alexander, Lena Al-Shammari, Joel Anderson, Jonny Anderson, Warren Askew, Karen Aslett **B** Arden Bashforth, Elisabeth Baxter, Yann Bell, Megan Berkle, Dan Biggs, Jocelyne Bisaillon, Russell Blackbourn, Stacey Boshier, Margaret Bouton, Simon & Lisa Brady, Mattes Brau, Kelly Brennan, Charlotte Briscoe, Angela & Grant Brown, Jenny Brown, Corina Browne, Tina Brumfield, Stefan Brunner, Mary Bryant, John Buchanan, David Burns, E J Butler, Yvonne Butler **C** Jonas Callmer, Kirsty Cambridge, Chris Carey, Claudio Cassara, Ray Chandler, Nicolas Chereau, Mindy Christie, Vanessa Clark, Claire Clements, Sarah Collinson, Kevin L Corr, Catherine Coulton, Wendy Cremin, Gabor Csonka, David Cuschieri, Natali Cvijeticanin **D** Dayne Davey, Fabiola de Moraaz Imans, Jeroen Decuyper, Lars Dehli, Bridget Dejong, Marital Denia, John Dick, Aiden Donegal, Tom Donnelly, Alastair Dow, Regina Du, Aoife Duggan, Jo Duthie **E** Philipp Ehrne, Kirk Evans, Joanne Everall **F** Matt Farnholtz, Guenter Fetter, Frederick Flagg, Karen Flam, Gemma Foster, Jade & Dave Fredericks, Bart Friederichs, Tim Frier, Hershel Frimer, Frank Froboese, Karen Fung **G** Fernando Garcia, Lia Genovese, Richard George, Jenny Gibson, Chris Gillard, Siow Yune Goh, Tony Gordon, Chris Grabe, Fred Green, Leslie Griffiths, Abha Gulati, Fabian Gumucio **H** Gernot Haidorfer, Sofie Håkansson,

Trevor Hale, Nicole Hannam, Matt Harding, Sebastian Hare, Mark Harkison, Matthew Harrup, Volker Heider, Thrudur Helgadottir, Sandra Hitz, Ben Hoffman, Carol Holley, George J Horiguchi, Wei Hu, Mark Hunnebell, Quentin & Ann Hunter, Sally Huskinson, Alice Hutchings **J** Karolien Joossens **K** Daniel Kahle, Simon Karsties, Claire Kent, James & Kasia Kilvington, Lex Kortekaas, Jochen Krauss, Marieke Krijnen, Paul Kyne **L** Chris & Jolene Laing, Michael Lamb, Colin Lamont, Martin Landers, Richard Langevin, Madeline Lasko, Uli Leikauf, Brian & Lorna Lewis, Ann Loh, Chris Louie, Katherine Lu, Sarah Lulofs, Therese Lundin, Elizabeth Lydon, Jessie Lyons **M** Bev Mackenzie, Jeanie Magee, Clive Magill, Gareth & Emma Maguire, Margarita Malkina, Ukirsari Manggalani, Calos Marcos, Fiona Mark, Mary Markotic, Silvia Maurer, Michel May, Lisa McCallum, Shane McCarthy, Casey McCartney, Angela McKay, Bianca-Lee Mclauchlan, Richard Mcneill, Kathy McRae, Melissa McVee, Luis Miguel Medianero, Stefan Meivers, Thet Naung Mg Mg, Chris Michael, Sabrina Mileto, John Moffat, Rainer Moor, John Moran, Kathy Morf, Susan Morley **N** Chris Naylor, Steve Newcomer, Brad Nieder, Philippa Nigg **O** Mary O'Connell, Alan O'Dowd, Dax Oliver, Audrey Osborn, Chris Owen **P** M D S Parco, Tara Patterson, Javier Paz, Jill Peary, Renate Pelzl, Amanda Peskin, Thekla Pesta, Gabby Phillips, Jonathan Phillips, Lorenzo Pilati, Ben Posil, Thomas Prestgaard, Janet Preston, Ceri Price, Ty Prichard, Mark Princi, Matthew Prousialkas, Graham Purse, Olli Puustinen **Q** Mark Quartley **R** Elizabeth Raddatz, Matthew Ridd, Patrik Rieckmann, Jamie Roach, Catherine Roberts, Karin Robnik, Steffen Rose, Barrett Ross, David Rostron, Anne Royden-Turner, Daniel Rozas, Denise Ruygrok, Shannon Ryan **S** Nurit Sadan, Georgia Salpa, Aurelie Salvaire, Sara Schirmer, Michael Schofield, Amy Seagrove, Marlene Searle, Wolfgang Seel, Mark Slatter, Peter Smith, Aity Soekidjo, Jan O Staal, Robert Stagg, Grzegorz Stefaniak, Jonathan Stephens, Rebecca Stewart, Marlene Strauch, Richard Sumner, Edward Sylvester, Julie Symons **T** Alvaro Amejeiras Taibo, Ming Tang, Kate Thompson, Melle Toering **V** Dena van Dalfsen, Bartjan van Hulten, Ruud van Zwet, Joanna Varela-Hughes, Eleni Vlahakis **W** Jeff Walters, Ben Watkins, Fabio Weibel, Wolfram Weidemann, Lars Welander, Merav Wheelhouse, Virginie Whiteway-Wilkinson, Theresa Wolters, Kevin Wootton **Y** Tsuyoki Yamagishi, Colin Young **Z** Ariel Zisman

ACKNOWLEDGMENTS

Many thanks to the following for the use of their content:

Globe on back cover ©Mountain high Maps 1993 Digital Wisdom, Inc.

Index

INDEX

INDEX

INDEX

000 Map pages
000 Location of photographs

INDEX

Tat Kuang Si 380
Tat Somphamit 405
Tek Chhoou Falls 106
websites, *see* Internet resources
Werapak Elosak mummy 338
West Papua 330
West Timor 300-4
  safe travel 300
  tours 301
whale sharks 619-20, 622
whale-watching 631
Whisky Village 380
White Beach (Boracay) 633
White Beach 622-3
white elephants 693
Wihaan Phra Mongkhon Bophit 728
wildlife 34, 131, 693, *see also* wildlife-
  spotting
  Brunei Darussalam 41
  Cambodia 59
  endangered species 694
  East Timor 131
  Indonesia 155
  Laos 350
  Malaysia 420
  Philippines 594-5
  reserves 646
  Thailand 693
  Vietnam 828
wildlife-spotting, *see also* wildlife
  Anggi Lakes 336
  animal observation hides 479-80
  monitor lizards 291
  Bohorok Orang-utan Viewing
    Centre 265
  Kersik Luwai Orchid Reserve 309
  Monkey Forest Sanctuary 224
  Phuket Gibbon Rehabilitation
    Centre 807
  Pusat Latihan Gajah 244-5
  rafflesia sanctuary 252

salt licks 479-80
sea turtles 511
Semenggoh Wildlife Centre 489
Sungai Kinabatangan 513
Taman Burung & Anggrek 335
Tambunan Rafflesia Reserve 506
Taman Pertanian Sabah 507
Thai Elephant Conservation Center
  747
safari 646
tours 481, 511, 646
Wimontok Mabel mummy 338
Wind Cave 498
windsurfing, *see also* surfing
  Boracay 633
  Mui Ne 884
  Nha Trang 880
Wisnu Kencana Cultural Park 221
Wolonjita 297
Wolowaru 297
women travellers 932-3
  Brunei Darussalam 52
  Cambodia 71, 124
  health 952
  Indonesia 287, 344
  Laos 414
  Malaysia 522
  Myanmar 587
  Philippines 655
  Singapore 683
  Thailand 822
Wonosobo 187
work 933, *see also* volunteering
  Cambodia 124
  Laos 414
  Myanmar 587
  Thailand 822
  Vietnam 920
Workers' Day 582
World Heritage sites
  Ayuthaya 726-30

Gunung Mulu National Park
  498-9
Halong Bay 851
Hoi An Old Town 872-4
Komodo 291-2
Luang Prabang 369-80
My Son 877
Puerto Galera 620-1
Rinca 291-2
Wat Phu Champasak 402
World War II Museum 724

X
Xanana Reading Room 134
Xe om 831
xich lo 831
Xieng Khuan (Buddha Park) 360
Xieng Khuang Province 383-6

Y
Yadana Man Aung Paya 551
Yamashita's Horde 593
Yangon 534-44, **536, 538, 540**
  accommodation 539-41
  attractions 535-7
  drinking 542-4
  emergency services 535
  entertainment 542
  food 541-2
  shopping 542
  travel to/from 535, 542-3
  travel within 543-4
Yeh Sanih 233
yoga 899-900
Yogyakarta 188-94, **189, 195, 191**
Yudhoyono, Susilo Bambang 153

Z
zoos
  Bandung Zoo 179
  Ragunan Zoo 168
  Singapore Zoological Gardens 669

THE LONELY PLANET STORY

The story begins with a classic travel adventure: Tony and Maureen Wheeler's 1972 journey across Europe and Asia to Australia. There was no useful information about the overland trail then, so Tony and Maureen published the first Lonely Planet guidebook to meet a growing need.

From a kitchen table, Lonely Planet has grown to become the largest independent travel publisher in the world, with offices in Melbourne (Australia), Oakland (USA) and London (UK). Today Lonely Planet guidebooks cover the globe. There is an ever-growing list of books and information in a variety of media. Some things haven't changed. The main aim is still to make it possible for adventurous travellers to get out there – to explore and better understand the world.

At Lonely Planet we believe travellers can make a positive contribution to the countries they visit – if they respect their host communities and spend their money wisely. Every year 5% of company profit is donated to charities around the world.

SEND US YOUR FEEDBACK

We love to hear from travellers – your comments keep us on our toes and help make our books better. Our well-travelled team reads every word on what you loved or loathed about this book. Although we cannot reply individually to postal submissions, we always guarantee that your feedback goes straight to the appropriate authors, in time for the next edition. Each person who sends us information is thanked in the next edition – and the most useful submissions are rewarded with a free book. See the Behind the Scenes section.

To send us your updates – and find out about Lonely Planet events, newsletters and travel news – visit our award-winning website: **www.lonelyplanet.com/feedback**.

Note: We may edit, reproduce and incorporate your comments in Lonely Planet products such as guidebooks, websites and digital products, so let us know if you don't want your comments reproduced or your name acknowledged. For a copy of our privacy policy, go to www.lonelyplanet.com/privacy.

Published by Lonely Planet Publications Pty Ltd
ABN 36 005 607 983

© Lonely Planet 2006

© photographers as indicated 2006

Cover photographs by Lonely Planet Images: John Banagan, Anders Blomqvist, Frank Carter and Richard I'Anson (front); kayaking in Thailand, Philip and Karen Smith (back). Many of the images in this guide are available for licensing from Lonely Planet Images: www.lonelyplanetimages.com

Printed through SNP Security Printing Pte Ltd at
KHL Printing Co Sdn Bhd Malaysia

LONELY PLANET OFFICES

Australia
Head Office
Locked Bag 1, Footscray, Victoria 3011
☎ 03 8379 8000, fax 03 8379 8111
talk2us@lonelyplanet.com.au

USA
150 Linden St, Oakland, CA 94607
☎ 510 893 8555, toll free 800 275 8555
fax 510 893 8572, info@lonelyplanet.com

UK
72–82 Rosebery Ave,
Clerkenwell, London EC1R 4RW
☎ 020 7841 9000, fax 020 7841 9001
go@lonelyplanet.co.uk